FORD

FORD THUNDERBIRD & MERCURY COUGAR 1983-96 REPAIR MANUAL

CHILTON'S

Senior Vice President — Ronald A. Hoxter

Publisher & Editor-In-Chief — Kerry A. Freeman, S.A.E.
Executive Editors — Dean F. Morgantini, S.A.E., W. Calvin Settle, Jr., S.A.E.
Managing Editor — Nick D'Andrea
Senior Editors — Jacques Gordon, Michael L. Grady, Ben Greisler, S.A.E., Debra McCall, Kevin M. G. Maher, Richard J. Rivele, S.A.E., Richard T. Smith, Jim Taylor, Ron Webb
Project Managers — Martin J. Gunther, Will Kessler, A.S.E., Richard Schwartz
Production Manager — Andrea Steiger
Product Systems Manager — Robert Maxey
Director of Manufacturing — Mike D'Imperio
Editors — Dawn M. Hoch, Christine L. Nuckowski

CHILTON BOOK COMPANY

ONE OF THE **DIVERSIFIED PUBLISHING COMPANIES**, A PART OF **CAPITAL CITIES/ABC, INC.**

Manufactured in USA

Chilton Way, Radnor, PA 19089
ISBN 0-8019-8818-7
Library of Congress Catalog Card No. 96-84548
1234567890 5432109876

Contents

Contents

SAFETY NOTICE

Proper service and repair procedures are vital to the safe, reliable operation of all motor vehicles, as well as the personal safety of those performing repairs. This manual outlines procedures for servicing and repairing vehicles using safe, effective methods. The procedures contain many NOTES, CAUTIONS and WARNINGS which should be followed along with standard procedures to eliminate the possibility of personal injury or improper service which could damage the vehicle or compromise its safety.

It is important to note that the repair procedures and techniques, tools and parts for servicing motor vehicles, as well as the skill and experience of the individual performing the work vary widely. It is not possible to anticipate all of the conceivable ways or conditions under which vehicles may be serviced, or to provide cautions as to all of the possible hazards that may result. Standard and accepted safety precautions and equipment should be used when handling toxic or flammable fluids, and safety goggles or other protection should be used during cutting, grinding, chiseling, prying, or any other process that can cause material removal or projectiles.

Some procedures require the use of tools specially designed for a specific purpose. Before substituting another tool or procedure, you must be completely satisfied that neither your personal safety, nor the performance of the vehicle will be endangered.

Although information in this manual is based on industry sources and is complete as possible at the time of publication, the possibility exists that some car manufacturers made later changes which could not be included here. While striving for total accuracy, Chilton Book Company cannot assume responsibility for any errors, changes or omissions that may occur in the compilation of this data.

PART NUMBERS

Part numbers listed in this reference are not recommendation by Chilton for any product by brand name. They are references that can be used with interchange manuals and aftermarket supplier catalogs to locate each brand supplier's discrete part number.

SPECIAL TOOLS

Special tools are recommended by the vehicle manufacturer to perform their specific job. Use has been kept to a minimum, but where absolutely necessary, they are referred to in the text by the part number of the tool manufacturer. These tools can be purchased, under the appropriate part number, from your local dealer or regional distributor, or an equivalent tool can be purchased locally from a tool supplier or parts outlet. Before substituting any tool for the one recommended, read the SAFETY NOTICE at the top of this page.

ACKNOWLEDGMENTS

The Chilton Book Company expresses appreciation to Ford Motor Company for their generous assistance.

1 GENERAL INFORMATION AND MAINTENANCE

HOW TO USE THIS BOOK

Chilton's Total Car Care manual for the Thunderbird and Cougar is intended to help you learn more about the inner workings of your vehicle while saving you money on its upkeep and operation.

The beginning of the book will likely be referred to the most, since that is where you will find information for maintenance and tune-up. The other sections deal with the more complex systems of your vehicle. Operating systems from engine through brakes are covered to the extent that the average do-it-yourselfer becomes mechanically involved. This book will not explain such things as rebuilding a differential for the simple reason that the expertise required and the investment in special tools make this task uneconomical. It will, however, give you detailed instructions to help you change your own brake pads and shoes, replace spark plugs, and perform many more jobs that can save you money, give you personal satisfaction and help you avoid expensive problems.

A secondary purpose of this book is a reference for owners who want to understand their vehicle and/or their mechanics better. In this case, no tools at all are required.

Where to Begin

Before removing any bolts, read through the entire procedure. This will give you the overall view of what tools and supplies will be required. There is nothing more frustrating than having to walk to the bus stop on Monday morning because you were short one bolt on Sunday afternoon. So read ahead and plan ahead. Each operation should be approached logically and all procedures thoroughly understood before attempting any work.

All sections contain adjustments, maintenance, removal and installation procedures, and in some cases, repair or overhaul procedures. When repair is not considered practical, we tell you how to remove the part and then how to install the new or rebuilt replacement. In this way, you at least save the labor costs. Backyard repair of some components is just not practical.

Avoiding Trouble

Many procedures in this book require you to "label and disconnect . . . " a group of lines, hoses or wires. Don't be lulled into thinking you can remember where everything goes — you won't. If you hook up vacuum or fuel lines incorrectly, the vehicle will run poorly, if at all. If you hook up electrical wiring incorrectly, you may instantly learn a very expensive lesson.

You don't need to know the official or engineering name for each hose or line. A piece of masking tape on the hose and a piece on its fitting will allow you to assign your own label such as the letter A or a short name. As long as you remember your own code, the lines can be reconnected by matching similar letters or names. Do remember that tape will dissolve in gasoline or other fluids; if a component is to be washed or cleaned, use another method of identification. A permanent felt-tipped marker can be very handy for marking metal parts. Remove any tape or paper labels after assembly.

Maintenance or Repair?

It's necessary to mention the difference between maintenance and repair. Maintenance includes routine inspections, adjustments, and replacement of parts which show signs of normal wear. Maintenance compensates for wear or deterioration. Repair implies that something has broken or is not working. A need for repair is often caused by lack of maintenance. Example: draining and refilling the automatic transmission fluid is maintenance recommended by the manufacturer at specific mileage intervals. Failure to do this can ruin the transmission/transaxle, requiring very expensive repairs. While no maintenance program can prevent items from breaking or wearing out, a general rule can be stated: MAINTENANCE IS CHEAPER THAN REPAIR.

Two basic mechanic's rules should be mentioned here. First, whenever the left side of the vehicle or engine is referred to, it is meant to specify the driver's side. Conversely, the right side of the vehicle means the passenger's side. Second, most screws and bolts are removed by turning counterclockwise, and tightened by turning clockwise.

Safety is always the most important rule. Constantly be aware of the dangers involved in working on an automobile and take the proper precautions. See the information in this section regarding SERVICING YOUR VEHICLE SAFELY and the SAFETY NOTICE on the acknowledgment page.

Avoiding the Most Common Mistakes

Pay attention to the instructions provided. There are 3 common mistakes in mechanical work:

1. Incorrect order of assembly, disassembly or adjustment. When taking something apart or putting it together, performing steps in the wrong order usually just costs you extra time; however, it CAN break something. Read the entire procedure before beginning disassembly. Perform everything in the order in which the instructions say you should, even if you can't immediately see a reason for it. When you're taking apart something that is very intricate, you might want to draw a picture of how it looks when assembled at one point in order to make sure you get everything back in its proper position. We will supply exploded views whenever possible. When making adjustments, perform them in the proper order; often, one adjustment affects another, and you cannot expect even satisfactory results unless each adjustment is made only when it cannot be changed by any other.
2. Overtorquing (or undertorquing). While it is more common for overtorquing to cause damage, undertorquing may allow a fastener to vibrate loose causing serious damage. Especially when dealing with aluminum parts, pay attention to torque specifications and utilize a torque wrench in assembly. If a torque figure is not available, remember that if you are using the right tool to perform the job, you will probably not have to strain yourself to get a fastener tight enough. The pitch of most threads

is so slight that the tension you put on the wrench will be multiplied many times in actual force on what you are tightening. A good example of how critical torque is can be seen in the case of spark plug installation, especially where you are putting the plug into an aluminum cylinder head. Too little torque can fail to crush the gasket, causing leakage of combustion gases and consequent overheating of the plug and engine parts. Too much torque can damage the threads or distort the plug, changing the spark gap.

There are many commercial products available for ensuring that fasteners won't come loose, even if they are not torqued just right (a very common brand is Loctite®). If you're worried about getting something together tight enough to hold, but loose enough to avoid mechanical damage during assembly, one of these products might offer substantial insurance. Before choosing a threadlocking compound, read the label on the package and make sure the product is compatible with the materials, fluids, etc. involved.

3. Crossthreading. This occurs when a part such as a bolt is screwed into a nut or casting at the wrong angle and forced. Crossthreading is more likely to occur if access is difficult. It helps to clean and lubricate fasteners, then to start threading with the part to be installed positioned straight in. Then, start the bolt, spark plug, etc. with your fingers. If you encounter resistance, unscrew the part and start over again at a different angle until it can be inserted and turned several times without much effort. Keep in mind that many parts, especially spark plugs, have tapered threads, so that gentle turning will automatically bring the part you're threading to the proper angle, but only if you don't force it or resist a change in angle. Don't put a wrench on the part until it's been tightened a couple of turns by hand. If you suddenly encounter resistance, and the part has not seated fully, don't force it. Pull it back out to make sure it's clean and threading properly.

Always take your time and be patient; once you have some experience, working on your vehicle may well become an enjoyable hobby.

TOOLS AND EQUIPMENT

See Figures 1, 2, 3, 4, 5, 6, 7, 8, 9, 10, 11, 12, 13 and 14

Naturally, without the proper tools and equipment it is impossible to properly service your vehicle. It would also be virtually impossible to catalog every tool that you would need to perform all of the operations in this book. Of course, It would be unwise for the amateur to rush out and buy an expensive set of tools on the theory that he/she may need one or more of them at some time.

The best approach is to proceed slowly, gathering a good quality set of those tools that are used most frequently. Don't be misled by the low cost of bargain tools. It is far better to spend a little more for better quality. Forged wrenches, 6 or 12-point sockets and fine tooth ratchets are by far preferable to their less expensive counterparts. As any good mechanic can tell you, there are few worse experiences than trying to work on a vehicle with bad tools. Your monetary savings will be far outweighed by frustration and mangled knuckles.

Begin accumulating those tools that are used most frequently: those associated with routine maintenance and tune-up. In addition to the normal assortment of screwdrivers and pliers, you should have the following tools:

- Wrenches/sockets and combination open end/box end wrenches in sizes from $^1/_8$–$^3/_4$ in. (8mm–19mm) depending on whether your vehicle uses standard or metric fasteners and a $^{13}/_{16}$ in. or $^5/_8$ in. spark plug socket (depending on plug type).

If possible, buy various length socket drive extensions. Universal-joint and wobble extensions can be extremely useful, but be careful when using them, as they can change the amount of torque applied to the socket.

- Jackstands for support.
- Oil filter wrench.
- Spout or funnel for pouring fluids.
- Grease gun for chassis lubrication (unless your vehicle is not equipped with any grease fittings — for details, please refer to information on Fluids and Lubricants found later in this section).
- Hydrometer for checking the battery (unless equipped with a sealed, maintenance-free battery).
- A container for draining oil and other fluids.
- Rags for wiping up the inevitable mess.

In addition to the above items there are several others that are not absolutely necessary, but handy to have around. These include Oil Dry® (or an equivalent oil absorbent gravel — such as cat litter) and the usual supply of lubricants, antifreeze and fluids, although these can be purchased as needed. This is a basic list for routine maintenance, but only your personal needs and desire can accurately determine your list of tools.

After performing a few projects on the vehicle, you'll be amazed at the other tools and non-tools on your workbench. Some useful household items are: a large turkey baster or siphon, empty coffee cans and ice trays (to store parts), ball of twine, electrical tape for wiring, small rolls of colored tape for tagging lines or hoses, markers and pens, a note pad, golf tees (for plugging vacuum lines), metal coat hangers or a roll of mechanics's wire (to hold things out of the way), dental pick or similar long, pointed probe, a strong magnet, and a small mirror (to see into recesses and under manifolds).

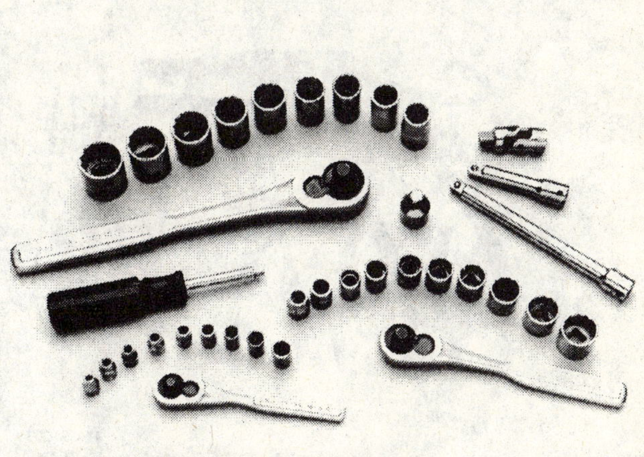

Fig. 1 All but the most basic procedures will require an assortment of ratchets and sockets

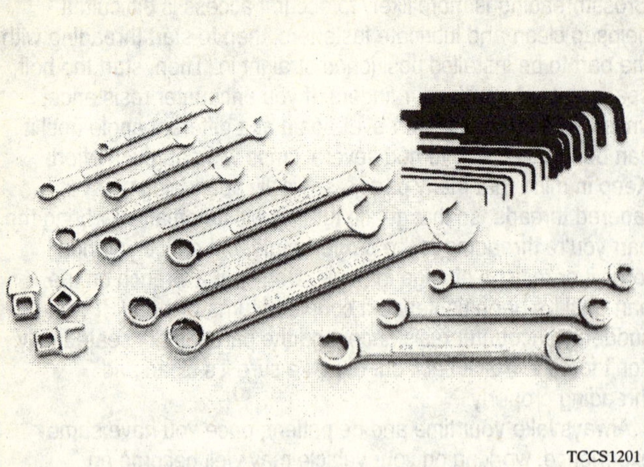

TCCS1201

Fig. 2 In addition to ratchets, a good set of wrenches and hex keys will be necessary

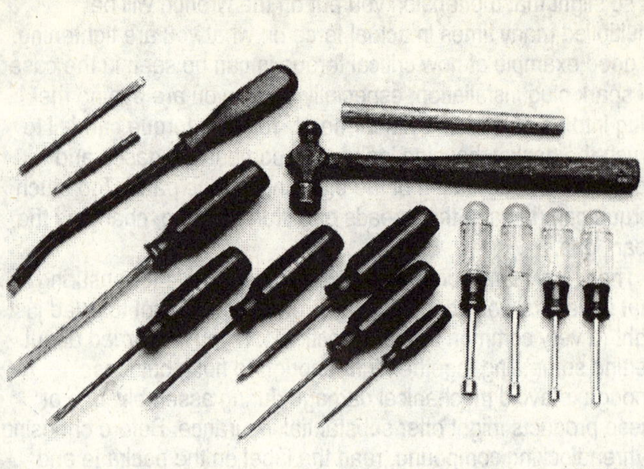

TCCS1204

Fig. 5 Various drivers, chisels and prybars are great tools to have in your toolbox

TCCS1202

Fig. 3 A hydraulic floor jack and a set of jackstands are essential for lifting and supporting the vehicle

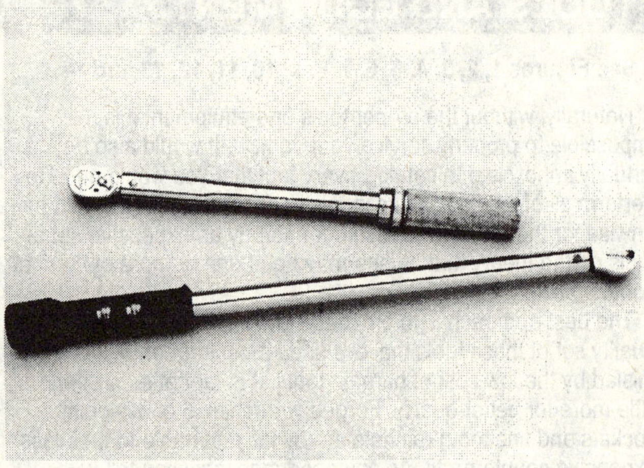

TCCS1205

Fig. 6 Many repairs will require the use of a torque wrench to assure the components are properly fastened

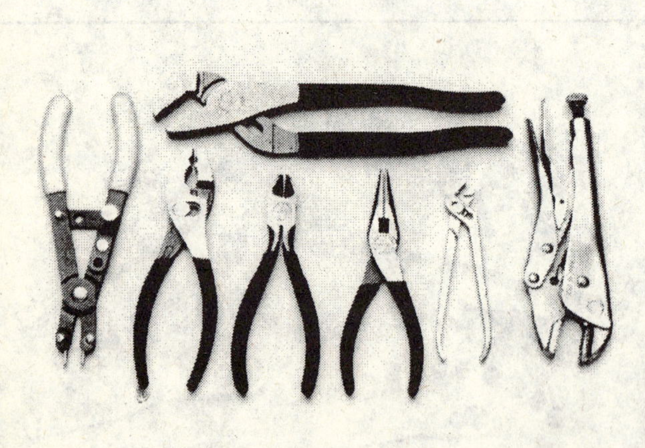

TCCS1203

Fig. 4 An assortment of pliers, grippers and cutters will be handy, especially for old rusted parts and stripped bolt heads

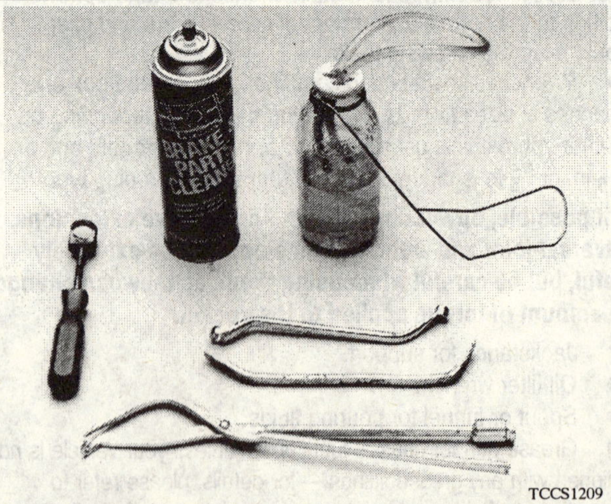

TCCS1209

Fig. 7 Although not always necessary, using specialized brake tools will save time

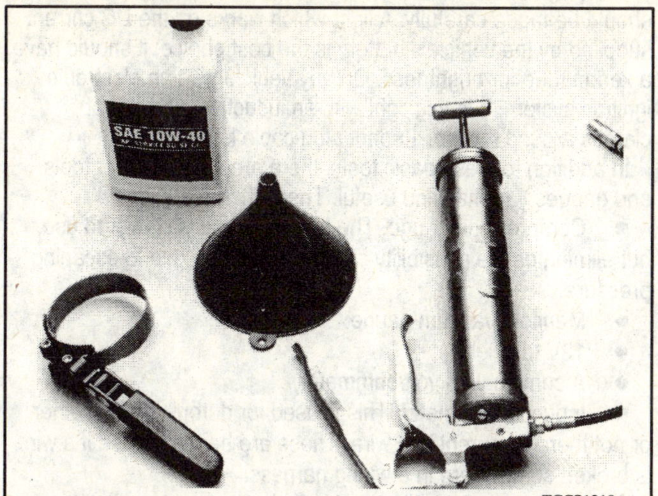

TCCS1210

Fig. 8 A few inexpensive lubrication tools will make maintenance easier

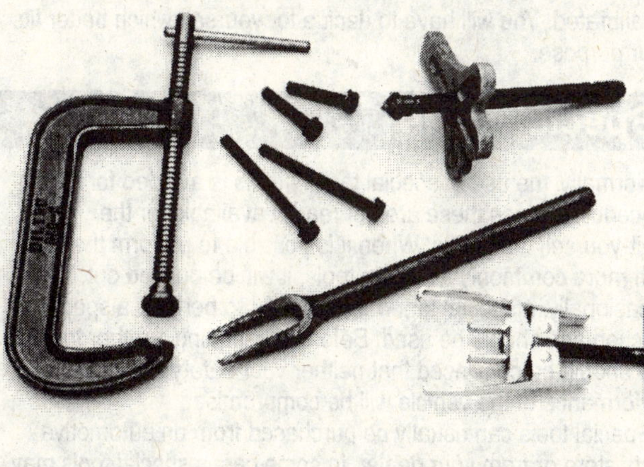

TCCS1211

Fig. 9 Various pullers, clamps and separator tools are needed for many larger, more complicated repairs

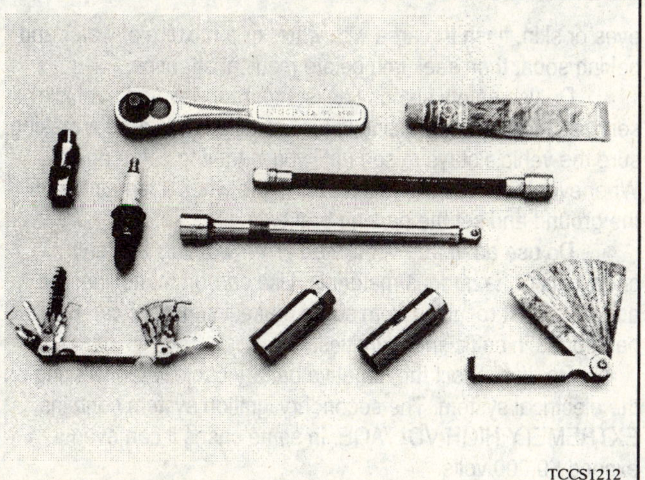

TCCS1212

Fig. 10 A variety of tools and gauges should be used for spark plug gapping and installation

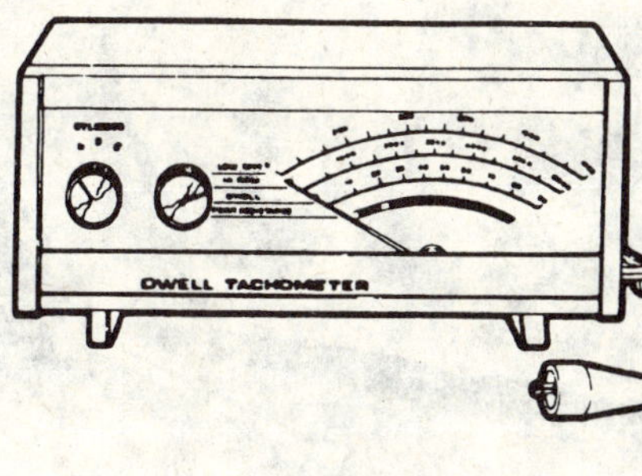

TCCS1001

Fig. 11 Dwell/tachometer unit (typical)

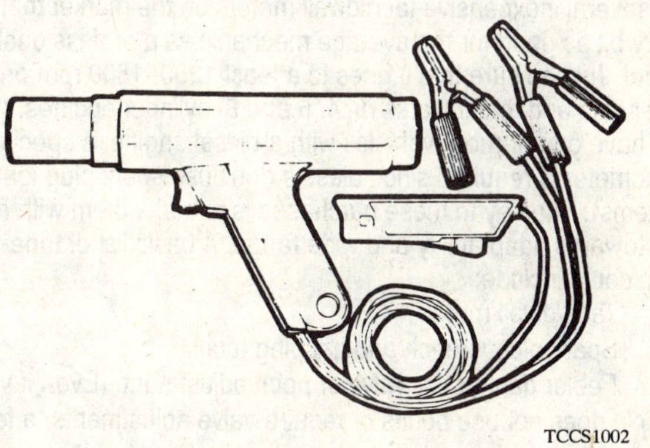

TCCS1002

Fig. 12 Inductive type timing light

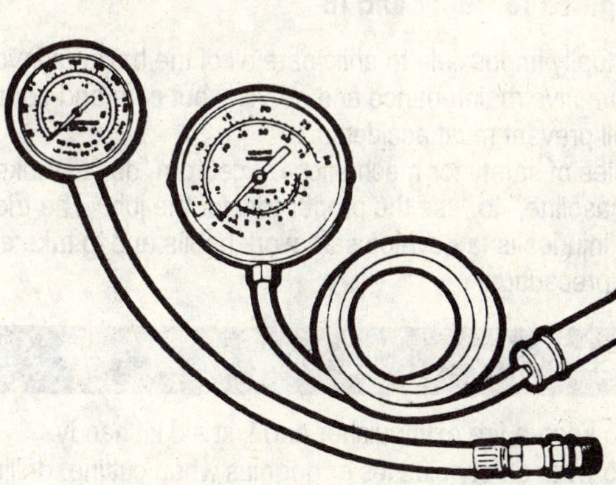

TCCS1003

Fig. 13 Compression gauge and a combination vacuum/fuel pressure test gauge

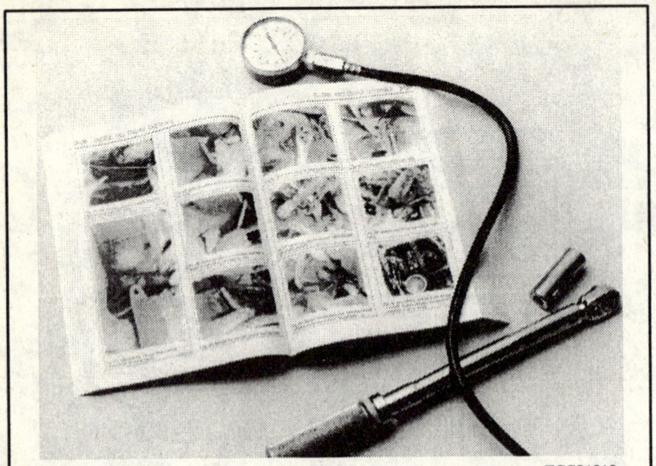
TCCS1213

Fig. 14 The most important tool you need to do the job is the proper information, so always have a Chilton Total Car Care manual handy

A more advanced set of tools, suitable for tune-up work, can be drawn up easily. While the tools are slightly more sophisticated, they need not be outrageously expensive. There are several inexpensive tach/dwell meters on the market that are every bit as good for the average mechanic as a professional model. Just be sure that it goes to a least 1200–1500 rpm on the tach scale and that it works on 4, 6 and 8-cylinder engines. (If you have one or more vehicles with a diesel engine, a special tachometer is required since diesels don't use spark plug ignition systems). The key to these purchases is to make them with an eye towards adaptability and wide range. A basic list of tune-up tools could include:

- Tach/dwell meter.
- Spark plug wrench and gapping tool.
- Feeler gauges for valve or point adjustment. (Even if your vehicle does not use points or require valve adjustments, a feeler gauge is helpful for many repair/overhaul procedures).

A tachometer/dwell meter will ensure accurate tune-up work on vehicles without electronic ignition. The choice of a timing light should be made carefully. A light which works on the DC current supplied by the vehicle's battery is the best choice; it should have a xenon tube for brightness. On any vehicle with an electronic ignition system, a timing light with an inductive pickup that clamps around the No. 1 spark plug cable is preferred.

In addition to these basic tools, there are several other tools and gauges you may find useful. These include:

- Compression gauge. The screw-in type is slower to use, but eliminates the possibility of a faulty reading due to escaping pressure.
- Manifold vacuum gauge.
- 12V test light.
- A combination volt/ohmmeter
- Induction Ammeter. This is used for determining whether or not there is current in a wire. These are handy for use if a wire is broken somewhere in a wiring harness.

As a final note, you will probably find a torque wrench necessary for all but the most basic work. The beam type models are perfectly adequate, although the newer click types (breakaway) are easier to use. The click type torque wrenches tend to be more expensive. Also keep in mind that all types of torque wrenches should be periodically checked and/or recalibrated. You will have to decide for yourself which better fits your purpose.

Special Tools

Normally, the use of special factory tools is avoided for repair procedures, since these are not readily available for the do-it-yourself mechanic. When it is possible to perform the job with more commonly available tools, it will be pointed out, but occasionally, a special tool was designed to perform a specific function and should be used. Before substituting another tool, you should be convinced that neither your safety nor the performance of the vehicle will be compromised.

Special tools can usually be purchased from an automotive parts store or from your dealer. In some cases special tools may be available directly from the tool manufacturer.

SERVICING YOUR VEHICLE SAFELY

See Figures 15, 16, 17 and 18

It is virtually impossible to anticipate all of the hazards involved with automotive maintenance and service, but care and common sense will prevent most accidents.

The rules of safety for mechanics range from "don't smoke around gasoline," to "use the proper tool for the job." The trick to avoiding injuries is to develop safe work habits and to take every possible precaution.

Do's

- Do keep a fire extinguisher and first aid kit handy.
- Do wear safety glasses or goggles when cutting, drilling, grinding or prying, even if you have 20-20 vision. If you wear glasses for the sake of vision, wear safety goggles over your regular glasses.
- Do shield your eyes whenever you work around the battery. Batteries contain sulfuric acid. In case of contact with the eyes or skin, flush the area with water or a mixture of water and baking soda, then seek immediate medical attention.
- Do use safety stands (jackstands) for any undervehicle service. Jacks are for raising vehicles; jackstands are for making sure the vehicle stays raised until you want it to come down. Whenever the vehicle is raised, block the wheels remaining on the ground and set the parking brake.
- Do use adequate ventilation when working with any chemicals or hazardous materials. Like carbon monoxide, the asbestos dust resulting from some brake lining wear can be hazardous in sufficient quantities.
- Do disconnect the negative battery cable when working on the electrical system. The secondary ignition system contains EXTREMELY HIGH VOLTAGE. In some cases it can even exceed 50,000 volts.
- Do follow manufacturer's directions whenever working with potentially hazardous materials. Most chemicals and fluids are poisonous if taken internally.

- Do properly maintain your tools. Loose hammerheads, mushroomed punches and chisels, frayed or poorly grounded electrical cords, excessively worn screwdrivers, spread wrenches (open end), cracked sockets, slipping ratchets, or faulty droplight sockets can cause accidents.
- Likewise, keep your tools clean; a greasy wrench can slip off a bolt head, ruining the bolt and often harming your knuckles in the process.
- Do use the proper size and type of tool for the job at hand. Do select a wrench or socket that fits the nut or bolt. The wrench or socket should sit straight, not cocked.
- Do, when possible, pull on a wrench handle rather than push on it, and adjust your stance to prevent a fall.
- Do be sure that adjustable wrenches are tightly closed on the nut or bolt and pulled so that the force is on the side of the fixed jaw.
- Do strike squarely with a hammer; avoid glancing blows.
- Do set the parking brake and block the drive wheels if the work requires a running engine.

Don'ts

- Don't run the engine in a garage or anywhere else without proper ventilation — EVER! Carbon monoxide is poisonous; it takes a long time to leave the human body and you can build up a deadly supply of it in your system by simply breathing in a little every day. You may not realize you are slowly poisoning yourself. Always use power vents, windows, fans and/or open the garage door.
- Don't work around moving parts while wearing loose clothing. Short sleeves are much safer than long, loose sleeves. Hard-toed shoes with neoprene soles protect your toes and give a better grip on slippery surfaces. Jewelry such as watches, fancy belt buckles, beads or body adornment of any kind is not safe working around a vehicle. Long hair should be tied back under a hat or cap.
- Don't use pockets for toolboxes. A fall or bump can drive a screwdriver deep into your body. Even a rag hanging from your back pocket can wrap around a spinning shaft or fan.
- Don't smoke when working around gasoline, cleaning solvent or other flammable material.
- Don't smoke when working around the battery. When the battery is being charged, it gives off explosive hydrogen gas.
- Don't use gasoline to wash your hands; there are excellent soaps available. Gasoline contains dangerous additives which can enter the body through a cut or through your pores. Gasoline also removes all the natural oils from the skin so that bone dry hands will suck up oil and grease.
- Don't service the air conditioning system unless you are equipped with the necessary tools and training. When liquid or compressed gas refrigerant is released to atmospheric pressure it will absorb heat from whatever it contacts. This will chill or freeze anything it touches. Although refrigerant is normally non-toxic, R-12 becomes a deadly poisonous gas in the presence of an open flame. One good whiff of the vapors from burning refrigerant can be fatal.
- Don't use screwdrivers for anything other than driving screws! A screwdriver used as an prying tool can snap when you least expect it, causing injuries. At the very least, you'll ruin a good screwdriver.
- Don't use a bumper or emergency jack (that little ratchet, scissors, or pantograph jack supplied with the vehicle) for anything other than changing a flat! These jacks are only intended for emergency use out on the road; they are NOT designed as a maintenance tool. If you are serious about maintaining your vehicle yourself, invest in a hydraulic floor jack of at least a $1^1/_2$ ton capacity, and at least two sturdy jackstands.

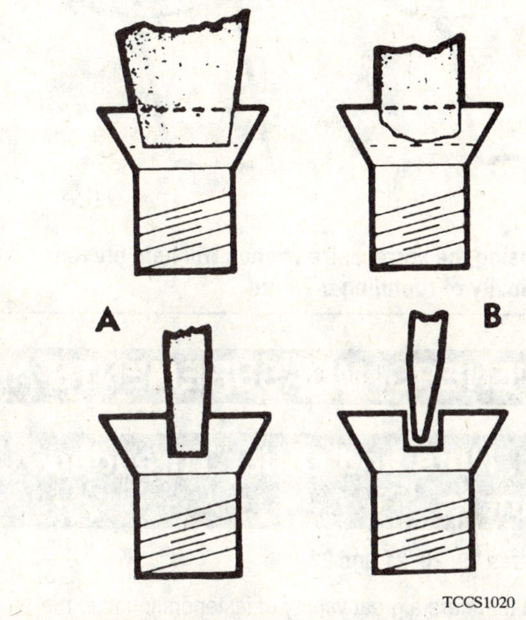

Fig. 15 Screwdrivers should be kept in good condition to prevent injury or damage which could result if the blade slips from the screw

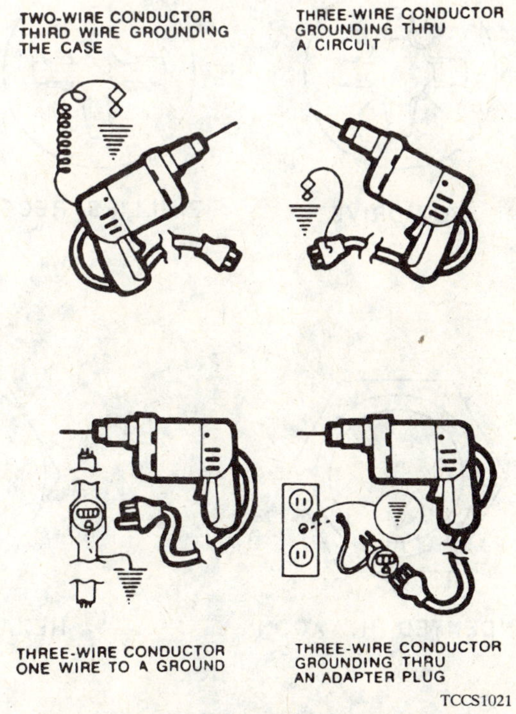

Fig. 16 Power tools should always be properly grounded

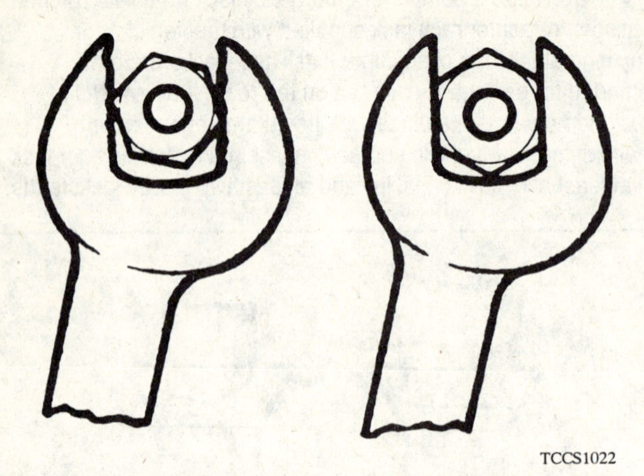

Fig. 17 Using the correct size wrench will help prevent the possibility of rounding-off a nut

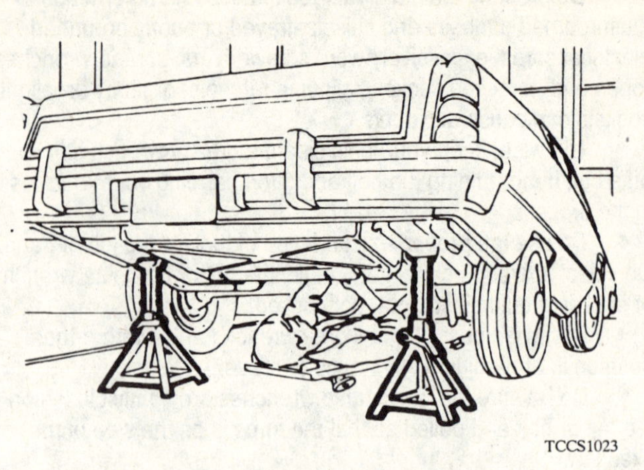

Fig. 18 NEVER work under a vehicle unless it is supported using safety stands (jackstands)

FASTENERS, MEASUREMENTS AND CONVERSIONS

Bolts, Nuts and Other Threaded Retainers

➧ See Figures 19, 20, 21 and 22

Although there are a great variety of fasteners found in the modern car or truck, the most commonly used retainer is the threaded fastener (nuts, bolts, screws, studs, etc). Most threaded retainers may be reused, provided that they are not damaged in use or during the repair. Some retainers (such as stretch bolts or torque prevailing nuts) are designed to deform when tightened or in use and should not be reinstalled.

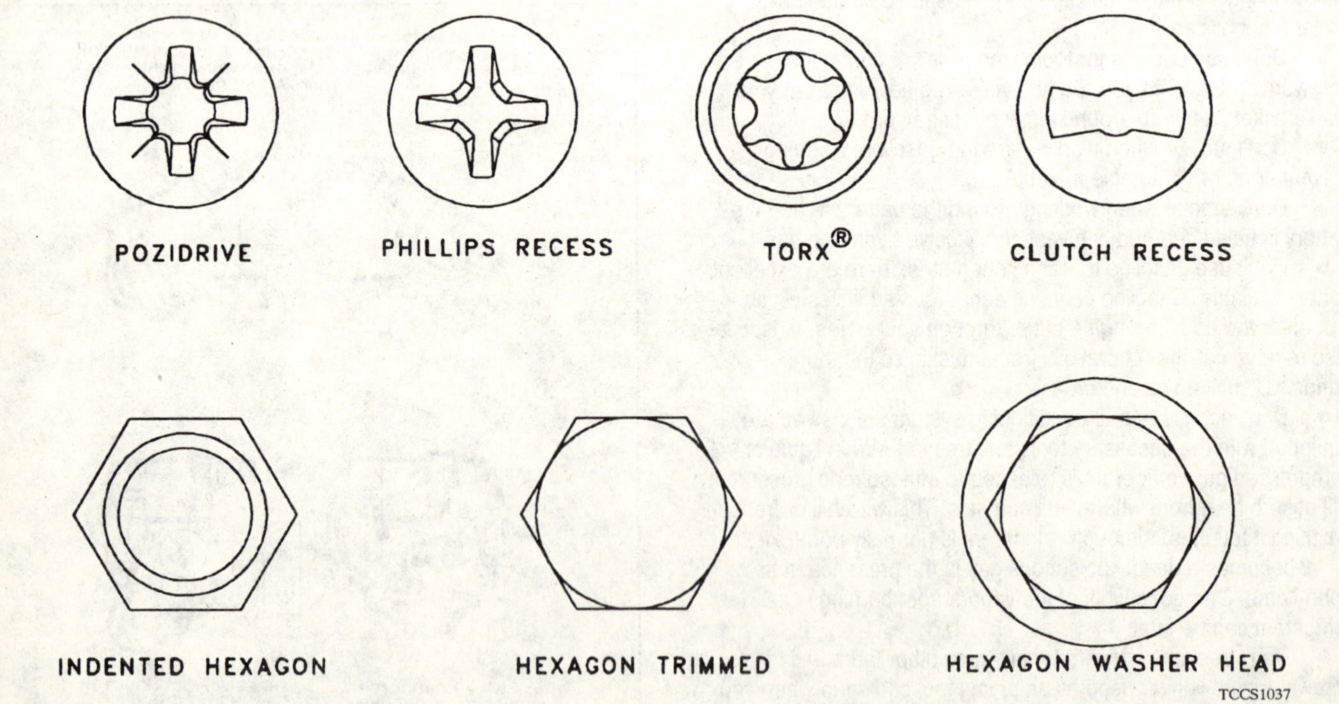

Fig. 19 Here are a few of the most common screw/bolt driver styles

Whenever possible, we will note any special retainers which should be replaced during a procedure. But you should always inspect the condition of a retainer when it is removed and replace any that show signs of damage. Check all threads for rust or corrosion which can increase the torque necessary to achieve the desired clamp load for which that fastener was originally selected. Additionally, be sure that the driver surface of the fastener has not been compromised by rounding or other damage. In some cases a driver surface may become only partially rounded, allowing the driver to catch in only one direction. In many of these occurrences, a fastener may be installed and tightened, but the driver would not be able to grip and loosen the fastener again. (This could lead to frustration down the line should that component ever need to be disassembled again).

If you must replace a fastener, whether due to design or damage, you must ALWAYS be sure to use the proper replacement. In all cases, a retainer of the same design, material and strength should be used. Markings on the heads of most bolts will help determine the proper strength of the fastener. The same material, thread and pitch must be selected to assure proper installation and safe operation of the vehicle afterwards.

Thread gauges are available to help measure a bolt or stud's thread. Most automotive and hardware stores keep gauges available to help you select the proper size. In a pinch, you can use another nut or bolt for a thread gauge. If the bolt you are replacing is not too badly damaged, you can select a match by finding another bolt which will thread in its place. If you find a nut which threads properly onto the damaged bolt, then use that nut to help select the replacement bolt. If however, the bolt you are replacing is so badly damaged (broken or drilled out) that its threads cannot be used as a gauge, you might start by looking for another bolt (from the same assembly or a similar location on your vehicle) which will thread into the damaged bolt's mounting. If so, the other bolt can be used to select a nut; the nut can then be used to select the replacement bolt.

In all cases, be absolutely sure you have selected the proper replacement. Don't be shy, you can always ask the store clerk for help.

****WARNING**

Be aware that when you find a bolt with damaged threads, you may also find the nut or drilled hole it was threaded into has also been damaged. If this is the case, you may have to drill and tap the hole, replace the nut or otherwise repair the threads. NEVER try to force a replacement bolt to fit into the damaged threads.

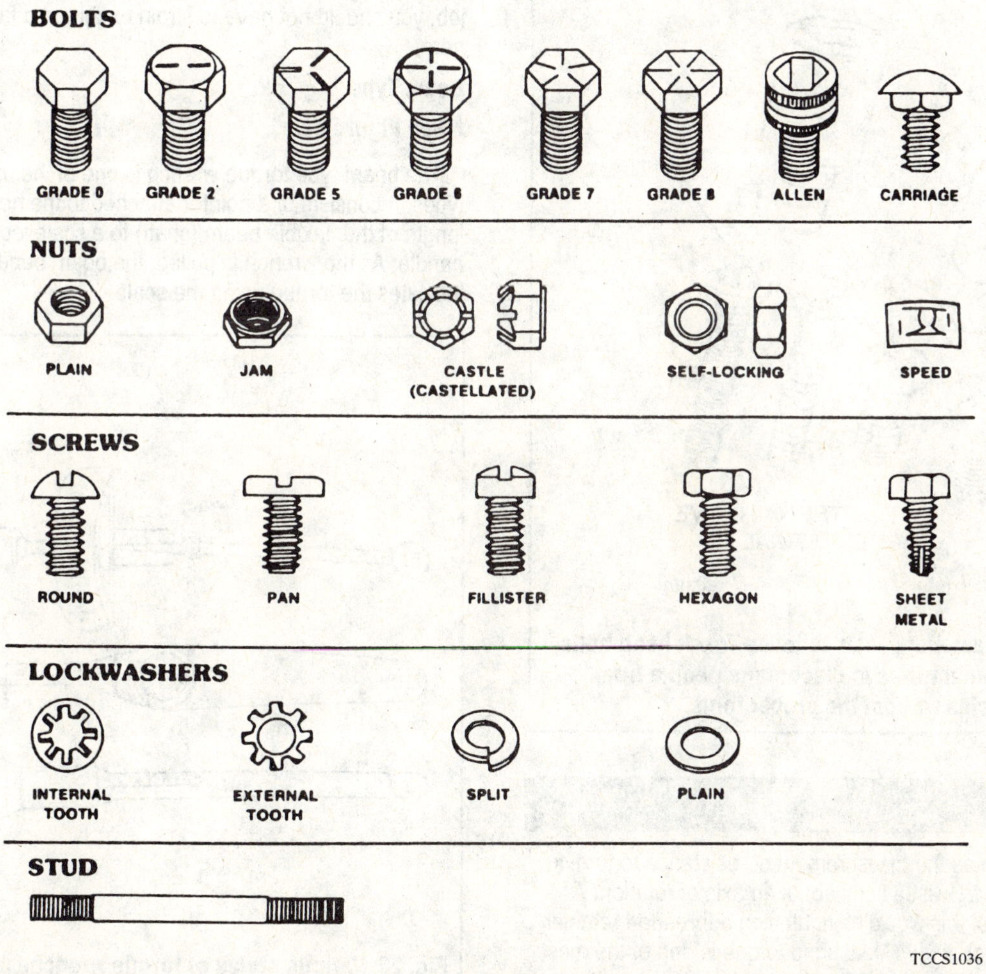

Fig. 20 There are many different types of threaded retainers found on vehicles

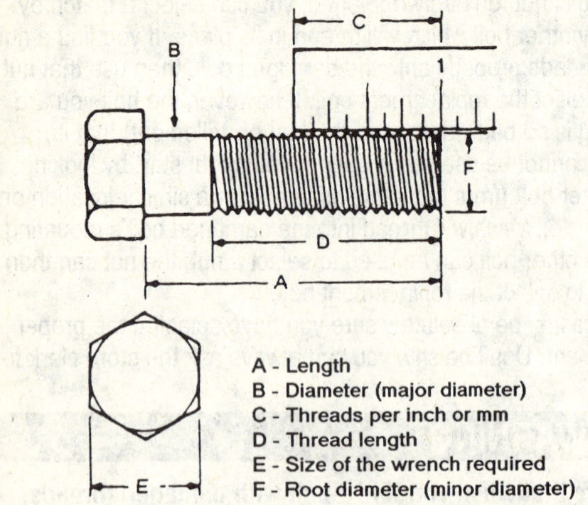

Fig. 21 Threaded retainer sizes are determined using these measurements

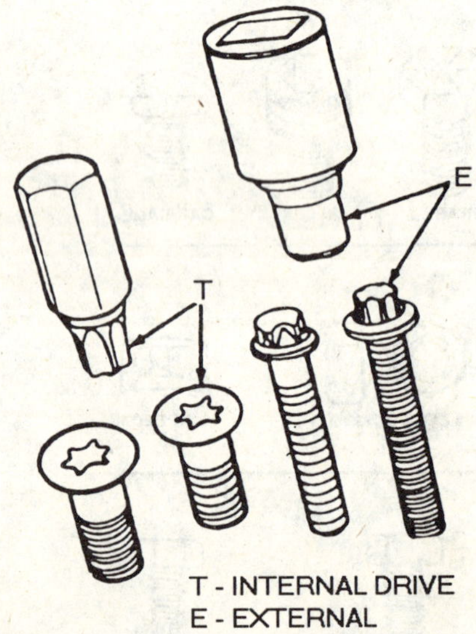

Fig. 22 Special fasteners such as these Torx® head bolts are used by manufacturers to discourage people from working on vehicles without the proper tools

Torque

Torque is defined as the measurement of resistance to turning or rotating. It tends to twist a body about an axis of rotation. A common example of this would be tightening a threaded retainer such as a nut, bolt or screw. Measuring torque is one of the most common ways to help assure that a threaded retainer has been properly fastened.

When tightening a threaded fastener, torque is applied in three distinct areas, the head, the bearing surface and the clamp load. About 50 percent of the measured torque is used in overcoming bearing friction. This is the friction between the bearing surface of the bolt head, screw head or nut face and the base material or washer (the surface on which the fastener is rotating). Approximately 40 percent of the applied torque is used in overcoming thread friction. This leaves only about 10 percent of the applied torque to develop a useful clamp load (the force which holds a joint together). This means that friction can account for as much as 90 percent of the applied torque on a fastener.

TORQUE WRENCHES

See Figure 23

In most applications, a torque wrench can be used to assure proper installation of a fastener. Torque wrenches come in various designs and most automotive supply stores will carry a variety to suit your needs. A torque wrench should be used any time we supply a specific torque value for a fastener. A torque wrench can also be used if you are following the general guidelines in the accompanying charts. Keep in mind that because there is no worldwide standardization of fasteners, the charts are a general guideline and should be used with caution. Again, the general rule of""if you are using the right tool for the job, you should not have to strain to tighten a fastener" applies here.

Beam Type

See Figure 24

The beam type torque wrench is one of the most popular types. It consists of a pointer attached to the head that runs the length of the flexible beam (shaft) to a scale located near the handle. As the wrench is pulled, the beam bends and the pointer indicates the torque using the scale.

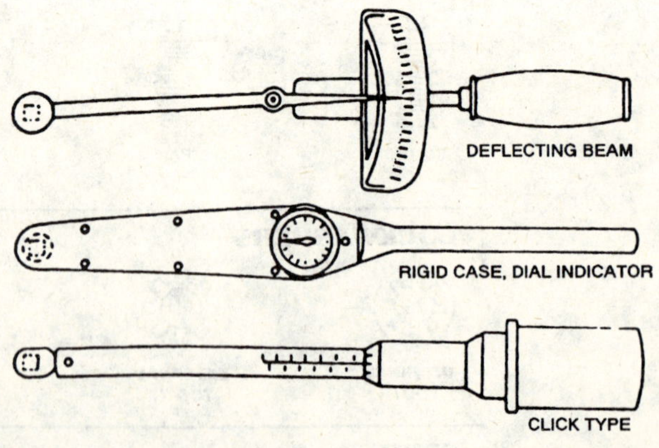

Fig. 23 Various styles of torque wrenches are usually available at your local automotive supply store

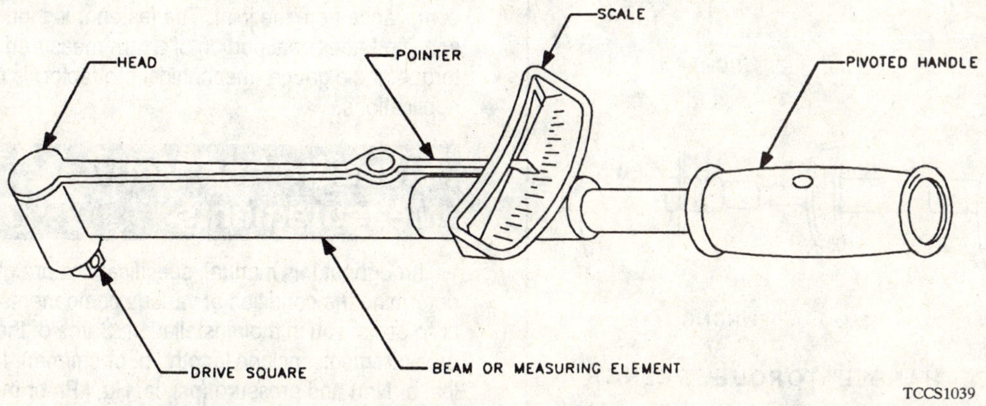

Fig. 24 Example of a beam type torque wrench

Click (Breakaway) Type

➧ **See Figure 25**

Another popular design of torque wrench is the click type. To use the click type wrench you pre-adjust it to a torque setting. Once the torque is reached, the wrench has a reflex signalling feature that causes a momentary breakaway of the torque wrench body, sending an impulse to the operator's hand.

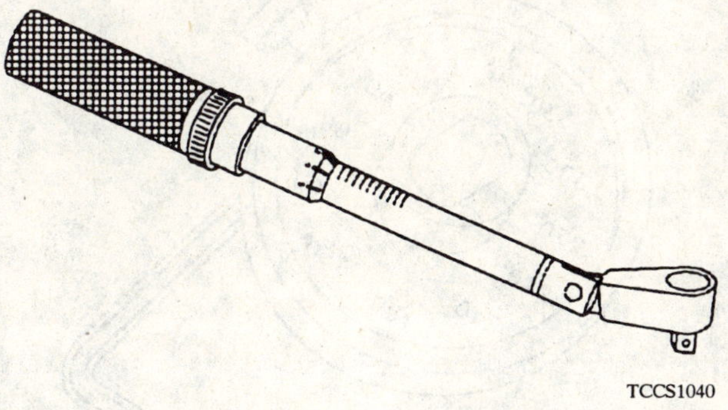

Fig. 25 A click type or breakaway torque wrench — note this one has a pivoting head

Pivot Head Type

➧ **See Figures 25 and 26**

Some torque wrenches (usually of the click type) may be equipped with a pivot head which can allow it to be used in areas of limited access. BUT, it must be used properly. To hold a pivot head wrench, grasp the handle lightly, and as you pull on the handle, it should be floated on the pivot point. If the handle comes in contact with the yoke extension during the process of pulling, there is a very good chance the torque readings will be inaccurate because this could alter the wrench loading point. The design of the handle is usually such as to make it inconvenient to deliberately misuse the wrench.

➥ **It should be mentioned that the use of any U-joint, wobble or extension will have an effect on the torque readings, no matter what type of wrench you are using. For the most accurate readings, install the socket directly on the wrench driver. If necessary, straight extensions (which hold a socket directly under the wrench driver) will have the least effect on the torque reading. Avoid any extension that alters the length of the wrench from the handle to the head/driving point (such as a crow's foot). U-joint or Wobble extensions can greatly affect the readings; avoid their use at all times.**

Rigid Case (Direct Reading)

➧ **See Figure 27**

A rigid case or direct reading torque wrench is equipped with a dial indicator to show torque values. One advantage of these wrenches is that they can be held at any position on the wrench without affecting accuracy. These wrenches are often preferred because they tend to be compact, easy to read and have a great degree of accuracy.

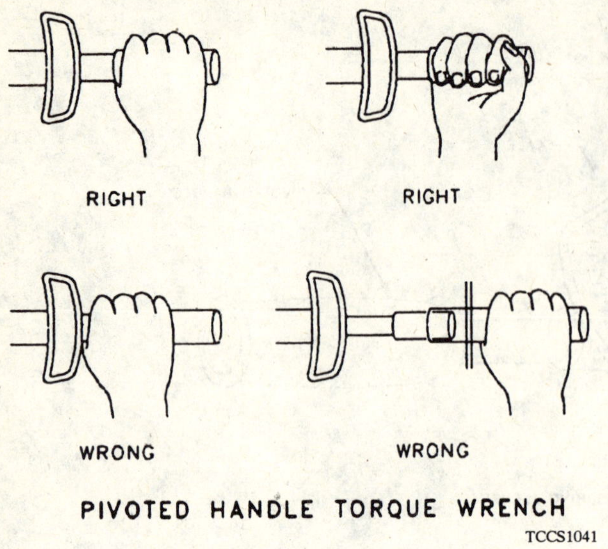

Fig. 26 Torque wrenches with pivoting heads must be grasped and used properly to prevent an incorrect reading

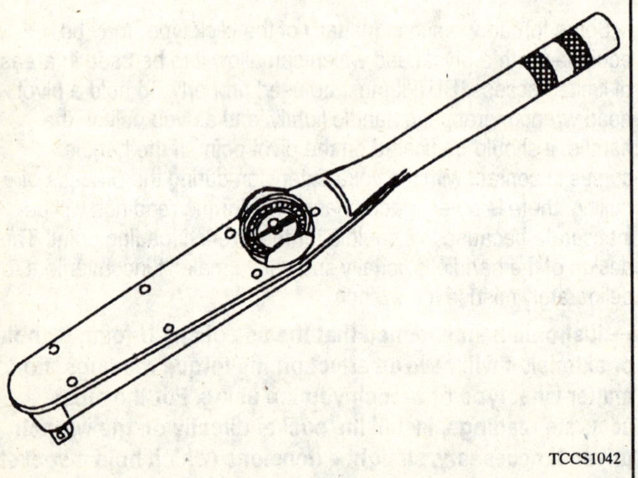

Fig. 27 The rigid case (direct reading) torque wrench uses a dial indicator to show torque

TORQUE ANGLE METERS

➧ See Figure 28

Because the frictional characteristics of each fastener or threaded hole will vary, clamp loads which are based strictly on torque will vary as well. In most applications, this variance is not significant enough to cause worry. But, in certain applications, a manufacturer's engineers may determine that more precise clamp loads are necessary (such is the case with many aluminum cylinder heads). In these cases, a torque angle method of installation would be specified. When installing fasteners which are torque angle tightened, a predetermined seating torque and standard torque wrench are usually used first to remove any compliance from the joint. The fastener is then tightened the specified additional portion of a turn measured in degrees. A torque angle gauge (mechanical protractor) is used for these applications.

Standard and Metric Measurements

Throughout this manual, specifications are given to help you determine the condition of various components on your vehicle, or to assist you in their installation. Some of the most common measurements include length (in. or cm/mm), torque (ft. lbs., inch lbs. or Nm) and pressure (psi, in. Hg, kPa or mm Hg). In most cases, we strive to provide the proper measurement as determined by the manufacturer's engineers.

Though, in some cases, that value may not be conveniently measured with what is available in your toolbox. Luckily, many of the measuring devices which are available today will have two scales so the Standard or Metric measurements may easily be taken. If any of the various measuring tools which are available to you do not contain the same scale as listed in the specifications, use the accompanying conversion factors to determine the proper value.

The conversion factor chart is used by taking the given specification and multiplying it by the necessary conversion factor. For instance, looking at the first line, if you have a measurement in inches such as""free-play should be 2 in." but your ruler reads only in millimeters, multiply 2 in. by the conversion factor of 25.4 to get the metric equivalent of 50.8mm. Likewise, if the specification was given only in a Metric measurement, for example in Newton Meters (Nm), then look at the center column first. If the measurement is 100 Nm, multiply it by the conversion factor of 0.738 to get 73.8 ft. lbs.

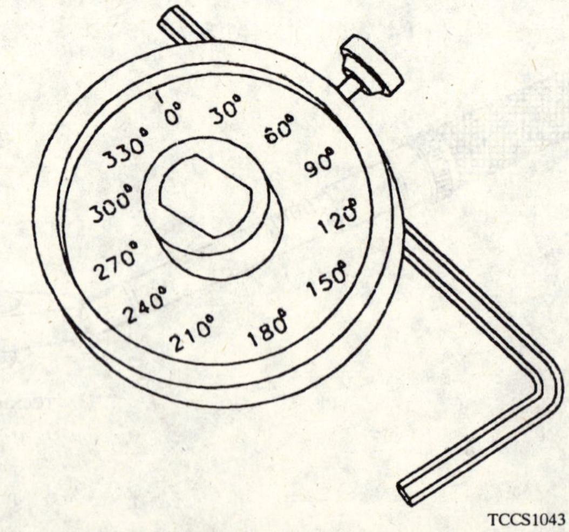

Fig. 28 Some specifications require the use of a torque angle meter (mechanical protractor)

CONVERSION FACTORS

LENGTH–DISTANCE

Inches (in.)	x 25.4	= Millimeters (mm)	x .0394	= Inches
Feet (ft.)	x .305	= Meters (m)	x 3.281	= Feet
Miles	x 1.609	= Kilometers (km)	x .0621	= Miles

VOLUME

Cubic Inches (in3)	x 16.387	= Cubic Centimeters	x .061	= in3
IMP Pints (IMP pt.)	x .568	= Liters (L)	x 1.76	= IMP pt.
IMP Quarts (IMP qt.)	x 1.137	= Liters (L)	x .88	= IMP qt.
IMP Gallons (IMP gal.)	x 4.546	= Liters (L)	x .22	= IMP gal.
IMP Quarts (IMP qt.)	x 1.201	= US Quarts (US qt.)	x .833	= IMP qt.
IMP Gallons (IMP gal.)	x 1.201	= US Gallons (US gal.)	x .833	= IMP gal.
Fl. Ounces	x 29.573	= Milliliters	x .034	= Ounces
US Pints (US pt.)	x .473	= Liters (L)	x 2.113	= Pints
US Quarts (US qt.)	x .946	= Liters (L)	x 1.057	= Quarts
US Gallons (US gal.)	x 3.785	= Liters (L)	x .264	= Gallons

MASS–WEIGHT

Ounces (oz.)	x 28.35	= Grams (g)	x .035	= Ounces
Pounds (lb.)	x .454	= Kilograms (kg)	x 2.205	= Pounds

PRESSURE

Pounds Per Sq. In. (psi)	x 6.895	= Kilopascals (kPa)	x .145	= psi
Inches of Mercury (Hg)	x .4912	= psi	x 2.036	= Hg
Inches of Mercury (Hg)	x 3.377	= Kilopascals (kPa)	x .2961	= Hg
Inches of Water (H_2O)	x .07355	= Inches of Mercury	x 13.783	= H_2O
Inches of Water (H_2O)	x .03613	= psi	x 27.684	= H_2O
Inches of Water (H_2O)	x .248	= Kilopascals (kPa)	x 4.026	= H_2O

TORQUE

Pounds–Force Inches (in–lb)	x .113	= Newton Meters (N·m)	x 8.85	= in–lb
Pounds–Force Feet (ft–lb)	x 1.356	= Newton Meters (N·m)	x .738	= ft–lb

VELOCITY

Miles Per Hour (MPH)	x 1.609	= Kilometers Per Hour (KPH)	x .621	= MPH

POWER

Horsepower (Hp)	x .745	= Kilowatts	x 1.34	= Horsepower

FUEL CONSUMPTION*

Miles Per Gallon IMP (MPG)	x .354	= Kilometers Per Liter (Km/L)
Kilometers Per Liter (Km/L)	x 2.352	= IMP MPG
Miles Per Gallon US (MPG)	x .425	= Kilometers Per Liter (Km/L)
Kilometers Per Liter (Km/L)	x 2.352	= US MPG

*It is common to covert from miles per gallon (mpg) to liters/100 kilometers (1/100 km), where mpg (IMP) x 1/100 km = 282 and mpg (US) x 1/100 km = 235.

TEMPERATURE

Degree Fahrenheit (°F)	= (°C x 1.8) + 32
Degree Celsius (°C)	= (°F – 32) x .56

TCCS1044

SERIAL NUMBER IDENTIFICATION

Vehicle

➧ See Figure 29

The serial number contains seventeen or more digits or letters. The first three give the world manufacturer code. The fourth is the type of restraint system. The fifth will remain the letter P. The sixth and seventh are the car line, series and body type. The eighth is the engine type. The ninth is a check digit. The tenth is the model year. The eleventh is the assembly plant. The last 6 digits of the vehicle identification number indicates the consecutive unit number of each unit built at each assembly plant. The consecutive unit numbers begin as follows: 100 001 through 600 000: Ford division vehicles, 600 001 through 999 999: Lincoln/Mercury division vehicles.

There are two locations of the vehicle identification number. One is on the driver's door jam. This label also has many other codes; so be sure to specifically find the word VIN on the tag. The other location of the identification number is on the lower left driver's side dash. As you look through the windshield, there is a long thin tag with the VIN number stamped on it.

Vehicle Certification Label

➧ See Figures 30 and 31

This label is affixed on the left hand front door lock panel or door pillar. The upper half of the label contains the name of the manufacturer, month and year of the manufacture, Gross Vehicle Weight Rating (GVWR), Gross Axle Weight Rating (GAWR) and certification statement.

The vehicle certification label also contains a 17 character vehicle identification number. This number is used for warranty identification of the vehicle and indicates: manufacturer, type of restraint system, line, series, body type, engine, model year and consecutive unit number.

The remaining information on this label consists of the following vehicle identification codes: color and body type, vinyl roof, molding and interior trim. Additional codes indicate vehicle equipped with air conditioning, radio type, sun roof type (if so equipped), as well as axle, transmission, spring, district sales office and special order codes.

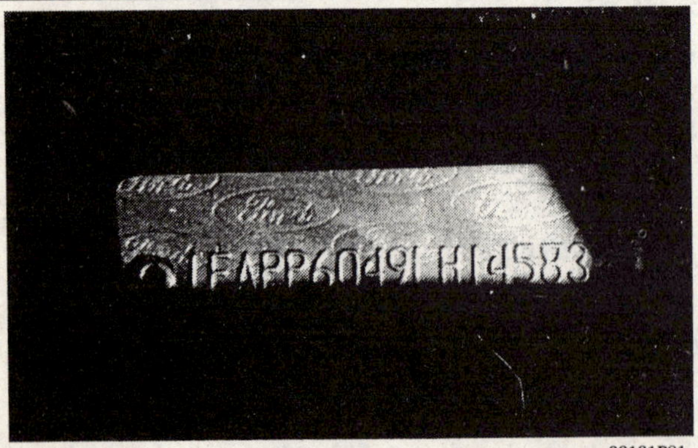

88181P01

Fig. 29 This 17 digit VIN is visible through the driver's side windshield

Engine

➧ See Figure 32

The engine identification number is located in the vehicle identification number. It will be the 8th digit of the serial number.

Transmission

➧ See Figures 33 and 34

The transmission identification tag is usually attached by the lower left extension attaching bolt or under the lower front intermediate servo cover bolt. The transmission identification code number is found on the bottom of the vehicle certification label. The transmission tag shows the model prefix and suffix, assembly part numbers, and build date code. The first line on the tag shows the transmission model prefix and suffix. A number appearing after the suffix indicates that internal parts have been changed after the initial production start up. For example, a PEE-FL model transmission that has been changed internally would read PEE-FL1. Both transmissions are basically the same, but some service parts in the PEE-FL1 transmission are slightly different than the PEE-FL transmission. Therefore, it is important that the codes on the transmission identification tag be checked when ordering parts or making inquires about the transmission.

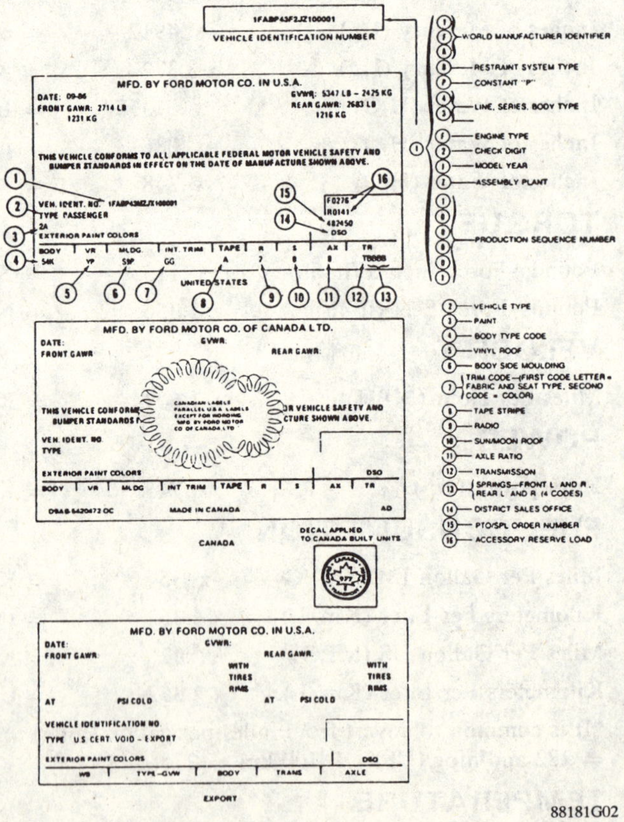

88181G02

Fig. 30 An example of the vehicle certification label — 1983–89 models

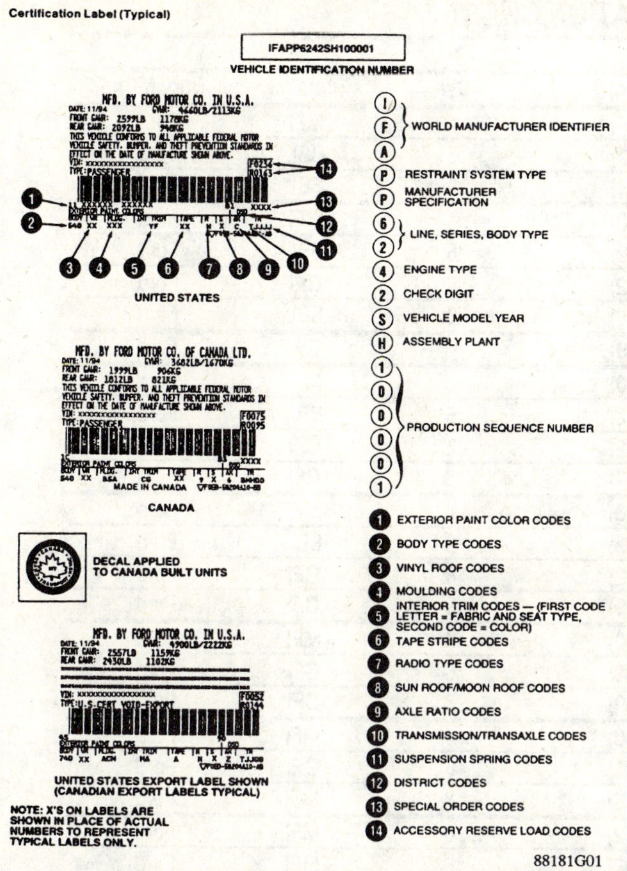

Fig. 31 An example of the vehicle certification label used on 1990–96 models

Drive Axle

➧ **See Figures 35 and 36**

The plant code on the axle identification tag is the official identifier. It is located under the cover-to-carrier bolt in the 12 o'clock position. The code for a particular axle assembly will not change as long as it never undergoes an external design change. If there is an internal change through the life of the axle, a suffix number will be added to the plant code.

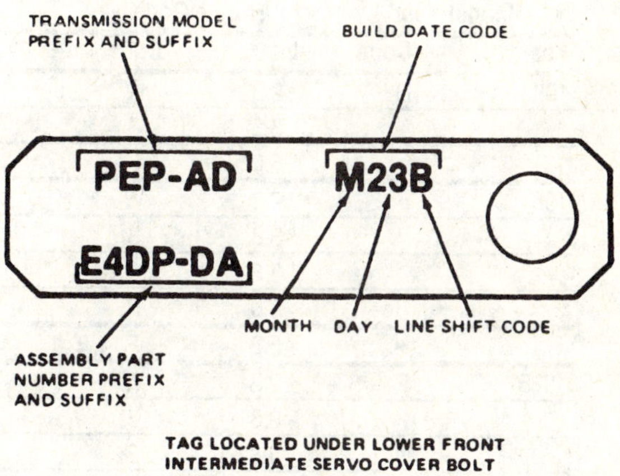

Fig. 33 Common transmission identification tag

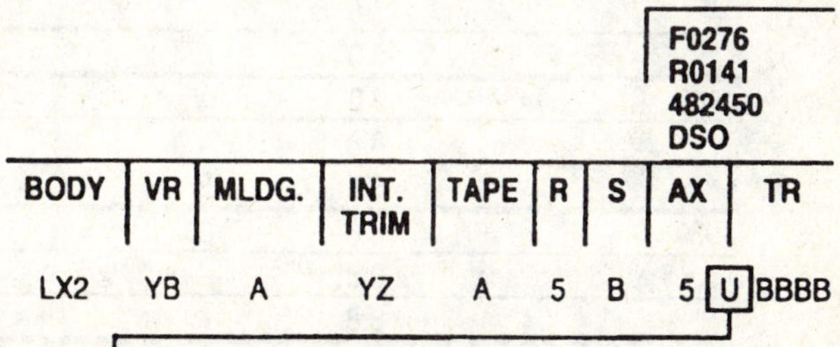

Code	Manual
2	5-Speed OD M5R2
	Automatic
U	4R70W

88181G04

Fig. 34 The transmission code on the certification label is identified by the digits located under the TR of the label

VIN POSITION 8

1FAPP62 [4] 2SH100001

VIN Code	Displacement		Cylinders	Fuel	Manufacturer
	Liter	CID			
4	3.8 SFI	232	V-6	Gasoline	Ford
R	3.8 SFI SC	232	V-6	Gasoline	Ford
W	4.6 SFI (2V)	281	V-8	Gasoline	Ford

88181G05

Fig. 32 The 8th digit of the VIN identifies the size and type of engine

VEHICLE IDENTIFICATION CHART

Model Year		Engine Code						
Year	Code	Liters	Code		Cu. In. (cc)	Cyl.	Fuel Sys.	Eng. Mfg.
1983	D	2.3	W	1	140 (2300)	4	MFI	Ford
		3.8	3		232 (3802)	6	BBL	Ford
		5.0	F		302 (4949)	8	BBL	Ford
1984	E	2.3	W	1	140 (2300)	4	MFI	Ford
		3.8	3		232 (3802)	6	BBL	Ford
		3.8	3		232 (3802)	6	CFI	Ford
		5.0	F		302 (4949)	8	BBL	Ford
		5.0	F		302 (4949)	8	CFI	Ford
1985	F	2.3	W	1	140 (2300)	4	MFI	Ford
		3.8	3		232 (3802)	6	BBL	Ford
		3.8	3		232 (3802)	6	CFI	Ford
		5.0	F		302 (4949)	8	CFI	Ford
1986	G	2.3	W	1	140 (2300)	4	MFI	Ford
		3.8	3		232 (3802)	6	BBL	Ford
		3.8	3		232 (3802)	6	CFI	Ford
		5.0	F		302 (4949)	8	CFI	Ford
1987	H	2.3	W	1	140 (2300)	4	MFI	Ford
		3.8	3		232 (3802)	6	CFI	Ford
		5.0	F		302 (4949)	8	CFI	Ford
1988	I	2.3	W	1	140 (2300)	4	MFI	Ford
		3.8	4		232 (3802)	6	CFI	Ford
		5.0	F		302 (4949)	8	MFI	Ford
1989	J	3.8	C		232 (3802)	6	MFI	Ford
		3.8	R	2	232 (3802)	6	MFI	Ford
		3.8	4		232 (3802)	6	SFI	Ford
1990	K	3.8	4		232 (3802)	6	SFI	Ford
		3.8	R	2	232 (3802)	6	MFI	Ford
1991	L	3.8	4		232 (3802)	6	SFI	Ford
		3.8	R	2	232 (3802)	6	MFI	Ford
		5.0	T		302 (4949)	8	MFI	Ford
1992	N	3.8	4		232 (3802)	6	SFI	Ford
		3.8	R	2	232 (3802)	6	SFI	Ford
		3.8	C	2	232 (3802)	6	SFI	Ford
		5.0	T		302 (4949)	8	MFI	Ford
1993	P	3.8	4		232 (3802)	6	SFI	Ford
		3.8	R	2	232 (3802)	6	SFI	Ford
		5.0	T		302 (4949)	8	MFI	Ford
1994	R	3.8	4		232 (3802)	6	SFI	Ford
		3.8	R	2	232 (3802)	6	SFI	Ford
		4.6	W	3	281 (4593)	8	SFI	Ford
1995	S	3.8	4		232 (3802)	6	SFI	Ford
		3.8	R	2	232 (3802)	6	SFI	Ford
		4.6	W	3	281 (4593)	8	SFI	Ford
1996	T	3.8	4		232 (3802)	6	SFI	Ford
		4.6	W	3	281 (4593)	8	SFI	Ford

BBL - Carburetor
CFI - Central fuel injection
MFI - Multipoint fuel injection
SFI - Sequential fuel injection
1 Turbo
2 Supercharged
3 (2V)-2 valve

88181C01

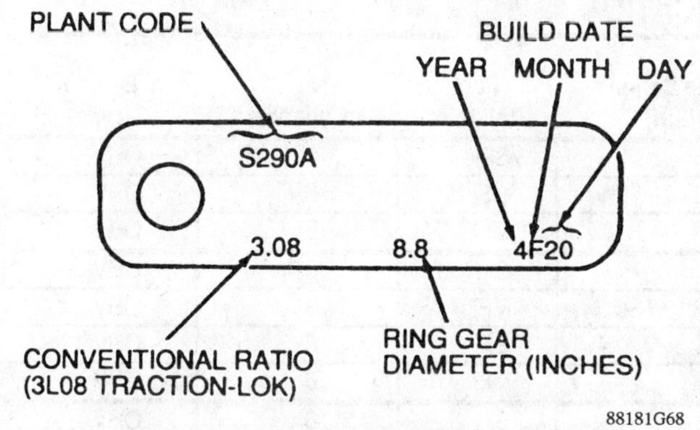

Fig. 35 The plant code is on a tag located on the cover-to-carrier bolt in the 12 o'clock position

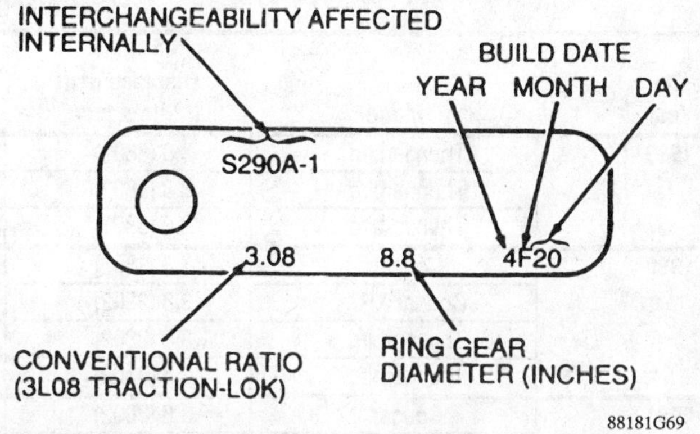

Fig. 36 A suffix is noted on the end of the plant code when an internal change is made to the axle

ENGINE IDENTIFICATION

Year	Model	Engine Displacement Liters (cc)	Engine Series (ID/VIN)	Fuel System	No. of Cylinders	Engine Type
1983	Cougar ①	2.3 (2300)	W	MFI	4	SOHC
	Cougar	3.8 (3802)	3	2BBL	6	OHV
	Cougar	5.0 (4949)	F	CFI	8	OHV
	Thunderbird ①	2.3 (2300)	W	MFI	4	SOHC
	Thunderbird	3.8 (3802)	3	2BBL	6	OHV
	Thunderbird	5.0 (4949)	F	CFI	8	OHV
1984	Cougar ①	2.3 (2300)	W	MFI	4	SOHC
	Cougar	3.8 (3802)	3	CFI	6	OHV
	Cougar	5.0 (4949)	F	CFI	8	OHV
	Thunderbird ①	2.3 (2300)	W	MFI	4	SOHC
	Thunderbird	3.8 (3802)	3	CFI	6	OHV
	Thunderbird	5.0 (4949)	F	CFI	8	OHV
1985	Cougar ①	2.3 (2300)	W	MFI	4	SOHC
	Cougar	3.8 (3802)	3	CFI	6	OHV
	Cougar	5.0 (4949)	F	CFI	8	OHV
	Thunderbird ①	2.3 (2300)	W	MFI	4	SOHC
	Thunderbird	3.8 (3802)	3	CFI	6	OHV
	Thunderbird	5.0 (4949)	F	CFI	8	OHV
1986	Cougar ①	2.3 (2300)	W	MFI	4	SOHC
	Cougar	3.8 (3802)	3	CFI	6	OHV
	Cougar	5.0 (4949)	F	CFI	8	OHV
	Thunderbird ①	2.3 (2300)	W	MFI	4	SOHC
	Thunderbird	3.8 (3802)	3	CFI	6	OHV
	Thunderbird	5.0 (4949)	F	CFI	8	OHV
1987	Cougar	3.8 (3802)	3	CFI	6	OHV
	Cougar	5.0 (4949)	F	CFI	8	OHV
	Thunderbird ①	2.3 (2300)	W	MFI	4	SOHC
	Thunderbird	3.8 (3802)	3	CFI	6	OHV
	Thunderbird	5.0 (4949)	F	CFI	8	OHV
1988	Cougar	3.8 (3802)	4	SFI	6	OHV
	Cougar	5.0 (4949)	F	MFI	8	OHV
	Thunderbird ①	2.3 (2300)	W	MFI	4	SOHC
	Thunderbird	3.8 (3802)	4	SFI	6	OHV
	Thunderbird	5.0 (4949)	F	MFI	8	OHV
1989	Cougar	3.8 (3802)	4	SFI	6	OHV
	Cougar ②	3.8 (3802)	C	MFI	6	OHV
	Cougar ②	3.8 (3802)	R	MFI	6	OHV

88181C03

ENGINE IDENTIFICATION

Year	Model	Engine Displacement Liters (cc)	Engine Series (ID/VIN)	Fuel System	No. of Cylinders	Engine Type
1989	Thunderbird	3.8 (3802)	4	SFI	6	OHV
	Thunderbird ②	3.8 (3802)	C	MFI	6	OHV
	Thunderbird ②	3.8 (3802)	R	MFI	6	OHV
1990	Cougar	3.8 (3802)	4	SFI	6	OHV
	Cougar XR7	3.8 (3802)	R	MFI	6	OHV
	Thunderbird	3.8 (3802)	4	SFI	6	OHV
	Thunderbird ②	3.8 (3802)	R	MFI	6	OHV
1991	Cougar	3.8 (3802)	4	SFI	6	OHV
	Cougar	5.0 (4943)	T	MFI	8	OHV
	Thunderbird	3.8 (3802)	4	SFI	6	OHV
	Thunderbird ②	3.8 (3802)	R	MFI	6	OHV
	Thunderbird	5.0 (4943)	T	MFI	8	OHV
1992	Cougar	3.8 (3802)	4	SFI	6	OHV
	Cougar	5.0 (4943)	T	MFI	8	OHV
	Thunderbird	3.8 (3802)	4	SFI	6	OHV
	Thunderbird ②	3.8 (3802)	C	SFI	6	OHV
	Thunderbird ②	3.8 (3802)	R	SFI	6	OHV
	Thunderbird	5.0 (4943)	T	MFI	8	OHV
1993	Cougar	3.8 (3802)	4	SFI	6	OHV
	Cougar	5.0 (4943)	T	MFI	8	OHV
	Thunderbird	3.8 (3802)	4	SFI	6	OHV
	Thunderbird ②	3.8 (3802)	R	SFI	6	OHV
	Thunderbird	5.0 (4949)	T	MFI	8	OHV
1994	Cougar	3.8 (3802)	4	SFI	6	OHV
	Cougar	4.6 (4593)	W	SFI	8	SOHC
	Thunderbird	3.8 (3802)	4	SFI	6	OHV
	Thunderbird ②	3.8 (3802)	R	SFI	6	OHV
	Thunderbird	4.6 (4593)	W	SFI	8	SOHC
1995	Cougar	3.8 (3802)	4	SFI	6	OHV
	Cougar	4.5 (4593)	W	SFI	8	SOHC
	Thunderbird	3.8 (3802)	4	SFI	6	OHV
	Thunderbird ②	3.8 (3802)	R	SFI	6	OHV
	Thunderbird	4.6 (4593)	W	SFI	8	SOHC
1996	Cougar	3.8 (2802)	4	SFI	6	OHV
	Cougar	4.6 (4593)	W	SFI	8	SOHC
	Thunderbird	3.8 (3802)	4	SFI	6	OHV
	Thunderbird	4.6 (4593)	W	SFI	8	SOHC

Note: There are early models in 1992 with the Vin code of C

BBL - Barrel carburetor
MFI - Multiport fuel injection
SFI - Sequential fuel injection
CFI - Central fuel injection
SOHC - Single overhead camshaft
OHV - Overhead valve
1 : Turbo
2 : Supercharged

88181C04

TRANSMISSION IDENTIFICATION

Year	Identification Code	Transmission Type
1983	4	80ET 4-speed
	C	C-5
	T	AOD
1984	2	T50D 5-speed
	V	C-3
	C	C-5
	T	AOD
1985	2	T50D 5-speed
	V	C-3
	C	C-5
	T	AOD
1986	2	T50D 5-speed
	V	C-3
	C	C-5
	T	AOD
1987	2	T50D 5-speed
	C	C-5
	T	AOD
	L	A4LD
1988	2	T50D 5-speed
	T	AOD
	L	A4LD
1989	2	M5R2 5-speed OD
	T	AOD
1990	2	M5R2 5-speed OD
	T	AOD
1991	2	M5R2 5-speed OD
	T	AOD
1992	2	M5R2 5-speed OD
	T	AOD
1993	W	M4R2 5-speed OD
	T	AOD
1994	W	M4R2 5-speed OD
	L	4R70W
1995	2	M5R2 5-speed OD
	U	4R70W
1996	L	4R70W

88181C02

ROUTINE MAINTENANCE AND TUNE-UP

Proper maintenance and tune-up is the key to long and trouble-free vehicle life, and the work can yield its own rewards. Studies have shown that a properly tuned and maintained vehicle can achieve better gas mileage than an out-of-tune vehicle. As a conscientious owner and driver, set aside a Saturday morning, say once a month, to check or replace items which could cause major problems later. Keep your own personal log to jot down which services you performed, how much the parts cost you, the date, and the exact odometer reading at the time. Keep all receipts for such items as engine oil and filters, so that they may be referred to in case of related problems or to determine operating expenses. As a do-it-yourselfer, these receipts are the only proof you have that the required maintenance was performed. In the event of a warranty problem, these receipts will be invaluable.

The literature provided with your vehicle when it was originally delivered includes the factory recommended maintenance schedule. If you no longer have this literature, replacement copies are usually available from the dealer. A maintenance schedule is provided later in this section, in case you do not have the factory literature.

Air Cleaner Element

All engines are equipped with a dry type, replaceable air filter element. The element should be replaced at the recommended intervals shown on the Maintenance Chart in this section. If your vehicle is operated under severely dusty conditions or severe operating conditions, more frequent changes are necessary. Inspect the element at least twice a year. Early spring and at the beginning of fall are good times for the inspection.

REMOVAL & INSTALLATION

Carbureted Engines

➧ **See Figure 37**

1. Disconnect all hoses, ducts and vacuum tubes from the air cleaner assembly.
2. Remove the top cover wing nut and grommet (if equipped). Remove any side bracket mount retaining bolts (if equipped). Remove the air cleaner assembly from the top of the carburetor or intake assembly.
3. Remove the cover and the element, wipe clean all inside surfaces of the air cleaner housing and cover. Check the condition of the mounting gasket (cleaner base-to-carburetor). Replace the mounting gasket if it is worn or broken.
4. Check for holes in the filter. Check the cleaner housing for signs of dirt or dust that has leaked through the filter element. Place a light on the inside of the element and look through the filter at the light. If no glow of light can be seen through the element material, replace the filter. If holes in the filter are apparent or signs of dirt leakage through the filter are noticed, replace the filter.

To install:

5. Reposition the cleaner assembly, element and cover on the carburetor or intake assembly.
6. Reconnect all hoses, duct and vacuum hoses removed. Install the wing nut finger-tight.

Fuel Injected Engines

➧ **See Figures 38, 39, 40, 41, 42, 43 and 44**

1. Disconnect all hoses, ducts vacuum tubes and wiring from the air cleaner assembly.
2. On the early models, remove the top cover wing nut and grommet (if equipped), remove the cover.
3. On the later models, release the 2 hold-down clips from the cover and position the air cleaner lid aside.
4. Remove the air cleaner element, wipe clean all inside surfaces of the air cleaner housing and cover. Check the condition of the mounting gasket (if so equipped). Replace the mounting gasket if it is worn or broken.

To install:

5. Reposition the air cleaner assembly, element and cover.
6. Reconnect all hoses, duct, vacuum hoses and wiring that was removed. Install the wing nut finger-tight, if so equipped.

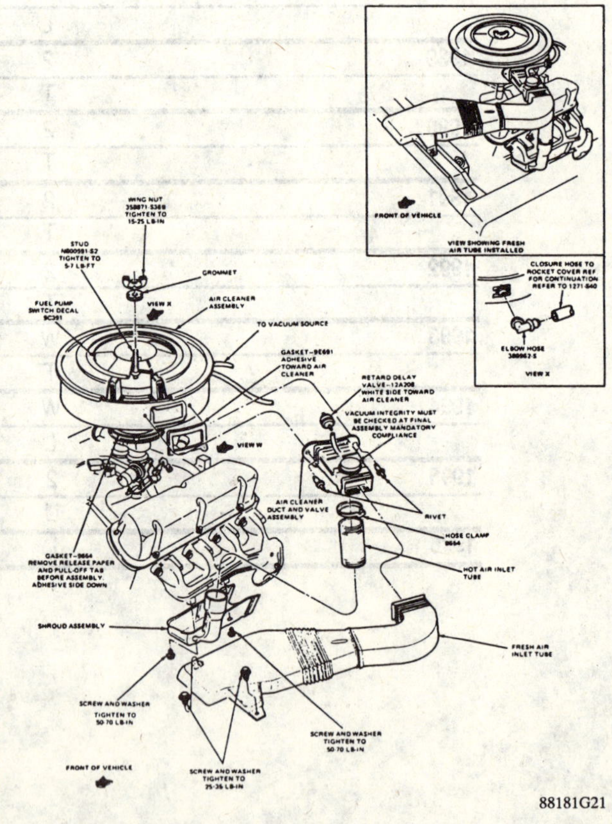

Fig. 37 Exploded view of the 1984–85 5.0L air cleaner assembly

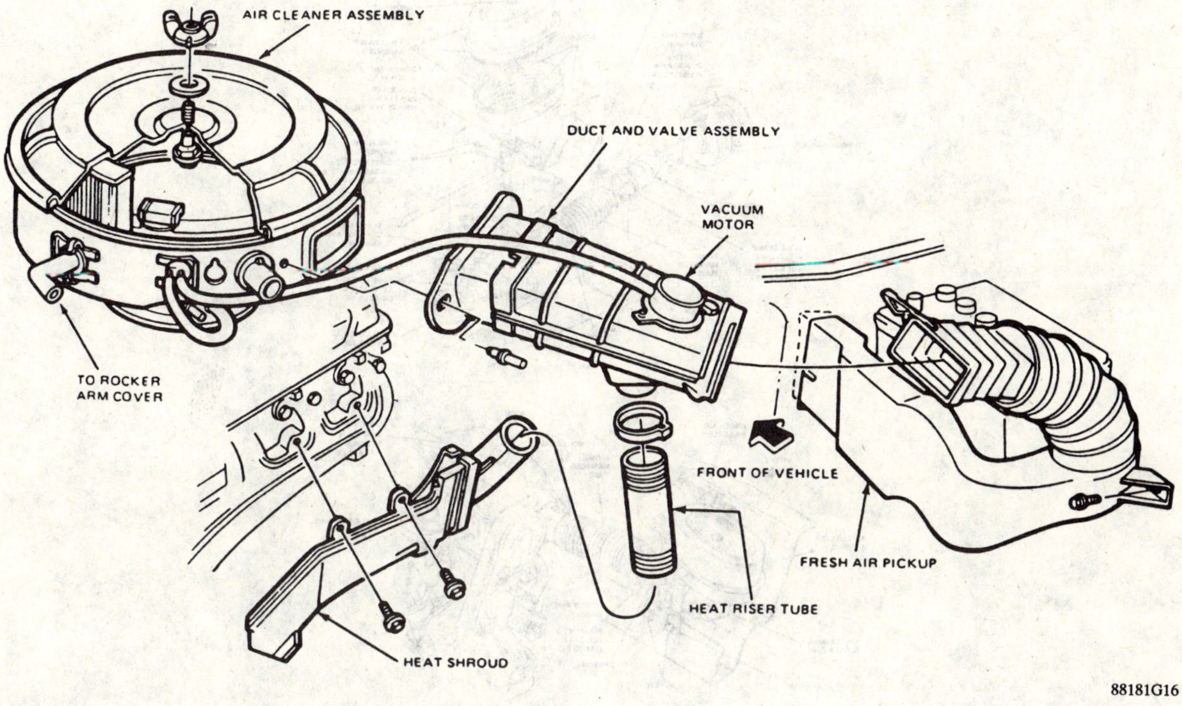

Fig. 38 Exploded view of the 1983 3.8L air cleaner assembly

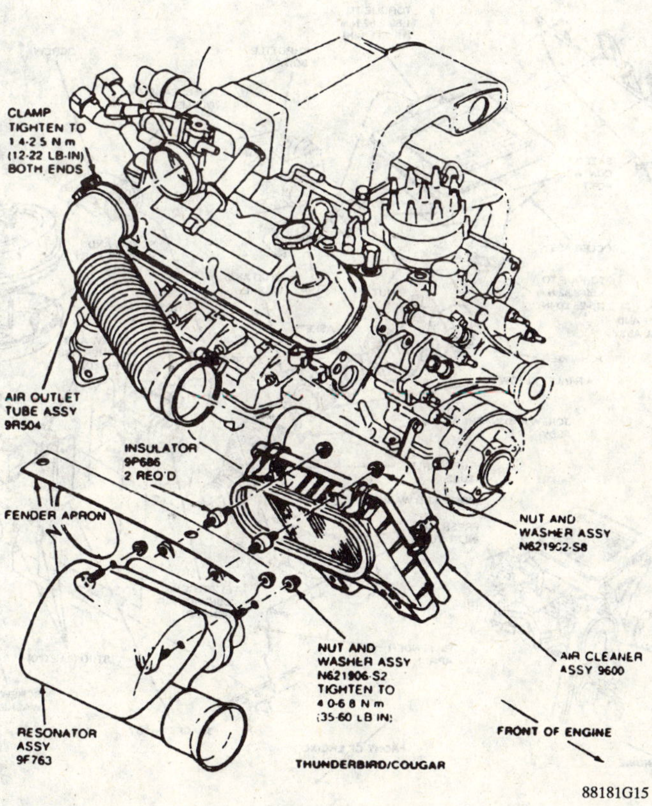

Fig. 39 Exploded view of the 1986–88 5.0L air cleaner assembly

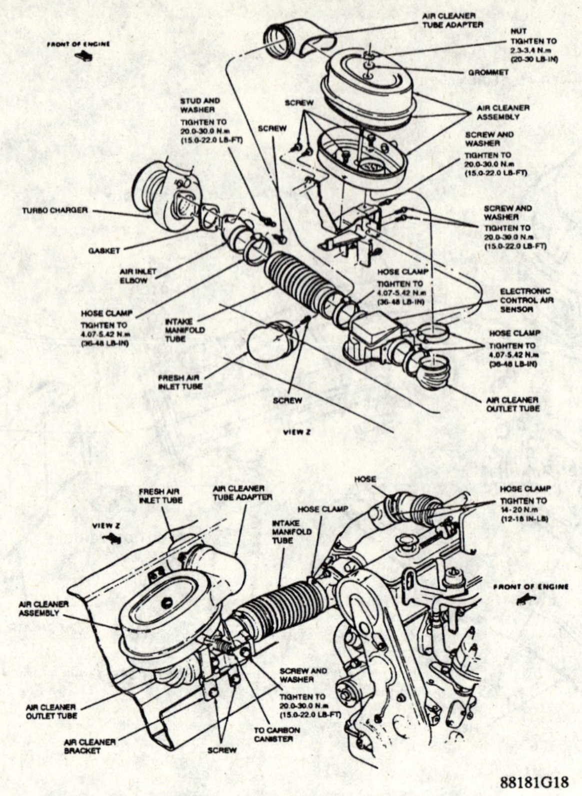

Fig. 40 Exploded view of the 1983–86 2.3L turbo air cleaner assembly

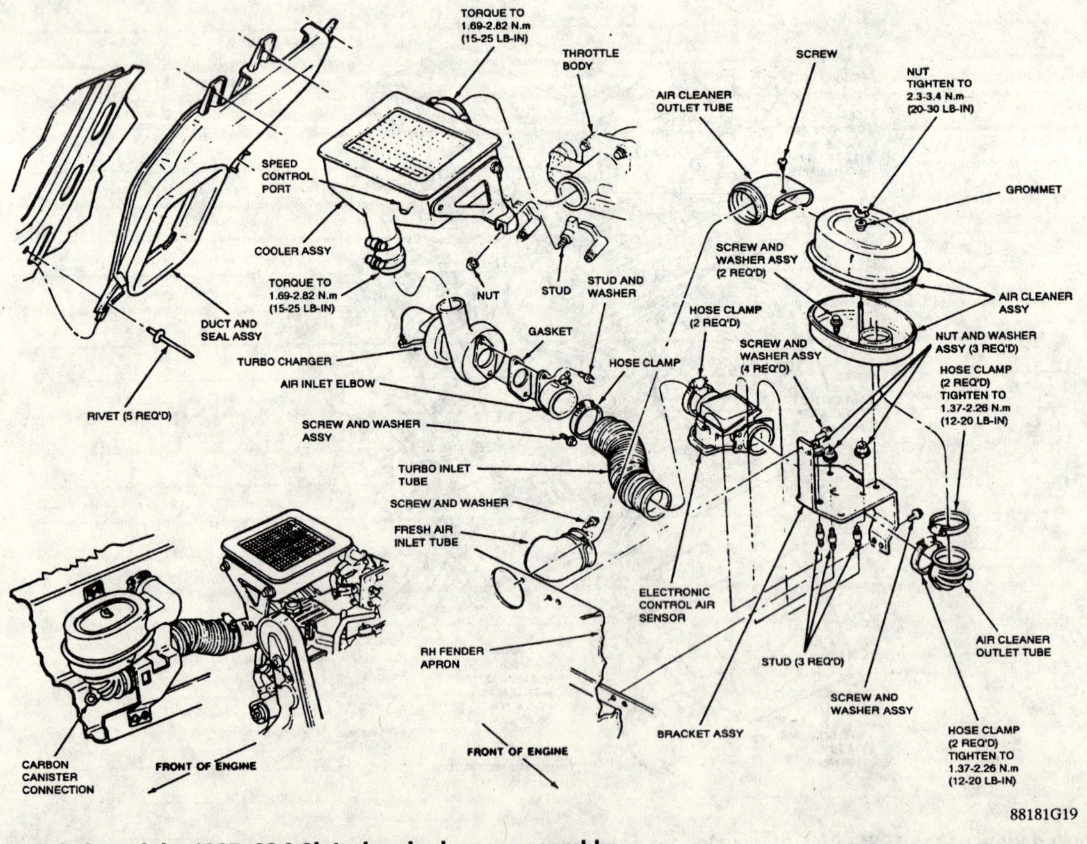

Fig. 41 Exploded view of the 1987–88 2.3L turbo air cleaner assembly

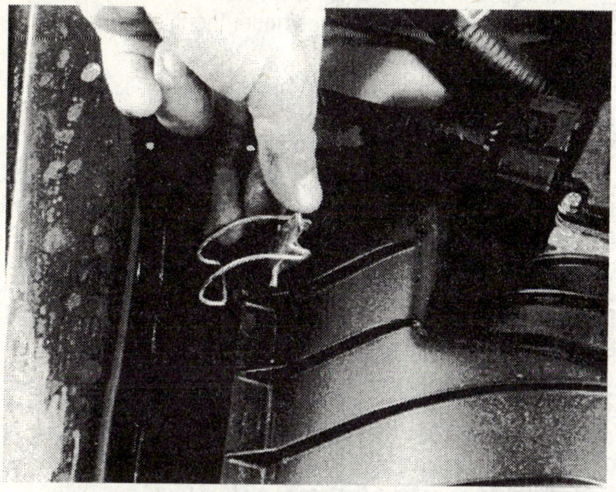

Fig. 42 Lift the clips up to release the lid

Fig. 43 Remove the lid and lift out the element

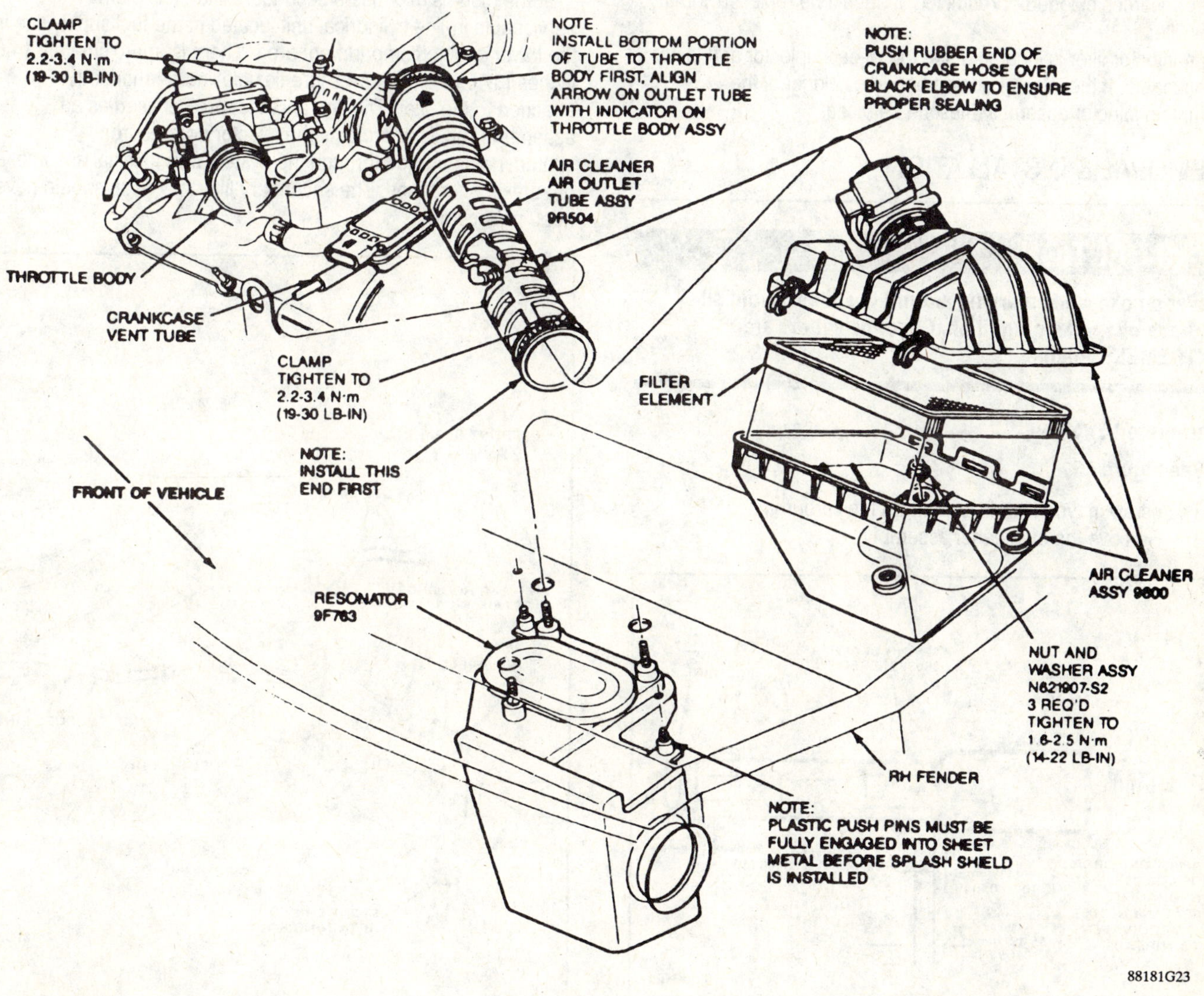

Fig. 44 Exploded view of the 3.8L supercharged air cleaner assembly

Fuel Filter

The fuel filter should be replaced, immediately, upon evidence of dirt in the fuel system. Regular replacement of the fuel filter should be every 30,000 miles (48,270 km). If the engine seems to be suffering from fuel starvation, remove the filter and blow through it to see if it is clogged. If air won't pass through the filter easily, or if dirt is visible in the inlet passage, replace the filter.

➝ A backup wrench is an open end wrench of the proper size used to hold a fuel filter or fitting in position while a fuel line is removed. A flared wrench is a special hex wrench with a narrow open end allowing the fuel line nut to be gripped tightly. A regular open end wrench may be substituted if used carefully so the fitting is not rounded.

The fuel filter on the carbureted models contains a screen to minimize the amount of contaminants entering the carburetor via the fuel system. The fuel filter is located in the carburetor.

The EFI model fuel filter provides extremely fine filtration to protect the small metering orifices of the injector nozzles. The filter is a one-piece construction which cannot be cleaned. If the filter becomes clogged or restricted, it should be replaced with a new filter.

An injector filter is located at the top of each injector and is not serviceable. If the injector screen becomes clogged, the complete injector assembly must be serviced.

REMOVAL & INSTALLATION

****CAUTION**

Never smoke when working around gasoline! Avoid all sources of sparks or ignition. Gasoline vapors are EXTREMELY volatile!

Carbureted Engines

➧ See Figure 45

The screw in type filter is located on the carburetor.

1. Remove the air cleaner assembly.
2. Remove the hose clamps and rubber connector hose.
3. Place some absorbent rags under the inlet fitting. Unscrew the filter from the carburetor.
4. Discard the filter and clamps.

To install:

5. Coat the threads of the new filter with non-hardening, gasoline-proof sealer and screw it into place by hand. Tighten it snugly with the wrench.
6. Install new fuel line and clamps.
7. Start the engine and check for leaks.

Fuel Injected Engines

➧ See Figures 46, 47, 48, 49, 50, 51 and 52

The filter used in these models is an in-line replaceable cartridge type. The filter has the capability of 50,000 miles (80,450 km) of maintenance free operation. Its function is to provide filtration to protect the small metering orifices of the injector nozzles. The filter is located downstream of the pump and is mounted on the chassis frame near the right rear wheel well. The filter and filter housing is protected by a metal stone shield.

Some models may use a secondary filter. It is a small serviceable in-line cylindrical unit located in the fuel supply line in the lower engine compartment area. There is approximately 14.5 inches (37 cm) of high pressure flexible line permanently attached to the filter. The line and filter are serviced as an assembly. This filter protects the injector nozzles from contaminates purged through the system during initial assembly or service operations. The secondary filter however, should never need replacement.

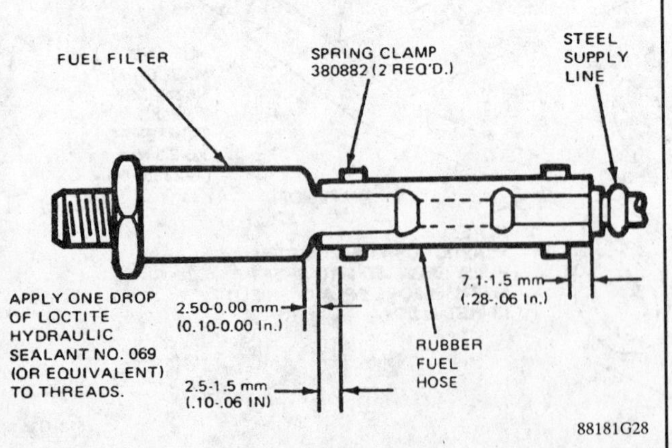

Fig. 45 Proper installation of the screw-in type with hose connections

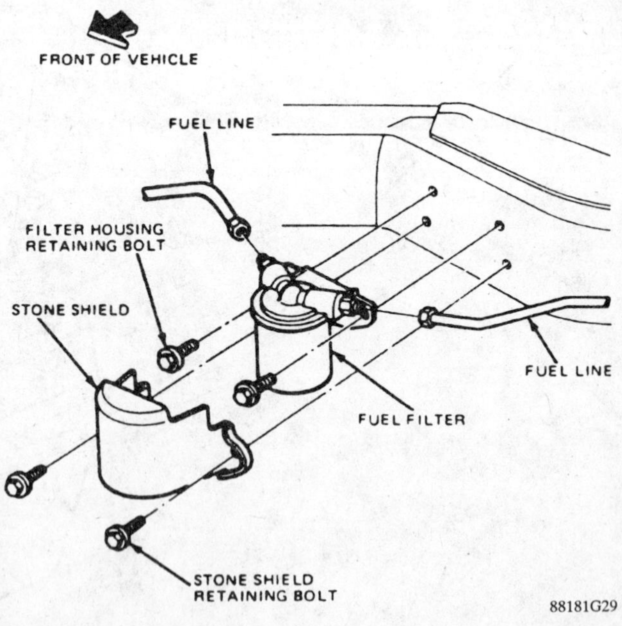

Fig. 46 Exploded view of the fuel filter mounting used on some fuel injected models

PRIMARY FILTER

1. Raise and support the rear end on jackstands.
2. With the engine **OFF**, depressurize the fuel system. Refer to Section 5.
3. Remove the stone shield from in front of the filter.
4. On models with flare fittings, unscrew them at both ends of the filter.
5. Remove the filter retaining screws from the filter bracket, then the filter from the frame rail.

To install:

6. Clean the gasket sealing surface of the filter housing adapter.
7. Lubricate the filter sealing surfaces and the housing threads with a light film of clean engine oil. Screw the filter onto the housing. Hand tighten the filter, then back off the filter to the point where the filter gasket just makes contact with the housing sealing surface.
8. Finally, tighten the filter element an additional $^5/_8$ to $^3/_4$ of a turn.
9. Install the stone shield. Lower the vehicle.
10. Start the engine and inspect the fuel filter for leaks.

88181P07

Fig. 49 . . . then lower and remove it

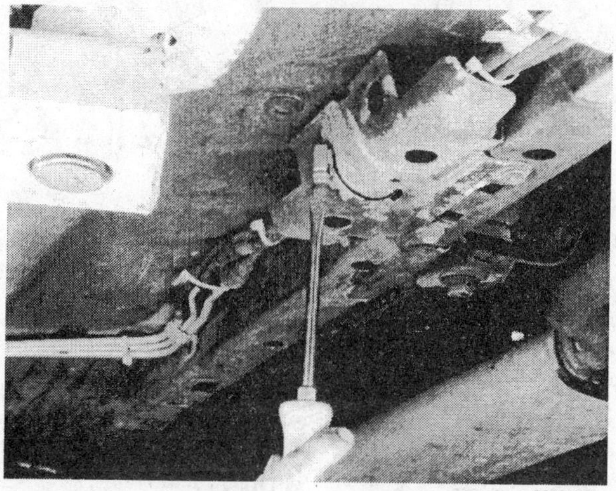

88181P05

Fig. 47 Remove the clamp surrounding the stone shield

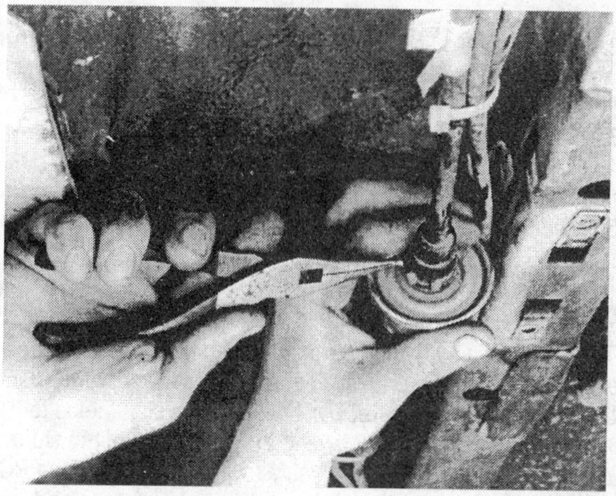

88181P08

Fig. 50 Remove the clamps retaining the lines to the filter

88181P06

Fig. 48 Unbolt the shield from the vehicle . . .

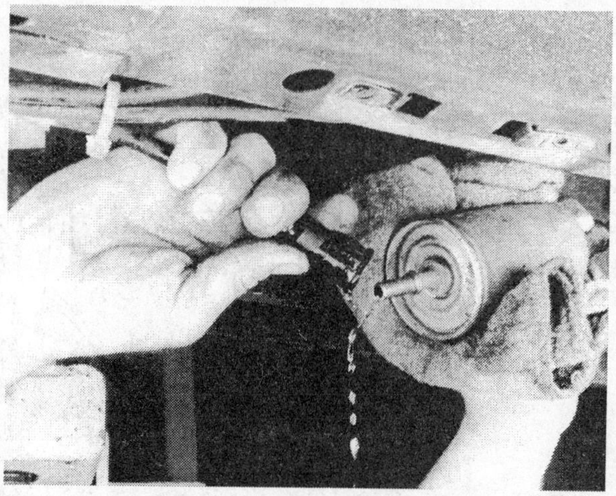

88181P09

Fig. 51 Slide the lines off the filter, watch for spillage

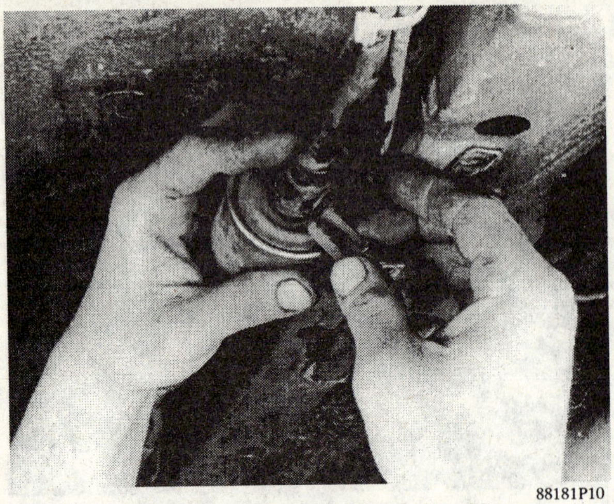

88181P10

Fig. 52 Use new clips when reinstalling the filter

SECONDARY FILTER

1. With the engine **OFF**, depressurize the fuel system. Refer to Section 5.
2. Remove the clips and slide the lines off of the filter ends to remove the unit.

To install:

3. Place a new filter into position.
4. Slide the fuel lines over the filter ends and place the clamps over the end/hose connections.
5. Start the engine and inspect the fuel filter for leaks.

PCV Valve

The PCV valve system vents combustion blow-by gases from the crankcase into the engine air intake where they are burned with the fuel and air mixture. The PCV valve system helps to keep the engine oil clean by ridding the crankcase of moisture and corrosive fumes. The PCV valve system consists of the PCV valve, its mounting grommet, the nipple in the air intake and the connecting hoses. On some engine applications, the PCV valve system is connected with the evaporative emission system.

The PCV valve controls the amount of vapors pulled into the intake manifold from the crankcase. It also acts as a check valve by preventing the flow of air from entering the crankcase in the opposite direction. The PCV valve limits the fresh air intake to suit the engine demand; it also serves to prevent combustion backfiring into the crankcase as well as protecting against crankcase explosions.

REMOVAL & INSTALLATION

PCV Valve

➧ See Figures 53, 54 and 55

1. On some models it may be necessary to remove the air cleaner outlet tube.
2. Disconnect the vacuum hose from the PCV valve.
3. Remove the PCV valve from its mounting grommet.

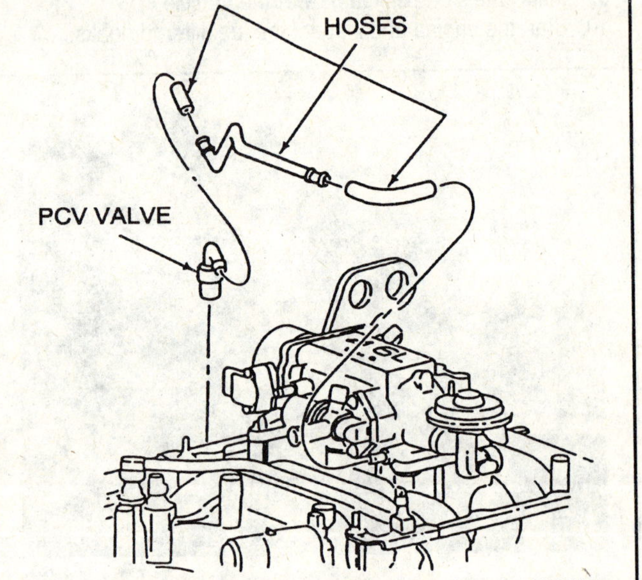

88181G35

Fig. 53 PCV location — 4.6L shown

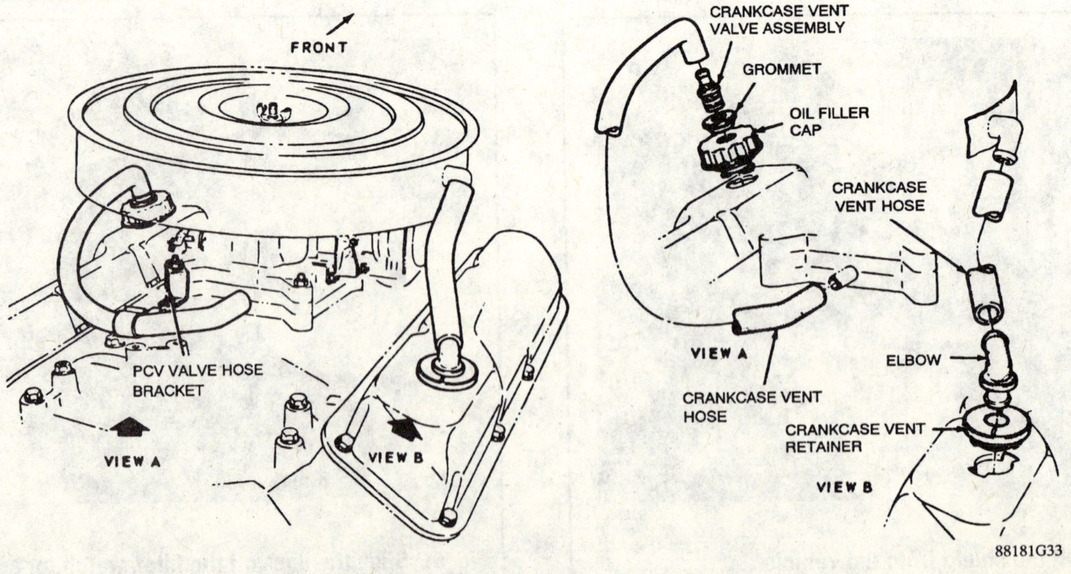

88181G33

Fig. 54 Exploded view of the PCV system — 1983 3.8L shown

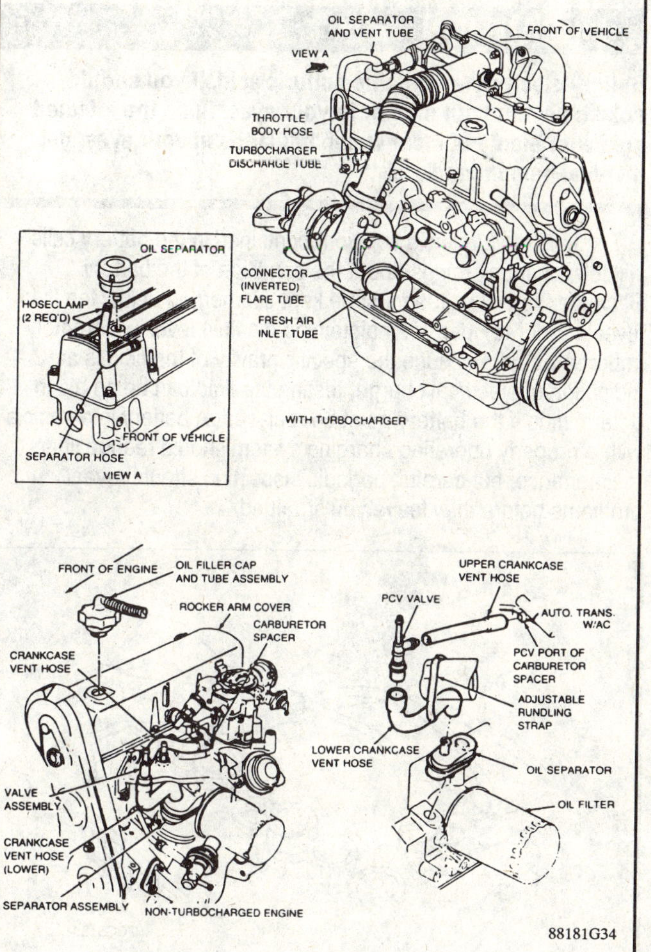

Fig. 55 Exploded view of the PCV system — 1984-87 2.3L turbo shown

To install:

4. Inspect the mounting grommet and PCV hose, replace if necessary.
5. Place a small amount of clean engine oil onto the valve end portion to be inserted into the grommet. Then insert.
6. Place the PCV hose on the exposed valve end.
7. If removed, install the air cleaner outlet tube.

Crankcase Ventilation Filter

➧ See Figure 56

Replace or inspect cleaner mounted crankcase ventilation filter (on models equipped) at the same time the air cleaner filter element is serviced. To replace the filter, simply remove the air cleaner top cover and pull the filter from its housing. Push a new filter into the housing and install the air cleaner cover. If the filter and plastic holder need replacement, remove the clip mounting the feed tube to the air cleaner housing (hose already removed) and remove the assembly from the air cleaner. Installation is the reverse of removal.

Evaporative Canister

SERVICING

➧ See Figure 57

The canister functions to cycle the fuel vapor from the fuel tank (and the float chamber on the carbureted models) into the intake manifold and eventually into the cylinders for combustion. The activated charcoal element within the canister acts as a storage device for the fuel vapor at times when the engine operating condition will not permit fuel vapor to burn efficiently.

Fuel vapors trapped in the sealed fuel tank are vented through the orifice's vapor valve assembly in the top of the tank. The vapors leave the valve assembly through a single vapor line and continue to the carbon canister for storage until they are purged to the engine for burning.

The carbon canister contains activated carbon, which absorbs the fuel vapor. The canister is located in the engine compartment or along the frame rail. The only required service for the evaporative emissions canister is a regular inspection of the canister. If the charcoal canister is gummed up, cracked or saturated with fuel, the entire canister should be replaced.

Battery

GENERAL MAINTENANCE

All batteries, regardless of type, should be carefully secured by a battery hold-down device. If this is not done, the battery terminals or casing may crack from stress applied to the battery during vehicle operation. A battery which is not secured may allow acid to leak out, making it discharge faster; such leaking corrosive acid can also eat away components under the hood. A battery that is not sealed must be checked periodically for electrolyte level. You cannot add water to a sealed maintenance-free battery (though not all maintenance-free batteries are sealed), but a sealed battery must also be checked for proper electrolyte level as indicated by the color of the built-in hydrometer "eye."

Keep the top of the battery clean, as a film of dirt can help completely discharge a battery that is not used for long periods. A solution of baking soda and water may be used for cleaning, but be careful to flush this off with clear water. DO NOT let any of the solution into the filler holes. Baking soda neutralizes battery acid and will de-activate a battery cell.

****CAUTION**

Always use caution when working on or near the battery. Never allow a tool to bridge the gap between the negative and positive battery terminals. Also, be careful not to allow a tool to provide a ground between the positive cable/terminal and any metal component on the vehicle. Either of these conditions will cause a short circuit leading to sparks and possible personal injury.

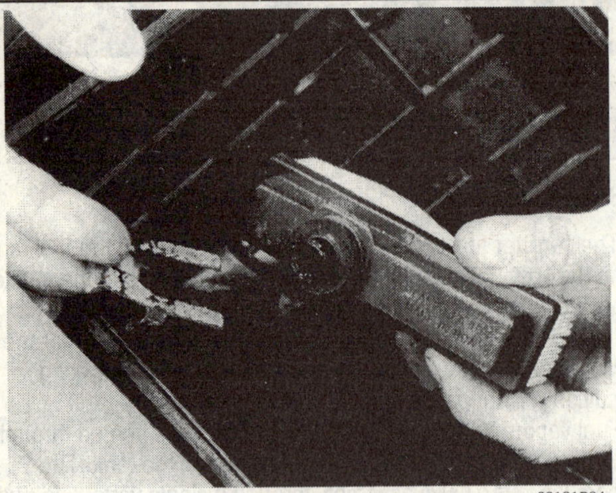

Fig. 56 To replace the holder and filter assembly, remove the clip mounting the feed tube

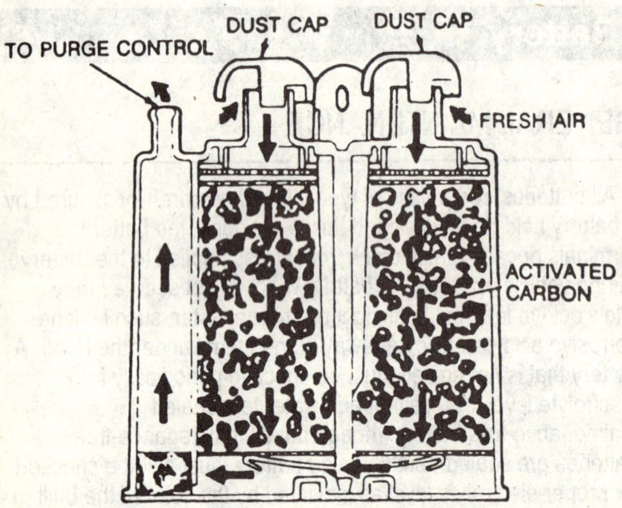

Fig. 57 Cutaway view of a common carbon canister

Batteries in vehicles which are not operated on a regular basis can fall victim to parasitic loads (small current drains which are constantly drawing current from the battery). Normal parasitic loads may drain a battery on a vehicle that is in storage and not used for 6–8 weeks. Vehicles that have additional accessories such as a cellular phone, an alarm system or other devices that increase parasitic load may discharge a battery sooner. If the vehicle is to be stored for 6–8 weeks in a secure area and the alarm system, if present, is not necessary, the negative battery cable should be disconnected at the onset of storage to protect the battery charge.

Remember that constantly discharging and recharging will shorten battery life. Take care not to allow a battery to be needlessly discharged.

BATTERY FLUID

➧ **See Figures 58, 59 and 60**

✱✱CAUTION

Battery electrolyte contains sulfuric acid. If you should splash any on your skin or in your eyes, flush the affected area with plenty of clear water. If it lands in your eyes, get medical help immediately.

The fluid (sulfuric acid solution) contained in the battery cells will tell you many things about the condition of the battery. Because the cell plates must be kept submerged below the fluid level in order to operate, maintaining the fluid level is extremely important. And, because the specific gravity of the acid is an indication of electrical charge, testing the fluid can be an aid in determining if the battery must be replaced. A battery in a vehicle with a properly operating charging system should require little maintenance, but careful, periodic inspection should reveal problems before they leave you stranded.

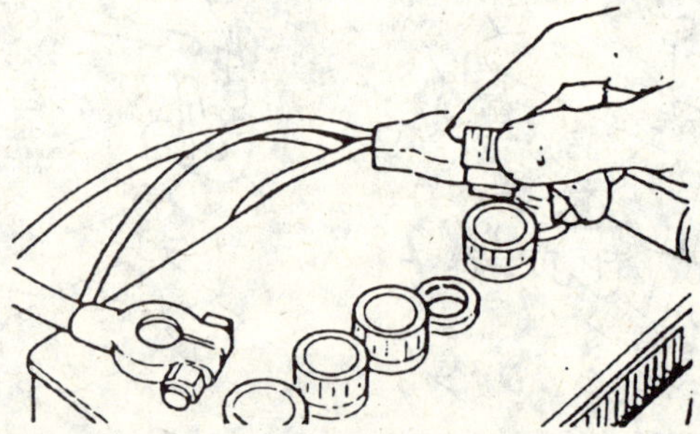

Fig. 58 On non-maintenance free batteries, the level can be checked through the case on translucent batteries; the cell caps must be removed on other models

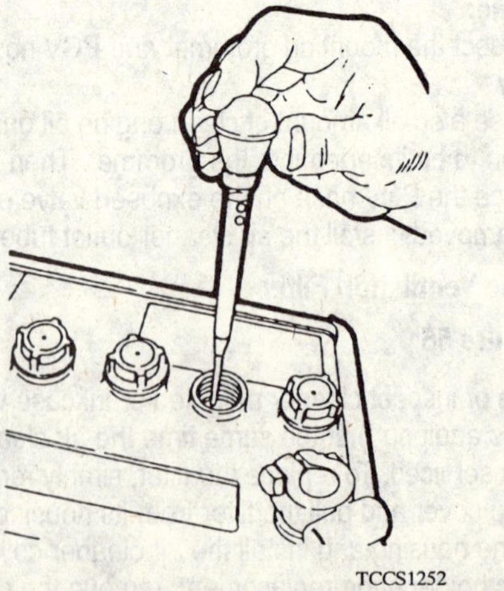

Fig. 59 Check the specific gravity of the battery's electrolyte with a hydrometer

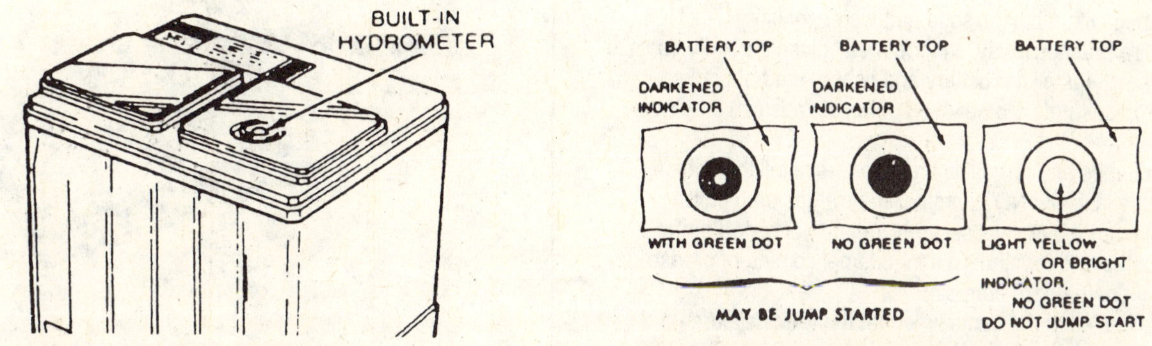

Location of indicator on sealed battery

Check the appearance of the charge indicator on top of the battery before attempting a jump start; if it's not green or dark, do not jump start the car

Fig. 60 A typical sealed (maintenance-free) battery with a built-in hydrometer — NOTE that the hydrometer eye may vary between battery manufacturers; always refer to the battery's label

Fluid Level

Check the battery electrolyte level at least once a month, or more often in hot weather or during periods of extended vehicle operation. On non-sealed batteries, the level can be checked either through the case on translucent batteries or by removing the cell caps on opaque-cased types. The electrolyte level in each cell should be kept filled to the split ring inside each cell, or the line marked on the outside of the case.

If the level is low, add only distilled water through the opening until the level is correct. Each cell is separate from the others, so each must be checked and filled individually. Distilled water should be used, because the chemicals and minerals found in most drinking water are harmful to the battery and could significantly shorten its life.

If water is added in freezing weather, the vehicle should be driven several miles to allow the water to mix with the electrolyte. Otherwise, the battery could freeze.

Although some maintenance-free batteries have removable cell caps for access to the electrolyte, the electrolyte condition and level on all sealed maintenance-free batteries must be checked using the built-in hydrometer "eye." The exact type of eye varies between battery manufacturers, but most apply a sticker to the battery itself explaining the possible readings. When in doubt, refer to the battery manufacturer's instructions to interpret battery condition using the built-in hydrometer.

➔ Although the readings from built-in hydrometers found in sealed batteries may vary, a green eye usually indicates a properly charged battery with sufficient fluid level. A dark eye is normally an indicator of a battery with sufficient fluid, but one which may be low in charge. And a light or yellow eye is usually an indication that electrolyte supply has dropped below the necessary level for battery (and hydrometer) operation. In this last case, sealed batteries with an insufficient electrolyte level must usually be discarded.

Specific Gravity

As stated earlier, the specific gravity of a battery's electrolyte level can be used as an indication of battery charge. At least once a year, check the specific gravity of the battery. It should be between 1.20 and 1.26 on the gravity scale. Most auto supply stores carry a variety of inexpensive battery testing hydrometers. These can be used on any non-sealed battery to test the specific gravity in each cell.

The battery testing hydrometer has a squeeze bulb at one end and a nozzle at the other. Battery electrolyte is sucked into the hydrometer until the float is lifted from its seat. The specific gravity is then read by noting the position of the float. If gravity is low in one or more cells, the battery should be slowly charged and checked again to see if the gravity has come up. Generally, if after charging, the specific gravity between any two cells varies more than 50 points (0.50), the battery should be replaced as it can no longer produce sufficient voltage to guarantee proper operation.

On sealed batteries, the built-in hydrometer is the only way of checking specific gravity. Again, check with your battery's manufacturer for proper interpretation of its built-in hydrometer readings.

CABLES

➧ See Figures 61, 62, 63, 64, 65 and 66

Once a year (or as necessary), the battery terminals and the cable clamps should be cleaned. Loosen the clamps and remove the cables, negative cable first. On batteries with posts on top, the use of a puller specially made for this purpose is recommended. These are inexpensive and available in most auto parts stores. Side terminal battery cables are secured with a small bolt.

Clean the cable clamps and the battery terminal with a wire brush, until all corrosion, grease, etc., is removed and the metal is shiny. It is especially important to clean the inside of the clamp (an old knife is useful here) thoroughly, since a small deposit of foreign material or oxidation there will prevent a sound electrical connection and inhibit either starting or charging. Special tools are available for cleaning these parts, one type for conventional top post batteries and another type for side terminal batteries.

Before installing the cables, loosen the battery hold-down clamp or strap, remove the battery and check the battery tray. Clear it of any debris, and check it for soundness (the battery tray can be cleaned with a baking soda and water solution). Rust should be wire brushed away, and the metal given a couple coats of anti-rust paint. Install the battery and tighten the hold-down clamp or strap securely. Do not overtighten, as this can crack the battery case.

After the clamps and terminals are clean, reinstall the cables, negative cable last; DO NOT hammer the clamps onto post batteries. Tighten the clamps securely, but do not distort them. Give the clamps and terminals a thin external coating of grease after installation, to retard corrosion.

Check the cables at the same time that the terminals are cleaned. If the cable insulation is cracked or broken, or if the ends are frayed, the cable should be replaced with a new cable of the same length and gauge.

TCCS1208

Fig. 63 Place the tool over the terminals and twist to clean the post

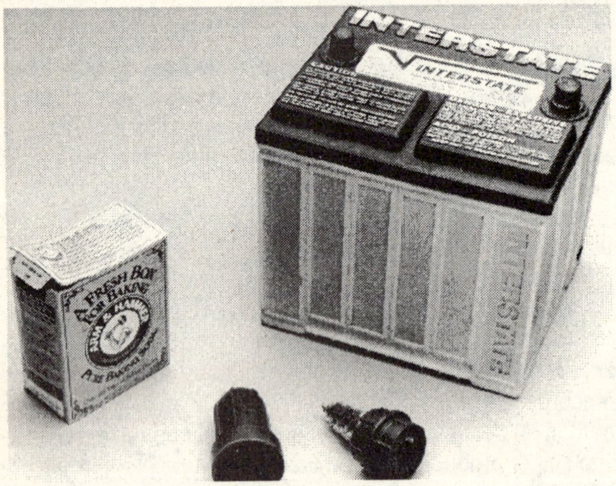

TCCS1206

Fig. 61 Maintenance is performed with household items and with special tools like this post cleaner

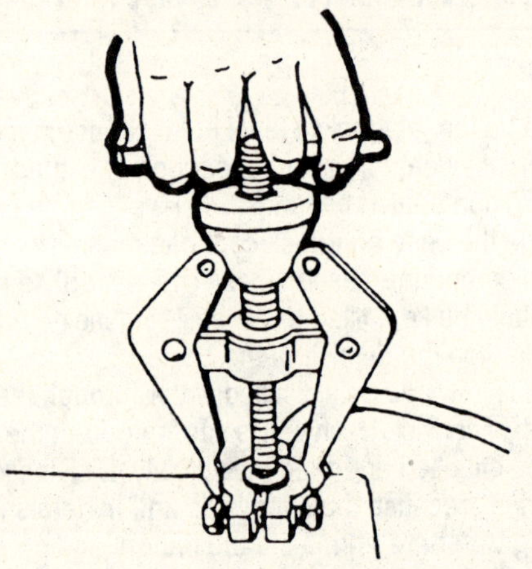

TCCS1254

Fig. 64 A special tool is available to pull the clamp from the post

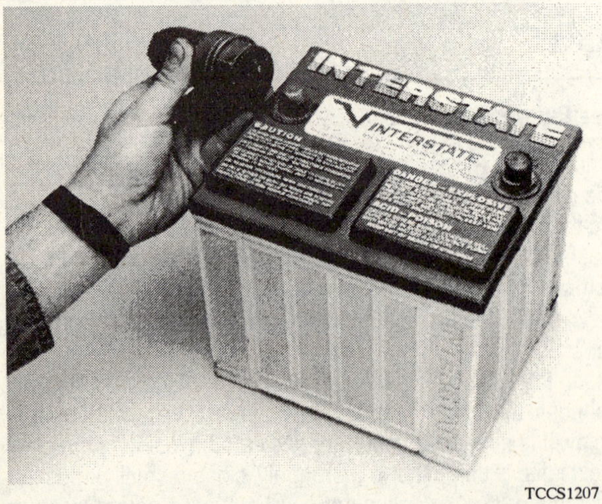

TCCS1207

Fig. 62 The underside of this special battery tool has a wire brush to clean post terminals

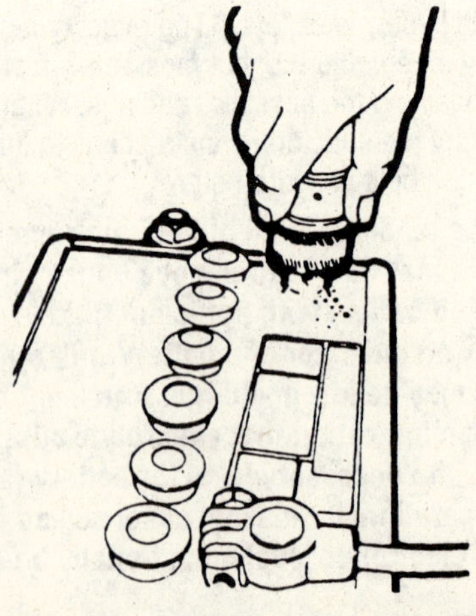

TCCS1255

Fig. 65 Clean the battery terminals until the metal is shiny

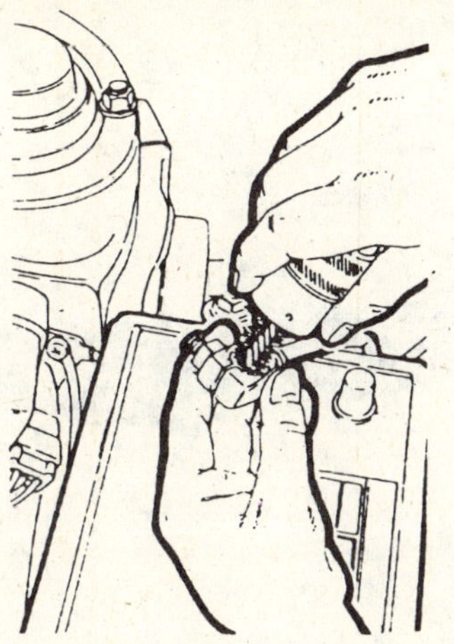
TCCS1256

Fig. 66 The cable ends should be cleaned as well

CHARGING

✻✻CAUTION

The chemical reaction which takes place in all batteries generates explosive hydrogen gas. A spark can cause the battery to explode and splash acid. To avoid serious personal injury, be sure there is proper ventilation and take appropriate fire safety precautions when connecting, disconnecting, or charging a battery and when using jumper cables.

A battery should be charged at a slow rate to keep the plates inside from getting too hot. However, if some maintenance-free batteries are allowed to discharge until they are almost "dead," they may have to be charged at a high rate to bring them back to "life." Always follow the charger manufacturer's instructions on charging the battery.

REPLACEMENT

When it becomes necessary to replace the battery, select one with a rating equal to or greater than the battery originally installed. Deterioration and just plain aging of the battery cables, starter motor, and associated wires makes the battery's job harder in successive years. The slow increase in electrical resistance over time makes it prudent to install a new battery with a greater capacity than the old.

Heat Riser

SERVICING

Some early models are equipped with exhaust control (heat riser) valves located near the head pipe connection in the exhaust manifold. These valves aid initial warm-up in cold weather by restricting exhaust gas flow slightly. The heat generated by this restriction is transferred to the intake manifold where it results in improved fuel vaporization.

The operation of the exhaust control valve should be checked every 6 months or 6,000 miles (9654 km). Make sure that the thermostatic spring is hooked on the stop pin and that the tension holds the valve shut. Rotate the counterweight by hand and make sure that it moves freely through about 90° of rotation. A valve which is operating properly will open when light finger pressure is applied (cold engine). Lubricate the shaft bushings with a mixture of penetrating oil and graphite. Operate the valve manually a few times to work in the lubricant.

Belts

INSPECTION

➧ See Figures 67, 68, 69, 70, 71 and 72

Inspect the belts for signs of glazing or cracking. A glazed belt will be perfectly smooth from slippage, while a good belt will have a slight texture of fabric visible. Cracks will usually start at the inner edge of the belt and run outward. All worn or damaged drive belts should be replaced immediately. It is best to replace all drive belts at one time, as a preventive maintenance measure, during this service operation.

ADJUSTMENTS

Except Serpentine Belts

✻✻WARNING

On models equipped with an electric cooling fan, disconnect the negative battery cable or fan motor wiring harness connector before replacing or adjusting drive belts. The fan may come on, under certain circumstances, even though the ignition is OFF.

Proper adjustment requires the use of the tension gauge. Since most people don't have the necessary gauge, a deflection method of adjustment is given. To assure proper belt tension, the following guidelines should be followed:

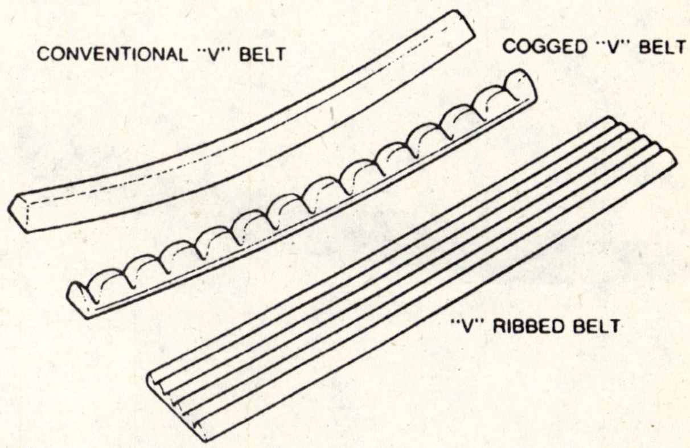

TCCS1218

Fig. 67 There are typically 3 types of accessory drive belts found on vehicles today

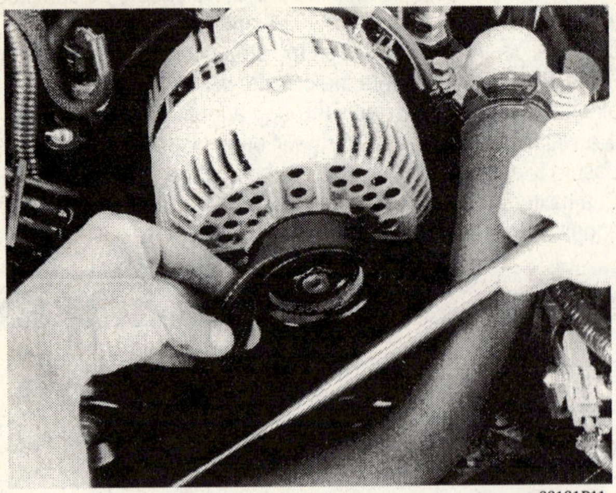

88181P11

Fig. 68 Inspect the belts for signs of glazing or cracking

TCCS1216

Fig. 71 The cover of this belt is worn, exposing the critical reinforcing cords to excessive wear

TCCS1214

Fig. 69 An example of a healthy drive belt

TCCS1217

Fig. 72 Installing too wide a belt can result in serious belt wear and/or breakage

TCCS1215

Fig. 70 Deep cracks in this belt will cause flex, building up heat that will eventually lead to belt failure

- Use belt tension gauge tool T63L-8620-A or equivalent.
- If a belt tension gauge is not obtainable, the belt deflection method may be used for conventional V and cogged V belts only.
- Locate a point on the belt midway between the two pulleys driven. Press firmly on the belt.

ALTERNATOR

See Figure 73

1. Position the ruler perpendicular to the drive belt at its longest straight run. Test the tightness of the belt by pressing it firmly with your thumb. The deflection should not exceed $^1/_4$ in. (6mm).
2. If the deflection exceeds $^1/_4$ in. (6mm), loosen the alternator mounting and adjusting arm bolts.
3. Place a 1 in. open-end or adjustable wrench on the adjusting ridge cast on the body, and pull on the wrench until the proper tension is achieved.
4. Holding the alternator in place to maintain tension, tighten the adjusting arm bolt. Recheck the belt tension. When the belt is properly tensioned, tighten the alternator mounting bolt.

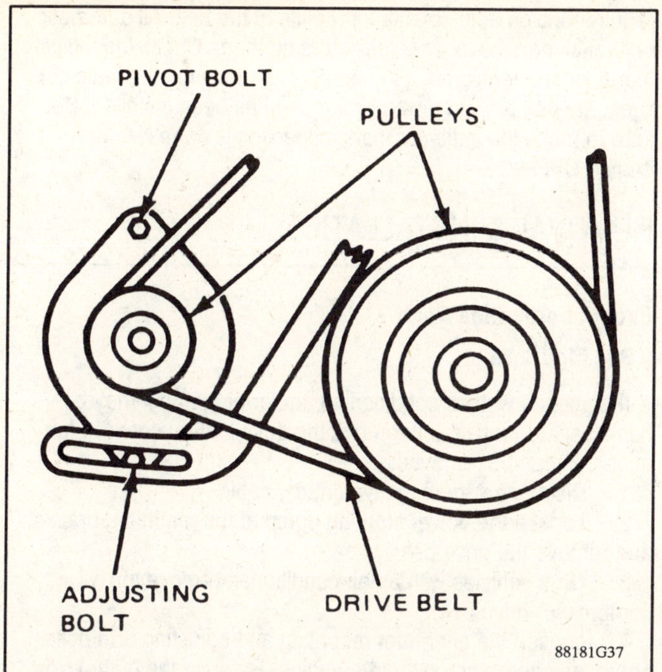

Fig. 73 Loosen the adjusting bolt to loosen or tighten the alternator belt

POWER STEERING — 2.3L ENGINE

1. Hold a ruler perpendicular to the drive belt at its longest run, test the tightness of the belt by pressing it firmly with your thumb. The deflection should not exceed 1/4 in. (6mm).
2. To adjust the belt tension, loosen the adjusting and mounting bolts on the front face of the steering pump cover plate (hub side).
3. Using a prybar or broom handle on the pump hub, move the power steering pump toward or away from the engine until the proper tension is reached. Do not pry against the reservoir as it is relatively soft and easily deformed.
4. Holding the pump in place, tighten the adjusting arm bolt and then recheck the belt tension. When the belt is properly tensioned tighten the mounting bolts.

POWER STEERING — EXCEPT 2.3L ENGINES

➧ See Figure 74

1. Position a ruler perpendicular to the drive belt at its longest run. Test the tightness of the belt by pressing it firmly with your thumb. The deflection should be about 1/4 in. (6mm).
2. To adjust the belt tension, loosen the three bolts in the three elongated adjusting slots at the power steering pump attaching bracket.
3. Turn the steering pump drive belt adjusting nut as required until the proper deflection is obtained. Turning the adjusting nut clockwise will increase tension and decrease deflection; counterclockwise will decrease tension and increase deflection.
4. Without disturbing the pump, tighten the three attaching bolts.

AIR CONDITIONING

➧ See Figure 75

1. Position a ruler perpendicular to the drive belt at its longest run. Test the tightness of the belt by pressing it firmly with your thumb. The deflection should not exceed 1/4 in. (6mm).
2. If the engine is equipped with an idler pulley, loosen the idler pulley adjusting bolt, insert a prybar between the pulley and the engine (or in the idler pulley adjusting slot), and adjust the tension accordingly. If the engine is not equipped with an idler pulley, the alternator must be moved to accomplish this adjustment, as outlined under Alternator Belt.
3. When the proper tension is reached, tighten the idler pulley adjusting bolt (if so equipped) or the alternator adjusting and mounting bolts.

AIR PUMP

➧ See Figure 76

1. Position a ruler perpendicular to the drive belt at its longest run. Test the tightness of the belt by pressing it firmly with your thumb. The deflection should be about 1/4 in. (6mm).

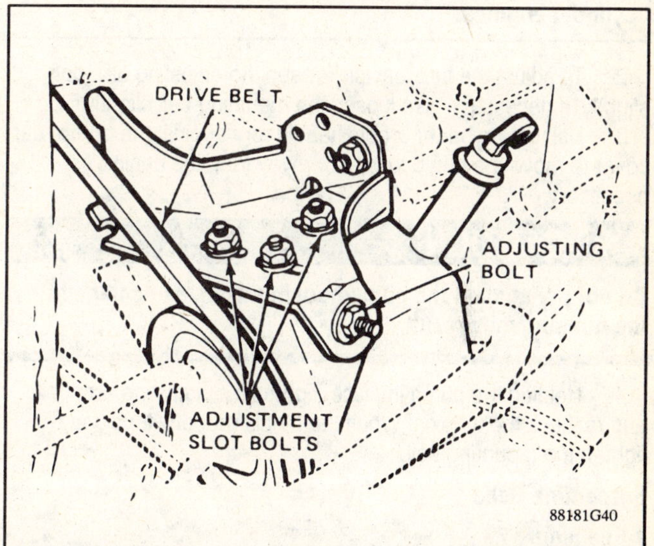

Fig. 74 Slider type power steering pump belt adjustment bolt locations

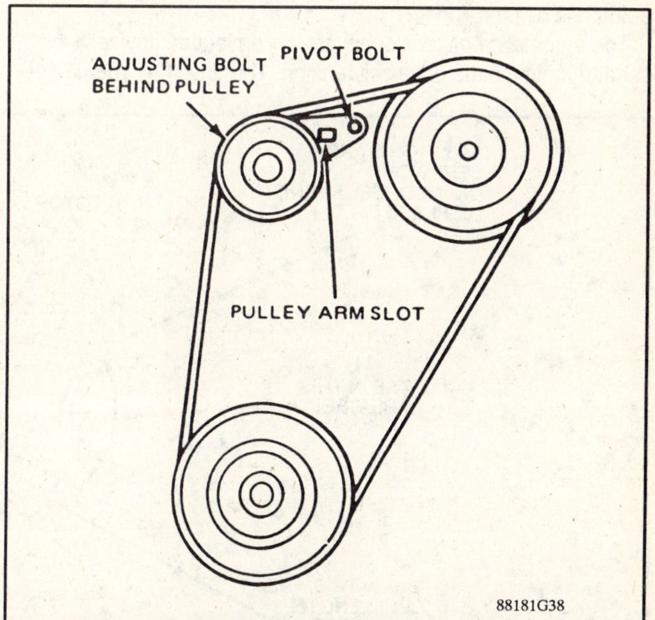

Fig. 75 Loosen the idler pulley adjusting bolt to loosen or tighten the air conditioning belt

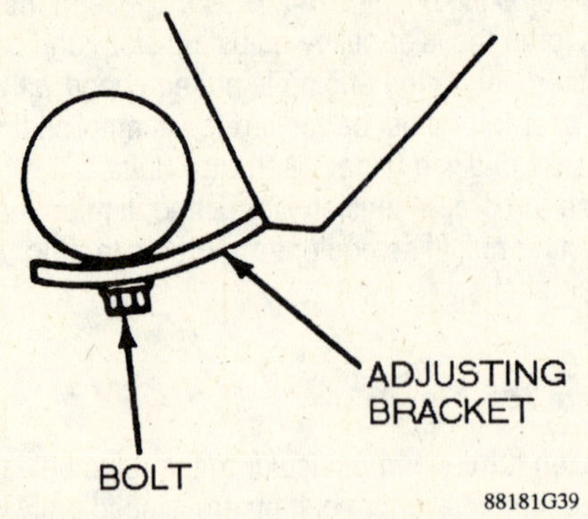

Fig. 76 Air pump adjustment points on the 6 and 8 cylinder engines

2. To adjust the belt tension, loosen the adjusting arm bolt slightly. If necessary, also loosen the mounting belt slightly.
3. Using a prybar or broom handle, pry against the pump rear cover to move the pump toward or away from the engine as necessary.

****CAUTION**

Do not pry against the pump housing itself, as damage to the housing may result.

4. Holding the pump in place, tighten the adjusting arm bolt and recheck the tension. When the belt is properly tensioned, tighten the mounting bolt.

Serpentine Belts

➧ See Figure 77

Most late models feature a single (some use a double), wide, ribbed V-belt that drives the water pump, alternator, and (on some models) the air conditioner compressor. These belts use an automatic belt tensioner.

The automatic belt tensioners are spring loaded devices which set and maintain the drive belt tension. The drive belt should not require tension adjustments for the life of the belt. All automatic belt tensioners have wear indicators on them. Check the indicator marks on the tensioner, if the mark is not between the indicator lines, the belt is worn or the wrong belt has been installed. Be sure to make the indicator mark inspection is done with the engine **OFF**.

REMOVAL & INSTALLATION

Except Serpentine Belts

➧ See Figure 78

If equipped with air conditioning and/or air pump it may be necessary to loosen and remove the drive belts before the fan drive belt can be removed.

1. Disconnect the negative battery cable.
2. Loosen the power steering pump at the mounting bracket and remove the drive belt.
3. On a vehicles with an air conditioner, remove the compressor drive belt.
4. Loosen the alternator mounting and adjusting arm bolts. Move the alternator toward the engine. Remove the belt(s) from the alternator and crankshaft pulleys, and lift them over the fan.

To install:

5. Place the belt(s) over the fan, insert the belt(s) in the water pump pulley, crankshaft pulley and alternator pulley grooves. Adjust the belt tension.
6. On a vehicle with an air conditioner, install and adjust the compressor drive belt tension.
7. Install the power steering pump drive belt and tighten the pump at the mounting bracket. Adjust the drive belt tension.

Serpentine Belts

➧ See Figures 79, 80, 81, 82, 83, 84, 85, 86, 87, 88, 89 and 90

To install a new belt, loosen the bracket lockbolt and/or idler pulley lockbolt, retract the belt tensioner with a prybar and slide the old belt off of the pulleys. Slip on a new belt and release the tensioner and tighten the lockbolt. The automatic spring powered tensioner eliminates the need for periodic adjustments.

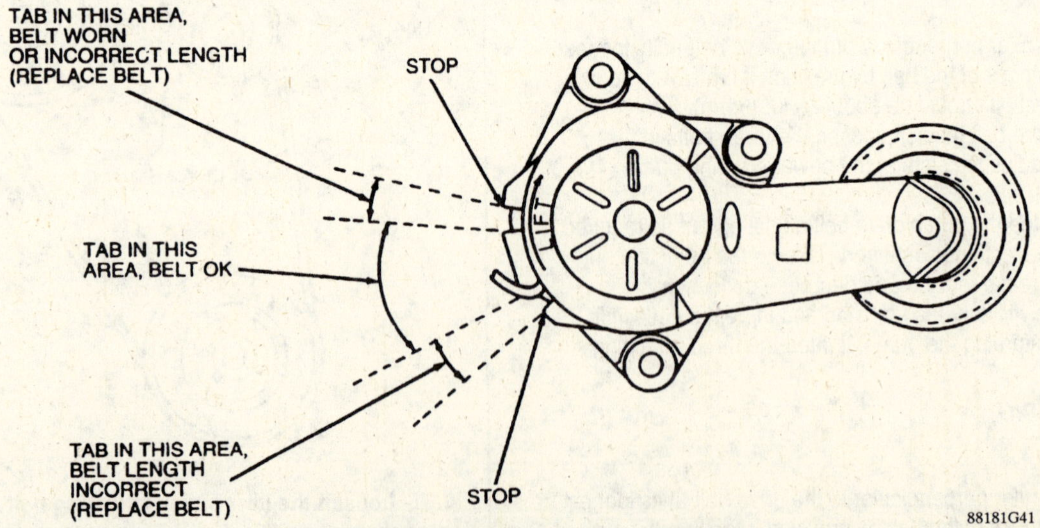

Fig. 77 Locate the area that the tab is on the adjuster to establish the life of the belt

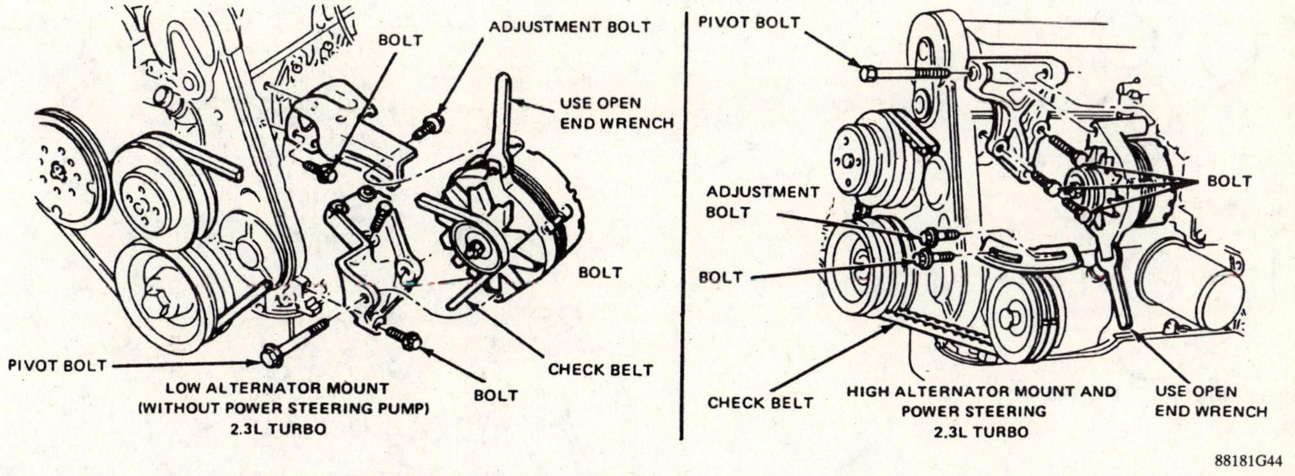

Fig. 78 Belt routing and adjustment — 1983-85 2.3L turbo engines

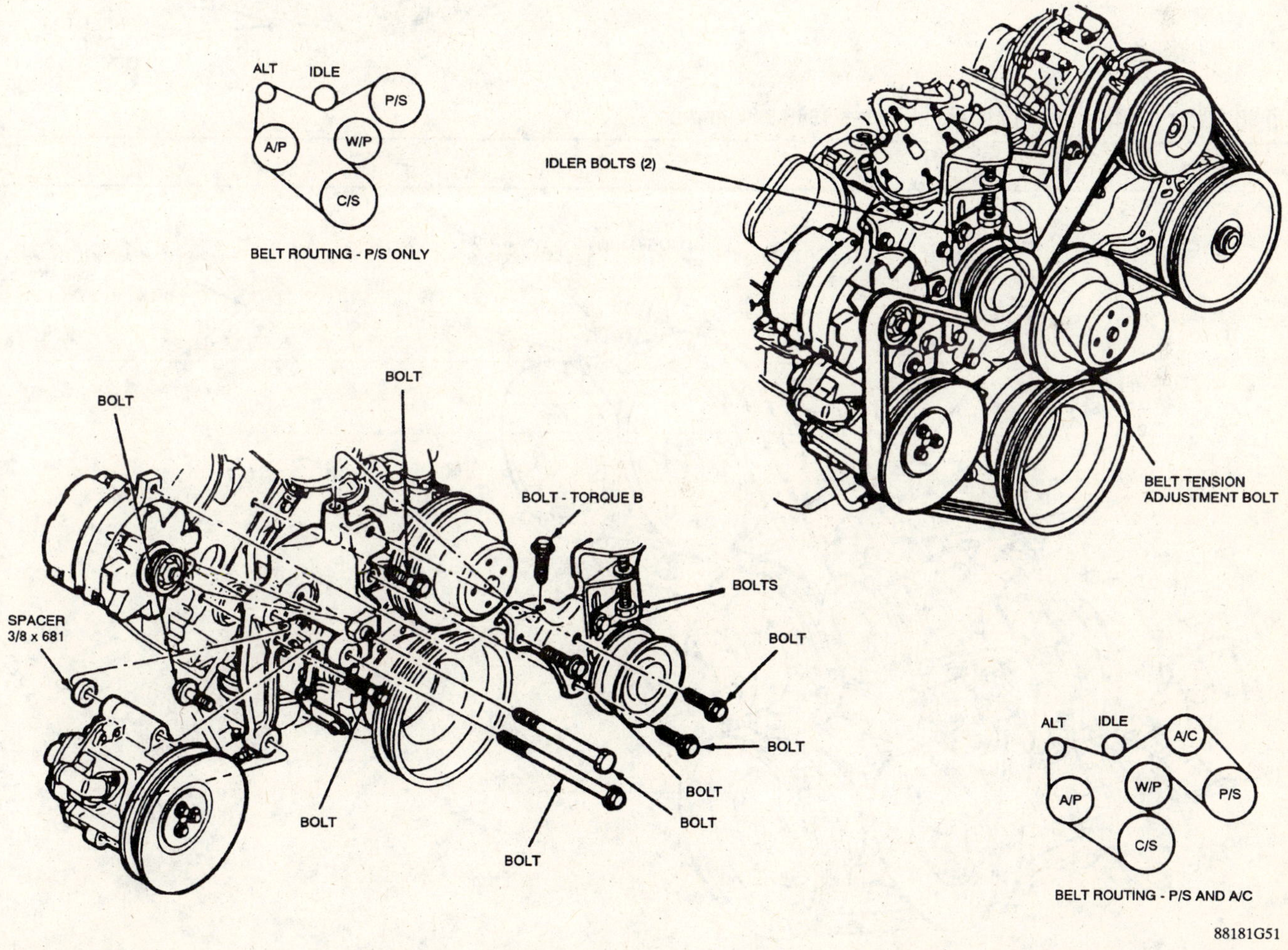

Fig. 79 Belt routing and adjustment points — 1983-86 3.8L engine

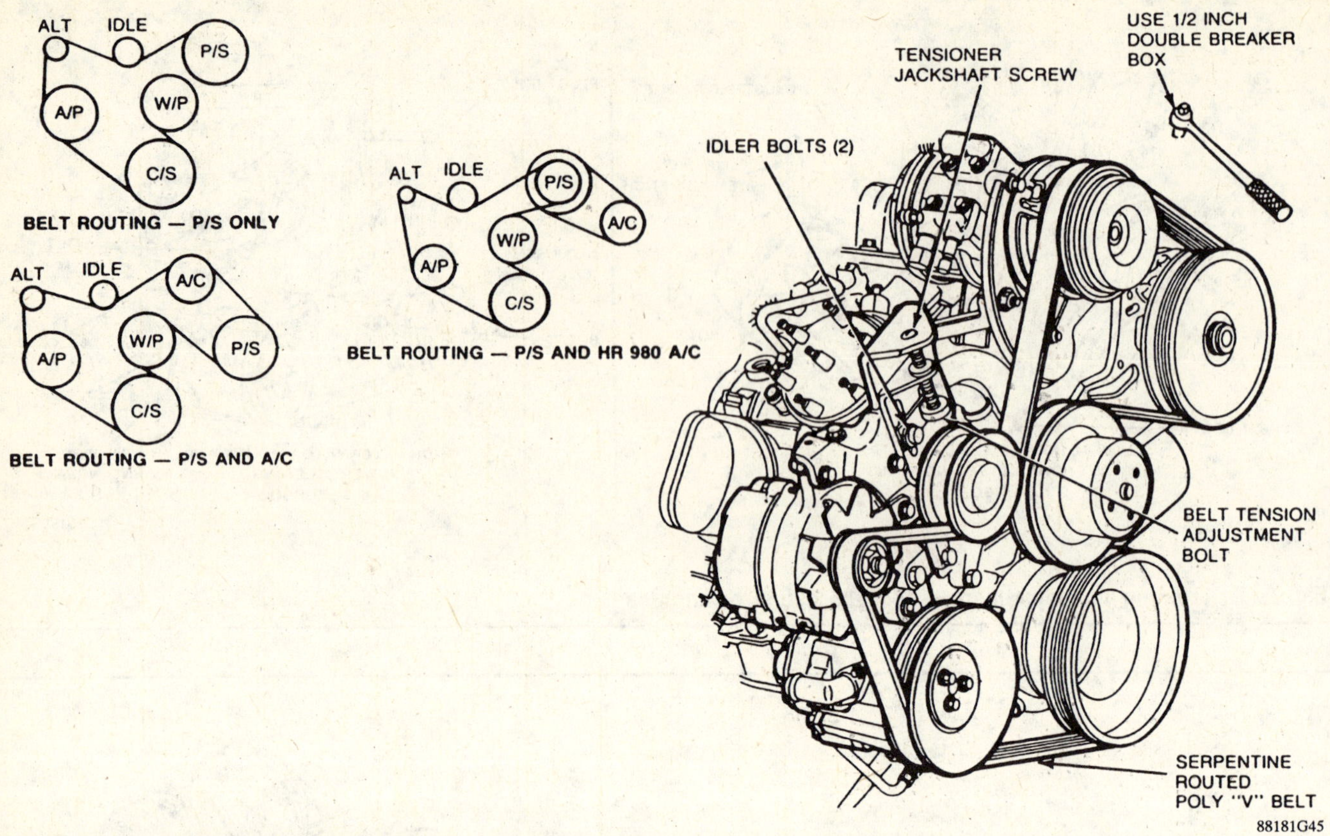

Fig. 80 Belt routing and adjustment points — 1985 3.8L engine

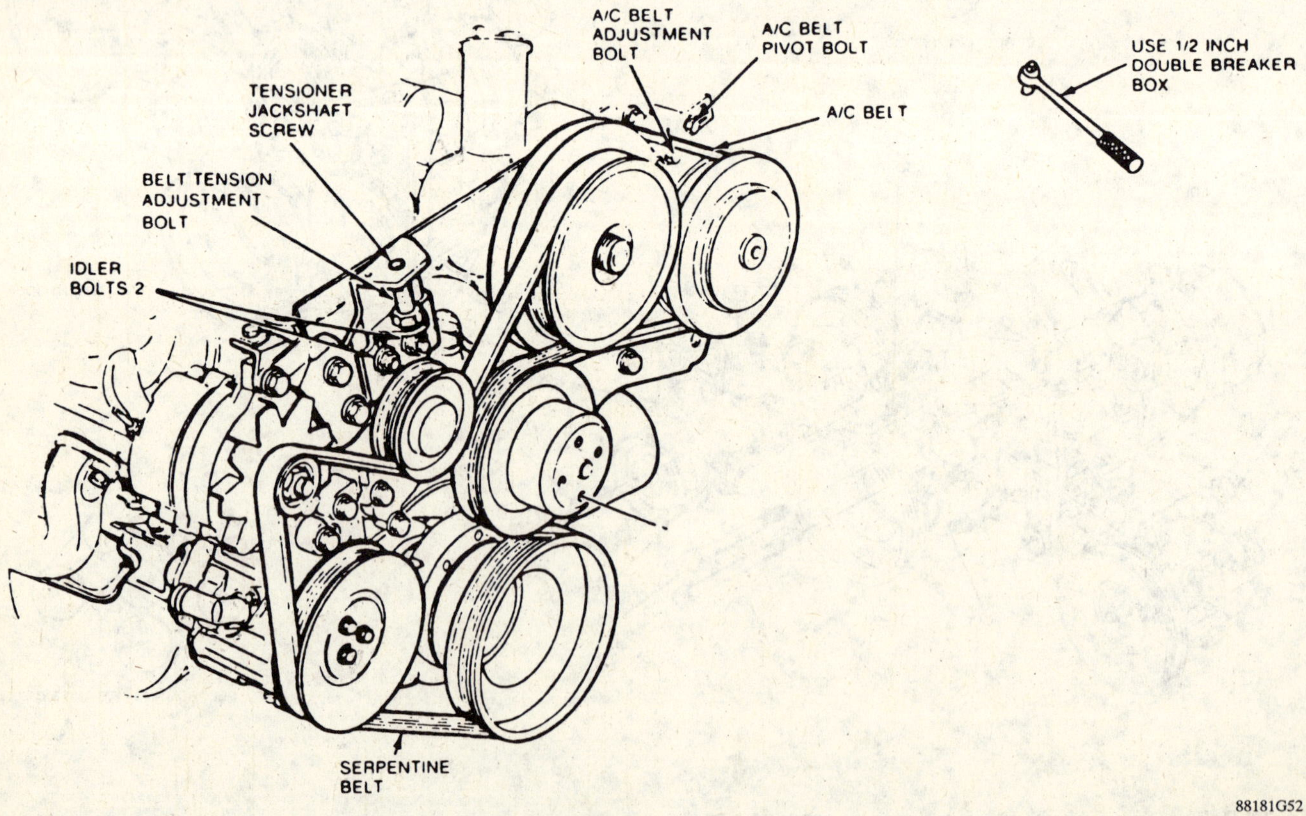

Fig. 81 Belt routing and adjustment points — 1987 3.8L engine

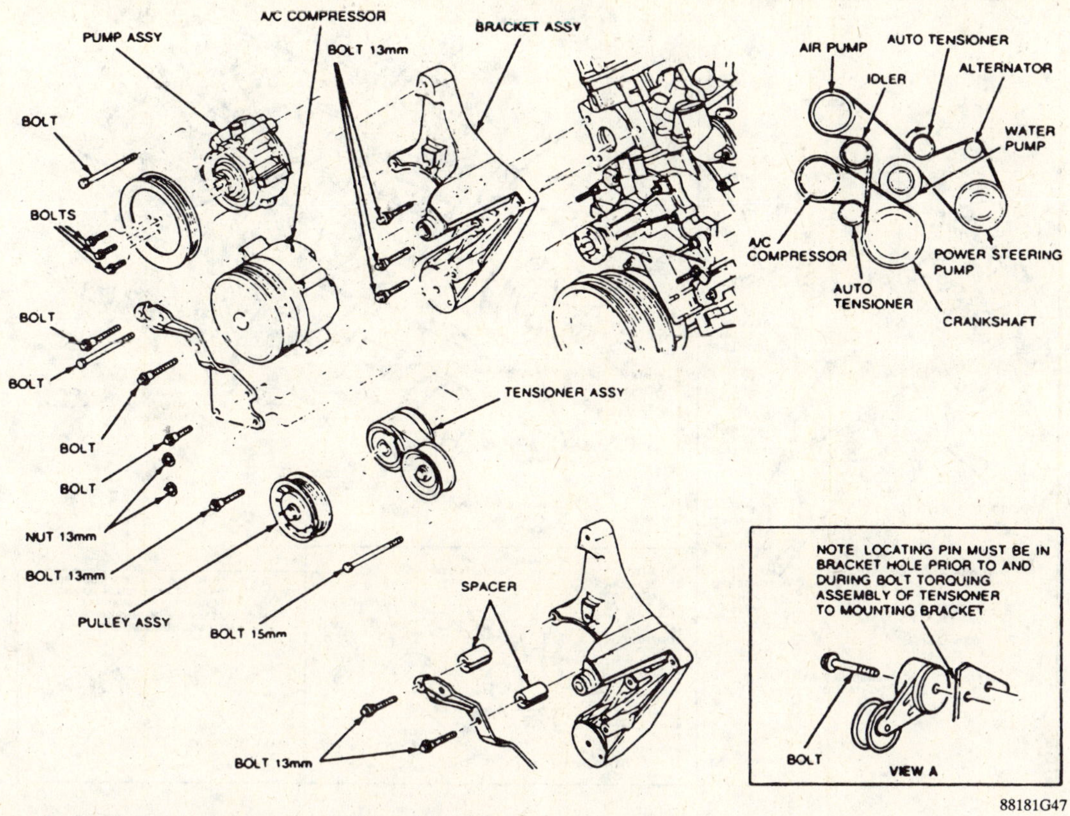

Fig. 82 Belt routing with dual tensioners — 1988 3.8L engine

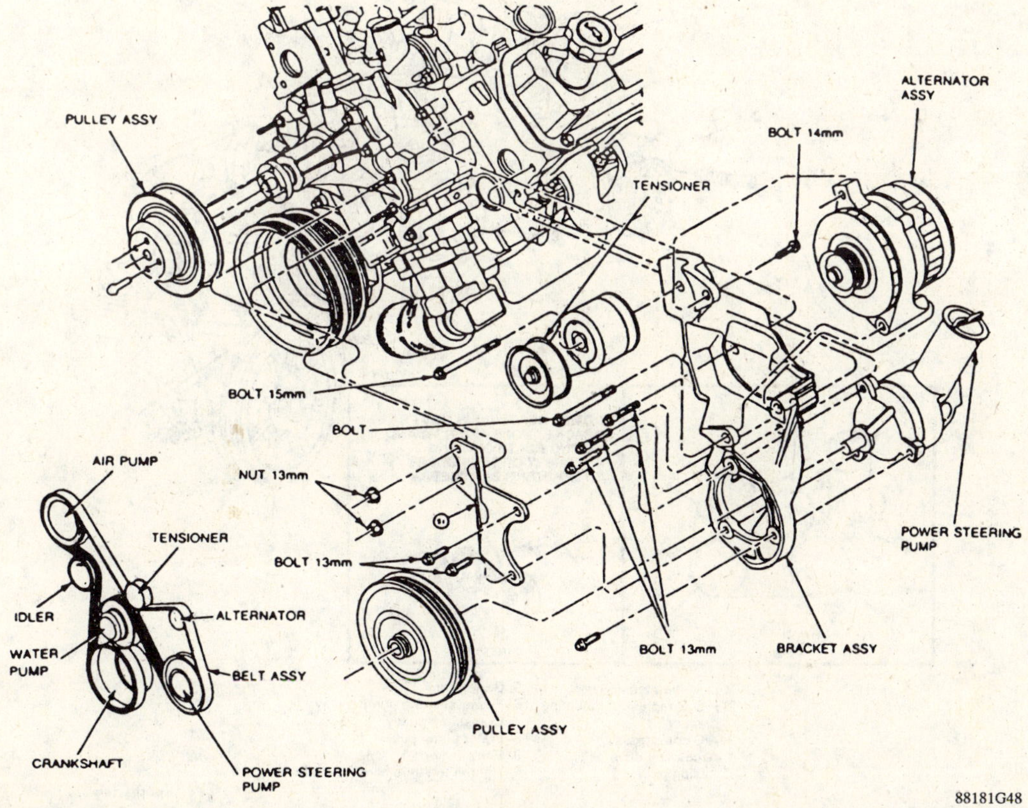

Fig. 83 Belt routing with single tensioner — 1988 3.8L engine

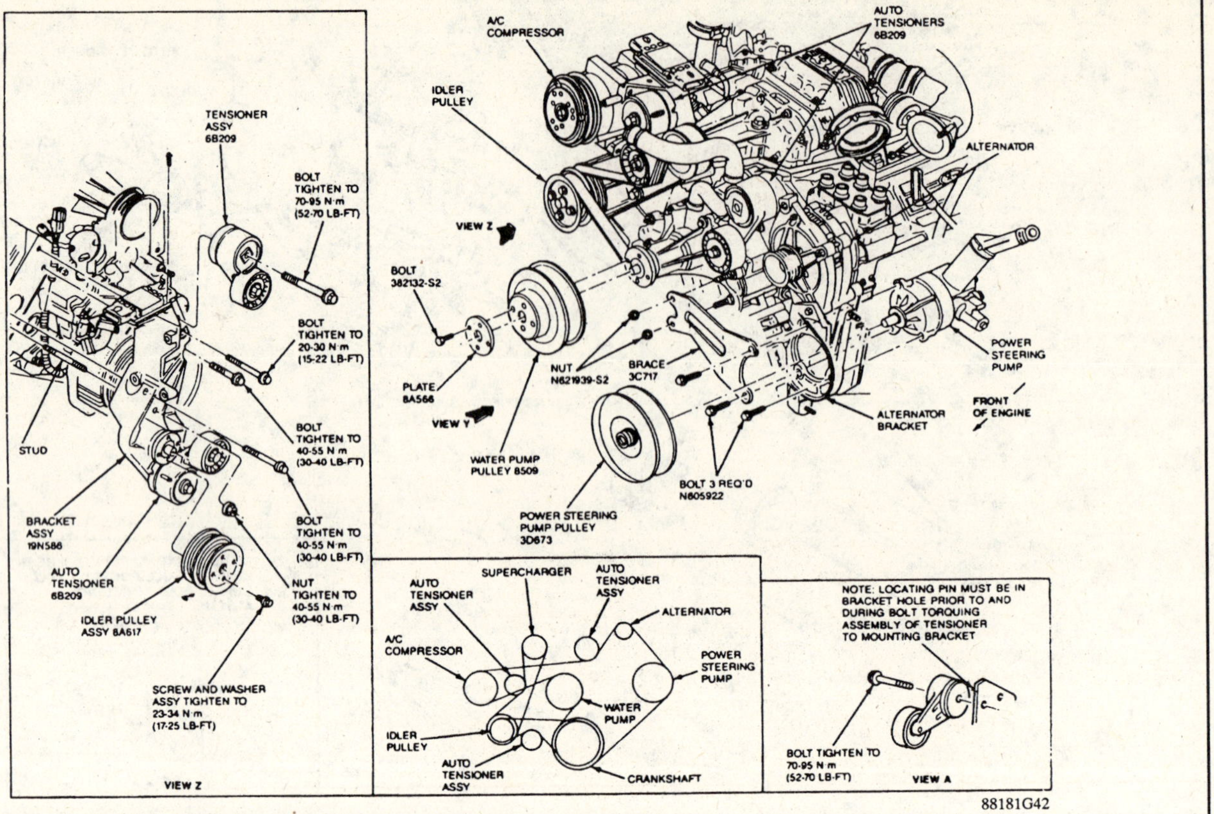

Fig. 84 Belt routing — 1989–91 3.8L supercharged engine

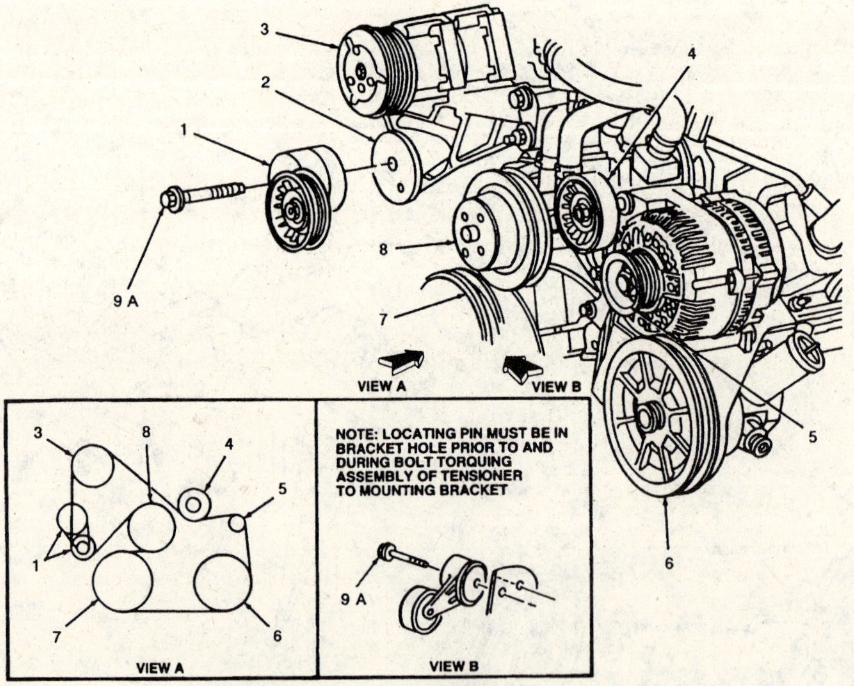

1. Drive belt tensioner
2. A/C compressor mounting bracket
3. A/C compressor
4. Accessory drive belt routing pulley
5. Generator
6. Power steering pump pulley
7. Crankshaft pulley
8. Water pump pulley
9. Bolt

A. Tighten to 70-95 N.m (52-70 lb-ft)

88181G55

Fig. 85 Belt routing — 1990–96 3.8L engine

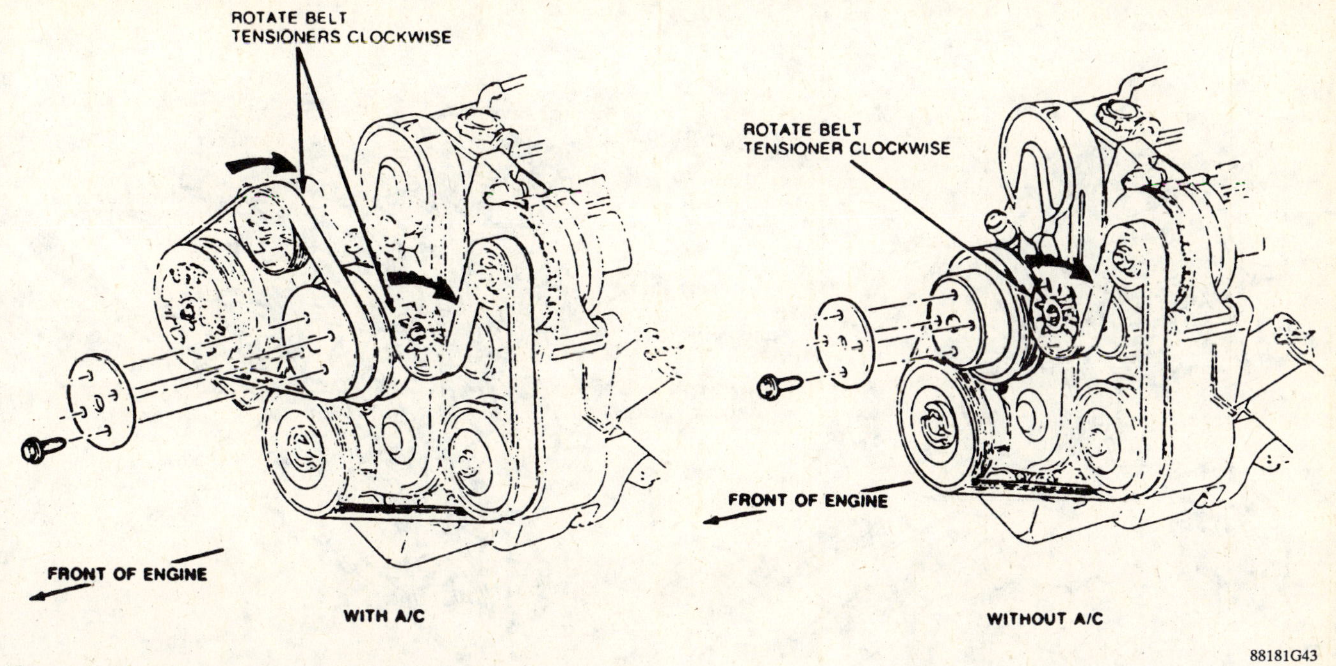

Fig. 86 Belt routing — 1987–88 2.3L turbocharged engine

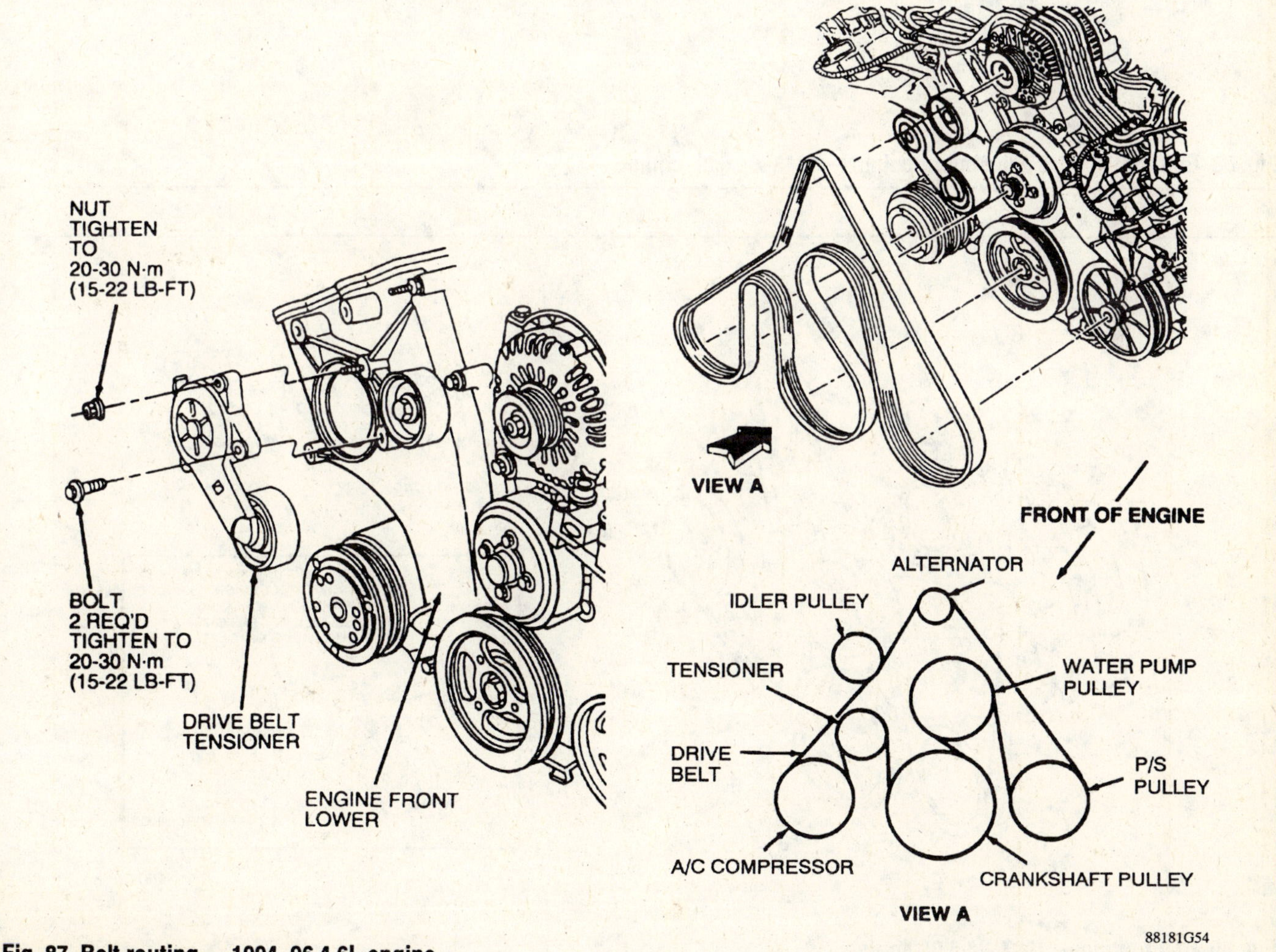

Fig. 87 Belt routing — 1994–96 4.6L engine

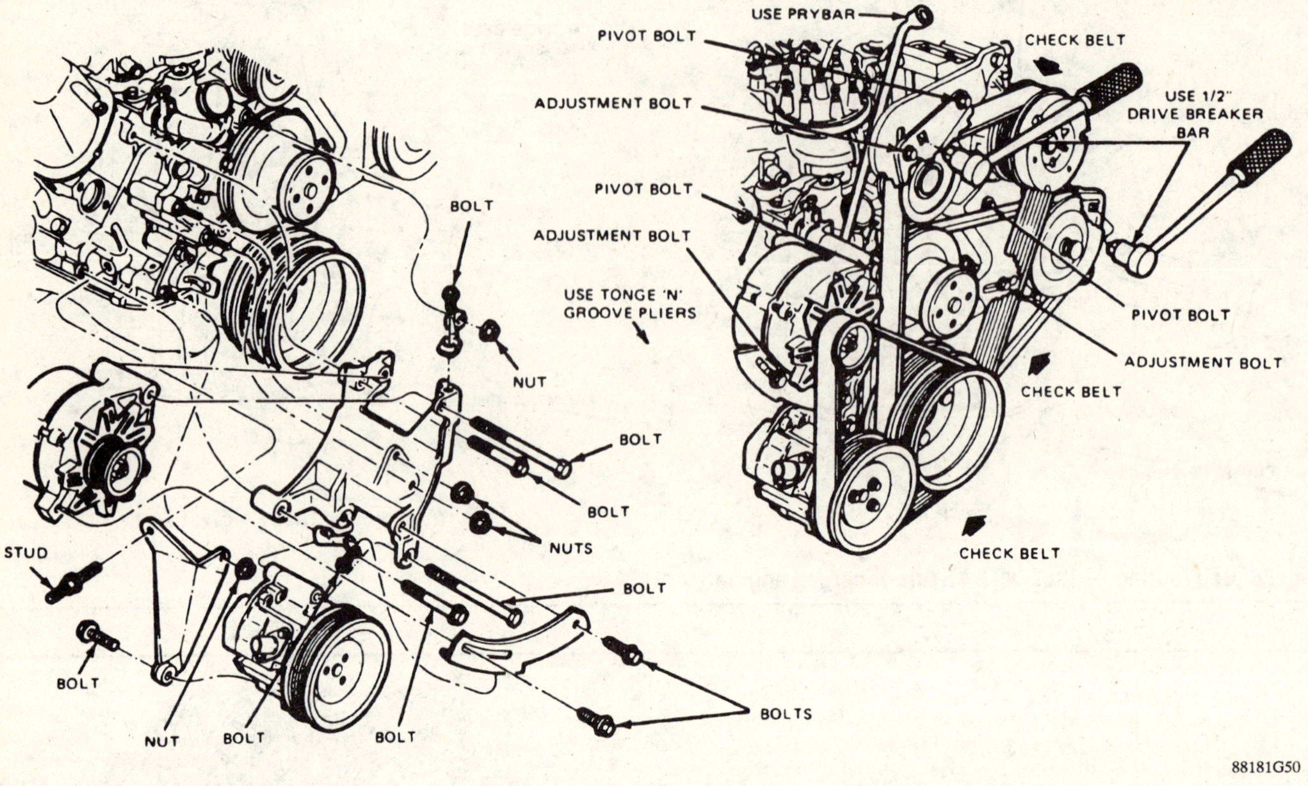

Fig. 88 Belt routing and adjustment points — 1983-86 5.0L engine

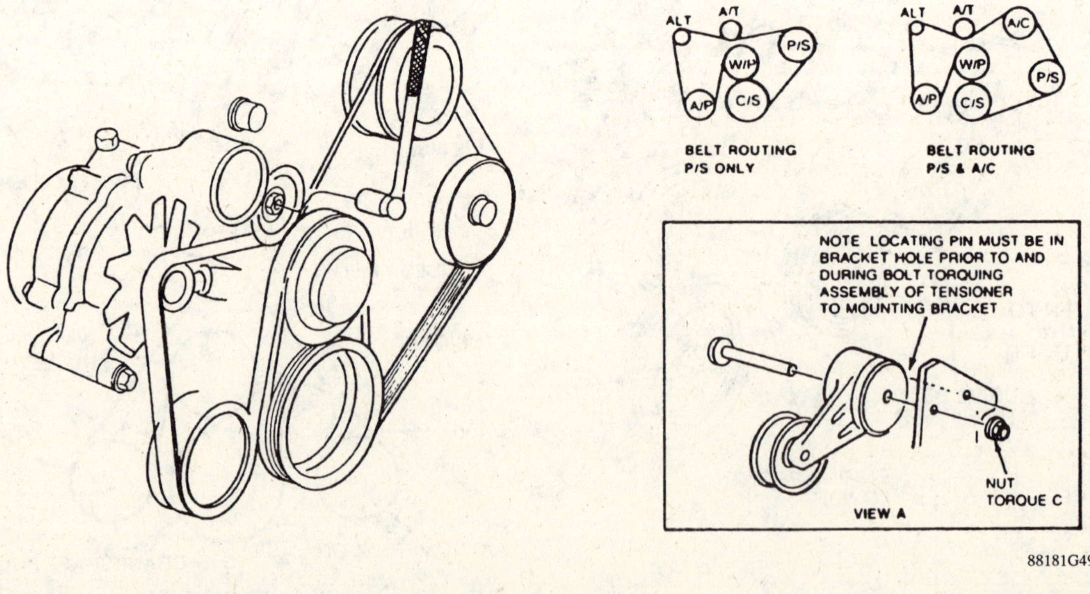

Fig. 89 Belt routing — 1987-88 5.0L engine

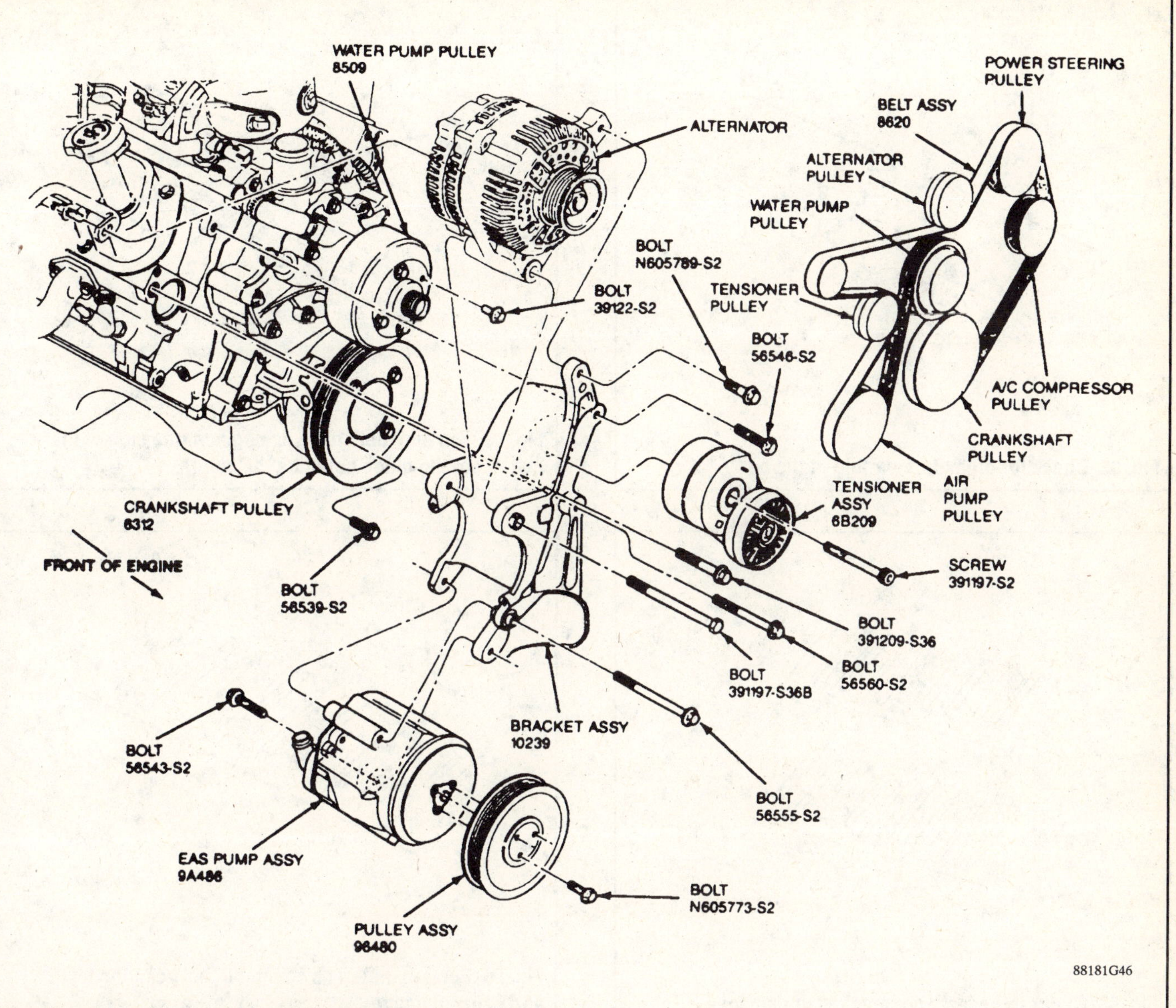

Fig. 90 Belt routing — 1991–93 5.0L engine

Timing Belts

INSPECTION

➧ **See Figures 91, 92, 93, 94, 95 and 96**

Ford recommends that the timing belt be replaced on vehicles that are used in extensive idling or low speed driving for long distances. Police, taxi and door-to-door deliveries are commonly used in this manner. The timing belt should be replaced every 60,000 miles (96,000 km) in these cases. If your vehicle has high milage, you may want to consider replacing the belt to prevent the possibility of having it snap. Or if your engine is being overhauled, inspect the belt for wear and replace if needed. In the event the belt does snap while you are driving, turn the engine **OFF** immediately. Section 3 has removal and installation procedures available.

Fig. 91 Do not bend, twist or turn the timing belt inside out. Never allow oil, water or steam to contact the belt

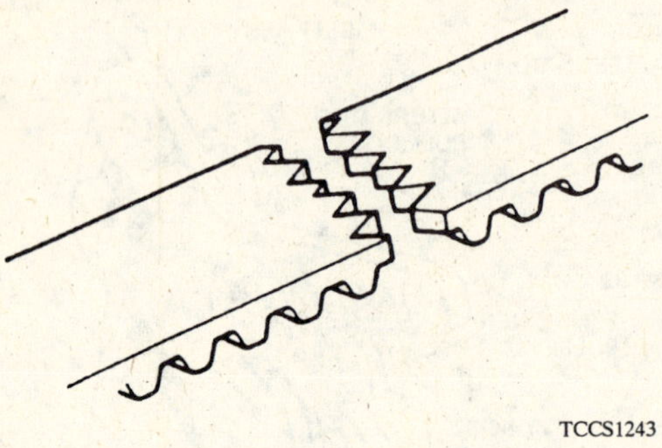

Fig. 92 Check for premature parting of the belt

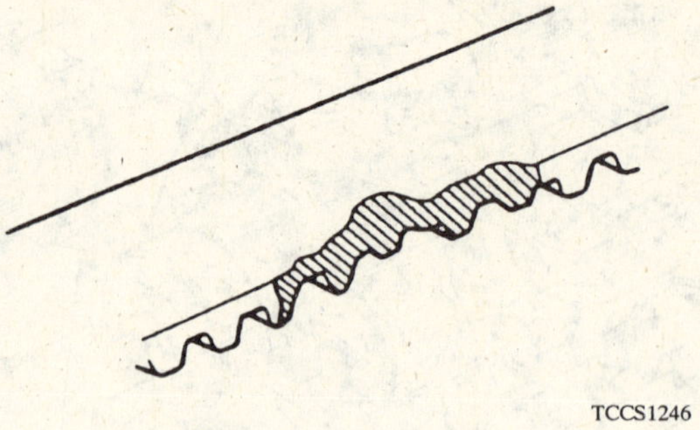

Fig. 95 You may only have damage on one side of the belt; if so, the guide could be the culprit

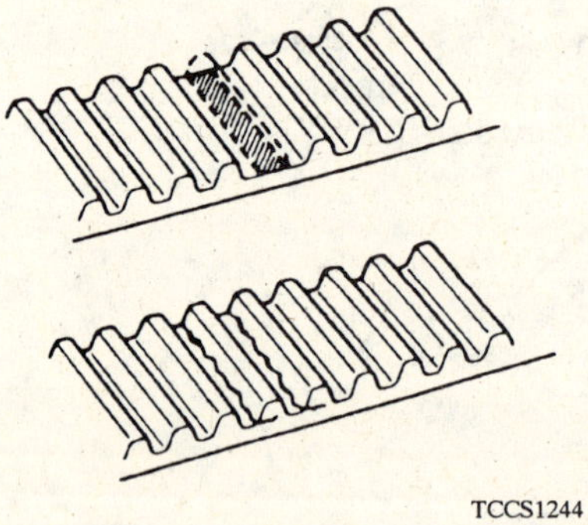

Fig. 93 Check if the teeth are cracked or damaged

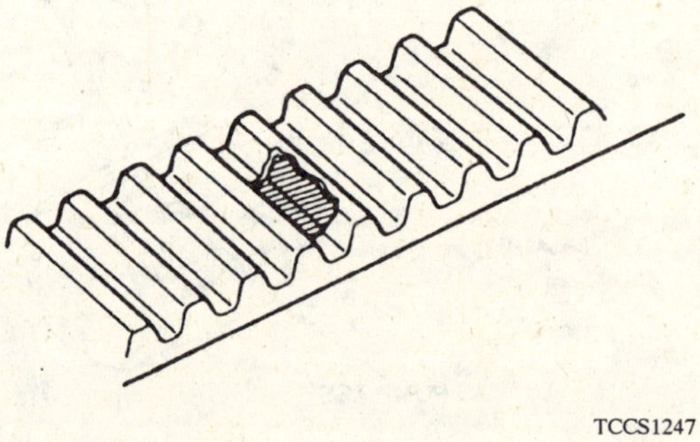

Fig. 96 Foreign materials can get in between the teeth and cause damage

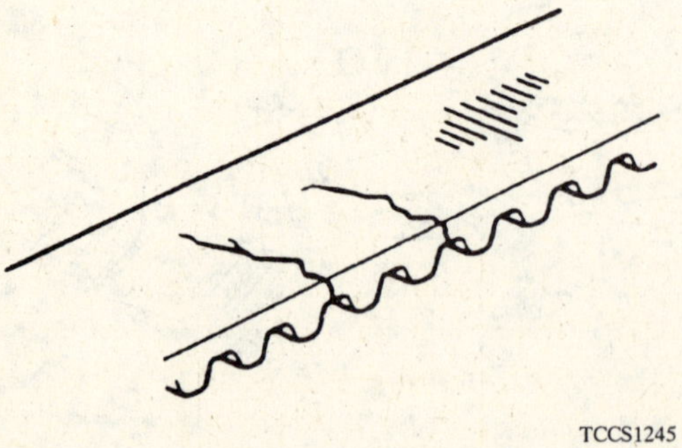

Fig. 94 Look for noticeable cracks or wear on the belt face

Hoses

INSPECTION

➧ See Figures 97, 98, 99 and 100

Upper and lower radiator hoses along with the heater hoses should be checked for deterioration, leaks and loose hose clamps at least every 15,000 miles (24,000 km). It is also wise to check the hoses periodically in early spring and at the beginning of the fall or winter when you are performing other maintenance. A quick visual inspection could discover a weakened hose which might have left you stranded if it had remained unrepaired.

Whenever you are checking the hoses, make sure the engine and cooling system are cold. Visually inspect for cracking, rotting or collapsed hoses, and replace as necessary. Run your hand along the length of the hose. If a weak or swollen spot is noted when squeezing the hose wall, the hose should be replaced.

TCCS1219

Fig. 97 The cracks developing along this hose are a result of age-related hardening

TCCS1220

Fig. 98 A hose clamp that is too tight can cause older hoses to separate and tear on either side of the clamp

TCCS1221

Fig. 99 A soft spongy hose (identifiable by the swollen section) will eventually burst and should be replaced

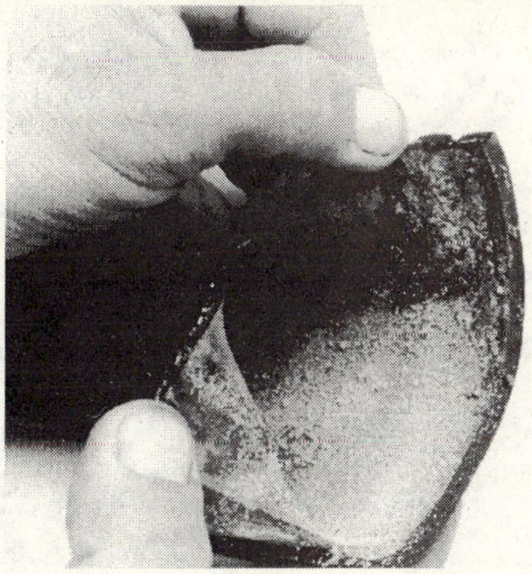

TCCS1222

Fig. 100 Hoses are likely to deteriorate from the inside if the cooling system is not periodically flushed

REMOVAL & INSTALLATION

➧ See Figure 101

1. Remove the radiator pressure cap.

****CAUTION**

Never remove the pressure cap while the engine is running, or personal injury from scalding hot coolant or steam may result. If possible, wait until the engine has cooled to remove the pressure cap. If this is not possible, wrap a thick cloth around the pressure cap and turn it slowly to the stop. Step back while the pressure is released from the cooling system. When you are sure all the pressure has been released, use the cloth to turn and remove the cap.

2. Position a clean container under the radiator and/or engine draincock or plug, then open the drain and allow the cooling system to drain to an appropriate level. For some upper hoses, only a little coolant must be drained. To remove hoses positioned lower on the engine, such as a lower radiator hose, the entire cooling system must be emptied.

****CAUTION**

When draining coolant, keep in mind that cats and dogs are attracted by ethylene glycol antifreeze, and are quite likely to drink any that is left in an uncovered container or in puddles on the ground. This will prove fatal in sufficient quantity. Always drain coolant into a sealable container. Coolant may be reused unless it is contaminated or several years old.

3. Loosen the hose clamps at each end of the hose requiring replacement. Clamps are usually either of the spring tension type (which require pliers to squeeze the tabs and loosen) or of the screw tension type (which require screw or hex drivers to loosen). Pull the clamps back on the hose away from the connection.
4. Twist, pull and slide the hose off the fitting, taking care not to damage the neck of the component from which the hose is being removed.

88181P12

Fig. 101 Spring tension type clamps require a pair of pliers to squeeze the tabs for removal

➥ If the hose is stuck at the connection, do not try to insert a screwdriver or other sharp tool under the hose end in an effort to free it, as the connection and/or hose may become damaged. Heater connections especially may be easily damaged by such a procedure. If the hose is to be replaced, use a single-edged razor blade to make a slice along the portion of the hose which is stuck on the connection, perpendicular to the end of the hose. Do not cut deeply to prevent damaging the connection. The hose can then be peeled from the connection and discarded.

5. Clean both hose mounting connections. Inspect the condition of the hose clamps and replace them, if necessary.

To install:

6. Dip the ends of the new hose into clean engine coolant to ease installation.
7. Slide the clamps over the replacement hose, then slide the hose ends over the connections into position.
8. Position and secure the clamps at least $^1/_4$ in. (6.35mm) from the ends of the hose. Make sure they are located beyond the raised bead of the connector.
9. Close the radiator or engine drains and properly refill the cooling system with the clean drained engine coolant or a suitable mixture of ethylene glycol coolant and water.
10. If available, install a pressure tester and check for leaks. If a pressure tester is not available, run the engine until normal operating temperature is reached (allowing the system to naturally pressurize), then check for leaks.

****CAUTION**

If you are checking for leaks with the system at normal operating temperature, BE EXTREMELY CAREFUL not to touch any moving or hot engine parts. Once temperature has been reached, shut the engine OFF, and check for leaks around the hose fittings and connections which were removed earlier.

CV Boots

INSPECTION

➧ See Figures 102 and 103

The CV (Constant Velocity) boots should should be checked for damage each time the oil is changed and any other time the vehicle is raised for service. These boots keep water, grime, dirt and other damaging matter from entering the CV-joints. Any of these could cause early CV-joint failure which can be expensive to repair. Heavy grease thrown around the inside of the rear wheel(s) and on the brakes can be an indication of a torn boot. Thoroughly check the boots for missing clamps and tears. If the boot is damaged, have it replaced immediately.

TCCS1011

Fig. 102 CV-Boots must be inspected periodically for damage

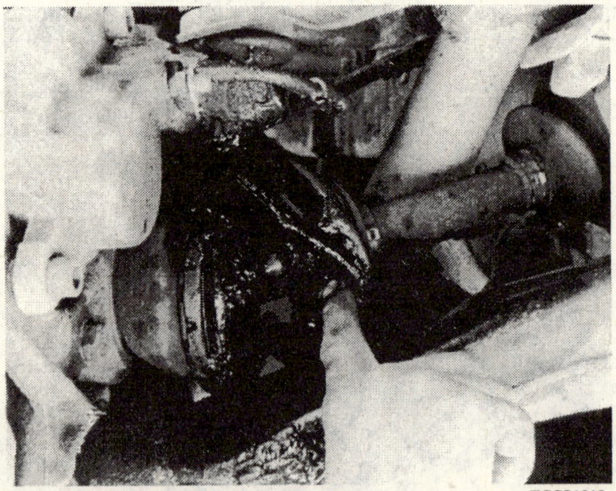

TCCS1010

Fig. 103 A torn boot should be replaced immediately

Spark Plugs

➧ See Figure 104

A typical spark plug consists of a metal shell surrounding a ceramic insulator. A metal electrode extends downward through the center of the insulator and protrudes a small distance. Located at the end of the plug and attached to the side of the outer metal shell is the side electrode. The side electrode bends in at a 90° angle so that its tip is just past and parallel to the tip of the center electrode. The distance between these two electrodes (measured in thousandths of an inch or hundredths of a millimeter) is called the spark plug gap.

The spark plug does not produce a spark but instead provides a gap across which the current can arc. The coil produces anywhere from 20,000 to 50,000 volts (depending on the type and application) which travels through the wires to the spark plugs. The current passes along the center electrode and jumps the gap to the side electrode, and in doing so, ignites the air/fuel mixture in the combustion chamber.

SPARK PLUG HEAT RANGE

➧ See Figure 105

Spark plug heat range is the ability of the plug to dissipate heat. The longer the insulator (or the farther it extends into the engine), the hotter the plug will operate; the shorter the insulator (the closer the electrode is to the block's cooling passages) the cooler it will operate. A plug that absorbs little heat and remains too cool will quickly accumulate deposits of oil and carbon since it is not hot enough to burn them off. This leads to plug fouling and consequently to misfiring. A plug that absorbs too much heat will have no deposits but, due to the excessive heat, the electrodes will burn away quickly and might possibly lead to preignition or other ignition problems. Preignition takes place when plug tips get so hot that they glow sufficiently to ignite the air/fuel mixture before the actual spark occurs. This early ignition will usually cause a pinging during low speeds and heavy loads.

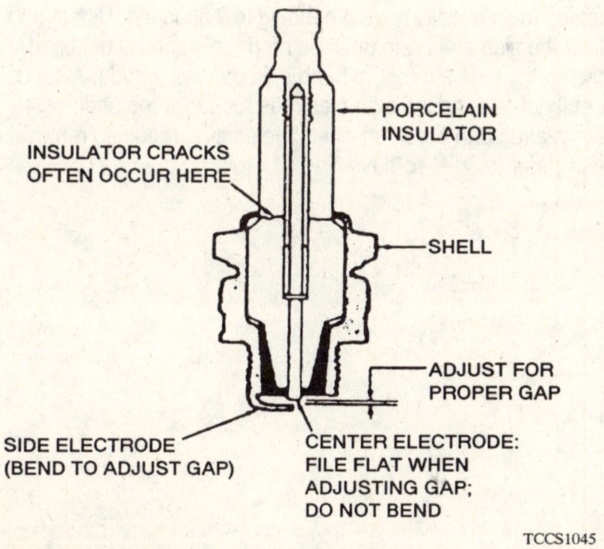

Fig. 104 Cross-section of a spark plug

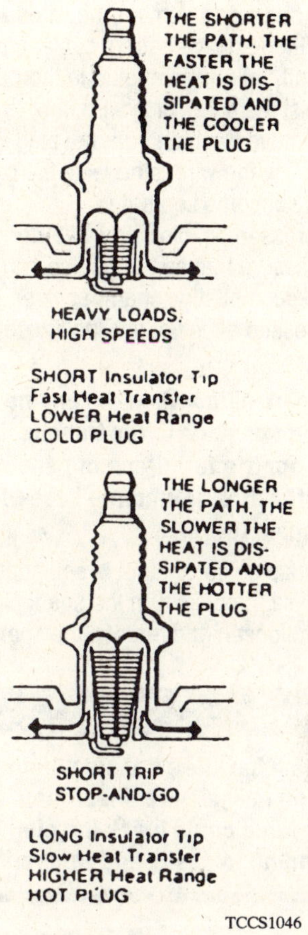

Fig. 105 Spark plug heat range

The general rule of thumb for choosing the correct heat range when picking a spark plug is: if most of your driving is long distance, high speed travel, use a colder plug; if most of your driving is stop and go, use a hotter plug. Original equipment plugs are generally a good compromise between the 2 styles and most people never have the need to change their plugs from the factory-recommended heat range.

REMOVAL & INSTALLATION

A non platinum set of spark plugs usually requires replacement after about 20,000-30,000 miles (32,000-48,000 km) depending on your style of driving. On the platinum spark plugs replace them at 60,000 miles (96,000 km). On normal operation plug gap increases about 0.001 in (0.025 mm) for every 2,500 miles (4000 km). As the gap increases, the plug's voltage requirement also increases. It requires a greater voltage to jump the wider gap and about two to three times as much voltage to fire the plug at high speeds than at idle. The improved air/fuel ratio control of modern fuel injection combined with the higher voltage output of modern ignition systems will often allow an engine to run significantly longer on a set of standard spark plugs, but keep in mind that efficiency will drop as the gap widens (along with fuel economy and power).

When you're removing spark plugs, work on one at a time. Don't start by removing the plug wires all at once, because, unless you number them, they may become mixed up. Take a minute before you begin and number the wires with tape.

1. Disconnect the negative battery cable, and if the vehicle has been run recently, allow the engine to thoroughly cool.
2. Carefully twist the spark plug wire boot to loosen it, then pull upward and remove the boot from the plug. Be sure to pull on the boot and not on the wire, otherwise the connector located inside the boot may become separated.
3. Using compressed air, blow any water or debris from the spark plug well to assure that no harmful contaminants are allowed to enter the combustion chamber when the spark plug is removed. If compressed air is not available, use a rag or a brush to clean the area.

Remove the spark plugs when the engine is cold, if possible, to prevent damage to the threads. If removal of the plugs is difficult, apply a few drops of penetrating oil or silicone spray to the area around the base of the plug, and allow it a few minutes to work.

4. Using a spark plug socket that is equipped with a rubber insert to properly hold the plug, turn the spark plug counterclockwise to loosen and remove the spark plug from the bore.

****WARNING**

Be sure not to use a flexible extension on the socket. Use of a flexible extension may allow a shear force to be applied to the plug. A shear force could break the plug off in the cylinder head, leading to costly and frustrating repairs.

To install:

5. Inspect the spark plug boot for tears or damage. If a damaged boot is found, the spark plug wire must be replaced.
6. Using a wire feeler gauge, check and adjust the spark plug gap. When using a gauge, the proper size should pass between the electrodes with a slight drag. The next larger size should not be able to pass while the next smaller size should pass freely.
7. Carefully thread the plug into the bore by hand. If resistance is felt before the plug is almost completely threaded, back the plug out and begin threading again. In small, hard to reach areas, an old spark plug wire and boot could be used as a threading tool. The boot will hold the plug while you twist the end of the wire and the wire is supple enough to twist before it would allow the plug to crossthread.

****WARNING**

Do not use the spark plug socket to thread the plugs. Always carefully thread the plug by hand or using an old plug wire to prevent the possibility of crossthreading and damaging the cylinder head bore.

8. Carefully tighten the spark plug. If the plug you are installing is equipped with a crush washer, seat the plug, then tighten about 1/4 turn to crush the washer. If you are installing a tapered seat plug, tighten the plug to specifications provided by the vehicle or plug manufacturer.
9. Apply a small amount of silicone dielectric compound to the end of the spark plug lead or inside the spark plug boot to prevent sticking, then install the boot to the spark plug and push until it clicks into place. The click may be felt or heard, then gently pull back on the boot to assure proper contact.

INSPECTION & GAPPING

See Figures 106, 107, 108, 109,110, 111, 112, 113, 114, 115 and 116

Check the plugs for deposits and wear. If they are not going to be replaced, clean the plugs thoroughly. Remember that any kind of deposit will decrease the efficiency of the plug. Plugs can be cleaned on a spark plug cleaning machine, which can sometimes be found in service stations, or you can do an acceptable job of cleaning with a stiff brush. If the plugs are cleaned, the electrodes must be filed flat. Use an ignition points file, not an emery board or the like, which will leave deposits. The electrodes must be filed perfectly flat with sharp edges; rounded edges reduce the spark plug voltage by as much as 50%.

Check spark plug gap before installation. The ground electrode (the L-shaped one connected to the body of the plug) must be parallel to the center electrode and the specified size wire gauge (please refer to the Tune-Up Specifications chart for details) must pass between the electrodes with a slight drag.

NEVER adjust the gap on a used platinum type spark plug.

Always check the gap on new plugs as they are not always set correctly at the factory. Do not use a flat feeler gauge when measuring the gap on a used plug, because the reading may be inaccurate. A round-wire type gapping tool is the best way to check the gap. The correct gauge should pass through the electrode gap with a slight drag. If you're in doubt, try one size smaller and one larger. The smaller gauge should go through easily, while the larger one shouldn't go through at all. Wire gapping tools usually have a bending tool attached. Use that to adjust the side electrode until the proper distance is obtained. Absolutely never attempt to bend the center electrode. Also, be careful not to bend the side electrode too far or too often as it may weaken and break off within the engine, requiring removal of the cylinder head to retrieve it.

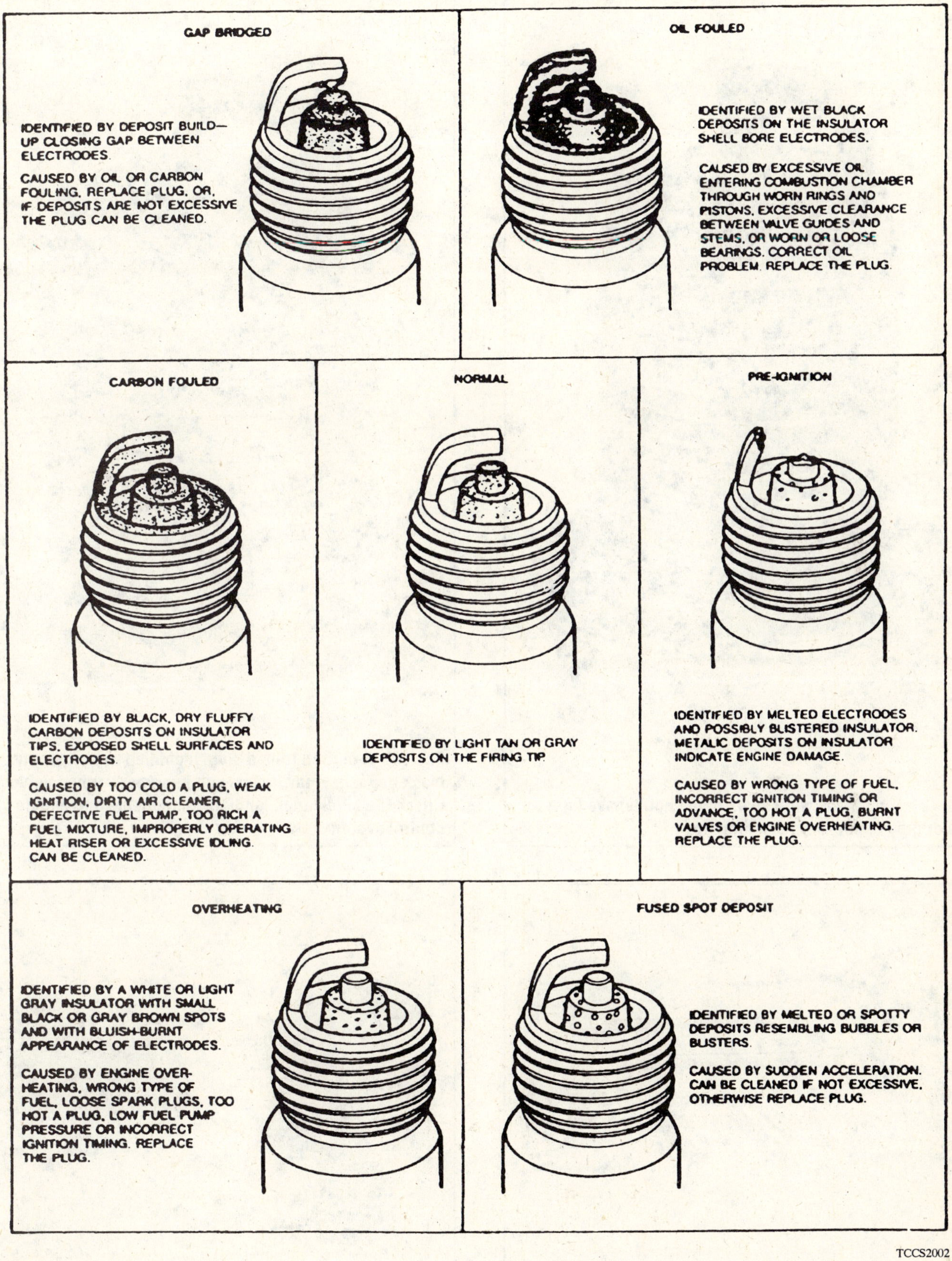

Fig. 106 Inspect the spark plug to determine engine running conditions

TCCS2135

Fig. 107 A normally worn spark plug should have light tan or gray deposits on the firing tip

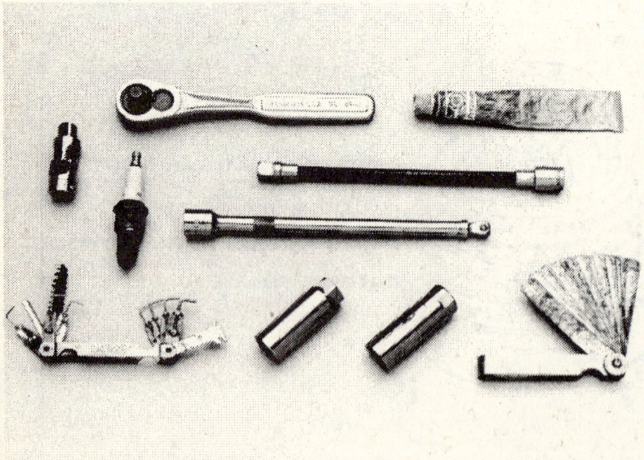

TCCS1212

Fig. 108 A variety of tools and gauges are needed for spark plug service

TCCS2136

Fig. 109 A carbon fouled plug, identified by soft, sooty, black deposits, may indicate an improperly tuned vehicle. Check the air cleaner, ignition components and engine control system

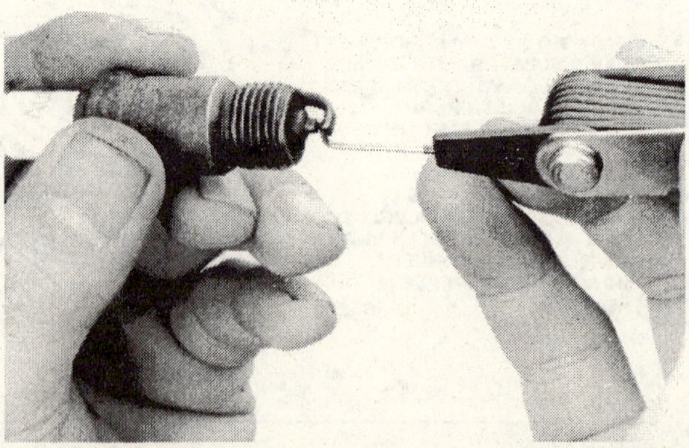

TCCS2903

Fig. 110 Checking the spark plug gap with a feeler gauge

TCCS2137

Fig. 111 A physically damaged spark plug may be evidence of severe detonation in that cylinder. Watch that cylinder carefully between services, as a continued detonation will not only damage the plug, but could also damage the engine

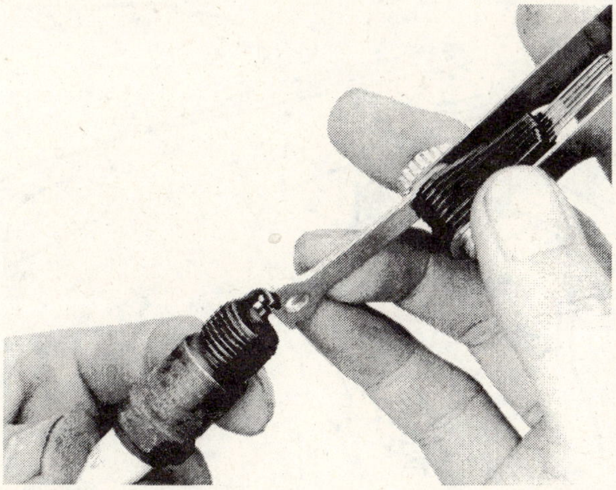

TCCS2904

Fig. 112 Adjusting the spark plug gap

TCCS2138

Fig. 113 An oil fouled spark plug indicates an engine with worn piston rings and/or bad valve seals allowing excessive oil to enter the chamber

TCCS2139

Fig. 114 This spark plug has been left in the engine too long, as evidenced by the extreme gap — Plugs with such an extreme gap can cause misfiring and stumbling accompanied by a noticeable lack of power

TCCS2140

Fig. 115 A bridged or almost bridged spark plug, identified by a build-up between the electrodes caused by excessive carbon or oil build-up on the plug

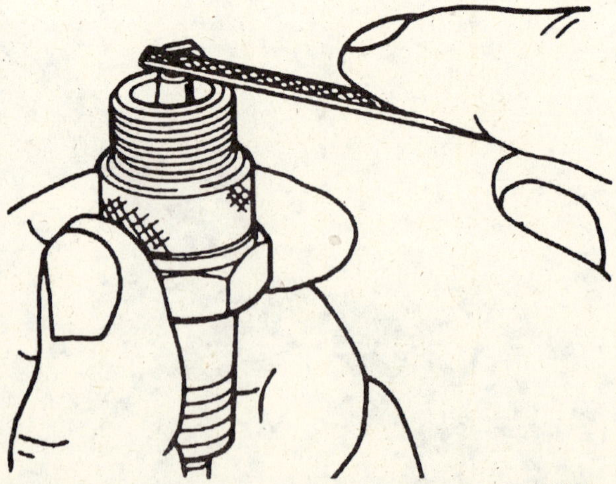

TCCS1141

Fig. 116 If the plug is in good condition, the electrode may be filed flat and reused

Spark Plug Wires

TESTING

➧ See Figures 117 and 118

At every tune-up/inspection, visually check the spark plug cables for burns cuts, or breaks in the insulation. Check the boots and the nipples on the distributor cap and/or coil. Replace any damaged wiring.

Every 50,000 miles (80,000 km) or 60 months, the resistance of the wires should be checked with an ohmmeter. Wires with excessive resistance will cause misfiring, and may make the engine difficult to start in damp weather.

To check resistance, remove the distributor cap, leaving the wires in place. Connect one lead of an ohmmeter to an electrode within the cap; connect the other lead to the corresponding spark plug terminal (remove it from the spark plug for this test). Replace any wire which shows a resistance over 30,000 ohms. The following resistance values are a function of length.

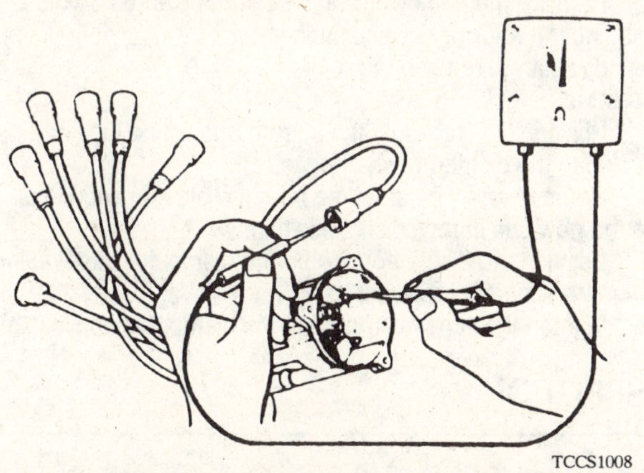

Fig. 117 Checking plug wire resistance through the distributor cap with an ohmmeter

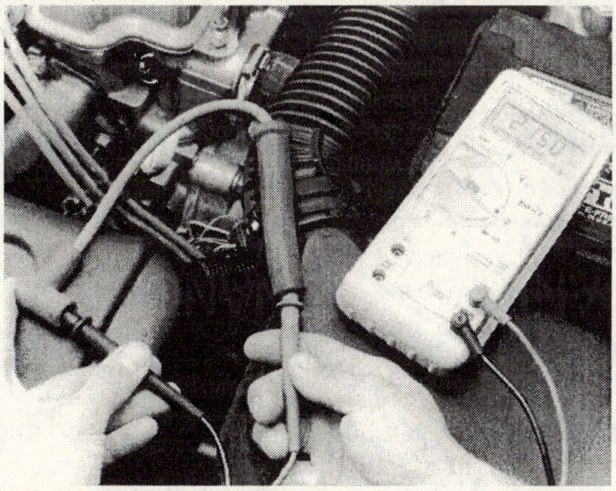

Fig. 118 Checking individual plug wire resistance with a digital ohmmeter

- 0-15 in. (0-38cm): 3000-10,000 ohms
- 15-25 in. (38-64cm): 4000-15,000 ohms
- 25-35 in. (64-89cm): 6000-20,000 ohms
- Over 35 in. (89cm): 25,000 ohms

It should be remembered that resistance is also a function of length; the longer the wire, the greater the resistance. Thus, if the wires on your car are longer than the factory originals, resistance will be higher, quite possibly outside these limits.

When installing new wires, replace them one at a time to avoid mixups. Start by replacing the longest one first. Install the boot firmly over the spark plug. Route the wire over the the same path as the original. Insert the nipple firmly onto the tower on the distributor cap, then install the cap cover and latches to secure the wires.

REMOVAL & INSTALLATION

➧ See Figure 119

1. Before removing high tension wires from the spark plugs, distributor cap or coil, inspect them for visible damage such as cuts, pinches, cracks or torn boots. Replace only wires that are damaged.
2. Remove the wires from the spark plugs, using a suitable spark plug wire removal tool (T74P-6666-A or equivalent).
3. Grasp and twist the spark plug wire boot back and forth, then pull the wire off the plug.

➥ Do not pull directly on the spark plug wire, or it may separate from its terminal inside the spark plug wire boot.

4. If it becomes necessary to remove the wires from the distributor cap or coil, grasp the boot by hand and remove with a twisting and pulling motion.

To install:

➥ Whenever an ignition wire is removed from a spark plug, ignition coil or distributor cap terminal, silicone compound must be applied to the spark plug wire boot before it is reconnected. Using a small clean tool, lightly coat the entire inner surface of the boot with Ford Silicone Dielectric Compound (D7AZ-19A331-A or equivalent).

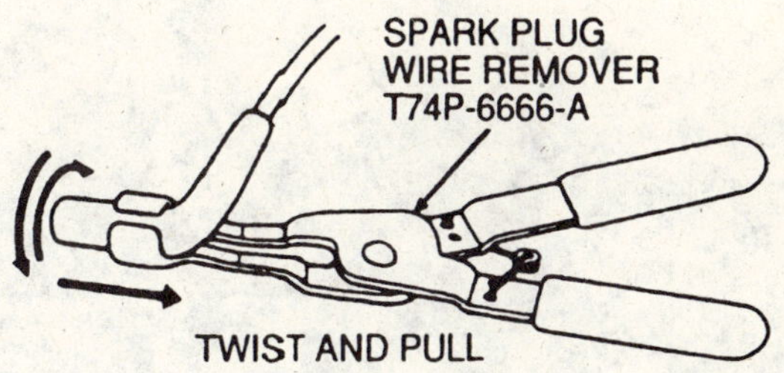

Fig. 119 A spark plug wire remover such as the T74P-6666-A will ease removal of the wires

5. When installing a new set of spark plug wires, replace the wires one at a time so there will be no mixup. Start by replacing the longest wire first. Install the boot firmly over the spark plug. Route the wire exactly the same as the original. Attach each wire to the proper terminal of the distributor cap. Check to ensure the wires are fully seated on the terminals. Repeat the process for each wire.
6. Remove the wire separators from the old wire set and install them on the new wire set in the same position.
7. Connect the wires to the proper spark plugs. Install the ignition coil wire. Check to ensure the wires are fully seated on the terminals.

Distributor Cap and Rotor

REMOVAL & INSTALLATION

➧ See Figures 120, 121 and 122

1. Disconnect the negative battery cable.

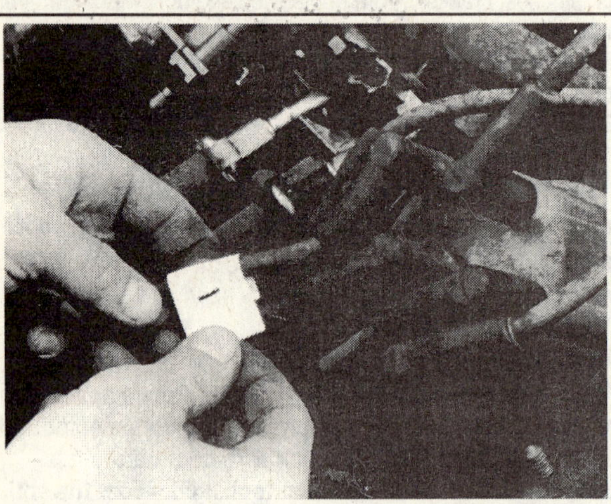

88181P13

Fig. 120 If necessary for removal, label each wire for installation purposes

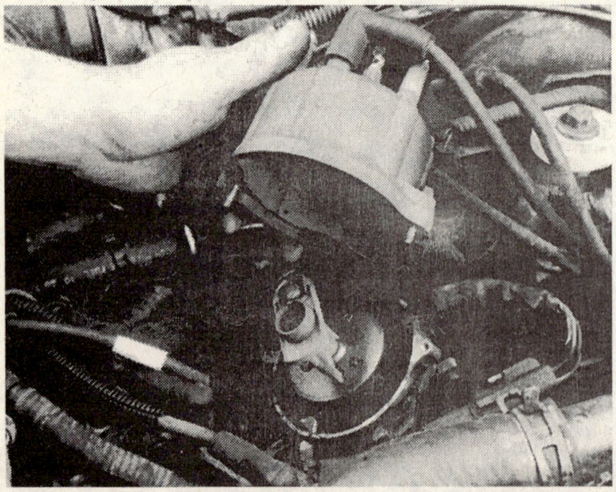

88181P14

Fig. 121 Pull the cap upward to avoid damaging the rotor

88181P15

Fig. 122 Pull the rotor straight up from the distributor shaft to remove

2. Label the spark plug wires.
3. Loosen the distributor cap hold-down screws or release the clamps.
4. Remove the cap by pulling it straight upwards. Avoid damaging the rotor points and spring.
5. If required, remove the rotor.

To install:

6. Position the rotor with the square and round locator pins matched to the distributor shaft plate.
7. Remove one wire at a time from the old cap and install onto the new cap in the correct position.
8. Position the distributor cap on the distributor base noting the square alignment locator.
9. Tighten the screws or engage the clamps as applicable.

INSPECTION

➧ See Figures 123 and 124

Clean the inside and outside of the cap surfaces with soap and water. Dry the cap with compressed air. Inspect it for cracks, broken carbon button or carbon tracks. Also inspect the terminals for dirt and corrosion.

Clean the distributor rotor with a soap and water solution. Dry the rotor with compressed air and inspect it for tip wear or damages.

****WARNING**

Do not bend the rotor spring or file the tip.

Replace the cap and rotor if any signs of damage or wear are noticed. It is advisable to replace them both in a set.

Ignition Timing

GENERAL INFORMATION

Ignition timing is the measurement in degrees of crankshaft rotation at the instant the spark plug fires while the piston is on its compression stroke.

Ideally, the air/fuel mixture in the cylinder will be ignited by the spark plug and just beginning its rapid expansion as the piston passes Top Dead Center (TDC) of the compression stroke. If this happens, the piston will be beginning the power stroke just as the compressed air/fuel mixture starts to burn and expand. The expansion (explosion) of the air/fuel mixture will then force the piston down on the power stroke and turn the crankshaft.

It takes a fraction of a second for the spark from the plug to completely ignite the mixture in the cylinder. Because of this, the spark plug must fire before the piston reaches TDC, if the mixture is to be completely ignited as the piston passes TDC. This measurement is given in degrees of crankshaft rotation before the piston reaches top dead center (BTDC). If the ignition timing setting for your engine is ten (10°) BTDC, this means that the spark plug must fire at the time when the piston for that cylinder is 10° before reaching the top of its compression stroke. However, this only holds true while your engine is at idle speed.

As the engine accelerates from idle, the speed of the engine (rpm, or revolutions per minute) increases. The increase in rpm means that the pistons are now traveling up and down much faster. Because of this, the spark plugs will have to fire even sooner if the mixture is to be completely ignited as the piston passes TDC. To accomplish this, the distributor incorporates means to advance the timing of the spark as engine speed increases.

If ignition timing is set too far advanced (BTDC), the ignition and expansion of the air/fuel mixture in the cylinder will try to force the piston down in the cylinder while it is still traveling upward. This causes engine "ping", a sound which resembles marbles being dropped into an empty tin can. If the ignition timing is too far retarded (after, or ATDC), the piston will have already started down on the power stroke when the air/fuel mixture ignites. This will cause the piston to be forced down only a portion of its travel, resulting in poor engine performance and lack of power.

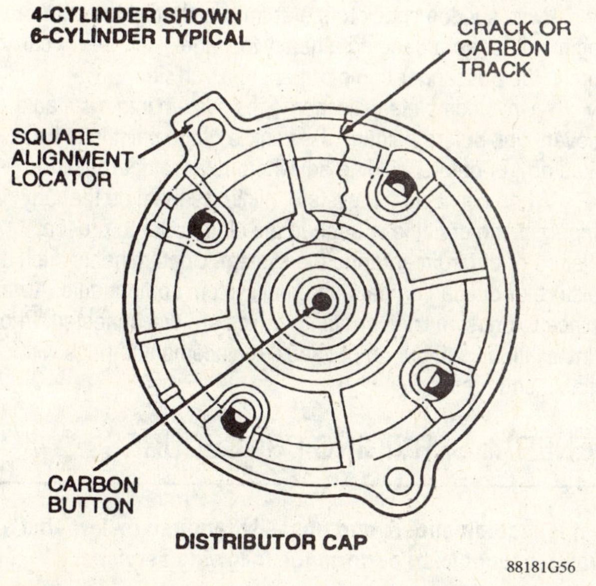

Fig. 123 Inspect the cap for cracks and corrosion

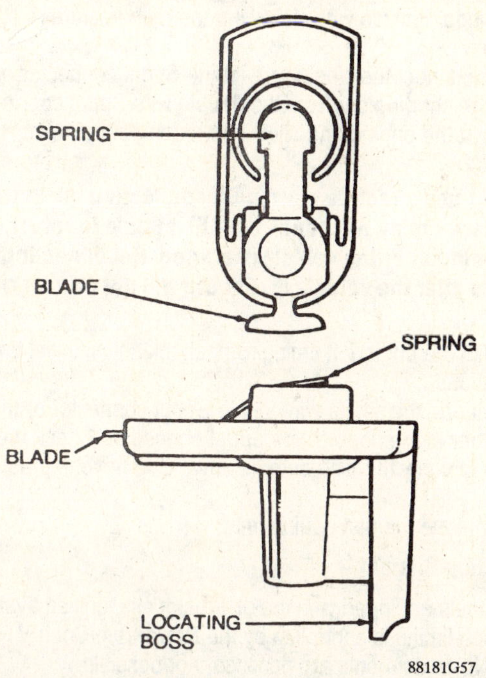

Fig. 124 The rotor blade and spring are the spots which would show the most wear and damage

INSPECTION & ADJUSTMENT

Dura Spark II Ignition System

This sytem is used on the 3.8l carburreted engines.

➥ If the following timing procedure differs from that found on the Vehicle's Emission Information label, use those found on the sticker. Always refer to the Vehicle Emission Information label for initial timing and spark plug specifications.

1. Place the transmission in **P** or **N**.
2. Turn all accessories off (A/C, heater...etc.).
3. Remove vacuum hoses from the distributor vacuum advance connection and plug them.
4. Connect an inductive timing light and tachometer to the No. 1 cylinder ignition wire (following the manufactures instructions).
5. If equipped with a barometric pressure switch, disconnect it from the ignition module and place a jumper wire across the pins at the ignition module connector.
6. Start the engine and allow it to reach operating temperature.
7. With the engine at timing rpm, check/adjust initial timing to specifications.
8. Remove the test equipments.
9. Unplug and reconnect the vacuum hoses.
10. Remove the jumper from the ignition module connector and engage it.

EEC-IV Thick Film Ignition System

This system is used on the fuel injected engines.

1. Place the transmission in **P** or **N**.
2. Turn all accessories off (A/C, heater...etc.).

3. Connect an inductive timing light and tachometer to the No. 1 cylinder ignition wire (following the manufactures instructions).
4. Disconnect the single wire in-line Spout connector or remove the shorting bar from the double wire Spout connector.
5. Start the engine and allow it to reach operating temperature.

➔ Do not use a remote starter. Disconnecting the start wire at the starter relay will cause the TFI module to revert to start mode timing after the vehicle is started. Reconnecting the start wire after the vehicle is running will not correct the timing.

6. With the engine at timing rpm, check/adjust initial timing to specifications.
7. Engage the single wire in-line Spout connector or the shorting bar to the double wire Spout connector. Check the timing advance to verify the distributor is advancing beyond the initial timing.
8. Remove the test equipments.

DIS Ignition System

On models equipped with the distributorless ignition system, the ignition timing is controlled by the Powertrain Control Module (PCM). No adjustments are necessary or possible.

Idle Speed and Mixture Adjustments

The idle speed and mixture adjustments are regulated by the computer control module. No routine adjustment is necessary. Refer to Section for any applicable adjustments.

Air Conditioning

➔ Be sure to consult the laws in your area before servicing the air conditioning system. In most areas, it is illegal to perform repairs involving refrigerant unless the work is done by a certified technician. Also, it is quite likely that you will not be able to purchase refrigerant without proof of certification.

SAFETY PRECAUTIONS

There are two major hazards associated with air conditioning systems and they both relate to the refrigerant gas. First, the refrigerant gas (R-12 or R-134a) is an extremely cold substance. When exposed to air, it will instantly freeze any surface it comes in contact with, including your eyes. The other hazard relates to fire (if your vehicle is equipped with R-12. Although normally non-toxic, the R-12 gas becomes highly poisonous in the presence of an open flame. One good whiff of the vapor formed by burning R-12 can be fatal. Keep all forms of fire (including cigarettes) well clear of the air conditioning system.

Because of the inherent dangers involved with working on air conditioning systems, these safety precautions must be strictly followed.

- Avoid contact with a charged refrigeration system, even when working on another part of the air conditioning system or vehicle. If a heavy tool comes into contact with a section of tubing or a heat exchanger, it can easily cause the relatively soft material to rupture.
- When it is necessary to apply force to a fitting which contains refrigerant, as when checking that all system couplings are securely tightened, use a wrench on both parts of the fitting involved, if possible. This will avoid putting torque on refrigerant tubing. (It is also advisable to use tube or line wrenches when tightening these flare nut fittings.)

➔ R-12 refrigerant is a chlorofluorocarbon which, when released into the atmosphere, can contribute to the depletion of the ozone layer in the upper atmosphere. Ozone filters out harmful radiation from the sun.

- Do not attempt to discharge the system without the proper tools. Precise control is possible only when using the service gauges and a proper A/C refrigerant recovery station. Wear protective gloves when connecting or disconnecting service gauge hoses.
- Discharge the system only in a well ventilated area, as high concentrations of the gas which might accidentally escape can exclude oxygen and act as an anesthetic. When leak testing or soldering, this is particularly important, as toxic gas is formed when R-12 contacts any flame.
- Never start a system without first verifying that both service valves are properly installed, and that all fittings throughout the system are snugly connected.
- Avoid applying heat to any refrigerant line or storage vessel. Charging may be aided by using water heated to less than 125°F (50°C) to warm the refrigerant container. Never allow a refrigerant storage container to sit out in the sun, or near any other source of heat, such as a radiator or heater.
- Always wear goggles to protect your eyes when working on a system. If refrigerant contacts the eyes, it is advisable in all cases to consult a physician immediately.
- Frostbite from liquid refrigerant should be treated by first gradually warming the area with cool water, and then gently applying petroleum jelly. A physician should be consulted.
- Always keep refrigerant drum fittings capped when not in use. If the container is equipped with a safety cap to protect the valve, make sure the cap is in place when the can is not being used. Avoid sudden shock to the drum, which might occur from dropping it, or from banging a heavy tool against it. Never carry a drum in the passenger compartment of a vehicle.
- Always completely discharge the system into a suitable recovery unit before painting the vehicle (if the paint is to be baked on), or before welding anywhere near refrigerant lines.
- When servicing the system, minimize the time that any refrigerant line or fitting is open to the air in order to prevent moisture or dirt from entering the system. Contaminants such as moisture or dirt can damage internal system components. Always replace O-rings on lines or fittings which are disconnected. Prior to installation coat, but do not soak, replacement O-rings with suitable compressor oil.

GENERAL SERVICING PROCEDURES

➔ It is recommended, and possibly required by law, that a qualified technician perform the following services.

GASOLINE ENGINE TUNE-UP SPECIFICATIONS

Year	Engine ID/VIN	Engine Displacement Liters (cc)	Spark Plugs Gap (in.)	Ignition Timing (deg.) MT	Ignition Timing (deg.) AT	Fuel Pump (psi)	Idle Speed (rpm) MT	Idle Speed (rpm) AT	Valve Clearance In.	Valve Clearance Ex.
1983	W	2.3 (2300) ①	0.034	10B	10B	36-42	750	750	HYD	HYD
	3	3.8 (3802)	0.044	10B	10B	6-8	600	600	HYD	HYD
	F	5.0 (4949)	0.050	-	10B	36-42	-	550	HYD	HYD
1984	W	2.3 (2300) ①	0.034	10B	10B	36-42	750	750	HYD	HYD
	3	3.8 (3802)	0.044	10B	10B	35-45	600	600	HYD	HYD
	F	5.0 (4949)	0.050	-	10B	6-8	-	550	HYD	HYD
1985	W	2.3 (2300) ①	0.034	10B	10B	36-42	750	750	HYD	HYD
	3	3.8 (3802)	0.044	10B	10B	35-45	600	600	HYD	HYD
	F	5.0 (4949)	0.050	-	10B	36-42	-	550	HYD	HYD
1986	W	2.3 (2300) ①	0.034	10B	10B	36-42	750	750	HYD	HYD
	3	3.8 (3802)	0.044	10B	10B	35-45	600	600	HYD	HYD
	F	5.0 (4949)	0.044	-	10B	36-42	-	550	HYD	HYD
1987	W	2.3 (2300) ①	0.034	10B	10B	36-42	750	750	HYD	HYD
	3	3.8 (3802)	0.044	10B	10B	35-45	600	600	HYD	HYD
	F	5.0 (4949)	0.044	-	10B	36-42	-	550	HYD	HYD
1988	W	2.3 (2300) ①	0.034	10B	10B	36-42	750	750	HYD	HYD
	4	3.8 (3802)	0.044	-	10B	35-45	550	550	HYD	HYD
	F	5.0 (4949)	0.044	-	10B	36-42	-	550	HYD	HYD
1989	4	3.8 (3802)	0.044	-	10B	35-45	550	550	HYD	HYD
	R	3.8 (3802)	0.054	10B	10B	35-45	550	550	HYD	HYD
1990	4	3.8 (3802)	0.054	10B	10B	35-45	550	550	HYD	HYD
	R	3.8 (3802)	0.054	10B	10B	35-45	550	550	HYD	HYD
1991	4	3.8 (3802)	0.054	10B	10B	35-45	550	550	HYD	HYD
	R	3.8 (3802)	0.054	10B	10B	35-45	550	550	HYD	HYD
	T	5.0 (4949)	0.054	-	10B	35-40	-	650	HYD	HYD
1992	4	3.8 (3802)	0.054	10B	10B	35-45	550	550	HYD	HYD
	R	3.8 (3802)	0.054	10B	10B	35-45	550	550	HYD	HYD
	T	5.0 (4949)	0.054	-	10B	35-40	-	650	HYD	HYD
1993	4	3.8 (3802)	0.054	10B	10B	35-45	550	550	HYD	HYD
	R	3.8 (3802)	0.054	②	②	35-45	550	550	HYD	HYD
	T	5.0 (4949)	0.054	-	10B	35-40	-	650	HYD	HYD
1994	4	3.8 (3802)	0.054	10B	10B	30-45	-	②	HYD	HYD
	R	3.8 (3802)	0.054	②	②	35-45	550	550	HYD	HYD
	W	4.6 (4593)	0.054	-	②	30-45	-	②	HYD	HYD
1995	4	3.8 (3802)	0.054	②	②	30-45	-	②	HYD	HYD
	R	3.8 (3802)	0.054	②	②	35-45	550	550	HYD	HYD
	W	4.6 (4593)	0.054	-	②	30-45	-	②	HYD	HYD
1996	4	3.8 (3802)	0.054	-	②	30-45	-	②	HYD	HYD
	W	4.6 (4593)	0.054	-	②	35-45	-	②	HYD	HYD

NOTE: The Vehicle Emission Control Information label often reflects specification changes made during production. The label figures must be used if they differ from those in this chart.

B - Before top dead center

HYD - Hydraulic

1 : Turbo

2 : Refer to Vehicle Emission Information label

88181C05

****WARNING**

Some of the vehicles covered by this manual may be equipped with R-134a refrigerant systems, rather than R-12. Be ABSOLUTELY SURE what type of system you are working on before attempting to add refrigerant. Use of the wrong refrigerant or oil will cause damage to the system.

The most important aspect of air conditioning service is the maintenance of a pure and adequate charge of refrigerant in the system. A refrigeration system cannot function properly if a significant percentage of the charge is lost. Leaks are common because the severe vibration encountered underhood in an automobile can easily cause a sufficient cracking or loosening of the air conditioning fittings; allowing, the extreme operating pressures of the system to force refrigerant out.

The problem can be understood by considering what happens to the system as it is operated with a continuous leak. Because the expansion valve regulates the flow of refrigerant to the evaporator, the level of refrigerant there is fairly constant. The receiver/drier stores any excess refrigerant, and so a loss will first appear there as a reduction in the level of liquid. As this level nears the bottom of the vessel, some refrigerant vapor bubbles will begin to appear in the stream of liquid supplied to the expansion valve. This vapor decreases the capacity of the expansion valve very little as the valve opens to compensate for its presence. As the quantity of liquid in the condenser decreases, the operating pressure will drop there and throughout the high side of the system. As the refrigerant continues to be expelled, the pressure available to force the liquid through the expansion valve will continue to decrease, and, eventually, the valve's orifice will prove to be too much of a restriction for adequate flow even with the needle fully withdrawn.

At this point, low side pressure will start to drop, and a severe reduction in cooling capacity, marked by freeze-up of the evaporator coil, will result. Eventually, the operating pressure of the evaporator will be lower than the pressure of the atmosphere surrounding it, and air will be drawn into the system wherever there are leaks in the low side.

Because all atmospheric air contains at least some moisture, water will enter the system mixing with the refrigerant and oil. Trace amounts of moisture will cause sludging of the oil, and corrosion of the system. Saturation and clogging of the filter/drier, and freezing of the expansion valve orifice will eventually result. As air fills the system to a greater and greater extent, it will interfere more and more with the normal flows of refrigerant and heat.

From this description, it should be obvious that much of the repairman's focus in on detecting leaks, repairing them, and then restoring the purity and quantity of the refrigerant charge. A list of general rules should be followed in addition to all safety precautions:

- Keep all tools as clean and dry as possible.
- Thoroughly purge the service gauges/hoses of air and moisture before connecting them to the system. Keep them capped when not in use.
- Thoroughly clean any refrigerant fitting before disconnecting it, in order to minimize the entrance of dirt into the system.
- Plan any operation that requires opening the system beforehand, in order to minimize the length of time it will be exposed to open air. Cap or seal the open ends to minimize the entrance of foreign material.
- When adding oil, pour it through an extremely clean and dry tube or funnel. Keep the oil capped whenever possible. Do not use oil that has not been kept tightly sealed.
- Purchase refrigerant intended for use only in automatic air conditioning systems.
- Completely evacuate any system that has been opened for service, or that has leaked sufficiently to draw in moisture and air. This requires evacuating air and moisture with a good vacuum pump for at least one hour. If a system has been open for a considerable length of time it may be advisable to evacuate the system for up to 12 hours (overnight).
- Use a wrench on both halves of a fitting that is to be disconnected, so as to avoid placing torque on any of the refrigerant lines.
- When overhauling a compressor, pour some of the oil into a clean glass and inspect it. If there is evidence of dirt, metal particles, or both, flush all refrigerant components with clean refrigerant before evacuating and recharging the system. In addition, if metal particles are present, the compressor should be replaced.
- Schrader valves may leak only when under full operating pressure. Therefore, if leakage is suspected but cannot be located, operate the system with a full charge of refrigerant and look for leaks from all Schrader valves. Replace any faulty valves.

Additional Preventive Maintenance

USING THE SYSTEM

The easiest and most important preventive maintenance for your A/C system is to be sure that it is used on a regular basis. Running the system for five minutes each month (no matter what the season) will help assure that the seals and all internal components remain lubricated.

ANTIFREEZE

➧ See Figure 125

In order to prevent heater core freeze-up during A/C operation, it is necessary to maintain a proper antifreeze protection. Use a hand-held antifreeze tester (hydrometer) to periodically check the condition of the antifreeze in your engine's cooling system.

➥ Antifreeze should not be used longer than the manufacturer specifies.

RADIATOR CAP

For efficient operation of an air conditioned vehicle's cooling system, the radiator cap should have a holding pressure which meets manufacturer's specifications. A cap which fails to hold these pressures should be replaced.

CONDENSER

Any obstruction of or damage to the condenser configuration will restrict the air flow which is essential to its efficient operation. It is therefore a good rule to keep this unit clean and in proper physical shape.

➥ Bug screens which are mounted in front of the condenser (unless they are original equipment) are regarded as obstructions.

TCCS1233

Fig. 125 An antifreeze tester can be use to determine the freezing and boiling level of the coolant in your vehicle

CONDENSATION DRAIN TUBE

This single molded drain tube expels the condensation, which accumulates on the bottom of the evaporator housing, into the engine compartment. If this tube is obstructed, the air conditioning performance can be restricted and condensation buildup can spill over onto the vehicle's floor.

SYSTEM INSPECTION

➥ R-12 refrigerant is a chlorofluorocarbon which, when released into the atmosphere, can contribute to the depletion of the ozone layer in the upper atmosphere. Ozone filters out harmful radiation from the sun.

The easiest and often most important check for the air conditioning system consists of a visual inspection of the system components. Visually inspect the air conditioning system for refrigerant leaks, damaged compressor clutch, compressor drive belt tension and condition, plugged evaporator drain tube, blocked condenser fins, disconnected or broken wires, blown fuses, corroded connections and poor insulation.

A refrigerant leak will usually appear as an oily residue at the leakage point in the system. The oily residue soon picks up dust or dirt particles from the surrounding air and appears greasy. Through time, this will build up and appear to be a heavy dirt impregnated grease. Most leaks are caused by damaged or missing O-ring seals at the component connections, damaged charging valve cores or missing service gauge port caps.

For a thorough visual and operational inspection, check the following:

1. Check the surface of the radiator and condenser for dirt, leaves or other material which might block air flow.
2. Check for kinks in hoses and lines. Check the system for leaks.
3. Make sure the drive belt is under the proper tension. When the air conditioning is operating, make sure the drive belt is free of noise or slippage.
4. Make sure the blower motor operates at all appropriate positions, then check for distribution of the air from all outlets with the blower on **HIGH**.

➥ Keep in mind that under conditions of high humidity, air discharged from the A/C vents may not feel as cold as expected, even if the system is working properly. This is because the vaporized moisture in humid air retains heat more effectively than does dry air, making the humid air more difficult to cool.

5. Make sure the air passage selection lever is operating correctly. Start the engine and warm it to normal operating temperature, then make sure the hot/cold selection lever is operating correctly.

DISCHARGING, EVACUATING AND CHARGING

Discharging, evacuating and charging the air conditioning system must be performed by a properly trained and certified mechanic in a facility equipped with refrigerant recovery/recycling equipment that meets SAE standards for the type of system to be serviced.

If you don't have access to the necessary equipment, we recommend that you take your vehicle to a reputable service station to have the work done. If you still wish to perform repairs on the vehicle, have them discharge the system, then take your vehicle home and perform the necessary work. When you are finished, return the vehicle to the station for evacuation and charging. Just be sure to cap ALL A/C system fittings immediately after opening them and keep them protected until the system is recharged.

Windshield Wipers

ELEMENT (REFILL) CARE AND REPLACEMENT

➧ See Figures 126, 127, 128, 129, 130, 131, 132, 133, 134 and 135

For maximum effectiveness and longest element life, the windshield and wiper blades should be kept clean. Dirt, tree sap, road tar and so on will cause streaking, smearing and blade deterioration if left on the glass. It is advisable to wash the windshield carefully with a commercial glass cleaner at least once a month. Wipe off the rubber blades with the wet rag afterwards. Do not attempt to move wipers across the windshield by hand; damage to the motor and drive mechanism will result.

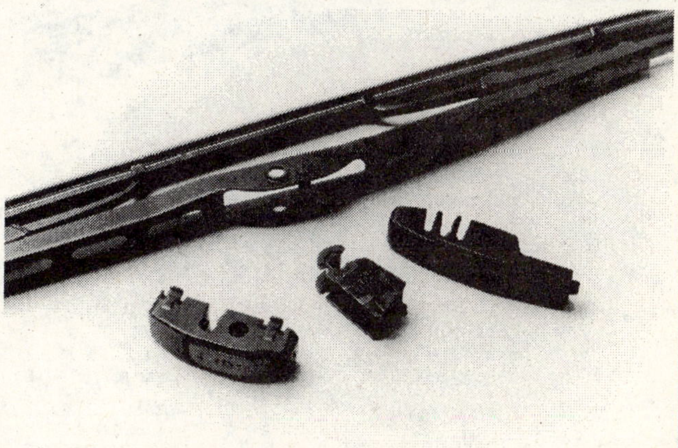

TCCS1223

Fig. 126 Bosch® wiper blade and fit kit

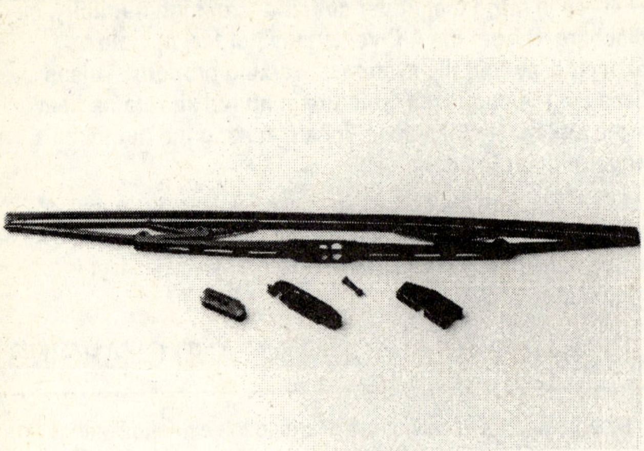

TCCS1224

Fig. 127 Lexor® wiper blade and fit kit

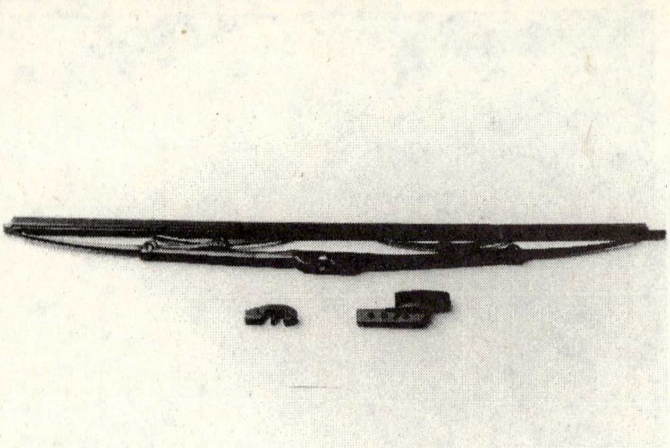

TCCS1227

Fig. 130 Tripledge® wiper blade and fit kit

TCCS1225

Fig. 128 Pylon® wiper blade and adaptor

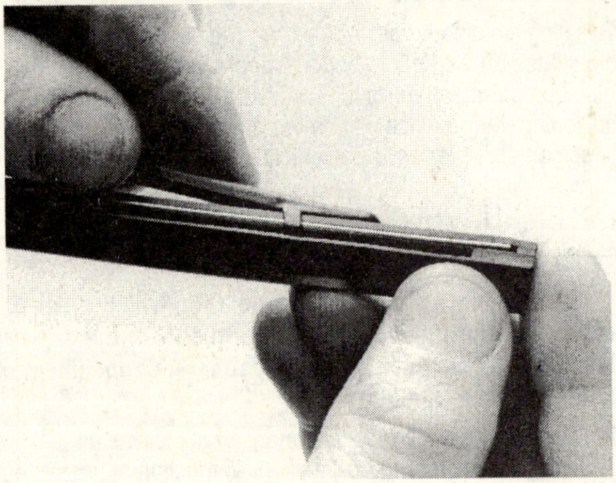

TCCS1228

Fig. 131 To remove and install a Lexor® wiper blade refill, slip out the old insert and slide in a new one

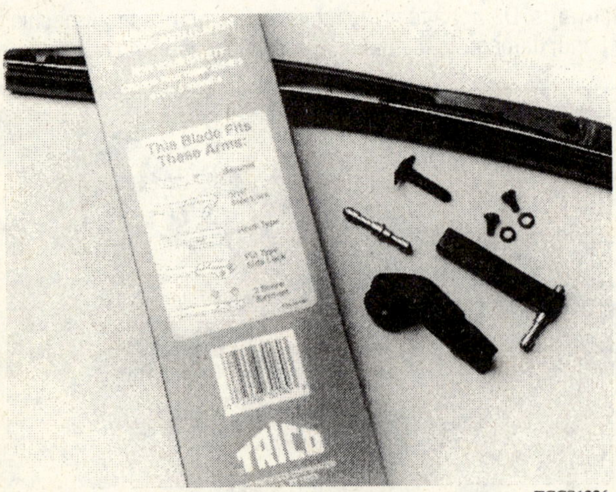

TCCS1226

Fig. 129 Trico® wiper blade and fit kit

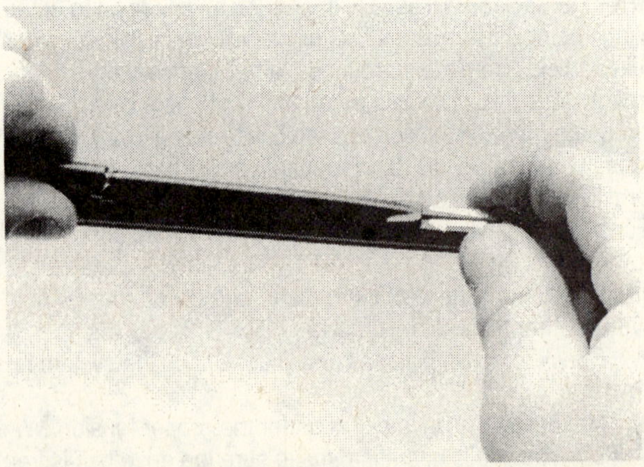

TCCS1229

Fig. 132 On Pylon® inserts, the clip at the end has to be removed prior to sliding the insert off. Don't forget to install the clip after the new insert is installed

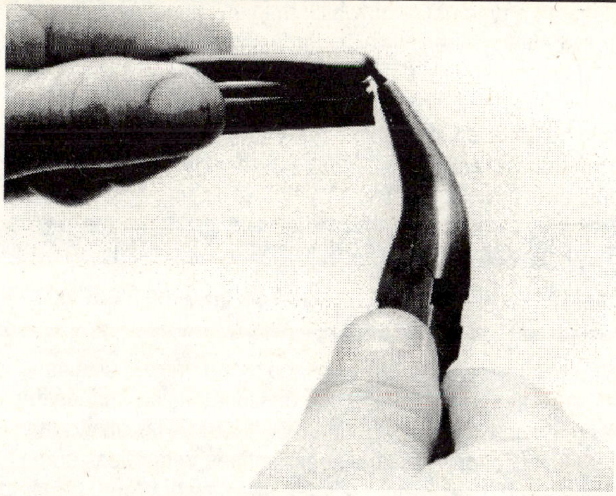

TCCS1230

Fig. 133 On Trico® wiper blades, the tab at the end of the blade must be turned up . . .

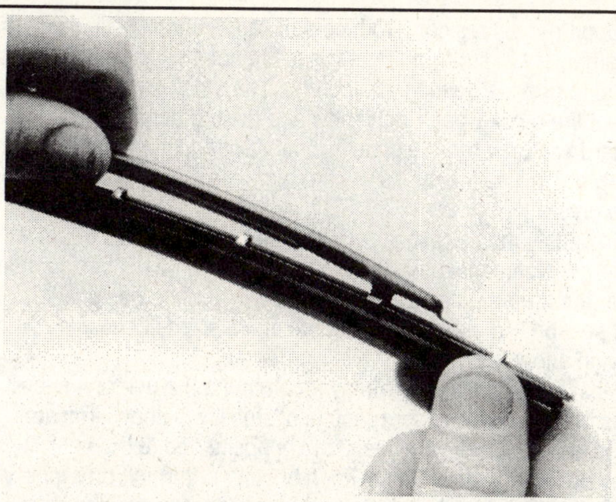

TCCS1231

Fig. 134 . . . then the insert can be removed. After installing the replacement insert, bend the tab back

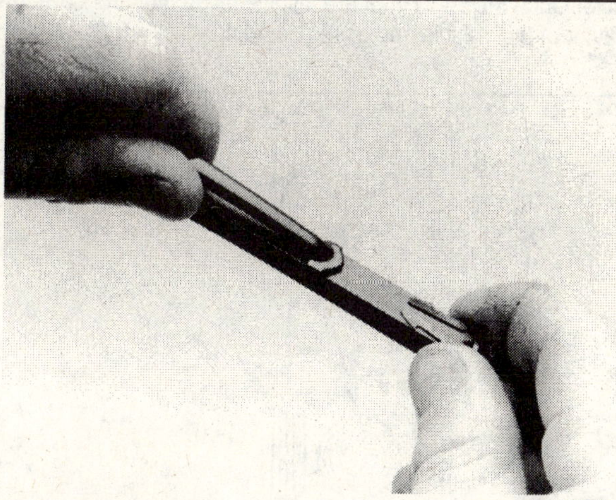

TCCS1232

Fig. 135 The Tripledge® wiper blade insert is removed and installed using a securing clip

To inspect and/or replace the wiper blade elements, place the wiper switch in the **LOW** speed position and the ignition switch in the **ACC** position. When the wiper blades are approximately vertical on the windshield, turn the ignition switch to **OFF**.

Examine the wiper blade elements. If they are found to be cracked, broken or torn, they should be replaced immediately. Replacement intervals will vary with usage, although ozone deterioration usually limits element life to about one year. If the wiper pattern is smeared or streaked, or if the blade chatters across the glass, the elements should be replaced. It is easiest and most sensible to replace the elements in pairs.

If your vehicle is equipped with aftermarket blades, there are several different types of refills and your vehicle might have any kind. Aftermarket blades and arms rarely use the exact same type blade or refill as the original equipment. Here are some typical aftermarket blades; not all may be available for your vehicle:

The Anco® type uses a release button that is pushed down to allow the refill to slide out of the yoke jaws. The new refill slides back into the frame and locks in place.

Some Trico® refills are removed by locating where the metal backing strip or the refill is wider. Insert a small screwdriver blade between the frame and metal backing strip. Press down to release the refill from the retaining tab.

Other types of Trico® refills have two metal tabs which are unlocked by squeezing them together. The rubber filler can then be withdrawn from the frame jaws. A new refill is installed by inserting the refill into the front frame jaws and sliding it rearward to engage the remaining frame jaws. There are usually four jaws; be certain when installing that the refill is engaged in all of them. At the end of its travel, the tabs will lock into place on the front jaws of the wiper blade frame.

Another type of refill is made from polycarbonate. The refill has a simple locking device at one end which flexes downward out of the groove into which the jaws of the holder fit, allowing easy release. By sliding the new refill through all the jaws and pushing through the slight resistance when it reaches the end of its travel, the refill will lock into position.

To replace the Tridon® refill, it is necessary to remove the wiper blade. This refill has a plastic backing strip with a notch about 1 in. (25mm) from the end. Hold the blade (frame) on a hard surface so that the frame is tightly bowed. Grip the tip of the backing strip and pull up while twisting counterclockwise. The backing strip will snap out of the retaining tab. Do this for the remaining tabs until the refill is free of the blade. The length of these refills is molded into the end and they should be replaced with identical types.

Regardless of the type of refill used, be sure to follow the part manufacturer's instructions closely. Make sure that all of the frame jaws are engaged as the refill is pushed into place and locked. If the metal blade holder and frame are allowed to touch the glass during wiper operation, the glass will be scratched.

Tires and Wheels

Common sense and good driving habits will afford maximum tire life. Fast starts, sudden stops and hard cornering are hard on tires and will shorten their useful life span. Make sure that you don't overload the vehicle or run with incorrect pressure in the tires. Both of these practices will increase tread wear.

➥ For optimum tire life, keep the tires properly inflated, rotate them often and have the wheel alignment checked periodically.

Inspect your tires frequently. Be especially careful to watch for bubbles in the tread or sidewall, deep cuts or underinflation. Replace any tires with bubbles in the sidewall. If cuts are so deep that they penetrate to the cords, discard the tire. Any cut in the sidewall of a radial tire renders it unsafe. Also look for uneven tread wear patterns that may indicate the front end is out of alignment or that the tires are out of balance.

TIRE ROTATION

➧ See Figure 136 and 137

Tires must be rotated periodically to equalize wear patterns that vary with a tire's position on the vehicle. Tires will also wear in an uneven way as the front steering/suspension system wears to the point where the alignment should be reset.

Rotating the tires will ensure maximum life for the tires as a set, so you will not have to discard a tire early due to wear on only part of the tread. Regular rotation is required to equalize wear.

When rotating "unidirectional tires," make sure that they always roll in the same direction. This means that a tire used on the left side of the vehicle must not be switched to the right side and vice-versa. These tires are marked on the sidewall as to the direction of rotation; observe the mark when reinstalling the tire(s).

Some styled or "mag" wheels may have different offsets front to rear. In these cases, the rear wheels must not be used up front and vice-versa. Furthermore, if these wheels are equipped with unidirectional tires, they cannot be rotated unless the tire is remounted for the proper direction of rotation.

➥ The compact or space-saver spare is strictly for emergency use. It must never be included in the tire rotation or placed on the vehicle for everyday use.

TIRE DESIGN

➧ See Figure 138

For maximum satisfaction, tires should be used in sets of four. Mixing of different types (radial, bias-belted, fiberglass belted) must be avoided. In most cases, the vehicle manufacturer has designated a type of tire on which the vehicle will perform best. Your first choice when replacing tires should be to use the same type of tire that the manufacturer recommends.

When radial tires are used, tire sizes and wheel diameters should be selected to maintain ground clearance and tire load capacity equivalent to the original specified tire. Radial tires should always be used in sets of four.

****CAUTION**

Radial tires should never be used on only the front axle.

When selecting tires, pay attention to the original size as marked on the tire. Most tires are described using an industry size code sometimes referred to as P-Metric. This allows the exact identification of the tire specifications, regardless of the manufacturer. If selecting a different tire size or brand, remember to check the installed tire for any sign of interference with the body or suspension while the vehicle is stopping, turning sharply or heavily loaded.

Snow Tires

Good radial tires can produce a big advantage in slippery weather, but in snow, a street radial tire does not have sufficient tread to provide traction and control. The small grooves of a street tire quickly pack with snow and the tire behaves like a billiard ball on a marble floor. The more open, chunky tread of a snow tire will self-clean as the tire turns, providing much better grip on snowy surfaces.

To satisfy municipalities requiring snow tires during weather emergencies, most snow tires carry either an M + S designation after the tire size stamped on the sidewall, or the designation "all-season." In general, no change in tire size is necessary when buying snow tires.

Most manufacturers strongly recommend the use of 4 snow tires on their vehicles for reasons of stability. If snow tires are fitted only to the drive wheels, the opposite end of the vehicle may become very unstable when braking or turning on slippery surfaces. This instability can lead to unpleasant endings if the driver can't counteract the slide in time.

Note that snow tires, whether 2 or 4, will affect vehicle handling in all non-snow situations. The stiffer, heavier snow tires will noticeably change the turning and braking characteristics of the vehicle. Once the snow tires are installed, you must re-learn the behavior of the vehicle and drive accordingly.

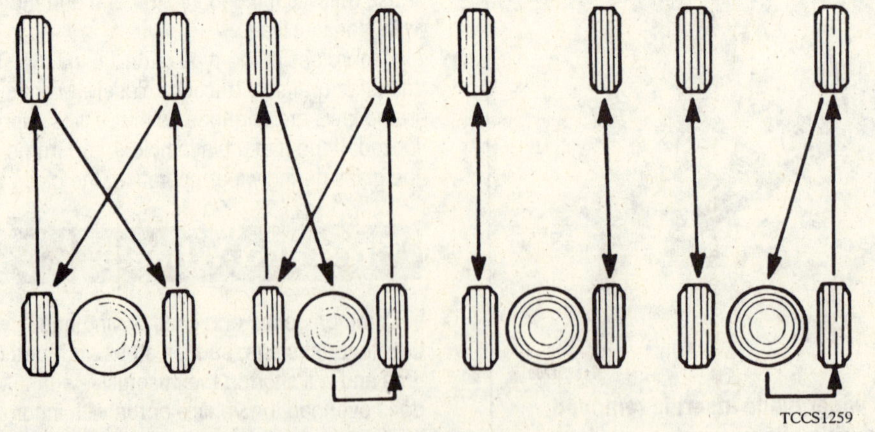

Fig. 136 Common tire rotation patterns for 4 and 5 wheel rotations

TCCS1234

Fig. 137 Unidirectional tires can only be rotated on the same side of the vehicle (front-to-rear). Such tires are identified by an arrow or the word "rotation"

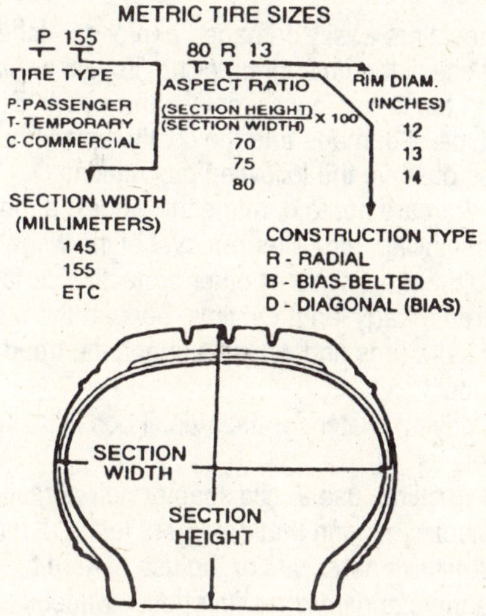

TCCS1261

Fig. 138 P-Metric tire coding

Consider buying extra wheels on which to mount the snow tires. Once done, the "snow wheels" can be installed and removed as needed. This eliminates the potential damage to tires or wheels from seasonal removal and installation. Even if your vehicle has styled wheels, see if inexpensive steel wheels are available. Although the look of the vehicle will change, the expensive wheels will be protected from salt, curb hits and pothole damage.

TIRE STORAGE

If they are mounted on wheels, store the tires at proper inflation pressure. All tires should be kept in a cool, dry place. If they are stored in the garage or basement, do not let them stand on a concrete floor; set them on strips of wood, a mat or a large stack of newspaper. Keeping them away from direct moisture is of paramount importance. Tires should not be stored upright, but in a flat position.

INSPECTION

See Figures 139, 140, 141, 142, 143 and 144

The importance of proper tire inflation cannot be overemphasized. A tire employs air as part of its structure. It is designed around the supporting strength of the air at a specified pressure. For this reason, improper inflation drastically reduces the tires's ability to perform as intended. A tire will lose some air in day-to-day use; having to add a few pounds of air periodically is not necessarily a sign of a leaking tire.

Two items should be a permanent fixture in every glove compartment: an accurate tire pressure gauge and a tread depth gauge. Check the tire pressure (including the spare) regularly with a pocket type gauge. Too often, the gauge on the end of the air hose at your corner garage is not accurate because it suffers too much abuse. Always check tire pressure when the tires are cold, as pressure increases with temperature. If you must move the vehicle to check the tire inflation, do not drive more than a mile before checking. A cold tire is generally one that has not been driven for more than three hours.

A plate or sticker is normally provided somewhere in the vehicle (door post, hood, tailgate or trunk lid)which shows the proper pressure for the tires. Never counteract excessive pressure build-up by bleeding off air pressure (letting some air out). This will cause the tire to run hotter and wear quicker.

TCCS1095

Fig. 139 Tires with deep cuts, or cuts which show bulging should be replaced immediately

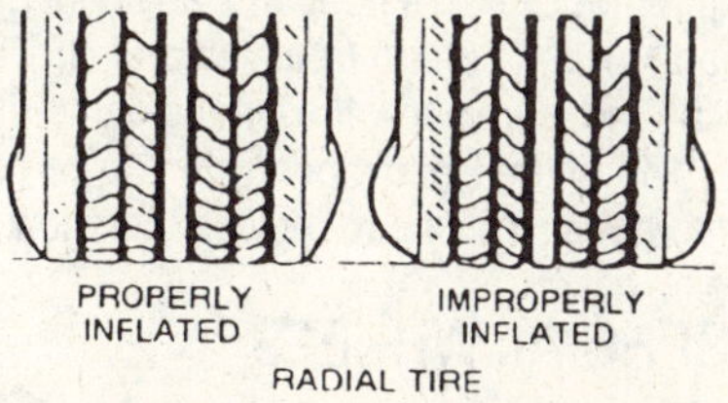

TCCS1263

Fig. 140 Radial tires have a characteristic sidewall bulge; don't try to measure pressure by looking at the tire. Use a quality air pressure gauge

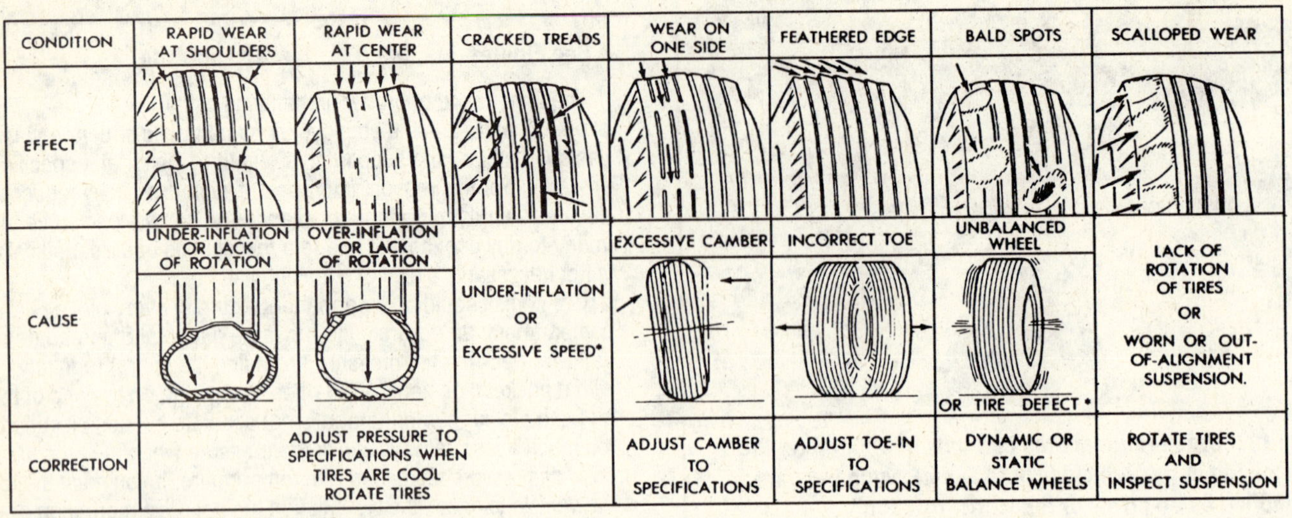

CONDITION	RAPID WEAR AT SHOULDERS	RAPID WEAR AT CENTER	CRACKED TREADS	WEAR ON ONE SIDE	FEATHERED EDGE	BALD SPOTS	SCALLOPED WEAR
EFFECT	1. 2.						
CAUSE	UNDER-INFLATION OR LACK OF ROTATION	OVER-INFLATION OR LACK OF ROTATION	UNDER-INFLATION OR EXCESSIVE SPEED*	EXCESSIVE CAMBER	INCORRECT TOE	UNBALANCED WHEEL OR TIRE DEFECT*	LACK OF ROTATION OF TIRES OR WORN OR OUT-OF-ALIGNMENT SUSPENSION.
CORRECTION	ADJUST PRESSURE TO SPECIFICATIONS WHEN TIRES ARE COOL ROTATE TIRES			ADJUST CAMBER TO SPECIFICATIONS	ADJUST TOE-IN TO SPECIFICATIONS	DYNAMIC OR STATIC BALANCE WHEELS	ROTATE TIRES AND INSPECT SUSPENSION

*HAVE TIRE INSPECTED FOR FURTHER USE.

TCCS1267

Fig. 141 Common tire wear patterns and causes

✻✻CAUTION

Never exceed the maximum tire pressure embossed on the tire! This is the pressure to be used when the tire is at maximum loading, but it is rarely the correct pressure for everyday driving. Consult the owner's manual or the tire pressure sticker for the correct tire pressure.

Once you've maintained the correct tire pressures for several weeks, you'll be familiar with the vehicle's braking and handling personality. Slight adjustments in tire pressures can fine-tune these characteristics, but never change the cold pressure specification by more than 2 psi. A slightly softer tire pressure will give a softer ride but also yield lower fuel mileage. A slightly harder tire will give crisper dry road handling but can cause skidding on wet surfaces. Unless you're fully attuned to the vehicle, stick to the recommended inflation pressures.

All tires made since 1968 have built-in tread wear indicator bars that show up as $^1/_2$ in. (13mm) wide smooth bands across the tire when $^1/_{16}$ in. (1.5mm) of tread remains. The appearance of tread wear indicators means that the tires should be replaced. In fact, many states have laws prohibiting the use of tires with less than this amount of tread.

You can check your own tread depth with an inexpensive gauge or by using a Lincoln head penny. Slip the Lincoln penny (with Lincoln's head upside-down) into several tread grooves. If you can see the top of Lincoln's head in 2 adjacent grooves, the tire has less than $^1/_{16}$ in. (1.5mm) tread left and should be replaced. You can measure snow tires in the same manner by using the "tails" side of the Lincoln penny. If you can see the top of the Lincoln memorial, it's time to replace the snow tire(s).

CARE OF SPECIAL WHEELS

If you have invested money in magnesium, aluminum alloy or sport wheels, special precautions should be taken to make sure your investment is not wasted and that your special wheels look good for the life of the vehicle.

Special wheels are easily damaged and/or scratched. Occasionally check the rims for cracking, impact damage or air leaks. If any of these are found, replace the wheel. But in order to prevent this type of damage and the costly replacement of a special wheel, observe the following precautions:

- Use extra care not to damage the wheels during removal, installation, balancing, etc. After removal of the wheels from the vehicle, place them on a mat or other protective surface. If they are to be stored for any length of time, support them on strips of wood. Never store tires and wheels upright; the tread may develop flat spots.
- When driving, watch for hazards; it doesn't take much to crack a wheel.
- When washing, use a mild soap or non-abrasive dish detergent (keeping in mind that detergent tends to remove wax). Avoid cleansers with abrasives or the use of hard brushes. There are many cleaners and polishes for special wheels.
- If possible, remove the wheels during the winter. Salt and sand used for snow removal can severely damage the finish of a wheel.
- Make certain the recommended lug nut torque is never exceeded or the wheel may crack. Never use snow chains on special wheels; severe scratching will occur.

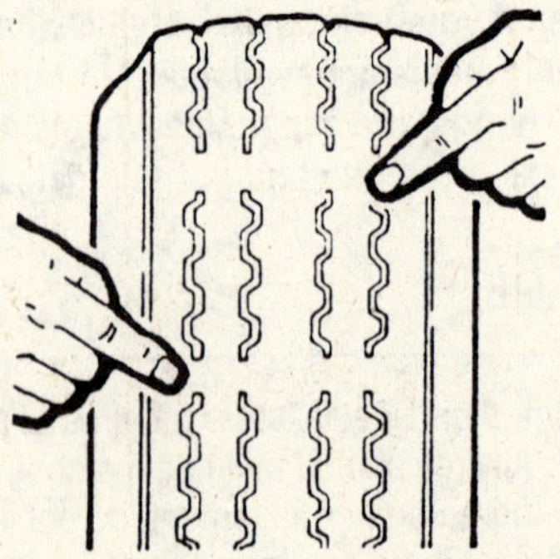

TCCS1265

Fig. 142 Tread wear indicators will appear when the tire is worn

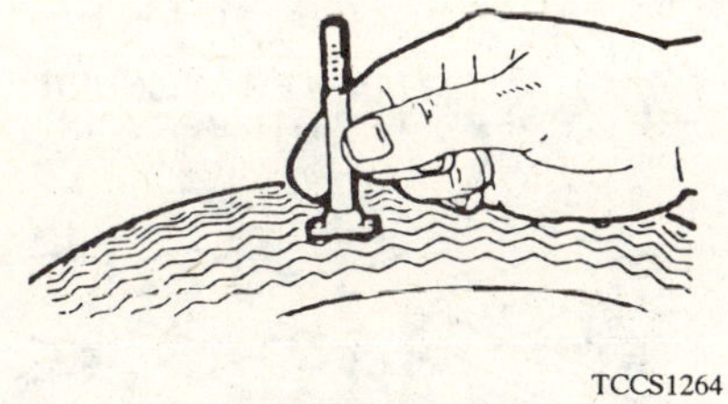

Fig. 143 Accurate tread depth indicators are inexpensive and handy

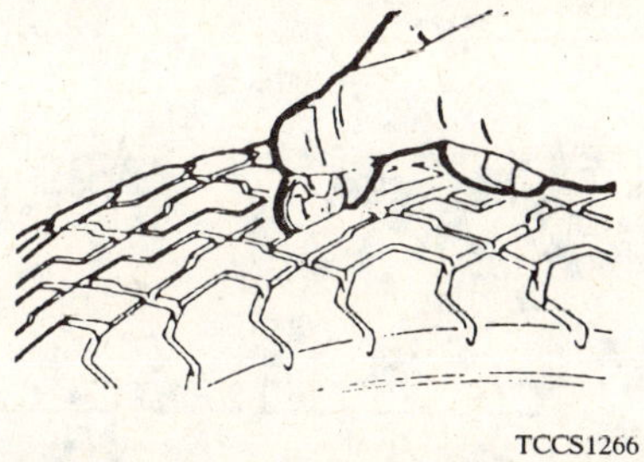

Fig. 144 A penny works well for a quick check of tread depth

FLUIDS AND LUBRICANTS

➧ See Figures 145, 146, 147, 148, 149 and 150

Fluid Disposal

Used fluids such as engine oil, transmission fluid, antifreeze and brake fluid are hazardous wastes and must be disposed of properly. Before draining any fluids, consult with your local authorities; in many areas waste oil, etc. is being accepted as a part of recycling programs. A number of service stations and auto parts stores are also accepting waste fluids for recycling.

Be sure of the recycling center's policies before draining any fluids, as many will not accept different fluids that have been mixed together.

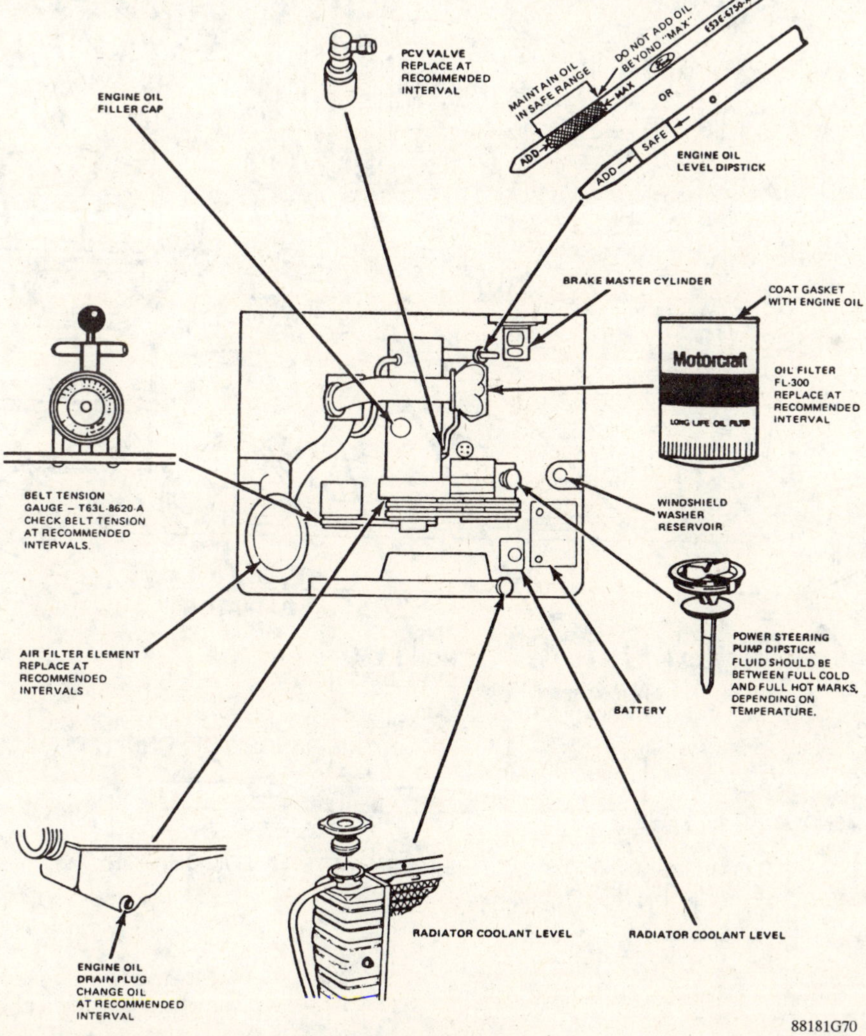

Fig. 145 Engine component service locations — 2.3L turbo engine shown

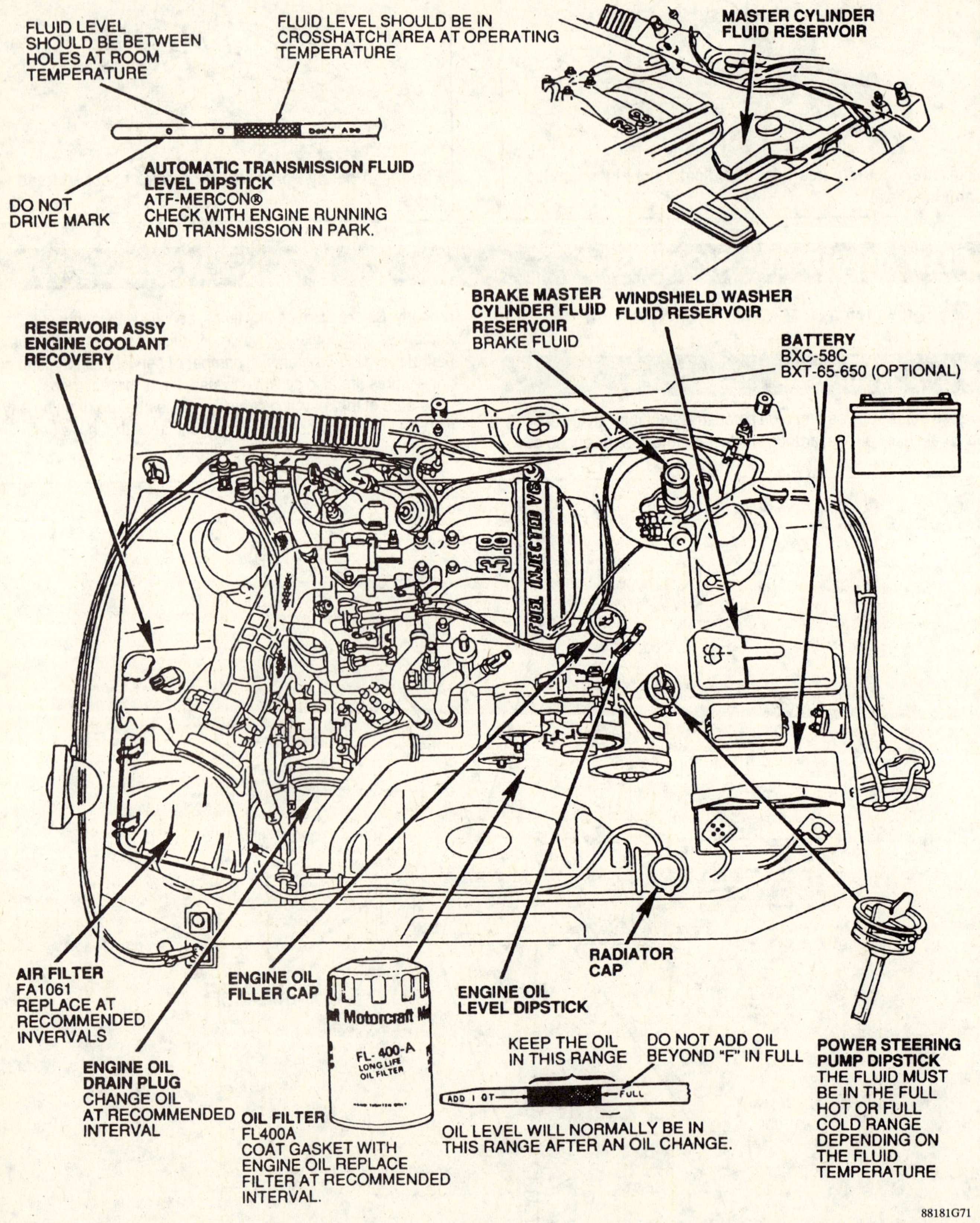

Fig. 146 Engine component service locations — 3.8L SFI engine shown

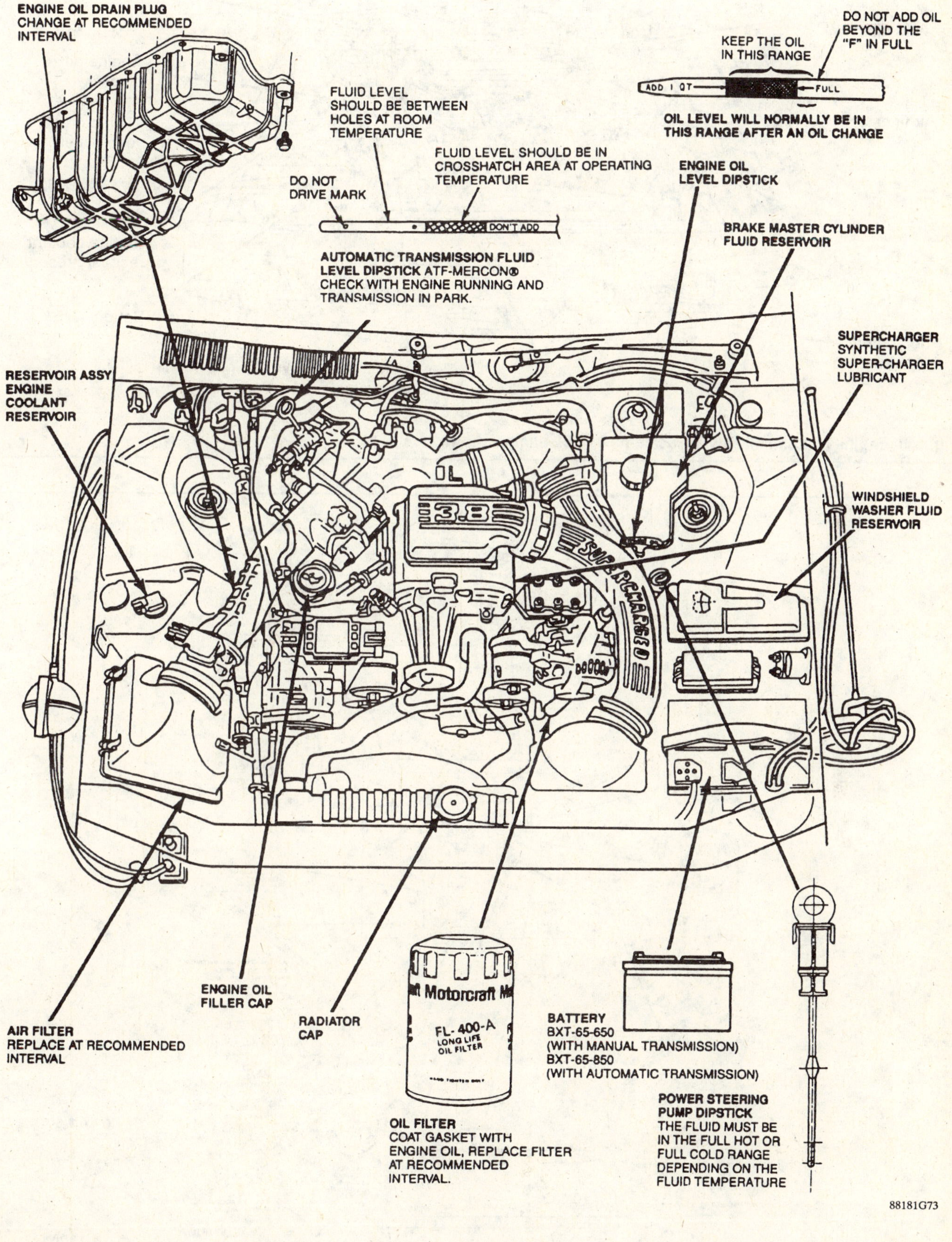

Fig. 147 Engine component service locations — 3.8L Supercharged engine shown

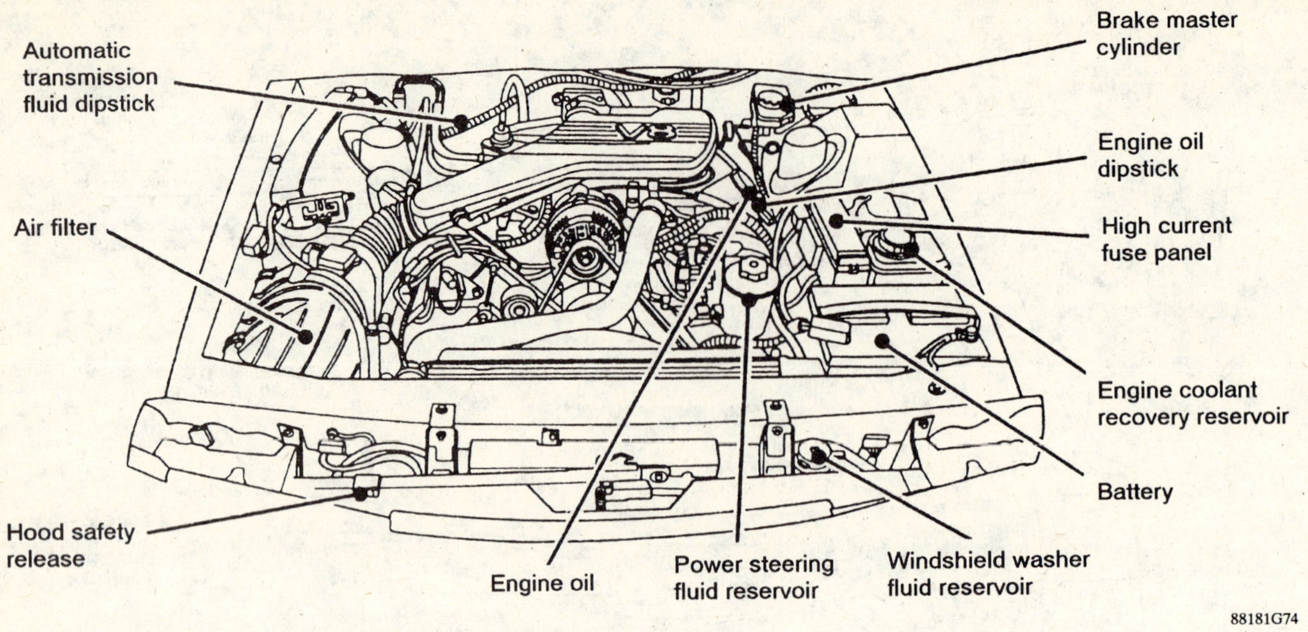

Fig. 148 Engine component service locations — 4.6L engine shown

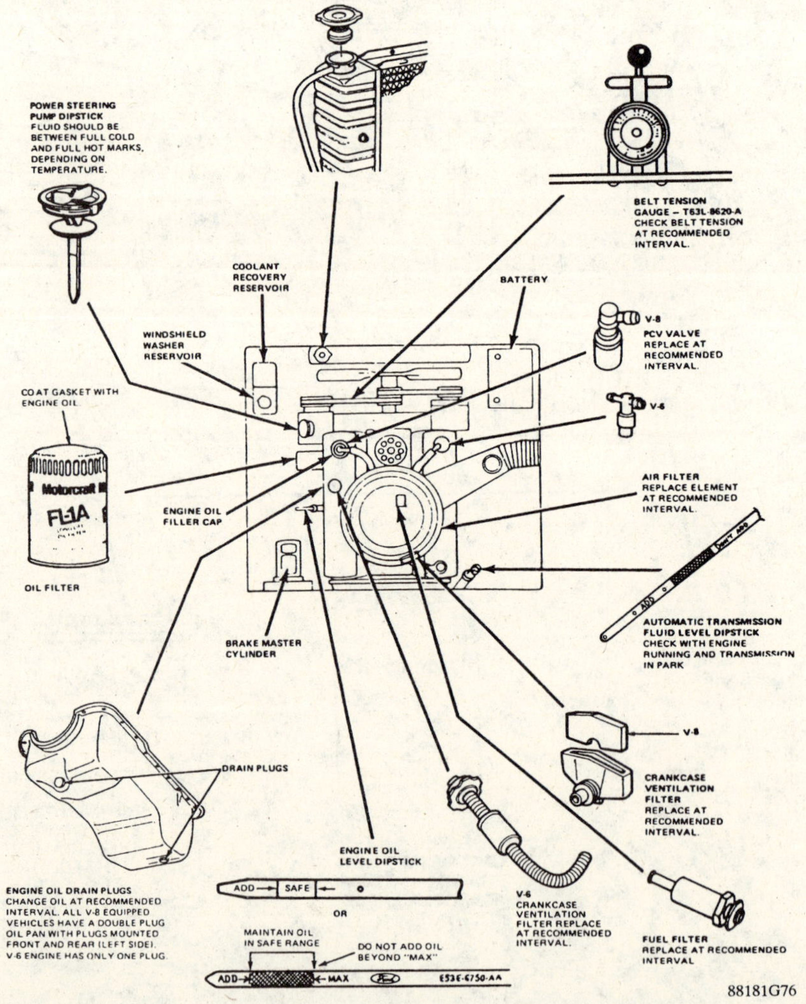

Fig. 149 Engine component service locations — 3.8L 2bbl engine shown

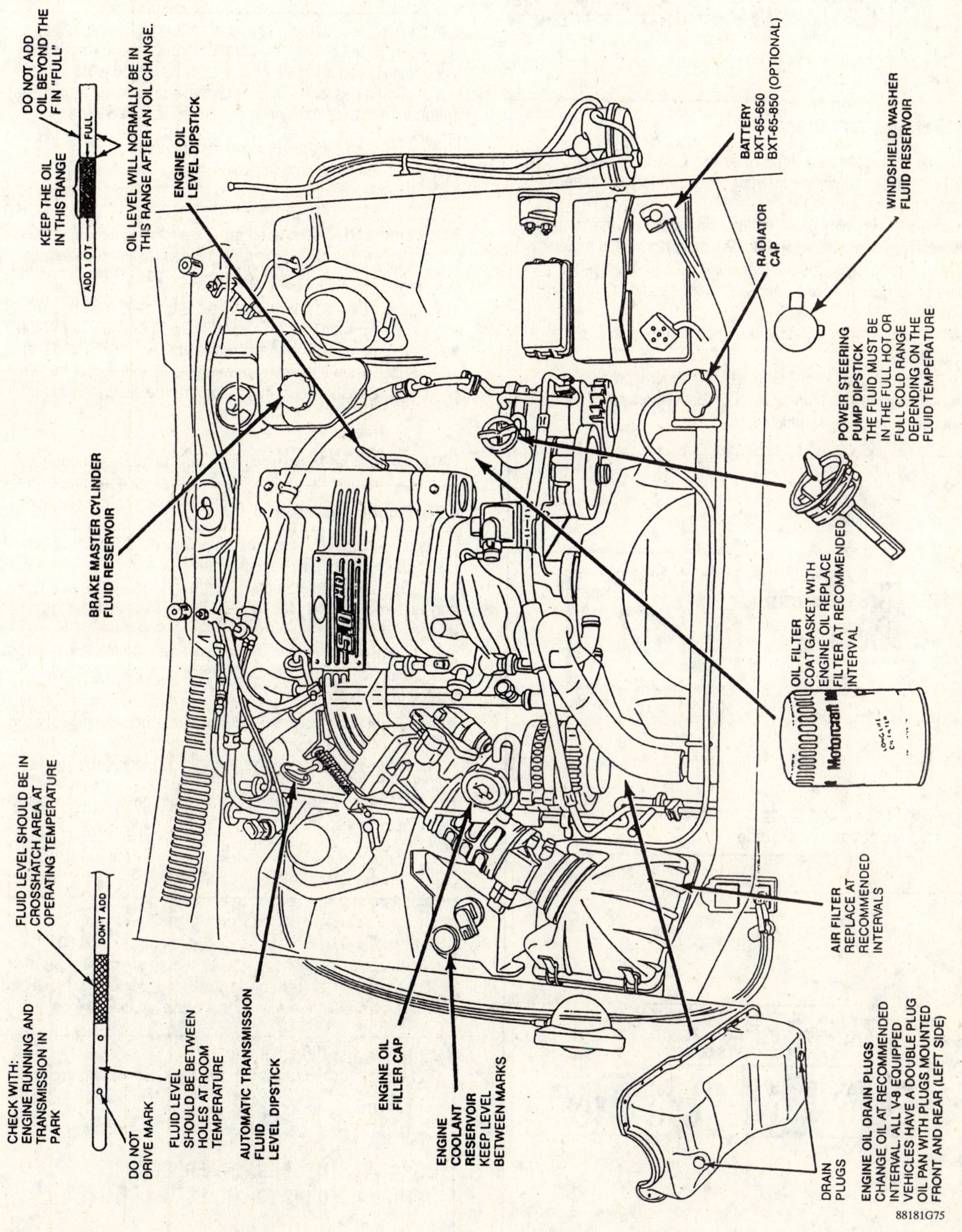

Fig. 150 Engine component service locations — 5.0L MFI HO engine shown

Fuel and Engine Oil Recommendations

FUEL

➧ See Figures 151 and 152

Unleaded gasoline having a Research Octane Number (RON) of 87-91 is recommended for your car. Refer to your owners manual for the exact RON.

Using a high quality unleaded gasoline may help maintain the driveability, fuel economy and emissions performance of your vehicle. A properly formulated gasoline will be comprised of well refined hydrocarbons and chemical additives and will perform the following.

- Minimize varnish, lacquer and other induction system deposits.
- Prevent gum formation or other deterioration.
- Protect the fuel tank and other fuel system components from corrosion or degradation.

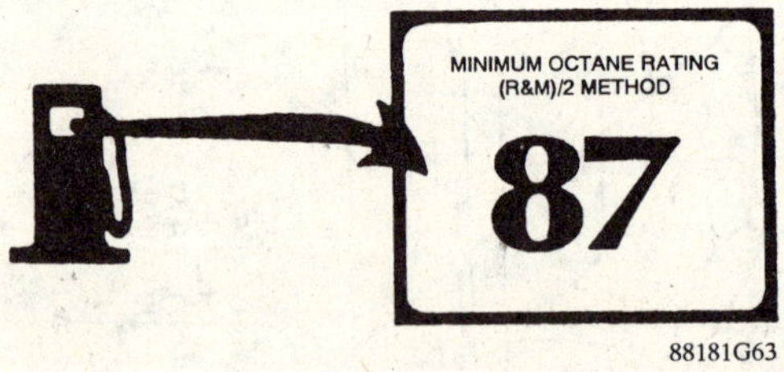

Fig. 151 The octane rating is located on a sticker at the gas pump, at your local station

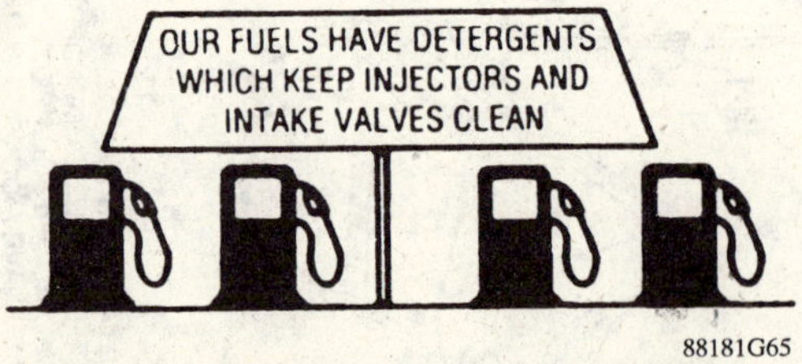

Fig. 152 Always use a fuel which keeps your intake valve system clean

- Provide the correct seasonally and geographically adjusted volatility. This will provide easy starting in the winter and avoid vapor lock in the summer. Avoid fuel system icing.

In addition, the fuel will be free of water debris and other impurities. Some driveability deterioration on multi-port electronically fuel injected vehicles can be traced to continuous use of certain gasolines which may have insufficient amounts of detergent additives to provide adequate deposit control protection.

OIL

➧ See Figures 153 and 154

Oil meeting API classification SH or latest superceding grade is recommended for use in your vehicle. Viscosity grades 10W-30 or 10W-40 are recommended on 1983 models. On 1984 and later models it is recommended that you use 5W-30 if you drive your vehicle in temperatures below 100°F (37°C) and 10W-30 for when you drive your vehicle in above 100°F (37°C) conditions. See the viscosity-to-temperature illustration in this section.

OIL LEVEL CHECK

➧ See Figures 155, 156 and 157

It is a good idea to check the engine oil each time or at least every other time you fill your gas tank.

1. Be sure your car is on level ground. Shut off the engine and wait for a few minutes to allow the oil to drain back into the oil pan.
2. Remove the engine oil dipstick and wipe clean with a rag.
3. Reinsert the dipstick and push it down until it is fully seated in the tube.
4. Remove the stick and check the oil level shown. If the oil level is below the lower mark, add one quart.
5. If you wish, you may carefully fill the oil pan to the upper mark on the dipstick with less than a full quart. Do not, however, add a full quart when it would overfill the crankcase (level above the upper mark on the dipstick). The excess oil will generally be consumed at an excessive rate even if no damage to the engine seals occurs.

Fig. 153 Look for the API oil identification label when choosing your engine oil

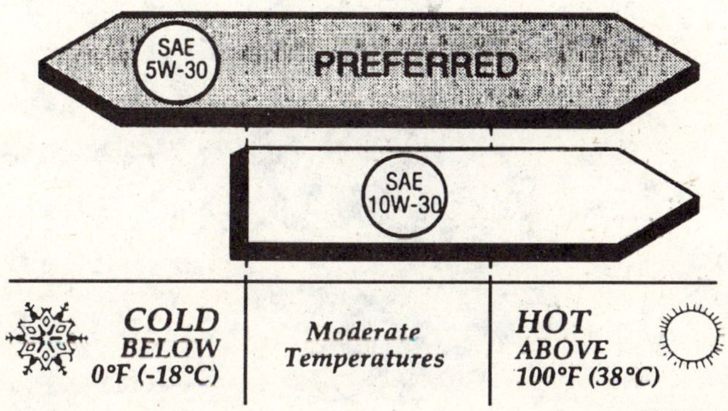

Fig. 154 Oil viscosity recommendations according to temperature

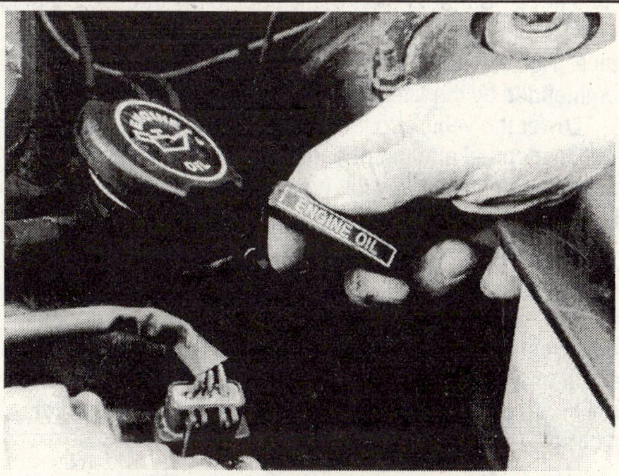

Fig. 155 The engine oil dipstick has the words imprinted on the handle on most vehicles

Fig. 156 To add oil, remove the filler cap . . .

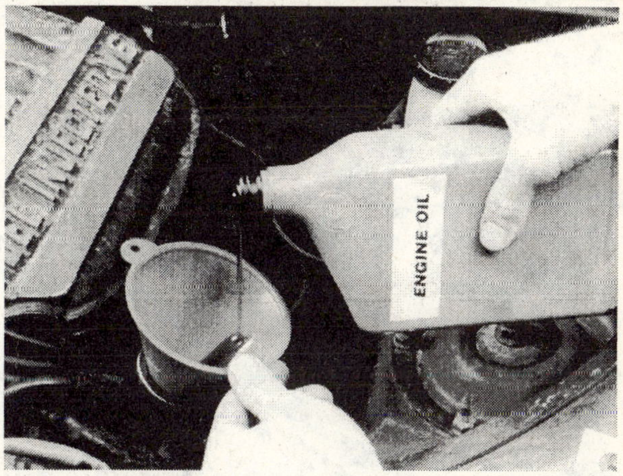

Fig. 157 . . . then using a funnel, top off with the correct type of oil to the crankcase

OIL AND FILTER CHANGE

➧ See Figures 158, 159, 160 and 161

The manufacturer recommends changing the engine oil and oil filter every 3 months or 3000 miles (5000 km). The engine oil and oil filter can be changed at 2000 miles (3200 km) or 2 month intervals if the driving conditions for your vehicle is done through severe dust and dirty conditions. Following these recommended intervals will help keep you car engine in good condition.

1. Make sure the engine is at normal operating temperature (this promotes complete draining of the old oil).

****CAUTION**

The EPA warns that prolonged contact with used engine oil may cause a number of skin disorders, including cancer! You should make every effort to minimize your exposure to used engine oil. Protective gloves should be worn when changing the oil. Wash your hands and any other exposed skin areas as soon as possible after exposure to used engine oil. Soap and water, or waterless hand cleaner should be used.

2. Apply the parking brake and block the wheels or raise and support the car evenly on jackstands.
3. Place a drain pan of about a gallon and a half capacity under the engine oil pan drain plug (DO NOT DRAIN OIL ONTO THE GROUND). Using the proper size wrench, loosen and remove the plug. Allow all the old oil to drain. Wipe the pan and the drain plug with a clean rag. Inspect the drain plug gasket, replace if necessary.
4. Reinstall and tighten the drain plug to 15–25 ft. lbs. (20–34 Nm) on all engines excluding the 4.6L. On the 4.6L engine tighten to 9–11 ft. lbs. (11–16 Nm). DO NOT OVERTIGHTEN.
5. Move the drain pan under the engine oil filter. Use a strap wrench and loosen the oil filter (do not remove), allow the oil to drain. Unscrew the filter the rest of the way by hand. Use a rag, if necessary, to keep from burning your fingers. When the filter comes loose from the engine, turn the mounting base upward to avoid spilling the remaining oil.

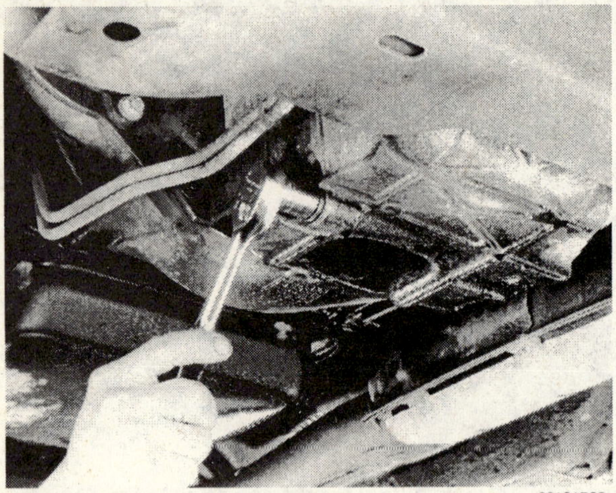
88181P20

Fig. 158 Locate the oil drain plug and loosen

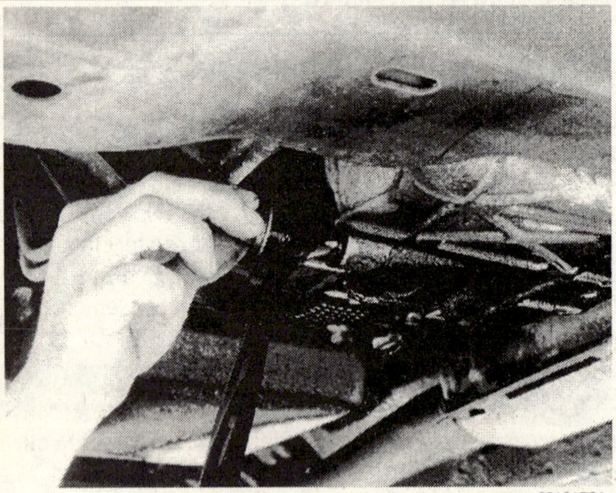
88181P21

Fig. 159 Stepping back, slowly remove the plug from the oil pan to allow the oil to flow out

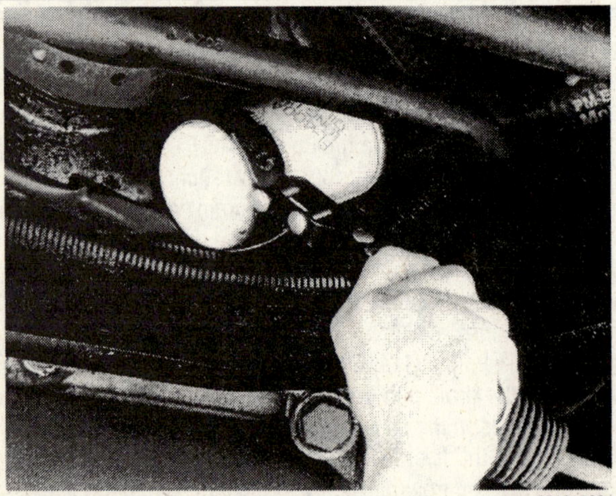
88181P22

Fig. 160 Using a strap type filter wrench, loosen the old filter

TCCS1901

Fig. 161 Before installing a new oil filter, lightly coat the rubber gasket with clean oil

6. Wipe the engine filter mount clean with a rag. Coat the rubber gasket on the new oil filter with clean engine oil, applying it with a finger. Carefully start the filter onto the threaded engine mount. Turn the filter until it touches the engine mounting surface. Tighten the filter, by hand, $^1/_2$ turn more or as recommended by the filter manufacturer.

7. Lower the vehicle to the ground. Refill the crankcase with the recommended amount of engine oil. Replace the filler cap and start the engine. Allow the engine to idle and check for oil leaks. Shut off the engine, wait for several minutes, then check the oil level with the dipstick. Add oil if necessary.

➥ Used oil has been determined to be hazardous to the environment. Recycling oil is the best way for disposal. Check local laws and recycle whenever possible. Store the used oil in a container made for that purpose until you can find a service station or garage that accepts used oil for recycling.

Manual Transmission

FLUID RECOMMENDATIONS

All of the Thunderbird and Cougar models use Dexron®II or Mercon® type fluid. A 85W/90 gear oil may be used in the T50D transmission in very warm climates or if gear/bearing noise is excessive.

LEVEL CHECK

The fluid level should be checked every 6 months or 6000 miles (9654 km), whichever comes first.

1. Park the car on a level surface, turn off the engine, apply the parking brake and block the wheels.
2. Remove the filler plug from the side of the transmission case with a proper sized wrench. The fluid level should be even with the bottom of the filler hole.
3. If additional fluid is necessary, add it through the filler hole using a siphon pump or squeeze bottle.
4. Install the filler plug; do not overtighten.

DRAIN AND REFILL

1. Place a suitable drain pan under the transmission.
2. Remove the filler plug.
3. Remove the drain plug and allow the gear lube to drain out.
4. Replace the drain plug.
5. Fill the transmission to the proper level with the required fluid.
6. Reinstall the filler plug.

Automatic Transmissions

FLUID RECOMMENDATIONS

- 1983-86 C3 — Dexron®II
- 1983-87 C5 — Type H
- 1983-92 AOD — Mercon®/Dexron®II
- 1987-88 A4LD — Mercon®/Dexron®II
- 1994-96 4R70W — Mercon®/Dexron®II

LEVEL CHECK

➧ **See Figures 162, 163 and 164**

It is very important to maintain the proper fluid level in an automatic transmission. If the level is either too high or too low, poor shifting operation and internal damage are likely to occur. For this reason a regular check of the fluid level is essential.

1. Drive the vehicle for 15-20 minutes to allow the transmission to reach operating temperature.
2. Park the car on a level surface, apply the parking brake and leave the engine idling. Shift the transmission and engage each gear, then place the gear selector in **P** (PARK).
3. Wipe away any dirt in the areas of the transmission dipstick to prevent it from falling into the filler tube. Withdraw the dipstick, wipe it with a clean, lint-free rag and reinsert it until it seats.

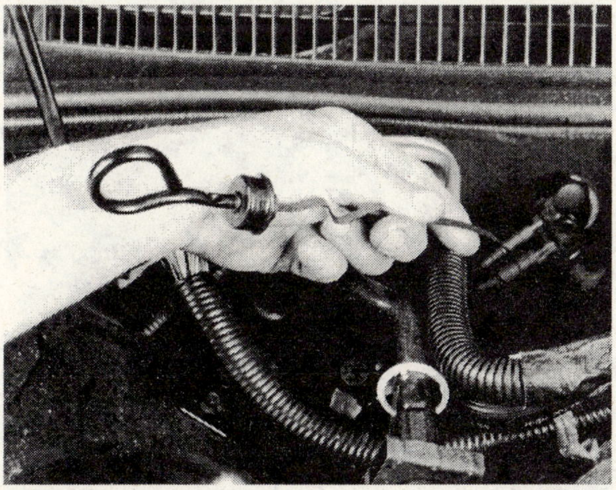
88181P23

Fig. 162 Withdraw the dipstick from the transmission filler tube

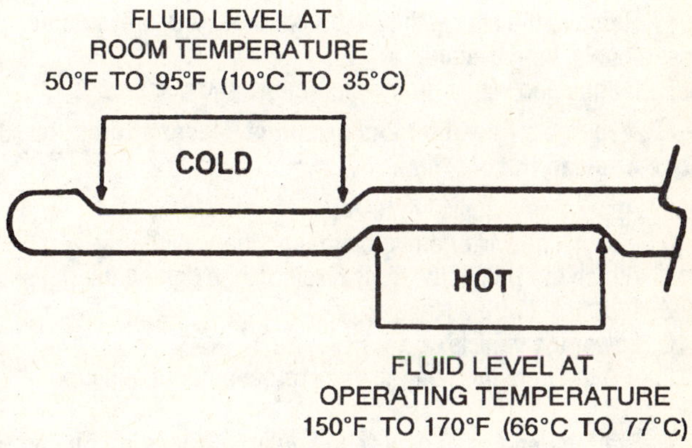

88181G67

Fig. 163 The temperature and level of the fluid determines where it will read on the dipstick

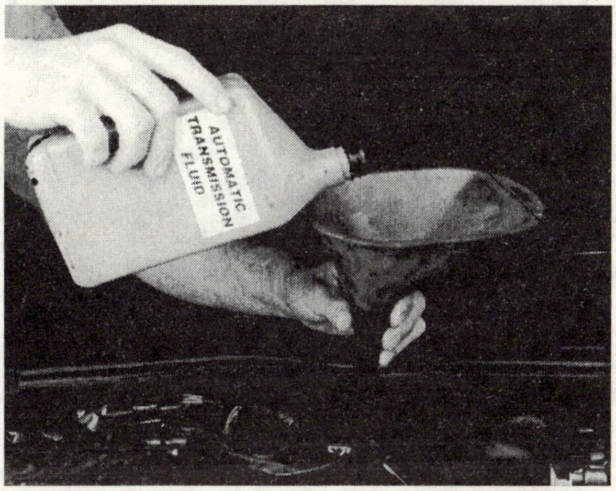

88181P24

Fig. 164 If necessary, use a funnel to add fluid to the transmission

4. Withdraw the dipstick and note the fluid level. It should be between the upper (FULL) mark and the lower (ADD) mark.
5. If the level is below the lower mark, use a funnel and add fluid in small quantities $\frac{1}{2}$ pint (0.25L) through the dipstick filler neck. Keep the engine running while adding fluid and check the level after each small amount. Do not overfill.

DRAIN AND REFILL

➧ **See Figures 165, 166, 167, 168 and 169**

1. Raise and safely support the vehicle.
2. Disconnect the fluid filler tube from the pan and allow the fluid to drain into an appropriate container.
3. Remove the transmission oil pan attaching bolts, pan and gasket. Allow the fluid to drain completely into an appropriate container before removing the pan.
4. Discard the old gasket.

5. Once the pan is removed, clean oil pan and mating surfaces.
6. Unscrew the filter from the valve body.
7. Remove the filter with both hands by pulling upwards on most models, then discard.
8. If equipped with a grommet, remove and discard.

➔ Always use a new filter and grommet. Never attempt to reuse or clean the old filter.

9. Apply a new gasket to the pan.
10. Install a new filter and grommet on the valve body.
11. Attach the pan to the transmission, then tighten the bolts to 10–16 ft. lbs. (13–22 Nm).
12. Lower the vehicle.
13. Fill the transmission with the correct amount and type fluid.
14. Start the engine and move the gear selector through shift pattern. Allow the engine to reach normal operating temperature.
15. Check the transmission fluid. Add fluid, if necessary, to maintain correct level.

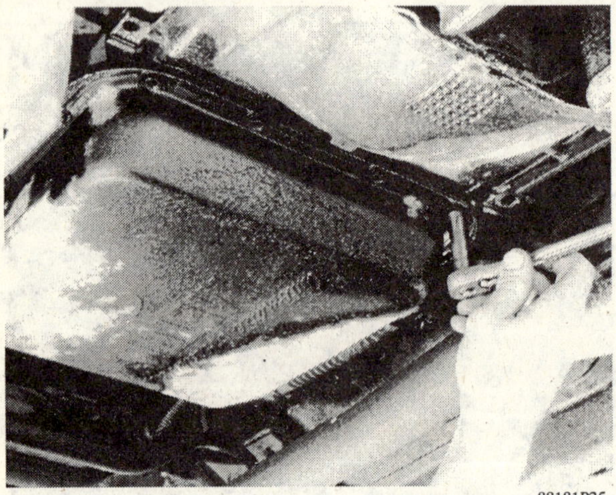

88181P25

Fig. 165 Remove the oil pan mounting bolts

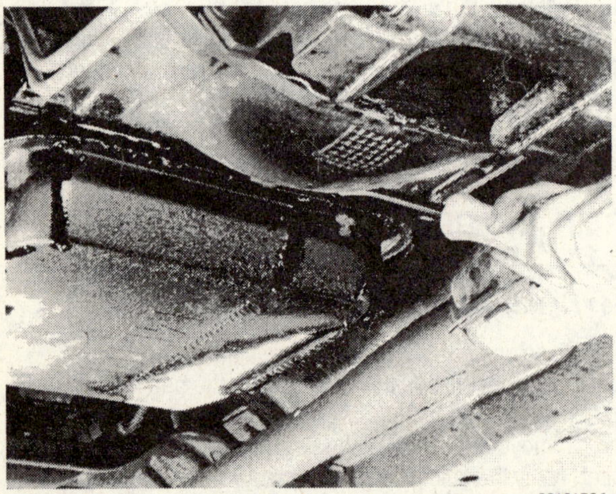

88181P26

Fig. 166 Carefully pry the pan to break loose the seal

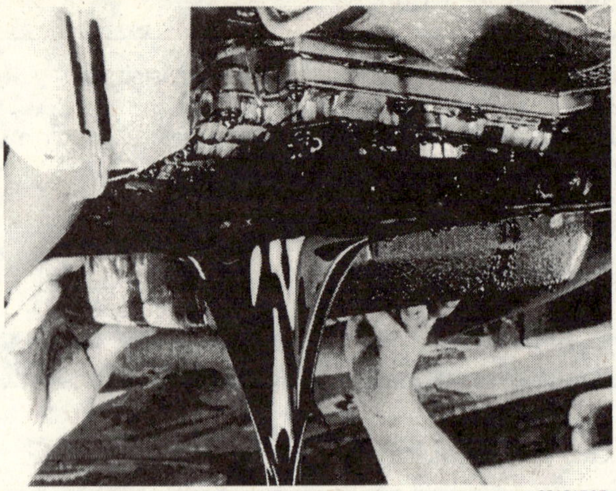

88181P27

Fig. 167 Lower the pan and allow the fluid to drain

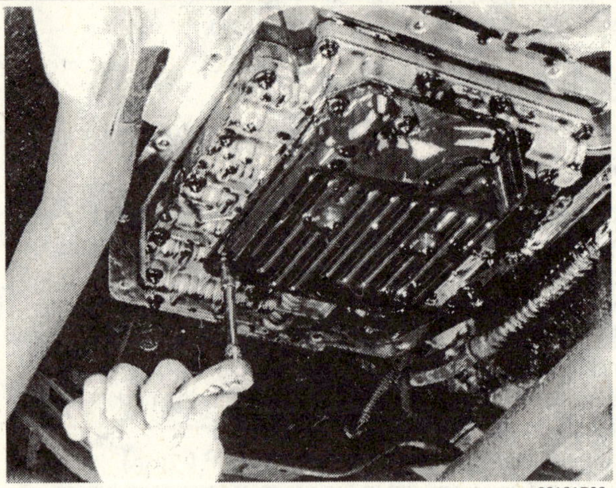

88181P28

Fig. 168 Unscrew the filter from the transmission valve body

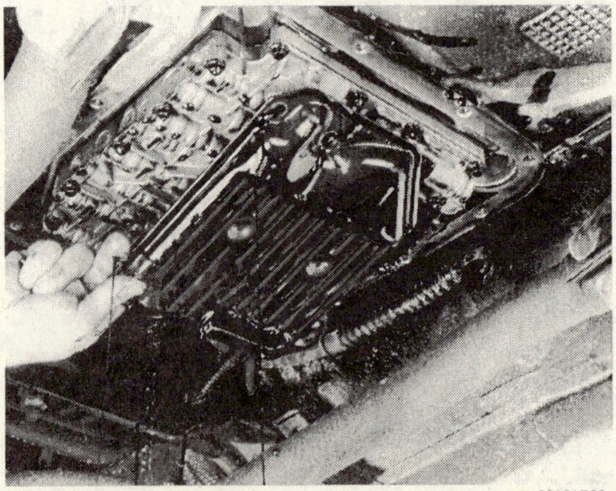

88181P29

Fig. 169 Discard the old filter once removed

Drive Axle

FLUID RECOMMENDATIONS

Like the manual transmission, the rear axle fluid should be checked every six months or 6000 miles (9654 km). A filler plug is provided near the center of the rear cover or on the upper (driveshaft) side of the gear case. Add SAE 85W/90/95 gear lube as required.

LEVEL CHECK

➧ See Figures 170, 171 and 172

1. Remove the plug and check to ensure that the fluid level is even with the bottom of the filler hole.
2. Add SAE 85W/90/95 gear lube as required.
3. If the vehicle is equipped with a limited slip rear axle, add the required special fluid.
4. Install the filler plug but do not overtighten.

DRAIN AND REFILL

Normal maintenance does not require changing the rear axle fluid. However, to do so, remove the rear drain plug (models equipped), the lower two cover bolts, or the cover. Catch the drained fluid in a suitable container.

If the rear cover was removed, clean the mounting surfaces of the cover and rear housing. Install a new gasket (early models) or (on late models) apply a continuous bead of Silicone Rubber Sealant (D6AZ-19562-AA or BA or the equivalent) around the rear housing face inside the circle of bolt holes. Install the cover and tighten the bolts to specifications. Parts must be assembled within a half hour after the sealant is applied. If the fluid was drained by removing the two lower cover bolts, apply sealant to the bolts before reinstallation. Fill the rear axle through the filler hole with the proper lube. Add friction modifier to limited slip models if required.

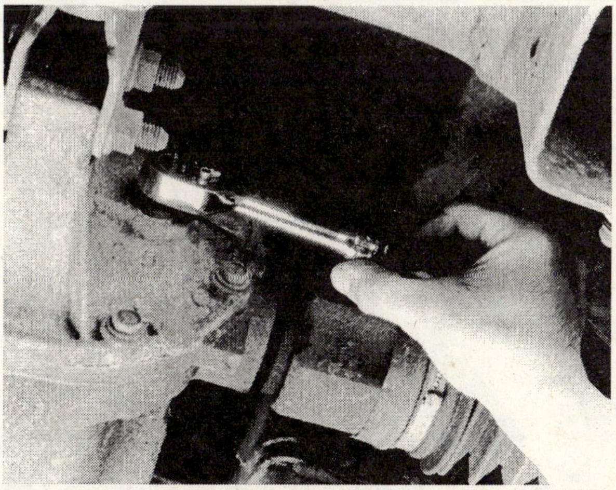

88181P34

Fig. 170 Use a proper sized ratchet to loosen the filler plug

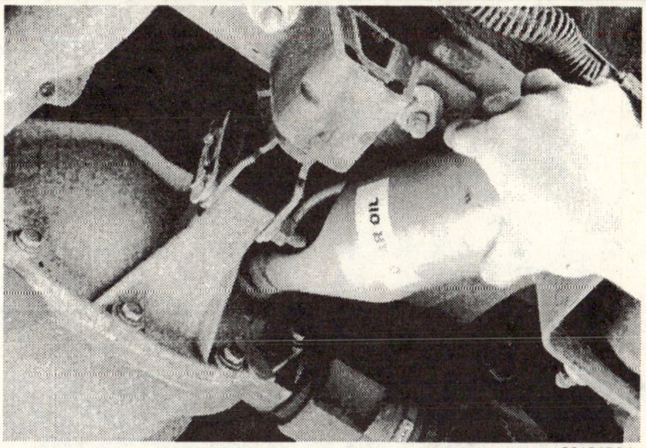

88181P36

Fig. 171 If necessary, add the proper fluid through the filler hole

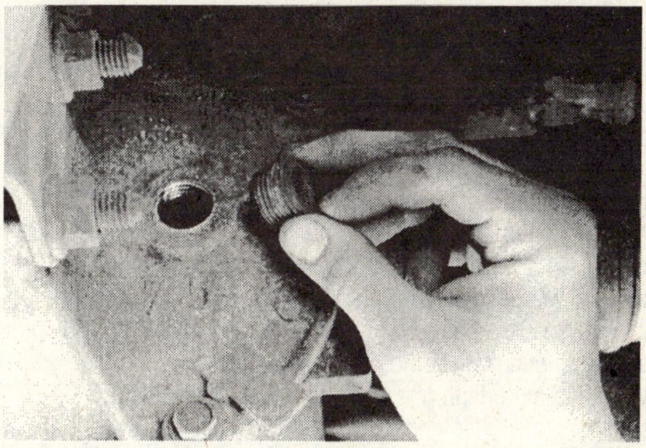

88181P35

Fig. 172 When installing the plug, first thread it in by hand

Cooling System

FLUID RECOMMENDATIONS

When additional coolant is required to maintain the proper level, always add a 50/50 mixture of antifreeze/coolant and water.

LEVEL CHECK

➧ See Figures 173

✱✱CAUTION

Exercise extreme care when removing the cap from a hot radiator. Wait a few minutes until the engine has time to cool somewhat, then wrap a thick towel around the radiator cap and slowly turn it counterclockwise to the first stop. Step back and allow the pressure to release from the cooling system. Then, when the steam has stopped venting, press down on the cap, turn it one more stop counterclockwise and remove the cap.

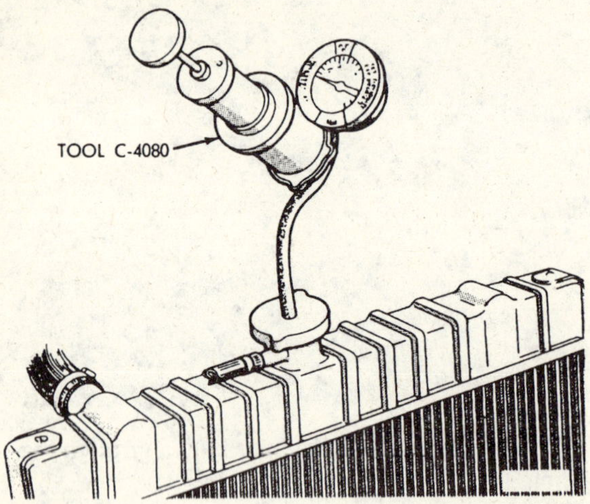

Fig. 173 Cooling systems should be pressure tested for leaks periodically

The coolant level in the radiator should be checked on a monthly basis, preferably when the engine is cold. On a cold engine, the coolant level should be maintained at one inch below the filler neck on vertical flow radiators, and $2\frac{1}{2}$ in. (63.5mm) below the filler neck at the **COLD FILL** mark on crossflow radiators. On the Coolant Recovery System, the level is maintained at the **COLD LEVEL** mark in the translucent plastic expansion bottle. Top up as necessary with a mixture of 50% water and 50% ethylene glycol antifreeze, to ensure proper rust, freezing and boiling protection. If you have to add coolant more often than once a month or if you have to add more than one quart at a time, check the cooling system for leads. Also check for water in the crankcase oil, indicating a blown cylinder head gasket.

DRAIN, FLUSH AND REFILL

See Figures 174, 175 and 176

****CAUTION**

When draining the coolant, keep in mind that cats and dogs are attracted by the ethylene glycol antifreeze, and are quite likely to drink any that is left in an uncovered container or in puddles on the ground. This will prove fatal in sufficient quantity. Always drain the coolant into a sealable container. Coolant should be reused unless it is contaminated or several years old.

Completely draining and refilling the cooling system every two years at least will remove accumulated rust, scale and other deposits.

Use a good quality antifreeze with water pump lubricants, rust inhibitors and other corrosion inhibitors along with acid neutralizers. Use a permanent type coolant that meets specification ESE-M97B44A or the equivalent.

1. Remove the radiator cap to relieve the pressure.
2. Drain the existing antifreeze and coolant. Open the radiator and engine drain petcocks (models equipped), or disconnect the bottom radiator hose, at the radiator outlet. Set the heater temperature controls to the full HOT position.

Before opening the radiator petcock, spray it with some penetrating lubricant.

3. Close the petcock or reconnect the lower hose and fill the system with water.
4. Add a can of quality radiator flush. If applicable, be sure the flush is safe to use in engines having aluminum components.
5. Idle the engine until the upper radiator hose gets hot.
6. Drain the system again.
7. Repeat this process until the drained water is clear and free of scale.
8. Close all petcocks and connect all the hoses.
9. If equipped with a coolant recovery system, flush the reservoir with water and leave empty.
10. Determine the capacity of your cooling system (see the capacity specification chart). Add a 50/50 mix of quality antifreeze (ethylene glycol) and water to provide the desired protection.
11. After adding the appropriate amount of coolant and water, start the engine. Add more fluid to top off while the engine is running.

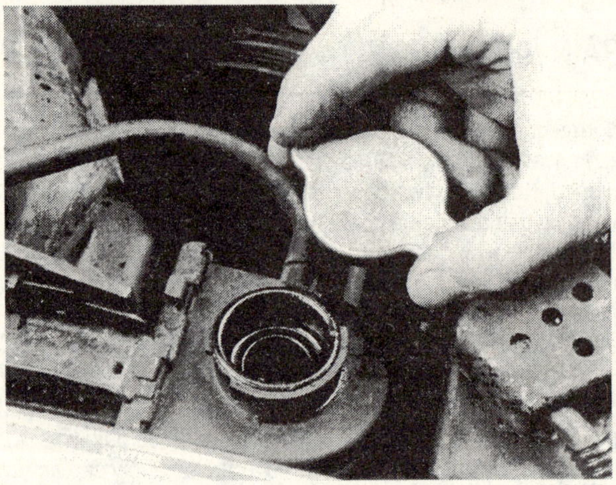

Fig. 174 Remove the radiator cap

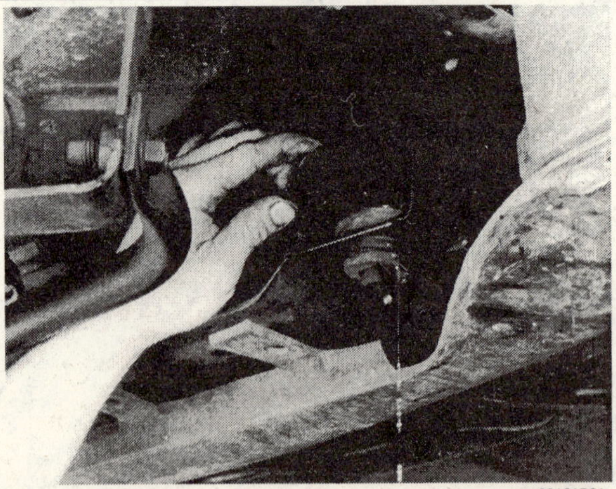

Fig. 175 Slowly turn the petcock at the bottom of the radiator to release the water/coolant mixture

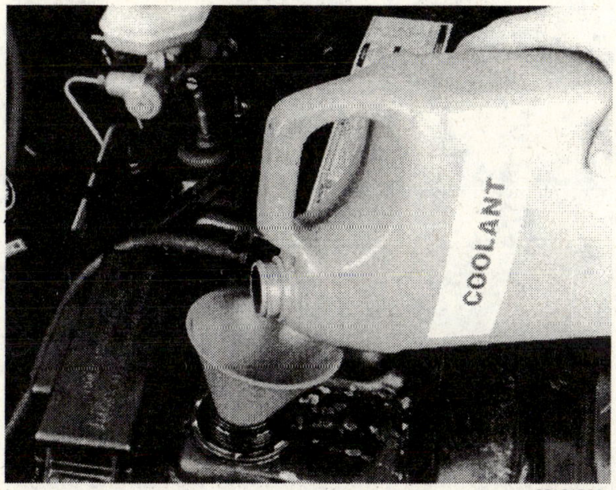

88181P33

Fig. 176 While the engine is running, top off the coolant level

SYSTEM INSPECTION

Most permanent antifreeze/coolant have a colored dye added which makes the solution an excellent leak detector. When servicing the cooling system, check for leakage at:

- All hoses and hose connections
- Radiator seams, radiator core, and radiator draincock
- All engine block and cylinder head freeze (core) plugs, and drain plugs
- Edges of all cooling system gaskets (head gaskets, thermostat gasket)
- Transmission fluid cooler
- Heating system components, water pump
- Check the engine oil dipstick for signs of coolant in the engine oil
- Check the coolant in the radiator for signs of oil in the coolant

Investigate and correct any indication of coolant leakage.

Check the Radiator Cap

➧ See Figure 177

While you are checking the coolant level, check the radiator cap for a worn or cracked gasket. If the cap doesn't seal properly, fluid will be lost and the engine will overheat.

A worn cap should be replaced with a new one.

Clean Radiator of Debris

➧ See Figure 178

Periodically clean any debris such as leaves, paper, insects, etc., from the radiator fins. Pick the large pieces off by hand. The smaller pieces can be washed away with water pressure from a hose.

Carefully straighten any bent radiator fins with a pair of needle nose pliers. Be careful, the fins are very soft. Don't wiggle the fins back and forth too much. Straighten them once and try not to move them again.

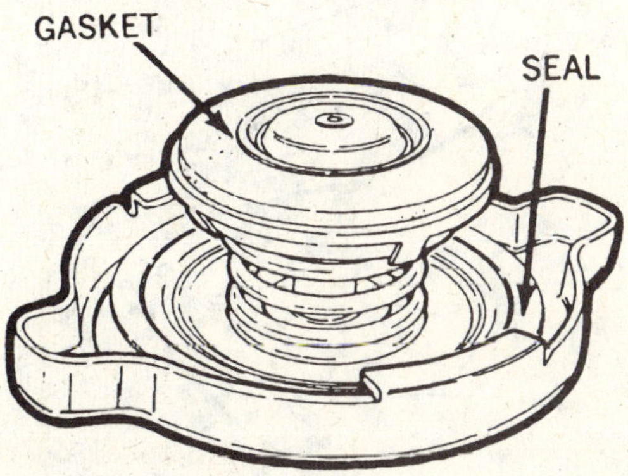

TCCS1079

Fig. 177 Be sure the rubber gasket on the radiator cap has a tight seal

CHECKING SYSTEM PROTECTION

A 50/50 mix of coolant concentrate and water will usually provide protection to −35°F (−37°C). Freeze protection may be checked by using a cooling system hydrometer. Inexpensive hydrometers (floating ball types) may be obtained from a local department store (automotive section) or an auto supply store. Follow the directions packaged with the coolant hydrometer when checking protection.

Brake Master Cylinder

FLUID RECOMMENDATIONS

Use only Heavy Duty Brake Fluid meeting DOT 3 specifications on the brake master cylinder.

LEVEL CHECK

The fluid in the brake master cylinder should be checked every 6 months or 6000 miles (9600 km).

Cast Iron Reservoir

1. Park the vehicle on a level surface and open the hood.
2. Pry the retaining spring bar holding the cover onto the master cylinder to one side.
3. Clean any dirt from the sides and top of the cover before removal. Remove the master cylinder cover and gasket.
4. Add fluid, if necessary, to within $^3/_8$ in. (10mm) of the top of the reservoir, or to the full level indicator (on models equipped).
5. Push the gasket bellows back into the cover. Reinstall the gasket and cover and position the retainer spring bar.

Plastic Reservoir

➧ See Figure 179

Check the fluid level on the side of the reservoir. If fluid is required, remove the filler cap and gasket from the reservoir. Fill the reservoir to the FULL line. Install the filler cap, making sure the gasket is properly seated in the cap.

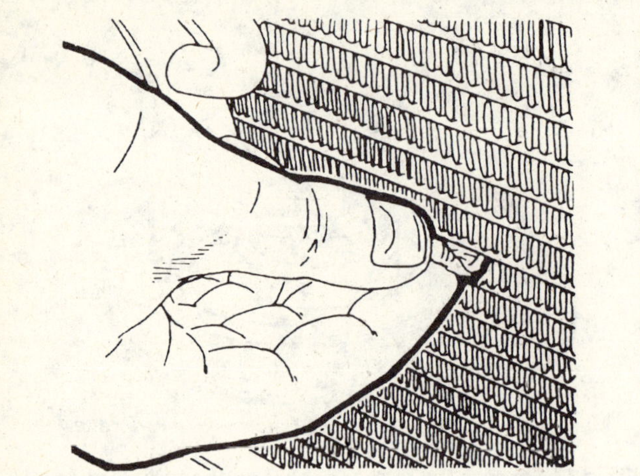
TCCS1081

Fig. 178 Periodically remove all debris from the radiator fins

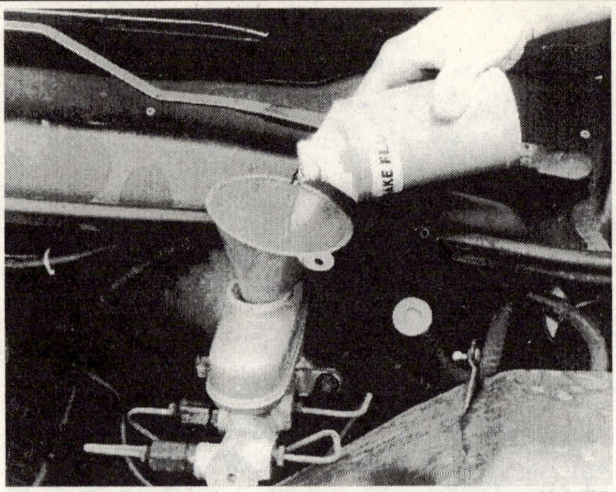
88181P37

Fig. 179 Always use a funnel to avoid spilling the brake fluid

Clutch Master Cylinder

FLUID RECOMMENDATIONS

Use only Heavy Duty Brake Fluid meeting DOT 3 specifications on the clutch master cylinder.

LEVEL CHECK

The fluid in the clutch master cylinder should be checked every 30,000 miles (50,000 km).

Plastic Reservoir

Check the fluid level on the side of the reservoir. If fluid is required, remove the filler cap and gasket from the reservoir. Fill the reservoir to the FULL line. Install the filler cap, making sure the gasket is properly seated in the cap.

Power Steering

FLUID RECOMMENDATION

Add power steering fluid; E6AZ-19582-AA or equivalent.

LEVEL CHECK

➧ See Figures 180 and 181

Check the power steering fluid level every 6 months or 6,000 miles (9600 km).

1. Park the vehicle on a level surface. Run the engine until normal operating temperature is reached.
2. Turn the steering all the way to the left and then all the way to the right several times. Center the steering wheel and shut off the engine.
3. Open the hood and check the power steering reservoir fluid level.

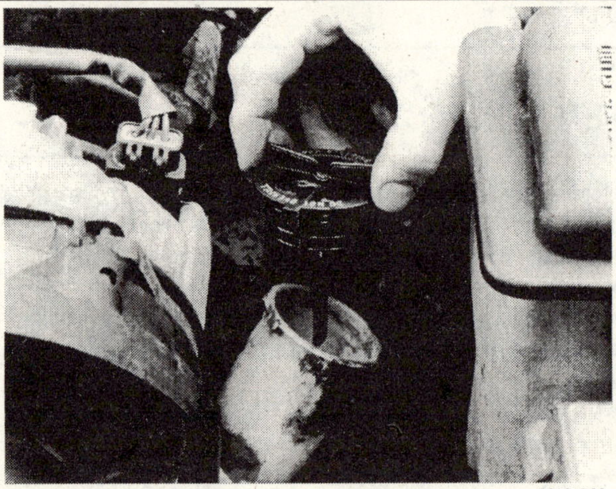
88181P38

Fig. 180 Remove the filler cap and wipe the dipstick clean, then reinsert and read the level

88181P39

Fig. 181 The level should be at any point below the FULL/MAX mark, but not below the ADD/MIN mark

4. Remove the filler cap and wipe the dipstick attached clean.
5. Re-insert the dipstick and tighten the cap. Remove the dipstick and note the fluid level indicated on the dipstick.
6. The level should be at any point below the FULL mark, but not below the ADD mark.
7. Add fluid as necessary. Do not overfill.

Chassis Greasing

➧ **See Figure 182**

BALL JOINTS

Ford does not require the ball joints to be lubricated on these models.

TIE ROD ENDS

Apply a small amount of chassis grease to the tie rods ends and check for wear.

CLUTCH LINKAGE

On models so equipped, apply a small amount of chassis grease to the pivot points of the clutch linkage.

AUTOMATIC TRANSMISSION LINKAGE

On models so equipped, apply a small amount of 10W engine oil to the kickdown and shift linkage at the pivot points.

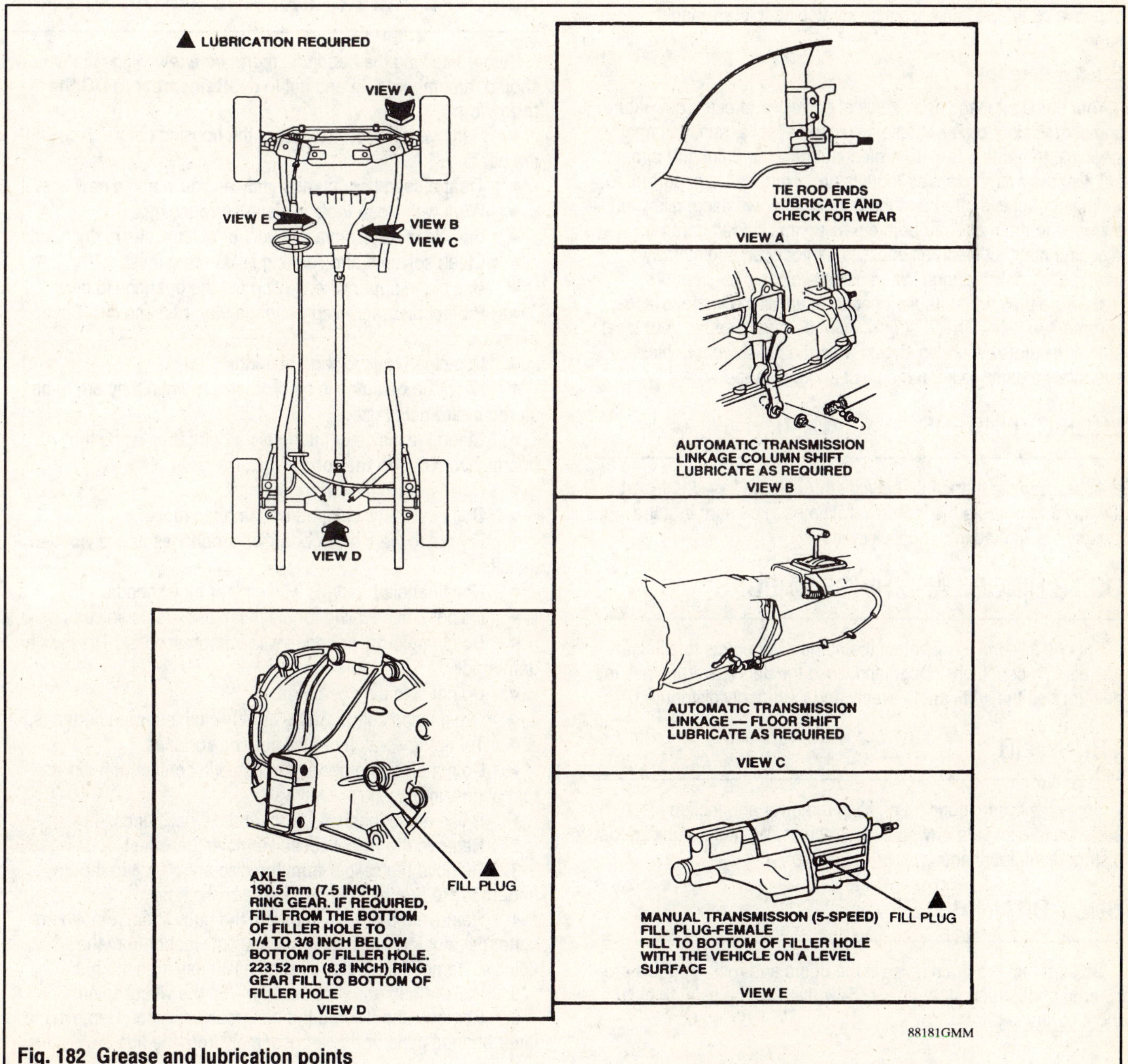

Fig. 182 Grease and lubrication points

PARKING BRAKE LINKAGE

At yearly intervals or whenever binding is noticeable in the parking brake linkage, lubricate the cable guides, levers and linkage with a suitable chassis grease.

Body Lubrication and Maintenance

CARE OF YOUR VEHICLE

Glass Surfaces

All glass surfaces should be kept clean at all times for safe driving. You should use a window cleaner, the same cleaner you use on windows in your home. Use caution and never use an abrasive cleaners, this will cause scratching to the window surfaces.

Exterior Care

Your car is exposed to all kinds of corrosive effects from nature and chemicals. Some of these are road salt, oils, rain, hail and sleet just to name a few. To protect not only the paint and trim, but also the many exposed mounts and fixtures, it is important to wash your vehicle often and thoroughly. After washing, allow all surfaces to drain and dry before parking in a closed garage. Washing may not clean all deposits off your car, so you may need additional cleaners. When using professional cleaners, make sure they are suitable for enamel/acrylic painted surfaces, chrome, tires etc.. These supplies can be purchased in your local auto parts store. You also should wax and polish your vehicle every few months to keep the paint in good shape.

LOCK CYLINDERS

Apply graphite lubricant sparingly through the key slot. Insert the key and operate the lock several times to be sure that the lubricant is worked into the lock cylinder.

DOOR HINGES AND HINGE CHECKS

Spray a silicone lubricant on the hinge pivot points to eliminate any binding conditions. Open and close the door several times to be sure that the lubricant is evenly and thoroughly distributed.

TRUNK LID

Spray a silicone lubricant on all of the pivot and friction surfaces to eliminate any squeaks or binds. Work the trunk lid to distribute the lubricant

BODY DRAIN HOLES

Be sure that the drain holes in the doors and rocker panels are cleared of obstruction. A small screwdriver can be used to clear them of any debris.

Front Wheel Bearings

➥ On the 1989–97 models, the front wheel bearings are of an integral hub/bearing design and are pregreased, sealed and require no scheduled maintenance. The bearings are preset and cannot be adjusted. If a bearing replacement is required for any repair, the hub and bearing must be replaced as an assembly. The bearings cannot be disassembled from the hub and serviced separately. No individual service seals, roller or races are available. The hub nut torque of 225–254 ft. lbs. (305–345 Nm), restricts bearing/hub relative movement and maintains axial position of the hub. For more information on this hub assembly removal, refer to Section 8 of this manual.

REMOVAL, REPACKING, AND INSTALLATION

Before handling the bearings, there are a few things that you should remember to do and not to do. **Remember to DO the following:**

- Remove all outside dirt from the housing before exposing the bearing.
- Treat a used bearing as gently as you would a new one.
- Work with clean tools in clean surroundings.
- Use clean, dry canvas gloves, or at least clean, dry hands.
- Clean solvents and flushing fluids are a must.
- Use clean paper when laying out the bearings to dry.
- Protect disassembled bearings from rust and dirt. Cover them up.
- Use clean rags to wipe bearings.
- Keep the bearings in oil-proof paper when they are to be stored or are not in use.
- Clean the inside of the housing before replacing the bearing.**Do NOT do the following:**
- Don't work in dirty surroundings.
- Don't use dirty, chipped or damaged tools.
- Try not to work on wooden work benches or use wooden mallets.
- Don't handle bearings with dirty or moist hands.
- Do not use gasoline for cleaning; use a safe solvent.
- Do not spin-dry bearings with compressed air. They will be damaged.
- Do not spin dirty bearings.
- Avoid using cotton waste or dirty cloths to wipe bearings.
- Try not to scratch or nick bearing surfaces.
- Do not allow the bearing to come in contact with dirt or rust at any time.

1. Raise and support the front end on jackstands.
2. Remove the wheel cover. Remove the wheel.
3. Remove the caliper from the disc and wire it to the underbody to prevent damage to the brake hose.
4. Remove the grease cap from the hub. Then, remove the cotter pin, nut lock, adjusting nut and flat washer from the spindle. Remove the outer bearing assembly from the hub.
5. Pull the hub and disc assembly off the wheel spindle.
6. Remove and discard the old grease retainer. Remove the inner bearing cone and roller assembly from the hub.

7. Clean all grease from the inner and outer bearing cups with solvent. Inspect the cups for pits, scratches, or excessive wear. If the cups are damaged, remove them with a drift.

8. Clean the inner and outer cone and roller assemblies with solvent and shake them dry. If the cone and roller assemblies show excessive wear or damage, replace them with the bearing cups as a unit.

9. Clean the spindle and the inside of the hub with solvent to thoroughly remove all old grease.

10. Covering the spindle with a clean cloth, brush all loose dirt and dust from the brake assembly. Remove the cloth carefully so as to not get dirt on the spindle.

11. If the inner and/or outer bearing cups were removed, install the replacement cups on the hub. Be sure that the cups seat properly in the hub.

12. It is imperative that all old grease be removed from the bearings and surrounding surfaces before repacking. The new lithium-based grease is not compatible with the sodium base grease used in the past.

13. Install the hub and disc on the wheel spindle. To prevent damage to the grease retainer and spindle threads, keep the hub centered on the spindle.

14. Install the outer bearing cone and roller assembly and the flat washer on the spindle. Install the adjusting nut.

15. Adjust the wheel bearings by tightening the adjusting nut to 17–25 ft. lbs. (23–34 Nm) with the wheel rotating to seat the bearing. Then back off the adjusting nut 1/2 turn. Retighten the adjusting nut to 10–28 inch lbs. (1–3 Nm). Install the locknut so that the castellations are aligned with the cotter pin hole. Install the cotter pin. Bend the ends of the cotter pin around the castellations of the locknut to prevent interference with the radio static collector in the grease cap. Install the grease cap.

****WARNING**

New bolts must be used when servicing floating caliper units. The upper bolt must be tightened first.

16. Install the wheels.

17. Install the wheel cover.

ADJUSTMENT

The front wheels each rotate on a set of opposed, tapered roller bearings. The grease retainer at the inside of the hub prevents lubricant from leaking into the brake drum.

1. Raise and support the front end on jackstands.
2. Remove the grease cap and remove excess grease from the end of the spindle.
3. Remove the cotter pin and nut lock.
4. Rotate the assembly while tightening the adjusting nut to 17-25 ft. lbs. (23-34 Nm) in order to seat the bearings.
5. Back off the adjusting nut 1/2, then retighten the adjusting nut to 10-28 inch lbs. (1-3 Nm).
6. Locate the nut lock on the adjusting nut so that the castellations on the lock are lined up with the cotter pin hole in the spindle.
7. Install the new cotter pin, bending the ends of the cotter pin around the castellated flange of the nut lock.
8. Check the wheel for proper rotation, then install the grease cap. If the wheel still does not rotate properly, inspect and clean or replace the wheel bearings and cups.

TRAILER TOWING

➧ See Figure 183

General Recommendations

Your vehicle was primarily designed to carry passengers and cargo. It is important to remember that towing a trailer will place additional loads on your vehicle's engine, drive train, steering, braking and other systems. However, if you decide to tow a trailer, using the proper equipment is a must.

Local laws may require specific equipment such as trailer brakes or fender mounted mirrors. Check your local laws.

Trailer Weight

The weight of the trailer is the most important factor. A good weight-to-horsepower ratio is about 35:1, 35 lbs. of Gross Combined Weight (GCW) for every horsepower your engine develops. Multiply the engine's rated horsepower by 35 and subtract the weight of the vehicle passengers and luggage. The number remaining is the approximate ideal maximum weight you should tow, although a numerically higher axle ratio can help compensate for heavier weight.

Hitch (Tongue) Weight

Calculate the hitch weight in order to select a proper hitch. The weight of the hitch is usually 9–11% of the trailer gross weight and should be measured with the trailer loaded. Hitches fall into various categories: those that mount on the frame and rear bumper, the bolt-on type, or the weld-on distribution type used for larger trailers. Axle mounted or clamp-on bumper hitches should never be used.

Check the gross weight rating of your trailer. Tongue weight is usually figured as 10% of gross trailer weight. Therefore, a trailer with a maximum gross weight of 2000 lbs. will have a maximum tongue weight of 200 lbs. Class I trailers fall into this category. Class II trailers are those with a gross weight rating of 2000–3000 lbs., while Class III trailers fall into the 3500–6000 lbs. category. Class IV trailers are those over 6000 lbs. and are for use with fifth wheel trucks, only.

When you've determined the hitch that you'll need, follow the manufacturer's installation instructions, exactly, especially when it comes to fastener torques. The hitch will subjected to a lot of stress and good hitches come with hardened bolts. Never substitute an inferior bolt for a hardened bolt.

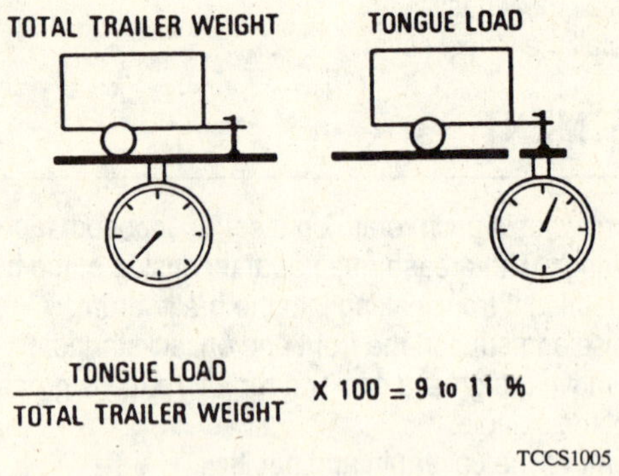

Fig. 183 Calculating proper tongue weight for your trailer

Cooling

ENGINE

Overflow Tank

One of the most common, if not THE most common, problems associated with trailer towing is engine overheating. If you have a cooling system without an expansion tank, you'll definitely need to get an aftermarket expansion tank kit, preferably one with at least a 2 quart capacity. These kits are easily installed on the radiator's overflow hose, and come with a pressure cap designed for expansion tanks.

Flex Fan

Another helpful accessory for vehicles using a belt-driven radiator fan is a flex fan. These fans are large diameter units designed to provide more airflow at low speeds, by using fan blades that have deeply cupped surfaces. The blades then flex, or flatten out, at high speed, when less cooling air is needed. These fans are far lighter in weight than stock fans, requiring less horsepower to drive them. Also, they are far quieter than stock fans. If you do decide to replace your stock fan with a flex fan, note that if your vehicle has a fan clutch, a spacer will be needed between the flex fan and water pump hub.

Oil Cooler

Aftermarket engine oil coolers are helpful for prolonging engine oil life and reducing overall engine temperatures. Both of these factors increase engine life. While not absolutely necessary in towing Class I and some Class II trailers, they are recommended for heavier Class II and all Class III towing. Engine oil cooler systems usually consist of an adapter, screwed on in place of the oil filter, a remote filter mounting and a multi-tube, finned heat exchanger, which is mounted in front of the radiator or air conditioning condenser.

TRANSMISSION

An automatic transmission is usually recommended for trailer towing. Modern automatics have proven reliable and, of course, easy to operate, in trailer towing. The increased load of a trailer, however, causes an increase in the temperature of the automatic transmission fluid. Heat is the worst enemy of an automatic transmission. As the temperature of the fluid increases, the life of the fluid decreases.

It is essential, therefore, that you install an automatic transmission cooler. The cooler, which consists of a multi-tube, finned heat exchanger, is usually installed in front of the radiator or air conditioning compressor, and hooked in-line with the transmission cooler tank inlet line. Follow the cooler manufacturer's installation instructions.

Select a cooler of at least adequate capacity, based upon the combined gross weights of the vehicle and trailer.

Cooler manufacturers recommend that you use an aftermarket cooler in addition to, and not instead of, the present cooling tank in your radiator. If you do want to use it in place of the radiator cooling tank, get a cooler at least two sizes larger than normally necessary.

➔ A transmission cooler can, sometimes, cause slow or harsh shifting in the transmission during cold weather, until the fluid has a chance to come up to normal operating temperature. Some coolers can be purchased with or retrofitted with a temperature bypass valve which will allow fluid flow through the cooler only when the fluid has reached above a certain operating temperature.

Handling A Trailer

Towing a trailer with ease and safety requires a certain amount of experience. It's a good idea to learn the feel of a trailer by practicing turning, stopping and backing in an open area such as an empty parking lot.

Towing

Before starting on a trip, practice turning, stopping and backing up in an area away from other traffic (such as a deserted shopping center parking lot) to gain experience in handling the extra weight and length of the trailer. Take enough time to get the feel of the vehicle/trailer combination under a variety of situations.

Skillful backing requires practice. Back up slowly with an assistant acting as a guide and watching for obstructions. Use both rear view mirrors. Place your hand at the bottom of the steering wheel and move it in the direction you want the rear of the trailer to swing. Make small corrections, instead of exaggerated ones, as a slight movement of the steering wheel will result in a much larger movement of the rear of the trailer.

Allow considerable more room for stopping when a trailer is attached to the vehicle. If you have a manual brake controller, lead with the trailer brakes when approaching a stop. Trailer brakes are also handy for correcting side sway. Just touch them for a moment without using your vehicle brakes and the trailer should settle down and track straight again.

To assist in obtaining good handling with the car/trailer combination, it is important that the trailer tongue load be maintained at approximately 10-15% of the loaded trailer weight.

Check everything before starting out on the road, then stop after you've traveled about 50 miles (80 km) and double-check the trailer hitch and electrical connections to make sure everything is still OK. Listen for sounds like chains dragging on the ground (indicating that a safety chain has come loose) and check your rear view mirrors frequently to make sure the trailer is still there and tracking properly. Check the trailer wheel lug nuts to make sure they're tight and never attempt to tow the trailer with a space saver spare installed on the car.

Remember that a car/trailer combination is more sensitive to cross winds and slow down when crossing bridges or wide open expanses in gusty wind conditions. Exceeding the speed limit while towing a trailer is not only illegal, it is foolhardy and invites disaster. A strong gust of wind can send a speeding car/trailer combination out of control.

Because the trailer wheels are closer than the towing vehicle wheels to the inside of a turn, drive slightly beyond the normal turning point when negotiating a sharp turn at a corner. Allow extra distance for passing other vehicles and downshift if necessary for better acceleration. Allow at least the equivalent of one vehicle and trailer length combined for each 10 mph of road speed.

Finally, remember to check the height of the loaded car/trailer, allowing for luggage racks, antenna, etc. mounted on the roof and take note of low bridges or parking garage clearances.

Wiring

Wiring the car for towing is fairly easy. There are a number of good wiring kits available and these should be used, rather than trying to design your own. All trailers will need brake lights and turn signals as well as tail lights and side marker lights. Most states require extra marker lights for overly wide trailers. Also, most states have recently required back-up lights for trailers, and most trailer manufacturers have been building trailers with back-up lights for several years.

Additionally, some Class I, most Class II and just about all Class III trailers will have electric brakes.

Add to this number an accessories wire, to operate trailer internal equipment or to charge the trailer's battery, and you can have as many as seven wires in the harness.

Determine the equipment on your trailer and buy the wiring kit necessary. The kit will contain all the wires needed, plus a plug adapter set which included the female plug, mounted on the bumper or hitch, and the male plug, wired into, or plugged into the trailer harness.

When installing the kit, follow the manufacturer's instructions. The color coding of the wires is standard throughout the industry.

One point to note, some domestic vehicles, and most imported vehicles, have separate turn signals. On most domestic vehicles, the brake lights and rear turn signals operate with the same bulb. For those vehicles with separate turn signals, you can purchase an isolation unit so that the brake lights won't blink whenever the turn signals are operated, or, you can go to your local electronics supply house and buy four diodes to wire in series with the brake and turn signal bulbs. Diodes will isolate the brake and turn signals. The choice is yours. The isolation units are simple and quick to install, but far more expensive than the diodes. The diodes, however, require more work to install properly, since they require the cutting of each bulb's wire and soldering in place of the diode.

One final point, the best kits are those with a spring loaded cover on the vehicle mounted socket. This cover prevents dirt and moisture from corroding the terminals. Never let the vehicle socket hang loosely. Always mount it securely to the bumper or hitch.

TOWING THE VEHICLE

Towing

See Figures 184 and 185

Whenever you are towing another vehicle, or being towed, make sure the chain or strap is sufficiently long and strong. Attach the chain securely at a point on the frame, shipping tie-down slots are provided on the front and rear of you car and should be used. Never attach a chain or strap to any steering or suspension part. Never try to start the vehicle when being towed, it might run into the back of the tow car. Do not allow too much slack in the tow line, the towed car could run over the line and damage to both cars could occur. If you car is being towed by a tow truck, the towing speed should be limited to 50 mph (80 km/h) with the driving wheels off the ground. If it is necessary to tow the car with the drive wheels on the ground, speed should be limited to no more then 35 mph (56 km/h) and the towing distance should not be greater than 50 miles (80 km).

Your vehicle may be towed by a wrecker from the front or rear as outlined in the following paragraphs. A 4 in. (102mm) x 4 in. (102mm) x 48 in. (122cm) wood pacer blocks and T-hook chains are required for proper towing to prevent damage to your vehicle. This equipment is commonly found on commercial wreckers. For flatbed towing, T-hook chains are required to prevent damage to the driveline or suspension components.

J-hook chains should not be used under any circumstances or your vehicle may be damaged.

As a general rule, vehicles should be towed with the driving wheels off the ground. To tow your vehicle in this manner, release the parking brake and place the transmission shift lever in the **NEUTRAL** position. Towing speed is limited to 50 mph (80 km/h) on smooth roads and 35 mph (56 km/h) on rough roads.

If it is necessary to tow a vehicle with an automatic transmission with the driving wheels on the ground, the transmission must be in proper working order. To tow your vehicle in this manner release the parking brake, place the shift lever in the **NEUTRAL** position and clamp the steering wheel in the straight ahead position with a steering wheel clamping device designed for towing service use. Do not exceed 35 mph (56 km/h) and a distance of 50 miles (80 km) or transmission damage could result.

If it is necessary to tow a vehicle with a manual transmission with the driving wheels on the ground, do not exceed 55 mph (88 km/h) but the distance is not limited. When ever towing from the rear, chains must not be attached forward of rear suspension arms or directly to the rear suspension arms. This could result in vehicle damage.

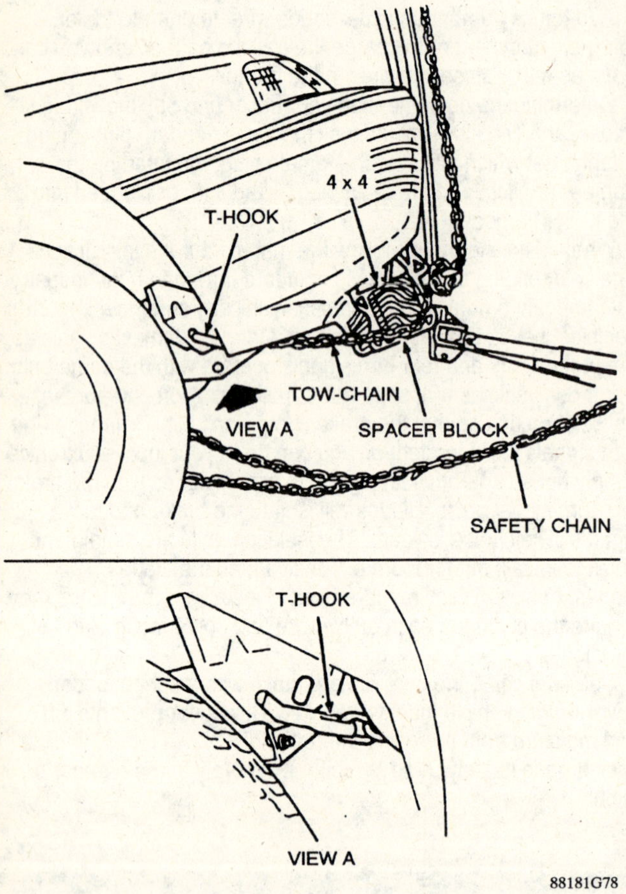

Fig. 184 Use spacer block pads under the front bumper. Put the tow chains on the outside of the blocks

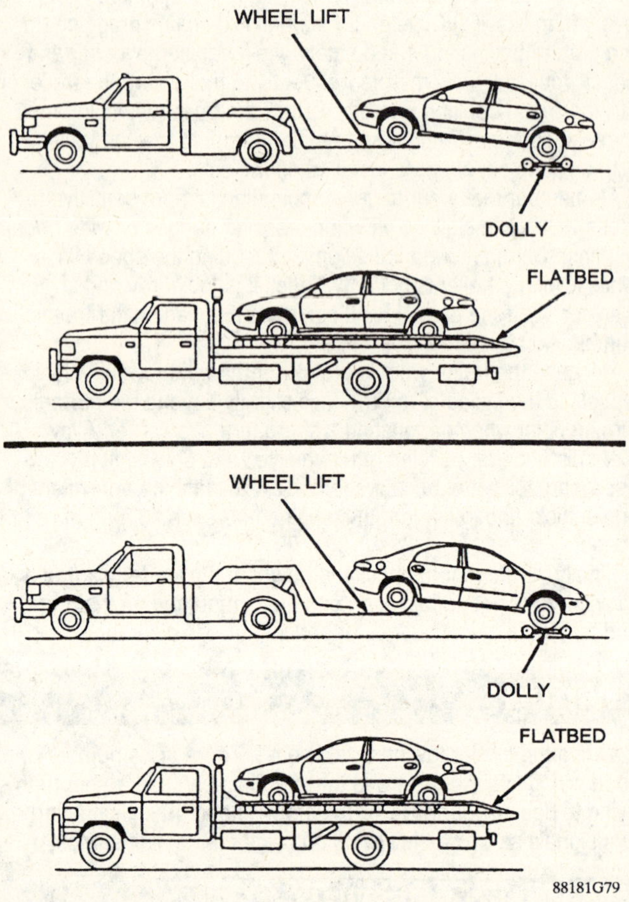

Fig. 185 Common tow truck operator car positioning

JUMP STARTING A DEAD BATTERY

➧ See Figure 186

Whenever a vehicle is jump started, precautions must be followed in order to prevent the possibility of personal injury. Remember that batteries contain a small amount of explosive hydrogen gas which is a by-product of battery charging. Sparks should always be avoided when working around batteries, especially when attaching jumper cables. To minimize the possibility of accidental sparks, follow the procedure carefully.

****CAUTION**

NEVER hook the batteries up in a series circuit or the entire electrical system will go up in smoke, especially the starter!

Jump Starting Precautions

- Be sure that both batteries are of the same voltage. Vehicles covered by this manual and most vehicles on the road today utilize a 12 volt charging system.
- Be sure that both batteries are of the same polarity (have the same terminal, in most cases NEGATIVE grounded).
- Be sure that the vehicles are not touching or a short could occur.
- On serviceable batteries, be sure the vent cap holes are not obstructed.
- Do not smoke or allow sparks anywhere near the batteries.
- In cold weather, make sure the battery electrolyte is not frozen. This can occur more readily in a battery that has been in a state of discharge.
- Do not allow electrolyte to contact your skin or clothing.

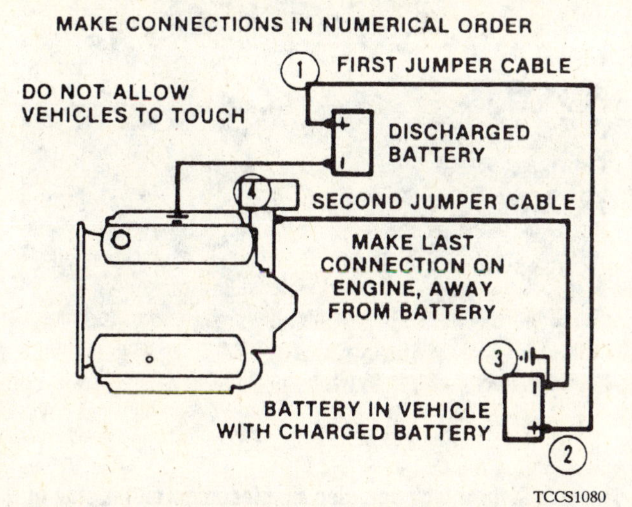

Fig. 186 Connect the jumper cables to the batteries and engine in the order shown

Jump Starting Procedure

1. Make sure that the voltages of the 2 batteries are the same. Most batteries and charging systems are of the 12 volt variety.
2. Pull the jumping vehicle (with the good battery) into a position so the jumper cables can reach the dead battery and that vehicle's engine. Make sure that the vehicles do NOT touch.
3. Place the transmissions/transaxles of both vehicles in **Neutral** (MT) or **P** (AT), as applicable, then firmly set their parking brakes.

➥ If necessary for safety reasons, the hazard lights on both vehicles may be operated throughout the entire procedure without significantly increasing the difficulty of jumping the dead battery.

4. Turn all lights and accessories OFF on both vehicles. Make sure the ignition switches on both vehicles are turned to the **OFF** position.
5. Cover the battery cell caps with a rag, but do not cover the terminals.
6. Make sure the terminals on both batteries are clean and free of corrosion or proper electrical connection will be impeded. If necessary, clean the battery terminals before proceeding.
7. Identify the positive (+) and negative (−) terminals on both batteries.
8. Connect the first jumper cable to the positive (+) terminal of the dead battery, then connect the other end of that cable to the positive (+) terminal of the booster (good) battery.
9. Connect one end of the other jumper cable to the negative (−) terminal on the booster battery and the final cable clamp to an engine bolt head, alternator bracket or other solid, metallic point on the engine with the dead battery. Try to pick a ground on the engine that is positioned away from the battery in order to minimize the possibility of the 2 clamps touching should one loosen during the procedure. DO NOT connect this clamp to the negative (−) terminal of the bad battery.

**CAUTION

Be very careful to keep the jumper cables away from moving parts (cooling fan, belts, etc.) on both engines.

10. Check to make sure that the cables are routed away from any moving parts, then start the donor vehicle's engine. Run the engine at moderate speed for several minutes to allow the dead battery a chance to receive some initial charge.
11. With the donor vehicle's engine still running slightly above idle, try to start the vehicle with the dead battery. Crank the engine for no more than 10 seconds at a time and let the starter cool for at least 20 seconds between tries. If the vehicle does not start in 3 tries, it is likely that something else is also wrong or that the battery needs additional time to charge.
12. Once the vehicle is started, allow it to run at idle for a few seconds to make sure that it is operating properly.
13. Turn ON the headlights, heater blower and, if equipped, the rear defroster of both vehicles in order to reduce the severity of voltage spikes and subsequent risk of damage to the vehicles' electrical systems when the cables are disconnected. This step is especially important to any vehicle equipped with computer control modules.
14. Carefully disconnect the cables in the reverse order of connection. Start with the negative cable that is attached to the engine ground, then the negative cable on the donor battery. Disconnect the positive cable from the donor battery and finally, disconnect the positive cable from the formerly dead battery. Be careful when disconnecting the cables from the positive terminals not to allow the alligator clips to touch any metal on either vehicle or a short and sparks will occur.

JACKING

➧ See Figures 187, 188, 189 and 190

Your vehicle was supplied with a jack for emergency road repairs. This jack is fine for changing a flat tire or other short term procedures not requiring you to go beneath the vehicle. If it is used in an emergency situation, carefully follow the instructions provided either with the jack or in your owner's manual. Do not attempt to use the jack on any portions of the vehicle other than specified by the vehicle manufacturer. Always block the diagonally opposite wheel when using a jack.

A more convenient way of jacking is the use of a garage or floor jack. You may use the floor jack at the specified points shown in following the illustrations.

Never place the jack under the radiator, engine or transmission components. Severe and expensive damage will result when the jack is raised. Additionally, never jack under the floorpan or bodywork; the metal will deform.

Whenever you plan to work under the vehicle, you must support it on jackstands or ramps. Never use cinder blocks or stacks of wood to support the vehicle, even if you're only going to be under it for a few minutes. Never crawl under the vehicle when it is supported only by the tire-changing jack or other floor jack.

➥ Always position a block of wood or small rubber pad on top of the jack or jackstand to protect the lifting point's finish when lifting or supporting the vehicle.

88181P40

Fig. 187 Place a floor jack in the center under the rear axle to raise the rear end

88181P41

Fig. 188 A floor jack can also be placed on either side of the rear under the coil springs

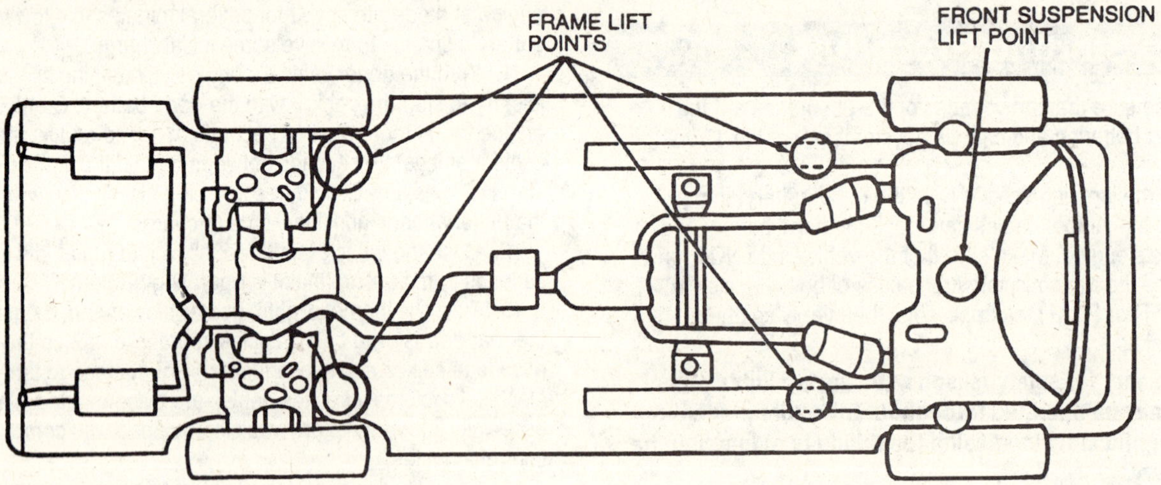

88181G80

Fig. 189 These five area points are recommended to support the vehicle for jacking purposes

Small hydraulic, screw, or scissors jacks are satisfactory for raising the vehicle. Drive-on trestles or ramps are also a handy and safe way to both raise and support the vehicle. Be careful though, some ramps may be too steep to drive your vehicle onto without scraping the front bottom panels. Never support the vehicle on any suspension member (unless specifically instructed to do so by a repair manual) or by an underbody panel.

Jacking Precautions

The following safety points cannot be overemphasized:

- Always block the opposite wheel or wheels to keep the vehicle from rolling off the jack.
- When raising the front of the vehicle, firmly apply the parking brake.
- When the drive wheels are to remain on the ground, leave the vehicle in gear to help prevent it from rolling.
- Always use jackstands to support the vehicle when you are working underneath. Place the stands beneath the vehicle's jacking brackets. Before climbing underneath, rock the vehicle a bit to make sure it is firmly supported.

88181P42

Fig. 190 Using a safety stand in conjunction with a floor jack is highly recommended

HOW TO BUY A USED VEHICLE

Many people believe that a two or three year old used car or truck is a better buy than a new vehicle. This may be true as most new vehicles suffer the heaviest depreciation in the first two years and, at three years old, a vehicle is usually not old enough to present a lot of costly repair problems. But keep in mind, when buying a non-warranted automobile, there are no guarantees. Whatever the age of the used vehicle you might want to purchase, this section and a little patience should increase your chances of selecting one that is safe and dependable.

Tips

1. First decide what model you want, and how much you want to spend.
2. Check the used car lots and your local newspaper ads. Privately owned vehicles are usually less expensive, however, you may not get a warranty that, in many cases, comes with a used vehicle purchased from a lot. Of course, some aftermarket warranties may not be worth the extra money, so this is a point you will have to debate and consider based on your priorities.
3. Never shop at night. The glare of the lights make it easy to miss faults on the body caused by accident or rust repair.
4. Try to get the name and phone number of the previous owner. Contact him/her and ask about the vehicle. If the owner of a lot refuses this information, look for a vehicle somewhere else.

A private seller can tell you about the vehicle and maintenance. But remember, there's no law requiring honesty from private citizens selling used vehicles. There is a law that forbids tampering with or turning back the odometer mileage. This includes both the private citizen and the lot owner. The law also requires that the seller or anyone transferring ownership of the vehicle must provide the buyer with a signed statement indicating the mileage on the odometer at the time of transfer.

5. You may wish to contact the National Highway Traffic Safety Administration (NHTSA) to find out if the vehicle has ever been included in a manufacturer's recall. Write down the year, model and serial number before you buy the vehicle, then contact NHTSA (there should be a 1-800 number that your phone company's information line can supply). If the vehicle was listed for a recall, make sure the needed repairs were made.
6. Refer to the Used Vehicle Checklist in this section and check all the items on the vehicle you are considering. Some items are more important than others. Only you know how much money you can afford for repairs, and depending on the price of the vehicle, may consider performing anv needed work yourself. Beware, however, of trouble in areas that will affect operation, safety or emission. Problems in the Used Vehicle Checklist break down as follows:

- Numbers 1-8: Two or more problems in these areas indicate a lack of maintenance. You should beware.
- Numbers 9-13: Problems here tend to indicate a lack of proper care, however, these can usually be corrected with a tune-up or relatively simple parts replacement.
- Numbers 14-17: Problems in the engine or transmission can be very expensive. Unless you are looking for a project, walk away from any vehicle with problems in 2 or more of these areas.

7. If you are satisfied with the apparent condition of the vehicle, take it to an independent diagnostic center or mechanic for a complete check. If you have a state inspection program, have it inspected immediately before purchase, or specify on the bill of sale that the sale is conditional on passing state inspection.
8. Road test the vehicle — refer to the Road Test Checklist in this section. If your original evaluation and the road test agree — the rest is up to you.

USED VEHICLE CHECKLIST

See Figure 191

The numbers on the illustrations refer to the numbers on this checklist.

1. Mileage: Average mileage is about 12,000-15,000 miles per year. More than average mileage may indicate hard usage or could indicate many highway miles (which could be less detrimental than half as many tough around town miles).
2. Paint: Check around the tailpipe, molding and windows for overspray indicating that the vehicle has been repainted.
3. Rust: Check fenders, doors, rocker panels, window moldings, wheelwells, floorboards, under floormats, and in the trunk for signs of rust. Any rust at all will be a problem. There is no way to permanently stop the spread of rust, except to replace the part or panel.

If rust repair is suspected, try using a magnet to check for body filler. A magnet should stick to the sheet metal parts of the body, but will not adhere to areas with large amounts of filler.

4. Body appearance: Check the moldings, bumpers, grille, vinyl roof, glass, doors, trunk lid and body panels for general overall condition. Check for misalignment, loose hold-down clips, ripples, scratches in glass, welding in the trunk, severe misalignment of body panels or ripples, any of which may indicate crash work.
5. Leaks: Get down and look under the vehicle. There are no normal leaks, other than water from the air conditioner condenser.
6. Tires: Check the tire air pressure. One old trick is to pump the tire pressure up to make the vehicle roll easier. Check the tread wear, open the trunk and check the spare too. Uneven wear is a clue that the front end may need an alignment.
7. Shock absorbers: Check the shock absorbers by forcing downward sharply on each corner of the vehicle. Good shocks will not allow the vehicle to bounce more than once after you let go.
8. Interior: Check the entire interior. You're looking for an interior condition that agrees with the overall condition of the vehicle. Reasonable wear is expected, but be suspicious of new seat covers on sagging seats, new pedal pads, and worn armrests. These indicate an attempt to cover up hard use. Pull back the carpets and look for evidence of water leaks or flooding. Look for missing hardware, door handles, control knobs, etc. Check lights and signal operations. Make sure all accessories (air conditioner, heater, radio, etc.) work. Check windshield wiper operation.
9. Belts and Hoses: Open the hood, then check all belts and hoses for wear, cracks or weak spots.

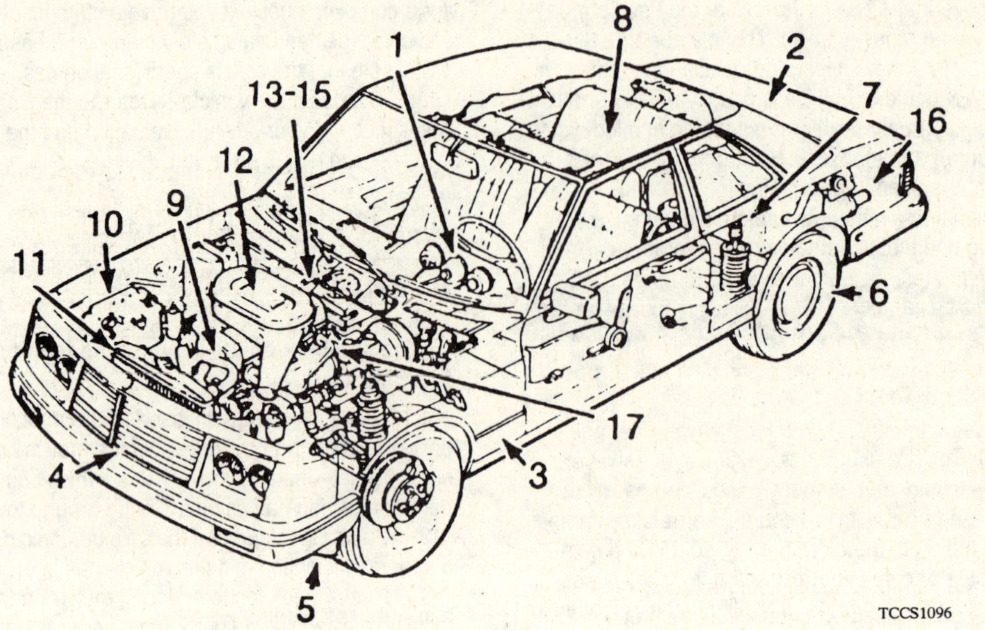

Fig. 191 Each of the numbered items should be checked when purchasing a used vehicle

10. Battery: Low electrolyte level, corroded terminals and/or cracked case indicate a lack of maintenance.
11. Radiator: Look for corrosion or rust in the coolant indicating a lack of maintenance.
12. Air filter: A severely dirty air filter would indicate a lack of maintenance.
13. Ignition wires: Check the ignition wires for cracks, burned spots, or wear. Worn wires will have to be replaced.
14. Oil level: If the oil level is low, chances are the engine uses oil or leaks. Beware of water in the oil (there is probably a cracked block or bad head gasket), excessively thick oil (which is often used to quiet a noisy engine), or thin, dirty oil with a distinct gasoline smell (this may indicate internal engine problems).
15. Automatic Transmission: Pull the transmission dipstick out when the engine is running. The level should read FULL, and the fluid should be clear or bright red. Dark brown or black fluid that has distinct burnt odor, indicates a transmission in need of repair or overhaul.
16. Exhaust: Check the color of the exhaust smoke. Blue smoke indicates, among other problems, worn rings. Black smoke can indicate burnt valves or carburetor problems. Check the exhaust system for leaks; it can be expensive to replace.
17. Spark Plugs: Remove one or all of the spark plugs (the most accessible will do, though all are preferable). An engine in good condition will show plugs with a light tan or gray deposit on the firing tip.

ROAD TEST CHECKLIST

1. Engine Performance: The vehicle should be peppy whether cold or warm, with adequate power and good pickup. It should respond smoothly through the gears.
2. Brakes: They should provide quick, firm stops with no noise, pulling or brake fade.
3. Steering: Sure control with no binding harshness, or looseness and no shimmy in the wheel should be expected. Noise or vibration from the steering wheel when turning the vehicle means trouble.
4. Clutch (Manual Transmission/Transaxle): Clutch action should give quick, smooth response with easy shifting. The clutch pedal should have free-play before it disengages the clutch. Start the engine, set the parking brake, put the transmission in first gear and slowly release the clutch pedal. The engine should begin to stall when the pedal is $\frac{1}{2}$–$\frac{3}{4}$ of the way up.
5. Automatic Transmission/Transaxle: The transmission should shift rapidly and smoothly, with no noise, hesitation, or slipping.
6. Differential: No noise or thumps should be present. Differentials have no normal leaks.
7. Driveshaft/Universal Joints: Vibration and noise could mean driveshaft problems. Clicking at low speed or coast conditions means worn U-joints.
8. Suspension: Try hitting bumps at different speeds. A vehicle that bounces excessively has weak shock absorbers or struts. Clunks mean worn bushings or ball joints.
9. Frame/Body: Wet the tires and drive in a straight line. Tracks should show two straight lines, not four. Four tire tracks indicate a frame/body bent by collision damage. If the tires can't be wet for this purpose, have a friend drive along behind you and see if the vehicle appears to be traveling in a straight line.

1983-88 MAINTENANCE SCHEDULE

SCHEDULE 1 — UNIQUE DRIVING CONDITIONS — GASOLINE ENGINES

Follow this Schedule if your driving habits FREQUENTLY include:

- Operating when outside temperatures remain **below freezing** and most trips are less than 5 miles (8 km).
- Operating during HOT WEATHER (above 90°F, 32°C) and:
  — Driving continuously in excess of normal highway speeds;
  — Driving in stop-and-go "rush hour" traffic.
- Towing a trailer, using a camper or car-top carrier or otherwise carryng heavy loads.
- Operating in severe dust conditions.
- Extensive idling, such as police, taxi or door-to-door delivery use.

SERVICE INTERVAL Perform at the months or distances shown, whichever comes first. Miles × 1000	3	6	9	12	15	18	21	24	27	30	33	36	39	42	45	48
Kilometers × 1000	4.8	9.6	14.4	19.2	24	28.8	33.6	38.4	43.2	48	52.8	57.6	62.4	67.2	72	76.8
EMISSION CONTROL SERVICE																
Change Engine Oil (every 3 months) or	X	X	X	X	X	X	X	X	X	X	X	X	X	X	X	X
Change Engine Oil Filter (every 3 months) or	X	X	X	X	X	X	X	X	X	X	X	X	X	X	X	X
Spark Plugs: Check/Regap (All)		X		X		X		X				X		X		X
Replace (Non-Turbo)										X						
Turbocharged Only-Replace					(X)					X					(X)	
Inspect Accessory Drive Belt(s)										X						
Check/Lube Exhaust Control Valve (if equipped)		(X)								(X)					(X)	
Replace Air Cleaner Filter (1)										X						
Replace Crankcase Emission Filter (1)										X						
Replace EGR Solenoid Filter (Six Cylinder 3.8L Engine Only)										X						
Check/Clean Choke Linkage — If Equipped										X						
Replace Engine Coolant, Check Hoses and Clamps EVERY 36 Months OR										X						
Check Engine Coolant Protection	ANNUALLY															
GENERAL MAINTENANCE																
Inspect Exhaust Heat Shields										X						
Change Automatic Transmission Fluid (2)										X						
Lubricate Steering and/or Suspension Linkage (All Cars)										X						
Lubricate Steering Linkage					X										X	

(1) If operating in severe dust, ask your dealer for proper replacement intervals.

(2) If your vehicle accumulates 5,000 miles (8 000 km) or more per month or is used in CONTINUOUS stop and go service, change every 30,000 miles (48 000 km) — not necessary for severe dust, short trips or extensive idling.

(X) All items with either a "X" or a "(X)" code are required t be performed in all states except California. For cars sold in California, only "X" items are REQUIRED to be performed. However, Ford recommends that you also perform maintenance on items designated by an "(X)" in order to achieve best vehicle operation.

88181C08

1983-88 MAINTENANCE SCHEDULE

SCHEDULE 2 — NORMAL DRIVING CONDITIONS — GASOLINE ENGINES

Follow this Schedule if, generally, you drive your vehicle on a daily basis for several miles and NONE OF THE UNIQUE DRIVING CONDITIONS SHOWN IN SCHEDULE I APPLY TO YOUR DRIVING HABITS.

SERVICE INTERVALS Perform at the months or distances shown, whichever comes first. Miles x 1000	7.5	15	22.5	30	37.5	45	52.5	60
Kilometers x 1000	12	24	36	48	60	72	84	96
EMISSIONS CONTROL SERVICE								
Four Cylinder: Change Engine Oil (Every 12 Months) or	X	X	X	X	X	X	X	X
Change Oil Filter (Every 12 Months) or	X	X	X	X	X	X	X	X
Six and Eight Cylinders: Change Engine Oil (Every 12 Months) or	X	X	X	X	X	X	X	X
Change Oil Filter (Every 12 Months) or	X		X		X		X	
Turbocharged Engines: Change Spark Plugs		(X)		X		(X)		X
Change Oil and Filter	(EVERY 5,000 MILES (8 000 km)							
(ALL ENGINES)								
Replace Spark Plugs				X				X
Inspect Accessory Drive Belt(s) TURBOCHARGED ONLY				X				X
Inspect Accessory Drive Belt(s)				X				X
Replace EGR Vacuum Solenoid Filter 3.8L								X
Check/Lube Exhaust Control Valve (if equipped)	(X)			(X)		(X)		(X)
Change Crankcase Emission Filter				X				X
Replace Air Cleaner Filter				X				X
Check/Clean Choke Linkage				X				X
Change Engine Coolant Every 36 Months or				X				X
Check Engine Coolant Protection	ANNUALLY							
GENERAL MAINTENANCE								
Check Exhaust Heat Shields				X				X
Lube Steering and/or Suspension				X				X

(X) All items with either an "X" or an "(X)" code are required to be performed in all states except California. For cars sold in California, only "X" items are REQUIRED to be performed. However, Ford recommends that you also perform maintenance on items designated by an "(X)" in order to achieve best vehicle operation.

88181C55

1989-96 MAINTENANCE SCHEDULE

SCHEDULE A

Follow this Schedule if your driving habits MAINLY include one or more of the following conditions:

- Short trips of less than 16 km (10 miles) when outside temperatures remain below freezing.
- Operating during HOT WEATHER
  — Driving in stop-and-go "rush hour" traffic.
- Towing a trailer, using a car-top carrier.
- Operating in severe dust conditions.
- Extensive idling, such as police, taxi or door-to-door delivery service.

SERVICE INTERVAL Perform at the months or distances shown, whichever comes first. Miles × 1000	3	6	9	12	15	18	21	24	27	30	33	36	39	42	45	48	51	54	57	60
Kilometers × 1000	4.8	9.6	14.4	19.2	24	28.8	33.6	38.4	43.2	48	52.8	57.6	62.4	67.2	72	76.8	81.6	86.4	91.2	96
EMISSION CONTROL SERVICE																				
Replace Engine Oil and Oil Filter Every 3 Months OR	X	X	X	X	X	X	X	X	X	X	X	X	X	X	X	X	X	X	X	X
Replace Spark Plugs										X										X
Replace Spark Plugs (Supercharged use Platinum Type)																				X
Check Supercharger Lubricant										X										X
Inspect Accessory Drive Belt(s)										X										X
Replace Air Cleaner Filter①										X										X
Replace Engine Coolant, EVERY 36 Months OR										X										X
Check Engine Coolant Protection, Hoses and Clamps	ANNUALLY																			
GENERAL MAINTENANCE																				
Lubricate Tie Rod Ends										X										X
Inspect Exhaust Heat Shields										X										X
Change Automatic Transmission Fluid②										X										X
Inspect Brake Pads and Rotors (front)③ (Front and Rear — Super Coupe/XR7)③										X										X
Inspect Brake Linings and Drums (Rear)③										X										X
Rotate Tires		X					X					X					X			

① If operating in severe dust, more frequent intervals may be required. Consult your dealer.
② Change automatic transmission fluid if your driving habits frequently include one or more of the following conditions:
- Operation during hot weather (above 32°C (90°F)) carrying heavy loads and in hilly terrain.
- Towing a trailer or using a car top carrier.
- Police, taxi or door-to-door delivery service.
- Vehicle accumulates 5,000 miles (8 000 km) or more per month or is used in CONTINUOUS stop-and-go service.

③ If your driving includes continuous stop-and-go driving or driving in mountainous areas, more frequent intervals may be required.
X All items designated by an X must be performed in all states.

88181C56

1989-96 MAINTENANCE SCHEDULE

SCHEDULE B

Follow Maintenance Schedule B if, generally, you drive your vehicle on a daily basis for farther than 16 km (10 miles) and NONE OF THE DRIVING CONDITIONS SHOWN IN SCHEDULE A APPLY TO YOUR DRIVING HABITS.

SERVICE INTERVALS Perform at the months or distances shown, whichever comes first. Miles x 1000	7.5	15	22.5	30	37.5	45	52.5	60
Kilometers x 1000	12	24	36	48	60	72	84	96
EMISSIONS CONTROL SERVICE								
Supercharged Engines — Change Oil and Filter	As Indicated by the Vehicle Maintenance Monitor, But Not Beyond Every 5,000 Miles (8 000 km) or 6 Months, Whichever Comes First							
Replace Engine Oil and Oil Filter As Indicated by the Vehicle Maintenance Monitor (if equipped), But Not Beyond Every 6 Months or 7,500 Miles Whichever Occurs First — Except Supercharged	X	X	X	X	X	X	X	X
Replace Spark Plugs — Except Supercharged				X				X
Replace Spark Plugs — Platinum Type Supercharged								X
Check Supercharger Lubricant				X				X
Replace Crankcase Emission Filter①				X				X
Inspect Accessory Drive Belt(s)				X				X
Replace Air Cleaner Filter①				X				X
Replace Engine Coolant Every 36 Months OR				X				X
Check Engine Coolant Protection, Hoses and Clamps	ANNUALLY							
GENERAL MAINTENANCE								
Lubricate Tie Rod Ends				X				X
Check Exhaust Heat Shields				X				X
Inspect Disc Brake Pads and Rotors (Front and Rear Super Coupe/XR7)②				X				X
Inspect Brake Linings and Drums (Rear)②				X				X
Rotate Tires	X		X		X		X	

① If operating in severe dust, more frequent intervals may be required. Consult your dealer.
② If your driving includes continuous stop-and-go driving or driving in mountainous areas, more frequent intervals may be required.

88181C57

CAPACITIES

Year	Model	Engine ID/VIN	Engine Displacement Liters (cc)	Engine Oil with Filter (qts.)	Transmission (pts.) 4-Spd	5-Spd	Auto.	Transfer Case (pts.)	Drive Axle Front (pts.)	Rear (pts.)	Fuel Tank (gal.)	Cooling System (qts.)
1983	Cougar	W	2.3 (2300)	5.0	4.5	4.8	-	-	-	3.25	18.0	8.7
	Cougar	3	3.8 (3802)	5.0	-	-	22.0	-	-	3.25	21.0	10.7
	Cougar	F	5.0 (4949)	5.0	-	-	22.0	-	-	3.25	20.0	13.4
	Thunderbird	W	2.3 (2300)	5.0	4.5	4.8	-	-	-	3.25	18.0	8.7
	Thunderbird	3	3.8 (3802)	5.0	-	-	22.0	-	-	3.25	21.0	10.7
	Thunderbird	F	5.0 (4949)	5.0	-	-	22.0	-	-	3.25	20.0	13.4
1984	Cougar	W	2.3 (2300)	5.0	4.5	4.8	-	-	-	3.25	18.0	8.7
	Cougar	3	3.8 (3802)	5.0	-	-	22.0	-	-	3.25	21.0	10.7
	Cougar	F	5.0 (4949)	5.0	-	-	22.0	-	-	3.25	20.0	13.4
	Thunderbird	W	2.3 (2300)	5.0	4.5	4.8	-	-	-	3.25	18.0	8.7
	Thunderbird	3	3.8 (3802)	5.0	-	-	22.0	-	-	3.25	21.0	10.7
	Thunderbird	F	5.0 (4949)	5.0	-	-	22.0	-	-	3.25	20.0	13.4
1985	Cougar	W	2.3 (2300)	5.0	4.5	4.8	-	-	-	3.25	18.0	8.7
	Cougar	3	3.8 (3802)	5.0	-	-	22.0	-	-	3.25	21.0	10.7
	Cougar	F	5.0 (4949)	5.0	-	-	22.0	-	-	3.25	20.0	13.4
	Thunderbird	W	2.3 (2300)	5.0	4.5	4.8	-	-	-	3.25	18.0	8.7
	Thunderbird	3	3.8 (3802)	5.0	-	-	22.0	-	-	3.25	21.0	10.7
	Thunderbird	F	5.0 (4949)	5.0	-	-	22.0	-	-	3.25	20.0	13.4
1986	Cougar	W	2.3 (2300)	5.0	4.5	4.8	-	-	-	3.25	18.0	8.7
	Cougar	3	3.8 (3802)	5.0	-	-	22.0	-	-	3.25	21.0	10.7
	Cougar	F	5.0 (4949)	5.0	-	-	22.0	-	-	3.25	20.0	13.4
	Thunderbird	W	2.3 (2300)	5.0	4.5	4.8	-	-	-	3.25	18.0	8.7
	Thunderbird	3	3.8 (3802)	5.0	-	-	22.0	-	-	3.25	21.0	10.7
	Thunderbird	F	5.0 (4949)	5.0	-	-	22.0	-	-	3.25	20.0	13.4
1987	Cougar	3	3.8 (3802)	5.0	-	-	22.0	-	-	3.25	21.0	10.7
	Cougar	F	5.0 (4949)	5.0	-	-	22.0	-	-	3.25	20.0	13.4
	Thunderbird	W	2.3 (2300)	5.0	4.5	4.8	-	-	-	3.25	18.0	8.7
	Thunderbird	3	3.8 (3802)	5.0	-	-	22.0	-	-	3.25	21.0	10.7
	Thunderbird	F	5.0 (4949)	5.0	-	-	22.0	-	-	3.25	20.0	13.4
1988	Cougar	4	3.8 (3802)	5.0	-	-	22.0	-	-	3.25	21.0	11.8
	Cougar	F	5.0 (4949)	5.0	-	-	22.0	-	-	3.25	20.0	13.4
	Thunderbird	W	2.3 (2300)	5.0	4.8	4.8	16.0	-	-	3.25	18.0	10.0
	Thunderbird	4	3.8 (3802)	5.0	-	-	22.0	-	-	3.25	21.0	11.8
	Thunderbird	F	5.0 (4949)	5.0	-	-	22.0	-	-	3.25	20.0	13.4
1989	Cougar	4	3.8 (3802)	5.0	-	-	22.0	-	-	3.75	21.0	11.8
	Cougar	C	3.8 (3802)	5.0	-	-	22.0	-	-	3.75	21.0	12.0
	Cougar	R	3.8 (3802)	5.0	-	-	22.0	-	-	3.75	21.0	13.4
	Thunderbird	4	3.8 (3802)	5.0	-	-	22.0	-	-	3.25	21.0	11.8
	Thunderbird	R	3.8 (3802) ①	5.0	-	6.3	24.0	-	-	3.25	18.8	11.8
	Thunderbird	C	3.8 (3802) ①	5.0	-	6.3	24.0	-	-	3.25	28.8	11.8
1990	Cougar	4	3.8 (3802)	5.0	-	-	22.0	-	-	3.25	21.0	11.8
	Cougar	R	3.8 (3802)	5.0	-	6.3	24.0	-	-	3.25	18.8	11.8
	Thunderbird	4	3.8 (3802)	5.0	-	-	22.0	-	-	3.25	21.0	11.8
	Thunderbird	R	3.8 (3802) ①	5.0	-	6.3	24.0	-	-	3.25	18.8	11.8

88181C06

88181C07

CAPACITIES

Year	Model	Engine ID/VIN	Engine Displacement Liters (cc)	Engine Oil with Filter (qts.)	Transmission (pts.) 4-Spd	Transmission (pts.) 5-Spd	Transmission (pts.) Auto.	Transfer Case (pts.)	Drive Axle Front (pts.)	Drive Axle Rear (pts.)	Fuel Tank (gal.)	Cooling System (qts.)
1991	Cougar	4	3.8 (3802)	5.0	-	-	22.0	-	-	3.25	21.0	11.8
	Cougar	R	3.8 (3802)	5.0	-	6.3	24.0	-	-	3.25	18.8	11.8
	Thunderbird	4	3.8 (3802)	5.0	-	-	22.0	-	-	②	21.0	11.8
	Thunderbird	R	3.8 (3802) ①	5.0	-	6.3	24.0	-	-	②	18.8	11.8
	Thunderbird	T	5.0 (4943)	5.0	-	-	24.6	-	-	②	19.0	14.1
1992	Cougar	4	3.8 (3802)	5.0	-	-	22.0	-	-	3.75	21.0	11.8
	Cougar	T	5.0 (4943)	5.0	-	-	24.6	-	-	3.75	19.0	14.1
	Thunderbird	4	3.8 (3802)	5.0	-	-	22.0	-	-	②	21.0	11.8
	Thunderbird	R	3.8 (3802) ①	5.0	-	6.3	24.0	-	-	②	18.8	11.8
	Thunderbird	T	5.0 (4943)	5.0	-	-	24.6	-	-	②	19.0	14.1
1993	Cougar	4	3.8 (3802)	5.0	-	-	22.0	-	-	②	21.0	11.8
	Cougar	T	5.0 (4943)	5.0	-	-	24.6	-	-	②	19.0	14.1
	Thunderbird	4	3.8 (3802)	5.0	-	-	22.0	-	-	②	21.0	11.8
	Thunderbird	R	3.8 (3802) ①	5.0	-	6.3	24.0	-	-	②	18.8	11.8
	Thunderbird	E	5.0 (4943)	5.0	-	-	24.6	-	-	②	19.0	14.1
1994	Cougar	4	3.8 (3802)	5.0	-	-	25.0	-	-	②	18.0	12.6
	Cougar	W	4.6 (4593)	5.0	-	-	25.0	-	-	②	18.0	14.1
	Thunderbird	4	3.8 (3802)	5.0	-	-	25.0	-	-	②	18.0	12.6
	Thunderbird	R	3.8 (3802) ①	5.0	-	6.3	25.0	-	-	②	18.0	12.5
	Thunderbird	W	4.6 (4593)	5.0	-	-	25.0	-	-	②	18.0	14.1
1995	Cougar	4	3.8 (3802)	5.0	-	-	27.2	-	-	②	18.0	12.6
	Cougar	W	4.6 (4593)	5.0	-	-	27.2	-	-	②	18.0	14.1
	Thunderbird	4	3.8 (3802)	5.0	-	-	27.2	-	-	②	18.0	12.6
	Thunderbird	R	3.8 (3802) ①	5.0	-	6.3	27.2	-	-	②	18.0	12.5
	Thunderbird	W	4.6 (4593)	5.0	-	-	27.2	-	-	②	18.0	14.1
1996	Cougar	4	3.8 (3802)	5.0	-	-	27.8	-	-	②	18.0	12.6
	Cougar	W	4.6 (4593)	5.3	-	-	27.8	-	-	②	18.0	14.1
	Thunderbird	4	3.8 (3802)	5.0	-	-	27.8	-	-	②	18.0	12.6
	Thunderbird	W	4.6 (4593)	5.3	-	-	27.8	-	-	②	18.0	14.1

1 Supercharged

2 7.5" limited slip axle: 2.75 pts.
7.50" axle: 3.0 pts.
8.80" axle: 3.25 pts.

ENGLISH TO METRIC CONVERSION: MASS (WEIGHT)

Current mass measurement is expressed in pounds and ounces (lbs. & ozs.). The metric unit of mass (or weight) is the kilogram (kg). Even although this table does not show conversion of masses (weights) larger than 15 lbs, it is easy to calculate larger units by following the data immediately below.

To convert ounces (oz.) to grams (g): multiply th number of ozs. by 28
To convert grams (g) to ounces (oz.): multiply the number of grams by .035

To convert pounds (lbs.) to kilograms (kg): multiply the number of lbs. by .45
To convert kilograms (kg) to pounds (lbs.): multiply the number of kilograms by 2.2

lbs	kg	lbs	kg	oz	kg	oz	kg
0.1	0.04	0.9	0.41	0.1	0.003	0.9	0.024
0.2	0.09	1	0.4	0.2	0.005	1	0.03
0.3	0.14	2	0.9	0.3	0.008	2	0.06
0.4	0.18	3	1.4	0.4	0.011	3	0.08
0.5	0.23	4	1.8	0.5	0.014	4	0.11
0.6	0.27	5	2.3	0.6	0.017	5	0.14
0.7	0.32	10	4.5	0.7	0.020	10	0.28
0.8	0.36	15	6.8	0.8	0.023	15	0.42

ENGLISH TO METRIC CONVERSION: TEMPERATURE

To convert Fahrenheit (°F) to Celsius (°C): take number of °F and subtract 32; multiply result by 5; divide result by 9
To convert Celsius (°C) to Fahrenheit (°F): take number of °C and multiply by 9; divide result by 5; add 32 to total

Fahrenheit (F)		Celsius (C)		Fahrenheit (F)		Celsius (C)		Fahrenheit (F)		Celsius (C)	
°F	°C	°C	°F	°F	°C	°C	°F	°F	°C	°C	°F
−40	−40	−38	−36.4	80	26.7	18	64.4	215	101.7	80	176
−35	−37.2	−36	−32.8	85	29.4	20	68	220	104.4	85	185
−30	−34.4	−34	−29.2	90	32.2	22	71.6	225	107.2	90	194
−25	−31.7	−32	−25.6	95	35.0	24	75.2	230	110.0	95	202
−20	−28.9	−30	−22	100	37.8	26	78.8	235	112.8	100	212
−15	−26.1	−28	−18.4	105	40.6	28	82.4	240	115.6	105	221
−10	−23.3	−26	−14.8	110	43.3	30	86	245	118.3	110	230
−5	−20.6	−24	−11.2	115	46.1	32	89.6	250	121.1	115	239
0	−17.8	−22	−7.6	120	48.9	34	93.2	255	123.9	120	248
1	−17.2	−20	−4	125	51.7	36	96.8	260	126.6	125	257
2	−16.7	−18	−0.4	130	54.4	38	100.4	265	129.4	130	266
3	−16.1	−16	3.2	135	57.2	40	104	270	132.2	135	275
4	−15.6	−14	6.8	140	60.0	42	107.6	275	135.0	140	284
5	−15.0	−12	10.4	145	62.8	44	112.2	280	137.8	145	293
10	−12.2	−10	14	150	65.6	46	114.8	285	140.6	150	302
15	−9.4	−8	17.6	155	68.3	48	118.4	290	143.3	155	311
20	−6.7	−6	21.2	160	71.1	50	122	295	146.1	160	320
25	−3.9	−4	24.8	165	73.9	52	125.6	300	148.9	165	329
30	−1.1	−2	28.4	170	76.7	54	129.2	305	151.7	170	338
35	1.7	0	32	175	79.4	56	132.8	310	154.4	175	347
40	4.4	2	35.6	180	82.2	58	136.4	315	157.2	180	356
45	7.2	4	39.2	185	85.0	60	140	320	160.0	185	365
50	10.0	6	42.8	190	87.8	62	143.6	325	162.8	190	374
55	12.8	8	46.4	195	90.6	64	147.2	330	165.6	195	383
60	15.6	10	50	200	93.3	66	150.8	335	168.3	200	392
65	18.3	12	53.6	205	96.1	68	154.4	340	171.1	205	401
70	21.1	14	57.2	210	98.9	70	158	345	173.9	210	410
75	23.9	16	60.8	212	100.0	75	167	350	176.7	215	414

TCCS1C01

ENGLISH TO METRIC CONVERSION: LENGTH

To convert inches (ins.) to millimeters (mm): multiply number of inches by 25.4

To convert millimeters (mm) to inches (ins.): multiply number of millimeters by .04

Inches	Decimals	Milli-meters	Inches to millimeters inches	mm	Inches	Decimals	Milli-meters	Inches to millimeters inches	mm
1/64	0.051625	0.3969	0.0001	0.00254	33/64	0.515625	13.0969	0.6	15.24
1/32	0.03125	0.7937	0.0002	0.00508	17/32	0.53125	13.4937	0.7	17.78
3/64	0.046875	1.1906	0.0003	0.00762	35/64	0.546875	13.8906	0.8	20.32
1/16	0.0625	1.5875	0.0004	0.01016	9/16	0.5625	14.2875	0.9	22.86
5/64	0.078125	1.9844	0.0005	0.01270	37/64	0.578125	14.6844	1	25.4
3/32	0.09375	2.3812	0.0006	0.01524	19/32	0.59375	15.0812	2	50.8
7/64	0.109375	2.7781	0.0007	0.01778	39/64	0.609375	15.4781	3	76.2
1/8	0.125	3.1750	0.0008	0.02032	5/8	0.625	15.8750	4	101.6
9/64	0.140625	3.5719	0.0009	0.02286	41/64	0.640625	16.2719	5	127.0
5/32	0.15625	3.9687	0.001	0.0254	21/32	0.65625	16.6687	6	152.4
11/64	0.171875	4.3656	0.002	0.0508	43/64	0.671875	17.0656	7	177.8
3/16	0.1875	4.7625	0.003	0.0762	11/16	0.6875	17.4625	8	203.2
13/64	0.203125	5.1594	0.004	0.1016	45/64	0.703125	17.8594	9	228.6
7/32	0.21875	5.5562	0.005	0.1270	23/32	0.71875	18.2562	10	254.0
15/64	0.234375	5.9531	0.006	0.1524	47/64	0.734375	18.6531	11	279.4
1/4	0.25	6.3500	0.007	0.1778	3/4	0.75	19.0500	12	304.8
17/64	0.265625	6.7469	0.008	0.2032	49/64	0.765625	19.4469	13	330.2
9/32	0.28125	7.1437	0.009	0.2286	25/32	0.78125	19.8437	14	355.6
19/64	0.296875	7.5406	0.01	0.254	51/64	0.796875	20.2406	15	381.0
5/16	0.3125	7.9375	0.02	0.508	13/16	0.8125	20.6375	16	406.4
21/64	0.328125	8.3344	0.03	0.762	53/64	0.828125	21.0344	17	431.8
11/32	0.34375	8.7312	0.04	1.016	27/32	0.84375	21.4312	18	457.2
23/64	0.359375	9.1281	0.05	1.270	55/64	0.859375	21.8281	19	482.6
3/8	0.375	9.5250	0.06	1.524	7/8	0.875	22.2250	20	508.0
25/64	0.390625	9.9219	0.07	1.778	57/64	0.890625	22.6219	21	533.4
13/32	0.40625	10.3187	0.08	2.032	29/32	0.90625	23.0187	22	558.8
27/64	0.421875	10.7156	0.09	2.286	59/64	0.921875	23.4156	23	584.2
7/16	0.4375	11.1125	0.1	2.54	15/16	0.9375	23.8125	24	609.6
29/64	0.453125	11.5094	0.2	5.08	61/64	0.953125	24.2094	25	635.0
15/32	0.46875	11.9062	0.3	7.62	31/32	0.96875	24.6062	26	660.4
31/64	0.484375	12.3031	0.4	10.16	63/64	0.984375	25.0031	27	690.6
1/2	0.5	12.7000	0.5	12.70					

ENGLISH TO METRIC CONVERSION: TORQUE

To convert foot-pounds (ft. lbs.) to Newton-meters: multiply the number of ft. lbs. by 1.3

To convert inch-pounds (in. lbs.) to Newton-meters: multiply the number of in. lbs. by .11

in lbs	N-m	in lbs	N-m	in lbs	N-m	in lbs	N-m	in lbs	N-m
0.1	0.01	1	0.11	10	1.13	19	2.15	28	3.16
0.2	0.02	2	0.23	11	1.24	20	2.26	29	3.28
0.3	0.03	3	0.34	12	1.36	21	2.37	30	3.39
0.4	0.04	4	0.45	13	1.47	22	2.49	31	3.50
0.5	0.06	5	0.56	14	1.58	23	2.60	32	3.62
0.6	0.07	6	0.68	15	1.70	24	2.71	33	3.73
0.7	0.08	7	0.78	16	1.81	25	2.82	34	3.84
0.8	0.09	8	0.90	17	1.92	26	2.94	35	3.95
0.9	0.10	9	1.02	18	2.03	27	3.05	36	4.07

TCCS1C02

2

ENGINE ELECTRICAL

BASIC ELECTRICAL THEORY

Understanding Electricity

For any electrical system to operate, there must be a complete circuit. This simply means that the power flow from the battery must make a full circle. When an electrical component is operating, power flows from the battery to the components, passes through the component (load) causing it to function, and returns to the battery through the ground path of the circuit. This ground may be either another wire or a metal part of the vehicle (depending upon how the component is designed).

BASIC CIRCUITS

➧ See Figures 1 and 2

Perhaps the easiest way to visualize a circuit is to think of connecting a light bulb (with two wires attached to it) to the battery. If one of the two wires was attached to the negative post (-) of the battery and the other wire to the positive post (+), the circuit would be complete and the light bulb would illuminate. Electricity could follow a path from the battery to the bulb and back to the battery. It's not hard to see that with longer wires on our light bulb, it could be mounted anywhere on the vehicle. Further, one wire could be fitted with a switch so that the light could be turned on and off. Various other items could be added to our primitive circuit to make the light flash, become brighter or dimmer under certain conditions, or advise the user that it's burned out.

Ground

Some automotive components are grounded through their mounting points. The electrical current runs through the chassis of the vehicle and returns to the battery through the ground (-) cable; if you look, you'll see that the battery ground cable connects between the battery and the body of the vehicle.

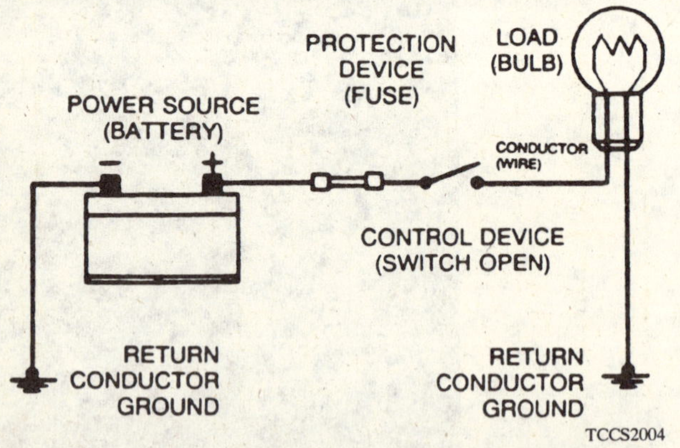

Fig. 1 Here is an example of a simple automotive circuit. When the switch is closed, power from the positive battery terminal flows through the fuse, then the switch and to the load (light bulb), the light illuminates and then, the circuit is completed through the return conductor and the vehicle ground. If the light did not work, the tests could be made with a voltmeter or test light at the battery, fuse, switch or bulb socket

Fig. 2 Damaged insulation can allow wires to break (causing an open circuit) or touch (causing a short)

Load

Every complete circuit must include a "load" (something to use the electricity coming from the source). If you were to connect a wire between the two terminals of the battery (DON'T do this, but take out word for it) without the light bulb, the battery would attempt to deliver its entire power supply from one pole to another almost instantly. This is a short circuit. The electricity is taking a short cut to get to ground and is not being used by any load in the circuit. This sudden and uncontrolled electrical flow can cause great damage to other components in the circuit and can develop a tremendous amount of heat. A short in an automotive wiring harness can develop sufficient heat to melt the insulation on all the surrounding wires and reduce a multiple wire cable to one sad lump of plastic and copper. Two common causes of shorts are broken insulation (thereby exposing the wire to contact with surrounding metal surfaces or other wires) or a failed switch (the pins inside the switch come out of place and touch each other).

Switches and Relays

Some electrical components which require a large amount of current to operate also have a relay in their circuit. Since these circuits carry a large amount of current (amperage or amps), the thickness of the wire in the circuit (wire gauge) is also greater. If this large wire were connected from the load to the control switch on the dash, the switch would have to carry the high amperage load and the dash would be twice as large to accommodate wiring harnesses as thick as your wrist. To prevent these problems, a relay is used. The large wires in the circuit are connected from the battery to one side of the relay and from the opposite side of the relay to the load. The relay is normally open, preventing current from passing through the circuit. An additional, smaller wire is connected from the relay to the control switch for the circuit. When the control switch is turned on, it grounds the smaller wire to the relay and completes its circuit. The main switch inside the relay closes, sending power to the component without routing the main power through the inside of the vehicle. Some common circuits which may use relays are the horn, headlights, starter and rear window defogger systems.

Protective Devices

It is possible for larger surges of current to pass through the electrical system of your vehicle. If this surge of current were to reach the load in the circuit, it could burn it out or severely damage it. To prevent this, fuses, circuit breakers and/or fusible links are connected into the supply wires of the electrical system. These items are nothing more than a built-in weak spot in the system. It's much easier to go to a known location (the fusebox) to see why a circuit is inoperative than to dissect 15 feet of wiring under the dashboard, looking for what happened.

When an electrical current of excessive power passes through the fuse, the fuse blows (the conductor melts) and breaks the circuit, preventing the passage of current and protecting the components.

A circuit breaker is basically a self repairing fuse. It will open the circuit in the same fashion as a fuse, but when either the short is removed or the surge subsides, the circuit breaker resets itself and does not need replacement.

A fuse link (fusible link or main link) is a wire that acts as a fuse. One of these is normally connected between the starter relay and the main wiring harness under the hood. Since the starter is usually the highest electrical draw on the vehicle, an internal short during starting could direct about 130 amps into the wrong places. Consider the damage potential of introducing this current into a system whose wiring is rated at 15 amps and you'll understand the need for protection. Since this link is very early in the electrical path, it's the first place to look if nothing on the vehicle works, but the battery seems to be charged and is properly connected.

TROUBLESHOOTING

See Figures 3, 4 and 5

Electrical problems generally fall into one of three areas:

- The component that is not functioning is not receiving current.
- The component is receiving power but is not using it or is using it incorrectly (component failure).
- The component is improperly grounded.

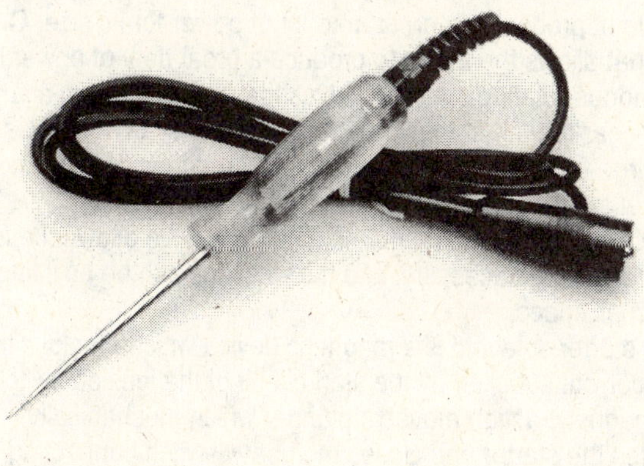

TCCS2006

Fig. 3 A 12 volt test light is useful when checking parts of a circuit for power

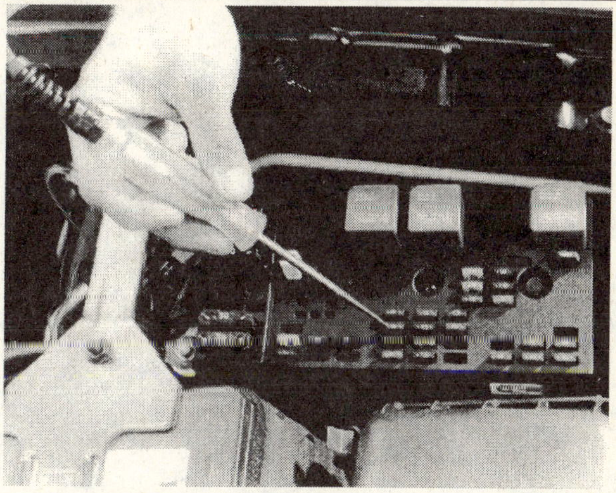

TCCS2007

Fig. 4 Here, someone is checking a circuit by making sure there is power to the component's fuse

The circuit can be can be checked with a test light and a jumper wire. The test light is a device that looks like a pointed screwdriver with a wire on one end and a bulb in its handle. A jumper wire is simply a piece of wire with alligator clips or special terminals on each end. If a component is not working, you must follow a systematic plan to determine which of the three causes is the villain.

1. Turn ON the switch that controls the item not working.

Some items only work when the ignition switch is turned ON.

2. Disconnect the power supply wire from the component.
3. Attach the ground wire of a test light or a voltmeter to a good metal ground.
4. Touch the end probe of the test light (or the positive lead of the voltmeter) to the power wire; if there is current in the wire, the light in the test light will come on (or the voltmeter will indicate the amount of voltage). You have now established that current is getting to the component.
5. Turn the ignition or dash switch **OFF** and reconnect the wire to the component.

If there was no power, then the problem is between the battery and the component. This includes all the switches, fuses, relays and the battery itself. The next place to look is the fusebox; check carefully either by eye or by using the test light across the fuse clips. The easiest way to check is to simply replace the fuse. If the fuse is blown, and upon replacement, immediately blows again, there is a short between the fuse and the component. This is generally (not always) a sign of an internal short in the component. Disconnect the power wire at the component again and replace the fuse; if the fuse holds, the component is the problem.

****WARNING**

DO NOT test a component by running a jumper wire from the battery UNLESS you are certain that it operates on 12 volts. Many electronic components are designed to operate with less voltage and connecting them to 12 volts could destroy them. Jumper wires are best used to bypass a portion of the circuit (such as a stretch of wire or a switch) that DOES NOT contain a resistor and is suspected to be bad.

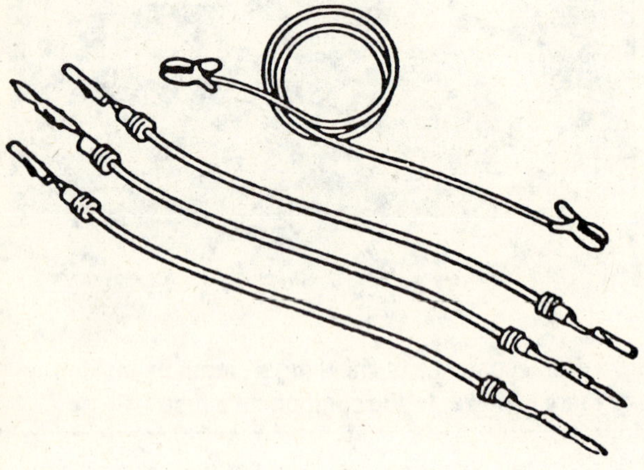

Fig. 5 Jumper wires with various connectors are handy for quick electrical testing

If all the fuses are good and the component is not receiving power, find the switch for the circuit. Bypass the switch with the jumper wire. This is done by connecting one end of the jumper to the power wire coming into the switch and the other end to the wire leaving the switch. If the component comes to life, the switch has failed.

****WARNING**

Never substitute the jumper for the component. The circuit needs the electrical load of the component. If you bypass it, you will cause a short circuit.

Checking the ground for any circuit can mean tracing wires to the body, cleaning connections or tightening mounting bolts for the component itself. If the jumper wire can be connected to the case of the component or the ground connector, you can ground the other end to a piece of clean, solid metal on the vehicle. Again, if the component starts working, you've found the problem.

A systematic search through the fuse, connectors, switches and the component itself will almost always yield an answer. Loose and/or corroded connectors, particularly in ground circuits, are becoming a larger problem in modern vehicles. The computers and on-board electronic (solid state) systems are highly sensitive to improper grounds and will change their function drastically if one occurs.

Remember that for any electrical circuit to work, ALL the connections must be clean and tight.

➥ For more information on Understanding and Troubleshooting Electrical Systems, please refer to Section 6 of this manual.

Battery, Starting and Charging Systems

BASIC OPERATING PRINCIPLES

Battery

The battery is the first link in the chain of mechanisms which work together to provide cranking of the automobile engine. In most modern vehicles, the battery is a lead/acid electrochemical device consisting of six 2v subsections (cells) connected in series so the unit is capable of producing approximately 12v of electrical pressure. Each subsection consists of a series of positive and negative plates held a short distance apart in a solution of sulfuric acid and water.

The two types of plates are of dissimilar metals. This sets-up a chemical reaction, and it is this reaction which produces current flow from the battery when its positive and negative terminals are connected to an electrical accessory such as a lamp or motor. The continued transfer of electrons would eventually convert the sulfuric acid to water, and make the two plates identical in chemical composition. As electrical energy is removed from the battery, its voltage output tends to drop. Thus, measuring battery voltage and battery electrolyte composition are two ways of checking the ability of the unit to supply power. During engine cranking, electrical energy is removed from the battery. However, if the charging circuit is in good condition and the operating conditions are normal, the power removed from the battery will be replaced by the alternator which will force electrons back through the battery, reversing the normal flow, and restoring the battery to its original chemical state.

Starting System

The battery and starting motor are linked by very heavy electrical cables designed to minimize resistance to the flow of current. Generally, the major power supply cable that leaves the battery goes directly to the starter, while other electrical system needs are supplied by a smaller cable. During starter operation, power flows from the battery to the starter and is grounded through the vehicle's frame/body or engine and the battery's negative ground strap.

The starter is a specially designed, direct current electric motor capable of producing a great amount of power for its size. One thing that allows the motor to produce a great deal of power is its tremendous rotating speed. It drives the engine through a tiny pinion gear (attached to the starter's armature), which drives the very large flywheel ring gear at a greatly reduced speed. Another factor allowing it to produce so much power is that only intermittent operation is required of it. Thus, little allowance for air circulation is necessary, and the windings can be built into a very small space.

The starter solenoid is a magnetic device which employs the small current supplied by the start circuit of the ignition switch. This magnetic action moves a plunger which mechanically engages the starter and closes the heavy switch connecting it to the battery. The starting switch circuit usually consists of the starting switch contained within the ignition switch, a neutral safety switch or clutch pedal switch, and the wiring necessary to connect these in series with the starter solenoid or relay.

The pinion, a small gear, is mounted to a one way drive clutch. This clutch is splined to the starter armature shaft. When the ignition switch is moved to the **START** position, the solenoid plunger slides the pinion toward the flywheel ring gear via a collar and spring. If the teeth on the pinion and flywheel match properly, the pinion will engage the flywheel immediately. If the gear teeth butt one another, the spring will be compressed and will force the gears to mesh as soon as the starter turns far enough to allow them to do so. As the solenoid plunger reaches the end of its travel, it closes the contacts that connect the battery and starter, then the engine is cranked.

As soon as the engine starts, the flywheel ring gear begins turning fast enough to drive the pinion at an extremely high rate of speed. At this point, the one-way clutch begins allowing the pinion to spin faster than the starter shaft so that the starter will not operate at excessive speed. When the ignition switch is released from the starter position, the solenoid is de-energized, and a spring pulls the gear out of mesh interrupting the current flow to the starter.

Some starters employ a separate relay, mounted away from the starter, to switch the motor and solenoid current on and off. The relay replaces the solenoid electrical switch, but does not eliminate the need for a solenoid mounted on the starter used to mechanically engage the starter drive gears. The relay is used to reduce the amount of current the starting switch must carry.

Charging System

The automobile charging system provides electrical power for operation of the vehicle's ignition system, starting system and all electrical accessories. The battery serves as an electrical surge or storage tank, storing (in chemical form) the energy originally produced by the engine driven generator. The system also provides a means of regulating output to protect the battery from being overcharged and to avoid excessive voltage to the accessories.

The storage battery is a chemical device incorporating parallel lead plates in a tank containing a sulfuric acid/water solution. Adjacent plates are slightly dissimilar, and the chemical reaction of the two dissimilar plates produces electrical energy when the battery is connected to a load such as the starter motor. The chemical reaction is reversible, so that when the generator is producing a voltage (electrical pressure) greater than that produced by the battery, electricity is forced into the battery, and the battery is returned to its fully charged state.

Newer automobiles use alternating current generators or alternators, because they are more efficient, can be rotated at higher speeds, and have fewer brush problems. In an alternator, the field usually rotates while all the current produced passes only through the stator winding. The brushes bear against continuous slip rings. This causes the current produced to periodically reverse the direction of its flow. Diodes (electrical one way valves) block the flow of current from traveling in the wrong direction. A series of diodes is wired together to permit the alternating flow of the stator to be rectified back to 12 volts DC for use by the vehicle's electrical system.

The voltage regulating function is performed by a regulator. The regulator is often built in to the alternator; this system is termed an integrated or internal regulator.

FIRING ORDERS

See Figures 6, 7, 8, 9 and 10

To avoid confusion, remove and tag the wires one at a time, for replacement.

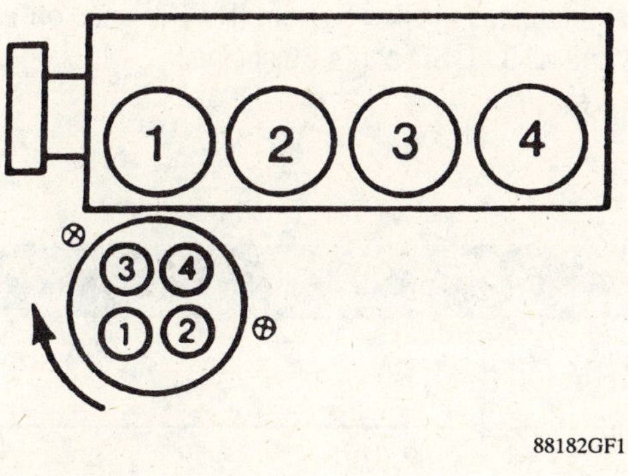

Fig. 6 2.3L Engine
Firing Order: 1-3-4-2
Distributor Rotation: Clockwise

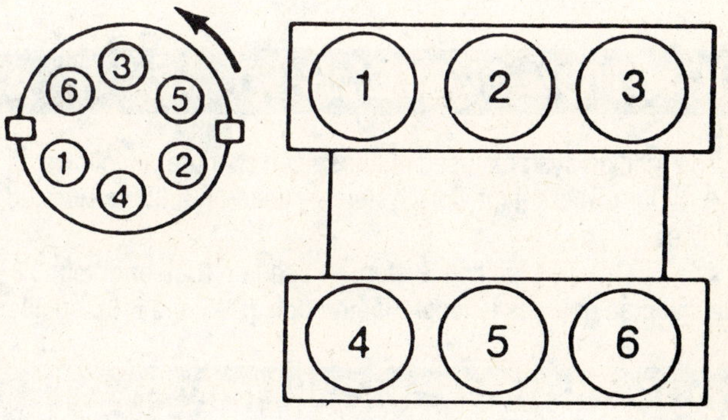

Fig. 7 3.8L Engine
Firing Order: 1-4-2-5-3-6
Distributor Rotation: Counterclockwise

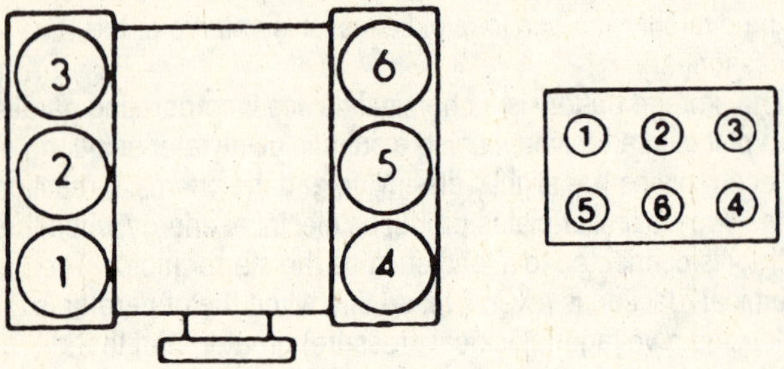

88182GF3

Fig. 8 3.8L Engine
Firing Order: 1-4-2-5-3-6
Distributorless Ignition System

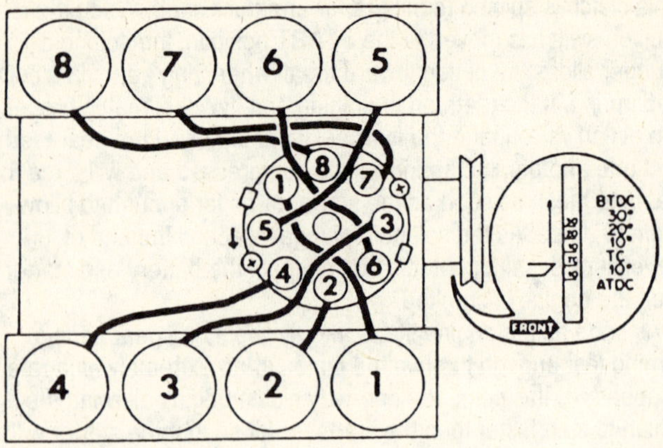

88182GF4

Fig. 9 5.0L Engine
Firing Order: 1-5-4-2-6-3-7-8
Distributor Rotation: Counterclockwise

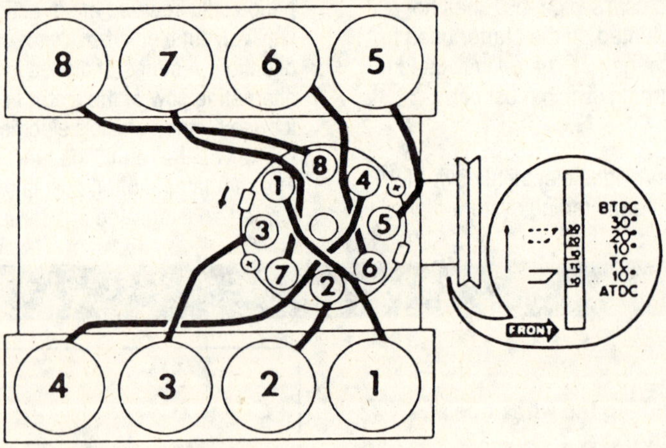

88182GF5

Fig. 10 5.0L Engine
Firing Order: 1-3-7-2-6-5-4-8
Distributor Rotation: Counterclockwise

IGNITION SYSTEMS

The ignition systems used on these vehicles are as follows:

- Dura Spark II Ignition System — used on 3.8L carbureted engines
- EEC-IV TFI Ignition System — used on 2.3L engines, 3.8L fuel injected engines (except SC) through 1995 and 5.0L engines
- Distributorless Ignition System (DIS) — used on 1996 3.8L (non-SC) and all 3.8L SC and 4.6L engines

DURA SPARK II IGNITION SYSTEM

General Information

➧ **See Figures 11 and 12**

The Dura Spark II ignition system was used on 3.8L carbureted vehicles. The Dura Spark II ignition system consists of the typical electronic primary and conventional secondary circuits, designed to carry higher voltages. The primary and secondary circuits consists of the following components:

PRIMARY CIRCUIT

- Battery
- Ignition switch
- Ballast resistor start bypass (wire)
- Ignition coil primary winding
- Ignition module
- Distributor stator assembly

SECONDARY CIRCUIT

- Battery
- Ignition switch
- Ignition coil secondary winding
- Distributor rotor
- Distributor cap
- Ignition wires
- Ballast resistor start bypass (wire)
- Spark plugs

The Dura Spark II system uses either a Dura Spark II module or the Universal Ignition Module (UIM).

The two different Duraspark II ignition modules can be identified by 2 connectors/blue grommet on the standard module and 3 connectors/yellow grommet on the UIM.

Both ignition modules perform the function of turning off current flow through the ignition coil in response to a control signal. In the Dura Spark II ignition system, this signal comes from the distributor stator assembly. Additionally, the Universal Ignition Module (UIM), can respond to another control signal from either an ignition barometric pressure switch or the Microprocessor Control Unit (MCU), depending upon the engine's calibration. In responding to this second control signal, the UIM provides additional spark timing control for certain operating conditions by turning off the ignition coil current flow at a different time than what would happen from just the distributor signal.

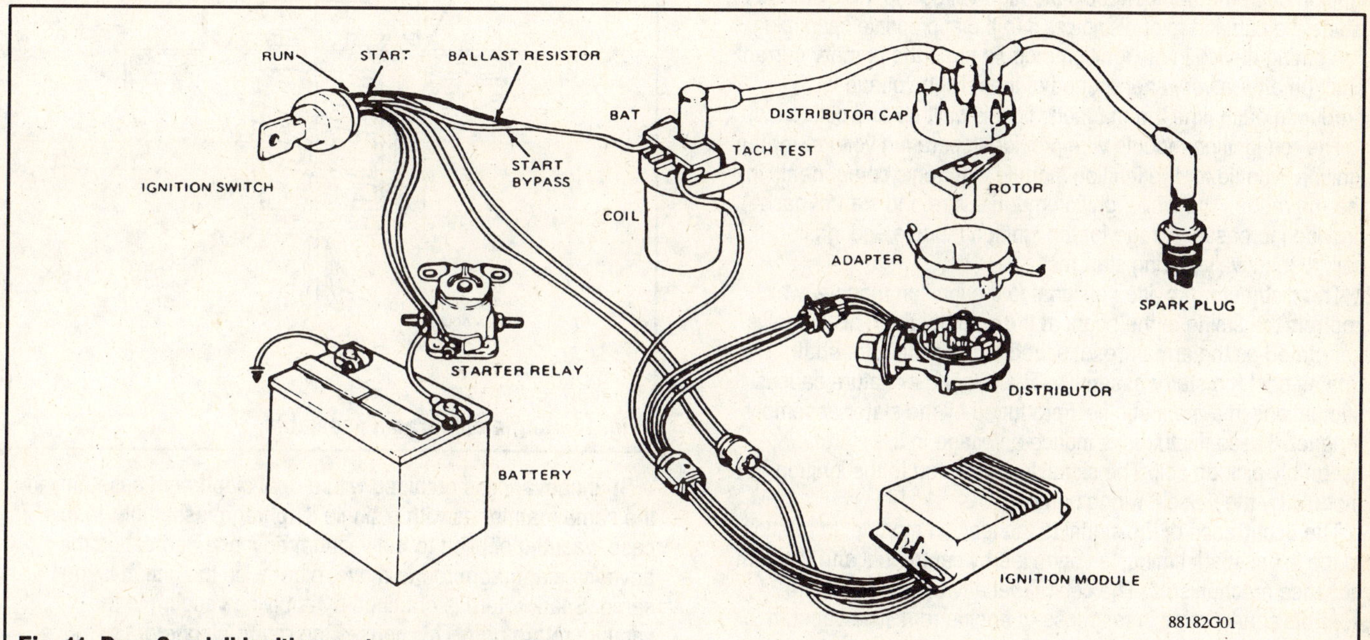

Fig. 11 Dura Spark II ignition system components

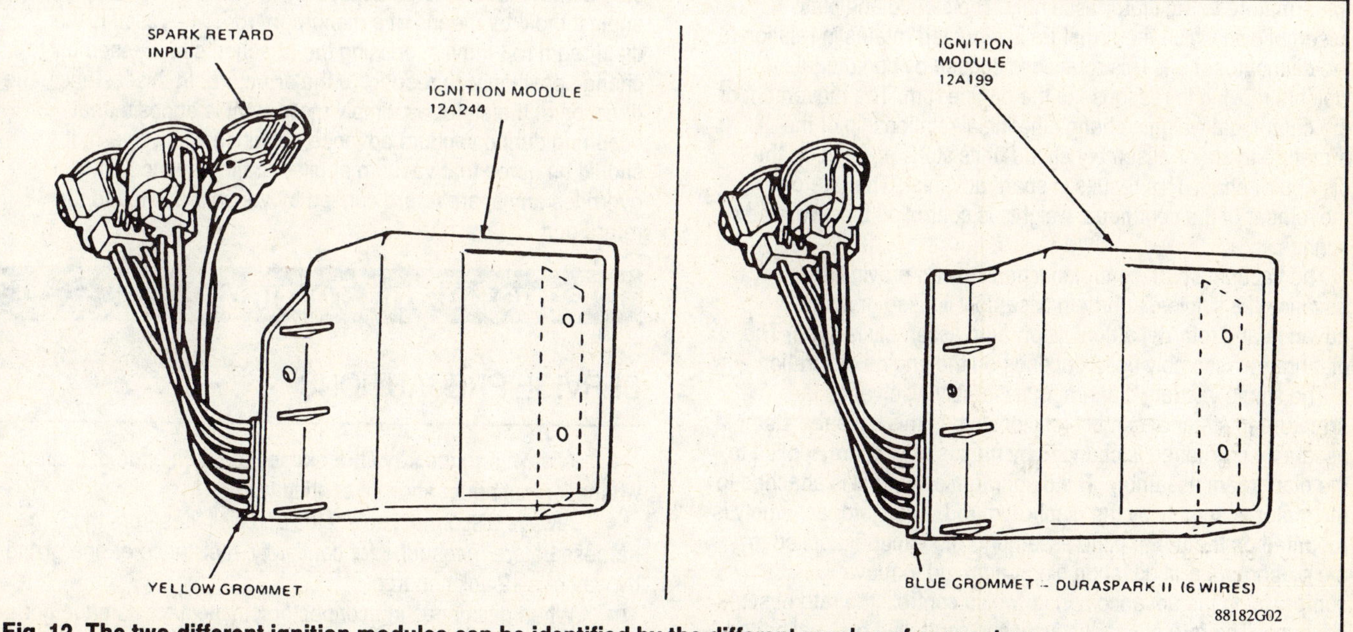

Fig. 12 The two different ignition modules can be identified by the different number of connectors

System Operation

See Figures 13, 14 and 15

With the ignition switch in the **RUN** position, the primary circuit current is directed from the battery, through the ignition switch, the ballast resistor, the ignition coil (in the positive side, out the negative side), the ignition module and back to the battery through the ignition system ground in the distributor. This current flow causes a magnetic field to be built up in the ignition coil. When the poles on the armature and the stator assembly align, the ignition module turns the primary current flow off, collapsing the magnetic field in the ignition coil. The collapsing field induces a high voltage in the ignition coil secondary windings. The ignition coil wire then conducts the high voltage to the distributor where the cap and rotor distributes it to the appropriate spark plug.

A timing device in the ignition module turns the primary current back on after a very short period of time. High voltage is produced each time the magnetic field is built up and collapsed.

The red ignition module wire provides operating voltage for the ignition module for the ignition module electronic components in the run mode. The white ignition module wire and start bypass provide increased voltage for the ignition module and ignition coil, respectively, during start mode.

The distributor provides a signal to the ignition module, which controls the timing of the spark at the spark plugs. This signal is generated as the armature, attached to the distributor shaft, rotates past the stator assembly. The rotating armature causes fluctuations in a magnetic field produced by the stator assembly magnet. These fluctuations induce a voltage in the stator assembly pick-up coil. The signal is connected to the ignition module by the vehicle wiring harness.

The occurrence of the signal to the ignition module, in relation to the initial spark timing, is controlled by centrifugal and vacuum advance mechanisms. The centrifugal advance mechanism controls spark timing in response to engine rpm. The vacuum advance mechanism controls spark timing in response to engine load.

The centrifugal advance mechanism varies the relationship of the armature to the stator assembly. The sleeve and plate assembly, on which the armature is mounted rotates in relation to the distributor shaft. This rotation is caused by centrifugal weights moving in response to the engine rpm. The movement of the centrifugal weights change the initial relationship of the armature to stator assembly ahead of its static position on the distributor shaft. This results in spark advance. The rate of movement of the centrifugal weights is controlled by calibrated springs.

The vacuum spark control mechanism can provide spark advance if a single diaphragm assembly is used or spark advance and retard if a dual diaphragm assembly is used. The diaphragm assembly used depends on the engine calibration.

The single vacuum diaphragm assembly also varies the armature to stator assembly relationship. In this case the stator assembly positioned is changed by means of vacuum applied to the diaphragm assembly. The diaphragm assembly is attached to the stator assembly by the diaphragm rod. The stator assembly is mounted on the upper plate assembly. The vacuum applied to the diaphragm and attached diaphragm rod to move, compressing the advance spring, which controls the rate of spark advance. The rate of spark advance is controlled by a calibrated spring.

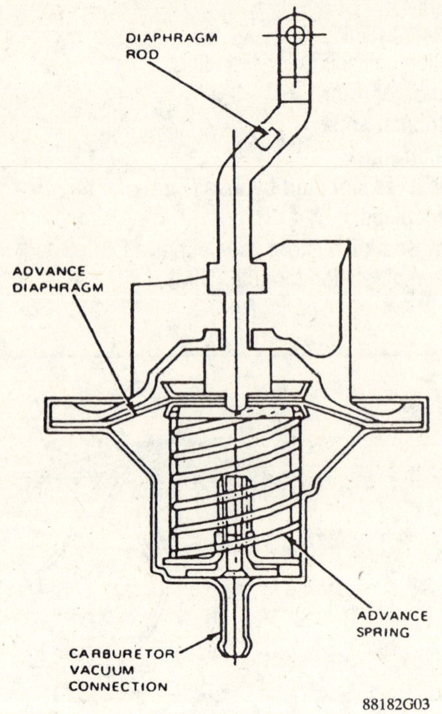

Fig. 13 Single diaphragm assembly

Spark advance is obtained with a dual diaphragm assembly in the same manner as with a single diaphragm assembly. In this case, vacuum applied to the vacuum advance port cause the advance diaphragm rod to move, other wise the action is the same. Spark retard is obtained by applying vacuum to the vacuum retard port. This causes the retard diaphragm to move, compressing the retard spring, which controls the rate of spark retard. Compressing the retard spring allows the diaphragm rod stop to move due to force applied by an advance spring pushing against the it by means of a diaphragm rod. The result is the diaphragm rod moves, causing the attached stator assembly to change position with respect to the armature. In this instance, the direction of the stator assembly movement is opposite that occurring during vacuum advance, resulting spark retard. It should be noted that vacuum applied to the advance port overrides any spark retard caused by vacuum applied to the retard port.

Diagnosis and Testing

SERVICE PRECAUTIONS

- Always turn the key **OFF** and isolate both ends of a circuit whenever testing for short or continuity.
- Always disconnect solenoids and switches from the harness before measuring for continuity, resistance or energizing by way of a 12 volts source.
- When disconnecting connectors, inspect for damaged or pushed-out pins, corrosion, loose wires, etc. Service if required.

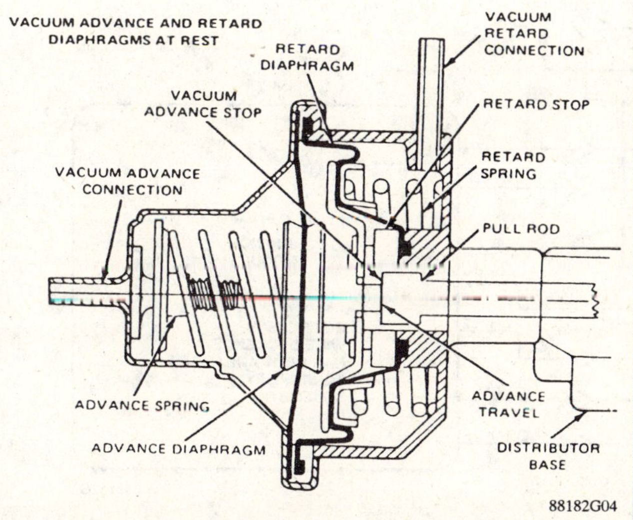

Fig. 14 Dual diaphragm assembly

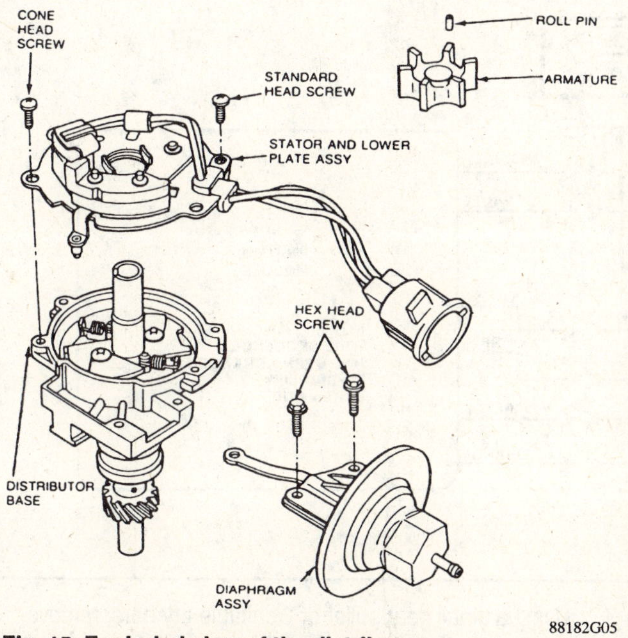

Fig. 15 Exploded view of the distributor

PRELIMINARY CHECKS

- Visually inspect the engine compartment to ensure that all vacuum lines and spark plug wires are properly routed and securely connected.
- Examine all wiring harnesses and connectors for insulation damage, burned, overheated, loose or broken conditions.
- Be certain that the battery is fully charged and all accessories **OFF** during the diagnosis.
- The tools needed during this diagnosis procedure will be a suitable spark tester, 12 volt test lamp, small straight pins and Volt/ohm meter.

➔ A spark plug with a broken side electrode is not sufficient to check for spark and may lead to incorrect results. All wire colors referred to in this part relate to the colors of the ignition module wires. When working with a wiring harness, the wire must be traced back to the ignition module for proper color identification. When instructed to inspect a wiring harness, both visual inspection and a continuity test should be performed. When making measurements on a wiring harness or connector, it is good practice to wiggle the wires while measuring.

SECONDARY SPARK TEST

1. Disconnect the secondary (high voltage) coil wire from the distributor cap and install a spark tester between the coil wire and ground.
2. Crank the engine. A good, strong spark should be noted at the spark tester. If spark is noted, but the engine will not start, check the spark plugs, spark plug wiring, and fuel system. If there is no spark at the tester:
   a. Check the ignition coil secondary wire resistance; it should be no more than 5,000 ohms per inch (25mm).
   b. Inspect the ignition coil for damage and/or carbon tracking.
   c. With the distributor cap removed, verify that the distributor shaft turns with the engine; if it does not, repair the engine as required.

Ignition Coil

TESTING

➧ See Figures 16 and 17

1. Follow the coil wire from the center terminal on the distributor cap to the end at the ignition coil. Make sure that the transmission is in Park (AT) or Neutral (MT) and that the ignition is turned **OFF**.
2. Separate the wiring harness connector from the ignition module at the distributor. Inspect for dirt, corrosion and/or damage. Reconnect the harness if no problems are found.
3. Attach a 12 volt DC test light between the coil TACH terminal and an engine ground, then crank the engine. If the light flashes or is continuous:
   a. Turn the ignition switch **OFF**.
   b. Detach the ignition coil connector on top of the coil and inspect for dirt, corrosion and/or damage.
   c. Using an ohmmeter, measure the ignition coil primary resistance from the BATT to the TACH terminals.
   d. The ohmmeter reading should be 0.8–1.6 ohms. If the reading is less than 0.8 ohms or greater than 1.6 ohms, the ignition coil should be replaced.
   e. Using an ohmmeter, measure the ignition coil secondary resistance from the BATT terminal to the high voltage terminal.
   f. The resistance should be 7,700–10,500 ohms. If the resistance is less that 7,700 ohms or greater than 10,500 ohms, replace the ignition coil.

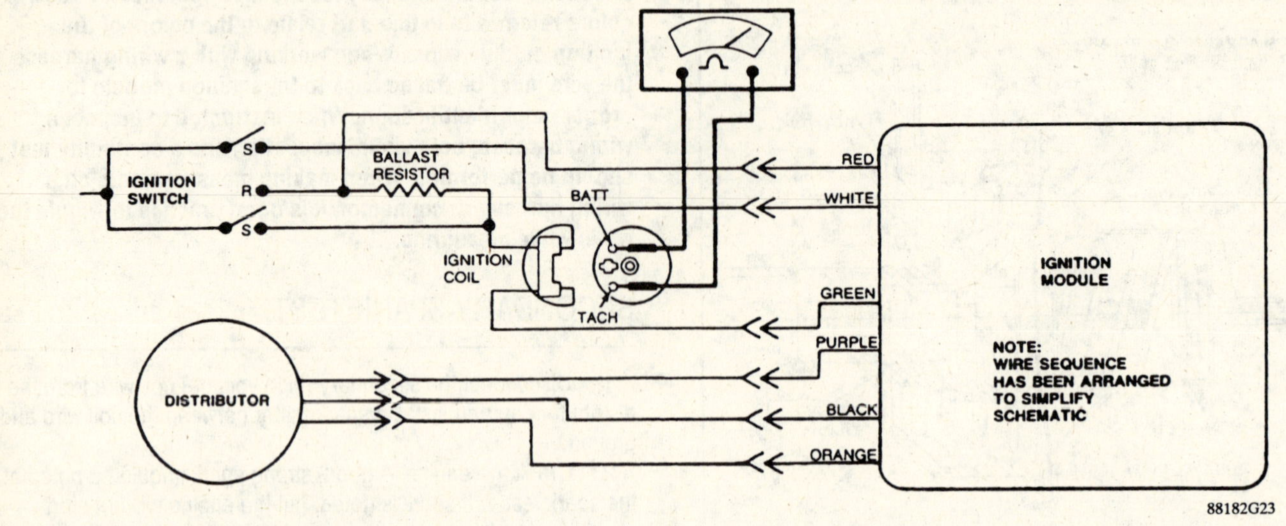

Fig. 16 Testing ignition coil primary resistance

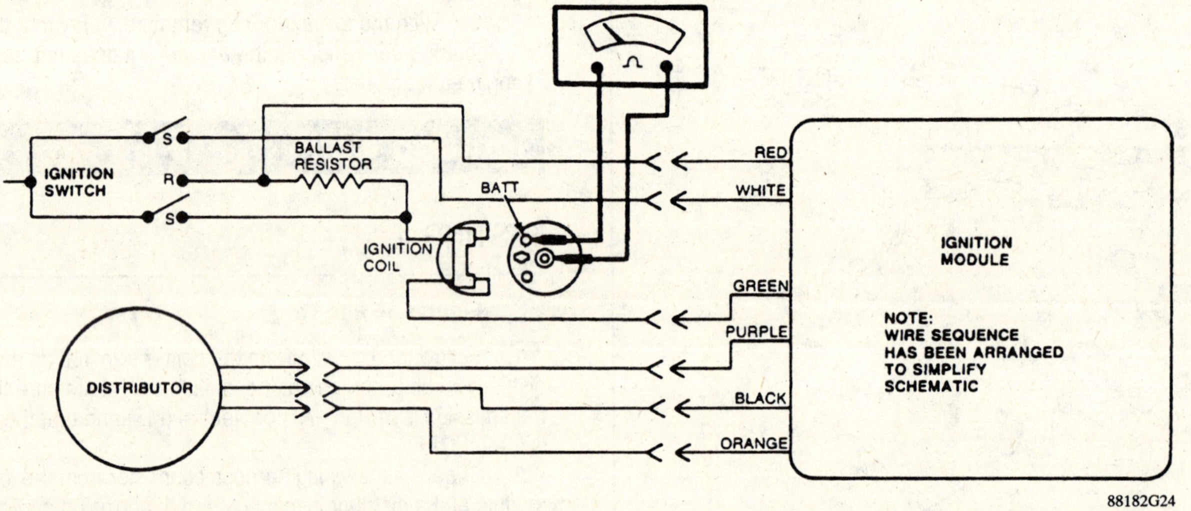

Fig. 17 Testing ignition coil secondary resistance

REMOVAL & INSTALLATION

1. Disconnect the negative battery cable.
2. Detach the coil electrical connector(s).
3. Unfasten the retainers, then remove the ignition coil from the vehicle.
4. Installation is the reverse of the removal procedure.

Stator Assembly

REMOVAL & INSTALLATION

1. Disconnect the negative battery cable.
2. Remove the distributor cap, rotor and adapter.
3. Separate the distributor connector from the wiring harness.
4. Using a small gear puller or 2 suitable pry bars, remove the armature from the sleeve and plate assembly. Use caution to avoid losing the roll pin.
5. Remove the two screws retaining the lower plate assembly and stator assembly to the distributor base. There are 2 different screws.
6. Remove the lower plate assembly and stator assembly from the distributor.
7. Remove the E-clip, flatwasher and wave washer securing the stator assembly to the lower plate assembly and separate the stator assembly from the lower plate assembly. Notice the installation of the wave washer.

To install:

8. Place the stator assembly on the lower plate assembly and install the wave washer (OUTER EDGES UP), flatwasher and E-clip.

9. Install the stator/lower plate assembly on the distributor base, while aligning the pin on the stator assembly in the diaphragm rod.
10. Install the two retaining screws .
11. There are 2 locating notches in the armature and install on sleeve and plate assembly with unused notch and new roll pin.
12. Connect the distributor to the wiring harness.
13. Replace the distributor rotor and cap. Check to ensure the ignition wires are secured in the distributor cap and spark plugs.
14. Connect the negative battery cable. Check the ignition timing.

Vacuum Diaphragm Assembly

REMOVAL & INSTALLATION

1. Disconnect the diaphragm assembly vacuum hoses.
2. Remove the 2 diaphragm assembly attaching screws (Note screws location).
3. Disengage the diaphragm rod from the stator assembly pin and remove the diaphragm assembly.

To install:

4. Adjust the new diaphragm assembly per manufacturer's instructions included with the new diaphragm.
5. Fit the diaphragm rod with the stator assembly pin.
6. Attach the diaphragm assembly and identification tag to the distributor base. Check to ensure the diaphragm rod is properly engaged with the stator assembly pin.
7. Connect the vacuum hoses.

Distributor Cap And Rotor

REMOVAL & INSTALLATION

➧ See Figure 18

1. Disconnect the negative battery cable.
2. If necessary for removal, tag and disconnect the spark plug wires from the distributor cap.
3. Loosen the distributor cap hold-down screws.
4. Remove the cap by pulling it cap straight up. Avoid damaging the rotor points and spring.
5. If required, remove the rotor by pulling it straight up.

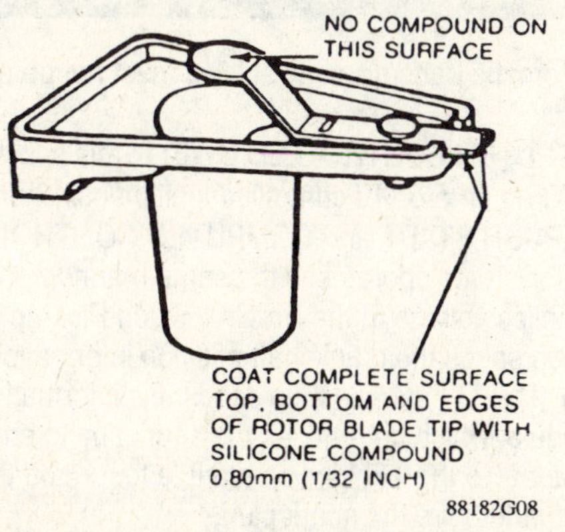

Fig. 18 Silicone compound application on the rotor

To install:

6. Apply a 1/32 in. (0.8mm) bead of a suitable silicone compound on the rotor as shown in the accompanying figure. Position the rotor with the square and round locator pins matched to the distributor shaft plate.
7. Position the distributor cap on the distributor base noting the square alignment locator. Tighten the hold-down screws to 17-23 inch lbs. (2.0-2.6 Nm).
8. If removed, attach the plug wires, noting the correct locations on the distributor cap.
9. Connect the negative battery cable, start the engine and check the timing. Adjust if necessary.

Distributor

REMOVAL

➧ See Figure 19

1. Disconnect the negative battery cable.

➥ Make sure to tag the spark plug wires if it necessary to disconnect them from the distributor cap.

2. Disconnect and plug the vacuum hose at the vacuum diaphragm.
3. Remove the distributor cap (if possible, DO NOT disconnect the wires from the cap) from the distributor and position it aside.
4. Separate the distributor connector from the wiring harness.
5. Rotate the engine to align the stator assembly pole and any armature pole.
6. Scribe a mark in the distributor body and the engine block to indicate position of the distributor in the engine and position the rotor.
7. Unfasten the distributor hold-down bolt and clamp, then carefully remove the distributor assembly from the engine. Be sure not to rotate the engine while the distributor is removed.

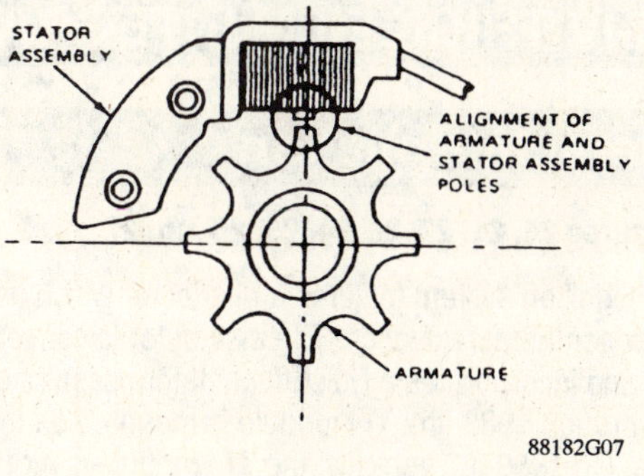

Fig. 19 Armature/stator assembly alignment

INSTALLATION

Engine Not Rotated

This condition exists if the engine has not been rotated while the distributor was removed.

1. If the old distributor is being installed, proceed as follows:
   a. Position the distributor in the engine with the rotor and distributor aligning with the previously scribed mark. Armature and stator assembly poles should also align if the distributor is fully seated in the block and properly installed.
   b. If necessary, connect the negative battery cable, and crank the engine to fully seat the distributor in the block.
   c. Install the distributor hold-down bolt and clamp, but do not tighten at this time.
2. If a new distributor is being installed, proceed as follows:
   a. Position the distributor in the engine with the rotor aligned with the previously scribed mark. If necessary, connect the negative battery cable, then crank the engine to full seat the distributor.
   b. Rotate the engine until the timing marks for correct initial timing align and the rotor is pointing at the No. 1 cap terminal.
   c. Rotate the distributor in the block to align the armature and stator assembly poles.
   d. Install the distributor hold-down bolt and clamp, but do not tighten at this time.

➥ If the armature and stator assembly poles cannot be aligned by rotating the distributor in the block, pull the distributor up out of the block enough to disengage the distributor gear. Rotate the distributor shaft to engage a different gear tooth and install the distributor.

3. Connect the distributor wiring harness. Install the distributor cap and tighten the mounting screws to 17–23 inch lbs., if so equipped. If necessary, attach the ignition wires as tagged during removal. Verify that the ignition wires are securely connected to the distributor cap and spark plugs.
4. Reconnect the negative battery cable and connect a suitable timing light and tachometer. Start the engine, letting it run until it reaches normal operating temperature.
5. Set the initial timing to the specifications given on the Vehicle Emission Control Information Decal located under the hood. Tighten down the distributor hold-down bolt to 17–25 ft. lbs. (23–34 Nm).
6. Recheck the initial timing and readjust as necessary.
7. Reconnect all vacuum lines and wire harness connectors. Reinstall and removed parts in the reverse order of the removal procedure.

Engine Rotated

This condition exists if the engine has been rotated with the distributor removed.

1. Rotate the engine until the No. 1 piston is on compression stroke.
2. Align the timing mark for correct initial timing.
3. Install the distributor with the rotor pointing at No. 1 terminal position in the cap and armature and stator assembly poles aligned.
4. Be sure that the oil pump intermediate shaft properly engages the distributor shaft. It may be necessary to crank the engine after the distributor gear is partially engaged in order to engage the oil pump intermediate shaft and fully seat the distributor in the engine block.
5. If it was necessary to crank the engine again, rotate the engine until the No. 1 piston is on top dead center of its compression stroke and align the timing marks for correct initial timing.
6. Rotate the distributor in the block to align the armature and stator assembly poles and verify that the rotor is pointing at the No. 1 terminal in the distributor cap.
7. Install the distributor hold-down bolt and clamp, but to not tighten at this time.
8. Connect the distributor wiring harness. Install the distributor cap and tighten the mounting screws to 17–23 inch lbs., if so equipped. If necessary, connect the ignition wires as tagged during removal. Verify that the ignition wires are securely connected to the distributor cap and spark plugs.
9. Reconnect the negative battery cable and connect a suitable timing light and tachometer. Start the engine letting it run until it reaches normal operating temperature.
10. Set the initial timing to the specifications given on the Vehicle Emission Control Information Decal located under the hood. Tighten down the distributor hold-down bolt to 17–25 ft. lbs. (23–34 Nm).
11. Recheck the initial timing and readjust as necessary.
12. Reconnect all vacuum lines and wire harness connectors.

EEC-IV THICK FILM INTEGRATED (TFI) IGNITION SYSTEM

General Information

➧ See Figures 20, 21, 22, 23, 24, 25, 26 and 27

The TFI ignition system features a distributor which uses no vacuum or centrifugal advance. The distributor is conventionally mounted and incorporates a Hall Effect stator assembly. On vehicles through 1988, the TFI module is mounted on the distributor. On 1989–93 vehicles, the TFI module is mounted remotely on the radiator support bracket and on 1994–95 vehicles, it is mounted on the front fender apron.

There are 2 type of TFI systems, and are as follows:

- PUSH START: this first TFI system featured a "push start" mode which allow manual transmission vehicles to be push started. Automatic transmission vehicles must not be push started.
- COMPUTER CONTROLLED DWELL: this second TFI system features an EEC-IV controlled ignition coil charge time.

Both the PUSH START and COMPUTER CONTROLLED DWELL TFI systems operates in the same manner. The TFI module supplies voltage to the Profile Ignition Pick-up (PIP) sensor, which sends the crankshaft position information to the TFI module. The TFI module then sends this information to the EEC-IV module, which determines the spark timing and sends an electronic signal to the TFI ignition module to turn off the coil and produce a spark to fire the spark plug.

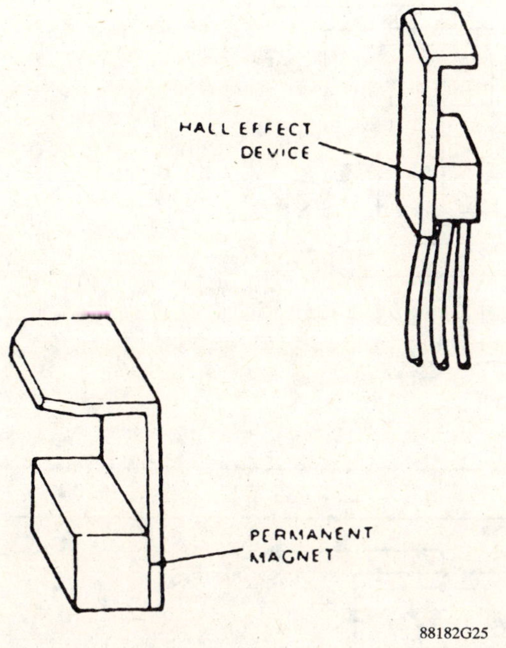

Fig. 20 Common Hall-Effect device

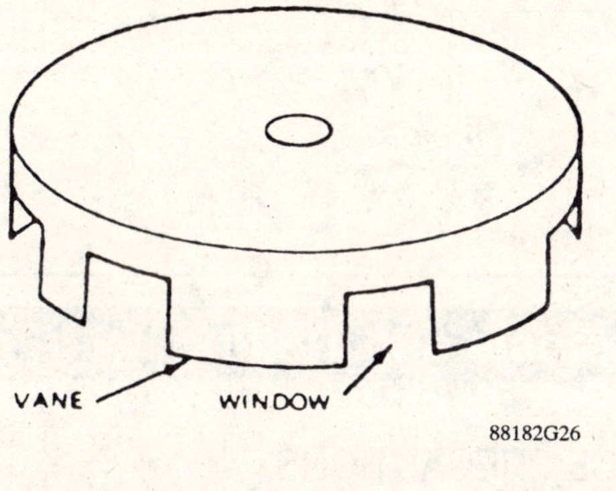

Fig. 21 View of the rotary vane cup

SYSTEM OPERATION

The operation of the universal distributor is accomplished through the Hall Effect stator assembly, causing the ignition coil to be switched off and on by the EEC-IV computer and TFI modules. The vane switch is encapsulated package consisting of a Hall sensor on one side and a permanent magnet on the other side.

A rotary armature (vane cup), made of ferrous metal, is used to trigger the Hall Effect switch. When the window of the armature is between the magnet and the Hall Effect device, a magnetic flux field is completed from the magnet through the Hall Effect device back to the magnet. As the vane passes through the opening, the flux lines are shunted through the vane and back to the magnet. A voltage is produced while the vane passes through the opening. When the vane clears the opening, the window causes the signal to go to 0 volts. The signal is then used by the EEC-IV system for crankshaft position sensing and the computation of the desired spark advance based on the engine demand and calibration. The voltage distribution is accomplished through a conventional rotor, cap and ignition wires.

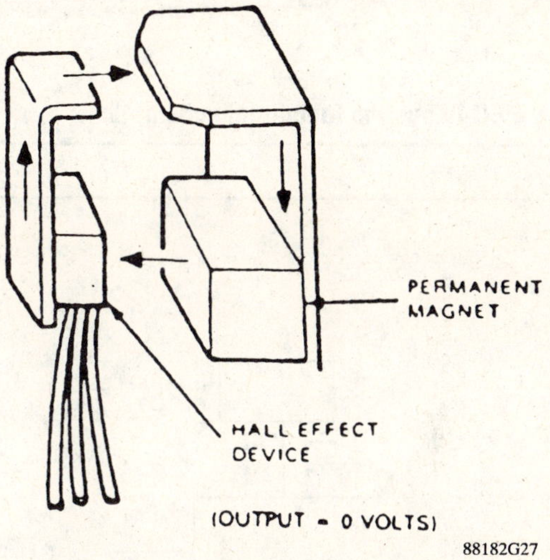

Fig. 22 Hall effect response to window

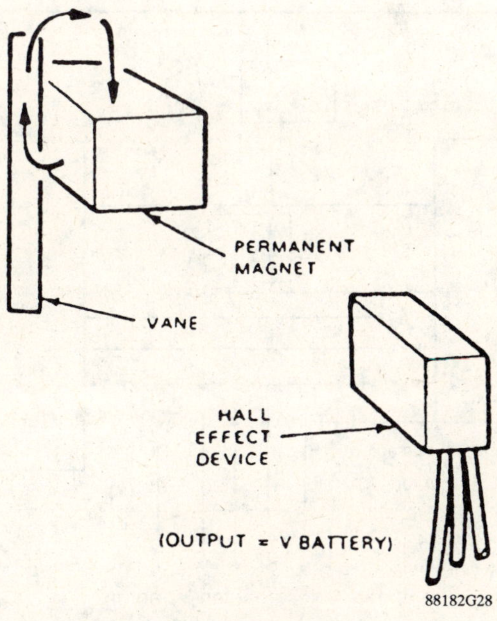

Fig. 23 Hall effect response to vane

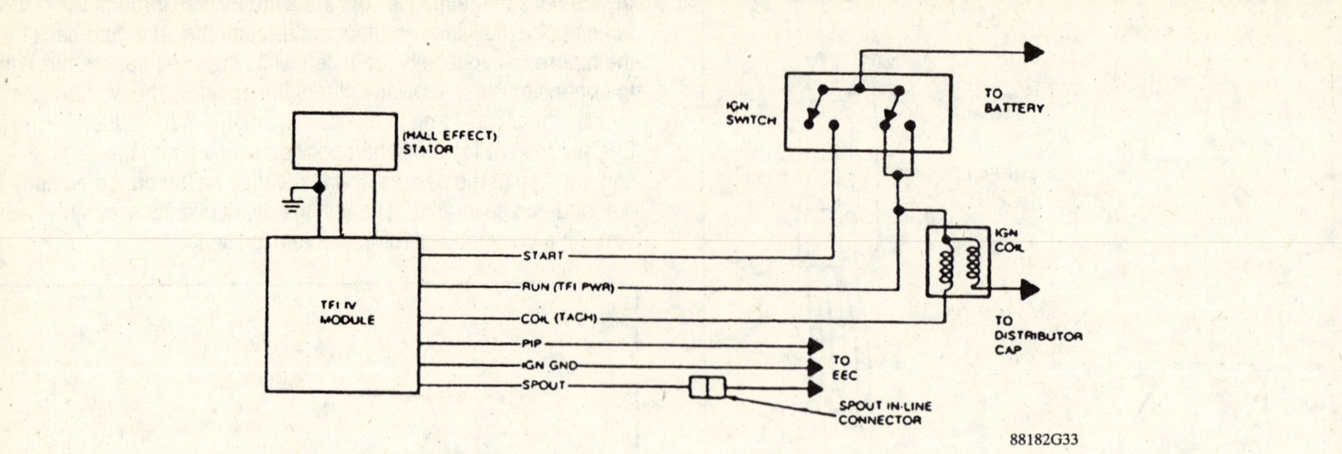

Fig. 24 EEC-IV system functional schematic

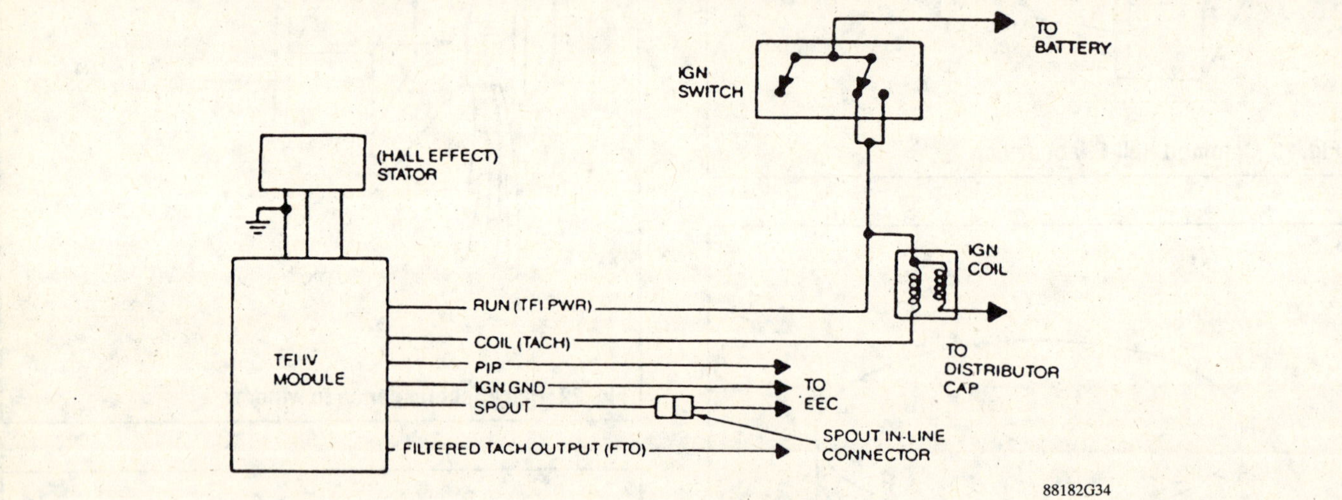

Fig. 25 Schematic of the EEC-IV system with Computer Controlled Dwell (CCD)

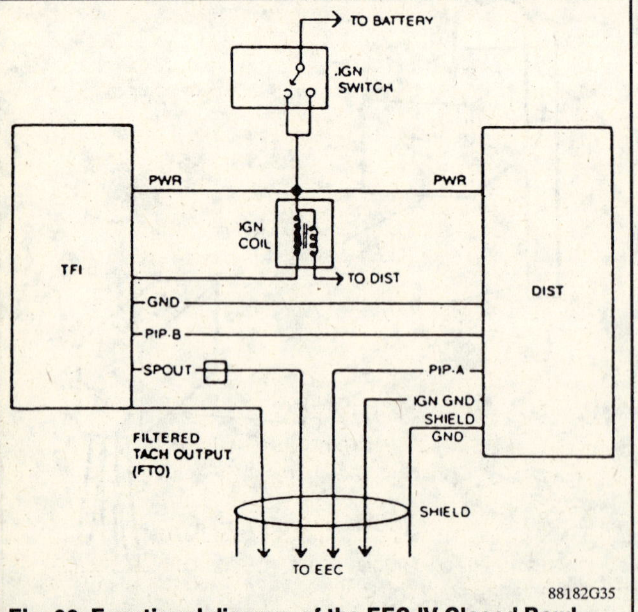

Fig. 26 Functional diagram of the EEC-IV Closed Bowl system with CCD

Diagnosis and Testing

SERVICE PRECAUTIONS

- Always turn the key **OFF** and isolate both ends of a circuit whenever testing for short or continuity.
- Never measure voltage or resistance directly at the processor connector.
- Always disconnect solenoids and switches from the harness before measuring for continuity, resistance or energizing by way of a 12 volts source.
- When disconnecting connectors, inspect for damaged or pushed-out pins, corrosion, loose wires, etc. Service if required.

PRELIMINARY CHECKS

1. Visually inspect the engine compartment to ensure that all vacuum lines and spark plug wires are properly routed and securely connected.

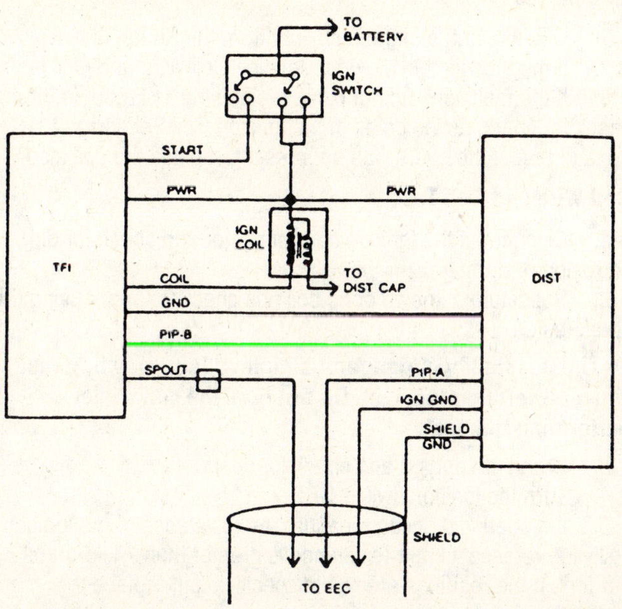

88182G36

Fig. 27 EEC-IV Closed bowl functional diagram

2. Examine all wiring harnesses and connectors for insulation damage, burned, overheated, loose or broken conditions. Check that the TFI module is securely fasten to the side of the distributor.
3. Be certain that the battery is fully charged and that all accessories should be **OFF** during the diagnosis.

INTERMITTENT DIAGNOSIS PROCEDURE

This procedure begins with a customer complaint. For example, the engine stops at unexpected times but can be restarted. When the technician must diagnose complaints of these nature, he must obtain as much information as possible directly from the customer about the conditions under which the problem occurs and the service history of the vehicle must be thoroughly reviewed to avoid repeat replacement of good components.

EEC-IV AND EEC-IV WITH COMPUTER CONTROLLED DWELL

Ignition Coil Secondary Voltage Test

➧ **See Figure 28**

CRANK MODE

1. Connect a spark tester between the ignition coil wire and a good engine ground.
2. Crank the engine and check for spark at the tester.
3. Turn the ignition switch **OFF**.
4. If no spark occurs, check the following:
   a. Inspect the ignition coil for damage or carbon tracking.
   b. Also, check that the distributor shaft is rotating, when the engine is being cranked.
   c. If the results in Steps a, and b are okay, go to Stator Test 1.
5. If a spark did occur, check the distributor cap and rotor for damage or carbon tracking. Go to Ignition Coil Secondary Voltage (Run Mode) test.

RUN MODE

1. Fully apply the parking brake. Place the gear shift lever in **P** (automatic transmission) or **N** (manual transmission).
2. Disconnect the **S** terminal wire at the starter relay. Then, attach a remote starter switch.
3. Turn the ignition switch to the **RUN** position.
4. Using the remote starter switch, crank the engine and check for spark.
5. Turn the ignition switch **OFF**.
6. If no spark occurs, go to the Wiring Harness test.
7. If a spark did occur, the problem is not in the ignition system.

Wiring Harness Test

➧ **See Figure 29**

1. Push the connector tabs and separate the wiring harness connector from the ignition module. Check for dirt, corrosion or damage.
2. Check that the **S** terminal wire at the starter relay is disconnected.
3. Measure the battery voltage.
4. Carefully insert a small straight pin in the appropriate terminal.

➥ Do not allow the straight pin to contact electrical ground, while performing this test.

5. Measure the voltage at the following points:
   a. TFI Without CCD: Terminal No. 3 (Run Circuit) – with ignition switch in **RUN** and **START**.
   b. TFI Without CCD: Terminal No. 4 (Start Circuit) – with ignition switch in **START**.
   c. TFI With CCD: Terminal No. 3 (Run Circuit) – with ignition switch in **RUN** and **START**.
6. Turn the ignition switch **OFF** and remove the straight pin.
7. Reconnect the **S** terminal wire at the starter relay.
8. If the results are within 90% of battery voltage, replace the TFI module.
9. If the results are not within 90% of battery voltage, inspect the wiring harness and connectors in the faulty circuit. Also, check for a faulty ignition switch.

Stator Test 1

1. Fully apply the parking brake. Place the gear shift lever in **P** (automatic transmission) or **N** (manual transmission).
2. Disconnect the harness connector at the TFI module and connect the TFI tester.
3. Disconnect the **S** terminal wire at the starter relay. Then, attach a remote starter switch.
4. Using the remote starter switch, crank the engine and check the status of the 2 LED lamps.
5. Remove the tester and remote switch.
6. Reconnect the wire at the starter relay and harness to the TFI module.
7. If the PIP light blink, go to the TFI module test.
8. If the PIP light did not blink, remove the distributor cap, crank the engine and check that the distributor shaft rotates. If okay, go to the Stator Test 2.

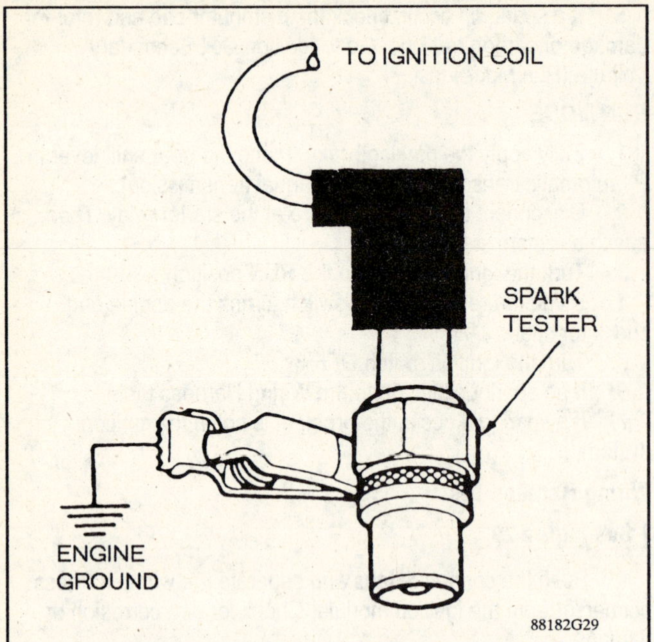

Fig. 28 Check for spark with a suitable spark tester

Stator Test 2

1. Remove the distributor from the engine. Remove the TFI module from the distributor.
2. Measure the resistance between the TFI module terminals, as follow:
   a. GND-PIP In — should be greater than 500 ohms.
   b. PIP PWR-PIP IN — should be less than 2 kilo-ohms.
   c. PIP PWR-TFI PWR — should be less than 200 ohms.
   d. GND-IGN GND — should be less than 2 ohms.
   e. PIP In-PIP — should be less than 200 ohms.
3. If the readings are within the specified value, replace the stator.
4. If the readings are not as specified, replace the TFI.

Module Test

1. Use the status of the tach light from the Stator Test 1.
2. If the tach light blink, go to Ignition Coil Wire and Coil test.
3. If the tach light did not blink, replace the TFI module, then check for spark, as indicated in the Ignition Coil Secondary Voltage test. If the spark was not present, replace the coil also.

Coil Wire and Coil Test

1. Disconnect the ignition coil connector and check for dirt, corrosion or damage.
2. Substitute a known good coil and check for spark using the spark tester.

➜ The possibility of dangerous high voltage may be present when performing this test. Do not hold the coil while performing this test.

3. Crank the engine and check for spark.
4. Turn the ignition switch **OFF**.
5. If a spark did occur, measure the resistance of the ignition coil wire, replace it if the resistance is greater than 7 kilo-ohms per foot. If the readings are within specification, replace the ignition coil.
6. If no spark occurs, the problem is not the coil. Go to the EEC-IV/TFI test.

EEC-IV/TFI Test

1. Disconnect the pin-in-line connector near the distributor.
2. Crank the engine.
3. Turn the ignition switch **OFF**.
4. If a spark did occur, check the PIP and ignition ground wires for continuity. If okay, the problem is not ignition.
5. If no spark occurs, check the voltage at the positive (+) terminal of the ignition coil, with the ignition switch in **RUN**.
6. If the reading is not within battery voltage, check for a worn or damaged ignition switch.
7. If the reading is within battery voltage, check for faults in the wiring between the coil and TFI module terminal No. 2 or any additional wiring or components connected to that circuit.

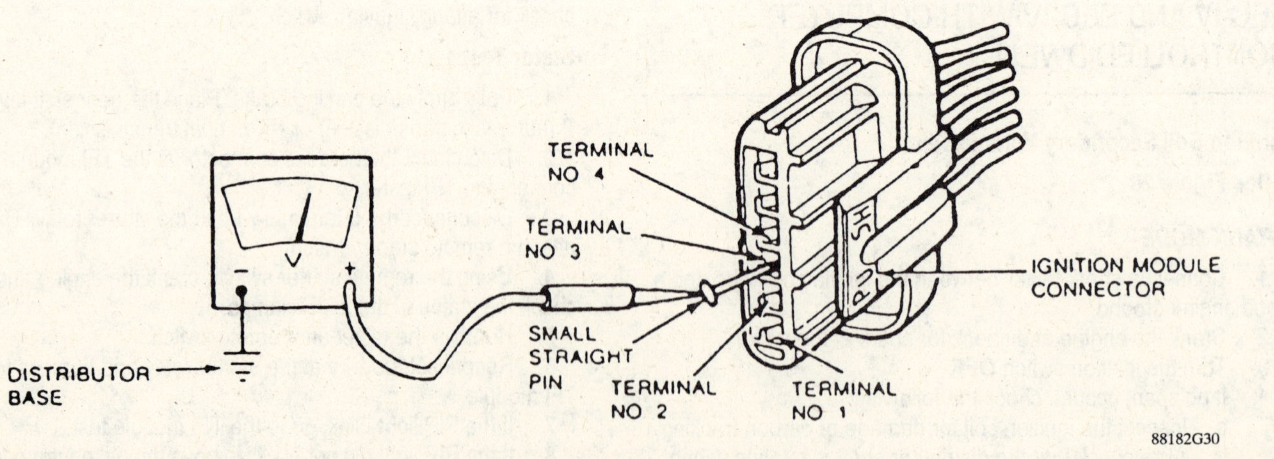

Fig. 29 Check the wiring harness at the ignition module connector

TFI WITH CLOSED BOWL DISTRIBUTOR

Ignition Coil Secondary Voltage Test

CRANK MODE

1. Connect a spark tester between the ignition coil wire and a good engine ground.
2. Crank the engine and check for spark at the tester.
3. Turn the ignition switch **OFF**.
4. If no spark occurs, check the following:
   a. Inspect the ignition coil for damage or carbon tracking.
   b. Also, check that the distributor shaft is rotating, when the engine is being cranked.
   c. If results in Steps a and b are okay, go to Stator Test 1.
5. If a spark did occur, check the distributor cap and rotor for damage or carbon tracking. Go to Ignition Coil Secondary Voltage (Run Mode) test.

RUN MODE

1. Fully apply the parking brake. Place the gear shift lever in **P** (automatic transmission) or **N** (manual transmission).
2. Disconnect the **S** terminal wire at the starter relay. Then, attach a remote starter switch.
3. Turn the ignition switch to the **RUN** position.
4. Using the remote starter switch, crank the engine and check for spark.
5. Turn the ignition switch **OFF**.
6. If no spark occurs, go to the Wiring Harness test.
7. If a spark did occur, the problem is not in the ignition system.

Wiring Harness Test

See Figure 30

1. Push the connector tabs and separate the wiring harness connector from the ignition module. Check for dirt, corrosion or damage.
2. Check that the **S** terminal wire at the starter relay is disconnected.
3. Measure the battery voltage.
4. Carefully insert a small straight pin in the appropriate terminal.

Do not allow the straight pin to contact electrical ground, while performing this test.

5. Measure the voltage at the following points:
   a. TFI Without CCD — Terminal No. 3 (Run Circuit); with ignition switch in **RUN** and **START**.
   b. TFI Without CCD — Terminal No. 4 (Start Circuit); with ignition switch in **START**.
   c. TFI With CCD — Terminal No. 3 (Run Circuit); with ignition switch in **RUN** and **START**.
6. Turn the ignition switch **OFF** and remove the straight pin.
7. Reconnect the **S** terminal wire at the starter relay.
8. If the results are within 90% of battery voltage, check for faults in the wiring between the coil and TFI module terminal No. 2 or any additional wiring or components connected to that circuit.
9. If the results are not within 90% of battery voltage, inspect the wiring harness and connectors in the faulty circuit. Also, check for a faulty ignition switch.

Stator Test 1

1. Separate the wiring harness connector from the distributor. Check for dirt, corrosion or damage.
2. Measure the resistance between the stator connector terminals 1 and 5.
3. If greater than 5 ohms, replace the stator.
4. If less than 5 ohms, measure the resistance between the stator connector terminal 2 and the distributor base. Also, measure the resistance between the stator connector terminal 6 and the distributor base.
5. If the resistance is greater than 1 ohm in each case, inspect the stator retaining screws. If okay, replace the stator.
6. If less than 1 ohms, go to Stator Test 2.

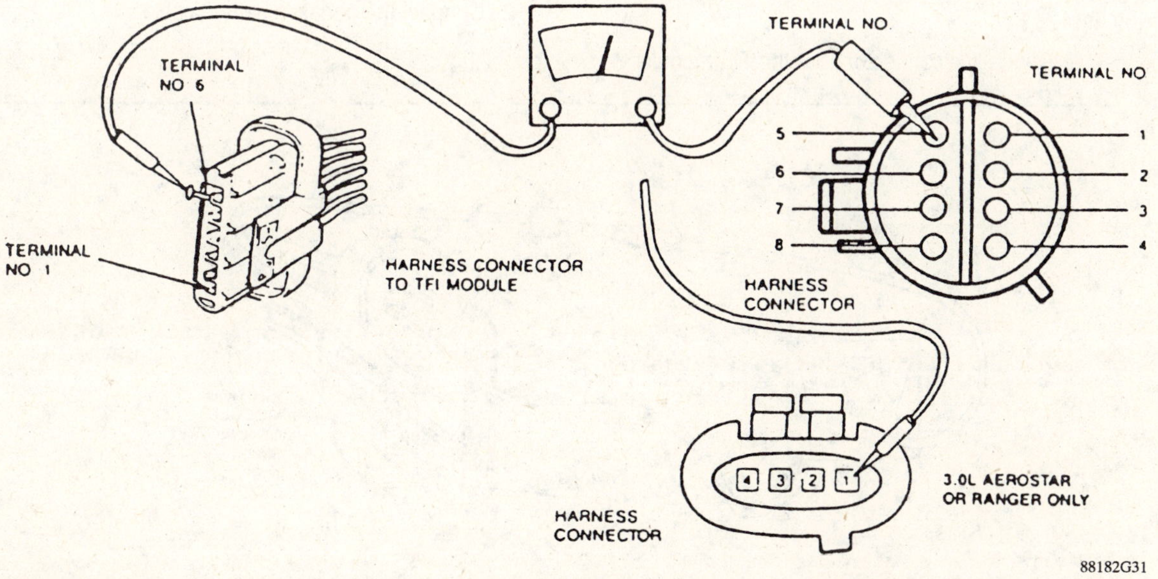

Fig. 30 Checking wiring harness; distributor-to-TFI module — EEC-IV closed bowl distributor

Stator Test 2

➧ See Figure 31

1. Fully apply the parking brake. Place the gear shift lever in **P** (automatic transmission) or **N** (manual transmission).
2. Disconnect the harness connector at the TFI module and connect the TFI tester.
3. Disconnect the **S** terminal wire at the starter relay. Then, attach a remote starter switch.
4. Using the remote starter switch, crank the engine and check the status of the 2 LED lamps.
5. Remove the tester and remote switch.
6. Reconnect the wire at the starter relay and harness to the TFI module.
7. If the PIP light blink, go to the TFI module test.
8. If the PIP light did not blink, replace the stator.

Module Test

1. Use the status of the tach light from the Stator test 2.
2. If the tach light blink, go to Ignition Coil Wire and Coil test.
3. If the tach light did not blink, replace the TFI module, then check for spark, as indicated in the Ignition Coil Secondary Voltage test. If the spark was not present, replace the coil also.

Coil Wire And Coil Test

1. Disconnect the ignition coil connector and check for dirt, corrosion or damage.
2. Substitute a known good coil and check for spark using the spark tester.

➜ The possibility of dangerous high voltage may be present when performing this test. Do not hold the coil while performing this test.

3. Crank the engine and check for spark.
4. Turn the ignition switch **OFF**.
5. If a spark did occur, measure the resistance of the ignition coil wire, replace it if the resistance is greater than 7 kilo-ohms per foot. If the readings are within specification, replace the ignition coil.
6. If no spark occurs, reconnect the coil connector and install the spark tester, then go to EEC-IV Wiring Test.

EEC-IV Wiring Test

1. Disconnect the pin-in-line connector near the TFI module.
2. Crank the engine.
3. If a spark did occur, check the PIP-A and ignition ground wires for continuity to the EEC system. If okay, the problem is not ignition.
4. If no spark occurs, check the wiring harness between the harness connector to the TFI module and the distributor. Service as required.

Ignition Coil

REMOVAL & INSTALLATION

➧ See Figure 32

1. Disconnect the negative battery cable.
2. Detach the engine control sensor wiring connector from the ignition coil and the radio ignition interference capacitor.
3. Tag and disconnect the ignition wires from the ignition coil.
4. Unfasten the ignition coil mounting bracket retaining bolts, then remove the bracket from the front side inner member.
5. Remove the ignition coil-to-bracket retaining screws and the ignition coil.
6. If necessary, unfasten the radio ignition interference capacitor retaining screw, then remove the radio ignition interference capacitor from the ignition coil mounting bracket.

To install:

7. Install the radio ignition interference capacitor to the mounting bracket and secure with the retaining screw. Tighten the screws to 25–35 inch lbs. (2.8–4.0 Nm).
8. Position the ignition coil, then install the ignition coil-to-bracket retaining screws and tighten to 25–35 inch lbs. (2.8–4.0 Nm).
9. Install the ignition coil mounting bracket on the front side inner member, then fasten with the retaining bolts and tighten to 15–22 ft. lbs. (20–30 Nm).
10. Connect the ignition wires to the coil, as tagged during removal.
11. Attach the engine control sensor wiring connector to the ignition coil and radio ignition interference capacitor.
12. Connect the negative battery cable.

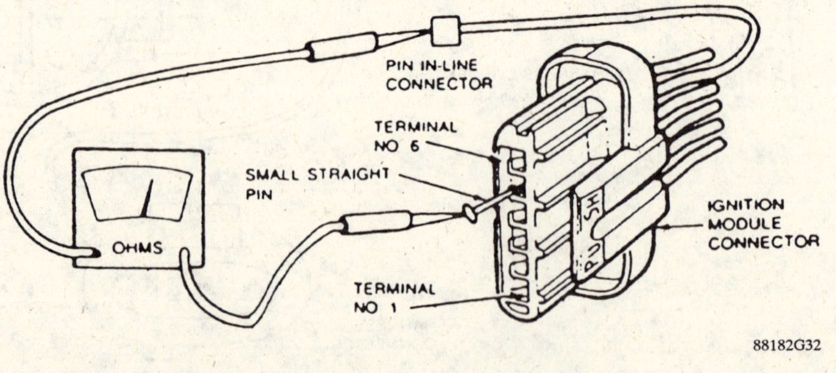

Fig. 31 Measuring resistance between the TFI module connector and inline pin

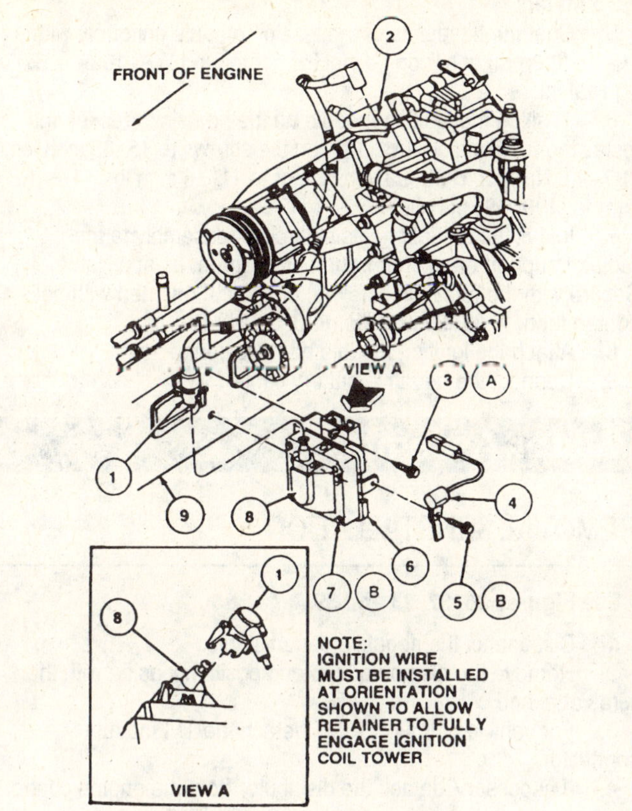

Item	Description
1	Ignition Wire
2	Distributor Cap
3	Bolt (2 Req'd)
4	Radio Ignition Interference Capacitor
5	Screw
6	Ignition Coil Mounting Bracket
7	Screw (4 Req'd)
8	Ignition Coil
9	Front Side Inner Member
A	Tighten to 20-30 N·m (15-22 Lb-Ft)
B	Tighten to 2.8-4.0 N·m (25-35 Lb-In)

88182G12

Fig. 32 Location of the ignition coil mounting — 1995 vehicle shown

TFI Ignition Module

REMOVAL & INSTALLATION

Vehicles Through 1988

➧ **See Figure 33**

1. Disconnect the negative battery cable.
2. Remove the distributor cap and position it aside with the wires attached.
3. Detach the TFI-ignition module electrical connector.
4. Remove the distributor from the engine and place on a workbench.
5. Remove the two ignition module retaining screws.
6. Slide the right side of the module down toward the distributor mounting flange and then back up. Then, slide the left side of the module down toward the distributor mounting flange and them back up. Continue alternating, side-to-side, until the module terminals are disengaged from the connector in the distributor base.
7. With the terminals completely disengaged, slide the module downward and gently pull the module away from the mounting surface.

****WARNING**

Do not attempt to lift the module from the mounting surface before moving the entire module toward the distributor flange as you will break the pins at the distributor/module connector.

To install:

8. Coat the metal base of the ignition module uniformly with suitable silicone compound, about $^1/_{32}$ in. (0.79mm) thick.
9. Place the TFI-module on the distributor base.
10. Carefully slide the TFI module assembly toward the distributor connector pins until the connector engages and the module screw holes line up with the tapped holes on the base.
11. Install the two module mounting screws and tighten to 15–35 inch lbs. (1.7–4.0 Nm).
12. Install the distributor in the engine, as outlined later in this section.
13. Position the distributor cap and tighten the cap mounting screws to 17–23 inch lbs. (2.0–2.6 Nm).
14. Attach the TFI-module harness connector.
15. Connect the negative battery cable, then start the engine. Using a timing light, check the ignition timing and adjust, if necessary.

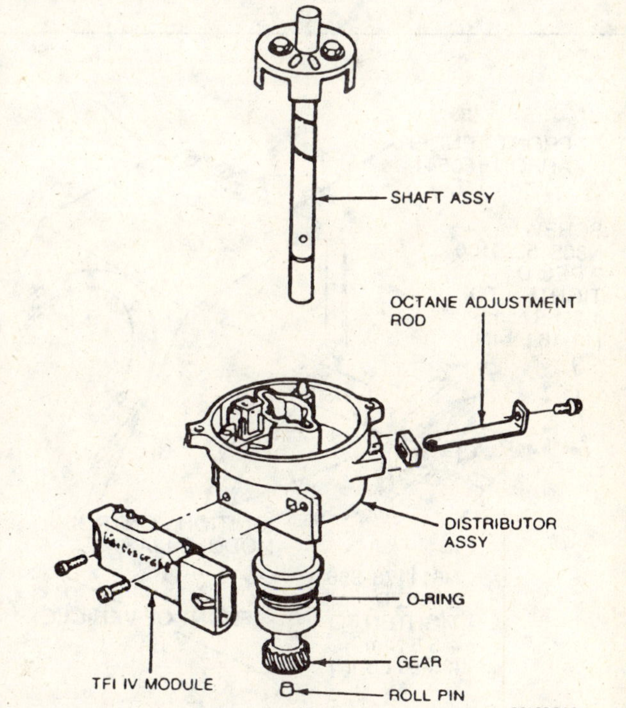

88182G09

Fig. 33 Through 1988, then ignition module is mounted directly on the distributor assembly

1989–95 Vehicles

➧ See Figures 34 and 35

1. Disconnect the negative battery cable
2. Detach the ignition module/ICM electrical connector.
3. Remove the screw(s) or bolts retaining the module heatsink/bracket assembly to the radiator support bracket for vehicles through 1993 or to the front fender apron for 1994–95 vehicles.
4. Unfasten the ignition module-to-heatsink retaining screws and remove the module.

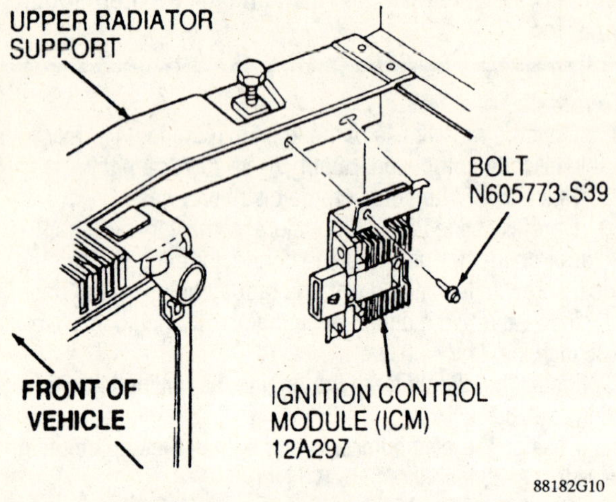

Fig. 34 The ignition module on 1989-93 vehicles, is located on the radiator support bracket

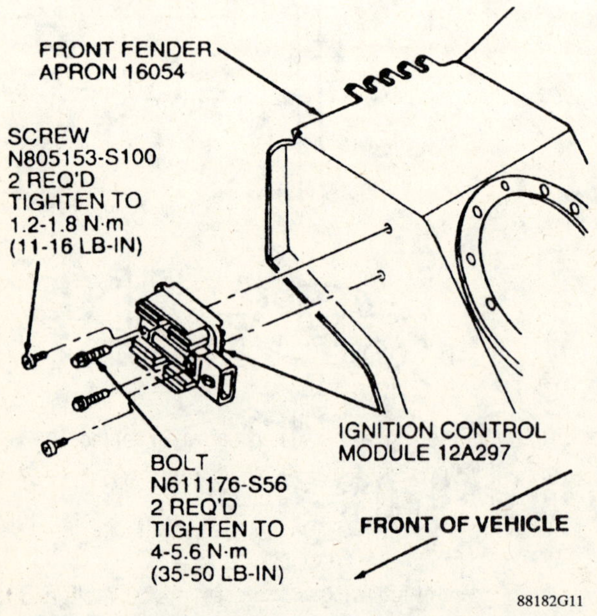

Fig. 35 On 1994–95 vehicles, the ignition module is mounted to the front fender apron

To install:

5. Coat the baseplate of the ignition module uniformly with a $^{1}/_{32}$ in. (0.8mm) of silicone dielectric compound WA-10 or equivalent.
6. Position the ignition module on the heatsink/bracket and install the retaining screws. Tighten the screws to 15–35 inch lbs. (1.7-4.0 Nm) for 1989–93 vehicles or to 11–16 inch lbs. (1.2–1.8 Nm) for 1994–95 vehicles.
7. Install the module heatsink/bracket assembly to the radiator support bracket or front fender apron, as applicable. Secure with the retaining screw(s) or bolts. If retained with bolts, tighten them to 35–50 inch lbs. (4.0–5.6 Nm).
8. Attach the ignition module harness connector.
9. Connect the negative battery cable.

Stator Assembly

REMOVAL & INSTALLATION

➧ See Figures 36, 37, 38 and 39

1. Disconnect the negative battery cable.
2. Remove the distributor cap and position it aside with the wires attached.
3. For vehicles through 1988, detach the TFI module connector.
4. If necessary, detach the distributor from the engine control sensor.
5. Remove the distributor assembly from the engine.
6. Remove the rotor.
7. If equipped, unfasten the two retaining screws and remove the module from the base. Wipe the grease from the base and module, keeping the surfaces free of dirt.

➥ Hold the gear to loosen the armature screws, do not hold the armature.

8. Mark the armature and distributor gear for orientation during installation.
9. Hold the distributor drive gear and remove the armature retaining screws. Remove the armature.
10. Remove the distributor gear retaining pins and discard, if equipped.
11. If equipped, remove the gear and gear collar.
12. Invert the distributor and place in the Axle Bearing/Seal Plate D84L-950-A/T75L-1165-B or equivalent arbor press. Press off the distributor gear from the shaft, using bearing removal tool D84L-950-A/D79L-4621-A or equivalent.
13. Clean and polish the shaft with emery paper. Wipe clean so that the shaft slides out freely from the distributor base. Remove the shaft.
14. Remove the octane rod retaining screw and retain, then remove the octane rod and retain.
15. Unfasten the stator assembly retaining screws and remove the stator from the top of the bowl.
16. Inspect the base bushing for wear or signs of excess heat concentration. If damaged, replace the entire distributor. Inspect the base O-ring for damage and replace, if necessary.

To install:

17. Position the stator assembly over the bushing and press to seat. Place the stator connector in position. The tab should fit in the notch on the base and the fastening eyelets aligned with the screw holes. Be certain the wires are positioned away from moving parts.

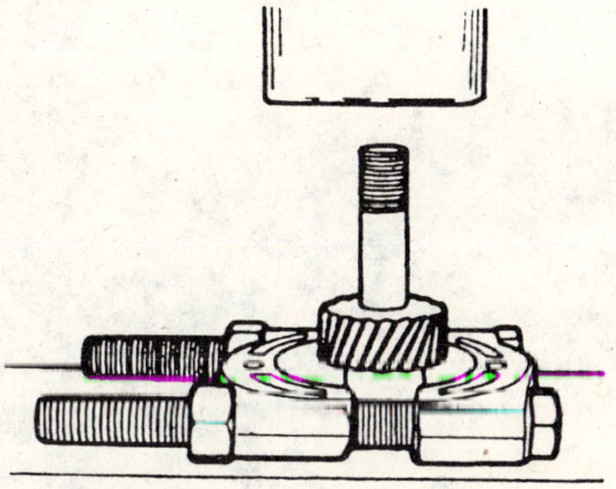

88182G13

Fig. 36 **Invert the distributor and place in an axle bearing/seal plate, then press the gear from the shaft using a suitable bearing removal tool**

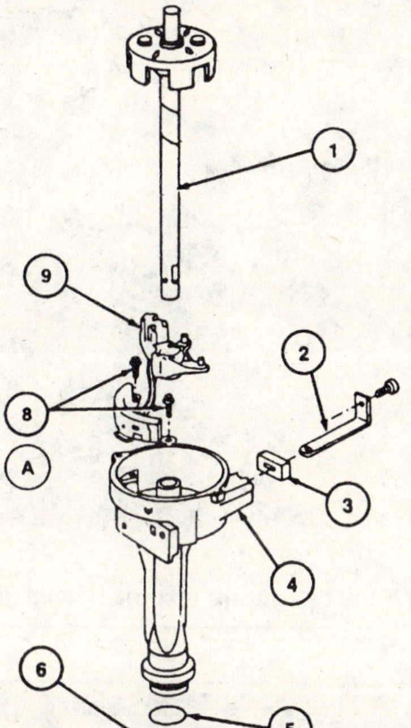

Item	Description
1	Shaft (Part of 12127)
2	Octane Rod (Part of 12127)
3	Grommet (Part of 12127)
4	Distributor
5	Distributor Base O-Ring
6	Thrust Collar (Part of 12127)
7	Gear (Part of 12127)
8	Screws (2 Req'd) (Part of 12127)
9	Distributor Stator
A	Tighten to 1.7-4.0 N·m (15-35 Lb-In)

88182G14

Fig. 37 Exploded view of the stator and related components

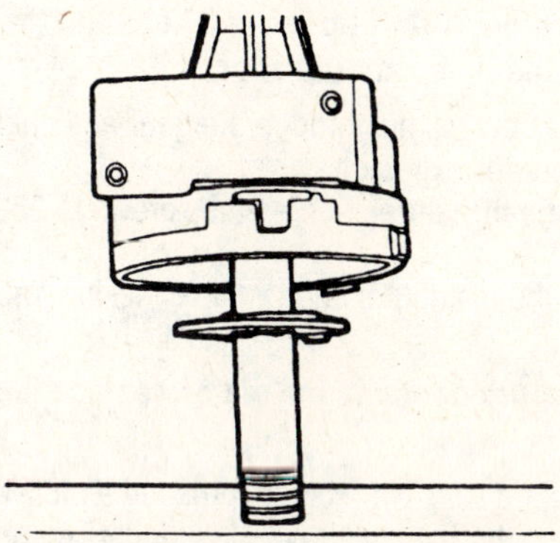

88182G15

Fig. 38 Invert the distributor and place on an arbor press plate

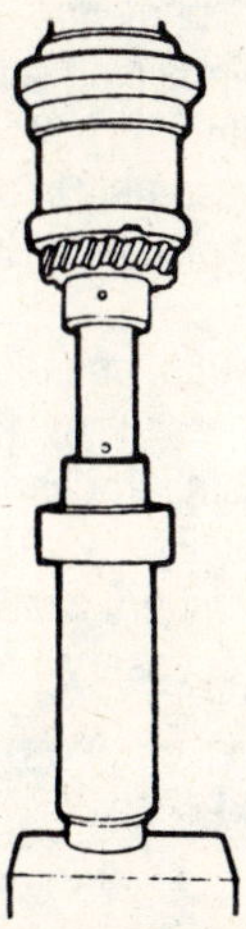

88182G16

Fig. 39 Place a 5/8 in. deep well socket over the shaft and gear and press the gear to align with the retainer pin hole

18. Install the stator retaining screws and tighten to 15–35 inch lbs. (1.7–4.0 Nm).
19. Install the octane rod, inserting the rod through the base hole. Place the end of the octane rod onto the same post as the original stator. Only one post should fit easily in the rod hole. Firmly seat the octane rod seal into the housing.
20. Apply a light coat of engine oil to the distributor shaft (do NOT overlubricate), beneath the armature. Insert the shaft through the base bushing.
21. Place the collar, if required, over the shaft and line up the mark on the armature and original drill hole. Use a drift punch to ensure proper alignment. If not present, go to step 24.
22. Insert a new roll pin through the collar and shaft. The pin should be flush with both sides of the collar when seated.
23. Position a 1/2 in. deep well socket over the shaft, invert and place in the arbor press.
24. Place the distributor gear on the shaft end. Make certain the mark on the armature align with the gear.

➜ The hole in the shaft and gear must be properly aligned to ensure ease of the roll pin.

25. Place a 5/8 in. deep well socket over the shaft and gear and press the gear to align with the original drill hole.

➥ If the gear holes do not align, the gear must be removed and repressed on. A drift punch will not align the holes. As in the collar, the holes should align.

26. Install a new roll pin through the gear and shaft. The pin should have proper extrusion.
27. Install the armature. Tighten the screws to 25–35 inch lbs. (2.8–40Nm).
28. Rotate the distributor shaft while checking for free movement.

➥ If the armature contacts the stator, replace the entire distributor.

29. If equipped with TFI module, proceed as follows:
    a. Wipe the back of the module and its mounting surface in the distributor clean. Coat the base of the TFI ignition module uniformly with a $^1/_{32}$ in. (0.8mm) of silicone compound (Silicone Dielectric Compound WA-10 or equivalent).
    b. Invert the distributor base so the stator connector is in full view. Then, insert the module. Be certain the 3 module pins are inserted into the stator connector.
    c. Install the module retaining screws and tighten to 15–35 inch lbs. (1.7–4.0 Nm).
30. Install the distributor assembly into the engine block.
31. If equipped, attach the distributor to the engine control sensor wiring.
32. For vehicles through 1988, connect the TFI module wiring harness.
33. Install the rotor and distributor cap. Tighten the cap mounting screws to 18–23 inch lbs. (2.0–2.6 Nm).
34. Connect the negative battery cable. Check the initial ignition timing and adjust if necessary.

Distributor

REMOVAL & INSTALLATION

➧ See Figures 40, 41, 42, 43, 44 and 45

1. Rotate the engine until the No. 1 piston is on TDC of its compression stroke.
2. Disconnect the negative battery cable.
3. Before removing the distributor cap, mark the position of the No. 1 wire tower on the distributor base for future reference.
4. If rotor removal is necessary, mark the position of the rotor to the distributor housing.
5. Scribe a mark in the distributor body and the engine block to indicate position of the distributor in the engine.
6. Remove the distributor hold-down bolt and clamp.
7. Loosen the distributor cap hold-down screws and remove the cap. Position the cap and wires out of the way.
8. Detach the distributor electrical connector.
9. Remove the distributor assembly from the engine. Be sure not to rotate the engine while the distributor is removed.

To install:

10. Make sure that the engine it still at TDC of its compression stroke.

➥ If the crankshaft was rotated, while the distributor was removed, it will be necessary to remove the No. 1 spark plug and rotate the engine clockwise until No. 1 piston is on the compression stroke. Align the timing pointer with TDC on the crankshaft damper.

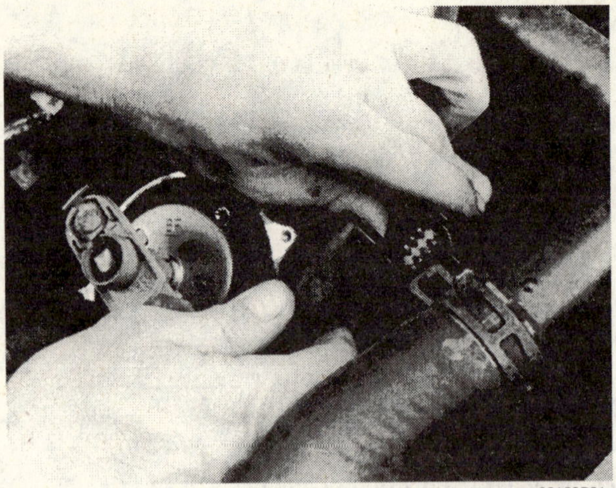
88182P01

Fig. 40 Detach the distributor electrical connector

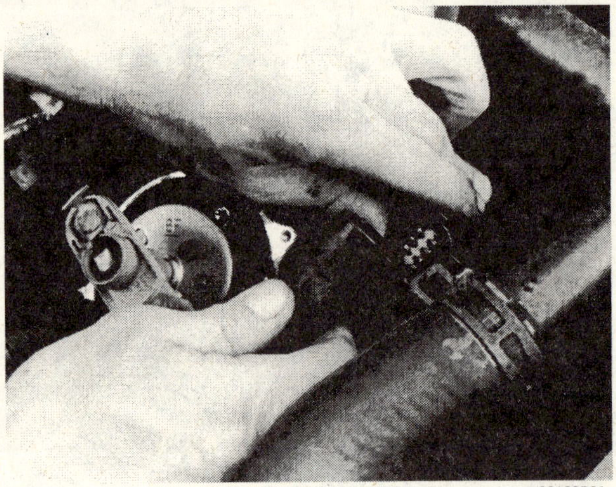
88182P01

Fig. 41 Detach the distributor electrical connector

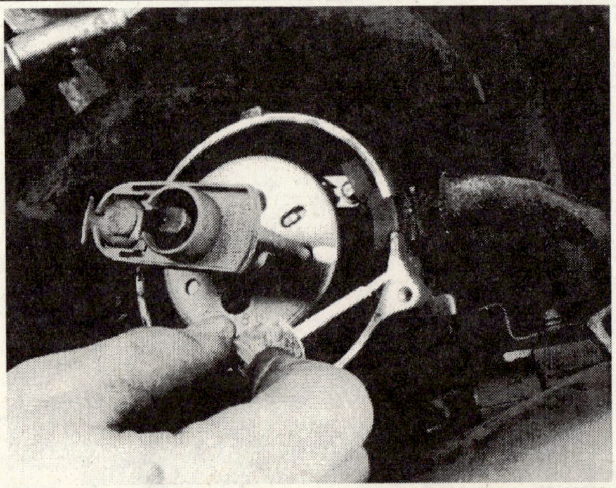
88182P02

Fig. 42 If removing the rotor, matchmark the position of the rotor to the distributor housing

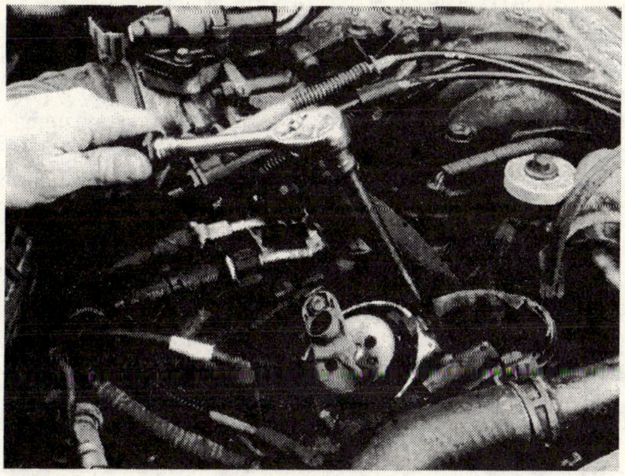

88182P03

Fig. 43 Unfasten the distributor hold-down bolt and clamp

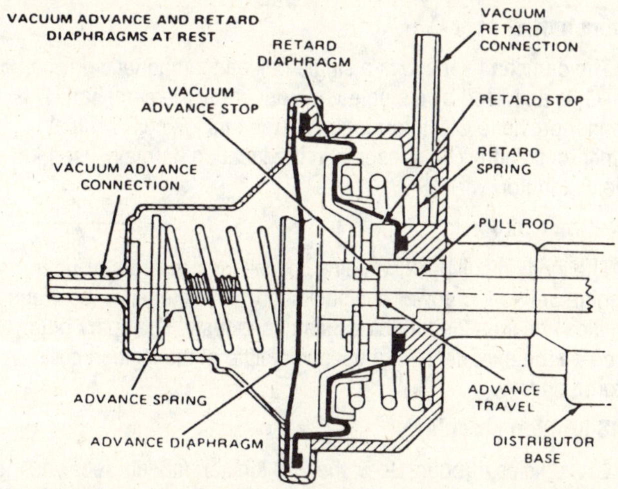

88182G04

Fig. 44 Carefully lift the distributor straight up, then . . .

88182P05

Fig. 45 . . . remove the distributor from the engine

11. Rotate the distributor shaft so the rotor points toward the mark on distributor housing, made previously.
12. Rotate the rotor slightly so the leading edge of the vane is centered in the vane switch stator assembly.
13. Rotate the distributor in the block to align the leading edge of the vane with the vane switch stator assembly. Make certain the rotor is pointing to the No. 1 mark on the distributor base.

If the vane and vane switch stator cannot be aligned by rotating the distributor in the cylinder block, remove the distributor enough to just disengage the distributor gear from the camshaft gear. Rotate the rotor enough to engage the distributor gear on another tooth of the camshaft gear. Repeat Step 7, if necessary.

14. Install the distributor hold-down clamp and bolt(s) and tighten slightly. Install the distributor cap and wires. Install the No. 1 spark plug, if removed.
15. Connect the negative battery cable. Check the initial ignition timing.
16. Tighten the hold-down clamp and recheck the timing. Adjust if necessary.

DISTRIBUTORLESS IGNITION SYSTEM (DIS)

General Information

The Distributorless Ignition System (DIS), also called the Electronic Ignition (EI) system, on later model vehicles, eliminates the conventional distributor and all its components, by using multiple ignition coils. Six cylinder engines use a six tower coil pack. Eight cylinder use two four tower coil packs. Each coil pack has 2 tach wires, 1 for each coil.

In the DIS ignition system, each coil fires 2 spark plugs at the same time. The plugs are paired so that the plug on the compression stroke fires, while the other plug is on its exhaust stroke. The next time the coil is fired, the plug that was on the exhaust will be on the compression and the one that was on the compression will be on the exhaust. The spark in the exhaust cylinder is wasted but little of the coil energy is lost.

The DIS ignition system consists of the following components:

- Crankshaft timing sensor
- Camshaft sensor
- DIS ignition module (vehicles through 1995)
- Ignition coil pack
- Spark angle portion of the EEC-IV module
- Powertrain Control Module (PCM)
- Related wiring

These engines use a camshaft and crankshaft sensor. These sensors are hall effect devices. A rotary vane cup (or wheel), made of ferrous metal is used to trigger the hall effect devices. The camshaft cup incorporates a single tooth and is driven by the camshaft. The signal from the camshaft sensor has 1 positive-going edge once every camshaft revolution. The crankshaft cup incorporates 3 teeth and causes the crankshaft sensor to generate 3 positive (PIP) edges every crankshaft revolution.

On 1996 vehicles, there is no longer a stand-alone Ignition Control Module (ICM). The ICM has been integrated into the PCM. The Profile Ignition Pickup (PIP), Spark Output

(SPOUT), Ignition Ground (IGN GND), and Ignition Diagnostic Monitor (IDM) have also been enclosed in the PCM. The functionality of the ignition remains the same.

SYSTEM OPERATION

EEC-IV Vehicles Through 1995

In the DIS ignition system the EEC-IV processor determines the spark angle using the PIP signal to establish base timing. Spout is provided by the EEC-IV processor to the DIS module and serves 2 purposes. The leading edge fires the coil and the trailing edge controls the dwell time. This feature is referred to as Computer Control Dwell (CCD).

The DIS module incorporates an Ignition Diagnostic Monitor (IDM). This is an output signal that provides diagnostic information concerning the ignition system to the EEC-IV processor for self-test. It is also the input signal for the vehicle's tachometer.

If the CID circuit fails and an attempt to start the engine is made, the DIS module will randomly select 1 of the coils to fire. If hard starting results, turning the key **OFF** and trying to restart will result in another guess. Several attempts may be needed until the proper coil is selected, allowing the vehicle to be started and driven until repairs can be made. The Failure Mode Effects Management (FMEM) system will try to keep the vehicle drivable despite certain EEC-IV system failures that prevent the EEC-IV processor from providing spark angle or dwell commands. The EEC-IV processor opens the SPOUT line and the DIS module fires the coils directly from the PIP input. This condition will result in a fixed spark angle of 10 degrees and a fixed dwell.

The DIS ignition module receives the PIP signal from the crankshaft sensor, the CID signals from the camshaft sensor and the Spout (spark out) signal is from the EEC-IV control module. During normal operation the PIP signal is sent to the EEC-IV control module from the crankshaft timing sensor and provides base timing and rpm information. The CID signal provides the DIS module with the information required to synchronize the ignition coils so that they are fired in the proper sequence.

When the window of the vane cup is located between the magnet and hall effect device, a magnetic flux field is completed. At this time the magnetic field is allow to travel from the permanent magnet through the hall effect device and back to the magnetic. This condition creates a low (0 volts) output signal. When the vane tooth is located between the magnet and hall effect device, the flux field is shunted through the vane and back to the magnetic. The output signal, during this time, will change from a low (0 volts) to high (source volts).

1996 EEC-V Vehicles

In the EI system, the Crankshaft Position (CKP) sensor is used to indicate the crankshaft position and speed information to the PCM. By sensing a missing tooth on a trigger wheel mounted on the crankshaft damper, the CKP is also able to identify a specific point in the travel of piston 1. The PCM uses the information from the CKP sensor to generate an internal Profile Ignition Pickup (PIP) signal.

Once the PIP signal is generated, fuel and spark functions are enabled. The calculated spark target is used internally by the PCM as a pulse width modulated digital signal called the Spark Output (SPOUT). The PCM decodes the SPOUT signal and fires the next spark at the commanded spark target. The PIP signal is also used to supply a clean, inverted signal (PIP) for tachometer operation.

The PCM also serves as an electric switch for the coil primary circuit. When the switch closes, current flows and a magnetic field expands around the primary coil. When the switch opens, current flows and a magnetic field expands around the primary coil. When the switch opens, the field collapses and causes the secondary coil to fire the spark plugs at high voltage. In addition, and Ignition Diagnostic Monitor (IDM) signal is transmitted on each spark firing. This signal communicates information by pulse width modulation.

SYSTEM COMPONENTS

Crankshaft Timing Sensor

The crankshaft sensor, is a single hall effect magnetic device. Its provides base timing and rpm signals to by the DIS and EEC-IV modules.

Camshaft Sensor

The camshaft sensor, is a single hall effect magnetic device, which is activated by a single vane driven by the camshaft. This sensor provides CID information for the ignition coil and fuel synchronization. The sensor is in the location normally used for the distributor.

Ignition Coil Pack

The ignition coil pack contains six coil towers for 6-cylinder engine or two four tower coil packs for 8-cylinder engines. Each ignition coil fires 2 spark plugs simultaneously. The spark plug fired on the exhaust stroke uses very little of the ignition coil's stored energy.

DIS Ignition Module

On vehicles through 1995, the DIS ignition module receives the PIP signal from the crankshaft sensor. The CID signal provides the DIS ignition module with the information required to synchronize the ignition coils so that they are fired in the proper sequence.

1996 vehicles do not have an ignition control module. The PCM determines the ignition coil ON and OFF times and calculates the desired spark angle signal.

Diagnosis and Testing

SERVICE PRECAUTIONS

- Always turn the key **OFF** and isolate both ends of a circuit whenever testing for short or continuity.
- Never measure voltage or resistance directly at the processor connector.
- Always disconnect solenoids and switches from the harness before measuring for continuity, resistance or energizing by way of a 12 volts source.
- When disconnecting connectors, inspect for damaged or pushed-out pins, corrosion, loose wires, etc. Service if required.

PRELIMINARY CHECKS

1. Visually inspect the engine compartment to ensure that all vacuum lines and spark plug wires are properly routed and securely connected.
2. Examine all wiring harnesses and connectors for insulation damage, burned, overheated, loose or broken conditions.
3. Be certain that the battery is fully charged and that all accessories should be **OFF** during the diagnosis.

Ignition Coil Pack

REMOVAL & INSTALLATION

See Figures 46, 47 and 48

1. Turn the ignition key **OFF** and disconnect the negative battery cable.
2. Detach the electrical harness connector(s) from the ignition coil pack and the radio ignition interference capacitors.
3. Disconnect the spark plug wires by squeezing the locking tabs and twisting while pulling upward to release the coil boot retainers.

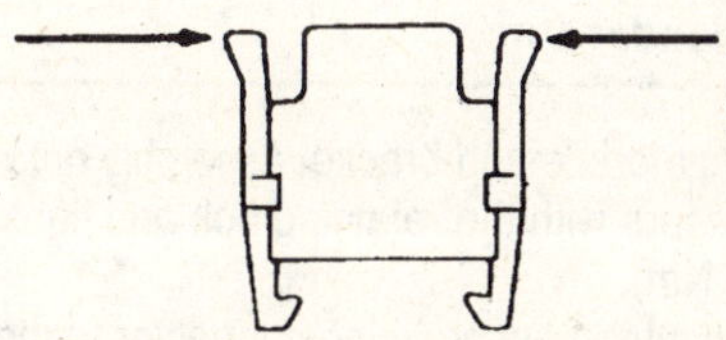

Fig. 46 You must squeeze the locking tabs on the spark plug wires to remove them from the coil

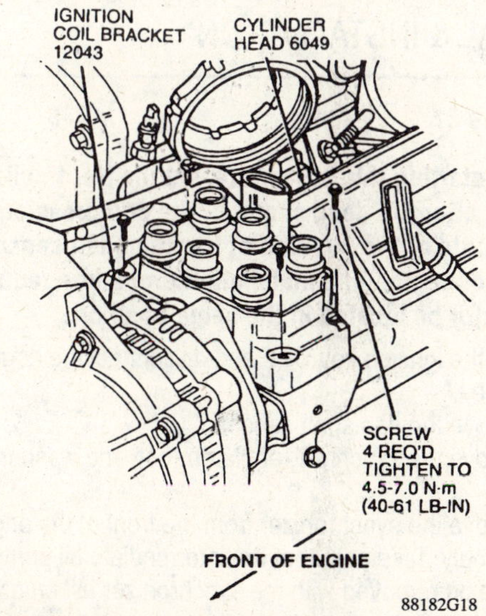

Fig. 47 Unfasten the screws, then remove the ignition coil — 1995 3.8L SC engine shown

4. Unfasten the ignition coil pack mounting screws, then remove the coil pack and radio ignition interference capacitors, if equipped.

If equipped, save the radio ignition interference capacitors for reinstallation with the ignition coils.

To install:

5. Position the coil pack and radio ignition interference capacitor (if equipped) to the mounting bracket. Secure with the retaining screws and tighten to 40–62 inch lbs. (5–7 Nm).

Apply a suitable silicone dielectric compound to the spark plug wire boots before connecting them to the coil.

6. Attach each spark plug wire to the ignition coil. Make sure the boots are properly seated.
7. Connect the engine control sensor wiring to the ignition coils and, if equipped, radio ignition interference capacitor.
8. Connect the negative battery cable.

Be sure to place some dielectric compound into each spark plug boot prior to installation of the spark plug wire.

DIS Ignition Module/Ignition Control Module (ICM)

REMOVAL & INSTALLATION

Vehicles Through 1993

See Figure 49

1. Turn the ignition key **OFF** and disconnect the negative battery cable.
2. Detach both electrical connectors at the ignition module. It may be necessary to press down on the locking tabs (where it is stamped PUSH) to remove the connector.
3. Unfasten the ignition module mounting bolts, then remove the module from the vehicle.

To install:

4. Apply a uniform coat of about 1/32 in. (0.08mm) or silicone dielectric compound to the mounting surface of the ignition module.
5. Position the module, then install the mounting bolts. Tighten the mounting bolts to 22–30 inch lbs. (2.5–3.5 Nm).
6. Attach both electrical connectors to the ignition module.
7. Connect the negative battery cable.

1994–95 Vehicles

See Figure 50

1. Disconnect the negative battery cable.
2. Detach the engine control sensor wiring connector from the ignition control module by pressing down on the locking tab where it is stamped PUSH, and remove the connector.
3. Remove the ignition module and the module bracket from the front fender apron.
4. Unfasten the two ignition module retaining screws, then remove the ignition module form the module bracket.

To install:

5. Install the ignition module onto the module bracket. Tighten the retaining screws to 24–33 inch lbs. (2.7–3.7 Nm).

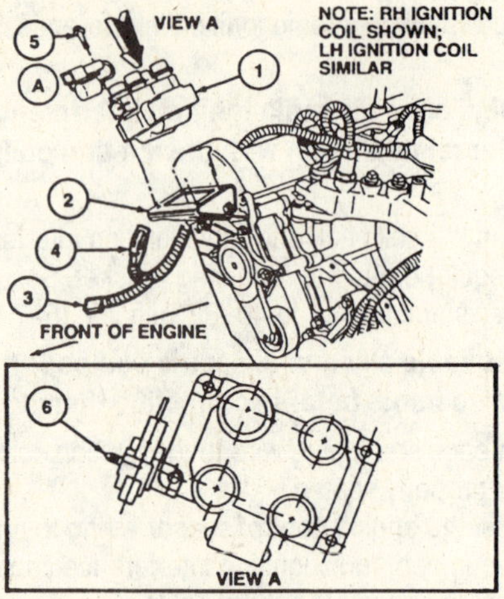

Item	Description
1	Ignition Coil (2 Req'd)
2	Ignition Coil Mounting Bracket (2 Req'd)
3	Radio Ignition Interference Capacitor Connector (Part of 12A581)
4	Ignition Coil Connector
5	Screw (8 Req'd)
6	Radio Ignition Interference Capacitor
A	Tighten to 5-7 N·m (40-61 Lb-In)

88182G19

Fig. 48 Ignition coil location and mounting — 1995 4.6L engine shown

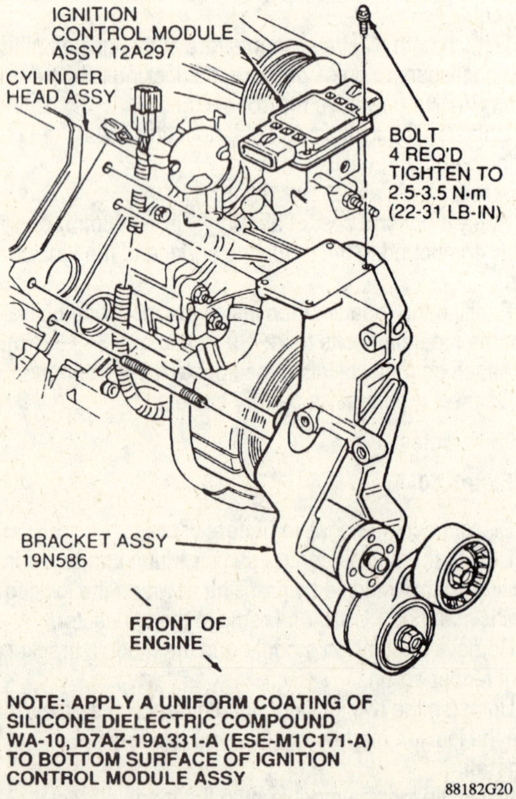

88182G20

Fig. 49 Ignition module (also referred to as DIS module or ICM) mounting — 1993 3.8L SC engine shown

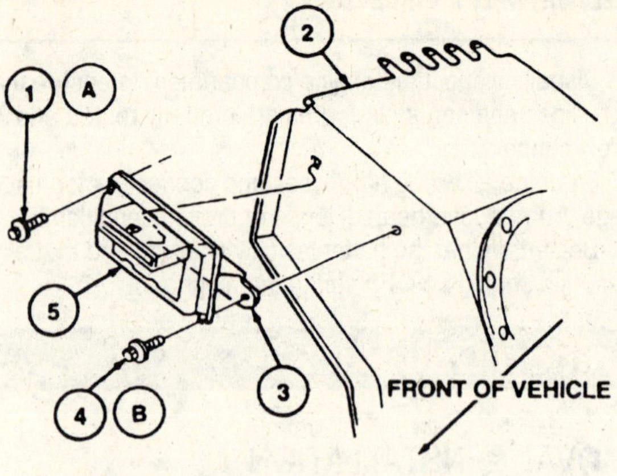

Item	Description
1	Screw (2 Req'd)
2	Front Fender Apron
3	Ignition Control Module Bracket
4	Bolt
5	Ignition Control Module
A	Tighten to 2.7-3.7 N·m (24-33 Lb-In)
B	Tighten to 4-5.6 N·m (35-50 Lb-In)

88182G21

Fig. 50 The ignition module on 1994-95 vehicles is mounted on the front fender apron

6. Position the ignition module and bracket assembly onto the front fender apron. Secure with the retaining bolt and tighten to 35-50 inch lbs. (4-5.6 Nm).
7. Attach the engine control sensor wiring connector to the ignition module.
8. Connect the negative battery cable.

Synchronizer Assembly

REMOVAL & INSTALLATION

➧ See Figure 51

➥ Prior to starting this procedure, set the No. 1 cylinder to 26 degrees after top dead center of the compression stroke. Then take note of the position of the camshaft sensor electrical connector. The installation procedure requires that the connector be located in the same position.

1. Turn the ignition key **OFF** and disconnect the negative battery cable.
2. Remove the camshaft sensor.
3. Remove the synchronizer clamp (bolt and washer assembly).
4. Remove the synchronizer from the front of the engine cover assembly. Take note that the intermediate oil pump drive shaft should be removed with the synchronizer assembly.

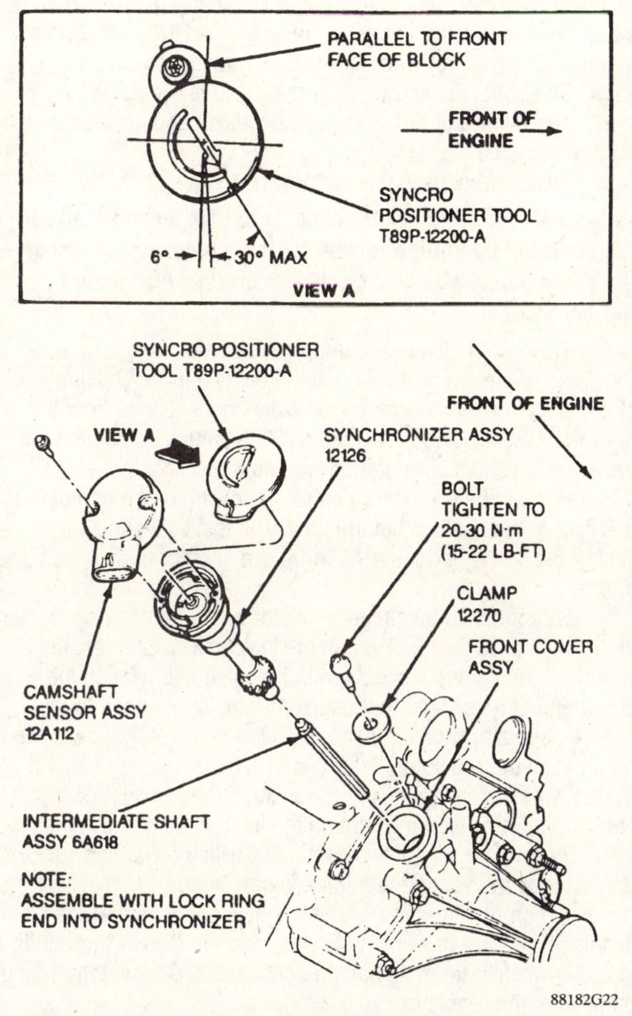

Fig. 51 Synchronizer assembly mounting. Note that 1994–96 vehicles do not utilize a synchronizer

To install:

If the replacement synchronizer does not contain a plastic locator cover tool, a special service tool such as synchro positioner T89P-12200-A or equivalent must be obtained prior to installation of the replacement synchronizer. Failure to follow this procedure will result in improper synchronizer alignment. This will result in the ignition system and fuel system being out of time with the engine, possibly causing engine damage.

5. If the replacement synchronizer does not contain a plastic locator cover tool, attach the synchro positioner tool T89P-12200-A or equivalent as follows:
   a. Engage the synchronizer vane into the radial slot of the tool. Rotate the tool on the synchronizer base until the tool boss engages the base notch.
   b. The cover tool should be square and in contact with the entire top surface of the synchronizer base.
6. Transfer the intermediate oil pump driveshaft from the old synchronizer to the new one.
7. Install the synchronizer assembly so that the gear engagement occurs when the arrow on the locator tool is pointed approximately 30 degrees counterclockwise from the front face of the engine block. This step will locate the camshaft sensor electrical connector in the pre-removal position.
8. Install the synchronizer base clamp, bolt and washer and torque the bolt to 15–22 ft. lbs. (20–30 Nm)
9. Remove the synchro positioner tool T89P-12200-A or equivalent.
10. Install the camshaft sensor.

➛ Make sure the camshaft sensor electrical connector is positioned properly (i.e. not contacting the A/C bracket or forward of the supercharger drive belt). Do not reposition the connector by rotating the synchronizer base. This will result in the ignition system and fuel system being out of time with the engine, possibly causing engine damage. Remove the synchronizer and repeat the installation procedure.

11. Connect the negative battery cable.

Crankshaft Position (CKP) Sensor

REMOVAL & INSTALLATION

For removal and installation of the Crankshaft Position (CKP) sensor, please refer to Section 4 of this manual.

Camshaft Position (CMP) Sensor

REMOVAL & INSTALLATION

For removal and installation of the Camshaft Position (CMP) sensor, please refer to Section 4 of this manual.

CHARGING SYSTEM

General Information

The automobile charging system provides electrical power for operation of the vehicle's ignition system, starting system and all electrical accessories. The battery serves as an electrical surge or storage tank, storing (in chemical form) the energy originally produced by the engine driven generator. The system also provides a means of regulating output to protect the battery from being overcharged and to avoid excessive voltage to the accessories.

The storage battery is a chemical device incorporating parallel lead plates in a tank containing a sulfuric acid/water solution. Adjacent plates are slightly dissimilar, and the chemical reaction of the two dissimilar plates produces electrical energy when the battery is connected to a load such as the starter motor. The chemical reaction is reversible, so that when the generator is producing a voltage (electrical pressure) greater than that produced by the battery, electricity is forced into the battery, and the battery is returned to its fully charged state.

Newer automobiles use alternating current generators or alternators, because they are more efficient, can be rotated at higher speeds, and have fewer brush problems. In an alternator, the field usually rotates while all the current produced passes only through the stator winding. The brushes bear against continuous slip rings. This causes the current produced to periodically reverse the direction of its flow. Diodes (electrical one way valves) block the flow of current from traveling in the wrong direction. A series of diodes is wired together to permit the alternating flow of the stator to be rectified back to 12 volts DC for use by the vehicle's electrical system.

The voltage regulating function is performed by a regulator. The regulator is often built in to the alternator; this system is termed an integrated or internal regulator.

Alternator Precautions

To avoid damage to the on-board computer, alternator and regulator, the following measures must be taken when working with the electrical system.

- If the battery is removed for any reason, make sure that it is reconnected with the correct polarity. Reversing the battery connections may result in damage to the one-way rectifiers.
- When utilizing a booster battery as a starting aid, always connect it as follows: positive to positive, and negative (booster battery) to a good ground on the engine of the car being started.
- Never use a fast charger as a booster to start cars with alternating current (AC) circuits
- When servicing the battery with a fast charger, always disconnect the car battery cables.
- Never attempt to polarize an alternator.
- Avoid long soldering times when replacing diodes or transistors. Prolonged heat is damaging to alternators.
- Do not use test lamps of more than 12 volts (V) for checking diode continuity.
- Do not short across or ground any of the terminals on the alternator.
- The polarity of the battery, alternator, and regulator must be matched and considered before making any electrical connections within the system.
- Never separate the alternator on an open circuit. Make sure that all connections within the circuit are clean and tight.
- Disconnect the battery terminals when performing any service on the electrical system. This will eliminate the possibility of accidental reversal of polarity.
- Disconnect the battery ground cable if arc welding is to be done on any part of the car.

Alternator

TESTING

There are many possible ways in which the charging system can malfunction. Often the source of a problem is difficult to diagnose, requiring special equipment and a good deal of experience. This is usually not the case, however, where the charging system fails completely and causes the dash board warning light to come on or the battery to become dead. To troubleshoot a complete system failure only two pieces of equipment are needed: a test light, to determine that current is reaching a certain point; and a current indicator (ammeter), to determine the direction of the current flow and its measurement in amps.This test works under three assumptions:

1. The battery is known to be good and fully charged.
2. The alternator belt is in good condition and adjusted to the proper tension.
3. All connections in the system are clean and tight.

➥ In order for the current indicator to give a valid reading, the car must be equipped with battery cables which are of the same gauge size and quality as original equipment battery cables.

4. Turn off all electrical components on the car. Make sure the doors of the car are closed. If the car is equipped with a clock, disconnect the clock by removing the lead wire from the rear of the clock. Disconnect the positive battery cable from the battery and connect the ground wire on a test light to the disconnected positive battery cable. Touch the probe end of the test light to the positive battery post. The test light should not light. If the test light does light, there is a short or open circuit on the car.
5. Disconnect the voltage regulator wiring harness connector at the voltage regulator. Turn on the ignition key. Connect the wire on a test light to a good ground (engine bolt). Touch the probe end of a test light to the ignition wire connector into the voltage regulator wiring connector. This wire corresponds to the **I** terminal on the regulator. If the test light goes on, the charging system warning light circuit is complete. If the test light does not come on and the warning light on the instrument panel is on, either the resistor wire, which is parallel with the warning light, or the wiring to the voltage regulator, is defective. If the test light does not come on and the warning light is not on, either the bulb is defective or the power supply wire form the battery through the ignition switch to the bulb has an open circuit. Connect the wiring harness to the regulator.
6. Examine the fuse link wire in the wiring harness from the starter relay to the alternator. If the insulation on the wire is cracked or split, the fuse link may be melted. Connect a test light to the fuse link by attaching the ground wire on the test light to an engine bolt and touching the probe end of the light to the bottom of the fuse link wire where it splices into the alternator output wire. If the bulb in the test light does not light, the fuse link is melted.
7. Start the engine and place a current indicator on the positive battery cable. Turn off all electrical accessories and make sure the doors are closed. If the charging system is working properly, the gauge will show a draw of less than 5 amps. If the system is not working properly, the gauge will show a draw of more than 5 amps. A charge moves the needle toward the battery, a draw moves the needle away from the battery. Turn the engine off.

➥ When the Message Center or electronic instrument cluster is initially powered-up (after a battery disconnect), the "computer" may be energized for as long as one minute causing a 0.25A current draw before returning to the normal 0.010–0.012A current draw. Therefore, it is important to allow at least one minute to pass (after ammeter hookup) before observing any current measurements.

8. Disconnect the wiring harness from the voltage regulator at the regulator at the regulator connector. Connect a male spade terminal (solderless connector) to each end of a jumper wire. Insert one end of the wire into the wiring harness connector which corresponds to the **A** terminal on the regulator. Insert the other end of the wire into the wiring harness connector which corresponds to the **F** terminal on the regulator. Position the connector with the jumper wire installed so that it cannot contact any metal surface under the hood. Position a current indicator gauge on the positive battery cable. Have an assistant start the engine. Observe the reading on the current indicator. Have your assistant slowly raise the speed of the engine to about 2,000 rpm or until the current indicator needle stops moving, whichever comes first. Do not run the engine for more than a short period of time in this condition. If the wiring harness connector or jumper wire becomes excessively hot during this test, turn off the engine and check for a grounded wire in the regulator wiring harness. If the current indicator shows a charge of about three amps less than the output of the alternator, the alternator is working properly. If the previous tests showed a draw, the voltage regulator is defective. If the gauge does not show the proper charging rate, the alternator is defective.

REMOVAL & INSTALLATION

Vehicles Through 1993

➧ **See Figures 52, 53, 54 and 55**

1. Disconnect the negative battery cable.
2. For all except side terminal alternators, disconnect the wire harness attachments from the integral alternator/regulator assembly.
3. Loosen the alternator pivot bolt, then remove the adjustment arm bolt from the alternator.
4. Disengage the alternator drive belt from the alternator pulley.
5. For side-terminal alternators, disconnect the wiring terminals from the back of the alternator. The stator and field wiring terminals are the push-on type. After depressing the lock tab, the push-on terminal should be pulled straight off the terminal to prevent damage.
6. Remove the alternator pivot bolt, then remove the alternator/regulator assembly.
7. If equipped, remove the alternator fan shield.

To Install:

8. Position the alternator/regulator assembly on the engine. Install the alternator pivot and adjuster arm bolts, but do not tighten the bolts until the belt is tensioned.
9. For side terminal alternators, connect the wiring terminals to the alternator. Tighten the nuts to the specifications shown in the accompanying figure.
10. Install the drive belt over the alternator pulley.
11. Adjust the belt tensioner, then tighten to the following specifications:
    a. 1983–88 vehicles: Tighten the adjusting bolt to 30–45 ft. lbs. (41–61 Nm) and the pivot bolt to 50–70 ft. lbs. (68–94 Nm).
    b. 1989–92 3.8L (base) engine: Tighten the adjustment arm bolt to 31–44 ft. lbs. (41–61 Nm) and the pivot bolt to 40–55 ft. lbs. (54–75 Nm).
    c. 1989–93 3.8L SC and 5.0L engines: Tighten the adjustment arm bolt to 15–22 ft. lbs. (20–30 Nm) and the pivot bolt to 30–40 ft. lbs. (40–55 Nm).
    d. 1993 3.8L (base) engine: Tighten the adjustment arm bolt to 23–31 ft. lbs. (30–43 Nm) and the pivot bolt to 45–56 ft. lbs. (61–77 Nm).
12. Check the belt tension using Belt Tensioner Gauge T63L-8620-A or equivalent. Apply pressure to the alternator front housing only when adjusting belt tension.
13. If not already done, connect the alternator wire harness.
14. If equipped, attach the alternator fan shield to the alternator assembly.
15. Connect the negative battery cable.

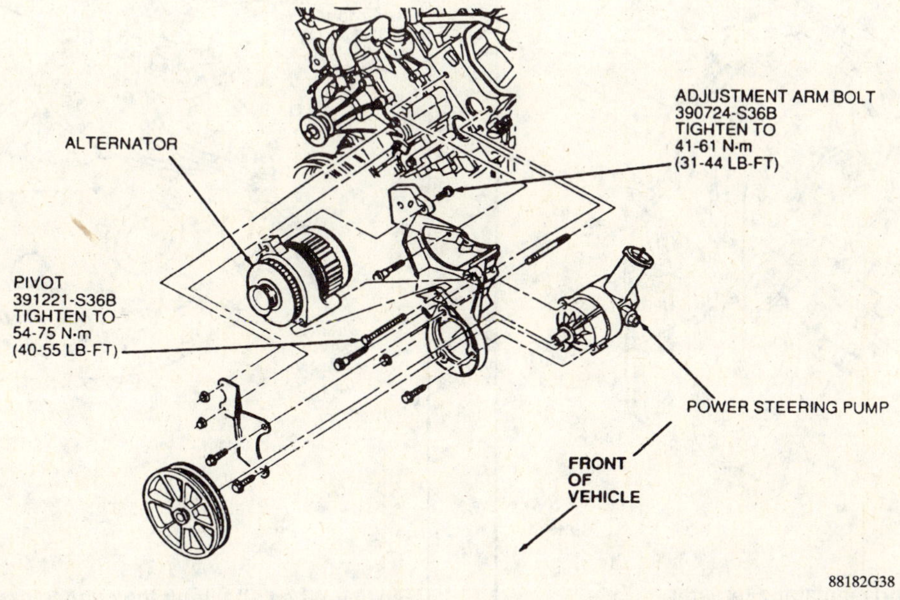

Fig. 52 Integral regulator/external fan alternator mounting — 1992 3.8L base engine shown

1994-96 Vehicles

See Figures 56, 57 and 58

1. Disconnect the negative battery cable.
2. Detach the wire harness attachments to the alternator/voltage regulator assembly.
3. Disengage the drive belt from the alternator pulley.
4. On the 4.6L engine, unfasten the alternator mounting bolts, then remove the alternator mounting bracket. On the 3.8L (non-SC) engines, remove the alternator mounting bolt.
5. Remove the alternator mounting bolts or pivot bolt, as applicable, then remove the alternator from the vehicle.

To install:

6. Position the alternator on the engine.
7. On the 3.8L SC engine, install the alternator pivot and upper mounting bolts but do not tighten the bolts until the drive belt is installed.
8. On the 4.6L engine, install the mounting bolts. Tighten the bolts to 15-22 ft. lbs. (20-30 Nm). On the 3.8L (non-SC) engines, install the pivot bolt. Tighten the pivot bolt to 30-40 ft. lbs. (40-55 Nm).
9. On the 4.6L engine, install the alternator mounting bracket and retaining bolts. Tighten the bolts to 70-106 inch lbs. (8-12 Nm). On the 3.8L (non-SC) engine, install the alternator mounting bolt and tighten to 15-22 ft. lbs. (20-30 Nm).
10. Install the drive belt over the alternator pulley.
11. On the 3.8L SC engines, tighten the upper alternator mounting bolts to 30-40 ft. lbs. (40-55 Nm) and the pivot bolt to 40-53 ft. lbs.)
12. Attach the engine control sensor wiring to the alternator/voltage regulator. Tighten the output terminal nut to 80-97 inch lbs. (9-11 Nm).
13. Connect the negative battery cable.

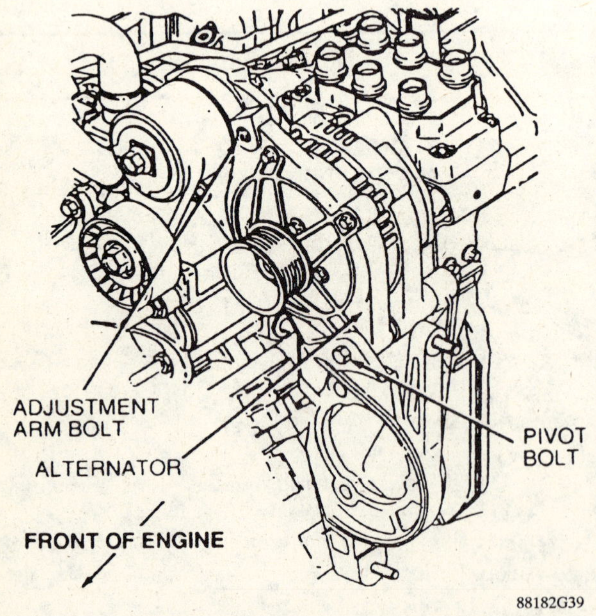

Fig. 53 Internal fan and regulator alternator mounting — 1993 3.8L SC engine shown

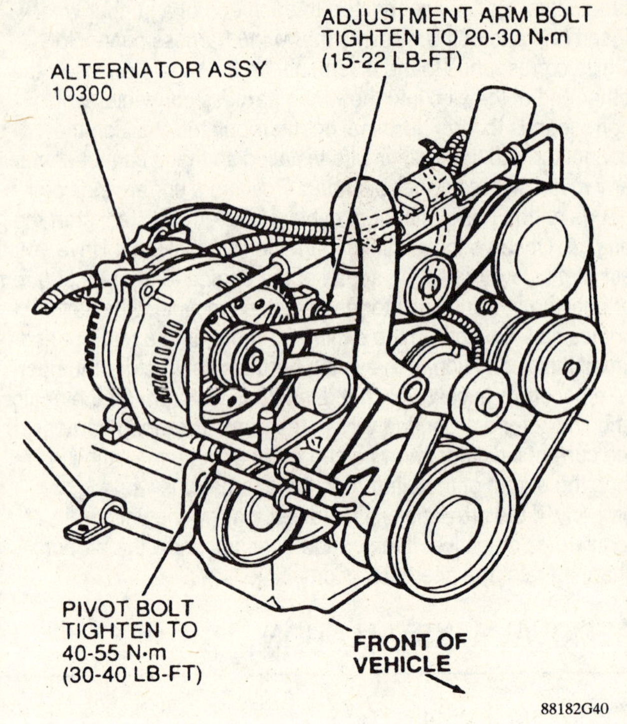

Fig. 54 Integral rear mounting regulator and internal fan alternator — 1992 5.0L engine shown

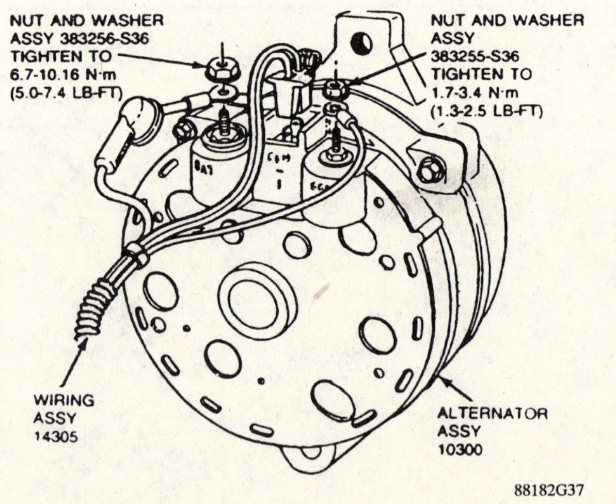

Fig. 55 When attaching the connectors on side-terminal alternators, make sure to tighten the nuts to specification

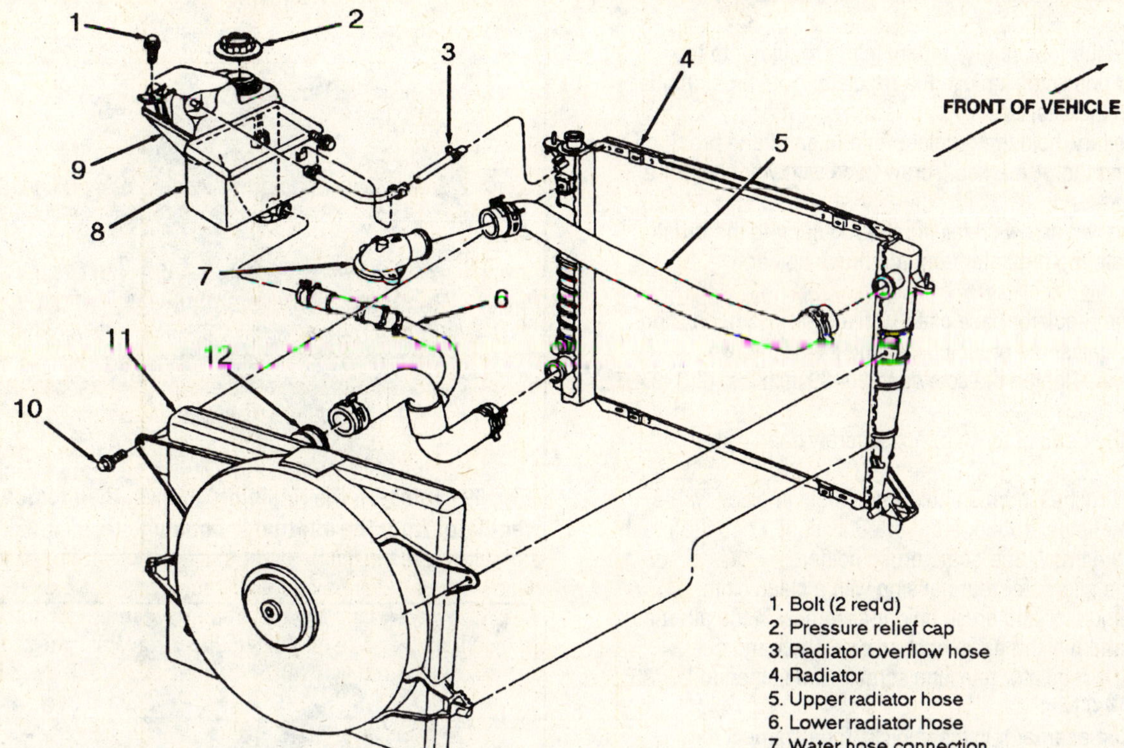

1. Bolt (2 req'd)
2. Pressure relief cap
3. Radiator overflow hose
4. Radiator
5. Upper radiator hose
6. Lower radiator hose
7. Water hose connection
8. Power distribution box
9. Radiator coolant recovery reservoir
10. Bolt (2 req'd)
    Tighten to 5.2-7.2 Nm
    (46-64 lb. in.)
11. Cooling fan motor and shroud assembly
12. Oil filter adapter

88183G41

Fig. 56 Alternator location and mounting — 1995 3.8L (non-SC) engine shown

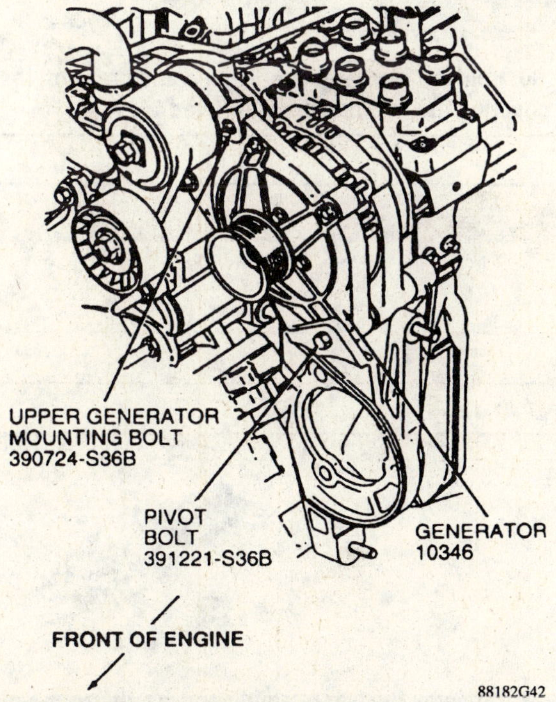

Fig. 57 Location of the alternator mounting and pivot bolts — 1995 3.8L SC engine shown

Voltage Regulator

REMOVAL & INSTALLATION

Electronic Regulator

1. Remove the battery ground cable. On models with the regulator mounted behind the battery, it is necessary to remove the battery hold-down, and move the battery.
2. Remove the regulator mounting screws.
3. Disconnect the regulator from the wiring harness.

To install:

4. Mount the regulator to the regulator mounting plate. The radio suppression condenser mounts under one mounting screw; the ground lead under the other mounting screw. Tighten the mounting screws.
5. If the battery was moved to gain access to the regulator, position the battery and install the hold-down. Connect the battery ground cable, and test the system for proper voltage regulation.

Integral Regulator

➧ **See Figures 59, 60, 61, 62, 63 and 64**

1. Disconect the battery ground cable.

2. Remove the alternator from the engine as described previously.

3. Remove the four screws retaining the regulator to the alternator rear housing. Remove the regulator, with brush holder attached, from the alternator.

4. If necessary, hold the regulator in one hand and break off the tab covering the, **A** marked, screw head with you hand or a prytool, if necessary.

5. Remove two screws retaining the regulator to the brush holder. Separate the regulator from the brush holder.

To Install:

6. Wipe the regulator base plate with a clean cloth, position the regulator against the brush holder and install the two retaining screws. Tighten the screws to 20–30 inch lbs. (2.3–3.4 Nm).

7. Cover the head of the **A** terminal screw head with electrical tape.

8. Locate brushes in brush holder and hold in place with a thin, flat piece of steel, rubber band or equivalent. Loop the brush leads toward the brush end of the brush holder.

9. Wipe the alternator rear housing with a clean cloth. Position the regulator and brush holder assembly in the alternator rear housing and pull the piece of steel or rubberband out.

10. Install the regulator retaining screws and tighten to 25–35 inch lbs. (2.8–4.0 Nm).

11. Install the alternator in the vehicle, then connect the negative battery cable.

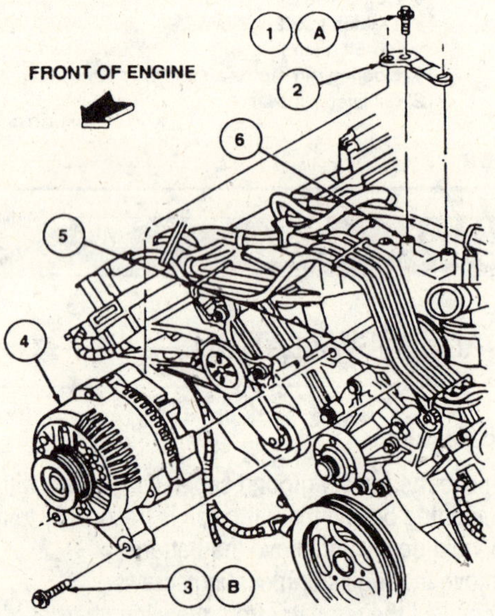

Item	Description
1	Generator Mounting Bracket Bolt (3 Req'd)
2	Generator Mounting Bracket
3	Generator Mounting Bolt (2 Req'd)
4	Generator
5	Cylinder Block
6	Intake Manifold
A	Tighten to 8-12 N·m (71-106 Lb-In)
B	Tighten to 20-30 N·m (15-22 Lb-Ft)

88182G43

Fig. 58 Alternator/regulator assembly mounting — 1995 4.6L engine shown

88182P06

Fig. 59 Unfasten the retaining screws, then remove the regulator from the alternator housing

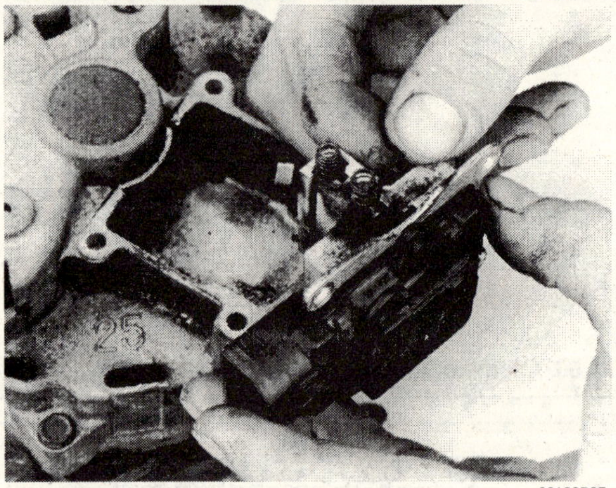

88182P07

Fig. 60 Hold the regulator in one hand and break off the tab covering the, A-marked, screw head

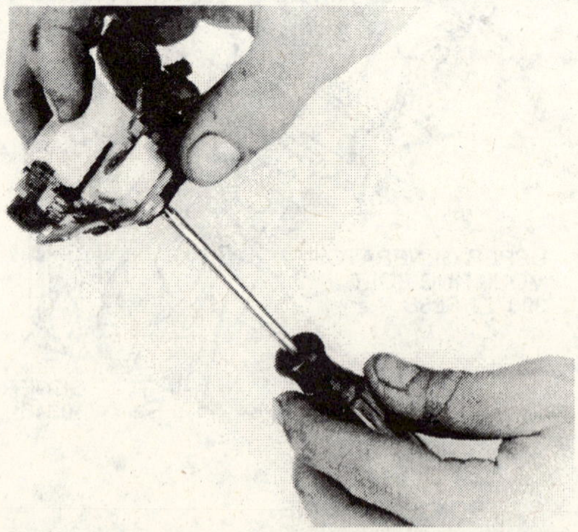

88182P08

Fig. 61 Unfasten the two retaining screws, then separate the regulator from the brush holder

88182P09

Fig. 62 Hold the brushes in place the brush holder with a rubber band, then position in the alternator housing

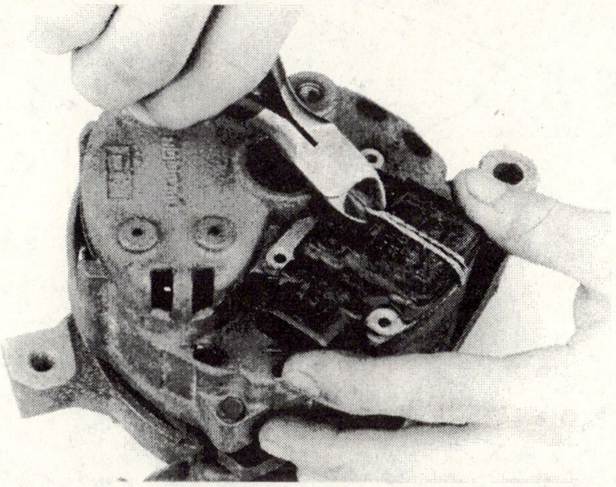

88182P10

Fig. 63 Use a suitable tool to cut the rubber band, . . .

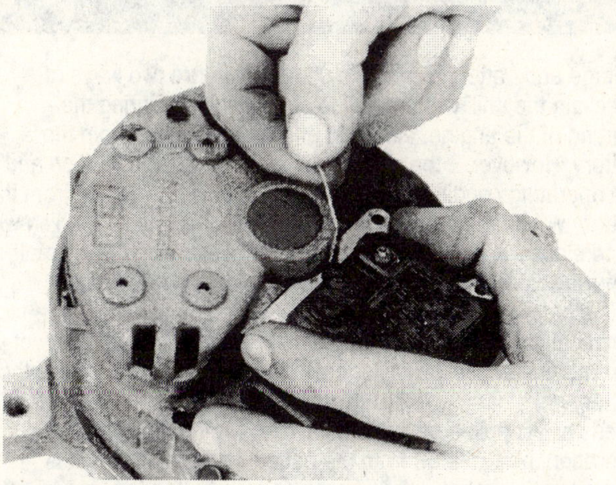

88182P11

Fig. 64 . . . then pull the rubber band from the alternator housing

Battery

REMOVAL & INSTALLATION

See Figures 65, 66, 67 and 68

1. Disconnect the negative, the the positive battery cables.

A mixture of baking soda and water will neutralize any battery acid corroded around the terminals.

2. Clean the battery terminals using an acid neutralizing solution and terminal cleaning brush.
3. Remove the hold-down screws/spacer retaining bolt, then remove the hold-down spacer from the battery tray.
4. Lift the battery from the vehicle. Using a suitable battery carrier may make the job of lifting the battery from the engine compartment easier.

To install:

5. Clean the cable terminals and battery hold-down clamp with a wire brush. Replace all cables or parts that are worn or frayed.
6. Clean the battery tray with a wire brush and scraper.
7. Place the battery in the tray with the positive and negative terminals in the same position as the previous battery. Tighten the retaining bolts/screws to 36–48 inch lbs. (4–6 Nm), but be careful not to overtighten the retainers.

When the battery is disconnected and reconnected, some abnormal driving symptoms may occur while the PCM relearns its adaptive strategy. The vehicle may need to be driven 10 miles or more to relearn the strategy.

8. Secure the positive, then the negative battery cables, being sure not to over tighten the cables. Apply petroleum jelly to the terminals. This will prevent buildup of oxidized acid on the terminals and the cable ends.
9. If not already done, install and tighten the nuts of the battery box.

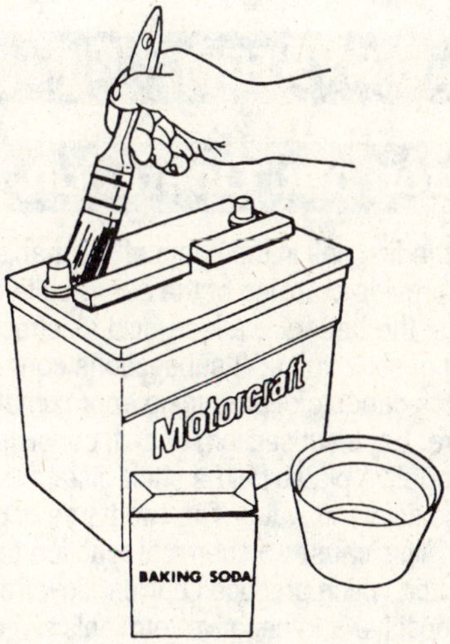

88182G44

Fig. 65 Clean the terminals with a baking soda and water solution to neutralize any battery acid

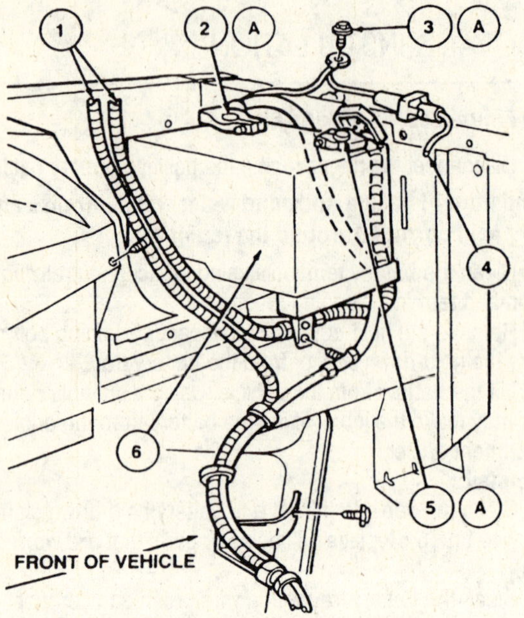

Item	Description
1	Positive Battery Cable
2	Battery Ground Cable
3	Screw
4	PCM Ground (Part of 12A581)
5	Positive Battery Cable Terminal (Part of 14300)
6	Battery
A	Tighten to 6-10 N·m (4-7 Lb-Ft)

88182G45

Fig. 66 View of the battery mounting — 1995 vehicle shown

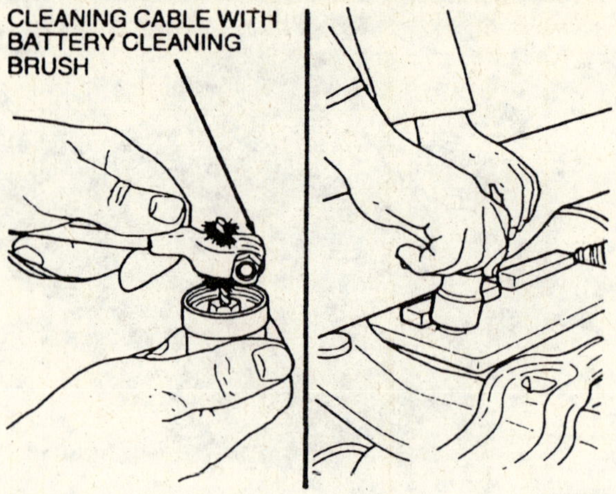

88182G46

Fig. 67 Make sure thoroughly clean the cables and cable terminals

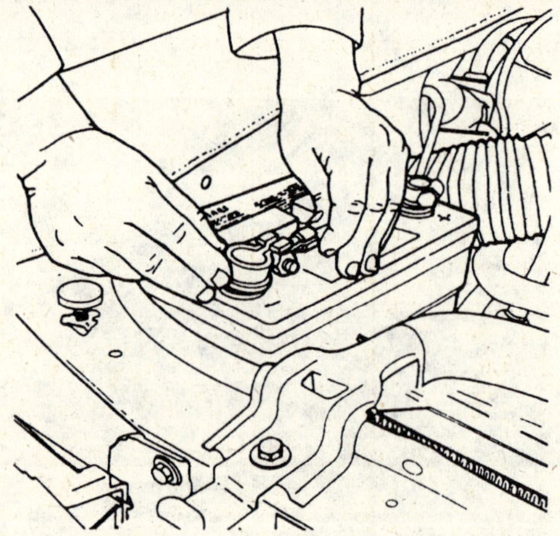

88182G47

Fig. 68 Secure the cables over the terminals, but DO NOT overtighten

STARTING SYSTEM

Description and Operation

The battery is the first link in the chain of mechanisms which work together to provide cranking of the automobile engine. In most modern cars, the battery is a lead-acid electrochemical device consisting of six 2 volt (2V) subsections connected in series so the unit is capable of producing approximately 12V of electrical pressure. Each subsection, or sell, consists of a series of positive and negative plates held a short distance apart in a solution of sulfuric acid and water. The two types of plates are of dissimilar metals. This causes a chemical reaction to be set up, and it is this reaction which produces current flow from the battery when its positive and negative terminals are connected to an electrical appliance such as a lamp or motor. The continued transfer of electrons would eventually convert the sulfuric acid in the electrolyte to water, and make the two plates identical in chemical composition. As electrical energy is removed from the battery, its voltage output tend to drop. Thus, measuring battery voltage and battery electrolyte composition are two ways of checking the ability of the unit to supply power. During the starting of the engine, electrical energy is removed from the battery. However, if the charging circuit is in good condition and the operating conditions are normal, the power removed from the battery will be replaced by the generator (or alternator) which will force electrons back through the battery, reversing the normal flow, and restoring the battery to its original chemical state.

The battery and starting motor are linked by very heavy electrical cables designed to minimize resistance to the flow of current. Generally, the major power supply cable that leaves the battery goes directly to the starter, while other electrical system needs are supplied by a smaller cable. During the starter operation, power flows from the battery to the starter and is grounded through the car's frame and the battery's negative ground strap.

The starting motor is a specially designed, direct current electric motor capable of producing a very great amount of power for its size. One thing that allows the motor to produce a great deal of power is its tremendous rotating speed. It drives the engine through a tiny pinion gear (attached to the starter's armature), which drives the very large flywheel ring gear at a greatly reduced speed. Another factor allowing it to produce so much power is that only intermittent operation is required of it. Thus, little allowance for air circulation is required, and the windings can be built into a very small space.

The starter solenoid is a magnetic device which employs the small current supplied by the starting switch circuit of the ignition switch. This magnetic action moves a plunger which mechanically engages the starter and electrically closes the heavy switch which connects it to the battery. The starting switch circuit consists of the starting switch contained within the ignition switch, a transmission neutral safety switch or clutch pedal switch, and the wiring necessary to connect these with the starter solenoid or relay.

A pinion, which is a small gear, is mounted to a one-way drive clutch. this clutch is splined to the starter armature shaft. When the ignition switch is moved to the start position, the solenoid plunger slides the pinion toward the flywheel ring gear via a collar and spring. If the teeth on the pinion and flywheel match properly, the pinion will engage the flywheel immediately. If the gear teeth butt one another, the spring will be compressed and will force the gears to mesh as soon as the starter turns far enough to allow them to do so. As the solenoid plunger reaches the end of its travel, it closes the contacts that connect the battery and starter and then the engine is cranked.

As soon as the engine starts, the flywheel ring gear begins turning fast enough to drive the pinion at an extremely high rate of speed. At this point, the one-way clutch begins allowing the pinion to spin faster that the starter shaft so that the starter will not operate at excessive speed. When the ignition switch is released from the starter position, the solenoid is de-energized, and a spring contained within the solenoid assembly pulls the gear out of mesh and interrupts the current flow to the starter.

Some starters employ a separate relay, mounted away from the starter, to switch the motor and solenoid current on and off. The relay thus replaces the solenoid electrical switch, but does not eliminate the need for a solenoid mounted on the starter used to mechanically engage the starter drive gears. The relay is used to reduce the amount of current the starting switch must carry.

All 1983-89 engines use a positive engagement starter which is activated via a remotely mounted relay. In 1990, only the Cougar with the 3.8L engine used the positive engagement starter. All other models use a gear reduced permanent magnet starter with an integral relay (solenoid). Beginning is 1991, all engines and models use the gear reduced starter.

The positive engagement starter system employs a starter relay (solenoid), usually mounted inside the engine compartment on a fender wall, to transfer battery current to the starter. The relay is activated by the ignition switch and, when engaged, it creates a direct current from the battery to the starter windings. Simultaneously, the armature begins to turn the starter drive is pushed out to engage the flywheel.

In the integral relay (solenoid) actuated starter system, battery current is first directed to a relay which is mounted on the starter case. The current closes the relay's contacts, which engages the drive pinion and directs current to the coil windings, causing the armature to rotate. While this system does not need a starter relay, some models were nevertheless equipped with one in order to simplify assembly procedures. These vehicles also have a connector link attached to the relay, which provides a hook up for the relay wire.

Starter

TESTING

Load Test

➧ See Figure 69

➥ Conduct this test if the starter motor cranks slowly and also to compare current to specifications.

1. Connect Rotunda Starting and Charging Tester (VAT-40) 070 00005 or equivalent and shown in the accompanying figure. Make sure that current is not flowing through ammeter and heavy duty carbon pile rheostat portion of the circuit (rheostat at maximum counterclockwise position).

➥ Make sure the ignition switch is in the OFF position and the S-terminal connector has been removed so the engine does not start.

2. Place the transmission in **NEUTRAL** (manual) or **PARK** (automatic). Crank the engine with the ignition switch **OFF** and determine the exact reading on a voltmeter. This test is accomplished by detaching the push-on connector S at the starter solenoid and by connecting a remote control starter switch from the positive battery terminal to the S-terminal of the starter solenoid.
3. Stop cranking the engine. Reduce the resistance of the carbon pile until the voltmeter indicates the same reading as that obtained while the starter motor cranked the engine. The ammeter will indicate starter current draw under load. Compare with the specifications in the Starter Specification Chart found in this section.

No-Load Test

➧ See Figure 70

The starter no-load test will uncover such conditions as open or shorted windings, or rubbing starter motor armature. The starter can be tested at no load, on the test bench only.

****CAUTION**

Make sure the starter motor is securely mounted in a bench vise while energizing, as the starter will move or jump during the test.

➥ A remote control starter switch should be used in the S-circuit for turning the starter motor ON and OFF during testing.

1. Remove the starter from the vehicle and mount securely in a suitable bench vise.
2. Make the test connections with the Rotunda Starting and Charging Tester 078-00005 or equivalent cables connector to the starer motors, large enough to carry high current (the same as in the vehicle). The starter motor will run at no-load. Be sure that no current is flowing through the ammeter (rheostat at maximum counterclockwise position). Determine the exact reading on a voltmeter.
3. Disconnect the starter motor from the battery. Then reduce the resistance of the rheostat until the voltmeter indicated the same reading as than obtained while the starter motor was running. The ammeter will indicate starter motor no-load current draw. Compare the result with the Starter Specifications Chart, located in this section.

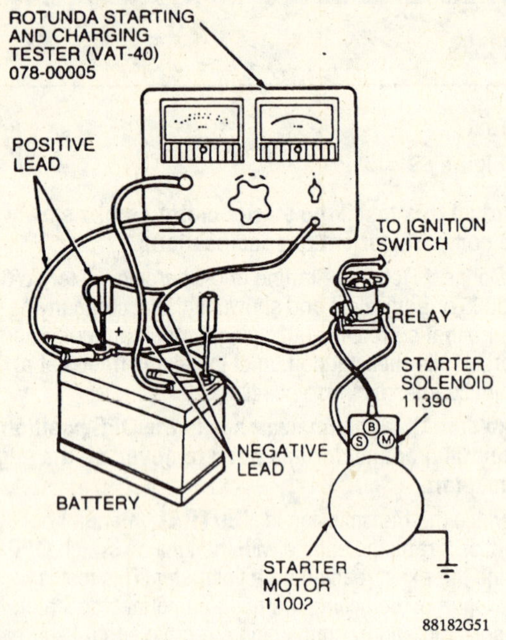

Fig. 69 Electrical connections for the starter "Load Test"

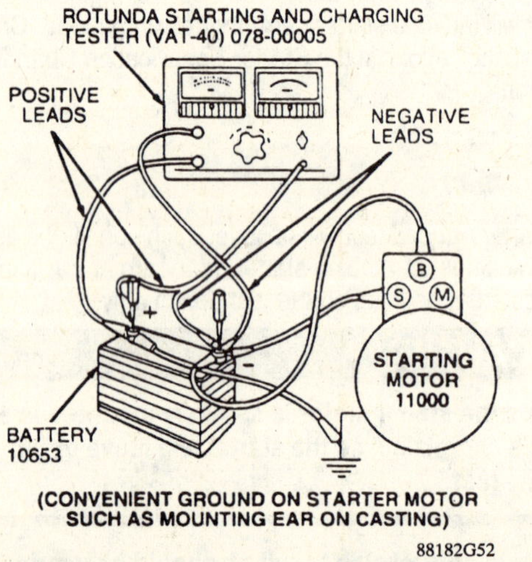

Fig. 70 Electrical connections for the starter "No-Load" test

4. If current exceeds specification, check for rubbing starter armature, bent output shaft, binding bushings, or shorts in the starter motor armature or brush holder.

REMOVAL & INSTALLATION

Positive Engagement Type Starter

➧ **See Figure 71 and 72**

1. Disconnect the negative battery cable.
2. Raise and safely support the vehicle with jackstands.
3. Tag and disconnect the wiring at the starter.
4. If necessary, turn the front wheels fully to the right. On some later models it will be necessary to remove the frame brace. On many models, it will be necessary to remove the two bolts retaining the steering idler arm to the frame to gain access to the starter.
5. Unfasten the starter mounting bolts, then remove the starter from the vehicle.

To install:

6. Position the starter motor to the engine, then secure with the retaining bolts. Tighten the mounting bolts to 12–15 ft. lbs. (16–20 Nm) on starters with 3 mounting bolts and 15–20 ft. lbs. (20–27 Nm) on starters with 2 mounting bolts.
7. If removed, tighten the idler arm retaining bolts to 28–35 ft. lbs. (38–47 Nm).
8. Connect the starter cable to the motor. Tighten to 70–110 inch lbs. (8–12 Nm).
9. Carefully lower the vehicle.
10. Connect the negative battery cable.

Gear Reduced Permanent Magnet Starter

➧ **See Figure 73**

****CAUTION**

When servicing the starter or performing any work around the starter motor, note that the heavy gauge input lead connected to the starter solenoid is hot at all times. Make sure the protective cap is installed over the terminal and is replaced after service.

1. Disconect the negative battery cable.
2. Raise and safely support the vehicle with jackstands.
3. Disconect starter cable and the push-on relay connector from solenoid.
4. Unfasten the starter retaining bolts, then remove the starter from the vehicle.

To install:

5. Position the starter motor to the engine and install the upper and lower bolts finger-tight. Begin with the top most bolt and work down, tighten the bolts to 15–20 ft. lbs. (20–27 Nm).
6. Attach the starter solenoid connector. Be careful to push straight on and make sure the connector locks in positions with a notable click or detent.
7. Install the starter cable nut to the starter solenoid B-terminal. Tighten to 80–124 inch lbs. (9–14 Nm). Replace the red starter solenoid safety cap.
8. Carefully lower the vehicle, then connect the negative battery cable.

RELAY (SOLENOID) REPLACEMENT

Remote Relay

➧ **See Figures 74 and 75**

1. Disconect the negative battery cable.
2. Tag and disconnect all wires from the relay.
3. Unfasten the two mounting screws attaching relay to fender, then remove the relay from the vehicle.
4. Installation is the reverse of removal. Tighten the relay retaining bolts to 70–110 inch lbs. (8.0–12.4 Nm).

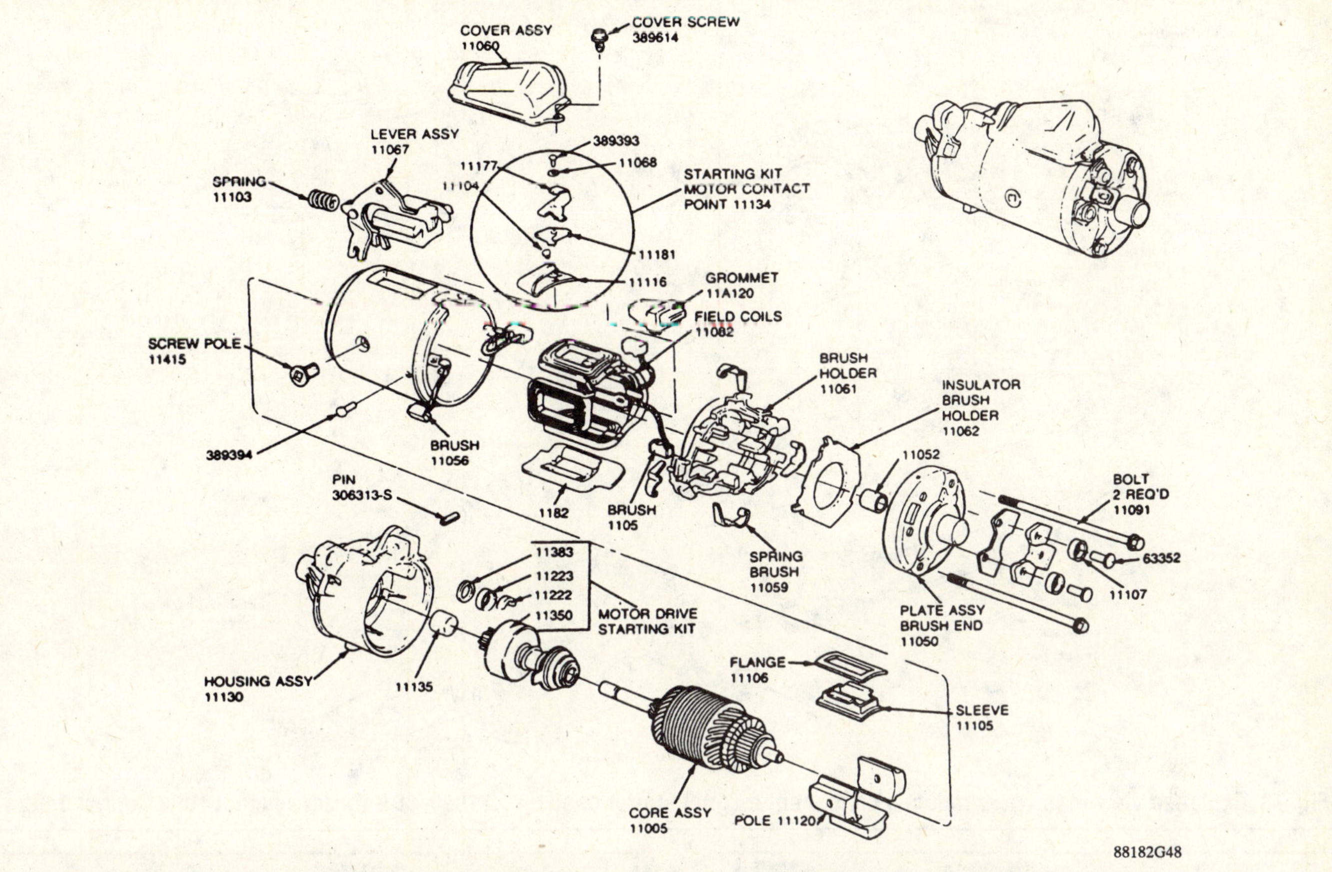

Fig. 71 Exploded view of a positive engagement starter — 1990 Cougar with 3.8L engine shown

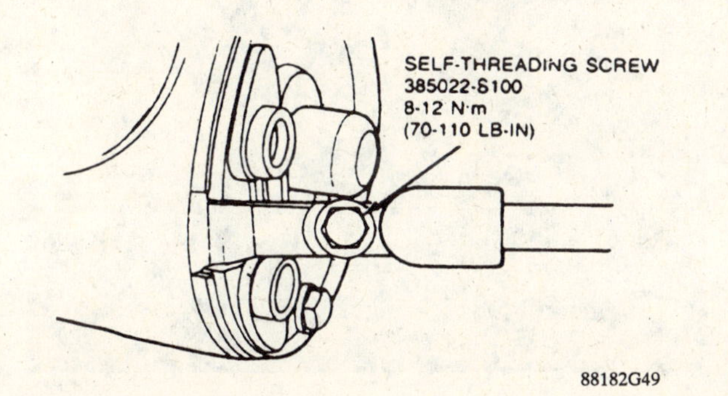

Fig. 72 Fasten the starter cable to the starter, then tighten to specification

Integral Relay

1. Disconnect the negative battery cable.
2. Remove the starter from the vehicle as outlined earlier in this section.
3. Detach the field coil connection from the solenoid motor terminal.
4. Remove the solenoid attaching screws, solenoid and plunger return spring. Rotate the solenoid 90° to remove it.

To install:

5. Install the return spring on the solenoid plunger and install the solenoid. Attach the two solenoid screws and tighten them to 84 inch lbs. (9.4 Nm). Apply a sealing compound to the junction of the solenoid case flange, gear and drive end housing.
6. Attach the motor field terminal to the solenoid, and tighten fasteners to 30 inch lbs. (3.4 Nm).
7. Install starter motor in vehicle as previously described.
8. Connect the negative battery cable.

Sending Units and Sensors

REMOVAL & INSTALLATION

Coolant Temperature

The coolant temperature sending unit is located on the, left side rear of the head on inline engines, and on front of the intake manifold on V6 and V8 engines. Disconnect the sensor wire and unscrew the sending unit, quickly thread the new unit into place (this will cause very little coolant fluid loss) tighten until the fluid stops leaking; to about 6–10 ft. lbs. (8–14 Nm). Connect the sensor wire and check for normal operation.

Oil Pressure

All Ford engines have the oil pressure sending unit mounted in the side of the engine block near the oil filter. A special socket is available to remove and install the unit. Disconnect the sensor wire, using the special socket remove the sending unit. Before installing the new sending unit, put Teflon® tape or equivalent on the threads, tighten unit to 10–15 ft. lbs. (14–20 Nm).

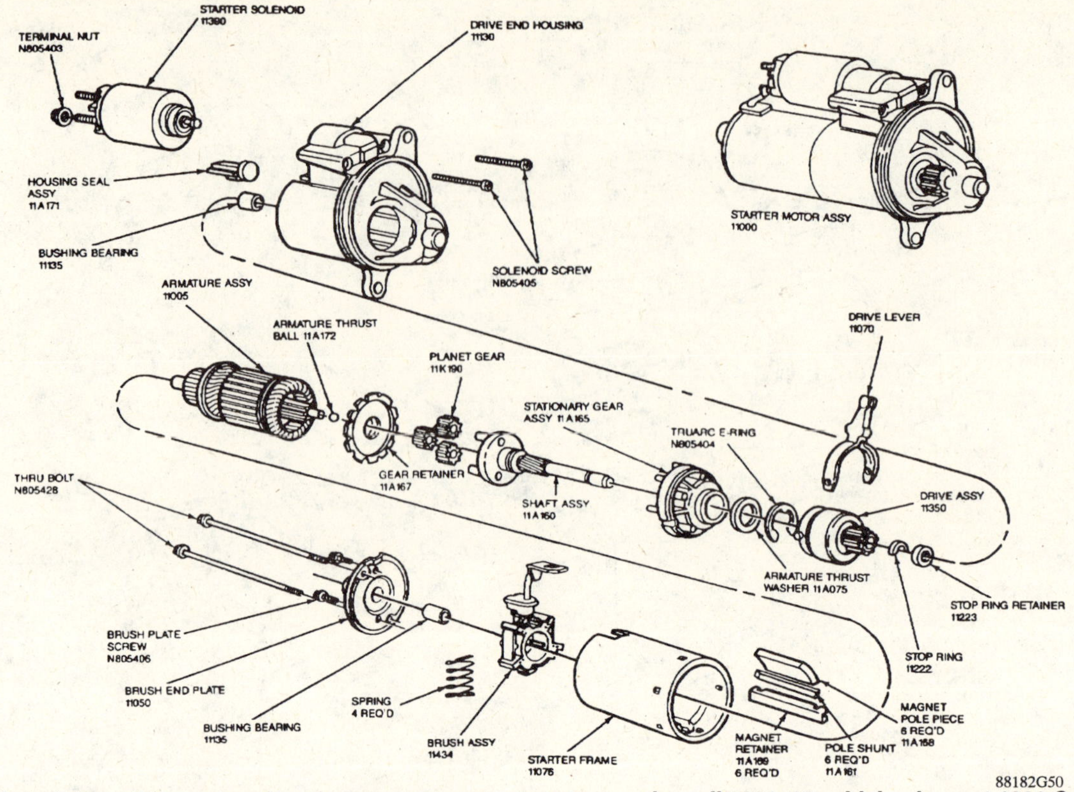

88182G50

Fig. 73 Exploded view of the gear reduced permanent magnet starter used on all 1990–96 vehicles (except 1990 Cougar 3.8L)

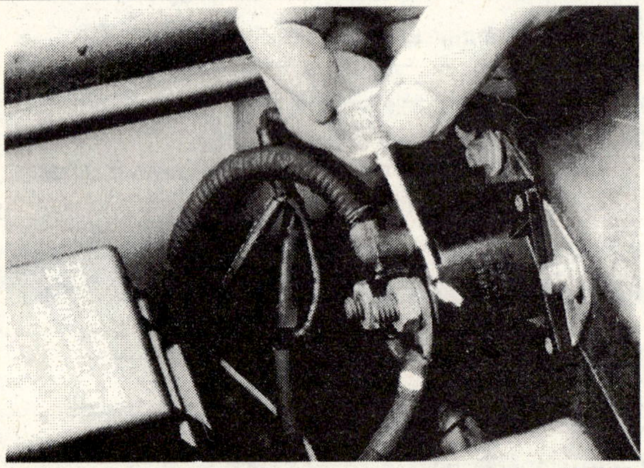
88182P12

Fig. 74 Make sure to tag or mark the connectors before detaching

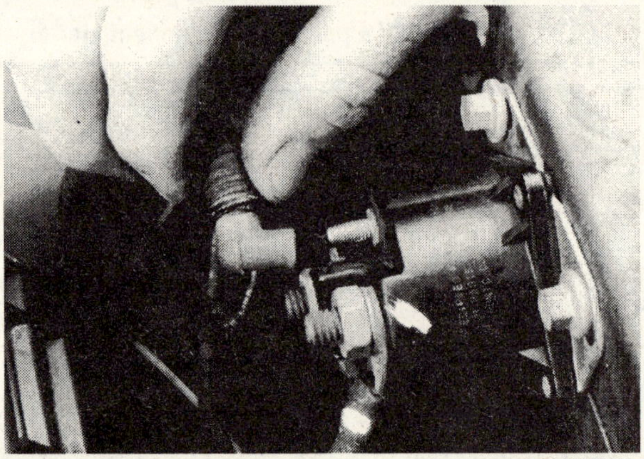
88182P13

Fig. 75 The remote mounted relay is located on the fender

STARTER SPECIFICATIONS

		Starter Motor					Starter Brushes	
Year	Diameter	Current Draw Under Normal Load	Normal Engine Cranking Speed	Min. Stall Torque @ 5 Volts	Max. Load	No Load	Mfg. Length	Spring Tension
1983-86	4 in.	150-250 Amps	180-250 RPM	9.5 ft. lbs. (12.9 Nm)	500 Amps	80	0.45 in. (11.4mm)	80 oz (22 N)
	4.5 in.	150-210 Amps	150-290 RPM	15.5 ft. lbs. (21 Nm)	670 amps	85	0.45 in. (11.4mm)	80 oz (22 N)
1987-89	4 in.	150-250 Amps	180-250 RPM	9.5 ft. lbs. (12.9 Nm)	500 Amps	80 Amps	0.45 in. (11.4mm)	80 oz (22 N)
1990-91	3 in.	140-200 Amps	130-180 RPM	11 ft. lbs. (15 Nm)	800	60-80 Amps	0.66 in (16.8mm)	64 oz (18 N)
1992-93	3 in.	130-220 Amps	140-220 RPM	11 ft. lbs. (15 Nm)	800 Amps	60-80 Amps	0.66 in. (16.8mm)	64 oz (18 N)
1994-96	3 in.	130-220 Amps	140-220 RPM	11 ft. lbs. (15 Nm)	800 Amps	60-80 Amps	0.55 in. (14mm)	64 oz (18 N)

88182CS1

3

ENGINE AND ENGINE OVERHAUL

ENGINE MECHANICAL

Engine Overhaul Tips

Most engine overhaul procedures are fairly standard. In addition to specific parts replacement procedures and specifications for your individual engine, this section is also a guide to acceptable rebuilding procedures. Examples of standard rebuilding practice are given and should be used along with specific details concerning your particular engine.

Competent and accurate machine shop services will ensure maximum performance, reliability and engine life. In most instances it is more profitable for the do-it-yourself mechanic to remove, clean and inspect the component, buy the necessary parts and deliver these to a shop for actual machine work.

On the other hand, much of the rebuilding work (crankshaft, block, bearings, piston rods, and other components) is well within the scope of the do-it-yourself mechanic's tools and abilities. You will have to decide for yourself the depth of involvement you desire in an engine repair or rebuild.

TOOLS

The tools required for an engine overhaul or parts replacement will depend on the depth of your involvement. With a few exceptions, they will be the tools found in a mechanic's tool kit (see Section 1 of this manual). More in-depth work will require some or all of the following:

- A dial indicator (reading in thousandths) mounted on a universal base
- Micrometers and telescope gauges
- Jaw and screw-type pullers
- Scraper
- Valve spring compressor
- Ring groove cleaner
- Piston ring expander and compressor
- Ridge reamer
- Cylinder hone or glaze breaker
- Plastigage®
- Engine stand

The use of most of these tools is illustrated in this chapter. Many can be rented for a one-time use from a local parts jobber or tool supply house specializing in automotive work.

Occasionally, the use of special tools is called for. See the information on Special Tools and the Safety Notice in the front of this book before substituting another tool.

INSPECTION TECHNIQUES

Procedures and specifications are given in this chapter for inspecting, cleaning and assessing the wear limits of most major components. Other procedures such as Magnaflux® and Zyglo® can be used to locate material flaws and stress cracks. Magnaflux® is a magnetic process applicable only to ferrous materials. The Zyglo® process coats the material with a fluorescent dye penetrant and can be used on any material.

Checking for suspected surface cracks can be more readily made using spot check dye. The dye is sprayed onto the suspected area, wiped off and the area sprayed with a developer. Cracks will show up brightly.

OVERHAUL TIPS

Aluminum has become extremely popular for use in engines, due to its low weight. Observe the following precautions when handling aluminum parts:

- Never hot tank aluminum parts (the caustic hot tank solution will eat the aluminum.
- Remove all aluminum parts (identification tag, etc.) from engine parts prior to the tanking.
- Always coat threads lightly with engine oil or anti-seize compounds before installation, to prevent seizure.
- Never overtorque bolts or spark plugs especially in aluminum threads.

Stripped threads in any component can be repaired using any of several commercial repair kits (Heli-Coil®, Microdot®, Keenserts®, etc.).

When assembling the engine, any parts that will be exposed to frictional contact must be prelubed to provide lubrication at initial start-up. Any product specifically formulated for this purpose can be used, but engine oil is not recommended as a prelube in most cases.

When semi-permanent (locked, but removable) installation of bolts or nuts is desired, threads should be cleaned and coated with Loctite® or another similar, commercial non-hardening sealant.

REPAIRING DAMAGED THREADS

➧ See Figures 1, 2, 3, 4 and 5

Several methods of repairing damaged threads are available. Heli-Coil® (shown here), Keenserts® and Microdot® are among the most widely used. All involve basically the same principle — drilling out stripped threads, tapping the hole and installing a prewound insert — making welding, plugging and oversize fasteners unnecessary.

Two types of thread repair inserts are usually supplied: a standard type for most inch coarse, inch fine, metric course and metric fine thread sizes and a spark lug type to fit most spark plug port sizes. Consult the individual tool manufacturer's catalog to determine exact applications. Typical thread repair kits will contain a selection of prewound threaded inserts, a tap (corresponding to the outside diameter threads of the insert) and an installation tool. Spark plug inserts usually differ because they require a tap equipped with pilot threads and a combined reamer/tap section. Most manufacturers also supply blister-packed thread repair inserts separately in addition to a master kit containing a variety of taps and inserts plus installation tools.

Before attempting to repair a threaded hole, remove any snapped, broken or damaged bolts or studs. Penetrating oil can be used to free frozen threads. The offending item can usually be removed with locking pliers or using a screw/stud extractor. After the hole is clear, the thread can be repaired, as shown in the series of accompanying illustrations and in the kit manufacturer's instructions.

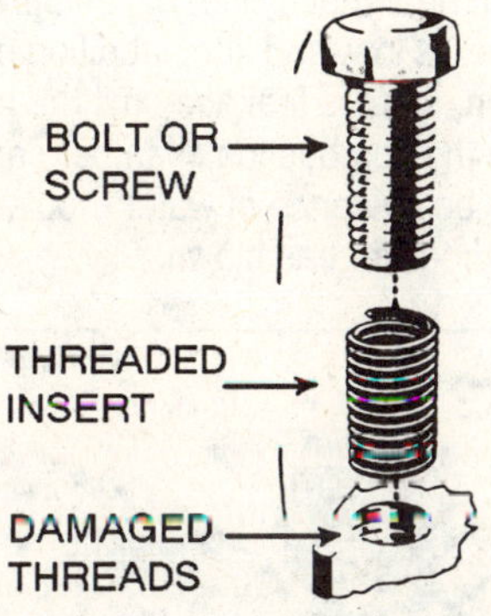

Fig. 1 Damaged bolt hole threads can be replaced with thread repair inserts

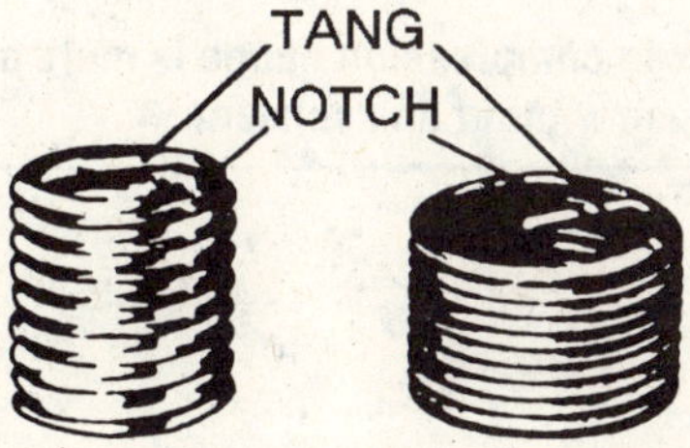

Fig. 2 Standard thread repair insert (left), and spark plug thread insert

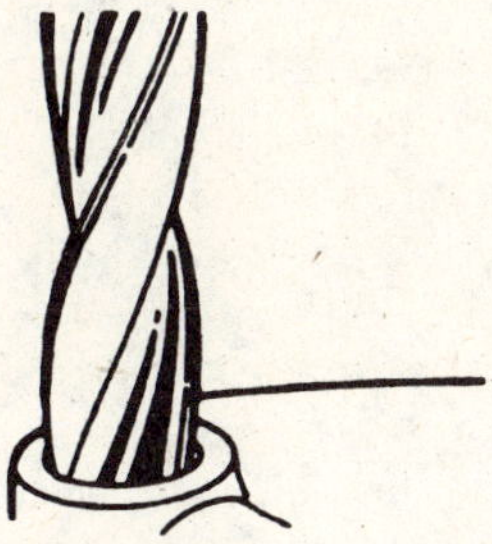

Fig. 3 Drill out the damaged threads with the specified size bit. Be sure to drill completely through the hole or to the bottom of a blind hole

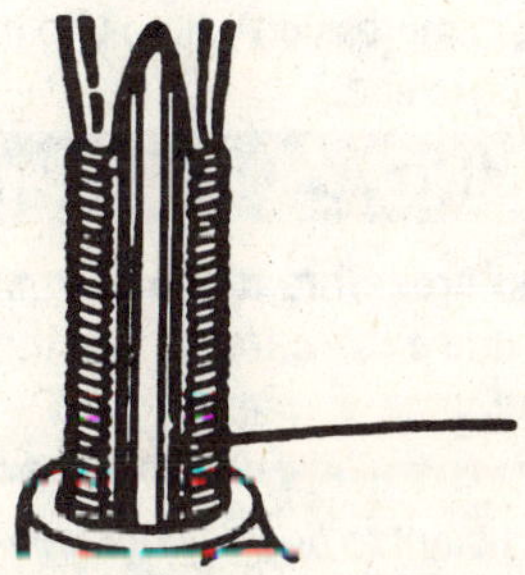

Fig. 4 Using the kit, tap the hole in order to receive the thread insert. Keep the tap well oiled and back it out frequently to avoid clogging the threads

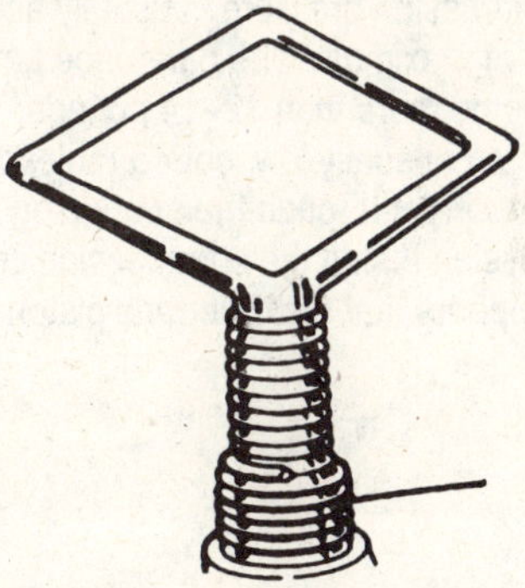

Fig. 5 Screw the insert onto the installer tool until the tang engages the slot. Thread the insert into the hole until it is $^1/_4$–$^1/_2$ turn below the top surface, then remove the tool and break off the tang using a punch

Checking Engine Compression

➧ See Figure 6

A noticeable lack of engine power, excessive oil consumption and/or poor fuel mileage measured over an extended period are all indicators of internal engine war. Worn piston rings, scored or worn cylinder bores, blown head gaskets, sticking or burnt valves and worn valve seats are all possible culprits here. A check of each cylinder's compression will help you locate the problems.

As mentioned in the Tools and Equipment section of Section 1, a screw-in type compression gauge is more accurate that the type you simply hold against the spark plug hole, although it takes slightly longer to use. It's worth it to obtain a more accurate reading. Follow the procedures below.

1. Warm up the engine to normal operating temperature.
2. Remove all the spark plugs.
3. Disconnect the high tension lead from the ignition coil.

4. On fully open the throttle either by operating the carburetor throttle linkage by hand or by having an assistant floor the accelerator pedal.

5. Screw the compression gauge into the no.1 spark plug hole until the fitting is snug.

****WARNING**

Be careful not to crossthread the plug hole. On aluminum cylinder heads use extra care, as the threads in these heads are easily ruined.

6. Ask an assistant to depress the accelerator pedal fully on both carbureted and fuel injected vehicles. Then, while you read the compression gauge, ask the assistant to crank the engine two or three times in short bursts using the ignition switch.

7. Read the compression gauge at the end of each series of cranks, and record the highest of these readings. Repeat this procedure for each of the engine's cylinders. Compare the highest reading of each cylinder to the compression pressure specification in the Tune-Up Specifications chart in Section 2. The specs in this chart are maximum values.

A cylinder's compression pressure is usually acceptable if it is not less than 80% of maximum. The difference between any two cylinders should be no more than 12–14 pounds.

8. If a cylinder is unusually low, pour a tablespoon of clean engine oil into the cylinder through the spark plug hole and repeat the compression test. If the compression comes up after adding the oil, it appears that the cylinder's piston rings or bore are damaged or worn. If the pressure remains low, the valves may not be seating properly (a valve job is needed), or the head gasket may be blown near that cylinder. If compression in any two adjacent cylinders is low, and if the addition of oil doesn't help the compression, there is leakage past the head gasket. Oil and coolant water in the combustion chamber can result from this problem. There may be evidence of water droplets on the engine dipstick when a head gasket has blown.

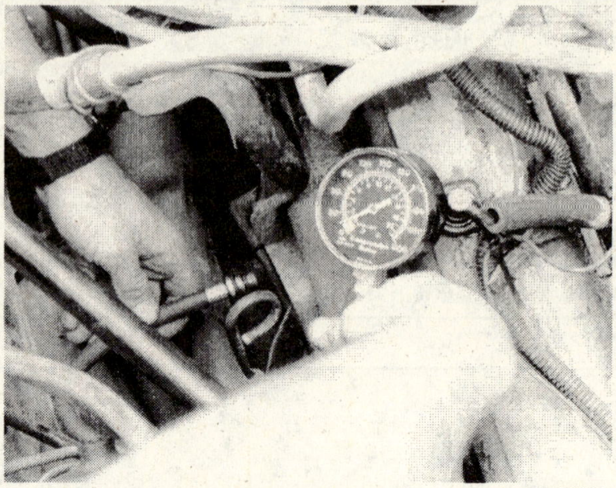

TCCS3801

Fig. 6 A screw-in compression gauge is more accurate and easier to use without an assistant

GENERAL ENGINE SPECIFICATIONS

Year	Engine ID/VIN	Engine Displacement Liters (cc)	Fuel System Type	Net Horsepower @ rpm	Net Torque @ rpm (ft. lbs.)	Net Bore x Stroke (in.)	Com-pression Ratio	Oil Pressure @ rpm
1983	W	2.3 (2300)	MFI-Turbo	145@4600	180@3600	3.78x3.13	8.0:1	40-60@2000
	3	3.8 (3802)	2 BBL	120@3600	250@1600	3.81x3.39	8.7:1	40-60@2000
	F	5.0 (4949)	2 BBL	132@3400	236@1800	4.00x3.00	8.4:1	40-60@2000
	F	5.0 (4949)	CFI	165@3200	250@1600	4.00x3.00	8.4:1	40-60@2000
1984	W	2.3 (2300)	MFI-Turbo	145@4600	180@3600	3.78x3.13	8.0:1	40-60@2000
	3	3.8 (3802)	2 BBL	120@3600	250@1600	3.81x3.39	8.7:1	40-60@2000
	F	5.0 (4949)	2 BBL	132@3400	236@1800	4.00x3.00	8.4:1	40-60@2000
	F	5.0 (4949)	CFI	165@3200	250@1600	4.00x3.00	8.4:1	40-60@2000
1985	W	2.3 (2300)	MFI-Turbo	145@4600	180@3600	3.78x3.13	8.0:1	40-60@2000
	3	3.8 (3802)	2 BBL	120@3600	250@1600	3.81x3.39	8.7:1	40-60@2000
	F	5.0 (4949)	2 BBL	132@3400	236@1800	4.00x3.00	8.4:1	40-60@2000
	F	5.0 (4949)	CFI	165@3200	250@1600	4.00x3.00	8.4:1	40-60@2000
1986	W	2.3 (2300)	MFI-Turbo	145@4600	180@3600	3.78x3.13	8.0:1	40-60@2000
	3	3.8 (3802)	2 BBL	120@3600	250@1600	3.81x3.39	8.7:1	40-60@2000
	3	3.8 (3802)	MFI	120@3600	250@1600	3.81x3.39	8.7:1	40-60@2000
	F	5.0 (4949)	2 BBL	132@3400	236@1800	4.00x3.00	8.4:1	40-60@2000
	F	5.0 (4949)	MFI	150@3200	270@1600	4.00x3.00	8.9:1	40-60@2000
1987	W	2.3 (2300)	MFI-Turbo	145@4600	180@3600	3.78x3.13	8.0:1	40-60@2000
	3	3.8 (3802)	MFI	120@3600	250@1600	3.81x3.39	8.7:1	40-60@2000
	F	5.0 (4949)	MFI	165@3200	250@1600	4.00x3.00	8.4:1	40-60@2000
1988	W	2.3 (2300)	MFI-Turbo	145@4600	180@3600	3.78x3.13	8.0:1	40-60@2000
	4	3.8 (3802)	MFI	120@3600	205@1600	3.81x3.39	8.7:1	40-60@2000
	F	5.0 (4949)	MFI	165@3200	250@1600	4.00x3.00	8.4:1	40-60@2000
1989	4	3.8 (3802)	MFI	120@3600	205@1600	3.81x3.39	8.7:1	40-60@2000
	R ①	3.8 (3802)	MFI	210@2000	315@2600	3.81x3.39	8.2:1	40-60@2000
	C ①	3.8 (3802)	MFI	210@2000	315@2600	3.81x3.39	8.2:1	40-60@2000
1990	4	3.8 (3802)	MFI	120@3600	205@1600	3.81x3.39	8.7:1	40-60@2000
	R ①	3.8 (3802)	MFI	210@2000	315@2600	3.81x3.39	8.2:1	40-60@2000
1991	4	3.8 (3802)	MFI	140@3800	215@2400	3.81x3.39	8.2:1	40-60@2000
	R ①	3.8 (3802)	MFI	210@2000	315@2600	3.81x3.39	8.2:1	40-60@2000
	T	5.0 (4949)	MFI	200@4000	275@3000	4.00x3.39	9.0:1	40-60@2000
1992	4	3.8 (3802)	MFI	140@3800	215@2400	3.81x3.39	8.2:1	40-60@2000
	R ①	3.8 (3802)	MFI	210@2000	315@2600	3.81x3.39	8.2:1	40-60@2000
	T	5.0 (4949)	MFI	200@4000	275@3000	4.00x3.39	9.0:1	40-60@2000
1993	4	3.8 (3802)	MFI	140@3800	215@2400	3.81x3.39	8.2:1	40-60@2000
	R ①	3.8 (3802)	MFI	210@2000	315@2600	3.81x3.39	8.2:1	40-60@2000
	T	5.0 (4949)	MFI	200@4000	275@3000	4.00x3.39	9.0:1	40-60@2000
1994	4	3.8 (3802)	SFI	140@3800	215@2400	3.81x3.39	8.2:1	40-60@2500
	R ①	3.8 (3802)	SFI	210@2000	315@2600	3.81x3.39	8.2:1	40-60@2500
	W	4.6 (4593)	SFI	②	③	3.55x3.5.4	9.0:1	20-45@2000
1995	4	3.8 (3802)	SFI	140@3800	215@2400	3.81x3.39	9.0:1	40-60@2500
	R ①	3.8 (3802)	SFI	210@2000	315@2600	3.81x3.39	8.2:1	40-60@2500
	W	4.6 (4593)	SFI	②	③	3.55x3.54	9.0:1	20-45@2000
1996	4	3.8 (3802)	SFI	145@4000	215@2750	3.81x3.39	9.0:1	40-60@2500
	W	4.6 (4593)	SFI	205@4250	280@3000	3.55x3.54	9.0:1	20-45@1500

BBL - Barrel carburetor
MFI - Multiport fuel injection
CFI - Central fuel injection
SFI - Sequential fuel injection

1: Supercharged
2: Single exhaust: 190@4250
Dual exhaust:: 210@4600
3: Single exhaust: 260@3200
Dual exhaust:: 270@3400

88183C01

VALVE SPECIFICATIONS

Year	Engine ID/VIN	Engine Displacement Liters (cc)	Seat Angle (deg.)	Face Angle (deg.)	Spring Test Pressure (lbs. @ in.)	Spring Installed Height (in.)	Stem-to-Guide Clearance (in.)		Stem Diameter (in.)	
							Intake	Exhaust	Intake	Exhaust
1983	W	2.3 (2300)	45	44	154@1.12	1.563	0.0010-0.0027	0.0015-0.0032	0.3420	0.3415
	3	3.8 (3802)	44.5	45.8	215@1.79	1.750	0.0010-0.0027	0.0015-0.0032	0.3420	0.3415
	F	5.0 (4949)	45	45	205@1.36	1.750	0.0010-0.0027	0.0015-0.0032	0.3420	0.3420
1984	W	2.3 (2300)	45	44	154@1.12	1.563	0.0010-0.0027	0.0015-0.0032	0.3420	0.3415
	3	3.8 (3802)	44.5	45.8	215@1.79	1.750	0.0010-0.0027	0.0015-0.0032	0.3420	0.3415
	F	5.0 (4949)	45	45	205@1.36	1.750	0.0010-0.0027	0.0015-0.0032	0.3420	0.3420
1985	W	2.3 (2300)	45	44	154@1.12	1.563	0.0010-0.0027	0.0015-0.0032	0.3420	0.3415
	3	3.8 (3802)	44.5	45.8	215@1.79	1.750	0.0010-0.0027	0.0015-0.0032	0.3420	0.3415
	F	5.0 (4949)	45	45	205@1.36	1.750	0.0010-0.0027	0.0015-0.0032	0.3420	0.3420
1986	W	2.3 (2300)	45	44	154@1.12	1.563	0.0010-0.0027	0.0015-0.0032	0.3420	0.3415
	3	3.8 (3802)	44.5	45.8	215@1.79	1.750	0.0010-0.0027	0.0015-0.0032	0.3420	0.3415
	F	5.0 (4949)	45	45	205@1.36	1.750	0.0010-0.0027	0.0015-0.0032	0.3420	0.3420
1987	W	2.3 (2300)	45	44	154@1.12	1.563	0.0010-0.0027	0.0015-0.0032	0.3420	0.3415
	3	3.8 (3802)	44.5	45.8	215@1.79	1.750	0.0010-0.0027	0.0015-0.0032	0.3420	0.3420
	F	5.0 (4949)	45	45	205@1.36	1.750	0.0010-0.0027	0.0015-0.0032	0.3420	0.3420
1988	W	2.3 (2300)	45	44	154@1.12	1.563	0.0010-0.0027	0.0015-0.0032	0.3420	0.3415
	4	3.8 (3802)	44.5	45.8	215@1.79	1.750	0.0010-0.0027	0.0015-0.0032	0.3420	0.3415
	F	5.0 (4949)	45	45	205@1.36	1.750	0.0010-0.0027	0.0015-0.0032	0.3420	0.3420
1989	4	3.8 (3802)	44.5	45.8	215@1.79	1.750	0.0010-0.0027	0.0015-0.0032	0.3420	0.3415
	C	3.8 (3802)	44.5	45.8	220@1.18	1.650	0.0010-0.0027	0.0015-0.0032	0.3420	0.3415
	R	3.8 (3802)	44.5	45.8	220@1.18	1.650	0.0010-0.0027	0.0015-0.0032	0.3420	0.3415
1990	4	3.8 (3802)	44.5	45.8	220@1.18	1.650	0.0010-0.0027	0.0015-0.0032	0.3420	0.3415
	R	3.8 (3802)	44.5	45.8	220@1.18	1.650	0.0010-0.0027	0.0015-0.0032	0.3420	0.3415

88183C03

VALVE SPECIFICATIONS

Year	Engine ID/VIN	Engine Displacement Liters (cc)	Seat Angle (deg.)	Face Angle (deg.)	Spring Test Pressure (lbs. @ in.)	Spring Installed Height (in.)	Stem-to-Guide Clearance (in.)		Stem Diameter (in.)	
							Intake	Exhaust	Intake	Exhaust
1991	4	3.8 (3802)	44.5	45.8	215@1.79	1.750	0.0010-0.0027	0.0015-0.0032	0.3420	0.3415
	R	3.8 (3802)	44.5	45.8	220@1.18	1.650	0.0010-0.0027	0.0015-0.0032	0.3420	0.3415
	T	5.0 (4949)	45	45	①	②	0.0010-0.0027	0.0015-0.0032	0.3420	0.3420
1992	4	3.8 (3802)	44.5	45.8	215@1.79	1.750	0.0010-0.0027	0.0015-0.0032	0.3420	0.3415
	R	3.8 (3802)	44.5	45.8	220@1.18	1.650	0.0010-0.0027	0.0015-0.0032	0.3420	0.3415
	T	5.0 (4949)	45	45	①	②	0.0010-0.0027	0.0015-0.0032	0.3420	0.3420
1993	4	3.8 (3802)	44.5	45.8	215@1.79	1.750	0.0010-0.0027	0.0015-0.0032	0.3420	0.3415
	R	3.8 (3802)	44.5	45.8	220@1.18	1.650	0.0010-0.0027	0.0015-0.0032	0.3420	0.3415
	T	5.0 (4949)	45	44	①	②	0.0010-0.0027	0.0015-0.0032	0.3420	0.3420
1994	4	3.8 (3802)	44.5	45.8	220@1.18	1.970	0.0010-0.0027	0.0015-0.0032	0.3415-0.3423	0.3410-0.3418
	R	3.8 (3802)	44.5	45.8	220@1.18	1.970	0.0010-0.0027	0.0015-0.0032	0.3415-0.3423	0.3410-0.3418
	W	4.6 (4593)	45	45.5	132@1.10	1.570	0.0008-0.0027	0.0018-0.0037	0.2746-0.2754	0.2736-0.2744
1995	4	3.8 (3802)	44.5	45.8	220@1.18	1.970	0.0010-0.0027	0.0015-0.0032	0.3415-0.3423	0.3410-0.3418
	R	3.8 (3802)	44.5	45.8	220@1.18	1.970	0.0010-0.0027	0.0015-0.0032	0.3415-0.3423	0.3410-0.3418
	W	4.6 (4593)	45	45.5	132@1.10	1..570	0.0008-0.0027	0.0018-0.0037	0.2746-0.2754	0.2736-0.2744
1996	4	3.8 (3802)	44.5	45.8	220@1.18	1.650	0.0010-0.0027	0.0015-0.0032	0.3415-0.3423	0.3410-0.3418
	W	4.6 (4593)	45	45.5	132@1.10	1.570	0.0008-0.0027	0.0018-0.0037	0.2746-0.2754	0.2736-0.2744

1: Measure spring free length and out of square.
Maximum allowable out-of-square: 0.642
Spring free length: Intake: 1.729, Exhaust: 1.847

2: Intake: 211-230@1.33
Exhaust: 200-226@1.15

88183C04

CAMSHAFT SPECIFICATIONS

All measurements given in inches.

Year	Engine ID/VIN	Engine Displacement Liters (cc)	Journal Diameter 1	2	3	4	5	Elevation In.	Ex.	Bearing Clearance	Camshaft End Play
1983	W	2.3 (2300)	1.7713-1.7720	1.7713-1.7720	1.7713-1.7720	1.7713-1.7720	1.7713-1.7720	0.4000	0.4000	0.0010-0.0030	0.0010-0.0070
	3	3.8 (3802)	2.0505-2.0515	2.0505-2.0515	2.0505-2.0515	2.0505-2.0515	2.0505-2.0515	0.2400	0.2410	0.0010-0.0030	①
	F	5.0 (4949)	2.0805-2.0815	2.0655-2.0665	2.0505-2.0515	2.0355-2.0365	2.0505-2.0515	0.2780	0.2830	0.0010-0.0030	0.0010-0.0070
1984	W	2.3 (2300)	1.7713-1.7720	1.7713-1.7720	1.7713-1.7720	1.7713-1.7720	1.7713-1.7720	0.4000	0.4000	0.0010-0.0030	0.0010-0.0070
	3	3.8 (3802)	2.0505-2.0515	2.0505-2.0515	2.0505-2.0515	2.0505-2.0515	2.0505-2.0515	0.2400	0.2410	0.0010-0.0030	①
	F	5.0 (4949)	2.0805-2.0815	2.0655-2.0665	2.0505-2.0515	2.0355-2.0365	2.0505-2.0515	0.2780	0.2830	0.0010-0.0030	0.0010-0.0070
1985	W	2.3 (2300)	1.7713-1.7720	1.7713-1.7720	1.7713-1.7720	1.7713-1.7720	1.7713-1.7720	0.4000	0.4000	0.0010-0.0030	0.0010-0.0070
	3	3.8 (3802)	2.0505-2.0515	2.0505-2.0515	2.0505-2.0515	2.0505-2.0515	2.0505-2.0515	0.2400	0.2410	0.0010-0.0030	①
	F	5.0 (4949)	2.0805-2.0815	2.0655-2.0665	2.0505-2.0515	2.0355-2.0365	2.0505-2.0515	0.2780	0.2830	0.0010-0.0030	0.0010-0.0070
1986	W	2.3 (2300)	1.7713-1.7720	1.7713-1.7720	1.7713-1.7720	1.7713-1.7720	1.7713-1.7720	0.4000	0.4000	0.0010-0.0030	0.0010-0.0070
	3	3.8 (3802)	2.0505-2.0515	2.0505-2.0515	2.0505-2.0515	2.0505-2.0515	2.0505-2.0515	0.2400	0.2410	0.0010-0.0030	①
	F	5.0 (4949)	2.0805-2.0815	2.0655-2.0665	2.0505-2.0515	2.0355-2.0365	2.0505-2.0515	0.2780 ②	0.2830 ②	0.0010-0.0030	0.0010-0.0070
1987	W	2.3 (2300)	1.7713-1.7720	1.7713-1.7720	1.7713-1.7720	1.7713-1.7720	1.7713-1.7720	0.4000	0.4000	0.0010-0.0030	0.0010-0.0070
	3	3.8 (3802)	2.0505-2.0515	2.0505-2.0515	2.0505-2.0515	2.0505-2.0515	2.0505-2.0515	0.2400	0.2410	0.0010-0.0030	①
	F	5.0 (4949)	2.0805-2.0815	2.0655-2.0665	2.0505-2.0515	2.0355-2.0365	2.0205-2.0515	0.2375 ②	0.2474 ②	0.0010-0.0030	0.0010-0.0070
1988	W	2.3 (2300)	1.7713-1.7720	1.7713-1.7720	1.7713-1.7720	1.7713-1.7720	1.7713-1.7720	0.4000	0.4000	0.0010-0.0030	0.0010-0.0070
	4	3.8 (3802)	2.0505-2.0515	2.0505-2.0515	2.0505-2.0515	2.0505-2.0515	2.0505-2.0515	0.2400	0.2410	0.0010-0.0030	①
	F	5.0 (4949)	2.0805-2.0815	2.0655-2.0665	2.0505-2.0515	2.0355-2.0365	2.0205-2.0515	0.2375 ②	0.2474 ②	0.0010-0.0030	0.0010-0.0070
1989	4	3.8 (3802)	2.0505-2.0515	2.0505-2.0515	2.0505-2.0515	2.0505-2.0515	2.0505-2.0515	0.2400	0.2410	0.0010-0.0030	①
	C	3.8 (3802)	2.0505-2.0515	2.0505-2.0515	2.0505-2.0515	2.0505-2.0515	2.0505-2.0515	0.2400	0.2410	0.0010-0.0030	①
	R	3.8 (3802)	2.0505-2.0515	2.0505-2.0515	2.0505-2.0515	2.0505-2.0515	2.0505-2.0515	0.2400	0.2410	0.0010-0.0030	①
1990	4	3.8 (3802)	2.0505-2.0515	2.0505-2.0515	2.0505-2.0515	2.0505-2.0515	2.0505-2.0515	0.2400-0.2450	0.2410-0.2490	0.0010-0.0030	①
	R	3.8 (3802)	2.0505-2.0515	2.0505-2.0515	2.0505-2.0515	2.0505-2.0515	2.0505-2.0515	0.2400-0.2450	0.2410-0.2590	0.0010-0.0030	①

88183C06

CAMSHAFT SPECIFICATIONS

All measurements given in inches.

Year	Engine ID/VIN	Engine Displacement Liters (cc)	Journal Diameter 1	2	3	4	5	Elevation In.	Ex.	Bearing Clearance	Camshaft End Play
1991	4	3.8 (3802)	2.0505-2.0515	2.0505-2.0515	2.0505-2.0515	2.0505-2.0515	2.0505-2.0515	0.2400-0.2450	0.2410-0.2590	0.0010-0.0030	①
	R	3.8 (3802)	2.0505-2.0515	2.0505-2.0515	2.0505-2.0515	2.0505-2.0515	2.0505-2.0515	0.2400-0.2450	0.2410-0.2590	0.0010-0.0030	①
	T	5.0 (4949)	2.0805-2.0815	2.0655-2.0665	2.0505-2.0515	2.0355-2.0365	2.0205-2.0515	0.2780	0.2780	0.0010-0.0030	0.0050-0.0090
1992	4	3.8 (3802)	2.0505-2.0515	2.0505-2.0515	2.0505-2.0515	2.0505-2.0515	2.0505-2.0515	0.2400-0.2450	0.2410-0.2450	0.0010-0.0030	②
	C	3.8 (3802)	2.0505-2.0515	2.0505-2.0515	2.0505-2.0515	2.0505-2.0515	2.0505-2.0515	0.2400-0.2450	0.2410-0.2450	0.0010-0.0030	②
	R	3.8 (3802)	2.0505-2.0515	2.0505-2.0515	2.0505-2.0515	2.0505-2.0515	2.0505-2.0515	0.2400-0.2450	0.2410-0.2450	0.0010-0.0030	②
	T	5.0 (4949)	2.0805-2.0815	2.0655-2.0665	2.0505-2.0515	2.0355-2.0365	2.0205-2.0515	0.2780	0.2780	0.0010-0.0030	0.0050-0.0090
1993	4	3.8 (3802)	2.0505-2.0515	2.0505-2.0515	2.0505-2.0515	2.0505-2.0515	2.0505-2.0515	0.2400-0.2450	0.2410-0.2450	0.0010-0.0030	②
	R	3.8 (3802)	2.0505-2.0515	2.0505-2.0515	2.0505-2.0515	2.0505-2.0515	2.0505-2.0515	0.2400-0.2450	0.2410-0.2590	0.0010-0.0030	②
	T	5.0 (4949)	2.0805-2.0815	2.0655-2.0665	2.0505-2.0515	2.0355-2.0365	2.0205-2.0515	0.2780	0.2780	0.0010-0.0030	0.0050-0.0090
1994	4	3.8 (3802)	2.0505-2.0515	2.0505-2.0515	2.0505-2.0515	2.0505-2.0515	2.0505-2.0515	0.2400-0.2450	0.2540-0.2590	0.0010-0.0030	0.0010-0.0060
	R	3.8 (3802)	2.0505-2.0515	2.0505-2.0515	2.0505-2.0515	2.0505-2.0515	2.0505-2.0515	0.2400-0.2450	0.2540-0.2590	0.0010-0.0030	0.0010-0.0060
	W	4.6 (4593)	1.0605-1.0615	1.0605-1.0615	1.0605-1.0615	1.0605-1.0615	1.0605-1.0615	0.2590	0.2590	0.0010-0.0030	0.0010-0.0060
1995	4	3.8 (3802)	2.0505-2.0515	2.0505-2.0515	2.0505-2.0515	2.0505-2.0515	2.0505-2.0515	0.2400-0.2450	0.2540-0.2590	0.0010-0.0030	0.0010-0.0060
	R	3.8 (3802)	2.0505-2.0515	2.0505-2.0515	2.0505-2.0515	2.0505-2.0515	2.0505-2.0515	0.2400-0.2450	0.2540-0.2590	0.0010-0.0030	0.0010-0.0060
	W	4.6 (4593)	1.0605-1.0615	1.0605-1.0615	1.0605-1.0615	1.0605-1.0615	1.0605-1.0615	0.2590	0.2590	0.0010-0.0030	0.0010-0.0060
1996	4	3.8 (3802)	2.0505-2.0515	2.0505-2.0515	2.0505-2.0515	2.0505-2.0515	2.0505-2.0515	0.2400-0.2450	0.2540-0.2590	0.0010-0.0030	0.0010-0.0060
	W	4.6 (4593)	1.0605-1.0615	1.0605-1.0615	1.0605-1.0615	1.0605-1.0615	1.0605-1.0615	0.2590	0.2590	0.0010-0.0030	0.0065-0.0684

NA - Not Available

1: Endplay is controlled by button and spring on camshaft end

2: Front and rear journals: 0.0014-0.0030

Center journals: 0.0026-0.0045

88183C07

CRANKSHAFT AND CONNECTING ROD SPECIFICATIONS

All measurements are given in inches.

Year	Engine ID/VIN	Engine Displacement Liters (cc)	Crankshaft Main Brg. Journal Dia.	Crankshaft Main Brg. Oil Clearance	Crankshaft Shaft End-play	Crankshaft Thrust on No.	Connecting Rod Journal Diameter	Connecting Rod Oil Clearance	Connecting Rod Side Clearance
1983	W	2.3 (2300)	2.3990-2.3982	0.0008-0.0015	0.0040-0.0080	3	2.0464-2.0472	0.0008-0.0015	0.0035-0.0105
	3	3.8 (3802)	2.5190	0.0001-0.0010	0.0040-0.0080	3	2.3103-2.3111	0.0008-0.0026	0.0047-0.0114
	F	5.0 (4949)	2.2482-2.2490	0.0004-0.0015	0.0040-0.0150	3	2.1228-2.1236	0.0008-0.0015	0.0100-0.0200
1984	W	2.3 (2300)	2.3990-2.3982	0.0008-0.0015	0.0040-0.0080	3	2.0464-2.0472	0.0008-0.0015	0.0035-0.0105
	3	3.8 (3802)	2.5190	0.0001-0.0010	0.0040-0.0080	3	2.3103-2.3111	0.0008-0.0026	0.0047-0.0114
	F	5.0 (4949)	2.2482-2.2490	0.0004-0.0015	0.0040-0.0150	3	2.1228-2.1236	0.0008-0.0015	0.0100-0.0200
1985	W	2.3 (2300)	2.3990-2.3982	0.0008-0.0015	0.0040-0.0080	3	2.0464-2.0472	0.0008-0.0015	0.0035-0.0105
	3	3.8 (3802)	2.5190	0.0001-0.0010	0.0040-0.0080	3	2.3103-2.3111	0.0008-0.0026	0.0047-0.0114
	F	5.0 (4949)	2.2482-2.2490	0.0004-0.0015	0.0040-0.0150	3	2.1228-2.1236	0.0008-0.0015	0.0100-0.0200
1986	W	2.3 (2300)	2.3990-2.3982	0.0008-0.0015	0.0040-0.0080	3	2.0464-2.0472	0.0008-0.0015	0.0035-0.0105
	3	3.8 (3802)	2.5190	0.0001-0.0010	0.0040-0.0080	3	2.3103-2.3111	0.0008-0.0026	0.0047-0.0114
	F	5.0 (4949)	2.2482-2.2490	0.0004-0.0015	0.0040-0.0150	3	2.1228-2.1236	0.0008-0.0015	0.0100-0.0200
1987	W	2.3 (2300)	2.3982-2.3990	0.0008-0.0015	0.0040-0.0080	3	2.0464-2.0472	0.0008-0.0015	0.0035-0.0105
	3	3.8 (3802)	2.5190	0.0001-0.0010	0.0040-0.0080	3	2.3103-2.3111	0.0008-0.0026	0.0047-0.0114
	F	5.0 (4949)	2.2482-2.2490	0.0004-0.0015	0.0040-0.0150	3	2.1228-2.1236	0.0008-0.0015	0.0100-0.0200
1988	W	2.3 (2300)	2.3982-2.3990	0.0008-0.0015	0.0040-0.0080	3	2.0464-2.0472	0.0008-0.0015	0.0035-0.0105
	4	3.8 (3802)	2.5189-2.5190	0.0010-0.0014	0.0040-0.0080	3	2.3103-2.3111	0.0010-0.0014	0.0047-0.0114
	F	5.0 (4949)	2.2482-2.2490	0.0004-0.0015	0.0040-0.0150	3	2.1228-2.1236	0.0008-0.0015	0.0100-0.0200
1989	4	3.8 (3802)	2.5189-2.5190	0.0010-0.0014	0.0040-0.0080	3	2.3103-2.3111	0.0010-0.0014	0.0047-0.0114
	C	3.8 (3802)	2.5186-2.5194	0.0009-0.0026	0.0040-0.0080	3	2.4226-2.4274	0.0008-0.0026	0.0047-0.0114
	R	3.8 (3802)	2.5186-2.5194	0.0009-0.0026	0.0040-0.0080	3	2.4226-2.4274	0.0008-0.0026	0.0047-0.0114

88183C09

CRANKSHAFT AND CONNECTING ROD SPECIFICATIONS

All measurements are given in inches.

Year	Engine ID/VIN	Engine Displacement Liters (cc)	Crankshaft				Connecting Rod		
			Main Brg. Journal Dia.	Main Brg. Oil Clearance	Shaft End-play	Thrust on No.	Journal Diameter	Oil Clearance	Side Clearance
1990	4	3.8 (3802)	2.5189-2.5190	0.0010-0.0014	0.0040-0.0080	3	2.3103-2.3111	0.0010-0.0014	0.0047-0.0114
	R	3.8 (3802)	2.5186-2.5194	0.0009-0.0026	0.0040-0.0080	3	2.4226-2.4274	0.0008-0.0026	0.0047-0.0114
1991	4	3.8 (3802)	2.5180 2.5190	0.0010-0.0014	0.0040-0.0080	3	2.3103-2.3111	0.0010-0.0014	0.0047-0.0114
	R	3.8 (3801)	①	②	0.0040-0.0080	3	2.3103-2.3111	0.0009-0.0027	0.0047-0.0140
	T	5.0 (4949)	2.2482-2.2490	0.0004-0.0015	0.0040-0.0150	3	2.1228-2.1236	0.0008-0.0015	0.0100-0.0200
1992	4	3.8 (3802)	2.5189-2.5190	0.0010-0.0014	0.0040-0.0080	3	2.3103-2.3111	0.0010-0.0014	0.0047-0.0114
	C	3.8 (3802)	2.5186-2.5194	0.0009-0.0026	0.0040-0.0080	3	2.4226-2.4274	0.0008-0.0026	0.0047-0.0114
	R	3.8 (3801)	①	②	0.0040-0.0080	3	2.3103-2.3111	0.0009-0.0027	0.0047-0.0140
	T	5.0 (4949)	2.2482-2.2490	0.0004-0.0015	0.0040-0.0150	3	2.1228-2.1236	0.0008-0.0015	0.0100-0.0200
1993	4	3.8 (3802)	2.5189-2.5190	0.0010-0.0014	0.0040-0.0080	3	2.3103-2.3111	0.0010-0.0014	0.0047-0.0114
	R	3.8 (3801)	①	②	0.0040-0.0080	3	2.3103-2.3111	0.0009-0.0027	0.0047-0.0140
	T	5.0 (4949)	2.2482-2.2490	0.0004-0.0015	0.0040-0.0150	3	2.1228-2.1236	0.0008-0.0015	0.0100-0.0200
1994	4	3.8 (3802)	2.5190-2.5198	0.0010-0.0014	0.0040-0.0080	3	2.3103-2.3111	0.0009-0.0027	0.0047-0.0140
	R	3.8 (3802)	①	②	0.0040-0.0080	3	2.3103-2.3111	0.0009-0.0027	0.0047-0.0140
	W	4.6 (4593)	2.6578-2.6598	0.0011-0.0025	0.0050-0.0100	5	2.0874-2.0891	0.0011-0.0027	0.0006-0.0177
1995	4	3.8 (3802)	2.5190-2.5198	0.0010-0.0014	0.0040-0.0080	3	2.3103-2.3111	0.0009-0.0027	0.0047-0.0140
	R	3.8 (3802)	①	②	0.0040-0.0080	3	2.3103-2.3111	0.0009-0.0027	0.0047-0.0140
	W	4.6 (4593)	2.6578-2.6598	0.0011-0.0025	0.0050-0.0100	5	2.0874-2.0891	0.0011-0.0027	0.0006-0.0177
1996	4	3.8 (3802)	2.5190-2.5198	0.0010-0.0024	0.0040-0.0080	3	2.3103-2.3111	0.0009-0.0027	0.0047-0.0140
	W	4.6 (4593)	2.6569-2.6576	0.0011-0.0026	0.0058-0.0119	5	2.0861-2.0867	0.0011-0.0027	0.0006-0.0177

1: Nos. 1-3: 2.5190-2.5198
No. 4: 2.55096-2.5104

2: Nos. 1-3: 0.0005-0.0023
No. 4: 0.0010-0.0028

88183C10

PISTON AND RING SPECIFICATIONS

All measurements are given in inches.

		Engine		Ring Gap			Ring Side Clearance		
Year	Engine ID/VIN	Displacement Liters (cc)	Piston Clearance	Top Compression	Bottom Compression	Oil Control	Top Compression	Bottom Compression	Oil Control
1983	W	2.3 (2300)	0.0030-0.0038	0.0100-0.0200	0.0100-0.0200	0.0150-0.0550	0.0020-0.0040	0.0020-0.0040	SNUG
	3	3.8 (3802)	0.0014-0.0032	0.0100-0.0220	0.0100-0.0220	0.0150-0.0550	0.0020-0.0040	0.0020-0.0040	SNUG
	F	5.0 (4949)	0.0018-0.0026	0.0200	0.0200	0.0550	0.0040	0.0040	SNUG
1984	W	2.3 (2300)	0.0030-0.0038	0.0100-0.0200	0.0100-0.0200	0.0150-0.0550	0.0020-0.0040	0.0020-0.0040	SNUG
	3	3.8 (3802)	0.0014-0.0032	0.0100-0.0220	0.0100-0.0220	0.0150-0.0550	0.0020-0.0040	0.0020-0.0040	SNUG
	F	5.0 (4949)	0.0018-0.0026	0.0200	0.0200	0.0550	0.0040	0.0040	SNUG
1985	W	2.3 (2300)	0.0030-0.0038	0.0100-0.0200	0.0100-0.0200	0.0150-0.0550	0.0020-0.0040	0.0020-0.0040	SNUG
	3	3.8 (3802)	0.0014-0.0032	0.0100-0.0220	0.0100-0.0220	0.0150-0.0550	0.0020-0.0040	0.0020-0.0040	SNUG
	F	5.0 (4949)	0.0018-0.0026	0.0200	0.0200	0.0550	0.0040	0.0040	SNUG
1986	W	2.3 (2300)	0.0030-0.0038	0.0100-0.0200	0.0100-0.0200	0.0150-0.0550	0.0020-0.0040	0.0020-0.0040	SNUG
	3	3.8 (3802)	0.0014-0.0032	0.0100-0.0220	0.0100-0.0220	0.0150-0.0550	0.0020-0.0040	0.0020-0.0040	SNUG
	F	5.0 (4949)	0.0018-0.0026	0.0200	0.0200	0.0550	0.0040	0.0040	SNUG
1987	W	2.3 (2300)	0.0030-0.0038	0.0100-0.0200	0.0100-0.0200	0.0150-0.0550	0.0020-0.0040	0.0020-0.0040	SNUG
	3	3.8 (3802)	0.0014-0.0032	0.0100-0.0220	0.0100-0.0220	0.0150-0.0550	0.0020-0.0040	0.0020-0.0040	SNUG
	F	5.0 (4949)	0.0018-0.0026	0.0200	0.0200	0.0550	0.0040	0.0040	SNUG
1988	W	2.3 (2300)	0.0030-0.0038	0.0100-0.0200	0.0100-0.0200	0.0150-0.0550	0.0020-0.0040	0.0020-0.0040	SNUG
	4	3.8 (3802)	0.0014-0.0032	0.0100-0.0220	0.0100-0.0220	0.0150-0.0550	0.0020-0.0040	0.0020-0.0040	SNUG
	F	5.0 (4949)	0.0018-0.0026	0.0200	0.0200	0.0550	0.0040	0.0040	SNUG
1989	4	3.8 (3802)	0.0014-0.0032	0.0100-0.0220	0.0100-0.0220	0.0150-0.0550	0.0020-0.0040	0.0020-0.0040	SNUG
	C	3.8 (3802)	0.0014-0.0047	0.0602-0.0610	0.0602-0.0610	0.1582-0.0602	0.0016-0.0034	0.0016-0.0034	SNUG
	R	3.8 (3802)	0.0014-0.0047	0.0602-0.0610	0.0602-0.0610	0.1582-0.0602	0.0016-0.0034	0.0016-0.0034	SNUG

88183C11

PISTON AND RING SPECIFICATIONS

All measurements are given in inches.

		Engine		Ring Gap			Ring Side Clearance		
Year	Engine ID/VIN	Displacement Liters (cc)	Piston Clearance	Top Compression	Bottom Compression	Oil Control	Top Compression	Bottom Compression	Oil Control
1990	4	3.8 (3802)	0.0014-0.0032	0.0100-0.0220	0.0100-0.0220	0.0150-0.0550	0.0020-0.0040	0.0020-0.0040	SNUG
	R	3.8 (3802)	0.0040-0.0045	0.0110-0.0120	0.0090-0.0200	0.0150-0.0580	0.0016-0.0034	0.0016-0.0034	SNUG
1991	4	3.8 (3802)	0.0014-0.0032	0.0100-0.0220	0.0100-0.0220	0.0150-0.0550	0.0020-0.0040	0.0020-0.0040	SNUG
	R	3.8 (3802)	0.0040-0.0045	0.0110-0.0120	0.0090-0.0200	0.0150-0.0580	0.0016-0.0034	0.0016-0.0034	SNUG
	T	5.0 (4949)	0.0030-0.0038	0.0100-0.0200	0.0100-0.0200	0.0150-0.0550	0.0020-0.0040	0.0020-0.0040	SNUG
1992	4	3.8 (3802)	0.0014-0.0032	0.0100-0.0220	0.0100-0.0220	0.0150-0.0550	0.0020-0.0044	0.0020-0.0040	SNUG
	C	3.8 (3802)	0.0014-0.0047	0.0602-0.0610	0.0602-0.0610	0.1582-0.0602	0.0016-0.0034	0.0016-0.0034	SNUG
	R	3.8 (3802)	0.0040-0.0045	0.0110-0.0120	0.0090-0.0200	0.0150-0.0580	0.0016-0.0034	0.0016-0.0034	SNUG
	T	5.0 (4949)	0.0030-0.0038	0.0100-0.0200	0.0100-0.0200	0.0150-0.0550	0.0020-0.0040	0.0020-0.0040	SNUG
1993	4	3.8 (3802)	0.0014-0.0032	0.0100-0.0220	0.0100-0.0220	0.0150-0.0550	0.0020-0.0040	0.0020-0.0040	SNUG
	R	3.8 (3802)	0.0040-0.0045	0.0110-0.0120	0.0090-0.0200	0.0150-0.0580	0.0016-0.0034	0.0016-0.0034	SNUG
	T	5.0 (4949)	0.0030-0.0038	0.0100-0.0200	0.0100-0.0200	0.0150-0.0550	0.0020-0.0040	0.0020-0.0040	SNUG
1994	4	3.8 (3802)	0.0014-0.0032	0.0110-0.0120	0.0100-0.0200	0.0150-0.0580	0.0016-0.0034	0.0016-0.0034	SNUG
	R	3.8 (3802)	0.0015-0.0032	0.0110-0.0120	0.0090-0.0200	0.0150-0.0580	0.0016-0.0034	0.0016-0.0034	SNUG
	W	4.6 (4593)	0.0003-0.0006	0.0090-0.0190	0.0090-0.0190	0.0060-0.0260	0.0016-0.0035	0.0012-0.0031	SNUG
1995	4	3.8 (3802)	0.0014-0.0032	0.0110-0.0120	0.0100-0.0200	0.0150-0.0580	0.0016-0.0034	0.0016-0.0034	SNUG
	R	3.8 (3802)	0.0004-0.0034	0.0110-0.0120	0.0090-0.0200	0.0150-0.0580	0.0016-0.0034	0.0016-0.0034	SNUG
	W	4.6 (4593)	0.0003-0.0006	0.0090-0.0190	0.0090-0.0190	0.0060-0.0260	0.0016-0.0035	0.0012-0.0031	SNUG
1996	4	3.8 (3802)	0.0014-0.0022	0.0110-0.0120	0.0100-0.0200	0.0150-0.0580	0.0016-0.0034	0.0016-0.0034	SNUG
	W	4.6 (4593)	0.0005-0.0010	0.0090-0.0190	0.0090-0.0190	0.0060-0.0260	0.0016-0.0035	0.0012-0.0031	SNUG

88183C12

TORQUE SPECIFICATIONS

All readings in ft. lbs.

Year	Engine ID/VIN	Engine Displacement Liters (cc)	Cylinder Head Bolts	Main Bearing Bolts	Rod Bearing Bolts	Crankshaft Damper Bolts	Flywheel Bolts	Manifold Intake	Manifold Exhaust	Spark Plugs	Lug Nut
1983	W	2.3 (2300)	①	②	③	100-120	54-64	14-21	16-23	5-10	95
	3	3.8 (3802)	④	65-81	31-36	85-100	75-85	⑤	15-22	5-11	95
	F	5.0 (4949)	65-72	60-70	19-24	70-90	75-85	23-25	18-24	10-15	95
1984	W	2.3 (2300)	①	②	③	100-120	54-64	14-21	16-23	5-10	95
	3	3.8 (3802)	④	65-81	31-36	85-100	75-85	⑤	15-22	5-11	95
	F	5.0 (4949)	65-72	60-70	19-24	70-90	75-85	23-25	18-24	10-15	95
1985	W	2.3 (2300)	①	②	③	100-120	54-64	14-21	16-23	5-10	95
	3	3.8 (3802)	④	65-81	31-36	85-100	75-85	⑤	15-22	5-11	95
	F	5.0 (4949)	65-72	60-70	19-24	70-90	75-85	23-25	18-24	10-15	95
1986	W	2.3 (2300)	①	②	③	100-120	54-64	14-21	16-23	5-10	95
	3	3.8 (3802)	⑥	65-81	31-36	85-100	75-85	⑤	15-22	5-11	95
	F	5.0 (4949)	65-72	60-70	19-24	70-90	75-85	23-25	18-24	10-15	95
1987	W	2.3 (2300)	①	②	③	100-120	54-64	⑦	16-23	5-10	95
	3	3.8 (3802)	⑥	65-81	31-36	85-100	75-85	⑤	15-22	5-11	95
	E	5.0 (4949)	65-72	60-70	19-24	70-90	75-85	23-25	18-24	10-15	95
1988	W	2.3 (2300)	①	②	③	100-120	54-64	⑦	16-23	5-10	95
	4	3.8 (3802)	⑥	65-81	31-36	85-100	75-85	⑤	15-22	5-11	95
	F	5.0 (4949)	65-72	60-70	19-24	70-90	75-85	23-25	18-24	10-15	95
1989	4	3.8 (3802)	⑥	65-81	31-36	85-100	75-85	⑤	15-22	5-11	95
	C	3.8 (3802)	⑥	65-81	31-36	85-100	75-85	⑧	15-22	5-11	95
	R	3.8 (3802)	⑥	65-81	31-36	85-100	75-85	⑧	15-22	5-11	95
1990	R	3.8 (3802)	⑩	65-81	31-36	103-132	54-64	⑧	15-22	5-11	95
	4	3.8 (3802)	⑥	65-81	31-36	85-100	75-85	⑨	15-22	5-11	95
1991	R	3.8 (3801)	⑩	65-81	31-36	103-132	54-64	①	15-22	5-11	95
	4	3. 8(3802)	⑥	65-81	31-36	85-100	75-85	⑨	15-22	5-11	95
	T	5.0 (4949)	65-72	60-70	19-24	70-90	75-85	23-25	18-24	10-15	95
1992	R	3.8 (3801)	⑩	65-81	31-36	103-132	54-64	①	15-22	5-11	95
	4	3.8 (3802)	⑥	65-81	31-36	85-100	75-85	⑨	15-22	5-11	95
	T	5.0 (4949)	65-72	60-70	19-24	70-90	75-85	23-25	18-24	10-15	95
1993	R	3.8 (3801)	⑩	65-81	31-36	103-132	54-64	①	15-22	5-11	95
	4	3.8 (3802)	⑥	65-81	31-36	85-100	75-85	⑨	15-22	5-11	95
	T	5.0 (4949)	65-72	60-70	19-24	70-90	75-85	23-25	18-24	10-15	95
1994	R	3.8 (3802)	⑫	65-81	31-36	103-132	54-64	⑩	15-22	7-15	95
	4	3.8 (3802)	⑫	65-81	31-36	103-132	54-64	⑩	15-22	7-15	95
	W	4.6 (4593)	⑬	⑮	⑮	114-121	54-64	15-22	15-22	7-15	95
1995	R	3.8 (3802)	⑩	65-81	31-36	103-132	54-64	⑫	15-22	7-15	95
	4	3.8 (3802)	⑬	65-81	31-36	103-132	54-64	⑫	15-22	7-15	95
	W	4.6 (4593)	⑭	⑮	⑯	114-121	54-64	15-22	15-22	7-15	95
1996	4	3.8 (3802)	⑬	82-88	⑰	103-132	54-64	⑫	23-26	7-15	95
	W	4.6 (4593)	⑱	⑮	⑯	114-121	54-64	15-22	14-16	7-15	95

88183C13

TORQUE SPECIFICATIONS

All readings in ft. lbs.

Year	Engine ID/VIN	Engine Displacement Liters (cc)	Cylinder Head Bolts	Main Bearing Bolts	Rod Bearing Bolts	Crankshaft Damper Bolts	Flywheel Bolts	Manifold		Spark Plugs	Lug Nut
								Intake	Exhaust		

NOTE: Always follow proper torque patterns

NOTE: Stretch bolts are used in all procedures that require rotating the fastener a certain number of degrees. The bolts stretch and cannot be reused. For reassembly, replace with new fasteners.

1: Step 1: 50-60 ft. lbs.
Step 2: 80-90 ft. lbs.

2: Step 1: 50-60 ft. lbs.
Step 2: 75-85 ft. lbs.

3: Step 1: 25-30 ft. lbs.
Step 2: 30-36 ft. lbs.

4: Step 1: 37 ft. lbs.
Step 2: 45 ft. lbs.
Step 3: 52 ft. lbs.
Step 4: 59 ft. lbs.

5: Step 1: 7 ft. lbs.
Step 2: 15 ft. lbs.
Step 3: 24 ft. lbs.

6: Step 1: 37 ft. lbs.
Step 2: 45 ft. lbs.
Step 3: 52 ft. lbs.
Step 4: 59 ft. lbs.

7: Step 1: 5-7 ft. lbs.
Step 2: 13-18 ft. lbs.

8: Step 1: 7.5 ft. lbs.
Step 2: 11 ft. lbs.

9: Step 1: 48-54 ft. lbs.
Step 2: 63-80 ft. lbs.

10: Step 1: 37 ft. lbs.
Step 2: 45 ft. lbs.
Step 3: 52 ft. lbs.
Step 4: 59 ft. lbs.
Step 5: Back off all bolts two to three turns
Step 6: Tighten to 48-55 ft.lbs.
Step 7: Rotate bolts and additional 90-110 degrees

11: Step 1: 11 ft. lbs.
Step 2: 18 ft. lbs.
Step 3: 24 ft. lbs.

12: Step 1: 22-26 ft. lbs.
Step 2: 33-36 ft. lbs.

13: Step 1: 15 ft. lbs.
Step 2: 29 ft. lbs.
Step 3: 37 ft. lbs.
Step 4: Loosen bolts and retorque as follows:
Long bolts: 11-18 ft. lbs.
Short bolts: 7-15 ft. lbs.
Step 5: Rotate 85-95 degrees

14: Step 1: 25-30 ft. lbs.
Step 2: Rotate each bolt 85-95 degrees
Step 3: Repeat Step 2

15: Step 1: Main bearing cap bolts: 22-25 ft. lbs.
Step 2: Rotate each bolts 85-95 degrees
Step 3: Main bearing cap adjusting screws:
4 ft. lbs. then 6.5-8.0 ft. lbs.
Step 4: Main bearing cap side bolts:
7 ft. lbs. then 14-17 ft. lbs.

16: Step 1: 12 ft. lbs.
Step 2: 85-95 degrees

17: 29 ft. lbs. plus 90-120 degrees

18: Step 1: 27-31 ft. lbs.
Step 2: Rotate 85-95 degrees
Step 3: Loosen bolts one turn
Step 4: 27-31 ft. lbs.
Step 5: Rotate 85-95 degrees
Step 6: Repeat Step 5

19: Step 1: Main bearing cap bolts: 27-31 ft. lbs.
Step 2: Rotate 85-95 degrees
Step 3: Main bearing cap adjusting screws:
4 ft. lbs. then 6.5-8.0 ft. lbs.
Step 4: Main beaing cap side bolts:
7 ft. lbs. then 14-17 ft. lbs.

88183C14

Engine

REMOVAL & INSTALLATION

2.3L Engine

1. Raise and support the hood. In many cases, it may be easier to matchmark the hood hinges and remove the hood from the vehicle.
2. Properly drain the engine cooling system and the oil from the crankcase.
3. Disconnect the zip tube from the turbocharger inlet. Remove the ground strap on the turbocharger inlet elbow.
4. Remove the air cleaner and exhaust manifold shroud.
5. Disconnect the negative battery cable.
6. Detach the upper and lower radiator hoses.
7. Remove the radiator and fan assembly. On vehicles equipped with an electric cooling fan, detach the fan electrical connector, then remove the fan and shroud assembly.
8. Disconnect the heater hose from the water pump.
9. Detach the electrical connectors from the alternator and starter. Disconnect the accelerator cable from the throttle body.

WARNING

When repositioning the compressor, DO NOT disconnect the refrigerant lines!

10. If equipped with A/C, remove the compressor from the mounting bracket and position it out of the way, leaving the refrigerant lines attached.
11. Disconnect and cap the power steering lines from the power steering pump.
12. Disconnect and plug the flexible fuel line at the fuel pump or fuel rail.

13. Detach the coil primary wire at the coil. Disconnect the oil pressure and water temperature sending unit wires from the units.
14. Remove the starter, as outlined in Section 2 of this manual.
15. Raise and safely support the vehicle.
16. Remove the flywheel or converter housing attaching bolts.
17. Disconnect the muffler inlet pipe at the turbocharger outlet pipe. Disconnect the engine right and left mounts at the No. 2 crossmember pedestals. Remove the flywheel or converter housing cover.
18. If equipped with a manual transmission, remove the flywheel housing lower attaching bolts.
19. If equipped with an automatic transmission, disconnect the converter from the flywheel. Disconnect the transmission oil cooler lines, if attached to the engine at the pan rail. Remove the converter housing cover lower attaching bolts.
20. Carefully lower the vehicle. Support the transmission and flywheel or converter housing with a jack.
21. Attach engine lifting hooks to the existing lifting brackets. Carefully lift the engine out of the engine compartment, using a suitable shop crane, then install the engine on a suitable work stand.

To install:

22. If removed, install the clutch. Carefully lower the engine into the engine compartment.
23. Make sure the studs on the turbocharger are aligned with the holes in the muffler inlet pipe.
24. If equipped with an automatic transmission, start the converter pilot into the crankshaft.
25. If equipped with a manual transmission, start the transmission main drive gear into the clutch disc. It may be necessary to adjust the position of the transmission in relation to the engine it the input shaft will not enter the clutch disc. If the engine hangs up after the shaft enters, turn the crankshaft in the clockwise direction slowly (transmission in gear) until the shaft splines mesh with the clutch disc splines.
26. Install the flywheel or converter housing upper attaching bolts. Remove the engine lifting sling hooks.
27. Carefully remove the jack from the transmission. Raise and safely support the vehicle.
28. Install the flywheel or converter housing lower attaching bolts.
29. If equipped with an automatic transaxle, attach the converter to the flexplate. Tighten the attaching nuts to 27–49 ft. lbs. (37–66 Nm).
30. Install the flywheel or converter housing dust cover.
31. Install the engine left and right mounts to the No. 2 crossmember pedestals. Tighten the nuts an bolts to 33–45 ft. lbs. (45–61 Nm).
32. Unplug the fuel line and connect it to the fuel pump or fuel rail. Install the turbocharger-to-muffler inlet pipe nuts.
33. Carefully lower the vehicle.
34. Connect the oil pressure and engine temperature sending unit wires. Attach the coil wires, then connect the accelerator cable.
35. Install the starter motor and attach the electrical connector. Connect the alternator wires and connect the heater hose to the water pump.
36. Connect the air inlet hose to the turbocharger. Connect the ground strap to the turbocharger inlet elbow.
37. Uncap and connect the power steering lines.
38. Install the pulley, fan and drive belt. Adjust the drive belt tension. If equipped with A/C, install the compressor on the mounting bracket and adjust the belt tension.
39. Install the fan and radiator. On vehicles equipped with an electric cooling fan, attach the electrical connector.
40. Attach the upper and lower radiator hoses. Fill and bleed the cooling system. Fill the crankcase with the proper grade and quantity of engine oil.
41. Connect the negative battery cable.
42. Start the engine and operate at fast idle. Inspect for fluid and/or vacuum leaks.
43. Either install or lower the hood assembly.

3.8L Engine

1983–87 VEHICLES (VIN 3 ENGINE)

1. Properly drain the engine cooling system.
2. Disconnect the negative battery cable.
3. If equipped with an underhood lamp, detach the wiring connector. Matchmark the hood hinges, then remove the hood.
4. Remove the air cleaner assembly, including the air intake duct and heat tube.
5. Unfasten the fan shroud attaching screws. Remove the fan/clutch assembly attaching bolts, then remove the fan/clutch assembly and shroud.
6. Loosen the accessory drive belt idler. Remove the drive belt and water pump pulley.
7. Disconnect the upper and lower radiator hoses at the radiator.
8. Detach the Thermactor hose from the downstream air tube check valve.
9. Remove the downstream air tube bracket attaching bolt at the rear of the right cylinder head.
10. Detach the coil secondary wire from the coil.
11. Remove the power steering pump mounting brackets' attaching bolts. Leave the hoses connected, then position the pump aside in a position to prevent the fluid from leaking out.
12. If equipped with A/C, remove the mounting bracket attaching bolts. Leaving the refrigerant lines attached, secure the compressor to the right shock tower.
13. Remove the alternator mounting bolts and position the alternator aside.
14. Disconnect the heater hoses from the heater tube and water pump.
15. If equipped with cruise control, disconnect the cable at the carburetor or fuel charging assembly, as applicable.
16. Tag and disconnect the necessary vacuum hoses.
17. Remove the screw attaching the engine ground strap to the dash panel.
18. Disconnect the transmission linkage at the carburetor or fuel charging assembly.
19. Disconnect the accelerator cable at the carburetor and remove the cable routing bracket attaching bolts from the intake manifold (two places).
20. Tag and detach any necessary electrical connectors.
21. Disconnect the fuel lines and PCV hose at the carburetor, or detach the flexible fuel lines from the steel lines over the rocker arm (valve) cover, as applicable.
22. Detach and plug the flexible fuel inlet line at the pump.
23. Remove the carburetor or fuel charging assembly, as applicable. Leaving the EGR spacer and phenolic gasket in place, install Engine Lifting Plate T75T–6000–A or equivalent over the carburetor/throttle body hold-down studs. Tighten the nuts securely.

✱✱WARNING

Because the intake manifold is aluminum and of lightweight design, all studs must be used to secure the lifting plate. DO NOT remove the engine with the transmission attached when using the lifting plate.

24. Raise and safely support the vehicle. Properly drain the engine oil.
25. Remove the dust shield from the transmission converter housing.
26. Remove the flex plate-to-torque converter attaching nuts.
27. Disconnect the battery cable from the starter motor. Unfasten the starter motor attaching bolts, then remove the starter.
28. Remove the transmission oil cooler line routing clip.
29. Unfasten the exhaust inlet pipe-to-exhaust manifold attaching nuts.
30. Disconnect the exhaust heat control valve vacuum line and remove the valve from the exhaust manifold studs, if equipped.
31. Remove the transmission-to-engine lower attaching bolts. There are two on each side.
32. Remove the engine mount-to-crossmember through bolts.
33. Carefully lower the vehicle.
34. Position a jack under the transmission. Raise the jack just enough to support the weight of the transmission.
35. Remove the two transmission-to-engine upper attaching bolts.
36. Position a protective cover, such as $^{1}/_{4}$ in. (6.4mm) plywood, between the engine and the radiator to prevent damage to the radiator.
37. Using a suitable shop crane, raise the engine slightly and carefully pull it away from the transmission. Carefully lift the engine out of the engine compartment (avoid bending or damaging the rear cover plate or other components). Install the engine on a suitable work stand.

To install:

➔ Lightly oil all bolt and stud threads before installation except those specifying special sealant.

38. With the EGR spacer and the phenolic gasket in position, install Engine Lifting plate T75T-6000-A or equivalent, over the carburetor/throttle body hold-down studs. Tighten the nuts securely.

✱✱WARNING

Because the intake manifold is aluminum and of lightweight design, all studs must be used to secure the lifting plate. DO NOT remove the engine with the transmission attached when using the lifting plate.

39. Using a suitable shop crane, hoist the engine from the work stand and carefully lower it into the vehicle.
40. With the exhaust heat control valve in place, align the engine insulators, exhaust manifolds-to-exhaust inlet pipes, transmission converter housing-to-cylinder block dowels and transmission converter-to-flywheel stud bolts.
41. Install the transmission-to-engine upper attaching bolts. Remove the shop crane and transmission jack.
42. Raise and safely support the vehicle.
43. Install the transmission-to-engine lower attaching bolts.
44. Install the engine mount-to-crossmember through bolts and tighten to 33-45 ft. lbs. (45-61 Nm).
45. Install the flex plate-to-torque converter attaching nuts and tighten to 20-30 ft. lbs. (28-40 Nm).
46. Install the dust shield on the transmission converter housing.
47. Fasten the exhaust inlet pipe-to-exhaust manifold attaching nuts. Tighten to 16-24 ft. lbs. (21-32 Nm).
48. If equipped, connect the heat control vacuum line.
49. Install the transmission oil cooler line routing clip.
50. Position the starter motor, install the attaching bolts and tighten to 15-20 ft. lbs. (20-27 Nm).
51. Connect the battery cable to the starter motor.
52. Attach the flexible fuel inlet line to the fuel pump and tighten securely.
53. Carefully lower the vehicle.
54. Remove the engine lifting plate.
55. Install the carburetor or fuel charging assembly and tighten the hold-down nuts to 12-15 ft. lbs (16-20 Nm).
56. Connect the fuel lines to the carburetor or fuel charging assembly and secure. Connect the flexible fuel lines to the steel lines over the rocker arm cover.
57. Connect the PCV hose at the carburetor.
58. Attach the accelerator cable and tighten the mounting bracket attaching bolts to 15-22 ft. lbs. (20-30 Nm).
59. If equipped with cruise control, connect the speed control cable at the carburetor/fuel charging assembly.
60. Attach the transmission linkage at the carburetor or fuel charging assembly.
61. If equipped with A/C, position the compressor and mounting brackets, then secure with the attaching bolts.
62. If equipped with power steering, position the pump and mounting brackets and secure with the attaching bolts.
63. If fuel injected, connect the hose to the downstream air tube check valve and clamp securely.
64. Connect the heater and radiator hoses.
65. Position the alternator and install the attaching bolts.
66. Connect the necessary vacuum lines and electrical connectors, as tagged during removal.
67. Fasten the engine ground strap to the dash panel.
68. Connect the ignition coil secondary wires.
69. Position the accessory drive belt over the pulleys.

➔ Examine the fan for possible cracks, separation or damage before installation. Replace the fan if necessary.

70. Install the water pump pulley, fan/clutch assembly and fan shroud. Cross-tighten the fan/clutch assembly retaining bolts to 12-18 ft. lbs. (16-24 Nm).
71. Place the fan shroud on the radiator, then install the attaching screws.
72. Position the accessory drive belt over the pump pulley and adjust the drive belt tension.
73. Fill the engine cooling system with the proper type and quantity of coolant. Fill the crankcase with the correct amount and type of engine oil.
74. Connect the negative battery cable, then install the hood assembly.
75. If equipped, connect the underhood light.
76. Start the engine and check for fluid and/or vacuum leaks.
77. Check the engine curb idle speed and adjust, if necessary.
78. Install the air cleaner assembly, including the air intake duct and heat tube.

1988-96 VEHICLES (VIN 4, C & R ENGINES)

➥ Supercharged engines require special procedures for removing and installing the charge air cooler/intercooler and tube assemblies.

1. If equipped with A/C, have a repair shop recover the refrigerant using the proper equipment.
2. Properly drain the engine cooling system.
3. Disconnect the negative battery cable.
4. Detach the wiring connector from the engine compartment lamp, then matchmark the hood hinges and remove the hood assembly.
5. Remove the left side cowl vent screen and wiper module assembly.
6. For non-SuperCharged (SC) engines, disconnect the alternator-to-voltage regulator wiring.
7. If equipped with a supercharged engine, remove the charge air cooler/intercooler inlet tube at the supercharger and charge air cooler/intercooler. Remove the bolt retaining the charge air cooler inlet tube to the alternator mounting bracket and remove the tube.
8. Remove the radiator upper sight shield.
9. Release the belt tension, then remove the drive belt.
10. Detach the air cleaner outlet tube.
11. Disconnect the cooling fan motor. Remove the cooling fan motor, fan blade and fan shroud as an assembly.
12. Remove the upper radiator hose.
13. If equipped with an automatic transmission, disconnect the oil cooler inlet tube and oil cooler tube.
14. Disconnect the heater water hoses. Disconnect the lower radiator hose at the water pump.
15. Unfasten the radiator retaining bolts, then remove the radiator. On supercharged engines, it will also be necessary to remove the two push pins retaining the charge air cooler to the radiator.
16. Disconnect the power steering pressure hose. On non-supercharged engines, remove the power steering pump and power steering pump bracket and position aside.
17. Disconnect the fuel charge wiring from the A/C clutch.
18. Detach and cap the A/C compressor lines. Unfasten the retaining bolts, then remove the A/C compressor.
19. Remove the coolant recovery reservoir.
20. Remove the wiring shield.
21. Unfasten the accelerator cable bracket and position it aside.
22. Proper relieve the fuel system pressure. Disconnect the fuel supply hose, then the fuel return hose.
23. Disconnect the PCM from the engine control sensor wiring and fuel charging wiring.
24. Tag and detach all necessary vacuum hoses.
25. On non-SC 49 state engine vehicles, disconnect the ground wire assembly and the coil wire. On the SC and non-SC California vehicles, disconnect the Ignition Control Module (ICM) at the wiring connector.
26. For SC engines, remove the ignition coil retaining screws, then position the ignition coil aside.
27. For SC engines, remove the nuts retaining the charge air cooler outlet tube to the charge air cooler to intake manifold adapter and charge air cooler outlet tube bracket and remove the charge air cooler outlet tube retaining bolts and nut at the alternator mounting bracket.
28. For SC engines, unfasten the alternator mounting bracket bolts, disconnect the alternator wiring and remove the alternator.
29. If equipped with a supercharged engine, remove the power steering pump and bracket and position it aside.
30. Disconnect the fuel vapor hose.
31. Detach one end of the throttle valve control actuating cable.
32. Raise and safely support the vehicle. Properly drain the engine oil.
33. For SC engines, remove the two nuts retaining the charge air cooler and remove the charge air cooler and cooler outlet tube.
34. Remove the dual converter Y-pipe-to-exhaust manifold nuts and remove the left exhaust manifold shield.
35. Detach the heated oxygen sensors.
36. Remove the inspection plug from the engine rear plate and remove the torque converter bolts, if equipped with an automatic transaxle.
37. Remove the engine-to-transmission bolts.
38. Remove the front engine support insulator through bolts. On the SC engine, remove the left front engine support insulator retaining strap bolt.

➥ If the crankshaft damper and pulley have to be separated, mark the damper and pulley so that they may be reassembled in the same relative position. This is important as the damper and pulley are initially balanced as a unit.

39. Remove the pulley from the damper.

➥ If the crankshaft damper is being replaced, check if the original crankshaft damper had balance pins installed on it. If so, new balance pins (EOSZ-6A328-A or equivalent) must be installed on the new crankshaft damper in the same position as the original crankshaft damper. The pulley must also be installed in the same relative position as originally installed.

40. Remove the starter motor.
41. Remove the ground cable and remove the starter motor wire harness retainers (right and left sides).
42. For the SC, disconnect the low oil level sensor.
43. Partially lower the vehicle.
44. Disconnect the oil pressure sensor.
45. Position a suitable floor jack under the transmission. Position a shop crane and attach to the engine lifting eyes.
46. Remove the engine assembly from the vehicle and place it on a suitable work stand.

To install:

➥ Lightly oil all bolt and stud bolt threads before installation except those specifying special sealant.

47. Install engine lifting equipment to the engine lifting eyes and remove the engine assembly from the work stand.
48. Position the engine assembly in the vehicle. Install two engine-to-transmission bolts.

➥ Seat the left side locating pin before seating the right side.

49. Lower the engine onto the front engine support insulators and remove the shop crane.
50. Remove the floor jack from under the transmission. Tighten two engine-to-transmission bolts.
51. Attach the oil pressure sensor electrical connector.
52. Raise and safely support the vehicle.
53. Install the remaining engine-to-transmission bolts. Tighten all bolts to 40-50 ft. lbs. (55-68 Nm).

54. Install the torque converter bolts and tighten to 20–34 ft. lbs. (27–46 Nm). Install the inspection plug to the engine rear plate.
55. Install and tighten the front engine support insulator through bolts and the left front engine support insulator retaining strap bolt.
56. Install the starter motor, as outlined in Section 2 of this manual.
57. Fasten the starter motor wire harness retainer, ground cable and transmission oil cooler line bracket.
58. Install the dual converter Y-pipe-to-exhaust manifold retaining nuts.
59. Install the pulley to the crankshaft damper. Tighten the bolts to 20–28 ft. lbs. (26–38 Nm).
60. Attach the heated oxygen sensor(s) at the wiring connector.
61. Install the oil bypass filter.
62. For SC engines, connect the low oil level sensor.
63. Carefully lower the vehicle.
64. Connect the throttle valve control actuating cable.
65. Attach the fuel vapor hose.
66. For SC engines, install the charge air cooler outlet tube, charge air cooler and power steering pump and bracket.
67. If equipped with a SC engine, install the alternator, connect the wiring and install the alternator mounting bracket bolts.
68. If equipped with a SC engine, install the charge air cooler outlet tube bolts at the power steering bracket and install the nuts retaining the charge air cooler outlet tube to the charge air cooler outlet tube bracket and charge air cooler to the intake manifold adapter.
69. For SC engines, install the ignition coil and retaining bolts.
70. Install the coolant recovery reservoir.
71. Attach the alternator-to-voltage regulator electrical wiring.
72. Connect the vacuum hoses, as tagged during removal.
73. Attach the engine control sensor wiring and the fuel charging wiring.
74. On non-SC 49 state engine vehicles, connect the ground wire assembly and coil wire. On SC and non-SC California engines, attach the ignition control module at the wiring connector.
75. Unplug and connect the fuel supply and return lines.
76. Install the accelerator cable bracket.
77. Fasten the wiring shield.
78. If equipped, install the A/C compressor. Tighten the retaining bolts to 30–45 ft. lbs. (41–61 Nm). Unplug and connect the compressor lines.
79. If equipped, connect the fuel charging wiring to the A/C clutch.
80. For non-SC engines, install the power steering pump and bracket. Connect the power steering hoses.
81. Install the radiator and retaining bolts. On SC engines, install the charge air cooler to the radiator and secure with the retaining push pins.
82. Connect the lower radiator hose to the water pump. Install the heater water hoses.
83. If equipped with an automatic transmission, install the oil cooler inlet tube and oil cooler tube.
84. Attach the upper radiator hose.
85. Install the cooling fan motor, fan blade, and fan shroud as an assembly. For SC engines, attach the cooling fan motor.
86. Position the drive belts (accessory/supercharger).
87. Install the radiator upper sight shield.
88. For SC engines, install the charge air cooler tube and bolts retaining the tube to the power steering bracket. Install the charge air cooler tube to the supercharger and charge air cooler.
89. Install the cowl vent screen and wiper module.
90. Install the hood, using the marks make during removal for alignment purposes.
91. Attach the engine compartment lamp wiring.
92. Connect the negative battery cable.
93. Refill the crankcase to the proper level with the specified type of engine oil. Properly fill the engine cooling system.
94. Bleed the power steering system. Start the engine and check the fluid levels, and for fluid/vacuum leaks.
95. If equipped with A/C, take the car to a certified repair shop to have the system evacuated, charged and leak tested.

4.6L Engine

➧ See Figure 7

1. If equipped with A/C, have a repair shop recover the refrigerant using the proper equipment.
2. Disconnect the negative battery cable.
3. Properly drain the engine cooling system.
4. Remove the air cleaner outlet tube, then remove the air cleaner assembly.
5. Remove the cooling fan motor, blade and shroud as an assembly.
6. Properly relieve the fuel system pressure, then disconnect and plug the fuel lines.
7. Detach the fuel charging wiring 42–pin connector and 8–pin connector, then position out of the way.
8. Disconnect the accelerator cable and speed control actuator with a suitable prytool.
9. Detach the fuel charging wiring and front vapor hose from the evaporative emission canister purge valve.
10. Disconnect the positive battery cable from the power distribution box.
11. Detach the vacuum supply hose from the throttle body adapter vacuum port.
12. Disconnect the transmission oil cooler tubes from the oil cooler.
13. Unfasten the upper radiator hose from the radiator. Disconnect the heater supply and return hoses.
14. If equipped, disconnect the A/C compressor inlet and outlet hoses from the compressor using Spring Lock Coupling Disconnect tool T81P–19623–G1 ($^3/_8$ in.) and T81P–19623–G2 ($^1/_2$ in.), or equivalent tools.
15. Detach the engine-to-frame wire from the dash panel.
16. Partially raise and safely support the vehicle.
17. Remove the front wheel and tire assemblies.
18. Detach the right and left front anti-lock sensor and bracket wiring connectors.
19. Remove the right and left front disc brake caliper bolts. Remove the calipers and support from the body using a piece of wire. DO NOT let the calipers hang by the brake hose.
20. Disconnect the right and left front suspension upper control arms.
21. Detach the front spring and shocks from the front suspension lower control arms.
22. Raise and safely support the vehicle. Properly drain the engine oil into a suitable container.
23. Disconnect the dual converter Y-pipe from the right and left exhaust manifolds and resonator.

24. Detach the shift cable and bracket.
25. Index the driveshaft centering socket yoke to the rear axle universal joint flange.
26. Remove the four bolts connecting the driveshaft centering socket yoke to the rear axle universal joint flange. Support the rear axle assembly with a jackstand.
27. Remove the two nut and bolt assemblies retaining the front of the rear axle to the rear sub-frame.
28. Loosen the rear differential bracket-to-body bolts, then lower.
29. Slide the driveshaft rearward until it is free of the extension housing.
30. Disconnect the lower hose from the radiator.
31. Loosen the spring clamps and remove the power steering hoses from the power steering oil cooler.
32. Detach the wiring connector bulkhead.
33. Support the front sub/frame using Rotunda Powertrain Lift 014-00765 and Adapter 014-00341 or equivalent.
34. Remove the rear engine support insulator retaining bolts.
35. Disconnect the steering coupling at the pinch bolt joint.
36. Remove the eight front sub-frame retaining bolts, then lower the engine and transmission from the vehicle.
37. Disconnect the power steering pressure and return hoses from the power steering pump.
38. Remove the engine wire harness retainers from the front sub-frame.
39. Remove the left and right front engine support insulator through bolts.
40. Install Rotunda Engine Lift Bracket Set 014-00334 or equivalent on the side of the left cylinder head as the front, as shown in the accompanying figure. Attach Rotunda Engine Lift Bracket Set 014-00334 or equivalent using two M-12 x 1.75 x 20mm bolts. Install Rotunda Engine Lift Bracket Set on the side of right cylinder head at the rear.
41. Connect a shop crane, to the lift brackets.
42. Raise the engine and transmission assembly and carefully separate the engine from the front sub-frame.
43. Remove the starter, as outlined in Section 2 of this manual.
44. Disconnect the transmission oil cooler tubes.
45. Remove the retaining nut from the transmission line stud-to-cylinder block.
46. Remove the transmission housing cover from the cylinder block to gain access to the torque converter retaining nuts. Rotate the crankshaft until each of the four nuts is accessible, then remove the nuts.
47. Lower the engine and transmission assembly to a level, stationary surface.
48. Detach the transmission wire harness connectors at the transmission.
49. Remove the six engine-to-transmission retaining bolts, then separate the engine from the transmission.
50. Position the engine on a suitable work stand, then remove the engine lifting equipment.

To install:

51. Install the Rotunda Engine Lifting Bracket set 014-00334 in the position described earlier in this procedure.
52. Connect a suitable shop crane to the lifting brackets, then remove the engine from the work stand.
53. Carefully lower the engine and align it to the transmission.

➥ Make sure the studs on the torque converter align with the holes in the flywheel.

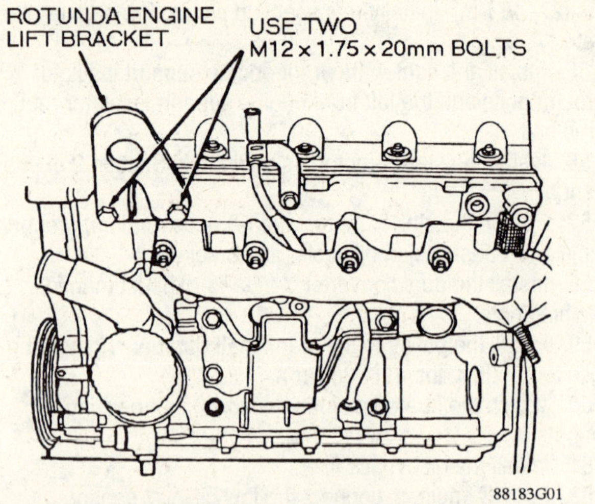

Fig. 7 Install the lift bracket on the side of the left cylinder head with the correct size bolts

54. Start the torque converter pilot into the flywheel and align the paint marks on the flywheel and torque converter.
55. Fully engage the engine to the transmission, then install the six retaining bolts. Tighten the bolts to 30-44 ft. lbs. (40-60 Nm).

➥ Rotate the crankshaft until each of the four nuts is accessible.

56. Install the four torque converter retaining nuts, then tighten to 22-25 ft. lbs. (30-35 Nm).
57. Fasten the transmission housing cover to the cylinder block.
58. Install the starter motor, as outlined in Section 2 of this manual.
59. Position the transmission case to the cylinder block bracket, then install the three bolts and one stud. Tighten the bolts and stud to 18-31 ft. lbs. (25-43 Nm).
60. Position the transmission oil cooler tube bracket to the transmission case-to-cylinder block bracket stud and install the retaining nut. Tighten the nut to 15-22 ft. lbs. (20-30 Nm).
61. Connect the transmission oil cooler tubes to the transmission. Attach the transmission wire harness connector to the transmission.
62. Raise the engine and transmission assembly with a suitable shop crane.
63. Carefully lower the engine and transmission assembly onto the front sub-frame.
64. Install the left and right front engine support insulator through bolts. Tighten the bolts to 15-22 ft. lbs. (20-30 Nm).
65. Fasten the engine wire harness retainers to the front sub-frame.
66. Connect the power steering pressure and return hoses to the power steering pump.
67. Remove the lift bracket from the cylinder heads.
68. Raise the engine, transmission and front sub-frame using Rotunda Powertrain Lift 014-00765 and Adapter 014-00341 or equivalent, into the vehicle.
69. Align the front sub-frame with the body and install the retaining bolts. Tighten to 70-96 ft. lbs. (95-130 Nm).
70. Connect the steering coupling at the pinch bolt joint.

71. Install the rear engine support insulator retaining bolts. Tighten to 15–22 ft. lbs. (20–30 Nm).
72. Remove the powertrain lift and position it out of the way.
73. Install the driveshaft to the transmission.
74. Lift the rear axle assembly into position.
75. Install the two nut and bolts assemblies retaining front of the rear axle assembly to the rear sub-frame. Tighten to 72–89 ft. lbs. (98–120 Nm).
76. Tighten the two rear axle differential insulator nuts to 75–94 ft. lbs. (102–127 Nm).
77. Align the driveshaft centering socket yoke to the rear axle universal joint flange, then install the four retaining bolts. Tighten to 70–96 ft. lbs. (95–130 Nm).
78. Connect the transmission shift linkage.
79. Position the front suspension lower arms to the front spring and shock and install the retaining bolt. Tighten to 118–162 ft. lbs. (160–220 Nm).
80. Connect the upper radiator hose.
81. Attach the power steering hoses to the power steering oil cooler.
82. Connect the engine-to-frame wire to the dash panel.
83. Install the dual converter Y-pipe.
84. Connect the front suspension upper arms to the front wheel knuckles. Tighten to 50–68 ft. lbs. (68–92 Nm).
85. Attach the front anti-lock sensor and bracket wiring connectors.
86. Install the disc brake calipers.
87. Install the front wheel and tire assemblies.
88. Carefully lower the vehicle.
89. Attach the A/C lines to the compressor.
90. Connect the transmission oil cooler tubes to the transmission fluid cooler.
91. Attach the upper radiator hose to the radiator.
92. Connect the heater supply and return hoses.
93. Attach the vacuum supply hose to the throttle body adapter vacuum port.
94. Connect the positive battery cable to the power distribution box.
95. Connect the fuel charging wiring and front vapor hose to the evaporative emission canister purge valve.
96. Attach the accelerator cable and cruise control actuator to the throttle body.
97. Fasten the 42–pin and 8–pin fuel charging wire connectors.
98. Connect the fuel lines.
99. Install the cooling fan motor, blade and shroud.
100. Install the air cleaner outlet tube and the engine air cleaner assembly.
101. Fill and bleed the engine cooling system.
102. Connect the negative battery cable.
103. Fill the crankcase with the proper type and amount of engine oil.
104. Start the engine and check for fluid and/or vacuum leaks.
105. If equipped, take the car to a certified repair shop to have the A/C system evacuated, charged and leak tested.

5.0L Engine

1983–88 VEHICLES (VIN F ENGINES)

The engine removal and installation procedures are for the engine only, without the transmission attached. Remove or disconnect parts of Thermactor system that will interfere with the removal or installation of the engine.

1. If equipped with A/C, have a repair shop recover the refrigerant using the proper equipment.
2. Disconnect the negative battery cable.
3. Properly drain the cooling system and crankcase.
4. Properly relieve the fuel system pressure.
5. Scribe a matchmark around the hood hinges, for installation purposes, then remove the hood.
6. Disconnect the battery ground cables from the engine block.
7. Remove the air intake duct assembly.
8. Disconnect the upper radiator hose from the coolant outlet housing and the lower radiator hose from the water pump.
9. If equipped, disconnect the transmission oil cooler lines from the radiator.
10. Unfasten the bolts attaching the fan shroud to the radiator, then remove the radiator. Remove the fan, spacer, belt pulley and shroud.
11. Remove the alternator bolts, then position the alternator out of the way.
12. Disconnect the oil pressure sending unit wire from the sending unit. Disconnect the low oil level sensor wire, if equipped, at the middle of the rear oil sump on the left side of the oil pan and the flexible fuel lines at the fuel tank line. Plug the fuel tank line.
13. Disconnect the accelerator cable from the throttle body. On automatic transmissions, disconnect the TV rod. If equipped, disconnect the cruise control cable.
14. If equipped, disconnect the throttle valve vacuum line from the intake manifold. Remove the transmission filler tube bracket from the cylinder block.
15. If equipped with A/C, remove the compressor.
16. Disconnect the power steering pump bracket from the cylinder head. Position the power steering pump out of the way and in a position that will prevent the fluid from leaking out.
17. Disconnect the brake vacuum line from the intake manifold.
18. Disconnect the heater hoses from the engine mounted heater tubes and intake manifold. Detach the coolant temperature sending unit wire from the unit.
19. Remove the flywheel or converter housing-to-engine upper bolts.
20. Detach the wiring harness at the two 10–pin connectors.
21. Raise and safely support the front of the vehicle.
22. Detach the starter electrical connector, then remove the starter from the vehicle.
23. Disconnect the muffler inlet pipes from the exhaust manifolds. Disconnect the engine support insulators from the chassis. If equipped detach the downstream Thermactor tubing and check valve from the right exhaust manifold stud.
24. Detach the transmission cooler lines from the retainer and remove the converter housing inspection cover. Disconnect the flywheel from the converter. Secure the converter assembly in the housing. Remove the remaining converter housing-to-engine bolts.
25. Carefully lower the vehicle, then support the transmission with a suitable jack. Attach a suitable shop crane to the lifting brackets on the exhaust manifolds.
26. Raise the engine slightly and carefully pull it from the transmission. Carefully lift the engine out of the engine compartment (avoid bending or damaging the rear cover plate or other components). Install the engine on a suitable work stand.

To install:

27. Attach the engine lifting sling and lifting brackets to the exhaust manifold. Carefully hoist the engine from the work stand.
28. Lower the engine carefully into the engine compartment. Make sure the exhaust manifolds are properly aligned with the muffler inlet pipes. Start the converter pilot into the crankshaft. Align the paint mark on the flywheel with the mark on the torque converter.
29. Install the flywheel or converter housing upper bolts. Make sure the dowels in the cylinder block engage the converter housing.
30. Install the engine support insulator to the chassis attaching fasteners.
31. Raise and safely support the front of the vehicle. Connect both muffler inlet pipes to the exhaust manifolds.
32. Install the starter, then attach the starter electrical connector.
33. Remove the retainer holding the converter in the housing. Attach the converter to the flex plate. Install the converter housing inspection cover. Install the remaining converter housing attaching bolts.
34. Remove the support from the transmission, then lower the vehicle.
35. Attach the wiring harness at the two 10-pin connectors.
36. Connect the coolant temperature sending unit wire. Connect the heater hose to the intake manifold. Connect the low oil sensor wire. Attach the metal heater tubes at the ECT, ACT and EGO sensors, if equipped.
37. Install the transmission filler tube bracket. Connect the manual shift rod and connect the retracting spring. If equipped, connect the throttle valve vacuum line.
38. Unplug the fuel tank line and connect the fuel line and oil pressure sending unit wire.
39. Install the pulley, belt, spacer and fan.
40. Position the alternator, then install the retaining bolts. Attach the alternator and battery ground connections. Adjust the belt tension to specifications.
41. If equipped with A/C, install the compressor.
42. Install the drive belt and power steering pump bracket. Install the bracket attaching bolts. Adjust the belt tension to specifications.
43. Connect the brake vacuum line.
44. Place the radiator shroud over the fan, if equipped. Connect the radiator upper and lower hoses. If equipped with an automatic transmission, connect the transmission fluid cooler lines. If equipped, install the shroud bolts and tighten to 24-48 inch lbs. (3-5 Nm).
45. Connect the heater hoses to the heater tubes.
46. Fill and bleed the engine cooling system. Fill the crankcase with the proper grade and amount of engine oil.
47. Adjust the transmission throttle linkage.
48. Connect the negative battery cable, then start the engine and run at a fast idle. Check the fluid levels and inspect for any fluid and/or vacuum leaks.
49. Install the air intake duct assembly.
50. Install the hood assembly.
51. If equipped, take the car to a certified repair shop to have the A/C system evacuated, charged and leak tested.

1991-93 VEHICLES (VIN T AND E ENGINES)

1. If equipped with A/C, have a repair shop recover the refrigerant using the proper equipment.
2. Properly drain the engine cooling system.
3. Disconnect the negative battery cable. Detach the underhood lamp wiring connector.
4. Remove the engine oil dipstick.
5. Scribe a matchmark around the hood hinges for installation reference, then remove the hood.
6. If equipped, disconnect and cap or plug the A/C compressor lines.
7. Detach the compressor clutch electrical connector and the power steering pressure switch.
8. Disconnect the alternator wiring harness from the alternator and position the harness aside.
9. Remove the fan shroud and fan assembly.
10. Disconnect the upper radiator hose.
11. Remove the air cleaner-to-throttle body tube assembly.
12. Disconnect the transmission oil cooler inlet and outlet tubes.
13. Detach the throttle and kickdown cables from the throttle body and remove the cable bracket retaining bolts. Position the cable and bracket assembly out of the way.
14. Tag and disconnect the following vacuum lines:
    - Upper intake manifold vacuum tee
    - A/C control panel vacuum supply hose
    - Secondary air injection valve
    - EGR external pressure valve (vacuum and electrical connections)
15. Remove the upper intake manifold, as outlined in this section.
16. Detach the main engine wiring harness at the dash panel (right side).
17. Disconnect the heater hoses at the engine.
18. Position the engine wiring harness so it can be removed with the engine.
19. Disconnect the wiring harness form the coil and distributor and position it out of the way.
20. Properly relieve the fuel system pressure. For details, please refer to Section 5 of this manual.
21. Disconnect and plug the fuel inlet and return hoses from the fuel supply manifold.
22. Detach the lower radiator hose from the water pump.
23. Unfasten the radiator retaining bolts, then remove the radiator.
24. Raise and safely support the vehicle, then properly drain the engine oil and remove the oil filter.
25. Remove the starter, as outlined in Section 2 of this manual.
26. Disconnect the heated O_2 sensor from the right and left catalytic converters.
27. Detach the battery ground cable from the left side of the engine.
28. On the right side of the engine, disconnect the bracket for the transmission cooler lines, engine-to-body ground straps and the starter motor wiring harness.
29. Remove the torque converter inspection cover and mark one of the converter studs to the flywheel for alignment during reassembly.
30. Remove the torque converter retaining nuts.
31. Remove the exhaust manifold heat shield at the left manifold flange and disconnect the exhaust pipe from the flange.
32. Disconnect the right side exhaust manifold flange.
33. Loosen the transmission mount retaining nut.

34. Remove the converter housing-to-engine bolts.
35. Remove the engine mount through bolts.

➥ It may be helpful to drain the power steering fluid before removing the lines.

36. Carefully lower the vehicle, then disconnect and plug the power steering fluid lines.
37. Support the transmission with a suitable floor jack.
38. Install a suitable engine lifting sling on the engine lifting eyes.
39. Using a shop crane, lift the engine assembly clear of the engine mounts and remove the engine assembly from the vehicle. Place the engine on a suitable work stand.

To install:

40. Install a suitable engine lifting sling on the engine lifting eyes and lift the engine from the work stand.
41. Carefully lower the engine into the engine compartment. Make sure the exhaust manifolds are properly aligned with the muffler inlet pipes.
42. Start the converter pilot into the crankshaft. Align the mark on the flywheel to the mark on the torque converter.
43. Position the retaining clip for the left side O_2 sensor wiring near the left side upper transmission-to-engine bolt.
44. Install the converter housing upper bolts. Make sure the dowels in the cylinder block engage the converter housing.
45. Raise and safely support the vehicle, then install the housing bolts.
46. Install the engine mount through bolts and tighten to 35–50 ft. lbs. (47–68 Nm).
47. Tighten the transmission mount retaining nut to 65–85 ft. lbs. (88–115 Nm).
48. Connect the right side exhaust manifold flange.
49. Attach the exhaust pipe to the left side exhaust manifold flange, then install the exhaust manifold heat shield.
50. Install the torque converter, then install the converter inspection cover.
51. On the right side of the engine, install the bracket for the transmission cooler lines, engine-to-body ground strap and the starter motor wiring harness.
52. Connect the battery ground cable to the left side of the engine.
53. Attach the O_2 sensors for the right and left catalytic converters.
54. Install the starter, as outlined in Section 2 of this manual.
55. Install a new engine oil filter, and install the drain plug, if still removed.
56. Carefully lower the vehicle, then unplug and connect the power steering lines.
57. Install the radiator. Attach the coolant overflow hose to the radiator.
58. Connect the lower radiator hose to the water pump.
59. Uncap and connect the fuel inlet and return hoses to the fuel supply manifold.
60. Position and connect the engine wiring harness for the coil and distributor.
61. Attach the engine wiring harness to the coil.
62. Connect the heater hoses at the engine.
63. Attach the main engine wiring harness connectors at the dash panel (right side).
64. Install the upper intake manifold.
65. Connect the following vacuum lines:
    - Upper intake manifold vacuum tee
    - A/C control panel vacuum supply hose
    - Secondary air injection valve
    - EGR external pressure valve (vacuum and electrical connections)
66. Connect the throttle and kickdown cables to the throttle body and install the cable bracket retaining bolts.
67. Attach the transmission oil cooler inlet and outlet tubes.
68. Install the upper radiator hose.
69. Install the fan assembly and fan shroud.
70. Connect the air cleaner-to-throttle body tube.
71. Position and connect the wiring harness for the alternator.
72. Attach the compressor clutch electrical connector.
73. If equipped, unplug and connect the A/C compressor lines.
74. Install the hood, using the marks made during removal for alignment purposes.
75. Attach the wiring connector for the underhood lamp.
76. Connect the negative battery cable.
77. Fill and bleed the engine cooling system and crankcase.
78. Fill and bleed the power steering fluid with the proper type and amount of fluid.
79. Install the oil dipstick.
80. Start the engine and check the fluid levels. Inspect for fluid and/or vacuum leaks.
81. If equipped, take the car to a certified repair shop to have the A/C system evacuated, charged and leak tested.

Rocker Arm (Valve) Cover

REMOVAL & INSTALLATION

2.3L Engine

➧ See Figure 8

1. Disconnect the negative battery cable..
2. Detach the air intake tube at the throttle body by disconnecting the metal tube from the turbocharger (there are two retaining bolts) and remove the clamp from the throttle body end.
3. Disconnect the PCV hose from the rear of the rocker arm cover.
4. Remove the throttle body assembly, as outlined in Section 5 of this manual.
5. Remove the eight retaining bolts, then remove the rocker arm (valve) cover. Clean all old gasket material from the cover and cylinder head gasket surfaces.

To install:

6. Coat the gasket surfaces of the rocker arm cover and cylinder head with Gasket and Seal Contact Adhesive D7AZ-19B508-A or equivalent. Allow to dry past the "wet" stage.
7. Install the guide pins, the position the rocker arm cover over the pins. Hand start two bolts, then remove the guide pins. Hand start the remaining bolts. Tighten the rocker arm cover bolts to 62–97 inch lbs. (7–11 Nm).
8. Install the throttle body, as outlined in Section 5 of this manual.
9. Attach the PCV hose to the rear of the rocker arm cover.
10. Connect the air intake tube.
11. Connect the negative battery cable, then start the engine and check for leaks.

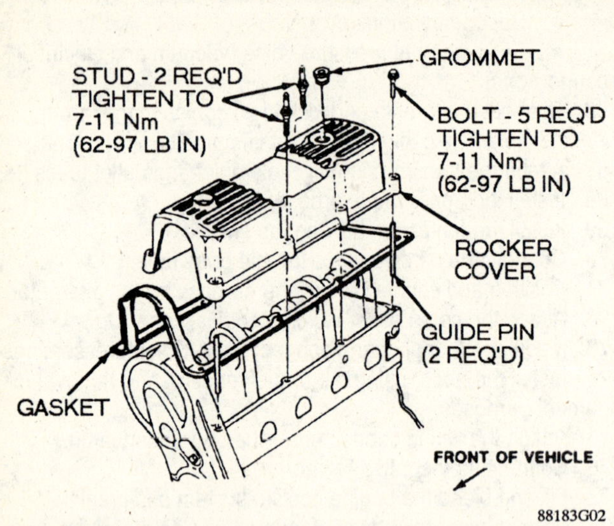

Fig. 8 After removing the throttle body, you can remove the rocker arm (valve) cover from the 2.3L engine

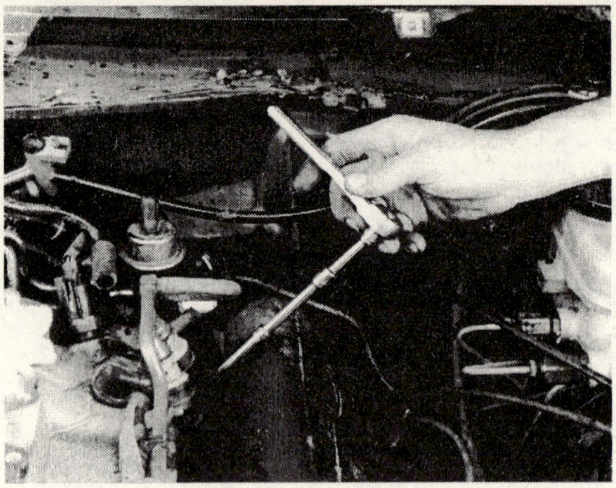

Fig. 9 Unfasten the retaining bolts, then . . .

Fig. 10 . . . remove the valve cover from the engine

Fig. 11 Remove the old gasket and replace with a new one during installation

3.8L Engine

See Figures 9, 10, 11 and 12

1. Disconnect the negative battery cable.
2. Tag and disconnect the spark plug wires. Remove the ignition wire routing clips from the valve cover retaining bolt studs.
3. If the left side valve cover is being removed, proceed as follows:
   a. Remove the oil filler cap.
   b. For SC engines, remove the charge air cooler/intercooler tubes.
   c. Remove the crankcase ventilation tube.
   d. For SC engines, disconnect the engine oil cooler inlet tube and hose.
4. If the right side valve cover is being removed, proceed as follows:
   a. Remove the PCV valve.
   b. For SC engines, remove the air cleaner outlet tube.
   c. For SC engines, remove the throttle body.
5. Unfasten the valve cover retaining screws/bolts, then remove the cover from the vehicle. Remove and discard the old gasket. Use a suitable solvent to carefully clean the old gasket material and/or dirt from the sealing surfaces.

To install:

Lightly oil all bolt and stud threads before installation.

6. Position a new gasket into the groove on the valve cover.
7. Place the cover on the cylinder head and install the retaining bolts. Note the location of the spark plug wire routing clip stud bolts. Tighten the retaining bolts to 7–9 ft. lbs. (9–12 Nm).
8. If the left side valve cover is being installed, proceed as follows:
   a. For SC engines, connect the engine oil cooler inlet tube and hose.
   b. Connect the crankcase ventilation tube.
   c. For SC engines, install the charge air cooler/intercooler tubes.
   d. Install the oil filler cap.

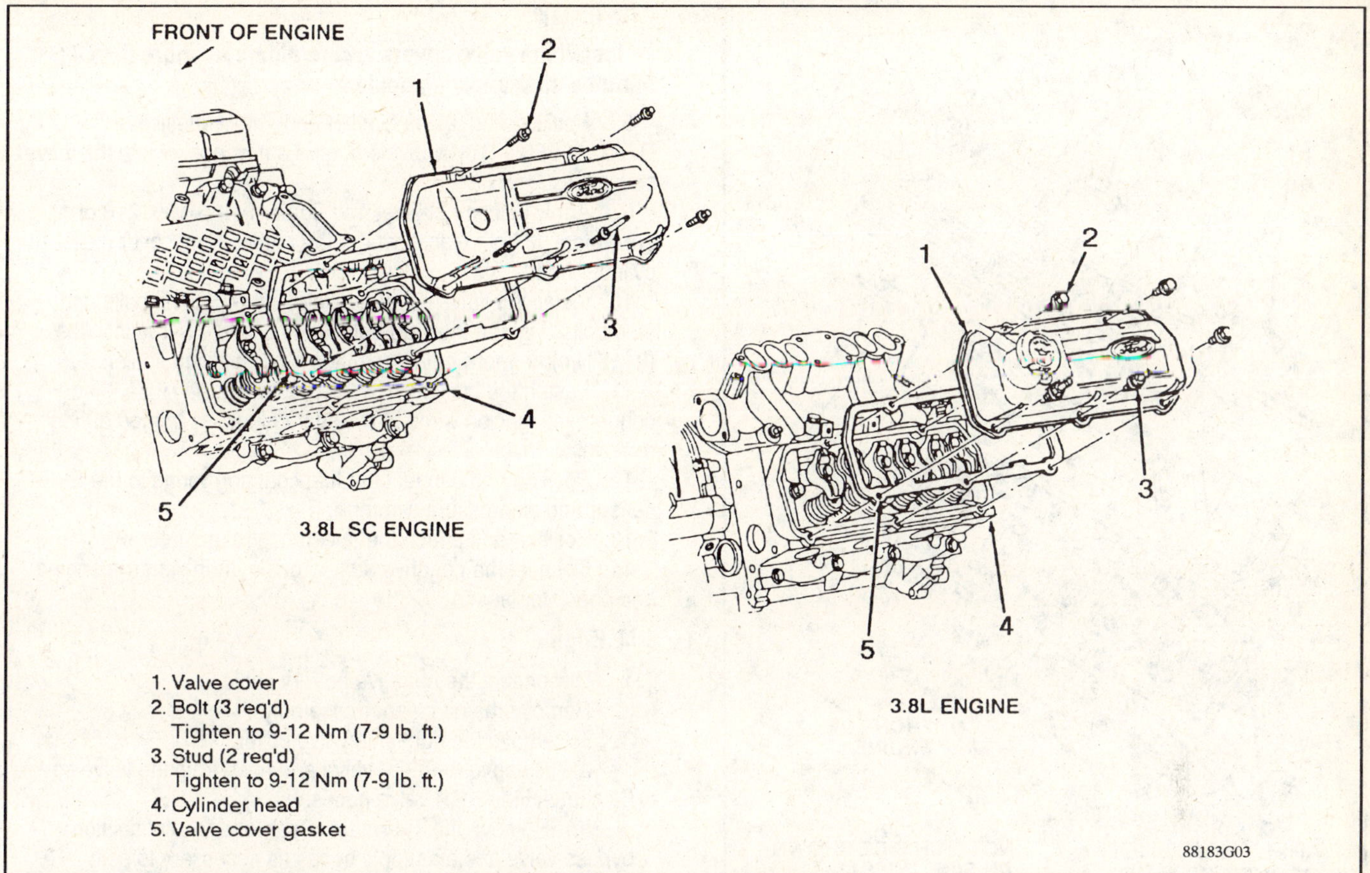

Fig. 12 Valve cover removal — 3.8L Super Charged (SC) and non-SC engines

9. If the right side valve cover is being installed, proceed as follows:
   a. For SC engines, install the throttle body.
   b. For SC engines, connect the air cleaner outlet tube.
   c. Install the PCV valve.
10. Install the spark plug wire routing clips, then connect the spark plug wires, as tagged during removal.
11. Connect the negative battery cable, then start the engine and check for leaks.

4.6L Engine

➧ See Figure 13

RIGHT SIDE

1. Disconnect the negative battery cable.
2. Remove the air cleaner outlet tube.
3. Detach the 42-pin connector and the 8-pin connector leading to the Mass Air Flow (MAF) sensor and Intake Air Temperature (IAT) sensor.
4. Remove the nut retaining the A/C line to the right front fender apron.
5. Lift the A/C line and feed the 42-pin connector under the line. Position the connector out of the way.
6. Properly relieve the fuel system pressure, as outlined in Section 5 of this manual. Disconnect the fuel lines.

➥ Do NOT pull on the ignition wires, as the wire may separate from the connector in the wire boot.

7. Tag and disconnect the ignition wires from the spark plugs.
8. Remove the ignition wires and the ignition wire separators from the valve cover studs, then position the wires out of the way.
9. Disconnect the PCV valve from the crankcase ventilation grommet, then position it out of the way.
10. Unfasten the bolts and stud bolts retaining the valve cover to the cylinder, then remove the valve cover. Remove and discard the gasket. Thoroughly clean and dry the gasket mating surfaces using Metal Surface Cleaner F4AZ-19A536-RA or equivalent.

To install:

➥ Install the valve covers and retainers no more than 4 minutes after applying sealant.

11. Position and, using Gasket and Trim Adhesive D7AZ-19B508-B or equivalent, glue a new gasket into the valve cover.
12. Apply Silicone Gasket and Sealer F1AZ-19562-B or equivalent, in both places where the engine front cover meets the cylinder head.
13. Install the valve cover gaskets, valve covers, bolts and stud bolts. Tighten the stud bolts and bolts to 71-106 inch lbs. (8-12 Nm) no more than 4 minutes after applying sealer.
14. Install the PCV valve into the crankcase ventilation grommet.
15. Fasten the ignition wire separators on the studs, then connect the ignition wires to the spark plugs, as tagged during removal.
16. Connect the fuel lines.
17. Position and attach the 42-pin and 8-pin connectors.
18. Position the A/C line, then install the retaining nut.
19. Connect the negative battery cable, then start the engine and check for leaks.

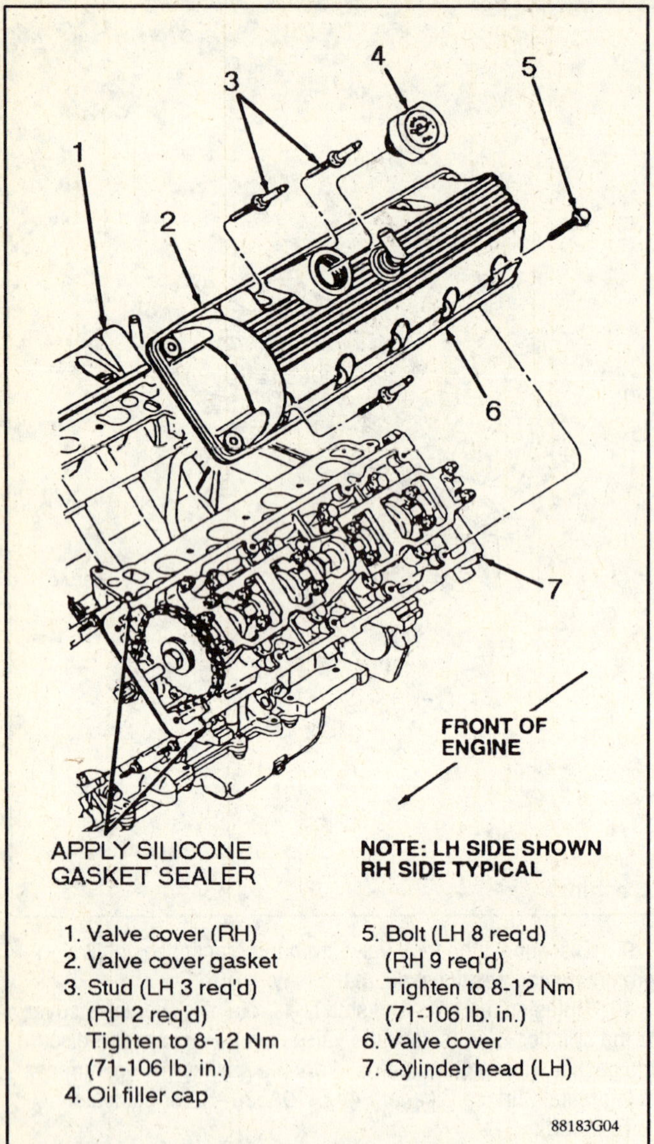

Fig. 13 Removal of the valve cover on the 4.6L engine — left side shown, right side similar

LEFT SIDE

1. Disconnect the negative battery cable.
2. Remove the air cleaner outlet tube.
3. Disconnect the speed control actuator from the throttle body, then position the actuator out of the way.
4. Detach the fuel charging wiring from the Electronic Variable Orifice (EVO) sensor and oil pressure sensor. Position the fuel charging wiring out of the way.

➥ Do NOT pull on the ignition wires, as the wire may separate from the connector in the wire boot.

5. Tag and disconnect the ignition wires from the spark plugs.
6. Remove the ignition wires and the ignition wire separators from the valve cover studs, then position the wires out of the way.
7. Unfasten the bolts and stud bolts retaining the valve cover to the cylinder head, then remove the valve cover.Remove and discard the gasket. Thoroughly clean and dry the gasket mating surfaces using Metal Surface Cleaner F4AZ-19A536-RA or equivalent.

To install:

➥ Install the valve covers and retainers no more than 4 minutes after applying sealant.

8. Position and, using Gasket and Trim Adhesive D7AZ-19B508-B or equivalent, glue a new gasket into the valve cover.
9. Apply Silicone Gasket and Sealer F1AZ-19562-B or equivalent, in both places where the engine front cover meets the cylinder head.
10. Install the valve cover gaskets, valve covers, bolts and stud bolts. Tighten the stud bolts and bolts to 71-106 inch lbs. (8-12 Nm) no more than 4 minutes after applying sealer.
11. Fasten the ignition wire separators on the studs, then connect the ignition wires to the spark plugs, as tagged during removal.
12. Position and connect the fuel charging wiring to the EVO sensor and oil pressure sensor.
13. Position and attach the speed control actuator.
14. Connect the negative battery cable, then start the engine and check for leaks.

5.0L Engine

1. Disconnect the negative battery cable.
2. Remove the air cleaner assembly.
3. To remove the right side valve cover:
   a. Remove the PCV valve and hose from the valve cover. Disconnect the EGR valve hoses.
   b. Remove the Thermactor®/secondary air injection bypass valve and air supply hoses as necessary to gain clearance.
   c. Tag and disconnect the spark plug wires from the plugs, using tool T74P-666-A or equivalent, with a twisting pulling motion. Twist and pull on the boots only, never on the wire. Position the wires and mounting bracket out of the way.
4. To remove the left side valve cover:
   a. Remove the spark plug wires and bracket.
   b. Remove the wiring harness and any vacuum hose from the bracket.
   c. Remove the upper intake manifold.
   d. Remove the valve cover mounting bolts and valve cover.
5. Remove the upper intake manifold.
6. Unfasten the valve cover mounting bolts, then remove the valve cover.
7. Clean all old gasket material from the valve cover and cylinder head mounting surfaces.

To install:

8. Use oil resistant sealing compound and a new valve cover gasket. Position a new valve cover gasket, making sure all the gasket tangs are engaged into the cover notches provided.
9. Position the valve cover(s) on the cylinder head. On the left side cover, install the bolts and wire loom clips. For vehicles through 1988, the cover is tightened in two steps. Tighten the bolts to 3-5 ft. lbs. (4-7 Nm) for vehicles through 1985, to 6-9 ft. lbs. (8-12 Nm) for 1986-88 vehicles or to 10-13 ft. lbs. (14-18 Nm) for 1991-92 vehicles, then two minutes later, tighten the bolts to the same specification. For 1993 vehicles, tighten the bolts to 12-15 ft. lbs. (16-20 Nm).
10. Install the upper intake manifold.
11. Install the crankcase ventilation hoses in the cover(s).

12. Install the spark plugs wires and bracket assembly on the rocker arm cover attaching stud. Connect the spark plug wires, as tagged during removal.
13. Install the air cleaner and intake duct assembly.
14. Install the Thermactor bypass valve and air supply hoses.
15. Connect the negative battery cable.

Rocker Arm (Cam Follower) and Hydraulic Lash Adjuster

REMOVAL & INSTALLATION

2.3L Engine

16. A special tool is required to compress the lash adjuster.
1. Remove the valve cover and associated parts as required.
2. Rotate the camshaft so that the base circle of the cam is against the cam follower you intend to remove.
3. Remove the retaining spring from the cam follower, if so equipped.
4. Using special tool T74P-6565-B or a valve spring compressor tool, collapse the lash adjuster and/or depress the valve spring, as necessary, and slide the cam follower over the lash adjuster and out from under the camshaft.
5. Install the cam follower in the reverse order of removal. Make sure that the lash adjuster is collapsed and released before rotating the camshaft.

Rocker Arm Shaft/Rocker Arms

REMOVAL & INSTALLATION

V6 and V8 Engines

1. Disconnect the negative battery cable.
2. Remove the rocker arm (valve) cover, as outlined earlier in this section.
3. Remove the rocker arm stud nut or bolt, fulcrum seat and rocker arm.
4. Lubricate all parts with heavy engine oil before installation.
5. When installing, rotate the crankshaft until the lifter is on the base of the cam circle (all the way down) and assemble the rocker arm.
6. Tighten the nut or bolt to 17-23 ft. lbs. (23-31 Nm).

➥ Some later engines use RTV sealant instead of valve cover gaskets.

Valve Lash

ADJUSTMENTS

2.3L Engine

➧ See Figure 14

The 2.3L engine is an overhead cam engine with hydraulic lash adjusters. These units are placed at the fulcrum point of the cam followers (rocker arms). Their action are similar to hydraulic tappets used in pushrod engines and are serviced in the same manner.

➥ Valve Arrangement (Front to Rear)...E-I-E-I-E-I-E-I

1. Position the camshaft so that the base circle of the lobe is facing the cam follower of the valve to be checked.
2. Using the appropriate tool (T74P-6565 or equivalent), slowly apply pressure to the cam follower until the lash adjuster is completely collapsed. Hold the follower in this position and insert the proper size feeler gauge between the base circle of the cam and the follower.
3. If the clearance is excessive, remove the cam follower and inspect for damage.
4. If the cam follower appears to be intact and not excessively worn, measure the valve spring assembled height to be sure the valve is not sticking.
5. If the valve spring assembled height is correct, check the dimensions of the camshaft.
6. If the camshaft dimensions are within specifications, remove, clean and test the lash adjuster.
7. Reinstall the lash adjuster and check the clearance. Replace any damaged or worn parts, as necessary.

3.8L and 4.6L Engines

The 3.8L and 4.6L engines are equipped with hydraulic tappets, providing automatic lash adjustment.

5.0L Engine

EXCEPT HIGH OUTPUT

➧ See Figures 15 and 16

1. Install an auxiliary starter switch.

➥ Turn the ignition switch OFF and remove the ignition key while performing this procedure.

2. Crank the engine until the No. 1 piston is on TDC after the compression stroke.
3. With the crankshaft in the positions designated in Steps 4, 5 and 6, position the tappet compressor tool (T71P-6513-B or equivalent) on the rocker arm.
   a. Slowly apply pressure to bleed down the tappet until the plunger is completely bottomed. Hold the tappet in this position and check the available clearance between the rocker arm and the valve stem tip with a feeler gauge.
   b. If the clearance is less than specified, install a shorter pushrod.
   c. If the clearance is greater than specified, install a longer pushrod.
4. With the No. 1 piston on TDC at the end of the compression stroke (POSITION 1), check the following valves:
   a. No. 1 Intake & No. 1 Exhaust
   b. No. 7 Intake & No. 5 Exhaust
   c. No. 8 Intake & No. 4 Exhaust
5. Rotate the crankshaft (POSITION 2) and check the following valves.
   a. No. 5 Intake & No. 2 Exhaust
   b. No. 4 Intake & No. 6 Exhaust
6. Rotate the crankshaft (POSITION 3) and check the following valves.
   a. No. 2 Intake & No. 7 Exhaust
   b. No. 3 Intake & No. 3 Exhaust
   c. No. 6 Intake & No. 8 Exhaust

HIGH-OUTPUT

1. Disconnect the "I terminal" and the "S terminal" from the starter relay.

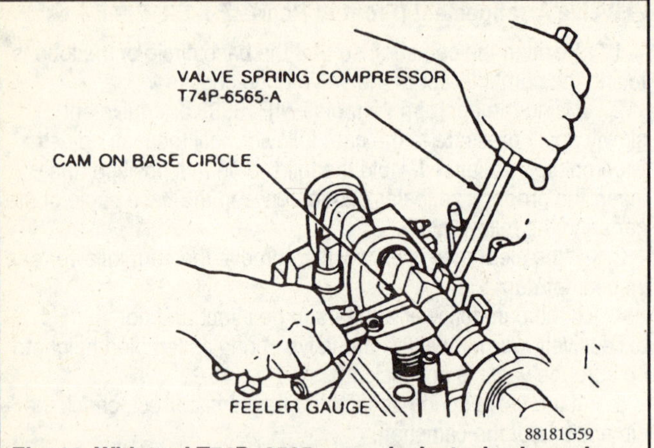

Fig. 14 With tool T74P-6565 or equivalent, slowly apply pressure to the cam follower until the lash adjuster is completely collapsed. Then insert a feeler gauge

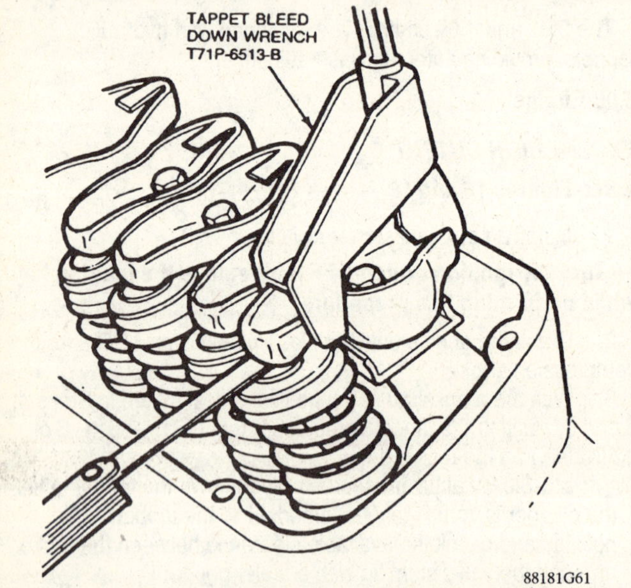

Fig. 15 With tool T71P-6513-B or equivalent, slowly apply pressure to the tappet until it has completely bottomed. Then insert a feeler gauge

2. Install an auxiliary starter switch between the battery and S terminals of the starter relay.

➥ Turn the ignition switch OFF and remove the ignition key while performing this procedure.

3. Crank the engine until the No. 1 piston is on TDC after the compression stroke.

4. With the crankshaft in the positions designated in Steps 5, 6 and 7, position the tappet compressor tool (T71P-6513-B or equivalent) on the rocker arm.

   a. Slowly apply pressure to bleed down the tappet until the plunger is completely bottomed. Hold the tappet in this position and check the available clearance between the rocker arm and the valve stem tip with a feeler gauge.

   b. If the clearance is less than specified, install a shorter pushrod.

   c. If the clearance is greater than specified, install a longer pushrod.

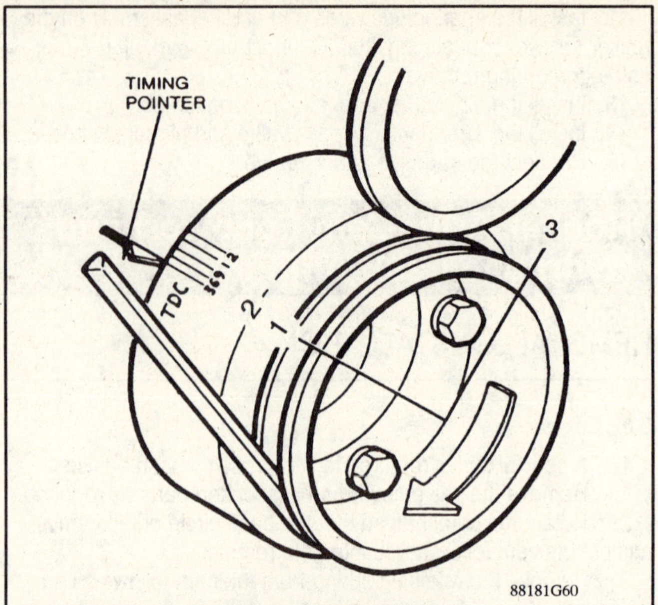

Fig. 16 Valve lash adjustment positions

5. With the No. 1 piston on TDC at the end of the compression stroke (POSITION 1), check the following valves:

   a. No. 1 Intake & No. 1 Exhaust
   b. No. 4 Intake & No. 3 Exhaust
   c. No. 8 Intake & No. 7 Exhaust

6. Rotate the crankshaft (POSITION 2) and check the following valves.

   a. No. 3 Intake & No. 2 Exhaust
   b. No. 7 Intake & No. 6 Exhaust

7. Rotate the crankshaft (POSITION 3) and check the following valves.

   a. No. 2 Intake & No. 4 Exhaust
   b. No. 5 Intake & No. 5 Exhaust
   c. No. 6 Intake & No. 8 Exhaust

Thermostat

REMOVAL & INSTALLATION

✱✱CAUTION

When draining the coolant, keep in mind that cats and dogs are attracted by the ethylene glycol antifreeze, and are quite likely to drink any that is left in an uncovered container or in puddles on the ground. This will prove fatal in sufficient quantity. Always drain the coolant into a sealable container. Coolant should be reused unless it is contaminated or several years old.

Except 2.3L Engine

➧ See Figure 17

1. Partially drain the cooling system so the coolant level is below the thermostat.

2. Disconnect the upper radiator hose at the thermostat housing.

3. Unfasten the two water outlet connection/thermostat housing retaining bolts, the remove the thermostat housing, thermostat and gasket or O-ring, as applicable.

To install:

4. Clean the mating surfaces of the housing and the engine to remove all old gasket material and sealer.

➥ To prevent incorrect installation of the thermostat, the hose/housing connection on all engine contains a locking recess into the thermostat is turned and locked. Install the thermostat with the bridge section in the connection. Turn the thermostat clockwise to lock it in position on the flats cast into the connection.

5. Position the thermostat, gasket or O ring and connection on the intake manifold. Install the retaining bolts and tighten to 15–22 ft. lbs. (20–30 Nm).
6. Connect the upper radiator hose to the housing/hose connection. Position a new hose clamp on the connection. Make sure the clamp is between the alignment marks on the hose.
7. Properly fill the cooling system with the correct type and quantity of coolant. Run the engine at operating temperature and check for leaks. Recheck the coolant level.

2.3L Engine

➧ See Figure 18

1. Partially drain the engine cooling system to a level below the thermostat.
2. Disconnect the heater return hose at the thermostat housing located on the left front lower side of the engine.
3. Unfasten the coolant outlet housing retaining bolts. Pull the housing away from the cylinder head or manifold sufficiently to provide access to the thermostat.
4. Remove the thermostat by rotating counterclockwise in the housing until the thermostat becomes free. Do not pry on the thermostat. Remove the gasket.

To install:

➥ To prevent incorrect installation of the thermostat, the hose/housing connection on all engine contains a locking recess into the thermostat is turned and locked. Install the thermostat with the bridge section in the connection. Turn the thermostat clockwise to lock it in position on the flats cast into the connection.

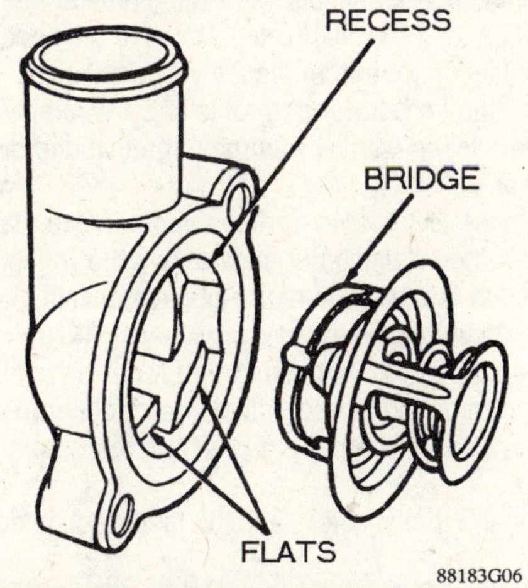

Fig. 17 Turn the thermostat clockwise to lock it in position on the flats cast into the connection

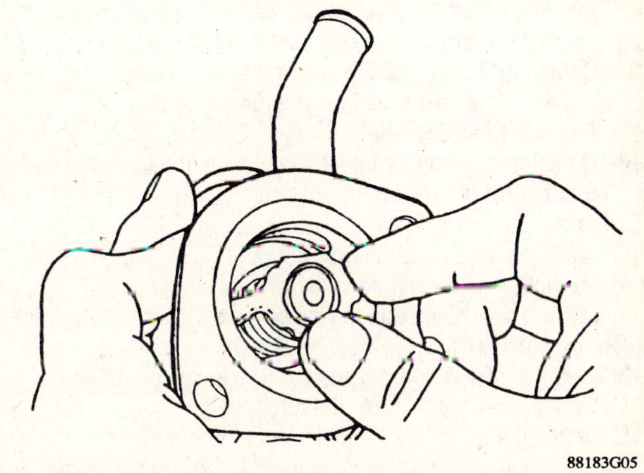

Fig. 18 On the 2.3L engine, rotate the thermostat counterclockwise to remove

5. Clean the mating surfaces of the outlet elbow and the engine to remove all old gasket material and sealer. Using an adhesive-type gasket cement, glue the gasket to the engine outlet. Coat the gasket surfaces of the outlet housing with gasket sealer. Position the thermostat in the outlet housing. The thermostat must be rotated clockwise to lock it in position. Be sure the full width of the heater outlet tube is visible within the thermostat port.
6. Position the coolant outlet elbow, then install the retaining bolts. Tighten the bolts to 12–15 ft. lbs. (16–20 Nm).
7. Connect the heater hoses to the thermostat housing.
8. Properly fill the cooling system with the correct type and quantity of coolant. Run the engine at operating temperature and check for leaks. Recheck the coolant level.

Intake Manifold

REMOVAL & INSTALLATION

****CAUTION**

When draining the coolant, keep in mind that cats and dogs are attracted by the ethylene glycol antifreeze, and are quite likely to drink any that is left in an uncovered container or in puddles on the ground. This will prove fatal in sufficient quantity. Always drain the coolant into a sealable container. Coolant should be reused unless it is contaminated or several years old.

2.3L Engine

➧ See Figure 19

UPPER INTAKE MANIFOLD

1. Properly relieve the fuel system pressure.
2. Disconnect the negative battery cable.
3. Remove the air cleaner and duct assembly.
4. Tag and detach the wiring at the Throttle Position (TP) sensor, air bypass valve, Knock Sensor (KS) and EGR valve.

5. Tag and disconnect all vacuum lines at the manifold.
6. Disconnect the throttle, speed control and kickdown cables. Unbolt the bracket and position it out of the way.
7. Detach the air intake and crankcase vent hoses.
8. Separate the cast tube from the turbocharger.
9. Remove the EGR tube.
10. Unfasten the 4 upper intake manifold mounting bolts and left off the manifold/throttle body assembly.

To install:

11. Clean all mating surfaces thoroughly. Take great care to avoid damaging the machined surfaces!
12. Place a new gasket on the lower manifold assembly, then tighten the bolts to 15-22 ft. lbs. (20-30 Nm).
13. Install the EGR tube. Tighten to 6-9 ft. lbs. (8-12 Nm).
14. Connect the cast tube to the turbocharger.
15. Attach the air intake manifold crankcase vent hoses.
16. Position the bracket, then connect the kickdown, speed control and throttle cables.
17. Connect the vacuum lines as tagged during removal.
18. Attach the wiring at the EGR valve, Knock sensor, air bypass valve and TP sensor.
19. Install the air cleaner and duct assembly.
20. Connect the negative battery cable.

LOWER INTAKE MANIFOLD

1. Properly relieve the fuel system pressure.
2. Disconnect the negative battery cable.
3. Properly drain the engine cooling system into a suitable container.
4. Remove the upper intake manifold/throttle body assembly.
5. Disconnect the coolant hose at the lower intake manifold.
6. Remove the fuel injector pulse dampening bracket.
7. Detach the fuel supply line quick-connect fitting.
8. Disconnect the fuel return line.
9. Detach the injector wiring.
10. Unfasten the 2 bolts and lift off the fuel supply manifold.
11. Remove the 8 retaining bolts, then lift off the lower intake manifold.

To install:

12. Clean all mating surfaces thoroughly. Take great care to avoid damaging the machined surfaces!
13. Position a new gasket, then install the lower manifold. Tighten the retaining bolts to 14-21 ft. lbs. (19-28 Nm).
14. Install the fuel supply manifold, then tighten the 2 bolts to 15-22 ft. lbs. (20-30 Nm).
15. Attach the injector wiring. Connect the fuel return line. Attach the fuel supply line quick-connect fitting.
16. Install the fuel injector pulse dampening bracket. Tighten the nuts to 15-22 ft. lbs. (20-30 Nm).
17. Attach the coolant hose at the lower intake manifold.
18. Install the upper intake manifold, as outlined in this section.
19. Properly fill the engine cooling system.
20. Connect the negative battery cable, then start the engine and check for leaks.

3.8L Engine

➧ See Figures 20, 21, 22, 23, 24, 25, 26, 27, 28 and 29

1. Disconnect the negative battery cable.
2. Remove the air cleaner assembly including the air intake duct and heat tube.
3. Disconnect the accelerator cable from the carburetor or throttle body, as applicable. If equipped, also disconnect the speed control cable.
4. Detach the transmission linkage at the carburetor or fuel charging assembly, as applicable.
5. Unfasten the retaining bolts from the accelerator cable bracket, then position the cables aside.
6. If equipped with an SC engine, remove the supercharger as follows:
   a. Remove the cowl vent screens.
   b. Tag and disconnect the right side spark plug wires from the ignition coil and move out of the way. Detach the fuel charging wiring connectors at the Idle Air Control (IAC) valve, Throttle Position (TP) sensor, and Intake Air Temperature (IAT) sensor.
   c. Tag and disconnect the vacuum lines from the supercharger bypass valve actuator and fuel pressure regulator. Detach the crankcase ventilation tube.
   d. Disconnect the EGR valve-to-exhaust manifold tubes from the EGR valve.
   e. Remove the EGR transducer.
   f. Remove the supercharger drive belt.
   g. Remove the charge air cooler inlet tube and outlet tube.
   h. Unfasten the three charge air cooler-to-intake manifold adapter retaining bolts.
   i. Remove the three supercharger retaining bolts, then lift the supercharger and charge air cooler-to-intake manifold adapter from the vehicle as a unit. Remove and discard the gasket, then clean all mating surfaces.
7. If equipped, disconnect the Thermactor air supply hose at the check valve. The valve is located at the back of the intake manifold.
8. Disconnect and plug the fuel lines from the carburetor or fuel charging assembly, as applicable.
9. Detach the upper radiator hose at the thermostat housing.
10. Disconnect the coolant bypass hose at the intake manifold.
11. Disconnect the heater tube at the intake manifold. Remove the heater hose at the rear of the heater tube. Loosen the hose clamp at the heater elbow and remove the heater tube with the hoses attached. On fuel injected engines, remove the heater tube with the fuel lines attached and position the assembly aside.
12. Tag and disconnect the vacuum lines at the carburetor/fuel charging assembly and the intake manifold.
13. Tag and detach all necessary electrical connectors.
14. If equipped with A/C, remove the compressor mounting bracket.
15. Disconnect one crankcase ventilation tube at the upper intake manifold and at the PCV valve. Remove the second crankcase ventilation tube from the left valve cover.
16. Remove the carburetor or throttle body assembly, as applicable. If equipped with a carburetor, remove and discard the phenolic gasket.
17. Remove the EGR valve from the upper intake manifold.
18. Unfasten the retaining nut and remove the wiring retainer bracket located at the left front of the intake manifold and set aside with the spark plug wires.
19. Unfasten the upper intake manifold retaining bolts and stud bolts, then remove the upper intake manifold from the vehicle. Remove and discard the gasket and thoroughly clean all mating surfaces.
20. Remove the fuel injectors and the fuel injection supply manifold.
21. Remove the heater water outlet tube.
22. Disconnect the upper radiator hose from the water hose connection.

✲✲WARNING

The intake manifold is sealed at each end with silicone sealer. To break the seal, it may be necessary to pry on the front of the intake manifold with a suitable prybar. If this is necessary, be careful not to damage the machined surfaces or engine oil and coolant leakage may occur.

23. Unfasten the lower intake manifold retaining bolts and stud bolts. Remove the lower intake manifold. Remove and discard the gasket and end seals and thoroughly clean all mating surfaces.

24. If the lower manifold is to be disassembled, perform the following:

a. Remove the water hose connection and thermostat.
b. Remove the ECT sensor.
c. Remove the heater elbow.
d. Remove all vacuum and electrical fittings.

To install:

➥ Lightly oil all retaining bolt and stud bolt threads before installation.

25. If the intake manifold was disassembled, perform the following:

a. Apply a coat of Pipe Sealant with Teflon® D8AZ-19554-A or equivalent to the threads of the EGR sensor, all vacuum fittings and heater elbows, if equipped.
b. Install the thermostat and water hose connection gasket. Install the water hose connection and tighten the retaining bolts to 15-22 ft. lbs. (20-30 Nm).

➥ Before applying sealer, clean the mating surfaces with Metal Surface Cleaner F4AZ-19A536-A or equivalent.

➥ The SC engine uses a graph-oil type intake manifold gasket.

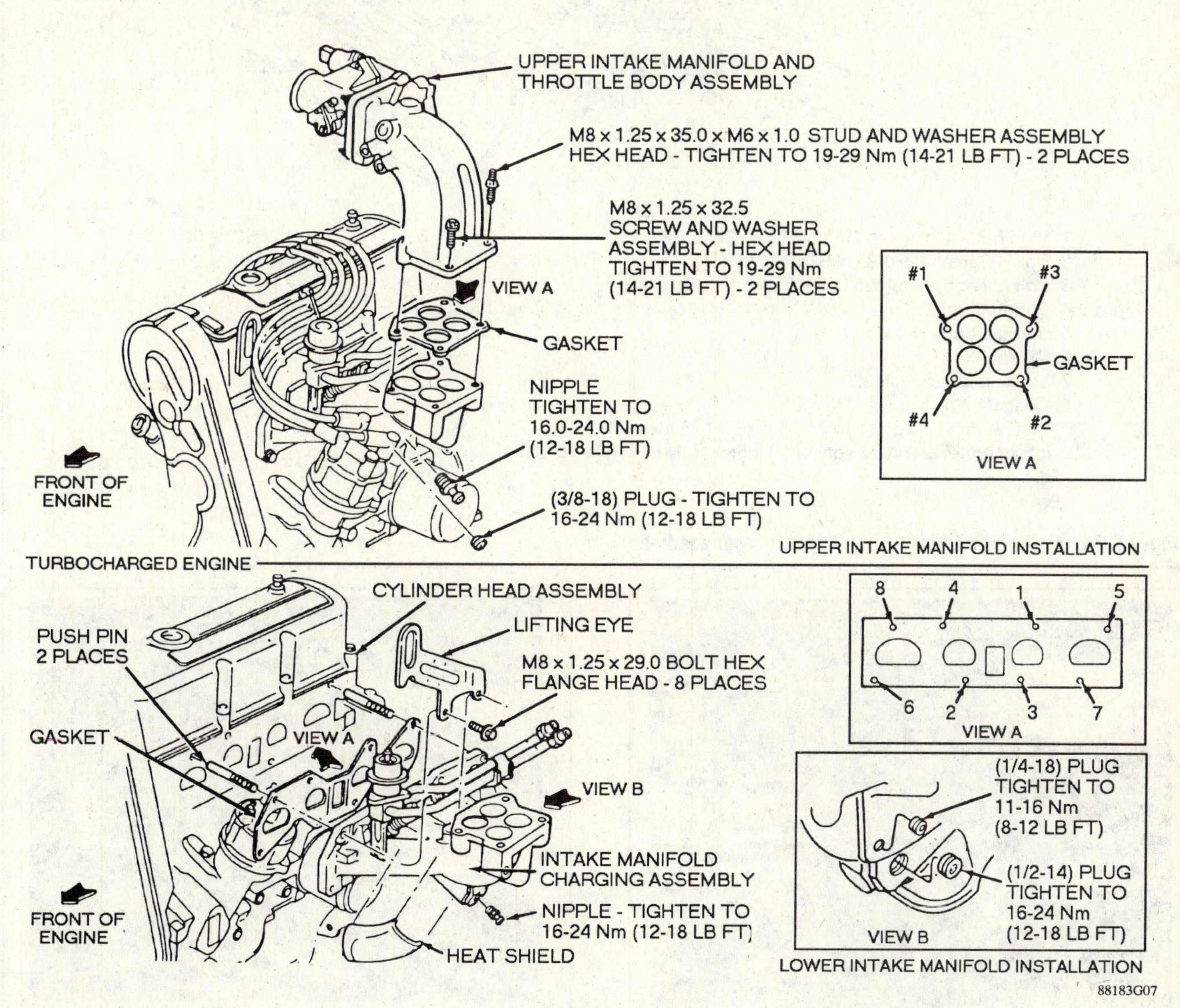

Fig. 19 Upper and lower intake manifold removal and installation — 2.3L engine

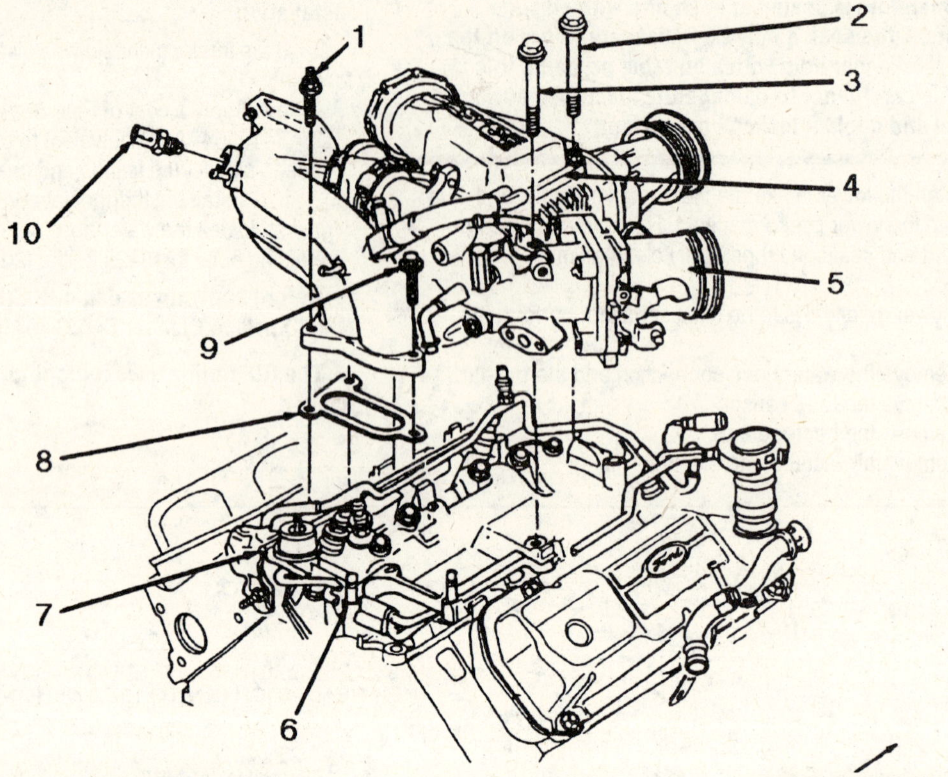

1. Stud bolt - Tighten to 26-38 Nm (20-28 lb. ft.)
2. Bolt - Tighten to 70-95 Nm (52-70 lb. ft.)
3. Bolt (2 req'd) - Tighten to 20-30 Nm (15-22 lb. ft.)
4. Supercharger
5. Throttle body
6. Guide pin
7. Lower intake manifold
8. Gasket
9. Bolt (2 req'd) - Tighten to 26-38 Nm (20-28 lb. ft.)
10. Intake air temperature sensor - Tighten to 8-13 Nm (6-10 lb. ft.)

88183G10

Fig. 20 Removal of the throttle body/supercharger assembly

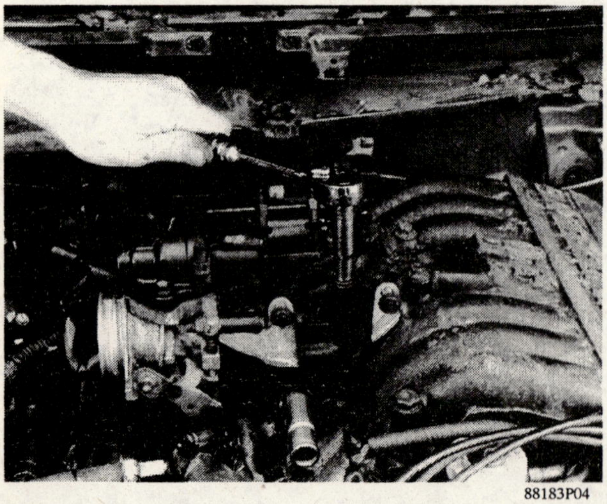

88183P04

Fig. 21 Unfasten the upper manifold bolts, then . . .

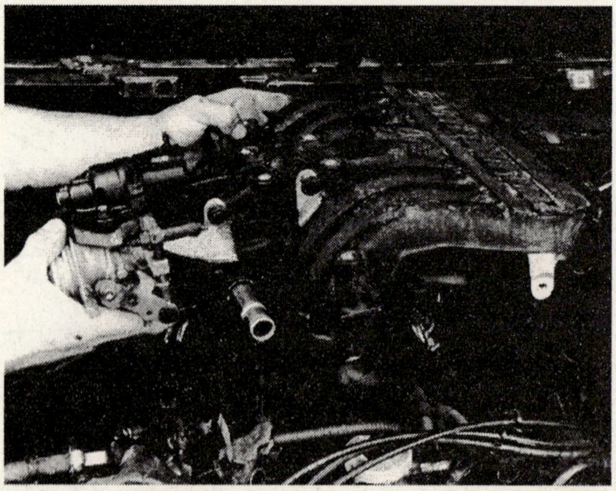

88183P05

Fig. 22 . . . remove the upper intake manifold (and throttle body) assembly — 3.8L non-SC engine shown

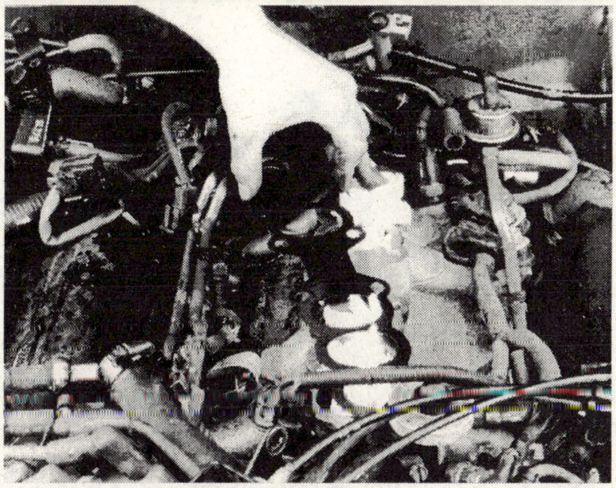

Fig. 23 Remove the upper intake manifold gasket, then clean the mating surfaces

Fig. 26 Remove and discard the lower manifold gasket, then thoroughly clean the gasket mating surfaces

Fig. 24 Unfasten the lower intake manifold retaining bolts, then . . .

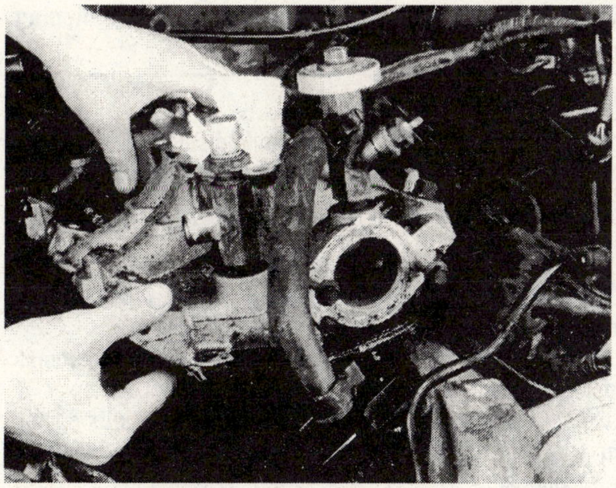

Fig. 25 . . . remove the lower manifold from the vehicle

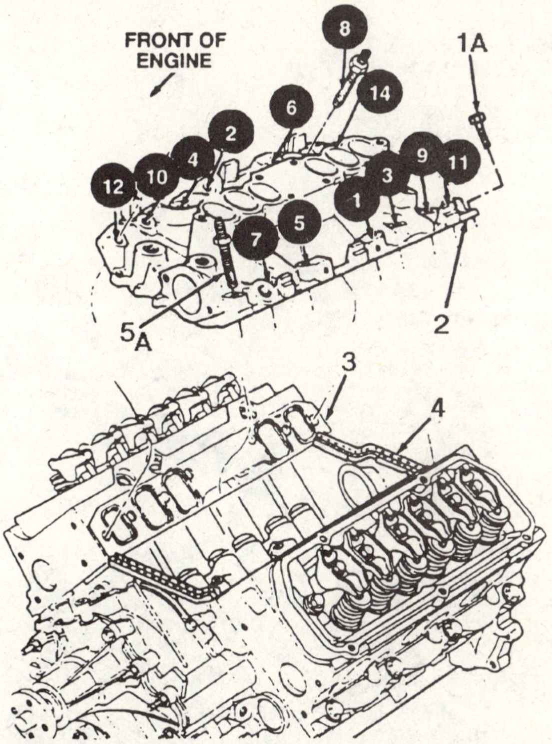

1. Bolt (12 req'd)
2. Lower intake manifold
3. Intake manifold gaskets
4. End seals
5. Stud bolt (2 req'd)

A. Tighten in sequence as shown in two steps:
18 Nm (13 lb. ft.)
22 Nm (16 lb. ft.)

88183G11

Fig. 27 Lower intake manifold tightening sequence — 3.8L non-SC engine

26. Apply a dab of Gasket and Trim Adhesive D7AZ-19B508-B or equivalent to each cylinder head mating surface. Press new intake manifold gasket into place, using location pins as necessary to aid in alignment.

➥ When using silicone rubber sealer, assembly must occur within 15 minutes after application or the sealer may start to set.

27. Apply a $^3/_4$ in (3-4mm) bead of Silicone Rubber D6AZ-19562-BA or equivalent, at each corner where the cylinder head joins the block. Install new front and rear intake manifold seals.

28. Carefully lower the lower intake manifold into position on the block and cylinder heads. Install the retainers in the original locations. Tighten in sequence to the following specifications, in two steps:

- Step 1: 13 ft. lbs. (18 Nm)
- Step 23: 16 ft. lbs. (22 Nm)

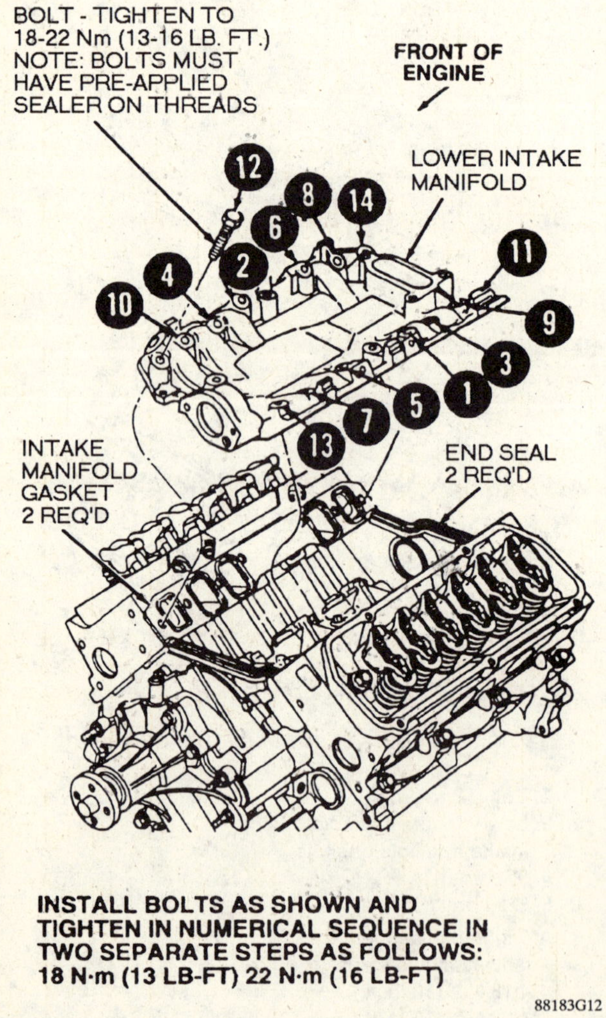

Fig. 28 Lower intake manifold tightening sequence — 3.8L SC engine

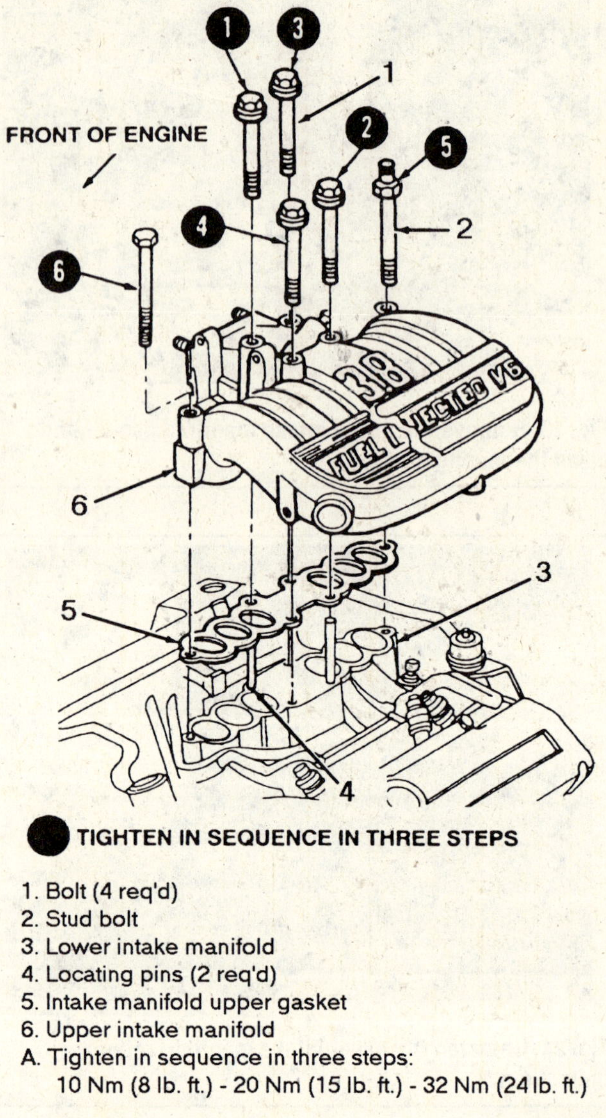

Fig. 29 Non-SC engine upper intake manifold tightening sequence

29. Install the heater water outlet tube so that the mounting bracket sits over the lower intake manifold stud bolt. Tighten the nut on the stud bolt to 15-22 ft. lbs. (20-30 Nm). Install and tighten the retaining bolt on the water pump to 6-8 ft. lbs. (8-11 Nm).

30. Install the fuel injectors and fuel supply manifold.

31. Connect the upper radiator hose to the water hose connection and tighten the clamp securely.

32. For non SC engines, position a new upper intake manifold upper gasket and upper intake manifold on top of the lower intake manifold. Install the bolts and stud bolts in their original locations, then tighten in the sequence shown to the following specifications:

a. Step 1: 8 ft. lbs. (15 Nm)
b. Step 2: 15 ft. lbs. (20 Nm)
c. Step 3: 24 ft. lbs. (32 Nm)

33. For SC engines, install the supercharger as follows:
a. Position a new gasket on the lower intake manifold.
b. Install the supercharger and charge air cooler to the intake manifold as a unit.
c. Tighten the two 8mm bolts to 15–22 ft. lbs. (20–30 Nm). Tighten the 12mm bolt to 52–70 ft. lbs. (70–95 Nm).
d. Install the three charge air cooler-to-intake manifold adapter retaining bolts. Tighten to 20–28 ft. lbs. (26–38 Nm).
e. Install the charge air cooler inlet tube and outlet tube as outlined.
f. Attach the EGR valve-to-exhaust manifold tube to the EGR valve.
g. Install the EGR transducer.
h. Install the accelerator cable bracket, then connect the accelerator cable. Tighten the bolt to 10–15 ft. lbs. (14–20 Nm).
i. Connect the vacuum lines to the supercharger bypass valve actuator and fuel pressure regulator.
j. Attach the right side spark plug wires, as tagged during removal.
k. Connect the fuel charging wiring connectors at the Idle Air Control (IAC) valve, Throttle Position (TP) sensor, and Intake Air Temperature (IAT) sensor.
l. Install the cowl vent screens.

34. Install the throttle body. Tighten the retaining nuts in a criss-cross pattern to 15–22 ft. lbs. (20–30 Nm).
35. Connect the rear crankcase ventilation tube at the positive crankcase ventilation valve on the upper intake manifold.
36. For non-SC engines, if equipped, install the A/C compressor mounting bracket. Tighten the retaining nut to 15–22 ft. lbs. (20–30 Nm).
37. If equipped, connect the speed control actuator cable.
38. Attach the throttle valve control actuating cable at the upper intake manifold.
39. For SC engines, install the supercharger and charge air cooler tubes.
40. Connect the negative battery cable.
41. Properly fill the engine cooling system.

4.6L Engine

➧ See Figures 30 and 31

1. Disconnect the negative battery cable.
2. Properly drain the engine cooling system into a suitable container.
3. Relieve the fuel system pressure, as outlined in Section 5, then disconnect and plug the fuel lines.
4. Remove the air cleaner outlet tube.
5. Release the drive belt tensioner, then remove the belt.

➥ Do NOT pull on the spark plug wires, as they may separate from the connector in the wire boot.

6. Tag and disconnect the spark plug wires.
7. Detach the spark plug wires and wire separators from the valve cover stud bolts.
8. Disconnect the fuel charging wiring from both ignition coils and Camshaft Position (CMP) sensor.
9. Unfasten the 4 bolts retaining the ignition coil to the coil brackets.
10. Detach the alternator wiring harness form the junction block at the front fender apron and from the alternator.
11. Unfasten the 4 bolts retaining the alternator mounting bracket to the intake manifold. Remove the bolts retaining the alternator to the cylinder head, then remove the alternator from the vehicle.
12. Raise and safely support the vehicle.

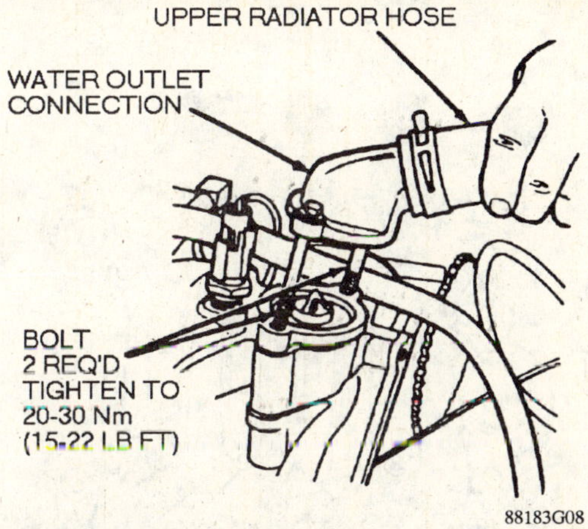

Fig. 30 Unfasten the two bolts, then remove the water hose connection and position aside

13. Disconnect the fuel charging wiring from the oil pressure sensor and EVO sensor, then position the wiring out of the way.
14. Disconnect the EGR valve-to-exhaust manifold tube from the right side exhaust manifold.
15. Carefully lower the vehicle.
16. Disconnect the accelerator cable and speed control actuator from the throttle body using a suitable pry tool.
17. Remove the accelerator cable bracket from the intake manifold and position it out of the way.
18. Disconnect the vacuum hose from the throttle body adapter vacuum port.
19. Disconnect the heater water hose.
20. Remove the 2 bolts retaining the water hose connection to the intake manifold and position the upper radiator hose and water hose connection out of the way.
21. Unfasten the 9 bolts retaining the intake manifold to the cylinder head, then remove the manifold. Remove and discard the gasket. Thoroughly clean the intake manifold and cylinder head mating surfaces.

To install:

➥ If a new intake manifold is being installed, transfer all necessary components onto the new manifold.

22. Position new intake manifold gaskets on the cylinder heads, then place the intake manifold on the heads. Install and tighten the 9 retaining bolts, in the sequence shown in the accompanying figure, to 15–22 ft. lbs. (20–30 Nm).
23. Replace the O-ring seal on the water hose connection. Position the water hose connection and upper radiator hose, and the 2 retaining bolts. Tighten the bolts to 15–22 ft. lbs. (20–30 Nm). Attach the heater water hose.
24. Connect the vacuum hose to the throttle body adapter vacuum port.
25. Install the accelerator cable bracket on the intake manifold, then connect the accelerator cable and speed control actuators to the throttle body.
26. Raise and safely support the vehicle.
27. Connect the EGR valve-to-exhaust manifold tube to the right side exhaust manifold, then tighten the nut to 26–33 ft. lbs. (35–45 Nm).
28. Attach the fuel charging wiring to the EVO sensor and oil pressure sensor.
29. Carefully lower the vehicle.
30. Position the alternator, then install the 2 retaining bolts. Tighten the bolts to 15–22 ft. lbs. (20–30 Nm).

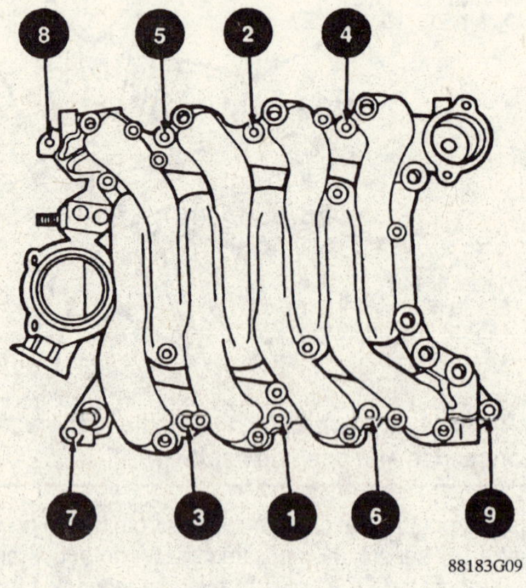

Fig. 31 Intake manifold bolt tightening sequence — 4.6L engine

31. Install the 2 bolts retaining the alternator rear mounting bracket to the intake manifold and tighten to 71–106 inch lbs. (8–12 Nm). Connect the alternator wiring harness to the alternator, right side front fender apron and junction block.

32. Position the spark plug wires and wire separators on the engine, then install the bolts retaining the ignition coil to the coil bracket. Tighten the bolts to 71–106 ft. lbs. (8–12 Nm). Connect the spark plug wires to the spark plugs, as tagged during removal. Attach the spark plug wire separators on the valve cover studs.

33. Connect the fuel charging wiring to both ignition coils and CMP sensor.

34. Install the drive belt.

35. Connect the air cleaner outlet tube.

36. Unplug and attach the fuel lines.

37. Connect the negative battery cable. Fill and bleed the engine cooling system. Check the engine oil level, and add if necessary. Start the engine and check for fluid and/or vacuum leaks.

5.0L Engine

➧ **See Figures 32, 33, 34, 35 and 36**

1. Disconnect the negative battery cable.

2. Properly drain the cooling system into a suitable container. Relieve the fuel system pressure, as outlined in Section 5 of this manual.

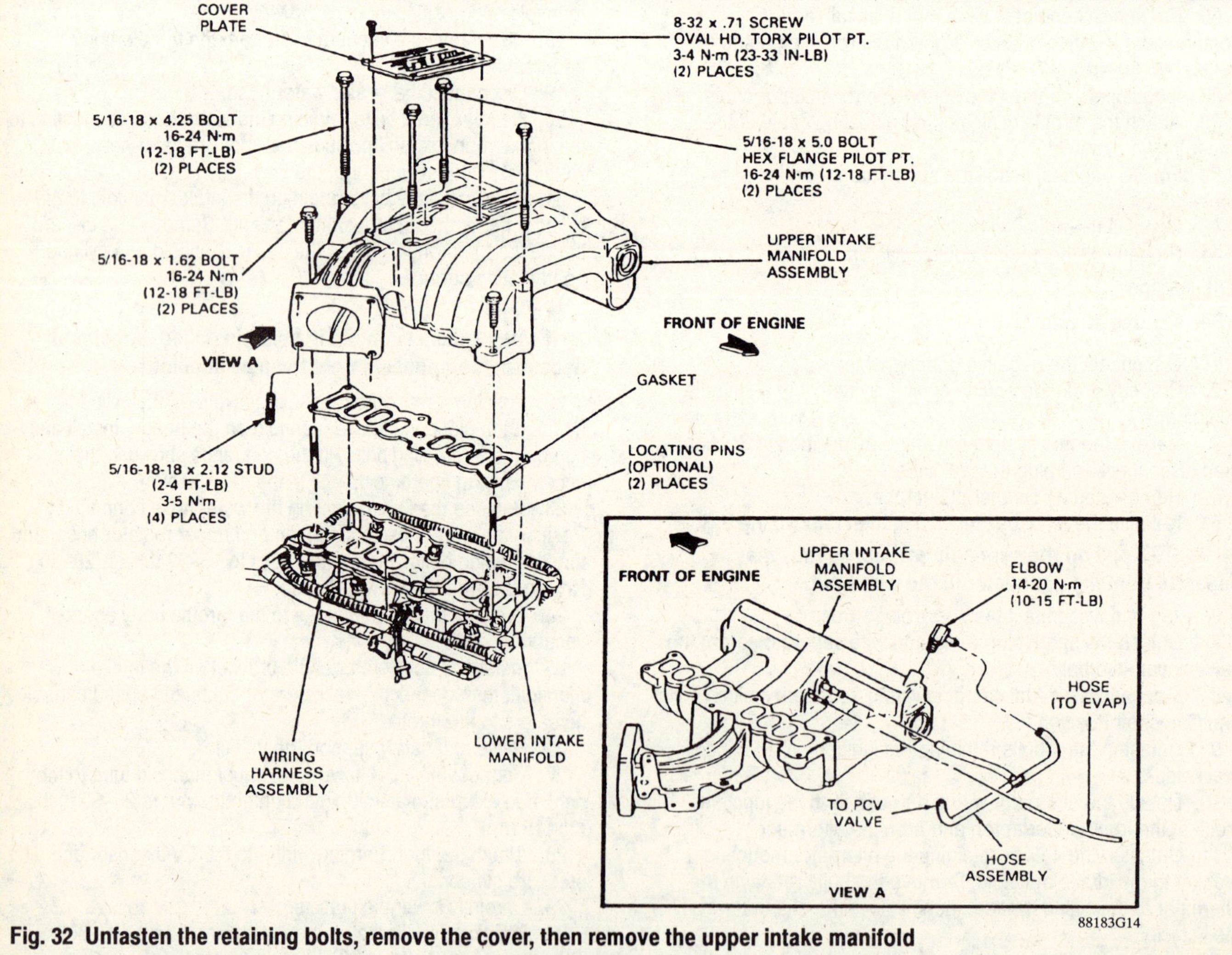

Fig. 32 Unfasten the retaining bolts, remove the cover, then remove the upper intake manifold

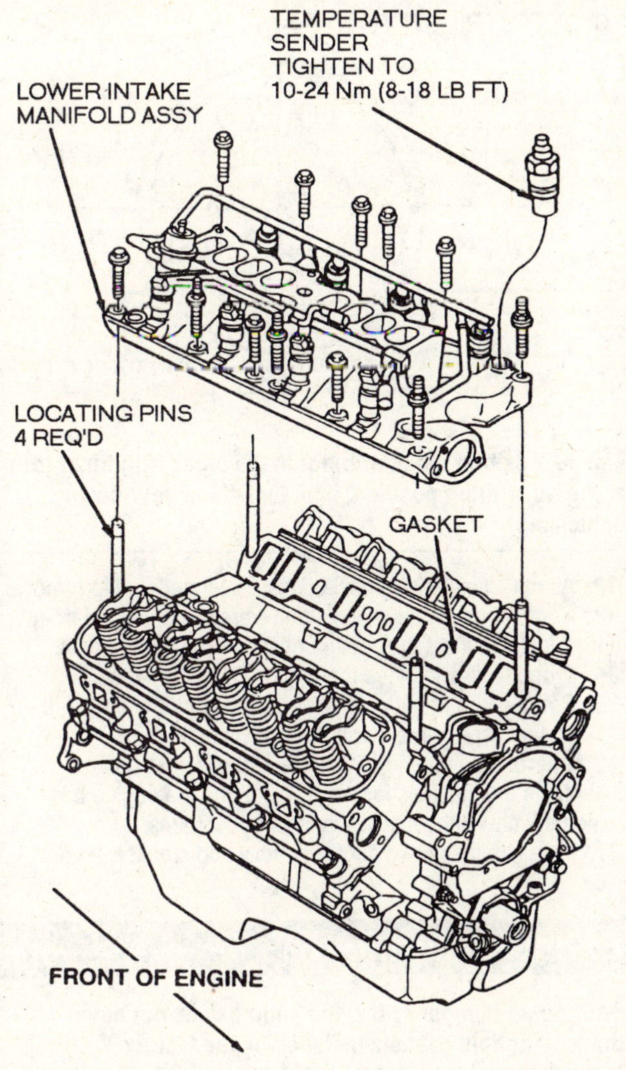

Fig. 33 Installing the lower intake manifold — 1993 5.0L engine shown

3. Remove the air intake duct assembly and crankcase vent hose.
4. Disconnect the accelerator cable and speed control linkage (if equipped) from the throttle body. Disconnect the TV cable from the the accelerator cable bracket.
5. Tag and disconnect the vacuum lines at the intake manifold fitting.
6. Tag and disconnect the spark plug wires from the spark plugs by pulling on the boots. Do NOT pull on the wires. Remove the wires and bracket assembly from the rocker arm (valve) cover attaching stud. Remove the distributor cap, adapter and spark plug wire assembly.
7. Disconnect and cap the fuel supply and return lines.
8. Detach the distributor wiring connector. Unfasten the distributor hold-down bolt, then remove the distributor.
9. Disconnect the radiator upper hose form the coolant outlet housing, and the water temperature sending unit wire at the sending unit. Disconnect the 2 throttle body cooler hoses.
10. Loosen the clamp on the water pump bypass hose at the coolant outlet housing and slide the hose off the outlet housing.
11. Tag and detach the wires at the ECT sensor, IAT sensor, TP sensor, IAC valve and EGR sensors. Disconnect the fuel charging assembly wiring.
12. Pull the PCV valve out of the grommet at the rear of the lower intake manifold or the rocker arm cover. Disconnect the fuel evaporative purge hose from the plastic connector at the front of the upper intake manifold.
13. Unfasten the upper intake manifold cover plate retaining screws/bolts, then remove the cover. Remove the upper intake manifold from the vehicle.
14. Remove the heater tube assembly from the lower intake manifold.

➥ It may be necessary to pry the intake manifold away from the cylinder head(s). Be careful to avoid damage to the gasket sealing surfaces.

15. Remove the lower intake manifold. Remove and discard the gaskets and seals and clean all gasket mating surfaces.
16. If necessary, remove the ignition coil and temperature sending unit. Transfer parts to the new manifold.

To install:

17. If the intake manifold was disassembled, install the temperature sending unit (threads coated with electrical conductive sealer). Position the thermostat in the coolant outlet housing. Coat the thermostat gasket with suitable sealer and position it on the coolant outlet housing. Install the coolant outlet housing. Install the ignition coil, if necessary.
18. Make sure the mating surfaces of the manifold and intake manifold are clean, then apply a $^{1}/_{8}$ in. (3.2mm) bead of Silicone Rubber D6AZ-19562-AA or equivalent at the points shown in the accompanying figure.

➥ This sealer sets up in 15 minutes, so it's important that assembly take place swiftly. Do NOT drip any sealer into the engine valley.

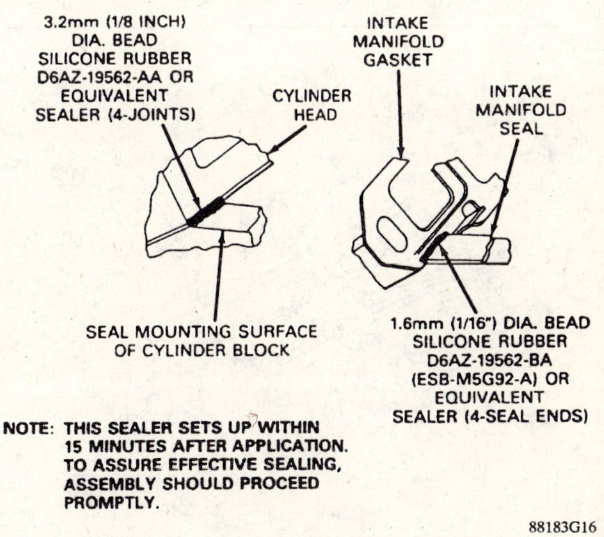

Fig. 34 Apply sealer to the cylinder head and intake manifold as shown

19. Position new seals on the cylinder block and new gaskets on the cylinder heads with the gaskets interlocked with the seal tabs. Make sure the holes in the gaskets are aligned with the holes in the cylinder heads.
20. Apply a $^1/_{16}$ in. (1.6mm) bead of sealer to the outer end of each intake manifold seal for the full width of the seal (four places).
21. Using guide pins ease installation, carefully lower the intake manifold into position on the block and heads. After the manifold is in place, run a finger around the seal area to be sure the seals are in place. If not, remove the manifold and reposition the seals.
22. Make sure the holes in the manifold gaskets and intake manifold are aligned. Remove the guide pins. Install the intake manifold retaining bolts, then tighten in sequence to the following specifications:
    Step 1: 8 ft. lbs. (11 Nm).
    Step 2: 16 ft. lbs. (22 Nm).
    Step 3: 23–25 ft. lbs. (31–34 Nm).
23. Install the heater tube assembly to the lower intake manifold.
24. Install the water pump bypass hose on the coolant outlet housing. Slide the clamp into position and tighten the clamp. Connect the hoses to the heater tubes, then tighten the clamps.
25. Attach the upper radiator hose. Connect the heater hose at the intake manifold.
26. Uncap and connect the fuel lines.
27. Rotate the crankshaft until the No. 1 piston is on TDC at the end of the compression stroke. Align the correct initial timing mark on the damper with the pointer. Position the distributor in the block with the rotor at the No. 1 firing position, then install the hold-down bolt/clamp.
28. Install the distributor cap. Position the spark plug wires in the harness brackets on the valve cover attaching stud, then connect the wires to the spark plugs as tagged earlier.
29. Install the upper intake manifold.
30. Connect the PCV/crankcase vent tube.
31. Attach the accelerator cable and cable bracket. Connect the TV cable and speed control (if equipped) to the throttle body.

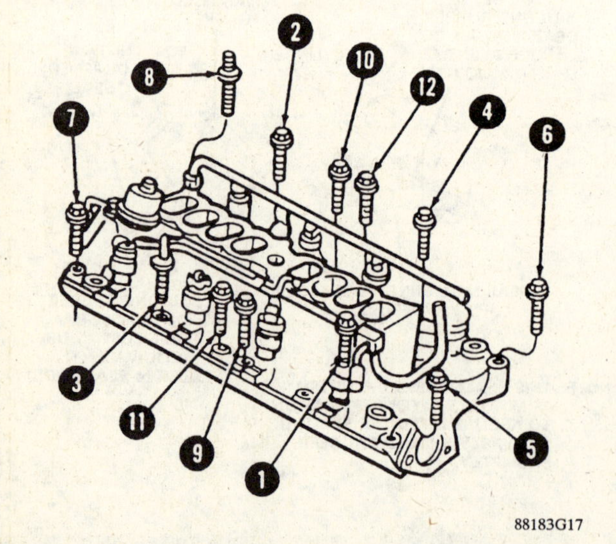

Fig. 35 The intake manifold bolts must be tightened in sequence

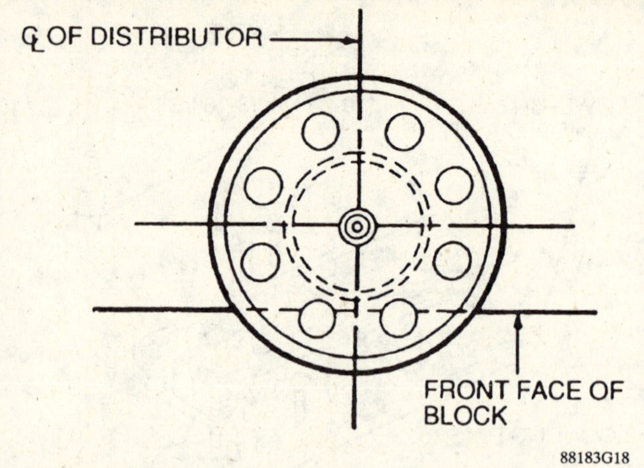

Fig. 36 Position the distributor in the block with the rotor at the No. 1 firing position, then install the hold-down bolt/clamp

32. Attach all electrical connections, as tagged during removal.
33. Connect any vacuum lines that were disconnected from the manifold. Connect the coolant hoses to the EGR spacer.
34. Properly fill and bleed the engine cooling system.
35. Connect the negative battery cable. Start the engine, then check and adjust (if necessary) the ignition timing.
36. Operate the engine at fast idle and check all hose connections and gaskets for leaks. When the the engine has warmed up, check the intake manifold bolt torques.
37. Install the air intake duct assembly and crankcase vent hose.

Exhaust Manifold

➔ **Although, in most cases, the engine does not have exhaust manifold gaskets installed by the factory, aftermarket gaskets are available from parts stores.**

REMOVAL & INSTALLATION

2.3L Engine

➧ **See Figure 37**

1. Disconnect the negative battery cable.
2. Remove the air cleaner assembly.
3. Remove the heat shroud from the exhaust manifold.
4. Remove the turbocharger, as outlined later in this section.
5. Place a block of wood under the exhaust pipe and disconnect the exhaust pipe from the exhaust manifold.
6. Unfasten the exhaust manifold attaching nuts/bolts, then remove the manifold.

To install:

7. Install a light coat of graphite grease on the exhaust manifold mating surface and position the manifold on the cylinder head.
8. Install the exhaust manifold attaching nuts and tighten them in the sequence shown in the accompanying illustration in two steps, as follows:
    Step 1: 15–17 ft. lbs. (20–23 Nm).
    Step 2: 20–30 ft. lbs. (27–40.5 Nm).

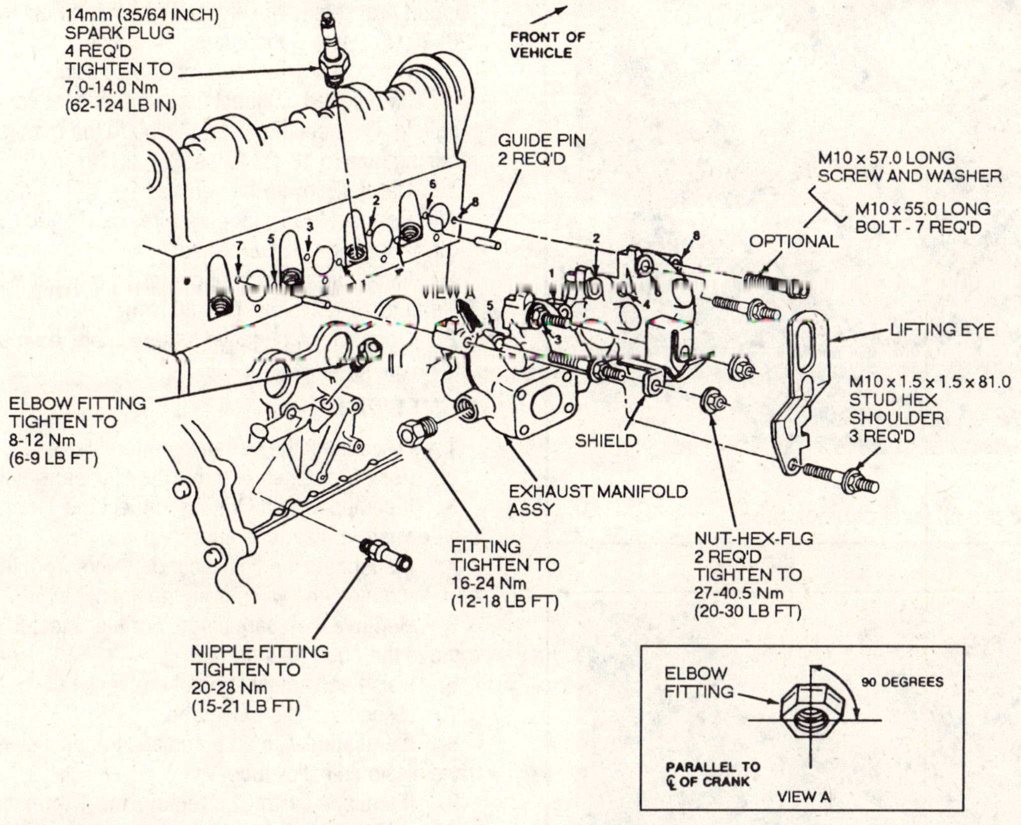

Fig. 37 Exhaust manifold installation and tightening sequence — 2.3L engine

9. Install the turbocharger assembly, as outlined later in this section.
10. Connect the exhaust pipe to the exhaust manifold and remove the wood support from under the pipe.
11. Install the air cleaner assembly.
12. Connect the negative battery cable.

3.8L Engine

See Figures 38, 39, 40, 41, 42 and 43

Supercharged engines require special procedures for removal and installation. Refer to the supercharger removal and installation procedure.

LEFT SIDE

1. Disconnect the negative battery cable.
2. For fuel injected engines, remove the oil level dipstick tube support bracket or tube, as necessary.
3. Detach the HEGO/HO_2 sensor at the wiring connector.
4. Tag and disconnect the spark plug wires.
5. Raise and safely support the vehicle.
6. Remove the manifold-to-exhaust pipe retaining nuts. If equipped, disconnect the exhaust heat control valve vacuum line.
7. Carefully lower the vehicle.
8. For SC engines, remove the intercooler tubes. Remove the oil cooler tube and dipstick tube support brackets from the studs.
9. Remove the exhaust manifold retaining bolts, then remove the manifold.

To install:

Lightly oil all bolt and stud threads before installation except those specifying special sealant.

10. Clean the mating surfaces of the exhaust manifold, cylinder head and exhaust pipe.

****CAUTION**

Do NOT allow anti-seize compound to enter the sensor flutes.

11. Coat the threads of the HEGO sensor with high temperature anti-seize compound. Install the sensor into the exhaust manifold and tighten to 28–33 ft. lbs. (37–45 Nm).
12. Position the exhaust manifold on the cylinder head. Install the pilot bolt (lower front bolt hole on No. 5 cylinder.

For 1996 vehicles, tighten the retaining bolts in the sequence shown in the accompanying figure.

13. Install the remaining manifold retaining bolts. Tighten the bolts to 15–22 ft. lbs. (20–30 Nm).

****WARNING**

A slight warpage in the exhaust manifold may cause a misalignment between the bolt holes in the head and the manifold. Elongate the holes in the manifold as necessary to correct the misalignment. Do NOT, however, elongate the lower front No. 5 cylinder hole on the left side, nor the lower rear No. 2 cylinder hole on the right side. These holes are used as alignment pilots.

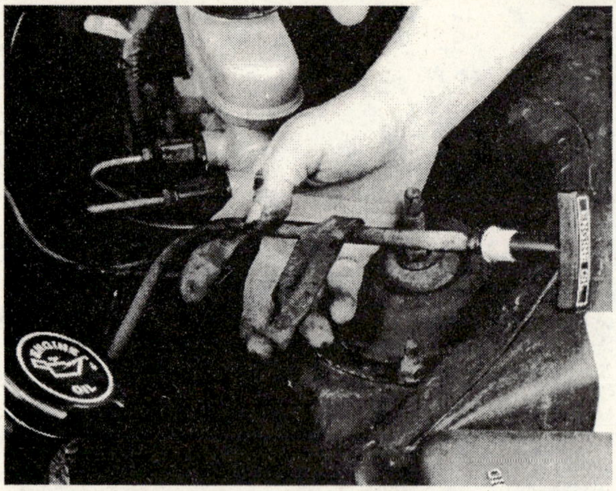

88183P07

Fig. 38 Remove the oil level dipstick tube

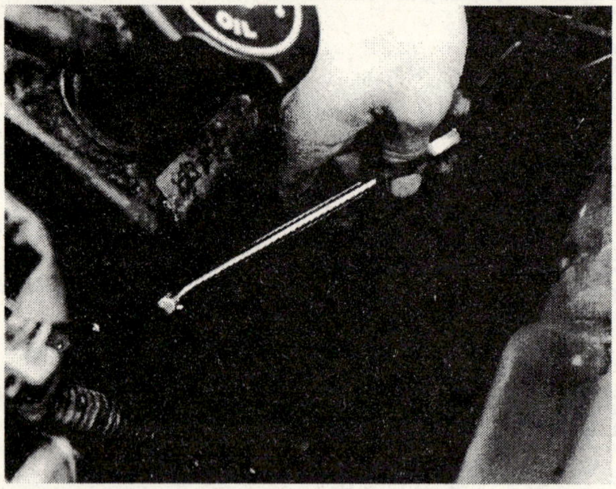

88183P08

Fig. 39 Using a suitable sized wrench, unfasten the retaining bolts, then . . .

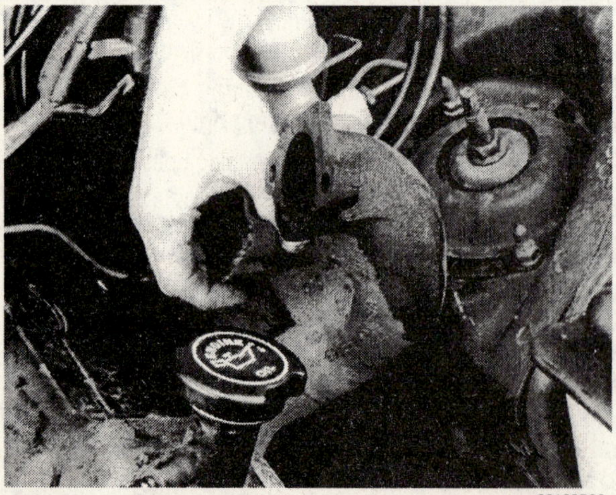

88183P09

Fig. 40 . . . remove the exhaust manifold from the vehicle.

14. For SC engines, install the dipstick tube and oil cooler tube support brackets to the studs. Tighten the nuts to 15–22 ft. lbs. (20–30 Nm). Install the intercooler tubes.
15. Raise and safely support the vehicle.
16. If equipped, connect the exhaust heat control valve to the manifold. Connect the exhaust pipe to the manifold. Tighten the retaining nuts to 16–23 ft. lbs. (21–32 Nm).
17. Carefully lower the vehicle.
18. Connect the spark plug wires as tagged during removal.
19. Attach the HEGO sensor.
20. Install the dipstick tube support bracket retaining nut. Tighten to 15–22 ft. lbs. (20–30 Nm).
21. Connect the negative battery cable, then start the engine and check for exhaust leaks.

RIGHT SIDE

1. Disconnect the negative battery cable.
2. For SC engines, remove the air cleaner inlet tube.
3. If equipped with CFI, disconnect the Thermactor hose form the downstream air tube check valve.
4. Disconnect the coil secondary wire from the coil, then tag and disconnect the wires from the spark plugs.
5. Remove the spark plugs. For fuel injected engines, remove the outer heat shroud.
6. Raise and safely support the vehicle.
7. Disconnect the EGR tube.
8. If equipped with an automatic transmission, remove the transmission dipstick tube.
9. If equipped with CFI, remove the Thermactor downstream air tube. Use EGR Clamp Cutter and Crimping tool T78P-9481-A or equivalent to cut the tube clamp at the underbody catalyst.
10. Remove the manifold-to-exhaust pipe retaining nuts.
11. Carefully lower the vehicle.
12. Unfasten the exhaust manifold retaining bolts, then remove the manifold assembly.

To install:

➥ Lightly oil all bolt and stud threads before installation except those specifying special sealant.

13. Clean the mating surfaces of the exhaust manifold, cylinder head and exhaust pipe.
14. Position the inner half of the heat shroud and exhaust manifold on the cylinder head. Start two retaining bolts.

➥ For 1996 vehicles, tighten the retaining bolts in the sequence shown in the accompanying figure.

15. Install the remaining retaining bolts. Tighten to 15–22 ft. lbs. (20–30 Nm).

****WARNING**

A slight warpage in the exhaust manifold may cause a misalignment between the bolt holes in the head and the manifold. Elongate the holes in the manifold as necessary to correct the misalignment. Do NOT, however, elongate the lower front No. 5 cylinder hole on the left side, nor the lower rear No. 2 cylinder hole on the right side. These holes are used as alignment pilots.

16. Raise and safely support the vehicle.
17. Connect the exhaust pipe to the manifold. Tighten the retaining nuts to 16–23 ft. lbs. (21–32 Nm).

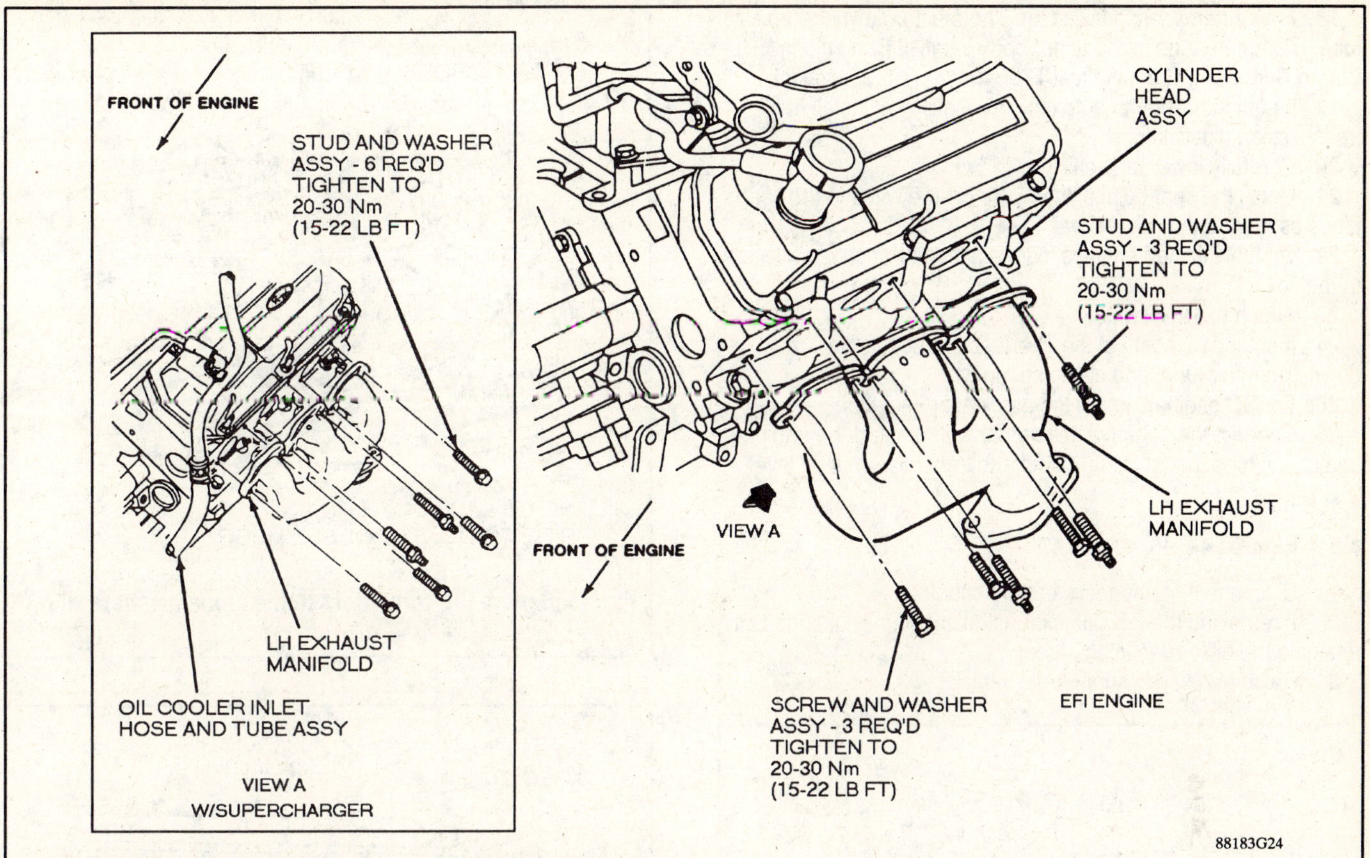

Fig. 41 Exhaust manifold removal — 1992 3.8L engine shown

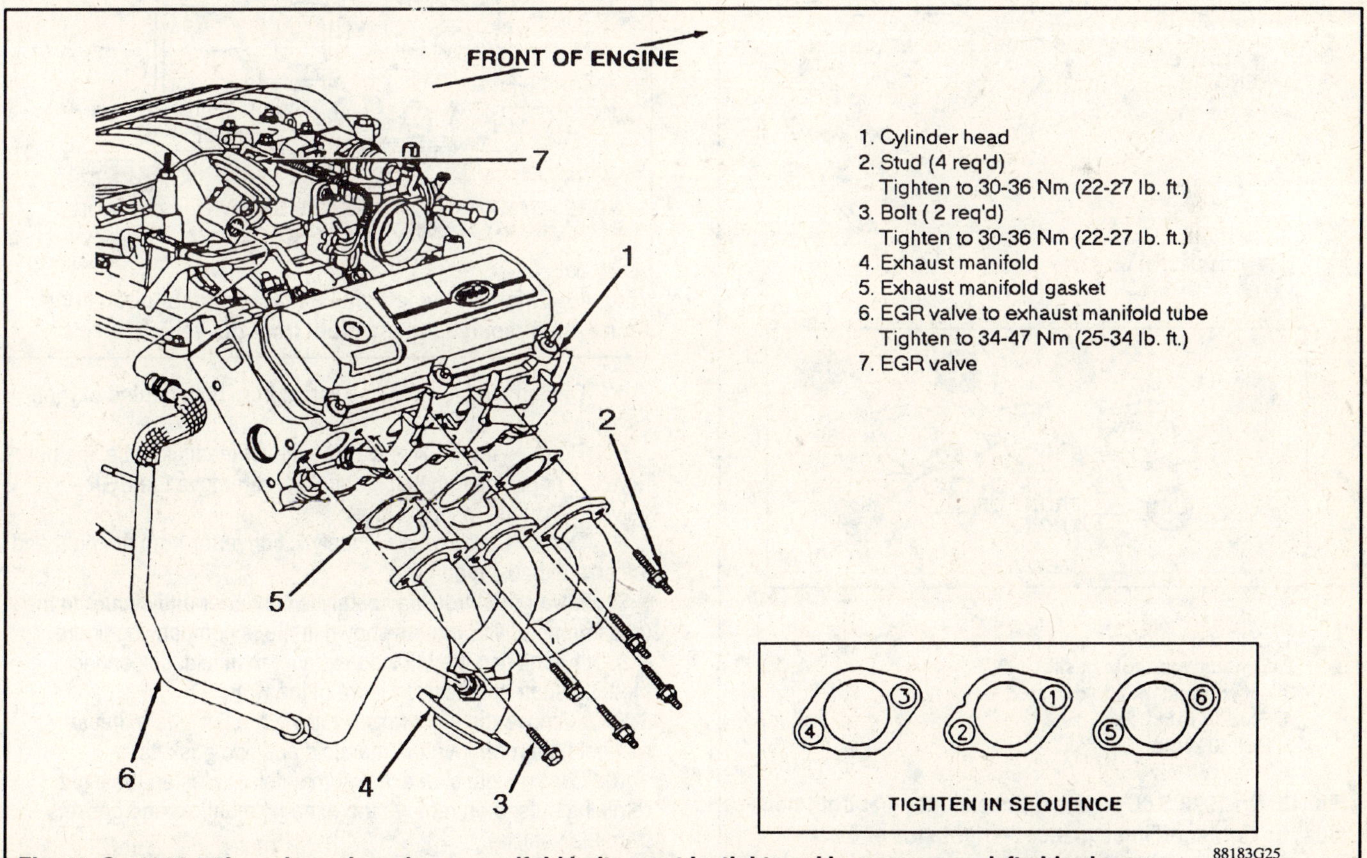

Fig. 42 On 1996 3.8L engines, the exhaust manifold bolts must be tightened in sequence — left side shown

18. For CFI engines, position the Thermactor downstream air tube. Clamp the tube to the under body catalyst fitting using EGR Clamp Cutter and Crimping tool T78P-9481-A or equivalent.
19. If equipped with an automatic transmission, install the transmission dipstick tube.
20. Carefully lower the vehicle.
21. Install the spark plugs, then connect the wires to the spark plugs as tagged during removal.
22. On fuel injected engines, connect the coil secondary wire to the coil.
23. Attach the EGR tube.
24. If equipped, connect the Thermactor hose to the downstream air tube, and clamp securely.
25. For SC engines, install the air cleaner inlet tube.
26. Connect the negative battery cable, then start the engine and check for exhaust leaks. Check the transmission fluid level.

4.6L Engine

➧ See Figures 44, 45, 46 and 47

1. Disconnect the negative battery cable.
2. If removing the left side exhaust manifold, remove the bolt retaining the oil level indicator tube.
3. Raise and safely support the vehicle.

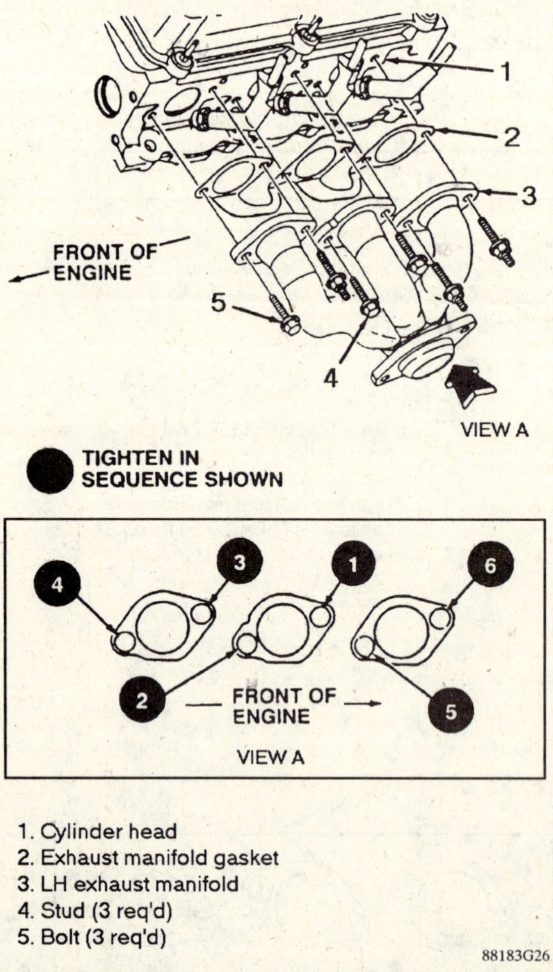

Fig. 43 On 1996 3.8L engines, the exhaust manifold bolts must be tightened in sequence — right side shown

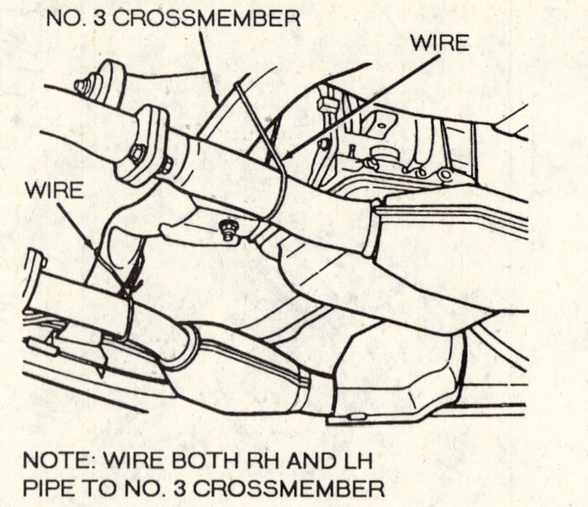

Fig. 44 Secure the converters to the crossmembers with wire

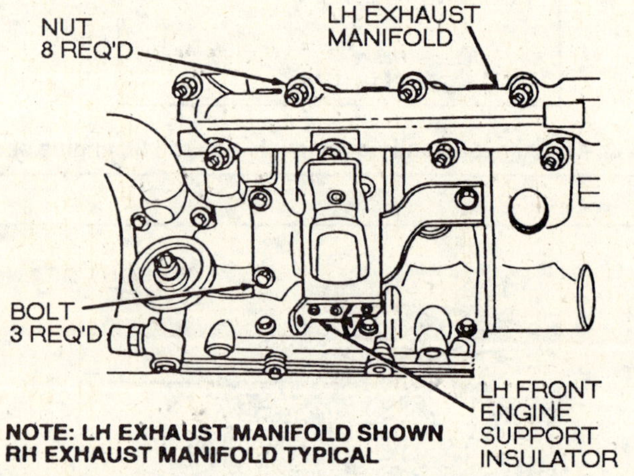

Fig. 45 Unfasten the left side exhaust manifold retaining nuts, then remove the manifold from the vehicle

4. Detach the fuel charging wiring from both heated oxygen sensors.
5. Remove the EGR valve-to-exhaust manifold tube line nut from the right side exhaust manifold and remove the EGR valve-to-exhaust manifold tube.
6. Detach the three-way catalytic converter from the right and left side exhaust manifolds.
7. Lower the three-way catalytic converter and secure to the crossmember with wire as shown in the accompanying figure.
8. If removing the left side exhaust manifold, disconnect the steering shaft and position it out of the way.
9. Remove the eight nuts retaining the left side exhaust manifold, then remove the manifold and two gaskets.
10. For the right side exhaust manifold, unfasten the eight retaining nuts, then remove the exhaust manifold and gaskets from the vehicle.

To install:

11. If the exhaust manifolds are being replaced, transfer the heated oxygen sensors to the replacement manifolds and tighten to 27-33 ft. lbs. (37-45 Nm). For the right side exhaust manifold, transfer the EGR valve tube to manifold connector and tighten to 33-48 ft. lbs. (45-65 Nm).
12. Thoroughly clean the mating surfaces of the exhaust manifolds and cylinder heads.
13. Position the exhaust manifold gaskets and right side exhaust manifold to the cylinder head and studs, then install the eight retaining nuts. Tighten, in the sequence shown in the accompanying figures, to 13-16 ft. lbs. (18-22 Nm).

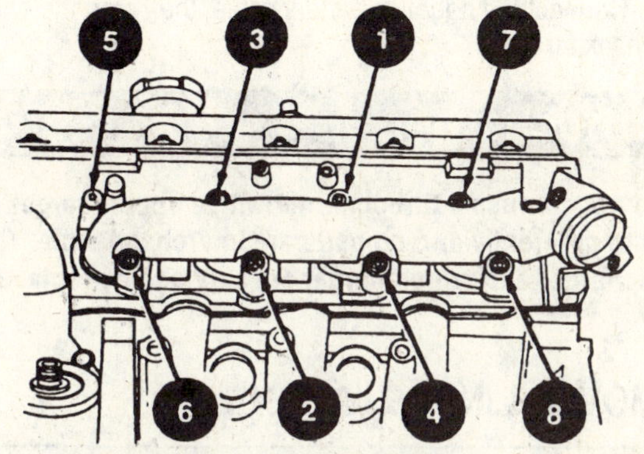

Fig. 46 Exhaust manifold tightening sequence — 1994-95 4.6L engine

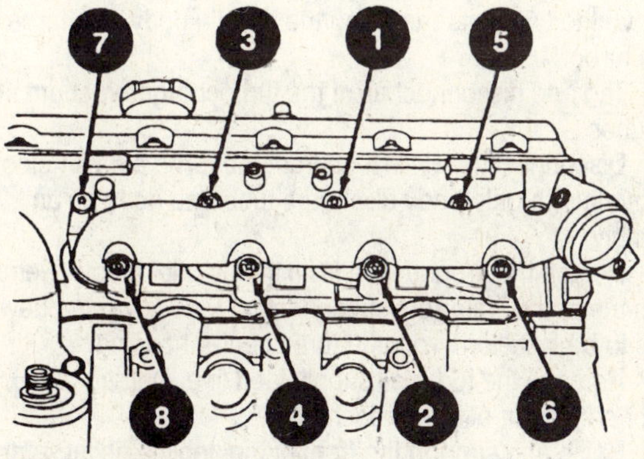

Fig. 47 Exhaust manifold tightening sequence — 1996 4.6L engine

14. Position the gaskets and the left side exhaust manifold to the cylinder head and studs, then install the eight retaining nuts. Tighten, in the sequence shown in the accompanying figures, to 13-16 ft. lbs. (18-22 Nm).
15. Position and connect the steering shaft.
16. Loosen the line nut at the EGR valve before installing the assembly into the vehicle. This will allow enough movement to align the EGR valve retaining bolts. Position and connect the EGR valve-to-exhaust tube to the exhaust manifold. Tighten the line nut to 26-33 ft. lbs. (35-45 Nm).

➥ Two through bolts are required on the left front engine support insulator and one through bolt is required on the right side from engine support insulator. Make sure the exhaust system clears the No. 3 crossmember.

17. Remove the wire, then position the three-way catalytic converter. Install the four nuts, then tighten to 20-30 ft. lbs. (27-41 Nm).
18. Connect the fuel charging wiring to the heated oxygen sensors.
19. Carefully lower the vehicle.
20. Connect the negative battery cable, then start the engine and check for leaks.

5.0L Engine

➧ See Figures 48, 49, 50 and 51

1. Disconnect the negative battery cable.
2. For the left side manifold, remove the oil level dipstick tube retaining nut, then pull the bracket off the manifold stud.
3. Raise and safely support the vehicle.
4. Remove the oil level dipstick tube assembly by carefully tapping upward on the tube.
5. For the left manifold, detach the HO_2S connector from the manifold.
6. Disconnect the exhaust manifolds from the muffler inlet pipe(s).
7. Carefully lower the vehicle.
8. Detach the electrical connector from the MAF sensor located on the air cleaner assembly.
9. Remove the air cleaner and inlet duct assembly.
10. Unfasten the nuts attaching the alternator rear brace to the exhaust manifold, then remove the brace.
11. Tag and disconnect the spark plug wires.
12. On the exhaust manifold, remove the Secondary Air Injection hose assembly and EGR valve-to-exhaust manifold tube.
13. Remove the retaining nuts and washers attaching the engine lifting eyes to the exhaust manifolds.

➥ The exhaust manifolds are removed from the vehicle out through the top of the engine compartment.

14. Unfasten the retaining bolts and washers and remove the exhaust manifolds.

To install:

15. Clean the mating surfaces of the manifolds and cylinder head(s). Clean the mounting flange of the exhaust manifold and muffler inlet pipe.
16. Position the exhaust manifold on the cylinder head with a new exhaust manifold gasket. Install the attaching bolts and washers, and working from the center to the ends, tighten the bolts to 26-32 ft. lbs. (32-43 Nm).

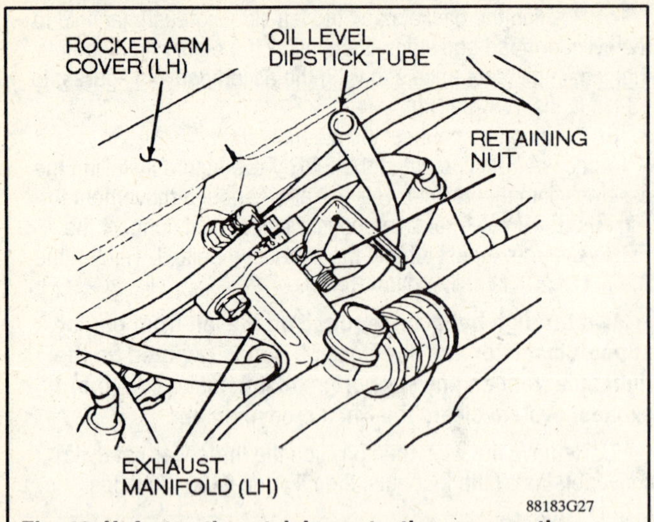

Fig. 48 Unfasten the retaining nuts, then remove the dipstick tube bracket

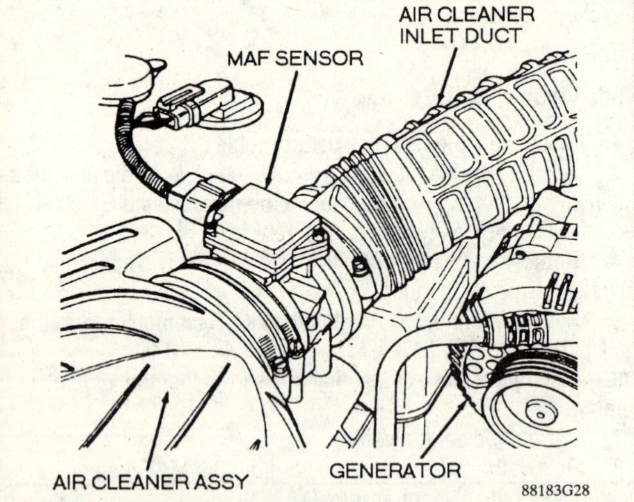

Fig. 49 The Mass Air Flow (MAF) sensor is located on the air cleaner assembly

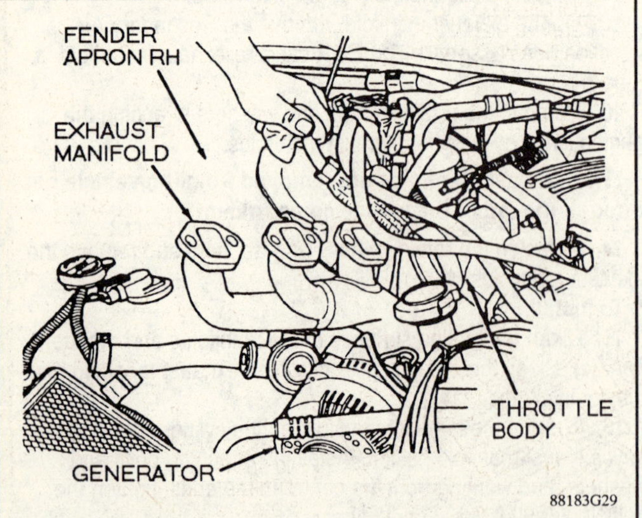

Fig. 50 Removing the right side exhaust manifold

17. Attach the engine lifting eyes to the exhaust manifold studs and tighten.
18. Install the oil level dipstick tube in the engine block and position the tube bracket to the exhaust manifold stud. Install the retaining nut.
19. Connect the spark plug wires, as tagged during removal.
20. On the right side exhaust manifold, install the secondary air injection control valve hose assembly, alternator rear brace and EGR valve-to-exhaust manifold tube.
21. Install the air cleaner and inlet duct assembly.
22. Attach the electrical connector to the MAF sensor on the air cleaner.
23. Raise the vehicle. Install the muffler inlet pipes.
24. On the left side, install the HO_2S wiring connector.
25. Carefully lower the vehicle.
26. Connect the negative battery cable, then start the engine and check for leaks.

Turbocharger

➜ Do not confuse a turbocharger with a supercharger. They operate differently and no parts are interchangeable. The turbocharger and supercharger are serviced by replacement only.

REMOVAL & INSTALLATION

➜ Before starting removal/service procedures, clean the area around the turbocharger with a non-caustic solution. Cover the openings of component connections to prevent the entry of dirt and foreign materials. Exercise care when handling the turbocharger not to nick, bend or in any way damage the compressor wheel blades.

1983–85 2.3L Engines

1. Disconnect the negative battery cable.
2. Properly drain the cooling system into a suitable container.
3. Loosen the upper clamp on the turbocharger inlet hose. Remove the two bolts mounting the throttle body discharge tube to the turbo.
4. Tag and disconnect all of the turbocharger vacuum hoses and tubes.
5. Disconnect the PCV tube from the turbo air inlet elbow. Remove the throttle body discharge tube and hose as an assembly.
6. Detach the ground wire from the air inlet elbow. Remove (disconnect) the water outlet connection (and fitting if a new turbo unit is to be installed) from the turbo center housing.
7. Remove the turbo oil supply feed line. Detach the oxygen sensor connector at the turbocharger.
8. Raise and support the front of the vehicle on jackstands. Disconnect the exhaust pipe from the turbocharger.
9. Disconnect the oil return line from the bottom of the turbocharger. Be careful not to damage or kink the line.
10. Detach the water inlet tube at the turbo center housing.
11. Remove the lower turbo mounting bracket-to-engine bolt. Lower the vehicle from the stands.
12. Unfasten the lower front mounting nut. Remove the three remaining mounting nuts evenly while sliding the turbocharger away from its mounting.

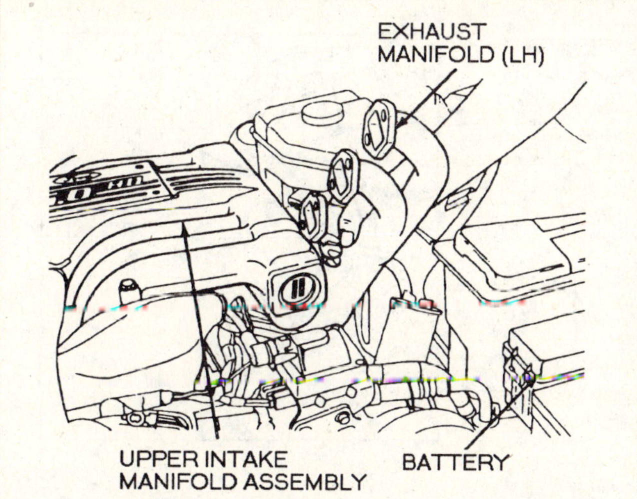

Fig. 51 Left side exhaust manifold removal

To install:

13. Position a new turbocharger mounting gasket in position with the bead side facing outward. Install the turbocharger in position over the four mounting studs.
14. Position the lower mounting bracket over the two bottom studs. Using new nuts, start the two lower then the two upper mountings. Do not tighten them completely at this time; allow for slight turbo movement.
15. Raise and support the front of the vehicle on jackstands.
16. Install and tighten the lower gasket and connect the return line. Tighten the mounting bolts to 14–21 ft. lbs. (19–28 Nm).
17. Connect the water inlet tube assembly. Install the exhaust pipe on the turbo. Tighten the mounting nuts to 25–35 ft. lbs. (34–47 Nm).
18. Lower the vehicle. Tighten the turbo mounting nut to 28–40 ft. lbs. (38–54 Nm).
19. Connect the water outlet assembly to the turbocharger, tighten the fasteners to 11–14 ft. lbs. (15–19 Nm). Hold the fitting with a wrench when tightening the line.
20. Install the air inlet tube to the turbo inlet elbow, then tighten the clamp.
21. Connect the PCV tube and all vacuum lines.
22. Attach the oxygen sensor and other wiring and lines.
23. Connect the oil supply line, then attach the intake tube. Fill the cooling system with the correct type and quantity of coolant.
24. Connect the negative battery cable. Start the engine and check for coolant leaks. Check vehicle operation.

****WARNING**

When installing the turbocharger, or after an oil and filter change, disconnect the distributor feed harness and crank the engine with the starter motor until the oil pressure light on the dash goes out. Oil pressure must be up before starting the engine.

1986–88 2.3L Engines

➧ See Figures 52, 53, 54, 55, 56, 57 and 58

1. Disconnect the negative battery cable.
2. Properly drain the cooling system into a suitable container.
3. Loosen the upper and lower clamps securing the hoses to the intercooler.
4. Disconnect the aspirator hoses at the intercooler and remove the nut securing the bracket to the engine.
5. Remove the intercooler by first lifting then pulling it out.
6. Tag and disconnect all of the vacuum hoses and tubes from the turbocharger. Detach the oxygen sensor connector.
7. Disconnect the PCV tube from the turbocharger air inlet elbow.
8. Loosen the clamp, then disconnect the air inlet tube from the inlet elbow.
9. Detach the ground wire from the turbocharger air inlet elbow, then remove the air inlet elbow.
10. Remove the water connections and fittings from the turbo center housing. Note that some coolant may drain from the engine block.
11. Remove the turbocharger oil supply feed line. Plug the oil inlet hole, to avoid debris from entering.

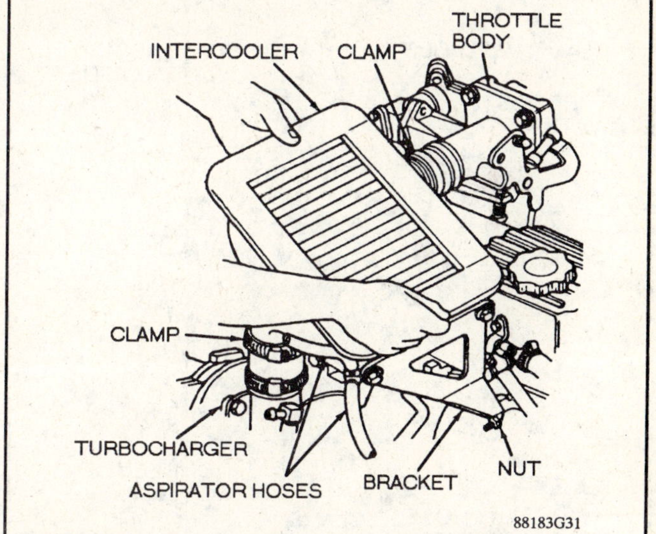

Fig. 52 To remove the intercooler, first lift, then pull the assembly out

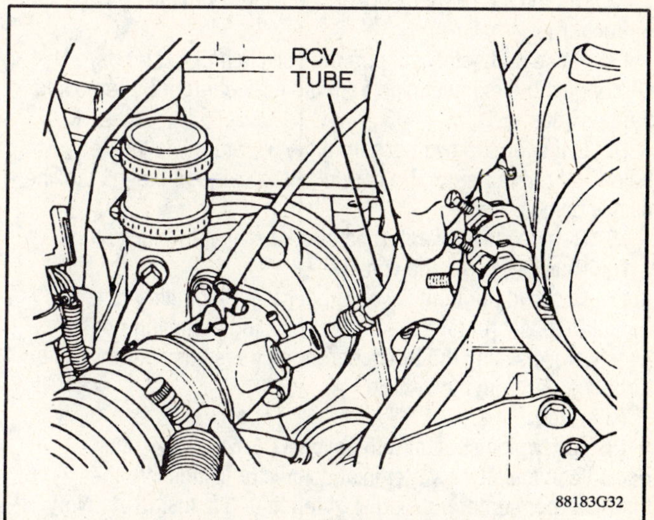

Fig. 53 Detach the PCV tube from the air inlet elbow

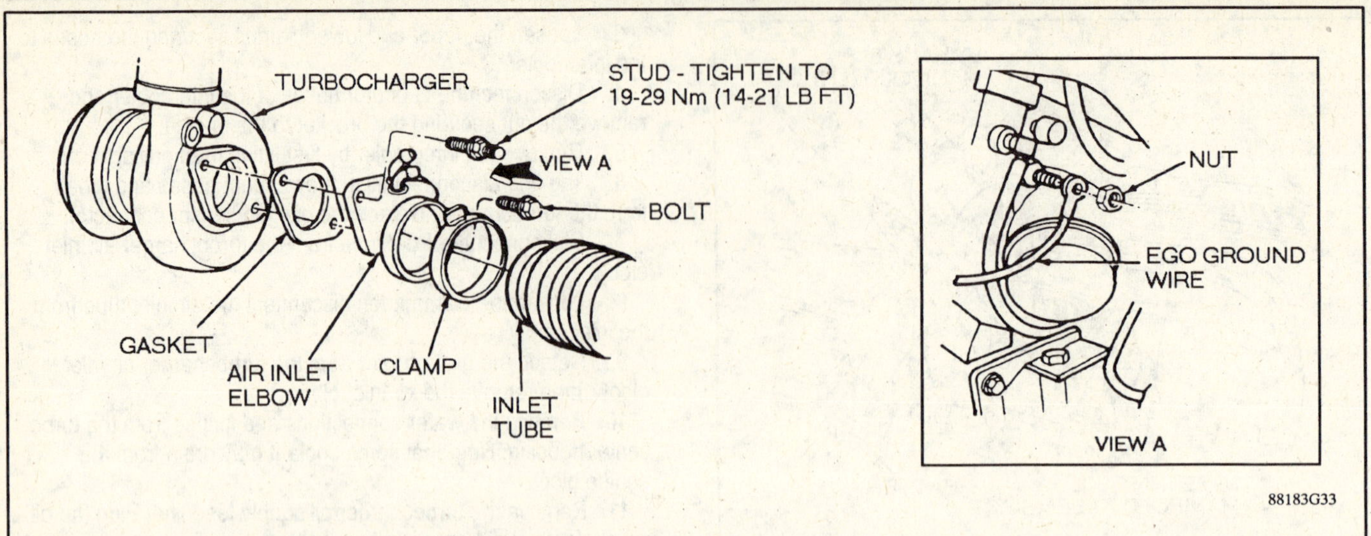

Fig. 54 Unfasten the clamp and remove the air inlet tube and elbow

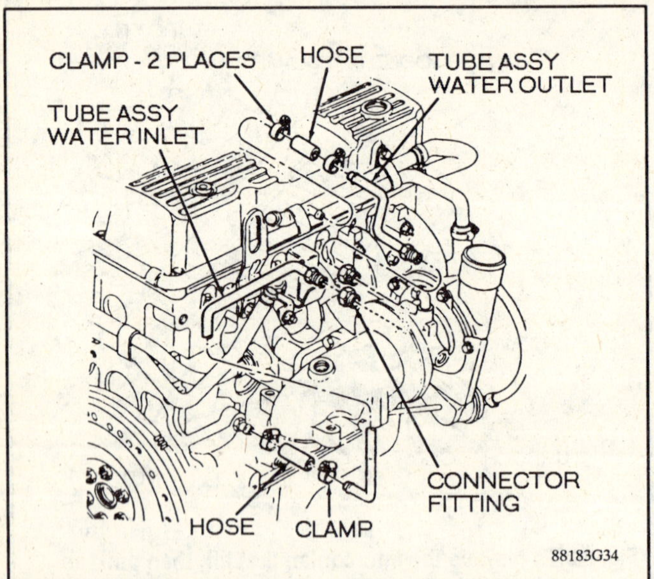

Fig. 55 Unfasten the water connections and fittings

12. Detach the oxygen sensor connector from the turbocharger.
13. Raise and safely support the vehicle on jackstands. Disconnect the exhaust pipe from the turbocharger by removing the two bolts.
14. Unfasten the two bolts from the oil return line located below the turbocharger. Be careful not to damage or kink the line as it is being removed.
15. Remove the lower turbocharger bracket-to-block stud.
16. Carefully lower the vehicle.
17. Remove the front lower turbocharger mounting nut. Simultaneously remove the three remaining mounting nuts evenly while sliding the turbocharger off the studs. Remove the turbocharger from the vehicle.

To install:

18. Apply pipe sealant with Teflon® D8AZ-19554-A or equivalent. Install the water inlet connector fittings into the turbocharger center housing. Tighten to 6-8 ft. lbs. (8-11 Nm) and rotate clockwise so that the fitting is within 5 degrees of vertical, pointing down.
19. Position a new turbocharger mounting gasket in position with the bead side facing outward. Install the turbocharger in position over the four mounting studs.
20. Install the turbocharger bracket on the two lower studs. Using new nuts, start the two lower then the two upper mountings. Do not tighten them completely at this time; allow for slight turbo movement.
21. Raise and safely support the vehicle on jackstands.
22. Install the lower bracket-to-block bolt. Tighten to 28-40 ft. lbs. (38-54 Nm).
23. Position a new oil return line gasket. Attach the oil return line to the turbocharger. Tighten the bolt to 14-21 ft. lbs. (19-29 Nm).
24. Connect the water inlet tube assembly to the inlet fitting at the turbocharger assembly. Tighten the hose clamp to 12-20 inch lbs. (1.4-2.3 Nm).
25. Attach the exhaust pipe to the turbocharger. Tighten the mounting nuts to 25-35 ft. lbs. (34-47 Nm).
26. Lower the vehicle.
27. Using four new nuts, tighten the turbocharger-to-exhaust manifold nuts to 28-40 ft. lbs. (38-54 Nm).
28. Connect the water tube assemblies to the fitting on the turbocharger, then tighten the fasteners to 8-12 ft. lbs. (11-16 ft. lbs.) using a backup wrench to hold the fitting while tightening the line.
29. Position a new gasket, then install the compressor inlet elbow. Tighten the bolts to 14-21 ft. lbs. (19-29 Nm).
30. Fasten the air inlet tube to the turbocharger inlet elbow. Tighten the hose clamp to 1.2-1.6 ft. lbs. (1.7-2.3 Nm).
31. Install the PCV tube fitting, then tighten the clamp to 15-20 inch lbs. (1.7-2.2 Nm).
32. Attach all vacuum lines, as tagged during removal.
33. Connect the oxygen sensor.
34. Attach the electrical ground wire to the air inlet elbow attaching stud.
35. Unplug the oil inlet hole. Connect the oil supply line. Tighten the fitting to 9-16 ft. lbs. (12-22 Nm).
36. Install the intercooler assembly. Tighten the clamps to 25-35 inch lbs. (2.9-3.9 Nm) and tighten the nut to 20-30 ft. lbs. (27-41 Nm).
37. Properly fill and bleed the cooling system.

38. Connect the negative battery cable. Start the engine and check for coolant leaks. Check vehicle operation.

****WARNING**

When installing the turbocharger, or after an oil and filter change, disconnect the distributor feed harness and crank the engine with the starter motor until the oil pressure light on the dash goes out. Oil pressure must be up before starting the engine.

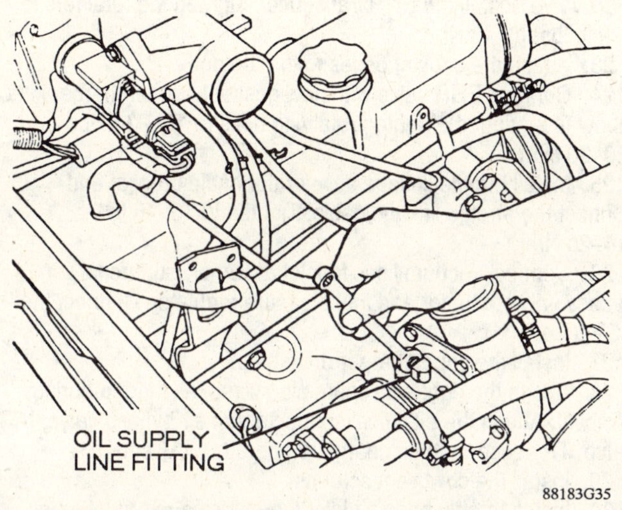

Fig. 56 After disconnect the oil supply feed line, plug it to avoid debris from entering

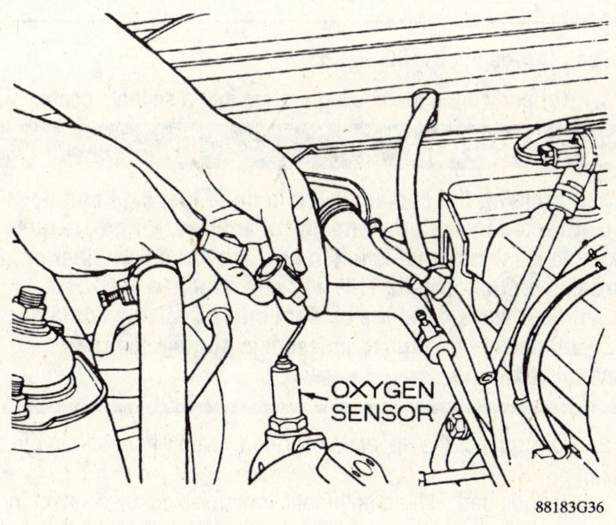

Fig. 57 Detach the oxygen sensor connector from the turbocharger

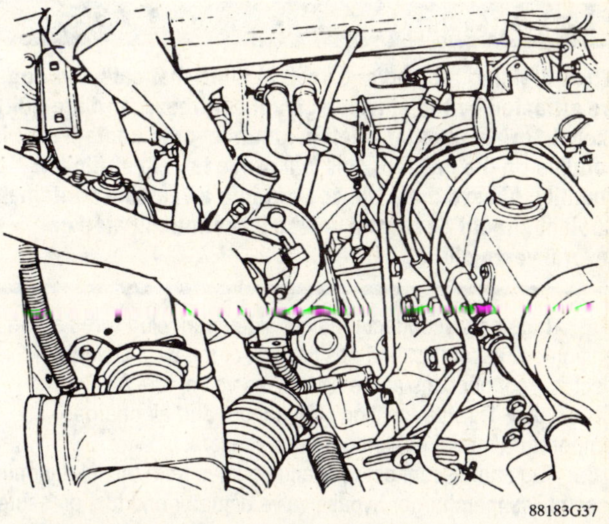

Fig. 58 Slide the turbocharger from the mounting studs, then remove from the vehicle

Supercharger

➥ Do not confuse the turbocharger with the supercharger, they operate differently and no parts are interchangeable. The turbocharger and supercharger are serviced by replacement only.

REMOVAL & INSTALLATION

3.8L (VIN C and R) Engines

➧ See Figure 59

➥ The supercharger is not a bolt-on option. It is part of an integrated engine system. Many components of the supercharged engine are not interchangeable with similar parts from a non-supercharged engine.

The supercharger has a self-contained oiling system that does not require a fluid change for the life of the vehicle. The fluid level should be checked at 30,000 mile intervals, or if visual signs of leakage occur. To check the oil, remove the Allen head plug located at the front of the supercharger. The oil should be at the bottom of the fill plug threads when cold. If the fluid level is low, add a synthetic supercharger fluid that meets or exceeds Ford specification ESE-M99C115-A

****CAUTION**

Before any supercharger service, clean the areas around the supercharger assembly. Cover all openings of the engine and supercharger while the supercharger is removed to prevent damage by foreign material.

1. Disconnect the negative battery cable.
2. Remove throttle body air inlet tube/air cleaner outlet tube.

3. Remove cowl vent screens.
4. Partially drain cooling system.

****CAUTION**

When draining the coolant, keep in mind that cats and dogs are attracted by the ethylene glycol antifreeze, and are quite likely to drink any that is left in an uncovered container or in puddles on the ground. This will prove fatal in sufficient quantity. Always drain the coolant into a sealable container. Coolant should be reused unless it is contaminated or several years old.

5. Tag and disconnect the right side spark plug wires at the ignition coil assembly, and position out of the way. Detach electrical connections at the air bypass valve, Idle Air Control (IAC) valve, Throttle Position (TP) sensor and air charger temperature/Intake Air Temperature sensors.
6. Tag and disconnect the vacuum lines from the inlet/plenum assembly/supercharger bypass valve actuator and fuel pressure regulator Detach the crankcase ventilation tube.
7. Disconnect the EGR valve-to-exhaust manifold tubes from the EGR valve. Remove EGR transducer from bracket and disconnect vacuum line (If so equipped).
8. Disconnect the throttle linkage at throttle body. Remove linkage bracket attaching bolts and position bracket out of the way. If equipped, disconnect the speed control cable.
9. If necessary, remove two EGR valve attaching bolts and move EGR valve away from the intake assembly.
10. Disconnect coolant hoses from throttle body.
11. Remove the supercharger drive belt.
12. Remove intercooler/charge air cooler inlet and outlet tubes.
13. Unfasten the three charge air cooler-to-intake manifold adapter retaining bolts.
14. Remove the three supercharger retaining bolts.
15. Lift the supercharger and charge air cooler/intercooler-to-intake manifold adapter from the vehicle as a unit.

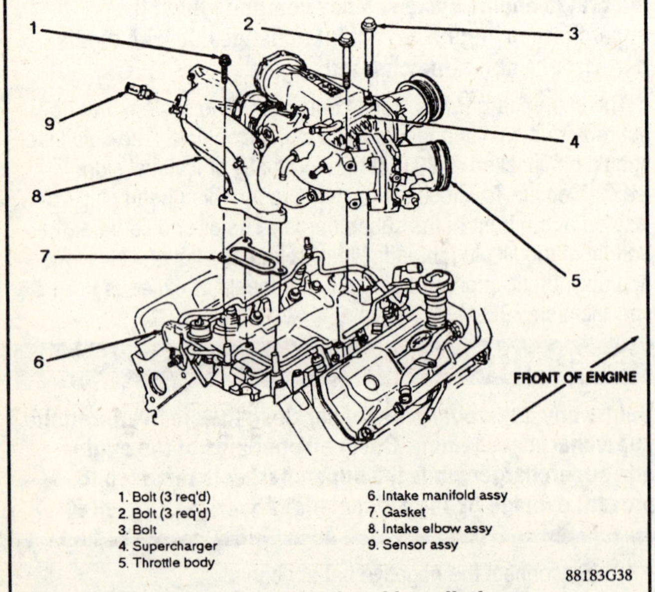

Fig. 59 Supercharger removal and installation

To install:

16. Clean and inspect the sealing surfaces of the supercharger outlet adapter, intake elbow, and intercooler/charge air cooler.
17. Position new gasket on intake manifold using guide pins, if available.
18. Install supercharger, throttle body and charger air cooler to the intake manifold as an assembly.
19. Tighten the two 8mm bolts to 15–22 ft. lbs. (20–30 Nm). Tighten the 12mm bolt to 52–70 ft. lbs. (70–95 Nm).
20. Install three intake elbow/charger air cooler-to-intake manifold adapter retaining nuts/bolts and tighten to 20–28 ft. lbs. (26–38 Nm).
21. Connect the charger air cooler inlet and outlet tubes.
22. Fasten the EGR valve-to-exhaust manifold tube to the EGR valve. Install the EGR transducer. Tighten the retainers to 6–9 ft. lbs. (8–13 Nm).
23. Attach the coolant hoses to throttle body.
24. Connect EGR valve with new gasket to supercharger inlet elbow (if equipped). Tighten retaining bolts to 15–22 ft. lbs. (20–30 Nm).
25. Install throttle linkage/accelerator cable bracket and connect the throttle linkage/cable. Tighten to 10–15 ft. lbs. (14–20 Nm).
26. Connect vacuum lines to inlet assembly/supercharger bypass valve actuator and fuel pressure regulator. Connect the PCV tube.
27. Install the supercharger drive belt.
28. Attach the right side spark plug wires, as tagged during removal. Attach the electrical connectors at air bypass valve, IAC valve, TP sensor and air charge temperature/IAT sensors.
29. Install the cowl vent screens.
30. Install throttle body air inlet tube/air cleaner outlet tube.
31. Properly refill the coolant to proper level.
32. Connect the negative battery cable. Start engine and check for proper operation.

Radiator

REMOVAL & INSTALLATION

See Figures 60, 61, 62 and 63

1. Properly drain the cooling system into a suitable container.

****CAUTION**

When draining the coolant, keep in mind that cats and dogs are attracted by the ethylene glycol antifreeze, and are quite likely to drink any that is left in an uncovered container or in puddles on the ground. This will prove fatal in sufficient quantity. Always drain the coolant into a sealable container. Coolant should be reused unless it is contaminated or several years old.

2. Disconnect the upper, lower and overflow hoses from the radiator.
3. If equipped with an automatic transmission, disconnect the transmission oil cooler inlet and outlet lines from the radiator. Plug the fittings/lines to prevent contamination of the transmission oil cooling system.

4. Depending on the model, remove the two top mounting bolts and remove the radiator and shroud assembly, remove the shroud mounting bolts and position the shroud out of the way, or remove the side mounting bolts. If the A/C condenser is attached to the radiator, remove the retaining bolts and position the condenser out of the way. DO NOT disconnect the refrigerant lines.

5. If equipped with an SC engine, remove the two bolts retaining the top of the air duct to the charge air cooler.

6. Unfasten the radiator attaching bolts or top brackets, then lift out the radiator.

To install:

7. If a new radiator is to be installed, transfer the petcock from the old radiator to the new one. If equipped with an automatic transmission, transfer the oil cooler line intermediate fittings to the new radiator, using Pipe Sealant with Teflon®.

8. Position the radiator and install the upper brackets, if equipped and tighten the mounting bolts securely.

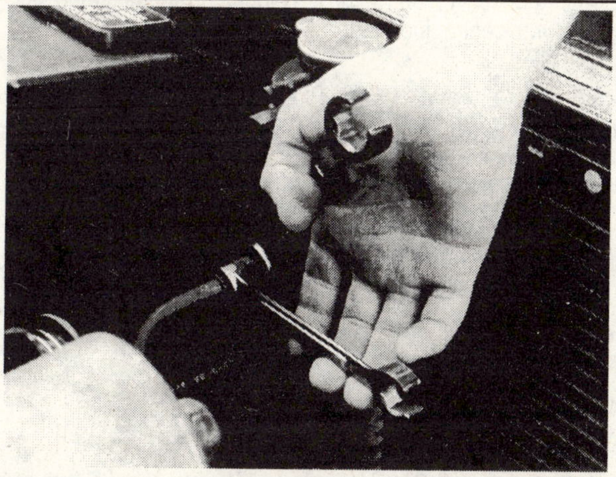

88183P10

Fig. 60 If equipped with an automatic transmission, you must disconnect the oil cooler lines; you must use a backup wrench to avoid stripping the fittings

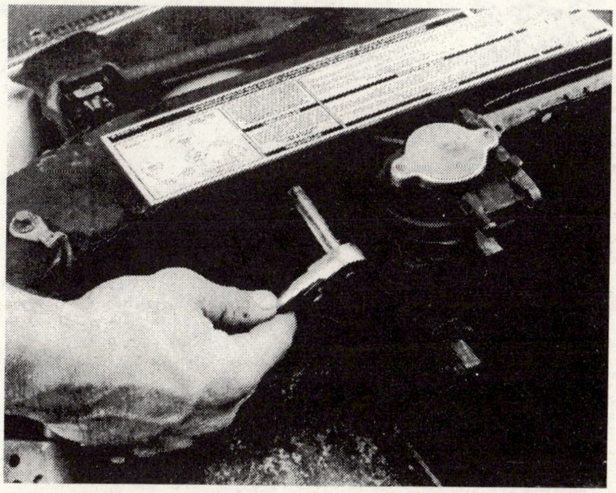

88183P11

Fig. 61 Unfasten the fan shroud retaining bolts

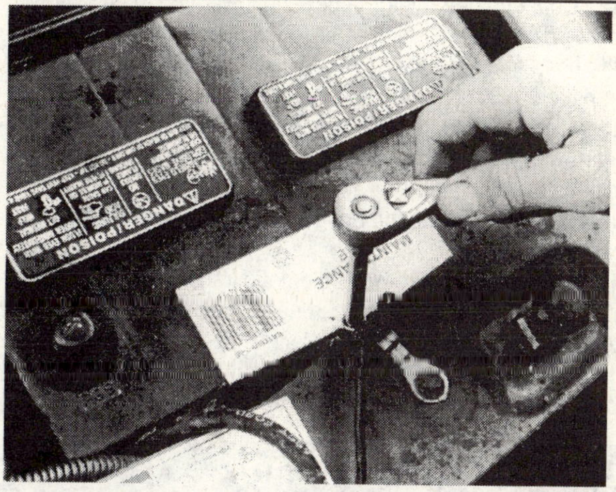

88183P12

Fig. 62 Remove the rest of the shroud or mounting bolts, then . . .

88183P13

Fig. 63 . . . lift and remove the radiator from the vehicle

9. If equipped with an SC engine, cut the retaining strap from the charge air cooler air duct. The duct should spring out from the radiator support assembly. Lift the top of the duct and insert the tabs into the bottom of the duct into the clips at the bottom of the charge air cooler. Install the two bolts that retaining the top of the duct to the charger air cooler.

10. On cars equipped with automatic transmissions, unplug and connect the oil cooler lines using a backup wrench. If equipped, tighten the tube nut on the line to 18–21 ft. lbs. (24.4–28.5 Nm).

11. Install the cooling fan motor, blade and/or shroud as necessary.

****CAUTION**

Make sure the clamps are beyond the bead and place in the center of the clamping surface of the connections. New screw-type hose clamps must be installed inside the hose alignment marks.

12. Connect the radiator upper and lower and the overflow hoses. Position the clamps at least 2 in. (50mm) from each end of the hose and slide the hose on the connections. Tighten the clamps to 20–30 inch lbs. (2.2–3.4 Nm).

13. Close the radiator petcock. Fill and bleed the cooling system with a 50/50 mix of the proper type and quantity of coolant and clean water.

14. Start the engine and bring it to operating temperature. Check for leaks.

15. On cars equipped with automatic transmissions, check the cooler lines for leaks and interference. Check the transmission fluid level.

16. Turn the engine off, then check the radiator and radiator coolant recovery reservoir fluid levels. Add if necessary.

Electric Cooling Fan

REMOVAL & INSTALLATION

See Figures 64, 65 and 66

Various models, are equipped with a bracket-mounted electric cooling fan that replaces the conventional water pump mounted fan.

Operation of the fan motor is dependent on engine coolant temperature and air conditioner compressor clutch engagement. The fan will run only when the coolant temperature is approximately 180° or higher, or when the compressor clutch is engaged. The fan, motor and mount can be removed as an assembly after disconnecting the wiring harnesses and mounting bolts.

****CAUTION**

The cooling fan is automatic and may come on at any time without warning even if the ignition is switched OFF. To avoid possible injury, always disconnect the negative battery cable when working near the electric cooling fan.

1. Disconnect the negative battery cable.
2. Detach the fan motor wire connector at the side of the fan shroud. Remove the male terminal connector retaining clip from the fan shroud mounting tab.
3. Remove the two fan shroud upper retaining bolts at the radiator support of radiator tanks.
4. If necessary, remove the mounting bracket attaching screws.
5. Lift the cooling fan motor/fan blade/shroud assembly past the radiator, disengaging the fan shroud from the two lower retaining clips.
6. Installation is the reverse of the removal procedure. On SC engines, tighten the fan shroud retaining bolts to 27–53 inch lbs. (3–6 Nm). On all other engines, tighten the fan shroud retaining bolts to 46–64 inch lbs. (5.2–7.2 Nm).

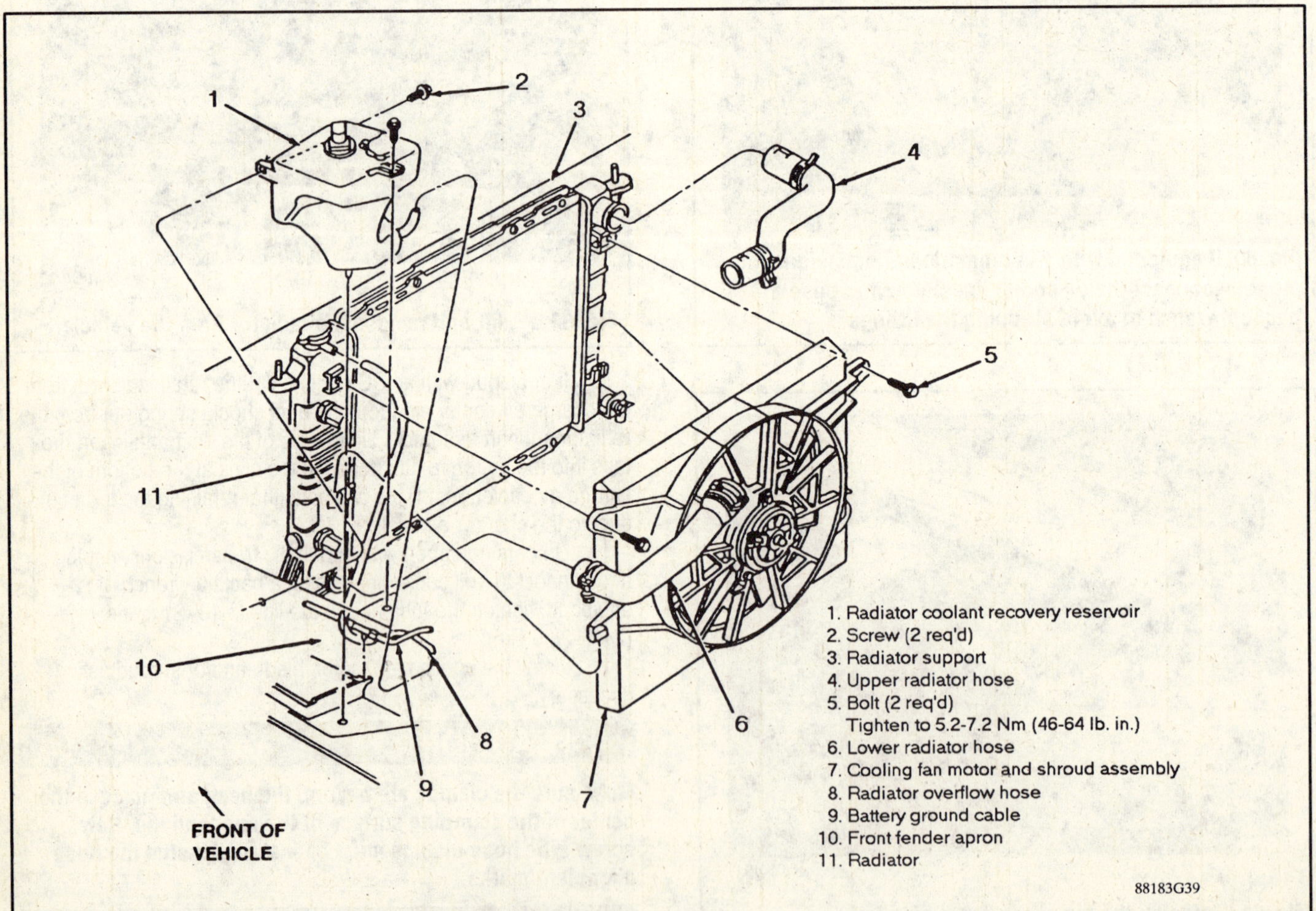

Fig. 64 Electric fan removal — 1995 3.8L engine shown

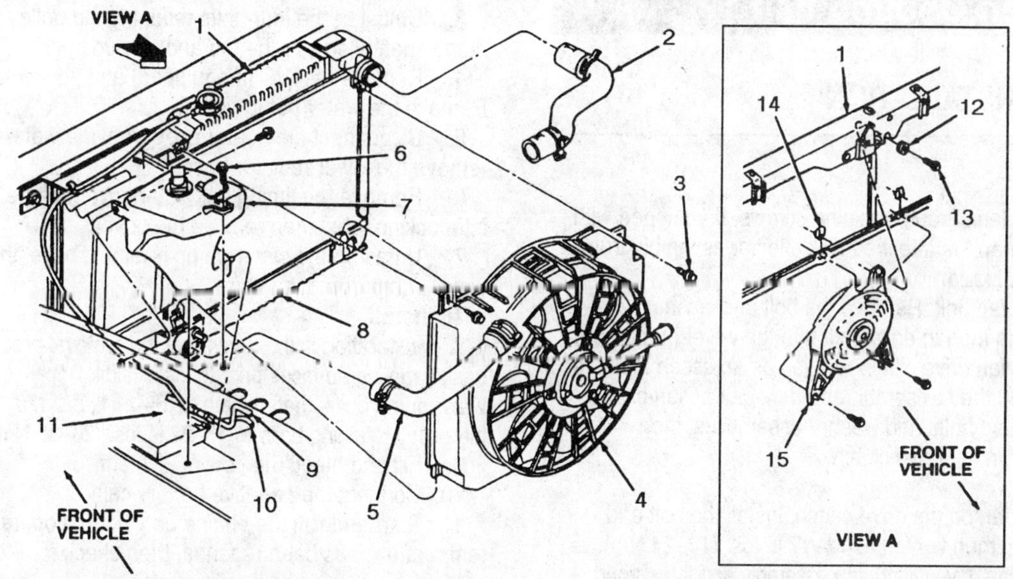

1. Radiator support
2. Upper radiator hose
3. Bolt (2 req'd) Tighten to 3-6 Nm (27-53 lb. in.)
4. Cooling fan, motor and shroud assembly
5. Lower radiator hose
6. Screw (2 req'd)
7. Radiator coolant recovery reservoir
8. Radiator
9. Battery ground cable
10. Radiator overflow hose
11. Front fender apron
12. Grommet
13. Bolt (3 req'd) Tighten to 3-6 Nm (27-53 lb. in.)
14. U-nut (2 req'd)
15. Auxiliary cooling fan

88183G40

Fig. 65 View of the electric fan mounting — 3.8L SC engine shown

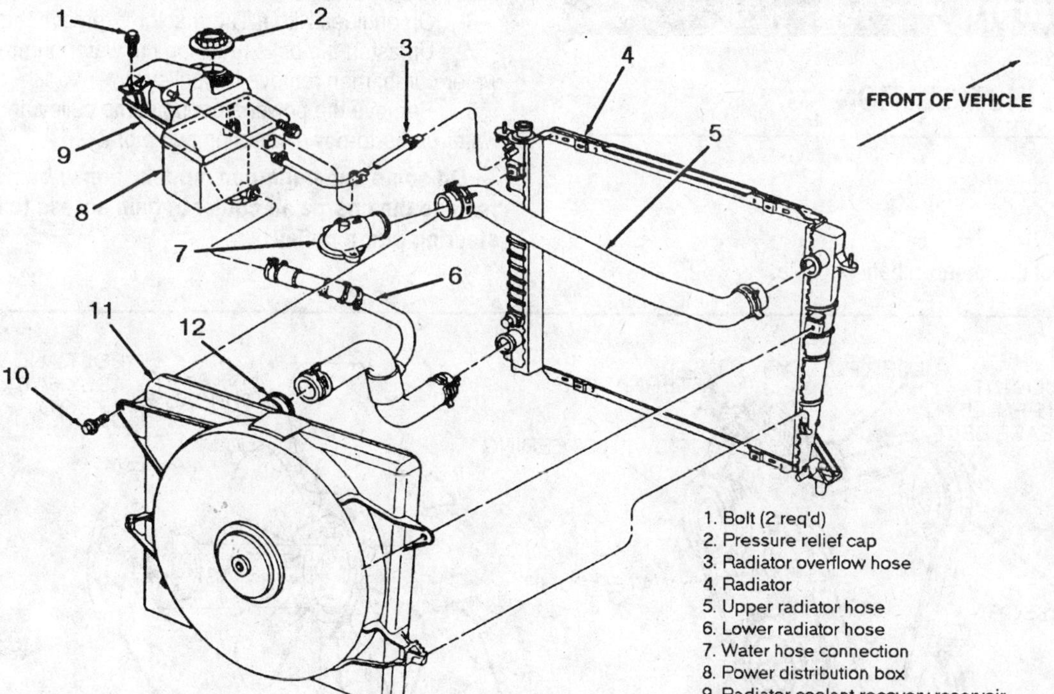

1. Bolt (2 req'd)
2. Pressure relief cap
3. Radiator overflow hose
4. Radiator
5. Upper radiator hose
6. Lower radiator hose
7. Water hose connection
8. Power distribution box
9. Radiator coolant recovery reservoir
10. Bolt (2 req'd) Tighten to 5.2-7.2 Nm (46-64 lb. in.)
11. Cooling fan motor and shroud assembly
12. Oil filter adapter

88183G41

Fig. 66 The fan/fan shroud assembly is usually secured with mounting bolts around the shroud

Belt-Driven Cooling Fan

REMOVAL & INSTALLATION

➧ See Figure 67

1. Remove the fan shroud retaining screws. If equipped with a 5.0L engine, unsnap the attached air deflector assembly from the subframe cross brace.
2. Remove the fan belt. Remove the bolt and washer assemblies retaining the fan drive clutch to the water pump hub.
3. Remove the fan drive clutch and fan as an assembly at the same time removing the fan shroud and deflector assembly. Unfasten the retaining bolts and washer assemblies, then separate the fan from the drive clutch.

To install:

4. Position the fan on the drive clutch. Install the bolt and washer assemblies, then tighten to 12–17 ft. lbs. (16–24 Nm).
5. Position the fan drive clutch, fan assembly and fan shroud, then bolt the fan and clutch assembly to the water pump hub. Install and tighten the clutch retaining bolt and water pump assemblies evenly and alternately to 15–22 ft. lbs. (20–30 Nm) for the 3.8L engine or to 36–47 ft. lbs. (48–65 Nm) for the 5.0L engine.
6. Install the fan belt. Align the fan shroud and adjust for equal fan-to-shroud radiator clearance but maintaining a minimum of 0.38 inch clearance to the fan tip on 5.0L engines.
7. Install and tighten the shroud retaining screws. On 5.0L engines, snap the air deflector assembly to the sub-frame cross brace.

Water Pump

REMOVAL & INSTALLATION

2.3L Engine

➧ See Figure 68

1. Disconnect the negative battery cable.
2. Properly drain the cooling system into a suitable container.
3. Unfasten the four bolts retaining the pulley to the water pump shaft. Remove the fan and shroud.
4. Remove the A/C (if equipped) and power steering belts. Remove the water pump pulley.
5. Disconnect the heater hose from the water pump, then remove the lower radiator hose.
6. Remove the timing belt outer cover bolt, release the interlocking tabs, then remove the cover.
7. Unfasten the water pump retaining bolts, then remove the water pump from the vehicle.

To install:

8. Installation is the reverse of the removal procedure. Clean all gasket mating surfaces prior to installation. Apply pipe sealant to the water pump bolts, then tighten to 15–21 ft. lbs. (20–30 Nm). Tighten the pulley retaining bolts to 15–22 ft. lbs. (20–30 Nm).
9. Fill and bleed the cooling system.
10. Connect the negative battery cable.
11. Start and run the engine until normal operating temperature has been reached, then check for leaks. Check the coolant level, and add if necessary.

3.8L Engine

➧ See Figures 69, 70 and 71

1. Disconnect the negative battery cable.
2. Properly drain the cooling system into a suitable container.
3. Remove the cooling fan and fan shroud, as outlined earlier in this section.
4. Release the belt tensioner, then remove the accessory drive belt(s).
5. If the vehicle is equipped with air conditioning, remove the idler pulley bracket and air conditioner drive belt.
6. On engines with a Thermactor®, remove the belt.
7. Unfasten the bolts retaining the water pump pulley to the water pump, then remove the pulley.
8. Remove the power steering pump pulley and remove the water pump-to-power steering pump brace.

➥ **On some supercharged models, it may be necessary to remove the charge air cooler to gain access to the power steering pump pulley.**

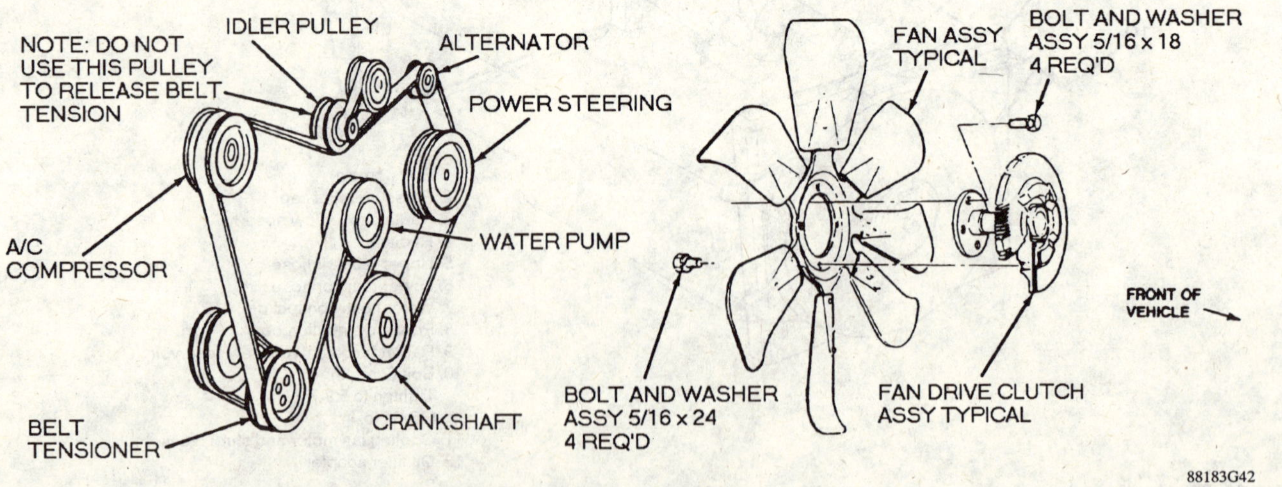

Fig. 67 Exploded view of the belt drive fan assembly — 1992 vehicle shown

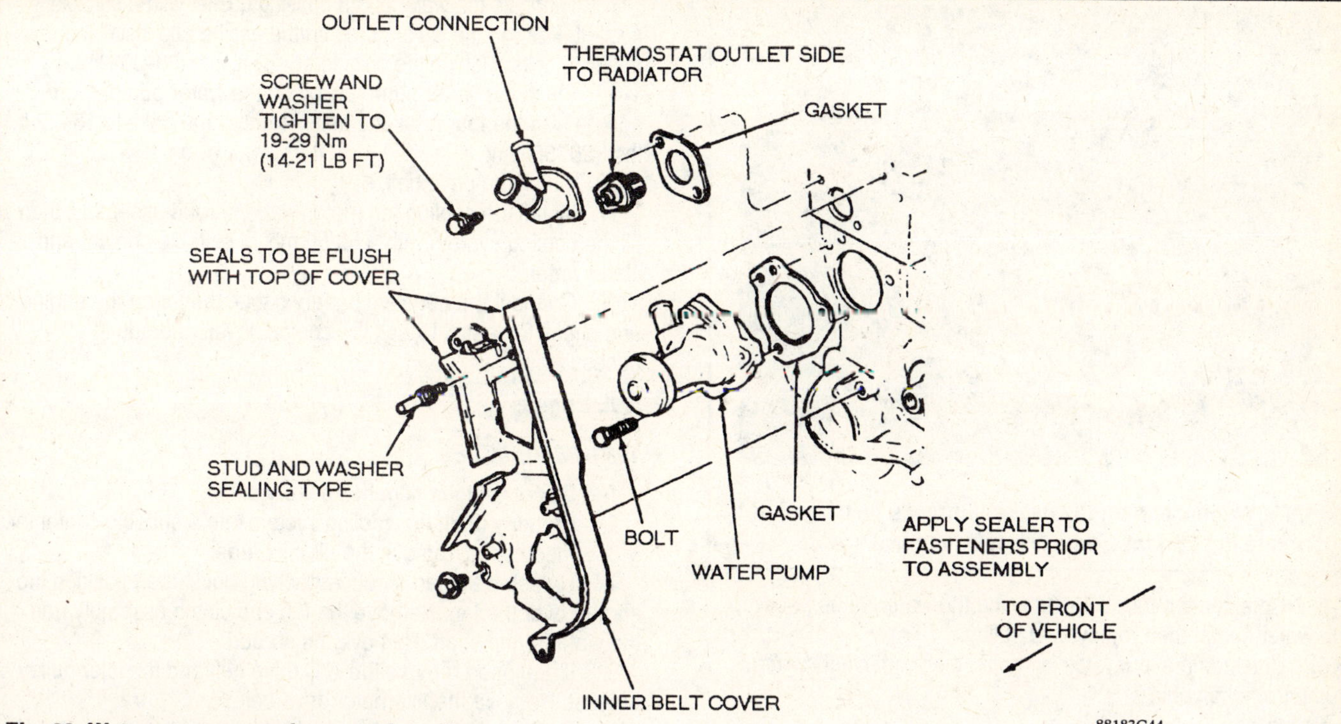

Fig. 68 Water pump mounting — 2.3L engine

9. Detach the water bypass hose at the water pump.
10. Disconnect the heater hose at the water pump and disconnect the lower radiator hose. On SC models, disconnect the oil cooler inlet tube and hose.
11. On SC vehicles, remove the Crankshaft Position (CKP) sensor upper shield.
12. Unfasten the bolts retaining the water pump to the engine, then remove the water pump from the vehicle.

To install:

13. Clean any gasket material from the pump mating surfaces. On engines equipped with a water pump backing plate, remove the plate, clean the gasket surfaces, install a new gasket and plate on the water pump.
14. Coat both sides of the new gasket with a water-resistant sealer, then position the gasket on the water pump housing.

Fig. 69 Unfasten the retaining bolts, then . . .

➥ **The use of gasket adhesive is recommended.**

15. Install the water pump, then tighten the retaining bolts, in the sequence shown in the accompanying figure, to 15–22 ft. lbs. (20–30 Nm).
16. On SC vehicles, install the CKP sensor upper shield.
17. Connect the water bypass hose at the water pump, then tighten the clamps (and oil cooler inlet tube and hose).
18. Attach the heater hose at the water pump and connect the lower radiator hose and tighten the clamps.
19. Install the power steering pump pulley and water pump-to-power steering pump brace. If removed, install the charge air cooler.
20. Install the water pump pulley and tighten the retaining bolts to 15–22 ft. lbs. (20–30 Nm).
21. On engines with a Thermactor®, install the belt.
22. If the vehicle is equipped with air conditioning, install the idler pulley bracket and air conditioner drive belt.
23. Install the accessory drive belt(s).
24. Install the cooling fan and shroud, as outlined earlier in this section.
25. Fill the engine cooling system with the proper type and quantity of coolant. Connect the negative battery cable.
26. Start and run the engine and inspect for leaks. Check the coolant level, and add if necessary.

4.6L Engine

➧ **See Figure 72**

1. Disconnect the negative battery cable.
2. Properly drain the engine cooling system into a suitable container.
3. Remove the cooling fan/motor/blade assembly, as outlined in this section.
4. Release the drive belt tension, then remove the belt.

88183P16

Fig. 70 When cleaning the gasket surfaces be careful not to gouge the surfaces, which may cause leakage

5. Unfasten the four bolts retaining the water pump pulley to the water pump, then remove the pulley.
6. Unfasten the four retaining bolts, then remove the water pump from the vehicle.

To install:

7. Replace the O-ring type water pump housing gasket and clean the sealing surfaces of the cylinder block
8. Lubricate the water pump housing gasket with a suitable coolant. Position the water pump on the engine and install the four retaining bolts. Tighten the bolts to 15–22 ft. lbs. (20–30 Nm).
9. Place the water pump pulley on the water pump, then secure with the four retaining bolts. Tighten the bolts to 15–22 ft. lbs. (20–30 Nm).
10. Install the drive belt.
11. Install the cooling fan motor/blade/shroud assembly, then fill the cooling system with a 50/50 mix of suitable coolant and clean water.
12. Connect the negative battery cable, then start the engine and check for leaks. Check the coolant level, and add if necessary.

5.0L Engine

1983–88 VEHICLES

1. Disconnect the negative battery cable.
2. Properly drain the cooling system into a suitable container.
3. If equipped, remove the air inlet tube.
4. Unfasten the fan shroud attaching bolts, then position the shroud over the fan. Remove the fan and clutch assembly from the water pump shaft. Remove the shroud.
5. If equipped remove the A/C drive belt and the idler pulley bracket. Remove the alternator drive belt.
6. Remove the power steering drive belt and the power steering pump. Do NOT disconnect the power steering pump lines.

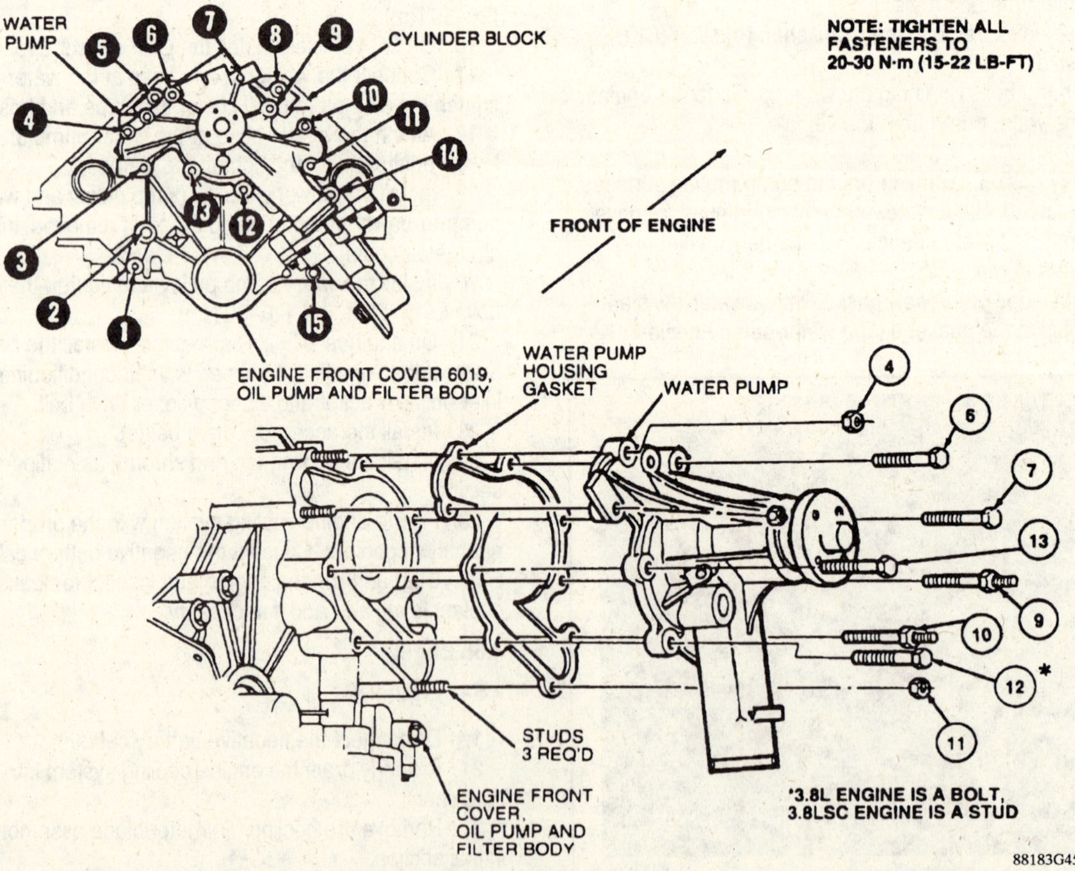

88183G45

Fig. 71 The water pump retaining bolts must be tightened in sequence to prevent possible coolant leakage

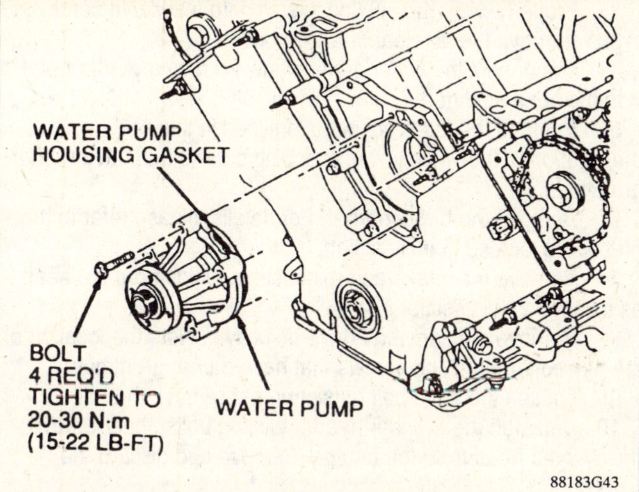

Fig. 72 After you remove the pulley, unfasten the bolts and remove the water pump from the vehicle

7. Remove all accessory brackets which attach to the water pump. Remove the water pump pulley.
8. Disconnect the radiator lower hose, heater hose, and water pump bypass hose at the water pump.
9. Unfasten the bolts that attach the pump to the cylinder front cover. Remove the pump and gasket. Discard the gasket.

To install:

10. Clean all gasket material from the mounting surfaces of the cylinder front cover and water pump.
11. Position a new gasket, coated on both sides with Perfect Seal sealing compound B5A-19554-A or equivalent, on the cylinder front cover. Position the water pump, then install the retaining bolts. Tighten the bolts to 12-18 ft. lbs. (16-24 Nm).
12. Connect the radiator hose, heater hose and water pump bypass hose at the water pump.
13. Install all the accessory brackets which attach to the water pump. Place the water pump pulley on the water pump shaft.
14. Install the power steering pump and drive belt. Install the alternator and drive belt. If equipped install the A/C idler pulley bracket and drive belt.
15. Position the fan shroud over the water pump pulley and install the fan drive clutch and fan. Install the shroud attaching bolts.
16. Adjust the drive belts to the specified belt tension.
17. Fill and bleed the cooling system. Connect the negative battery cable.
18. Start and run the engine until it reaches normal operating temperature, then inspect for leaks. Check the coolant level and add if necessary.

1991-93 VEHICLES

See Figures 73 and 74

1. Disconnect the negative battery cable.
2. Properly drain the cooling system into a suitable container.

The fan and clutch assembly is removed by turning the nut counterclockwise.

3. Remove the fan and clutch assembly from the water pump shaft using Fan Clutch Holding Tool T84T-6312-C and Fan Clutch Nut Wrench T84T-6312-D, or equivalent tools, and position the fan and clutch assembly in the fan shroud.
4. Remove the fan shroud and fan/clutch as an assembly.
5. Loosen the water pump pulley bolts.
6. Remove the accessory drive belt by rotating the tensioner away from the belt by using pulley retaining bolts only.
7. Remove the water pump pulley.
8. Disconnect the lower radiator hose, heater hose and water pump bypass hose at the water pump.
9. Unfasten the bolts that attach the pump to the cylinder front cover. Remove the pump and gasket, then discard the gasket.

To install:

10. Clean all gasket material from the mating surfaces of the cylinder front cover and the water pump.
11. Position a new gasket, coated on both sides with Perfect Seal sealing compound B5A-19554-A or equivalent, on the cylinder front cover. Position the water pump, then install the retaining bolts. Tighten the bolts to 12-18 ft. lbs. (16-24 Nm).
12. Connect the radiator hose, heater hose and water pump bypass hose at the water pump.

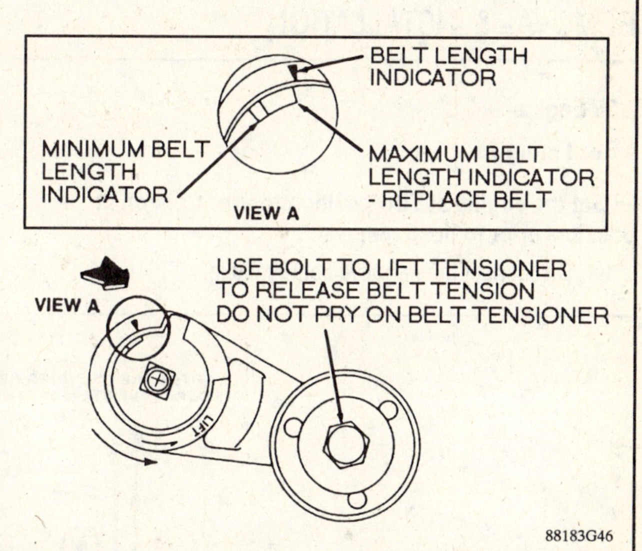

Fig. 73 Rotate the tensioner away from the belt to remove the drive belt

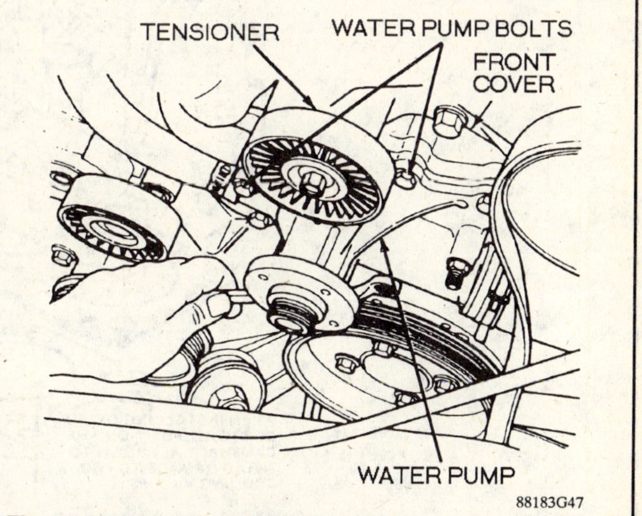

Fig. 74 Unfasten the retaining bolts, then remove the water pump from the vehicle

13. Install the water pump pulley and tighten the bolts hand-tight.
14. Install the accessory drive belt and tighten the water pump pulley bolts.
15. Position the fan and clutch assembly in the fan shroud, then install the shroud.
16. Install the fan drive clutch and fan using Fan Clutch Holding tool T84T-6312-C and Fan Clutch Nut Wrench T84T-6312-D, or equivalent tools.
17. Connect the upper radiator hose.
18. Fill and bleed the cooling system. Connect the negative battery cable.
19. Start and run the engine until it reaches normal operating temperature, then inspect for leaks. Check the coolant level and add if necessary.

Cylinder Head

REMOVAL & INSTALLATION

2.3L Engine

➧ See Figure 75

➥ Set the engine at TDC position for No. 1 piston, if possible prior to head removal.

1. Disconnect the negative battery cable.
2. Properly drain the cooling system into a suitable container.
3. Remove the air cleaner assembly.
4. Disconnect the water outlet elbow from the cylinder head with the hose attached.
5. Remove the valve cover, as outlined in this section. Note the location of the valve cover attaching screws that have rubber grommets.
6. Remove the turbocharger. For details, please refer to the procedure located in this section.
7. Remove the intake and exhaust manifolds from the head, as outlined in this section.
8. Remove the camshaft drive belt cover. Note the location of the belt cover attaching screws that have rubber grommets.
9. Loosen the drive belt tensioner and remove the belt.
10. Unfasten the cylinder head attaching bolts, then remove the cylinder head from the engine. Remove and discard the gasket.
11. Clean all gaskets material and carbon from the top of the cylinder block and pistons and from the bottom of the cylinder head.

To install:

12. Position a new cylinder head gasket on the engine. Rotate the camshaft so that the head locating pin is at the five o'clock position to avoid damage to the valves and pistons.
13. If they are available, cut the heads off of two old cylinder head bolts to use as guide studs. Thread the studs into the engine block at opposite corners.

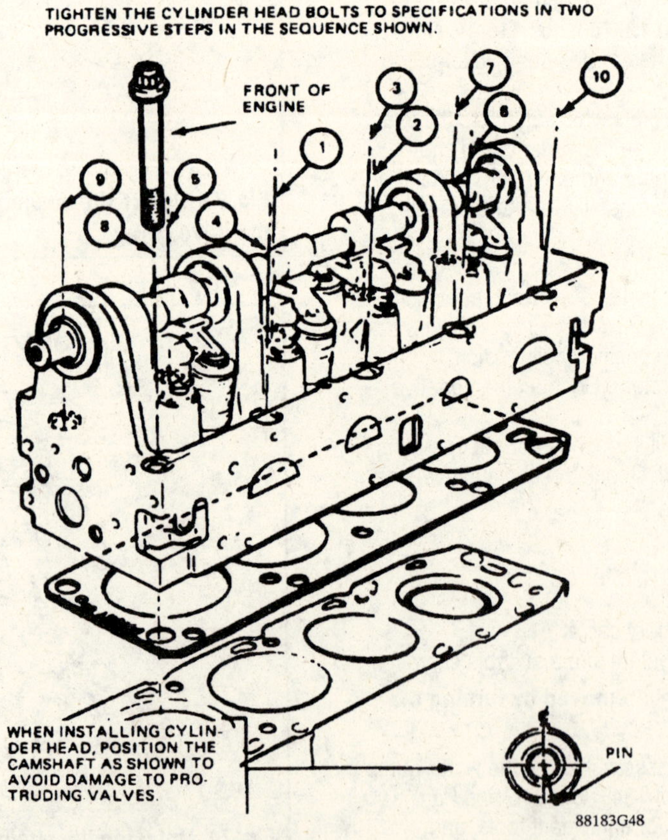

Fig. 75 Cylinder head bolt tightening sequence — 2.3L engine

14. Fit the gasket onto the block, then set the head into place. Remove the guide studs. Apply a non-hardening gasket sealer to the bolt threads, then install the bolts finger tight.
15. Using a torque wrench, tighten the head bolts, in the sequence shown in the illustration, first to 50-60 ft. lbs. (68-81 Nm), then to 80-90 ft. lbs. (108-122 Nm).
16. Install the camshaft drive belt.
17. Install the camshaft drive belt cover and its attaching bolts. Make sure the rubber grommets are installed on the bolts. Tighten the bolts to 6-13 ft. lbs. (8-18 Nm).
18. Install the water outlet elbow and a new gasket on the engine and tighten the attaching bolts to 12-15 ft. lbs. (16-20 Nm).
19. Install the intake and exhaust manifolds and the turbocharger.
20. Install the air cleaner and the valve cover.
21. Fill the cooling system.
22. Connect the negative battery cable, then start and run the engine and inspect for leaks. Check the coolant level and add if necessary.

3.8L Engine

➧ See Figures 76, 77, 78, 79, 80 and 81

➥ Cylinder head bolts must be replaced any time they are removed. The bolts are designed to stretch when tightened to the proper angle torque and may break or loosen if torqued a second time. Do NOT use the old bolts over again.

1. Disconnect the negative battery cable.

✻✻CAUTION

Fuel injection systems remain under pressure, even after the engine has been shut OFF. The fuel system pressure must be relieved before disconnecting any fuel lines. Failure to do so may result in fire and/or personal injury.

2. Properly relieve the fuel system pressure. Drain the cooling system into a suitable container.
3. Remove the air cleaner assembly including the air intake duct and heat tube.
4. Loosen the accessory drive belt idler. Remove the drive belt.

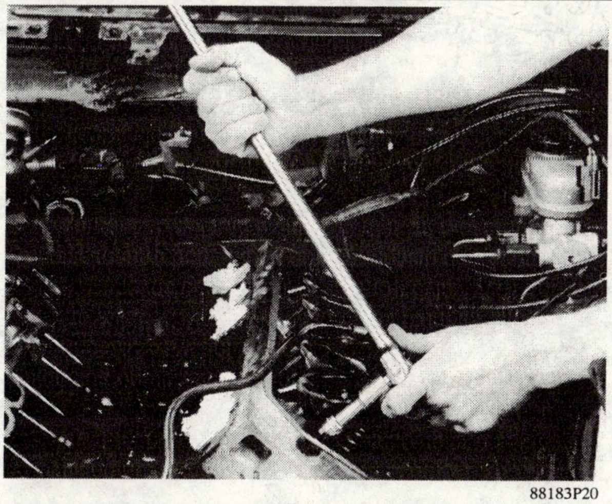

88183P20

Fig. 76 Unfasten and discard the cylinder head bolts, then . . .

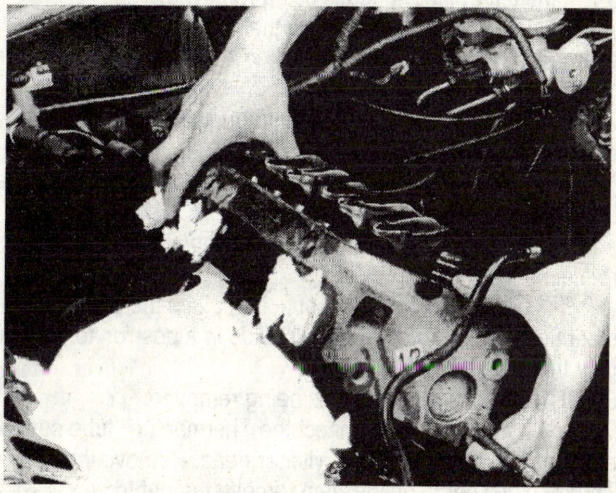

88183P21

Fig. 77 . . . remove the head from the vehicle

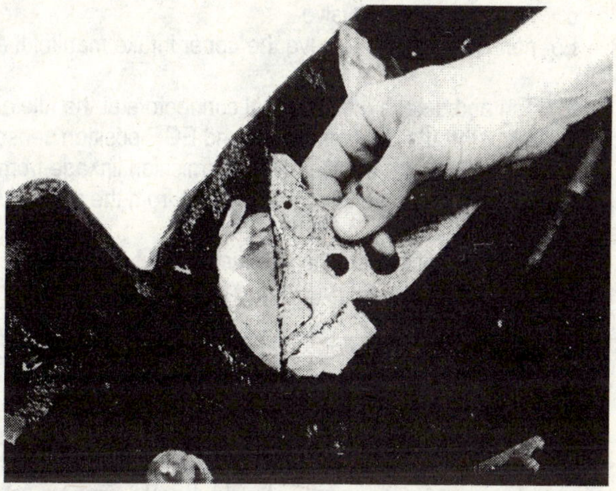

88183P22

Fig. 78 Remove and discard the cylinder head gasket

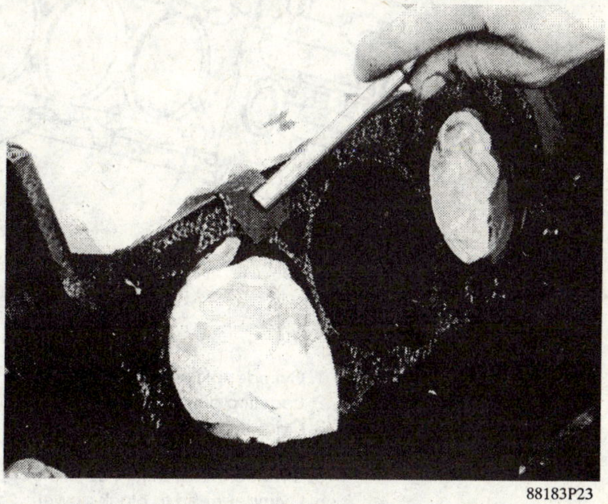

88183P23

Fig. 79 Use a suitable gasket scraper to clean the mating surfaces

5. If the left cylinder head is being removed:
a. For SC engines, remove the charge air cooler and charge air cooler tubes.
b. Remove the oil fill cap.
c. Remove the power steering pump front mounting bracket attaching bolts.
d. Remove the alternator assembly and accessory drive belt main idler.
e. Remove the power steering pump/alternator bracket retaining bolts.
f. Leaving the hoses connected, place the power steering pump/alternator bracket aside in a position to prevent fluid from leaking out.
6. If the right cylinder head is being removed:
a. If equipped, disconnect the Thermactor® tube support bracket from the rear of the cylinder head. Remove the Thermactor® pump pulley, then remove the pump.
b. If equipped, remove the A/C compressor belt and main drive belt.
c. If equipped, remove the compressor mounting bracket retaining bolts. Leave the hoses connected, then position the compressor aside.
d. Remove the PCV valve.
7. For non-SC engines, remove the upper intake manifold, as follows:
a. Tag and detach the electrical connectors at the idle air bypass valve, throttle position sensor and EGR position sensor.
b. Disconnect the throttle and transmission linkage from the throttle body. Remove the cable bracket from the manifold and position the bracket and cables aside.
c. Tag and disconnect the vacuum lines at the upper manifold vacuum tree, EGR valve and fuel pressure regulator.
d. Detach the PCV hose from the fitting at the rear of the upper manifold.
e. Unfasten the retaining bolts, then remove the upper intake manifold.
8. For SC engines, remove the supercharger, as outlined in this section.
9. Remove the valve (rocker arm) cover attaching screws. Loosen the silicone rubber gasketing material by inserting a putty knife under the cover flange. Work the cover loose and remove. The plastic rocker arm covers will break if excessive prying is applied.
10. Remove the fuel rail and lower intake manifold.
11. Remove the exhaust manifold(s).
12. Loosen the rocker arm fulcrum attaching bolts enough to allow the rocker arm to be lifted off the pushrod and rotated to one side.
13. Remove the pushrods. Make sure to identify the position of each rod. They must be installed in their original position during assembly.
14. Unfasten the cylinder head attaching bolts and discard.
15. Remove the cylinder head(s). Remove and discard the old cylinder head gasket(s). Clean all gasket mating surfaces.
16. Check the flatness of the cylinder head gasket surface using a straight-edge and a feeler gauge. The allowable warpage is 0.003 in. for every 6.0 inches. Do not machine more than 0.010 in.

To install:

↱ Lightly oil all bolt and stud bolt threads before installation except those entering coolant passages.

17. Position new head gasket(s) on the cylinder block using the dowels for alignment.
18. Place the cylinder heads on the block.

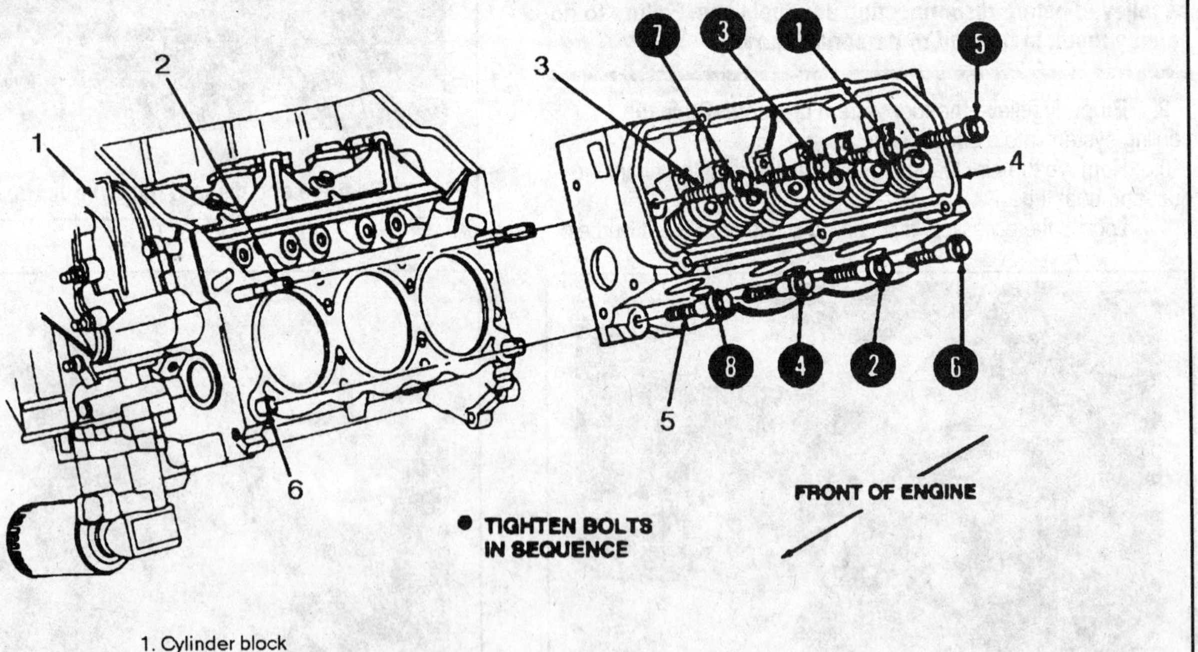

1. Cylinder block
2. Locating pin (2)
3. Cylinder head bolt (4 each side)
4. Cylinder head
5. Cylinder head bolt (4 each side)
6. Cylinder head to block dowel

88183G49

Fig. 80 The cylinder head bolts may NOT be reused and must be tightened in sequence — 3.8L engine

✱✱CAUTION

Always use new cylinder head bolts to assure a leak-tight assembly. Torque retention with used bolts can vary, which may result in coolant or compression leakage at the cylinder head mating surface area.

19. Install new cylinder head bolts hand-tight.
20. For vehicles through 1992 and all SC engines, tighten the bolts, in the sequence shown in the accompanying figure to:
    a. 37 ft. lbs. (50 Nm)
    b. 45 ft. lbs. (60 Nm)
    c. 52 ft. lbs. (70 Nm)
    d. 59 ft. lbs. (80 Nm)
21. For 1993–96 vehicles, except SC engines, tighten the bolts, in the sequence shown in the accompanying figure to:
    a. 15 ft. lbs. (20 Nm)
    b. 29 ft. lbs. (40 Nm)
    c. 37 ft. lbs. (50 Nm)

➛ Do NOT loosen more than one bolt at a time.

22. For non SC engines, loosen each bolt in the torque sequence, on at a time, 2–3 turns, then :
    a. Tighten each long bolt to 11–18 ft. lbs. (15–25 Nm), then rotate an additional 90 degrees.
    b. Tighten each short bolt to 7–15 ft. lbs. (10–20 Nm), then rotate an additional 90 degrees.
23. For SC engines, loosen each bolt in sequence 2–3 turns, then torque to 48–55 ft. lbs. (67–75 Nm). Rotate each bolt in sequence an additional 90–110 degrees.

➛ When the cylinder head attaching bolts have been tightened using the above sequential procedure, it is not necessary to retighten the bolts after extended engine operation. However, the bolts can be checked for tightness if desired.

24. Lubricate each pushrod in heavy engine oil and install them in their original positions. Rotate the rocker arm into position.
25. For each valve, rotate the crankshaft until the lifter rests on the base circle of the camshaft lobe (pushrod all the way down), then tighten the fulcrum bolt to 43 inch lbs. (5 Nm). The fulcrum must be fully seated and the pushrod must be seated in the rocker arm socket before final tightening.

88183P24

Fig. 81 The head bolts must be tightened to the correct sequence to prevent leakage

✱✱WARNING

Fulcrums must be fully seated in cylinder head and pushrods must be seated in rocker arm sockets prior to final tightening.

26. Lubricate all rocker arm assemblies with heavy engine oil, then tighten the fulcrum bolts to 19–25 ft. lbs. (25–35 Nm). For final tightening, the camshaft may be in any position.

➛ If the original valve train components are being installed, a valve clearance check is not required. If a component has been replaced, perform a valve clearance check.

27. Install the exhaust manifold(s).
28. Install the lower intake manifold and the fuel rail.
29. Position a new gasket and the valve cover on the cylinder head, then install the attaching bolts. Note the location of the spark plug routing clip stud bolts. Tighten the attaching bolts to 80–106 inch lbs. (9–12 Nm).
30. Install the upper intake manifold or the supercharger, as applicable.
31. If removed, install the spark plugs. Connect the spark plug wires to the spark plugs.
32. If the left cylinder head is being installed:
    a. Install the oil fill cap.
    b. Install the alternator/power steering pump mounting bracket.
    c. Install the alternator assembly,.
    d. Install the main accessory drive belt tensioner assembly.
    e. Install the power steering pump assembly.
    f. Install the power steering pump support bracket.
    g. If equipped with an SC engine, install the charge air cooler tubes and charge air cooler.
33. If the right cylinder head is being installed:
    a. Install the PCV valve.
    b. If equipped with A/C, install the compressor mounting and support brackets and install the compressor.
    c. If equipped, install the Thermactor® pump and pump pulley.
    d. If equipped, install the accessory drive belt idler pulley.
    e. If equipped, install the Thermactor air control valve or idle air bypass hose. Tighten the clamps securely to the air pump assembly.
34. Install the accessory drive belt. If equipped, attach the Thermactor tube(s) support bracket to the rear of the cylinder head. Tighten the attaching bolts to 30–40 ft. lbs. (40–55 Nm).
35. Connect the cable to the battery negative terminal.
36. Fill and bleed the cooling system with the specified coolant.

✱✱WARNING

This engine has an aluminum cylinder head and requires a compatible coolant formulation to avoid radiator damage.

37. Start the engine and check for coolant, fuel, and oil leaks.
38. Check and, if necessary, adjust the curb idle speed.
39. Install the air cleaner assembly including the air intake duct and heat tube.

4.6L Engines

➧ See Figures 82, 83, 84, 85, 86 and 87

✻✻CAUTION

Fuel injection systems remain under pressure, even after the engine has been turned OFF. The fuel system pressure must be relieved before disconnecting any fuel lines. Failure to do so may result in fire and/or personal injury.

➥ The cylinder head bolts are a torque-to-yield design and cannot be reused. Before beginning this procedure, make sure new cylinder head bolts are available.

1. Disconnect the negative battery cable.
2. Properly drain the cooling system into a suitable container.
3. Remove the cooling fan and shroud assembly.
4. Relieve the fuel system pressure as follows:
   a. Remove the fuel tank fill cap to relieve the pressure in the fuel tank.
   b. Remove the cap from the Schrader valve located on the fuel injection supply manifold.
   c. Attach Fuel Pressure Gauge T80L-9974-B or equivalent, to the Schrader valve and drain the fuel through the drain tube into a suitable container.
   d. After the fuel system pressure is relieved, remove the fuel pressure gauge and install the cap on the Schrader valve.
5. Remove the engine air cleaner outlet tube.
6. Remove the windshield wiper governor (module).
7. Release the drive belt tensioner and remove the accessory drive belt.
8. Tag and disconnect the ignition wires from the spark plugs. Disconnect the ignition wire brackets from the cylinder head cover studs and are move the two bolts retaining the ignition wire tray to the ignition coil brackets.
9. Remove the bolt retaining the A/C pressure line to the right-hand ignition coil bracket.

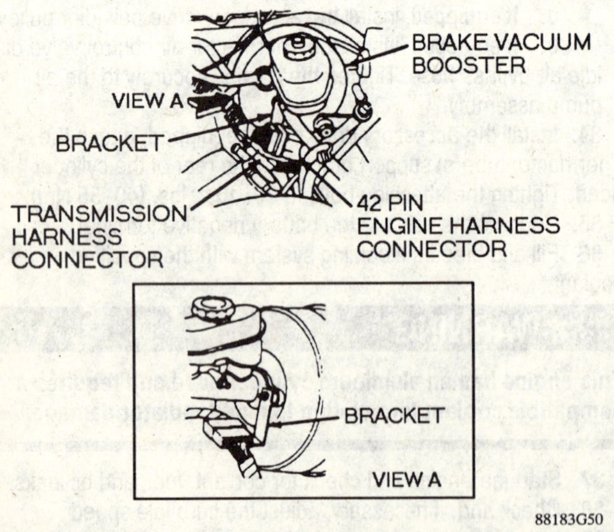

Fig. 82 Detach the engine and transmission electrical connectors from the bracket on the brake booster

10. Disconnect the wiring to both ignition coils and the Camshaft Position (CMP) sensor.
11. Remove the nuts retaining the ignition coil brackets to the engine front cover. Slide the ignition coil brackets ignition wire assemblies off the mounting studs and remove from the vehicle.
12. Remove the water pump pulley.
13. Disconnect the alternator wiring harness from the junction block, fender apron and alternator. Unfasten the bolts retaining the alternator to the intake manifold and cylinder block, then remove the alternator.
14. Disconnect the positive battery cable at the power distribution box. Remove the retaining bolt from the positive battery cable bracket located on the side of the right-hand cylinder head.
15. Detach the vent hose from the canister purge solenoid and position the positive battery cable out of the way. Disconnect the canister purge solenoid vent hose from the PCV valve and remove the PCV valve from the cylinder head cover.
16. Remove and disconnect the engine and transmission harness connectors from the retaining bracket on the power brake booster.
17. Detach the Crankshaft Position (CKP) sensor, A/C compressor clutch and canister purge solenoid electrical connectors.
18. Raise and safely support the vehicle.
19. Remove the bolts retaining the power steering pump to the cylinder block and engine front cover. The front lower bolt on the power steering pump will not come all the way out. Wire the power steering pump out of the way.
20. Remove the engine oil pan and oil pan gasket.
21. Remove the crankshaft pulley retaining bolts and remove the pulley, using Damper Remover T58P-6316-D or equivalent.
22. Detach the power steering control valve actuator and oil pressure sensor wiring connector and position out of the way.
23. Disconnect the EGR tube from the right hand exhaust manifold.
24. Detach the exhaust pipes from the exhaust manifolds. Lower the exhaust pipes and hang with wire from the crossmember.
25. Remove the bolt retaining the starter wiring harness to the rear of the right-hand cylinder head.
26. Carefully lower the vehicle.
27. Unfasten the bolts and stud bolts retaining the cylinder head covers to the cylinder head and remove the covers.
28. Disconnect the accelerator and cruise control cables. Remove the accelerator cable bracket from the intake manifold and position out of the way.
29. Tag and disconnect the vacuum hose from the throttle body elbow vacuum port, both Heated Oxygen Sensors (HO_2S) and the heater water hose.

➥ The two thermostat housing bolts also retain the intake manifold.

30. Unfasten the two bolts retaining the thermostat housing to the intake manifold and position the upper hose and thermostat housing out of the way.
31. Unfasten the 9 bolts retaining the intake manifold to the cylinder heads and remove the intake manifold and gaskets.
32. Remove the 7 stud bolts and 4 bolts retaining the engine front cover to the engine, then remove the front cover.
33. Remove both timing chains.

✱✱WARNING

This is not a freewheeling engine. Cam Positioning Tools T92P-6256-A or equivalent, must be installed on the camshafts to prevent the camshafts from rotating. Do not rotate the camshafts or crankshaft with the timing chains removed or the valves will contact the pistons.

34. Unfasten the 10 bolts retaining the left-hand cylinder head to the cylinder block and remove the head. The lower rear cylinder head bolt must stay in the cylinder head until the cylinder head is removed due to a lack of clearance for removal in the vehicle. Use a rubber band to secure the cylinder head bolt in the cylinder head during removal and installation of the cylinder head and to prevent the bolt from damaging the cylinder block or head gasket.

35. Clean all gasket mating surfaces. Check the cylinder heads and block for flatness. Check the head for scratches near the coolant passages and combustion chambers that could provide leak paths.

To install:

36. Rotate the crankshaft counterclockwise 45 degrees. The crankshaft keyway should be at the 9 o'clock position viewed from the front of the engine. This ensures that all pistons are below the top of the engine block deck face.

37. Rotate the camshaft to a stable position where the valves do not extend below the head face.

38. Position new cylinder head gaskets on the block. Install new bolts in the lower rear bolt holes on both cylinder heads and retain with rubber bands, as explained during the removal procedure.

➥ **New cylinder head bolts must be used whenever the cylinder head is removed and reinstalled. The cylinder head bolts are a torque-to-yield design and cannot be reused.**

39. Position the cylinder heads on the cylinder block dowels, being careful not to score the surface of the head face. Apply clean oil to the new cylinder head bolts, remove the rubber bands from the lower rear bolts and install all bolts hand-tight.

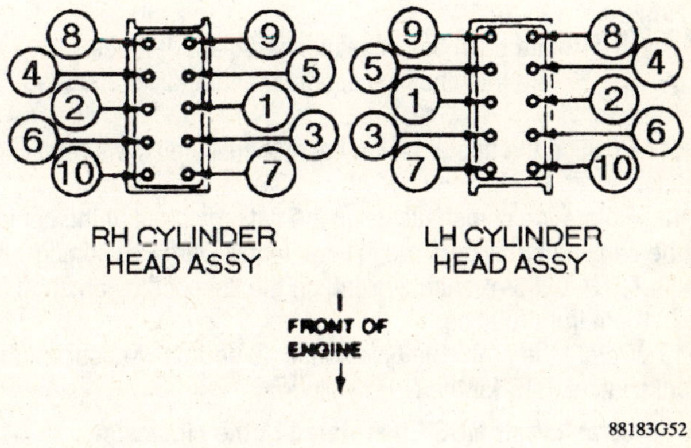

Fig. 84 Cylinder head bolt torque sequence — 4.6L engine

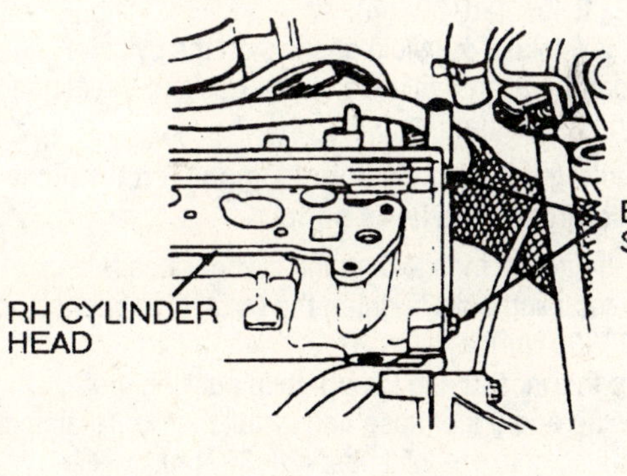

Fig. 85 Heater return retaining bolt location

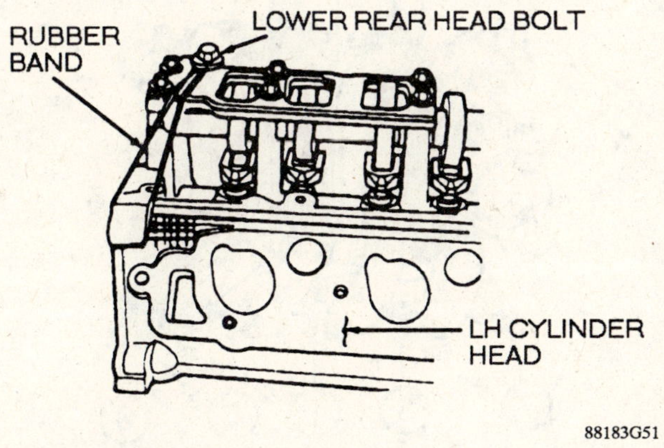

Fig. 83 Use a rubber band to hold the lower rear head bolt away from the cylinder block

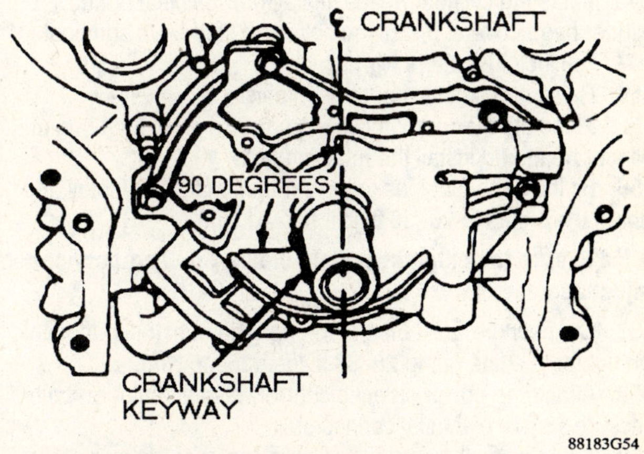

Fig. 86 Crankshaft positioning for installation of the cylinder heads

40. Tighten the new cylinder head bolts as follows:
   a. Torque the bolts in sequence, to 22-30 ft. lbs. (30-40 Nm).
   b. Rotate each bolt in sequence 85-95 degrees.
   c. Rotate each bolt in sequence and additional 85-95 degrees.
41. Position the heater return hose, then install the 2 retaining bolts.
42. Rotate the camshafts using the flats matched at the center of the camshaft until both are in time. Install Cam Positioning Tools T91P-6256-A or equivalent, on the flats of the camshaft to keep them from rotating.
43. Rotate the crankshaft clockwise 45 degrees to position the crankshaft at TDC for the No. 1 cylinder.

➥ The crankshaft MUST be rotated in the clockwise direction any only as far as TDC.

44. Install both timing chains.
45. Install a new engine front cover and gasket. Apply silicone sealer to the lower corners of the cover where it meets the junction of the engine oil pan and cylinder block and to the points where the cover contacts the junction of the cylinder block and the heads.
46. Install the engine front cover and the stud bolts and bolts. Tighten to 15-22 ft. lbs. (20-30 Nm).
47. Position new intake manifold gaskets on the cylinder heads. Make sure the alignment tabs on the gaskets are aligned with the holes in the cylinder heads.

➥ Before installing the intake manifold, inspect it for nicks and cuts that could provide leaks paths.

48. Position the intake manifold on the cylinder heads and secure with the retaining bolts. Tighten the bolts, in sequence, to 15-22 ft. lbs. (20-30 Nm).
49. Install the thermostat and O-ring, then position the thermostat housing and upper hose and install the two retaining bolts. Tighten the bolts to 15-22 ft. lbs. (20-30 Nm).
50. Connect the heater water hose and both HO_2S sensors.
51. Attach the vacuum hose to the throttle body adapter vacuum port.
52. Install the accelerator cable bracket on the intake manifold and connect the accelerator and cruise control cables to the throttle body.
53. Apply silicone sealer to both places where the engine front cover meets the cylinder heads. Install new gaskets on the cylinder head covers. Install the bolts and stud bolts and tighten to 71-106 inch lbs. (8-12 Nm).
54. Raise and safely support the vehicle.
55. Place the starter motor wiring harness on the right hand cylinder head and install the retaining bolt.
56. Fit the exhaust pipes to the exhaust manifold. Install and tighten the 4 nuts to 20-30 ft. lbs. (27-41 Nm).

➥ Make sure the exhaust system clears No. 3 crossmember. Adjust as necessary.

57. Connect the EGR tube to the right-hand exhaust manifold and tighten the line nut to 26-33 ft. lbs. (35-45 Nm).
58. Attach the power steering control valve actuator and oil pressure sensor electrical connectors.
59. Apply a small amount of silicone sealer in the rear of the keyway on the crankshaft pulley. Position the pulley on the crankshaft, making sure the crankshaft key and keyway are aligned.
60. Using Damper Installer T74P-6316-B or equivalent, install the crankshaft pulley. Install the pulley bolt and washer and tighten to 114-121 ft. lbs. (155-165 Nm).
61. Install the engine oil pan and a new gasket.
62. Place the power steering pump in position on the cylinder block and install 4 retaining bolts. Tighten the bolts to 15-22 ft. lbs. (20-30 Nm).
63. Carefully lower the vehicle.
64. Attach the A/C compressor, CKP sensor and canister purge solenoid electrical connectors.
65. Connect the engine and transmission harness connectors install on the retaining bracket on the power brake booster.
66. Install the PCV valve in the right hand cylinder head cover and connect the canister purge solenoid vent hose.
67. Position the positive battery cable harness on the right-hand cylinder head and install the bolt retaining the cable bracket to the cylinder head. Connect the positive battery cable at the power distribution box and battery.
68. Position the alternator and install the two retaining bolts. Tighten the bolts to 15-22 ft. bs. (20-30 Nm). Install the 2 bolts retaining the alternator brace to the intake manifold and tighten to 6-8 ft. lbs. (8-12 Nm).
69. Install the water pump pulley and tighten the bolts to 15-22 ft. lbs. (20-30 Nm).
70. Position the ignition coil brackets and ignition wire assemblies onto the mounting studs. Install the 7 nuts retaining the ignition coil brackets to the engine front cover and tighten to 15-22 ft. lbs. (20-30 Nm).
71. Install the 2 bolts retaining the ignition wire tray to the ignition coil bracket and tighten to 71-106 inch lbs. (8-12 Nm). Attach both ignition coil and CMP sensor harness connectors.
72. Place the A/C pressure line on the right-hand ignition coil bracket and install the retaining bolt. Connect the ignition wires to the spark plugs and install the bracket onto the cylinder head cover studs.
73. Install the accessory drive belts and the windshield wiper governor.
74. Attach the fuel supply and return lines.
75. Install the cooling fan and shroud.

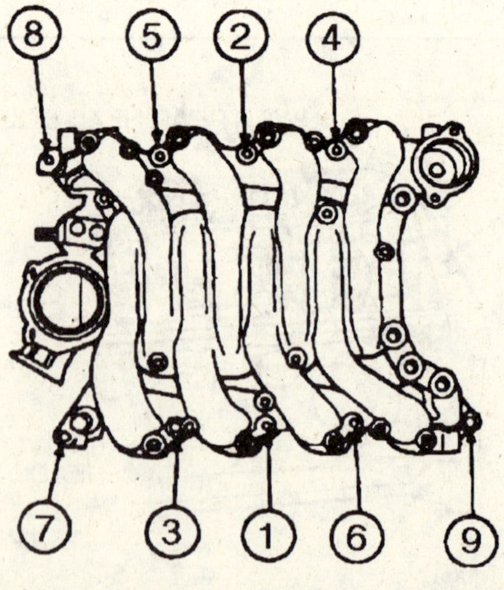

Fig. 87 Intake manifold bolt tightening sequence — 4.6L engine

76. Fill the engine cooling system, then install the engine air cleaner outlet tube.
77. Connect the negative battery cable.
78. Check all fluid levels. Replace the engine oil and filter if the oil is contaminated.
79. Start the engine and bring to normal operating temperature while checking for leaks.
80. Road test the vehicle and check for proper engine operation.

5.0L Engine

See Figure 88

1. If equipped, have the A/C system discharged at a reputable repair shop.
2. Disconnect the negative battery cable.
3. Properly drain the cooling system into a suitable container.
4. Relieve the fuel system pressure as follows:
   a. Remove the fuel tank fill cap to relieve the pressure in the fuel tank.
   b. Remove the cap from the Schrader valve located on the fuel injection supply manifold.
   c. Attach Fuel Pressure Gauge T80L-9974-B or equivalent, to the Schrader valve and drain the fuel through the drain tube into a suitable container.
   d. After the fuel system pressure is relieved, remove the fuel pressure gauge and install the cap on the Schrader valve.
5. Remove the upper and lower intake manifold and throttle body assembly.
6. If the A/C compressor is in the way of a cylinder head that is to be removed, proceed as follows:
   a. Disconnect and plug the refrigerant lines at the compressor. Cap the openings on the compressor.
   b. Detach the electrical connector from the compressor.
   c. Remove the compressor and necessary mounting brackets.
7. If the left cylinder head is to be removed, disconnect the power steering pump bracket from the cylinder head and remove the drive belt from the pump pulley. Position the pump out of the way in a position that will prevent the oil from draining out.
8. Disconnect the oil level dipstick tube bracket from the exhaust manifold stud, if necessary.
9. If the right cylinder head is to be removed, on some vehicles it is necessary to disconnect the alternator mounting bracket from the cylinder head.
10. Remove the Thermactor crossover tube from the rear of the cylinder heads. If equipped, remove the fuel lines from the clip at the front of the right cylinder head.
11. Raise and safely support the vehicle. Disconnect the exhaust manifolds from the muffler inlet pipes. Carefully lower the vehicle.
12. Remove the rocker arm fulcrum bolts and the pushrods. Keep these in order; they must be installed into their original locations.
13. Unfasten the cylinder head attaching bolts, then remove the cylinder heads. Only if necessary, remove the exhaust manifolds to gain access to the lower bolts. Remove and discard head gaskets.
14. Clean all gasket mating surfaces. Check the flatness of the cylinder head using a straight-edge and a feeler gauge. The cylinder head must not be warped any more than 0.003 in in any 6.0 inch span; 0.006 overall.

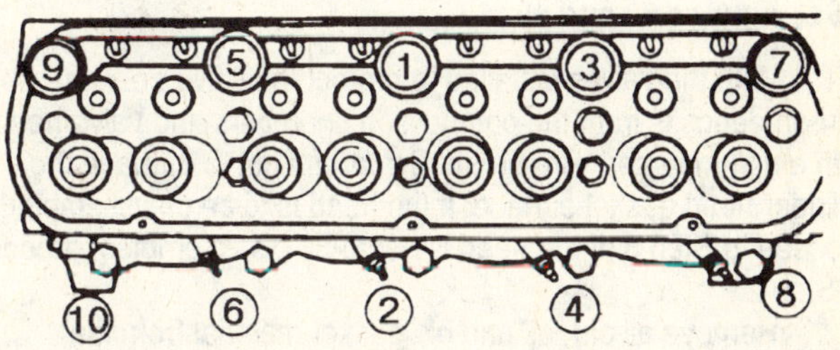

Fig. 88 Cylinder head bolt tightening sequence — 5.0L engine

To install:

15. Position the new cylinder head gasket over the dowels on the block. Position the cylinder heads on the block and install the attaching bolts.
16. Tighten the bolts in sequence in 2 steps, first to 55–65 ft. lbs. (75–88 Nm), then to 65–72 ft. lbs. (88–97 Nm).

When the cylinder head bolts have been tightened following this procedure, it is not necessary to retighten the bolts after extended operation.

17. If removed, install the exhaust manifolds with new gaskets and tighten the bolts to 18–24 ft. lbs. (24–32 Nm).
18. Clean the pushrods, making sure the oil passages are clean. Check the ends of the pushrods for warpage. Visually check the pushrods straightness or check for runout using a dial indicator. Replace pushrods as necessary.
19. Apply lithium grease to the ends of the pushrods and install them in their original locations. Position the rocker arms over the pushrods and the valves.
20. Before tightening each fulcrum bolt, make sure the lifter is on the base circle of the camshaft (pushrod all the way down by rotating the crankshaft as needed. Tighten the fulcrum bolt to 18–25 ft. lbs. (24–32 Nm).

If all the original valve train parts are reinstalled, a valve clearance check is not necessary. If any valve train components are replaced, a valve clearance check must be performed.

21. Install new rocker arm cover gaskets on the cover, then install the covers on the cylinder heads.
22. Raise and safely support the vehicle. Connect the exhaust manifolds to the muffler inlet pipes. Carefully lower the vehicle.
23. If necessary, install the A/C compressor and brackets. Unplug and connect the refrigerant lines and electrical connector to the compressor.
24. If necessary, install the alternator bracket.
25. If the left cylinder head was removed, install the power steering pump.
26. Install the drive belts. Install the Thermactor tube at the rear of the cylinder heads.
27. Install the intake manifold. Fill and bleed the cooling system.
28. Connect the negative battery cable, start the engine and bring to normal operating temperature. Inspect for leaks, and check all fluid levels.
29. If necessary, take the vehicle to a reputable repair shop the have the A/C system evacuated and charged.

CLEANING AND INSPECTION

➧ See Figures 89 and 90

1. With the valves installed to protect the valve seats, remove carbon deposits from the combustion chambers and valve heads with a drill-mounted wire brush. Be careful not to damage the cylinder head gasket surface. If the head is to be disassembled, proceed to Step 3. If the head is not to be disassembled, proceed to Step 2.
2. Remove all dirt, oil and old gasket material from the cylinder head with solvent. Clean the bolt holes and oil passages. Be careful not to get solvent on the valve seals, as the solvent may damage them. If available, dry the cylinder head with compressed air. Check the head for cracks or other damage, and check the gasket surface for burrs, nicks and flatness. If you are in doubt about the heads serviceability, consult a reputable automotive machine shop.
3. Remove the valves, springs and retainers, then clean the valve guide bores with a suitable wire brush. Remove all dirt, oil and old gasket material from the cylinder head with solvent. Clean the bolt holes and the oil passage.

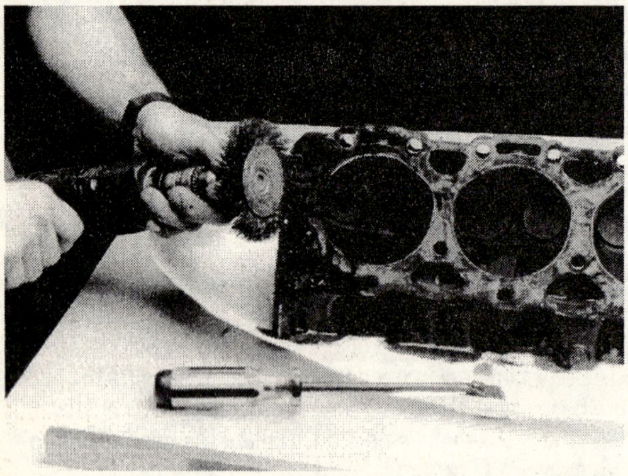

TCCS3133

Fig. 89 An electric drill equipped with a wire wheel will expedite complete gasket removal

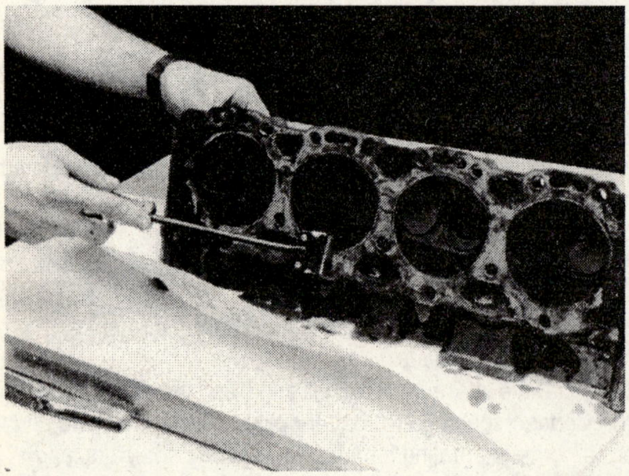

TCCS3132

Fig. 90 Use a gasket scraper to remove the bulk of the old head gasket from the mating surface

4. Remove all deposits from the valves with a wire brush or buffing wheel. Inspect the valves as described later in this section.
5. Check the head for cracks using a dye penetrant in the valve seat area and ports, head surface and top. Check the gasket surface for burrs, nicks and flatness. If you are in doubt about the heads serviceability, consult a reputable automotive machine shop.

➥ If the cylinder head was removed due to an overheating condition and a crack is suspected, do not assume that the head is not cracked because a crack is not visually found. A crack can be so small that it cannot be easily seen by eye, but can pass coolant when the engine is at operating temperature. Consult an automotive machine shop that has pressure testing equipment to make sure the head is not cracked.

RESURFACING

➧ See Figures 91 and 92

Whenever the cylinder head is removed, check the flatness of the cylinder head gasket surfaces as follows:

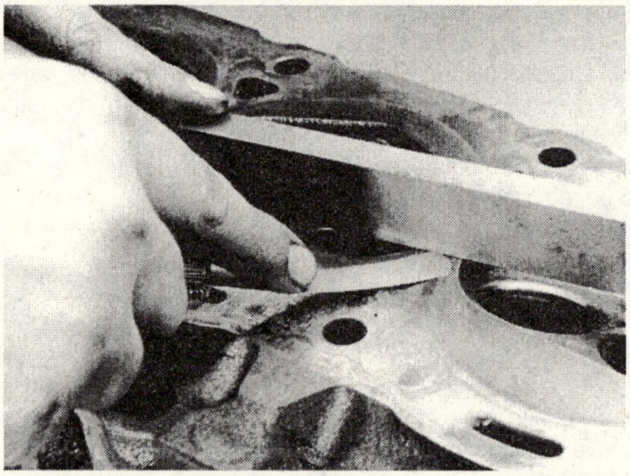

TCCS3918

Fig. 91 Check the cylinder head for flatness across the head surface

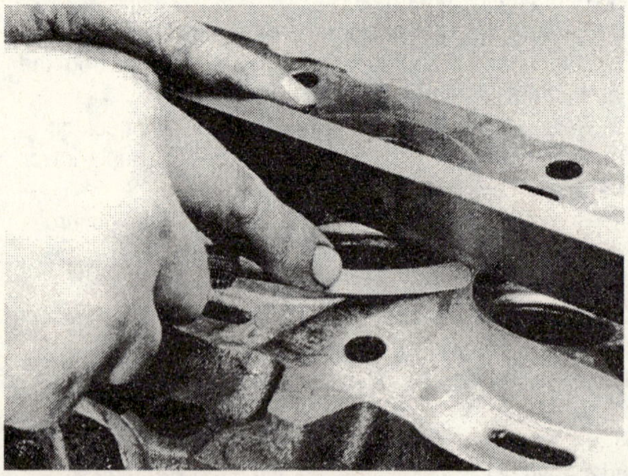

TCCS3919

Fig. 92 Checks should be made both straight across the head and both diagonals

1. Make sure all the dirt and old gasket material has been cleaned from the cylinder head. Any foreign material left on the head gasket surface can cause a false measurement.

2. Place a straight-edge laterally and diagonally across the gasket surface of the cylinder head (in the positions shown in the figures). Using feeler gauges, determine the clearance at the center of the straightedge.

3. If the warpage exceeds 0.003 in. (0.08mm) in a 6 in. (152mm) span, or 0.006 in. (0.15mm) over the total length, the cylinder head must be resurfaced, but Do NOT exceed 0.010 in. (0.254mm) stock removal from the original head gasket surface.

Valves

REMOVAL & INSTALLATION

See Figures 93, 94, 95, 96, 97, 98 and 99

1. Remove the cylinder head from the vehicle, as outlined earlier in this section.
2. Block the head on its side, or install a pair of head-holding brackets made especially for valve removal.
3. Use a socket slightly larger than the valve stem and keepers, place the socket over the valve stem and gently hit the socket with a plastic hammer to break loose any varnish buildup.
4. Remove the valve keepers, retainer, spring shield and valve spring using a valve spring compressor (the locking C-clamp type is the easiest kind to use).
5. Put the parts in a separate container numbered for the cylinder being worked on; do not mix them with other parts removed.
6. Remove and discard the valve stem oil seals. A new seal will be used at assembly time.
7. Remove the valves from the cylinder head and place them, in order, through numbered holes punched in a stiff piece of cardboard or wood valve holding stick.

The exhaust valve stems, on some engines, are equipped with small metal caps. Take care not to lose the caps. Make sure to reinstall them at assembly time. Replace any caps that are worn.

TCCS3809

Fig. 94 A magnet may be helpful in removing the valve keepers

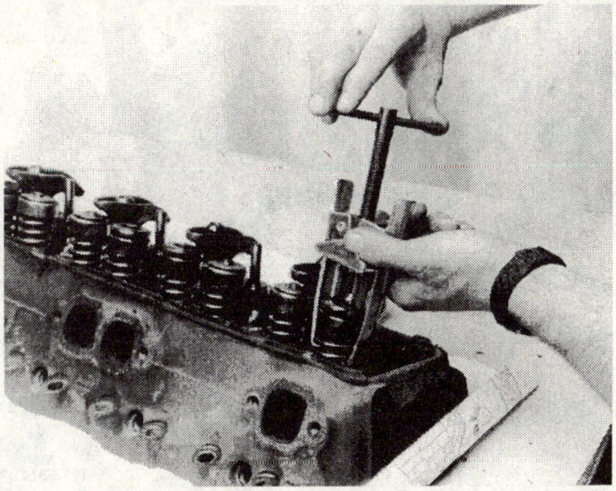

TCCS3137

Fig. 93 Use a valve spring compressor tool to relieve spring tension from the valve caps

TCCS3139

Fig. 95 Be careful not to lose the valve keepers

8. Use an electric drill and rotary wire brush to clean the intake and exhaust valve ports, combustion chamber and valve seats. In some cases, the carbon will need to be chipped away. Use a blunt pointed drift for carbon chipping. Be careful around the valve seat areas.

9. Use a wire valve guide cleaning brush and safe solvent to clean the valve guides.

10. Clean the valves with a revolving wire brush. Heavy carbon deposits may be removed with the blunt drift.

➔ When using a wire brush to clean carbon on the valve ports, valves etc., be sure that the deposits are actually removed, rather than burnished.

11. Wash and clean all valve springs, keepers, retaining caps etc., in safe solvent.

12. Clean the head with a brush and some safe solvent and wipe dry.

13. Check the head for cracks. Cracks in the cylinder head usually start around an exhaust valve seat because it is the hottest part of the combustion chamber. If a crack is suspected but cannot be detected visually have the area checked with dye penetrant or other method by the machine shop.

TCCS3810

Fig. 96 Remove the spring from the valve stem in order to access the seal

TCCS3811

Fig. 97 Remove the valve stem seal from the cylinder head

TCCS3141

Fig. 98 Invert the cylinder head and withdraw the valve from the cylinder head bore

TCCS3802

Fig. 99 A wire wheel may be used to clean the combustion chambers of carbon deposits

14. Inspect the valves, guides, springs and seats, then machine or replace parts, as necessary.

To install:

15. Lubricate the valve stems with clean engine oil.
16. Install the valve seals and springs.
17. Install the valves in the cylinder head, one at a time, as numbered.
18. Install the spring caps, and compress the springs.
19. With the valve keeper groove exposed above the compressed valve spring, wipe some vasoline around the groove. This will retain the keepers as you release the spring compressor.
20. Using needle nose pliers (or your fingers), carefully place the keepers in the grooves. The grease should hold the keepers in place. Slowly release the spring compressor; the valve cap will raise up as the compressor is released, retaining the keeper.
21. Install the cylinder head(s).

INSPECTION

➧ **See Figures 100, 101, 102, 103 and 104**

➥ **Excessive valve stem-to-bore clearance will cause excessive oil consumption and may cause valve breakage. Insufficient clearance will result in noisy and sticky functioning of the valve and disturb engine smoothness.**

Inspect the valve faces and seats (in the head) for pits, burned spots and other evidence of poor seating. Valves that are pitted must be refaced to the proper angle. Valves that are warped excessively must be replaced. When a valve head that is warped excessively is refaced, a knife edge will be ground on part or all of the valve head due to the amount of material that must be removed to completely reface the valve. Knife edges lead to breakage, burning or preignition due to heat localizing on the knife edge. If the edge of the valve head is less than $^1/_{32}$ in. (1mm) after machining, replace the valve. We recommend that all machine work be performed by a reputable machine shop.

Make sure the valve stem is not bent. The valve may be rolled on a flat surface such as a mirror or glass. An even better indication of valve stem bending can be determined by carefully chocking the stem into an electric drill. Use the drill to spin the stem while you watch the valve head. A bent stem will be obvious by the wobbling of the head. Be very careful if this method is used. If the valve stem is not properly chocked in position it could come flying out of the drill and cause injury.

Some of the engines covered in this guide are equipped with valve rotators, which double as valve spring caps. In normal operation the rotators put a certain degree of wear on the tip of the valve stem; this wear appears as concentric rings on the stem tip. However, if the rotator is not working properly, the wear may appear as straight notches or **X** patterns across the valve stem tip. Whenever the valves are removed from the cylinder head, the tips should be inspected for improper pattern, which could indicate valve rotator problems. Valve stem tips will have to be ground flat if rotator patterns are severe.

Check the valve stem for scoring and burned spots. If not noticeably scored or damaged, clean the valve stem with solvent to remove all gum and varnish. Clean the valve guides using solvent and an expanding wire type valve guide cleaner. Check the valve stem-to-guide clearance in one or more of the following manners, but do not rely on the visual inspection alone:

1. A visual inspection can give you a fairly good idea if the guide, valve stem or both are worn. Insert the valve into the guide until the valve head is slightly away from the valve seat. Wiggle the valve sideways. A small amount of wobble is normal, excessive wobble means a worn guide and/or valve stem.

➥ **If a dial indicator and micrometer are not available to you, take your cylinder head and valves to a reputable machine shop of inspection.**

2. If a dial indicator is on hand, mount the indicator so that gauge stem is 90° to the valve stem as close to the top of the valve guide as possible. Move the valve from the seat, and measure the valve guide-to-stem clearance by rocking the stem back and forth to actuate the dial indicator. Measure the valve stem using a micrometer and compare to specifications to determine whether stem or guide is causing excessive clearance.
3. If both a ball gauge and a micrometer are available, first, measure the inside diameter of the valve guide bushing at three locations using the ball gauge. Second, use the micrometer to measure the stem diameter. Finally, subtract the valve stem diameter from the corresponding valve guide inside diameter to arrive at the valve clearance. If clearance is greater than specification, the valve and guide bushing must be replaced.

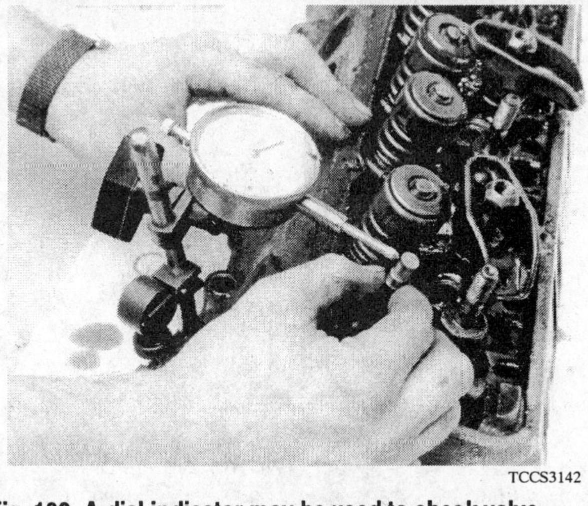

TCCS3142

Fig. 100 A dial indicator may be used to check valve stem-to-guide clearance

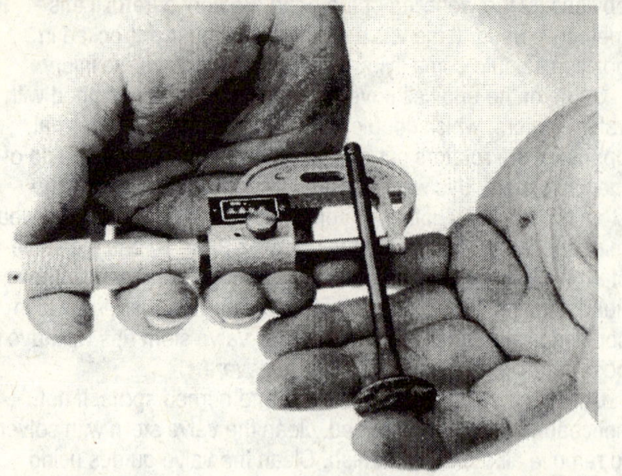
TCCS3910

Fig. 101 Use a micrometer to measure the valve stem diameter

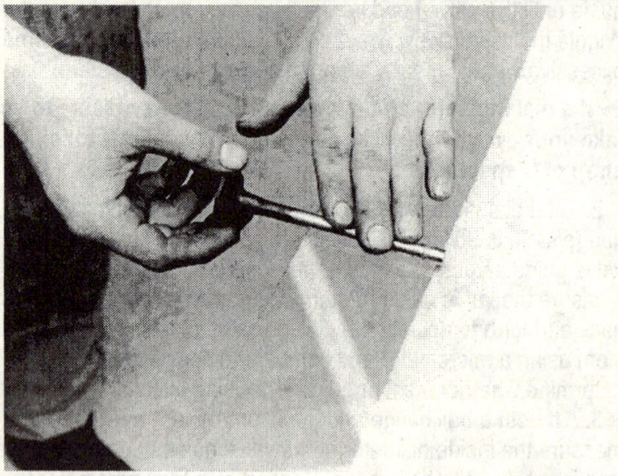
TCCS3144

Fig. 102 Valve stems may be rolled on a flat surface to check for bends

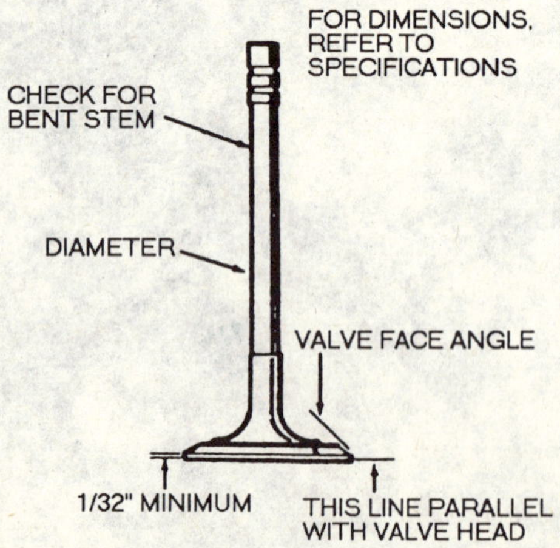

88183G71

Fig. 103 Valve inspection and measurement

88183G72

Fig. 104 A run-out (dial) gauge is used to check valve seat concentricity

The valve guide, if worn, must be repaired before the valve seats can be resurfaced. A new valve guide should be installed or, in some cases, knurled. Consult the automotive machine shop.

If the valve guide is okay, measure the valve seat concentricity using a runout gauge. Follow the manufacturer's instructions. If runout is excessive, reface or replace the valve and machine or replace the valve seat.

Valves and seats must always be machined together. Never use a refaced valve on a valve seat that has not been machined; never use a valve that has not been refaced on a machined valve seat.

VALVE REFACING

All valve grinding operations should be performed by a qualified machine shop; only the valve lapping operation is recommended to be performed by the home mechanic.

Valve Lapping

See Figure 105

When valve faces and seats have been refaced, or if they are determined to be in good condition, the valves may have to be lapped to ensure efficient sealing when the valve closes against the seat. But, modern metals used in valves/seats and the extremely accurate machining available today may preclude the need to lap. Consult your machinist to determine if lapping is necessary. If so, proceed as follows:

1. Invert the cylinder head so that the combustion chambers are facing upward.
2. Lightly lubricate the valve stems with clean engine oil and coat the valve seats with valve lapping compound. Install the valves in the cylinder head as numbered.
3. Moisten and attach the suction cup of a valve lapping tool to a valve head.
4. Rotate the tool between your palms, changing position and lifting the tool often to prevent grooving. Lap the valve until a smooth polished seat is evident (you may have to add a bit more compound after some lapping is done).

Fig. 105 Lapping the valves by hand

5. Remove the valve and tool, then remove ALL traces of the grinding compound with a solvent-soaked rag or rinse the head with solvent.

➥ Valve lapping can also be done by fastening a suction cup to a piece of drill rod in a hand egg-beater type drill. Proceed as above, using the drill as a lapping tool. Due to the higher speeds involved when using the hand drill, care must be exercised to avoid grooving the seat. Lift the tool and change direction of rotation often.

Valve Stem Seals

REPLACEMENT

Cylinder Head Installed

➧ See Figures 106 and 107

The valve stem seals on most engines covered by this manual may be replaced with the cylinder head either on or off the engine. The removal procedure with the cylinder head installed utilizes compressed air in the cylinder to hold the valve in place and keep it from dropping into the cylinder once the valve keeper, cap and spring are removed.

➥ If air pressure is lost while the valve keepers are removed, the valve will drop into the cylinder. If this happens, the cylinder head must be removed in order to recover the valve.

1. Disconnect the negative battery cable.
2. Remove the rocker arm cover.

➥ The cylinder must be at TDC of its compression stroke in order to follow this procedure. On the compression stroke, the cylinder's valves will be closed allowing the air pressure to hold the valve in position. The engine must therefore be turned slightly for each cylinder's valve seals.

3. Remove the rocker arm and pushrod assemblies from the cylinders for which the valves are being serviced.
4. Remove the spark plug from the cylinder which is on its compression stroke and install a spark plug air fitting adapter with an in-line gauge set between the adapter and air compressor. Apply compressed air to hold the valve in place.
5. For the 4.6L engine, install Valve Spring Spacer T91P-6565-AH or equivalent, between the valve spring coils.
6. Compress the valve spring using a suitable compressor tool and remove the valve keeper. Carefully release the spring tension, then remove the valve cap and spring.

➥ If the air pressure has forced the piston to the bottom of the cylinder, any removal of air pressure will allow the valves to fall into the cylinder. A rubber band, tape or string wrapped around the end of the valve stem will prevent this.

7. Remove the old seal using a suitable removal tool.

To install:

8. Install the new seal using the valve stem seal tool.
9. Install the valve spring and cap.
10. For the 4.6L engine, install Valve Spring Spacer T91P-6565-AH or equivalent, between the valve spring coils.
11. Compress the spring and install the valve keeper.
12. When the valve springs are properly installed, remove the valve spring compressor and spacer, if used. Release the pressure from the cylinder using the gauge set, then remove the spark plug adapter.
13. Install the spark plug and turn the engine sufficiently to work on the next cylinder. Repeat the above steps until all seals are replaced.
14. Install the rocker arm and pushrod assemblies, then install the rocker cover and connect the negative battery cable.

Cylinder Heads Removed

The valve stem oil seals are replaced as a part of normal valve service any time the valve stems are removed from the cylinder head. Refer to the valve procedure in this section for seal removal and installation when the cylinder head has been removed from the vehicle.

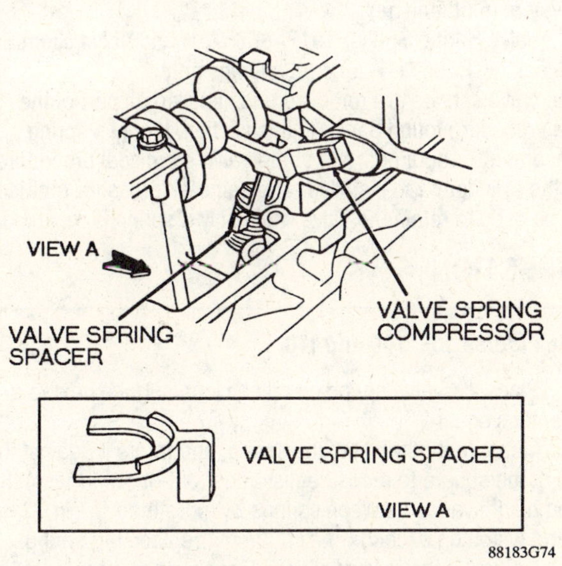

Fig. 106 Compressing the valve spring and the spring spacer tool used for the 4.6L engine

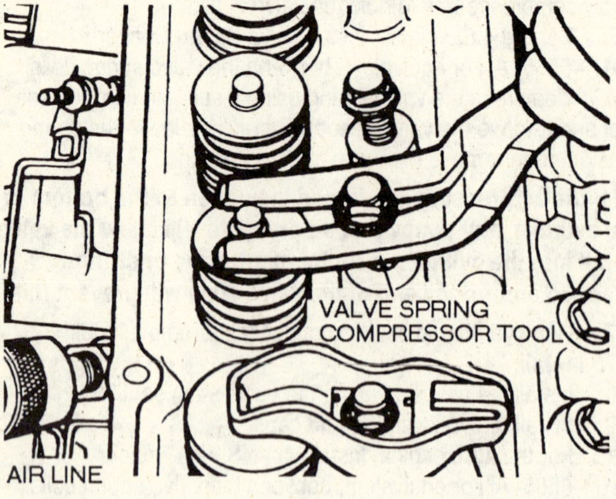

Fig. 107 Compressing the valve spring for stem seal removal

Valve Springs

REMOVAL & INSTALLATION

Removal or installation of the valve springs requires use of the following tools:

- Valve Spring Compressor tool No. T74P-6565-A or equivalent (2.3 and 4.6L engines)
- Valve Spring Compressor tool No. T81P-6513-A or equivalent (3.8L engine)
- Valve Spring Compressor tool No. T70P-6049-A or equivalent (5.0L engine)
- Valve Spring Spacer T91P-6565-AH and Valve Stem Seal Replacer T91P-6571-A for 4.6L engines only

The valve springs are removed and installed as part of the valve procedure found earlier in this section. If only a spring replacement is required, refer to the valve stem seal procedure with the cylinder head installed. The same air pressure method may be used to retain the valve while only a spring is replaced.

INSPECTION

See Figures 108, 109 and 110

1. Place the valve spring on a flat, clean surface next to a carpenter's square.
2. Measure the height of the spring, and rotate it against the edge of the square to measure distortion (out-of-roundness). If spring height varies between springs by more than $^1/_{16}$ in. (2mm) or if the distortion exceeds $^1/_{16}$ in. (2mm), replace the spring.

A valve spring tester is needed to test spring test pressure, so the valve springs must usually be taken to a professional machine shop for this test. Spring pressure at the installed and/or compressed height is checked, depending on the specification.

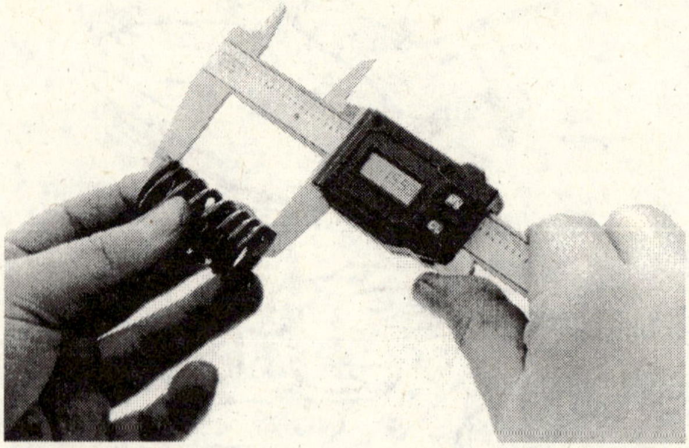

Fig. 108 A caliper gauge may be used to check the valve spring free-length

Valve Seats

REMOVAL & INSTALLATION

Due to the high degree of precision and special equipment required, valve seat replacement should be left to an automotive machine shop. Seat replacement procedures vary depending on whether the engine is equipped with cast iron or aluminum heads. Iron heads use a valve seat which is originally an integral part of the head. To replace these, a bore must be cut in the head which will accept an insert. The bore must be drilled to exacting specifications for the insert to work.

Aluminum cylinder heads are already equipped with valve seat inserts. There are various methods to replace these inserts, and although most are similar, the specifications are unique to each cylinder head application. The following procedure can be construed as what is generally acceptable for aluminum cylinder heads; the actual method employed should be the decision of the machinist.

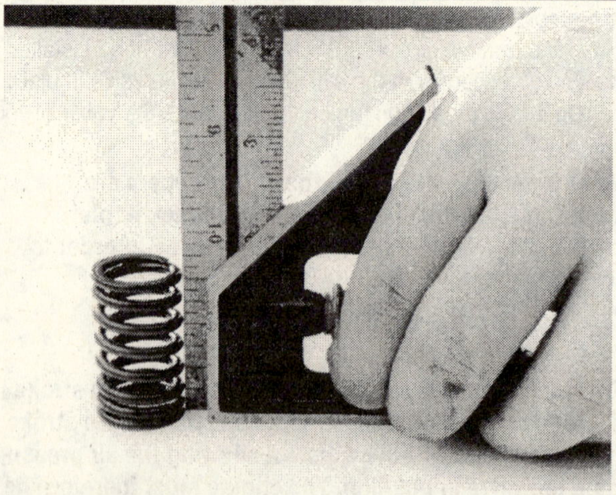

Fig. 109 Check the valve spring for squareness on a flat surface, a carpenters square can be used

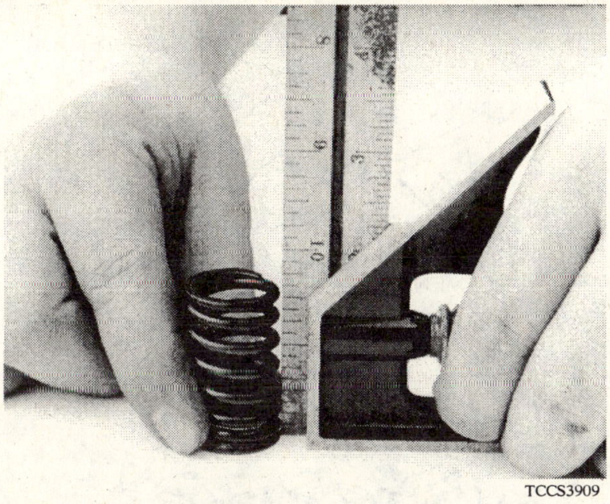

Fig. 110 The valve spring should be straight up and down when placed like this

The replaceable inserts can be removed by cutting them out to within a few thousandths of their outside diameter and then collapsing the remainder. Another method sometimes used to remove aluminum head seat inserts is to heat the head to a high temperature and drive the seat out.

Upon installation, the new seat may be installed with the aluminum cylinder head heated to a high temperature, then the seat, which is at room temperature or slightly chilled, is pressed into the head. The aluminum head is then allowed to cool and as it does, it contracts and grips the seat. In certain applications, the new seat may be driven in with both the head and seat at room temperature. The calculated press-fit interference will then retain the seat in the head.

Valve Guides

Worn valve guides can, in most cases, be reamed to accept a valve with an oversized stem. Valve guides that are not excessively worn or distorted may, in some cases, be knurled rather than reamed. However, if the valve stem is worn reaming for an oversized valve stem is the answer since a new valve would be required.

Knurling is a process in which metal is displaced and raised, thereby reducing clearance. Knurling also produces excellent oil control. The possibility of knurling instead of reaming the valve guides should be discussed with reputable machinist or engine specialist.

Oil Pan

REMOVAL & INSTALLATION

✱✱CAUTION

The EPA warns that prolonged contact with used engine oil may cause a number of skin disorders, including cancer! You should make every effort to minimize your exposure to used engine oil. Protective gloves should be worn when changing the oil. Wash your hands and any other exposed skin areas as soon as possible after exposure to used engine oil. Soap and water, or waterless hand cleaner should be used. Recycle used engine oil; check local laws.

2.3L Engine

1. Disconnect the negative battery cable.
2. Raise and safely support the vehicle.
3. Drain the crankcase into a suitable container. If equipped, detach the low oil level sensor.
4. Remove the right and left engine support bolts and nuts or through-bolts.
5. Using a jack, raise the engine as far as it will go. Place blocks of wood between the mounts and the No. 2 crossmember pedestal brackets. Remove the jack.
6. Remove the steering gear retaining nuts and bolts. Unfasten the bolt retaining the steering flex coupling to the steering gear. Position the steering gear forward and down.
7. Remove the shake brace.
8. Disconnect the starter cable, then remove the starter.
9. Remove the engine rear support-to-crossmember nuts.
10. Position a jack under the transmission and raise it.
11. Unfasten the oil pan retaining bolts and reinforcements. Remove the oil pump and lay it in the oil pan. Remove the oil pan. Clean the pan mating surfaces.

To install:

12. Remove and clean the oil pickup tube and screen assembly. After cleaning, reinstall.
13. Position a new oil pan gasket to the oil pan with gasket and Seal Contact Adhesive D7AZ-19B508-A or equivalent.
14. Place the pump in the oil pan, then install the pump when the pan is in position. Position the oil pan to the cylinder block. Place the reinforcements and install the retaining bolts. Tighten to 90–120 inch lbs. (10–13.5 Nm).
15. Lower the jack under the transmission and install the crossmember nuts. Remove the jack.

➥ Crossmember nuts should not be tightened until the front bolts are tightened to aid alignment of the powertrain.

16. Replace the oil filter.
17. If equipped, attach the low oil level sensor.
18. Position the flex coupling on the steering gear and install the retaining bolt.
19. Install the steering gear.
20. Install the shake brace. Install the starter and connect the starter cable.
21. Raise the engine enough to remove the wood blocks. Lower the engine and remove the jack. Install the engine support bolts and nuts and tighten to 33–45 ft. lbs. (45–61 Nm).
22. Lower the vehicle and fill the crankcase with oil and the cooling system with coolant.
23. Connect the negative battery cable. Start the engine and check for leaks.

3.8L Engine

1983–88 VEHICLES

➧ See Figure 111

1. Disconnect the negative battery cable.
2. Remove the air cleaner assembly including the air intake duct.

3. Unfasten the fan shroud attaching bolts, then position the shroud back over the fan.
4. Remove the oil level dipstick. If equipped with a low oil level sensor, remove the retainer clip at the sensor. Detach the electrical connector from the sensor.
5. Raise and safely support the vehicle.
6. Remove the exhaust manifold-to-exhaust pipe attaching nuts.
7. Drain the crankcase into a suitable container, then remove the oil filter.
8. Remove the bolts attaching the shift linkage bracket to the transmission bell housing. If necessary, remove the starter motor for more clearance.
9. Disconnect the transmission cooler lines at the radiator.
10. Unfasten the four converter cover retaining bolts, then remove the cover.
11. Disconnect the steering flex coupling. Unfasten the two bolts attaching the steering gear to the main crossmember, then let the steering gear rest on the frame away from the oil pan.
12. Remove the through bolts attaching the front engine insulator to the chassis.
13. Remove the nut and washer assembly attaching the front engine insulator to the chassis.
14. Raise the engine 2–3 in. (50–80mm) and insert wood blocks between the engine mounts and the vehicle frame.

➥ It may be necessary to raise the engine as much as 5 inches (127mm) to provide adequate pan-to-crossmember clearance. When raising the engine, watch the clearance between the transmission dipstick tube and the Thermactor® downstream air tube. If the tubes contact before adequate pan-to-crossmember clearance is provided, lower the engine and remove the transmission dipstick tube and the downstream air tube. Manual Clamp Cutter T78P-9481-A or equivalent, will be needed to disconnect the tube from the catalyst.

15. Remove the oil pan attaching bolts. Work the oil pan loose, then remove it from the vehicle.
16. Lower the oil pan onto the crossmember. Remove the oil pickup tube attaching nut. Lower the pickup tube/screen assembly into the pan and remove the oil pan through the front of the vehicle.
17. Remove the oil pan gasket and discard.

To install:

➥ When using silicone rubber sealer, assembly must occur within 15 minutes after sealer application. After this time, the sealer may start to set-up, and its sealing effectiveness may be reduced.

18. Clean the gasket surfaces on the cylinder block, oil pan and oil pick-up tube.
19. Trial fit the oil pan to the cylinder block. Ensure enough clearance has been provided to allow the oil pan to be installed without the sealant being scraped off when the pan is positioned under the engine. Remove the oil pan.

✱✱CAUTION

Make sure to use adequate ventilation when applying the gasket adhesive.

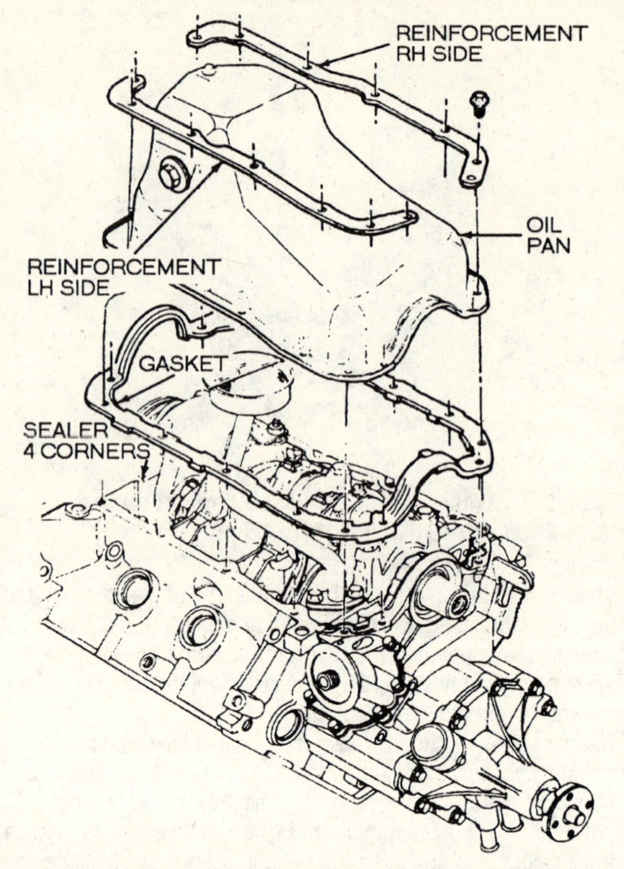

Fig. 111 Exploded view of the oil pan and gasket assemblies — 1983–88 3.8L engine

20. Install the oil pan gasket as follows:
a. Apply a thin film of GE pressure sensitive adhesive PSA-6574 or equivalent to the block rails front cover, rear bearing cap and block side of gasket.

➥ The gasket taps go to the block side.

b. Allow the adhesive to become tacky, then apply a $^1/_8$ in. (3–4mm) bead of Silicone Rubber D6AZ-19562-A or equivalent to the joints between the front cover and the block.
c. Apply a $^1/_6$ in. (4–5mm) bead of Silicone Rubber D6AZ-19562-A or equivalent, into the groove where the main bearing cap meets the block.
d. Immediately position the oil pan gasket against the engine block and press into position, being careful not to press out the sealant beads applied in Step c.

21. Install the oil pan, as follows:
a. Place the oil pickup tube/screen assembly in the oil pan.
b. Position the oil pan.
c. Position the oil pickup tube/screen with a new gasket. Install the tube attaching bolts and support bracket attaching nut. Tighten the attaching bolt to 15–22 ft. lbs. (20–30 Nm) and support bracket nut to 30–40 ft. lbs. (40–55 Nm).
d. Install the left and right side oil pan reinforcements and retaining bolts. Tighten the pan bolts to 80–105 inch lbs. (9–12 Nm).

22. Raise the engine, remove the wood blocks supporting the engine.

23. Install the front mount and damper attaching bolts. Tighten to 33–45 ft. lbs. (45–61 Nm).

24. Position the steering gear on the main crossmember. Install two attaching bolts. Connect the steering flex coupling and tighten the retaining nuts.

25. Position the shift linkage bracket and install the attaching bolts.

26. Connect the transmission cooler lines at the radiator.

27. If removed, install the transmission dipstick tube and the Thermactor® downstream air tube. Clamp cutter and Crimping tool T78P-9481-A or equivalent will be needed to connect the air tube to the catalyst.

28. Raise and safely support the vehicle.

29. Install a new oil filter.

30. Attach the exhaust manifold to the exhaust pipe and tighten the retaining nuts.

31. Carefully lower the vehicle.

32. If equipped, attach the low level oil sensor connector, then install the sensor with the retaining clip.

33. Position the fan shroud on the radiator and install the retaining bolts.

34. Connect the negative battery cable.

35. Fill the crankcase with the proper type and amount of oil.

36. Start the engine and check the fluid levels in the transmission. Check for engine oil, and transmission fluid leaks.

37. Install the air cleaner assembly, including the air intake duct.

1989-96 VEHICLES

See Figure 112

1. Disconnect the negative battery cable.
2. Remove the air cleaner outlet tube.
3. Unfasten the two bolts retaining the radiator upper sight shield, then position the shield aside.
4. Remove hood weather seal.
5. Remove the wiper pivot arms.
6. Remove LH cowl vent screen and wiper module.
7. On SC engines, remove intercooler/charge air cooler tubes.
8. Install Three Bar Engine Lifting Support D88L-6000-A or equivalent.
9. Raise and safely support the vehicle.
10. Remove the front engine support insulator through bolt. On SC, also remove LH front engine support/mount retaining strap bolt.
11. Partially lower the vehicle. Raise the engine with the lifting support tool.
12. Raise and safely support the vehicle. Remove the starter motor assembly.
13. Position a drain pan, drain the engine oil, then remove the filter.
14. Remove the starter motor wire, ground strap and oil cooler inlet tube (automatic transmission only).

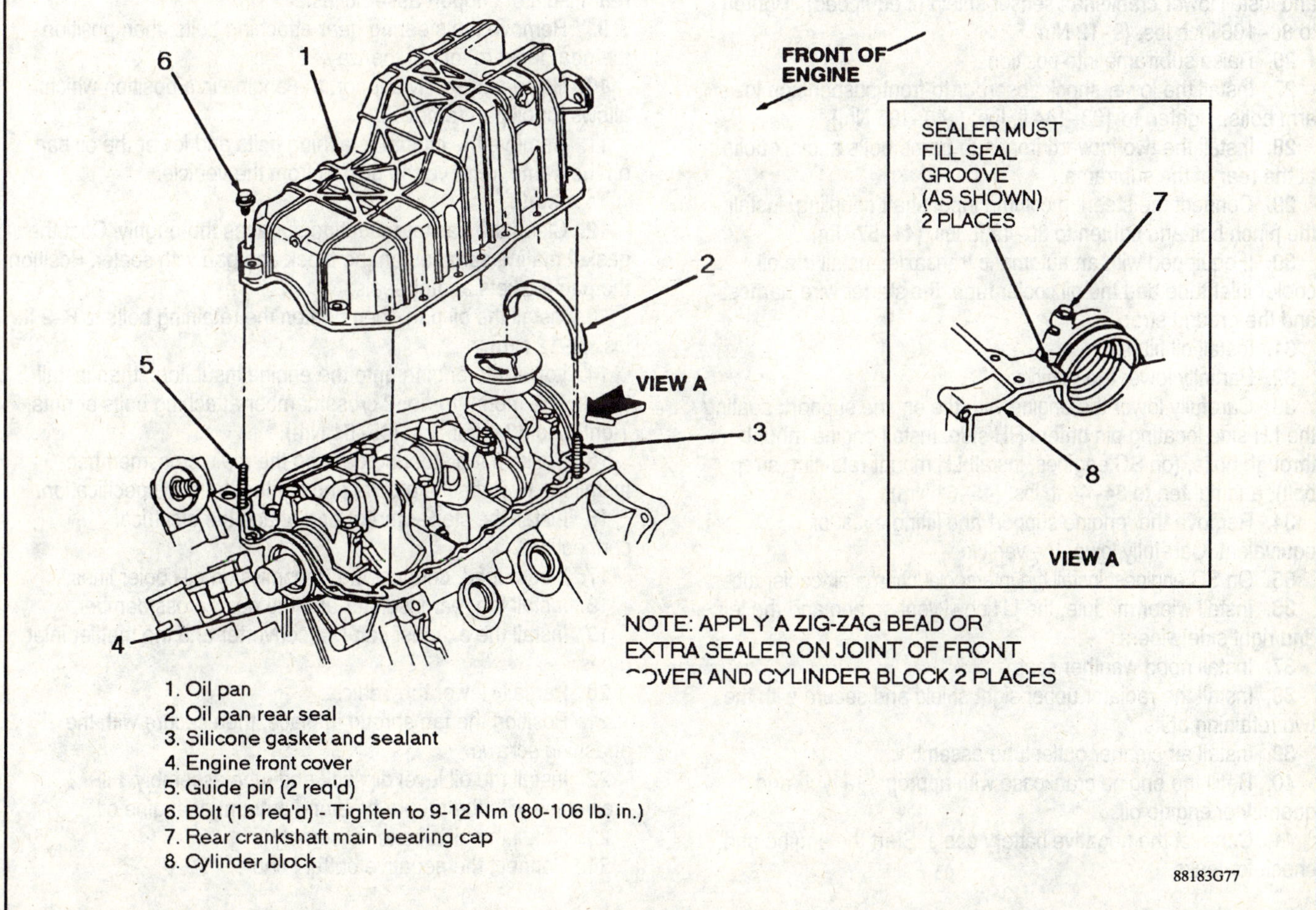

Fig. 112 Exploded view of the oil pan mounting — 1995 3.8L engine shown

15. Unfasten oil pan-to-bell housing bolts and Crankshaft Position (CKP) sensor lower shield retaining bolts (if equipped).
16. Remove the remaining oil pan retaining bolts.
17. Remove steering shaft pinch bolts and separate steering shaft.
18. Position transmission jack under front of the front subframe. Remove the six rearward bolts on front of subframe, then loosen the two forward subframe bolts.
19. Remove lower shock absorber-to-control arm bolts and nuts (both sides).

➥ It is necessary to remove the front wheels, brake calipers, anti-lock sensors, power steering pressure lines and all wiring harness clips from subframe to allow lowering of subframe.

20. Lower the front subframe.
21. Remove oil pan then empty any residual oil from the pan.

To install:

22. Clean mating surfaces of oil pan and cylinder block.
23. Apply a bead of RTV silicone gasket sealer to oil pan.

➥ When using silicone rubber (RTV) sealer, assembly must occur within 15 minutes after sealer application. After this time, the sealer may start to set up, and its sealing effectiveness may be reduced.

24. Fit oil pan to block to ensure enough clearance has been provided, to allow oil pan to be installed without sealant being scraped off, under cylinder block assembly.
25. Install oil pan retaining bolts at cylinder block, bell housing and install lower crankshaft sensor shield (if equipped). Tighten to 80–106 inch lbs. (9–12 Nm).
26. Raise subframe into position.
27. Install the lower shock absorber-to-front suspension lower arm bolts. Tighten to 103–144 ft. lbs. (140–195 Nm).
28. Install the two forward front sub-frame bolts and six bolts at the rear of the subframe.
29. Connect the steering column input shaft coupling, install the pinch bolt and tighten to 30–42 ft. lbs. (41–57 Nm).
30. If equipped with an automatic transaxle, install the oil cooler inlet tube and the oil cooler tube, the starter wire harness and the ground strap.
31. Install oil filter.
32. Partially lower the vehicle.
33. Carefully lower the engine with the engine support, seating the LH side locating pin before RH side. Install engine mount through bolts, (on SC engines, install LH mount retaining strap bolt), and tighten to 34–44 ft. lbs. (45–61 Nm).
34. Remove the engine support and lifting eyes, or equivalent. Carefully lower the vehicle.
35. On SC engines, install the intercooler/charge air cooler tubes.
36. Install wiper module, the LH cowl vent screen and the left and right side wipers.
37. Install hood weather seal.
38. Install the radiator upper sight shield and secure with the two retaining bolts.
39. Install air cleaner outlet tube assembly.
40. Refill the engine crankcase with appropriate type and quantity of engine oil.
41. Connect the negative battery cable. Start the engine and check for leaks.

5.0L Engine

1983–88 VEHICLES

➧ See Figure 113

✽✽WARNING

On vehicles equipped with a dual sump oil pan, both drain plugs must be removed to thoroughly drain the crankcase. When raising the engine for oil pan removal clearance, drain the cooling system, disconnect the hoses, check the fan-to-radiator clearance when jacking. Remove the radiator if clearance is inadequate.

1. Disconnect the negative battery cable.
2. Remove the oil level indicator from the left side of the cylinder block.
3. Remove the air cleaner tube assembly.
4. Remove the fan shroud retaining bolts, then position the shroud over the fan.
5. Raise and safely support the vehicle. Properly drain the engine oil.
6. Remove the starter motor retaining bolts and electrical connections, then remove the starter from the vehicle.
7. Remove the exhaust catalyst converter and muffler inlet pipes.
8. Unfasten the engine mount-to-no. 2 crossmember attaching bolts or nuts. Remove the no. 3 crossmember and the rear insulator support assemblies.
9. Remove the steering gear attaching bolts, then position the gear forward, out of the way.
10. Raise and safely support the engine in a position which allows for oil pan removal.
11. Remove the oil pan attaching bolts and lower the oil pan on the frame, remove the oil pan from the vehicle.

To install:

12. Clean the gasket mounting surfaces thoroughly. Coat the gasket mating surfaces on the block and pan with sealer. Position the pan gaskets and/or seals.
13. Install the oil pan, then tighten the retaining bolts to 6–9 ft. lbs. (9–12 Nm).
14. Lower the engine onto the engine insulators, then install the engine mount-to-no. 2 crossmember attaching bolts or nuts. Tighten to 33–45 ft. lbs. (45–61 Nm).
15. Position the steering gear on the main crossmember. Install the two attaching bolts and tighten them to specification.
16. Install the starter motor and attach the electrical connections.
17. If equipped, connect the transmission oil cooler lines.
18. Install the rear insulator and the no. 3 crossmember.
19. Install the exhaust catalyst converter and the muffler inlet pipes.
20. Partially lower the vehicle.
21. Position the fan shroud in place, then secure with the attaching screws.
22. Install the oil level dipstick and tube assembly. Fill crankcase with the proper type and amount of engine oil.
23. Install the air cleaner assembly.
24. Connect the negative battery cable.

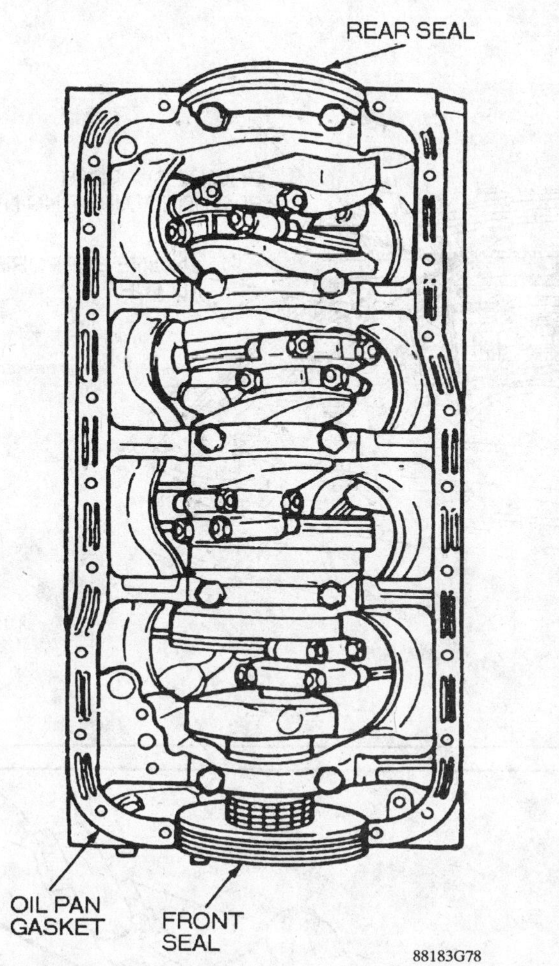

Fig. 113 After applying sealer to the mating surfaces, position the gasket(s) and/or seal(s) — 1988 5.0L engine shown

25. Apply the parking brake and while holding a foot on the brake, start the engine and allow to run for a few minutes. Turn the engine OFF and check for oil leaks.

1991–93 VEHICLES

➧ See Figures 114, 115, 116, 117, 118, 119, 120, 121 and 122

1. Disconnect the negative battery cable.
2. Remove the oil level dipstick.
3. Detach the air filter cover retaining clips to allow free movement when the engine is raised.
4. Install Engine Support Fixture D88L-6000-A or equivalent.
5. Raise and safely support the vehicle.

➥ It is recommended to use an engine hoist to lift the engine. Although wooden blocks and a jack will work, it may not provide enough room to remove the subframe and oil pan safely.

6. Properly drain the engine oil, then remove the oil filter.
7. Unfasten the engine mount through bolts.
8. Loosen the transmission mount nut to allow the mount to move the when the engine is raised.
9. Unfasten the two bolts retaining the radiator shroud to the radiator, then pull the shroud loose from the lower retaining clips.
10. Partially lower the vehicle.
11. Carefully raise the engine, about two inches, with the support fixture.
12. Raise and safely support the vehicle.
13. Remove the power steering cooler line retaining clips.
14. Remove the bolt securing the transmission lines to the engine block (right hand side).
15. If equipped, detach the electrical connector from the low oil level sensor.
16. Unfasten the oil pan retaining bolts.
17. Remove the steering shaft pinch bolt, then separate the shaft from the power steering rack assembly.
18. Position two jackstands under the engine support subframe.
19. Unfasten the lower strut-to-control arm bolts and nuts on both sides.
20. While supporting the engine subframe on the jackstands, remove the six rearward bolts on the subframe. Loosen the two forward bolts on the subframe, then lower the subframe.

➥ It is necessary to remove the front wheels, brake calipers, anti-lock sensors, power steering pressure lines and all wiring harness clips from subframe to allow lowering of subframe.

21. Remove oil pan. Empty any residual oil from the oil pan.

To install:

22. Clean mating surfaces of oil pan and cylinder block.

➥ The following procedure allows the gasket to stick to the engine block to insure correct gasket position during assembly. Do NOT apply and adhesive to the oil pan, or the oil pan side of the gasket. If adhesive is applied too thick, it will take longer to dry.

23. Apply a thin coat of Silicone Gasket Adhesive E6AZ-19562-A or equivalent, to the engine block and to the engine block side of a new oil pan gasket. Allow the adhesive to set-up for about 5 minutes, before positioning the gasket to the engine.
24. Position the oil pan to the engine. Install all the pan bolts hand tight, then tighten the $^{1}/_{4}$ inch pan bolt to 80–120 inch lbs. and the $^{5}/_{16}$ inch oil pan bolts to 12–18 ft. lbs. (16–24 Nm).

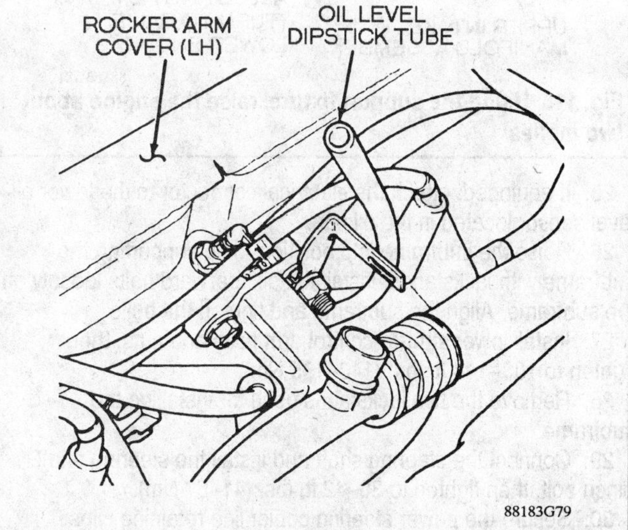

Fig. 114 Remove the oil dipstick, which is located near the left side valve cover

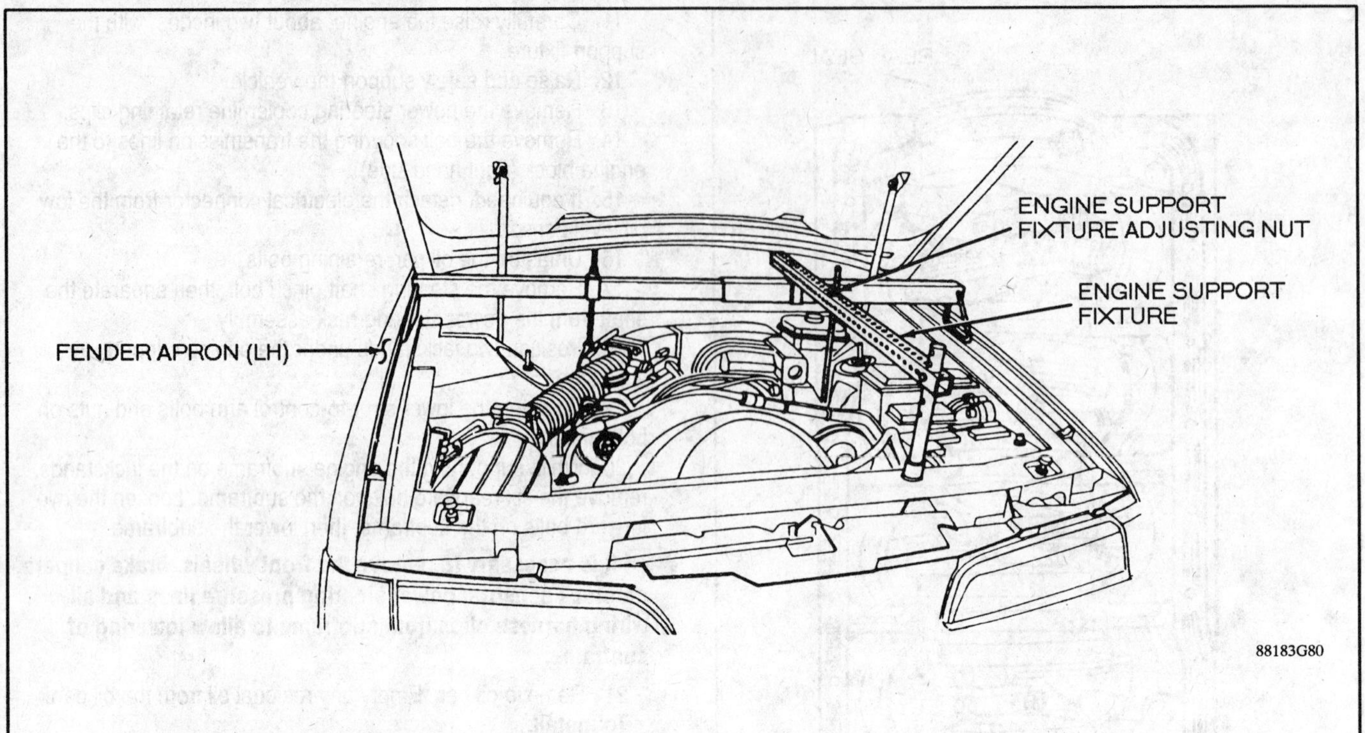

Fig. 115 Properly install a suitable engine support fixture

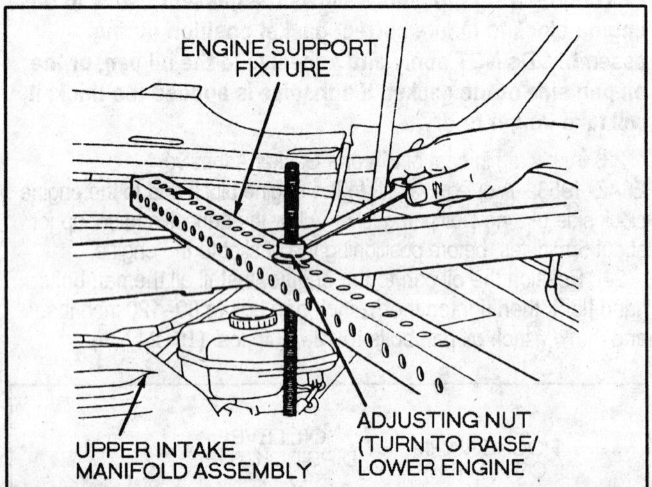

Fig. 116 Using the support fixture, raise the engine about two inches

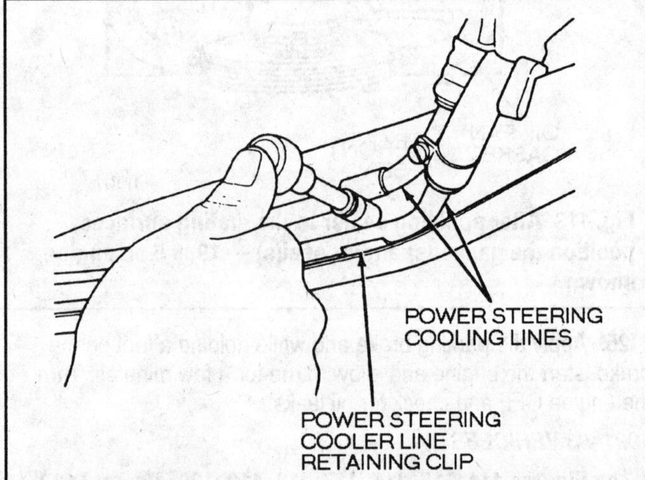

Fig. 117 Use a suitable socket to remove the power steering line clips

25. If equipped, attach the electrical connector to the lower oil level sensor located in the oil pan.
26. Raise the subframe into position while supporting the subframe with jackstands, install the six rearward bolts loosely on the subframe. Align the subframe and tighten the bolts.
27. Install lower strut-to-control arm bolts and nuts, then tighten to 103–144 ft. lbs. (140–195 Nm).
28. Remove the two jackstands used for installing the subframe.
29. Connect the steering shaft and install the steering shaft pinch bolt, then tighten to 30–42 ft. lbs. (41–57 Nm).
30. Secure the power steering cooler line retaining clips.
31. Carefully lower the vehicle.
32. Lower the engine onto the engine mounts, then remove the support fixture.
33. Raise and safely support the vehicle.
34. Tighten the transmission mount nut to 65–85 ft. lbs. (88–115 Nm).
35. Install the engine mount through-bolts and tighten.
36. Carefully lower the vehicle.
37. Position the radiator fan shroud into the lower retaining clips, then install the two bolts retaining the shroud to the radiator.
38. Attach the air filter cover retaining clips.
39. Fill the engine with the proper type and quantity of oil. Install the engine oil dipstick.
40. Connect the negative battery cable. Start engine and check for leaks.

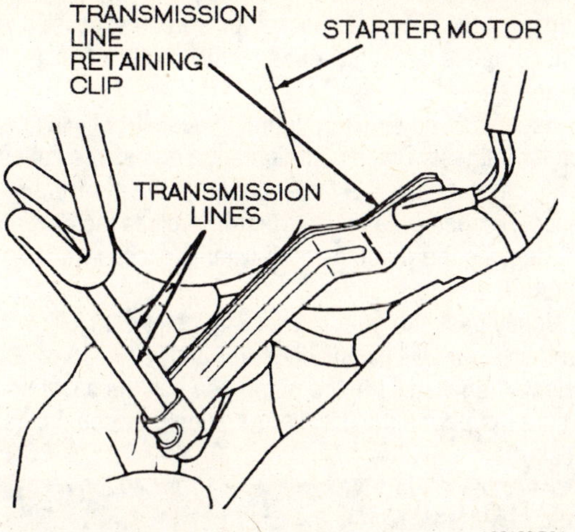

Fig. 118 Unfasten the bolt holding the transmission lines to the engine block

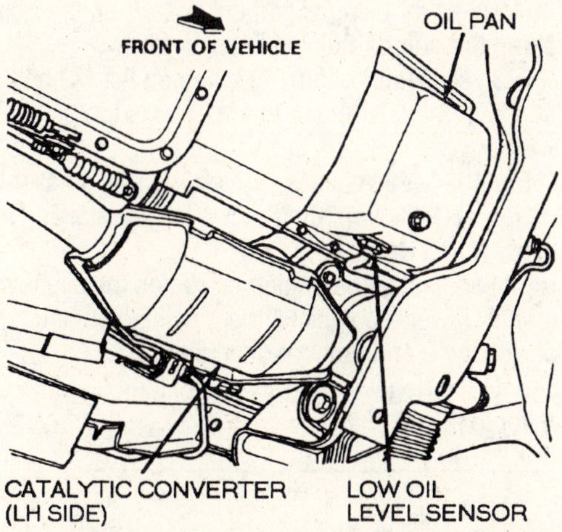

Fig. 119 Detach the connector from the low oil level sensor

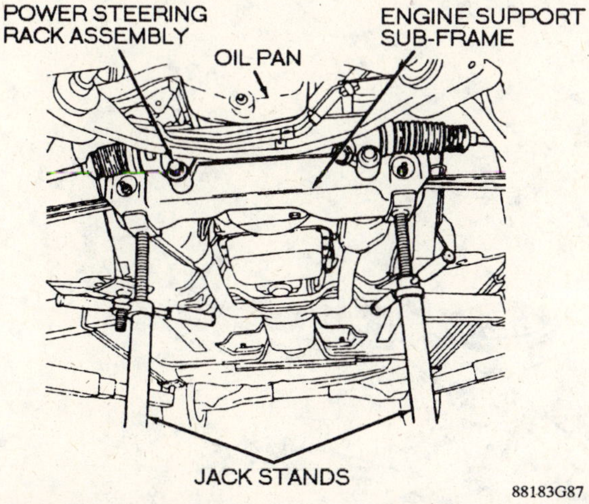

Fig. 120 Put two jackstands or transmission jacks under the front of the subframe

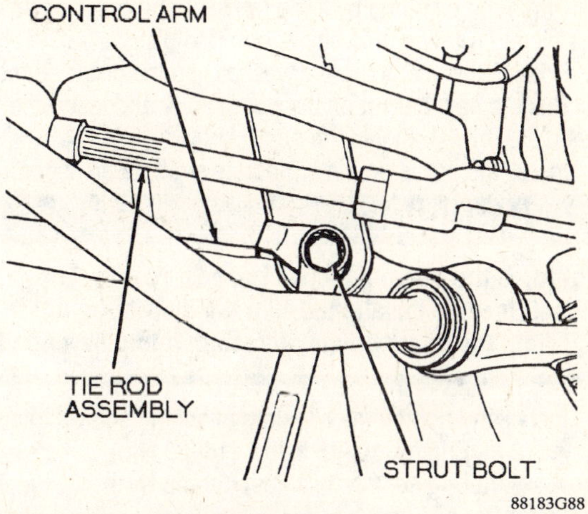

Fig. 121 Use an open-ended wrench to remove the lower strut-to-control arm bolts and nuts

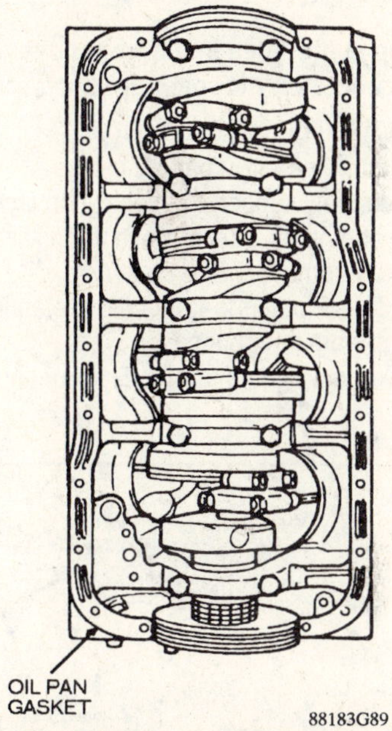

Fig. 122 Apply the adhesive to the engine block, NOT to the oil pan or pan side of the gasket

Oil Pump

REMOVAL & INSTALLATION

2.3L and 5.0L Engines

➧ **See Figures 123 and 124**

1. Disconnect the negative battery cable.
2. Remove the oil pan.
3. Remove the oil pump inlet tube and screen assembly.
4. Unfasten the oil pump attaching bolts, then remove the oil pump gasket and the intermediate shaft.

To install:

5. Prime the oil pump by filling the inlet and outlet ports with engine oil and rotating the shaft of pump to distribute it.
6. Position the intermediate driveshaft into the distributor socket.
7. Place a new gasket on the pump body and insert the intermediate driveshaft into the pump body.
8. Install the pump and intermediate shaft as an assembly.

****WARNING**

Do not force the pump if it does not seat readily. The driveshaft may be misaligned with the distributor shaft. To align, rotate the intermediate driveshaft into a new position.

9. Install and tighten the oil pump attaching screws to:
   - 2.3L Engine: 12–15 ft. lbs. (16–20 Nm)
   - 5.0L Engine: 22–32 ft. lbs. (30–43 Nm)
10. Install the oil pan.
11. Connect the negative battery cable, then start the engine and check for leaks.

3.8L Engine

See Figure 125

The oil pump is mounted in the front cover assembly. Oil pan removal is necessary for pick-up tube/screen replacement or service.

1. Disconnect the negative battery cable.
2. Raise and safely support the vehicle on jackstands.
3. Drain the engine oil, then remove the oil filter.
4. If necessary, remove the oil cooler.
5. Unfasten the oil pump-to-front cover retaining bolts, then remove the pump from the front cover.
6. Lift the two pump gears from their mounting pocket in the front cover.
7. Clean all gasket mounting surfaces.
8. Inspect the mounting pocket for wear. If excessive wear is present, complete timing cover assembly replacement is necessary.
9. Inspect the cover/filter mounting gasket-to-timing cover surface for flatness. Place a straightedge across the flat and check the clearance with a feeler gauge. If the measured clearance exceeds 0.004 in. (0.10mm), replace the cover/filter mount. Replace the pump gears if wear is excessive.

To install:

10. Lightly pack the gear pocket with petroleum jelly or coat all gear surfaces with Oil Conditioner D9AZ-19579-CA or equivalent, then install the the pump gears in the cover pocket. Make sure the petroleum jelly fills all voids between the gears and pockets.

****WARNING**

Failure to properly coat the oil pump gears may result in failure of the pump to prime when the engine is started.

11. Position the pump body O-ring seal and install the pump body to the front cover using alignment dowels on the front cover.
12. Tighten the pump retaining bolts as follows
    a. For vehicles through 1993, tighten the M8 bolts to 18–22 ft. lbs. (25–30 Nm) and the M10 bolts to 30–40 ft. lbs. (40–55 Nm).
    b. For 1994–96 vehicles, tighten the four smaller bolts to 15–22 ft. lbs. (20–30 Nm) and the two larger retaining bolts to 6–11 ft. lbs. (8–15 Nm).
13. If removed, install the engine oil cooler. Install the oil filter.
14. Carefully lower the vehicle, then refill the engine crankcase with the correct type and amount of engine oil.
15. Connect the negative battery cable, then start the engine and check for leaks.

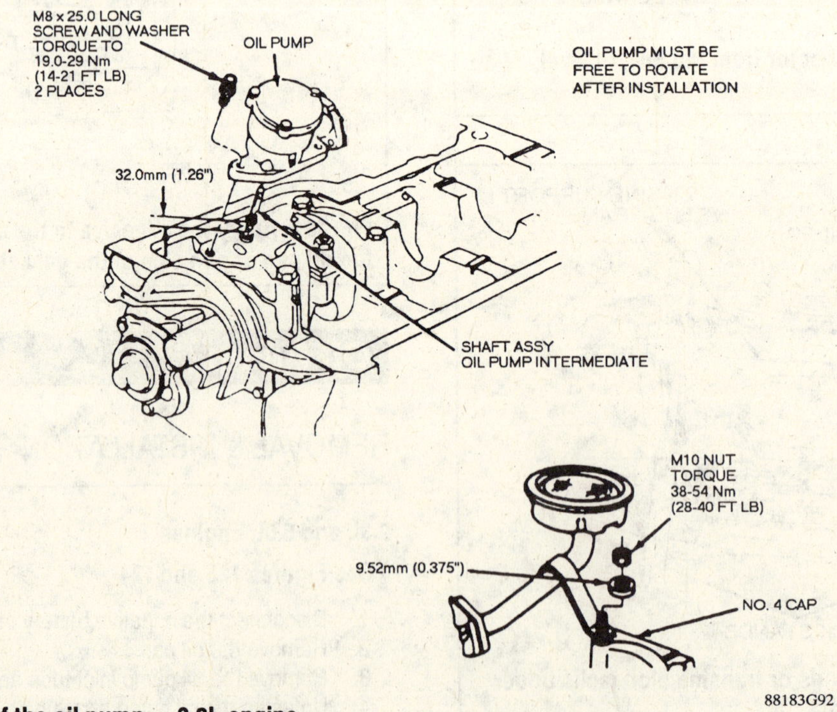

Fig. 123 Installation of the oil pump — 2.3L engine

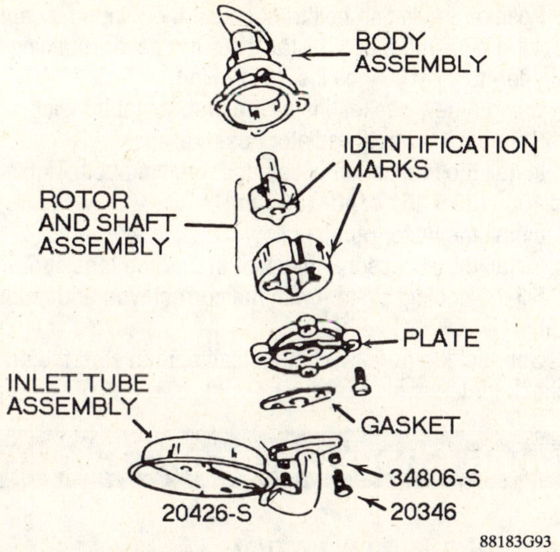

Fig. 124 Exploded view of the oil pump assembly — 5.0L engine

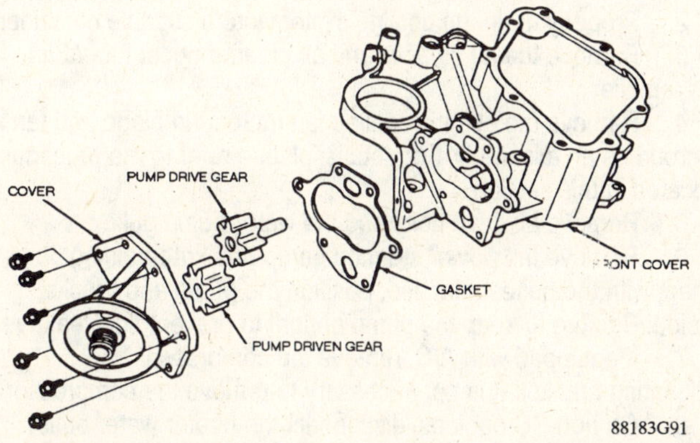

Fig. 125 Exploded view of the oil pump and gears — 3.8L engine

4.6L Engine

➧ **See Figure 126**

1. Disconnect the negative battery cable.
2. Remove the valve covers, engine front cover and the oil pan.
3. Remove the timing chains.
4. Remove the 2 bolts retaining the oil pickup tube to the oil pump and remove the bolt retaining the oil pickup tube to the main bearing stud spacer. Remove the pickup tube.
5. Unfasten the 4 bolts retaining the oil pump to the cylinder block, then remove the oil pump.

To install:

6. Rotate the inner rotor of the oil pump to align with the flats on the crankshaft and install the oil pump flush with the cylinder block.
7. Install the four retaining bolts, then tighten to 71-106 inch lbs. (8-12 Nm).
8. Clean the oil pickup tube and replace the O-ring.

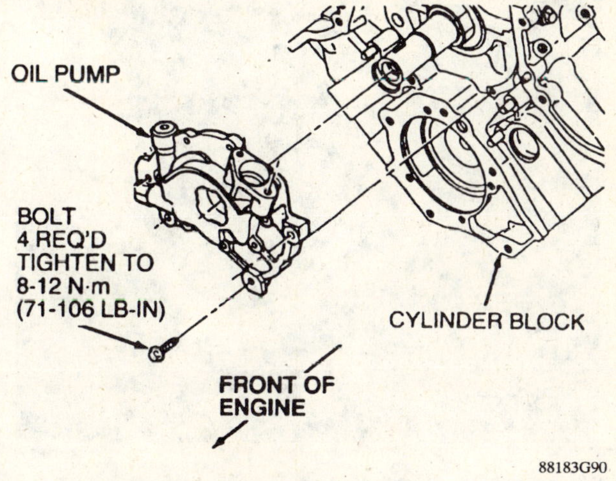

Fig. 126 Position the pump flush with the cylinder block, then install and tighten the retaining bolts — 4.6L engine

9. Place the pickup tube on the oil pump and hand-start the 2 retaining bolts. Install the bolt retaining the pickup tube to the main bearing stud spacer hand-tight. Tighten the pick-up tube-to-oil pump bolts to 72-106 inch lbs. (8-12 Nm). Tighten the pickup tube-to-main bearing stud spacer bolt to 15-22 ft. lbs. (20-30 Nm).
10. Install a new the oil filter.
11. Install the timing chains.
12. Install the oil pan, engine front cover, and valve covers.
13. Fill the crankcase with the proper type and quantity of engine oil.
14. Connect the negative battery cable, then start the engine and check for leaks.

Crankshaft Damper

REMOVAL & INSTALLATION

➧ **See Figures 127 and 128**

1. Disconnect the negative battery cable.
2. Remove the fan shroud, as required.
3. If necessary, drain the cooling system and remove the radiator.
4. Remove drive belts from pulley.
5. On those engines with a separate pulley, remove the retaining bolts and separate the pulley from the vibration damper.
6. Remove the vibration damper/pulley retaining bolt from the crankshaft end.
7. Using a puller, remove the damper/pulley from the crankshaft.

To install:

8. Align the key slot of the pulley hub to the crankshaft key.
9. Complete the assembly in the reverse order of removal. Tighten the retaining bolts to specifications, as follows:
    a. 2.3L engines: 100-120 ft. lbs. (136-162 Nm).
    b. 3.8L engines: 103-132 ft. lbs. (140-180 Nm)
    c. 5.0L engines: 70-90 ft. lbs. (95-122 Nm).
10. Connect the negative battery cable, then start the engine and check for proper engine operation.

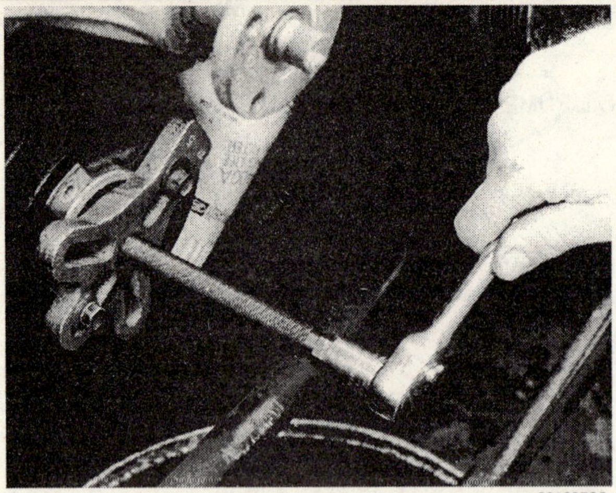

88183P25

Fig. 127 Use a suitable puller to remove the damper from the crankshaft — 1990 3.8L engine shown

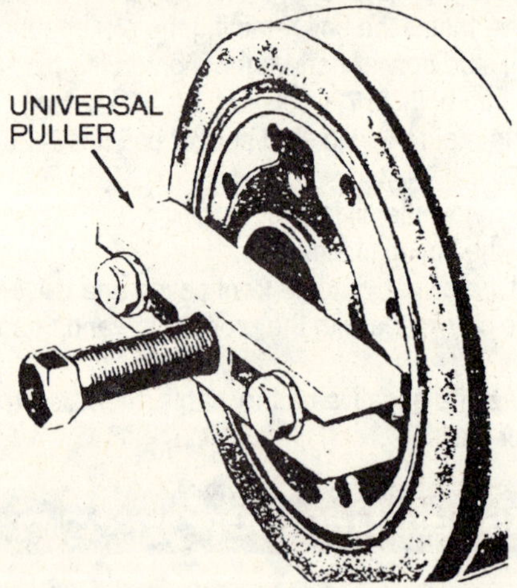

88183G94

Fig. 128 There are several types of pullers to remove the crankshaft (vibration) damper from the crankshaft

Timing Belt Cover

REMOVAL & INSTALLATION

2.3L Engine

1. Disconnect the negative battery cable.
2. Properly drain the engine cooling system.
3. Unfasten the four water pump pulley bolts.
4. Remove the automatic belt tensioner and accessory drive belt(s).
5. Disconnect the upper radiator hose.
6. Unfasten the crankshaft pulley bolt, then remove the pulley.
7. Remove the thermostat housing and gasket.
8. Remove the timing belt outer cover retaining bolt(s). Release the cover interlocking tabs, if equipped, then remove the cover from the vehicle.

To install:

9. Position the timing belt front cover. If equipped, snap the interlocking tabs into place. Install the outer cover retaining bolts, then tighten to 71–106 inch lbs. (8–12 Nm).
10. Using a new gasket, install the thermostat housing.
11. Connect the upper radiator hose.
12. Install the crankshaft pulley and retaining bolt. Tighten the bolt to 103–133 ft. lbs. (140–180 Nm).
13. Install the water pump pulley.
14. Install the accessory drive belt(s) and the tensioner.
15. Fill the cooling system with the correct type and amount of coolant.
16. Connect the negative battery cable, then start the engine and check for leaks.

Timing Chain Cover and Seal

REMOVAL & INSTALLATION

3.8L Engine

See Figures 129 and 137

1. Disconnect the negative battery cable
2. Properly drain the cooling system into a suitable container.
3. Remove the air cleaner and air cleaner outlet tube/duct assemblies.
4. Remove the electric cooling fan motor, fan blade and fan shroud as an assembly. For details, please refer to the procedure located in this section.
5. Remove all drive belts and the water pump pulley.
6. Remove the power steering pump bracket retaining bolts, then, with the hoses attached, position the pump and bracket aside. Be sure to keep the pump upright to prevent fluid leakage.
7. If equipped with A/C, remove the compressor front mounting bracket. It is not necessary to remove the compressor.
8. On non-SC engines, disconnect the heater water outlet tube and the water bypass hose from the water pump.
9. Disconnect the upper radiator hose at the thermostat housing.
10. Detach the ignition coil wire from the distributor cap and remove the cap with the ignition wires attached.
11. For non-SC engines, remove the hold-down clamp and lift the distributor out of the engine front cover. For SC engines, remove the hold-down clamp and remove the Camshaft Position (CMP) sensor from the engine front cover.
12. If equipped with a tripminder, remove the fuel flow meter support bracket. The fuel lines will support the flow meter.
13. Raise and safely support the vehicle using jackstands.

If the crankshaft damper and pulley have to be separated, mark the damper and pulley so that they may be reassembled in the same relative position. This is important as the damper and pulley are initially balanced as a unit.

14. Remove the crankshaft damper using Crankshaft Damper Remover T58P-6316-D and Vibration Damper Remover Adapter T82L-6316-B or equivalent pullers.
15. For carbureted vehicles, remove the fuel pump shield. disconnect the fuel line from the carburetor at the fuel pump. Remove the mounting bolts and the fuel pump. Position pump out of the way with tank line still attached.

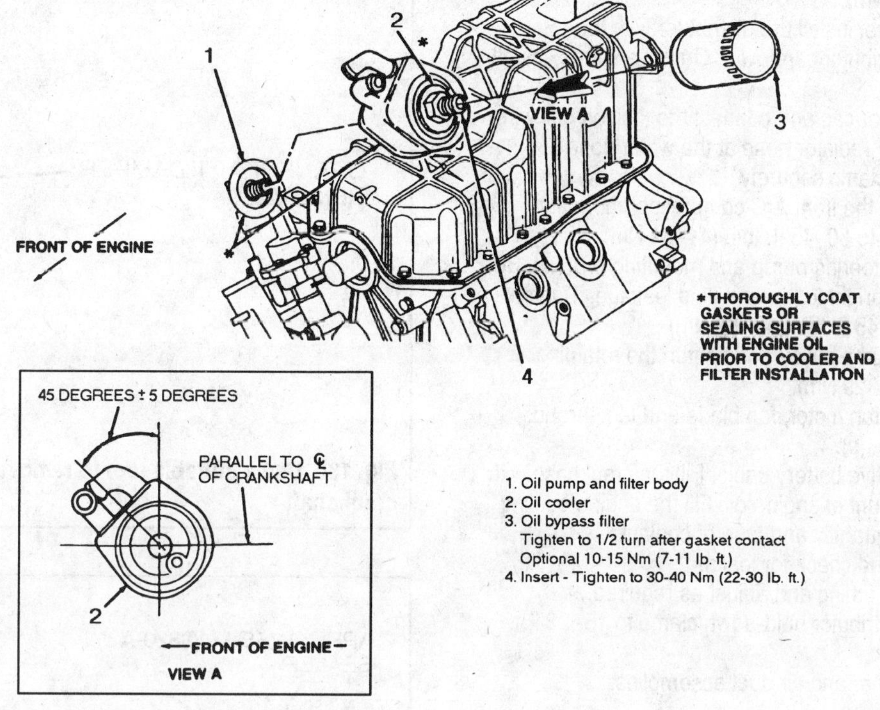

Fig. 129 Remove the oil filter and oil cooler (if equipped)

16. Drain the engine oil and remove the oil filter and the oil cooler (if equipped).
17. Disconnect the lower radiator hose at the water pump.
18. Unfasten the oil pan mounting bolts and remove the oil pan.

➥ The front cover cannot be removed without lowering the oil pan, or possible engine oil leakage may occur.

19. Carefully lower the car from the jackstands.
20. Remove the front cover mounting bolts. It is not necessary to remove the water pump from the engine front cover.

➥ Do not overlook the engine front cover retaining bolt, located behind the oil pump and filter body. The engine front cover will break if pried upon and all retaining bolts are not removed.

21. Remove the engine front cover and water pump as an assembly. Remove and discard the front cover gasket.

To install:

➥ Lightly oil all bolt and stud bolt threads before installation except those specifying special sealant.

22. Clean all gasket surfaces on the front cover, cylinder block, fuel pump and oil pan.
23. If reusing the engine front cover, install a new front cover oil seal. If a new front cover is to be installed:
    a. Install the oil pump, oil filter adapter and intermediate shaft from the old cover.
    b. Remove the water pump from the old cover.
    c. Clean the mounting surface, install a new mounting gasket and the pump on the new front cover. Tighten the water pump attaching bolts to 15–22 ft. lbs. (20–30 Nm).

➥ Gasket and trim adhesive D7AZ-19B508-B or equivalent is recommended to hold the new front cover gasket in position while the front cover is installed.

24. Position a new front cover gasket on the front of the engine and install the cover and water pump assemblies, using the dowels for proper alignment. Tighten the front cover bolts to 15–22 ft. lbs. (20–30 Nm).
25. Raise and safely support the vehicle. Install the oil pan.
26. Connect the lower radiator hose to the water pump. Make sure to tighten the clamp securely.
27. Install the oil filter.
28. If equipped with a carbureted engine, install the fuel pump, then connect the fuel line at the carburetor and at the fuel pump.

✻✻WARNING

When installing the fuel pump, turn the crankshaft 180° to position the fuel pump drive eccentric away from the fuel pump arm. Failure to turn the drive eccentric away from the pump arm can cause stress on the pump mounting threads and strip them out when installing the pump.

29. Coat the crankshaft front seal sealing surface with clean engine oil. Apply a small amount os Silicone Gasket and Sealant F1AZ-19562-A or equivalent, to the crankshaft keyway.
30. Position the crankshaft key in the crankshaft keyway. Install the crankshaft damper using Damper Front Cover Seal Replacer T82L-6316-A or equivalent. Install the damper retaining washer and bolt, then tighten the bolt to 103–132 ft. lbs. (140–180 Nm).
31. Fasten the pulley to the damper, then tighten the retaining bolts to 20–28 ft. lbs. (26–38 Nm).
32. Install the fuel pump shield.
33. Carefully lower the vehicle.
34. If equipped with an SC engine, connect the water bypass hose. Tighten the clamp securely. On non-SC engines, install the

heater water outlet tube to the water pump. Tighten the retaining bolt to 6-8 ft. lbs. (8-11 Nm).

35. On non-SC engines, install the distributor with the rotor pointing at the No. 1 distributor cap tower. On SC engines, install the CMP sensor.
36. Install the distributor cap and connect the ignition coil wire.
37. Connect the upper radiator hose at the water hose connection. Tighten the clamp securely.
38. If equipped, install the front A/C compressor mounting bracket bolts and tighten to 30-45 ft. lbs. (41-61 Nm).
39. Install the power steering pump and mounting bracket. Be sure to keep the pump upright to prevent fluid leakage. Tighten the retaining bolts to 30-45 ft. lbs. (40-62 Nm).
40. Install the water pump pulley and tighten the retaining bolts to 16-21 ft. lbs. (21-29 Nm).
41. Install the cooling fan motor, fan blade and fan shroud.
42. Install the drive belt(s).
43. Connect the negative battery cable. Fill the crankcase with the proper type and amount of engine oil. Fill the engine cooling system with the correct quantity and type of coolant.
44. Start the engine and check for leaks.
45. Check the ignition timing and adjust as required. If equipped, tighten the distributor hold-down clamp to 15-22 ft. lbs. (20-30 Nm).
46. Install the air cleaner and air duct assemblies.

4.6L Engine

See Figures 130, 131 and 132

1. Disconnect the negative battery cable.

The valve covers, oil pan and oil pan gasket must be removed prior to the engine front cover or possible engine damage and/or leakage may occur upon reassembly.

2. Remove the cooling fan motor/fan blade and shroud assembly.
3. Loosen the water pump pulley bolts.
4. Remove the drive belt and the water pump pulley.
5. Raise and safely support the vehicle.
6. Remove the bolts retaining the power steering pump to the cylinder block and engine front cover. Note that the front lower bolt on the pump will not come all the way out. Wire the power steering pump out of the way. DO NOT disconnect the fluid lines.
7. Remove the oil pan and gasket, as outlined in this section.
8. Remove the crankshaft pulley retaining bolt and washer from the crankshaft.
9. Install Crankshaft Damper Remover T58P-6316-D on the crankshaft pulley, then pull the pulley from the crankshaft.
10. Carefully lower the vehicle.
11. Unfasten the bolts retaining the power steering fluid reservoir of the left side coil bracket, then position the reservoir out of the way.
12. Remove the right and left side valve covers, as outlined in this section.
13. Detach the fuel charging wiring from both ignition coils and Camshaft Position (CMP) sensor.
14. Unfasten the three bolts retaining the right side ignition coil bracket to the engine front cover.
15. Remove the left side ignition coil from the bracket, then lay it on the top of the engine.
16. Unfasten the three nuts retaining the left side ignition coil bracket to the engine front cover.

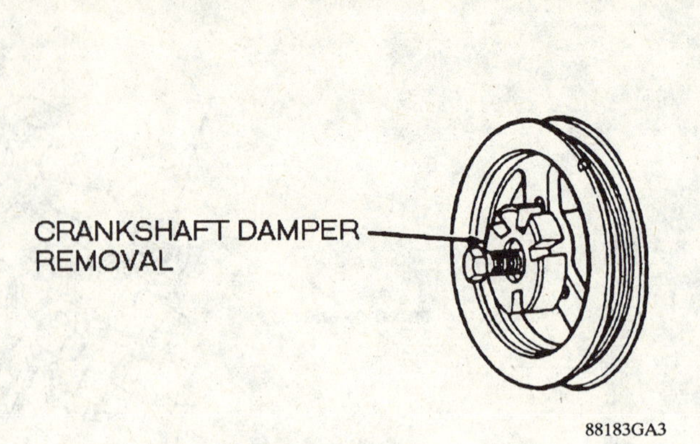

Fig. 130 Use a suitable tool to remove the pulley from the crankshaft

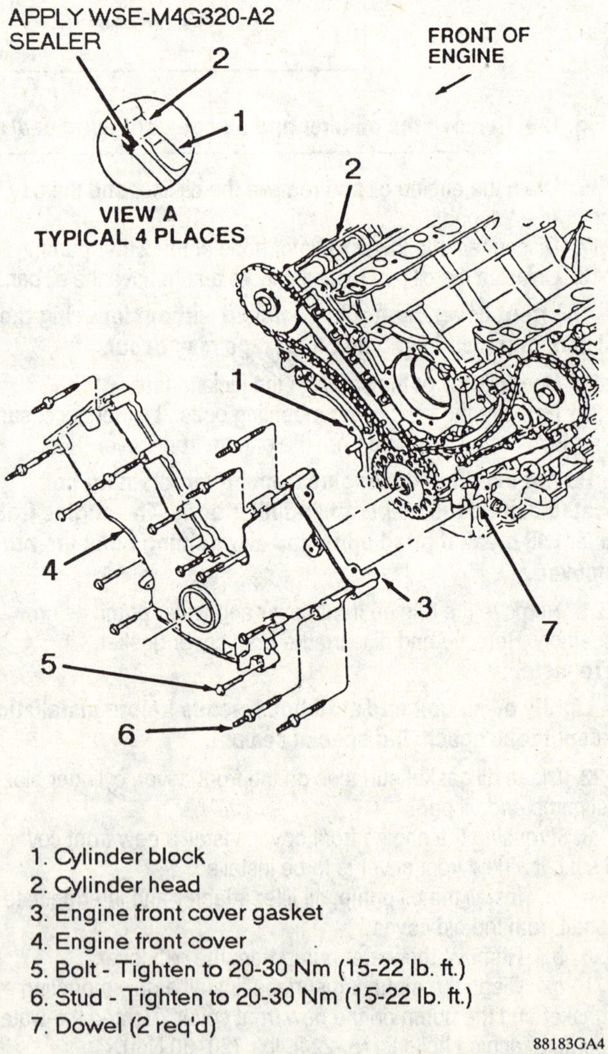

Fig. 131 Unfasten the retainers, then remove the front cover from the engine

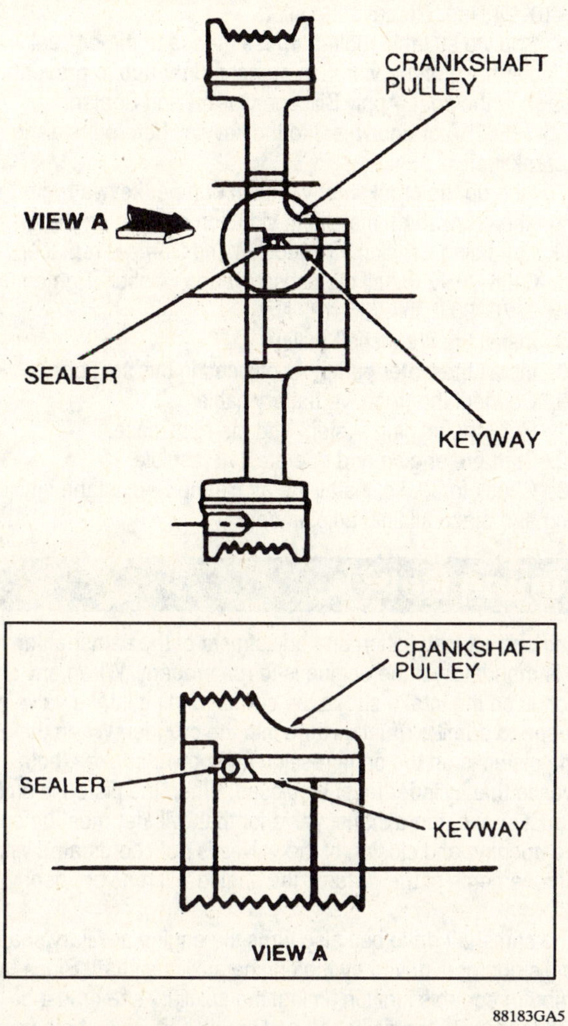

Fig. 132 Apply sealer to the end of the keyway and crankshaft pulley

17. Slide the right side ignition coil bracket and ignition wires off the mounting studs and lay the assembly on top of the engine. Remove the bolts and retaining belt idler pulley, then remove the pulley.
18. Detach the fuel charging wiring from the Crankshaft Position (CKP) sensor.
19. Unfasten the seven stud bolts and four bolts retaining the engine front cover, then remove the cover from the vehicle.

To install:

20. Clean all dirt, oil and/or sealant from the engine front cover, cylinder heads and cylinder block sealing surfaces. The surfaces must be clean and dry before applying sealant.
21. Replace the crankshaft front seal and engine front cover gasket (three each).
22. Apply a 0.32–0.47 inch (8–12mm) bead of Silicone Gasket Sealant F1AZ-19562-B or equivalent, to the locations shown in the accompanying illustration. Install the engine front cover and retainers in no more than four minutes after applying sealer.
23. Install the studs and bolts retaining the engine front cover to the engine in the locations shown in the accompanying figure. Tighten to 15–22 ft. lbs. (20–30 Nm) no more than four minutes after applying sealer.
24. Connect the fuel charging wiring to the CKP sensor.
25. Install the right side ignition coil bracket and ignition wires as an assembly. Tighten the nuts to 15–22 ft. lbs. (20–30 Nm).
26. Install the left side ignition coil bracket. Tighten the nuts to 15–22 ft. lbs. (20–30 Nm). Install the left side ignition coil and wires as an assembly.
27. Position and install the power steering fluid reservoir.
28. Attach the fuel charging wiring to both ignition coils and CMP sensors.
29. Install the valve covers, as outlined earlier in this section.
30. Raise and safely support the vehicle.
31. Make sure the surfaces is clean, then apply Silicone Gasket and Sealant F1AZ-19562-B or equivalent to the end of the keyway and crankshaft pulley.
32. Position the crankshaft pulley on the crankshaft. Make sure the crankshaft key and keyway are aligned.
33. Using Crankshaft Damper Replacer T47P-6316-B or equivalent, install the crankshaft pulley.
34. Install the crankshaft pulley bolt and retaining washer. Tighten the bolt to 114–121 ft. lbs. (155–165 Nm).
35. Install the oil pan as outlined in this section.
36. Position the power steering pump on the engine, then install the four retaining bolts. Tighten the bolts to 15–22 ft. lbs. (20–30 Nm).
37. Carefully lower the vehicle.
38. Install the water pump pulley and secure with the four bolts. Tighten the bolts to 15–22 ft. lbs. (20–30 Nm).
39. Install the drive belt.
40. Install the cooling fan motor/fan blade and fan shroud assembly.
41. Connect the negative battery cable, then start the engine and check for leaks.

5.0L Engines

➧ See Figures 133 and 134

1. Disconnect the negative battery cable.
2. Drain the cooling system into a suitable container.
3. Refer to the Water Pump removal procedure in this section. Perform all steps, but leave the pump attached to the front cover.

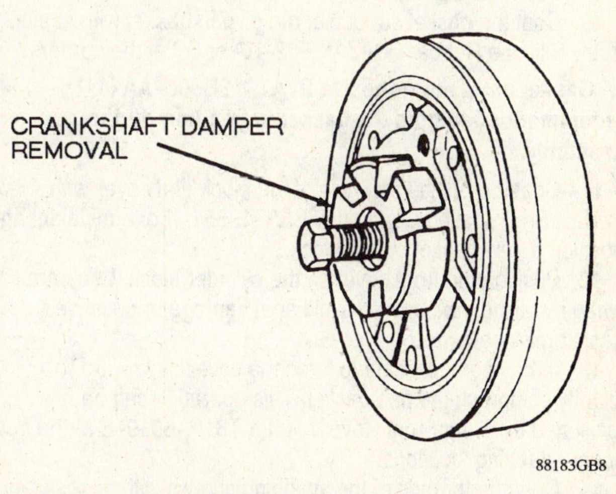

Fig. 133 Use a suitable puller to remove the crankshaft (vibration) damper

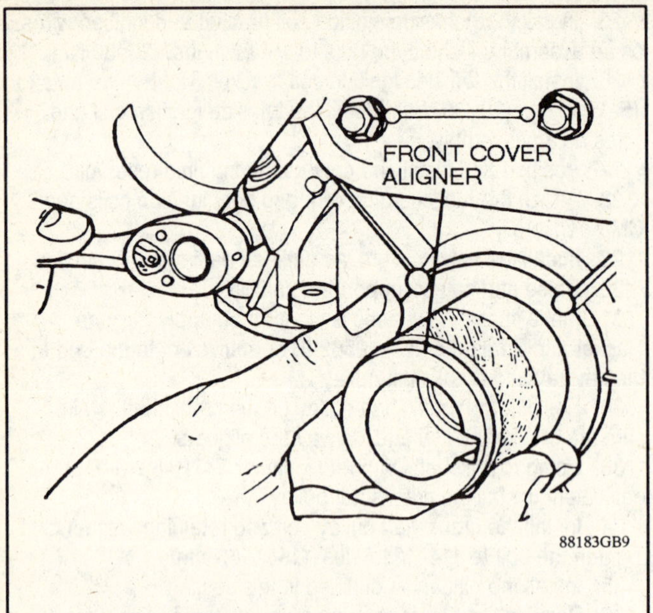

Fig. 134 Use the aligner tool to ease cover installation

4. Drain the oil from the crankcase.
5. Remove the crankshaft pulley from the crankshaft vibration damper. Remove the damper attaching capscrew and washer. Install Crankshaft Damper Remover T58P-6316-D, or equivalent, on the crankshaft vibration damper. Remove the damper.

➥ Cover the front oil pan opening while the cover assembly is off to prevent foreign material from entering the pan.

6. Unfasten the oil pan-to-front cover attaching bolts. Carefully separate the front cover from the oil pan gasket. Remove the front cover and water pump as an assembly. If a new front cover is to be installed, remove the water pump from the old front cover and transfer to the new cover.
7. Remove and discard the front cover gasket.

To install:

8. Clean the front cover and mating surfaces of old gasket material. Install a new oil seal in the cover. Use a seal driver tool, if available.
9. Lubricate the timing chain with engine oil.
10. Coat the gasket surface of the oil pan gasket with sealer. Apply Silicone Rubber D6AZ-19562-AA or BB at the corners.

➥ Gasket and Trim Adhesive D7AZ-19B508-AA is recommended to hold the gasket in position during assembly.

11. Coat the gasket surfaces of the block and cover with Perfect Seal Sealing Compound B5A-19554-A or equivalent and position a new gasket on the block.
12. Position the front cover on the cylinder block. Use care when installing the cover to avoid seal damage or possible gasket mislocation.
13. It may be necessary to force the cover downward to slightly compress the pan gasket. This operation can be facilitated by using Front Cover Aligner T61P-6019-B at the front cover attaching locations.
14. Coat the threads of the attaching screws with oil resistant Pipe Sealant with Teflon® and install the screws. While pushing on the alignment tool, tighten the oil pan-to-cover attaching screws to 12-18 ft. lbs. (16-24 Nm).
15. Tighten the cover-to-block attaching screws to 12-18 ft. lbs. (16-24 Nm). Remove the pilot.
16. Apply a suitable multi-purpose grease to the oil seal rubbing surface of the vibration damper inner hub to prevent damage to the seal. Apply Silicone Gasket and Sealant F1AZ-19562-A or equivalent to the keyway before installing on the crankshaft.
17. Line up the crankshaft vibration damper keyway with the key on the crankshaft. Install the vibration damper on the crankshaft using Crankshaft Sprocket and Damper replacer T52L-6306-AEE. Install the capscrew and washer. Tighten the screw to 70-90 ft. lbs. (95-122 Nm).
18. Install the crankshaft pulley.
19. Install the water pump, as outlined in this section.
20. Connect the negative battery cable.
21. Refill the cooling system and the crankcase.
22. Start the engine and operate it at fast idle.
23. Check for leaks, install the air cleaner. Adjust the ignition timing and make all final adjustments.

Timing Belt

The correct installation and adjustment of the camshaft drive belt is mandatory if the engine is to run properly. When any given piston is on the intake stroke the corresponding intake valve must be open to admit air/fuel mixture into the cylinder. When the same piston is on the compression and power strokes, both valves in that cylinder must be closed. When the piston is on the exhaust stroke, the exhaust valve for that cylinder must be open. If the opening and closing of the valves is not coordinated with the movements of the pistons, the engine will run very poorly, if at all.

The camshaft drive belt also turns the engine auxiliary shaft. The distributor is driven by the engine auxiliary shaft. Since the distributor controls ignition timing, the auxiliary shaft must be coordinated with the camshaft and crankshaft, since both valves in any given cylinder must be closed and the piston in that cylinder near the top of the compression stroke when the spark plug fires.

Due to this complex interrelationship between the camshaft, the crankshaft and the auxiliary shaft, the cogged pulleys on each component must be aligned when the camshaft drive belt is installed.

REMOVAL & INSTALLATION

➧ See Figures 135 and 136

1. Set the engine to TDC as described in the troubleshooting section. The crankshaft and camshaft timing marks should align with their respective pointers and the distributor rotor should point to the No. 1 plug tower.
2. Disconnect the negative battery cable, then properly drain the engine cooling system.
3. Remove the timing belt front cover, as outlined in this section.
4. Loosen the belt tensioner adjustment screw, position belt tensioner tool T74P-6254-A or equivalent, on the tension spring roll pin and release the belt tensioner. Tighten the adjustment screw to hold the tensioner in the released position.

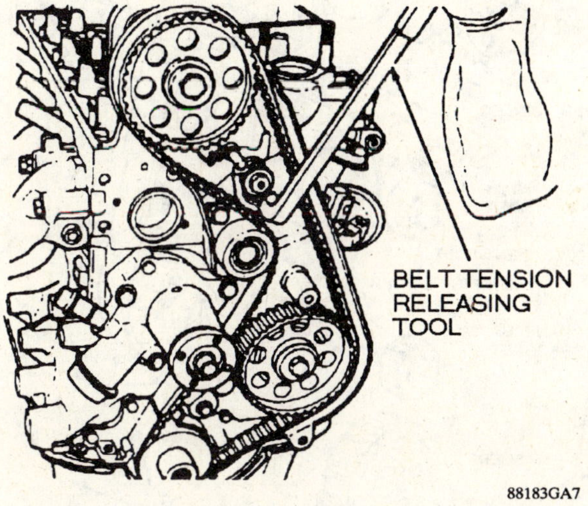

Fig. 135 Use the suitable tool to release belt tension

5. Remove the crankshaft pulley, hub and belt guide. Remove the timing belt. If the belt is to be reused, mark the direction of rotation so it may be reinstalled in the same direction.

To install:

6. Position the crankshaft sprocket to align with the TDC mark and the camshaft sprocket to align wit the camshaft timing pointer.
7. Install the timing belt over the crankshaft sprocket, then counterclockwise over the auxiliary shaft and the camshaft sprockets. Align the belt fore-and-aft so that it is centered on the sprockets.
8. Loosen the tensioner adjustment bolt to allow the tensioner to move against the belt. If the spring does not have enough tension to move the roller against the belt, it may be necessary to manually push the roller against the belt and tighten the bolt.
9. To make sure the belt does not jump time during rotation in the next step, remove a spark plug from each cylinder.
10. Rotate the crankshaft two complete turns in the direction of normal rotation to remove any slack from the belt. Tighten the tensioner adjustment to 29-40 ft. lbs. (40-55 Nm) and pivot bolts to 14-22 ft. lbs. (20-30 Nm). Check the alignment of the timing marks.
11. Install the crankshaft belt guide. Install the crankshaft pulley and tighten the retaining bolt.
12. Install the timing belt front cover, spark plugs and remaining components.
13. Fill the cooling system, then connect the negative battery cable. Start the engine and check for proper operation. Check the coolant level and add if necessary. Check and adjust the ignition timing, if necessary.

Timing Chain

REMOVAL & INSTALLATION

3.8L Engine

1983-87 VEHICLES

➧ See Figures 137, 138 and 139

1. Disconnect the negative battery cable.
2. Remove the timing chain front cover, as outlined earlier in this section.
3. Remove the timing indicator. Remove the front cover and water pump assembly.
4. Remove the camshaft thrust button and spring from the end of the camshaft. Remove the camshaft sprocket attaching bolts.
5. Remove the camshaft sprocket, crankshaft sprocket and timing chain by pulling forward evenly on both sprockets. If the crankshaft sprocket is difficult to remove, position two small prybars, one on each side, behind the sprocket and pry forward.

To install:

6. Clean all gasket surfaces on the front cover, cylinder block, fuel pump and oil pan.
7. Install a new front cover oil seal. If a new front cover is to be installed:
    a. Install the oil pump, oil filter adapter and intermediate shaft from the old cover.
    b. Remove the water pump from the old cover.
    c. Clean the mounting surface, install a new mounting gasket and the pump on the new front cover. Pump attaching bolt torque is 13-22 ft. lbs.
8. Rotate the crankshaft, if necessary, to bring No. 1 piston to TDC with the crankshaft keyway at the 12 o'clock position.
9. Lubricate the timing chain with motor oil. Install the chain over the two gears making sure the marks on both gears are positioned across from each other. Install the gears and chain on the cam and crankshaft. Install the camshaft mounting bolts. Tighten the bolts to 15-22 ft. lbs. (20-30 Nm).
10. Install the camshaft thrust button and spring. Lubricate the thrust button with polyethylene grease before installation.

****WARNING**

The thrust button and spring must be bottomed in the camshaft seat and must not be allowed to fall out during front cover installation.

11. Position a new cover gasket on the front of the engine and install the cover and water pump assemblies. Install the timing indicator. Torque the front cover bolts to 15-22 ft. lbs. (20-30 Nm).
12. Install the remaining components as outlined under the Timing Chain Front Cover procedure, located in this section.
13. Connect the negative battery cable. Fill the crankcase with the proper type and amount of engine oil. Fill the engine cooling system with the correct quantity and type of coolant.
14. Start the engine and check for leaks.

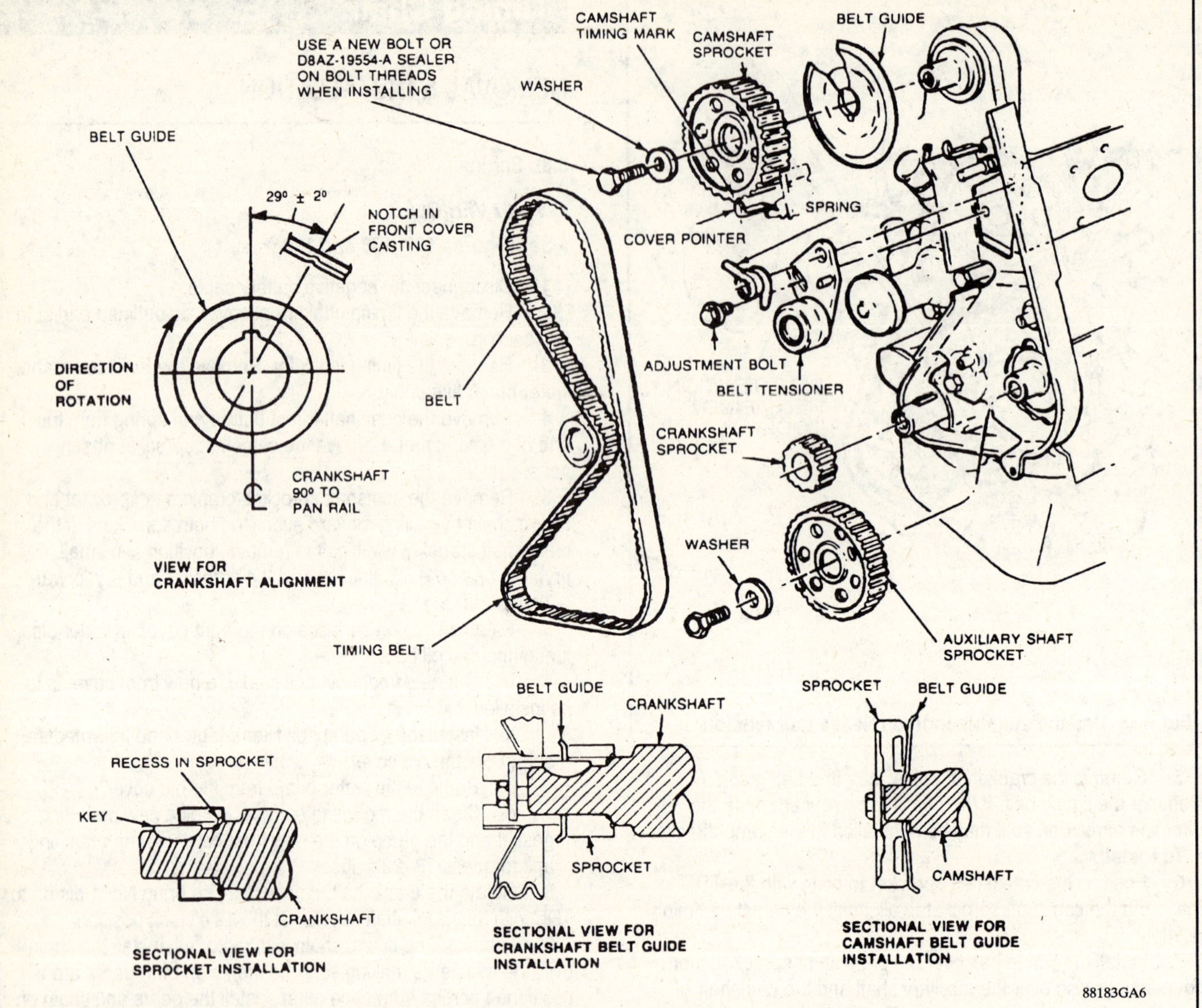

Fig. 136 Exploded view of the timing belt, sprockets and related components — 2.3L engine

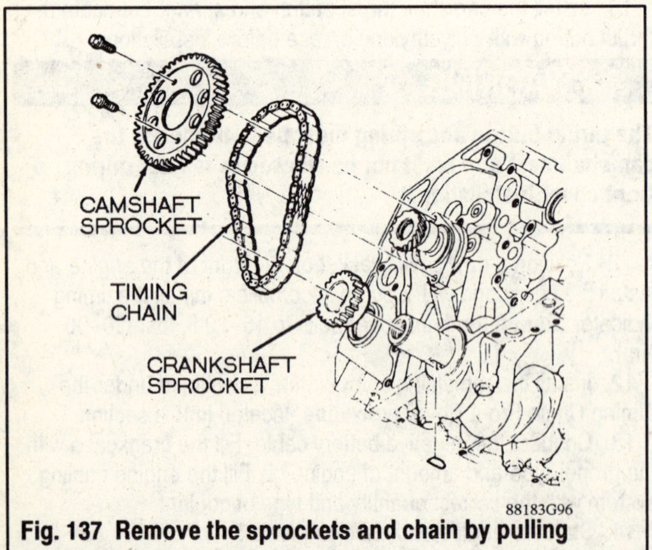

Fig. 137 Remove the sprockets and chain by pulling forward evenly on both sprockets

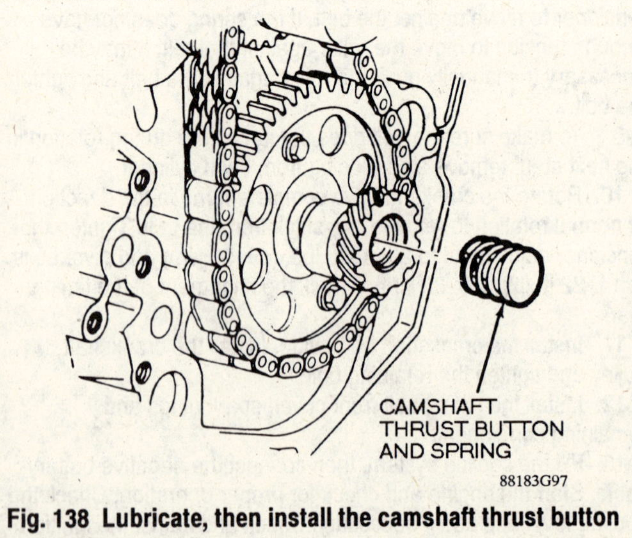

Fig. 138 Lubricate, then install the camshaft thrust button and spring

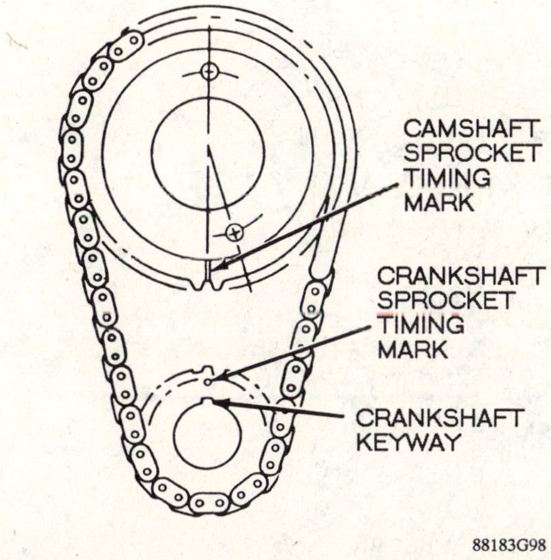

Fig. 139 Timing mark alignment — 1983-87 3.8L engines

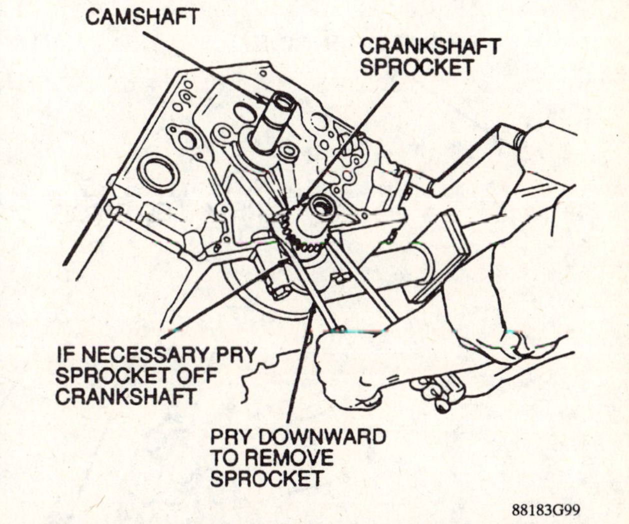

Fig. 140 If the crankshaft sprocket is difficult to remove, pry the sprocket off the shaft using a pair of prytools positioned on both sides of the crankshaft sprocket

1988-96 VEHICLES

➧ See Figures 140, 141 and 142

1. Disconnect the negative battery cable.
2. Remove the timing chain front cover, as outlined earlier in this section.
3. Unfasten the camshaft sprocket retainer bolt and washer from the end of the camshaft.
4. Remove the distributor drive gear.
5. Remove the camshaft and crankshaft sprockets and the timing chain by pulling forward evenly on both sprockets. If the crankshaft sprocket is difficult to remove, position two small prybars, one on each side, behind the sprocket and pry forward.

➥ The engine front cover contains the oil pump gears and water pump. If a new engine front cover is to be installed, remove the water pump and oil pump gears from the oil engine front cover.

6. Remove the timing chain vibration damper from the front of the cylinder block. This requires pulling back on the ratcheting mechanism, then install the pin through the hole in the bracket to relieve tension.

To install:

7. Rotate the crankshaft, as necessary to bring No. 1 piston to TDC with the crankshaft keyway at the 12 o'clock position.
8. Lubricate the timing chain with motor oil.
9. Install the camshaft and crankshaft sprockets and the timing chain. Make sure the timing marks line up across from each other.
10. Install the bolt and washer assembly at the end of the camshaft. Tighten the bolt to 30-37 ft. lbs. (41-50 Nm).
11. Install the remaining components as outlined under the Timing Chain Front Cover procedure, located in this section.
12. Connect the negative battery cable. Fill the crankcase with the proper type and amount of engine oil. Fill the engine cooling system with the correct quantity and type of coolant.
13. Start the engine and check for leaks.

4.6L Engine

➧ See Figures 143, 144, 145, 146, 147, 148, 149, 150 and 151

✱✱WARNING

At no time, when the timing chain(s) are removed and the cylinder head installed, may the crankshaft and/or camshafts be rotated. Failure to heed this warning will result in valve and/or piston damage.

Because this is not a free-wheeling engine, if it has "jumped free" there will be damage to the valves and/or pistons and will require the removal of the cylinder heads. The camshaft sprockets should only be disassembled from the camshafts when one of the components is being replaced.

1. Disconnect the negative battery cable.
2. Remove the valve covers, oil pan and timing chain front cover, as outlined in this section.
3. Remove the Crankshaft Position (CKP) sensor pulse wheel.
4. Rotate the engine to No. 1 Top Dead Center (TDC).

➥ This will prevent accidental rotations of the camshafts.

5. Install Cam Positioning Tool Adapters T92P-6256-A and Cam Positioning Tools T91P-6256-A on the flats of the camshafts.
6. Unfasten the two bolts retaining the right-side timing chain tensioner to the cylinder, then remove the tensioner.
7. Remove the right-side timing chain tensioner arm.
8. Remove the two bolts retaining the right-side timing chain guide to the cylinder head and remove the timing chain guide.
9. Remove the right-side timing chain from the camshaft and crankshaft sprockets.

➥ Cam Positioning Tool Adapters T92P-6256-A and Cam Positioning Tools T91P-6256-A MUST be installed on the camshaft to prevent it from turning.

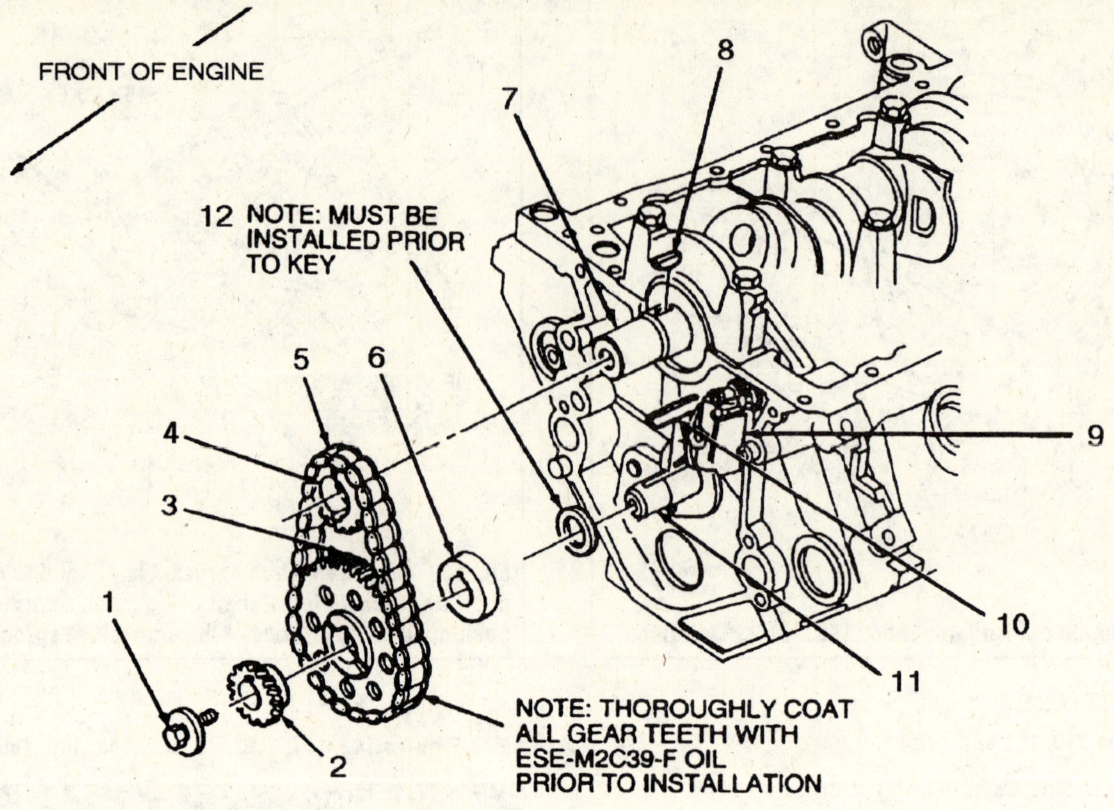

1. Camshaft sprocket retaining bolt and washer Tighten to 40-50 Nm (30-37 lb. ft.)
2. Distributor drive gear
3. Camshaft sprocket
4. Crankshaft sprocket
5. Timing chain
6. Engine balance shaft gear spacer
7. Crankshaft
8. Crankshaft key
9. Timing chain vibration damper
10. Camshaft sprocket key
11. Camshaft
12. Camshaft sprocket spacer

88183GA1

Fig. 141 Timing chain and sprocket removal — 1995 3.8L engine shown

10. Remove the two bolts retaining the left-side timing chain tensioner to the cylinder head, then remove the timing chain tensioner.
11. Remove the left-side timing chain tensioner arm.
12. Unfasten the two bolts retaining the left-side timing chain guide to the cylinder head and remove the timing chain guide.
13. Remove the left-side timing chain from the camshaft and crankshaft sprockets.
14. If necessary, remove the camshaft and crankshaft sprockets.

****WARNING**

Do NOT rotate the crankshaft and/or camshafts or engine damage may occur.

15. Inspect the plastic running face on the timing chain tensioner arms and timing chain guides. If worn or damaged, remove and clean the oil pan and oil pump screen cover and tube.

➥ If the engine has "jumped time", make sure that all repairs to the engine components and/or valve train have been made. Then, rotate the engine counterclockwise 45 degrees. This will position all pistons below the top of the deck face. Install the cylinder heads as outlined.

To install:

➥ Cam Positioning Tool Adapters T92P-6256-A and Cam Positioning Tools T91P-6256-A MUST be installed on the camshaft to prevent it from turning.

16. Install the timing chain guides (both sides) and secure with the retaining bolts. Tighten the bolts to 71-106 inch lbs. (8-12 Nm).
17. If removed, position the left-side camshaft sprocket spacer and sprocket on the camshaft.
18. Install the washer and the camshaft sprocket retaining bolt, but do not tighten at this time.
19. If removed, position the right-side camshaft sprocket spacer and sprocket on the camshaft.
20. Install the washer and the camshaft sprocket retaining bolt, but do not tighten at this time.

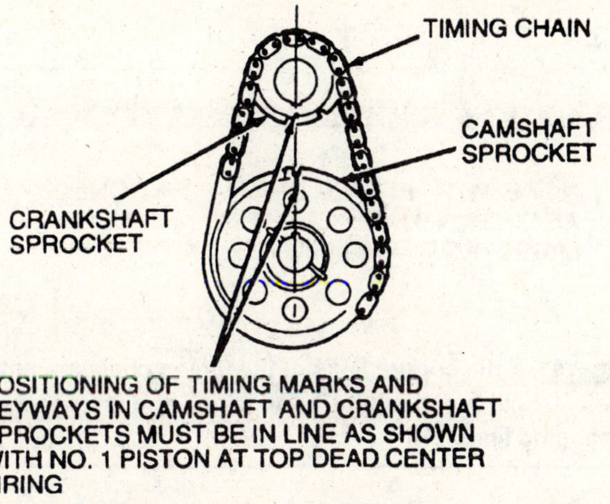

88183GA2

Fig. 142 When installing the timing chain, make sure the timing marks line up across from each other

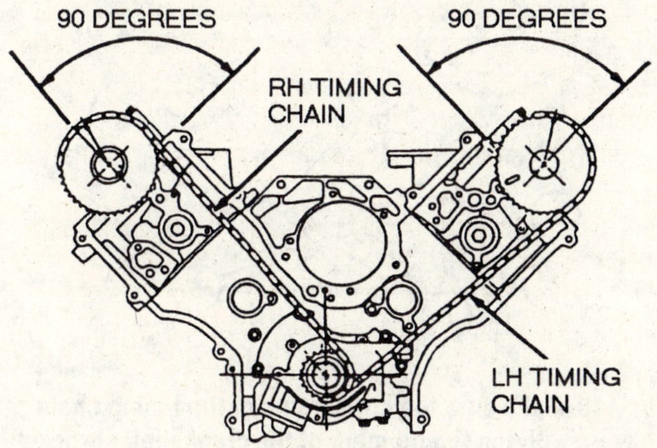

88183GA8

Fig. 143 Rotate the engine to TDC

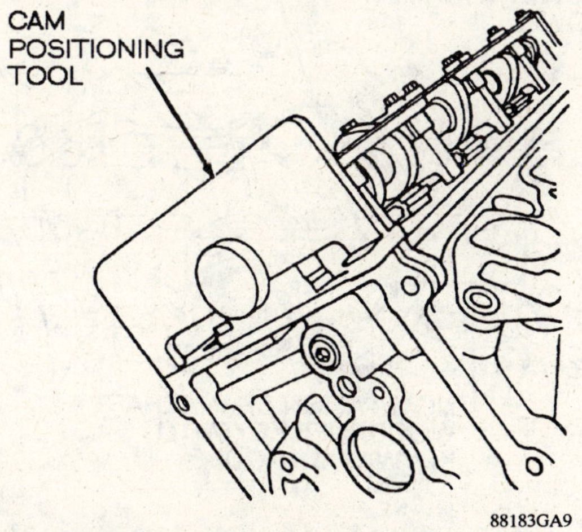

88183GA9

Fig. 144 These tools MUST be installed to prevent accidental rotation of the camshafts

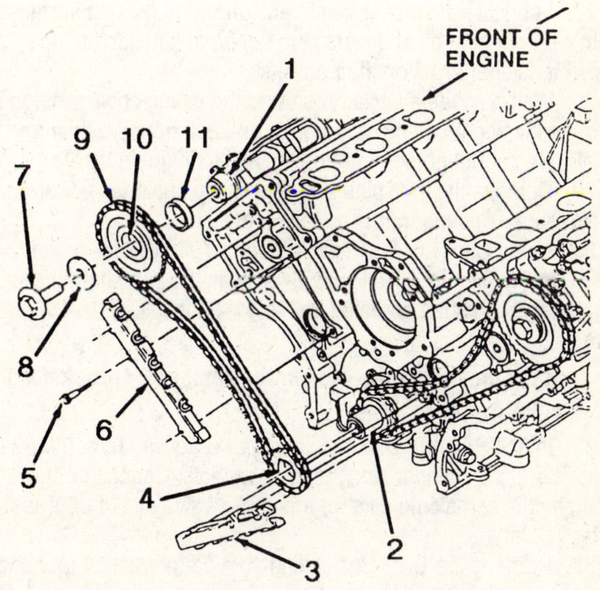

1. Camshaft
2. Crankshaft
3. Timing chain guide (LH)
4. Crankshaft sprocket (2 req'd)
5. Bolt (2 req'd each side)
   Tighten to 8-12 Nm (71-106 lb. in.)
6. Timing chain guide (RH)
7. Bolt (1 req'd each side)
   Tighten to 110-130 Nm (81-95 lb. ft.)
8. Washer (1 req'd each side)
9. Timing chain
10. Camshaft sprocket (RH)
11. Camshaft sprocket spacer
    (1 req'd each side)

88183GB1

Fig. 145 Installation of the left and right side timing chains and guides

→ Crankshaft sprockets are identical. They may be installed only one way. Refer to the accompanying illustration for proper crankshaft sprocket installation.

21. If removed, install the left-side crankshaft sprocket.
22. Install the left-side timing chain on the crankshaft sprocket. Make sure the copper link of the timing chain lines up with the timing mark of the crankshaft sprocket.
23. If removed, install right-side crankshaft sprocket. Install the right-side timing chain on the camshaft sprocket. Make sure the copper link of the timing chain lines up with the timing mark of the camshaft sprocket.
24. Install the right-side timing chain on the crankshaft sprocket. Make sure the copper link of the timing chain lines up with the timing mark of the crankshaft sprocket.
25. Install the right and left-side tensioners and secure with two bolts on each. Tighten the bolts to 15–22 ft. lbs. (20–30 Nm).

26. Install Crankshaft Holding Tool T93P-6303-A over the crankshaft and engine front cover alignment dowel, to position the crankshaft.

27. Lubricate the timing chain tensioner arm contact surfaces with clean engine oil and install the right and left-side timing chain tensioner arms on their dowels.

28. With a suitable C-clamp around the timing chain tensioner arm and timing chain guide. remove all slack from the timing chain. Be careful not to bend the timing chain guide.

29. Remove the lock pins from the timing chain tensioners and make sure all timing marks are aligned.

30. Using Cam Position Tool Adapters T92P-6256-A and Cam Positioning Tool T91P-6256-A, align the camshaft, then tighten the camshaft sprocket bolt to 81-95 ft. lbs. (110-130 Nm).

If not at maximum lift, loosen the camshaft sprocket bolt and repeat steps 26-29.

31. Install Rotunda Dial Indicator with Bracketry 014-00282 or equivalent, ins cylinder No. 1 spark plug hole. Check that the camshaft is at maximum lift for the intake valve at 114 degrees after TDC.

32. Remove the Cam Positioning Tool Adapters and Tool and Crankshaft Holding Tool.

33. Install the timing chain front cover, oil pan and valve covers, as outlined in this section.

34. Fill the crankcase with the proper type and quantity of engine oil.

35. Connect the negative battery cable, then start the engine and check for leaks and proper operation.

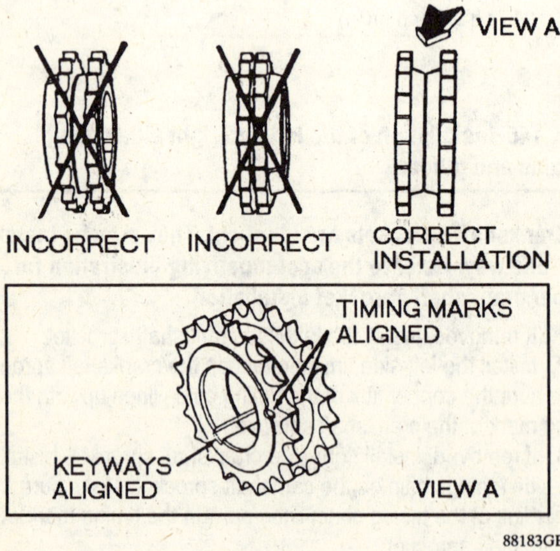

Fig. 146 Make sure the tapered part of the crankshaft sprocket faces away from the cylinder block

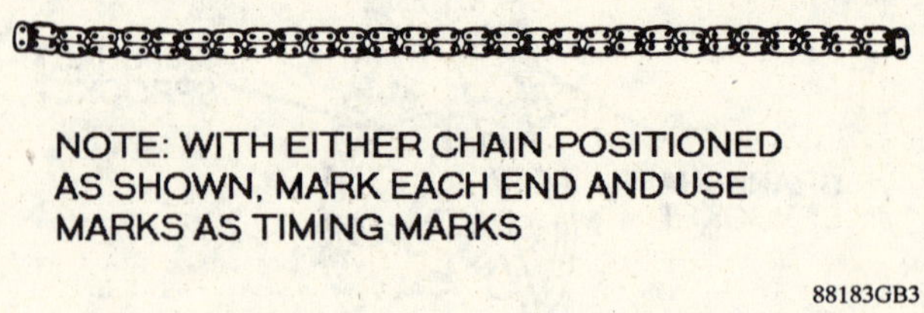

Fig. 147 If the copper links of the timing chain are not visible, split both timing chains in half and mark thethe opposing links

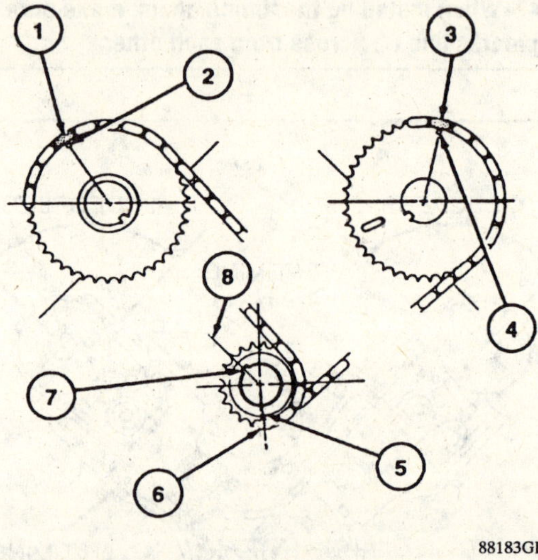

Fig. 148 Make sure the copper link of the timing chain lines up with the timing mark of the crankshaft sprocket

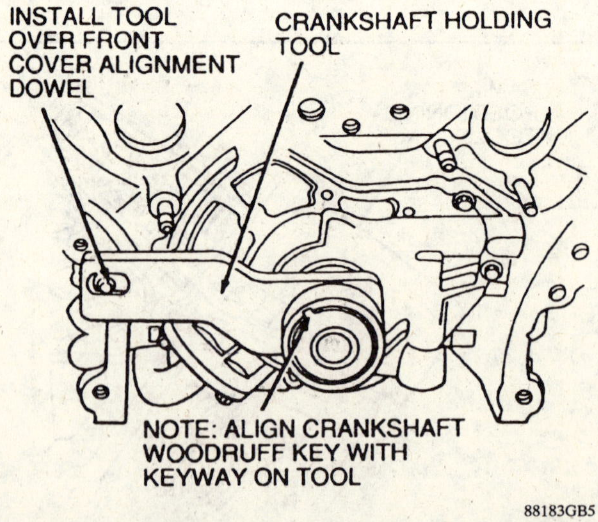

Fig. 149 To position the crankshaft, position the holding tool over the crankshaft and engine front cover alignment dowel

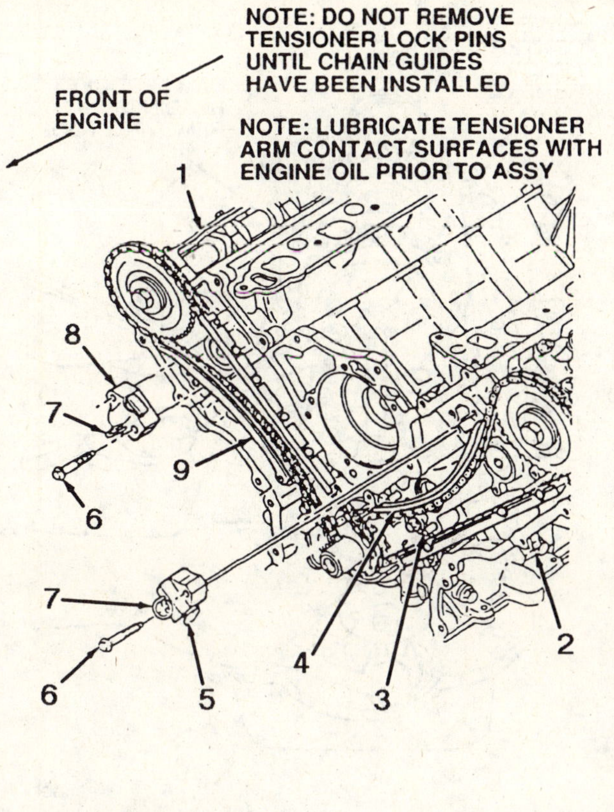

1. Cylinder head (RH)
2. Cylinder head (LH)
3. Dowel
4. Timing chain tensioner arm (LH)
5. Timing chain tensioner (LH)
6. Bolt (2 req'd) - Tighten to 20-30 Nm (15-22 lb. ft.)
7. Lock pin
8. Timing chain tensioner (RH)
9. Timing chain tensioner arm (RH)

88183GB6

Fig. 150 Installation of the timing chain tensioners

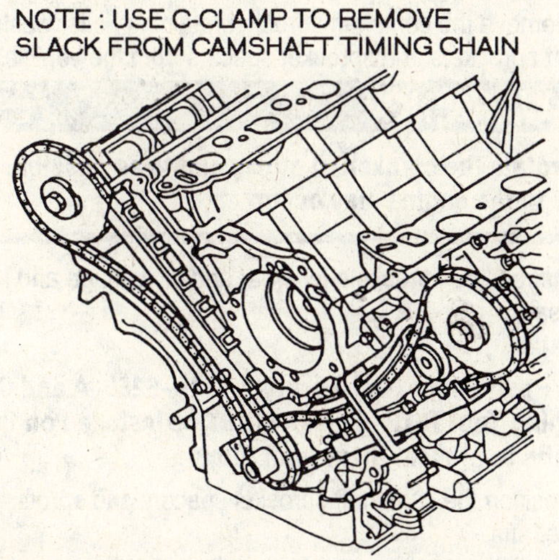

88183GB7

Fig. 151 You must remove any timing chain slack

5.0L Engine

➧ See Figures 152 and 153

1. Disconnect the negative battery cable.
2. Remove the timing chain front cover, as outlined earlier in this section.
3. Crank the engine until the timing marks on the sprockets are positioned.
4. Remove the camshaft sprocket capscrew and washer. Slide both sprockets and the timing chain forward, and remove then as an assembly.

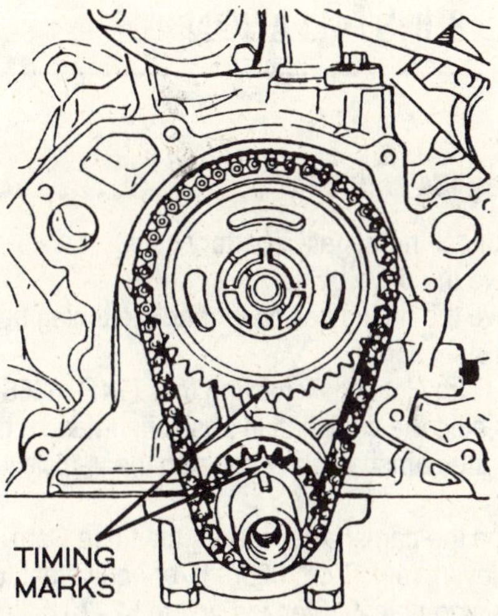

88183GC1

Fig. 152 Crank the engine until the timing marks on the sprockets are positioned

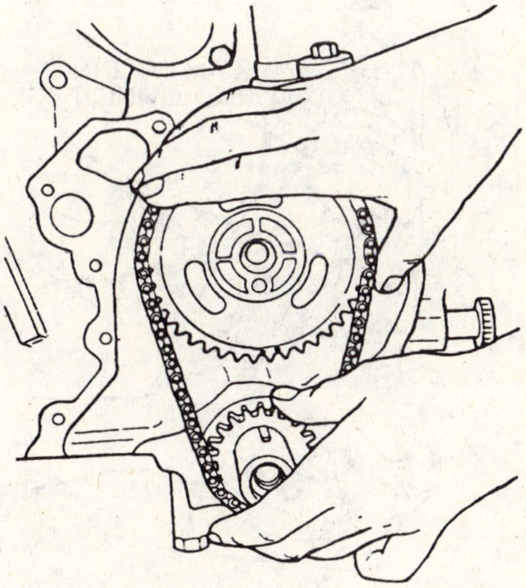

88183GC2

Fig. 153 Carefully slide the timing chain and sprockets off as an assembly

To install:

5. Position the sprockets and timing chain on the camshaft and crankshaft simultaneously. Make sure the timing marks on the sprockets are positioned.
6. Install the washer and camshaft sprocket capscrew. Tighten the capscrew to 40-45 ft. lbs. (54-61 Nm).
7. Install the front cover as outlined earlier in this section.
8. Connect the negative battery cable.
9. Start the engine and operate it at fast idle.
10. Check for leaks, install the air cleaner. Adjust the ignition timing and make all final adjustments.

Camshaft Sprocket

REMOVAL & INSTALLATION

2.3L Engine

➧ See Figures 154 and 155

1. Disconnect the negative battery cable.
2. Remove the drive belt(s).
3. Remove the timing belt cover and the timing belt, as outlined in this section.
4. Using Cam Holding/Removing tool T74P-6256-B, or equivalent to hold the camshaft in position, unfasten the bolts, then remove the camshaft sprocket from the vehicle.

To install:

5. Position the camshaft sprocket, then use Cam Holding/Removing tool T74P-6256-B, or equivalent to install the sprocket retaining bolt. Tighten the bolt to 52-70 ft. lbs. (70-95 Nm).
6. Install the timing belt and cover, as outlined earlier in this section.
7. Install the drive belt(s).
8. Connect the negative battery cable.

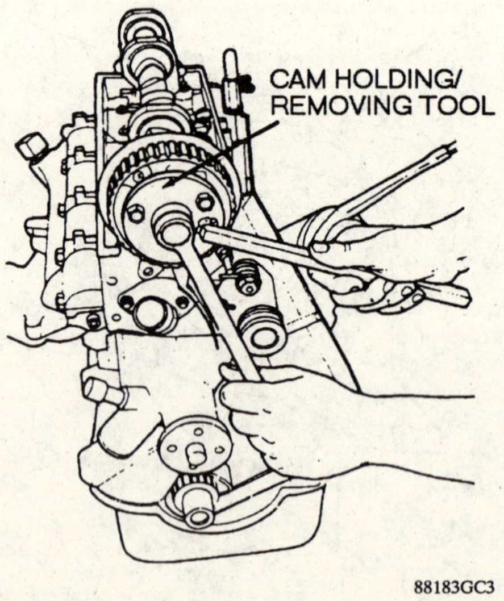

Fig. 154 With the cam holding tool in place, unfasten the sprocket retaining bolt

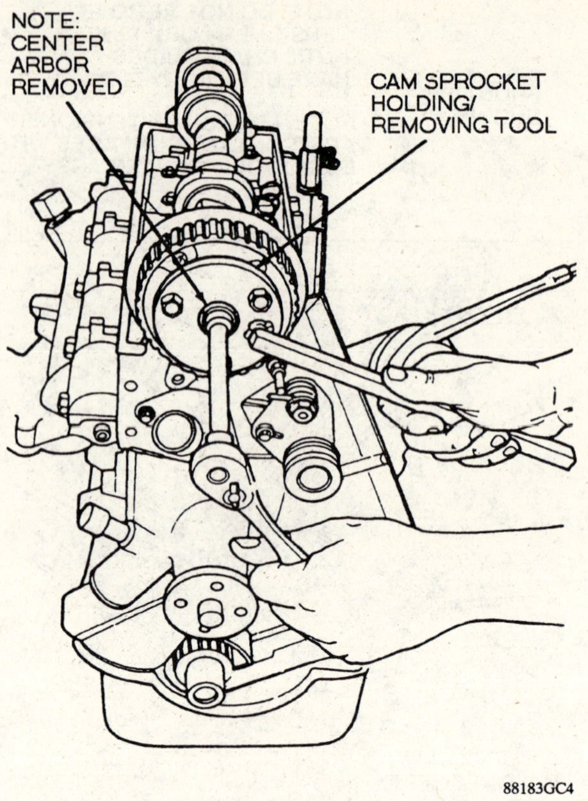

Fig. 155 An extension will be necessary when installing the camshaft sprocket retaining bolt

4.6L Engine

➧ See Figure 156

1. Disconnect the negative battery cable.
2. Remove the timing chains and tensioners as outlined earlier in this section.
3. If necessary, remove the crankshaft sprockets from the crankshaft.

➥ Cam Positioning Tool Adapters T92P-6256-A and Cam Positioning Tool T91P-6256-A MUST be installed on the camshafts to prevent them from turning.

4. Remove the camshaft sprocket retaining bolts, washers, camshaft sprockets and sprocket spacers from the vehicle.

****WARNING**

Do not rotate the crankshaft or camshafts as possible damage to the engine may occur.

5. Inspect the sprockets for wear and/or damage and replace if necessary.

To install:

➥ Cam Positioning Tool Adapters T92P-6256-A and Cam Positioning Tool T91P-6256-A MUST be installed on the camshafts to prevent them from turning.

6. Position the camshaft sprocket spacers and sprockets on the camshafts.
7. Install the washers and camshaft sprocket retaining bolts, but do not tighten at this time.

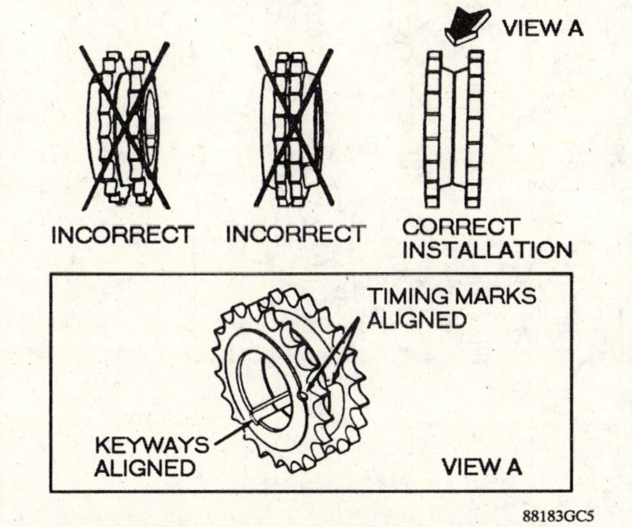

Fig. 156 Correct crankshaft sprocket installation

Crankshaft sprockets are identical and may be installed in only one way.

8. Install the crankshaft sprockets onto the crankshaft.
9. Install the timing chains and tensioners, as outlined earlier in this section.
10. Connect the negative battery cable.

Camshaft

REMOVAL & INSTALLATION

****CAUTION**

When draining the coolant, keep in mind that cats and dogs are attracted by the ethylene glycol antifreeze, and are quite likely to drink any that is left in an uncovered container or in puddles on the ground. This will prove fatal in sufficient quantity. Always drain the coolant into a sealable container. Coolant should be reused unless it is contaminated or several years old.

2.3L Engine

See Figure 157

The following procedure covers camshaft removal and installation with the cylinder head on or off the engine. If the cylinder head has been removed start at Step 9.

1. Properly drain the cooling system into a suitable container.
2. Remove the air cleaner assembly and disconnect the negative battery cable.
3. Tag and disconnect the spark plug wires from the plugs, detach the retainer from the valve cover, then position the wires out of the way.
4. Label and disconnect the rubber vacuum lines as necessary.
5. Remove all drive belts.
6. Unfasten the alternator mounting bracket-to-cylinder head mounting bolts, then position the bracket and alternator out of the way.
7. Disconnect the upper radiator hose. Remove the radiator shroud.
8. Remove the fan blades and water pump pulley and fan shroud. Remove the cam belt and valve covers.
9. Align the engine timing marks at TDC. Remove the timing belt, as outlined earlier in this section.
10. Raise and safely support the vehicle on jackstands.
11. Remove the front engine mount bolts.
12. Disconnect the lower radiator hose from the radiator. If equipped, disconnect and plug the automatic transmission cooler lines.
13. Position a piece of wood on a floor jack and carefully raise the engine as far as it will go. Place blocks of wood between the engine mounts and crossmember pedestals.
14. Remove the rocker arms, as described earlier in this section.
15. Remove the camshaft drive gear and belt guide using a suitable puller. Remove the front oil seal with a sheet metal screw and slide hammer.
16. Remove the camshaft retainer located on the rear mounting stand, by removing the two bolts.
17. Remove the camshaft by carefully withdrawing it toward the front of the engine. Caution should be used to prevent damage to the cam bearings, lobes and journals.

To install:

18. Check the camshaft journals and lobes for wear. Inspect the cam bearings. If they are worn, the cylinder head must be removed for new bearings to be installed by a machine shop.
19. Install the camshaft. Caution should be used to prevent damage to the cam bearings, lobes and journals. Coat the camshaft with heavy clean engine oil before sliding it into the cylinder head.
20. Install the camshaft retainer located on the rear mounting stand.
21. Install a new front oil seal.
22. Install the camshaft drive gear and belt guide. Apply a coat of sealer or Teflon® tape to the cam drive gear bolt before installation.
23. Install the rocker arms, as described earlier in this section.
24. Remove the blocks of wood between the engine mounts and crossmember pedestals and carefully lower the engine onto the mounts.
25. Carefully lower the vehicle.
26. Install the front engine mount bolts.
27. Connect the lower radiator hose at the radiator.
28. Unplug and connect the automatic transmission cooler lines.
29. Align the engine timing marks at TDC.
30. Install the cam drive belt.
31. Install the cam belt and valve covers.
32. Install the fan blades and water pump pulley and fan shroud.
33. Connect the upper radiator hose.
34. Install the alternator and mounting bracket on the cylinder head.
35. Install all drive belts.
36. Attach the spark plug wires to the plugs, as tagged during removal.

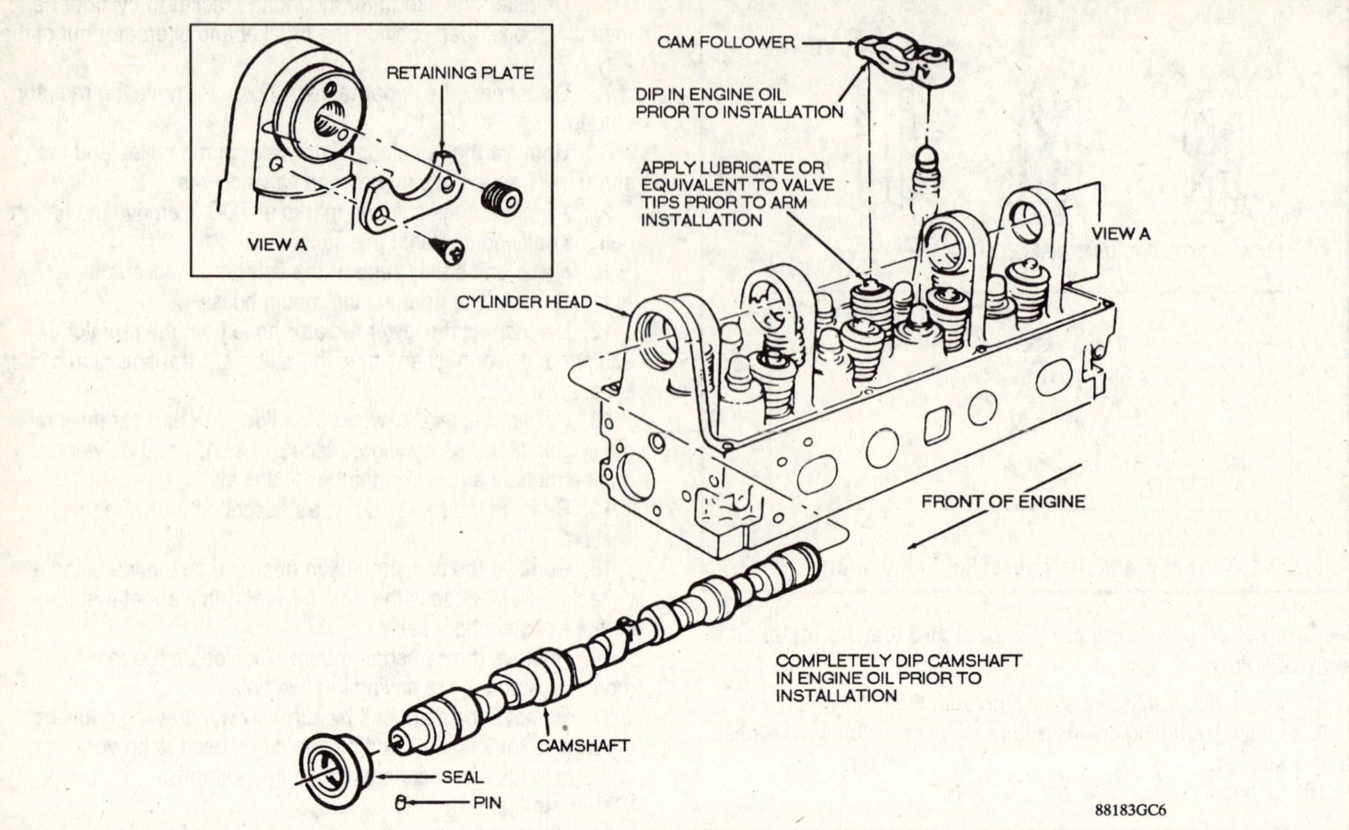

Fig. 157 Exploded view of the camshaft removal and related components

37. Fasten the plug wires to the retainer on the valve cover.
38. Connect the rubber vacuum lines, as labelled during removal.
39. Fill the cooling system with the correct type and amount of coolant.
40. Install the air cleaner assembly.
41. Connect the negative battery cable, then start the engine and check for leaks and/or proper operation.

****WARNING**

After any procedure requiring removal of the rocker arms, each lash adjuster must be fully collapsed after assembly, then released. This must be done before the camshaft is turned. See Valve Clearance — Hydraulic Valve Lash Adjusters.

3.8L Engine

See Figure 158

1. Disconnect the negative battery cable. Properly drain the cooling system and engine oil into suitable containers.
2. Remove or reposition the radiator, as necessary.
3. If equipped with A/C, remove the A/C condenser core, auxiliary cooling fan motor/fan assembly and fan shroud as an assembly.
4. Remove the radiator grille.
5. Remove the intake manifold, as outlined earlier in this section.
6. Remove the valve tappets, valve tappet guide plates and tappet guide plate and retainer. Make sure to keep all parts in order for reassembly.
7. Remove the timing chain front cover and timing chain as previously described in this section.
8. Remove the camshaft sprocket and engine balance shaft gear spacer.
9. As outlined earlier, remove the oil pan from the vehicle.
10. Remove the camshaft thrust plate or button and spring, then carefully remove the camshaft by pulling toward the front of the engine. Be careful not to damage the camshaft bearing surfaces and lobes.
11. Inspect the camshaft for damage and replace if necessary.

To install:

Lightly oil all bolt and stud bolt threads before installation, except those specifying special sealant.

12. Inspect the camshaft rear bearing cover for damage or leakage and replace if necessary.
13. Before installing, lubricate the camshaft lobes and bearing surfaces with Engine Assembly Lubricant D9AZ-19579, or equivalent.
14. Install the camshaft, being careful not to damage the bearing surfaces and lobes while sliding it into position.
15. Position the camshaft thrust plate with the groove towards the cylinder block. Tighten the bolts to 71-124 inch lbs.l (8-14 Nm).
16. Install the engine balance shaft gear spacer, timing chain, camshaft sprocket and timing chain front cover.
17. Install the oil pan, as outlined earlier in this section.
18. Install the valve tappet guide plate and retainer, valve tappet guide plates and valve tappets.
19. As outlined in this section, install the intake manifold.
20. Install the radiator grille.

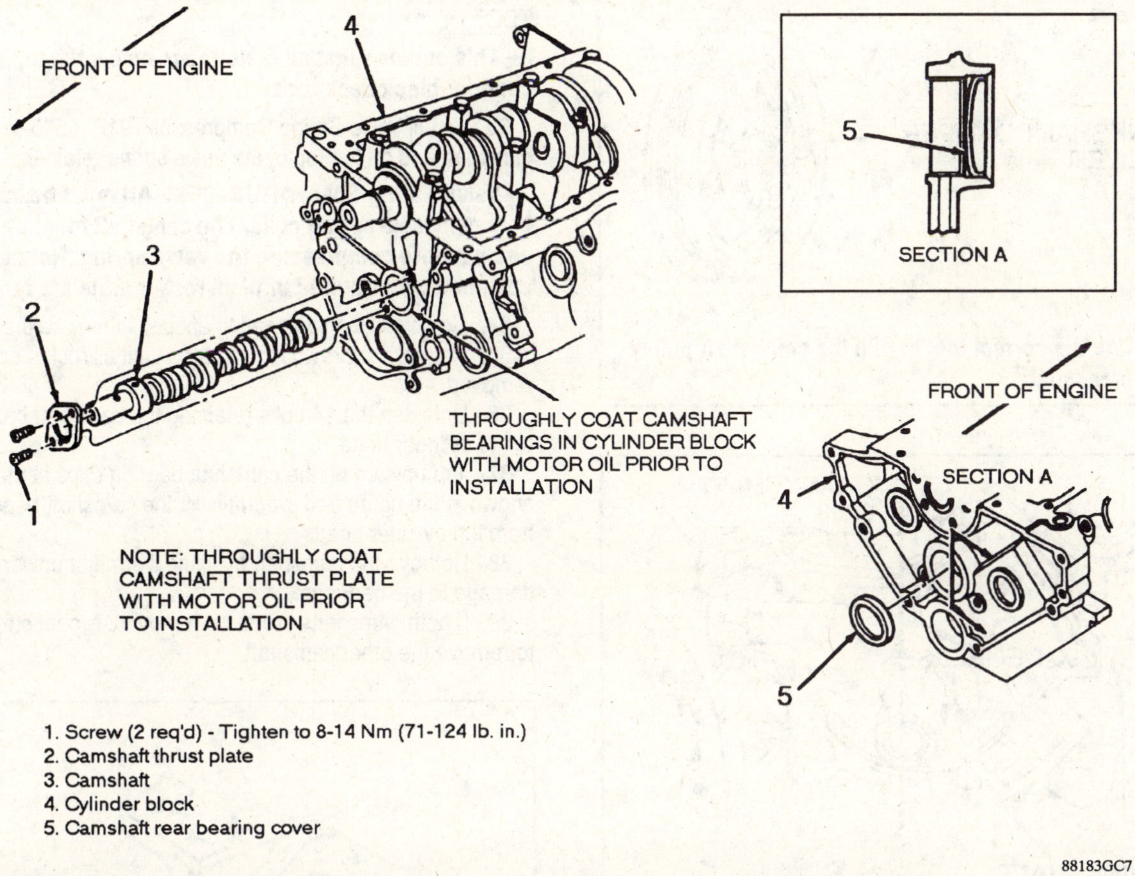

Fig. 158 When removing the camshaft, make sure not to damage the bearing surfaces or cam lobes

21. If equipped with A/C, install the A/C condenser core.
22. Install the radiator and cooling fan motor/blade and fan shroud assembly.
23. Fill the crankcase and cooling system to the proper levels with the correct type of fluids.
24. Connect the negative battery cable, then start the engine and check for leaks and/or proper operation. Check the fluid levels and add if necessary.

4.6L Engine

See Figures 159, 160, 161, 162, 163, 164 and 165

1. Disconnect the negative battery cable.
2. Remove the cooling fan motor/fan blade and fan shroud assembly.
3. Properly relieve the fuel system pressure, as outlined in Section 5 of this manual.
4. Disconnect the fuel lines.
5. Remove the air cleaner outlet tube.
6. Release the tensioner, then remove the drive belt.

****WARNING**

Do NOT pull on the spark plug wire, as it may separate from the connector in the wire boot.

7. Tag and disconnect the spark plug wires from the plugs. Detach the spark plug wire and brackets from the valve cover studs.
8. Unfasten the two bolts retaining the spark plug wire separator to the ignition coil bracket.
9. Disconnect the fuel charging wiring from both ignition coils and Camshaft Position (CMP) sensor.
10. Remove the three nuts retaining the right side ignition coil bracket to the engine front cover. Remove the ignition coil bracket, ignition coil and wires from the vehicles as an assembly.
11. Unfasten the bolts retaining the power steering oil reservoir to the left side ignition coil bracket and position the reservoir out of the way.
12. Remove the left side ignition coil from the bracket and remove from the vehicle as an assembly with the wires.
13. Unfasten the three nuts retaining the left side ignition coil bracket to the engine front cover, then remove the bracket.
14. Remove the water pump pulley.
15. Remove the PCV valve from the valve cover and position out of the way.
16. Detach the fuel charging wiring at the 42-pin connector and 8-pin connect leading to the Mass Air Flow (MAF) sensor.
17. Remove the nut retaining the A/C line to the right front fender apron.
18. Lift the A/C line and feed the 42-pin connector under the line. Position the connector aside.
19. Disconnect the fuel charging wiring from the Crankshaft Position (CKP) sensor, A/C clutch and EVAP canister purge valves.
20. Raise and safely support the vehicle.

The front lower bolt on the power steering pump will not come all the way out.

21. Remove the bolts retaining the power steering pump to the cylinder block and engine front cover.

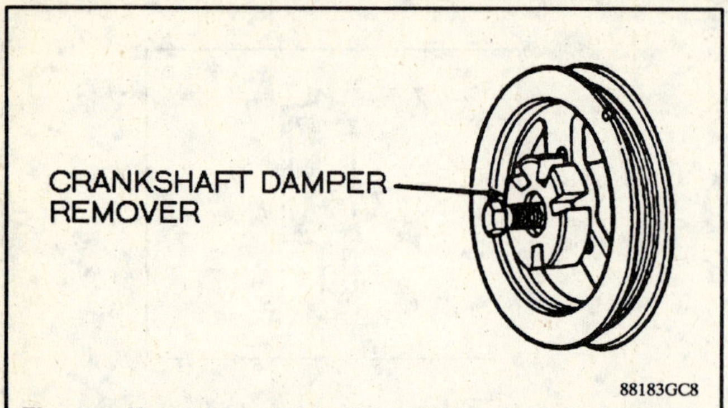

Fig. 159 Use the correct tool to pull the crankshaft pulley from the crankshaft

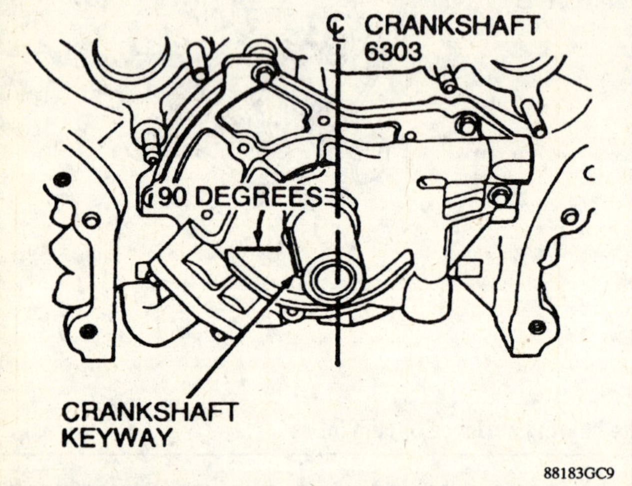

Fig. 160 Rotate the crankshaft counterclockwise 45 degrees from TDC.

22. Wire the power steering pump out of the way.
23. Remove the oil pan and gasket as outlined.
24. Remove the crankshaft pulley bolt and retaining washer from the crankshaft.
25. Install Crankshaft Damper Remover T58P-6316-D on the crankshaft pulley and pull the crankshaft pulley from the crankshaft.
26. Position a suitable drain pan under the oil filter, then remove the filter.
27. Disconnect the fuel charging wiring from the EVO sensor and oil pressure sensor.
28. Remove the oil filter adapter and position the fuel charging wiring out of the way.
29. Unfasten the nine bolts and two stud bolts retaining the right side valve cover to the cylinder head and remove the valve cover.
30. Unfasten the eight bolts and three stud bolts retaining the left side valve cover to the cylinder head, then remove the valve cover.
31. Remove the timing chain cover and timing chains, as outlined earlier in this section.

****WARNING**

Crankshaft must be in this position prior to rotating camshafts or damage to the pistons and/or valve train will result.

32. Rotate the crankshaft counterclockwise 45 degrees from TDC.

This ensures that all pistons are below the top of the cylinder block deck face.

33. Install Valve Spring Compressor T91P-6565-A under the camshaft and on the top of the valve spring retainer.

Valve Spring Spacer T91P-6565-AH must be installed between valve spring coils. The camshaft must be at base circle before compressing the valve spring. Rotate the camshafts as required until all rocker arms are removed.

34. Compress the valve spring enough to remove the rocker arm.
35. Repeat the previous two steps until all rocker arms are removed.
36. Unfasten the 14 bolts retaining the camshaft bearing caps to the cylinder head.
37. Tap upward on the camshaft bearing caps at the position shown in the figure and gradually lift the camshaft bearing caps from the cylinder head.
38. Remove the camshaft by lifting it straight upward to avoid damage to the bearings.
39. If both camshafts are to be removed, repeat steps 33–38 to remove the other camshaft.

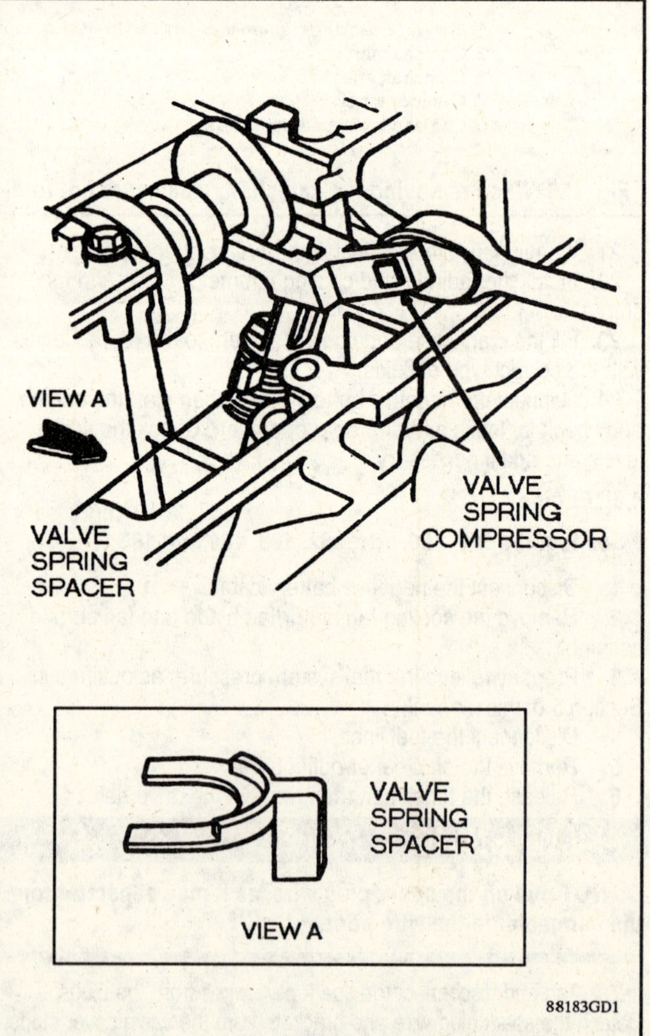

Fig. 161 Install a suitable valve spring compressor

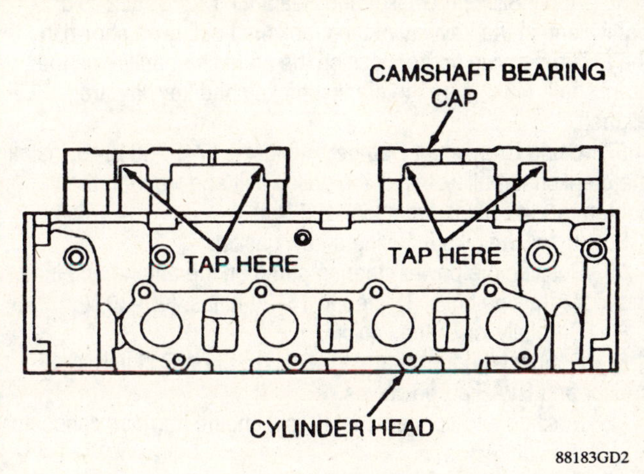

Fig. 162 Positions to tap for bearing removal

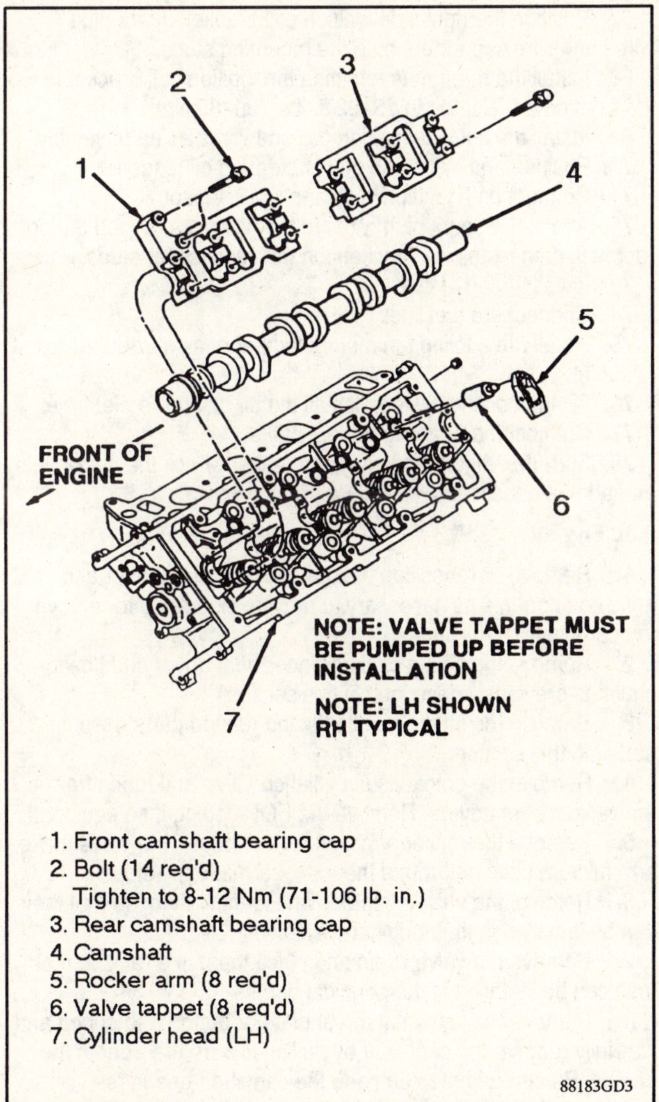

Fig. 163 Camshaft removal and installation — 4.6L engine

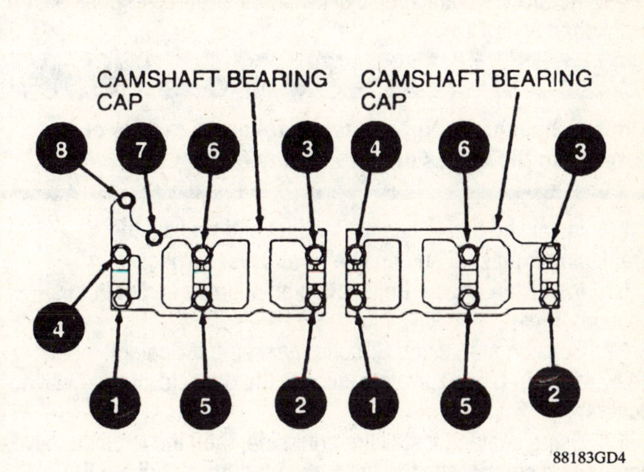

Fig. 164 Camshaft bearing bolt tightening sequence

To install:

40. Clean and inspect the valve cover, engine front cover and cylinder head sealing surfaces.

➡ **Steps 41-48 will install only one camshaft. If both camshafts are being serviced, repeat steps 41-48 to install the other camshaft.**

41. Position the camshaft on the cylinder head. Apply oil to the journals and lobed of the camshaft.
42. Install and seat the camshaft bearing caps. Hand-start the 14 bolts.

➡ **Each camshaft bearing bolt is tightened individually.**

43. Tighten the camshaft bearing bolts, in sequence to 71-106 inch lbs. (8-12 Nm). Loosen the 14 bolts about two turns or until the head of the bolt is free. The camshaft should turn freely with a slight drag. Retighten all bolts, in sequence, to 71-106 inch lbs. (8-12 Nm).
44. Check camshaft end-play using Rotunda Dial Indicator with Bracketry 014-00282 or equivalent.
45. If necessary, install Camshaft Position Tool Adapters T92P-6256-A and Cam Position Tool T91P-6256-A on the flats of the camshaft and install the camshaft sprocket spacer and camshaft sprocket. Install the bolt and washer and tighten to 81-95 ft. lbs. (110-130 Nm).

➡ **Valve Spring Spacer T91P-6565-AH must be installed between the valve spring coils and the camshaft MUST be at base circle prior to compressing the valve spring. Rotate the camshaft as necessary until all rocker arms are installed.**

46. Install Valve Spring Compressor T91P-6565-A under the camshaft and on top of the valve spring retainer. Install the valve tappet.
47. Compress the valve spring far enough to install the rocker arm.
48. Repeat steps 45-47 until all rocker arms are installed. Remove the valve spring spacer.

✲✲WARNING

The crankshaft must only be rotated in the clockwise direction and only as far as Top Dead Center (TDC).

49. Rotate the crankshaft clockwise 45 degrees to position the crankshaft at TDC.

✲✲WARNING

Timing chain procedures must be followed exactly or damage to the valves or pistons may result.

50. Install the timing chains. Inspect and replace the crankshaft front seal and engine front cover as necessary.
51. Install the engine front cover, as outlined earlier in this section.
52. Position and, using Silicone Gasket and Sealant F1AZ-19562-B or equivalent, secure the gaskets into the valve covers.
53. Using sealant, install the right side, then the left side valve covers and secure with the bolts and stud bolts. Tighten the 71-106 inch lbs. (8-12 Nm), no more than four minutes after applying sealer.
54. Raise and safely support the vehicle.
55. Connect the fuel charging wiring to the EVO sensor and oil pressure sensor.

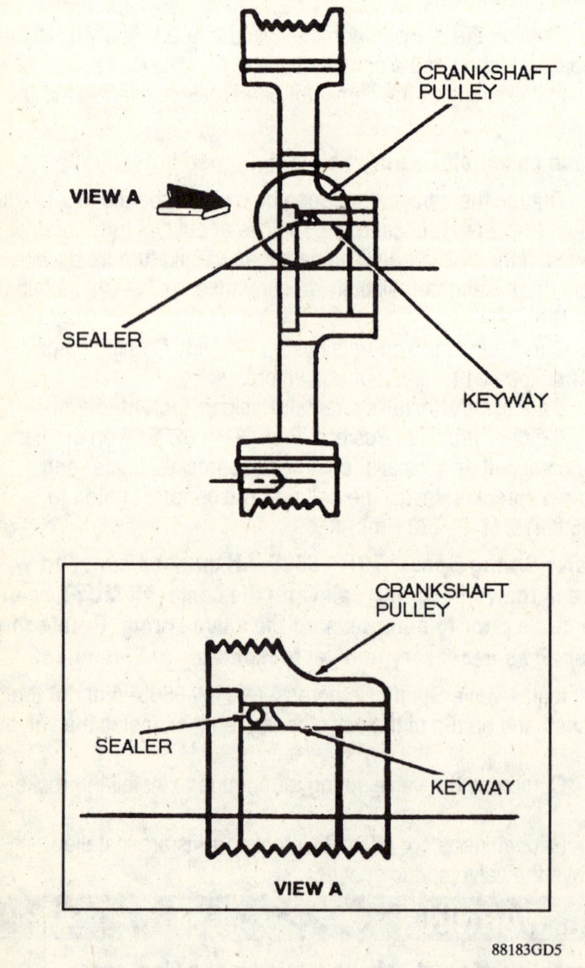

Fig. 165 Apply sealer to the crankshaft pulley keyway

56. Apply Silicone Gasket and Sealant F1AZ-19562-B or equivalent, in the keyway of the crankshaft pulley as shown in the accompanying figure. position the crankshaft pulley on the crankshaft. Make sure the crankshaft key and keyway are aligned.
57. Using Crankshaft Damper Replacer, T74P-6316-B, install the crankshaft pulley. Install the pulley bolt and washer, then tighten to 114-121 ft. lbs. (155-165 Nm).
58. Install the oil pan, using a new gasket.
59. Position the power steering pump on the engine and install the four retaining bolts. Tighten to 15-22 ft. lbs. (20-30 Nm).
60. Carefully lower the vehicle.
61. Connect the fuel charging wiring to the A/C clutch, CKP sensor and EVAP purge valves.
62. Position and connect the 42-pin engine harness connector and 8-pin connector.
63. Position the A/C line and install the retaining nut.
64. Install the PCV valve in the right side valve cover.
65. Connect the vent hose to the EVAP canister purge valve.
66. Install the water pump pulley and tighten the bolts to 15-22 ft. lbs. (20-30 Nm).
67. Position the right side ignition coil bracket, spark plug wires and wire separators onto the mounting studs.
68. Install the three nuts retaining the ignition coil bracket to the front cover. Tighten to 15-22 ft. lbs. (20-30 Nm).
69. Install the left side ignition coil and wires as an assembly.
70. Position and install the power steering oil reservoir.
71. Connect both ignition coils and CMP sensor.
72. Attach the spark plug wires to the plugs, as tagged during removal, then install the brackets on the valve cover studs.
73. Install the drive belt.
74. Connect the fuel lines.
75. Install the cooling fan motor/blade and fan shroud assembly.
76. Fill the cooling system. Install the air cleaner outlet tube.
77. Connect the negative battery cable.
78. Start the engine and check for leaks. Check the fluid levels and add as necessary.

5.0L Engine

1. Remove or reposition the radiator, A/C condenser and grille components as necessary to provide clearance to remove the camshaft.
2. Remove the timing chain/cylinder front cover and timing chain as previously described in this section.
3. Remove the intake manifolds and related parts described earlier in this section.
4. Remove the crankcase ventilation valve and tubes from the valve rocker covers. Remove the EGR cooler, if so equipped.
5. Remove the rocker arm covers and loosen the valve rocker arm fulcrum bolts and rotate the rocker arms to the side.
6. Remove the valve pushrods and identify them so that they can be installed in their original positions.
7. Remove the valve lifters and place them in a rack so that they can be installed in their original bores.
8. Remove the camshaft thrust plate or button and spring and carefully remove the camshaft by pulling toward the front of the engine. Be careful not to damage the camshaft bearings.

To install:

9. Before installing, oil the camshaft journals with heavy engine oil SG and apply Lubriplate® or equivalent to the lobes. Carefully slide the camshaft through the bearings.

10. Install the camshaft thrust plate with the groove towards the cylinder block.
11. Lubricate the lifters with heavy SG engine oil and install in their original bores.
12. Apply Lubriplate® or equivalent to the valve stem tips and each end of the pushrods. Install the pushrods in their original position.
13. Lubricate the rocker arms and fulcrum seats with heavy SG engine oil and position the rocker arms over the push rods.
14. Install all other parts previously removed.
15. Fill the crankcase and cooling system and adjust the timing.

INSPECTION

Degrease the camshaft using safe solvent, clean all oil grooves. Visually inspect the cam lobes and bearing journals for excessive wear. If a lobe is questionable, check all lobes and journals with a micrometer.

Measure the lobes from nose to base and again at 90°. The lift is determined by subtracting the second measurement from the first. If all exhaust lobes and all intake lobes are not identical, the camshaft must be reground or replaced. Measure the bearing journals and compare to specifications. If a journal is worn there is a good chance that the cam bearings are worn too, requiring replacement.

If the lobes and journals appear intact, place the front and rear cam journals in V-blocks and rest a dial indicator on the center journal. Rotate the camshaft to check for straightness. If deviation exceeds 0.001 in. (0.025mm), replace the camshaft.

Auxiliary Shaft

REMOVAL & INSTALLATION

2.3L Engine

➧ See Figure 166

1. Disconnect the negative battery cable.
2. Remove the camshaft drive belt cover.
3. Remove the drive belt. Remove the auxiliary shaft sprocket. A puller may be necessary to remove the sprocket.
4. Remove the distributor and fuel pump.
5. Remove the auxiliary shaft cover and thrust plate.
6. Withdraw the auxiliary shaft from the block.

****WARNING**

The distributor drive gear and the fuel pump eccentric on the auxiliary shaft must not be allowed to touch the auxiliary shaft bearings during removal and installation. Completely coat the shaft with oil before sliding it into place.

To install:

7. Slide the auxiliary shaft into the housing and insert the thrust plate to hold the shaft.
8. Install a new gasket and auxiliary shaft cover.

➔ The auxiliary shaft cover and cylinder front cover share a gasket. Cut off the old gasket around the cylinder cover and use half of the new gasket on the auxiliary shaft cover.

9. Fit a new gasket on the fuel pump and install the pump.

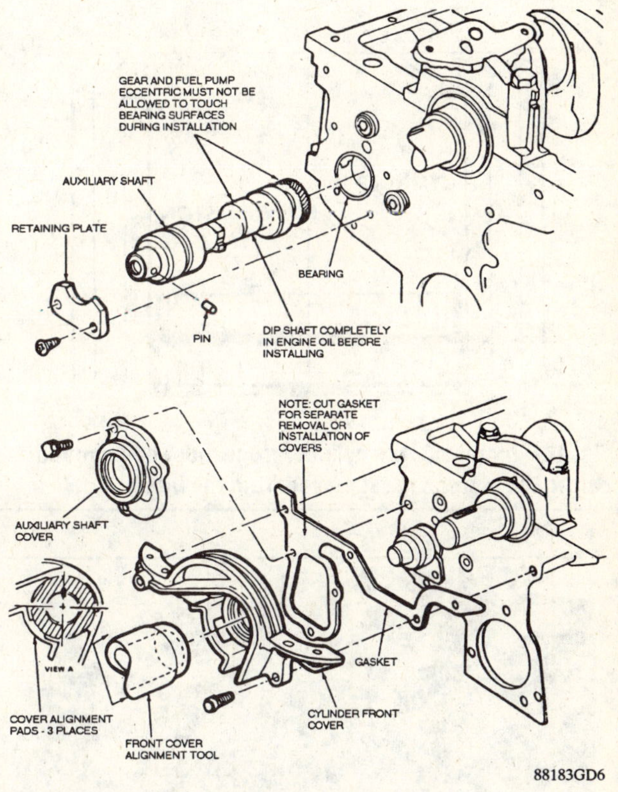

Fig. 166 Auxiliary shaft removal and installation — 2.3L engine

10. Insert the distributor and install the auxiliary shaft sprocket.
11. Align the timing marks and install the drive belt.
12. Install the drive belt cover.
13. Connect the negative battery cable.
14. Check the ignition timing.

Pistons and Connecting Rods

REMOVAL

➧ See Figures 167, 168, 169, 170, 171 and 172

Although in some cases the pistons and connecting rods may be removed with the engine still in the vehicle, it is rarely worth the aggravation, especially when you are not working with a lift. On vehicles where this is possible (cylinder head and oil pan removal are both possible with the engine installed and there is sufficient working clearance) take EXTREME care to assure no dirt or contamination is allowed into the cylinders during assembly and installation.

Before removing the pistons, the top of the cylinder bore must be examined for a ridge. A ridge at the top of the bore is the result of normal cylinder wear, caused by the piston rings only traveling so far up the bore in the course of the piston stroke. If the ridge can be felt by hand; it must be removed before the pistons are removed.

1. Remove cylinder head or heads.
2. Remove the oil pan.

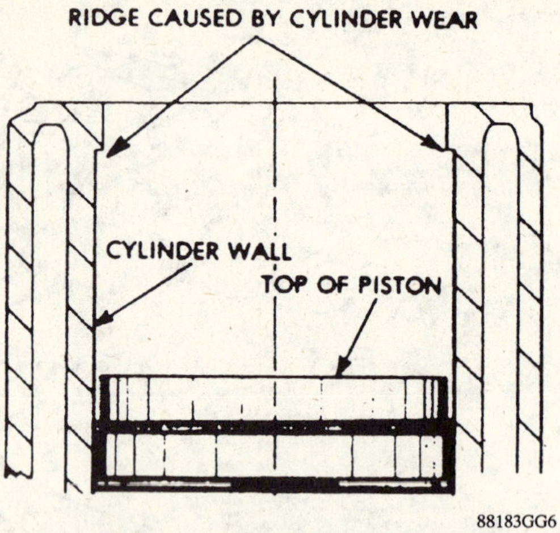

Fig. 167 If present, the cylinder ridge must be removed before the pistons are removed from the block

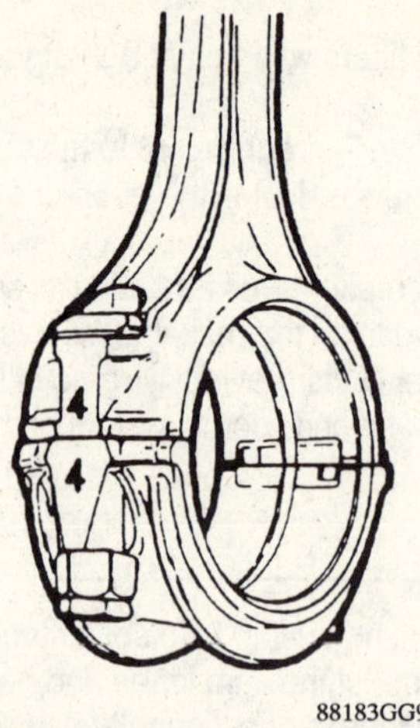

Fig. 170 Match the connecting rods to their cylinders using a number stamp

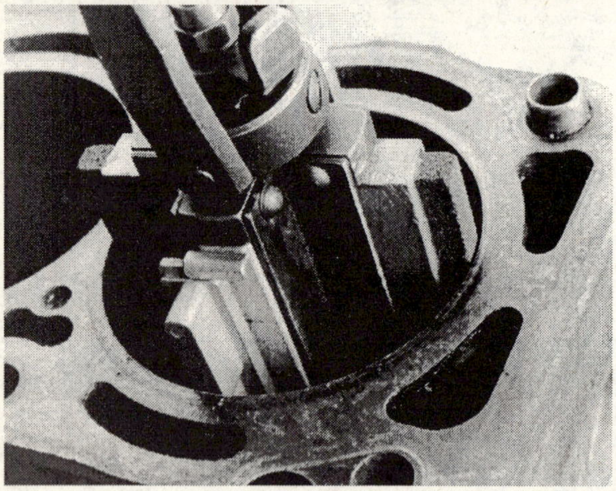

Fig. 168 Removing the ridge from the cylinder bore using a ridge cutter

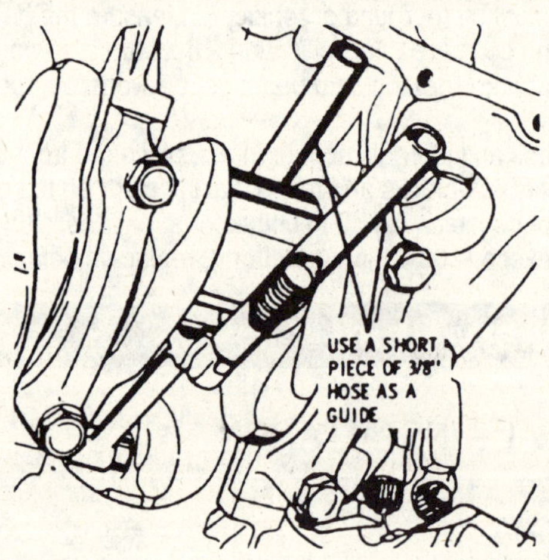

Fig. 171 Cut lengths of rubber hose for connecting rod bolt guides

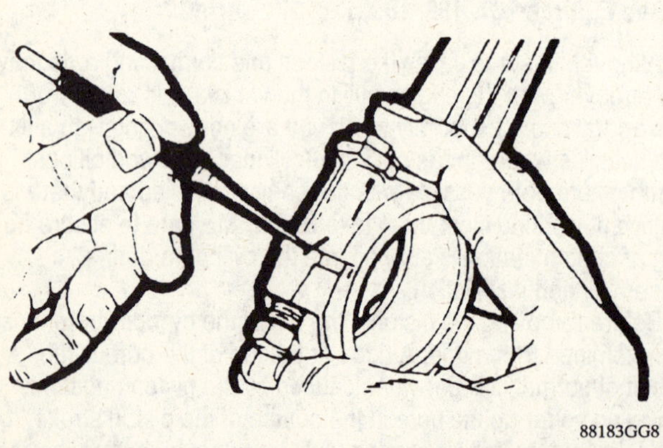

Fig. 169 Match connecting rods to their caps using a scribe mark

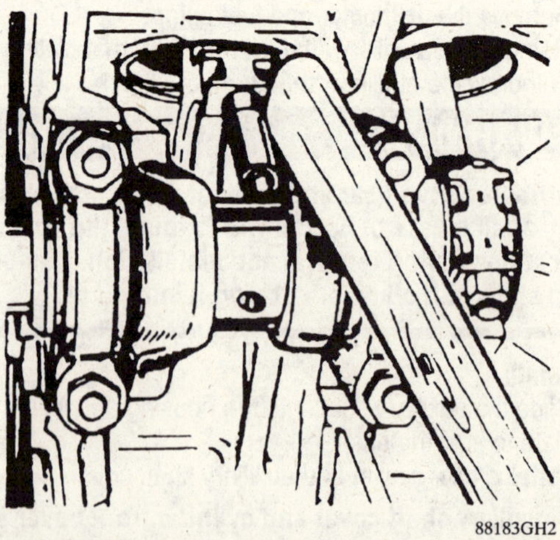

Fig. 172 Carefully tap the piston and rod assembly out using a wooden hammer handle

3. If necessary, remove the oil pump assembly.
4. Matchmark the connecting rod cap to the connecting rod with a scribe; each cap must be reinstalled on its proper rod in the proper direction. Remove the connecting rod bearing cap and the rod bearing. Number the top of each piston with silver paint or a felt-tip pen for reference during assembly.
5. Cut lengths of $^3/_8$ in. (10mm) diameter hose to use as rod bolt guides. Install the hose over the threads of the rod bolts, to prevent the bolt threads from damaging the crankshaft journals and cylinder walls when the piston is removed.
6. Squirt some clean engine oil onto the cylinder wall from above, until the wall is coated. Carefully push the piston and rod assembly up and out of the cylinder by tapping on the bottom of the connecting rod with a wooden hammer handle.
7. Place the rod bearing and cap back on the connecting rod, and install the nuts temporarily.
8. Remove remaining pistons in similar manner.
9. Clean and inspect the engine block, the crankshaft, the pistons and the connecting rods.

CLEANING AND INSPECTION

See Figures 173, 174, 175, 176, 177 and 178

Pistons

A piston ring expander is necessary for removing piston rings without damaging them; any other method (screwdriver blades, pliers, etc.) usually results in the ring being bent, scratched or distorted, or the piston itself being damaged. When the rings are removed, clean the piston grooves using an appropriate ring groove cleaning tool, using care not to cut too deeply. Make sure that all the oil ring holes and slots are clean. Thoroughly clean all carbon and varnish from the piston with a suitable cleaning solvent. DO NOT WIRE BRUSH ANY PART OF THE PISTON.

****WARNING**

Do not use a wire brush or caustic solvent (acids, etc.) on pistons. Inspect the pistons for scuffing, scoring, cracks, pitting, or excessive ring groove wear. If these are evident, the piston must be replaced.

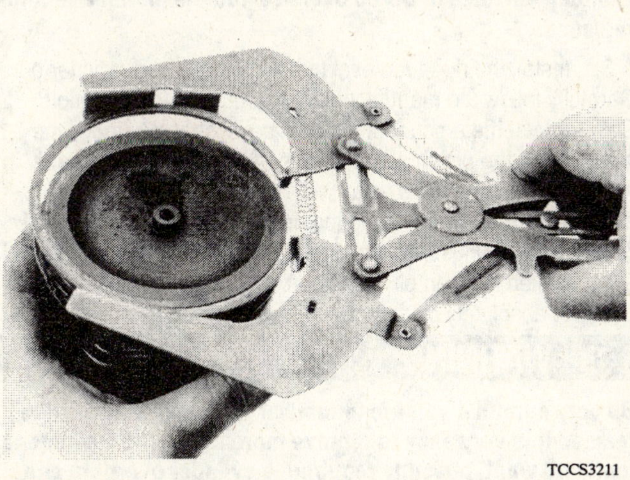

TCCS3211

Fig. 173 Use a ring expander tool to remove the piston rings

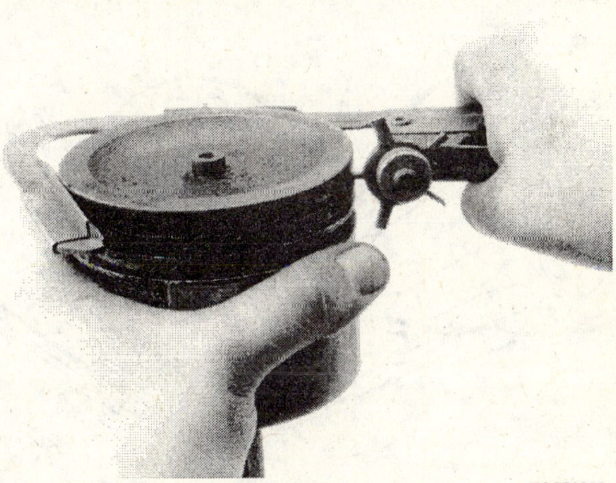

TCCS3208

Fig. 174 Clean the piston grooves using a ring groove cleaner

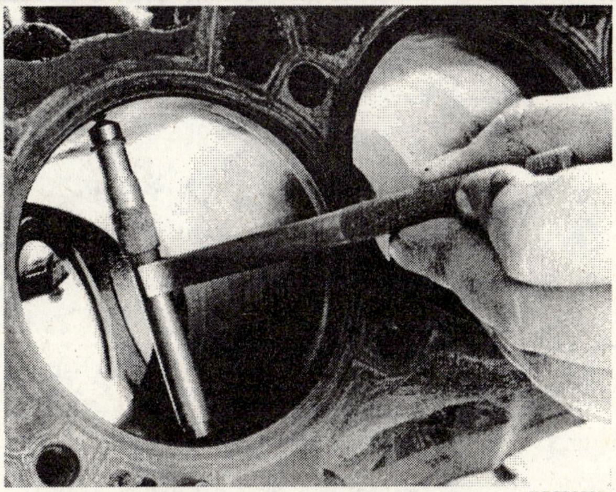

TCCS3209

Fig. 175 A telescoping gauge may be used to measure the cylinder bore diameter

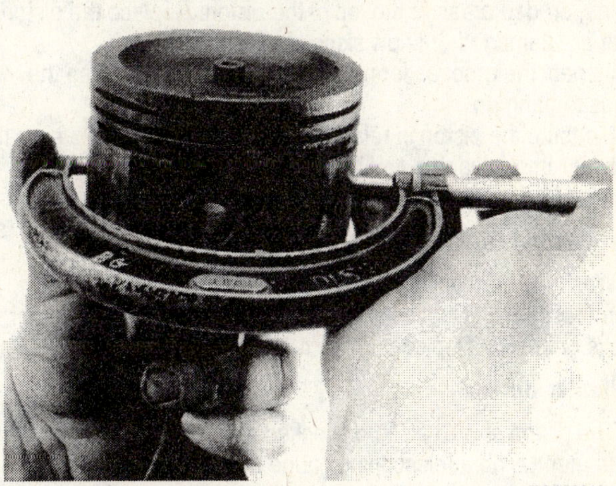

TCCS3210

Fig. 176 Measure the piston's outer diameter using a micrometer

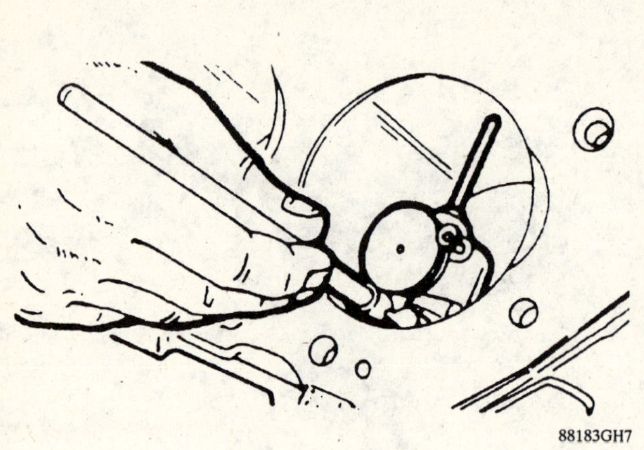

Fig. 177 The cylinder bore may also be measured using a dial gauge

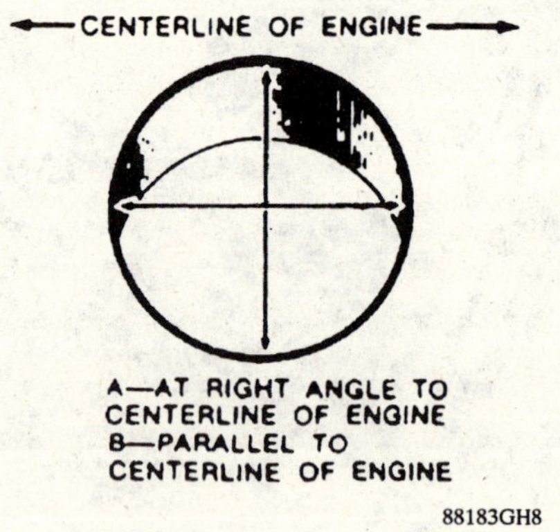

Fig. 178 Cylinder bore measuring points

Inspect the piston for cracked ring lands, scuffed or damaged skirts, eroded areas at the top of the piston. Replace the pistons that are damaged or show signs of excessive wear.

Inspect the grooves for nicks of burrs that might cause the rings to hang up.

Measure the piston in relation to cylinder diameter. Refer to the cylinder bore cleaning and inspection procedures later in this section.

Connecting Rods

Wash the connecting rods in cleaning solvent and dry with compressed air. Check for twisted or bent rods and inspect for nicks or cracks. Replace connecting rods that are damaged.

Cylinder Bores

The piston should also be checked in relation to the cylinder diameter. Using a telescoping gauge and micrometer, or a dial gauge, measure the cylinder bore diameter perpendicular (90 degrees) to the piston pin, about 1–2$^1/_2$ in. (25–64mm) below the cylinder block deck (surface where the block mates with the heads). Then, with the micrometer, measure the piston perpendicular to its wrist pin on the skirt. The difference between the two measurements is the piston clearance.

If the clearance is within specifications or slightly below (after the cylinders have been bored or honed), finish-honing is all that is necessary, If the clearance is excessive, try to obtain a slightly larger piston to bring the clearance within specifications. If this is not possible, obtain the first oversize piston and hone the cylinder or (if necessary) bore the cylinder to size. Generally, if the cylinder bore is tapered more than 0.005 in. (0.127mm) or is out-of-round more than 0.003 in. (0.0762mm), it is advisable to rebore for the smallest possible oversize piston and rings. After measuring, mark the pistons with a felt-tip pen for reference and for assembly.

➥ Boring of the cylinder block should be performed by a reputable machine shop with the proper equipment. In some cases, clean-up honing can be done with the cylinder block in the vehicle, but most excessive honing and all cylinder boring MUST BE done with the block stripped and removed from the vehicle.

RIDGE REMOVAL & HONING

➧ See Figures 179 and 180

1. Before the piston is removed from the cylinder, check for a ridge at the top of the cylinder bore. This ridge occurs because the piston ring does not travel all the way to the top of the bore, thereby leaving an unworn portion of the bore surface.
2. Clean away any carbon buildup at the top of the cylinder with sand paper, in order to see the extent of the ridge more clearly. If the ridge is slight, it will be safe to remove the pistons without damaging the rings or piston ring lands. If the ridge is severe, and easily catches your fingernail, it will have to be removed using a ridge reamer.

➥ A severe ridge is an indication of excessive bore wear. Before removing the piston, check the cylinder bore diameter with a bore gauge, as explained in the cleaning and inspection procedure. Compare your measurement with engine specification. If the bore is excessively worn, the cylinder will have to bored oversize and the piston and rings replaced.

3. Install the ridge removal tool in the top of the cylinder bore. Carefully follow the manufacturer's instructions for operation. Only remove the amount of material necessary to remove the ridge. Place the piston at the bottom of its stroke, and cover it with a rag. Cut the ridge away with the ridge reamer, using extreme care to avoid cutting too deeply. Remove the rag, and remove the cuttings that remain on the piston with a magnet and a rag soaked in clean oil. Make sure the piston top and cylinder bore are absolutely clean before moving the piston.

✲✲WARNING

Be very careful if you are unfamiliar with operating a ridge reamer. It is very easy to remove more cylinder bore material than you want, possibly requiring a cylinder overbore and piston replacement that may not have been necessary.

Fig. 179 Removing cylinder glazing using a flexible hone

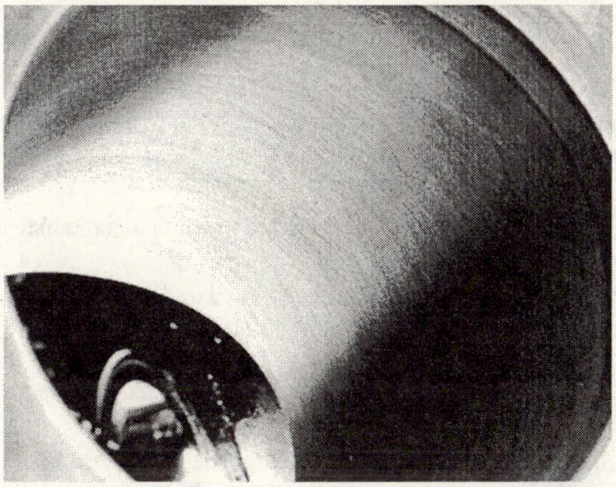

Fig. 180 A properly cross-hatched cylinder bore

4. After the piston and connecting rod assembly have been removed, check the clearances as explained earlier in this section under the cleaning and inspection procedure, to determine whether boring and honing or just light honing are required. If boring is necessary, consult an automotive machine shop. If light honing is all that is necessary, proceed with the next step.
5. Honing is best done with the crankshaft removed, to prevent damage to the crankshaft and to make the post-honing cleaning easier, as the honing process will scatter metal particles. However, if you do not want to remove the crankshaft, position the connecting rod journal for the cylinder being honed as far away from the bottom of the cylinder bore as possible, and wrap a shop cloth around the journal.
6. Honing can be done either with a flexible glaze breaker type hone or with a rigid hone that has honing stones and guide shoes. The flexible hone removes the least amount of metal, and is especially recommended if your piston-to-cylinder bore clearance is on the loose side. The flexible hone is useful to provide a finish on which the new piston rings will seat. A rigid hone will remove more material than the flexible hone and requires more operator skill.
7. Regardless of which type of hone you use, carefully follow the manufacturer's instructions for operation.
8. The hone should be moved up and down the bore at sufficient speed to obtain a uniform finish. A rigid hone will provide a definite cross-hatch finish; operate the rigid hone at a speed to obtain a 45–65 degree included angle in the cross-hatch. The finish marks should be clean but not sharp, free from embedded particles and torn or folded metal.
9. Periodically during the honing procedure, thoroughly clean the cylinder bore and check the piston-to-bore clearance with the piston for that cylinder.
10. After honing is completed, thoroughly wash the cylinder bores and the rest of the engine with hot water and detergent. Scrub the bores well with a stiff bristle brush and rinse thoroughly with hot water. Thorough cleaning is essential, for if any abrasive material is left in the cylinder bore, it will rapidly wear the new rings and the cylinder bore. If any abrasive material is left in the rest of the engine, it will be picked up by the oil and carried throughout the engine, damaging bearings and other parts.
11. After the bores are cleaned, wipe them down with a clean cloth coated with light engine oil, to keep them from rusting.

PISTON PIN REPLACEMENT

****WARNING**

Do not use a wire brush or caustic solvent (Acids, etc.) on pistons. Inspect the pistons for scuffing, scoring, cracks, pitting, or excessive ring groove wear. If these are evident, the piston must be replaced.

➧ See Figures 181, 182, 183 and 184

The engines covered by this manual utilize a piston and pin assembly which is pressed together. Disassembly will require an arbor press, a suitable support and the proper drivers.

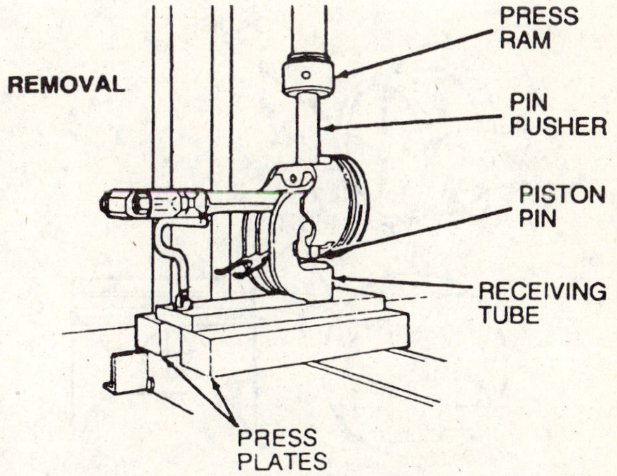

Fig. 181 Use the suitable tool to press the pin from the piston

Use care at all times when handling and servicing the connecting rods and pistons. To prevent possible damage to these units, DO NOT clamp the rod or piston in a vise since they may become distorted. DO NOT allow the pistons to strike one another, against hard objects or bench surfaces, since distortion of the piston contour or nicks in the soft aluminum material may result.

1. Using an arbor press, a fixture/support assembly and Tool T68P–6135– a or equivalent piston pin removal tool, place the piston assembly in the fixture/support tool and press the pin from the piston assembly.

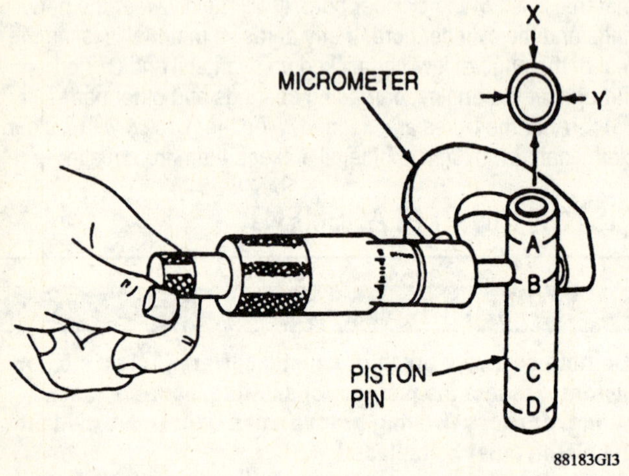

Fig. 182 Use a micrometer to inspect the piston pin diameter in the X and Y directions at points A, B, C and D

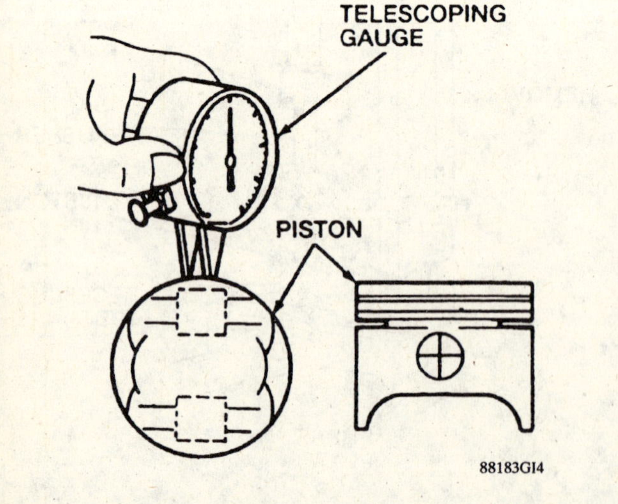

Fig. 183 Measure each piston pin hole diameter at the four points shown

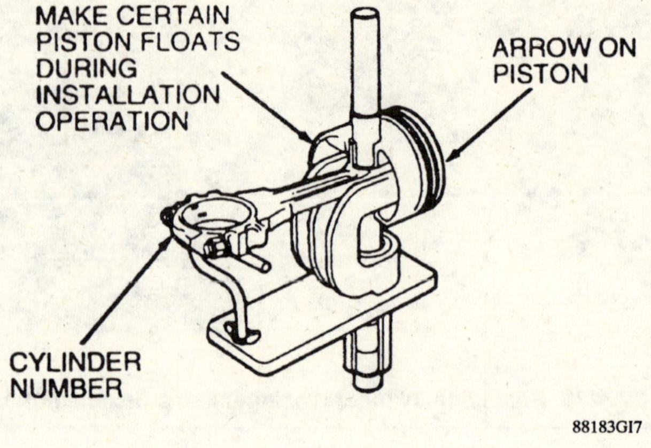

Fig. 184 Using an arbor press and the pin remover and replacer, press the piston pin through the piston until the pin is centered

➥ The piston and the piston pin are a matched set which are not serviced separately.

2. Using a suitable solvent, wash the varnish and oil from the parts, then inspect the parts for scuffing or wear.
3. Using a micrometer, measure the diameter of the piston pin. Using an inside micrometer or a dial bore gauge, measure the diameter of the piston bore.

➥ If the piston pin-to-piston clearance is in excess of 0.001 in. (0.0254mm), replace the piston and piston pin assembly.

To install:

4. Lubricate the piston pin and the piston bore with engine oil.
5. Install the piston pin into the piston assembly, use an arbor press, the fixture/support assembly tool and the piston pin installation tool, then press the piston pin into the piston/connecting rod assembly.

➥ When installing the piston pin into the piston/connecting rod assembly and the installation tool bottoms onto the support assembly, DO NOT exceed 5000 lbs. of pressure or structural damage may occur to the tool.

6. Install the piston/connecting rod assembly into the engine block.

PISTON RING REPLACEMENT

Piston Ring End-Gap

Piston ring end-gap should be checked while the rings are removed from the pistons. Incorrect end gap indicates the wrong size rings are being used; ring breakage could occur and engine damage could result.

Squirt clean engine oil into the cylinder, then carefully compress and insert the piston rings to be used in a cylinder, one at a time, into that cylinder. Position the rings approximately 1 in. (25.4mm) below the deck of the block at a point where bore diameter is smallest. The ring can be carefully positioned using the top of the piston, this will assure that the ring is properly squared to the cylinder walls. Measure the ring end-gap with a feeler gauge, and compare to the piston and ring chart earlier in this chapter. Carefully pull the ring out of the cylinder and, if a larger clearance is necessary, replace the piston ring.

Piston Ring Side Clearance Check

➧ See Figure 185

Check the pistons to see that the ring grooves and oil return holes have been properly cleaned. Slide a piston ring into its groove, and check the side clearance with a feeler gauge. On used pistons, make sure you insert the gauge between the ring and its lower land (lower edge of the groove), because any wear that occurs forms a step at the inner portion of the lower land. If the piston grooves have worn to the extent that relatively high steps exist on the lower land, the piston should be replaced, because these will interfere with the operation of the new rings and ring clearance will be excessive. Piston rings are not furnished in oversize widths to compensate for ring groove wear.

Ring Installation

➧ See Figures 186, 187, 188 and 189

Install the rings on the piston, lowest ring first, using a piston ring expander. There is a high risk of breaking or distorting the rings, or scratching the piston, if the rings are installed by hand or other means.

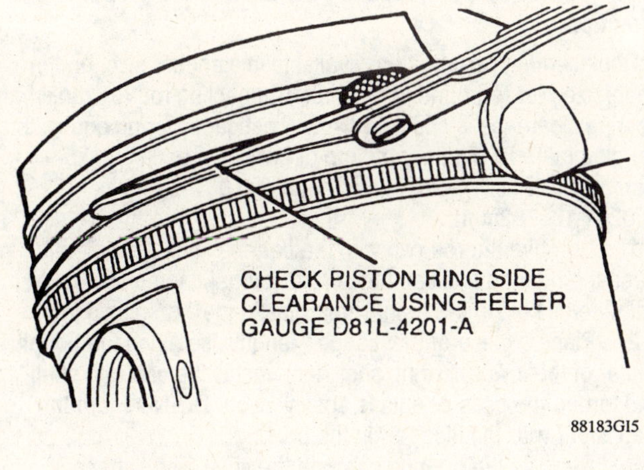

Fig. 185 Checking piston ring side clearance using a feeler gauge

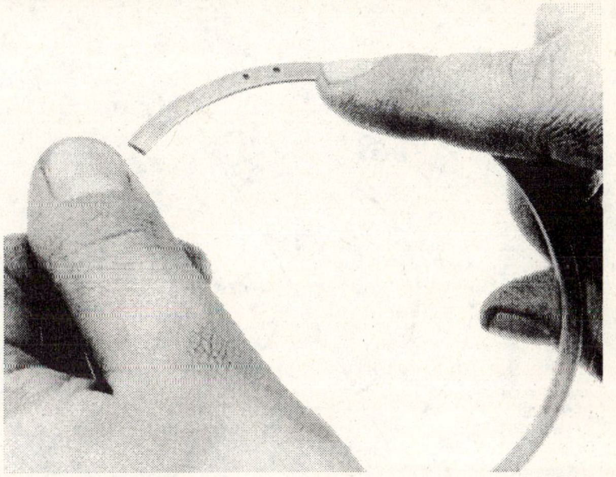

Fig. 186 Most rings are marked to show which side should face upward

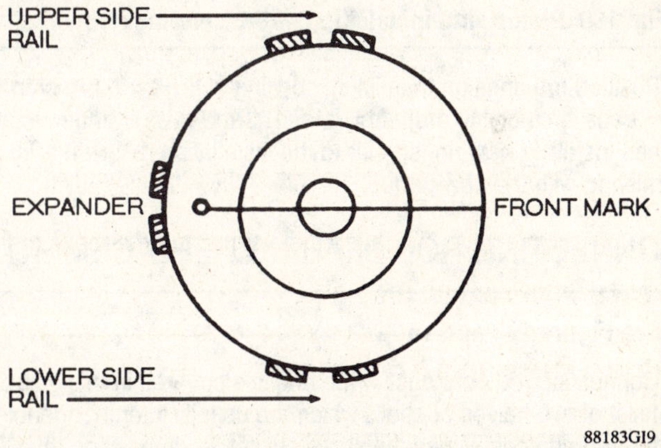

Fig. 187 Install the oil ring expander and two rails by hand. Position the oil ring rail and expander gaps as shown — 4.6L engine

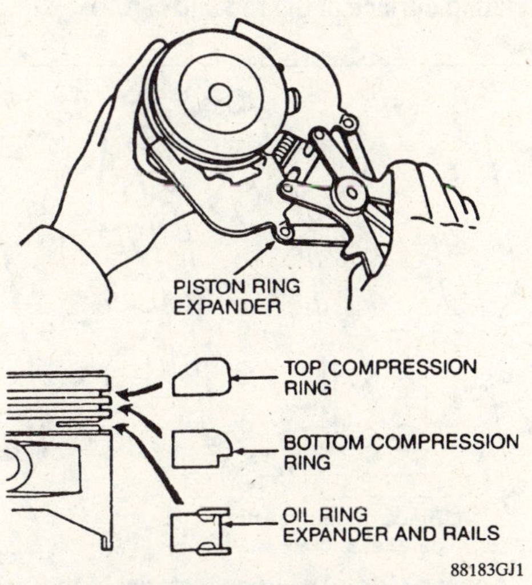

Fig. 188 Installing the piston rings — 4.6L engine

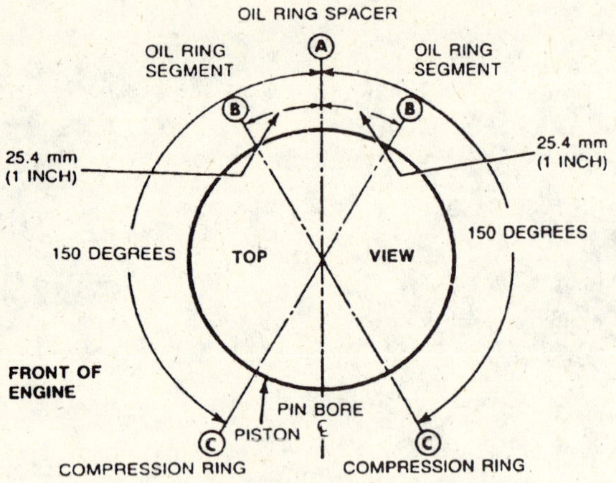

CAUTION: Install the piston with the indentation notch in the piston head toward the front of the engine.

88183GJ2

Fig. 189 Piston ring installation — 5.0L engine shown

Position the rings on the piston; spacing of the various piston ring gaps is crucial to proper oil retention and even cylinder wear. When installing new rings, refer to the installation diagram furnished with the new parts.

CONNECTING ROD BEARING REPLACEMENT

➧ See Figure 190 and 191

Connecting rod bearings for the engines covered in this guide consist of two halves or shells which are usually interchangeable in the rod and cap. When the shells are placed in position, the ends extend slightly beyond the rod and cap surfaces so that when the rod bolts are torqued the shells will be clamped tightly in place to insure positive seating and to prevent turning. A tang holds the shells in place.

➥ The ends of the bearing shells must never be filed flush with the mating surface of the rod and cap.

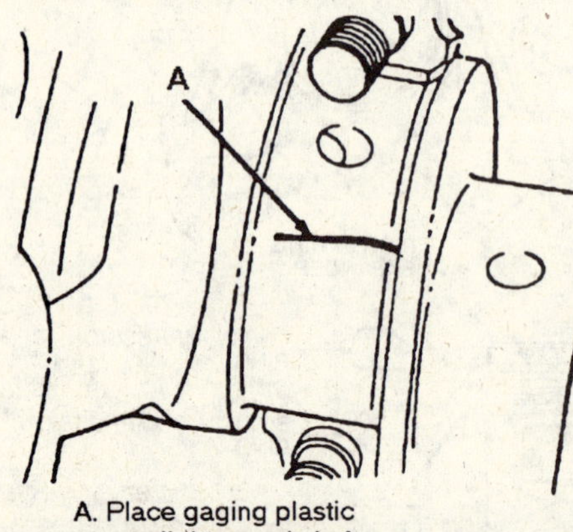

88183GJ3

Fig. 190 Apply a strip of gauging material to the connecting rod journal or the bearing

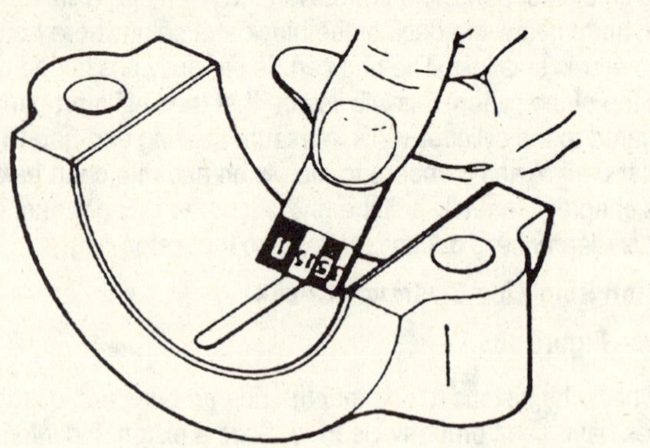

88183GJ4

Fig. 191 Remove the bearing cap and compare the gauging material to the scale provided with the package (check the journal if the material was applied there)

If a rod bearing becomes noisy or is worn so that its clearance on the crank journal is sloppy, a new bearing of the correct undersize must be selected and installed since there is no provision for adjustment.

✻✻WARNING

Under no circumstances should the rod end or cap be filed to adjust the bearing clearance, nor should shims of any kind be used.

Inspect the rod bearings while the rod assemblies are out of the engine. If the shells are scored or show flaking, they should be replaced. If they are in good shape check for proper clearance on the crank journal (see below). Any scoring or ridges on the crank journal means the crankshaft must be replaced, or reground and fitted with undersized bearings.

➥ Make sure connecting rods and their caps are kept together, and that the caps are installed in the proper direction.

Replacement bearings are available in standard size, and in undersizes for reground crankshaft. Connecting rod-to-crankshaft bearing clearance is checked using Plastigage® or an equivalent gauging material at either the top or bottom of each crank journal. The Plastigage® has a range of 0.001–0.003 in. (0.0254–0.0762mm).

1. Remove the rod cap with the bearing shell. Completely clean the bearing shell and the crank journal, then blow any oil from the oil hole in the crankshaft; Plastigage® is soluble in oil.
2. Place a piece of Plastigage® lengthwise along the bottom center of the lower bearing shell, then install the cap with shell and torque the bolts or nuts to specification. DO NOT turn the crankshaft with Plastigage® in the bearing.
3. Remove the bearing cap with the shell. The flattened Plastigage® will be found sticking to either the bearing shell or crank journal. Do not remove it yet.
4. Use the scale printed on the Plastigage® envelope to measure the flattened material at its widest point. The number within the scale which most closely corresponds to the width of the Plastigage® indicates bearing clearance in thousandths of an inch.

5. Check the specifications chart earlier this section for the desired clearance. It is advisable to install a new bearing if clearance exceeds 0.003 in. (0.0762mm); however, if the bearing is in good condition and is not being checked because of bearing noise, bearing replacement is not necessary.
6. If you are installing new bearings, try a standard size, then each undersize in order until one is found that is within the specified limits when checked for clearance with Plastigage®. Each undersize shell has its size stamped on it.
7. When the proper size shell is found, clean off the Plastigage® and oil the bearing thoroughly, then reinstall the cap with its shell and torque the rod fasteners to specification.

➥ With the proper bearing selected and the nuts torqued, it should be possible to move the connecting rod back and forth freely on the crank journal as allowed by the specified connecting rod end clearance. If the rod cannot be moved, either the rod bearing is too far undersize or the rod is misaligned.

INSTALLATION

➧ See Figures 192 and 193

➥ The following procedure requires the use of a ring compressor tool such as J-8037 or equivalent, and the ring expander (removal/installation) tool mentioned earlier.

Assemble the piston, connecting rod and rings as detailed earlier in this section.

1. Make sure that the connecting rod big-end bearings (including the end cap) are of the correct size and are properly installed.
2. Fit rubber hoses over the connecting rod bolts to protect the crankshaft journals, as done during removal. Coat the rod bearings with clean oil.

➥ It is a good idea to lightly coat the walls of the cylinder bore with clean engine oil during assembly.

3. Using the proper ring compressor tool, compress the rings around the piston head, then insert the piston assembly into the cylinder so that the notch (or other mark) in the top of the piston faces the front of the engine. This assumes that the dimple(s) or other markings on the connecting rods are in correct relation to the piston marking(s). The marks made during disassembly should serve as a guide here.
4. From beneath the engine, coat each crank journal with clean oil. Pull the connecting rod, with the bearing shell in place, into position against the crank journal.
5. Remove the rubber hoses from the studs. Install the bearing cap (with bearing shell) onto the connecting rod and the cap nuts. Torque the connecting rod cap nuts to the following:
   - 2.3L engine: 1st step to 25–30 ft. lbs. (34–41 Nm), then 2nd step to 30–36 ft. lbs. (41–49 Nm)
   - 3.8L engine: 31–36 ft. lbs. (41–49 Nm)
   - 4.6L engine: 29–34 ft. lbs. (40–45 Nm), plus a 85–95 degree additional rotation
   - 5.0L engine: 19–24 ft. lbs. (26–32 Nm)

➥ When more than one rod and piston assembly is being installed, the connecting rod cap attaching nuts should only be tightened enough to keep each rod in position until all have been installed. This will ease the installation of the remaining piston assemblies.

6. Check the clearance between the sides of the connecting rods and the crankshaft using a feeler gauge. Spread the rods slightly with a small prybar and insert the gauge. If clearance is below the minimum tolerance, the rod may be machined to provide adequate clearance. If clearance is excessive, substitute an unworn rod, and recheck. If clearance is still outside specifications, the crankshaft must be welded and reground, or replaced.
7. If removed, install the oil pump
8. Install the oil pan.
9. Install the cylinder head(s), as applicable.
10. If removed, install the engine to the vehicle.

TCCS3914

Fig. 192 Using a wooden hammer handle, carefully tap the piston down through the ring compressor and into the cylinder bore

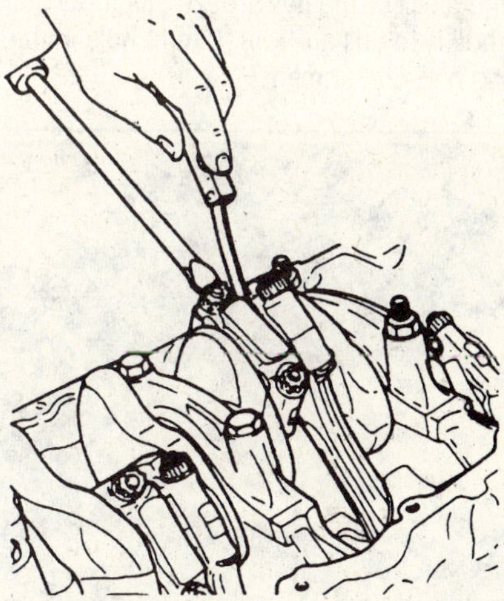

88183GJ6

Fig. 193 Check the connecting rod side clearance using a feeler gauge. A small prybar should be used to carefully spread the connecting rods.

Freeze Plugs

On most cast iron blocks, round metal plugs are used to seal coolant jackets. These plugs allow for a certain amount of water and block expansion should water (without anti-freeze) ever be left in the coolant system. Although the cooling system should NEVER be filled with plain water only, an emergency and unavailability of coolant could force the situation to occur.

In the event that water only is placed in the cooling system and the engine is subject to sub-freezing temperatures, it is likely that the water will freeze and expand. It is also quite possible that the block will expand and crack. If you are lucky though, the expansion may only cause freeze plugs to become dislodged.

During engine block overhaul, it is standard procedure to remove and replace all of the freeze plugs.

REMOVAL & INSTALLATION

➧ **See Figures 194 and 195**

1. Disconnect the negative battery cable, then properly drain the engine cooling system.
2. If equipped, remove the engine coolant drain plugs (located at the bottom of the block usually near the oil pan rail) and drain the coolant from the block. If the engine is not equipped with coolant drain plugs, drill a small hole in the leaking freeze plug and allow any remaining coolant to drain.
3. Remove any components that restrict access to the freeze plug or, if necessary, remove the engine from the vehicle for access to the freeze plug(s).

****CAUTION**

Always wear proper eye protection when using a chisel, especially when attempting to dislodge a freeze plug.

4. Using a chisel, tap the bottom edge of the freeze plug to cock it in the bore. Remove the plug using pliers, but be careful not to score the block or the new freeze plug may not fit well. An alternate method is to drill an $^1/_8$ in. (3mm) hole in the plug and remove it using a slide hammer.

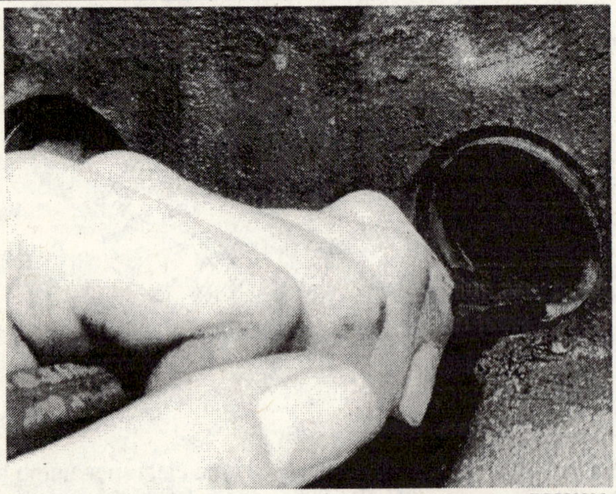

TCCS3905

Fig. 194 Using a punch and hammer, the freeze plug can be cocked and loosened in the block

TCCS3906

Fig. 195 Once the freeze plug has been cocked, it can be removed from the block

To install:

5. Clean the bore of any debris and make sure it is free of any deep scratches which could cause a leak.

➥ Some auto part stores may offer easy to install freeze plugs consisting of a grommet with metal plates and an adjustment bolt. These plugs are positioned, then the bolt is tightened to expand the grommet sealing the block bore. Although these might be handy to get the vehicle home quickly, they should not be installed as a permanent fix.

6. Freeze plugs are interference fitted to the block. Make sure you have the proper plug size and an equalled sized driver. The proper sized driver will ease the installation process by preventing the plug from cocking in the bore as it is driven into position.
7. Coat the plug with sealant, then position it in the bore and drive it into position.
8. Install all remaining components on the engine, as applicable.
9. Connect the negative battery cable and properly refill the engine cooling system, then check for leaks.

Block Heater

REMOVAL & INSTALLATION

1. Disconnect the negative battery cable, then properly drain the engine cooling system.
2. If equipped, remove the engine coolant drain plugs (located at the bottom of the block near the oil pan rail) and drain the coolant from the block. If the engine is not equipped with coolant drain plugs, be ready to catch the coolant that will likely drain from the block when the block heater is removed.
3. Disconnect the block heater electrical connector.
4. Loosen the block heater retaining screw and remove the block heater from the engine.
5. **To install:**
6. Coat the block heater O-ring with engine oil and clean the block heater hole of rust.
7. Install the block heater and tighten the retaining screw.
8. Connect the negative battery cable and properly refill the engine cooling system, then check for leaks.

Rear Main Oil Seal

Replacing a rear main seal can be a formidable task. Before replacing the seal, care should be taken in determining the exact source of the leak. Various manufacturers produce a fluorescent dye oil additive which can be added to your crankcase. The engine is run, allowing the dyed oil to leak from the same source, then a black light is used to illuminate the leak so it can be traced.

REMOVAL & INSTALLATION

➥ Some 1983 3.8L engines, may be equipped with a split-type two piece rear main seal. All other engines have a one piece seal.

Split-Type Seal

➧ See Figures 196 and 197

➥ The rear oil seal installed in these engines is a rubber type (split-lip) seal.

1. Disconnect the negative battery cable.
2. Remove the oil pan, and, if required, the oil pump.
3. Loosen all the main bearing caps allowing the crankshaft to lower slightly.

****WARNING**

The crankshaft should not be allowed to drop more than $^1/_{32}$ in. (0.8mm).

4. Remove the rear main bearing cap and remove the seal from the cap and block. Be very careful not to scratch the sealing surface. Remove the old seal retaining pin from the cap, if equipped. It is not used with the replacement seal.

To install:

5. Carefully clean the seal grooves in the cap and block with solvent.
6. Soak the new seal halves in clean engine oil.
7. Install the upper half of the seal in the block with the undercut side of the seal toward the front of the engine. Slide the seal around the crankshaft journal until $^3/_8$ in. (9.5mm) protrudes beyond the base of the block.
8. Tighten all the main bearing caps (except the rear main bearing) to 65–81 ft. lbs. (88–110 Nm).
9. Install the lower seal into the rear cap, with the undercut side facing the front of the engine. Allow $^3/_8$ in. (9.5mm) of the seal to protrude above the surface, at the opposite end from the block seal.
10. Squeeze a $^1/_{16}$ in. (1.6mm) bead of silicone sealant onto the areas shown in the accompanying figure.
11. Install the rear main bearing cap, secure with the retaining bolts and tighten to 65–81 ft. lbs. (88–110 Nm).
12. Install the oil pump and pan.
13. Fill the crankcase with oil, the connect the negative battery cable.
14. Start the engine and inspect for leaks. Check the oil level, and add if necessary.

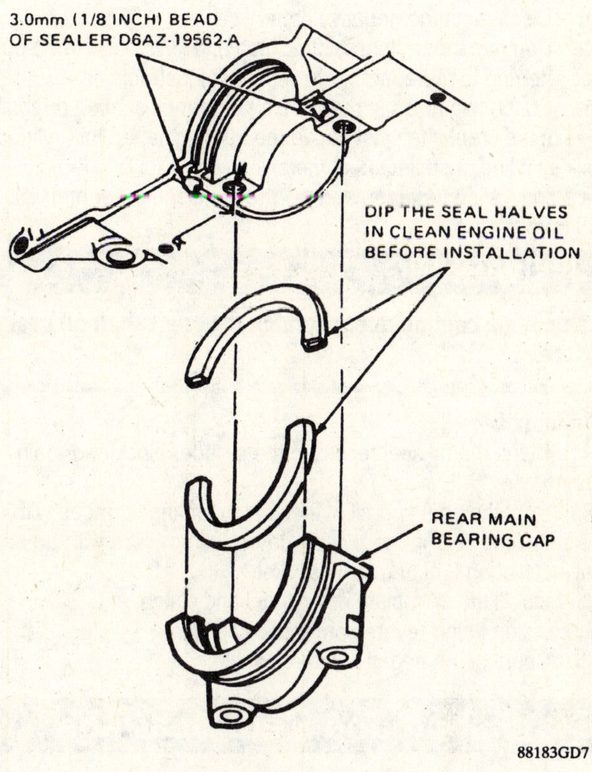

Fig. 196 A two piece split seal was used on some early model 3.8L engines

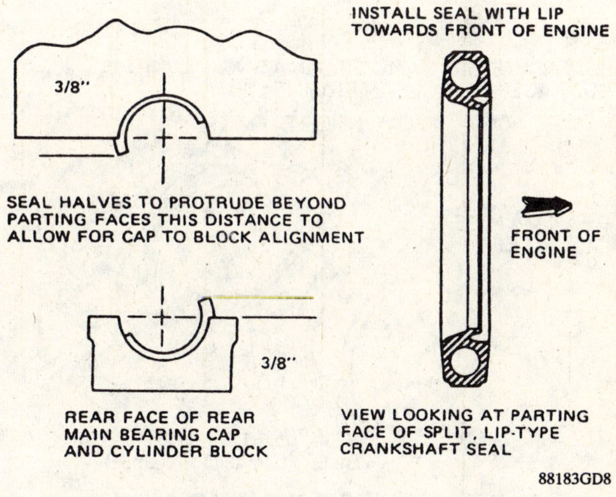

Fig. 197 Proper installation of the split-type rear main oil seal

One-Piece Seal

➧ **See Figure 198**

1. Disconnect the negative battery cable.
2. Remove the transmission, clutch and flywheel or driveplate after referring to the appropriate section for instructions.
3. Punch two holes in the crankshaft rear oil seal on opposite sides of the crankshaft just above the bearing cap to the cylinder block split line. Install a sheet metal screw in each of the holes or use a small slide hammer, and pry the crankshaft rear main oil seal from the block.

****WARNING**

Use extreme caution not to scratch the crankshaft oil seal surface.

To install:

4. Clean the oil seal recess in the cylinder block and main bearing cap.
5. Coat the seal and all of the seal mounting surfaces with oil and install the seal in the recess, driving it into place with an oil seal installation tool or a large socket.
6. Install the driveplate or flywheel and clutch, and transmission in the reverse order of removal.
7. Connect the negative battery cable.

Crankshaft and Main Bearings

REMOVAL & INSTALLATION

➧ **See Figures 199, 200 and 201**

1. Remove the engine from the vehicle and place on a suitable workstand.
2. Drain the crankcase and the cylinder block.

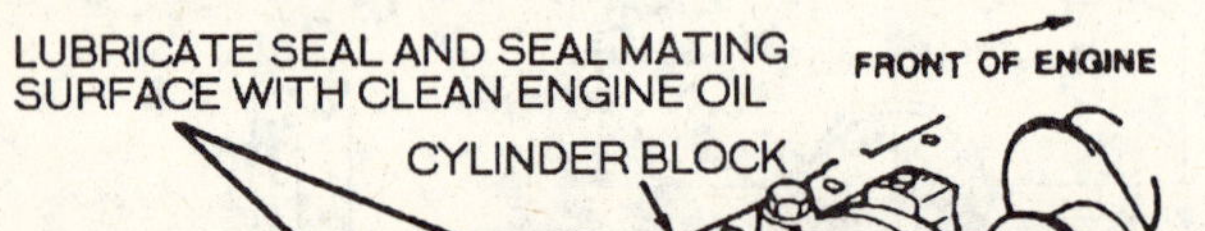

Fig. 198 One piece rear main oil seal installation — 2.3L engine shown

3. Tag and disconnect the spark plug wires at the spark plugs, then remove the wires from the ignition harness brackets on the valve covers. If necessary, remove the distributor cap and spark plug wire assembly.
4. Remove the spark plugs to allow easy rotation of the crankshaft.
5. Remove the oil pan. If necessary remove the oil pump.
6. Remove the engine front cover and water pump (if necessary) as an assembly.
7. If equipped, remove the distributor drive gear.
8. Remove the crankshaft sprocket, camshaft sprocket(s) and timing chain.
9. Remove the flywheel and the engine rear plate.
10. If equipped, remove and discard the 1-piece rear main seal.

➥ **Each connecting rod cap MUST be identified so it can be installed in its original position during assembly.**

11. Remove the connecting rod caps. Turn the crankshaft as necessary to position the connecting rod in the low point of travel before removing the connecting rod cap. After removing the connecting rod cap, push the piston into the cylinder block bore. Make sure the crankshaft journals are not damaged.
12. Remove the crankshaft main bearing caps.

****WARNING**

Be sure to handle the crankshaft carefully to prevent damage to the finished bearing surfaces.

13. Carefully lift the crankshaft out of the cylinder block to avoid damage to the bearing surfaces.
14. If equipped, remove the split-type crankshaft rear oil seal, then discard.

To install:

****WARNING**

Any contaminants on a bearing surface will cause damage to the crankshaft journals.

15. Lightly oil all bolt and stud bolts threads before installation. Make sure all crankshaft bearing surfaces and main bearings are clean.
16. If the crankshaft main bearing journals have been refinished to definite undersize, remove the crankshaft main bearings from the cylinder block and main bearing caps.
17. Install new crankshaft main bearings. Make sure the tabs on the main bearings engage the slots in the main bearing caps and cylinder block.
18. Install the upper half of the split-type rear main seal. Make sure the crankshaft rear oil seal groove in the cylinder block is clean. Carefully lower the crankshaft into position in the cylinder block. Take care not to damage the crankshaft main bearing.
19. Make sure the crankshaft split-type rear oil seal groove in the rear crankshaft main bearing cap is clean.

➥ **When using sealer, assembly must occur within 15 minutes after sealer application. After this time, the sealer may start to set-up, and its sealing effectiveness may be reduced.**

20. Apply a $^{1}/_{8}$ in. (3mm) bead of Silicone Rubber to the rear main bearing cap-to-cylinder block parting line.

21. Install the lower half of the split-type rear main seal.

22. Lubricate the bearing surfaces with Engine Assembly Lubricant D9AZ-19579-D or equivalent. Install the main bearing caps and retaining bolts, except for the 5.0L engine. For the 5.0L engine, install all bearing caps, except the thrust bearing cap (no. 3 bearing).

23. For the 2.3L engine, tighten the main bearing cap retaining bolts in two steps, as follows:

a. Step 1: to 50–60 ft. lbs. (68–81 Nm)

b. Step 2: to 75–85 ft. lbs. (102–115 Nm)

24. For the 3.8L engine, tighten the main bearing cap retaining bolts as follows:

a. Wedge a prybar between the cylinder block web and the crankshaft cheek in front of the No. 3 crankshaft main bearing. Do NOT jam the prybar into position. Carefully tap on the prybar until it holds the crankshaft toward the front of the engine.

b. Tighten the main bearing cap bolts to 65–81 ft. lbs. (88–110 Nm) for vehicles through 1994 or to 81–89 ft. lbs. (110–120 Nm) for 1995–96 vehicles, then remove the prybar.

25. For the 4.6L engine, tighten the main bearing cap bolt 1/2 turn, after the gasket contacts the sealing surface.

26. For the 5.0L engine, tighten the main bearing cap retaining bolts, except the thrust bearing cap (No. 3) to 60–70 ft. lbs. (81–95 Nm). Install the thrust bearing cap with the bolts finger-tight.

27. For the 5.0L engine, pry the crankshaft forward against the thrust surface of the upper half of the bearing. Hold the crankshaft forward and pry the thrust bearing cap to the rear. This will align the thrust surfaces of both halves of the bearing. Retain the forward pressure on the crankshaft, then tighten the thrust cap bolts to 60–70 ft. lbs. (81–95 Nm). Force the crankshaft toward the rear of the engine.

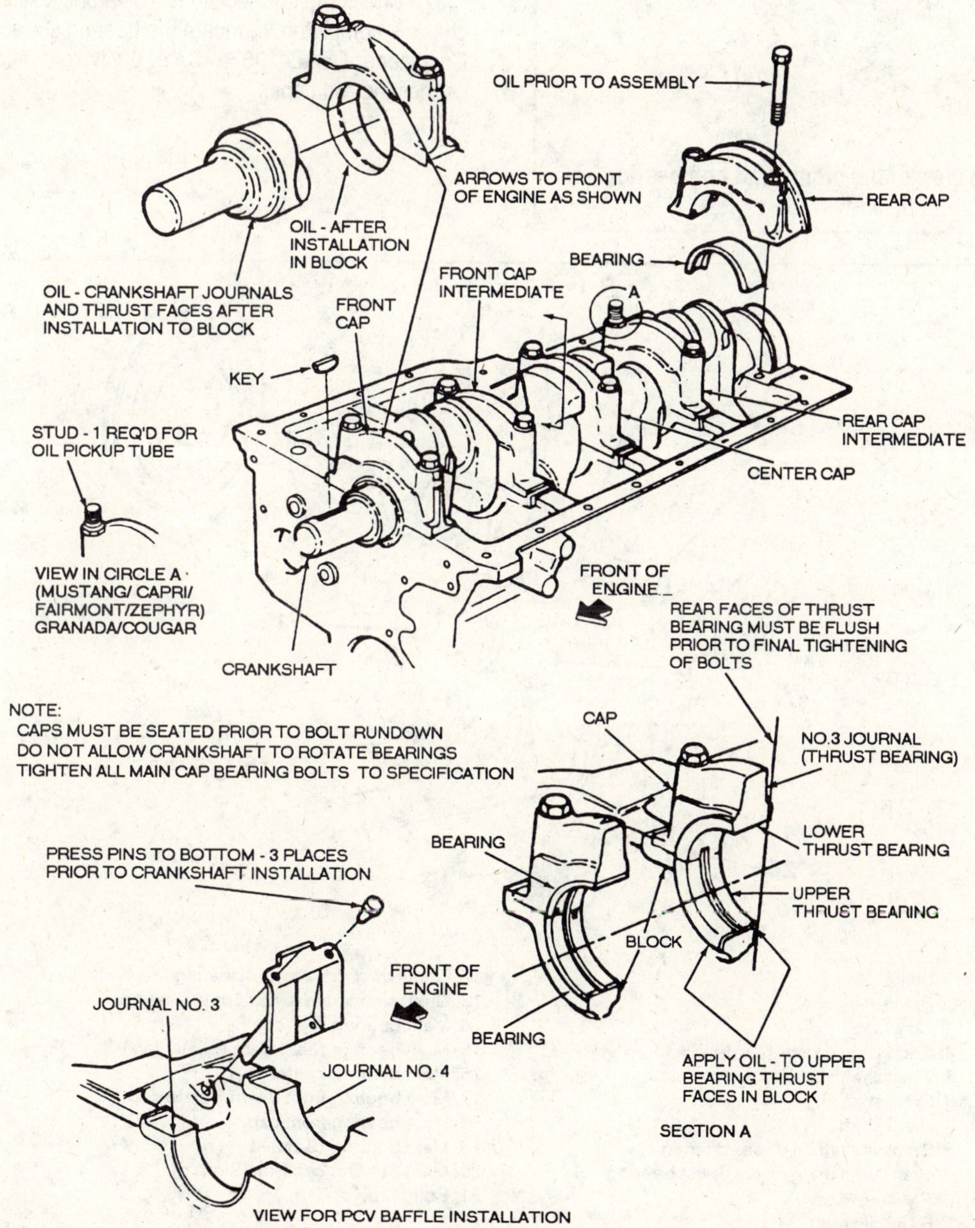

Fig. 199 Crankshaft and main bearing installation — 2.3L engine

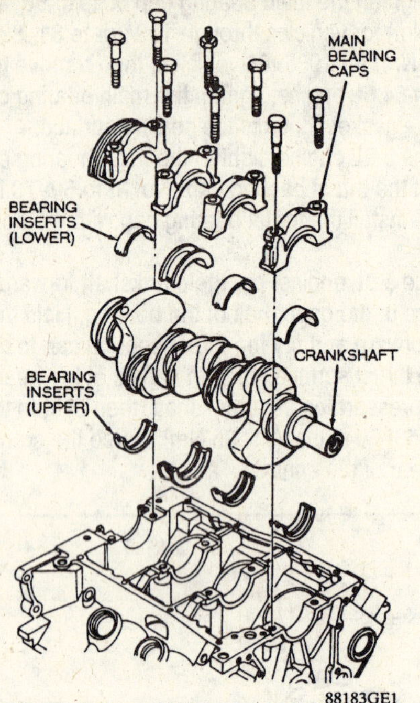

Fig. 200 Exploded view of the crankshaft and bearing assemblies — 3.8L engine shown

28. Check the crankshaft end-play, as follows:
   a. Pry against the No. 2 main bearing cap and check the crankshaft end play in both directions as shown in the accompanying figure.
   b. If end play exceeds specifications, grind the crankshaft and install an oversize crankshaft thrust main bearing or replace the crankshaft and crankshaft thrust main bearing.
29. Install the one-piece crankshaft rear oil seal.
30. If the crankshaft connecting rod journals have been refinished to a definite undersize, remove the bearing inserts from the connecting rods and rod caps. Install new bearings. Make sure the tabs on the insert securely engage the slot in the cap and rod.
31. Rotate the crankshaft as necessary to bring each crankshaft throw to the lowest point of travel. Pull the piston downward until the connecting rod seats on the crank throw and install the rod caps.
32. Check the connecting rod clearance. After each clearance check is completed, lubricate the bearing surfaces with Oil Conditioner D9AZ-19579-CA or equivalent before installing the connecting rod caps.

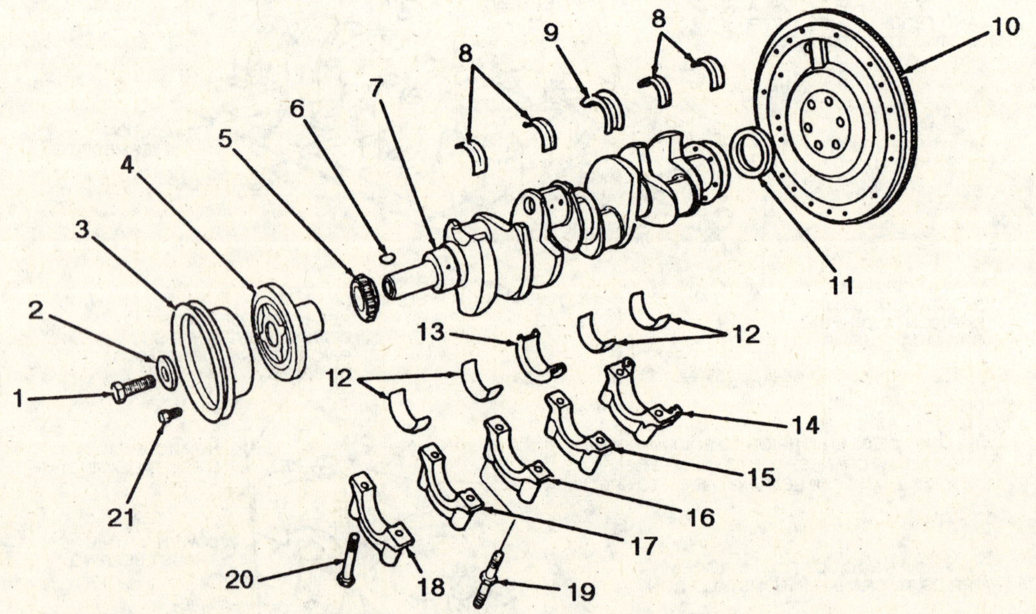

1. Bolt
2. Damper washer
3. Crankshaft pulley
4. Crankshaft damper
5. Crankshaft sprocket
6. Crankshaft key
7. Crankshaft
8. Crankshaft main upper bearing
9. Crankshaft main upper thrust bearing
10. Flywheel assy
11. Rear oil seal
12. Crankshaft main lower bearing
13. Crankshaft main lower thrust bearing
14. Main bearing rear cap
15. Main bearing rear intermediate cap
16. Main bearing center cap
17. Main bearing front intermediate cap
18. Main bearing front cap
19. Main bearing cap stud
20. Main bearing cap bolt (9 req'd)
21. Bolt (4 req'd)

88183GE2

Fig. 201 View of the crankshaft and bearings — 5.0L engine shown

33. Tighten the connecting rod retaining nuts, as follows:
- 2.3L Engine: Step 1 to 25-30 ft. lbs. (34-41 Nm), then Step 2 to 30-36 ft. lbs. (41-49 Nm)
- 3.8L Engine: tighten the nuts to 31-36 ft. lbs. (41-49 Nm), back off the nuts two or three turns, then final tighten to 31-36 ft. lbs. (41-49 Nm)
- 4.6L Engine: tighten to 29-34 ft. lbs. (40-45 Nm), plus an additional 85-95 degree rotation
- 5.0L Engine: tighten the nuts to 19-24 ft. lbs. (26-32 Nm)

34. Install the timing chain and front cover (water pump) assembly, as outlined earlier in this section.
35. If equipped, install the distributor drive gear.
36. Install the oil pan and, if necessary, the oil pump.
37. Install the rear cover plate and flywheel, as outlined.
38. Install the spark plugs, distributor cap (if equipped), then connect the wires to the spark plugs as tagged during removal.
39. Retighten the lower intake manifold, as outlined in this section.
40. Install the engine into the vehicle.
41. Fill the engine cooling system and crankcase to the proper levels with the correct types of fluids.
42. Connect the negative battery cable, then start the engine and check for proper operation.

CLEANING AND INSPECTION

See Figures 202, 203, 204 and 205

1. Clean the crankshaft with solvent and a brush. Clean the oil passages with a brass brush, then blow them out with compressed air.
2. Inspect the crankshaft for obvious damage or wear. Check the main and connecting rod journals for cracks, scratches, grooves or scores. Inspect the crankshaft oil seal surfaces for nicks, sharp edges or burrs that could damage the oil seal or cause premature seal wear.
3. If the crankshaft passes a visual inspection, check journal runout using a dial indicator. Support the crankshaft in V-blocks, then check runout as shown. Compare to the specifications shown at the end of this section.
4. Measure the main and connecting rod journals for wear, out-of-roundness or taper, using a micrometer. Measure in at least 4 places around each journal and compare your findings with the journal diameter specifications.
5. If the crankshaft fails any inspection for wear or damage, it must be reground or replaced.

BEARING REPLACEMENT

See Figures 206 and 207

The following procedure requires the use of Plastigage® or a micrometer set consisting of inside and outside micrometers, and a dial indicator.

1. Inspect the bearings for scoring, chipping or other wear.
2. Inspect the crankshaft journals as detailed in the Cleaning and Inspection procedure.
3. If the crankshaft journals appear usable, clean them and the bearing shells until they are completely free of oil. Blow any oil from the oil hole in the crankshaft.

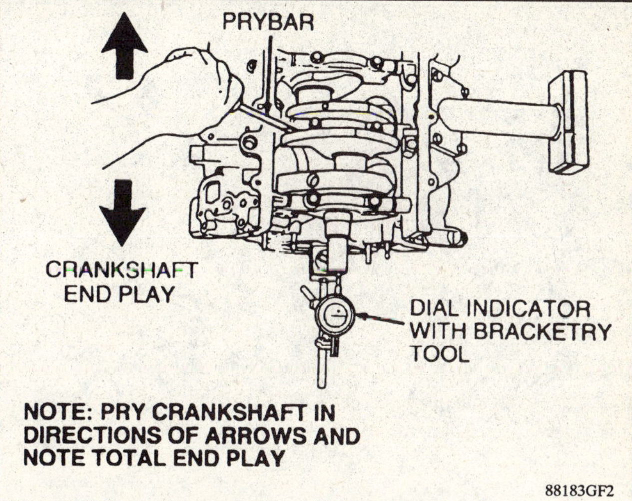

Fig. 202 Pry against the No. 2 main bearing cap to check the crankshaft end play in both directions

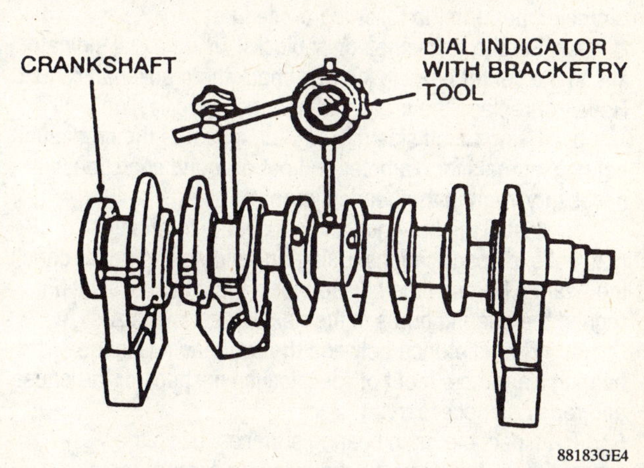

Fig. 203 Use the proper type of dial indicator to check for excessive crankshaft runout

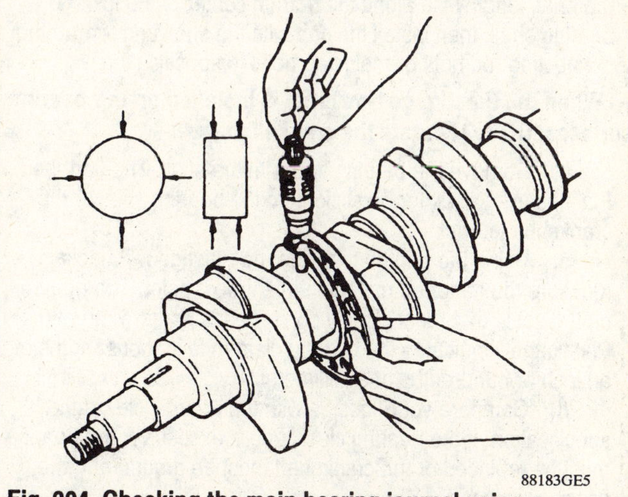

Fig. 204 Checking the main bearing journal using a micrometer

Fig. 205 Checking main bearing bore diameter with bearings installed

4. To check the crankshaft/rod bearing clearances using a micrometer, perform the following procedures:
   a. Set the crankshaft on V-blocks. Using a dial indicator set on the center bearing journal, check the crankshaft runout. Repair or replace the crankshaft if out of specification.
   b. Using an outside micrometer, measure the crankshaft bearing journals for diameter and out-of-round conditions; if necessary, regrind the bearing journals.
   c. Install the bearings and caps, then torque the nuts/bolts to specifications. Using an inside micrometer, check the bearing bores in the engine block. If out of specification, regrind the bearing bores to the next largest oversize.
   d. The difference between the two readings is the bearing clearance. If out of specification, inspect for the cause and repair as necessary.
5. To inspect the main bearing surfaces, using the Plastigage® method, perform the following procedures:

➥ NOTE: The journal surfaces and bearing shells must be completely free of oil to get an accurate reading with Plastigage®.

   a. Place a strip of Plastigage® or equivalent gauging material, lengthwise along the bottom center of the lower bearing shell, then install the cap with the shell and torque the connecting rod nuts or main cap bolts to specification.

➥ When the Plastigage® material is installed on the bearing surfaces, DO NOT rotate the crankshaft.

   b. Remove the bearing cap with the shell. The flattened Plastigage® will either be sticking to the bearing shell or the crankshaft journal.
   c. Using the printed scale on the Plastigage® package, measure the flattened material at its widest point. The number on the scale that most closely corresponds to the width of the Plastigage® indicates the bearing clearance in thousandths of an inch or hundredths of a millimeter.
   d. Compare your findings with the bearing clearance specification. If the bearing clearance is excessive, the bearing must be replaced or the crankshaft must be ground and the bearing replaced.

➥ NOTE: Bearing shell sets over standard size are available to correct excessive bearing clearance.

   e. After clearance measurement is completed, be sure to remove the Plastigage® from the crankshaft and/or bearing shell.
   f. For final bearing shell installation, make sure the connecting rod and rod cap and/or cylinder block and main cap bearing saddles are clean and free of nicks or burrs. Install the bearing shells in the bearing saddles, making sure the shell tangs are seated in the notches.

TCCS3243

Fig. 206 Apply a strip of gauging material to the bearing, then install and torque the cap

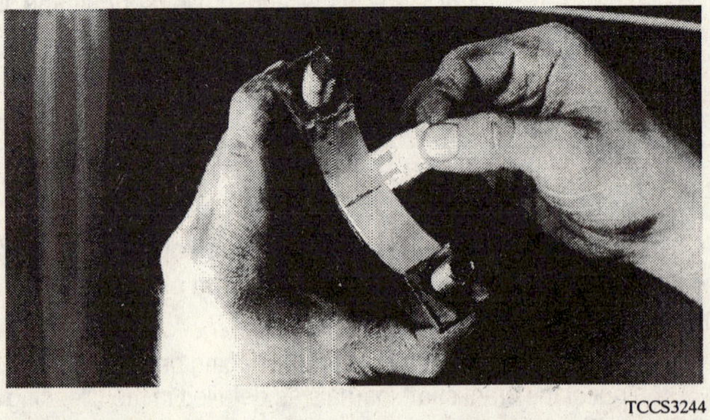

TCCS3244

Fig. 207 As with the connecting rod bearings, remove the cap and compare the gauging material to the provided scale

➥ NOTE: Be careful when handling any plain bearings. Your hands and the working area should be clean. Dirt is easily embedded in the bearing surface and the bearings are easily scratched or damaged.

Flywheel/Flex Plate and Ring Gear

REMOVAL & INSTALLATION

➥ The ring gear is replaceable only on engines mated with a manual transmission. Engines with automatic transmissions have ring gears which are welded to the flex plate.

1. Remove the transmission, as outlined in Section 7 of this manual.
2. Remove the clutch, if equipped, or torque converter from the flywheel. The flywheel bolts should be loosened a little at a time in a cross pattern to avoid warping the flywheel. On cars with manual transmissions, replace the pilot bearing in the end of the crankshaft if removing the flywheel.
3. The flywheel should be checked for cracks and glazing. It can be resurfaced by a machine shop.
4. If the ring gear is to be replaced, drill a hole in the gear between two teeth, being careful not to contact the flywheel surface. Using a cold chisel at this point, crack the ring gear and remove it.

To install:

5. Polish the inner surface of the new ring gear and heat it in an oven to about 600°F (316°C). Quickly place the ring gear on the flywheel and tap it into place, making sure that it is fully seated.

****WARNING**

Never heat the ring gear past 800°F (426°C), or the tempering will be destroyed.

6. Position the flywheel on the end of the crankshaft. Most flywheels will only attach to the crankshaft in one position, as the bolt holes are unevenly spaced and/or the crankshaft is fitted with a dowel pin. Install the bolts and tighten to specification using a criss-cross pattern.
7. Install the clutch or torque converter.
8. Install the transmission and transfer case.

EXHAUST SYSTEM

➧ See Figures 208, 209, 210, 211, 212, 213, 214, 215, 216, 217, 218, 219, 220 and 221

General Information

➥ Safety glasses should be worn at all times when working on or near the exhaust system. Older exhaust systems will almost always be covered with loose rust particles which will shower you when disturbed. These particles are more than a nuisance and could injure your eye.

Whenever working on the exhaust system always keep the following in mind:

- Check the complete exhaust system for open seams, holes loose connections, or other deterioration which could permit exhaust fumes to seep into the passenger compartment.
- The exhaust system is usually supported by free-hanging rubber mountings which permit some movement of the exhaust system, but does not permit transfer of noise and vibration into the passenger compartment. Do not replace the rubber mounts with solid ones.
- Before removing any component of the exhaust system, ALWAYS squirt a liquid rust dissolving agent onto the fasteners for ease of removal. A lot of knuckle skin will be saved by following this rule. It may even be wise to spray the fasteners and allow them to sit overnight.

****CAUTION**

Allow the exhaust system to cool sufficiently before spraying a solvent exhaust fasteners. Some solvents are highly flammable and could ignite when sprayed on hot exhaust components.

- Annoying rattles and noise vibrations in the exhaust system are usually caused by misalignment of the parts. When aligning the system, leave all bolts and nuts loose until all parts are properly aligned, then tighten, working from front to rear.
- When installing exhaust system parts, make sure there is enough clearance between the hot exhaust parts and pipes and hoses that would be adversely affected by excessive heat. Also make sure there is adequate clearance from the floor pan to avoid possible overheating of the floor.

****CAUTION**

When working on exhaust systems, ALWAYS wear protective goggles! Avoid working on a hot exhaust system as catalytic converters reach high temperatures after only a short period of engine operation!

Muffler

REMOVAL & INSTALLATION

➥ The following applies to exhaust systems using clamped joints. Some models, use welded joints at the muffler. These joints will, of course, have to be cut.

2.3L Engine

VEHICLES WITH A SINGLE MUFFLER

1. Disconnect the negative battery cable.
2. Carefully raise the vehicle at the frame lift points to allow the axle full downward travel. This will provide the clearance necessary to remove and replace the muffler and pipe.

88183P26

Fig. 208 Under-vehicle view of the dual converter Y-pipe — 1990 3.8L engine shown

88183P27

Fig. 209 View of the exhaust pipe running to the muffler — 1990 3.8L engine shown

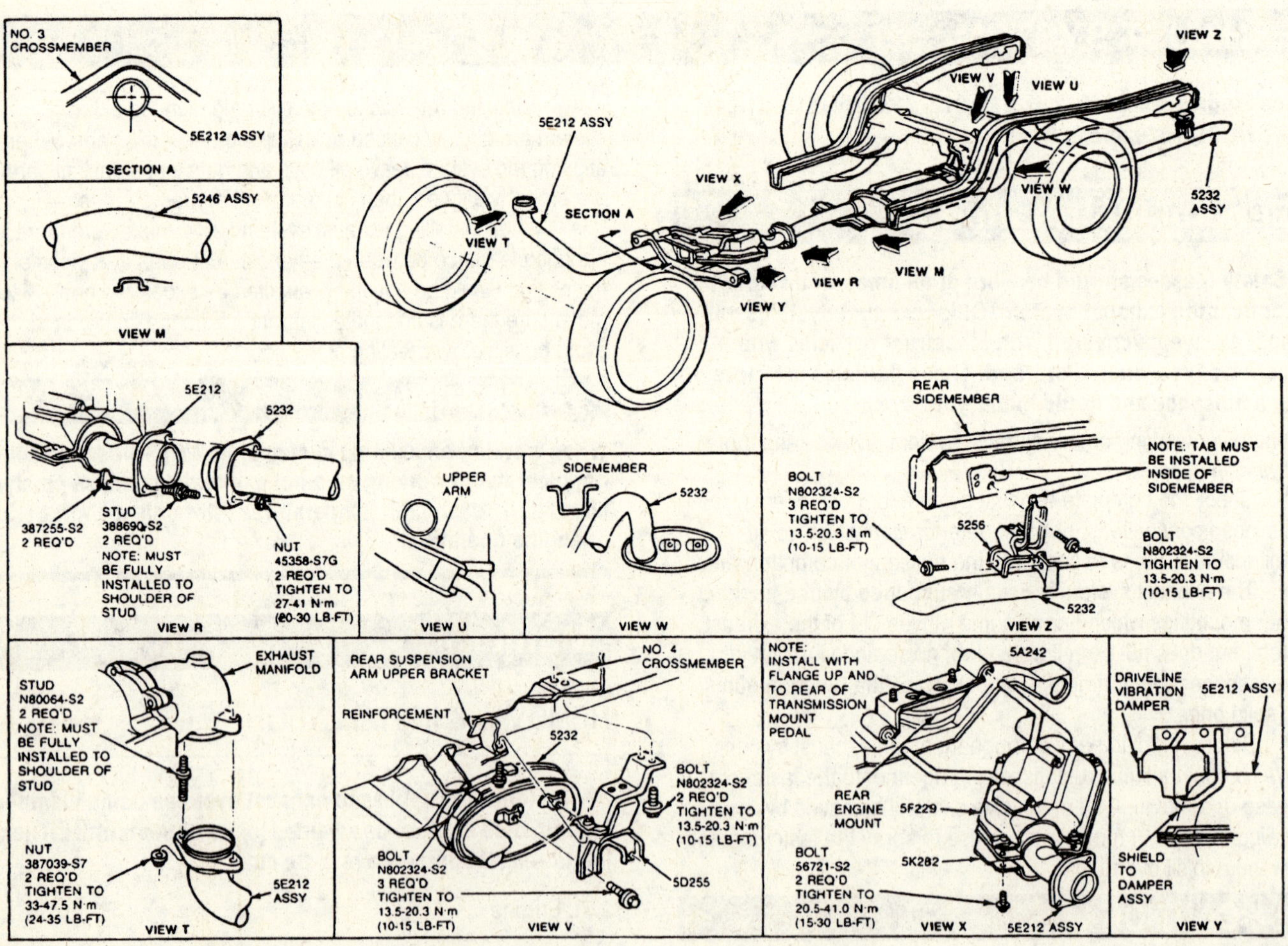

88183GF3

Fig. 210 View of the exhaust system — 2.3L engine with single muffler shown

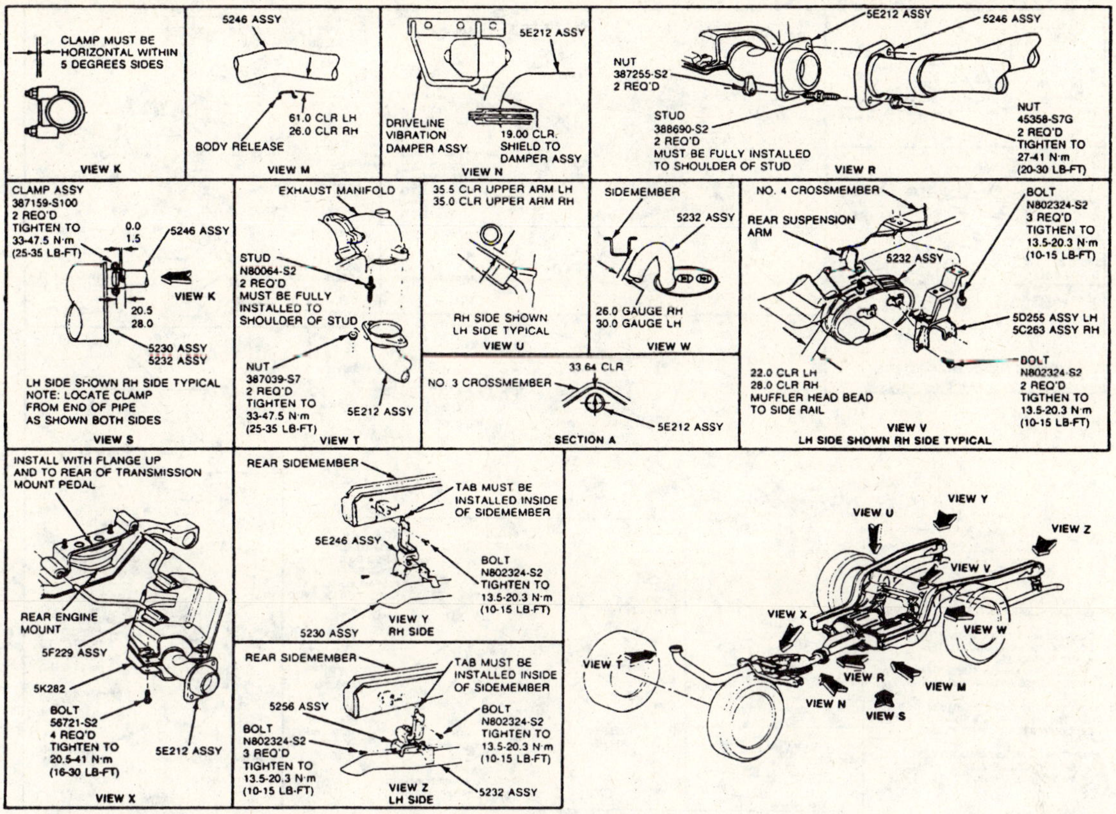

Fig. 211 View of the exhaust system — 2.3L engine with dual mufflers shown

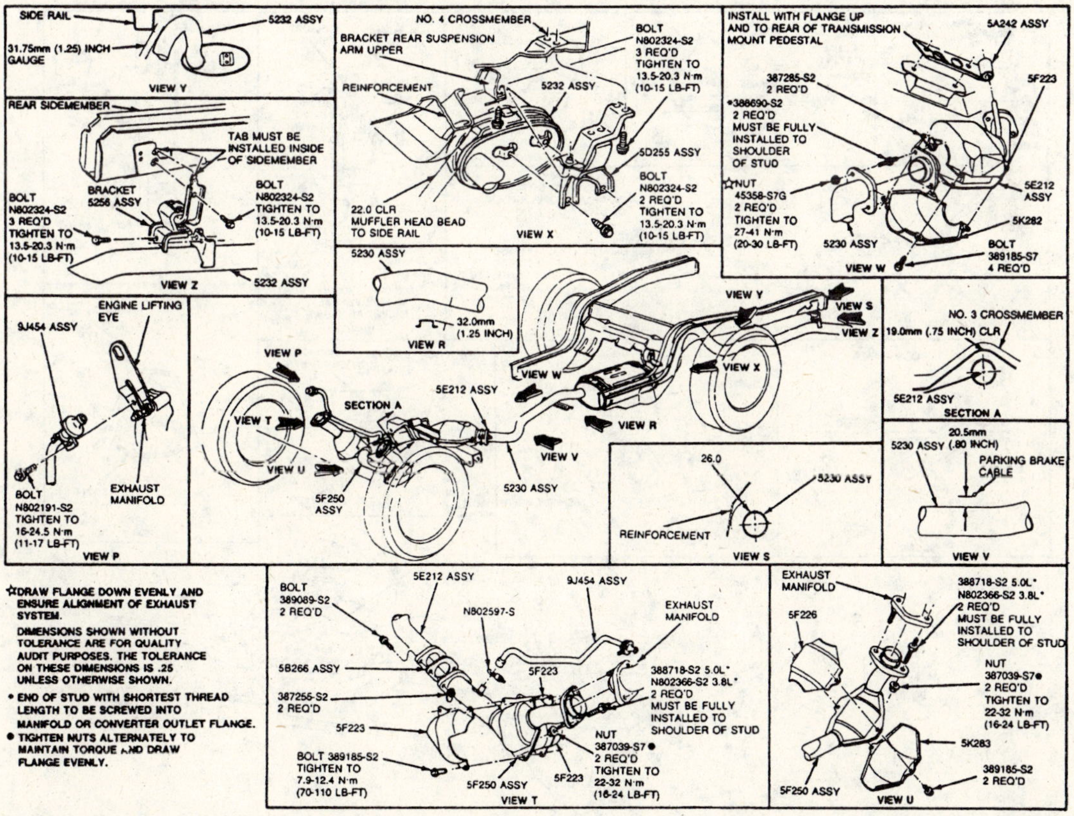

Fig. 212 Exhaust system and alignment specifications — 3.8L engine through 1988 shown

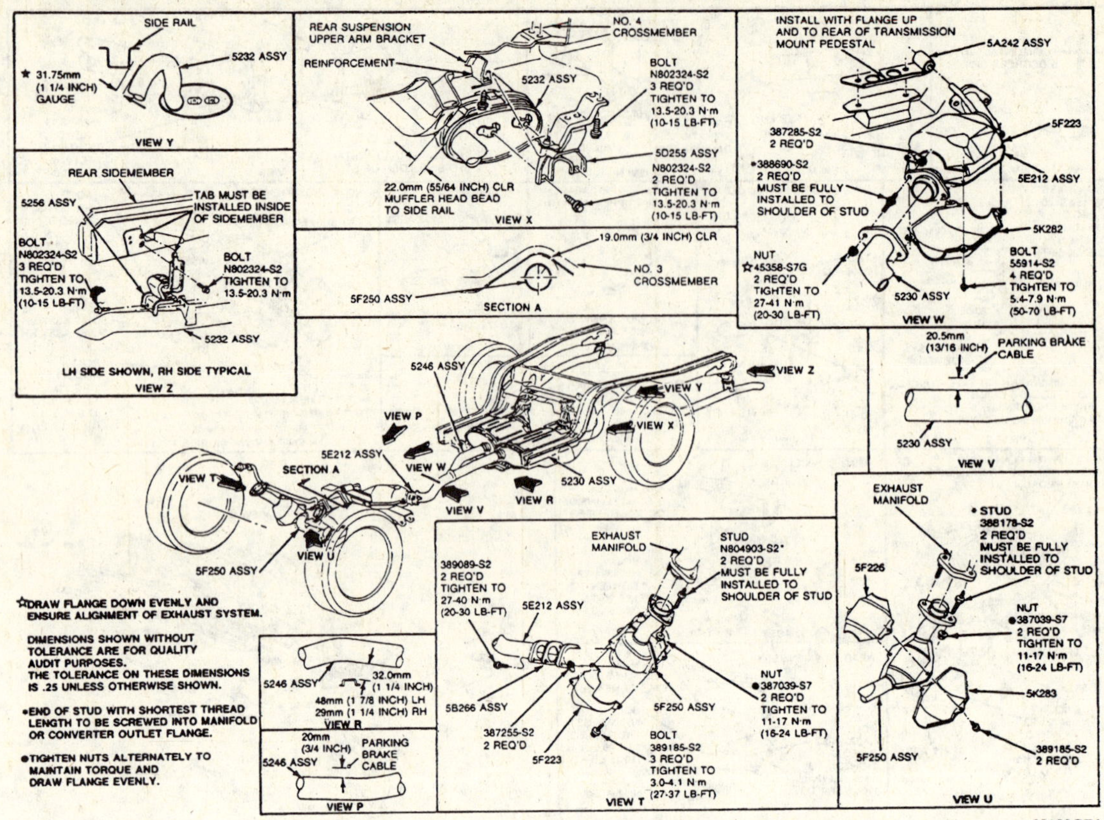

88183GF6

Fig. 213 Exhaust system and alignment specifications — 5.0L engine through 1988 shown

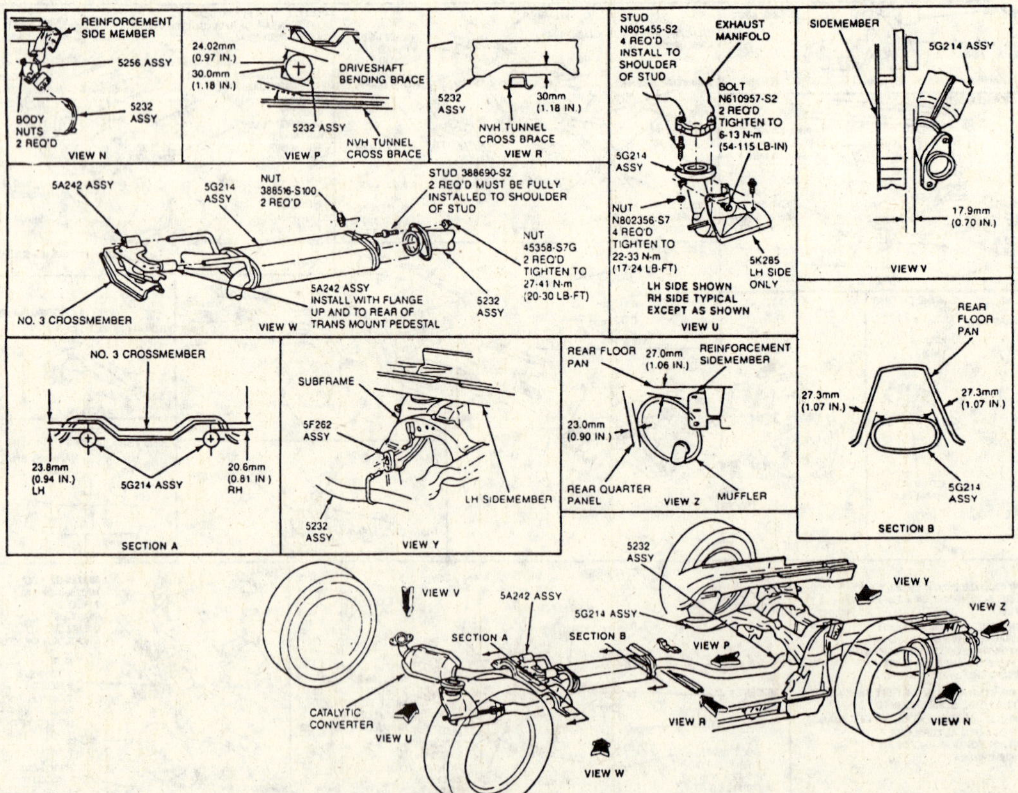

88183GF7

Fig. 214 View of the exhaust system and tightening specifications — 1993 3.8L non-SC engine shown

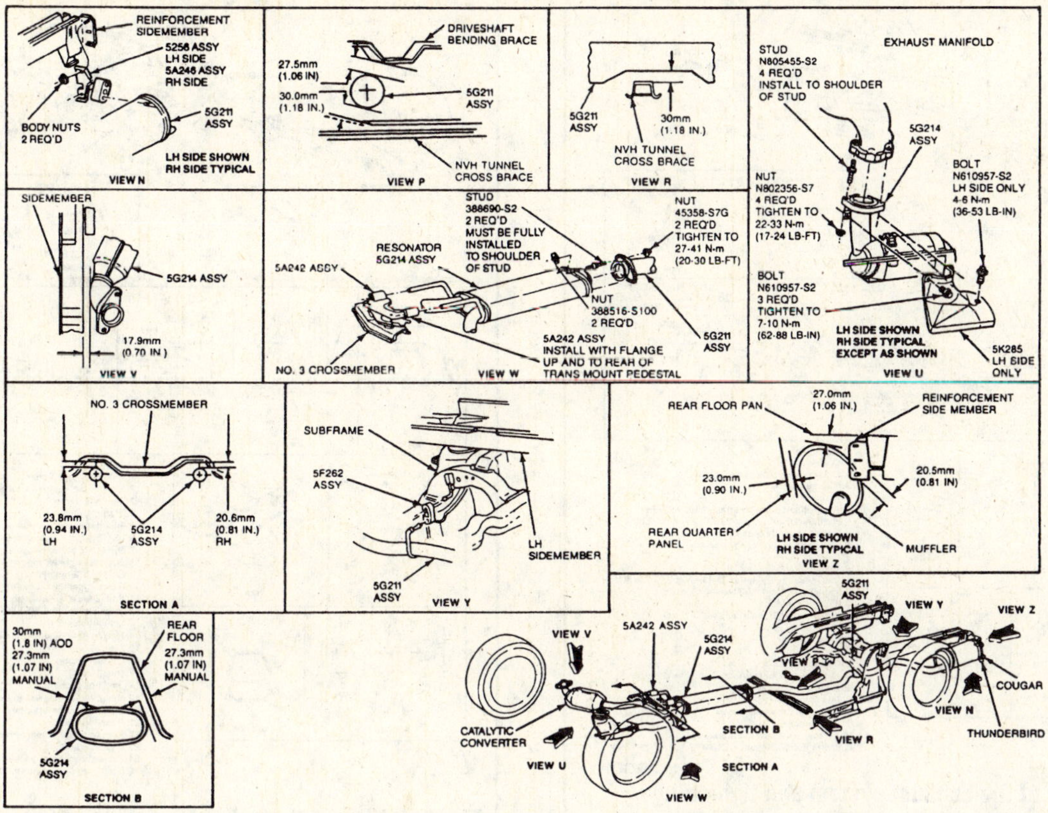

88183GF8

Fig. 215 View of the exhaust system and tightening specifications — 1993 3.8L SC engine shown

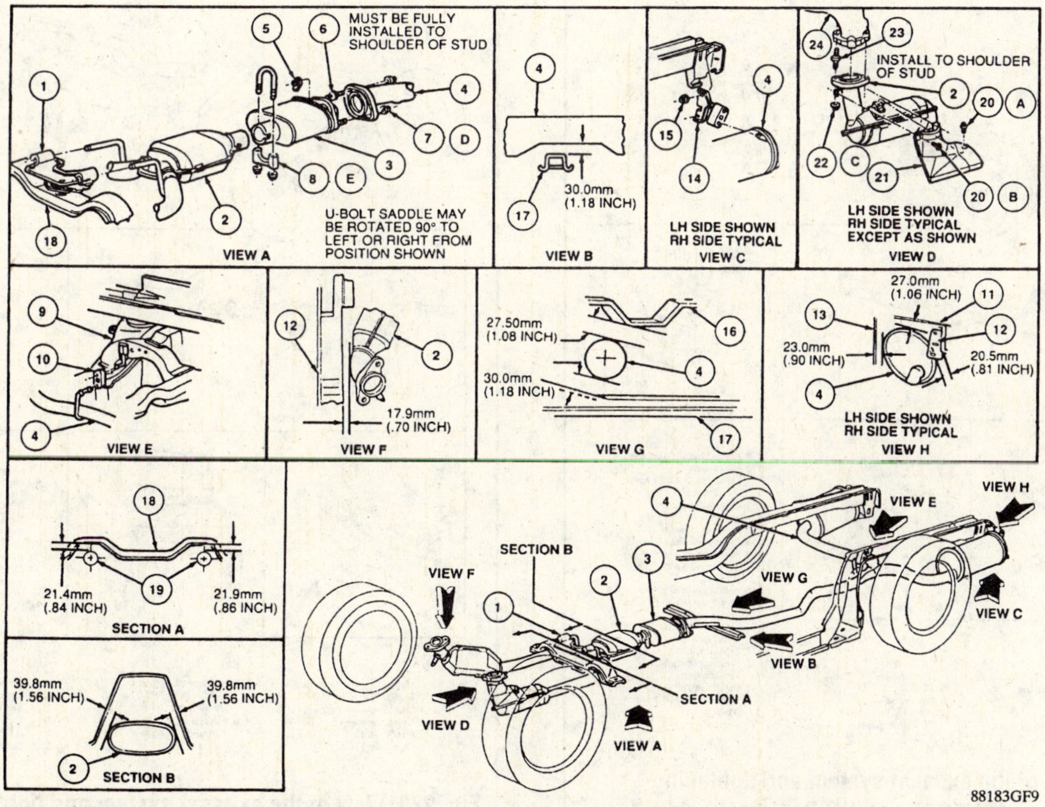

88183GF9

Fig. 216 View of the exhaust system and tightening specifications — 1993 5.0L engine shown

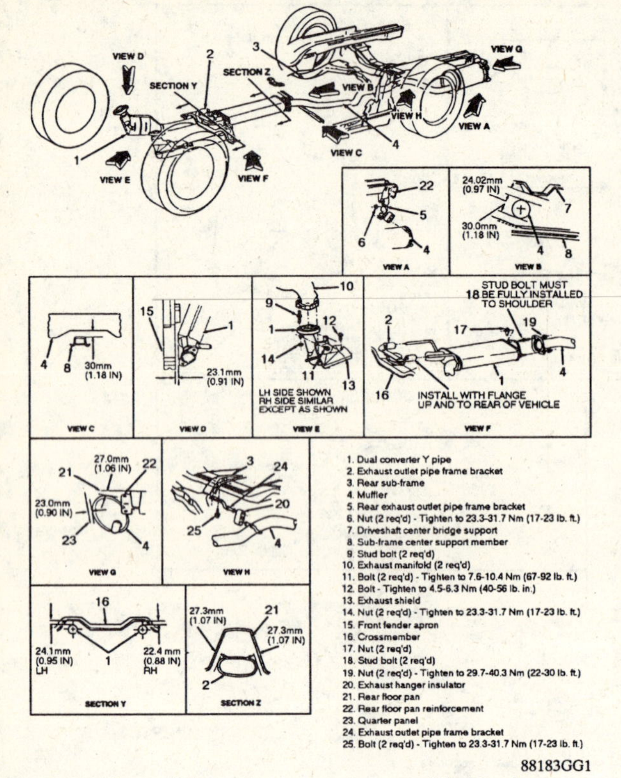

Fig. 217 View of the exhaust system and tightening specifications — 1995 3.8L non-SC (except California) engine shown

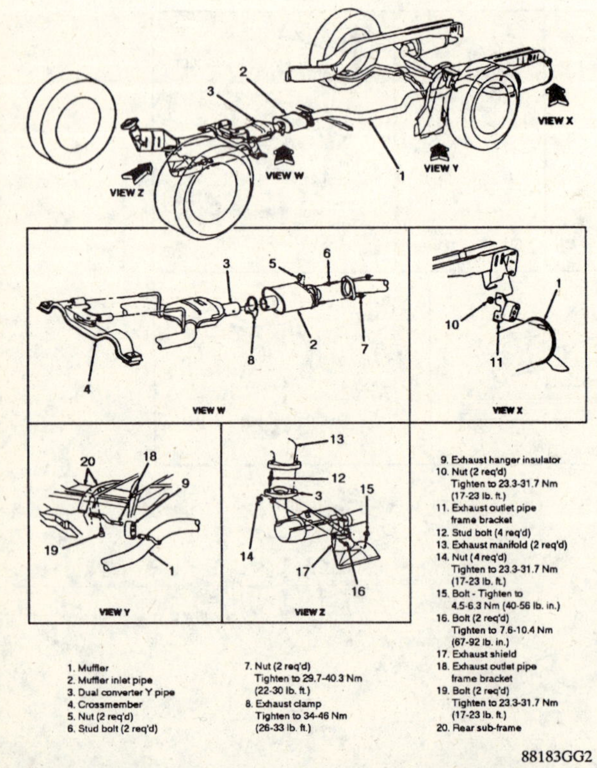

Fig. 218 View of the exhaust system and tightening specifications — 1995 3.8L non-SC California engine shown

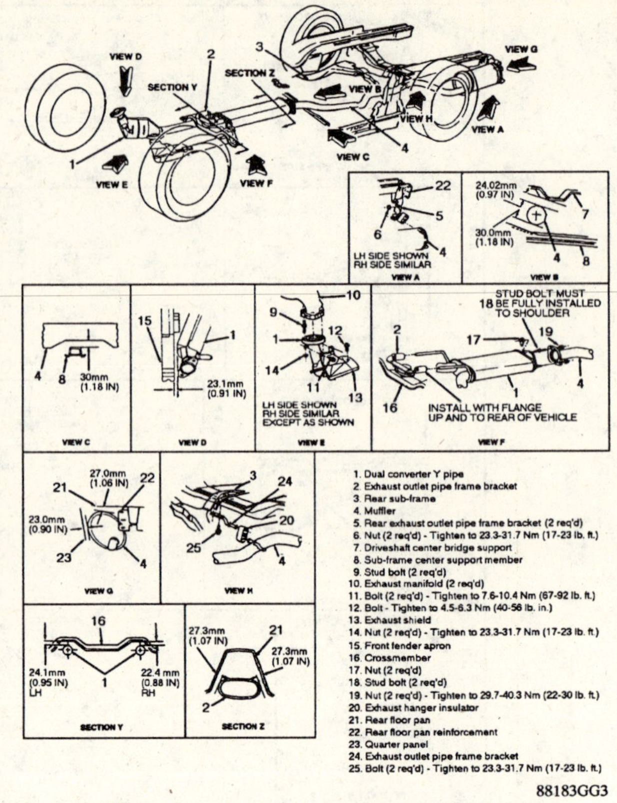

Fig. 219 View of the exhaust system and tightening specifications — 1995 3.8L SC engine with A/T shown

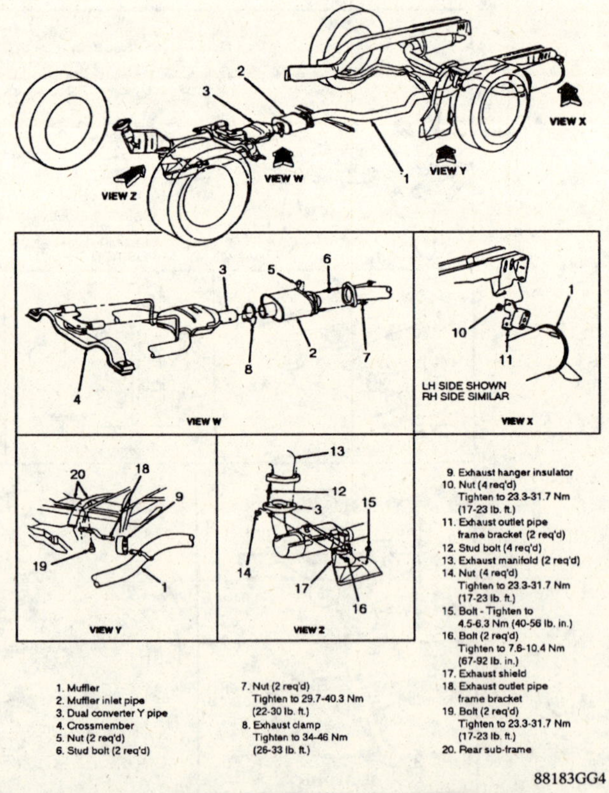

Fig. 220 View of the exhaust system and tightening specifications — 1995 3.8L SC engine with M/T shown

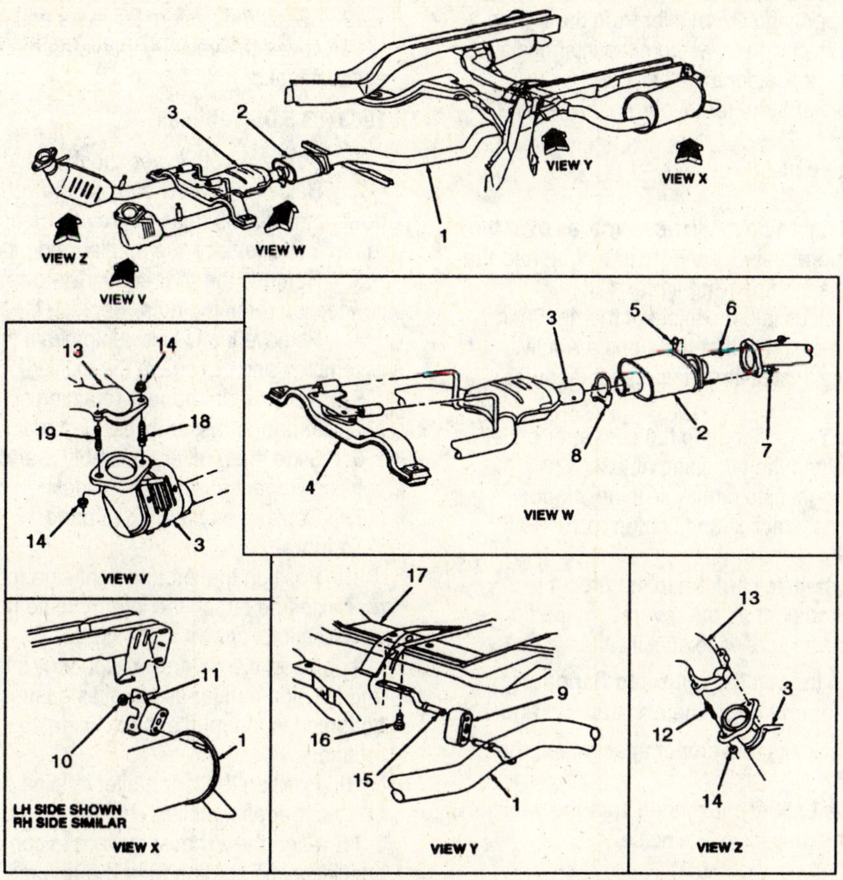

1. Muffler
2. Muffler inlet pipe
3. Dual converter Y pipe
4. Crossmember
5. Nut (2 req'd)
6. Stud bolt (2 req'd)
7. Nut (2 req'd) Tighten to 29.7-40.3 Nm (22-30 lb. ft.)
8. Exhaust clamp Tighten to 34-46 Nm (26-33 lb. ft.)
9. Exhaust hanger insulator
10. Nut (4 req'd) Tighten to 23.3-31.7 Nm (17-23 lb. ft.)
11. Exhaust outlet pipe frame bracket (2 req'd)
12. Stud bolt (2 req'd)
13. Exhaust manifold (2 req'd)
14. Nut (4 req'd) Tighten to 23.3-31.7 Nm (17-23 lb. ft.)
15. Exhaust outlet pipe frame bracket
16. Bolt (2 req'd) Tighten to 23.3-31.7 Nm (17-23 lb. ft.)
17. Rear sub-frame
18. Stud bolt
19. Stud bolt

88183GG5

Fig. 221 View of the exhaust system and tightening specifications — 1995 4.6L engine

3. Unfasten the rear converter-to-muffler pipe flange connection attaching nuts.
4. Remove both lower shock absorber attachments.
5. Remove the attaching screws from the tailpipe bracket to disengage the rear hanger.
6. Slide the muffler assembly rearward to disconnect it from the catalytic converter.
7. Unfasten the intermediate hanger-to-muffler support attaching screws. Remove the muffler from the vehicle. Replace any damaged parts.

To install:

➥ Transfer any heat or grass shields to new parts. The muffler heat shield is banded to the muffler body. New service clamps MUST be used for reassembly.

8. Position the muffler assembly over the rear axle and attach the intermediate support bracket. Tighten to specifications shown in the accompanying figure.
9. Position the muffler inlet pipe flange on the converter flange. Install but do not tighten the attaching nuts.
10. Position the muffler rear support bracket and tighten the two retaining screws to specifications shown in the accompanying figure.
11. Align the exhaust system to conform to the proper clearance specifications. Starting from the muffler inlet pipe connection, tighten all nuts and screws to specification.
12. Assembly the lower shock absorber attachments.
13. Check the system for leaks and proper attachment, then carefully lower the vehicle.
14. Connect the negative battery cable, then start the vehicle and check for leaks and/or exhaust system noise.

VEHICLES WITH DUAL MUFFLERS

1. Disconnect the negative battery cable.
2. Remove both lower shock absorber attachments.
3. Carefully raise the vehicle at the frame lift points to allow the axle full downward travel. This will provide the clearance necessary to remove and replace the muffler and pipe.
4. Remove the rear converter-to-reverse Y-pipe flange connection attaching nuts. Replace if necessary.

5. Unfasten the U-bolt clamps from the right and left side muffler assemblies, then disengage the muffler from the Y-pipe.
6. Remove the hanger attaching screws from the intermediate and rear hanger assemblies. Repeat for the other side.
7. Slide the muffler rearward and remove from the vehicle. Repeat for the other side.
8. Replace any damage parts.

To install:

9. Position the left and right side muffler assemblies over the rear axle, then attach the intermediate hangers and tighten to the specifications shown in the accompanying figure.
10. Insert reverse Y-pipe legs into the inlets of the right and left side muffler assemblies ensuring that the stops are fully bottomed in the muffler slots. Install the retainer, but do not tighten at this time.
11. Position the reverse Y-pipe flange to the converter outlet flange. Install but do not tighten the attaching nuts.
12. Position the left and right side muffler tailpipe support bracket to the rear hanger assemblies and tighten to 10–15 ft. lbs. (14–20 Nm).
13. Align the exhaust system to conform to the proper clearance specifications. Starting from the reverse Y-pipe flange connection, tighten all nuts and screws to specification.

➥ It may be necessary to loosen the manifold flange connection in order to properly align the exhaust system.

14. Check the for system leaks and proper attachment, then carefully lower the vehicle.
15. Connect the negative battery cable, then start the vehicle and check for leaks and/or exhaust system noise.

1983–88 3.8L Vehicles

1. Disconnect both rear shock absorber lower mounting bolts.
2. Raise and support the car on jackstands placed under the frame, to allow the rear axle to lower to the full limit of its travel, WITHOUT STRETCHING THE BRAKE HOSE.
3. Unbolt the muffler inlet flange from the converter outlet flange.
4. Remove the tailpipe support bracket from the rear hanger, if required. If equipped with a resonator, this bracket will be attached to the back of the resonator.
5. Remove the muffler support bracket attaching screws.
6. Slide the muffler and resonator assembly rearward to disconnect it from the catalytic converter flange, then forward to remove from the vehicle.

To install:

➥ Transfer any heat or grass shields to new parts. The muffler heat shield is "banded" to the muffler body. New service clamps must be used in assembly.

7. Position the muffler and install the muffler support bracket attaching screws. Do not tighten the screws at this time.
8. Install the tailpipe support bracket to the rear hanger, if required. Do not tighten the screws at this time.
9. Position the muffler inlet pipe to the converter and install the attaching nuts. Do not tighten the nuts at this time.
10. Align the exhaust system to conform to clearance specifications.
11. With the system held to alignment specification:
    a. Tighten the support bracket attaching screws to specification as shown in the figure.
    b. Tighten the muffler inlet pipe flange attaching nuts equally to specification.
12. Install both shock absorber attachments and tighten.
13. Check the system for leaks and proper alignment.
14. Lower the vehicle, then start the engine and check for exhaust leaks.

1983–88 5.0L Vehicles

1. Remove both lower shock absorber attachments.
2. Raise and safely support the vehicle to allow the axle full downward travel. This will provide clearance necessary to remove and replace the muffler and pipe.
3. Remove the rear converter-to-reverse Y-pipe flange connection retaining nuts. Replace if necessary.
4. Remove the U-bolt clamps from the right and left side muffler assemblies and disengage the muffler form the reverse Y-pipe.
5. Remove the hanger retaining screws from the intermediate and rear hanger assemblies. Repair for the other side.
6. Slide the muffler assembly rearward and remove from the vehicle. Repeat for the other side.
7. Replace any damaged parts.

To install:

8. Position the left and right side muffler assemblies over the rear axle and attach the intermediate hangers. Tighten to specifications shown in the figure.
9. Insert the reverse Y-pipe legs into the inlets of the right and left side muffler assemblies ensuring that the stops are fully bottomed in the muffler slots. Install but do not tighten the retainers.
10. Position the left muffler tailpipe support brackets to the rear hanger assemblies. Tighten to specification.
11. Align the exhaust system to conform to proper clearance specifications starting from the reverse Y-flange connection, tighten all nuts and screws to specification.

➥ Sometimes it may be necessary to loosen the manifold flange connection in order to properly align the exhaust system.

12. Check the system for leaks, then carefully lower the vehicle.

1989–96 Vehicles

1. Raise and support the car on jackstands placed under the frame.
2. Remove the nuts retaining the muffler inlet pipe flange to the resonator outlet flange.
3. Remove the muffler support brackets/hanger rods from all hanger insulators.
4. Slide muffler assembly rearward to disconnect it from the catalytic converter flange, and remove from vehicle.
5. Replace any damaged parts.

To install:

6. Position the muffler and install the muffler support brackets/hanger rods into all hanger insulators.
7. With the muffler assembly support by hangers, install the inlet flange over the resonator outlet flange studs. Install, but do not tighten, the retaining nuts.
8. Align the exhaust system to conform to clearance specifications.
9. With the system held to alignment specification, tighten the muffler inlet pipe flange attaching nuts equally to 20–30 ft. lbs. (27–41 Nm).
10. Check the system for leaks and proper alignment, then carefully lower the vehicle.

Front Exhaust Pipe

REMOVAL & INSTALLATION

2.3L Engine

1. Raise and safely support the front of the vehicle with jackstands.
2. Support the muffler with a wire.
3. Unbolt the inlet pipe from the converter inlet flange.
4. Remove the inlet pipe-to-exhaust manifold flange.

To install:

5. Installation is the reverse of removal.
6. Always use new clamps. Always install parts loosely, then align the system, making sure that all clearances between the system parts and surrounding components are adequate. Tighten the clamp nuts to 35 ft. lbs. (47 Nm) and the flange nuts to 30 ft. lbs. (41 Nm).
7. Carefully lower the vehicle, then start the engine and check for exhaust leaks.

3.8L and 5.0L Engines

1983–88 VEHICLES

1. Raise and support the front end on jackstands.
2. Remove the clamp attaching the Y-pipe to the converter inlet pipe.
3. Unbolt the Y-pipe flanges from the exhaust manifolds.
4. Remove the Y-pipe.
5. **To install:**
6. Installation is the reverse of removal.
7. Always use new clamps. Always replace the pipe ends-to-manifold packings.
8. Always install all parts loosely and align the system, making sure that all clearances among the system parts and surrounding components are adequate.
9. Tighten the clamp nuts to 35 ft. lbs. (47 Nm) and the flange nuts to 30 ft. lbs. (41 Nm).

Catalytic Converter

REMOVAL & INSTALLATION

2.3L Engine

1. Disconnect the downstream injection air hose at the check valve.
2. Raise and support the front end on jackstands.
3. Remove the nuts attaching the converter inlet pipe to the exhaust manifold.
4. Unfasten the nuts attaching the converter outlet flange to the muffler.
5. Remove the upper and lower heat shields.
6. Remove the converter from the vehicle.

To install:

7. Installation is the reverse of removal.
8. Always use new clamps. Always replace the pipe ends-to-manifold packings.
9. Always install all parts loosely and align the system, making sure that all clearances between the system parts and surrounding components are adequate. Torque the flange nuts to 30 ft. lbs. (41 Nm) and the manifold nuts to 35 ft. lbs. (47 Nm).

1983 3.8L And 5.0L Engines

1. Raise and support the car on jackstands.
2. If the converters are the air-injected, dual type, disconnect the air injection tube from the cover.
3. Unbolt the Y-pipe flanges from the converter flanges.
4. Unbolt the converter flange at the manifolds.
5. Slide the inlet pipe rearward until the converters can be removed. Separate the flanges and remove the converters.

To install:

6. Installation is the reverse of removal.
7. Always use new clamps. Always replace the pipe ends-to-manifold packings.
8. Always install all parts loosely and align the system, making sure that all clearances between the system parts and surrounding components are adequate.
9. Tighten the flange nuts to 30 ft. lbs. (41 Nm) and the manifold nuts to 35 ft. lbs. (47 Nm).

1984–88 3.8L And 1986–87 5.0L Engines

1. Raise and support the front end on jackstands.
2. Remove the bolts attaching the Y-pipe to the converter inlet flange.
3. Remove the nuts attaching the muffler inlet pipe to the converter outlet flange.
4. Separate the catalytic converter inlet and outlet flange connections.
5. Remove the converter.
6. Installation is the reverse of removal. Always use new clamps. Always replace the pipe ends-to-manifold packings. Always install all parts loosely and align the system, making sure that all clearances between the system parts and surrounding components are adequate. Torque the flange nuts to 30 ft. lbs.; the manifold nuts to 35 ft. lbs.

1984–85 5.0L Engines

1. Raise and support the car on jackstands.
2. Disconnect the air injection tube from the cover.
3. Unbolt the Y-pipe flanges from the converter flanges.
4. Unbolt the converter flange at the muffler.
5. Slide the inlet pipe rearward until the converters can be removed. Separate the flanges and remove the converters.

To install:

6. Installation is the reverse of removal.
7. Always use new clamps. Always replace the pipe ends-to-manifold packings.
8. Always install all parts loosely and align the system, making sure that all clearances between the system parts and surrounding components are adequate.
9. Torque the flange nuts to 30 ft. lbs. (41 Nm). and the manifold nuts to 35 ft. lbs. (47 Nm).

1989–96 Vehicles 3.8L, 4.6L And 5.0L Engines

1. Raise and safely support the car on jackstands.
2. If equipped, detach the heated oxygen sensors at the wiring harness connectors.

3. Remove two nuts retaining the muffler assembly inlet flange to the resonator outlet flange. Disengage muffler inlet flange from resonator outlet flange studs.

4. Remove three screws retaining the left converter shield.

5. Unfasten the four nuts retaining converter pipe flanges to the exhaust manifolds.

6. Slide the converter and resonator assembly rearward to disengage the hanger rods from the hanger insulators. Remove the converter and insulator assembly.

7. On 5.0L engines, remove resonator from converter assembly by loosening U-bolt clamp and pulling resonator from converter.

8. Replace any damaged parts.

To install:

9. On 5.0L slide resonator over converter so the converter is bottomed into resonator. Position U-bolt and tighten to 25–35 ft. lbs. (34–47 Nm).

10. Engage hanger rods of converter and resonator assembly with transmission mount hanger insulators. Slide converter and resonator assembly forward.

11. Position the converter inlet pipe flanges to the exhaust manifold and install new retaining nuts. Do not tighten the nuts at this time.

12. Align the converter and resonator assembly to conform to all clearance specifications. Tighten all manifold nuts to 17–24 ft. lbs. (22–33 Nm).

13. Position the left side converter shield and tighten the retaining bolts to 54–115 inch lbs. (6–13 Nm).

14. With the muffler assembly supporter by hangers, install the muffler inlet flange over the resonator outlet flange studs. Install but do not tighten the retaining nuts.

15. Align the muffler and conform to clearance specifications. Tighten the flange nuts to 20–30 ft. lbs. (27–40 Nm).

16. Attach the heated oxygen sensors to the wiring harness connectors.

17. Carefully lower the vehicle, then start the engine and check for exhaust leaks.

4

EMISSION CONTROLS

AIR POLLUTION

The earth's atmosphere, at or near sea level, consists approximately of 78 percent nitrogen, 21 percent oxygen and 1 percent other gases. If it were possible to remain in this state, 100 percent clean air would result. However, many varied sources allow other gases and particulates to mix with the clean air, causing our atmosphere to become unclean or polluted.

Some of these pollutants are visible while others are invisible, with each having the capability of causing distress to the eyes, ears, throat, skin and respiratory system. Should these pollutants become concentrated in a specific area and under certain conditions, death could result due to the displacement or chemical change of the oxygen content in the air. These pollutants can also cause great damage to the environment and to the many man made objects that are exposed to the elements.

To better understand the causes of air pollution, the pollutants can be categorized into 3 separate types, natural, industrial and automotive.

Natural Pollutants

Natural pollution has been present on earth since before man appeared and continues to be a factor when discussing air pollution, although it causes only a small percentage of the overall pollution problem. It is the direct result of decaying organic matter, wind born smoke and particulates from such natural events as plain and forest fires (ignited by heat or lightning), volcanic ash, sand and dust which can spread over a large area of the countryside.

Such a phenomenon of natural pollution has been seen in the form of volcanic eruptions, with the resulting plume of smoke, steam and volcanic ash blotting out the sun's rays as it spreads and rises higher into the atmosphere. As it travels into the atmosphere the upper air currents catch and carry the smoke and ash, while condensing the steam back into water vapor. As the water vapor, smoke and ash travel on their journey, the smoke dissipates into the atmosphere while the ash and moisture settle back to earth in a trail hundreds of miles long. In some cases, lives are lost and millions of dollars of property damage result.

Industrial Pollutants

Industrial pollution is caused primarily by industrial processes, the burning of coal, oil and natural gas, which in turn produce smoke and fumes. Because the burning fuels contain large amounts of sulfur, the principal ingredients of smoke and fumes are sulfur dioxide and particulate matter. This type of pollutant occurs most severely during still, damp and cool weather, such as at night. Even in its less severe form, this pollutant is not confined to just cities. Because of air movements, the pollutants move for miles over the surrounding countryside, leaving in its path a barren and unhealthy environment for all living things.

Working with Federal, State and Local mandated regulations and by carefully monitoring emissions, big business has greatly reduced the amount of pollutant introduced from its industrial sources, striving to obtain an acceptable level. Because of the mandated industrial emission clean up, many land areas and streams in and around the cities that were formerly barren of vegetation and life, have now begun to move back in the direction of nature's intended balance.

Automotive Pollutants

The third major source of air pollution is automotive emissions. The emissions from the internal combustion engines were not an appreciable problem years ago because of the small number of registered vehicles and the nation's small highway system. However, during the early 1950's, the trend of the American people was to move from the cities to the surrounding suburbs. This caused an immediate problem in transportation because the majority of suburbs were not afforded mass transit conveniences. This lack of transportation created an attractive market for the automobile manufacturers, which resulted in a dramatic increase in the number of vehicles produced and sold, along with a marked increase in highway construction between cities and the suburbs. Multi-vehicle families emerged with a growing emphasis placed on an individual vehicle per family member. As the increase in vehicle ownership and usage occurred, so did pollutant levels in and around the cities, as suburbanites drove daily to their businesses and employment, returning at the end of the day to their homes in the suburbs.

It was noted that a smoke and fog type haze was being formed and at times, remained in suspension over the cities, taking time to dissipate. At first this "smog," derived from the words "smoke" and "fog," was thought to result from industrial pollution but it was determined that automobile emissions shared the blame. It was discovered that when normal automobile emissions were exposed to sunlight for a period of time, complex chemical reactions would take place.

It is now known that smog is a photo chemical layer which develops when certain oxides of nitrogen (NOx) and unburned hydrocarbons (HC) from automobile emissions are exposed to sunlight. Pollution was more severe when smog would become stagnant over an area in which a warm layer of air settled over the top of the cooler air mass, trapping and holding the cooler mass at ground level. The trapped cooler air would keep the emissions from being dispersed and diluted through normal air flows. This type of air stagnation was given the name "Temperature Inversion."

TEMPERATURE INVERSION

In normal weather situations, surface air is warmed by heat radiating from the earth's surface and the sun's rays. This causes it to rise upward, into the atmosphere. Upon rising it will cool through a convection type heat exchange with the cooler upper air. As warm air rises, the surface pollutants are carried upward and dissipated into the atmosphere.

When a temperature inversion occurs, we find the higher air is no longer cooler, but is warmer than the surface air, causing the cooler surface air to become trapped. This warm air blanket can extend from above ground level to a few hundred or even a few thousand feet into the air. As the surface air is trapped, so are the pollutants, causing a severe smog condition. Should this stagnant air mass extend to a few thousand feet high, enough air movement with the inversion takes place to allow the smog layer to rise above ground level but the pollutants still cannot dissipate. This inversion can remain for days over an area, with the smog level only rising or lowering from ground level to a few hundred feet high. Meanwhile, the pollutant levels increase, causing eye irritation, respiratory problems, reduced visibility, plant damage and in some cases, even disease.

This inversion phenomenon was first noted in the Los Angeles, California area. The city lies in terrain resembling a basin and with certain weather conditions, a cold air mass is held in the basin while a warmer air mass covers it like a lid.

Because this type of condition was first documented as prevalent in the Los Angeles area, this type of trapped pollution was named Los Angeles Smog, although it occurs in other areas where a large concentration of automobiles are used and the air remains stagnant for any length of time.

HEAT TRANSFER

Consider the internal combustion engine as a machine in which raw materials must be placed so a finished product comes out. As in any machine operation, a certain amount of wasted material is formed. When we relate this to the internal combustion engine, we find that through the input of air and fuel, we obtain power during the combustion process to drive the vehicle. The by-product or waste of this power is, in part, heat and exhaust gases with which we must dispose.

The heat from the combustion process can rise to over 4000°F (2204°C). The dissipation of this heat is controlled by a ram air effect, the use of cooling fans to cause air flow and a liquid coolant solution surrounding the combustion area to transfer the heat of combustion through the cylinder walls and into the coolant. The coolant is then directed to a thin-finned, multi-tubed radiator, from which the excess heat is transferred to the atmosphere by 1 of the 3 heat transfer methods, conduction, convection or radiation.

The cooling of the combustion area is an important part in the control of exhaust emissions. To understand the behavior of the combustion and transfer of its heat, consider the air/fuel charge. It is ignited and the flame front burns progressively across the combustion chamber until the burning charge reaches the cylinder walls. Some of the fuel in contact with the walls is not hot enough to burn, thereby snuffing out or quenching the combustion process. This leaves unburned fuel in the combustion chamber. This unburned fuel is then forced out of the cylinder and into the exhaust system, along with the exhaust gases.

Many attempts have been made to minimize the amount of unburned fuel in the combustion chambers due to quenching, by increasing the coolant temperature and lessening the contact area of the coolant around the combustion area. However, design limitations within the combustion chambers prevent the complete burning of the air/fuel charge, so a certain amount of the unburned fuel is still expelled into the exhaust system, regardless of modifications to the engine.

AUTOMOTIVE EMISSIONS

Before emission controls were mandated on internal combustion engines, other sources of engine pollutants were discovered along with the exhaust emissions. It was determined that engine combustion exhaust produced approximately 60 percent of the total emission pollutants, fuel evaporation from the fuel tank and carburetor vents produced 20 percent, with the final 20 percent being produced through the crankcase as a by-product of the combustion process.

Exhaust Gases

The exhaust gases emitted into the atmosphere are a combination of burned and unburned fuel. To understand the exhaust emission and its composition, we must review some basic chemistry.

When the air/fuel mixture is introduced into the engine, we are mixing air, composed of nitrogen (78 percent), oxygen (21 percent) and other gases (1 percent) with the fuel, which is 100 percent hydrocarbons (HC), in a semi-controlled ratio. As the combustion process is accomplished, power is produced to move the vehicle while the heat of combustion is transferred to the cooling system. The exhaust gases are then composed of nitrogen, a diatomic gas (N_2), the same as was introduced in the engine, carbon dioxide (CO_2), the same gas that is used in beverage carbonation, and water vapor (H_2O). The nitrogen (N_2), for the most part, passes through the engine unchanged, while the oxygen (O_2) reacts (burns) with the hydrocarbons (HC) and produces the carbon dioxide (CO_2) and the water vapors (H_2O). If this chemical process would be the only process to take place, the exhaust emissions would be harmless. However, during the combustion process, other compounds are formed which are considered dangerous. These pollutants are hydrocarbons (HC), carbon monoxide (CO), oxides of nitrogen (NOx) oxides of sulfur (SOx) and engine particulates.

HYDROCARBONS

Hydrocarbons (HC) are essentially fuel which was not burned during the combustion process or which has escaped into the atmosphere through fuel evaporation. The main sources of incomplete combustion are rich air/fuel mixtures, low engine temperatures and improper spark timing. The main sources of hydrocarbon emission through fuel evaporation on most vehicles used to be the vehicle's fuel tank and carburetor float bowl.

To reduce combustion hydrocarbon emission, engine modifications were made to minimize dead space and surface area in the combustion chamber. In addition, the air/fuel mixture was made more lean through the improved control which feedback carburetion and fuel injection offers and by the addition of external controls to aid in further combustion of the hydrocarbons outside the engine. Two such methods were the addition of air injection systems, to inject fresh air into the exhaust manifolds and the installation of catalytic converters, units that are able to burn traces of hydrocarbons without affecting the internal combustion process or fuel economy.

To control hydrocarbon emissions through fuel evaporation, modifications were made to the fuel tank to allow storage of the fuel vapors during periods of engine shut-down. Modifications were also made to the air intake system so that at specific times during engine operation, these vapors may be purged and burned by blending them with the air/fuel mixture.

CARBON MONOXIDE

Carbon monoxide is formed when not enough oxygen is present during the combustion process to convert carbon (C) to carbon dioxide (CO_2). An increase in the carbon monoxide (CO) emission is normally accompanied by an increase in the hydrocarbon (HC) emission because of the lack of oxygen to completely burn all of the fuel mixture.

Carbon monoxide (CO) also increases the rate at which the photo chemical smog is formed by speeding up the conversion of nitric oxide (NO) to nitrogen dioxide (NO_2). To accomplish this, carbon monoxide (CO) combines with oxygen (O_2) and nitric oxide (NO) to produce carbon dioxide (CO_2) and nitrogen dioxide (NO_2). ($CO + O_2 + NO = CO_2 + NO_2$).

The dangers of carbon monoxide, which is an odorless and colorless toxic gas are many. When carbon monoxide is inhaled into the lungs and passed into the blood stream, oxygen is replaced by the carbon monoxide in the red blood cells, causing a reduction in the amount of oxygen supplied to the many parts of the body. This lack of oxygen causes headaches, lack of coordination, reduced mental alertness and, should the carbon monoxide concentration be high enough, death could result.

NITROGEN

Normally, nitrogen is an inert gas. When heated to approximately 2500°F (1371°C) through the combustion process, this gas becomes active and causes an increase in the nitric oxide (NO) emission.

Oxides of nitrogen (NOx) are composed of approximately 97–98 percent nitric oxide (NO). Nitric oxide is a colorless gas but when it is passed into the atmosphere, it combines with oxygen and forms nitrogen dioxide (NO_2). The nitrogen dioxide then combines with chemically active hydrocarbons (HC) and when in the presence of sunlight, causes the formation of photo-chemical smog.

Ozone

To further complicate matters, some of the nitrogen dioxide (NO_2) is broken apart by the sunlight to form nitric oxide and oxygen. (NO_2 + sunlight = NO + O). This single atom of oxygen then combines with diatomic (meaning 2 atoms) oxygen (O_2) to form ozone (O_3). Ozone is one of the smells associated with smog. It has a pungent and offensive odor, irritates the eyes and lung tissues, affects the growth of plant life and causes rapid deterioration of rubber products. Ozone can be formed by sunlight as well as electrical discharge into the air.

The most common discharge area on the automobile engine is the secondary ignition electrical system, especially when inferior quality spark plug cables are used. As the surge of high voltage is routed through the secondary cable, the circuit builds up an electrical field around the wire, which acts upon the oxygen in the surrounding air to form the ozone. The faint glow along the cable with the engine running that may be visible on a dark night, is called the "corona discharge." It is the result of the electrical field passing from a high along the cable, to a low in the surrounding air, which forms the ozone gas. The combination of corona and ozone has been a major cause of cable deterioration. Recently, different and better quality insulating materials have lengthened the life of the electrical cables.

Although ozone at ground level can be harmful, ozone is beneficial to the earth's inhabitants. By having a concentrated ozone layer called the "ozonosphere," between 10 and 20 miles (16–32 km) up in the atmosphere, much of the ultra violet radiation from the sun's rays are absorbed and screened. If this ozone layer were not present, much of the earth's surface would be burned, dried and unfit for human life.

OXIDES OF SULFUR

Oxides of sulfur (SOx) were initially ignored in the exhaust system emissions, since the sulfur content of gasoline as a fuel is less than $^1/_{10}$ of 1 percent. Because of this small amount, it was felt that it contributed very little to the overall pollution problem. However, because of the difficulty in solving the sulfur emissions in industrial pollution's and the introduction of catalytic converter to the automobile exhaust systems, a change was mandated. The automobile exhaust system, when equipped with a catalytic converter, changes the sulfur dioxide (SO_2) into the sulfur trioxide (SO_3).

When this combines with water vapors (H_2O), a sulfuric acid mist (H_2SO_4) is formed and is a very difficult pollutant to handle since it is extremely corrosive. This sulfuric acid mist that is formed, is the same mist that rises from the vents of an automobile battery when an active chemical reaction takes place within the battery cells.

When a large concentration of vehicles equipped with catalytic converters are operating in an area, this acid mist may rise and be distributed over a large ground area causing land, plant, crop, paint and building damage.

PARTICULATE MATTER

A certain amount of particulate matter is present in the burning of any fuel, with carbon constituting the largest percentage of the particulates. In gasoline, the remaining particulates are the burned remains of the various other compounds used in its manufacture. When a gasoline engine is in good internal condition, the particulate emissions are low but as the engine wears internally, the particulate emissions increase. By visually inspecting the tail pipe emissions, a determination can be made as to where an engine defect may exist. An engine with light gray or blue smoke emitting from the tail pipe normally indicates an increase in the oil consumption through burning due to internal engine wear. Black smoke would indicate a defective fuel delivery system, causing the engine to operate in a rich mode. Regardless of the color of the smoke, the internal part of the engine or the fuel delivery system should be repaired to prevent excess particulate emissions.

Diesel and turbine engines emit a darkened plume of smoke from the exhaust system because of the type of fuel used. Emission control regulations are mandated for this type of emission and more stringent measures are being used to prevent excess emission of the particulate matter. Electronic components are being introduced to control the injection of the fuel at precisely the proper time of piston travel, to achieve the optimum in fuel ignition and fuel usage. Other particulate after-burning components are being tested to achieve a cleaner emission.

Good grades of engine lubricating oils should be used, which meet the manufacturers specification. Cut-rate oils can contribute to the particulate emission problem because of their low flash or ignition temperature point. Such oils burn prematurely during the combustion process causing emission of particulate matter.

The cooling system is an important factor in the reduction of particulate matter. The optimum combustion will occur, with the cooling system operating at a temperature specified by the manufacturer. The cooling system must be maintained in the same manner as the engine oiling system, as each system is required to perform properly in order for the engine to operate efficiently for a long time.

Crankcase Emissions

Crankcase emissions are made up of water, acids, unburned fuel, oil fumes and particulates. These emissions are classified as hydrocarbons (HC) and are formed by the small amount of unburned, compressed air/fuel mixture entering the crankcase from the combustion area (between the cylinder walls and piston rings) during the compression and power strokes. The head of the compression and combustion help to form the remaining crankcase emissions.

Since the first engines, crankcase emissions were allowed into the atmosphere through a road draft tube, mounted on the lower side of the engine block. Fresh air came in through an open oil filler cap or breather. The air passed through the crankcase mixing with blow-by gases. The motion of the vehicle and the air blowing past the open end of the road draft tube caused a low pressure area (vacuum) at the end of the tube. Crankcase emissions were simply drawn out of the road draft tube into the air.

To control the crankcase emission, the road draft tube was deleted. A hose and/or tubing was routed from the crankcase to the intake manifold so the blow-by emission could be burned with the air/fuel mixture. However, it was found that intake manifold vacuum, used to draw the crankcase emissions into the manifold, would vary in strength at the wrong time and not allow the proper emission flow. A regulating valve was needed to control the flow of air through the crankcase.

Testing, showed the removal of the blow-by gases from the crankcase as quickly as possible, was most important to the longevity of the engine. Should large accumulations of blow-by gases remain and condense, dilution of the engine oil would occur to form water, soots, resins, acids and lead salts, resulting in the formation of sludge and varnishes. This condensation of the blow-by gases occurs more frequently on vehicles used in numerous starting and stopping conditions, excessive idling and when the engine is not allowed to attain normal operating temperature through short runs.

Evaporative Emissions

Gasoline fuel is a major source of pollution, before and after it is burned in the automobile engine. From the time the fuel is refined, stored, pumped and transported, again stored until it is pumped into the fuel tank of the vehicle, the gasoline gives off unburned hydrocarbons (HC) into the atmosphere. Through the redesign of storage areas and venting systems, the pollution factor was diminished, but not eliminated, from the refinery standpoint. However, the automobile still remained the primary source of vaporized, unburned hydrocarbon (HC) emissions.

Fuel pumped from an underground storage tank is cool but when exposed to a warmer ambient temperature, will expand. Before controls were mandated, an owner might fill the fuel tank with fuel from an underground storage tank and park the vehicle for some time in warm area, such as a parking lot. As the fuel would warm, it would expand and should no provisions or area be provided for the expansion, the fuel would spill out of the filler neck and onto the ground, causing hydrocarbon (HC) pollution and creating a severe fire hazard. To correct this condition, the vehicle manufacturers added overflow plumbing and/or gasoline tanks with built in expansion areas or domes.

However, this did not control the fuel vapor emission from the fuel tank. It was determined that most of the fuel evaporation occurred when the vehicle was stationary and the engine not operating. Most vehicles carry 5–25 gallons (19–95 liters) of gasoline. Should a large concentration of vehicles be parked in one area, such as a large parking lot, excessive fuel vapor emissions would take place, increasing as the temperature increases.

To prevent the vapor emission from escaping into the atmosphere, the fuel systems were designed to trap the vapors while the vehicle is stationary, by sealing the system from the atmosphere. A storage system is used to collect and hold the fuel vapors from the carburetor (if equipped) and the fuel tank when the engine is not operating. When the engine is started, the storage system is then purged of the fuel vapors, which are drawn into the engine and burned with the air/fuel mixture.

EMISSION CONTROLS

See Figure 1

There are three basic sources of automotive pollution in the modern internal combustion engine. They are the crankcase with its accompanying blow-by vapors, the fuel system with its evaporation of unburned gasoline, and the combustion chambers with their resulting exhaust emissions. Pollution arising from the incomplete combustion of fuel generally falls into three categories: hydrocarbons (HC), carbon monoxide (CO), and oxides of nitrogen (NOx).

All vehicles (covered in this book) have an Emissions Control Information Decal, mounted on the radiator support or possibly on the air cleaner housing. Always refer to this decal when performing service to the emission controls.

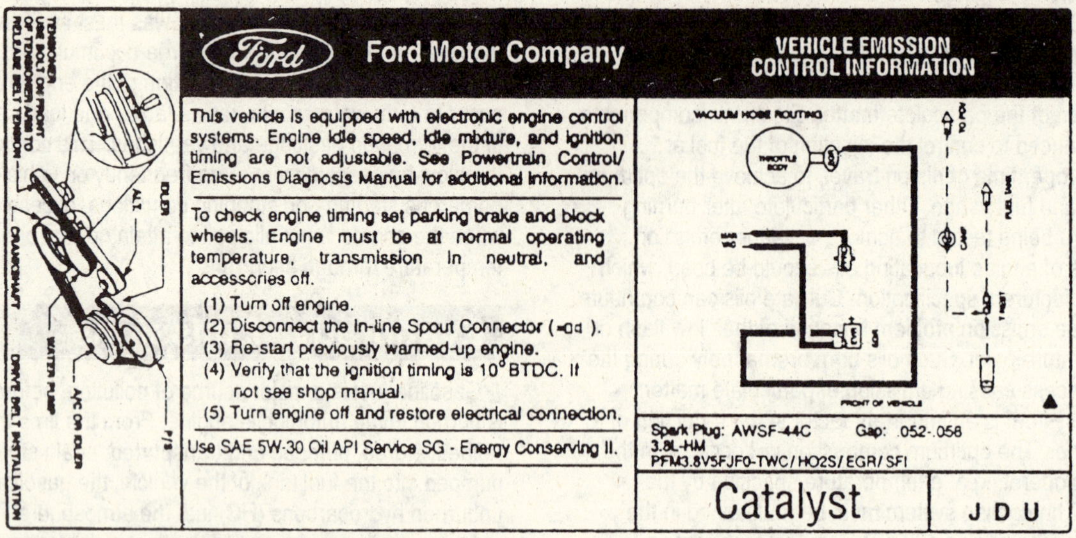

88184G02

Fig. 1 Common Emissions Control Information Decal

Crankcase Ventilation System

OPERATION

➧ See Figures 2 and 3

All models covered in this book are equipped with a positive crankcase ventilation (PCV) system. The system vents harmful combustion blow-by fumes from the crankcase into the engine air intake for burning with the fuel/air mixture. The PCV valve prevents combustion backfiring into the crankcase and serves the engine upon demand by limiting the fresh air intake. The PCV valve also controls the amount of blow-by vapors that are allowed into the intake manifold from the crankcase. The PCV valve also acts as a one-way check valve and prevents air from entering the the crankcase in the opposite direction. The PCV valve system maximizes oil cleanliness by venting moisture and corrosive fumes from the crankcase. The PCV valve system is connected with the evaporative emission system on some vehicles. Do not remove the PCV valve system from the engine. Doing so will adversely affect fuel economy and engine ventilation and may result in shortened engine life.

SYSTEM INSPECTION

1. Visually inspect the components of the PCV valve system. Check for loose, leaking, clogged or damaged hoses. Check for high oil consumption, rough idle or slow starting.
2. Check both hoses for flow restriction or leakage. Inspect the hoses for cracks, splitting, kinking or poor grommet fit.
3. Inspect the ventilation filter for excessive oil consumption.
4. If a component is suspected as a cause of malfunction, replace it before proceeding. If components check out okay, proceed to component testing.

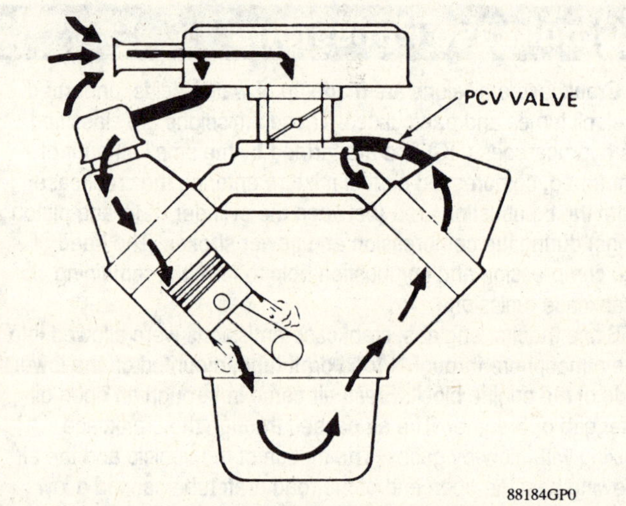

88184GP0

Fig. 2 PCV system operation — early models shown

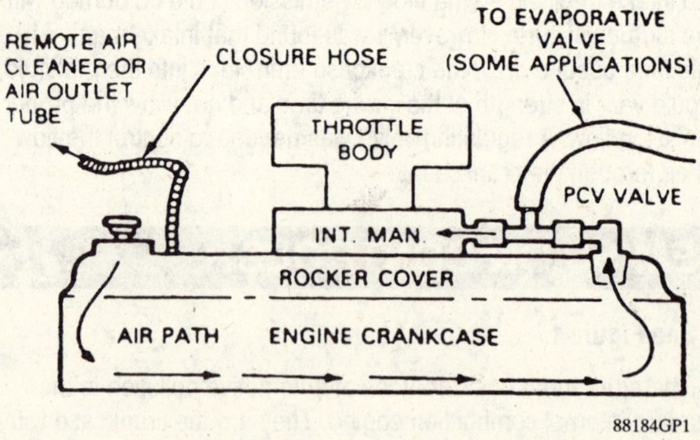

88184GP1

Fig. 3 PCV system operation — late models shown

COMPONENT TESTING

PCV Valve

➧ **See Figure 4**

1. Remove the PCV valve from the grommet and shake the valve. If the valve rattles when shaken, reinstall and proceed to the next step. If it does not rattle, it is sticking and should be replaced.
2. Start the engine and bring it to normal operating temperature.
3. Disconnect the hose from the remote air cleaner or air outlet tube.
4. Place a stiff piece of paper over the hose end and wait 1 minute. If the vacuum holds the paper in place, the system is okay. Reconnect the hose. If the paper is not held in place, the system is plugged or the Evaporative Emission Valve is leaking (if equipped). If valve is suspected of leaking, proceed to the next step.
5. Disconnect the evaporative hose, if equipped and cap the connector.
6. Place a stiff piece of paper over the hose end/nipple and wait 1 minute. If the vacuum holds the paper in place, proceed to the evaporative emission system testing.
7. If the paper is not held in place, check the system for vacuum leaks or obstructions. Inspect the oil cap, PCV valve, hoses, grommets and valve cover for bolt tighten/gasket leak.

REMOVAL & INSTALLATION

PCV Valve

➧ **See Figures 5 and 6**

1. On some engines it may be necessary to remove the air cleaner outlet tube.
2. Remove the PCV valve from the mounting grommet in the valve cover.
3. Disconnect the hose from the valve and remove the valve from the vehicle.
4. Inspect the hoses and grommet for deterioration. Replace if necessary.

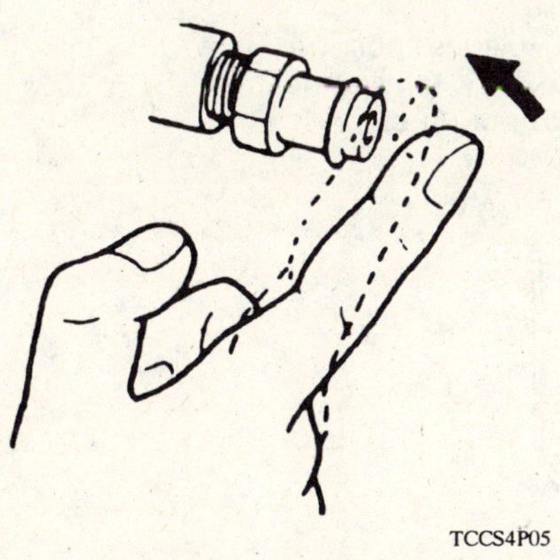

Fig. 4 Check the PCV valve for vacuum at idle

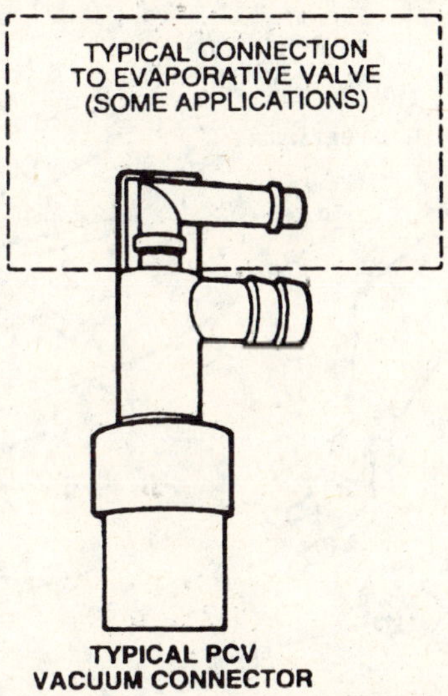

Fig. 5 PCV valves on Thunderbirds and Cougars usually have two vacuum connections

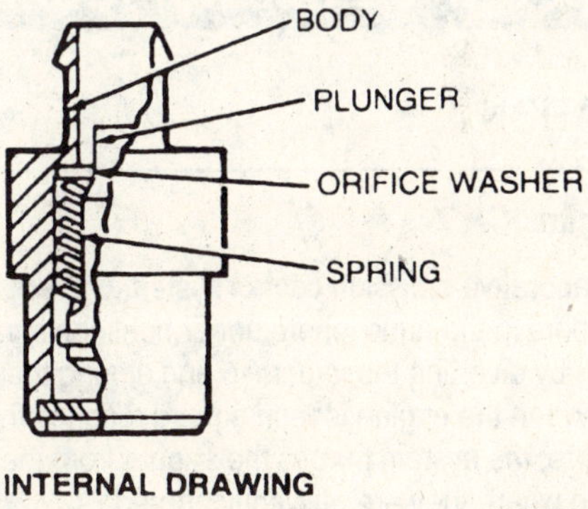

Fig. 6 Inner view of the PCV valve

To install:

5. Install a new PCV valve into the valve cover grommet.
6. Attach the hose to the valve.
7. If removed, install the air cleaner outlet tube.

Ventilation Filter

➧ **See Figure 7**

1. Disconnect the PCV hose at the air cleaner by unsnapping the elbow from the retainer clip or sliding off the hose from the PCV filter adapter.
2. Remove the air cleaner body top.
3. Remove the ventilation filter retainer clip and filter retainer from the air cleaner body.
4. Remove the filter from the retainer and clean out the retainer.

To install:

5. Install a new filter into the filter retainer pack.
6. Position the filter assembly into the air cleaner body with the retainer clip.
7. Attach the hose to the air cleaner assembly.
8. Place the air cleaner cap on the air cleaner body and secure.

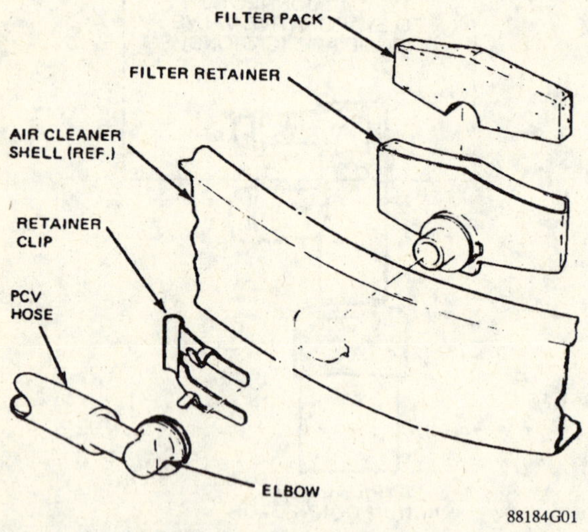

Fig. 7 The ventilation filter is secured in the air cleaner body by a retainer clip

Evaporative Emission Controls

OPERATION

➧ **See Figure 8**

The evaporative emission control system prevents the escape of fuel vapors to the atmosphere under hot soak and engine off conditions by diverting the vapors to and storing them in a carbon canister. When the engine is running and reaches the proper temperature, the system purges the vapors from the canister to the engine where they are efficiently burned.

The evaporative emission control system consists of the carbon canister, the CANP purge control solenoid(s), purge valve(s), the fuel tank vapor hose, and the fuel vapor return line.

SYSTEM INSPECTION

1. Inspect the canister hose and inlet nipple for blockage.
2. Inspect fuel evaporative emission system for blockage.
3. Inspect the vapor tube and the hoses for kinks or pinched areas.
4. Inspect the vapor hose routing between the fuel tank and the body for kinks or pinched areas.

REMOVAL & INSTALLATION

Carbon Canister

The carbon canister stores the fuel vapor by absorbing it until it is returned to the engine to be burned. There should be no liquid in the canister.

1. Disconnect the canister purge hose from the air cleaner fitting.
2. Loosen the canister retaining bracket and lift out the canister.

To install:

3. Attach the canister to the retaining bracket.
4. Connect the purge hose to the air cleaner fitting.

Fuel Tank Vapor Valve

➧ **See Figures 9 and 10**

The fuel tank vapor valve vents the fuel vapor from the tank to the carbon canister for storage. The valve is located in the upper area of the fuel tank.

1. Disconnect the negative battery cable.
2. Raise and safely support the vehicle.
3. Remove the fuel tank from the vehicle.
4. Disconnect the hoses and remove the vapor valve from the grommet in the fuel tank.

To install:

5. Install the vapor valve to the tank and attach the hoses.
6. Install the tank in the vehicle.
7. Check for leaks.
8. Lower the vehicle. Connect the negative battery cable.

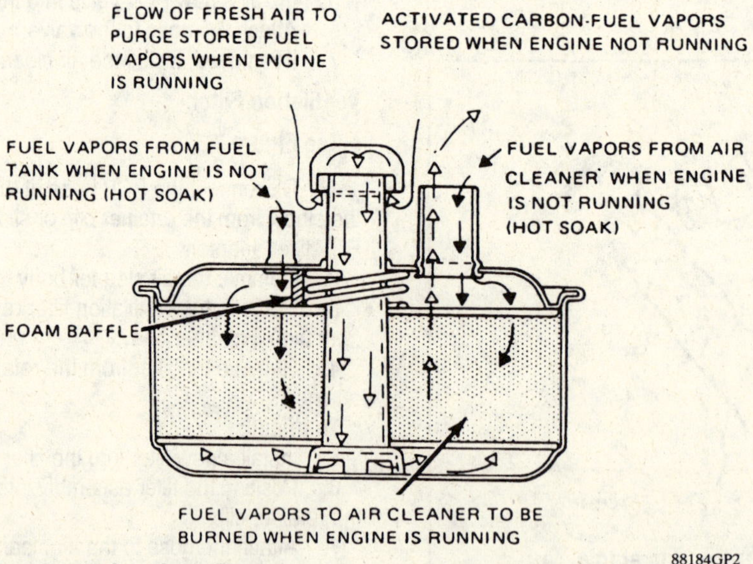

Fig. 8 Evaporative emissions control canister flow

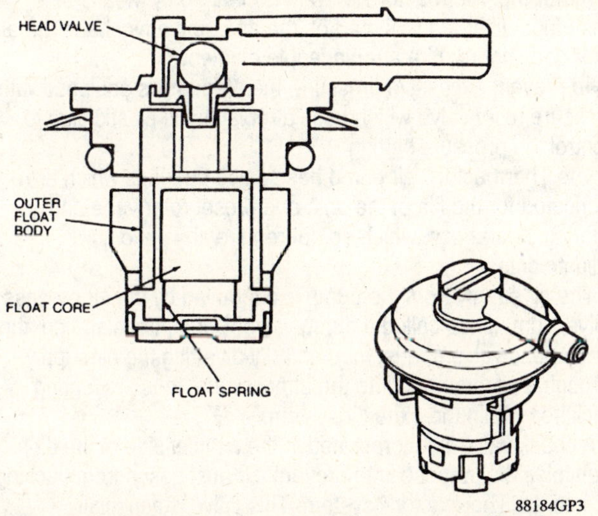

Fig. 9 The fuel vapor valve controls vapor entering the tank delivery line

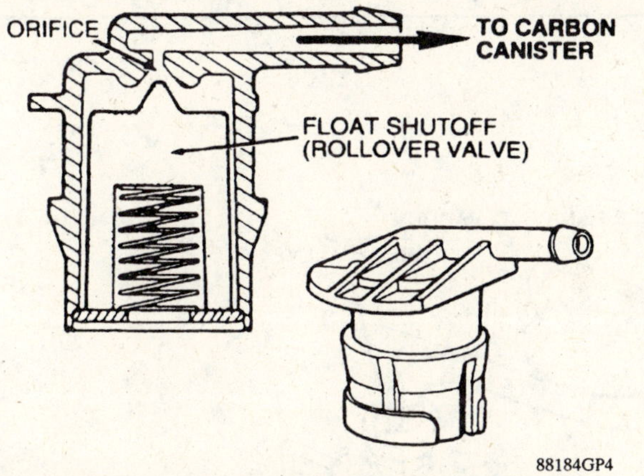

Fig. 10 In the rollover position the spring pushes the float closed

Ported Vacuum Switch (PVS)

➧ See Figure 11

The Ported Vacuum Switch (PVS) turns the purge vacuum valve on as the engine warms up. It also allows the purge valve to close when the engine is turned off and the vacuum is lost.

Vapor Management (VMV) Valve

➧ See Figure 12

The Vapor Management (VMV) valve is the part of the emissions system that is controlled by the PCM. This valve controls the flow of vapors purging from the carbon canister to the intake manifold during various engine operating modes. The VMV is normally a closed valve.

Thermactor® Air Injector System

OPERATION

➧ See Figures 13, 14 and 15

This system is found in most models sold in the 50 states.

The Thermactor® emission control system makes use of a belt-driven air pump to inject fresh air into the hot exhaust stream through the engine exhaust ports. The result is the extended burning of those fumes which were not completely ignited in the combustion chamber, and the subsequent reduction of some of the hydrocarbon and carbon monoxide content of the exhaust emissions into harmless carbon dioxide and water.

The Thermactor® system is composed of the following components:

1. Air supply pump (belt-driven)
2. Air by-pass valve
3. Check valves
4. Air manifolds (internal or external)
5. Air supply tubes (on external manifolds only).

3-PORT PVS OPERATION

- **EGR/CSC** – switches EGR vacuum from EGR system to distributor advance with cold engine.
- **Cold Start Spark Advance (CSSA)** – supplies manifold vacuum to distributor below 125° F. coolant temperature.
- **Coolant Spark Control (CSC)** – cuts off distributor advance below hot engine temperature.
- **Cooling PVS** – switches advance vacuum from spark port to manifold vacuum if engine overheats.

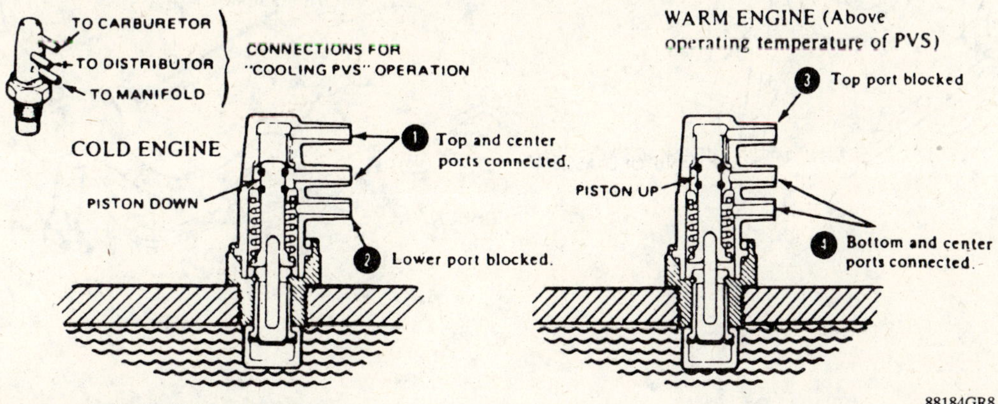

Fig. 11 Ported Vacuum Switch (PVS) operation

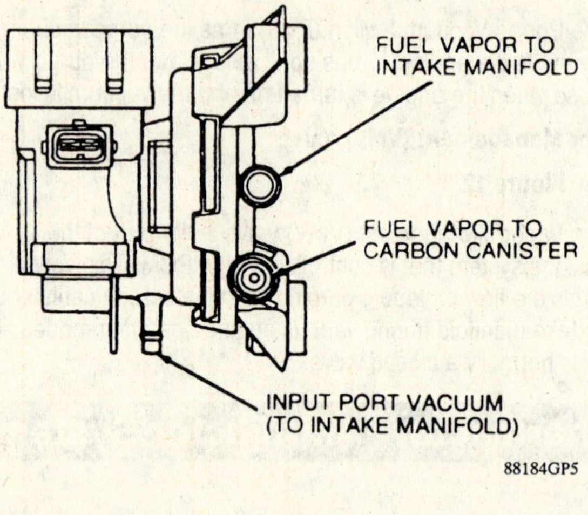

Fig. 12 The vapor management valve has three openings for vapors

Air for the Thermactor® system is cleaned by means of a centrifugal filter fan mounted on the air pump driveshaft. The air filter does not require a replaceable element.

To prevent excessive pressure, the air pump is equipped with a pressure relief valve which uses a replaceable plastic plug to control the pressure setting.

The Thermactor® air pump has sealed bearings which are lubricated for the life of the unit, and preset rotor vane and bearing clearances, which do not require any periodic adjustments.

The air supply from the pump is controlled by the air by-pass valve, sometimes called a dump valve. During deceleration, the air by-pass valve opens, momentarily diverting the air supply through a silencer and into the atmosphere, thus preventing backfires within the exhaust system.

A check valve is incorporated in the air inlet side of the air manifolds. Its purpose is to prevent exhaust gases from backing up into the Thermactor® system. This valve is especially important in the event of drive belt failure, and during deceleration, when the air by-pass valve is dumping the air supply.

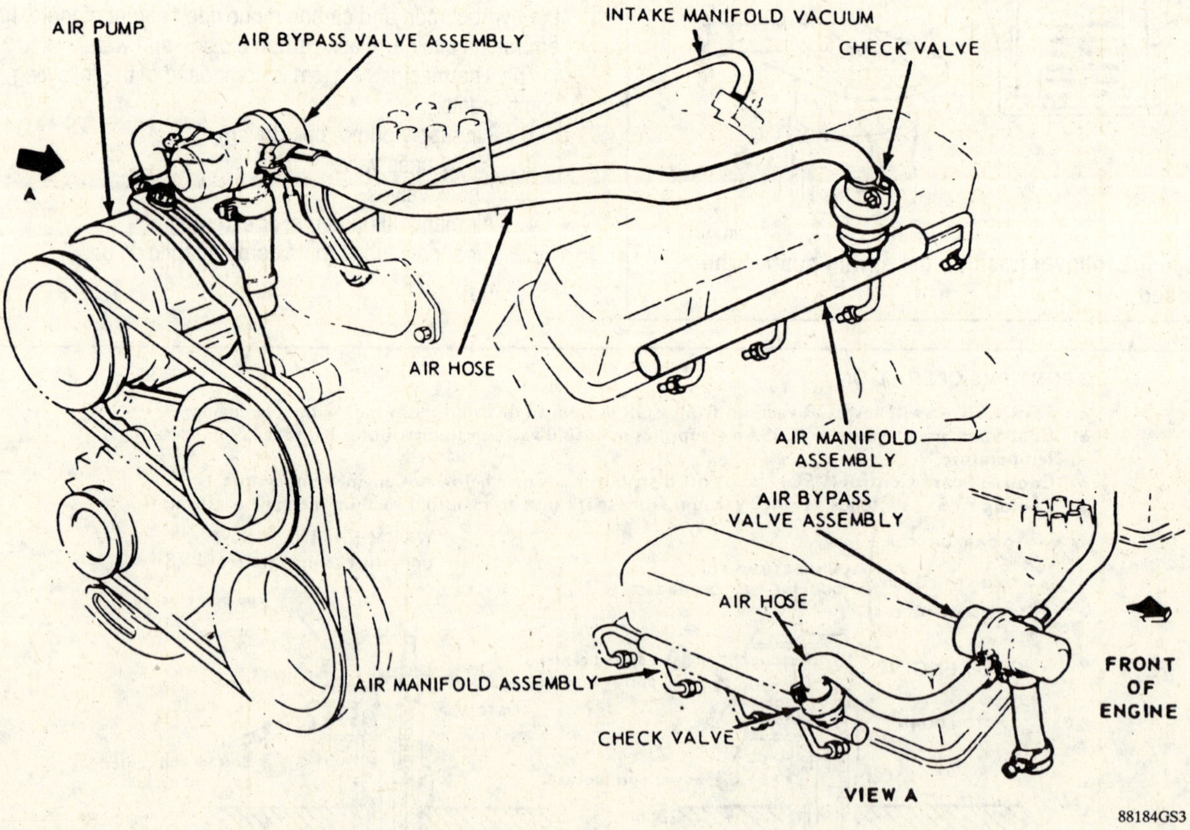

Fig. 13 Thermactor system — early 3.8L engines

The air manifolds and air supply tubes channel the air from the Thermactor® air pump into the exhaust ports of each cylinder, thus completing the cycle of the Thermactor® system.

SYSTEM INSPECTION

The entire Thermactor® system should be checked periodically. Use the following procedure to determine if the system is functioning properly.

1. Remove air cleaner, if necessary.
2. Inspect all components of the Thermactor® system for any loose connections or other abnormal conditions. Repair or replace them as necessary.
3. Inspect the air pump drive belt for wear and tension. Adjust or replace them as necessary.
4. With the transmission in neutral or park and the parking brake on, start engine and bring to normal operating temperature.
5. Stop the engine. Connect a tachometer to the engine. Remove the air supply hose at the check valve. If the engine has two check valves, remove both air supply hoses at the check valves and plug off one hose. Position the open hose so that the air blast emitted is harmlessly dissipated.
6. Start the engine and accelerate to 1,500 rpm. Place hand over the open hose. Air flow should be heard and felt. If not air flow is noted, the air bypass valve is defective and should be replaced. The procedure is outlined later in this section.
7. Let the engine speed return to normal idle. Pinch off and remove the vacuum hose from the bypass valve. Accelerate the engine to 1,500 rpm. With hand held over the open end of the check valve hose (same as Step 6), virtually no air flow should be felt or heard.

➥ If air flow is noted, the bypass valve is defective and is to be replaced.

8. Let the engine speed return to normal idle and reinstall the vacuum hose on the by-pass valve vacuum hose nipple. Check hose routing to be sure it is not pinched or restricting normal vacuum signal flow.
9. With hand held over the open end of the check valve hose (same as Step 6), rapidly increase the engine speed to approximately 2,500 rpm. Immediately release the throttle for the engine to return to normal idle. Air flow should be felt and/or heard to momentarily diminish or go to zero during the deceleration. If the air flow does not momentarily diminish or go to zero repeat the above using an engine speed of 3,000–3,200 rpm.
10. If air flow does not momentarily diminish or stop during the deceleration from 3,000–3,200 rpm, the vacuum differential control valve should be replaced. Omit this step if the system is not equipped with a differential vacuum valve.
11. Accelerate the engine to 1,500 rpm and check for any exhaust gas leakage at the check valve. There should be virtually no pressure felt or heard when hand is held over the open end of the check valve for approximately 15 seconds. If excessive leakage is noted, replace the check valve(s).

✻✻CAUTION

The check valve may be hot and capable of causing a burn if the hands are not protected.

12. If the engine is equipped with two check valves, repeat step 10 on the second valve.
13. Stop the engine and remove all the test equipment. Reconnect all the related components. Reinstall the air cleaner, if removed.

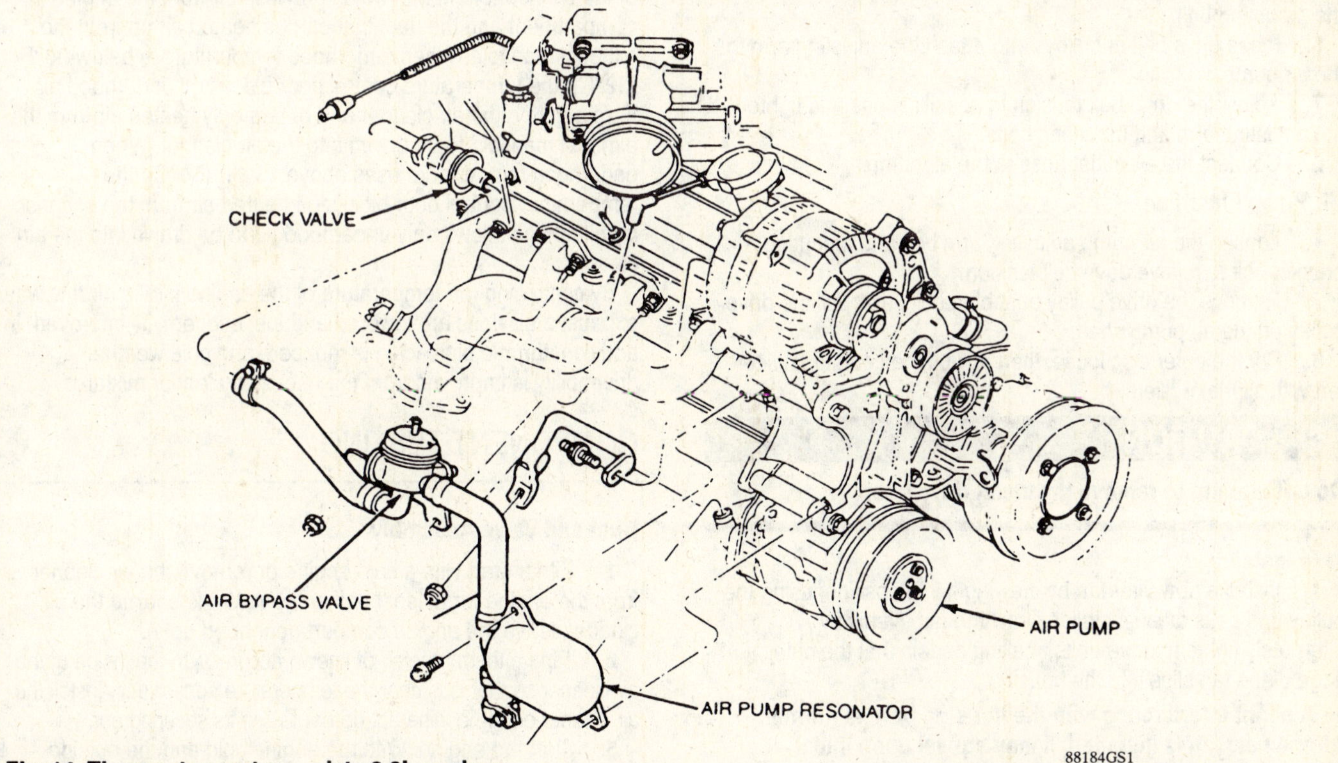

Fig. 14 Thermactor system — late 3.8L engines

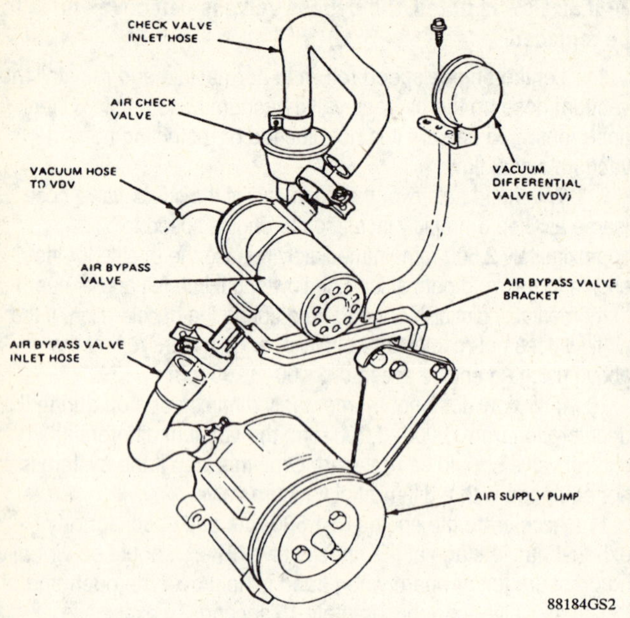

Fig. 15 Thermactor system components

REMOVAL & INSTALLATION

Air Pump

1. Disconnect the air outlet hose at the air pump.
2. Loosen the pump belt tension adjuster.
3. Disengage the drive belt.
4. Remove the mounting bolt and air pump.

To install:

5. Position the air pump on the mounting bracket and install the mounting bolt.
6. Place drive belt in pulleys and attach the adjusting arm to the air pump.
7. Adjust the drive belt tension to specifications and tighten the adjusting arm and mounting bolts.
8. Connect the air outlet hose to the air pump.

Air Pump Filter Fan

1. Loosen the air pump adjusting arm bolt and mounting bracket bolt to relieve drive belt tension.
2. Remove the drive pulley attaching bolts and pull the drive pulley off the air pump shaft.
3. Pry the outer disc loose, then pull off the centrifugal filter fan with slip-joint pliers.

****CAUTION**

Do not attempt to remove the metal drive hub.

To install:

4. Install a new filter fan by drawing it into position, using the pulley and bolts as an installer. Draw the fan evenly by alternately tightening the bolts, making certain that the outer edge of the fan slips into the housing.

➥ A slight interference with the housing bore is normal. After a new fan is installed, it may squeal upon initial operation, until its outer diameter sealing lip has worn in, which may require 20 to 30 miles of operation.

Check Valve

1. Disconnect the air supply hose at the valve. Use a $1^1/_4$ in. crowfoot wrench, the valve has a standard, right hand pipe thread.
2. Clean the threads on the air manifold adapter with a wire brush. Do not blow compressed air through the check valve in either direction.

To install:

3. Install the check valve and tighten.
4. Connect the air supply hose.

Air By-Pass Valve

1. Disconnect the air and vacuum hoses at the air by-pass valve body.
2. Installation is the reverse of removal. Position the air by-pass valve, and connect the respective hoses.

Vacuum Differential Control Valve

1. Remove the hose connections.
2. Unbolt the valve at its mounting bracket.

To install:

3. Attach the valve to its mounting bracket and tighten.
4. Attach the hose to the valve.

Heated Air Intake System

OPERATION

The heated air intake portion of the air cleaner consists of a thermostat, or bimetal switch and vacuum motor, and a spring-loaded temperature control door in the snorkel of the air cleaner. The temperature control door is located between the end of the air cleaner snorkel which draws in air from the engine compartment and the duct that carries heated air up from the exhaust manifold. When underhood temperature is below 90°F (32°C), the temperature control door blocks off underhood air from entering the air cleaner and allows only heated air from the exhaust manifold to be drawn into the air cleaner. When underhood temperature rises above 130°F (54°C), the temperature control door blocks off heated air from the exhaust manifold and allows only underhood air to be drawn into the air cleaner.

By controlling the temperature of the engine intake air this way, exhaust emissions are lowered and fuel economy is improved. In addition, throttle plate icing is reduced, and cold weather driveability is improved from the necessary leaner mixtures.

COMPONENT TESTING

Duct and Valve Assembly

1. Either start with a cold engine or remove the air cleaner from the engine for at least half an hour. While cooling the air cleaner, leave the engine compartment hood open.
2. Tape a thermometer, of known accuracy, to the inside of the air cleaner so that is is near the temperature sensor unit. Install the air cleaner on the engine but do not fasten its securing nut.
3. Start the engine. With the engine cold and the outside temperature less than 90°F (32°C), the door should in the **HEAT ON** position (closed to outside air).

4. Operate the throttle lever rapidly to $^1/_2$–$^3/_4$ of its opening and release it. The air door should open to allow outside air to enter and then close again.

5. Allow the engine to warm up to normal temperature. Watch the door. When it opens to the outside air, remove the cover from the air cleaner. The temperature should be over 90°F (32°C) and no more than 130°F (54°C); 105°F (41°C) is about normal. If the door does not work within these temperature ranges, or fails to work at all, check for linkage or door binding.

If binding is not present and the air door is not working, proceed with the vacuum tests given below. If these indicate no faults in the vacuum motor and the door is not working, the temperature sensor is defective and must be replaced.

Vacuum Motor

Be sure that the vacuum hose that runs between the temperature switch and the vacuum motor is not pinched by the retaining clip under the air cleaner. This could prevent the air door from closing.

1. Check all the vacuum lines and fittings for leaks. Correct any leaks. If none are found, proceed with the test.
2. Remove the hose which runs from the sensor to the vacuum motor. Run a hose directly from the manifold vacuum source to the vacuum motor.
3. If the motor closes the air door, it is functioning properly and the temperature sensor is defective.
4. If the motor does not close the door and no binding is present in its operation, the vacuum motor is defective and must be replaced.

If an alternator vacuum source is applied to the motor, insert a vacuum gauge in the line by using a T-fitting. Apply at least 9 in.Hg of vacuum in order to operate the motor.

REMOVAL & INSTALLATION

Temperature Operated Duct and Valve Assembly

1. Remove the hex-head cap screws which secure the air intake duct and valve assembly to the air cleaner.
2. Remove the air intake duct and valve assembly from the engine.
3. If inspection reveals that the valve plate is sticking or the thermostat is malfunctioning, remove the thermostat and valve plates as follows:
    a. Detach the valve plate tension spring from the valve plate using long-nose pliers.
    b. Loosen the thermostat locknut and unscrew the thermostat from the mounting bracket.
    c. Grasp the valve plate and withdraw it from the cut.

To install:

4. Install the air intake duct and valve assembly on the shroud tube.
5. Connect the air intake duct and valve assembly the air cleaner and tighten the hex-head retaining cap screws.
6. If it was necessary to disassemble the thermostat and air duct and valve, assembly the unit as follows: Install the locknut on the thermostat, and screw the thermostat into the mounting bracket. Install the valve plate tension spring on the valve plate and duct.
7. Install the vacuum override motor (if applicable) and check for proper operation.

Vacuum Operated Duct and Valve Assembly

1. Disconnect the vacuum hose at the vacuum motor.
2. Remove the hex-head cap screws which secure the air intake duct and valve assembly to the air cleaner.
3. Remove the duct and valve assembly from the engine.

To install:

4. Position the duct and valve assembly to the air cleaner and heat stove tube. Install the attaching cap screws.
5. Connect the vacuum line at the vacuum motor.

Exhaust Gas Recirculation System

OPERATION

See Figures 16, 17 and 18

All models are equipped with an exhaust gas recirculation (EGR) system which reintroduces the exhaust gas into the combustion cycle. This process lowers the combustion temperatures and reduces the formation of oxides of nitrogen. There are several systems that are utilized on the Thunderbird and the Cougar.

One of the systems used is the Pressure Feedback Electronic (PFE) system. The PFE is a subsonic closed loop system that controls the EGR flow rate by monitoring the pressure drop across a remotely mounted sharp edged orifice. A pressure transducer serves as the feedback device. Controlled pressure is varied by valve modulation using vacuum output of the EGR Vacuum Regulator (EVR) solenoid. In the PFE system the EGR valve serves only as a pressure regulator rather than a flow metering device.

Another system used is the Electronic EGR (EEGR) valve system. This system is required in EEC systems where the EGR flow is controlled according to the demands made by the computer through the EGR Valve Position (EVP) sensor attached to the valve. The valve is operated by a vacuum signal from the electronic vacuum regulator. The regulator actuates the valve diaphragm as supply vacuum overcomes the spring load. This in turn lifts the pintle off of it's seat which allows the exhaust gas to recirculate. The amount of flow is proportional to the pintle position. The EVP sensor on the valve sends a signal of its position to the PCM.

The ported EGR valve is operated by a vacuum signal which in turn actuates the valve diaphragm. As the vacuum increases sufficiently to overcome the power spring, the valve opens to allow EGR flow. The vacuum that reaches the EGR valve is controlled by the EGR Vacuum Regulator (EVR) or the Pressure Feedback EGR transducer (PFE), depending on the system application.

The Differential Pressure Feedback EGR (DPFE) system is continuously monitored by the On Board Diagnostic II (OBDII) system for component integrity. The systems functionally faults that can cause the emission levels to exceed the Federal regulations. When the OBDII monitor determines that a failure had occurred, the Malfunction Indicator Lamp (MIL) illuminates to warn the driver and a trouble code is stored in the memory.

Differential Pressure Feedback (DPFE) Sensor

The DPFE sensor is a ceramic capacitive type pressure transducer which monitors the differential pressure across a metering orifice located in the orifice tube assembly. The sensor receives this signal through two hoses called the downstream pressure hose (REF SIGNAL) and the upstream pressure hose HI SIGNAL). The HI and REF signals are marked on the DPFE sensor outputs a voltage proportional to the pressure drop across the metering orifice and supplies it to the PCM as a EGR flow rate feedback.

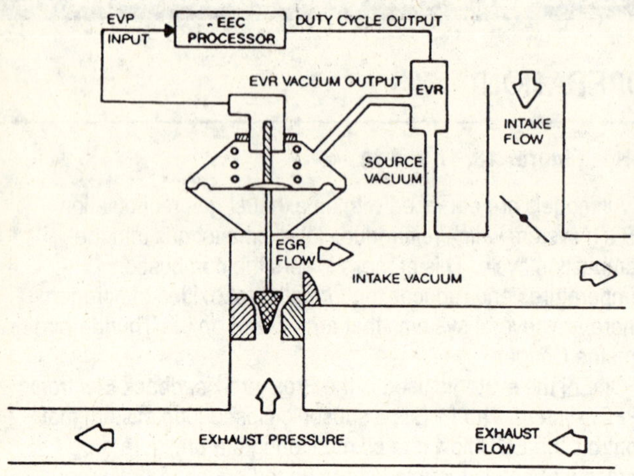

88184GR2

Fig. 16 Electronic EGR system schematic

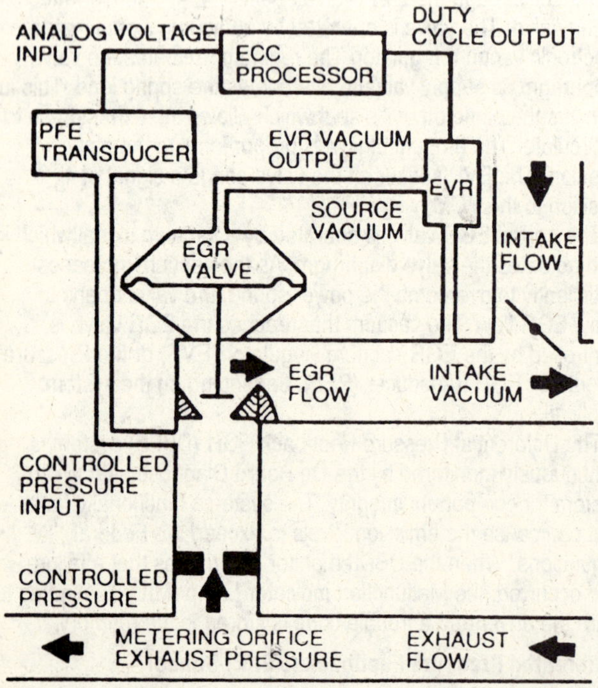

88184GR3

Fig. 17 The pressure feedback EGR system schematic

Electronic Vacuum Regulator Solenoid

The Electronic Vacuum Regulator Solenoid (EVR) solenoid is an electromagnetic device which is used to regulate the vacuum supply to the EGR valve. The solenoid contains a coil which magnetically controls the position of a disc to regulate the vacuum. As the duty cycle to the coil increases, the vacuum signal is passed the the EVR solenoid to the EGR valve which also increases. Vacuum not directed to the EGR valve is vented through the EVR solenoid vent to the atmosphere. When a 0 percent duty cycle or no electrical signal applied, the EVR solenoid allows some vacuum to pass, but not enough to open the EGR valve.

REMOVAL & INSTALLATION

Ported EGR

See Figure 19

1. Disconnect the negative battery cable.
2. Tag and disconnect the vacuum line from the EGR valve.
3. Remove the mounting bolts and remove the EGR valve.
4. Scrape the old gasket off of the engine mating area.

To install:

5. Attach the EGR valve with a new gasket and tighten.
6. Attach the vacuum lines to the valve.
7. Connect the negative battery cable.

Electronic EGR

The electronic EGR valve is vacuum operated. When the vacuum signal becomes strong enough, the pintle is lifted off of it's seat which allows the exhaust gas to recirculate. The main difference between the ported EGR valve and the electronic EGR valve is that there is a EGR valve position sensor mounted on top of the electronic EGR valve. The EVP sensor must be serviced separately from the EGR valve. The electronic EGR valve is not serviceable.

1. Disconnect the negative battery cable.
2. Disconnect the vacuum line from the EGR valve.
3. Remove the mounting bolts and remove the EGR valve.
4. Remove the EVP sensor from the EGR valve.
5. Remove any old gasket material from the engine mating area.

To install:

6. Attach the EVP sensor to the EGR valve.
7. Install the EGR valve to the engine with a new gasket and tighten.
8. Attach the vacuum line to the valve.
9. Connect the negative battery cable.

Pressure Feedback Electronic (PFE) Transducer

The PFE EGR transducer converts exhaust pressure into proportional voltage which is digitized by the PCM. The PCM utilizes the signal from the PFE to maintain optimum EGR flow.

1. Disconnect the negative battery cable.
2. Detach the electrical connector and exhaust pressure line from the transducer.
3. Remove the transducer from the vehicle.

To install:

4. Attach the transducer to the engine and tighten the mounting bolt.
5. Attach the electrical connector and exhaust pressure line to the transducer.

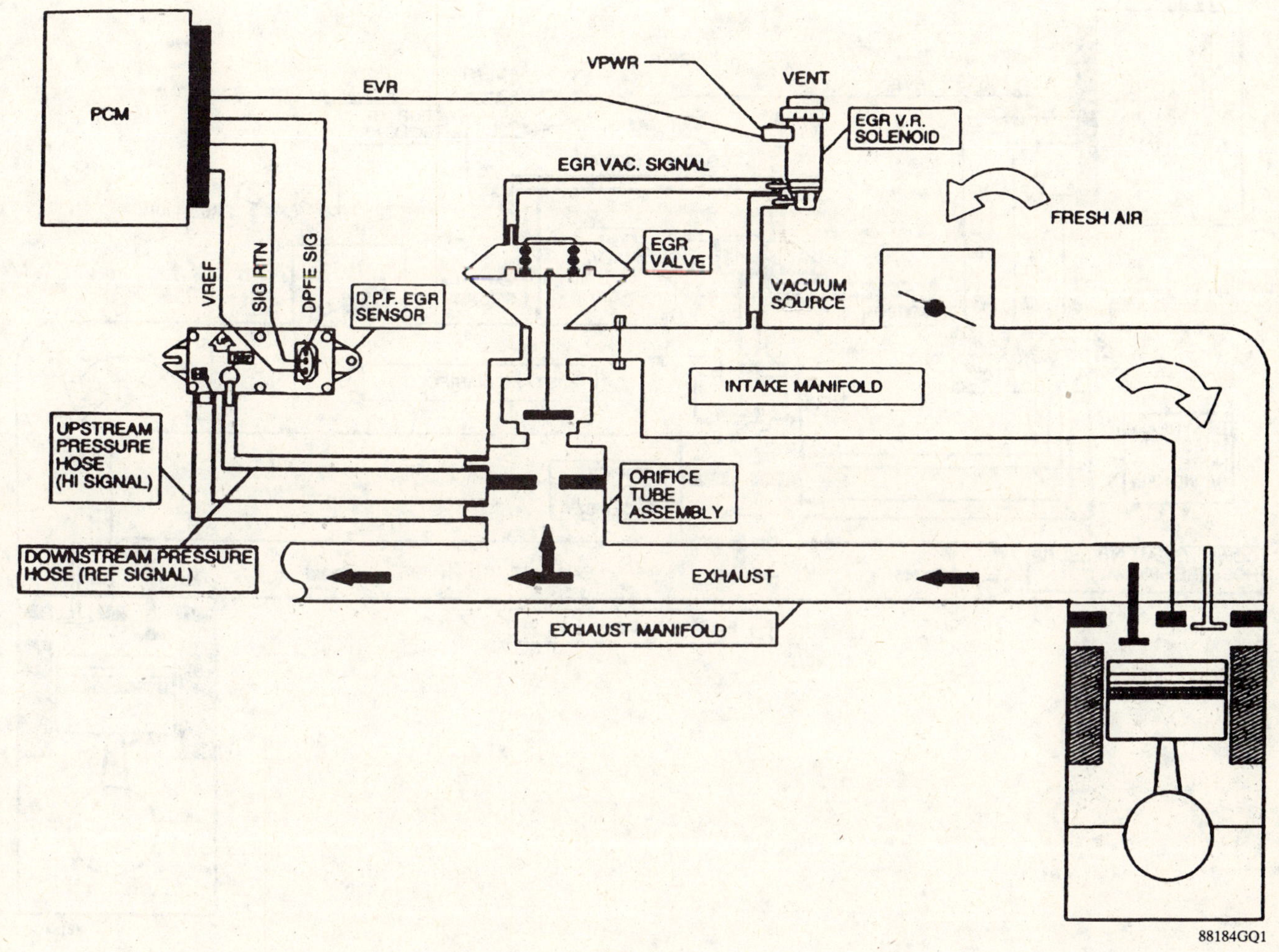

Fig. 18 Electronic vacuum regulator solenoid with testing schematics

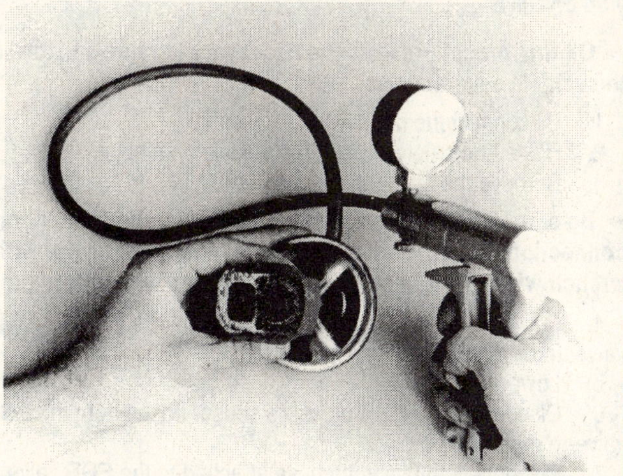

Fig. 19 Some EGR valves may be tested using a vacuum pump by watching for diaphragm movement

Differential Pressure Feedback EGR

3.8L ENGINE

➧ See Figure 20

1. Disconnect the negative battery cable.
2. Disconnect the PCV hose from the air cleaner.
3. Remove the air cleaner outlet tube from the throttle body and mass air flow sensor.
4. Disconnect the emission vacuum control hose from the valve.
5. Separate the fuel charging wiring from the EGR pressure sensor.
6. Disconnect the EGR pressure sensor hose(s) from the valve-to-exhaust manifold tube.
7. Remove the transducer mounting bracket retainers. Remove the pressure sensor and transducer mounting bracket from the engine.
8. Disconnect the EGR valve-to-exhaust manifold tube from the EGR valve.

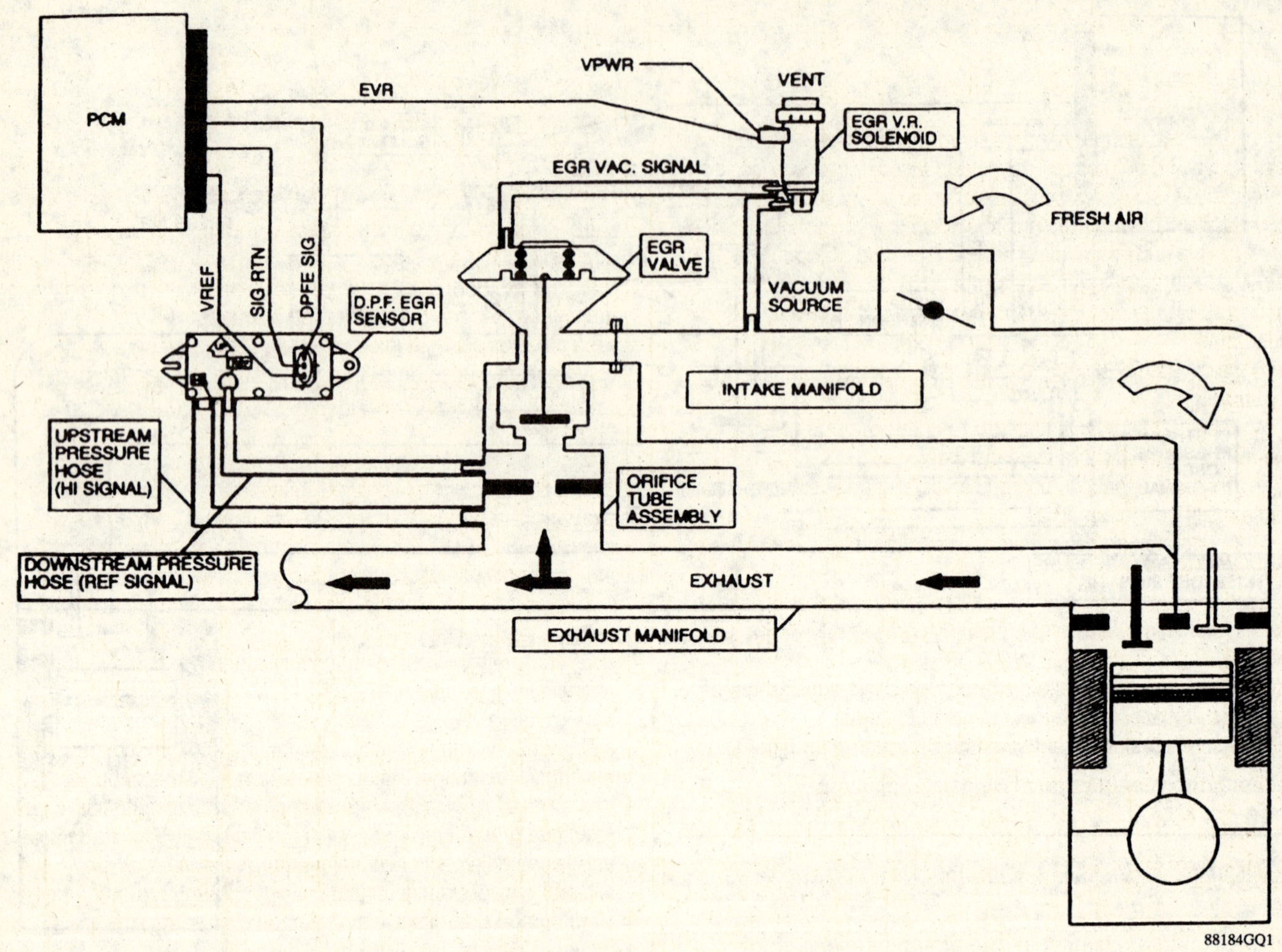

Fig. 20 Differential pressure feedback EGR system diagram

9. Remove the valve bolts and valve from the vehicle.
10. Discard the old gasket and clean the mating areas.

To install:

11. Apply a heat resistant sealer on the gasket and mating areas of the valve.
12. Attach the valve with gasket on the engine and tighten the mounting bolts to 15-22 ft. lbs. (20-30 Nm).
13. Attach the EGR valve-to-exhaust manifold tube to the EGR valve and tighten the bolts to 26-33 ft. lbs. (35-45 Nm).
14. Attach the pressure sensor and transducer mounting bracket to the engine. Install the transducer mounting bracket retainers.
15. Connect the EGR pressure sensor hose(s) to the valve-to-exhaust manifold tube.
16. Attach the fuel charging wiring to the EGR pressure sensor.
17. Connect the emission vacuum control hose to the valve.
18. Install the air cleaner outlet tube to the throttle body and mass air flow sensor.
19. Connect the PCV hose to the air cleaner.
20. Connect the negative battery cable.

4.6L ENGINE

→ On this procedure it will be necessary to raise and lower the vehicle several times.

1. Disconnect the negative battery cable.
2. Raise and safely support the vehicle on a hoist.
3. Remove the air cleaner outlet tube.

→ Be careful not to damage the EGR valve tube-to-manifold connection. Hold the valve tube-to manifold connector with a wrench while disconnecting the EGR valve-to manifold tube.

4. Disconnect the EGR valve-to-manifold tube from the EGR valve and valve tube-to manifold connector.
5. Lower the vehicle.
6. Disconnect the EGR pressure sensor hoses from the EGR valve-to manifold tube.
7. Disconnect the vacuum hose attached to the EGR valve.
8. Unbolt the EGR valve.
9. Remove the valve, gasket and valve-to manifold tube from the engine.
10. Clean the gasket mating areas.

To install:

11. Position the valve-to manifold tube into the EGR valve and loosely connect the valve-to-manifold tube nut.
12. Position the EGR valve gasket, valve and valve-to-manifold nut on the engine.
13. Install the mounting bolts for the EGR valve-to intake manifold. Tighten to 15–22 ft. lbs. (20–30 Nm).
14. Connect the vacuum hose to the EGR valve.
15. Connect the pressure sensor hoses to the EGR valve-to-manifold.
16. Raise and support the vehicle.
17. Hold the valve tube-to manifold connector with a wrench while tightening the EGR valve-to manifold tube nut.
18. Connect the EGR valve-to-exhaust manifold tube to the EGR valve tube-to-manifold connector. Tighten the tube nuts to 26–33 ft. lbs. (35–45 Nm).
19. Lower the vehicle.
20. Install the air cleaner outlet tube.
21. Connect the negative battery cable.

EGR Control Solenoid

The EGR control solenoid is located on a bracket attached to the lower intake manifold. On the 3.8L supercharged engines, the EGR vacuum regulator control is located on the rear of the left cylinder head mounted on a bracket.

3.8L ENGINE

1. Disconnect the fuel charging wiring from the EGR vacuum regulator control.
2. Disconnect the main emission vacuum control connector from EGR vacuum regulator control.
3. Remove the retaining nuts and the EGR vacuum regulator control from the mounting bracket.

To install:

4. Attach the vacuum regulator control to the mounting bracket with the nuts.
5. Connect the main emission vacuum control connector to the EGR vacuum regulator control.
6. Attach the fuel wiring to the EGR vacuum regulator control.

4.6L ENGINE

1. Disconnect the fuel charging wiring from the EGR vacuum regulator control.
2. Disconnect the emission vacuum control connector from the EGR vacuum regulator control
3. Remove the retaining nut and EGR vacuum regulator control from the transducer mounting bracket located at the rear of the lower intake manifold.
4. Reverse to install. Tighten the retaining nut for the EGR vacuum regulator to 40–61 inch lbs. (5–7 Nm).

EGR Pressure Sensor

3.8L ENGINE

1. Disconnect the negative battery cable.
2. Disconnect the PCV hose from the air cleaner.
3. Remove the air cleaner outlet tube from the throttle body and mass air flow sensor.
4. Disconnect the emission vacuum control hose from the valve.
5. Separate the fuel charging wiring from the EGR pressure sensor.
6. Disconnect the EGR pressure sensor hose(s) from the valve-to-exhaust manifold tube.
7. Remove the transducer mounting bracket retainers. Remove the pressure sensor and transducer mounting bracket from the engine.

To install:

8. Attach the pressure sensor and transducer mounting bracket to the engine. Install the transducer mounting bracket retainers.
9. Connect the EGR pressure sensor hose(s) to the valve-to-exhaust manifold tube.
10. Attach the fuel charging wiring to the EGR pressure sensor.
11. Connect the emission vacuum control hose to the valve.
12. Install the air cleaner outlet tube to the throttle body and mass air flow sensor.
13. Connect the PCV hose to the air cleaner.
14. Connect the negative battery cable.

4.6L ENGINE

1. Disconnect the fuel charging wiring from the EGR pressure sensor.
2. Tag and disconnect the hoses at the pressure sensor.
3. Remove the EGR sensor mounting bolts and separate the sensor from the transducer mounting bracket.

To install:

4. Attach the sensor to the transducer mounting bracket, tighten the bolts to 40–61 inch lbs. (5–7 Nm).
5. Attach the hoses to the pressure sensor.
6. Connect the fuel charging wiring to the EGR pressure sensor.

3.8L Thunderbird/Cougar

Electrical Schematic

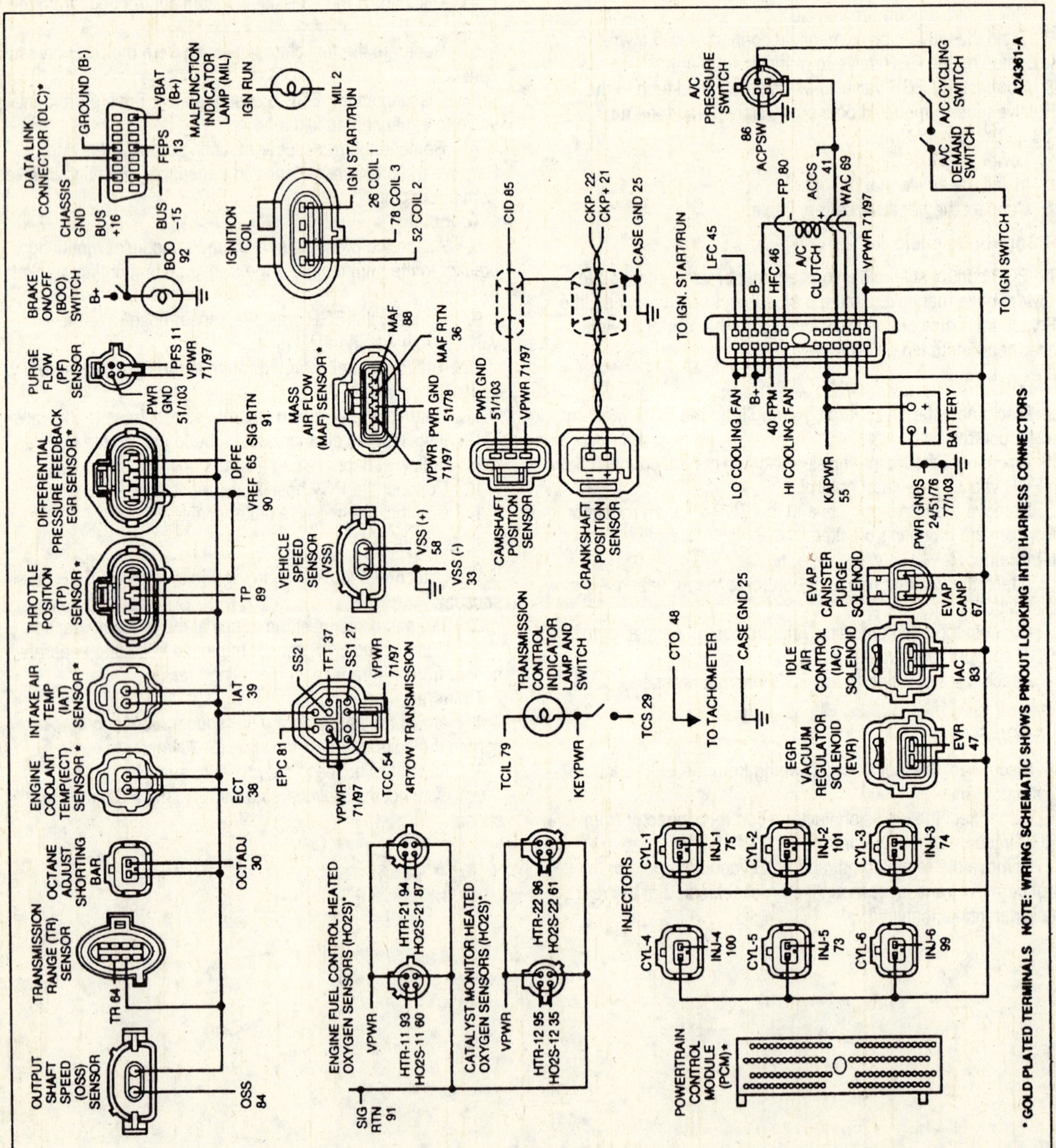

88184CMM

3.8L Thunderbird/Cougar

Powertrain Control Module (PCM) Connector Pin Usage

Pin	CKT	Wire Color	Application	Abbreviation
1	315	P/O	Shift Solenoid 2	SS2
2	658	PK/LG	Malfunction Indicator Lamp	MIL
11	91	P/W	Purge Flow Sensor	PFS
13	107	P	Flash EPROM power supply	FEPS
15	915	PK/LB	BUS (-)	BUS-
16	914	T/O	BUS (+)	BUS+
21	349	DB	Crankshaft Position Sensor	CKP +
22	350	GY	Crankshaft Position Sensor	CKP -
24	570	BK/W	Power Ground	PWR GND
25	57	BK	Case Ground	Case Gnd
26	526	DB/LG	Coil Driver 1	CD1
27	237	O/Y	Shift Solenoid 1	SS1
29	224	T/W	Transmission Control Switch	TCS
30	242	DG	Octane Adjust	OCT ADJ
33	676	PK/O	Vehicle Speed Sensor (-)	VSS-
35	392	R/LG	Heated Oxygen Sensor-12 (R-Right)	HO2S-12
36	968	T/LB	Mass Air Flow Sensor Return	MAF RTN
37	923	O/BK	Transmission Fluid Temperature Sensor	TFT
38	354	LG/R	Engine Coolant Temperature Sensor	ECT
39	743	GY	Intake Air Temperature Sensor	IAT
40	787	PK/BK	Fuel Pump Monitor	FPM
41	883	PK/LB	A/C Cycling Switch	ACCS
45	197	T/O	Low Fan Control	LFC
46	639	LG/P	High Fan Control	HFC
47	360	BR/PK	EGR Vacuum Regulator Solenoid	EVR
51	570	BK/W	Power Ground	PWR GND
52	527	R/LB	Coil Driver 2	CD2
54	924	BR/O	Torque Converter Clutch Solenoid	TCC
55	37	Y	Keep Alive Power	KAPWR
58	679	GY/BK	Vehicle Speed Sensor (+)	VSS +
60	74	GY/LB	Heated Oxygen Sensor-11 (F-Right)	HO2S-11
61	393	P/LG	Heated Oxygen Sensor-22 (R-Left)	HO2S-22
64	199	LB/Y	Transmission Range Sensor	TR
65	352	BR/LG	Differential Pressure Feedback EGR Sensor	DPFE
67	101	GY/Y	Canister Purge Solenoid	CANP
69	331	PK/Y	Wide Open Throttle A/C Cut-off	WAC
71	361	R	Vehicle Power	VPWR
73	559	T/BK	Injector-5	INJ 5

(Continued)

88184CMN

3.8L Thunderbird/Cougar

Pin	CKT	Wire Color	Application	Abbreviation
74	557	BR/Y	Injector-3	INJ 3
75	555	T	Injector-1	INJ 1
76	570	BK/W	Power Ground	PWR GND
77	570	BK/W	Power Ground	PWR GND
78	528	PK/W	Coil Driver 3	CD3
79	911	W/LG	Transmission Control Indicator Lamp	TCIL
80	926	LB/O	Fuel Pump Control	FP
81	925	W/Y	Electronic Pressure Control	EPC
83	264	W/LB	Idle Air Control Solenoid	IAC
84	970	DG/W	Turbine Shaft Speed Sensor	TSS
85	795	DG	Cylinder Identification	CID
86	439	T/LG	A/C Pressure Switch	ACPSW
87	94	R/BK	Heated Oxygen Sensor-21 (F-Left)	HO2S-21
88	967	LB/R	Mass Air Flow Sensor	MAF
89	355	GY/W	Throttle Position Sensor	TP
90	351	BR/W	Vehicle Reference Voltage	VREF
91	359	GY/R	Signal Return	SIG RTN
92	511	LG	Brake On/Off Switch	BOO
93	387	R/W	Heater-11 HO2S (F-Right)	HTR-11
94	388	Y/LB	Heater-21 HO2S (F-Left)	HTR-21
95	389	W/BK	Heater-12 HO2S (R-Right)	HTR-12
96	390	T/Y	Heater-22 HO2S (R-Left)	HTR-22
97	361	R	Vehicle Power	VPWR
99	560	LG/O	Injector-6	INJ 6
100	558	BR/LB	Injector-4	INJ 4
101	556	W	Injector-2	INJ 2
103	570	BK/W	Power Ground	PWR GND

88184CMP

3.8L Thunderbird/Cougar

Constant Control Relay Module (CCRM) Schematic

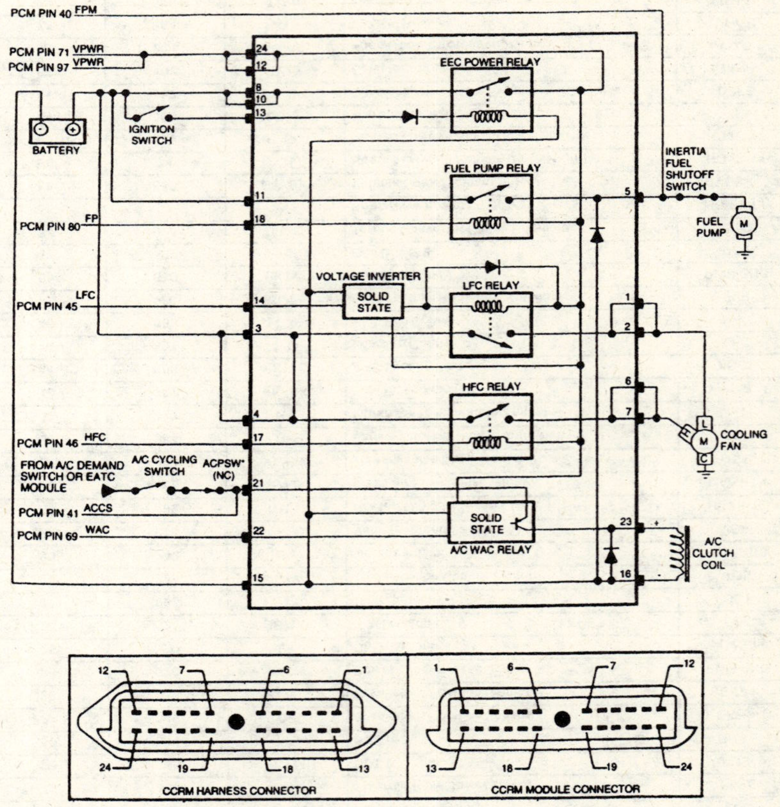

*High pressure contacts of the dual function A/C Pressure Switch (ACPSW)

88184CMQ

Pin	CKT	Wire Color	Application	Abbreviation
1	228	DB	Power to Low Speed Fan	PTLSF.
2	228	DB	Power to Low Speed Fan	PTLSF
3	38	BK/O	Battery Positive	B+
4	38	BK/O	Battery Positive	B+
5	787	PK/BK	Power to Fuel Pumps	PTP
6	181	BR/O	Power to High Speed Fan	PTHSF
7	181	BR/O	Power to High Speed Fan	PTHSF
8	37	Y	Battery to EEC Relay	B+
11	175	BK/Y	Battery to Fuel Pump Relay	B+
12	361	R	Vehicle Power	VPWR
13	16	R/LG	Key Power	KEY PWR
14	197	T/O	Low Fan Control	LFC
15	57	BK	Power Ground	PWR GND
16	321	GY/W	A/C Clutch Ground	ACC GND
17	639	LG/P	High Fan Control	HFC
18	926	LB/O	Fuel Pump Control	FP
21	883	PK/LB	A/C Cycling Switch	ACCS
22	331	PK/Y	WOT A/C Cut-off	WAC
23	347	BK/Y	Power to A/C Clutch	PTAC
24	361	R	Vehicle Power	VPWR

88184CMR

4.6L Thunderbird/Cougar

Powertrain Control Module (PCM) Connector Pin Usage

Pin	CKT	Wire Color	Application	Abbreviation
1	315	P/O	Shift Solenoid 2	SS2
2	658	PK/LG	Malfunction Indicator Lamp	MIL
11	91	P/W	Purge Flow Sensor	PF
13	107	P	Flash EPROM power supply	FEPS
15	915	PK/LB	BUS (-)	BUS-
16	914	T/O	BUS (+)	BUS+
21	349	DB	Crankshaft Position Sensor	CKP +
22	350	GY	Crankshaft Position Sensor	CKP -
24	570	BK/W	Power Ground	PWR GND
25	57	BK	Case Ground	Case Gnd
26	526	DB/LG	Coil Driver 1	CD1
27	237	O/Y	Shift Solenoid 1	SS1
29	224	T/W	Transmission Control Switch	TCS
30	242	DG	Octane Adjust	OCT ADJ
33	676	PK/O	Vehicle Speed Sensor (-)	VSS-
35	392	R/LG	Heated Oxygen Sensor-12 (R-Right)	HO2S-12
36	968	T/LB	Mass Air Flow Sensor Return	MAF RTN
37	923	O/BK	Transmission Fluid Temperature Sensor	TFT
38	354	LG/R	Engine Coolant Temperature Sensor	ECT
39	743	GY	Intake Air Temperature Sensor	IAT
40	787	PK/BK	Fuel Pump Monitor	FPM
41	883	PK/LB	A/C Cycling Switch	ACCS
45	197	T/O	Low Fan Control	LFC
46	639	LG/P	High Fan Control	HFC
47	360	BR/PK	EGR Vacuum Regulator Solenoid	EVR
51	570	BK/W	Power Ground	PWR GND
52	527	R/LB	Coil Driver 2	CD2
54	924	BR/O	Torque Converter Clutch Solenoid	TCC
55	37	Y	Keep Alive Power	KAPWR
58	679	GY/BK	Vehicle Speed Sensor (+)	VSS +
60	74	GY/LB	Heated Oxygen Sensor-11 (F-Right)	HO2S-11
61	393	P/LG	Heated Oxygen Sensor-22 (R-Left)	HO2S-22
64	199	LB/Y	Transmission Range Sensor	TR
65	352	BR/LG	Differential Pressure Feedback EGR Sensor	DPFE
67	101	GY/Y	Canister Purge Solenoid	CANP
69	331	PK/Y	Wide Open Throttle A/C Cut-off	WAC
71	361	R	Vehicle Power	VPWR
73	559	T/BK	Injector-5	INJ 5

(Continued)

88184CMS

4.6L Thunderbird/Cougar

Pin	CKT	Wire Color	Application	Abbreviation
74	557	BR/Y	Injector-3	INJ 3
75	555	T	Injector-1	INJ 1
76	570	BK/W	Power Ground	PWR GND
77	570	BK/W	Power Ground	PWR GND
78	528	PK/W	Coil Driver 3	CD3
79	911	W/LG	Transmission Control Indicator Lamp	TCIL
80	926	LB/O	Fuel Pump Control	FP
81	925	W/Y	Electronic Pressure Control	EPC
83	264	W/LB	Idle Air Control Solenoid	IAC
84	970	DG/W	Turbine Shaft Speed Sensor	TSS
85	795	DG	Cylinder Identification	CID
86	439	T/LG	A/C Pressure Switch	ACPSW
87	94	R/BK	Heated Oxygen Sensor-21 (F-Left)	HO2S-21
88	967	LB/R	Mass Air Flow Sensor	MAF
89	355	GY/W	Throttle Position Sensor	TP
90	351	BR/W	Vehicle Reference Voltage	VREF
91	359	GY/R	Signal Return	SIG RTN
92	511	LG	Brake On/Off Switch	BOO
93	387	R/W	Heater-11 HO2S (F-Right)	HTR-11
94	388	Y/LB	Heater-21 HO2S (F-Left)	HTR-21
95	389	W/BK	Heater-12 HO2S (R-Right)	HTR-12
96	390	T/Y	Heater-22 HO2S (R-Left)	HTR-22
97	361	R	Vehicle Power	VPWR
99	560	LG/O	Injector-6	INJ 6
100	558	BR/LB	Injector-4	INJ 4
101	556	W	Injector-2	INJ 2
103	570	BK/W	Power Ground	PWR GND
104	529	R/Y	Coil Driver 4	CD4

88184CMT

4.6L Thunderbird/Cougar

Constant Control Relay Module (CCRM) Schematic

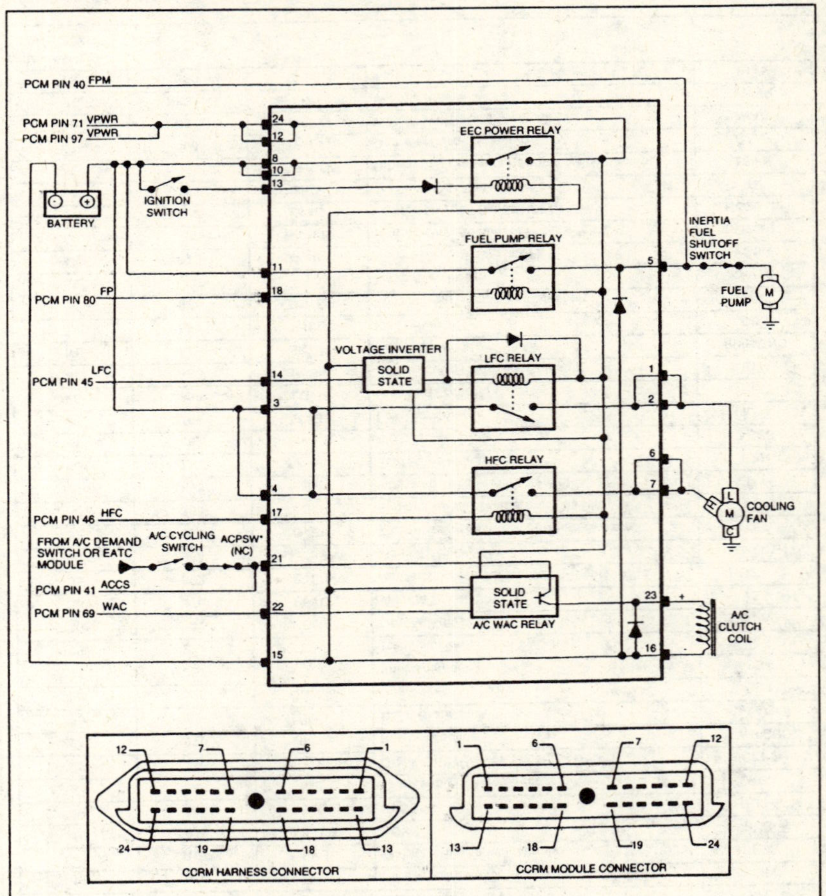

*High pressure contacts of the dual function A/C Pressure Switch (ACPSW)

88184CMU

4.6L Thunderbird/Cougar

Constant Control Relay Module (CCRM) Connector Pin Usage

Pin	CKT	Wire Color	Application	Abbreviation
1	228	DB	Power to Low Speed Fan	PTLSF
2	228	DB	Power to Low Speed Fan	PTLSF
3	38	BK/O	Battery Positive	B+
4	38	BK/O	Battery Positive	B+
5	787	PK/BK	Power to Fuel Pumps	PTP
6	181	BR/O	Power to High Speed Fan	PTHSF
7	181	BR/O	Power to High Speed Fan	PTHSF
8	37	Y	Battery to EEC Relay	B+
11	175	BK/Y	Battery to Fuel Pump Relay	B+
12	361	R	Vehicle Power	VPWR
13	16	R/LG	Key Power	KEY PWR
14	197	T/O	Low Fan Control	LFC
15	57	BK	Power Ground	PWR GND
16	321	GY/W	A/C Clutch Ground	ACC GND
17	639	LG/P	High Fan Control	HFC
18	926	LB/O	Fuel Pump Control	FP
21	883	PK/LB	A/C Cycling Switch	ACCS
22	331	PK/Y	WOT A/C Cut-off	WAC
23	347	BK/Y	Power to A/C Clutch	PTAC
24	361	R	Vehicle Power	VPWR

88184CMV

EGR VALVE CLEANING

➧ **See Figure 21**

If the EGR valve is serviceable, remove the EGR valve for cleaning. Do not strike or pry on the valve diaphragm housing or supports, as this may damage the valve operating mechanism and/or change the valve calibration. Check orifice hole in the EGR valve body for deposits. A small hand drill of no more than 0.060 in. (1.5mm) diameter may be used to clean the hole if plugged. Extreme care must be taken to avoid enlarging the hole or damaging the surface of the orifice plate.

Catalytic Converter System

➧ **See Figure 22**

Catalytic converters convert noxious emissions of hydrocarbons (HC) and carbon monoxide (CO) into harmless carbon dioxide and water. The reaction takes place inside the reactor(s) at great heat using platinum or palladium metals as the catalyst. The 5 in. (127mm) diameter units are installed in the exhaust system ahead of the mufflers. They are designed, if the engine is properly tuned, to last 50,000 miles or more before replacement.

There are different types of catalytic converters for your vehicle. The most common type used on vehicles today is the Three Way Catalytic Converter (TWC). This converter contains either platinum and rhodium to pallidadium and rhodium. The TWC converter catalyzes the oxidation reactions of the unburned hydrocarbons and carbon monoxide and the reduction reaction of oxides of nitrogen. The three way conversion only occurs with the air fuel/ratio near stoichiometry.

➥ **Lead-free gasoline must be used on all converter equipped vehicles.**

A Catalytic converter should last you almost the lifetime of your vehicle if taken care of. You should never allow your engine run at an idle for long periods of time. This can overheat the converter and shorten the life.

Emission Service Lights

RESETTING

➥ **Thunderbirds and Cougars do not use an emission maintenance reminder light. Starting in 1985, a SERVICE interval reminder light was used.**

At approximately every 5000 (8046 km) or 7500 miles (12,070 km), (depending on engine application) the word **SERVICE** will appear on the electronic display for the first 1500 miles (2414 km) to remind you that it is time for the regular vehicle service interval maintenance (refer to maintenance chart in Section 1).

To reset the service interval reminder light for another interval. With engine running, press the **TRIP** and **TRIP RESET** buttons at the same time. Hold the buttons down until 3 beeps are heard to verify that the service reminder has been reset.

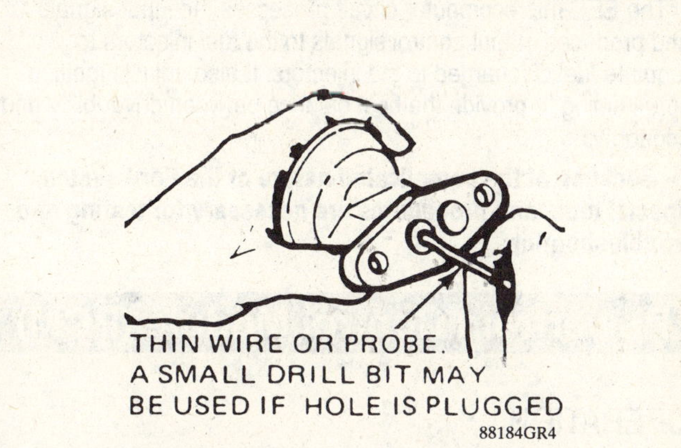

Fig. 21 Check the orifice in the EGR valve for deposits, then clean if necessary

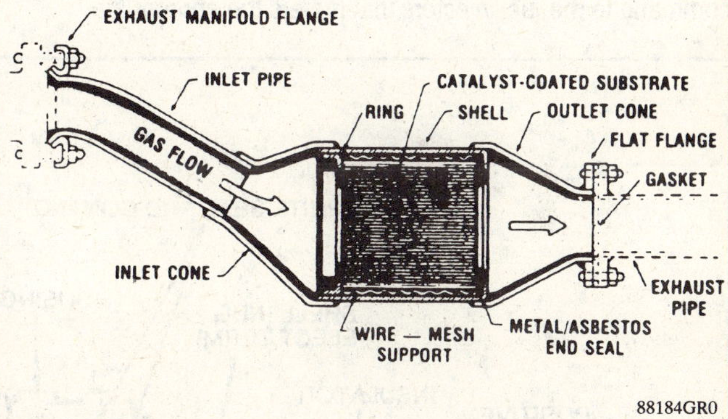

Fig. 22 Sectional view of a catalytic converter

ELECTRONIC ENGINE CONTROLS

Electronic Engine Control (EEC)

All CFI and MFI engines use the EEC system. The heart of the EEC system is a micro-processor called an Powertrain Control Module (PCM). The PCM receives data from a number of sensors and other electronic components (switches, relay, etc.). Based on information received and information programmed in the PCM's memory, it generates output signals to control various relay, solenoids and other actuators. The PCM in the EEC system has calibration modules located inside the assembly that contain calibration specifications for optimizing emissions, fuel economy and drive ability. The calibration module is called a PROM.

A potentiometer senses the position of the vane airflow meter in the engine's air induction system and generates a voltage signal that varies with the amount of air drawn into the engine. A sensor in the area of the vane airflow meter measures the temperature of the incoming air and transmits a corresponding electrical signal. Another temperature sensor inserted in the engine coolant tells if the engine is cold or warmed up. And a switch that senses throttle plate position produces electrical signals that tell the control unit when the throttle is closed or wide open.

A special probe (oxygen sensor) in the exhaust manifold measures the amount of oxygen in the exhaust gas, which is in indication of combustion efficiency, and sends a signal to the control unit. The sixth signal, crankshaft position information, is transmitted by a sensor integral with the new-design distributor.

The EEC microcomputer circuit processes the input signals and produces output control signals to the fuel injectors to regulate fuel discharged to the injectors. It also adjusts ignition spark timing to provide the best balance between driveability and economy.

Because of the complicated nature of the Ford system, special tools and procedures are necessary for testing and troubleshooting.

Powertrain Control Module (PCM)

OPERATION

The Powertrain Control Module (PCM) performs many functions on your car. The module accepts information from various engine sensors and computes the required fuel flow rate necessary to maintain the correct amount of air/fuel ratio throughout the entire engine operational range.

Based on the information that is received and programmed into the PCM's memory, the PCM generates output signals to control relays, actuators and solenoids. The PCM also sends out a command to the fuel injectors that meters the appropriate quantity of fuel. The module automatically senses and compensates for any changes in altitude when driving your vehicle.

REMOVAL & INSTALLATION

1. Disconnect the negative battery cable.
2. Remove the right cowl trim panel.
3. Disconnect the module wiring leading to the unit.
4. Remove the control unit from the bracket by pulling the unit downwards.

To install:

5. Attach the module to the bracket.
6. Attach the wiring to the module.
7. Install the right cowl trim panel.
8. Connect the negative battery cable.

Oxygen Sensors

OPERATION

See Figure 23

The oxygen sensor supplies the computer with a signal which indicates a rich or lean condition during engine operation. The input information assists the computer in determining the proper air/fuel ratio. The oxygen sensor is threaded into the exhaust manifold or exhaust pipes on all vehicles. Heated oxygen sensors are used on some models to allow the engine to reach the closed loop faster.

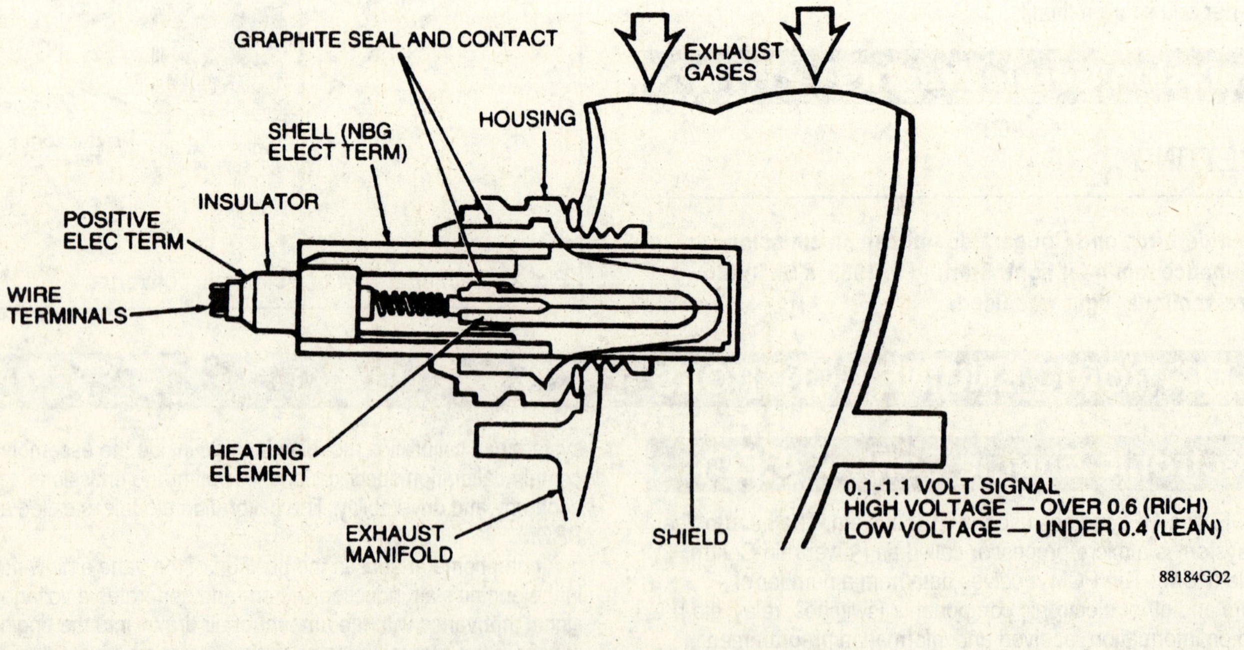

Fig. 23 Common oxygen sensor location — heated type shown

TESTING

➧ **See Figure 24**

1. Disconnect the Oxygen Sensor (O_2S).
2. On heated O_2S sensors, measure the resistance between PWR and GND terminals of the sensor. If the reading is about 6 ohms at 68°F (20°C). the sensor's heater element is okay.
3. With the O_2S connected and engine running, measure voltage with DVOM between terminals O_2S and **SIG RTN** (GND) of the oxygen sensor connector. If the voltage readings are about equal to those in the table, the sensor is okay.

REMOVAL & INSTALLATION

➥ The 4.6L engine uses four heated oxygen sensors for the engine control system. The heated sensors are located in the dual converter and pipe. On the 3.8L engines, there are two sensors, one is located in the left exhaust manifold and the other in the dual converter Y pipe.

1. Disconnect the negative battery cable.
2. Raise and safely support the vehicle.

Condition	Voltage—Between Terminals HO2S and SIG RTN
Ignition **ON**, engine **OFF**	0V
Idle (cold)	0V
Idle (warm)	0–1.0V
Acceleration	0.5–1.0V
Deceleration	0–0.5V

88184GZA

Fig. 24 The heated oxygen sensor voltage table

3. Disconnect the heated oxygen sensor from the engine control sensor wiring.

➥ If excessive force is needed to remove the sensors, lubricate the sensors with penetrating oil prior to removal.

4. Remove the sensors from the Y pipe or left manifold with a sensor removal tool T94P-9472-A or equivalent.

To install:

5. Install the sensor in its correct location, tighten to 26–34 ft. lbs. (36–46 Nm).
6. Connect the sensor electrical wiring.
7. Lower the vehicle.
8. Connect the negative battery cable.

Idle Air Control (IAC) Valve

OPERATION

➧ **See Figure 25**

The Idle Air Control (IAC) valve control the engine idle speed and dashpot functions. The valve is located on the throttle body on the 2.3L, 3.8L and 5.0L engines, and on the intake manifold on the 4.6L engines. This valve allows air to bypass the throttle plate. The amount of air is determined by the Powertrain Control Module (PCM) and controlled by a duty cycle signal.

TESTING

1. Make sure the ignition key is **OFF**.
2. Disconnect the air control valve.
3. Use an ohmmeter to measure the resistance between the terminals of the valve solenoid.

➥ Due to the diode in the solenoid, place the ohmmeter positive lead on the VPWR pin and the negative lead on the ISC pin.

4. If the resistance is not 7-13 ohms replace the air control valve.

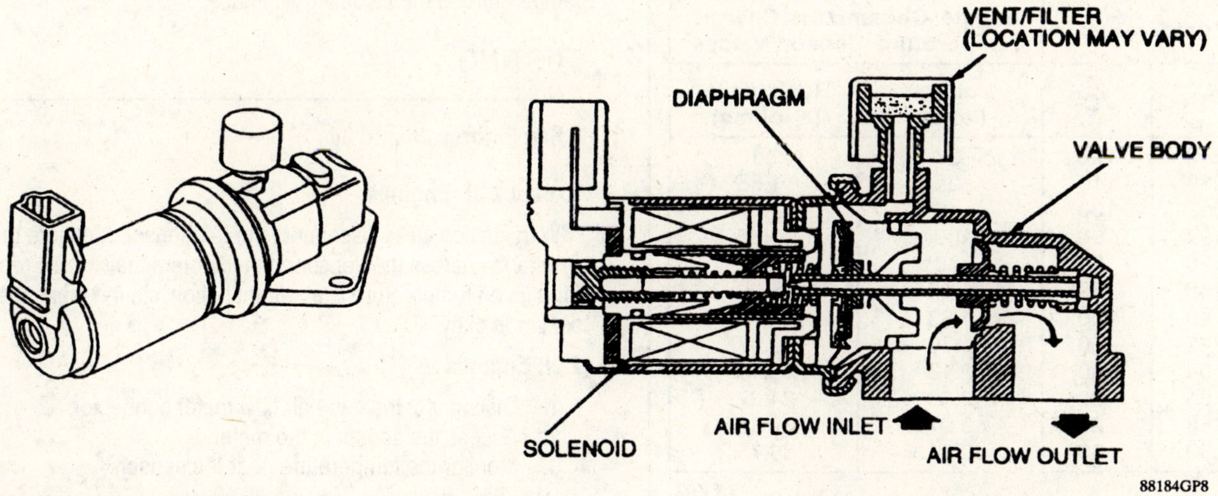

88184GP8

Fig. 25 Idle Air Control (IAC) valve on 4.6L engines

SSREMOVAL & INSTALLATION

1. Disconnect the negative battery cable.
2. Disconnect the engine wiring to the IAC sensor.
3. Remove the two retaining screws for the valve.
4. Remove the IAC valve and discard of the old gasket.

To install:

5. Clean the area of old gasket material.
6. Using a new gasket, attach the IAC valve to the engine. Tighten the retaining screws to 71–102 inch lbs. (8–12 Nm) on the 2.3L, 3.8L and 5.0L engines and 7 ft. lbs. (10 Nm) on the 4.6L engines.
7. Connect the IAC valve wiring to the unit.
8. Connect the negative battery cable.

Engine Coolant Temperature (ECT) Sensor

OPERATION

The engine coolant temperature sensor changes the resistance in response to the engine coolant temperature. The sensor decreases the resistance as the surrounding temperature increases. This provides a signal to the PCM that indicates the engine coolant temperature.

TESTING

➧ See Figures 26 and 27

1. Disconnect the temperature sensor.
2. Connect an ohmmeter between the sensor terminals and set the ohmmeter scale on 200,000 ohms.
3. Measure the resistance with the engine off and cool and with the engine running and warmed up. Compare the resistance values obtained with the chart.
4. Replace the sensor if the readings are incorrect.

Temperature		Engine Coolant/Air Charge Temperature Sensor Values	
°F	°C	Voltage (volts)	Resistance (K ohms)
248	120	.27	1.18
230	110	.35	1.55
212	100	.46	2.07
194	90	.60	2.80
176	80	.78	3.84
158	70	1.02	5.37
140	60	1.33	7.70
122	50	1.70	10.97
104	40	2.13	16.15
86	30	2.60	24.27
68	20	3.07	37.30
50	10	3.51	58.75

88184GZP

Fig. 26 ACT, IAT and ECT temperature sensor value chart

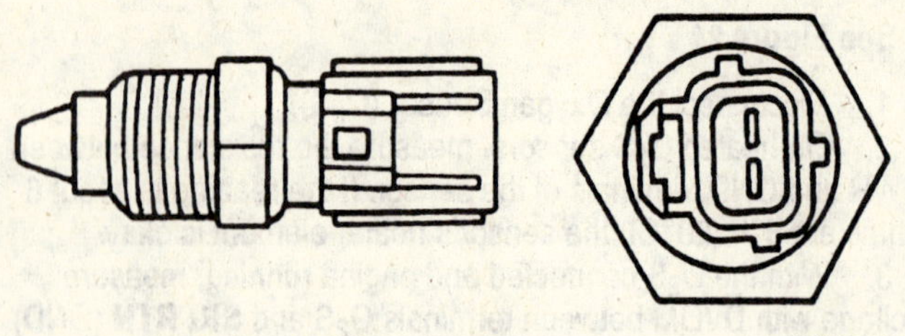

88184GQ5

Fig. 27 Check the resistance between the twp terminals

REMOVAL & INSTALLATION

1. Drain the engine cooling system slightly.
2. Disconnect the negative battery cable.
3. Detach the wiring connection from the sensor.
4. Remove the coolant temperature sensor from the intake manifold.
5. Clean the sensor area of any debris.

To install:

6. Install a new sensor into the intake manifold. Tighten the 6–14 ft. lbs. (8–19 Nm).
7. Attach the sensor wiring to the unit.
8. Connect the negative battery cable.
9. Fill the engine cooling system with a 50/50 coolant water mixture.
10. Start the engine and top off the cooling system.

Intake Air Temperature (IAT) Sensor

OPERATION

The Intake Air Temperature (IAT) sensor changes the resistance in response to the intake air temperature. The sensor resistance decreases as the surrounding air temperature increases. This provides a signal to the PCM indicating the temperature of the incoming air intake.

TESTING

➧ See Figures 26 and 28

Except 2.3L Engines

With ignition **OFF**, disconnect the IAT sensor. Measure the resistance across the sensor connector terminals. If the reading for a given temperature is about that shown in the table, the IAT sensor is okay.

2.3L Engines

1. Disconnect the vane air flow meter connector.
2. Access the sensor in the meter.
3. Monitor the temperature near the sensor.

➥ If using a hot air gun to heat the sensor, be careful not to melt any plastic or rubber components.

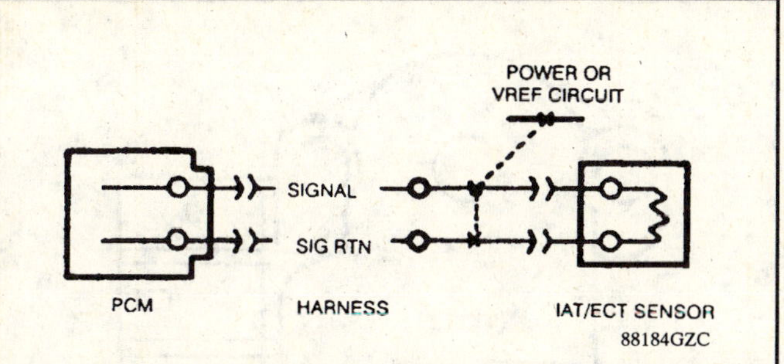

Fig. 28 The intake air temperature (IAT) sensor circuit

4. Measure the resistance between the meter black/white terminal and the meter pink/black terminal and record.
5. Compare the resistance readings with the chart. If the readings are incorrect, replace the sensor.

REMOVAL & INSTALLATION

2.3L Engines

The air temperature sensor is an integral component of the vane air flow meter. If the temperature sensor is defective, the vane air flow meter must be replaced.

3.8L and 5.0L Engines

1. Disconnect the negative battery cable.
2. Disconnect the wiring to the IAT.
3. Remove the sensor from the intake manifold.

To install:

4. Clean the sensor area. Install the sensor into the intake manifold and tighten to 6–8 ft. lbs. (8–13 Nm).
5. Attach the wiring to the unit.
6. Connect the negative battery cable.

4.6L Engine

1. Disconnect the negative battery cable.
2. Disconnect the wiring to the IAT.
3. Remove the sensor from the air cleaner cover.

To install:

4. Clean the sensor area. Install the sensor into the air cleaner cover.
5. Attach the wiring to the unit.
6. Connect the negative battery cable.

Mass Air Flow (MAF) Sensor

OPERATION

The Mass Air Flow (MAF) sensor directly measures the mass of the air flowing into the engine. The sensor output is an analog signal ranging from about 0.5–5.0 volts. The signal is used by the PCM to calculate the injector pulse width. The sensing element is a thin platinum wire wound on a ceramic bobbin and coated with glass. This "hot wire" is maintained at 392°F (200°C) above the ambient temperature as measured by a constant "cold wire". The MAF sensor is located in the outlet side of the air cleaner lid assembly on all models except the 1995–96 4.6L and 1996 3.8L engines. On the 1995–96 4.6L and 1996 3.8L engines, the sensor is located between the air cleaner and the throttle body.

TESTING

➧ See Figure 29

Except 1995–96 4.6L and 1996 3.8L Engines

1. With engine running, use DVOM to verify there is at least 10.5 volts between terminals A and B of the MAF sensor connector. This indicates the power input to the sensor is okay.
2. With engine running, use DVOM to measure voltage between MAF sensor connector terminals C and D. If the readings are about as indicated in the table, the sensor is okay. The readings may vary based on vehicle load and temperature.

1995–96 4.6L and 1996 3.8L Engines

➧ See Figures 30 and 31

1. With engine running, use DVOM to verify there is at least 10.5 volts between terminals A and B of the MAF sensor connector. This indicates the power input to the sensor is okay.
2. With engine running, use DVOM to measure voltage between MAF sensor connector terminals C and D. If the reading is about 0.34–1.96 volts at idle, the sensor is okay.

Engine Condition	Signal Voltage—Sensor Terminals C and D
Idle	0.60V
20 mph	1.10V
40 mph	1.70V
60 mph	2.10V

88184GZK

Fig. 29 The Mass Air Flow (MAF) sensor — conditions vs. signal table

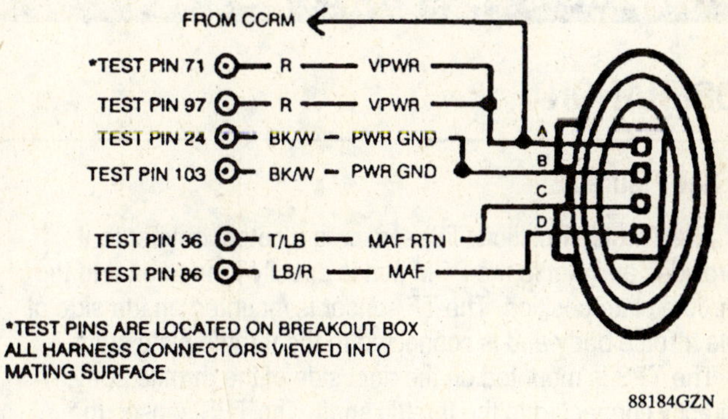

Fig. 30 The mass air flow (MAF) sensor — conditions vs. signal table except 1995–96 4.6L and 1996 3.8L engines

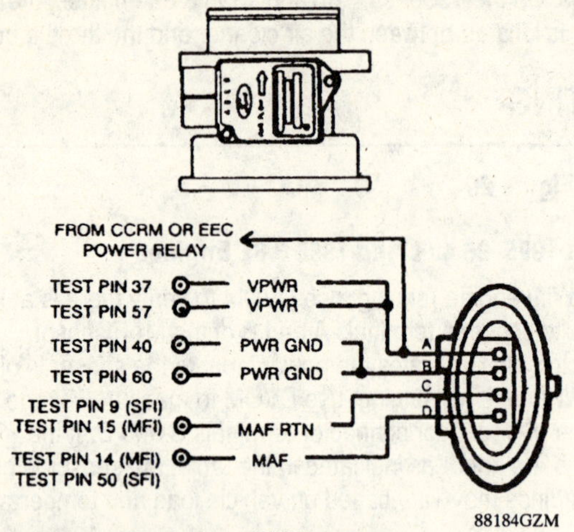

Fig. 31 The mass air flow (MAF) sensor connector — 1995-96 4.6L and 1996 3.8L engines

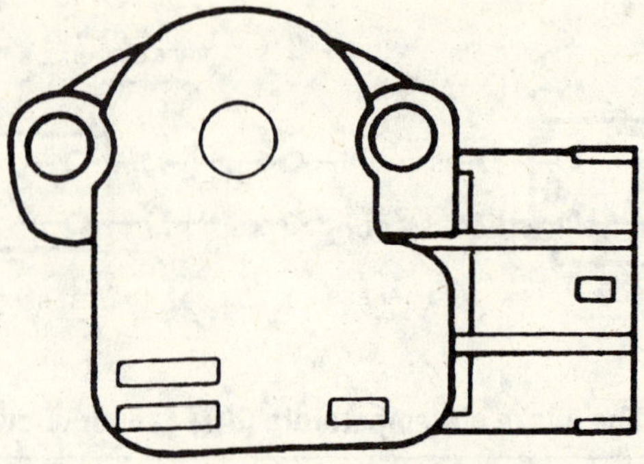

Fig. 32 Throttle position sensor for a 3.8L engine — 1996 shown

REMOVAL & INSTALLATION

****CAUTION**

The mass air flow sensor hot wire sensing element and housing are calibrated as a unit and must be serviced as a complete assembly. Do not damage the sensing element or possible failure of the sensor may occur.

1. Disconnect the negative battery cable.
2. Disconnect the engine control sensor wiring from the MAF sensor.
3. Loosen the engine air cleaner outlet tube clamps and the engine air cleaner cover.
4. Disconnect the mass air flow sensor.

To install:

5. Install the MAF sensor to the vehicle.
6. Install the air cleaner cover and tighten the outlet tube clamps to 12–22 inch lbs. (1–3 Nm).
7. Attach the engine control sensor wiring to the sensor.
8. Connect the negative battery cable.

Throttle Position (TP) Sensor

OPERATION

See Figure 32

The Throttle Position (TP) sensor is a potentiometer that provides a signal to the PCM that is directly proportional to the throttle plate position. The TP sensor is mounted on the side of the throttle body and is connected to the throttle plate shaft.

The TPS is mounted on the right side of the throttle body, directly connected to the throttle shaft. The TPS senses the throttle movement and position and transmits an appropriate electrical signal to the PCM. These signals are used by the PCM to adjust the air/fuel mixture, spark timing and EGR operation according to engine load at idle, part throttle, or full throttle. The TPS is nonadjustable.

TESTING

1. Disconnect the negative battery cable.
2. Remove the PCM and connect a breakout box to the PCM and harness.
3. Probe terminals 89 and 90 with an ohmmeter.
4. Slowly rotate the throttle shaft and monitor the ohmmeter for a continuous change in resistance. Any sudden changes in resistance indicates an open or substrate sensor.
5. Reconnect the negative battery cable.
6. Turn the ignition switch **ON** and using a voltmeter, measure the voltage between terminals 89 and 90 of the breakout box. The specification is 0.8 volts on the 2.3L, 3.8L and 5.0L engines or 0.9 volts on the 4.6L engine.
7. If the voltage is outside the standard value or if it does not change smoothly, inspect the circuit wiring and/or replace the throttle position sensor.

REMOVAL & INSTALLATION

2.3L and 3.8L (Except SC) Engines

EXCEPT 1996 3.8L ENGINES

1. Disconnect the throttle position sensor from the wiring harness.
2. Matchmark the sensor and throttle body.
3. Remove the two retaining screws.
4. Remove the throttle position sensor.

To install:

5. Align the matchmarks and install the sensor.
6. Tighten the sensor screws 11–16 inch lbs. (1–2 Nm).

This throttle position sensor is not adjustable.

3.8L (SC) Engine

EXCEPT 1996 3.8L ENGINES

1. Disconnect the negative battery cable.
2. Disconnect the idle bypass valve wiring.
3. Remove the lower IBV bolt and loosen the upper. Rotate the valve out of the way to gain access to the TPS bolts.

4. Disconnect the TPS wiring and remove the bolts.
5. Remove the sensor.

To install:

6. Attach the sensor and tighten the screws to 26 inch lbs. (3 Nm).; and the IBV bolts to 70–100 inch lbs. (8–11 Nm).
7. Attach the wiring to the sensor.
8. Connect the negative battery cable.

3.8L and 4.6L Engines

1995-95 4.6L AND 1996 3.8L ENGINES

1. Disconnect the negative battery cable.
2. Detach the wiring leading to the sensor.
3. Remove the two screws retaining the sensor to the throttle body.
4. Remove the TP sensor.

To install:

5. Install the sensor with the retaining screws. Tighten the screws to 25–34 inch lbs. (3–4 Nm).
6. Attach the wire to the sensor.
7. Connect the negative battery cable.

5.0L Engines

1. Disconnect the TPS wiring harness.
2. Matchmark the TPS and throttle body.
3. Remove the 2 retaining screws and the sensor.

To install:

4. If the sensor had a bushing, it must be reused. Install the bushing with the larger diameter facing outwards.
5. Install the TPS on the throttle shaft and rotate the sensor 10–20° counterclockwise to align the bolt holes.
6. Install the bolts and tighten them to 11–15 inch lbs. (1–2 Nm).
7. Cycle the throttle to the wide open position. It should return without interference.
8. Connect the wiring.
9. Connect the negative battery cable.

Camshaft Position (CMP) Sensor

OPERATION

The distributor stator or Camshaft Position Sensor, is a single Hall effect magnetic switch. This is activated by a single vane. This is driven by by the camshaft.

The distributor stator or Camshaft Position sensor provides the camshaft position information. The sensor also provides what is called the CMP signal. This signal is used by the powertrain control module (PCM) for fuel synchronization.

On the 4.6L engines, the Camshaft Position (CMP) sensor is a variable reluctance sensor that is triggered by the high-point mark on the camshaft sprocket.

TESTING

See Figures 33 and 34

Three Wire Sensors

1. With the ignition **OFF**, disconnect the CMP sensor. With the ignition **ON** and the engine **OFF**, measure the voltage between sensor harness connector VPWR and PWR GND terminals (refer to the figure). If the reading is greater than 10.5 volts, the power circuit to the sensor is okay.
2. With the ignition **OFF**, install breakout box. Connect CMP sensor and ECM. Using DVOM on AC and scale set to monitor less than 5 volts, measure voltage between breakout box terminals 24 and 40 with the engine running at varying RPM. If the voltage reading varies more than 0.1 volt AC, the sensor is okay.

Two Wire Sensors

1. With the ignition **OFF**, install breakout box.
2. Connect CMP sensor and ECM.
3. Using DVOM on AC scale and set to monitor less than 5 volts, measure voltage between breakout box terminals 24 and 46 with the engine running at varying RPM. If the voltage reading varies more than 0.1 volt AC, the sensor is okay.

REMOVAL & INSTALLATION

Except 4.6L Engines

****CAUTION**

Prior to removing the camshaft position sensor, set the No. 1 cylinder to 26° after top dead center of the compression stroke. Note the position of the sensor electrical connection. When installing the sensor, the connection must be in the exact position on installation.

1. Disconnect the negative battery cable.
2. Remove the ignition coil, radio capacitor and ignition coil bracket.
3. Remove the camshaft position sensor retaining screw and sensor.
4. Remove the retaining bolt and hold-down clamp.
5. The oil pump intermediate shaft should be removed with the camshaft sensor housing. Remove the housing from the front engine cover.

To install:

****CAUTION**

If the camshaft position sensor housing does not contain a plastic locator cover tool, a special service tool such as T89P-12200-A or equivalent must be obtained prior to installation. Failure to follow this procedure may result in improper stator alignment. This will result in the fuel system being out of time with the engine, possibly causing engine damage.

→ If the plastic locator cover is not attached to the replacement camshaft position sensor, attach a synchro positioning tool T89P-12200-A or equivalent. To do so perform the following.

6. Engage the sensor housing vane into the radial slot of the tool.
   a. Rotate the tool on the camshaft sensor housing until the tool boss engages notch in the sensor housing.
   b. The cover tool should be square and in contact with the entire top surface of the camshaft position sensor housing.

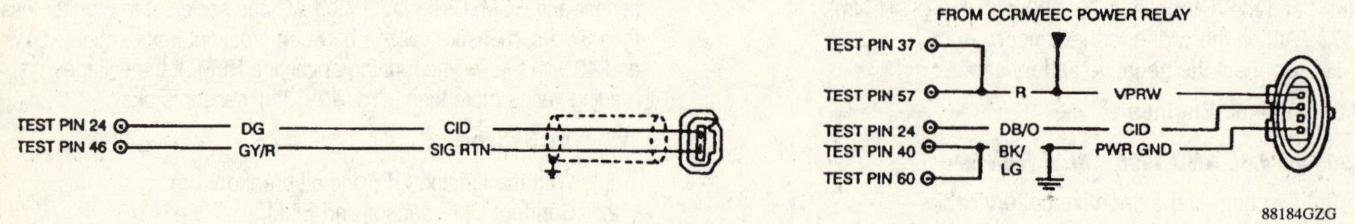

Fig. 33 Camshaft position sensor schematics — except 1995-96 4.6L and 1996 3.8L engines

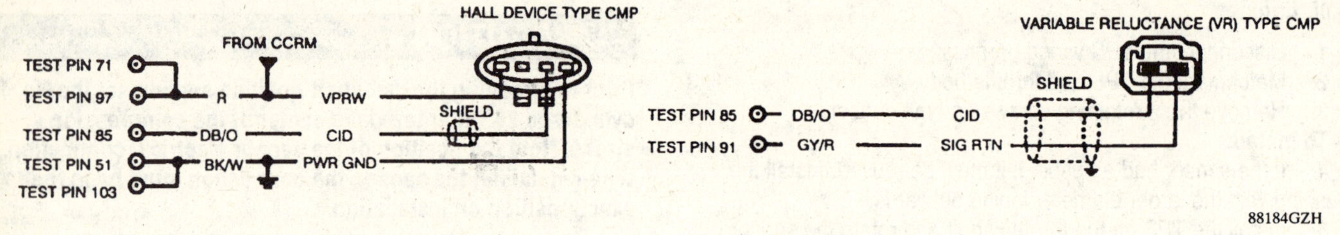

Fig. 34 Camshaft position sensor schematics — 1995-96 4.6L and 1996 3.8L engines

7. Transfer the oil pump intermediate shaft from the old camshaft position sensor housing to the replacement sensor housing.
8. Install the camshaft sensor housing so that the drive gear engagement occurs when the arrow on the locator tool is pointed approximately 30° counterclockwise from the face of the cylinder block. This will locate the sensor electrical connector in the removal procedure.
9. Install the hold-down clamp and bolt, then tighten the bolt to 15–22 ft. lbs. (20–30 Nm).
10. Remove the synchro positioning tool.

****CAUTION**

If the sensor connector is positioned correctly, DO NOT reposition the connector by rotating the sensor housing. This will result in the fuel system being out of time with the engine. This could possibly cause engine damage. Remove the sensor housing and repeat the installation procedure beginning with step one.

11. Install the sensor and retaining screws, tighten the screws to 22–31 inch lbs. (2–4 Nm).
12. Connect the engine control sensor wiring connector to the sensor.
13. Install the ignition coil bracket, radio ignition capacitor and ignition coil.
14. Connect the negative battery cable.

4.6L Engine

1. Disconnect the negative battery cable.
2. Disconnect the engine control sensor wiring from the camshaft position sensor.
3. Remove the sensor retaining screw and the sensor from the front of the engine front cover.

To install:

4. Make sure the camshaft position sensor mounting surface is clean and the O-ring is positioned correctly.
5. Position the sensor, then install the retaining screw and tighten to 71–106 inch lbs. (8–12 Nm).

****CAUTION**

Do not overtighten the screw.

6. Connect the sensor wiring to the sensor.
7. Connect the negative battery cable.

Barometric/Manifold Absolute Pressure Sensors (B/MAP)

OPERATION

The B/MAP sensor used on 3.8L engines is separate from the barometric sensor and is located on the left fender panel in the engine compartment. The barometric sensor signals the PCM of changes in atmospheric pressure and density to regulate calculated air flow into the engine. The MAP sensor monitors and signals the PCM of changes in intake manifold pressure which result from engine load, speed and atmospheric pressure changes.

The Manifold Absolute Pressure (MAP) sensor measures the pressure in the intake manifold and sends a variable frequency signal to the Powertrain Control Module (PCM). When the ignition is **ON** and the engine **OFF**, the MAP sensor will indicate the barometric pressure in the intake manifold.

TESTING

➧ See Figures 35, 36 and 37

1. Connect **MAP/BARO** tester to sensor connector and sensor harness connector. With ignition **ON** and engine **OFF**, use DVOM to measure voltage across tester terminals. If the tester's 4-6 volts indicator is ON, the reference voltage input to the sensor is okay.
2. If the DVOM voltage reading is as indicated in the table, the sensor is okay.

REMOVAL & INSTALLATION

1. Disconnect the negative battery cable.
2. Disconnect the electrical wiring and the vacuum line from the sensor.
3. Remove the sensor mounting bolts and remove the sensor.

To install:

4. Install the sensor with the mounting bolts and tighten.
5. Attach the electrical wiring lead to the sensor.
6. Attach the vacuum line to the sensor.
7. Connect the negative battery cable.

Approximate Altitude (Feet)	Signal Voltage (±0.04V)
0	1.59
1000	1.56
2000	1.53
3000	1.50
4000	1.47
5000	1.44
6000	1.41
7000	1.39

88184GZD

Fig. 35 The manifold absolute pressure (MAP) sensor altitude vs. signal voltage — except 1995-96 4.6L and 1996 3.8L engines

Transmission Range Position	Resistance—Ohms
Park	3770–4607
Reverse	1304–1593
Neutral	660–807
Overdrive	361–442
Drive	190–232
First	78–95

88184GZE

Fig. 36 The manifold absolute pressure (MAP) sensor position vs. resistance — 1995-96 4.6L and 1996 3.8L engines

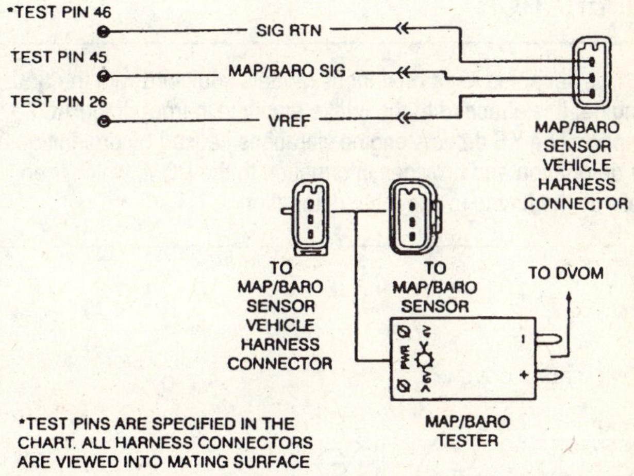

88184GZF

Fig. 37 Barometric/Manifold Absolute Pressure Sensors (B/MAP) circuit and tester — except 1995-96 4.6L and 1996 3.8L engines

Crankshaft Position (CP) Sensor

OPERATION

➧ See Figure 38

The Crankshaft Position (CP) sensor, located inside the front cover is used to determine crankshaft position and crankshaft rpm.

TESTING

➧ See Figure 39

Using DVOM on the AC scale and set to monitor less than 5 volts, measure voltage between the sensor Cylinder Identification (CID) terminal and ground. The sensor is okay if the voltage reading varies more than 0.1 volt AC with the engine running at varying RPM.

REMOVAL & INSTALLATION

1. Disconnect the negative battery cable.
2. Loosen the water pump pulley bolts, then remove the accessory drive belt is necessary.
3. Disconnect the wiring to the crankshaft position sensor. Remove the sensor mounting bolt, then remove the sensor.

To install:

4. Install the sensor and connect the wiring. Tighten the mounting bolt to 71–106 inch lbs. (8–12 Nm).
5. Install the accessory drive belt if removed. Tighten the water pump pulley bolts as described in Section 1.
6. Connect the negative battery cable.

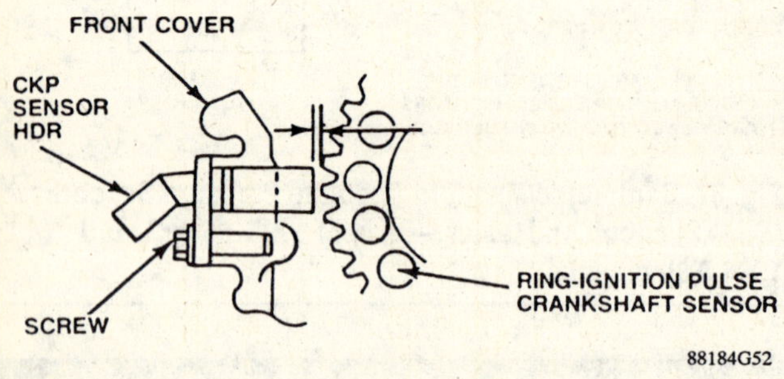

Fig. 38 Common crankshaft position sensor

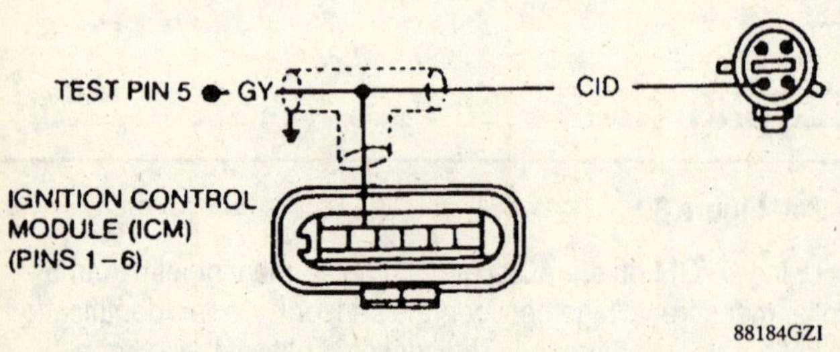

Fig. 39 Crankshaft position sensor schematics

Knock Sensor (KS)

OPERATION

This sensor is used on various models equipped with the 3.8L engine. It is attached to the intake manifold in front of the ACT sensor. The KS detects engine vibrations caused by preignition or detonation and provides information to the PCM, which then retards the timing to eliminate detonation.

TESTING

1. With ignition **ON** and engine **OFF**, measure voltage between KS connector terminals. If voltage reading is 2.4–2.6 volts, the circuit between the ECM and KS is okay.
2. With engine running at idle and 3000 rpm, measure voltage using a DVOM on the AC setting between the KS terminals. If the AC voltage reading increases as the rpm increases, the sensor is okay.

REMOVAL & INSTALLATION

1. Disconnect the negative battery cable.
2. Disconnect the electrical wiring from the sensor.
3. Remove the sensor from the front of the ACT sensor.

To install:

4. Attach the KS to the front of the ACT sensor.
5. Attach the electrical connector to the sensor.
6. Connect the negative battery cable.

EGR Valve Position (EVP) Sensor

OPERATION

The EGR Valve Position (EVP) system uses an electronic EGR valve to control the flow of exhaust gases. The Powertrain Control Module (PCM) monitors the flow by means of an EVP sensor and regulates the electronic EGR valve accordingly. The valve is operated by a vacuum signal from the EGR Vacuum Regulator (EVR) solenoid which actuates the valve diaphragm.

As the supply vacuum overcomes the spring load, the diaphragm is actuated. This lifts the pintle off its seat and allows exhaust gases to flow. The amount of flow is proportional to the pintle position. The EVP sensor, mounted on the valve, sends an electronic signal representing pintle position to the ECM.

TESTING

1. Disconnect the EVP sensor connector. With the ignition **ON** and the engine **OFF**, measure the voltage between **VREF** (red) and **SIG RTN** (dark green) terminals of EVP sensor harness connector. If the voltage is 4.0–6.0 volts, the power circuits to the sensor are okay.
2. Reconnect the EVP sensor. With the ignition **ON** and the engine **OFF**, measure the voltage between EVP sensor terminals EVP and **SIG RTN** (dark green). If the voltage reading is 0.67 volts or less, the sensor is okay.

REMOVAL & INSTALLATION

1. Disconnect the negative battery cable.
2. Disconnect the electrical connector from the sensor.
3. Remove the sensor mounting nuts and remove the sensor from the EGR valve.

To install:

4. Attach the sensor to the EGR valve and tighten the mounting nuts.
5. Connect the sensor electrical lead to the sensor.
6. Connect the negative battery cable.

EEC-IV TROUBLE CODES

- These procedures apply only to vehicles equipped with fourth generation Electronic Engine Controls (EEC-IV). This is found on all models except 1995–96 4.6L and 1996 3.8L engines
- The Key On Engine Off and Engine Running self tests detect faults that are present at the time of testing. Intermittent faults that have occurred in the last 80 (40 for some applications) warm-up cycles are detected during continuous self test and stored in the EEC-IV memory
- Vehicles with a Malfunction Indicator Light (MIL) concern must run quick test and address all service codes present
- If all phases of the quick test result in a Pass, it is likely that the problem is non EEC-IV related and will be found elsewhere
- After service, rerun quick test to ensure that service was effective

General Information

All vehicles have self-diagnostic capabilities. Malfunctions in the engine control system are found through the Self-Test procedure. Vehicles using the EEC-IV system use a Self-Test divided into 3 specialized tests: Key On Engine Off Self-Test, Engine Running Self-Test and Continuous Self-Test. The Self-Test is not a conclusive test by itself, but is used as a part of a functional Quick Test diagnostic procedure. The PCM stores the Self-Test program in its permanent memory. When activated, it checks the EEC-IV system by testing it's memory integrity and processing capability and verifies that various sensors and actuators are connected and operating properly. The Key On Engine Off and Engine Running Self-Tests are functional tests which only detect faults present at the time of the Self-Test. Continuous Self-Test is an ongoing test that stores fault information in Keep Alive Memory (KAM) for retrieval at a later time.

Fault information is communicated through the Self-Test service codes. These service codes are 2–digit or 3–digit numbers representing the results of the Self-Test. The 3–digit numbers start in the 1991 models. The service codes are transmitted on the Self-Test output line found in the vehicle Self-Test connector. They are in the form of timed pulses and are read on a voltmeter, STAR or SUPER STAR II tester and the malfunction indicator light.

VEHICLE PREPARATION

1. Apply the parking brake, place the transaxle shift lever firmly into **P** on automatic transaxle or neutral on manual transaxles and block the drive wheels.
2. Turn all electrical loads such as the radio, lights, blower fan, etc. OFF.

Using The Star Or Super Star II Tester

➥ The STAR tester cannot be used to read 3–digit service codes. If the STAR tester is used on a 3–digit service code application, the display will be blank. The SUPER STAR II tester must be used to read 3–digit service codes.

After hooking up the STAR tester and turning on it's power switch, the tester will run a display check and the numerals **88** will begin to flash in the display window. A steady **00** will then appear, indicating that the STAR tester is ready. To receive service codes, press the button on the front of the STAR tester. The button will latch down and a colon will appear in the display window in front of the **00** numerals. The colon must be displayed to receive the service codes.

If it is desired to clear the display window during the Self-Test, turn **OFF** the vehicle's engine, press the tester's button once to unlatch it, then press the button again to latch down the button.

Connect the STAR or SUPER STAR II tester as follows:

1. Turn the ignition key **OFF**.
2. Connect the color coded adapter cable to the STAR tester.
3. Connect the adapter cable leads to the proper Self-Test connectors.
4. Ground the adapter cable for vehicles using the SUPER STAR II tester.
5. Slide the SUPER STAR II tester switch to the EEC-IV position, according to the vehicle system.

Using The Analog Voltmeter

Service codes will be represented by pulsing or sweeping movements of the voltmeter's needle across the dial face of the voltmeter. Therefore, a single digit number of 3 will be reported by 3 needle sweeps. However, a service code is represented by a 2–digit or 3–digit number, such as 23. As a result, the Self-Test service code of 23 will appear on the voltmeter as 2 needle sweeps, then after a 2 second pause, the needle will sweep 3 times.

Connect the analog voltmeter as follows:

1. Turn the ignition key **OFF**.
2. Set the voltmeter on a DC voltage range to read from 0–20 volts.
3. On all EEC-IV vehicles, connect the voltmeter from the battery positive post to the Self-Test output pin of the large Self-Test connector. On all others Connect the positive voltmeter lead to the EEC STO line and the negative lead to engine ground and jumper the EEC STI to ground.

Using The Indicator Light

During the Self-Test a service code is reported by the malfunction indicator light. It will represent itself as a flash on the CHECK ENGINE or SERVICE ENGINE SOON light on the dash panel. A single digit number of 3 will be reported by 3 flashes. However, a service code is represented by a 2–digit or 3–digit number, such as 23. As a result, the Self-Test service code of 23 will appear on the MIL light as 2 flashes, then, after a 2 second pause, the light will flash 3 times.

READING CODES

Key On Engine Off Self-Test

Start the engine and let it run until it reaches normal operating temperature. Turn the engine **OFF** and activate the Self-Test.

1. If using the STAR tester, proceed as follows:

a. Latch the center button in the down position.
b. Place the ignition key in the **ON** position.
c. Record all service codes displayed.

2. If using the SUPER STAR II tester, proceed as follows:
a. Latch the center button in the **TEST** position.
b. Turn the ignition key **ON**.
c. Turn the tester **ON**, the tester will sound and **888** will be displayed for 2 seconds.
d. Unlatch and relatch the center test button. After all codes are received, unlatch the center button to review all codes retained in tester memory.

➛ The SUPER STAR II tester has a mode switch. The tester will only display 3-digit service codes in fast code mode. If slow code mode is used on 3-digit service code applications, the display will be blank.

3. If using the analog voltmeter jumper the STI to the SIG RTN at the Self-Test connectors and turn the ignition key and the voltmeter **ON**. Observe the needle for any code indications and record.
4. If using the malfunction indicator light connect the jumper wire from STI to the SIG RTN at the Self-Test connectors and turn the ignition switch **ON**. Service codes will be flashed on the MIL light.

Engine Running Self-Test

1. Deactivate the Self-Test.
2. Start and run the engine at 2000 rpm for 2 minutes.
3. Turn the engine **OFF** and wait 10 seconds.
4. Activate the Self-Test.
5. Start the engine.
6. Record all service codes displayed.

➛ Engine identification codes are issued at the beginning of the Engine Running Self-Test and are 1-digit numbers represented by the number of pulses sent out. The engine identification code is equal to 1/2 the number of engine cylinders. Two pulses equals 4 cylinders. The identification codes are used to verify that the proper processor is installed and that the Self-Test has been entered.

CLEARING CODES

➛ Do not disconnect the battery to clear continuous memory codes. This will erase the Keep Alive Memory (KAM) information which may cause a driveability concern.

1. Run the Key On Engine Off Self-Test.
2. When the service codes begin to be displayed, deactivate the Self-Test as follows:
a. STAR tester: unlatch the center button to the UP position.
b. Analog voltmeter, MIL, Continental message center: remove the jumper wire from between the Self-Test Input (STI) connector and the signal return pin of the Self-Test connector.
c. The continuous memory codes will be erased from the PCM memory.

TEST STEP	RESULT ▶	ACTION TO TAKE
1.0 VISUAL CHECK		
• Check vacuum hoses for damage and proper connection. • Check EEC-IV system wiring harness for proper connections. • **Are all visual checks OK?**	Yes ▶ No ▶	GO to Quick Test Step 2.0. SERVICE as necessary.
2.0 VEHICLE PREPARATION AND EQUIPMENT HOOKUP		
• Apply parking brake. • Place shift lever firmly in PARK (NEUTRAL for manual transmissions). • Block drive wheels. • Turn off all electrical loads. • Connect appropriate test equipment to the Self-Test connector in order to run Self-Test. • **Is vehicle prepared to run Self-Test?**	Yes ▶ No ▶	GO to Quick Test Step 3.0. REPEAT this test step.

88184C10

TEST STEP	RESULT ▶	ACTION TO TAKE
3.0 PERFORM KOEO SELF-TEST		
• Start engine and idle until vehicle is at operating temperature. **NOTE: If engine does not start or stalls after starting, continue to perform KOEO Self-Test.** • Key off, wait 10 seconds. • Activate Self-Test. • Key on, engine off. • Record all KOEO and Continuous Memory Codes received. • **Is a PASS code "11" or "111" present in KOEO? (11/111-10-any code)**	Yes ▶	**If Malfunction Indicator Light (MIL) is on:** GO to Continuous Memory code charts, **If engine runs rough or idles rough:** GO to Pinpoint Test Step [S2], except DIS/EDIS vehicles, GO to Quick Test Step [3.1]. **If engine is a no start:** GO to Pinpoint Test Step [A1], except EDIS vehicles, GO to Pinpoint Test Step [AA1]. **If these symptoms are not present:** GO to Quick Test Step [4.0], except 7.3L diesel, GO to Quick Test Step [5.0].
	No ▶	**If KOEO service codes are received:** GO to KOEO code charts, **If no service codes are received:** GO to Pinpoint Test Step [QA1].

88184C11

TEST STEP	RESULT ▶	ACTION TO TAKE
3.1 CHECK FOR CONTINUOUS MEMORY SERVICE CODES 45, 46, 48, 215, 216, 217, 232, OR 238		
• For DIS/EDIS vehicles only. • **Were Continuous Memory service codes 45, 46, 48, 215, 216, 217, 232 or 238 received during KOEO Self-Test?**	Yes ▶	GO to DIS or EDIS diagnostics.
	No ▶	GO to Pinpoint Test Step [S2].
4.0 COMPUTED TIMING CHECK		
• Key off, wait 10 seconds • Activate Engine Running Self-Test. • Start engine. **NOTE: If additional information is required for Engine Running Self-Test, refer to Quick Test** **If engine starts but stalls or stalls during Self-Test, GO to Pinpoint Test Step [S1].** **Engine Running Service Code 98/998 indicates vehicle is in Failure Mode Effects Management (FMEM) and DID NOT PASS KOEO On-Demand/Continuous Memory Self-Test. Engine Running Self-Test cannot be performed while in FMEM. Rerun KOEO Self-Test, Quick Test Step [3.0].** • Check computed timing after the last service code has been displayed. The timing will remain fixed for two minutes, unless Self-Test is deactivated. **NOTE: Computed timing is equal to base timing plus 20 degrees BTDC with 3 degrees tolerance. See vehicle decal for correct base timing.** • **Is computed timing within specs?**	Yes ▶	Go to Quick Test Step [5.0].
	No ▶	**For EDIS:** GO to Pinpoint Test Step [PC2]. **For DIS:** Go to Pinpoint Test Step [PB2]. **For TFI:** Go to Pinpoint Test Step [PA2].

88184C12

TEST STEP	RESULT ▶	ACTION TO TAKE
5.0 PERFORM ENGINE RUNNING SELF-TEST		
• Deactivate Self-Test. • Start engine and idle until vehicle is at operating temperature. • Turn engine off. • Activate Engine Running Self-Test. • Start engine. • Record all service codes displayed. **NOTE: Engine Running Service Code 98/998 indicates vehicle is in Failure Mode Effects Management (FMEM) and DID NOT PASS KOEO On-Demand/Continuous Memory Self-Test. Engine Running Self-Test cannot be performed while in FMEM. Rerun KOEO Self-Test, Quick Test Step 3.0.** • **Is a PASS Code (11 or 111) received during Engine Running Self-Test?**	Yes ▶	**If any Continuous Memory service codes were received in Quick Test Step 3.0:** GO to Continuous Memory code charts **If a Continuous Memory PASS Code (11/111) was received in Quick Test Step 3.0 and no symptoms are present:** EEC-IV diagnostic testing is complete. **If a Continuous Memory PASS Code (11/111) was received in Quick Test Step 3.0 and symptoms are present:** GO to Diagnosis By Symptom chart Quick Test Step 12.0.
	No ▶	**If Engine Running service codes are received:** GO to Engine Running code charts, Quick **If no service codes are received:** GO to Pinpoint Test Step QA1.

88184C14

12.0 DIAGNOSIS BY SYMPTOM
SPECIAL NOTES: • Verify that a **Pass Code 11/111** was received in Key On Engine Off, Engine Running and Continuous Self-Tests before continuing with this test. • If a symptom is present and the EEC system is suspected, Go to Diagnosis By Symptom charts. If the EEC system is not suspected, GO to Diagnostic Routines.

88184C15

1984–88 2.3L EFI TURBOCHARGED ENGINE SERVICE CODES

Code		Explanation
11	O/R/C	System pass
12	R	Rpm unable to reach upper test limit
13	R	Rpm unable to reach lower test limit
14	C	PIP circuit failure
15	O	ROM test failure
15	C	Power interrupted to keep alive memory
18	C	Loss of tach input to ECU, spout grounded
21	O/R	ECT sensor input out of test range
22	O/R/C	BP sensor input out of test range
23	O/R	TP sensor input out of test range
24	O/R	VAT sensor input out of test range
25	R	KS sensor not detected during test
26	O/R	VAF sensor input out of self-test range
34	R	Insufficient EGR flow
35	R	Rpm too low for EGR test
41	R	EGO/HEGO circuit shows system lean
41	C	No EGO/HEGO switching detected, system lean
42	R	EGO/HEGO shows system rich
42	C	No EGO/HEGO switching detected, system rich
51	O/C	ECT sensor input exceeds test maximum
53	O/C	TP sensor input exceeds test maximum
54	O/C	VAT sensor input exceeds test maximum
61	O/C	ECT test sensor input below test minimum
63	O/C	TP sensor below test minimum
64	O/C	VAT sensor input below test minimum
66	O/C	VAF sensor input below test minimum
67	O	Neutral drive switch open. A/C input high
67	C	Clutch switch circuit failure
71	C	Software re-initialization detected
72	C	Power interrupt detected
73	R	Insufficient TP output change during test
76	R	Insufficient VAF output change during test
77	R	Wide open throttle not sensed during test
No Code		Unable to run self-test or output codes [1]
Code not listed		Does not apply to vehicle being tested [1]

O—Key On, Engine Off
R—Engine running
C—Continuous Memory
1 Refer to system diagnostics

88184C16

1984–87 3.8L CFI ENGINE SERVICE CODES

Code		Explanation
11	O/R/C	System pass
12	R	Rpm unable to reach upper test limit
13	R	Rpm unable to reach lower test limit
14	C	PIP circuit failure
15	O	ROM test failure
15	C	Power interrupted to keep alive memory
18	C	Loss of tach input to ECU, spout grounded
18	R	Spout circuit open
19	O	Failure of EEC power supply
21	O/R	ECT sensor input out of test range
22	O/R/C	MAP sensor input out of test range
23	O/R/C	TP sensor input out of test range
24	O/R	ACT sensor input out of test range
29	C	Insufficent input from vehicle speed sensor
31	O/R/C	PFE circuit below minimum voltage
32	R/C	EGR valve not seated
33	R/C	EGR valve not opening
34	O	Defective PFE sensor
34	R/C	Excess exhaust back pressure
35	O/R/C	PFE circuit above maximum voltage
39	C	AXOD by-pass clutch not applying properly
41	R	EGO/HEGO circuit shows system lean (right side HEGO)
41	C	No EGO/HEGO switching detected, system lean (right side HEGO)
42	R	EGO/HEGO shows system rich (right side HEGO)

88184C17

1984–87 3.8L CFI ENGINE SERVICE CODES

51	O/C	ECT sensor input exceeds test maximum
52	O	PSPS circuit open
52	R	PSPS always open or always closed
53	O/C	TP sensor input exceeds test maximum
54	O/C	ACT sensor input exceeds test maximum
57	C	AXOD neutral pressure switch failed open
59	C	AXOD 4/3 pressure switch failed open
59	O	AXOD 4/3 pressure switch failed closed
61	O/C	ECT test sensor input below test minimum
63	O/C	TP sensor below test minimum
64	O/C	ACT sensor input below test minimum
67	O	Neutral drive switch open. A/C input high [4]
67	O	AXOD neutral pressure switch failed closed
68	O/R/C	AXOD temperature switch failed open
69	C	AXOD 3/4 pressure switch failed open
69	O	AXOD 3/2 pressure switch failed closed
70	C	EEC-IV data transmission link failed
71	C	Cluster control assembly circuit failed
72	C	Message center control circuit failed
74	R	Brake on/off circuit open, not on during test
79	O	A/C on during self-test
83	C	High speed electro drive fan circuit failure
84	O	EGR VAC regulator circuit failure
85	O	Canister purge circuit failure
87	O/C	Fuel pump primary circuit failure
88	O	Electro drive fan circuit failure
89	O	AXOD lock-up solenoid circuit failure
91	R	HEGO sensor circuit shows system lean (left side HEGO)
91	C	No HEGO switching sensed (left side HEGO)
92	R	HEGO sensor circuit shows system rich
95	O/C	Fuel pump secondary circuit failure

88184C18

1986–87 5.0L SEFI ENGINE SERVICE CODES

Code		Explanation
12	R	Rpm unable to reach upper test limit
13	R	Rpm unable to reach lower test limit
14	C	PIP circuit failure
15	O/C	Power interrupted to keep alive memory
16	R	Rpm too low to perform test
18	C	Loss of ignition signal to ECU—ignition grounded, spout, PIP, IDM
19	O	Failure of EEC power supply
21	O/R	ECT sensor input out of test range
22	O/R/C	MAP sensor input out of test range
23	O/R	TP sensor input out of test range
24	O/R	ACT sensor input out of test range
29	C	Insufficent input from vehicle speed sensor
31	O/R/C	EVP circuit below minimum voltage
32	O/R/C	EVP voltage below closed limit
33	R/C	EGR valve not opening
34	O/R/C	EVP voltage above closed limit
35	O/R/C	EVP circuit above maximum voltage
41	R	EGO/HEGO circuit shows system lean (right side HEGO)
42	R	EGO/HEGO shows system rich (right side HEGO)
44	R	Thermactor air system inoperative (cyl. 1–4)
45	R	Thermactor air upstream during self-test
46	R	Thermactor air not bypassed during self-test
51	O/C	ECT sensor input exceeds test maximum
53	O/C	TP sensor input exceeds test maximum
54	O/C	ACT sensor input exceeds test maximum
61	O/C	ECT test sensor input below test minimum
63	O/C	TP sensor below test minimum
64	O/C	ACT sensor input below test minimum
67	O	Neutral drive switch open. A/C input high
81	O	Air management 2 circuit failure
82	O	Air management 1 circuit failure
84	O	EGR VAC regulator circuit failure
85	O	Canister purge circuit failure
87	O	Fuel pump primary circuit failure
91	R	HEGO sensor circuit shows system lean (left side HEGO)
92	R	HEGO sensor circuit shows system rich (left side HEGO)
94	R	Thermactor air system inoperative (cyl. 5–8)
98	R	Hard fault is present
No Code		Unable to run self-test or output codes [1]
Code not listed		Does not apply to vehicle being tested [1]

O—Key On, Engine Off
R—Engine running
C—Continuous Memory
1 Refer to system diagnostics

88184C19

1988 5.0L SEFI ENGINE SERVICE CODES

Code		Explanation
11	O/R/C	System pass
12	R	Rpm unable to reach upper test limit
13	R	Rpm unable to reach lower test limit
14	C	PIP circuit failure
15	O	ROM test failure
15	C	Power interrupted to keep alive memory
16	R	Rpm too low to perform test
18	C	Loss of tach input to ECU, spout grounded
18	R	Spout circuit open
19	O	Failure of EEC power supply
21	O/R	ECT sensor input out of test range
22	O/R/C	MAP sensor input out of test range
23	O/R	TP sensor input out of test range
24	O/R	ACT sensor input out of test range
29	C	Insufficent input from vehicle speed sensor
31	O/R/C	EVP circuit below minimum voltage
32	O/R/C	EVP voltage below closed limit
33	R/C	EGR valve not opening
34	O/R/C	EVP voltage above closed limit
35	O/R/C	EVP circuit above maximum voltage
41	R	EGO/HEGO circuit shows system lean (right side HEGO)
41	C	No EGO/HEGO switching detected, system lean (right side HEGO)
42	R	EGO/HEGO shows system rich (right side HEGO)
44	R	Thermactor air system inoperative (cyl. 1–4)
45	R	Thermactor air upstream during self-test
46	R	Thermactor air not bypassed during self-test
51	O/C	ECT sensor input exceeds test maximum
53	O/C	TP sensor input exceeds test maximum
54	O/C	ACT sensor input exceeds test maximum
61	O/C	ECT test sensor input below test minimum
63	O/C	TP sensor below test minimum
64	O/C	ACT sensor input below test minimum
67	O	Neutral drive switch open. A/C input high
74	R	Brake on/off circuit open, not on during test
75	R	Brake on/off circuit closed, always high
79	O	A/C on during self-test
81	O	Air management 2 circuit failure
82	O	Air management 1 circuit failure
84	O	EGR VAC regulator circuit failure
85	O	Canister purge circuit failure
87	O/C	Fuel pump primary circuit failure
91	R	HEGO sensor circuit shows system lean (left side HEGO)
91	C	No HEGO switching sensed (left side HEGO)
92	R	HEGO sensor circuit shows system rich (left side HEGO)
94	R	Thermactor air system inoperative (cyl. 5–8)
98	R	Hard fault is present
No Code		Unable to run self-test or output codes [1]
Code not listed		Does not apply to vehicle being tested [1]

O—Key On, Engine Off
R—Engine running
C—Continuous Memory
1 Refer to system diagnostics

88184C20

1989–90 3.8L SEFI ENGINE SERVICE CODES

Code		Explanation
11	O/R/C	System pass
12	R	Rpm unable to reach upper test limit
13	R	Rpm unable to reach lower test limit
14	C	PIP circuit failure
15	O	ROM test failure
15	C	Power interrupted to keep alive memory
18	C	Loss of tach input to ECU, spout grounded
18	R	Spout circuit open
19	O	Failure of EEC power supply
21	O/R	ECT sensor input out of test range
22	O/R/C	MAP sensor input out of test range
23	O/R/C	TP sensor input out of test range
24	O/R	ACT sensor input out of test range
29	C	Insufficent input from vehicle speed sensor
31	O/R/C	PFE circuit below minimum voltage
32	R/C	EGR valve not seated
33	R/C	EGR valve not opening
34	O	Defective PFE sensor
34	R/C	Excess exhaust back pressure
35	O/R/C	PFE circuit above maximum voltage
41	R	EGO/HEGO circuit shows system lean (right side HEGO)
41	C	No EGO/HEGO switching detected, system lean (right side HEGO)
42	R	EGO/HEGO shows system rich (right side HEGO)
51	O/C	ECT sensor input exceeds test maximum
53	O/C	TP sensor input exceeds test maximum
54	O/C	ACT sensor input exceeds test maximum
61	O/C	ECT test sensor input below test minimum
63	O/C	TP sensor below test minimum
64	O/C	ACT sensor input below test minimum
74	R	Brake on/off circuit open, not on during test
79	O	A/C on during self-test
84	C	EGR VAC regulator circuit failure
85	O	Canister purge circuit failure
87	O/C	Fuel pump primary circuit failure
91	R	HEGO sensor circuit shows system lean (left side HEGO)
91	C	No HEGO switching sensed (left side HEGO)
92	R	HEGO sensor circuit shows system rich (left side HEGO)
95	O/C	Fuel pump secondary circuit failure
96	O/C	Fuel pump secondary circuit failure
98	R	Hard fault is present
No Code		Unable to run self-test or output codes [1]
Code not listed		Does not apply to vehicle being tested [1]

O—Key On, Engine Off
R—Engine running
C—Continuous Memory
1 Refer to system diagnostics

88184C21

1989–90 3.8L SEFI SUPERCHARGED ENGINE SERVICE CODES

Code		Explanation
11	O/R/C	System pass
12	R	Rpm unable to reach upper test limit
13	R	Rpm unable to reach lower test limit
14	C	PIP circuit failure
15	O	ROM test failure
15	C	Power interrupted to keep alive memory
18	C	Loss of tach input to ECU, spout grounded
18	R	Spout circuit open
19	C	CID sensor input failed
21	O/R	ECT sensor input out of test range
22	O/R/C	BP sensor input out of test range
23	O/R	TP sensor input out of test range
24	O/R	ACT sensor input out of test range
25	R	KS sensor not detected during test
26	O/R	MAF sensor input out of self-test range
29	C	Insufficient input from vehicle speed sensor
31	O/R/C	PFE circuit below minimum voltage
32	R/C	EGR valve not seated
33	R/C	EGR valve not opening
34	O	Defective PFE sensor
34	R/C	Excess exhaust back pressure
35	O/R/C	PFE circuit above maximum voltage
41	R	EGO/HEGO circuit shows system lean (right side HEGO)
41	C	No EGO/HEGO switching detected, system lean (right side HEGO)
42	R	EGO/HEGO shows system rich (right side HEGO)
45	C	DIS coil Pack 3 circuit failure
46	C	DIS coil Pack 1 circuit failure
48	C	DIS coil Pack 2 circuit failure
49	C	Spout signal defaulted to 10 degrees BTDC
51	O/C	ECT sensor input exceeds test maximum
52	O	PSPS circuit open
52	R	PSPS always open or always closed
53	O/C	TP sensor input exceeds test maximum
54	O/C	ACT sensor input exceeds test maximum
56	O/C	MAF sensor input exceeds test maximum
61	O/C	ECT test sensor input below test minimum
63	O/C	TP sensor below test minimum
64	O/C	ACT sensor input below test minimum
66	C	MAF sensor input below test minimum
67	O	Neutral drive switch open. A/C input high
67	C	Clutch switch circuit failure
72	R	Insufficient BP change during test
73	R	Insufficient TP output change during test
74	R	Brake on/off circuit open, not on during test

88184C22

1989–90 3.8L SEFI SUPERCHARGED ENGINE SERVICE CODES

77	R	Wide open throttle not sensed during test
79	O	A/C on during self-test
82	O	Supercharger bypass circuit failure
83	O	High speed electro drive fan circuit failure
84	O	EGR VAC regulator circuit failure
85	O	Canister purge circuit failure
87	O/C	Fuel pump primary circuit failure
88	O	Electro drive fan circuit failure
91	R	HEGO sensor circuit shows system lean (left side HEGO)
91	C	No HEGO switching sensed (left side HEGO)
92	R	HEGO sensor circuit shows system rich (left side HEGO)
96	O/C	Fuel pump secondary circuit failure
98	R	Hard fault is present
No Code		Unable to run self-test or output codes [1]
Code not listed		Does not apply to vehicle being tested [1]

O—Key On, Engine Off
R—Engine running
C—Continuous Memory
1 Refer to system diagnostics

88184C23

1991–92 3.8L SEFI ENGINE SERVICE CODES

SERVICE CODE		SERVICE CODE DEFINITION
111	orc	▶ System Pass
112	oc	▶ Air Charge Temp (ACT) Sensor circuit below minimum voltage/ 254°F indicated
113	oc	▶ Air Charge Temp (ACT) Sensor circuit above maximum voltage/ −40°F indicated
114	or	▶ Air Charge Temp (ACT) higher or lower than expected during KOEO, KOER
116	or	▶ Engine Coolant Temp (ECT) higher or lower than expected during KOEO, KOER
117	oc	▶ Engine Coolant Temp (ECT) sensor circuit below minimum voltage/ 254°F indicated
118	oc	▶ Engine Coolant Temp (ECT) Sensor circuit above maximum voltage/ −40°F indicated
121	orc	▶ Closed throttle voltage higher or lower than expected
122	oc	▶ Throttle Position (TP) Sensor circuit below minimum voltage
123	oc	▶ Throttle Position (TP) Sensor circuit above maximum voltage
124	c	▶ Throttle Position (TP) Sensor voltage higher than expected
125	c	▶ Throttle Position (TP) Sensor voltage lower than expected
129	r	▶ Insufficient Mass Air Flow (MAF) change during Dynamic Response Test
136	r	▶ Lack of Oxygen Sensor (HEGO) switches, indicates lean (LEFT SIDE)
137	r	▶ Lack of Oxygen Sensor (HEGO) switches, indicates lean (LEFT SIDE)
139	c	▶ No Oxygen Sensor (HEGO) switches detected (LEFT SIDE)
144	c	▶ No Oxygen Sensor (HEGO) Switches detected (RIGHT SIDE)
157	c	▶ Mass Air Flow (MAF) sensor circuit below minimum voltage
158	oc	▶ Mass Air Flow (MAF) sensor circuit above maximum voltage
159	or	▶ Mass Air Flow (MAF) higher or lower than expected during KOEO, KOER
167	r	▶ Insufficient throttle position change during Dynamic Response Test
171	c	▶ Fuel system at adaptive limits, Oxygen Sensor (HEGO) unable to switch (RIGHT SIDE)
172	rc	▶ Lack of Oxygen Sensor (HEGO) switches, indicates lean (RIGHT SIDE)
173	rc	▶ Lack of Oxygen Sensor (HEGO) switches, indicates rich (RIGHT SIDE)
175	c	▶ Fuel system at adaptive limits, Oxygen Sensor (HEGO) unable to switch (LEFT SIDE)
176	c	▶ Lack of Oxygen Sensor (HEGO) switches, indicates lean (LEFT SIDE)
177	c	▶ Lack of Oxygen Sensor (HEGO) switches, indicates rich (LEFT SIDE)
179	c	▶ Fuel system at lean adaptive limit at part throttle, system rich (RIGHT SIDE)
181	c	▶ Fuel system at rich adaptive limit at part throttle, system lean (RIGHT SIDE)
182	c	▶ Fuel system at lean adaptive limit at idle, system rich (RIGHT SIDE)
183	c	▶ Fuel system at rich adaptive limit at idle, system lean (RIGHT SIDE)
184	c	▶ Mass Air Flow (MAF) higher than expected
185	c	▶ Mass Air Flow (MAF) lower than expected
186	c	▶ Injector pulse width higher or MAF lower than expected
187	c	▶ Injector pulse width lower or MAF higher than expected
188	c	▶ Fuel system at lean adaptive limit at part throttle, system rich (LEFT SIDE)
189	c	▶ Fuel system at rich adaptive limit at part throttle, system lean (LEFT SIDE)
191	c	▶ Fuel system at lean adaptive limit at idle, system rich (LEFT SIDE)
192	c	▶ Fuel system at rich adaptive limit at idle, system lean (LEFT SIDE)
211	c	▶ Profile Ignition Pickup (PIP) circuit fault
212	c	▶ Loss of Ignition Diagnostic Monitor (IDM) input to EEC processor/SPOUT circuit grounded
213	r	▶ SPOUT circuit open
326	rc	▶ PFE circuit voltage lower than expected
327	orc	▶ PFE circuit below minimum voltage
332	rc	▶ Insufficient EGR flow detected
335	o	▶ PFE sensor voltage higher or lower than expected during KOEO
336	rc	▶ Exhaust Pressure high/PFE circuit voltage higher than expected
337	orc	▶ PFE circuit above maximum voltage
411	r	▶ Cannot control RPM during KOER low RPM check
412	r	▶ Cannot control RPM during KOER high RPM check
452	c	▶ Insufficient input from Vehicle Speed Sensor (VSS)
511	o	▶ EEC processor Read Only Memory (ROM) test failure
512	c	▶ EEC processor Keep Alive Memory (KAM) test failure
522	o	▶ Vehicle not in PARK or NEUTRAL during KOEO
525	o	▶ Indicates vehicle in gear / AC on
536	oc	▶ Brake On/Off (BOO) circuit failure / not actuated during KOER
538	r	▶ Insufficient RPM change during KOER Dynamic Response Test
539	o	▶ AC ON/Defrost ON during KOEO
542	oc	▶ Fuel pump secondary circuit failure
543	oc	▶ Fuel pump secondary circuit failure
556	oc	▶ Fuel pump relay primary circuit failure
558	o	▶ EGR Vacuum Regulator (EVR) circuit failure
565	o	▶ Canister Purge (CANP) circuit failure
998	r	▶ Hard fault present****FMEM Mode****

KEY: o = Key On Engine Off (KOEO) r = Engine Running (ER) c = Continuous Memory

88184C24

1991–92 3.8L SEFI SUPERCHARGED ENGINE SERVICE CODES

SERVICE CODE		SERVICE CODE DEFINITION
111	orc	▶ System PASS
112	oc	▶ Air Charge Temp (ACT) sensor circuit below minimum voltage/ 254°F indicated
113	oc	▶ Air Charge Temp (ACT) sensor circuit above maximum voltage/ −40°F indicated
114	or	▶ Air Charge Temp (ACT) higher or lower than expected during KOEO, KOER
116	or	▶ Engine Coolant Temp (ECT) higher or lower than expected during KOEO, KOER
117	oc	▶ Engine Coolant Temp (ECT) sensor circuit below minimum voltage/ 254°F indicated
118	oc	▶ Engine Coolant Temp (ECT) sensor circuit above maximum voltage/ −40°F indicated
121	orc	▶ Closed throttle voltage higher or lower than expected
122	oc	▶ Throttle Position (TP) Sensor circuit below minimum voltage
123	oc	▶ Throttle Position (TP) Sensor circuit above maximum voltage
124	c	▶ Throttle Position (TP) Sensor voltage higher than expected
125	c	▶ Throttle Position (TP) Sensor voltage lower than expected
126	orc	▶ BP sensor higher or lower than expected
129	r	▶ Insufficient Mass Air Flow (MAF) change during Dynamic Response Test
136	r	▶ Lack of Oxygen Sensor (HEGO) switches, indicates lean (LEFT SIDE)
137	r	▶ Lack of Oxygen Sensor (HEGO) switches, indicates rich (LEFT SIDE)
139	c	▶ No Oxygen Sensor (HEGO) switches detected (LEFT SIDE)
144	c	▶ No Oxygen Sensor (HEGO) switches detected (RIGHT SIDE)
157	c	▶ Mass Air Flow (MAF) sensor circuit below minimum voltage
158	oc	▶ Mass Air Flow (MAF) sensor circuit above maximum voltage
159	or	▶ Mass Air Flow (MAF) higher or lower than expected during KOEO, KOER
167	r	▶ Insufficient throttle position change during Dynamic Response Test
171	c	▶ Fuel system at adaptive limits, Oxygen Sensor (HEGO) unable to switch (RIGHT SIDE)
172	rc	▶ Lack of Oxygen Sensor (HEGO) switches, indicates lean (RIGHT SIDE)
173	rc	▶ Lack of Oxygen Sensor (HEGO) switches, indicates rich (RIGHT SIDE)
175	c	▶ Fuel system at adaptive limits, Oxygen Sensor (HEGO) unable to switch (LEFT SIDE)
176	c	▶ Lack of Oxygen Sensor (HEGO) switches, indicates lean (LEFT SIDE)
177	c	▶ Lack of Oxygen Sensor (HEGO) switches, indicates rich (LEFT SIDE)
179	c	▶ Fuel system at lean adaptive limit at part throttle, system rich (RIGHT SIDE)
181	c	▶ Fuel system at rich adaptive limit at part throttle, system lean (RIGHT SIDE)
182	c	▶ Fuel system at lean adaptive limit at idle, system rich (RIGHT SIDE)
183	c	▶ Fuel system at rich adaptive limit at idle, system lean (RIGHT SIDE)
184	c	▶ Mass Air Flow (MAF) higher than expected
185	c	▶ Mass Air Flow (MAF) lower than expected
186	c	▶ Injector pulse width higher than expected
187	c	▶ Injector pulse width lower than expected
188	c	▶ Fuel system at lean adaptive limit at part throttle, system rich (LEFT SIDE)
189	c	▶ Fuel system at rich adaptive limit at part throttle, system lean (LEFT SIDE)
191	c	▶ Fuel system at lean adaptive limit at idle, system rich (LEFT SIDE)
192	c	▶ Fuel system at rich adaptive limit at idle, system lean (LEFT SIDE)
211	c	▶ Profile Ignition Pickup (PIP) circuit fault
212	c	▶ Loss of Ignition Diagnostic Monitor (IDM) input to EEC processor/SPOUT circuit grounded
213	r	▶ SPOUT circuit open
214	c	▶ Cylinder Identification (CID) circuit failure
215	c	▶ EEC processor detected coil 1 primary circuit failure
216	c	▶ EEC processor detected coil 2 primary circuit failure
217	c	▶ EEC processor detected coil 3 primary circuit failure
219	c	▶ Spark timing defaulted to 10 degrees-SPOUT circuit open
225	r	▶ Knock not sensed during Dynamic Response Test
341	o	▶ Octane adjust service pin in use
411	r	▶ Cannot control rpm during KOER low rpm check
412	r	▶ Cannot control rpm during KOER high rpm check
452	c	▶ Insufficient input from Vehicle Speed Sensor (VSS)
511	o	▶ EEC Processor Read Only Memory (ROM) test failure
512	c	▶ EEC Processor Keep Alive Memory (KAM) test failure
522	o	▶ Vehicle not in PARK or NEUTRAL during KOEO
525	o	▶ Indicates vehicle in gear / AC ON
528	c	▶ Clutch switch circuit failure
536	rc	▶ Brake On/Off (BOO) circuit failure / not actuated during KOER
538	r	▶ Insufficient rpm change during KOER Dynamic Response Test
539	o	▶ AC On/Defrost On during KOEO
542	oc	▶ Fuel pump secondary circuit failure
543	oc	▶ Fuel pump secondary circuit failure
556	oc	▶ Fuel pump relay primary circuit failure
558	o	▶ EGR Vacuum Regulator (EVR) circuit failure
563	o	▶ High Speed-Electro Drive Fan (HEDF) circuit failure
564	o	▶ Electro-Drive Fan (EDF) circuit failure
565	o	▶ Canister Purge (CANP) circuit failure
998	r	▶ Hard fault present****FMEM mode****

KEY: o = Key On Engine Off (KOEO) r = Engine Running (ER) c = Continuous Memory

88184C25

1991–92 5.0L SEFI ENGINE SERVICE CODES

SERVICE CODE			SERVICE CODE DEFINITION
111	orc	▶	System PASS
112	oc	▶	ACT indicated 254°F/circuit grounded
113	oc	▶	ACT indicated −40°F/circuit open
114	or	▶	ACT out of Self-Test range
116	or	▶	ECT out of Self-Test range
117	oc	▶	ECT indicated 254°F/circuit grounded
118	oc	▶	ECT indicated −40°F/circuit open
121	orc	▶	TP out of Self-Test range
122	oc	▶	TP circuit below minimum voltage
123	oc	▶	TP circuit above maximum voltage
124	c	▶	TP circuit output higher than expected
125	c	▶	TP circuit output lower than expected
129	r	▶	Insufficient MAF change during Dynamic Response Test
136	r	▶	HEGO sensor indicates system lean (Left Side)
137	r	▶	HEGO sensor indicates system rich (Left Side)
139	c	▶	No HEGO switching detected (Left Side)
144	c	▶	No HEGO switching detected (Right Side)
157	c	▶	MAF circuit below minimum voltage
158	oc	▶	MAF circuit above maximum voltage
159	or	▶	MAF out of Self-Test range
167	r	▶	Insufficient TP change during Dynamic Response Test
171	c	▶	No HEGO switching detected/adaptive fuel at limit (Right Side)
172	rc	▶	HEGO sensor indicates system lean (Right Side)
173	rc	▶	HEGO sensor indicates system rich (Right Side)
174	c	▶	HEGO switching time is slow (Right Side)
175	c	▶	No HEGO switching detected/adaptive fuel at limit (Left Side)
176	c	▶	HEGO sensor indicates system lean (Left Side)
177	c	▶	HEGO sensor indicates system rich (Left Side)
178	c	▶	HEGO switching time is slow (Left Side)
179	c	▶	Adaptive fuel lean limit is reached (Right Side)
181	c	▶	Adaptive fuel rich limit is reached (Right Side)
182	c	▶	Adaptive fuel lean limit is reached at idle (Right Side)
183	c	▶	Adaptive fuel rich limit is reached at idle (Right Side)
184	c	▶	MAF circuit output higher than expected
185	c	▶	MAF circuit output lower than expected
186	c	▶	Injector pulsewidth higher than expected
187	c	▶	Injector pulsewidth lower than expected
188	c	▶	Adaptive fuel lean limit is reached (Left Side)
189	c	▶	Adaptive fuel rich limit is reached (Left Side)
191	c	▶	Adaptive fuel lean limit is reached at idle (Left Side)
192	c	▶	Adaptive fuel rich limit is reached at idle (Left Side)
211	c	▶	PIP circuit failure
212	c	▶	IDM circuit failure/SPOUT circuit grounded
213	r	▶	SPOUT circuit open
311	r	▶	Thermactor air system inoperative (Right Side)
313	r	▶	Thermactor air not bypassed during Self-Test
314	r	▶	Thermactor air system inoperative (Left Side)
327	orc	▶	EVP circuit output below minimum
328	orc	▶	EVP voltage below closed limit
332	rc	▶	EGR valve opening not detected (SONIC)
334	orc	▶	EVP voltage above closed limit (SONIC)
337	orc	▶	EVP circuit above maximum voltage
411	r	▶	Cannot control rpm during Self-Test low rpm check
412	r	▶	Cannot control rpm during Self-Test high rpm check
452	c	▶	Insufficient input from the Vehicle Speed Sensor (VSS)
511	o	▶	EEC processor Read Only Memory (ROM) test failed
512	c	▶	EEC processor Keep Alive Memory (KAM) test failed
513	o	▶	Failure in EEC processor internal voltage
522	o	▶	Indicates vehicle in gear
538	r	▶	Operator error (Dynamic response/Cylinder Balance Test)
539	o	▶	A/C on/Defrost on during Self-Test
542	oc	▶	Fuel pump secondary circuit failure
543	oc	▶	Fuel pump secondary circuit failure
552	o	▶	Air Management 1 (AM1) circuit failure
556	oc	▶	Fuel pump primary circuit failure
558	o	▶	EGR Vacuum Regulator (EVR) circuit failure
565	o	▶	Canister Purge Solenoid (CANP) circuit failure
998	r	▶	Hard fault is present − FMEM mode
NO CODES		▶	Unable to initiate Self-Test or unable to output Self-Test codes
CODES NOT LISTED		▶	Service codes displayed are not applicable to the vehicle being tested

KEY: o = Key On Engine Off (KOEO) r = Engine Running (ER) c = Continuous Memory

88184C26

EEC-IV Diagnostic Trouble Code (DTC) Charts

Diagnostic Trouble Code (DTC)	Application	Section 6A Pinpoint Test Step GO to Direction		
		KOEO	ER	CONT
No DTC's	All	QA1	QA1	QA1
11	All	Pass	Pass	Pass
12	All	—	KE1	—
13	All	—	KE15	—
14	7.3L Diesel	—	—	DJ1
14	All Others	—	—	NA1
15	All	Replace PCM		QB1
16	All	—	KE1	—
18	All	—	PA1	NA3
19	All	Replace PCM		—
21	All	DA1	DA1	—
22	Mustang	DF1	DF1	DF90
22	All Others	DF1	DF7	DF90
23	7.3L Diesel	DQ1	DQ1	—
23	All Others	DH2	DH1	—
24	All	DA1	DA1	—
25	All	—	DG1	—
26	E-Series/F-Series Trucks, Bronco	TE1	TE1	—
26	All Others	DC1	DC1	—
29	E-Series/F-Series Truck, Bronco	—	—	DS1
29	All Others	—	—	DP1
31	All	DN1	DN1	DN90
32	All	DN25	DN25	DN90
33	7.3L Diesel	—	—	DQ97
33	All Others	—	DN40	DN110
34	All	DN20	DN20	DN115
35	All	DN5	DN5	DN90
41	All	—	H1	H1
42	All	—	H1	—
43	All	—	—	DQ100
44	All	—	KC1	—
45	All	—	KC1	—
46	All	—	KC1	—
47	All	TB1	—	
49	All	—	—	TG90
51	All	DA10	—	DA90
52	All	FF1	FF5	—
53	7.3L Diesel	DQ2	—	DQ90

(Continued)

88184C27

Diagnostic Trouble Code (DTC)	Application	Section 6A Pinpoint Test Step GO to Direction		
		KOEO	ER	CONT
53	All Others	DH3	—	DH90
54	All	DA10	—	DA90
56	E-Series/F-Series Trucks, Bronco	TE10	—	TG90
56	All Others	DC21	—	DC21
57	All	KP1	—	—
59	All	—	—	TG90
61	All	DA20	—	DA90
62	All	—	—	TG90
63	7.3L Diesel	DQ10	—	DQ94
63	All Others	DH10	—	DH94
64	All	DA20	—	DA90
65	All	—	TB2	—
66	E-Series/F-Series Trucks, Bronco	TE20	—	TG90
66	All Others	—	—	DC10
67	All E-Series/F-Series Trucks and Bronco except 4.9L M/T	KM40	—	TG90
67	All Others	TA1	—	TA1
68	All	—	—	TE100
69	All	—	—	TG90
72	All	—	DF10	—
73	All	—	DH20	—
74	All	—	FD1	—
75	All	—	FD10	—
77	All	—	M1	—
79	All	KM40	—	—
81	All	KC8	—	DF11
82	All	KC8	—	—
84	All	DN10	—	—
85	All	KD6	—	—
86	All	TC1	—	—
87	All	J1	—	J95
89	All	TC1	—	—
91	All	TC1	H1	H1
92	All	TC1	H1	—
93	All	TC1	—	—
94	All	TC1	KC1	—
95	All	J10	—	J90 .
96	All	J20	—	J93

88184C28

Diagnostic Trouble Code (DTC)	Application	Section 6A Pinpoint Test Step GO to Direction		
		KOEO	ER	CONT
97	All	TB3	—	—
98	All	TC10		
99	All	TC10	—	TG90
Codes Not Listed	All	QA1	QA1	QA1

88184CLY

EEC-IV Diagnostic Trouble Code (DTC) Charts

Diagnostic Trouble Code (DTC)	Application	Section 6A Pinpoint Test Step Go to Direction		
		KOEO	ER	Cont
No DTC's	All	QA1	QA1	QA1
111	All	Pass	Pass	Pass
112	All	DA20	—	DA90
113	All	DA10	—	DA90
114	All	DA1	DA1	—
116	All	DA1	DA1	—
117	All	DA20	—	DA90
118	All	DA10	—	DA90
121	All	DH2	DH1	G1
122	All	DH10	—	DH94
123	All	DH3	—	DH90
124	All	—	—	G1
125	All	—	—	G1
126	All	DF1	DF1	DF90
128	All	—	—	DF11
129	All Cars, Ranger, Aerostar, Explorer, 5.0L SFI E-Series	—	DC13	—
129	All Other Trucks	—	DF10	—
136	3.0L FF Taurus	—	HB1	—
136	All Others	—	H1	—
137	3.0L FF Taurus	—	HB1	—
137	All Others	—	H1	—
138	All	—	HB26	—
139	All	—	—	H1
144	All	—	—	H1
157	All	—	—	DC10
158	All	DC21	—	DC21
159	All	DC1	DC1	—
167	All	—	DH20	—
171	3.0L FF Taurus	—	—	HB1
171	All Others	—	—	H1
172	3.0L FF Taurus	—	HB1	HB1
172	All Others	—	H1	H1
173	3.0L FF Taurus	—	HB1	HB1
173	All Others	—	H1	H1
174	All	—	—	H1
175	3.0L FF Taurus	—	—	HB1
175	All Others	—	—	H1

(Continued)

88184C29

EEC-IV Diagnostic Trouble Code (DTC) Charts

Diagnostic Trouble Code (DTC)	Application	Section 6A Pinpoint Test Step Go to Direction		
		KOEO	ER	Cont
176	3.0L FF Taurus	—	—	HB1
176	All Others	—	—	H1
177	3.0L FF Taurus	—	—	HB1
177	All Others	—	—	H1
178	All	—	—	H1
179	All	—	—	HA1
181	All	—	—	HA1
182	All	—	—	HA1
183	All	—	—	HA1
184	All	—	—	G5
185	All	—	—	G5
186	All	—	—	G7
187	All	—	—	G7
188	All	—	—	HA15
189	All	—	—	HA1
191	All	—	—	HA15
192	All	—	—	HA1
193	All	DE1	—	—
194	All	—	—	H5
195	All	—	—	H5
211	Distributor Ignition (DI)	—	—	NA1
211	Electronic Ignition (EI)-Low Data Rate	—	—	NB1
211	Electronic Ignition (EI)-High Data Rate	—	—	NC1
212	3.0L SFI, 5.0L SFI E-Series and 7.0L MFI Truck	—	—	NA2
212	Distributor Ignition (DI)—All Other Trucks	—	—	NA3
212	Distributor Ignition (DI)—All Other Cars	—	—	NA2
212	Electronic Ignition (EI)-Low Data Rate except 2.3L Mustang	—	—	NB2
212	2.3L Mustang	—	—	*Section 8A
212	Electronic Ignition (EI)-High Data Rate	—	—	NC3
213	Distributor Ignition (DI)	—	PA1	—
213	Electronic Ignition (EI)-Low Data Rate	—	PB1	—
213	Electronic Ignition (EI)-High Data Rate	—	PC1	—
214	All	—	—	DR1
215	All	—	—	*Section 8A
216	All	—	—	*Section 8A
217	All	—	—	*Section 8A
218	All	—	—	*Section 8A
219	All	—	—	PB10

(Continued)

88184C30

EEC-IV Diagnostic Trouble Code (DTC) Charts

Diagnostic Trouble Code (DTC)	Application	Section 6A Pinpoint Test Step Go to Direction		
		KOEO	ER	Cont
222	All	—	—	*Section 8A
223	All	—	—	*Section 8A
224	All	—	—	*Section 8A
225	All	—	DG1	—
226	All	NC2	—	—
232	All	—	—	*Section 8A
238	All	—	—	*Section 8A
311	All	—	KC1	—
312	All	—	KC1	—
313	All	—	KC1	—
314	All	—	KC1	—
326	2.0L Probe	—	—	DB10
326	3.0L Taurus (Flex Fuel) 3.8L Taurus/Sable (Calif) 3.2L Taurus SHO, Town Car, Mark VIII 4.0L SFI Ranger/Explorer	—	DL22	—
326	All Others	—	DL20	DL90
327	2.0L Probe	—	—	DB1
327	Mustang, 5.0L Thunderbird/Cougar, E/F Series, Bronco, Ranger (49 States)	DN1	DN1	DN90
327	3.0L Taurus Flex Fuel 3.8L Taurus/Sable (Calif) 3.2L Taurus SHO, Town Car, Mark VIII 4.0L Ranger/Explorer (Calif)	DL1	DL22	DL90
327	All Others	DL1	DL21	DL90
328	All	DN25	DN25	DN90
332	2.0L Probe	—	—	DB20
332	Mustang, 5.0L Thunderbird/Cougar, E/F Series, Bronco, Ranger (49 States)	—	DN40	DN110
332	All Others	—	DL30	DL90
334	All	DN20	DN20	DN115
335	All	DL8	—	—
336	3.0L Taurus Flex Fuel 3.8L Taurus/Sable (Calif) 3.2L Taurus SHO, Town Car, Mark VIII 4.0L SFI Ranger/Explorer	—	DL50	DL90
336	All Others	—	DL25	DL90
337	2.0L Probe	—	—	DB5
337	Mustang, 5.0L Thunderbird/Cougar, E/F Series, Bronco, Ranger (49 States)	DN5	DN5	DN90

(Continued)

88184C31

EEC-IV Diagnostic Trouble Code (DTC) Charts

Diagnostic Trouble Code (DTC)	Application	Section 6A Pinpoint Test Step Go to Direction		
		KOEO	ER	Cont
337	3.0L Taurus Flex Fuel 3.8L Taurus/Sable (Calif) 3.2L Taurus SHO, Town Car, Mark VIII 4.0L SFI Ranger/Explorer	DL5	DL50	DL90
337	All Others	DL5	DL25	DL90
338	All	—	—	DA100
339	All	—	—	DA101
341	All	KP1	—	—
411	All	—	KE15	—
412	All	—	KE1	—
452	Aerostar, E-Series/F-Series Trucks, Bronco	—	—	DS1
452	All Others	—	—	DP1
511	All		Replace PCM	
512	All	—	—	QB1
513	All		Replace PCM	
519	2.0L Probe	FF10	—	—
519	All Others	FF1	—	—
521	2.0L Probe	—	FF20	—
521	All Others	—	FF5	—
522	Continental, Taurus/Sable except 3.0L SHO, Crown Victoria/Grand Marquis with AODE, Town Car, Mark VIII	TD1	—	—
522	All Others	TA1	—	—
524	3.0L Taurus SHO	X98	—	X110
524	Mark VIII	XB135	—	XB150
524	3.0L Taurus Flex Fuel (FF)	X88	—	X110
525	All	TA1	—	TA1
528	All	—	—	TA1
529	All	—	—	ML25
533	All	—	—	ML25
536	All	—	FD1	FD90
538	All	—	M1	—
539	2.0L Probe	KM70	—	—
539	All Others	KM40	KM40	—
542	2.3L Mustang, Tempo/Topaz, Taurus/Sable, Continental	X80	—	X105
542	Mark VIII	XB120	—	XB155
542	All Others	J10	—	J90
543	Tempo/Topaz, 2.3L Mustang, Taurus/Sable, Continental	X90	—	X110
543	Mark VIII	XB135	—	XB150

(Continued)

88184C32

EEC-IV Diagnostic Trouble Code (DTC) Charts

Diagnostic Trouble Code (DTC)	Application	Section 6A Pinpoint Test Step Go to Direction		
		KOEO	ER	Cont
543	All Others	J20	—	J93
551	All	KT1	—	—
552	All	KC8	—	—
553	All	KC8	—	—
554	All	KN1	—	—
556	Tempo/Topaz, 2.3L Mustang, Taurus/Sable, Continental	X70	—	X115
556	Mark VIII	XB110	—	XB150
556	All Others	J1	—	J95
557	3.0L Taurus SHO	X70	—	X115
557	Taurus Flex Fuel (FF)	X75	—	X115
558	Mustang, 5.0L Thunderbird/Cougar, E/F Series, Bronco, Ranger (49 States)	DN10	—	—
558	2.0L Probe	KA1	—	—
558	All Others	DL11	—	—
559	All	KM60	—	—
563	Escort/Tracer, 2.0L Probe	KF1	—	—
563	All Others	X15	—	—
564	Escort/Tracer, 2.0L Probe	KF1	—	—
564	All Others	X20	—	—
565	3.0L Taurus Flexible Fuel (FF)	KB1	—	—
565	All Others	KD6	—	—
566	All	TC1	—	—
569	All	KD6	—	—
578	All	—	—	XB40
579	All	—	—	XB50
581	All	—	—	XB20
582	All	XB30	—	—
583	All	—	—	XB135
584	All	—	—	XB15
585	All	—	—	XB70
586	All	—	—	XB80
587	All	XB170	—	XB170
617	All	—	—	TG90
618	All	—	—	TG90
619	All	—	—	TG90
621	Escort/Tracer	TC20	—	TC30
621	All Others	TC1	—	—
622	Escort/Tracer	TC20	—	TC30

(Continued)

88184C33

EEC-IV Diagnostic Trouble Code (DTC) Charts

Diagnostic Trouble Code (DTC)	Application	Section 6A Pinpoint Test Step Go to Direction		
		KOEO	ER	Cont
622	All Others	TC1	—	—
624	All	TC10	—	TG90
625	All	TC10	—	TG90
626	All	TC1	—	—
627	All	TC1	—	—
628	All	—	—	TG90
629	All	TC1	—	TG90
631	All	TB3	—	—
632	All	—	TB2	—
633	All	TB1	—	—
634	Escort/Tracer	—	—	TD10
634	E-Series/F-Series Trucks, Bronco	TD1	—	TD1
634	All Others	TD1	—	TG90
636	All	TE1	TE1	—
637	Escort/Tracer	TE10	—	TE90
637	All Others	TE10	—	TG90
638	Escort/Tracer	TE20	—	TE90
638	All Others	TE20	—	TG90
639	Escort/Tracer	—	TF10	TF95
639	All Others	—	TF1	TF90
641	Escort/Tracer	TC20	—	TC30
641	All Others	TC1	—	—
643	All	TC20	—	TC30
645	All	—	—	TG90
646	All	—	—	TG90
647	All	—	—	TG90
648	All	—	—	TG90
649	All	—	—	TG90
651	All	—	—	TG90
652	All	TC1	—	—
654	All	TD1	—	—
656	All	—	—	TG90
657	All	—	—	TE100
998	All	TC10		[2]
DTC's Not Listed	All	QA1	QA1	QA1

TA18834A

2 *Refer to these EEC-IV DTC Charts for direction to diagnose the Continuous DTC received during Key On Engine Off Self-Test.*

88184C34

EEC-IV Diagnostic Trouble Code (DTC) Charts

Diagnostic Trouble Code (DTC)	Application	Section 6A Pinpoint Test Step GO to Direction		
		KOEO	ER	CONT
No DTCs	All	QA1	QA1	QA1
11	All	Pass	Pass	Pass
14	All	—	—	DJ1
15	All	Replace PCM		QB1
19	All	Replace PCM		—
22	All	DF1	DF7	DF90
23	All	DQ1	DQ1	—
26	All	TE1	TE1	—
29	All	—	—	DS1
33	All	—	—	DQ97
47	All	TB1	—	—
49	All	—	—	TG90
53	All	DQ2	—	DQ90
56	All	TE10	—	TG90
59	All	—	—	TG90
62	All	—	—	TG90
63	All	DQ10	—	DQ94·
65	All	—	TB2	—
66	All	TE20	—	TG90
67	All	KM40	—	TG90
68	All	—	—	TE100
69	All	—	—	TG90
74	All	—	FD1	—
86	All	TC1	—	—
89	All	TC1	—	—
91	All	TC1	—	—
92	All	TC1	—	—
93	All	TC1	—	—
94	All	TC1	KC1	—
97	All	TB3	—	—
98	All	TC10	See note "1" below	
99	All	TC10	—	TG90
Codes Not Listed	All	QA1	QA1	QA1

1 — Refer to these EEC-IV DTC Charts for direction to diagnose the Continuous DTC received during Key On Engine Off Self-Test.

88184C35

EEC-IV Diagnostic Trouble Code (DTC) Charts

Diagnostic Trouble Code (DTC)	Application	Section 6A Pinpoint Test Step Go to Direction		
		KOEO	ER	Cont
No DTC's	All	QA1	QA1	QA1
111	All	Pass	Pass	Pass
112	All	DA20	—	DA90
113	All	DA10	—	DA90
114	All	DA1	DA1	—
116	All	DA1	DA1	—
117	All	DA20	—	DA90
118	All	DA10	—	DA90
121	All	DH2	DH1	G1
122	All	DH10	—	DH94
123	All	DH3	—	DH90
124	All	—	—	G1
125	All	—	—	G1
126	E/F Series with MAP Sensor	DF1	DF7	DF90
126	All Others	DF1	DF1	DF90
128	All	—	—	DF11
129	All Cars, Ranger, Aerostar, Explorer, 5.0L SFI E-Series	—	DC13	—
129	All Other Trucks	—	DF10	—
136	3.0L Taurus (Flex Fuel)	—	HB1	—
136	All Others	—	H1	—
137	3.0L Taurus (Flex Fuel)	—	HB1	—
137	All Others	—	H1	—
139	All	—	—	H1
141	All	—	HB1	—
144	All	—	—	H1
157	All	—	—	DC10
158	All	DC21	—	DC21
159	All	DC1	DC1	—
167	All	—	DH20	—
171	3.0L Taurus (Flex Fuel)	—	—	HB1
171	All Others	—	—	H1
172	3.0L Taurus (Flex Fuel)	—	HB1	HB1
172	All Others	—	H1	H1
173	3.0L Taurus (Flex Fuel)	—	HB1	HB1
173	All Others	—	H1	H1
174	All	—	—	H1
175	3.0L Taurus (Flex Fuel)	—	—	HB1

(Continued)

88184C36

EEC-IV Diagnostic Trouble Code (DTC) Charts

Diagnostic Trouble Code (DTC)	Application	Section 6A Pinpoint Test Step Go to Direction		
		KOEO	ER	Cont
175	All Others	—	—	H1
176	3.0L Taurus (Flex Fuel)	—	—	HB1
176	All Others	—	—	H1
177	3.0L Taurus (Flex Fuel)	—	—	HB1
177	All Others	—	—	H1
178	All	—	—	H1
179	All	—	—	HA1
181	All	—	—	HA1
184	All	—	—	G5
185	All	—	—	G5
186	All	—	—	G7
187	All	—	—	G7
188	All	—	—	HA1
189	All	—	—	HA1
193	All	DE1	—	—
194	All	—	—	H5
195	All	—	—	H5
211	Distributor Ignition (DI)	—	—	NA1
211	Electronic Ignition (EI)-2.3L Ranger and Taurus SHO	—	—	NB1
211	Electronic Ignition (EI)-All Others	—	—	NC1
212	Distributor Ignition (DI)	—	—	NA2
212	Electronic Ignition (EI)-2.3L Ranger and Taurus SHO	—	—	NB2
212	Electronic Ignition (EI)-All Others	—	—	NC3
213	Distributor Ignition (DI)	—	PA1	—
213	Electronic Ignition (EI)-2.3L Ranger and Taurus SHO	—	PB1	—
213	Electronic Ignition (EI)-All Others	—	PC1	—
214	All	—	—	DR1
215	All	—	—	Section 8A
216	All	—	—	Section 8A
217	All	—	—	Section 8A
218	All	—	—	Section 8A
219	All	—	—	PB10
222	All	—	—	Section 8A
223	All	—	—	Section 8A
224	All	—	—	Section 8A
225	All	—	DG1	—

(Continued)

88184C37

EEC-IV Diagnostic Trouble Code (DTC) Charts

Diagnostic Trouble Code (DTC)	Application	Section 6A Pinpoint Test Step Go to Direction		
		KOEO	ER	Cont
226	All	NC2	—	—
232	All	—	—	Section 8A
238	All	—	—	Section 8A
244	All	—	DR1	—
311	All	—	KC1	—
312	All	—	KC1	—
313	All	—	KC1	—
314	All	—	KC1	—
326	Probe	—	—	DB10
326	DPFE (Thunderbird/Cougar (Calif) 3.8L Taurus/Sable (Calif), Thunderbird SC, 3.2L Taurus SHO, Town Car, Mark VIII, Crown Victoria/Grand Marquis (Calif), Ranger/Explorer, 3.0L Taurus (Flex Fuel))	—	DL22	—
326	PFE (All Others)	—	DL20	DL90
327	Probe M/T (49 State)	—	—	DB1
327	Probe CD4E, M/T (Calif)	DD1	DD1	DD90
327	EVP (Mustang, E/F Series)	DN1	DN1	DN90
327	DPFE (Thunderbird/Cougar (Calif), 3.8L Taurus/Sable (Calif), Thunderbird SC, 3.2L Taurus SHO, Town Car, Mark VIII Crown Victoria/Grand Marquis (Calif), Ranger/Explorer, 3.0L Taurus (Flex Fuel))	DL1	DL22	DL90
327	PFE (All Others)	DL1	DL21	DL90
328	All	DN25	DN25	DN90
332	Probe M/T (49 State)	—	—	DB20
332	Probe CD4E, M/T (Calif)	—	DD30	DD100
332	EVP (Mustang, E/F Series)	—	DN40	DN110
332	DPFE/PFE (All Others)	—	DL30	DL90
334	All	DN20	DN20	DN115
335	All	DL8	—	—
336	DPFE (Thunderbird/Cougar (Calif), 3.8L Taurus/Sable (Calif), Thunderbird SC 3.2L Taurus SHO, Town Car, Mark VIII, Crown Victoria/Grand Marquis (Calif), Ranger/Explorer, 3.0L Taurus (Flex Fuel))	—	DL50	DL90
336	PFE (All Others)	—	DL25	DL90
337	Probe M/T (49 State)	—	—	DB5
337	Probe CD4E, M/T (Calif)	DD10	DD10	DD90
337	EVP (Mustang, E/F Series)	DN5	DN5	DN90

(Continued)

88184C38

EEC-IV Diagnostic Trouble Code (DTC) Charts

Diagnostic Trouble Code (DTC)	Application	Section 6A Pinpoint Test Step Go to Direction		
		KOEO	ER	Cont
337	DPFE (Thunderbird/Cougar (Calif), 3.8L Taurus/Sable (Calif), Thunderbird SC, 3.2L Taurus SHO, Town Car, Mark VIII Crown Victoria/Grand Marquis (Calif), Ranger/Explorer, 3.0L Taurus (Flex Fuel))	DL5	DL50	DL90
337	PFE (All Others)	DL5	DL25	DL90
338	All	—	—	DA100
339	All	—	—	DA101
341	All	KP1	—	—
381	All	—	—	X130
411	All	—	KE15	—
412	All	—	KE1	—
415	All	—	—	KE30
416	All	—	—	KE35
452	Aerostar, E-Series/F-Series Trucks, Bronco	—	—	DS1
452	All Others	—	—	DP1
511	All	Replace PCM		
512	All	—	—	QB1
513	All	Replace PCM		
519	Probe	FF10	—	—
519	All Others	FF1	—	—
521	Probe	—	FF20	—
521	All Others	—	FF5	—
522	MLP Sensors (Mustang, Thunderbird/Cougar, Continental, Taurus/Sable except 3 0L SHO, Crown Victoria/Grand Marquis, Town Car, Mark VIII, 2.0L Probe with CD4E, 5.0L E/F Series, 5.0L Bronco)	TD1	—	—
522	All Others	TA1	—	—
524	3.0L Taurus SHO	X90	—	X110
524	3.0L Taurus (Flex Fuel)	X88	—	X110
524	Mark VIII	XB135	—	XB150
525	All	TA1	—	TA1
528	All	—	—	TA1
529	All	—	—	ML25
532	All	—	—	ML25
533	All	—	—	ML25
536	All	—	FD1	FD90
538	All	—	M1	—
539	Probe	KM70	—	—

(Continued)

88184C39

EEC-IV Diagnostic Trouble Code (DTC) Charts

Diagnostic Trouble Code (DTC)	Application	Section 6A Pinpoint Test Step Go to Direction		
		KOEO	ER	Cont
539	All Others	KM40	KM40	—
542	CCRM (Tempo/Topaz, Mustang, Taurus/Sable, Thunderbird/Cougar, Continental)	X80	—	X105
542	VCRM (Mark VIII)	XB120	—	XB155
542	All Others	J10	—	J90
543	CCRM (Tempo/Topaz, Mustang, Taurus/Sable, Thunderbird/Cougar, Continental)	X90	—	X110
543	VCRM (Mark VIII)	XB135	—	XB150
543	All Others	J20	—	J93
551	All	KT1	—	—
552	All	KC9	—	—
553	All	KC9	—	—
554	All	KN1	—	—
556	CCRM (Tempo/Topaz, Mustang, Taurus/Sable, Thunderbird/Cougar, Continental)	X70	—	X115
556	VCRM (Mark VIII)	XB110	—	XB150
556	All Others	J1	—	J95
557	3.0L Taurus (Flex Fuel)	X165	—	X115
557	All Others	X70	—	X115
558	EVP (Mustang, E/F Series)	DN10	—	—
558	Probe	KA1	—	—
558	DPFE/PFE (All Others)	DL11	—	—
559	All	KM60	—	—
562	All	X10	—	—
563	Escort/Tracer, Probe	KF1	—	—
563	All Others	X15	—	—
564	Escort/Tracer, Probe	KF1	—	—
564	All Others	X20	—	—
565	3.0L Taurus (Flex Fuel)	KB1	—	—
565	All Others	KD6	—	—
566	All	TC1	—	—
569	All	KD6	—	—
571	All	DD20	—	—
572	All	DD20	—	—
578	All	—	—	XB40
579	All	—	—	XB50
581	All	—	—	XB20
582	All	XB30	—	—
583	All	—	—	XB135
584	All	—	—	XB15

(Continued)

88184C40

EEC-IV Diagnostic Trouble Code (DTC) Charts

Diagnostic Trouble Code (DTC)	Application	Section 6A Pinpoint Test Step Go to Direction		
		KOEO	ER	Cont
585	All	—	—	XB70
586	All	—	—	XB80
587	All	XB170	—	XB170
617	All	—	—	TG90
618	All	—	—	TG90
619	All	—	—	TG90
621	Escort/Tracer	TC20	—	TC30
621	All Others	TC1	—	—
622	Escort/Tracer	TC20	—	TC30
622	All Others	TC1	—	—
623	All	TB3	—	—
624	All	TC10	—	TG90
625	All	TC10	—	TG90
626	All	TC1	—	—
627	All	TC1	—	—
628	All	—	—	TG90
629	All	TC1	—	TG90
631	All	TB3	—	—
632	All	—	TB2	—
633	All	TB1	—	—
634	Escort/Tracer	—	—	TD10
634	E-Series/F-Series Trucks, Bronco	TD1	—	TD1
634	All Others	TD1	—	TG90
636	All	TE1	TE1	—
637	Escort/Tracer	TE10	—	TE90
637	All Others	TE10	—	TG90
638	Escort/Tracer	TE20	—	TE90
638	All Others	TE20	—	TG90
639	Escort/Tracer	—	TF10	TF95
639	All Others	—	TF1	TF90
641	Escort/Tracer	TC20	—	TC30
641	All Others	TC1	—	—
643	All	TC20	—	TC30
645	All	—	—	TG90
646	All	—	—	TG90
647	All	—	—	TG90
648	All	—	—	TG90
649	All	—	—	TG90

(Continued)

88184C41

EEC-IV Diagnostic Trouble Code (DTC) Charts

Diagnostic Trouble Code (DTC)	Application	Section 6A Pinpoint Test Step Go to Direction		
		KOEO	ER	Cont
651	All	—	—	TG90
652	All	TC1	—	—
653	All	—	TB2	—
654	All	TD1	—	—
656	All	—	—	TG90
657	All	—	—	TE100
659	All	—	—	TG90
667	All	—	—	TG90
668	All	—	—	TG90
675	All	—	—	TG90
676	All	Go to Transmission Group of the Service Manual; Diagnosis by Symptom Chart		
677	All	Go to Transmission Group of the Service Manual; Diagnosis by Symptom Chart		
691	All	—	—	TB1
998	All	TC10	See note "2" below	
DTCs Not Listed	All	QA1	QA1	QA1

2 — Refer to these EEC-IV DTC Charts for direction to diagnose the Continuous DTC received during Key On Engine Off Self-Test.

TA18634B

88184C42

EEC-IV Diagnostic Trouble Code (DTC) Charts

Diagnostic Trouble Code (DTC)	Application	Section 6A Pinpoint Test Step Go to Direction		
		KOEO	ER	Cont
No DTCs / Module not responding	All	QA1	QA1	QA1
111	All	Pass	Pass	Pass
112	All	DA20	—	DA90
113	All	DA10	—	DA90
114	All	DA1	DA1	—
116	All	DA1	DA1	—
117	All	DA20	—	DA90
118	All	DA10	—	DA90
121	All	DH2	DH1	G1
122	All	DH10	—	DH94
123	All	DH3	—	DH90
124	All	—	—	G1
125	All	—	—	G1
126	E/F Series with MAP Sensor	DF1	DF7	DF90
126	All Others	DF1	DF1	DF90
128	All	—	—	DF11
129	MAF	—	DC13	—
129	All Others	—	DF10	—
136	3.0L Taurus (Flex Fuel)	—	HB1	—
136	All Others	—	H1	—
137	3.0L Taurus (Flex Fuel)	—	HB1	—
137	All Others	—	H1	—
139	All	—	—	H1
141	All	—	HB1	—
144	All	—	—	H1
157	All	—	—	DC10
158	All	DC22	—	DC22
159	All	DC1	DC1	—
167	All	—	DH20	—
171	3.0L Taurus (Flex Fuel)	—	—	HB1
171	All Others	—	—	H1
172	3.0L Taurus (Flex Fuel)	—	HB1	HB1
172	All Others	—	H1	H1
173	3.0L Taurus (Flex Fuel)	—	HB1	HB1
173	All Others	—	H1	H1
174	All	—	—	H1
175	3.0L Taurus (Flex Fuel)	—	—	HB1

(Continued)

88184C43

EEC-IV Diagnostic Trouble Code (DTC) Charts

Diagnostic Trouble Code (DTC)	Application	Section 6A Pinpoint Test Step Go to Direction		
		KOEO	ER	Cont
175	All Others	—	—	H1
176	3.0L Taurus (Flex Fuel)	—	—	HB1
176	All Others	—	—	H1
177	3.0L Taurus (Flex Fuel)	—	—	HB1
177	All Others	—	—	H1
178	All	—	—	H1
179	All	—	—	HA1
181	All	—	—	HA1
184	All	—	—	G7
185	All	—	—	G7
186	All	—	—	G9
187	All	—	—	G9
188	All	—	—	HA1
189	All	—	—	HA1
193	All	DE1	—	—
194	All	—	—	H5
195	All	—	—	H5
211	Distributor Ignition (DI)	—	—	NA1
211	Electronic Ignition (EI) Taurus SHO	—	—	NB1
211	Electronic Ignition (EI)-All Others	—	—	NC1
212	Distributor Ignition (DI)	—	—	NA2
212	Electronic Ignition (EI) Taurus SHO	—	—	NB2
212	Electronic Ignition (EI)-All Others	—	—	NC3
213	Distributor Ignition (DI)	—	PA1	—
213	Electronic Ignition (EI) Taurus SHO	—	PB1	—
213	Electronic Ignition (EI)-All Others	—	PC1	—
214	All	—	—	DR1
215	All	—	—	Section 8A
216	All	—	—	Section 8A
217	All	—	—	Section 8A
218	All	—	—	Section 8A
219	All	—	—	PB10
222	All	—	—	Section 8A
224	All	—	—	Section 8A
225	All	—	DG1	—
226	All	NC2	—	—
232	All	—	—	Section 8A
238	All	—	—	Section 8A

(Continued)

88184C44

EEC-IV Diagnostic Trouble Code (DTC) Charts

Diagnostic Trouble Code (DTC)	Application	Section 6A Pinpoint Test Step Go to Direction		
		KOEO	ER	Cont
244	All	—	DR1	—
311	All	—	KC1	—
312	All	—	KC1	—
313	All	—	KC1	—
314	All	—	KC1	—
326	Probe	—	—	DB10
326	DPFE	—	DL22	—
326	PFE	—	DL20	DL90
327	Probe	DD1	DD1	DD90
327	EVP	DN1	DN1	DN90
327	DPFE	DL1	DL22	DL90
327	PFE	DL1	DL21	DL90
328	All	DN25	DN25	DN90
332	Probe	—	DD30	DD100
332	EVP	—	DN40	DN110
332	DPFE/PFE	—	DL30	DL90
334	All	DN20	DN20	DN115
335	All	DL8	—	—
336	DPFE	—	DL50	DL90
336	PFE	—	DL25	DL90
337	Probe	DD10	DD10	DD90
337	EVP (Mustang, E/F Series)	DN5	DN5	DN90
337	DPFE	DL5	DL50	DL90
337	PFE	DL5	DL25	DL90
338	All	—	—	DA100
339	All	—	—	DA101
341	All	KP1	—	—
381	All	—	—	X130
411	All	—	KE15	—
412	All	—	KE1	—
452	Aerostar, E-Series/F-Series Trucks, Bronco	—	—	DS1
452	All Others	—	—	DP1
511	All	Replace PCM		
512	All	—	—	QB1
513	All	QD1	QD1	QD1
519	Probe	FF10	—	—
519	2.0L Contour/Mystique	DT1	DT1	DT1
519	All Others	FF1	—	—
521	Probe	—	FF20	—

(Continued)

88184C45

EEC-IV Diagnostic Trouble Code (DTC) Charts

Diagnostic Trouble Code (DTC)	Application	Section 6A Pinpoint Test Step Go to Direction		
		KOEO	ER	Cont
521	2.0L Contour/Mystique	—	DT	—
521	All Others	—	FF5	—
522	TR Sensors	TD1	—	—
522	All Others	TA1	—	—
524	3.0L Taurus SHO	X90	—	X110
524	3.0L Taurus (Flex Fuel)	X88	—	X110
524	Mark VIII	XB135	—	XB150
525	All	TA1	—	TA1
528	All	—	—	TA1
529	All	—	—	ML25
532	All	—	—	ML25
533	All	—	—	ML25
536	All	—	FD1	FD90
538	All	—	M1	—
539	Probe	KM70	—	—
539	All Others	KM40	KM40	—
542	CCRM	X80	—	X105
542	VCRM	XB120	—	XB155
542	All Others	J10	—	J90
543	CCRM	X90	—	X110
543	VCRM	XB135	—	XB150
543	All Others	J20	—	J93
551	All	KT1	—	—
552	All	KC9	—	—
553	All	KC9	—	—
554	All	KN1	—	—
556	CCRM	X70	—	X115
556	VCRM	XB110	—	XB150
556	All Others	J1	—	J95
557	3.0L Taurus (Flex Fuel)	X165	—	X115
557	All Others	X70	—	X115
558	EVP	DN10	—	—
558	DPFE/PFE	DL11	—	—
559	All	KM60	—	—
562	All	X10	—	—
563	CCRM	X15	—	—
563	All Others	KF1	—	—
564	CCRM	X20	—	—
564	All Others	KF1	—	—

(Continued)

88184C46

EEC-IV Diagnostic Trouble Code (DTC) Charts

Diagnostic Trouble Code (DTC)	Application	Section 6A Pinpoint Test Step Go to Direction		
		KOEO	ER	Cont
565	3.0L Taurus (Flex Fuel), 4.0L Explorer, 5.8L SFI	KB1	—	—
565	All Others	KD6	—	—
566	All	TC1	—	—
569	All	KD6	—	—
571	All	DD20	—	—
572	All	DD20	—	—
578	All	—	—	XB40
579	All	—	—	XB50
581	All	—	—	XB20
582	All	XB30	—	—
583	All	—	—	XB135
584	All	—	—	XB15
585	All	—	—	XB70
586	All	—	—	XB80
587	All	XB170	—	XB170
593	All	H40	—	H40
617	All	—	—	TG90
618	All	—	—	TG90
619	All	—	—	TG90
621	Escort/Tracer	TC20	—	TC30
621	All Others	TC1	—	—
622	Escort/Tracer	TC20	—	TC30
622	All Others	TC1	—	—
623	All	TB3	—	—
624	All	TC10	—	TG90
625	All	TC10	—	TG90
626	All	TC1	—	—
627	All	TC1	—	—
628	All	—	—	TG90
629	All	TC1	—	TG90
631	All	TB3	—	—
632	All	—	TB2	—
633	Explorer	TB10	—	—
633	All Others	TB1	—	—
634	Escort/Tracer	—	—	TD10
634	E-Series/F-Series Trucks, Bronco	TD1	—	TD1
634	All Others	TD1	—	TG90
636	All	TE1	TE1	—

(Continued)

88184C47

EEC-IV Diagnostic Trouble Code (DTC) Charts

Diagnostic Trouble Code (DTC)	Application	Section 6A Pinpoint Test Step Go to Direction		
		KOEO	ER	Cont
637	Escort/Tracer	TE10	—	TE90
637	All Others	TE10	—	TG90
638	Escort/Tracer	TE20	—	TE90
638	All Others	TE20	—	TG90
639	Escort/Tracer	—	TF10	TF95
639	All Others	—	TF1	TF90
641	Escort/Tracer	TC20	—	TC30
641	All Others	TC1	—	—
643	All	TC20	—	TC30
645	All	—	—	TG90
646	All	—	—	TG90
647	All	—	—	TG90
648	All	—	—	TG90
649	All	—	—	TG90
651	All	—	—	TG90
652	All	TC1	—	—
653	All	—	TB2	—
654	All	TD1	—	—
656	All	—	—	TG90
657	All	—	—	TE100
659	All	—	—	TG90
667	All	TD1	TD1	TG90
668	All	TD1	TD1	TG90
675	All	—	—	TG90
676	All	Go to Transmission Group of the Service Manual; Diagnosis by Symptom Chart		
677	All	Go to Transmission Group of the Service Manual; Diagnosis by Symptom Chart		
691	Explorer	—	—	TE10
691	All Others	—	—	TB1
692	All	Go to Transmission Group of the Service Manual; Diagnosis by Symptom Chart		
998	All	TC10	See note "2" below	
DTCs Not Listed	All	QA1	QA1	QA1

2 — Refer to these EEC-IV DTC Charts for direction to diagnose the Continuous DTC received during Key On Engine Off Self-Test.

88184C48

EEC-V TROUBLE CODES

General Information

Ford developed the EEC-V system on the 1995–96 models in response to the increased diagnostic requirements for the California Air Resource Board. The regulations developed by the Environmental Protection Agency are designated as the OBD II system.

The OBDII is similar to the OBD I system but not identical. The OBD I requires that the malfunction indicator lamp (MIL) illuminates to inform the driver when an emissions component or monitored system fails. The MIL also lights up to indicate when the PCM is operating in hardware limiting operating strategy (HLOS).

The EEC-V is a evolutionary development from the EEC-IV. None of the components involved are actually new, only the applications have changed.

The only component that has been added is another heated Oxygen Sensor (HO_2S located behind the catalyst. These downstream sensors are called the Catalyst Monitor sensors (CSM). This means that there are four sensors instead of two.

Data Link Connector (DLC)

See Figure 40

The DLC on the EEC-V is located on the passenger's side of the vehicle, beneath the instrument panel, and the right of the console.

The DLC is rectangular in design and capable of allowing access to 16 terminals. The connector has keying features that allow easy connection. The test equipment and the DLC have a latching feature to ensure a good mated connection.

Reading Codes

When diagnosing the OBD II EEC-V system, the New Generation Star (NGS) tester or generic scan tool may be used to retrieve codes, view the system operating specifications or test the system components.

Clearing Codes

PCM RESET

The PCM reset mode allows the scan tool to clear any emission related diagnostic information from the PCM. When resetting the PCM, a DTC P1000 will be stored until all OBD II system monitors or components have been tested to satisfy a Trip without any other faults occurring.

The following items occur when the the PCM Reset is performed:

- The DTC is cleared
- The freeze frame data is cleared
- The oxygen sensor test data is cleared
- The status of the OBD II system monitors is reset
- A DTC P1000 code is set

PCM fault codes may be cleared by using the scan tool or disconnecting the negative battery cable for a minimum of 15 seconds.

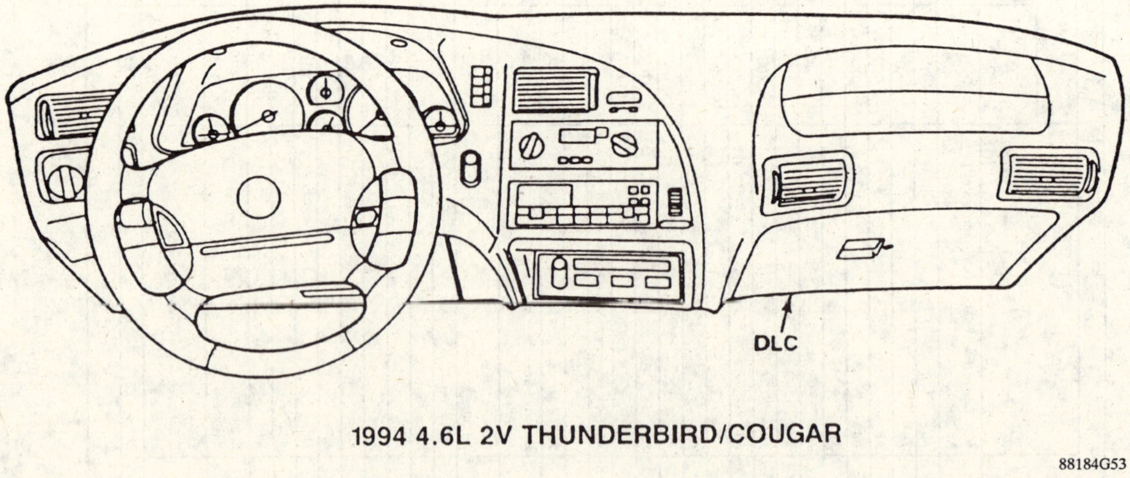

Fig. 40 The data link connector is located on the passengers side of the vehicle, beneath the instrument panel

KEEP ALIVE MEMORY (KAM) RESET

The Keep Alive Memory (KAM) contains the adaptive factors used by the processor to compensate for component tolerances and wear. It should not be routinely cleared during diagnosis. If and emissions related part is replaced during repair, the KAM must be cleared. Failure to clear the KAM may cause severe driveability problems since the correction factor for the old component will be applied to the new component.

To clear the KAM disconnect the negative battery cable for at least 5 minuets. After the memory is cleared and the battery is reconnected, the vehicle must be driven a couple of miles so that the PCM may relearn the needed correction factors. The distance to be driven depends on the engine and vehicle, but all drives should include steady throttle cruise on the open roads. Certain driveability problems may be noted during the drive because the adaptive factors are not yet functioning.

Key On Engine Off (KOEO)

A series of characters must be entered into the scan tool to perform this test. The codes are listed below and must be entered as such to perform the test correctly. See the manufacture of the scan tool for any additional instructions.

1. Perform the necessary vehicle preparation and visual inspection.
2. Connect the scan tool to the DLC.
3. Turn the ignition to the ON position but DO NOT start the engine.
4. Verify that the scan tool is connected and communicating correctly by entering the OBD II system readiness test. All scan tools are required to automatically enter this test once communication is established between the tool and the PCM.
5. Enter the following string of information to initiate the KOEO self test.
6. Enter the four strings separately and in the order shown. All of the string ID numbers must match in the order shown.
   a. 04, 31, 21, C4 103381, 9E 00 445443287329 20 8042 20 8062 20 8082 A851 FF, 2E
   b. 03, 32, 22FF, C4 10220202, 9E 00 434E54 20 8061 A961 00 04, EA
   c. 02, 32, 21, C4 10328100, 9E 00 574149 54 20 8081 A181 61 03, 5E
   d. 01, 32, 21, C4 103181, 9E 00 53544155254 20 8081 A 181 00 02, 54
7. Turn the ignition OFF to end the test cycle.

Key On Engine Running (KOER)

A series of characters must be entered into the scan tool to perform this test. The codes are listed below and must be entered as such to perform the test correctly. See the manufacture of the scan tool for any additional instructions.

1. Perform the necessary vehicle preparation and visual inspection.
2. Connect the scan tool to the DLC.
3. Turn the ignition to the ON position and start the engine.
4. Verify that the scan tool is connected and communicating correctly by entering the OBD II system readiness test. All scan tools are required to automatically enter this test once communication is established between the tool and the PCM.
5. Enter the following string of information to initiate the KOEO self test.
6. Enter the four strings separately and in the order shown. All of the string ID numbers must match in the order shown.
7. After the test begins, cycle the brake and Transmission Control (TCS) switches if equipped.
   a. 08, 31, 21, C4103382, 9E 00 445443287329 20 8042 20 8062 20 8082 A851 FF, 33
   b. 07, 32, 22FF, C410220202, 9E 00 434E54 20 8061 A961 00 08, F2
   c. 06, 32, 21, C4 10328200, 9E 00 574149 54 20 8081 A181 61 07, 67
   d. 05, 32, 21, C4 103182, 9E 00 5354415254 20 8081 A181 00 06, 5D
8. Turn the ignition OFF to end the test cycle.

Continuous Memory

1. Perform the necessary vehicle preparation and visual inspection.
2. Connect the scan tool to the DLC.
3. Turn the key to the **ON** position or start the vehicle. This may depend on the pinpoint manual instructions for the type of data requested.
4. Verify the tool is connected properly and communicating.
5. Enter the following string of characters to retrieve all the continuous DTC's (DTC CNT).
   a. 09, 2C, 21, C4 1 0 13,, 9E 00 44 54 43 20 43 4E 54 20 8B 44, B2
6. The scan tool will display all the continuous DTC's.

Powertrain Diagnostic Trouble Code (DTC) Charts

Diagnostic Trouble Code (DTC)	Application	Key On Engine Off	Key On Engine Running	Continuous Memory
P0102	All	—	DC6	DC6
P0103	All	DC20	DC20	DC20
P0106	Probe	—	—	HH1
P0107	Probe	—	—	HH10
P0108	Probe	—	—	HH20
P0112	All	DA20	DA20	DA90
P0113	All	DA10	DA10	DA90
P0117	All	DA20	DA20	DA90
P0118	All	DA10	DA10	DA90
P0121	All	—	DH22	DH22
P0122	All	DH11	DH11	DH11
P0123	All	DH8	DH8	DH8
P0125	All	—	—	DA100
P0131	All	—	—	H27
P0132	All	H10	H10	H10
P0133	All	—	—	H20
P0135	NG Crown Victoria	HA30	HA30	HA30
	All Others	H30	H30	H30
P0136	Ranger, 3.0L Windstar, 4.0L Explorer and 4.6L Continental	—	—	H90
	All Others	—	—	H80
P0138	All	H10	H10	H10
P0141	NG Crown Victoria	HA30	HA30	HA30
	All Others	H30	H30	H30
P0151	All	—	—	H27
P0152	All	H10	H10	H10
P0153	All	—	—	H20
P0155	NG Crown Victoria	HA30	HA30	HA30
	All Others	H30	H30	H30
P0156	Ranger, 3.0L Windstar, 4.0L Explorer and 4.6L Continental	—	—	H90
	All Others	—	—	H80
P0158	All	H10	H10	H10
P0161	NG Crown Victoria	HA30	HA30	HA30
	All Others	H30	H30	H30
P0171	NG Crown Victoria	HA41	HA41	HA41
	All Others	—	—	H41
P0172	NG Crown Victoria	HA41	HA41	HA41
	All Others	—	—	H41

(Continued)

88184C49

Powertrain Diagnostic Trouble Code (DTC) Charts

Diagnostic Trouble Code (DTC)	Application	Key On Engine Off	Key On Engine Running	Continuous Memory
P0174	NG Crown Victoria	HA41	HA41	HA41
	All Others	—	—	H41
P0175	NG Crown Victoria	HA41	HA41	HA41
	All Others	—	—	H41
P0176	All	—	DE1	DE20
P0182	NG Crown Victoria	DB4	DB4	DB7
P0183	NG Crown Victoria	DB1	DB1	DB7
P0187	NG Crown Victoria	DB4	DB4	DB7
P0188	NG Crown Victoria	DB1	DB1	DB7
P0191	NG Crown Victoria	DD11	DD11	—
P0192	NG Crown Victoria	DD1	DD1	DD9
P0193	NG Crown Victoria	DD6	DD6	DD9
P0222	All	HT1	HT1	HT1
P0223	All	HT10	HT10	HT10
P0230	w/ CCRM (except Continental)	X150	X150	X200
	Continental NG Crown Victoria Mark VIII All Others	KB30 KC1 XB90 KA1	KB30 KC1 XB90 KA1	KB30 KC40 XB150 KA40
P0231	w/ CCRM (except 4.6L 4V Mustang	X180	X180	X195
	4.6L 4V Mustang NG Crown Victoria Mark VIII All Others	X180 KC20 XB115 KA20	X180 KC20 XB115 KA20	X194 KC35 XB160 KA35
P0232	w/ CCRM	X170	X170	X190
	NG Crown Victoria Mark VIII All Others	KC10 XB100 KA10	KC10 XB100 KA10	KC30 XB155 KA30
P0300	All	—	HD1	HD1
P0301	All	—	HD1	HD1
P0302	All	—	HD1	HD1
P0303	All	—	HD1	HD1
P0304	All	—	HD1	HD1
P0305	All	—	HD1	HD1
P0306	All	—	HD1	HD1
P0307	All	—	HD1	HD1
P0308	All	—	HD1	HD1
P0320	Distributor Ignition	—	—	JG1
	3.0L Windstar All Others	— —	— —	NA1 NC1
P0325	All	—	DG1	DG1

(Continued)

88184C50

Powertrain Diagnostic Trouble Code (DTC) Charts

Diagnostic Trouble Code (DTC)	Application	Key On Engine Off	Key On Engine Running	Continuous Memory
P0326	All	—	DG1	DG1
P0330	All	—	DG1	DG1
P0331	All	—	DG1	DG1
P0340	All	—	—	DR1
P0350	2.3L Ranger	—	—	JE20
P0350	All Other 4 Cylinders	—	—	JE1
	3.0L Windstar	—	—	JC1
	All Other 6 Cylinders	—	—	JE60
	3.4L Taurus SHO	—	—	JF1
	All Other 8 Cylinders	—	—	JE90
P0351	2.3L Ranger	—	—	JE20
	All Other 4 Cylinders	—	—	JE1
	3.0L Windstar	—	—	JC1
	All Other 6 Cylinders	—	—	JE60
	3.4L Taurus SHO	—	—	JF1
	All Other 8 Cylinders	—	—	JE90
P0352	2.3L Ranger	—	—	JE20
	All Other 4 Cylinders	—	—	JE1
	3.0L Windstar	—	—	JC1
	All Other 6 Cylinders	—	—	JE60
	3.4L Taurus SHO	—	—	JF1
	All Other 8 Cylinders	—	—	JE90
P0353	3.0L Windstar	—	—	JC1
	All Other 6 Cylinders	—	—	JE60
	3.4L Taurus SHO	—	—	JF1
	All Other 8 Cylinders	—	—	JE90
P0354	3.4L Taurus SHO	—	—	JF1
	All Other 8 Cylinders	—	—	JE90
P0355	3.4L Taurus SHO	—	—	JF1
P0356	3.4L Taurus SHO	—	—	JF1
P0357	3.4L Taurus SHO	—	—	JF1
P0358	3.4L Taurus SHO	—	—	JF1
P0385	Distributor Ignition	—	DK1	DK1
P0400	Probe	—	—	HH70
	All Others	HE130	HE130	HE130
P0401	5.0L Explorer	HJ30	HJ30	HJ30
	All Others	—	—	HE70
P0402	5.0L Explorer	HJ40	HJ40	HJ40
	All Others	—	HE20	HE20
P0411	Electric Pump	HM7	HM7	HM7
	Mechanical Pump	HM40	HM40	HM40
P0413	All	HM75	HM75	HM75
P0414	All	HM75	HM75	HM75

(Continued)

88184C51

Powertrain Diagnostic Trouble Code (DTC) Charts

Diagnostic Trouble Code (DTC)	Application	Key On Engine Off	Key On Engine Running	Continuous Memory
P0416	All	HM75	HM75	HM75
P0417	All	HM75	HM75	HM75
P0420	All	—	—	HF1
P0421	Probe	—	—	HF1
P0430	All	—	—	HF1
P0431	Probe	—	—	HF1
P0440	Probe	—	—	HV10
P0442	All	—	—	HX1
P0443	Taurus / Sable	HX7	HX7	HX6
	Crown Victoria / Grand Marquis, Town Car, 4.0L Explorer, 4.2L / 4.6L F-Series			
	Probe	HV1	HV1	HV1
	All Others	HW1	HW1	HW38
P0446	All	—	—	HX13
P0452	All	—	HX22	HX22
P0453	All	—	HX28	HX28
P0455	All	—	—	HX40
P0500	Contour, Mystique	—	—	DP5
	Taurus SHO	—	—	DF1
	Aerostar, E / F-Series, Bronco	—	—	DJ1
	All Others	—	—	DP1
P0503	Aerostar, E / F-Series, Bronco	—	—	DJ1
	All Others	—	—	DP20
P0505	All	—	KE2	—
P0552	All	—	DT1	DT1
P0553	All	—	DT1	DT1
P0603	All	QB1	—	—
P0605	All	Replace PCM	Replace PCM	Replace PCM
P0703	All	—	—	FD3
P0704	Ranger, Explorer	—	—	TA1
	Escort / Tracer, Probe	TA5	—	TA5
	Contour / Mystique	TA5	—	TA5
	E / F-Series, Bronco	TA5		TA5
	All Others	—	—	TA9
P0705	Escort, Tracer	TD7	TD7	—
	All Others	TD1	TD1	—
P0707	Escort / Tracer	—	—	TD7
	All Others	—	—	TD1
P0708	Escort, Tracer	—	—	TD7
	All Others	—	—	TD1

(Continued)

88184C52

Powertrain Diagnostic Trouble Code (DTC) Charts

Diagnostic Trouble Code (DTC)	Application	Key On Engine Off	Key On Engine Running	Continuous Memory
P0712	All	TE1	TE1	TE90
P0713	All	TE10	TE10	TE100
P0715	Escort, Tracer	—	TF10	TF10
	All Others	—	TF1	TF1
P0720	All	—	—	TF1
P0721	All	—	—	TF7
P0731	Escort/Tracer	—	—	TC9
	All Others	—	—	TC1
P0732	Escort/Tracer	—	—	TC9
	All Others	—	—	TC1
P0733	Escort/Tracer	—	—	TC9
	All Others	—	—	TC1
P0734	Escort/Tracer	—	—	TC9
	All Others	—	—	TC1
P0736	All	—	—	TD1
P0741	Escort/Tracer	—	—	TC9
	All Others	—	—	TC5
P0743	Escort/Tracer	TC9	TC9	TC9
	All Others	TC5	TC5	TC5
P0746	All	—	—	TC5
P0750	Escort/Tracer	TC9	TC9	TC9
	All Others	TC1	TC1	TC1
P0751	Escort/Tracer	—	—	TC9
	All Others	—	—	TC1
P0755	Escort/Tracer	TC9	TC9	TC9
	All Others	TC1	TC1	TC1
P0756	Escort/Tracer	—	—	TC9
	All Others	—	—	TC1
P0760	Escort/Tracer	TC9	TC9	TC9
	All Others	TC1	TC1	TC1
P0761	Escort/Tracer	—	—	TC9
	All Others	—	—	TC1
P0781	Escort/Tracer	—	—	TC9
	All Others	—	—	TC1
P0782	Escort/Tracer	—	—	TC9
	All Others	—	—	TC1
P0783	Escort/Tracer	—	—	TC9
	All Others	—	—	TC1
P0784	Escort/Tracer	—	—	TC9

(Continued)

88184C53

Powertrain Diagnostic Trouble Code (DTC) Charts

Diagnostic Trouble Code (DTC)	Application	Key On Engine Off	Key On Engine Running	Continuous Memory
P1224	All	HT40	HT40	HT40
P1230	All	XB130	—	XB162
P1231	All	XB135	—	—
P1232	All	X160	X160	X205
P1233	All	KB1	KB1	KB1
P1234	All	KB1	KB1	KB1
P1235	Continental	KB30	KB30	KB30
	Mark VIII	XB140	XB140	XB170
P1236	Continental	KB30	KB30	KB30
	Mark VIII	XB140	XB140	XB170
P1237	All	KB47	KB47	KB47
P1238	All	KB47	KB47	KB47
P1260	All	—	—	QD1
P1270	All	—	—	ND1
P1288	All	DL1	DL1	—
P1289	All	DL10	DL10	DL90
P1290	All	DL20	DL20	DL90
P1299	All	—	—	DL100
P1351	Distributor Ignition	—	—	JG50
	3.0L Windstar All Others	— —	— —	NA2 NC2
P1352	6 Cylinder	—	—	JC1
	8 Cylinder All Integrated EI	— —	— —	JC30 JE1
P1353	6 Cylinder	—	—	JC1
	8 Cylinder All Integrated EI	— —	— —	JC30 JE1
P1354	6 Cylinder	—	—	JC1
	8 cylinder All Integrated EI	— —	— —	JC30 JE1
P1355	8 Cylinder All Integrated EI	— —	— —	JC30 JE1
P1356	3.0L Windstar	—	—	NA3
P1358	3.0L Windstar	NA3	—	NA2
	All Others	NC2	—	NC2
P1359	Distributor Ignition	—	JG60	JG60
	3.0L Windstar All others	— —	MC1 MD1	MC1 MD1
P1364	6 Cylinder	—	—	JC1
	8 Cylinder All Integrated EI	— —	— —	JC30 JE1

(Continued)

88184C54

Powertrain Diagnostic Trouble Code (DTC) Charts

Diagnostic Trouble Code (DTC)	Application	Key On Engine Off	Key On Engine Running	Continuous Memory
	All Others	—	—	TC1
P1000	All	See Note 1	See Note 1	QC1
P1001	All	—	QA1	—
P1100	All	—	—	DC2
P1101	All	DC2	DC1	—
P1112	All	—	—	DA90
P1116	All	DA1	DA1	—
P1117	All	—	—	DA90
P1120	All	DH3	DH3	DH3
P1121	All	—	—	DH15
P1124	All	DH1	DH1	—
P1125	All	—	—	DH20
P1127	NG Crown Victoria	HA90	HA90	HA90
	All Others	—	H100	—
P1128	NG Crown Victoria	HA100	HA100	HA100
	All Others	—	H110	—
P1129	NG Crown Victoria	HA100	HA100	HA100
	All Others	—	H110	—
P1130	NG Crown Victoria	HA40	HA40	HA40
	All Others	H40	H40	H40
P1131	NG Crown Victoria	HA40	HA40	HA40
	All Others	H40	H40	H40
P1132	NG Crown Victoria	HA40	HA40	HA40
	All Others	H40	H40	H40
P1137	NG Crown Victoria	—	HA80	—
	All Others	—	H80	—
P1138	NG Crown Victoria	—	HA80	—
	All Others	—	H80	—
P1150	NG Crown Victoria	HA40	HA40	HA40
	All Others	H40	H40	H40
P1151	NG Crown Victoria	HA40	HA40	HA40
	All Others	H40	H40	H40
P1152	NG Crown Victoria	HA40	HA40	HA40
	All Others	H40	H40	H40
P1157	NG Crown Victoria	—	HA80	—
	All Others	—	H80	—
P1158	NG Crown Victoria	—	HA80	—
	All Others	—	H80	—
P1220	All	HT20	HT20	HT20

(Continued)

88184C55

Powertrain Diagnostic Trouble Code (DTC) Charts

Diagnostic Trouble Code (DTC)	Application	Key On Engine Off	Key On Engine Running	Continuous Memory
P1390	All	FG1	—	—
P1400	Probe	HH30	HH30	HH30
	5.0L Explorer All Others	HJ1 HE1	HJ1 HE1	HJ1 HE1
P1401	Probe	HH40	HH40	HH40
	5.0L Explorer All Others	HJ10 HE10	HJ10 HE10	HJ10 HE10
P1405	All	—	—	HE50
P1406	All	—	—	HE60
P1407	Probe	—	—	HE70
P1408	Probe	—	HH50	—
	All Others	—	HE71	—
P1409	5.0L Explorer	HJ20	HJ20	HJ20
	All Others	HE110	HE110	HE120
P1411	All	HM40	HM40	HM40
P1413	All	HM18	HM18	HM18
P1414	All	HM25	HM25	HM25
P1442	All	—	—	HX1
P1443	Escort/Tracer, Mustang, Thunderbird/Cougar, Aerostar, Ranger, 7.5L F-Series	—	—	HW7
	All others	—	—	HW6
P1444	All	—	—	HW27
P1445	All	—	—	HW31
P1450	All	—	—	HX56
P1452	All	—	—	HX56
P1455	All	—	—	HX40
P1460	CCRM	X105	X105	X120
	Probe All Others	KM60 KM1	KM60 KM1	KM30 KM30
P1461	All	DS1	DS1	DS1
P1462	All	DS10	DS10	DS10
P1463	All	—	—	DS20
P1464	CCRM	X124	X124	—
	VLCM Escort, Tracer, Probe All Others	XB75 KM70 KM19	XB75 KM70 KM19	— — —
P1469	All	—	—	X115
P1473	All	XB20	—	—
P1474	CCRM	X20	X20	X30

(Continued)

88184C56

Powertrain Diagnostic Trouble Code (DTC) Charts

Diagnostic Trouble Code (DTC)	Application	Key On Engine Off	Key On Engine Running	Continuous Memory
	Escort/Tracer	KF1	KF1	KF15
	All Others	KF1	KF1	KF10
P1479	CCRM	X15	X15	X35
	All Others	KF1	KF1	KF20
P1480	All	X45	X45	X75
P1481	All	X50	X50	X50
P1483	All	XB10	XB10	XB10
P1484	All	XB1	XB1	XB1
P1500	Aerostar, E/F Series, Bronco	—	—	DJ1
	All Others	—	—	DP25
P1501	Aerostar, E/F Series, Bronco	DJ1	DJ1	—
	All Others	—	DP15	—
P1504	All	KE2	KE2	KE2
P1505	All	KE25	KE25	KE25
P1506	All	—	KE20	KE20
P1507	All	—	KE2	KE2
P1512	All	—	—	HU15
P1513	All	—	—	HU15
P1516	All	HU15	—	HU15
P1517	All	HU15	—	HU15
P1518	All	HU15	HU15	HU15
P1519	All	HU15	—	HU15
P1520	All	HU15	HU15	HU15
P1530	All	XB50	XB50	XB50
P1537	All	HU15	HU15	HU15
P1538	All	HU15	HU15	HU15
P1539	All	XB40	XB40	XB40
P1550	All	—	DT1	DT1
P1605	All	QB1	—	—
P1625	All	XB60	XB60	XB65
P1626	All	XB60	XB60	XB65
P1650	All	FF1	FF1	—
P1651	All	—	FF1	FF1
P1701	All	—	—	TD1
P1703	All	FD2	FD1	—
P1705	Escort/Tracer	TD7	TD7	—
	All Others	TD1	TD1	—
P1709	Escort/Tracer (M.T.), Probe, Contour/Mystique	TA5	—	—

(Continued)

88184C57

Powertrain Diagnostic Trouble Code (DTC) Charts

Diagnostic Trouble Code (DTC)	Application	Key On Engine Off	Key On Engine Running	Continuous Memory
	All Others	TA1	—	—
P1709	Escort/Tracer (A.T.), Probe, Contour/Mystique	TD7	—	—
P1711	All	TE20	TE20	—
P1728	All	—	—	See Note 3
P1729	Ranger/Explorer	—	—	TG1
	All Others	—	—	TG6
P1741	All	—	—	See Note 3
P1742	All	—	—	See Note 3
P1743	All	—	—	See Note 3
P1744	All	—	—	See Note 3
P1746	All	TC1	—	TC1
P1747	All	TC1	—	TC1
P1749	All	—	—	TC1
P1751	Escort/Tracer	—	—	TC9
	All Others	—	—	TC1
P1754	All	TC1	—	TC1
P1756	Escort/Tracer	—	—	TC9
	All Others	—	—	TC1
P1761	Escort/Tracer	—	—	TC9
	All Others	—	—	TC1
P1780	All	—	TB1	—
P1781	Ranger, Explorer	TG1	—	—
	All Others	TG6	—	—
P1783	All	—	—	TE110
P1784	All	—	—	See Note 3
P1785	All	—	—	See Note 3
P1786	All	—	—	See Note 3
P1787	All	—	—	See Note 3
P1788	All	TC1	—	TC1
P1789	All	TC1	—	TC1
U1021	All	XB180	XB180	XB180
U1039	All	—	—	See Note 2
U1051	All	—	—	See Note 2
U1073	All	XB180	XB180	XB180
U1131	All	XB180	XB180	XB180

(Continued)

88184C58

Powertrain Diagnostic Trouble Code (DTC) Charts

Diagnostic Trouble Code (DTC)	Application	Key On Engine Off	Key On Engine Running	Continuous Memory
U1135	All	—	—	See Note 2
U1256	All	XB180	XB180	XB180
U1451	All	—	—	See Note 2

Note 1: DTC P1000 is ignored in KOEO AND KOER Self-Test. Disregard the P1000 and continue as directed.

Note 2: Go to the 1996 Continental Service Manual, section Module Communication Network.

Note 3: Go to the Transmission Service Manual, Diagnosis by Symptom Chart.

88184C59

VACUUM DIAGRAMS

Following are vacuum diagrams for most of the engine and emissions package combinations covered by this manual. Because vacuum circuits will vary based on various engine and vehicle options, always refer first to the vehicle emission control information label, if present. Should the label be missing, or should vehicle be equipped with a different engine from the vehicle's original equipment, refer to the diagrams below for the same or similar configuration.

If you wish to obtain a replacement emissions label, most manufacturers make the labels available for purchase. The labels can usually be ordered from a local dealer.

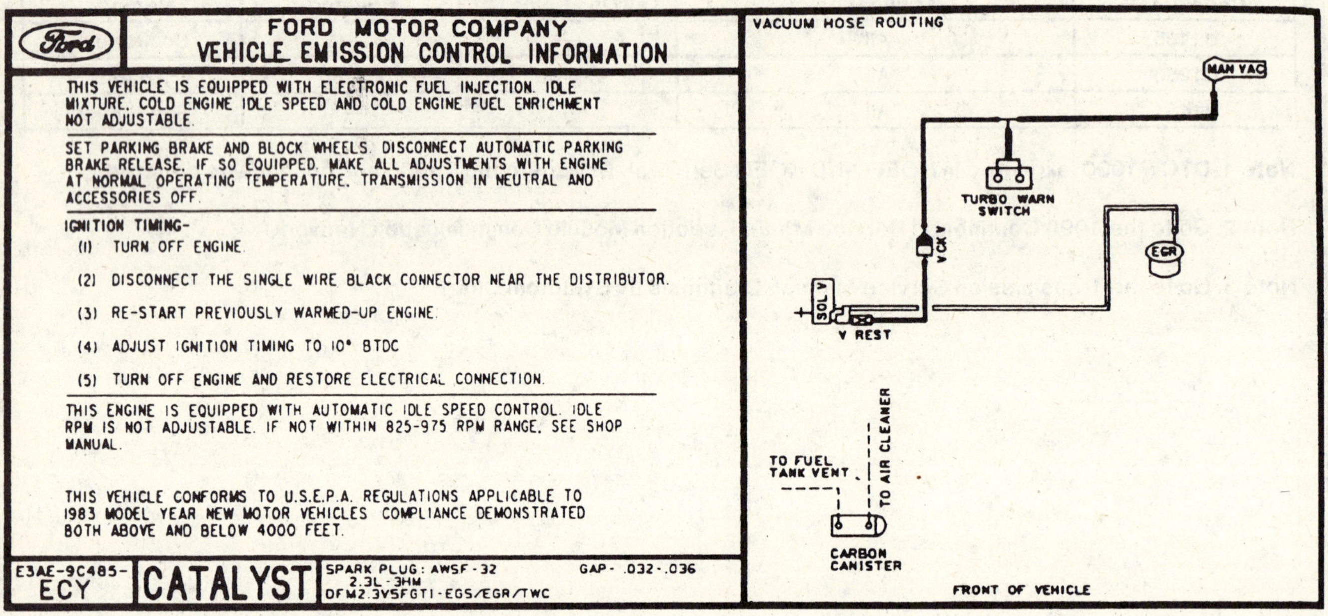

FORD MOTOR COMPANY
VEHICLE EMISSION CONTROL INFORMATION

THIS VEHICLE IS EQUIPPED WITH ELECTRONIC FUEL INJECTION. IDLE MIXTURE, COLD ENGINE IDLE SPEED AND COLD ENGINE FUEL ENRICHMENT NOT ADJUSTABLE.

SET PARKING BRAKE AND BLOCK WHEELS. DISCONNECT AUTOMATIC PARKING BRAKE RELEASE, IF SO EQUIPPED. MAKE ALL ADJUSTMENTS WITH ENGINE AT NORMAL OPERATING TEMPERATURE, TRANSMISSION IN NEUTRAL AND ACCESSORIES OFF.

IGNITION TIMING-
(1) TURN OFF ENGINE.
(2) DISCONNECT THE SINGLE WIRE BLACK CONNECTOR NEAR THE DISTRIBUTOR.
(3) RE-START PREVIOUSLY WARMED-UP ENGINE.
(4) ADJUST IGNITION TIMING TO 10° BTDC
(5) TURN OFF ENGINE AND RESTORE ELECTRICAL CONNECTION.

THIS ENGINE IS EQUIPPED WITH AUTOMATIC IDLE SPEED CONTROL. IDLE RPM IS NOT ADJUSTABLE. IF NOT WITHIN 825-975 RPM RANGE, SEE SHOP MANUAL.

THIS VEHICLE CONFORMS TO U.S.E.P.A. REGULATIONS APPLICABLE TO 1983 MODEL YEAR NEW MOTOR VEHICLES COMPLIANCE DEMONSTRATED BOTH ABOVE AND BELOW 4000 FEET.

E3AE-9C485- ECY | CATALYST | SPARK PLUG: AWSF-32 GAP-.032-.036 2.3L-3HM DFM2.3V5FGT1-EGS/EGR/TWC

Fig. 41 Vehicle Emission Label 1983 2.3L engine — 3-05E-R10

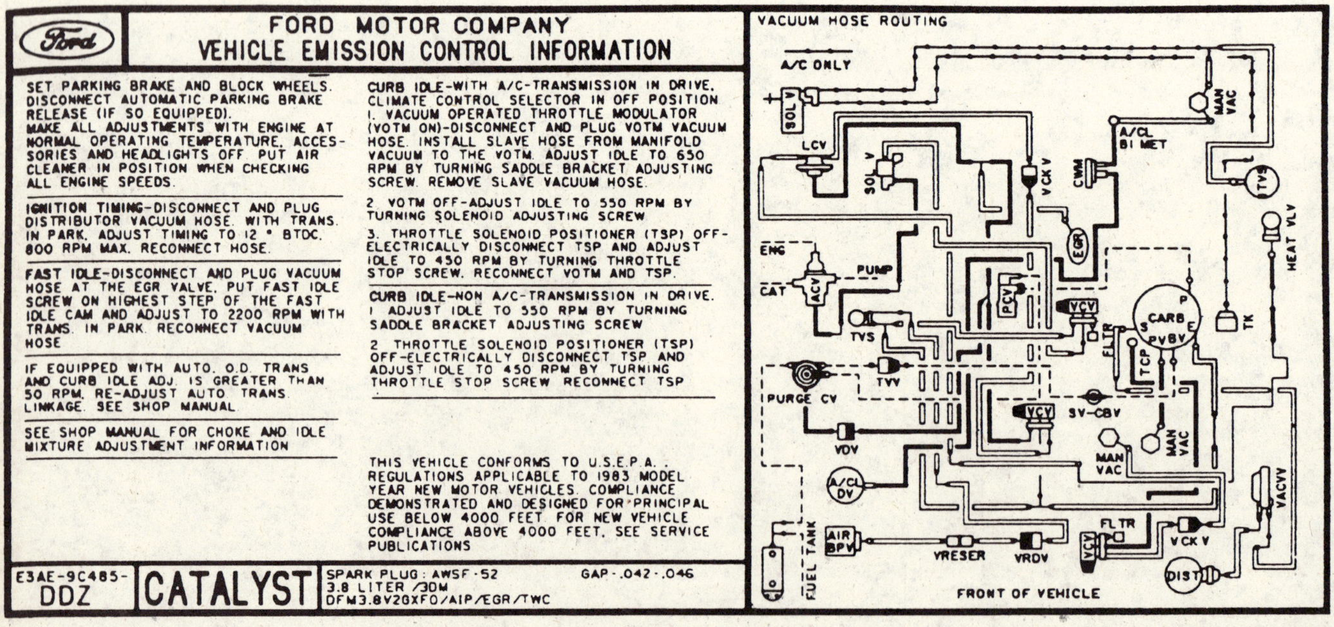

FORD MOTOR COMPANY
VEHICLE EMISSION CONTROL INFORMATION

SET PARKING BRAKE AND BLOCK WHEELS. DISCONNECT AUTOMATIC PARKING BRAKE RELEASE (IF SO EQUIPPED). MAKE ALL ADJUSTMENTS WITH ENGINE AT NORMAL OPERATING TEMPERATURE, ACCESSORIES AND HEADLIGHTS OFF. PUT AIR CLEANER IN POSITION WHEN CHECKING ALL ENGINE SPEEDS.

IGNITION TIMING-DISCONNECT AND PLUG DISTRIBUTOR VACUUM HOSE. WITH TRANS. IN PARK, ADJUST TIMING TO 12 ° BTDC, 800 RPM MAX. RECONNECT HOSE.

FAST IDLE-DISCONNECT AND PLUG VACUUM HOSE AT THE EGR VALVE. PUT FAST IDLE SCREW ON HIGHEST STEP OF THE FAST IDLE CAM AND ADJUST TO 2200 RPM WITH TRANS. IN PARK. RECONNECT VACUUM HOSE

IF EQUIPPED WITH AUTO. O.D. TRANS AND CURB IDLE ADJ. IS GREATER THAN 50 RPM, RE-ADJUST AUTO. TRANS. LINKAGE. SEE SHOP MANUAL.

SEE SHOP MANUAL FOR CHOKE AND IDLE MIXTURE ADJUSTMENT INFORMATION

CURB IDLE-WITH A/C-TRANSMISSION IN DRIVE. CLIMATE CONTROL SELECTOR IN OFF POSITION
1. VACUUM OPERATED THROTTLE MODULATOR (VOTM ON)-DISCONNECT AND PLUG VOTM VACUUM HOSE. INSTALL SLAVE HOSE FROM MANIFOLD VACUUM TO THE VOTM. ADJUST IDLE TO 650 RPM BY TURNING SADDLE BRACKET ADJUSTING SCREW. REMOVE SLAVE VACUUM HOSE.
2. VOTM OFF-ADJUST IDLE TO 550 RPM BY TURNING SOLENOID ADJUSTING SCREW
3. THROTTLE SOLENOID POSITIONER (TSP) OFF-ELECTRICALLY DISCONNECT TSP AND ADJUST IDLE TO 450 RPM BY TURNING THROTTLE STOP SCREW. RECONNECT VOTM AND TSP.

CURB IDLE-NON A/C-TRANSMISSION IN DRIVE.
1 ADJUST IDLE TO 550 RPM BY TURNING SADDLE BRACKET ADJUSTING SCREW
2 THROTTLE SOLENOID POSITIONER (TSP) OFF-ELECTRICALLY DISCONNECT TSP AND ADJUST IDLE TO 450 RPM BY TURNING THROTTLE STOP SCREW RECONNECT TSP

THIS VEHICLE CONFORMS TO U.S.E.P.A. REGULATIONS APPLICABLE TO 1983 MODEL YEAR NEW MOTOR VEHICLES. COMPLIANCE DEMONSTRATED AND DESIGNED FOR PRINCIPAL USE BELOW 4000 FEET. FOR NEW VEHICLE COMPLIANCE ABOVE 4000 FEET, SEE SERVICE PUBLICATIONS

E3AE-9C485- DDZ | CATALYST | SPARK PLUG: AWSF-52 GAP-.042-.046 3.8 LITER /30M DFM3.8V2GXFO/AIP/EGR/TWC

Fig. 42 Vehicle Emission Label 1983 3.8L engine — 3-14B-R00

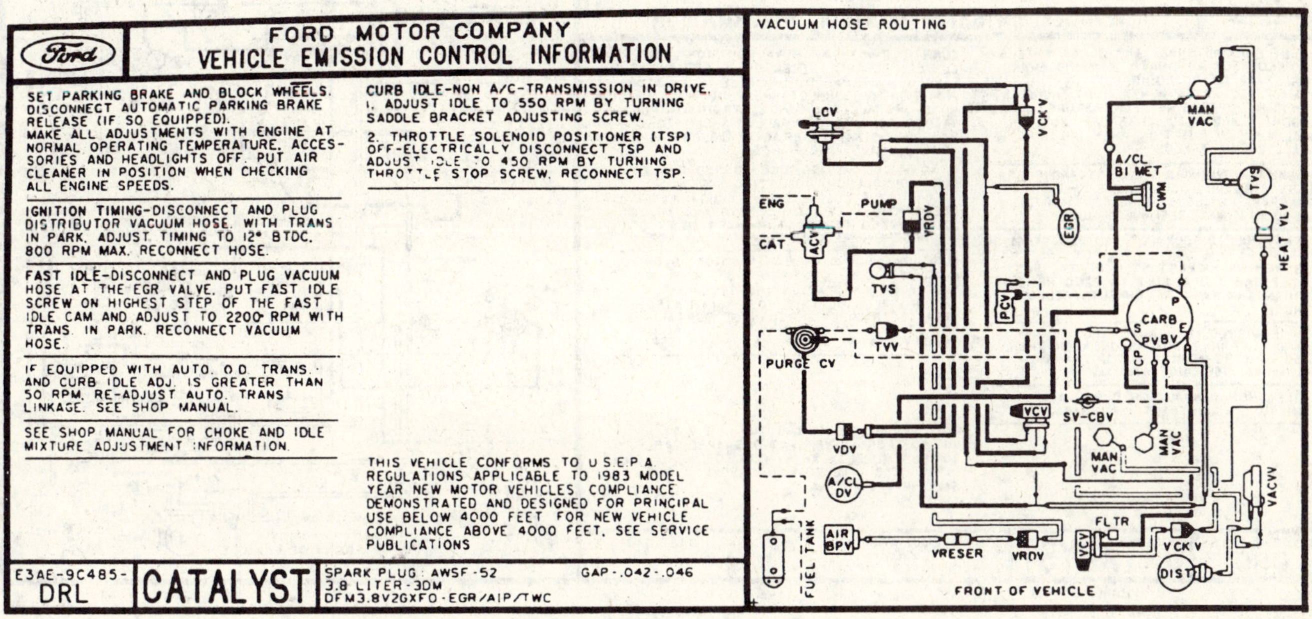

88184GH2

Fig. 43 Vehicle Emission Label 1983 3.8L engine — 3-14B-R11

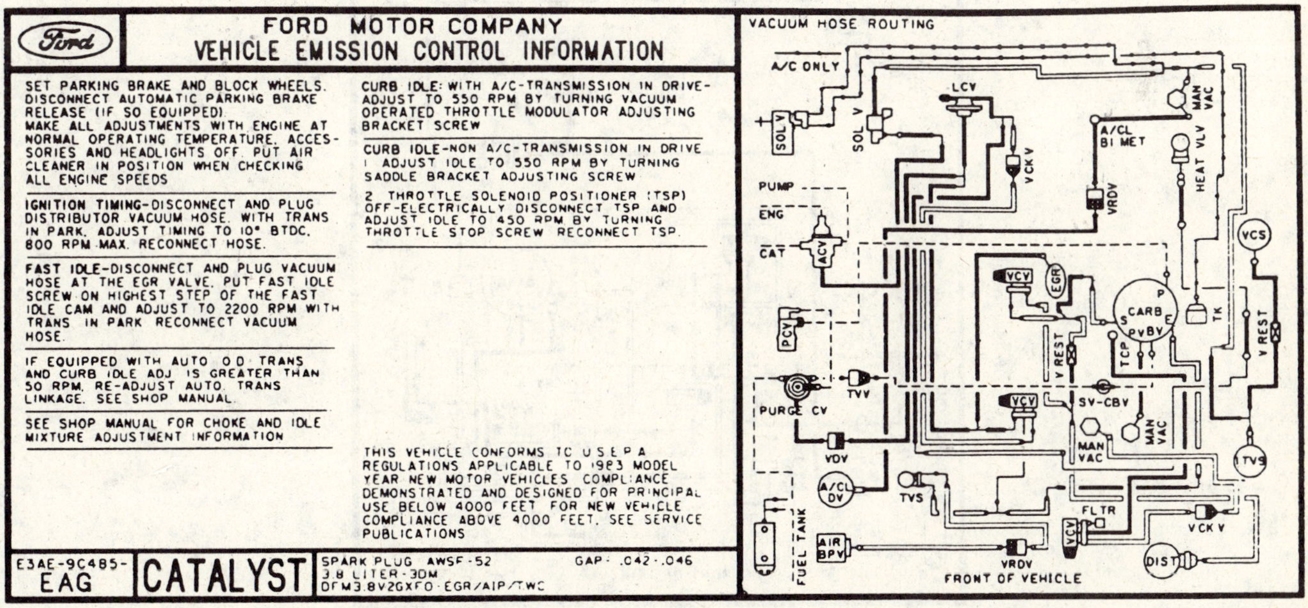

88184GH3

Fig. 44 Vehicle Emission Label 1983 3.8L engine — 3-14C-R10

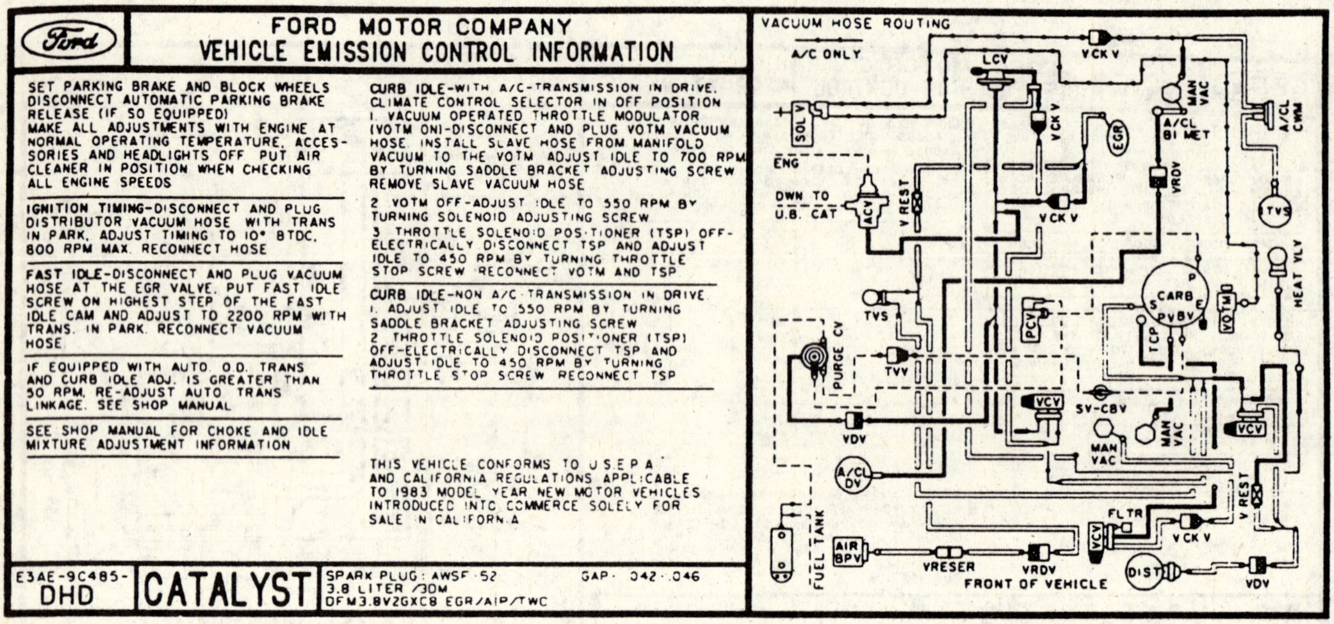

88184GH5

Fig. 45 Vehicle Emission Label 1983 3.8L engine — 3-14N-R04

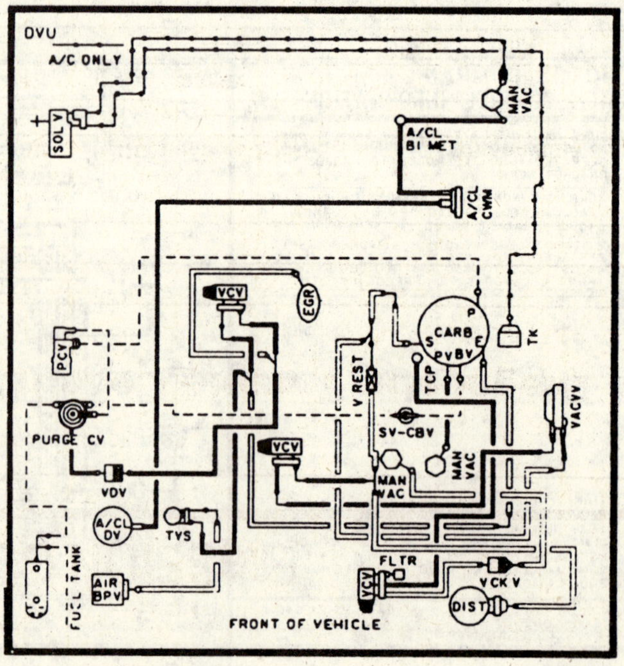

88184GH6

Fig. 46 Vehicle Emission Label 1983 3.8L engine — 3-14G-R11

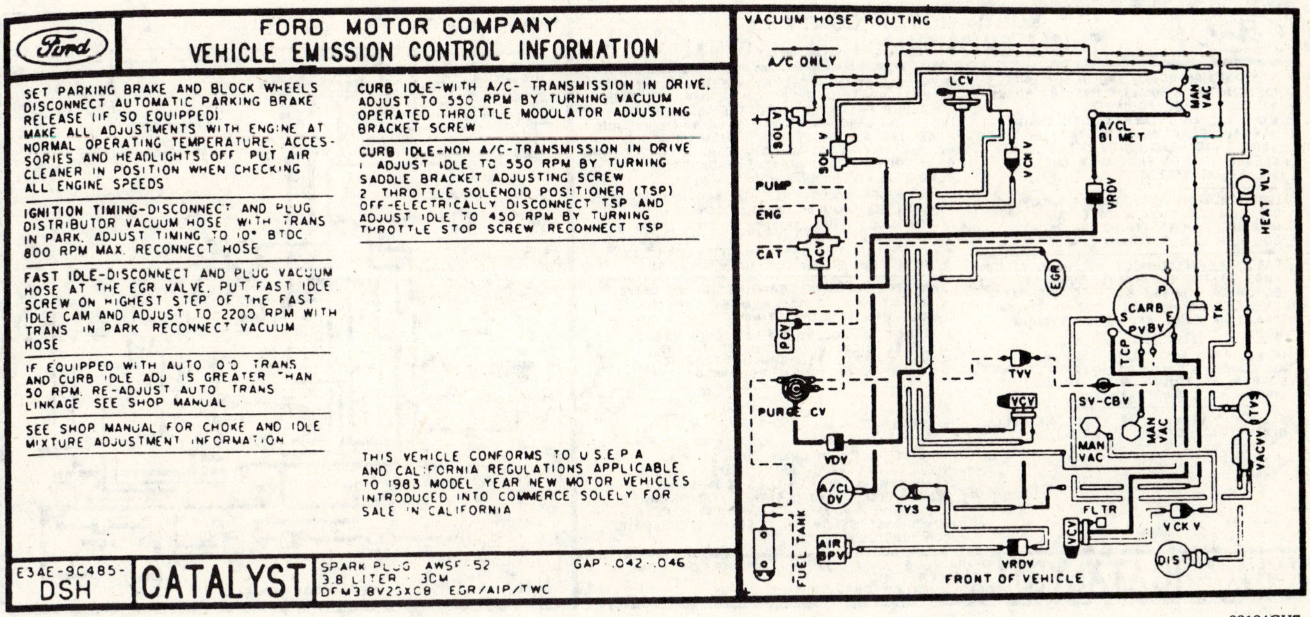

88184GH7

Fig. 47 Vehicle Emission Label 1983 3.8L engine — 3-14Q-R11

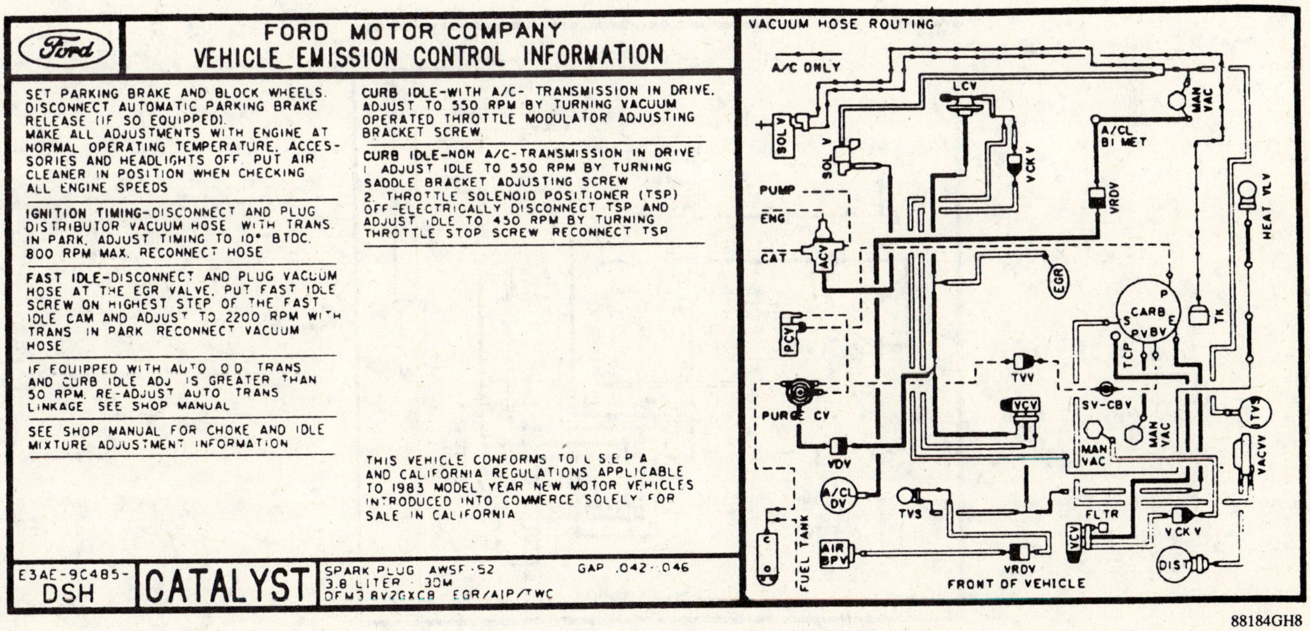

88184GH8

Fig. 48 Vehicle Emission Label 1983 3.8L engine — 3-14Q-R10

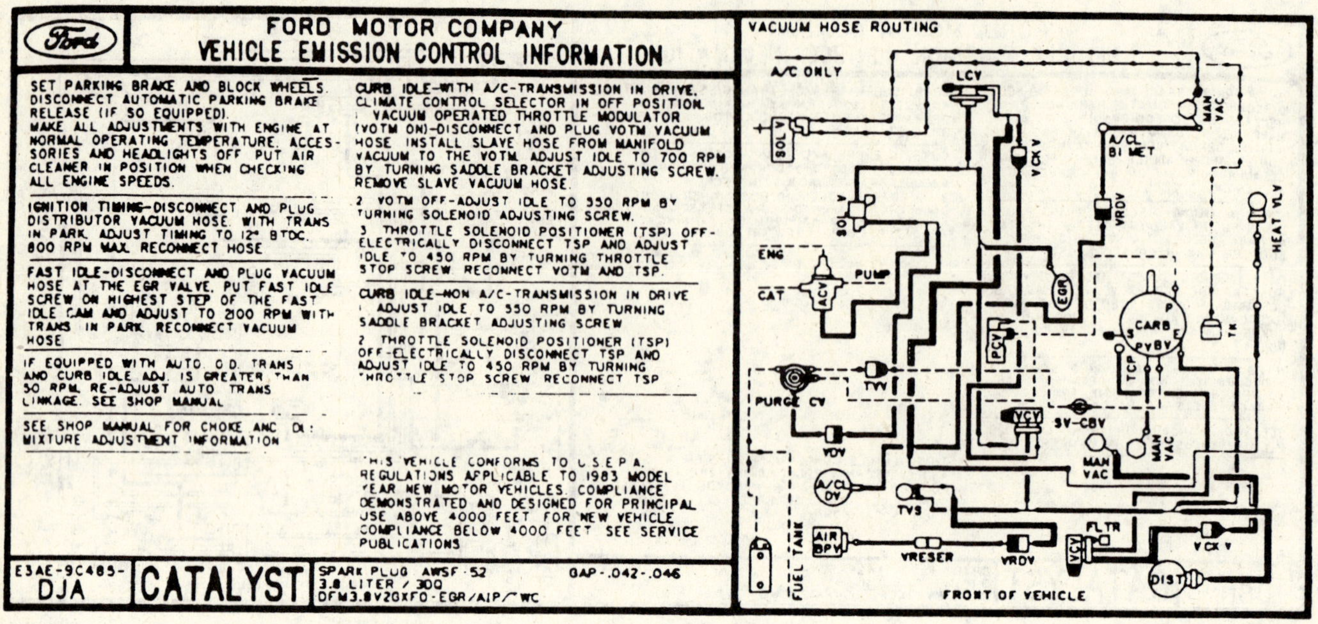

88184GH9

Fig. 49 Vehicle Emission Label 1983 3.8L engine — 3-14X-R00

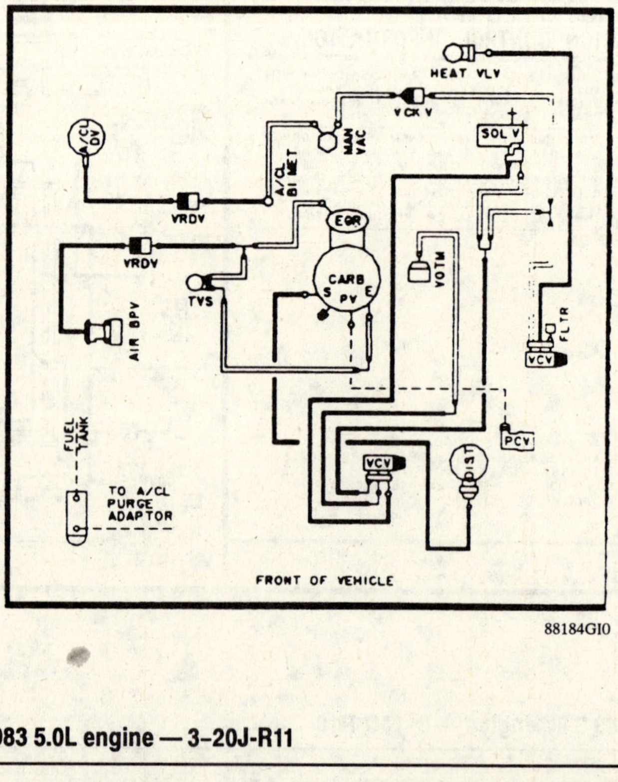

88184GI0

Fig. 50 Vehicle Emission Label 1983 5.0L engine — 3-20J-R11

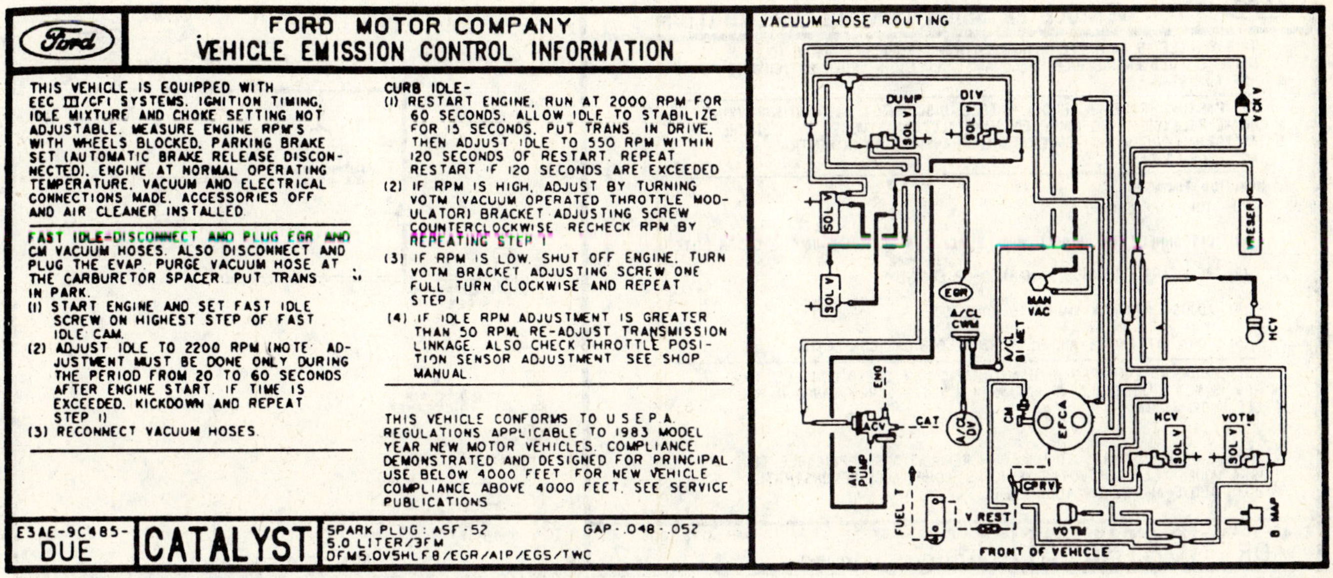

88184GI1

Fig. 51 Vehicle Emission Label 1983 5.0L engine — 3-22D-R00

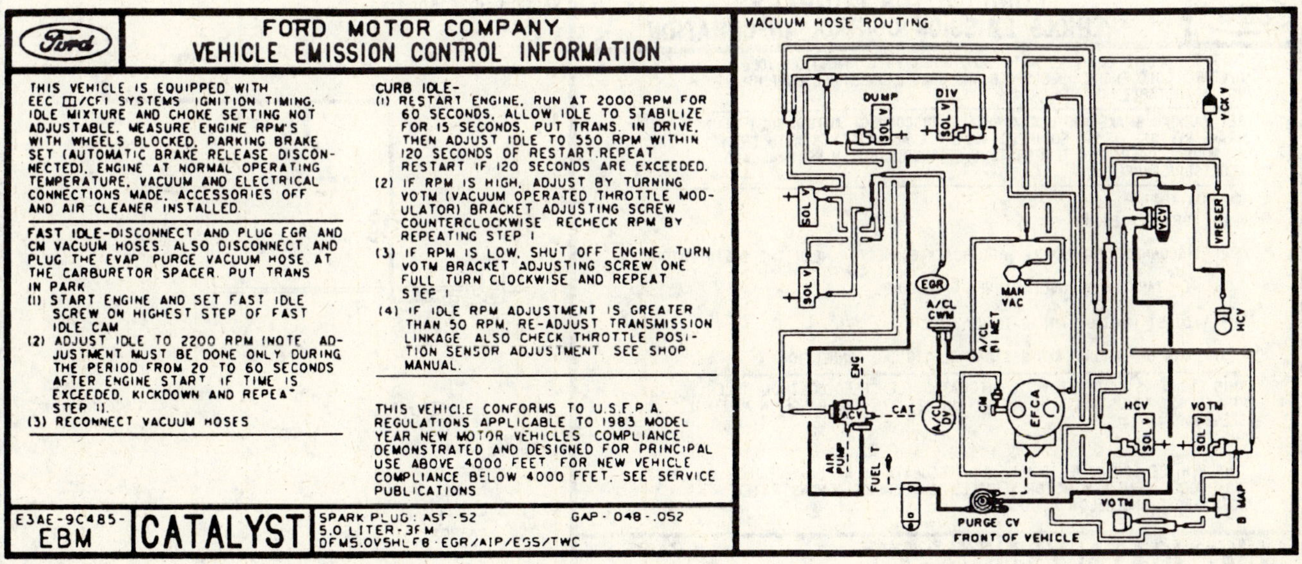

88184GI2

Fig. 52 Vehicle Emission Label 1983 5.0L engine — 3-22W-R00

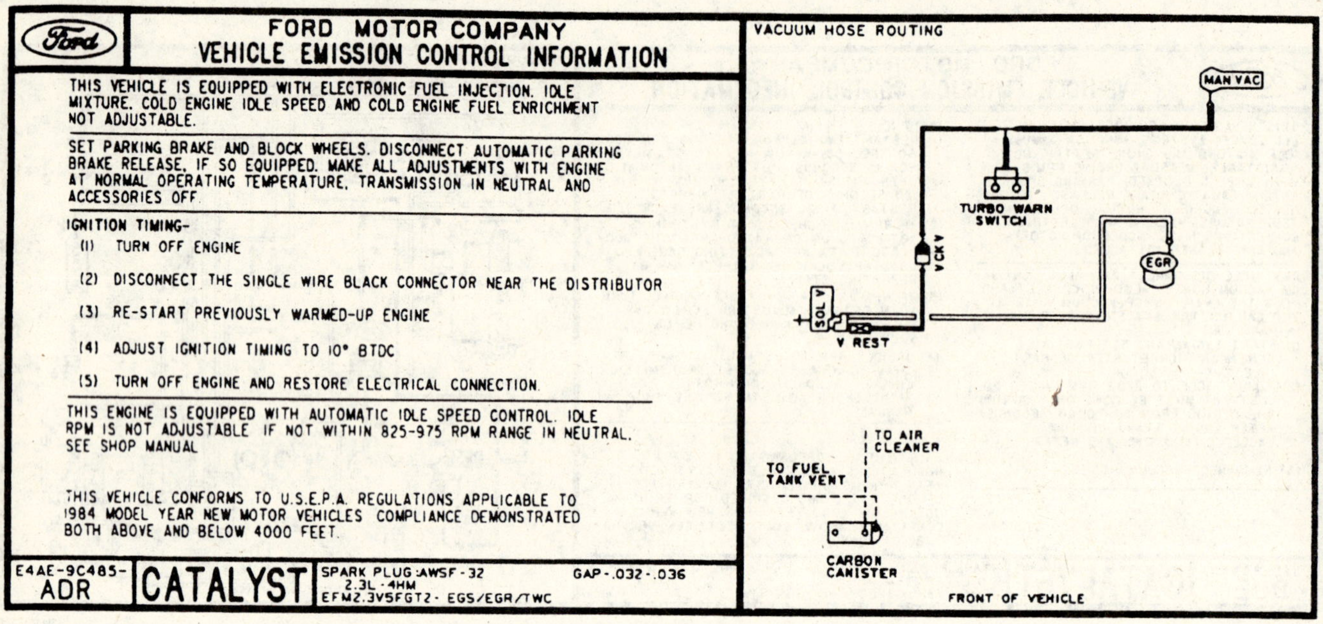

88184GI3

Fig. 53 Vehicle Emission Label 1984 2.3L engine — 3-05E-R12

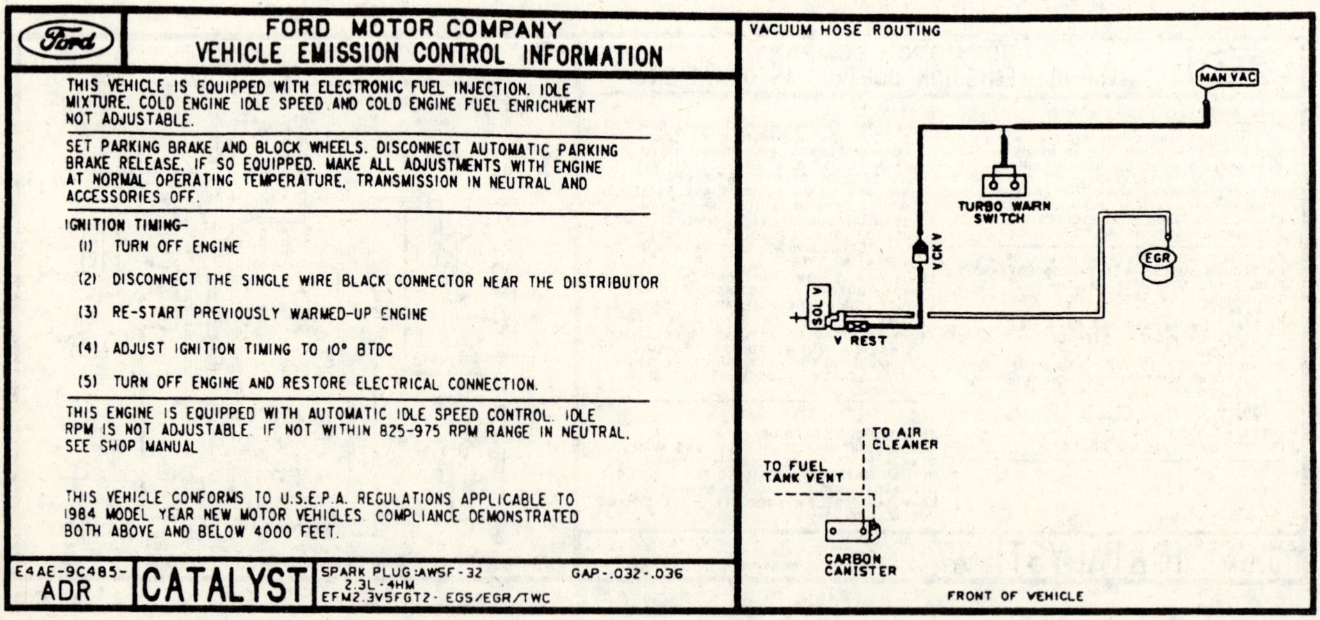

88184GI4

Fig. 54 Vehicle Emission Label 1984 2.3L engine — 4-06E-R00

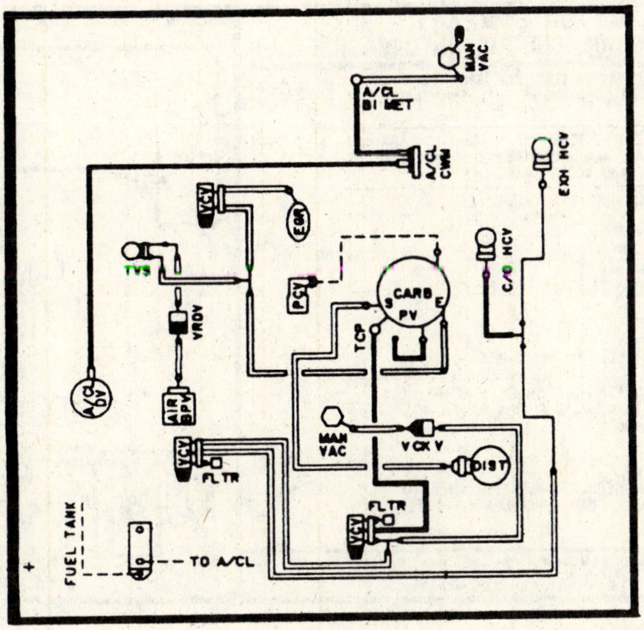

88184GI5

Fig. 55 Vehicle Emission Label 1984 3.8L engine — 4-14G-R03

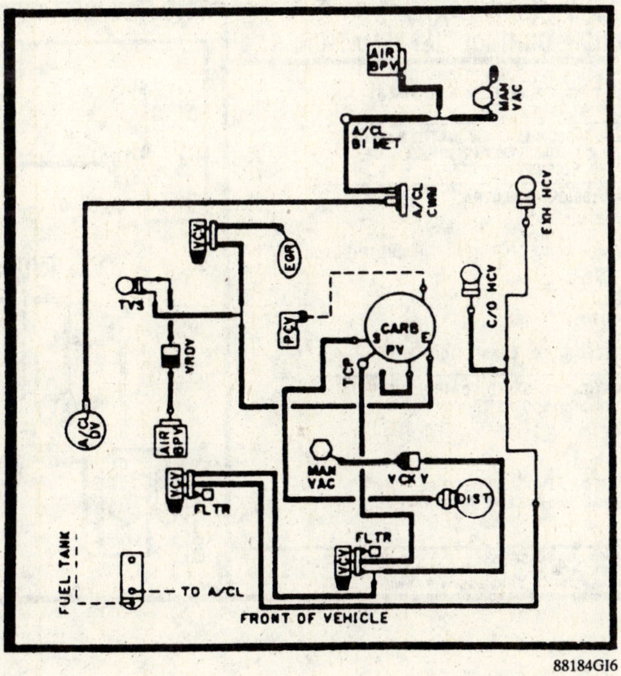

88184GI6

Fig. 56 Vehicle Emission Label 1984 3.8L engine — 4-14G-R10

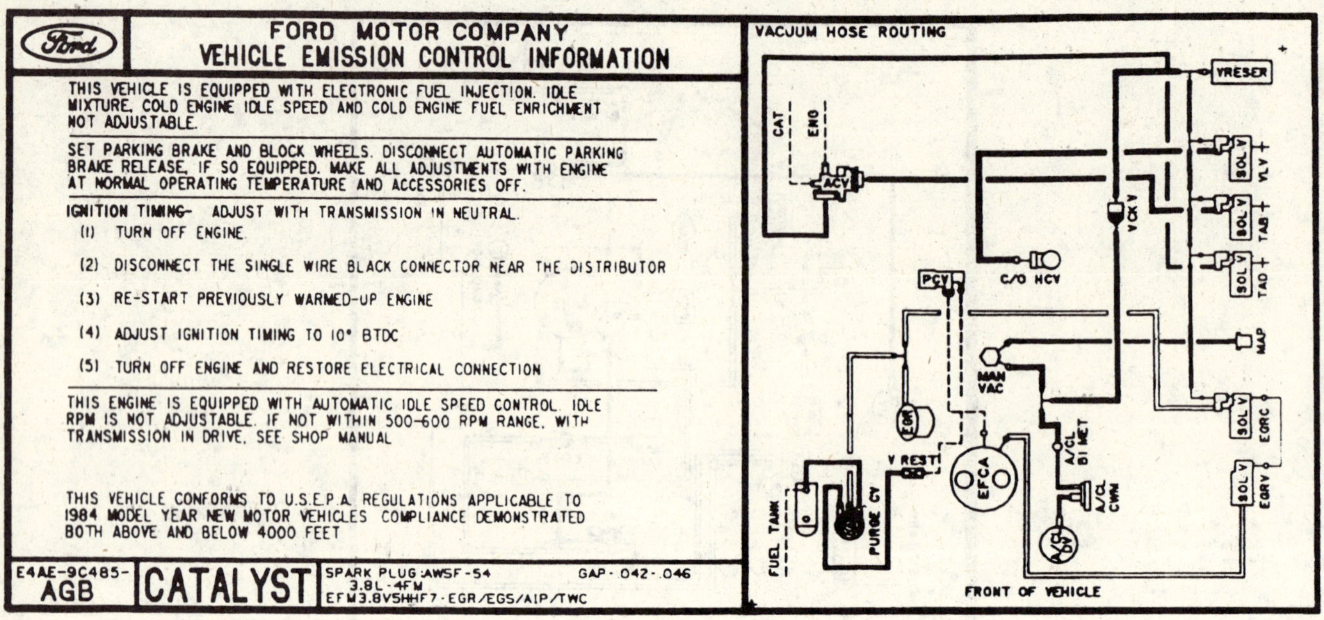
FORD MOTOR COMPANY
VEHICLE EMISSION CONTROL INFORMATION

THIS VEHICLE IS EQUIPPED WITH ELECTRONIC FUEL INJECTION. IDLE MIXTURE, COLD ENGINE IDLE SPEED AND COLD ENGINE FUEL ENRICHMENT NOT ADJUSTABLE.

SET PARKING BRAKE AND BLOCK WHEELS. DISCONNECT AUTOMATIC PARKING BRAKE RELEASE, IF SO EQUIPPED. MAKE ALL ADJUSTMENTS WITH ENGINE AT NORMAL OPERATING TEMPERATURE AND ACCESSORIES OFF.

IGNITION TIMING- ADJUST WITH TRANSMISSION IN NEUTRAL.
(1) TURN OFF ENGINE.
(2) DISCONNECT THE SINGLE WIRE BLACK CONNECTOR NEAR THE DISTRIBUTOR
(3) RE-START PREVIOUSLY WARMED-UP ENGINE
(4) ADJUST IGNITION TIMING TO 10° BTDC
(5) TURN OFF ENGINE AND RESTORE ELECTRICAL CONNECTION

THIS ENGINE IS EQUIPPED WITH AUTOMATIC IDLE SPEED CONTROL. IDLE RPM IS NOT ADJUSTABLE. IF NOT WITHIN 500-600 RPM RANGE, WITH TRANSMISSION IN DRIVE, SEE SHOP MANUAL

THIS VEHICLE CONFORMS TO U.S.E.P.A. REGULATIONS APPLICABLE TO 1984 MODEL YEAR NEW MOTOR VEHICLES COMPLIANCE DEMONSTRATED BOTH ABOVE AND BELOW 4000 FEET

E4AE-9C485- AGB
CATALYST
SPARK PLUG:AWSF-54 GAP-.042-.046
3.8L-4FM
EFM3.8V5HHF7-EGR/EGS/AIP/TWC

88184GI7

Fig. 57 Vehicle Emission Label 1984 3.8L engine — 4-16B-R00

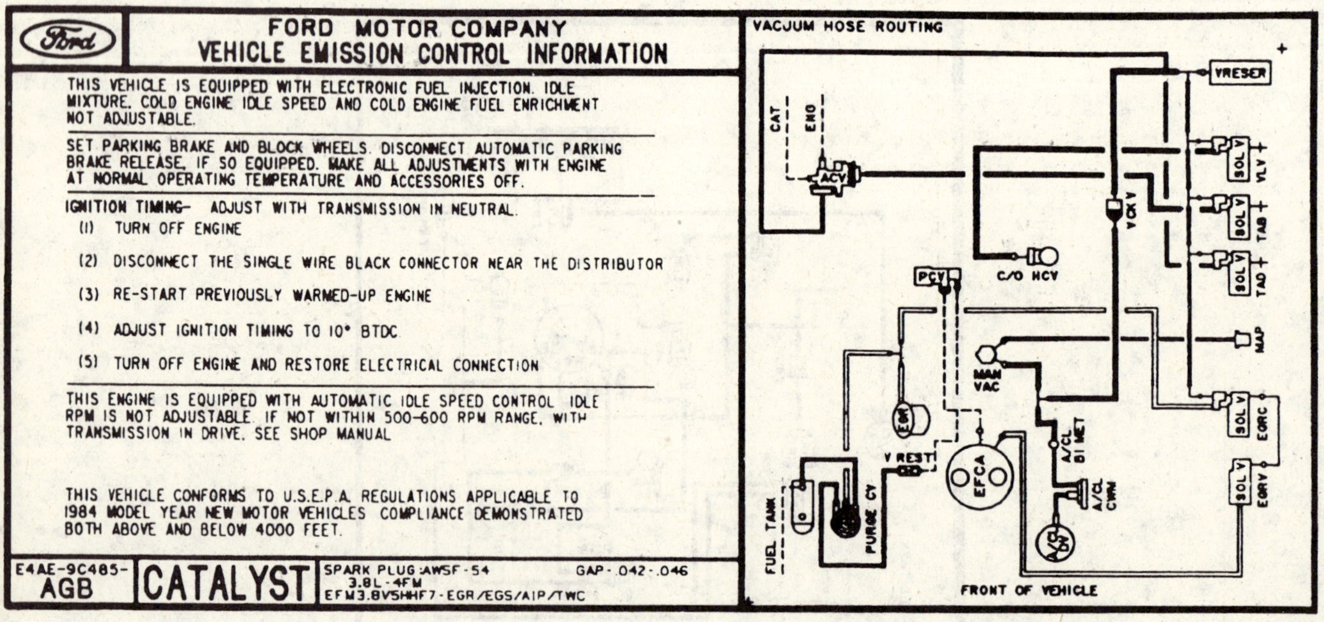
FORD MOTOR COMPANY
VEHICLE EMISSION CONTROL INFORMATION

THIS VEHICLE IS EQUIPPED WITH ELECTRONIC FUEL INJECTION. IDLE MIXTURE, COLD ENGINE IDLE SPEED AND COLD ENGINE FUEL ENRICHMENT NOT ADJUSTABLE.

SET PARKING BRAKE AND BLOCK WHEELS. DISCONNECT AUTOMATIC PARKING BRAKE RELEASE, IF SO EQUIPPED. MAKE ALL ADJUSTMENTS WITH ENGINE AT NORMAL OPERATING TEMPERATURE AND ACCESSORIES OFF.

IGNITION TIMING- ADJUST WITH TRANSMISSION IN NEUTRAL.
(1) TURN OFF ENGINE
(2) DISCONNECT THE SINGLE WIRE BLACK CONNECTOR NEAR THE DISTRIBUTOR
(3) RE-START PREVIOUSLY WARMED-UP ENGINE
(4) ADJUST IGNITION TIMING TO 10° BTDC
(5) TURN OFF ENGINE AND RESTORE ELECTRICAL CONNECTION

THIS ENGINE IS EQUIPPED WITH AUTOMATIC IDLE SPEED CONTROL. IDLE RPM IS NOT ADJUSTABLE. IF NOT WITHIN 500-600 RPM RANGE, WITH TRANSMISSION IN DRIVE, SEE SHOP MANUAL

THIS VEHICLE CONFORMS TO U.S.E.P.A. REGULATIONS APPLICABLE TO 1984 MODEL YEAR NEW MOTOR VEHICLES COMPLIANCE DEMONSTRATED BOTH ABOVE AND BELOW 4000 FEET.

E4AE-9C485- AGB
CATALYST
SPARK PLUG:AWSF-54 GAP-.042-.046
3.8L-4FM
EFM3.8V5HHF7-EGR/EGS/AIP/TWC

88184GI8

Fig. 58 Vehicle Emission Label 1984 3.8L engine — 4-16B-R10

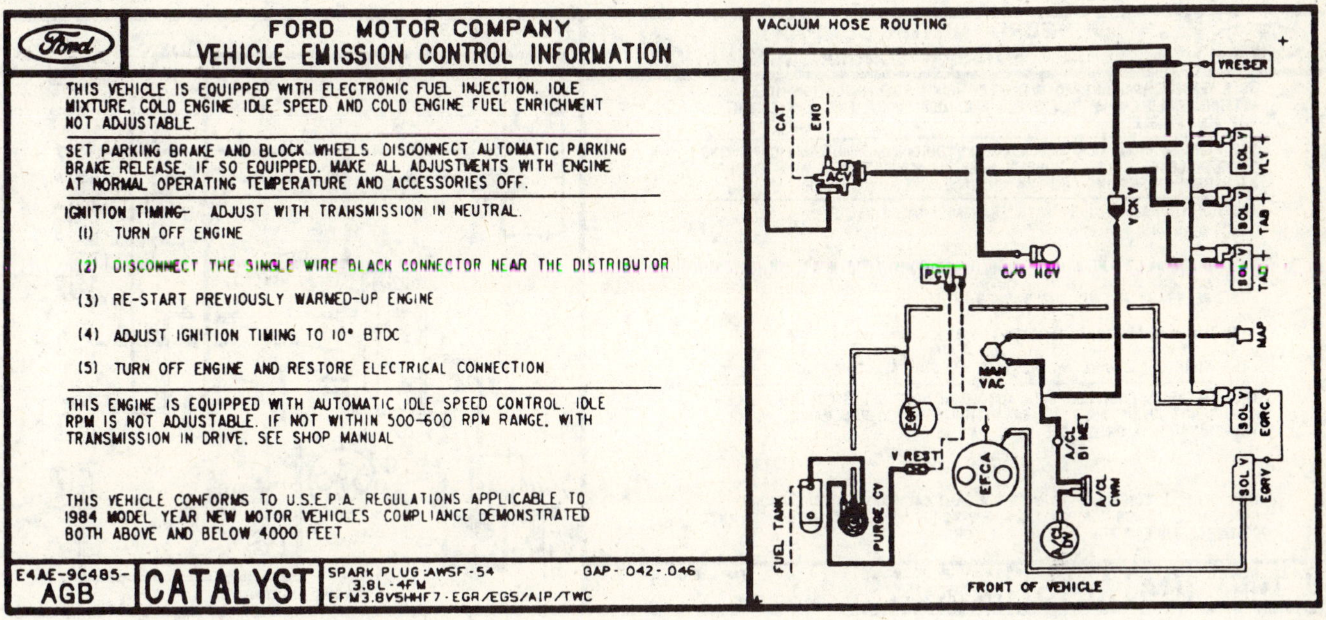

88184GI9

Fig. 59 Vehicle Emission Label 1984 3.8L engine — 4-16F-R00

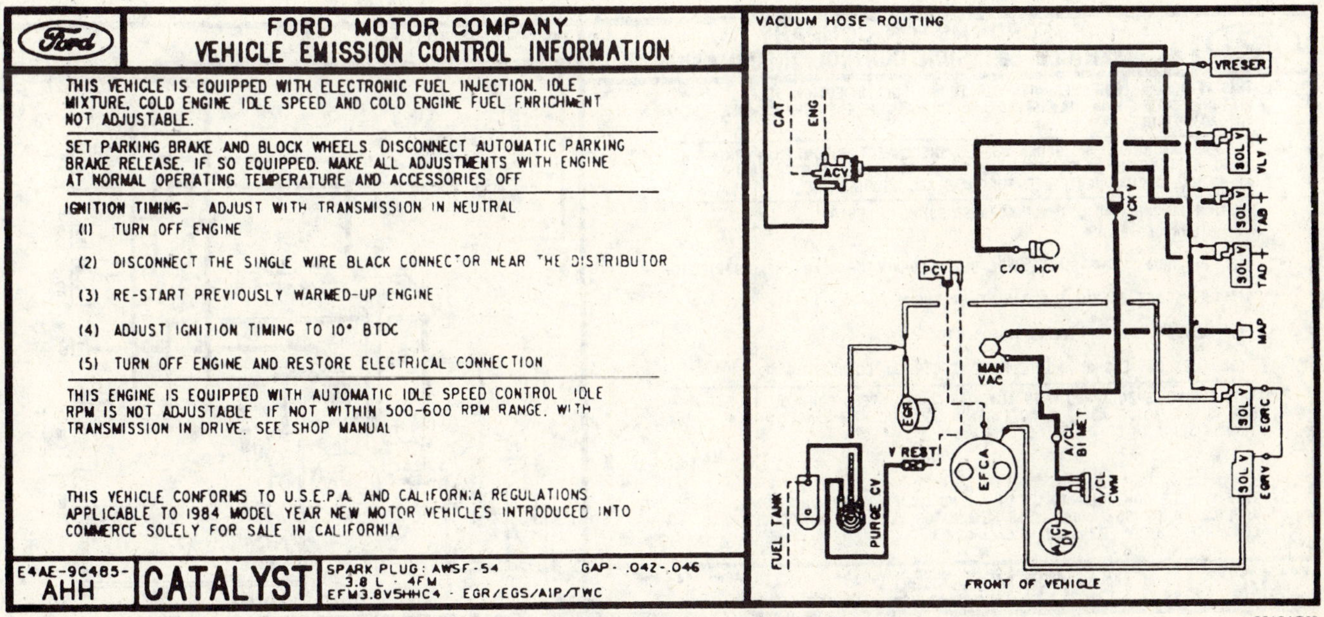

88184GJ0

Fig. 60 Vehicle Emission Label 1984 3.8L engine — 4-16N-R00

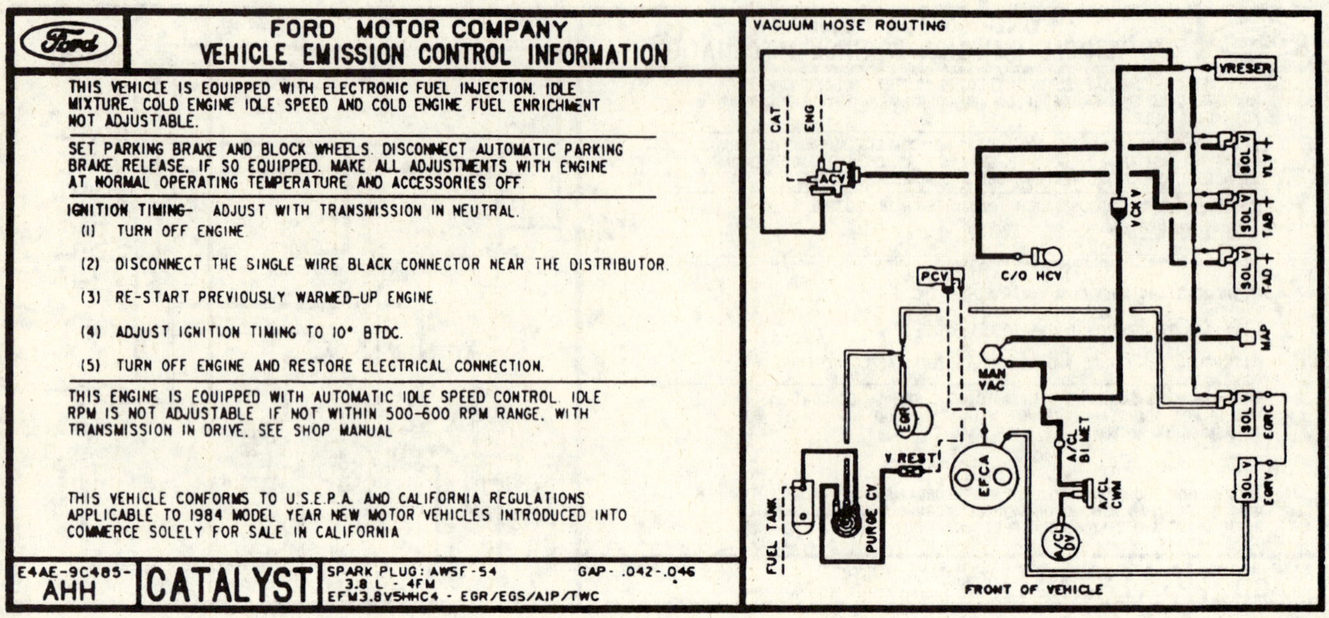

88184GJ1

Fig. 61 Vehicle Emission Label 1984 3.8L engine — 4-16N-R10

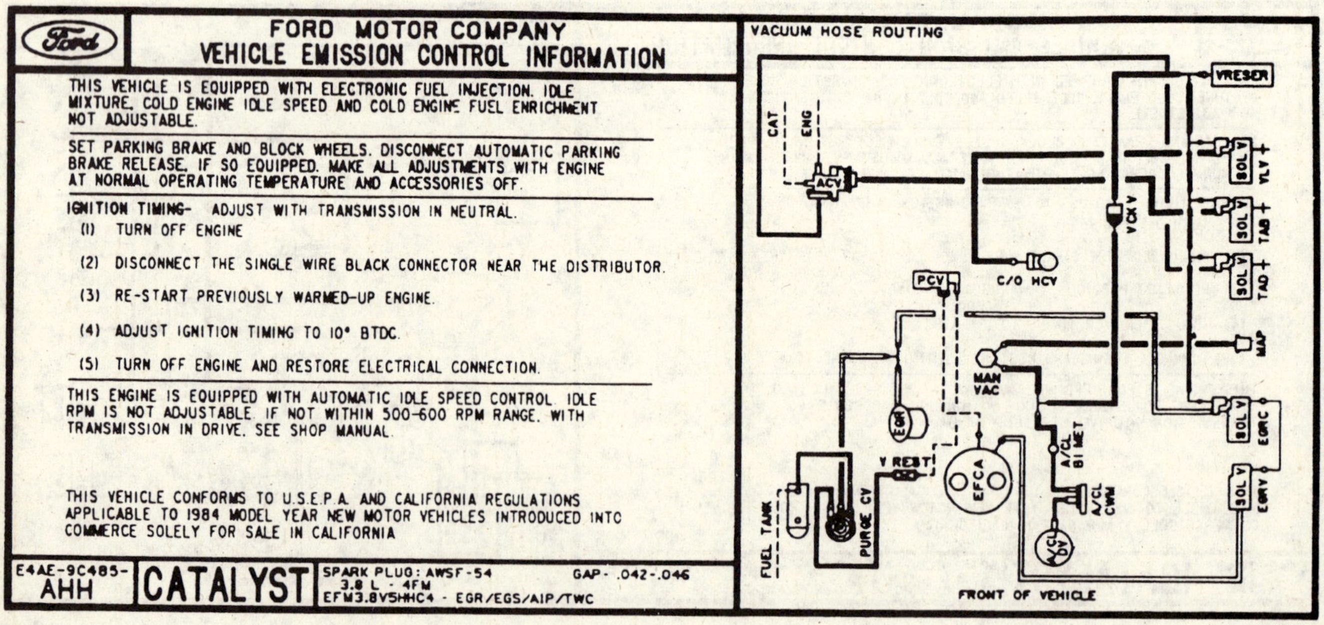

88184GJ2

Fig. 62 Vehicle Emission Label 1984 3.8L engine — 4-16S-R00

FORD MOTOR COMPANY
VEHICLE EMISSION CONTROL INFORMATION

THIS VEHICLE IS EQUIPPED WITH EEC III/EFI SYSTEM. IGNITION TIMING, IDLE MIXTURE AND CHOKE SETTING NOT ADJUSTABLE. MEASURE ENGINE RPM'S WITH WHEELS BLOCKED, PARKING BRAKE SET (AUTOMATIC BRAKE RELEASE DISCONNECTED), ENGINE AT NORMAL OPERATING TEMPERATURE, VACUUM AND ELECTRICAL CONNECTIONS MADE, ACCESSORIES OFF AND AIR CLEANER INSTALLED.

FAST IDLE-DISCONNECT AND PLUG EGR AND CM VACUUM HOSES. ALSO DISCONNECT AND PLUG THE EVAP. PURGE VACUUM HOSE AT THE CARBURETOR SPACER. PUT TRANS IN PARK.

(1) START ENGINE AND SET FAST IDLE SCREW ON HIGHEST STEP OF FAST IDLE CAM.
(2) ADJUST IDLE TO 2200 RPM (NOTE: ADJUSTMENT MUST BE DONE ONLY DURING THE PERIOD FROM 20 TO 60 SECONDS AFTER ENGINE START. IF TIME IS EXCEEDED KICKDOWN AND REPEAT STEP 1)
(3) RECONNECT VACUUM HOSES

CURB IDLE-
(1) RESTART ENGINE. RUN AT 2000 RPM FOR 60 SECONDS, ALLOW IDLE TO STABILIZE FOR 15 SECONDS. PUT TRANS IN DRIVE. THEN ADJUST IDLE TO 550 RPM WITHIN 120 SECONDS OF RESTART. REPEAT RESTART IF 120 SECONDS ARE EXCEEDED
(2) IF RPM IS HIGH, ADJUST BY TURNING VOTM (VACUUM OPERATED THROTTLE MODULATOR) BRACKET ADJUSTING SCREW COUNTERCLOCKWISE, RECHECK RPM BY REPEATING STEP 1.
(3) IF RPM IS LOW, SHUT OFF ENGINE. TURN VOTM BRACKET ADJUSTING SCREW ONE FULL TURN CLOCKWISE AND REPEAT STEP 1
(4) IF IDLE RPM ADJUSTMENT IS GREATER THAN 50 RPM, RE-ADJUST TRANSMISSION LINKAGE. ALSO CHECK THROTTLE POSITION SENSOR ADJUSTMENT. SEE SHOP MANUAL

FIRNG ORDER-1-5-4-2-6-3-7-8

THIS VEHICLE CONFORMS TO U.S.E.P.A AND CALIFORNIA REGULATIONS APPLICABLE TO 1984 MODEL YEAR NEW MOTOR VEHICLES INTRODUCED INTO COMMERCE SOLELY FOR SALE IN CALIFORNIA

E4AE-9C485-AKC | CATALYST | SPARK PLUG ASF-52 GAP .048-.052 5.0 L - 4FM EFM5.0V5HBC4 EGR/EGS/AIP/TWC

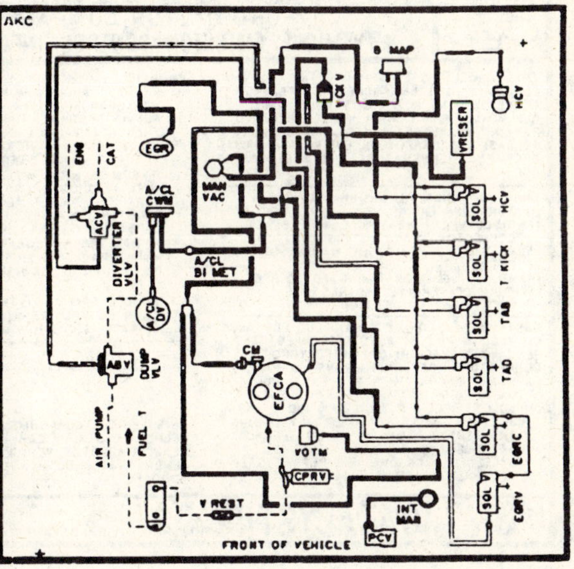

88184GJ3

Fig. 63 Vehicle Emission Label 1984 5.0L engine — 3-22D-R00

FORD MOTOR COMPANY
VEHICLE EMISSION CONTROL INFORMATION

THIS VEHICLE IS EQUIPPED WITH EEC IV/CFI SYSTEMS. IDLE MIXTURE AND CHOKE SETTING NOT ADJUSTABLE. MAKE ALL ADJUSTMENTS WITH WHEELS BLOCKED, PARKING BRAKE SET (AUTOMATIC BRAKE RELEASE DISCONNECTED), ENGINE AT NORMAL OPERATING TEMPERATURE AND ACCESSORIES OFF

IGNITION TIMING - TRANS IN PARK
(1) TURN OFF ENGINE
(2) DISCONNECT THE SINGLE WIRE/BLACK CONNECTOR NEAR THE DISTRIBUTOR
(3) RE-START PREVIOUSLY WARMED-UP ENGINE
(4) ADJUST IGNITION TIMING TO 10° BTDC
(5) TURN OFF ENGINE AND RESTORE ELECTRICAL CONNECTION

FAST IDLE-DISCONNECT AND PLUG EGR AND CM VACUUM HOSES. ALSO DISCONNECT AND PLUG VOTM (VACUUM OPERATED THROTTLE MODULATOR) HOSE. PUT TRANS IN PARK
(1) START ENGINE THEN SET FAST IDLE SCREW ON HIGHEST STEP OF FAST IDLE CAM
(2) ADJUST IDLE TO 2200 RPM (NOTE: ADJUSTMENT MUST BE DONE ONLY DURING THE PERIOD FROM 20 TO 60 SECONDS AFTER ENGINE START. IF TIME IS EXCEEDED, KICKDOWN AND REPEAT STEP 1)
(3) RECONNECT VACUUM HOSES

CURB IDLE-
(1) RESTART ENGINE. RUN AT 2000 RPM FOR 60 SECONDS. ALLOW IDLE TO STABILIZE FOR 15 SECONDS. PUT TRANS IN DRIVE. THEN ADJUST IDLE TO 550 RPM WITHIN 105 SECONDS OF RESTART. REPEAT RESTART IF 105 SECONDS ARE EXCEEDED
(2) IF RPM IS HIGH, ADJUST BY TURNING VOTM (VACUUM OPERATED THROTTLE MODULATOR) BRACKET ADJUSTING SCREW COUNTERCLOCKWISE. RECHECK RPM BY REPEATING STEP 1
(3) IF RPM IS LOW, SHUT OFF ENGINE. TURN VOTM BRACKET ADJUSTING SCREW ONE FULL TURN CLOCKWISE AND REPEAT STEP 1
(4) IF IDLE RPM ADJUSTMENT IS GREATER THAN 50 RPM, RE-ADJUST TRANSMISSION LINKAGE. SEE SHOP MANUAL

FIRING ORDER 5 4 2 6 3 7 8

THIS VEHICLE CONFORMS TO U.S.E.P.A REGULATIONS APPLICABLE TO 1984 MODEL YEAR NEW MOTOR VEHICLES. COMPLIANCE DEMONSTRATED BOTH ABOVE AND BELOW 4000 FEET

E4AE-9C485-ALM | CATALYST | SPARK PLUG ASF 52 GAP .048-.052 5.0 L 4FM EFM5.0V5HBF7 EGR/EGS/AIP/TWC

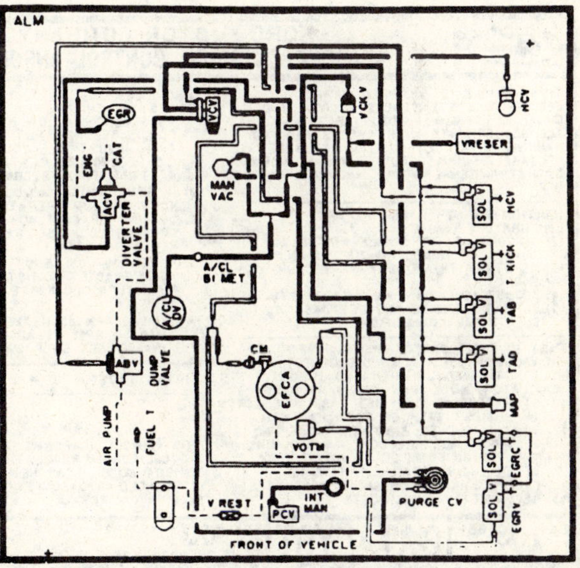

88184GJ4

Fig. 64 Vehicle Emission Label 1984 5.0L engine — 4-22F-R00

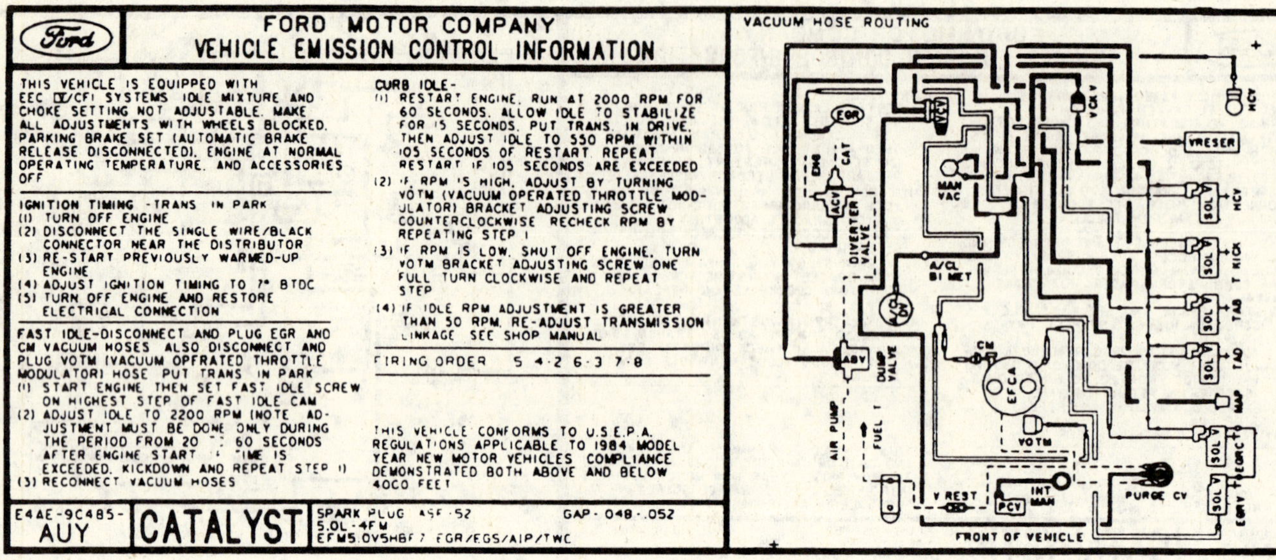

FORD MOTOR COMPANY
VEHICLE EMISSION CONTROL INFORMATION

THIS VEHICLE IS EQUIPPED WITH EEC IV/CFI SYSTEMS. IDLE MIXTURE AND CHOKE SETTING NOT ADJUSTABLE. MAKE ALL ADJUSTMENTS WITH WHEELS BLOCKED, PARKING BRAKE SET (AUTOMATIC BRAKE RELEASE DISCONNECTED), ENGINE AT NORMAL OPERATING TEMPERATURE, AND ACCESSORIES OFF

IGNITION TIMING - TRANS IN PARK
(1) TURN OFF ENGINE
(2) DISCONNECT THE SINGLE WIRE/BLACK CONNECTOR NEAR THE DISTRIBUTOR
(3) RE-START PREVIOUSLY WARMED-UP ENGINE
(4) ADJUST IGNITION TIMING TO 7° BTDC
(5) TURN OFF ENGINE AND RESTORE ELECTRICAL CONNECTION

FAST IDLE-DISCONNECT AND PLUG EGR AND CM VACUUM HOSES. ALSO DISCONNECT AND PLUG VOTM (VACUUM OPERATED THROTTLE MODULATOR) HOSE. PUT TRANS. IN PARK
(1) START ENGINE THEN SET FAST IDLE SCREW ON HIGHEST STEP OF FAST IDLE CAM
(2) ADJUST IDLE TO 2200 RPM (NOTE: ADJUSTMENT MUST BE DONE ONLY DURING THE PERIOD FROM 20 TO 60 SECONDS AFTER ENGINE START. IF TIME IS EXCEEDED, KICKDOWN AND REPEAT STEP 1)
(3) RECONNECT VACUUM HOSES

CURB IDLE-
(1) RESTART ENGINE, RUN AT 2000 RPM FOR 60 SECONDS. ALLOW IDLE TO STABILIZE FOR 15 SECONDS. PUT TRANS. IN DRIVE. THEN ADJUST IDLE TO 550 RPM WITHIN 105 SECONDS OF RESTART. REPEAT RESTART IF 105 SECONDS ARE EXCEEDED
(2) IF RPM IS HIGH, ADJUST BY TURNING VOTM (VACUUM OPERATED THROTTLE MODULATOR) BRACKET ADJUSTING SCREW COUNTERCLOCKWISE. RECHECK RPM BY REPEATING STEP 1
(3) IF RPM IS LOW, SHUT OFF ENGINE, TURN VOTM BRACKET ADJUSTING SCREW ONE FULL TURN CLOCKWISE AND REPEAT STEP 1
(4) IF IDLE RPM ADJUSTMENT IS GREATER THAN 50 RPM, RE-ADJUST TRANSMISSION LINKAGE. SEE SHOP MANUAL

FIRING ORDER 5-4-2-6-3-7-8

THIS VEHICLE CONFORMS TO U.S.E.P.A. REGULATIONS APPLICABLE TO 1984 MODEL YEAR NEW MOTOR VEHICLES. COMPLIANCE DEMONSTRATED BOTH ABOVE AND BELOW 4000 FEET

E4AE-9C485-AUY CATALYST SPARK PLUG ASF-52 GAP .048-.052
5.0L-4FM
EFM5.0V5HBF7 EGR/EGS/AIP/TWC

88184GJ5

Fig. 65 Vehicle Emission Label 1984 5.0L engine — 4-22F-R10

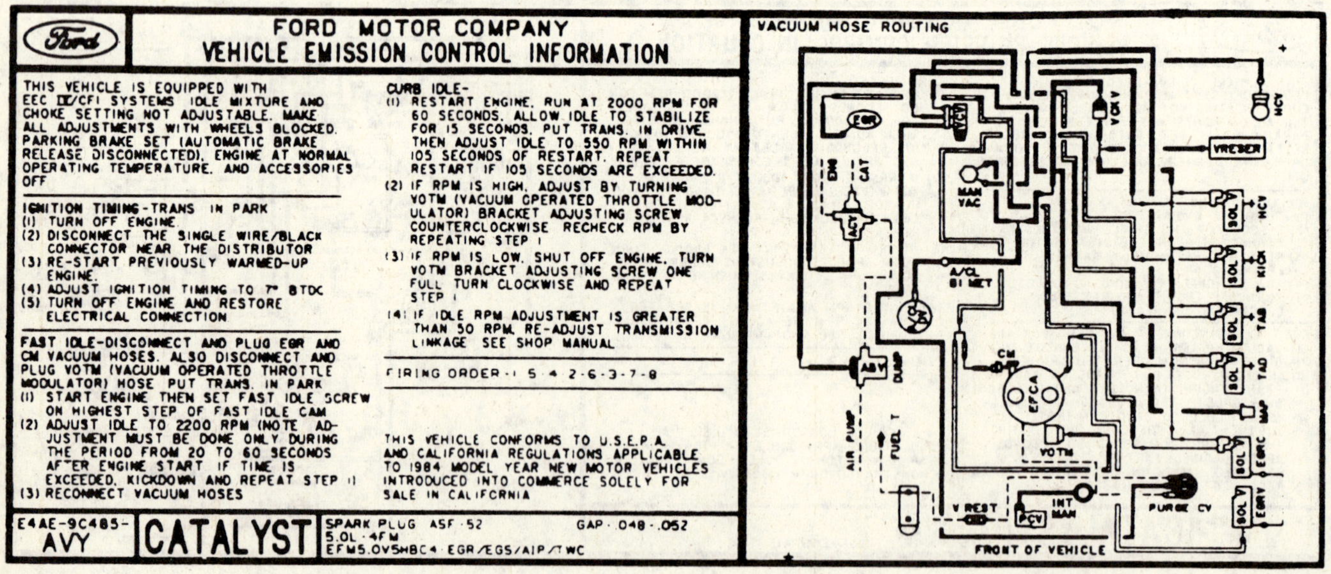

FORD MOTOR COMPANY
VEHICLE EMISSION CONTROL INFORMATION

THIS VEHICLE IS EQUIPPED WITH EEC IV/CFI SYSTEMS. IDLE MIXTURE AND CHOKE SETTING NOT ADJUSTABLE. MAKE ALL ADJUSTMENTS WITH WHEELS BLOCKED, PARKING BRAKE SET (AUTOMATIC BRAKE RELEASE DISCONNECTED), ENGINE AT NORMAL OPERATING TEMPERATURE, AND ACCESSORIES OFF

IGNITION TIMING-TRANS IN PARK
(1) TURN OFF ENGINE
(2) DISCONNECT THE SINGLE WIRE/BLACK CONNECTOR NEAR THE DISTRIBUTOR
(3) RE-START PREVIOUSLY WARMED-UP ENGINE
(4) ADJUST IGNITION TIMING TO 7° BTDC
(5) TURN OFF ENGINE AND RESTORE ELECTRICAL CONNECTION

FAST IDLE-DISCONNECT AND PLUG EGR AND CM VACUUM HOSES. ALSO DISCONNECT AND PLUG VOTM (VACUUM OPERATED THROTTLE MODULATOR) HOSE. PUT TRANS. IN PARK
(1) START ENGINE THEN SET FAST IDLE SCREW ON HIGHEST STEP OF FAST IDLE CAM
(2) ADJUST IDLE TO 2200 RPM (NOTE: ADJUSTMENT MUST BE DONE ONLY DURING THE PERIOD FROM 20 TO 60 SECONDS AFTER ENGINE START. IF TIME IS EXCEEDED, KICKDOWN AND REPEAT STEP 1)
(3) RECONNECT VACUUM HOSES

CURB IDLE-
(1) RESTART ENGINE, RUN AT 2000 RPM FOR 60 SECONDS. ALLOW IDLE TO STABILIZE FOR 15 SECONDS. PUT TRANS. IN DRIVE. THEN ADJUST IDLE TO 550 RPM WITHIN 105 SECONDS OF RESTART. REPEAT RESTART IF 105 SECONDS ARE EXCEEDED.
(2) IF RPM IS HIGH, ADJUST BY TURNING VOTM (VACUUM OPERATED THROTTLE MODULATOR) BRACKET ADJUSTING SCREW COUNTERCLOCKWISE. RECHECK RPM BY REPEATING STEP 1
(3) IF RPM IS LOW, SHUT OFF ENGINE, TURN VOTM BRACKET ADJUSTING SCREW ONE FULL TURN CLOCKWISE AND REPEAT STEP 1
(4) IF IDLE RPM ADJUSTMENT IS GREATER THAN 50 RPM, RE-ADJUST TRANSMISSION LINKAGE. SEE SHOP MANUAL

FIRING ORDER-1-5-4-2-6-3-7-8

THIS VEHICLE CONFORMS TO U.S.E.P.A. AND CALIFORNIA REGULATIONS APPLICABLE TO 1984 MODEL YEAR NEW MOTOR VEHICLES INTRODUCED INTO COMMERCE SOLELY FOR SALE IN CALIFORNIA

E4AE-9C485-AVY CATALYST SPARK PLUG ASF-52 GAP .048-.052
5.0L-4FM
EFM5.0V5HBC4 EGR/EGS/AIP/TWC

88184GJ6

Fig. 66 Vehicle Emission Label 1984 5.0L engine — 4-22T-R10

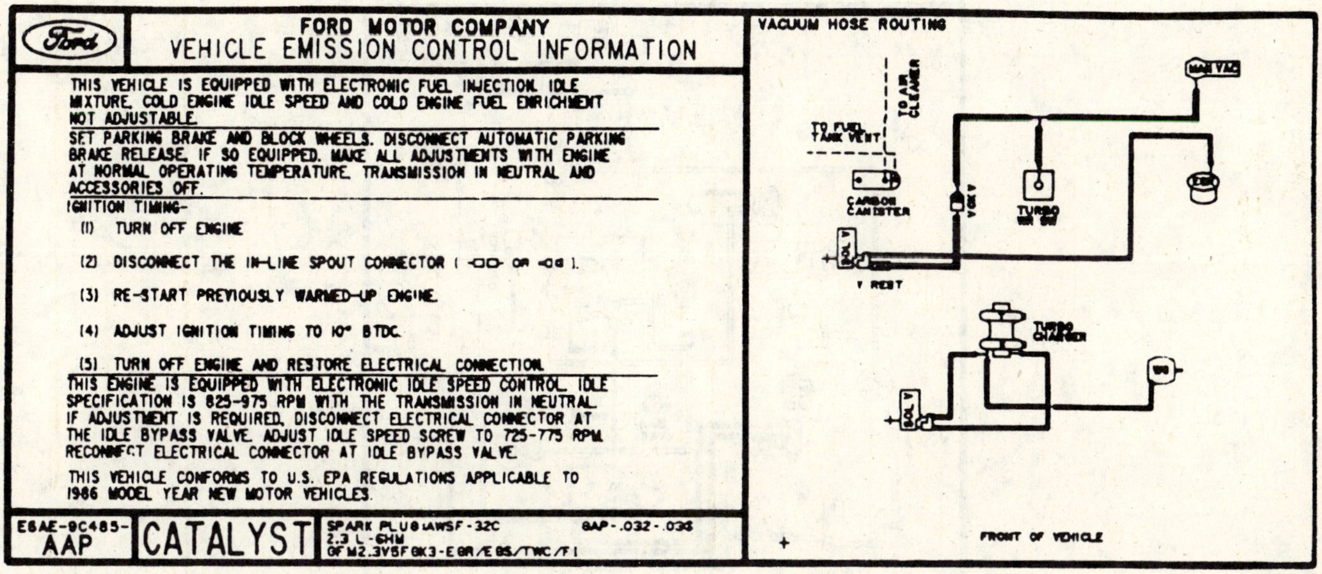
FORD MOTOR COMPANY
VEHICLE EMISSION CONTROL INFORMATION

THIS VEHICLE IS EQUIPPED WITH ELECTRONIC FUEL INJECTION. IDLE MIXTURE, COLD ENGINE IDLE SPEED AND COLD ENGINE FUEL ENRICHMENT NOT ADJUSTABLE.

SET PARKING BRAKE AND BLOCK WHEELS. DISCONNECT AUTOMATIC PARKING BRAKE RELEASE, IF SO EQUIPPED. MAKE ALL ADJUSTMENTS WITH ENGINE AT NORMAL OPERATING TEMPERATURE, TRANSMISSION IN NEUTRAL AND ACCESSORIES OFF.

IGNITION TIMING-

(1) TURN OFF ENGINE

(2) DISCONNECT THE IN-LINE SPOUT CONNECTOR (-□□- OR -□◁).

(3) RE-START PREVIOUSLY WARMED-UP ENGINE.

(4) ADJUST IGNITION TIMING TO 10° BTDC.

(5) TURN OFF ENGINE AND RESTORE ELECTRICAL CONNECTION.

THIS ENGINE IS EQUIPPED WITH ELECTRONIC IDLE SPEED CONTROL. IDLE SPECIFICATION IS 825-975 RPM WITH THE TRANSMISSION IN NEUTRAL. IF ADJUSTMENT IS REQUIRED, DISCONNECT ELECTRICAL CONNECTOR AT THE IDLE BYPASS VALVE. ADJUST IDLE SPEED SCREW TO 725-775 RPM. RECONNECT ELECTRICAL CONNECTOR AT IDLE BYPASS VALVE.

THIS VEHICLE CONFORMS TO U.S. EPA REGULATIONS APPLICABLE TO 1986 MODEL YEAR NEW MOTOR VEHICLES.

E6AE-9C485-AAP | CATALYST | SPARK PLUG AWSF-32C 2.3 L-6HM GFM2.3V5FGK3-EGR/EBS/TWC/FI | GAP-.032-.036

88184GJ7

Fig. 67 Vehicle Emission Label 1985-86 2.3L engine — 5-05E-R00

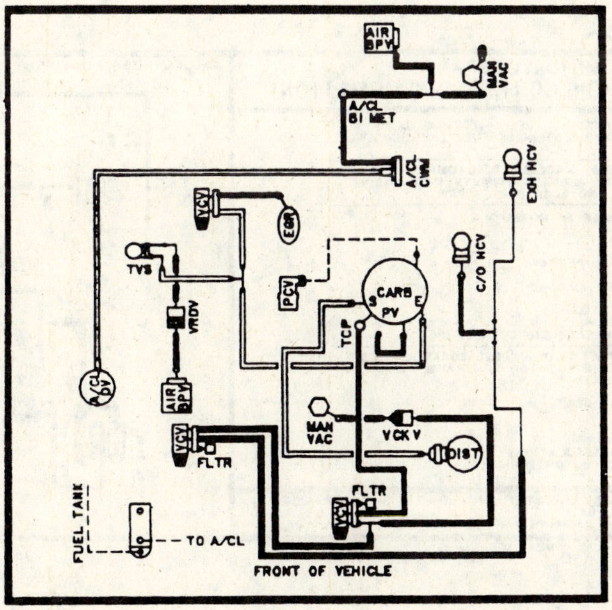

88184GJ9

Fig. 68 Vehicle Emission Label 1986 2.3L T/C engine — 6-06E-R01

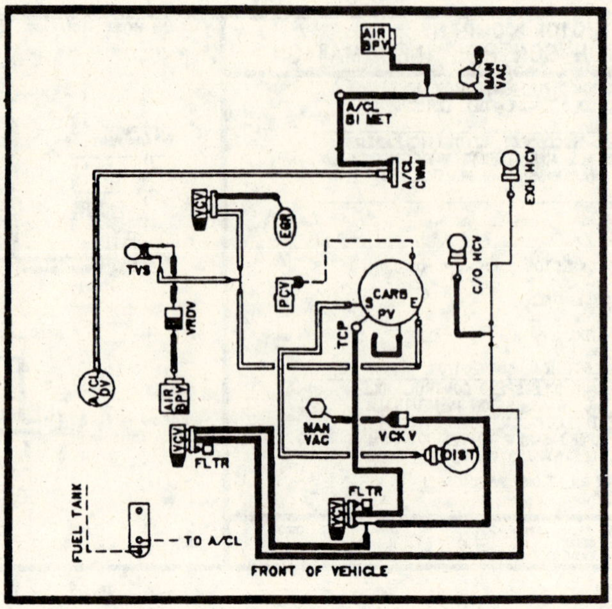

88184GJ9

Fig. 69 Vehicle Emission Label 1985–86 3.8L engine — 5-14G-R10

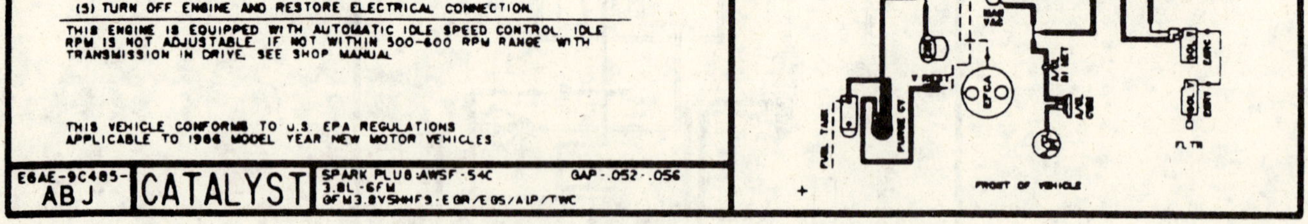
FORD MOTOR COMPANY
VEHICLE EMISSION CONTROL INFORMATION

THIS VEHICLE IS EQUIPPED WITH ELECTRONIC FUEL INJECTION. IDLE MIXTURE, COLD ENGINE IDLE SPEED AND COLD ENGINE FUEL ENRICHMENT NOT ADJUSTABLE.

SET PARKING BRAKE AND BLOCK WHEELS. DISCONNECT AUTOMATIC PARKING BRAKE RELEASE, IF SO EQUIPPED. MAKE ALL ADJUSTMENTS WITH ENGINE AT NORMAL OPERATING TEMPERATURE AND ACCESSORIES OFF

IGNITION TIMING- ADJUST WITH TRANSMISSION IN NEUTRAL
(1) TURN OFF ENGINE
(2) DISCONNECT THE IN-LINE SPOUT CONNECTOR
(3) RE-START PREVIOUSLY WARMED-UP ENGINE.
(4) ADJUST IGNITION TIMING TO 10° BTDC.
(5) TURN OFF ENGINE AND RESTORE ELECTRICAL CONNECTION.

THIS ENGINE IS EQUIPPED WITH AUTOMATIC IDLE SPEED CONTROL. IDLE RPM IS NOT ADJUSTABLE. IF NOT WITHIN 500-600 RPM RANGE WITH TRANSMISSION IN DRIVE, SEE SHOP MANUAL

THIS VEHICLE CONFORMS TO U.S. EPA REGULATIONS APPLICABLE TO 1986 MODEL YEAR NEW MOTOR VEHICLES

E6AE-9C485-ABJ | CATALYST | SPARK PLUG:AWSF-54C 3.8L-6FM GFM3.8V5HHF9-EGR/EOS/AIP/TWC | GAP-.052-.056

88184GK0

Fig. 70 Vehicle Emission Label 1985–86 3.8L engine — 5-16B-R10

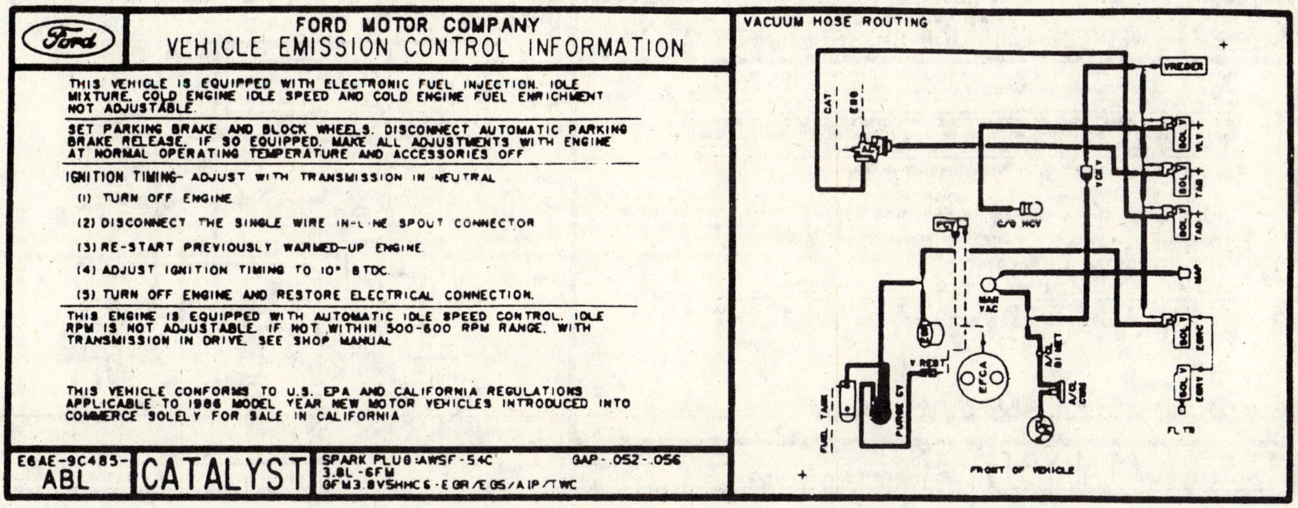

88184GK1

Fig. 71 Vehicle Emission Label 1985-86 3.8L engine — 5-16N-R11

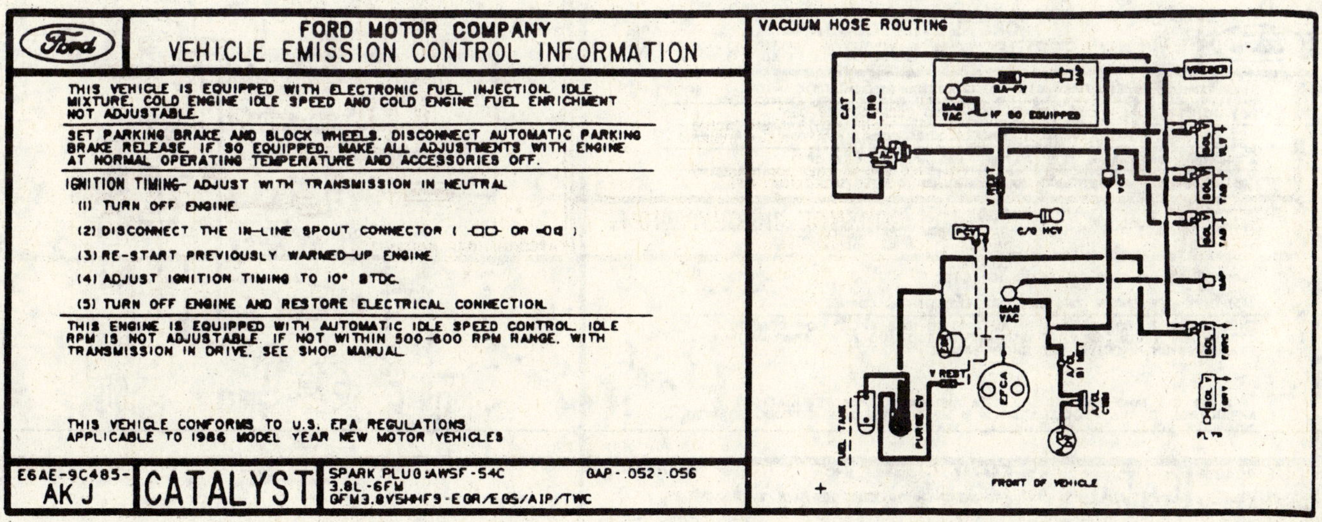

88184GK2

Fig. 72 Vehicle Emission Label 1986 3.8L engine — 6-16B-R02

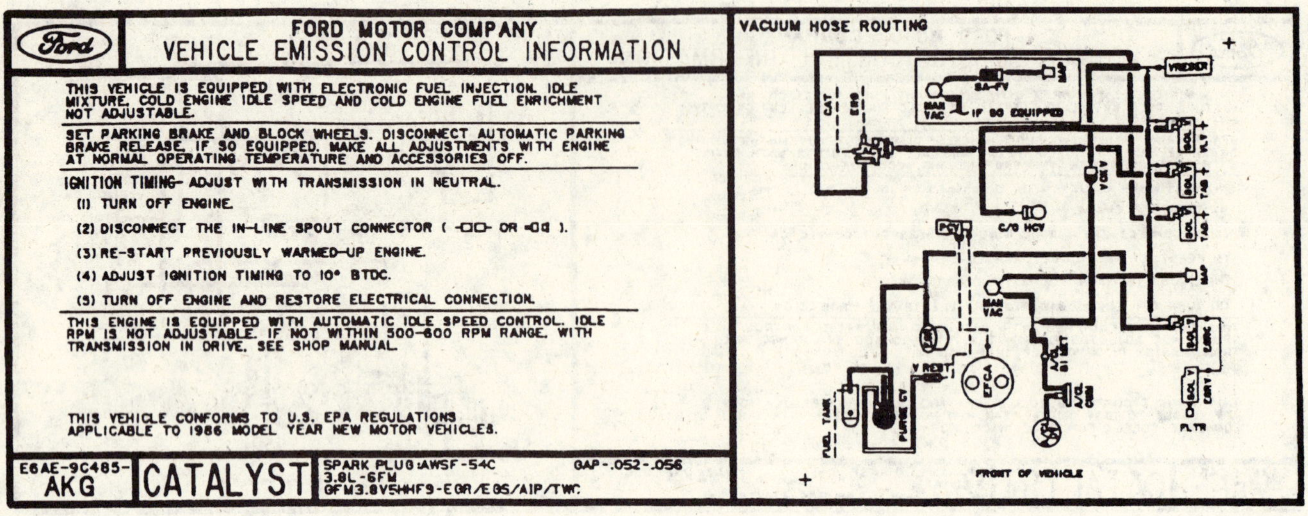

88184GKZ

Fig. 73 Vehicle Emission Label 1986 3.8L engine — 6-16B-R10

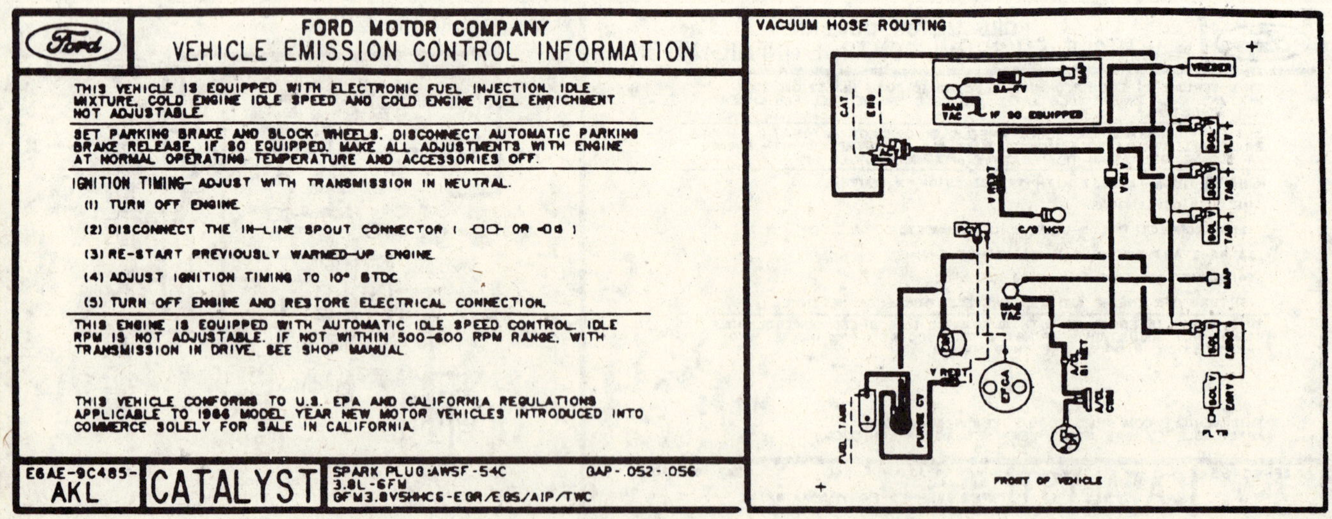

88184GK3

Fig. 74 Vehicle Emission Label 1986 3.8L engine — 6-16N-R02

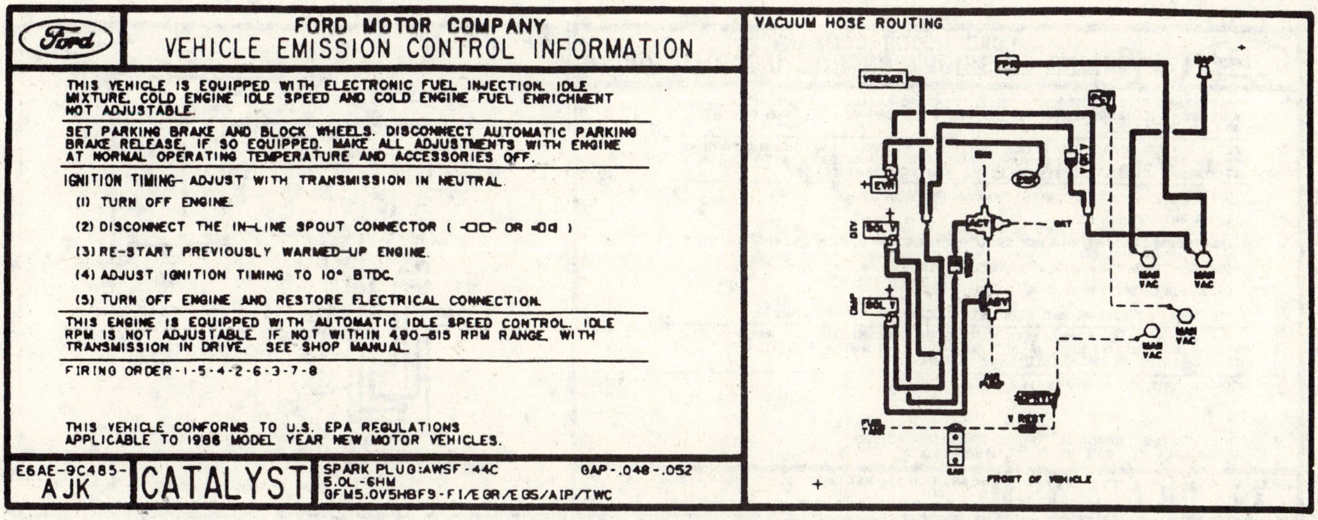

88184GK4

Fig. 75 Vehicle Emission Label 1986 5.0L engine — 6-22D-R22

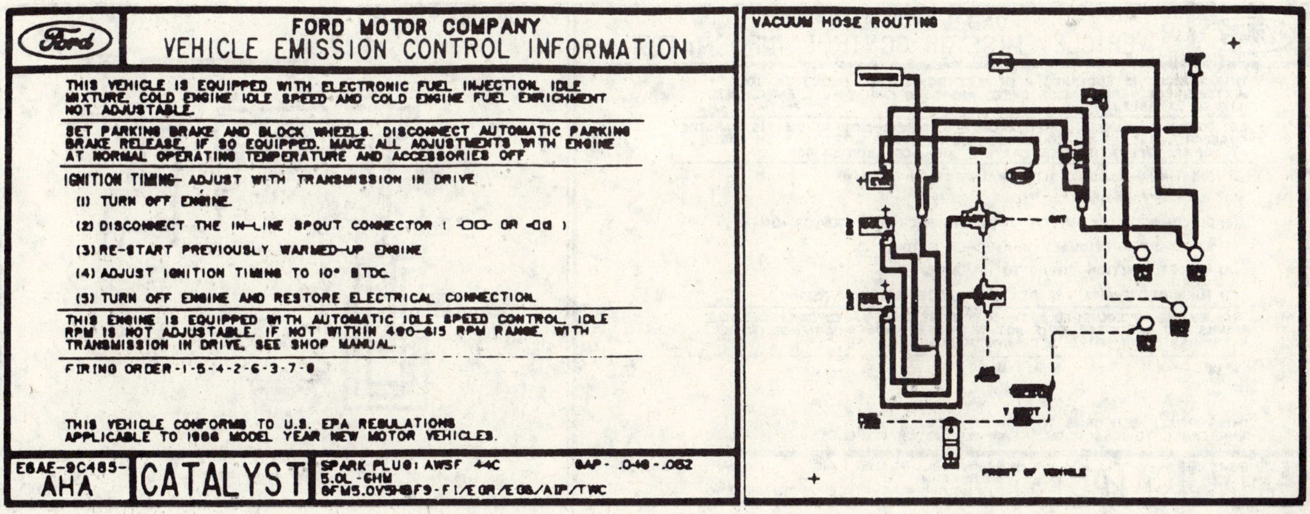

88184GK9

Fig. 76 Vehicle Emission Label 1986 5.0L engine — 6-22D-R11

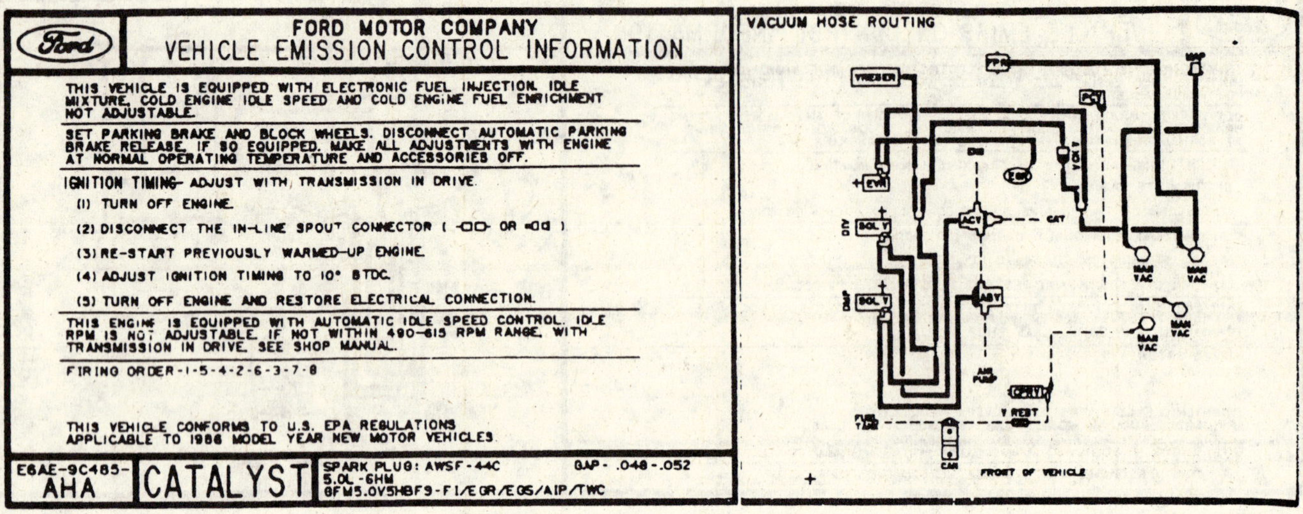

88184GL0

Fig. 77 Vehicle Emission Label 1986 5.0L engine — 6-22D-R10

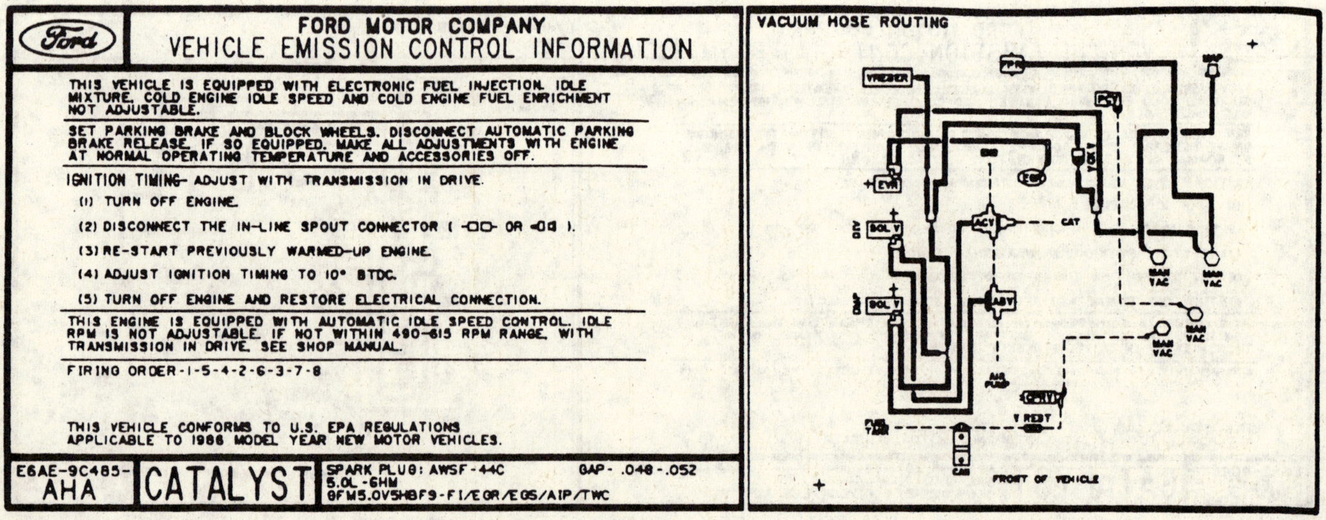

88184GL1

Fig. 78 Vehicle Emission Label 1986 5.0L engine — 6-22F-R00

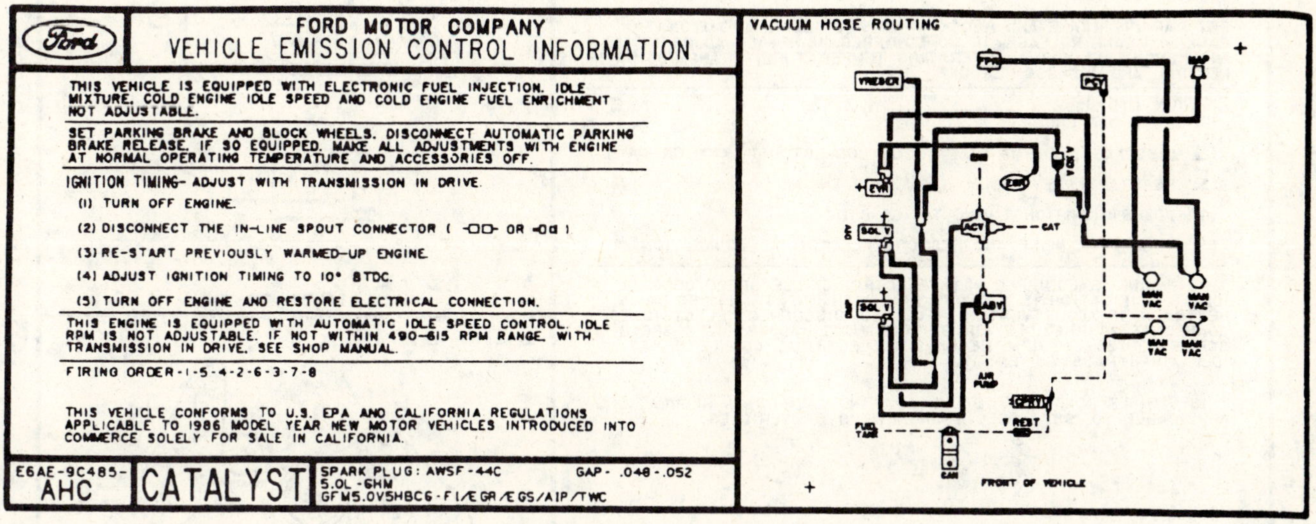

88184GL2

Fig. 79 Vehicle Emission Label 1986 5.0L engine — 6-22T-R00

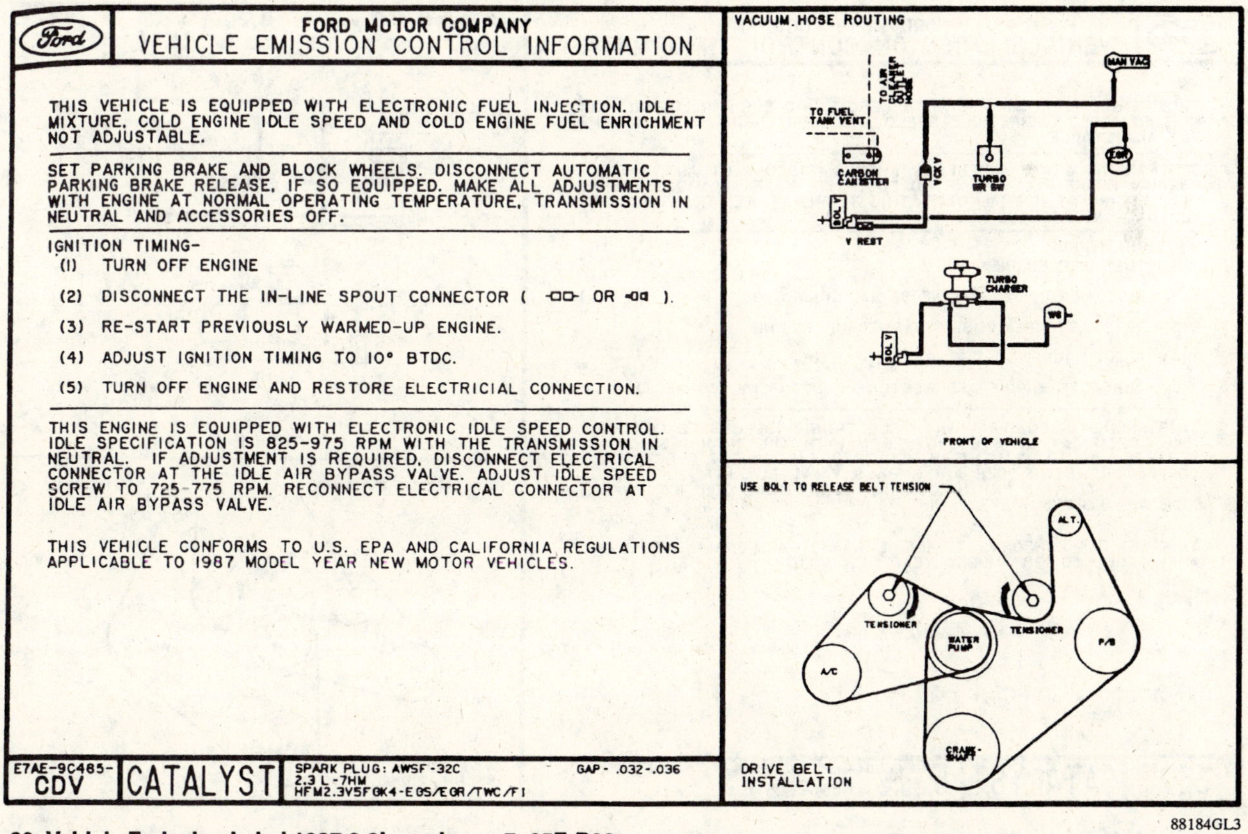

88184GL3

Fig. 80 Vehicle Emission Label 1987 2.3L engine — 7-05E-R00

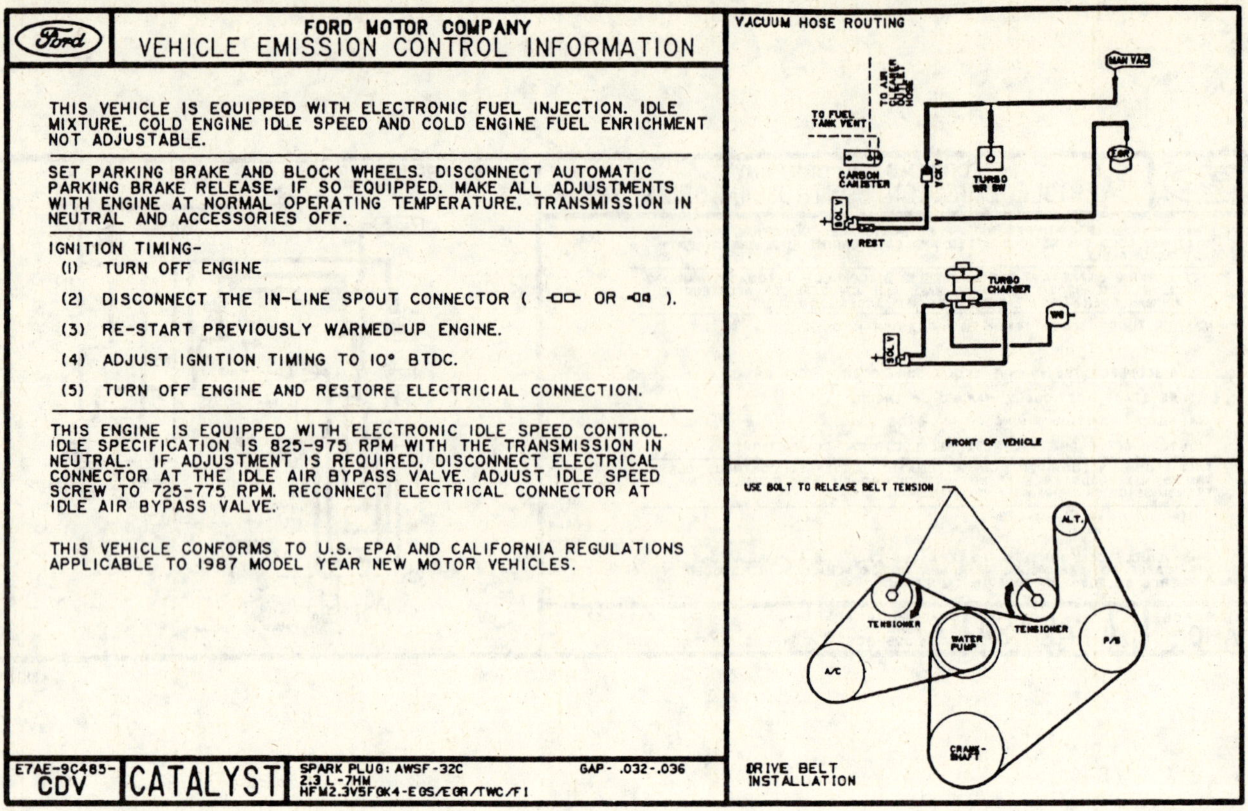

FORD MOTOR COMPANY
VEHICLE EMISSION CONTROL INFORMATION

THIS VEHICLE IS EQUIPPED WITH ELECTRONIC FUEL INJECTION. IDLE MIXTURE, COLD ENGINE IDLE SPEED AND COLD ENGINE FUEL ENRICHMENT NOT ADJUSTABLE.

SET PARKING BRAKE AND BLOCK WHEELS. DISCONNECT AUTOMATIC PARKING BRAKE RELEASE, IF SO EQUIPPED. MAKE ALL ADJUSTMENTS WITH ENGINE AT NORMAL OPERATING TEMPERATURE, TRANSMISSION IN NEUTRAL AND ACCESSORIES OFF.

IGNITION TIMING-
(1) TURN OFF ENGINE
(2) DISCONNECT THE IN-LINE SPOUT CONNECTOR (-□□- OR -□□).
(3) RE-START PREVIOUSLY WARMED-UP ENGINE.
(4) ADJUST IGNITION TIMING TO 10° BTDC.
(5) TURN OFF ENGINE AND RESTORE ELECTRICIAL CONNECTION.

THIS ENGINE IS EQUIPPED WITH ELECTRONIC IDLE SPEED CONTROL. IDLE SPECIFICATION IS 825-975 RPM WITH THE TRANSMISSION IN NEUTRAL. IF ADJUSTMENT IS REQUIRED, DISCONNECT ELECTRICAL CONNECTOR AT THE IDLE AIR BYPASS VALVE. ADJUST IDLE SPEED SCREW TO 725-775 RPM. RECONNECT ELECTRICAL CONNECTOR AT IDLE AIR BYPASS VALVE.

THIS VEHICLE CONFORMS TO U.S. EPA AND CALIFORNIA REGULATIONS APPLICABLE TO 1987 MODEL YEAR NEW MOTOR VEHICLES.

E7AE-9C485-CDV CATALYST SPARK PLUG: AWSF-32C GAP-.032-.036
2.3 L-7HM
HFM2.3V5FGK4-EGS/EGR/TWC/FI

88184GL4

Fig. 81 Vehicle Emission Label 1987 2.3L engine — 7-05E-R10

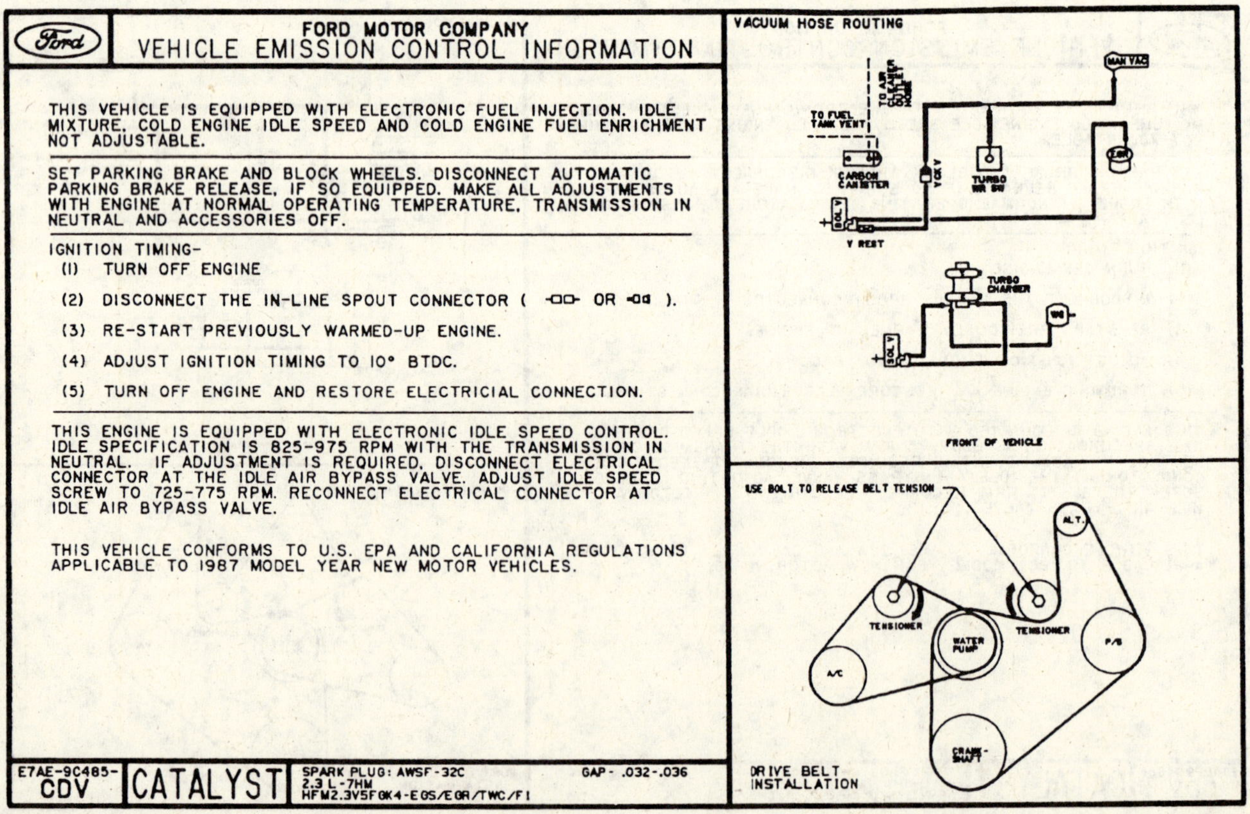

FORD MOTOR COMPANY
VEHICLE EMISSION CONTROL INFORMATION

THIS VEHICLE IS EQUIPPED WITH ELECTRONIC FUEL INJECTION. IDLE MIXTURE, COLD ENGINE IDLE SPEED AND COLD ENGINE FUEL ENRICHMENT NOT ADJUSTABLE.

SET PARKING BRAKE AND BLOCK WHEELS. DISCONNECT AUTOMATIC PARKING BRAKE RELEASE, IF SO EQUIPPED. MAKE ALL ADJUSTMENTS WITH ENGINE AT NORMAL OPERATING TEMPERATURE, TRANSMISSION IN NEUTRAL AND ACCESSORIES OFF.

IGNITION TIMING-
(1) TURN OFF ENGINE
(2) DISCONNECT THE IN-LINE SPOUT CONNECTOR (-□□- OR -□□).
(3) RE-START PREVIOUSLY WARMED-UP ENGINE.
(4) ADJUST IGNITION TIMING TO 10° BTDC.
(5) TURN OFF ENGINE AND RESTORE ELECTRICIAL CONNECTION.

THIS ENGINE IS EQUIPPED WITH ELECTRONIC IDLE SPEED CONTROL. IDLE SPECIFICATION IS 825-975 RPM WITH THE TRANSMISSION IN NEUTRAL. IF ADJUSTMENT IS REQUIRED, DISCONNECT ELECTRICAL CONNECTOR AT THE IDLE AIR BYPASS VALVE. ADJUST IDLE SPEED SCREW TO 725-775 RPM. RECONNECT ELECTRICAL CONNECTOR AT IDLE AIR BYPASS VALVE.

THIS VEHICLE CONFORMS TO U.S. EPA AND CALIFORNIA REGULATIONS APPLICABLE TO 1987 MODEL YEAR NEW MOTOR VEHICLES.

E7AE-9C485-CDV CATALYST SPARK PLUG: AWSF-32C GAP-.032-.036
2.3 L-7HM
HFM2.3V5FGK4-EGS/EGR/TWC/FI

88184GL5

Fig. 82 Vehicle Emission Label 1987 2.3L engine — 7-06E-R10

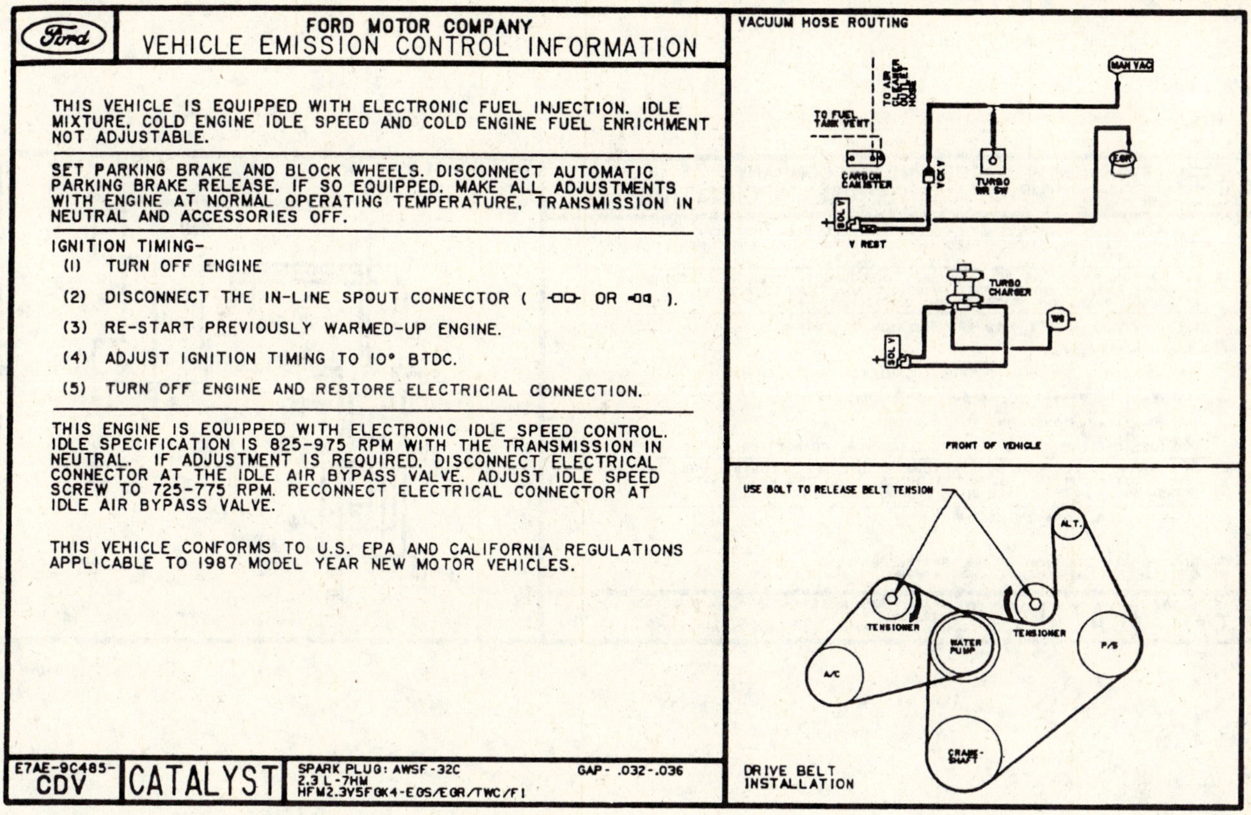

88184GL6

Fig. 83 Vehicle Emission Label 1987 2.3L engine — 7-06E-R11

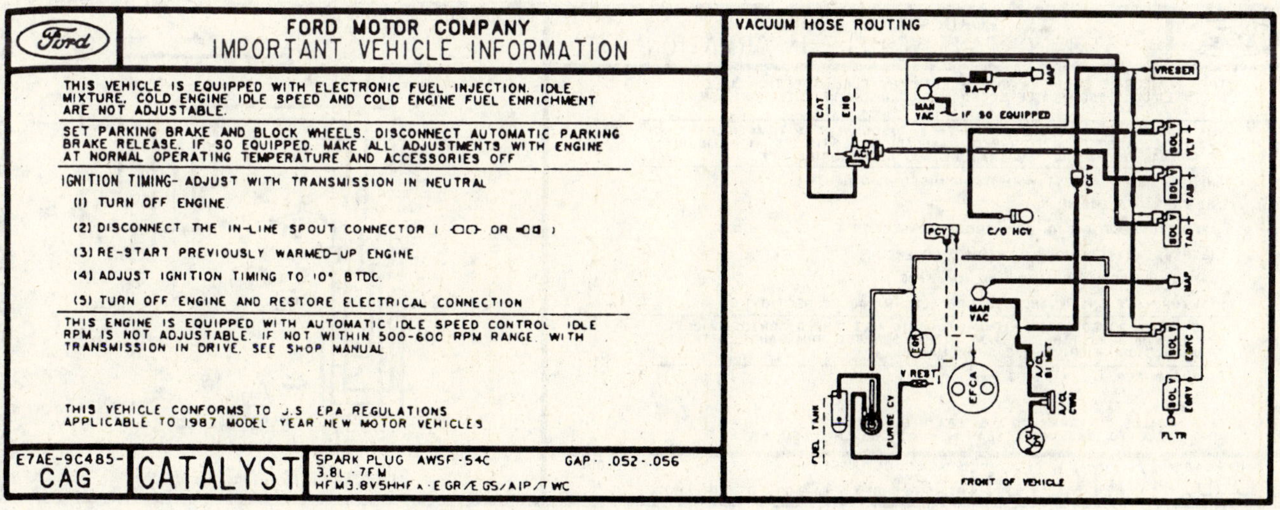

88184GL7

Fig. 84 Vehicle Emission Label 1987 3.8L engine — 7-16A-R00

FORD MOTOR COMPANY
IMPORTANT VEHICLE INFORMATION

THIS VEHICLE IS EQUIPPED WITH ELECTRONIC FUEL INJECTION. IDLE MIXTURE, COLD ENGINE IDLE SPEED AND COLD ENGINE FUEL ENRICHMENT NOT ADJUSTABLE.

SET PARKING BRAKE AND BLOCK WHEELS. DISCONNECT AUTOMATIC PARKING BRAKE RELEASE, IF SO EQUIPPED. MAKE ALL ADJUSTMENTS WITH ENGINE AT NORMAL OPERATING TEMPERATURE AND ACCESSORIES OFF.

IGNITION TIMING- ADJUST WITH TRANSMISSION IN NEUTRAL

(1) TURN OFF ENGINE

(2) DISCONNECT THE IN-LINE SPOUT CONNECTOR (-□□- OR =□□)

(3) RE-START PREVIOUSLY WARMED-UP ENGINE

(4) ADJUST IGNITION TIMING TO 10° BTDC.

(5) TURN OFF ENGINE AND RESTORE ELECTRICAL CONNECTION.

THIS ENGINE IS EQUIPPED WITH AUTOMATIC IDLE SPEED CONTROL. IDLE RPM IS NOT ADJUSTABLE. IF NOT WITHIN 525-650 RPM RANGE, WITH TRANSMISSION IN DRIVE, SEE SHOP MANUAL

FIRING ORDER-1-5-4-2-6-3-7-8

THIS VEHICLE CONFORMS TO U.S. EPA REGULATIONS APPLICABLE TO 1987 MODEL YEAR NEW MOTOR VEHICLES

E7AE-9C485- CAM | CATALYST | SPARK PLUG: AWSF-44C GAP- .048-.052 5.0L-7HM HFM5.0V5HBFX - FI/EGR/EGS/AIP/TWC

VACUUM HOSE ROUTING

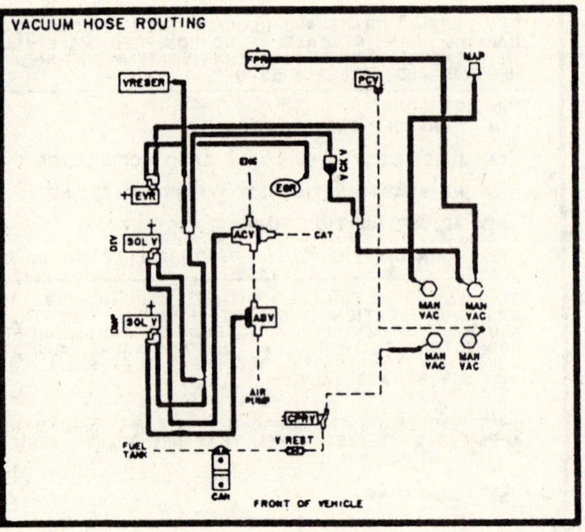

88184GL8

Fig. 85 Vehicle Emission Label 1987 3.8L engine — 7-22D-R00

FORD MOTOR COMPANY
IMPORTANT VEHICLE INFORMATION

THIS VEHICLE IS EQUIPPED WITH ELECTRONIC FUEL INJECTION. IDLE MIXTURE, COLD ENGINE IDLE SPEED AND COLD ENGINE FUEL ENRICHMENT NOT ADJUSTABLE.

SET PARKING BRAKE AND BLOCK WHEELS. DISCONNECT AUTOMATIC PARKING BRAKE RELEASE, IF SO EQUIPPED. MAKE ALL ADJUSTMENTS WITH ENGINE AT NORMAL OPERATING TEMPERATURE AND ACCESSORIES OFF.

IGNITION TIMING- ADJUST WITH TRANSMISSION IN NEUTRAL.

(1) TURN OFF ENGINE

(2) DISCONNECT THE IN-LINE SPOUT CONNECTOR (-□□- OR =□□).

(3) RE-START PREVIOUSLY WARMED-UP ENGINE

(4) ADJUST IGNITION TIMING TO 10° BTDC

(5) TURN OFF ENGINE AND RESTORE ELECTRICAL CONNECTION.

THIS ENGINE IS EQUIPPED WITH AUTOMATIC IDLE SPEED CONTROL. IDLE RPM IS NOT ADJUSTABLE. IF NOT WITHIN 525-650 RPM RANGE, WITH TRANSMISSION IN DRIVE. SEE SHOP MANUAL

FIRING ORDER-1-5-4-2-6-3-7-8

THIS VEHICLE CONFORMS TO U.S. EPA REGULATIONS APPLICABLE TO 1987 MODEL YEAR NEW MOTOR VEHICLES

E7AE-9C485- CDD | CATALYST | SPARK PLUG: AWSF-44C GAP- .048 - .052 5.0L-7HM HFM5.0V5HBFX - FI/EGR/EGS/AIP/TWC

VACUUM HOSE ROUTING

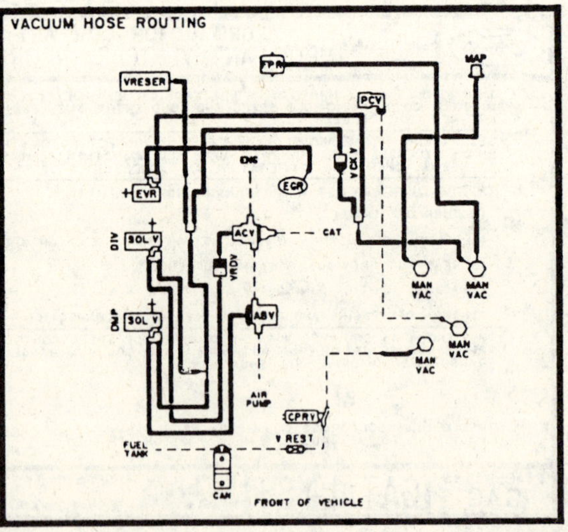

88184GL9

Fig. 86 Vehicle Emission Label 1987 3.8L engine — 7-22F-R00

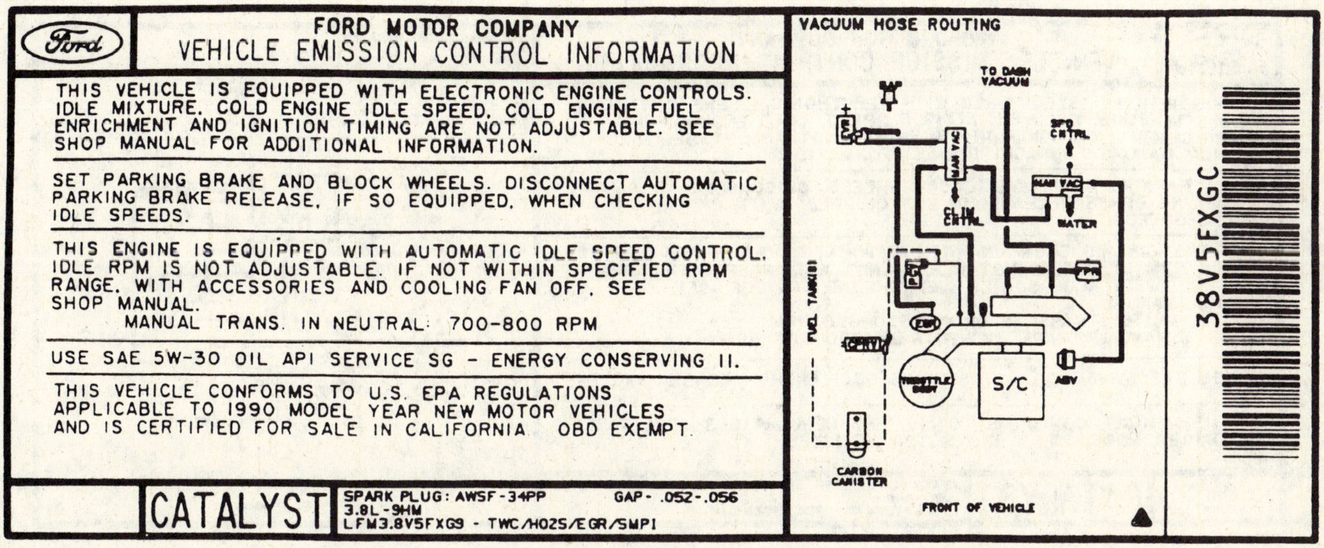

88184GM0

Fig. 87 Vehicle Emission Label 1989-90 3.8L S/C engine — 9-15A-R12

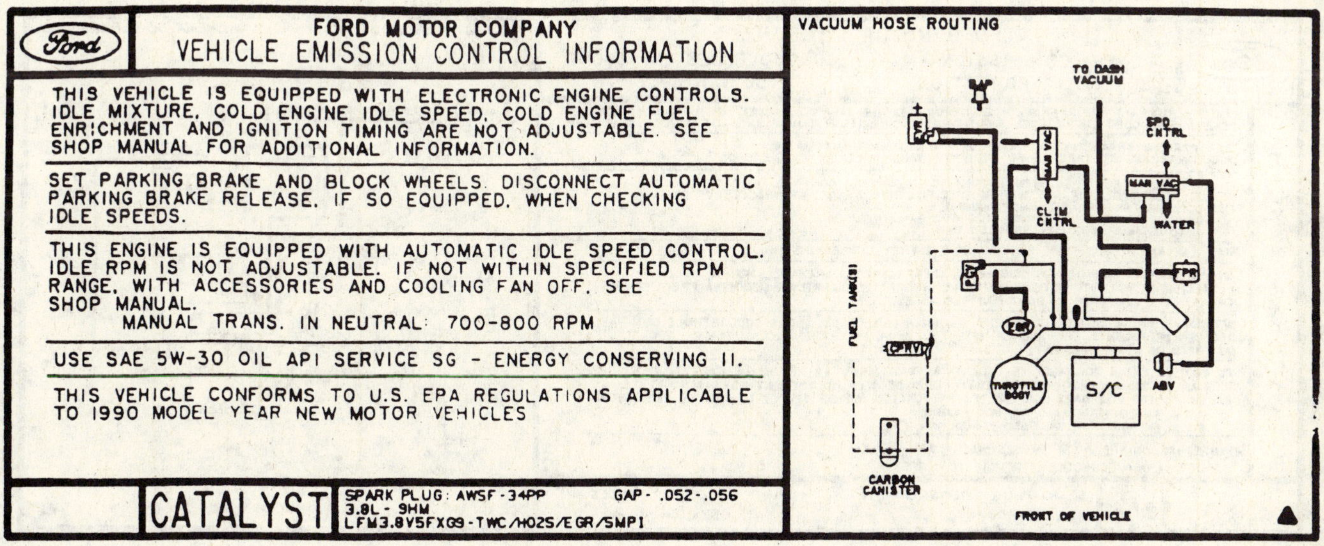

88184GM1

Fig. 88 Vehicle Emission Label 1989-90 3.8L S/C engine — 9-15A-R12

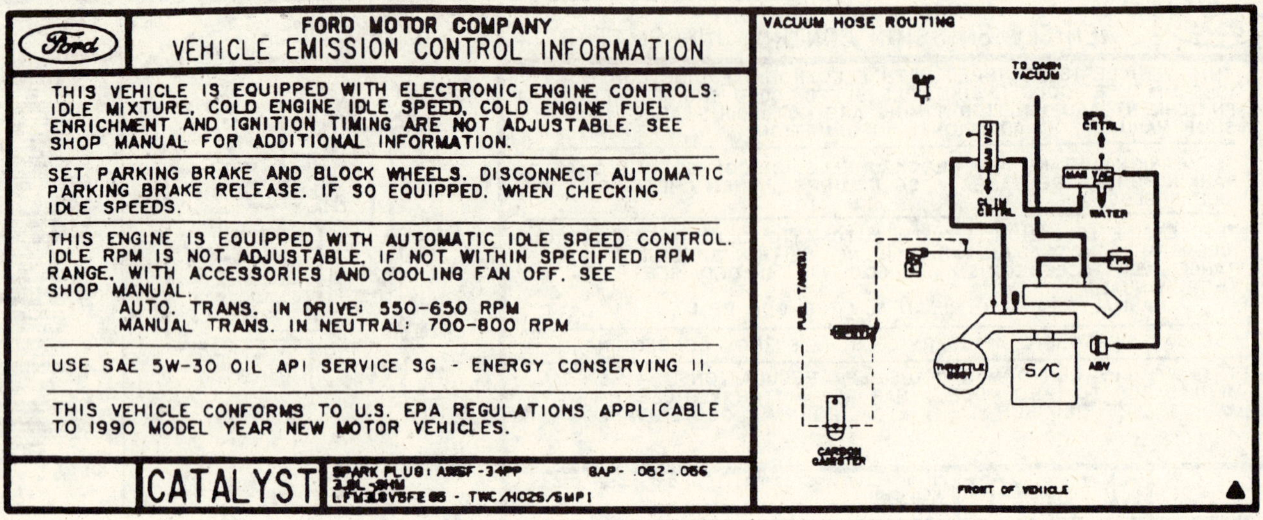

88184GM2

Fig. 89 Vehicle Emission Label 1989-90 3.8L S/C engine — 9-15A-R11

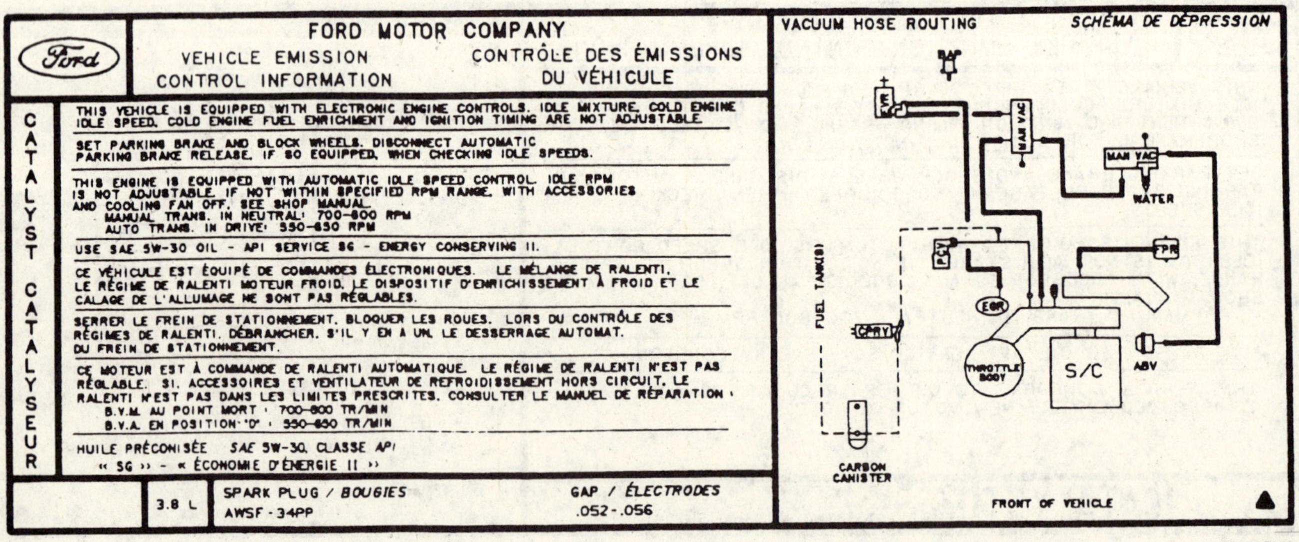

88184GM3

Fig. 90 Vehicle Emission Label 1989-90 3.8L S/C engine — 0-16G-R10

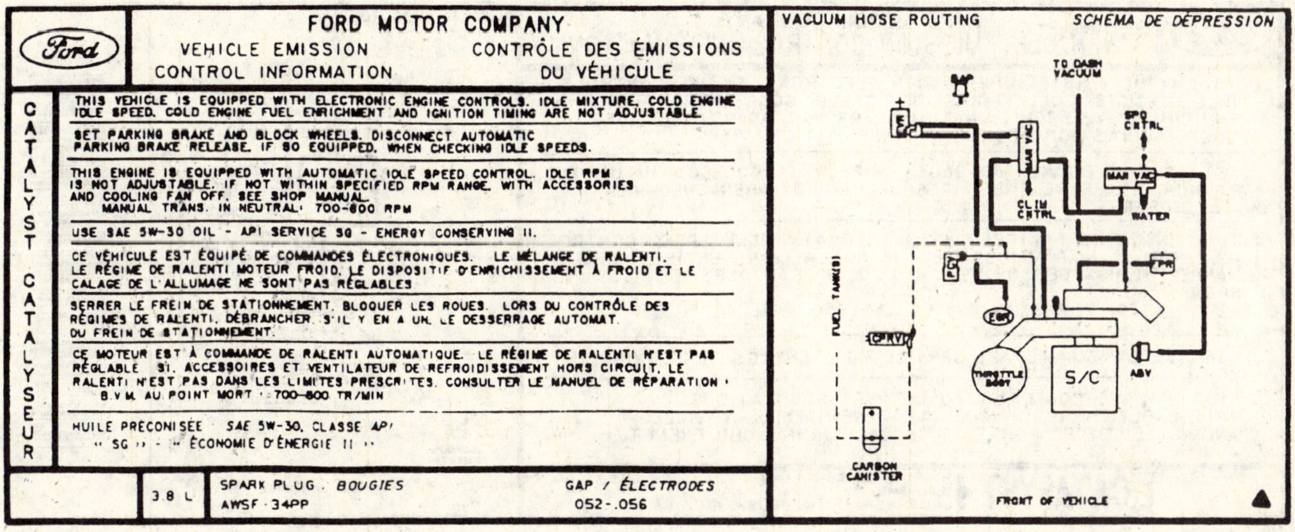
FORD MOTOR COMPANY
VEHICLE EMISSION CONTROL INFORMATION
CONTRÔLE DES ÉMISSIONS DU VÉHICULE

CATALYST CATALYSEUR

THIS VEHICLE IS EQUIPPED WITH ELECTRONIC ENGINE CONTROLS. IDLE MIXTURE, COLD ENGINE IDLE SPEED, COLD ENGINE FUEL ENRICHMENT AND IGNITION TIMING ARE NOT ADJUSTABLE.

SET PARKING BRAKE AND BLOCK WHEELS. DISCONNECT AUTOMATIC PARKING BRAKE RELEASE, IF SO EQUIPPED, WHEN CHECKING IDLE SPEEDS.

THIS ENGINE IS EQUIPPED WITH AUTOMATIC IDLE SPEED CONTROL. IDLE RPM IS NOT ADJUSTABLE. IF NOT WITHIN SPECIFIED RPM RANGE, WITH ACCESSORIES AND COOLING FAN OFF, SEE SHOP MANUAL.
MANUAL TRANS. IN NEUTRAL: 700-800 RPM

USE SAE 5W-30 OIL - API SERVICE SG - ENERGY CONSERVING II.

CE VÉHICULE EST ÉQUIPÉ DE COMMANDES ÉLECTRONIQUES. LE MÉLANGE DE RALENTI, LE RÉGIME DE RALENTI MOTEUR FROID, LE DISPOSITIF D'ENRICHISSEMENT À FROID ET LE CALAGE DE L'ALLUMAGE NE SONT PAS RÉGLABLES

SERRER LE FREIN DE STATIONNEMENT, BLOQUER LES ROUES. LORS DU CONTRÔLE DES RÉGIMES DE RALENTI, DÉBRANCHER, S'IL Y EN A UN, LE DESSERRAGE AUTOMAT. DU FREIN DE STATIONNEMENT.

CE MOTEUR EST À COMMANDE DE RALENTI AUTOMATIQUE. LE RÉGIME DE RALENTI N'EST PAS RÉGLABLE. SI, ACCESSOIRES ET VENTILATEUR DE REFROIDISSEMENT HORS CIRCUIT, LE RALENTI N'EST PAS DANS LES LIMITES PRESCRITES, CONSULTER LE MANUEL DE RÉPARATION :
B.V.M. AU POINT MORT : 700-800 TR/MIN

HUILE PRÉCONISÉE : SAE 5W-30, CLASSE API « SG » - « ÉCONOMIE D'ÉNERGIE II »

3.8 L | SPARK PLUG / BOUGIES AWSF-34PP | GAP / ÉLECTRODES 052-.056

88184GM4

Fig. 91 Vehicle Emission Label 1989–90 3.8L S/C engine — 9-15A-R12

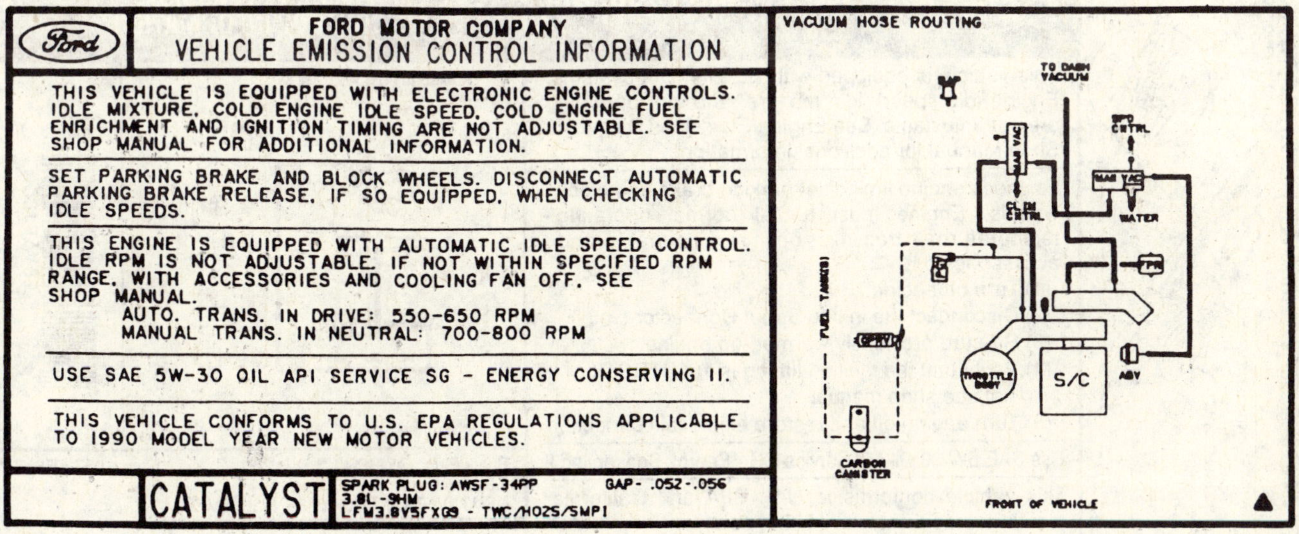
FORD MOTOR COMPANY
VEHICLE EMISSION CONTROL INFORMATION

THIS VEHICLE IS EQUIPPED WITH ELECTRONIC ENGINE CONTROLS. IDLE MIXTURE, COLD ENGINE IDLE SPEED, COLD ENGINE FUEL ENRICHMENT AND IGNITION TIMING ARE NOT ADJUSTABLE. SEE SHOP MANUAL FOR ADDITIONAL INFORMATION.

SET PARKING BRAKE AND BLOCK WHEELS. DISCONNECT AUTOMATIC PARKING BRAKE RELEASE, IF SO EQUIPPED, WHEN CHECKING IDLE SPEEDS.

THIS ENGINE IS EQUIPPED WITH AUTOMATIC IDLE SPEED CONTROL. IDLE RPM IS NOT ADJUSTABLE. IF NOT WITHIN SPECIFIED RPM RANGE, WITH ACCESSORIES AND COOLING FAN OFF, SEE SHOP MANUAL.
AUTO. TRANS. IN DRIVE: 550-650 RPM
MANUAL TRANS. IN NEUTRAL: 700-800 RPM

USE SAE 5W-30 OIL API SERVICE SG - ENERGY CONSERVING II.

THIS VEHICLE CONFORMS TO U.S. EPA REGULATIONS APPLICABLE TO 1990 MODEL YEAR NEW MOTOR VEHICLES.

CATALYST | SPARK PLUG: AWSF-34PP GAP- .052-.056
3.8L-SHM
LFM3.8V5FXG9 - TWC/HO2S/SMPI

88184GM5

Fig. 92 Vehicle Emission Label 1989–90 3.8L S/C engine — 9-16A-R11

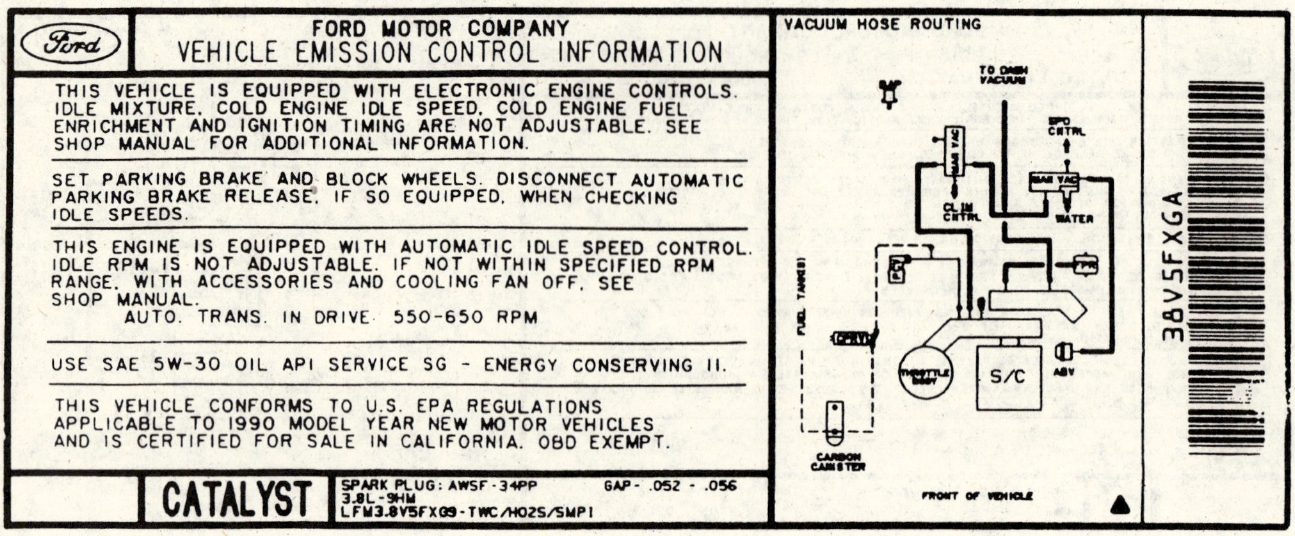

88184GM6

Fig. 93 Vehicle Emission Label 1989-90 3.8L S/C engine — 9-16A-R11

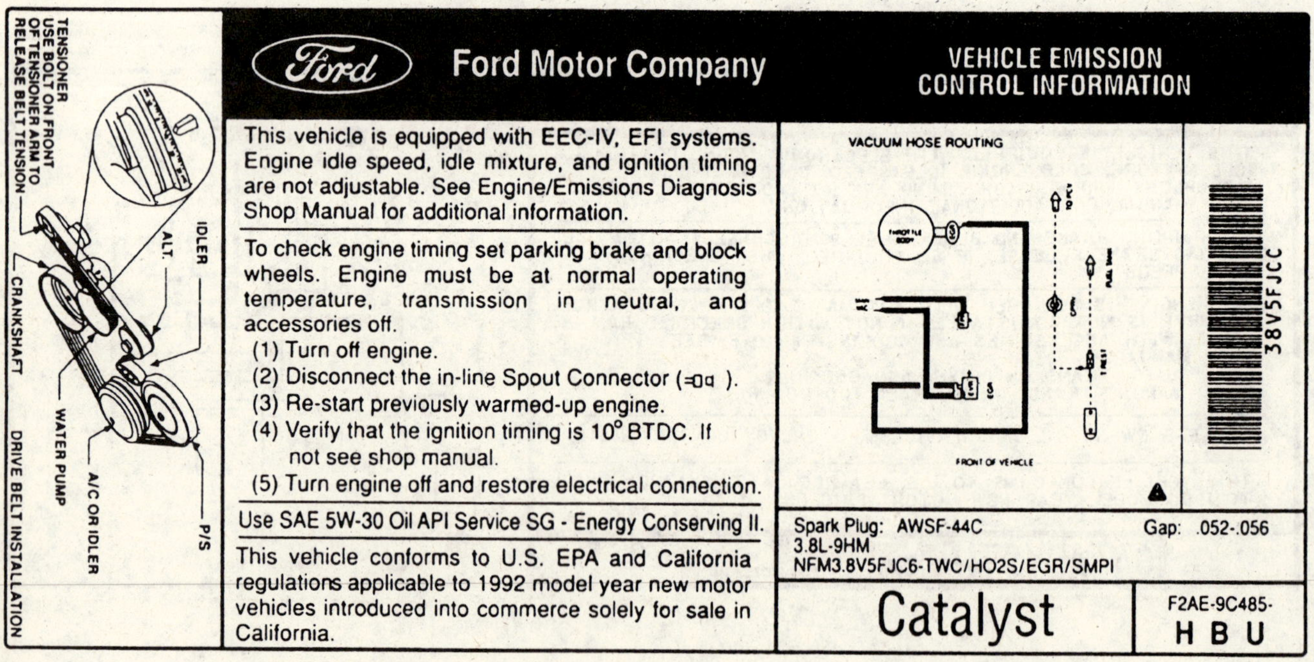

88184GA0

Fig. 94 Vehicle Emission Label 1992 3.8L engine — 2-16Q-R10

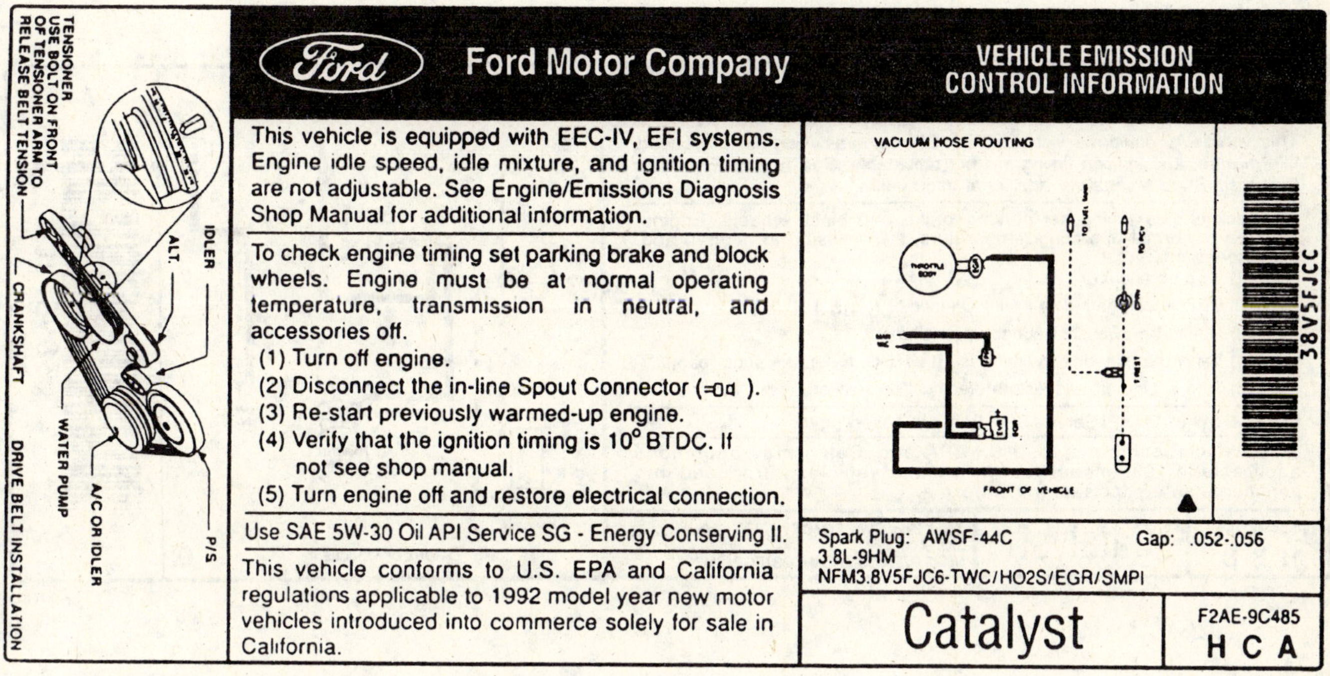

88184GA1

Fig. 95 Vehicle Emission Label 1992 3.8L engine — 2-16R-R05

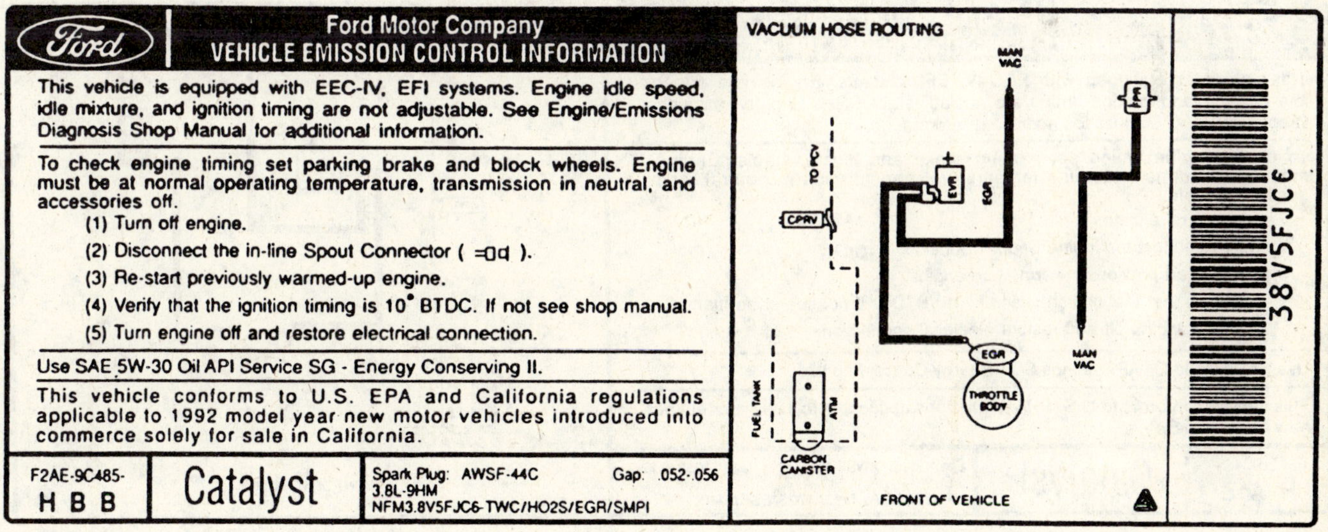

88184GA2

Fig. 96 Vehicle Emission Label 1992 3.8L engine — 2-16T-R00

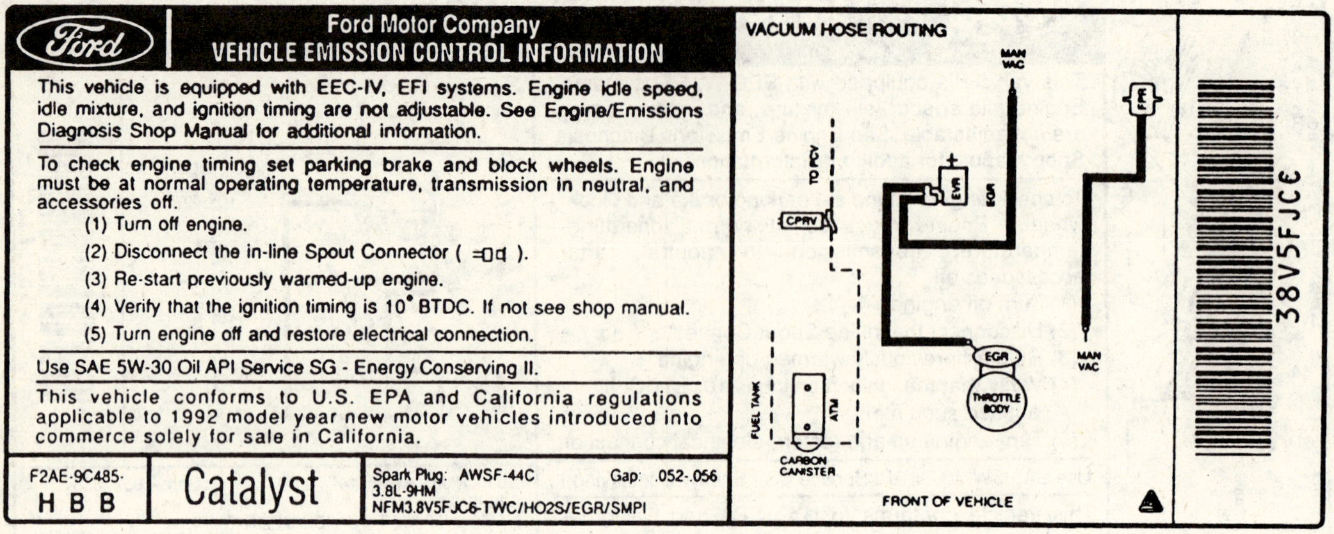

88184GA3

Fig. 97 Vehicle Emission Label 1992 3.8L engine — 2-16T-R10

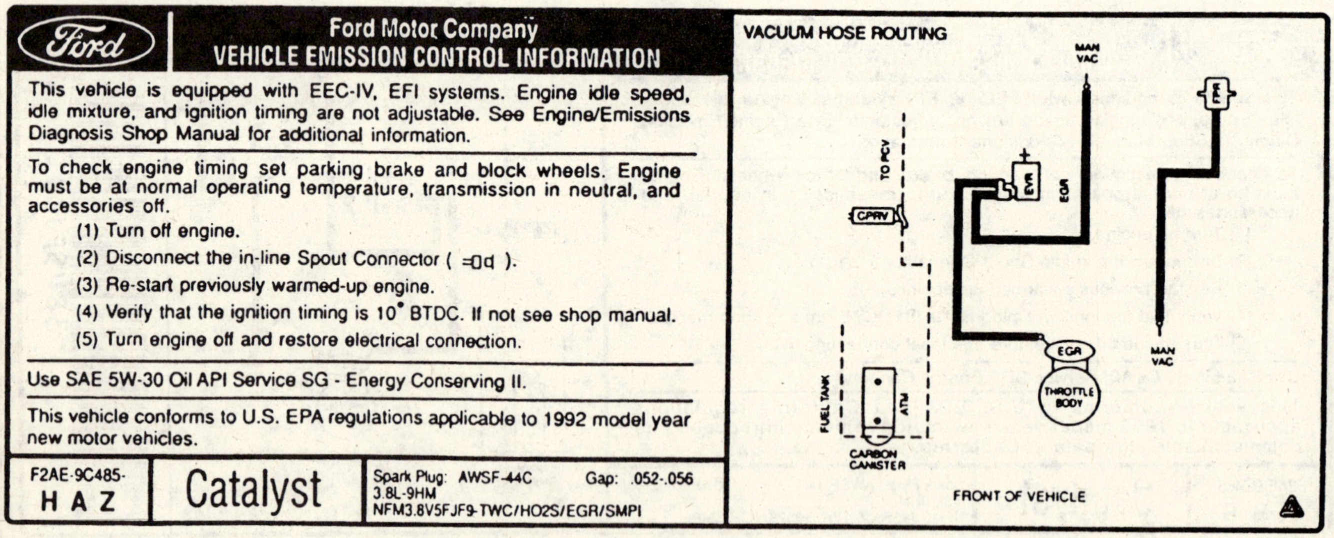

88184GA4

Fig. 98 Vehicle Emission Label 1992 3.8L engine — 2-16F-R00

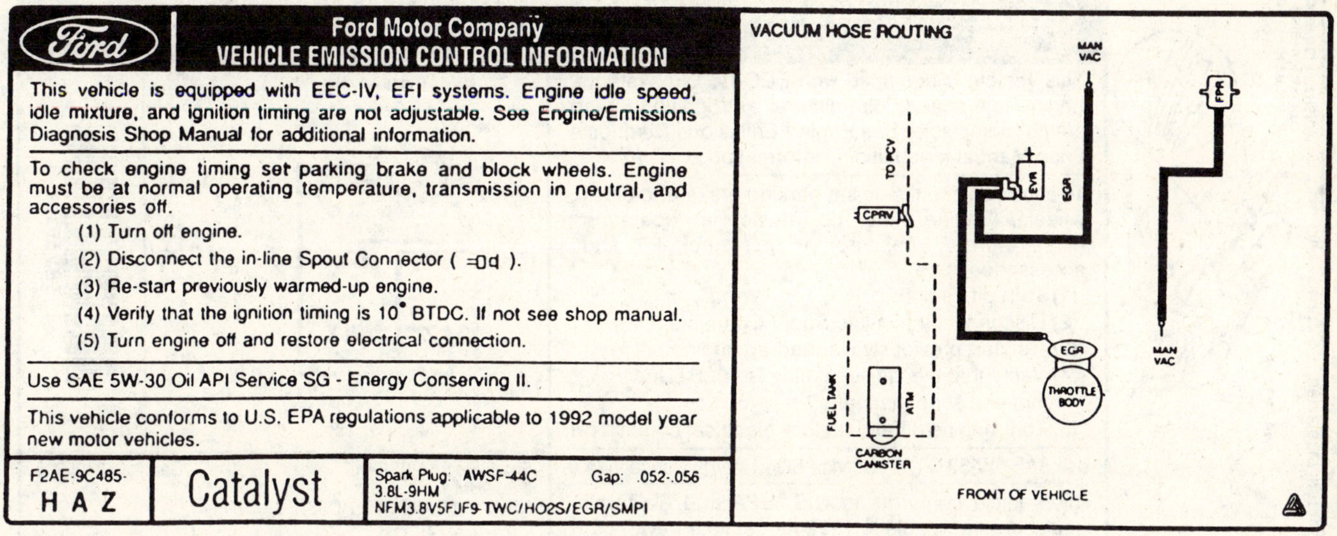

88184GA6

Fig. 99 Vehicle Emission Label 1992 3.8L engine — 2-16F-R10

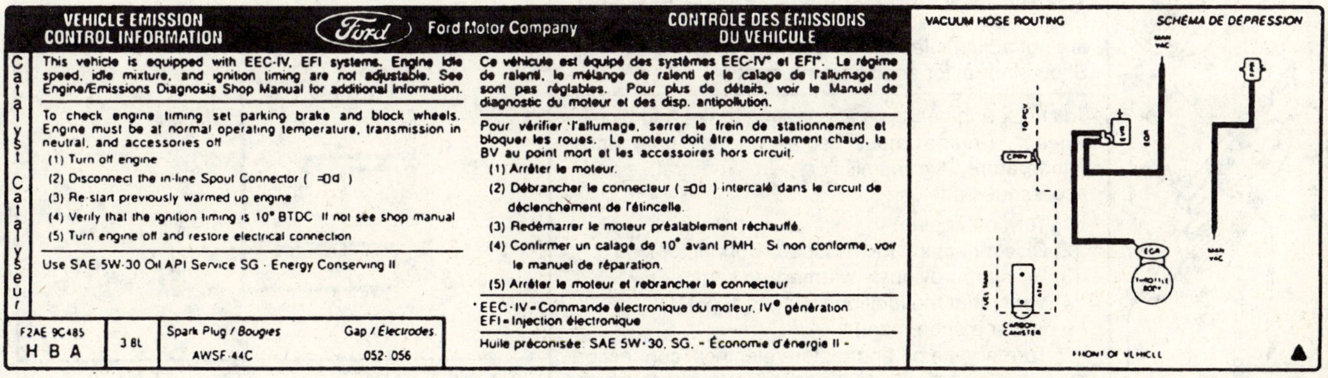

88184GA7

Fig. 100 Vehicle Emission Label 1992 3.8L engine — 2-16F-R10

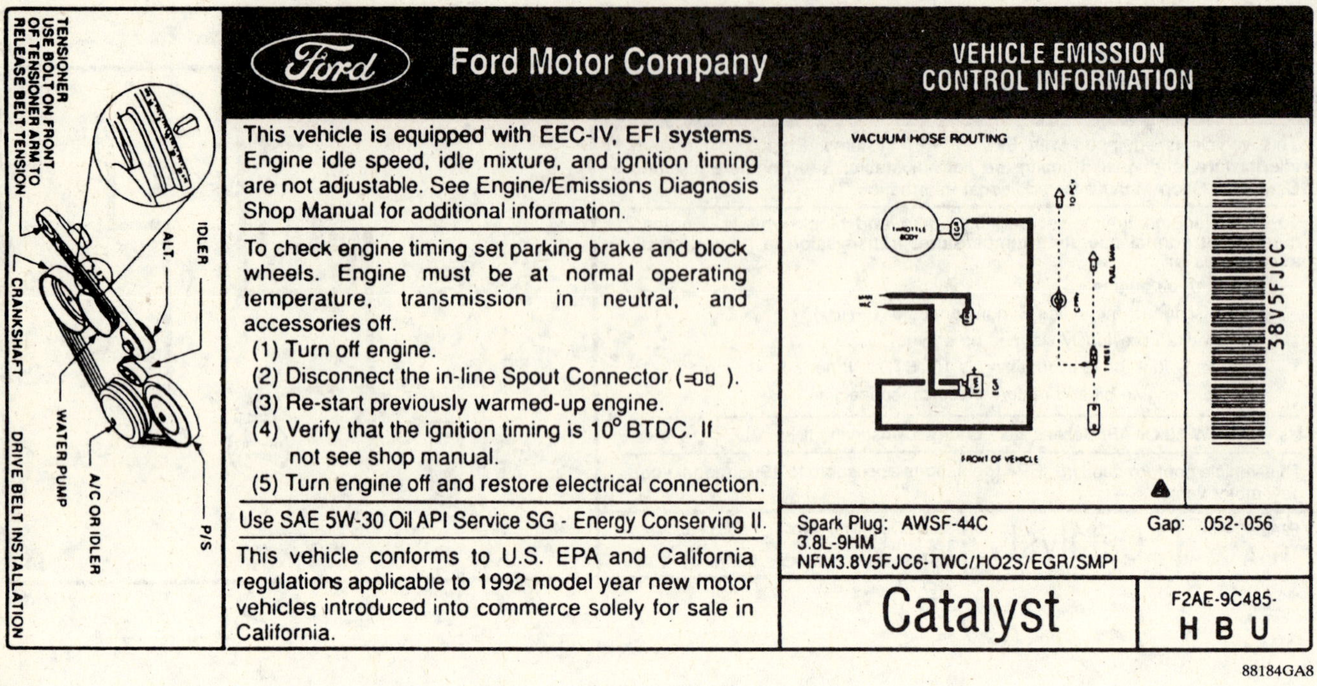

Fig. 101 Vehicle Emission Label 1992 3.8L engine — 2-16Q-R00

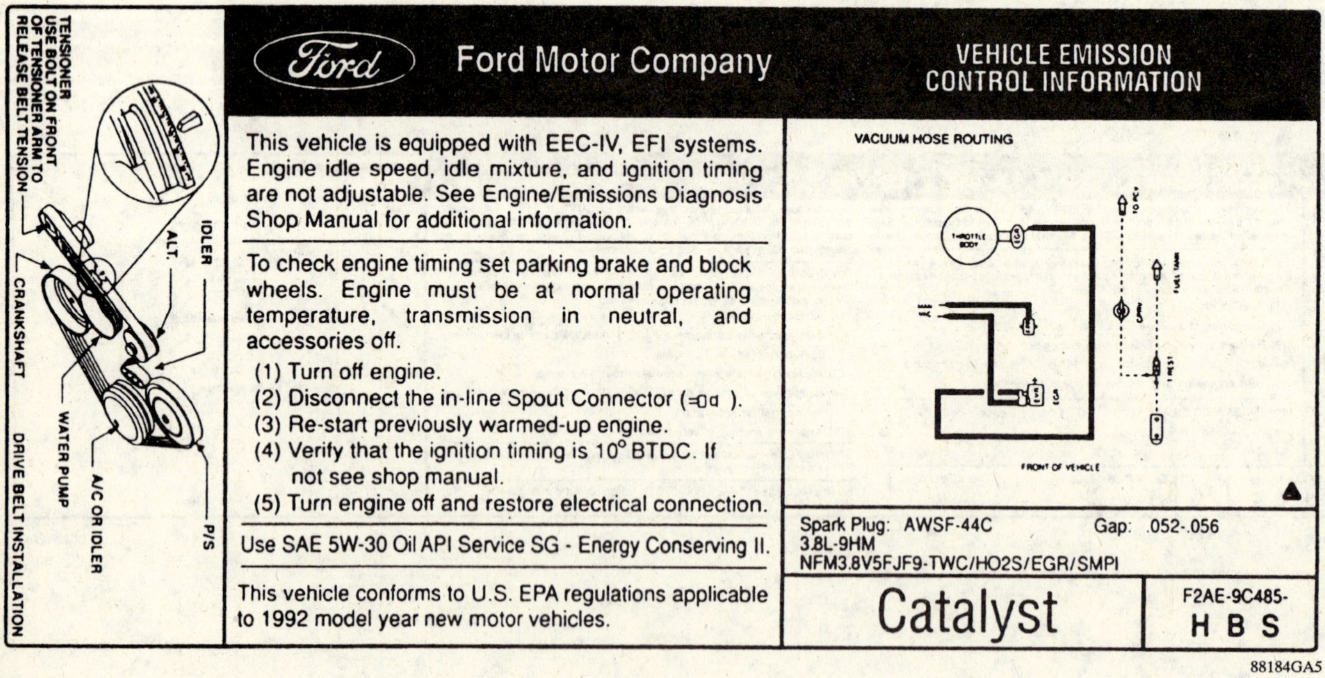

Fig. 102 Vehicle Emission Label 1992 3.8L engine — 2-16C-R00

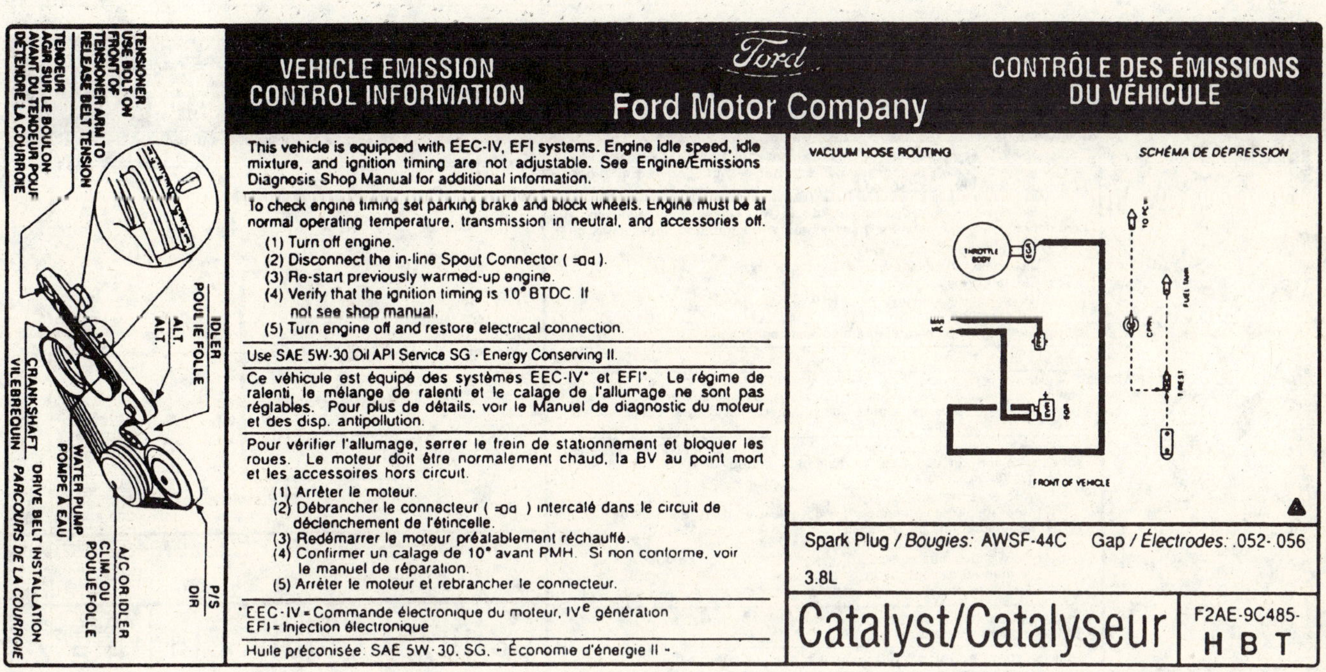

VEHICLE EMISSION CONTROL INFORMATION

Ford

Ford Motor Company

CONTRÔLE DES ÉMISSIONS DU VÉHICULE

This vehicle is equipped with EEC-IV, EFI systems. Engine idle speed, idle mixture, and ignition timing are not adjustable. See Engine/Emissions Diagnosis Shop Manual for additional information.

To check engine timing set parking brake and block wheels. Engine must be at normal operating temperature, transmission in neutral, and accessories off.

(1) Turn off engine.
(2) Disconnect the in-line Spout Connector (=□ɑ).
(3) Re-start previously warmed-up engine.
(4) Verify that the ignition timing is 10° BTDC. If not see shop manual.
(5) Turn engine off and restore electrical connection.

Use SAE 5W-30 Oil API Service SG - Energy Conserving II.

Ce véhicule est équipé des systèmes EEC-IV* et EFI*. Le régime de ralenti, le mélange de ralenti et le calage de l'allumage ne sont pas réglables. Pour plus de détails, voir le Manuel de diagnostic du moteur et des disp. antipollution.

Pour vérifier l'allumage, serrer le frein de stationnement et bloquer les roues. Le moteur doit être normalement chaud, la BV au point mort et les accessoires hors circuit.

(1) Arrêter le moteur.
(2) Débrancher le connecteur (=□ɑ) intercalé dans le circuit de déclenchement de l'étincelle.
(3) Redémarrer le moteur préalablement réchauffé.
(4) Confirmer un calage de 10° avant PMH. Si non conforme, voir le manuel de réparation.
(5) Arrêter le moteur et rebrancher le connecteur.

*EEC-IV = Commande électronique du moteur, IVe génération
EFI = Injection électronique

Huile préconisée: SAE 5W-30, SG, - Économie d'énergie II -.

Spark Plug / *Bougies:* AWSF-44C Gap / *Électrodes:* .052-.056

3.8L

Catalyst/Catalyseur

F2AE-9C485-
H B T

88184GA9

Fig. 103 Vehicle Emission Label 1992 3.8L engine — 2-16C-R00

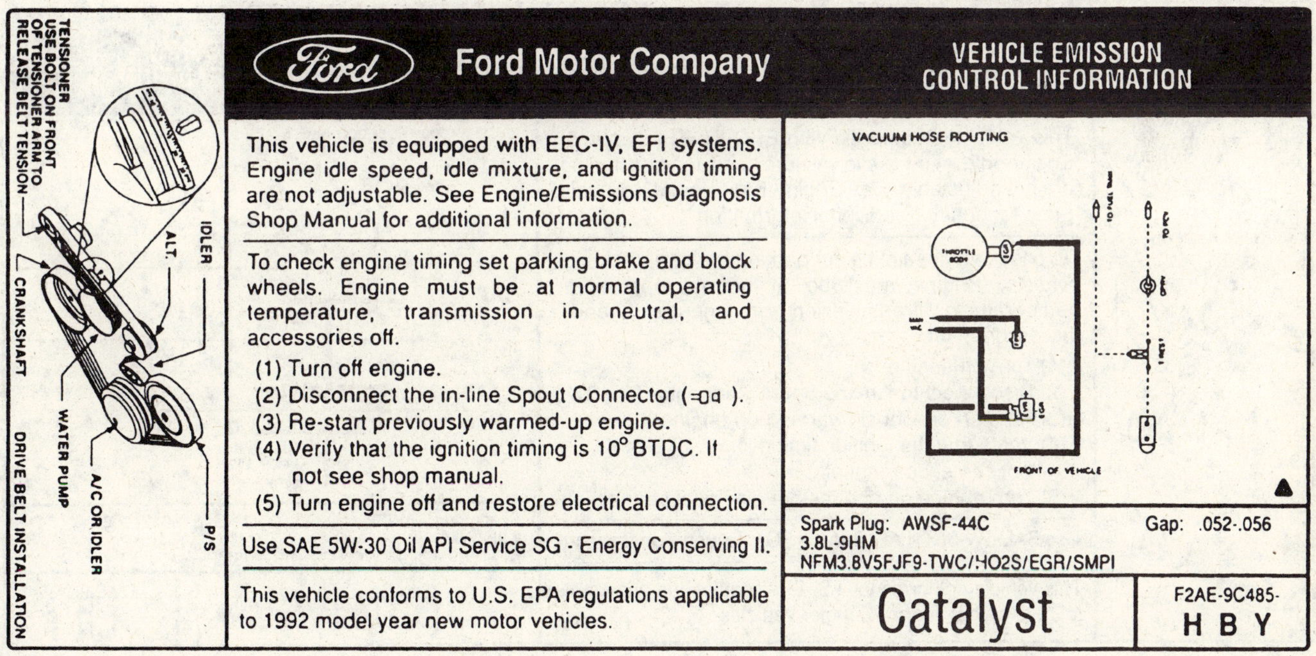

Ford

Ford Motor Company

VEHICLE EMISSION CONTROL INFORMATION

This vehicle is equipped with EEC-IV, EFI systems. Engine idle speed, idle mixture, and ignition timing are not adjustable. See Engine/Emissions Diagnosis Shop Manual for additional information.

To check engine timing set parking brake and block wheels. Engine must be at normal operating temperature, transmission in neutral, and accessories off.

(1) Turn off engine.
(2) Disconnect the in-line Spout Connector (=□ɑ).
(3) Re-start previously warmed-up engine.
(4) Verify that the ignition timing is 10° BTDC. If not see shop manual.
(5) Turn engine off and restore electrical connection.

Use SAE 5W-30 Oil API Service SG - Energy Conserving II.

This vehicle conforms to U.S. EPA regulations applicable to 1992 model year new motor vehicles.

Spark Plug: AWSF-44C Gap: .052-.056
3.8L-9HM
NFM3.8V5FJF9-TWC/HO2S/EGR/SMPI

Catalyst

F2AE-9C485-
H B Y

88184GB0

Fig. 104 Vehicle Emission Label 1992 3.8L engine — 2-16D-R05

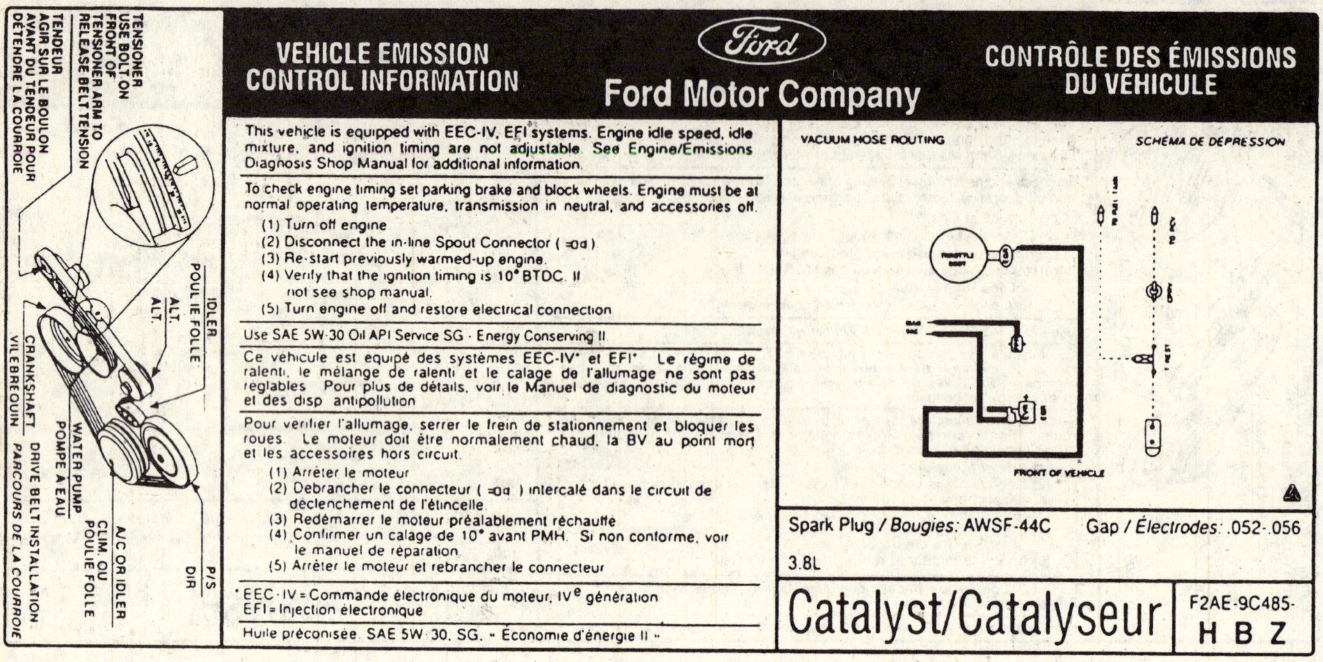

88184GB1

Fig. 105 Vehicle Emission Label 1992 3.8L engine — 2-16D-R05

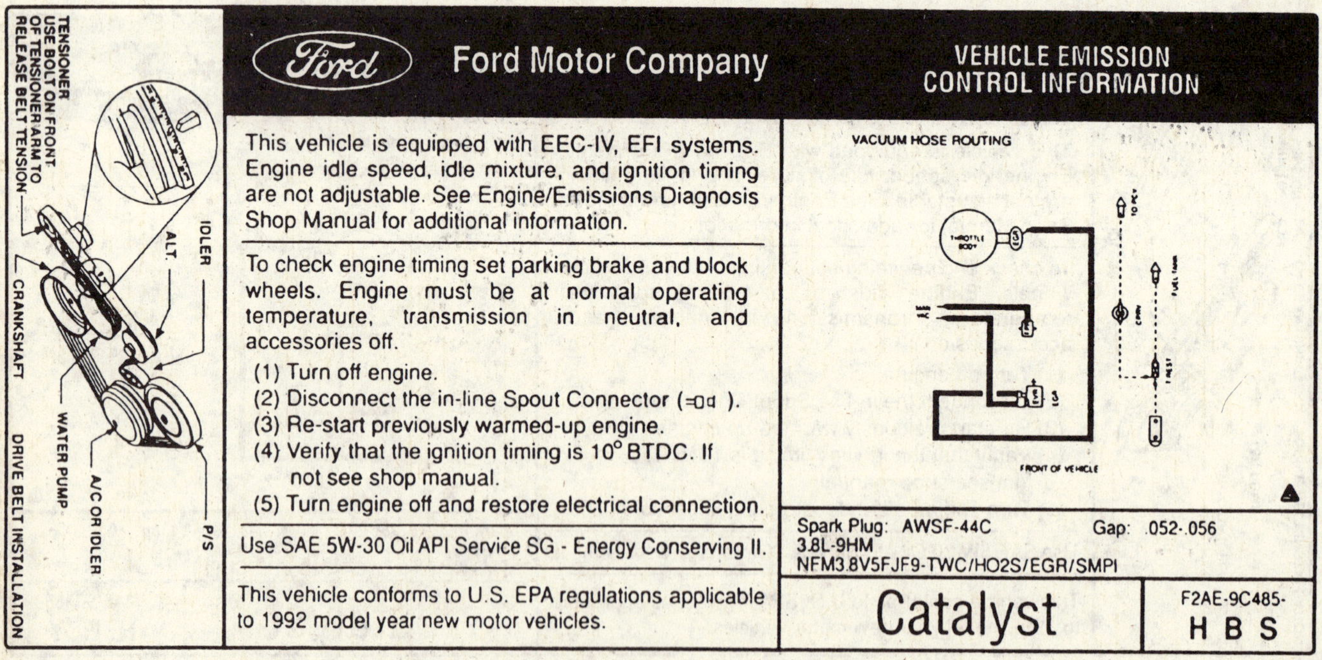

88184GB2

Fig. 106 Vehicle Emission Label 1992 3.8L engine — 2-16B-R00

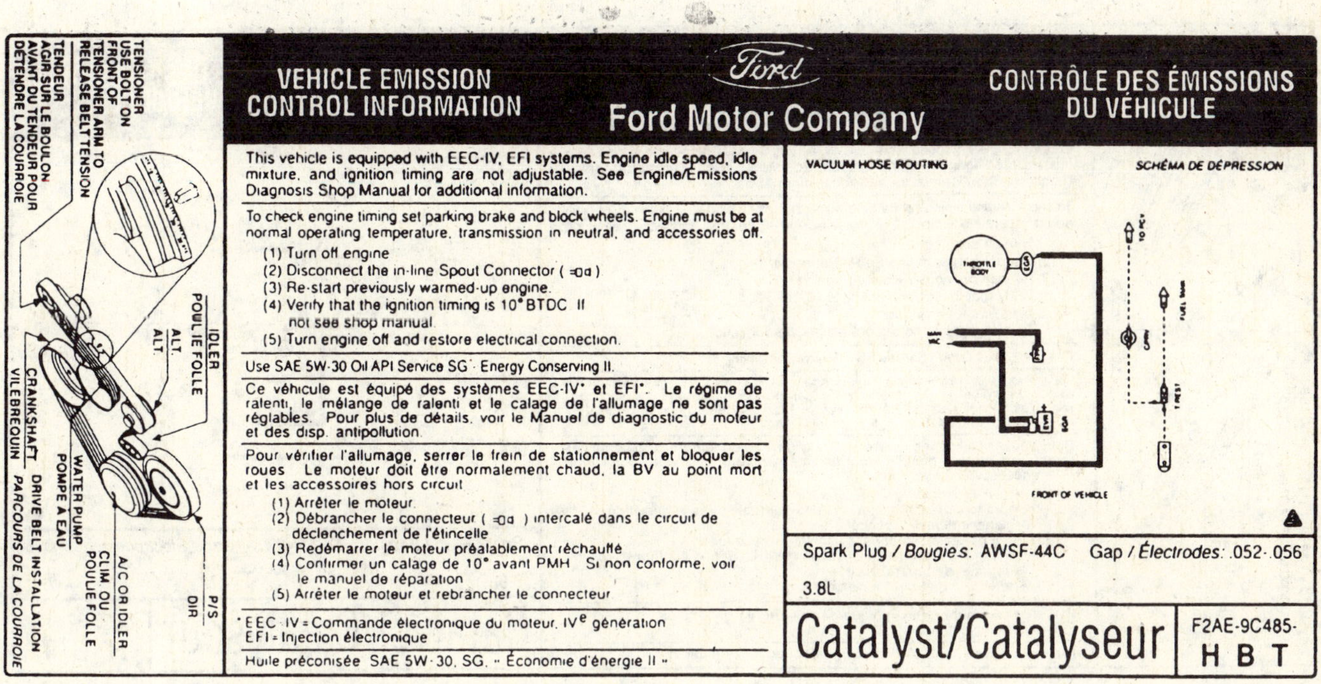
VEHICLE EMISSION CONTROL INFORMATION

Ford Motor Company

CONTRÔLE DES ÉMISSIONS DU VÉHICULE

This vehicle is equipped with EEC-IV, EFI systems. Engine idle speed, idle mixture, and ignition timing are not adjustable. See Engine/Emissions Diagnosis Shop Manual for additional information.

To check engine timing set parking brake and block wheels. Engine must be at normal operating temperature, transmission in neutral, and accessories off.

(1) Turn off engine
(2) Disconnect the in-line Spout Connector (=Dd)
(3) Re-start previously warmed-up engine.
(4) Verify that the ignition timing is 10° BTDC If not see shop manual.
(5) Turn engine off and restore electrical connection.

Use SAE 5W-30 Oil API Service SG · Energy Conserving II.

Ce véhicule est équipé des systèmes EEC-IV* et EFI*. Le régime de ralenti, le mélange de ralenti et le calage de l'allumage ne sont pas réglables. Pour plus de détails, voir le Manuel de diagnostic du moteur et des disp. antipollution.

Pour vérifier l'allumage, serrer le frein de stationnement et bloquer les roues. Le moteur doit être normalement chaud, la BV au point mort et les accessoires hors circuit.

(1) Arrêter le moteur.
(2) Débrancher le connecteur (=Dd) intercalé dans le circuit de déclenchement de l'étincelle
(3) Redémarrer le moteur préalablement réchauffé.
(4) Confirmer un calage de 10° avant PMH. Si non conforme, voir le manuel de réparation
(5) Arrêter le moteur et rebrancher le connecteur

*EEC-IV = Commande électronique du moteur, IVe génération
EFI = Injection électronique

Huile préconisée SAE 5W-30, SG, « Économie d'énergie II »

Spark Plug / *Bougies*: AWSF-44C Gap / *Électrodes*: .052-.056

3.8L

Catalyst/Catalyseur

F2AE-9C485-
H B T

88184GB3

Fig. 107 Vehicle Emission Label 1992 3.8L engine — 2-16B-R00

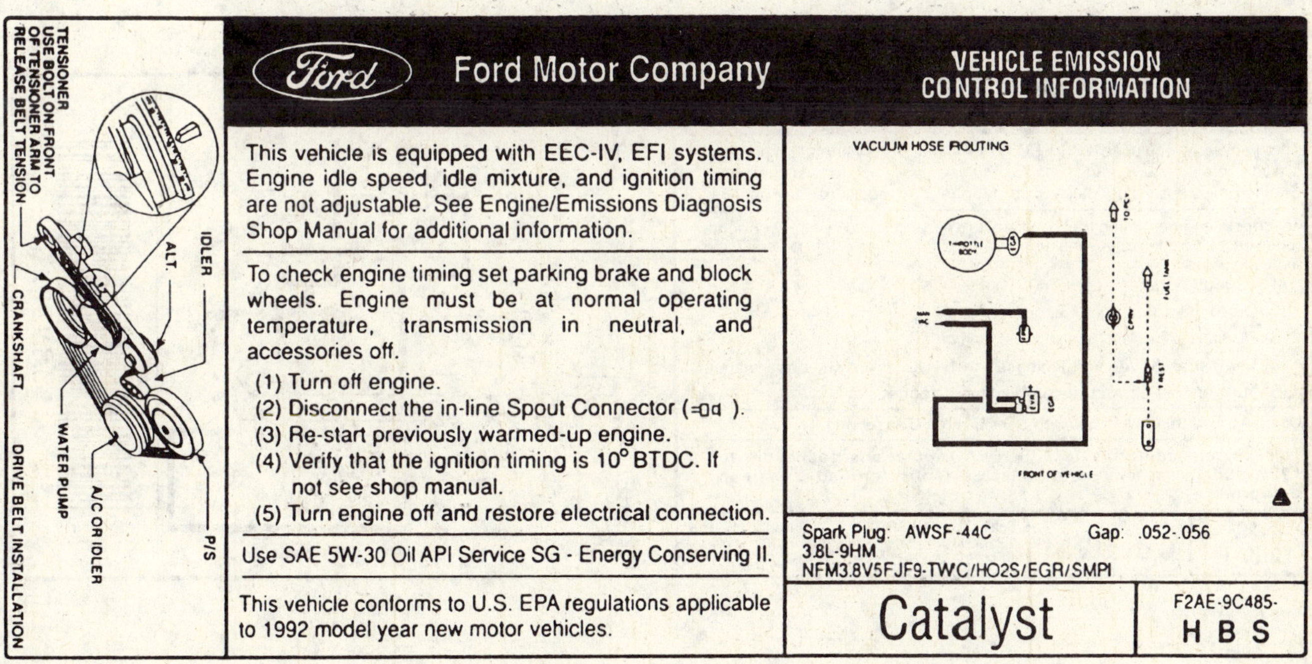
Ford Motor Company

VEHICLE EMISSION CONTROL INFORMATION

This vehicle is equipped with EEC-IV, EFI systems. Engine idle speed, idle mixture, and ignition timing are not adjustable. See Engine/Emissions Diagnosis Shop Manual for additional information.

To check engine timing set parking brake and block wheels. Engine must be at normal operating temperature, transmission in neutral, and accessories off.

(1) Turn off engine.
(2) Disconnect the in-line Spout Connector (=Dd).
(3) Re-start previously warmed-up engine.
(4) Verify that the ignition timing is 10° BTDC. If not see shop manual.
(5) Turn engine off and restore electrical connection.

Use SAE 5W-30 Oil API Service SG - Energy Conserving II.

This vehicle conforms to U.S. EPA regulations applicable to 1992 model year new motor vehicles.

Spark Plug: AWSF-44C Gap: .052-.056
3.8L-9HM
NFM3.8V5FJF9-TWC/HO2S/EGR/SMPI

Catalyst

F2AE-9C485-
H B S

88184GB4

Fig. 108 Vehicle Emission Label 1992 3.8L engine — 2-16B-R10

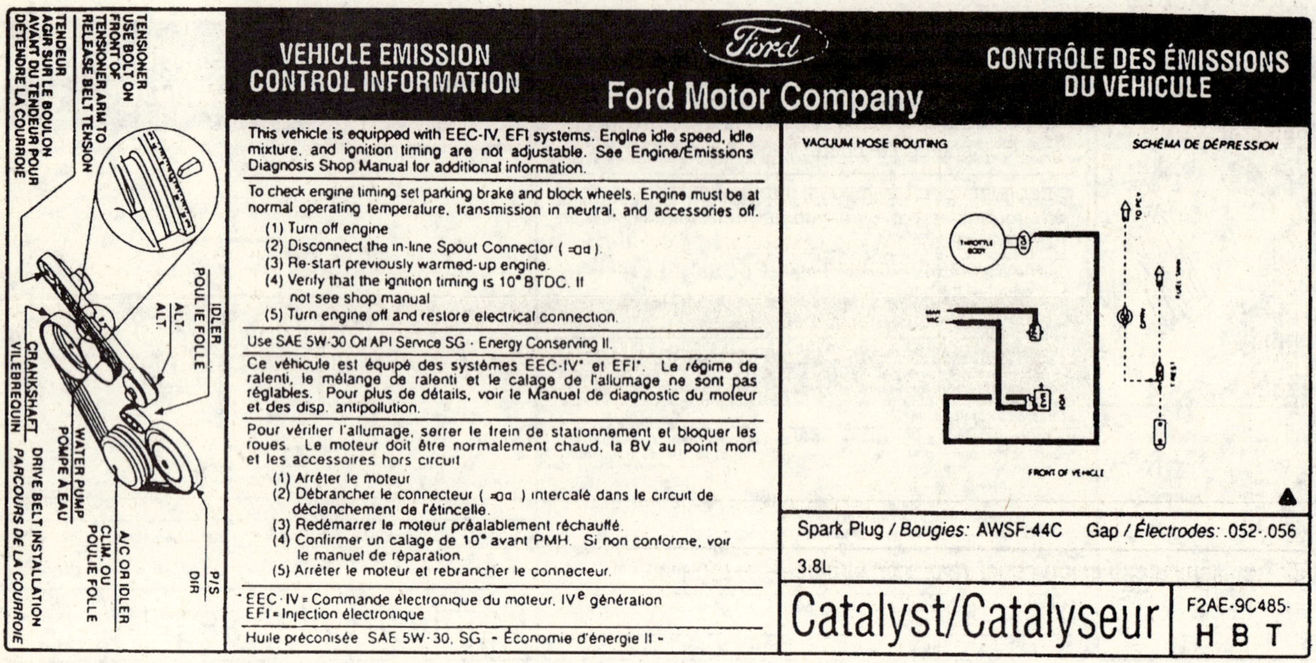

88184GB5

Fig. 109 Vehicle Emission Label 1992 3.8L engine — 2-16B-R10

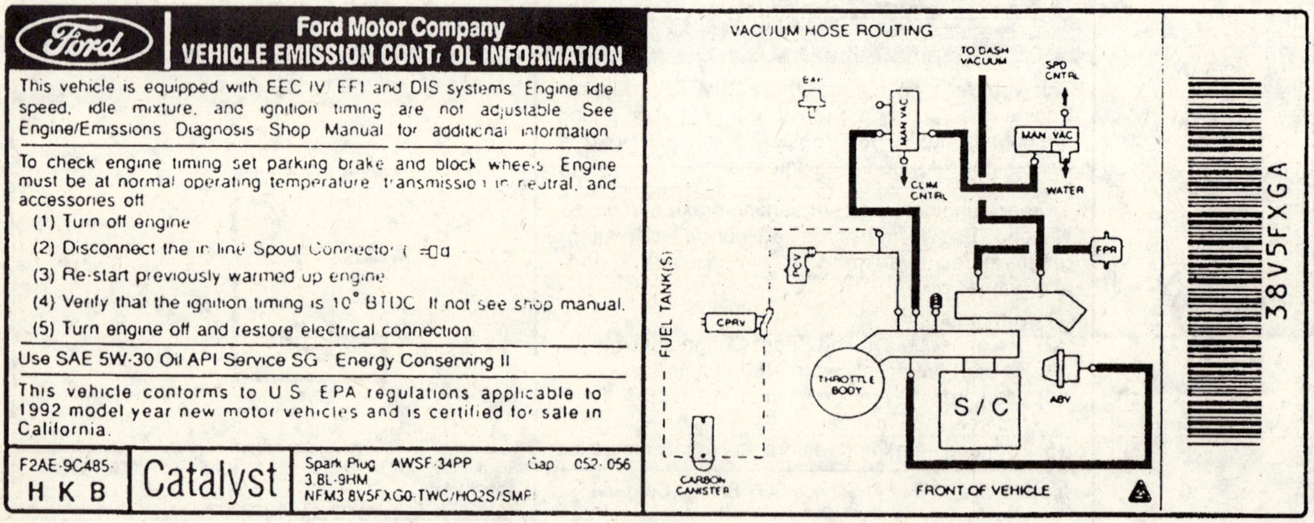

88184GB6

Fig. 110 Vehicle Emission Label 1992 3.8L SC engine — 2-16A-R12

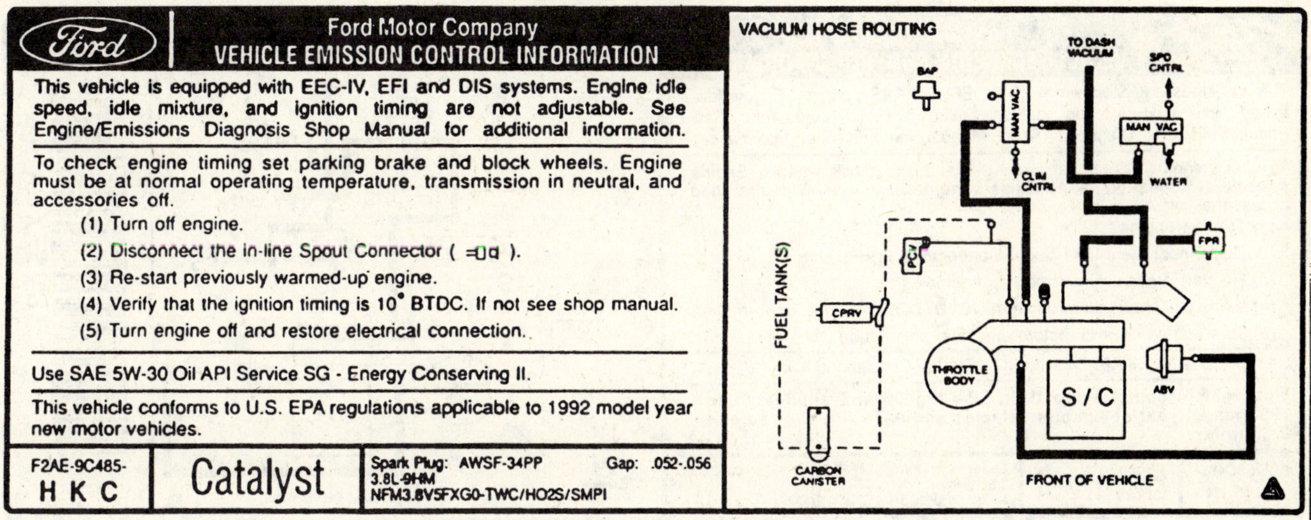

88184GB7

Fig. 111 Vehicle Emission Label 1992 3.8L SC engine — 2-16A-R12

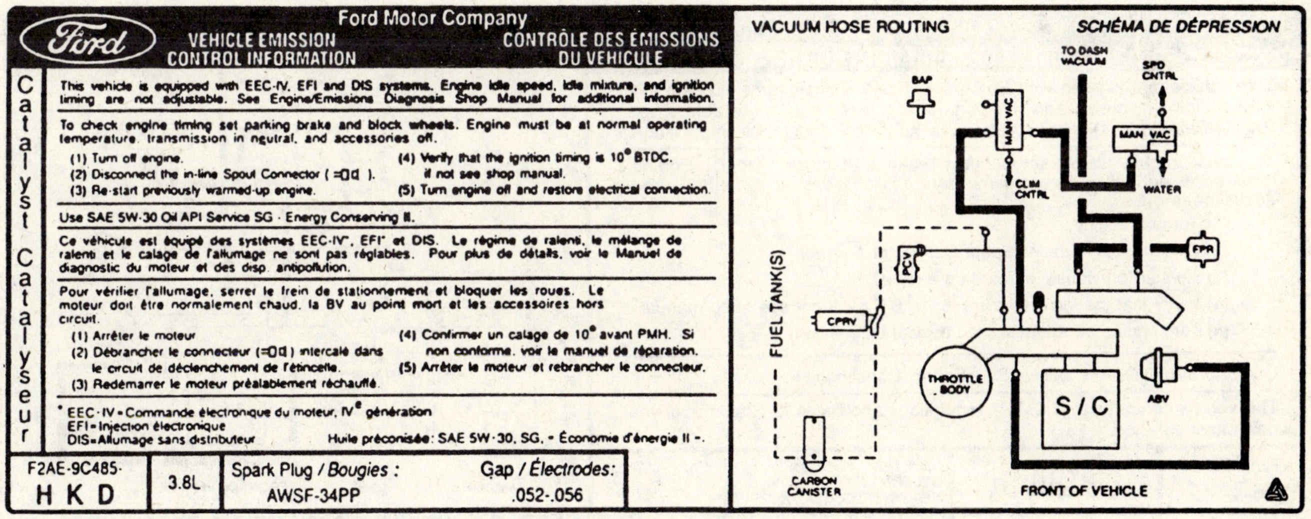

88184GB8

Fig. 112 Vehicle Emission Label 1992 3.8L SC engine — 2-16A-R12

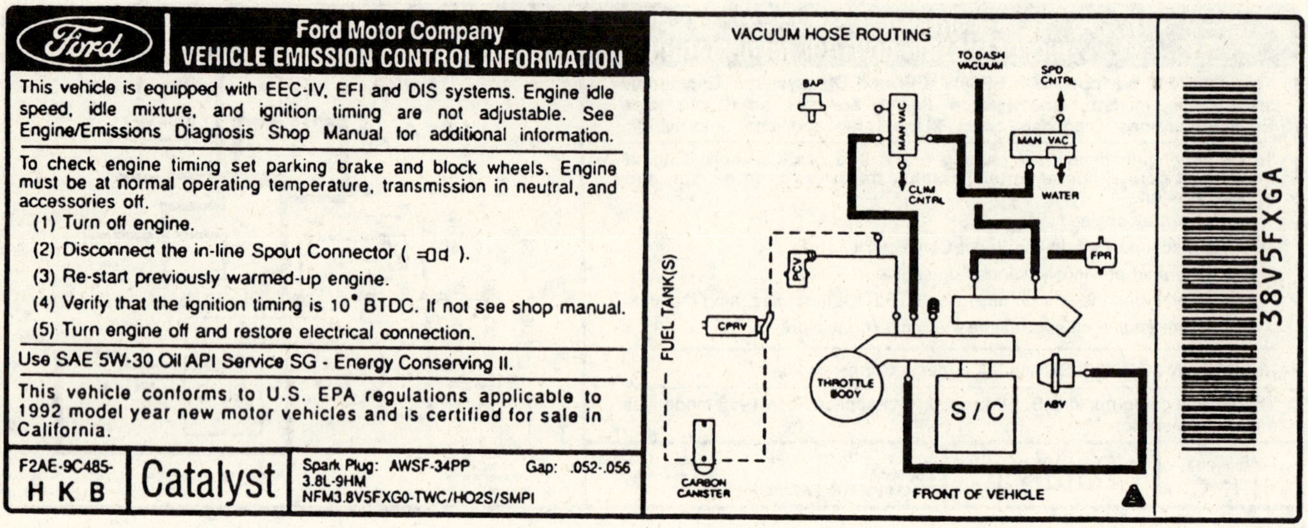

Ford Motor Company
VEHICLE EMISSION CONTROL INFORMATION

This vehicle is equipped with EEC-IV, EFI and DIS systems. Engine idle speed, idle mixture, and ignition timing are not adjustable. See Engine/Emissions Diagnosis Shop Manual for additional information.

To check engine timing set parking brake and block wheels. Engine must be at normal operating temperature, transmission in neutral, and accessories off.

(1) Turn off engine.
(2) Disconnect the in-line Spout Connector ( ).
(3) Re-start previously warmed-up engine.
(4) Verify that the ignition timing is 10° BTDC. If not see shop manual.
(5) Turn engine off and restore electrical connection.

Use SAE 5W-30 Oil API Service SG - Energy Conserving II.

This vehicle conforms to U.S. EPA regulations applicable to 1992 model year new motor vehicles and is certified for sale in California.

F2AE-9C485-
H K B

Catalyst

Spark Plug: AWSF-34PP Gap: .052-.056
3.8L-9HM
NFM3.8V5FXG0-TWC/HO2S/SMPI

88184GB9

Fig. 113 Vehicle Emission Label 1992 3.8L SC engine — 2-15A-R10

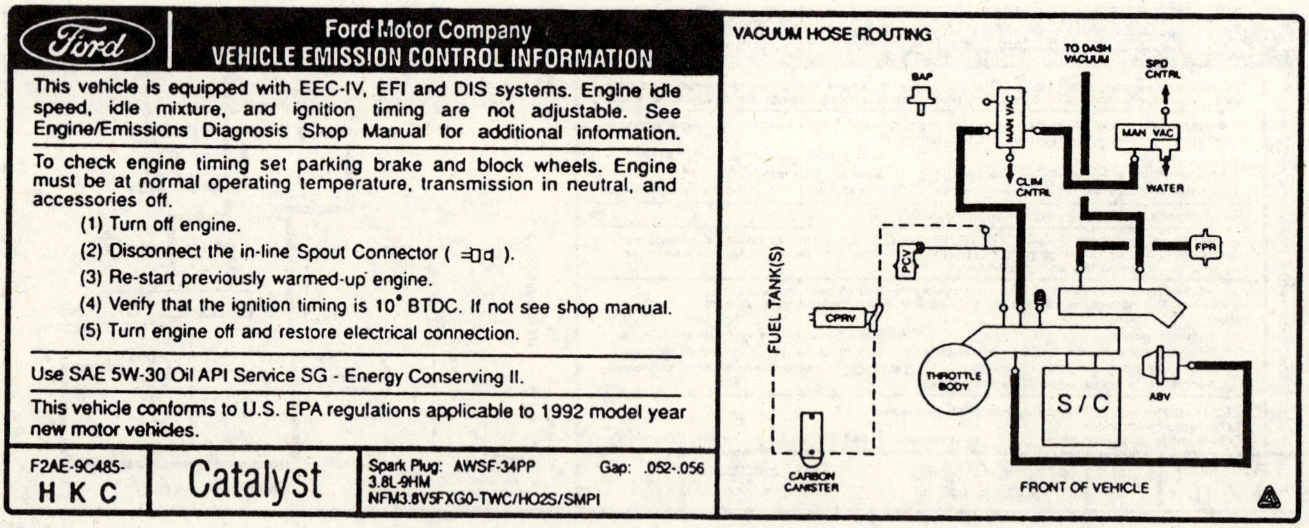

Ford Motor Company
VEHICLE EMISSION CONTROL INFORMATION

This vehicle is equipped with EEC-IV, EFI and DIS systems. Engine idle speed, idle mixture, and ignition timing are not adjustable. See Engine/Emissions Diagnosis Shop Manual for additional information.

To check engine timing set parking brake and block wheels. Engine must be at normal operating temperature, transmission in neutral, and accessories off.

(1) Turn off engine.
(2) Disconnect the in-line Spout Connector ( ).
(3) Re-start previously warmed-up engine.
(4) Verify that the ignition timing is 10° BTDC. If not see shop manual.
(5) Turn engine off and restore electrical connection.

Use SAE 5W-30 Oil API Service SG - Energy Conserving II.

This vehicle conforms to U.S. EPA regulations applicable to 1992 model year new motor vehicles.

F2AE-9C485-
H K C

Catalyst

Spark Plug: AWSF-34PP Gap: .052-.056
3.8L-9HM
NFM3.8V5FXG0-TWC/HO2S/SMPI

88184GC0

Fig. 114 Vehicle Emission Label 1992 3.8L SC engine — 2-15A-R10

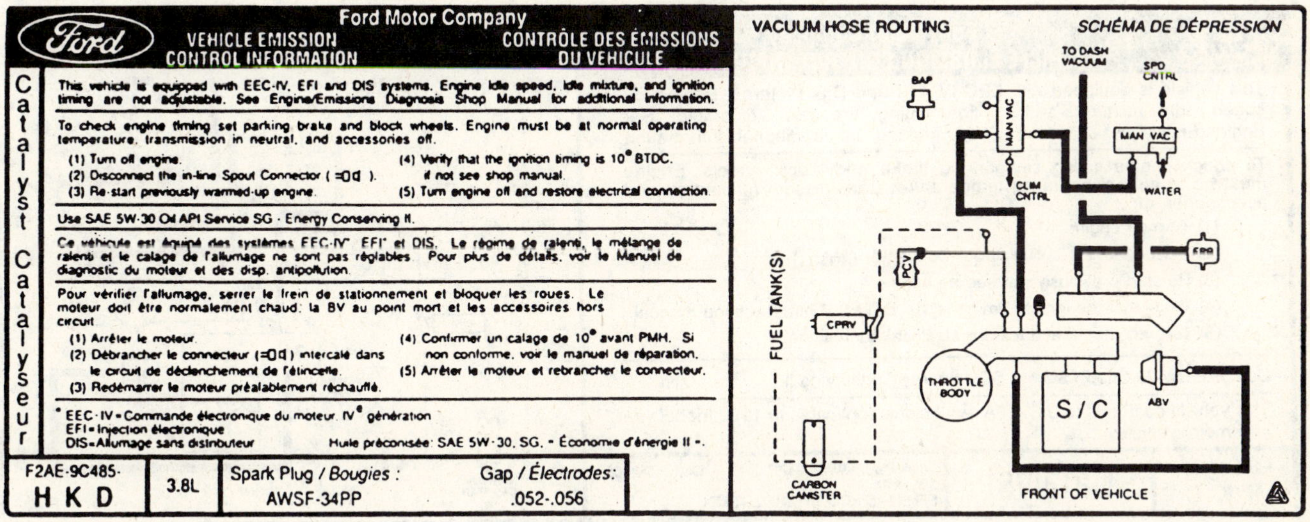

88184GC1

Fig. 115 Vehicle Emission Label 1992 3.8L SC engine — 2-15A-R12

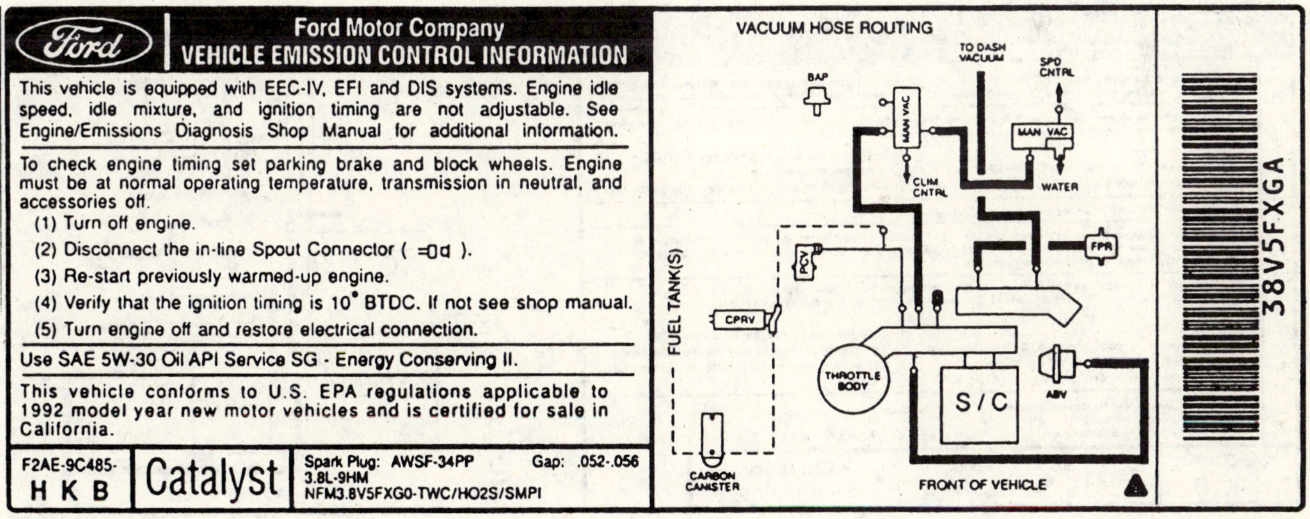

88184GC2

Fig. 116 Vehicle Emission Label 1992 3.8L SC engine — 2-15A-R10

Ford Motor Company
VEHICLE EMISSION CONTROL INFORMATION

This vehicle is equipped with EEC-IV, EFI and DIS systems. Engine idle speed, idle mixture, and ignition timing are not adjustable. See Engine/Emissions Diagnosis Shop Manual for additional information.

To check engine timing set parking brake and block wheels. Engine must be at normal operating temperature, transmission in neutral, and accessories off.

(1) Turn off engine.
(2) Disconnect the in-line Spout Connector (=▯ᑯ).
(3) Re-start previously warmed-up engine.
(4) Verify that the ignition timing is 10° BTDC. If not see shop manual.
(5) Turn engine off and restore electrical connection.

Use SAE 5W-30 Oil API Service SG - Energy Conserving II.

This vehicle conforms to U.S. EPA regulations applicable to 1992 model year new motor vehicles.

F2AE-9C485- H K C	Catalyst	Spark Plug: AWSF-34PP Gap: .052-.056 3.8L-9HM NFM3.8V5FXG0-TWC/HO2S/SMPI

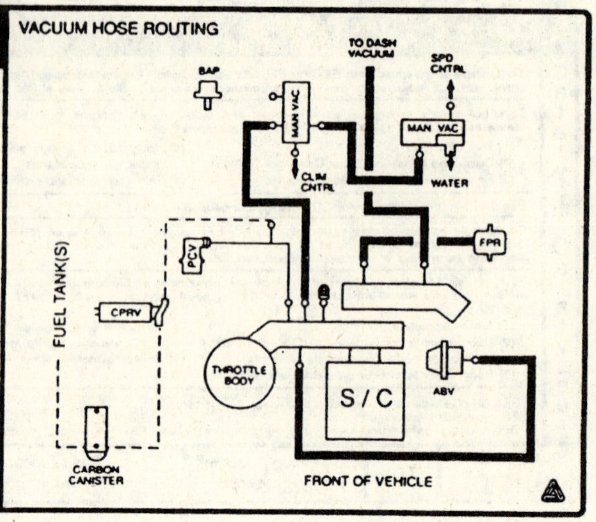

88184GC3

Fig. 117 Vehicle Emission Label 1992 3.8L SC engine — 2-15A-R12

Ford Motor Company
VEHICLE EMISSION CONTROL INFORMATION — CONTRÔLE DES EMISSIONS DU VEHICULE

Catalyst Catalyseur

This vehicle is equipped with EEC-IV, EFI and DIS systems. Engine idle speed, idle mixture, and ignition timing are not adjustable. See Engine/Emissions Diagnosis Shop Manual for additional information.

To check engine timing set parking brake and block wheels. Engine must be at normal operating temperature, transmission in neutral, and accessories off.

(1) Turn off engine.
(2) Disconnect the in-line Spout Connector (=▯ᑯ)
(3) Re-start previously warmed-up engine.
(4) Verify that the ignition timing is 10° BTDC. If not see shop manual.
(5) Turn engine off and restore electrical connection.

Use SAE 5W-30 Oil API Service SG - Energy Conserving II.

Ce véhicule est équipé des systèmes EEC-IV*, EFI* et DIS. Le régime de ralenti, le mélange de ralenti et le calage de l'allumage ne sont pas réglables. Pour plus de détails, voir le Manuel de diagnostic du moteur et des disp. antipollution.

Pour vérifier l'allumage, serrer le frein de stationnement et bloquer les roues. Le moteur doit être normalement chaud, la BV au point mort et les accessoires hors circuit.

(1) Arrêter le moteur
(2) Débrancher le connecteur (=▯ᑯ) intercalé dans le circuit de déclenchement de l'étincelle
(3) Redémarrer le moteur préalablement réchauffé
(4) Confirmer un calage de 10° avant PMH. Si non conforme, voir le manuel de réparation.
(5) Arrêter le moteur et rebrancher le connecteur.

* EEC-IV = Commande électronique du moteur, IVe génération
EFI = Injection électronique
DIS = Allumage sans distributeur

Huile préconisée: SAE 5W-30, SG, - Économie d'énergie II -.

F2AE-9C485- H K D	3.8L	Spark Plug / *Bougies* : AWSF-34PP	Gap / *Électrodes:* .052-.056

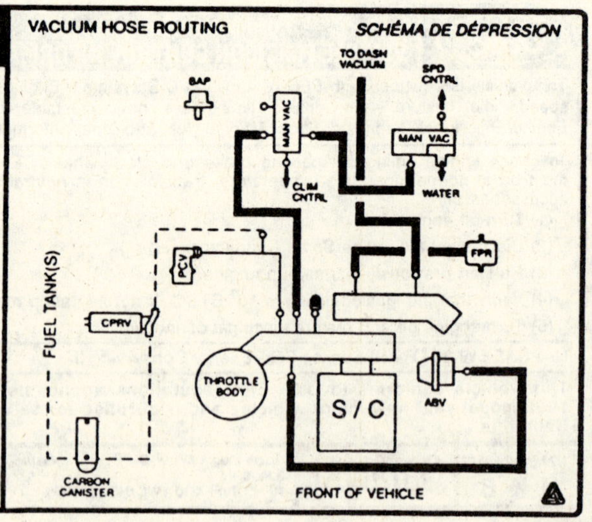

88184GC4

Fig. 118 Vehicle Emission Label 1992 3.8L SC engine — 2-15A-R12

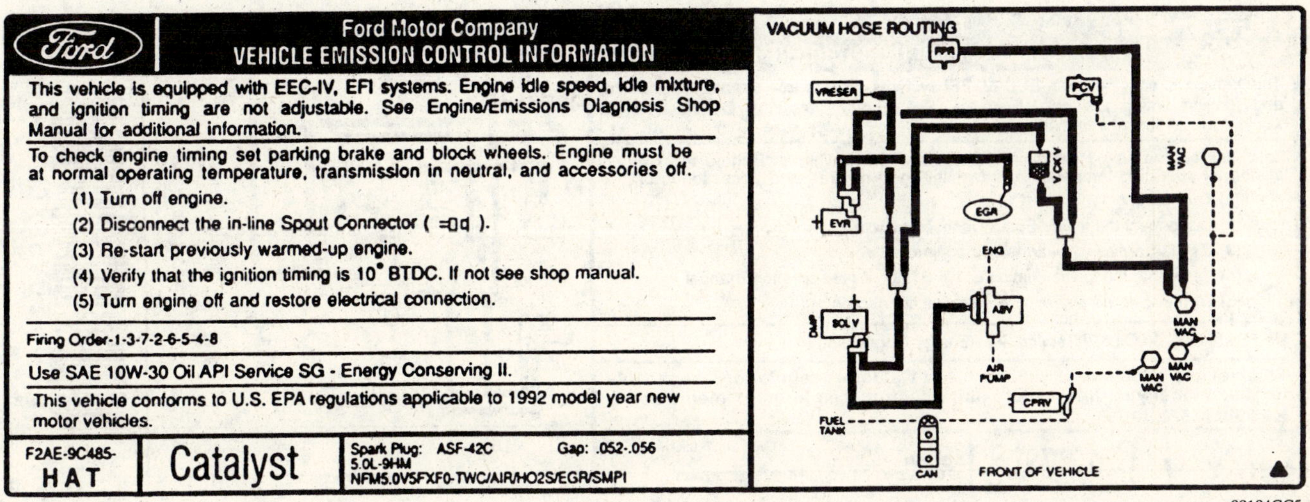

88184GC5

Fig. 119 Vehicle Emission Label 1992 5.0L HO engine — 2-16A-R12

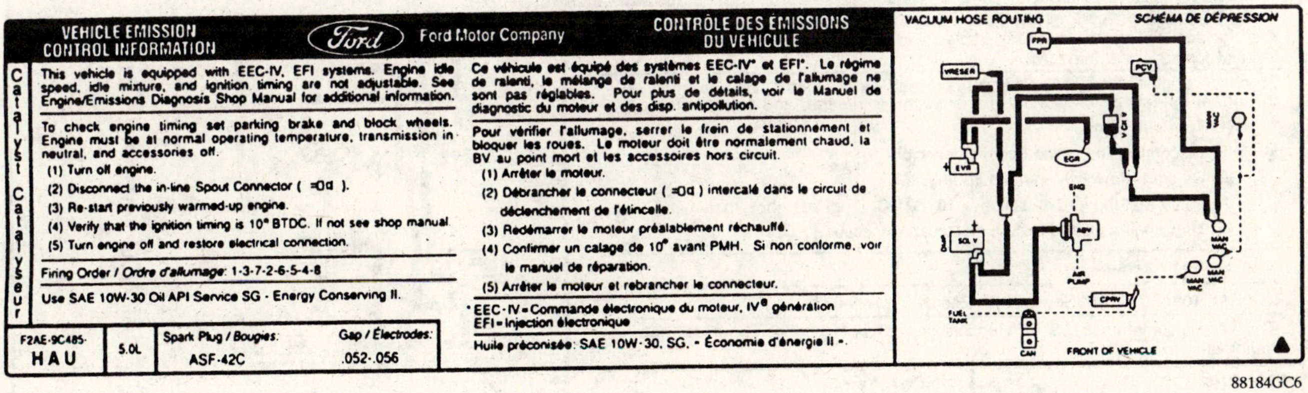

88184GC6

Fig. 120 Vehicle Emission Label 1992 5.0L HO engine — 1-22F-R00

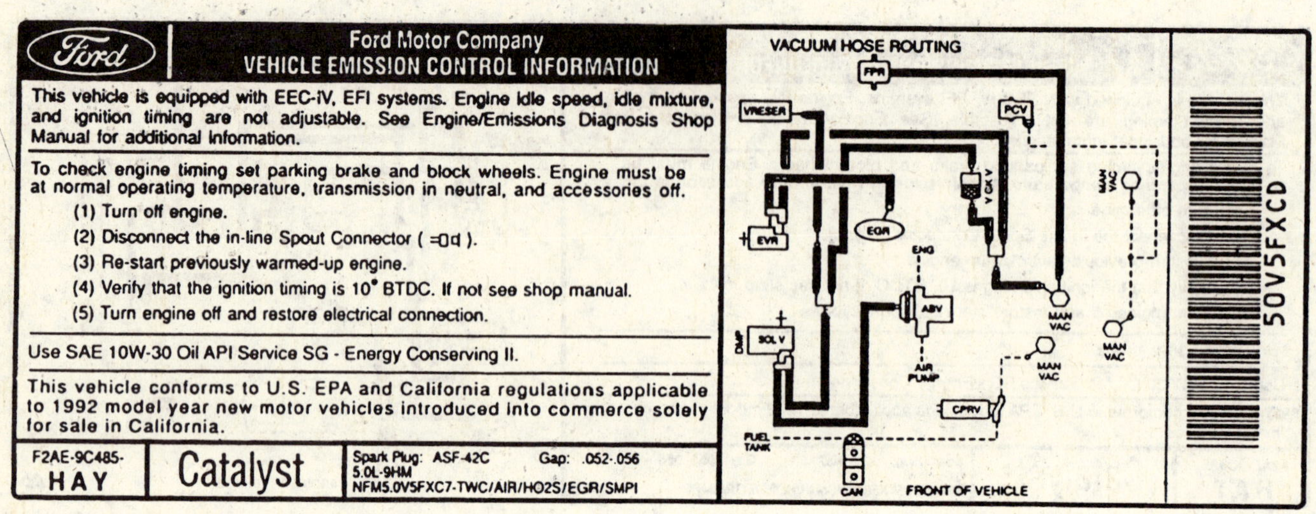

Ford Motor Company
VEHICLE EMISSION CONTROL INFORMATION

This vehicle is equipped with EEC-IV, EFI systems. Engine idle speed, idle mixture, and ignition timing are not adjustable. See Engine/Emissions Diagnosis Shop Manual for additional information.

To check engine timing set parking brake and block wheels. Engine must be at normal operating temperature, transmission in neutral, and accessories off.

(1) Turn off engine.
(2) Disconnect the in-line Spout Connector (=0d).
(3) Re-start previously warmed-up engine.
(4) Verify that the ignition timing is 10° BTDC. If not see shop manual.
(5) Turn engine off and restore electrical connection.

Use SAE 10W-30 Oil API Service SG - Energy Conserving II.

This vehicle conforms to U.S. EPA and California regulations applicable to 1992 model year new motor vehicles introduced into commerce solely for sale in California.

F2AE-9C485- HAY	Catalyst	Spark Plug: ASF-42C Gap: .052-.056 5.0L-9HM NFM5.0V5FXC7-TWC/AIR/HO2S/EGR/SMPI

88184GC7

Fig. 121 Vehicle Emission Label 1992 5.0L HO engine — 1-22T-R00

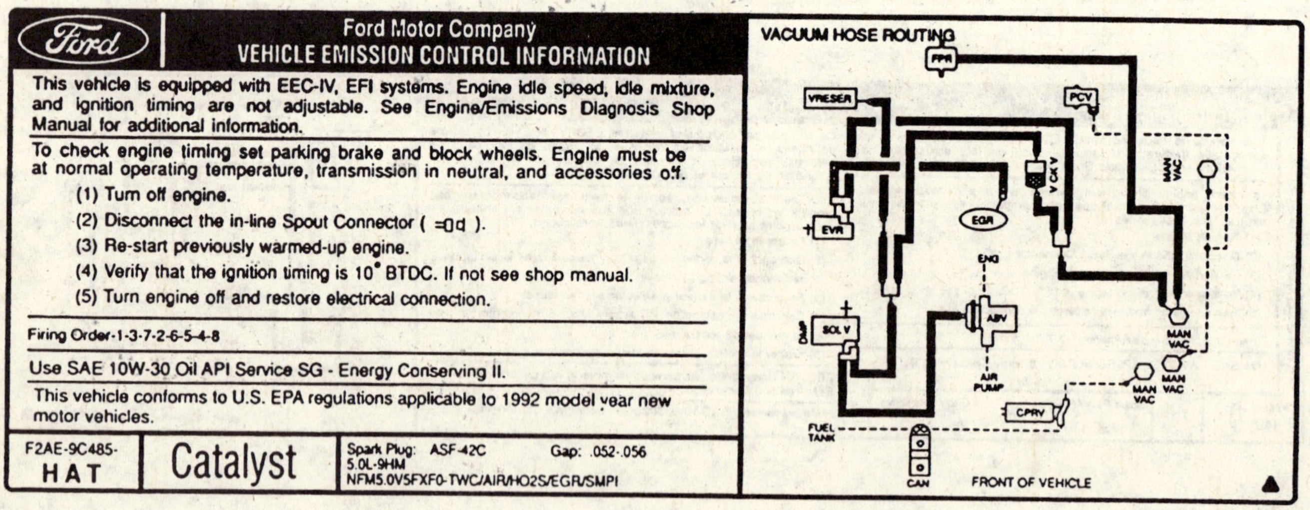

Ford Motor Company
VEHICLE EMISSION CONTROL INFORMATION

This vehicle is equipped with EEC-IV, EFI systems. Engine idle speed, idle mixture, and ignition timing are not adjustable. See Engine/Emissions Diagnosis Shop Manual for additional information.

To check engine timing set parking brake and block wheels. Engine must be at normal operating temperature, transmission in neutral, and accessories off.

(1) Turn off engine.
(2) Disconnect the in-line Spout Connector (=0d).
(3) Re-start previously warmed-up engine.
(4) Verify that the ignition timing is 10° BTDC. If not see shop manual.
(5) Turn engine off and restore electrical connection.

Firing Order-1-3-7-2-6-5-4-8

Use SAE 10W-30 Oil API Service SG - Energy Conserving II.

This vehicle conforms to U.S. EPA regulations applicable to 1992 model year new motor vehicles.

F2AE-9C485- HAT	Catalyst	Spark Plug: ASF-42C Gap: .052-.056 5.0L-9HM NFM5.0V5FXF0-TWC/AIR/HO2S/EGR/SMPI

88184GC8

Fig. 122 Vehicle Emission Label 1992 5.0L HO engine — 2-22G-R00

VEHICLE EMISSION CONTROL INFORMATION — Ford Motor Company — **CONTRÔLE DES ÉMISSIONS DU VEHICULE**

Catalyst Catalyseur

This vehicle is equipped with EEC-IV, EFI systems. Engine idle speed, idle mixture, and ignition timing are not adjustable. See Engine/Emissions Diagnosis Shop Manual for additional information.

To check engine timing set parking brake and block wheels. Engine must be at normal operating temperature, transmission in neutral, and accessories off.

(1) Turn off engine.
(2) Disconnect the in-line Spout Connector (=⊡ɑ).
(3) Re-start previously warmed-up engine.
(4) Verify that the ignition timing is 10° BTDC. If not see shop manual.
(5) Turn engine off and restore electrical connection.

Firing Order / *Ordre d'allumage*: 1-3-7-2-6-5-4-8

Use SAE 10W-30 Oil API Service SG - Energy Conserving II

Ce véhicule est équipé des systèmes EEC-IV* et EFI*. Le régime de ralenti, le mélange de ralenti et le calage de l'allumage ne sont pas réglables. Pour plus de détails, voir le Manuel de diagnostic du moteur et des disp. antipollution.

Pour vérifier l'allumage, serrer le frein de stationnement et bloquer les roues. Le moteur doit être normalement chaud, la BV au point mort et les accessoires hors circuit.

(1) Arrêter le moteur.
(2) Débrancher le connecteur (=⊡ɑ) intercalé dans le circuit de déclenchement de l'étincelle.
(3) Redémarrer le moteur préalablement réchauffé.
(4) Confirmer un calage de 10° avant PMH. Si non conforme, voir le manuel de réparation.
(5) Arrêter le moteur et rebrancher le connecteur.

* EEC-IV = Commande électronique du moteur, IV® génération
EFI = Injection électronique

Huile préconisée: SAE 10W-30, SG. - Économie d'énergie II -.

F2AE-9C485-HAU	5.0L	Spark Plug / *Bougies* ASF-42C	Gap / *Électrodes* 052-056

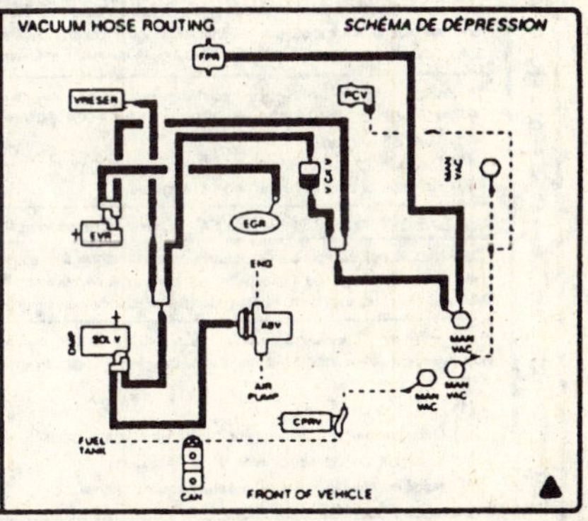

88184GC9

Fig. 123 Vehicle Emission Label 1992 5.0L HO engine — 2-22G-R00

Ford Motor Company
VEHICLE EMISSION CONTROL INFORMATION

This vehicle is equipped with electronic engine control systems. Engine idle speed, idle mixture, and ignition timing are not adjustable. See Powertrain Control/Emissions Diagnosis Manual for additional information.

To check engine timing set parking brake and block wheels. Engine must be at normal operating temperature, transmission in neutral, and accessories off.

(1) Turn off engine.
(2) Disconnect the in-line Spout Connector (=⊡ɑ)
(3) Re-start previously warmed-up engine.
(4) Verify that the ignition timing is 10° BTDC. If not see shop manual.
(5) Turn engine off and restore electrical connection.

Use SAE 5W-30 Oil API Service SG - Energy Conserving II

This vehicle conforms to U.S. EPA regulations applicable to 1993 model year new motor vehicles.

F3AE-9C485-J F A	Catalyst	Spark Plug AWSF-34PF 3.8L-HM PFM3.8V5FXG2-TWC/HO2S/SF.	Gap 052-056

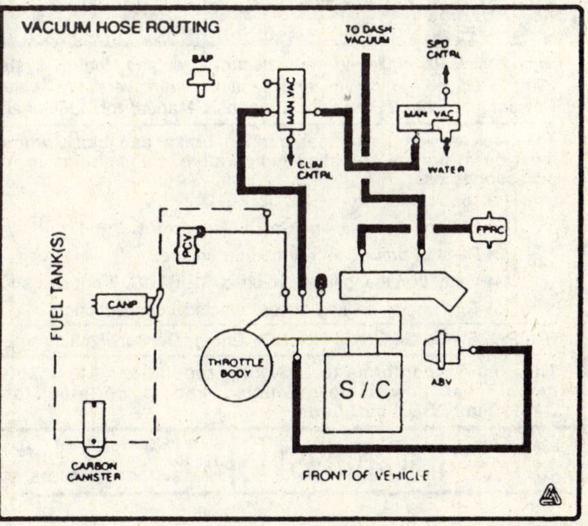

88184GD0

Fig. 124 Vehicle Emission Label 1993 3.8L VIN-R engine — 2-15A-R10

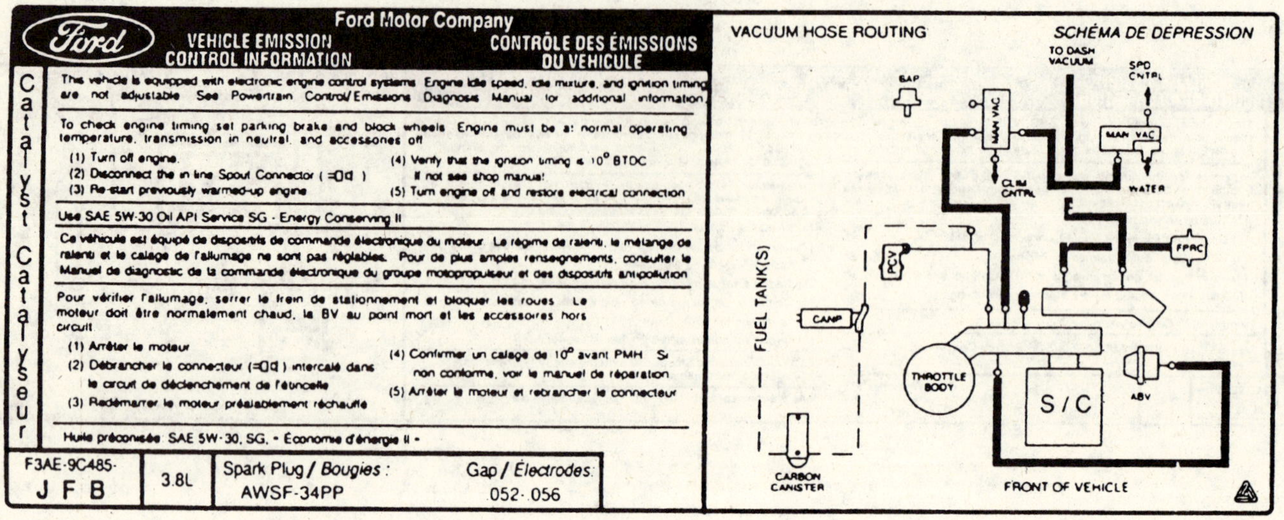

88184GD1

Fig. 125 Vehicle Emission Label 1993 3.8L VIN-R engine — 2-15A-R10

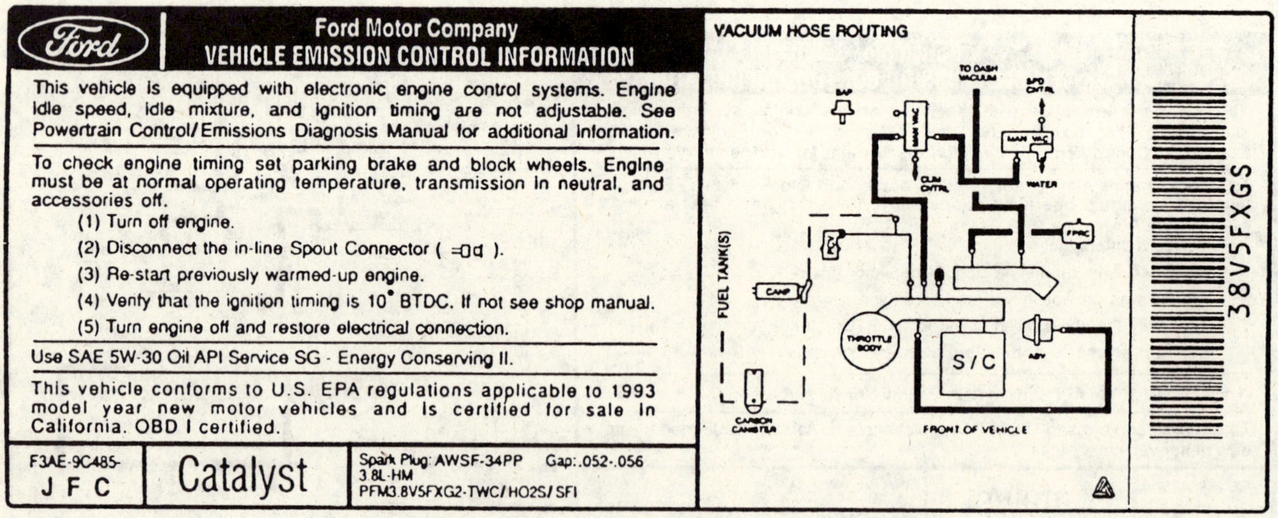

88184GD2

Fig. 126 Vehicle Emission Label 1993 3.8L VIN-R engine — 2-15A-R10

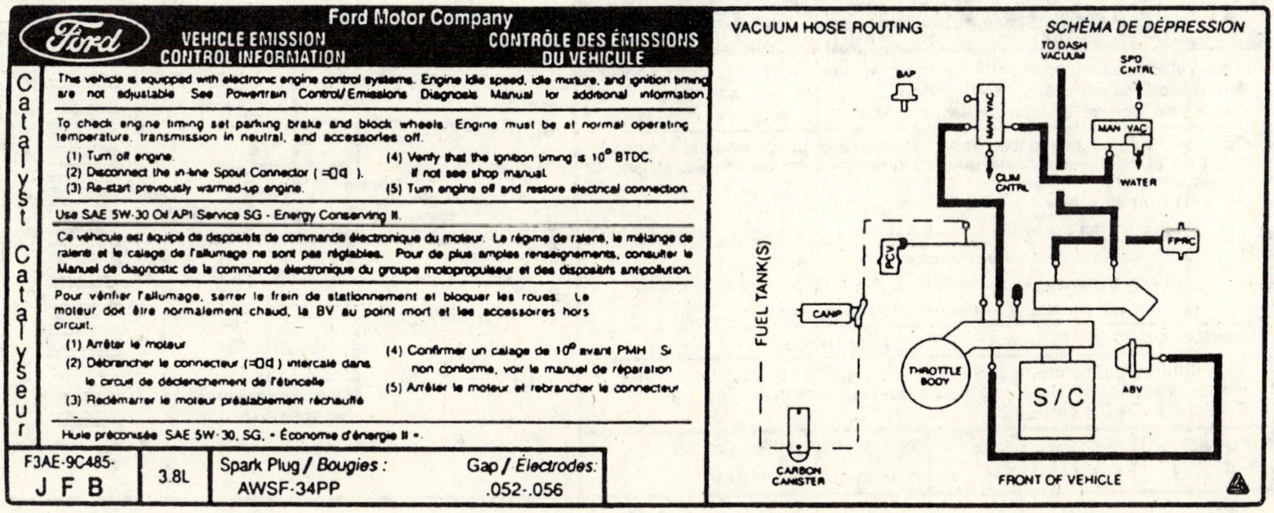

88184GD3

Fig. 127 Vehicle Emission Label 1993 3.8L VIN-R engine — 2–16A-R10

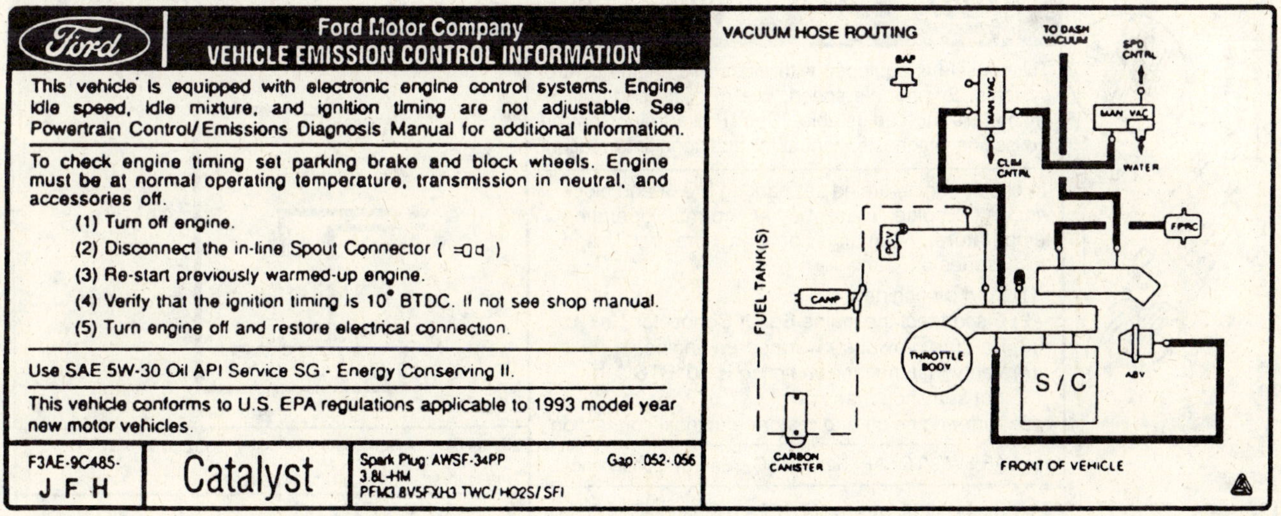

88184GD4

Fig. 128 Vehicle Emission Label 1993 3.8L VIN-R engine — 2–16A-R10

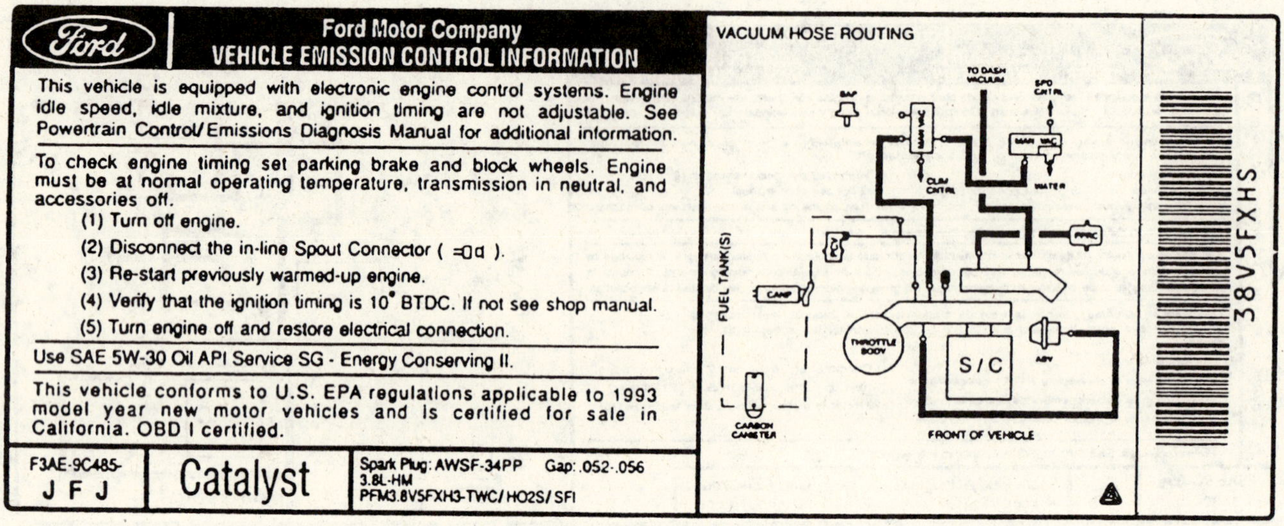
Ford Motor Company
VEHICLE EMISSION CONTROL INFORMATION

This vehicle is equipped with electronic engine control systems. Engine idle speed, idle mixture, and ignition timing are not adjustable. See Powertrain Control/Emissions Diagnosis Manual for additional information.

To check engine timing set parking brake and block wheels. Engine must be at normal operating temperature, transmission in neutral, and accessories off.

(1) Turn off engine.
(2) Disconnect the in-line Spout Connector (=0d).
(3) Re-start previously warmed-up engine.
(4) Verify that the ignition timing is 10° BTDC. If not see shop manual.
(5) Turn engine off and restore electrical connection.

Use SAE 5W-30 Oil API Service SG - Energy Conserving II.

This vehicle conforms to U.S. EPA regulations applicable to 1993 model year new motor vehicles and is certified for sale in California. OBD I certified.

F3AE-9C485-
J F J

Catalyst

Spark Plug: AWSF-34PP Gap: .052-.056
3.8L-HM
PFM3.8V5FXH3-TWC/HO2S/SFI

88184GD5

Fig. 129 Vehicle Emission Label 1993 3.8L VIN-R engine — 2-16A-R10

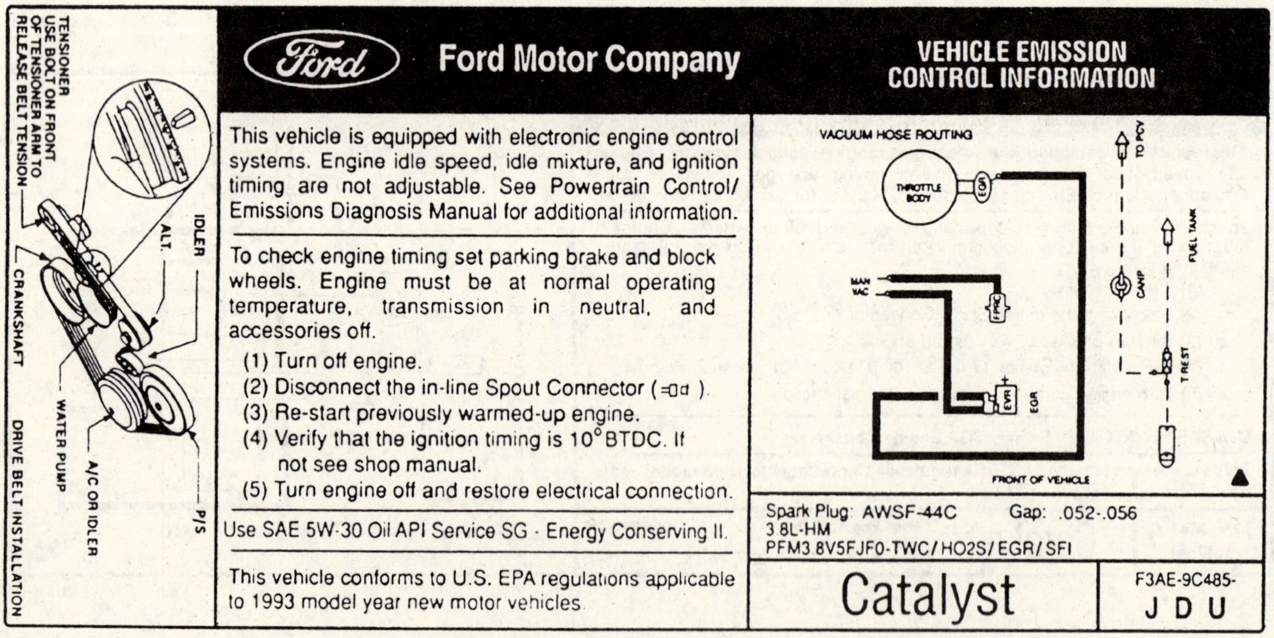

Ford Motor Company
VEHICLE EMISSION CONTROL INFORMATION

This vehicle is equipped with electronic engine control systems. Engine idle speed, idle mixture, and ignition timing are not adjustable. See Powertrain Control/Emissions Diagnosis Manual for additional information.

To check engine timing set parking brake and block wheels. Engine must be at normal operating temperature, transmission in neutral, and accessories off.

(1) Turn off engine.
(2) Disconnect the in-line Spout Connector (=0d).
(3) Re-start previously warmed-up engine.
(4) Verify that the ignition timing is 10° BTDC. If not see shop manual.
(5) Turn engine off and restore electrical connection.

Use SAE 5W-30 Oil API Service SG - Energy Conserving II.

This vehicle conforms to U.S. EPA regulations applicable to 1993 model year new motor vehicles.

Spark Plug: AWSF-44C Gap: .052-.056
3.8L-HM
PFM3.8V5FJF0-TWC/HO2S/EGR/SFI

Catalyst

F3AE-9C485-
J D U

88184GD6

Fig. 130 Vehicle Emission Label 1993 3.8L VIN-4 engine — 2-16B-R11

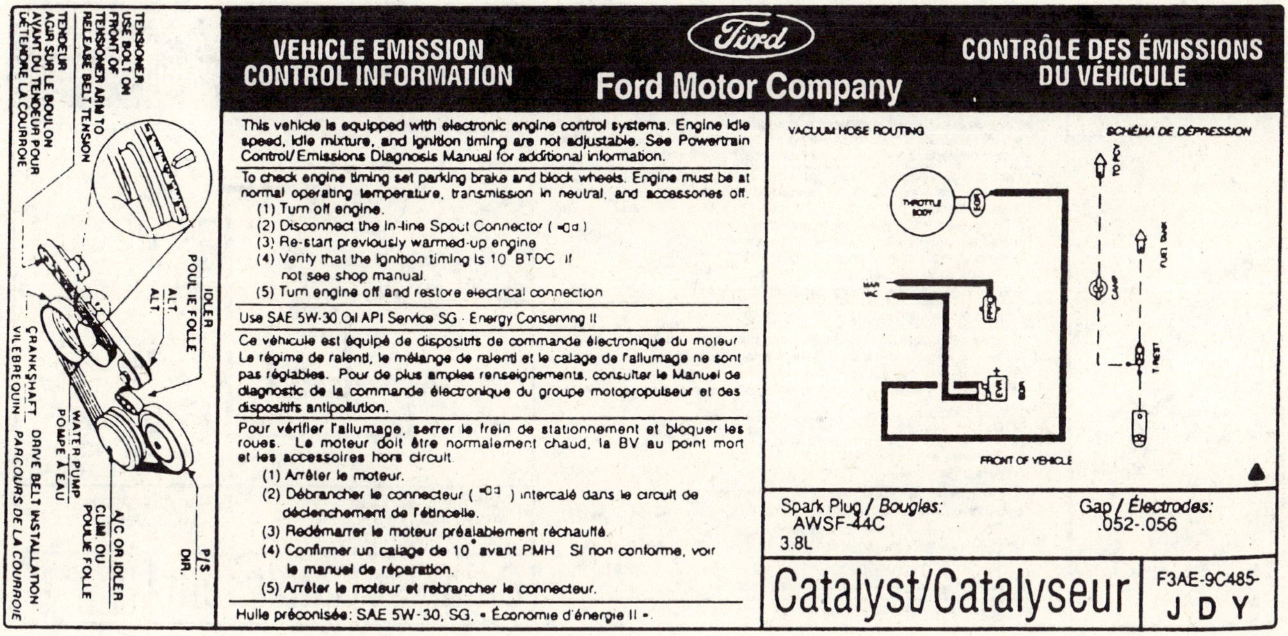

88184GD7

Fig. 131 Vehicle Emission Label 1993 3.8L VIN-4 engine — 2-16B-R11

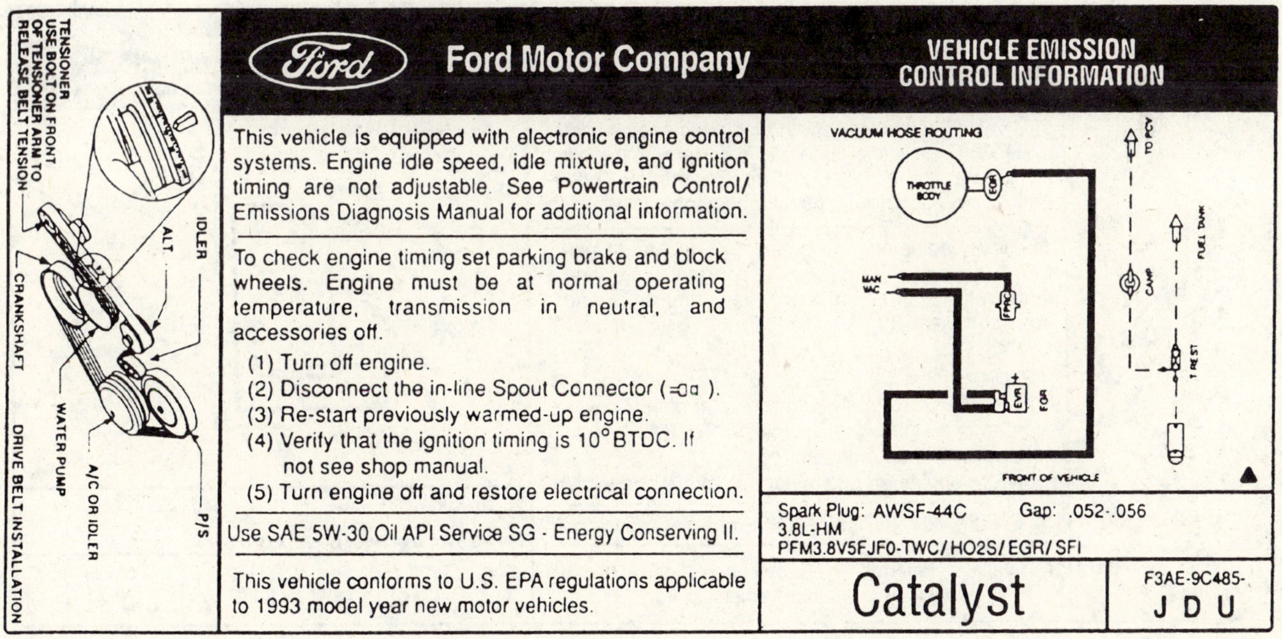

88184GD8

Fig. 132 Vehicle Emission Label 1993 3.8L VIN-4 engine — 2-16C-R11

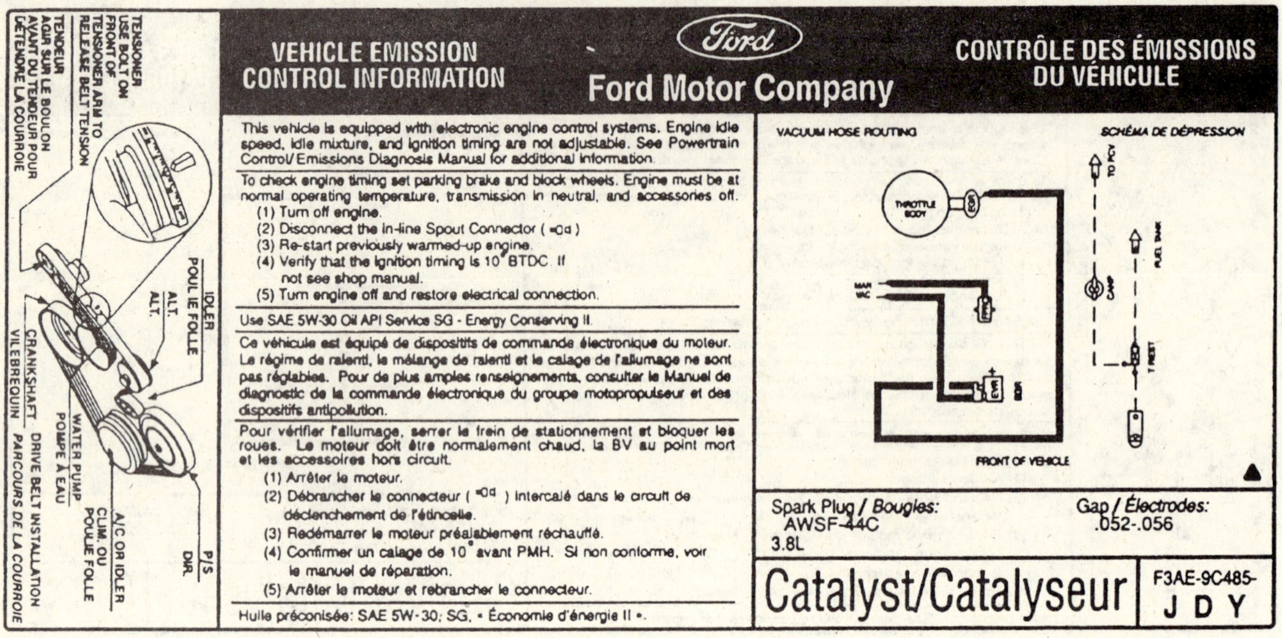

88184GD9

Fig. 133 Vehicle Emission Label 1993 3.8L VIN-4 engine — 2-16C-R11

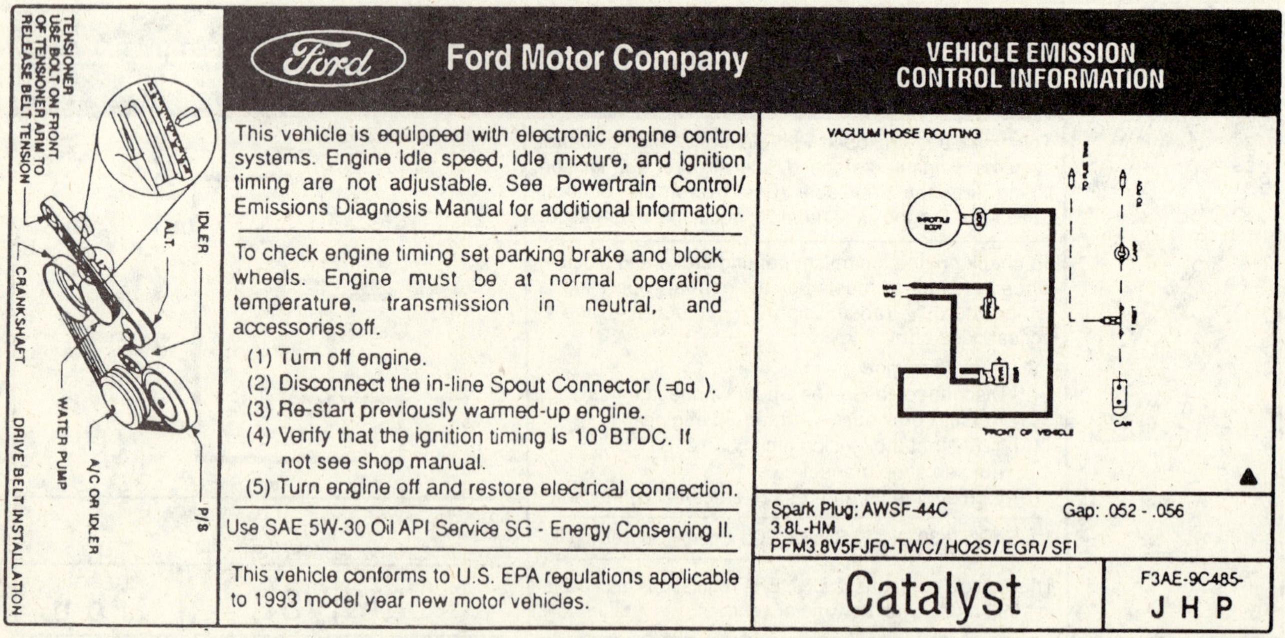

88184GE0

Fig. 134 Vehicle Emission Label 1993 3.8L VIN-4 engine — 2-16D-R10

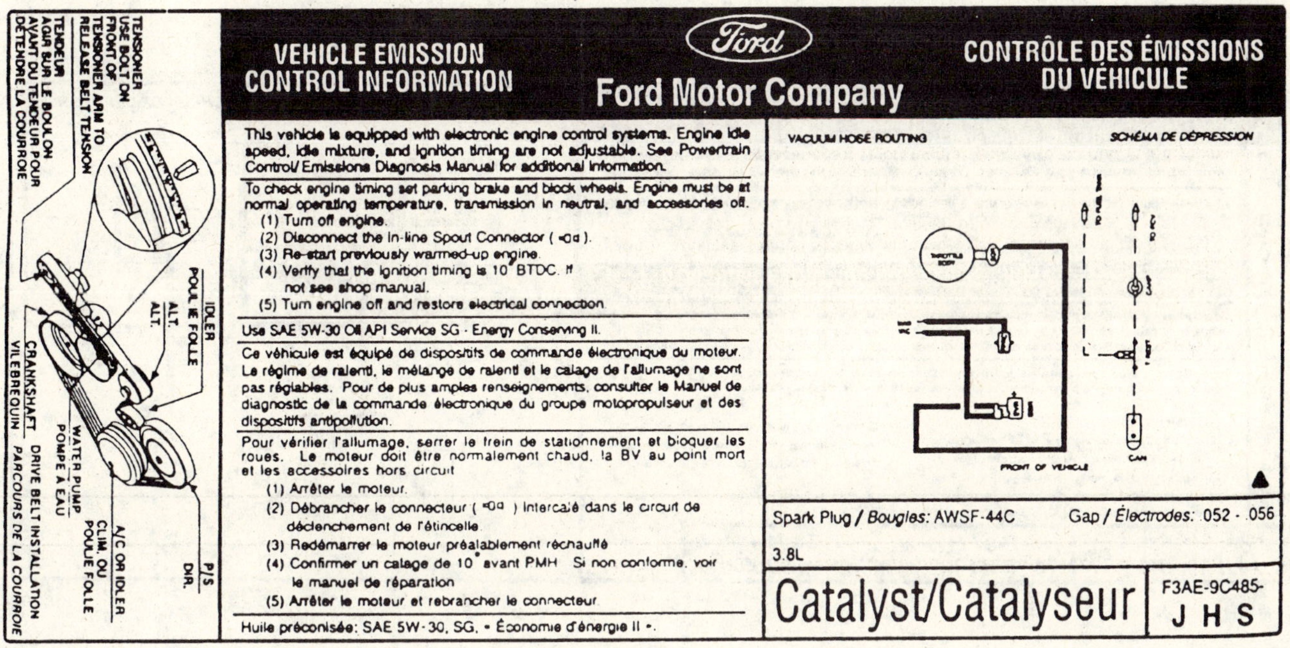

88184GE1

Fig. 135 Vehicle Emission Label 1993 3.8L VIN-4 engine — 2-16D-R10

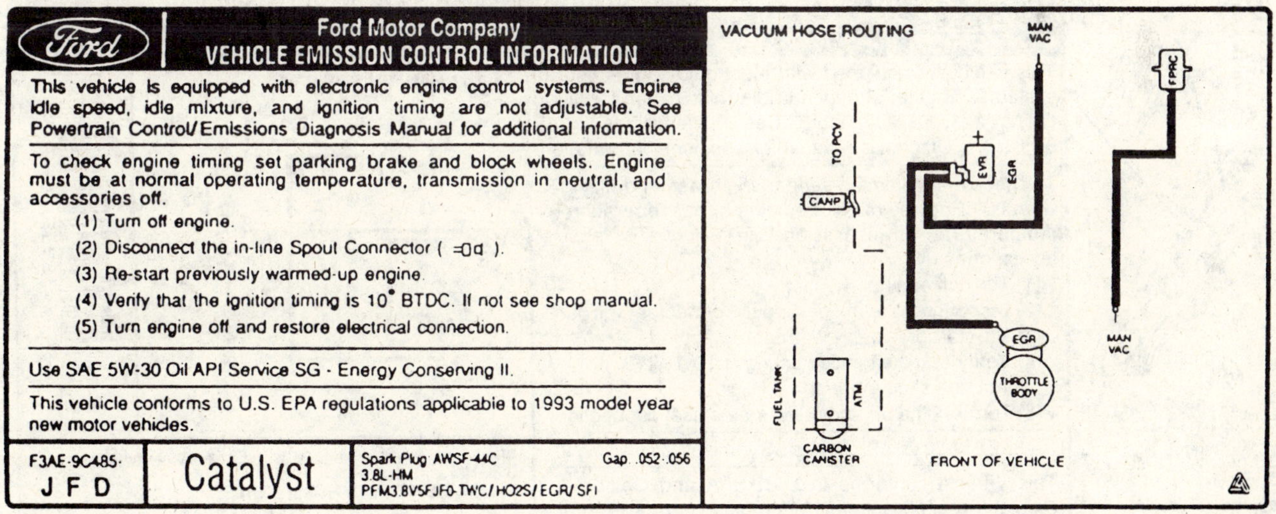

88184GE2

Fig. 136 Vehicle Emission Label 1993 3.8L VIN-4 engine — 2-16F-R10

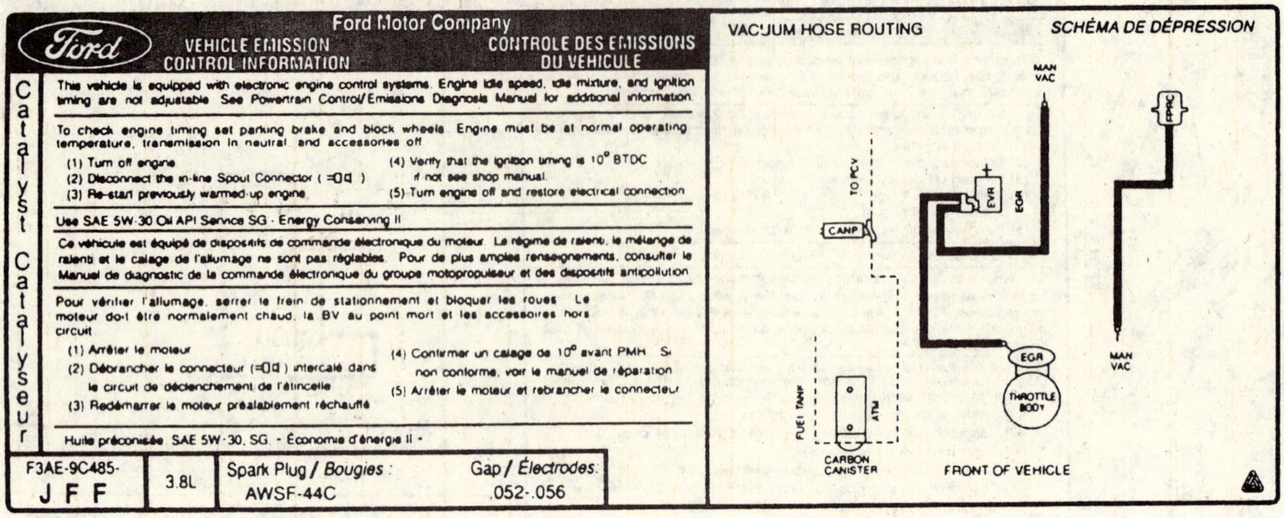

Fig. 137 Vehicle Emission Label 1993 3.8L VIN-4 engine — 2-16F-R10

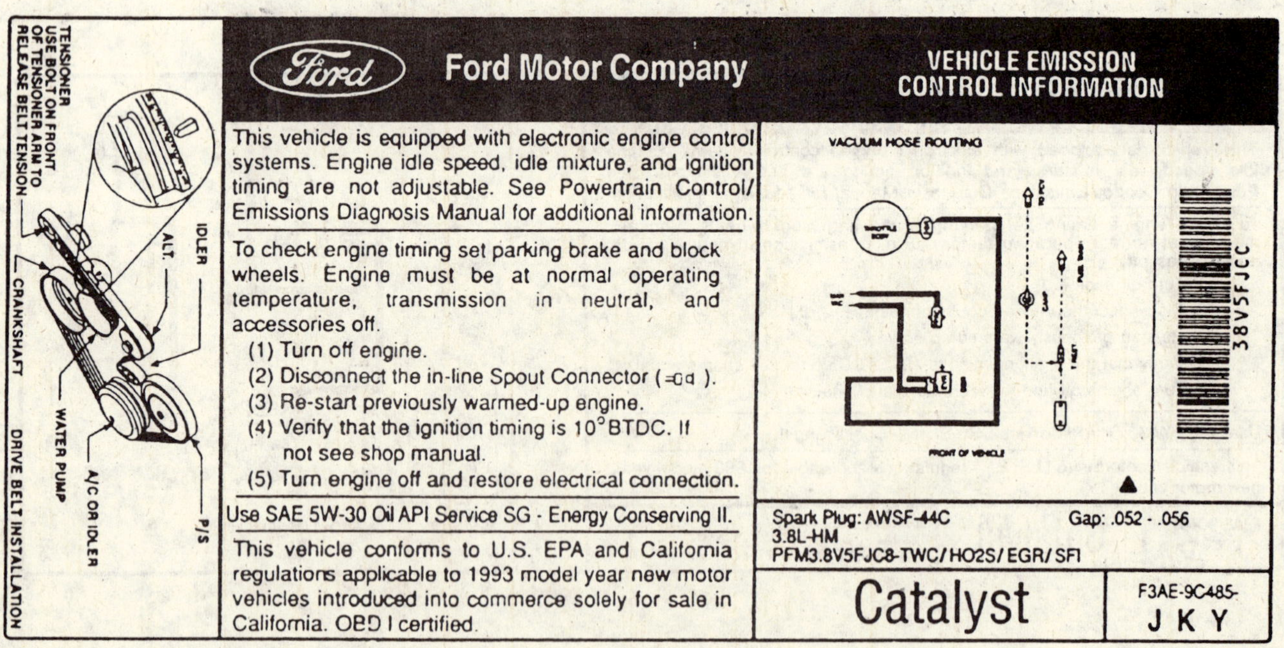

Fig. 138 Vehicle Emission Label 1993 3.8L VIN-4 engine — 2-16Q-R11

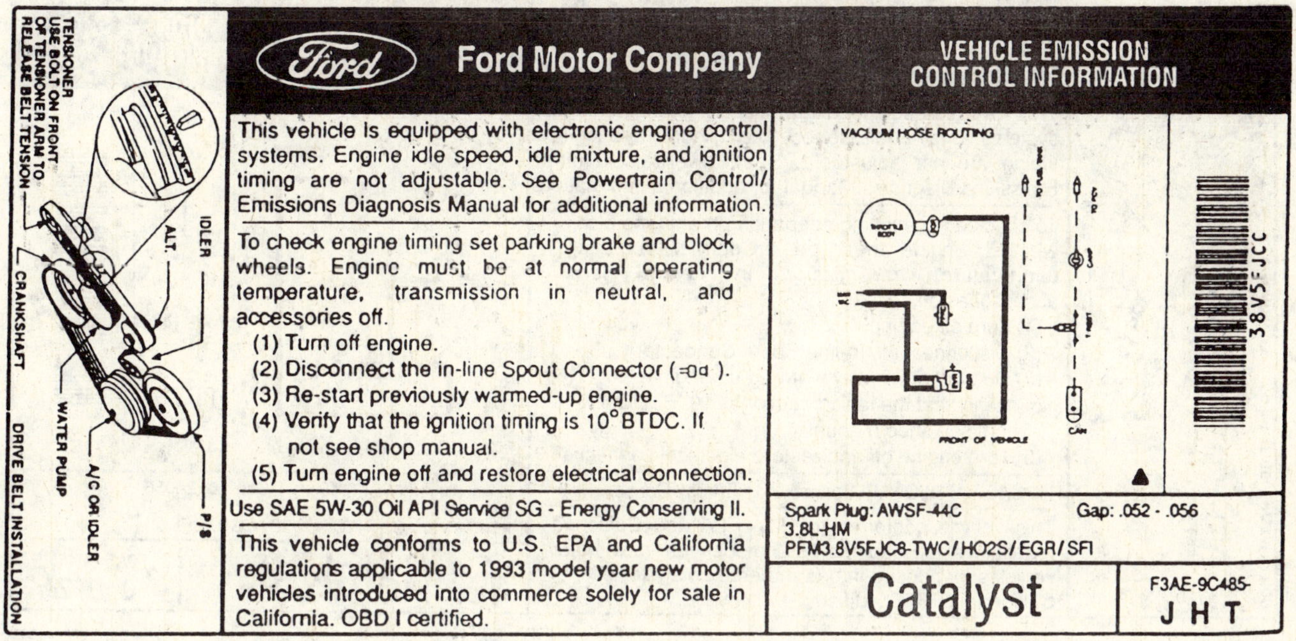

88184GE5

Fig. 139 Vehicle Emission Label 1993 3.8L VIN-4 engine — 2-16R-R10

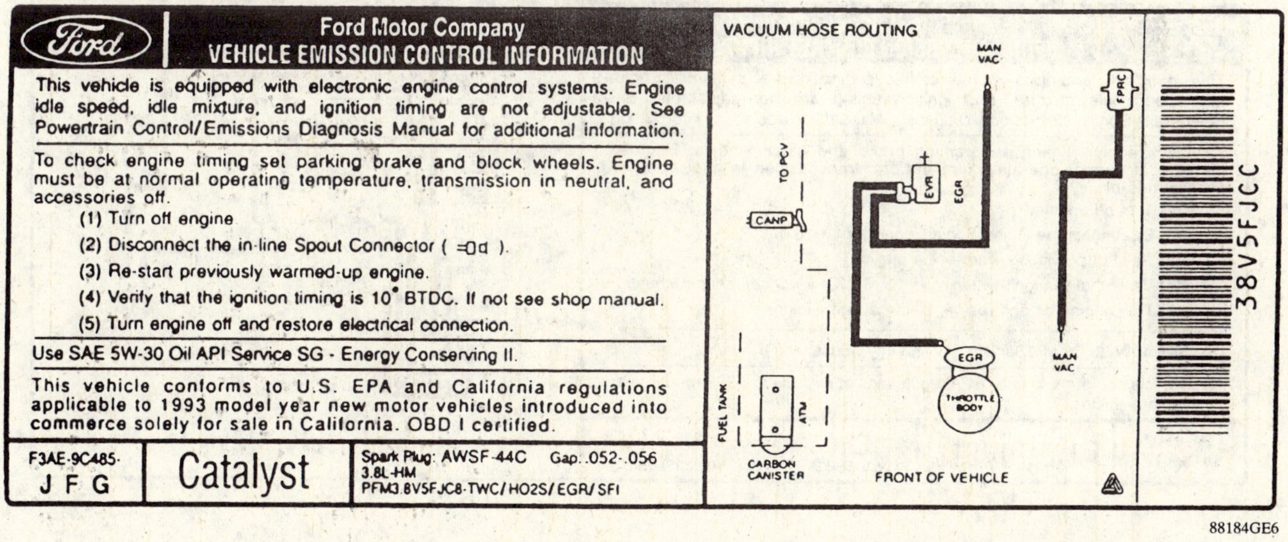

88184GE6

Fig. 140 Vehicle Emission Label 1993 3.8L VIN-4 engine — 2-16T-R10

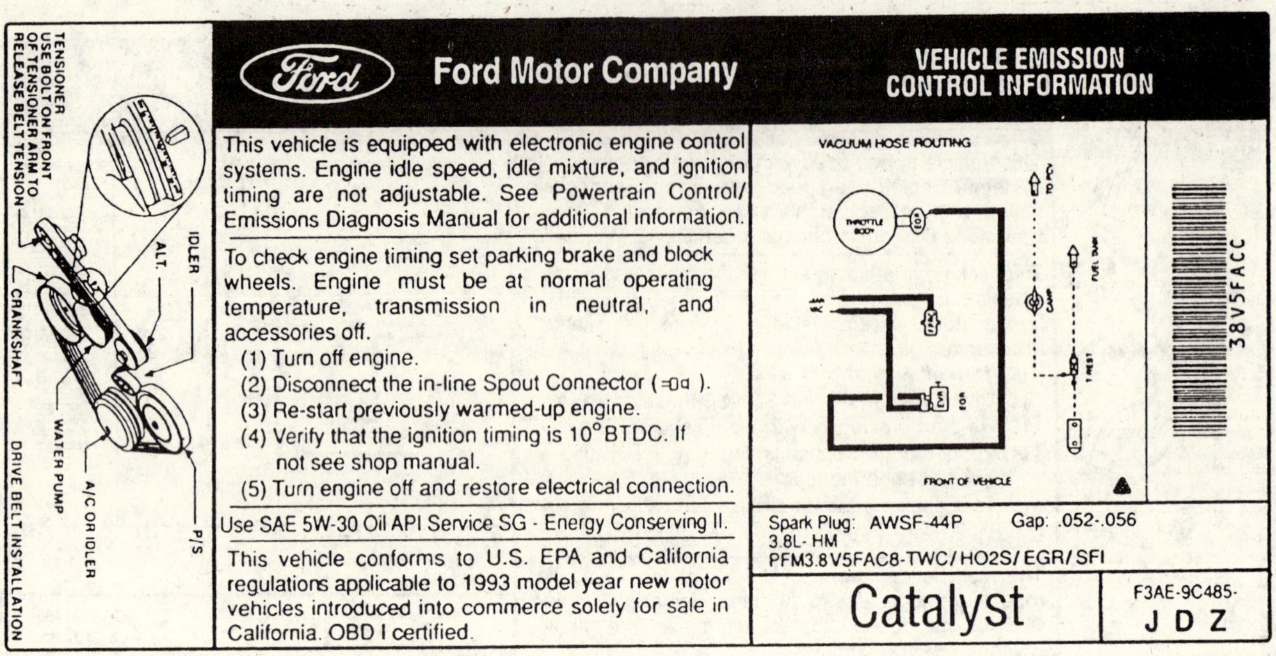

88184GE7

Fig. 141 Vehicle Emission Label 1993 3.8L VIN-4 engine — 3-16Q-R10

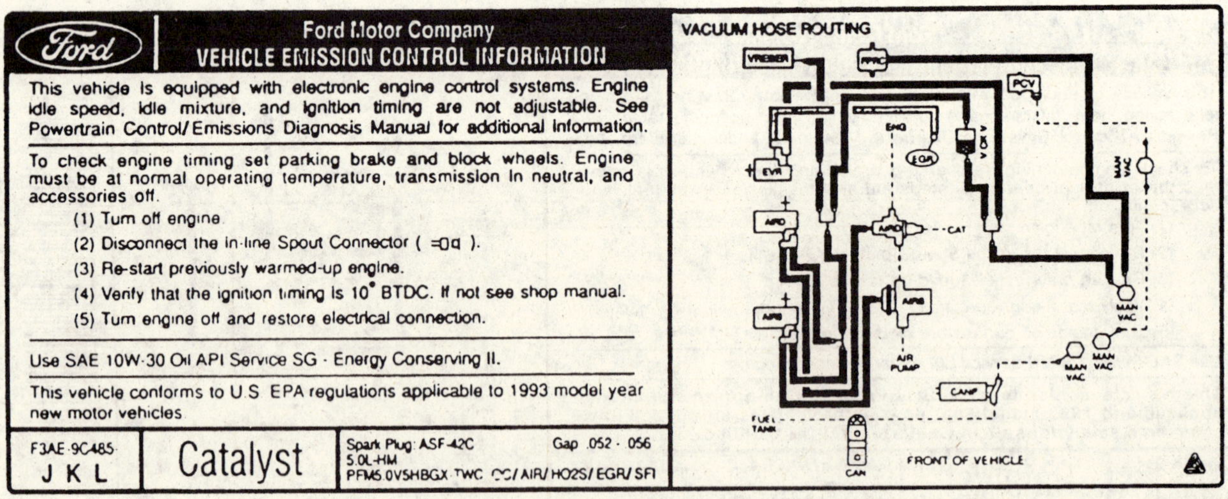

88184GE8

Fig. 142 Vehicle Emission Label 1993 5.0L VIN-T engine — 9-21A-R00

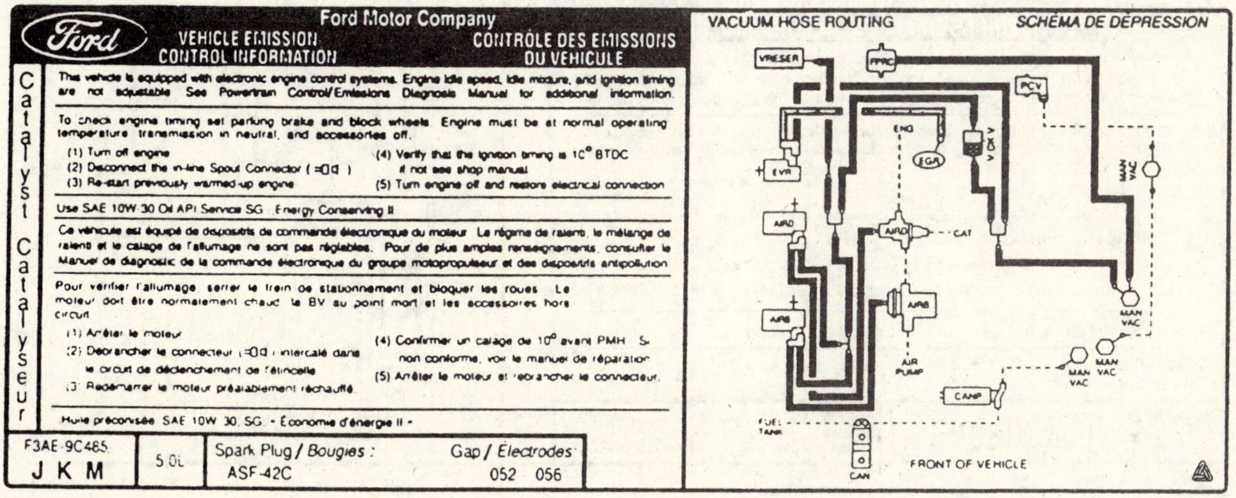

88184GE9

Fig. 143 Vehicle Emission Label 1993 5.0L VIN-T engine — 9-21A-R00

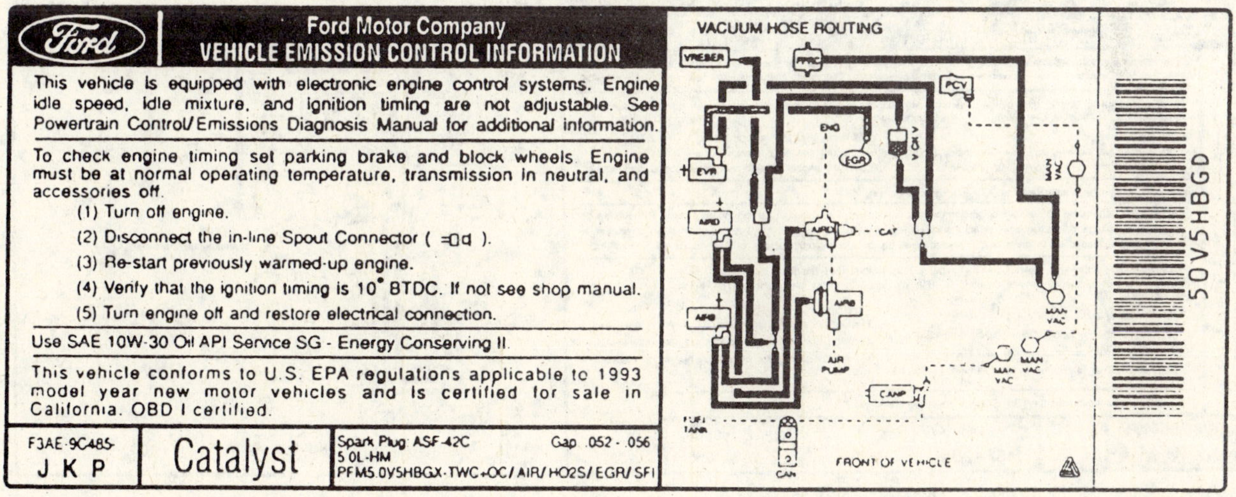

88184GF0

Fig. 144 Vehicle Emission Label 1993 5.0L VIN-T engine — 9-21A-R00

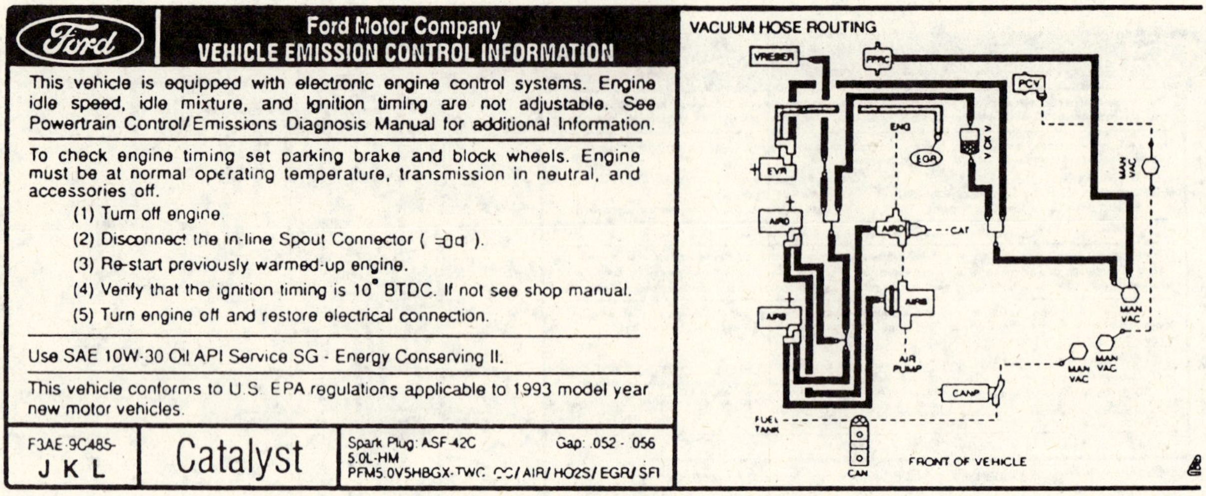

88184GF1

Fig. 145 Vehicle Emission Label 1993 5.0L VIN-T engine — 9-21C-R00

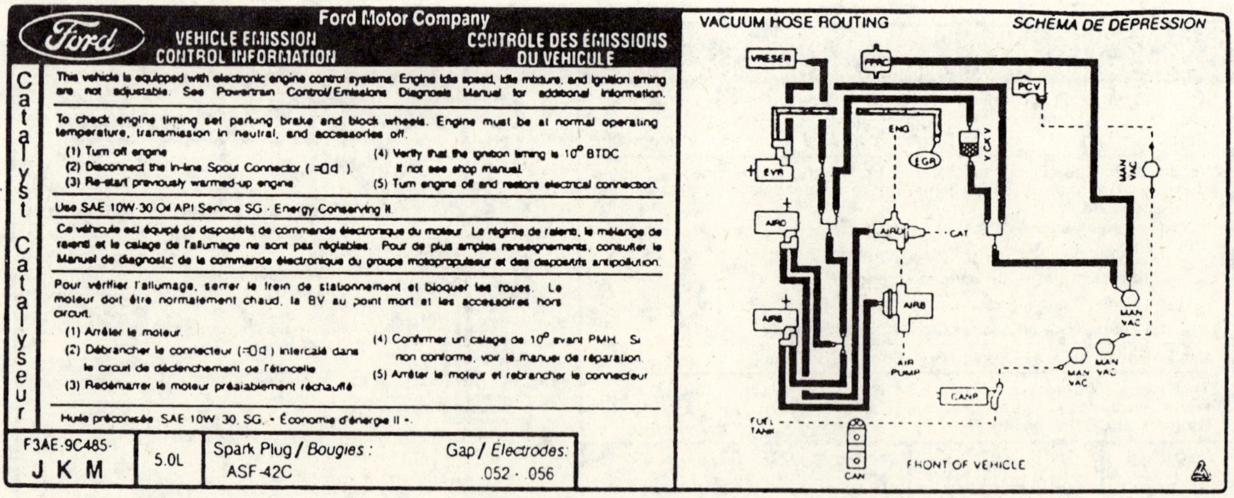

88184GF2

Fig. 146 Vehicle Emission Label 1993 5.0L VIN-T engine — 9-21C-R00

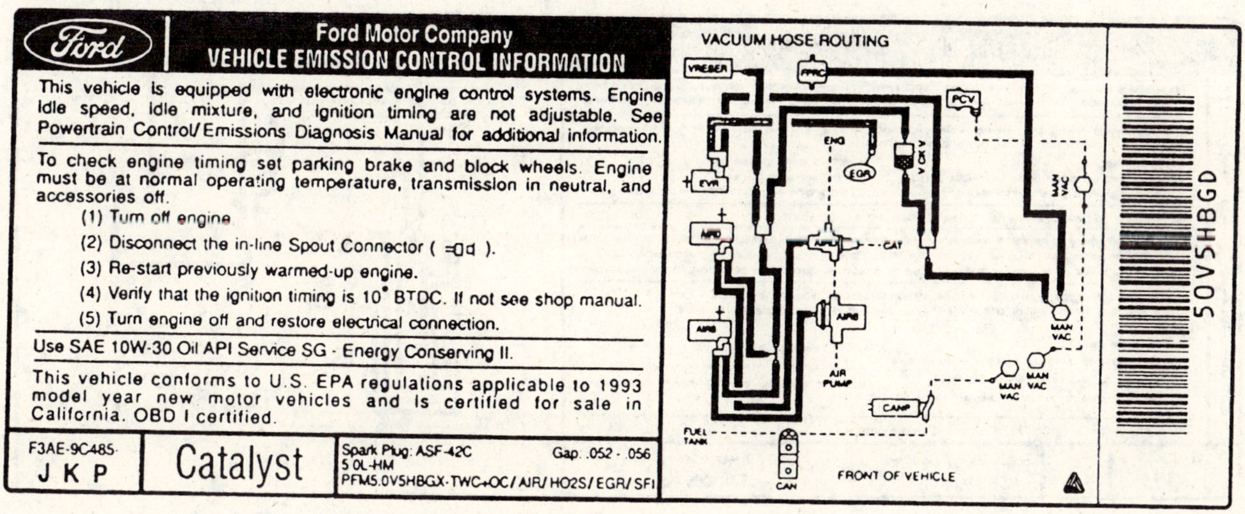

Ford Motor Company
VEHICLE EMISSION CONTROL INFORMATION

This vehicle is equipped with electronic engine control systems. Engine idle speed, idle mixture, and ignition timing are not adjustable. See Powertrain Control/Emissions Diagnosis Manual for additional information.

To check engine timing set parking brake and block wheels. Engine must be at normal operating temperature, transmission in neutral, and accessories off.

(1) Turn off engine.
(2) Disconnect the in-line Spout Connector (=▢d).
(3) Re-start previously warmed-up engine.
(4) Verify that the ignition timing is 10° BTDC. If not see shop manual.
(5) Turn engine off and restore electrical connection.

Use SAE 10W-30 Oil API Service SG - Energy Conserving II.

This vehicle conforms to U.S. EPA regulations applicable to 1993 model year new motor vehicles and is certified for sale in California. OBD I certified.

F3AE-9C485-
J K P

Catalyst

Spark Plug: ASF-42C Gap: .052 - .056
5.0L-HM
PFM5.0V5HBGX-TWC+OC/AIR/HO2S/EGR/SFI

88184GF3

Fig. 147 Vehicle Emission Label 1993 5.0L VIN-T engine — 9-21C-R00

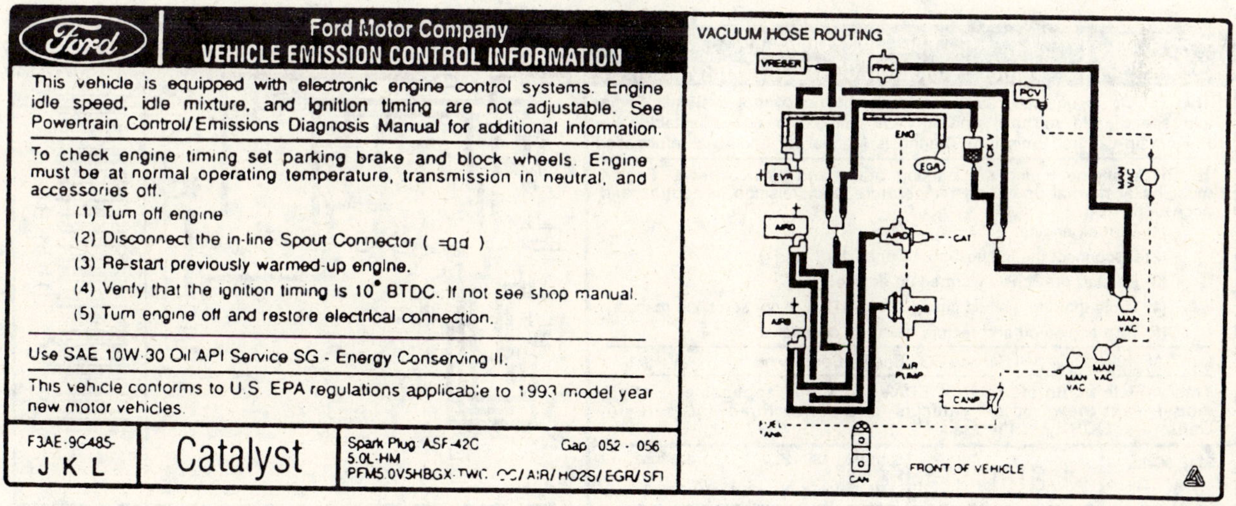

Ford Motor Company
VEHICLE EMISSION CONTROL INFORMATION

This vehicle is equipped with electronic engine control systems. Engine idle speed, idle mixture, and ignition timing are not adjustable. See Powertrain Control/Emissions Diagnosis Manual for additional information.

To check engine timing set parking brake and block wheels. Engine must be at normal operating temperature, transmission in neutral, and accessories off.

(1) Turn off engine
(2) Disconnect the in-line Spout Connector (=▢d)
(3) Re-start previously warmed-up engine.
(4) Verify that the ignition timing is 10° BTDC. If not see shop manual.
(5) Turn engine off and restore electrical connection.

Use SAE 10W-30 Oil API Service SG - Energy Conserving II.

This vehicle conforms to U.S. EPA regulations applicable to 1993 model year new motor vehicles.

F3AE-9C485-
J K L

Catalyst

Spark Plug: ASF-42C Gap: .052 - .056
5.0L-HM
PFM5.0V5HBGX-TWC+OC/AIR/HO2S/EGR/SFI

88184GF4

Fig. 148 Vehicle Emission Label 1993 5.0L VIN-T engine — 9-22A-R00

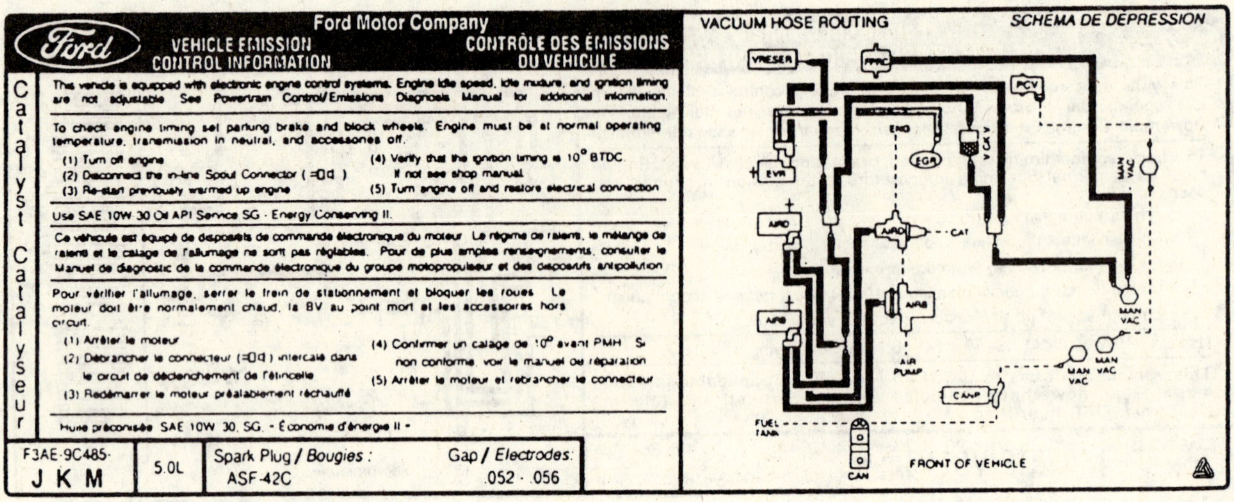

88184GF5

Fig. 149 Vehicle Emission Label 1993 5.0L VIN-T engine — 9-22A-R00

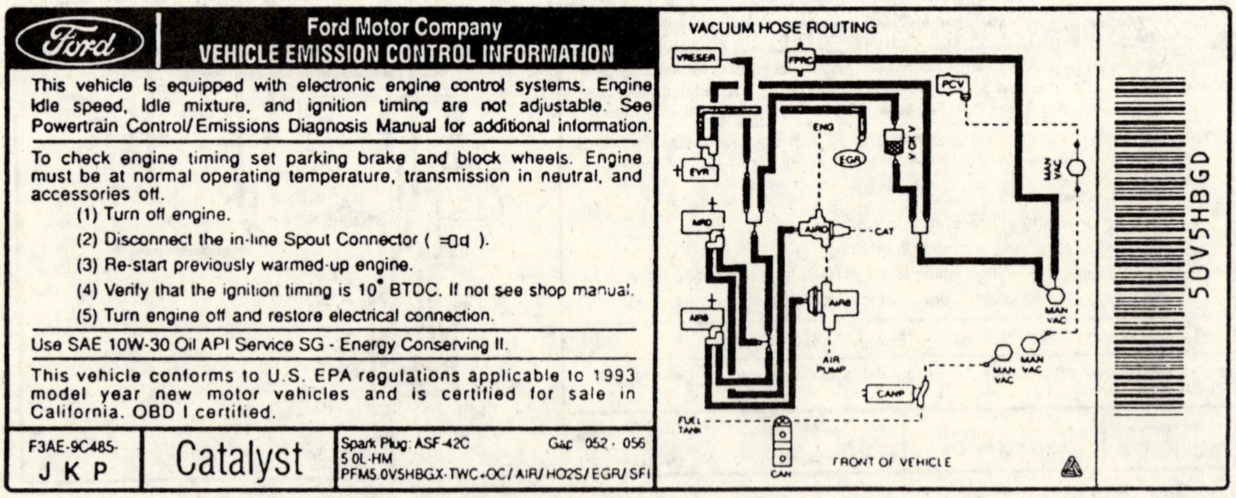

88184GF6

Fig. 150 Vehicle Emission Label 1993 5.0L VIN-T engine — 9-22A-R00

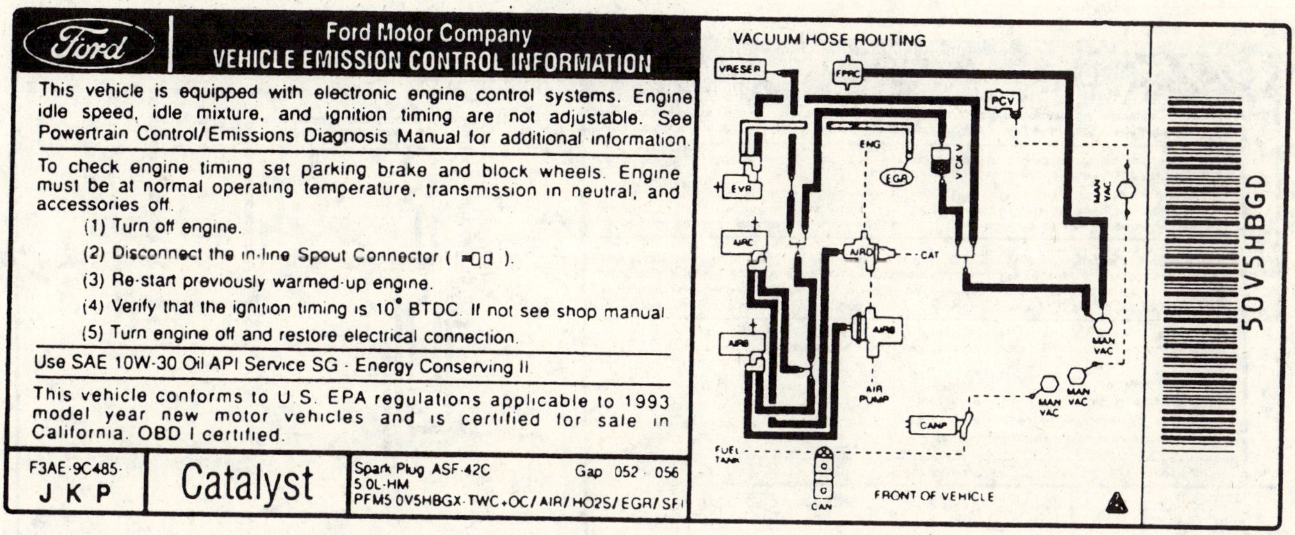

Ford Motor Company
VEHICLE EMISSION CONTROL INFORMATION

This vehicle is equipped with electronic engine control systems. Engine idle speed, idle mixture, and ignition timing are not adjustable. See Powertrain Control/Emissions Diagnosis Manual for additional information.

To check engine timing set parking brake and block wheels. Engine must be at normal operating temperature, transmission in neutral, and accessories off.

(1) Turn off engine.
(2) Disconnect the in-line Spout Connector ( ).
(3) Re-start previously warmed-up engine.
(4) Verify that the ignition timing is 10° BTDC. If not see shop manual.
(5) Turn engine off and restore electrical connection.

Use SAE 10W-30 Oil API Service SG - Energy Conserving II

This vehicle conforms to U.S. EPA regulations applicable to 1993 model year new motor vehicles and is certified for sale in California. OBD I certified.

F3AE-9C485-
J K P

Catalyst

Spark Plug ASF-42C Gap .052 - .056
5.0L-HM
PFM5.0V5HBGX-TWC+OC/AIR/HO2S/EGR/SFI

88184GF8

Fig. 151 Vehicle Emission Label 1993 5.0L VIN-N engine — 3-22A-R10

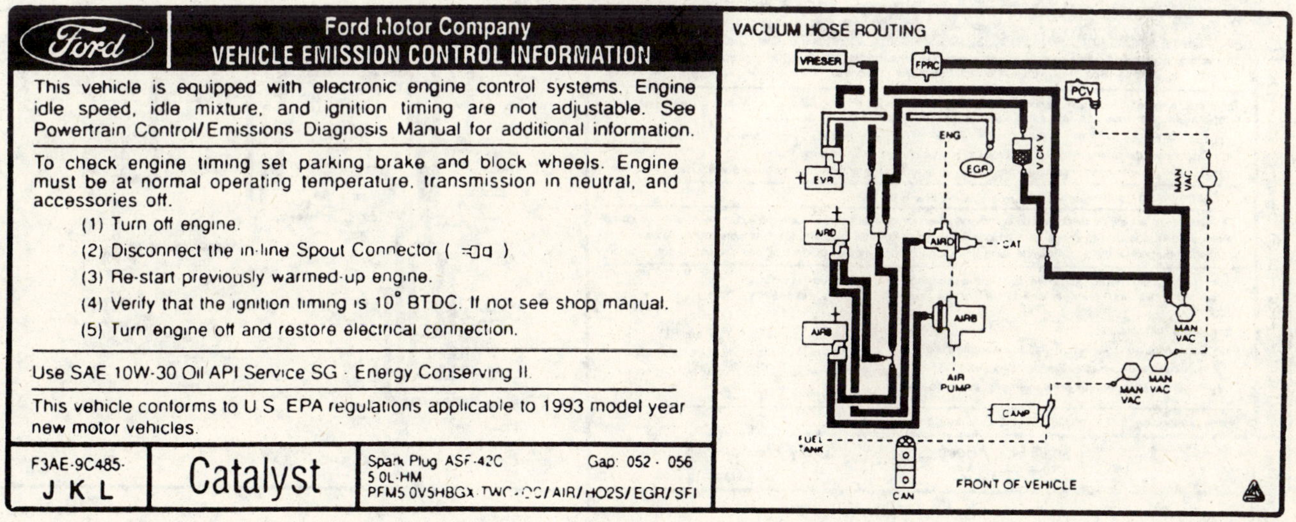

Ford Motor Company
VEHICLE EMISSION CONTROL INFORMATION

This vehicle is equipped with electronic engine control systems. Engine idle speed, idle mixture, and ignition timing are not adjustable. See Powertrain Control/Emissions Diagnosis Manual for additional information.

To check engine timing set parking brake and block wheels. Engine must be at normal operating temperature, transmission in neutral, and accessories off.

(1) Turn off engine.
(2) Disconnect the in-line Spout Connector ( ).
(3) Re-start previously warmed-up engine.
(4) Verify that the ignition timing is 10° BTDC. If not see shop manual.
(5) Turn engine off and restore electrical connection.

Use SAE 10W-30 Oil API Service SG - Energy Conserving II.

This vehicle conforms to U.S. EPA regulations applicable to 1993 model year new motor vehicles.

F3AE-9C485-
J K L

Catalyst

Spark Plug ASF-42C Gap .052 - .056
5.0L-HM
PFM5.0V5HBGX-TWC+OC/AIR/HO2S/EGR/SFI

88184GF9

Fig. 152 Vehicle Emission Label 1993 5.0L VIN-N engine — 3-22A-R10

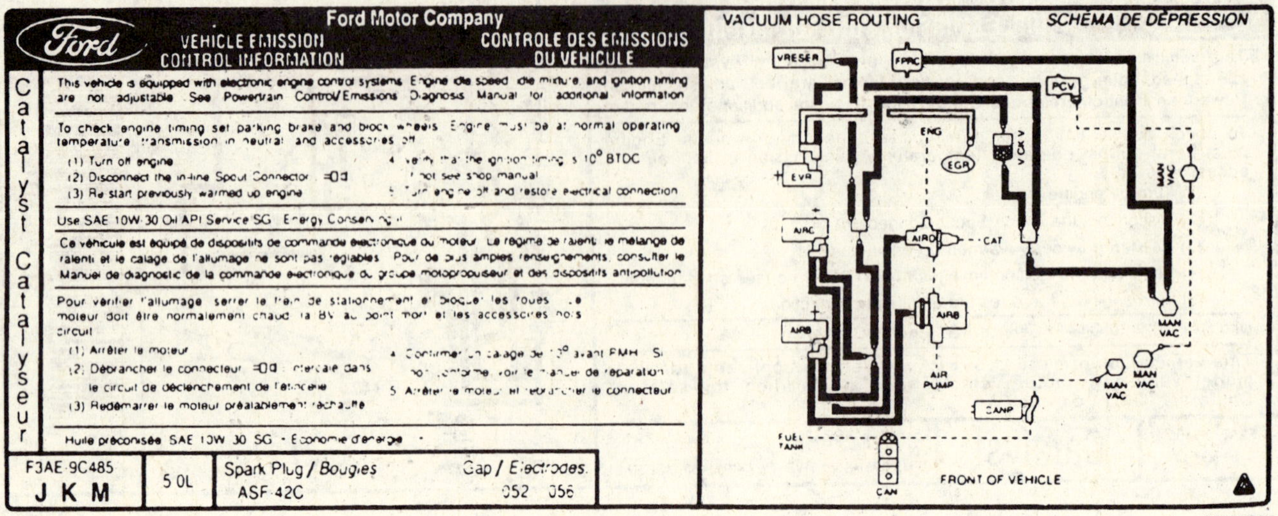

88184GG0

Fig. 153 Vehicle Emission Label 1993 5.0L VIN-N engine — 3-22A-R10

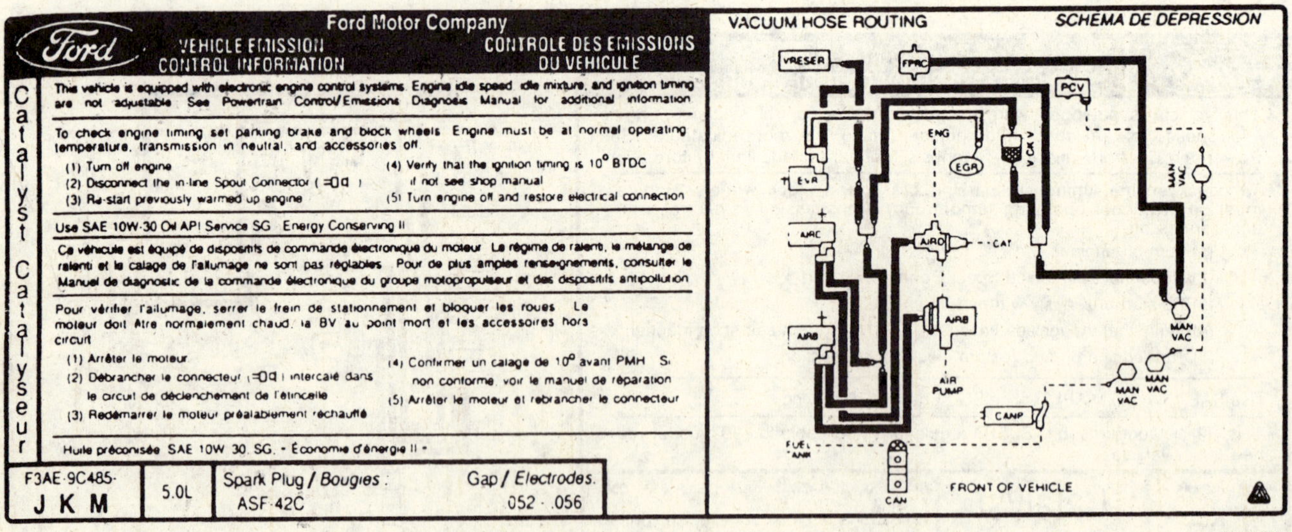

88184GG1

Fig. 154 Vehicle Emission Label 1993 5.0L VIN-N engine — 3-21C-R10

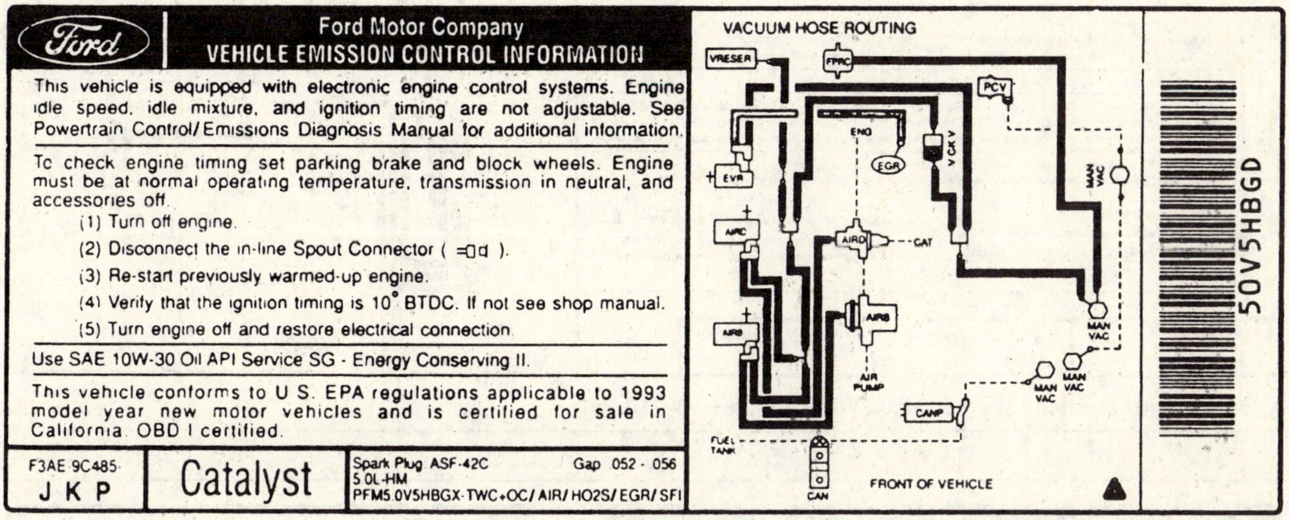

88184GG2

Fig. 155 Vehicle Emission Label 1993 5.0L VIN-N engine — 3-21C-R10

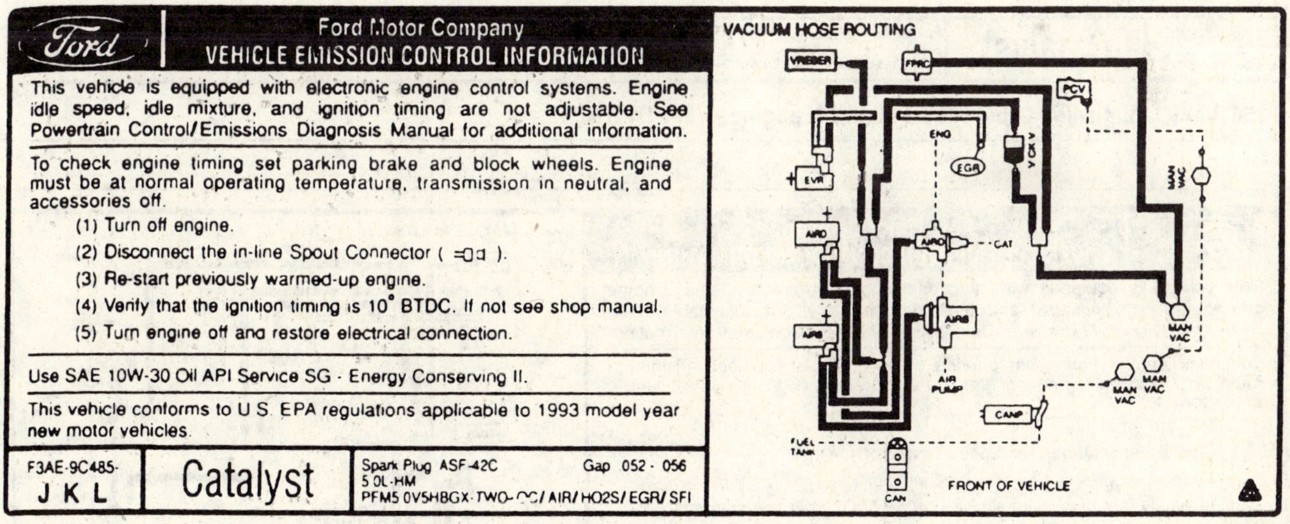

88184GG3

Fig. 156 Vehicle Emission Label 1993 5.0L VIN-N engine — 3-21A-R10

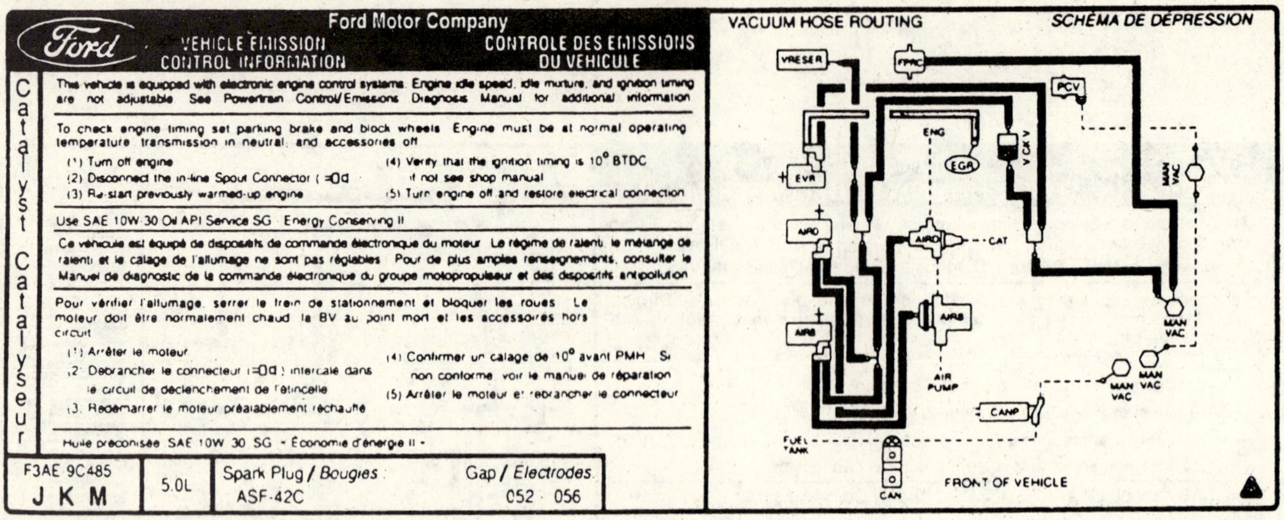

Ford Motor Company
VEHICLE EMISSION CONTROL INFORMATION — CONTROLE DES EMISSIONS DU VEHICULE

Catalyst — Catalyseur

This vehicle is equipped with electronic engine control systems. Engine idle speed, idle mixture, and ignition timing are not adjustable. See Powertrain Control/Emissions Diagnosis Manual for additional information.

To check engine timing set parking brake and block wheels. Engine must be at normal operating temperature, transmission in neutral, and accessories off.

(1) Turn off engine
(2) Disconnect the in-line Spout Connector ( )
(3) Re-start previously warmed-up engine
(4) Verify that the ignition timing is 10° BTDC. If not see shop manual.
(5) Turn engine off and restore electrical connection

Use SAE 10W-30 Oil API Service SG - Energy Conserving II

Ce véhicule est équipé de dispositifs de commande électronique du moteur. Le régime de ralenti, le mélange de ralenti et le calage de l'allumage ne sont pas réglables. Pour de plus amples renseignements, consulter le Manuel de diagnostic de la commande électronique du groupe motopropulseur et des dispositifs antipollution.

Pour vérifier l'allumage, serrer le frein de stationnement et bloquer les roues. Le moteur doit être normalement chaud, la BV au point mort et les accessoires hors circuit.

(1) Arrêter le moteur
(2) Débrancher le connecteur ( ) intercalé dans le circuit de déclenchement de l'étincelle
(3) Redémarrer le moteur préalablement réchauffé
(4) Confirmer un calage de 10° avant PMH. Si non conforme, voir le manuel de réparation
(5) Arrêter le moteur et rebrancher le connecteur

Huile préconisée SAE 10W 30 SG - Économie d'énergie II -

F3AE 9C485 JKM	5.0L	Spark Plug / *Bougies* ASF-42C	Gap / *Electrodes* 052 - 056

Fig. 157 Vehicle Emission Label 1993 5.0L VIN-N engine — 3-21A-R10

88184GG4

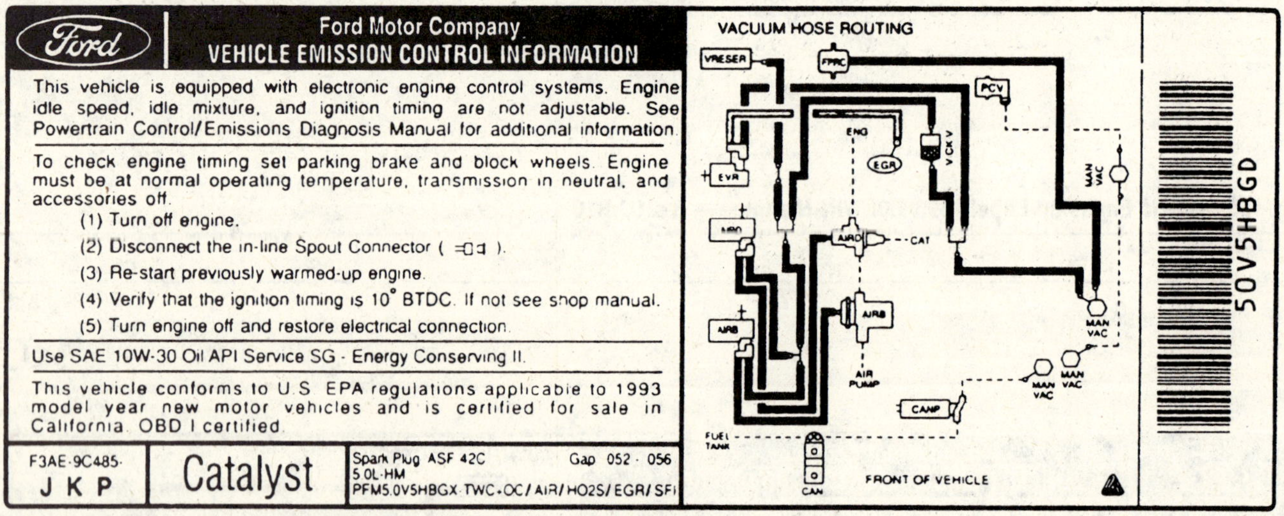

Ford Motor Company
VEHICLE EMISSION CONTROL INFORMATION

This vehicle is equipped with electronic engine control systems. Engine idle speed, idle mixture, and ignition timing are not adjustable. See Powertrain Control/Emissions Diagnosis Manual for additional information.

To check engine timing set parking brake and block wheels. Engine must be at normal operating temperature, transmission in neutral, and accessories off.

(1) Turn off engine.
(2) Disconnect the in-line Spout Connector ( ).
(3) Re-start previously warmed-up engine.
(4) Verify that the ignition timing is 10° BTDC. If not see shop manual.
(5) Turn engine off and restore electrical connection.

Use SAE 10W-30 Oil API Service SG - Energy Conserving II.

This vehicle conforms to U.S. EPA regulations applicable to 1993 model year new motor vehicles and is certified for sale in California. OBD I certified.

F3AE-9C485- JKP	Catalyst	Spark Plug ASF 42C Gap 052 - 056 5.0L-HM PFM5.0V5HBGX-TWC+OC/AIR/HO2S/EGR/SFI

Fig. 158 Vehicle Emission Label 1993 5.0L VIN-N engine — 3-21A-R10

88184GG5

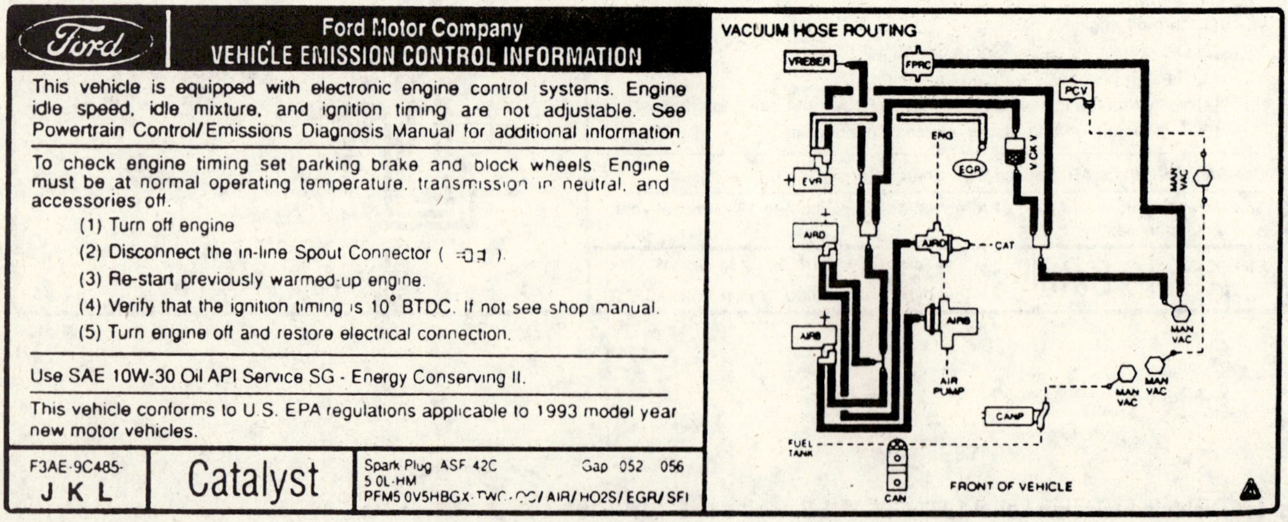

Ford Motor Company
VEHICLE EMISSION CONTROL INFORMATION

This vehicle is equipped with electronic engine control systems. Engine idle speed, idle mixture, and ignition timing are not adjustable. See Powertrain Control/Emissions Diagnosis Manual for additional information

To check engine timing set parking brake and block wheels. Engine must be at normal operating temperature, transmission in neutral, and accessories off.

(1) Turn off engine
(2) Disconnect the in-line Spout Connector ( ).
(3) Re-start previously warmed-up engine.
(4) Verify that the ignition timing is 10° BTDC. If not see shop manual.
(5) Turn engine off and restore electrical connection.

Use SAE 10W-30 Oil API Service SG - Energy Conserving II.

This vehicle conforms to U.S. EPA regulations applicable to 1993 model year new motor vehicles.

F3AE-9C485- JKL	Catalyst	Spark Plug ASF 42C Gap 052 - 056 5.0L-HM PFM5.0V5HBGX-TWC-OC/AIR/HO2S/EGR/SFI

Fig. 159 Vehicle Emission Label 1993 5.0L VIN-N engine — 3-21C-R10

88184GG6

5

FUEL SYSTEM

BASIC FUEL SYSTEM DIAGNOSIS

When there is a problem starting or driving a vehicle, two of the most important checks involve the ignition and the fuel systems. The questions most mechanics attempt to answer first, "is there spark?" and "is there fuel?" will often lead to solving most basic problems. For ignition system diagnosis and testing, please refer to the information on engine electrical components and ignition systems found earlier in this manual. If the ignition system checks out (there is spark), then you must determine if the fuel system is operating properly (is there fuel?).

FUEL LINES AND FITTINGS

Quick-Connect Fuel Line Fittings

REMOVAL & INSTALLATION

There are 3 methods used to connect the fuel lines and fuel system components: the hairpin clip push connect fitting, the duck bill clip push connect fitting and the spring lock coupling. Each requires a different procedure to disconnect and connect.

Hairpin Clip Push Connect Fitting

➧ See Figure 1

1. Inspect the visible internal portion of the fitting for dirt accumulation. If more than a light coating of dust is present, clean the fitting before disassembly.
2. Some adhesion between the seals in the fitting and the tubing will occur with time. To separate, twist the fitting on the tube, then push and pull the fitting until it moves freely on the tube.

➥ Use care when separating 90 degree elbow connectors, as excessive side loading could break the connector body.

3. Remove the hairpin clip from the fitting by first bending and breaking the shipping tab. Next, spread the 2 clip legs by hand about 1/8 in. each to disengage the body and push the legs into the fitting. Lightly pull the triangular end of the clip and work it clear of the tube and fitting.

➥ Do not use hand tools to complete this operation.

4. Grasp the fitting and pull in an axial direction to remove the fitting from the tube.
5. After disassembly, inspect and clean the tube end sealing surfaces. The tube end should be free of scratches and corrosion that could provide leak paths. Inspect the inside of the fitting for any internal parts such as O-rings and spacers that may have been dislodged from the fitting. Replace any damaged connector.

To connect:

6. Install a new connector if damage was found. Insert a new clip into any 2 adjacent openings with the triangular portion pointing away from the fitting opening. Install the clip until the legs of the clip are locked on the outside of the body. Piloting with an index finger is necessary.
7. Before installing the fitting on the tube, wipe the tube end with a clean cloth. Inspect the inside of the fitting to make sure it is free of dirt and/or obstructions.
8. Apply a light coating of engine oil to the tube end. Align the fitting and tube axially and push the fitting onto the tube end. When the fitting is engaged, a definite click will be heard. Pull on the fitting to make sure it is fully engaged.

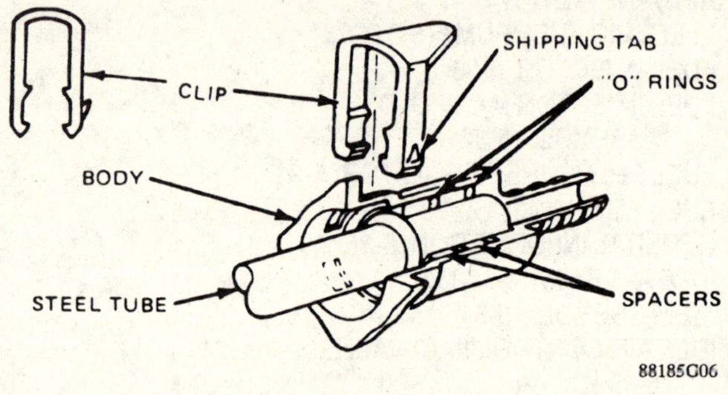

Fig. 1 Push connect fitting with a hair pin clip

Duck Bill Clip Push Connect Fitting

➧ See Figures 2, 3 and 4

1. Inspect the visible internal portion of the fitting for dirt accumulation. If more than a light coating of dust is present, clean the fitting before disassembly.
2. Some adhesion between the seals in the fitting and the tubing will occur with time. To separate, twist the fitting on the tube, then push and pull the fitting until it moves freely on the tube.
3. Align the slot on push connect disassembly tool T82L-9600-AH or equivalent, with either tab on the clip, 90 degrees from the slots on the side of the fitting and insert the tool. This disengages the duck bill retainer from the tube.
4. Holding the tool and the tube with one hand, pull the fitting away from the tube.

➥ Use hands only. Only moderate effort is required if the tube has been properly disengaged.

5. After disassembly, inspect and clean the tube end sealing surfaces. The tube end should be free of scratches and corrosion that could provide leak paths. Inspect the inside of the fitting for any internal parts such as O-rings and spacers that may have been dislodged from the fitting. Replace any damaged connector.

6. Some fuel tubes have a secondary bead which aligns with the outer surface of the clip. These beads can make tool insertion difficult. If there is extreme difficulty, use the following disassembly method:

a. Using pliers with a jaw width of 0.2 in. (5mm) or less, align the jaws with the openings in the side of the fitting case and compress the portion of the retaining clip that engages the fitting case. This disengages the retaining clip from the case. Often one side of the clip will disengage before the other. The clip must be disengaged from both openings.

b. Pull the fitting off the tube by hand only. Only moderate effort is required if the retaining clip has been properly disengaged.

c. After disassembly, inspect and clean the tube end sealing surfaces. The tube end should be free of scratches and corrosion that could provide leak paths. Inspect the inside of the fitting for any internal parts such as O-rings and spacers that may have been dislodged from the fitting. Replace any damaged connector.

d. The retaining clip will remain on the tube. Disengage the clip from the tube bead and remove.

To connect:

7. Install a new connector if damage was found. Install the new replacement clip into the body by inserting 1 of the retaining clip serrated edges on the duck bill portion into one side of the window openings. Push on the other side until the clip snaps into place.

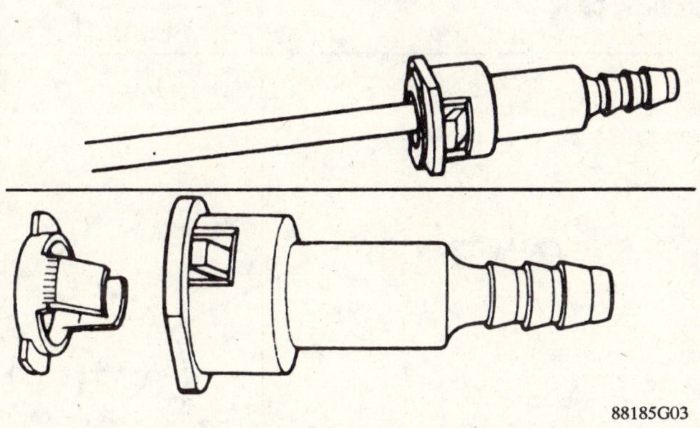

Fig. 2 Push connect type with a duck bill clip fitting

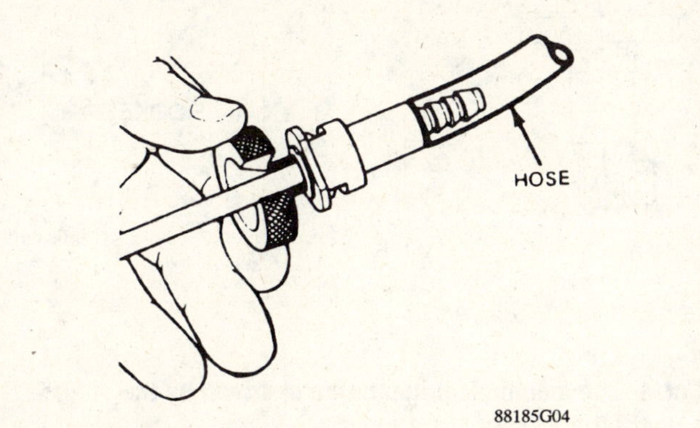

Fig. 3 Connector removal using a T82-9600-AH tool

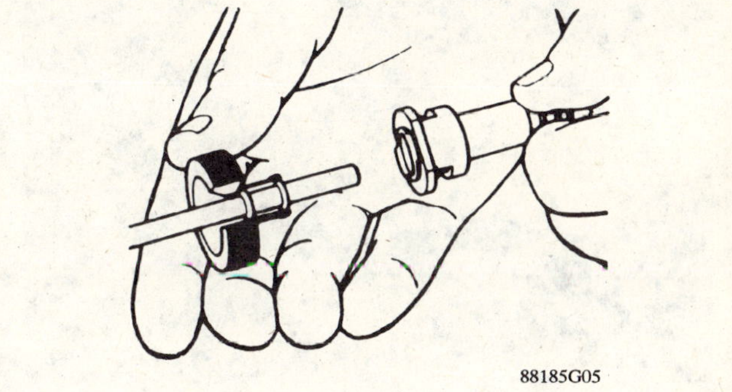

Fig. 4 Pull off the push connect fitting

8. Before installing the fitting on the tube, wipe the tube end with a clean cloth. Inspect the inside of the fitting to make sure it is free of dirt and/or obstructions.

9. Apply a light coating of engine oil to the tube end. Align the fitting and tube axially and push the fitting onto the tube end. When the fitting is engaged, a definite click will be heard. Pull on the fitting to make sure it is fully engaged.

Spring Lock Coupling

➧ **See Figures 5, 6 and 7**

The spring lock coupling is a fuel line coupling held together by a garter spring inside a circular cage. When the coupling is connected together, the flared end of the female fitting slips behind the garter spring inside the cage of the male fitting. The garter spring and cage then prevent the flared end of the female fitting from pulling out of the cage. As an additional locking feature, most vehicles have a horseshoe shaped retaining clip that improves the retaining reliability of the spring lock coupling.

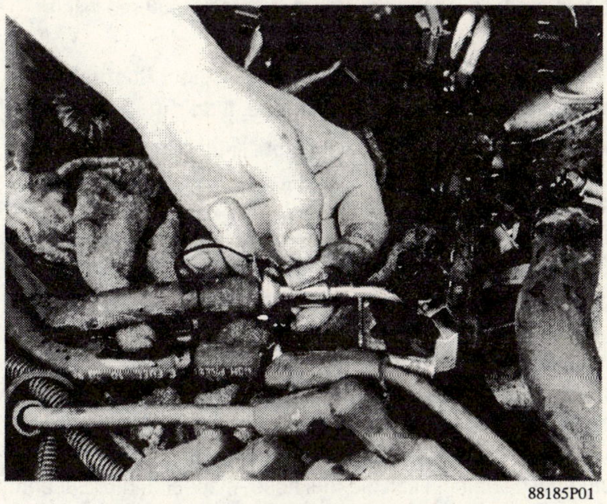

Fig. 5 Remove the clip retaining the hose to the line

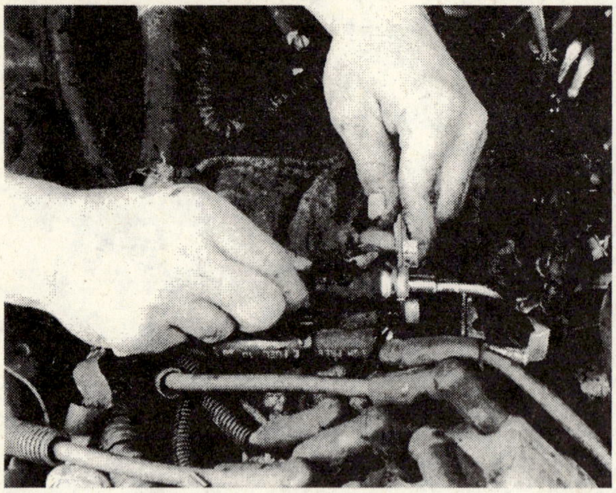

88185P02

Fig. 6 Separate the line from the hose

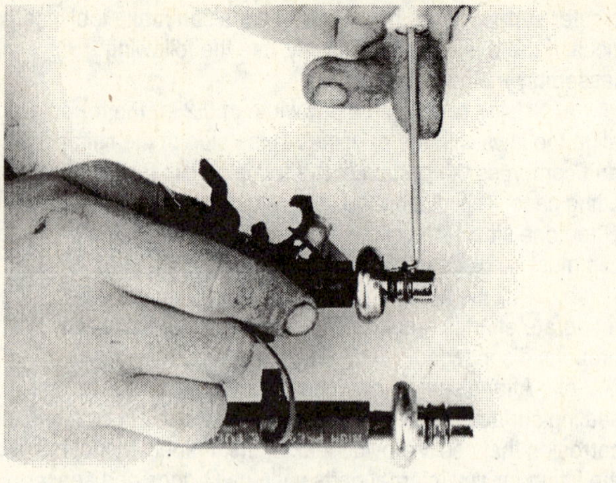

88185P03

Fig. 7 Replace the O-rings from the fuel line fittings

CARBURETED FUEL SYSTEM

Mechanical Fuel Pump

REMOVAL & INSTALLATION

See Figure 8

Before removing the pump, rotate the engine so that the low point of the cam lobe is against the pump arm. This can be determined by rotating the engine with the fuel pump mounting bolts loosened slightly. When tension (resistance) is removed from the arm, proceed.

1. Loosen the threaded fuel line connection(s) with the proper size flared nut wrench, then retighten snugly. Do not remove the lines at this time.
2. Loosen the mounting bolts one to two turns. Apply force with your hands to loosen the fuel pump if the gasket is stuck. Rotate the engine, by nudging the starter, until the pump cam lobe is near its low position. The tension on the pump will be greatly reduced at the low cam position.

The outlet line is pressurized. Disconnect the fuel pump inlet line, the outlet vapor return line, if so equipped.

3. Remove the pump attaching bolts, then the pump and gasket. Clean the mating areas well.

To Install:

4. Install the attaching bolts into the pump, then install a new gasket on the bolts. Position the pump to the mounting pad. Turn the bolts alternately and evenly, then tighten to 12–15 ft. lbs. (16–20 Nm).
5. Install the fuel outlet line. If it is a threaded connection, start fitting by hand to avoid any crossthreading. Tighten the fitting to 20–24 ft. lbs. (15–18 Nm).
6. Install the inlet line and fuel vapor return line, if removed. Using new clamps, install the fuel hose. Inspect and replace any cracked or damaged fuel hoses.
7. Check that all connections are intact, then start the engine and inspect for leaks. Run the engine for approximately 2 minutes.
8. Stop the engine and check all the pump and fuel line connections for any leaks. Inspect for any oil leaks at the pump mounting pad.

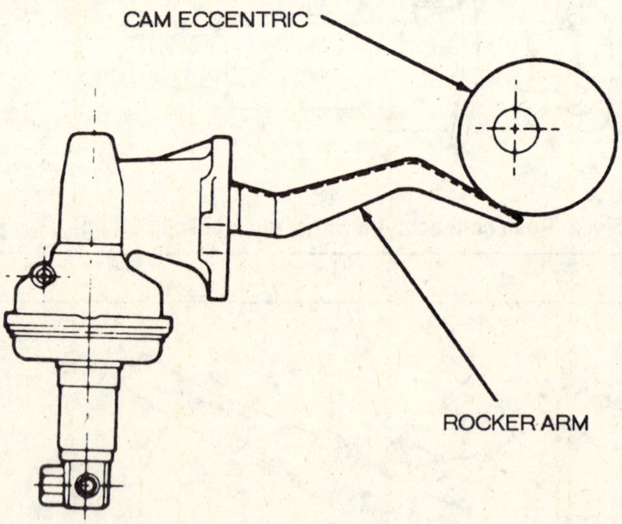

88185G01

Fig. 8 The mechanical fuel pump is driven by the camshaft

TESTING

➧ See Figure 9

No adjustments may be made to the fuel pump. Before removing and replacing the old fuel pump, the following test may be made while the pump is still installed on the engine.

1. If a fuel pressure gauge is available, connect the gauge to the engine and operate the engine until the pressure stops rising. Stop the engine and take the reading. If the reading is within the specifications given in the Tune-Up Specifications chart in Section 2, the malfunctions is not in the fuel pump. Also check the pressure drop after the engine is stopped. A large pressure drop below the minimum specification indicates leaky valves. If the pump proves to be satisfactory, check the tank and inlet line.
2. If a fuel pressure gauge is not available, disconnect the fuel line at the pump outlet, place a vessel beneath the pump outlet, and crank the engine. A good pump will force the fuel out of the outlet in steady spurts. One pint in 25–30 seconds is a good flow. A worn diaphragm spring may not provide proper pumping action.
3. As a further test, disconnect and plug the fuel line from the tank at the pump, and hold your thumb over the pump inlet. If the pump is functioning properly, a suction indicates that the pump diaphragm is leaking, or that the diaphragm linkage is worn.
4. Check the crankcase for gasoline. A ruptured diaphragm may leak fuel into the engine.

Carburetors

ADJUSTMENTS

Motorcraft 2150

IDLE SPEED

1. Place the transmission in **P** or **N**.
2. Allow the engine to operate until normal operating temperature is reached.
3. Turn all accessories off.
4. Check/adjust curb idle rpm:
   a. On non-air conditioning equipped vehicles, adjust the saddle bracket adjusting screw.
   b. On air conditioning equipped vehicles, adjust the hex head screw protruding from the rear of the TSP housing.
5. Slightly rev the engine momentarily. Recheck the curb idle and readjust, if required.

FAST IDLE

➧ See Figure 10

1. Place the transmission in Neutral or Park position.
2. Bring the engine to normal operating condition.
3. Disconnect the vacuum hose at the EGR valve and plug.

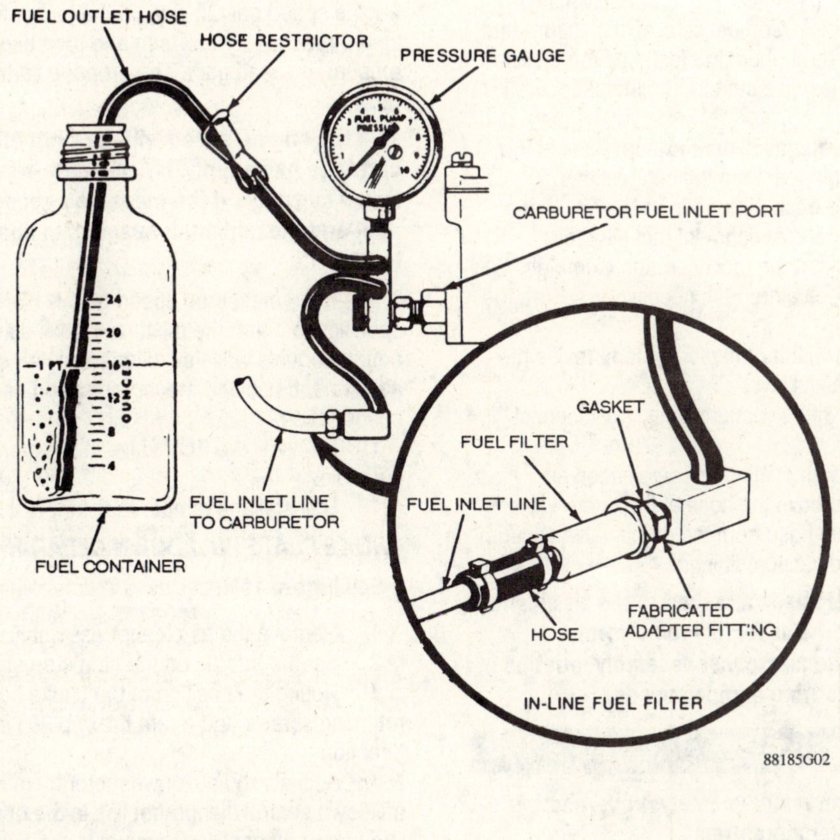

Fig. 9 Fuel pump pressure and capacity test equipment

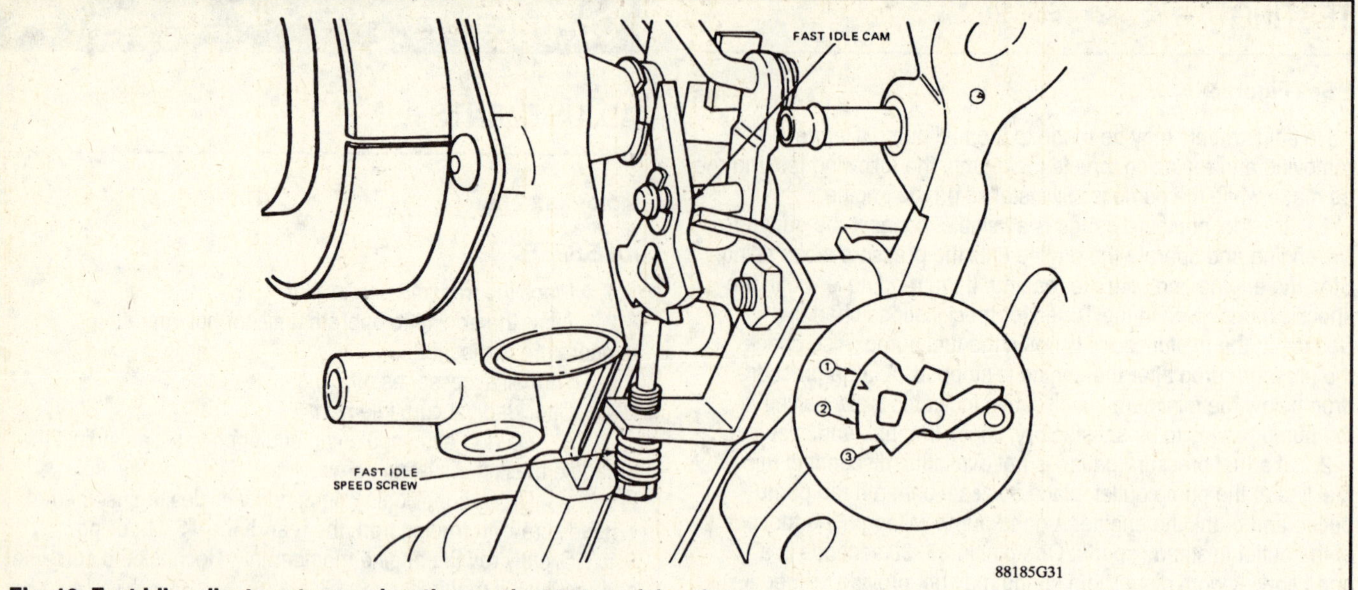

Fig. 10 Fast idle adjustment screw location on the 2150 model carburetor

4. Place the fast idle cam adjustment on the specified step of the fast idle cam. Check and adjust the fast idle rpm to specification.
5. Rev the engine momentarily, place the fast idle on the specified step and then recheck the fast idles RPM.
6. Remove the plug from the EGR vacuum hose, then reconnect.

IDLE MIXTURE

1. Set the parking brake and block the drive wheels.
2. Connect a tachometer (Rotunda 20362 or equivalent).
3. If equipped with a Hot Idle Compensator (HIC), insure that it remains in closed position throughout the test. Idle the vehicle on the kickdown step of the fast idle cam for 3 minutes to ensure the HIC valve is closed.
4. Disconnect the fuel evaporative purge return hose at the engine and air cleaner, if equipped. Plug the connections.
5. Disconnect the flexible fresh air tube from the air cleaner duct or adaptor. Using a propane enrichment tool (Rotunda T75L-9600 or equivalent), insert the tool hose approximately $^3/_4$ of the way into the duct or fresh air tube. If necessary, secure the hose with tape.
6. On vehicles equipped with thermactor system, revise the dump valve vacuum hoses as follows:
   a. For dump valves with 2 vacuum fittings, disconnect and plug the hoses.
   b. For dump valves with 1 fitting or combination air bypass/air control valve, remove the hose at the dump valve and plug it. Connect a slave hose from the dump valve vacuum fitting to an intake manifold vacuum fitting.

Leave all vacuum signal hoses attached to the air cleaner assembly when relocating the assembly to perform carburetor adjustments. The air cleaner assembly must be in place, however, when measuring engine speeds.

****CAUTION**

Prolonged engine idling can result in catalyst overheating and excessive underbody temperatures.

7. Verify the ignition timing and curb idle is set to specifications.
8. Remove the PCV valve from the grommet and allow it to draw underhood air during the idle mixture check. Locate the crankcase vent hose and disconnect it at the air cleaner, allowing the in-line fixed orifice to vent to underhood air.
9. With the transmission in **N**, run the engine at approximately 2500 rpm for 15 seconds before each mixture check.
10. Gradually open the propane tool valve and watch for engine speed gain, if any, on the tachometer. When the engine speed reaches a maximum and then begins to drop off, note the amount of speed gain. The propane cartridge must be in vertical position.

If the engine speed will not drop off, check the propane cartridge gas supply. If necessary, repeat Steps 9 and 10 with a new cartridge. If the measured speed gain is 0 rpm (no rpm rise) and the minimum speed gain specification is 0 rpm, go to Step 13.

11. If the measured speed gain is higher than the speed gain specification, turn the mixture screws counter clockwise (rich) in equal amounts while simultaneously repeating the mixture adjustment, until the measured speed rise meets the reset rpm specification.
12. Reinstall the PCV valve in the grommet and adjust the curb idle.
13. Reinstall the tamper resistant feature.

CHOKE PLATE PULLDOWN CLEARANCE

See Figure 11

1. Remove the air cleaner assembly.
2. Set the throttle on the stop step of the fast idle cam.
3. Noting the position of the choke housing cap, loosen the retaining screws and rotate the cap 90° in the rich (closing) direction.
4. Activate the pulldown motor by manually forcing the pulldown control diaphragm link in the direction of applied vacuum or by applying vacuum to the external vacuum tube.

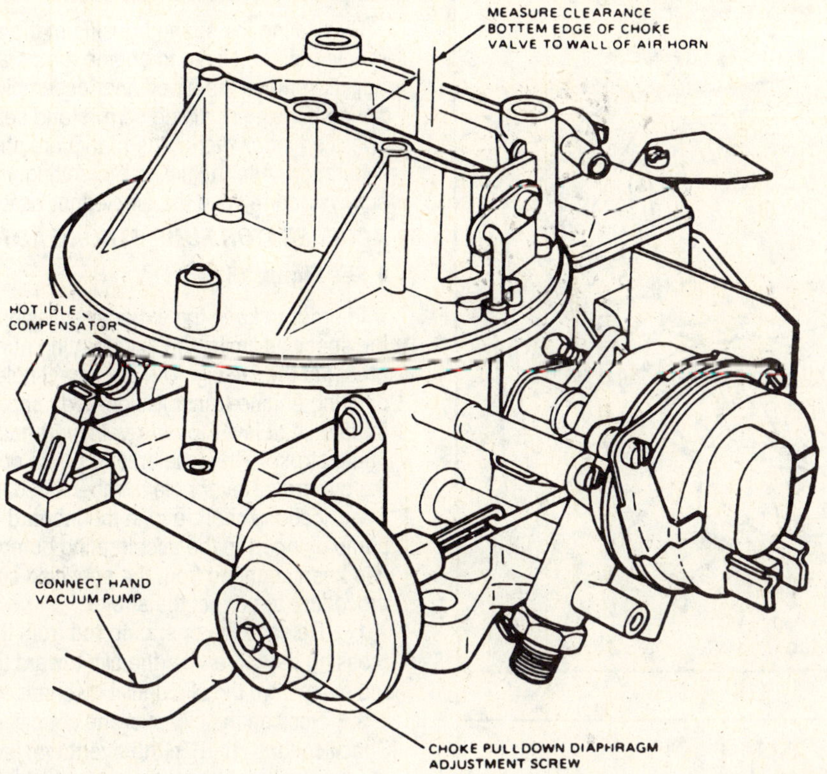

Fig. 11 Adjusting the choke plate pulldown

5. Using a drill gauge of the specified diameter, measure the clearance between the choke plate and the center of the air horn wall nearest the fuel bowl.
6. To adjust, reset the diaphragm stop on the end of the choke pulldown diaphragm.
7. After adjusting, reset the choke housing cap to the specified notch. Check and reset fast idle speed, if necessary. Install the air cleaner.

FLOAT LEVEL ADJUSTMENT — DRY

➧ See Figures 12 and 13

This preliminary setting of the float level adjustment must be done with the carburetor removed from the engine.

1. Remove the air horn and see that the float is raised and the fuel inlet needle is seated. Check the distance between the top surface of the main body (with the gasket removed) and the top surface of the float. Depress the float tab to seat the fuel inlet needle. Take a measurement near the center of the float, at a point $^1/_8$ in. (3mm) from the free end. If you are using a prefabricated float gauge, place the gauge in the corner of the enlarged end section of the fuel bowl. The gauge should touch the float near the end, but not on the end radius.
2. If necessary, bend the tab on the end of the float to bring the setting within the specified limits.

FLOAT LEVEL ADJUSTMENT — WET

➧ See Figure 14

1. Bring the engine to its normal operating temperature, park the car on as nearly level a surface as possible, and stop the engine.
2. Remove the air cleaner assembly from the carburetor.
3. Remove the air horn retaining screws and the carburetor identification tag. Leave the air horn and gasket in position on the carburetor main body. Start the engine, let it idle for several minutes, rotate the air horn out of the way, and remove the gasket to provide access to the float assembly.

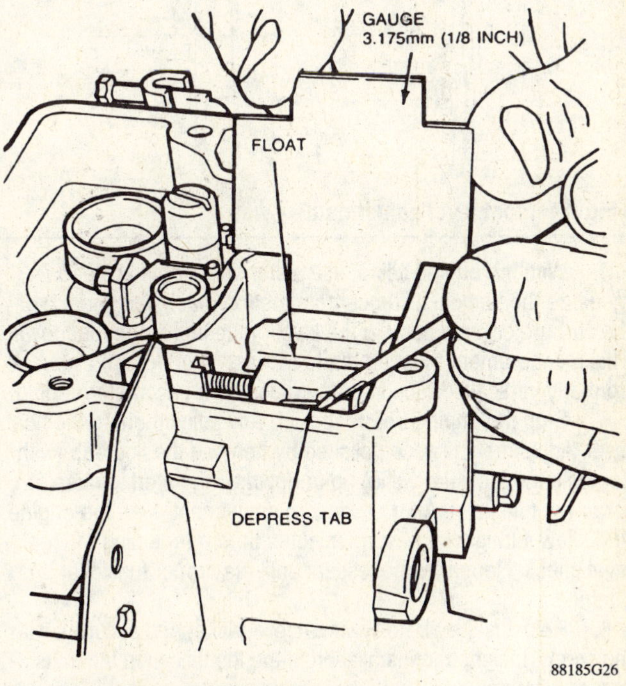

Fig. 12 Float level adjustment — dry

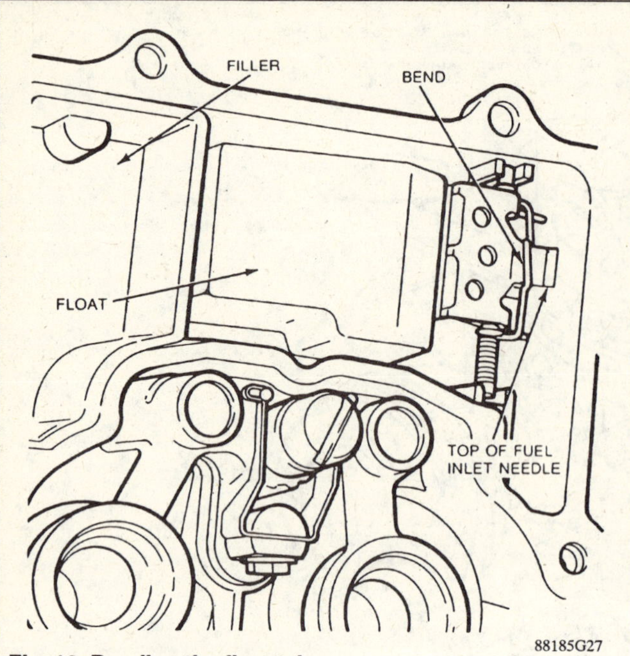

88185G27

Fig. 13 Bending the float tab

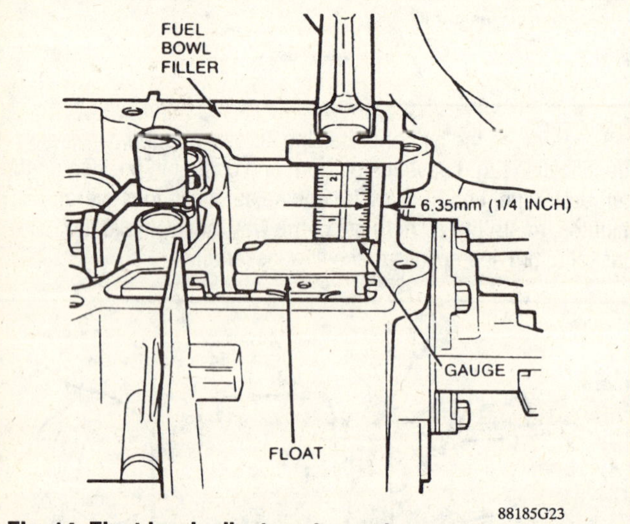

88185G23

Fig. 14 Float level adjustment — wet

4. With the engine idling, use a standard depth scale to measure the vertical distance from the top machined surface of the carburetor main body to the level of the fuel in the fuel bowl. This measurement must be made at least $^{1}/_{4}$ in. (6mm) away from any vertical surface in order to assure an accurate reading.
5. Stop the engine before making any adjustment to the float level. Adjustment is accomplished by bending the float tab (with contacts the fuel inlet valve) up or down as required to raise or lower the fuel level. After making an adjustment, start the engine, and allow it to idle for several minutes before repeating the fuel level check. Repeat as necessary until the proper fuel level is attained.
6. Reinstall the air horn with a new gasket and secure it with the screw. Include the installation of the identification tag in its proper location.
7. Check the idle speed, fuel mixture, and dashpot adjustments. Install the air cleaner assembly.

AUTOMATIC CHOKE HOUSING

By rotating the spring housing of the automatic choke, the reaction of the choke to engine temperature can be controlled. To adjust, remove the air cleaner assembly, loosen the thermostatic spring housing retaining screws and set the spring housing to the specified index mark. The marks are shown in the accompanying illustration. After adjusting the setting, tighten the retaining screws and replace the air cleaner assembly to the carburetor.

ACCELERATOR PUMP STROKE ADJUSTMENT

➧ **See Figure 15**

In order to keep the exhaust emission level of the engine within the specified limits, the accelerating pump stroke has been preset at the factory. The additional holes are provided for differing engine-transmission-body applications only. The primary throttle shaft lever (overtravel lever) has four holes to control the pump stroke. The accelerating pump operating rod should be in the overtravel lever hole number listed in the Carburetor Specifications chart, and in the inboard hole (hole closest to the pump plunger) in the accelerating pump link. If the pump stroke has been changed from the specified settings, use the following procedure to correct the stroke.

1. Release the operating rod from the retaining clip by pressing the tab end of the clip toward the rod while pressing the rod away from the clip until it disengages.
2. Position the clip over the specified hole (see Carburetor Specifications chart) in the overtravel lever. Press the ends of the clip together and insert the operating rod through the clip and the overtravel lever. Release the clip to engage the rod.

ANTI-STALL DASHPOT ADJUSTMENT

Having made sure that the engine idle speed and mixture are correct and that the engine is at normal operating temperature, loosen the anti-stall dashpot locking nut (see accompanying illustration). With the throttle held closed, depress the plunger with a screwdriver blade and measure the clearance between the throttle lever and the plunger tip. If the clearance is not as specified in the Carburetor Specifications chart, turn the dashpot until the proper clearance is obtained between the throttle lever and the plunger tip. After tightening the locking nut, recheck the adjustment.

KICKER SET SPEED

1. Place the transmission in the Neutral or Park position.
2. Bring the engine to the normal operating temperature.
3. Place the A/C-heater selector in the OFF position.
4. Disconnect and plug the vacuum hose at the VOTM kicker.
5. Connect the external vacuum source providing a minimum of 33.7 kPA (10 in-Hg) to the VOTM kicker.
6. Place the transmission selector in the specified position.
7. Check and adjust the VOTM kicker on the rpm, if the adjustment is required. Adjust the VOTM saddle bracket adjustment screw.
8. Remove the external vacuum source, remove the plug from the VOTM kicker hose and reconnect.
9. Reset the curb idle.

ELECTRIC CHOKE — OPERATIONAL TEST

➧ **See Figures 16, 17 and 18**

All carbureted models use an electrically assisted choke to reduce exhaust emissions of carbon monoxide during warm-up. The system consists of a choke cap, a thermostatic spring, a bimetal sensing disc (switch) and a ceramic positive temperature coefficient (PTC) heater.

The choke is powered from the center tap of the alternator, so that current is constantly applied to the temperature sensing disc. The system is grounded through the carburetor body. At temperatures below approximately 60°F (16°C), the switch is open and no current is supplied to the ceramic heater, thereby resulting in normal unassisted thermostatic spring choke action. When the temperature rises above 60°F (16°C), the temperature sensing disc closes and current is supplied to the heater, which in turn, acts on the thermostatic spring. Once the heater starts, it causes the thermostatic spring to pull the choke plate(s) open within 1½ minutes, which is sooner than it would open if non-assisted.

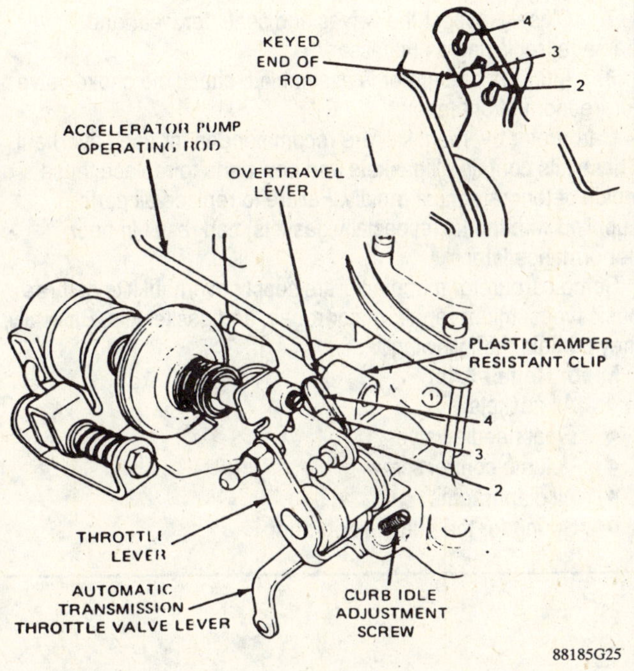

Fig. 15 Accelerating pump stroke adjustment

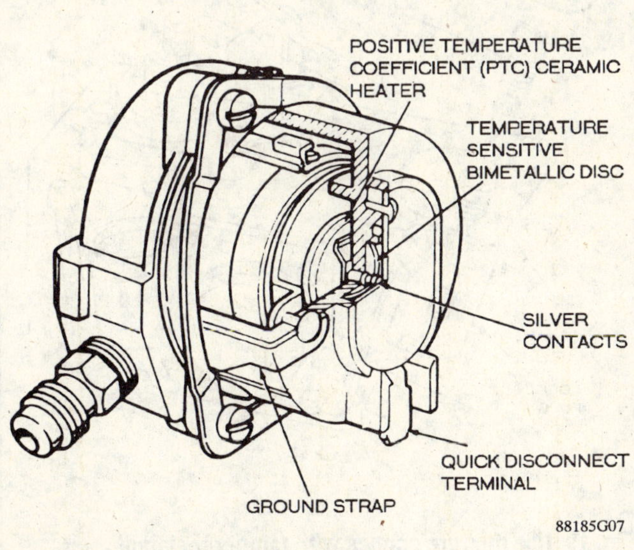

Fig. 16 Electric choke components

Fig. 17 Electric choke hookup

1. Detach the electrical lead from the choke cap.
2. Use a jumper lead to connect the terminal on the choke cap and the wire terminal, so that the electrical circuit is still completed.
3. Start the engine.
4. Hook up a test light between the connector on the choke lead and ground.
5. The test light should glow. If it does not, current is not being supplied to the electrically assisted choke.
6. Connect the test light between the terminal on the alternator and the terminal on the choke cap. If the light now glows, replace the lead, since it is not passing current to the choke assist.

****CAUTION**

Do not ground the terminal on the alternator while performing Step 6.

7. If the light still does not glow, the fault lies somewhere in the electrical system. Check the system out. If the electrically assisted choke receives power but still does not appear to be functioning properly, reconnect the choke lead and proceed with the rest of the test.
8. Tape the bulb end of the thermometer to the metallic portion of the choke housing.
9. If the electrically assisted choke operates below 55°F (13°C), it is defective and must be replaced.
10. Allow the engine to warm up to 80–100°F (27–38°C); at these temperatures the choke should operate for about 1½ minutes.
11. If it does not operate for this length of time, check the bimetallic spring to see if it is connected to the tang on the choke lever.
12. If the spring is connected and the choke is not operating properly, replace the cap assembly.

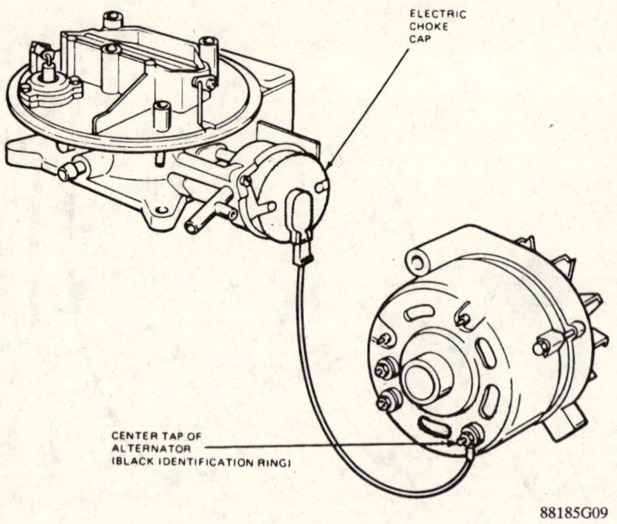

Fig. 18 The electric choke has wiring that attaches to the alternator

OVERHAUL

➧ See Figure 19

Efficient carburetion depends greatly on careful cleaning and inspection during overhaul, since dirt, gum, water, or varnish in or on the carburetor parts are often responsible for poor performance.

Overhaul your carburetor in a clean, dust free area. Carefully disassemble the carburetor, referring often to the exploded views. Keep all similar and look-alike parts segregated during the disassembly and cleaning to avoid accidental interchange during assembly. Make a note of all jet sizes.

When the carburetor is disassembled, wash all parts (except diaphragms, electric choke units, pump plunger, and any other plastic, leather, fiber, or rubber parts) in clean carburetor solvent. Do not leave parts in the solvent any longer than is necessary to sufficiently loosen the deposits. Excessive cleaning may remove the special finish from the float bowl and choke valve bodies, leaving these parts unfit for service. Rinse all parts in clean solvent and blow them dry with compressed air or allow them to air dry. Wipe clean all cork, plastic, leather, and fiber parts with a clean, lint-free cloth.

Blow out all passages and jets with compressed air and be sure that there are no restrictions or blockages. never use wire of similar tools to clean jets, fuel passages, or air bleeds. Clean all jets and valves separately to avoid accidental interchange.

Check all parts for wear or damage. If wear or damage is found, replace the defective parts. Especially check the following:

1. Check the float needle and seat for wear. If wear is found, replace the complete assembly.
2. Check the float hinge pin for wear and the float(s) for dents or distortion. Replace the float if fuel has leaked into it.
3. Check the throttle and choke shaft bores for wear or an out-of-round condition. Damage or wear to the throttle arm, shaft, or shaft bore will often require replacement of the throttle body. These parts require a close tolerance of fit; wear may allow air linkage, which could affect starting and idling.

➥ Throttle shafts and bushings are not included in overhaul kits. They can be purchased separately.

4. Inspect the idle mixture adjusting needles for burrs for grooves. Any such condition requires replacement of the needle, since you will not be able to obtain a satisfactory idle.
5. Test the accelerator pump check valves. They should pass air one way but not the other. Test for proper seating by blowing and sucking on the valve. Replace the valve is necessary. If the valve is satisfactory, wash the valve again to remove breath moisture.
6. Check the bowl cover for warped surfaces with a straightedge.
7. Closely inspect the valves and seats for wear and damage, replacing as necessary.
8. After the carburetor is assembled, check the choke valve for freedom of operation.

Carburetor overhaul kits are recommended for each overhaul. These kits contain all gaskets and new parts to replace those which deteriorate most rapidly. Failure to replace all parts supplied with the kit (especially gaskets) can result in poor performance later.

Some carburetor manufacturers supply overhaul kits of three basic types: minor repair; major repair; and gasket kits. Basically, they contain the following:

Minor Repair Kits:

- All gaskets
- Float needle valve
- Volume control screw
- All diaphragms
- Spring for the pump diaphragm

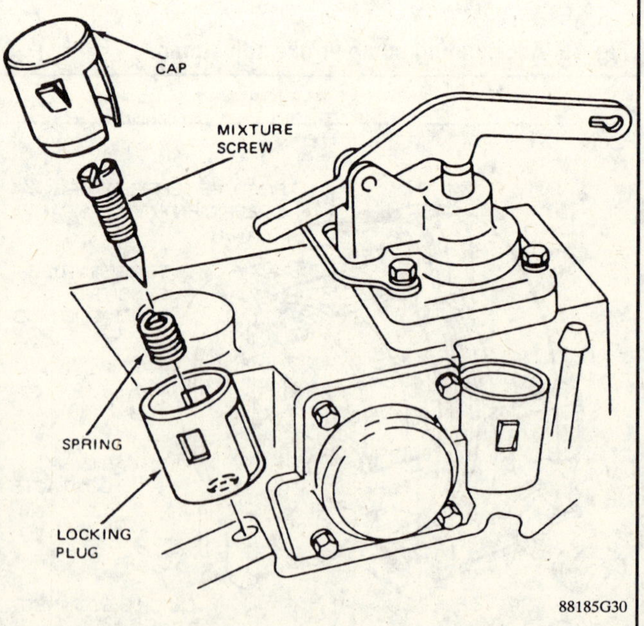

Fig. 19 Idle mixture screws with tamper resistant caps — 2150 models shown

Major Repair Kits:

- All jets and gaskets
- All diaphragms
- Float needle valve
- Volume control screw
- Pump ball valve
- Float
- Complete intermediate rod
- Intermediate pump lever
- Some cover hold-down screws and washers

Gasket Kits:

- All gaskets

After cleaning and checking all components, reassemble the carburetor, using new parts and referring to he exploded view. When reassembling, make sure that all screws and jets are tight in their seats, but do not overtighten as the tops will be distorted. Tighten all screws gradually, in rotation. Do not tighten needle valves into their seats; uneven jetting will result. Always use new gaskets. Be sure to adjust the float level when reassembling.

Motorcraft 2150

➧ See Figures 20, 21, 22, 23, 24, 25 and 26

1. Remove the air cleaner anchor screw.
2. Remove the automatic choke control rod retainer.
3. Remove the airhorn attaching screws, lockwashers and the carburetor identification tag. Remove the airhorn and the airhorn gasket.
4. Remove the choke control rod by loosening the screw that secures the choke shaft lever to the choke shaft. Remove the rod from the airhorn. Slide the plastic dust seal out of the airhorn.
5. Remove the staking marks on the choke plate attaching screws and remove the screws. Remove the choke plate by sliding it out of the shaft from the top of the airhorn. Remove any burrs around screw holes prior to removing the choke shaft. Slide the choke shaft out of the airhorn.
6. Remove the two attaching screws on the choke pulldown diaphragm assembly from the bracket, disconnect the vacuum supply tube, disconnect the E-clip at the rod and remove the pulldown diaphragm.
7. Remove the fast idle cam retainer.
8. Center punch the choke cap retaining screw heads and using a $^{1}/_{4}$ in. (6mm) drill, drill the screw heads deep enough to remove the retainer from the choke cap. Remove the remaining portion of the choke cap screws with small locking pliers.
9. Remove the choke housing assembly retaining screws. Remove the choke housing assembly, gasket and the fast idle cam and rod from the fast idle cam lever.
10. Remove the choke lever retaining screw and washer. Disconnect the choke control rod from the choke lever. Remove the choke lever and fast idle cam lever from the choke housing.
11. With a screwdriver, pry the float shaft retainer from the fuel inlet seat. Remove the float, float shaft retainer and fuel inlet needle assembly. Remove the retainer and float shaft from the float lever. Remove the fuel bowl filler.
12. Remove the fuel inlet needle, seat, filter screen and the main jets.
13. Remove the booster venturi screw (accelerator pump discharge), booster and metering rod assembly and gasket. Remove the filter screen from the booster venturi screw. Invert the main body and catch the weight and ball. Remove the lift spring retaining clip and spring, separate the lift rod assembly from the booster. Do not disassemble the metering rod hanger from the lift rod.
14. Remove the accelerator pump link and rod assembly. Remove the temperature compensated valve assembly.
15. Remove the accelerator pump cover attaching screws. Remove the accelerator pump cover, diaphragm assembly and spring.
16. If it is necessary to remove the Elastomer valve, grasp it firmly and pull it out. An Elastomer valve must be replaced whenever it has been removed.
17. Invert the main body and remove the enrichment valve cover and the gasket. Remove the enrichment valve with a box wrench or socket wrench. Remove the enrichment valve gasket and discard it.
18. To remove the idle fuel mixture screws and springs, support the area under the limiter plug and using a pointed tool directed at the tang, lightly tap the plug forward.
19. If necessary, remove the nut and washer securing the fast idle adjusting lever assembly to the throttle shaft, and remove the lever assembly. If necessary, remove the idle screw and the spring from the fast idle adjusting lever.
20. Remove the throttle positioner, if so equipped.
21. If it is necessary to remove the throttle plates, lightly scribe the throttle plates along the throttle shaft and mark each plate in its corresponding bore with a number for proper installation. File off the staked portion of the throttle plate screws prior to their removal. Remove any burrs on the throttleshaft caused by the screw removal to prevent scoring of the throttle shaft bores as the throttle shaft is withdrawn. Catch the mechanical high speed cam located on the throttle shaft between the throttle plates.
22. Remove the three screws that attach the aneroid assembly to the main body (if altitude compensated) and remove the assembly.

To install:

23. Slide the throttle shaft assembly into the main body until it begins to enter the high speed bleed cam slot in the body. Holding the cam by the edge of the point, hold it in the slot and rotate the throttle shaft until it will pass through the cam. Rotate the shaft clockwise until the throttle lever clears the boss for the throttle solenoid positioners Off idle screw. Continue inserting the shaft into proper position, rotating as necessary to properly position the cam.
24. Refer to the lines scribed on the throttle plates and install the throttle plates in their proper location with the screws snug, but not tight. Always use new screws when installing throttle plates.
25. Close the throttle plates. Invert the main body, and hold it up to the light. Little to no light should show between the throttle plates and bores. Tap the plates lightly with a screwdriver handle to seat them. Hold the throttle plates closed and tighten the screws and stake them by crimping the exposed threads with diagonal cutters.
26. If the aneroid was separated from the metering valve assembly, position a new gasket and the aneroid on the valve and install the attaching screws. Using a new gasket position the aneroid assembly to the main body and install the four attaching screws.
27. Place the fast idle adjusting lever assembly on the throttle shaft and install the retaining washer and nut, tighten to 25 inch lbs. (3 Nm). If necessary install the fast idle screw and spring on the fast idle adjusting lever.
28. Invert the main body. Install the enrichment valve and new gasket with a wrench and tighten to 110 inch lbs.

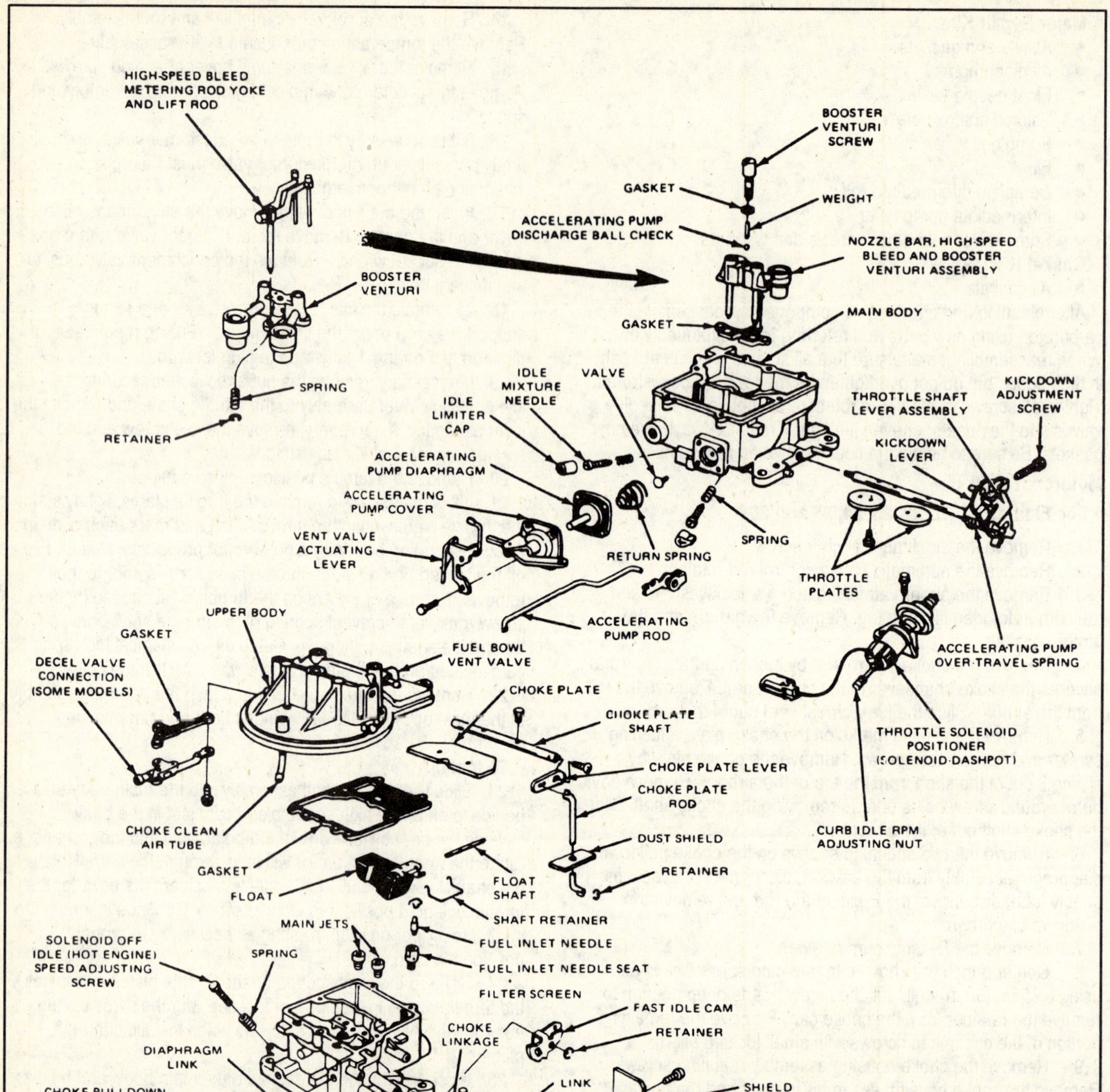

Fig. 20 Exploded view of the Motorcraft 2150 carburetor

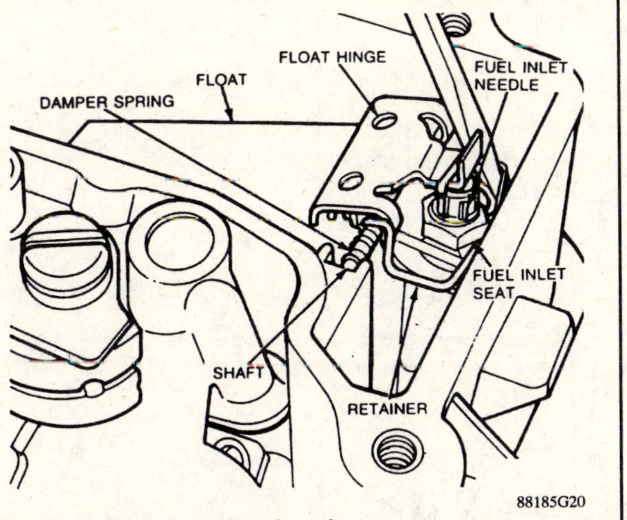

Fig. 21 Float shaft retainer location

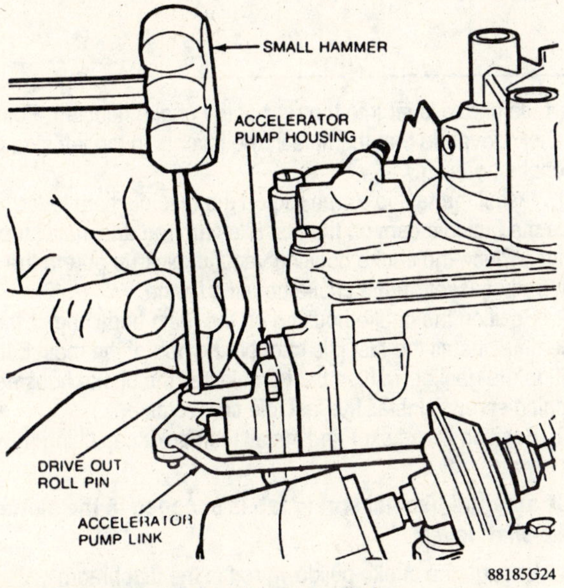

Fig. 22 Drive out the accelerator roll pin

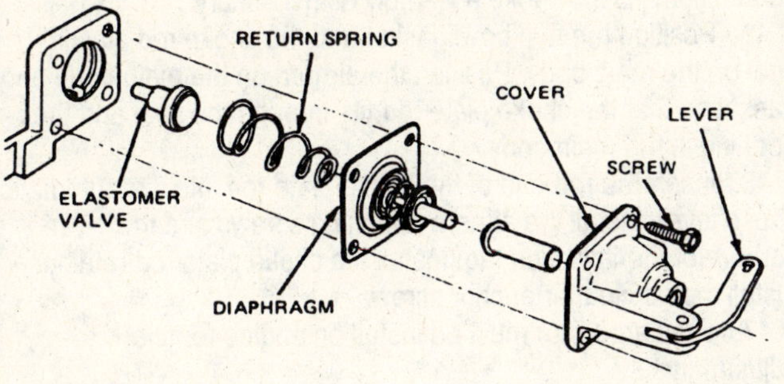

Fig. 23 The Elastomer valve is located in the accelerator pump

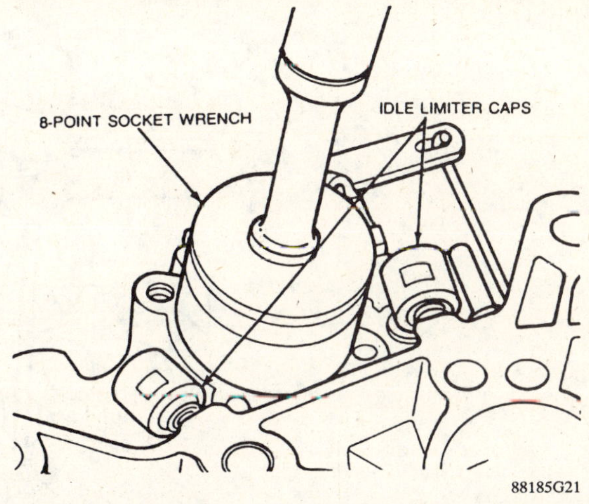

Fig. 24 The enrichment valve may need a socket wrench to remove it

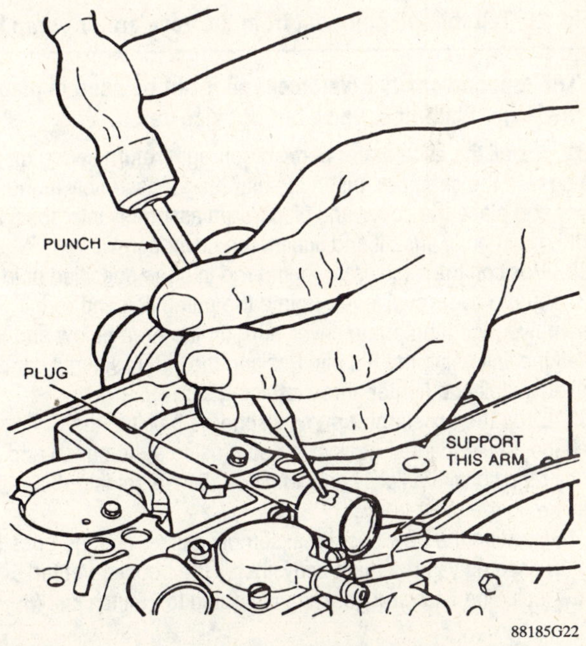

Fig. 25 To remove the idle fuel mixture screws and springs, support the area under the limiter plug and using a pointed tool directed at the tang, lightly tap the plug forward

29. Install the idle mixture adjusting screws and springs. Turn the screws in gently with your fingers until they just touch the seat, then back them out $1\frac{1}{2}$ turns. Install the enrichment valve cover and new gasket. The cover must be installed with the limiter stops engaged in the plugs.

30. If the Elastomer valve was removed, lightly lubricate the tip of the new Elastomer valve and insert the tip into the accelerator pump cavity center hole. Using a pair of needle nosed pliers, reach into the fuel bowl and grasp the valve tip. Pull the valve in until it seats in the pump cavity wall and cut off the tip forward of the retaining shoulder. Remove the tip from the bowl.

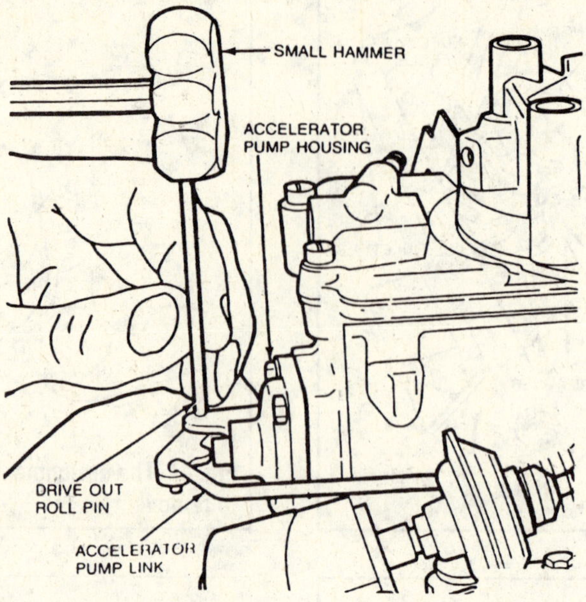

Fig. 26 Tap the roll point out from the accelerator pump linkage

➥ The reduced cavity Elastomer valve can be used in place of the larger Elastomer valve but not vice-versa.

31. Install the accelerator pump diaphragm return spring on the boss in the chamber. Insert the diaphragm assembly in the cover and place the cover and diaphragm assembly into position on the main body. Install and tighten the cover screws.
32. Position the accelerator pump rod into the specified hole on the pump overtravel lever. Rotate the pump link and rod assembly toward the pump cover, support the area below and install the link using the roll pin. Position the TCP assembly and gasket, install and tighten three retaining screws.
33. Drop the accelerator pump discharge ball into the passage, stake the ball against the seat using a flat punch and gently tapping with a light hammer. Drop the weight into the passage in the main body.
34. Position the new booster assembly gasket and the booster venturi assembly in the main body. Install the booster venturi screw including filter and gasket and tighten to 75 inch lbs. (8 Nm).
35. Install the main jets, be sure the right jets are installed. Install the fuel inlet seat, filter screen, baffle and new gasket.
36. Install the fuel inlet needle assembly in the fuel inlet seat.
37. Slide the float shaft into the float lever. Position the float shaft retainer on the float shaft.
38. Insert the float assembly into the fuel bowl and hook the float lever tab under the fuel inlet needle assembly. Place the float damper spring on the shaft. Insert the float shaft into its guides at the sides of the fuel bowl. Install the fuel bowl filler.
39. With a screwdriver, position the float shaft retainer in the groove on the fuel inlet needle seat. Check and set the float level setting , ensure that the float does not interfere with the Elastomer valve.
40. Position the fast idle cam lever on the thermostatic choke shaft and lever assembly. The bottom of the fast idle cam lever adjusting screw must rest against the tang on the choke lever. Insert the choke lever into the rear of the choke housing. Position the choke lever so that the hole in the lever is to the left side of the choke housing.
41. Install the fast idle cam rod on the fast idle cam lever. Place the fast idle cam on the fast idle cam rod and install the retainer. Place the choke housing vacuum pick-up port to the main body gasket on the choke housing flange.
42. Position the choke housing on the main body and at the same time, install the fast idle cam on the hub of the main body. Position the gasket, with sealant and install the choke housing attaching screws. Install the fast idle cam retainer.
43. Position the gasket and install the choke cap using new breakaway screws.

➥ Be sure the bimetal spring tab is engaged in the slotted choke shaft lever.

44. Engage the choke pulldown rod in the diaphragm assembly link. Rotate the assembly to align the mounting bracket with the main body casting. Attach the pulldown rod and install the E-clip. Install and tighten the two attaching screws. Connect the vacuum supply tube to the correct vacuum base tube connection. Adjust choke assembly as necessary.
45. Position the fuel bowl gasket and the choke rod plastic seal on the main body. Position the airhorn on the main body and gasket so that the choke plate rod fits through the seal and the opening in the main body.
46. Insert the rod end of the choke plate rod into the automatic choke lever. Install the airhorn attaching screws and the carburetor identification tag. Install the choke plate rod retainer. Install the air cleaner anchor screw.
47. The carburetor must be install on engine for final adjustments.

Carburetor ID

➧ See Figure 27

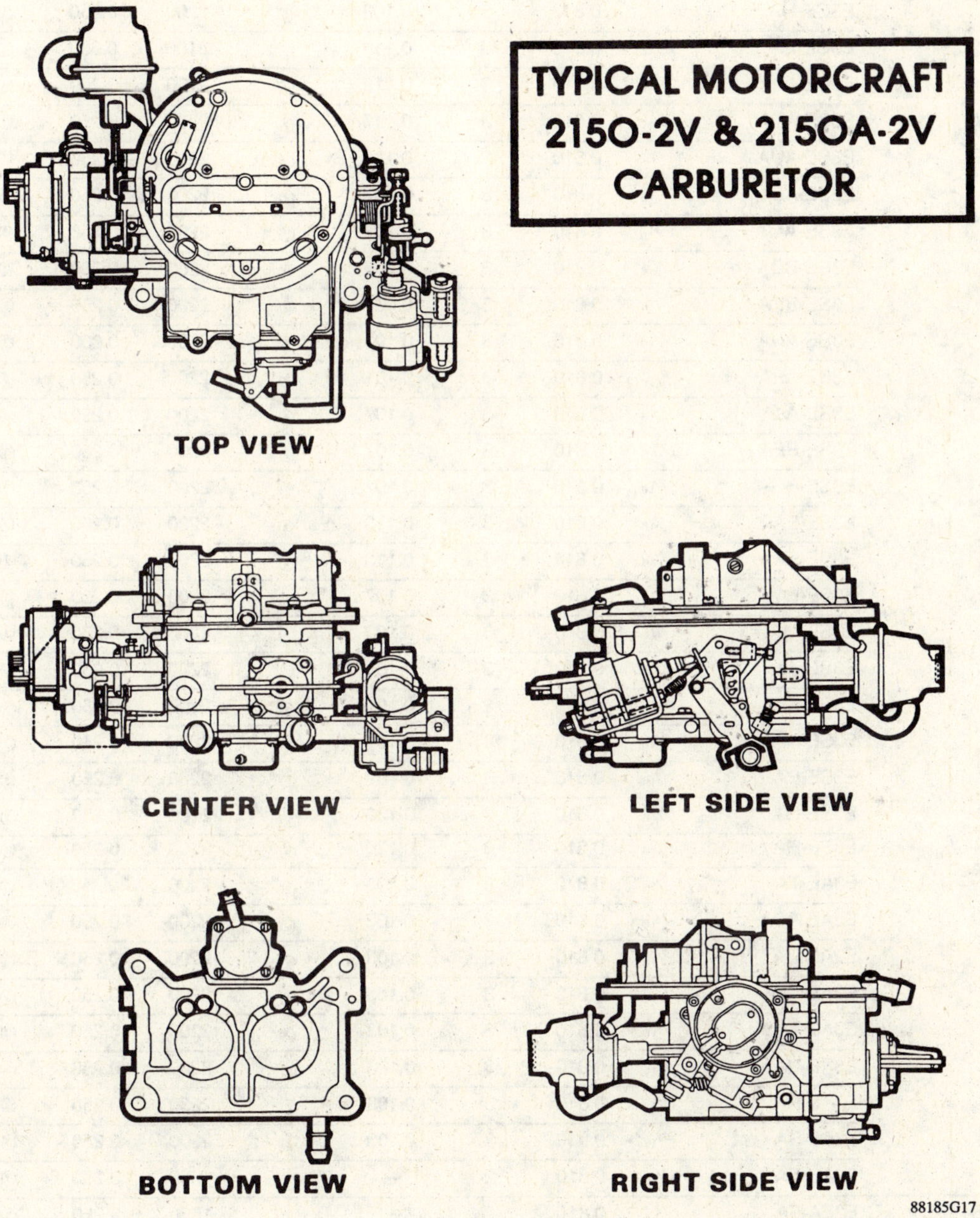

Fig. 27 Carburetor identification Model 2150

Autolite (Motorcraft) 2150 Specifications

Year	(9510)* Carburetor Identification	Dry Float Level (in.)	Wet Float level (in.)	Pump Setting Hole #①	Choke Plate Pulldown (in.)	Fast Idle Cam Linkage Clearance (in.)	Fast Idle (rpm)	Dechoke (in.)	Choke Setting
1983	E3CE-AA	7/16	0.810	3	0.103	②	2200	0.250	③
	E3CE-BA	7/16	0.810	3	0.103	②	2200	0.250	③
	E3CE-GA	7/16	0.810	3	0.103	②	2200	0.250	③
	E3CE-HA	7/16	0.810	3	0.103	②	2200	0.250	③
	E3CE-EA	7/16	0.810	3	0.113	②	2100	0.250	③
	E3CE-FA	7/16	0.810	3	0.113	②	2100	0.250	③
	E3SE-ATA	7/16	0.810	3	0.113	②	2200	0.250	③
	E3SE-AUA	13/16	0.810	3	0.113	②	2200	0.250	③
	E3SE-ALA	7/16	0.810	3	0.107	②	2200	0.250	③
	E3SE-AMA	7/16	0.810	3	0.107	②	2200	0.250	③
	E3SE-BDA	7/16	0.810	3	0.107	②	2200	0.250	③
	E3SE-BEA	7/16	0.810	3	0.107	②	2200	0.250	③
	E3SE-ANA	7/16	0.810	3	0.101	②	2200	0.250	③
	E3SE-APA	7/16	0.810	3	0.101	②	2200	0.250	③
	E3SE-AJA	7/16	0.810	3	0.107	②	2200	0.250	③
	E3SE-BFA	7/16	0.810	3	0.107	②	2200	0.250	③
	E3SE-BGA	7/16	0.810	3	0.107	②	2200	0.250	③
	E3SE-EA	7/16	0.810	3	0.113	②	2200	0.250	③
	E3SE-FA	7/16	0.810	3	0.113	②	2200	0.250	③
	E3SE-LA	7/16	0.810	3	0.107	②	2200	0.250	③
	E3SE-MA	7/16	0.810	3	0.107	②	2200	0.250	③
	E3SE-JA	7/16	0.810	3	0.101	②	2200	0.250	③
	E3SE-KA	7/16	0.810	3	0.101	②	2200	0.250	③
	E3SE-NA	7/16	0.810	3	0.107	②	2200	0.250	③
	E3SE-PA	7/16	0.810	3	0.107	②	2200	0.250	③
	E3SE-GA	7/16	0.810	3	0.120	②	2100	0.250	③
	E3SE-HA	7/16	0.810	3	0.120	②	2100	0.250	③
	E3AE-TA	7/16	0.810	3	0.103	②	2200	0.250	③
	E3AE-ADA	7/16	0.810	3	0.103	②	2200	0.250	③
	E2AE-UA	7/16	0.810	3	0.103	②	2200	0.250	③
	E3AE-AEA	7/16	0.810	3	0.103	②	2200	0.250	③
	E3AE-TA	7/16	0.810	3	0.103	②	2200	0.250	③
	E3AE-UA	7/16	0.810	3	0.103	②	2200	0.250	③
	E3AE-RA	7/16	0.810	3	0.103	②	2200	0.250	③
	E3AE-SA	7/16	0.810	3	0.103	②	2200	0.250	③
	E3AE-EA	7/16	0.810	2	—	②	1550	0.250	③
1984–85	E3EA-EA	7/16	0.810	2	—	②	1550	0.250	③
	E4CE-AA	7/16	0.810	3	0.103	②	2200	0.250	2NR
	E4CE-BA	7/16	0.810	3	0.103	②	2200	0.250	2NR
	E4SE-CA	7/16	0.810	3	0.103	②	2200	0.250	③
	E4SE-DA	7/16	0.810	3	0.103	②	2200	0.250	③
	E5AE-CA	7/16	0.810	2	—	②	1550	0.250	③

*Basic carburetor number for Ford products
① With link in inboard hole of pump lever
② Opposite V-notch
③ V-notch

88185C11

CENTRAL FUEL INJECTION

General Information

➧ **See Figures 28, 29, 30 and 31**

Central Fuel Injection (CFI) is a throttle body injection system in which two fuel injectors are mounted in a common throttle body, spraying fuel down through the throttle valves at the bottom of the body and into the intake manifold.

Fuel is supplied from the fuel tank by a high pressure, in-tank fuel pump. The fuel passes through a filter and is sent to the throttle body where a regulator keeps the fuel delivery pressure at a constant 39 psi. The two fuel injectors are mounted vertically above the throttle plates and are connected in line with the fuel pressure regulator. Excess fuel supplied by the pump, but not needed by the engine, is returned to the fuel tank by a steel fuel return line.

The fuel injection system is linked with and controlled by the Electronic Engine Control (EEC) system.

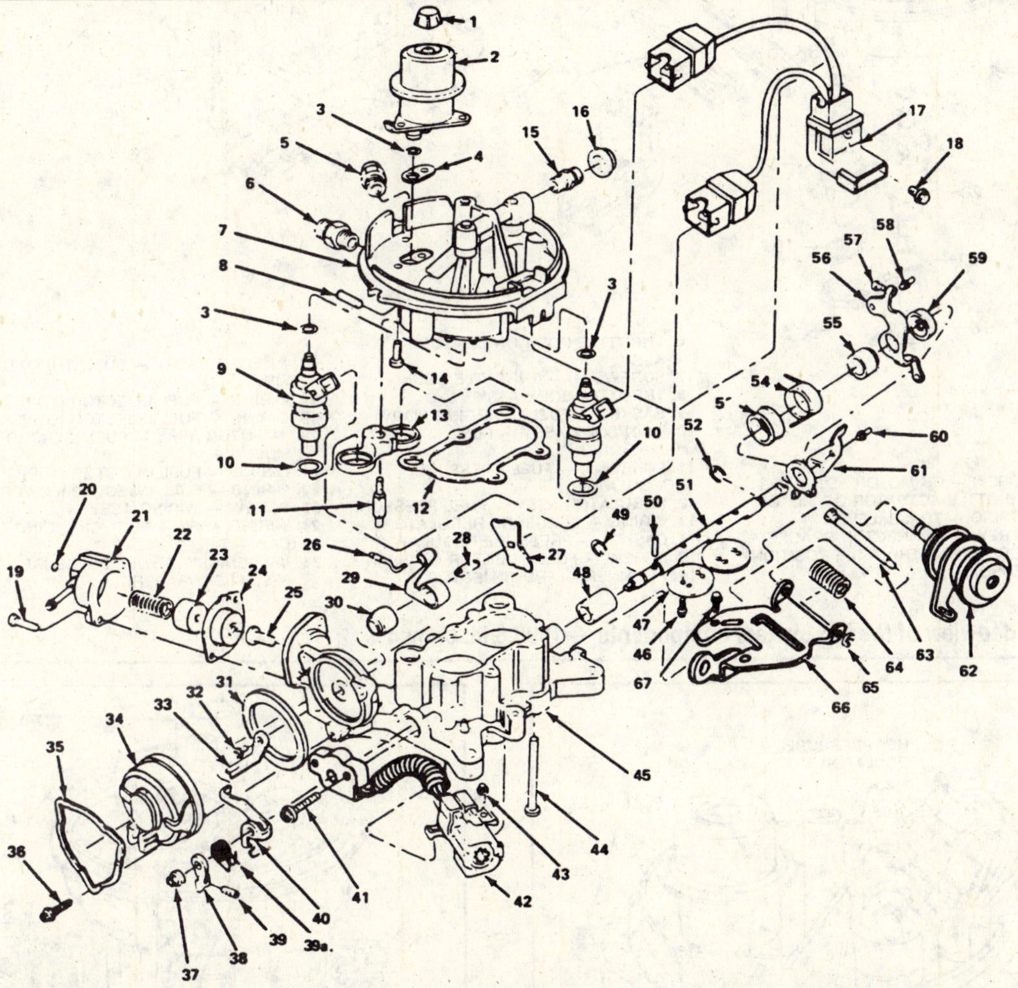

Legend:

1. PLUG – FUEL PRESSUHE REGULATOR ADJUSTING SCREW
2. REGULATOR ASSEMBLY – FUEL PRESSURE
3. SEAL – 5/16 x .070 "O" RING
4. GASKET – FUEL PRESSURE REGULATOR
5. CONNECTOR – 1/4 PIPE TO 1/2-20
6. CONNECTOR – 1/8 PIPE TO 9/16-16
7. BODY – FUEL CHARGING MAIN
8. PLUG – 1/16 x 27 HEADLESS HEX
9. INJECTOR ASSEMBLY – FUEL
10. SEAL – 5/8 x .103 "O" RING
11. SCREW – FUEL INJECTOR RETAINING
12. GASKET – FUEL CHARGING BODY
13. RETAINER – FUEL INJECTOR
14. SCREW M5.0 x 20.0 PAN HEAD
15. VALVE ASSEMBLY – DIAGNOSTIC VALVE
16. CAP – FUEL PRESSURE RELIEF VALVE
17. WIRING ASSEMBLY – FUEL CHARGING
18. SCREW – M3.5 x 1.27 x 12.7 PAN HEAD
19. SCREW & WASHER – M4 x 7.0 20.00
20. BALL – LEAD SHOT .26 - .24 DIA.
21. COVER ASSEMBLY – CONTROL DIAPHRAGM
22. SPRING – CONTROL MODULATOR
23. RETAINER – PULLDOWN DIAPHRAGM
24. DIAPHRAGM – PULLDOWN CONTROL
25. ADJUSTER – PULLDOWN CONTROL
26. ROD – FAST IDLE CONTROL
27. CAM – FAST IDLE
28. SHAFT – CHOKE HOUSING
29. POSITIONER – FAST IDLE CONTROL ROD
30. BUSHING – CHOKE HOUSING
31. GASKET – THERMOSTAT HOUSING
32. SCREW & WASHER – M3.5 x 0.6 x 6 PAN HEAD
33. LEVER – CHOKE THERMOSTAT
34. HOUSING ASSEMBLY – THERMOSTAT
35. RETAINER – HOUSING ASSEMBLY
36. SCREW
37. NUT & WASHER ASSEMBLY – .7-6H HEX
38. LEVER – FAST IDLE CAM ADJUSTER
39. SCREW – NO. 10 - 32 x .50 SET SLOTTED HEAD

39a. FAST IDLE PICK-UP LEVER RETURN SPRING

40. LEVER – FAST IDLE
41. SCREW & WASHER – M4.07 x 22.0 PAN HEAD
42. THROTTLE POSITION SENSOR
43. SCREW – M4 x .7 x 14.0 HEX WASHER TAP
44. SCREW – M5 x .7 x 55.0
45. BODY – FUEL CHARGING – THROTTLE
46. SCREW – M3 x 0.5 x 7.4 HEX WASHER HEAD
47. PLATE – THROTTLE
48. BEARING – THROTTLE CONTROL LINKAGE
49. "E" RING – 7/32 RETAINING
50. PIN – SPRING COILED
51. SHAFT – THROTTLE
52. "C" RING – THROTTLE SHAFT BUSHING
53. BEARING – THROTTLE CONTROL LINKAGE
54. SPRING – THROTTLE RETURN
55. BUSHING – ACCELERATOR PUMP OVER TRAVEL SPRING
56. LEVER – TRANSMISSION LINKAGE
57. SCREW – M4 x 0.7 x 7.6
58. PIN – TRANSMISSION LINKAGE LEVER
59. SPACER – THROTTLE SHAFT
60. BALL – THROTTLE LEVER
61. LEVER – THROTTLE
62. POSITIONER ASSEMBLY – THROTTLE
63. SCREW – 1/4 - 28 x 2.53 HEX HEAD ADJUSTING
64. SPRING – THROTTLE POSITIONER RETAINING
65. "E" RING – RETAINING
66. BRACKET – THROTTLE POSITIONER
67. SCREW – M5 x 8 x 14.0 HEX WASHER TAP

88185G40

Fig. 28 Exploded view of the CFI system components

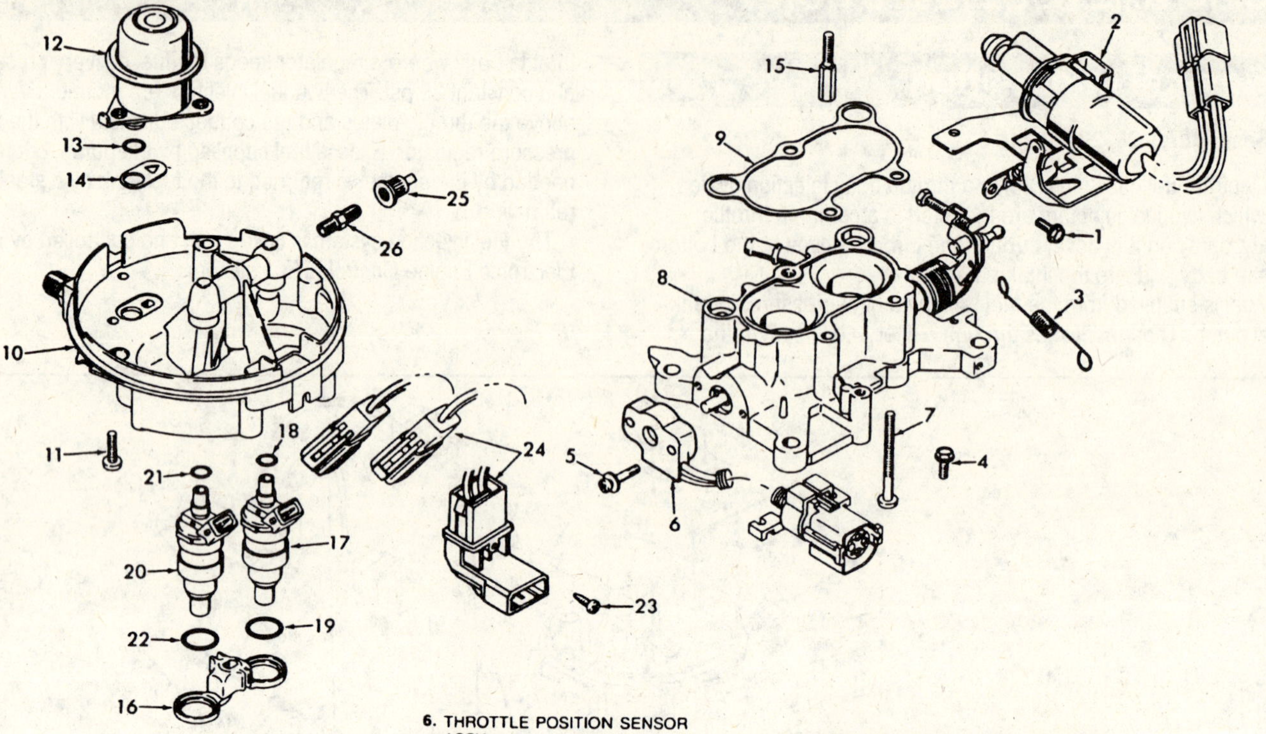

REF. NO.

1. SCREW — DC MOTOR ACTUATOR
2. THROTTLE ACTUATOR DC MOTOR
3. SPRING — TRANS. LEVER
4. SCREW — CONNECTOR BRACKET
5. SCREW (2) — THROTTLE POSITION SENSOR
6. THROTTLE POSITION SENSOR ASSY
7. SCREWS (4) — THROTTLE BODY
8. THROTTLE BODY ASSY
9. GASKET — FUEL CHARGING BODY
10. MAIN BODY ASSY — FUEL CHARGING
11. SCREW (3) — FUEL PRESSURE REGULATOR
12. REGULATOR ASSY — FUEL PRESSURE
13. O-RING — PRESSURE REGULATOR
14. GASKET — PRESSURE REGULATOR
15. SCREW — FUEL INJECTOR RETAINING
16. RETAINER — FUEL INJECTOR'S
17. INJECTOR ASSY — FUEL (THROTTLE SIDE)
18. O-RING — FUEL INJECTOR (TOP)
19. O-RING — FUEL INJECTOR (LOWER)
20. INJECTOR ASSY — FUEL (SENSOR SIDE)
21. O-RING — FUEL INJECTOR (TOP)
22. O-RING — FUEL INJECTOR (LOWER)
23. SCREW — WIRING ASSY
24. WIRING ASSY — FUEL CHARGING
25. CAP — RELIEF VALVE
26. VALVE ASSY — FUEL PRESSURE RELIEF (SCHRADER)

88185G60

Fig. 29 Exploded view of the CFI system components — 1995 3.8L shown

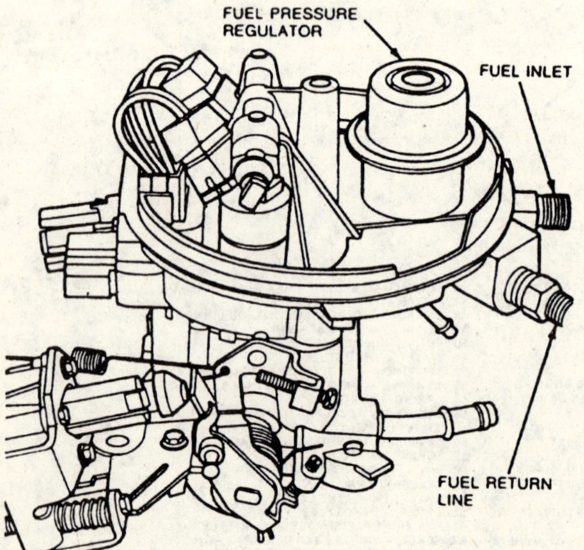

88185G41

Fig. 30 Left side view of the 3.8L CFI throttle body assembly

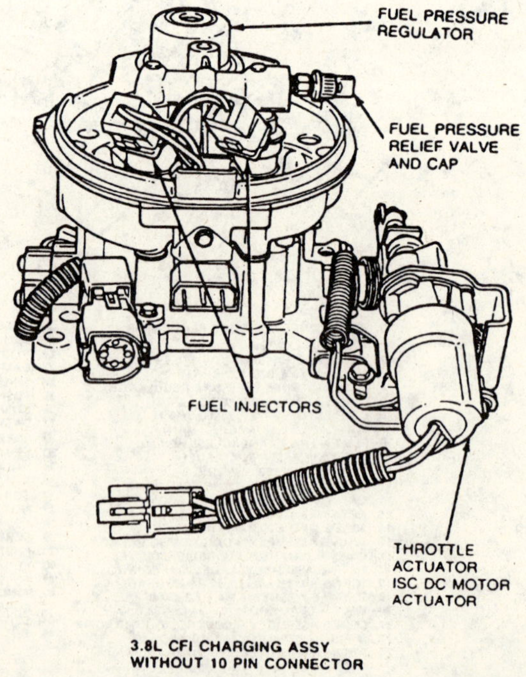

88185G42

Fig. 31 Front view of the 3.8L CFI throttle body assembly

Relieving Fuel System Pressure

Fuel supply lines on all fuel injected engines will remain pressurized for some period of time after the engine is shut **OFF**. This pressure must be relieved before servicing the fuel system. Pressure is relieved through the fuel pressure relief valve. To relieve the fuel system pressure, first remove the fuel tank cap to relieve pressure in the tank, then remove the cap on the fuel pressure relief valve, located on the fuel rail. Attach fuel pressure gauge T80L-9974-A or equivalent, and drain the system through the drain tube into a suitable container. Remove the fuel pressure gauge and replace the cap on the relief valve.

Electric Fuel Pump

REMOVAL & INSTALLATION

Models equipped with a high output injected or turbocharged injected engine are equipped with two electric pumps. A low pressure pump is mounted in the tank and a high pressure pump is externally mounted.

All other models are equipped with a single, in-tank, high pressure fuel pump.

****CAUTION**

Before servicing any part of the fuel injection it is necessary to depressurize the system. A special tool is available for testing and bleeding the system.

1983-84 Low Pressure In-Tank Pump

See Figures 32 and 33

1. Disconnect the negative battery cable.

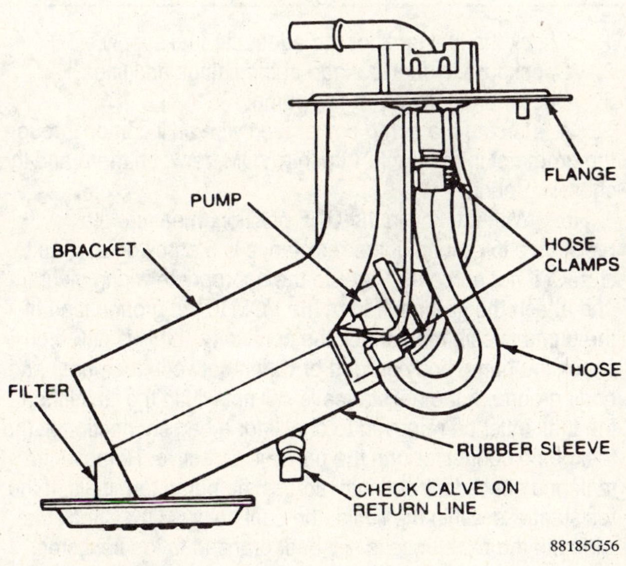

Fig. 32 Low pressure in-tank electric fuel pump — 1983-84 3.8L and 5.0L engines

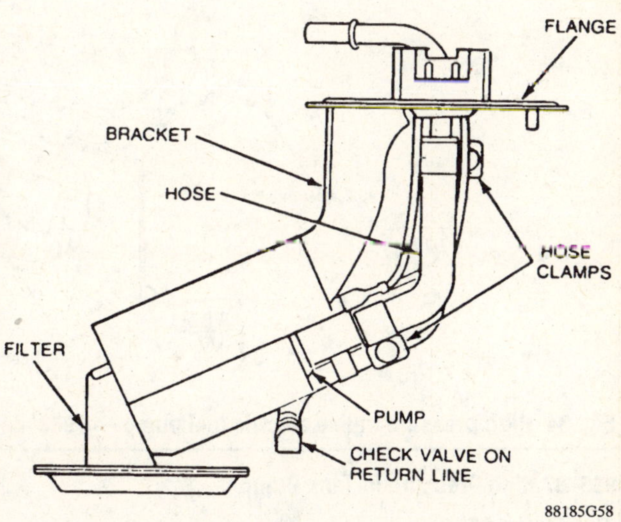

Fig. 33 Low pressure in-tank electric fuel pump — 2.3 turbo engine

2. Depressurize the system and drain as much gas from the tank by pumping out through the filler neck.
3. Raise and support the rear end on jackstands.
4. Disconnect the fuel supply, return and vent lines at the right and left side of the frame.
5. Disconnect the wiring to the fuel pump.
6. Support the gas tank, loosen and remove the mounting straps. Remove the gas tank.
7. Disconnect the lines and harness at the pump flange.
8. Clean the outside of the mounting flange and retaining ring. Turn the fuel pump lock ring counterclockwise and remove.
9. Remove the fuel pump.

To Install:

10. Clean the mounting surfaces. Put a light coat of grease on the mounting surfaces and on the new sealing ring. Install the new fuel pump.
11. Installation is in the reverse order of removal. If you have a single high pressure pump system, fill the tank with at least 10 gals. of gas. Turn the ignition key **ON** for three seconds. Repeat 6 or 7 times until the fuel system is pressurized. Check for any fitting leaks. Start the engine and check for leaks.

1983-84 High Pressure External Pump

See Figure 34

1. Disconnect the negative battery cable.
2. Depressurize the fuel system.
3. Raise and support the rear of the vehicle on jackstands.
4. Disconnect the inlet and outlet fuel lines.
5. Disconnect the electrical harness connection.
6. Bend down the retaining tab and remove the pump from the mounting bracket ring.
7. Install in reverse order, make sure the pump is indexed correctly in the mounting bracket insulator.

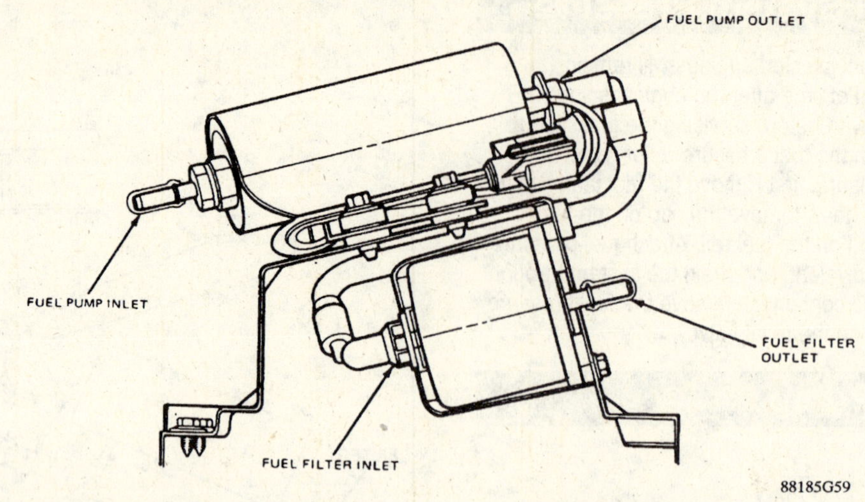

Fig. 34 High pressure in-line electric fuel pump — 1983–84 3.8L and 5.0L engines

1985–87 High Pressure In-Tank Pump

See Figure 35

1. Depressurize the system.
2. Disconnect the negative battery cable.
3. Drain as much gas from the tank by pumping out through the filler neck as possible.
4. Raise and support the rear end on jackstands.
5. Disconnect the filler hose, fuel supply, return and vent lines at the right and left side of the frame. On some models the gas tank must be lowered to gain access to the fuel and vent lines.
6. Disconnect the wiring to the fuel pump.

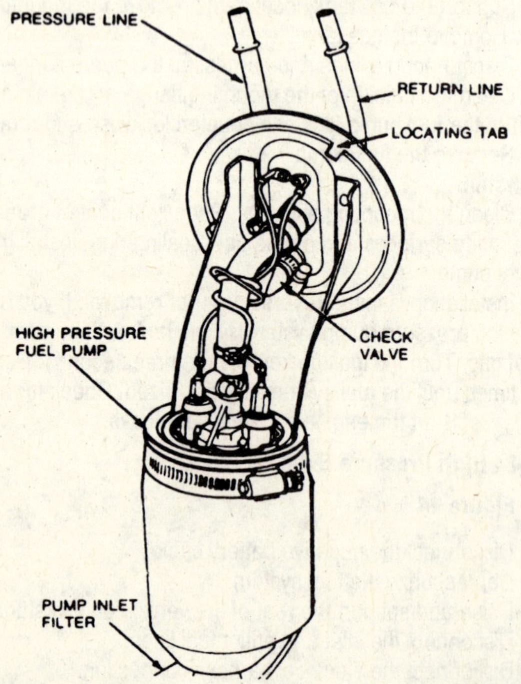

Fig. 35 High pressure in-tank electric fuel pump — 1984 3.8L and 5.0L engines

7. Support the gas tank, loosen and remove the mounting straps. Remove the gas tank. On some models the exhaust pipe and shield must be removed first.
8. Disconnect the lines and harness at the pump flange.
9. Clean the outside of the mounting flange and retaining ring. Turn the fuel pump lock ring counterclockwise and remove.
10. Remove the fuel pump.

To install:

11. Clean the mounting surfaces. Put a light coat of grease on the mounting surfaces and on the new sealing ring. Install the new fuel pump.
12. Installation is in the reverse order of removal. If you have a single high pressure pump system, fill the tank with at least 10 gals. of gas. Turn the ignition key **ON** for three seconds. Repeat 6 or 7 times until the fuel system is pressurized. Check for any fitting leaks. Start the engine and check for leaks.

TESTING

1. Check the fuel tank for the adequate fuel supply.
2. Check for any fuel leakage at the fittings and lines.
3. Check for continuity at the pump:
    a. Locate the pump power feed wire as it comes through the grommet in the trunk. Attach a VOM between there and the chassis ground.
    b. With the key in the **OFF** position, measure the resistance to ground, if the resistance is 5 ohms or less, go to step C. if not proceed. Refer to the appropriate wiring diagram and attach the ground lead of the VOM to the ground lead of the pump circuit, then check the continuity. If this is OK, then check the pump body ground or wiring between the pump and body ground. If the resistance is still not within the limits then the tank must be removed to check for a bad connection at the fuel pump connector or if the pump is defective. Remove the tank and check for continuity across the pump terminals. If the resistance is within the limits, the continuity is OK. Check the wiring. If the resistance is still bad, proceed to the next step.
    c. Set the meter to read the voltage and turn the ignition **ON**. The voltage should rise to 10 volts or more for one second, then return to 0. If the voltage is not within specification, check the electrical circuit and service as needed.

4. Check the fuel pump pressure and flow:
   a. Attach a pressure gage tool T80L-9974-A or equivalent to the fuel diagnostic valve.
   b. As a primary check, turn the ignition **ON**, and check the pressure gage reading. The gage should read between 30-40 psi (2.7-275 kPa). If the pump is operating properly and other system components are OK, continue.
   c. Disconnect the fuel return line at the fuel rail.
   d. Connect a hose from the rail fitting to a calibrated container of at least one quart.
   e. Locate and replace with the modified relay. Take the ground lead to a convenient location of the vehicle and ground it. This should make the pump run. Energize the pump for ten seconds.
   f. Allow the fuel to drain from the return hose into the container, then observe the volume.
   g. The pump is operating properly if:

- The pressure reaches 35-45 psi (241-310 kPa)
- Fuel flow is a minimum of 5.6 oz. (170ml) in 10 seconds
- The fuel pressure remains a minimum of 30 psi (207 kPa) immediately after de-energization

   h. If all three conditions are met, the pump is operating normally. Check the engine and possible electrical problems.
   i. If the pressure is met but the flow is not, check for a clogged fuel filter and/or supply hoses. After correcting any of these problems and the conditions are still not met, replace the pump.
   j. If both pressure and flow are good but the pressure will not remain after de-enterization, check for leaking injectors or regulator. If both check OK, then replace the pump.
   k. If no flow or pressure is seen, the fuel system should be checked as in step i. If no trouble is found, replace the pump.

Throttle Body

GENERAL INFORMATION

Air and Fuel Control

The throttle body assembly is comprised of six individual components which perform the job of mixing the air and fuel to the ideal ratio for controlling exhaust emissions and providing performance and economy. The six components are: air control, fuel injector nozzles, fuel pressure regulator, fuel pressure diagnostic valve, cold engine speed control, and throttle position sensor.

Air Control

Air flow to the engine is controlled by two butterfly valves mounted in a two piece, die-cast aluminum housing called the throttle body. The butterfly valves, or throttle valves, are identical in design to the throttle plates of a conventional carburetor and are actuated by a similar linkage and pedal cable arrangement.

Fuel Injector Nozzles

The fuel injector nozzles are mounted in the throttle body and are electromechanical devices which meter and atomize the fuel delivered to the engine. The injector valve bodies consist of a solenoid actuated pintle and needle valve assembly. An electrical control signal from the EED electronic processor activates the solenoid causing the pintle to move inward off its seat and allowing fuel to flow. the fuel flow through the injector is controlled by the amount of time the injector solenoid holds the pintle off its seat.

Fuel Pressure Regulator

The fuel pressure regulator is mounted on the throttle body. The regulator smooths out fuel pressure drops from the fuel pump. It is not sensitive to back pressure in the return line to the tank.

A second function of the pressure regulator is to maintain fuel supply pressure upon engine and fuel pump shut down. The regulator acts as a check valve and traps fuel between itself and the fuel pump. This promotes rapid start ups and helps prevent fuel vapor formation in the lines, or vapor lock. The regulator makes sure that the pressure of the fuel at the injector nozzles stays at a constant 39 psi.

Fuel Pressure Diagnostic Valve

A Schrader-type diagnostic pressure valve is located at the top of the throttle body. This valve can be used by service personnel to monitor fuel pressure, bleed down the system pressure prior to maintenance and to bleed out air which may have been introduced during assembly or filter servicing. A special Ford Tool (T80L-9974-A) is used to accomplish these procedures.

CAUTION

Under no circumstances should compressed air be forced into the fuel system using the diagnostic valve.

Cold Engine Speed Control

The cold engine speed control serves the same purpose as the fast idle speed device on a carbureted engine, which is to raise engine speed during cold engine idle. A throttle stop cam positioner is used. the cam is positioned by a bimetal spring and an electric heating element. The cold engine speed control is attached to the throttle body. As the engine heats up, the fast idle cam on the cold engine speed control is gradually repositioned by the bimetal spring, heating element and EEC computer until normal idle speed is reached. The EEC computer automatically kicks down the fast idle cam to a lower step (lower engine speed) by supplying vacuum to the automatic kickdown motor which physically moves the high speed cam a predetermined time after the engine starts.

Throttle Position Sensor

This sensor is attached to the throttle body and is used to monitor changes in throttle plate position. the throttle position sensor sends this information to the computer, which uses it to select proper air/fuel mixture, spark timing and EGR control under different engine operating conditions.

Fuel System Inertia Switch

In the event of a collision, the electrical contacts in the inertia switch open and the fuel pump automatically shuts off. The fuel pump will shut off even if the engine does not stop running. The engine, however, will stop a few seconds after the fuel pump stops. It is not possible to restart the engine until the inertia switch is manually reset. The switch is located in the luggage compartment on the left hinge support on all models to 1988. 1989-91 models, LH lower back panel in luggage compartment. To reset, depress both buttons on the switch at the same time (Some models use only one button).

****CAUTION**

Do not reset the inertia switch until the complete fuel system has been inspected for leaks.

ON-CAR SERVICE

➥ Diagnostic and test procedures on the EEC-III and EEC-IV electronic control system require special test equipment. Have the testing done by a professional.

Fuel Pressure Tests

The diagnostic pressure valve (Schrader type) is located at the top of the Fuel charging main body. This valve provides a convenient point for service personnel to monitor fuel pressure, bleed down the system pressure prior to maintenance, and to bleed out air which may become trapped in the system during filter replacement. A pressure gauge with a adapter is required to perform pressure tests.

****CAUTION**

Under no circumstances should compressed air be forced into the fuel system using the diagnostic valve. Depressing the pin in the diagnostic valve will relieve system pressure by expelling fuel into the throttle body.

System Pressure Test

Testing fuel pressure requires the use of a special pressure gauge (T80L-9974-A or equivalent) that attaches to the diagnostic pressure tap on the fuel charging assembly. Depressurize the fuel system before disconnecting any lines.

1. Disconnect the fuel return line at the throttle body (in-tank high pressure pump) and connect the hose to a 1 quart calibrated container. Connect a pressure gauge.
2. Disconnect the electrical connector at the fuel pump. The connector is located ahead of fuel tank (in-tank high pressure pump) or just forward of pump outlet (in-line high pressure pump). Connect an auxiliary wiring harness to the connector of the fuel pump. Energize the pump for 10 seconds by applying 12 volts to the auxiliary harness connector, allowing the fuel to drain into the calibrated container. Note the fuel volume and pressure gauge reading.
3. Correct fuel pressure should be 35-45 psi (241-310 kPa). Fuel volume should be 10 oz. in 10 seconds (minimum) and fuel pressure should maintain a minimum of 30 psi (206 kPa) immediately after pump cut-off.

If the pressure condition is met, but the fuel flow is not, check for blocked filter(s) and fuel supply lines. After correcting the problem, repeat the test procedure. If the fuel flow is still inadequate, replace the high pressure pump. If the flow specification is met but the pressure is not, check for a worn or damaged pressure regulator valve on the throttle body. If both the pressure and fuel flow specifications are met, but the pressure drops excessively after de-energizing, check for a leaking injector valve(s) and/or pressure regulator valve. If the injector valves and pressure regulator valve are okay, replace the high pressure pump. If no pressure or flow is seen in the fuel system, check for blocked filters and fuel lines. If no trouble is found, replace the in-line fuel pump, in-tank fuel pump and the fuel filter inside the tank.

Fuel Injector Pressure Test

1. Connect pressure gauge T80L-9974-A, or equivalent, to the fuel pressure test fitting. Disconnect the coil connector from the coil. Disconnect the electrical lead from one injector and pressurize the fuel system. Disable the fuel pump by disconnecting the inertia switch or the fuel pump relay and observe the pressure gauge reading.
2. Crank the engine for 2 seconds. Turn the ignition **OFF** and wait 5 seconds, then observe the pressure drop. If the pressure drop is 2-16 psi (14-110 kPa), the injector is operating properly. Reconnect the injector, activate the fuel pump, then repeat the procedure for other injector.
3. If the pressure drop is less than 2 psi (14 kPa) or more than 16 psi (110 kPa), switch the electrical connectors on injectors and repeat the test. If the pressure drop is still incorrect, replace the disconnected injector with one of the same color code, then reconnect both injectors properly and repeat the test.
4. Disconnect and plug the vacuum hose at EGR valve. It may be necessary to disconnect the idle speed control (3.8L) or the throttle kicker solenoid (5.0L) and use the throttle body stop screw to set the engine speed. Start and run the engine at 1,800 rpm (2,000 rpm on 1984 and later models). Disconnect the left injector electrical connector. Note the rpm after the engine stabilizes (around 1,200 rpm). Reconnect the injector and allow the engine to return to high idle.
5. Perform the same procedure for the right injector. Note the difference between the rpm readings of the left and right injectors. If the difference is 100 rpm or less, check the oxygen sensor. If the difference is more than 100 rpm, replace both injectors.

REMOVAL & INSTALLATION

1. Remove the air cleaner assembly.
2. Release the pressure from the fuel system at the diagnostic valve on the throttle body using SST T80L-9974-A or equivalent.
3. Disconnect the throttle cable and transmission valve lever.
4. Disconnect the fuel, vacuum and electrical connections.

➥ Either the multi or single ten pin connections may be encountered. To disconnect the electrical ten pin connectors, push in or squeeze on the right side lower locking tab while pulling up on the connection. Multi connectors disconnect by pulling apart. The ISC connector tab must be moved out while pulling them apart.

5. Remove the throttle body assembly retaining nuts, then remove the unit.
6. Remove the mounting gasket from the intake manifold.

To install:

7. Clean the gasket mounting surfaces and place a spacer and gaskets on the intake manifold. Position the throttle body assembly on the spacer and gasket.
8. Secure the throttle body assembly with the retaining nut, tighten to 10 ft. lbs. (14 Nm). To prevent any leakage, distortion or damage to the throttle body flange, snug the nuts, then in an alternately fashion; tighten each nut in a criss-cross pattern.
9. Connect the fuel line, electrical connections, throttle cable and all emission lines.
10. Start the engine, check for leaks. Adjust the engine idle if necessary.

DISASSEMBLY AND ASSEMBLY

➧ **See Figures 36, 37, 38, 39, 40, 41, 42, 43, 44, 45, 46 and 47**

1. Remove the air cleaner mounting stud in order to separate the upper body from the throttle body.
2. Turn the fuel charging assembly (throttle body) over and remove the four screws from the bottom of the throttle body.
3. Separate the throttle body (lower half) from the main body (upper half).
4. Remove the old gasket. If it is stuck and scraping is necessary, use only a plastic or wood scraper. Take care not to damage the gasket surfaces.
5. Remove the three pressure regulator mounting screws. Remove the pressure regulator.
6. Disconnect the electrical connectors at each injector by pulling outward on the connector and not on the wire. Loosen, but do not remove the wiring harness retaining screw. Push in on the harness tab's to remove it from the upper body.
7. Remove the fuel injector retaining screw. Remove the injection retainer.
8. Pull the injectors, one at a time, from the upper body. Mark the injectors for identification. They must be reinstalled in the same position (choke or throttle side). Each injector is equipped with a small O-ring. If the O-ring does not come out with the injector, carefully pick out of body.
9. Remove the fuel diagnostic valve assembly.
10. Remove the choke cover by drilling the retaining rivets. A $^1/_8$ in. (3mm) or No. 30 drill is required. A choke mounting kit for installation is available from Ford.
11. Remove the choke cap retaining ring, choke cap and gasket. Remove the thermostat lever screw and lever. Remove the fast idle cam assembly and control rod positioner.
12. Hold the control diaphragm cover in position and remove the two mounting screws. Carefully remove the cover, spring and pull down diaphragm.
13. Remove the fast idle retaining nut, fast idle cam adjuster lever, fast idle lever and E-clip.

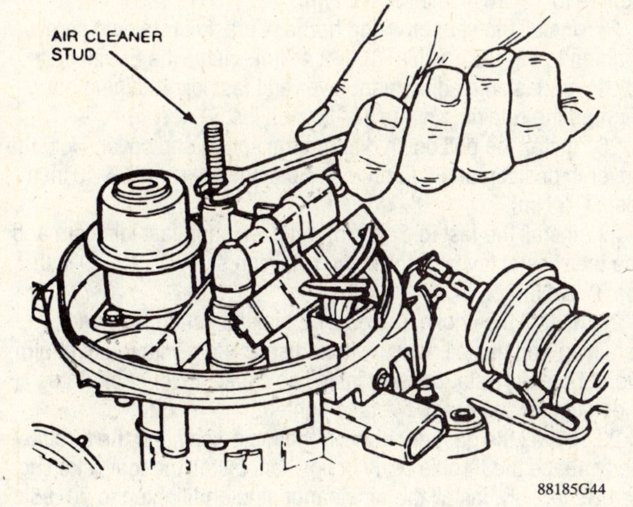

Fig. 36 Remove the air cleaner stud

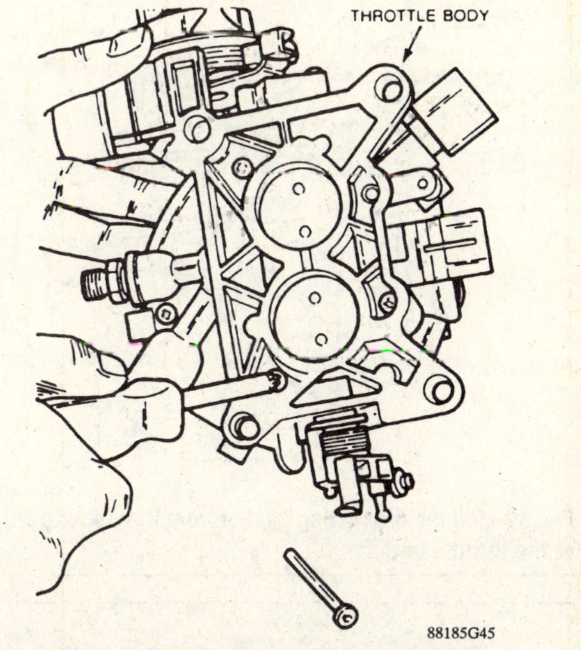

Fig. 37 Unscrew the four retaining screws from the bottom of the throttle body

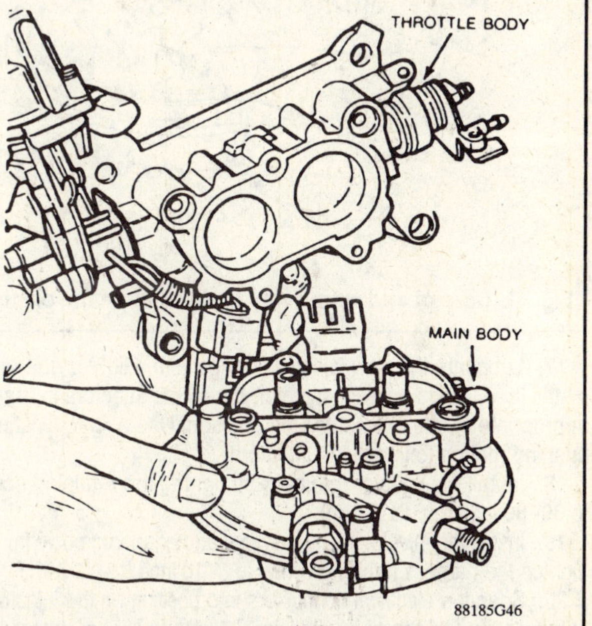

Fig. 38 Separate the upper and lower throttle bodys halves

14. Remove the potentiometer (sensor) connector bracket retaining screw. Mark the throttle body and throttle position sensor for correct installation position. Remove the throttle sensor retaining screws and slide the sensor off of the throttle shaft. Remove the throttle positioner retaining screw and remove the throttle positioner.

To install:

15. Perform any necessary cleaning or repair.
16. Assemble the upper body by first installing the fuel diagnostic fuel pressure valve assembly.

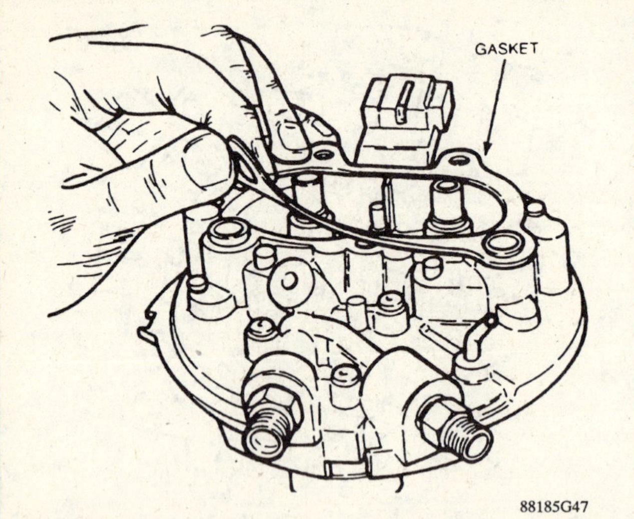

Fig. 39 Pull the old mating gasket from the upper portion of the throttle body

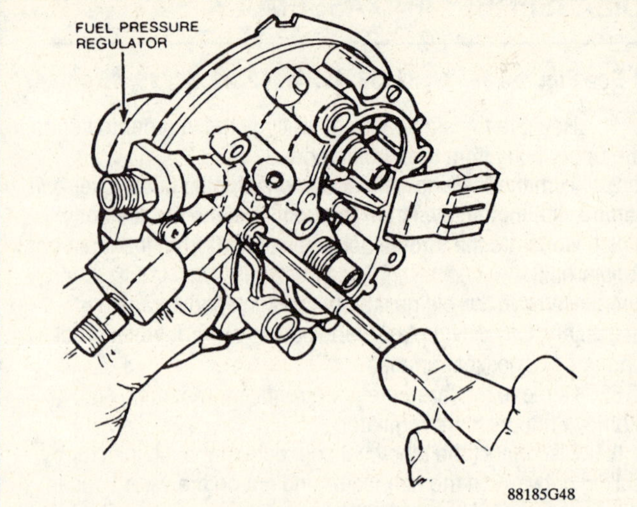

Fig. 40 Remove the three pressure regulator mounting screws

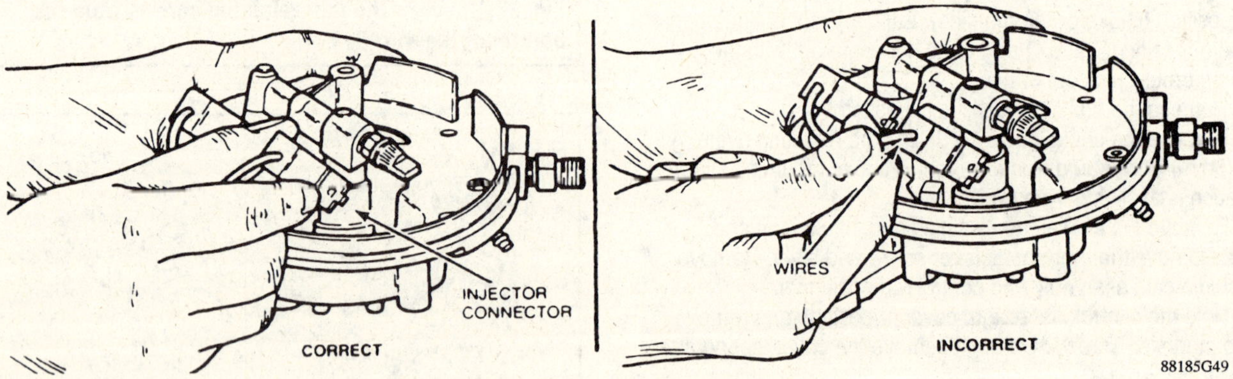

Fig. 41 Correct and wrong way to disconnect the electrical wiring to the injector

17. Lubricate the new injector O-rings with a light grade oil. Install the O-rings on each injector. Install the injectors in their appropriate choke or throttle side position. Use a light, twisting, pushing motion to install the injectors.

18. Install the injector retainer and tighten the retaining screw to 30–60 inch lbs. (3–7 Nm).

19. Install the injector wiring harness and snap into position. Tighten the harness retaining screw to 8–10 inch lbs. (0.8–1.1 Nm).

20. Snap the electrical connectors into position on the injectors. Lubricate the fuel pressure regulator O-ring with light oil. Install the O-ring and new gasket on the regulator. Install the regulator and tighten retaining screws to 27–40 inch lbs. (2–4 Nm).

21. Install the throttle positioner onto the throttle body. Tighten the retaining screw to 32–44 inch lbs. (3–5 Nm).

22. Hold the throttle sensor (potentiometer) with the location identification mark (see the last removal step) in the 12 o'clock position. The two rotary tangs should be at 3 o'clock and 9 o'clock positions.

23. Slide the sensor onto the throttle shaft with the identification mark still in the 12 o'clock position. Hold the sensor firmly against the throttle body.

24. Rotate the sensor until the identification marks on the sensor and body are aligned. Install the retaining screws and tighten to 13–18 inch lbs. (1–2 Nm).

25. Install the sensor wiring harness bracket retaining screw. Tighten to 18–22 inch lbs. (2.0–2.4 Nm). Install the E-clip, fast idle lever, fast idle adjustment lever and fast idle retaining nut. Tighten the retaining nut to 16–20 inch lbs. (1–2 Nm)

26. Install the pull down diaphragm, spring and cover. Hold the cover in position and tighten the retaining screws to 13–19 inch lbs. (1–2 Nm).

27. Install the fast idle control rod positioner, fast idle cam and the thermostat lever. Tighten the retaining screw to 13–19 inch lbs. (1–2 Nm).

28. Install the choke cap gasket, bimetal spring, cap and retaining ring. Install new rivets and snug them with the rivet gun. Do not break rivets. Loosely install so choke cover can rotate. Index choke and break rivets to tighten.

29. Install the gasket between the main body and the throttle body. Place the throttle body in position. Install the four retaining screws loosely. Install the air cleaner stud and tighten to 70–95 inch lbs. (8–10 Nm). Tighten the four retaining screws.

30. The rest of the assembly is in the reverse order of disassembly.

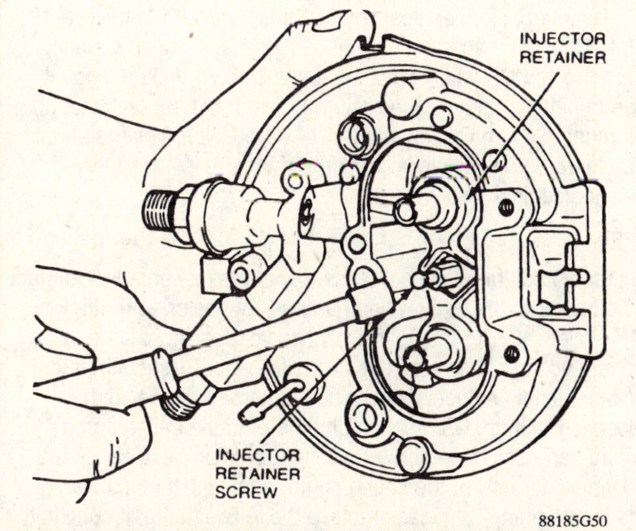

Fig. 42 Remove the fuel injector retainer from the unit

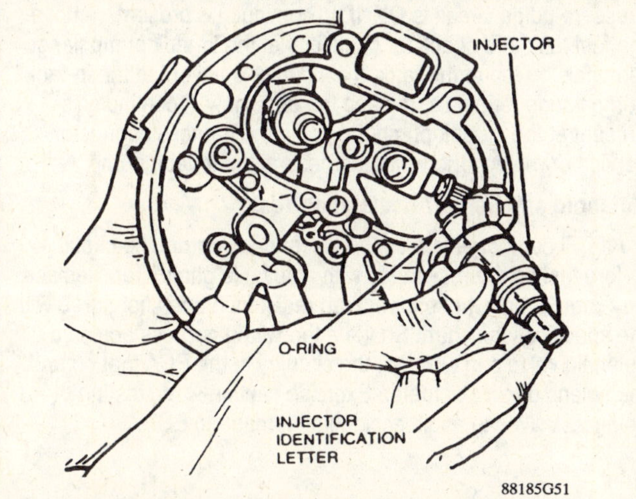

Fig. 43 Each injector has a mark, but you should tag them to ensure correct positioning on installation

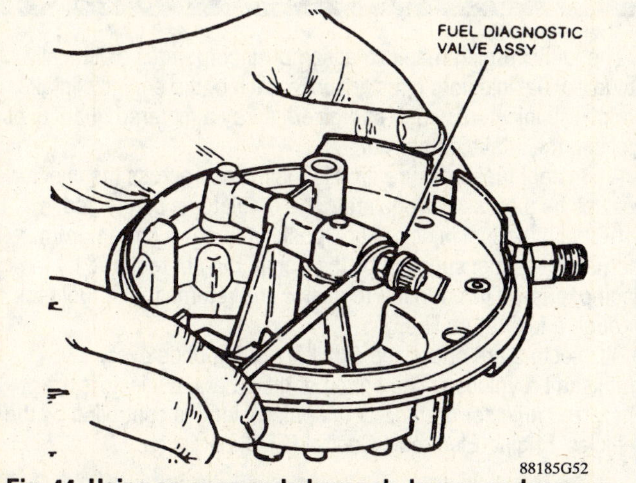

Fig. 44 Using an open ended wrench, loosen and remove the diagnostic valve assembly

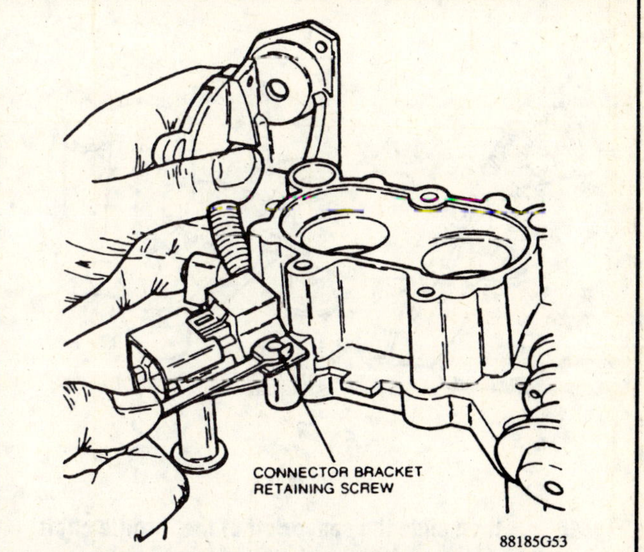

Fig. 45 Remove the throttle sensor retaining screws . . .

ADJUSTMENTS

1. Place the transmission in **P** or **N**.
2. Allow the engine to operate until normal operating temperature is reached.
3. Turn all accessories off.
4. Shut the engine **OFF**. Restart the engine, run at 2000 rpm for 60 seconds in **N** and let the engine idle stabilized for 15 seconds before checking or adjusting the curb idle rpm.
5. Have and assistant place the transmission in **R** and check/adjust the curb idle rpm. If adjustment is necessary, use the saddle bracket adjusting screw.
6. Check/adjust the Throttle Position Sensor (TPS), refer to Section 4.

CFI COMPONENT TESTS

➥ Complete CFI system diagnosis requires the use of special test equipment. Have the system tested professionally.

Before beginning any component testing, always check the following:

- Check the ignition and fuel systems to ensure there is fuel and spark.
- Remove the air cleaner assembly and inspect all vacuum and pressure hoses for proper connection to fittings. Check for damaged or pinched hoses.
- Inspect all sub-system wiring harnesses for proper connections to the EGR solenoid valves, injectors, sensors, etc.
- Check for loose or detached connectors and broken or detached wires. Check that all terminals are seated firmly and are not corroded. Look for partially broken or frayed wires or any shorting between the wires.
- Inspect the sensors for physical damage. Inspect the vehicle electrical system. Check the battery for full charge and cable connections for tightness.
- Inspect the relay connector and make sure the ECA power relay is securely attached and making a good ground connection.

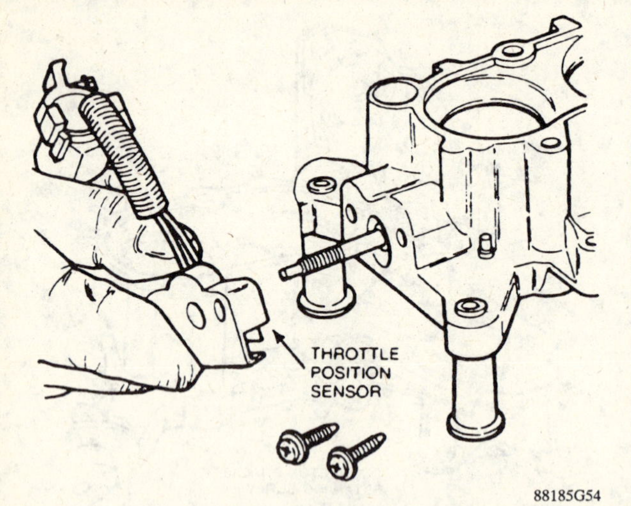

Fig. 46 . . . then slide the sensor off of the throttle shaft

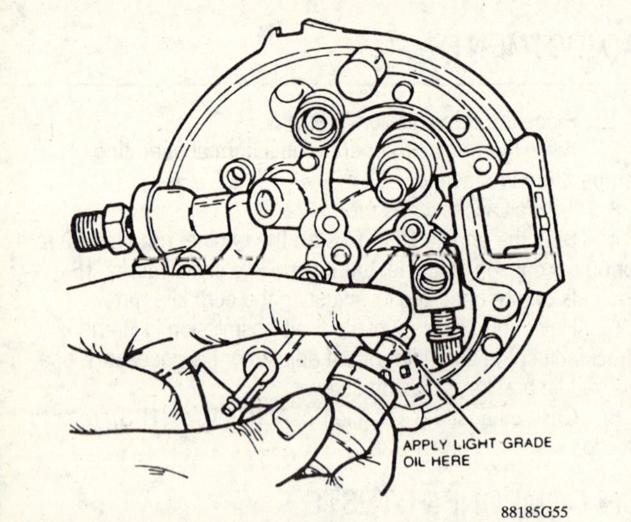

Fig. 47 Lubricate the new injector O-rings with a light grade oil, then install the O-rings on each injector

High Pressure In-Tank Pump

Disconnect the electrical connector just forward of the fuel tank. Connect a voltmeter to the body wiring harness connector. Turn the key **ON** while watching the voltmeter. Voltage should rise to battery voltage, then return to zero after about 1 second. Momentarily turn the key to the **START** position. Voltage should rise to about 8 volts while cranking. If voltage is not specified, check electrical system.

High Pressure In-Line & Low Pressure In-Tank Pumps

Disconnect the electrical connector at the fuel pumps. Connect a voltmeter to the body wiring harness connector. Turn the key **ON** while watching the voltmeter. The voltage should rise to battery voltage, then return to zero after about 1 second. If the voltage is not as specified, check the inertia switch and the electrical system. Connect an ohmmeter to the in-line pump wiring harness connector. If no continuity is present, check the continuity directly at the in-line pump terminals. If no continuity at the in-line pump terminals, replace the in-line pump. If continuity is present, service or replace the wiring harness.

Connect an ohmmeter across the body wiring harness connector. If continuity is present (about 5 ohms), the low pressure pump circuit is OK. If no continuity is present, remove the fuel tank and check for continuity at the in-tank pump flange terminals on top of the tank. If continuity is absent at the in-tank pump flange terminals, replace the assembly. If continuity is present at the in-tank pump but not in the harness connector, service or replace the wiring harness at the in-tank pump.

Solenoid and Sensor Resistance Tests

All CFI components must be disconnected from the circuit before testing the resistance with a suitable ohmmeter. Replace any component whose measured resistance does not agree with the specifications chart. Shorting the wiring harness across a solenoid valve can burn out the circuitry in the ECA that control the solenoid valve actuator. Exercise caution when testing the solenoid valves to avoid accidental damage to ECA.

MULTI-POINT INJECTION (EFI) AND SEQUENTIAL FUEL INJECTION (SEFI)

General Information

➧ See Figures 48, 49, 50, 51, 52, 53 and 54

The Electronic Fuel Injector System (EFI) is classified as a multi-point, pulse time, mass air flow (EFI) or speed density control (SEFI) fuel injection system.

An on board vehicle electronic engine control (EEC) computer accepts inputs from various engine sensors to compute the required fuel flow rate necessary to maintain a prescribed air/fuel ratio throughout the entire engine operational range. The computer then outputs a command to the fuel injectors to meter the approximate quantity of fuel.

The fuel charging manifold assembly incorporates electrically actuated fuel injectors directly above each of the engine's intake ports. The injectors, when energized, spray a metered quantity of fuel into the intake air stream.

A constant fuel pressure drop is maintained across the injector nozzles by a pressure regulator. The regulator is connected in series with the fuel injectors and positioned down stream from them. Excess fuel supplied by the pump, but not required by the engine, passes through the regulator and returns to the fuel tank through a fuel return line.

All injectors are energized simultaneously, once every crankshaft revolution. The period of time that the injectors are energized (injector on-time or the pulse width) is controlled by the vehicles' Engine Electronic Control (EEC) computer.

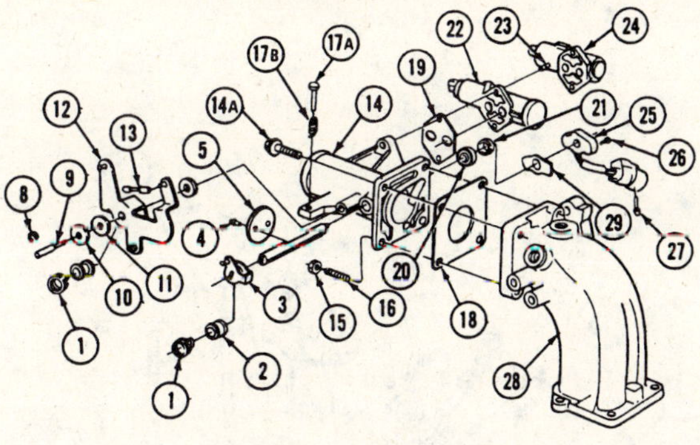

ITEM	PART NAME
1	SPRING — CARBURETOR THROTTLE RETURN
2	BUSHING — ACCELERATOR PUMP OVERTRAVEL SPRING (2)
3	LEVER — ENGINE THROTTLE
4	SCREW — M4 X .7 X 8
5	PLATE — AIR INTAKE CHARGE THROTTLE
6	SHAFT — AIR INTAKE CHARGE THROTTLE
7	SPRING — SECONDARY THROTTLE RETURN
8	E-RING
9	HUB — THROTTLE CONTROL
10	SPACER
11	WASHER — NYLON (2)
12	LEVER — THROTTLE CONTROL
13	ROD — ENGINE SECONDARY THROTTLE CONTROL
14	BODY — AIR INTAKE CHARGE THROTTLE
14A	BOLT M8 X 1.25 X 30 HEX FLANGE HEAD 2 REQ'D
15	NUT — M8 2 REQ'D
16	STUD — M8 X 42.5 2 REQ'D
17A	SCREW THROTTLE STOP
17B	SPRING — THROTTLE RETURN CONTROL
18	GASKET — AIR CHARGE CONTROL TO INTAKE MANIFOLD
19	GASKET — AIR BYPASS VALVE
20	SEAL — THROTTLE CONTROL SHAFT
21	BUSHING — CARBURETOR THROTTLE SHAFT
22	VALVE ASSY — THROTTLE AIR BYPASS
23	BOLT — M6 X 1.0 X 20 HEX HEAD FLANGE
24	VALVE ASSY — THROTTLE AIR BYPASS (ALT.)
25	POTENTIOMETER THROTTLE POSITION
26	SCREW AND WASHER ASSY M4 X 22
27	SCREW — M4 X 0.7 X 14.0 HEX. WASHER TAP
28	MANIFOLD — INTAKE UPPER
29	GASKET TPS

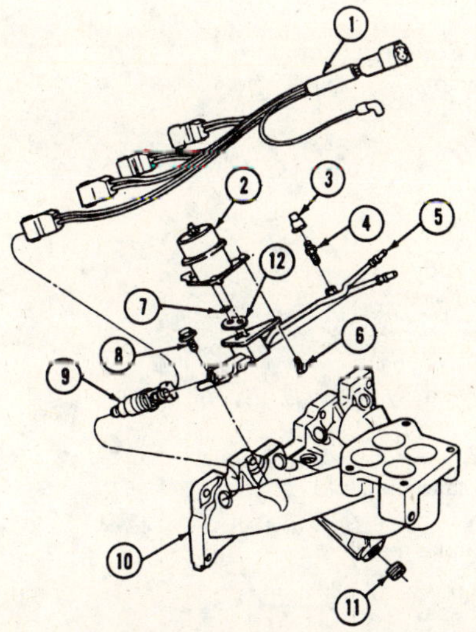

ITEM	PART NAME
1	WIRING HARNESS — FUEL CHARGING
2	REGULATOR ASSY — FUEL PRESSURE SSURE
3	CAP — FUEL PRESSURE RELIEF
4	VALVE ASSY — FUEL PRESSURE RELIEF
5	MANIFOLD ASSY — FUEL INJECTION FUELD SUPPLY
6	SCREW — M5 X 0.8 X 10 SOCKET HEAD 3 REQ'D
7	SEAL — 5/16 X .070 O-RING
8	BOLT (2 REQ'D)
9	INJECTOR ASSY — FUEL 4 REQ'D
10	MANIFOLD — INTAKE LOWER
11	PLUG
12	GASKET — FUEL PRESSURE REGULATOR

88185G77

Fig. 48 Exploded view of the EFI injection system components — 1985-86 2.3L engine

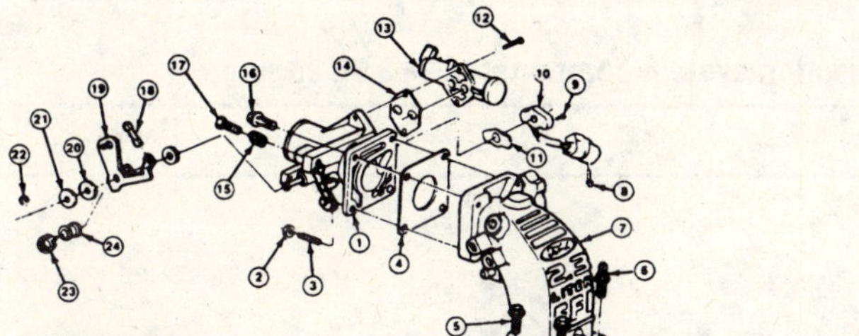

1. Throttle body assy
2. Nut—throttle body retaining
3. Stud—throttle body retaining
4. Gasket—throttle body to intake manifold
5. Screw—upper to lower manifold
6. Stud—upper to lower manifold
7. Manifold—intake upper
8. Screw—tps bracket retaining
9. Screw—tps retaining
10. Throttle pos'n sensor
11. Gasket—throttle pos'n sensor
12. Screw—air bypass valve retaining
13. Air bypass valve
14. Gasket—air bypass valve
15. Spring—idle screw
16. Screw—throttle stop
17. Bolt—throttle body retaining
18. Rod—secondary throttle
19. Lever assy—throttle control (a/t)
20. Washer—sec throttle control lever
21. Spacer—sec throttle control lever
22. Ring—sec throttle lever retaining
23. Spring—carb throttle return
24. Bushing—accel pump o'travel
25. Gasket—upper to lower manifold
26. Manifold assy—intake lower
27. Nipple
28. Screw—fuel pressure regulator
29. Manifold assy—fuel rail
30. Valve assy—fuel pressure relief
31. Valve cap
32. Harness—electric fuel connector
33. Regulator assy
34. Gasket—fuel regulator
35. Seal—O-ring—fuel press reg
36. Screw—fuel rail to lower manifold
37. Injector assy
38. Gasket—lower intake manifold to engine
39. Lifting eye
40. Fuel pulse dampener
41. Screw—fuel pulse dampener

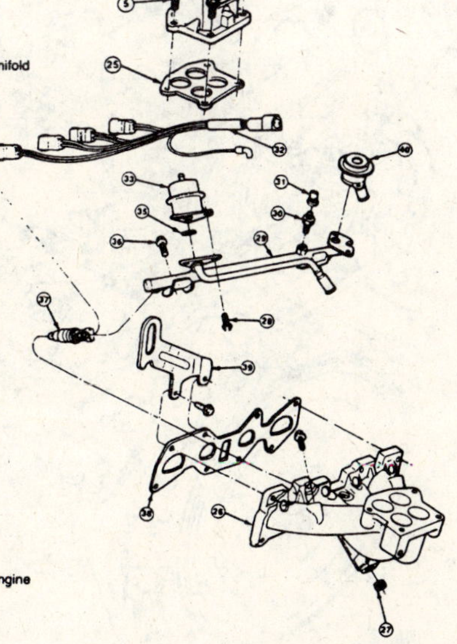

88185G90

Fig. 49 Exploded view of the EFI injection system components — 1987-88 2.3L engine

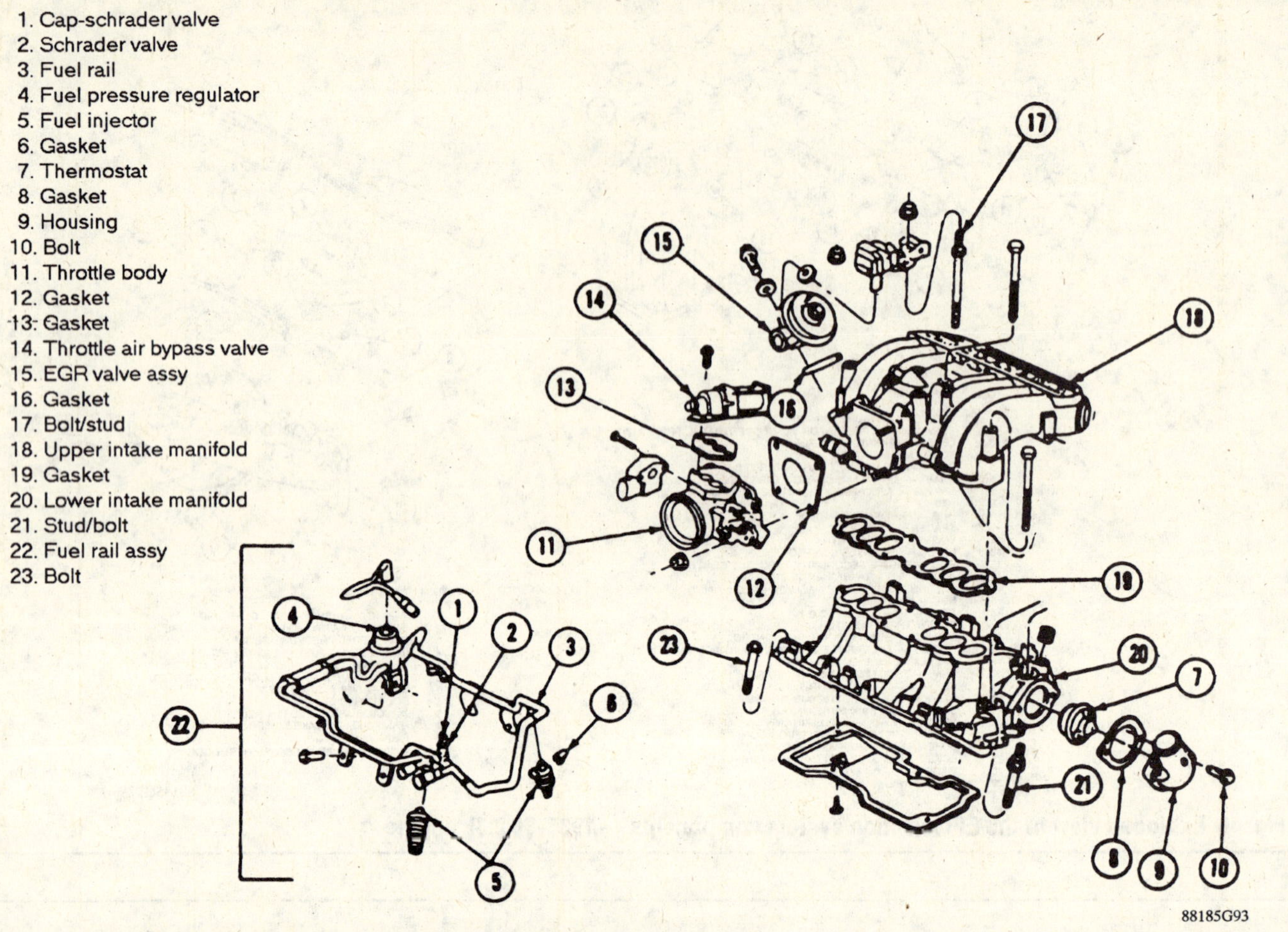

Fig. 50 Exploded view of the EFI injection system components — 3.8L engine

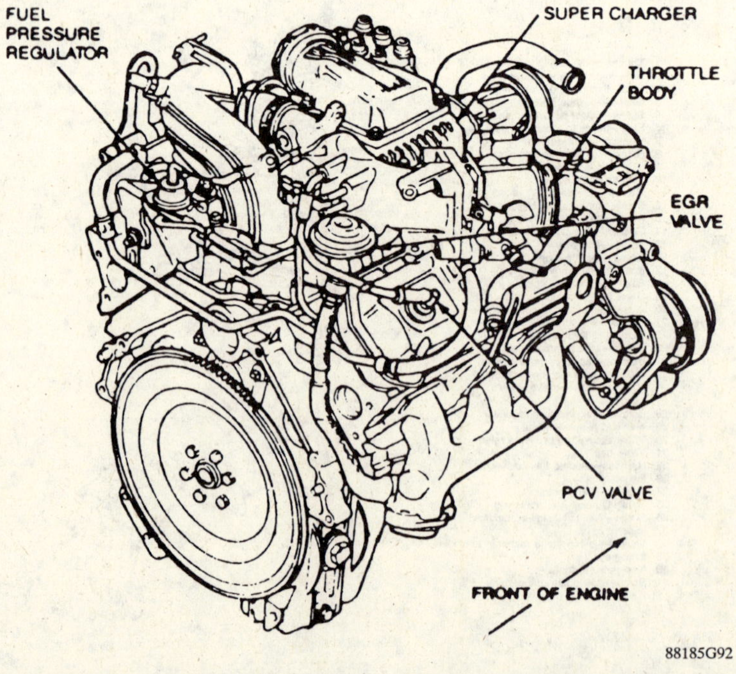

Fig. 51 Exploded view of the EFI injection system components — 3.8L Supercharged engine

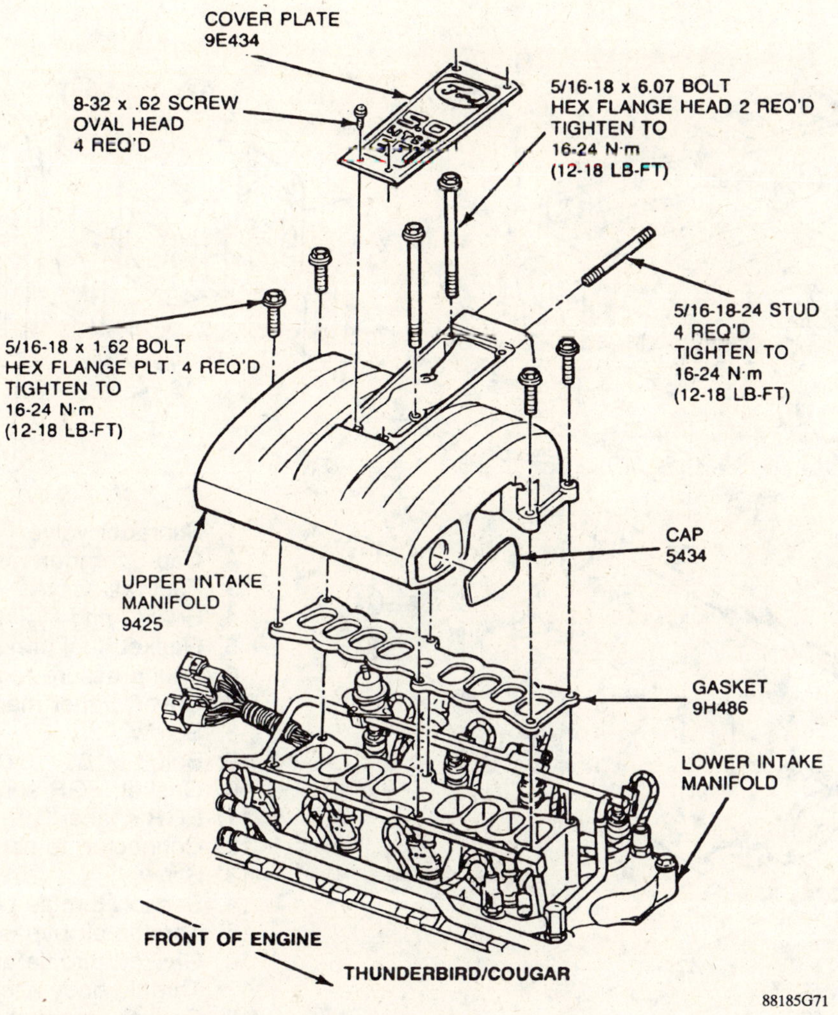

Fig. 52 Exploded view of the SEFI injection manifolds — 5.0L engine

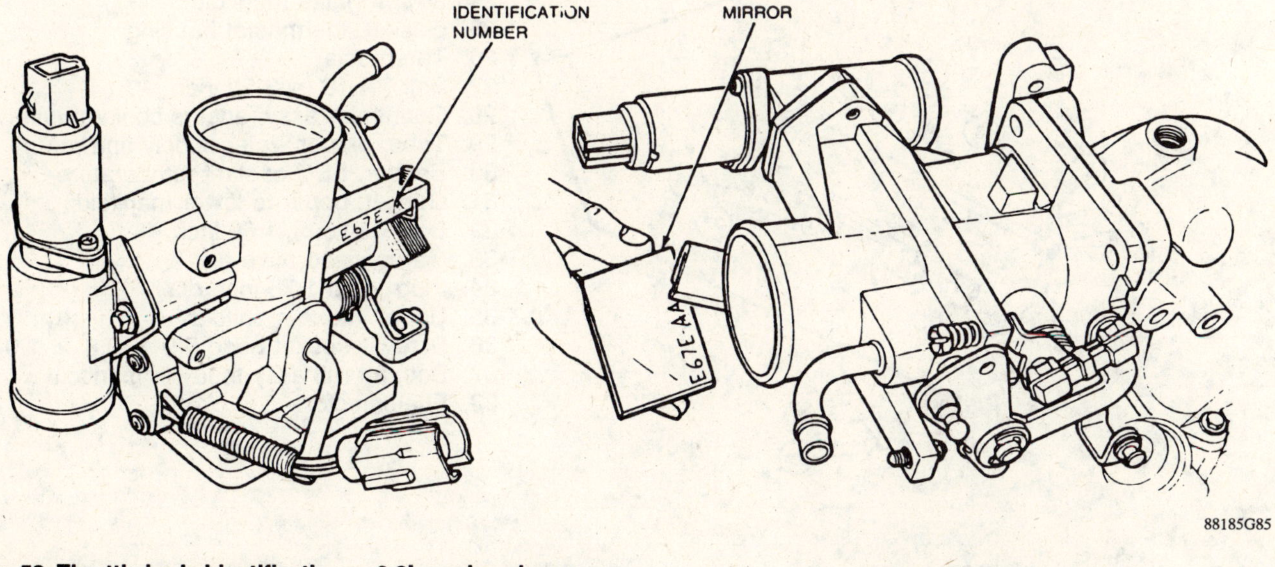

Fig. 53 Throttle body identification — 2.3L engine shown

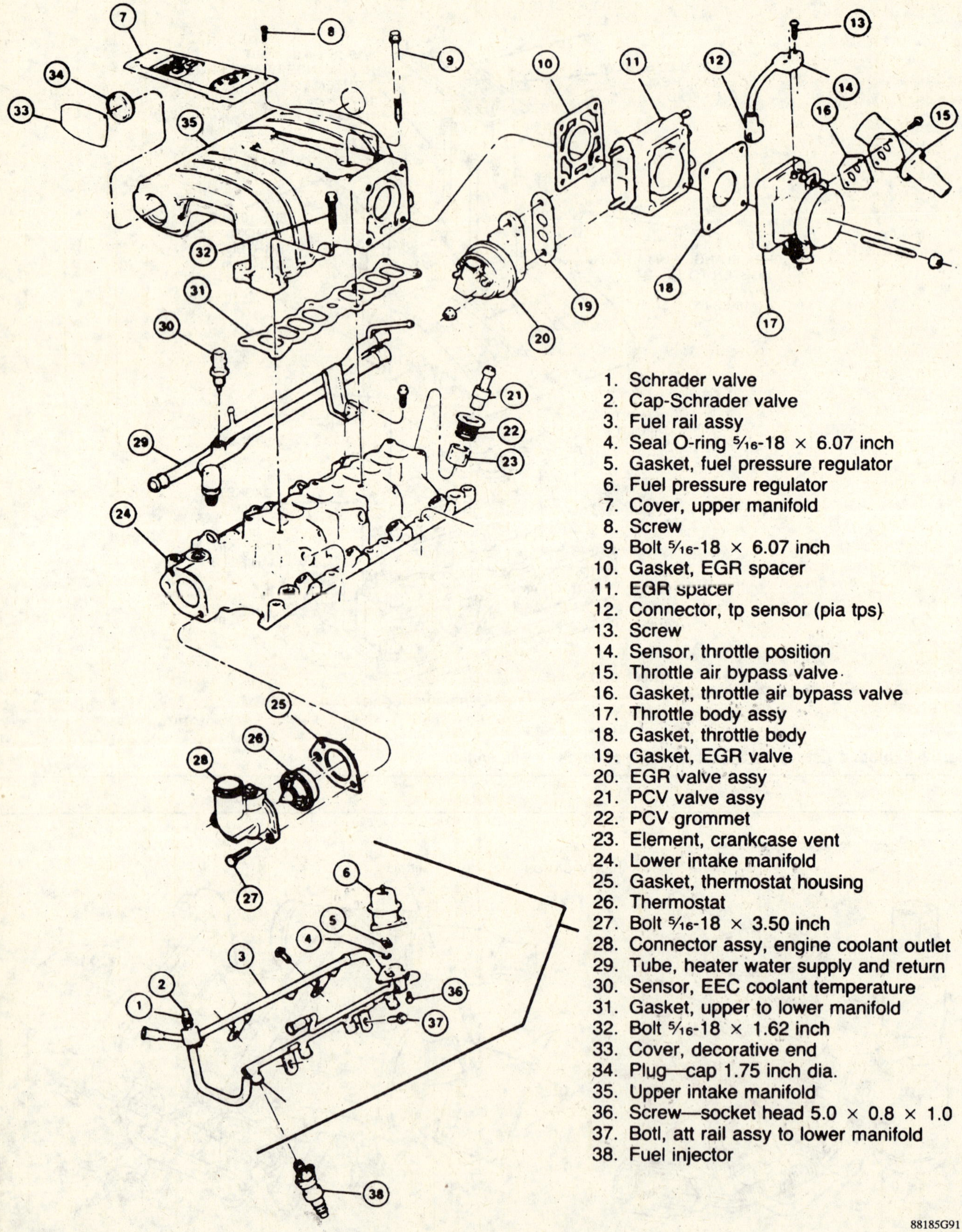

1. Schrader valve
2. Cap-Schrader valve
3. Fuel rail assy
4. Seal O-ring 5/16-18 × 6.07 inch
5. Gasket, fuel pressure regulator
6. Fuel pressure regulator
7. Cover, upper manifold
8. Screw
9. Bolt 5/16-18 × 6.07 inch
10. Gasket, EGR spacer
11. EGR spacer
12. Connector, tp sensor (pia tps)
13. Screw
14. Sensor, throttle position
15. Throttle air bypass valve
16. Gasket, throttle air bypass valve
17. Throttle body assy
18. Gasket, throttle body
19. Gasket, EGR valve
20. EGR valve assy
21. PCV valve assy
22. PCV grommet
23. Element, crankcase vent
24. Lower intake manifold
25. Gasket, thermostat housing
26. Thermostat
27. Bolt 5/16-18 × 3.50 inch
28. Connector assy, engine coolant outlet
29. Tube, heater water supply and return
30. Sensor, EEC coolant temperature
31. Gasket, upper to lower manifold
32. Bolt 5/16-18 × 1.62 inch
33. Cover, decorative end
34. Plug—cap 1.75 inch dia.
35. Upper intake manifold
36. Screw—socket head 5.0 × 0.8 × 1.0
37. Botl, att rail assy to lower manifold
38. Fuel injector

88185G91

Fig. 54 Exploded view of the SEFI injection system components — 5.0L engine

Relieving Fuel System Pressure

Fuel supply lines on all fuel injected engines will remain pressurized for some period of time after the engine is shut **OFF**. This pressure must be relieved before servicing the fuel system. Pressure is relieved through the fuel pressure relief valve. To relieve the fuel system pressure, first remove the fuel tank cap to relieve pressure in the tank, then remove the cap on the fuel pressure relief valve, located on the fuel rail. Attach fuel pressure gauge T80L-9974-A or equivalent, and drain the system through the drain tube into a suitable container. Remove the fuel pressure gauge and replace the cap on the relief valve.

Electric Fuel Pump

REMOVAL & INSTALLATION

Non-Supercharged

1. Disconnect the negative battery cable and properly relieve the fuel system pressure.
2. Remove the fuel tank and place it on a bench.
3. Remove any dirt that has accumulated around the fuel pump retaining flange so it will not enter the tank during pump removal and installation.
4. Turn the fuel pump locking ring counterclockwise and remove the locking ring.
5. Remove the fuel pump and bracket assembly. Remove and discard the seal ring.

To install:

6. Clean the fuel pump mounting flange, fuel tank mounting surface and seal ring groove.
7. Apply a light coating of grease on a new seal ring to hold it in place during assembly and install in the seal ring groove.
8. Install the fuel pump and bracket assembly carefully to ensure the filter is not damaged. Make sure the locating keys are in the keyways and the seal ring remains in the groove.
9. Hold the pump assembly in place and install the locking ring finger-tight. Make sure all the locking tabs are under the tank lock ring tabs.
10. Rotate the locking ring clockwise until the ring is against the stops.
11. Install the fuel tank in the vehicle. Add a minimum of 10 gallons of fuel to the tank and check for leaks.
12. Install a suitable fuel pressure gauge on the valve on the fuel rail.
13. Turn the ignition switch from **OFF** to **ON** for 3 seconds. Repeat this procedure 5-10 times until the pressure gauge shows at least 35 psi. Check for fuel leaks.
14. Remove the pressure gauge, start the engine and check for leaks.

PRESSURE TESTING

1. Relieve the fuel system pressure and connect a fuel pressure gauge to the valve on the fuel rail.
2. Ground the fuel pump lead of the self-test connector through a jumper wire at the **FP** lead.
3. Turn the ignition key to the **RUN** position to operate the fuel pump.
4. Observe the fuel pressure gauge. The indicated pressure should be 35-40 psi.
5. Remove the fuel pressure gauge and the jumper wire.

Fuel Pressure Regulator

REMOVAL & INSTALLATION

➧ See Figures 55, 56, 57, 58 and 59

The fuel pressure regulator is attached to the fuel supply manifold assembly downstream of the fuel injectors. It regulates the fuel pressure supplied to the injectors. The regulator is a diaphragm operated relief valve in which one side of the diaphragm senses fuel pressure and the other side is subjected to intake manifold pressure. The nominal fuel pressure is established by a spring preload applied to the diaphragm. Balancing one side of the diaphragm with manifold pressure maintains a constant fuel pressure drop across the injectors. Fuel, in excess of that used by the engine, is bypassed through the regulator and returns to the fuel tank.

****WARNING**

Before attempting this procedure, depressurize the fuel system.

1. Remove the vacuum line at the pressure regulator.
2. Remove the three Allen retaining screws from the regulator housing.
3. Remove the pressure regulator, gasket and O-ring. Discard the gasket and inspect the O-ring for deterioration.

****WARNING**

If scraping is necessary be careful not to damage the gasket surface.

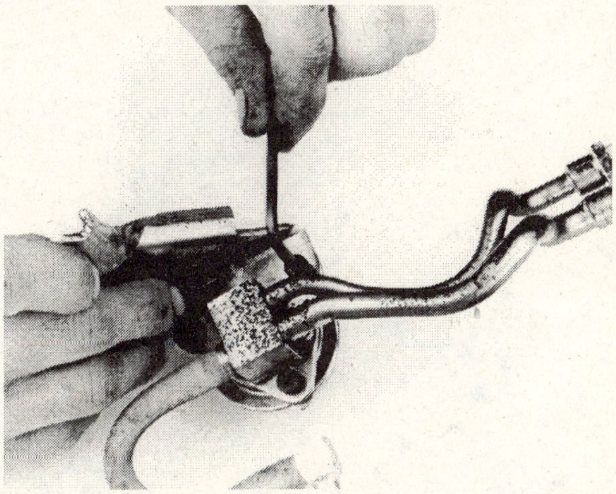

88185P60

Fig. 55 Separate the pressure regulator from the fuel rail

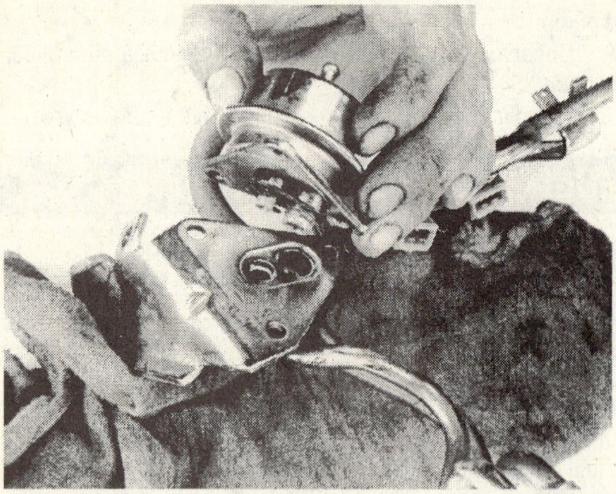

Fig. 56 Lift the regulator off of the mating surface . . .

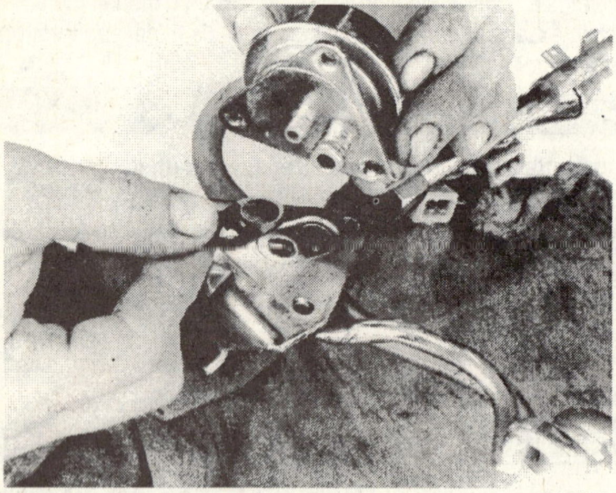

Fig. 57 . . . remove the gasket . . .

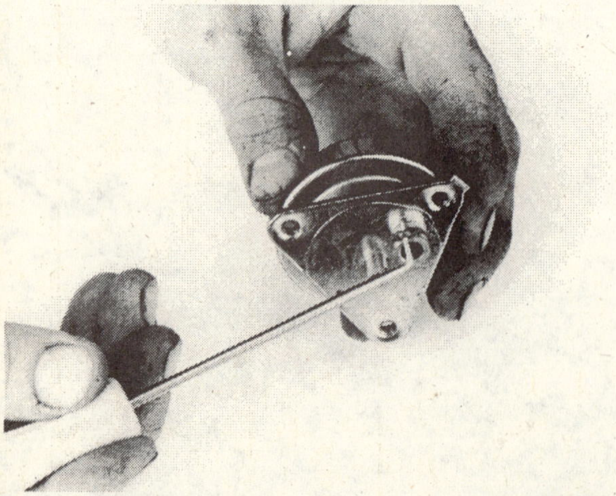

Fig. 58 . . . then the O-ring

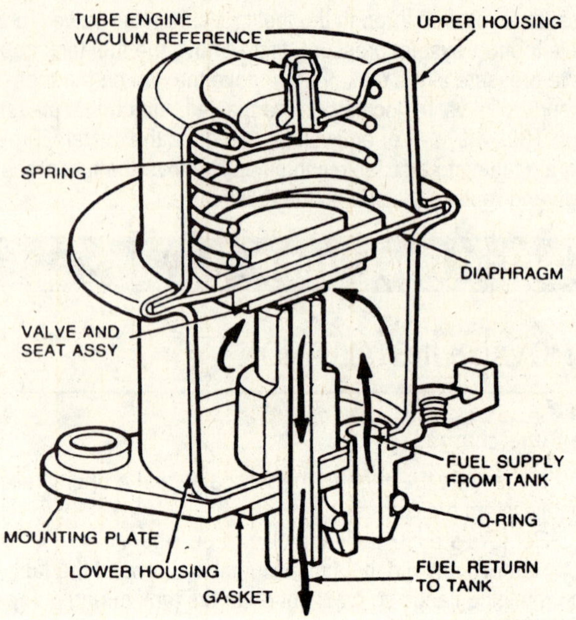

Fig. 59 The pressure regulator is attached to the supply manifold downstream of the injectors on the 5.0L engine

4. Lubricate the O-ring with light oil prior to installation.
5. Ensure the gasket surfaces of the fuel pressure regulator and fuel rail assembly are clean.
6. Install the new O-ring and gasket on the regulator.
7. Using new allen head screws, install the pressure regulator on the fuel rail assembly, tighten the screws 27–40 inch lbs. (3–4 Nm).
8. Install the vacuum line to the regulator.
9. With the injector wiring disconnected, turn the ignition system to **RUN** and allow the system to pressurize. Check for leaks. Connect the wiring, run the engine at idle for 2 minutes. Turn the engine off and check for leaks.

Fuel Injector Manifold Assembly

REMOVAL & INSTALLATION

The fuel supply manifold assembly is the component that delivers high pressure fuel from the vehicle fuel supply line to the fuel injectors. The assembly consists of a single preformed tube or stamping with four injector connector, a mounting flange for the fuel pressure regulator, a pressure relief valve for diagnostic testing or field service fuel system pressure bleed down and mounting attachments which locate the fuel manifold assembly and provide fuel injector retention.

2.3L Engine

1. Remove the fuel tank cap. Release the pressure from the fuel system.
2. Disconnect the fuel supply and return lines.
3. Disconnect the wiring harness from the injectors.
4. Disconnect the vacuum line from the fuel pressure regulator valve.
5. Remove the two fuel injector manifold retaining bolts.
6. Carefully disengage the manifold from the fuel injectors. Remove the manifold.
7. Installation is the reverse of removal. Tighten the fuel manifold bolts 15–22 ft. lbs. (20–30 Nm).

3.8L, Exc. SC and 5.0L Engines

See Figure 60

1. Remove the fuel tank cap and relieve the fuel system pressure.
2. Remove the upper intake manifold.
3. Disconnect the fuel inlet and return quick-disconnect couplings.
4. Remove the fuel pressure regulator.
5. Remove the retaining bolts and injection manifold with the injectors attached.

To install:

6. Position the injection manifold making sure all injectors are pushed into a fully seated position.
7. Install the retaining bolts while holding the injection manifold down and tighten the bolts to 87 inch lbs. (9 Nm) on the 3.8L; 71–106 inch lbs. (8–12 Nm) on the 5.0L.
8. Install all remaining parts. With the injector wiring disconnected, turn the ignition system to **RUN** and allow the system to pressurize. Check for leaks. Connect the wiring, run the engine at idle for 2 minutes. Turn the engine off and check for leaks.

3.8L SC Engine

1. Remove the fuel tank cap and relieve the fuel system pressure.
2. Remove the supercharger/throttle body assembly, intercooler tubes, intercooler and intake elbow.
3. Disconnect the fuel inlet and return quick-disconnect couplings.
4. Remove the fuel pressure regulator.
5. Remove the retaining bolts and injection manifold with the injectors attached.

To install:

6. Position the injection manifold making sure all injectors are pushed into a fully seated position.
7. Install the retaining bolts while holding the injection manifold down and tighten the bolts to 71–97 inch lbs. (8–11 Nm).
8. Install all remaining parts. With the injector wiring disconnected, turn the ignition system to **RUN** and allow the system to pressurize. Check for leaks. Connect the wiring, run the engine at idle for 2 minutes. Turn the engine off and check for leaks.

88185P65

Fig. 60 Fuel injection manifold with injectors attached

Pressure Relief Valve

REMOVAL & INSTALLATION

See Figure 61

1. If the fuel charging assembly is mounted on the engine, the fuel system must be depressurized.
2. Using an open end wrench or suitable deep well socket, remove the pressure relief valve from the injection manifold.
3. Install the pressure relief valve and cap. Tighten the valve 48–84 inch lbs. (5–9 Nm). Tighten the cap tp 4–6 inch lbs. (0.5–0.7 Nm).

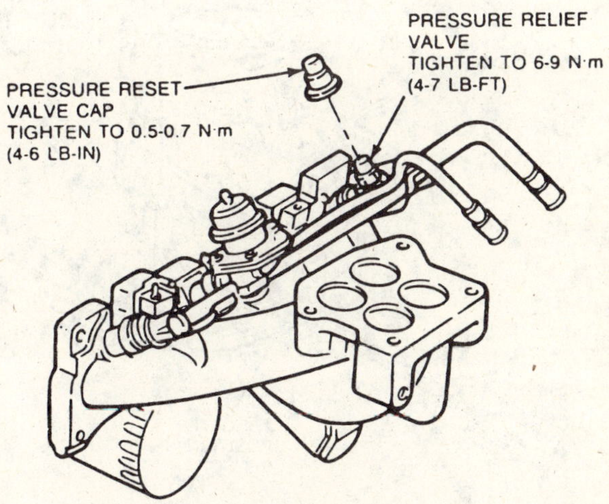

88185G83

Fig. 61 Tightening specifications on the fuel pressure relief valve and cap

Throttle Position Sensor

REMOVAL & INSTALLATION

2.3L and 3.8L Except SC Engine

➧ See Figure 62

1. Disconnect the throttle position sensor from the wiring harness.
2. Matchmark the sensor and throttle body.
3. Remove the two retaining screws.
4. Remove the throttle position sensor.
5. Installation is the reverse of removal.
6. Align the matchmarks.
7. Tighten the sensor screws 11-16 inch lbs. (15-22 Nm).

➥ This throttle position sensor is not adjustable on these engines.

3.8L SC Engine

1. Disconnect the idle air control (IAC) valve wiring.
2. Remove the lower IAC bolt and loosen the upper. Rotate the valve out of the way to gain access to the TPS bolts.
3. Disconnect the TPS wiring and remove the bolts.
4. Remove the sensor.
5. Installation is the reverse of removal. Tighten the TPS screws to 26 inch lbs. (35 Nm); the IAC bolts to 70-100 inch lbs. (8-11 Nm).

➥ This throttle position sensor is not adjustable on this engine.

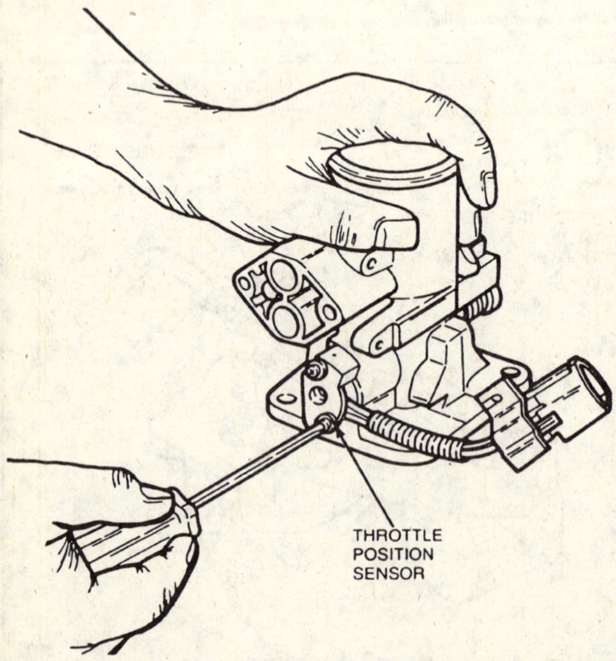

Fig. 62 Throttle position sensor retaining screw removal — 2.3L engine shown

5.0L Engine

➧ See Figure 63

1. Disconnect the TPS wiring harness.
2. Matchmark the TPS and throttle body.
3. Remove the 2 retaining screws and the sensor.

To install:

4. If the sensor had a bushing, it must be reused. Install the bushing with the larger diameter facing outwards.
5. Install the TPS on the throttle shaft and rotate the sensor 10-20° counterclockwise to align the bolt holes.
6. Install the bolts and tighten them to 11-15 inch lbs. (15-20 Nm).
7. Cycle the throttle to the wide open position. It should return without interference.
8. Connect the wiring.

Idle Air By-pass Valve Assembly

REMOVAL & INSTALLATION

2.3L, 3.8L and 5.0L Engines

➧ See Figure 63

1. Disconnect the air bypass valve assembly connector from the wiring harness.
2. Remove the two air bypass valve retaining screws.
3. Remove the air bypass valve and gasket.

****WARNING**

If necessary to remove the gasket by scraping, be careful not to damage the gasket surface.

4. Installation is the reverse of removal. Tighten the air bypass valve assembly 70-100 inch lbs. (8-11 Nm).

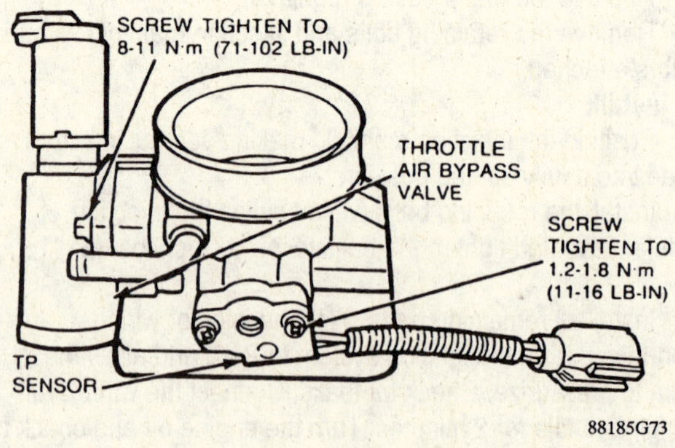

Fig. 63 Throttle position sensor and air bypass valve assembly — 5.0L engine

Idle Air Control (IAC) Valve

REMOVAL & INSTALLATION

1. Disconnect the idle air control valve assembly connector from the wiring harness.
2. Remove the retaining screws from the valve.
3. Remove the IAC valve and gasket.

To install:

4. Clean the gasket mating surfaces.
5. Install the valve using a new gasket, tighten the retaining screws to 71-101 inch lbs. (8-12 Nm).

Air Intake Throttle Body

REMOVAL & INSTALLATION

The throttle body assembly controls air flow to the engine through a single butterfly-type valve. The throttle position is controlled by conventional cable/cam throttle linkage. The body is a single piece die casting made of aluminum. It has a single bore with an air bypass channel around the throttle plate. This by-pass channel controls both cold and warm engine idle air flow control as regulated by an air bypass valve assembly mounted directly to the throttle body. The valve assembly is an electromechanical device controlled by the EEC computer. It incorporates a linear actuator which positions a variable area metering valve.

Other features of the air throttle body assembly include:

- An adjustment screw to set the throttle plate at a minimum idle airflow position.
- A preset stop to locate the WOT position.
- A throttle body mounted throttle position sensor.
- A PCV fresh air source (4 and 8-cylinder) located upstream of the throttle plate.
- Individual ported vacuum taps (as required) for PCV and EVAP control signals.

2.3L Engine

See Figures 64 and 65

1. Remove the four throttle body nuts. Make sure that the throttle position sensor connector and the air by-pass valve connector have been disconnected from the harness. Disconnect the air cleaner outlet tube.
2. Remove the throttle bracket.
3. Carefully separate the throttle body from the upper intake manifold.
4. Identify and disconnect the vacuum hoses.
5. Remove and discard the gasket between the throttle body and the upper intake manifold.

****WARNING**

If scraping is necessary, be careful not to damage the gasket surfaces, or allow any material to drop into the manifold.

6. Installation is the reverse of removal. Tighten the throttle body-to-upper intake manifold nuts 12-15 ft. lbs. (16-20 Nm).

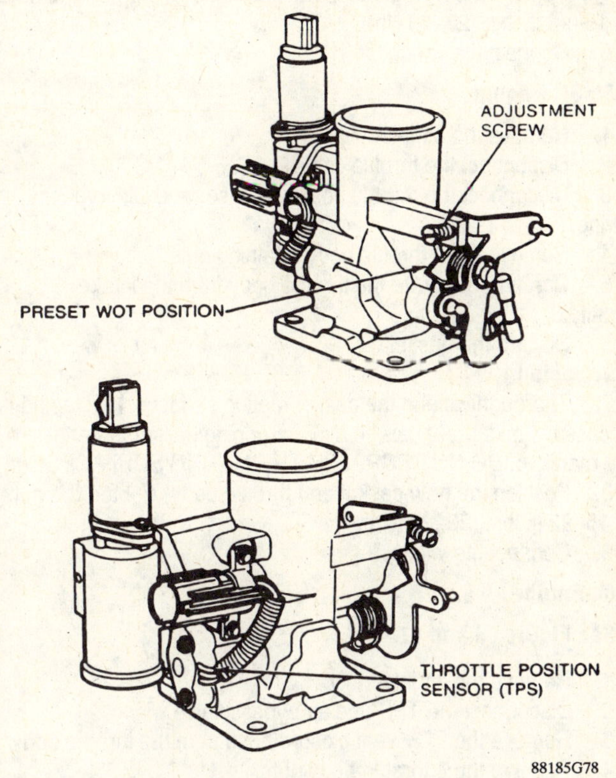

Fig. 64 Air throttle body assembly adjustment screw and sensor locations — 2.3L engine

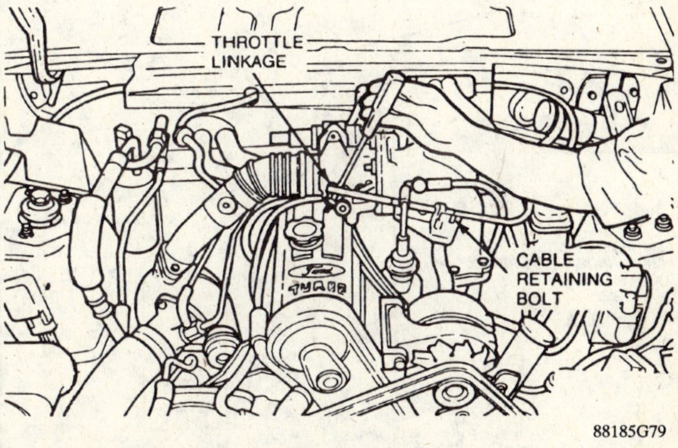

Fig. 65 Disconnect the throttle linkage

3.8L Engine Except SC

1. Remove the air inlet duct.
2. Disconnect the throttle position sensor and idle bypass wiring.
3. Remove the 4 throttle body retaining nuts.
4. Carefully separate the throttle body from the intake manifold.
5. Discard the gasket.

To install:

6. Thoroughly clean the gasket mating surfaces. If scraping is necessary, take great care to avoid dropping gasket material into the manifold. DO NOT SCRATCH THE MATING SURFACES!

7. Position the new gasket and throttle body. Tighten the nuts to 15–22 ft. lbs. (20–29 Nm).
8. Connect the wiring.

3.8L SC Engine

1. Remove the air inlet duct.
2. Disconnect the throttle cable.
3. Disconnect the throttle position sensor and idle bypass wiring.
4. Remove the 4 throttle body retaining nuts.
5. Carefully separate the throttle body from the intake manifold.
6. Discard the gasket.

To install:

7. Thoroughly clean the gasket mating surfaces. If scraping is necessary, take great care to avoid dropping gasket material into the manifold. DO NOT SCRATCH THE MATING SURFACES!
8. Position the new gasket and throttle body. Tighten the nuts to 15–22 ft. lbs. (20–29 Nm).
9. Connect the wiring.

5.0L Engine

➧ See Figure 66 and 67

1. Remove the air inlet duct.
2. Disconnect the TPS and air bypass valve wiring.
3. Remove the PCV vent closure hose from the throttle body.
4. Remove the 4 throttle body nuts.

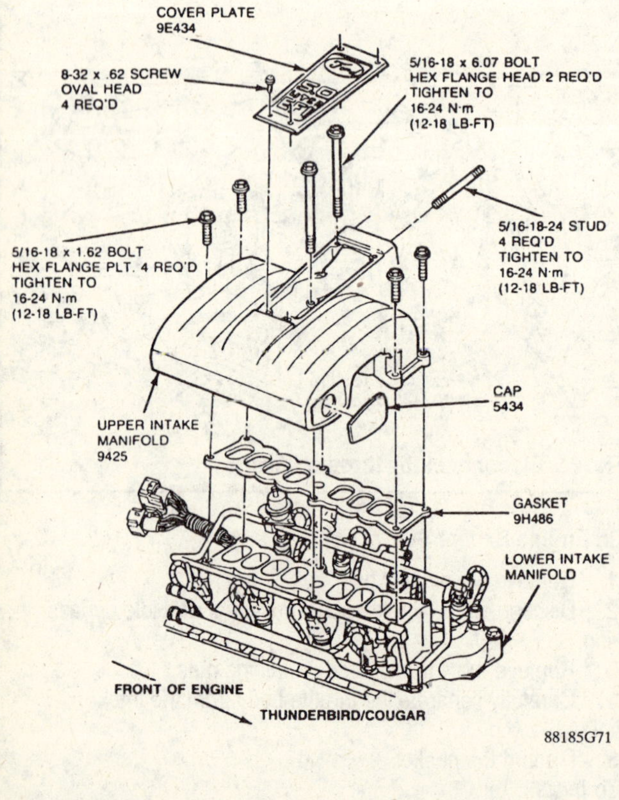

Fig. 66 Exploded view of the SEFI injection system components — 5.0L engine

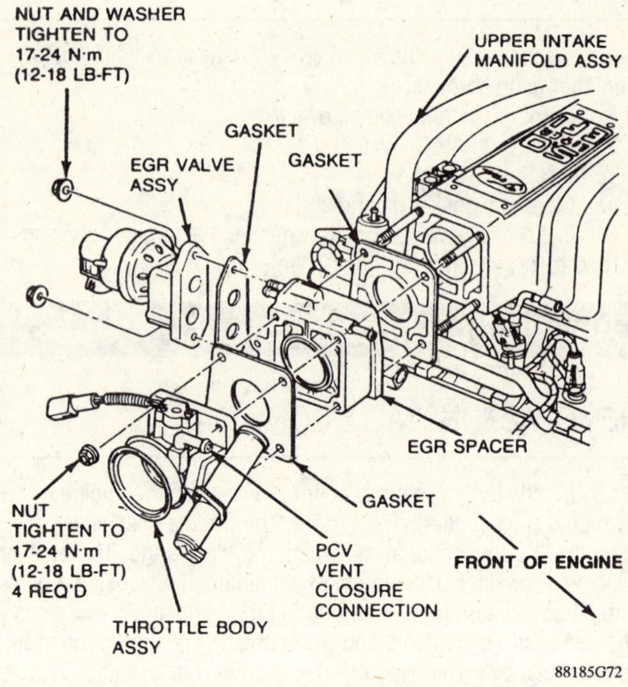

Fig. 67 Exploded view of the air intake throttle body assembly — 5.0L engine

5. Carefully remove the throttle body from the EGR spacer and discard the gasket.

To install:

6. Clean the gasket mating surfaces thoroughly. If scraping is necessary, take great care to avoid dropping gasket material into the manifold. DO NOT SCRATCH THE MATING SURFACES!
7. Position the new gasket and throttle body. Tighten the nuts to 12–17 ft. lbs. (16–23 Nm).
8. Connect the PCV hose.
9. Connect the wiring.

Upper Intake Manifold

REMOVAL & INSTALLATION

2.3L Engine

➧ See Figures 68 and 69

1. Disconnect the air cleaner outlet tube from the air intake throttle body.
2. Unplug the throttle position sensor from the wiring harness.
3. Unplug the air by-pass valve connector.
4. Remove the three upper manifold retaining bolts.
5. Remove the upper manifold assembly.
6. Remove and discard the gasket from the lower manifold assembly.

****WARNING**

If scraping is necessary, be careful not to damage gasket surfaces, or allow any material to drop into the lower manifold.

7. Installation is the reverse of removal. Tighten the upper intake manifold bolts 15 22 ft. lbs. (20–30 Nm). Use a new gasket between the manifolds.

3.8L Engine Except SC

➥ For SC engines, see Section 3 under Supercharger.

1. Depressurize the fuel system.
2. Remove the air inlet duct.
3. Disconnect the wiring at the:
   - Idle air bypass valve
   - Throttle position sensor
   - EGR position sensor
4. Disconnect the throttle linkage and transmission kickdown linkage.

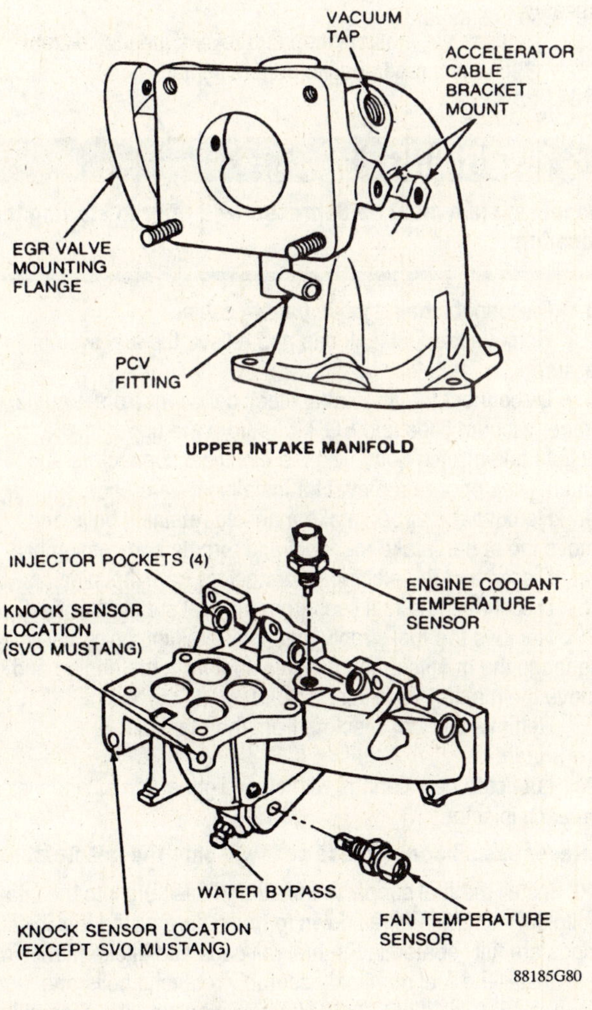

Fig. 68 Upper and lower intake manifold assemblies — 2.3L engine

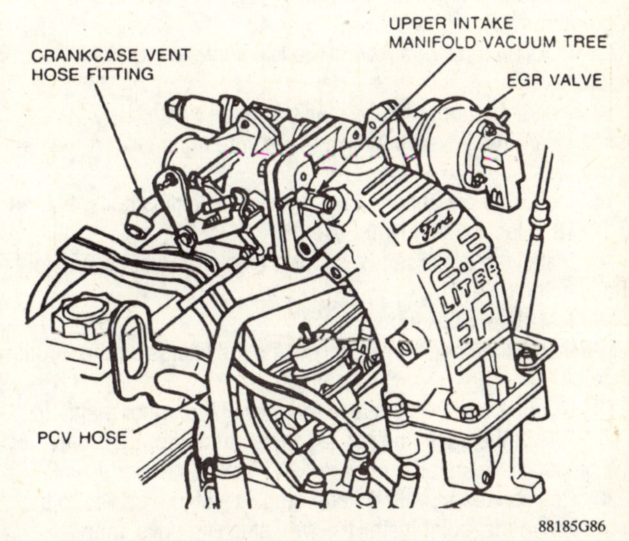

Fig. 69 Upper manifold attached to the engine with hoses connected — 2.3L engine

5. Remove the 2 bolts and position the bracket and cables out of the way.
6. Tag and disconnect all vacuum lines at the manifold.
7. Disconnect the PCV hose.
8. Remove the 6 manifold attaching bolts.
9. Carefully lift the manifold and throttle body assembly from the lower manifold. Discard the gasket.

To install:

10. Clean the gasket mating surfaces thoroughly. DO NOT SCRATCH THEM! Position a new gasket on the lower manifold.
11. Position the upper manifold and install the bolts. Make sure the gasket hasn't moved. Tighten the bolts to 24 ft. lbs. (32 Nm).
12. Connect the vacuum hoses, cable and fuel lines. Tighten the cable bracket bolts to 13 ft. lbs. (17 Nm).
13. Connect the wiring.

5.0L Engine

1. Disconnect the electrical connectors at the air bypass valve, throttle position sensor and EGR position sensor.
2. Separate the throttle linkage at the throttle ball and transmission linkage from the throttle body.
3. Remove the bolts securing bracket and the intake manifold and position the bracket with the cables out of the way.
4. Tag and disconnect the upper intake manifold vacuum fitting connections by disconnecting all of the vacuum lines to the vacuum tree, vacuum lines to the EGR valve, and vacuum line to the fuel pressure regulator.
5. Disconnect the PCV system by separating the hose from the fitting at the rear of the upper manifold.
6. Remove the two canister purge lines from the fittings on the throttle body.
7. Disconnect the EGR tube from the EGR valve by removing the flange nut.
8. Remove the bolt securing the upper intake support bracket to the upper manifold.
9. Remove the six upper intake manifold retaining bolts.
10. Remove the upper intake and throttle body as an assembly from the lower intake manifold.

To install:

11. Clean and inspect the mounting faces of the lower and upper manifolds.
12. Position a new gasket on the lower intake manifold mounting face.
13. Install the upper intake manifold and throttle body assembly on the lower manifold, make sure the gasket remains in place.
14. Install the six upper intake manifold retaining bolts, tighten to 12–18 ft. lbs. (16–24 Nm).
15. Install the upper intake support bracket-to-upper manifold attaching bolt.
16. Install the EGR tube.
17. Install the canister purge lines on the fittings on the throttle body.
18. Connect the PCV hose to the rear of the upper manifold.
19. Attach the vacuum lines to the vacuum tree, EGR valve and pressure regulator.
20. Position the throttle linkage bracket with the cables to the upper intake manifold. Install the two attaching bolts, then tighten. Connect the throttle cable and transmission cable to the throttle body.
21. Attach the electrical connectors at the air bypass valve, TPS sensor, and EGR position sensor.

Fuel Injector

REMOVAL & INSTALLATION

➧ See Figures 70 and 71

The fuel injector nozzles are electromechanical devices which both meter and atomize fuel delivered to the engine. The injectors are mounted in the lower intake manifold and are positioned so that their tips are directing fuel just ahead of the engine intake valves. The injector bodies consist of a solenoid actuated pintle and needle valve assembly. An electrical control signal from the Electronic Engine Control unit activates the injector solenoid causing the pintle to move inward off the seat,

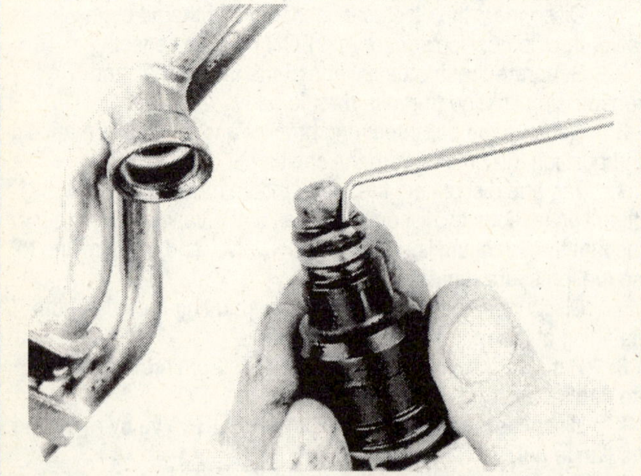

88185P66

Fig. 70 Remove the O-ring from the lower portion of the injector

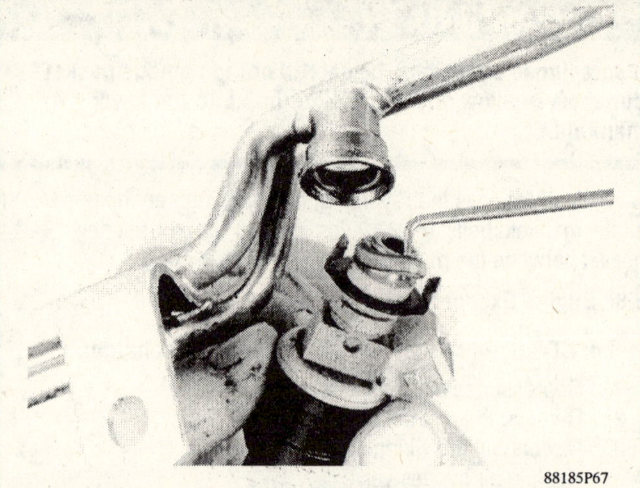

88185P67

Fig. 71 Remove the O-ring from the upper portion of the injector

allowing fuel to flow. Since the injector flow orifice is fixed and the fuel pressure drop across the injector tip is constant, fuel flow to the engine is regulated by how long the solenoid is energized. Atomization is obtained by contouring the pintle at the point where the fuel separates.

2.3L Engine

➧ See Figure 72

✻✻WARNING

The fuel system must be depressurized prior to starting this procedure.

1. Disconnect the negative battery cable.
2. Remove the fuel tank cap and relieve the fuel system pressure.
3. Disconnect the air intake, electrical connectors, throttle linkage, vacuum lines and EGR tube from the upper intake manifold and throttle body. Tag the electrical connectors and vacuum lines prior to removal for installation reference.
4. Remove the upper intake manifold retaining bolts and remove the upper intake manifold and throttle body assembly.
5. Disconnect the electrical connectors from the injectors.
6. Disconnect the fuel lines from the fuel supply manifold.
7. Remove the fuel supply manifold retaining bolts, carefully disengage the manifold and fuel injectors from the engine and remove the manifold and injectors.
8. Remove the fuel injectors from the manifold.

To install:

9. Lubricate new O-rings with clean light grade oil and install 2 on each injector.

➥ Never use silicone grease as it will clog the injectors.

10. Install the fuel supply manifold and injectors into the intake manifold. Push the fuel rail down to make sure all the fuel injector O-rings are fully seated in the fuel rail cups and intake manifold.
11. Install the fuel manifold assembly retaining bolts and tighten to 15–22 ft. lbs. (20–30 Nm) while holding the assembly down.

12. Connect the fuel lines to the manifold assembly.
13. After the fuel rail assembly has been installed and before the fuel injector wire connectors have been connected, connect the negative battery cable and turn the key to the **ON** position. This will cause the fuel pump to run for 2–3 seconds and pressurize the system.
14. Check for fuel leaks, especially where the fuel injector is installed into the fuel rail.
15. Disconnect the negative battery cable.
16. Install the upper intake manifold in the reverse order of removal. Tighten the retaining bolts, in sequence, to 15–22 ft. lbs. (20–30 Nm).
17. Connect the fuel injector wire connectors.
18. Connect the negative battery cable. Start the engine and let it idle.
19. Turn the engine **OFF** and check for fuel leaks.

3.8L Engine

EXCEPT SUPERCHARGED ENGINE

1. Disconnect the negative battery cable.
2. Remove the fuel tank cap and relieve the fuel system pressure.
3. Disconnect the electrical connectors at the idle air bypass valve, TP sensor and EGR position sensor.
4. Disconnect the throttle linkage at the throttle ball and the transmission linkage from the throttle body.
5. Remove the 2 bolts securing the bracket to the intake manifold and position the bracket with the cables aside.
6. Disconnect all the vacuum lines and PCV from the upper intake manifold and throttle assembly. Tag all lines prior to removal for ease of reinstallation.
7. Remove the upper intake manifold retaining bolts and remove the upper intake manifold and throttle body assembly.
8. Disconnect the fuel lines from the fuel rail assembly.
9. Remove the fuel pressure regulator.
10. Disconnect the electrical connectors from the fuel injectors. Remove the injector retaining clips, as required.
11. Remove the fuel rail retaining bolts. Carefully disengage the fuel rail from the fuel injectors and remove the fuel rail.

➥ It may be easier to remove the injectors with the fuel rail as an assembly.

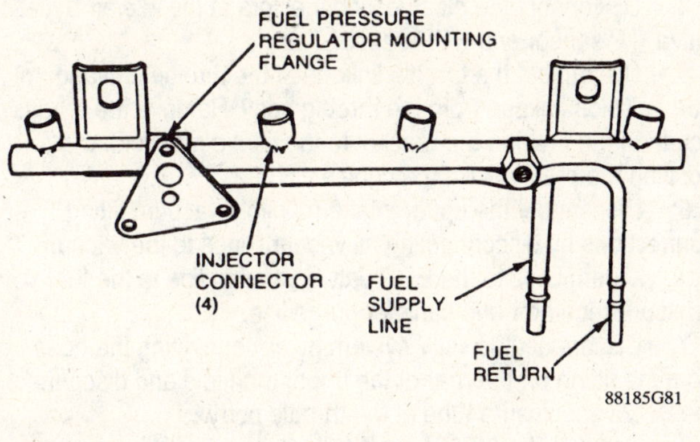

Fig. 72 Exploded view of the fuel supply manifold assembly — 2.3L engine

12. Grasping the injector body, pull while gently rocking the injector from side-to-side to remove the injector from the fuel rail or the intake manifold.
13. Inspect the pintle protection cap (plastic hat) and washer for signs of deterioration. Replace the complete injector, as required. If the cap is missing, look for it in the intake manifold.

➥ The pintle protection cap is not available as a separate part.

To install:

14. Lubricate new O-rings with light grade oil and install 2 on each injector.

➥ Never use silicone grease as it will clog the injectors.

15. Install the injectors in the intake manifold using a light, twisting pushing motion.
16. Install the fuel rail, pushing it down to ensure all injector O-rings are fully seated in the fuel rail cups and intake manifold.
17. Install the retaining bolts while holding the fuel rail down and tighten to 87 inch lbs. (10 Nm). Reinstall the injector retaining clips, as required.
18. Install the fuel pressure regulator retaining bolt and tighten to 15–22 ft. lbs. (20–30 Nm).
19. Connect the fuel lines to the fuel rail.
20. With the injector wiring disconnected, connect the negative battery cable and turn the ignition to the **RUN** position to allow the fuel pump to pressurize the system. Check for fuel leaks.
21. Disconnect the negative battery cable.
22. Connect the fuel injector wiring harness.
23. Install the upper intake manifold and throttle body assembly by reversing the removal procedure. Tighten the upper intake manifold retaining bolts to 24 ft. lbs. (32 Nm).
24. Connect the negative battery cable, start the engine and check for fuel leaks.

SUPERCHARGED ENGINE

1. Disconnect the negative battery cable.
2. Remove the fuel tank cap and relieve the fuel system pressure.
3. Remove the supercharger assembly.
4. Disconnect the fuel lines from the fuel rail assembly.
5. Remove the 4 fuel rail assembly retaining bolts and remove the fuel pressure regulator bracket retaining bolt.
6. Disconnect the electrical connectors from the injectors.
7. Carefully disengage the fuel rail from the fuel injectors and remove the fuel rail.

➥ It may be easier to remove the injectors with the fuel rail as an assembly.

8. Grasping the injector body, remove the injector from the fuel rail or intake manifold by pulling while gently rocking the injector from side-to-side.
9. Inspect the pintle protection cap (plastic hat) and washer for signs of deterioration. Replace the complete injector, as required. If the cap is missing, look for it in the intake manifold.

➥ The pintle protection cap is not available as a separate part.

To install:

10. Lubricate new O-rings with light grade oil and install 2 on each injector.

➥ Never use silicone grease as it will clog the injectors.

11. Install the injectors, using a light, twisting, pushing motion.

12. Place the fuel rail assembly over each of the injectors and seat the injectors into the fuel rail.

➥ It may be easier to seat the injectors in the fuel rail and then seat the entire assembly in the lower intake manifold.

13. Install the fuel rail assembly retaining bolts and tighten to 70–97 inch lbs. (8–11 Nm). Install the fuel pressure regulator bracket retaining bolt and tighten to 15–22 ft. lbs. (20–30 Nm).
14. Install the supercharger assembly.
15. Connect the negative battery cable. Turn the ignition from **OFF** to **ON** several times without starting the engine to check for fuel leaks. Check all connections at the fuel rail and injectors.
16. Start the engine and warm to operating temperature. Check for fuel or coolant leaks.

4.6L Engine

➧ See Figure 73

1. Disconnect the negative battery cable.
2. Remove the fuel tank cap and relieve the fuel system pressure.

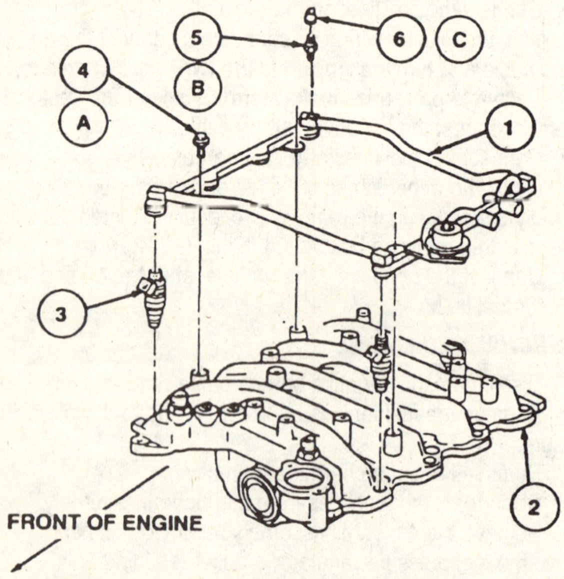

Item	Part Number	Description
1	9F792	Fuel Injection Supply Manifold
2	9424	Intake Manifold
3	9F593	Fuel Injector
4	N804394-S8M	Bolt (4 Req'd)
5	9H321	Fuel Pressure Relief Valve
6	9H323	Fuel Pressure Relief Valve Cap
A	—	Tighten to 8-12 N·m (71-106 Lb-In)
B	—	Tighten to 7.75 N·m (69 Lb-In)
C	—	Tighten to 0.6 N·m (5.3 Lb-In)

88185G87

Fig. 73 Fuel rail assembly — 4.6L engine

3. Disconnect the vacuum line at the pressure regulator.
4. Disconnect the fuel lines from the fuel rail.
5. Disconnect the electrical connectors from the injectors.
6. Remove the fuel rail assembly retaining bolts.
7. Carefully disengage the fuel rail from the fuel injectors and remove the fuel rail.

➥ It may be easier to remove the injectors with the fuel rail as an assembly.

8. Grasping the injector body, pull while gently rocking the injector from side-to-side to remove the injector from the fuel rail or intake manifold.
9. Inspect the pintle protection cap and washer for signs of deterioration. Replace the complete injector, as required. If the cap is missing, look for it in the intake manifold.

➥ The pintle protection cap is not available as a separate part.

To install:

10. Lubricate new O-rings with light grade oil and install 2 on each injector.

➥ Never use silicone grease as it will clog the injectors.

11. Install the injectors using a light, twisting, pushing motion.
12. Install the fuel rail, pushing it down to ensure all injector O-rings are fully seated in the fuel rail cups and intake manifold.
13. Install the retaining bolts while holding the fuel rail down and tighten to 71–106 inch lbs. (8–12 Nm).
14. Connect the fuel lines to the fuel rail and the vacuum line to the pressure regulator.
15. With the injector wiring disconnected, connect the negative battery cable and turn the ignition switch to the **RUN** position to allow the fuel pump to pressurize the system.
16. Check for fuel leaks.
17. Disconnect the negative battery cable.
18. Connect the electrical connectors to the fuel injectors.
19. Connect the negative battery cable and start the engine. Let it idle for 2 minutes.
20. Turn the engine **OFF** and check for leaks.

5.0L Engine

➧ See Figures 74, 75 and 76

1. Disconnect the negative battery cable.
2. Remove the fuel tank cap and relieve the fuel system pressure.
3. Partially drain the cooling system into a suitable container.
4. Disconnect the electrical connectors at the idle air bypass valve, TP sensor and EGR sensor.
5. Disconnect the throttle linkage at the throttle ball and transmission linkage from the throttle body. Remove the 2 bolts securing the bracket the bracket to the intake manifold and position the bracket with the cables aside.
6. Disconnect the upper intake manifold vacuum fitting connections by disconnecting all vacuum lines to the vacuum tree, vacuum lines to the EGR valve, vacuum line to the fuel pressure regulator and canister purge line.
7. Disconnect the PCV system by disconnecting the hose from the fitting on the rear of the upper manifold and disconnect the PCV vent closure tube at the throttle body.
8. Remove the 2 EGR coolant lines from the fittings on the EGR spacer.
9. Remove the 6 upper intake manifold retaining bolts.

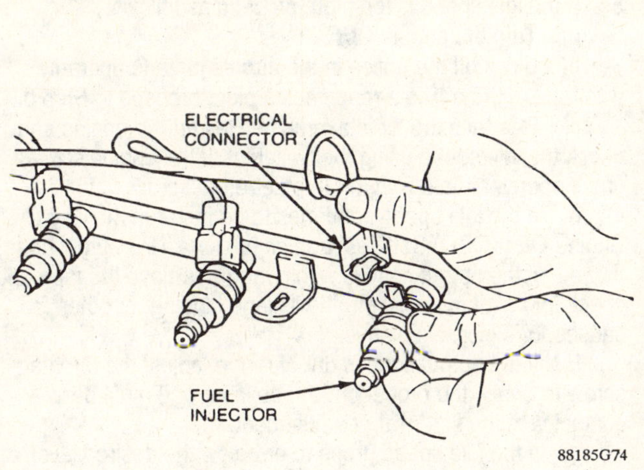

Fig. 74 Carefully remove the electrical harness from the individual injectors

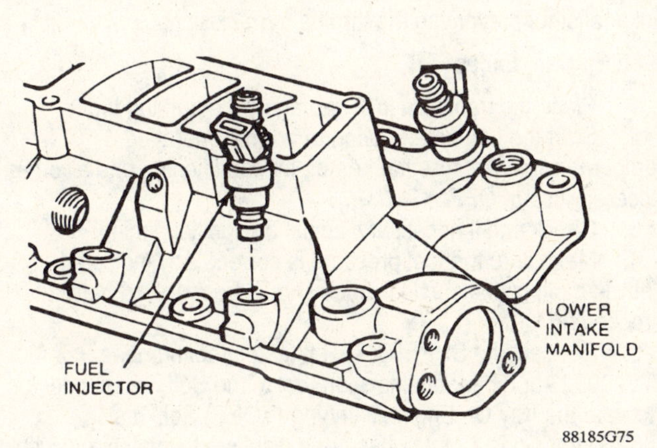

Fig. 75 Grasping the injector body, pull up while gently rocking the injector from side-to-side to remove the injector from the fuel rail or intake manifold

10. Remove the upper intake and throttle body as an assembly from the lower intake manifold.
11. Disconnect the fuel lines from the fuel rail.
12. Remove the 4 fuel rail assembly retaining bolts.
13. Disconnect the electrical connectors from the injectors.
14. Carefully disengage the fuel rail from the fuel injectors.

➦ It may be easier to remove the injectors with the fuel rail as an assembly.

15. Grasping the injector body, pull up while gently rocking the injector from side-to-side to remove the injector from the fuel rail or intake manifold.
16. Inspect the pintle protection cap (plastic hat) and washer for signs of deterioration. Replace the complete injector, as required. If the cap is missing, look for it in the intake manifold.

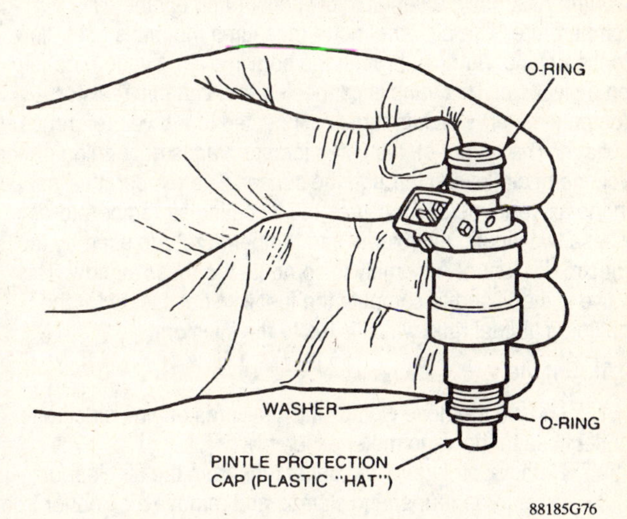

Fig. 76 Inspect the plastic hat and washer for signs of deterioration

➦ The pintle protection cap is not available as a separate part.

To install:

17. Lubricate new O-rings with light grade oil and install 2 on each injector.

➦ Never use silicone grease as it will clog the injectors.

18. Install the injectors using a light, twisting, pushing motion.
19. Install the fuel rail, pushing it down to ensure all the injector O-rings are fully seated in the fuel rail cups and intake manifold.
20. Install the retaining bolts while holding the fuel rail down and tighten to 70–105 inch lbs. (8–12 Nm).
21. Connect the fuel lines to the fuel rail.
22. With the injector wiring disconnected, connect the negative battery cable and turn the ignition switch to the **RUN** position to allow the fuel pump to pressurize the system.
23. Check for fuel leaks.
24. Disconnect the negative battery cable.
25. Connect the electrical connectors to the injectors.
26. Install the upper intake manifold and throttle body assembly by reversing the removal procedure. Tighten the retaining bolts to 12–17 ft. lbs. (16–24 Nm).
27. Refill the cooling system and connect the negative battery cable.
28. Start the engine and let it idle for 2 minutes. Turn the engine **OFF** and check for leaks.

Air Vane Meter

REMOVAL & INSTALLATION

The air vane meter assembly is located between the air cleaner and the throttle body on the 4-2.3L engine, and is mounted on a bracket near the left shock tower. The vane air meter contains two sensors which furnish input to the Electronic

Control Assembly: a vane airflow sensor and a vane air temperature. The air vane meter measures the mass of air flow to the engine. Air flow through the body moves a vane mounted on a pivot pin. This vane is connected to a variable resistor (potentiometer) which in turn is connected to a 5 volt reference voltage. The output of this potentiometer varies depending on the volume of air flowing through the sensor. The temperature sensor in the air vane meter measures the incoming air temperature. These two inputs, air volume and temperature, are used by the Electronic Control Assembly to compute the mass air flow. This valve is then used to compute the fuel flow necessary for the optimum air/fuel ratio which is fed to the injectors.

2.3L Engine

1. Loosen the hose clamp which secures engine air cleaner outlet hose to the vane meter assembly.
2. Remove air intake and outlet tube from the air cleaner.
3. Disengage four spring clamps and remove air cleaner front cover and air cleaner filter panel.
4. Remove the two screw and washer assemblies which secure the air meter to its bracket. Remove the vane air meter assembly.
5. Installation is the reverse of removal.

Idle Speed

ADJUSTMENT

2.3L Engine

On the most models you will need a scan tool to do the idle speed adjustment.

1. Connect the SUPER STAR II tester, tool number 007-00028 or other suitable scan tool to the Self-Test connector. Activate the Key On Engine Running (KOER) Self-Test.
2. After Code 1 or 111 has been displayed, unlatch and within 4 seconds, latch the STI button.
3. A single pulse code indicates the entry mode, then observe the Self-Test Output (STO) on the tester for the following:
    a. A constant tone, solid light or **STO LO** readout means the base idle speed is within the correct range. To exit the test, unlatch the STI button, then wait 4 seconds for reinitialization. After 10 minutes, the tool will exit by itself.
    b. A beeping tone, flashing light or **STO LO** readout at 8 Hz indicates the Throttle Position Sensor (TPS) is out of range due to over adjustment. Adjustment may be required.
    c. A beeping tone, flashing light or **STO LO** readout at 4 Hz indicates the base idle speed is too fast and adjustment is required. Proceed to Step 5.
    d. A beeping tone, flashing light or **STO LO** readout at 1 Hz indicates the base idle speed is too low and adjustment is required. Proceed to Step 4.
4. If the idle speed is too low, check for the presence of a throttle plate orifice plug. If there is no plug, turn the throttle screw clockwise until the conditions in Step 3a exist. If there is a plug from previous service, remove the plug and then adjust the screw in either direction, as required. The screw must be in contact with the lever pad after adjustment.
5. If the idle speed is too high, proceed as follows:
    a. Turn the engine **OFF**.
    b. Block off the orifice in the throttle plate temporarily with tape. If the orifice already has a plug, proceed to Step d.
    c. Reattach the air intake hose. Restart the engine and check the idle speed using the Self-Test. If the engine stalled, crack open the plate with the throttle return screw.
    d. If the idle speed continues to be fast, run the Key On Engine Off (KOEO) Self-Test and check for a TPS output code.
    e. If the output code is within range, remove the tape and check for vacuum leaks, throttle linkage binding, or other causes for excessive high idle.
    f. If the output code is out of range, adjust the throttle screw to obtain the proper code. The lever pad must be in contact with the screw after adjustment.
    g. If the idle speed drops to or below the desired level, as indicated by the Self-Test Output tone, turn the engine **OFF**, disconnect the air cleaner hose and remove the tape.
    h. Install the proper plug in the throttle plate orifice.
    i. Reconnect the air cleaner hose. Start the engine and turn the throttle plate stop screw clockwise until the conditions in Step 3a exist. Do not turn the screw counterclockwise as this may cause the throttle plate to stick at idle.
6. Run the KOEO Self-Test for proper TPS output code.
7. Make sure the throttle is not stuck in the bore and the linkage is not preventing the throttle from closing.

3.8L Engine, Except SC

1. Place the transaxle in **P** and apply the parking brake.
2. Start the engine and bring to normal operating temperature. Make sure the heater, air conditioning and all other accessories are OFF.
3. Check and if necessary, adjust the ignition timing.
4. Make sure the fuel pressure is correct. Any indicated vehicle malfunction service codes should be resolved before proceeding further.
5. Connect the SUPER STAR II tester, tool number 007-00028 or other suitable scan tool to the Self-Test connector. Activate the Key On Engine Running (KOER) Self-Test.
6. After Code 1 or 111 has been displayed, unlatch and within 4 seconds, latch the STI button.
7. A single pulse code indicates the entry mode, then observe the Self-Test Output (STO) on the tester for the following:
    a. A constant tone, solid light or **STO LO** readout means the base idle speed is within the correct range. To exit the test, unlatch the STI button, then wait 4 seconds for reinitialization. After 10 minutes, the tool will exit by itself.
    b. A beeping tone, flashing light or **STO LO** readout at 8 Hz indicates the Throttle Position Sensor (TPS) is out of range due to over adjustment. Adjustment may be required.
    c. A beeping tone, flashing light or **STO LO** readout at 4 Hz indicates the base idle speed is too fast and adjustment is required. Proceed to Step 9.
    d. A beeping tone, flashing light or **STO LO** readout at 1 Hz indicates the base idle speed is too low and adjustment is required. Proceed to Step 8.
8. If the idle speed is too low, check for the presence of a throttle plate orifice plug. If there is no plug, turn the throttle screw clockwise until the conditions in Step 7a exist. If there is a plug from previous service, remove the plug and then adjust the screw in either direction, as required. The screw must be in contact with the lever pad after adjustment.

9. If the idle speed is too high, proceed as follows:
a. Turn the engine **OFF**.
b. Block off the orifice in the throttle plate temporarily with tape. If the orifice already has a plug, proceed to Step d.
c. Reattach the air intake hose. Restart the engine and check the idle speed using the Self-Test. If the engine stalled, crack open the plate with the throttle return screw.
d. If the idle speed continues to be fast, run the Key On Engine Off (KOEO) Self-Test and check for a TPS output code.
e. If the output code is within range, remove the tape and check for vacuum leaks, throttle linkage binding, or other causes for excessive high idle.
f. If the output code is out of range, adjust the throttle screw to obtain the proper code. The lever pad must be in contact with the screw after adjustment.
g. If the idle speed drops to or below the desired level, as indicated by the Self-Test Output tone, turn the engine **OFF**, disconnect the air cleaner hose and remove the tape.
h. Install the proper plug in the throttle plate orifice.
i. Reconnect the air cleaner hose. Start the engine and turn the throttle plate stop screw clockwise until the conditions in Step 7a exist. Do not turn the screw counterclockwise as this may cause the throttle plate to stick at idle.

10. Run the KOEO Self-Test for proper TPS output code.
11. Make sure the throttle is not stuck in the bore and the linkage is not preventing the throttle from closing.
12. Check the Throttle Valve (TV) pressure adjustment.

3.8L SC Engine

1. Place the transaxle in **P** and apply the parking brake.
2. Start the engine and bring to normal operating temperature. Make sure the heater, air conditioning and all other accessories are OFF.
3. Check and if necessary, adjust the ignition timing.
4. Make sure the fuel pressure is correct. Any indicated vehicle malfunction service codes should be resolved before proceeding further.
5. Connect the SUPER STAR II tester, tool number 007-00028 or other suitable scan tool to the Self-Test connector. Activate the Key On Engine Running (KOER) Self-Test.
6. After Code 1 or 111 has been displayed, unlatch and within 4 seconds, latch the STI button.
7. A single pulse code indicates the entry mode, then observe the Self-Test Output (STO) on the tester for the following:
a. A constant tone, solid light or **STO LO** readout means the base idle speed is within the correct range. To exit the test, unlatch the STI button, then wait 4 seconds for reinitialization. After 10 minutes, the tool will exit by itself.
b. A beeping tone, flashing light or **STO LO** readout at 8 Hz indicates the Throttle Position Sensor (TPS) is out of range due to over adjustment. Adjustment may be required.
c. A beeping tone, flashing light or **STO LO** readout at 4 Hz indicates the base idle speed is too fast and adjustment is required. Proceed to Step 9.
d. A beeping tone, flashing light or **STO LO** readout at 1 Hz indicates the base idle speed is too low and adjustment is required. Proceed to Step 8.

8. If the idle speed is too low, do not clean the throttle body. Turn the air trim screw counterclockwise until the conditions in Step 7a are satisfied.
9. If the idle speed is too high, do not clean the throttle body. Turn the air trim screw clockwise until the conditions in Step 7a are satisfied.

4.6L Engine

The idle speed is not adjustable on the 4.6L engine

5.0L Engine

1. Place the transaxle in **P** and apply the parking brake.
2. Start the engine and bring to normal operating temperature. Make sure the heater, air conditioning and all other accessories are OFF.
3. Check and if necessary, adjust the ignition timing.
4. Make sure the fuel pressure is correct. Any indicated vehicle malfunction service codes should be resolved before proceeding further.
5. Connect the SUPER STAR II tester tool 007-00028 or other suitable scan tool, to the Self-Test connector. Activate the Key On Engine Running (KOER) Self-Test.
6. After Code 1 or 111 has been displayed, unlatch and within 4 seconds, latch the STI button.
7. A single pulse code indicates the entry mode, then observe the Self-Test Output (STO) on the tester for the following:
a. A constant tone, solid light or **STO LO** readout means the base idle speed is within the correct range. To exit the test, unlatch the STI button, then wait 4 seconds for reinitialization. After 10 minutes, the tool will exit by itself.
b. A beeping tone, flashing light or **STO LO** readout at 8 Hz indicates the Throttle Position Sensor (TPS) is out of range due to over adjustment. Adjustment may be required.
c. A beeping tone, flashing light or turn the air trim screw counterclockwise until the conditions in Step 7a are satisfied.

8. If the idle speed is too high, do not clean the throttle body. Turn the air trim screw clockwise until the conditions in Step 7a are satisfied.

Idle Mixture Adjustment

The idle mixture is controlled by the electronic control unit and cannot be adjusted.

Fuel Tank

✻✻WARNING

NEVER SMOKE AROUND OR NEAR GASOLINE! GASOLINE VAPORS ARE EXTREMELY FLAMMABLE! EVEN THE PROXIMITY OF LIGHTED SMOKING MATERIAL CAN CAUSE AN EXPLOSION AND FIRE!

REMOVAL & INSTALLATION

1983-92 Models

➥ **Before disconnecting any fuel line, relieve the pressure from the fuel system. On 3.8L and 5.0L engines with CFI, relieve the system pressure at the pressure relief valve**

mounted on the throttle body. Special tool T80L-9974-A, or its equivalent, is needed for this procedure.

1. On the 2.3L turbocharged engines with EFI this valve is located in the flexible fuel supply tube approximately 12 inches (305mm) back from where it connects to the engine fuel rail on the left side of the engine compartment.
2. On the 3.8L and 5.0L with EFI, the valve is located in the metal engine fuel line at the right front corner of the engine.
3. Before opening the fuel system on EFI engines:
   a. Remove the fuel tank cap.
   b. Disconnect the vacuum hose from the fuel pressure regulator located on the engine fuel rail.
   c. Using a hand vacuum pump, apply about 25 in.Hg to the pressure regulator. Fuel pressure will be released into the fuel tank through the fuel return hose.
4. Raise and support the rear end on jackstands.
5. Disconnect the battery ground cable.
6. Siphon off as much gasoline as possible into an approved container.

➥ On cars with fuel injection, the fuel tank has small reservoirs inside to maintain the fuel level at or near the fuel pick-up. These reservoirs are difficult to drain in as much as they may block the siphoning hose. You'll have to try different angle and repeated attempts with the siphoning hose. Be patient.

7. Place a pan under the fuel fill hose and disconnect the fuel filler hose at the tank. Pour any drained fuel into an approved container.

➥ On 1989-92 models the exhaust pipe and exhaust shields must be removed from car first, refer to Engine section for proper removal and installation procedures

8. Place a floor jack, cushioned with a length of wood, under the fuel tank.
9. Remove the fuel tank strap nuts and lower the fuel tank just enough to disconnect the fuel liquid and vapor lines, and the fuel sending unit wire.
10. Remove the air deflector from the tank retaining straps. The deflector is retained with pop rivets.
11. On cars cars equipped with a metal retainer which fastens the filler pipe to the tank, remove the screw attaching the retainer to the fuel tank flange.
12. Continue lowering the tank once all lines are disconnected, and remove it from the car.
13. Installation is the reverse of removal. The fuel vapor line should be retaped in position in the ribbed channel atop the tank.

1993-96 Models

1. Disconnect the negative battery cable and relieve the fuel system pressure.
2. Siphon or pump as much fuel as possible out through the fuel filler pipe.

➥ All vehicles have reservoirs inside the fuel tank to maintain fuel near the fuel pickup during cornering and under low fuel operating conditions. These reservoirs could block siphon tubes or hoses from reaching the bottom of the fuel tank. Repeated attempts using different hose orientations can overcome this obstacle.

3. Raise and safely support the vehicle.
4. Remove the exhaust pipe and exhaust shield, if equipped. Disconnect the fuel fill and vent hoses connecting the filler pipe to the tank. Disconnect one end of the vapor crossover hose at the rear over the driveshaft.
5. If equipped with a metal retainer that fastens the filler pipe to the fuel tank, remove the screw attaching the retainer to the fuel tank flange.
6. Disconnect the fuel lines and the electrical connector to the fuel tank sending unit. On some vehicles, these are inaccessible on top of the tank. In these cases they must be disconnected with the tank partially removed.
7. Place a safety support under the fuel tank and remove the bolts from the fuel tank straps. Allow the straps to swing out of the way. Be careful not to deform the fuel tank.
8. Partially remove the tank and disconnect the fuel lines and electrical connector from the sending unit, if required.
9. Remove the tank from the vehicle.

To install:

10. Raise the fuel tank into position in the vehicle. Connect the fuel lines and sending unit electrical connector if it is necessary to connect them before the tank is in the final installed position.
11. Lubricate the fuel filler pipe with water base tire mounting lubricant and install the tank onto the filler pipe, then bring the tank into final position. Be careful not to deform the tank.
12. Bring the fuel tank straps around the tank and start the retaining nut or bolt..Align the tank with the straps. If equipped, make sure the fuel tank shields are installed with the straps and are positioned correctly on the tank. Align the tank with the driveshaft.
13. Check the hoses and wiring mounted on the tank top to make sure they are correctly routed and will not be pinched between the tank and body. Make sure the fuel vent hose is positioned above the vent retainer and not contacting the driveshaft.
14. Tighten the fuel tank strap retaining nuts or bolts to 22-30 ft. lbs. (29-41 Nm).
15. If not already connected, connect the fuel hoses and lines which were disconnected. Make sure the fuel supply, fuel return, if present, and vapor vent connections are made correctly. If not already connected, connect the sending unit electrical connector.
16. Install the exhaust pipe shield, if equipped, and exhaust pipe.
17. Lower the vehicle. Replace the fuel that was drained from the tank. Check all connections for leaks.

6

CHASSIS ELECTRICAL

UNDERSTANDING AND TROUBLESHOOTING ELECTRICAL SYSTEMS

Over the years import and domestic manufacturers have incorporated electronic control systems into their production lines. In fact, electronic control systems are so prevalent that all new cars and trucks built today are equipped with at least one on-board computer. These electronic components (with no moving parts) should theoretically last the life of the vehicle, provided that nothing external happens to damage the circuits or memory chips.

While it is true that electronic components should never wear out, in the real world malfunctions do occur. It is also true that any computer-based system is extremely sensitive to electrical voltages and cannot tolerate careless or haphazard testing/service procedures. An inexperienced individual can literally cause major damage looking for a minor problem by using the wrong kind of test equipment or connecting test leads/connectors with the ignition switch **ON**. When selecting test equipment, make sure the manufacturer's instructions state that the tester is compatible with whatever type of system is being serviced. Read all instructions carefully and double check all test points before installing probes or making any test connections.

The following section outlines basic diagnosis techniques for dealing with automotive electrical systems. Along with a general explanation of the various types of test equipment available to aid in servicing modern automotive systems, basic repair techniques for wiring harnesses and connectors are also given. Read the basic information before attempting any repairs or testing. This will provide the background of information necessary to avoid the most common and obvious mistakes that can cost both time and money. Although the replacement and testing procedures are simple in themselves, the systems are not, and unless one has a thorough understanding of all components and their function within a particular system, the logical test sequence these systems demand cannot be followed. Minor malfunctions can make a big difference, so it is important to know how each component affects the operation of the overall system in order to find the ultimate cause of a problem without replacing good components unnecessarily. It is not enough to use the correct test equipment; the test equipment must be used correctly.

Safety Precautions

**CAUTION

Whenever working on or around any electrical or electronic systems, always observe these general precautions to prevent the possibility of personal injury or damage to electronic components.

- Never install or remove battery cables with the key **ON** or the engine running. Jumper cables should be connected with the key **OFF** to avoid power surges that can damage electronic control units. Engines equipped with computer controlled systems should avoid both giving and getting jump starts due to the possibility of serious damage to components from arcing in the engine compartment if connections are made with the ignition **ON**.
- Always remove the battery cables before charging the battery. Never use a high output charger on an installed battery or attempt to use any type of "hot shot" (24 volt) starting aid.
- Exercise care when inserting test probes into connectors to insure good contact without damaging the connector or spreading the pins. Always probe connectors from the rear (wire) side, NOT the pin side, to avoid accidental shorting of terminals during test procedures.
- Never remove or attach wiring harness connectors with the ignition switch **ON**, especially to an electronic control unit.
- Do not drop any components during service procedures and never apply 12 volts directly to any component (like a solenoid or relay) unless instructed specifically to do so. Some component electrical windings are designed to safely handle only 4 or 5 volts and can be destroyed in seconds if 12 volts are applied directly to the connector.
- Remove the electronic control unit if the vehicle is to be placed in an environment where temperatures exceed approximately 176°F (80°C), such as a paint spray booth or when arc/gas welding near the control unit location.

Understanding Basic Electricity

Understanding the basic theory of electricity makes electrical troubleshooting much easier. Several gauges are used in electrical troubleshooting to see inside the circuit being tested. Without a basic understanding, it will be difficult to understand testing procedures.

THE WATER ANALOGY

Electricity is the flow of electrons — hypothetical particles thought to constitute the basic stuff of electricity. Many people have been taught electrical theory using an analogy with water. In a comparison with water flowing in a pipe, the electrons would be the water. As the flow of water can be measured, the flow of electricity can be measured. The unit of measurement is amperes, frequently abbreviated amps. An ammeter will measure the actual amount of current flowing in the circuit.

Just as the water pressure is measured in units such as pounds per square inch, electrical pressure is measured in volts. When a voltmeter's two probes are placed on two live portions of an electrical circuit with different electrical pressures, current will flow through the voltmeter and produce a reading which indicates the difference in electrical pressure between the two parts of the circuit.

While increasing the voltage in a circuit will increase the flow of current, the actual flow depends not only on voltage, but on the resistance of the circuit. The standard unit for measuring circuit resistance is an ohm, measured by an ohmmeter. The ohmmeter is somewhat similar to an ammeter, but incorporates its own source of power so that a standard voltage is always present.

CIRCUITS

An actual electric circuit consists of four basic parts. These are: the power source, such as a generator or battery; a hot wire, which conducts the electricity under a relatively high voltage to the component supplied by the circuit; the load, such as a lamp, motor, resistor or relay coil; and the ground wire, which carries the current back to the source under very low voltage. In such a circuit the bulk of the resistance exists between the point where the hot wire is connected to the load, and the point where the load is grounded. In an automobile, the vehicle's frame or body, which is made of steel, is used as a part of the ground circuit for many of the electrical devices.

Remember that, in electrical testing, the voltmeter is connected in parallel with the circuit being tested (without disconnecting any wires) and measures the difference in voltage between the locations of the two probes; that the ammeter is connected in series with the load (the circuit is separated at one point and the ammeter inserted so it becomes a part of the circuit); and the ohmmeter is self-powered, so that all the power in the circuit should be off and the portion of the circuit to be measured contacted at either end by one of the probes of the meter.

For any electrical system to operate, it must make a complete circuit. This simply means that the power flow from the battery must make a complete circle. When an electrical component is operating, power flows from the battery to the component, passes through the component causing it to perform it to function (such as lighting a light bulb) and then returns to the battery through the ground of the circuit. This ground is usually (but not always) the metal part of the vehicle on which the electrical component is mounted.

Perhaps the easiest way to visualize this is to think of connecting a light bulb with two wires attached to it to your vehicle's battery. The battery in your vehicle has two posts (negative and positive). If one of the two wires attached to the light bulb was attached to the negative post of the battery and the other wire was attached to the positive post of the battery, you would have a complete circuit. Current from the battery would flow out one post, through the wire attached to it and then to the light bulb, where it would pass through causing it to light. It would then leave the light bulb, travel through the other wire, and return to the other post of the battery.

AUTOMOTIVE CIRCUITS

The normal automotive circuit differs from this simple example in two ways. First, instead of having a return wire from the bulb to the battery, the light bulb return the current to the battery through the chassis of the vehicle. Since the negative battery cable is attached to the chassis and the chassis is made of electrically conductive metal, the chassis of the vehicle can serve as a ground wire to complete the circuit. Secondly, most automotive circuits contain switches to turn components on and off.

Some electrical components which require a large amount of current to operate also have a relay in their circuit. Since these circuits carry a large amount of current, the thickness of the wire in the circuit (gauge size) is also greater. If this large wire were connected from the component to the control switch on the instrument panel, and then back to the component, a voltage drop would occur in the circuit. To prevent this potential drop in voltage, an electromagnetic switch (relay) is used. The large wires in the circuit are connected from the vehicle battery to one side of the relay, and from the opposite side of the relay to the component. The relay is normally open, preventing current from passing through the circuit. An additional, smaller wire is connected from the relay to the control switch for the circuit. When the control switch is turned on, it grounds the smaller wire from the relay and completes the circuit.

SHORT CIRCUITS

If you were to disconnect the light bulb (from the previous example of a light-bulb being connected to the battery by two wires) from the wires and touch the two wires together (please take our word for this; don't try it), the result will be a shower of sparks. A similar thing happens (on a smaller scale) when the power supply wire to a component or the electrical component itself becomes grounded before the normal ground connection for the circuit. To prevent damage to the system, the fuse for the circuit blows to interrupt the circuit — protecting the components from damage. Because grounding a wire from a power source makes a complete circuit — less the required component to use the power — the phenomenon is called a short circuit. The most common causes of short circuits are: the rubber insulation on a wire breaking or rubbing through to expose the current carrying core of the wire to a metal part of the car, or a shorted switch.

Some electrical systems on the vehicle are protected by a circuit breaker which is, basically, a self-repairing fuse. When either of the described events takes place in a system which is protected by a circuit breaker, the circuit breaker opens the circuit the same way a fuse does. However, when either the short is removed from the circuit or the surge subsides, the circuit breaker resets itself and does not have to be replaced as a fuse does.

Troubleshooting

When diagnosing a specific problem, organized troubleshooting is a must. The complexity of a modern automobile demands that you approach any problem in a logical, organized manner. There are certain troubleshooting techniques that are standard:

1. Establish when the problem occurs. Does the problem appear only under certain conditions? Were there any noises, odors, or other unusual symptoms?
2. Isolate the problem area. To do this, make some simple tests and observations; then eliminate the systems that are working properly. Check for obvious problems such as broken wires, dirty connections or split/disconnected vacuum hoses. Always check the obvious before assuming something complicated is the cause.
3. Test for problems systematically to determine the cause once the problem area is isolated. Are all the components functioning properly? Is there power going to electrical switches and motors? Is there vacuum at vacuum switches and/or actuators? Is there a mechanical problem such as bent linkage or loose mounting screws? Performing careful, systematic checks will often turn up most causes on the first inspection without wasting time checking components that have little or no relationship to the problem.
4. Test all repairs after the work is done to make sure that the problem is fixed. Some causes can be traced to more than one component, so a careful verification of repair work is important in order to pick up additional malfunctions that may cause a problem to reappear or a different problem to arise. A blown fuse, for example, is a simple problem that may require more than another fuse to repair. If you don't look for a problem that caused a fuse to blow, a shorted wire (for example) may go undetected.

Experience has shown that most problems tend to be the result of a fairly simple and obvious cause, such as loose or corroded connectors or air leaks in the intake system. This makes careful inspection of components during testing essential to quick and accurate troubleshooting.

BASIC TROUBLESHOOTING THEORY

Electrical problems generally fall into one of three areas:

- The component that is not functioning is not receiving current.
- The component itself is not functioning.
- The component is not properly grounded.

Problems that fall into the first category are by far the most complicated. It is the current supply system to the component which contains all the switches, relay, fuses, etc.

The electrical system can be checked with a test light and a jumper wire. A test light is a device that looks like a pointed screwdriver with a wire attached to it. It has a light bulb in its handle. A jumper wire is a piece of insulated wire with an alligator clip attached to each end.

If a light bulb is not working, you must follow a systematic plan to determine which of the three causes is the villain.

1. Turn on the switch that controls the inoperable bulb.
2. Disconnect the power supply wire from the bulb.
3. Attach the ground wire to the test light to a good metal ground.
4. Touch the probe end of the test light to the end of the power supply wire that was disconnected from the bulb. If the bulb is receiving current, the test light will go on.

➛ If the bulb is one which works only when the ignition key is turned on (turn signal), make sure the key is turned on.

If the test light does not go on, then the problem is in the circuit between the battery and the bulb. As mentioned before, this includes all the switches, fuses, and relays in the system. Turn to a wiring diagram and find the bulb on the diagram. Follow the wire that runs back to the battery. The problem is an open circuit between the battery and the bulb. If the fuse is blown and, when replaced, immediately blows again, there is a short circuit in the system which must be located and repaired. If there is a switch in the system, bypass it with a jumper wire. This is done by connecting one end of the jumper wire to the power supply wire into the switch and the other end of the jumper wire to the wire coming out of the switch. If the test light illuminates with the jumper wire installed, the switch or whatever was bypassed is defective.

➛ Never substitute the jumper wire for the bulb, as the bulb is the component required to use the power from the power source.

5. If the bulb in the test light goes on, then the current is getting to the bulb that is not working in the car. This eliminates the first of the three possible causes. Connect the power supply wire and connect a jumper wire from the bulb to a good metal ground. Do this with the switch which controls the bulb works with jumper wire installed, then it has a bad ground. This is usually caused by the metal area on which the bulb mounts to the vehicle being coated with some type of foreign matter.
6. If neither test located the source of the trouble, then the light bulb itself is defective.

The above test procedure can be applied to any of the components of the chassis electrical system by substituting the component that is not working for the light bulb. Remember that for any electrical system to work, all connections must be clean and tight.

TEST EQUIPMENT

➛ Pinpointing the exact cause of trouble in an electrical system can sometimes only be accomplished by the use of special test equipment. The following describes different types of commonly used test equipment and explains how to use them in diagnosis. In addition to the information covered below, the tool manufacturer's instructions booklet (provided with the tester) should be read and clearly understood before attempting any test procedures.

Jumper Wires

Jumper wires are simple, yet extremely valuable, pieces of test equipment. They are basically test wires which are used to bypass sections of a circuit. The simplest type of jumper wire is a length of multi-strand wire with an alligator clip at each end. Jumper wires are usually fabricated from lengths of standard automotive wire and whatever type of connector (alligator clip, spade connector or pin connector) that is required for the particular vehicle being tested. The well equipped tool box will have several different styles of jumper wires in several different lengths. Some jumper wires are made with three or more terminals coming from a common splice for special purpose testing. In cramped, hard-to-reach areas it is advisable to have insulated boots over the jumper wire terminals in order to prevent accidental grounding, sparks, and possible fire, especially when testing fuel system components.

Jumper wires are used primarily to locate open electrical circuits, on either the ground (-) side of the circuit or on the hot (+) side. If an electrical component fails to operate, connect the jumper wire between the component and a good ground. If the component operates only with the jumper installed, the ground circuit is open. If the ground circuit is good, but the component does not operate, the circuit between the power feed and component may be open. By moving the jumper wire successively back from the lamp toward the power source, you can isolate the area of the circuit where the open is located. When the component stops functioning, or the power is cut off, the open is in the segment of wire between the jumper and the point previously tested.

You can sometimes connect the jumper wire directly from the battery to the hot terminal of the component, but first make sure the component uses 12 volts in operation. Some electrical components, such as fuel injectors, are designed to operate on about 4 volts and running 12 volts directly to the injector terminals can cause damage.

By inserting an in-line fuse holder between a set of test leads, a fused jumper wire can be used for bypassing open circuits. Use a 5 amp fuse to provide protection against voltage spikes. When in doubt, use a voltmeter to check the voltage input to the component and measure how much voltage is normally being applied.

✻✻CAUTION

Never use jumpers made from wire that is of lighter gauge than that which is used in the circuit under test. If the jumper wire is of too small a gauge, it may overheat and possibly melt. Never use jumpers to bypass high resistance loads in a circuit. Bypassing resistance's, in effect, creates a short circuit. This may, in turn, cause damage and fire. Jumper wires should only be used to bypass lengths of wire.

Unpowered Test Lights

The 12 volt test light is used to check circuits and components while electrical current is flowing through them. It is used for voltage and ground tests. Twelve volt test lights come in different styles but all have three main parts; a ground clip, a probe, and a light. The most commonly used 12 volt test lights have pick-type probes. To use a 12 volt test light, connect the ground clip to a good ground and probe wherever necessary with the pick. The pick should be sharp so that it can be probed into tight spaces.

✻✻CAUTION

Do not use a test light to probe electronic ignition spark plug or coil wires. Never use a pick-type test light to probe wiring on computer controlled systems unless specifically instructed to do so. Any wire insulation that is pierced by the test light probe should be taped and sealed with silicone after testing.

Like the jumper wire, the 12 volt test light is used to isolate opens in circuits. But, whereas the jumper wire is used to bypass the open to operate the load, the 12 volt test light is used to locate the presence of voltage in a circuit. If the test light glows, you know that there is power up to that point; if the 12 volt test light does not glow when its probe is inserted into the wire or connector, you know that there is an open circuit (no power). Move the test light in successive steps back toward the power source until the light in the handle does glow. When it glows, the open is between the probe and point which was probed previously.

➥ The test light does not detect that 12 volts (or any particular amount of voltage) is present; it only detects that some voltage is present. It is advisable before using the test light to touch its terminals across the battery posts to make sure the light is operating properly.

Self-Powered Test Lights

The self-powered test light usually contains a 1.5 volt penlight battery. One type of self-powered test light is similar in design to the 12 volt unit. This type has both the battery and the light in the handle, along with a pick-type probe tip. The second type has the light toward the open tip, so that the light illuminates the contact point. The self-powered test light is a dual purpose piece of test equipment. It can be used to test for either open or short circuits when power is isolated from the circuit (continuity test). A powered test light should not be used on any computer controlled system or component unless specifically instructed to do so. Many engine sensors can be destroyed by even this small amount of voltage applied directly to the terminals.

Voltmeters

A voltmeter is used to measure voltage at any point in a circuit, or to measure the voltage drop across any part of a circuit. It can also be used to check continuity in a wire or circuit by indicating current flow from one end to the other. Analog voltmeters usually have various scales on the meter dial and a selector switch to allow the selection of different voltages. The voltmeter has a positive and a negative lead. To avoid damage to the meter, always connect the negative lead to the negative (-) side of the circuit (to ground or nearest the ground side of the circuit) and connect the positive lead to the positive (+) side of the circuit (to the power source or the nearest power source). Note that the negative voltmeter lead will always be black and that the positive voltmeter will always be some color other than black (usually red).

Depending on how the voltmeter is connected into the circuit, it has several uses. A voltmeter can be connected either in parallel or in series with a circuit and it has a very high resistance to current flow. When connected in parallel, only a small amount of current will flow through the voltmeter current path; the rest will flow through the normal circuit current path and the circuit will work normally. When the voltmeter is connected in series with a circuit, only a small amount of current can flow through the circuit. The circuit will not work properly, but the voltmeter reading will show if the circuit is complete or not.

Ohmmeters

The ohmmeter is designed to read resistance (which is measured in ohms or Ω) in a circuit or component. Although there are several different styles of ohmmeters, all analog meters will usually have a selector switch which permits the measurement of different ranges of resistance (usually the selector switch allows the multiplication of the meter reading by 10, 100, 1000, and 10,000). A calibration knob allows the meter to be set at zero for accurate measurement. Since all ohmmeters are powered by an internal battery, the ohmmeter can be used as a self-powered test light. When the ohmmeter is connected, current from the ohmmeter flows through the circuit or component being tested. Since the ohmmeter's internal resistance and voltage are known values, the amount of current flow through the meter depends on the resistance of the circuit or component being tested.

The ohmmeter can be used to perform a continuity test for opens or shorts (either by observation of the meter needle or as a self-powered test light), and to read actual resistance in a circuit. It should be noted that the ohmmeter is used to check the resistance of a component or wire while there is no voltage applied to the circuit. Current flow from an outside voltage source (such as the vehicle battery) can damage the ohmmeter, so the circuit or component should be isolated from the vehicle electrical system before any testing is done. Since the ohmmeter uses its own voltage source, either lead can be connected to any test point.

➥ When checking diodes or other solid state components, the ohmmeter leads can only be connected one way in order to measure current flow in a single direction. Make sure the positive (+) and negative (-) terminal connections are as described in the test procedures to verify the one-way diode operation.

In using the meter for making continuity checks, do not be concerned with the actual resistance readings. Zero resistance, or any ohm reading, indicates continuity in the circuit. Infinite resistance indicates an open in the circuit. A high resistance reading where there should be none indicates a problem in the circuit. Checks for short circuits are made in the same manner as checks for open circuits except that the circuit must be isolated from both power and normal ground. Infinite resistance indicates no continuity to ground, while zero resistance indicates a dead short to ground.

Ammeters

An ammeter measures the amount of current flowing through a circuit in units called amperes or amps. Amperes are units of electron flow which indicate how fast the electrons are flowing through the circuit. Since Ohms Law dictates that current flow in a circuit is equal to the circuit voltage divided by the total circuit resistance, increasing voltage also increases the current level (amps). Likewise, any decrease in resistance will increase the amount of amps in a circuit. At normal operating voltage, most circuits have a characteristic amount of amperes, called "current draw" which can be measured using an ammeter. By referring to a specified current draw rating, measuring the amperes, and comparing the two values, one can determine what is happening within the circuit to aid in diagnosis. An open circuit, for example, will not allow any current to flow so the ammeter reading will be zero. More current flows through a heavily loaded circuit or when the charging system is operating.

An ammeter is always connected in series with the circuit being tested. All of the current that normally flows through the circuit must also flow through the ammeter; if there is any other path for the current to follow, the ammeter reading will not be accurate. The ammeter itself has very little resistance to current flow and therefore will not affect the circuit, but it will measure current draw only when the circuit is closed and electricity is flowing. Excessive current draw can blow fuses and drain the battery, while a reduced current draw can cause motors to run slowly, lights to dim and other components to not operate properly. The ammeter can help diagnose these conditions by locating the cause of the high or low reading.

Multimeters

Different combinations of test meters can be built into a single unit designed for specific tests. Some of the more common combination test devices are known as Volt/Amp testers, Tach/Dwell meters, or Digital Multimeters. The Volt/Amp tester is used for charging system, starting system or battery tests and consists of a voltmeter, an ammeter and a variable resistance carbon pile. The voltmeter will usually have at least two ranges for use with 6, 12 and/or 24 volt systems. The ammeter also has more than one range for testing various levels of battery loads and starter current draw. The carbon pile can be adjusted to offer different amounts of resistance. The Volt/Amp tester has heavy leads to carry large amounts of current and many later models have an inductive ammeter pickup that clamps around the wire to simplify test connections. On some models, the ammeter also has a zero-center scale to allow testing of charging and starting systems without switching leads or polarity. A digital multimeter is a voltmeter, ammeter and ohmmeter combined in an instrument which gives a digital readout. These are often used when testing solid state circuits because of their high input impedance (usually 10 megohms or more).

The tach/dwell meter that combines a tachometer and a dwell (cam angle) meter is a specialized kind of voltmeter. The tachometer scale is marked to show engine speed in rpm and the dwell scale is marked to show degrees of distributor shaft rotation. In most electronic ignition systems, dwell is determined by the control unit, but the dwell meter can also be used to check the duty cycle (operation) of some electronic engine control systems. Some tach/dwell meters are powered by an internal battery, while others take their power from the vehicle battery in use. The battery powered testers usually require calibration (much like an ohmmeter) before testing.

TESTING

Open Circuits

To use the self-powered test light or a multimeter to check for open circuits, first isolate the circuit from the vehicle's 12 volt power source by disconnecting the battery or wiring harness connector. Connect the test light or ohmmeter ground clip to a good ground and probe sections of the circuit sequentially with the test light. (start from either end of the circuit). If the light is out/or there is infinite resistance, the open is between the probe and the circuit ground. If the light is on/or the meter shows continuity, the open is between the probe and end of the circuit toward the power source.

Short Circuits

By isolating the circuit both from power and from ground, and using a self-powered test light or multimeter, you can check for shorts to ground in the circuit. Isolate the circuit from power and ground. Connect the test light or ohmmeter ground clip to a good ground and probe any easy-to-reach test point in the circuit. If the light comes on or there is continuity, there is a short somewhere in the circuit. To isolate the short, probe a test point at either end of the isolated circuit (the light should be on/there should be continuity). Leave the test light probe engaged and open connectors, switches, remove parts, etc., sequentially, until the light goes out/continuity is broken. When the light goes out, the short is between the last circuit component opened and the previous circuit opened.

➔ The battery in the test light and does not provide much current. A weak battery may not provide enough power to illuminate the test light even when a complete circuit is made (especially if there are high resistance's in the circuit). Always make sure that the test battery is strong. To check the battery, briefly touch the ground clip to the probe; if the light glows brightly the battery is strong enough for testing. Never use a self-powered test light to perform checks for opens or shorts when power is applied to the electrical system under test. The 12 volt vehicle power will quickly burn out the light bulb in the test light.

Available Voltage Measurement

Set the voltmeter selector switch to the 20V position and connect the meter negative lead to the negative post of the battery. Connect the positive meter lead to the positive post of the battery and turn the ignition switch **ON** to provide a load. Read the voltage on the meter or digital display. A well charged battery should register over 12 volts. If the meter reads below

11.5 volts, the battery power may be insufficient to operate the electrical system properly. This test determines voltage available from the battery and should be the first step in any electrical trouble diagnosis procedure. Many electrical problems, especially on computer controlled systems, can be caused by a low state of charge in the battery. Excessive corrosion at the battery cable terminals can cause a poor contact that will prevent proper charging and full battery current flow.

Normal battery voltage is 12 volts when fully charged. When the battery is supplying current to one or more circuits it is said to be "under load." When everything is off the electrical system is under a "no-load" condition. A fully charged battery may show about 12.5 volts at no load; will drop to 12 volts under medium load; and will drop even lower under heavy load. If the battery is partially discharged the voltage decrease under heavy load may be excessive, even though the battery shows 12 volts or more at no load. When allowed to discharge further, the battery's available voltage under load will decrease more severely. For this reason, it is important that the battery be fully charged during all testing procedures to avoid errors in diagnosis and incorrect test results.

Voltage Drop

When current flows through a resistance, the voltage beyond the resistance is reduced (the larger the current, the greater the reduction in voltage). When no current is flowing, there is no voltage drop because there is no current flow. All points in the circuit which are connected to the power source are at the same voltage as the power source. The total voltage drop always equals the total source voltage. In a long circuit with many connectors, a series of small, unwanted voltage drops due to corrosion at the connectors can add up to a total loss of voltage which impairs the operation of the normal loads in the circuit. The maximum allowable voltage drop under load is critical, especially if there is more than one high resistance problem in a circuit because all voltage drops are cumulative. A small drop is normal due to the resistance of the conductors.

INDIRECT COMPUTATION OF VOLTAGE DROPS

1. Set the voltmeter selector switch to the 20 volt position.
2. Connect the meter negative lead to a good ground.
3. While operating the circuit, probe all loads in the circuit with the positive meter lead and observe the voltage readings. A drop should be noticed after the first load. But, there should be little or no voltage drop before the first load.

DIRECT MEASUREMENT OF VOLTAGE DROPS

1. Set the voltmeter switch to the 20 volt position.
2. Connect the voltmeter negative lead to the ground side of the load to be measured.
3. Connect the positive lead to the positive side of the resistance or load to be measured.
4. Read the voltage drop directly on the 20 volt scale.

Too high a voltage indicates too high a resistance. If, for example, a blower motor runs too slowly, you can determine if perhaps there is too high a resistance in the resistor pack. By taking voltage drop readings in all parts of the circuit, you can isolate the problem. Too low a voltage drop indicates too low a resistance. Take the blower motor for example again. If a blower motor runs too fast in the MED and/or LOW position, the problem might be isolated in the resistor pack by taking voltage drop readings in all parts of the circuit to locate a possibly shorted resistor.

HIGH RESISTANCE TESTING

1. Set the voltmeter selector switch to the 4 volt position.
2. Connect the voltmeter positive lead to the positive post of the battery.
3. Turn on the headlights and heater blower to provide a load.
4. Probe various points in the circuit with the negative voltmeter lead.
5. Read the voltage drop on the 4 volt scale. Some average maximum allowable voltage drops are:

- FUSE PANEL: 0.7 volts
- IGNITION SWITCH: 0.5 volts
- HEADLIGHT SWITCH: 0.7 volts
- IGNITION COIL (+): 0.5 volts
- ANY OTHER LOAD: 1.3 volts

➥ **Voltage drops are all measured while a load is operating; without current flow, there will be no voltage drop.**

Resistance Measurement

The batteries in an ohmmeter will weaken with age and temperature, so the ohmmeter must be calibrated or "zeroed" before taking measurements. To zero the meter, place the selector switch in its lowest range and touch the two ohmmeter leads together. Turn the calibration knob until the meter needle is exactly on zero.

➥ **All analog (needle) type ohmmeters must be zeroed before use, but some digital ohmmeter models are automatically calibrated when the switch is turned on. Self-calibrating digital ohmmeters do not have an adjusting knob, but its a good idea to check for a zero readout before use by touching the leads together. All computer controlled systems require the use of a digital ohmmeter with at least 10 megohms impedance for testing. Before any test procedures are attempted, make sure the ohmmeter used is compatible with the electrical system or damage to the on-board computer could result.**

To measure resistance, first isolate the circuit from the vehicle power source by disconnecting the battery cables or the harness connector. Make sure the key is **OFF** when disconnecting any components or the battery. Where necessary, also isolate at least one side of the circuit to be checked in order to avoid reading parallel resistance's. Parallel circuit resistance's will always give a lower reading than the actual resistance of either of the branches. When measuring the resistance of parallel circuits, the total resistance will always be lower than the smallest resistance in the circuit. Connect the meter leads to both sides of the circuit (wire or component) and read the actual measured ohms on the meter scale. Make sure the selector switch is set to the proper ohm scale for the circuit being tested to avoid misreading the ohmmeter test value.

****WARNING**

Never use an ohmmeter with power applied to the circuit. Like the self-powered test light, the ohmmeter is designed to operate on its own power supply. The normal 12 volt automotive electrical system current could damage the meter!

Wiring Harnesses

The average automobile contains about 1/2 mile of wiring, with hundreds of individual connections. To protect the many wires from damage and to keep them from becoming a confusing tangle, they are organized into bundles, enclosed in plastic or taped together and called wiring harnesses. Different harnesses serve different parts of the vehicle. Individual wires are color coded to help trace them through a harness where sections are hidden from view.

Automotive wiring or circuit conductors can be in any one of three forms:

1. Single strand wire
2. Multi-strand wire
3. Printed circuitry

Single strand wire has a solid metal core and is usually used inside such components as alternators, motors, relays and other devices. Multi-strand wire has a core made of many small strands of wire twisted together into a single conductor. Most of the wiring in an automotive electrical system is made up of multi-strand wire, either as a single conductor or grouped together in a harness. All wiring is color coded on the insulator, either as a solid color or as a colored wire with an identification stripe. A printed circuit is a thin film of copper or other conductor that is printed on an insulator backing. Occasionally, a printed circuit is sandwiched between two sheets of plastic for more protection and flexibility. A complete printed circuit, consisting of conductors, insulating material and connectors for lamps or other components is called a printed circuit board. Printed circuitry is used in place of individual wires or harnesses in places where space is limited, such as behind instrument panels.

Since automotive electrical systems are very sensitive to changes in resistance, the selection of properly sized wires is critical when systems are repaired. A loose or corroded connection or a replacement wire that is too small for the circuit will add extra resistance and an additional voltage drop to the circuit. A ten percent voltage drop can result in slow or erratic motor operation, for example, even though the circuit is complete. The wire gauge number is an expression of the cross-section area of the conductor. The most common system for expressing wire size is the American Wire Gauge (AWG) system.

Gauge numbers are assigned to conductors of various cross-section areas. As gauge number increases, area decreases and the conductor becomes smaller. A 5 gauge conductor is smaller than a 1 gauge conductor and a 10 gauge is smaller than a 5 gauge. As the cross-section area of a conductor decreases, resistance increases and so does the gauge number. A conductor with a higher gauge number will carry less current than a conductor with a lower gauge number.

➔ Gauge wire size refers to the size of the conductor, not the size of the complete wire. It is possible to have two wires of the same gauge with different diameters because one may have thicker insulation than the other.

12 volt automotive electrical systems generally use 10, 12, 14, 16 and 18 gauge wire. Main power distribution circuits and larger accessories usually use 10 and 12 gauge wire. Battery cables are usually 4 or 6 gauge, although 1 and 2 gauge wires are occasionally used. Wire length must also be considered when making repairs to a circuit. As conductor length increases, so does resistance. An 18 gauge wire, for example, can carry a 10 amp load for 10 feet without excessive voltage drop; however if a 15 foot wire is required for the same 10 amp load, it must be a 16 gauge wire.

An electrical schematic shows the electrical current paths when a circuit is operating properly. It is essential to understand how a circuit works before trying to figure out why it doesn't. Schematics break the entire electrical system down into individual circuits and show only one particular circuit. In a schematic, no attempt is made to represent wiring and components as they physically appear on the vehicle; switches and other components are shown as simply as possible. Face views of harness connectors show the cavity or terminal locations in all multi-pin connectors to help locate test points.

If you need to backprobe a connector while it is on the component, the order of the terminals must be mentally reversed. The wire color code can help in this situation, as well as a keyway, lock tab or other reference mark.

WIRING REPAIR

Soldering is a quick, efficient method of joining metals permanently. Everyone who has the occasion to make wiring repairs should know how to solder. Electrical connections that are soldered are far less likely to come apart and will conduct electricity much better than connections that are only "pig-tailed" together. The most popular (and preferred) method of soldering is with an electrical soldering gun. Soldering irons are available in many sizes and wattage ratings. Irons with higher wattage ratings deliver higher temperatures and recover lost heat faster. A small soldering iron rated for no more than 50 watts is recommended, especially on electrical systems where excess heat can damage the components being soldered.

There are three ingredients necessary for successful soldering; proper flux, good solder and sufficient heat. A soldering flux is necessary to clean the metal of tarnish, prepare it for soldering and to enable the solder to spread into tiny crevices. When soldering, always use a rosin core solder which is non-corrosive and will not attract moisture once the job is finished. Other types of flux (acid core) will leave a residue that will attract moisture and cause the wires to corrode. Tin is a unique metal with a low melting point. In a molten state, it dissolves and alloys easily with many metals. Solder is made by mixing tin with lead. The most common proportions are 40/60, 50/50 and 60/40, with the percentage of tin listed first. Low priced solders usually contain less tin, making them very difficult for a beginner to use because more heat is required to melt the solder. A common solder is 40/60 which is well suited for all-around general use, but 60/40 melts easier and is preferred for electrical work.

Soldering Techniques

Successful soldering requires that the metals to be joined be heated to a temperature that will melt the solder, usually 360–460°F (182–238°C). Contrary to popular belief, the purpose of the soldering iron is not to melt the solder itself, but to heat the parts being soldered to a temperature high enough to melt the solder when it is touched to the work. Melting flux-cored solder on the soldering iron will usually destroy the effectiveness of the flux.

➥ Soldering tips are made of copper for good heat conductivity, but must be "tinned" regularly for quick transference of heat to the project and to prevent the solder from sticking to the iron. To "tin" the iron, simply heat it and touch the flux-cored solder to the tip; the solder will flow over the hot tip. Wipe the excess off with a clean rag, but be careful as the iron will be hot.

After some use, the tip may become pitted. If so, simply dress the tip smooth with a smooth file and "tin" the tip again. Flux-cored solder will remove oxides but rust, bits of insulation and oil or grease must be removed with a wire brush or emery cloth. For maximum strength in soldered parts, the joint must start off clean and tight. Weak joints will result in gaps too wide for the solder to bridge.

If a separate soldering flux is used, it should be brushed or swabbed on only those areas that are to be soldered. Most solders contain a core of flux and separate fluxing is unnecessary. Hold the work to be soldered firmly. It is best to solder on a wooden board, because a metal vise will only rob the piece to be soldered of heat and make it difficult to melt the solder. Hold the soldering tip with the broadest face against the work to be soldered. Apply solder under the tip close to the work, using enough solder to give a heavy film between the iron and the piece being soldered, while moving slowly and making sure the solder melts properly. Keep the work level or the solder will run to the lowest part and favor the thicker parts, because these require more heat to melt the solder. If the soldering tip overheats (the solder coating on the face of the tip burns up), it should be retinned. Once the soldering is completed, let the soldered joint stand until cool. Tape and seal all soldered wire splices after the repair has cooled.

Wire Harness Connectors

Most connectors in the engine compartment or that are otherwise exposed to the elements are protected against moisture and dirt which could create oxidation and deposits on the terminals.

These special connectors are weather-proof. All repairs require the use of a special terminal and the tool required to service it. This tool is used to remove the pin and sleeve terminals. If removal is attempted with an ordinary pick, there is a good chance that the terminal will be bent or deformed. Unlike standard blade type terminals, these weather-proof terminals cannot be straightened once they are bent. Make certain that the connectors are properly seated and all of the sealing rings are in place when connecting leads. On some models, a hinge-type flap provides a backup or secondary locking feature for the terminals. Most secondary locks are used to improve connector reliability by retaining the terminals if the small terminal lock tangs are not positioned properly.

Molded-on connectors require complete replacement of the connection. This means splicing a new connector assembly into the harness. All splices should be soldered to insure proper contact. Use care when probing the connections or replacing terminals in them as it is possible to short between opposite terminals. If this happens to the wrong terminal pair, it is possible to damage certain components. Always use jumper wires between connectors for circuit checking and never probe through weatherproof seals.

Open circuits are often difficult to locate by sight because corrosion or terminal misalignment are hidden by the connectors. Merely wiggling a connector on a sensor or in the wiring harness may correct the open circuit condition. This should always be considered when an open circuit or a failed sensor is indicated. Intermittent problems may also be caused by oxidized or loose connections. When using a circuit tester for diagnosis, always probe connections from the wire side. Be careful not to damage sealed connectors with test probes.

All wiring harnesses should be replaced with identical parts, using the same gauge wire and connectors. When signal wires are spliced into a harness, use wire with high temperature insulation only. It is seldom necessary to replace a complete harness. If replacement is necessary, pay close attention to insure proper harness routing. Secure the harness with suitable plastic wire clamps to prevent vibrations from causing the harness to wear in spots or contact any hot components.

➥ Weatherproof connectors cannot be replaced with standard connectors. Instructions are provided with replacement connector and terminal packages. Some wire harnesses have mounting indicators (usually pieces of colored tape) to mark where the harness is to be secured.

In making wiring repairs, its important that you always replace damaged wires with wiring of the same gauge as the wire being replaced. The heavier the wire, the smaller the gauge number. Wires are color-coded to aid in identification and whenever possible the same color coded wire should be used for replacement. A wire stripping and crimping tool is necessary to install solderless terminal connectors. Test all crimps by pulling on the wires; it should not be possible to pull the wires out of a good crimp.

Wires which are open, exposed or otherwise damaged are repaired by simple splicing. Where possible, if the wiring harness is accessible and the damaged place in the wire can be located, it is best to open the harness and check for all possible damage. In an inaccessible harness, the wire must be bypassed with a new insert, usually taped to the outside of the old harness.

When replacing fusible links, be sure to use fusible link wire, NOT ordinary automotive wire. Make sure the fusible segment is of the same gauge and construction as the one being replaced and double the stripped end when crimping the terminal connector for a good contact. The melted (open) fusible link segment of the wiring harness should be cut off as close to the harness as possible, then a new segment spliced in as described. In the case of a damaged fusible link that feeds two harness wires, the harness connections should be replaced with two fusible link wires so that each circuit will have its own separate protection.

➥ Most of the problems caused in the wiring harness are due to bad ground connections. Always check all vehicle ground connections for corrosion or looseness before performing any power feed checks to eliminate the chance of a bad ground affecting the circuit.

Hard-Shell Connectors

Unlike molded connectors, the terminal contacts in hard-shell connectors can be replaced. Weatherproof hard-shell connectors with the leads molded into the shell have non-replaceable terminal ends. Replacement usually involves the use of a special terminal removal tool that depresses the locking tangs (barbs) on the connector terminal and allows the connector to be removed from the rear of the shell. The connector shell should be replaced if it shows any evidence of burning, melting, cracks, or breaks.

Replace individual terminals that are burnt, corroded, distorted or loose.

The insulation crimp must be tight to prevent the insulation from sliding back on the wire when the wire is pulled. The insulation must be visibly compressed under the crimp tabs, and the ends of the crimp should be turned in for a firm grip on the insulation.

The wire crimp must be made with all wire strands inside the crimp. The terminal must be fully compressed on the wire strands with the ends of the crimp tabs turned in to make a firm grip on the wire. Check all connections with an ohmmeter to insure a good contact. There should be no measurable resistance between the wire and the terminal when connected.

Fusible Links

The fuse link is a short length of special, Hypalon (high temperature) insulated wire, integral with the engine compartment wiring harness and should not be confused with standard wire. It is several wire gauges smaller than the circuit which it protects. Under no circumstances should a fuse link replacement repair be made using a length of standard wire cut from bulk stock or from another wiring harness.

To repair any blown fuse link use the following procedure:

1. Determine which circuit is damaged, its location and the cause of the open fuse link. If the damaged fuse link is one of three fed by a common No. 10 or 12 gauge feed wire, determine the specific affected circuit.
2. Disconnect the negative battery cable.
3. Cut the damaged fuse link from the wiring harness and discard it. If the fuse link is one of three circuits fed by a single feed wire, cut it out of the harness at each splice end and discard it.
4. Identify and procure the proper fuse link with butt connectors for attaching the fuse link to the harness.

Heat shrink tubing must be slipped over the wire before crimping and soldering the connection.

5. To repair any fuse link in a 3-link group with one feed:
   a. After cutting the open link out of the harness, cut each of the remaining undamaged fuse links close to the feed wire weld.
   b. Strip approximately $^1/_2$ in. (13mm) of insulation from the detached ends of the two good fuse links. Insert two wire ends into one end of a butt connector, then carefully push one stripped end of the replacement fuse link into the same end of the butt connector and crimp all three firmly together.

Care must be taken when fitting the three fuse links into the butt connector as the internal diameter is a snug fit for three wires. Make sure to use a proper crimping tool. Pliers, side cutters, etc. will not apply the proper crimp to retain the wires and withstand a pull test.

   c. After crimping the butt connector to the three fuse links, cut the weld portion from the feed wire and strip approximately $^1/_2$ in. (13mm) of insulation from the cut end. Insert the stripped end into the open end of the butt connector and crimp very firmly.
   d. To attach the remaining end of the replacement fuse link, strip approximately $^1/_2$ in. (13mm) of insulation from the wire end of the circuit from which the blown fuse link was removed, and firmly crimp a butt connector or equivalent to the stripped wire. Then, insert the end of the replacement link into the other end of the butt connector and crimp firmly.
   e. Using rosin core solder with a consistency of 60 percent tin and 40 percent lead, solder the connectors and the wires at the repairs then insulate with electrical tape or heat shrink tubing.
6. To replace any fuse link on a single circuit in a harness, cut out the damaged portion, strip approximately $^1/_2$ in. (13mm) of insulation from the two wire ends and attach the appropriate replacement fuse link to the stripped wire ends with two proper size butt connectors. Solder the connectors and wires, then insulate.
7. To repair any fuse link which has an eyelet terminal on one end such as the charging circuit, cut off the open fuse link behind the weld, strip approximately $^1/_2$ in. (13mm) of insulation from the cut end and attach the appropriate new eyelet fuse link to the cut stripped wire with an appropriate size butt connector. Solder the connectors and wires at the repair, then insulate.
8. Connect the negative battery cable to the battery and test the system for proper operation.

Do not mistake a resistor wire for a fuse link. The resistor wire is generally longer and has print stating, "Resistor-don't cut or splice."

When attaching a single No. 16, 17, 18 or 20 gauge fuse link to a heavy gauge wire, always double the stripped wire end of the fuse link before inserting and crimping it into the butt connector for positive wire retention.

Add-On Electrical Equipment

The electrical system in your vehicle is designed to perform under reasonable operating conditions without interference between components. Before any additional electrical equipment is installed, it is recommended that you consult your dealer or a reputable repair facility that is familiar with the vehicle and its systems.

If the vehicle is equipped with mobile radio equipment and/or mobile telephone, it may have an effect upon the operation of any on-board computer control modules. Radio Frequency Interference (RFI) from the communications system can be picked up by the vehicle's wiring harnesses and conducted into the control module, giving it the wrong messages at the wrong time. Although well shielded against RFI, the computer should be further protected by taking the following measures:

- Install the antenna as far as possible from the control module. For instance, if the module is located behind the center console area, then the antenna should be mounted at the rear of the vehicle.
- Keep the antenna wiring a minimum of eight inches away from any wiring running to control modules and from the module itself. NEVER wind the antenna wire around any other wiring.
- Mount the equipment as far from the control module as possible. Be very careful during installation not to drill through any wires or short a wire harness with a mounting screw.
- Insure that the electrical feed wire(s) to the equipment are properly and tightly connected. Loose connectors can cause interference.
- Make certain that the equipment is properly grounded to the vehicle. Poor grounding can damage expensive equipment.

Mechanical Test Equipment

VACUUM GAUGE

Most gauges are graduated in inches of mercury (in.Hg), although a device called a manometer reads vacuum in inches of water (in. H_2O). The normal vacuum reading usually varies between 18 and 22 in.Hg at sea level. To test engine vacuum, the vacuum gauge must be connected to a source of manifold vacuum. Many engines have a plug in the intake manifold which can be removed and replaced with an adapter fitting. Connect the vacuum gauge to the fitting with a suitable rubber hose or, if no manifold plug is available, connect the vacuum gauge to any device using manifold vacuum, such as EGR valves, etc. The vacuum gauge can be used to determine if enough vacuum is reaching a component to allow its actuation.

HAND VACUUM PUMP

Small, hand-held vacuum pumps come in a variety of designs. Most have a built-in vacuum gauge and allow the component to be tested without removing it from the vehicle. Operate the pump lever or plunger to apply the correct amount of vacuum required for the test specified in the diagnosis routines. The level of vacuum in inches of Mercury (in.Hg) is indicated on the pump gauge. For some testing, an additional vacuum gauge may be necessary.

Intake manifold vacuum is used to operate various systems and devices on late model vehicles. To correctly diagnose and solve problems in vacuum control systems, a vacuum source is necessary for testing. In some cases, vacuum can be taken from the intake manifold when the engine is running, but vacuum is normally provided by a hand vacuum pump. These hand vacuum pumps have a built-in vacuum gauge that allow testing while the device is still attached to the component. For some tests, an additional vacuum gauge may be necessary.

BATTERY CABLES

➧ See Figure 1

**WARNING

Make sure the battery cables are connected to the correct battery terminals. Reverse polarity will damage the electrical components, particularly the (expensive) engine control module.

In most cases to work on many portions of your vehicle, it is necessary to disconnect the battery cables from the terminals so not to damage any components or cause harm to yourself with a jolt of electricity.

1. Start by making sure the ignition is **OFF**.

➥ When disconnecting the battery cables, always remove the negative terminal first.

2. Use the correct size wrenches to loosen the terminal hardware. If this is not done you may strip a nut and cause more aggravation than you may want on a Sunday evening!
3. If necessary, use a puller tool which is designed to remove the terminal from the battery post.
4. Lift the negative terminal off the battery post, then the positive.

**CAUTION

Do not allow the battery cables to touch during or after removal!

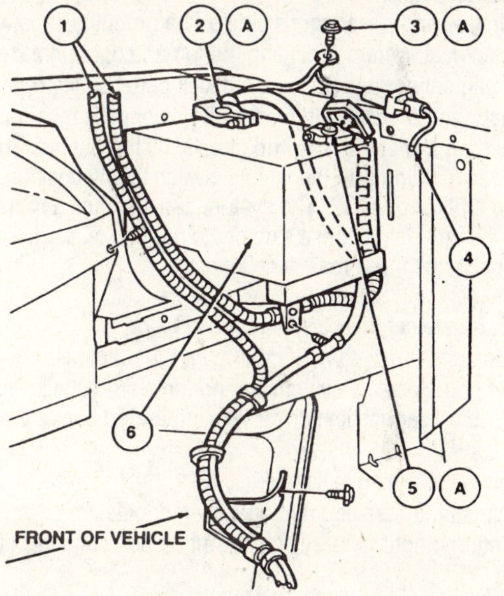

1. Positive Battery Cable
2. Battery Ground Cable
3. Screw
4. PCM Ground (Part of 12A581)
5. Positive Battery Cable Terminal (Part of 14300)
6. Battery
A. Tighten to 6-10 N·m (4-7 Lb-Ft)

88186G01

Fig. 1 Common battery cable routing — 1995 shown

SUPPLEMENTAL RESTRAINT SYSTEM (AIR BAG)

General Information

SYSTEM OPERATION

➧ **See Figures 2, 3 and 4**

The air bag system is designed to operate in frontal or front angled collisions. The system will activate in a crash with severe frontal deceleration, more sever than hitting a parked car of similar size and weight at 28 mph (45 km/h). The system will sense the severity of the crash rather than vehicle speed so some frontal collisions at speeds above 28 mph (45 km/h) may not be severe enough to require inflation.

The Supplemental Air Bag Restraint System is designed to provide increased collision protection for the front seat occupants in addition to that provided by the three-point seat belt system.

The seat belts are used to obtain the best protection and to receive the full advantages of the supplemental air bag.

The Supplemental Air Bag Restraint System consists of two basic subsystems:

- Drivers and passenger's side air bag module assemblies
- Electrical system, including the left and right primary crash front air bag sensor and bracket, left kick panel safing rear air bag sensor and bracket and the air bag diagnostic monitor.

The air bag system is powered directly by the battery. Tho system can function with the ignition switch in any position, including OFF and LOCK. The system can also function when the driver's and passenger's side seats are unoccupied. The system performs three main functions:

- Detects on impact
- Carries electrical current to the igniters
- Monitors the system to determine the readiness

The air bag electrical system components are as follows:

- Air bag diagnostic monitor with integrated back-up power supply
- Air bag warning indicator
- Wiring harness and air bag sliding contact
- Left and right primary crash front air bag sensors with brackets
- Left kick panel safing rear air bag sensor and bracket
- An igniter within the driver's and passenger's side air bag modules

SYSTEM COMPONENTS

Drivers Side

AIR BAG MODULE

➧ **See Figure 5**

The driver's side air bag module is serviced as an assembly. It is mounted in the center of the steering wheel. The module consists of the following components:

- Inflator
- Air bag
- Mounting plate and retainer ring
- Steering wheel trim cover

INFLATOR

The inflator assembly is not a serviceable item.

When the sensors close, signaling a crash, the electrical current flows to the air bag inflator. Inside the inflator, an igniter converts the electrical energy to thermal energy (heat). This causes the ignition of the inflator gas generant.

This ignition reaction combusts the sodium azide\copper oxide gas generant in the inflator, producing nitrogen gas, which in turn inflates the air bag.

AIR BAG

The driver's side air bag is constructed of neoprene coated nylon and is 26.5 inches (673mm) in diameter. The air bag fills to a volume of about 1.94 cubic feet (0.059 cubic meters) in approximately 40 milliseconds. The air bag assembly is not a serviceable item. You must replace it with a new one when involved in any type of crash whether it has inflated or not.

STEERING WHEEL TRIM COVER

The steering wheel trim cover encases the driver's side air bag module. The trim has molded-in tear seams that separate to allow inflation of the air bag. The trim cover is a component of the air bag module and is not a serviceable item.

Passengers Side

AIR BAG MODULE

The passenger's side air bag module is serviced as an assembly. It is mounted in the right position of the instrument panel above the glove compartment. The module consists of the following components:

- Inflator
- Air bag
- Reaction housing with mounting hardware
- Trim cover

INFLATOR

The inflator assembly is not a serviceable item. Inside the inflator, an igniter converts the electrical energy to thermal energy (heat). This causes the gas generant to ignite, as with the driver's side. This ignition reaction combusts the sodium azide\copper oxide gas generant in the inflator, producing nitrogen gas, which in turn inflates the air bag.

Since the passenger's side air bag module is much larger than the driver's side module, it contains more gas generant in a different inflator configuration to produce more nitrogen gas.

AIR BAG

The passenger's side air bag is constructed of ripstop nylon. The air bag fills to a volume of 8 cubic feet (0.227 cubic meters. The air bag assembly is not a serviceable item. You must replace it with a new one when involved in any type of crash whether it has inflated or not.

REACTION HOUSING

The steel reaction housing supplies support for the inflator. The housing provides a reaction surface for the passenger's side air bag module. It is used to attach the trim cover. The reaction housing contains mounting brackets that attach the passenger's air bag module to the instrument panel. This is not a serviceable item.

Fig. 2 Air bag warning labels are very important for your own personal safety

TRIM COVER

The thermo-plastic trim cover is textured and painted to match the surface of the instrument panel. It is constructed with a molded-in tear seam that separates when the air bag is inflated and hinges out of the way during deployment. The trim cover retains the air bag in the reaction housing during the operation of the vehicle and is not a serviceable item.

Air Bag Diagnostic Monitor

The air bag diagnostic monitor continually monitors all air bag system components and wiring connections for possible faults in the system. The monitor will display a diagnostic trouble code on the air bag warning indicator if it detects a fault in the air bag system while the ignition switch is in the **RUN** position.

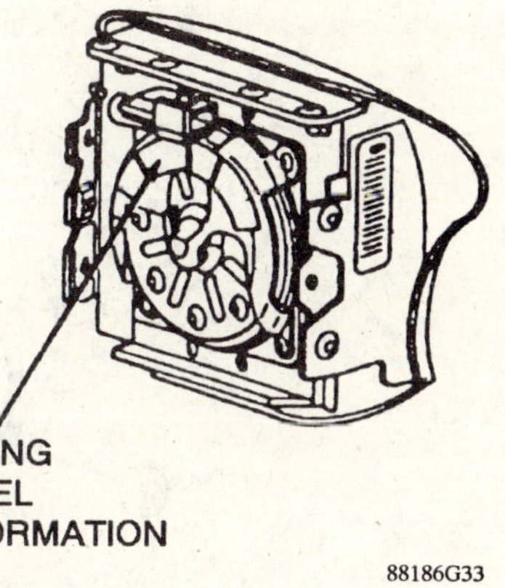

Fig. 3 The back of the driver's air bag has a warning label

The monitor performs system diagnostics which is its main function. The air bag diagnostic monitor does not deploy the air bags in the event of a crash! Crash sensors are hard wired to the air bags, and therefore, the sensors determine when to deploy the bags.

The air bag diagnostic monitor illuminates the air bag warning light for approximately six seconds when the ignition switch is turned to RUN and then turns off. This indicates that the air bag warning indicator is operational. If the air bag warning light does not illuminate or if it stays on or flashes at any time, a fault has been detected by the air bag diagnostic monitor.

Sensors

➧ **See Figure 6**

The sensors are an electrical switch which reacts to impacts according to direction and force. It discriminates between impacts that require air bag deployment and impacts that do not . When an impact occurs that requires deployment, the sensor contacts close, completing the electrical circuit necessary for the system to operate.

The sensors are located in the vehicle in several places. A primary crash sensor and bracket are located on the left and right front radiator supports. The safing rear air bag sensor is located in the left kick panel in the passenger's compartment. The safing and one of the primary sensors must be activated simultaneously to inflate the air bag.

SERVICE PRECAUTIONS

****WARNING**

Always wear safety glasses when servicing an air bag vehicle and handling the air bag to avoid possible injury.

- Carry a live air bag with the bag and trim cover pointed away from your body.
- Place a live air bag on a bench or other surface with the trim cover up, away from the surface.

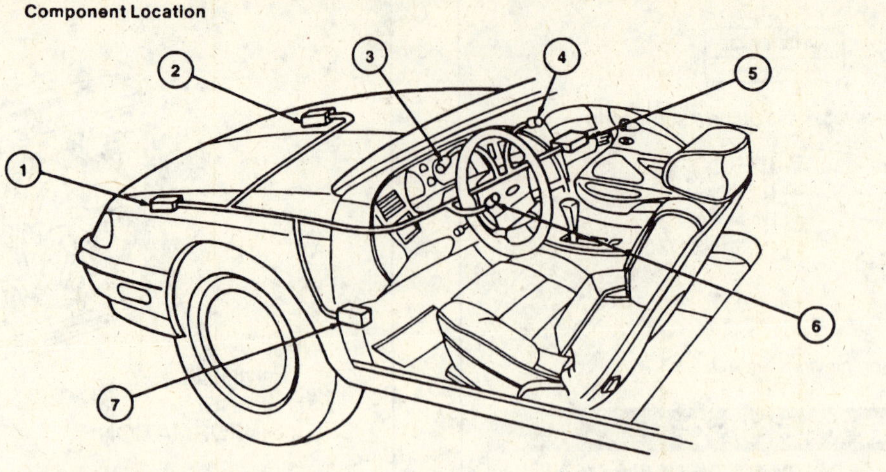

Fig. 4 Component locations for the air bag system

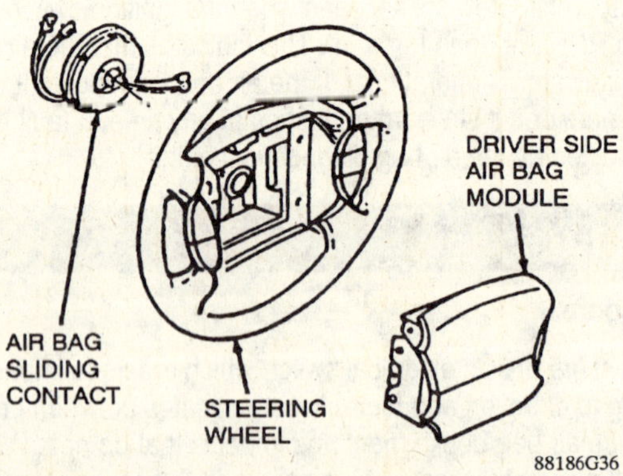

Fig. 5 The driver's side air bag module is located in the steering wheel front cover

- After deployment, the air bag surface may contain deposits of sodium hydroxide. This is a product of the gas generant combustion that is irritating to the skin.
- Wash your hands immediately with a mild soap after handling a deployed air bag.
- You can only replace, NOT service the crash sensors, sliding contact, diagnostic monitor and air bag modules.
- If the air bag module has a discolored or damaged trim cover deployment door it must be replaced. Do not attempt to paint it, any paint applied may damage the cover material. This could affect the air bag performance during deployment, which could cause personal injury.
- Never probe the connectors on the air bags. This may result in air bag deployment.
- All component replacement must be done with the negative battery cable disconnected for as minimum of one minute before service or replacement is attempted.

DISARMING THE SYSTEM

➧ See Figure 7

A special service tool is required to perform thic procedure, Rotunda Air Bag Simulator 105-00010 or equivalent

1. Disconnect the negative battery cable.

****WARNING**

The back-up power supply must be depleted before any air bag component service is performed. To deplete the back-up power supply energy, disconnect the negative battery cable for a minimum of one minute before service or replacement is attempted.

2. Wait one minute. This is required for the back-up power supply in the air bag diagnostic monitor to deplete its stored energy.

****WARNING**

Place the air bag module on a bench with the trim cover facing up to avoid personal injury.

3. Remove the two back cover plugs and remove the two bolt and washer assemblies retaining the driver's air bag module assembly to the steering wheel. Disconnect the air bag harness at the bag. Remove the driver's air bag module from the steering wheel.
4. Connect the Rotunda Air Bag Simulator 105-00010 or equivalent to the vehicle harness at the top of the steering column.
5. Remove the passenger's side air bag module assembly . The connector will contain the 614 (GY/O) and 616 (PK/BK) circuits. Install the Rotunda Air Bag Simulator 105-00010 or equivalent on the harness connector in place of the passenger's side air bag module assembly.
6. Connect the negative battery cable.

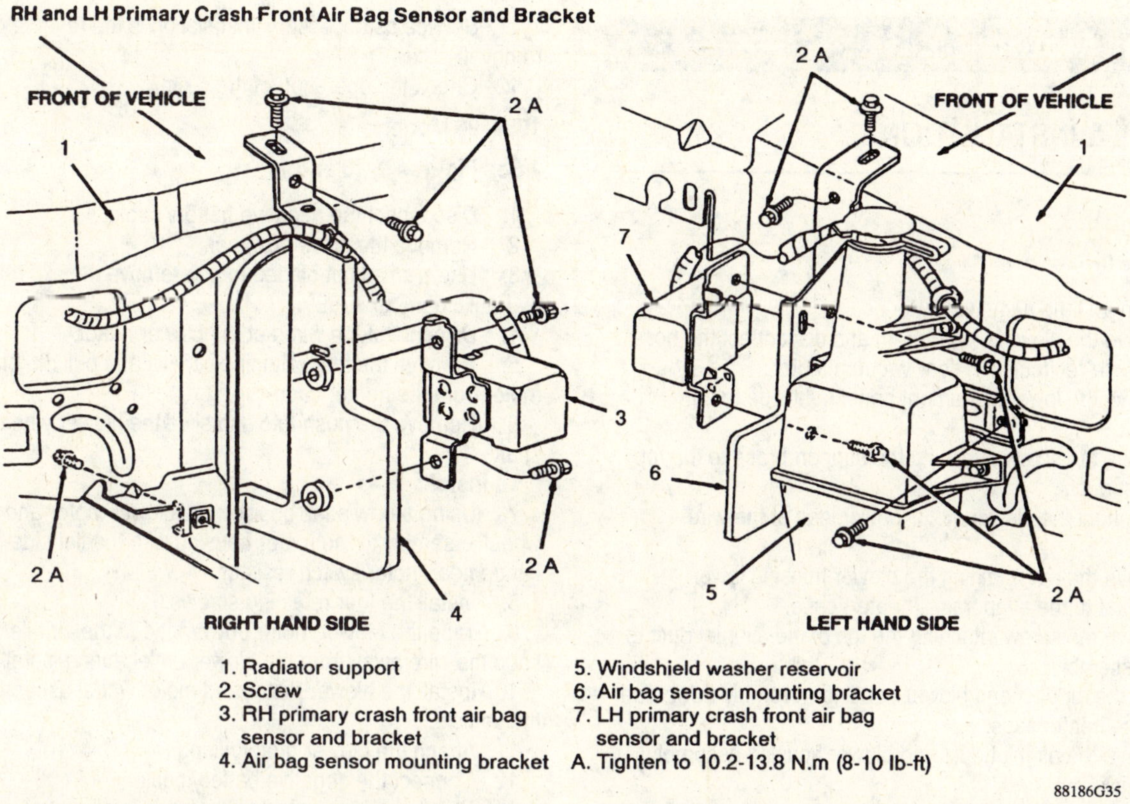

Fig. 6 Location of the left and right side air bag sensors

ARMING THE SYSTEM

****WARNING**

The air bag simulators must be removed and the air bags reconnected when the system is reactivated to avoid non-deployment in a collision resulting in possible personal injury.

1. Disconnect the negative battery cable.
2. Wait one minute, this is required for the back-up power supply in the air bag diagnostic monitor to deplete its stored energy.
3. Remove the air bag simulator from the air bag sliding contact connector at the top of the steering column. Reconnect the driver's side air bag module assembly. Position the driver's air bag module on the steering wheel and secure with the two bolts and washers. Tighten the bolt and washer assembly to 8–10 ft. lbs. (10–14 Nm).
4. Remove the air bag simulator wire from the vehicle harness connector. Reconnect and install the passenger's side air bag module assembly.
5. Connect the negative battery cable.
6. Turn the ignition switch from the OFF to RUN and visually monitor the air bag warning indicator. The light will illuminate continuously for approximately six seconds and then turn off. If a fault occurs, the air bag indicator will either fail to light, remain lighted continuously or flash. The flashing may not occur until approximately 16 seconds after the ignition switch has been turned from OFF to RUN. This is the time needed for the air bag diagnostic monitor to complete testing the system. If the air bag indicator is inoperative, an air bag system fault exists, a tone will sound in a pattern of five sets of five beeps. If this occurs, the air bag indicator will need to be serviced before further diagnostics can be done.

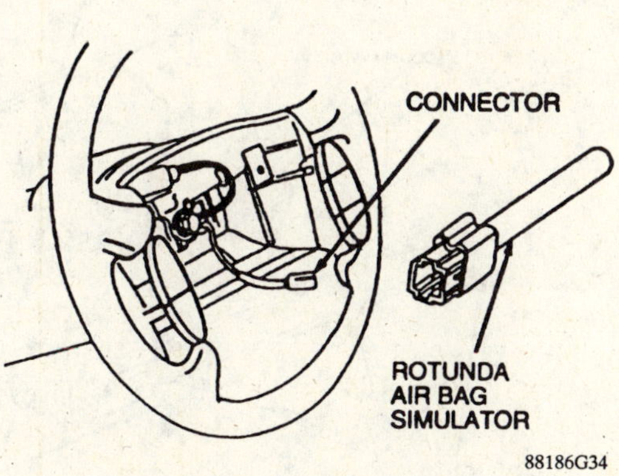

Fig. 7 Connect the Rotunda Air Bag Simulator 105-00010 or equivalent to the vehicle harness at the top of the steering column

HEATER

Blower Motor

REMOVAL & INSTALLATION

1983-88 Models

➧ **See Figure 8**

1. Disconnect the negative battery cable.
2. Remove the glove compartment and disconnect the hose from the outside-recirculation door vacuum motor.
3. Remove the lower instrument panel right side to cowl attaching bolt.
4. Remove the screw attaching the support brace to the top of the air inlet duct.
5. Disconnect the blower motor power lead at the wire connector.
6. Remove the nut retaining the blower housing lower support bracket to the evaporator (heater) case.
7. Remove the screw attaching the top of the air inlet duct to the heater assembly.
8. Move the air duct and blower housing assembly down and away from the heater case.
9. Remove the air inlet duct and blower housing assembly from the vehicle.
10. Remove the blower motor mounting plate screws and remove the blower motor and wheel assembly from the housing.
11. Service as necessary. Installation is the reverse of removal.
12. Check the operation of the system.

1989-96 Models

➧ **See Figures 9, 10 and 11**

1. Disconnect the negative battery cable.
2. Remove the glove box liner.
3. Use a small flat bladed tool to remove the clip retaining the hydraulic damper strut.
4. Disconnect the wires at the blower motor.
5. Remove the four retaining screws and pull the blower motor from the heater case.
6. Remove the pushnuts and slide the blower wheel from the shaft.

To install:

7. Using a new seal, position the blower motor and motor wheel assembly to the motor housing with the flat side of the flange near motor switch resistor.
8. Install the four retaining screws.
9. Tape the blower motor power lead to the air inlet duct to keep the wire away from the blower outlet during installation.
10. Install the blower motor and motor wheel assembly into the vehicle.
11. Attach the blower motor wiring.
12. Connect the negative battery cable.
13. Check the blower motor operation in all speeds.
14. Install the glove compartment liner.
15. Check the operation of the system.

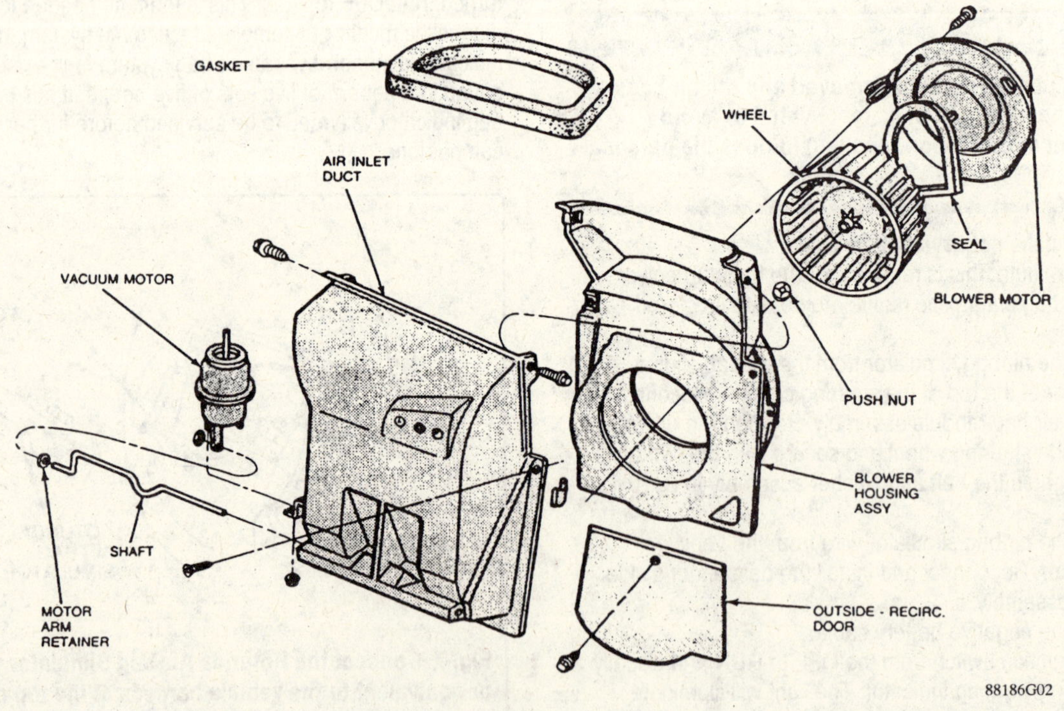

Fig. 8 Exploded view of the blower motor unit — 1983-88 models

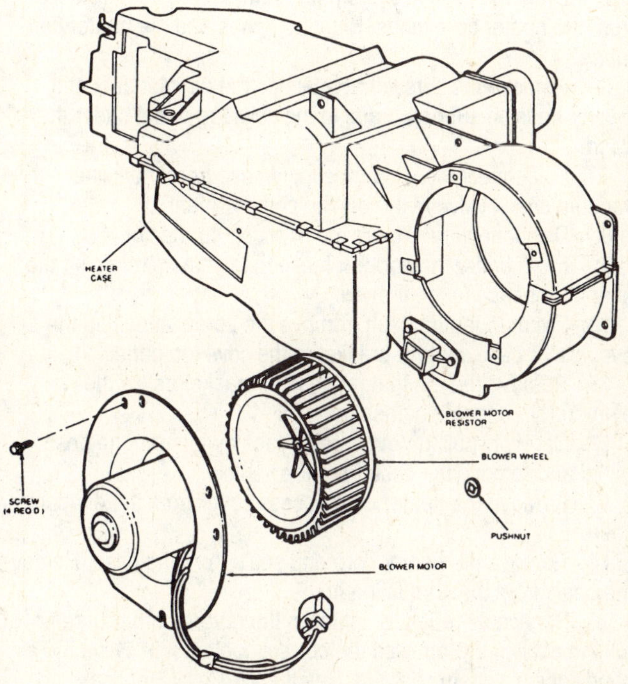

88186G03

Fig. 9 Exploded view of the blower motor unit — 1989-96 models

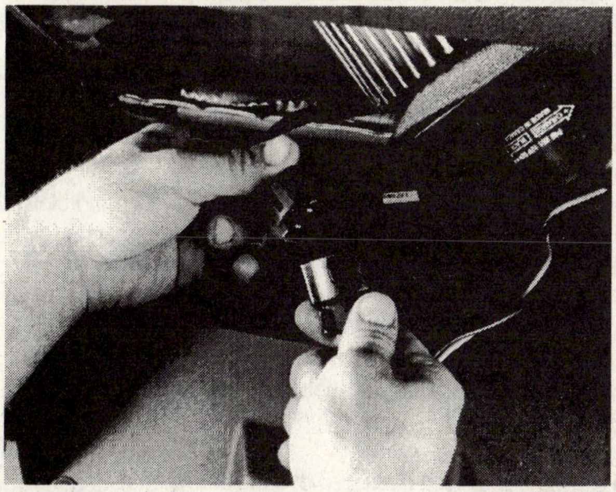

88186P02

Fig. 10 Disconnect the wiring attached to the blower motor

Heater Core

REMOVAL & INSTALLATION

****CAUTION**

When draining the coolant, keep in mind that cats and dogs are attracted by the ethylene glycol antifreeze, and are quite likely to drink any that is left in an uncovered container or in puddles on the ground. This will prove fatal in sufficient quantity. Always drain the coolant into a sealable container. Coolant should be reused unless it is contaminated or several years old.

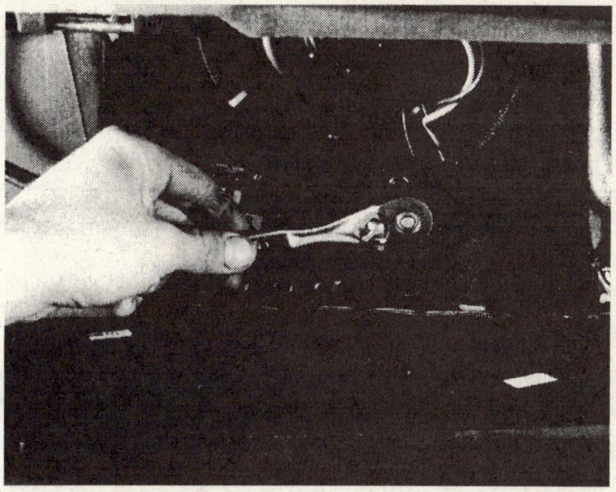

88186P01

Fig. 11 Remove the retaining screws that mount the motor to the heater unit

1983-88 Without A/C

➧ **See Figure 12**

1. Disconnect the negative battery cable.
2. Drain the cooling system.
3. Remove the instrument panel. Refer to Section 10, Instrument Panel Removal and Installation.
4. Disconnect the heater hoses from the heater core tubes. Plug the heater hoses and core tubes to prevent coolant spillage during removal.
5. Working under the hood at the firewall, remove the two nuts retaining the evaporator (heater) case to the dash.
6. From under the dash, remove the screws attaching the heater assembly support bracket and air inlet duct support bracket to the top cowl panel.
7. Remove the nut retaining the bracket at the left end of the heater assembly to the dash panel, and the nut retaining the bracket below the case to the dash panel.
8. Carefully pull the heater assembly away from the dash panel to gain access to the screws that retain the heater core access cover to the evaporator (heater) case.
9. Remove the cover retaining screws and the cover.
10. Lift the heater core and seals from the case. Remove the seals from the core tubes.

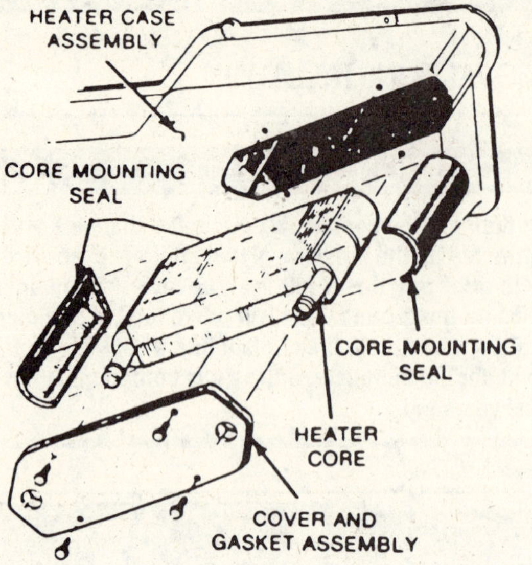

Fig. 12 Exploded view of the heater core on vehicles without A/C — 1983-88 models

11. Install the heater core in the reverse order of removal. Fill the system with the correct coolant mix.
12. Check the operation of the system.

1983-88 Air Conditioned Models

****CAUTION**

When draining the coolant, keep in mind that cats and dogs are attracted by the ethylene glycol antifreeze, and are quite likely to drink any that is left in an uncovered container or in puddles on the ground. This will prove fatal in sufficient quantity. Always drain the coolant into a sealable container. Coolant should be reused unless it is contaminated or several years old.

WITH MANUAL AIR CONDITIONING

See Figure 13

Heater core removal requires instrument panel and heater/evaporator case assembly removal.

1. Disconnect the negative battery cable.
2. Remove the instrument panel. Refer to Section 10, Instrument Panel Removal and Installation.

****WARNING**

Removal of the heater/air conditioner (evaporator) housing, if necessary, requires evacuation of the air conditioner refrigerant. This operation requires special tools and a thorough familiarity with automotive refrigerant systems. Failure to follow proper safety precautions may cause personal injury. If you are not familiar with these systems, it is recommended that discharging and charging of the A/C system be performed by an experienced professional mechanic.

3. Discharge the air conditioning system at the service access gauge port locate on the suction line. See the WARNING notice.
4. Once the air conditioning system has been discharged, remove the high and low pressure hoses. Use a second wrench to hold the fittings when loosening the lines. Plug the hose openings to prevent dirt and moisture from entering.
5. Drain the cooling system and remove the heater hoses from the heater core tubes. Plug the hoses and the heater core tubes.
6. Remove the screw that attaches the air inlet duct and blower housing support brace to the cowl top panel under the dash.
7. Disconnect the vacuum supply hose from the inline vacuum check valve in the engine compartment.
8. Disconnect the blower motor wiring connector.
9. From under the hood, remove the two nuts retaining the evaporator case to the firewall.
10. From under the dash, remove the screw attaching the evaporator case support bracket to the cowl top panel.
11. Remove the nut that retains the bracket below the evaporator case to the dash panel.
12. Carefully pull the evaporator case away from the dash panel and remove the case from the vehicle.
13. Remove the heater core access cover from the evaporator case.
14. Remove the heater core and seals from the case. Remove the seals from the core fitting tubes.
15. Service as required. Install in the reverse order of removal. Fill the cooling system with the correct coolant mix. Have the air conditioning system charged. See the WARNING notice.

WITH AUTOMATIC TEMPERATURE CONTROL

Core removal requires instrument panel and evaporator case assembly removal.

1. Disconnect the negative battery cable.
2. Remove the instrument panel. Refer to Section 10, Instrument Panel Removal and Installation.
3. Discharge the air conditioning system at the service access gauge port located on the suction line. See the WARNING notice.
4. Once the air conditioning system has been discharged, remove the high and low pressure hoses. Use a second wrench to hold the receiver fittings when loosening the lines. Plug the hose openings to prevent dirt and moisture from entering.
5. Drain the cooling system and remove the heater hoses from the heater core tubes. Plug the hoses and heater core tubes.
6. Remove the screw attaching the air inlet duct and blower housing assembly support brace to the top cowl panel under the dash.
7. Disconnect the vacuum supply hose from the inline vacuum check valve and the vacuum hose from the TBL (Thermal Blower Lockout Switch) in the engine compartment.
8. Disconnect the blower motor wiring connector.
9. From under the hood, remove the two nuts retaining the evaporator case to the firewall.
10. From under the dash, remove the screw attaching the evaporator case support bracket to the cowl top panel.
11. Remove the screw retaining the bracket below the evaporator case and dash panel.

12. Carefully pull the evaporator case assembly away from the dash panel and remove the assembly from the vehicle.
13. Remove the heater core access cover screws and the cover.
14. Lift the heater core and seals from the case assembly.
15. Remove the seals from the core.
16. Service as required. Install in the reverse order of removal. Fill the cooling system with the correct mixture of coolant. Have the air conditioning system recharged. See WARNING notice!

1989-93 Models

See Figure 14

The instrument panel must be removed to remove the heater assembly.

1. Disconnect the negative battery cable.
2. Disconnect the underhood wiring at the left side of dash panel.
3. Disengage the wiring connector from the dash panel and push the wiring harness into the passenger compartment.
4. Remove the steering column lower trim cover by removing the three screws at the bottom, one screw on the left side, and pull to disengage the five snap-in retainers across top.
5. Remove the six screws retaining steering column lower opening reinforcement, and remove it from the instrument panel.
6. Remove the steering column upper and lower shrouds, and disconnect the wiring from the steering column.
7. Remove the shift interlock switch.
8. Disconnect the steering column lower universal joint.
9. Support the steering column and remove the four nuts retaining column to the support bracket. Remove the column from the vehicle.
10. Remove the one screw retaining the left side of the instrument panel to the parking brake bracket.
11. Reinstall the steering column lower opening reinforcement using only four screws (one in each corner).

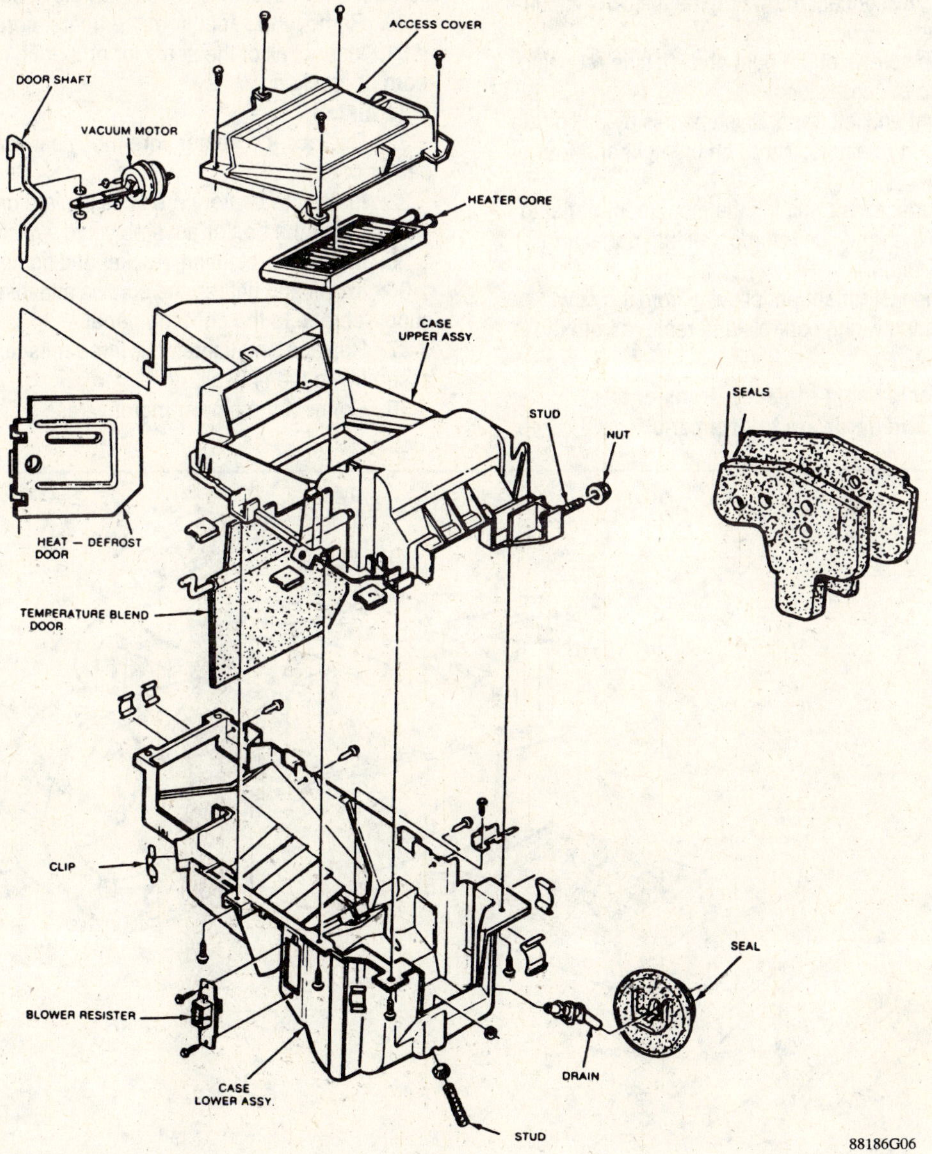

Fig. 13 Exploded view of the heater unit — 1983-84 models

➥ Reinforcement prevents instrument panel from twisting when being removed from vehicle.

12. Remove the right and left cowl side trim panels.
13. To remove the console assembly from vehicle:
    a. Open the console door and remove the container and mat to gain access to the two console-to-floorpan retaining screws. Then remove the screws.
    b. Remove the gear shift knob on the 5-speed transmission only.
    c. Remove the two rear finish panel retaining screws. Tilt the finish panel forward, disconnect the electrical connectors and remove the panel.
    d. Remove the two front console-to-instrument panel retaining screws and remove the console.
14. Remove the two nuts retaining the center of instrument panel to the floor (tunnel).
15. Open the glove compartment, squeeze the sides of the bin and lower it to the full open position.
16. From underneath the instrument panel and through glove compartment opening, disconnect the wiring, heater, A/C vacuum lines and control cables.
17. Remove the two screws at the right and left side retaining the instrument panel to the cowl sides.
18. Remove the right and left upper finish panels by pulling up to disengage the snap-in retainers. Three on the right and four on the left sides.
19. Remove the four screws retaining the instrument panel to the cowl top. Remove the right and left roof rail trim panel and the door frame weatherstrip.
20. Carefully pull the instrument panel away from the cowl. Disconnect any remaining wiring controls and remove from the vehicle.

➥ If instrument panel is being replaced, transfer all components, wiring and hardware to new panel.

21. Remove the right side instrument panel brace located above the heater case and attached to the cowl.
22. Drain the engine coolant from the cooling system and remove the hoses from the heater core. Plug the hoses and the core.
23. Disconnect the vacuum supply hose (black) from the inline vacuum check valve in the engine compartment.
24. Disconnect the blower motor wire harness from the resistor and motor lead.
25. Working under the hood, remove the three nuts retaining the heater assembly to the firewall.
26. In the passenger compartment, remove the screw attaching the heater assembly support bracket to the cowl top panel.
27. Remove the one screw retaining the bracket below the heater assembly to the dash panel.
28. Carefully pull the heater assembly away from the dash panel and remove the assembly from vehicle.
29. Remove the four heater core access cover attaching screws, and the access cover from the case.
30. Remove the seal from the heater core tubes.
31. Inspect all of the seals for proper fit, replace if they are worn or cracked.

To install:

32. Replace the heater core tube seal when installing the heater core.
33. Install the heater core access plate and tighten the screws.
34. Place the heater assembly into vehicle.
35. Install the retaining bracket and tighten the screw.
36. Install and tighten the screws attaching heater assembly support brace to the cowl top panel.
37. Replace and tighten the three nuts that secure the heater assembly to the firewall.
38. Connect the blower motor wires.

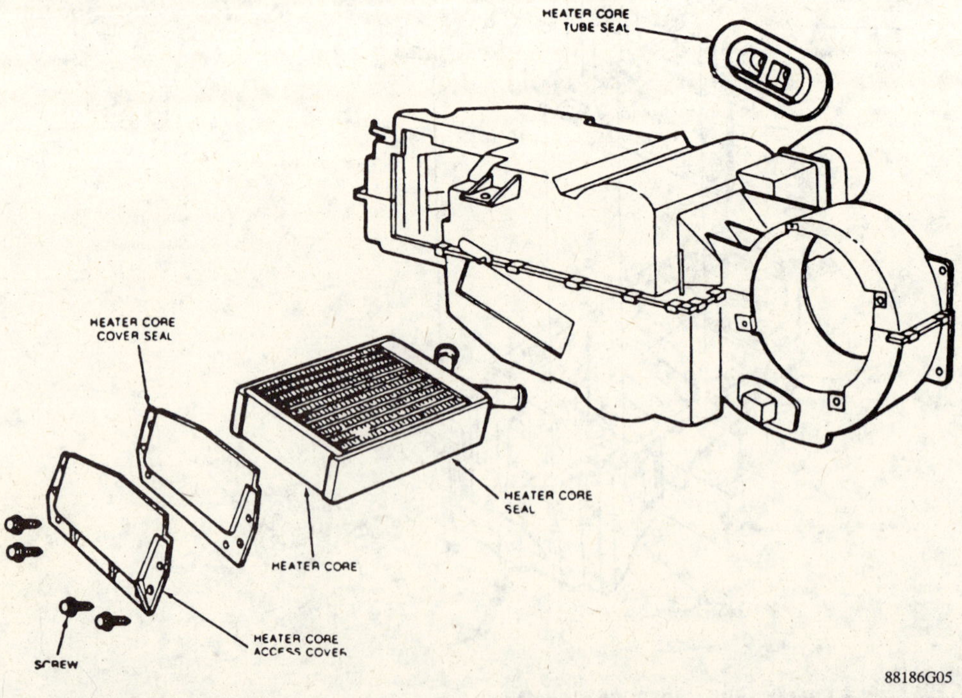

Fig. 14 Exploded view of the heater core

39. Connect the vacuum supply line.
40. Connect the heater hoses and tighten clamps. If possible, pressure check the cooling system before installing the instrument panel.
41. Install the instrument panel and steering column. Before installing the final trim pieces, connect the battery cables and make sure all systems function properly.
42. Refill cooling system using proper engine coolant.

1994-96 Models

➥ The instrument panel and steering column must be removed to remove the heater assembly. Two people are required to remove the assembly from the vehicle.

1. Disconnect negative battery cable. Disconnect positive battery cable and wait one minute for air bag diagnostic monitor to deplete the backup power supply.
2. Loosen main wiring connector bolt in the engine compartment at the left side of dash panel and separate connectors.
3. Remove radio antenna stanchion and disconnect cable from base of the radio antenna stanchion.
4. Remove both the right hand and left hand windshield side garnish mouldings.

➥ Do not remove safety belt retaining bolts in next step.

5. Remove the screws retaining both the right and left front door scuff plates and remove the front door opening weather-strips from body flanges.
6. Remove the right and left cowl side trim panels.
7. Remove the steering column cover by removing the three screws along the bottom and pull on the cover to unsnap the three clips across the top of the instrument panel steering column cover.
8. Remove the ignition switch lock cylinder.
9. Remove the four screws retaining the steering column shrouds together and remove the steering column shrouds.
10. Install the ignition switch lock cylinder to prevent the steering wheel from turning.
11. Disconnect the wiring connectors at the turn signal and windshield wiper switch.
12. Remove the one screw and A/C evaporator register duct from under the steering column tube.
13. Disconnect the wiring connectors at the bottom of the steering column tube.
14. Remove the pinch bolt attaching the steering column tube to the steering column lower yoke and slightly spread the joint with a screwdriver.
15. While supporting the steering column tube, remove the four steering column tube retaining nuts.
16. Remove the interlock cable retaining screws and shift actuator cable fitting.
17. Carefully remove the steering column tube from the vehicle.
18. Loosen the main wiring connector bolt at the left side of the steering column opening and separate the connectors.
19. Disconnect the stoplight switch wiring connector. On the manual transmission, disconnect the clutch pedal position switch wiring connector.
20. Pull back the floor carpet as required on the left and right sides of the vehicle and disconnect the window regulator safety relay switch wiring, and the powertrain control module from the main wiring.
21. Open the glove compartment to the stop, unsnap the hydraulic lift from the right side.
22. Remove the three screws at the bottom retaining the glove compartment door hinge and glove compartment to the instrument panel.
23. Remove the glove compartment.
24. Reach through the glove compartment opening and disconnect the wiring and vacuum hoses/connector from the heater-A/C evaporator housing.
25. Disconnect the wiring connector from the speed control amplifier and bracket assembly.
26. Remove floor console panel:
    a. Open the console panel glove compartment door to access screws to console finish panel.
    b. Remove the two screws, and lift the rear of the console finish panel to unsnap retainers.
    c. Reach under the console finish panel and disconnect wires to fog lamp and ride control switches (if equipped) and cigar lighter socket and retainer.
    d. Lift the rear of the console finish panel and slide rearward to release the two front locating tabs, remove console finish panel.
    e. With the console panel door open, remove the console glove compartment mat.
    f. Remove the center screw from the console (rear of shifter) bin, then lift the bin from the console panel. Disconnect the luggage compartment door release switch and fuel filler door lock switch (if equipped).
    g. Remove the two screws from the bottom of the console panel bin to floor pan.
    h. Remove the two cups and screws. Remove the floor console panel.
    i. Remove the two screws retaining the front of the floor console panel to the instrument panel. Disconnect the remaining wires (main jumper wire) and main wiring, then lift the console panel from the vehicle.

➥ Protect the instrument panel surface during next step.

27. Using a putty knife or similar tool, insert under the left or right corner of the instrument panel upper finish panel and pry up on the instrument panel upper finish panel to release one snap clip.
28. Unsnap the remaining four clips pulling up by hand, working toward the opposite side of the vehicle.
29. Remove the two nuts retaining the left side of the instrument panel to the cowl side.
30. Remove the two nuts and one bolt retaining the instrument panel to the console bracket.
31. Remove the nut attaching the right side of the instrument panel to cowl side.

➥ The following steps require two people.

32. Remove the six bolts retaining the top of the instrument panel to the dash panel.
33. Carefully pull the instrument panel away from the windshield glass while checking for and disconnecting any remaining wiring connectors. Disengage the antenna wire grommet from the sheet metal and pull the radio antenna lead in cable through.
34. Remove the right side instrument panel brace located above the heater case and attached to the cowl.

35. Drain the engine coolant from the cooling system, then remove the hoses from the heater core. Plug the hoses and the core.
36. Properly discharge the air conditioning system into freon recovery equipment.
37. Disconnect the vacuum supply hose (black) from the inline vacuum check valve in the engine compartment.
38. Disconnect the blower motor wire harness from the resistor and motor lead.
39. Working under the hood, remove the three nuts retaining the heater assembly to the firewall.
40. In the passenger compartment, remove the screw attaching the heater assembly support bracket to the cowl top panel.
41. Remove the one screw retaining the bracket below the heater assembly to the dash panel.
42. Carefully pull the heater assembly away from the dash panel and remove the assembly from vehicle.
43. Remove the four heater core access cover attaching screws, and the access cover from the case.
44. Remove the seal from the heater core tubes.
45. Inspect all seals for proper fit, replace if worn or cracked.

To install:

46. Replace the heater core tube seal.
47. Install the heater core and the access plate, then tighten the screws.
48. Place the heater assembly into vehicle.
49. Install the retaining bracket and tighten screw.
50. Install and tighten the screws attaching the heater assembly support brace to the cowl top panel.
51. Replace and tighten the three nuts that secure the heater assembly to the firewall.
52. Connect the blower motor wires.
53. Connect the vacuum supply line.
54. Connect the heater hoses and tighten the clamps. Pressure test the cooling system to check the heater core installation.
55. Carefully place instrument panel to windshield glass while connecting wiring connectors.
56. Install the six bolts retaining the top of the instrument panel to dash panel.
57. Install the nut attaching the right side of the instrument panel to cowl side.
58. Install the two nuts and one bolt retaining the instrument panel to the console bracket.
59. Install the two nuts retaining the left side of the instrument panel to cowl side.
60. Snap the clips in place, working toward the opposite side of the vehicle.
61. Install the floor console panel.
62. Connect the wiring harness to the speed control amplifier and bracket assembly.
63. Reach through the glove compartment opening and connect the wiring and vacuum hoses/connector from the heater-A/C evaporator housing.
64. Install the glove compartment.
65. Install the three screws at the bottom retaining the glove compartment door hinge and glove compartment to the instrument panel.
66. Open the glove compartment to the stop, snap in the hydraulic lift from the right side.
67. Connect the window regulator safety relay switch wiring and the powertrain control module from the main wiring.
68. Attach the stoplight switch wiring connector and on manual transmission. Connect the clutch pedal position switch wiring.
69. Carefully install the steering column tube into the vehicle.
70. Install the interlock cable retaining screws and shift actuator cable fitting.
71. While supporting the steering column tube, install the four steering column tube retaining nuts.
72. Install the pinch bolt attaching the steering column tube to steering column lower yoke.
73. Connect the wiring at the bottom of the steering column tube.
74. Install the one screw and A/C evaporator register duct from under the steering column tube.
75. Connect the wiring at the turn signal and windshield wiper switch.
76. Remove the ignition switch lock cylinder which was temporarily installed to prevent the steering wheel from turning.
77. Install the four screws retaining the steering column shrouds together, then install the steering column shrouds.
78. Install the ignition switch lock cylinder.
79. Install the steering column.
80. Install the right and left cowl side trim panels.
81. Install the screws retaining both right and left front door scuff plates, then install the front door opening weather-strips to body flanges.
82. Install both the right hand and left hand windshield side garnish mouldings.
83. Install the radio antenna stanchion and connect cable to base of the radio antenna stanchion.
84. Connect the main wiring and tighten bolt.
85. Connect the battery cables.
86. Refill the cooling system using proper engine coolant.
87. Evacuate and recharge the air conditioning system.

Control Panel

REMOVAL & INSTALLATION

1983 Models

➧ See Figure 15

1. Disconnect the negative battery cable.
2. Remove the 4 control assembly-to-instrument panel screws.
3. Pull the control panel towards you.
4. Disconnect the wiring from the panel connectors.
5. Disconnect the vacuum harness and the temperature control cable from the control panel.

To install:

6. Attach the vacuum harness and control cables to the unit.

➡ Push on the vacuum harness retaining nut, DO NOT TRY TO SCREW IT ON!

7. Connect the wiring to the control assembly.
8. Insert the unit into the dash, tighten the four mounting screws.
9. Connect the negative battery cable.
10. Adjust the cables as necessary.

1984–88 Models

➧ See Figures 16 and 17

1. Disconnect the negative battery cable.
2. Remove the temperature control knob from the lever shaft (on 1985 and later models only).
3. Remove the instrument cluster opening finish panel.
4. Remove the 4 screws attaching the control panel to the instrument panel.
5. Pull the control panel out and disconnect the wiring from the control panel.
6. Disconnect the vacuum harness and the temperature control cable from the control panel.

To install:

7. Attach the vacuum harness and temperature control cable to the control panel.

➥ Remember that the vacuum harness nut is a pushnut. It does not screw on.

8. Connect the wiring to the control unit.
9. Insert the unit into the dash, tighten the four screws to retain the unit in the vehicle.

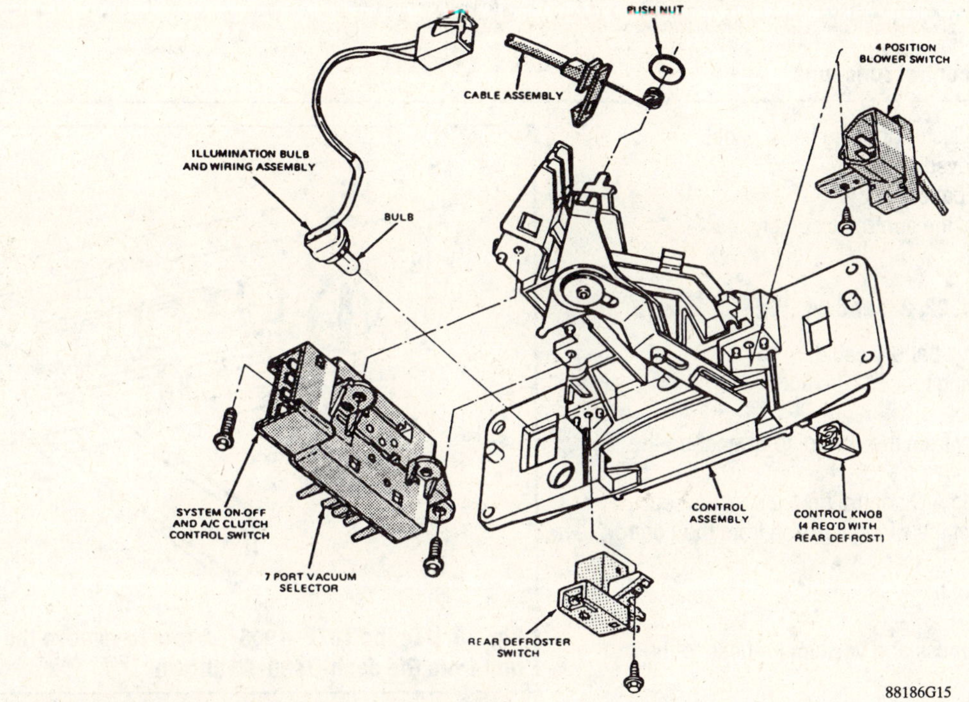

Fig. 15 Automatic temperature control unit — 1983 models

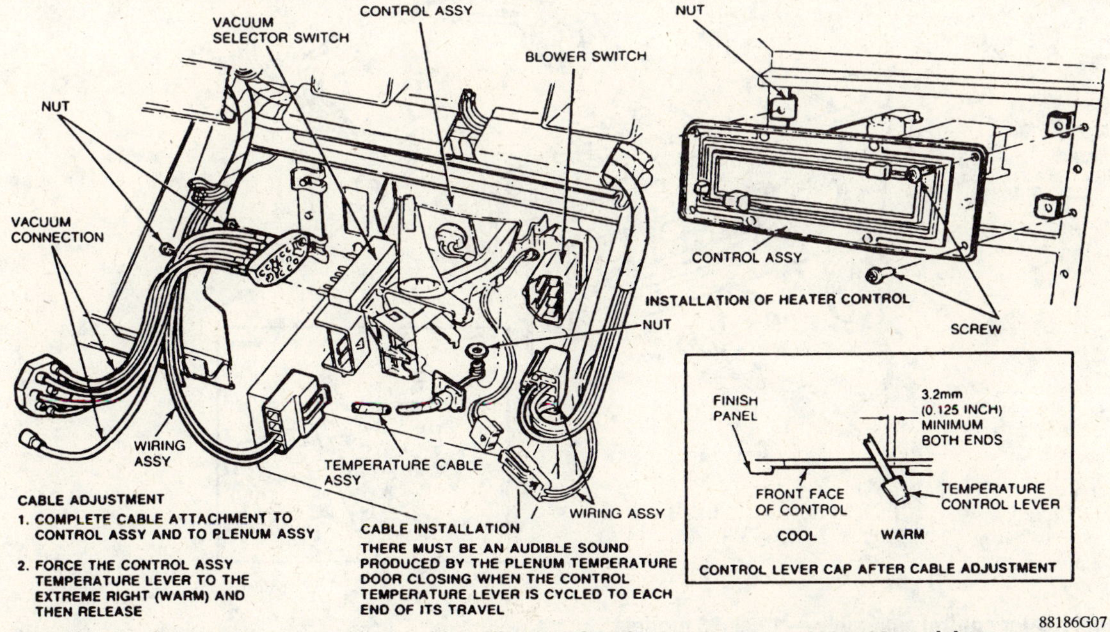

Fig. 16 Exploded view of the heater control assembly with associated components — 1984–88 models

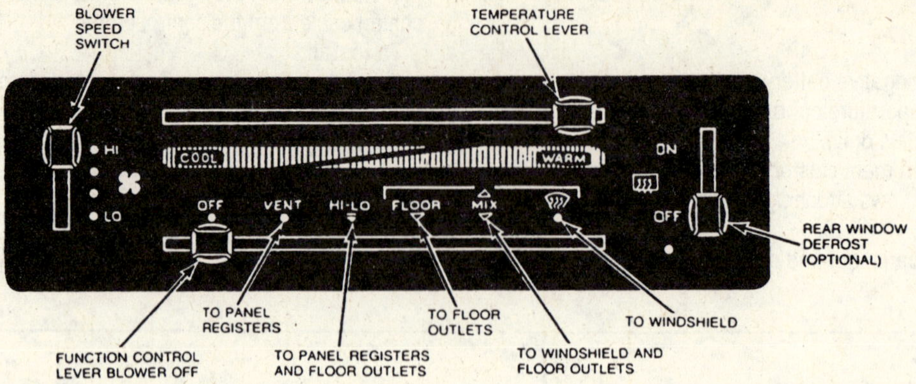

Fig. 17 Common heater control functions

10. Install the instrument cluster opening finish panel.
11. Install the knob if removed.
12. Connect the negative battery cable.
13. Check the operation of the control assembly.

1989-96 Models

➧ See Figures 18, 19, 20, 21, 22, 23, and 24

1. Disconnect the negative battery cable.
2. Insert the radio removing tool T87P-19061-A or equivalent in the retaining clip.
3. Apply a side load away from the control to disengage the clips.
4. Pull the semi-automatic A/C control from the instrument panel opening and disconnect the wiring harness from the control assembly.
5. Disconnect the vacuum harness.

To install:

6. Connect the wiring harness and vacuum harness to the control assembly.

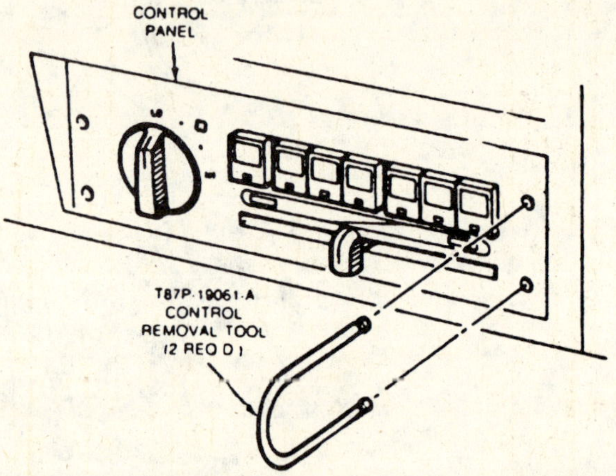

Fig. 18 Use the T87P-19061-A tool to remove the control unit from the dash-1989-93 shown

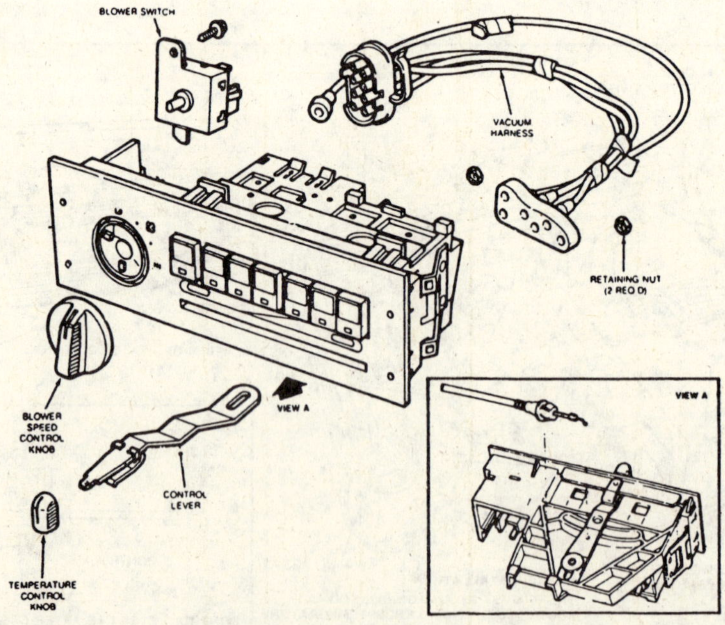

Fig. 19 Manual heater control assembly — 1989-93 models

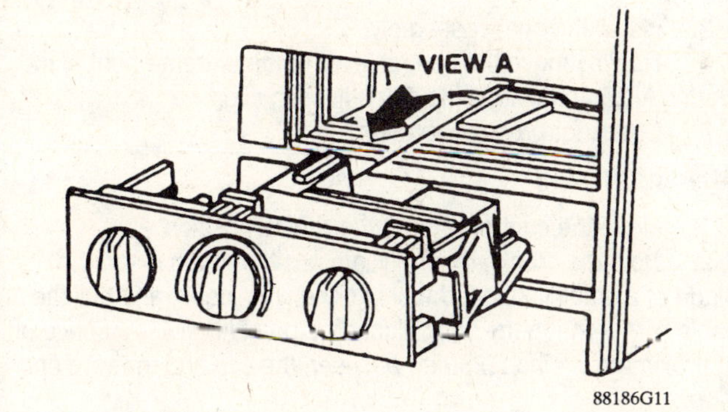

Fig. 20 Manual A/C heater control assembly — 1994-96 models

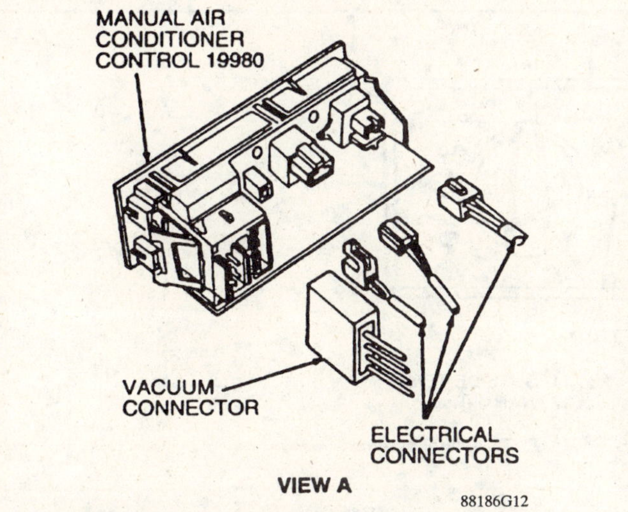

Fig. 21 Manual A/C heater control wiring harness connections — 1994-96 models

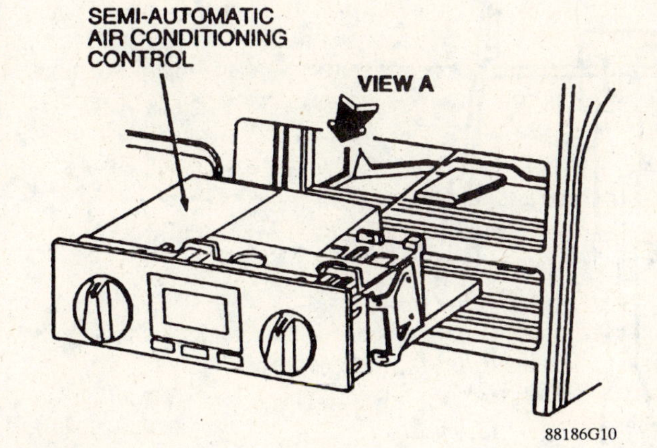

Fig. 22 Semi-automatic A/C heater control assembly — 1994-96 models

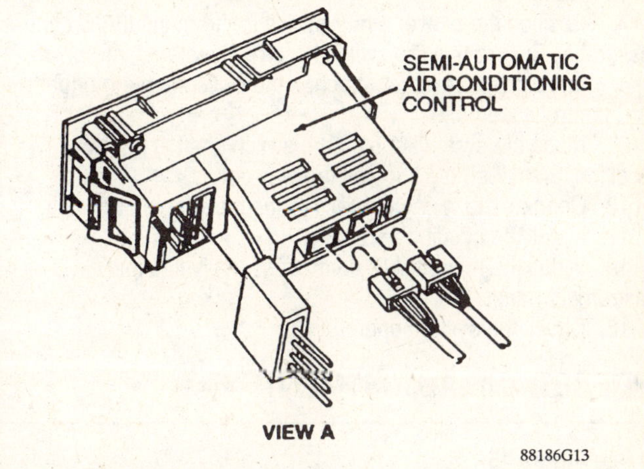

Fig. 23 Semi-automatic A/C heater control wiring harness connections — 1994-96 models

7. Position the control assembly into the instrument panel opening. Engage it into the track in the instrument panel, then push the unit in until it latches firmly into place.
8. Connect the negative battery cable.
9. Check the system for proper operation.

Blower Switch

REMOVAL & INSTALLATION

Without Climate Control

1. Disconnect the negative battery cable.
2. Remove the control assembly from the instrument panel.
3. Remove the switch knob.
4. Remove the screw from the underside of the control assembly, attaching the switch to the control assembly.
5. Disconnect the wire connector from the switch and remove the switch.

To Install:

6. Position the switch in the control assembly making sure the pins are inserted into the holes of the switch mounting plate.
7. Install the screw to attach the switch to the control assembly.
8. Connect the wire harness connector to the switch.
9. Install the control assembly in the instrument panel.
10. Place the switch knob on the switch shaft and push the knob all the way on.
11. Check the system for proper operation.

With Climate Control

1. Remove the climate control assembly.
2. Place the blower motor switch in the **LO** position, then pull the knob off of the switch shaft.
3. Detach the wiring connector from the heater blower motor switch.
4. Remove the circuit board cover.
5. Remove the one screw that retains the blower motor switch to the manual A/C control assembly.
6. Rotate the blower motor switch to disengage the locking tab. Pull the blower motor switch away from the housing, disengaging the knob.

To install:

7. Position the blower motor switch in the manual A/C control assembly. Ensure that the switch is correctly rotated into place.
8. Install the screw that attaches the switch to the manual A/C control assembly.
9. Place the switch knob on the switch shaft in the **LO** position, then push the knob all the way on.
10. Connect the wiring harness to the blower motor switch.
11. Install the circuit board cover.
12. Install the manual A/C control assembly into the instrument panel.
13. Check the system operation.

PRESET AND ADJUSTMENT

➧ See Figure 25

Before installation

1. Insert the blade of a small tool into the wire end loop (crank arm end) of the control cable.
2. Grip the self adjusting clip with a pair of pliers, then slide it down the control wire away from the loop approximately 1 inch (25mm).
3. Install the cable assembly.
4. Rapidly move the control lever to the extreme right of the slot (WARM) to position the self adjusting clip.
5. Check for proper operation.

After installation

1. Move the control lever to the COOL position.
2. Hold the crank arm firmly into position, then insert the blade of a small flatbladed tool into the wire loops, and pull the cable wire through the self adjusting clip until there is a space of approximately 1 inch (25mm) between the clip and the wire end loop.
3. Rapidly move the control lever to the extreme right of the slot (WARM) to position the self adjusting clip.
4. Check for proper operation.

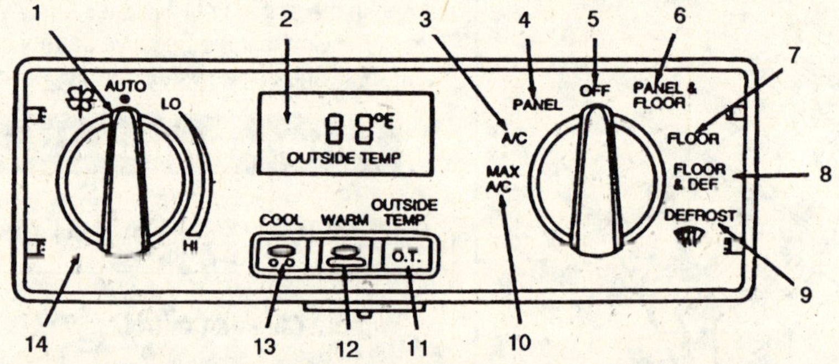

1. Blower switch (part of 19C933)
2. Digital display window (part of 19C933)
3. A/C
4. PANEL
5. OFF
6. PANEL and FLOOR
7. FLOOR
8. FLOOR and DEFROST
9. DEFROST
10. MAX A/C
11. OUTSIDE TEMP
12. WARM (Red)
13. Cool (Blue)
14. SATC control assembly

88186G09

Fig. 24 Semi-automatic A/C heater control knobs — 1994-96 models

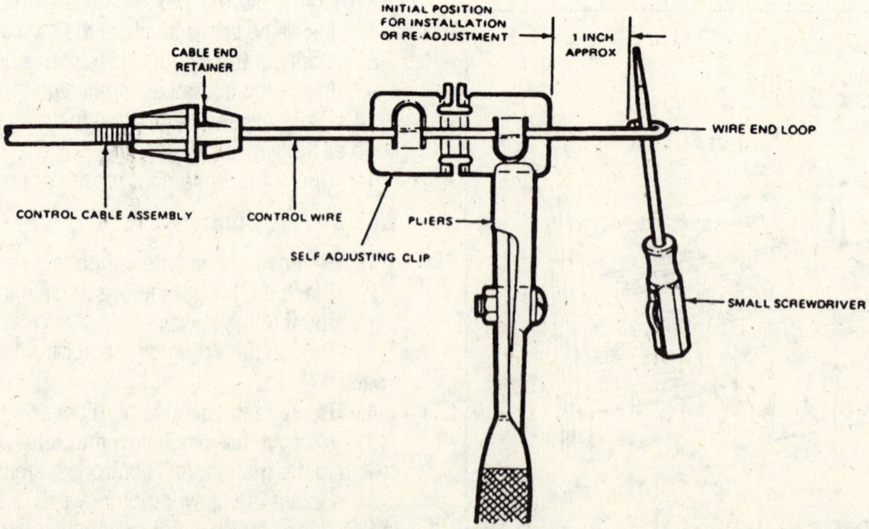

88186G46

Fig. 25 Adjustment procedure for the temperature control cable

AIR CONDITIONER

Although this section covers the removal and installation of the various components of the A/C, it is recommended that an approved SAE Recycling/Recovery A/C unit be used to discharge and charge the system. Refer to Section 1 for the proper procedures.

Compressor

REMOVAL & INSTALLATION

****CAUTION**

The compressed refrigerant used in air conditioning system expands into the atmosphere at a temperature of -21.7°F (-30°C) or lower. This will freeze any surface, including your eyes, that it contacts. In addition, the refrigerant decomposes into a poisonous gas in the presence of a flame, and is harmful to Earth's atmosphere. If discharging A/C system is necessary use an EPA safety approved Recovery/Recycling system, refer to Section 1.

FS-6 Axial Compressor

1983 WITH 3.8L ENGINE

➧ See Figure 26

1. Discharge the refrigerant system. See Section 1.
2. Disconnect the two refrigerant lines from the compressor. Cap the openings immediately!
3. Remove tension from the drive belt. Remove the belt
4. Disconnect the clutch wire at the connector.
5. Remove the bolt attaching the support brace to the front brace and the nut attaching the support brace to the intake manifold. Remove the support brace.
6. Remove the two bolts attaching the rear support to the bracket.
7. Remove the bolt attaching the compressor tab to the front brace and the two bolts attaching the compressor front legs to the bracket.
8. Remove the compressor.
9. Installation is the reverse of removal. Use new O-rings coated with clean refrigerant oil at all fittings. New, replacement compressors contain 10 oz. of refrigerant oil. Prior to installation, pour off 4 oz. of oil. This will maintain the oil charge in the system. Evacuate, charge and leak test the system.
10. Check the operation of the system.

1983-93 5.0L MODELS WITH MANUAL AIR CONDITIONING

➧ See Figures 27 and 28

1. Discharge the refrigerant system. See Section 1.
2. Disconnect the two refrigerant lines from the compressor. Cap the openings immediately!
3. Remove tension from the drive belt. Remove the belt
4. Disconnect the clutch wire at the connector.
5. Remove the two nuts from the rear support bracket. Remove the three bolts from the front bosses on the bracket. On 1985-86 models, remove one bolt from the front of the tubular brace and remove the tubular brace.
6. Rotate the compressor towards the left side of the engine compartment until the compressor upper boss clears the support.
7. Remove the compressor and rear support as an assembly.
8. Installation is the reverse of removal. Use new O-rings coated with clean refrigerant oil at all fittings. New, replacement compressors contain 10 oz. of refrigerant oil. Prior to installation, pour off 4 oz. of oil. This will maintain the oil charge in the system. Evacuate, charge and leak test the system.

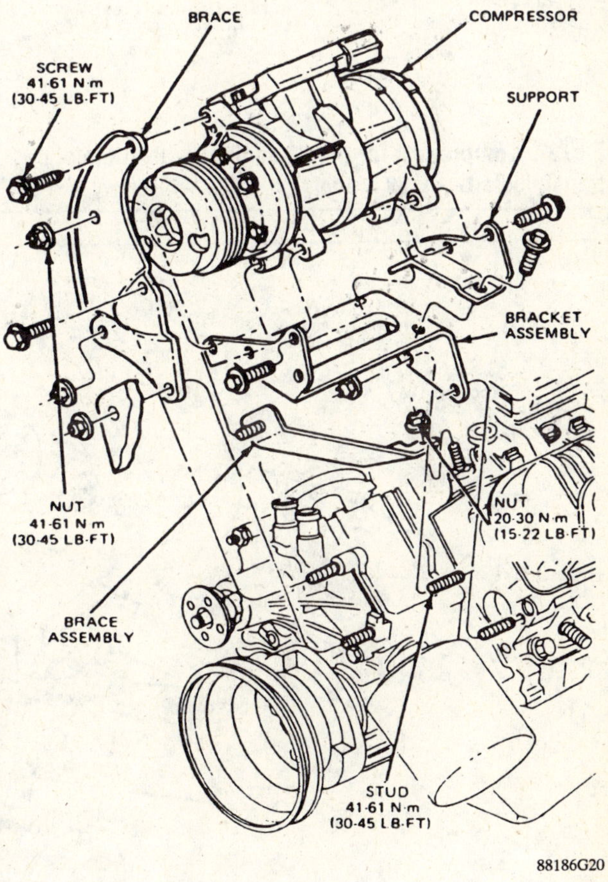

Fig. 26 A/C compressor mounting 3.8L FS-6

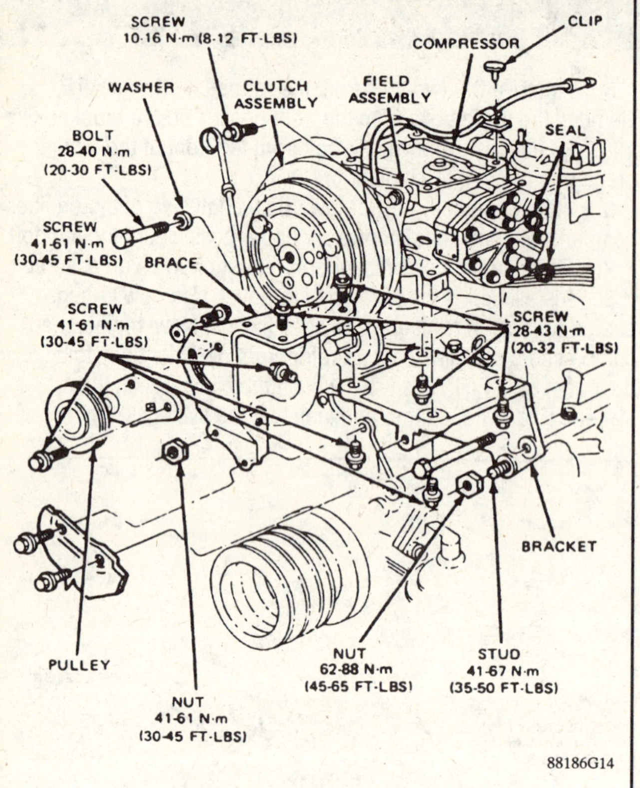

Fig. 27 Compressor for the V8 engines with automatic transmission — 1983 models

1986–93 5.0L MODELS WITH AUTOMATIC TEMPERATURE CONTROL

➧ **See Figure 29**

1. Discharge the refrigerant system. See Section 1.
2. Disconnect the two refrigerant lines from the compressor. Cap the openings immediately!
3. Remove tension from the drive belt. Remove the belt
4. Disconnect the clutch wire at the connector.
5. Remove the two bolts attaching the rear compressor brace to the power steering pump support. Remove the three bolts attaching the front bosses of the compressor to the power steering pump and the compressor brace.
6. Remove the compressor and rear support as an assembly.

To install:

➥ New, replacement compressors contain 10 fl. oz. of refrigerant oil. Prior to installation, pour off 4 fl. oz. of oil. This will maintain the oil charge in the system.

7. Place the compressor into position.
8. Install all bolts finger-tight before tightening any of them. Use new O-rings coated with clean refrigerant oil at all fittings.
9. Install the two bolts attaching the rear compressor brace to the power steering pump support. Install the three bolts attaching the front bosses of the compressor to the power steering pump and the compressor brace.
10. Connect the clutch wire at the connector.
11. Install the compressor belt.
12. Connect the two refrigerant lines to the compressor.
13. Evacuate, charge and leak test the system.
14. Check the operation of the system.

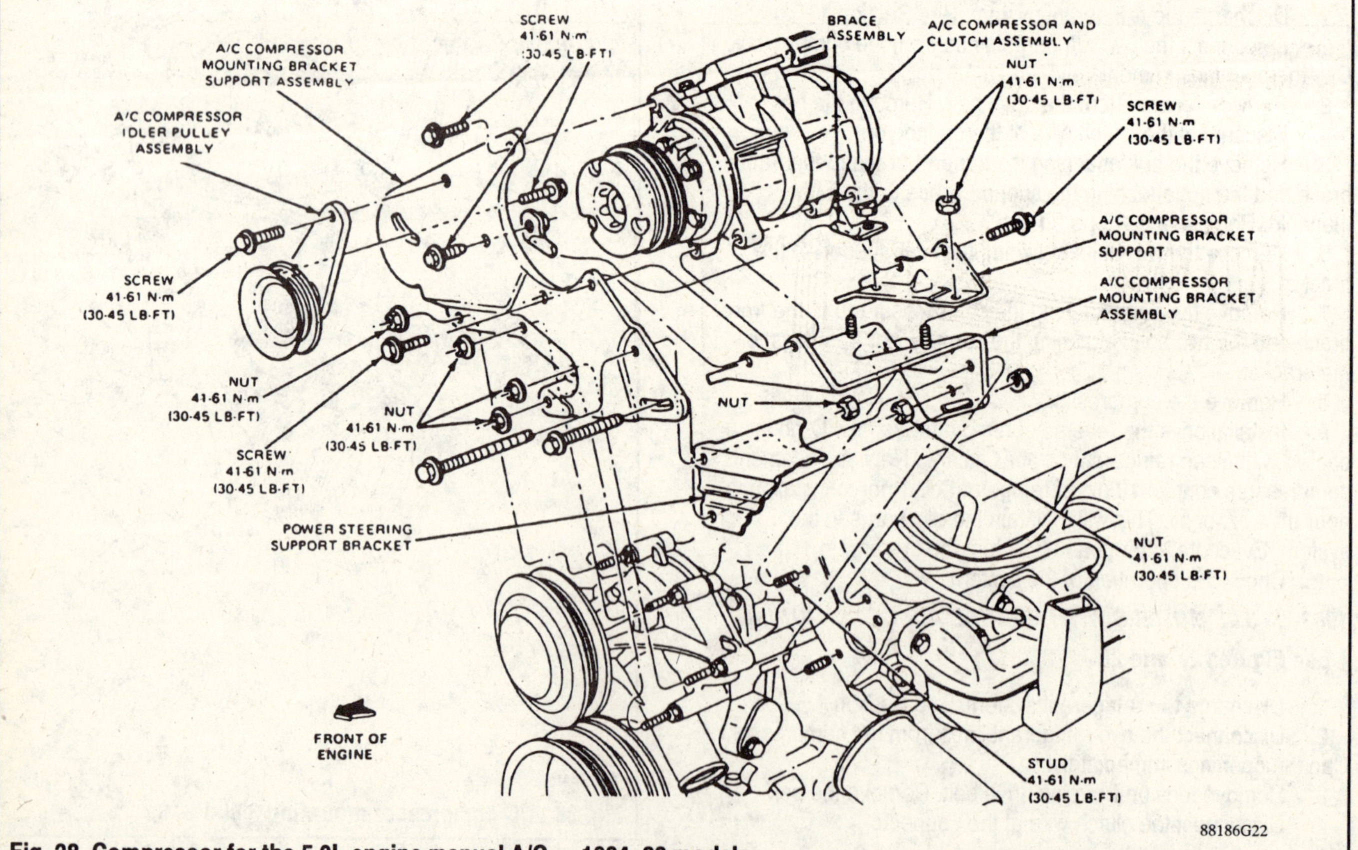

Fig. 28 Compressor for the 5.0L engine manual A/C — 1984–88 models

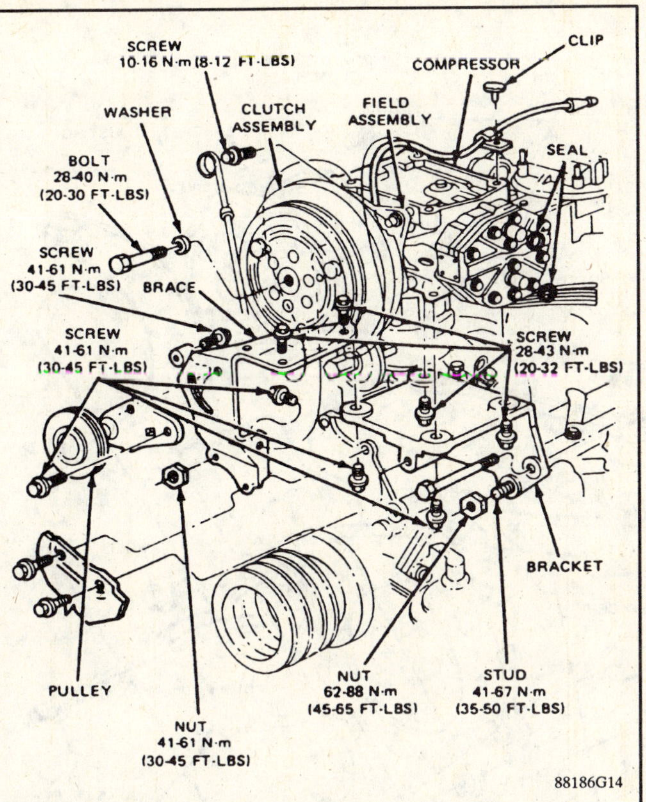

Fig. 29 Exploded view of the compressor for the 5.0L engine with automatic temperature control — 1985–88 models

HR-980 Radial Compressor

1983–92 WITH 2.3L, 3.8L ENGINES AND MANUAL AIR CONDITIONING

See Figures 30 and 31

1. Discharge the refrigerant system. See Section 1.
2. Disconnect the two refrigerant lines from the compressor. Cap the openings immediately!
3. Remove the bolt and washer from the adjusting bracket and remove the drive belts.
4. Remove the bolt attaching the compressor bracket to the compressor lower mounting lug.
5. Remove the compressor.

To install:

If a new compressor is being installed, it contains 8 fl. oz. of refrigerant oil. Prior to installing the compressor, drain 4 fl. oz. of the oil from the compressor. This will maintain the oil charge in the system.

6. Place the compressor into position, then loosely attach the mounting bolts.
7. Place the drive belt onto the compressor, then tighten the mounting bolts and the adjusting bolt.
8. Install new O-rings to the refrigerant lines. Only use new O-rings, coat them with refrigerant oil. Attach the lines in their proper places.
9. Evacuate, charge and leak test the system.
10. Check the belt adjustment again.
11. Test the operation of the system.
12. Check the operation of the system.

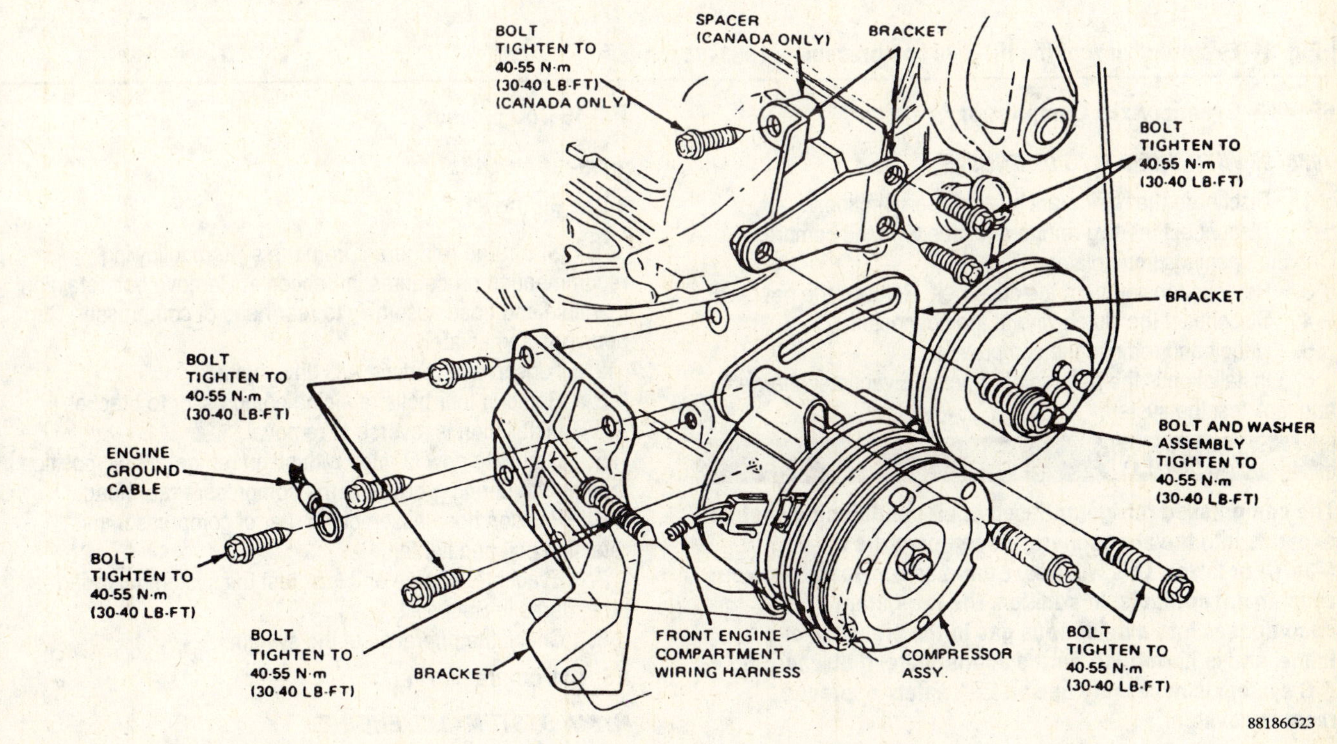

Fig. 30 Exploded view of the compressor for the 2.3L turbo engines — 1983–84 models

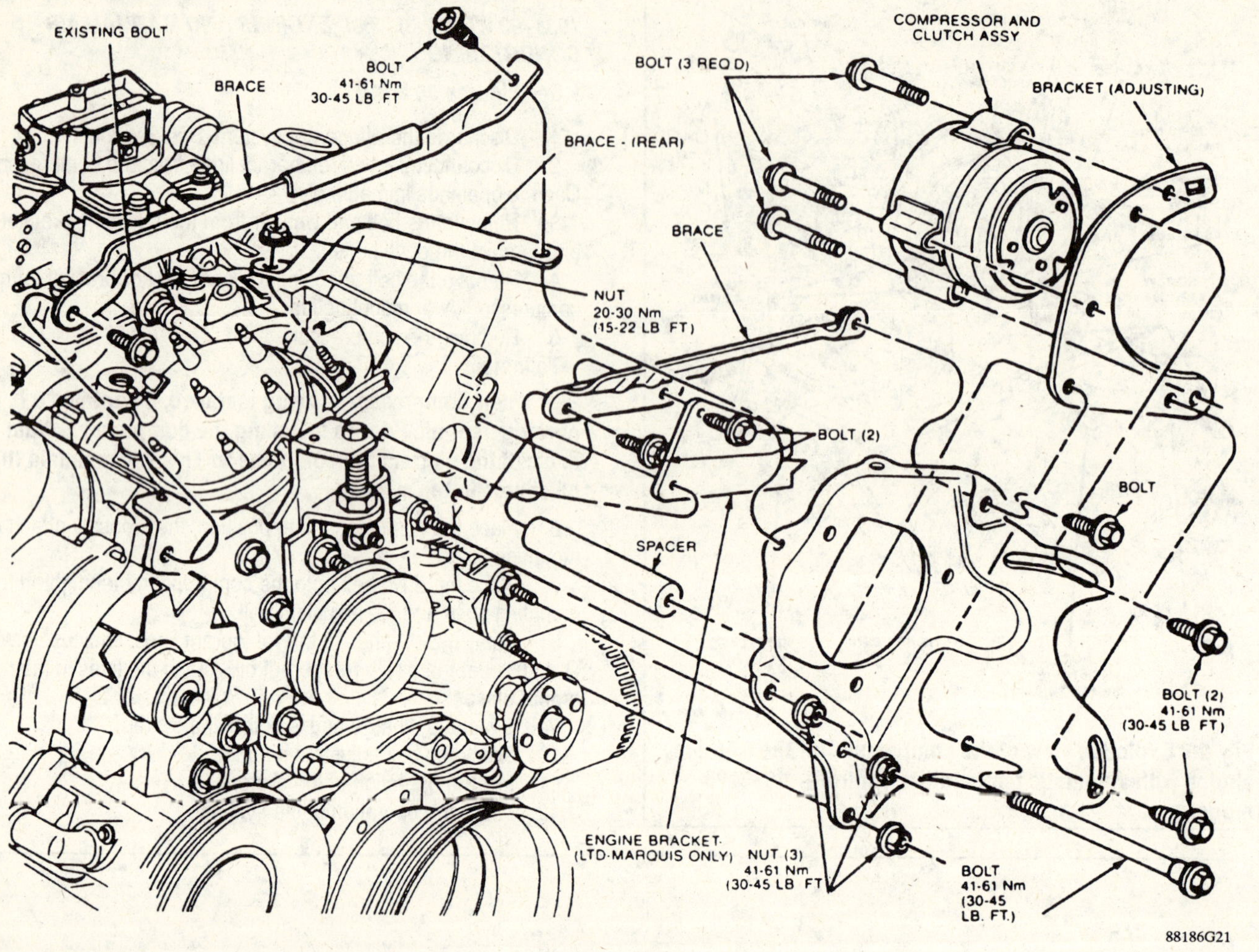

Fig. 31 Exploded view of the HR-980 compressor — 1983-88 models

6P148 3-Cylinder Axial Compressor

1986-93 WITH THE 3.8L, 5.0L ENGINE

1. Discharge the refrigerant system. See Section 1.
2. Disconnect the two refrigerant lines from the compressor. Cap the openings immediately!
3. Remove tension from the drive belt. Remove the belt
4. Disconnect the clutch wire at the connector.
5. Unbolt and remove the compressor.
6. Installation is the reverse of removal. Evacuate, charge and leak test the system.

✻✻CAUTION

The compressed refrigerant used in air conditioning system expands into the atmosphere at a temperature of -21.7°F (-30°C) or lower. This will freeze any surface, including your eyes, that it contacts. In addition, the refrigerant decomposes into a poisonous gas in the presence of a flame, and is harmful to Earths atmosphere. If discharging A/C system is necessary use an EPA safety approved recovery system.

FX-15 Compressor

1988-92 MODELS

➧ See Figure 32

1. Discharge refrigerant from the system following recommended procedures in Section 1. Remove bolt retaining manifold and hose assembly to rear head of compressor. Cap openings immediately.
2. Loosen and remove A/C drive belt.
3. Remove four bolts retaining compressor to bracket.
4. Installation is reverse of removal.
5. Lubricate new O-rings with clean refrigerant oil, position them in the O-ring grooves of the compressor rear head.
6. Position hose assembly to rear of compressor install retaining bolt and tighten.
7. Evacuate, charge and leak test the system following procedures in Section 1.
8. Check the operation of the system.

FS-10 Compressor

R134A SYSTEM-3.8L ENGINE

➧ See Figures 33 and 34

Replacement of the suction accumulator/drier is necessary when the A/C compressor is replaced. The A/C evaporator core orifice should be replaced whenever the A/C compressor is replaced due to lack of performance.

1. Discharge the system following the recommended service procedures in Section 1. Observe all of the safety precautions.
2. Remove the A/C compressor drive belt.
3. Disconnect the A/C clutch wires at the compressor clutch field coil connector on the compressor.
4. Remove the suction/discharge manifold and tube assembly from the compressor. Cap the suction and discharge ports in the manifold and tube assembly and compressor to prevent any entry of moisture and dirt.
5. Remove the four bolts retaining the compressor to the mounting bracket, then remove the compressor from the vehicle.

To install:

6. Install compressor oil into the unit, 7 oz. (207 ml).
7. Position the compressor on the mounting bracket, then install the four bolts, tighten to 31–44 ft. lbs. (41–61 Nm).
8. Remove the protective caps, then install the suction and discharge\ manifold and tube assembly on the compressor. tighten the retaining bolts to 12–17 ft. lbs. (17–23 Nm)
9. Connect the A/C clutch wires to the clutch field coil connector.
10. Install the A/C compressor drive belt.
11. Perform a leak test, evacuate and charge the system following the recommended service procedures. Be sure to observe all safety precautions.
12. Check the operation of the system.

4.6L ENGINE

1. Disconnect the engine cooling fan wire assembly.
2. Unscrew the cooling fan and remove.
3. Remove the engine drive belt.
4. Disconnect the A/C compressor wire assembly.
5. Remove the upper compressor retaining bolts.
6. Safely raise and support the vehicle.
7. Disconnect the knock sensor.
8. Remove the lower compressor bolts.
9. Remove the A/C manifold and tube.
10. Remove the compressor.

To install:

11. Position and install the lower compressor retaining bolts. Tighten the bolts to 31–44 ft. lbs. (41–61 Nm).
12. Attach the knock sensor wiring.
13. Lower the vehicle.
14. Install the upper compressor retaining bolts. Tighten the bolts to 31–44 ft. lbs. (41–61 Nm).
15. Install the A/C manifold and tube. Tighten the bolts to 12–17 ft. lbs. (17–23 Nm).
16. Install the drive belt.
17. Position and install the cooling fan retaining screw.
18. Connect the engine cooling fan wire.
19. Evacuate, charge and leak test the system following the recommended service procedures. Observe all safety precautions.
20. Check the systems operation.

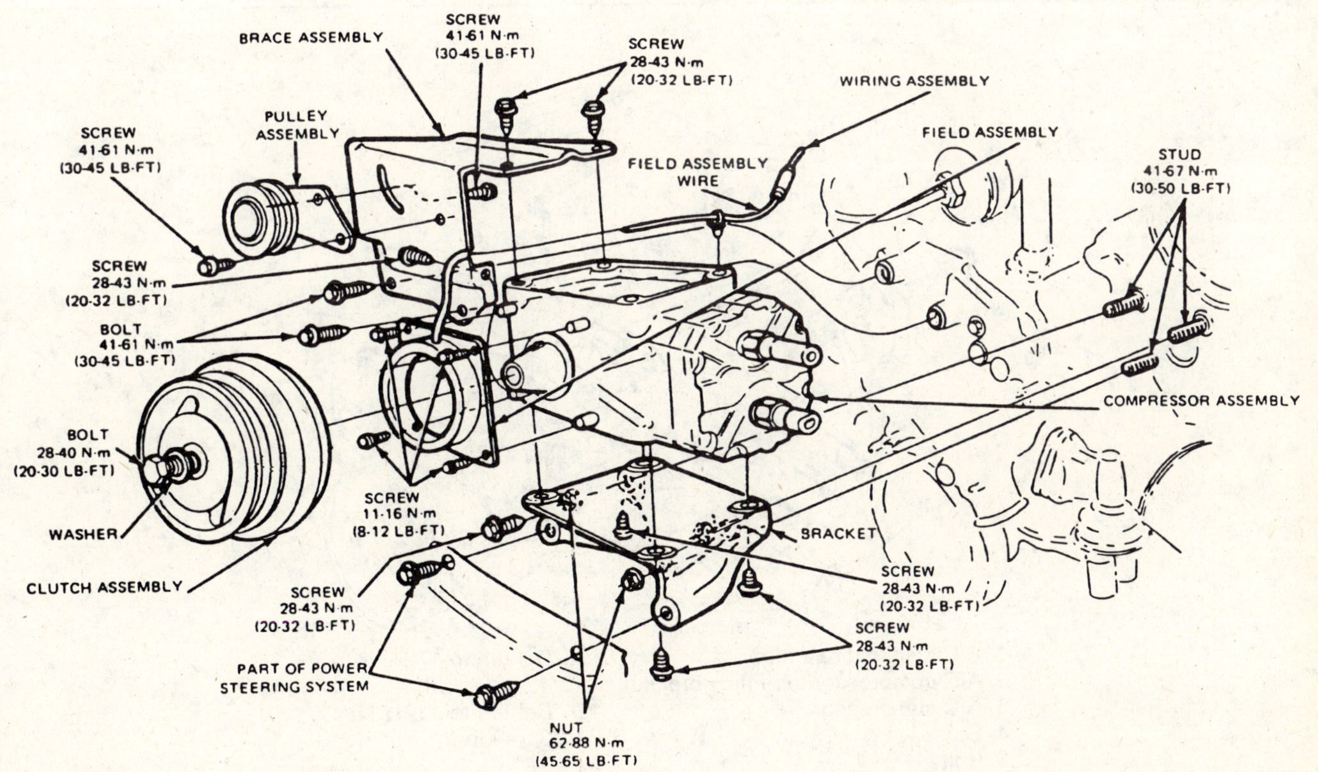

Fig. 32 Exploded view of the compressor

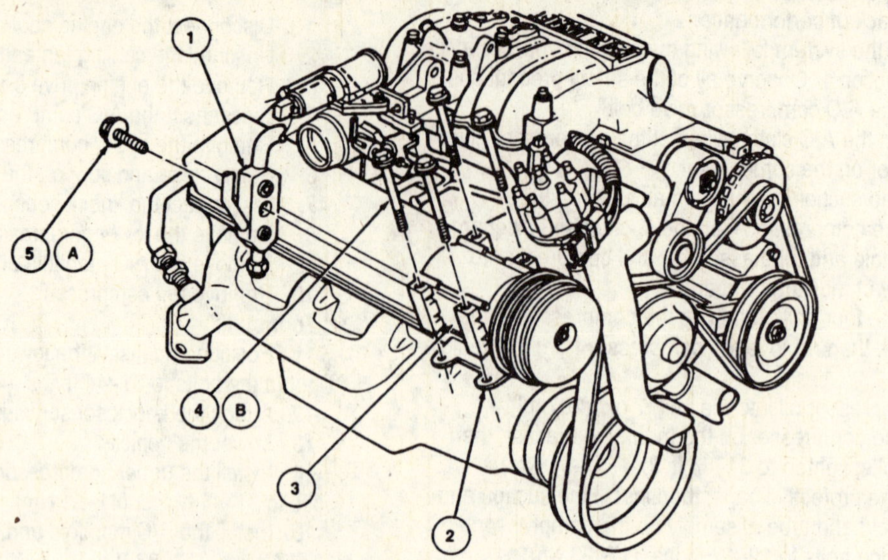

1. A / C Manifold and Tube
2. A / C Compressor Mounting Bracket
3. A / C Compressor
4. Bolt
5. Bolt

A. Tighten to 17-23 N·m (12.5-17 Lb-Ft)
B. Tighten to 41-61 N·m (31-44 Lb-Ft)

88186G28

Fig. 33 Exploded view of the FS-10 compressor for the 3.8L engine, exc SC

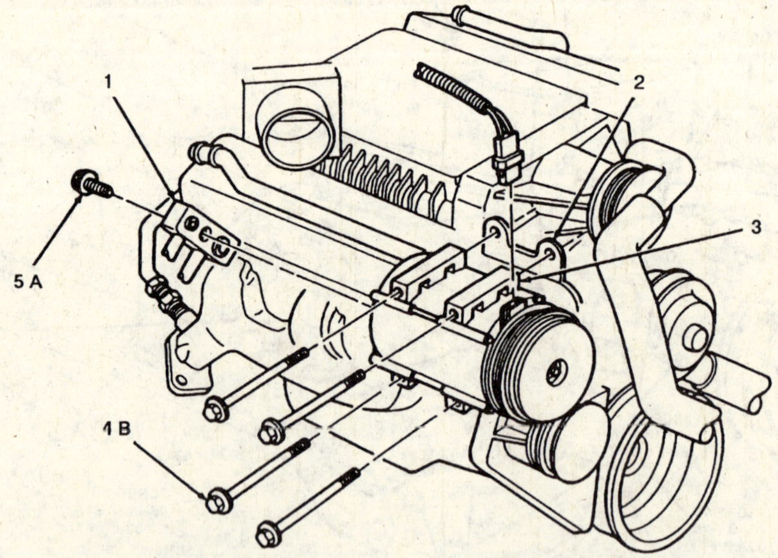

1. A/C manifold and tube
2. A/C compressor mounting bracket
3. A/C compressor
4. Bolt
5. Bolt

A. Tighten to 17-23 N.m (12.5-17 lb-ft)
B. Tighten to 41-61 N.m (31-44 lb-ft)

88186G27

Fig. 34 Exploded view of the FS-10 compressor for the 3.8L Supercharged engine

Condenser

REMOVAL & INSTALLATION

****CAUTION**

The compressed refrigerant used in air conditioning system expands into the atmosphere at a temperature of -21.7°F (-30°C) or lower. This will freeze any surface, including your eyes, that it contacts. In addition, the refrigerant decomposes into a poisonous gas in the presence of a flame, and is harmful to Earth's atmosphere. If discharging A/C system is necessary use an EPA safety approved recovery system.

1983–94 Models

➧ See Figure 35

1. Discharge the system. See Section 1.
2. Remove the battery.
3. Disconnect the refrigerant lines at the condenser and cap all openings immediately!

➥ The fittings are spring-lock couplings and a special tool, T81P-19623-G, should be used. The larger opening end of the tool is for 1/2 in. discharge lines; the smaller end for 3/8 in. liquid lines. To operate the tool, close the tool and push the tool into the open side of the cage to expand the garter spring and release the female fitting. If the tool is not inserted straight, the garter spring will cock and not release. After the garter spring is released, pull the fittings apart.

4. Remove the 4 bolts securing the condenser to the supports and remove the condenser.

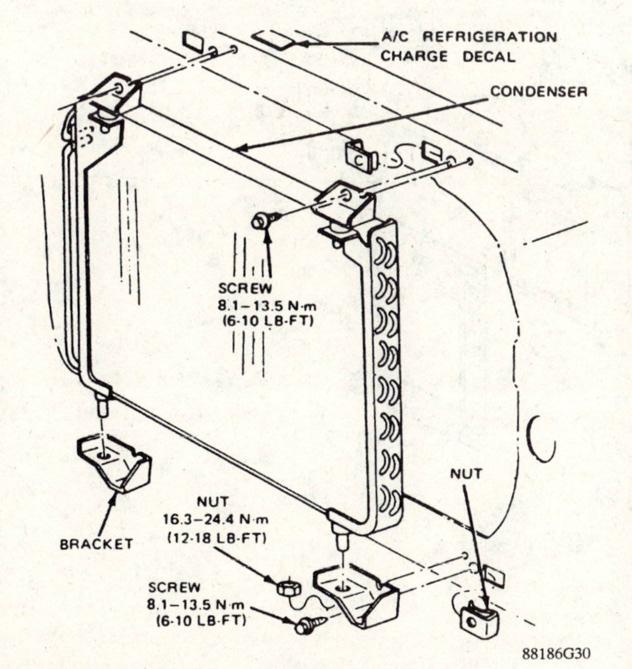

Fig. 35 Common mounting of the condenser

5. Installation is the reverse of removal. Always use new O-rings coated with clean refrigerant oil at the pipe fittings. To connect the couplings, check to ensure that the garter spring is In the cage of the male fitting. Make sure the fittings are clean. Install new O-rings made for this purpose. Lubricate the O-rings with clean refrigerant oil and push the male and female fittings together until the garter spring snaps into place over the female fitting. Evacuate, charge and leak test the system. See Section 1.
6. Check the operation of the system.

1995–96 Models

When working on a condenser core, it is necessary to replace the suction/accumulator drier.

1. Discharge the refrigerant from the A/C system at the service access gauge port valve located on the suction line.
2. Disconnect the negative battery cable.
3. Drain the cooling system.
4. Remove the radiator.
5. Disconnect the two refrigerant lines at the fittings on the right side of the A/C condenser core.
6. Remove the screws retaining retaining the condenser core to the radiator supports, then remove the condenser core from the vehicle.

To install:

7. Position the core assembly to the radiator supports. Install the retaining screws, tighten to 24–36 inch lbs. (3–4 Nm).
8. Connect the refrigerant lines to the A/C condenser core assembly.
9. Install the radiator.
10. Fill the cooling system.
11. Connect the battery cable.
12. Evacuate, charge and leak test the system following the recommended service procedures. Observe all safety precautions.
13. Check the systems operation.

Evaporator Core

REMOVAL & INSTALLATION

****CAUTION**

When draining the coolant, keep in mind that cats and dogs are attracted by the ethylene glycol antifreeze, and are quite likely to drink any that is left in an uncovered container or in puddles on the ground. This will prove fatal in sufficient quantity. Always drain the coolant into a sealable container. Coolant should be reused unless it is contaminated or several years old.

1983–84 Models

➧ See Figure 36

1. Discharge the system at the service access port located on the suction line. See Section 1.
2. Remove the instrument panel and lay it on the front seat. Refer to Section 10.
3. Drain the cooling system and disconnect the heater hoses at the core tubes.

4. Disconnect the refrigerant lines using back-up wrenches at each fitting. Cap all openings immediately!

5. Disconnect the wiring at the blower, and the ATC wiring on cars with electronic automatic temperature control. Remove the screw attaching the air inlet duct and blower housing assembly support brace to the cowl top panel.

6. Disconnect the black vacuum supply hose at the check valve, in the engine compartment, and, on cars with automatic temperature control, the vacuum hoses at the TBL switch, also in the engine compartment.

7. In the engine compartment, remove the 2 nuts retaining the evaporator case to the firewall.

8. In the passenger compartment, remove the screw attaching the evaporator case support bracket to the cowl top panel.

9. Remove the screw retaining the bracket below the case, to the firewall.

10. Carefully pull the case away from the firewall and remove the case from the car.

11. Remove the air inlet duct and blower housing from the case.

12. Remove the screws and snap-clips securing the halves of the case and separate the case halves.

13. Lift out the evaporator core and seal from the lower case half.

To install:

14. Assembly and installation is the reverse of removal and disassembly.

15. Always use new O-rings coated with clean refrigerant oil.

16. Make sure that the core seal fits over the case lower half edge.

17. Make sure that the temperature blend door and heat/defrost door are properly positioned.

18. Always use new sealer between the case halves.

19. Make sure that the drain hose is not kinked.

20. When everything is back together, turn on the blower and check for air leaks around the case.

21. Evacuate, charge and leak test the system. See Section 1.

1985 (All) and 1986-88 with Manual Air Conditioning

1. Discharge the system at the service access port located on the suction line. See Section 1.

2. Remove the instrument panel and lay it on the front seat.

3. Drain the cooling system and disconnect the heater hoses at the core tubes.

4. Disconnect the refrigerant lines using back-up wrenches at each fitting. Cap all openings immediately!

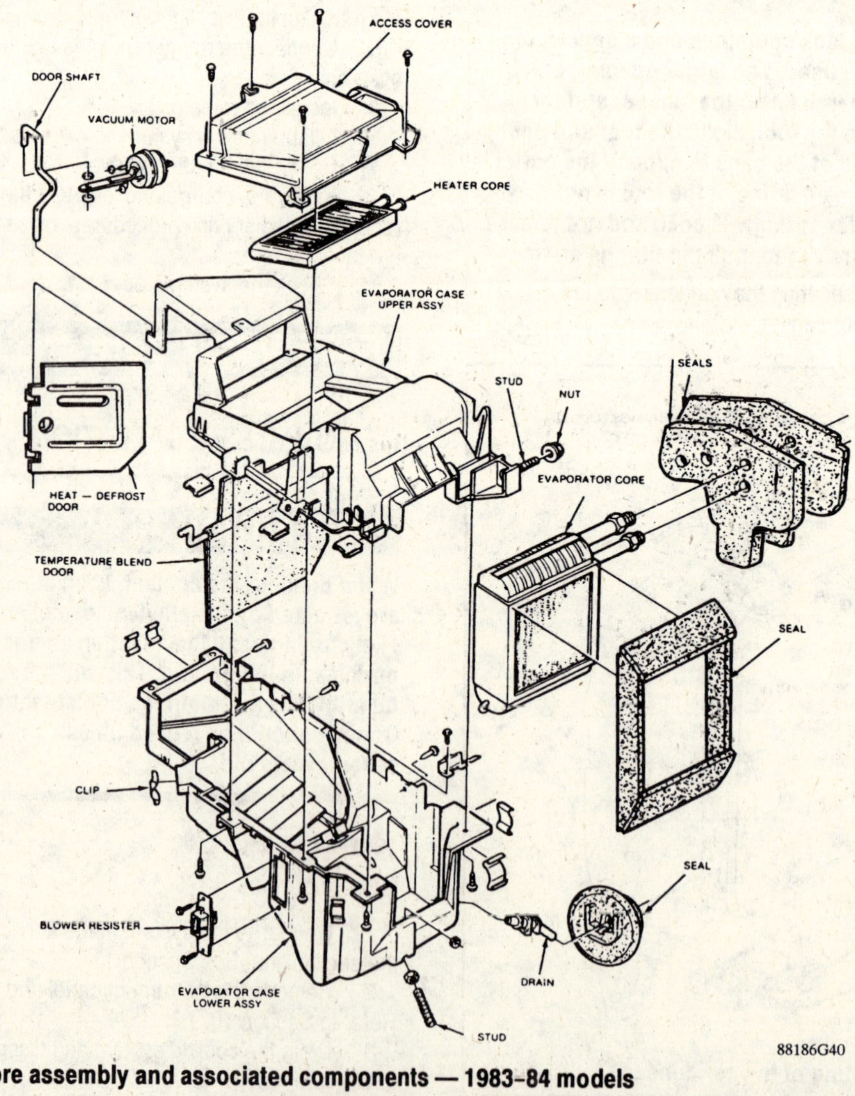

Fig. 36 Evaporator core assembly and associated components — 1983-84 models

5. Disconnect the liquid line and accumulator/drier inlet tube from the evaporator core at the firewall. Cap all openings immediately.
6. Disconnect the wiring at the blower, and the ATC wiring on cars with electronic automatic temperature control.
7. Remove the screw attaching the air inlet duct and blower housing assembly support brace to the cowl top panel.
8. Disconnect the black vacuum supply hose at the check valve, in the engine compartment, and, on cars with automatic temperature control, the vacuum hoses at the TBL switch, also in the engine compartment.
9. In the engine compartment, remove the 2 nuts retaining the evaporator case to the firewall.
10. In the passenger compartment, remove the screw attaching the evaporator case support bracket to the cowl top panel.
11. Remove the screw retaining the bracket below the case, to the firewall.
12. Carefully pull the case away from the firewall and remove the case from the car.
13. Remove the air inlet duct from the case.
14. Remove the foam seal from the core tubes.
15. Drill a $^{11}/_{16}$ in. (5mm) hole in both upright tabs on top of the evaporator case.
16. Using a small saw blade, cut the top of the case, between the raised outlines.
17. Remove the blower motor resistor from the case.
18. Fold the cut-out flap back from the opening and lift the core from the case.

To install:

19. Transfer the foam seals to the new core.
20. Position the core in the case and fold back the cut-out portion.
21. Install a spring nut on each of the two upright tabs. Be sure that the hole in the spring nut is aligned with the $^{11}/_{16}$ in. (5mm) hole drilled in the tab flange.
22. Install a screw in each spring nut through the hole in the tab or flange to secure the cut-out cover in the closed position. Tighten the screws.
23. Seal the cut-out edges with caulk.
24. Assembly and installation is the reverse of removal and disassembly.
25. Always use new O-rings coated with clean refrigerant oil.
26. Make sure that the core seal fits over the case lower half edge.
27. Make sure that the drain hose is not kinked.
28. When everything is back together, turn on the blower and check for air leaks.
29. Evacuate, charge and leak test the system. See Section 1.

1986–88 with Automatic Temperature Control

➧ See Figure 37

1. Discharge the system at the service access port located on the suction line. See Section 1.
2. Disconnect the negative battery cable.
3. Remove the air cleaner.
4. Drain the cooling system and disconnect the heater hoses at the core tubes. It may be necessary to blow the coolant from the core with compressed air.
5. Disconnect the wiring harness at the clutch cycling pressure switch, located on top of the suction accumulator/drier.
6. Disconnect the liquid line and accumulator/drier inlet tube from the evaporator core tubes, using back-up wrenches at each fitting. Cap all openings immediately!
7. Working under the hood, remove the 2 nuts retaining the accumulator/drier bracket to the dash panel.
8. Position the accumulator/drier and liquid line aside and remove the 2 evaporator assembly retaining nuts.
9. In the passenger compartment, remove the steering column opening cover from the instrument panel.
10. Remove the right and left sound insulators from the instrument panel.
11. Remove the right and left cowl trim panels.
12. Remove the ashtray from the instrument panel.
13. Remove the 2 screws attaching the lower center of the instrument panel to the floor brace.
14. Remove the steering column shroud.
15. Disconnect the transmission indicator cable from the steering column.
16. Remove the instrument panel pad.
17. Remove the steering column-to-brake pedal support retaining nuts and lay the steering column down against the front seat.
18. Remove the nut attaching the instrument panel to the brake pedal support and steering column support.
19. Remove the instrument panel attaching screws and lay the panel on the front seat.
20. Disconnect the blower motor and blower motor speed control harnesses.
21. Disconnect the automatic temperature control sensor hose and elbow at the evaporator case.
22. Disconnect the automatic temperature control harness at the control assembly.
23. Disconnect the antenna cable from the radio and from the strap retaining cable at the case.
24. Using a sharp knife, carefully slit the carpet on top of the transmission tunnel from the firewall straight back to the instrument panel support bracket.
25. Fold the carpet back to expose the rear seat duct.
26. Using a hot-knife, cut the top and side from the rear seat heat duct and remove the top from the floor duct.
27. Remove the 3 evaporator attaching screws and lift the evaporator assembly from the car.
28. Remove the air inlet duct and blower housing from the case.
29. Remove the screws and snap-clips securing the halves of the case and separate the case halves.
30. Lift out the evaporator core and seal from the lower case half.
31. Assembly and installation is the reverse of removal and disassembly.

To install:

32. Position the evaporator assembly on the firewall and install the 3 attaching screws in the passenger compartment. DO NOT TIGHTEN THESE SCREWS AT THIS TIME!
33. Install the 2 nuts that retain the evaporator to the firewall in the engine compartment.
34. Now tighten all the attaching fasteners.
35. Make sure that the drain hose is not kinked.
36. Always use new O-rings coated with clean refrigerant oil.
37. When connecting the refrigerant lines, make ALL connections loosely BEFORE tightening any of them.

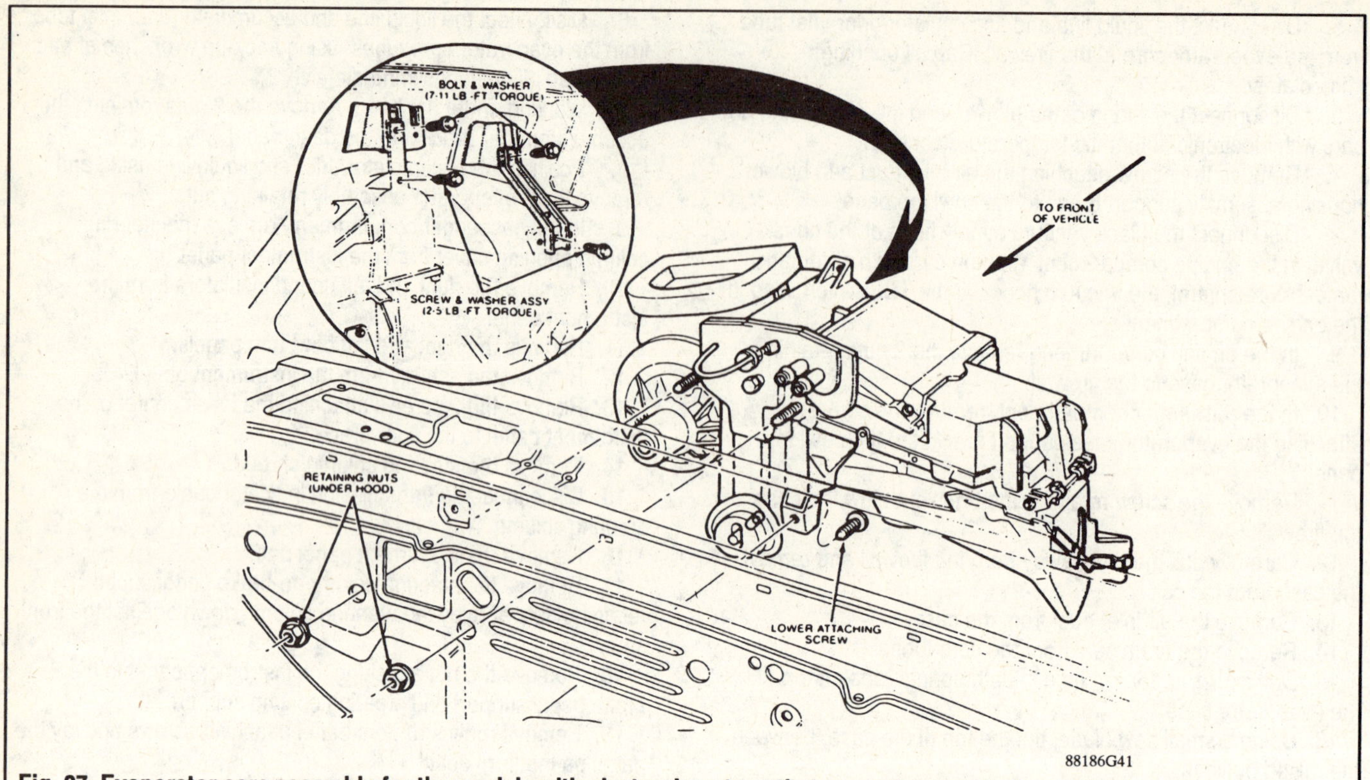

Fig. 37 Evaporator core assembly for the models with electronic automatic temperature control — 1987 shown

38. Make sure that the core seal fits over the case lower half edge.
39. Always use new sealer between the case halves.
40. When everything is back together, turn on the blower and check for air leaks around the case.
41. Evacuate, charge and leak test the system. See Section 1.

1989-94 Models

1. Remove the instrument panel and lay it on the front seat.
2. Discharge refrigerant from A/C system.
3. Remove the high and low pressure hoses and cap the openings to prevent dirt and moisture from entering.
4. Disconnect the liquid line and accumulator/drier inlet tube from the evaporator core at the dash panel and cap the lines.
5. Remove suction accumulator/drier and bracket. If necessary, remove throttle cable bracket and position out of way.
6. Disconnect heater hoses from heater core. Plug hoses and cap heater core tubes to prevent coolant loss during removal of evaporator case.
7. Disconnect vacuum supply hose (black) from the inline vacuum check valve in the engine compartment.
8. Working under the hood, remove three nuts retaining the evaporator case to the dash panel.
9. In the passenger compartment, remove the screw attaching the evaporator case support bracket to the cowl top panel.
10. Remove one nut retaining the bracket below the evaporator case to the dash panel.
11. Carefully pull the evaporator case away from the dash panel and remove assembly from vehicle.
12. Remove three screws and pull air inlet duct away from evaporator case.
13. With a small saw, cut the top of the evaporator case between the dotted lines and make sure all burrs are removed from cut edges.
14. Remove evaporator core from the case.
15. Hold the cover against the case firmly and drill five $^{11}/_{16}$ in. (5mm) diameter holes for the retaining screws.

To install:

16. Install new evaporator into the case.
17. Run a bead of caulk/sealer between evaporator case and service cover.
18. Install the service cover and five retaining screws onto the evaporator case.
19. Position air inlet duct on case and install three screws.
20. Install evaporator case into dash panel, reverse of the removal procedures.
    a. Make sure that the drain hose is not kinked.
    b. Always use new O-rings coated with clean refrigerant oil.
    c. When connecting the refrigerant lines, make ALL connections loosely BEFORE tightening any of them.
    d. Make sure that the core seal fits over the case lower half edge.
    e. Always use new sealer between the case halves.
    f. When everything is back together, turn on the blower and check for air leaks around the case.
    g. Evacuate, charge and leak test the system. See Section 1.

1995-96 Models R134A

➔ When working on a evaporator core, it is necessary to replace the suction/accumulator drier. Before replacing the evaporator core, it must be leak tested in the vehicle to verify that it is leaking.

1. Remove the evaporator housing. Refer to the procedure earlier in this section.
2. Separate the heater core from the A/C evaporator housing.
3. Remove the A/C recirculating air duct.

4. Remove the vacuum hose harness from its mounting points on the evaporator housing.
5. Remove the heater air damper door vacuum control motor.
6. Remove the heater blower motor resistor.
7. Remove the blower motor.
8. Remove the heater outlet floor duct.
9. Remove the A/C evaporator drain tube seal from the housing.

To install:

10. Attach the A/C evaporator drain tube seal to the core housing.
11. Install the heater outlet floor duct.
12. Install the blower motor and fan cage assembly.
13. Attach the heater blower motor resistor.
14. Install the heater air damper door vacuum control motor.
15. Place the vacuum hose harness, and attach to the mounting points on the evaporator housing.
16. Install the A/C recirculating air duct.
17. Install the heater core to the A/C evaporator housing.
18. Reinstall the evaporator housing assembly in the vehicle.
19. Evacuate, charge and leak test the system. See Section 1.
20. Check the operation of the system.

Control Panel

REMOVAL & INSTALLATION

1983 Automatic Temperature Control

1. Disconnect the negative battery cable.
2. On Thunderbird and XR-7, remove the radio knobs.
3. On the Thunderbird and XR-7, open the ashtray and remove the 2 screws attaching the center finish panel to the instrument panel at the ashtray opening.
4. Pull the lower edge of the center finish panel away from the instrument panel and disengage the upper tabs of the finish panel from the instrument panel.
5. Remove the 4 screws attaching the control panel to the instrument panel.
6. Pull the control panel towards you about $^1/_2$ in. (13mm). Insert a screwdriver and remove the control panel harness connector locator from the hole in the instrument panel.
7. Pull the control panel from the instrument panel and disconnect the wire connectors from the control panel.
8. Disconnect the vacuum harness and temperature control cable from the control panel. Discard the pushnuts.

To install:

➥ If the lamp wires become disconnected during the panel removal, put the clips back on the controls before installing the panel.

9. Connect the vacuum harness and temperature control cable to the control panel.
10. Push the control panel into the instrument panel after connecting the wiring to the control panel.
11. Screw the control panel to the instrument panel.
12. Install center finish panel on the instrument panel.
13. If removed, attach the 2 screws for the center finish panel to the instrument panel in the ashtray opening.
14. Install the radio knobs.
15. Connect the negative battery cable.

1983-88 with Manual Air Conditioning

1. Disconnect the negative battery cable.
2. Remove the temperature control knob from the lever shaft (on 1985-88 models).
3. Remove the center finish panel (if equipped).
4. Remove the 4 screws attaching the control panel to the instrument panel.
5. Pull the control panel out and disconnect the wiring from the control panel.
6. Disconnect the vacuum harness and the temperature control cable from the control panel.

To install:

➥ Remember that the vacuum harness nut is a pushnut. It does not screw on.

7. Connect the vacuum harness and the temperature control cable to the control panel.
8. Place the control panel into position and connect the wiring.
9. Screw on the control panel to the instrument panel.
10. Install the center finish panel (if equipped).
11. Install the temperature control knob to the lever shaft (on 1985-88 models).
12. Connect the negative battery cable.

1984-86 with Automatic Temperature Control

1. Disconnect the negative battery cable.
2. Remove the radio knobs.
3. Open the ashtray and remove the 2 screws attaching the center finish panel to the instrument panel at the ashtray opening.
4. Pull the lower edge of the center finish panel away from the instrument panel and disengage the upper tabs of the finish panel from the instrument panel.
5. Remove the 4 screws attaching the control panel to the instrument panel.
6. Pull the control panel towards you about $^1/_2$ in. (13mm). Insert a screwdriver and remove the control panel harness connector locator from the hole in the instrument panel.
7. Pull the control panel from the instrument panel and disconnect the wire connectors from the control panel.
8. Disconnect the vacuum harness and temperature control cable from the control panel. Discard the pushnuts.
9. Installation is the reverse of removal. If the lamp wires become disconnected during the panel removal, put the clips back on the controls before installing the panel.

1987-88 with Automatic Temperature Control

1. Disconnect the negative battery cable.
2. Remove the 4 screws attaching the center finish panel to the instrument panel.
3. Remove the 4 screws attaching the control panel to the instrument panel.
4. Pull the control panel towards you and remove the control panel harness connectors by disengaging the latches on the bottom of the control unit.
5. Disengage the rear window defroster switch connector.
6. Pull the control panel from the instrument panel and disconnect the wire connectors from the control panel.
7. Disconnect the vacuum harness and temperature control cable from the control panel. Discard the pushnuts.

8. Installation is the reverse of removal. If the lamp wires become disconnected during the panel removal, put the clips back on the controls before installing the panel.

1989–96 Models

➧ See Figures 38, 39, 40 and 41

1. Disconnect the negative battery cable.
2. Insert removal tool T87P-19061-A (or equivalent) into retaining clip access holes.
3. Apply a side load away from the control to disengage clips.
4. Pull the control assembly from the instrument panel opening and disconnect the wire connectors from the control assembly.
5. Disconnect the vacuum harness and the temperature control cable from the control assembly.

To install:

➥ Remember that the vacuum harness nuts are pushnuts. They do not screw on.

6. Connect the wiring and the vacuum harness to the control assembly.
7. Position the control assembly in the instrument panel opening. Engage it in the track in the instrument panel, then push it in unit it latches firmly in place.
8. Connect the negative battery cable.
9. Check the system operation.

Blower Switch

REMOVAL & INSTALLATION

1. Remove the climate control assembly.
2. Place blower control knob in the **LOW** position and pull the knob off the switch shaft.
3. Disconnect the wiring to the switch.
4. If necessary, remove the circuit board cover.
5. Remove one screw retaining the switch to the control assembly.
6. Rotate the switch to disengage locking tab, and pull switch away from housing, disengaging the knob.

To install:

7. Position the switch in the control assembly. Ensure that the switch is correctly into place.
8. Install the screw to attach the switch to the control assembly.
9. Place the switch knob on the switch shaft in the **LOW** position and push the knob all the way on.
10. Connect the wire harness connector to the switch.
11. If removed, install the circuit board cover.
12. Install the control assembly into the instrument panel and check for proper operation.

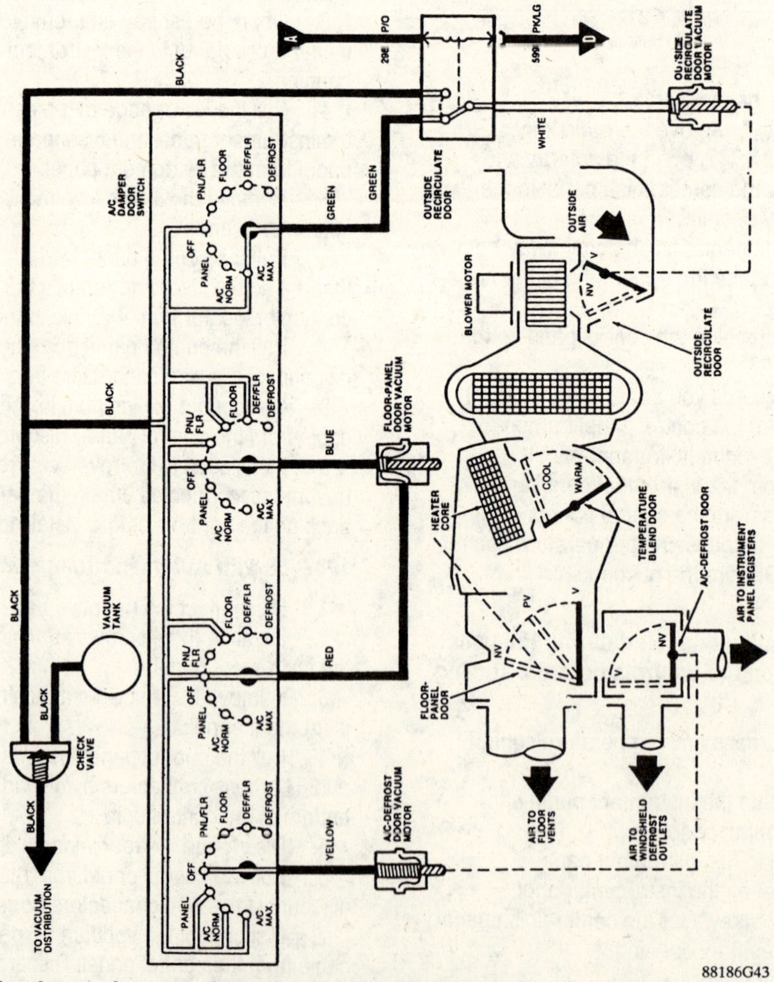

Fig. 38 Vacuum diagram for the semi-automatic temperature control system

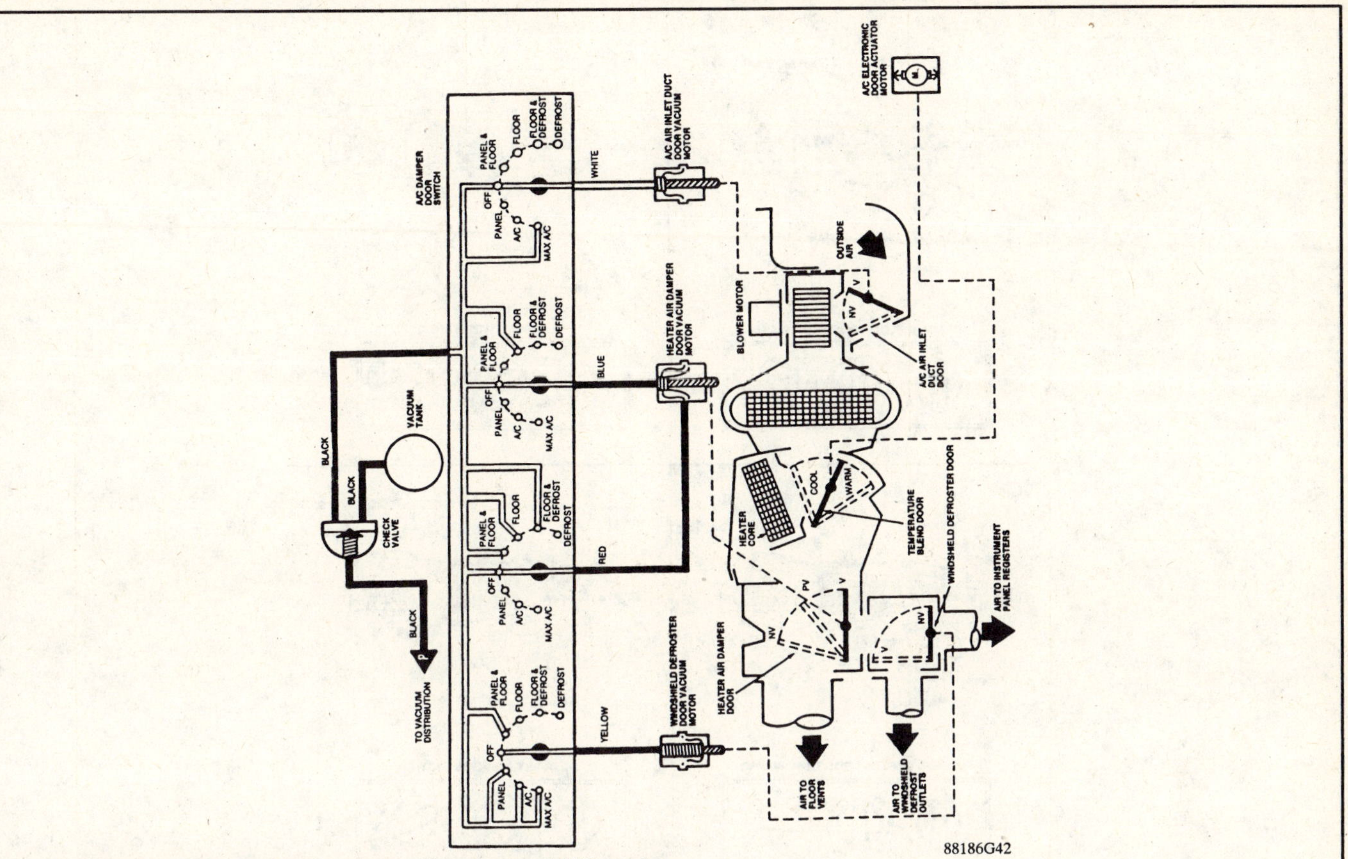

Fig. 39 Vacuum diagram for the manual heating and A/C system

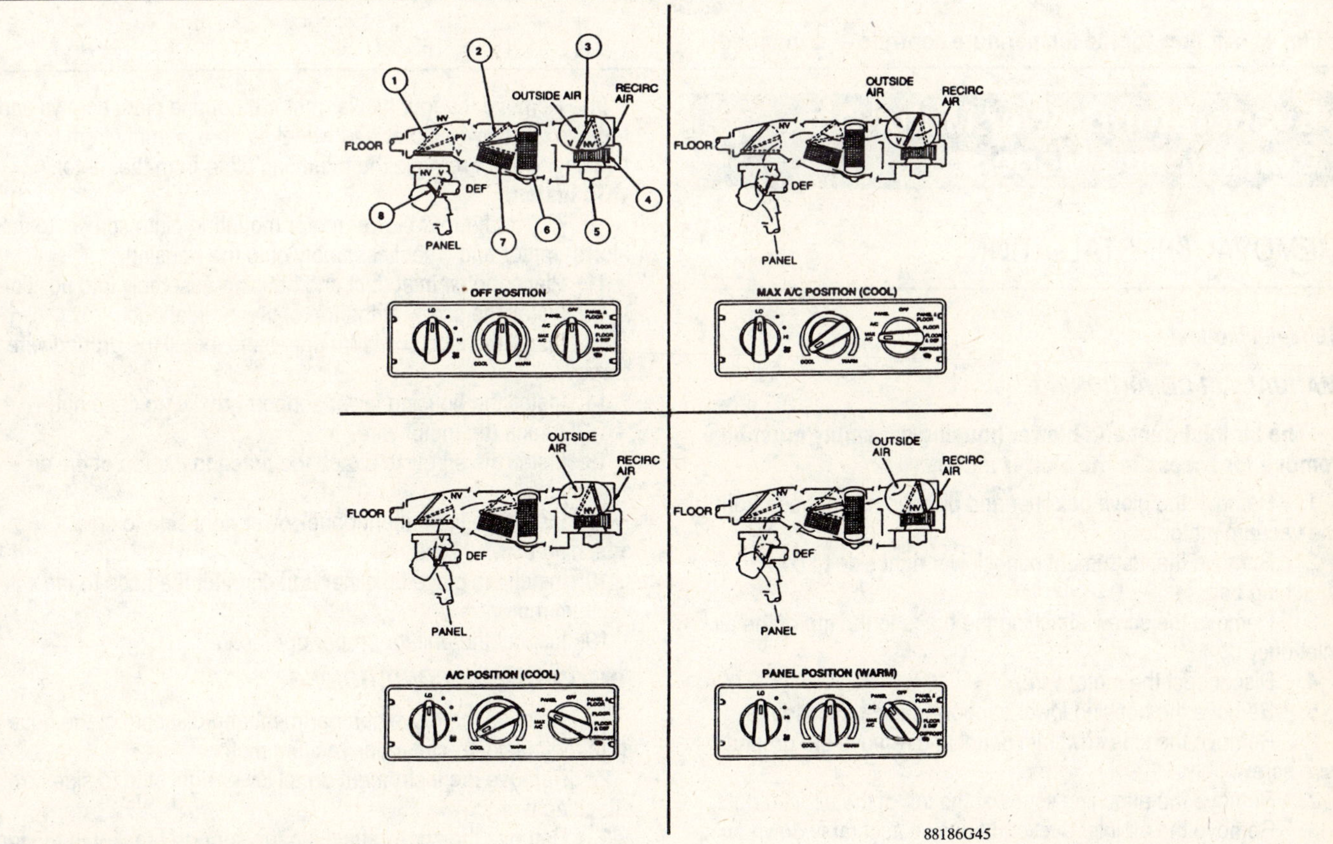

Fig. 40 Air flow for the temperature controls

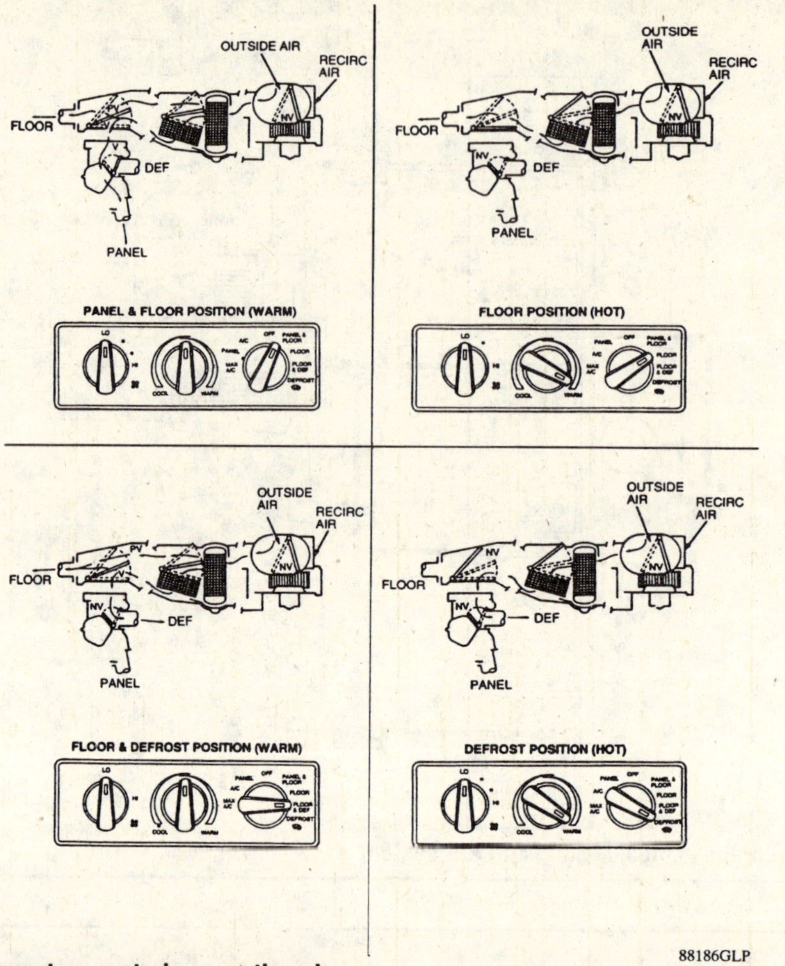

Fig. 41 Air flow for the temperature controls — continued

Evaporator Blower Motor Air Conditioned Models

REMOVAL & INSTALLATION

1983–88 Models

MANUAL AIR CONDITIONING

➥ The air inlet duct and blower housing assembly must be remove for access to the blower motor.

1. Remove the glove box liner and disconnect the hose from the vacuum motor.
2. Remove the instrument panel lower right side to cowl attaching bolt.
3. Remove the screw attaching the brace to the top of the air inlet duct.
4. Disconnect the motor wire.
5. Remove the housing lower support bracket to case nut.
6. Remove the side cowl trim panel and remove the ground wire screw.
7. Remove the attaching screw at the top of the air inlet duct.
8. Remove the air inlet duct and housing assembly down an away from the evaporator case.
9. Remove the four blower motor mounting plate screws and remove the blower motor and wheel as an assembly from the housing. Do not remove the mounting plate from the motor.

To install:

10. Attach the four blower motor mounting plate screws to the blower motor and wheel assembly onto the housing.
11. Place the air inlet duct and housing assembly into position.
12. Install the screw at the top of the air inlet duct.
13. Install the side cowl trim panel and install the ground wire screw.
14. Install the housing lower support bracket to case nut.
15. Attach the motor wire.
16. Install the screw to attach the brace to the top of the air inlet duct.
17. Install the instrument panel lower right side to cowl attaching bolt.
18. Install the glove box liner and connect the hose to the vacuum motor.
19. Inspect the unit for proper operation.

AUTOMATIC AIR CONDITIONING

1. Remove the glove compartment and disconnect the hose from the outside/recirc. door vacuum motor.
2. Remove the instrument panel lower right side to side cowl attaching bolt.
3. Remove the screw attaching the support bracket to the top of the air duct.

4. Disconnect the power lead for the blower motor at the wire connector.
5. Remove the nut retaining the blower motor housing lower support bracket to the evaporator case.
6. Remove the side cowl trim panel.
7. Remove the screw attaching the top of the air inlet duct to the evaporator case.
8. Move the air inlet duct and blower housing assembly down and away from the evaporator case. Remove the assembly.
9. Remove the blower plate mounting screws and remove the blower motor and wheel assembly.

To install:

10. Install the blower plate mounting screws to attach the blower motor and wheel assembly.
11. Place the air inlet duct and blower housing assembly into position.
12. Install the screw on the top of the air inlet duct.
13. Install the side cowl trim panel.
14. Tighten the nut retaining the blower motor housing lower support bracket to the evaporator case.
15. Attach the power lead for the blower motor at the wire connector.
16. Tighten the screw attaching the support bracket to the top of the air duct.
17. Install the instrument panel lower right side to side cowl attaching bolt.
18. Install the glove compartment and connect the hose to the outside/recirc. door vacuum motor.

1989–93 Models

1. Disconnect the negative battery cable.
2. Remove glove box liner.
3. Disconnect the blower motor wire connector.
4. Remove four screws and pull the blower motor and wheel assembly out of the heater case.
5. Remove the push nuts from the motor shaft and slide the wheel off the shaft.
6. Inspect the motor assembly to case assembly seal. If damaged replace seal.

To install:

7. Install the motor assembly into the case assembly.
8. Install the wheel onto the shaft using a push nut to keep it into place.
9. Tighten the four screws to keep the motor into place.
10. Attach the blower motor wiring connector.
11. Install the glove box liner.
12. Connect the negative battery cable.
13. Test the operation of the unit.

Accumulator/Drier

REMOVAL & INSTALLATION

REPLACEMENT GUIDELINES

➧ See Figure 42

Replacement of the suction accumulator/drier is necessary anytime a major component of the A/C system is replaced. A major component includes condenser, compressor, evaporator core or a refrigerant hose/line. An orifice tube or O-ring is not considered a major component, but the orifice tube should be replaced whenever the compressor is replaced.

In addition, the accumulator/drier should also be replaced if one of the following conditions exists:

- The accumulator/drier is perforated (cracked or damaged)
- The refrigerant system has been opened to the atmosphere for a period of time longer than required to make a minor repair
- There is evidence of moisture in the system such as internal corrosion of metal refrigerant lines or the refrigerant oil is thick and dark.

1. Discharge the A/C system using an approved Recycling/Recovery unit. Refer to Section 1.
2. Disconnect the inlet and outlet lines at the accumulator. Cap the ends to prevent any dirt or moisture from entering the system.
3. Disconnect the wiring harness connector for the A/C cycling switch on top of the accumulator/drier (if equipped).
4. Remove the bracket retaining accumulator in place and remove the accumulator.
5. Drain the oil from the accumulator/drier into a suitable measuring container.

➥ It may be necessary to drill two $^1/_2$ (12.5mm) holes into the bottom of the accumulator/drier to ensure that all of the oil has drained out.

6. Add the same amount of new refrigerant oil plus two fluid ounces to the new accumulator/drier. Use only oil specified for vehicle application.

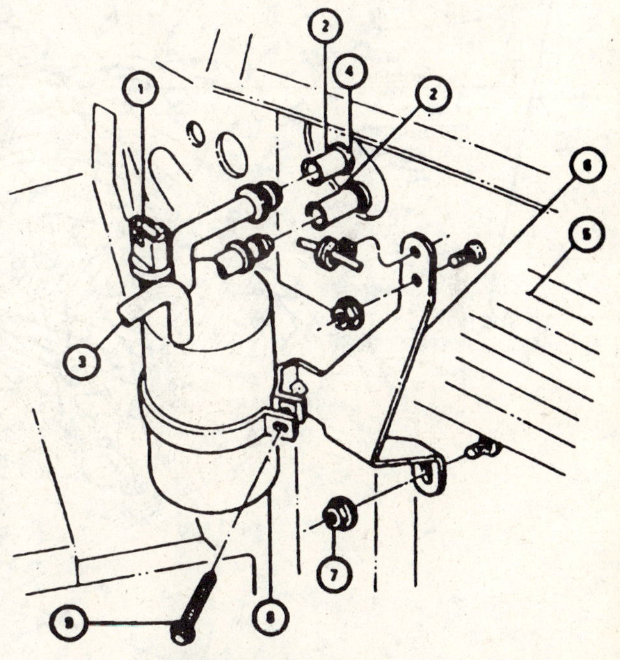

ITEM	DESCRIPTION
1	CLUTCH CYCLING PRESSURE SWITCH CONNECTOR
2	FEMALE END SLC
3	TO COMPRESSOR
4	FROM EVAPORATOR
5.	DASH PANEL
6.	BRACKET ASSY - 19D606
7	NUT (2 REQ'D) - N800907-S2
8	SUCTION ACCUMULATOR/DRIER - 19C913 ON 3.8 EFI ON 3.8L S/C ENGINE - 19E847
9	SCREW - 42152-S2

88186G47

Fig. 42 Accumulator/drier with the clutch cycling switch assembly

To install:

7. Position the accumulator/drier in the vehicle, then route the suction hose to the compressor.
8. Using new O-rings, lubricated with clean refrigerant oil, connect the accumulator/drier inlet tube to the evaporator.
9. Evacuate, charge and leak test the system. See Section 1.
10. Check the system for proper operation.

Refrigerant Lines

REMOVAL & INSTALLATION

See Figures 43, 44, 45, 46, 47, 48 and 49

Whenever a refrigerant line is replaced it is necessary to replace the accumulator/drier also.

1. Discharge the A/C system using an approved Recycling/Recovery unit. Refer to Section 1.
2. Disconnect and remove the refrigerant line at the condenser, evaporator and compressor using the disconnect procedure for spring lock couplings.
3. Remove the refrigerant line.

To install:

4. Route the new refrigerant line with protective caps installed.
5. Connect the refrigerant line into the system using new O-rings lubricated with clean specified refrigerant oil.
6. Evacuate, charge and leak test the system with refrigerant following procedures in Section 1.

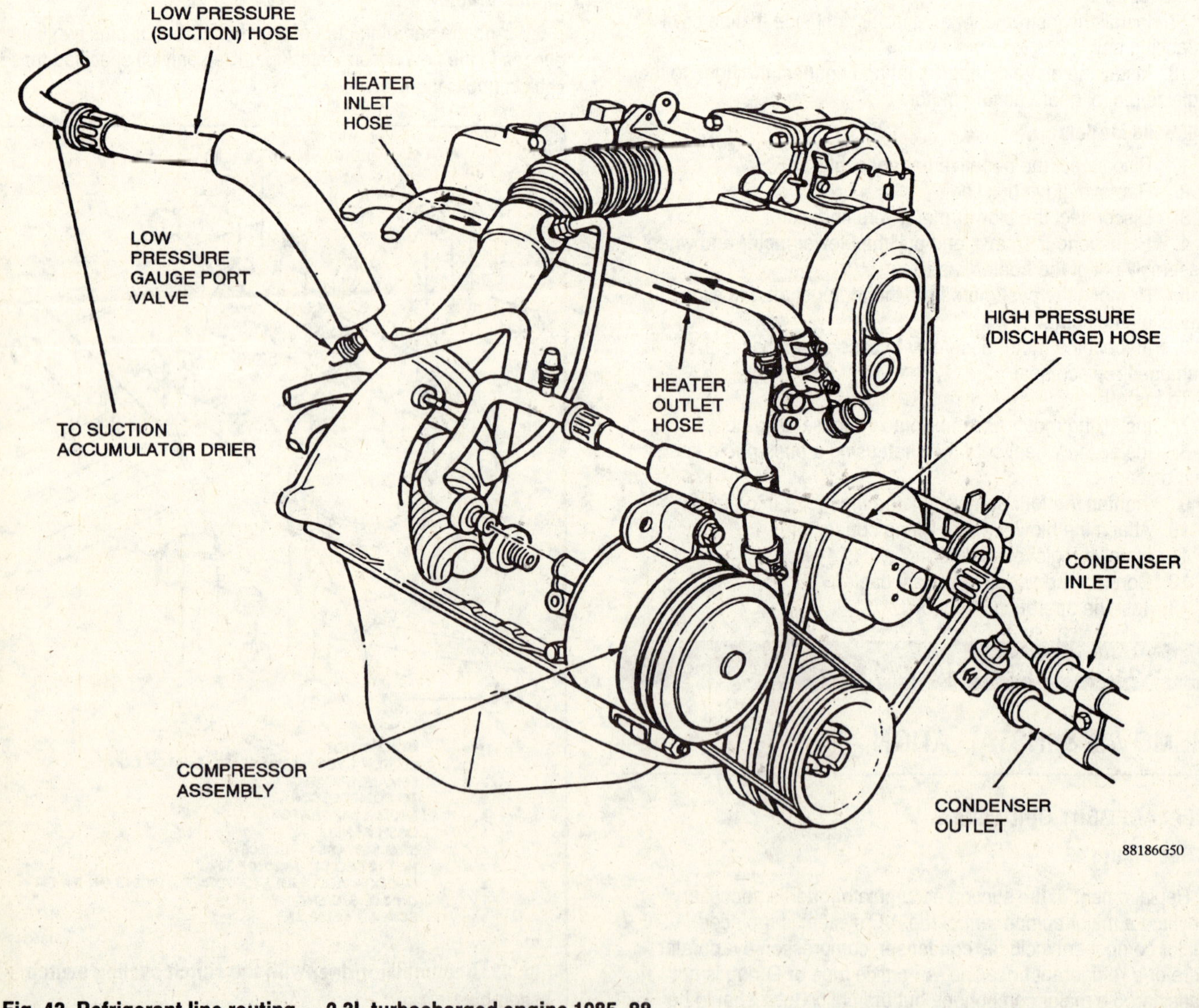

Fig. 43 Refrigerant line routing — 2.3L turbocharged engine 1985-88

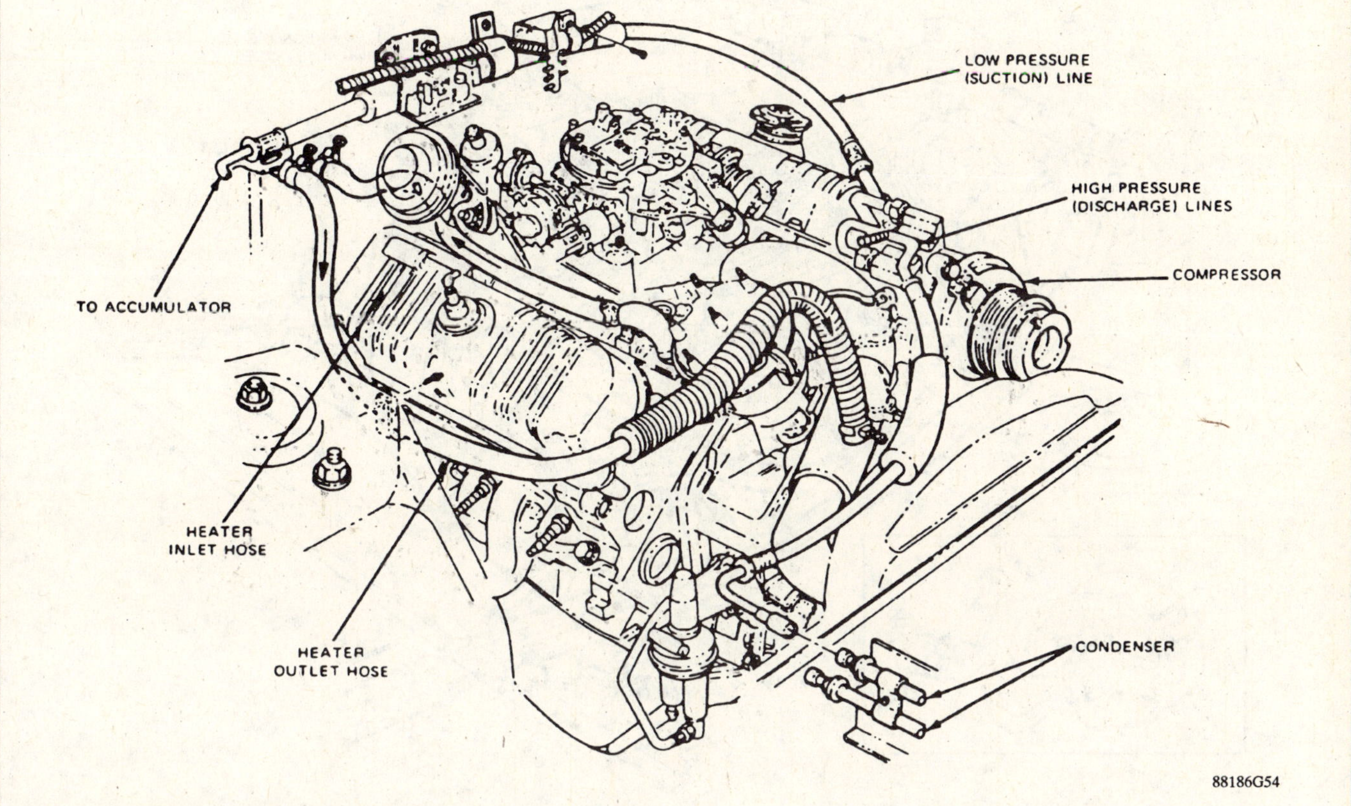

Fig. 44 Refrigerant line routing — through 1988 3.8L engine

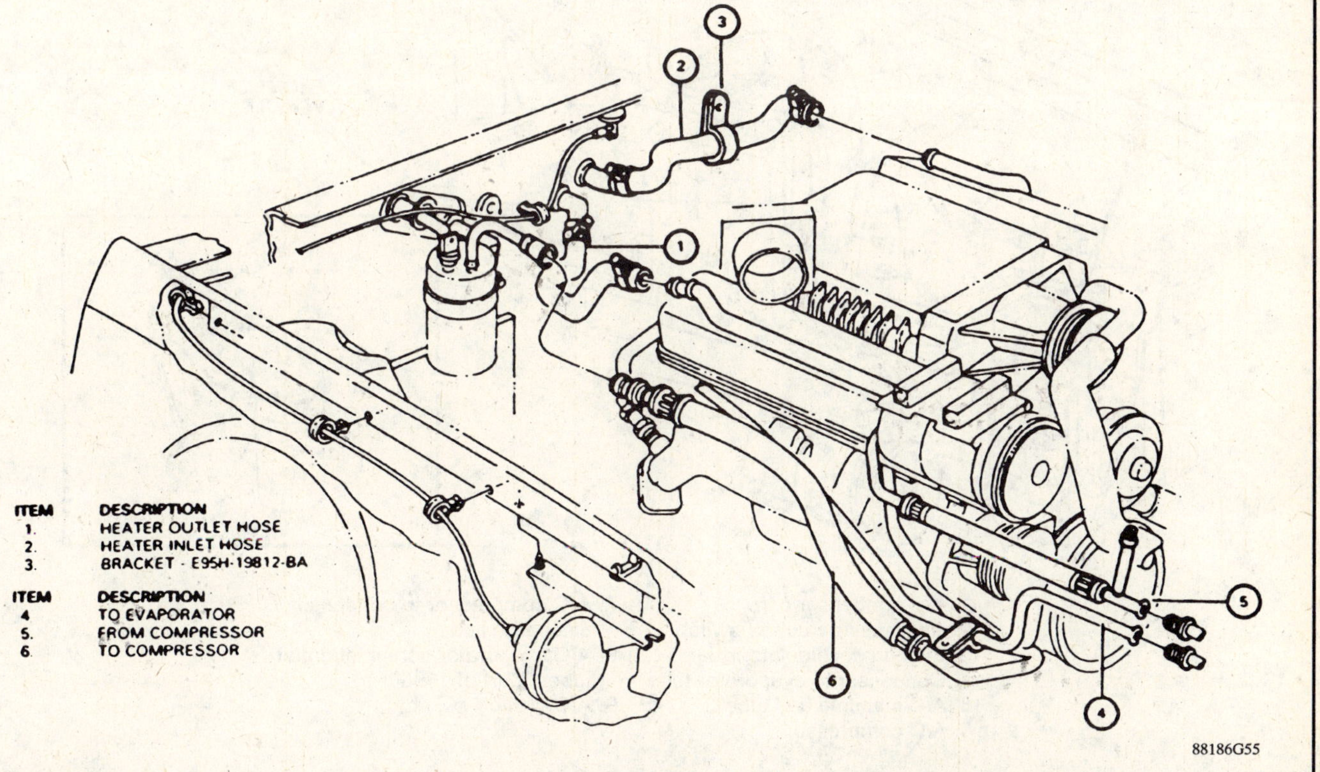

Fig. 45 Refrigerant line routing — 1989–95 3.8L supercharged engine

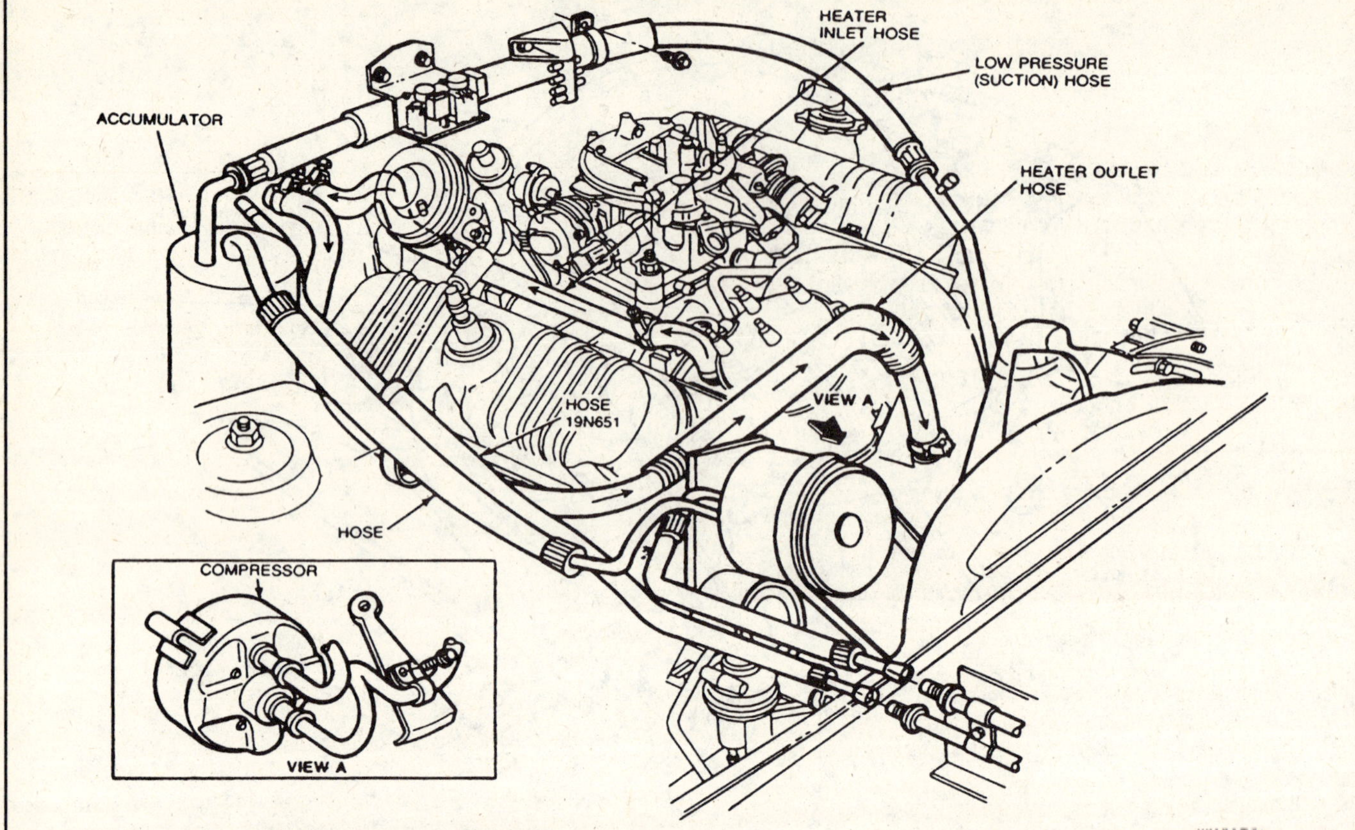

Fig. 46 Refrigerant line routing — 3.8L engine 1989–96 exc SC

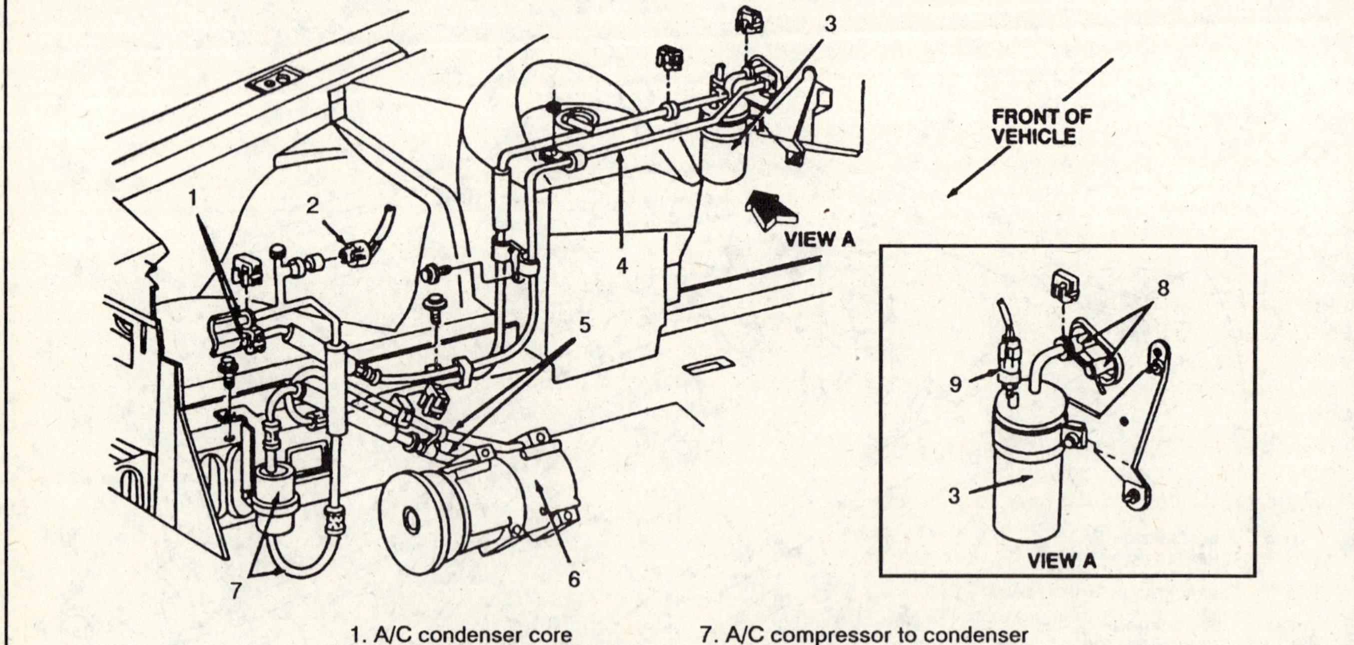

1. A/C condenser core
2. A/C pressure cut-off switch
3. Suction accumulator/drier
4. Condenser to evaporator tube
5. A/C manifold and tube
6. A/C compressor
7. A/C compressor to condenser discharge line
8. A/C evaporator core inlet/outlet tubes (part of 19860)
9. A/C cycling switch

88186G53

Fig. 47 Refrigerant line routing with manual A/C — 4.6L engine

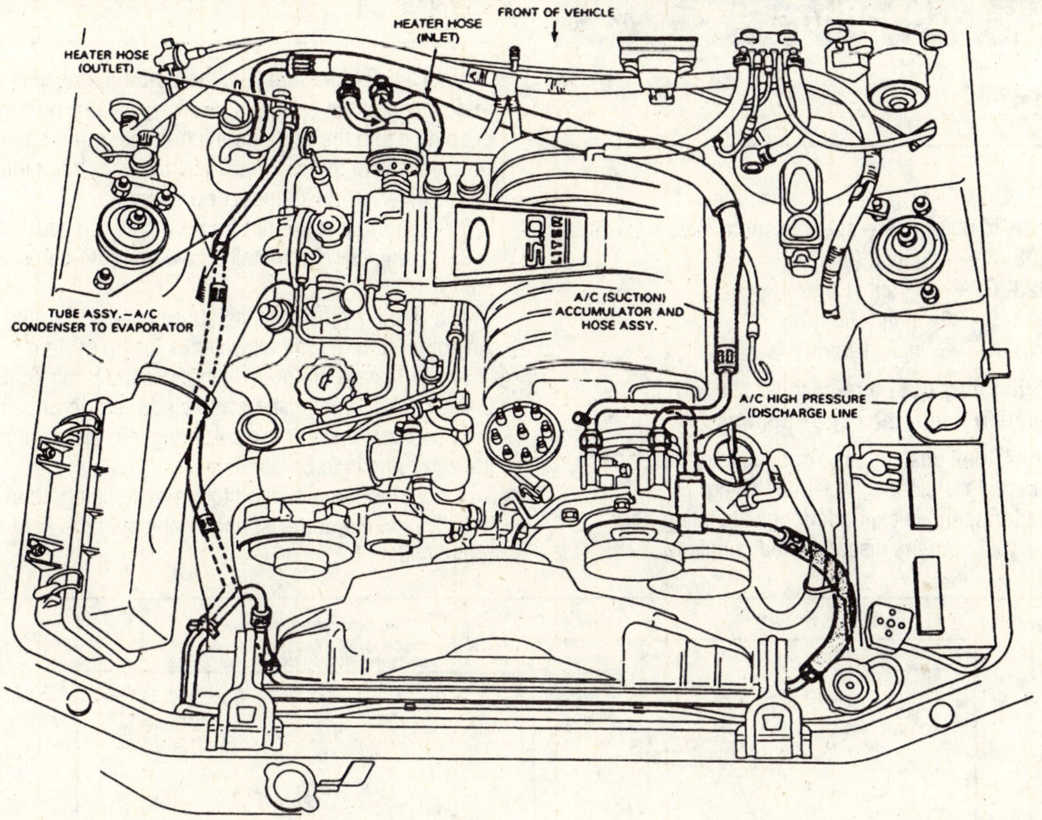

Fig. 48 Refrigerant line routing — through 1989 5.0L engine

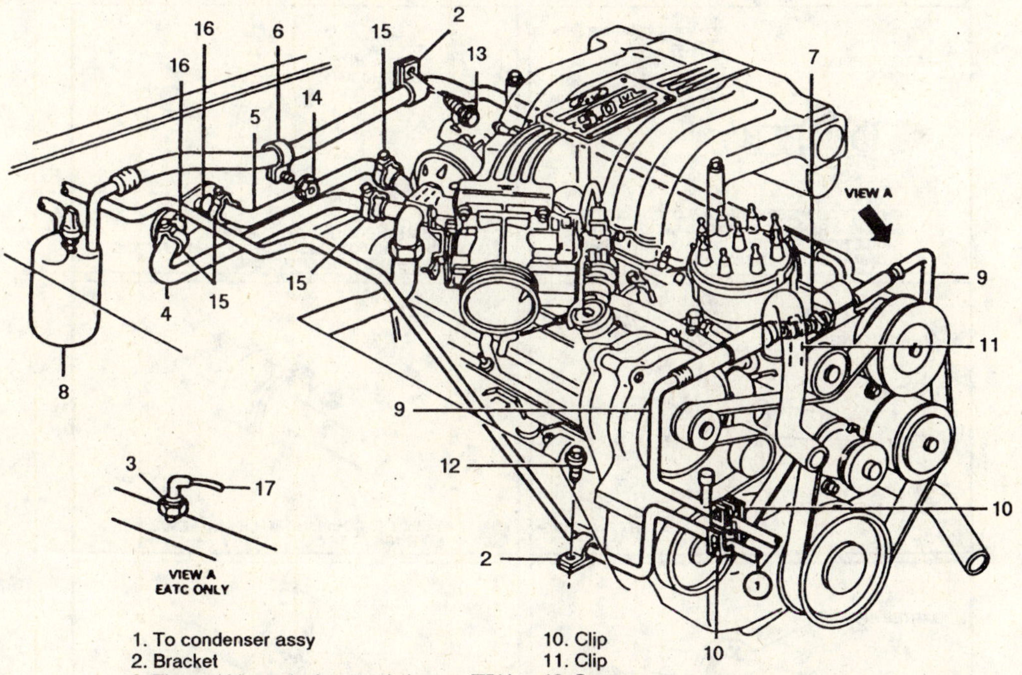

1. To condenser assy
2. Bracket
3. Thermal blower lock-out switch assy (TBL)
4. Heater hose inlet
5. Heater hose outlet
6. Bracket
7. Clip
8. Accumulator & switch assy
9. A/C compressor to condenser tube assy
10. Clip
11. Clip
12. Screw
13. Screw
14. Nut & washer assy
15. Post clamp
16. Lubricant (apply to heater hose prior to installation)
17. Wiring assy

Fig. 49 Refrigerant line routing — 1991–92 5.0L engine

Spring Lock Couplings

DISCONNECT

➧ See Figure 50

It will be necessary to obtain a few special service tools such as:

- T81P-19623-G1 — 3/8 inch (9mm)
- T81P-19623-G2 — 1/2 inch (12mm)
- T83P-19623-C — 5/8 inch (16mm)
- T85L-19623-A — 3/4 inch (19mm)

➛ The garter spring may not be released if the tool is cocked while pushing it into the cage opening.

1. Close the tool, then push into the open side of the cage to expand the garter spring. Release the female fitting.
2. After the garter spring is expanded, pull the fitting apart.
3. Remove the tool from the disconnected coupling.

CONNECT

1. Check to ensure that the garter spring is in the cage of the male fitting. If the spring is missing, install a new spring by pushing it into the cage opening. If the garter spring is damaged, remove it from the cage with a small wire hook (do not use a screwdriver), then install a new spring.
2. Clean all of the dirt from both Of the coupling pieces.
3. Lubricate and install a new green O-ring seals on the male fitting.
4. Use only the specified green seals from the manufacture. Any other O-ring may allow leaks IN the system.
5. Lubricate the male fitting, green O-ring seals and the inside of the female fitting with clean refrigerant oil.
6. Install a plastic indicator ring into the cage opening if the indicator ring is to be used.
7. Fit the female fitting to the male fitting, then push and twist slightly until the garter spring snaps over the flared end of the female fitting.

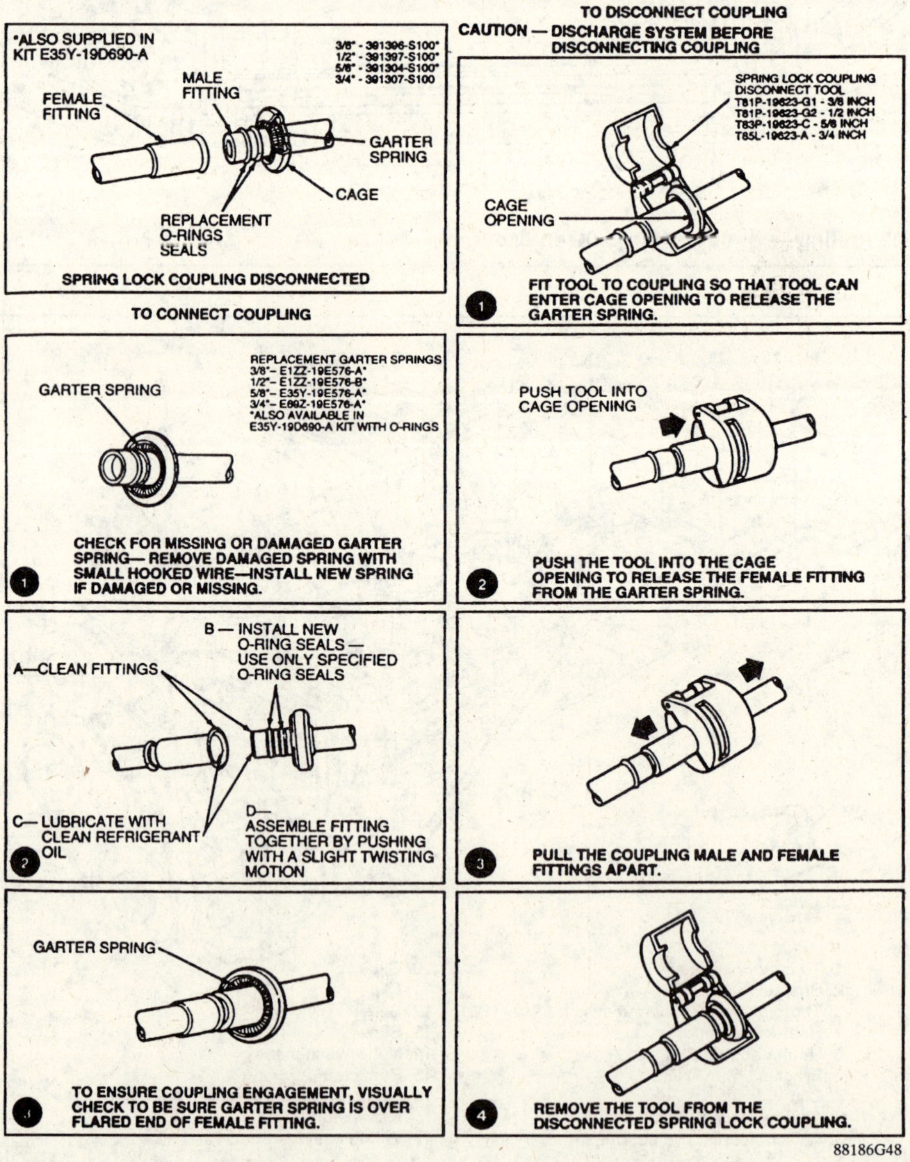

Fig. 50 Spring lock coupling installation procedure

8. If the plastic indicator ring is used, it will snap out of the cage opening when the coupling is connected to the indicated engagement.
9. If the indicator ring is not to be used, check the coupling engagement by making sure the garter spring is over the flared end of the female fitting.

Control Cables

REMOVAL & INSTALLATION

1. Remove the control assembly from the instrument panel.
2. Remove the pushnut retaining the cable end loop on the temperature lever arm. Then, disconnect the cable housing from the control assembly.
3. Disconnect the temperature cable from the plenum temperature blend door crank arm and the cable mounting bracket.
4. Note how the cable was routed, and remove the cable from the vehicle.

To install:

5. Check to be sure the self adjusting clip is at least 1 inch from the end loop of the control cable.
6. Route the cable behind the instrument panel and connect the control cable to the mounting bracket on the plenum.
7. Install the self adjusting clip on the temperature blend door crank arm.
8. Connect the loop end of the control cable to the temperature lever arm on the control assembly. Snap the cable housing into place at the control assembly.
9. Install a push nut to retain the cable end loop on the temperature lever arm.
10. Install the control assembly in the instrument panel.
11. Force the temperature lever to the extreme right end of the slot (warm position) to position the self adjusting clip on the control cable.
12. Check controls for proper operation.

PRESET AND ADJUSTMENT

➧ **See Figure 51**

Before Installation

1. Insert the blade of a small tool into the wire end loop (crank arm end) of the control cable.
2. Grip the self adjusting clip with a pair of pliers, then slide it down the control wire away from the loop approximately 1 inch (25.4mm).
3. Install the cable assembly.
4. Rapidly move the control lever to the extreme right of the slot (WARM) to position the self adjusting clip.
5. Check for proper operation.

After Installation

1. Move the control lever to the **COOL** position.
2. Hold the crank arm firmly into position, then insert the blade of a small flatbladed tool into the wire loops, and pull the cable wire through the self adjusting clip until there is a space of approximately 1 inch (25.4mm) between the clip and the wire end loop.
3. Rapidly move the control lever to the extreme right of the slot **WARM** to position the self adjusting clip.
4. Check for proper operation.

Vacuum Selector Switch

REMOVAL & INSTALLATION

1. Remove the control assembly from the instrument panel.
2. Remove the two screws retaining the vacuum switch to the control assembly.
3. On later models it is necessary to bend back two snap tabs on the bottom of control housing to release vacuum switch from control assembly.

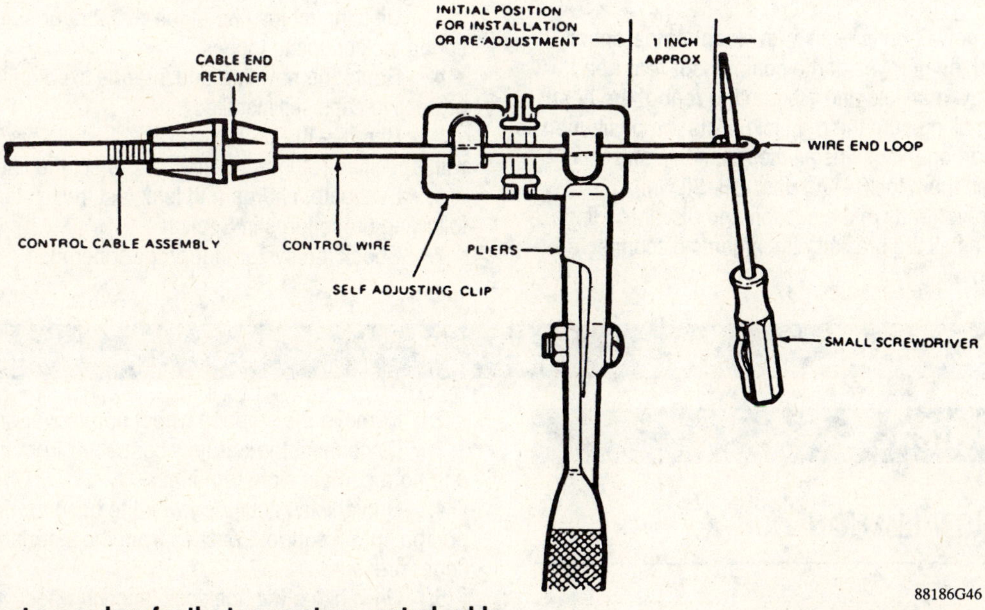

Fig. 51 Adjustment procedure for the temperature control cable

To Install:

4. Position the vacuum selector switch to the control housing, ensure selector switch snaps into place and the housing mounting pins are inserted into the holes of the selector switch.
5. Install the two screws to attach the vacuum switch to the control assembly.
6. Install the control assembly in instrument panel and check for proper operation.

Compressor Relief Valve

REMOVAL & INSTALLATION

1. Discharge the refrigerant from the system. This should be performed at an authorized service center.
2. Remove the A/C pressure relief valve deflector from the valve.
3. Remove the valve from the A/C manifold and tube.

To install:

4. Use new O-rings and lubricate them with clean refrigerant oil.
5. Install the O-rings to the compressor rear head. Install the valve to the manifold and tube.
6. Attach the deflector to the valve.
7. Evacuate, charge and leak test the system with refrigerant following procedures in Section 1.

A/C Manifold and Tube

REMOVAL & INSTALLATION

1. Discharge the refrigerant from the system. This should be performed at an authorized service center.
2. Disconnect the other ends of the suction and discharge lines. Remove any bracket attachments, then remove the A/C manifold and tube assembly from the vehicle.

To install:

3. Lubricate the new O-rings seals with clean refrigerant oil, then position them in the grooves of the compressor rear head.
4. Position the A/C manifold and tube on the rear of the head of the compressor, making sure the manifold pilots are positioned in the compressor port openings. Install the manifolds and tube retaining bolt. Tighten them to 13–17 ft. lbs. (18–23 Nm).
5. Connect the other ends of the suction and discharge lines using new O-rings. Install the bracket attachments disconnected previously during removal.
6. Evacuate, charge and leak test the system with refrigerant following procedures in Section 1.

Cycling Clutch Switch

REMOVAL & INSTALLATION

1. Discharge the A/C system using an approved Recycling/Recovery unit. Refer to Section 1.
2. Disconnect the wire harness connector from the pressure switch.
3. Unscrew the pressure switch from the top of the suction accumulator/drier.

To Install:

4. Lubricate the O-ring on the accumulator nipple with clean refrigerant oil.
5. Screw the pressure switch on the accumulator nipple and tighten the switch. Hand tighten switch if a plastic nipple is used.
6. Connect the wire connector to the pressure switch.
7. Evacuate, charge and leak test the system with refrigerant following procedures in Section 1.
8. Check the pressure switch for leaks and proper operation.

Orifice Tube

REMOVAL & INSTALLATION

➥ The fix orifice tube located in the liquid line cannot be serviced in detail as a component of the line. If replacement is necessary, the line and tube must be replaced as an assembly.

1. Discharge the A/C system using an approved Recycling/Recovery unit. Refer to Section 1.
2. Disconnect the refrigerant line at the condenser outlet connection using spring lock coupling removal tools.
3. Disconnect the line at the evaporator core using the same spring lock coupling tools.
4. Route the new line and integral fixed orifice tube with the protective caps still installed.
5. Remove the protective caps. Install new O-rings lubricated with specified refrigerant oil and connect the lines to the fittings.
6. Evacuate, charge and leak test the system with refrigerant following procedures in Section 1.
7. Check the system for proper operation.

CRUISE CONTROL

Control Switches

REMOVAL & INSTALLATION

Without Air Bags

1. Disconnect the negative battery cable.
2. Remove the steering wheel horn cover and pad assembly.
3. Disconnect the harness connector from the speed control and horn contact plate terminal.
4. On vehicles equipped with the base model steering wheel, pry the speed control switches from the steering wheel using finger pressure.
5. On vehicles with the sport steering wheel, remove the 4 screws attaching the speed control switches to the steering wheel.

6. Remove the speed control switch and harness assembly.

To install:

7. On vehicles equipped with the base model steering wheel, position the speed control switches into the steering wheel and snap into place.
8. On vehicles with the sport steering wheel, position the speed control switches into the steering wheel and install the 4 attaching screws.
9. Connect the wire harness to the terminal on the contact plate.
10. Connect the horn wires to the terminals on the horn cover and press the horn cover onto the steering wheel.

➥ Ensure that the wire harness does not interfere with cover installation.

11. Position the pad and cover assembly and snap into place.
12. Connect the negative battery cable and check system operation.

With Air Bags

1. Disconnect the negative battery cable.
2. Disconnect the positive battery cable and wait one minute for the backup power supply to deplete its stored energy.
3. Remove the two back cover plugs. Remove the two screw and washer assemblies retaining the driver's side air bag module to the steering wheel.
4. Disconnect the air bag electrical connection from the air bag sliding contact connector.

****WARNING**

Place the air bag module on a bench with the trim cover facing up.

5. Remove the driver's side air bag module from the steering wheel.
6. Disconnect the harness connector from the speed control.
7. Disconnect the horn switch wire.
8. Remove the retaining screws from the cruise control actuator switch.
9. Carefully pry away the right side of the steering wheel back cover to allow enough clearance to remove the right speed control switch wiring from the steering wheel. Repeat for the left side., then remove the actuator switch.

To install:

10. Position the cruise control actuator switch onto the steering wheel, then install the screws.

****CAUTION**

Make sure that the wires are positioned so that there is no interference when installing the air bag module.

11. Connect all of the harness wiring, then route them into the steering wheel cavity. Install the wire organizer.
12. Position the driver's side air bag module on the steering wheel, then connect the air bag sliding contact.
13. Install the driver's side air bag module on the steering wheel, and install the screws and washers assemblies. Tighten to 8–10 ft. lbs. (10–14 Nm).
14. Install the two back cover plugs.
15. Connect the positive battery cable.
16. Connect the negative battery cable.
17. Check the operation of the cruise control actuator switch.
18. Prove out the air bag system.

Speed Sensor

REMOVAL & INSTALLATION

➧ See Figure 52

1. Raise and safely support vehicle on jackstands.
2. Loosen the retaining nut holding the sensor in the transmission.
3. Remove the driven gear with the sensor from the transmission.
4. Disconnect the electrical connector from the speed sensor.
5. Disconnect the speedometer cable by pulling it out of the speed sensor.

➥ Do not attempt to remove the spring retainer clip with the speedometer in the sensor.

To install:

6. Position the driven gear on the speed sensor. Install the gear retainer.
7. Connect the electrical connector.

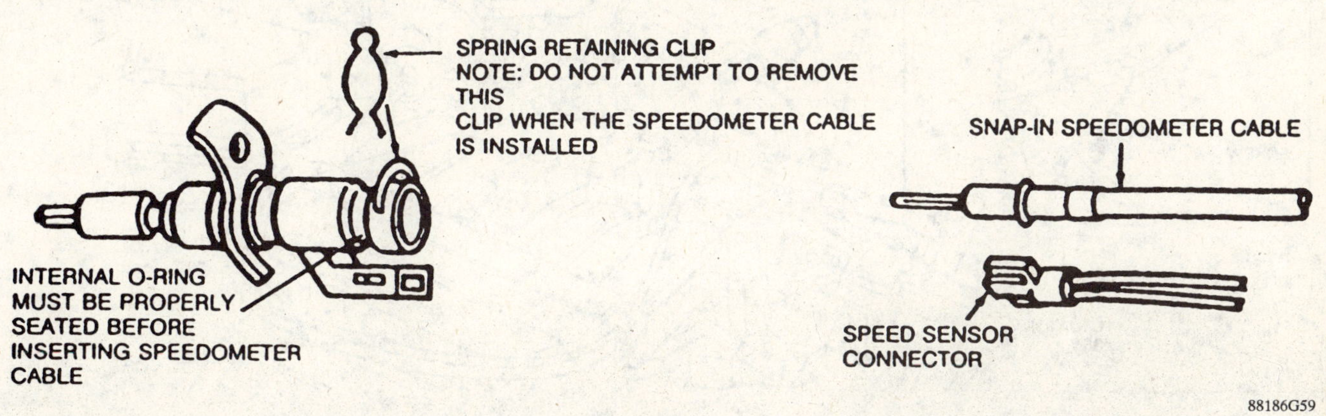

Fig. 52 The speed sensor is a vital part in the cruise control system

8. Ensure that the internal O-ring is properly seated in the sensor housing. Snap the speedometer cable into the sensor housing.
9. Insert the sensor assembly into the transmission housing and tighten the retaining nut to 36–54 inch lbs. (4–6 Nm). Lower the vehicle and check system operation.

Amplifier

REMOVAL & INSTALLATION

The amplifier is located on the brake pedal on some models, and behind the glove box, under the evaporator housing on others.

1. Disconnect the negative battery cable.
2. Remove the amplifier assembly hardware.
3. Disconnect the 2 amplifier assembly electrical connectors.
4. Remove the amplifier assembly from the its mounting area.

To Install:

5. Place the amplifier assembly into position and connect the electrical connectors.
6. Install the amplifier assembly hardware. Tighten the amplifier to its mounting bracket to 12–21 inch lbs. (1–3 Nm).
7. Connect the negative battery cable.

Servo

REMOVAL & INSTALLATION

See Figure 53

1. Disconnect the negative battery cable.
2. Disconnect the actuator cable from the accelerator cable.
3. Disconnect the servo wire at wiring harness connector near the radiator support.
4. Raise and safely support the left front side of vehicle on jackstands.
5. Remove the left front wheel and inner fender splash shield.
6. Remove the vacuum hoses from the servo assembly.
7. Remove the screws holding the servo mounting bracket to the brace.
8. Remove the nuts from the actuator cable cover at the servo. Remove the cable, cover and rubber boot.
9. Remove the nuts attaching the servo to the mounting bracket.

To install:

10. Attach the bolt assemblies two the front of the servo.
11. Attach the servo to mounting bracket with the nuts and tighten to 45-65 inch lbs. (5-7 Nm).
12. Install the servo rubber boot.

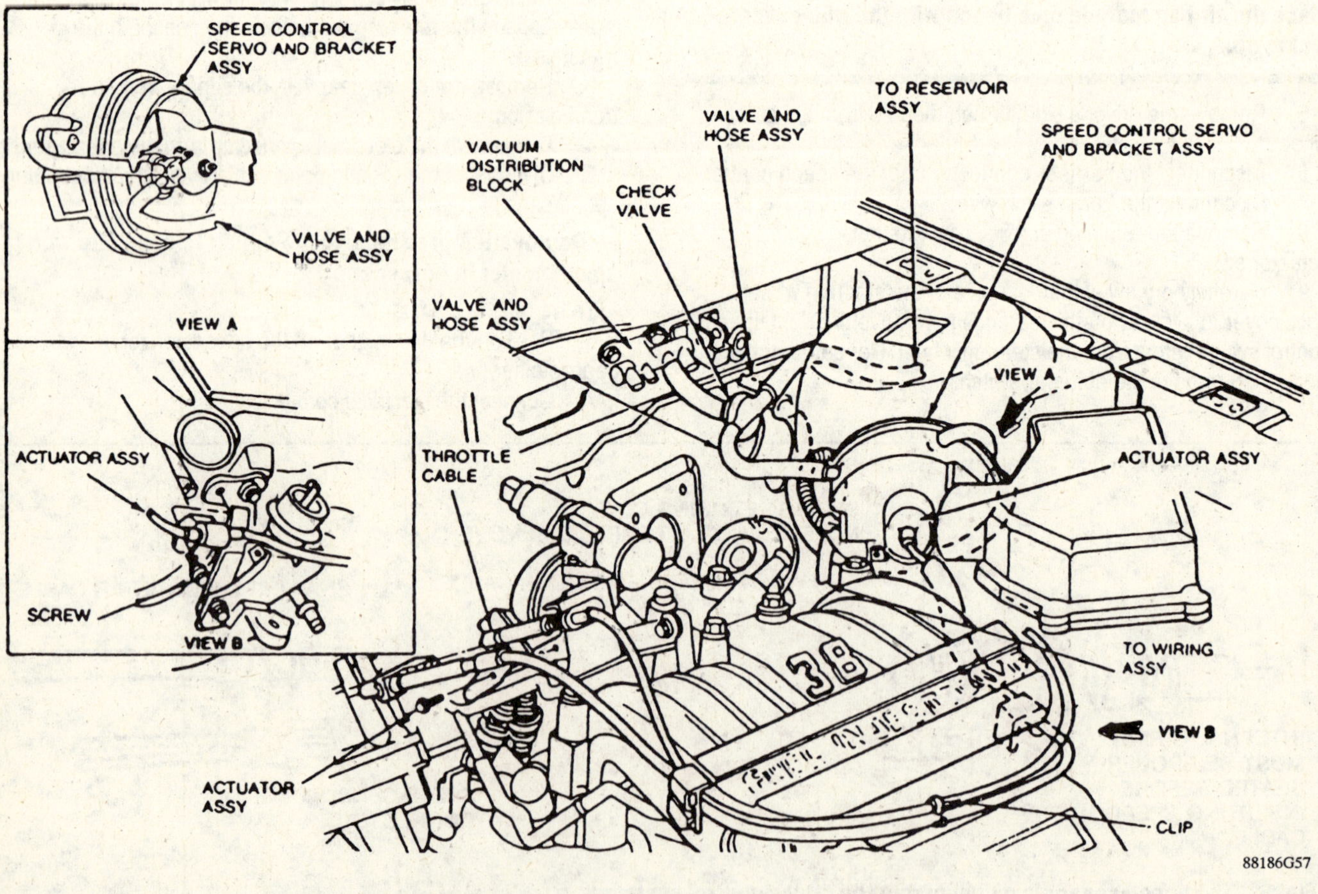

Fig. 53 Common location of the cruise control components

13. Attach the actuator cable to the servo plunger. Attach the cable cover to the servo with the nuts and tighten to 45–65 inch lbs. (5–7 Nm).
14. Attach the servo and bracket to the brace with screws.
15. Attach the vacuum hoses to the servo. Ensure the vacuum hoses are connected in the correct position. Adjust the servo boot to protect the servo.
16. Install the inner fender splash shield, install the wheel and lower the vehicle.
17. Connect the servo wire harness connector near the radiator support.
18. Connect the speed control actuator cable to the accelerator cable.
19. Connect the negative battery cable and check system operation.

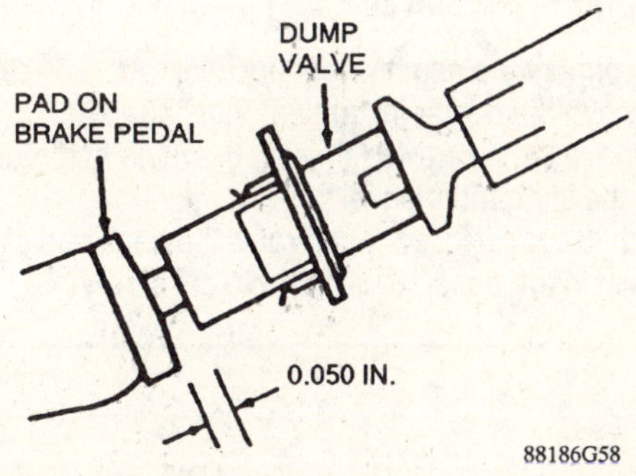

Fig. 54 The vacuum dump valve needs to be adjusted to allow no vacuum leaks in the system

Vacuum Dump Valve

REMOVAL & INSTALLATION

➧ See Figure 54

1. Remove the vacuum hose from valve.
2. Remove the valve from the bracket.

To install:

3. Attach the valve to the bracket.
4. Attach the hose to the valve.
5. Adjust the vacuum dump valve so that it is closed (no vacuum leak) when the brake pedal is up (brakes released) and open when brake pedal is depressed.

ENTERTAINMENT SYSTEMS

Radio Receiver

REMOVAL & INSTALLATION

There are many types of radio, cassette and CD models for the Thunderbird and Cougars throughout the years. The procedures should be pretty standard on most of these types of units. However it is impossible to show you all of the units themselves.

1983–85 exc. Digital Radio

➧ See Figures 55 and 56

1. Disconnect the negative battery cable.
2. Remove the radio knobs (pull off). Remove the center trim panel.
3. Remove the radio mounting plate screws. Pull the radio towards the front seat to disengage it from the lower bracket.
4. Disconnect the radio and antenna connections.
5. Remove the radio. Remove the nuts and washers as necessary.
6. The rest of installation is the reverse of removal.

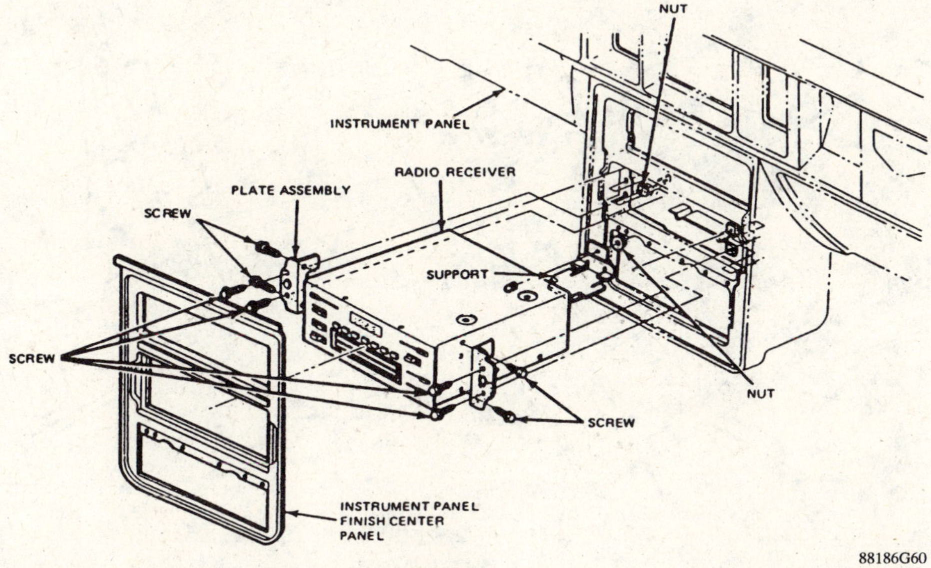

Fig. 55 Thunderbird and XR-7 radio installation — 1983 models

1983–88 Digital Radio

➧ See Figures 57, 58 and 59

1. Disconnect the negative battery cable.
2. Remove the center instrument trim panel.
3. Remove the 4 screws retaining the radio and mounting bracket to the instrument panel.
4. Push the radio forward and raise the back end slightly to clear the clip in the panel. Pull the radio out slowly.
5. Disconnect the antenna and wiring.

To install:

6. Attach the antenna and wiring to back of the unit..
7. Insert the radio into the dash, tighten the mounting screws to the bracket to retain the unit.
8. Connect the negative battery cable.
9. Test the unit for proper operation
10. If the system works well, install the center trim panel.

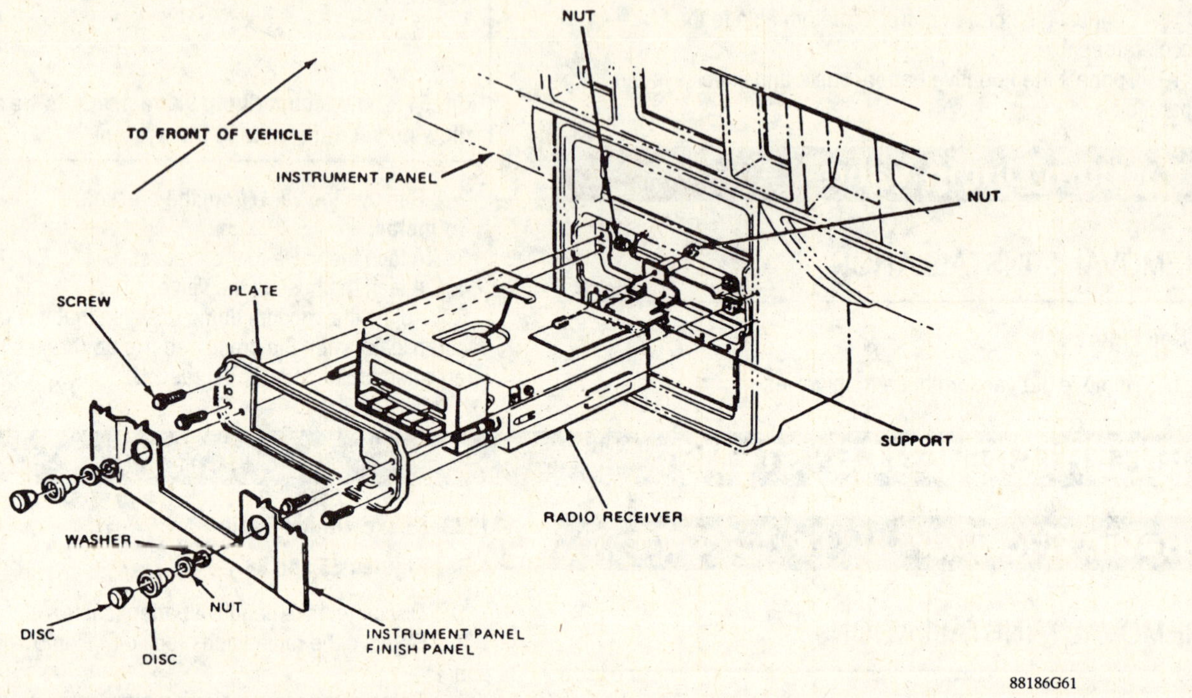

Fig. 56 Radio with cassette installation — 1983 models

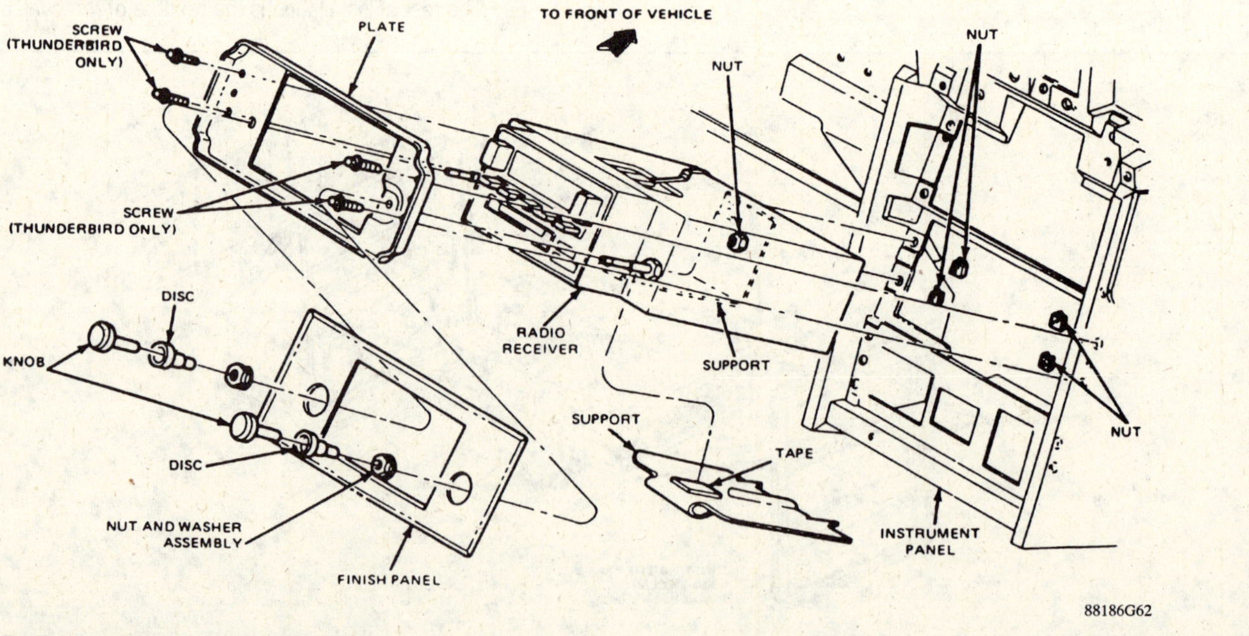

Fig. 57 Radio installation — 1984–86 models

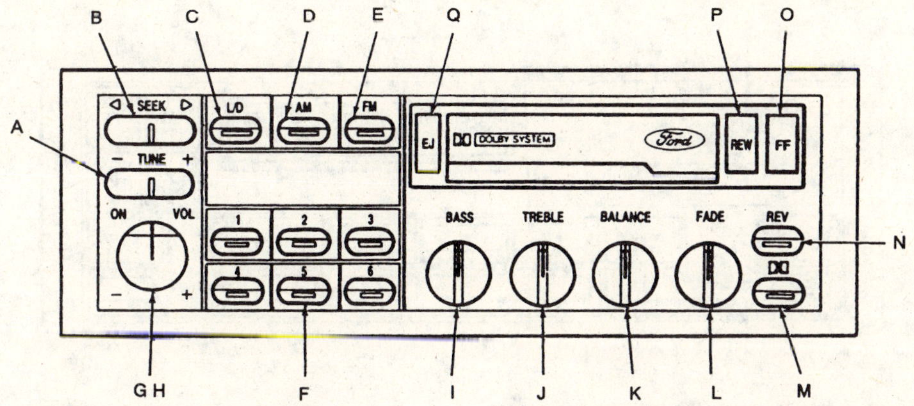

The features described are identical on all the radios (where applicable).

A. **Tune** up or down to the next channel (.2 mHz in FM, 10 kHz in AM).

B. **Seek** up or down to the next listenable station.

C. **LOCAL/DISTANT:** Toggles between local and Distant mode. Only displays LOC in Local mode (Distant mode not displayed). Local mode is for use in metropolitan areas and only on strong signal stations.

D. Pushing AM enables AM mode. AM will be displayed. Six AM memories.

E. Pushing FM enables FM mode. Pushing FM again will toggle between FM1 and FM2. Six FM memories in FM1 and another six in FM2. FM1 or FM2 will be displayed.

F. To store a station depress **MEMORY** button and hold for two seconds (sound will disappear and come back after two seconds). To recall a station, depress MEMORY button and release.

G. **VOLUME/ON-OFF:** (Thunderbird/Cougar), Push to turn on, push again to turn off. Turn control clockwise to increase volume.

H. **VOLUME/ON-OFF/CLOCK CONTROL:** (Mustang), Rotate to turn on radio and increase volume. Push to change display mode or push and hold to set time. Refer to clock operation.

I. **BASS:** Rotate clockwise for more bass and counterclockwise for less bass.

J. **TREBLE:** Rotate clockwise for more treble and counterclockwise for less treble.

K. **BALANCE:** Adjusts sound between LH side and RH side of vehicle.

L. **FADE:** Adjusts sound between front and rear of vehicle.

M. **DOLBY:** Press for playing tapes recorded using the Dolby® System. Press again to deactivate.

N. **REVERSE:** Press to change direction of cassette tape.

O. **FAST FORWARD:** Press to fast advance the program being played.

P. **FAST REWIND:** Press to change direction of tape and fast rewind.

Q. **EJECT:** Press to eject cassette.

88186G63

Fig. 58 Electronic radio with cassette — 1988 shown

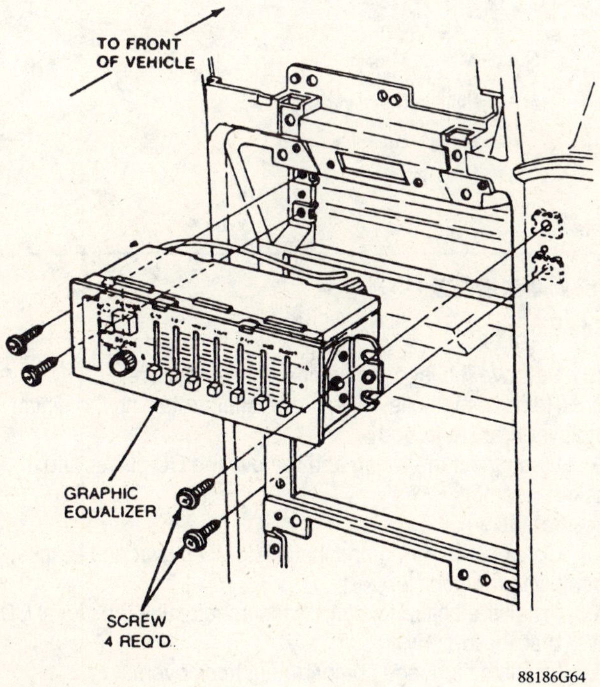

88186G64

Fig. 59 Graphic equalizer — 1988 shown

1989-96 Radio and Tape Player

➧ See Figures 60, 61, 62, 63, 64 and 65

➝ A special tool, number T87P-19061-A or equivalent, must be used in order to remove radio components with out damage to unit.

1. Disconnect negative battery cable.
2. Insert two removal tools T87P-19061-A or equivalent into the radio face plates holes, until tension of spring clips is felt.
3. Flex outward on both sides simultaneously and pull radio out.
4. Disconnect wiring connectors and antenna cable.

To install:

5. Attach the antenna and wiring to back of the unit..
6. Insert the radio into the dash, then push on the radio until the clips "click".
7. Connect the negative battery cable.
8. Test the unit for proper operation

CD Player

DASH MOUNTED

➧ See Figures 66

1. Disconnect negative battery cable.
2. Insert two removal tools T87P-19061-A or equivalent into holes, until tension of spring clips is felt.

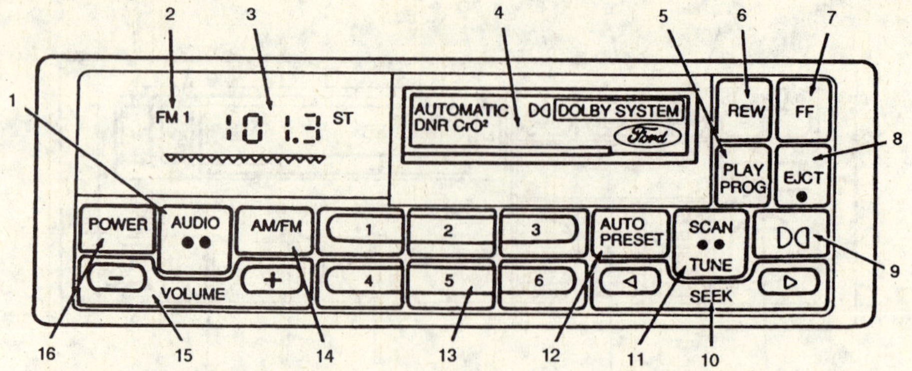

1. Audio button (bass, treble, speaker balance and speaker fade control)
2. AM/FM band indicator
3. Radio station frequency indicator
4. Tape opening
5. Play program button
6. Rewind button
7. Fast forward button
8. Eject button
9. Dolby button
10. Seek button
11. Scan/tune button
12. Auto preset button
13. Memory buttons
14. AM/FM band selector
15. Volume button
16. Power button

88186G70

Fig. 60 Premium Analog Cassette (PAC) and CCDJ radio chassis assembly — 1995 models

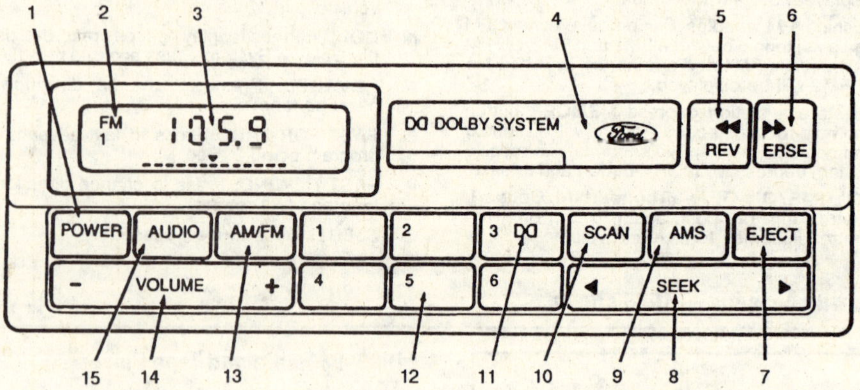

1. Power button
2. AM/FM band indicator
3. Radio station frequency indicator
4. Tape opening
5. Reverse button
6. Reverse button
7. Eject button
8. Seek button
9. Automatic music search (AMS) button
10. Scan button
11. Dolby button
12. Memory buttons
13. AM/FM band selector
14. Volume button
15. Audio button (bass, treble, speaker balance, and speaker fade control)

88186G71

Fig. 61 Electronic Cassette System (ECS) radio chassis — 1995 models

3. Flex outward on both sides simultaneously and pull CD player out.
4. Disconnect wiring connectors and ground strap.
5. Remove rear support

➥ If gear shift on console interferes with removal and installation, set parking brake and place in L1 or L2 for automatic transmission and 2nd or 4th gear for manual transmission.

To install:

6. Install the rear support.
7. Connect the wiring and ground strap for the radio unit.
8. Insert the radio/CD player unit into the dash, until the clips "click".
9. Connect the negative battery cable.
10. Test the system.

TRUNK MOUNTED

➧ See Figure 67

1. Remove the luggage compartment trim covers.
2. Remove the bolts, nuts and washers retaining the digital CD player bracket-to-body.
3. Disconnect the wiring and remove the CD player and bracket assembly.

To install:

4. Connect the wiring and install the CD player and bracket assembly to the vehicle.
5. Install the bolts, nuts and washers retaining the digital CD player bracket-to-body.
6. Install the luggage compartment trim covers.
7. Test the system.

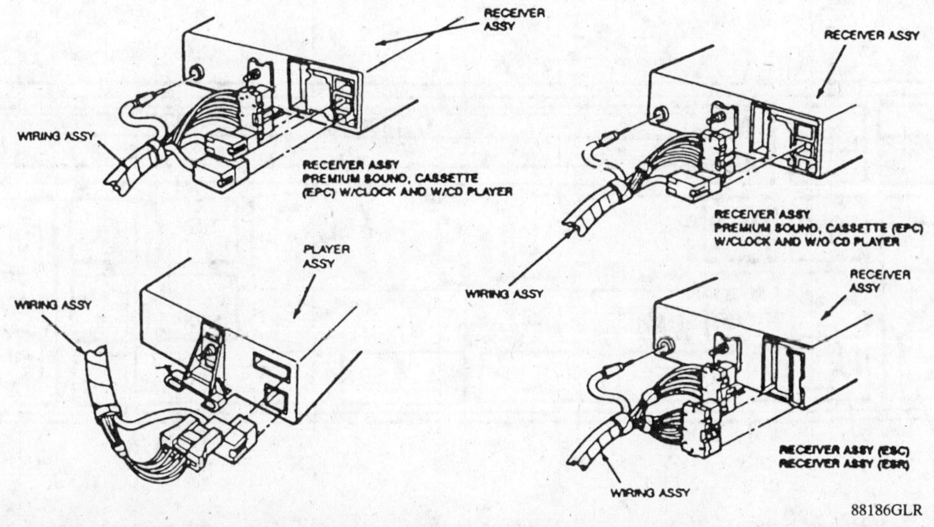

Fig. 62 Radio wiring harness types on some models — 1989–96 models

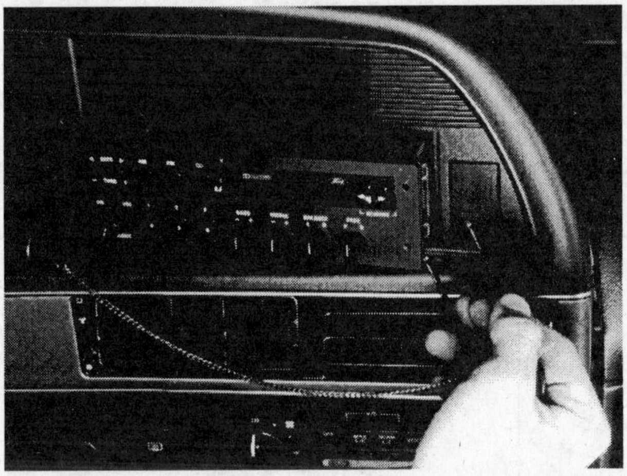

Fig. 63 Using the special radio removal tool, detach the unit from the dash

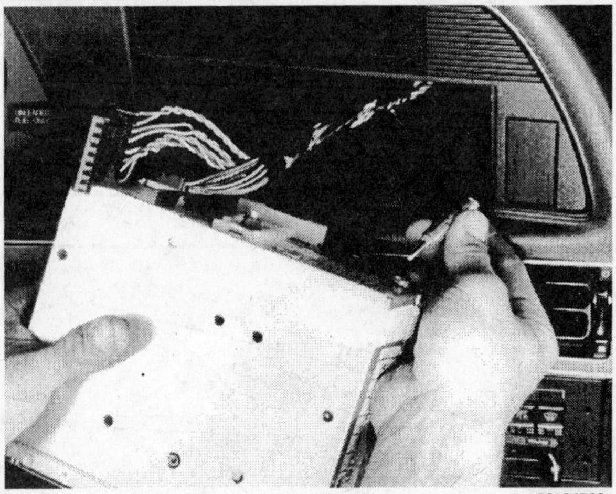

Fig. 65 The antenna cable is attached to the rear of the radio, disconnect it

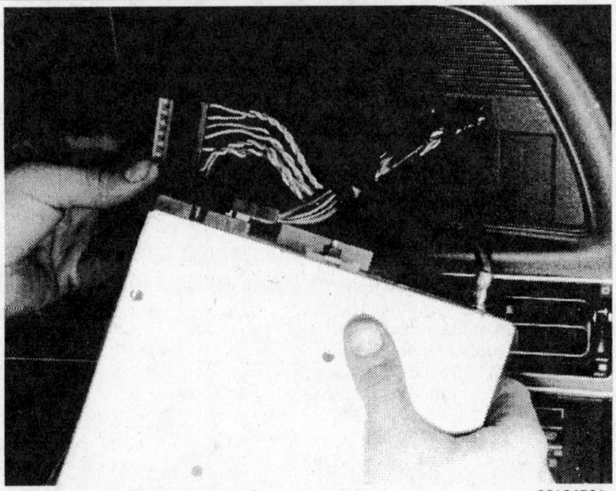

Fig. 64 Pull the electrical harness from the back of the radio assembly

Premium Sound System

➥ Premium sound amplifier and JBL amplifier removal and installation procedures are the same.

1. Remove the screw retaining relay panel in luggage compartment and swing panel down.
2. Press on the four retainers and lift amplifier assembly panel.
3. Disconnect electrical connectors and ground wire and remove assembly.

To install:

4. Attach the electrical connectors and ground wire to the unit.
5. Install the unit, then tighten the amplifier assembly panel.
6. Install the relay panel in the luggage compartment.

Subwoofer Assembly

➧ See Figure 68

1. Disconnect power/body electrical connector and signal feed from JBL amplifier.

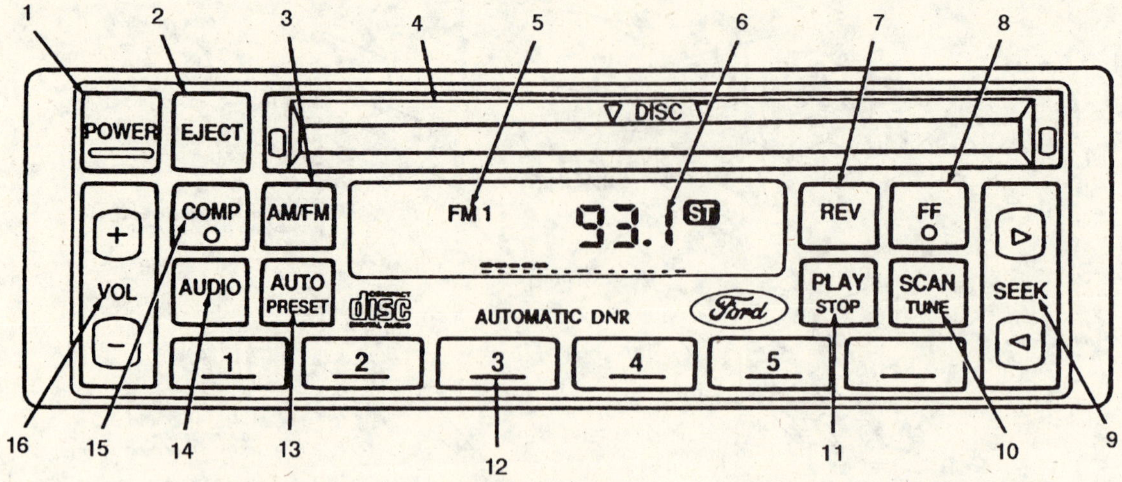

1. Power button
2. Eject button
3. AM/FM band selector
4. Disc loading slot
5. AM/FM band indicator
6. Radio station frequency indicator
7. Reverse button
8. Forward button
9. Seek button
10. Scan/tune button
11. Play/stop button
12. Preset station buttons
13. Auto preset button
14. Audio button (bass, treble, speaker balance and speaker fade control)
15. Compression button
16. Volume button

88186G74

Fig. 66 The CD player is incorporated in with the radio unit on these models — 1994-96 models

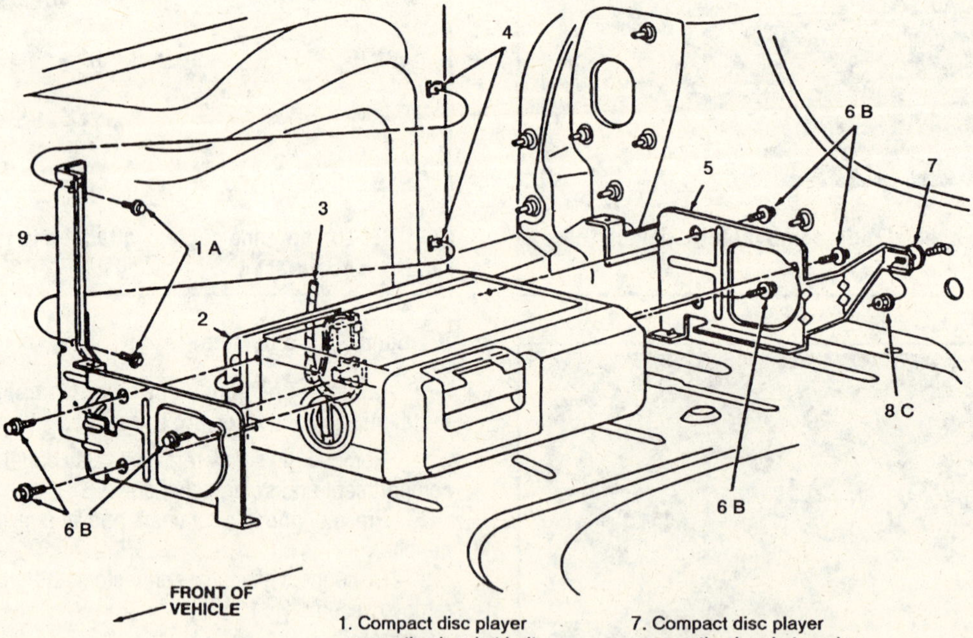

1. Compact disc player mounting bracket bolt (2 req'd)
2. Digital audio compact disc player
3. Radio amplifier wiring
4. J nut (2 req'd)
5. RH rear compact disc player mounting bracket
6. Digital audio compact disc player retaining bolt (6 req'd)
7. Compact disc player mounting bracket washer
8. Compact disc player mounting bracket nut
9. LH front compact disc player mounting bracket

A. Tighten to 2.7-3.7 N.m (23.9-32.7 lb-in)
B. Tighten to 1.6-2.2 N.m (14.2-19.5 lb-in)

88186G75

Fig. 67 When a CD unit requires more than one disc, your system will be installed in the trunk — 1995-96 models

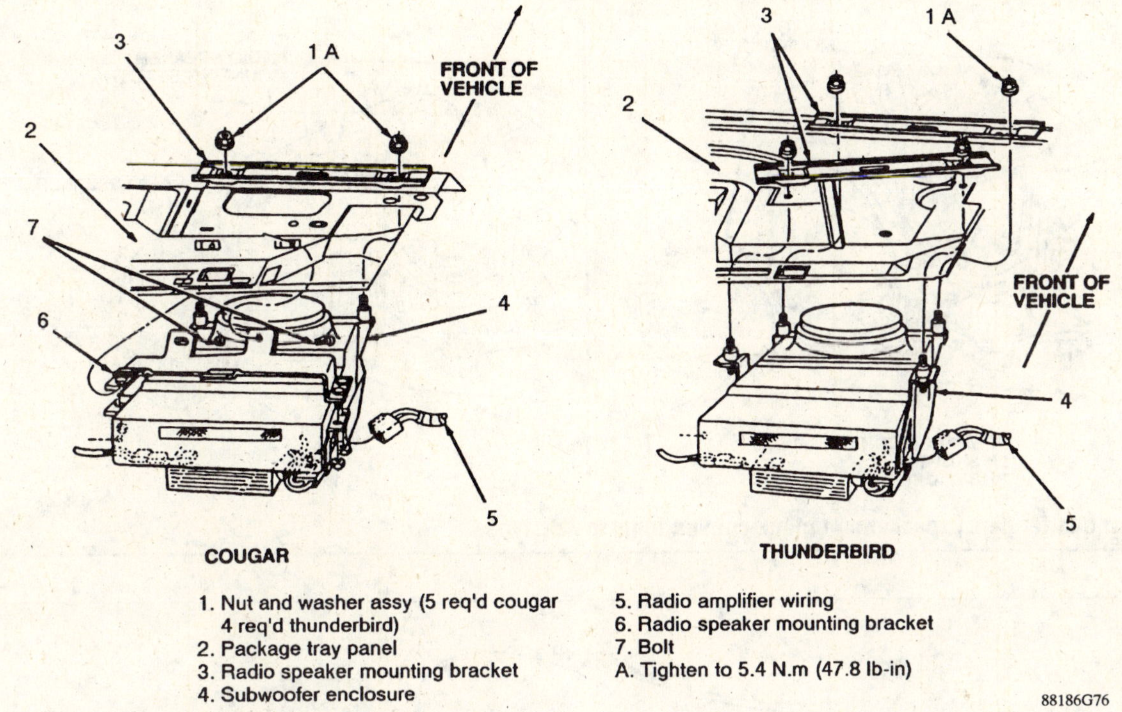

Fig. 68 JBL subwoofer assembly mounting — 1989–96 models

2. Remove the four attaching nuts and lower subwoofer assembly, taking care not to damage cover.

To install:

3. Attach the electrical harness to the unit, then place into position.
4. Make sure the four studs are aligned through subwoofer assembly.
5. Remove the four speaker retaining screws.

Speakers

REMOVAL & INSTALLATION

Door Mounted

➧ **See Figure 69**

1. Remove the door trim panel.
2. Disconnect the speaker lead wire connector and remove speaker.

To Install:

3. Connect the speaker lead wire connector.
4. Position speaker to the door panel. Ensure that a watershield protector has been installed first.
5. Install attaching screws.
6. Install door panel on door and check speaker operation.

Rear Quarter Mounted

➧ **See Figures 70 and 71**

1. Remove the screws or unsnap retaining speaker grille cover and remove the cover.
2. Remove the screws retaining the speaker to mount.
3. Disconnect the speaker lead wire connector and remove speaker.

To install:

4. Connect the speaker lead to the unit.
5. Insert the speaker into the quarter panel, then tighten the mounting screws to 24–32 inch lbs. (2–4 Nm).
6. Place the speaker cover into position and snap shut or screw tight.
7. Check the operation of the speaker.

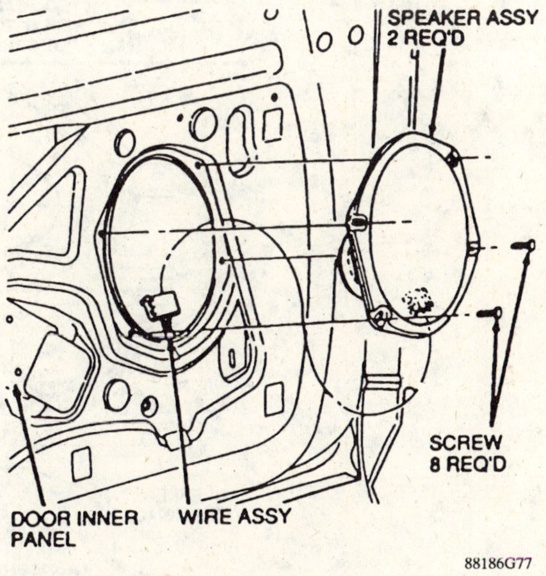

Fig. 69 Door mounted speakers are typically the same on most models

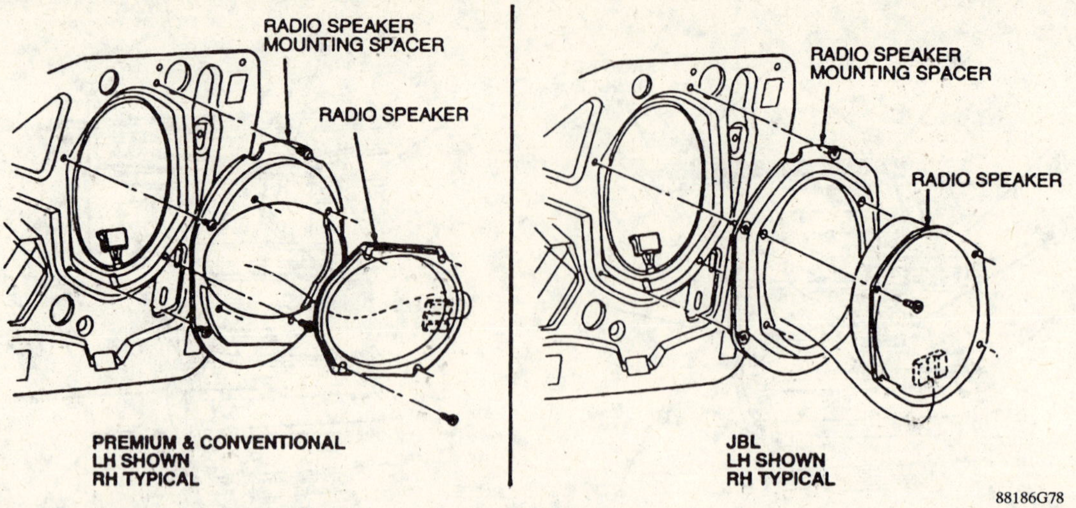

Fig. 70 Rear quarter panel speaker mounting, conventional to JBL types

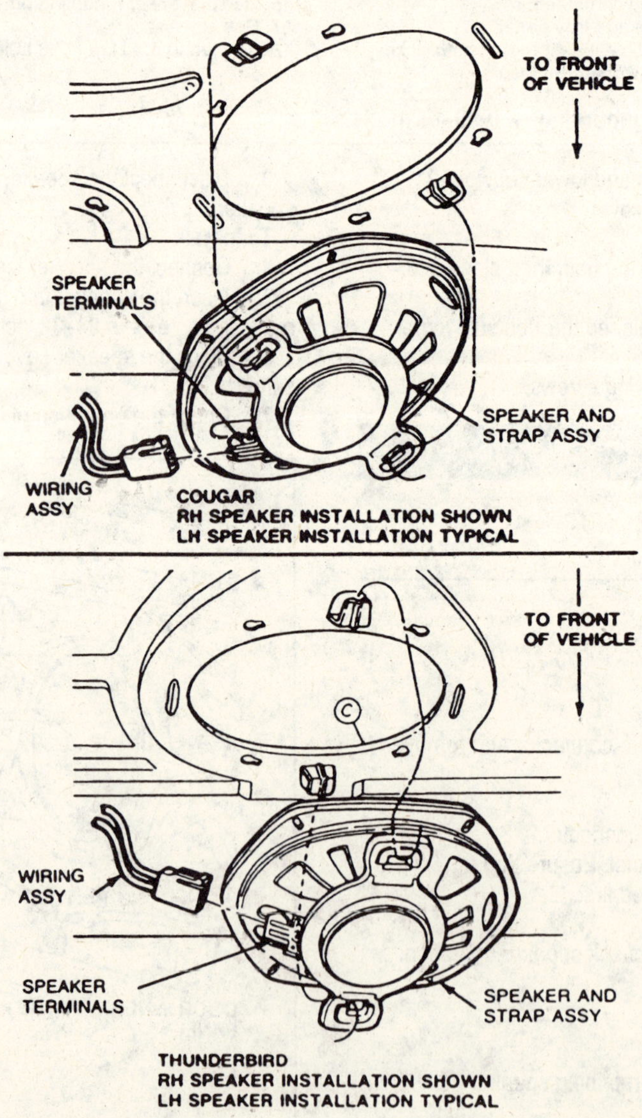

Fig. 71 Rear seat package tray mounted speakers

MOBILE PHONE UNIT

Telephone Microphone

REMOVAL & INSTALLATION

➧ **See Figure 72**

1. Remove the mobile phone microphone from the roof trim panel at the windshield.
2. Disconnect and lower the roof trim panel on the right side just enough to allow the removal of the microphone cable clips at the roof outer structure.
3. Remove the right roof side inner front moulding.
4. Remove the cowl side trim panel.
5. Pull the carpet back along the right side of the vehicle.
6. Remove the microphone cable from the wiring shields.
7. Remove the rear seat.
8. Remove the right quarter trim panel.
9. Pull the microphone cable into the trunk from the passenger's side.
10. Unhook the pushpin retaining the relay panel.
11. Unhook the two relay panel side retaining clips, then lower the relay panel.
12. Disconnect the cable connector from the module phone transceiver. Open the connector and verify which wiring belongs to the mobile telephone microphone. Cut the phone wiring 3-4 inches (76-102mm) from the connector. Splice the cable wiring into the old wiring.

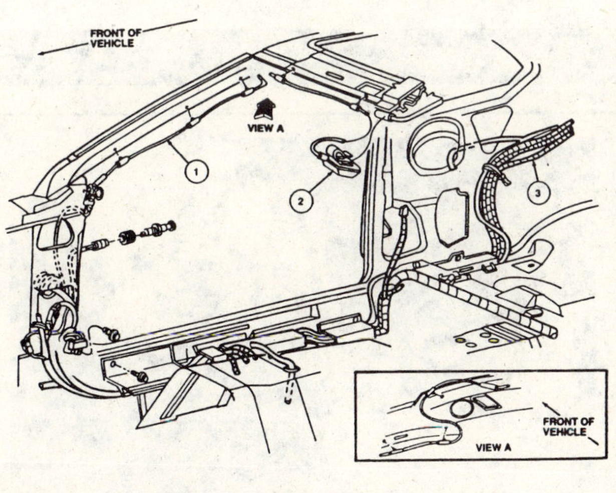

Fig. 72 Mobile telephone microphone — 1995-96 models

13. To install, reverse the procedure.
14. Check the operation of the unit.

Phone Transceiver

REMOVAL & INSTALLATION

➧ **See Figure 73**

1. Unhook the pushpin retaining relay panel on the driver's side in the trunk.
2. Unhook the relay panel side retaining clips, then lower the relay panel.
3. Push back the transceiver retaining clips, then remove the phone transceiver.
4. Disconnect the transceiver electrical connection and antenna cable.
5. Reverse the procedure to install.
6. Check the operation of the unit.

Telephone Antenna

REMOVAL & INSTALLATION

➧ **See Figure 74 and 75**

1. Disconnect the multi function control antenna cable from the interior antenna hose.

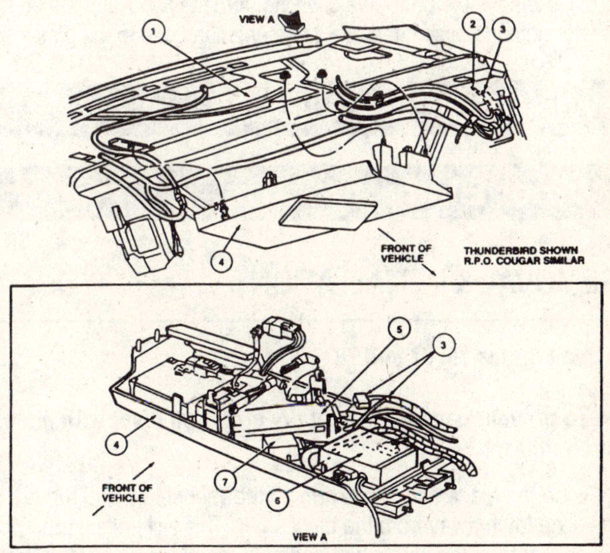

Fig. 73 Exploded view of the mobile phone components

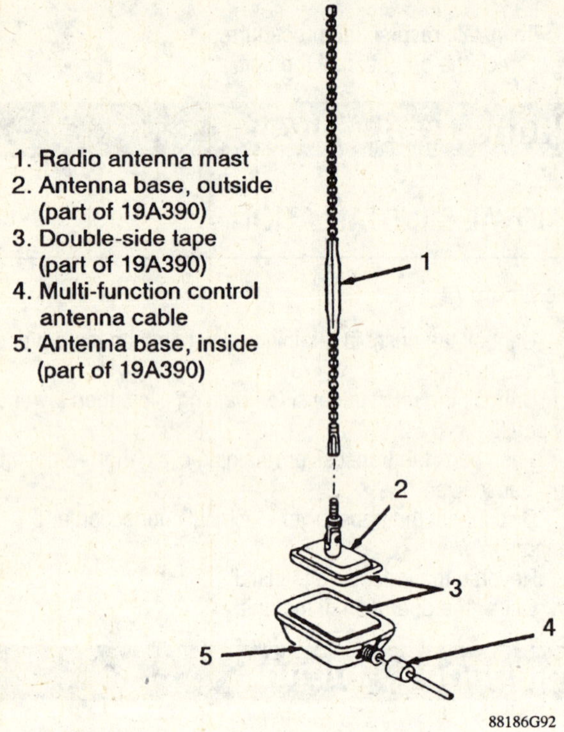

Fig. 74 Mobile phone antenna assembly

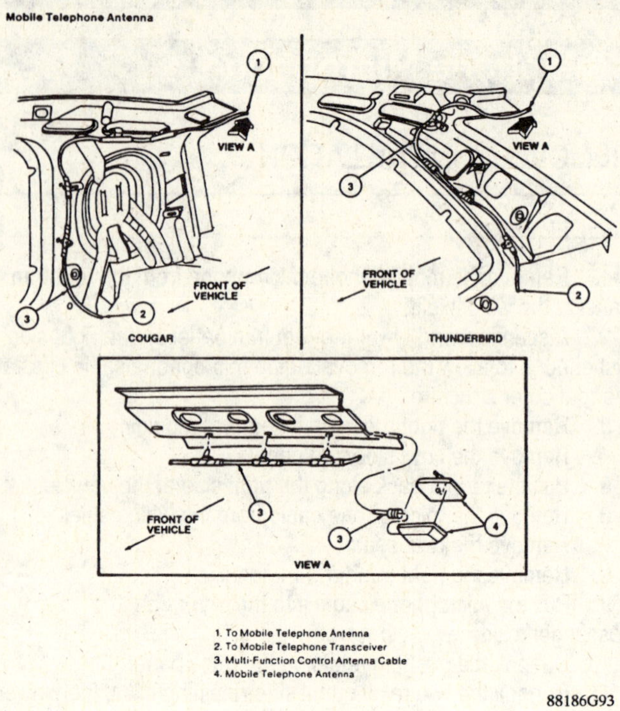

Fig. 75 Mobile phone antenna routing

2. Cut the two-way tape retaining the base to the glass. Remove the base by pulling on it by hand. Do not pry on the glass.
3. Remove the antenna mast from the exterior antenna base.

To install:

4. Clean the two-way tape from the inside and outside of the glass.
5. Remove the protective covering from the two-way tape on the interior antenna base, then attach the antenna base to the glass.
6. Connect the multi-function control antenna cable to the interior antenna case.
7. Remove the protective covering from the two-way tape on the exterior antenna base, then attach the antenna base to the glass directly over the interior base.
8. Install the antenna mast to the exterior antenna base.

WINDSHIELD WIPERS

Wiper Blade and Arm

REMOVAL & INSTALLATION

➧ See Figures 76, 77 and 78

➥ To prevent damage, do not pry arm from pivot with metal or sharp tool.

Raise the blade end of the arm off the windshield and move the slide latch away from the pivot shaft. This will unlock the wiper arm from the pivot shaft and hold the blade end of the arm off of the glass at the same time. The wiper arm can now be pulled off of the pivot shaft without the aid of any tools.

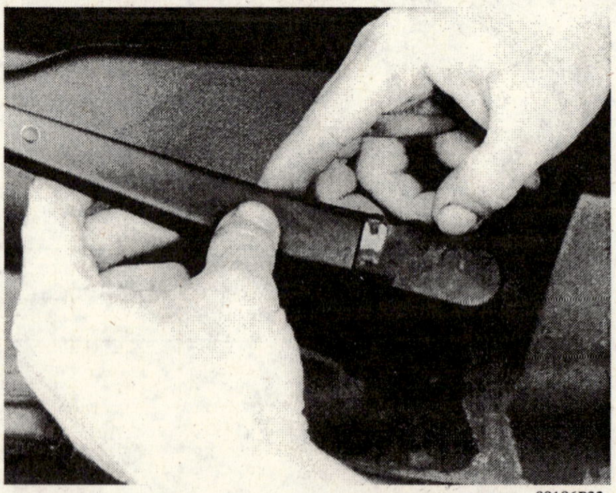

Fig. 76 Raise the wiper arm off of the windshield

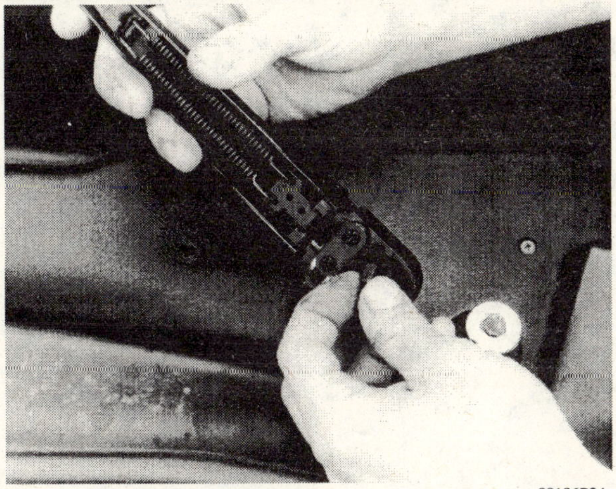
88186P34

Fig. 77 Move the slide latch away from the pivot shaft. This will unlock the wiper arm from the pivot shaft

To install, position the auxiliary arm over the pivot pin, (on 1989 and later models align the keyway on the pivot shaft) hold it down and push the main arm head over the pivot shaft. Ensure pivot shaft is in position, and that the blade assembly is positioned to the correct dimension. Hold the main arm head onto the pivot shaft while raising the blade end of the wiper arm and push the slide latch into the lock under the pivot shaft. Then, lower the blade to the windshield. If the blade does not touch the windshield, the slide latch is not completely in place.

Windshield Wiper Motor

REMOVAL & INSTALLATION

1983–88 Models

See Figure 79

1. Turn the ignition switch to the **ON** position. Turn the wiper switch on. When the blades are straight up on the windshield, turn the key switch **OFF**.
2. Disconnect the negative battery cable. Remove the arm and blade assemblies.
3. Remove the left side leaf guard screen or cowl assembly. Disconnect the linkage drive arm from the wiper motor after removing the retaining clip.
4. Disconnect the electrical wiring harness connector from the wiper motor. Remove the wiper motor mounting bolts and the motor.
5. Install in the reverse order of removal. Before installing the arm and blade assemblies, turn on the key and allow the motor to cycle. Turn the wiper control switch off so that the drives and motor will stop in the park position. Install the arm and blade assemblies.
6. Check the operation of the system.

1989–96 Models

See Figures 80, 81, 82, 83, 84, 85, 86, 87, 88 and 89

1. Disconnect the negative battery cable. With the wipers in the **PARK** position remove the arm and blade assemblies.

The internal permanent magnets used in the wiper motor are a ceramic (glass-like) material. Care must be exercised in handling the motor to avoid damaging the magnets. The motor must not be struck or tapped with a hammer or other object.

2. Remove the cowl vent screens. On some models it may be necessary to remove the cowl top extension-to-hood seal.
3. Remove vacuum manifolds from wiper module.
4. Disconnect wiring connections.
5. Remove the screws and nut from wiper module, then remove the wiper module.
6. Disconnect the linkage drive arm from the motor crankpin after removing the clip.
7. Remove the wiper motor's three attaching nuts. Pull the motor from the opening.

Before installing the arm and blade assembly on the pivot shaft, cycle motor and turn off switch to ensure that it is in PARK position.

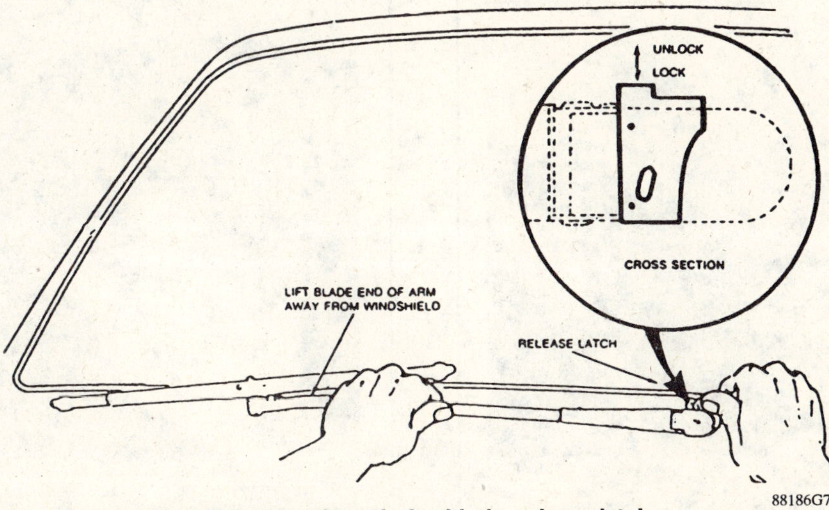

88186G73

Fig. 78 Removing the wiper arm and blade from the pivot shaft with the release latch

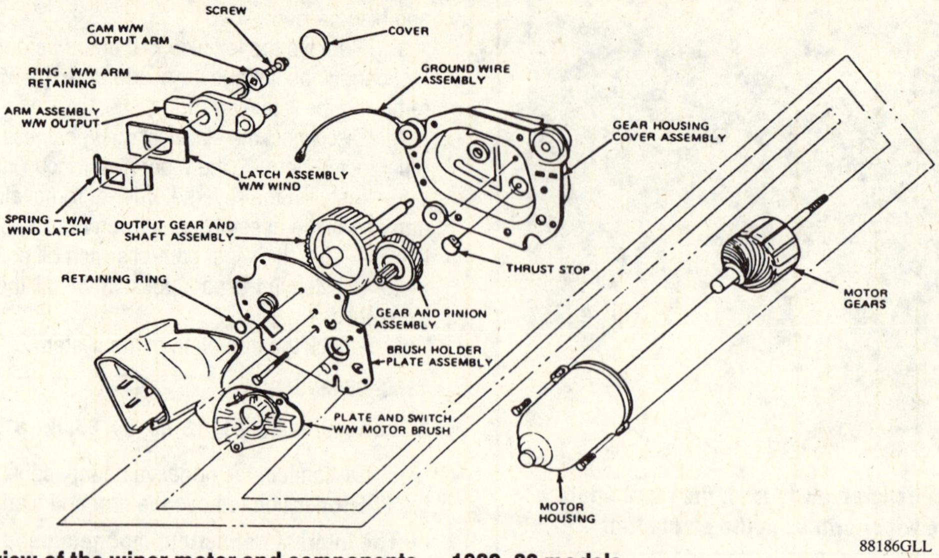

Fig. 79 Exploded view of the wiper motor and components — 1983-88 models

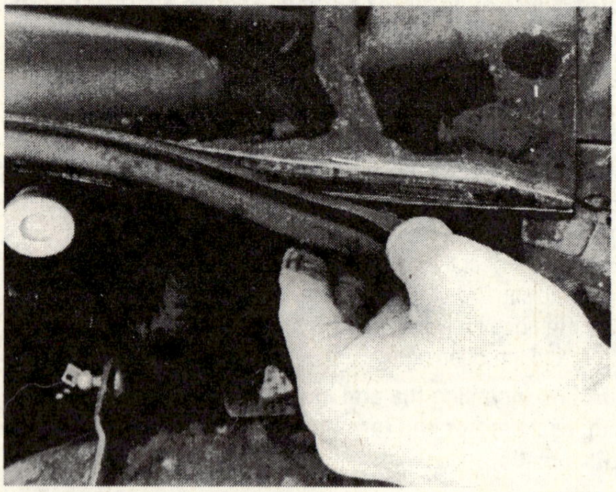

Fig. 80 Remove the cowl vent seal if necessary

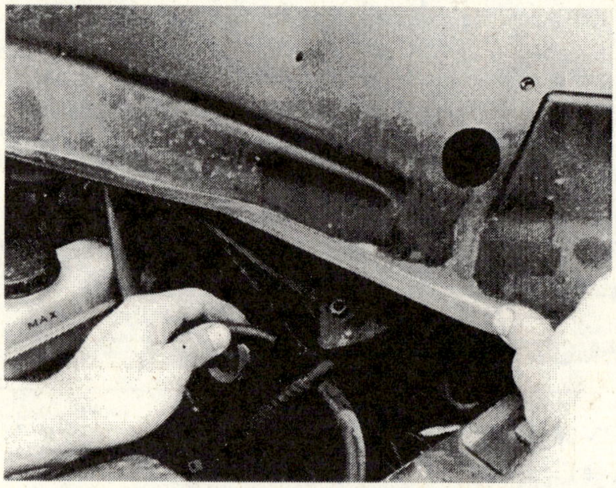

Fig. 82 Detach the vacuum lines from the wiper module

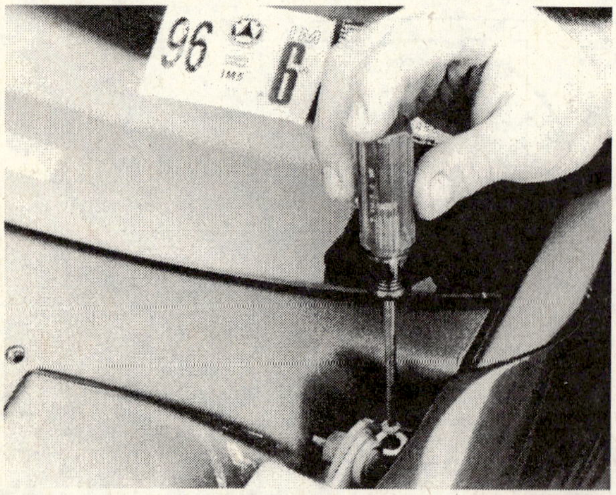

Fig. 81 Unscrew the cowl vent screen

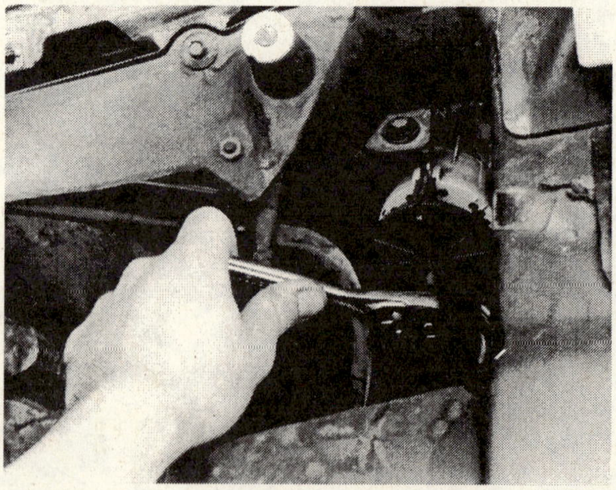

Fig. 83 Unbolt the wiper module . . .

88186P38

Fig. 84 . . . then remove the wiper module from the vehicle

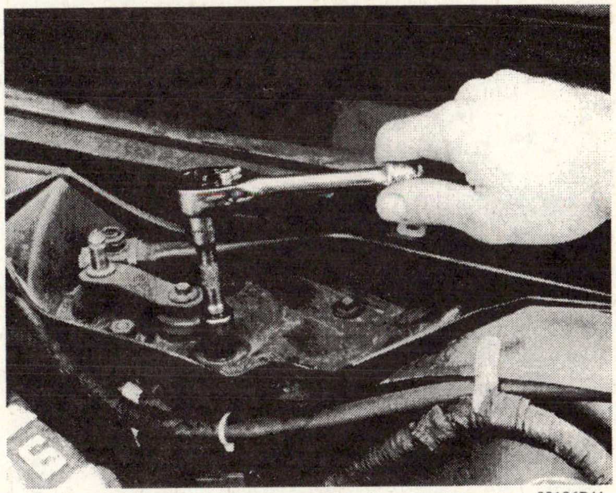

88186P41

Fig. 87 Unbolt the motor

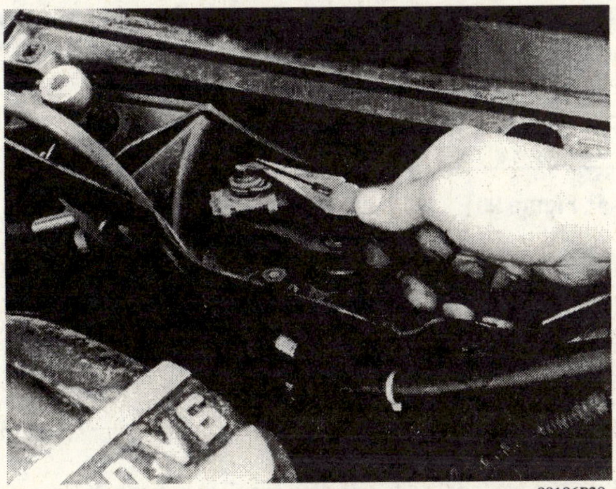

88186P39

Fig. 85 Remove the wiper linkage clip from the crank arm

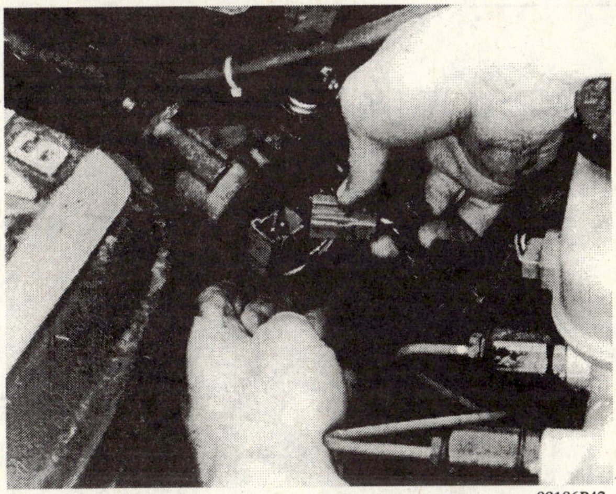

88186P42

Fig. 88 Detach the wiring harness from the motor . . .

88186P40

Fig. 86 Lift the linkage off the shaft

88186P43

Fig. 89 . . . then lift the motor out of the engine compartment

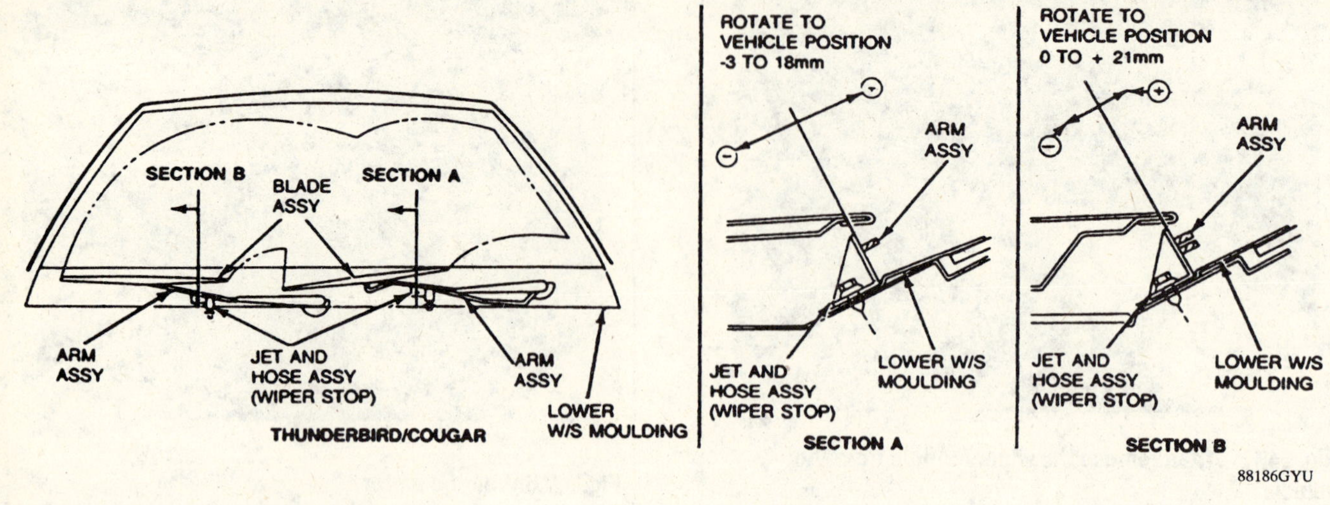

Fig. 90 Wiper height distance on most models

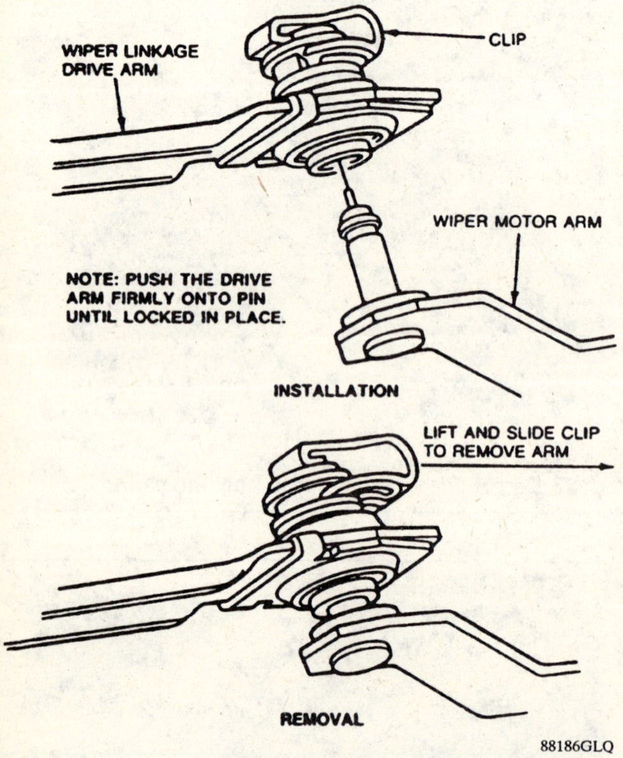

Fig. 91 Linkage components and installation procedure

To install:

8. Position the wiper in the cowl, then install the retaining bolts and nuts. Tighten the bolts to 91–122 inch lbs. (10–14 Nm).
9. Connect the windshield wiper mounting arm and pivot shaft to the windshield wiper motor. Ensure the clip is on the motor mounting arm and pivot shaft and is then secured to the motor. Install the mounting arm and pivot shaft by pulling until the clip snaps into place.
10. Installation is reverse of removal. Check the operation of the system.

Wiper Linkage

REMOVAL & INSTALLATION

➧ **See Figure 90**

1983 Models

1. Disconnect the battery ground.
2. Remove the right wiper arm from the pivot shaft.
3. Remove the cowl top grille attaching screw and lift off the grille.
4. Disconnect the linkage drive arm from the motor crankpin after removing the clip.
5. Remove the 2 bolts retaining the right pivot shaft to the cowl and remove the large nut, washer and spacer from the left pivot shaft.
6. Installation is the reverse of removal. Torque the pivot shaft retaining bolts to 84 inch lbs. (9 Nm) and the large nut to 110 inch lbs. (12 Nm).
7. Check the distance of the wiper blade and the bottom of the windshield.
8. Check the operation of the system.

1984–96 Models

➧ **See Figures 91 and 92**

1. Turn the wipers **ON** and, when the blades are in the straight up position, turn the ignition switch **OFF**.
2. Remove the wiper arms from the pivot shafts.
3. Disconnect the battery ground.
4. Remove the left and right cowl top grilles.
5. Disconnect the linkage drive arm from the motor crankpin after removing the clip.
6. Remove the pivot shafts attaching screws.
7. Installation is the reverse of removal. Torque the pivot fasteners to 110 inch lbs. (12 Nm).
8. Check the operation of the system.

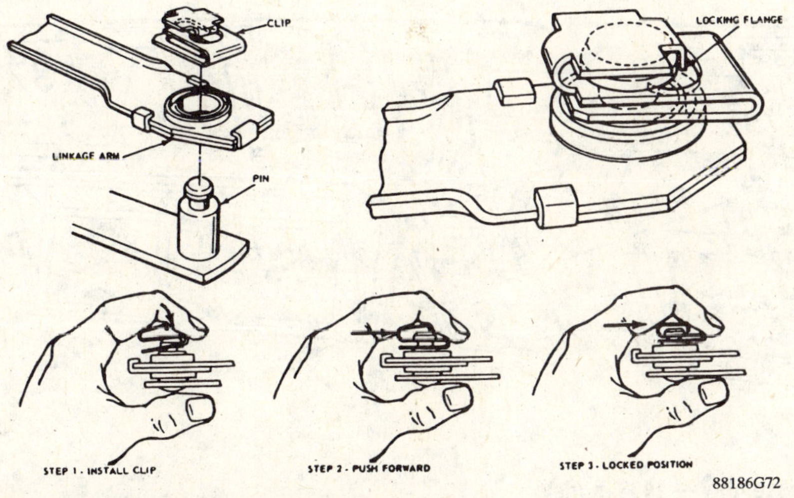

Fig. 92 Removing or installing the wiper linkage connecting clips

Washer Pump and Reservoir

REMOVAL & INSTALLATION

1. Remove the washer pump retaining screws.
2. Remove the reservoir hose to drain the fluid.
3. Disconnect the electrical connection.
4. Remove the washer reservoir from the vehicle.
5. Remove the pump from the reservoir.

To install:

6. Install the pump into the grommet. Check for deterioration of the grommet.
7. Secure the reservoir to the vehicle.
8. Connect the electrical wiring to the pump and attach the hose.
9. Check the operation of the unit.

INSTRUMENTS AND SWITCHES

Instrument Cluster

REMOVAL & INSTALLATION

****WARNING**

Extreme care must be exercised during the removal and installation of the instrument cluster and dash components to avoid damage or breakage. Wooden paddles should be used to separate dash components, if required. Tape or cover dash areas that may be damaged by the removal and installation of the dash components.

During the removal and installation procedures, slight variations may be required from the general outline, to facilitate the removal and installation of the instrument panel and cluster components, due to slight changes from model year to model year.

1983 Models

STANDARD CLUSTER

➧ See Figure 93

1. Disconnect the negative battery cable.
2. Disconnect the speedometer cable.
3. Remove the instrument panel trim cover and steering column lower shroud.
4. Remove the attaching screw holding the transmission indicator quadrant cable bracket to the steering column. Disconnect the cable loop from the pin on the steering column.
5. Remove the cluster retaining screws.
6. Remove the cluster from the instrument panel.
7. Reverse the removal procedure to install.

ELECTRONIC CLUSTER

➧ See Figure 94

1. Disconnect the negative battery cable.
2. Remove the instrument panel trim cover and steering column lower shroud.
3. Remove the cluster retaining screws.
4. Remove the attaching screw holding the transmission indicator quadrant cable bracket to the steering column. Disconnect the cable loop from the pin on the steering column.
5. Pull the cluster away from the instrument panel and disconnect the speedometer cable.
6. Disconnect the electrical connections from the cluster. Disconnect the ground wire.
7. Remove the cluster from the instrument panel.
8. Reverse the removal procedure to install.

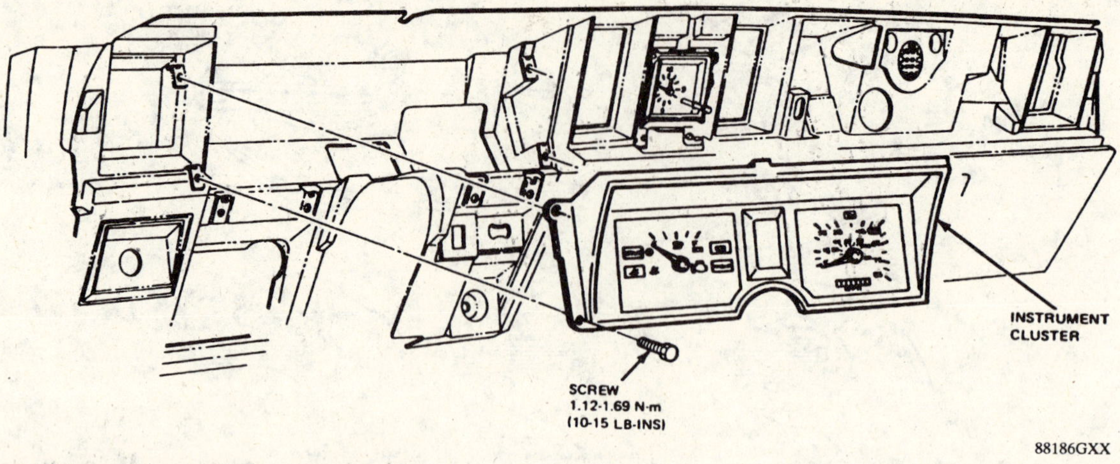

Fig. 93 Standard cluster assembly — 1983 models

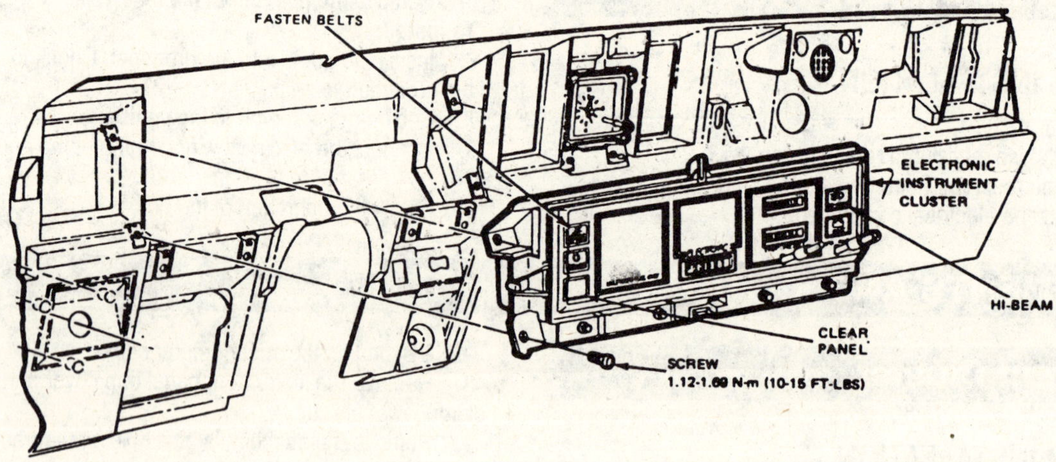

Fig. 94 Electronic instrument cluster — 1983 models

1984 Models

STANDARD CLUSTER

1. Disconnect the battery ground.
2. Remove the steering column shroud.
3. Remove the 4 cluster trim retaining screws and lift off the trim.
4. Remove the 6 cluster-to-instrument panel screws.
5. Pull the cluster out and disconnect the speedometer cable.
6. Disconnect the electrical connectors and remove the cluster.
7. Installation is the reverse of removal.

ELECTRONIC CLUSTER

1. Disconnect the negative battery cable.
2. Remove the 4 lower instrument panel trim cover screws.
3. Remove the steering column cover.
4. Remove the 6 cluster trim panel retaining screws.
5. Remove the 4 cluster-to-instrument panel attaching screws.
6. Remove the attaching screw from the transmission selector cable bracket. Disconnect the cable loop from the pin on the steering column.
7. Pull the cluster away from the instrument panel and disconnect the speedometer cable.
8. Disconnect the electrical connections from the cluster. Disconnect the ground wire.
9. Remove the cluster from the instrument panel.
10. Reverse the removal procedure to install.

1985-88 Models

STANDARD CLUSTER

➧ See Figure 95

1. Disconnect the battery ground.
2. Remove the 2 lower trim covers.
3. Remove the steering column cover.
4. Disconnect the shift selector bracket and cable assembly from the column.

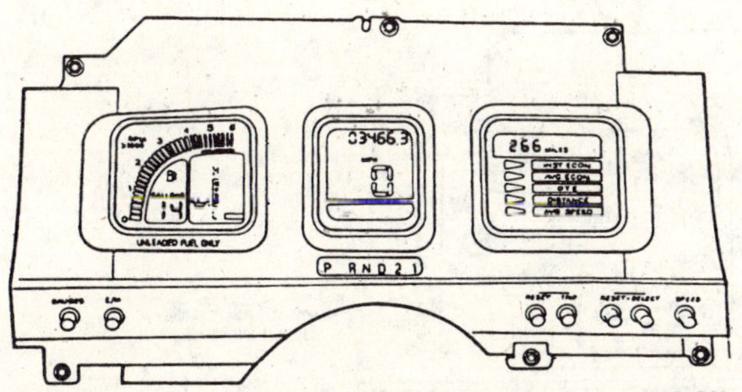

Fig. 95 Base electronic instrument cluster non-turbo coupe — 1984–88

5. Move the shift lever and remove the cluster trim panel.
6. Remove the 4 cluster mounting screws.
7. Pull the bottom of the cluster toward the steering wheel.
8. Reach behind the cluster and unplug the 2 connectors.
9. Swing the bottom of the cluster out and remove the cluster.
10. Install the components in the reverse order of removal.
11. Check the operation of the system.

TURBO COUPE CLUSTER

See Figure 96

1. Disconnect the battery ground.
2. Remove the steering column shroud.
3. Remove the 10 cluster trim screws and lift off the trim.
4. Remove the 4 cluster-to-instrument panel screws and pull the cluster out slightly.
5. Disconnect the cluster connectors.
6. Pull the boost gauge rubber tube off of the gauge nipple.
7. Remove the cluster.

To install:

8. Install the cluster in the dash.
9. Attach the boost gauge rubber tube onto the gauge nipple.
10. Attach the cluster connectors.
11. Secure the 4 cluster-to-instrument panel screws.
12. Tighten the 10 cluster trim screws.
13. Install the steering column shroud.
14. Connect the battery ground.
15. Check the operation of the system.

ELECTRONIC CLUSTER

See Figure 97

1. Disconnect the negative battery cable.
2. Remove the 2 lower instrument panel trim covers.
3. Remove the steering column cover.
4. Disconnect the shift selector bracket and cable at the column.
5. Move the shift lever and remove the cluster trim panel.
6. Remove the 4 cluster-to-instrument panel attaching screws.
7. Pull the bottom of the cluster toward the steering wheel.
8. Reach behind the cluster and disconnect the electrical connections.
9. Swing the bottom of the cluster out and away from the instrument panel.
10. Installation is the reverse of removal.

1989–93 Models

STANDARD CLUSTER

See Figures 98, 99 and 100

1. Disconnect negative battery cable.
2. Remove two retaining screws from cluster trim panel and remove panel.
3. Remove four cluster mounting screws, and pull bottom of cluster toward steering wheel.
4. Reaching behind and underneath cluster, unplug two connectors. For Super Coupe and XR-7 disconnect vacuum line for boost gauge.
5. Swing bottom of cluster out to clear top of steering column shroud and remove.
6. Installation is reverse of removal by inserting top of cluster, under crash pad leaving the bottom out, first.

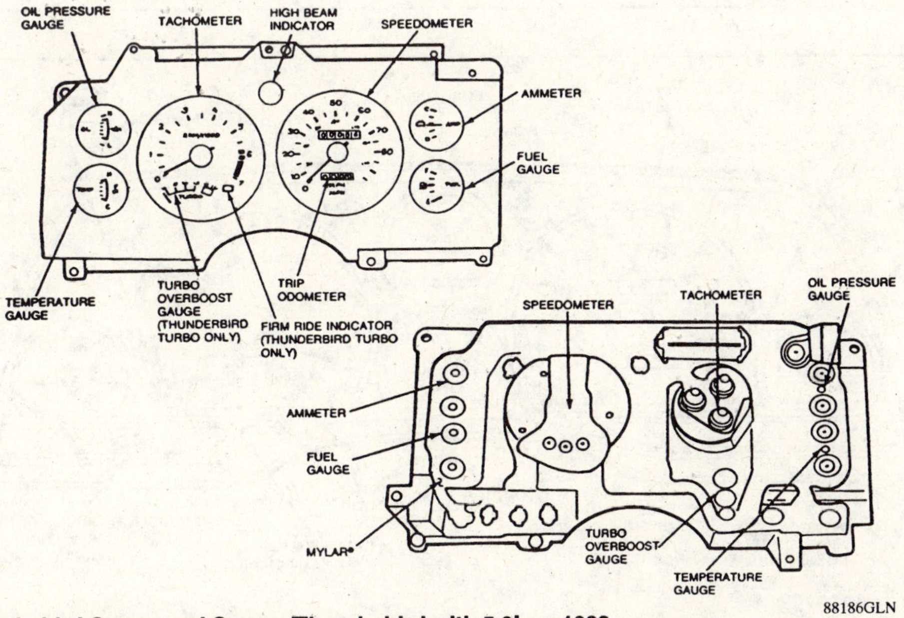

Fig. 96 Analog Thunderbird Coupe and Cougar/Thunderbird with 5.0L — 1988

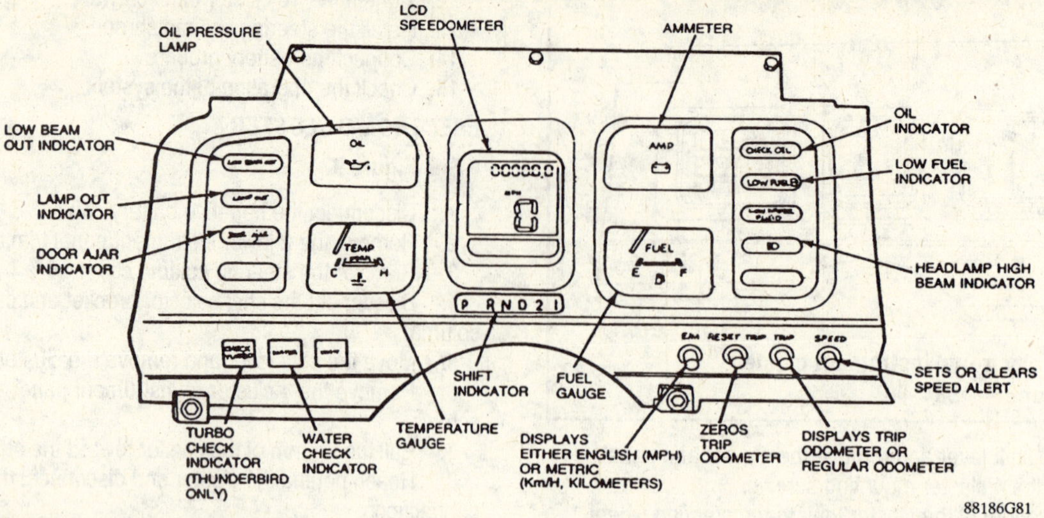

Fig. 97 Base electronic cluster — 1984-88

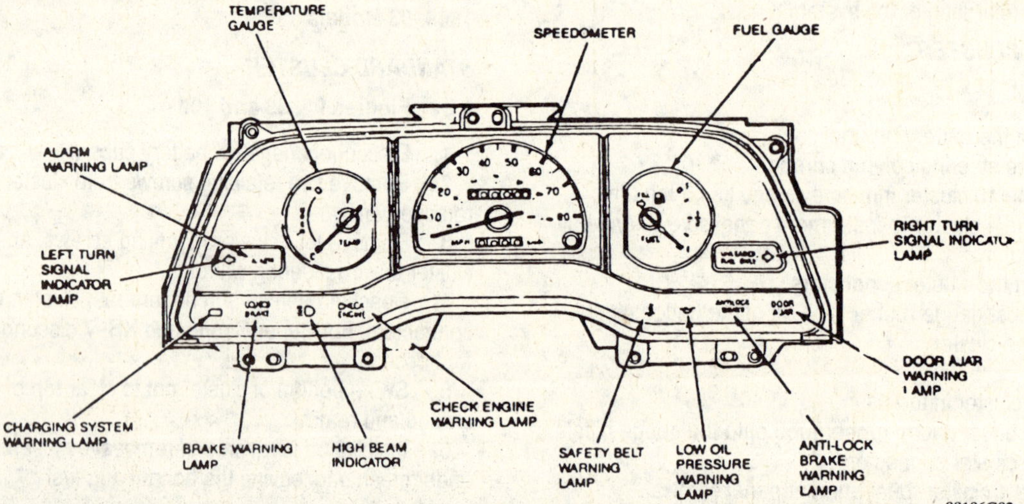

Fig. 98 Base electronic cluster — 1989-93

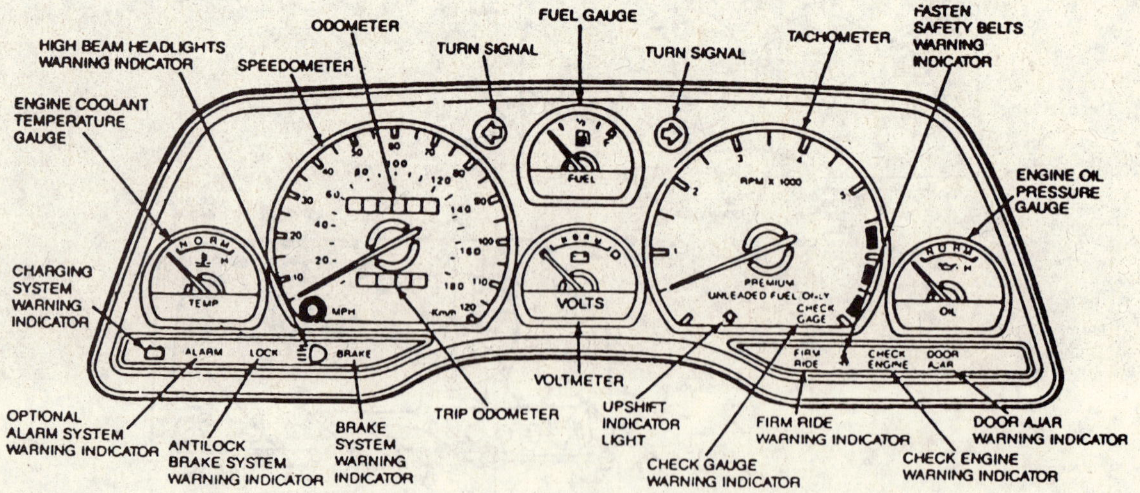

Fig. 99 Sport cluster — 1989-93

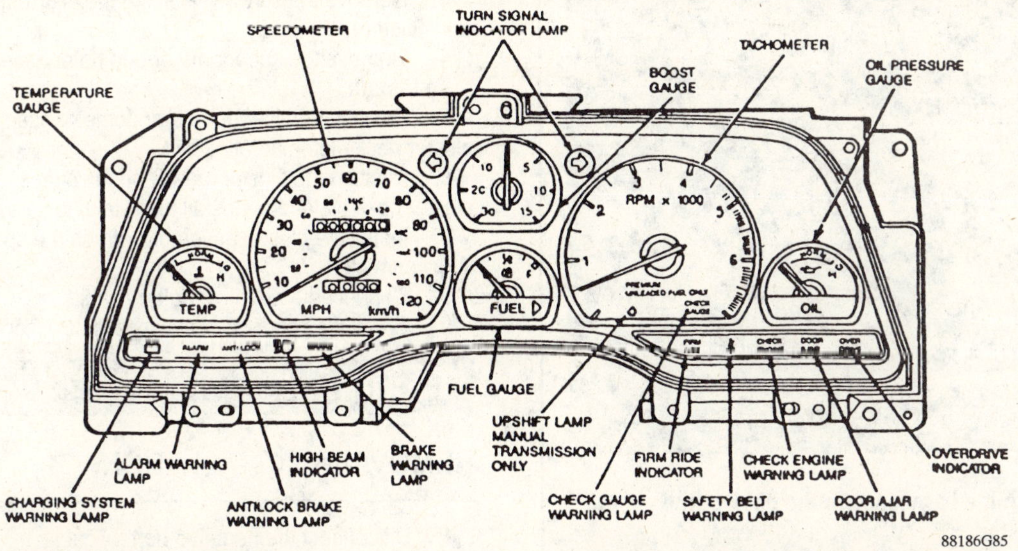

88186G85

Fig. 100 Super Coupe cluster — 1989-93

ELECTRONIC CLUSTER

➧ See Figures 101, 102 and 103

➛ The electronics with in the cluster are not serviceable. The cluster should be disassembled only to repair plastic defects or servicing other components where the cluster has to be removed to gain access to the component(s).

1. Disconnect negative battery cable.
2. Remove headlamp knob.
3. Remove cluster finish panel by removing two screws on upper inside surface.
4. Carefully pull away finish panel while detaching spring clips surrounding the finish panel.
5. Unplug connector on rear of switch assembly. If equipped, disconnect autolamp module.

➛ To prevent scratching and or damage to cluster assembly and steering column shroud, place a clean, soft cloth over steering column shroud, and lens of cluster assembly.

6. Remove the four cluster retaining screws, and pull bottom of cluster towards steering wheel.
7. Reaching behind and underneath cluster unplug two connectors.
8. Swing bottom of cluster out to clear top from crash pad and remove.
9. Installation is reverse of removal by inserting top of cluster, under crash pad leaving the bottom out, first.

1994-96 Models

➧ See Figures 104, 105 and 106

1. Disconnect the negative battery cable.
2. Remove the screws holding the instrument panel reinforcement.
3. Remove the screws holding the instrument panel lower shield.
4. Remove the fasteners that hold the steering wheel column. Gently lower the steering column.
5. Remove the fasteners that hold the instrument panel finish panel, then gently pry it off.

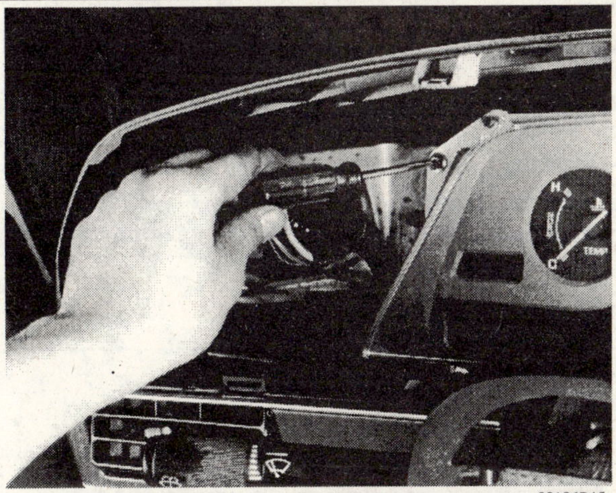
88186P45

Fig. 101 Remove the attaching screws for the instrument cluster

88186P46

Fig. 102 Lift the instrument cluster from the dash

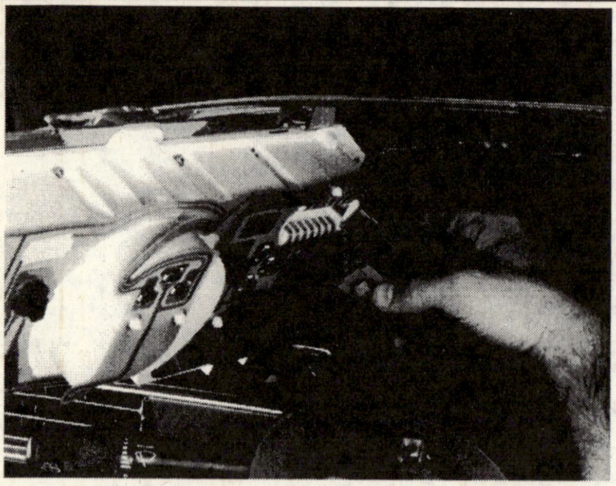

88186P47

Fig. 103 Detach the harnesses in the back of the instrument cluster

6. Remove the four cluster retaining screws. Do not remove the screws from the instrument panel main lens and cluster mask.
7. Slide the cluster to the right of the panel opening and unhook the panel harness from the back of the cluster.
8. Remove the instrument cluster from the panel.
9. To install, reverse the removal procedure, Tighten the cluster retaining screws to 18–27 inch lbs. (2–3 Nm).

Speedometer/Odometer

REMOVAL & INSTALLATION

1. Disconnect the negative battery cable.
2. Remove the instrument cluster assembly. On some models it will be necessary to disconnect the speedometer cable.
3. Remove the screws retaining the instrument cluster mask and cluster main lens.
4. Remove the speedometer/odometer assembly.

To install:

5. Position the speedometer/odometer assembly in the cluster back plate and attach.
6. Position the cluster mask and main lens to the instrument cluster back plate, then install the retaining screws.
7. Install the cluster assembly. Attach the speedometer cable if disconnected.
8. Connect the negative battery cable.
9. Check the operation of the speedometer/odometer assembly.

Tachometer

REMOVAL & INSTALLATION

1. Disconnect the negative battery cable.
2. Remove the instrument cluster.
3. Remove the screws retaining the mask and lens to the cluster back plate, then remove the mask and lens.
4. Remove the screws retaining the mask on the cluster back plate, then remove the mask.
5. Remove the screws retaining the tachometer on the cluster back plate, then remove the tachometer.

To install:

6. Position the tachometer to the cluster back plate, then install the retaining screws or nuts.
7. Position the lens and mask to the back plate, then install the retaining screws.
8. Install the cluster.
9. Connect the negative battery cable.
10. Check the operation of the gauge.

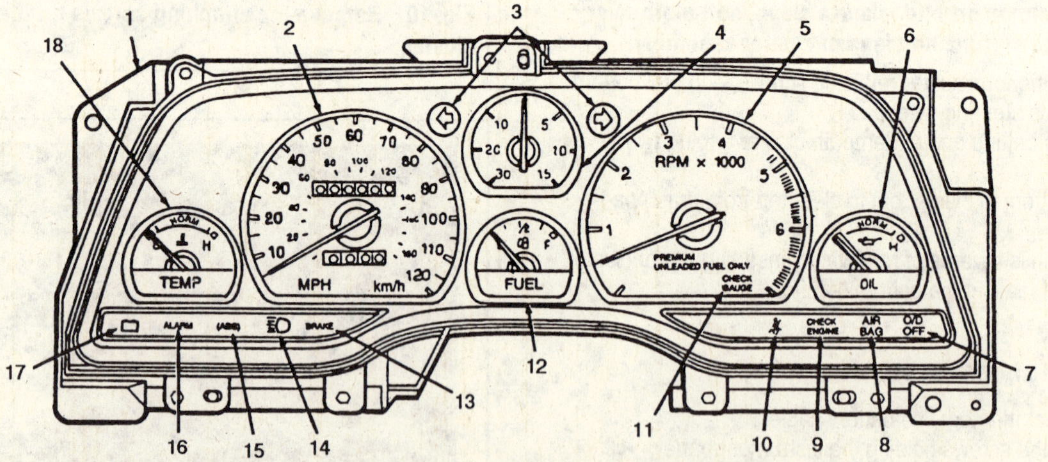

1. Instrument cluster
2. Speedometer
3. Turn signal indicators (part of 10849)
4. Supercharger boost gauge (part of 9305)
5. Tachometer
6. Oil pressure gauge
7. Overdrive indicator (part of 10849)
8. Air bag indicator (part of 10849)
9. Malfunction indicator lamp (MIL) (part of 10849)
10. Safety belt warning indicator (part of 10849)
11. Check gauge indicator (part of 17360)
12. Fuel gauge
13. Brake indicator (part of 10849)

88186G87

Fig. 104 Instrument cluster — 1995-96 Thunderbird Super Coupe

Speedometer Cable

REMOVAL & INSTALLATION

➧ See Figures 107 and 108

➥ Depending on year and model, some dash panels or the instrument cluster may require removal to gain access to the rear of the speedometer.

1. Reach up behind the speedometer and depress the flat, quick-disconnect tab, while pulling back on the cable.
2. If the inner cable is broken, raise and support the car and remove the cable-to-transmission clamp and pull the cable from the transmission.
3. Pull the core from the cable.
4. Installation is the reverse of removal. Lubricate the core with speedometer cable lubricant prior to installation.

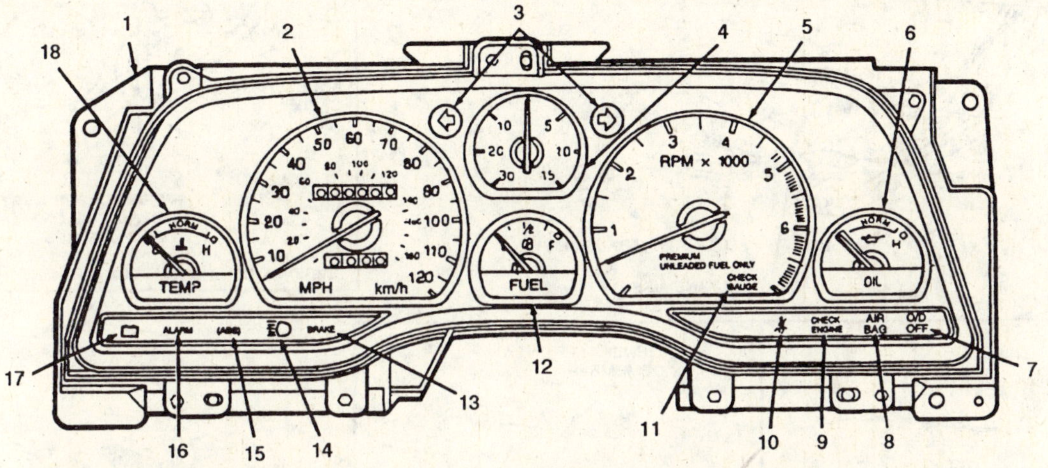

1. Instrument cluster
2. Speedometer
3. Turn signal indicators (part of 10849)
4. Supercharger boost gauge (part of 9305)
5. Tachometer
6. Oil pressure gauge
7. Overdrive indicator (part of 10849)
8. Air bag indicator (part of 10849)
9. Malfunction indicator lamp (MIL) (part of 10849)
10. Safety belt warning indicator (part of 10849)
11. Check gauge indicator (part of 17360)
12. Fuel gauge
13. Brake indicator (part of 10849)

88186G87

Fig. 105 Instrument cluster — 1995-96 Thunderbird Super Coupe

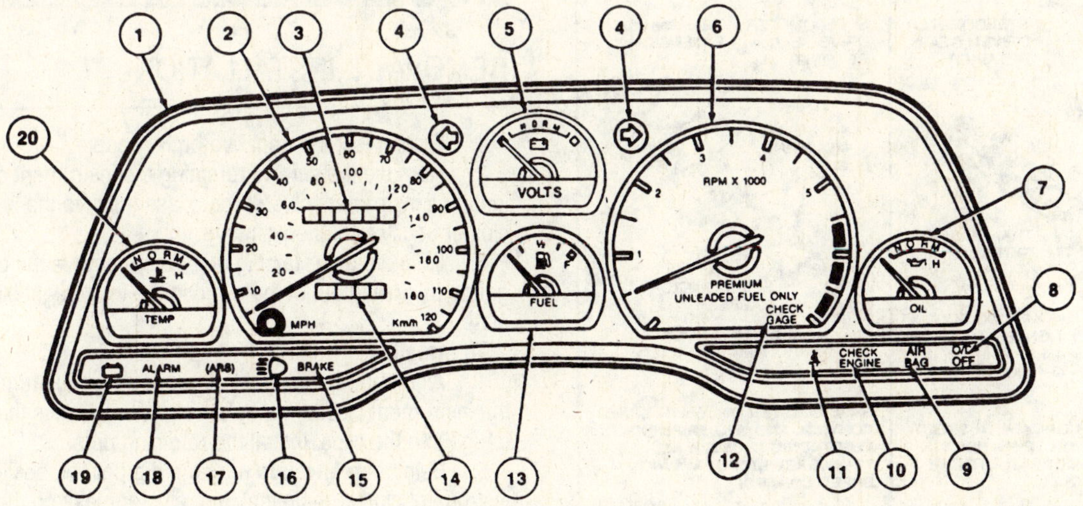

88186G88

Fig. 106 Instrument cluster — 1995-96 excluding Thunderbird Super Coupe

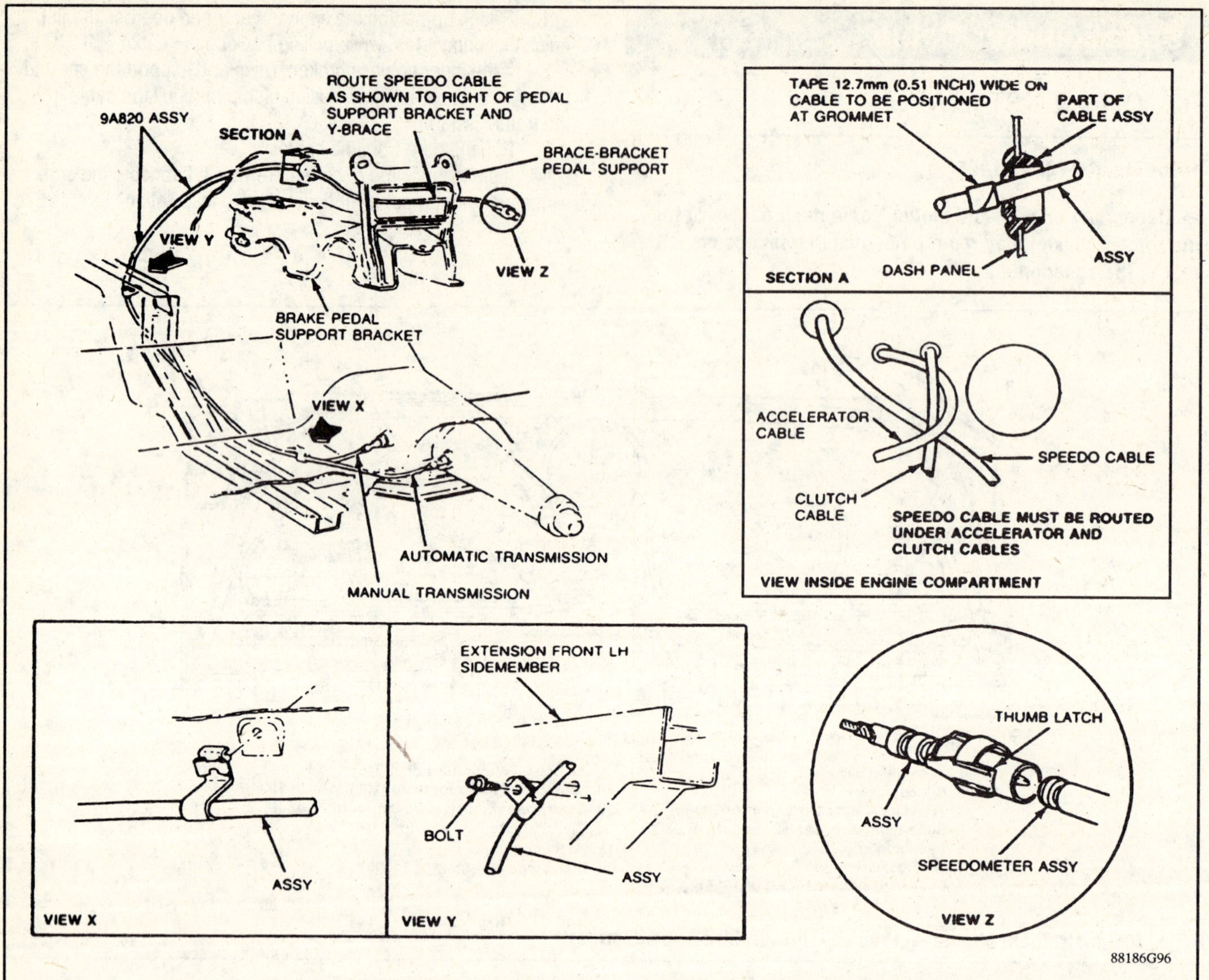

Fig. 107 Speedometer routing on most models — 1988 shown

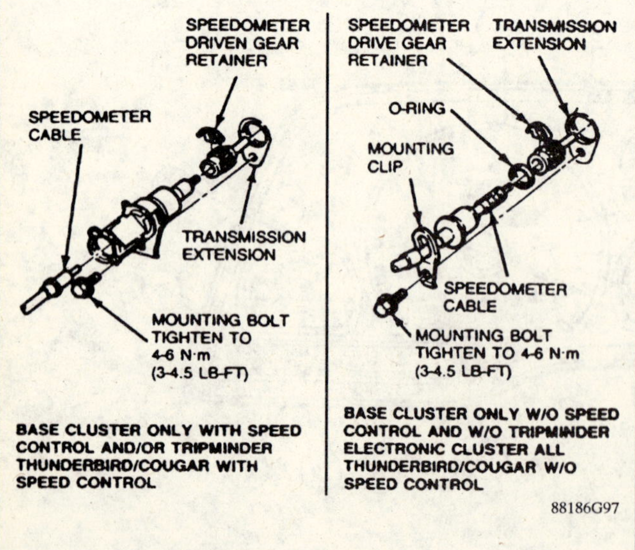

Fig. 108 Speedometer cable to transmission mounting

Oil Pressure Gauge

REMOVAL & INSTALLATION

1. Disconnect the negative battery cable.
2. Remove the screws retaining the instrument cluster main lens and instrument cluster mask assembly to the instrument cluster back plate, then remove.
3. Remove the retaining nuts, then remove the oil pressure gauge by pulling out of the clip[s in the instrument cluster back plate.

To install:

4. Align the replacement oil pressure gauge terminals with the instrument cluster backplate clips, then press the oil pressure gauge into the clips. Install the retaining nuts.
5. Being careful not to damage the pointer, position the instrument cluster main lens and cluster mask on the cluster back plate. Install the retaining screws.
6. Connect the negative battery cable.
7. Check the operation of the gauge.

Fuel Gauge

REMOVAL & INSTALLATION

1. Disconnect the negative battery cable.
2. Remove the instrument cluster assembly.
3. Remove the screws retaining the cluster main lens and the cluster mask on the cluster.
4. Remove the gauge.

To install:

5. Install the components in the reverse order of removal.
6. Check the operation of the gauge.

Temperature Gauge

REMOVAL & INSTALLATION

➧ **See Figure 109**

1. Remove the screws retaining the instrument cluster main lens and instrument cluster mask assembly to the instrument cluster back plate and remove.
2. Pull out the main dial assembly from the cluster back plate.
3. Remove the screws retaining the instrument cluster temperature gauge from the main dial.
4. Remove the temperature gauge from the main dial assembly.

To install:

5. Position the temperature gauge on the main dial assembly.
6. Install the retaining screws and tighten.
7. Install the main dial assembly into the cluster back plate aligning the assembly over the proper guides.
8. Position the cluster main lens and cluster mask assembly on the cluster back plate. Attach with the retaining screws.
9. Check the operation of the gauge.

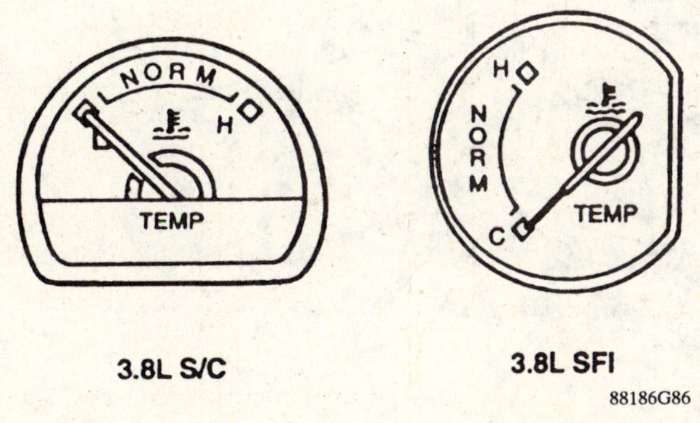

Fig. 109 Common temperature gauge on the 3.8L engine vehicles

Gauge Amplifier

REMOVAL & INSTALLATION

1. Remove the instrument cluster.
2. Grasp the cluster gauge amplifier on the outside far edges. Avoid touching the circuit board components
3. Push the connector tab in and slide the instrument cluster gauge amplifier out.

To install:

4. Position the cluster gauge amplifier in the guides. Line up the terminals over the center of the instrument cluster circuit connections. Push the cluster gauge amplifier until it clicks into place.
5. Install the cluster assembly.
6. Check the operation of the gauge.

Voltmeter

REMOVAL & INSTALLATION

1. Remove the two retaining screws from the cluster trim panel.
2. Remove the cluster trim assembly.
3. Remove the screws that attach the lens and mask assemblies to the back plate.
4. Remove the lens and mask assemblies.
5. Remove the voltmeter gauge assembly from the back plate.

To install:

6. Install the gauge onto the back plate assembly.
7. Install the lens and mask assemblies.
8. Install the cluster trim assembly.
9. Check the operation of the gauge.

Supercharger Boost/Battery Voltage Gauges

REMOVAL & INSTALLATION

The Supercharger boost and battery voltage gauges are part of the fuel gauge assembly.

1. Remove the instrument cluster assembly.
2. Remove the fuel gauge assembly.

To install:

3. Install the fuel gauge assembly.
4. Install the instrument cluster assembly.

Printed Circuit Board

REMOVAL & INSTALLATION

1. Disconnect the negative battery cable.
2. Remove the instrument cluster assembly.

3. Remove the retaining screws from the cluster mask lens and mask assembly, then remove the main lens and cluster mask.
4. Remove the gauges and speedometer assembly. On the Supercharged vehicles, remove the one retaining screw holding the cluster back plate to boost gauge.
5. Depress the clip on the instrument printed circuit board, then remove the printed circuit from the cluster back plate.
6. Remove the miniature bulb assemblies.
7. Remove the clip assembly by squeezing on each side and pushing them through the instrument cluster back plate.
8. Remove the instrument cluster printed board from the cluster back plate.

To install:

9. Position the cluster circuit board over the locating pins on the cluster back plate.
10. Push the clips through the instrument cluster back plate.

You should hear a click when the clips lock into position.

11. Install the miniature bulb assemblies.
12. Install the gauges and speedometer assembly. On the Supercharged vehicles, install the one retaining screw through the cluster back plate into the boost gauge.
13. Position the cluster mask and main lens assemblies on the locating pins, then install the retaining screws.
14. Install the instrument cluster assembly.
15. Connect the negative battery cable.

Windshield Wiper Switch

REMOVAL & INSTALLATION

1. Disconnect the negative battery cable.
2. Remove the split steering column cover retaining screws.
3. Separate the two halves and remove the wiper switch retaining screws.
4. Disconnect the wire connector and remove the wiper switch.

To install:

5. Attach the wire connector to the wiper switch.
6. Attach the wiper switch to the column unit with the mounting screws.
7. Install the split steering column.
8. Connect the negative battery cable.

Headlight Switch

REMOVAL & INSTALLATION

1983–84 Models

1. Disconnect the negative battery cable.
2. Pull the switch to the full **ON** position.
3. Reach up under the instrument panel and, while depressing the release button, pull the knob out of the switch.
4. Unscrew the switch bezel and pull the switch from the instrument panel.
5. Unplug the wiring.
6. Installation is the reverse of removal.

1985–88 Models

See Figure 110

1. Disconnect the negative battery cable.
2. Remove the headlamp switch lens screws and lift off the lens.
3. Remove the switch attaching screws and pull the switch out from the instrument panel.

On cars equipped with Auto Lamp/Auto Dimmer, remove the control.

4. Disconnect the wiring and remove the switch.

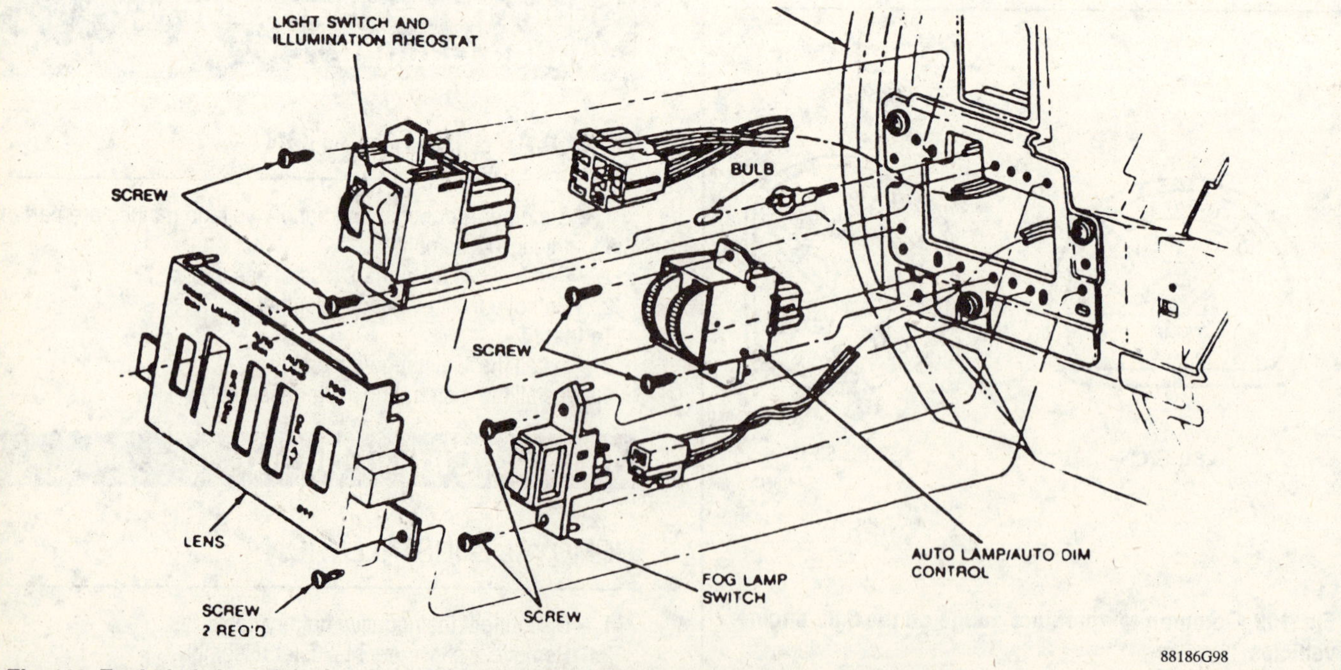

Fig. 110 Exploded view of the headlamp switch and associated components — 1987 shown

To install:

5. Attach the wiring to the switch assembly.
6. Install the switch to the instrument panel with the retaining screws.
7. Install the headlamp switch lens.
8. Connect the negative battery cable.

1989-92 Models

➧ **See Figure 111**

1. Disconnect the negative battery cable.
2. Remove the two cluster finish panel retaining screws.
3. Pull off the headlamp switch knob.
4. Remove the cluster finish panel. It snaps off. Disconnect electrical connector to dimmer sensor assembly.
5. Using the opening in the instrument panel, depress the shaft release button on switch and remove shaft.
6. Remove headlamp switch retaining nut and pull switch through opening to disconnect the wiring connector.
7. Installation is the reverse of removal.

Clock

REMOVAL & INSTALLATION

➧ **See Figure 112**

1. Disconnect the negative battery cable.
2. Remove two center radio speaker grille retaining screws and remove grille, if so equipped. On other models it may be necessary to remove the instrument panel upper finish panel.
3. Remove three retaining screws attaching the clock to the instrument panel.
4. Remove clock from opening and disconnect the electrical connection.

To install:

5. Attach the electrical connection to the clock unit.
6. Install the clock into the instrument panel assembly, attaching it with the retaining screws.
7. If removed, install the speaker grille assemblies. Install the instrument panel upper finish panel.

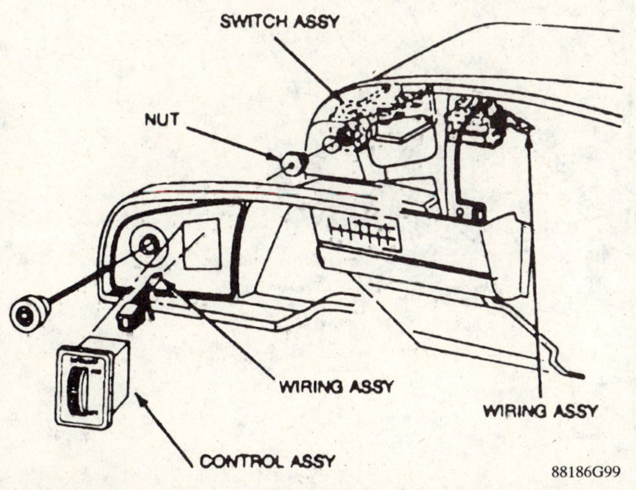

Fig. 111 The headlamp switch is mounted on the driver's side of the instrument panel — 1988-92 models

Fig. 112 Setting the clock in the dash — 1994-96 models

8. Connect the negative battery cable.

Back-up Light Switch

REMOVAL & INSTALLATION

➥ **Before replacing a back-up light switch, be sure to check the condition of the bulbs first.**

Since all back-up light switches are operated by the transmission shift lever, replacement procedures differ according to mounting location of the selector lever and type of transmission used.

Column Mounted Automatic Transmission

1. Disconnect the back-up light switch wires at the plug connector. On vehicles so equipped, disconnect the two parking brake release vacuum hoses.
2. Remove the two screws, securing the back-up light switch to the steering column and lift the switch from the column.
3. Check column to ensure that the metal switch actuator is secured to the shift tube and that it is seated as far forward against the shift tube bearing as possible. Also check for a broken or damaged actuator.

➥ **Before installing a new switch, check to see that the drive position gauge is inserted in the drive pinning hole. If the pin is missing, align the two holes on top of switch and install a No. 43 drill or a 0.092–0.093 in. (2.34–2.36mm) gauge pin.**

4. While holding the selector lever against the stop in the drive detent position, place the switch on the column and install the two attaching screws.
5. Remove the gauge pin (or equivalent). Connect switch wires to plug connector and connect the two parking brake release vacuum hoses (if equipped).

Manual Transmission

1. Raise and support the vehicle.
2. Disconnect the electrical wiring at the back-up lamp switch.
3. Remove the back-up lamp switch from the transmission extension housing.

To install:

4. Install the switch to the extension housing, tighten to 20–35 ft. lbs. (27–47 Nm).
5. Attach the electrical wiring to the switch assembly.
6. Lower the vehicle.

LIGHTING

Headlights

REMOVAL & INSTALLATION

All Except 1987 and Later Aerodynamic Headlamps

➧ **See Figures 113 and 114**

1. If the car is equipped with movable headlamp covers, close the bypass valve to raise the headlamp covers. The valve is located in the vacuum lines near the reservoir and left fender.
2. On cars without movable headlamp doors, remove the headlamp door retaining screws and remove the doors.
3. Remove the headlamp trim mounting screws and remove the trim.
4. Remove the retaining ring screws and remove the retaining ring from the headlamp. Pull the headlamp out and unplug it.
5. Installation is the reverse of removal.
6. Turn the lights on to check for proper operation.

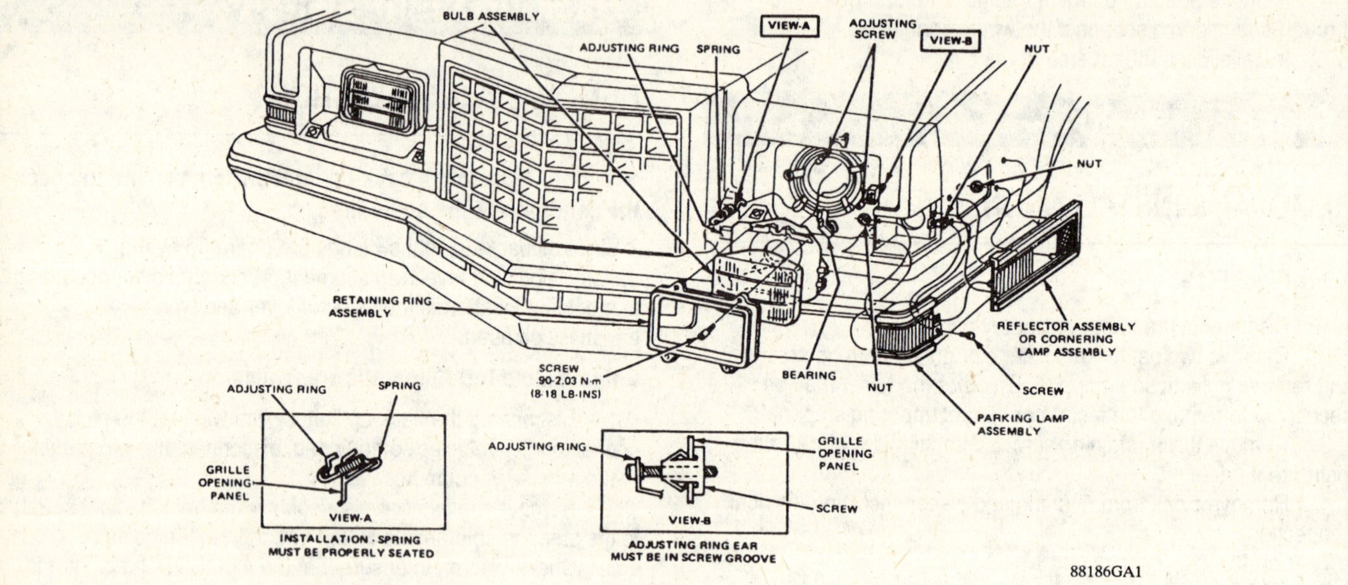

Fig. 113 Exploded view of the headlamp system — 1983 models

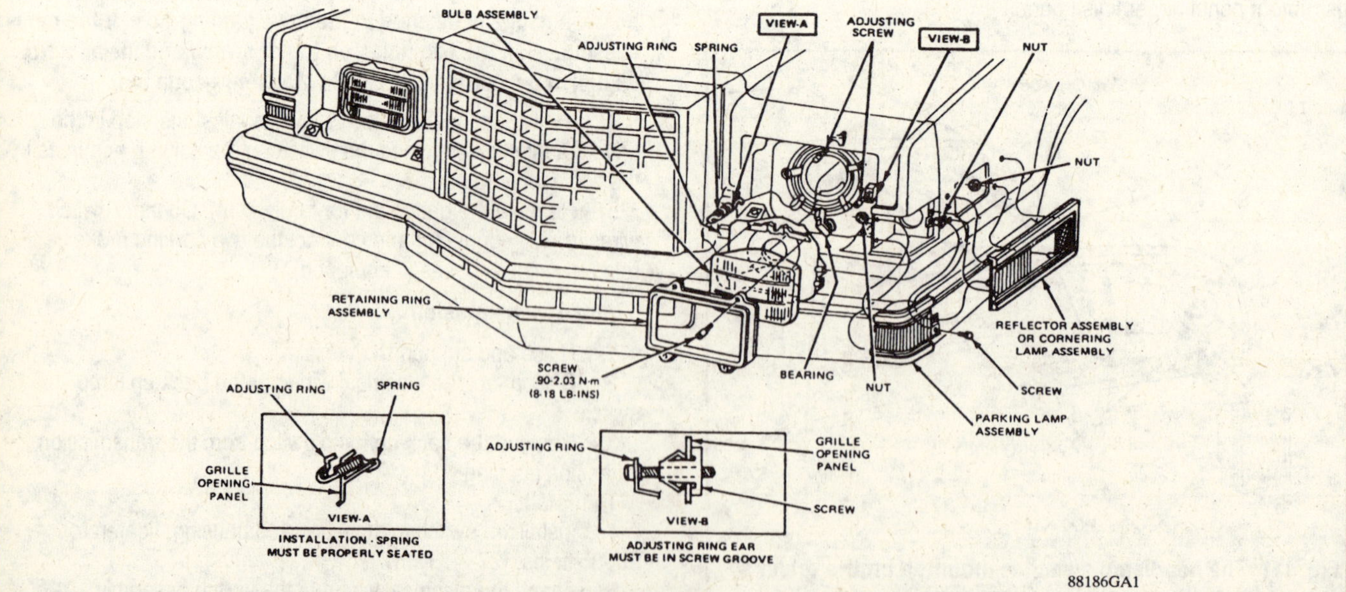

Fig. 114 Exploded view of the headlamp system — 1984-86 models

1987-96 Aerodynamic Headlamps

BULB ASSEMBLY

➧ See Figure 115 and 116

✲✲CAUTION

The halogen bulb contains pressurized gas. If the bulb is dropped or scratched it will shatter. Also, avoid touching the bulb glass with your bare fingers. Grasp the bulb only by its plastic base. Oil from bare skin will cause hot spots on the glass surface and lead to premature burnout. If you do touch the glass, clean it with alcohol prior to installation.

1. Make sure that the headlamp switch is **OFF**.
2. Raise the hood. The bulb protrudes from the rear of the headlamp assembly.
3. Unplug the electrical connector from the bulb.

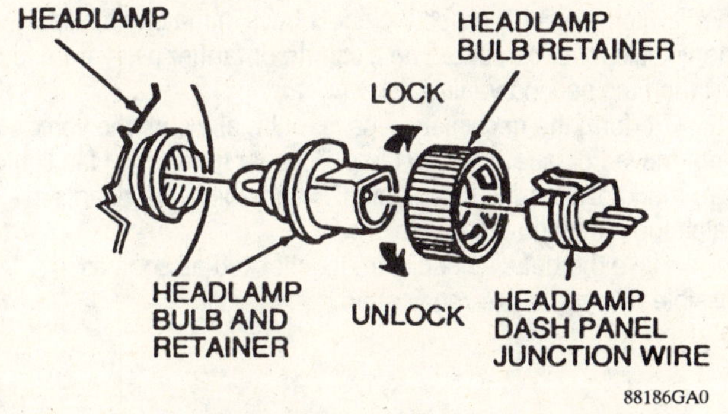

Fig. 115 The headlamp bulb on the aerodynamic type is retained with a bulb retainer ring

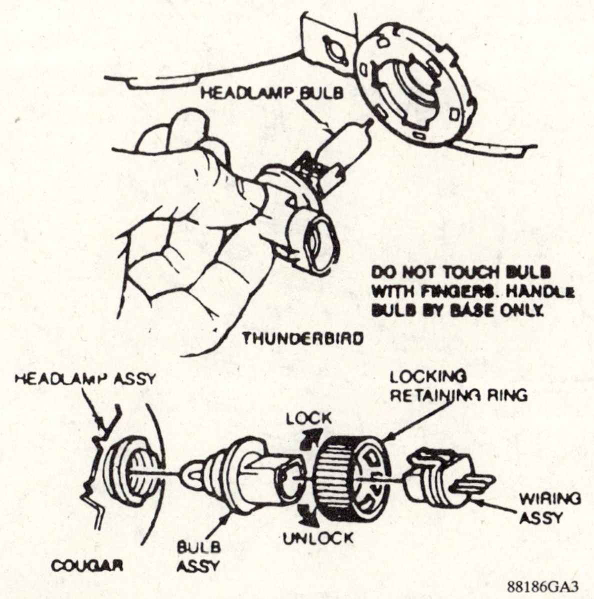

Fig. 116 Headlamp bulb replacement on the aerodynamic type bulb

4. Rotate the bulb retaining ring $^1/_8$ turn counterclockwise and remove it.
5. Pull the bulb straight back out of its socket. Don't rotate it.

To install:

6. When installing the bulb, push it into position, turning it slightly right or left to align the grooves in the forward part of the base with the tabs in the socket. When they are aligned, push the bulb firmly into position until the mounting flange on the base contacts the rear face of the socket.

➥ When servicing the headlamp bulb, energize the bulb only while it is contained within the headlamp body.

7. Slip the bulb retaining ring over the plastic base until it contacts the rear of the socket. Lock the ring into the socket by rotating it clockwise until you feel a stop.
8. Push the connector onto the bulb until it snaps into position.
9. Turn the headlamps on and make sure that they work properly. If the headlamp was correctly aimed before replacement, you should not need to adjust it.

1988 MODELS

➧ See Figure 117

1. Make sure that the headlamp switch is **OFF**.
2. Raise the hood. The bulb protrudes from the rear of the headlamp assembly.
3. Unplug the electrical connector from the bulb.
4. Remove the 3 nuts and washers from the rear of the headlamp.
5. Push forward on the headlamp at the bulb socket. It may be necessary to loosen the parking lamp and cornering lamp fasteners.
6. Remove the 3 clips which attach the headlamp to the black ring by prying them out from the base with a flat-bladed screwdriver.
7. Installation is the reverse of removal. Make sure that the black rubber shield is securely crimped on the headlamp.
8. Turn the lights on to check for proper operation.

1989-96 MODELS

➧ See Figure 118

1. Make sure the headlamp switch and time delay switch are in the off position.
2. Raise hood and disconnect wiring from each of the two bulbs.
3. Using snapring pliers, spread the three metal retainers attaching lamp assembly to grille opening panel, from the rear of panel. Pull straight upward to disengage and remove metal retainers.
4. Remove the lamp assembly from vehicle, then remove the bulbs. Reverse the procedure to install.
5. Turn the lights on to check for proper operation.

➥ A correctly aimed headlamp normally need not be re-aimed after installation of a new bulb. A burned out bulb should not be removed from the headlamp until just before a replacement bulb is to be installed. Removal of bulb for an extended period of time may allow contaminants such as, dust, moisture, smoke, etc. to enter the headlamp body and affect performance of the headlamp.

AIMING

The headlights must be properly aimed to provide the best, safest road illumination. The lights should be checked for proper aim and adjusted as necessary. Certain state and local authorities have requirements for headlight aiming; these should be checked before adjustment is made.

Headlight adjustment may be temporarily made using a wall, as described below, or on the rear of another vehicle. When adjusted, the lights should not glare in oncoming car or truck windshields, nor should they illuminate the passenger compartment of vehicles driving in front of you. These adjustments are rough and should always be fine-tuned by a repair shop which is equipped with headlight aiming tools. Improper adjustments may be both dangerous and illegal.

For most vehicles, horizontal and vertical aiming of each sealed beam unit is provided by two adjusting screws which move the retaining ring and adjusting plate against the tension of a coil spring. There is no adjustment for focus; this is done during headlight manufacturing.

➥ Because the composite headlight assembly is bolted into position, no adjustment should be necessary or possible. Some applications however may be bolted to an adjuster plate or may be retained used adjusting screws. If so, follow this procedure when adjusting the lights, BUT always have the adjustment checked by a reputable shop.

Before removing the headlight bulb or disturbing the headlamp in any way, note the current settings in order to make adjusting the headlights upon reassembly easier. If the high or low beam setting of the old lamp still works, this can be done using the wall of a garage or a building:

1. Park the vehicle on a level surface, with the fuel tank no more than 1/2 full and with the vehicle empty of all extra cargo (unless normally carried). The vehicle should be facing a wall which is no less the 6 feet high and 12 feet wide. The front of the vehicle should be about 25 feet from the wall.

➥ The vehicle's fuel tank should be about half full when adjusting the headlights. Tires should be properly inflated.

2. If this is be performed outdoors, it is advisable to wait until dusk in order to properly see the headlight beams on the wall. If done in a garage, darken the area around the wall as much as possible by closing shades or hanging cloth over the windows.
3. Turn the headlights **ON** and mark the wall at the center of each light's low beam, then switch on the brights and mark the center of each light's high beam. A short length of masking tape which is visible from the front of the vehicle may be used. Although marking all 4 positions is advisable, marking 1 position from each light should be sufficient.
4. If neither beam on 1 side of the vehicle is working, park another like-sized vehicle in the exact spot where the car was and mark the beams using the same side light on that vehicle. Then switch the vehicle's so the car is back in the original spot. The vehicle must be parked no closer to or farther away from the wall than the second vehicle.
5. Perform the necessary repairs, but make sure the vehicle is not moved or is returned to the exact spot from which the lights were marked. Turn the headlights **ON** and adjust the beams to match the marks on the wall.
6. Have the headlight adjustment checked as soon as possible by a reputable repair shop.

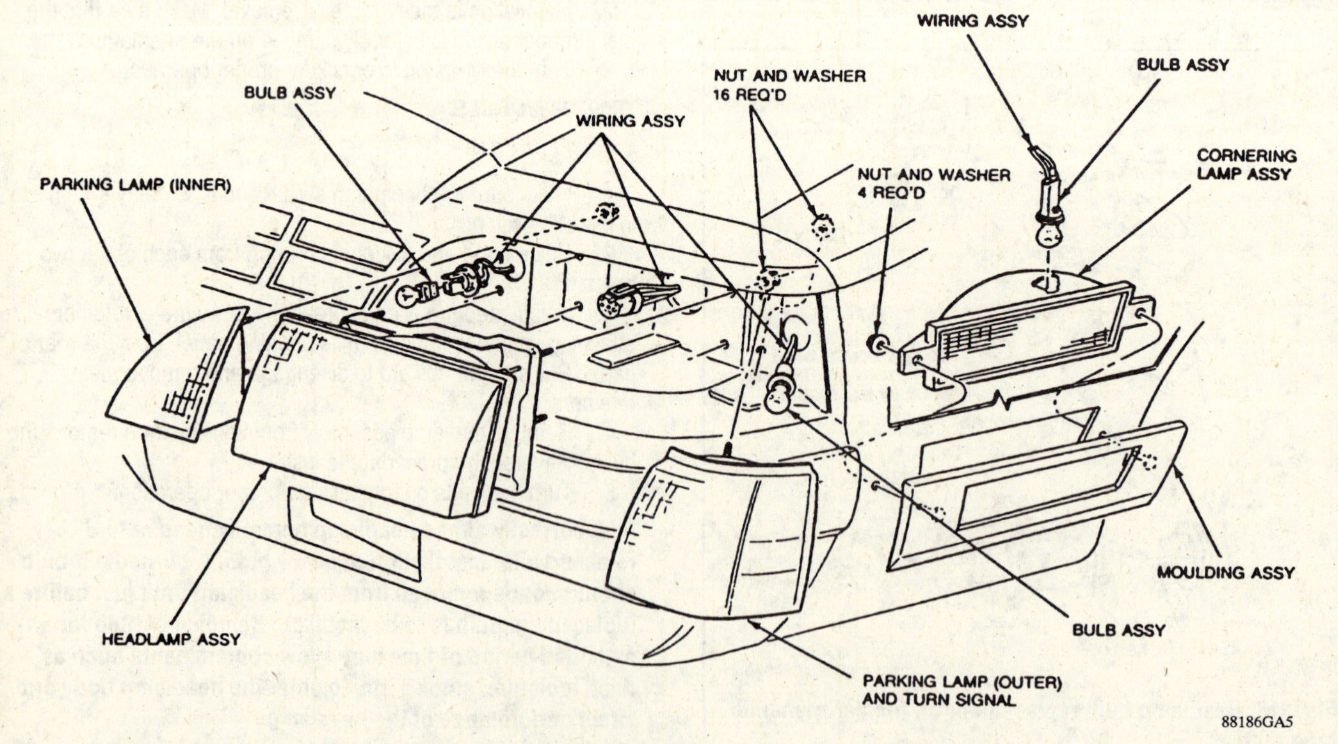

Fig. 117 Exploded view of the headlamp system — 1988 models

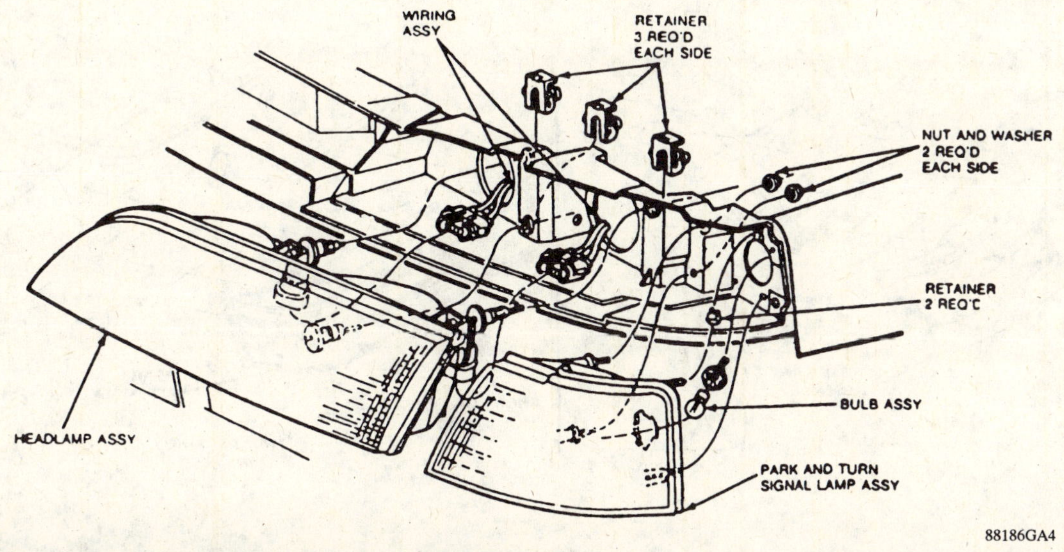

Fig. 118 Exploded view of the headlamp system — 1989-96 models

Signal and Marker Lights

REMOVAL & INSTALLATION

Front Parking and Turn Signal Lamps

➧ See Figure 119

1. Remove the nuts that retain the lamp on the back of the fender.
2. Pull the lamp forward and remove the socket assembly. Slide the lamp from the vehicle.

To install:

3. Place the lamp socket into the lens assembly.
4. Insert the lamp assembly on the vehicle and tighten the mounting nuts.
5. Turn the lights on to check for proper operation.

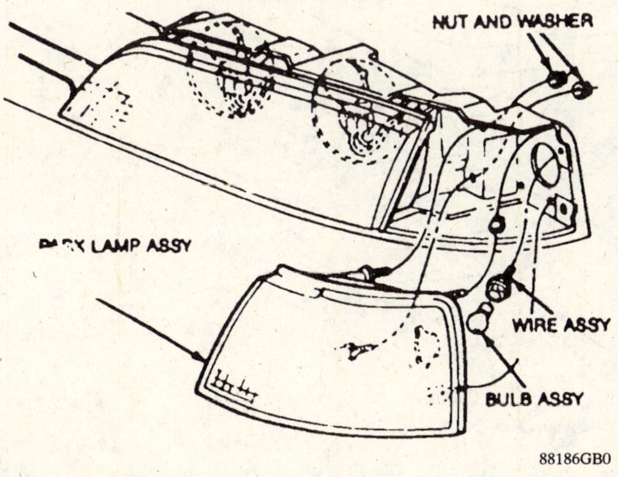

Fig. 119 Front turn signal assembly — 1989-92 models

BULBS

To replace the bulbs on the 1983 XR-7, reach behind the bumper and remove the socket from the lamp to replace the bulb. On the 1983 Thunderbird, reach behind the lamp and remove the 4 attaching nuts. Pull the lamp out and remove the screw from the parking lamp and the nut from the headlamp cover. Replace the bulb. On the 1984-87 models, reach behind the fender and remove the 2 nuts securing the assembly to the fender, pull out the assembly and replace the bulb.

Rear Turn Signal, Brake and Parking Lamps

BUTYL SEAL TYPE

To remove the rear tail lamp lens on some models, you need to only carefully pry off the lens from the lamp body. These types of lenses are attached with a butyl seal. When you remove the lens, be sure to clean all of the old seal from the lamp body prior to applying more sealer. Once the new sealer is applied, press the lens on the body firmly and hold for approximately 10-20 seconds. Do not apply pressure to the middle of the lens, this could cause the lens to break from the pressure.

RETAINED TYPE

➧ See Figures 120, 121, 122, 123, 124, 125 and 126

1. Remove the luggage compartment front cover as necessary.
2. Remove the nuts that attach the rear lamp to the lower back panel.
3. Remove the lamp from the vehicle.

To install:

4. Place the lamp into position. Tighten the nuts to 3-5 ft. lbs. (4-7 Nm).
5. Install the luggage compartment front cover.
6. Turn the lights on to check for proper operation.

All bulb sockets can be accessed from inside the trunk. In some models, the trunk trim panel will have to be removed first. To remove lamp assembly, remove retaining nuts from inside luggage compartment pull out all bulb sockets and remove assembly. Check sealant gaskets before reinstallation of assembly.

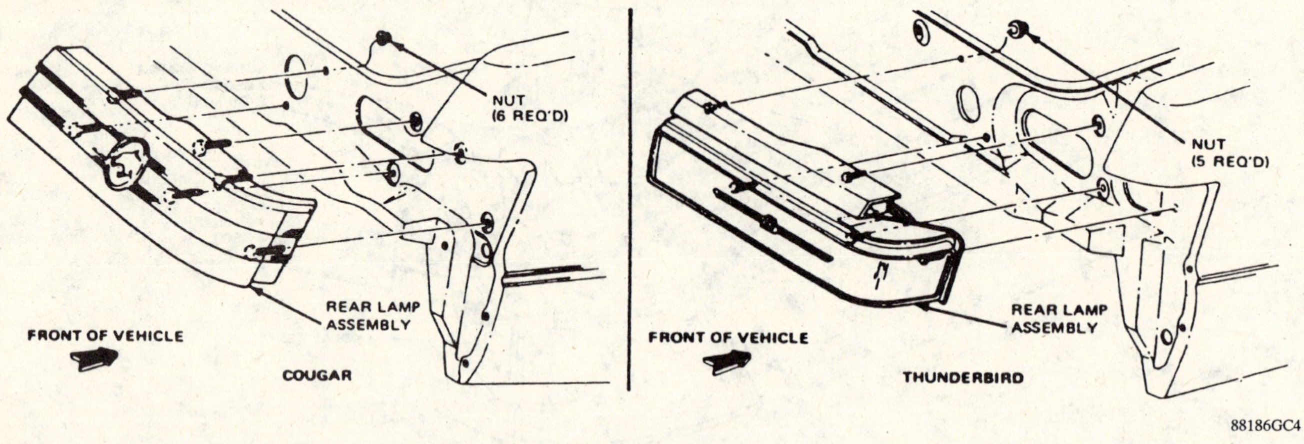

Fig. 120 Exploded view of the rear tail lamp assembly — 1983–87 models

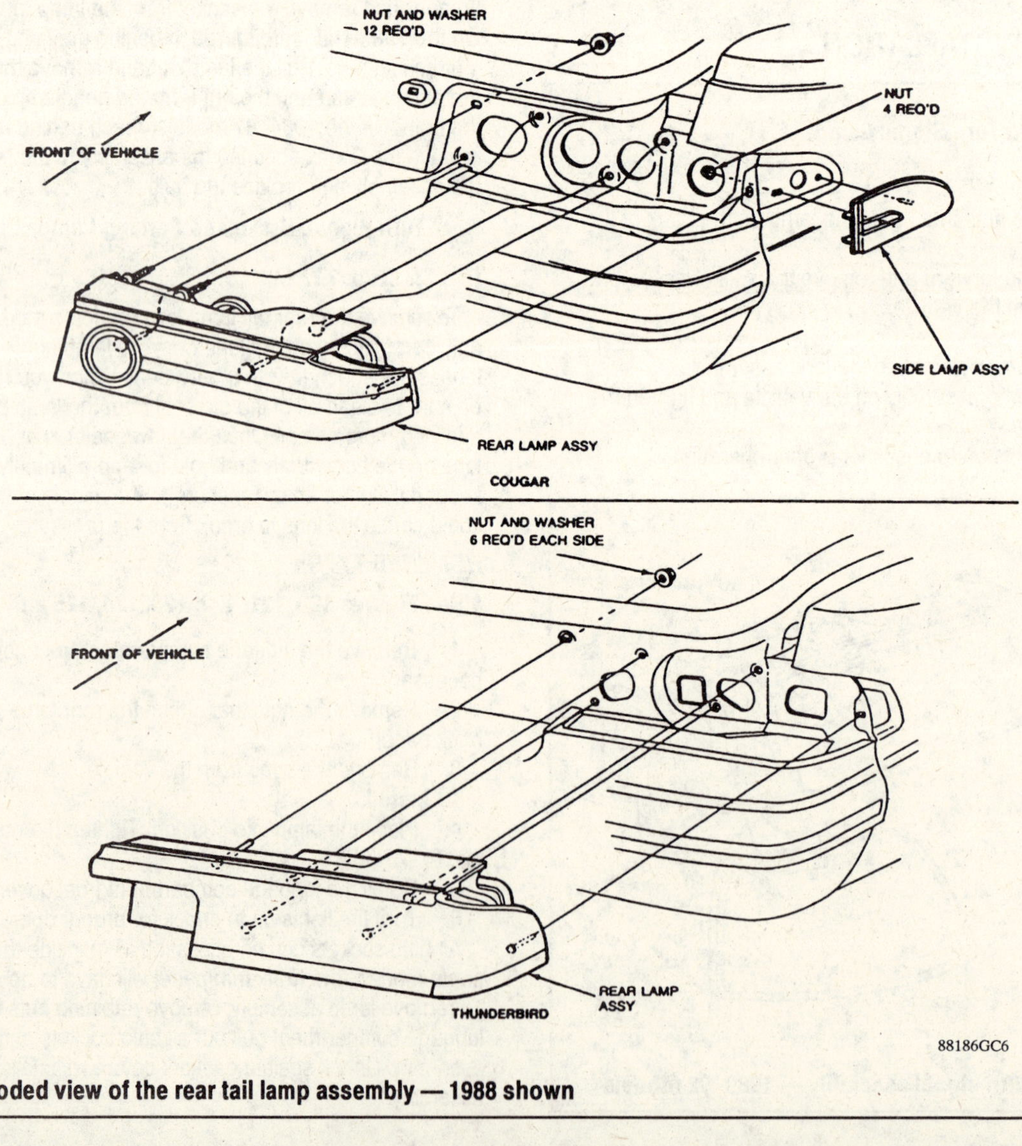

Fig. 121 Exploded view of the rear tail lamp assembly — 1988 shown

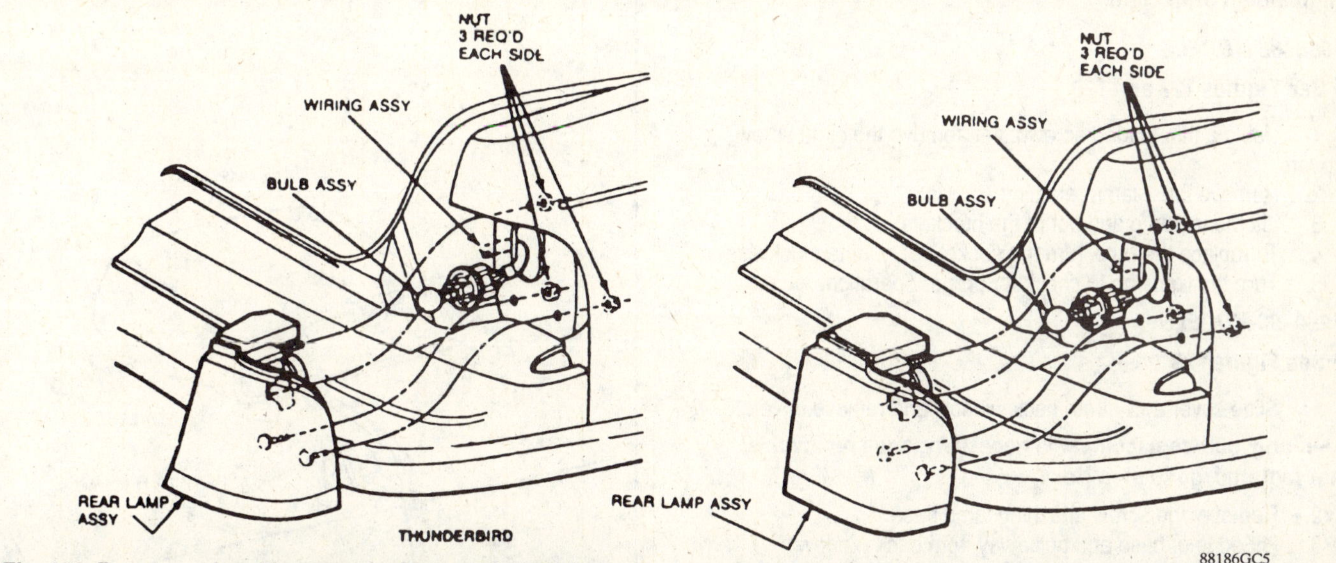

Fig. 122 Rear turn signal lamp assembly — 1989–93 shown

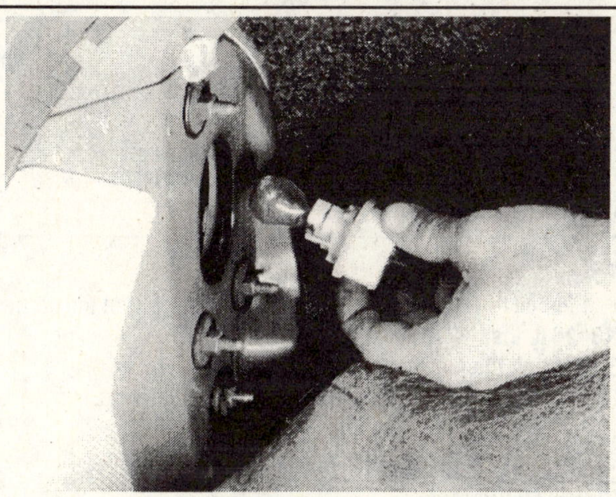
88186P83

Fig. 123 Turn the rear bulb socket to release it from the lamp unit

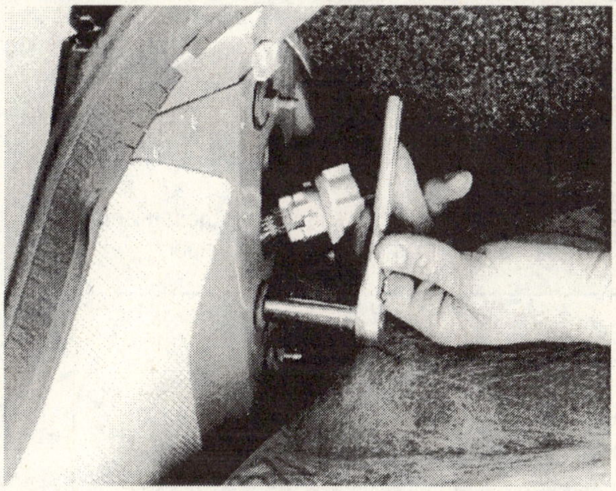
88186P85

Fig. 125 Unbolt the rear side marker . . .

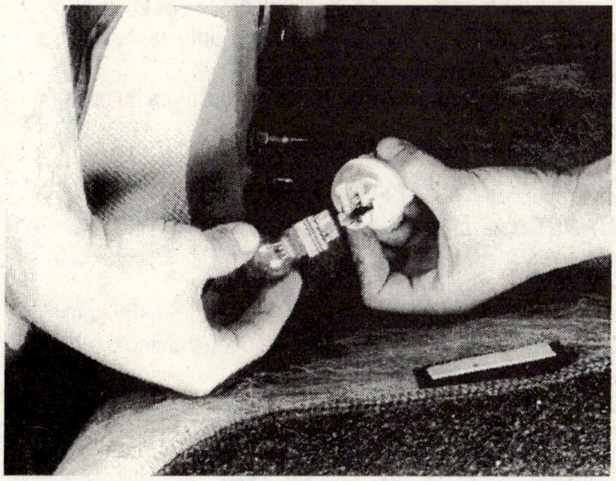
88186P84

Fig. 124 Pull the bulb from the socket to replace

88186P86

Fig. 126 . . . pull the lamp from the outside of the vehicle to remove

High Mount Stop Light

1986-88 MODELS

See Figures 127 and 128

1. Using a thin-bladed screwdriver, remove the lamp screw covers.
2. Remove the 2 lamp retaining screws.
3. Lift the lamp up and out of the brackets.
4. To replace the bulb, turn the socket 45° counterclockwise.
5. Turn the lights on to check for proper operation.

1989-96 MODELS

See Figure 129

1. Slide cover away from back window and remove cover.

If only bulb replacement is necessary, base removal is not required, go to step No. 4.

2. Remove one screw attaching lamp base.
3. Lift edge of base and pull away from back window.
4. Rotate and remove the two bulb and socket assemblies from lamp base.
5. Installation is the reverse of removal.
6. Turn the lights on to check for proper operation.

Fog Lamps

See Figures 130, 131, 132 and 133

1. Disconnect the headlamp dash panel junction wire from the fog lamp assembly.
2. Remove the two screws that retain the fog lamps.
3. Pull the fog lamps from the front bumper.

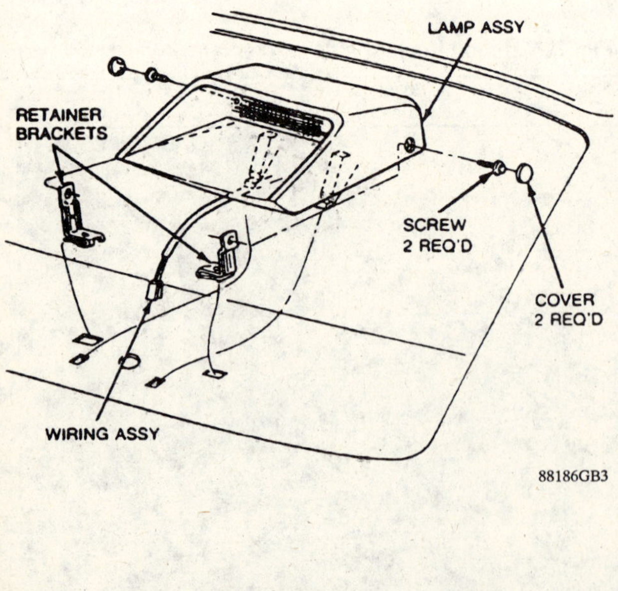

Fig. 127 Exploded view of the high mount lamp system — 1986-88 Thunderbird

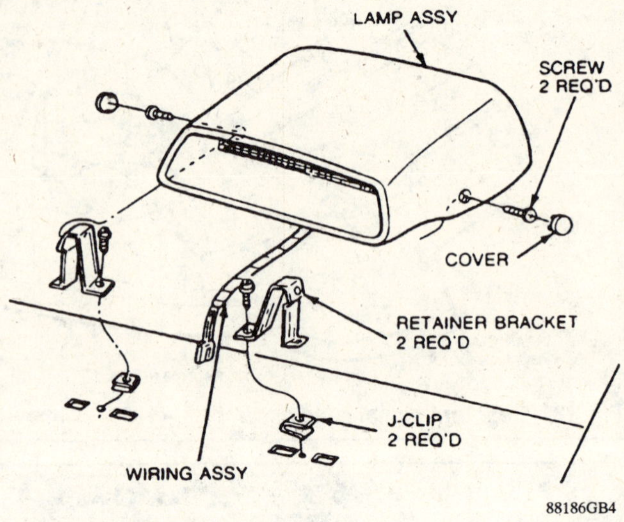

Fig. 128 Exploded view of the high mount lamp system — 1986-88 Cougar

To install:

4. Install the fog lamp to the front bumper, tighten the screws to 13-20 ft. lbs. (17-27 Nm).
5. Attach the junction wire to the lamp assembly.
6. Turn the lights on to check for proper operation.

Dome/Map Lamp

CEILING MOUNTED

See Figures 134, 135, 136, 137 and 138

1. Carefully squeeze the lens inwards to release the locking tabs.
2. Remove the lens from the lamp body.
3. Pull the wedge base bulb directly out of its socket.
4. Remove the screws that retain the lamp assembly to its mounting area.
5. Lower the lamp assembly, then replace the bulbs from the rear of the lamp.
6. Install in the reverse order of removal.
7. Check the operation of the lamp for proper operation.

WITHOUT MAP LIGHTS

See Figure 138

1. Carefully remove the dome lamp lens from the housing.
2. Remove the lamp screws retaining the unit to the body of the vehicle.
3. Replace the bulb if necessary.

To install:

4. Install the lamp unit to the ceiling of the vehicle and tighten the mounting screws.
5. Install the lens to the housing.

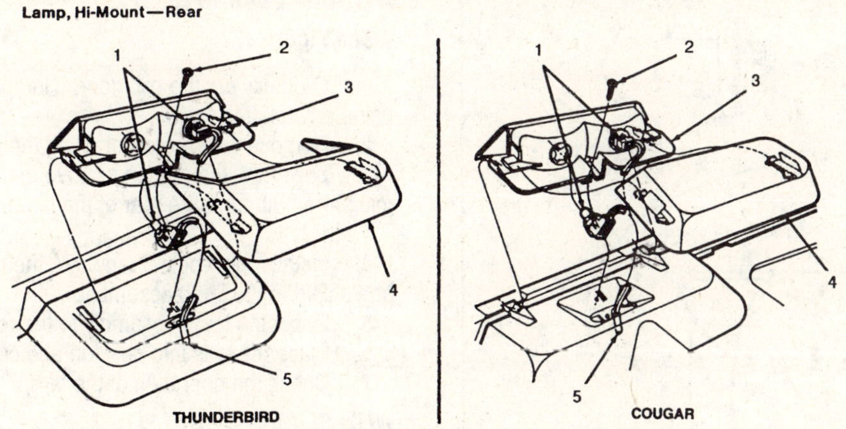

1. Miniature bulb
2. Screw
3. Rear hi-mount lamp
4. Rear hi-mount lamp cover
5. Rear lamp wiring hi-mount stoplamp wiring

88186GB1

Fig. 129 Exploded view of the hi-lamp mount lamp system — 1989–96 models

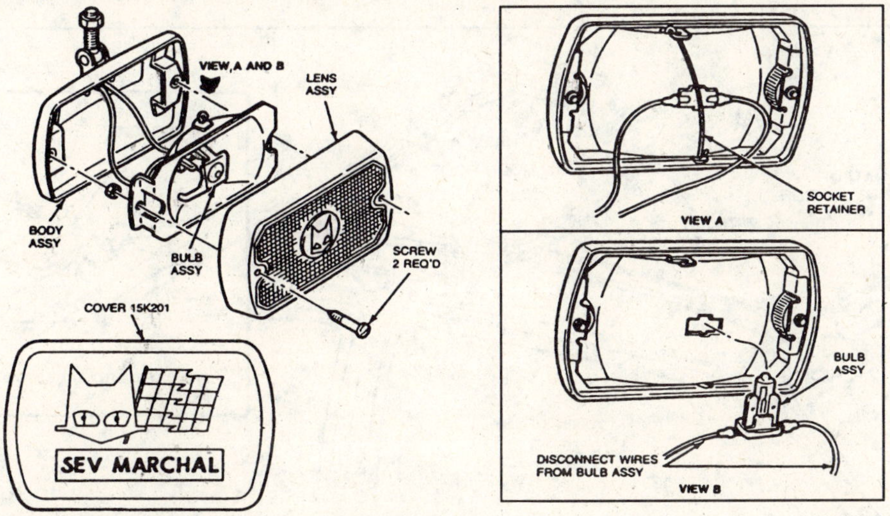

88186GA6

Fig. 130 Exploded view of the fog lamp system — 1988 models

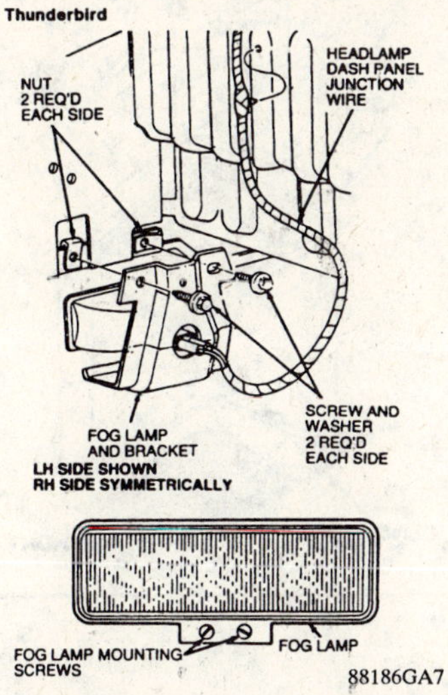

88186GA7

Fig. 131 Fog lamp wiring routing — 1995 shown

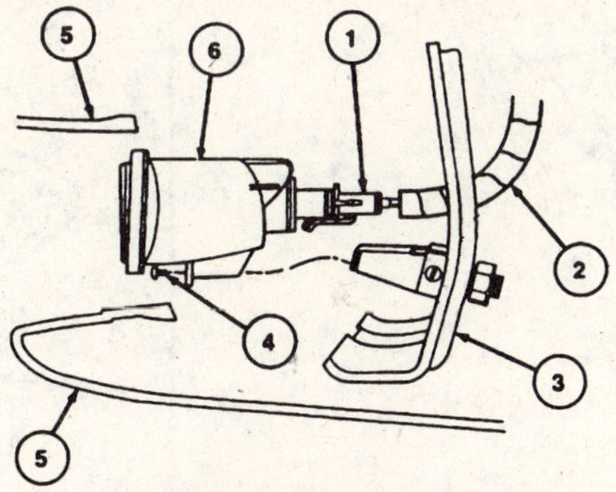

1. Connector (Part of 14290)
2. Headlamp Dash Panel Junction Wire
3. Mounting Bracket
4. Screw
5. Front Bumper Cover
6. Fog Lamp

88186GA8

Fig. 132 Fog lamps components

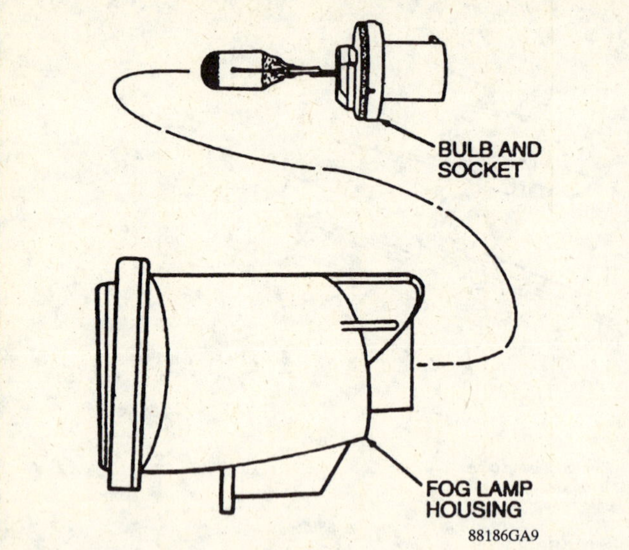

Fig. 133 The fog lamp bulb slides into the rear of the lens assembly

WITHOUT SLIDING ROOF

See Figure 137

1. Carefully pry the pillar/dome lamp lens from the lamp using a flatbladed tool.
2. Remove the screws retaining the lamp to the roof panel.
3. Lower the lamp, then remove the reflector heatshield and miniature bulb from the rear of the lamp.

To install:

4. Install a new bulb if required, then attach the reflector heatshield to the lamp assembly.
5. Install the lamp assembly to the roof panel.
6. Place the lens into position and carefully snap it in.
7. Check the operation of the lamp.

WITH SLIDING ROOF

See Figure 138

1. Carefully pry the pillar/dome lamp lens from the lamp using a flatbladed tool.
2. Carefully pry the switch bezel from the lamp assembly.

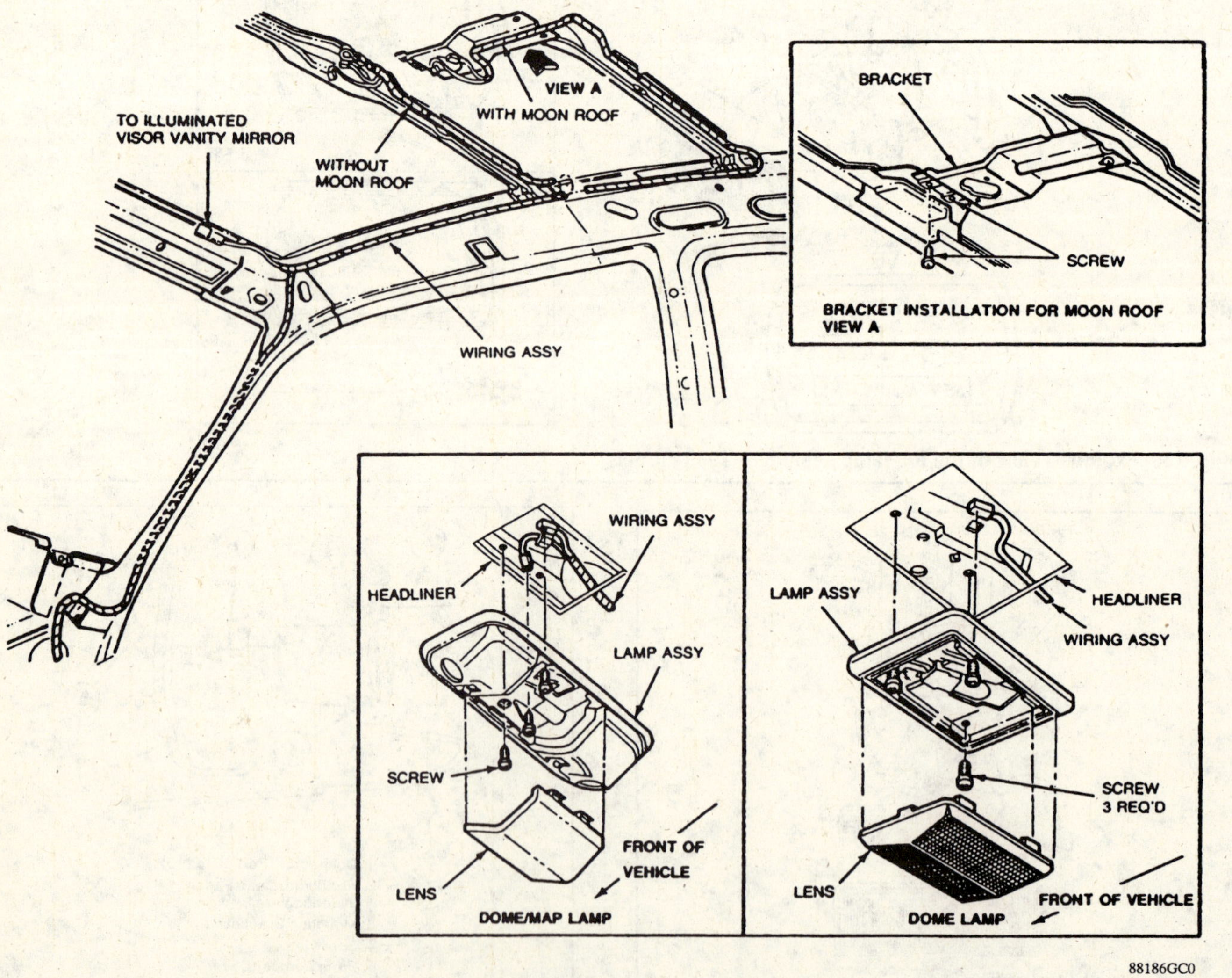

Fig. 134 Exploded view of the dome lamp with and without map light — 1983-88 models

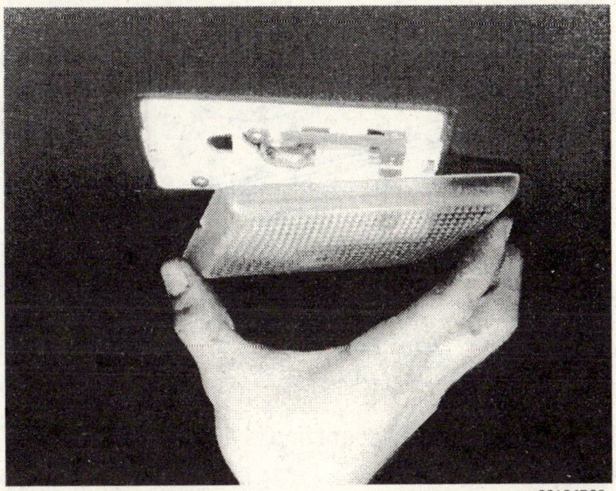

88186P80

Fig. 135 Unsnap the lens off of the ceiling mounting area

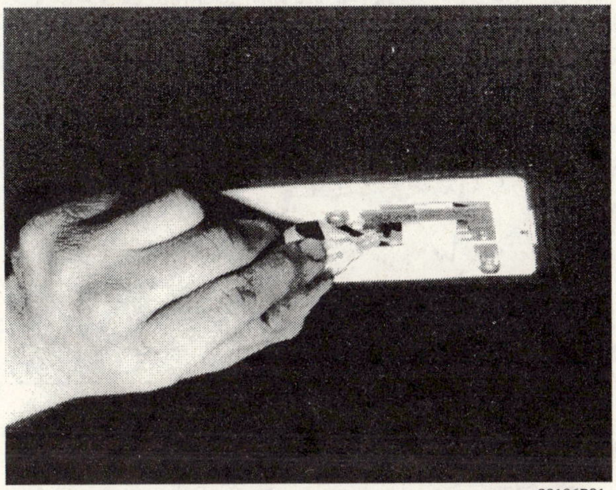

88186P81

Fig. 136 Remove the bulb and inspect for any damage

3. Remove the screws retaining the lamp to the interior roof.
4. Lower the lamp, then remove miniature bulb from the rear of the lamp.

To install:

5. Install a new bulb if required.
6. Install the lamp assembly on the roof panel. Install the switch bezel on the lamp assembly.
7. Place the lens into position and carefully snap it in.
8. Check the operation of the lamp.

Coach Lamps

See Figure 139

1. Remove the rear interior quarter trim panels, if necessary. See Section 10. This will allow you to gain access to the nuts attaching the lamp to the C-pillar.
2. Remove the socket and nuts that attach the lamp to the C-pillar, then remove the lamp.
3. Pull the lamp socket from the lamp assembly and replace the bulb if necessary.

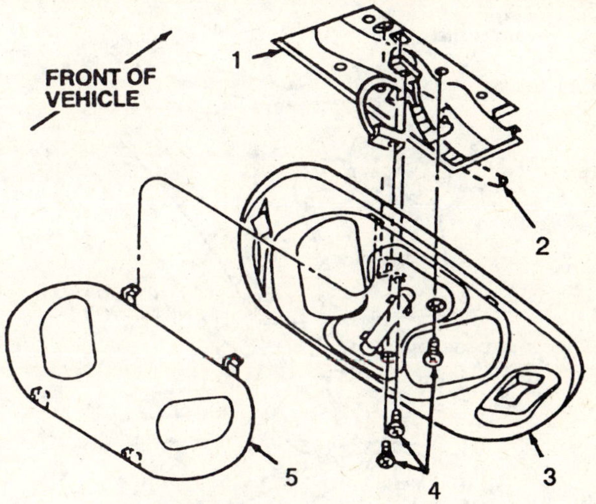

1. Roof headlining
2. Inside rear view mirror wiring
3. Interior lamp
4. Screws (3 req'd)
5. Interior lamp switch bezel

88186GB6

Fig. 137 Exploded view of the dome lamp without a sliding roof — 1994-96 models

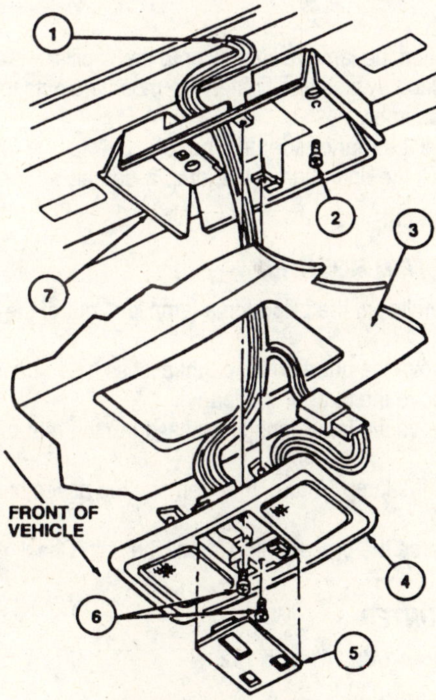

1. Inside Rear View Mirror Wiring
2. Screw (2 Req'd)
3. Roof Headlining
4. Interior Lamp
5. Interior Lamp Switch Bezel
6. Screw (2 Req'd)
7. Power Moonroof Dome Lamp Roof Support

88186GB7

Fig. 138 Exploded view of the dome lamp with a sliding roof — 1994-96 models

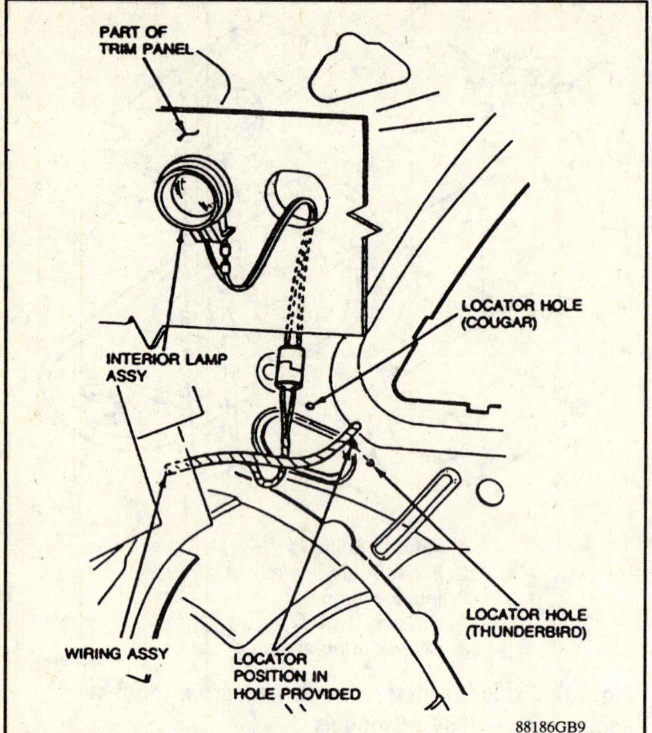

Fig. 139 The coach lamp is located in the rear interior trim panels — 1988 shown

To install:

4. Position the lamp assembly onto the C-pillar with the socket in place. Attach and tighten the mounting nuts to retain the lamp assembly.
5. Install the rear quarter trim panel.
6. Check the operation of the lamp assembly.

Courtesy Lamp

QUARTER TRIM MOUNTED

1. Carefully pry the pillar/dome lamp lens out of the quarter trim panel.
2. Remove the quarter trim panel access hole opening plate.
3. Remove the quarter trim panel.
4. Remove the lamp wiring harness from the rear of the lamp assembly.
5. Turn the lamp $^{1}/_{4}$ turn, then remove the assembly from the panel.
6. Reverse the procedure to install the unit. Check the operation.

DOOR MOUNTED

➧ See Figures 140, 141 and 142

1. Disconnect the negative battery cable.
2. Insert a flatbladed tool between the interior lamp lens tab and the interior lamps. This is the clear portion of the lower edge of the interior lamp lens. Gently twist the tool until the tab clears the lamp body, then rotate the tool down while maintaining a twist force on the tab.
3. Remove the interior lamp lens.
4. Grasp the bulb with your thumb and index finger, then pull the bulb from the socket. Do not twist the bulb.
5. Install the parts in the reverse order of removal.
6. Check the operation of the lamp.

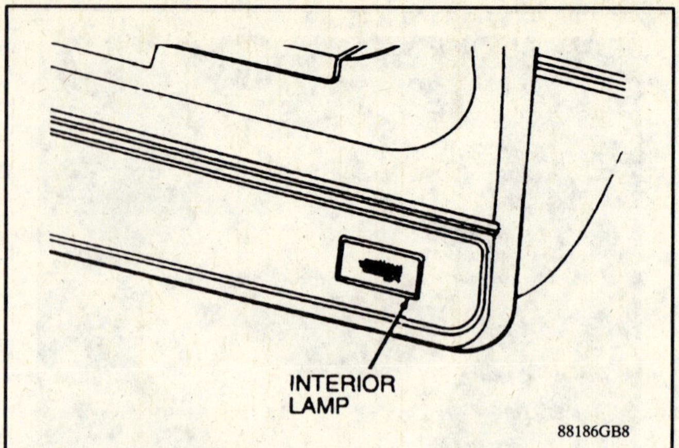

Fig. 140 The courtesy door lamp is a small lamp mounted in the door

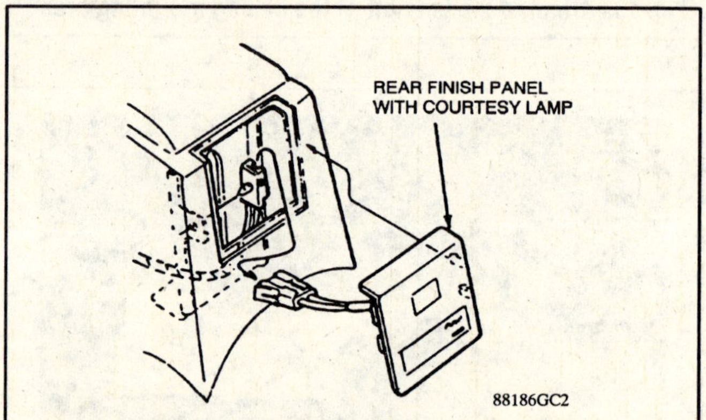

Fig. 141 Courtesy lamps located in the rear of the console — 1988 shown

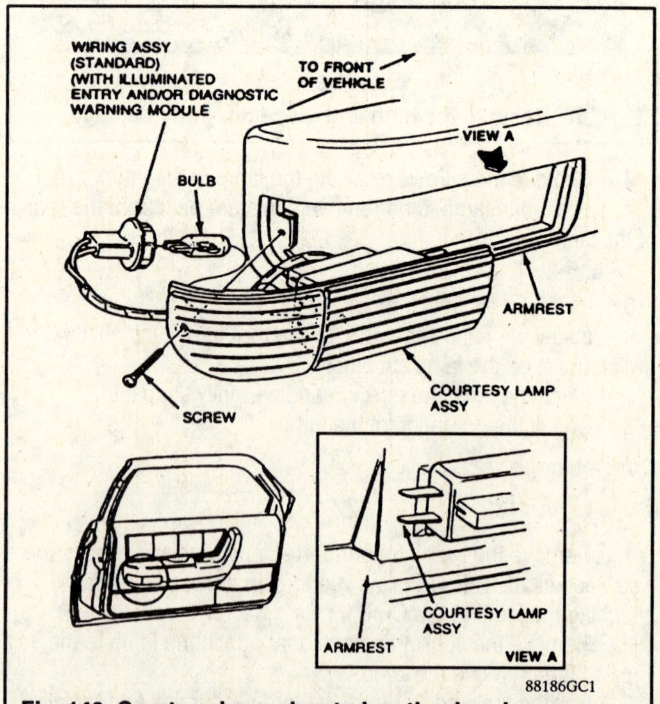

Fig. 142 Courtesy lamps located on the door lower arm rest panel type — 1988 shown

LIGHT BULB APPLICATIONS — 1983–86 MODELS

Function	Number of Bulbs	Trade Number
Exterior Illumination		
Headlamps — Lo Beam	2	H4656**
Headlamps — Hi Beam	2	H4651
Front Park/Turn	2	1157
Front Side Marker	2	194
Rear Side Marker	2	194
Back-Up Light	2	1156
High Mount Stop Lamp	2	912
License Plate	2	194
Tail/Stop/Turn	4	157
Cornering (Opt.)	2	1156
Ornament (Coach) (Opt.)	2	Electro Panel
Interior Illumination		
Turn Signal Indicator	2	194
Fan Nomenclature	1	1892
Heater Control Nomenclature	1	161
A/C Control Nomenclature	1	161
Electric Rear Window Defroster	1	2162
Glove Compartment (Opt.)	1	1816
Ashtray	1	1892
Instrument Panel Clock	1	194
High Beam Indicator	1	194
Warning Lamps — All	(1 each)	194
Instrument Cluster Illumination		
Standard Cluster	6	194
Standard Cluster	2	Halogen #2033*
Turbo Cluster	6	194
Electronic Cluster	1	Mini #37
Electronic Cluster	6	194
Electronic Cluster	6	Halogen #2033*
Dome Lamp	1	906
Dome/Map Lamp	1/2	912/105
Trunk Compartment (Opt.)	1	89
Engine Compartment (Opt.)	1	89
Automatic Transmission "PRND21" Indicator	1	1893
Anti-Theft Warning Lamp	1	***
Armrest Courtesy Lamp	2	904
Radio Lamps		
AM/FM Stereo		
General Illumination	6	7152
Dial Illumination	1	936
AM/FM Stereo Cassette		
General Illumination	6	7152
Dial Illumination	1	936
Pilot (Dial Illumination)		
AM/FM/Stereo	1	1893
AM/FM/Stereo/Cassette	2	1893
Stereo Indicator Lamp	N/A	—

*Replace with Ford Part Number D20B-18C622-AB or equivalent, if available (Bulb is an integral part of assembly).

**Substitution of headlamp bulbs other than original equipment or equivalent may result in false warning or no warning in the lamp outage warning indicator system.

***E3SB-10C915-AA — RPO (Throw away unit) (Bulb not replaceable)

****E5SF-13B765-CB — Requires cleaning only — no handling of glass.

88186C50

LIGHT BULB APPLICATIONS — 1987–88 MODELS

FUNCTION	NUMBER OF BULBS	TRADE NUMBER
Exterior Illumination		
Headlamps—Lo Beam, Hi Beam	2	9004[1]
Foglamps (Turbo Coupe)	2	H3
Front Park/Turn	2	2357NA
Park Lamp	2	2458NA
Rear Side Marker	2	904
Backup Lamp	2	1156
High Mount Brakelamp	2	912
License Plate	2	194
Tail/Stop/Turn	4	2458
Cornering Lamp (Opt.)	2	1156
Taillamp Only	2	194
Interior Illumination		
Turn Signal Indicator	2	194/37[4]
Fan Nomenclature	1	1892
Heater Control Nomenclature	1	161
A/C Control Nomenclature	1	161
Defroster		
Ashtray	1	161
Courtesy Lamps	2	904
Door	2	194
Floor Console	2	194
Instrument Panel	2	89
Visor Vanity Light	4	168
Keyless Entry Switch	3	731
High Beam Indicator	1	194/37[4]
Warning Lights—All (Opt.)	(1 each)	194/37[4]
Instrument Cluster Illumination		
Standard Cluster	6	194
Standard Cluster	2	Halogen #2033[2]
Performance Cluster Sport Turbo Coupe	6	194
Electronic Cluster (Opt.)	9	Mini #37
Electronic Cluster (Opt.)	4	194
Electronic Cluster (Opt.)	6	Halogen #2033[3]

88186C51

LIGHT BULB APPLICATIONS — 1989-93 MODELS

FUNCTION	NUMBER OF BULBS	TRADE NUMBER
Exterior Illumination		
Headlamps—Lo Beam/Hi Beam	2	9006/9005(1)
Foglamps (Super Coupe)	2	H3
Front Park/Turn/Side Marker	2	2458NA
Backup Lamp	2	2456
High Mount Stoplamp	2	921
License Plate	2	194
Tail/Stop/Turn/Side Marker	2	2458
Cornering Lamp	2	2456
Interior Illumination	2	194
Turn Signal Indicator	2	194/37(4)
Fan Nomenclature	1	1892
Heater Control Nomenclature	1	161
A/C Control Nomenclature	1	161
EATC	2	37
Ashtray	1	161
Glove Compartment	1	194
Courtesy Lamps	2	904
Door	2	168
Floor Console	1	T1895
Instrument Panel	2	89
Keyless Entry Switch	3	731
High Beam Indicator	1	194/37(4)
Warning Lights—All (Opts)	(1 each)	194/37(4)
Instrument Cluster Illumination		
Standard Cluster	6	1904
Standard Cluster	2	Xenon A7742 (3)
Performance Cluster (Sport and Super Coupe)	6	194
Electronic Cluster (Opt.)	9	Mini #37
Electronic Cluster (Opt.)	4	194
Electronic Cluster (Opt.)	6	Xenon A7742(3)

88186C52

LIGHT BULB APPLICATIONS — 1989-93 MODELS (continued)

FUNCTION	NUMBER OF BULBS	TRADE NUMBER
Dome Lamp	1	906
Dome/Map Lamp (Opt.)	1/2	912/105(4)
Trunk Compartment	1	98
Engine Compartment (Opt.)	1	98
Automatic Transmission Indicator	1	1893
Radio Pilot Light		
AM/FM/MPX (ESR)	6	7152
AM/FM/CASS (ESR)	6	7152
Graphic Equalizer	2	7373
Radio LCD Backlight		
AM/FM/MPX (ESR)	1	936
AM/FM/CASS (ESR)	1	936

(1) Substitution of headlamp bulbs other than original equipment or equivalent may result in false warning or no warning in the lamp outage warning indicator system.
(2) E3SB-10C915-AA—RPO (Throw away unit.) (Bulb not replaceable.)
(3) E5SF-13B765-CB—Refer bulb replacement to dealer
(4) Optional Replacement Bulb

88186C53

LIGHT BULB APPLICATIONS — 1994-96 THUNDERBIRD

Function	Trade number
Exterior lights	
Rear	
Tail lamp, brakelamp, turn lamp side marker	3157
Front	
Parklamp, turn lamp, side marker	3157NA**
Backup lamp	3156
Fog lamp (Super Coupe)	880
License plate lamp	194
High-mounted brakelamp	921
Headlamps	
Lo beam/Hi beam	9007
Interior lights	
Luggage compartment lamp	912
Dome lamp	912
Dome/map lamp	
Dome	912
Map	105
Courtesy lamps	98
Door courtesy lamp	168
Floor console storage bin lamp	T-1865
Engine compartment lamp (opt.)	906
Visor vanity	194
Instrument panel lights	
Glove compartment	194
Instrument courtesy lights	89
High beam indicator	194
Floor console ashtray lamp	1893
Floor console cigar lighter lamp	161
Radio illumination	•
Warning lights (all)	194
Turn signal indicator	194
Fan	1892
"PRND21" bulb	194
Heater or Heater A/C	37
Automatic climate control	37
Keyless entry switch	713
Instrument cluster lights	
Standard	194/37
Performance (sport and super coupe)	194

**NA means Natural Amber
• Refer bulb replacement to a Ford authorized radio service center.

88186C54

LIGHT BULB APPLICATIONS — 1994-96 COUGAR

Function	Trade number
Exterior lights	
Rear	
Tail lamp, brakelamp, turn lamp side marker	3157
Front	
Parklamp, turn lamp, side marker	3157NA**
Backup lamp	3156
License plate lamp	194
High-mounted brakelamp	921
Headlamps	
Lo beam/Hi beam	9007
Interior lights	
Luggage compartment lamp	912
Dome lamp	912
Dome/map lamp	
Dome	912
Map	105
Courtesy lamps	98
Door courtesy lamp	168
Floor console storage bin lamp	T1865
Floor console ashtray lamp	1893
Visor vanity lamp (opt.)	194
Engine compartment lamp (opt.)	906
Instrument panel lights	
Glove compartment	194
High beam indicator	194
Cigar lighter lamp	161
Radio illumination	•
Warning lights (all)	194
Turn signal indicator	194
Fan	1892
"PRND21" bulb	194
Heater or Heater A/C	37
Semi automatic climate control	37
Instrument cluster lights	
Mechanical	194/37

**NA means Natural Amber
• Refer bulb replacement to a Ford authorized radio service center.

88186C55

TRAILER WIRING

Wiring the vehicle for towing is fairly easy. There are a number of good wiring kits available and these should be used, rather than trying to design your own.

All trailers will need brake lights and turn signals as well as tail lights and side marker lights. Most areas require extra marker lights for overwide trailers. Also, most areas have recently required back-up lights for trailers, and most trailer manufacturers have been building trailers with back-up lights for several years.

Additionally, some Class I, most Class II and just about all Class III trailers will have electric brakes. Add to this number an accessories wire, to operate trailer internal equipment or to charge the trailer's battery, and you can have as many as seven wires in the harness.

Determine the equipment on your trailer and buy the wiring kit necessary. The kit will contain all the wires needed, plus a plug adapter set which includes the female plug, mounted on the bumper or hitch, and the male plug, wired into, or plugged into the trailer harness.

When installing the kit, follow the manufacturer's instructions. The color coding of the wires is usually standard throughout the industry. One point to note: some domestic vehicles, and most imported vehicles, have separate turn signals. On most domestic vehicles, the brake lights and rear turn signals operate with the same bulb. For those vehicles with separate turn signals, you can purchase an isolation unit so that the brake lights won't blink whenever the turn signals are operated, or, you can go to your local electronics supply house and buy four diodes to wire in series with the brake and turn signal bulbs. Diodes will isolate the brake and turn signals. The choice is yours. The isolation units are simple and quick to install, but far more expensive than the diodes. The diodes, however, require more work to install properly, since they require the cutting of each bulb's wire and soldering in place of the diode.

One, final point, the best kits are those with a spring loaded cover on the vehicle mounted socket. This cover prevents dirt and moisture from corroding the terminals. Never let the vehicle socket hang loosely; always mount it securely to the bumper or hitch.

CIRCUIT PROTECTION

Fuses

REPLACEMENT

➧ **See Figures 143 and 144**

A fuse panel is used to house the numerous fuses protecting the various branches of the electrical system and is normally the most accessible. The mounting of the fuse panel is either on the left side of the passenger compartment, under the dash, on the side kick panel or on the firewall to the left of the steering column. Certain models will have the fuse panel exposed while other models will have it covered with a removable trim cover.

Fuses are simply snapped in and out for replacement. Always replace a fuse with one of the same amp rating. On plug type fuses, the color will also be the same.

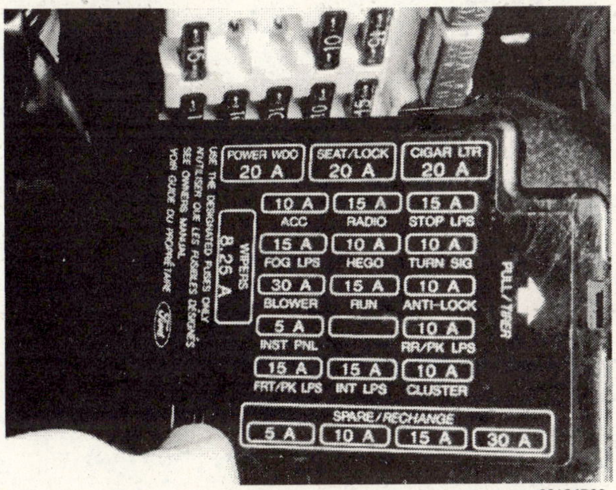

88186P90

Fig. 143 Unsnap the fuse box cover from the housing

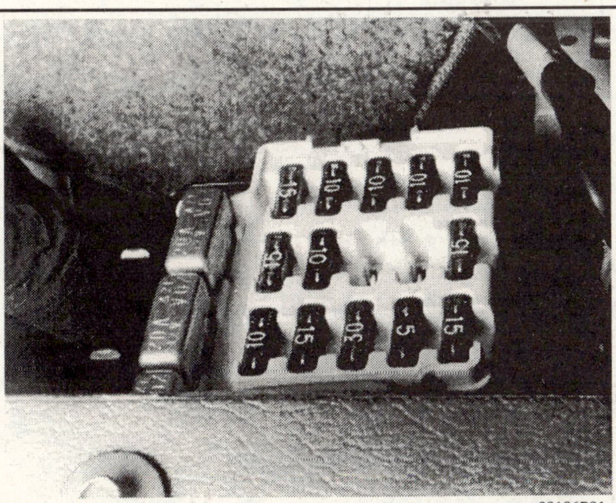

88186P91

Fig. 144 Be sure to replace the fuse that is bad with the correct size fuse!!

Fusible Links and Circuit Breakers

REPLACEMENT

➧ **See Figures 145 and 146**

A fuse link is a short length of insulated wire, integral with the engine compartment wiring harness. It is several wire gauges smaller than the circuit it protects and is located inline directly from the positive terminal of the battery.

When heavy current flows or when a short to ground occurs in the wiring harness, the fuse link burns out and protects the alternator or wiring. Production fuse links are color coded:

- 12 gauge: Gray
- 14 gauge: Dark Green
- 16 gauge: Black
- 18 gauge: Brown
- 20 gauge: Dark Blue

➥ **Replacement fuse link color coding may vary from production fuse link color coding.**

Circuit breakers are used on certain electrical components requiring high amperage, such as the headlamp circuit, electrical seats and/or windows to name a few. The advantage of the circuit breaker is its ability to open and close the electrical circuit as the lead demands, rather than the necessity of a part replacement, should the circuit be opened with another protective device in line.

Flashers

REPLACEMENT

➧ **See Figure 147**

The flasher unit can be found under the dash panel attached to a bracket on the right side steering column opening reinforcement. On some models, the flasher plugs into the fuse panel.

The flasher can be removed by pressing the plastic retaining clip and pulling straight rearward. Align the new flasher housing with bracket and push forward until it snaps into the bracket

➥ **Never unplug or plug in a flasher unit while it is in the ON mode. Damage could occur to fuses, light bulbs, and/or the flasher unit being installed.**

88186P92

Fig. 145 There is another fuse box located near the battery. This may contain your flashers and circuit breakers

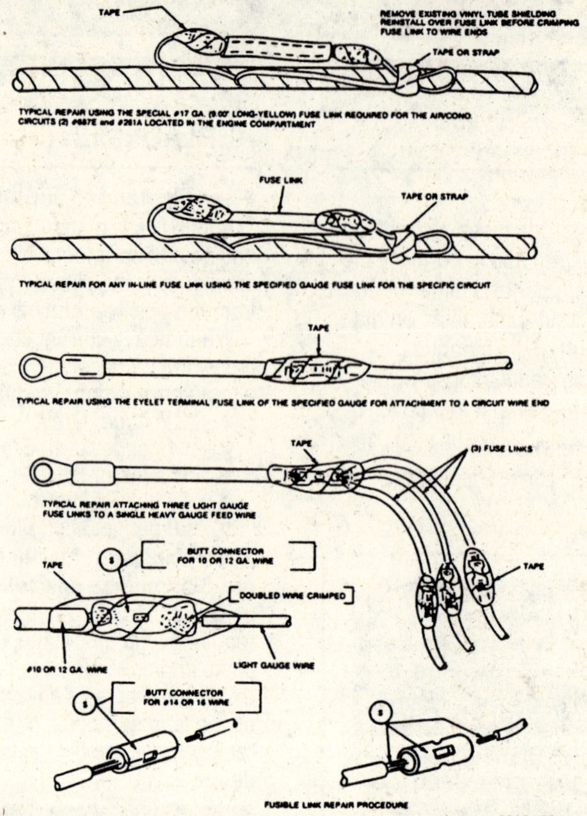

88186GM1

Fig. 146 Fusible link repair procedures

F = Front R = Rear ● = Lights off ○ = Lights on

Problem		Solution
Turn signals light, but do not flash	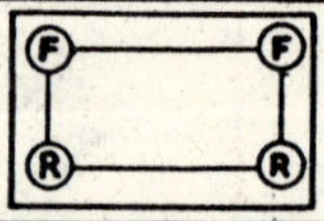	• Replace the flasher
No turn signals light on either side	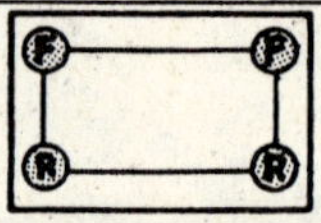	• Check the fuse. Replace if defective. • Check the flasher by substitution • Check for open circuit, short circuit or poor ground
Both turn signals on one side don't work	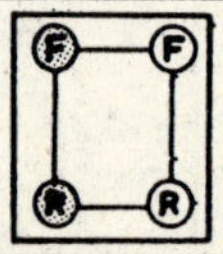	• Check for bad bulbs • Check for bad ground in both housings
One turn signal light on one side doesn't work	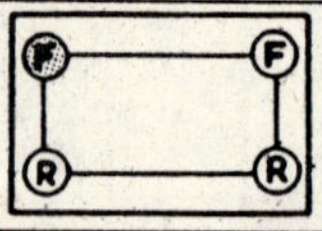	• Check and/or replace bulb • Check for corrosion in socket. Clean contacts. • Check for poor ground at socket
Turn signal flashes too fast or too slow	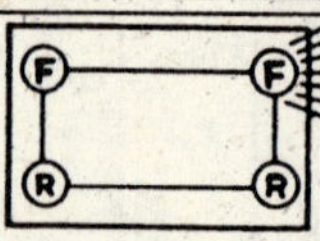	• Check any bulb on the side flashing too fast. A heavy-duty bulb is probably installed in place of a regular bulb. • Check the bulb flashing too slow. A standard bulb was probably installed in place of a heavy-duty bulb. • Check for loose connections or corrosion at the bulb socket
Indicator lights don't work in either direction		• Check if the turn signals are working • Check the dash indicator lights • Check the flasher by substitution

88186GM2

Fig. 147 Turn signal and flasher problems

FUSE PANEL APPLICATION — 1983–85 MODELS

Position	Description	Color	Circuit Protected
1	15 Amp. Fuse	Light Blue	Stop Lamps, Hazard Warning Lamps, Speed Control Module and Cornering Lamp Relays
2	6 Amp. C.B.	—	Windshield Wiper, Windshield Washer Pump, Interval Wiper
3	Spare	—	(Not Used)
4	15 Amp. Fuse	Light Blue	Taillamps, Parking Lamps, Side Marker Lamps, Instrument Cluster Illumination Lamps, License Lamps, A/C and Heater Illumination, Radio Illumination, Digital Clock Illumination, Autolamp Relay

88186C57

Position	Description	Color	Circuit Protected
5	15 Amp. Fuse	Light Blue	Turn Signal Lamps, Back-Up Lamps, Illumination Entry, Keyless Entry Module
6	20 Amp. Fuse	Yellow	A/C Clutch, Heated Backlite Relay Timer, Trunk Lid Release, Speed Control Module, Electronic Digital Clock Display, Graphic Warning Display Module, Illuminated Entry, AntiTheft Module
7	15 Amp. Fuse	—	Fog Lamps (Turbo Only)
8	15 Amp. Fuse	Light Blue	Courtesy Lamps, Key Warning Buzzer, Illuminated Entry Module, Analog Clock
9	30 Amp. Fuse	Light Green	A/C Heater Blower Motor
10	20 C.B.	—	Horn, Cigar Lighter
11	20 Amp. Fuse	Yellow	Radio, Tape Player, Premium Sound, Power Antenna
12	20 Amp. C.B.	—	Power Seat, Power Locks, Keyless Entry Fuel Filler Door
13	5 Amp. Fuse	Tan	Instrument Cluster Illumination Lamps, Radio, Climate Control
14	20 Amp. C.B.	—	Power Windows
15	10 Amp. Fuse	Red	On cars with optional Lamp Outage System, Taillamps, Rear Side Markers, License Lamps

88186C58

Position	Description	Color	Circuit Protected
16	20 Amp. Fuse	Yellow	Flash-to-Pass
17	15 Amp. Fuse	Light Blue	Electronic Cluster, Tripminder Display Module Fuel Gauge on Non-Electronic Cluster
18	10 Amp. Fuse	Red	Warning Indicator Lamps, Throttle Solenoid Positioner, Low Fuel Module, Dual Timer Chime, Tachometer, Washer Fluid Level Indicator

3 fuses for optional anti-theft system located in the luggage compartment near the package tray in fuse holders:

- 20 amp fuse to protect headlamps wiring.
- 20 amp fuse to protect horn circuit & feed circuit to module.
- 15 amp fuse to protect marker & taillamp wiring.

88186C59

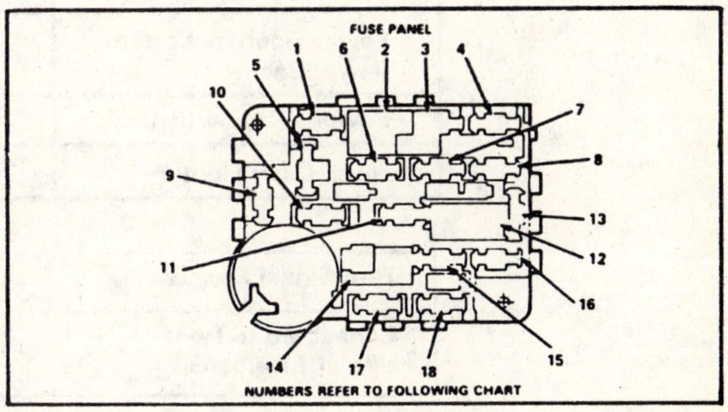

88186C57

FUSE LINK AND CIRCUIT BREAKER APPLICATION — 1983–85 MODELS

Circuit	Circuit Protection Rating	Location
Lamp Feed	16 GA Fuse Link	Near Starter Motor Relay
Ignition Feed	16 GA Fuse Link	Near Starter Motor Relay
Charging Circuit	14 GA Fuse Link	Near Starter Motor Relay
Heated Backlite	16 GA Fuse Link	Near Starter Motor Relay
Engine Compartment Lamp	20 GA Fuse Link	Near Starter Motor Relay
Electric Cooling Fan	20 GA Fuse Link	Near Starter Motor Relay
Electric Fan Control Unit	20 GA Fuse Link	Near Starter Motor
Windshield Wiper/ Washer	6 Amp. C.B.	Fuse Panel
Headlights, High Beam Indicator	22 Amp. C.B.	Part of Headlight Switch
Power Door Locks and Power Seats	20 Amp. C.B.	Fuse Panel
Power Window (2-Dr.)	20 Amp. C.B.	Fuse Panel
Horn, Cigar Lighter	20 Amp. C.B.	Fuse Panel

Turn Signal Flasher	Hazard Flasher
Connected to front side of fuse panel.	Connected to rear side of fuse panel.

NOTE—To replace turn signal or hazard flasher, disengage flasher units from the fuse panel.

88186C60

FUSE PANEL APPLICATION — 1986 MODELS

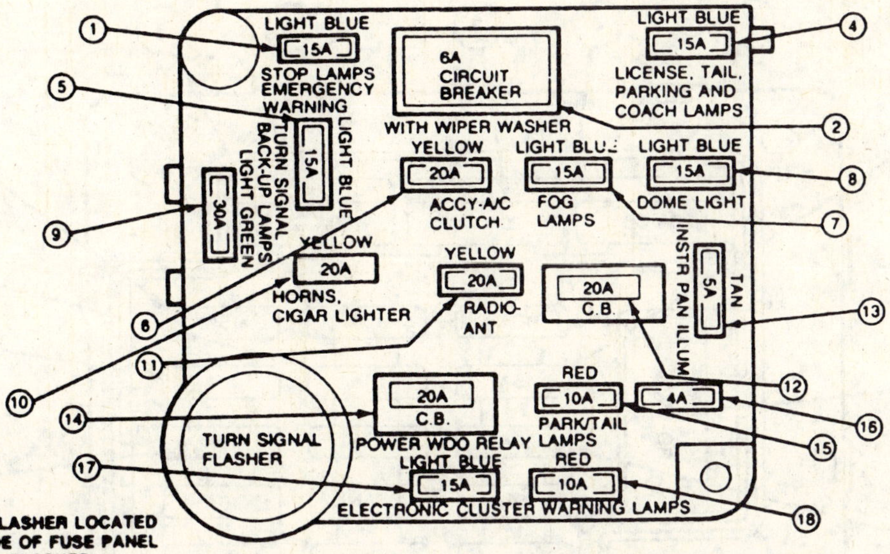

NOTE: EMERGENCY FLASHER LOCATED ON THE REVERSE SIDE OF FUSE PANEL BEHIND TURN SIGNAL FLASHER.

CAVITY NUMBER	SYSTEMS
1	STOP LAMPS, HAZARD WARNING LAMPS, SPEED CONTROL MODULE, CORNERING LAMP RELAY
2	WINDSHIELD WIPER, WINDSHIELD WASHER PUMP, INTERVAL WIPER MODULE
4	TAILLAMPS, PARKING LAMPS, SIDE MARKER/COACH LAMPS, CLUSTER ILLUMINATION LAMPS, LICENSE LAMPS, DIGITAL CLOCK ILLUMINATOR, A/C AND HEATER ILLUMINATION, RADIO ILLUMINATION
5	TURN SIGNAL LAMPS, BACK-UP LAMPS, ILLUMINATE/ KEYLESS ENTRY/DAY/NIGHT MIRRORS, TURBO BUZZER
6	HEATED BACKLIGHT CONTROL DECK LID RELEASE, ELECTRONIC CHIMES MODULE, LAMP OUTAGE AND CORNERING LAMPS/ELECTRONIC DIGITAL CLOCK DISPLAY, TRIPMINDER, ILLUMINATED ENTRY, ANTI-THEFT MODULE, RADIO AND CLUSTER ILLUMINATION, REAR READING LAMPS
7	FOG LAMPS (TURBO ONLY)
8	COURTESY LAMPS, KEY WARNING BUZZER, ILLUMINATED ENTRY MODULE, REMOTE ELECTRIC MIRRORS, ELECTRONIC RADIO MEMORY, CLOCK, CLUSTER MEMORY, GLOVE COMPARTMENT LAMP, ANTI-THEFT RELAY
9	A/C-HEATER BLOWER MOTOR
10	HORN, CIGAR LIGHTER, FLASH-TO-PASS, FUEL FILLER DOOR, SPEED CONTROL
11	RADIO, TAPE PLAYER, POWER ANTENNA, PREMIUM SOUND AMPLIFIER
12	POWER SEAT, DOOR LOCKS, KEYLESS ENTRY
13	INSTRUMENT CLUSTER, RADIO, CLIMATE CONTROL, INSTRUMENT PANEL ILLUMINATION
14	POWER WINDOWS, POWER MOON ROOF
15	TAIL/PARK LAMPS, COACH LAMPS, LICENSE LAMPS
16	EATC MEMORY
17	ELECTRONIC CLUSTER TRIPMINDER DISPLAY MODULE, FUEL GAUGE ON NON-ELECTRONIC CLUSTER, A/C CLUTCH, SPEED CONTROL MODULE, GRAPHIC WARNING DISPLAY MODULE
18	WARNING INDICATOR LAMPS, AUTO LAMP SYSTEM ELECTRONIC CHIMES; LOW WASHER FLUID LEVEL LAMP, LOW FUEL MODULE/THROTTLE SOLENOID POSITIONER, LOW OIL RELAY, TACHOMETER, FLASH-TO-PASS RELAY

***THE VISOR MIRROR USES TWO FUSES: A 15-AMP FUSE LOCATED IN THE FUSE PANEL AND A 2-AMP FUSE LOCATED IN THE VISOR ASSEMBLY. THE GARAGE DOOR OPENER IS NOT FUSED WITHIN THE VISOR.**

88186C61

FUSE PANEL APPLICATION — 1989–93 MODELS

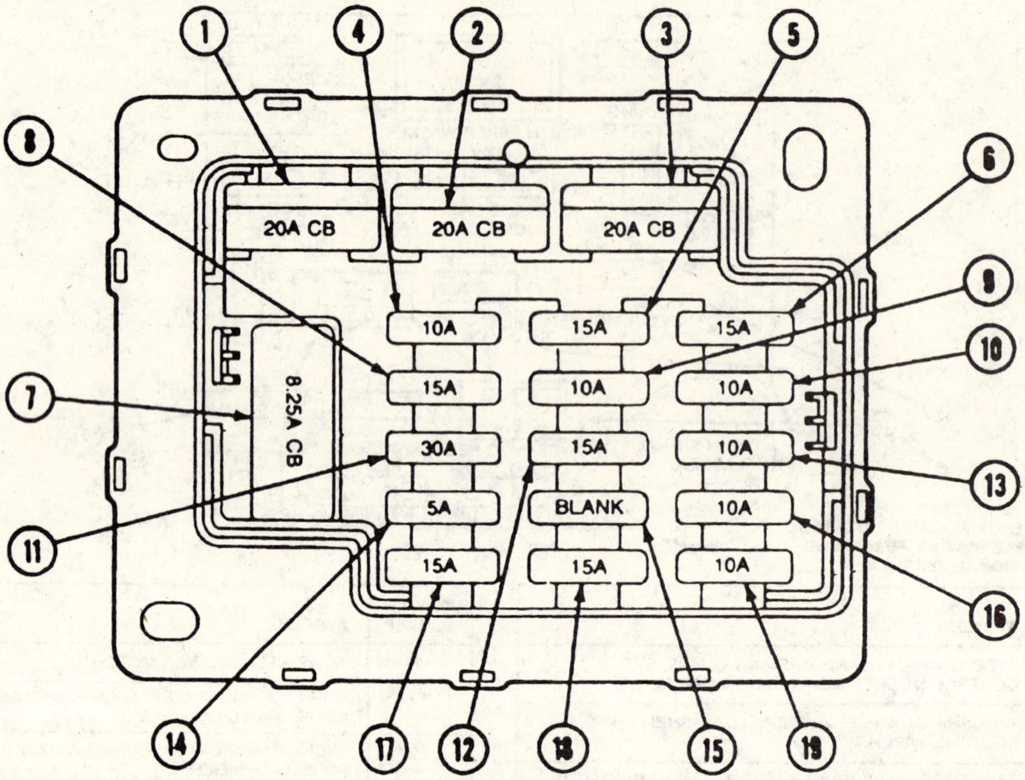

FUSE PANEL

Cavity Number	Systems
1	Deck lid solenoid, RH power window, LH power window, moon roof motor
2	Fuel door release solenoid, RH power seat, LH power seat, LH power door lock, RH power door lock
3	Cigar lighter, high beam
4	Radio LCD, autolamp dimmer control, anti-theft module, chime
5	Radio, power antenna motor
6	Stoplamps, hi-mount stoplamps, EEC module
7	Wiper motor, washer motor, IWW module
8	Fog lamps
9	HEGO sensors
10	Backup lamps, flasher
11	Blower motor
12	A/C clutch, heated rear window switch, VMM module, engine coolant level sensor, EIC feed, EVO test, steering sensor, ride control mode switch, ride control module, ride control relay, washer level sensor, auto day/nite mirror, parking brake illumination, keyless entry illumination module, daytime running lamps, performance cluster ride control lamp
13	Anti-lock motor relay coil
14	PRNDL lamp, VMM, EIC switch, EIC, rear defrost switch, A/C/heat selector switch, radio, radio LCD, compact disc LCD
15	Not used
16	Rear park lamps, license lamps
17	Chime, front park lamps, LCD illumination relay (coil)
18	Instrument panel courtesy lamp, glove box lamp, anti-theft lamp in cluster, daytime running lamps module, engine compartment lamp, map lamp, console lamp, power mirrors, keyless entry module, vanity lamps, luggage compartment lamp, door courtesy lamp, C-pillar courtesy lamp, dome lamp
19	Chime, autolamp lite sensor, chime, anti-lock module, cluster

88186C62

FUSE PANEL APPLICATION — 1993 T-BIRD AND 1989–94 COUGAR

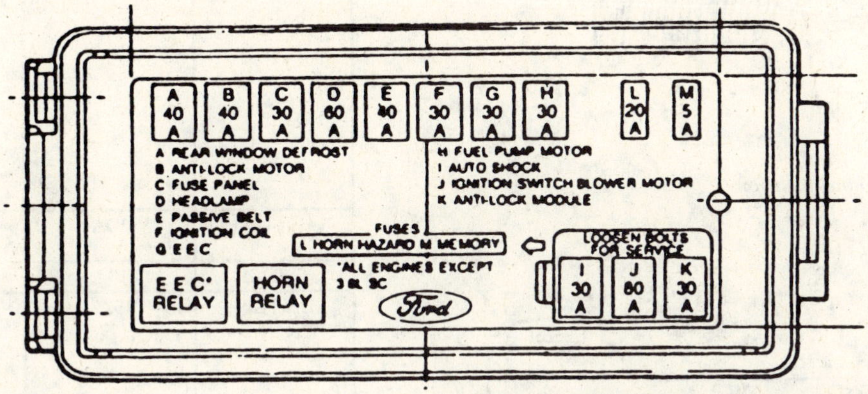

HIGH CURRENT FUSE PANEL

THE HIGH CURRENT FUSE PANEL IS LOCATED IN THE ENGINE COMPARTMENT ON THE LH FENDER APRON.

WARNING — ALWAYS DISCONNECT THE BATTERY BEFORE SERVICING HIGH CURRENT FUSES. FORD RECOMMENDS THAT HIGH CURRENT FUSES BE REPLACED BY A QUALIFIED TECHNICIAN.

CAVITY	FUSE RATING	COLOR	CIRCUIT PROTECTED
A	40 Amp	Green	Rear Window Defroster
B	40 Amp	Green	Anti-Lock Motor
C	40 Amp	Green	Fuse Panel
D	60 Amp	Yellow	Headlamp
E	40 Amp	Green	Passive Restraints
F	30 Amp	Pink	Ignition Coil
G	30 Amp	Pink	Electronic Engine Control
H	30 Amp	Pink	Fuel Pump Motor
I	30 Amp	Pink	Auto Shock
J	60 Amp	Black	Ignition Switch/Blower Motor
K	30 Amp	Pink	Anti-Lock Module
L	20 Amp	Yellow	Horn/Hazard
M	5 Amp	Tan	Memory

88186C63

FUSE PANEL APPLICATION — 1994–96 T-BIRD AND 1995–96 COUGAR

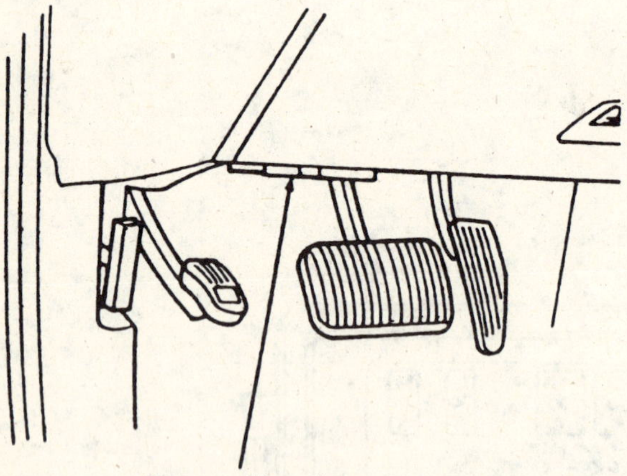

Fuse panel location

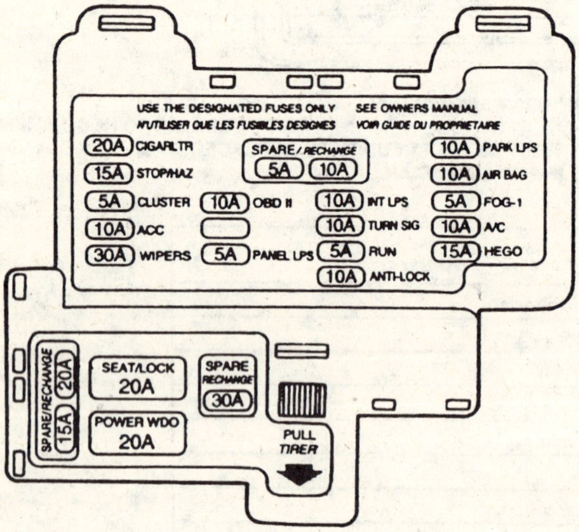

88186C64

The instrument panel fuses, circuit breakers and relays

Fuse/CB Location	Fuse Amp Rating	Description
Run	5A	• Cluster • Defrost switch • Coolant level sensor • Washer level sensor • DRL module • EVO test • EVO steering sensor • ARC (EVO) module • ARC switch • Hard ride relay • Soft ride relay • Auto mirror • EATC blend door • Air bag module • Overdrive cancel switch • Brake shift solenoid
Anti-Lock	10A	• Main ABS relay • ABS module
OBD-II	10A	• OBD-II test connector
Panel Lps.	5A	• Cluster illumination • Phone switch illumination • Rear defrost switch illumination • A/C switch-manual illumination • PRND21 illumination • Ashtray light • EATC illumination • Clock illumination • Radio illumination
Cigar Ltr.	20A	• Lighter • Flash to pass
Stop/Haz.	15A	• Speed control module • ABS module • Brake shift interlock • High mount brake lamp • Stop lamps • Flashers
Cluster	5A	• Cluster (gauges) • Cluster (ABS) • Cluster (air bags) • Chime • Autolamp sensor

88186C65

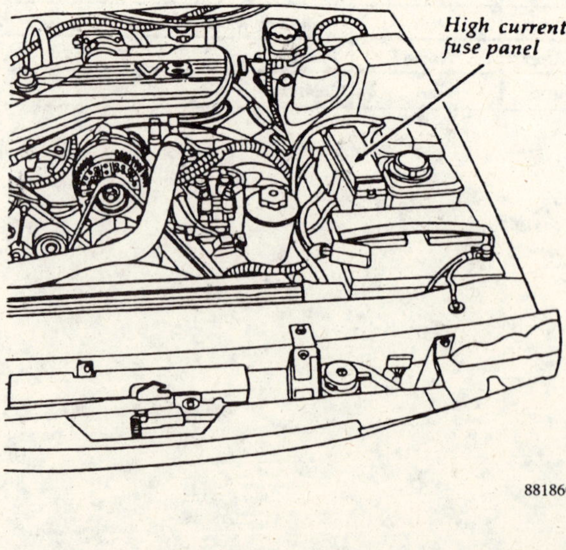

88186C67

FUSE PANEL APPLICATION — 1994–96 T-BIRD AND 1995–96 COUGAR

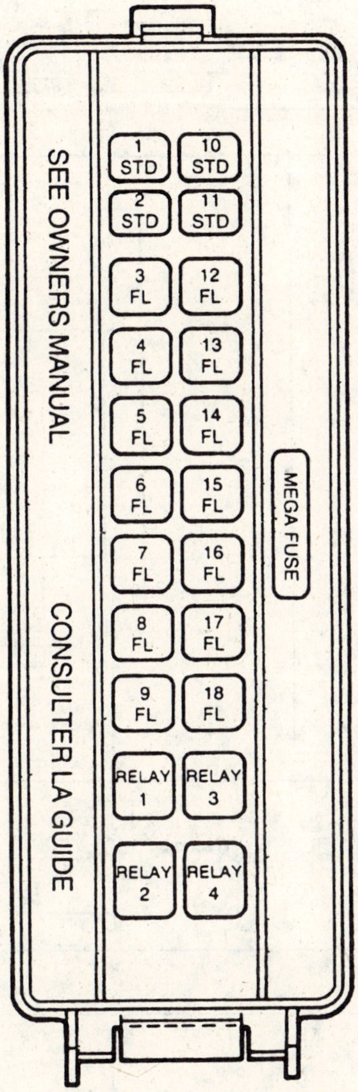

88186C68

Fuse/Relay Location	High Current Fuse Amp Rating	Description
1 STD	15A	• DRL module fog lamps
2 STD	5A	• Memory
3 FL	20A	• Ignition coil
4 FL	20A	• Autoshock
5 FL	60A	• Engine fan
6 FL	40A	• ABS motor
7 FL	60A	• Headlamps
8 FL	20A	• ABS module
9 FL	60A	• Ignition switch
10 STD	15A	• Horn
11 STD	15A	• Generator
12 FL	40A	• Fuse panel
13 FL	20A	• Fuel pump
14 FL	40A	• Rear defrost
15 FL	20A	• Electronic engine control (EEC) module
16 FL	30A	• Pusher fan
17 FL	60A	• Blower motor
18 FL	—	Not Used
Relay 1	—	Not Used
Relay 2	—	• Horn
Relay 3	—	Not Used
Relay 4	—	• ABS
Mega Fuse	175A	• Power distribution box

88186C69

WIRING DIAGRAMS

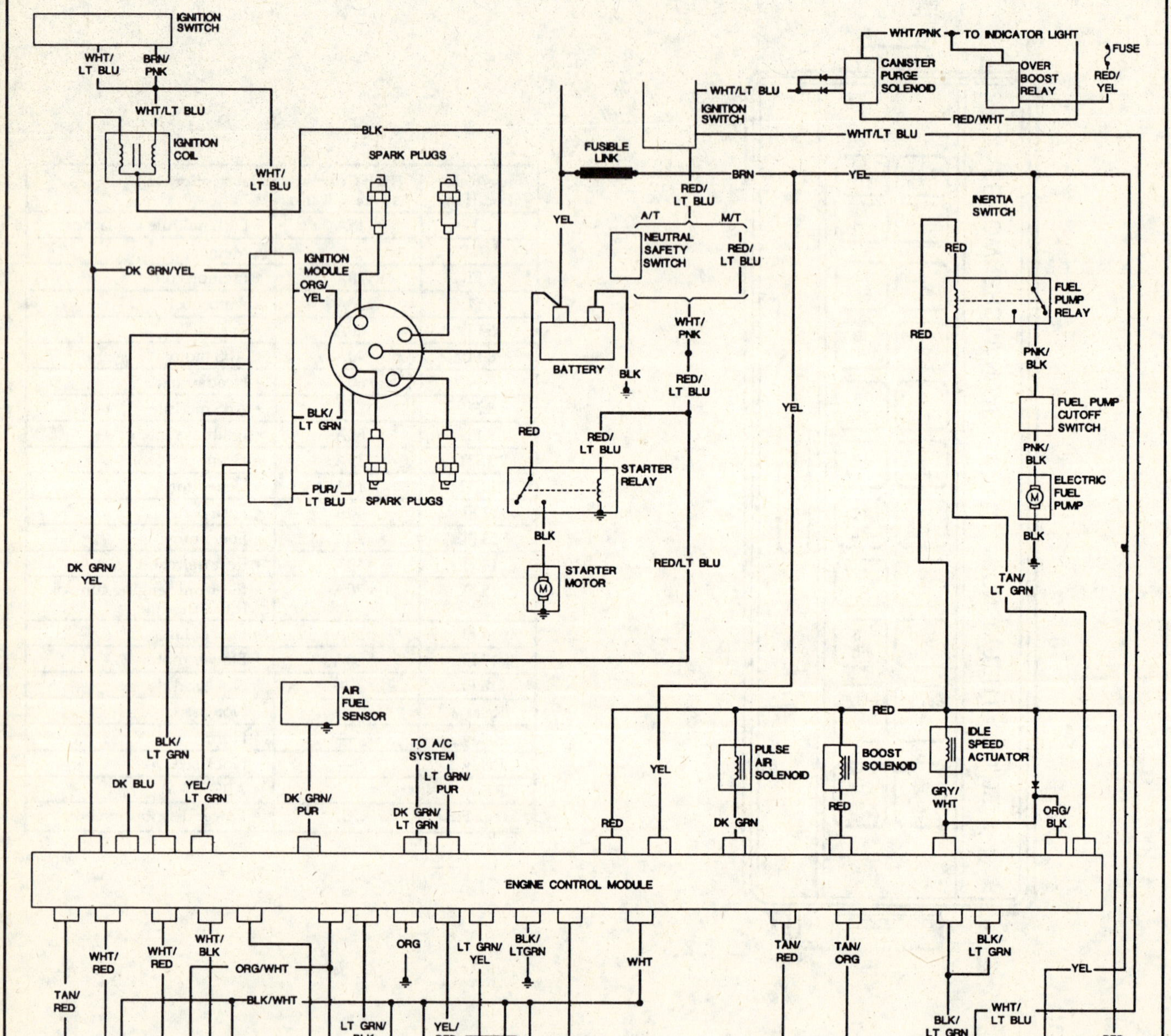

Fig. 148 Engine wiring — 1983 2.3L Turbo

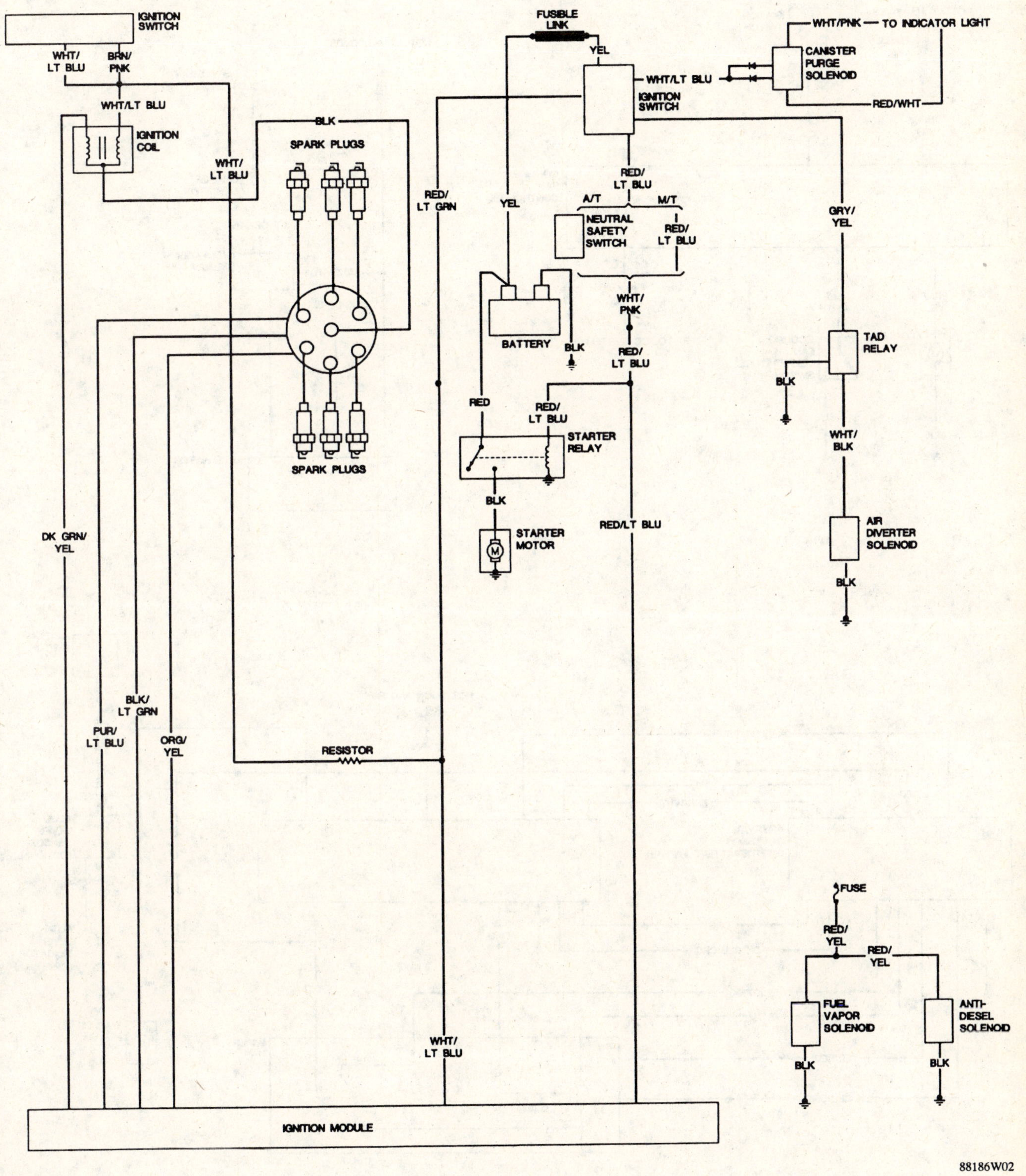

Fig. 149 Engine wiring — 1983 3.8L

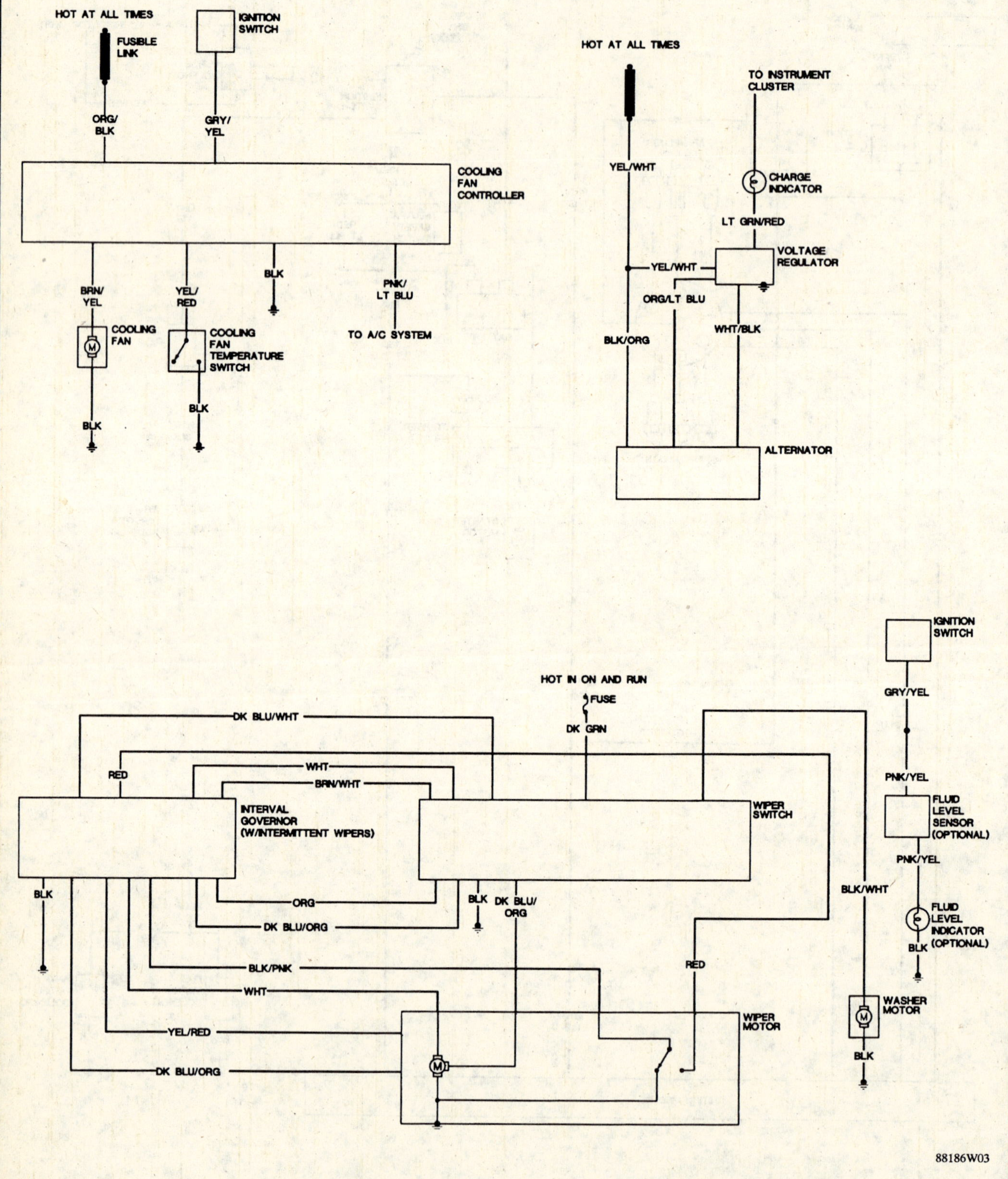

Fig. 150 Chassis wiring — 1983

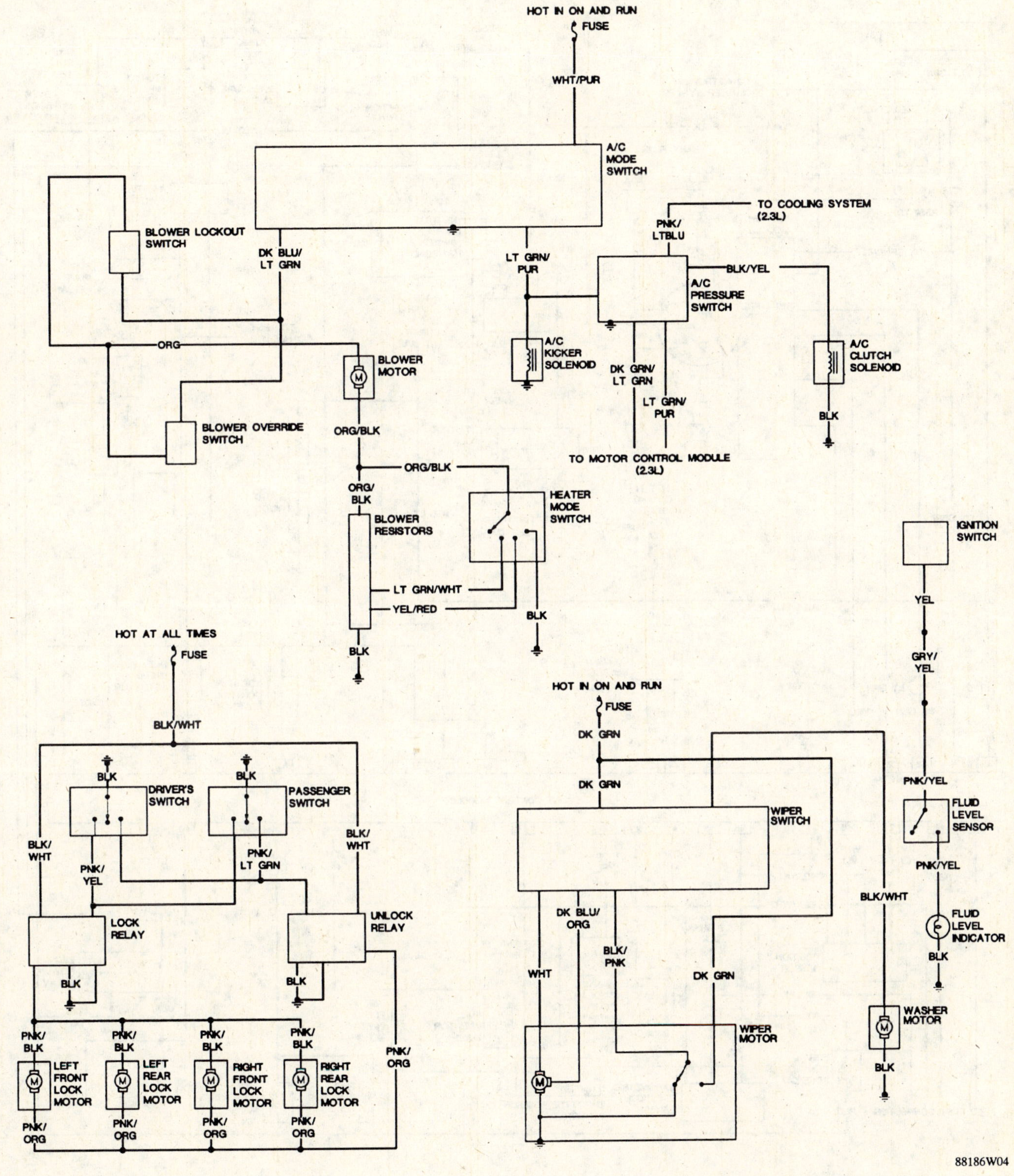

Fig. 151 Chassis wiring — 1983 continued

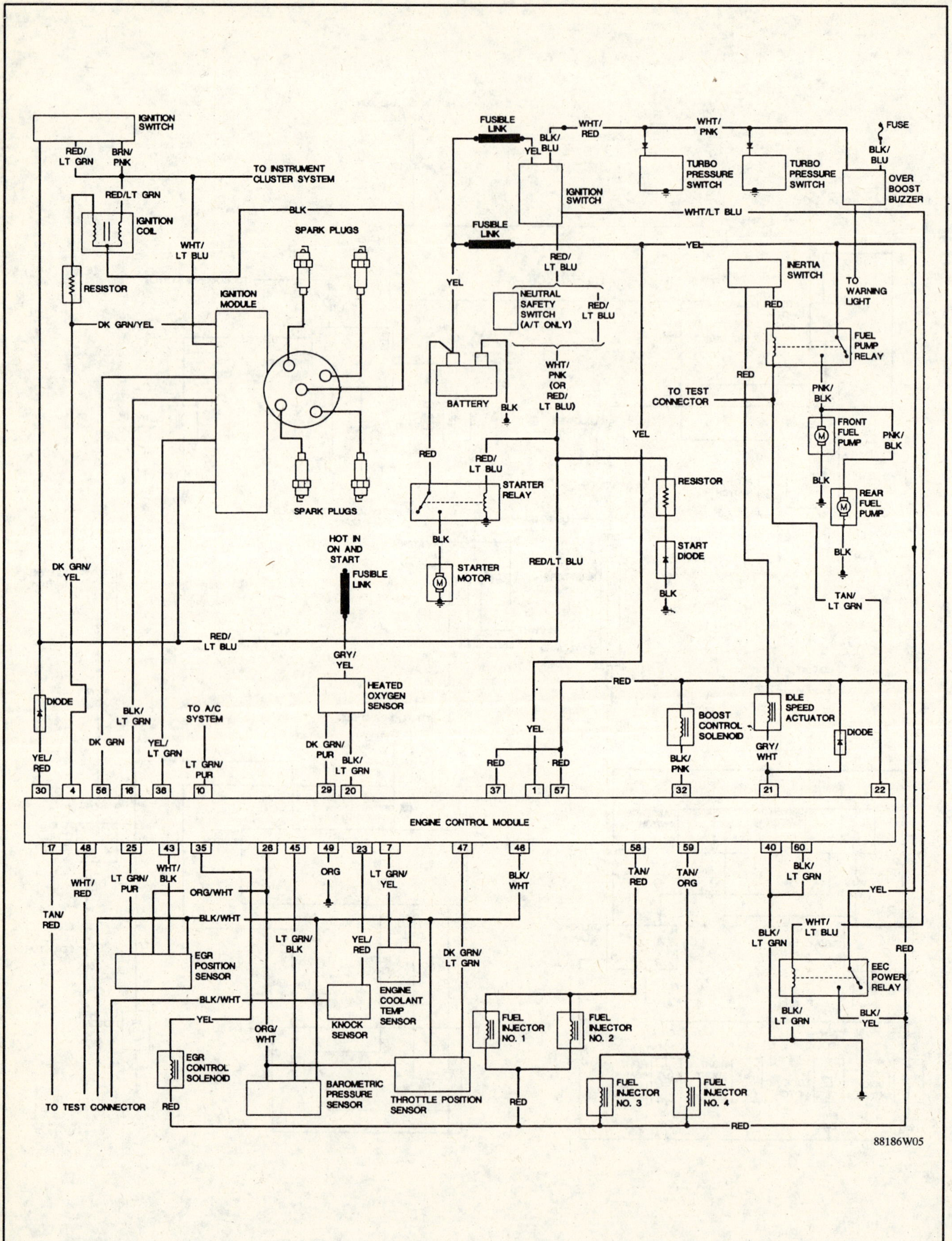

Fig. 152 Engine wiring — 1984 2.3L turbo

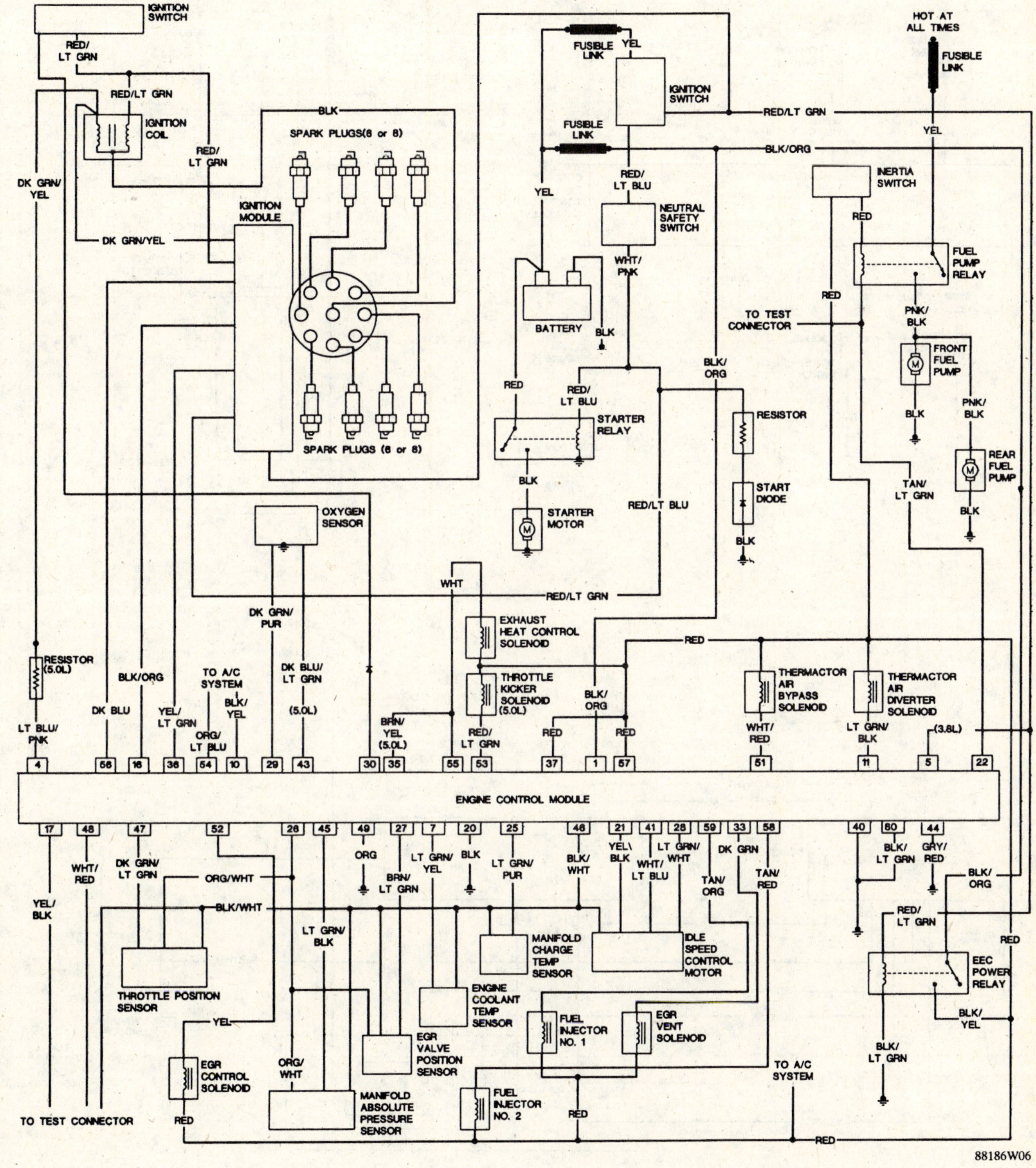

Fig. 153 Engine wiring — 1984 3.8L and 5.0L

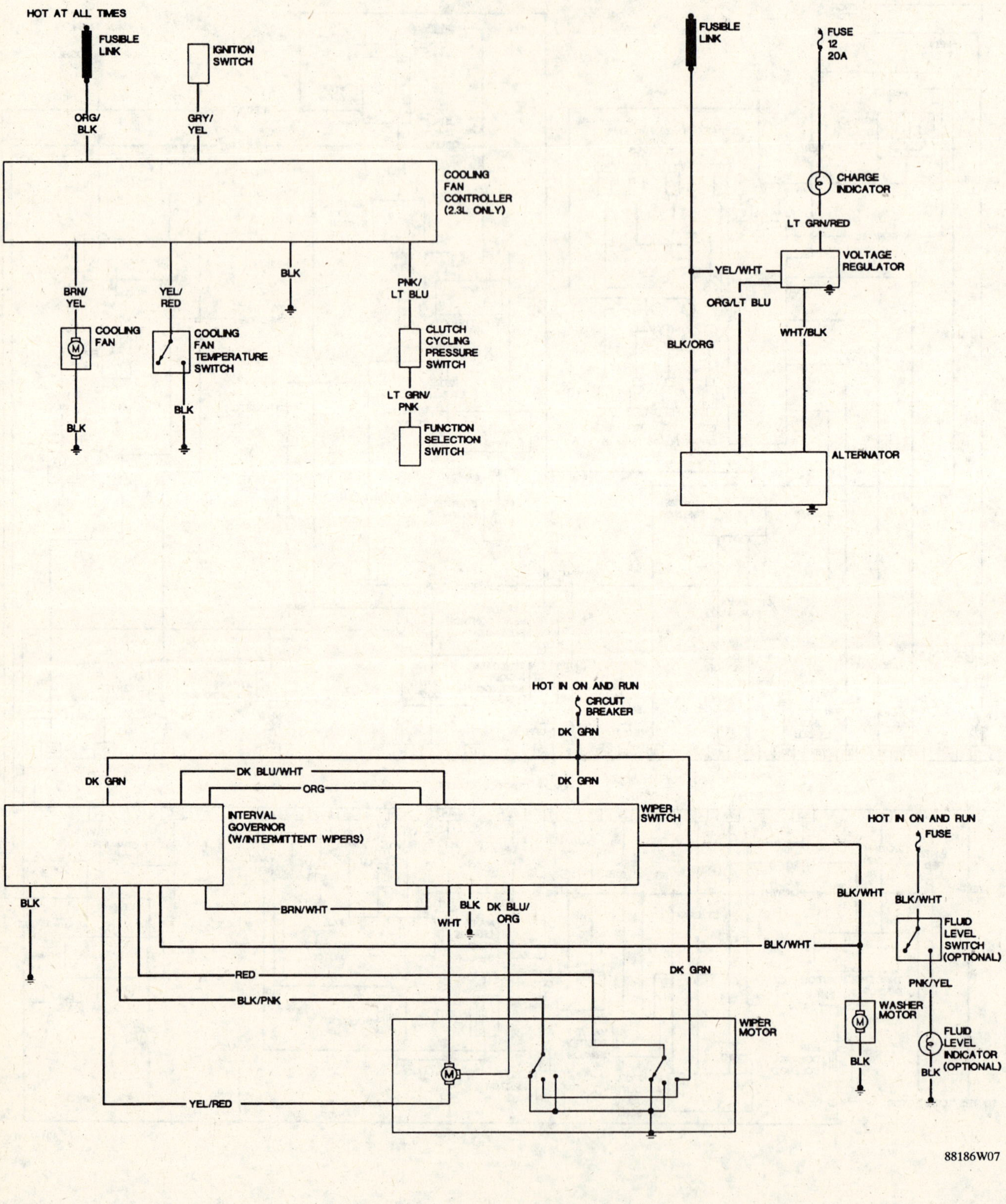

Fig. 154 Chassis wiring — 1984

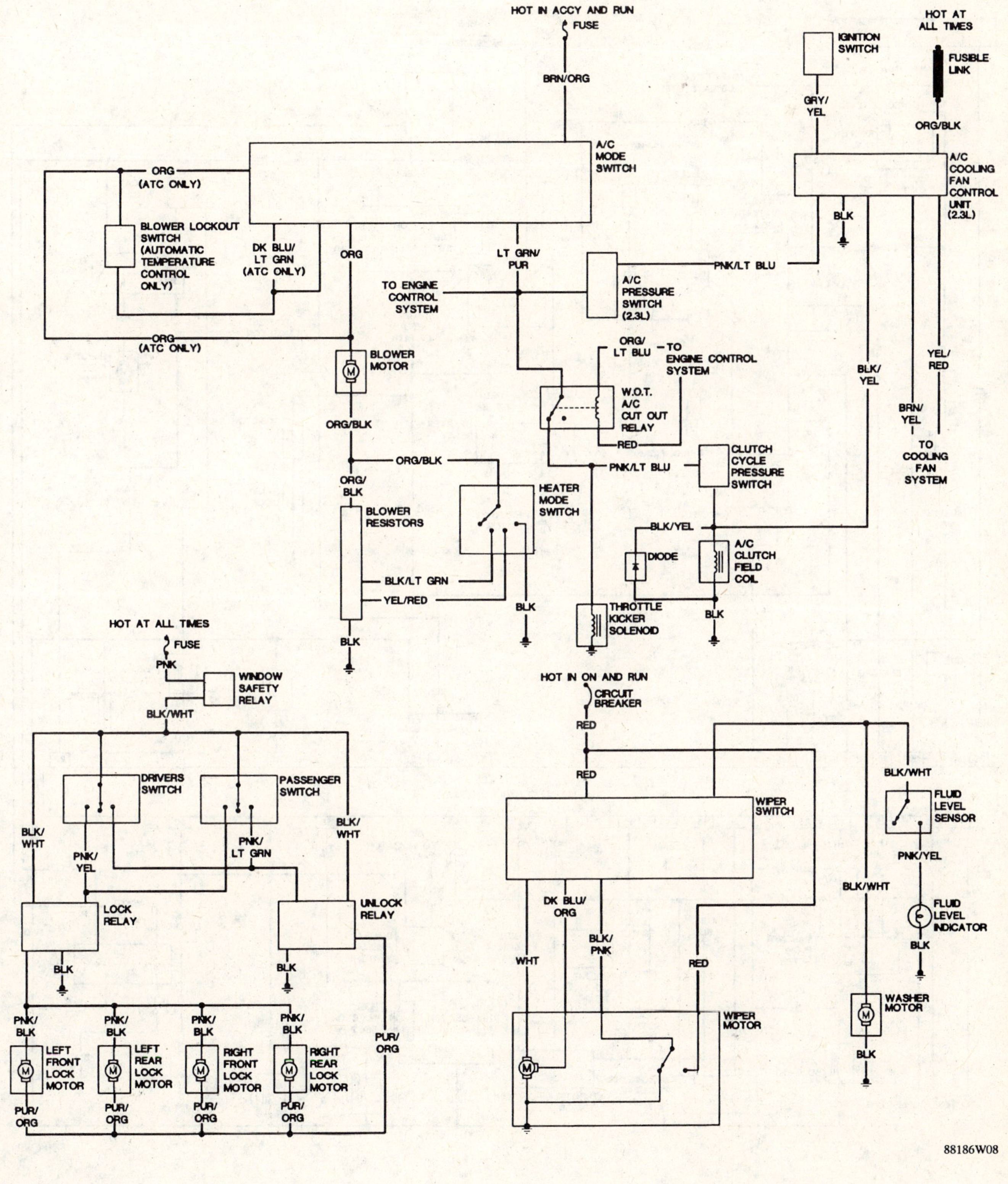

Fig. 155 Chassis wiring — 1984 continued

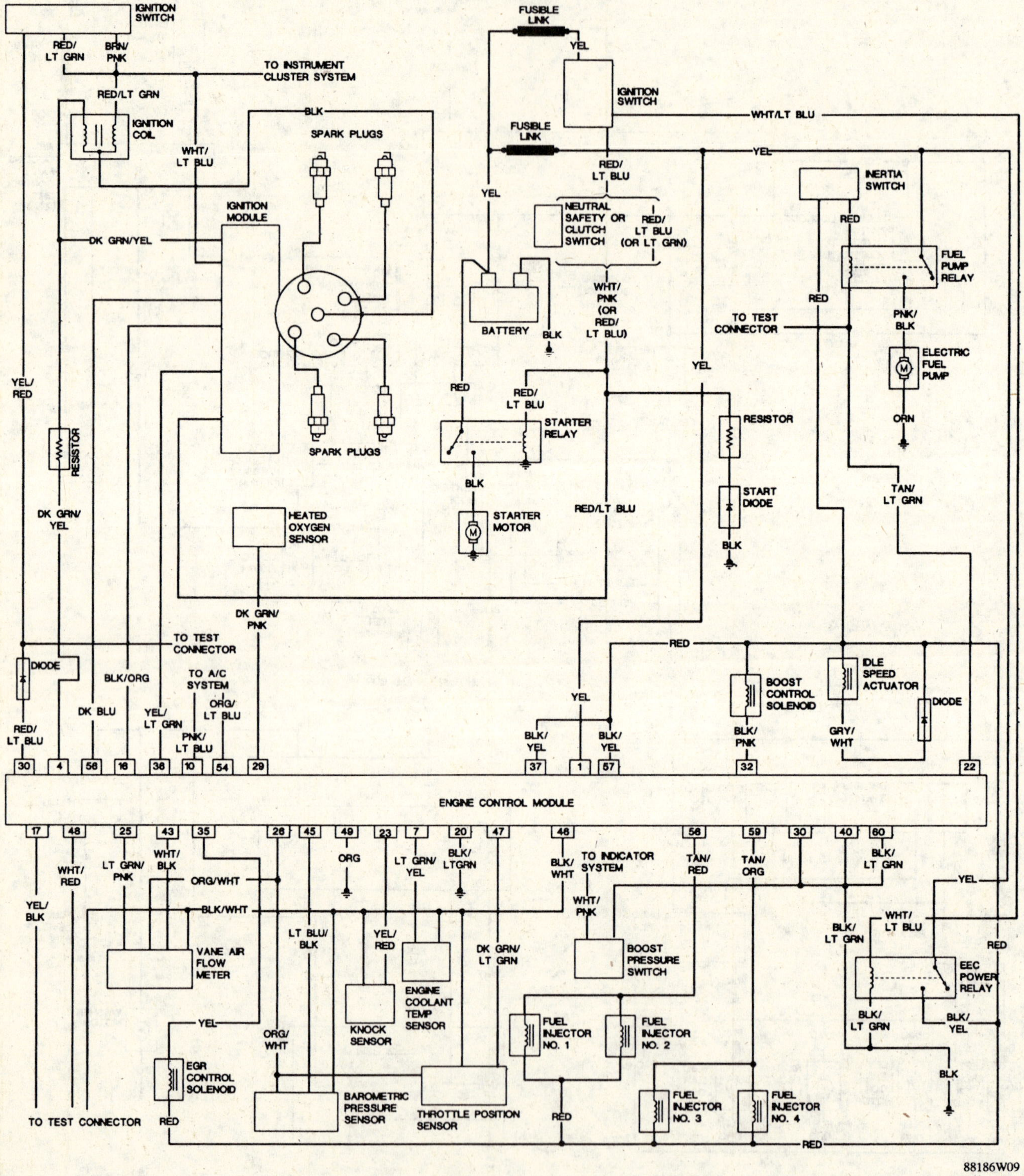

Fig. 156 Engine wiring — 1985 2.3L Turbo

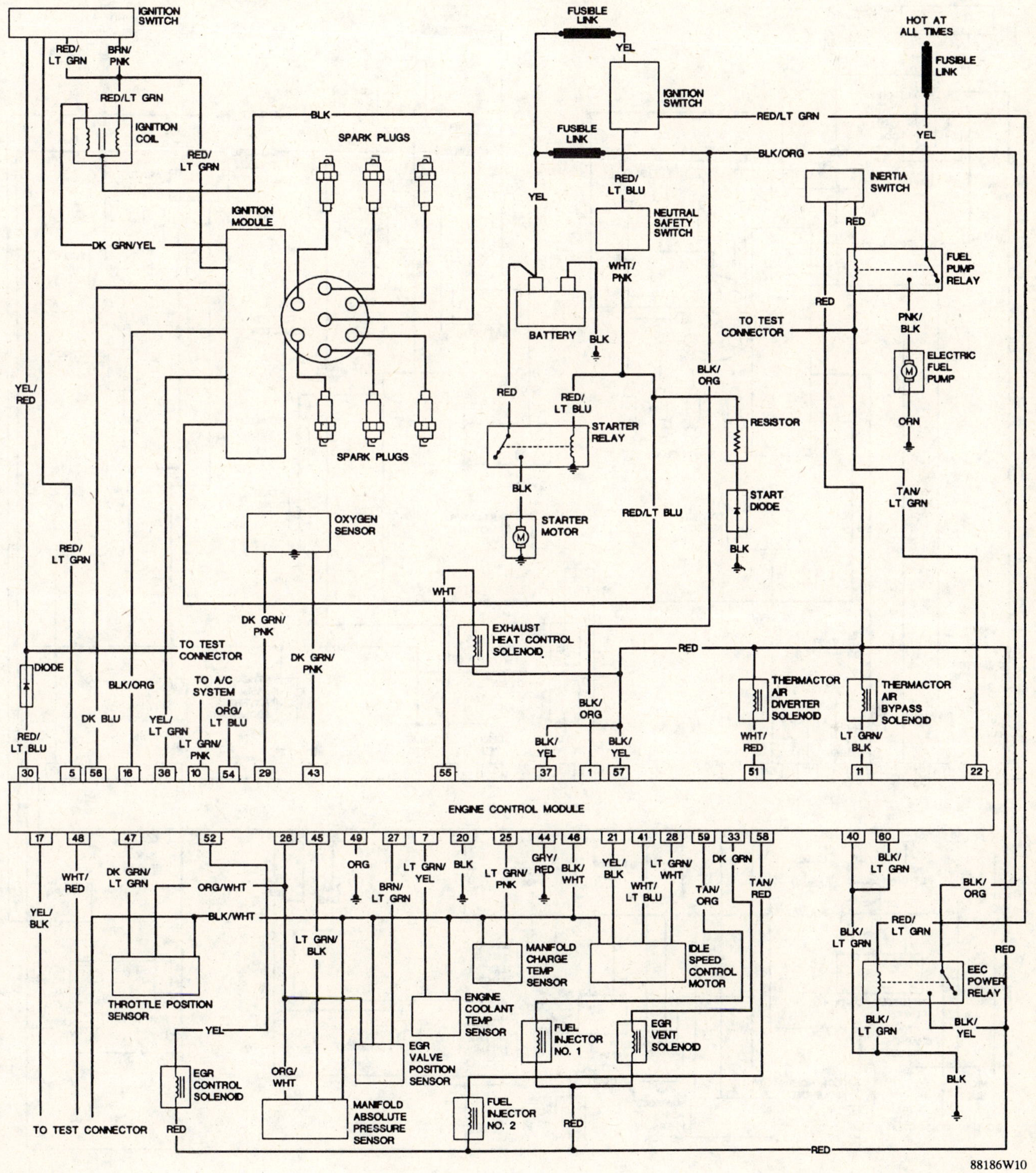

Fig. 157 Engine wiring — 1985 3.8L

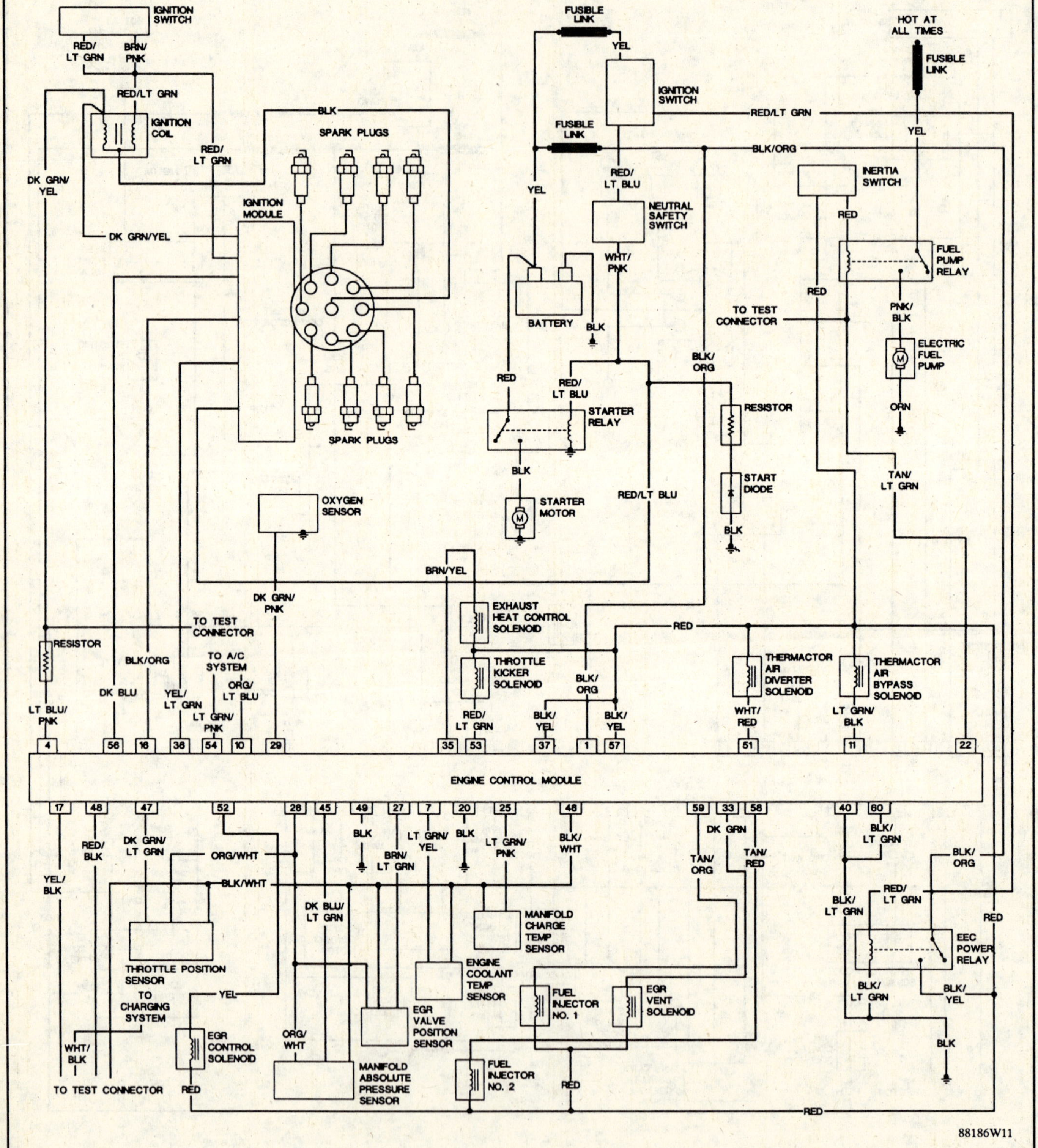

88186W11

Fig. 158 Engine wiring — 1985 5.0L

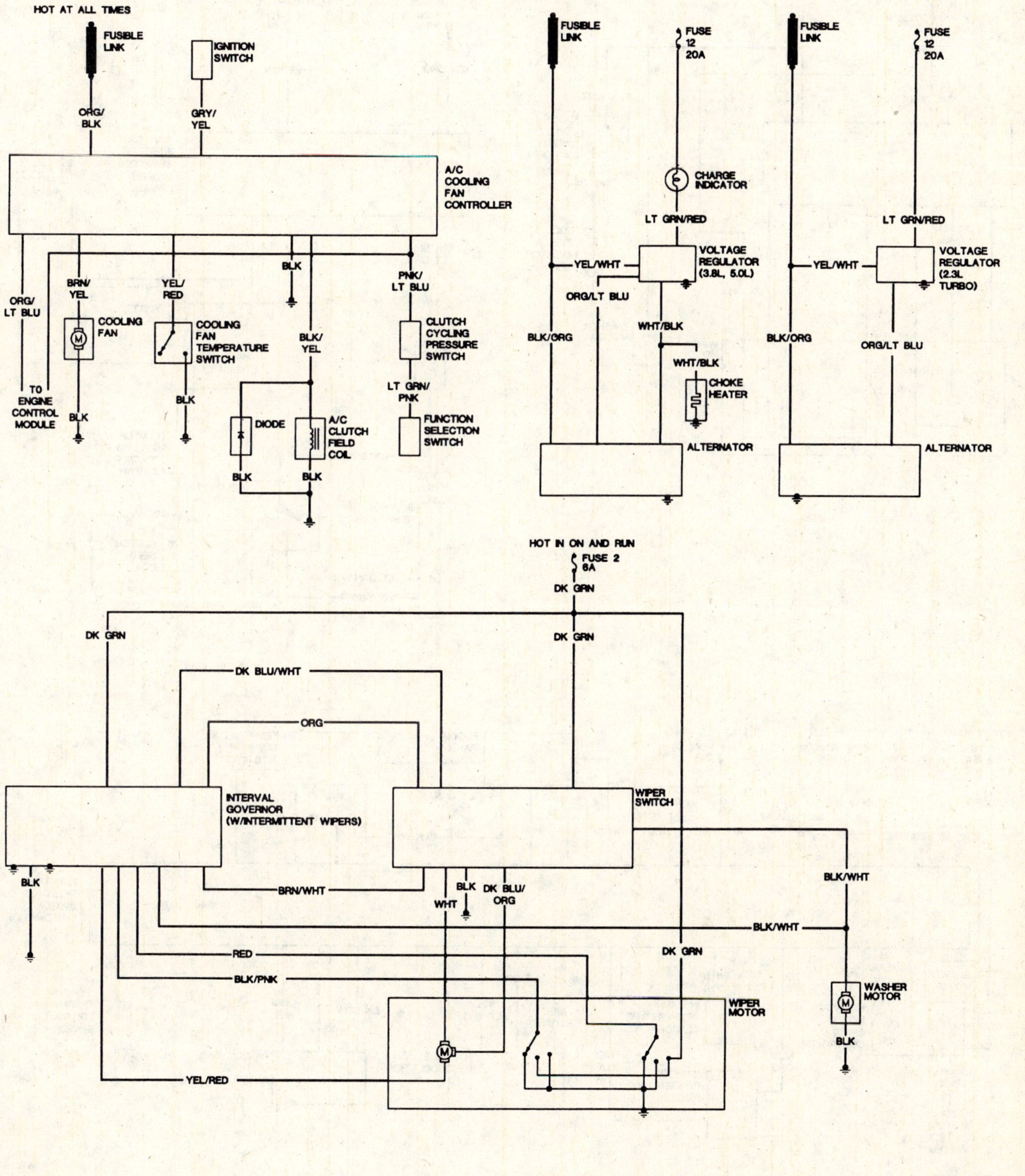

Fig. 159 Chassis wiring — 1985

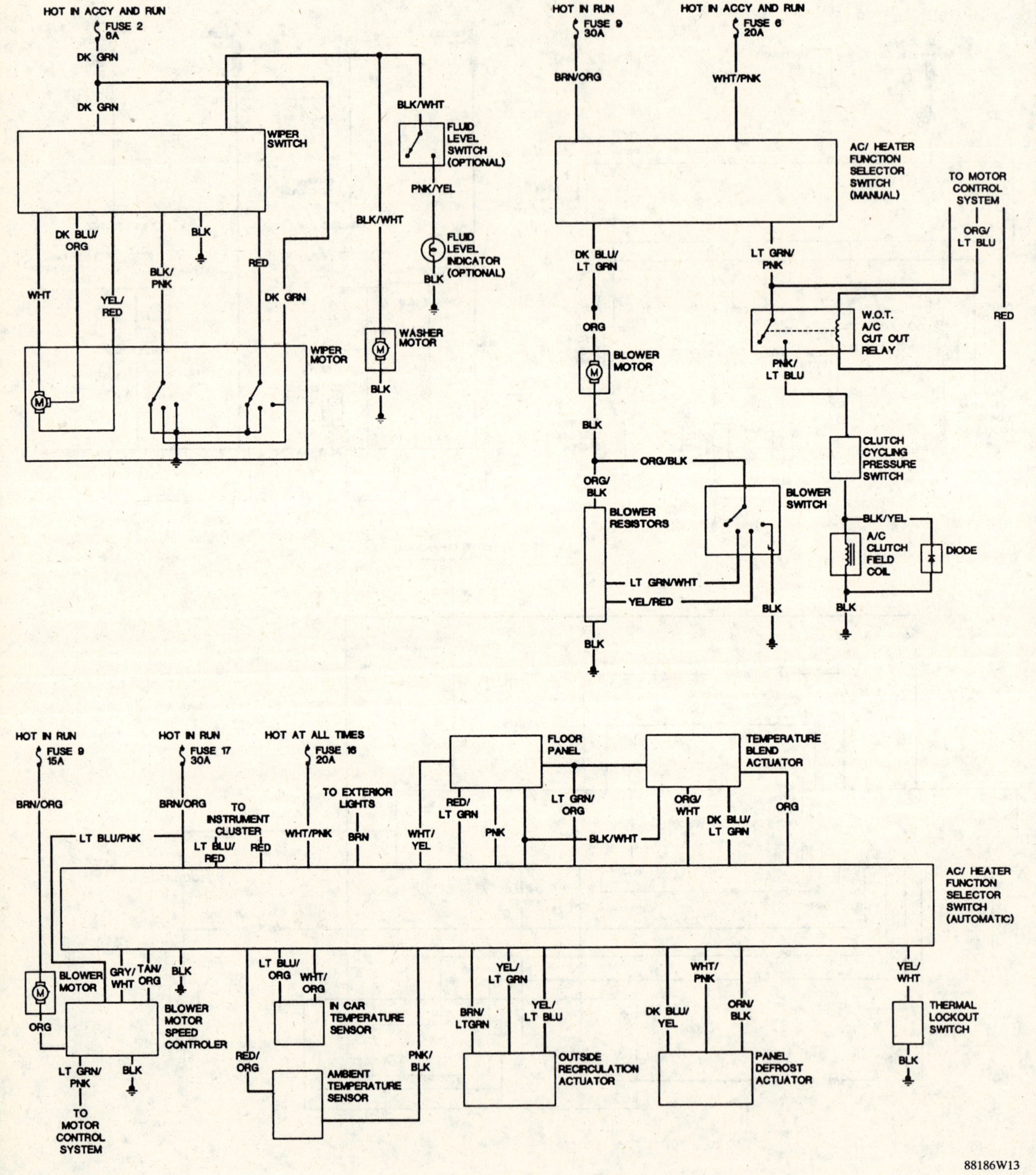

Fig. 160 Chassis wiring — 1985 continued

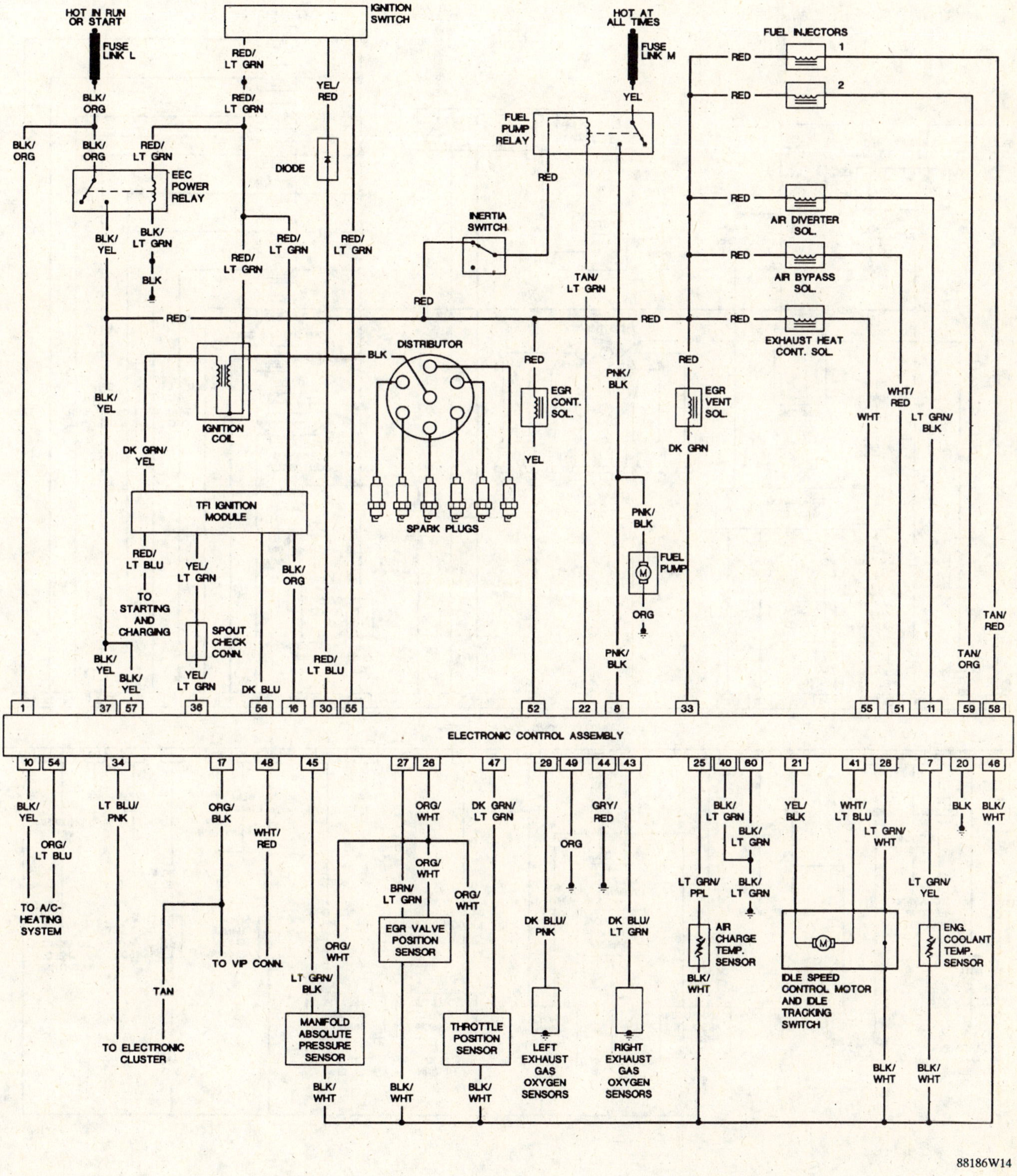

Fig. 161 Engine wiring — 1986–87 3.8L

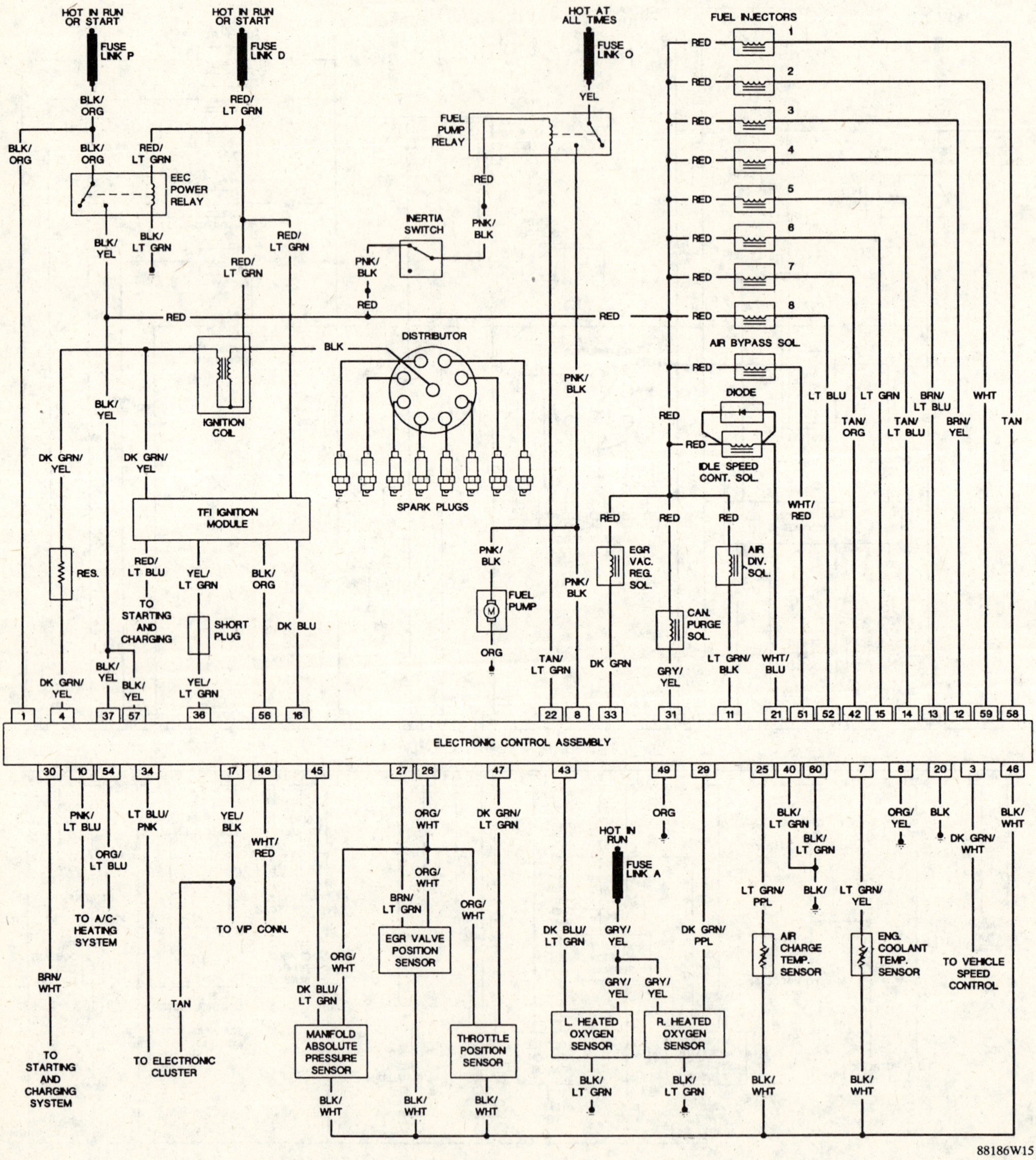

Fig. 162 Engine wiring — 1986–88 5.0L

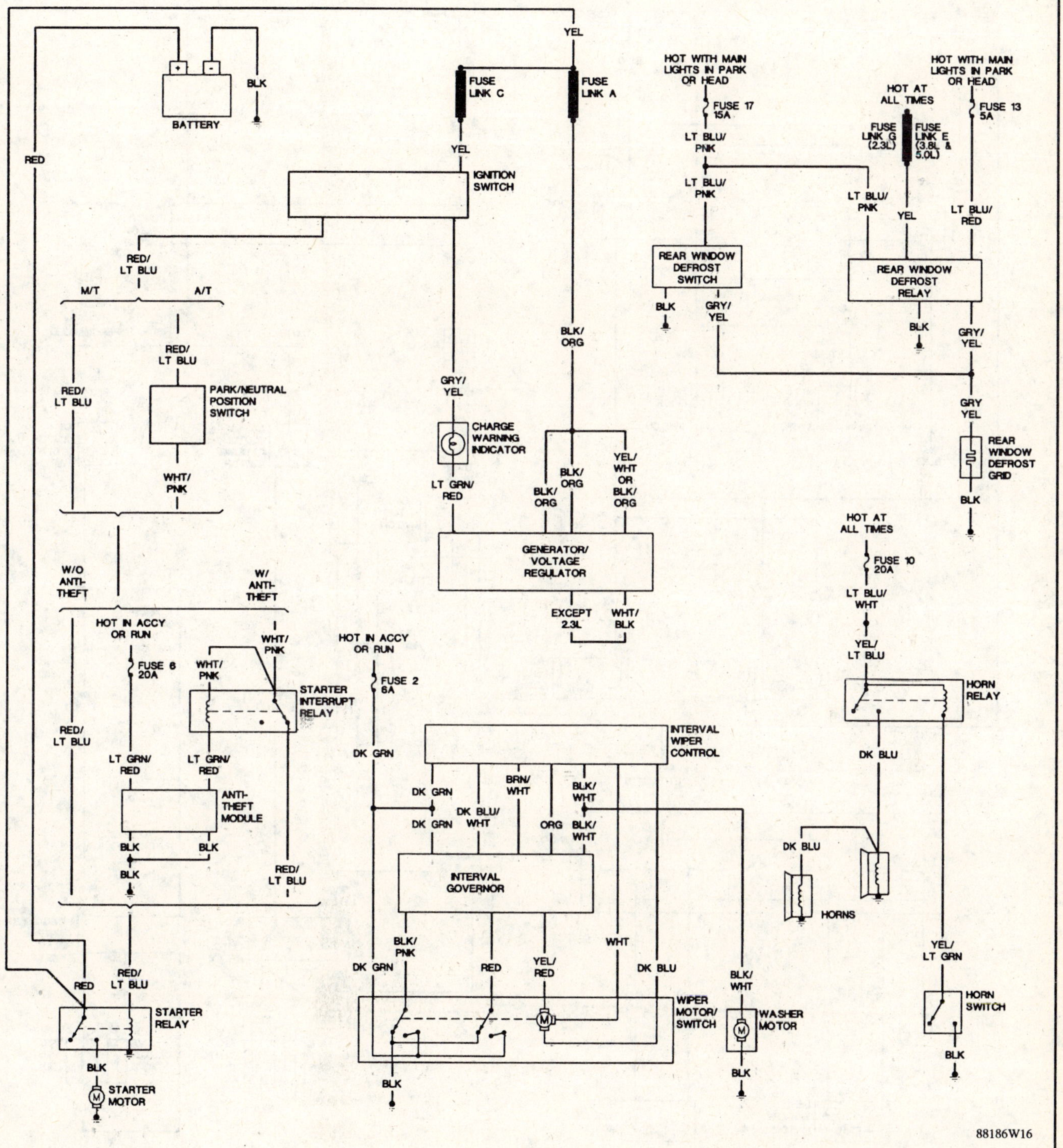

Fig. 163 Chassis wiring — 1986–88

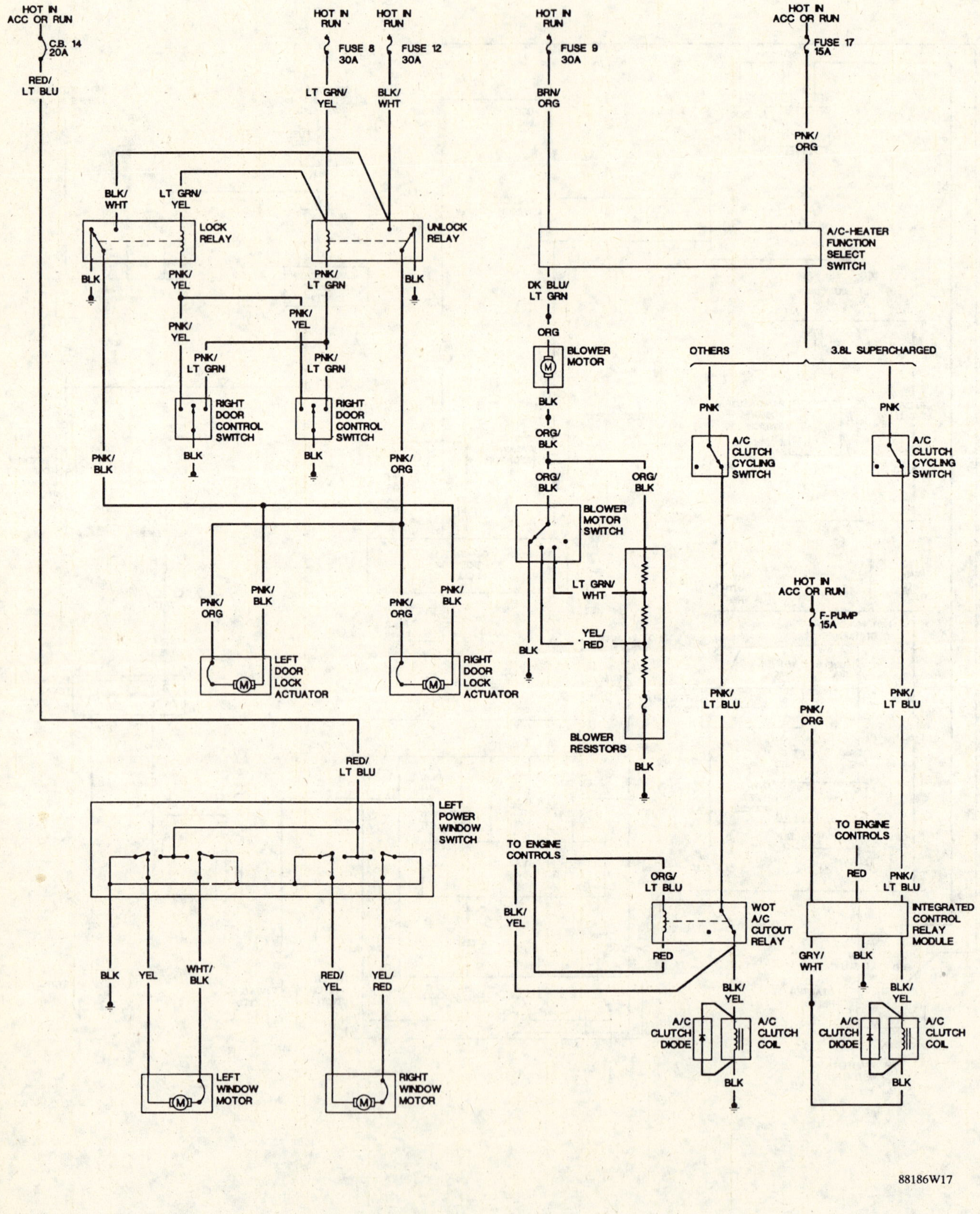

Fig. 164 Chassis wiring — 1986-88 continued

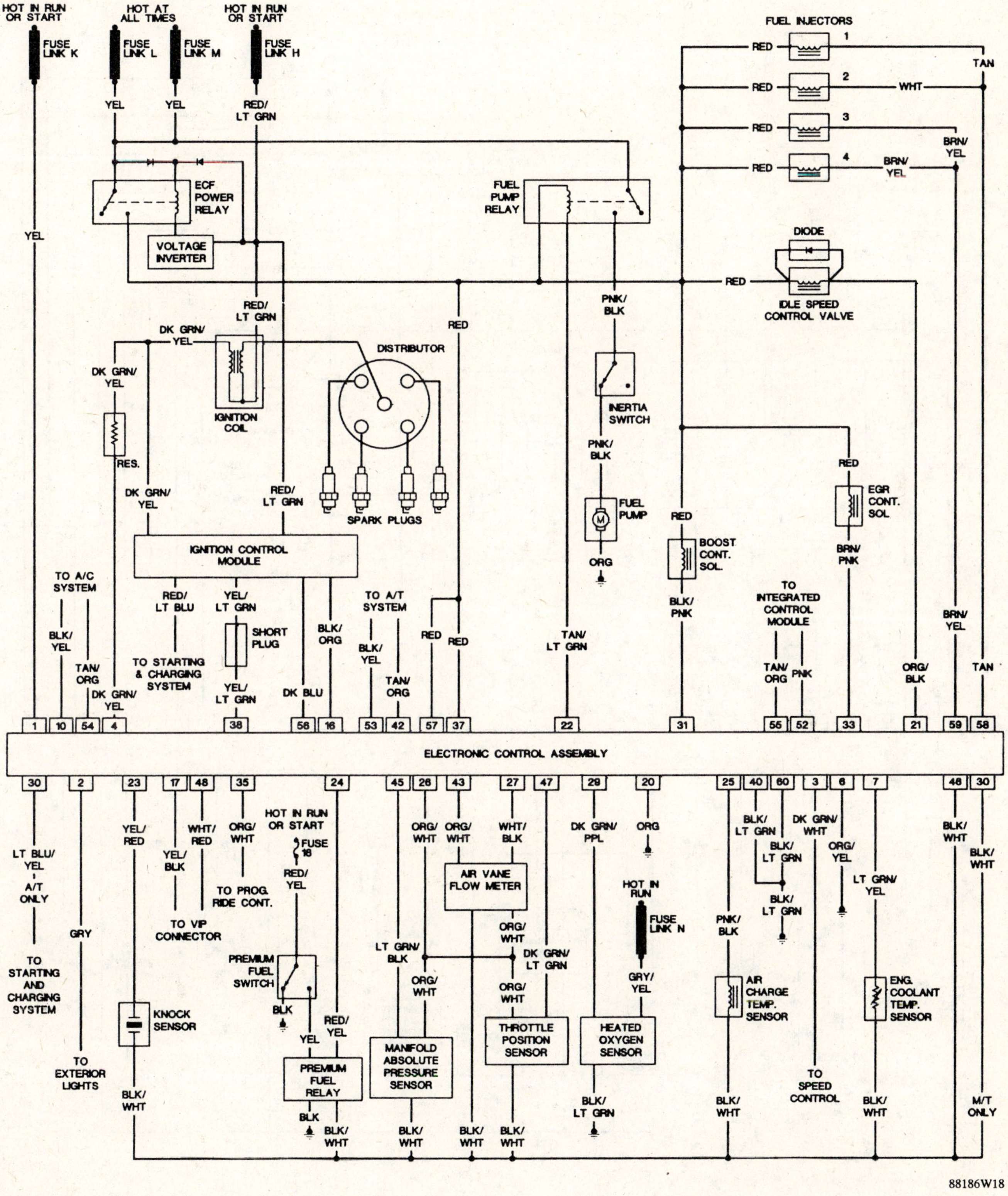

Fig. 165 Engine wiring — 1986–88 2.3L Turbo

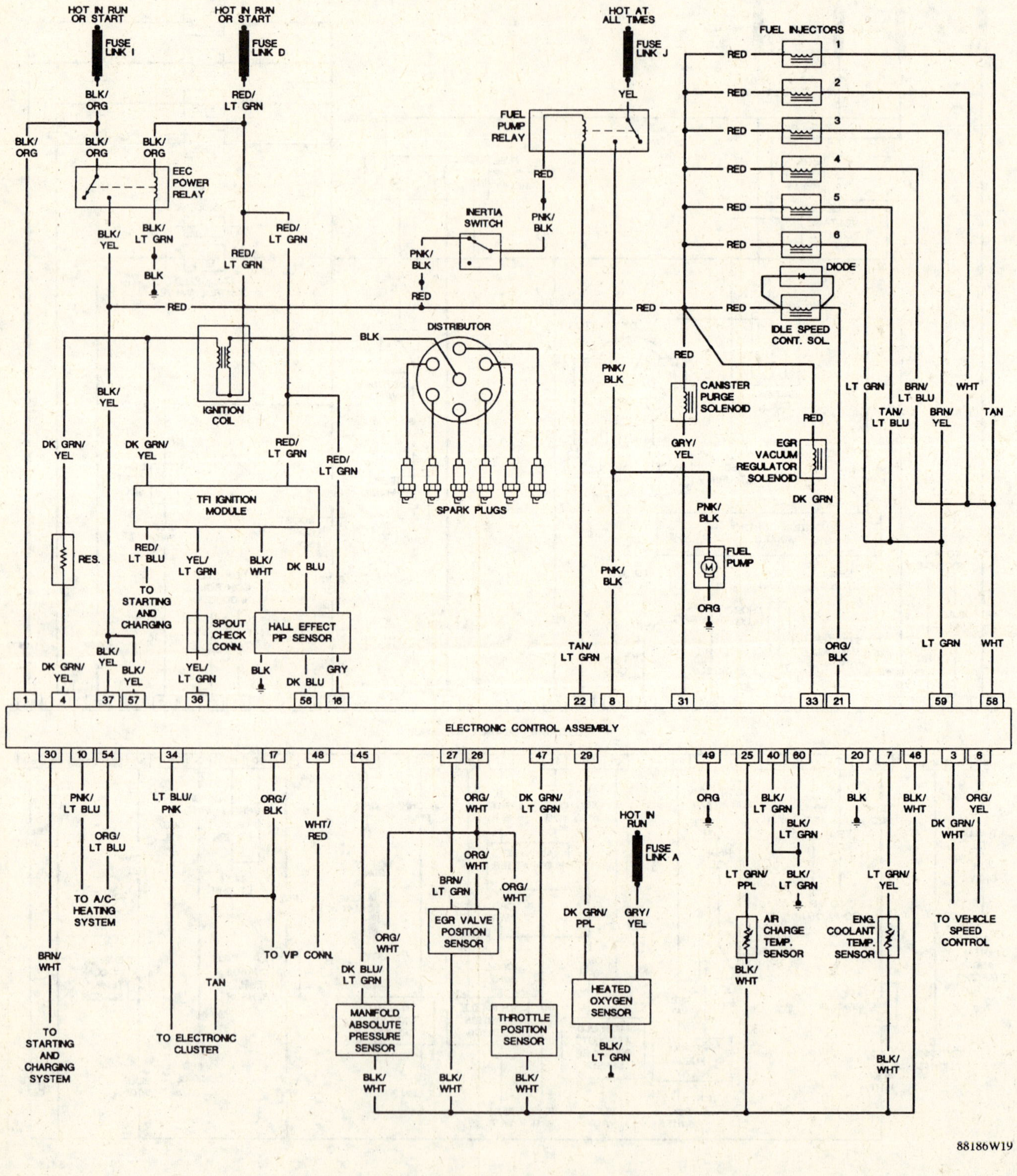

Fig. 166 Engine wiring — 1988 3.8L

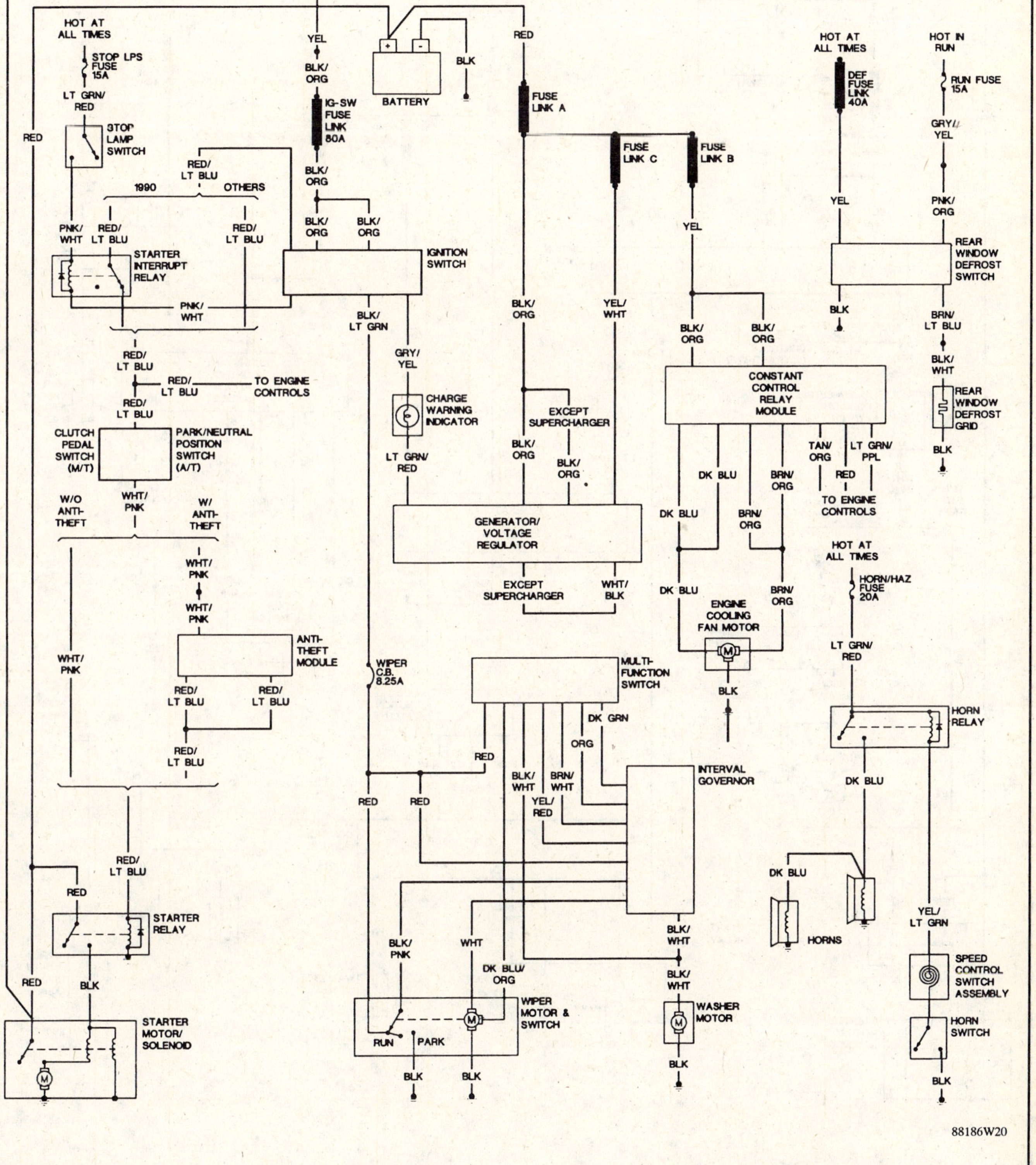

Fig. 167 Chassis wiring — 1989–90

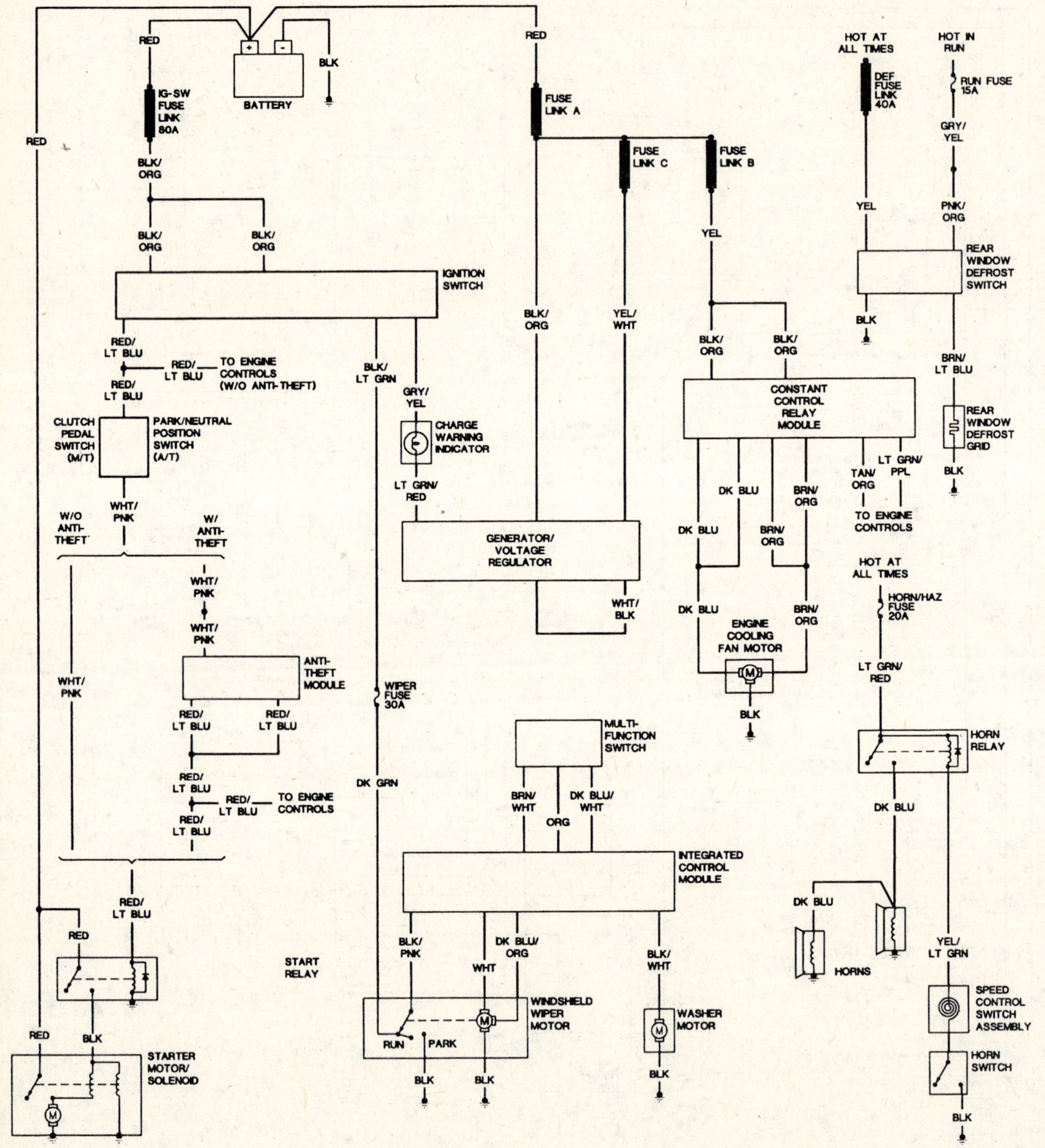

Fig. 168 Chassis wiring — 1991–93

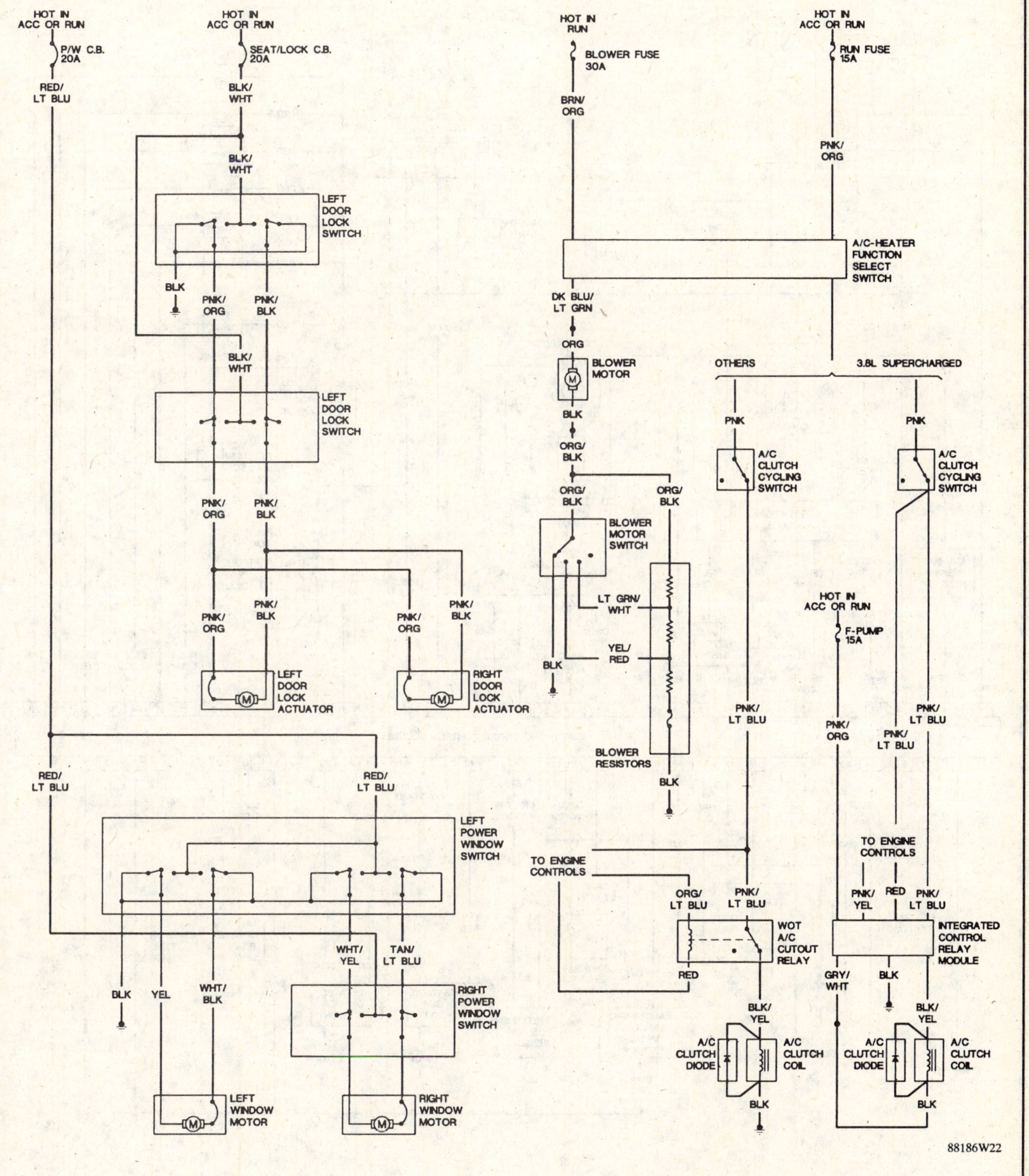

Fig. 169 Chassis wiring — 1989–93 continued

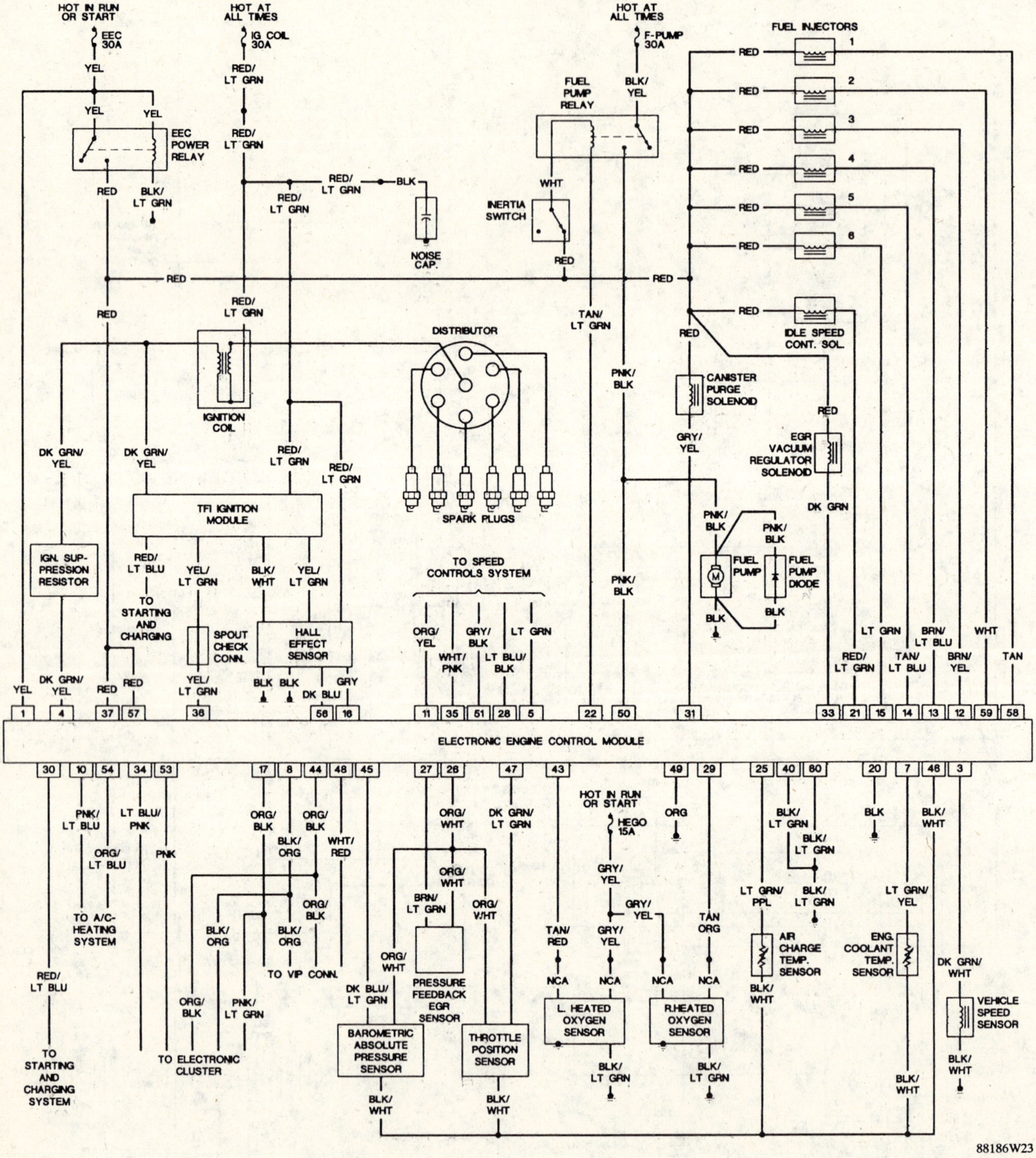

Fig. 170 Engine wiring — 1989-90 3.8L without supercharger

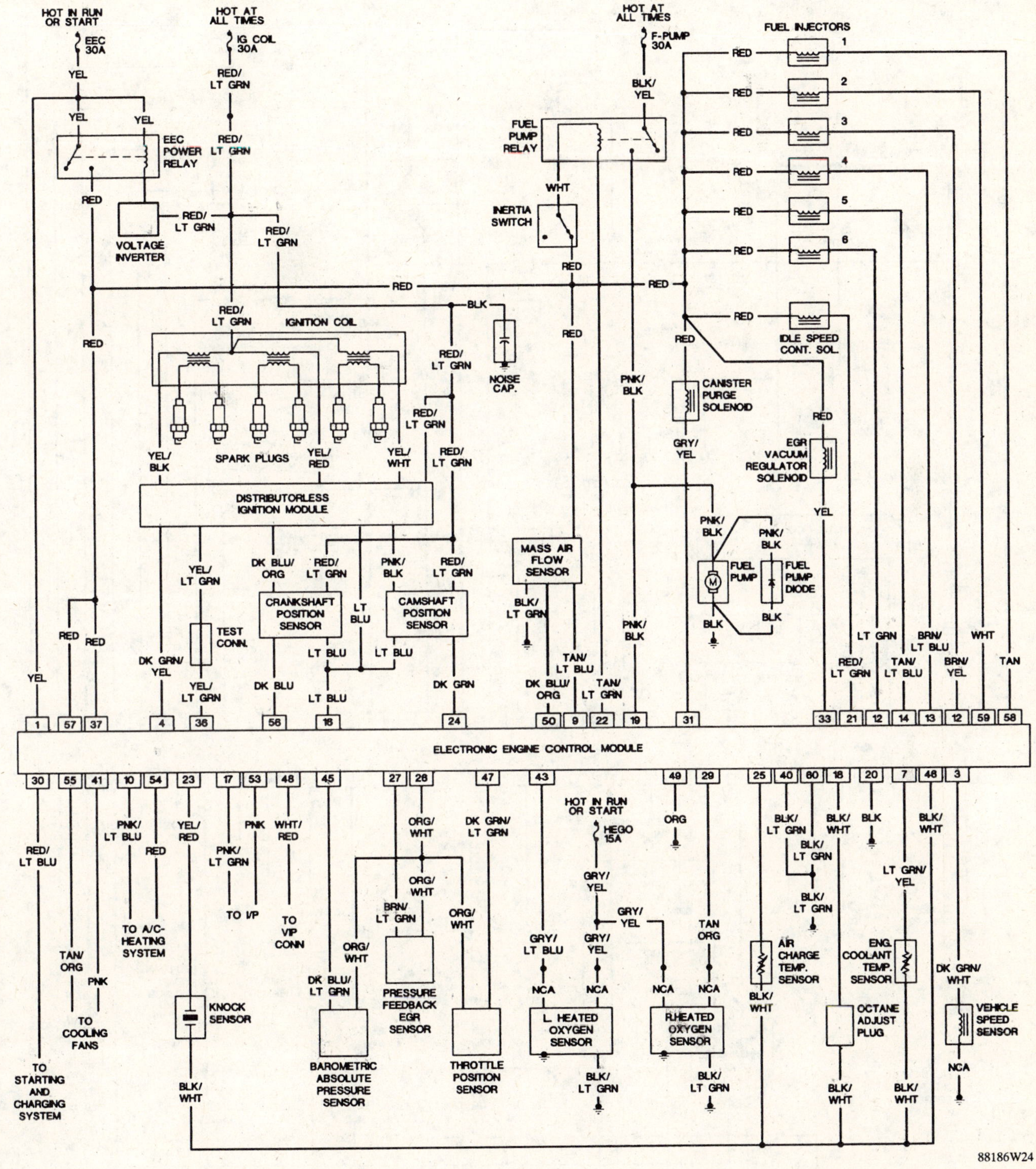

Fig. 171 Engine wiring — 1989-90 3.8L supercharged

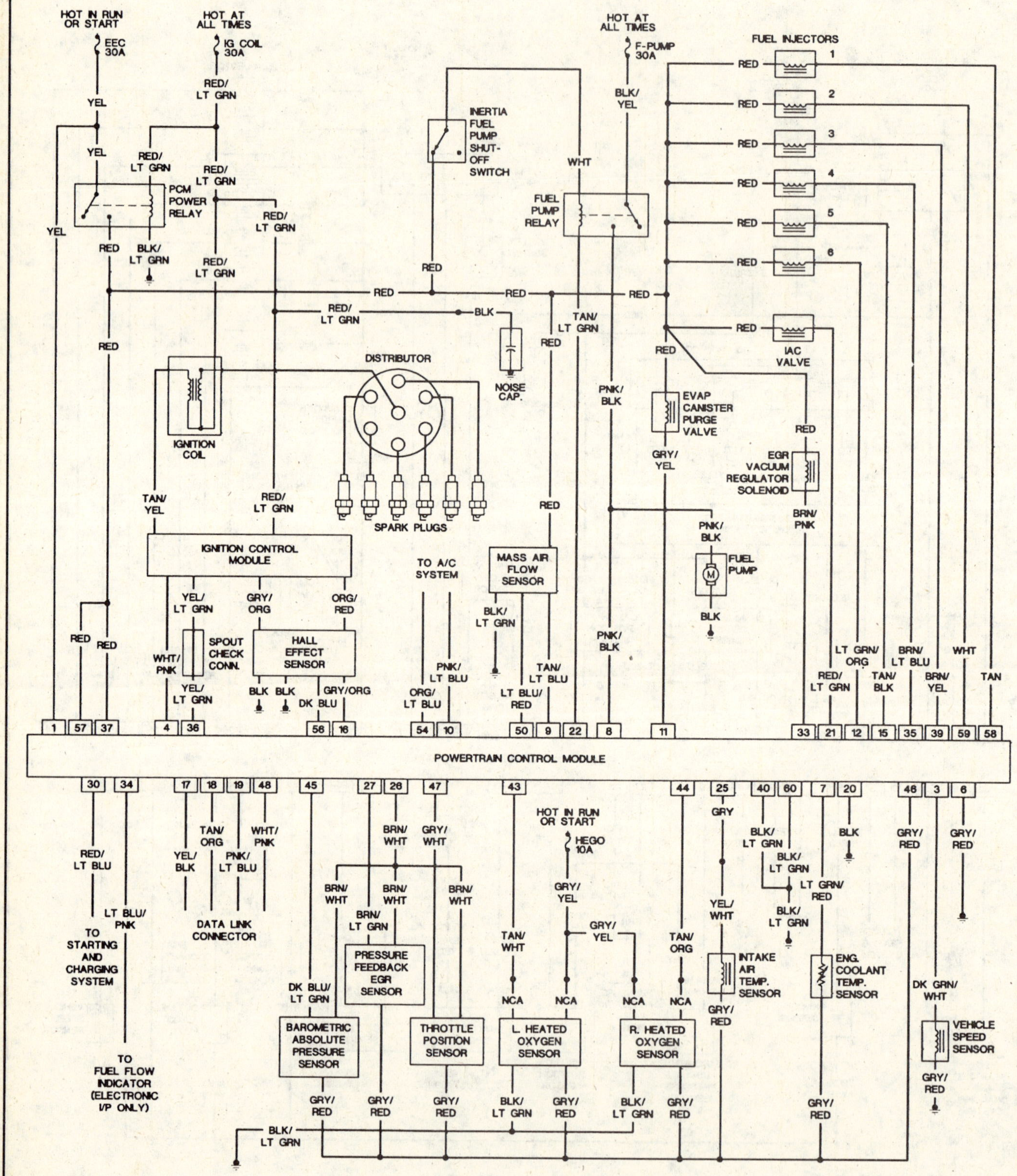

Fig. 172 Engine wiring — 1991-93 3.8L

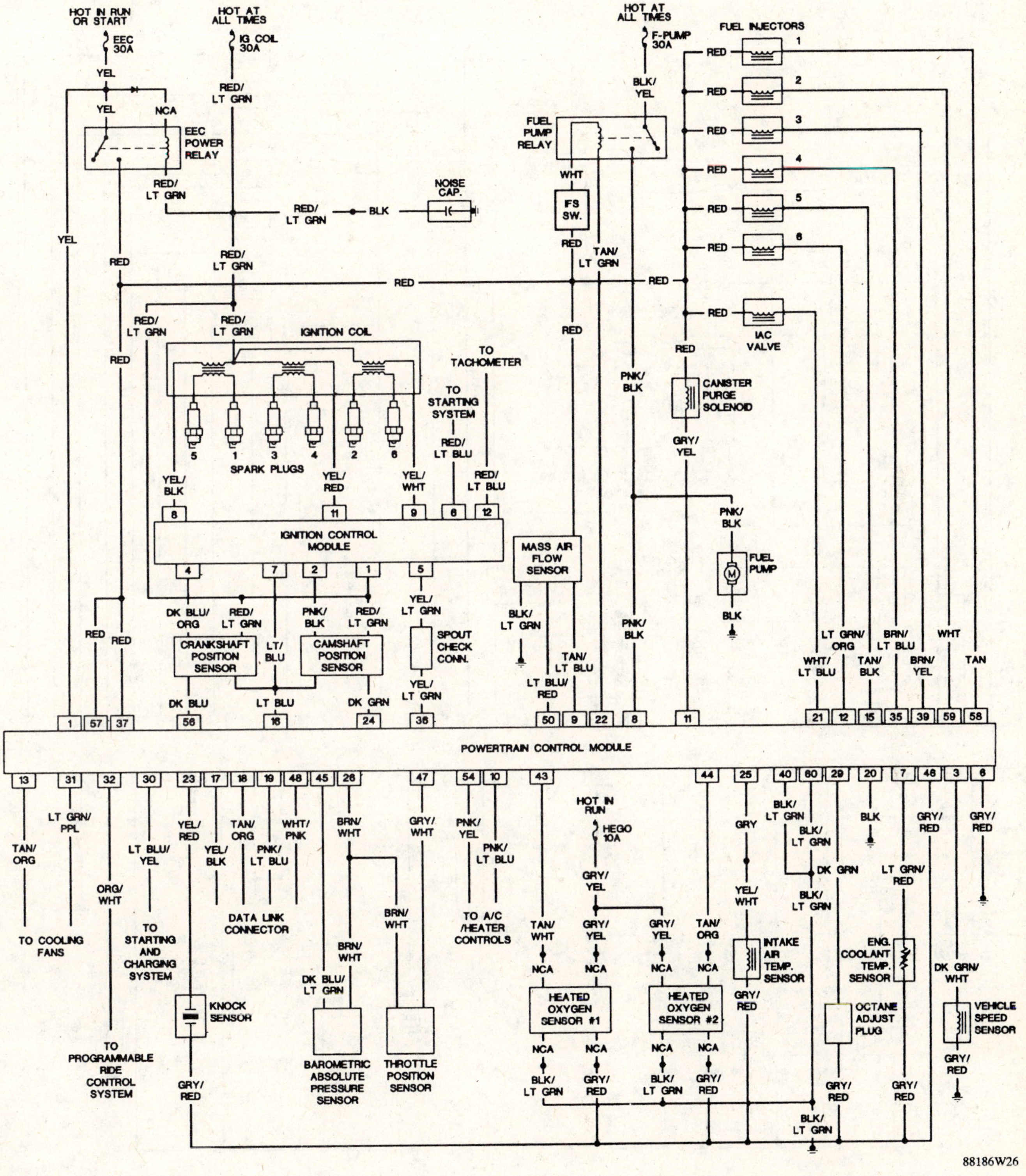

Fig. 173 Engine wiring — 1991-93 3.8L supercharged

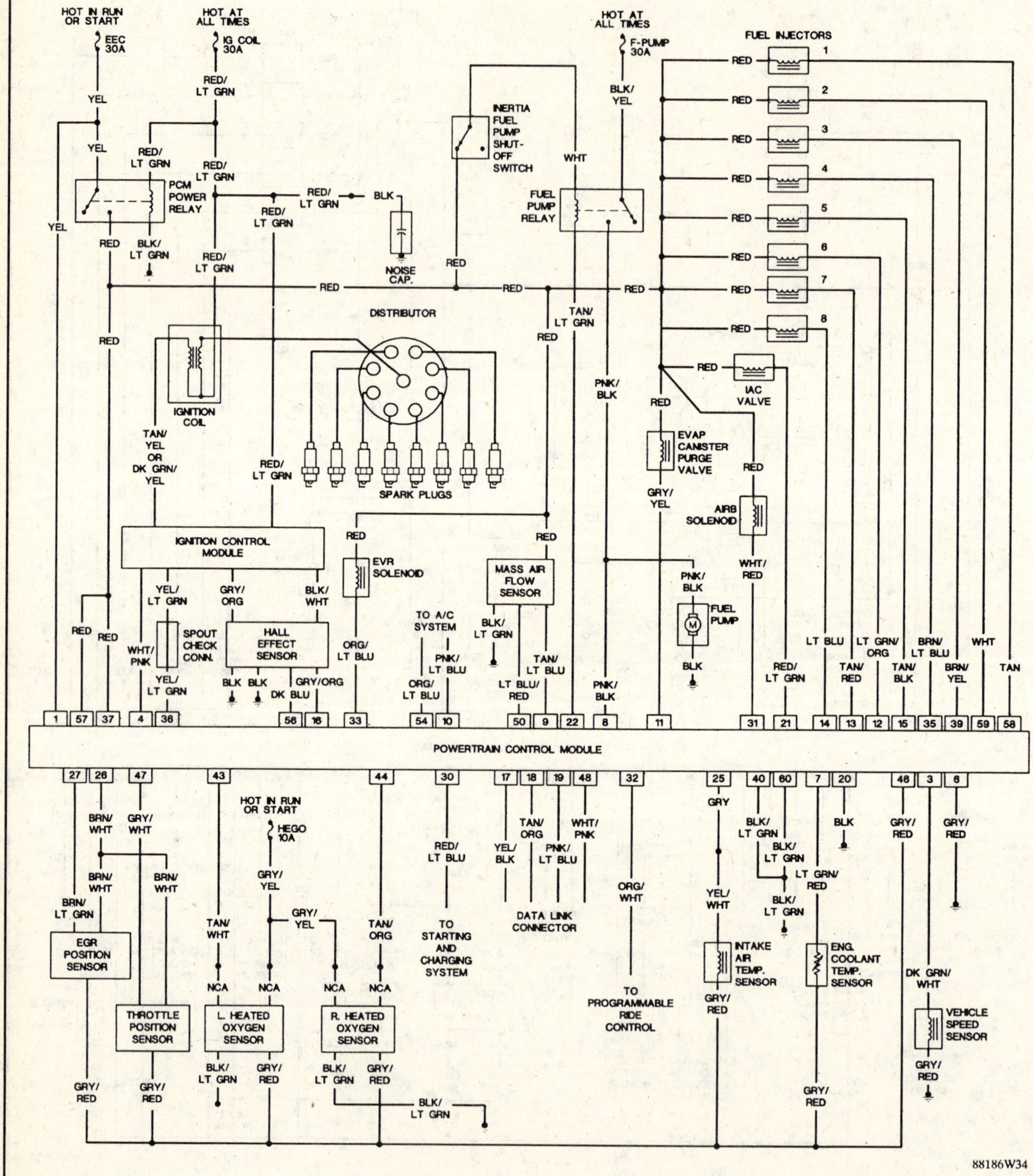

Fig. 174 Engine wiring — 1991–93 5.0L

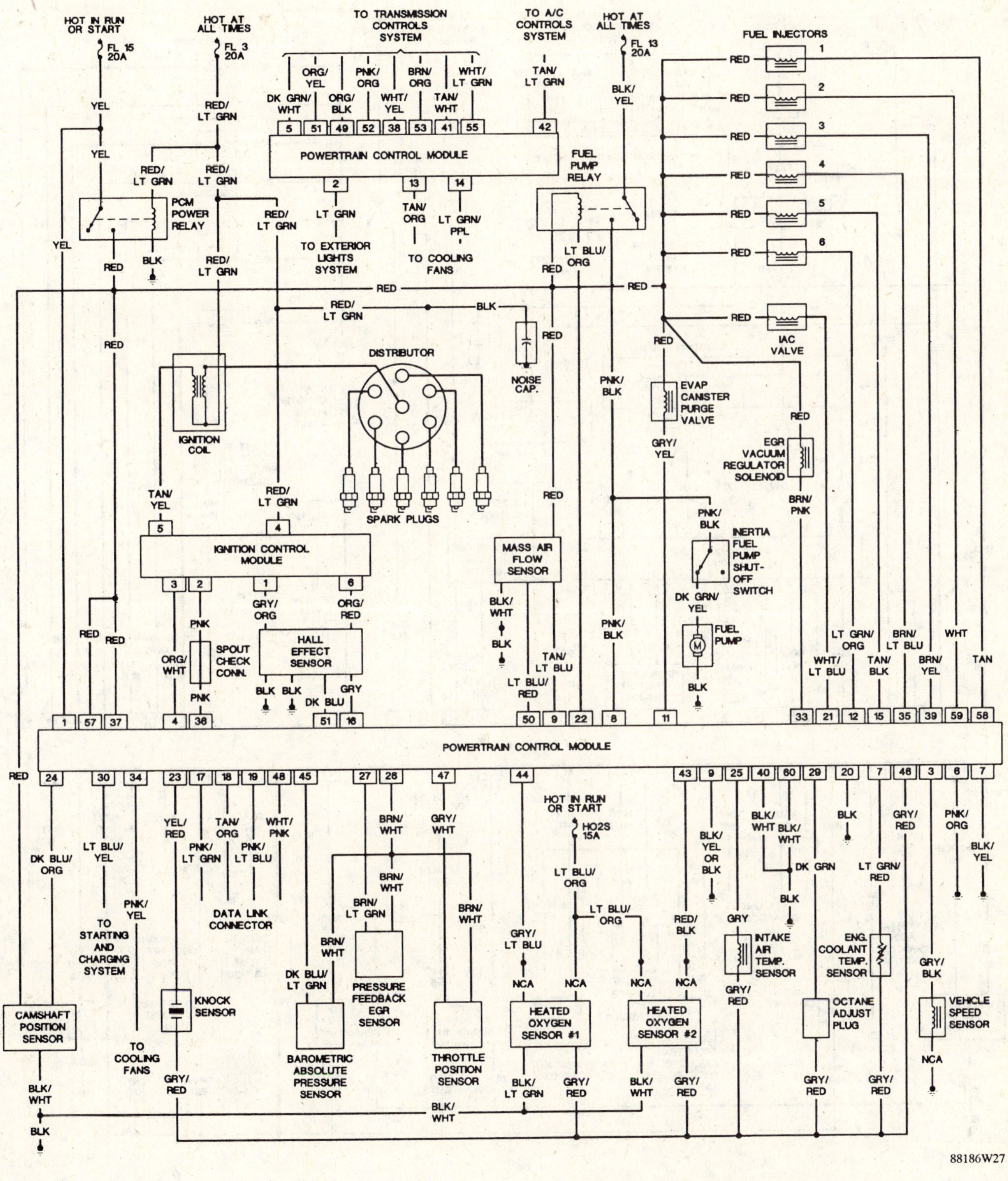

Fig. 175 Engine wiring — 1994–95 3.8L with distributor

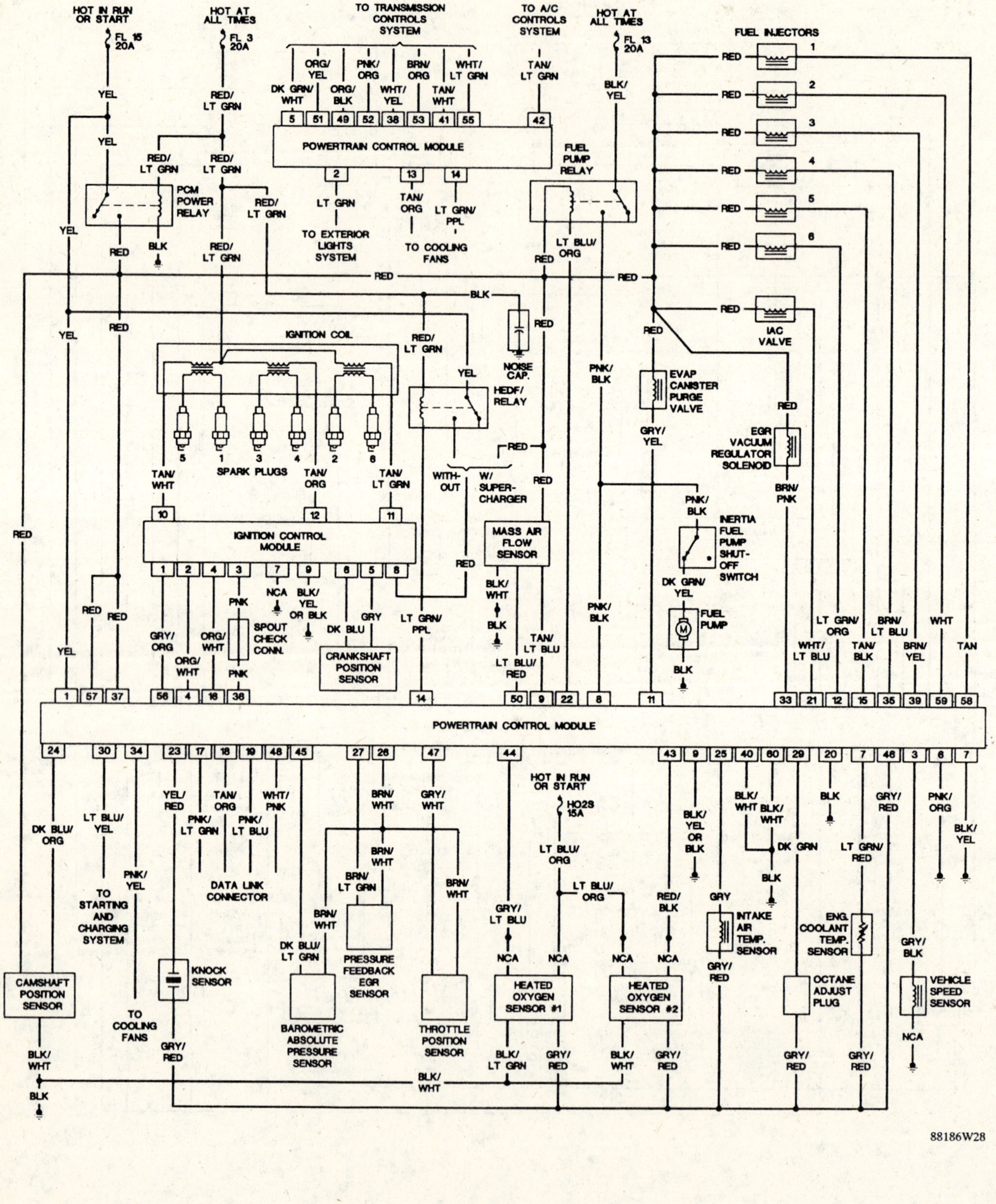

Fig. 176 Engine wiring — 1994–95 3.8L supercharged and 3.8 without distributor

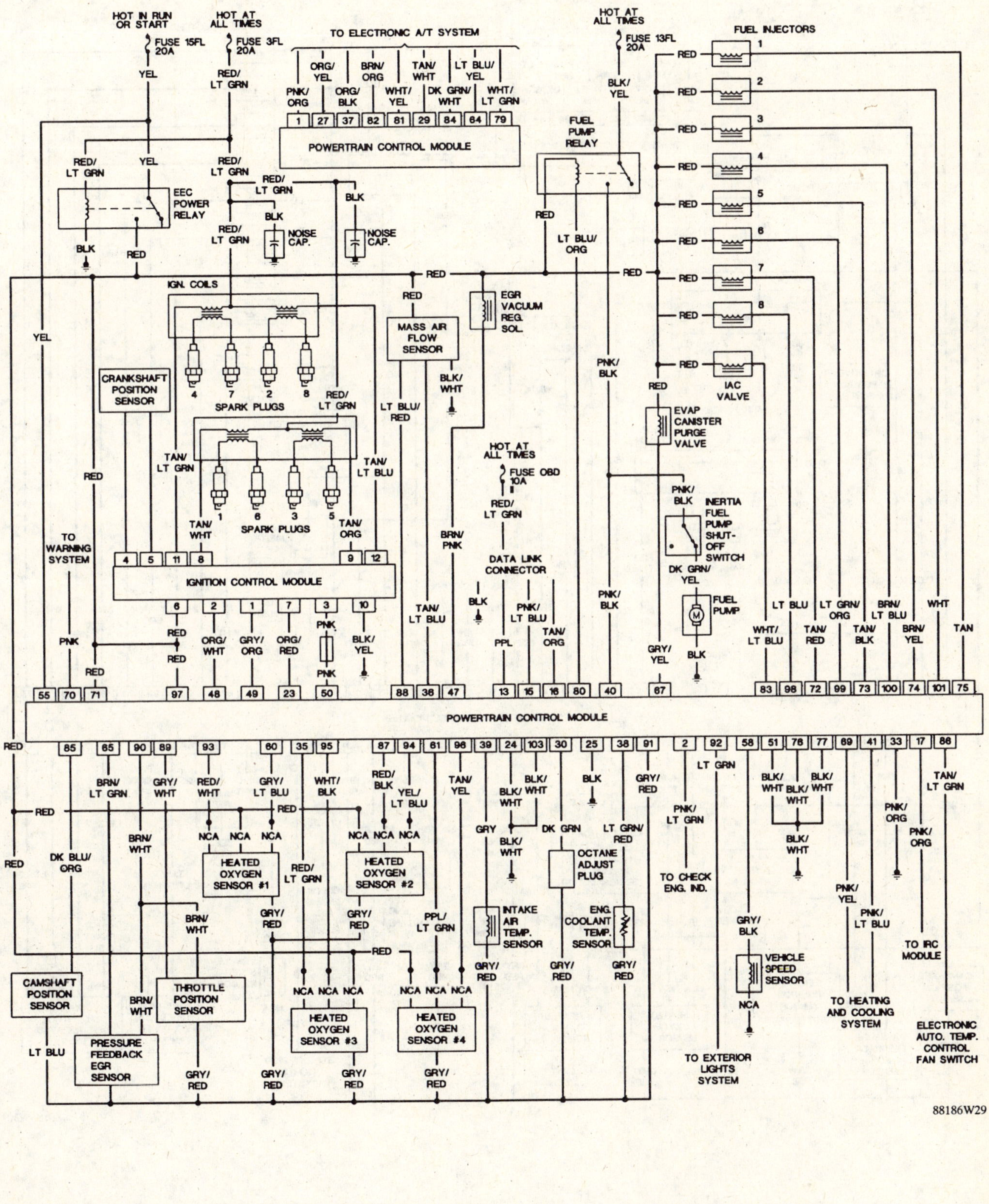

Fig. 177 Engine wiring — 1994–95 4.6L

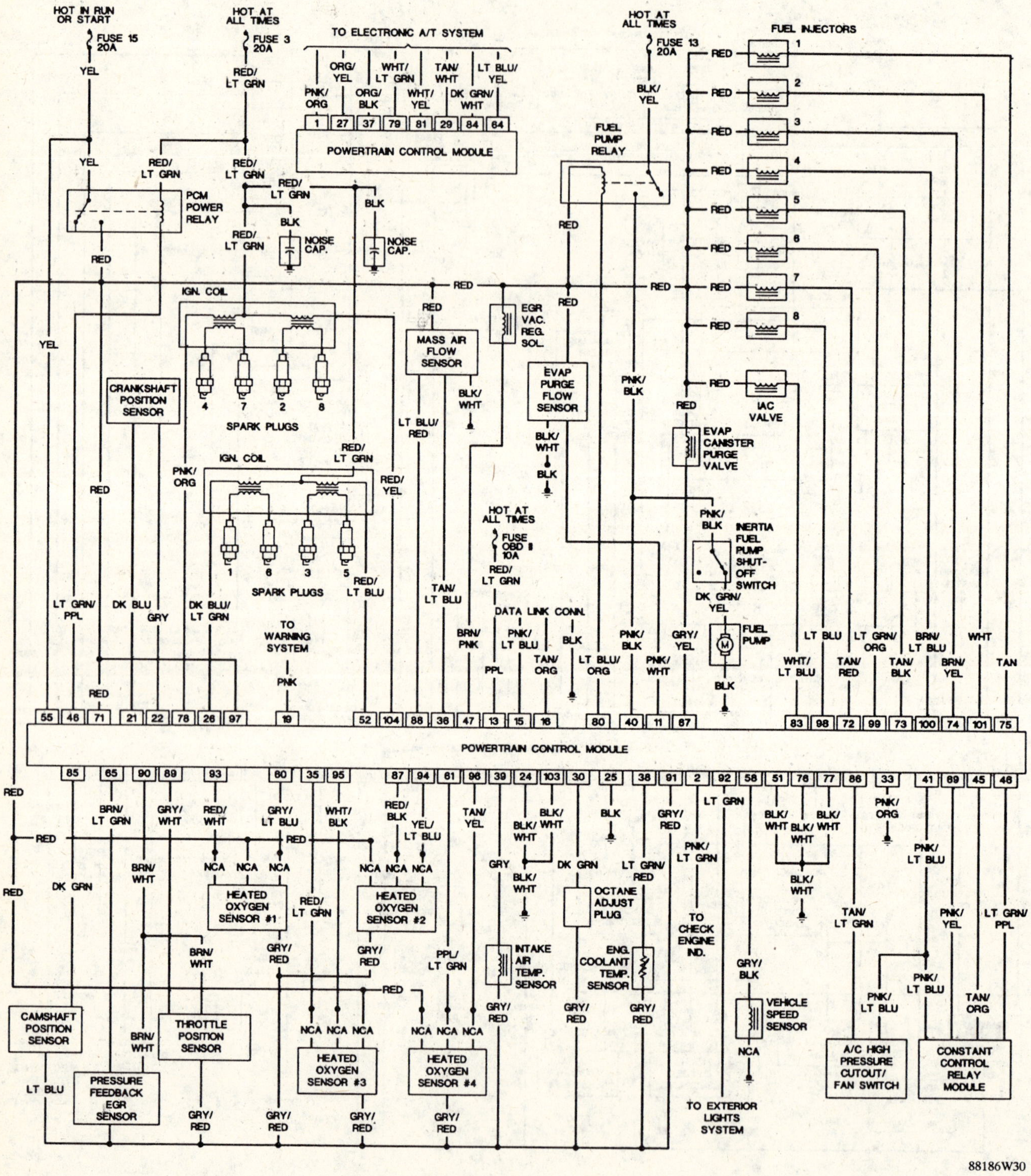

Fig. 178 Engine wiring — 1996 4.6L

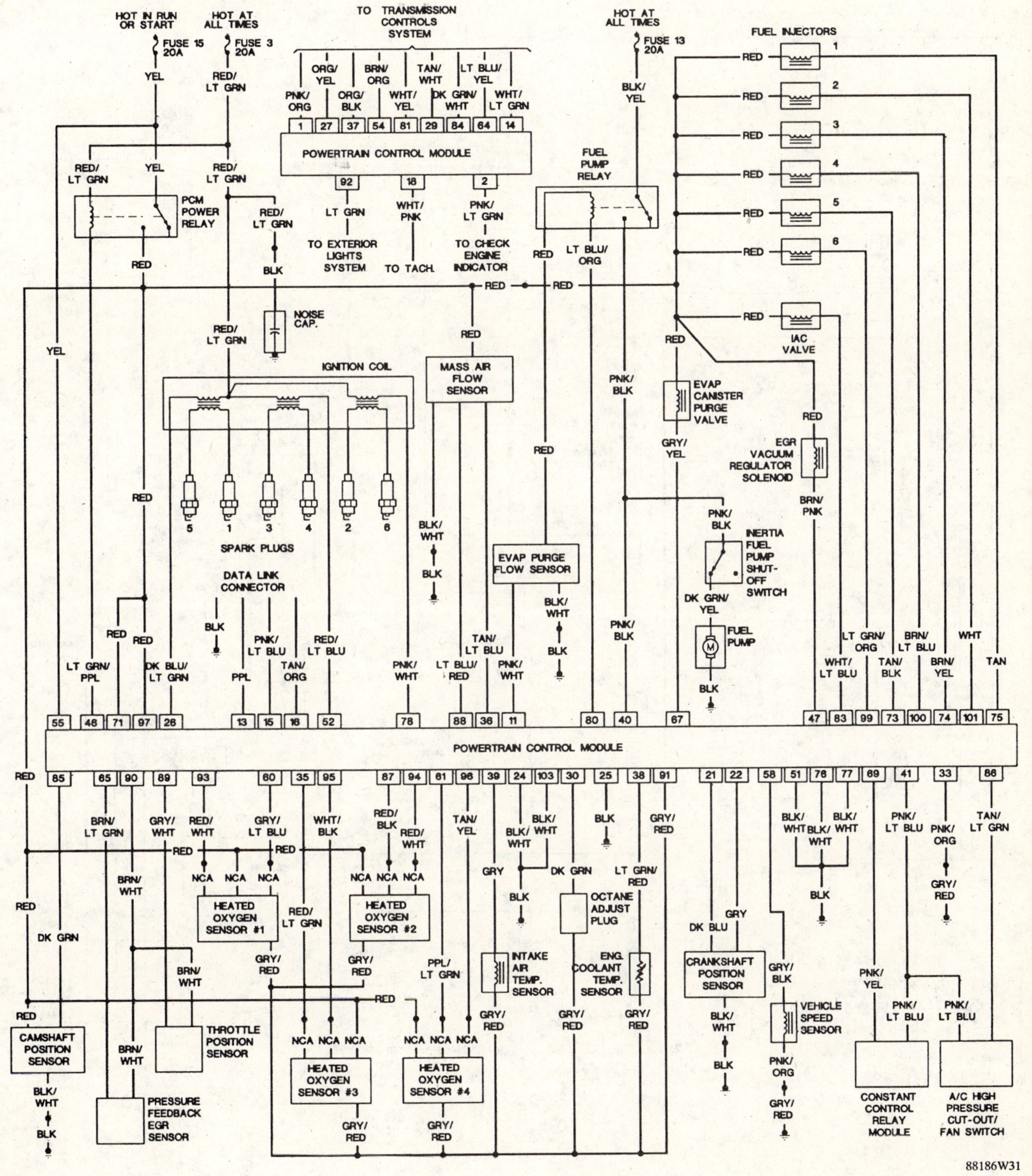

Fig. 179 Engine wiring — 1996 4.6L

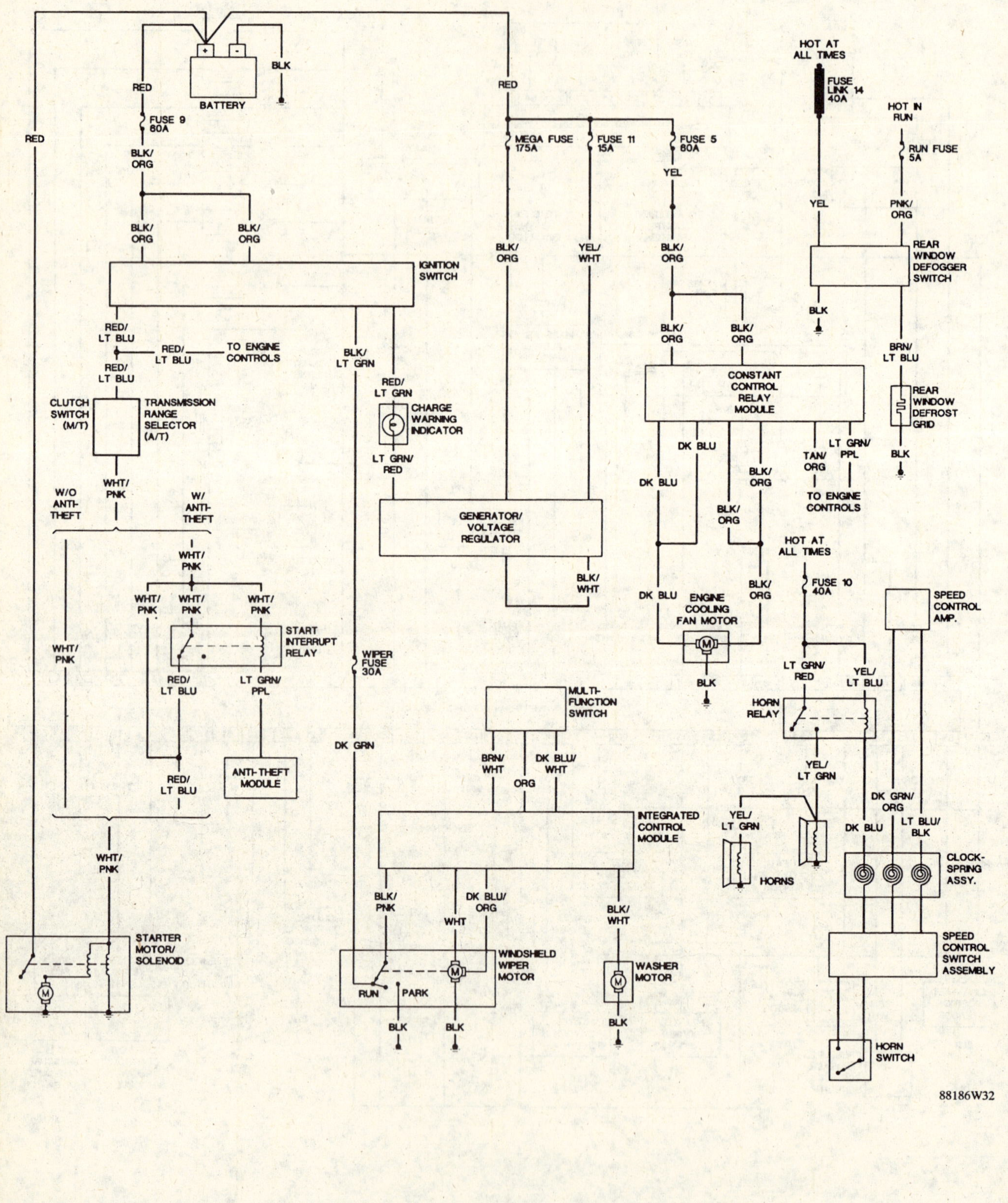

Fig. 180 Chassis wiring — 1994–96

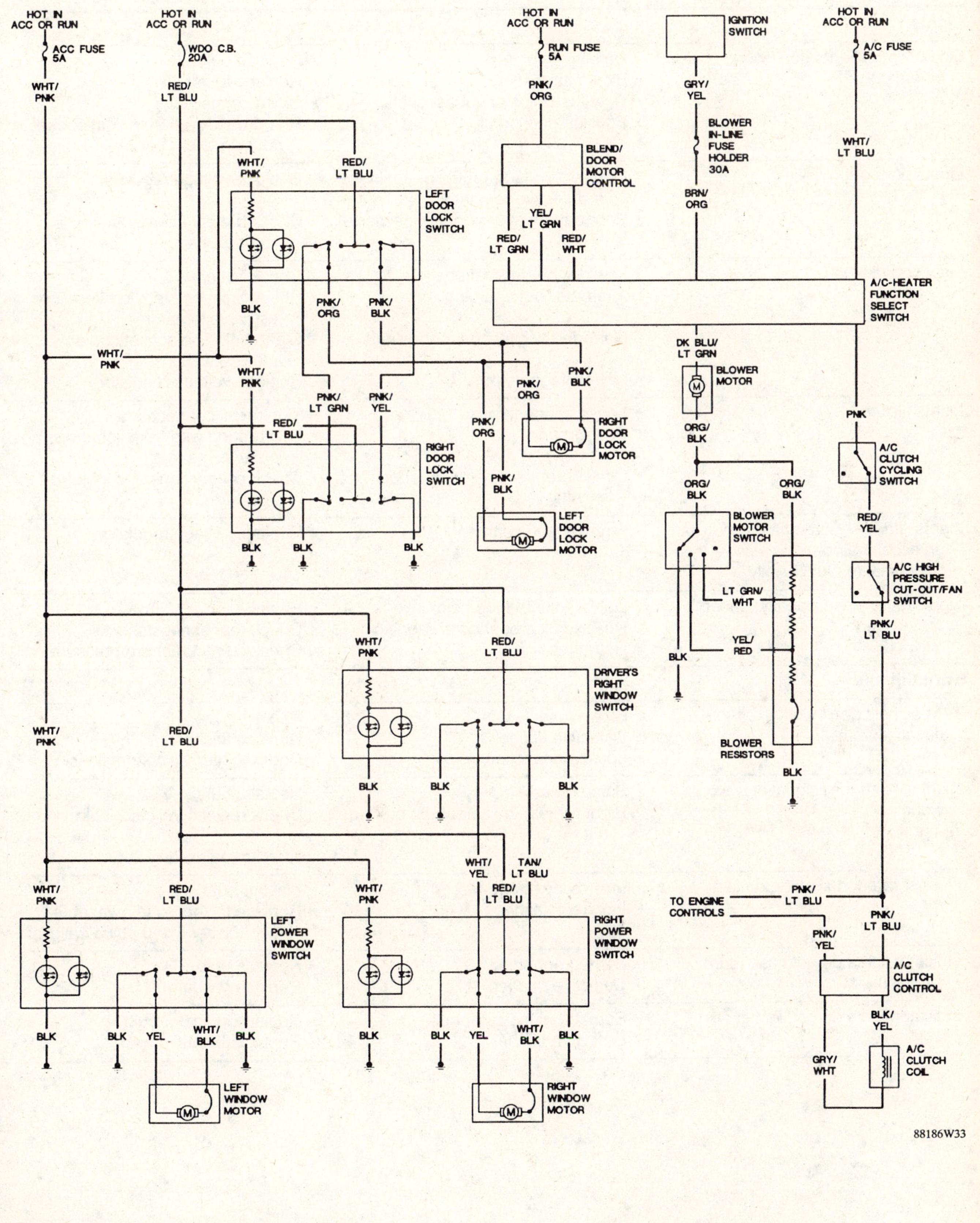

Fig. 181 Chassis wiring — 1994–96 continued

Troubleshooting Basic Lighting Problems

Problem	Cause	Solution
Lights		
One or more lights don't work, but others do	• Defective bulb(s) • Blown fuse(s) • Dirty fuse clips or light sockets • Poor ground circuit	• Replace bulb(s) • Replace fuse(s) • Clean connections • Run ground wire from light socket housing to car frame
Lights burn out quickly	• Incorrect voltage regulator setting or defective regulator • Poor battery/alternator connections	• Replace voltage regulator • Check battery/alternator connections
Lights go dim	• Low/discharged battery • Alternator not charging • Corroded sockets or connections • Low voltage output	• Check battery • Check drive belt tension; repair or replace alternator • Clean bulb and socket contacts and connections • Replace voltage regulator
Lights flicker	• Loose connection • Poor ground • Circuit breaker operating (short circuit)	• Tighten all connections • Run ground wire from light housing to car frame • Check connections and look for bare wires
Lights "flare"—Some flare is normal on acceleration—if excessive, see "Lights Burn Out Quickly"	• High voltage setting	• Replace voltage regulator
Lights glare—approaching drivers are blinded	• Lights adjusted too high • Rear springs or shocks sagging • Rear tires soft	• Have headlights aimed • Check rear springs/shocks • Check/correct rear tire pressure
Turn Signals		
Turn signals don't work in either direction	• Blown fuse • Defective flasher • Loose connection	• Replace fuse • Replace flasher • Check/tighten all connections
Right (or left) turn signal only won't work	• Bulb burned out • Right (or left) indicator bulb burned out • Short circuit	• Replace bulb • Check/replace indicator bulb • Check/repair wiring
Flasher rate too slow or too fast	• Incorrect wattage bulb • Incorrect flasher	• Flasher bulb • Replace flasher (use a variable load flasher if you pull a trailer)
Indicator lights do not flash (burn steadily)	• Burned out bulb • Defective flasher	• Replace bulb • Replace flasher
Indicator lights do not light at all	• Burned out indicator bulb • Defective flasher	• Replace indicator bulb • Replace flasher

88186C70

7

DRIVE TRAIN

MANUAL TRANSMISSION

Understanding the Manual Transmission

Because of the way an internal combustion engine breathes, it can produce torque (or twisting force) only within a narrow speed range. Most overhead valve pushrod engines must turn at about 2500 rpm to produce their peak torque. Often by 4500 rpm, they are producing so little torque that continued increases in engine speed produce no power increases.

The torque peak on overhead camshaft engines is, generally, much higher, but much narrower.

The manual transmission and clutch are employed to vary the relationship between engine RPM and the speed of the wheels so that adequate power can be produced under all circumstances. The clutch allows engine torque to be applied to the transmission input shaft gradually, due to mechanical slippage. The vehicle can, consequently, be started smoothly from a full stop.

The transmission changes the ratio between the rotating speeds of the engine and the wheels by the use of gears. 4-speed or 5-speed transmissions are most common. The lower gears allow full engine power to be applied to the rear wheels during acceleration at low speeds.

The clutch driveplate is a thin disc, the center of which is splined to the transmission input shaft. Both sides of the disc are covered with a layer of material which is similar to brake lining and which is capable of allowing slippage without roughness or excessive noise.

The clutch cover is bolted to the engine flywheel and incorporates a diaphragm spring which provides the pressure to engage the clutch. The cover also houses the pressure plate. When the clutch pedal is released, the driven disc is sandwiched between the pressure plate and the smooth surface of the flywheel, thus forcing the disc to turn at the same speed as the engine crankshaft.

The transmission contains a mainshaft which passes all the way through the transmission, from the clutch to the driveshaft. This shaft is separated at one point, so that front and rear portions can turn at different speeds.

Power is transmitted by a countershaft in the lower gears and reverse. The gears of the countershaft mesh with gears on the mainshaft, allowing power to be carried from one to the other. Countershaft gears are often integral with that shaft, while several of the mainshaft gears can either rotate independently of the shaft or be locked to it. Shifting from one gear to the next causes one of the gears to be freed from rotating with the shaft and locks another to it. Gears are locked and unlocked by internal dog clutches which slide between the center of the gear and the shaft. The forward gears usually employ synchronizers; friction members which smoothly bring gear and shaft to the same speed before the toothed dog clutches are engaged.

Identification

There are two types of manual transmissions used on these vehicles. There was no manual transmission offered in 1983. The T5OD 5-speed manual transmission was used from 1984-88, and the M5R2 5-speed manual transmission was used on 1989 and later models. The T5OD 5-speed utilizes a separate bell housing where as on the M5R2 5-speed transmission, the bell housing is an integral part of the transmission. Removal and installation procedures are the same except where noted. For more information regarding manual transmission identification, please refer to Section 1 of this manual.

Adjustments

LINKAGE

Neither of these units has any adjustment points. However, on some models when the shifter becomes loose or sloppy feeling, the shifter insert bushing can be replaced to tighten the feel of the shifter.

Shift Lever and Boot Assembly

REMOVAL & INSTALLATION

T5OD Manual Transmission

See Figure 1

1. Disconnect the negative battery cable.
2. Remove the four bolts attaching the shift boot to the floorpan.
3. Remove the two bolts attaching the the shift lever to the transmission.

To install:

4. Install the two bolts attaching the shift lever to the transmission. Tighten the bolts to 23-32 ft. lbs. (31-43 Nm).

The shift lever bolts must only be install in one direction; from the left side of the shift lever.

5. Install the four bolts attaching the shift boot to the floor pan, then tighten to 3-7 ft. lbs. (4.1-9.5 Nm).
6. Connect the negative battery cable.

M5R2 Manual Transmission

See Figure 2

1. Disconnect the negative battery cable.
2. Unscrew the gearshift lever knob.
3. Remove the center console panels.
4. Unfasten the console retaining clip from the underside of the upper gearshift lever boot.
5. Remove the upper gearshift lever boot.
6. Unfasten the two retaining screws, then remove the gearshift lever.
7. Remove the four retaining screws, then remove the lower gearshift lever boot.

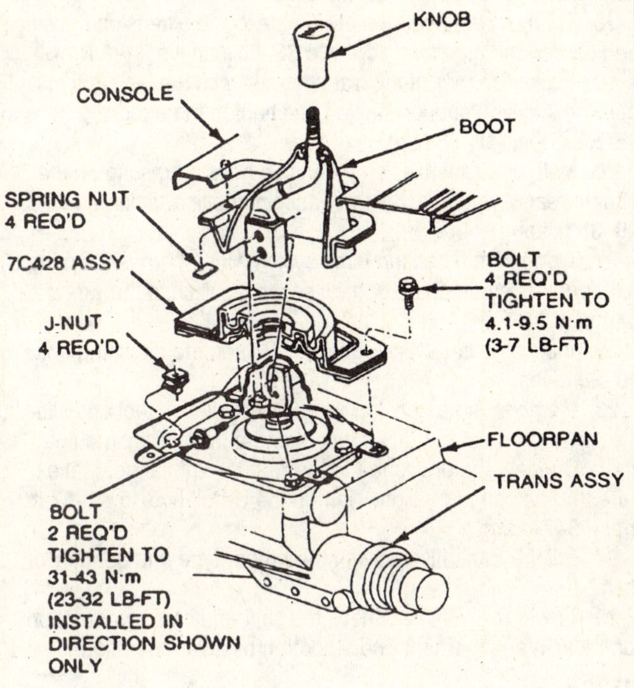

88187G01

Fig. 1 The shift boot and lever are secured to the floorpan with bolts

To install:

8. Position the lower gearshift lever boot and secure with the four retaining screws.
9. Install the gearshift lever and the two retaining screws.
10. Fasten the upper gearshift lever boot.
11. Install the console retaining clip from the underside of the upper gearshift lever boot.
12. Install the center console panels.
13. Install the gearshift lever knob by hand-tightening clockwise, then turn the gearshift lever knob 180 degrees to lock, and line up shift pattern.

Back-Up Light Switch

REMOVAL & INSTALLATION

1. Place the shift lever in neutral.
2. Raise and safely support the car on jackstands.
3. Unplug the electrical connector at the switch.
4. Unscrew the switch from the transmission extension housing.

To install:

5. Screw the new switch into place on the extension housing, then tighten it to 60 inch lbs. (6.7 Nm).
6. Attach the electrical wiring to the switch.
7. Carefully lower the vehicle.
8. Connect the negative battery cable, then check the switch for proper operation.

Extension Housing Seal

REMOVAL & INSTALLATION

1. Raise and safely support vehicle on jack stands.
2. Place a suitable container under the rear end of the transmission. Remove the propeller drive shaft.
3. Using an extension housing seal removal tool No. T74P-77248-A, remove the rear seal.

To install:

4. Using a seal installing tool No.T61L-7657-A, install the new seal.
5. Install the propeller driveshaft. Check fluid level in transmission fill as necessary.
6. Lower vehicle and check for leaks.

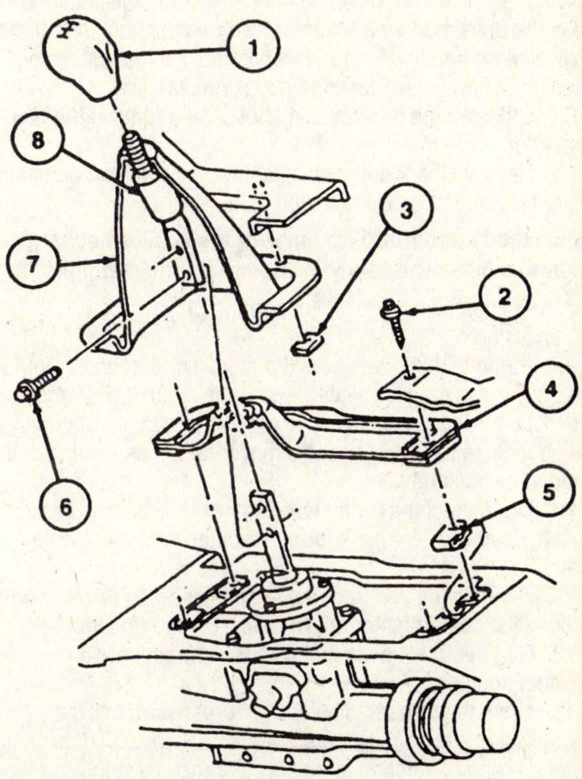

1. Gearshift lever knob
2. Lower dust boot retaining screw
3. Upper dust boot retaining clip
4. Lower gearshift lever boot
5. Retaining clip
6. Gearshift lever retaining screw
7. Upper gearshift lever boot
8. Gearshift lever

88187G05

Fig. 2 View of the gear shift lever and boot assembly mounting — 1995 M5R2 transmission shown

Transmission

REMOVAL & INSTALLATION

****CAUTION**

The clutch driven disc contains asbestos, which has been determined to be a cancer causing agent. Never clean clutch surfaces with compressed air! Avoid inhaling any dust from any clutch surface! When cleaning clutch surfaces, use a commercially available brake cleaning fluid.

T5OD 5-Speed Transmission

1. Disconnect the negative battery cable.
2. Raise and support the vehicle safely.
3. Matchmark the driveshaft for reassembly in the same relative position.
4. Disconnect the driveshaft from the rear U-joint flange. Slide the driveshaft off the transmission output shaft and install an extension housing seal installation tool into the extension housing to prevent lubricant from leaking out.
5. Unfasten the four retaining bolts, then remove the catalytic converter.
6. Remove the 2 nuts attaching the rear transmission support to the crossmember. Remove the bolts.

➥ On the Thunderbird Coupe with the 2.3L turbocharged engine, remove the catalytic converter and inlet pipe.

7. Using a suitable jack, support the engine and transmission.
8. Remove the 2 nuts from the crossmember bolts. Remove the bolts, raise the jack slightly and remove the crossmember.
9. Lower the transmission to expose the 2 bolts securing the shift handle to the shift tower. Remove the 2 nuts and bolts, then remove the shift handle.
10. Disconnect the wiring harness from the backup lamp switch. On the 5.0L engine, disconnect the neutral sensing switch.
11. Remove the bolt from the speedometer cable retainer and remove the speedometer driven gear from the transmission.
12. Remove the 4 bolts that secure the transmission to the flywheel housing.
13. Move the transmission and jack rearward until the transmission input shaft clears the flywheel housing. If necessary, lower the engine enough to obtain clearance for removing the transmission.

➥ Do not depress the clutch while the transmission is removed.

To install:

14. Make sure the mounting surface of the transmission and flywheel housing are clean and free of dirt, paint and burrs.
15. Install 2 guide pins in the flywheel housing lower mounting bolt holes. Raise the transmission and move forward on the guide pins until the input shaft splines enter the clutch hub splines and the case is positioned against the flywheel housing.
16. Install the 2 upper transmission-to-flywheel housing mounting bolts snug and remove the 2 guide pins. Install the 2 lower mounting bolts and tighten all the bolts to 45–65 ft. lbs. (61–88 Nm).
17. Raise the transmission with a jack until the shift handle can be secured to the shift tower. Install and tighten the attaching bolts and washers to 23–32 ft. lbs. (31–43 Nm).
18. Connect the speedometer cable to the extension housing and tighten the attaching screw to 36–54 inch lbs. (4–6 Nm).
19. Raise the rear of the transmission with the jack and install the transmission support. Install and tighten the attaching bolts to 36–50 ft. lbs. (48–68 Nm).
20. With the transmission extension housing resting on the engine rear support, install the attaching bolts and tighten to 25–35 ft. lbs. (38–48 Nm).
21. Connect the backup lamp switch wiring harness. On the 5.0L engine, connect the neutral sensing switch to the wiring harness.
22. Install the catalytic converter. Tighten the attaching bolts to 20–30 ft. lbs. (27–41 Nm).
23. Remove the extension housing installation tool and slide the forward end of the driveshaft over the transmission output shaft. Connect the driveshaft to the rear U-joint flange. Make sure the matchmarks align. Tighten the U-bolt nuts to 42–57 ft. lbs. (56–77 Nm).
24. Fill the transmission with the proper type and quantity of fluid.
25. Lower the vehicle. Check the shift and crossover motion for full shift engagement and smooth crossover operation.

M5R2 5-Speed

➧ See Figures 3, 4 and 5

1. Disconnect the negative battery cable.
2. Shift transmission into the Neutral position.
3. Remove the gearshift lever knob.
4. Remove the console top cover.
5. Remove the two shift control selector lever and housing retaining bolts, then remove the shift lever.
6. Raise and safely support the vehicle with jackstands.
7. Remove the drain plug, then drain the oil from the transmission into a suitable container.
8. Remove the body reinforcement in front of the axle.
9. Disconnect the rear exhaust assembly from the resonator.

➥ If not marked, mark the rear driveshaft centering socket yoke and circular companion flange so that the driveshaft can be installed in its original position.

10. Remove the four bolts retaining the driveshaft axle to the circular companion flange.
11. Position a suitable jackstand under the front of the axle housing and remove the forward retaining nuts, and bushings.
12. Loosen the rear retaining nuts to allow the axle to tilt for driveshaft removal.
13. Pull the vent tube from the hole in the subframe.
14. Lower the front of the axle housing with the axle stand and slide the driveshaft out of the transmission above the axle housing. Let the driveshaft rest on the front driveshaft support and axle assembly.

****WARNING**

Be very careful when positioning the driveshaft so as not to nick, burr or contaminate the driveshaft yoke or companion flange.

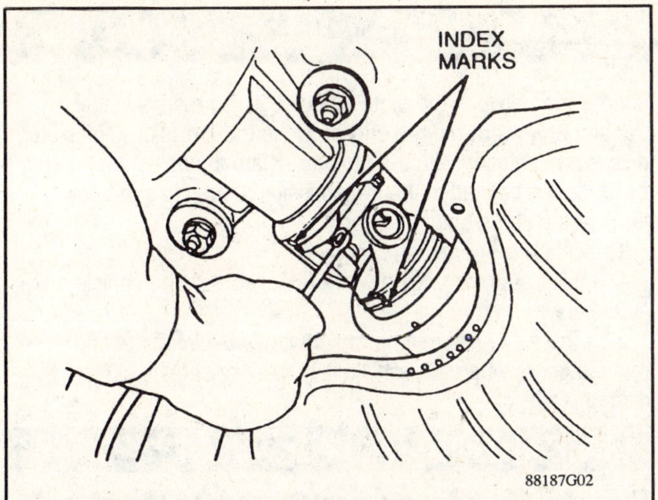

Fig. 3 **Unfasten the four driveshaft axle-to-circular companion flange bolts**

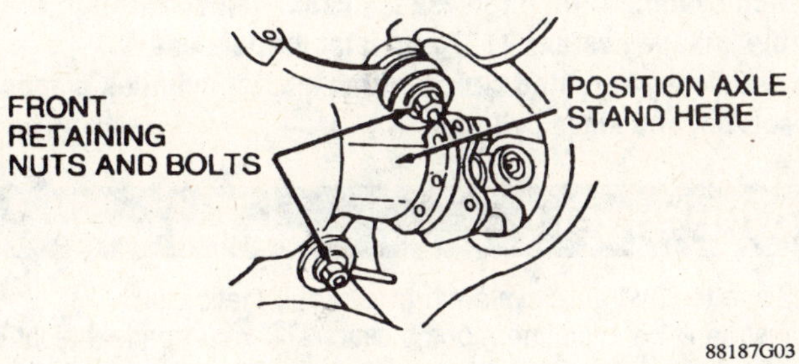

Fig. 4 **With an axle stand under the front of the housing, remove the front nuts and bolts**

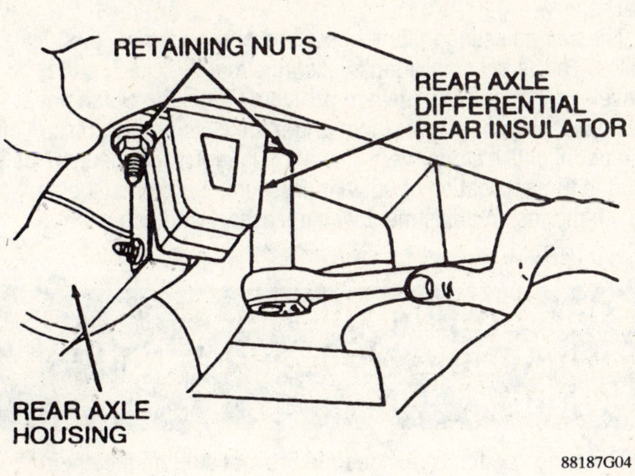

Fig. 5 **To allow the front of the axle to tilt for driveshaft removal, loosen the rear retaining nuts**

15. Remove the catalytic converter assembly.
16. Disconnect the hydraulic clutch line.
17. Detach the electrical connectors.
18. Remove the starter. For details, please refer to the procedure in Section 2 of this manual.
19. With the full weight of the transmission on the crossmember, remove the transmission mount nut using a 21mm socket.
20. Position a suitable transmission jack under the transmission.
21. Remove the crossmember.
22. Remove the bellhousing-to-engine bolts.
23. Move the transmission to the rear until the input shaft clears the engine flywheel, then carefully lower the transmission from the vehicle.

To install:

24. Secure the transmission assembly on the transmission jack. Install the guide studs in the engine block and raise the transmission until the input shaft splines are aligned with the clutch disc splines.
25. Slide the transmission forward on the guide studs until it is positioned in the vehicle.
26. Install the bellhousing/flywheel-to-engine retaining bolts. Tighten to 28–38 ft. lbs. (38–51 Nm).
27. Install the crossmember. Tighten the bolts to 35–50 ft. lbs. (47–68 Nm).
28. Remove the transmission jack.
29. Attach the electrical connectors.
30. Connect the hydraulic clutch line.
31. Install the starter, as outlined in Section 2 of this manual.
32. Install the catalytic converter assembly.
33. Slide the driveshaft into transmission.

➥ Lubricate the yoke splines with Premium Long-Life Grease C1AZ-19590-E (ESA-MIC75-B) or equivalent.

34. Raise the axle housing with the axle stand and install the bushings and retaining nuts. Tighten the retaining nuts to 68–100 ft. lbs. (92–136 Nm). Remove the axle stand.
35. Position the vent tube in hole of subframe.
36. Align the driveshaft centering socket yoke and circular companion flange, then install the retaining bolts. Tighten to 71–95 ft. lbs. (95–129 Nm).
37. Connect the exhaust pipe/muffler assembly to the resonator.
38. Add 5 ounces of Additive Friction Modifier C8AZ-19B546-A or equivalent, and fill to a total of 6.3 pts. (3L) with Synthetic MERCON® transmission fluid E6AZ-19582-B or equivalent.

➥ Apply Pipe Sealant with Teflon® to the fill plug threads in a clockwise position before installing the plug.

39. Install the transmission case plug, and fill/drain plug gasket. Tighten to 29–43 ft. lbs. (40–58 Nm) using a 24mm socket.
40. Carefully lower the vehicle.
41. Position the shifter and install the retaining bolts. Tighten to 18–24 ft. lbs. (24–33 Nm).
42. Install the console top cover.
43. Install the shifter knob.
44. Connect the battery ground cable.

CLUTCH

Understanding the Clutch

The purpose of the clutch is to disconnect and connect engine power at the transmission. A vehicle at rest requires a lot of engine torque to get all that weight moving. An internal combustion engine does not develop a high starting torque (unlike steam engines) so it must be allowed to operate without any load until it builds up enough torque to move the vehicle. To a point, torque increases with engine rpm. The clutch allows the engine to build up torque by physically disconnecting the engine from the transmission, relieving the engine of any load or resistance.

The transfer of engine power to the transmission (the load) must be smooth and gradual; if it weren't, drive line components would wear out or break quickly. This gradual power transfer is made possible by gradually releasing the clutch pedal. The clutch disc and pressure plate are the connecting link between the engine and transmission. When the clutch pedal is released, the disc and plate contact each other (the clutch is engaged) physically joining the engine and transmission. When the pedal is pushed in, the disc and plate separate (the clutch is disengaged) disconnecting the engine from the transmission.

Most clutch assemblies consists of the flywheel, the clutch disc, the clutch pressure plate, the throw out bearing and fork, the actuating linkage and the pedal. The flywheel and clutch pressure plate (driving members) are connected to the engine crankshaft and rotate with it. The clutch disc is located between the flywheel and pressure plate, and is splined to the transmission shaft. A driving member is one that is attached to the engine and transfers engine power to a driven member (clutch disc) on the transmission shaft. A driving member (pressure plate) rotates (drives) a driven member (clutch disc) on contact and, in so doing, turns the transmission shaft.

There is a circular diaphragm spring within the pressure plate cover (transmission side). In a relaxed state (when the clutch pedal is fully released) this spring is convex; that is, it is dished outward toward the transmission. Pushing in the clutch pedal actuates the attached linkage. Connected to the other end of this is the throw out fork, which hold the throw out bearing. When the clutch pedal is depressed, the clutch linkage pushes the fork and bearing forward to contact the diaphragm spring of the pressure plate. The outer edges of the spring are secured to the pressure plate and are pivoted on rings so that when the center of the spring is compressed by the throw out bearing, the outer edges bow outward and, by so doing, pull the pressure plate in the same direction – away from the clutch disc. This action separates the disc from the plate, disengaging the clutch and allowing the transmission to be shifted into another gear. A coil type clutch return spring attached to the clutch pedal arm permits full release of the pedal. Releasing the pedal pulls the throw out bearing away from the diaphragm spring resulting in a reversal of spring position. As bearing pressure is gradually released from the spring center, the outer edges of the spring bow outward, pushing the pressure plate into closer contact with the clutch disc. As the disc and plate move closer together, friction between the two increases and slippage is reduced until, when full spring pressure is applied (by fully releasing the pedal) the speed of the disc and plate are the same. This stops all slipping, creating a direct connection between the plate and disc which results in the transfer of power from the engine to the transmission. The clutch disc is now rotating with the pressure plate at engine speed and, because it is splined to the transmission shaft, the shaft now turns at the same engine speed.

The clutch is operating properly if:

1. It will stall the engine when released with the vehicle held stationary.
2. The shift lever can be moved freely between 1st and reverse gears when the vehicle is stationary and the clutch disengaged.

**CAUTION

The clutch driven disc may contain asbestos, which has been determined to be a cancer causing agent. Never clean clutch surfaces with compressed air! Avoid inhaling any dust from any clutch surface! When cleaning clutch surfaces, use a commercially available brake cleaning fluid.

➥ Models through 1986 employ a mechanically actuated clutch system. Clutch release is accomplished through a cable linkage system. 1987 and later models use a hydraulically actuated clutch with a master cylinder, plastic reservoir, and slave cylinder.

Adjustment

Since the hydraulic system provides automatic clutch adjustment, no adjustment of the clutch linkage or pedal height is required on vehicles with the master and slave cylinder actuator system.

LINKAGE

Vehicles not equipped with a hydraulic clutch actuator system (1983–86) are equipped with a linkage or cable system which have self-adjusting cable clutches. No adjustments are necessary.

The self-adjusting feature should be checked every 5,000 miles. This is accomplished by insuring that the clutch pedal travels to the top of its upward position. Grasp the clutch pedal with your hand or put your foot under the clutch pedal, pull up on the pedal until it stops. Very little effort is required (about 10 lbs.) During the application of upward pressure, a click may be heard which means an adjustment was necessary and has been accomplished.

Starter/Clutch Interlock SwitchClutch Pedal Position Switch

The clutch switch is designed to prevent starting the engine unless the clutch pedal is fully depressed. The switch is connected between the ignition switch and the starter motor relay coil and maintains an open circuit with the clutch pedal up (clutch engaged).

The switch is designed to self-adjust automatically the first time the clutch pedal is pressed to the floor. The self-adjuster consists of a two-piece clip snapped together over a serrated rod. When the plunger or rod is extended, the clip bottoms out on the switch body and allows the rod to ratchet over the serrations to a position determined by the clutch pedal travel limit. In this way, the switch is set to close the starter circuit when the clutch is pressed all the way to the floor (clutch disengaged).

TESTING CONTINUITY

1. Disconnect inline wiring connector at jumper harness.
2. Using a test lamp or continuity tester, check that switch is open with clutch pedal up (clutch engaged), and closed at approximately 1 in. (25mm) from the clutch pedal full down position (clutch disengaged).
3. If switch does not operate, check to see if the self-adjusting clip is out of position on the rod. It should be near the end of the rod.
4. If the self-adjusting clip is out of position, remove and reposition the clip to about 1 in. (25mm) from the end of the rod.
5. Reset the switch by pressing the clutch pedal to the floor.
6. Repeat Step 2. If switch is damaged, replace it.

REMOVAL & INSTALLATION

Vehicles Through 1986

See Figure 6

1. Disconnect the negative battery cable.
2. Detach the wiring connector.
3. Remove the retaining pin from the clutch pedal.
4. Remove the switch bracket attaching screw.
5. Lift the switch and bracket assembly upward to disengage tab from pedal support.
6. Move the switch outward to disengage actuating rod eyelet from clutch pedal pin and remove switch from vehicle.

To install:

Always install the switch with the self-adjusting clip about 1 in. (25.4mm) from the end of the rod. The clutch pedal must be fully up (clutch engaged). Otherwise, the switch may be misadjusted.

7. Place the eyelet end of the rod onto the pivot pin.
8. Swing the switch assembly around to line up hole in the mounting boss with the hole in the bracket.
9. Install the attaching screw.
10. Replace the retaining pin in the pivot pin.
11. Attach the wiring connector.
12. Connect the negative battery cable.

1987-88 Vehicles

1. Disconnect the negative battery cable.
2. Remove the switch bracket mounting nuts.
3. Detach the switch electrical connector.
4. Remove the switch and bracket assembly.
5. Installation is the reverse of the removal procedure.

1989-95 Vehicles

See Figure 7

1. Disconnect the negative battery cable.
2. Detach the wiring harness form the clutch pedal position switch.
3. Remove the C-clip from the clutch pedal pin. Slide the push rod off the pin.
4. Remove the C-clip from the end of the clutch pedal rod.
5. Remove the push rod from the clutch pedal position switch.
6. Detach the switch from the mounting bracket.

To install:

7. Install the clutch pedal position switch on the plastic switch mounting bracket.
8. Slide the push rod through the clutch pedal position switch and plastic bracket to ensure proper alignment.
9. Install the C-clip on the end of the push rod.
10. Install the push rod on the clutch pedal pin and install the C-clip.

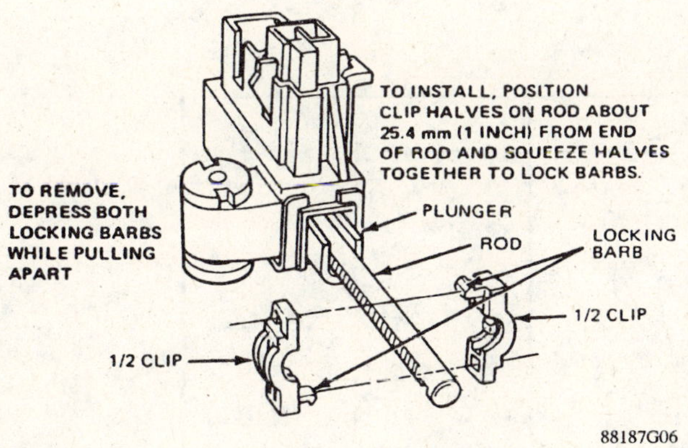

Fig. 6 Starter/clutch interlock switch self-adjuster clip installation — 1986 vehicle shown

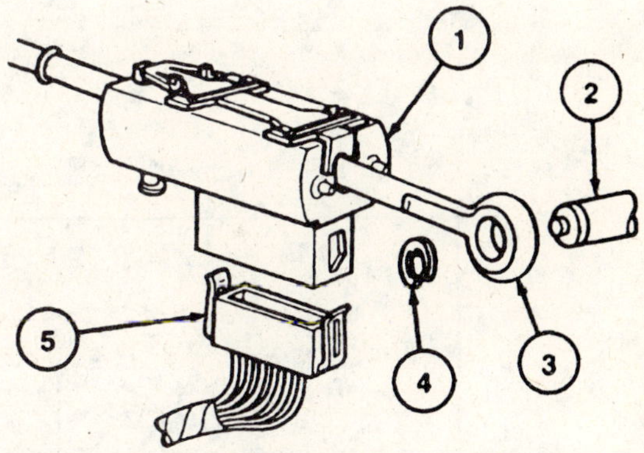

1. Clutch pedal position switch
2. Clutch pedal pin
3. Clutch interlock rod
4. C-clip
5. Wiring harness

88187G56

Fig. 7 Clutch pedal position switch removal — 1995 vehicle shown

11. Attach the wiring harness.
12. Connect the negative battery cable, then test for proper operation.

Clutch Pedal

REMOVAL & INSTALLATION

Vehicles Through 1986

➧ See Figure 8

1. Disconnect the negative battery cable.
2. Remove the starter/clutch interlock switch, as outlined earlier in this section.
3. Remove the clutch pedal attaching nut, then pull the pedal off the clutch pedal shaft.

To install:

4. Align the square hole of the clutch pedal with the clutch pedal shaft and push the clutch pedal on.
5. Install the clutch pedal attaching nut, then tighten to 17-26 ft. lbs. (23-36 Nm).
6. Install the starter/clutch interlock switch, as outlined earlier in this section.
7. Connect the negative battery cable, and check for proper operation.

1987-95 Vehicles

➧ See Figure 9

1. Disconnect the battery ground cable.
2. Disconnect the clutch and starter interlock harness from the switch.
3. Disconnect the master cylinder push rod from the clutch pedal. Rotate master cylinder 45 degrees counterclockwise to release it from the dash panel. It is not necessary to remove the master cylinder from the vehicle.
4. Remove the pedal support retaining nuts at the dash panel.
5. Remove the bolt attaching pedal support to the cowl. Remove the pedal and support from the vehicle.
6. To remove the pedal from the support, remove the clutch and starter switch, remove the nut attaching clutch pedal to support.

To install:

7. Install the clutch pedal to support. Tighten the retaining nut to 15-19 ft. lbs (20-27 Nm). Be sure the pedal bushings are in place.
8. Install the clutch and starter switch.
9. Position pedal assembly in vehicle, loosely attach the bolt through the support in the cowl.
10. Install the three pedal assembly retaining nuts to dash panel and tighten nuts to 16-22 ft. lbs. (21-30 Nm).
11. Tighten the cowl retaining bolt to 18.8-25.4 ft. lbs. (25.5-34.5 Nm).

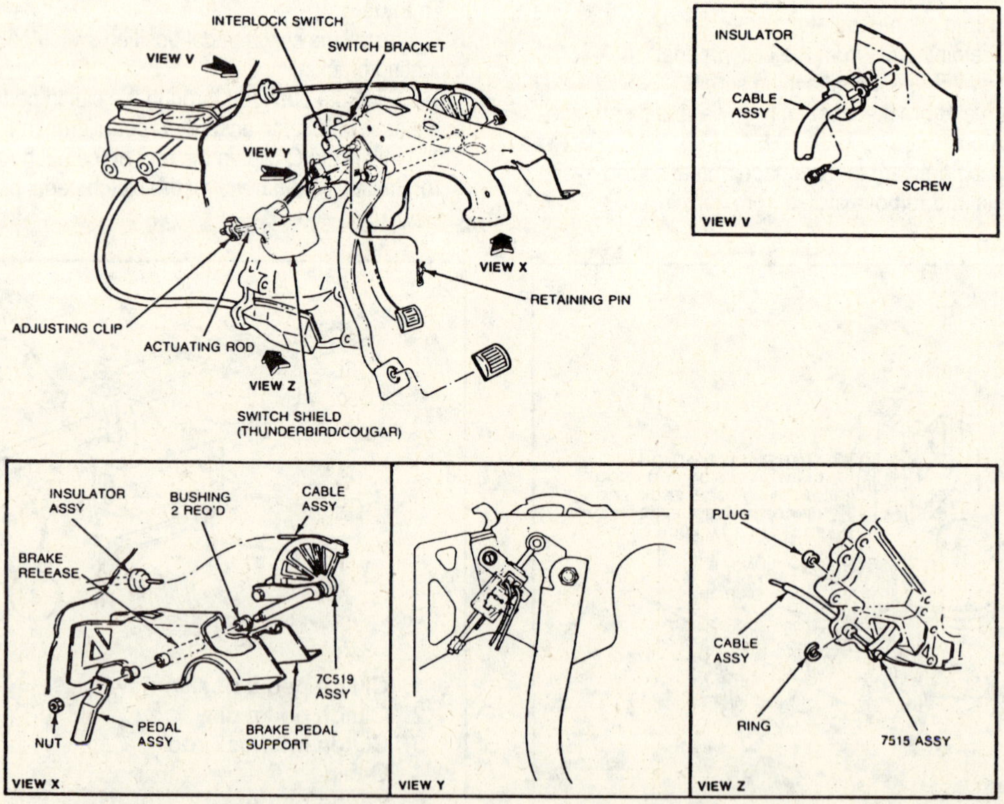

Fig. 8 Clutch pedal assembly removal and installation and related components — 1986 vehicle shown

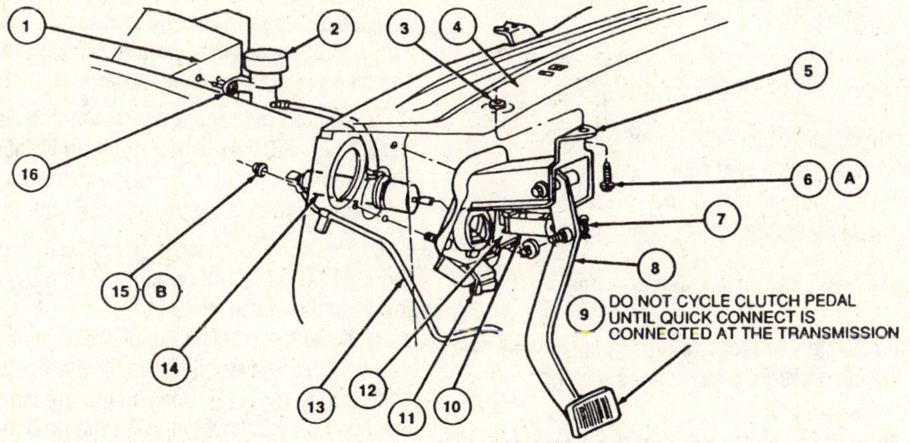

Item	Description
1	LH Shock Tower
2	Clutch Fluid Reservoir and Tube
3	Weld Nut
4	Cowl
5	Pedal Bracket Assy
6	Bolt
7	Clutch Interlock Rod
8	Clutch Pedal Assy
9	Pedal Pad
10	Clutch Pedal Position Switch

Item	Description
11	Clutch Pedal Stop
12	Clutch Pedal Position Switch Mounting Bracket
13	Clutch Slave Cylinder to Clutch Master Cylinder Tube
14	Clutch Master Cylinder
15	Nut
16	Push Pins
A	Tighten to 25.5-34.5 N·m (18.8-25.4 Lb-Ft)
B	Tighten to 21-30 N·m (16-22 Lb-Ft)

88187G55

Fig. 9 Clutch pedal removal and installation — 1995 vehicle shown

12. Install master cylinder to dash panel by rotating 45 degrees clockwise into locking position.
13. Attach master cylinder push rod to the clutch pedal.
14. Connect the wiring harness to the clutch/starter switch.
15. Connect the negative battery cable, and check for proper operation.

Clutch Cable Assembly

REMOVAL & INSTALLATION

➧ See Figure 8

1. Lift the clutch pedal to its upward most position to disengage the pawl and quadrant. Push the quadrant forward, unhook the cable from the quadrant and allow to slowly swing rearward.
2. Open the hood and remove the screw that holds the cable assembly isolator to the dash panel.
3. Pull the cable through the dash panel and into the engine compartment. On 2.3L and 5.0L engines, remove cable bracket screw from fender apron.
4. Raise and safely support the vehicle.
5. Remove the dust cover from the bell housing.
6. Remove the clip retainer holding the cable assembly to the bell housing.
7. Slide the ball on the end of the cable assembly through the hole in the clutch release lever and remove the cable.
8. Remove the dash panel isolator from the cable.

To install:

9. Install the dash panel isolator on the cable assembly.
10. Insert the cable through the hole in the bell housing and through the hole in the clutch release lever. Slide the ball on the end of the cable assembly away from the hole in the clutch release lever.
11. Install the clip retainer that holds the cable assembly to the bell housing.
12. Install the dust shield on the bell housing.
13. Push the cable assembly into the engine compartment and lower the vehicle. On 2.3L and 5.0L engines, install cable bracket screw in fender apron.
14. Push the cable assembly into the hole in the dash panel and secure the isolator with a screw.
15. Install the cable assembly by lifting the clutch pedal to disengage the pawl and quadrant, then, pushing the quadrant forward, hook the end of the cable over the rear of the quadrant.
16. Depress clutch pedal several times to adjust cable.

Driven Disc and Pressure Plate

➝ Models through 1986 employ a mechanically actuated clutch. Clutch release is accomplished through a cable linkage system. 1987 and later models use a hydraulically actuated clutch with a master cylinder, plastic reservoir, and slave cylinder

REMOVAL & INSTALLATION

➧ See Figures 10, 11, 12, 13 and 14

1. Disconnect the negative battery cable.

2. If equipped with a hydraulic clutch system, disconnect the master cylinder from the clutch pedal.
3. Raise and safely support the vehicle.
4. Remove the starter, as outlined in Section 2 of this manual.
5. If equipped with a hydraulic clutch, disconnect the hydraulic coupling at the transmission with Clutch Coupling Tool T88T-70522-A, or equivalent, by sliding the white plastic sleeve. Slide the sleeve toward the clutch slave cylinder and apply a slight tug on the tube.
6. Remove the transmission, as outlined earlier in this section.
7. Mark the cover and flywheel to facilitate reassembly in the same position. Loosen the six pressure plate cover attaching bolts evenly to release the spring pressure.

➥ The pressure plate is held in place with only the retaining bolts. Support the pressure plate before removing the last retaining bolt.

8. Remove the six attaching bolts while holding the pressure plate cover. Remove the pressure plate and clutch disc.

****WARNING**

Do not depress the clutch pedal while the transmission is removed.

To install

9. Before installing the clutch, clean the flywheel surface and pressure plate with a suitable commercial alcohol base solvent. Do NOT use cleaners with a petroleum base. Inspect the flywheel and pressure plate for wear, scoring, or burn marks (blue color). Light scoring and wear may be cleaned up with emery paper; heavy wear may require refacing of the flywheel or replacement of the damaged parts.

➥ The clutch disc must be assembled so that the FW SIDE or FLYWHEEL SIDE stamped notation is facing toward the engine. The three clutch pressure plate-to-flywheel dowels and the flywheel must be properly aligned with the pressure plate.

10. Position the clutch disc on the flywheel so that Clutch Aligner T74P-7137-K or equivalent, can enter the pilot bearing and align the clutch disc.
11. When reinstalling the original clutch pressure plate and cover, align the assembly and flywheel according to the marks made during removal. Position the pressure plate and cover assembly on the flywheel, align the pressure plate and disc and install the retaining bolts that fasten the assembly to the flywheel. To avoid pressure plate cover distortion, alternately tighten the cover bolts in sequence as shown until fully seated. Then, tighten the bolts to 29 ft. lbs. (39 Nm) in the sequence shown in the accompanying figure.
12. Remove the clutch alignment tool.
13. Align the clutch disc with the pilot bushing. Torque cover bolts to 12–14 ft. lbs. (16–19 Nm).
14. Install the transmission assembly.
15. If equipped, connect the coupling by pushing the male coupling into the slave cylinder female coupling. Connect the hydraulic clutch master cylinder push rod to the clutch pedal.
16. If necessary, bleed the clutch hydraulic system.
17. Connect the negative battery cable.

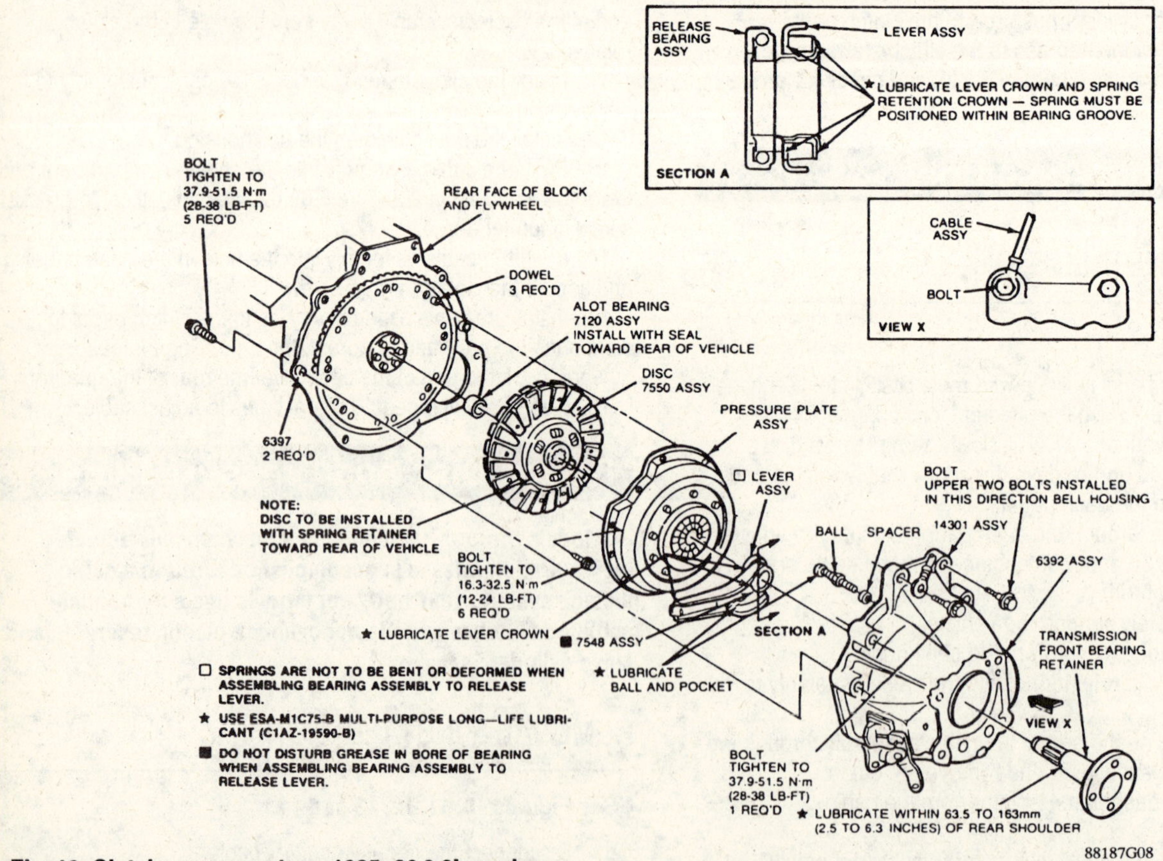

Fig. 10 Clutch components — 1985–86 2.3L engine

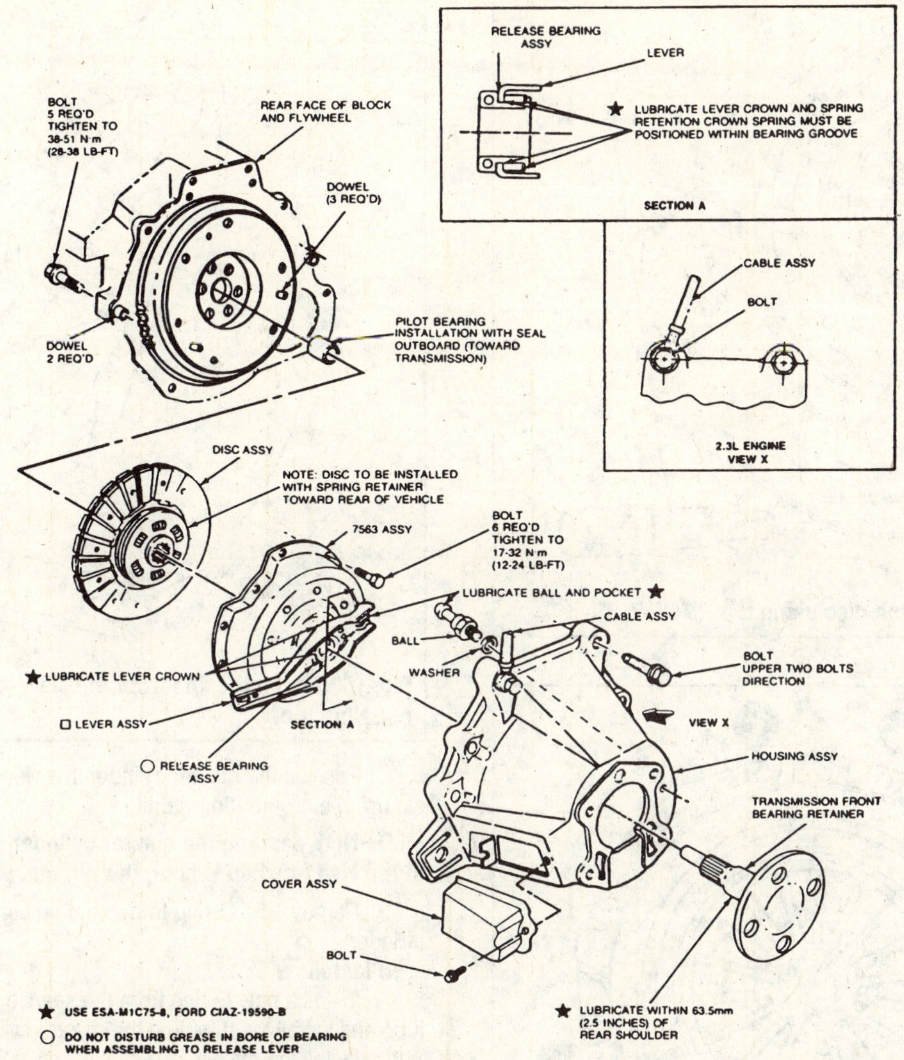

Fig. 11 Clutch removal and installation on 1987-88 2.3L engines

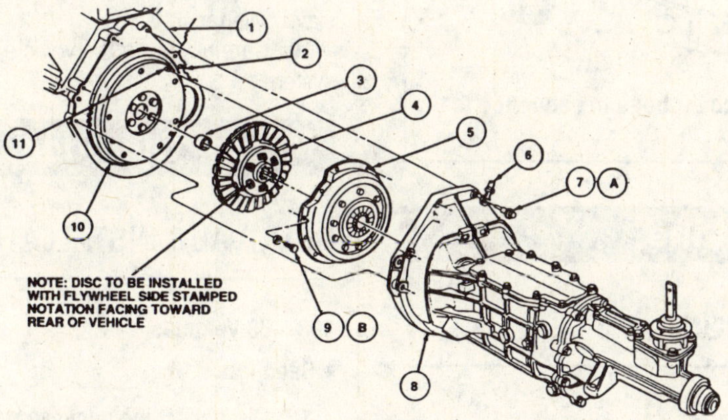

1. Cylinder block
2. Flywheel housing to block dowel (2 req'd)
3. Pilot bearing
4. Clutch disc
5. Clutch pressure plate
6. Dash panel ground cable
7. Bolt (6 req'd)
8. Transmission
9. Bolt and washer assembly (6 req'd)
10. Flywheel
11. Clutch pressure plate-to-flywheel dowel

A. Tighten to 54-64 Nm (40-49 lb-ft)
B. Tighten to 27-39 Nm (20-28 lb-ft)

88187G10

Fig. 12 Clutch components — 1995 vehicle shown

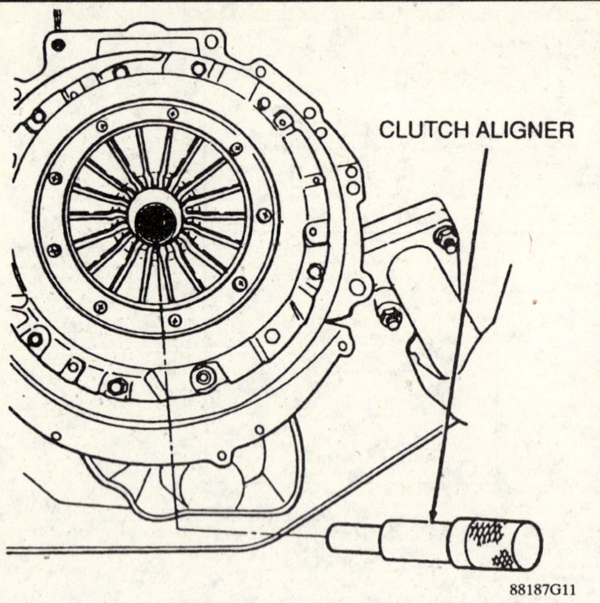

Fig. 13 Align the clutch disc using tool T74P-7137-K

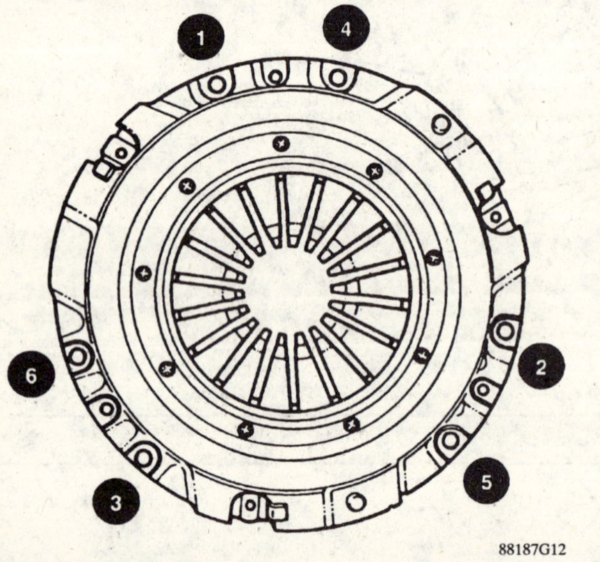

Fig. 14 You must tighten the cover bolts in sequence to prevent warpage

Clutch Hydraulic Line

REMOVAL & INSTALLATION

➧ See Figure 15

1. Raise and safely support the vehicle.
2. To disconnect the line from the slave cylinder fitting only, depress the white retainer bushing with Clutch Coupling Tool T88T-70522-A or equivalent, while pulling slightly on the line.
3. If the line is to be removed from the vehicle, the clutch master cylinder must be removed and the push rod disconnected from the clutch pedal.

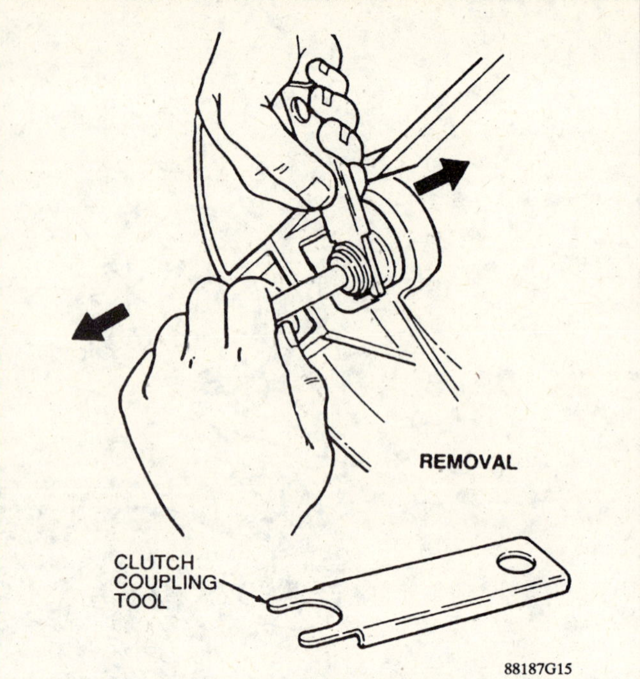

Fig. 15 Detach the line from the slave cylinder with the coupling tool

4. Position the master cylinder in a vise and drive out the roll pin using a $^{7}/_{64}$ in. (3mm) drift.

➥ Do NOT damage the master cylinder while it is being held in the vise or when driving the pin out.

5. Remove the O-ring from the tube connection of the master cylinder.

To install:

6. Install a new O-ring from the service kit onto the clutch tube and install the tube into the master cylinder.
7. Install the roll pin.

➥ Use care not to damage the master cylinder.

8. Install the master cylinder.
9. Push the male connector onto the female connector of the slave cylinder.
10. Carefully lower the vehicle, then bleed the hydraulic system.

Master Cylinder

REMOVAL & INSTALLATION

1987-88 Vehicles

➧ See Figure 16

1. Disconnect the negative battery cable.
2. Remove the slave cylinder as outlined later in this section.
3. Unfasten the two retaining nuts, then remove the master cylinder reservoir.
4. Disengage the pushrod from the clutch pedal.
5. Remove the master cylinder by carefully turning it 45° clockwise and gently pulling it out.
6. If necessary, remove the hydraulic pressure line.

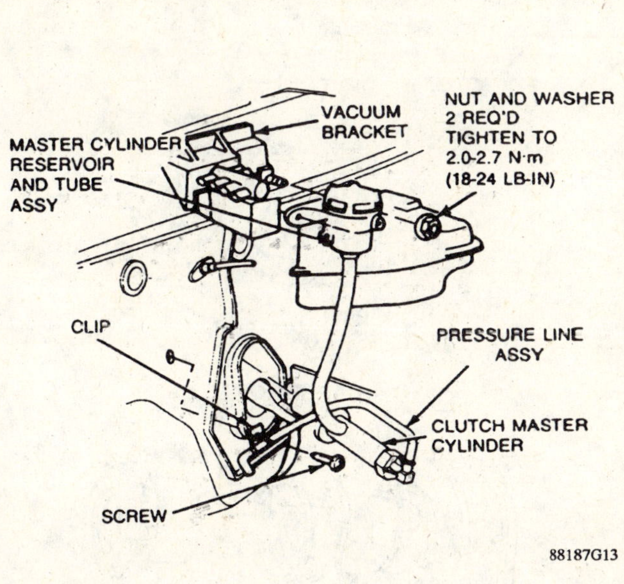

Fig. 16 Clutch master cylinder mounting — 1988 vehicle shown

To install:

7. Installation is the reverse of the removal procedure.
8. Fill the clutch master cylinder with the fresh clean DOT 3 brake fluid.
9. If the pressure line was removed, bleed the hydraulic system.
10. Connect the negative battery cable.

1989-95 Vehicles

➧ **See Figure 17**

1. Disconnect the negative battery cable.
2. Disconnect the clutch pedal from the pushrod.
3. Detach the clutch hydraulic line (slave cylinder-to-master cylinder tube) as outlined in this section.
4. Remove the two push pins retaining the clutch master cylinder reservoir to the left side shock tower.
5. Rotate the master cylinder 45° counterclockwise, then carefully pull the master cylinder through the dash panel. Note the routing of the hydraulic line to the slave cylinder before removing the master cylinder from the engine compartment.

To install:

6. Position the master cylinder in the engine compartment, then route the hydraulic line to the slave cylinder.
7. Install the master cylinder on the dash panel by turning it 45° clockwise to seat.
8. Install the master cylinder fluid reservoir.
9. Connect the hydraulic line.
10. Attach the pushrod to the clutch pedal.
11. Connect the negative battery cable.
12. Fill the reservoir and bleed the hydraulic system.

Slave Cylinder

REMOVAL & INSTALLATION

1987-88 Vehicles

➧ **See Figure 18**

➫ **Do NOT depress the clutch pedal while the slave cylinder is removed from the clutch housing.**

1. Disconnect the negative battery cable.
2. Remove the self-tapping screw, then remove the slave cylinder dust cover.
3. Unlatch the slave cylinder from the transmission housing bracket.
4. Place a drip pan under the cylinder and disconnect and cap the fluid line.

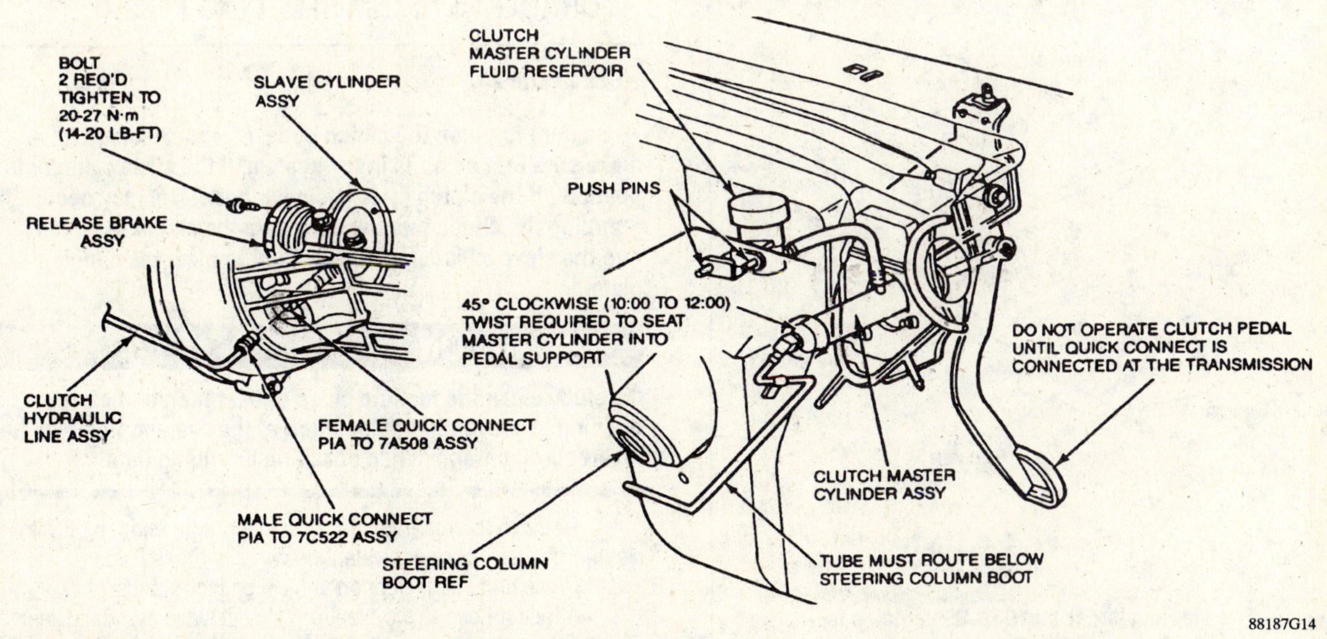

Fig. 17 Master cylinder and reservoir mounting — 1989-95 vehicles

To install:

5. Uncap and connect the hydraulic line to the slave cylinder.
6. Attach the slave cylinder to the transmission housing bracket.
7. Position the slave cylinder dust cover, then secure with the self-tapping screw.
8. Connect the negative battery cable.
9. Fill the master cylinder with the appropriate fluid, then bleed the clutch system.

1989-95 Vehicles

➧ **See Figure 19**

1. Disconnect the negative battery cable.
2. Detach the clutch master cylinder pushrod from the clutch pedal.
3. Raise and safely support the vehicle.
4. Disconnect the slave cylinder-to-master cylinder tube using the Clutch Coupling tool, as outlined earlier.
5. Remove the transmission from the vehicle.
6. Unfasten the slave cylinder retaining bolts, then remove the slave cylinder from the vehicle.

To install:

7. Position the slave cylinder over the input shaft, aligning the bleeder screw and line coupling with the holes in the transmission housing.
8. Install the slave cylinder retaining bolts and tighten to 15-19 ft. lbs. (20-27 Nm).
9. Install the transmission.
10. Attach the slave cylinder-to-master cylinder hydraulic tube/line.
11. Carefully lower the vehicle.
12. Connect the master cylinder pushrod to the clutch pedal.
13. Connect the negative battery cable, then bleed the clutch system.

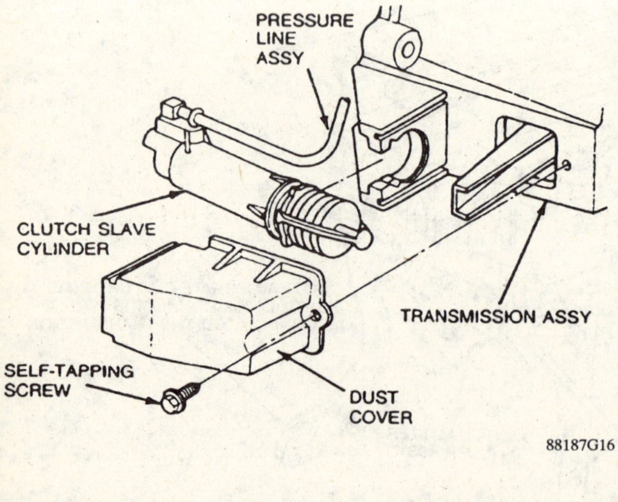

Fig. 18 The slave cylinder on 1987-88 vehicles is mounted on the transmission, under a dust cover

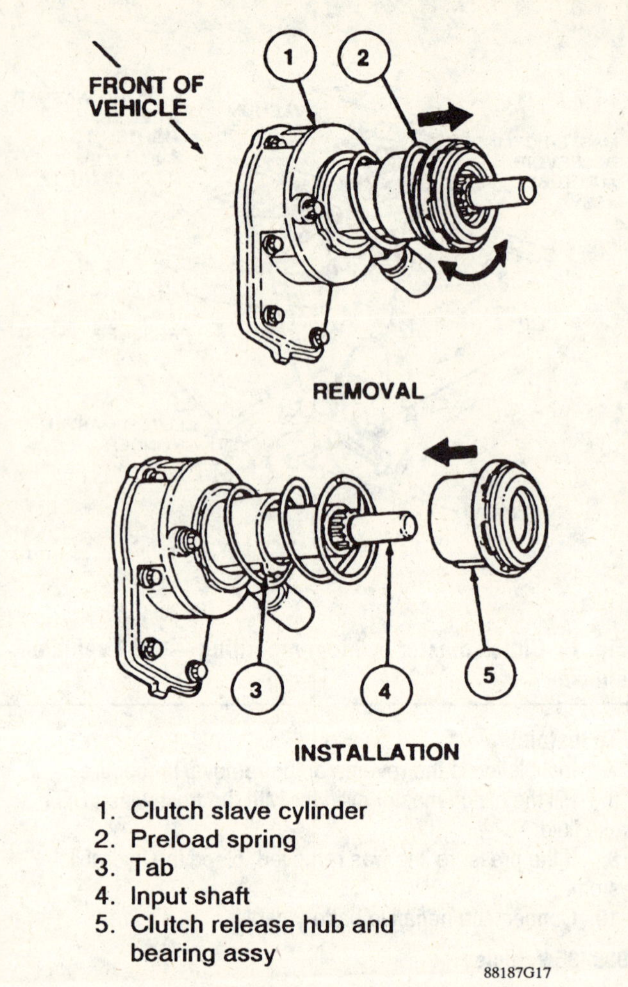

Fig. 19 On 1989-95 vehicles, you must remove the transmission to access the slave cylinder

HYDRAULIC SYSTEM BLEEDING

➧ **See Figure 20**

➥ **Be sure to pump the clutch pedal at least 30 times to make sure that no air is in the system. If the slave cylinder is pushed off the clutch plate, a similar pedal feel may occur. Pumping the clutch pushes fluid from the clutch reservoir into the slave cylinder, pushing it out to meet the clutch plate.**

✻✻CAUTION

Carefully clean the top and sides of the reservoir before opening to prevent contamination of the system. Remove the reservoir diaphragm when checking or adding fluid.

1. Remove the reservoir cap and diaphragm and top off with clean, fresh DOT 3 or equivalent heavy duty brake fluid.
2. Raise and safely support vehicle on jack stands.
3. Attach a hose to the bleeder valve at slave cylinder. Clear (Tygon) hose is recommended by the manufacturer to observe all air bubbles.

Keep the clutch master cylinder full at all times; this will prevent air from being pulled into the hydraulic system.

4. While the clutch pedal is being depressed, slightly open the bleeder valve. Observe air bubbles in clutch fluid at end of hose.
5. Close the bleeder valve before releasing the clutch pedal.
6. Repeat the previous two steps as many times as necessary until no air bubbles can be seen in the reservoir.
7. Carefully lower the vehicle and top off the reservoir. Install the diaphragm and reservoir cap.
8. Road test the vehicle for proper operation. If hard shifting, low reserve, or weak pedal are noticed, repeat the bleeding procedure.

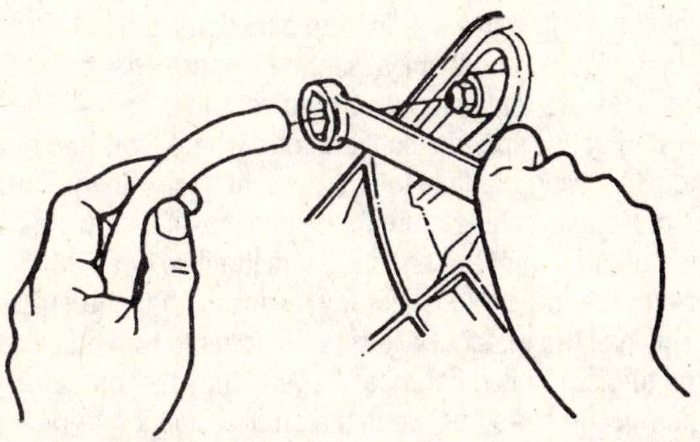

88187G18

Fig. 20 Attach a length of clear hose to the bleeder valve at the slave cylinder

AUTOMATIC TRANSMISSION

Understanding Automatic Transmissions

The automatic transmission allows engine torque and power to be transmitted to the rear wheels within a narrow range of engine operating speeds. It will allow the engine to turn fast enough to produce plenty of power and torque at very low speeds, while keeping it at a sensible rpm at high vehicle speeds (and it does this job without driver assistance). The transmission uses a light fluid as the medium for the transmission of power. This fluid also works in the operation of various hydraulic control circuits and as a lubricant. Because the transmission fluid performs all of these functions, trouble within the unit can easily travel from one part to another. For this reason, and because of the complexity and unusual operating principles of the transmission, a very sound understanding of the basic principles of operation will simplify troubleshooting.

TORQUE CONVERTER

See Figure 21

The torque converter replaces the conventional clutch. It has three functions:

1. It allows the engine to idle with the vehicle at a standstill, even with the transmission in gear.
2. It allows the transmission to shift from range-to-range smoothly, without requiring that the driver close the throttle during the shift.
3. It multiplies engine torque to an increasing extent as vehicle speed drops and throttle opening is increased. This has the effect of making the transmission more responsive and reduces the amount of shifting required.

The torque converter is a metal case which is shaped like a sphere that has been flattened on opposite sides. It is bolted to the rear end of the engine's crankshaft. Generally, the entire metal case rotates at engine speed and serves as the engine's flexplate.

The case contains three sets of blades. One set is attached directly to the case. This set forms the torus or pump. Another set is directly connected to the output shaft, and forms the turbine. The third set is mounted on a hub which, in turn, is mounted on a stationary shaft through a one-way clutch. This third set is known as the stator.

A pump, which is driven by the converter hub at engine speed, keeps the torque converter full of transmission fluid at all times. Fluid flows continuously through the unit to provide cooling.

Under low speed acceleration, the torque converter functions as follows:

The torus is turning faster than the turbine. It picks up fluid at the center of the converter and, through centrifugal force, slings it outward. Since the outer edge of the converter moves faster than the portions at the center, the fluid picks up speed.

The fluid then enters the outer edge of the turbine blades. It then travels back toward the center of the converter case along the turbine blades. In impinging upon the turbine blades, the fluid loses the energy picked up in the torus.

If the fluid was now returned directly into the torus, both halves of the converter would have to turn at approximately the same speed at all times, and torque input and output would both be the same.

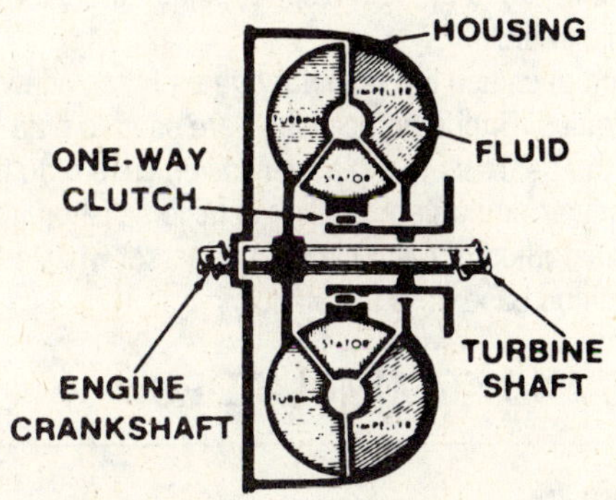

TCCS7011

Fig. 21 The torque converter housing is rotated by the engine's crankshaft, and turns the impeller — The impeller then spins the turbine, which gives motion to the turbine shaft, driving the gears

In flowing through the torus and turbine, the fluid picks up two types of flow, or flow in two separate directions. It flows through the turbine blades, and it spins with the engine. The stator, whose blades are stationary when the vehicle is being accelerated at low speeds, converts one type of flow into another. Instead of allowing the fluid to flow straight back into the torus, the stator's curved blades turn the fluid almost 90° toward the direction of rotation of the engine. Thus the fluid does not flow as fast toward the torus, but is already spinning when the torus picks it up. This has the effect of allowing the torus to turn much faster than the turbine. This difference in speed may be compared to the difference in speed between the smaller and larger gears in any gear train. The result is that engine power output is higher, and engine torque is multiplied.

As the speed of the turbine increases, the fluid spins faster and faster in the direction of engine rotation. As a result, the ability of the stator to redirect the fluid flow is reduced. Under cruising conditions, the stator is eventually forced to rotate on its one-way clutch in the direction of engine rotation. Under these conditions, the torque converter begins to behave almost like a solid shaft, with the torus and turbine speeds being almost equal.

PLANETARY GEARBOX

➧ See Figures 22, 23 and 24

The ability of the torque converter to multiply engine torque is limited. Also, the unit tends to be more efficient when the turbine is rotating at relatively high speeds. Therefore, a planetary gearbox is used to carry the power output of the turbine to the driveshaft.

Planetary gears function very similarly to conventional transmission gears. However, their construction is different in that three elements make up one gear system, and, in that all three elements are different from one another. The three elements are: an outer gear that is shaped like a hoop, with teeth cut into the inner surface; a sun gear, mounted on a shaft and located at the very center of the outer gear; and a set of three planet gears, held by pins in a ring-like planet carrier, meshing with both the sun gear and the outer gear. Either the outer gear or the sun gear may be held stationary, providing more than one possible torque multiplication factor for each set of gears. Also, if all three gears are forced to rotate at the same speed, the gearset forms, in effect, a solid shaft.

Most automatics use the planetary gears to provide various reductions ratios. Bands and clutches are used to hold various portions of the gearsets to the transmission case or to the shaft on which they are mounted. Shifting is accomplished, then, by changing the portion of each planetary gearset which is held to the transmission case or to the shaft.

SERVOS AND ACCUMULATORS

➧ See Figure 25

The servos are hydraulic pistons and cylinders. They resemble the hydraulic actuators used on many other machines, such as bulldozers. Hydraulic fluid enters the cylinder, under pressure, and forces the piston to move to engage the band or clutches.

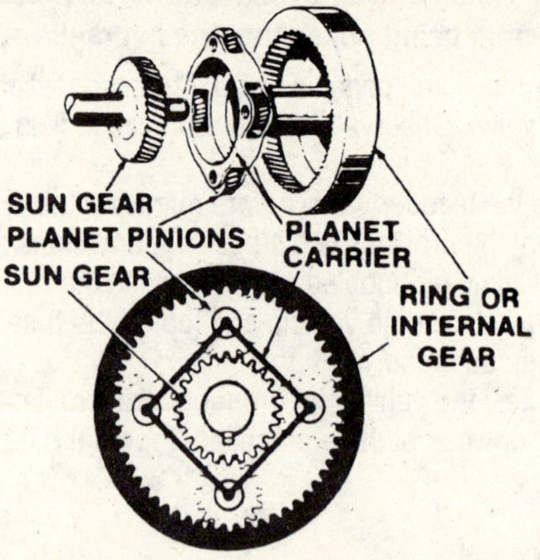

Fig. 22 Planetary gears work in a similar fashion to manual transmission gears, but are composed of three parts

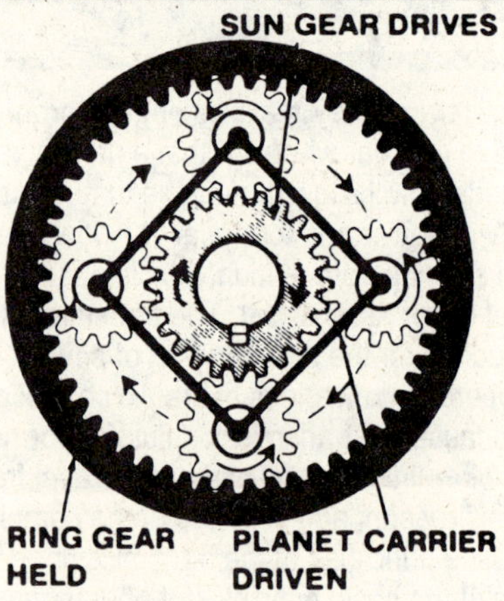

Fig. 23 Planetary gears in the maximum reduction (low) range. The ring gear is held and a lower gear ratio is obtained

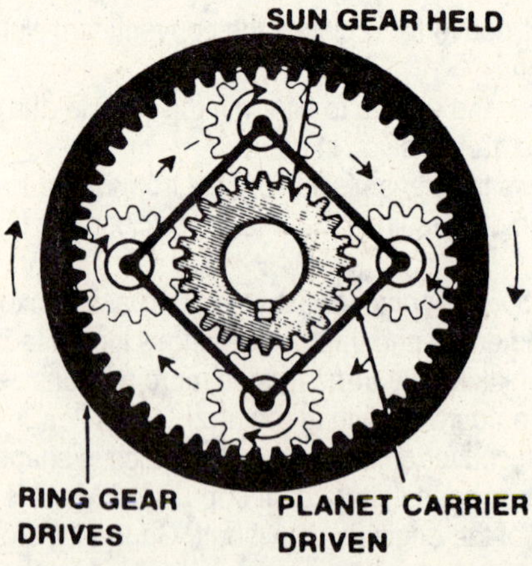

Fig. 24 Planetary gears in the minimum reduction (drive) range. The ring gear is allowed to revolve, providing a higher gear ratio

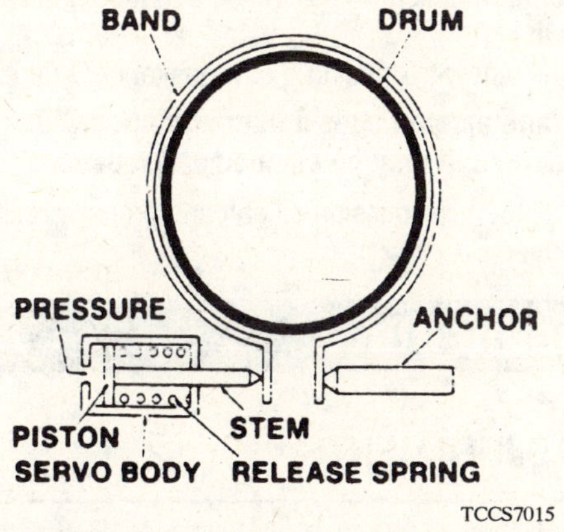

Fig. 25 Servos, operated by pressure, are used to apply or release the bands, to either hold the ring gear or allow it to rotate

The accumulators are used to cushion the engagement of the servos. The transmission fluid must pass through the accumulator on the way to the servo. The accumulator housing contains a thin piston which is sprung away from the discharge passage of the accumulator. When fluid passes through the accumulator on the way to the servo, it must move the piston against spring pressure, and this action smooths out the action of the servo.

HYDRAULIC CONTROL SYSTEM

The hydraulic pressure used to operate the servos comes from the main transmission oil pump. This fluid is channeled to the various servos through the shift valves. There is generally a manual shift valve which is operated by the transmission selector lever and an automatic shift valve for each automatic upshift the transmission provides.

Many new transmissions are electronically controlled. On these models, electrical solenoids are used to better control the hydraulic fluid. Usually, the solenoids are regulated by an electronic control module.

There are two pressures which affect the operation of these valves. One is the governor pressure which is effected by vehicle speed. The other is the modulator pressure which is effected by intake manifold vacuum or throttle position. Governor pressure rises with an increase in vehicle speed, and modulator pressure rises as the throttle is opened wider. By responding to these two pressures, the shift valves cause the upshift points to be delayed with increased throttle opening to make the best use of the engine's power output.

Most transmissions also make use of an auxiliary circuit for downshifting. This circuit may be actuated by the throttle linkage the vacuum line which actuates the modulator, by a cable or by a solenoid. It applies pressure to a special downshift surface on the shift valve or valves.

The transmission modulator also governs the line pressure, used to actuate the servos. In this way, the clutches and bands will be actuated with a force matching the torque output of the engine.

Identification

There are 5 different automatic transmissions used on theses vehicles: C3, C5, A4LD, AOD and 4R70W. For automatic transmission identification information, please refer to Section 1 of this manual.

Fluid Pan

Refer to Section 1 for current fluid requirements.

REMOVAL & INSTALLATION

See Figures 26 and 27

1. Raise and safely support the vehicle on jackstands.
2. Place a drain pan under the transmission.
3. Loosen the pan attaching bolts and drain the fluid from the transmission.

Always place used fluids and oils into a sealed storage container and take to an approved recycling collection facility. Never dump used fluids or oils on the ground or in a trash receptacle. Contamination to the environment can and will occur.

4. When the fluid has drained to the level of the pan flange, remove the remaining pan bolts working from the rear and both sides of the pan to allow it to drop and drain slowly.
5. Some AOD transmissions will have a plastic plunger type plug floating loosely in the pan when draining the fluid. It is of no importance and was used in the assembly process of the transmission. Discard it before reinstallation of pan.
6. When all of the fluid has drained, remove the pan and clean it thoroughly. discard the pan gasket. If equipped, remove the pan magnet.

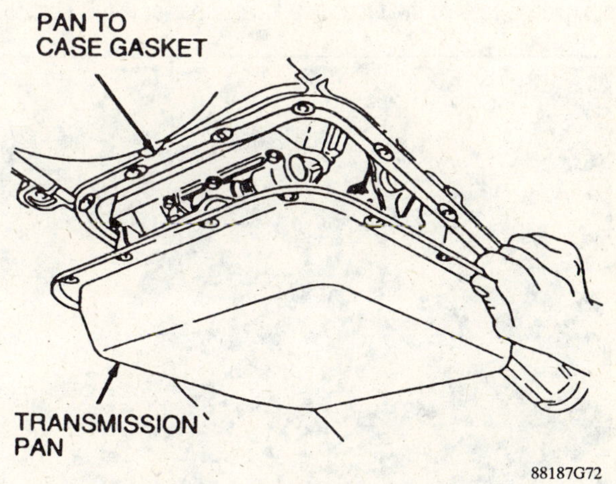

Fig. 26 Unfasten the remaining bolts, then remove the transmission fluid pan from the vehicle

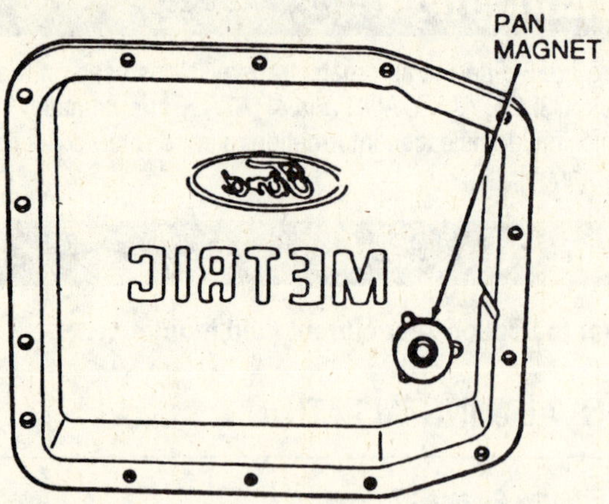

88187G73

Fig. 27 On some vehicles, such as this 1995, you must remove and clean the pan magnet

To install:

7. Place a new gasket on the pan, then install the pan on the transmission. If equipped, don't forget to install the pan magnet. Tighten the pan attaching bolts as follows:
   - C3 and C5 Transmissions: 12–16 ft. lbs. (16–22 Nm)
   - A4LD Transmissions: 8–10 ft. lbs. (11–13.5 Nm)
   - AOD Transmissions: 71–119 inch lbs. (8–13 Nm)
   - 4R70W Transmissions: 9–11 ft. lbs. (12–15 Nm)
8. Add the correct type and quantity of fluid to the transmission through the filler tube.
9. Lower the vehicle. Start the engine and move the gear selector through shift pattern. Allow the engine to reach normal operating temperature.
10. Check the transmission fluid. Add fluid, if necessary, to maintain correct level.

FILTER SERVICE

See Figure 28

1. Remove the transmission oil pan and drain the fluid. For details, please refer to the procedure located earlier in this section.

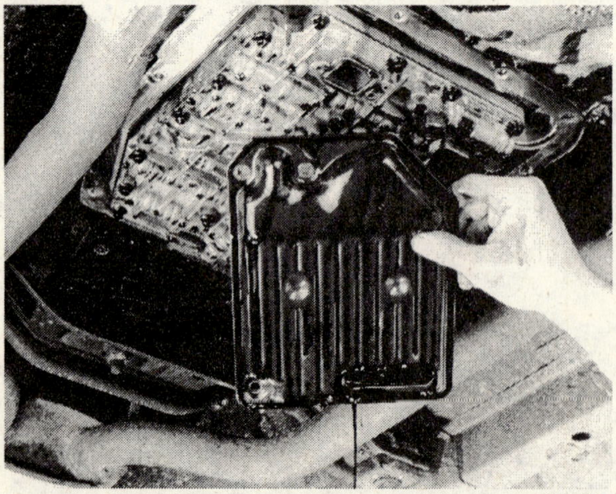

88187P01

Fig. 28 After the pan is removed, you can remove the transmission fluid filter

2. Remove the screen and the filter from the valve body. Most screens are retained using a fastener; through some may use an interference fit between the screen tube and valve body.

To install:

3. Install a new filter using a new gasket or O-ring.

If the transmission uses a filter equipped with a fully exposed screen, it may be cleaned and reused.

4. Install the transmission oil pan and properly refill the transmission.

Adjustments

BAND ADJUSTMENTS

No external adjustments are possible on AOD or 4R70W transmissions.

C3 Front Band

See Figure 29

1. Wipe clean the area around the adjusting screw on the side of the transmission, near the left front corner of the transmission.
2. Remove the adjusting screw locknut and discard it.
3. Install a new locknut on the adjusting screw but do not tighten it.
4. Tighten the adjusting screw to exactly 10 ft. lbs. (13.5 Nm).
5. Back off the adjusting screw exactly 2 turns.
6. Hold the adjusting screw so that it does not turn and tighten the adjusting screw locknut to 35–45 ft. lbs. (47–61 Nm).

C5 Intermediate Band

See Figure 30

1. Clean all the dirt from the adjusting screw and remove and discard the locknut.
2. Install a new locknut on the adjusting screw. Using a torque wrench, tighten the adjusting screw to 10 ft. lbs. (13.5 Nm).

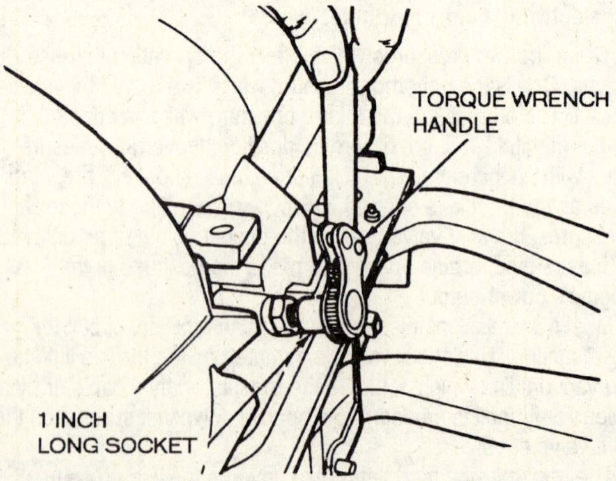

88187G57

Fig. 29 Front band adjustment — C3 transmissions

88187G58

Fig. 30 Intermediate band adjustment — C5 transmissions

3. Back off the adjusting screw exactly $4^1/_4$ turns.
4. Hold the adjusting screw steady and tighten the locknut to 35 ft. lbs. (47 Nm).

C5 Low-Reverse Band

➧ See Figure 31

1. Clean all dirt from around the band adjusting screw, and remove and discard the locknut.
2. Install a new locknut of the adjusting screw. Using a torque wrench, tighten the adjusting screw to 10 ft. lbs. (13.5 Nm).
3. Back off the adjusting screw exactly 3 full turns.
4. Hold the adjusting screw steady and tighten the locknut to 35 ft. lbs. (47 Nm).

A4LD Overdrive and Intermediate Band

➧ See Figures 32 and 33

Both band adjustment screws are located on the left side of transmission, the front being the overdrive band and the rear being the intermediate band adjustment screw. Both adjustment screws use the same procedure for adjustment.

1. Remove and discard locking nut from adjustment screw.
2. Install a new locking nut but do not tighten.
3. Using a torque wrench, tighten the adjusting screw to 10 ft. lbs. (13.5 Nm).
4. Back off adjusting screw exactly 2 turns.
5. Hold adjusting screw from turning. Tighten locknut to 35–45 ft. lbs. (47–61 Nm).

SHIFT LINKAGE ADJUSTMENT

Column Shift

➧ See Figures 34, 35, 36 and 37

1. With the engine off, place the gear selector in the D (Drive) position, or OD (Overdrive) position (AOD). Either hang a weight on the shifter or have an assistant sit in the car and hold the selector against the stop.
2. Loosen the adjusting nut or clamp at the shift lever so that the shift rod is free to slide. On models with a shift cable, remove the nut from the transmission lever and disconnect the cable from the transmission.
3. Place the manual shift lever on the transmission in the D (Drive) or OD (Overdrive) position. This is the second detent position from the full counterclockwise position.
4. Tighten the adjusting bolt. On cars with a cable, position the cable end on the transmission lever stud, aligning the flats. Tighten the adjusting nut.
5. Check the pointer alignment and transmission operation for all selector positions. If not correct, adjust linkage.

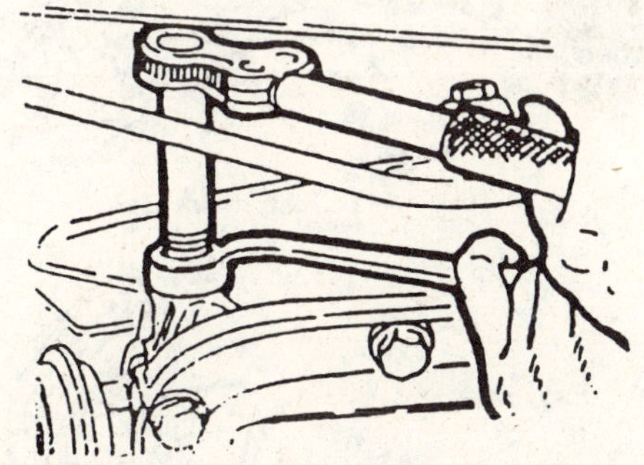
88187G59

Fig. 31 Low-reverse band adjustment — C5 transmissions

88187G60

Fig. 32 A4LD overdrive band adjustment

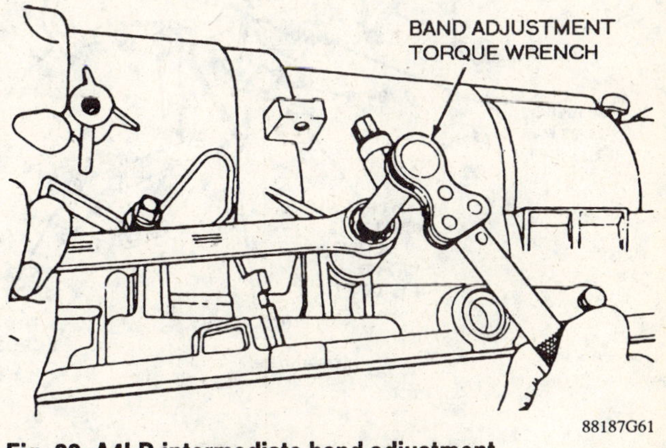

88187G61

Fig. 33 A4LD intermediate band adjustment

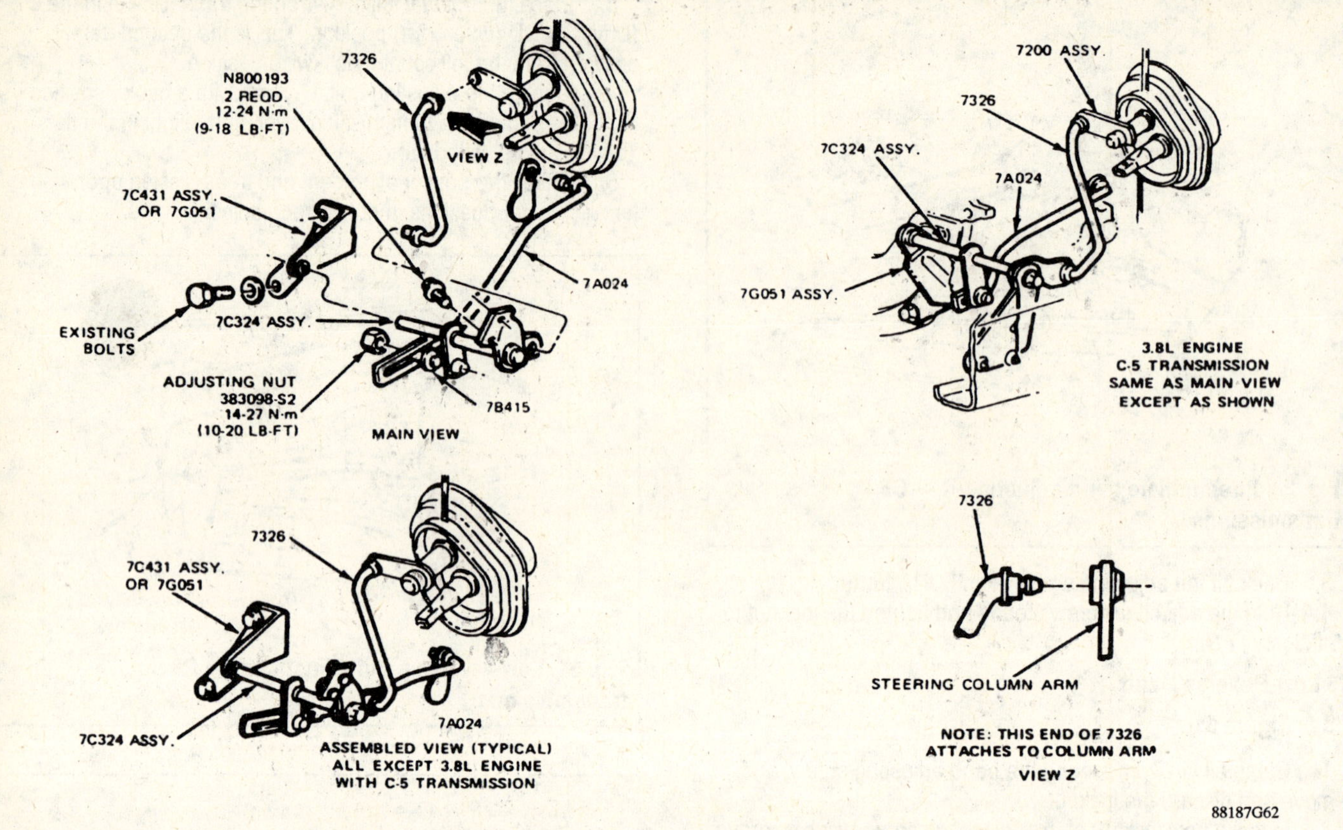

Fig. 34 Manual linkage on column shift — 1983 vehicles, except AOD transmissions

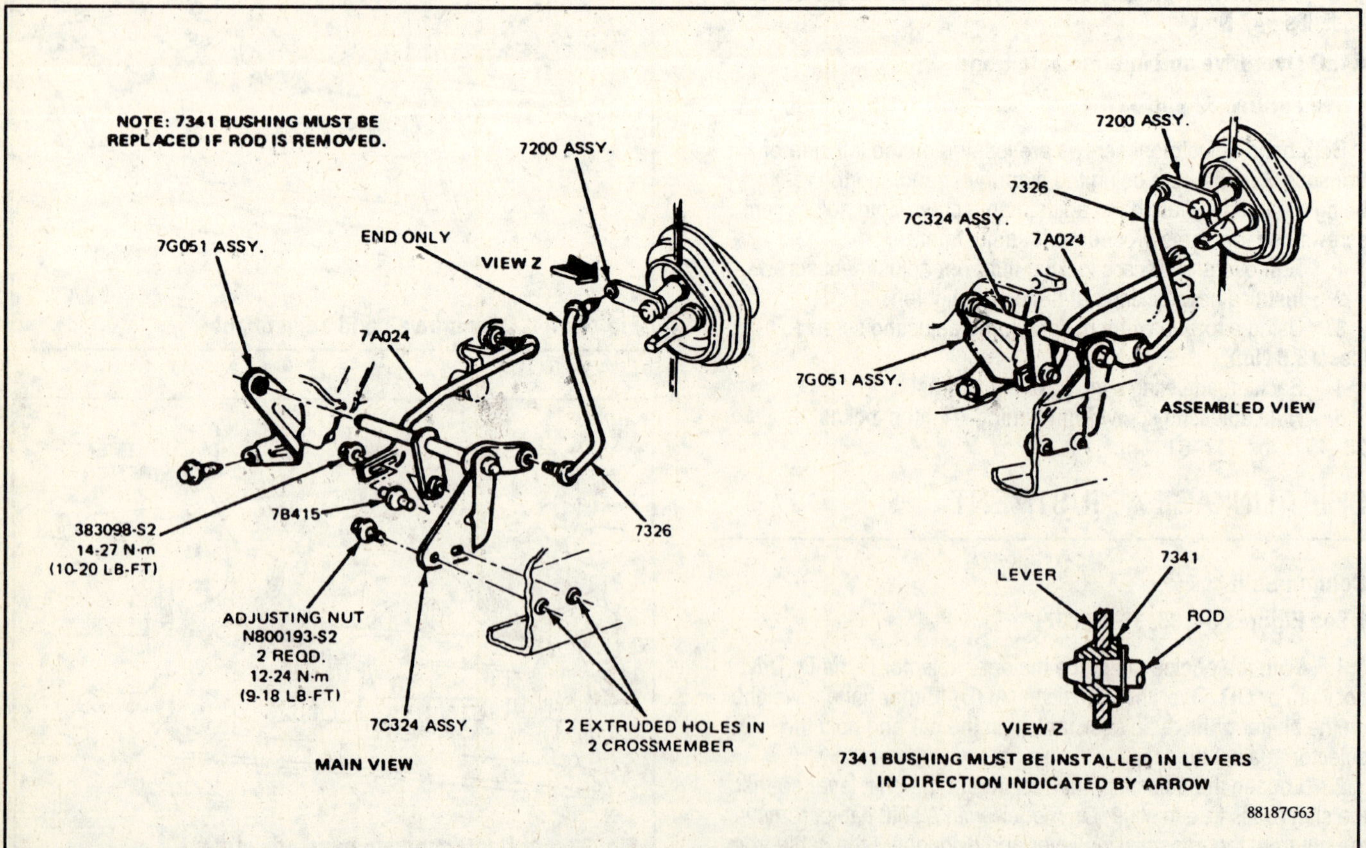

Fig. 35 Manual linkage on column shift — 1983 vehicles with AOD transmissions

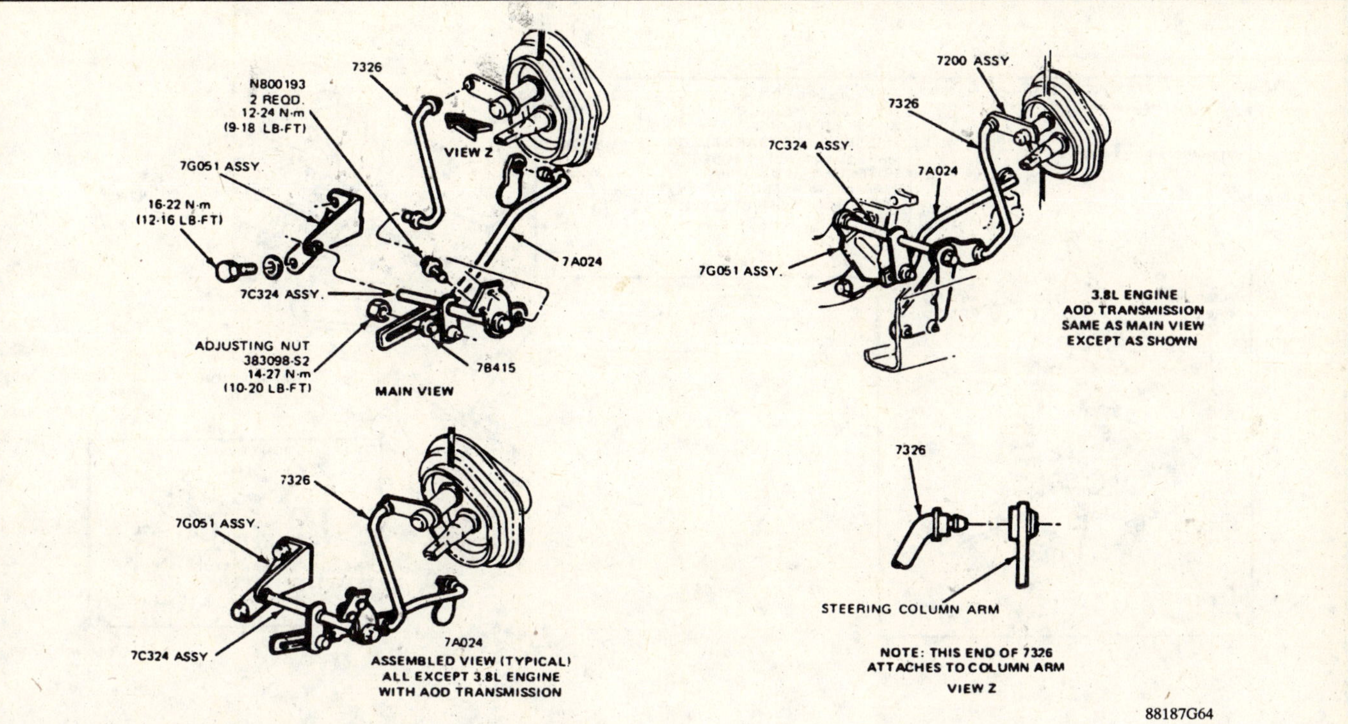

Fig. 36 Manual linkage on 1984–86 column shift models

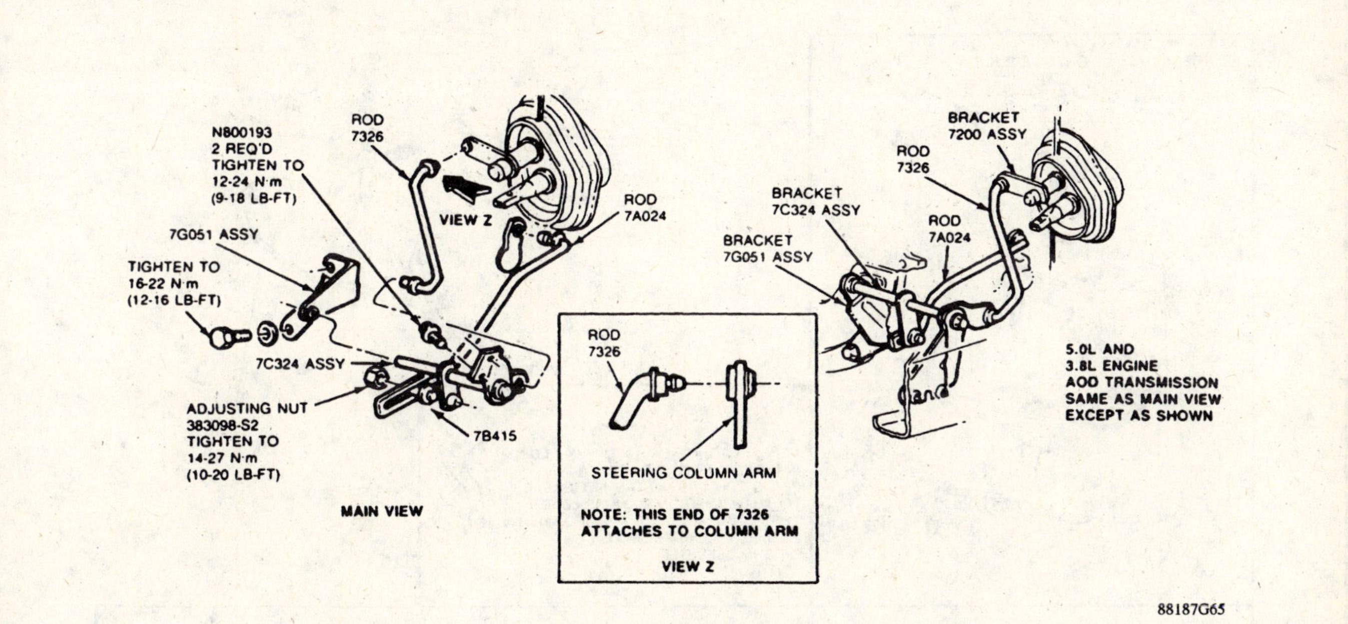

Fig. 37 Manual linkage on 1987–88 column shift vehicles with AOD transmissions

Floor or Console Shift

➧ See Figures 38, 39, 40, 41 and 42

1. Place the transmission shift lever in D (OD for AOD transmission).
2. Raise the vehicle and loosen the manual lever shift rod retaining nut. Move the transmission lever to D or OD position. D is the second detent, OD is the third from the full counterclockwise position.
3. With the transmission shift lever and transmission manual lever in position, tighten the nut at point A to 14–19 ft. lbs. (19–26 Nm).
4. Check transmission operation for all selector lever detent positions.

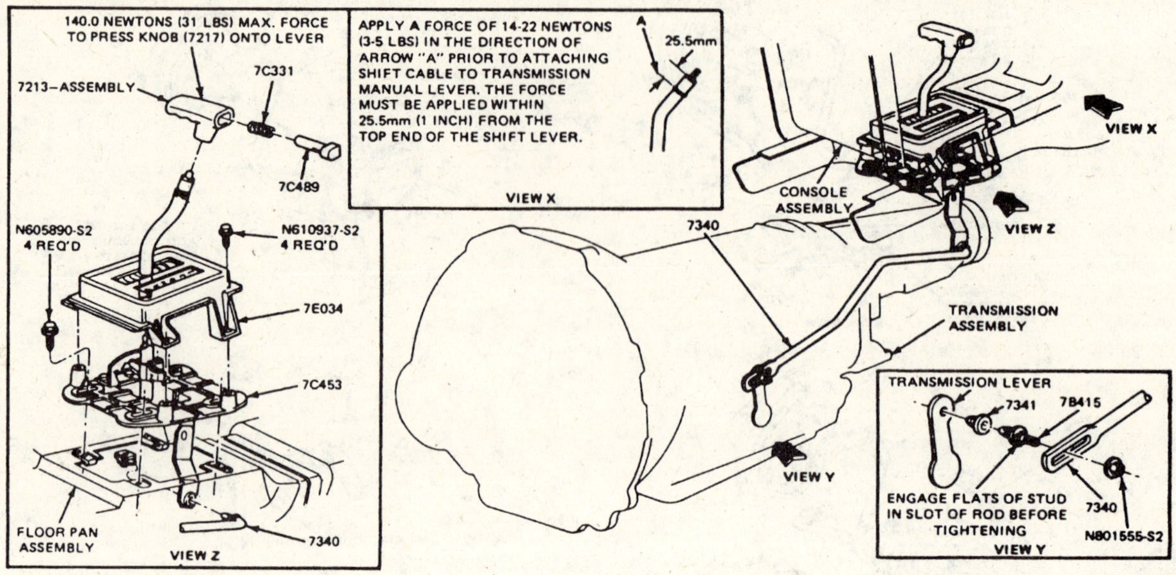

88187G66

Fig. 38 Manual linkage on 1984–86 floor shift Turbo vehicles

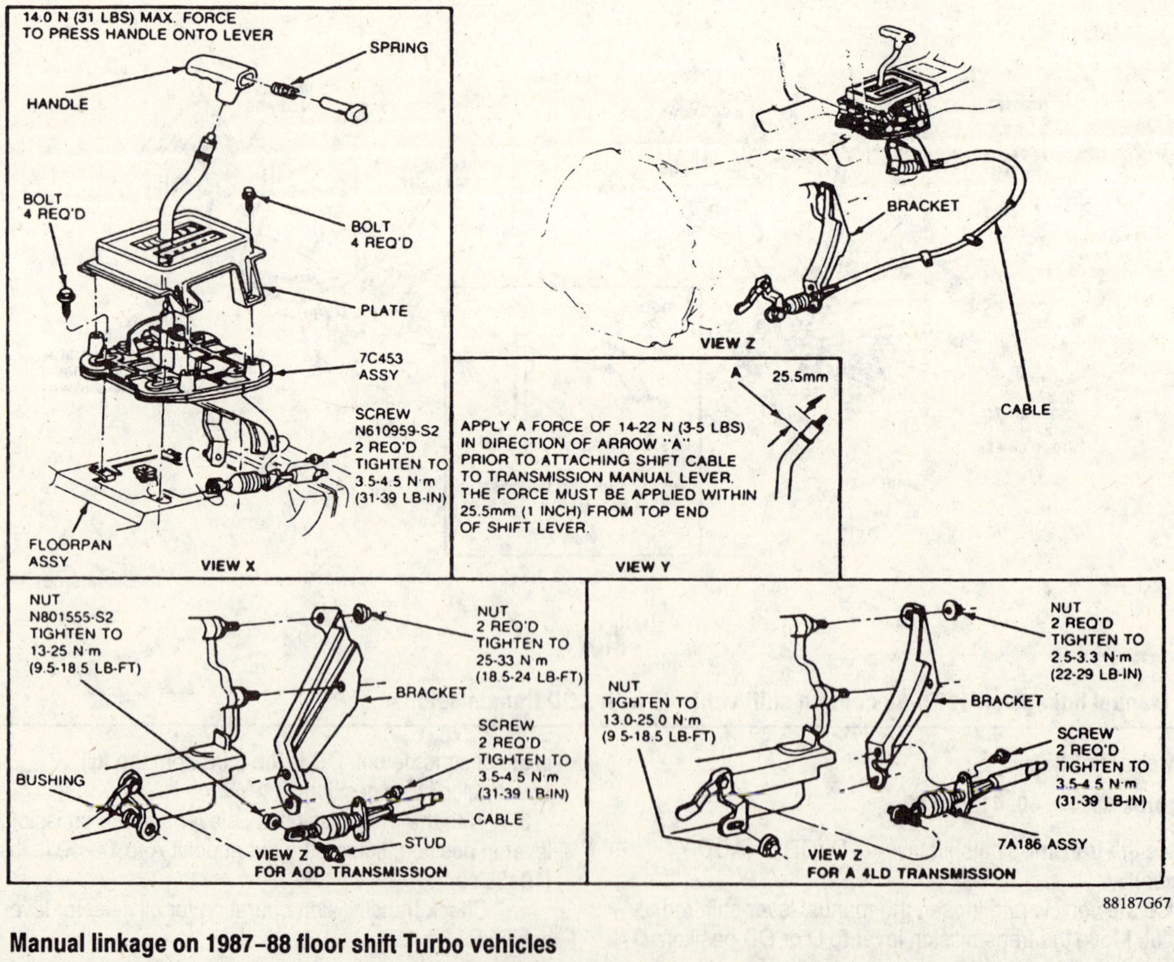

88187G67

Fig. 39 Manual linkage on 1987–88 floor shift Turbo vehicles

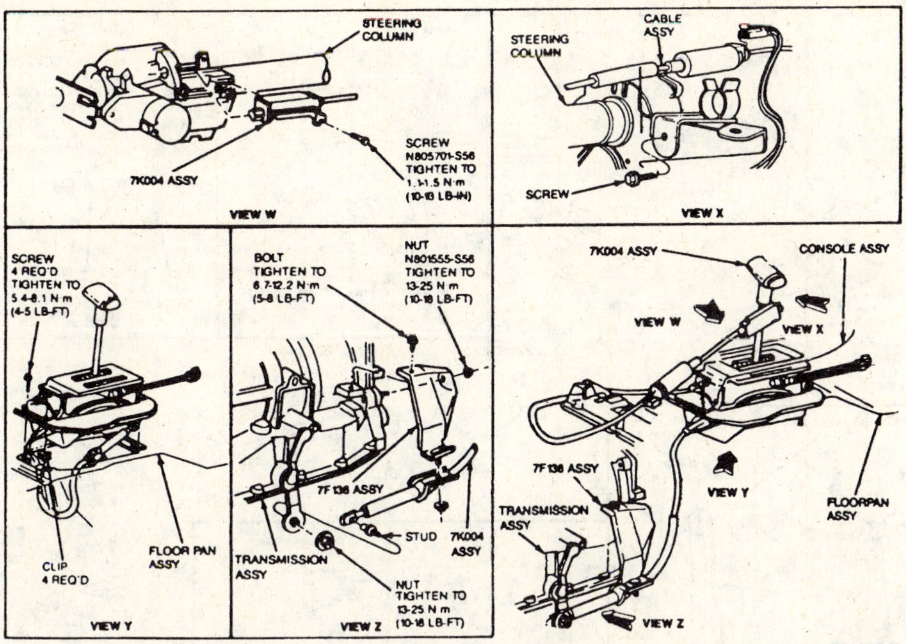

88187G68

Fig. 40 View of the manual linkage routing (cable type) — 1989–93 vehicles

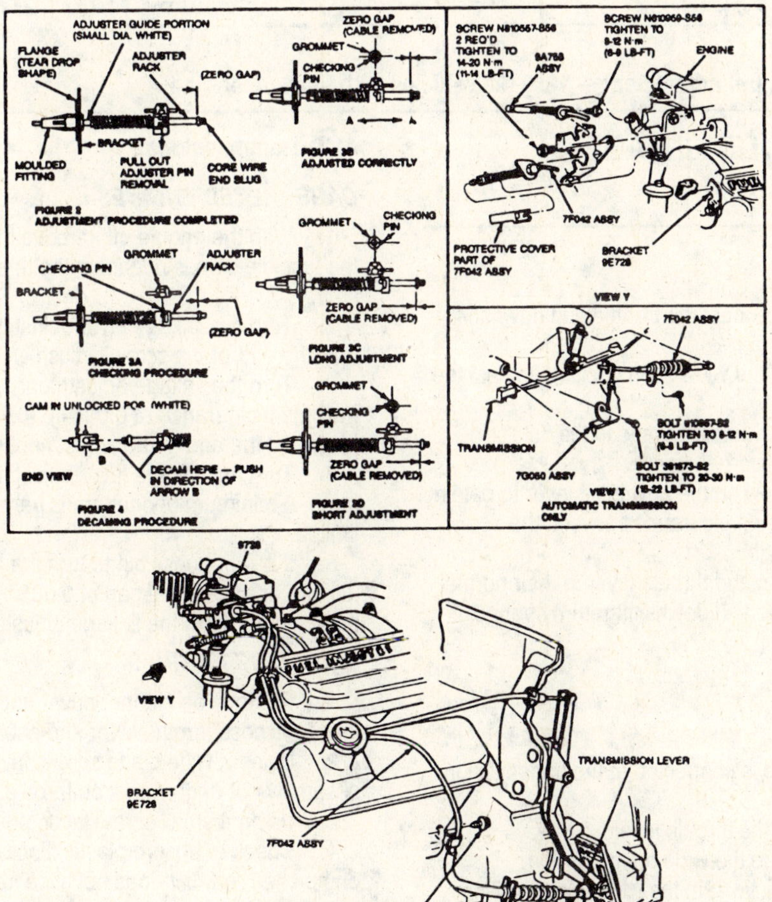

88187G69

Fig. 41 Automatic shift control adjustment — 1989–93 vehicles with the 3.8L engine

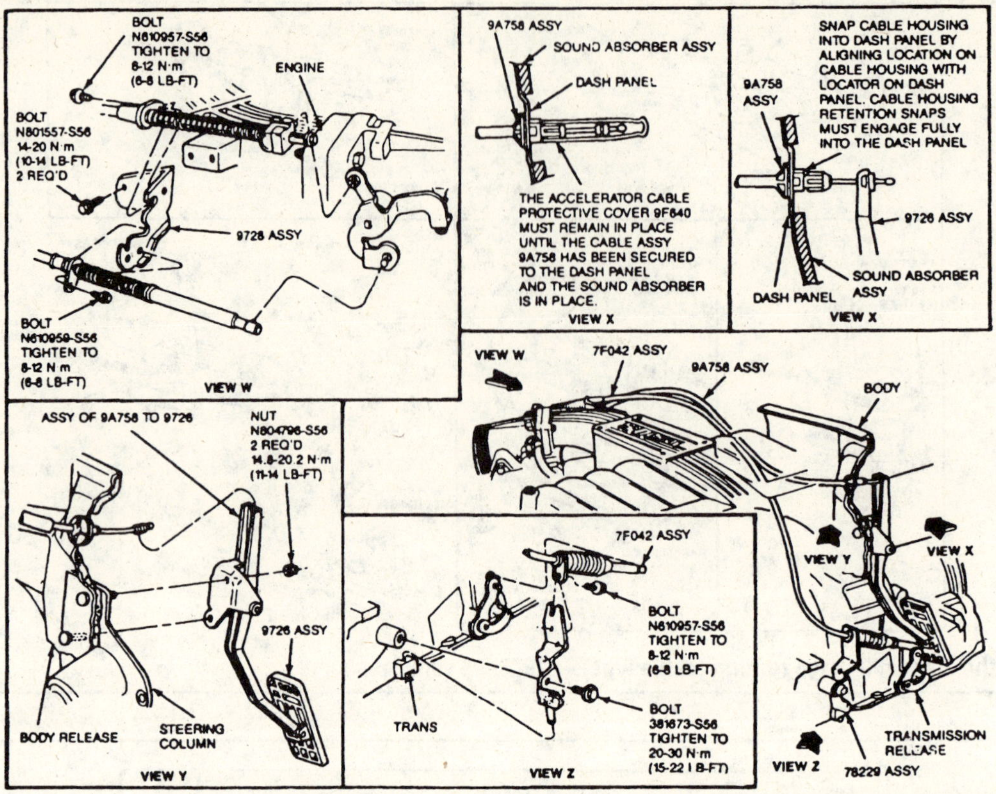

Fig. 42 Automatic shift control adjustment — 1989–93 vehicles with the 5.0L engine

DOWNSHIFT (THROTTLE) LINKAGE ADJUSTMENT

C3 And C5 Transmissions

1. With the engine off, disconnect the throttle and downshift return springs, if equipped.
2. Hold the throttle lever in the wide open position against the stop.
3. Hold the transmission downshift linkage in the full downshift position against the internal stop.
4. Turn the adjustment screw on the downshift lever to obtain 0.010–0.080 in. (0.254–2.032mm) clearance between the screw tip and the throttle shaft lever tab.
5. Release the transmission and throttle lever to their normal free positions. Install the throttle and downshift return springs, if removed.

A4LD Transmissions

➧ **See Figure 43**

1. Make sure that the cable is connected at the transmission kickdown lever.
2. Disconnect the cable at the throttle lever.
3. Rotate the throttle lever to the wide open position.
4. While holding the throttle lever in the wide open position, attach the cable, install the clip and push the locking lever into place.

AOD Transmissions

CARBURETED ENGINES

1. With the engine off, remove the air cleaner and make sure the fast idle cam is released; the throttle lever must be at the idle stop.
2. Turn the linkage lever adjusting screw counterclockwise until the end of the screw is flush with the face of the lever.
3. Turn the linkage adjustment screw in until there is a maximum clearance of 0.005 in. (0.127mm) between the throttle lever and the end of the adjustment screw.
4. Turn the linkage lever adjusting screw clockwise three full turns. A minimum of one turn is permissible if the screw travel is limited.
5. If it is not possible to turn the adjusting screw at least one full turn or if the initial gap of 0.005 in. (0.127mm) could not be obtained, perform the linkage adjustment at the transmission.

EFI AND SC ENGINES

1. Remove air cleaner cover and inlet tube from throttle body inlet to access throttle lever and cable assembly.
2. Using a wide blade screw driver, pry grooved pin on cable assembly out of grommet on throttle body lever.
3. Using a small screwdriver, push out white locking tab.
4. Check to ensure plastic block with pin and tab slides freely on notched rod. If it does not slide freely, the white tab may not be pushed out far enough.
5. While holding throttle lever firmly against its idle stop, push grooved pin into grommet on throttle lever as far as it will go.
6. Install air cleaner cover and air inlet tube.

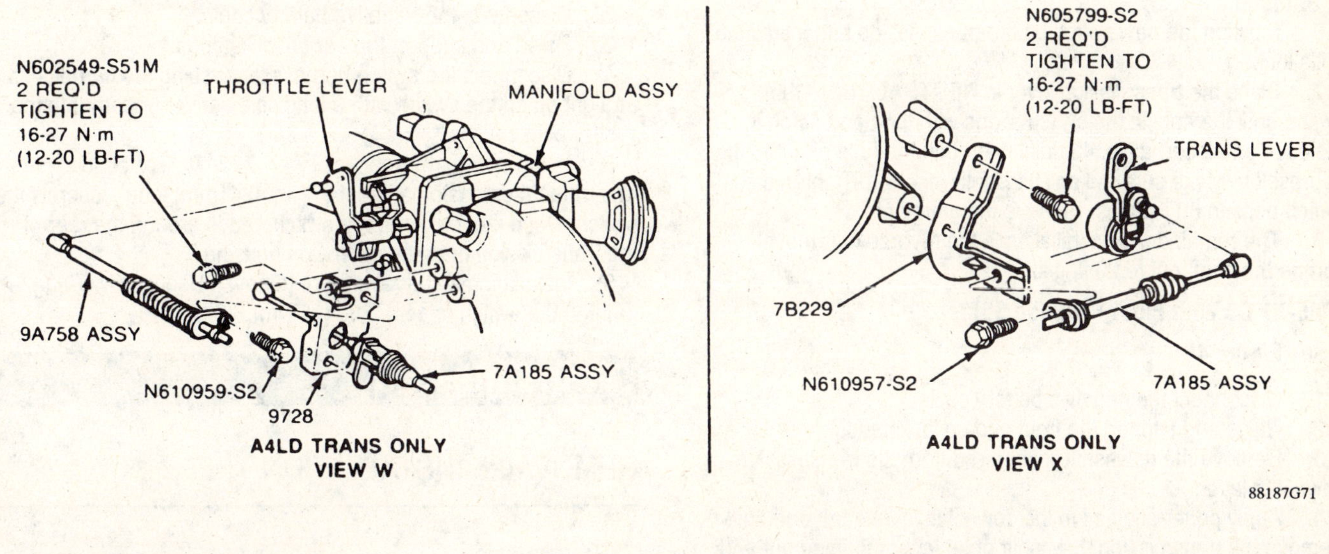

Fig. 43 A4LD downshift linkage

AOD Alternate Method

CARBURETED ENGINES ONLY

If you are unable to adjust the throttle valve control linkage at the carburetor, as described above, proceed as follows.

1. At the transmission, loosen the 8 mm bolt on the throttle (TV) control rod sliding trunnion block. Make sure the trunnion block slides freely on the control rod.
2. Push up on the lower end of the TV control rod to insure that the carburetor linkage lever is held against the throttle lever. When the pressure is released, the control rod must stay in position.
3. Force the TV control lever on the transmission against its internal stop. While maintaining pressure tighten the trunnion block bolt. Make sure the throttle lever is at the idle stop.

AOD IDLE SPEED ADJUSTMENT

Whenever it is necessary to adjust the idle speed by more than 50 rpm either above or below the factory specifications, the adjustment screw on the linkage lever at the carburetor should be used. $1\frac{1}{2}$ turns either way will change the idle speed by 50–100 rpm; $2\frac{1}{2}$ turns either way will change the idle speed by 100–150 rpm.

On models with EFI or SC engines an Air Bypass valve is used and idle setting does not effect TV cable adjustment

After making any idle speed adjustments, make sure the linkage lever and throttle lever are in contact with the throttle lever at its idle stop and verify that the shift lever is in N (neutral).

Back-Up Light Switch

Vehicles with column mounted shifters are covered in the previous Section. Vehicles with a floor mounted shifter incorporate the back-up light switch with the neutral start switch. For those vehicles, see the Neutral Start Switch procedure located in this section.

Neutral Start Switch

REMOVAL & INSTALLATION

See Figure 44

The neutral safety switch on C3 and A4LD transmission is non-adjustable.

1983–84 C5 With Floor Mounted Shifter

1. Raise and support the front end on jackstands.
2. Remove the downshift linkage rod from the transmission downshift lever.
3. Apply penetrating oil to the downshift lever shaft and nut. Remove the transmission downshift outer lever retaining nut and lever.

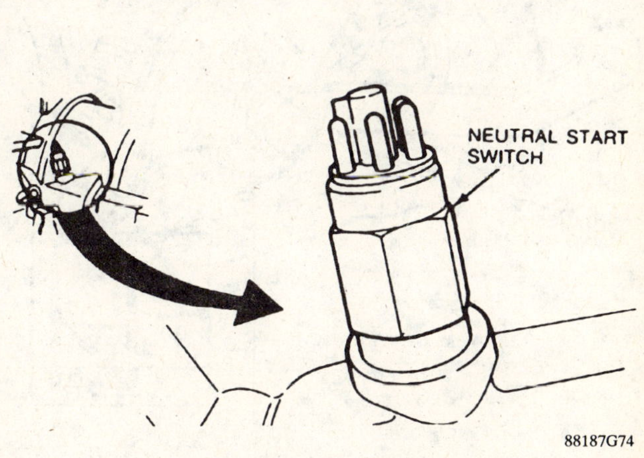

Fig. 44 Neutral start switch used on the C3, AOD and A4LD

4. Remove the 2 switch attaching screws.
5. Unplug the connector and remove the switch.

To install:

6. Position the new switch on the transmission and install the bolts loosely.
7. Place the transmission lever in NEUTRAL, rotate the switch until the hole in the switch aligns with the depression in the case and insert a No. 43 drill bit through the hole and into the depression. Make sure the drill bit is fully inserted. Tighten the switch bolts to 60 inch lbs. Remove the gauge pin.
8. The remainder of installation is the reverse of removal. Torque the shaft nut to 20 ft. lbs.

1985-87 C5 With Floor Mounted Shifter

➧ See Figure 45

1. Disconnect the negative battery cable.
2. Raise and support the front end on jackstands.
3. Remove the downshift linkage rod from the transmission downshift lever.
4. Apply penetrating oil to the downshift lever shaft and nut. Remove the transmission downshift outer lever retaining nut and lever.
5. Remove the 2 switch attaching screws.
6. Unplug the connector and remove the switch.

To install:

7. Position the new switch on the transmission and install the bolts loosely.
8. Place the transmission lever in NEUTRAL, rotate the switch until the hole in the switch aligns with the depression in the case and insert a No. 43 drill bit through the hole and into the depression. Make sure the drill bit is fully inserted. Tighten the switch bolts to 60 inch lbs. (7.3 Nm). Remove the gauge pin.
9. The remainder of installation is the reverse of removal. Tighten the shaft nut to 20 ft. lbs. (27 Nm).
10. Connect the negative battery cable.

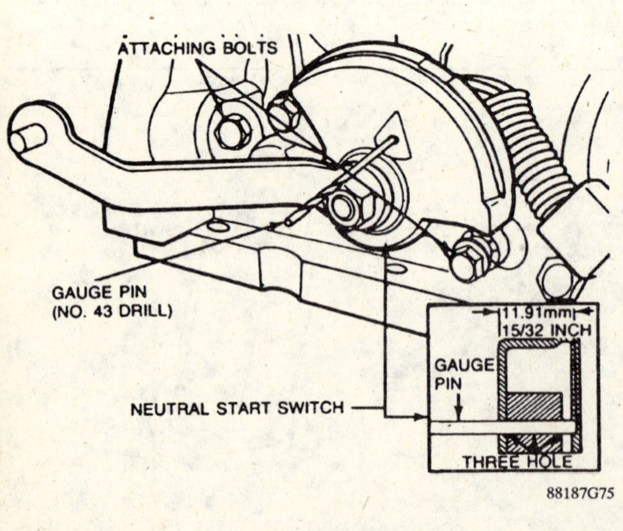

Fig. 45 Neutral start switch adjustment — C5 transmission

1985-93 AOD With Floor Mounted Shifter

1. Place the selector lever in the MANUAL LOW position.
2. Disconnect the negative battery cable.
3. Raise and support the car on jackstands.
4. Disconnect the switch harness by pushing the harness straight up off the switch with a long screwdriver underneath the rubber plug section.
5. Using special tool socket T74P-77247-A, or equivalent, on a ratchet extension at least $9^1/_2$ in. (241mm) long, unscrew the switch. Once the tool is on the switch, reach around the rear of the transmission over the extension housing.
6. Installation is the reverse of removal. Use a new O-ring. Tighten the switch to 11 ft. lbs. (15 Nm).

Transmission

REMOVAL & INSTALLATION

C3 Transmission

➧ See Figure 46

1. Disconnect the negative battery cable.
2. Raise and safely support the vehicle.
3. Place a drain pan under the transmission fluid pan. Starting at the rear of the pan and working toward the front, loosen the attaching bolts and allow the fluid to drain. Then remove all of the pan attaching bolts except two at the front, to allow the fluid to further drain. After all the fluid has drained, install two bolts on the rear side of the pan to temporarily hold it in place.
4. Remove the converter drain plug access cover and adapter plate bolts from the lower end of the converter housing.
5. Remove the four flexplate-to-converter attaching nuts. Crank the engine to turn the converter to gain access to the nuts, using a wrench on the crankshaft pulley attaching bolt. On 2.3L engines, never turn the engine backwards.
6. Crank the engine until the converter drain plug is accessible and remove the plug. Place a drain pan under the converter to catch the fluid. After all the fluid has been drained from the converter, reinstall the plug and tighten to 20-30 ft. lbs. (28-40 Nm).
7. Remove the driveshaft and install the extension housing seal replacer tool in the extension housing.
8. Remove the speedometer cable from the extension housing.
9. Disconnect the shift rod at the transmission manual lever using Shift Linkage Grommet Remover T84P-7341-A or equivalent. Disconnect the downshift rod at the transmission downshift lever.
10. Remove the starter-to-converter housing attaching bolts and position the starter out of the way.
11. Disconnect the neutral start switch wires from the switch.
12. Remove the vacuum line from the transmission vacuum unit.
13. Position a transmission jack under the transmission and raise it slightly.
14. Remove the engine rear support-to-crossmember nut.
15. Remove the crossmember-to-frame side support attaching bolts and remove the crossmember.

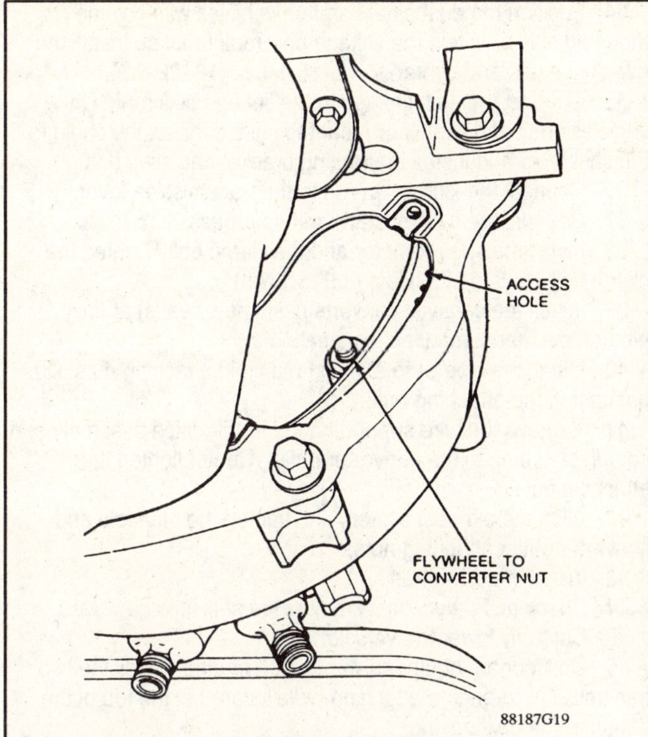

Fig. 46 Converter hub-to-flange position — C3 transmission

16. Remove the inlet pipe steady rest from the inlet pipe and rear engine support; then disconnect the muffler inlet pipe at the exhaust manifold and secure it.
17. Lower the jack under the transmission and allow the transmission to hang.
18. Position a jack to the front of the engine and raise the engine to gain access to the two upper converter housing-to-engine attaching bolts.
19. Disconnect the oil cooler lines at the transmission. Plug all openings to keep out dirt.
20. Remove the lower converter housing-to-engine attaching bolts.
21. Remove the transmission filter tube.
22. Secure the transmission to the jack with a safety chain.
23. Remove the two upper converter housing-to-engine attaching bolts. Move the transmission to the rear and down to remove it from under the vehicle.

To install:

24. Tighten the converter drain plug to 20–30 ft. lbs. (28–40 Nm). if not previously done.
25. Position the converter to the transmission making sure the converter hub is fully engaged in the pump gear. The dimension given in the accompanying illustration is for guidance only. It does not indicate engagement.
26. With the converter properly installed, place the transmission on the jack and secure with safety chain.
27. Rotate the converter so the drive studs and drain plug are in alignment with their holes in the flexplate.
28. With the transmission mounted on a transmission jack, move the converter and transmission assembly forward into position being careful not to damage the flexplate and the converter pilot.
29. During this move, to avoid damage, do not allow the transmission to get into a nosed down position as this will cause the converter to move forward and disengage from the pump gear. The converter must rest squarely against the flexplate. This indicates that the converter pilot is not binding in the engine crankshaft.
30. Install the two upper converter housing-to-engine attaching bolts and tighten to 28–38 ft. lbs.
31. Remove the safety chain from the transmission.
32. Insert the filler tube in the stub tube and secure it to the cylinder block with the attaching bolt. Tighten the bolt to 28–38 ft. lbs. If the stub tube is loosened or dislodged, it should be replaced.
33. Install the oil cooler lines in the retaining clip at the cylinder block. Connect the lines to the transmission case.
34. Remove the jack supporting the front of the engine.
35. Position the muffler inlet pipe support bracket to the converter housing and install the four lower converter housing-to-engine attaching bolts. Tighten the bolts to 28–38 ft. lbs. (38–51 Nm).
36. Raise the transmission. Position the crossmember to the frame side supports and install the attaching bolts. Tighten the bolts to 30–40 ft. lbs. (41–54 Nm).
37. Lower the transmission and install the rear engine support-to-crossmember nut. Tighten the nut to 30–40 ft. lbs. (41–54 Nm).
38. Remove the transmission jack.
39. Install the vacuum hose on the transmission vacuum unit. Install the vacuum line into the retaining clip.
40. Connect the neutral start switch plug to the switch.
41. Install the starter and tighten the attaching bolts.
42. Install the four flexplate-to-converter attaching nuts.
43. Install the converter drain plug access cover and adaptor plate bolts. Tighten the bolts to 15–20 ft. lbs. (20–30 Nm).
44. Connect the muffler inlet pipe to the exhaust manifold.
45. Connect the transmission shift rod to the manual lever.
46. Connect the downshift rod to the downshift lever.
47. Connect the speedometer cable to the extension housing.
48. Install the driveshaft. Tighten the companion flange U-bolt attaching nuts to 30 ft. lbs. (41 Nm).
49. Adjust the manual and downshift linkage as required.
50. Carefully lower the vehicle, then connect the negative battery cable.
51. Fill the transmission to the proper level with Dexron®II. Pour in 5 qts. (4.7L) of fluid; then run the engine and add fluid as required.
52. Check the transmission, converter assembly and oil cooler lines for leaks.

C5 Transmission

1. Open the hood and install protective covers on the fenders.
2. Disconnect the battery negative cable.
3. On Cougars equipped with a 3.8L engine, remove the air cleaner assembly.
4. Remove the fan shroud attaching bolts and position the shroud back over the fan.
5. On Cougars equipped with a 3.8L engine, loosen the clamp and disconnect the Thermactor® air injection hose at the catalytic converter check valve. The check valve is located on the right side of the engine compartment near the dash panel.
6. On Cougars equipped with a 3.8L engine, remove the two transmission-to-engine attaching bolts located at the top of the transmission bell housing. These bolts are accessible from the engine compartment.

7. Raise and safely support the vehicle.
8. Remove the driveshaft.
9. Disconnect the muffler inlet pipe from the catalytic converter outlet pipe. Support the muffler/pipe assembly by wiring it to a convenient underbody bracket.
10. Remove the nuts attaching the exhaust pipe(s) to the exhaust manifold(s).
11. Pull back on the catalytic coverts to release the converter hangers from the mounting bracket.
12. Remove the speedometer clamps bolt and pull the speedometer out of the extension housing.
13. Separate the neutral start switch harness connector.
14. Detach the kick down rod at the transmission lever.
15. Disconnect the shift linkage at the linkage bellcrank using Shift Linkage Grommet Remover T84P-7341-A or equivalent. On vehicles equipped with floor mounted shift, remove the shift cable routing bracket attaching bolts and disconnect the cable at the transmission lever.
16. Remove the converter dust shield.
17. Remove the torque converter to drive plate attaching nuts. To gain access to the converter nuts, turn the crankshaft and drive plate using a ratchet handle and socket on the crankshaft pulley attaching bolt.
18. Remove the starter attaching bolts.
19. Loosen the nuts attaching the rear support to the No. 3 crossmember.
20. Position a transmission jack under the transmission oil pan. Secure the transmission to the jack with a safety chain.
21. Remove the through bolts attaching the No. 3 crossmember to the body brackets.
22. Lower the transmission enough to allow access to the cooler line fittings. Disconnect the cooler lines.
23. On Cougars, remove the (4) remaining transmission-to-engine attaching bolts (2 each side). On all models, remove the (6) transmission-to-engine attaching bolts.
24. Pull the transmission back to disengage the converter studs from the drive plate. Lower the transmission out of the vehicle.

To install:

25. Raise the transmission into the vehicle. As the transmission is being slowly raised into position, rotate the torque converter until the studs and drain plug are aligned with the holes in the drive plate.
26. Move the converter/transmission assembly forward against the back of the engine. Make sure the converter studs engage the drive plate and that the transmission dowels on the back of the engine engage the bolts holes in the bellhousing.
27. On Cougars equipped with a 3.8L engine, install four transmission-to-engine attaching bolts (2 each side). On all other models, install the (6) transmission-to-engine attaching bolts. Tighten the attaching bolts to 40–50 ft. lbs. (55–67 Nm).
28. Connect the cooler lines.
29. Raise the transmission and install the No. 3 crossmember through bolts. Tighten the attaching nuts to 20–30 ft. lbs. (30–41 Nm).
30. Remove the safety chain and transmission jack.
31. Tighten the rear support attaching nuts to 30–50 ft. lbs. (41–68 Nm).
32. Position the starter and install the attaching bolts.
33. Install the torque converter to drive plate attaching nuts. Tighten the attaching nuts to 20–30 ft. lbs. (30–41 Nm).
34. Position the dust shield and on vehicles with column mounted shift, position the linkage bellcrank bracket. Install the attaching bolts and tighten to 12–16 ft. lbs. (16–22 Nm).
35. Connect the shift linkage to the linkage bellcrank. On vehicles equipped with floor mounted shift, connect the cable to the shift lever and install the routing bracket attaching bolt.
36. Connect the kick down rod to the transmission lever.
37. Connect the neutral start switch harness.
38. Install the speedometer and the clamp bolt. Tighten the clamp bolt to 35–54 inch lbs. (3.9–6.1 Nm).
39. Install the catalytic converts using new seal(s) at the pipe(s) to exhaust manifold connection(s).
40. Install the pipe(s) to exhaust manifold attaching nuts. Do not tighten the attaching nuts.
41. Remove the wire supporting the muffler/pipe assembly and connect the pipe to the converter outlet. Do not tighten the attaching nuts.
42. Align the exhaust system and tighten the manifold and converter outlet attaching nuts.
43. Install the driveshaft.
44. Check and if necessary, adjust the shift linkage.
45. Carefully lower the vehicle.
46. On Cougars equipped with a 3.8L engine, install the two transmission-to-engine attaching bolts located at the top of the transmission bellhousing.
47. On Cougars equipped with a 3.8L engine, connect the Thermactor® air injection hose to the converter check valve.
48. Position the fan shroud and install the attaching bolts.
49. On Cougars equipped with a 3.8L engine, install the air cleaner assembly.
50. Connect the battery negative cable.
51. Start the engine. Make sure the engine cranks only when the selector lever is positioned in the neutral (N) or Park (P) detent.
52. Fill the transmission with type H fluid.
53. Raise the vehicle and inspect for fluid leaks.

Automatic Overdrive (A4LD) Transmission

See Figures 47, 48, 49, 50, 51, 52, 53, 54 and 55

1. Disconnect the negative battery cable.
2. Raise and safely support the vehicle.
3. Place a drain pan under transmission fluid pan. Starting at the rear of pan and working toward front, loosen attaching bolts and allow fluid to drain. Finally remove all the pan attaching bolts except two at the front, to allow the fluid to further drain. With fluid drained install to bolts on the rear side of the pan to temporarily hold it in place.
4. Remove the converter access cover and adapter plate bolts from the lower left side of converter housing.
5. Remove the four flexplate-to-converter attaching nuts by placing a 22mm socket and breaker bar on the crankshaft pulley attaching (center) bolt. Rotate pulley clockwise (as viewed from front) to gain access to each of the nuts.

Never rotate a 2.3L engine in the counterclockwise direction (as viewed from the front) serious engine damage can occur!

6. Scribe a mark indexing the driveshaft to axle flange, disconnect the driveshaft from the rear axle and slide shaft rearward from the transmission. Install Extension Housing Seal Replacer T74P-77052-A or equivalent in the extension housing to prevent fluid leakage.

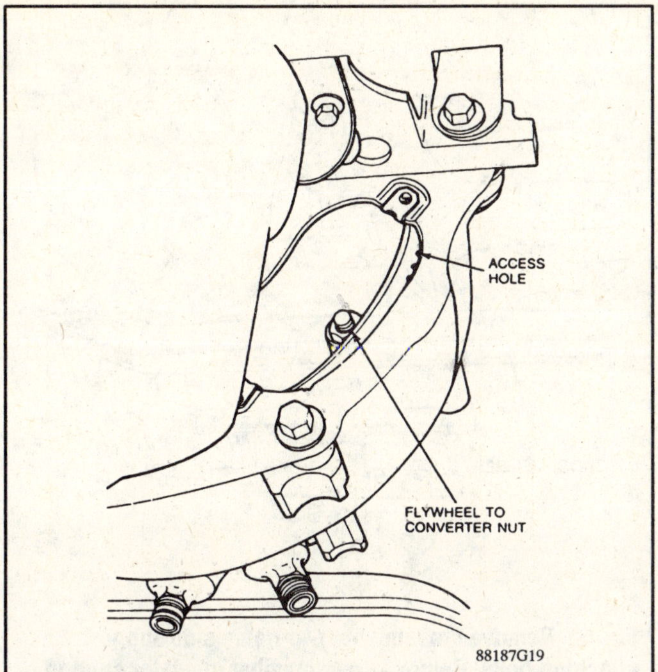

Fig. 47 Rotate the pulley clockwise to access each flexplate-to-converter nut

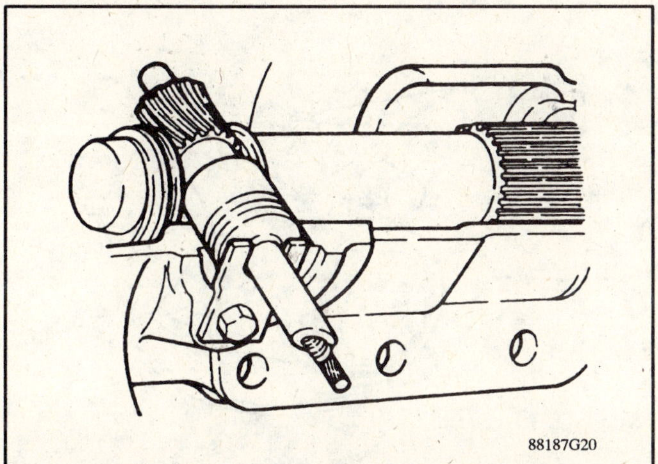

Fig. 48 Remove the driveshaft and install a suitable seal installation tool to prevent fluid from leaking out

7. Disconnect and remove speedometer sensor from extension housing.

8. Disconnect shift cable from transmission manual lever and retainer bracket (mounted at extension housing). Disconnect downshift cable at transmission downshift lever. Depress tab on cable downshift retainer and remove downshift cable from bracket.

9. Remove starter-to-converter housing attaching bolts and position out of the way.

10. Tag and detach the neutral start switch wires, converter clutch solenoid and the 3-4 shift solenoid connector.

11. Remove vacuum line from transmission vacuum modulator.

12. Position a transmission jack under transmission and raise it slightly.

13. Remove the engine rear support-to-crossmember bolts.

→ Certain models require the removal of some or all exhaust system components, before transmission can be removed from vehicle. Check for clearance and remove exhaust pipe or catalytic converter before removing crossmember.

14. Remove crossmember-to-frame side support attaching bolts. Remove crossmember insulator support and damper.

15. Lower jack under transmission and allow transmission to hang.

16. Position a jack under the front of the engine. Raise engine to gain access to two upper converter housing-to-engine attaching bolts.

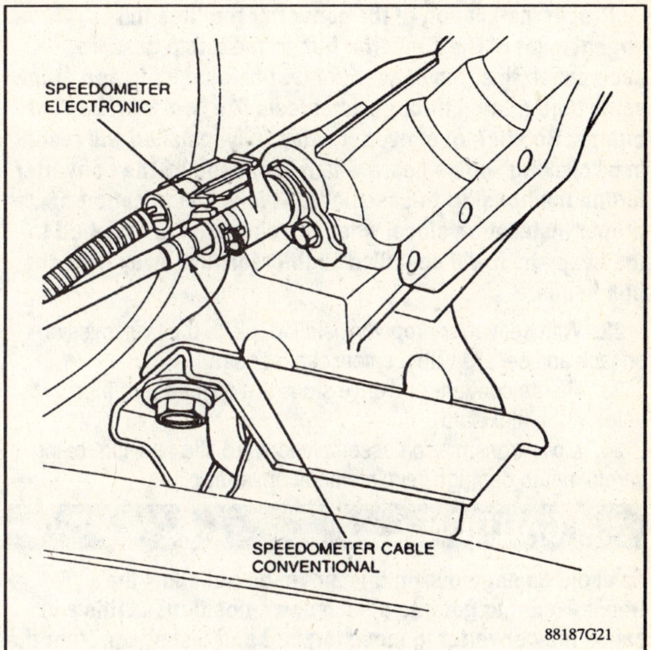

Fig. 49 Detach, then remove the speedometer sensor

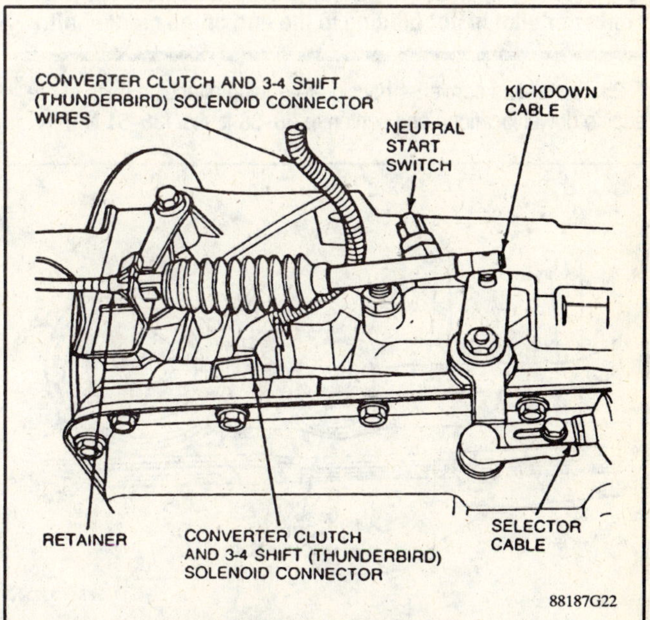

Fig. 50 Tag and disconnect the neutral start switch, converter clutch and the 3-4 shift solenoid wiring

17. Disconnect oil cooler lines from fittings at transmission and plug all openings to keep dirt out.

18. Remove the lower converter housing-to-engine attaching bolts and remove transmission filler tube.

19. Secure transmission to the jack with a safety chain or strap.

20. Remove the two upper converter housing-to-engine attaching bolts. Slide the transmission to the rear so it disengages from the dowel pins and the converter is disengaged from the flexplate.

21. Lower and remove transmission from vehicle. If necessary, remove the torque converter from vehicle.

To install:

Proper installation of the converter requires full engagement of the converter hub in the pump gear. To accomplish this, the converter must be pushed in and at the same time rotated through what feels like two "notches" or bumps. Rotation of converter when fully installed will result in a "clicking" noise heard which is caused by the converter hitting the housing-to-case bolts. This is an indication of proper installation since, when the converter is attached to the flexplate, it will be pulled slightly forward away from the bolt heads.

22. With converter properly installed, place the transmission on jack and secure with a safety chain or strap.

23. Rotate converter so drive studs are aligned with there holes in the flexplate.

24. Move transmission assembly forward into position, being careful not to damage flexplate and converter pilot.

****CAUTION**

To avoid damage during this move, do not allow the transmission to get into a nose down position, as this will cause the converter to move forward and disengage from the pump gear. The converter housing is piloted into position by dowels in the rear of the engine block. The converter must rest squarely against the flexplate. This indicates that the converter pilot is not binding in the end of the crankshaft.

25. Install two converter housing-to-engine attaching bolts at the engine dowel locations and tighten to 28–38 ft. lbs. (38–51 Nm).

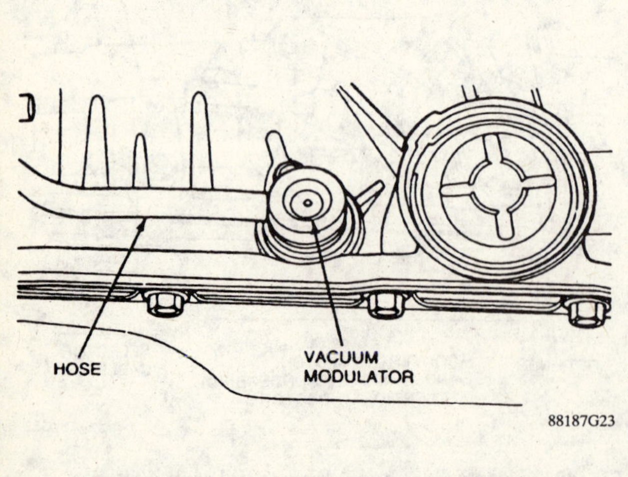

Fig. 51 Detach the vacuum line from the modulator

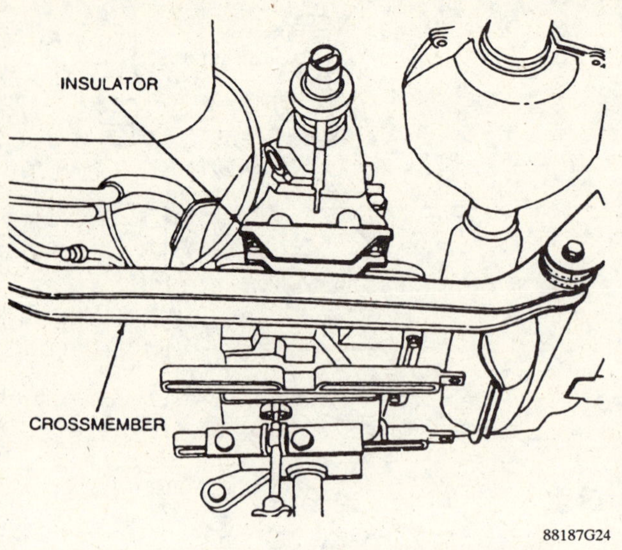

Fig. 52 Remove crossmember-to-frame side support attaching bolts. Remove crossmember insulator support and damper

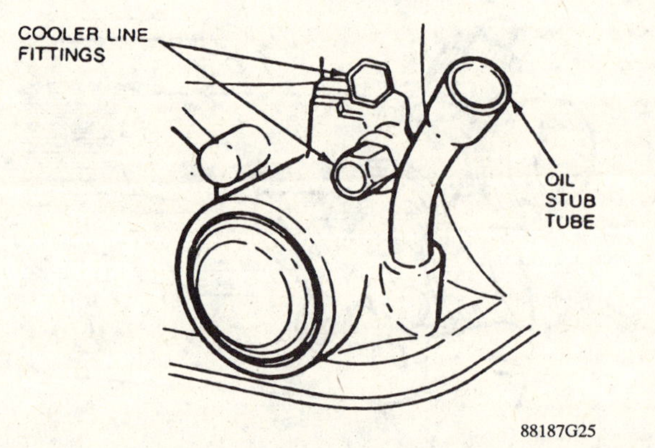

Fig. 53 Detach and plug the transmission oil cooler lines

26. Install the remaining housing-to-engine attaching bolts and tighten to 28–38 ft. lbs. (38–51 Nm).

27. Remove the safety chain or strap from the transmission.

28. Insert the filler tube into the stub tube and secure it to cylinder block with attaching bolt and tighten to 28–38 ft. lbs. (38–51 Nm).

If stub tube becomes loose or dislodged, it should be replaced.

29. Install the fluid cooler lines into the retaining clip at cylinder block. connect fittings to the transmission case.

30. Raise the transmission. Position the crossmember, insulator, support and damper to frame side supports. Install attaching bolts and tighten to 20–30 ft. lbs. (30–41 Nm).

31. Align and lower transmission to install rear engine support nut and tighten to 60–80 ft. lbs. (81–108 Nm).

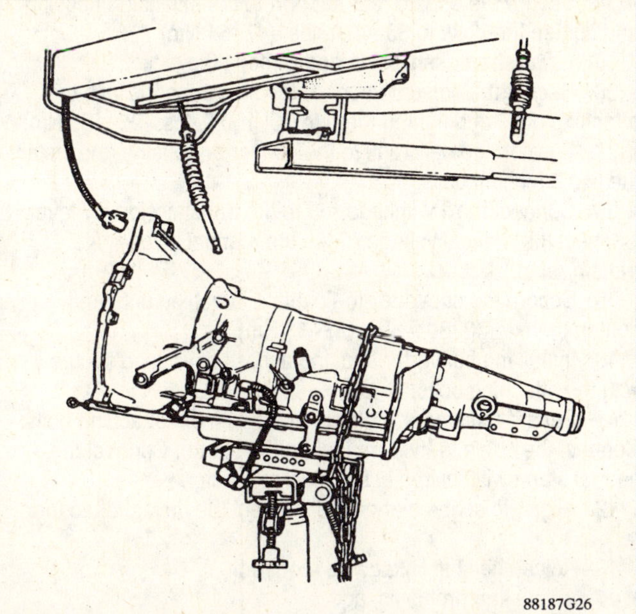

Fig. 54 Carefully lower the transmission from the vehicle, then . . .

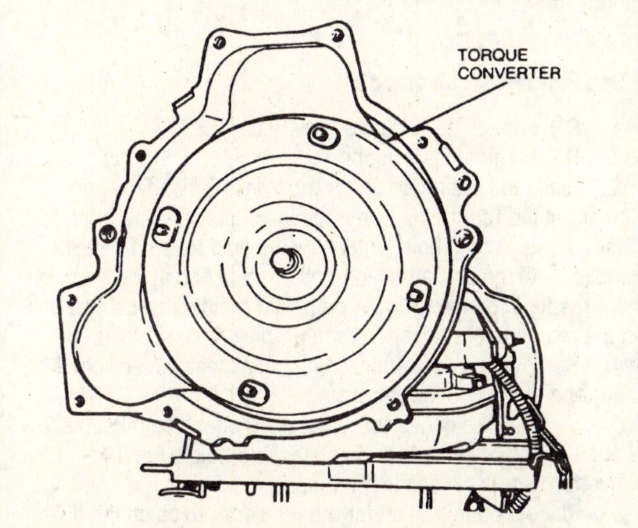

Fig. 55 . . . if necessary, remove the torque converter

32. Install vacuum hose onto vacuum unit and into retaining clip.
33. Connect plug to neutral start switch. Connect converter clutch solenoid wires and 3-4 shift solenoid wires.
34. Install starter and tighten attaching bolts to 15-20 ft. lbs. (20-27 Nm).
35. Install the four flexplate-to-converter attaching nuts and tighten to 20-34 ft. lbs. (27-46 Nm).
36. Install the converter access cover, adapter plate bolts and tighten to 12-16 ft. lbs. (16-22 Nm).
37. Reconnect any exhaust system components that were disconnected for transmission removal.
38. Position selector cable in bracket on transmission extension housing. Press the end of cable onto ball stud on lower portion of selector lever and install retaining clip on bracket.
39. Connect downshift cable to downshift lever. Install speedometer sensor and connect wiring.
40. Align the scribe marks on driveshaft to the rear axle companion flange and tighten attaching nuts to 70-95 ft. lbs. (95-129 Nm).
41. Adjust manual and downshift linkage as required. Lower vehicle.
42. Fill the transmission to the correct level with Mercon® or equivalent fluid. Start the engine and shift the transmission to all ranges, then recheck the fluid level.

Automatic Overdrive (AOD) Transmission

1983-89 VEHICLES

➧ See Figure 56

1. Disconnect the negative battery cable.
2. Raise and safely support the vehicle.
3. Place a suitable drain pan under the transmission fluid pan. Starting at the rear of the pan and working toward the front, loosen the attaching bolts and allow the fluid to drain. Finally remove all of the pan attaching bolts except two at the front, to allow the fluid to further drain. With fluid drained, install two bolts on the rear side of the pan to temporarily hold it in place.
4. Remove the converter drain plug access cover from the lower end of the converter housing.
5. Remove the converter-to-flexplate attaching nuts. place a wrench on the crankshaft pulley attaching bolt to turn the converter to gain access to the nuts.
6. Place a drain pan under the converter to catch the fluid. With the wrench on the crankshaft pulley attaching bolts, turn the converter to gain access to the converter drain plug and remove the plug. After the fluid has been drained, reinstall the plug.
7. Scribe a mark indexing the driveshaft to axle flange, disconnect the driveshaft from the rear axle and slide shaft rearward from the transmission. Install a seal installation tool in the extension housing to prevent fluid leakage.
8. Disconnect the cable from the terminal on the starter motor. Remove the three attaching bolts and remove the starter motor. Disconnect the neutral start switch wires at the plug connector.
9. Remove the rear mount-to-crossmember attaching bolts and the two crossmember-to-frame attaching bolts.
10. Remove the two engine rear support-to-extension housing attaching bolts.
11. Disconnect the TV linkage rod from the transmission TV lever. Disconnect the manual rod from the transmission manual lever at the transmission.
12. Remove the two bolts securing the bellcrank bracket to the converter housing.
13. Raise the transmission with a transmission jack to provide clearance to remove the crossmember. Remove the rear mount from the crossmember and remove the crossmember from the side supports.
14. Lower the transmission to gain access to the oil cooler lines.
15. Disconnect each oil line from the fittings on the transmission using Cooler Line Disconnect Tool T86P-77265-AH or equivalent.
16. Disconnect the speedometer cable from the extension housing.
17. Remove the bolt that secures the transmission fluid filler tube to the cylinder block. Lift the filler tube and the dipstick from the transmission.
18. Secure the transmission to the jack with the chain.

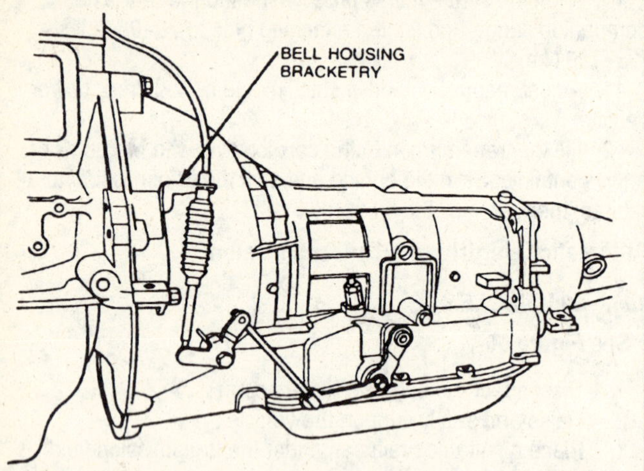

Fig. 56 Unfasten the two bellcrank bracket-to-converter housing bolts

19. Remove the converter housing-to-cylinder block attaching bolts.
20. Carefully move the transmission and converter assembly away from the engine and, at the same time, lower the jack to clear the underside of the vehicle.
21. Remove the converter and mount the transmission in Bench Mounted Holding Fixture T57L-500-B, or equivalent holding fixture.

To install:

22. Tighten the converter drain plug to 8–28 ft. lbs. (11–38 Nm).
23. Position the converter on the transmission, making sure the converter drive flats are fully engaged in the pump gear by rotating the converter.
24. With the converter properly installed, place the transmission on the jack. Secure the transmission to the jack with a chain.
25. Rotate the converter until the studs and drain plug are in alignment with the holes in the flexplate.

****WARNING**

Lubricate the pilot bushing with a suitable chassis grease.

26. Align the yellow balancing marks on converter and flexplate.
27. Move the converter and transmission assembly forward into position, using care not to damage the flexplate and the converter pilot. The converter must rest squarely against the flexplate. This indicates that the converter pilot is not binding in the engine crankshaft.
28. Install and tighten the converter housing-to-engine attaching bolts to 40–50 ft. lbs. (55–68 Nm), making sure that the vacuum tube retaining clips are properly positioned.
29. Remove the safety chain from around the transmission.
30. Install a new O-ring on the lower end of the transmission filler tube. Insert the tube in the transmission case and secure the tube to the engine with the attaching bolts.
31. Connect the speedometer cable to the extension housing.
32. Connect the oil cooler lines to the right side of the transmission case. Tighten the lines to 24–31 Nm).
33. Position the crossmember on the side supports. Position the rear mount on the crossmember and install the attaching bolt and nut.
34. Secure the engine rear support to the extension housing and tighten the bolts to 35–40 ft. lbs. (47–54 Nm).
35. Lower the transmission and remove the jack.
36. Secure the crossmember to the side supports with the attaching bolts and tighten them to 70–100 ft. lbs. (95–136 Nm).
37. Position the bellcrank to the converter housing and install the two attaching bolts.
38. Connect the TV linkage rod to the transmission TV lever. Connect the manual linkage rod to the manual lever at the transmission.
39. Secure the converter-to-flexplate attaching nuts and tighten them to 20–30 ft. lbs. (27–41 Nm).
40. Install the converter housing access cover and secure it with the attaching bolts.
41. Secure the starter motor in place with the attaching bolts. Connect the cable to the terminal on the starter. Connect the neutral start switch wires at the plug connector.
42. Align the scribe marks and connect the driveshaft to the rear axle.
43. Adjust the shift linkage as required.
44. Adjust the throttle linkage.
45. Carefully lower the vehicle, then connect the negative battery cable.
46. Fill the transmission to the correct level with Mercon® or equivalent fluid. Start the engine and shift the transmission to all ranges, then recheck the fluid level.

1990–93 VEHICLES

➧ See Figures 57, 58 and 59

1. Disconnect the negative battery cable.
2. Raise and safely support the vehicle.
3. Place the drain pan under the transmission fluid pan. Starting at the rear of the pan and working toward the front, loosen the attaching bolts and allow the fluid to drain. Finally remove all of the pan attaching bolts except two at the front, to allow the fluid to further drain. With fluid drained, install two bolts on the rear side of the pan to temporarily hold it in place.
4. Remove the converter drain plug access cover from the lower end of the converter housing.
5. Remove the converter-to-flexplate attaching nuts. place a wrench on the crankshaft pulley attaching bolt to turn the converter to gain access to the nuts.
6. Place a drain pan under the converter to catch the fluid. With the wrench on the crankshaft pulley attaching bolts, turn the converter to gain access to the converter drain plug and remove the plug. After the fluid has been drained, reinstall the plug.
7. Remove the catalytic converter assembly.
8. Remove the body reinforcement.
9. Remove the exhaust pipe and muffler assembly.
10. To maintain balance, matchmark the rear driveshaft yoke and the companion flange so the driveshaft can be installed in its original position.
11. Remove the four bolts retaining the driveshaft to the companion flange.
12. Loosen the differential housing assembly rear mounting nuts about 0.25 inch (6.4mm).
13. Position a suitable jackstand stand under the front of the differential housing and remove the forward mounting nuts and bushings. Pull the tube from the vent hole in the subframe.

➥ Use care when positioning the driveshaft so not to nick, burr of contaminate the driveshaft yoke and companion flange.

14. Lower the front of the differential housing with the axle stand and slide the driveshaft out of the transmission above the axle housing. Let the driveshaft rest on the front driveshaft support and axle assembly.

15. Disconnect the cable from the terminal on the starter motor. Unfasten the three retaining bolts, then remove the starter motor. Detach the neutral start switch wires at the plug connector.

16. Remove the rear mount-to-crossmember retaining bolts and the two crossmember-to-frame retaining bolts.

17. Remove the two engine rear support-to-extension housing retaining bolts.

18. Disconnect the TV linkage rod or cable from the transmission TV lever ball stud. Disconnect the cable from the bellcrank lever stud and remove the self-tapping bolt from the bell housing bracketry.

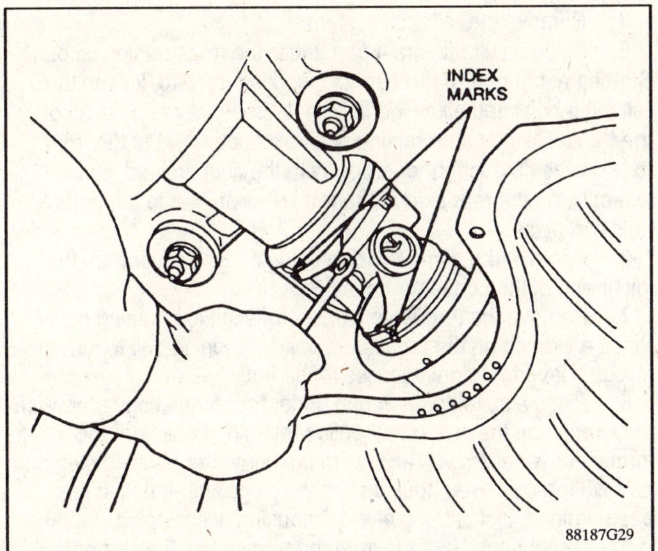

Fig. 57 Unfasten the 4 driveshaft-to-companion flange bolts

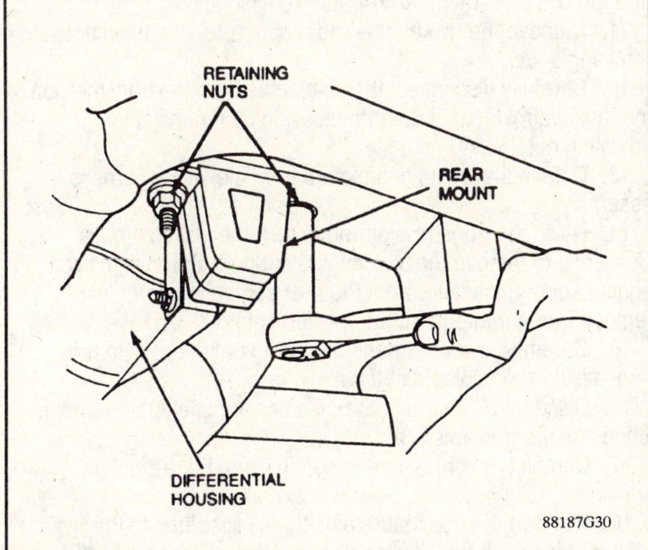

Fig. 58 Loosen the differential housing assembly rear nuts approximately 1/4 inch

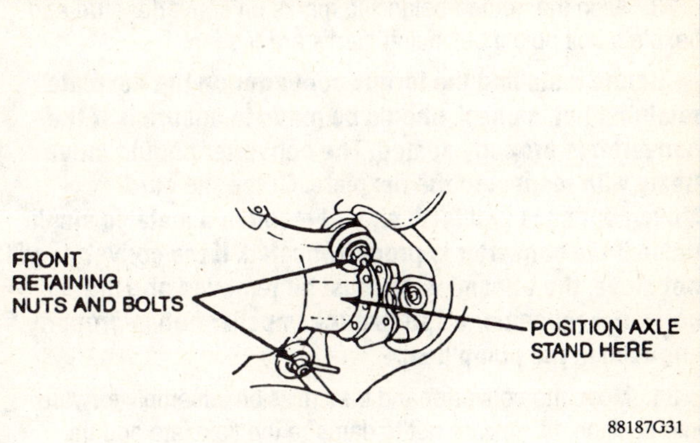

Fig. 59 Location for axle stand positioning

19. Carefully disconnect the manual cable form the transmission manual lever at the transmission. Remove the cable mounting bracket from the case using Grommet Remover T84P-7341-A or equivalent.

20. Remove the two bolts retaining the bellcrank bracket to the converter housing.

➥ **Disconnect and remove any interfering exhaust system components.**

21. Raise the transmission with a transmission jack to provide clearance to remove the crossmember. Remove the rear mount from the crossmember and remove the crossmember from the side supports.

22. Lower the transmission for access to the oil cooler lines. Detach and plug each oil line from the fittings on the transmission.

23. Disconnect the speedometer cable from the extension housing.

24. Remove the bolt that retains the transmission fluid filler tube to the cylinder block. Lift the filler tube and the dipstick from the transmission.

25. Secure the transmission to the jack with a chain.

26. Remove the converter housing-to-cylinder block retaining bolts.

27. Carefully move the transmission and converter assembly away from the engine and, at the same time, lower the jack to clear the underside of the vehicle.

28. Remove the converter and mount the transmission in Bench Mounted Holding Fixture T57L-500-B, or equivalent holding fixture.

To install:

29. Tighten the converter drain plug to 8-28 ft. lbs. (11-38 Nm).

➥ **Lubricate the pilot with suitable chassis grease.**

30. Position the converter on the transmission, making sure the converter drive flats are fully engaged in the pump gear by rotating the converter.

31. With the converter properly installed, place the transmission on the jack. Secure the transmission to the jack with a chain.

32. Rotate the converter until the studs and drain plug are in alignment with the holes in the flexplate.

33. Align the orange balancing marks on converter stud and flexplate bolt hole if balancing marks are present.

➥ Before installing the torque converter on the flexplate retaining nut, a check should be made to ensure that the converter is properly seated. The converter should move freely with respect to the flexplate. Grasp the stud. Movement back and forth should result in a metallic clank noise if the converter is properly seated. If the converter will not move, the transmission must be removed and the converter repositioned so that the impeller hub is properly engaged in the pump gear.

34. Move the converter and transmission assembly forward into position, using care not to damage the flexplate and the converter pilot. The converter must rest squarely against the flexplate. This indicates that the converter pilot is not binding in the engine crankshaft.
35. Install and tighten the converter housing-to-engine attaching bolts to 40–50 ft. lbs. (55–68 Nm).
36. Remove the safety chain from around the transmission.
37. Install a new O-ring on the lower end of the transmission filler tube. Insert the tube in the transmission case and secure the tube to the engine with the attaching bolts.
38. Connect the speedometer cable to the extension housing.
39. Connect the oil cooler lines to the right side of the transmission case. Tighten the lines to 12–18 ft. lbs. (16–24 Nm).
40. Position the crossmember on the side supports. Position the rear mount on the crossmember and install the attaching bolt and nut. Tighten the nut to 65–84 ft. lbs. (88–115 Nm).
41. Secure the engine rear support to the extension housing and tighten the bolts to 51–70 ft. lbs. (68–95 Nm).
42. Lower the transmission and remove the jack.
43. Secure the crossmember to the side supports with the attaching bolts and tighten them to 70–100 ft. lbs. (95–136 Nm).
44. Connect the TV linkage rod to the transmission TV lever. Connect the manual linkage rod to the manual lever at the transmission.
45. Secure the converter-to-flexplate attaching nuts and tighten them to 12–16 ft. lbs. (16–22 Nm).
46. Install the converter housing access cover and secure it with the attaching bolts. Tighten the bolts to 12–16 ft. lbs. (16–22 Nm).
47. Secure the starter motor in place with the attaching bolts. Connect the cable to the terminal on the starter. Connect the neutral start switch wires at the plug connector.
48. Slide the driveshaft into the transmission.
49. Raise the differential housing with the axle stand and install the bushings and retaining nuts. Tighten to 68–100 ft. lbs. (92–136 Nm). Remove the axle stand.
50. Tighten the differential assembly rear retaining nuts to 122–156 ft. lbs. (165–211 Nm).
51. Position the vent tube in the hole of the subframe.

➥ Lubricate the yoke splines with Premium Long Life Grease, or equivalent.

52. Align the driveshaft yoke and companion flange and install the retaining bolts. Tighten to 70–95 ft. lbs. (95–129 Nm).
53. Install the catalytic converter, exhaust pipe and muffler and the body reinforcement.
54. Carefully lower the vehicle, then connect the negative battery cable.
55. Fill the transmission to the correct level with Mercon® or equivalent fluid. Start the engine and shift the transmission to all ranges, then recheck the fluid level.
56. Adjust the manual shift linkage as required. Adjust the TV linkage.

4R70W Transmission

1994–95 VEHICLES

♦ See Figure 60

1. Disconnect the negative battery cable.
2. Raise and safely support the vehicle.
3. Disconnect the driveshaft from the rear axle assembly and slide the shaft rearward from the transmission. To maintain driveshaft balance, mark the rear driveshaft yoke and rear axle universal joint flange so the driveshaft can be installed in its original position.
4. Remove the exhaust system.
5. Place a suitable drain pan under the transmission oil pan. Starting at the rear of the pan and working forward, loosen the retaining bolts and allow the fluid to drain. Finally remove all of the transmission pan retaining bolts except the two at the front, to allow the fluid to further drain. With the fluid drained, install two bolts on the rear side of the transmission pan to temporarily hold it in place.
6. Remove the converter drain plug access cover from the lower end of the converter housing.
7. Remove the torque converter-to-flexplate retaining nuts. Place a wrench on the crankshaft pulley retaining bolt to turn the torque converter to gain access to the nuts.
8. Place a suitable drain pan under the torque converter. With the wrench on the crankshaft pulley retaining bolts, turn the torque converter to gain access to the converter housing plug and remove the converter housing access plug. After the fluid has been drained, install the converter housing access plug.
9. Disconnect the cable from the terminal on the starter motor. Unfasten the retaining bolts, then remove the starter. Detach the park/neutral position start switch wires at the plug connector.
10. Remove the rear mount-to-crossmember retaining bolts and the two crossmember-to-frame retaining bolts.
11. Remove the two engine rear support-to-extension housing retaining bolts.
12. Carefully disconnect the shift cable from the transmission manual control lever at the transmission by removing the adjusting nut.
13. Detach the wiring connectors from the wiring harness assembly.
14. Raise the transmission with a suitable jack to provide clearance to remove the rear engine support. Remove the rear engine support insulator from the rear engine support and remove the rear support from the side support.
15. Carefully lower the transmission to gain access to the transmission oil cooler inlet tube.
16. Disconnect the transmission oil cooler inlet tube from the fittings on the transmission.
17. Detach the vehicle speed sensor from the extension housing.
18. Remove the bolt that retains the oil filler tube to the cylinder block. Lift the oil filler tube and the oil lever indicator from the transmission.

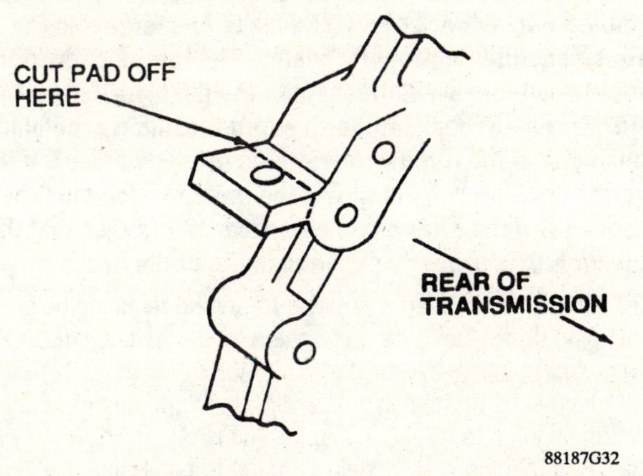

Fig. 60 For 1994 vehicles, you must use a hacksaw to cut the transmission pad off the left side of the converter housing

19. Secure the transmission to the jack with a chain.
20. Remove the converter housing-to-cylinder block retaining bolts.
21. For 1994 vehicles, remove the transmission pad from the left side of the converter housing using a hacksaw.
22. Carefully move the transmission and torque converter away from the engine and, at the same time, lower the jack to clear the underside of the vehicle.

To install:

23. Tighten the converter housing plug to 21-23 ft. lbs. (28-30 Nm).

➥ Make sure the lubricate the pilot with chassis grease.

24. Position the torque converter on the transmission, ensuring the converter drive flats are fully engaged in the pump gear by rotating the torque converter.
25. With the torque converter properly installed, place the transmission on a jack. Secure the transmission to the jack with a chain.
26. Rotate the torque converter until the studs and converter housing access plug are in alignment with the holes in the flexplate.
27. If present, align the orange balancing marks on the converter stud and flexplate bolt hole.
28. Move the torque converter and transmission assembly forward into position, using care not to damage the flexplate and the converter pilot. The torque converter face must rest squarely against the flexplate. This indicates that the converter pilot is not binding in the engine crankshaft.

➥ Before installing the crankshaft to the flexplate retaining nut, a check should be make to ensure that the torque converter is properly seated. The torque converter should move freely with respect to the flexplate. Grasp the stud. Movement back and forth should result in a metallic clank noise if the torque converter is properly seated. If the torque converter will not move, the transmission must be removed and the torque converter repositioned so that the impeller hub is properly engaged in the pump gear.

29. Connect the EGR tube to the torque converter assembly.
30. Position the transmission to the engine and install the retaining bolts. Tighten the bolts to 40-50 ft. lbs. (50-68 Nm).
31. Install the nuts retaining the torque converter to the flexplate. Tighten the nuts to 20-34 ft. lbs. (27-46 Nm).
32. Install the starter and the oil fill tube.
33. Connect the transmission shift selector mounting bracket.
34. Install the transmission rear engine support assembly. Tighten the bolts to 64-81 ft. lbs. (87-110 Nm).
35. Install the vehicle speed sensor and electrical connector.
36. Remove the transmission jack from under the vehicle.
37. Position the driveshaft yoke inside the extension housing.
38. Connect both transmission oil cooler inlet tube and oil cooler tube. Tighten to 15-19 ft. lbs. (20-26 ft. lbs.).
39. Raise the rear axle housing, then install the retaining nuts.
40. Install the driveshaft and secure with the retaining bolts.
41. Install the exhaust system components.
42. Carefully lower the vehicle, then connect the negative battery cable.
43. Fill the transmission with the proper type and amount of fluid.
44. Start the engine and check transmission operation.

1996 VEHICLES

1. Disconnect the negative battery cable.
2. Raise and safely support the vehicle.
3. Properly drain the transmission fluid.
4. Remove any exhaust system components necessary for transmission removal.
5. Remove the converter access cover and adapter plate bolts from the engine oil pan.

****WARNING**

Be careful not to damage the cooler lines.

➥ Never rotate the crankshaft pulley in a counterclockwise direction.

6. Remove the four flexplate-to-converter retaining nuts by placing a 22mm socket and breaker bar on the crankshaft pulley retaining bolt. Rotate the crankshaft pulley clockwise to gain access to each of the nuts.
7. Remove the driveshaft.
8. Disconnect and remove the vehicle speed sensor from the extension housing.
9. Place a suitable drain pan under the torque converter. With the wrench on the crankshaft pulley retaining bolt, turn the torque converter to gain access to the converter housing access plug and remove. After the fluid has been drained, install the converter housing access plug.
10. Carefully disconnect the shift cable form the transmission manual control lever at the transmission by removing the adjusting nut.
11. Detach the wiring harness electrical connectors.
12. Unfasten the starter-to-converter housing retaining bolts, then position the starter out of the way.
13. Position a transmission jack under the transmission and raise it slightly.
14. Remove the engine rear support-to-crossmember bolts.
15. Remove the crossmember-to-frame side support retaining bolts and remove the engine and transmission support insulator and engine and transmission support and engine damper mounting body bracket.
16. Lower the jack under the transmission and allow the transmission to hang.

17. Position a jack to the front of the engine and raise the engine to gain access to the two upper converter housing-to-engine retaining bolts.
18. Disconnect and plug the transmission cooler lines form the transmission.
19. Remove the lower converter housing-to-engine retaining bolts.
20. Remove the transmission fluid filler tube.
21. Secure the transmission to the jack with a safety chain.

➥ If the transmission is to be removed for a period of time, support the engine with a safely stand and wood block.

22. Remove the two upper converter housing-to-engine retaining bolts. Move the transmission to the rear so it disengages from the dowel pins and the torque converter is disengaged from the flexplate. Carefully lower the transmission from the vehicle.
23. Remove the torque converter from the transmission.

To install:

24. Tighten the converter housing drain plug to 21-22 ft. lbs. (28-30 Nm).
25. Proper installation of the torque converter requires full engagement of the converter hub in the pump gear. To accomplish this, the converter must be pushed and at the same time rotated through what feels like two""notches" or bumps.
26. With the torque converter properly installed, place the transmission on a jack and secure with safety chain.
27. Rotate the torque converter so the drive studs and converter housing access plug are in alignment with their holes in the flexplate.

**WARNING

During this move, to avoid damage, do not allow the transmission to get into a nose-down position as this will cause the torque converter to move forward and disengage from the pump gear. The converter housing is piloted into position by dowels in the rear of the engine block. The torque converter must rest squarely against the flexplate. This indicates that the converter pilot is not binding in the engine crankshaft.

28. If present, align the orange balancing marks on the converter stud and flexplate bolt hole.
29. With the transmission mounted on a transmission jack, move the torque converter and transmission assembly forward into position, being careful not to damage the flexplate and the converter pilot. The torque converter face must rest squarely against the flexplate. This indicates that the converter pilot is not binding in the engine crankshaft.

➥ Before installing the torque converter housing-to-flexplate retaining nut, a check should be make to ensure that the torque converter is properly seated. The torque converter should move freely with respect to the flexplate. Grasp the stud. Movement back and forth should result in a metallic clank noise if the torque converter is properly seated. If the torque converter will not move, the transmission must be removed and the torque converter repositioned so that the impeller hub is properly engaged in the pump gear.

30. Install two converter housing-to-engine retaining bolts at the engine dowel locations and tighten to 40-50 ft. lbs. (50-68 Nm).
31. Install the remaining converter housing-to-engine retaining bolts and tighten to 40-50 ft. lbs. (50-68 Nm).
32. Remove the safety chain from the transmission.
33. Install the fluid filler tube and secure it to the cylinder block with the retaining bolt. Tighten the bolt to 28-38 ft. lbs. (38-51 Nm). If the fluid filler tube is loose in the case, it should be replaced.
34. Unplug and connect the cooler lines to the transmission case. Tighten the lines to 15-19 ft. lbs. (20-26 Nm).
35. Remove the jack supporting the front of the engine.
36. Raise the transmission. Position the engine and transmission support insulator and engine and transmission support and engine damper mounting body bracket to the frame side support and install the retaining bolts.
37. Lower the transmission and install the rear engine support-to-crossmember nut.
38. Remove the transmission jack.
39. Attach the transmission wiring harness.
40. Install the starter motor.
41. Install the four flexplate-to-converter retaining nuts. Tighten to 20-33 ft. lbs. (27-46 Nm).
42. Install the converter access cover and cover plate bolts on the engine oil pan. Tighten to 12-16 ft. lbs. (16-22 Nm).
43. Install any exhaust system components that were removed.
44. Install the vehicle speed sensor, then connect the wiring.
45. Install the driveshaft.
46. Remove the safety stands and carefully lower the vehicle.
47. Connect the negative battery cable.
48. Fill the transmission with the proper type and amount of fluid.
49. Start the engine and check transmission operation. Inspect for transmission, torque converter assembly and oil cooler lines for leaks.

DRIVELINE

Driveshaft and U-Joints

The driveshaft is the means by which the power from the engine and transmission (in the front of the car) is transferred to the differential and rear axles, and finally to the rear wheels.

The driveshaft assembly incorporates two universal joints, one at each end, and a slip yoke at the front end of the assembly, which fits into the back of the transmission.

All driveshafts are balanced when installed in a car. It is therefore imperative that before applying undercoating to the chassis, the driveshaft and universal joint assembly be completely covered to prevent the accidental application of undercoating to the surfaces, and the subsequent loss of balance.

The universal joints are of a lube-for-life design, on 1989-92 models. The universal joints are equipped with a nylon thrust washer at the base of the bearing cup. This thrust washer controls end play, positions the needle bearings and improves grease movement in the bearing chamber.

➥ **Other type universal joints should not be used in place of this type. Driveshaft imbalance and vibration will result.**

REMOVAL AND INSTALLATION

1983–88 Vehicles

➧ See Figure 61

The procedure for removing the driveshaft assembly, complete with universal joint and slip yoke, is as follows:

1. Raise and safely support the vehicle.
2. Mark the relationship of the rear driveshaft yoke and the drive pinion flange of the axle. If the original yellow alignment marks are visible, there is no need for new marks. The purpose of this marking is to facilitate installation of the assembly in its exact original position, thereby maintaining proper balance.
3. Remove the four bolts or U-clamps which hold the rear universal joint to the pinion flange. Wrap tape around the loose bearing caps in order to prevent them from falling off the spider.
4. Pull the driveshaft toward the rear of the vehicle until the slip yoke clears the transmission housing and the seal. Plug the hole at the rear of the transmission housing or place a container under the opening to catch any fluid which might leak.
5. Carefully inspect the rubber seal on the output shaft and the seal in end of the transmission extension housing. Replace them if they are damaged.
6. Examine the lugs on the axle pinion flange and replace the flange if the lugs are shaved or distorted.

To install:

7. Coat the yoke spline with special-purpose lubricant. The Ford part number for this lubricant if B8A-19589-A.
8. Remove the plug from the rear of the transmission housing.
9. Insert the yoke into the transmission housing and onto the transmission output shaft. Make sure that the yoke assembly does not bottom on the output shaft with excessive force.
10. Locate the marks which you made on the rear driveshaft yoke and the pinion flange prior to removal of the driveshaft assembly. Install the driveshaft assembly with the marks properly aligned.
11. Install the U-bolts and nuts or bolts which attach the universal joint to the pinion flange. Tighten the U-bolt nuts to 8–15 ft. lbs. (11–20 Nm). Tighten the flange bolts to 70–95 ft. lbs. (95–129 Nm).
12. Carefully lower the vehicle.

➥ **Always check transmission fluid levels after removal and installation of driveshaft.**

1989–96 Vehicles

➧ See Figures 62, 63, 64, 65, 66, 67, 68, 69, 70, 71, 72, 73, 74 and 75

1. Disconnect the negative battery cable.
2. Properly drain the fuel tank into a suitable container.
3. Raise and safely support vehicle on jack stands.
4. Remove the crossmember/fuel tank modification shield and pipe kit on the forward side of the fuel tank.
5. Disconnect the outlet pipe from the muffler. Lower the pipe and support with wire.
6. Remove the exhaust hanger insulator from exhaust pipe hanger stud.

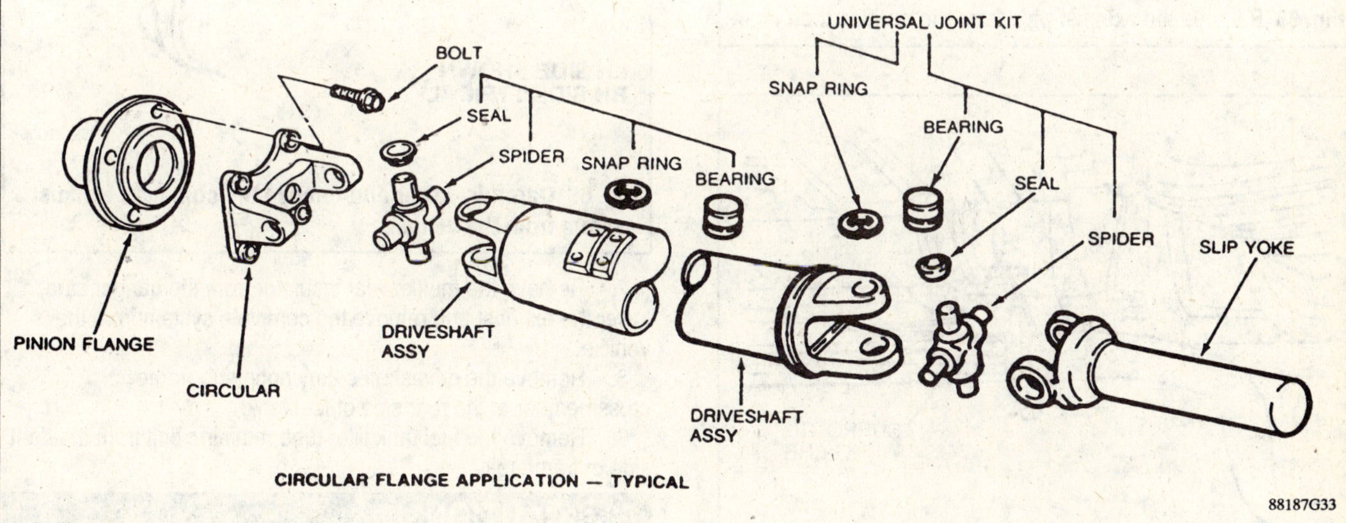

Fig. 61 Exploded view of the driveshaft and U-joints — 1988 vehicle shown

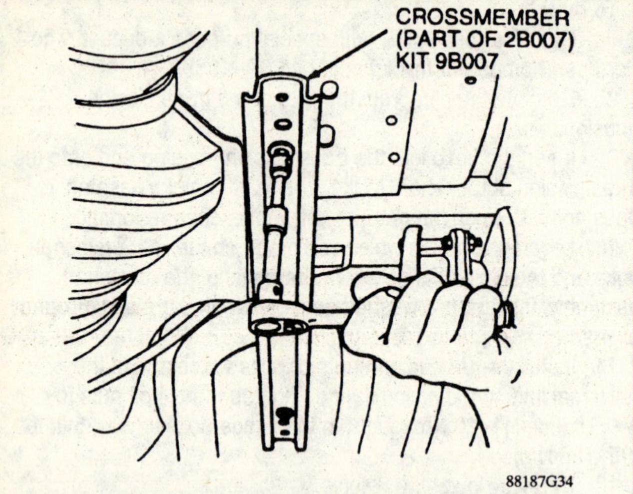

Fig. 62 Unfasten the retaining bolts, then remove the crossmember from the forward side of the fuel tank

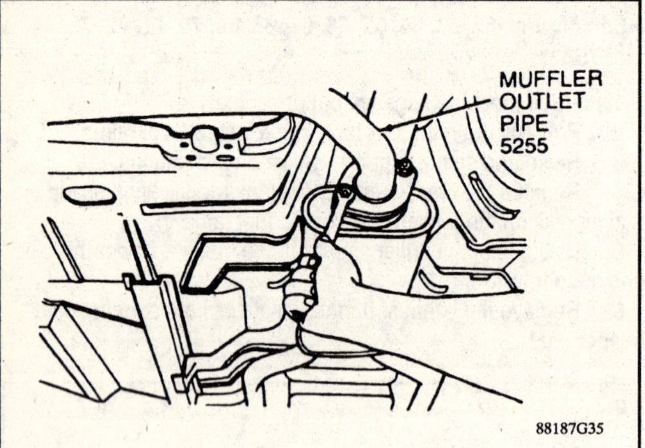

Fig. 63 Remove the exhaust pipe from the muffler, then . . .

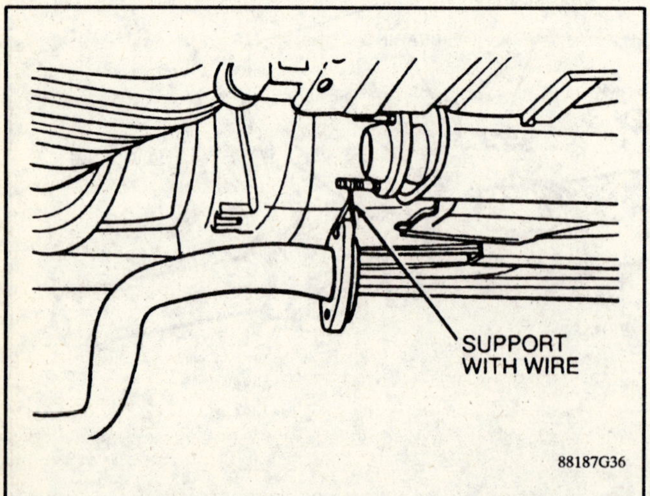

Fig. 64 . . . lower the pipe and secure it with a piece of wire

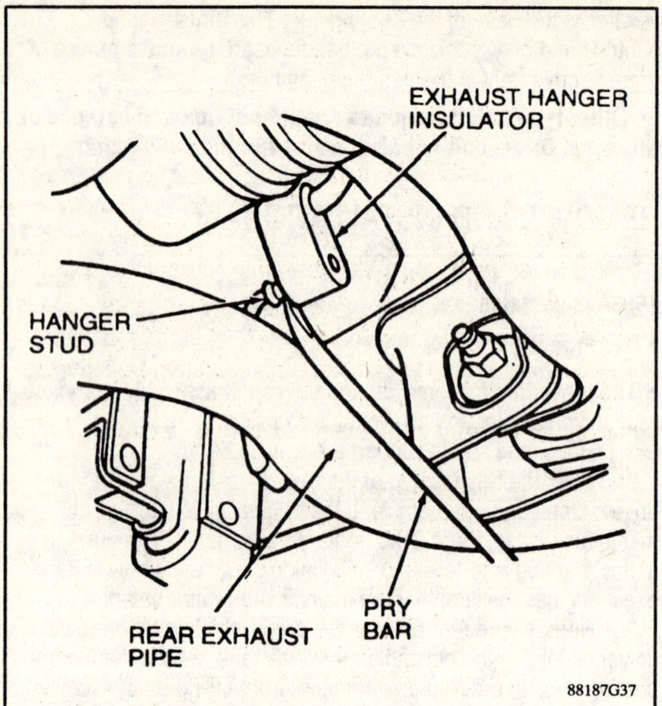

Fig. 65 Remove the exhaust hanger insulator from exhaust pipe hanger stud

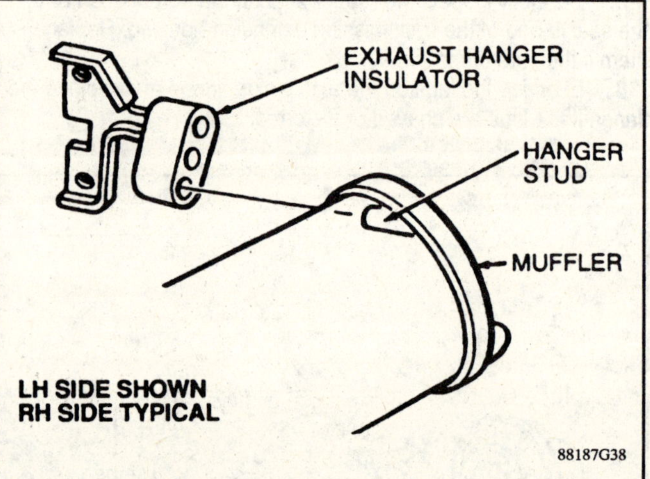

Fig. 66 Carefully lower and remove the complete exhaust system from the vehicle

7. Remove the muffler rear insulator from the hanger stud, lower the exhaust and remove the complete system from the vehicle.

8. Remove the driveshaft safety hoop/sub-frame crossmember at the rear side of fuel tank.

9. Remove the fuel tank filler tube retaining bolt from the right side of frame rail.

****CAUTION**

Use care not to damage the fuel tank to prevent a fuel leak.

10. Being careful not to damage the fuel tank, place a transmission jack under tank.

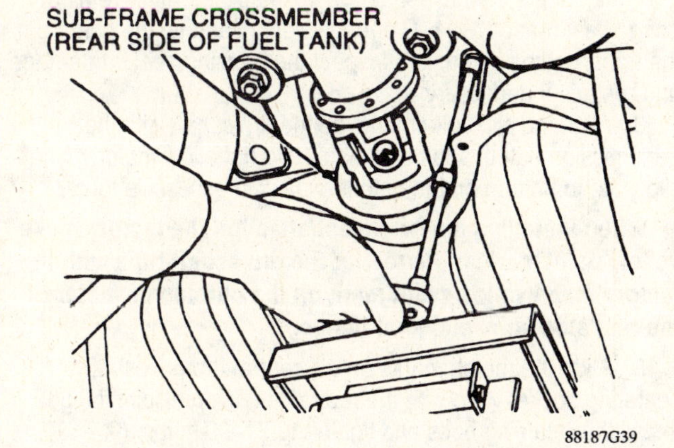

Fig. 67 Remove the sub-frame crossmember from the rear side of the fuel tank

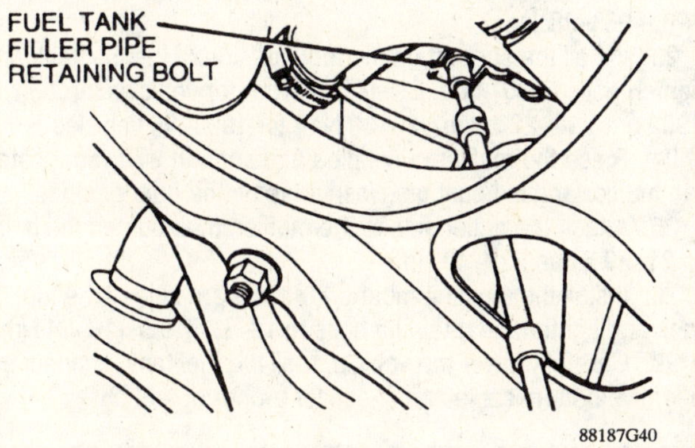

Fig. 68 Unfasten the fuel tank filler tube bolt

Fig. 69 When supporting the fuel tank, be very careful not to damage the fuel tank

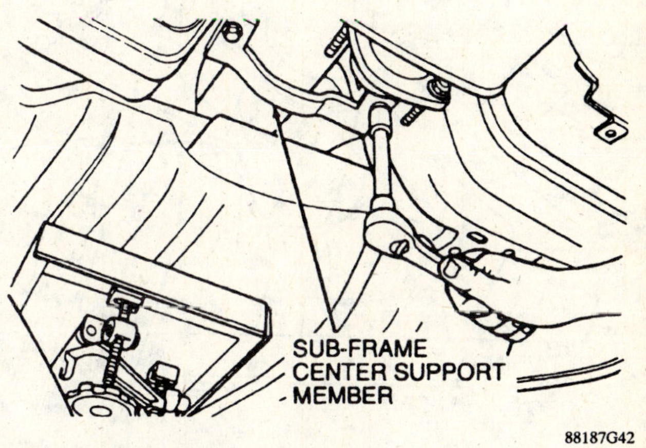

Fig. 70 Remove the sub-frame center support from the forward side of the fuel tank

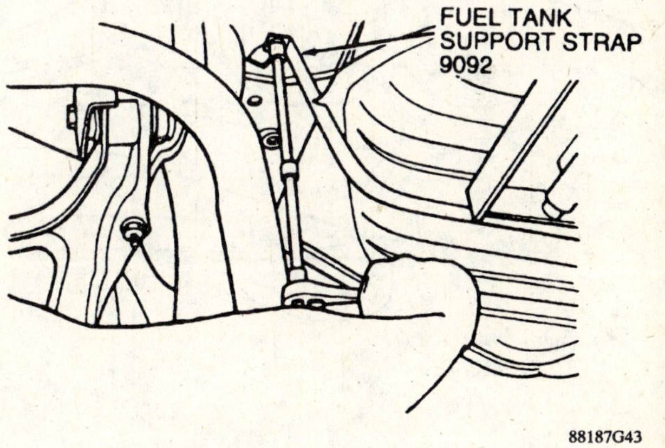

Fig. 71 Remove the fuel tank straps, then carefully lower the tank about 6 inches

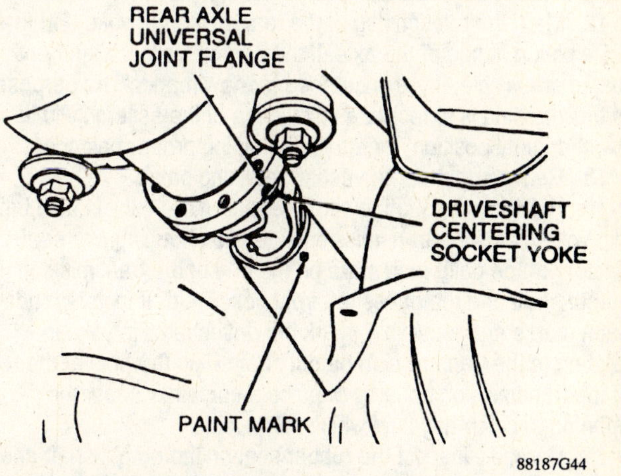

Fig. 72 If there are no factory-made marks, mark the relationship between the rear driveshaft yoke and the drive pinion flange of the axle

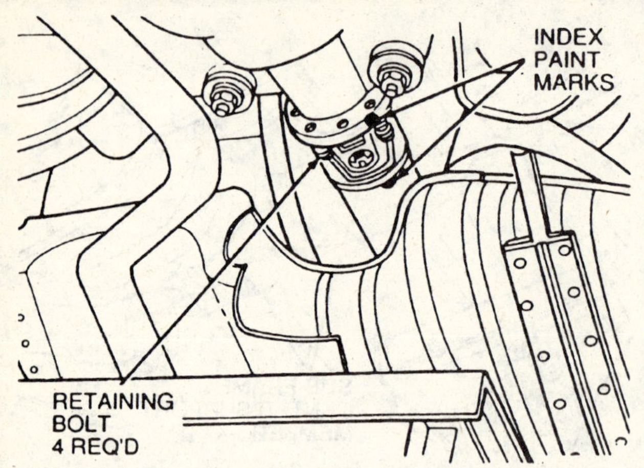

Fig. 73 Unfasten and remove the driveshaft retaining bolts

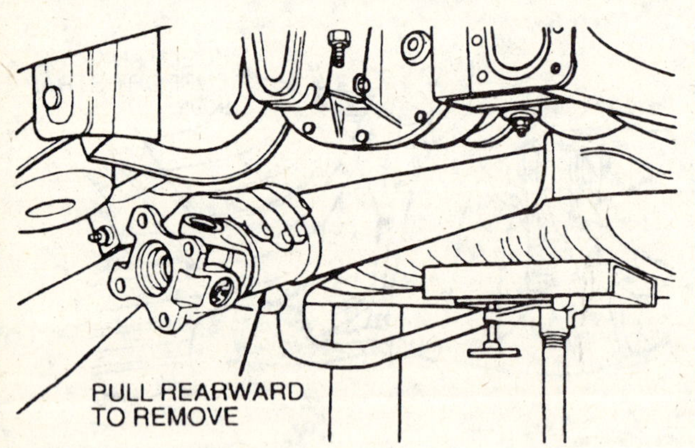

Fig. 74 Remove the driveshaft by carefully pulling it rearward

11. Remove the sub-frame center support on the forward side of fuel tank. Remove the fuel tank support straps, then carefully lower the fuel tank approximately 6 inches (15cm).
12. Mark the relationship of the rear driveshaft yoke and the drive pinion flange of the axle. If the original yellow alignment marks are visible, there is no need for new marks. The purpose of this marking is to facilitate installation of the assembly in its exact original position, thereby maintaining proper balance.
13. Remove the four driveshaft retaining bolts.
14. Pull the driveshaft toward the rear of the vehicle until the slip yoke clears the transmission extension housing and seal. Factory made paint marks are on the end of the transmission output shaft and the driveshaft front yoke weld. If factory made paint marks are not visible, mark the driveshaft slip yoke in relation to the transmission output shaft. Plug the hole at the rear of the transmission housing or place a container under the opening to catch any fluid which might leak.
15. Carefully inspect the rubber seal on the output shaft and the seal in end of the transmission extension housing. Replace them if they are damaged.
16. Examine the lugs on the axle pinion flange and replace the flange if the lugs are shaved or distorted.

To install:

17. Lubricate the driveshaft slip yoke splines with Premium Long Life Grease XG-1-C or equivalent. Remove the plug from the transmission extension. Inspect the housing seal for damage and replace if necessary.
18. Align the slip yoke marks on the driveshaft with the transmission output shaft and install. Do not allow the driveshaft slip yoke to bottom on the output shaft with excessive force.

➜ When installing a new driveshaft, align the factory make yellow paint mark at the rear of the driveshaft tube with the factory made yellow paint mark on the outside diameter of the rear axle universal joint flange.

19. Align the match marks on the rear of the driveshaft centering socket yoke with the rear axle universal joint flange. Install the retaining bolts and tighten to 71-95 ft. lbs. (95-130 Nm).
20. Carefully raise the fuel tank, then install the support straps and tighten the retaining bolts to 21-30 ft. lbs. (29-41 Nm).
21. Install the fuel tank fill tube retaining bolt and tighten to 24-32 inch lbs. (2.7-3.7 Nm).
22. Install the driveshaft safety hoop/sub-frame crossmember, then tighten the retaining bolts to 30-44 ft. lbs. (41-60 Nm) for vehicles through 1992 or to 14-22 ft. lbs. (20-30 Nm) for 1993-96 vehicles.
23. Install the support on the forward side of the fuel tank and tighten bolts to 30-44 ft. lbs. (41-60 Nm) for vehicles through 1992 or to 14-22 ft. lbs. (20-30 Nm) for 1993-96 vehicles.
24. Raise the muffler outlet pipe and support with wire. Install the muffler and exhaust pipe insulators on the hanger studs.
25. Attach the outlet pipe to the muffler, then tighten the bolts to 21-29 ft. lbs. (28-40 Nm).
26. Install the crossmember on the forward side of the fuel tank and tighten the retaining bolts to 12-17 ft. lbs. (16-24 Nm).
27. Carefully lower the vehicle, refill the fuel tank, connect the negative battery cable and check for proper operation.

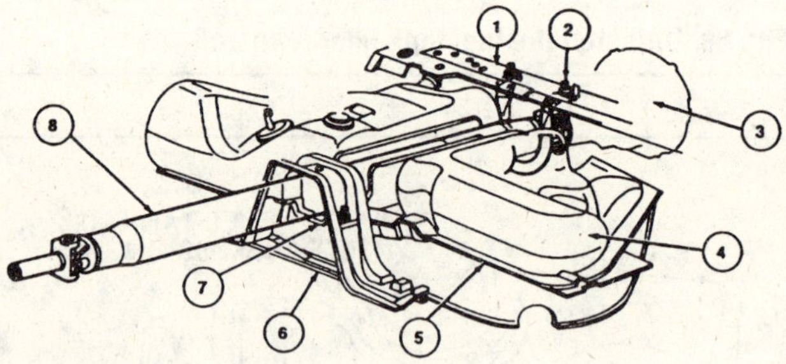

1. Body
2. Sub-frame crossmember
3. Rear axle housing
4. Fuel tank
5. Crossmember
6. Fuel tank modification shield and pipe kit
7. Sub-frame center support member
8. Driveshaft

88187G47

Fig. 75 Driveshaft removal and installation — 1995 vehicle shown

U-JOINT REPLACEMENT

➧ See Figures 76, 77, 78, 79, 80, 81 and 82

✻✻WARNING

Do NOT clamp the driveshaft in the jaws of a vise or similar holding fixture. Denting or cracking may result, causing driveshaft failure.

1. Remove the driveshaft from the vehicle and place on a suitable work bench. Be careful not to damage the tube.
2. Before disassembly, mark the positions of the driveshaft components relative to the driveshaft tube. All components must be reassembled in the same relationship for proper balance.
3. Clamp U-Joint tool T74P-4635, or equivalent in a vise.
4. Remove the four snaprings which retain the bearings.
5. Position the driveshaft slip yoke in U-Joint tool T74P-4635-C or equivalent, then press out the bearing. If the bearing cup cannot be pressed all the way out, remove it with vise grips, or suitable locking pliers.

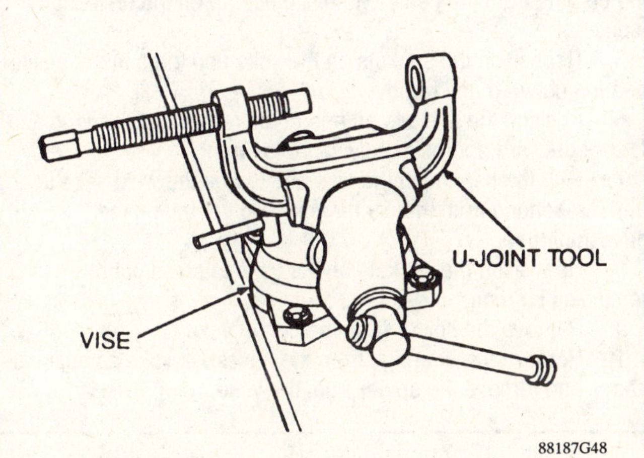

Fig. 76 Clamp the proper U-Joint tool into a suitable vise

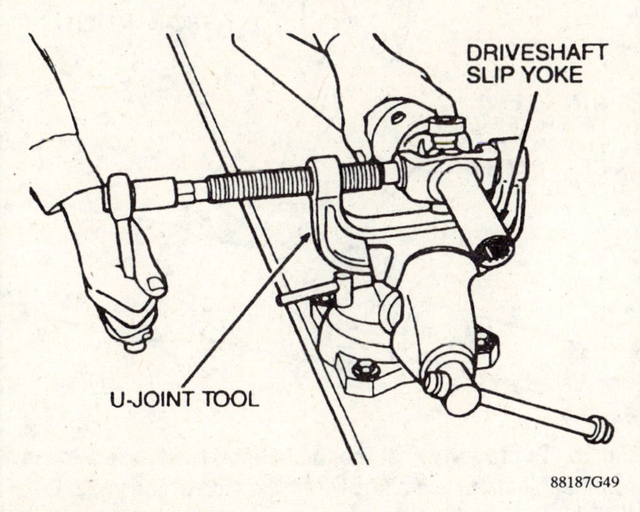

Fig. 77 Position the slip yoke in the U-joint tool

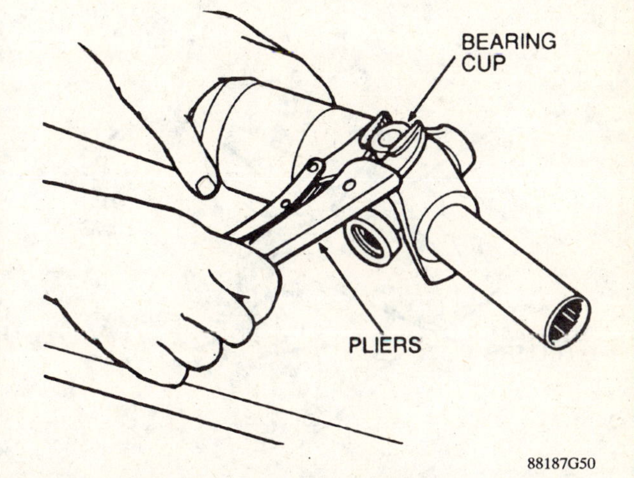

Fig. 78 If it cannot be pressed all the way out, use a pair of locking pliers to remove the bearing

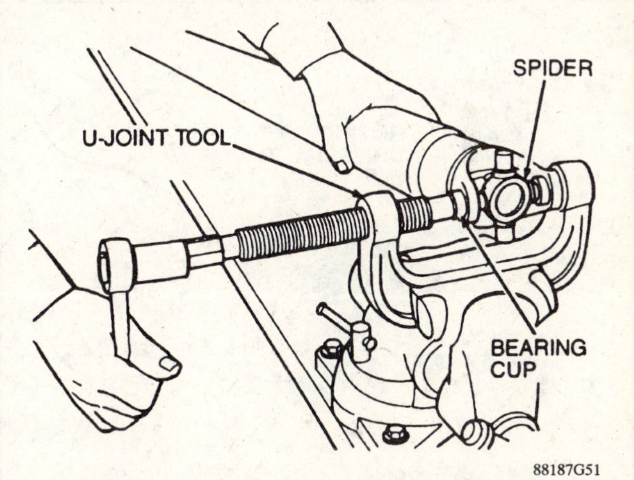

Fig. 79 Use the U-joint tool to press in a new bearing cup

6. Reposition the driveshaft slip yoke in the U-Joint tool 180 degrees to press on the spider and remove the remaining bearing cup from the opposite side.
7. Remove the driveshaft slip yoke from the spider.
8. Remove the remaining bearing cups and spiders from the driveshaft in the same way.
9. Clean all dirt, debris and/or foreign matter from the driveshaft slip yoke area at each end of the driveshaft.
10. Repeat Steps 1-9 to remove the driveshaft centering socket yoke.

To install:

➥ Universal joint service kits are to be installed as complete assemblies only. Do not mix components from the other universal joints.

11. Start a new bearing cup into the driveshaft slip yoke of a the driveshaft.
12. Position a new spider in the driveshaft slip yoke and press the new bearing cup $^{1}/_{4}$ in. (6mm) below the outer surface of the yoke using U-Joint tool T74P-4635-C or equivalent.
13. Remove the U-joint tool, then install a new snapring.

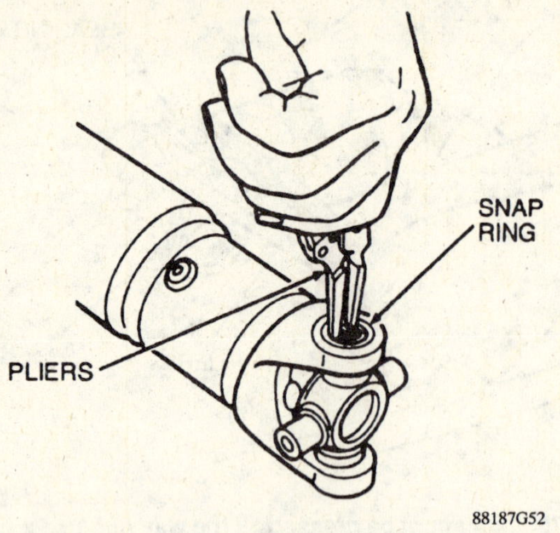

Fig. 80 Install a new snapring using suitable pliers

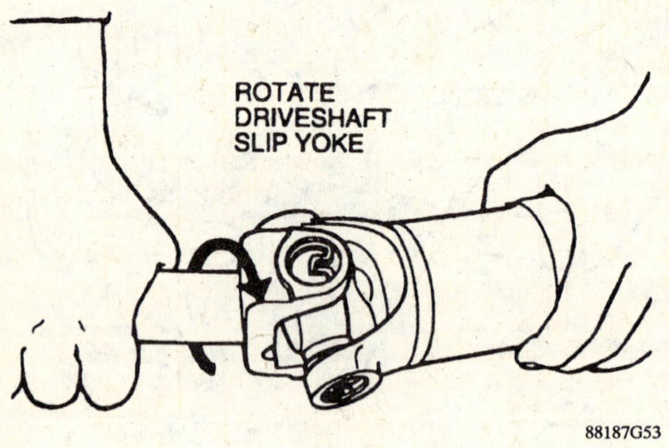

Fig. 81 Check the driveshaft for any binding before installing it in the vehicle

14. Start a new bearing into the opposite side of the yoke. Check the needles for proper position.

15. Position the driveshaft in U-Joint tool T74P-4635-C, then press on the bearing until the opposite bearing cup, which you have just installed, contacts the inner surface of the snapring.

➥ Assemble the rear axle shaft universal joint using the yellow snap rings supplied in the kit. If difficulty is encountered with the yellow snap rings, install the black rings suppled with the kit.

16. Remove the U-joint tool, then install a new snapring on the second bearing. Check the snapring for proper seating.

17. Install the driveshaft slip yoke, remaining bearing cups, spider, driveshaft centering socket yoke and snaprings in the same manner.

18. Check the rear axle shaft universal joints for freedom of movement. If misalignment of any part is causing a bind, a sharp rap on the side of the yoke with a brass or plastic hammer should seat the bearing needle and provide the desired freedom of movement. Care should be exercised to firmly support the shaft end during this operation, as well as to prevent blows to the bearings themselves. Make sure the rear axle shaft universal joints are free to rotate easily without binding before installing the driveshaft.

19. Repeat steps 11-19 to install the driveshaft centering socket yoke.

20. Install the driveshaft in the vehicle.

DOUBLE CARDAN JOINT REPLACEMENT (REAR)

1. Working at the rear axle end of the shaft, mark the position of the spiders, the center yoke, and the centering socket yoke as related to the companion flange. The spiders must be assembled with the bosses in their original position to provide proper clearances.
2. Using a large vise or an arbor press and a socket smaller than the bearing cap on one side and a socket larger than the bearing cap on the other side, drive one of the bearings in toward the center of the universal joint, which will force the opposite bearing out.
3. Remove the driveshaft from the vise.
4. Tighten the bearing in the vise and tap on the yoke to free the bearing from the center yoke. Do not tap on the driveshaft tube.
5. Reposition the sockets on the yoke and force the opposite bearing outward and remove it.
6. Position the sockets on one of the remaining bearings and force it outward approximately $^3/_8$ in. (9.5mm).
7. Grip the bearing in the vise and tap on the weld yoke to free the bearing from the center yoke. Do not tap on the driveshaft tube.
8. Reposition the sockets on the yoke to press out the remaining bearing.
9. Remove the spider from the center yoke.
10. Remove the bearings from the driveshaft yoke as outlined above and remove the spider from the yoke.

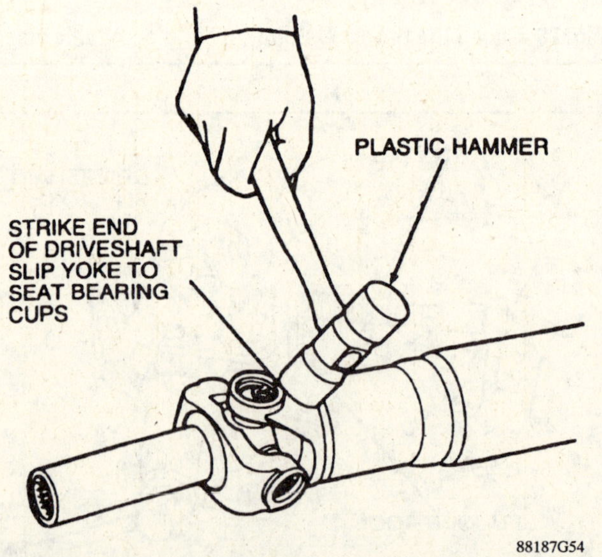

Fig. 82 To properly seat the the bearing cups, use a brass or plastic hammer to sharply rap the side of the yoke. Do NOT hit the bearings themselves

11. Insert a suitable tool into the centering ball socket located in the companion flange and pry out the rubber seal. Remove the retainer, three piece ball seat, washer and spring from the ball socket.

12. Inspect the centering ball socket assembly for worn or damaged parts. If any damage is evident replace the entire assembly.

To install:

13. Insert the spring, washer, three piece ball seat and retainer into the ball socket.

14. Using a suitable tool, install the centering ball socket seal.

15. Position the spider in the driveshaft yoke. Make sure the spider bosses are in the same position as originally installed. Press in the bearing cups with the sockets and vise. Install the internal snaprings provided in the repair kit.

16. Position the center yoke over the spider ends and press in the bearing cups. Install the snaprings.

17. Install the spider in the companion flange yoke. Make sure the spider bosses are in the position as originally installed. Press on the bearing cups and install the snaprings.

18. Position the center yoke over the spider ends and press on the bearing cups. Install the snaprings.

REAR AXLE

Understanding Drive Axles

The drive axle is a special type of transmission that reduces the speed of the drive from the engine and transmission and divides the power to the wheels. Power enters the axle from the driveshaft via the companion flange. The flange is mounted on the drive pinion shaft. The drive pinion shaft and gear which carry the power into the differential turn at engine speed. The gear on the end of the pinion shaft drives a large ring gear the axis of rotation of which is 90 degrees away from that of the pinion. The pinion and gear reduce the gear ratio of the axle, and change the direction of rotation to turn the axle shafts which drive both wheels. The axle gear ratio is found by dividing the number of pinion gear teeth into the number of ring gear teeth.

The ring gear drives the differential case. The case provides the two mounting points for the ends of a pinion shaft on which are mounted two pinion gears. The pinion gears drive the two side gears, one of which is located on the inner end of each axle shaft.

By driving the axle shafts through this arrangement, the differential allows the outer drive wheel to turn faster than the inner drive wheel in a turn.

The main drive pinion and the side bearings, which bear the weight of the differential case, are shimmed to provide proper bearing preload, and to position the pinion and ring gears properly.

****WARNING**

The proper adjustment of the relationship of the ring and pinion gears is critical. It should be attempted only by those with extensive equipment and/or experience.

Limited-slip differentials include clutches which tend to link each axle shaft to the differential case. Clutches may be engaged either by spring action or by pressure produced by the torque on the axles during a turn. During turning on a dry pavement, the effects of the clutches are overcome, and each wheel turns at the required speed. When slippage occurs at either wheel, however, the clutches will transmit some of the power to the wheel which has the greater amount of traction. Because of the presence of clutches, limited-slip units require a special lubricant.

There are also two types of axles used. The conventional type, where as the axle and carrier housing is a one piece unit and moves up and down with the suspension. The independent type, where as the carrier housing is a separate unit mounted to the frame and does not move, the axles (halfshafts) contain constant velocity (CV) joints which allow the axles to flex with suspension movement. 1989 and later vehicles employ the independent type rear axle.

Determining Axle Ratio

The drive axle is said to have a certain axle ratio. This number (usually a whole number and a decimal fraction) is actually a comparison of the number of gear teeth on the ring gear and the pinion gear. For example, a 4.11 rear means that theoretically, there are 4.11 teeth on the ring gear and one tooth on the pinion gear or, put another way, the driveshaft must turn 4.11 times to turn the wheels once. Actually, on a 4.11 rear, there might be 37 teeth on the ring gear and 9 teeth on the pinion gear. By dividing the number of teeth on the pinion gear into the number of teeth on the ring gear, the numerical axle ratio (4.11) is obtained. This also provides a good method of ascertaining exactly what axle ratio one is dealing with.

Another method of determining gear ratio is to jack up and support the car so that both rear wheels are off the ground. Make a chalk mark on the rear wheel and the driveshaft. Put the transmission in neutral. Turn the rear wheel one complete turn and count the number of turns that the driveshaft makes. The number of turns that the driveshaft makes in one complete revolution of the rear wheel is an approximation of the rear axle ratio.

Axle Shaft, Bearing and Seal

The axle type and ratio are stamped on a plate attached to a rear housing cover bolt. All 1983-88 axles are C-lock type axles. All 1989-96 axles are halfshaft type axles.

REMOVAL & INSTALLATION

Bearings must be pressed on and off the shaft with an arbor press. Unless you have access to one, it is inadvisable to attempt any repair work on the axle shaft bearing assemblies.

1983-88 Vehicles

See Figures 83, 84, 85 and 86

1. Raise and safely support the rear of the vehicle.
2. Remove the wheels and tire assembly.

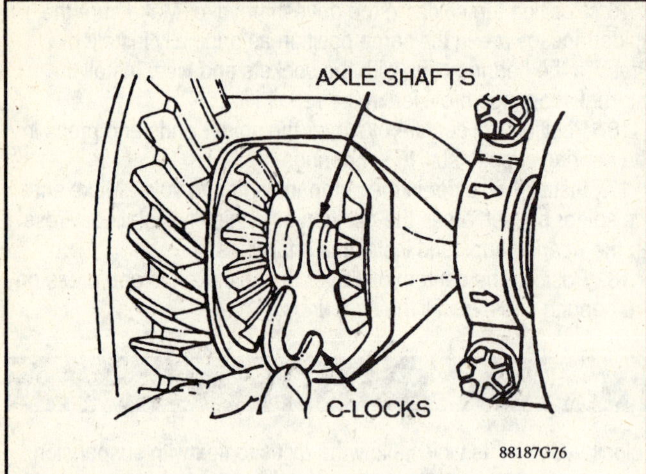

Fig. 83 Removing the C-lock from the axle shaft

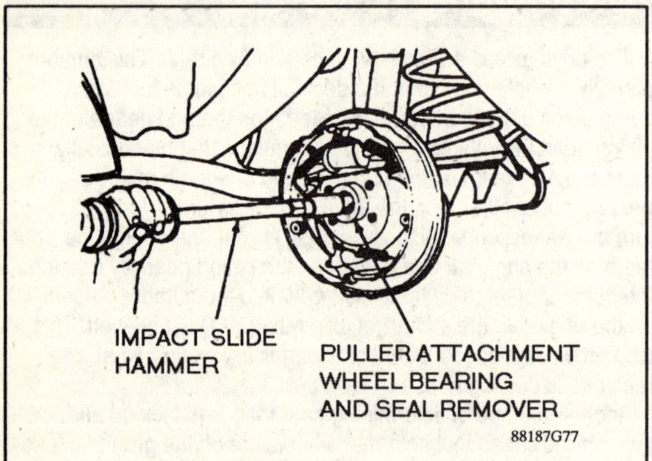

Fig. 84 Axle seal and bearing removal — 1983-88 vehicles

3. Remove the brake drum or disc brake caliper, as applicable.
4. If equipped, remove the anti-lock speed sensor.
5. Clean all dirt from around the axle housing cover. Place a suitable drain pan under the housing cover . Remove the axle housing cover and allow the rear axle lubricant to drain.
6. Remove the housing cover and gasket, if used.
7. Position jackstands under the rear frame member and lower the axle housing. This is done to give easy access to the inside of the differential.
8. Working through the opening in the differential case, remove the side gear pinion shaft lockbolt and the side gear pinion shaft.
9. Push the axle shafts inward and remove the C-locks from the inner end of the axle shafts. Temporarily replace the shaft and lockbolt to retain the differential gears in position.
10. Remove the axle shaft from the housing.
11. Place Bearing Remover T85L-1225-AH or equivalent, into the axle shaft housing bore and position the tangs behind the axle bearing. Remove the axle bearing and axle seal as an assembly with a slide hammer installed on the bearing removal tool. Be sure the seal is not damaged by the splines on the axle shaft.

➥ Two types of bearings are used on some axles, one with a press fit and the other a slip fit. A loose fitting bearing does not necessarily indicate excessive wear.

12. Inspect the axle shaft housing and axle shafts for burrs or other irregularities. Replace any worn or damaged parts. A light yellow color on the bearing journal of the axle shaft is normal, and does not require replacement of the axle shaft. Slight pitting and wear is also normal.

To install:

13. Lightly coat the wheel bearing rollers with axle lubricant. Install the bearings in the axle housing bore using Bearing Installer T78P-1225-A, or equivalent. Make sure the bearing seats firmly against the shoulder in the housing.
14. Wipe all lubricant from the oil seal bore, before installing the seal. Inspect the original seals for wear. If necessary, these may be replaced with new seals, which are prepacked with lubricant and do not require soaking. If the seals are dry, apply a suitable wheel bearing grease between the lips of the axle seal.
15. Install the axle seal using Seal Installer T78P-1177-A or equivalent.

➥ Installation of the seal without the proper tool can cause distortion and seal leakage. Seals may be color coded for side identification. Do not interchange seals from side to side, if they are coded.

16. Remove the lock bolt/pin and pinion shaft. Carefully slide the axle shafts into place. Be careful that you do not damage the seal with the splined end of the axle shaft. Engage the splined end of the shaft with the differential side gears.
17. Install the axle shaft C-locks on the bottom end of the axle shaft splines and seat the C-lock in the counterbore of the differential side gears by pulling the axle shaft in an outward direction.
18. Rotate the differential pinion gears until the differential pinion shaft can be installed. Apply a suitable thread locking compound to the threads on the lock pin and install the lock pin securing the differential pinion shaft. Tighten to 15-30 ft. lbs. (20-41 Nm).
19. Check the rear axle housing vent, making sure it is not plugged. A plugged vent can cause excessive pressure to build in the axle housing and leaking seals will result.

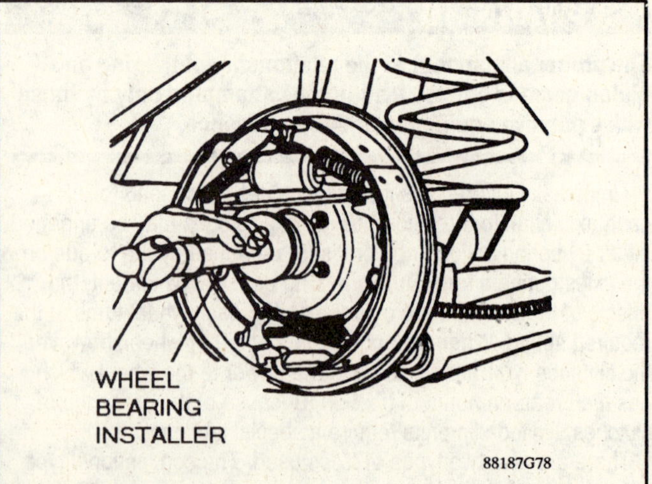

Fig. 85 Install the axle bearing on a vehicle with drum brakes — 1983-88 vehicles

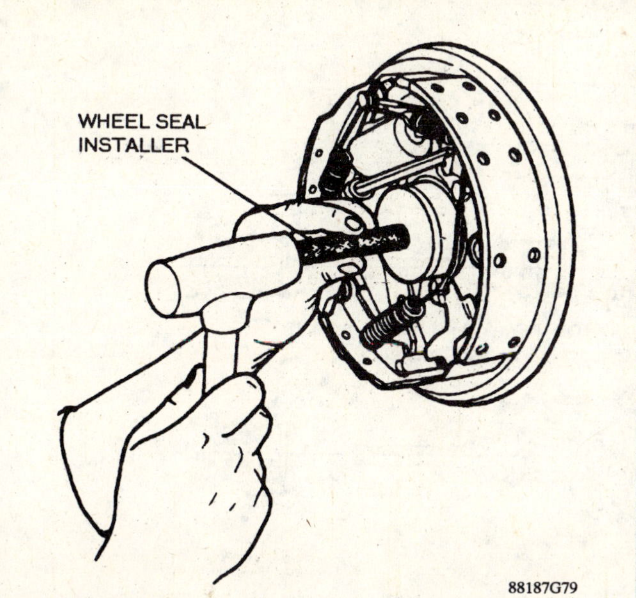

Fig. 86 Installation of the axle seal — 1983-88 vehicles with drum brakes

20. Clean the axle housing cover and the housing mating surface.
21. Apply a bead of silicone sealer to the axle housing cover and install the cover and retaining bolts. Tighten the bolts to 18-28 ft. lbs. (24-38 Nm).

➥ Some axle housing covers use a gasket instead of silicone sealer. Use the same type of gasket as removed.

22. Add a suitable rear axle lubricant to bring the level to approximately $^1/_2$ in. (13mm) below the fill hole. For traction-lock equipped vehicles, a suitable friction modifier must also be added.
23. Install the brake drum or disc brake rotor and caliper, as applicable.
24. If equipped, install the anti-lock brake sensor.
25. Install the wheel and tire assembly.
26. If the brake system was opened, bleed the rear brakes.
27. Carefully lower the vehicle.
28. Road test the vehicle and check for leaks and proper operation.

1989-96 Vehicles

➧ See Figures 87 and 88

➥ The bearings must be pressed on and off the shaft using an arbor press.

1. Raise and safely support the rear of the vehicle with jackstands.
2. Remove the wheel, tire, and brake drum. With disc brakes, remove the caliper, retainer, nuts and rotor. New anchor plate bolts will be needed for reassembly.
3. Remove the nuts holding the retainer plate in the backing plate, or axle shaft retainer bolts from the housing. Disconnect the brake line with drum brakes.
4. Remove the retainer and install nuts, finger-tight, to prevent the brake backing plate from being dislodged.
5. Pull out the axle shaft and bearing assembly, using a slide hammer.
6. On models with a tapered roller bearing, the tapered cup will normally remain in the axle housing when the shaft is removed. The cup must be removed from the housing to prevent seal damage when the shaft is reinstalled. The cup can be removed with a slide hammer and an expanding puller.

✱✱WARNING

If end-play is found to be excessive, the bearing should be replaced. Shimming the bearing is not recommended as this ignores end-play of the bearing itself and could result in improper bearing seating.

7. Using a chisel, nick the bearing retainer in 3 or 4 places. The retainer does not have to be cut, but merely collapsed sufficiently to allow the bearing retainer to be slid from the shaft.

To install:

8. Press off the bearing and install the new one by pressing it into position. With tapered bearings, place the lubricated seal and bearing on the axle shaft (cup rib ring facing the flange). make sure that the seal is the correct length. Disc brake seal rims are black, drum brake seal rims are grey. Press the bearing and seal onto the shaft.
9. Press on the new retainer.

➥ Do not attempt to press the bearing and the retainer on at the same time.

10. To replace the seal on ball bearing models:
    a. Remove the seal from the housing with an expanding cone type puller and a slide hammer. The seal must be replaced whenever the shaft is removed.
    b. Wipe a small amount of sealer onto the outer edge of the new seal before installation; do not put sealer on the sealing lip.
    c. Press the seal into the housing with a seal installation tool.
11. Assemble the shaft and bearing in the housing, being sure that the bearing is seated properly in the housing. On ball bearing models, be careful not to damage the seal with the shaft. With tapered bearings, first install the tapered cup on the bearing, and lubricate the outer diameter of the cup and the seal with axle lube. Then install the shaft and bearing assembly into the housing.
12. Install the retainer, drum or rotor and caliper, wheel and tire. Bleed the brakes.

Pinion Oil Seal

REMOVAL & INSTALLATION

➧ See Figures 89 and 90

➥ This procedure disturbs the pinion bearing preload which must be reset for a correct repair. Do not attempt this procedure without a new pinion nut, inch pound torque wrench, rear axle universal joint flange holding tool and a pinion seal installation tool.

1. Raise and safely support the vehicle.
2. Place jackstands under the rear axle housing.
3. Remove both wheel and tire assemblies.

● Other than the rear axle cv joint boot, the outboard CV joint is serviced only as an assembly with the outboard CV joint/interconnecting shaft.

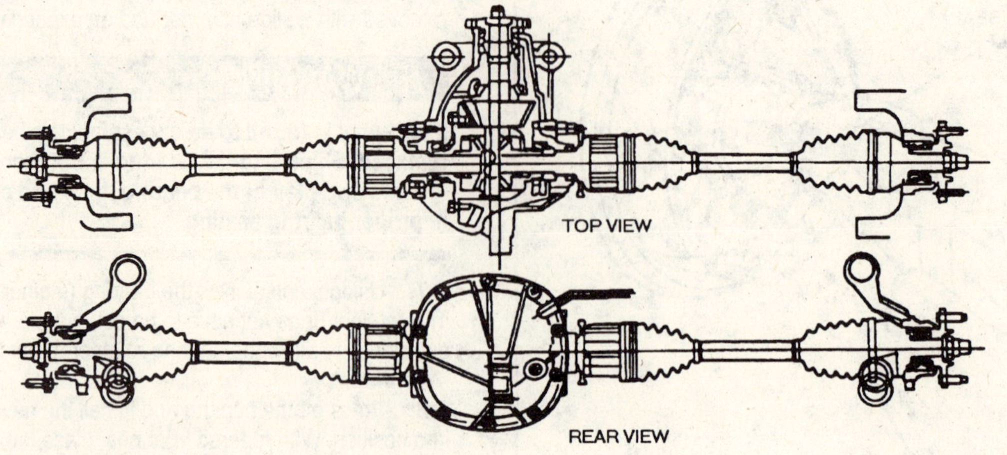

Fig. 87 Rear axle housing and halfshafts — 1989-96 vehicles

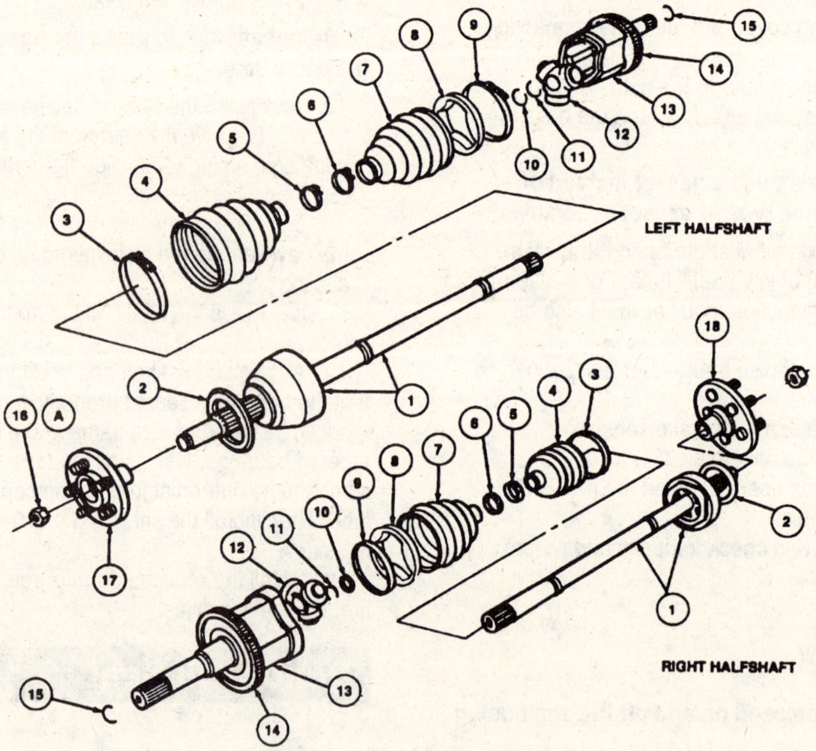

1. Outboard CV joint/interconnecting shaft
2. Halfshaft dust seal
3. Boot clamp(large outboard)
4. Rear axle CV joint boot(outboard)
5. Boot clamp(small inboard)
6. Boot clamp(small inboard)
7. Rear axle CV joint boot(inboard)
8. TriLobe insert
9. Boot clamp(large inboard)
10. Rear axle shaft joint assy retaining ring
11. Rear axle shaft retaining u-washer
12. Tripod assy
13. Inboard CV joint stub shaft pilot bearing housing
14. Rear brake anti-lock sensor indicator
15. "C" clip
16. Axle nut
17. Hub left shaft
18. Hub right shaft

88187G81

Fig. 88 Exploded view of the rear axle shaft assembly — 1989-96 vehicles

4. Remove the brake drums or calipers, as applicable.
5. Mark the driveshaft and yoke for reassembly in the same location.
6. Disconnect the driveshaft from the rear yoke.
7. Place an inch pound (Nm) torque wrench with a suitable socket on the pinion nut. Record the torque required to maintain rotation of the pinion through several revolutions.
8. Install Flange Holding Tool T78P-4851-A or equivalent on the rear axle universal joint flange. Remove the pinion nut while holding the flange stationary. Discard the pinion nut.
9. Clean the area around the pinion seal. Place a suitable drain pan under the pinion seal.
10. Mark the pinion shaft in relationship to the axle joint flange for assembly reference.
11. Remove the rear axle joint flange using Companion Flange Remover T65L-4851-B or equivalent.
12. Carefully place a suitable prytool under the flange of the pinion seal and strike with a hammer to wedge the prying tool between the seal and the axle housing. Pry on the flange of the pinion seal to raise the flange enough the grasp with suitable gripping pliers and remove the pinion seal.

To install:

13. Clean the seal seating area in the axle housing.
14. Before installing the new seal, coat the lip of the seal with a suitable wheel bearing grease, if not pre-greased.
15. Place the pinion seal on Pinion Seal Installer T79P-4676-A or equivalent and install the pinion seal into the axle housing using a hammer.
16. Check the axle universal joint flange for burrs and remove if found.
17. Apply a small amount of rear axle lubricant to the rear axle universal joint flange splines.
18. Align the index marks made on the axle universal joint flange and pinion shaft, then install the flange onto the shaft.
19. Install Flange Holding Tool T78P-4851-A or equivalent, on the rear axle universal joint flange. Rotate the pinion shaft while tightening the pinion nut the ensure proper pinion bearing seating.

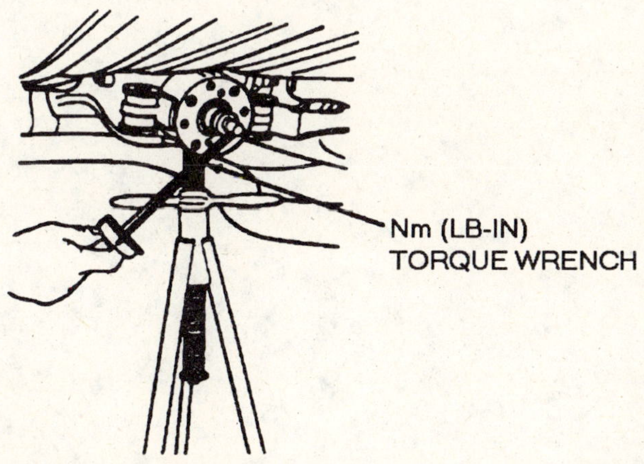

Fig. 89 Measuring the pinion bearing preload requires the use of a inch pound torque wrench

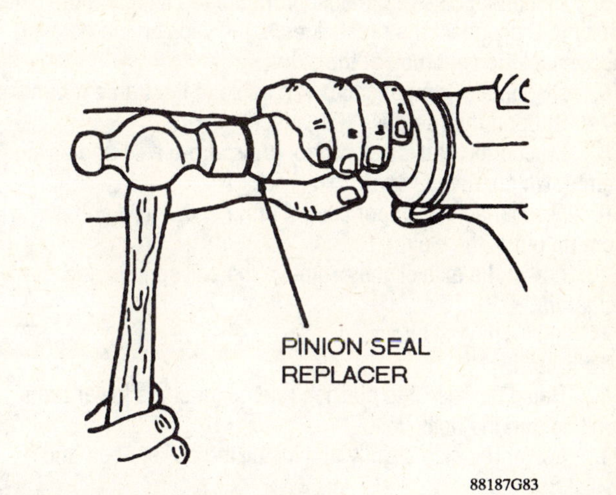

Fig. 90 Pinion seal installation

20. Take frequent pinion bearing torque preload readings until the original recorded reading is reached. Tighten the nut in small increments to avoid overtightening.
21. If the originally recorded pinion bearing preload is less than 8-14 inch lbs. (0.9-1.6 Nm) with original pinion bearing or 16-29 inch lbs. (1.8-3.2 Nm) with new pinion bearings, tighten the pinion nut to these readings.

Never back off the pinion nut to reduce pinion preload. If reduced preload is required, a new collapsible pinion spacer and pinion nut must be installed.

22. Install the driveshaft, aligning the index marks made during disassembly.
23. Add the proper rear axle lubricant to bring the level to approximately 1/2 in. (13mm) below the fill hole, if needed. Install the fill plug.
24. Check the rear axle housing vent, making sure it is not plugged. A plugged vent can cause excessive pressure to build in the axle housing and leaking seals may result.
25. Install the rear brake drums or calipers, as applicable.
26. Install the wheel and tire assemblies. Tighten the lug nuts in a star pattern to 85-105 ft. lbs. (115-142 Nm).
27. If the brake system was opened, bleed the rear brakes.
28. Remove the jackstands, then carefully lower the vehicle.
29. Road test the vehicle and check for leaks and proper operation.

Axle Housing Assembly

REMOVAL & INSTALLATION

1983-88 Vehicles

1. Raise the vehicle and support it on jackstands placed under the frame.
2. Remove the rear wheels.
3. Place an indexing mark on the rear yoke and driveshaft, and disconnect the shaft.
4. Disconnect the shock absorbers from the axle tubes. Disconnect the stabilizer bar at the axle bracket, on vehicles so equipped.

5. Disconnect the brake hose from the tee fitting on the axle housing. Disconnect the brake lines at the clips on the housing. Disconnect the vent tube at the axle.
6. Disconnect the parking brake cable at the frame mounting.
7. Support the rear axle with a jack.
8. Disconnect the lower control arms at the axle and swing them down out of the way.
9. Disconnect the upper control arms at the axle and swing them up out of the way.
10. Lower the axle slightly, remove the coil springs and insulators.
11. Lower the axle housing.

To install:

12. Raise the axle into position and connect the lower arms. Don't tighten the bolts yet.
13. Lower the axle slightly and install the coil springs and insulators.
14. Raise the axle and connect the upper control arms. Don't tighten the bolts yet.
15. Connect the parking brake cable at the frame mounting.
16. Connect the brake hose at the tee fitting on the axle housing.
17. Connect the vent tube at the axle. Apply thread locking compound to the threads.
18. Connect the stabilizer bar at the axle bracket, on vehicles so equipped.
19. Connect the shock absorbers from the axle tubes.
20. Connect the driveshaft.
21. Install the rear wheels.
22. Lower the vehicle.
23. Once the car is back on its wheels, observe the following torques:
    - Lower arm bolts: 100 ft. lbs.
    - Lower shock absorber nuts: 55 ft. lbs.
    - Upper arm bolts: 100 ft. lbs.

****WARNING**

Bleed and adjust the brakes accordingly.

Differential Carrier

REMOVAL & INSTALLATION

1989-96 Vehicles

1. Raise and support vehicle, remove driveshaft and only the right side halfshaft.
2. Using a transmission jack to support differential housing, remove the rear mount retaining bolts and remove rear mount from the housing cover.
3. Remove the front retaining nuts, bolts, bushings and washers.
4. Using a halfshaft removal tool, T89P-3514-A or equivalent, push tool towards carrier to release CV joint stub shaft from gear.
5. While lowering axle assembly, move assembly to the right to disengage stub shaft from housing and install plug tool T89P-4850-B or equivalent into left side of housing.

To install:

➥ Whenever halfshafts are removed from differential housing always install new oil seals in housing and circlips on stub shafts before reassembly.

6. Lightly lubricate left side stub shaft. Position differential housing on jack, raise enough to align left side CV joint stub shaft.Using extreme care push into differential side gear until circlip engages.
7. Raise housing into position. Install bushings, washers, bolts and nuts in front mounting holes. Tighten to 68-100 ft. lbs.
8. Install rear mount onto housing cover and tighten to 80-100 ft. lbs.
9. Install rear mount-to-crossmember retaining bolts and nuts. Tighten to 122-156 ft. lbs.
10. Replace the driveshaft and right side halfshaft using the procedures outlined previously.
11. Check differential oil level, fill as necessary.

8

SUSPENSION AND STEERING

WHEELS

Wheels must be replaced when they are bent, dented, heavily rusted, have air leaks or enlongated bolt holes. Replacement wheels must be equal to the original equipment wheels in load capacity, diameter, width, offset and mounting configuration. An improper wheel may affect wheel bearing life, ground and tire clearance, speedometer and odometer misreadings.

Corrosion buildup can result in wheels sticking to the axle or rotor flange. To help prevent this from happening, spray wheel center and wheel stud nuts with a good penetrating oil. Once the wheel has been removed, clean the axle/rotor flange and wheel bore with a wire brush, steel wool or other suitable material. Spread a thin coat of disc brake caliper grease on the wheel bore, but do not put grease on the wheel studs. Use spray penetrating lubricant on the wheel studs.

- To avoid injury from vehicles with a Traction-Lok® axle, NEVER run the engine with only one wheel off the ground, such as changing a tire. The wheel still on the ground could cause the vehicle to move.
- Never allow hoists or jacks to contact the axle housing, halfshafts or CV joints.
- Do not attempt to use jack pressure on either front or rear bumpers of any Unitized Bodied vehicle.
- The mini spare is provided only for temporary emergency use. Do not use as a regular tire. Service or replace the regular tire as soon as possible.

Wheels

REMOVAL & INSTALLATION

****CAUTION**

The service jack provided with the vehicle is only intended to be used in an emergency, for changing a deflated tire. Never use the service jack to hoist the vehicle for any other service.

See Figure 1

1. Using the end of the lug wrench, either remove the wheel cover or carefully pry off the wheel cover applique, as applicable.
2. If equipped, remove the wheel locking nut.
3. Loosen the remaining lug nuts with the wheel on the ground, then raise and safely support the vehicle. If you are working at home (not on a roadside emergency) support the car safely using jackstand(s).
4. Remove the lug nuts, then remove the wheel and tire assembly.

If the wheel is stuck or rusted on the hub, make all the lug nuts finger-tight, then back each one off 2 turns. Put the car back on the ground and rock it side to side. Get another person to help, if necessary. This is far safer than hitting a stuck wheel with the vehicle on a jack or jackstands.

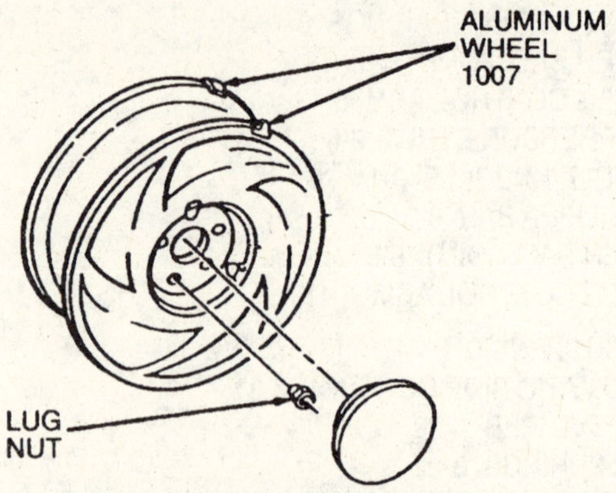

Fig. 1 On aluminum wheels, you must remove the center wheel cover to access the lug nuts

To install:

5. Clean the wheel bore and bolt holes as necessary.
6. Position wheel and tire assembly onto the axle or hub.
7. Install the lug nuts hand-tight.
8. Carefully lower the vehicle, then tighten the lug nuts in a rotation, skipping every other one. Always use a torque wrench to avoid uneven tightening. Tighten the lug nuts (including the locking nut, if so equipped) to 80–105 ft. lbs. (115–142 Nm).
9. Install the wheel cover, ensuring that the valve stem is positioned correctly, if so equipped.

Wheel Lug Studs

REMOVAL AND INSTALLATION

1. Raise and support the vehicle safely.
2. Remove the wheel.
3. Remove the brake assembly. On disc brake systems remove the rotor.
4. For vehicles equipped with disc brake systems, place the rotor in a press and remove the stud. On drum brake systems, use a portable press or a soft faced hammer to remove the stud.

To Install:

5. For disc brake systems, press the stud into place. Install the rotor.
6. On drum brake systems, use several washers and the lug nut to draw the stud into place.
7. Ensure that the head of the stud is seated tightly against the back of the hub or rotor.
8. Install the brake assembly and wheel. Tighten lug nuts to 80–105 ft. lbs. (115–142 Nm).
9. Lower vehicle and test drive. Check lug nut torque after driving vehicle a short distance.

FRONT SUSPENSION

On 1983–88 vehicles, the front suspension design utilizes MacPherson struts with coil springs mounted between the lower arm and a spring pocket in the No. 2 crossmember. The shock struts are non-repairable, and must be replaced as a unit. The ball joints lower suspension arm bushings are not separately serviced, and they also must be replaced by replacing the suspension arm assembly. The ball joint seal can be replaced separately.

On 1989–96 vehicles the front suspension design utilizes coil springs mounted over the MacPherson struts. The struts are non-repairable, and must be replaced as a unit. The suspension geometry features high caster angle and negative camber for outstanding handling and improved tire wear characteristics. Again the lower control arm bushings, lower and upper ball joints cannot be serviced individually, but as a unit with their control arms respectively.

Coil Springs

**CAUTION

Always use extreme caution when working with coil springs. Make sure the vehicle is supported safely.

REMOVAL & INSTALLATION

See Figures 2, 3, 4, 5 and 6

1983–88 Vehicles

1. Raise the front of the vehicle and place safety stands under both sides of the jack pads just back of the lower control arms so the lower control arms hang free.
2. Remove the wheel and tire assembly.
3. Remove the brake caliper and support out of the way with a piece of wire.
4. Disconnect the tie rod from the steering spindle, using Tie Rod End Remover Tool-3290-D or equivalent.
5. Detach the stabilizer bar link from the lower control arm.
6. Unfasten the steering gear bolts, if necessary, and move the steering gear out of the way so that the suspension arm bolt can be removed.
7. Use Spring Compressor Tool T82P-5310-A or equivalent, to place the upper plate in position into the spring pocket cavity on the crossmember. The hooks on the plate should be facing the center of the vehicle.
8. Install the compression rod into the lower arm spring pocket hole, through the coil spring, into the upper plate.
9. Install the lower plate, lower ball nut, thrust washer and bearing, and forcing nut onto the compression rod.
10. Tighten the forcing nut on the compressor tool until a drag on the nut is felt.
11. Remove the suspension arm-to-crossmember nuts and bolts. The compressor tool forcing nut may have to be tightening or loosened for easy bolt removal.

If a new spring is to be installed, mark the position of the upper and lower plates on the spring with chalk. Measure the compressed length of the spring as well as the amount of the spring curvature to assist in the compressing and installation of a new spring.

12. Loosen the compression rod forcing nut until the spring tensioner is relieved, then remove the forcing nut.
13. Remove the compression rod and the coil spring from the vehicle.

To install:

14. Place the insulator on the top of the spring. Position the spring into the lower arm spring pocket.

Make sure the spring pigtail is positioned between the two holes in the lower arm spring pocket.

15. Position the spring into the upper spring seat in the crossmember.
16. Insert the compression rod through the control arm and spring, then hook it to the upper plate. The upper plate is installed with the hooks facing the center of the vehicle.
17. Tighten the forcing nut, position the lower arm into the crossmember, then install new lower arm-to-crossmember bolts and nuts, but do not tighten at this time.
18. Remove the spring compressor tool from the vehicle.
19. With a suitable jack, raise the suspension arm to a normal position. Tighten the lower arm-to-crossmember attaching nuts to 110–150 ft. lbs. (149–203 Nm). Remove the jack.
20. Install the steering gear-to-crossmember bolts and nuts, if removed. Hold the bolts, then tighten to nuts to 90–100 ft. lbs. (122–136 Nm).

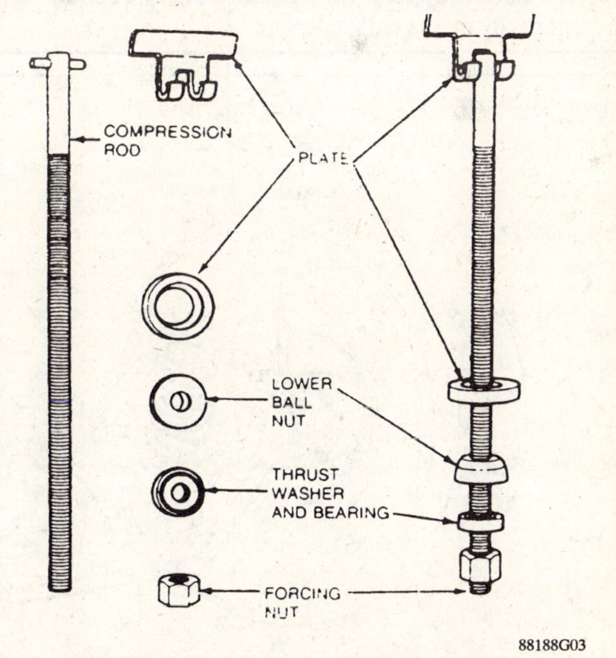

Fig. 2 Make sure to use the correct type of spring compressor tool

21. Connect the stabilizer bar link to the lower suspension arm. Tighten the attaching nut to 8–12 ft. lbs. (12–16 Nm).

22. Position the tie rod assembly into the steering spindle, then install the retaining nut. Tighten the nut to 35 ft. lbs. (47 Nm), and continue tightening the nut to align the next castellation with the cotter pin hole in the stud. Install a new cotter pin.

23. Install the wheel and tire assembly, then carefully lower the vehicle.

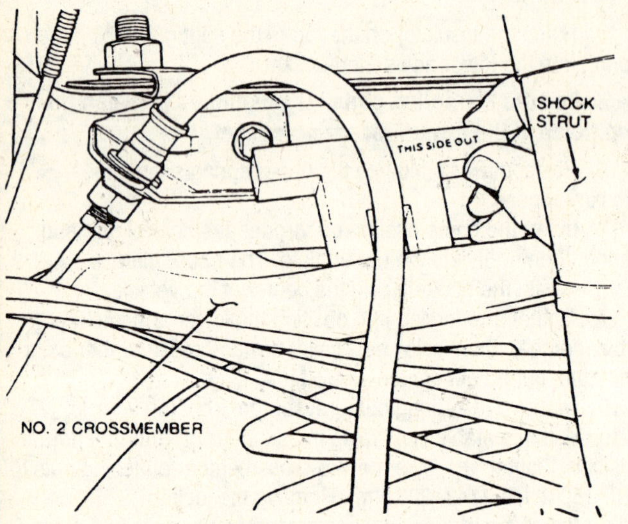

88188G04

Fig. 3 Place the upper plate in position into the spring pocket cavity on the crossmember

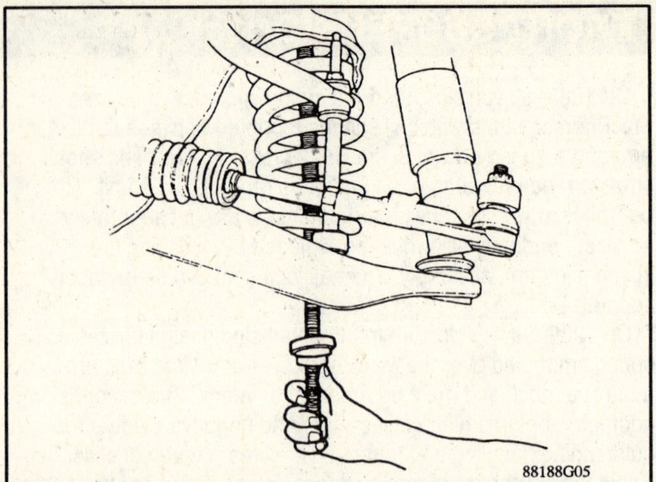

88188G05

Fig. 4 View of the spring compressor inserted through the control arm

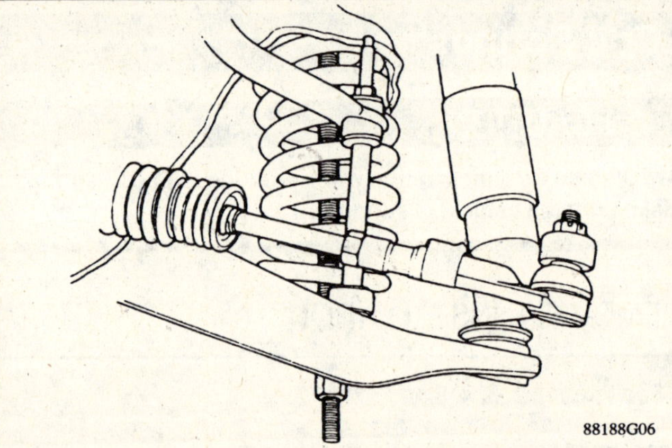

88188G06

Fig. 5 View of the spring compressor with the control arm and spring in position after tension is relieved

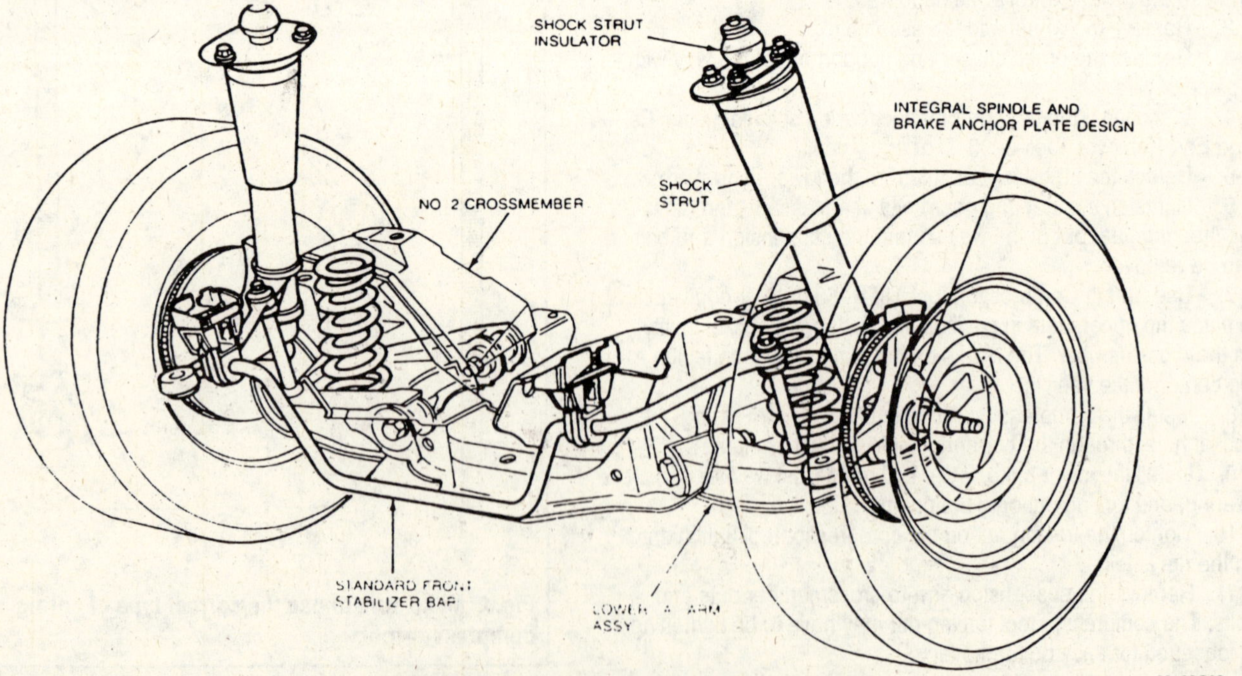

88188G02

Fig. 6 View of the coil springs and related front suspension components — 1983–88 vehicles

1989-96 Vehicles

See Figures 7, 8 and 9

The following procedures are used for removal and installation of the coil springs and MacPherson struts, since they are removed together; one can not be removed without the other.

1. If equipped, remove plastic front shock cover cup at the front shock absorber mounting bracket.
2. If equipped, remove the electronic automatic ride actuator and actuator mounting washer at top strut mount in engine compartment.
3. Unfasten the three upper shock retaining nuts and collar plate/seal from the mounting studs in the engine compartment.
4. Raise and safely support the vehicle with jackstands.
5. Remove the tire and wheel assembly.
6. Remove the lower strut mounting bolt and nut.
7. Remove nut at the stabilizer link upper mounting stud.

****WARNING**

Be very careful to avoid damage to the ball joint seal. If the seal is damaged, the stabilizer bar link assembly must be replaced.

8. Separate the link from the front wheel spindle using Ball Joint Separator/Remover D88L-3006-A, or equivalent.
9. Support lower control arm assembly with a transmission jack, or equivalent.
10. Raise the control arm and spindle with the jack, until the stabilizer link can be completely separated from the wheel spindle. Position the stabilizer link out of the way.
11. Remove the front wheel spindle-to-upper control arm ball joint attaching nut and bolt and discard.
12. Carefully lower the jack to separate the spindle from the upper control arm. Do not allow the spindle to hang free, support it with a piece of wire or other means.
13. Remove support from lower control arm and remove shock absorber/strut and spring assembly from vehicle.

To install:

14. Position the shock absorber and upper mount assembly over the lower control arm. Insert the lower shock bolt into the lower control arm.
15. Using a jack, raise the lower control arm and strut/shock absorber into position, aligning the upper strut mounting studs with the holes.
16. Remove the wire holding the spindle and position the spindle to the upper control arm. Raise the lower control arm with the jack and attach the spindle to the upper control arm ball joint using a new attaching bolt and nut. Tighten the nut to 50-68 ft. lbs. (68-92 Nm).
17. Position the stabilizer bar link and lower spindle assembly until link is in position to install the nut onto link. Tighten to 30-39 ft. lbs. (40-55 Nm).
18. Remove the jack from the lower control arm.
19. Install the lower strut nut, but do not tighten at this time.
20. Install tire and wheel assembly, then tighten the lug nuts to 85-105 ft. lbs. (115-142 Nm), using a torque wrench.
21. Carefully lower the vehicle, making sure the upper strut mounting studs are aligned with holes.
22. Install the shock absorber housing seal and three nuts to the upper mounting studs. Tighten to 17-22 ft. lbs. (22-31 Nm).
23. Install the washer, nut and install the electronic actuator, if equipped. Tighten the nut to 28-39 ft. lbs. (37-54 Nm).
24. Install the plastic shock absorber/strut cover cup, if equipped.

****WARNING**

To prevent front suspension lower arm strut bushing wind-up, the lower shock nut must be tightened with the vehicle weight on the wheels.

25. Neutralize the lower control arm bushings by pushing down on the front of the vehicle and releasing. Tighten the lower shock absorber/strut nut to 125-170 ft. lbs. (170-230 Nm).

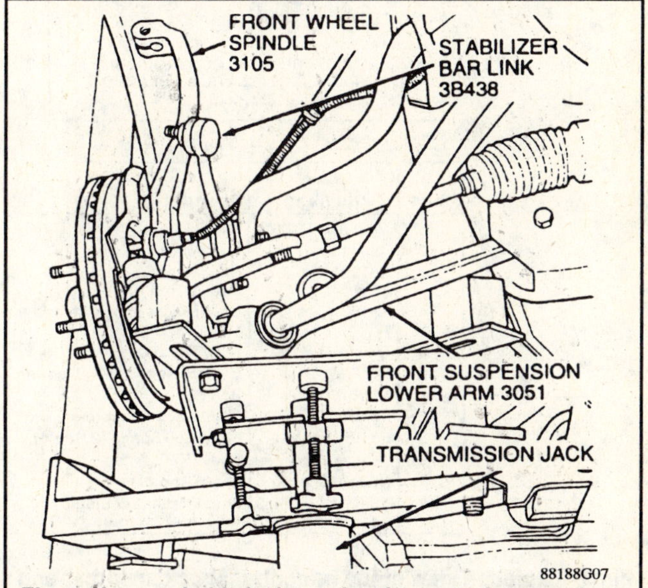

Fig. 7 Use a suitable jack to raise the control arm and spindle so the stabilizer link can be removed

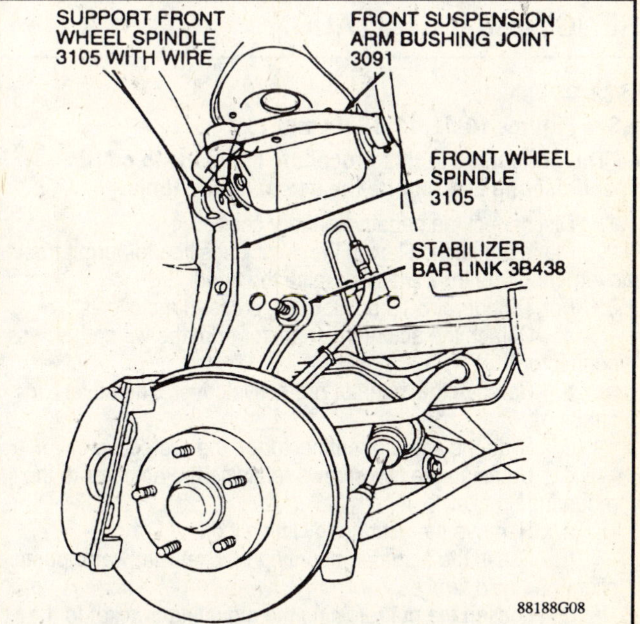

Fig. 8 Support the spindle with a piece of wire; do NOT let it hang free

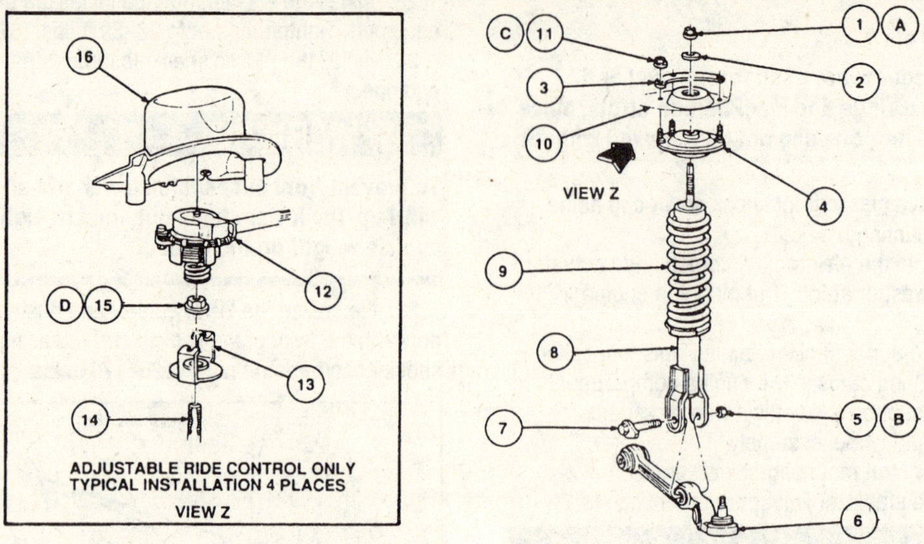

Item	Part Number	Description
1	N805377-S100	Nut (2 Req'd)
2	18041	Washer (2 Req'd)
3	18T003	Shock Absorber Housing Seal (2 Req'd)
4	18183	Upper Front Shock Absorber Mounting Bracket (2 Req'd)
5	N805476-S160	Nut (2 Req'd)
6	3079	Front Suspension Lower Arm
7	N806798-S56	Bolt (2 Req'd)
8	18124	Front Shock Absorber
9	5310	Front Coil Spring (2 Req'd)
10	—	Body (Ref)
11	N801310-S100	Nut (6 Req'd)
12	18B012	Shock Absorber Electronic Actuator (2 Req'd)

Item	Part Number	Description
13	18171	Actuator Washer (4 Req'd)
14	18124	Front Shock Absorber
15	N805377-S100	Nut (2 Req'd for Base Vehicles) (4 Req'd for Ride Control Vehicles)
16	18A179	Front Shock Absorber Strut Cover Cup
A	—	Tighten to 50-71 N·m (37-52 Lb-Ft)
B	—	Tighten to 170-230 N·m (125-170 Lb-Ft)
C	—	Tighten to 22-31 N·m (17-22 Lb-Ft)
D	—	Tighten to 37-54 N·m (28-39 Lb-Ft)

88188G09

Fig. 9 Exploded view of the front strut/shock absorber and spring removal — 1989-96 vehicles

MacPherson Strut

REMOVAL & INSTALLATION

1983-88 Vehicles

See Figures 10, 11, 12, 13, 14 and 15

The bolts used in this procedure are made to metric specifications and require the use of metric tools.

1. Disconnect the negative battery cable.
2. Place the ignition key in the unlock position to permit free movement of the front wheels. Raise the hood.
3. For Thunderbird Turbo Coupes, proceed as follows:
   a. Detach the actuator connector from the wiring harness connector.
   b. Remove the actuator protective cover. The cover snaps off.
   c. Slide the actuator connector off the protective cover.
   d. Unfasten the two screws retaining the actuator to the mounting bracket.
   e. Remove the actuator by lifting it off.
   f. Grasp the actuator mounting bracket with water pump pliers and hold firmly.
   g. Loosen the nut retaining the mounting bracket to the shock absorber, then remove the nut and mounting bracket.
   h. Install the nut onto the shock absorber.

****WARNING**

DO NOT move or raise the vehicle after removing the bracket retaining nut. If the shock absorber must be removed, install the nut onto the shock.

4. Raise the vehicle by the lower control arms until the wheels are just off the ground. From the engine compartment, remove and discard the three 12mm upper mount retaining nuts.

****WARNING**

The vehicle should not be driven with these nuts removed. Do NOT remove the pop-rivet holding the camber plate in position.

5. If the upper mount is to be replaced, loosen the 16mm strut rod nut.
6. Continue to raise the front of the vehicle by the lower control arms, then position safety stands under the frame jacking pads, behind the wheels.
7. Remove the tire and wheel assembly.
8. Remove the brake caliper, and rotate out of position.
9. Remove the two lower nuts attaching the strut to the spindle, leaving the bolts in place. Carefully remove both spindle-to-strut bolts, push the bracket free of the spindle, then remove the strut.

10. Compress the strut to clear the upper mount of the body mounting pad. Lift the strut up from the spindle to compress the rod, then pull down and remove the strut.

11. If necessary, remove the upper mount and jounce bumper from the strut.

To install:

12. If removed, install the upper mount and jounce bumper on the strut.

13. Position the three upper mount studs into the body mounting pad and camber plate, then start three new nuts.

14. With the rod half extended, place the rod through the upper mount and hand start the mount as soon as possible.

15. Extend the strut and position into the spindle.

16. Install two new lower mounting bolts and hand start the nuts. Remove the suspension load from the lower control arms by carefully lowering the vehicle. Tighten the lower mounting nuts to 140–200 ft. lbs. (190–271 Nm).

17. Raise the suspension control arms, then tighten the three new upper mounting nuts inside the engine compartment to 50–70 ft. lbs. (68–102 Nm).

18. For Thunderbird Turbo Coupes, perform the following:

a. Install the actuator mounting bracket on the shock absorber. Make sure the flats on the bracket and shock absorber line up.

b. Rotate the mounting bracket to align with the inner edge of the fender.

c. Install the retaining nut onto the shock absorber.

d. Grasp the mounting bracket with water pump pliers and hold firmly.

e. Tighten the nut to 60–75 ft. lbs. (81–102 Nm). Make sure the alignment of the mounting bracket to the fender is maintained while tightening the nut.

f. Install the actuator on the mounting bracket. Make sure the flats of the actuator and shock absorber are aligned.

g. Rotate the actuator to align the screw attaching holes in the mounting bracket.

h. Install the two actuator-to-mounting bracket attaching screws. Tighten the screws to 10–14 inch lbs. (1.1–1.6 Nm).

i. Fasten the actuator wiring connector onto the protective cover.

j. Position the actuator wiring in front of and under the actuator.

k. Install the wiring in the cutout in the protective cover.

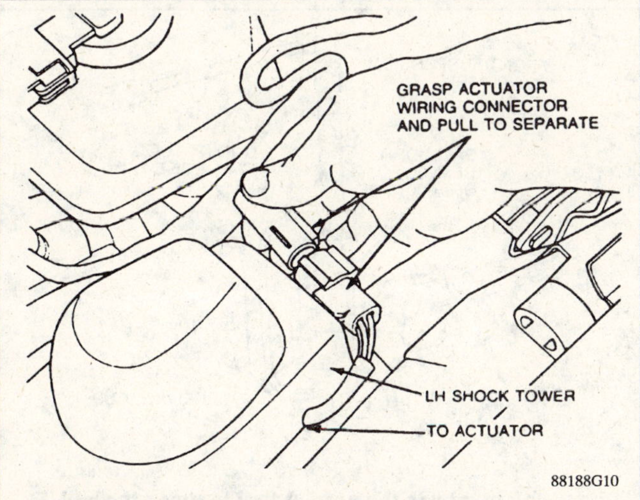

Fig. 10 For Thunderbird Turbo Coupes, detach the connector from the actuator wiring harness

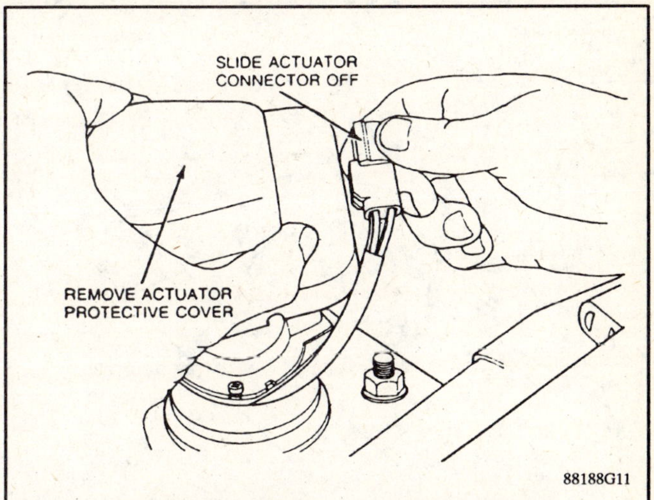

Fig. 11 Remove the protective cover, then slide the actuator connector from the cover

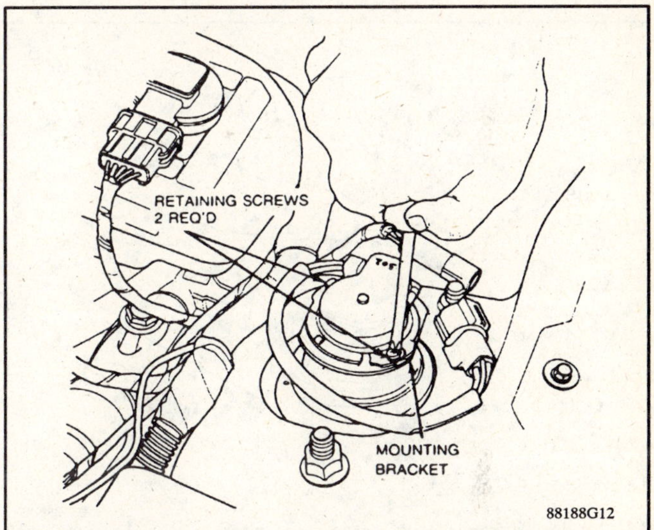

Fig. 12 Unfasten the two actuator-to-mounting bracket screws, then . . .

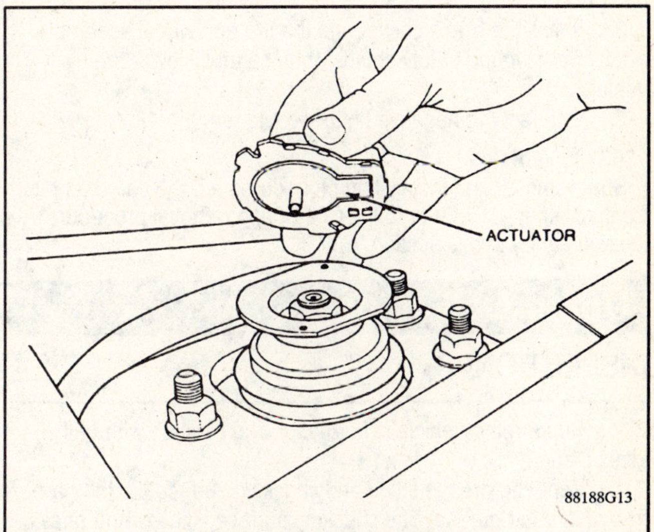

Fig. 13 . . . remove the actuator by lifting it off

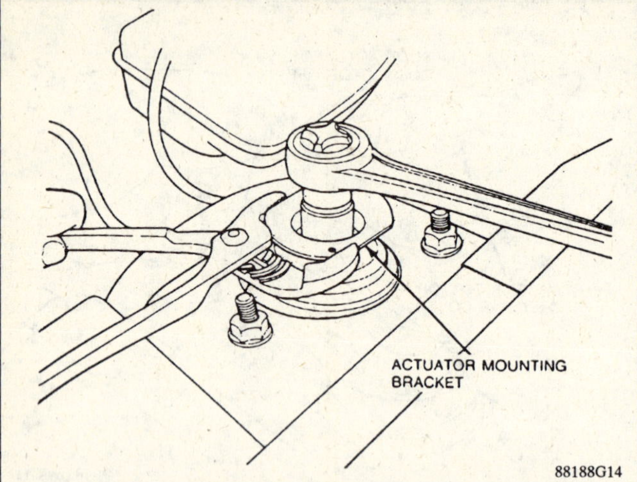

Fig. 14 While holding the mounting bracket with suitable pliers, loosen the mounting bracket-to-shock absorber nut

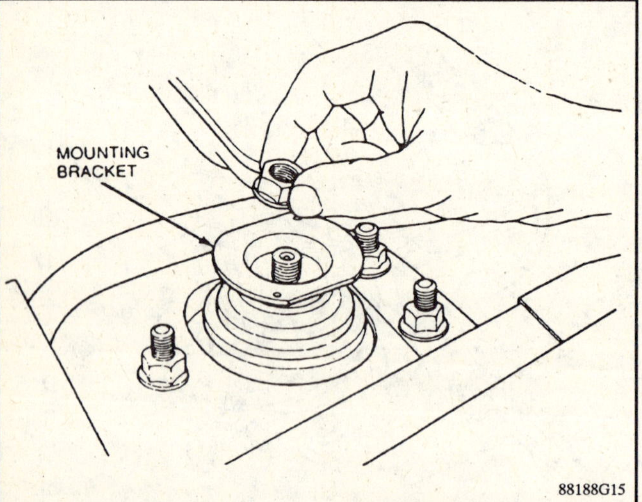

Fig. 15 Remove the nut and mounting bracket

19. If necessary, tighten the 16mm strut rod nut to 55–92 ft. lbs. (75–125 Nm).
20. Install the brake caliper and the tire and wheel assembly.
21. Remove the safety stands, then carefully lower the vehicle.
22. Connect the negative battery cable.

1989–96 Vehicles

Strut removal and installation procedures are the same as for front coil spring. Refer to to the Coil Spring removal procedure located earlier in this section.

Upper Ball Joint

INSPECTION

1. Support the vehicle in normal driving position with ball joints loaded.
2. Wipe the grease fitting and checking surface, so they are free of dirt and grease. The checking surface is the round boss into which the grease fitting is threaded.
3. The checking surface should project outside the cover. If the checking surface is inside the cover, replace the lower arm assembly.

REMOVAL AND INSTALLATION

Upper ball joints are not replaceable. The upper ball joint is part of the upper control arm bushing joint and is not serviced separately. If the upper ball joints are found to be defective, the entire upper control arm bushing joint assembly must be replaced.

Lower Ball Joint

INSPECTION

1. Support the vehicle in normal driving position with ball joints loaded.
2. Wipe the grease fitting and checking surface, so they are free of dirt and grease. The checking surface is the round boss into which the grease fitting is threaded.
3. The checking surface should project outside the cover. If the checking surface is inside the cover, replace the lower arm assembly.

REMOVAL AND INSTALLATION

See Figures 16 and 17

1. Raise and safely support the vehicle.
2. Remove the lower control arm as outlined later in this section.
3. Remove and discard the ball joint boot seal.
4. Clamp the lower control arm in a suitable vise.
5. Press out the lower control arm ball joint using Ball Joint Remover D89P-3010-A, Receiving Cup D84P-3395-A4, and U-Joint Tool T74P-4635-C, or equivalents. A suitable press may be used in place of the U-Joint tool, to press the ball joint out.

To install:

When installing a new lower ball joint, it is advisable that the protective cover be left in place during installation to protect the ball joint seal. It may be necessary to cut off the end of the cover to allow it to pass through the receiving cup.

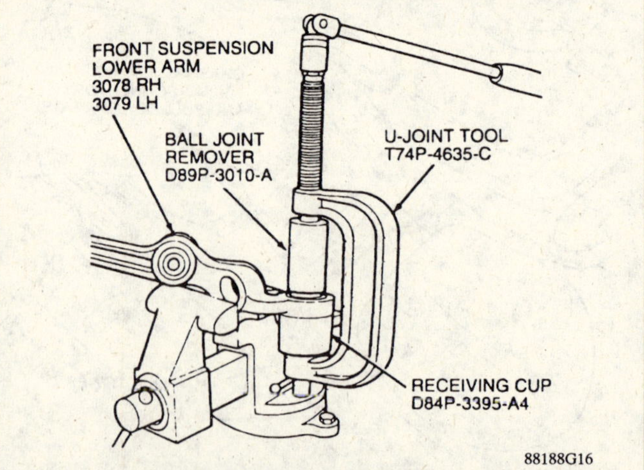

Fig. 16 You must use the correct tool to press the ball joint out from the lower control arm

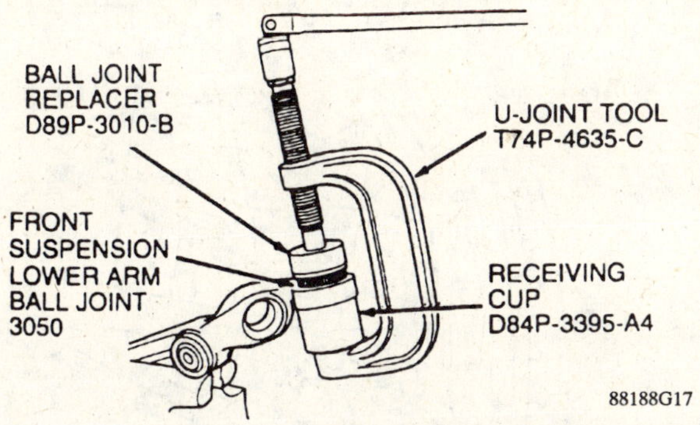

Fig. 17 Installation of the lower ball joint. Note that several special tools are needed for this job

6. Install the ball joint with a Ball Joint Replacer D89P-3010-A, Receiving Cup D84P-3395-A4 and U-Joint Tool T74P-4635-C. A press may be used instead of the U-Joint tool.
7. Discard the protective cover and check the ball joint to make sure that it is fully seated in the control arm.
8. Inspect the ball seal and ensure that it is free of cuts or tears.
9. Install the lower control arm as outlined in this Section.
10. Carefully lower the vehicle.
11. Have the wheel alignment checked by a reputable repair shop.

Stabilizer Bar

REMOVAL & INSTALLATION

1983-88 Vehicles

1. Raise and safely support the front end of the vehicle with jackstands.
2. Disconnect the stabilizer bar from each stabilizer link and both stabilizer insulator attaching clamps. Remove the stabilizer bar assembly.
3. Remove the adapter brackets from the clamps.
4. Cut the worn insulators form the stabilizer bar.

To install:

5. Coat the necessary parts of the stabilizer bar and the inside diameter of the stabilizer bar insulator with Rubber Lubricant E25Y-19553-A or equivalent and slide the insulators onto the stabilizer bar.
6. Install the adapter brackets on the clamps.
7. Using a new nut and bolt, secure each end of the stabilizer bar to the lower suspension arm. Tighten the nuts to 6-12 ft. lbs. (8-16 Nm).
8. Using new bolts, clamp the stabilizer bar to the attaching brackets on the side rail. Tighten the retaining bolts to 37-50 ft. lbs. (50-68 Nm).
9. Carefully lower the vehicle.

1989-93 Vehicles

1. Remove the air inlet tube.
2. Remove the stabilizer bar retaining bracket bolts and retaining brackets.
3. Remove the serpentine drive belt.
4. Raise and safely support vehicle on jackstands.
5. Remove the front tire and wheel assemblies.
6. Remove the crankshaft vibration damper pulley.
7. Remove the cotter pins and castellated nuts from the outer tie rod ends. Separate the tie rod ends from the spindle using a tie rod end removal tool.
8. Remove transmission oil cooler line bracket.
9. Remove the stabilizer bar retaining nuts from the lower link.
10. Remove the bar link from the stabilizer bar using joint separator D88L-3006-A or equivalent.

****CAUTION**

Use extreme care when separating the link from the sway bar as not to damage the ball joint seal. If seal becomes damaged, the link assembly must be replaced

11. Remove the stabilizer bar from the vehicle, through the right wheel opening and remove bushings from bar.

To install:

12. Install the bushings onto the stabilizer bar and position bar into vehicle through the right side wheel opening.
13. Attach the stabilizer links to the bar and tighten the retaining nuts to 40-55 ft. lbs. (54-74 Nm).
14. Install the transmission oil cooler line bracket.
15. Install the tie rod ends to the spindles. Tighten the nuts to 35-53 ft. lbs. (47-72 Nm) and install new cotter pins.
16. Install the crankshaft damper.
17. Install front tires and wheels and lower vehicle off the jackstands.
18. Install the stabilizer bar brackets and retaining nuts, tighten to 40-55 ft. lbs. (54-74 Nm).
19. Install the serpentine belt and air inlet tube.

1994-96 Vehicles

See Figures 18, 19, 20 and 21

MOUNTING BRACKET INSULATOR

1. Disconnect the negative battery cable.
2. For 1995-96 vehicles, remove the front subframe, as follows:
   a. Install Engine Lifting Brackets D91P-6001-A or equivalent.
   b. Install Three Bar Engine Support D88L-6000-A or equivalent to the engine lifting brackets.
   c. Raise and safely support the vehicle.
   d. Remove the front engine support insulator through bolts.

****WARNING**

Raise the engine carefully so as not to damage the lines and hoses at the rear of the engine.

   e. Raise the engine and support it with Three Bar Engine Support D88L-6000-A, or equivalent.
   f. Remove the front wheel and tire assemblies.
   g. Remove the tie rod end from the front wheel spindles.
   h. Remove the stabilizer bar link from the front wheel spindles.
   i. Remove the lower front shock absorber retaining bolts.
   j. Remove the front suspension lower arm strut from the front suspension lower arms.
   k. Remove the front suspension the front suspension lower arm inner pivot-to-front subframe retainer bolts.
   l. Remove the steering coupling pinch bolt and disconnect the steering coupling.

m. Drain the power steering fluid into a suitable container.

n. Disconnect and cap the power steering return line and pressure hoses.

o. Remove the power steering oil cooler from the body side rail.

p. Remove the wire harnesses and/or the wire harness clips from the front subframe.

q. Safely support the front subframe with adjustable jacks at the four points.

r. Remove the 8 front subframe-to-body retaining bolts.

s. With the help of an assistant, carefully lower the adjustable jacks and allow the front subframe to lower.

t. If replacing the subframe, place the subframe on the floor or a bench and transfer the power steering rack, front suspension lower arm struts, front suspension lower arms and the front stabilizer bar to the new subframe. Also, transfer the reinforcement rod and tighten to 72–97 ft. lbs. (97–132) to the new subframe.

3. Remove the air cleaner outlet tube.
4. Remove the stabilizer bar bracket bolts and the stabilizer bar brackets.
5. Remove the drive belt.
6. If not already done, raise and safely support the vehicle, then remove the front wheel and tire assemblies.
7. Remove the crankshaft vibration damper.
8. If not already done, remove the cotter pins and castellated nuts from the tie rod ends. Discard the cotter pins. Separate the tie rod ends from the front wheel spindles using Tie Rod End Puller TOOL-3290-D or equivalent.
9. Remove the transmission oil cooler line clip.

****WARNING**

Be very careful not to damage the ball joint seal. If the seal is damaged, replace the stabilizer link kit assembly.

10. Remove the front stabilizer bar-to-lower stabilizer bar retaining nuts.
11. Remove the stabilizer bar link from the front stabilizer bar using Ball Joint Remover D88L-3006-A or equivalent.
12. Remove the front stabilizer bar through the right wheel opening.
13. Remove the lower control arm stabilizer bar insulators from the front stabilizer bar.

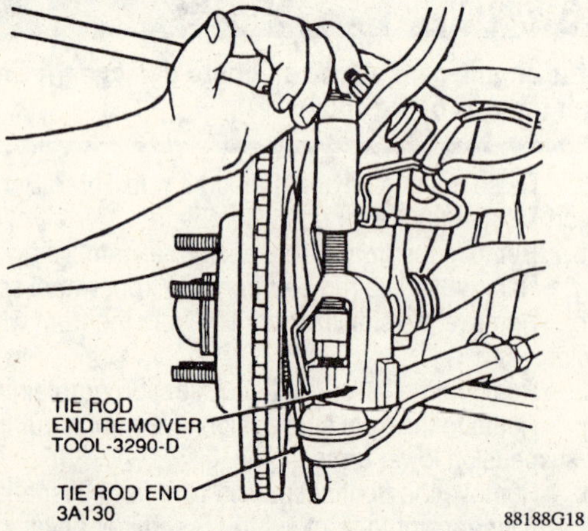

Fig. 18 Use the special tool to detach the tie rod ends from the spindles

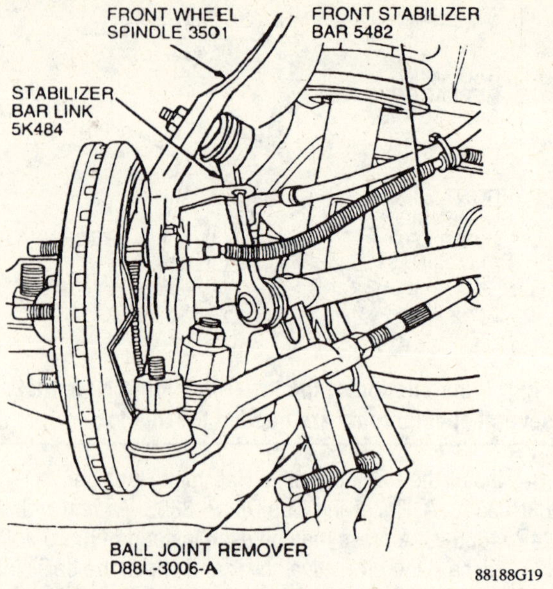

Fig. 19 Unfasten the stabilizer bar link from the bar using a ball joint removal tool

To install:

14. Install the lower control arm stabilizer bar insulators onto the front stabilizer bar.
15. Position the front stabilizer bar into the vehicle.
16. Attach the stabilizer bar link to the front stabilizer bar. Tighten the retaining nuts to 29–39 ft. lbs. (40–55 Nm).
17. Install the stabilizer bar brackets and retaining bolts. Tighten to 39–53 ft. lbs. (53–72 Nm).
18. Install the transmission oil cooler line clip.
19. For 1994 vehicles, attach the tie rod ends to the front wheel spindles. Tighten the nuts to 39–53 ft. lbs. (53–73 Nm). Install new cotter pins.
20. Install the crankshaft vibration damper.
21. For 1994 vehicles, install the front wheel and tire assemblies. Tighten the lug nuts to 85–105 ft. lbs. (115–142 Nm).
22. For 1994 vehicles, carefully lower the vehicle.
23. Install the serpentine drive belt.
24. Install the air cleaner outlet tube.
25. If removed, install the front subframe, as follows:

a. With the help of an assistant, position the front subframe to the body and hand start the 8 retaining bolts into the mating body cage nuts.

➜ Do not tighten the front subframe-to-body bolts at this time as the subframe must be aligned to the body before tightening the retainers.

b. Using an adjustable jack, carefully raise the subframe into contact with the bottom of the body side rails.

c. Install a $^{3}/_{4}$ in. (19mm) outside diameter pipe into body front left and right front subframe and body alignment holes. Tighten one bolt at each corner.

d. Remove the alignment tools, then tighten the 8 bolts to 72–97 ft. lbs. (97–132 Nm).

e. Install the wire harness clips and/or harnesses to the front subframe.

f. Install the power steering oil cooler on the body side rail. Uncap and connect the power steering pressure hose and return line hoses.

g. Connect the steering coupling and install the pinchbolt. Tighten the bolt to 21–30 ft. lbs. (28–40 Nm).

h. Attach the stabilizer bar links to the spindles and tighten to 41–55 ft. lbs. (55–75 Nm).

i. Install the tie rod end to the to the wheel spindles and tighten to 39–54 ft. lbs. (53–73 Nm).

j. Install the front suspension lower arm pivots onto the subframe. Tighten to 92–125 ft. lbs. (125–170 Nm).

k. Install the front suspension lower arm struts onto the left and right side front suspension lower arms and tighten to 89–118 ft. lbs. (120–160 Nm).

l. Connect the front shock absorber of the right and left front suspension lower arm and tighten to 103–144 ft. lbs. (140–195 Nm).

m. Install the tire and wheel assemblies.

n. Carefully lower the vehicle partway.

The left side front engine support insulator (with locating pin) must seat first.

o. Lower the engine onto the front engine support insulators, then raise and safely support the vehicle.

p. Install the front engine support insulator through bolts. On 3.8L engines, tighten to 35–50 ft. lbs. (47–68 Nm). On 4.6L engines, tighten the bolts to 35–46 ft. lbs. (47–63 Nm).

q. Carefully lower the vehicle, then remove the engine support and lifting bracket.

r. Check and fill the power steering fluid. Bleed the power steering system, as outlined in this section.

26. Connect the negative battery cable. Have the front end alignment checked at a reputable repair shop.

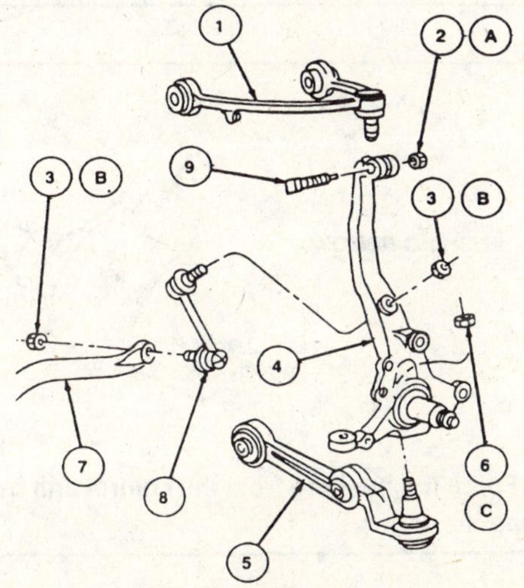

Item	Part Number	Description
1	3085	Upper Front Suspension Arm Bushing Joint
2	N805475-S150	Nut (2 Req'd)
3	N807145-S7	Nut (2 Req'd)
4	3105	Front Wheel Spindle
5	3079	Front Suspension Lower Arm
6	N805477 -S1050-C	Nut (2 Req'd)
7	5482	Front Stabilizer Bar
8	5K484	Stabilizer Bar Link (2 Req'd)
9	N806579-S150	Bolt (2 Req'd)
A	—	Tighten to 68-92 N·m (50-68 Lb-Ft)
B	—	Tighten to 40-55 N·m (29-39 Lb-Ft)
C	—	Tighten to 113-153 N·m (83-113 Lb-Ft)

88188G21

Fig. 20 Exploded view of the stabilizer bar and related components — 1996 vehicle shown

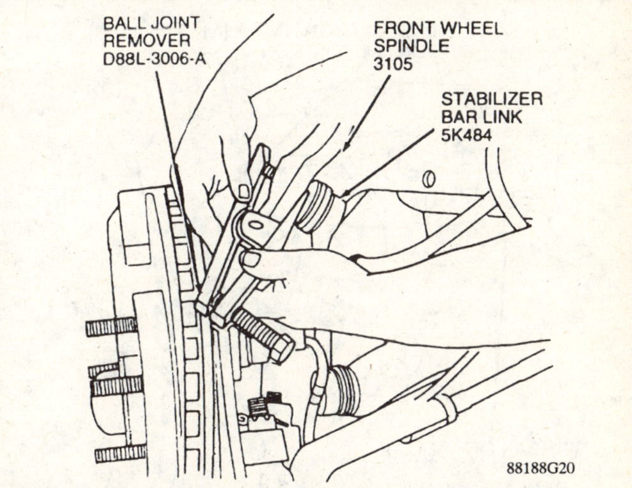

Fig. 21 Using the ball joint remover to separate the link studs from the steering knuckle

BAR LINK ASSEMBLY

1. Raise and safely support the vehicle.
2. Remove the nuts from the stabilizer bar link.

✻✻WARNING

Be very careful not to damage the ball joint seal. If the seal is damaged, replace the stabilizer link kit assembly.

3. Separate the link studs from the front steering knuckle/spindle and front stabilizer bar using Ball Joint Remover D88L-3006-A or equivalent.

To install:

4. Install the stabilizer bar link to the front wheel spindle/knuckle and front stabilizer bar. Tighten the retaining nuts to 29–39 ft. lbs. (40–55 Nm).
5. Carefully lower the vehicle.

Upper Control Arm

REMOVAL & INSTALLATION

1989–96 Vehicles

See Figure 22

The following procedure is the same for both the right and left side upper control arm.

1. Raise and safely support vehicle on jackstands.
2. Remove the tire and wheel assembly.
3. Remove and discard the upper spindle-to-ball joint bolt and nut. Slightly spread spindle at the slot opening to remove the ball joint from spindle.
4. Lower vehicle enough to gain access to the upper control arm pivot bolts.
5. Break off the small metal flags from the pivot bolt heads.

A 6-point socket must be used on the bolts due to the fact that the corners of the heads have been shaved off. Discard the nuts and bolts after removing them. Replacement bolts do not require metal flags.

6. Remove the upper control arm/upper control arm bushing joint bolts, then remove the control arm from the vehicle.

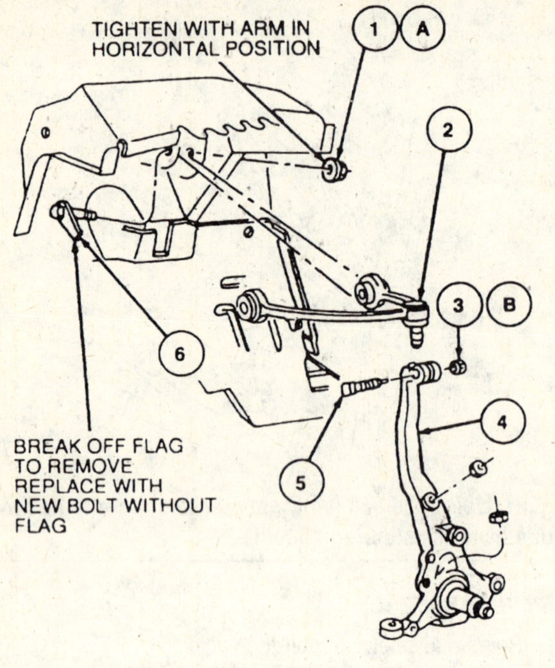

Item	Part Number	Description
1	N805470-S160	Nut (4 Req'd)
2	3085	Upper Front Suspension Arm Bushing Joint
3	N805475-S150	Nut (2 Req'd)
4	3105	Front Wheel Spindle
5	N806579-S150	Bolt (2 Req'd)
6	N805461-S150	Bolt (4 Req'd)
A	—	Tighten to 88-119 N·m (65-88 Lb-Ft)
B	—	Tighten to 68-92 N·m (50-68 Lb-Ft)

88188G22

Fig. 22 Upper control arm, also referred to as the upper front suspension arm bushing joint, removal

➥ If nuts cannot be torqued due to limited access on some models, tighten the bolts to 81–88 ft. lbs.

7. Raise and safely support the vehicle.
8. Attach spindle to to the upper control arm/arm bushing joint. Install a new bolt and nut (install the bolt through front to rear), and tighten nut to 50–68 ft. lbs. (68–92 Nm).
9. Install tire and wheel assembly, then carefully lower the vehicle.

CONTROL ARM BUSHING REPLACEMENT

1989–93 Vehicles

➧ See Figures 23, 24, 25 and 26

1. Remove the upper control arm as outlined previously.
2. Assemble Collets T89P-5638-C1, Bushing Installer T89P-5638-C3, Bushing Remover T89P-5638-D and Forcing Screw T78P-5638-A1, or equivalent, on the control arm over the bushing.
3. Assemble the tools so that the bushing will be forced outward (away from the head of the forcing screw).
4. Ensure the collet fits between the bushing flange and control arm surface.
5. Tighten the screw to force bushing out of the control arm.

To Install:

6. Position the Forcing Screw, Bushing Remover, Bushing Installer (T89P-5638-E) and the new new bushing on the outer side of the control arm. Position the Bushing Installer T89P-5638-C3 on the inside of the control arm, lining up the grooves in the installer with the ridge on the control arm.
7. Tighten the screw until the halves of the installer bottom out against each other.
8. Install the upper control arm as outlined previously.

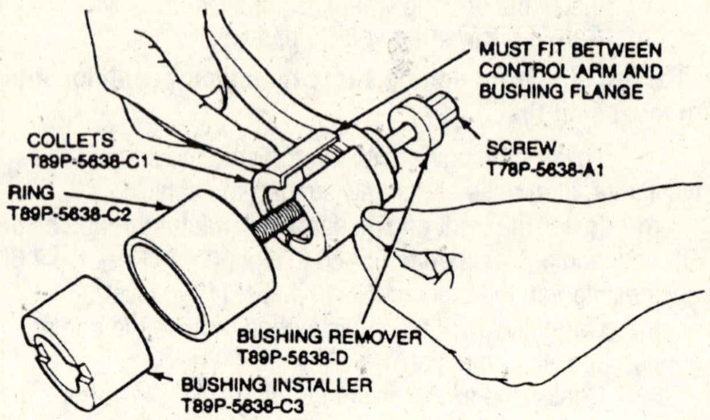

88188G23

Fig. 23 Make sure the properly assembly the required tools

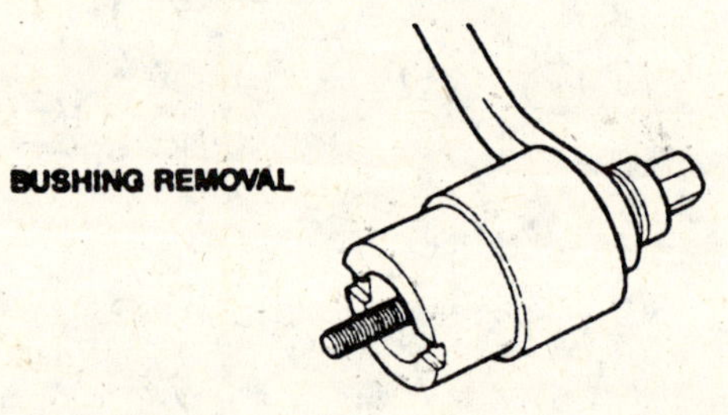

88188G24

Fig. 24 Force the bushing from the control arm by tightening the screw

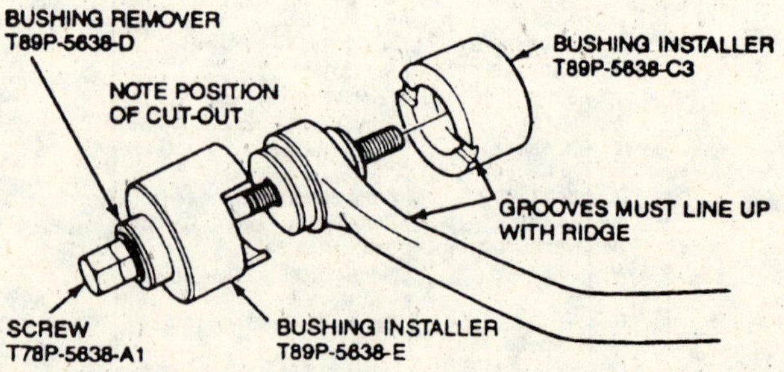

88188G25

Fig. 25 Install the tools and new control arm bushing as shown

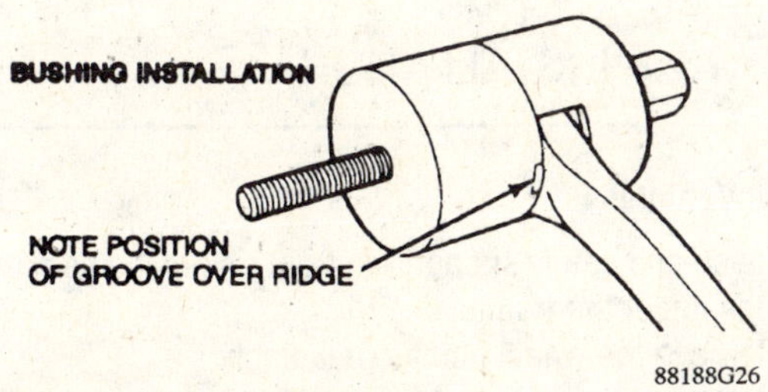

Fig. 26 Tighten the screw until the halves of the bushing installer bottom out against one another

1994–96 Vehicles

The upper control arm bushings on these vehicles are part of the upper control arm bushing joint. Replacement of the bushings require replacement of the complete upper control arm/bushing joint assembly.

Lower Control Arm

REMOVAL & INSTALLATION

1983–88 Vehicles

1. Raise the front of the vehicle and position safety stands under both sides of the jack pads, just to the rear of the lower arms.
2. Remove the wheel and tire assembly.
3. Disconnect the stabilizer bar link from the lower arm.
4. If necessary for access, remove the disc brake caliper and wire it out of the way, then remove the rotor and dust shield.
5. Disconnect the tie rod assembly from the steering spindle/knuckle using Tie Rod End Remover TOOL-3290-D or equivalent.
6. Remove the steering gear bolts and position out of the way so the control arm bolt my be removed.
7. Remove and discard the cotter pin from the ball joint stud nut, and loosen the ball joint nut one or two turns. Do NOT remove the nut at this time.
8. Tap the spindle/knuckle boss sharply to relieve the stud pressure.
9. Use Spring Compressor Tool T82P-5310-A or equivalent to place the upper plate in position into the spring pocket cavity on the crossmember. The hooks on the plate should be facing toward the center of the vehicle.
10. Install the compression rod into the lower arm spring pocket hole, through the coil spring, into the upper plate.
11. Install the lower plate, lower ball nut, thrust washer and bearing, and forcing nut, onto the compression rod.
12. Tighten the forcing nut onto the compressor tool until a drag on the nut is felt.
13. Remove and discard the ball joint stud nut, and raise the entire stud and spindle/knuckle assembly. Wire it out of the way to obtain working room.
14. Remove and discard the control arm-to-crossmember retaining nuts and bolts. The compressor tool may have to be tightened or loosened for easy bolt removal.
15. Loosen the compression rod forcing nut until spring tension is relieved, then remove the forcing nut, lower control arm and coil spring.

To install:

16. Place the insulator on the top of the spring. Position the spring into the lower arm spring pocket.

➥ Make sure the spring pigtail is positioned between the two holes in the lower arm spring pocket.

17. Position the spring and lower control arm onto the compression rod.
18. Tighten the forcing nut and position the lower control arm into the crossmember.
19. Install new lower control arm-to-crossmember bolts and nuts, but do not tighten yet.
20. Remove the wire from the strut and spindle/knuckle assembly, pull the assembly down and attach to the ball joint stud. Install a new ball joint stud nut, but do not tighten yet.
21. With a suitable jack, raise the control arm to a normal attitude position. Remove the compressor tool.
22. With the jack still in place, tighten the lower arm-to-crossmember attaching nuts to 110–150 ft. lbs. (149–203 Nm).
23. Tighten the ball joint stud nut to 100–120 ft. lbs. (149–203 Nm). Tighten the nut to align the holes, then install a new cotter pin. Carefully lower the vehicle and remove the jack.
24. Install the brake dust shield, rotor and caliper, if removed.
25. Install the steering gear-to-crossmember bolts and nuts, if removed. Hold the bolts and tighten them to 90–100 ft. lbs. (122–135 Nm).
26. Position the tie rod assembly into the steering spindle, then install the retaining nut. Tighten the nut to 35 ft. lbs. (47 Nm) and continue tightening the nut to align the next castellation with the cotter pin hole in the stud. Install a new cotter pin.
27. Connect the stabilizer bar link to the lower control arm. Tighten the attaching nut to 9–12 ft. lbs. (12–16 Nm).
28. Install the wheel and tire assembly.
29. Remove the safety stands and carefully lower the vehicle.

1989–96 Vehicles

➧ See Figure 27

1. Raise and safely support vehicle on jackstands.
2. Remove the tire and wheel assembly.
3. Loosen the lower ball joint nut 3 or 4 turns.
4. Rap on spindle with a heavy hammer, just enough to separate the ball joint from the spindle. Leave the nut on the ball joint.
5. Support the spindle by a wire or other means to prevent excessive sagging of the upper control arm.
6. Matchmark the position of the camber adjustment cam.

✻✻WARNING

Do not hold tension strut, with a wrench on any curved part of strut. Use only the flat spots, as damage to the tension strut may result.

7. Hold the lower control arm strut by the flats with a wrench, then remove the nut retaining the lower control arm strut to the control arm bushing joint and discard.
8. Remove the lower shock attaching bolt and nut.
9. Remove the pivot (camber) bolt and nut.

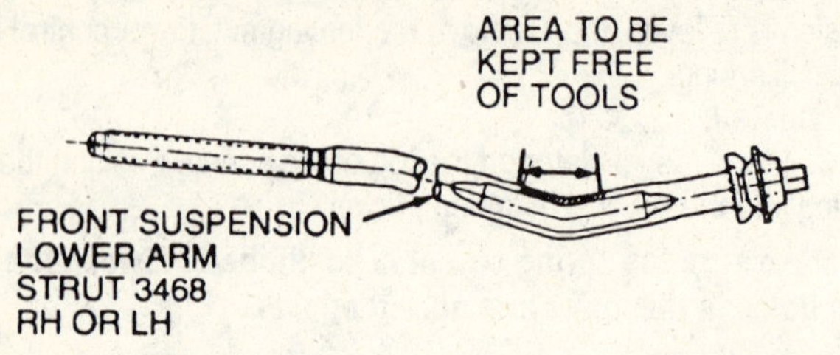

Fig. 27 Do not hold the strut, with a wrench on the curved part of the strut

10. Remove the nut from the lower ball joint, then remove lower control arm.

To install:

11. Position the lower control arm in vehicle and loosely install the pivot (camber) bolt and nut.
12. Install the tension strut insulator bushings and loosely install the attaching nut.
13. Install the ball joint nut loosely.
14. Install the lower shock bolt and nut but do not tighten at this time.
15. Tighten the ball joint nut to 83–113 ft. lbs. (113–153 Nm) and install a new cotter pin.
16. Tighten the tension strut control arm nut to 83–113 ft. lbs. (113–153 Nm).

**CAUTION

Do not hold tension strut, with a wrench on any curved part of strut. Use only the flat spots, as damage to the tension strut may result.

17. Remove the wire or other type of support holding the spindle.
18. Install the tire and wheel assembly. Tighten the lug nuts, with a torque wrench, to 85–105 ft. lbs. (115–142 Nm).
19. Carefully lower the vehicle.
20. Push down on the front of the vehicle and release to neutralize the suspension. Tighten the lower shock nut to 125–170 ft. lbs. (170–230 Nm).
21. Align the camber marks at the pivot bolt and tighten nut to 83–113 ft. lbs. (113–153 Nm).

➥ If the lower control arm was replaced, the alignment must be checked.

CONTROL ARM BUSHING REPLACEMENT

➧ See Figures 28 and 29

1. Remove the lower control arm as outlined previously.
2. Press out the lower control arm mounting bolt bushing with Bushing Remover T78P-5638-A5, Receiving Cup T78P-5638-A4 and Forcing Screw T78P-5638-A1.

To install:

3. Install a new lower control arm bushing into the lower control arm from the front of the control arm using Bushing Replacers T78P-5638-A and T89P-5493-B, Forcing Screw T78P-5638-A1 and Forcing Screw Washer T79P-5638-A6. Turn the Forcing Screw until it bottoms.
4. Install the lower control arm, as outlined earlier in this section.
5. Have the front alignment checked by a reputable repair shop.

Spindle/Knuckle

REMOVAL & INSTALLATION

1983–88 Vehicles

1. Raise and safely support the front end of the vehicle on jackstands under the frame.
2. Remove the wheel and tire assembly.
3. Remove the caliper and suspend it out of the way, with wire.
4. Remove the hub and rotor.
5. Remove the rotor dust shields.
6. Unbolt the stabilizer link from the lower control arm.
7. Using a separator, disconnect the tie rod ends from the spindle.
8. Remove and discard the cotter pin from the ball joint stud nut, and loosen the ball joint stud nut a few turns. Don't remove it at this time!

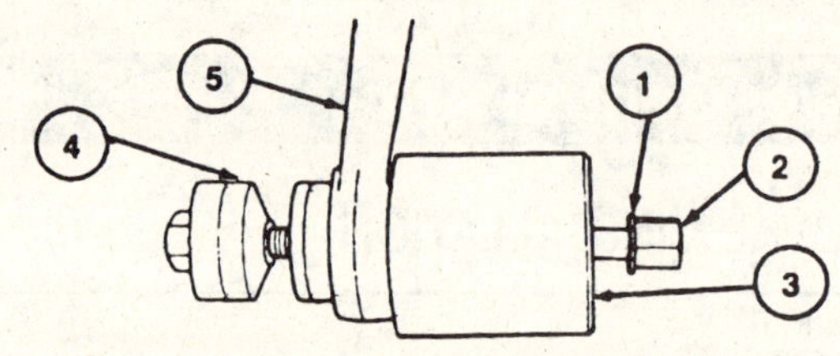

Item	Part Number	Description
1	T78P-5638-A6	Forcing Screw Washer
2	T78P-5638-A1	Forcing Screw
3	T78P-5638-A4	Receiving Cup
4	T78P-5638-A5	Bushing Remover
5	3051	Front Suspension Lower Arm

88188G27

Fig. 28 Use the specified tools to press the bushing out

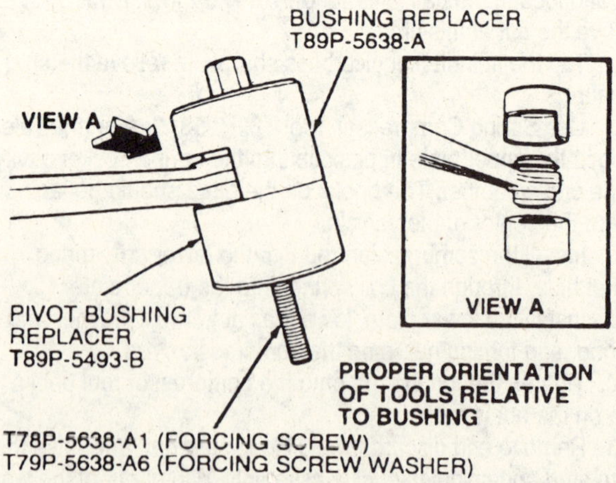

Fig. 29 After installing the tools, turn the forcing screw until it bottoms

9. Using a hammer, tap the spindle boss sharply to relieve stud pressure.
10. Support the lower control arm with a floor jack, compress the coil spring and remove the stud nut.
11. Remove the two bolts and nuts attaching the spindle to the shock strut. Compress the shock strut until working clearance is obtained.
12. Remove the spindle assembly.

To install:

13. Place the spindle on the ball joint stud, and install the stud nut, but don't tighten it yet.
14. Lower the shock strut until the attaching holes are aligned with the holes in the spindle. Install two new bolts and nuts.
15. Tighten the ball stud nut to 100–120 ft. lbs. (136–163 Nm) and install a new cotter pin. Do NOT back off the nut to align the holes. Tighten the nut to align the holes.
16. Tighten the shock strut-to-spindle attaching nuts to 150–180 ft. lbs. (203–244 Nm) for 1983–85 cars; 140–200 ft. lbs. (190–271 Nm) for 1986–88 cars.
17. Carefully lower the floor jack.
18. Install the stabilizer links. Tighten the nuts to 6–12 ft. lbs. (8–16 Nm).
19. Attach the tie rod ends and tighten the nuts to 35–47 ft. lbs. (47–64 Nm).
20. The remainder of installation is the reverse of the removal procedure.
21. Have the alignment checked at a reputable repair shop.

1989–96 Vehicles

See Figures 30, 31 and 32

1. Raise and safely support the vehicle on jackstands.
2. Remove tire and wheel assembly.
3. Mark the brake rotor and wheel hub bolt so the rotor can be install in the same position as original for rotor runout. Remove the brake caliper and support with wire, then remove the rotor.

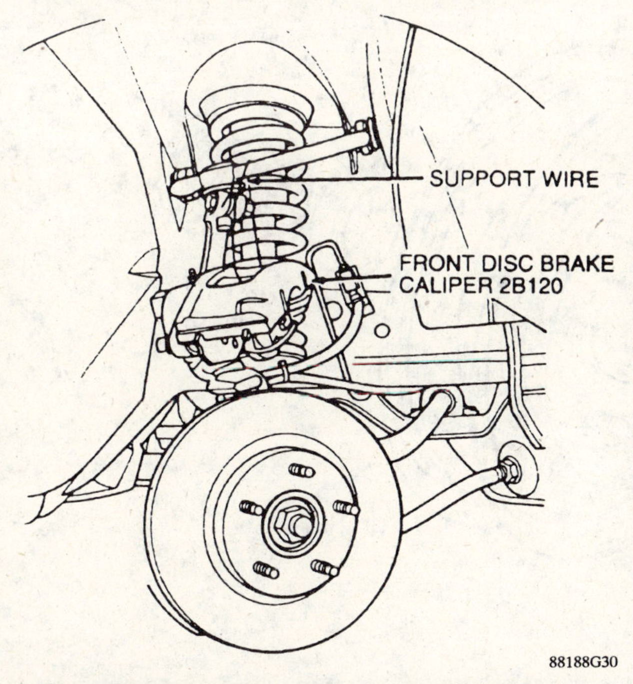

Fig. 30 Support the caliper with wire out of the way, as not to hang by the brake line.

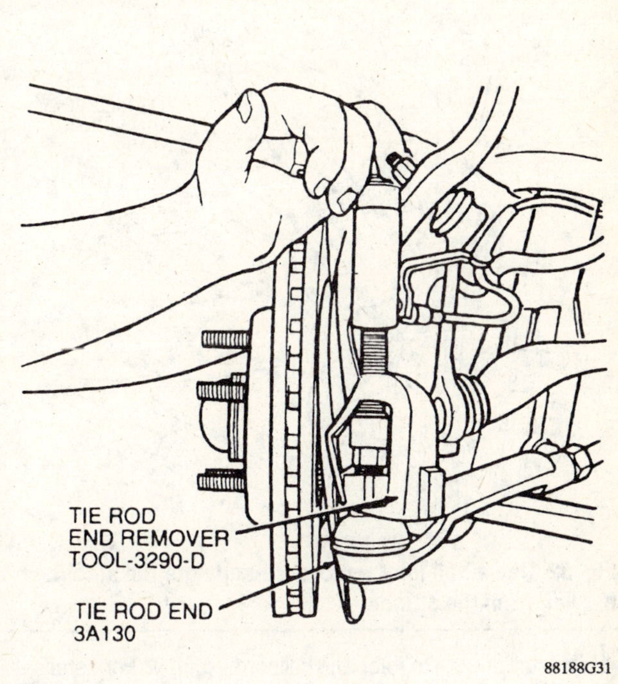

Fig. 31 Separate the tie rod end from the spindle

Do not disconnect the brake fluid line. Support brake caliper with wire. Do not let the caliper hang by, or bend the fluid line.

4. Remove the hub and bearing assembly.
5. If equipped, remove the anti-lock brake sensor and position out of the way.
6. Remove the cotter pin and loosen the castellated nut from the tie rod end. Using a tie rod removal tool, separate the tie rod end from spindle and remove nut.

****WARNING**

Be very careful to avoid damage to the ball joint seal. If the seal is damaged, the stabilizer bar link must be replaced.

7. Remove the stabilizer bar link from spindle using a joint separator D88L-3006-A or equivalent.
8. Loosen the lower ball joint nut three to four turns, then rap on the spindle with a hammer to separate ball joint from spindle and remove and discard the nut.
9. Remove the upper spindle-to-upper control arm bolt and nut. Discard the bolt and nut.
10. Spread the upper slot enough to remove the spindle from vehicle.

To install:

11. Position the spindle on the lower control arm and attach the upper control arm to the spindle.
12. Install a new bolt and nut (front to back) into spindle to hold the upper control arm and tighten to 50–65 ft. lbs. (68–88 Nm).
13. Install a new nut onto the lower ball joint and tighten to 83–113 ft. lbs. (113–153 Nm).
14. Install the hub and bearing assembly and hand-tighten.

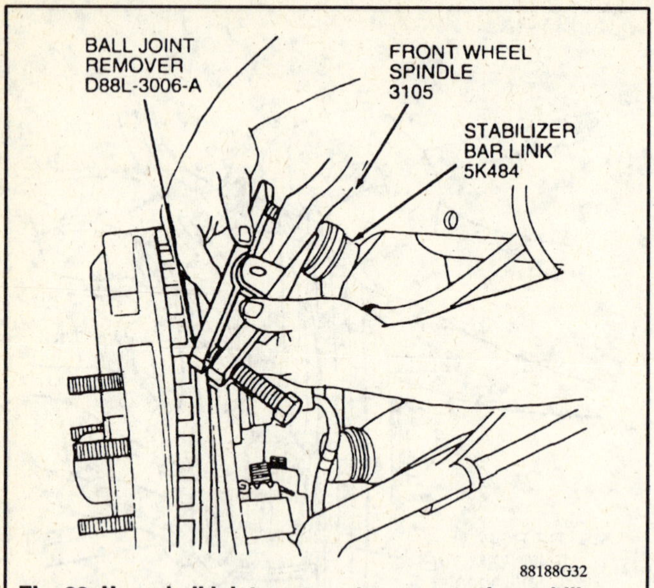

Fig. 32 Use a ball joint remover to separate the stabilizer bar link from the spindle

15. Install the brake rotor and caliper assembly. For details, please refer to Section 9 of this manual.
16. Install and adjust the anti-lock brake sensor. For details, please refer to Section 9 of this manual.
17. Install the stabilizer bar link to the spindle and tighten nut to 29–39 ft. lbs. (40–55 Nm).
18. Attach the tie rod end to the spindle and install the nut. Tighten the nut to 39–53 ft. lbs. (53–73 Nm). If the nut does not line up with the holes, continue to tighten the nut until the nut lines up with the holes. Install a new cotter pin.
19. Install the tire and wheel assembly, then carefully lower the vehicle.
20. Tighten the wheel hub retainer to 236–250 ft. lbs. (320–340 Nm). Install a new hub grease cap, using a suitable tool as not to distort or damage the cap.

Front Wheel Bearings

REMOVAL & INSTALLATION

1983–88 Vehicles

➧ See Figures 33, 34, 35, 36 and 37

Each front hub has an inner and outer bearing, with a grease retainer (seal) on the inside of hub. The outer bearing is held in place by nut and retainer washer with a cotter pin. Both inner and outer bearings are replaceable.

1. Loosen the wheel lug nuts.
2. Raise and safely support vehicle on jackstands.
3. Remove tire and wheel assembly.
4. Remove the disc brake caliper assembly. Tie the caliper assembly out of the way, do NOT let assembly hang by the brake line.
5. Remove the grease cap from center of hub.
6. Remove the cotter pin, nut locking ring, adjusting nut and washer. Wipe off all excess grease from spindle.
7. Wiggle rotor assembly back and forth, enough for the outer bearing to slide out and remove.
8. Pull the hub and rotor off the spindle.
9. Remove the grease retainer using removal tool Tool-1175-AC or equivalent. Discard grease retainer.
10. Remove inner bearing cone and roller assembly. Thoroughly clean both roller assemblies, and inspect for damage or worn parts. Replace parts as necessary.

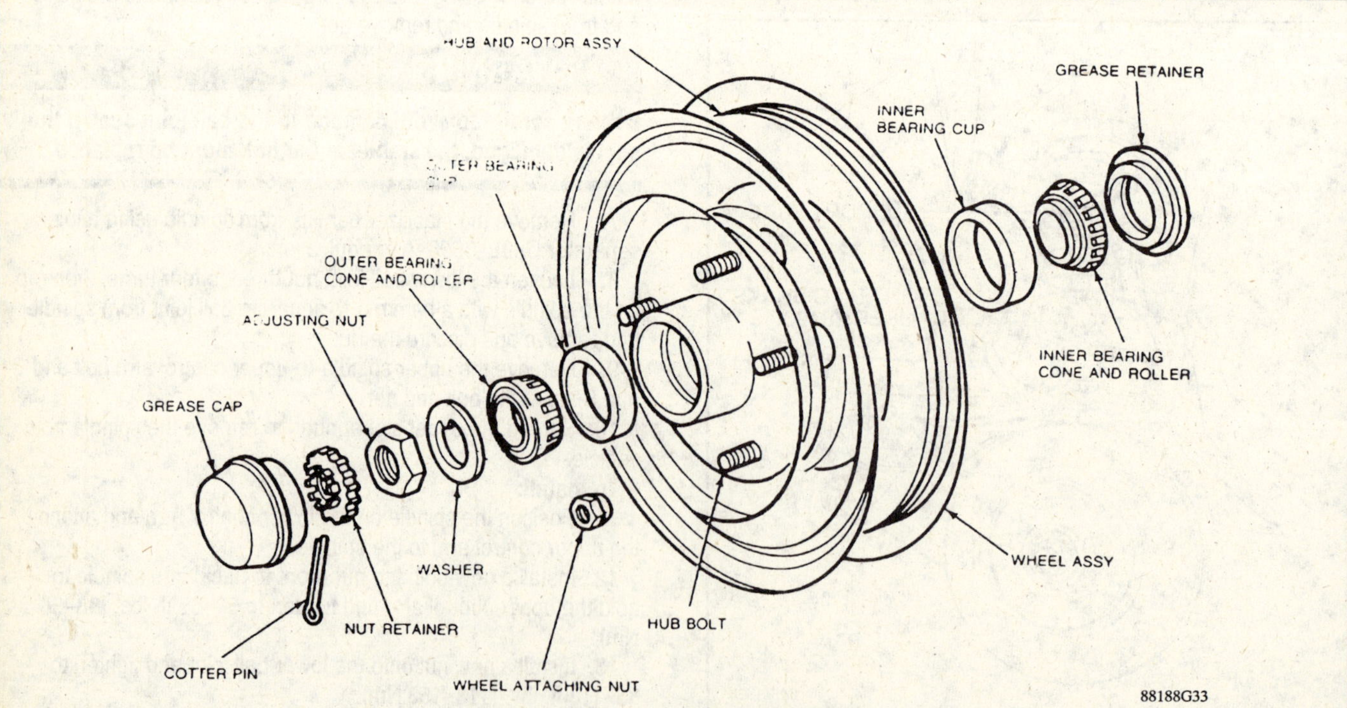

Fig. 33 Exploded view of the front wheel bearing assembly — 1983–88 vehicles

11. Clean and inspect the bearing cups inside hub assembly. If the cups are to be replaced use bearing cup puller T77F-1102-A or equivalent. Be sure to seat the new cups properly into the hub assembly.

↱ When removing or installing bearing cups on rotor, use a block of wood to rest the rotor on. This will prevent damage to the wheel studs.

To install:

12. Pack the bearing cone and roller assemblies with Long Life Multi-purpose grease, C1AZ-19590-B or equivalent with a bearing packer. If a bearing packer is not available, pack as much grease as possible by hand into bearing assembly and grease the cup surfaces also.

13. Place the inner bearing assembly into rotor onto cup. Apply a light film of grease to the lip of the new grease retainer seal and install into rotor assembly. Be sure that the seal is seated flush with back of the rotor hub.

↱ When installing the grease retainer, use a block of wood to rest the rotor on. This will prevent damage to the wheel studs.

14. Install the hub and rotor assembly onto the spindle, keeping the hub centered to prevent damage to the retainer and spindle threads.

15. Install the outer bearing assembly and flat washer. Install the adjusting nut finger tight.

16. While rotating the hub tighten the adjusting nut to 17-25 ft. lbs. (23-34 Nm). Back the nut off $^1/_2$ turn, using an inch pound torque wrench, tighten adjusting nut to 10-28 inch lbs. (1.1-3.2 Nm).

17. Place the nut locking ring on adjusting nut aligning the castellated flange with the cotter pin hole in spindle.

18. Install a new cotter pin, bending the ends around spindle and install the center hub dust cap.

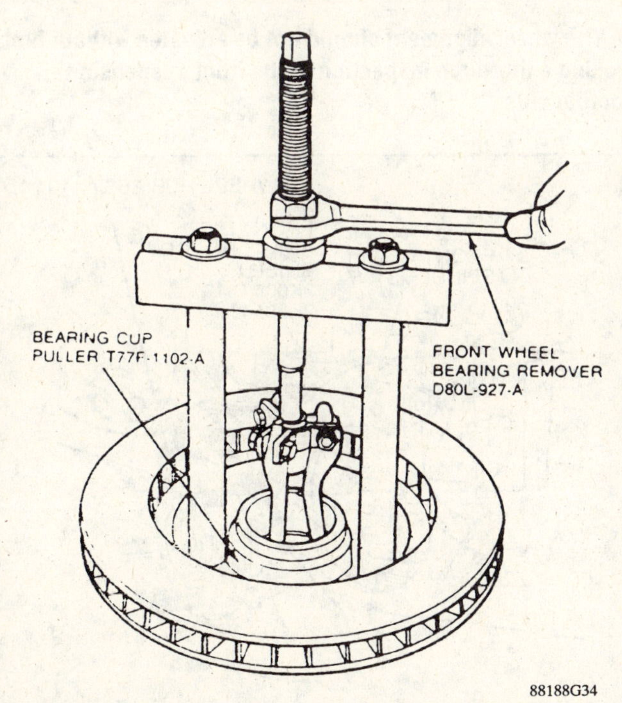

Fig. 34 Removing the wheel bearing cups — 1983-88 vehicles

19. Install the brake caliper, the tire and wheel assembly, then lower the vehicle.

↱ Before driving vehicle pump the brake pedal a few times to ensure proper brake pedal pressure to brakes.

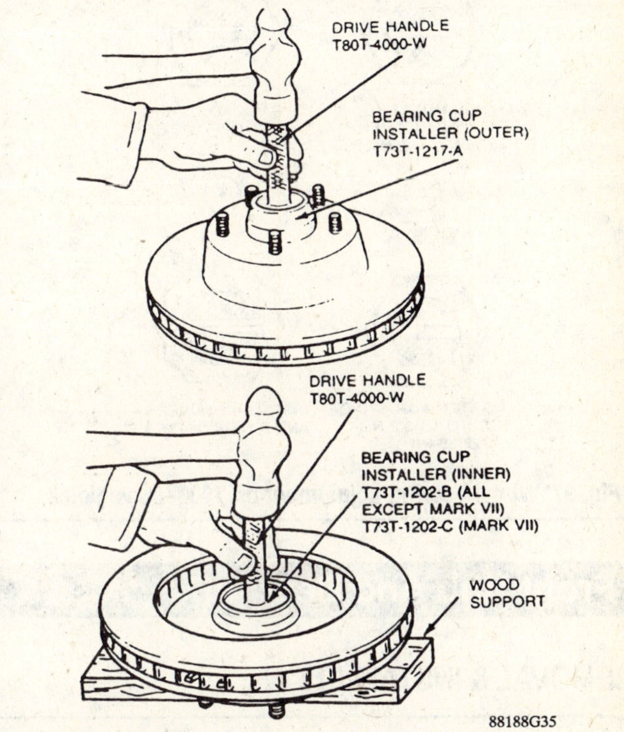

Fig. 35 Installing the wheel bearing cups — 1983-88 vehicles

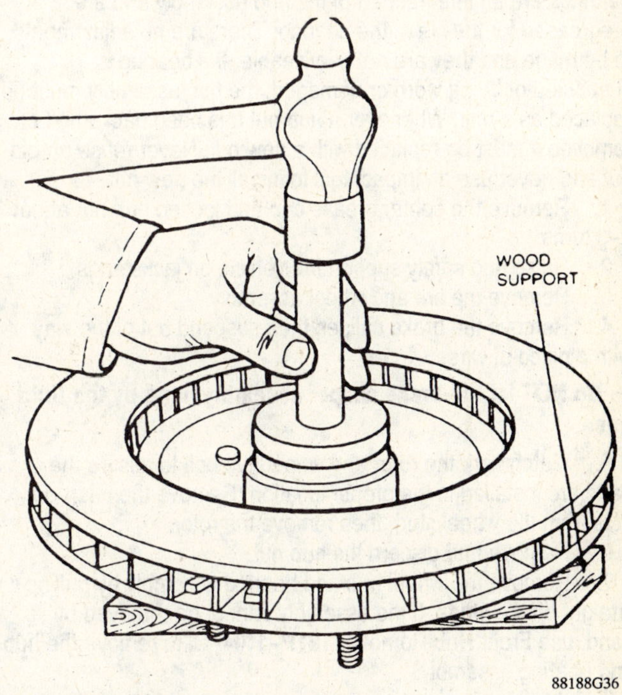

Fig. 36 Installation of the grease retainer — 1983-88 vehicles

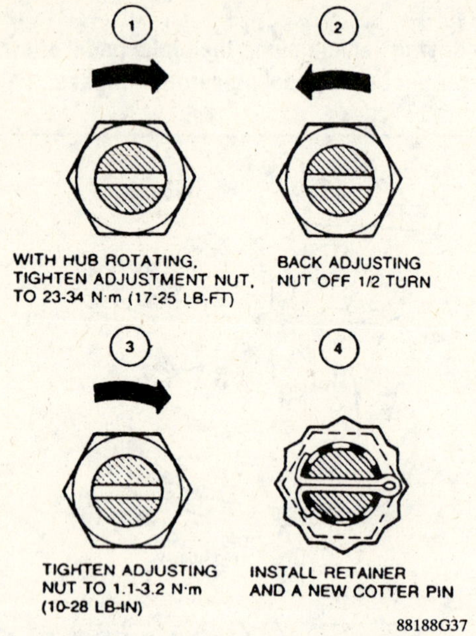

Fig. 37 Wheel bearing adjustment on 1983–88 vehicles

Front Hub And Bearing

REMOVAL & INSTALLATION

1989–96 Vehicles

➧ See Figure 38

The front wheel bearings are of the hub type design. The bearings are an integral part of the hub assembly and are pregreased for the life of the bearing. There are no adjustments to be made and they are not serviceable. If a bearing is suspected of being worn or damaged, the hub assembly must be replaced as a unit. Whenever a hub nut has been backed off or removed it must be replaced with a new nut. Never reuse an old nut and never use an impact tool to install the new nut.

1. Remove the center grease cap and loosen hub nut about 2–3 turns.
2. Raise and safely support the vehicle on jackstands.
3. Remove the tire and wheel assembly.
4. Remove the brake caliper, then suspend out of the way with a piece of wire.

➜ Do NOT let the brake caliper assembly hang by the fluid hose.

5. Matchmark the rotor and wheel hub bolt to assure the parts are installed in the proper location. Remove the push-on nuts from the wheel stud, then remove the rotor.
6. Remove and discard the hub nut.
7. Remove the wheel hub and bearing assembly by pulling it straight off the studs. If the assembly cannot be removed by hand, use Front Hub Remover T81P–1104–C, to remove the hub and bearing assembly.

To install:

8. Install hub and bearing assembly and a new hub nut. Only hand-tighten the nut at this time.
9. Install the rotor and push-on nuts. Make sure the rotor marks line up with the hub bolt marks.
10. Install brake caliper assembly. For details, please refer to the procedure located in Section 9 of this manual.
11. Install the tire and wheel assembly. Tighten the wheel lug nuts to 85–105 ft. lbs. (115–142 Nm) using a torque wrench.
12. Carefully lower the vehicle.
13. Tighten the center hub nut to 238–250 ft. lbs. and install a new hub grease cap, using a suitable tool as not to distort of damage the cap.

➜ Once torque has been applied to hub nut, do not back off the nut for any reason. The hub nut must be replaced with a new nut each time the nut has been loosened. Serious damage and or personal injury will occur if the hub nut is not replaced.

Front End Alignment

➧ See Figure 39

➜ The procedure for checking and adjusting front wheel alignment requires specialized equipment and professional skills. The following descriptions and adjustment procedures are for general reference only.

Front wheel alignment is the position of the front wheels relative to each other and to the vehicle. It is determined, and must be maintained to provide safe, accurate steering with minimum tire wear. Many factors are involved in wheel alignment and adjustments are provided to return those that might change due to normal wear to their original value. The factors which determine wheel alignment are dependent on one another; therefore, when one of the factors is adjusted, the others must be adjusted to compensate.

Descriptions of these factors and their affects on the car are provided below.

➜ The wheel alignment should not be adjusted without first making a thorough inspection of the front suspension components.

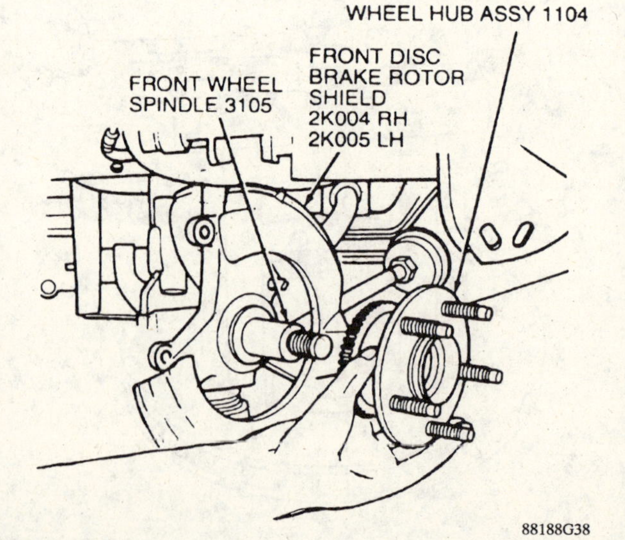

Fig. 38 If you can't remove the hub and bearing by hand, use a suitable hub puller

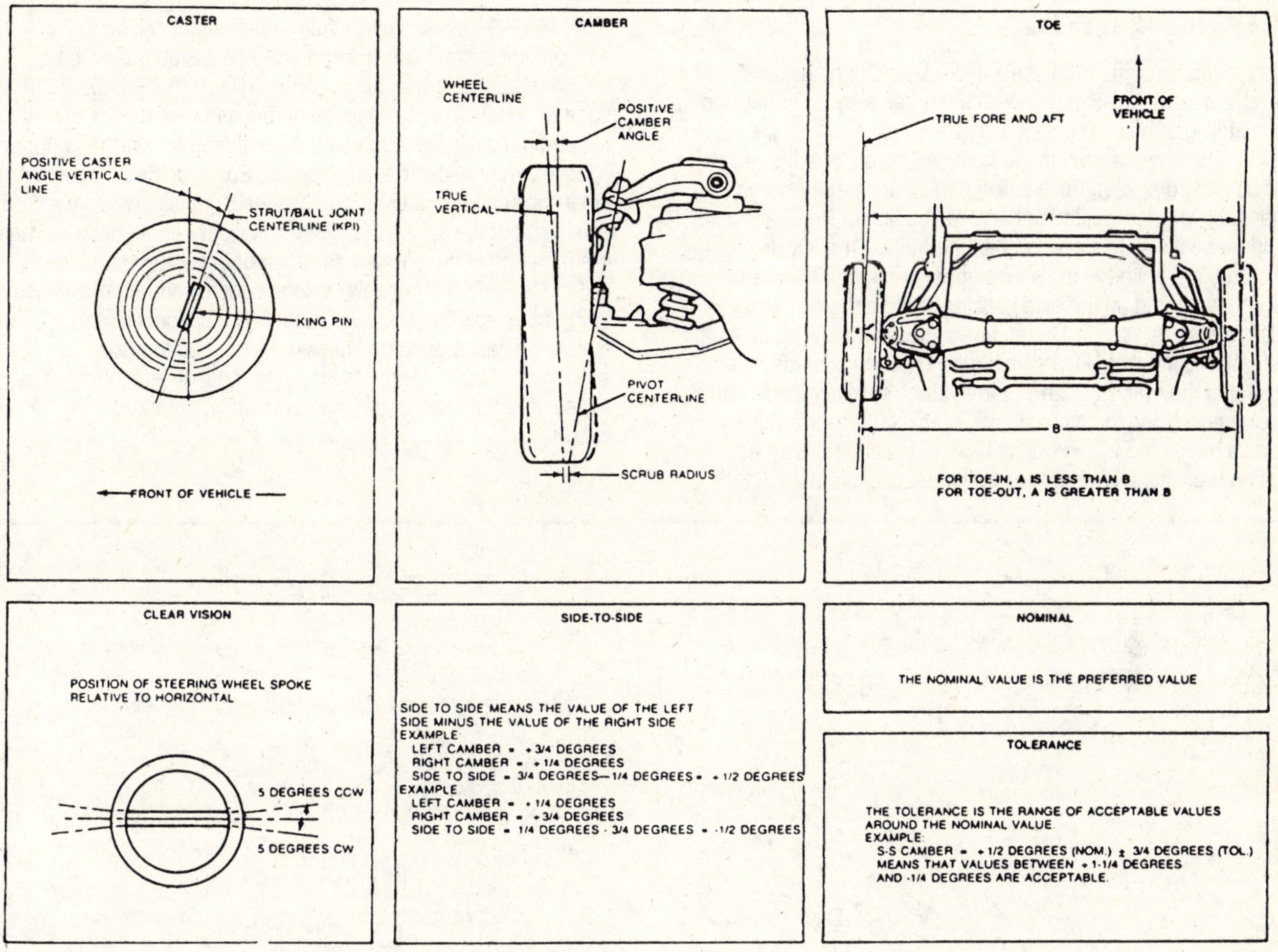

88188G39

Fig. 39 Diagram of camber, caster and toe-in

CAMBER

Camber angle is the number of degrees that the centerline of the wheel is inclined from the vertical. Camber reduces loading of the outer wheel bearing and improves the tire contact patch while cornering.

CASTER

Caster angle is the number of degrees that a line drawn through the steering knuckle pivots is inclined from the vertical, toward the front or rear of the car (when viewed from the side of the car). Caster improves the directional stability and decreases susceptibility to crosswinds or road surface deviations.

TOE-IN

Toe-in is the difference of the distance between the centers of the front and rear of the front wheels. It is most commonly measured in inches, but is occasionally referred to as an angle between the wheels. Toe-in is necessary to compensate for the tendency of the wheels to deflect rearward while in motion. Due to this tendency, the wheels of a vehicle, with properly adjusted toe-in, are traveling straight forward when the vehicle itself is traveling straight forward, resulting in directional stability and minimum tire wear.

Steering wheel spoke misalignment is often an indication of incorrect front end alignment. Care should be exercised when aligning the front end to maintain steering wheel spoke position. When adjusting the tie rod ends, adjust each an equal amount (in the opposite direction) to increase or decrease toe-in. If, following toe-in adjustment, further adjustments are necessary to center the steering wheel spokes, adjust the tie rod ends an equal amount in the same direction.

REAR SUSPENSION

➧ **See Figures 40, 41 and 42**

All models through 1988 use a 4-link coil spring suspension. The axle housing is suspended from the frame by an upper and lower trailing arm and a shock absorber at each side of the vehicle. These arms pivot in the frame members and the rear axle housing brackets. Each coil spring is mounted between a lower seat which is welded to the axle housing or lower arm and an upper seat which is integral with the frame. The shock absorbers are bolted to the spring upper seats at the top and brackets mounted on the axle housing at the bottom. The upper trailing arms are attached to the frame crossmember brackets at the front and brackets located near the outer ends of the axle housing at the rear. Both lower arms attach similarly to the frame side members and the axle housing brackets. A rear stabilizer bar attached to the frame side rail brackets and the two axle housing brackets is available as optional equipment.

All 1989–96 models use a fully independent coil spring suspension system which is mounted on a rubber isolated subframe. Large lower control arms (H-arm configuration) are used to oppose torque reaction on braking and acceleration. A toe compensator link controls toe-out during braking. The upper control arm provides camber control. Epoxy coated, variable rate, steel coil springs are used on all models. Insulators are used on either end of the spring for added isolation. Although the springs are mounted in the same manner on both the Base and the Super Coupe/XR-7 models, unique spring load/rate provisions are used to suit the particular model. The suspension also features a cast aluminum knuckle that carries the rear suspension loads, connects the upper and lower control arms, houses the halfshaft bearing and provides a mount for the brakes.

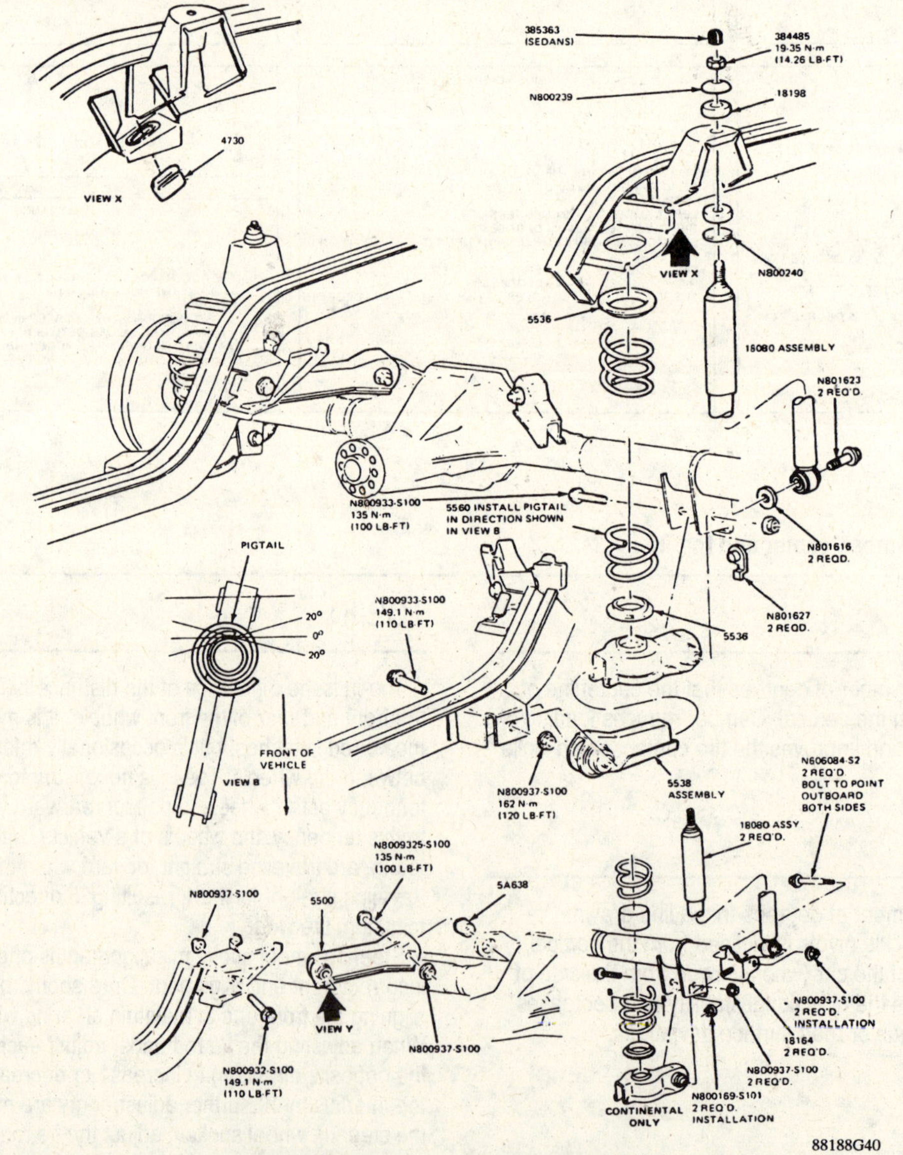

Fig. 40 Exploded view of the rear suspension components — 1983–86 vehicles

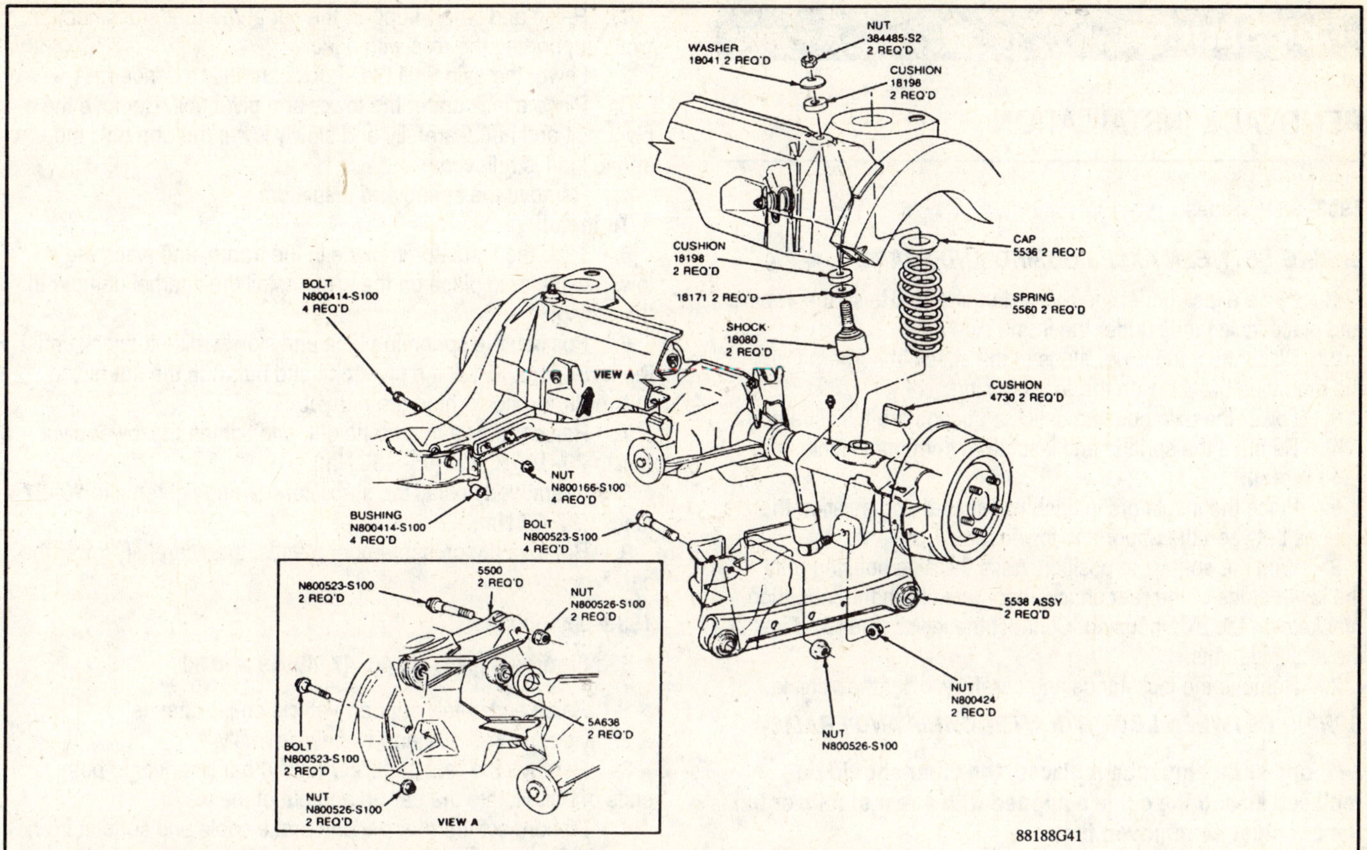

88188G41

Fig. 41 Exploded view of the rear suspension components — 1987–88 vehicles

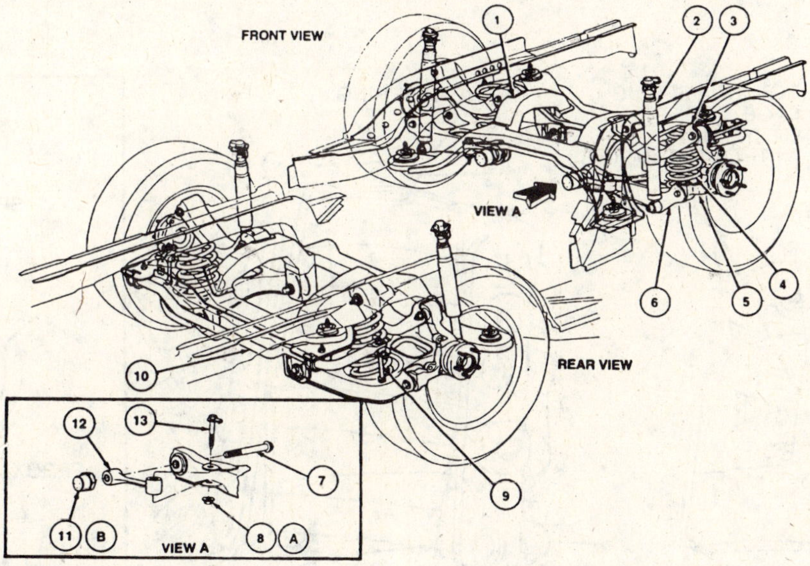

Item	Part Number	Description
1	—	Sub-Frame Assy
2	18125	Rear Shock Absorber
3	5500	Upper Rear Suspension Arm and Bushing
4	5560	Rear Spring
5	5A969	Rear Wheel Knuckle
6	5500	Rear Suspension Arm and Bushing
7	N805467-S160	Bolt (2 Req'd)
8	N805479-S1050C	Nut

Item	Part Number	Description
9	5C488	Rear Stabilizer Bar Link and Bushing
10	5A772	Rear Stabilizer Bar
11	N805646-S161	Nut (w/Cap) (2 Req'd)
12	5A972	Rear Suspension Compensator Link
13	N806066-S160	Bolt (2 Req'd)
A	—	Tighten to 149-201 N·m (110-148 Lb-Ft)
B	—	Tighten to 225-275 N·m (166-202 Lb-Ft)

88188G42

Fig. 42 Exploded view of the rear suspension components — 1989–96 vehicles

Coil Springs

REMOVAL & INSTALLATION

1983-88 Vehicles

SPRING BETWEEN AXLE HOUSING AND FRAME

1. Place a jack under the rear axle housing. Raise the vehicle and place jackstands under the frame side rails.
2. Disconnect the lower studs of the shock absorbers from the mounting brackets on the axle housing.
3. Lower the axle housing until the springs are fully seated.
4. Remove the springs and insulators from the vehicle.

To install:

5. Place the insulators in each upper seat and position the springs between the upper and lower seats.
6. With the springs in position, raise the axle housing until the lower studs of the rear shock absorbers reach the mounting brackets on the axle housing. Connect the lower studs and install the attaching nuts.
7. Remove the jackstands and carefully lower the vehicle.

SPRING BETWEEN LOWER CONTROL ARM AND FRAME

➥ If one spring must be replaced, the other should be replaced also. If the car is equipped with a rear stabilizer bar, the bar must be removed first.

1. Raise and safely support the car at the rear crossmember, while supporting the axle with a jack.
2. Lower the axle until the shocks are fully extended.
3. Place a jack under the lower arm pivot bolt. Remove the pivot bolt and nut. Carefully and slowly lower the arm until the spring load is relieved.
4. Remove the spring and insulators.

To install:

5. Tape the insulator in place in the frame, and place the lower insulator in place on the arm. Install the internal damper in the spring.
6. Position the spring in place and slowly raise the jack under the lower arm. Install the pivot bolt and nut, with the nut facing outwards. Do not tighten the nut yet.
7. Raise the axle to curb height, and tighten the lower pivot bolt to 70-100 ft. lbs. (95-135 Nm).
8. If removed, install the stabilizer bar and tighten it to 20-27 ft. lbs. (27-37 Nm).
9. Remove the crossmember stands, then carefully lower the car.

1989-96 Vehicles

➧ See Figures 43, 44, 45, 46, 47, 48, 49 and 50

1. Raise and safely support vehicle on jackstands.
2. Remove rear tire and wheel assembly.
3. Remove the rear stabilizer (sway) bar link nuts at both ends of bar. Rotate the bar up and out of the way.
4. Disconnect the rear parking brake cable and conduit from the caliper.

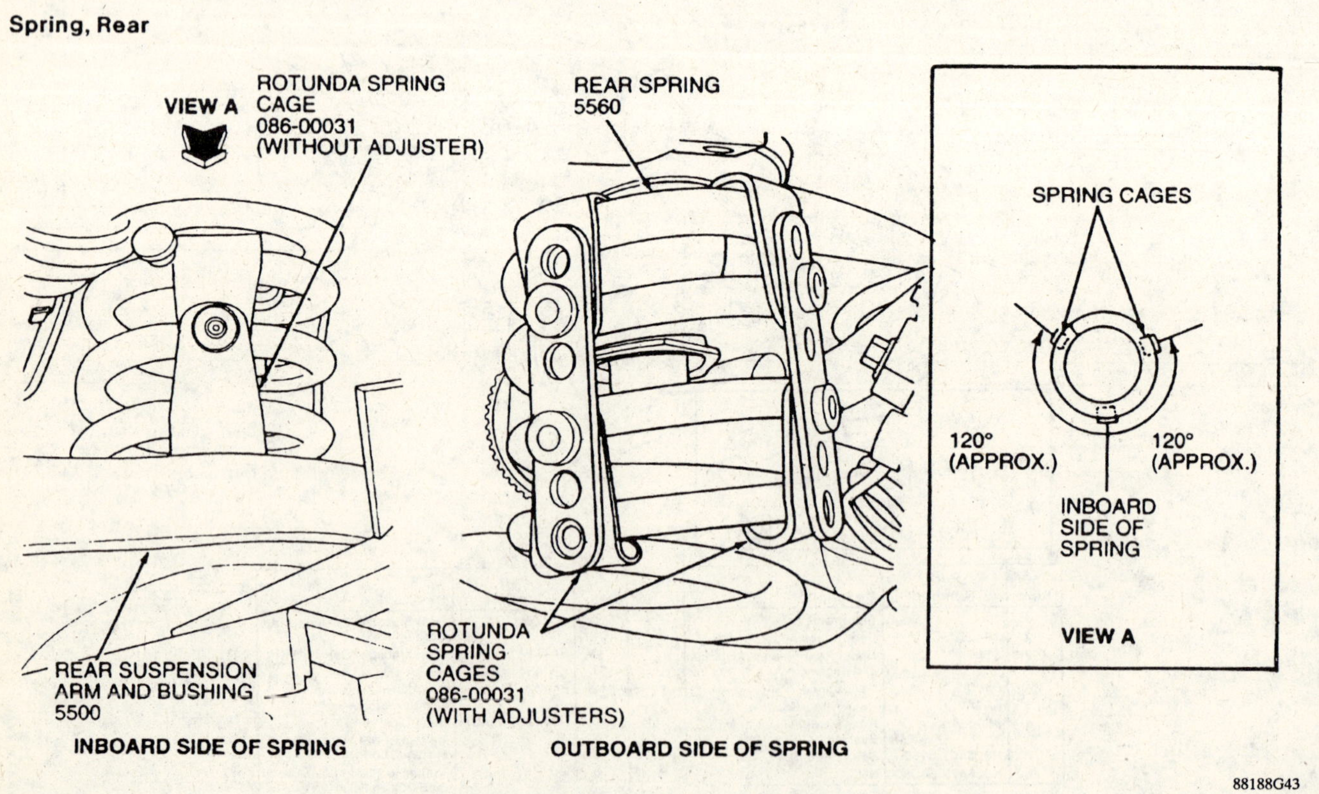

Fig. 43 Installation of the spring cages on the coil spring

5. Install three Rotunda Spring Cages 086-00031 or equivalent, to the rear spring, as follows:

a. Install one spring cage without an adjuster link to the inboard side (the innermost "bend" of the spring).

b. Install two more spring cages, with adjusters, at 120° angles ($^1/_3$ of the way each around spring) to the previously installed cage.

6. Place a transmission jack or suitable stand under the lower control arm as far outboard as possible.

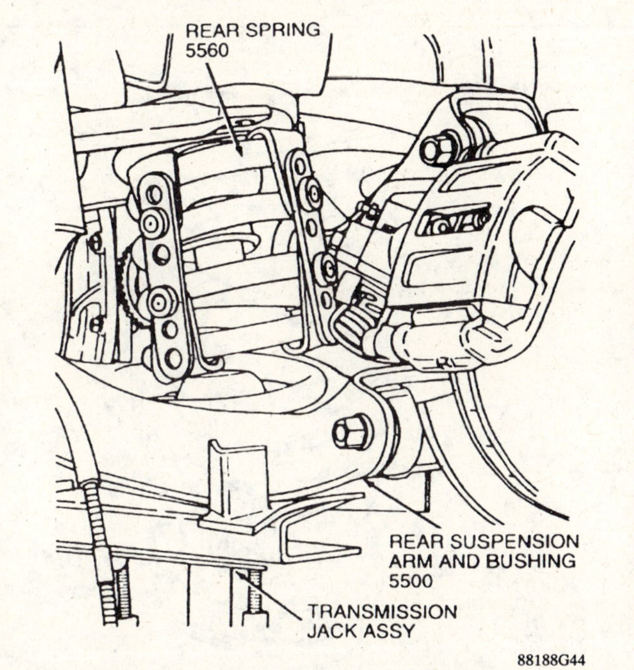

Fig. 44 Place a transmission jack under the lower control arm as far outboard as possible

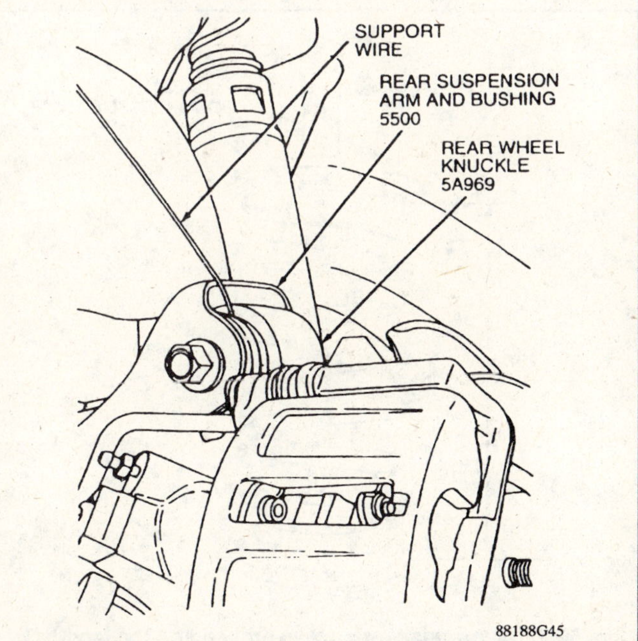

Fig. 45 Wire the upper control arm to the body to support the knuckle

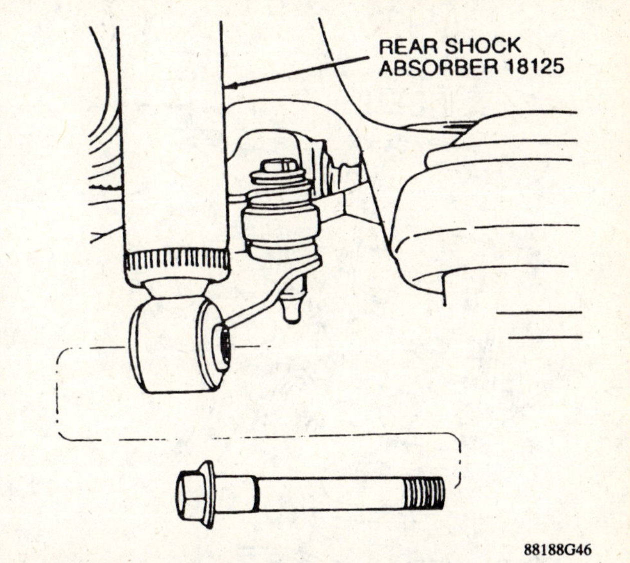

Fig. 46 Remove the lower shock absorber bolt, washer and nut

7. Support the rear knuckle by using a wire or other suitable means to support the upper control arm to the frame or body.

8. Remove the lower strut/shock mounting bolt, washer and nut.

Control arms must not be lowered until pivot bolts are loose. Do not attempt to remove plastic cap on the front of the pivot nut.

9. Mark the toe adjustment cam-to-subframe position with a suitable marker. Loosen both inboard pivot bolts on lower control arm.

10. Remove the two bolts and nuts attaching the lower control arm to the knuckle.

11. Lower the control arm by carefully lowering the support jack. Make sure the spring cages are properly seated on spring as the control arm is lowered.

12. Remove the jack, pull the control arm down fully by hand, then remove the coil spring with the cages in place.

13. If necessary, remove the spring center mounting insulators.

To install:

If new springs are to be installed, or cages removed from old spring, measure the length of the spring (with cages still installed and spring compressor installed), install a spring compressor D78P-5310-A or equivalent into the spring and compress the spring. Remove the spring cages and then the spring compressor. Install the spring compressor into the new spring and compress to previously measured length, or 10.5 in. (267mm). Install the spring cages and remove the spring compressor.

14. Install spring center mounting insulators, if removed.

15. Place spring, with cages installed, onto upper and lower control arm seats. The cage with no adjuster must face inward and cages must be closer to the bottom of spring. The spring pigtails can be in any position.

16. Position two jackstands under the front bumper reinforcement. This will prevent the vehicle from lifting off of the supporting stands at the rear of the car.

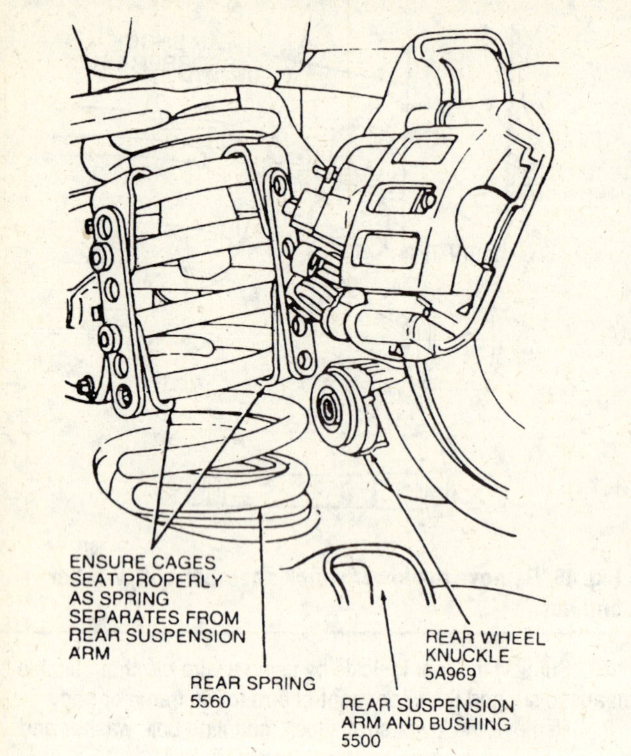

Fig. 47 While lowering the jack, make sure the spring cages are properly seated on the spring

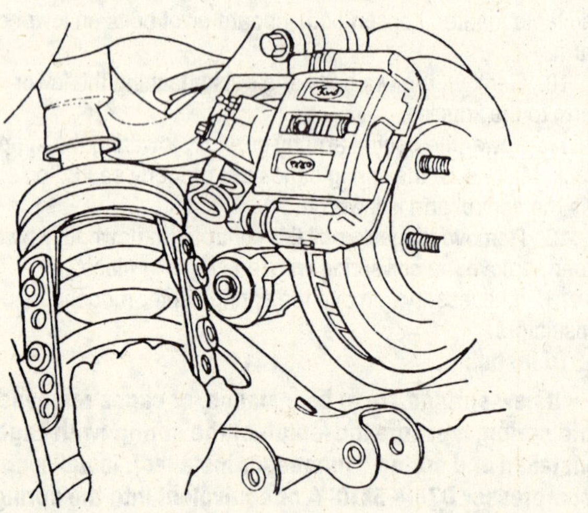

Fig. 48 Remove the rear spring with the cages in place

17. Position the jack under the lower control arm and raise enough to line up mounting holes, ensuring that the spring seats properly.
18. Install the bolts and nuts attaching the control arm to the knuckle and tighten bolts to 110–148 ft. lbs. (149–201 Nm).
19. Remove the wire, or other means of support, holding the upper control arm assembly.
20. Install the lower strut/shock bolt and nut, tighten nut to 83–113 ft. lbs. (113–153 Nm).
21. Remove the jack from under the control arm, and remove the spring cages.
22. Connect the parking brake cable to brake caliper assembly.
23. Install the stabilizer (sway) bar links and attaching nuts at both ends of bar.
24. Set toe adjustment cam to the mark previously made on removal.
25. Tighten lower front control arm-to-subframe nut to 166–202 ft. lbs. (225–275 Nm). Tighten the lower rear control arm-to-subframe nut to 142–191 ft. lbs. 192–259 Nm).
26. Carefully lower vehicle, then have the alignment checked.

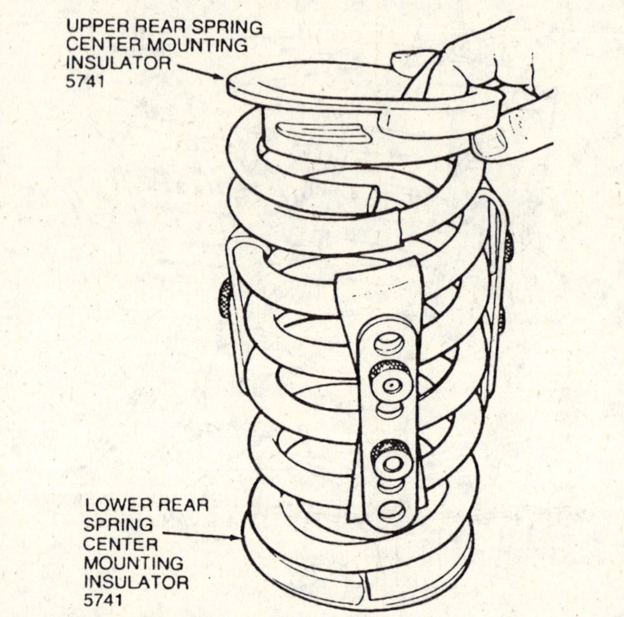

Fig. 49 Remove the spring center mounting insulators, if necessary

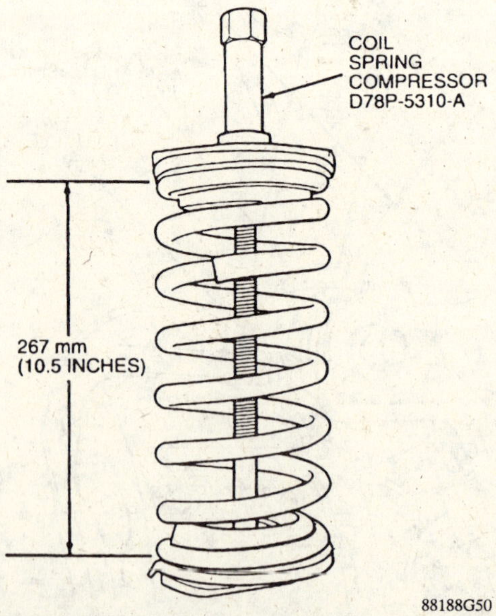

Fig. 50 If the original spring was broken and the length not known, compress the spring to about 10.5 inches (not including the insulators)

Shock Absorber

REMOVAL & INSTALLATION

➥ Purge a new shock of air by repeatedly extending it in its normal position and compressing it while inverted.

1983–88 Vehicles

➧ See Figures 51 and 52

SPRING BETWEEN LOWER CONTROL ARM AND FRAME

1. For Thunderbird Turbo Coupes, perform the following:
   a. Remove the luggage compartment side trim panel.
   b. Detach the actuator wiring connector from the harness connector.
   c. Squeeze the two actuator retaining tabs firmly inward with one hand and lift the actuator off the mounting bracket with the other hand.
   d. Grasp the mounting bracket with water pump pliers and hold firmly.
   e. While holding the mounting bracket, loosen the bracket attaching nut.
   f. Remove the mounting bracket.
   g. Install the mounting bracket retaining nut.

****WARNING**

Do NOT move or raise the vehicle after the nut is removed. If the shock absorber is being removed, make sure to install the mounting bracket retaining nut.

2. Remove the upper attaching nut, washer, and insulator. Access is through the trunk on sedans or side panel trim covers on station wagons and hatchbacks. Sedan studs have rubber caps.
3. Raise the car. Compress the shock to clear the upper tower. Remove the lower nut and washer; remove the shock.

To install:

4. Purge the shock of air and compress. Place the lower mounting eye over the lower stud and install the washer and a new locking nut. Do not tighten the nut yet.
5. Place the insulator and washer on the upper stud. Extend the shock, install the stud through the upper mounting hole.
6. Tighten the lower mounting nut to 45–60 ft. lbs. (61–81 Nm).
7. Carefully lower the car. Install the outer insulator and washer on the upper stud, and install a new nut. Tighten to 19–27 ft. lbs. (26–37 Nm).
8. For Thunderbird Turbo Coupes, perform the following:
   a. Align the flats on the mounting bracket with the flats on the shock stud. Install the mounting bracket.
   b. Install the nut on the shock absorber, if not already done.
   c. Grasp the mounting bracket with water pump pliers and tighten the bracket retaining nut. Tighten the nut to 15–21 ft. lbs. (20–28 Nm).
   d. Grasp the actuator by the retaining tabs, then install the actuator on the mounting bracket by pushing down on the plastic retainer tabs.
   e. Attach the actuator wiring connector.
9. Install the trim panel on station wagons and hatchbacks or the rubber cap on sedans.

SPRING BETWEEN AXLE HOUSING AND FRAME

1. Raise the vehicle and install jackstands.
2. Remove the shock absorber outer attaching nut, washer and insulator from the stud at the top side of the spring upper seat. Compress the shock sufficiently to clear the spring seat hole, and remove the inner insulator and washer from the upper attaching stud.
3. Remove the locknut and disconnect the shock absorber lower stud at the mounting bracket on the axle housing. Remove the shock absorber.

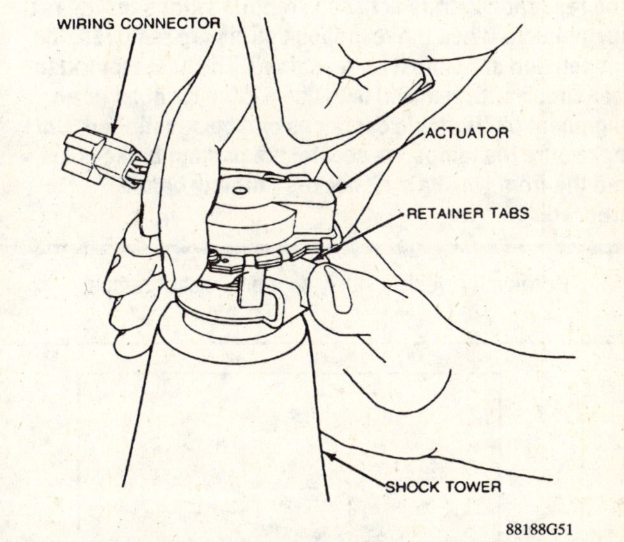

Fig. 51 Squeeze the two actuator retaining tabs firmly inward with one hand and lift the actuator off the mounting bracket with the other hand

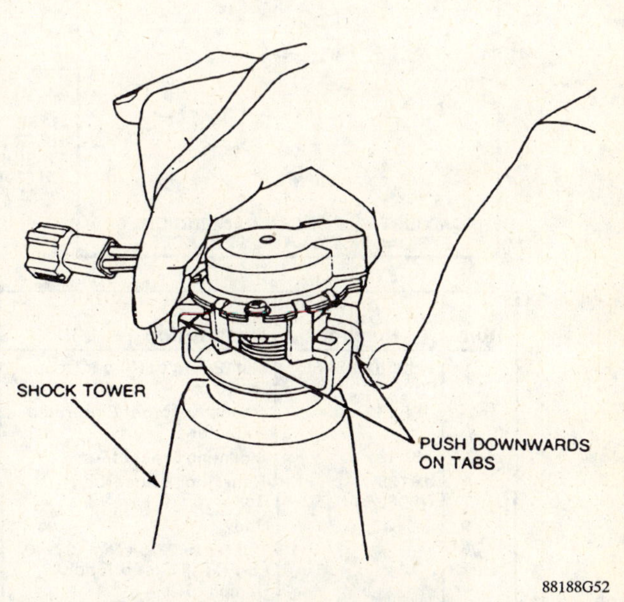

Fig. 52 Install the actuator to the mounting bracket by pushing down on the plastic retainer tabs

To install:

4. Position a new inner washer and insulator on the upper attaching stud. Place the upper stud in the hole in the upper spring seat. While maintaining the shock in this position, install a new outer insulator, washer, and nut on the stud from the top side of the spring upper seat.

5. Extend the shock absorber. Locate the lower stud in the mounting bracket hole on the axle housing and install the locknut.

1989–96 Vehicles

➧ See Figure 53

****WARNING**

The rear shock/struts act as the rebound stops for the rear suspension. When the rear shock/struts are removed, the suspension arms must be restrained. The best method for rear shock/strut removal is to use a drive on hoist or an alignment pit. Portable car ramps can be substituted, But make sure the ramps are secure, the parking brake is set, and the front wheels are chocked properly before proceeding.

1. Position the vehicle safely on a pit, hoist or ramps.

****WARNING**

These vehicles are equipped with gas-pressurized shock absorbers which will extend unassisted. DO NOT apply heat or flame to the shock absorber tube during removal.

2. Remove the side trim panels from inside luggage compartment.

3. If equipped with an Automatic Ride Control, perform the following:

   a. Detach the actuator wiring connector from harness connector.

   b. Squeeze the two actuator retaining tabs firmly inward with one hand and lift actuator off with the other hand, if so equipped.

   c. Using water pump pliers, grasp the mounting bracket and hold firmly. loosen attaching nut and remove mounting bracket, if so equipped.

4. Remove top attaching nut washer and insulator.

5. Remove the lower shock/strut mounting bolt and remove shock/strut.

To install:

6. Properly prime the new shock/strut by inverting and collapsing, then releasing the shock/strut to its fully extended position.

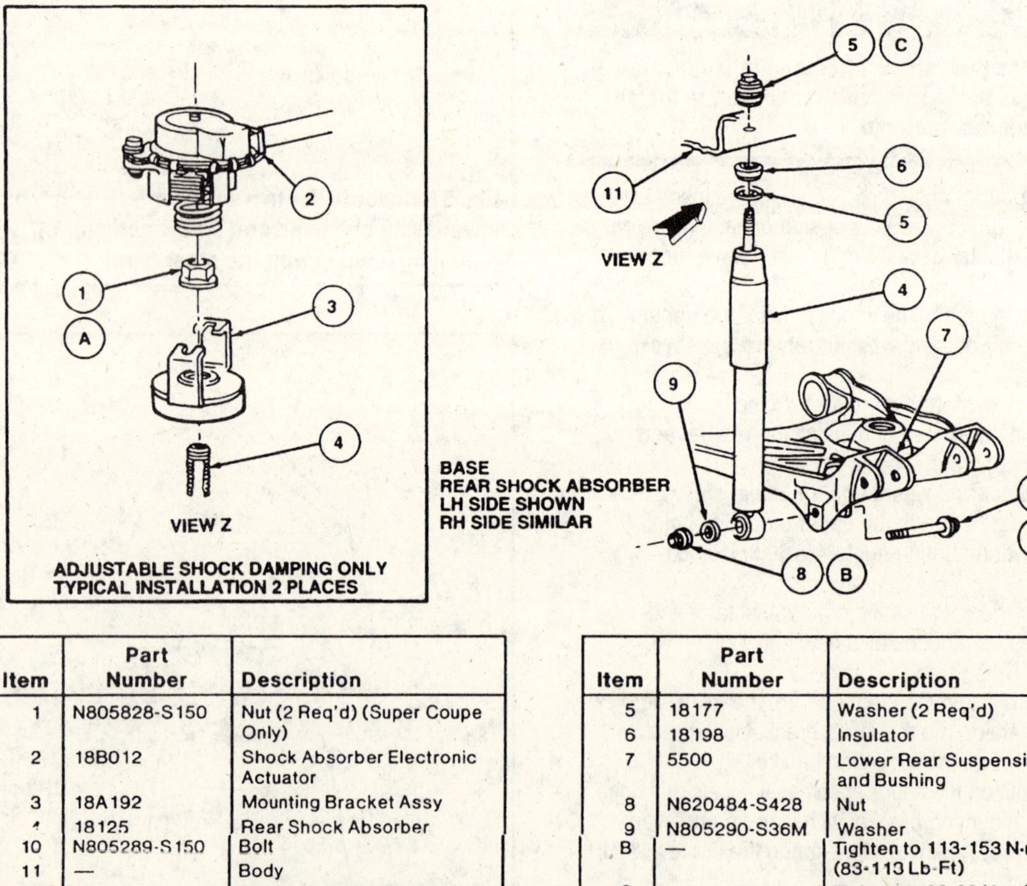

Item	Part Number	Description
1	N805828-S150	Nut (2 Req'd) (Super Coupe Only)
2	18B012	Shock Absorber Electronic Actuator
3	18A192	Mounting Bracket Assy
4	18125	Rear Shock Absorber
10	N805289-S150	Bolt
11	—	Body
A	—	Tighten to 37-54 N·m (27-40 Lb-Ft) (All Except Shock Damping)

Item	Part Number	Description
5	18177	Washer (2 Req'd)
6	18198	Insulator
7	5500	Lower Rear Suspension Arm and Bushing
8	N620484-S428	Nut
9	N805290-S36M	Washer
B	—	Tighten to 113-153 N·m (83-113 Lb-Ft)
C	—	Tighten to 60-80 N·m (44-58 Lb-Ft)

88188G53

Fig. 53 Rear shock absorber mounting — 1995 vehicle shown

When replacing shock/strut on an Automatic Ride Control equipped vehicle, an exact replacement automatic adjustable shock/strut must be used. Failure to do so will result in a vehicle that will handle poorly, and could lead to a potentially dangerous situation.

7. Place the inner washer and insulator on the upper retaining stud. Place the shock/strut up into position in upper mounting hole. Compress shock enough to install the lower mounting bolt and nut, then tighten the nut to 83-113 ft. lbs. (113-153 Nm).
8. With the upper end of the shock absorber protruding through the body shock tower hole, install the insulator, washer and nut on top of shock/strut, inside luggage compartment.

Automatic ride control shock absorbers (Super Coupe and XR7) use a separate nut whereas the base vehicles use the assembly consisting of the crimped on nut. For the ride control assembly, hold one of the tags on the washer securing the joint to prevent the shock rod from rotating during installation. Base vehicle shock absorbers have a hex on the end of the piston rod to prevent the rod from turning while the nut is being torqued. Tighten the nuts to 27-40 ft. lbs. (37-54 Nm) on the ride control shock absorber or to 44-58 ft. lbs. (60-80 Nm) on base vehicles.

9. If equipped with Automatic Ride Control, perform the following:
   a. Align the flats on mounting bracket with flats on the shock stud, and install mounting bracket.
   b. Install nut onto stud. Tabs on mounting bracket must be aligned in a fore and aft direction before tightening of nut.
   c. Using water pump pliers, grasp the mounting bracket firmly (if so equipped) and tighten the bracket retaining nut to 27-35 ft. lbs. (37-47 Nm).
   d. Grasp the actuator by the retaining tabs, install onto mounting bracket by pushing down on the retainer tabs.
   e. Connect the actuator wiring connector, and harness mating connector. Slide the connector onto the rail and push into secured position.

The actuator assembly may be difficult to install if the plastic becomes eccentric to actuator driving shaft. If this happens; loosen the two mounting screws, allowing the actuator to float with respect to the locator and install onto the shock. Tighten the two screws, if so equipped.

10. Install luggage compartment, and lower vehicle.

Upper Control Arms

REMOVAL & INSTALLATION

1983-88 Vehicles

See Figure 54 and 55

If one arm requires replacement, replace the other one also.

1. Raise and safely support the vehicle at the rear crossmember.
2. Remove and discard the upper control arm-to-axle pivot bolts and nut.

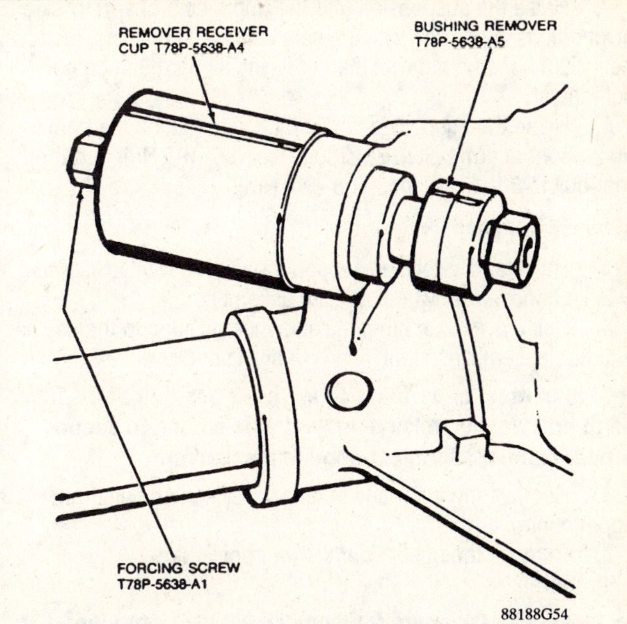

Fig. 54 Upper control arm bushing removal — 1983-88 vehicles

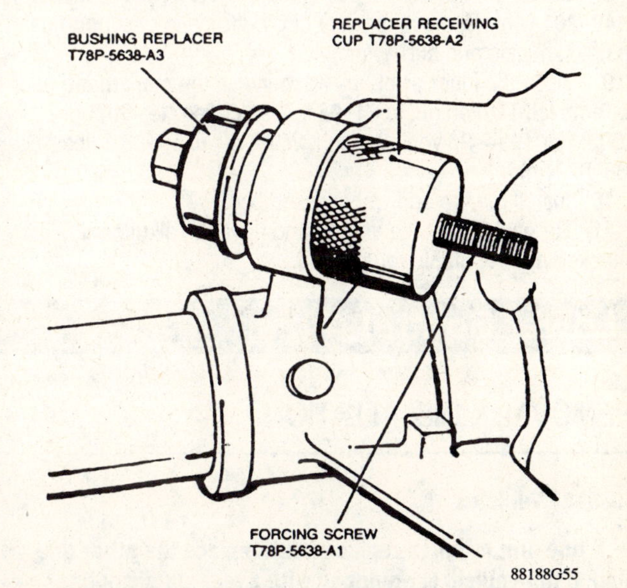

Fig. 55 Install the bushing assembly into the bushing ear of the rear axle

3. Remove and discard the upper control arm-to-frame pivot bolt and nut. Remove the upper control arm from the vehicle.
4. If the upper control arm bushing is to be replaced, use Bushing Remover and Installer Set T78P-5638-A place the upper control arm axle bushing remover tool in position, then remove the bushing assembly.
5. Use the installer tool, shown in the accompanying figure to install the bushing assembly into the bushing ear of the rear axle.

To install:

6. Place the upper control arm into the bracket of the body side rail. Insert a new control arm-to-frame pivot bolt and nut with the nut facing outboard. Do not tighten the nut yet.

7. Raise the suspension until the upper control arm-to-axle pivot hole is in position with the hole in the axle bushing. Install a new pivot bolt and nut with the nut facing inboard, but do not tighten yet.

8. Raise the suspension to curb height. Tighten the front upper control arm bolt to 70–100 ft. lbs. (95–135 Nm) and the rear bolt to 80–105 ft. lbs. (108–142 Nm).

1989–96 Vehicles

1. Raise and safely the support the vehicle with jackstands.
2. Remove rear wheel and tire assembly.
3. Using a wire, or other suitable means, support the knuckle and hub assembly so that it can not swing outward.

➥ It is of great importance to mark the position of the inner pivot bolt washer, relative to the frame mount, to ensure proper camber alignment upon reinstallation.

4. Remove the inner and outer pivot bolts and nuts from the upper control arm.
5. Remove the upper control arm from vehicle.

To install:

➥ Inspect all fasteners for damage, pitting, corrosion, stretching, etc. Replace fasteners as necessary.

6. Install the upper control arm into its position.
7. Install the inner pivot bolt and nut loosely.
8. Install the outer pivot bolt and tighten to 110–148 ft. lbs. (149–201 Nm). Remove the wire or other means of support used to hold knuckle and hub assembly.
9. Align the inner pivot bolt washer with the mark made prior to removal. Tighten nut to 81–98 ft. lbs. for vehicles through 1993. For 1994–96 vehicles, tighten the nut to 50–68 ft. lbs. (68–92 Nm).
10. Install the tire and wheel assembly.
11. Carefully lower the vehicle and have the alignment checked at a reputable repair shop.

Lower Control Arms

REMOVAL & INSTALLATION

1983–88 Vehicles

➥ If one arm requires replacement, replace the other one also. If the vehicle is equipped with a rear stabilizer bar, remove the bar.

1. Raise the vehicle and safely support the body at the rear crossmember.
2. Lower the vehicle until the rear shocks are fully extended.

➥ The axle must be supported by a transmission jack or jackstands.

3. Place a transmission jack under the lower control arm-to-axle pivot bolt. Remove and discard the bolt and nut. Lower the transmission slowly until the coil spring can be removed.
4. Remove and discard the lower control arm-to-frame pivot bolt and nut, then remove the lower control arm.

To install:

5. Position the lower control arm into the front arm bracket. Insert a new arm-to-frame pivot bolt and nut with the nut facing outwards. Do not tighten at this time.
6. Install the coil spring. Holding the spring into position, use the transmission jack under the rear of the lower control arm. Raise the jack until the arm is in position. Insert a new, arm-to-axle pivot bolt and nut with the nut facing outward. Do not tighten at this time.
7. Lower the transmission jack. Raise the axle with a suitable jack to curb height. Tighten the lower arm front bolt to 80–105 ft. lbs. (108–142 Nm) and the rear pivot bolt to 70–100 ft. lbs. (95–135 Nm).
8. If equipped, install the rear stabilizer bar.
9. Remove the crossmember supports, then carefully lower the vehicle.

1989–96 Vehicles

➧ See Figure 56

1. Raise and safely support vehicle on jackstands.
2. Remove the rear coil spring as outlined previously in this section.
3. Remove the inner control arm pivot bolts and nuts and remove arm assembly.
4. Remove the toe compensating link from control arm.

To install:

5. Inspect all fasteners for pitting, corrosion, stretching, thread conditioning, etc. Reuse fasteners only if in good condition.

➥ If the plastic cap on the large nut, used on the inner front part of control arm, is damaged, loose or missing, replace the nut.

6. Install the toe compensating link on control arm.
7. Place lower control arm on subframe, install bolts and nuts loosely.
8. Tighten the toe compensating link nut to 110–148 ft. lbs. (149–201 Nm).
9. Install the coil spring and attach outer lower control arm as previously described.
10. Carefully lower the vehicle, then have the alignment checked.

Stabilizer Bar

REMOVAL & INSTALLATION

1983–88 Vehicles

➧ See Figure 57

1. Raise and support the rear end on jackstands.
2. Remove and discard the four bolts and stamped nuts attaching the stabilizer bar to the brackets in the lower control arms.
3. Remove the stabilizer bar from the vehicle.

To install:

4. Install four new stamped nuts on the stabilizer bar over each attaching hole.
5. Align the four holes in the stabilizer bar with the holes in the brackets in the lower control arms.
6. Install four new bolts. Tighten bolts to 33–51 ft. lbs. (45–71 Nm).
7. Visually inspect the installation to be sure there is adequate clearance between the stabilizer bar and the lower control arm.

➥ Make sure the stabilizer bar is not installed upside down. A color code is provided on the bar (passenger side only) as an aid for proper position.

8. Carefully lower the vehicle.

1989–96 Vehicles

1. Raise and safely support vehicle on jackstands.
2. Remove both rear wheel and tire assemblies.
3. Remove both stabilizer bar link and bushing upper retaining bolts and nuts.
4. Remove both stabilizer bar bracket-to-frame bolts.
5. Remove the rear muffler hanger retaining nuts.
6. Remove the stabilizer bar from vehicle. Remove the bushings/insulator if necessary.

To install:

7. If removed, install the stabilizer bar bushings/insulator.
8. Place the stabilizer bar into position on vehicle.
9. Install the stabilizer bar bracket bolts loosely.
10. Install the rear muffler hanger retaining nuts.
11. Position the bar ends onto the bar links and install the link retaining bolts and nuts.
12. Tighten the link retaining nuts to 35–47 ft. lbs. (46.7–63.3 Nm).
13. Tighten the stabilizer bar mounting bracket bolts to 25–34 ft. lbs. (34–46 Nm).
14. Install the wheel and tire assemblies.
15. Lower the vehicle.

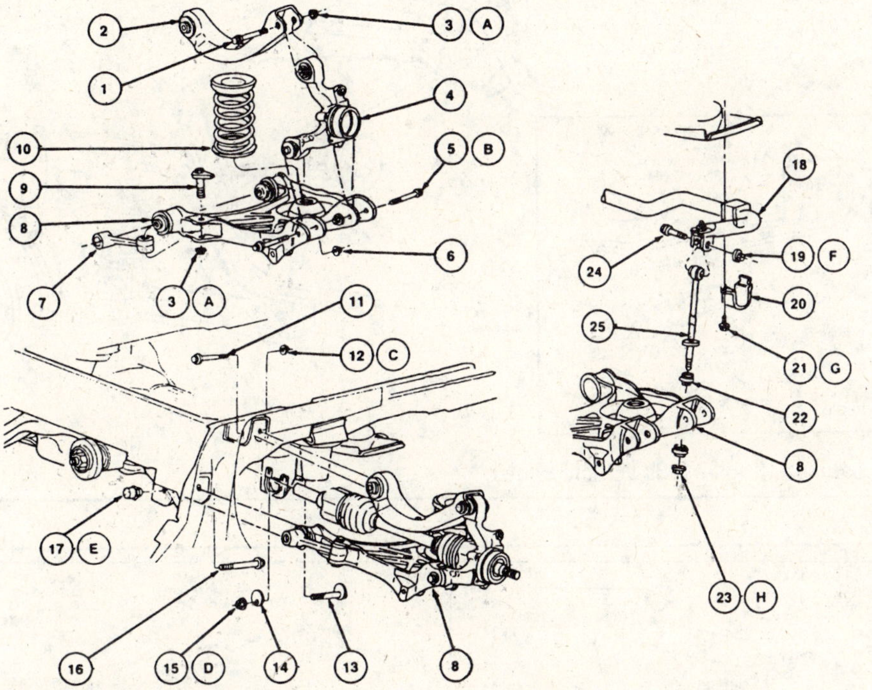

Item	Part Number	Description
1	N805618-S1050C	Bolt
2	5500	Upper Rear Suspension Arm and Bushing (2 Req'd Each Side)
3	N805479-S1050C	Nut
4	5A968	Rear Wheel Knuckle
5	N806365-S1050	Bolt (2 Req'd)
6	N806364-S1050	Nut (2 Req'd)
7	5A972	Rear Suspension Compensator Link
8	5A648	Lower Rear Suspension Arm and Bushing
9	N806066-S160	Bolt (1 Req'd Each Side)
10	5560	Rear Spring
11	N805678-S160	Bolt (2 Req'd)
12	N807144-S7	Nut (2 Req'd)
13	5K751	Rear Suspension Arm Adjusting Cam Kit (2 Req'd)

(Continued)

Item	Part Number	Description
14	5K751	Cam Assy (2 Req'd) (Part of 5K751)
15	N806082-S160	Nut (2 Req'd)
16	N805467-S160	Bolt (2 Req'd)
17	N805646-S161	Nut (2 Req'd)
18	5A772	Rear Stabilizer Bar
19	N805676-S150	Nut (2 Req'd)
20	5486	Stabilizer Bar Bracket
21	N805462-S160	Bolt (1 Req'd Each Side)
22	5493	Lower Suspension Arm Stabilizer Bar Insulator (2 Req'd)
23	N806001-S160	Nut (2 Req'd)
24	N805739-S150	Bolt (2 Req'd)
25	5C486	Link Assy
A	—	Tighten to 149-201 N·m (110-148 Lb-Ft)
B	—	Tighten to 113-153 N·m (83-113 Lb-Ft)

Item	Part Number	Description
C	—	Tighten to 68-92 N·m (50-68 Lb-Ft)
D	—	Tighten to 192-259 N·m (141-191 Lb-Ft)
E	—	Tighten to 225-275 N·m (166-202 Lb-Ft)

(Continued)

Item	Part Number	Description
F	—	Tighten to 46.7-63.3 N·m (35-47 Lb-Ft)
G	——	Tighten to 34-46 N·m (25-34 Lb-Ft)
H	—	Tighten to 10.2-13.8 N·m (8-10 Lb-Ft)

88188G56

Fig. 56 Lower control arm (suspension arm) mounting — 1995 vehicle shown

Axle Damper

REMOVAL & INSTALLATION

2.3L Turbocharged Thunderbird and Cougar Only

➧ See Figure 58

1. Raise and safely support vehicle on jackstands.
2. Support the rear axle housing with suitable jack or stands.
3. Remove the wheel and tire assembly.
4. Remove the front axle damper attaching nut and pivot bolt.
5. Remove the rear axle damper attaching nut.
6. Remove the axle damper and washers.

To install:

7. Install the washers axle damper on the rear mounting bracket stud.
8. Install the rear attaching nut but do not tighten.
9. Position the damper into front mounting bracket and install the pivot bolt and attaching nut.
10. Tighten both attaching nuts to 55–70 ft. lbs.
11. Install the wheel and tire assembly.
12. Lower the vehicle.

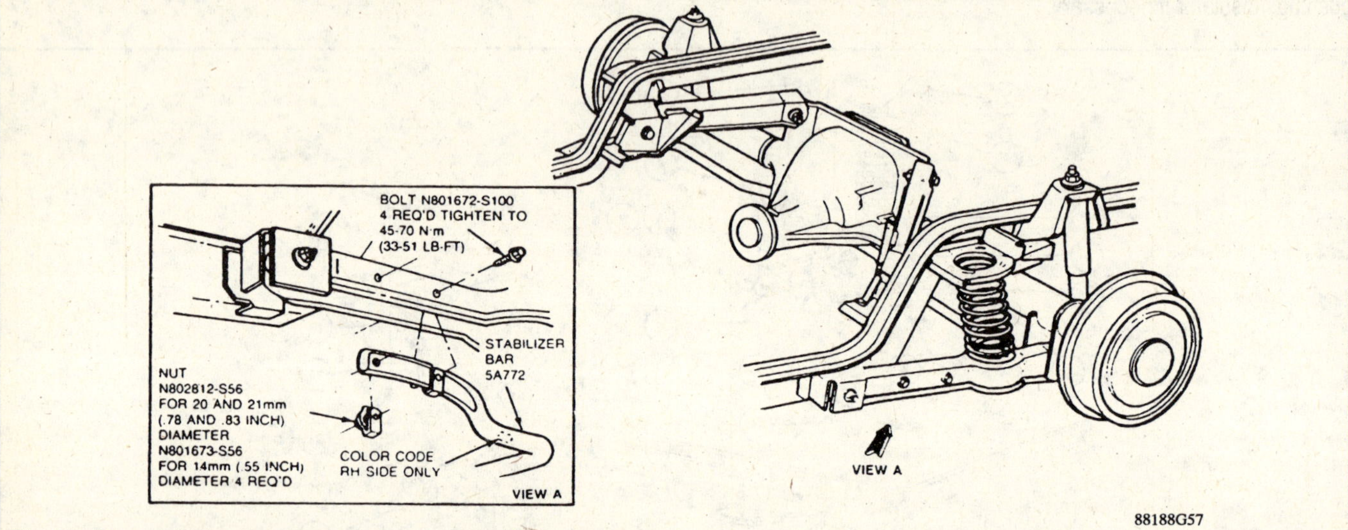

Fig. 57 Rear stabilizer bar mounting — 1988 vehicle shown

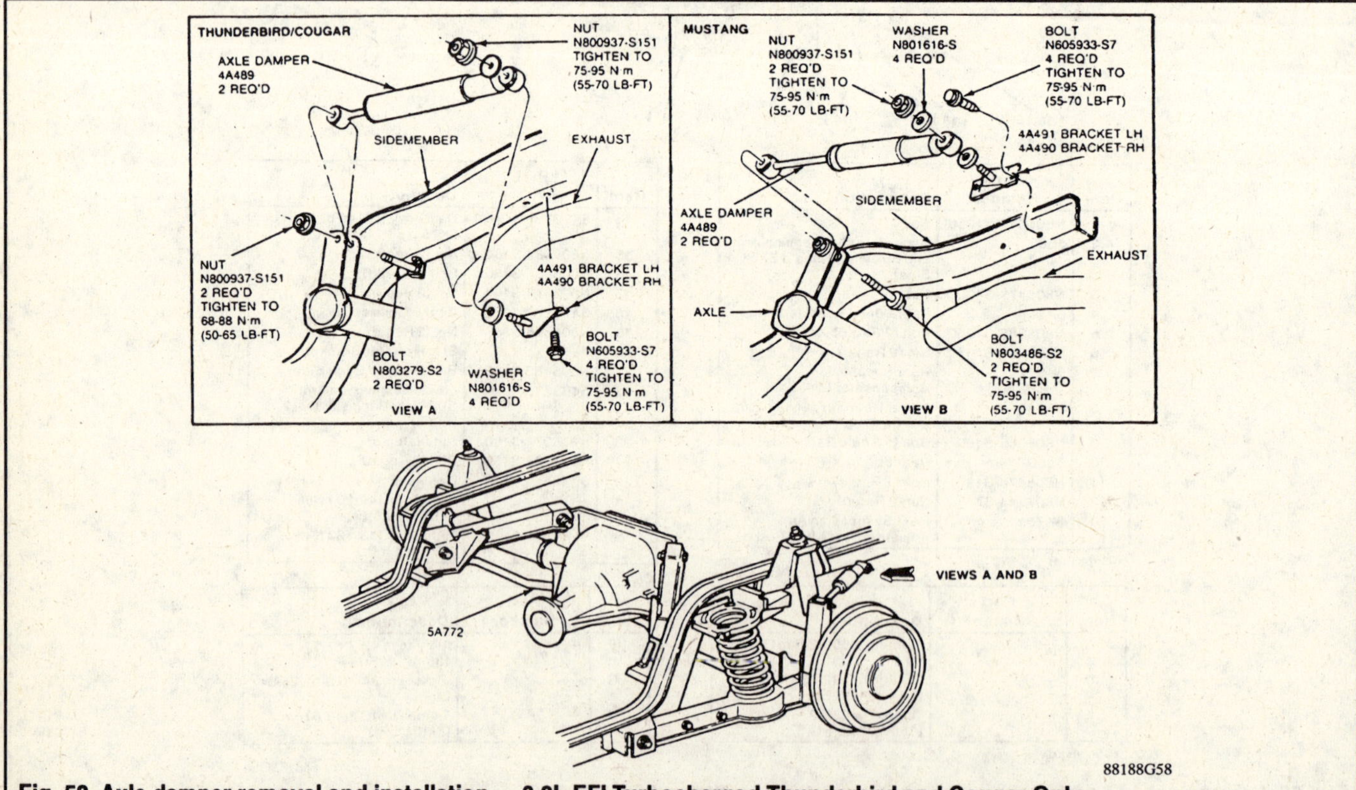

Fig. 58 Axle damper removal and installation — 2.3L EFI Turbocharged Thunderbird and Cougar Only

Automatic Ride Control

The Automatic Ride Control (ARC) feature is standard on the Super Coupe and XR-7. The ARC provides the selection of either a firm (sport) suspension tuning or an automatic ride control. The system is activated by using the rocker switch mounted on the center console to the right of the driver's seat.

With the ride control switch in the FIRM position, the ARC computer adjusts the shock/strut damping to provide a firm (sport) suspension tuning.

Switched to the AUTO position, the ARC computer adjusts the shock/strut damping to provide a soft ride during normal driving conditions. The automatic ride control (ARC) computer instantly changes suspension tuning to firm during hard braking, acceleration, cornering or high speed to provide improved handling. To accomplish this task, the ARC computer uses sensors on the following items:

- Brake line hydraulic pressure (above 400 psi)
- Throttle position (90 percent full throttle)
- Supercharger "boost" (relative to acceleration)
- Steering wheel angle (cornering above 0.35g lateral acceleration)
- Vehicle speed (above 83 mph)

The shock/strut damping will return to the softer ride position about 7 seconds after these conditions are no longer present, providing vehicle speed has dropped below 74 mph.

There is a green FIRM RIDE indicator lamp located in the lower right corner of the instrument panel. This lamp will illuminate when ever the suspension is firm, even if the switch is in the AUTO position. In the event of a system malfunction, the lamp will flash on and off. Moving the ride control switch between positions will usually clear any false or intermittent malfunction indications. Any malfunctions not cleared by this procedure should be checked by a qualified mechanic.

REMOVAL & INSTALLATION

Actuator and Mounting Bracket

1. Position the vehicle on a level area, set the parking brake and turn the ignition lock cylinder to the **OFF** position. On rear actuator, remove the side trim panel in luggage compartment for access.
2. Disconnect the actuator connector.
3. Remove the actuator protective cover. A slot is provided for use with a pry bar.
4. Slide actuator connector off protective cover. Squeeze actuator retaining tabs firmly inward with one hand and lift actuator off mounting bracket with the other hand.
5. Grasp piston rod end with a 9mm socket. Loosen the nut retaining actuator mounting bracket to shock absorber with a 19m wrench while holding socket.
6. Remove the nut and mounting bracket. Remove shock as required.

To install:

7. Install the actuator mounting bracket on the shock. Ensure the flat on the bracket and flat on the shock piston rod align.
8. Install the retaining nut on the shock.
9. Grasp the mounting bracket with water pump pliers and tighten nut to 27–35 ft. lbs. (37–47 Nm).

➥ The actuator assembly may be difficult to install if the plastic becomes eccentric to actuator driving shaft. If this happens; loosen the two mounting screws allowing the actuator to float with respect to the locator and install onto the shock. Tighten the two screws, if so equipped.

10. Install actuator on mounting bracket. Properly route wiring for connector.
11. Install protective cover by positioning retaining features on cover over the three shock absorber upper mounting studs. With a firm blow to the top of the cover, cover will snap in place.
12. Connect the actuator electrical connector.

Brake Sensor Switch

The brake sensor switch is located behind the left wheel well, below the master cylinder.

1. Raise and support the vehicle safely.
2. Disconnect the wiring connector from sensor switch.
3. Lower the vehicle.
4. Unscrew the sensor switch from the brake control valve body.

To install:

5. Ensure O-ring seal is on switch before installing. Install sensor switch and tighten to 8–10 ft. lbs. (11–14 Nm).
6. Raise vehicle. Connect wiring connector to sensor switch.
7. Lower vehicle.
8. Bleed front brake system.

Speed Sensor

The speed sensor is located on the transmission.

1. Raise and support the vehicle safely.
2. Remove the bolt retaining speed sensor mounting clip to transmission.
3. Remove sensor and driven gear from transmission.
4. Disconnect electrical connector from speed sensor.
5. Remove driven gear retainer and remove driven gear from sensor.

To install:

6. Position drive gear to speed sensor. Install gear retainer.
7. Connect electrical connector.
8. Ensure that internal O-ring is properly seated in the sensor housing.
9. Insert sensor assembly into transmission housing. Install retainer bolt.
10. Lower vehicle.

Steering Sensor and Ring

The steering sensor is located at the lower end of the steering column. It may be removed with the column in or out of the vehicle. The sensor and sensor ring are separate items.

1. Disconnect the electrical connector from the wiring harness.
2. Remove the sensor electrical connector from the bracket under the instrument panel.
3. Remove the retaining screws and remove the sensor.
4. To remove the sensor ring, perform the following steps:
   a. Remove the steering column.
   b. Remove the steering shaft from the column to remove the sensor ring.

To install:

5. To install the sensor ring, perform the following steps:
   a. Install the steering shaft in the column to install the sensor ring.
   b. Install the steering column.
6. Install the sensor, then fasten with the retaining screws.
7. Install the sensor electrical connector on the bracket under the instrument panel.
8. Connect the electrical connector to the wiring harness.

Rear Wheel Bearings and Hub

REMOVAL & INSTALLATION

➧ See Figures 59, 60, 61, 62, 63, 64, 65, 66, 67, 68, 69 and 70

****WARNING**

Do NOT begin this procedure unless a new hub retainer nut is available. Once removed, this part cannot be reused during assembly. Its torque holding and/or retention capability is greatly diminished during removal.

1. Remove the wheel cover/hub cover from the wheel and tire assembly, then loosen the lug nuts.
2. Remove and discard the hub nut and washer.
3. Raise and safely support the vehicle, then remove the wheel and tire assembly.
4. Pull back on the parking brake cable release lever and, at the same time, pull on the cable. This action will relax the cable so it can be removed from the brake caliper or backing plate.
5. For vehicles equipped with disc brakes, remove the parking brake from the caliper.
6. For vehicles with disc brakes, remove the caliper and support from the brake junction bracket with a piece of wire.

****WARNING**

Do NOT stretch, kink or twist the brake hose!

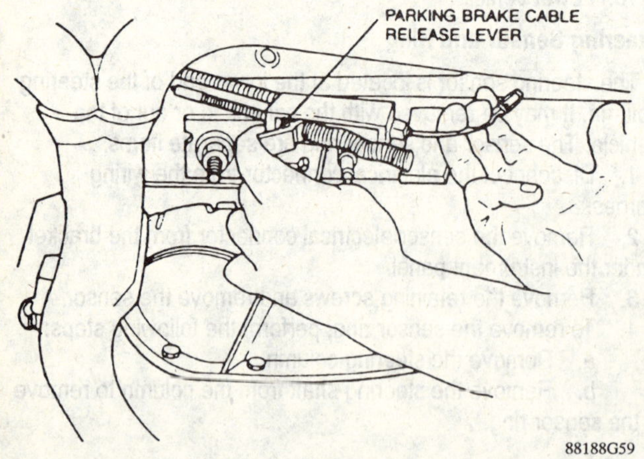

Fig. 59 Simultaneously, pull back on the parking brake cable release lever and pull on the cable

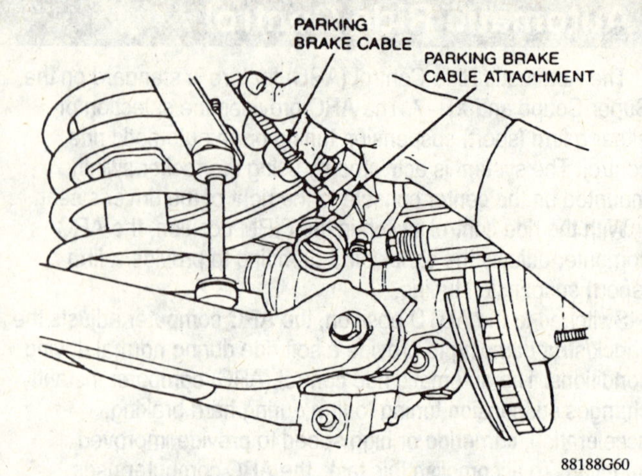

Fig. 60 Remove the parking brake cable from the brake caliper

7. Remove the push-on nuts, then remove the brake rotor or drum assembly, as applicable.
8. For vehicles with disc brakes, remove the three bolts retaining the splash shield to the knuckle, then remove the splash shield.
9. For vehicles with drum brakes, disconnect the parking brake cable and disconnect the brake lines from the wheel cylinder.
10. Remove the upper control arm nut and bolt.
11. Wire the upper control arm to the body to prevent damage to the CV-joint boots when the knuckle and hub assembly is removed.
12. Attach Hub Remover/Replacer T81P-1104-C or equivalent to the hub studs, as shown in the accompanying figure. Turn the wrench counterclockwise until the halfshaft is free in the hub.
13. Using a paint marker, mark the position of the control arm in relation to the knuckle with the bushings in relaxed position. Failure to mark the position will cause bushing wind-up upon assembly and incorrect ride height. These conditions can cause misalignment and premature tire wear.

➥ **When the upper control arm bolt is removed from the knuckle, the lower arm bushings will return to the relaxed position.**

14. If the knuckle is to be replaced, note the approximate angle of the knuckle in the relaxed position by measuring the distance from the upper bushing to any convenient point on the vehicle body.
15. Remove the lower control arm-to-knuckle retaining bolts and nuts, then remove the knuckle and hub assembly from the halfshaft.
16. Place the rear wheel knuckle and hub assembly into a suitable vise.
17. For vehicles equipped with drum brakes, remove the brake shoes and linings, shoe hold-down spring, and adjuster from the brake backing plate. Remove the four screws that retain the brake backing plate to the knuckle.

➥ **There are two methods to remove the hub from the bearing.**

18. Method One: Position a 2-3 Jaw Puller D80L-1013-A and Step Plate Adapter D80L-630-5 or equivalent on the knuckle and press out the hub from the knuckle assembly.

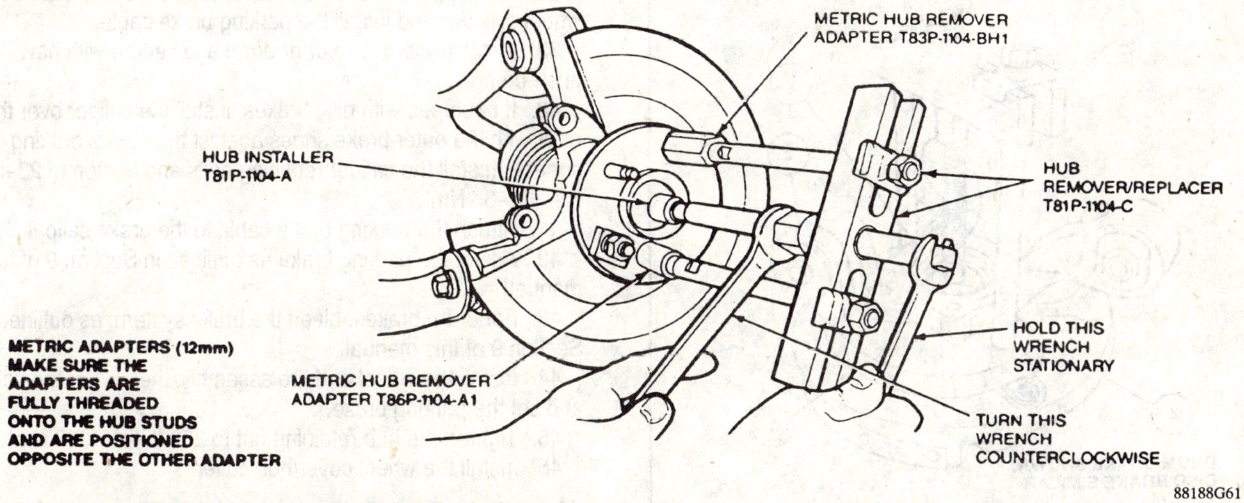

Fig. 61 Attach a suitable hub removal tool to the hub studs

19. Method Two: Position Rear Hub Remover T89P-1225-AH between the knuckle and the brake backing plate. Assembly Hub Remover/Replacer T81P-1104-C and Step Plate Adapter D80L-630-5 or equivalent. While forcing the nut below the crossbar, hold the forcing screw and turn the forcing nut to remove the hub from the knuckle.
20. Remove the brake backing plate.
21. Remove the bearing retainer snapring.
22. Place the knuckle and bearing on a press bed using Hub Support T89P-1104-A and Front Hub Bearing Remover/Replacer T83P-1104-AH2 and press the wheel bearing out of the knuckle.

To install:

23. Place the knuckle on the press bed and position the wheel bearing in the bearing bore of the knuckle.
24. Use Bearing Replacer T86P-1104-A3 to press the bearing into the knuckle.
25. Install the bearing retainer snapring.
26. Position the brake backing plate on the knuckle. Install the four retaining bolts and tighten to 44-60 ft. lbs. (59.5-80.5 Nm).
27. Place the knuckle on the Hub Support T89P-1104-A and position on the press bed plate.
28. If equipped with drum brakes, install the brake shoes and linings, brake shoe hold-down springs and adjuster to the backing plate.
29. Position the hub on the wheel bearing and, using Front Hub Bearing Remover/Replacer T83P-1104-AH4, press the rear hub into the rear wheel bearing.
30. Prior to hub/bearing/knuckle installation replace the bearing dust seal on the outboard CV-joint with a new seal.
31. Install a new dust seal, making sure the seal flange faces outboard toward the bearing. Use Spindle/Axle Installer T83T-3132-A1 and Bearing Dust Seal Replacer T89P-1249-A or equivalent.
32. Place the knuckle and hub assembly on the halfshaft splines and install the lower control arm-to-knuckle bolts and nuts.
33. Position the knuckle so that the index marks on the bushing line up with the marks on the control arm. If a new knuckle is being installed, set the knuckle at the approximate angle noted during removal before tightening the bolts.

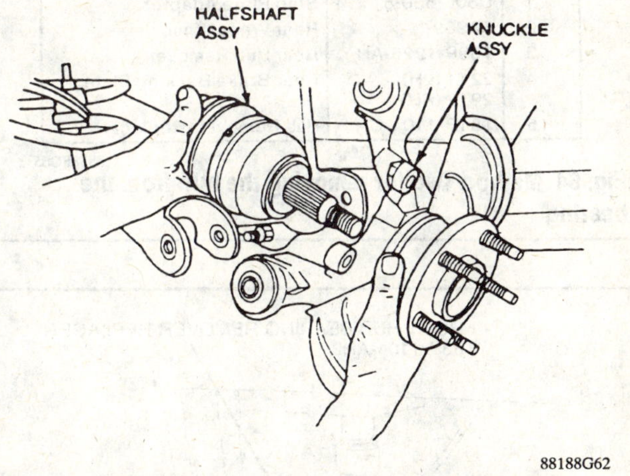

Fig. 62 Remove the knuckle/hub assembly from the halfshaft

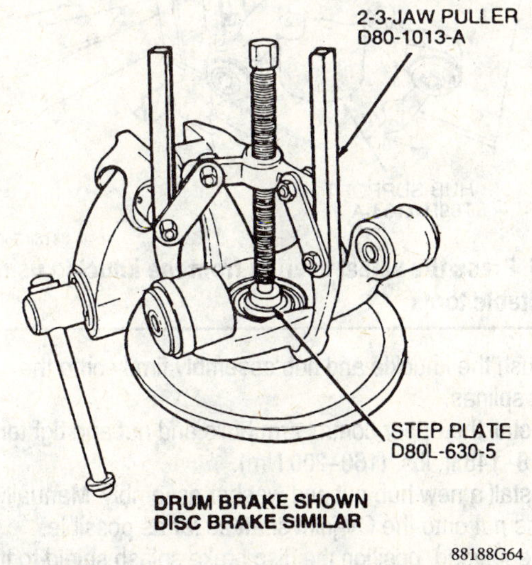

Fig. 63 Method One for removing the hub from the bearing

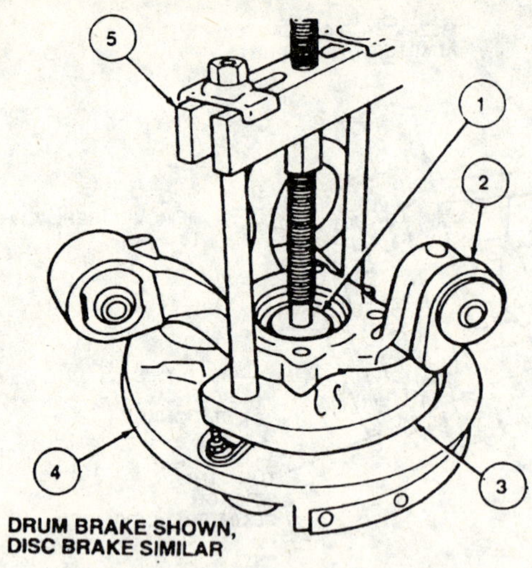

Item	Part Number	Description
1	D80L-630-5	Step Plate Adapter
2	5A969	Rear Wheel Knuckle
3	T89P-1225-AH	Rear Hub Remover
4	2211 (LH) 2212 (RH)	Rear Brake Backing Plate
5	T81P-1104-C	Hub Remover/Replacer

88188G65

Fig. 64 Method Two for removing the hub from the bearing

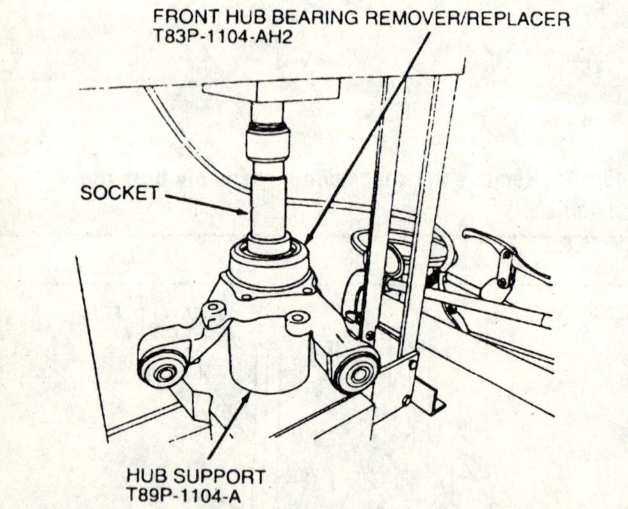

88188G66

Fig. 65 Press the wheel bearing from the knuckle using the suitable tools

34. Push the knuckle and hub assembly firmly onto the halfshaft splines.
35. Install the upper control arm bolts and nut and tighten the nut to 118–148 ft. lbs. (160–200 Nm).
36. Install a new hub nut and washer assembly. Manually thread the nut onto the CV-joint shaft as far as possible.
37. If equipped, position the disc brake splash shield to the knuckle assembly and install the three retaining bolts. Tighten the bolts to 45–59 ft. lbs. (61–81 Nm).
38. If equipped with drum brakes, attach the brake tube to the wheel cylinder and install the parking brake cable.
39. Install the brake rotor or drum and secure with new push-on nuts.
40. If equipped with disc brakes, install the caliper over the rotor with the outer brake shoes against the rotor's braking surface. Install the caliper retaining bolts and tighten to 23–26 ft. lbs. (31–35 Nm).
41. Attach the parking brake cable to the brake caliper.
42. Adjust the parking brake as outlined in Section 9 of this manual.
43. For drum brakes, bleed the brake system, as outlined in Section 9 of this manual.
44. Install the wheel and tire assembly, then lower the vehicle and set the parking brake.
45. Tighten the hub retaining nut to 250 ft. lbs. (340 Nm).
46. Install the wheel cover/hub cover.

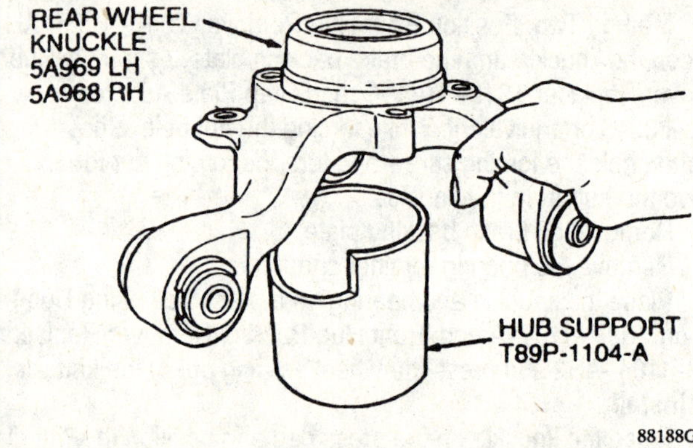

88188G67

Fig. 66 Place the knuckle on the Hub Support T89P-1104-A and position on the press bed plate

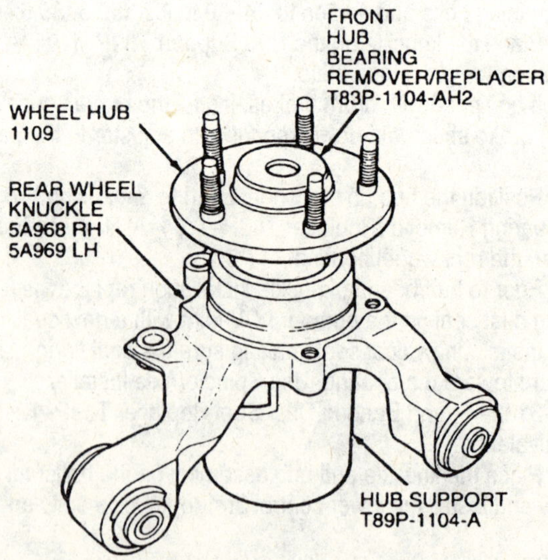

88188G68

Fig. 67 Position the hub on the wheel bearing and press the rear hub into the rear wheel bearing, using a suitable tool

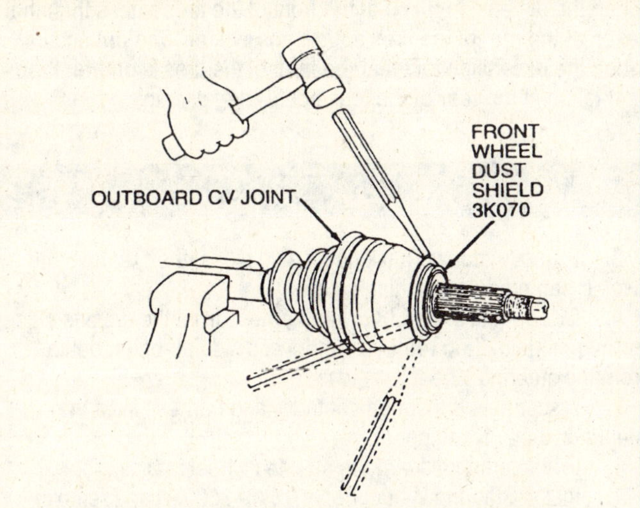

Fig. 68 Removing the outboard CV-joint dust seal

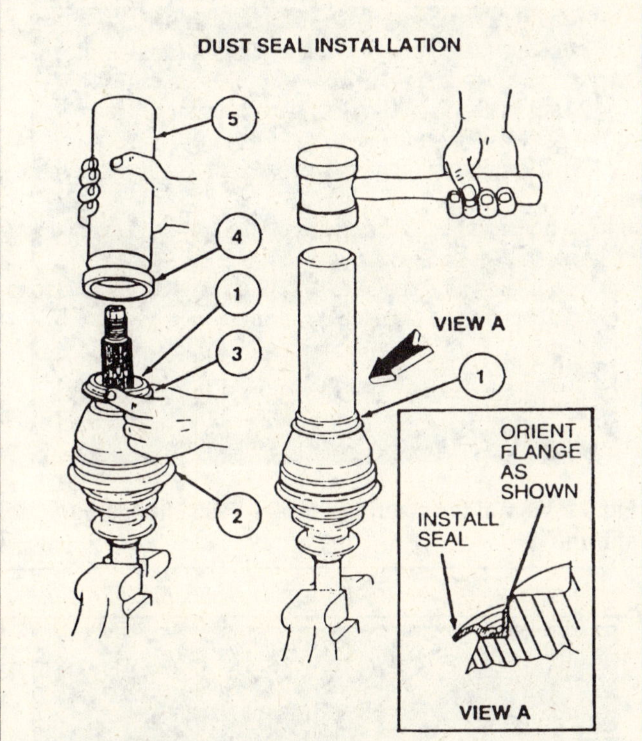

NOTE: CLAMP HALFSHAFT IN VISE AND INSTALL DUST SEAL USING DRIVE TUBE T83T-3132-A1 AND BEARING DUST SEAL REPLACER T89P-1249-A WITH SEAL FLANGE FACING OUTBOARD.

Item	Part Number	Description
1	3K070	Dust Seal
2	4B436	Outboard Halfshaft Joint
3	—	Seal Flange
4	T89P-1249-A	Bearing Dust Seal Replacer
5	T83T-3132-A1	Spindle / Axle Seal Installer

88188G70

Fig. 69 Install a new dust seal on the outboard CV-joint

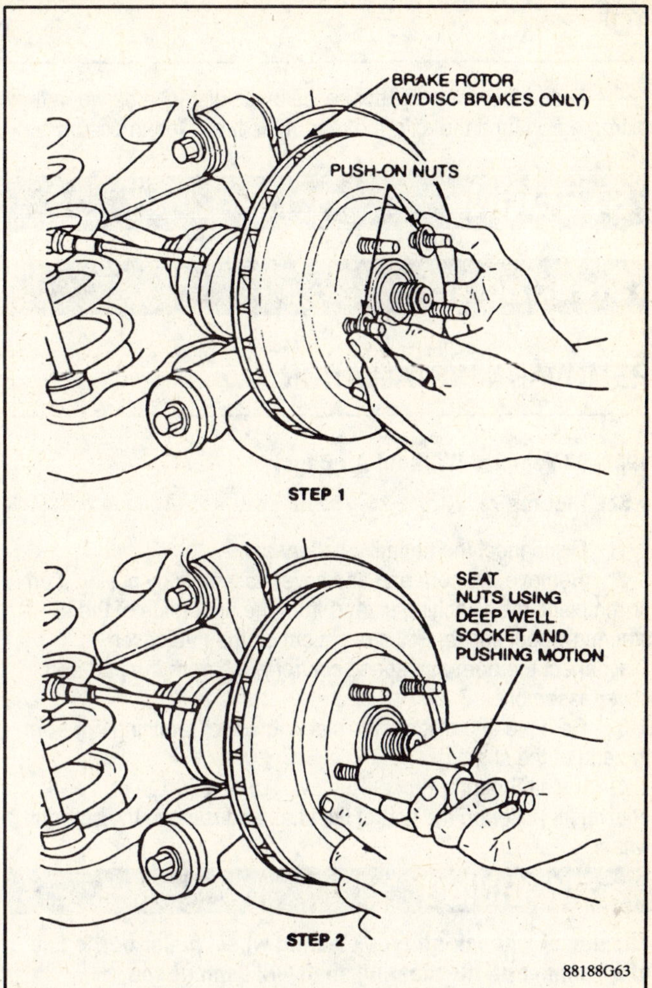

Fig. 70 Install the rotor or drum, then secure with new push-on nuts

Rear Wheel Alignment

For 1983–88 vehicles, there are no alignment adjustments for the rear wheels. For 1989–96 vehicles, the camber and toe are adjustable on the rear of these vehicles. If any parts were removed or replaced on the rear suspension, have the wheel alignment checked and adjusted at a qualified alignment shop.

CAMBER

Camber angle is the number of degrees that the centerline of the wheel is inclined from the vertical. Camber reduces loading of the outer wheel bearing and improves the tire contact patch while cornering.

CASTER

Caster angle is the number of degrees that a line drawn through the suspension knuckle pivots is inclined from the vertical, toward the front or rear of the car (when viewed from the side of the car). Caster improves the directional stability and decreases susceptibility to crosswinds or road surface deviations.

TOE

Toe-in and toe-out is the difference in the distance between the extreme front and the extreme rear of the tires. Toe-in occurs when the dimension taken at the front of the tires is less than that taken at the rear of the tires equals positive toe. Toe-out occurs when the dimension taken at the front of the tires is greater than that taken at the rear of the tires equals negative toe.

STEERING

Steering Wheel

REMOVAL & INSTALLATION

1983–93 Vehicles (Without Air Bags)

➧ See Figures 71, 72, 73, 74, 75 and 76

1. Disconnect the negative battery cable.
2. Remove the horn pad and cover assembly by pulling it off or removing the attaching screws from the underside of the steering wheel spoke. Pull straight out on the hub cover. Disconnect the horn and speed control wires from the pad and cover assembly.
3. Remove and discard the steering wheel retaining nut from the end of the shaft.
4. Install Steering Wheel Remover T67L-3600-A or equivalent puller on the end of the shaft and remove the steering wheel.

✻✻WARNING

The use of a knock-off type steering wheel puller or the use of a hammer on the steering shaft will damage the collapsible column.

To install:

5. Lubricate the upper surface of the steering shaft upper bushing with white grease. Transfer all serviceable parts to the new steering wheel.
6. Position the steering wheel on the shaft so that the alignment marks line up. Install a locknut and torque it to 23–33 ft. lbs. (31–45 Nm). Connect the horn wires.
7. Install the horn button or ring by turning it clockwise or connect the horn and speed control wires, install the horn pad and cover.
8. Connect the negative battery cable, then check for proper operation.

1994–96 Vehicles (With Air Bags)

➧ See Figures 77 and 78

1. Center the front wheels in the straight ahead position.

✻✻CAUTION

The backup power supply must be disconnected before any air bag component is serviced. Failure to do so may result in personal injury

2. Disconnect the negative, then the positive battery cables. Wait one minute for the air bag diagnostic monitor to deplete its stored energy.
3. Remove the two back cover side plugs, then remove the two air bag module retaining screws.
4. Disconnect the air bag wire harness from the driver's side air bag module, then remove the driver's side air bag module from the steering wheel.
5. Disconnect the speed control wiring harness from the steering wheel, if equipped.
6. Remove and discard the steering wheel retaining bolt.
7. Install Steering Wheel Puller T67L-3600-A and remove the steering wheel. Route the air bag sliding contact assembly wire harness through the steering wheel as the wheel is lifted off the steering gear input worm gear and rack.

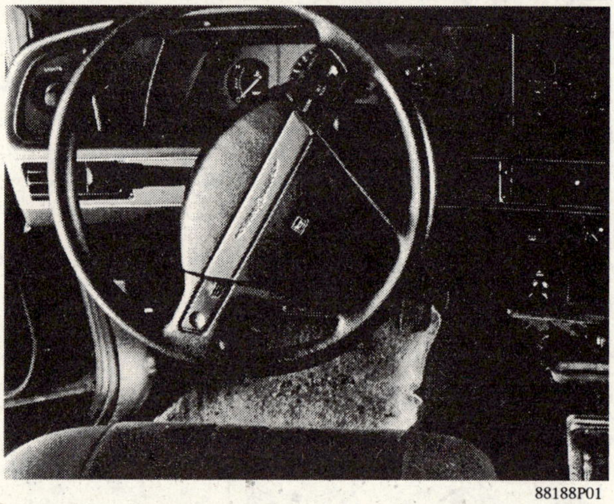

88188P01

Fig. 71 View of the steering wheel — 1990 Thunderbird shown

88188P02

Fig. 72 On some vehicles, you can remove the horn pad by simply pulling it off

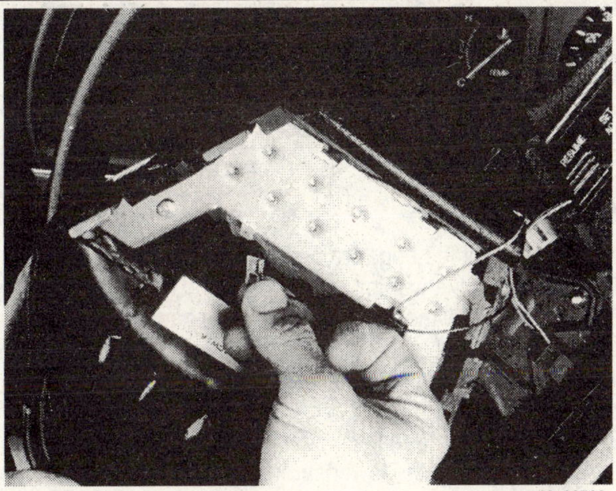

88188P03

Fig. 73 Detach the electrical connectors from the horn pad

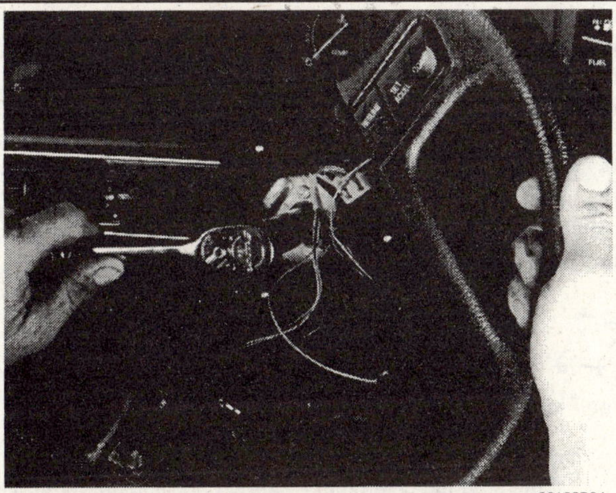

88188P04

Fig. 74 Remove, then discard the steering wheel retaining nut

88188P05

Fig. 75 Install a suitable steering wheel puller, then . . .

88188P06

Fig. 76 . . . remove the steering wheel from the shaft

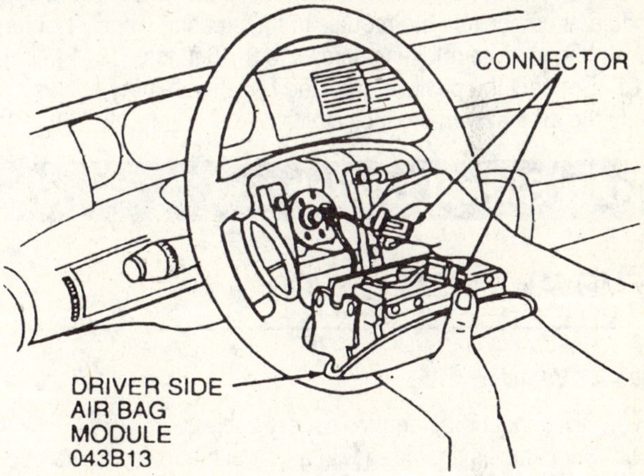

88188G71

Fig. 77 Detach the air bag wiring, then remove the module from the steering wheel

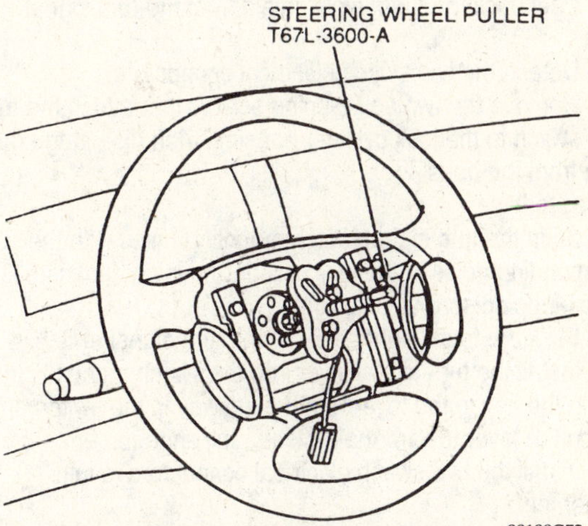

88188G72

Fig. 78 Install a suitable steering wheel puller, then remove the wheel from the vehicle

To install:

8. Make sure the vehicle's front wheels are still in the straight ahead position.

****WARNING**

Make sure the wiring does not get trapped between the steering wheel and air bag sliding contact, as damage to the sliding contact wiring may occur.

9. Route the air bag sliding contact wire harness through the steering wheel opening at the three o'clock position and position the steering wheel on the steering gear input worm gear and rack. The steering wheel and steering gear input worm gear and rack alignment marks should be aligned. Be sure the air bag sliding contact wire is not pinched.
10. Install a new steering wheel retaining bolt, then tighten to 23–33 ft. lbs. (31–48 Nm).
11. Attach the speed control wire harness to the steering wheel, then snap the connector assembly into the steering wheel clip.
12. Connect the air bag wire harness to the driver side air bag module, then position the module to the steering wheel. Tighten the air bag module retaining screws to 8–10 ft. lbs. (10–14 Nm).
13. Connect the positive, then the negative battery cables. Verify the air bag warning indicator.

Turn Signal Switch

REMOVAL & INSTALLATION

1983–88 Vehicles

1. Disconnect the negative battery cable.
2. For vehicles equipped with a tilt column, remove the upper extension shroud by unsnapping the shroud from the retaining clip at the 9 o'clock position.
3. Remove the two trim shroud halves by removing the attaching screws.
4. Remove the turn signal lever by pulling and twisting it straight out from the switch.
5. Peel back the foam sight shield from the turn signal switch.
6. Detach the two switch electrical connectors.
7. Remove the two self-tapping screws that attach the turn signal switch to the lock cylinder housing, then disengage the switch from the housing.

To install:

8. Align the turn signal switch mounting holes with the corresponding holes in the lock cylinder housing and install the two self-tapping screws until tight.
9. Stick the foam sight shield to the turn signal switch.
10. Install the turn signal lever into the switch manually by aligning the key to the lever with the keyway in the switch and pushing the lever toward the switch to full engagement.
11. Install the two switch electrical connectors to full engagement.
12. Install the steering column trim shroud(s).
13. Connect the negative battery cable, then test the switch.

Multi-Function Switch

REMOVAL & INSTALLATION

1989–93 Vehicles

1. Disconnect the negative ground cable.
2. Remove the lower left side finish panel retaining bolts.
3. Carefully pull the finish panel to disengage the retaining clips.
4. Remove the left side reinforcement panel retaining bolts and remove the panel.
5. Remove the steering column lower shroud retaining screws, then remove the lower shroud.
6. Remove the steering column retaining nuts.
7. Remove the steering column upper shroud.
8. Detach the multi-function switch electrical connector.
9. Remove the multi-function switch retaining bolts, then remove the switch.

To install:

10. Position the switch and install the retaining bolts.
11. Attach the electrical wiring connector to the switch.
12. Install the steering column upper shroud.
13. Position the steering column and install the retaining nuts.
14. Position the lower shroud and install the retaining screws.
15. Install the side reinforcement panel and secure with the retaining bolts.
16. Position the side finish panel and install the bolts.
17. Connect the negative battery cable, then check switch operation.

1994–96 Vehicles

See Figure 79

1. Disconnect the negative battery cable.
2. Tilt the steering column to its lowest position, then remove the tilt steering column lock lever.
3. Remove the ignition switch lock cylinder, as outlined in this section.
4. Unfasten the shroud screws, then remove the upper and and lower steering column shrouds.
5. Remove the two self-tapping screws retaining the multi-function switch to the steering column tube flange. Disengage the switch from the steering column tube flange.
6. Detach the two switch electrical connectors.

To install:

7. Install the two electrical connectors to full engagement.
8. Align the multi-function switch mounting holes with the corresponding holes in the steering column tube flange. Install the two self-tapping screws, making sure to start the screws in the previously tapped holes. Tighten the screws to 18–26 inch lbs. (2–3 Nm).
9. Install the upper and lower steering column shrouds, then secure with the retaining screws.
10. Install the ignition switch lock cylinder.
11. Install the tilt steering lock lever.
12. Connect the negative battery cable, then check the steering column for proper operation.

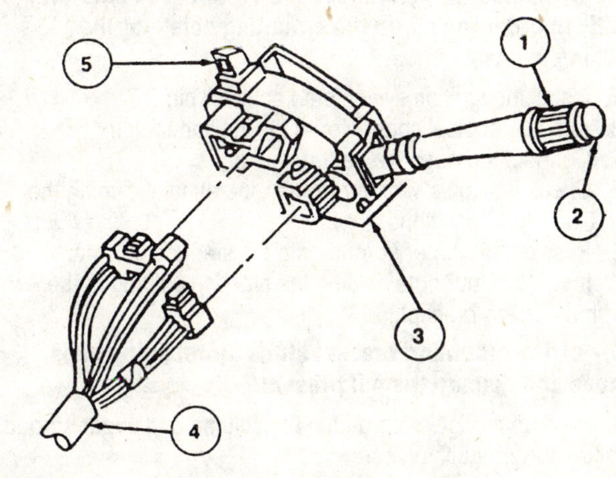

Item	Part Number	Description
1	—	Windshield Wiper Control Switch (Part of 13K359)
2	—	Windshield Washer Switch (Part of 13K359)
3	13K359	Multi-Function Switch
4	—	Part of 14401
5	—	Hazard Flasher Switch (Part of 13K359)

88188G75

Fig. 79 Multi-function switch and related components — 1994–96 vehicles

Ignition Switch

REMOVAL & INSTALLATION

1983–88 Vehicles

➧ See Figure 80

1. Disconnect the negative battery cable.
2. On vehicles with tilt columns, remove the upper extension shroud by unsnapping the shroud from the retaining clip at the 9 o'clock position.
3. Remove the trim shroud halves.
4. Disconnect the switch wiring.
5. On 1983–85 vehicles, drill out the break-off head bolts attaching the switch to the lock cylinder with a 1/8 in. (3mm) drill bit. Remove the remainder of the bolts with a screw extractor.
6. On 1986–88 vehicles, remove the bolts securing the switch to the lock cylinder housing.
7. Disengage the switch from the actuator pin.

To install:

8. Slide the switch carrier to the ON RUN position. New replacement switches will be in this position.
9. Turn the key to the ON RUN position.
10. Position the switch on the actuator pin. It may be necessary to move the switch slightly back and forth to align the switch mounting holes with the column lock housing threaded holes.

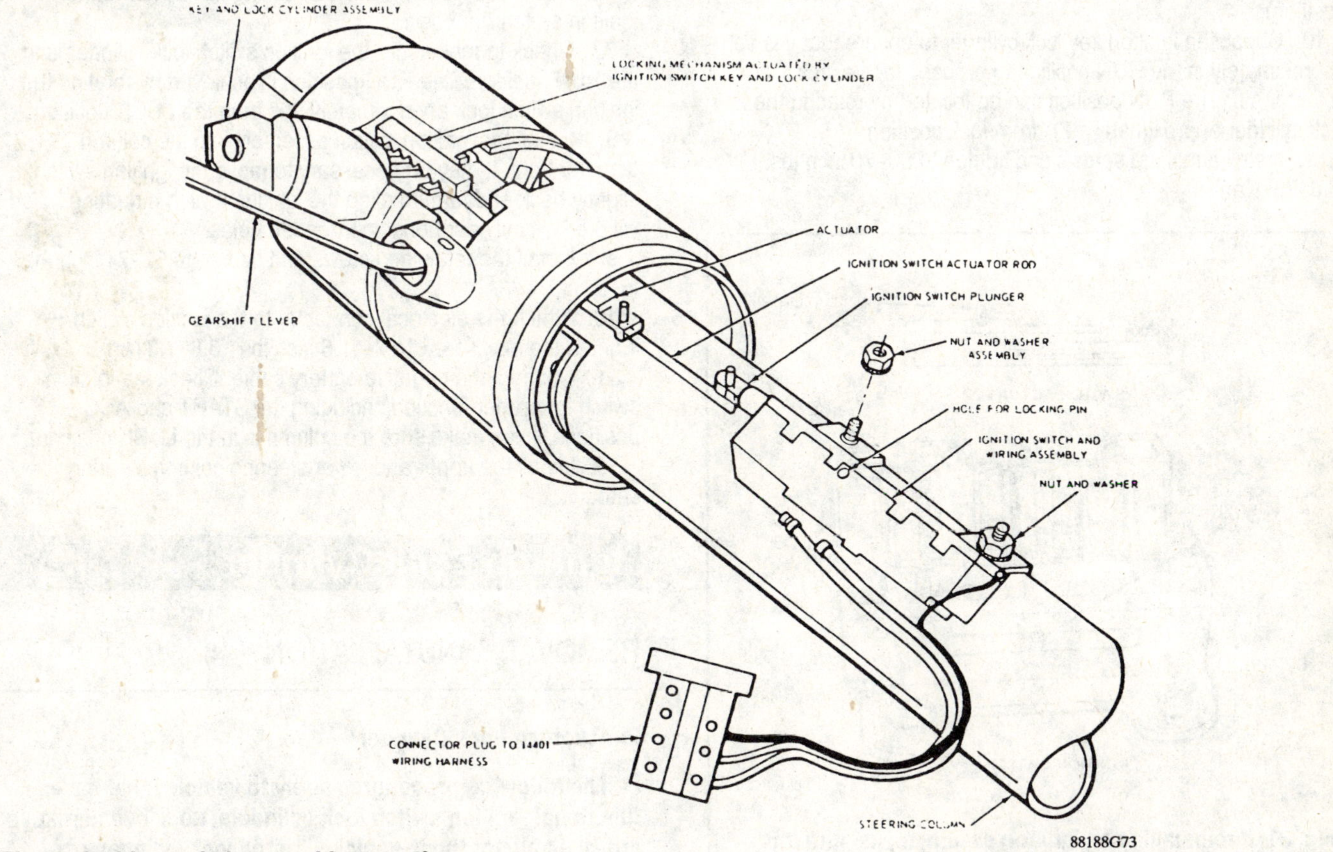

Fig. 80 Ignition switch assembly mounting

11. On 1983–85 cars, install new break-off bolts and hand tighten them.
12. On 1986–88 cars, install the bolts and tighten them to 50–60 inch lbs. (5.6–6.9 Nm).
13. Push the switch towards the steering wheel, parallel with the column, to remove any slack between the bolts and the switch slots.
14. While holding the switch in this position, tighten the bolts until the heads break off.
15. Remove the drill bit or packaging pin.
16. Connect the switch electrical wiring.
17. The remainder of installation is the reverse of the removal procedure.

1989–93 Vehicles

See Figure 81

1. Disconnect the negative battery cable.
2. Remove the three steering column shroud screws and remove the lower shroud.
3. Remove the four nuts holding the steering column assembly to the column mounting bracket, and lower the column enough to reach the ignition switch retaining screws.
4. Remove the upper shroud.
5. Detach ignition switch electrical connector.
6. Rotate the ignition key lock cylinder to the run position.
7. Remove the two attaching screws retaining the switch-to-lock cylinder housing.
8. Disengage and remove ignition switch from the actuator pin.

To install:

9. Ensure the actuator pin slot in ignition switch is in the RUN position (a new switch assembly comes preset in the RUN position).
10. Check the ignition key lock cylinder to ensure that it is set approximately in the RUN position to properly locate lock actuator pin. The RUN position can be located by rotating the key lock cylinder approximately 90° from lock position.
11. Install attaching screws and tighten to 50–70 inch lbs. (5.6–7.9 Nm).

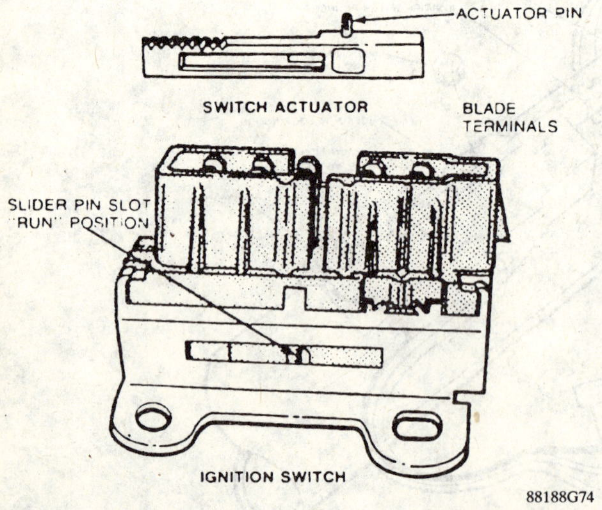

Fig. 81 If reinstalling an ignition switch, make sure it is set in the RUN position

It may be necessary to move the switch back and forth slightly in order to line up the mounting holes for the attaching screws.

12. Install the ignition switch onto actuator pin.
13. Attach electrical connector to the ignition switch.
14. Connect the negative battery cable.
15. Check ignition switch for proper operation, including the START and ACC positions.
16. Position the upper shroud onto the steering column.
17. Install the four nuts holding the steering column to the column mounting bracket.

Check the mounting bracket studs for retaining clips. Remove and discard them if present.

18. Position the lower shroud to the column and upper shroud. Install the three attaching screws.

1994–96 Vehicles

1. Disconnect the negative battery cable. Remove the upper steering column shroud by removing the self-tapping screws.
2. Unfasten the four bolts retaining the lower steering column shroud, then remove the shroud.
3. Remove the lock screw, then detach the ignition switch electrical connector.
4. Rotate the ignition switch lock cylinder to the RUN position.
5. Remove the two screws retaining the ignition switch, then disengage the ignition switch from the actuator.

To install:

A new replacement switch will be set in the RUN position as received.

6. Adjust the ignition switch by sliding the carrier to the ignition switch run position.
7. Check to make sure the ignition switch lock cylinder is in the RUN position. The RUN position is achieved by rotating the ignition switch lock approximately 90° from the LOCK position.
8. Install the ignition switch assembly into the column actuator hole. It may be necessary to move the ignition switch slightly back and forth to align the ignition switch mounting holes wit the lock cylinder housing threaded holes.
9. Install the retaining screws and tighten to 53–71 inch lbs. (6–8 Nm).
10. Attach the electrical connector to the ignition switch. Tighten the lock screw to 7–11.5 inch lbs. (0.8–1.3 Nm).
11. Connect the negative battery cable. Check the ignition switch for proper function, including the START and ACC positions. Also, make sure the column is in the LOCK position.
12. Install the upper and lower steering column steering shrouds.

Ignition Lock Cylinder

REMOVAL & INSTALLATION

Functioning Lock Cylinder

The following procedures apply to vehicles that have functional ignition switch lock cylinders. Lock cylinder keys are available for these vehicles, or the lock cylinder key numbers are known and the proper key can be made.

1983–93 VEHICLES

➧ **See Figures 82 and 83**

1. Disconnect the negative battery cable.
2. On tilt columns, remove the upper extension shroud by unsnapping the shroud from the retaining clip at the 9 o'clock position.
3. Remove the trim shroud halves.
4. Unplug the wire connector at the key warning switch.
5. Place the shift lever in PARK and turn the key to RUN.
6. Place a 1/8 in. (3mm) wire pin in the hole in the casting surrounding the lock cylinder and depress the retaining pin while pulling out on the cylinder.

To install:

7. When installing the cylinder, turn the lock cylinder to the RUN position and depress the retaining pin, then insert the lock cylinder into its housing in the flange casting. Assure that the cylinder is fully seated and aligned in the interlocking washer before turning the key to the OFF position. This will allow the cylinder retaining pin to extend into the cylinder cast housing hole.
8. The remainder of installation is the reverse of the removal procedure.
9. Connect the negative battery cable and check for proper operation.

1994–96 VEHICLES

➧ **See Figure 84**

1. Disconnect the negative battery cable.
2. Turn the ignition switch lock cylinder to the **RUN** position.
3. Place a 1/8 in. (3.17mm) diameter wire pin or small drift punch in the hole in the upper steering column shroud under the ignition switch lock cylinder. Press the retaining pin while pulling out of the ignition switch lock cylinder to remove it from the steering column tube flange.

To install:

4. Install the ignition lock cylinder by turning it to the **RUN** position and pressing the retaining pin. Insert the ignition lock cylinder into the steering column tube flange. Make sure the lock cylinder is fully seated and aligned in the interlocking washer before turning the key to the **OFF** position. This will permit the cylinder retaining pin to extend into the steering column tube flange hole.
5. Rotate the ignition lock cylinder, using the ignition key, to ensure correct mechanical operation in all positions.
6. Connect the negative battery cable.

Non-Functioning Lock Cylinder

➥ **The following procedure applies to vehicles in which the ignition lock is inoperative and the lock cylinder cannot be rotated due to a lost or broken lock key, the key number is not known, or the lock cap is damaged and/or broken to the extent that the lock cylinder cannot be rotated.**

1983–93 VEHICLES

1. Disconnect the battery ground.
2. Remove the steering wheel.
3. On tilt columns, remove the upper extension shroud by unsnapping the shroud from the retaining clip at the 9 o'clock position.
4. Remove the steering column trim shrouds.
5. Disconnect the wiring at the key warning switch.
6. Using a 1/8 in. (3mm) drill bit, mounted in a right angle drive drill adapter, drill out the retaining pin, going no deeper than 1/2 in. (13mm).
7. Tilt the column to the full down position. Place a chisel at the base of the ignition lock cylinder cap and using a hammer, break away the cap from the lock cylinder.
8. Using a 3/8 in. (9.5mm) drill bit, drill down the center of the ignition lock cylinder key slot about 1 3/4 in. (44mm), until the lock cylinder breaks loose from the steering column cover casting.
9. Remove the lock cylinder and the drill shavings from the housing.
10. Remove the upper bearing snapring washer and steering column lock gear.

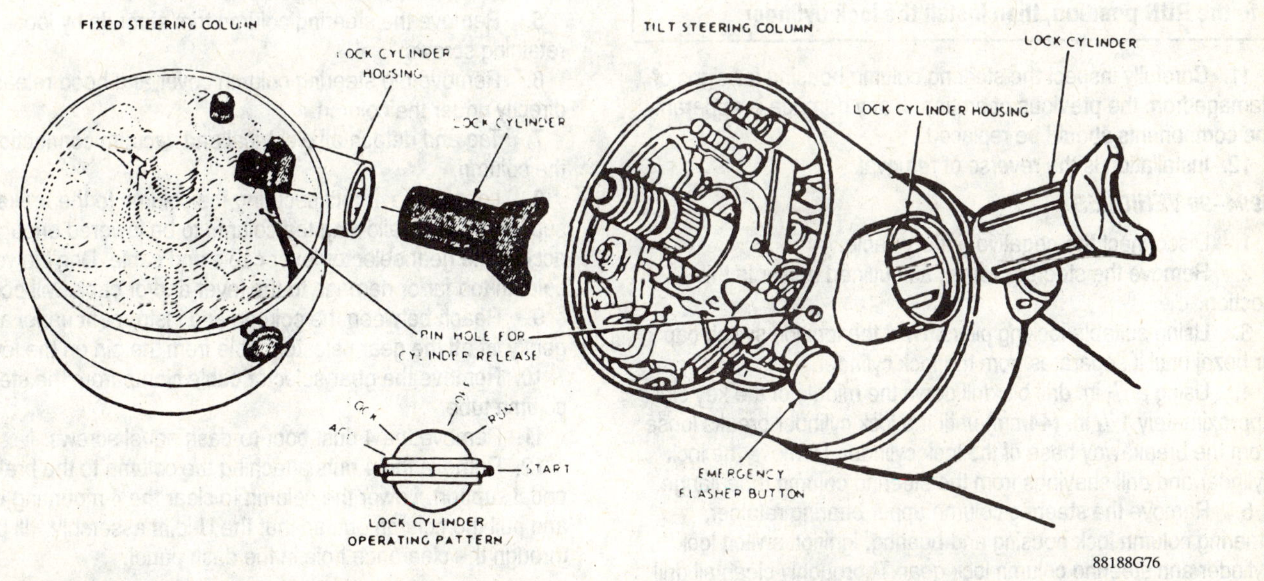

Fig. 82 Lock cylinder replacement on vehicles equipped with tilt column — 1983–93 vehicles

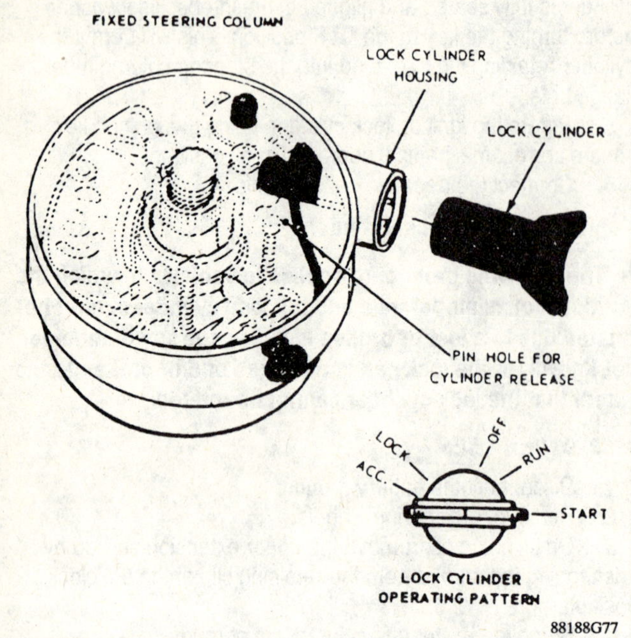

Fig. 83 Lock cylinder replacement on vehicles equipped with a fixed column — 1983-93 vehicles

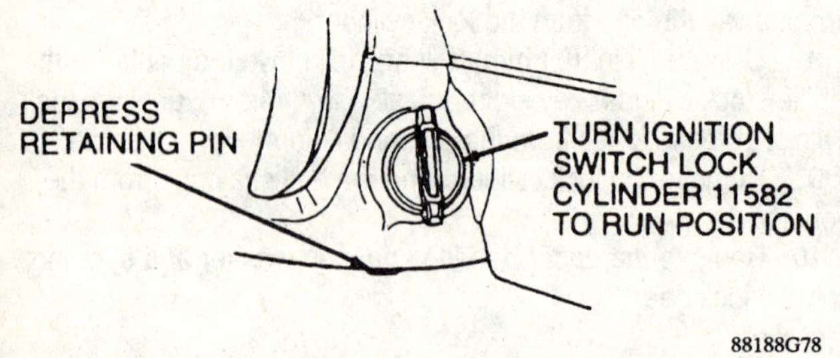

Fig. 84 Depress the retaining pin, turn the lock cylinder to the RUN position, then install the lock cylinder

11. Carefully inspect the steering column housing for signs of damage from the previous operation. If any damage is apparent, the components should be replaced.
12. Installation is the reverse of removal.

1994-96 VEHICLES

1. Disconnect the negative battery cable.
2. Remove the steering wheel, as outlined earlier in this section.
3. Using suitable locking pliers, twist the ignition switch cap or bezel until it separates from the lock cylinder.
4. Using a $^3/_8$ in. drill bit, drill down the middle of the key slot approximately 1$^3/_4$ in. (44mm) until the lock cylinder breaks loose from the breakaway base of the lock cylinder. Remove the lock cylinder and drill shavings from the steering column tube flange.
5. Remove the steering column upper bearing retainer, steering column lock housing and bearing, ignition switch lock cylinder and steering column lock gear. Thoroughly clean all drill shavings and other foreign materials from the casting.
6. Carefully inspect the steering column tube flange for damage. If there is damage, the steering column tube flange must be replaced.

To install:

7. If necessary, replace the steering column tube flange.
8. Install the steering column lock gear and ignition switch lock cylinder.
9. Install the trim and electrical parts.
10. Install a new ignition switch lock cylinder as outlined earlier in this section.
11. Install the steering wheel.
12. Connect the negative battery cable, then check the lock cylinder for proper operation.

Steering Column

REMOVAL & INSTALLATION

1983-88 Vehicles

➧ See Figures 85, 86, 87 and 88

COLUMN SHIFT

1. Disconnect the negative battery cable.
2. Remove the two nuts that attach the flexible coupling to the flange on the steering input shaft. Disengage the safety strap and bolt assembly from the flexible coupling. Disconnect the transmission shift rod from the transmission control selector lever.

➥ Column-type automatic transmission linkage uses oil impregnated plastic grommets to connect the rods and levers. Whenever a grommet-type connection is changed, the grommets should be replaced.

3. Remove the grommet and replace with a new one using Shift Linkage Insulator Tool T67P-7341-A or equivalent. For limited work space applications, use Shift Linkage Grommet Remover T84P-7341-A.
4. Remove the steering wheel.
5. Remove the steering column trim shrouds by loosening the retaining screws.
6. Remove the steering column cover and hood release lever directly under the column.
7. Tag and detach all electrical and vacuum connections at the column.
8. Loosen the 4 nuts securing the column to the brake pedal support bracket, allowing the column to be lowered enough to access the gear selector lever cable and cable. Don't lower the column too far or damage to the lever and/or cable will occur!
9. Reach between the column and instrument panel and gently lift off the gear selector cable from the pin on the lever.
10. Remove the gear selector cable clamp from the steering column tube.
11. Remove the 4 dust boot-to-dash panel screws.
12. Remove the 4 nuts attaching the column to the brake pedal support. Lower the column to clear the 4 mounting bolts and pull the column out, so that the U-joint assembly will pass through the clearance hole in the dash panel.

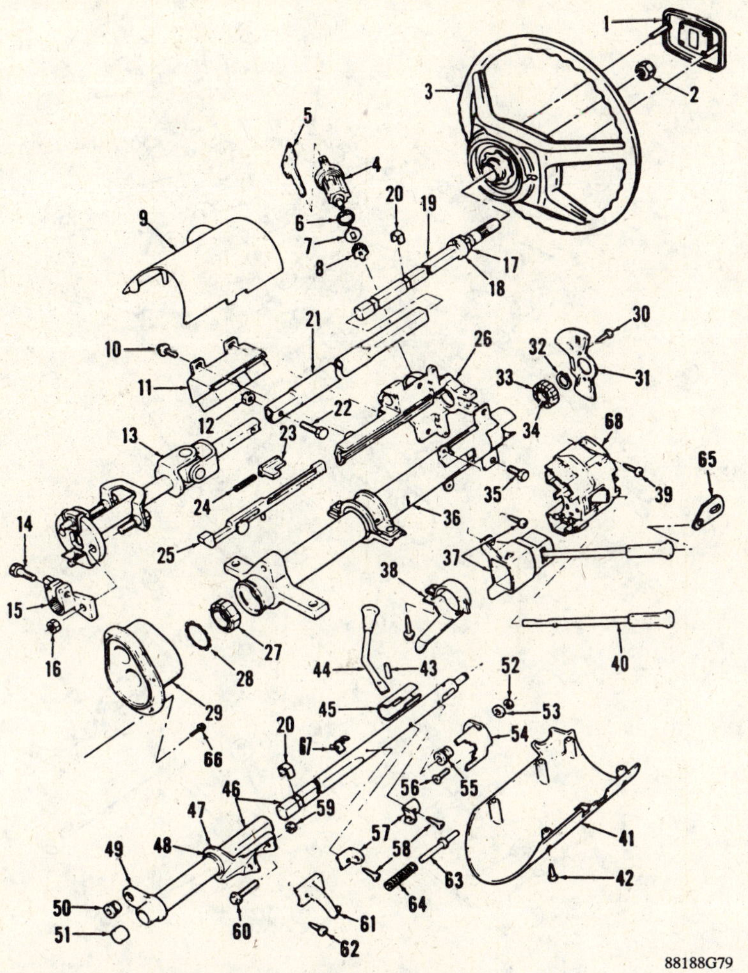

Fig. 85 Exploded view of a non-tilt steering column — 1983-84 vehicles

1. Emblem assy.
2. Nut—⅝-18 hex
3. Wheel assy.—stng.
4. Lock cyl.—(body)
5. Key—(body)
6. Ring
7. Bearing
8. Gear—stng. col. lock
9. Shroud—upper
10. Bolt (break off head) (2 req'd.)
11. Switch assy.—ignition
12. Nut—7/16-14 hex lock
13. Shaft assy.—stng. col. lower
14. Bolt—⅜-24 × 1.22
15. Flange—stng. shaft lower
16. Nut—⅜-16 hex lock
17. Cam—turn sig. turn off
18. Lock—stng. col. position
19. Shaft—stng. gear upper
20. Anti-rattle clips (4 req'd.)
21. Shaft—stng. gear lower
22. Bolt—7/16-14 × 1.50 hex
23. Pawl—stng. col. lock
24. Spring—stng. col. lock
25. Actuator assy.—stng. col. lock
26. Housing—stng. col. lock cyl.
27. Bearing assy.—stng. gear shaft lower
28. Ring—stng. gear shaft lower bearing retainer
29. Boot assy.—stng. col.
30. Screw—no. 8-18 × .62 pan hd. tap (2 req'd.)
31. Retainer—stng. col. upper bearing
32. Retainer—stng. col. upper bearing
33. Sleeve—stng. col. upper bearing
34. Bearing assy.—stng. col. upper
35. Bolt—m8 × 1.25 hex hd. (2 req'd.)
36. Tube assy.—col. outer
37. Wash/wipe switch & screws (body)
38. Bracket & cable assy.—trans. cont. selector (body)
39. Screw—no. 8-18 × .62 pan hd. tap (2 req'd.)
40. Handle & shank assy.—turn sig. switch
41. Shroud—stng. col. lower
42. Screw—no. 8-18 × 1.50 pan hd. tap (4 req'd.)
43. Pin—5mm spring coiled
44. Lever assy.—trans. cont. selector
45. Cover—trans. cont. sel. lever opening
46. Tube assy.—trans. cont. selector
47. Bracket—trans. gear shift support
48. Bushing—trans. gear shift shaft
49. Arm—trans. cont. selector
50. Insulator—stng. gear shaft
51. Seal—stng. gear shaft
52. Ring—5/16 retainer (external)
53. Washer—8.23 flat
54. Insert—trans. control selector position
55. Bearing—trans. gear shift lever socket
56. Screw—m5—0.8 × 12.5 flat head (3 req'd.)
57. Retainer—stng. col. lever (2 req'd.)
58. Screw 4mm—0.7 × 12.7 type "D" oval (2 req'd.)
59. Nut—5/16-18 hex prevail torque (2 req'd.)
60. Bolt—5/16-18 × 1.50 flg. pilot (2 req'd.)
61. Lever—trans. gear shift selector
62. Screw—no. 8—32 × .50 hex wshr. hd.
63. Plunger—trans. control selector lever
64. Spring—trans. control selector lever return
65. Foam cover
66. Screw (4 req'd.)
67. Spacer clip
68. Switch assy.—turn signal

88188G80

Fig. 86 Exploded view of a non-tilt steering column (continued) — 1983-84 vehicles

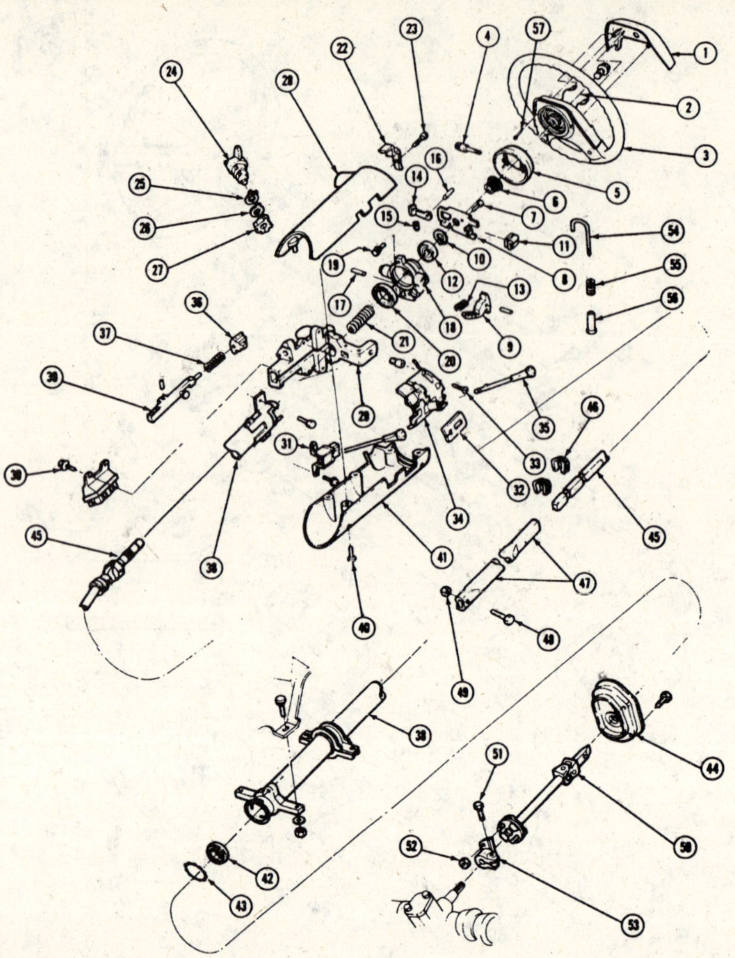

88188GA0

Fig. 87 Exploded view of a tilt steering column — 1985-88 vehicles

1. Emblem assy.
2. Bolt
3. Wheel assy.—strng.
4. Handle & shank assy. tilt strng. wheel lever
5. Extension—strng. col. shroud
6. Spring—strng. col. upper bearing
7. Screw
8. Plate strng. col. clip retainer
9. Lever strng. col. link
10. Ring ¾ retaining type
11. Clip—strng. col. shroud
12. Bearing assy.—strng. col. upper
13. Pin 4mm × 25.6 straight round end
14. Release lever
15. Spring—strng. col. release lever
16. Pin—4mm × 5.75
17. Pivot pin
18. Flange casting
19. Bumpers
20. Bearing assy.—strng. col. upper
21. Position spring
22. Cover—strng. col. lock actuator
23. Screw no. 8-18 × .62 pan head tapping
24. Lock cyl. (body)
25. Ring 24 × 1.07 retainer type
26. Bearing
27. Gear—strng. col. lock
28. Shroud—upper
29. Housing—strng. col. lock cyl.
30. Bolt (break off head) (2 req'd.)
31. Wash/wipe switch & screws (body)
32. Foam cover—turn signal & w/w switch
33. Screw no. 8-18 × .62 pan head tap (2 req'd.)
34. Turn signal switch
35. Handle & shank assy.—turn sig. switch
36. Pawl—strng. col. lock
37. Spring—strng. col. lock
38. Tube assy. col. outer
39. Actuator assy.—strng. col. lock
40. Screw no. 8-18 × 1.50 pan head tap (5 req'd.)
41. Shroud—strng. col. lower
42. Bearing assy.—strng. gear shaft lower
43. Ring—strng. gear shaft lower bearing retainer
44. Boot assy.—strng. col.
45. Shaft assy.—strng. col. upper
46. Anti-rattle clips (2 req'd.)
47. Shaft—strng. gear lower
48. Bolt ⁷⁄₁₆-14 × 1.50 hex
49. Nut ⁷⁄₁₆-14 hex lock
50. Shaft assy.—strng. col. lower
51. Bolt—⅜-24 × 1.22
52. Nut ⅜-16 hex lock
53. Flange—strng. shaft lower
54. Lever—strng. col. lock actuator
55. Spring—strng. col. lock
56. Knob—strng. col. lock actuator
57. Screw—strng. wheel

88188GA1

Fig. 88 Exploded view of a tilt steering column (continued) — 1985-88 vehicles

To install:

13. Install the steering column by inserting the U-joint assembly and lower shift cane through the opening in the dash panel. Be careful not to damage the column during installation.
14. Align the four bolts on the brake pedal support with the mounting holes on the column collar and bracket. Attach the nuts loosely, so that the column will hang with a clearance between the column and the instrument panel.
15. Install the selector cable clamp loosely.
16. Reach between the steering column and instrument panel, then attach the gear selector cable by slipping the loop on the cable over the cleat on the lever.
17. Tighten the 4 column-to-brake pedal support nuts to 20–37 ft. lbs. (27–50 Nm).
18. Move the shift selector to the DRIVE position, against the drive stop. Rotate the selector bracket clockwise or counterclockwise until the selector pointer in the cluster centers on the letter **D**. Tighten the bracket nut.
19. Attach the electrical and vacuum connectors.
20. Install the safety strap and bolt on the flange on the steering input flange.
21. Install the 2 nuts connecting the steering shaft to the flexible coupling. Tighten the nuts to 20–37 ft. lbs. (27–50 Nm). The safety strap must be properly positioned to avoid metal-to-metal contact. The flexible coupling must not be distorted when the nuts are tightened. Pry the shaft up or down to allow a +/–$^{1}/_{8}$ in. (3mm) insulator flatness.
22. Connect the shift rod to the shift lever on the lower end of the steering column. Make sure the grommet is replaced.
23. The remainder of installation is the reverse of removal. Adjust the shift linkage.

FLOOR SHIFT

1. Disconnect the negative battery cable.
2. Remove the two nuts that attach the flexible coupling to the flange on the steering input shaft.
3. Disengage the safety strap and bolt from the flexible coupling.
4. Remove the steering column trim shrouds by removing the self-tapping screws.
5. Remove the steering wheel.
6. Remove the steering column cover and hood release lever, directly under the column.
7. Tag and detach all electrical and vacuum connections at the column.
8. Unfasten the 4 screws that attach the dust boot to the dash panel.
9. Remove the 4 nuts securing the column to the brake pedal support bracket, Lower the column to clear the four mounting bolts, and pull the column out, so that the U-joint assembly passes through the clearance hole in the dash panel.

To install:

10. Install the steering column by inserting the U-joint assembly through the opening in the dash panel. Be careful not to damage the column during installation.
11. Under the instrument panel, align the four bolts on the brake pedal support with the mounting holes on the column collar and bracket. Attach the nuts and tighten to 20–37 ft. lbs. (27–50 Nm).
12. Attach the electrical and vacuum connectors.
13. Install the safety strap and bolt on the flange on the steering input flange.
14. Install the 2 nuts connecting the steering shaft to the flexible coupling. Tighten the nuts to 20–37 ft. lbs. (27–50 Nm). The safety strap must be properly positioned to avoid metal-to-metal contact. The flexible coupling must not be distorted when the nuts are tightened. Pry the shaft up or down to allow a +/–$^{1}/_{8}$ in. (3mm) insulator flatness.
15. Engage the dust boot to the base of the steering column to the dash panel opening. Install the four screws that attach the dust boot to the dash panel.
16. Install the steering wheel.
17. Install the steering column trim shrouds.
18. Install the hood release mechanism and steering column cover beneath the steering column.
19. Connect the negative battery cable.

1989–93 Vehicles

➧ See Figure 89

➥ All steering column components are assembled with self-locking fasteners. They are used to prevent loosening due to vibrations during normal operation of vehicle. If replacement becomes necessary, use fasteners of the same part number or type.

1. Disconnect the negative battery cable.
2. Remove the lower left side finish panel retaining bolts.
3. Carefully pull the lower left side finish panel to disengage the retaining clips.
4. Remove the lower left side reinforcement panel retaining bolts and remove the panel.
5. Remove the upper and lower steering column shroud covers.
6. Disengage the ignition key courtesy lamp wire connector.
7. Detach the cruise control wire connector.
8. Disconnect the ignition switch wire connector.
9. Detach the multi-function switch wire connector.
10. If equipped, detach the ARC steering shock/strut sensor wire connector.
11. Remove the steering universal shaft pinch bolt.
12. Remove the steering column retaining bolts.
13. Detach the hazard warning wire connector.
14. Remove the starter interlock switch retaining screw and remove the switch.
15. Remove the steering column from vehicle.

To install:

16. Position the steering column in vehicle and install one retaining nut loosely.
17. Install the starter interlock switch.
18. Connect the hazard warning wire connector.
19. Install the steering column upper shroud.
20. Align the steering column universal.
21. Install the remaining steering column retaining nuts.
22. Install the universal pinch bolt and tighten to 30–42 ft. lbs. (41–57 Nm).
23. If equipped, connect the ARC steering shock/strut sensor wire connector.
24. Attach the multi-function switch wire connector.
25. Connect the ignition switch wire connector.
26. Attach the cruise control wire connector.
27. Connect the ignition key courtesy lamp wire connector.
28. Position column harness wiring and secure them in place.
29. Install the lower column shroud and retaining screws.

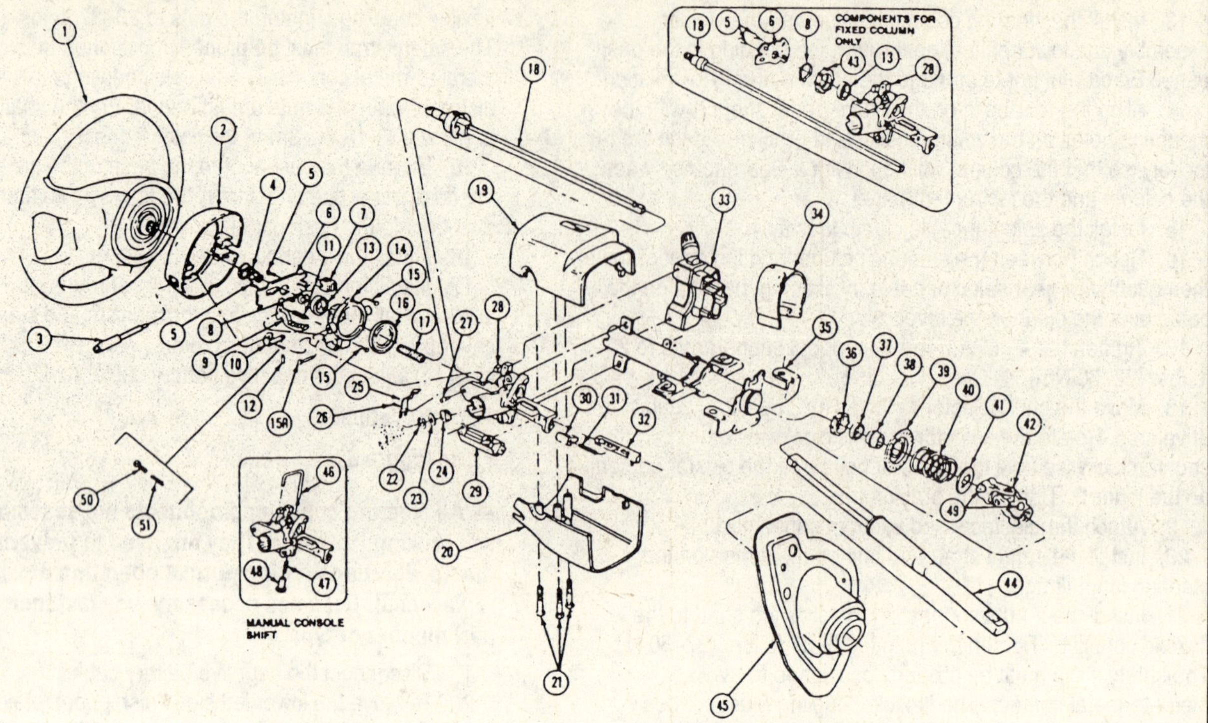

1 Steering Wheel Assembly
2 Steering Column Shroud Extension
3 Tilt Wheel Handle and Shank Assembly
4 Upper Bearing Spring
5 Retainer Plate Screws
6 Steering Column Clip Retainer Plate
7 Shroud Clip
8 Retaining Clip
9 Steering Column Lever Link
10 Release Lever
11 Position Lock Spring
12 Pin
13 Upper Bearing Assembly
14 Flange Housing
15 Rubber Bumpers
15A Pin
16 Bearing Assembly
17 Position Spring
18 Shaft Assembly
19 Upper Shroud
20 Lower Shroud
21 Screws
22 Retainer
23 Bearing
24 Lock Gear
25 Lock Actuator Cover
26 Screw
27 Pivot Pin
28 Lock Cylinder Housing
29 Ignition Switch Assembly
30 Steering Column Lock Pawl
31 Steering Column Lock Spring
32 Steering Column Lock Actuator Assembly
33 Multi-Function Switch Assembly
34 Shield
35 Steering Column Tube Assembly
36 Lower Bearing Sleeve
37 Lower Column Shaft Bearing
38 Sleeve
39 Sensor Ring
40 Sensor Ring Spring
41 Spring Retainer Ring
42 Lower Column Shaft Assembly
43 Upper Bearing
44 Intermediate Shaft
45 Lower Column Boot Assembly
46 Lock Actuator Lever (Manual Trans. Only)
47 Lock Actuator Spring
48 Lock Actuator Knob
49 Bolt
50 Cap
51 Spring

88188G81

Fig. 89 Exploded view of the steering column — 1989–93 vehicles

30. Position the lower left side reinforcement panel and secure with the retaining bolts.
31. Position the lower left side finish panel and install the retaining bolts.
32. Connect the negative battery cable, and check the operation of all the steering column's components.

1994–96 Vehicles

➧ See Figures 90, 91, 92, 93 and 94

➥ All steering column components are assembled with fasteners that are designed with a thread locking system to prevent loosening due to vibrations during normal operation of vehicle. If replacement becomes necessary, use fasteners of the same part number or type.

✻✻WARNING

Do not remove the steering column tube, steering wheel and air bag module as an assembly from the vehicle unless the steering column is locked to prevent rotation, or the lower end of the steering shaft should be wired in such a way to prevent the steering wheel from being rotated.

1. Make sure the vehicle's wheels are in the straight ahead position. Disconnect the negative, then the positive battery cables. Wait one minute for the air bag diagnostic monitor to deplete the air bag power supply.
2. Remove the steering wheel, as outlined earlier in this section.

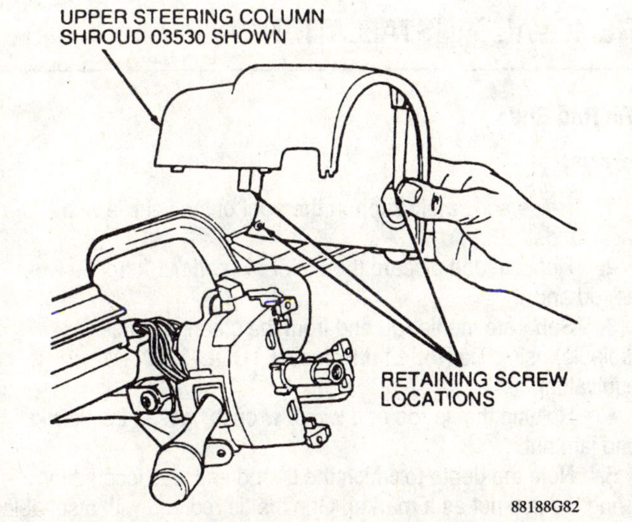

Fig. 90 Unfasten the retaining screws, then lower upper and lower column shrouds

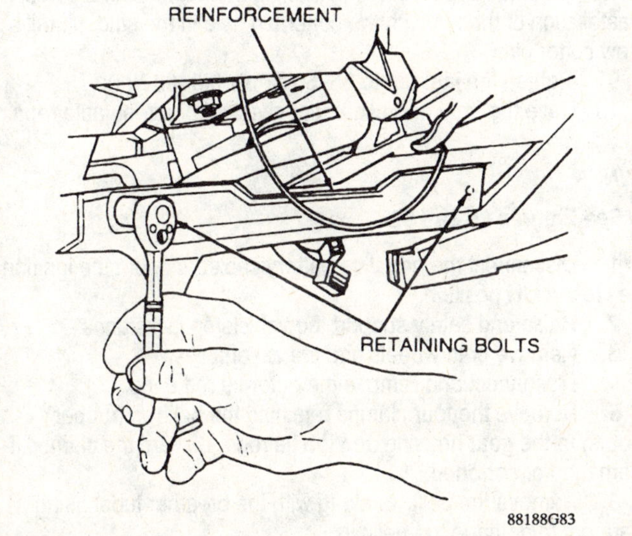

Fig. 91 Remove the instrument panel reinforcement

3. Remove the right and left side lower mouldings from the instrument panel by pulling up and snapping out of the retainers.
4. Remove the instrument panel lower trim cover.
5. Remove the air bag sliding contact.
6. Unscrew, then remove the tilt steering column lock lever.
7. Rotate the lock cylinder to the **RUN** position. Using a $^1/_8$ in. drift, press the ignition switch lock cylinder retaining pin through the access hole and remove the lock cylinder.
8. Remove the four retaining screws from the lower steering column shroud, then remove the upper and lower shrouds.
9. Remove the instrument panel reinforcement.
10. Remove the two retaining screws, then set the multi-function switch aside.
11. Remove the pinch bolt from the steering column lower yoke.
12. While supporting the steering column, remove the four column retaining nuts.
13. Remove the shift lock actuator retaining screws and the cable end assembly.
14. Remove the steering column from the vehicle.

To install:

15. Place the steering column through the dash panel, aligning the steering column tube boot with the retaining studs.
16. Install the ignition/shifter interlock cable retaining screws and cable end assembly. Tighten to 12–17 inch lbs. (1.4–2.0 Nm).
17. Align the steering column lower yoke with the lower steering column shaft. Install one bolt and tighten to 31–41 ft. lbs. (41–56 Nm).
18. Install the multi-function switch and secure with the two retaining screws. Tighten the screw to 18–26 inch lbs. (2–3 Nm).
19. Attach all electrical connectors.
20. Install the instrument panel reinforcement brace. Secure with the two bolts and tighten to 25–38 Nm).
21. Install the upper and lower steering column shrouds and secure with the four retaining screws.
22. Fasten the lower instrument panel cover.
23. Snap the right and left side instrument panel mouldings into place.
24. Install the ignition switch lock cylinder assembly.
25. Install the tilt steering column lock lever onto the steering actuator housing.
26. Install the air bag sliding contact and secure with the retaining screws. Tighten to 18–26 inch lbs. (2–3 Nm).
27. Install the steering wheel onto the steering shaft. Install a new bolt and tighten to 23–33 ft. lbs. (31–48 Nm).
28. Position the air bag module to the steering wheel and secure with the two retaining screws. Tighten the screws to 8–10 ft. lbs. (10–14 Nm).
29. Connect the positive, then the negative battery cables. Verify the air bag warning indicator.

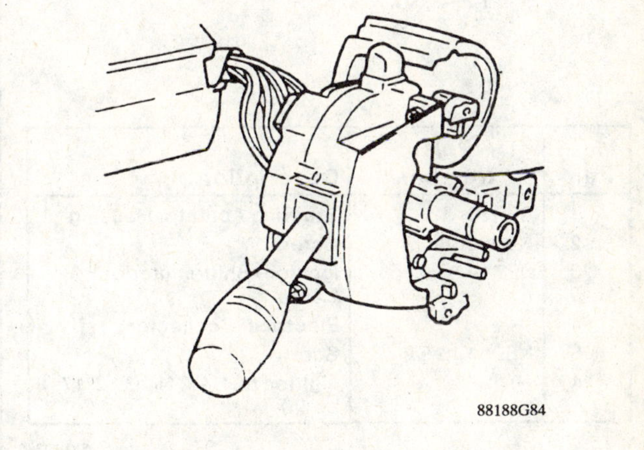

Fig. 92 Unfasten the switch retaining screws, then remove the multi-function switch

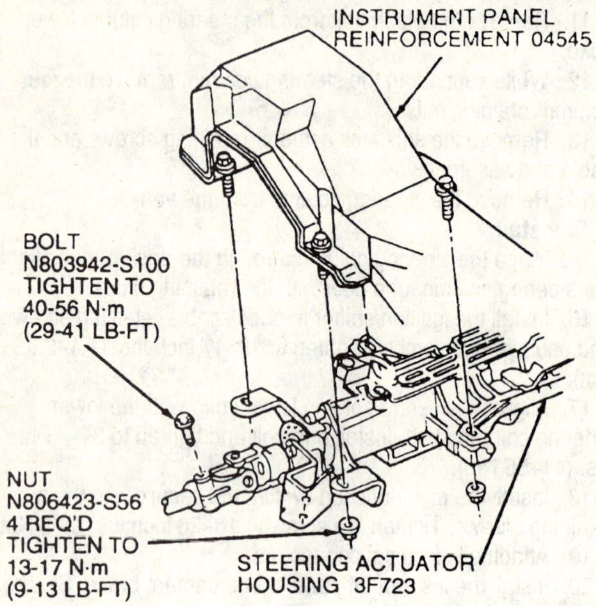

Fig. 93 While supporting the steering column, remove the four column retaining nuts

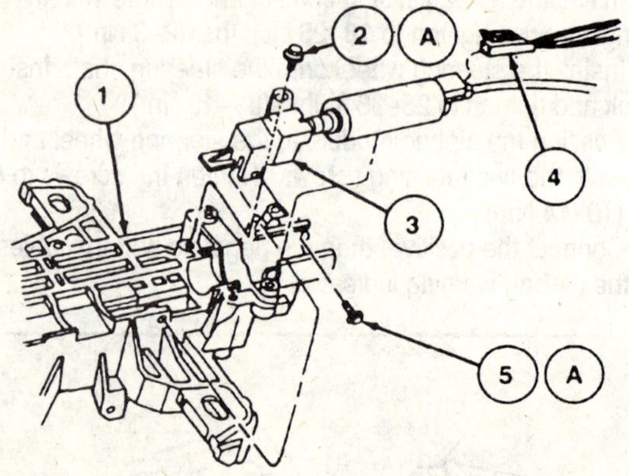

Item	Part Number	Description
1	3F723	Steering Actuator Housing
2	N806038-S2	Screw
3	3F719	Ignition / Shifter Interlock Cable
4	—	Electrical Connector
5	N805138-S2	Screw
A	—	Tighten to 1.4-2 N·m (12-17 Lb-In)

88188G86

Fig. 94 Remove the shift lock actuator retaining screws and the cable end assembly

Steering Linkage

REMOVAL & INSTALLATION

Tie Rod Ends

OUTER

1. Raise and safely support the front of the vehicle with jackstands.
2. Remove and discard the cotter pin and nut from the worn tie rod end.
3. Separate the tie rod end from the steering knuckle (spindle) using Tie Rod End Remover TOOL-3290-D or equivalent.
4. Holding the tie rod end with a wrench, loosen the tie rod end jam nut.
5. Note the depth to which the tie rod end was located by using the jam nut as a marker. Grip the tie rod end with a suitable pair of pliers, then remove the tie rod end.

To install:

6. Clean the tie rod end threads. Thread the tie rod ends to the same depth as the removed tie rod end.
7. Place the tie rod end into the steering knuckle (spindle). Make sure the wheels are in the straight ahead position.
8. Install a new nut on the tie rod end. Tighten the nut to 39 ft. lbs. (53 Nm), and continue tightening the nut to align the next castellation of the nut with the cotter pin hole in the stud. Install a new cotter pin.
9. Tighten the jam nut to 35–50 ft. lbs. (48–68 Nm).
10. Have the front end alignment checked at a reputable repair shop.

INNER

➧ **See Figures 95 and 96**

1. Disconnect the negative battery cable, and turn the ignition key to the **ON** position.
2. Raise and safely support the vehicle on jackstands.
3. Remove both wheels and tire assemblies.
4. Disconnect and remove the outer tie rod ends.
5. Remove the four clamps retaining the bellows (rubber boots) to the gear housing and the tie rods. Discard the clamps if damaged or corroded.
6. Remove the bellows along with the breather tube, using care not to damage the bellows.
7. Remove the coiled lock pins from inner tie rod ball joint, using a locknut pin removal tool D81P-3504-N or equivalent.
8. Turn the steering towards the right enough to expose a few rack teeth. Hold the rack with an adjustable wrench (on end teeth only), while loosening tie rod ball joints with a nut wrench T74P-3504-U or equivalent.

➝ Some gear assemblies may contain one or two rack travel restrictors on each side of the rack. The restrictors are split nylon washers and, if required, can easily be removed from the rack following tie rod removal. Restrictors may be reused unless heavily worn.

To install:

9. Turn the gear against or near left side stop and hold rack with an adjustable wrench nearest the rack end. Tighten each tie rod ball joint separately, using nut wrench T74P-3504-U or equivalent.

10. Thoroughly clean the rack and housing of any foreign material. Any abrasive material is extremely harmful to the high pressure oil seals in the rack.

➥ **Apply some gear grease to the groove on the tie rods where the bellows clamp to the rod. This allows for toe adjustments without damaging the bellows (rubber boots).**

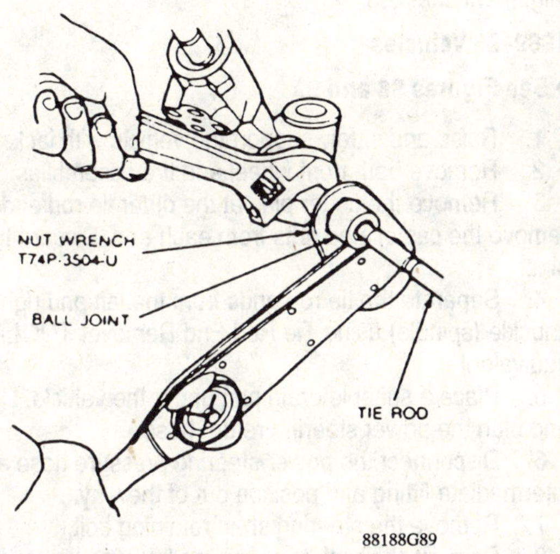

Fig. 95 Inner tie rod end removal/installation tool

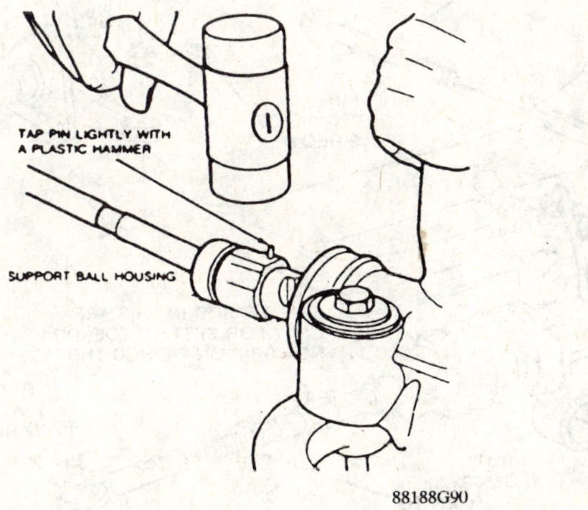

Fig. 96 Inner tie rod end installation

11. Install the breather tube and the bellows into position on the housing and tie rods.

12. Install new clamps onto the bellows.

13. Install the jam nuts and place a small amount of grease on the threads of the tie rods.

14. Install the outer tie rod ends.

15. Install the wheels and tires assemblies.

16. Carefully lower the vehicle, connect the negative battery cable, and have the alignment checked at a reputable repair shop.

Power Rack And Pinion Steering Gear

ADJUSTMENTS

The power rack and pinion steering gear provides for only one service adjustment. The gear must be removed from the vehicle to perform this adjustment.

Rack Yoke Plug Preload

1. Clean the exterior of the steering gear thoroughly.

2. Install two long bolts and washers through the bushing, and attach to the bench mounted holding fixture, Tool T57L-500-B or equivalent.

3. Do not remove the external pressure lines, unless they are leaking or damaged. If these lines are removed, they must be replaced with new lines.

4. Drain the power steering fluid by rotating the input shaft lock-to-lock twice using Tool T74P-3505-R or equivalent. Cover ports on valve housing with shop cloth while draining gear.

5. Insert an inch-pound torque wrench with maximum capacity of 30-60 inch lbs. into the input shaft torque adapter, Tool T74P-3504-R or equivalent. Position the adapter and wrench on the input shaft splines.

6. Loosen the yoke plug locknut with wrench, Tool T78P-3504-H or equivalent.

7. Loosen yoke plug with a $^{3}/_{4}$ in. socket wrench.

8. With the rack at the center of travel, tighten the yoke plug to 45-50 inch lbs. Clean the threads of the yoke plug prior to tightening to prevent a false reading.

9. Back off the yoke plug approximately $^{1}/_{8}$ turn (44° minimum to 54° maximum) until the torque required to initiate and sustain rotation of the input shaft is 7-18 inch lbs.

10. Place Tool T78P-3504-H or equivalent on the yoke plug locknut. While holding the yoke plug, tighten the locknut to 44-66 ft. lbs. Do not allow the yoke plug to move while tightening or the preload will be affected. Recheck input shaft torque after tightening locknut.

11. If the external pressure lines were removed, they must be replaced with new service line. Remove the copper seals from the housing ports prior to installation of new lines.

REMOVAL & INSTALLATION

1983-88 Vehicles

➧ **See Figure 97**

1. Disconnect the negative battery cable.

2. Remove the one bolt retaining the flexible coupling to the input shaft.
3. Leave the ignition key in the **ON** position, and raise the vehicle on a hoist.
4. Remove the two tie rod end retaining cotter pins and nuts. Separate the studs from the spindle arms, using the ball joint separator tool.
5. Support the steering gear, and remove the two nuts, insulator, washers, and bolts retaining the steering gear to the No. 2 crossmember. Lower the gear slightly to permit access to the pressure and return line fittings.
6. Disconnect the pressure and return lines from the steering gear valve housing. Plug the lines and parts in the valve housing to prevent entry of dirt.
7. Remove the steering gear assembly from the vehicle.

To install:

8. Support and position the steering gear, so that the pressure and return line fittings can be connected to the valve housing. Tighten the fittings to 15–20 ft. lbs. (20–27 Nm). The design allows the hoses to swivel when tightened properly. Do not attempt to eliminate looseness by overtightening, since this can cause damage to the fittings.

The rubber insulators must be pushed completely inside the gear housing before the installation of the gear housing on the No. 2 crossmember.

9. No gap is allowed between the insulator and the face of the gear boss. A rubber lubricant should be used to facilitate proper installation of the insulators in the gear housing. Insert the input shaft into the flexible coupling, and position the steering gear to the No. 2 crossmember. Install the two bolts, insulator washers, and nuts. Tighten the two nuts to 80–100 ft. lbs. (108–136 Nm).
10. Connect the tie rod ends to the spindle arms, and install the two retaining nuts. Tighten the nuts to 35–45 ft. lbs. (47–61 Nm), then, after tightening to specification, tighten the nuts to their nearest cotter pin castellation, and install two new cotter pins.
11. Lower the vehicle, and install the one bolt retaining the flexible coupling to the input shaft. Tighten the bolt to 18–23 ft. lbs. (24–31 Nm).
12. Turn the ignition key to the **OFF** position.
13. Connect the negative battery cable.
14. Remove the coil wire.
15. Fill the power steering pump reservoir.
16. Engage the starter, and cycle the steering wheel to distribute the fluid. Check the fluid level and add as required.
17. Install the coil wire, start the engine, and cycle the steering wheel. Check for fluid leaks.
18. If the tie rod ends were loosened, have the wheel alignment checked.

1989–96 Vehicles

See Figures 98 and 99

1. Raise and safely support the vehicle with jackstands.
2. Remove both front wheel and tire assemblies.
3. Remove the cotter pins at the outer tie rod ends, then remove the castellated nuts from each end. Discard the cotter pins.
4. Separate the tie rod ends from the left and right side knuckle (spindle) using Tie Rod End Remover TOOL–3290–D or equivalent.
5. Place a suitable drain pan under the vehicle. Disconnect and plug the power steering return hose.
6. Disconnect the power steering pressure hose at the intermediate fitting and position out of the way.
7. Remove the steering shaft retaining bolt.
8. Remove the rack-to-subframe bolts and nuts. Access the nuts through the hole in the front crossmember.

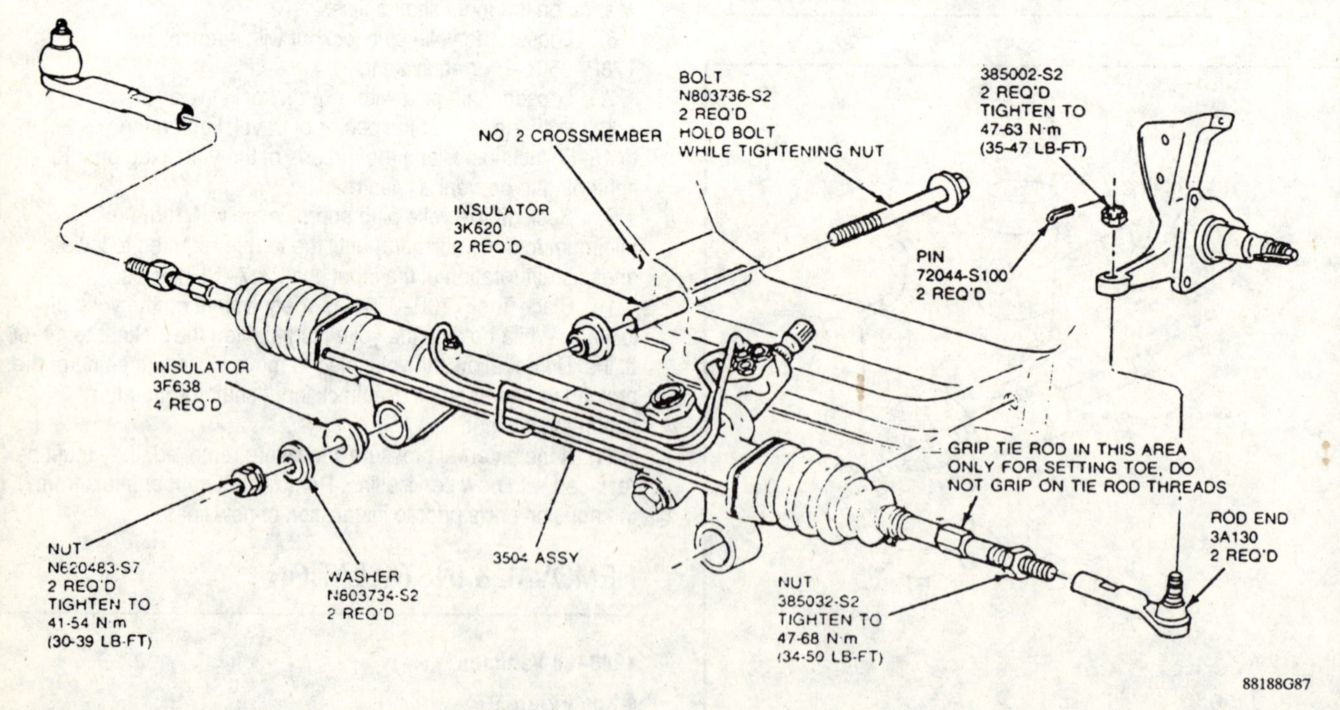

Fig. 97 Power steering gear assembly — 1983-88 vehicles

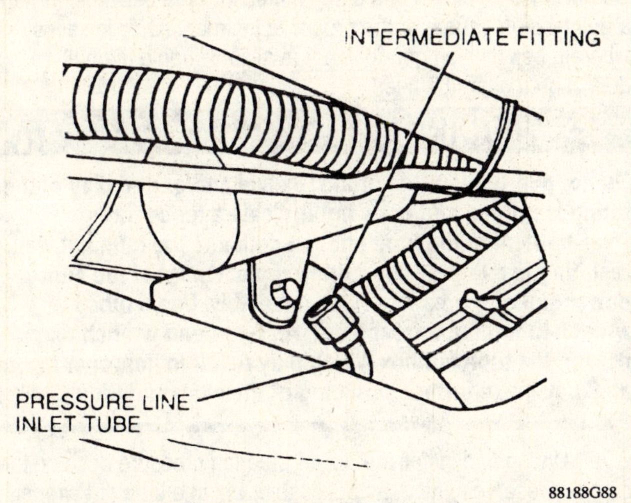

Fig. 98 Disconnect the power steering pressure hose at the intermediate fitting and position out of the way

9. Lower the power steering short rack as necessary, to remove the pressure line inlet tube. Remove and discard the plastic seal on the inlet tube.

10. Cut the tie strap securing the power steering pressure hose to each tube.

11. Remove the power steering short rack from the vehicle.

To install:

12. Install a new seal on the pressure line.

13. Install the steering gear insulator from the rear side of the steering gear housing, making sure they are fully seated. Use a suitable rubber lubricant to aid in installation.

14. Install and position the power steering short rack to the front crossmember.

15. Install the pressure line in the intermediate fitting.

16. Align the steering gear input shaft to allow the power steering short rack to completely seat on the front crossmember.

17. Install the steering gear input shaft retaining bolts and nuts. Tighten the bolts to 100–144 ft. lbs. (135–195 Nm).

18. Install the steering shaft flex coupling retaining bolt and tighten to 30–42 ft. lbs. (41–57 Nm).

19. Secure the power steering pressure hose to the power steering left turn pressure hose with a new tie strap.

20. Connect the power steering pressure hose.

21. Attach the power steering return hose, then tighten the clamp to 12–18 ft. lbs. (1.4–2.0 Nm).

22. Install the outer tie rod ends to the left and right knuckles and install castellated nuts at each ends. Tighten the nuts to 39 ft. lbs. (53 Nm). Continue to tighten the nuts until the castellations line up with the stud bores.

23. Install new cotter pins through the stud bores at each tie rod end.

24. Install both wheel and tire assemblies. Tighten the lug nuts to 85–105 ft. lbs. (115–142 Nm).

25. Carefully lower the vehicle, then fill the power steering system with the correct amount and type of fluid.

26. Connect the negative battery cable, then have the alignment checked at a reputable repair shop.

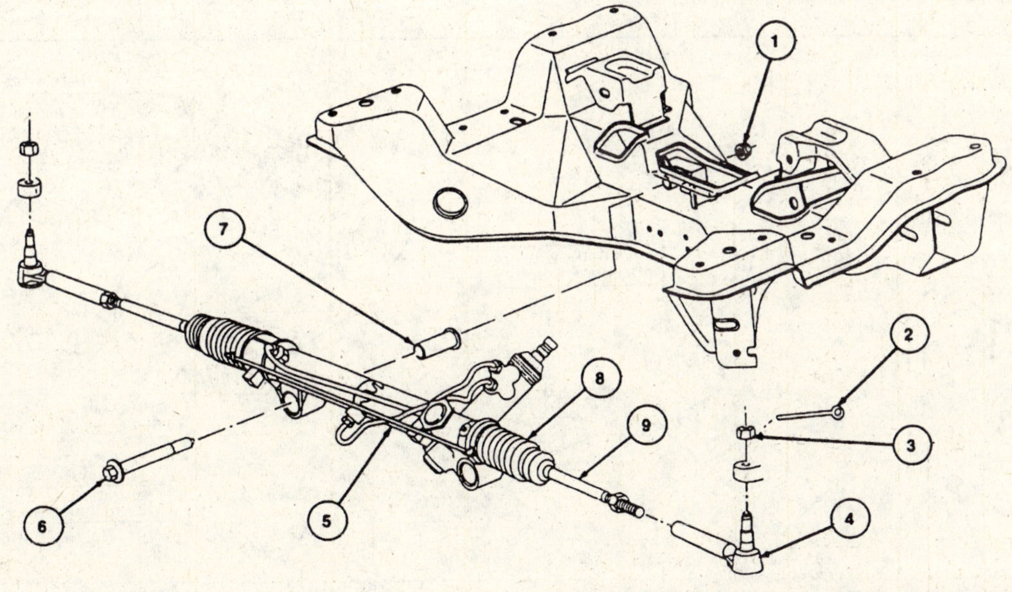

Item	Part Number	Description
1	N800237-S100	Nut (2 Req'd)
2	72044-S36	Pin
3	385002-S2	Nut (2 Req'd)
4	3A130	Tie Rod End
5	3L547	Power Steering Short Rack
6	N806254-S119	Bolt and Washer Assy (2 Req'd)

Item	Part Number	Description
7	3C716	Steering Gear Insulator (2 Req'd)
8	3332	Tie Rod Bellows (2 Req'd)
9	3280	Front Wheel Spindle Tie Rod (2 Req'd)

88188G91

Fig. 99 Power steering gear assembly — 1995 vehicle shown

Power Steering Pump

REMOVAL & INSTALLATION

Except 4.6L Engines

See Figures 100, 101, 102, 103 and 104

On supercharged engines the intercooler/charge air cooler tubes must be removed to gain access to the power steering pump.

1. Disconnect the negative battery cable.
2. Drain as much fluid as possible from the pump reservoir by disconnecting the fluid return hose at the reservoir and draining the fluid into a suitable container.
3. Disconnect and cap the power steering pressure hose.

If vehicle is equipped with a serpentine belt, remove the belt at this time.

4. Remove the mounting bolts from the front of the pump. After removal, move the pump inward to loosen the belt tension and remove the belt from the pulley. Some 1989 and later models require the removal of the pulley from the pump. Remove the power steering pump from the vehicle.

To install:

5. Position the power steering pump on the mounting bracket and install the mounting bolts and nuts. Tighten the nuts to 30–45 ft. lbs. (40–62 Nm). If removed, install the pulley.
6. Put the drive belt over the pulley and move the pump outward against the belt until the proper belt tension is obtained. Do not pry against the pump body. Measure the belt tension with a belt tension gauge for the proper adjustment. Only in cases where a belt tension gauge is not available should the belt deflection method be used.

****WARNING**

Do not overtighten this fitting. Swivel and/or end play of the fitting is normal and does not indicate a loose fitting. Over-tightening the tube nut can collapse the tube nut wall, resulting in a leak and requiring replacement of the entire power steering pressure hose assembly. Use a tube nut wrench to tighten the tube nut. An open-end wrench may deform the tube nut hex which may result in improper torque and may make further servicing of the system difficult.

7. Uncap and install the power steering pressure hose on the pump or reservoir fitting, as applicable. Using a tube nut wrench adapter on your torque wrench, NOT an open-end wrench, tighten to 20–25 ft. lbs. (27–34 Nm).
8. Connect the power steering return hose to the pump, then tighten the clamp.
9. Fill the power steering reservoir with the correct amount and type of fluid.
10. Install the serpentine belt, if so equipped.
11. Install the supercharger intercooler, if so equipped.
12. Use the start-up procedure after power steering fluid reservoir or steering rack overhaul.
13. Connect the negative battery cable, then start engine and check for leaks.

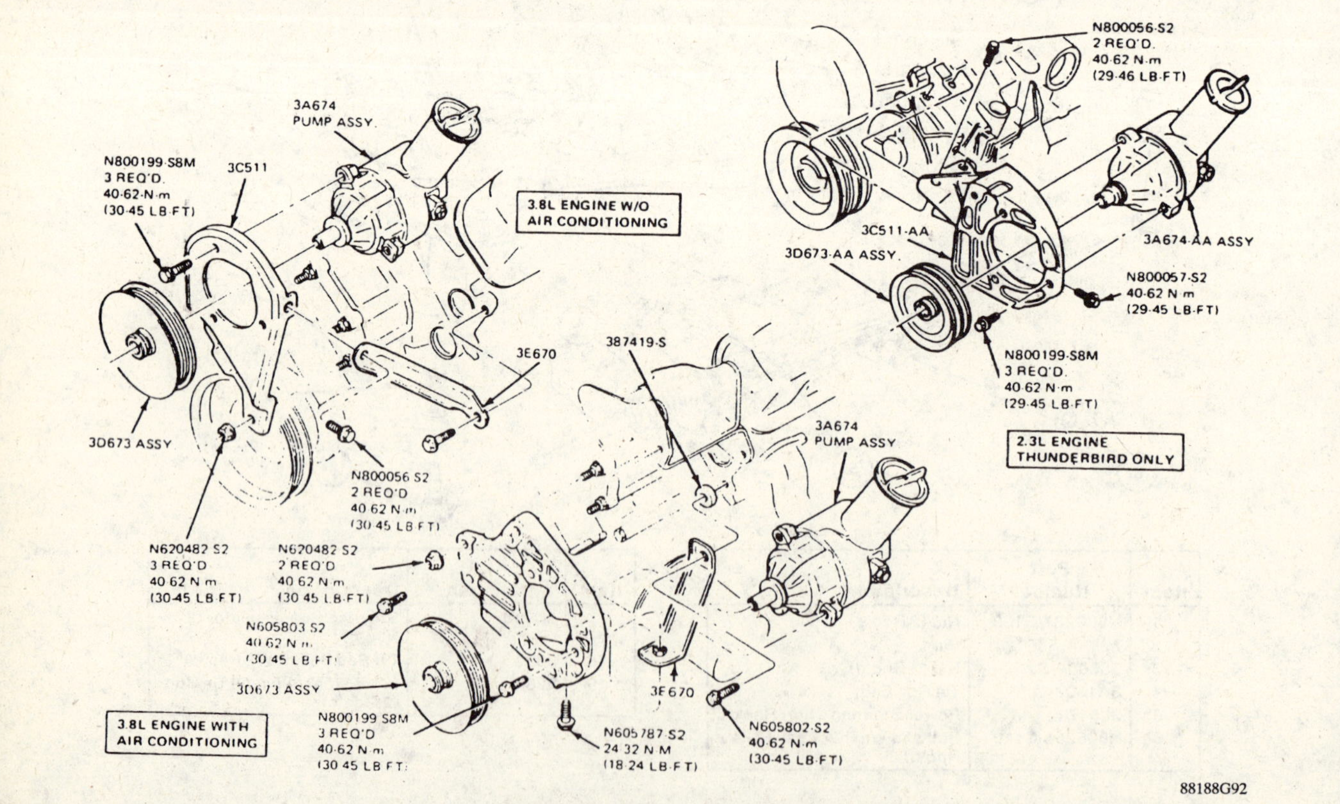

Fig. 100 Power steering pump mounting — 1983–84 vehicles with 2.3L and 3.8L engines

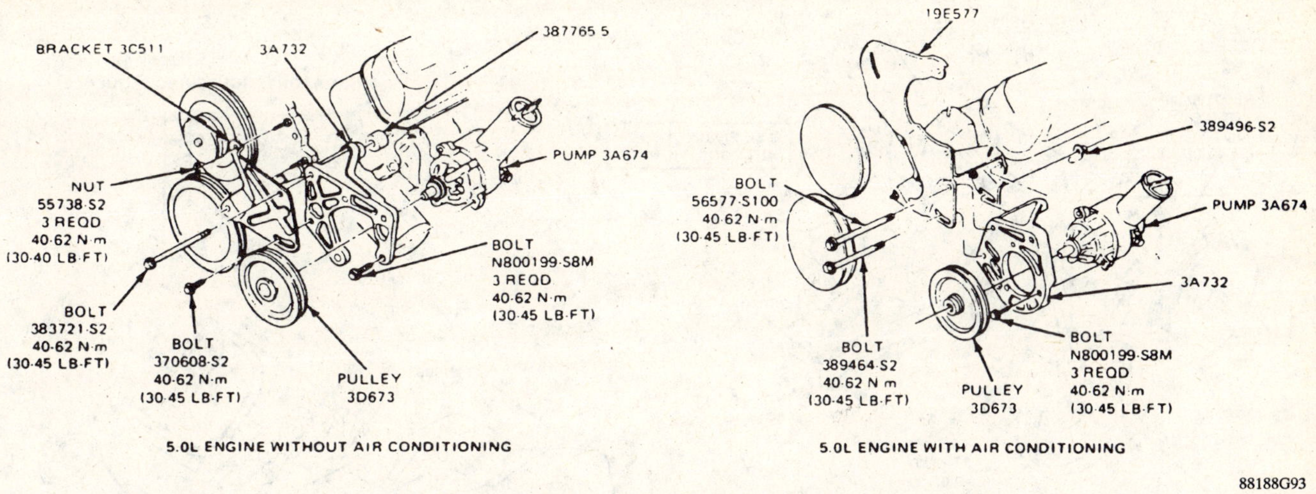

Fig. 101 Power steering pump removal and installation — 1983–84 vehicles with the 5.0L engine

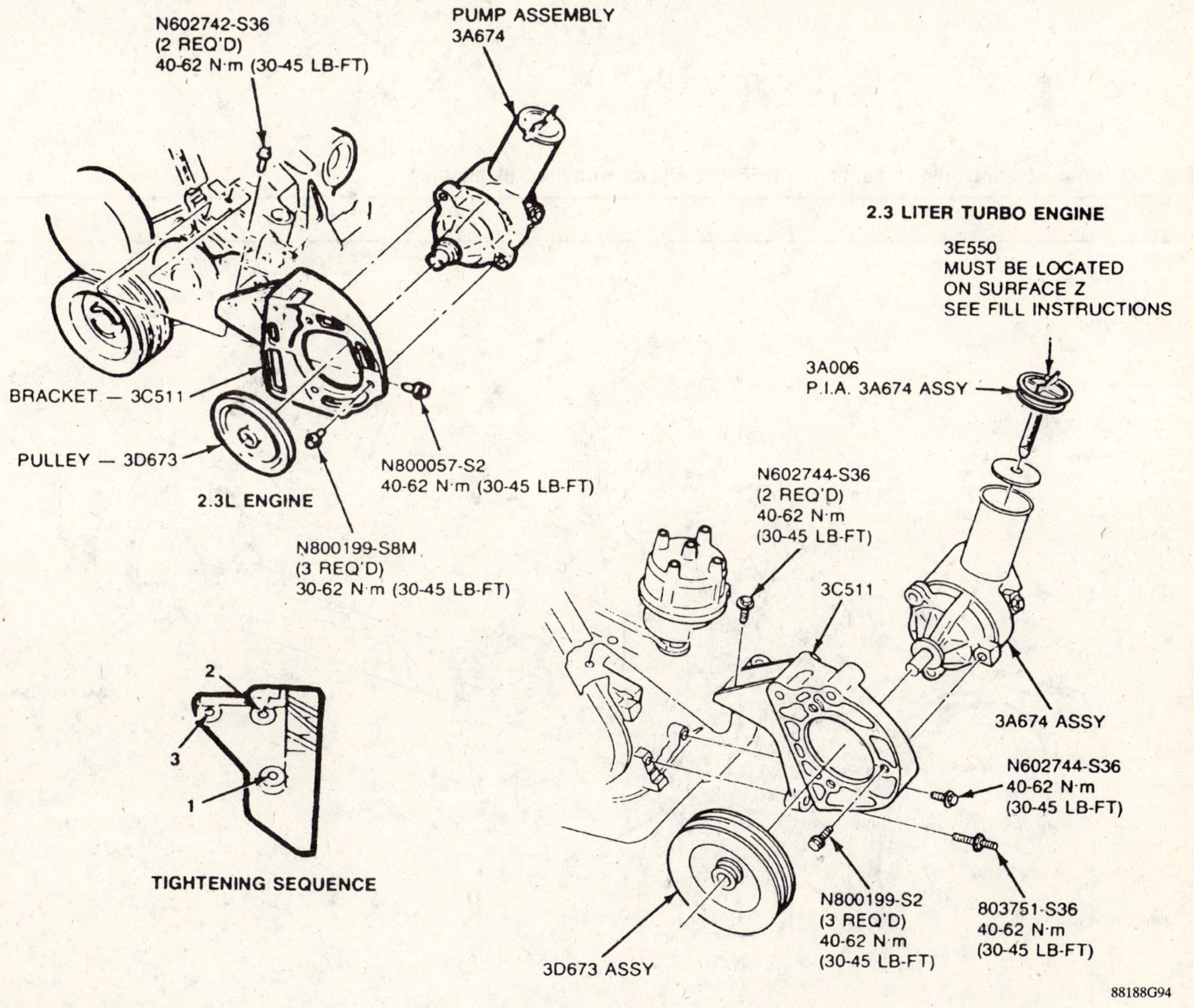

Fig. 102 Power steering pump mounting — 1985–88 vehicles with the 2.3L engine

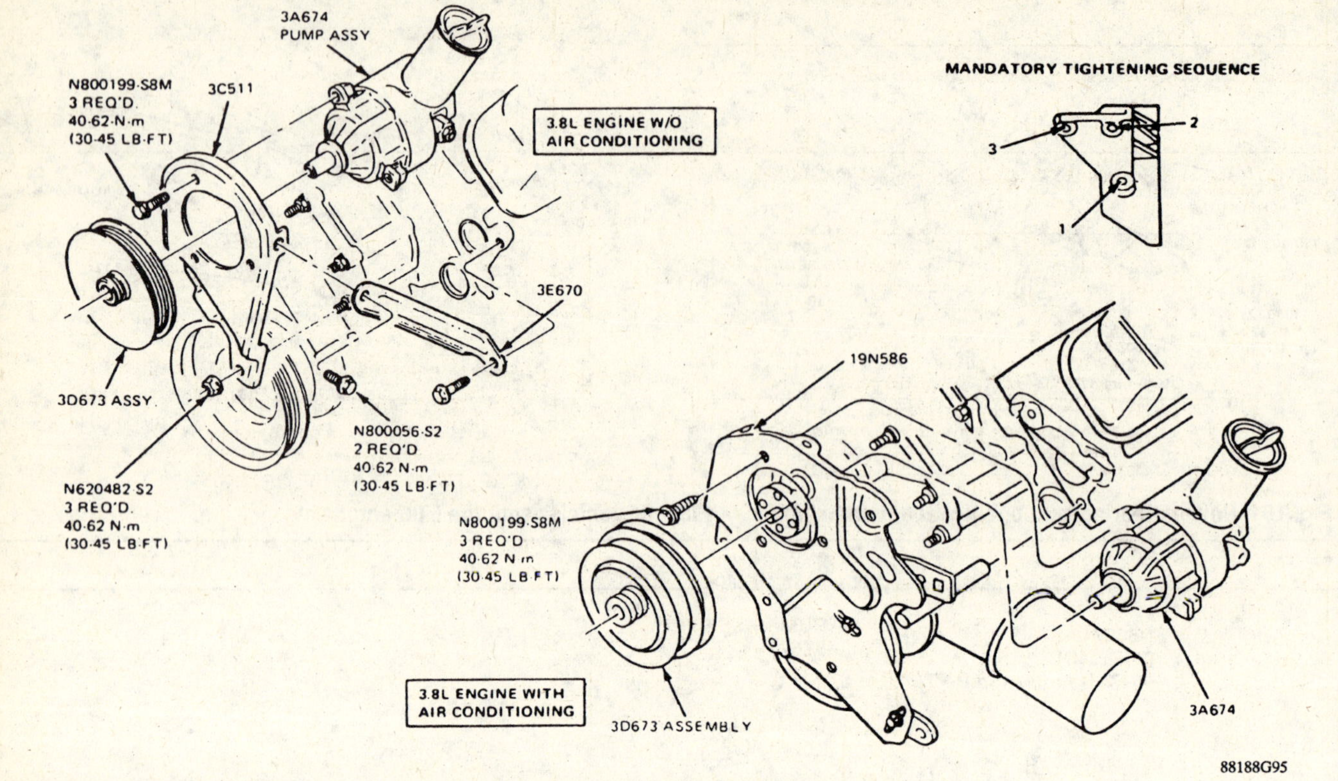

Fig. 103 Power steering pump mounting — 1985–88 vehicles with the 3.8L engine

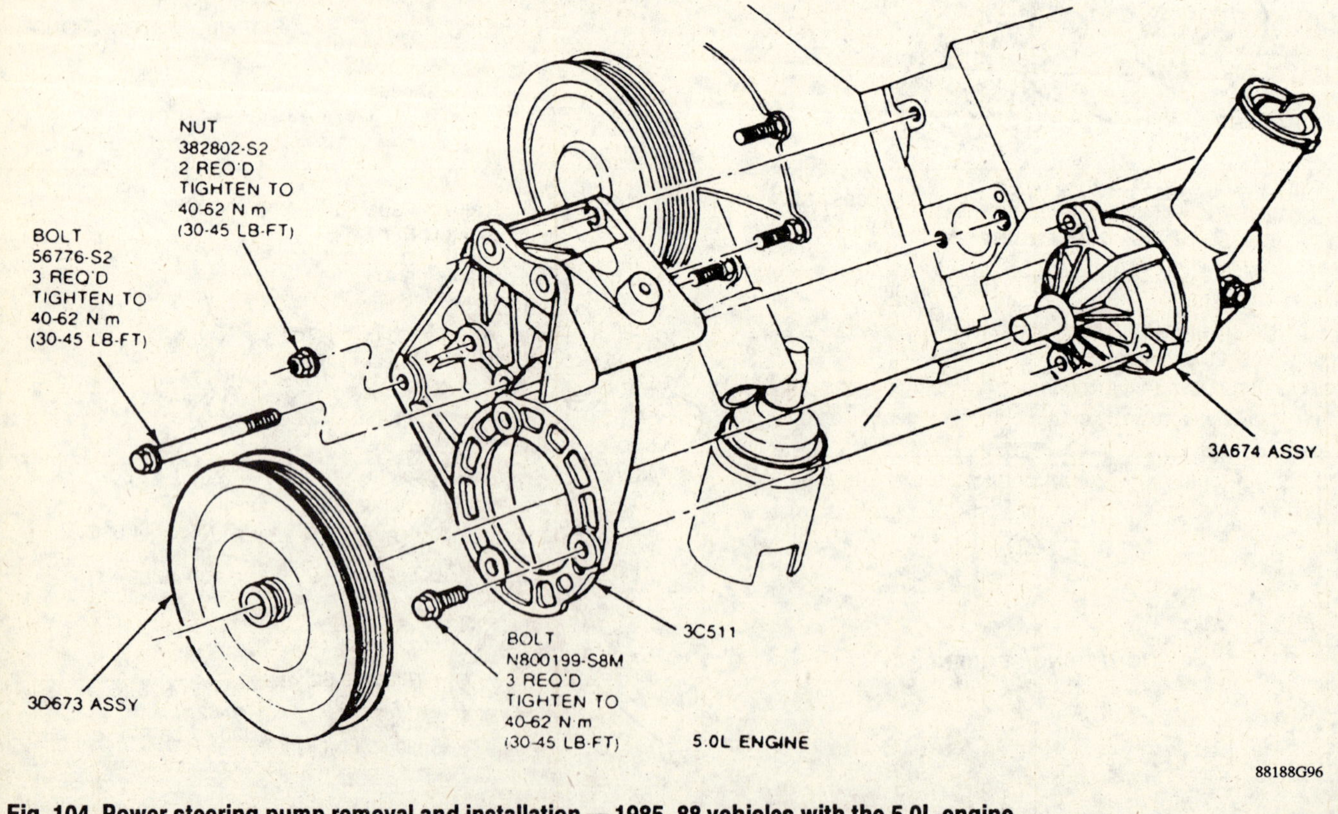

Fig. 104 Power steering pump removal and installation — 1985–88 vehicles with the 5.0L engine

4.6L Engine

➧ **See Figure 105**

1. To remove power steering fluid from the reservoir, disconnect the power steering return hose at the cooler return tube connection and drain the fluid into a suitable container.
2. Remove the power steering pressure hose from the power steering pump outlet, then drain the fluid into a suitable container.
3. Disconnect the drive belt from the power steering pump pulley, remove the four retaining bolts, then remove the power steering pump and pulley assembly.
4. Place the pump and pulley in a suitable vise, then separate the pulley from the pump using Steering Pump Pulley Remover T69L-10300-B or equivalent on the pulley hub.

To install:

➥ Before installing the pump, remove the shipping tube nut from the housing, if equipped.

5. Install the pulley to the power steering pump using Steering Pump Pulley Replacer T91P-3A733-A or equivalent.
6. Place the power steering pump on the mounting bosses of the engine block and install the bolts at the side of the pump. Tighten the bolts to 15–22 ft. lbs. (20–30 Nm).
7. Install the drive belt.

****WARNING**

Do not overtighten this fitting. Swivel and/or end play of the fitting is normal and does not indicate a loose fitting. Over-tightening the tube nut can collapse the tube nut wall, resulting in a leak and requiring replacement of the entire power steering pressure hose assembly. Use a tube nut wrench to tighten the tube nut. An open-end wrench may deform the tube nut hex which may result in improper torque and may make further servicing of the system difficult.

8. Install the power steering pressure hose to the pump fitting. Tighten the nut with a tube wrench adapter on your torque wrench, NOT an open end wrench. Tighten the nut to 40–54 ft. lbs. (57–73 Nm).
9. Connect the power steering pump hose to the cooler return tube, and reposition the hose clamp to the pump inlet fitting.

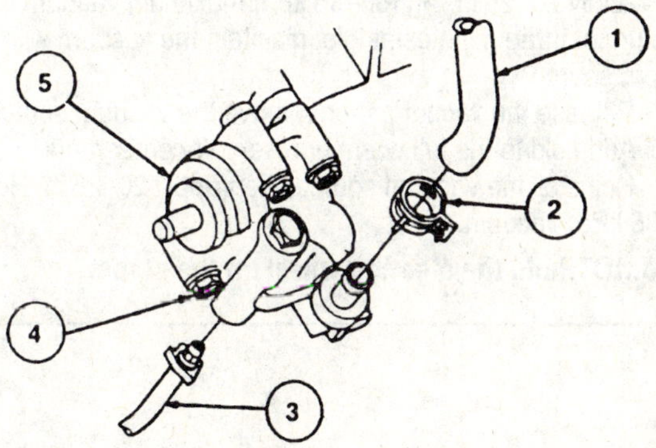

Item	Part Number	Description
1	3691	Power Steering Reservoir Pump Hose
2	3C750	Clamp
3	3A719	Power Steering Pressure Hose
4	N806176-S2	Bolt (4 Req'd)
5	3A674	Power Steering Pump

88188G97

Fig. 105 View of the power steering pump — 4.6L engine

BLEEDING

Fluid Level Top-Off Procedure

1. Check and fill the pump reservoir to the dipstick FULL COLD or remote reservoir center mark with the correct type of power steering fluid.
2. Disable the ignition by disconnecting the ignition coil wire.
3. Crank the engine for 30 seconds, check the fluid level, then add if necessary.

➥ Do NOT hold the steering wheel on the stops.

4. Crank the engine for 30 seconds while cycling the steering wheel lock-to-lock.
5. Check the fluid level and add, if required.

Start-Up Procedure After Power Steering Pump or Gear Service

After engine start-up, follow these steps to eliminate excessive steering system noise due to air trapped in the system during service.

1. Disable the ignition by disconnecting the ignition coil wire.
2. Raise and safely support the front end of the vehicle.
3. Fill the power steering fluid reservoir with the correct type and amount of power steering fluid.
4. Crank the engine with the starter motor and add power steering fluid until the level remains constant.

➥ The front wheels MUST be off the ground during lock-to-lock rotation of the steering wheel.

5. While cranking the engine, rotate the steering wheel from lock-to-lock.
6. Check the fluid level and add, if necessary.
7. Connect the ignition coil wire.
8. Start the engine and allow it to run for several minutes.
9. Rotate the steering wheel from lock-to-lock.
10. Turn the engine OFF, then check the fluid level and add, if necessary.
11. If air is still present, purge the system of air using the Air Purge With External Vacuum procedure.
12. Carefully lower the vehicle.

Air Purge With External Vacuum Source

➧ **See Figure 106**

Air trapped in the power steering system, which causes a whine or moaning noise, can be removed by using a power steering pump air evacuator assembly (devac tool). Use the Rotunda Vacuum Tester 021-00014 or equivalent.

1. Tightly insert the rubber stopper of the air evacuator assembly into the power steering pump reservoir.
2. Reattach the connection used to disable the ignition, then start the engine.
3. Apply 20–25 in. Hg (68–85 kPa) maximum vacuum for a minimum of three minutes at idle; maintain the vacuum with the vacuum source.
4. Release the vacuum, then remove the vacuum source.
5. Add fluid to the full warm or reservoir center mark.
6. Reinstall the vacuum source, then apply 20–25 in. Hg (68–85 kPa) vacuum.

➡ **Do NOT hold the steering wheel on the stops.**

7. Cycle the steering wheel from lock-to-lock every 30 seconds for about 5 minutes.
8. Shut the engine off, release the vacuum, then remove the vacuum source.
9. Add fluid if necessary, install the dipstick or reservoir cap.

➡ **Do NOT hold the steering wheel on the stops.**

10. Cycle the steering wheel from lock-to-lock every 30 seconds for about 5 minutes.
11. Check for oil leaks at all connections.
12. In severe cases, it may be necessary to repeat the air purge procedure.

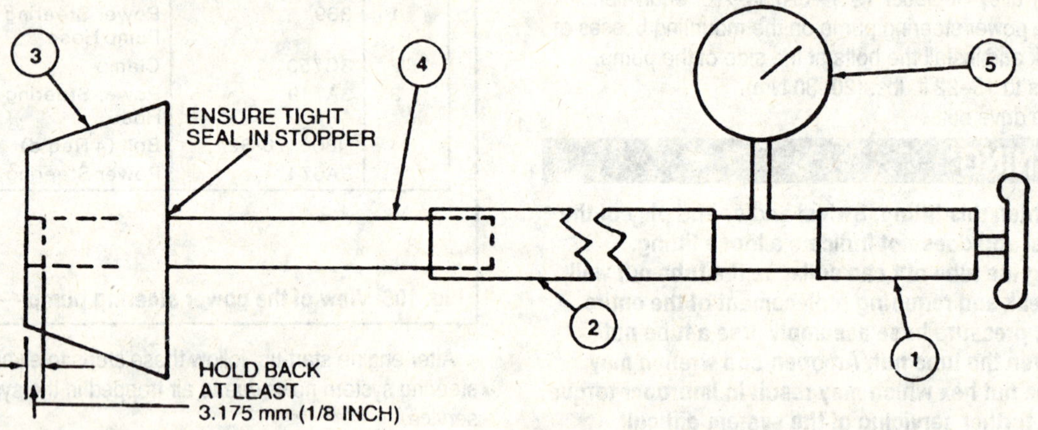

Item	Part Number	Description
1	021-00014	Rotunda Vacuum Source
2	—	Vacuum Hose
3		Rubber Stopper Cap No. 7 for CIII No. 11 for CII

Item	Part Number	Description
4	—	Tubing—Plexiglass, Steel or Copper (6.35-7.93 mm (1/4-5/16 inch))
5	—	Vacuum Gauge

88188G98

Fig. 106 Tightly insert the rubber stopper of the air evacuator assembly into the power steering pump reservoir

9

BRAKES

BRAKE OPERATING SYSTEM

Adjustments

DRUM BRAKES

➧ **See Figure 1**

The rear brakes are automatically adjusted while driving the vehicle. Manual brake adjustment is required only after the rear brake shoes and linings have been replaced, or if the adjuster has malfunctioned and has been repaired or replaced. Perform the manual adjustment with the brake drum removed, using Brake Adjustment Gauge D81L-1103-A or equivalent.

1. Raise and safely support the rear end of the vehicle on jackstands.
2. Remove the tire and wheel assembly, then remove the brake drum.
3. Apply a small quantity of Disc Brake Caliper Slide Grease D7AZ-19590-A or equivalent, to the points where the shoes contact the rear brake backing plate. Do NOT get any lubricant on the lining.
4. Determine the inside diameter of the brake drum braking surface using Brake Adjustment Gauge D81L-1103-A or equivalent.
5. Adjust the brake shoe and lining diameter to fit the gauge. Line up the brake shoes and linings vertically so that the flats on the bottom of the rear brake shoes and linings are aligned approximately 0.05 in. (1.5mm) above the bottom of the brake shoe and lining abutment plate before setting the gauge diameter. Hold the automatic brake shoe adjusting lever out of engagement while rotating the adjusting screw. If necessary, lubricate. Make sure the adjusting screw rotates freely.
6. Rotate Brake Adjustment Gauge D81L-1103-A or equivalent around the rear brake shoe and lining to ensure proper seating.
7. Install the brake drum, as outlined later in this section.
8. Install the tire and wheel assembly, then install the wheel cover and nut covers, as applicable.
9. After the rear brake shoes and linings have been properly adjusted, check the operation of the brakes by making several stops from varying forward speeds.

Brake Light Switch

REMOVAL & INSTALLATION

➧ **See Figure 2**

1. Disconnect the negative battery cable.

➥ **The locking tab on the connector must be lifted before the connector can be removed.**

2. Raise the locking tab and unplug the wiring harness at the switch.
3. Remove the hairpin clip from the stud and slide the switch up and down. Remove the switch and washers from the pedal.

➥ **It is not necessary to remove the pushrod from the stud.**

To install:

4. Installation is the reverse of removal. Position the U-shaped side nearest the pedal and directly over/under the pin. Slide the switch up and down trapping the pushrod and bushing between the switch sideplates.
5. Connect the negative battery cable.

Brake Pedal

REMOVAL & INSTALLATION

Vehicles Without ABS

➧ **See Figure 3**

1. Disconnect the negative battery cable.
2. Detach the stop lamp/brake light switch wire connector from the switch.
3. If equipped with a manual transmission, remove the clutch cable from clutch pedal.
4. Loosen the three pedal support retaining nuts at the dash panel. Remove the pushrod retainer and nylon washer. Slide the stop lamp switch outboard along the brake pedal pin just far enough for the outer hole of the switch frame to clear the pin.
5. Remove the switch by sliding it downward. Remove the black stop lamp switch bushing from the pushrod.
6. Remove the locknut from the pivot bolt. Pull the pivot bolt out, then remove the brake pedal from the vehicle.

To install:

7. Apply a coating of SAE 10W-40 engine oil to the bushings. Locate the bushings and pivot spacer in the brake pedal hub.
8. Position the brake pedal assembly in the pedal support. Install the pivot bolt, locknut and tighten to 10-20 ft. lbs. (13.5-27 Nm).

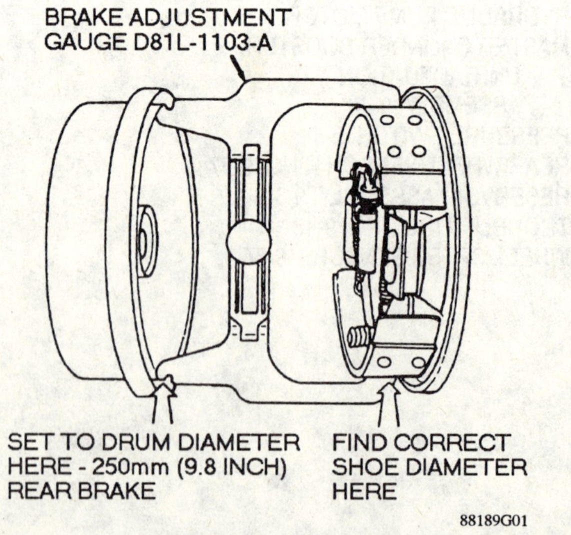

Fig. 1 Rear drum brake adjustment using the correct tool

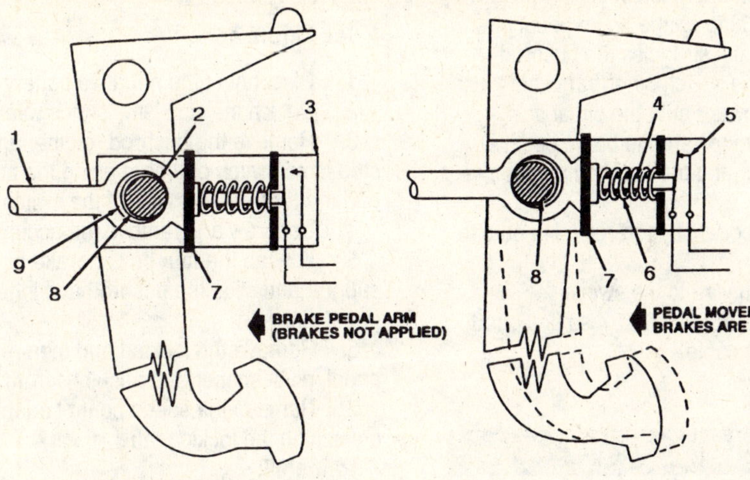

1. Power brake booster push rod
2. Brake pedal arm pin
3. Stoplight switch
4. Pin
5. Contacts
6. Spring
7. Switch pressure plate
8. Brake master cylinder push rod bushing
9. Brake master cylinder push rod spacer

88189G02

Fig. 2 Brake light (stop light) switch mounting — 1995 vehicle shown

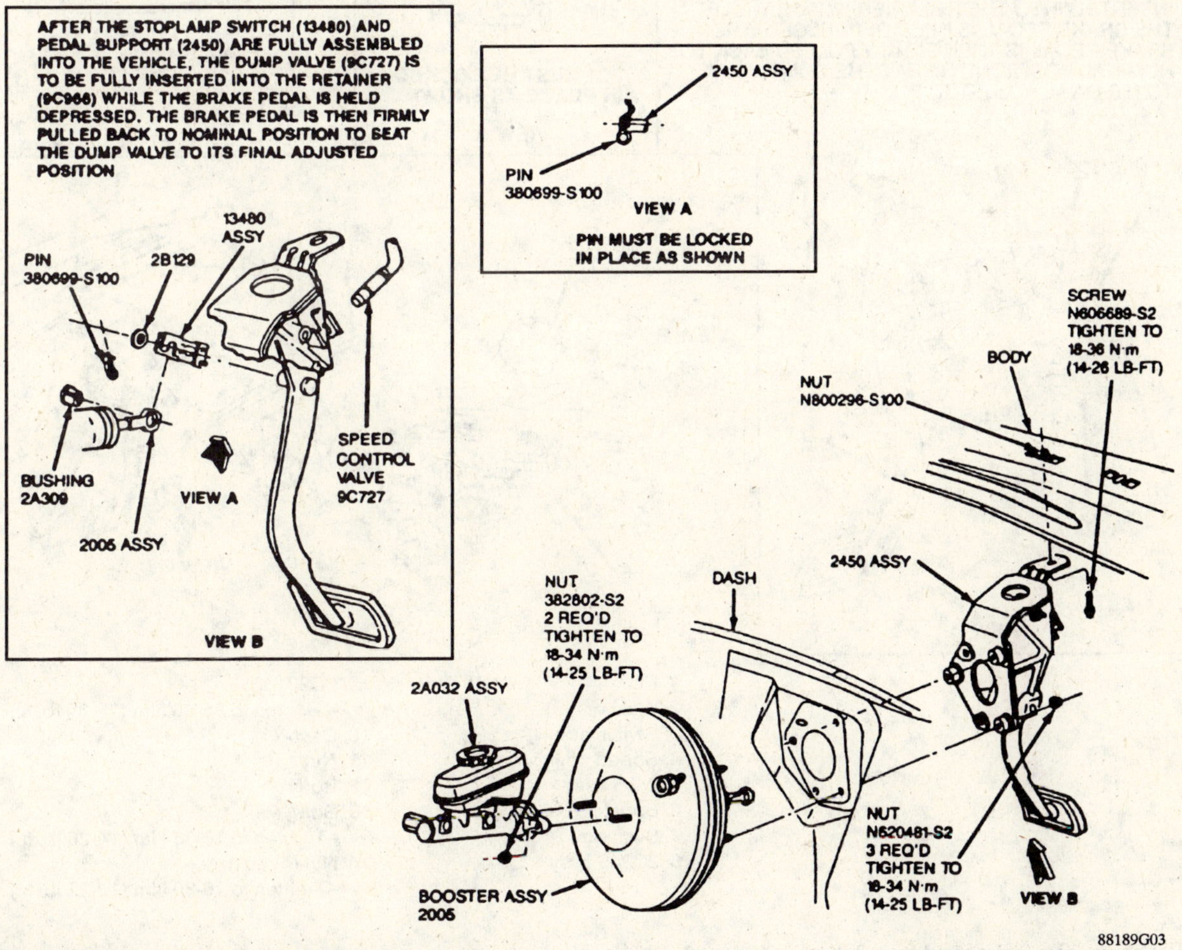

88189G03

Fig. 3 Brake pedal mounting — vehicles without ABS

9. Install the inner nylon washer, the master cylinder pushrod and the black stop lamp switch bushing on the brake pedal pin. Position the stop lamp switch so that it straddles the pushrod with the slot on the pedal pin and the switch outer frame hole just clearing the pin. Slide the switch upward onto the pin and pushrod. Slide the assembly inboard toward the brake pedal arm.

10. Install the outer nylon washer and the pushrod retainer. Lock the retainer securely.

11. Install and tighten the three pedal support retaining nuts to 12–22 ft.lbs. (16–30 Nm).

12. Connect the stop lamp switch wire to the switch.

13. Attach the clutch cable to the clutch pedal, if so equipped.

14. Connect the negative battery cable.

Vehicles With ABS

****CAUTION**

Before servicing any component which contains high pressure, it is mandatory that the pressure be discharged from the hydraulic system. To discharge system, turn the ignition switch OFF and pump the brake pedal a minimum of 20 times until an increase in pedal force can be felt.

1989–92 VEHICLES

➧ See Figure 4

1. Disconnect the negative battery cable.
2. Detach the stop lamp switch wire connector from the switch.
3. Remove the pushrod retainer and nylon washer. Slide the stop lamp switch outboard along the brake pedal pin just far enough for the outer hole of the switch frame to clear the pin.
4. Unscrew and remove the accumulator.
5. Loosen the four power brake booster nuts at the pedal support and slide the pushrod and inner nylon washer off the pedal pin.
6. Remove the locknut and then remove the pivot bolt, brake pedal, pivot spacer and bushings from the pedal support.
7. Remove the speed control adapter, if so equipped by unlatching the locking tab.

To install:

8. Apply a coating of SAE 10W–40 engine oil to the bushings. Locate the bushings and pivot spacer in the brake pedal hub.
9. Position the brake pedal assembly in the pedal support, install the pivot bolt, locknut and tighten to 10–20 ft. lbs. (13.5–27 Nm).

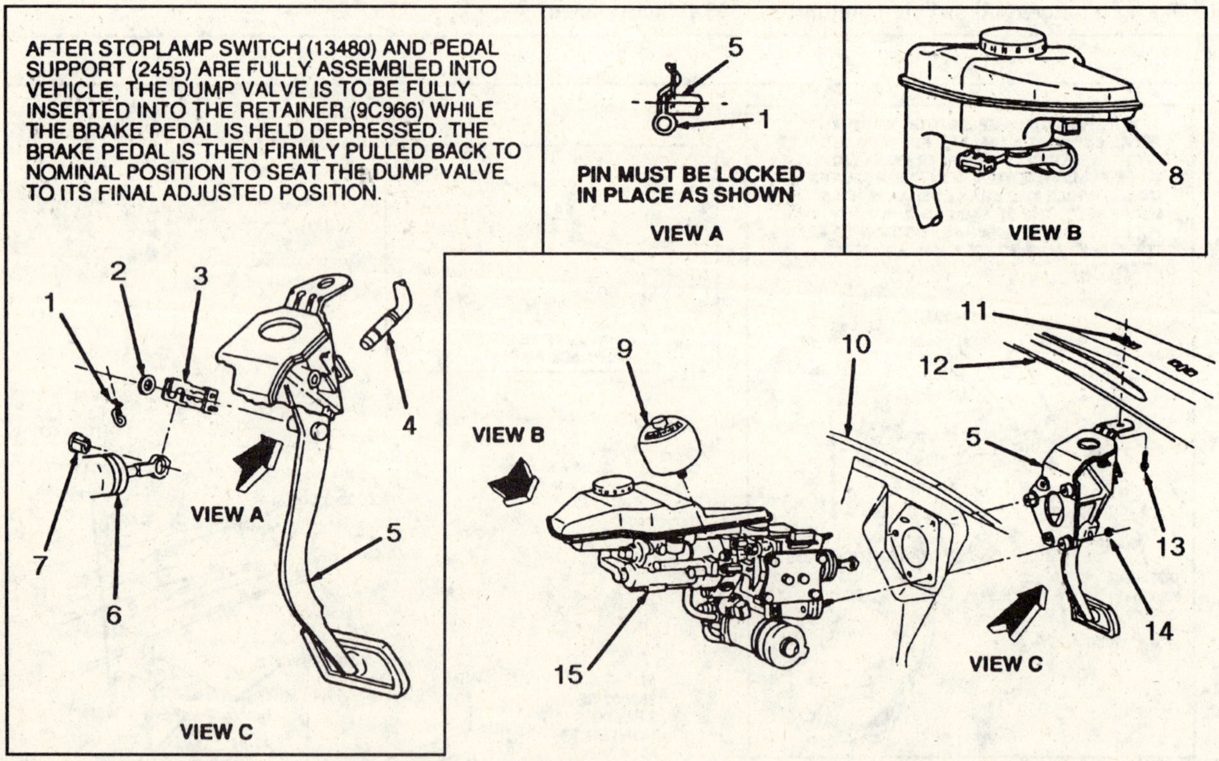

1. Pin
2. Washer
3. Switch assy
4. Speed control valve
5. 2455 assy
6. Booster assy
7. Bushing
8. 2C246 assy
9. 2C231
   - Tighten to 36-46 Nm (26-34 lb. ft.)
10. Dash
11. Nut
12. Body
13. Bolt
    - Tighten to 18-36 Nm (14-26 lb. ft.)
14. Nut (4 req'd)
    - Tighten to 16-30 Nm (12-22 lb. ft.)

88189G04

Fig. 4 Brake pedal removal and installation — 1989–92 vehicles

10. Install the inner nylon washer or speed control adapter, if so equipped, the master cylinder pushrod and the black stop lamp switch bushing on the brake pedal pin. Position the stop lamp switch so that it straddles the pushrod with the slot on the pedal pin and the switch outer frame hole just clearing the pin. Slide the switch upward onto the pin and pushrod. Slide the assembly inboard toward the brake pedal arm.

11. Install the outer nylon washer and the pushrod retainer. Lock the retainer securely.

12. Install and tighten the master cylinder or booster retaining nuts to 12–22 ft. lbs. (16–30 Nm).

13. Install the accumulator.

14. Attach the stop lamp switch wire to the switch.

15. Connect the negative battery cable.

1993–96 VEHICLES

➧ **See Figure 5**

1. Disconnect the negative battery cable.
2. Detach the stoplight switch connector from the switch.
3. Loosen the three pedal support retaining nuts at the dash panel.
4. Remove the pushrod retainer and brake master cylinder pushrod spacer.
5. Slide the stoplight switch outboard along the brake pedal pin just far enough for the outer hose of the switch frame to clear the pin.
6. Remove the stoplight switch by sliding it off the pin.
7. Remove the brake master cylinder pushrod bushing from the pushrod.
8. Remove the locknut from the pivot bolt. Pull the pivot bolt out, and remove the brake pedal.

To install:

9. Apply a coating of SAE 10W-40 engine oil to the bushings. Locate the bushings and pivot spacer in the brake pedal hub.

10. Position the brake pedal assembly in the pedal support bracket, and install the pivot bolt. Install the locknut and tighten the nut to 10–20 ft. lbs. (14–27 Nm). Make sure the brake pedal can swing freely while not being too loose side-to-side. If there is too much free play side-to-side, increase the locknut torque. The brake pedal must continue swing freely. If the brake pedal cannot swing freely, reduce the locknut torque without going below 10 ft. lbs. (14 Nm).

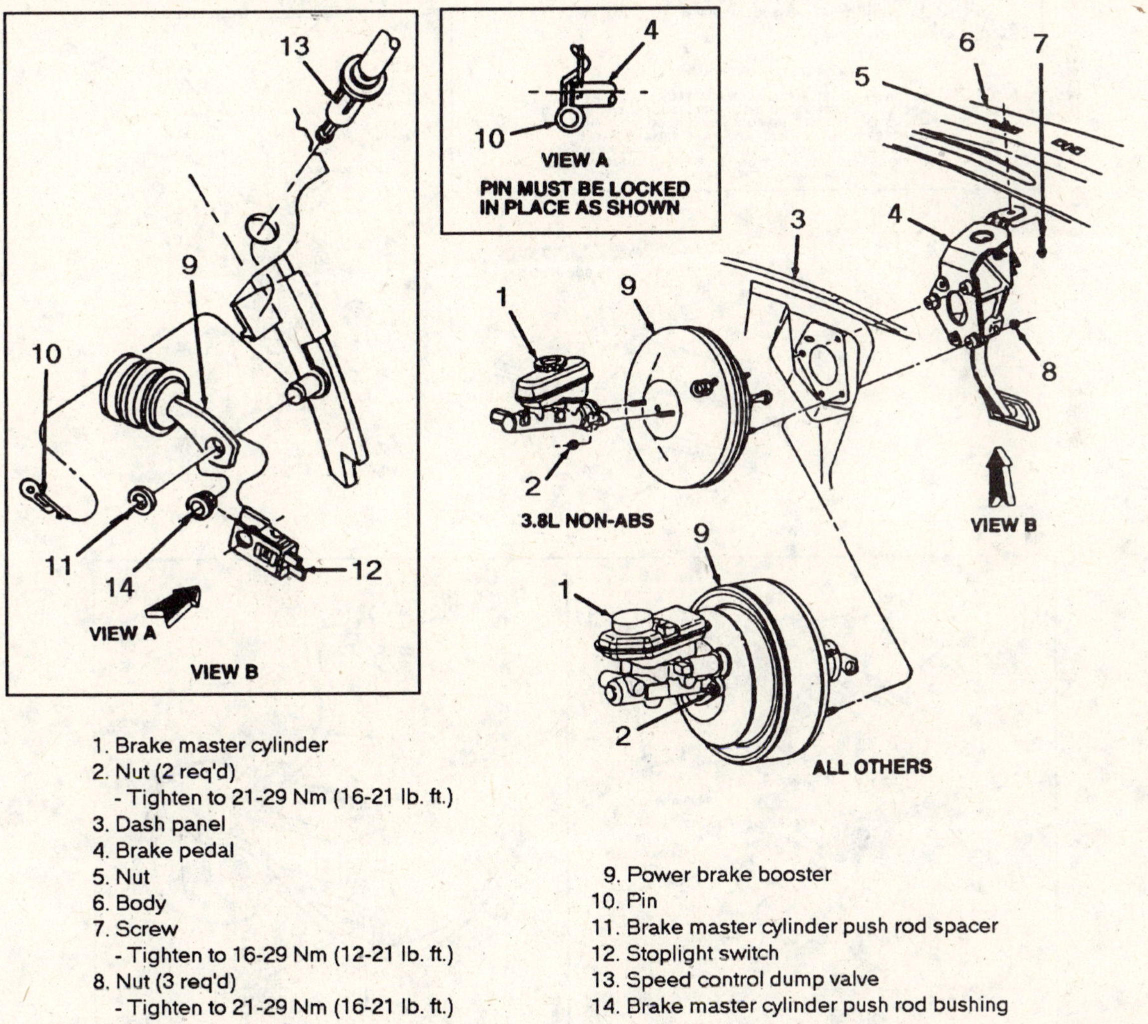

1. Brake master cylinder
2. Nut (2 req'd)
   - Tighten to 21-29 Nm (16-21 lb. ft.)
3. Dash panel
4. Brake pedal
5. Nut
6. Body
7. Screw
   - Tighten to 16-29 Nm (12-21 lb. ft.)
8. Nut (3 req'd)
   - Tighten to 21-29 Nm (16-21 lb. ft.)
9. Power brake booster
10. Pin
11. Brake master cylinder push rod spacer
12. Stoplight switch
13. Speed control dump valve
14. Brake master cylinder push rod bushing

88189G05

Fig. 5 Brake pedal mounting and related components — 1995 vehicle shown

11. Install the master cylinder pushrod, and the master cylinder pushrod bushing on the brake pedal pin. The large diameter portion of the pushrod bushing must not be between the pushrod and pedal arm.

12. Position the stoplight switch so it straddles the pushrod with the slot on the pedal pin and the switch outer frame holes just clearing the pin. Slide the stoplight switch onto the pin and pushrod. Slide the assembly toward the brake pedal arm. Install the brake master cylinder pushrod spacer and the pushrod retainer. Lock the retainer securely.

13. Tighten the three pedal support nuts to 16–21 ft. lbs. (21–29 Nm).

14. Attach the stoplight switch wire to the switch.

15. Connect the negative battery cable.

Master Cylinder

REMOVAL & INSTALLATION

Except Vehicles With ABS

See Figures 6, 7, 8 and 9

1. Disconnect the negative battery cable.
2. Apply the brake pedal several times to exhaust all the vacuum in the system.
3. Detach and cap the brake lines from the master cylinder.

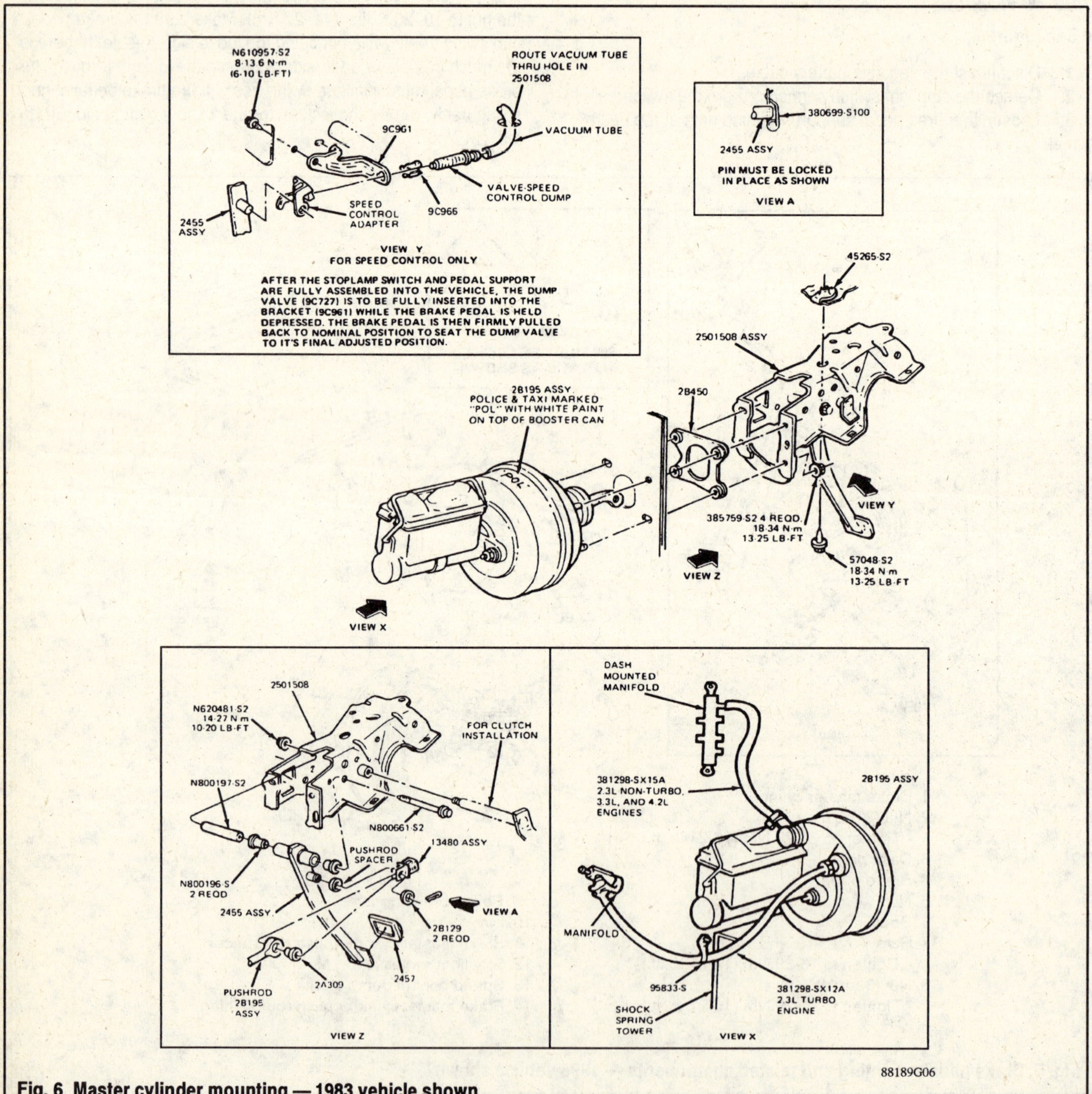

Fig. 6 Master cylinder mounting — 1983 vehicle shown

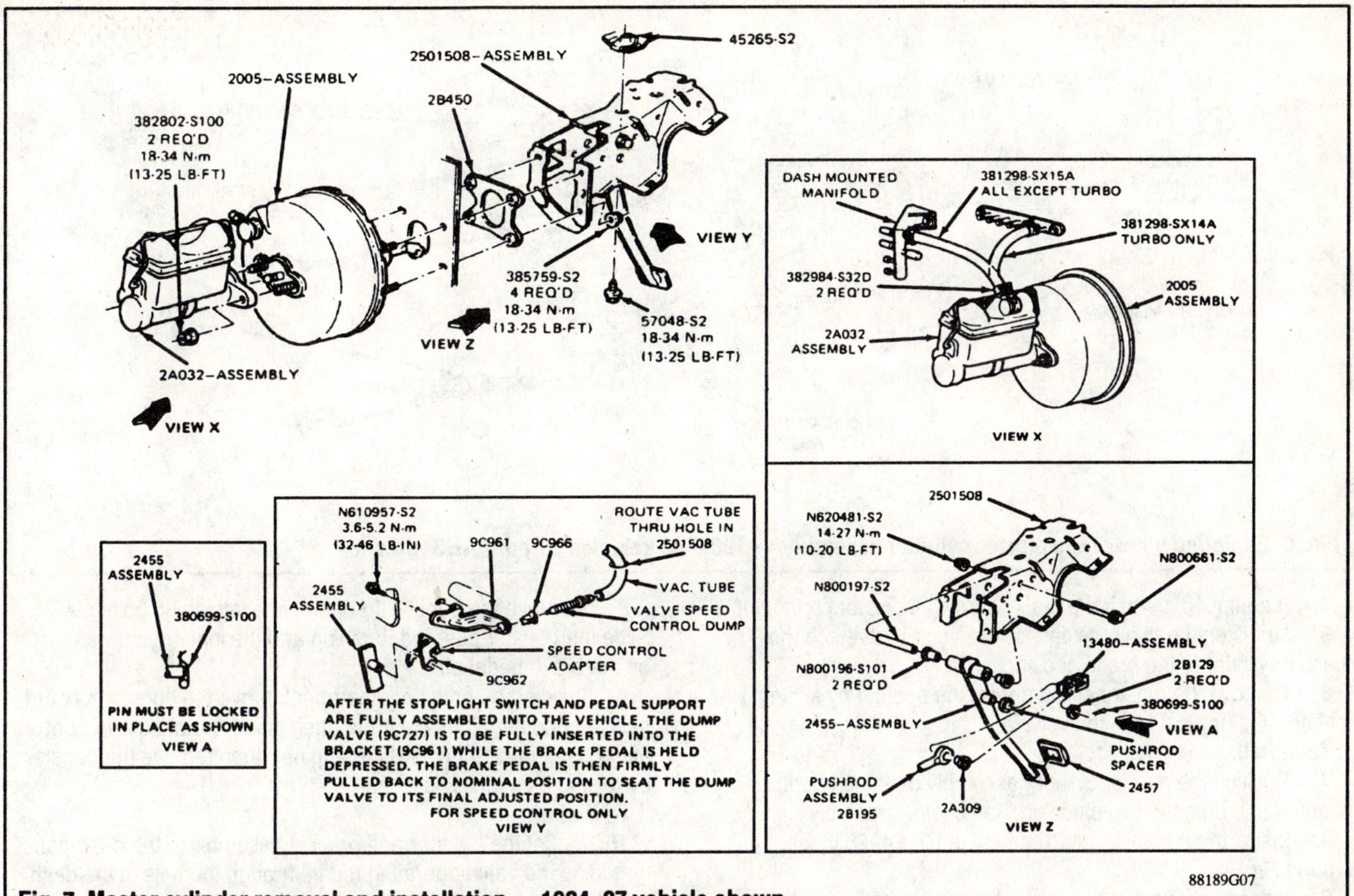

Fig. 7 Master cylinder removal and installation — 1984–87 vehicle shown

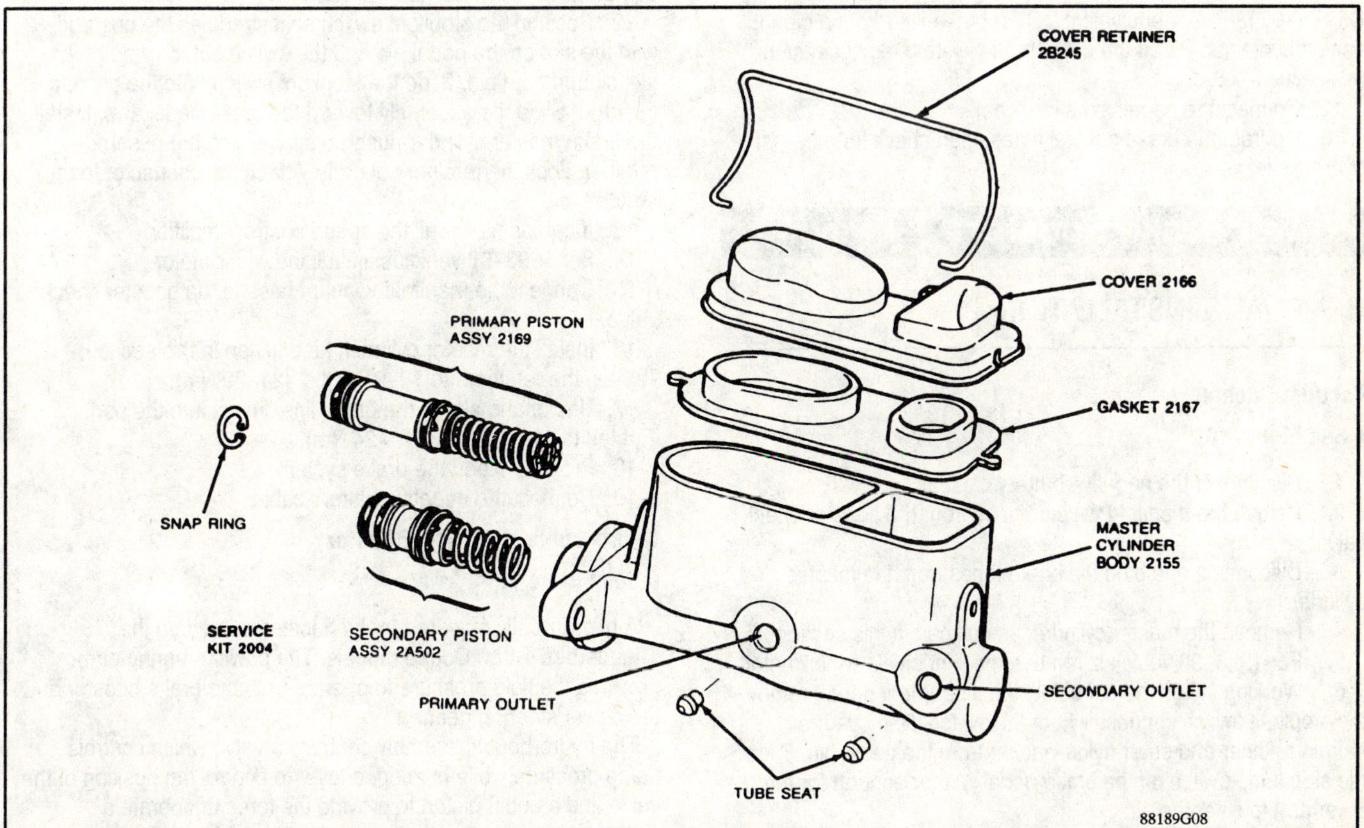

Fig. 8 Exploded view of the master cylinder assembly — 1983–86 vehicles

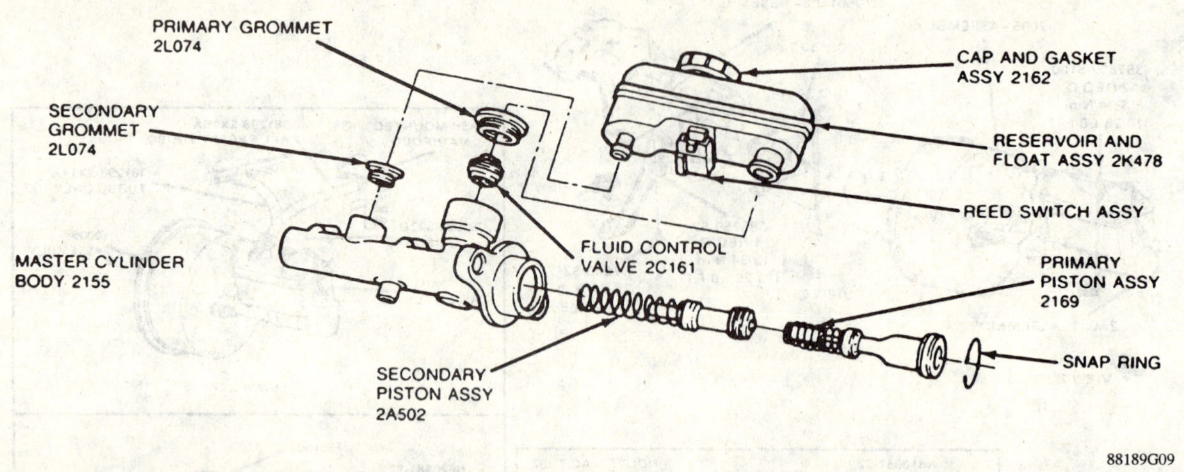

Fig. 9 Exploded view of the master cylinder assembly — 1987-96 vehicles without ABS shown

4. If equipped, detach the brake warning indicator connector.
5. Unfasten the two nuts and lockwashers that attach the master cylinder to the brake booster.
6. Remove the master cylinder from the booster by sliding it forward and upward from the vehicle.

To install:

7. Position the master cylinder assembly over the booster pushrod and onto the two studs on the booster assembly.
8. Install the retaining nuts, then tighten to 14-25 ft. lbs. (18-34 Nm).
9. Uncap and connect the brake lines to the master cylinder.
10. If equipped, connect the brake warning indicator.
11. Fill the master cylinder with Heavy Duty Brake Fluid C6AZ-19542-AA or equivalent DOT 3 brake fluid from a clean, sealed container. Bleed the entire brake system, as outlined in this section.
12. Connect the negative battery cable.
13. Operate the brake several times, then check for external hydraulic leaks.

Power Brake Booster

REMOVAL & INSTALLATION

Vacuum Booster

➧ **See Figure 10**

1. Disconnect the negative battery cable.
2. Detach the manifold vacuum hose from the booster check valve.
3. Disconnect and plug the brake tubes from the master cylinder.
4. Remove the master cylinder, as outlined in this section.
5. For 1993-96 vehicles, remove the windshield wiper motor.
6. Working inside the car below the instrument panel, remove the stoplight switch connector from the switch. Remove the hairpin retainer and outer nylon washer from the pedal pin. Slide the stop lamp switch off the brake pedal just far enough for the outer arm to clear the pin.
7. If equipped, remove the speed amplifier.
8. Remove the booster-to-dash panel attaching bolts/nuts. Slide the booster pushrod, bushing and the inner nylon washer off the brake pedal pin.
9. Inside the engine compartment, move the booster forward until the booster studs clear the dash panel. Rotate the front of the booster inward (toward the engine), then remove the booster by raising it up until it is clear.

To install:

10. Mount the booster and bracket assembly to the dash panel by sliding the valve operating rod in through the hole in the dash panel.
11. Install the booster-to-dash panel retaining nuts/bolts and tighten to 16-21 ft. lbs. (21-29 Nm).
12. Position the stoplight switch so it straddles the pushrod with the slot on the pedal pin and the switch outer frame holes just clearing the pin. Slide the stoplight switch onto the pin and pushrod. Slide the assembly toward the brake pedal arm. Install the brake master cylinder pushrod spacer and the pushrod retainer. Lock the retainer securely. Attach the connector to the switch.
13. If equipped, install the speed control amplifier.
14. For 1993-96 vehicles, install the wiper motor.
15. Connect the manifold vacuum hose to the booster check valve.
16. Install the master cylinder, as outlined in this section. Tighten the retainers to 16-21 ft. lbs. (21-29 Nm).
17. Uncap and attach the brake line fittings into the ports. Tighten to 11-17 ft. lbs. (14-24 Nm).
18. Properly bleed the brake system.
19. Connect the negative battery cable.

Hydro-Boost Hydraulic Booster

➧ **See Figure 11**

A hydraulically powered brake booster is used on the Thunderbird Turbo Coupe models. The power steering pump provides the fluid pressure to operate both the brake booster and the power steering gear.

The hydro-boost assembly contains a valve which controls pump pressure while braking, a lever to control the position of the valve and a boost piston to provide the force to operate a conventional master cylinder attached to the front of the booster.

The hydro-boost also has a reserve system, designed to store sufficient pressurized fluid to provide at least 2 brake applications in the event of insufficient fluid flow from the power steering pump. The brakes can also be applied unassisted if the reserve system is depleted.

Before removing the hydro-boost, discharge the accumulator by making several brake applications until a hard pedal is felt.

1. Disconnect the negative battery cable.
2. Working from inside the vehicle, below the instrument panel, disconnect the pushrod from the brake pedal. Disconnect the stoplight switch wires at the connector. Remove the hairpin retainer. Slide the stoplight switch off the brake pedal far enough for the switch outer hole to clear the pin. Remove the switch from the pin. Slide the pushrod, nylon washers and bushing off the brake pedal pin.
3. Open the hood and remove the nuts attaching the master cylinder to the hydro-boost. Remove the master cylinder. Secure it to one side without disturbing the hydraulic lines.
4. Disconnect the pressure, steering gear and return lines from the booster. Plug the lines to prevent the entry of dirt.
5. Remove the nuts attaching the hydro-boost. Remove the booster from the firewall, sliding the pushrod link out of the engine side of the firewall.

To install:

6. Install the hydro-boost on the firewall and install the attaching nuts.
7. Install the master cylinder on the booster.
8. Connect the pressure, steering gear and return lines to the booster.
9. Working below the instrument panel, install the nylon washer, booster pushrod and bushing on the brake pedal pin. Install the switch so that it straddles the pushrod with the switch slot on the pedal pin and the switch outer hole just clearing the pin. Slide the switch completely onto the pin and install the nylon washer. Attach these parts with the hairpin retainer. Connect the stoplight switch wires and install the wires in the retaining clip.
10. Connect the negative battery cable.
11. Remove the coil wire so that the engine will not start. Fill the power steering pump and engage the starter. Apply the brakes with a pumping action. Do not turn the steering wheel until air has been bled from the booster.
12. Check the fluid level and add as required. Start the engine and apply the brakes, checking for leaks. Cycle the steering wheel.
13. If a whine type noise is heard, suspect fluid aeration. Refer to the Power Steering bleeding procedure in Section 8.

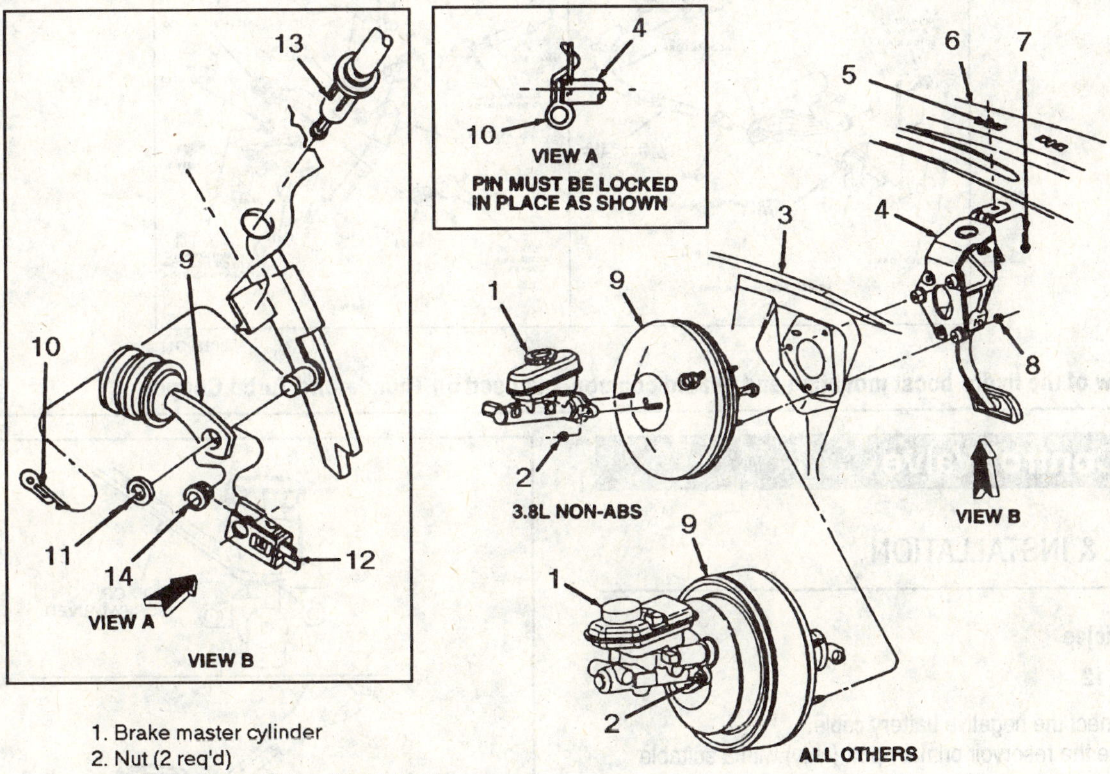

1. Brake master cylinder
2. Nut (2 req'd)
   - Tighten to 21-29 Nm (16-21 lb. ft.)
3. Dash panel
4. Brake pedal
5. Nut
6. Body
7. Screw
   - Tighten to 16-29 Nm (12-21 lb. ft.)
8. Nut (3 req'd)
   - Tighten to 21-29 Nm (16-21 lb. ft.)
9. Power brake booster
10. Pin
11. Brake master cylinder push rod spacer
12. Stoplight switch
13. Speed control dump valve
14. Brake master cylinder push rod bushing

88189G10

Fig. 10 Power brake booster removal — 1995 vehicle shown

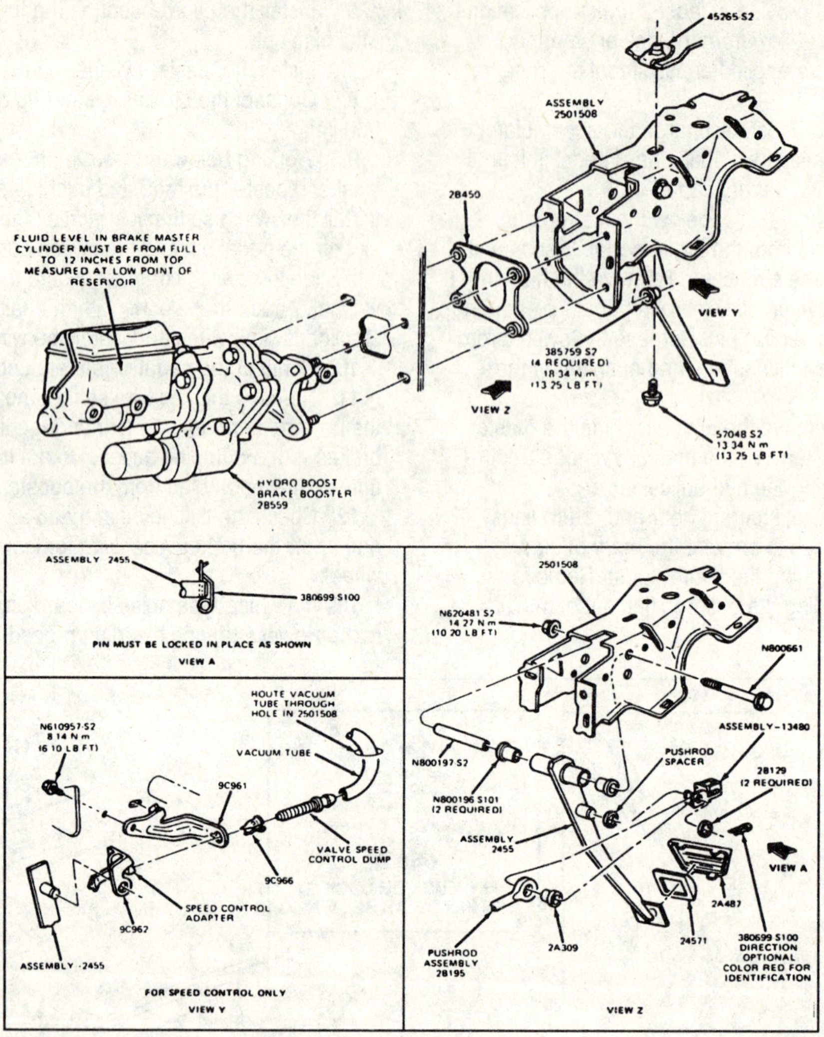

88189G11

Fig. 11 View of the hydro-boost mounting and related components used on Thunderbird Turbo Coupes

Fluid Control Valve

REMOVAL & INSTALLATION

1983–88 Vehicles

See Figure 12

1. Disconnect the negative battery cable.
2. Remove the reservoir primary port (only) with a suitable prytool.
3. Rotate the reservoir out of the way and remove the sealing grommet from the casting.
4. With a 12mm socket, remove the fluid control valve. Inspect for contamination under the seal or in the center orifice.

The fluid control valve is serviced as an assembly only. Do not attempt to service this unit.

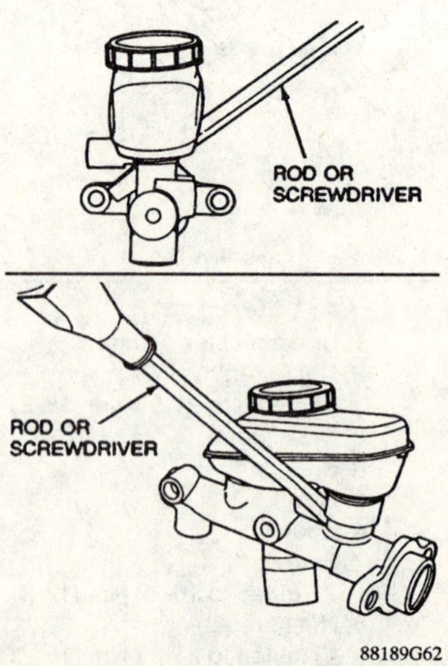

88189G62

Fig. 12 Use a suitable prytool to remove the reservoir primary port

To install:

****CAUTION**

Do NOT operate the brakes until the reservoir is installed and filled, or the primary brake system will have to be bled.

5. Install a new fluid control valve. Tighten to 97-115 inch lbs. (11-13 Nm).
6. Lubricate a new grommet with clean brake fluid and install it in the primary port.
7. Install the reservoir in the new grommet.
8. Refill the reservoir. Connect the negative battery cable.

Brake Pressure Control Valve

REMOVAL & INSTALLATION

1983-88 Vehicles

1. Disconnect all brake tubes from the brake control valve assembly.
2. Remove the nut that retains the valve on the fender apron. Remove the assembly from the vehicle.

➥ The brake pressure control valve is serviced as an assembly only.

To install:

3. Position the brake control valve assembly at the fender apron holes. Install the nut for the fender apron mounting. Tighten to 7-11 ft. lbs. (10-14 Nm).
4. Attach all brake tubes to the control valve assembly. Tighten the tube nut to 10-18 ft. lbs. (14-24 Nm).
5. Properly bleed the brake system, as outlined in this section.

1989-92 Vehicles

1. Disconnect the primary or secondary brake tube as necessary.
2. Loosen and remove the pressure control valve from the master cylinder housing.

To install:

3. Install the pressure control valve in the master cylinder housing port and tighten securely.
4. Attach the brake tube(s) and tighten to 10-18 ft. lbs. (14-24 Nm).
5. Properly fill and bleed the brake system, as outlined in this section.

1993-96 Vehicles

WITHOUT ABS

1. Disconnect the brake tube from the brake pressure control valve.
2. Loosen and remove the pressure control valve from the master cylinder housing.

To install:

3. Install the pressure control valve in the master cylinder housing port and tighten securely.
4. Attach the brake tube to the valve, then tighten to 10-18 ft. lbs. (14-24 Nm).
5. Properly fill and bleed the brake system, as outlined in this section.

WITH ABS

1. Disconnect the brake inlet tubes and the rear tubes from the brake pressure control valve.
2. Remove the screw that retains the brake pressure control valve assembly to the frame, then remove the assembly from the vehicle.

To install:

3. Position the brake pressure control valve assembly on the inner floor side member. Install one retaining screw for the frame mounting.
4. Connect the rear brake outlet tubes to the brake pressure control valve. Tighten the tube nut to 10-18 ft. lbs. (14-24 Nm).
5. Attach the inlet tubes to the brake pressure control valve. Tighten the tube nut to 10-18 ft. lbs. (14-24 Nm).
6. Properly fill and bleed the brake system, as outlined in this section.

Pressure Differential Warning Valve

A pressure differential warning valve is incorporated in the hydraulic system. The signal from this valve consists of a warning light on the dashboard activated by a differential pressure switch located below the master cylinder. The signal indicates a hydraulic pressure differential between the front and rear brakes of 80-150 psi, and should warn the driver that a hydraulic failure has occurred.

After repairing and bleeding any part of the hydraulic system the warning light may remain on due to the pressure differential valve remaining in the off-center position. To centralize the valve a pressure difference must be created in the opposite branch of the hydraulic system that was repaired or bled last.

➥ Front wheel balancing of cars equipped with disc brakes may also cause a pressure differential in the front branch of the system.

VALVE CENTERING PROCEDURE

1. Turn the ignition to either the **ACC** or **ON** position.
2. Check the fluid level in the master cylinder reservoirs. Fill to within $^1/_4$ in. (6mm) of the top if necessary.
3. Depress the brake pedal firmly. The valve will centralize itself causing the brake warning light to go out.
4. Turn the ignition off.
5. Prior to driving the vehicle, check the operation of the brakes and obtain a firm pedal.

Proportioning Valve

On vehicles equipped with front disc and rear drum brakes, a proportioning valve is an important part of the system. On cars through 1988, it is installed in the hydraulic line to the rear brakes. On 1989-96 cars, it is in the control valve assembly. Its function is to maintain the correct proportion between line pressures to the front and rear brakes. No attempt at adjustment of this valve should be made, as adjustment is preset and tampering will result in uneven braking action.

To assure correct installation when replacing the valve, the outlet to the rear brakes is stamped with the letter **R**.

Brake Hoses and Pipes

REMOVAL & INSTALLATION

The hydraulic brake lines and brake linings are to be inspected at the recommended intervals in the maintenance schedule. Follow the steel tubing from the master cylinder to the flexible hose fitting at each wheel. If a section of the tubing is found to be damaged, replace the entire section with tubing of the same type (steel, not copper), size, shape, and length. When installing a new section of brake tubing, flush clean brake fluid or denatured alcohol through to remove any dirt or foreign material from the line. Be sure to flare both ends to provide sound, leak-proof connections. When bending the tubing to fit the underbody contours, be careful not to kink or crack the line. Torque all hydraulic connections to 10–15 ft. lbs. (13.5-20 Nm).

Flexible Hoses

Check the flexible brake hoses that connect the steel tubing to each wheel cylinder. Replace a hose if it shows any signs of softening, cracking, or other damage. When installing a new front brake hose, position the hose to avoid contact with other chassis parts. Place a new copper gasket over the hose fitting and thread the hose assembly into the front wheel cylinder. A new rear brake hose must be positioned clear of the exhaust pipe or shock absorber. Thread the hose into the rear brake tube connector. When installing either a new front or rear brake hose, engage the opposite end of the hose to the bracket on the frame. Install the horseshoe type retaining clip and connect the tube to the hose with the tube fitting nut.

Always bleed the system after hose or line replacement. Before bleeding, make sure that the master cylinder is topped up with high temperature, extra heavy duty fluid of at least SAE 70R3 quality.

Steel Pipes

See Figure 13

When replacing steel brake pipes, always use the double-walled steel piping which is designed to withstand high pressure and resist corrosion. Also, it is important to make sure that the pipe is of the same size to assure both a proper fit and proper brake operation.

****CAUTION**

Never use copper tubing. It is subject to fatigue, cracking, and/or corrosion, which will result in brake line failure.

Whenever possible, try to work with brake lines that are already cut to the length needed. These lines are available at most auto parts stores and have machine made flares, the quality of which is hard to duplicate with most of the available inexpensive flaring kits.

When the brakes are applied, there is a great deal of pressure developed in the hydraulic system. An improperly formed flare can leak with a resultant loss of stopping power. If you have never formed a double-flare, take time to familiarize yourself with the flaring kit; practice forming double-flares on scrap tubing until you are satisfied with the results.

1. Obtain the recommended bulk $^{3}/_{16}$ in. double wall steel brake tubing and the correct standard tube nuts for $^{3}/_{16}$ in. tubing.

The outside diameter of the line is used to specify size.

2. Using a tubing cutter, cut the tubing to the proper length. Clean burrs after cutting. The correct length may be determined by measuring the line to be replaced using a length of cord, then adding $^{1}/_{8}$ in. (1.2mm) for each flare.

Make sure the fittings are installed and oriented correctly before flaring both ends of the line.

3. Place a tube nut onto the tube in the correct direction, then flare the tube with an SAE inverted flare or a metric ISO flare using Brake Line Flaring Tool D81L-2269-A, or equivalent. Carefully follow the instructions included with the tool. Repeat on the opposite end of the tube.
4. Bend the replacement tube to match the removed tube using a tubing bender. When the replacement brake tube is installed, maintain adequate clearance to metal edges and moving or vibrating parts.
5. Clean the brake tube by flushing with clean brake fluid. Install the brake tube, then tighten the tube nuts to specification using an inch lb. torque wrench.
6. Bleed the brake system.

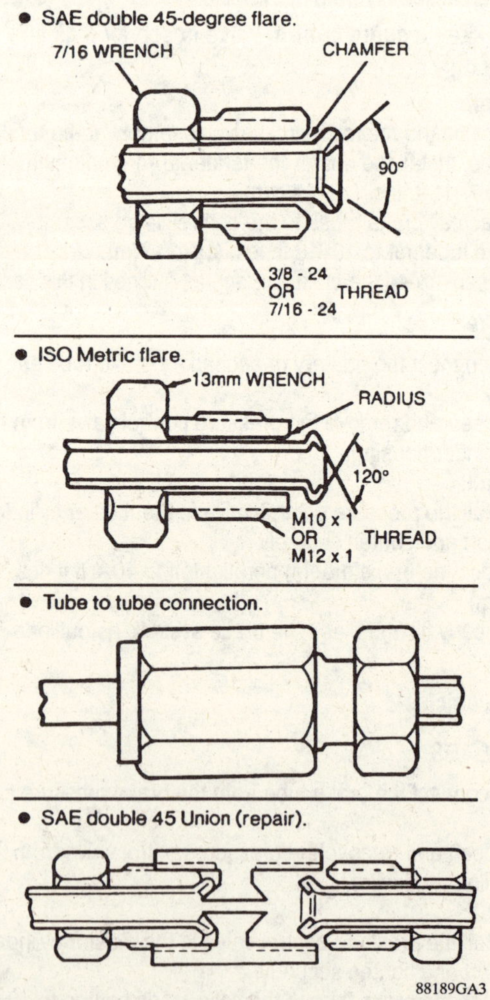

Fig. 13 Commonly used types of brake line flared connections

Bleeding the Hydraulic System

➥ If equipped with ABS, see the appropriate section for ABS System Bleeding.

When any part of the hydraulic system has been disconnected for service or replacement, air may enter the system causing a spongy pedal action. Bleed the hydraulic system, after it has been properly connected to ensure that all air has been expelled.

➥ Since the front and rear hydraulic systems are independent of each other, if it is known that only one system has air in it, only that system has to be bled.

PROCEDURE

Manual Bleeding

➧ **See Figure 14**

1. Clean all dirt from the master cylinder filler cap.
2. If the master cylinder is known or suspected to have air in the bore, it must be bled BEFORE any of the wheel cylinders or calipers. To bleed the master cylinder, loosen the upper secondary left front outlet fitting approximately $^3/_4$ of a turn.
3. Have an assistant depress the brake pedal slowly through its full travel. Close the outlet fitting and let the pedal return slowly to the fully released position. Wait 5 seconds and then repeat the operation until all air bubbles disappear.
4. Loosen the upper primary right front outlet fitting about $^3/_4$ of a turn. Repeat Step 3 with the right front outlet fitting.
5. To continue to bleed the brake system, remove the rubber dust cap from the wheel cylinder bleeder fitting or caliper fitting at the right rear side of the vehicle. Check to make sure the wheel cylinder bleeder screw is positioned at the upper half of the front caliper. If not, the caliper is located on the wrong side. Place a suitable box wrench on the bleeder fitting, then attach a rubber drain tube to the fitting. The end of the tube should fit snugly around the bleeder fitting.
6. Submerge the free end of the tube in a container partially filled with clean brake fluid, then loosen the fitting about $^3/_4$ of a turn.

88189P18

Fig. 14 Submerge the free end of the brake tube in a container partly filled with clean brake fluid, then loosen the fitting about $^3/_4$ of a turn

7. Have an assistant push the brake pedal down slowly through its full travel. Close the bleeder fitting and allow the pedal to slowly return to its full release position. Wait 5 seconds, then repeat the procedure until no bubbles appear at the submerged end of the bleeder tube.
8. When the fluid is completely free of air bubbles, close the bleeder fitting, then remove the bleeder tube. Install the rubber dust cap on the bleeder fitting.
9. Repeat this procedure in the following sequence: left front, left rear and right front. Refill the master cylinder reservoir after each wheel cylinder or caliper has been bled, then install the master cylinder cover and gasket. When brake bleeding is completed, the fluid level should be filled to the maximum level indicated on the reservoir using clean brake fluid from a sealed container.
10. Always make sure the disc brake pistons are returned to their normal positions by depressing the brake pedal several times until normal pedal travel is established. If the pedal feels spongy, repeat the bleeding procedure.

Pressure Bleeding

For pressure bleeding, use Rotunda Brake Bleeder 104-00064 or equivalent. Always bleed the longest line first. The bleeder tank should contain enough new brake fluid to complete the braking operation. Use only DOT 3 brake fluid from a new, sealed container. Never reuse brake fluid that has been drained from the hydraulic system. The pressure bleeder tank should be charged with 10-30 psi (69-206 kPa) of air pressure.

1. Clean all dirt from the reservoir filler cap and surrounding area.

➥ NEVER exceed 50 psi (344 kPa) of air pressure to prevent system damage.

2. Remove the master cylinder filler cap, then fill the reservoir with fluid to the MAX fill line. Following the manufacturer's instructions, install the pressure bleeder adapter tool to the master cylinder reservoir, then attach the bleeder tank hose to the fitting on the adapter.
3. If all wheel cylinders are to be bled, start with the right-hand rear brake wheel cylinder. Remove the dust cap from the right rear caliper bleeder fitting. Attach a rubber drain tube to the fitting, making sure the tube fits snugly.
4. Open the valve on the bleeder tank to admit pressurized brake fluid to the master cylinder reservoir.
5. Submerge the free end of the tube in a container partly filled with clean brake fluid, then loosen the wheel cylinder bleeder screw.
6. When the air bubbles cease to appear in the fluid at the submerged end of the bleeder tube, close the wheel cylinder bleeder screw, then remove the tube. Tighten to 7.5-8.9 ft. lbs. (10-12 Nm). Replace the rubber dust cap on the wheel cylinder bleeder screw.
7. Repeat Steps 3-6 at the left front disc brake caliper.
8. Next, repeat Steps 4, 5 and 6 at the left rear wheel cylinder or caliper, and then the right front disc brake caliper.
9. When the bleeding procedure is finished, close the bleeder tank valve, then remove the hose from the adapter fitting.
10. After disc brake service, make sure the disc brake pistons are returned to their normal positions and that the brake shoe and lining assemblies are properly seated. This is accomplished by depressing the brake pedal a few times until normal pedal travel is established.
11. Remove the pressure bleeder adapter tool from the master cylinder. Fill the master cylinder reservoir to the proper level using clean brake fluid from a sealed container.

FRONT DISC BRAKES

Brake Pads

**CAUTION

Some brake shoes contain asbestos, which has been determined to be a cancer causing agent. Never clean the brake surfaces with compressed air! Avoid inhaling any dust from any brake surface! When cleaning brake surfaces, use a commercially available brake cleaning fluid.

REMOVAL & INSTALLATION

1983–88 Vehicles

See Figures 15 and 16

1. Disconnect the negative battery cable.
2. Remove the master cylinder cap. Remove brake fluid until the larger of the two reservoirs is half full. Discard this fluid.
3. Raise and safely support the vehicle.
4. Remove the wheel and tire assembly. Be careful to avoid damage to or interference with the caliper splash shield or bleeder screw fitting.
5. Lift the caliper assembly from the integral spindle/anchor plate and rotor. Remove the outer shoe from the caliper assembly.
6. Remove the inner shoe and lining assembly. This could require a force as high as 20–30 lbs. (90–135 N) Inspect both rotor braking surfaces. Minor scoring or building of lining material does not require machining or replacement of the rotor.

Never let the caliper hang from the brake hose.

7. Suspend the caliper inside the fender housing with a wire hooked through the outer leg hole of the caliper. Be careful not to damage the caliper or stretch the brake hose.
8. Use a 4 in. (102mm) C-clamp and a block of wood $2^3/_4$ in. x 1 in. and approximately $^3/_4$ in. thick (70mm x 25mm x 19mm) to seat the caliper hydraulic piston in its bore. This must be done to provide clearance for the caliper assembly to fit over the rotor when installed. Remove the C-clamp from the caliper (the caliper piston will remain seated in its bore).

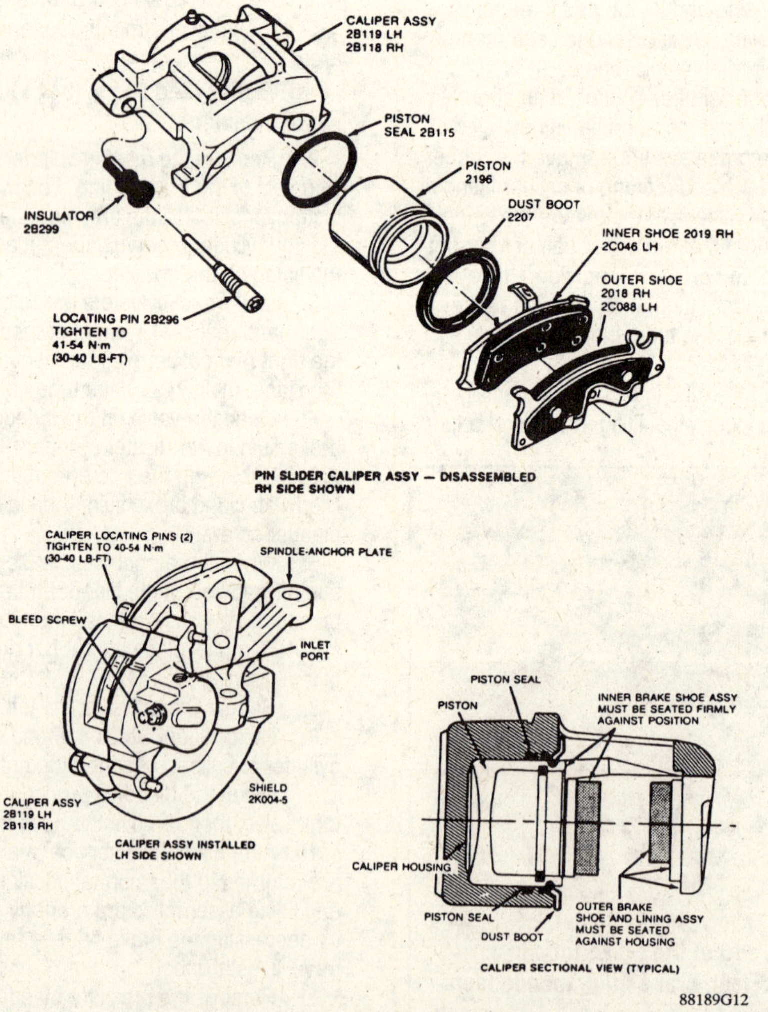

Fig. 15 Front disc brake components for 1983–88 vehicles, except 1986–88 2.3L Thunderbird Turbo Coupes

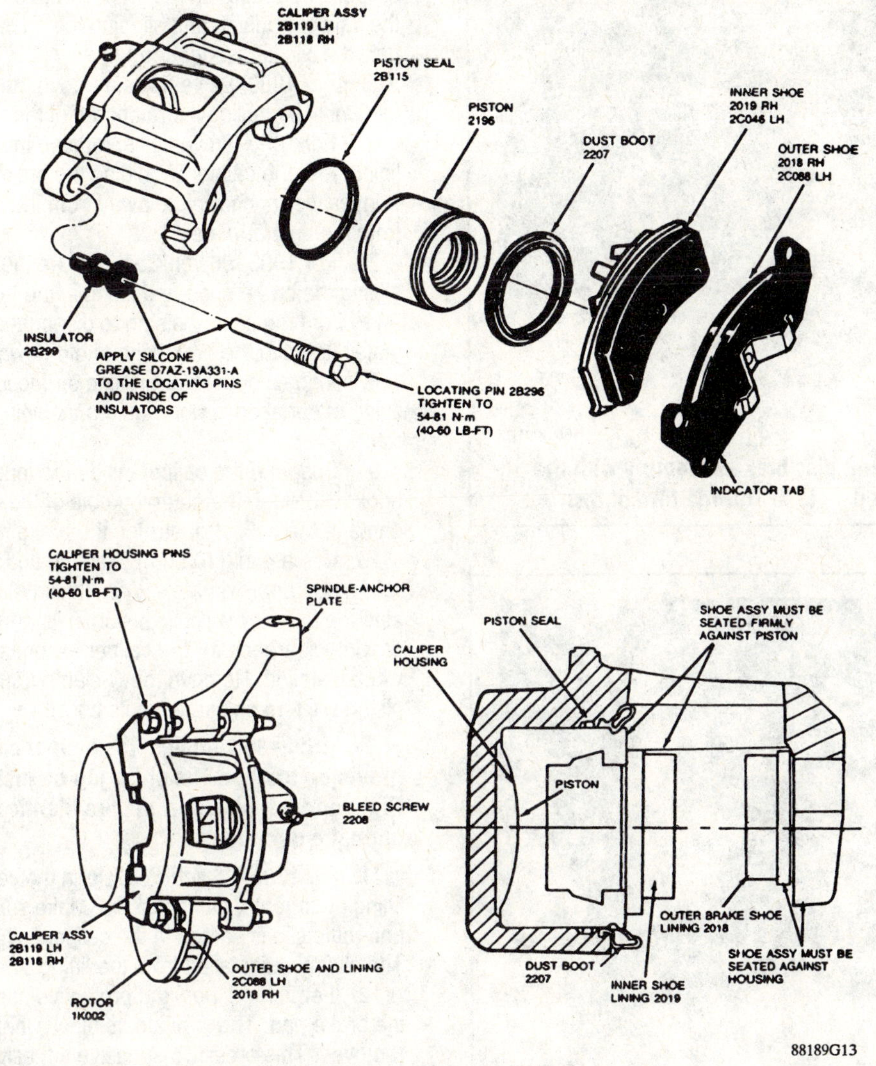

Fig. 16 Front disc brake components for 1986–88 Thunderbird Turbo Coupes

To install:

9. Install the inner shoe and lining assembly. All vehicles, have a separate anti-rattle clip and insulator that must be installed to the inner shoe and lining prior to their assembly to the caliper. The inner shoes are marked LH or RH and must be installed in the proper caliper. Also, care should be taken not to bend the anti-rattle clips too far in the piston or distortion and rattles can result.

10. Install the correct outer brake shoe and lining assembly (RH/LH), making sure that the clip and/or buttons located on the shoe are properly seated. The outer shoe can be identified as right hand or left hand by the war indicator which must always be installed toward the front of the vehicle or by a LH or RH mark.

****WARNING**

Make certain that the two round torque buttons on all vehicles, are seated solidly in the two holes of the outer caliper leg and that the shoe is held tightly against the housing by the spring clip. If the buttons are not seated, a temporary loss of brakes may occur!

11. Install the caliper, as outlined later in this section.

12. Install the wheel and tire assembly; tighten the lug nuts to 80–105 ft. lbs. (108–142 Nm).

13. Carefully lower the vehicle, then connect the negative battery cable.

14. Pump the brake pedal prior to moving the vehicle to position the brake linings.

15. Road test the vehicle.

1989–96 Vehicles

➧ See Figures 17, 18, 19, 20 and 21

1. Remove the master cylinder cap. Remove brake fluid until the reservoir is half full. Discard this fluid.

2. Raise and safely support the vehicle. Remove the wheels. Be careful to avoid damage to, or interference with, the caliper splash shield or bleeder screw fitting.

➥ It is not necessary to disconnect the hydraulic fluid line from the caliper to remove the brake pads.

3. Remove the caliper, as outlined later in this section, but do not disconnect the fluid line.

88189P01

Fig. 17 View of the front disc brake assembly with the wheel and tire removed — 1990 Thunderbird shown

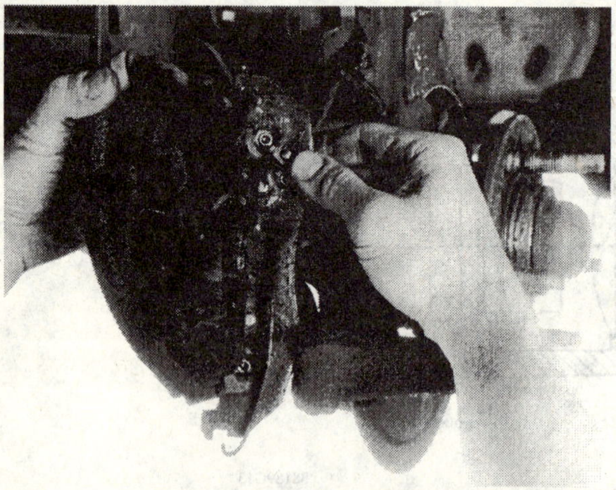

88189P02

Fig. 18 Remove the outboard brake pad, then . . .

88189P03

Fig. 19 . . . remove the inboard pad from the caliper — 1990 Thunderbird with the rotor already removed

4. For 1989–92 vehicles, remove the outer shoe from the caliper by pushing on the shoe to move the locating buttons from the caliper housing and slipping the shoe down the caliper leg until the clip is disengaged.
5. For 1989–92 vehicles, remove the inner shoe and lining assembly by pulling it straight out of the piston.
6. For 1993–96 vehicles, remove the outer brake shoe and lining from the caliper by sliding the brake shoe and lining in the front caliper anchor plate away from the outer leg to disengage it from the anchor plate.
7. For 1993–96 vehicles, remove the inner shoe and lining, sliding the brake shoe and lining in the front caliper anchor plate away from the caliper piston to disengage it from the anchor plate. Remove the brake shoe hold-down spring.
8. Inspect both rotor braking surfaces. Minor scoring of the lining material does not require machining or replacement of the rotor.
9. Suspend the caliper inside the fender housing with a wire hooked through the outer leg hole of the caliper. Be careful not to damage the caliper or stretch the brake hose.
10. Use a 4 in. (102mm) C-clamp and a block of wood $2^3/_4$ in. x 1 in. and approximately $^3/_4$ in. thick (70mm x 25mm x 19mm) to seat the caliper hydraulic piston in its bore. This must be done to provide clearance for the caliper assembly to fit over the rotor when installed. Remove the C-clamp from the caliper (the caliper piston will remain seated in its bore).

➥ For 1993–96 vehicles, the caliper casting has the provision to allow the spring to be installed only one way. Right and left side springs are identical but installed in opposite directions.

11. For 1993–96 vehicles, clean the caliper legs and shoe and lining abutments, as necessary. Make sure the brake pad anti-rattle clip is seated in the caliper lining inspection opening. The clip must installed from the lining side.
12. If equipped, peel the protective paper from the insulator on the brake pad. The insulator is black when the paper has been removed. This pressure-sensitive adhesive insulator functions to reduce noise. Care should be taken to avoid contamination on the adhesive surface before installing the pad in the caliper.
13. For vehicles through 1992, place the inner shoe in the caliper. Take care to avoid bending the shoe clips during installation in the piston. If the clips are bent, rattles will occur.

✱✱CAUTION

Damage to the boot and seal will occur if the 3-fingered clip is not visually verified to be resting on the inside rim of the piston prior to snapping it into place.

14. For vehicles through 1992, install the outer shoe, making sure that the clips are properly engaged.
15. For 1993–96 vehicles, engage the brake shoe and lining in the caliper anchor plate by first engaging the side opposite the caliper anti-rattle clip. Press the other end of the brake shoe and lining assembly to compress the anti-rattle clip and engage the brake shoe and lining in the anchor. Install the inner and outer shoe and linings (pads) in this manner.
16. Install the caliper, as outlined later in this section.
17. Install the wheel and tire assembly. Hand-tighten the lug nuts.
18. Carefully lower the vehicle, then tighten the lug nuts to 80–105 ft. lbs. (108–142 Nm).

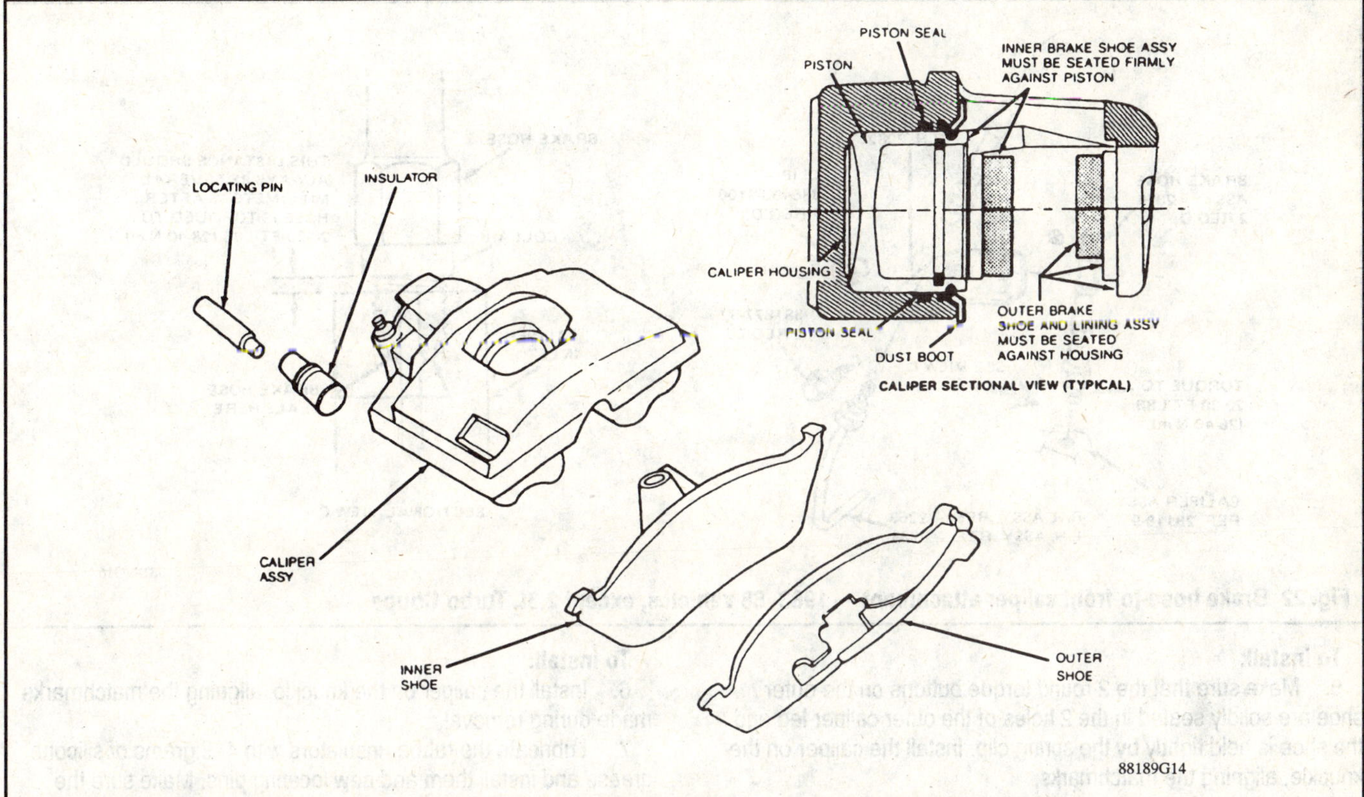

Fig. 20 View of the caliper and the brake shoe and lining assemblies — 1989–92 vehicles

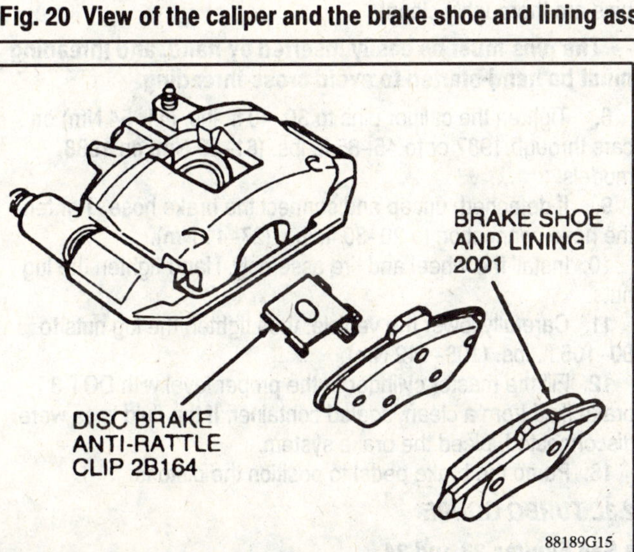

Fig. 21 Some vehicles are equipped with a disc brake anti-rattle clip — 1995 vehicle shown

19. Refill the master cylinder to the proper level with DOT 3 brake fluid from a fresh, sealed container.
20. Pump the brake pedal to seat the pads and position the piston.

INSPECTION

1. Raise the vehicle until the wheel and tire clear the floor. Place safety stands under the vehicle.
2. Remove the wheel cover, if equipped. Remove the wheel and tire from the hub and disc.
3. Visually inspect the shoe and lining assemblies. If the lining material has worn to a thickness of 0.030 in. (0.762mm) or less, or if the lining is contaminated with brake fluid, replace all pad assemblies on both front wheels. Make all thickness measurements across the thinnest section of the pad assembly. A slight taper on a used lining should be considered normal.
4. The caliper should be visually checked. If excess leakage is evident, the caliper should be replaced.
5. Install the wheel and hub assembly.

Brake Caliper

REMOVAL & INSTALLATION

1983–84 Vehicles

See Figure 22

1. Raise and safely support the front end on jackstands.
2. Remove the wheel and tire assembly.
3. Matchmark the caliper and knuckle for installation reference.

If the caliper is being removed for any purpose other than replacement or rebuilding, don't disconnect the brake line. Just suspend the caliper out of the way.

4. If the caliper is being replaced or rebuilt, disconnect the brake hose from the caliper and plug or cap the hose end to prevent fluid loss and contamination.
5. Remove the caliper locating pins, then lift the caliper off the rotor.

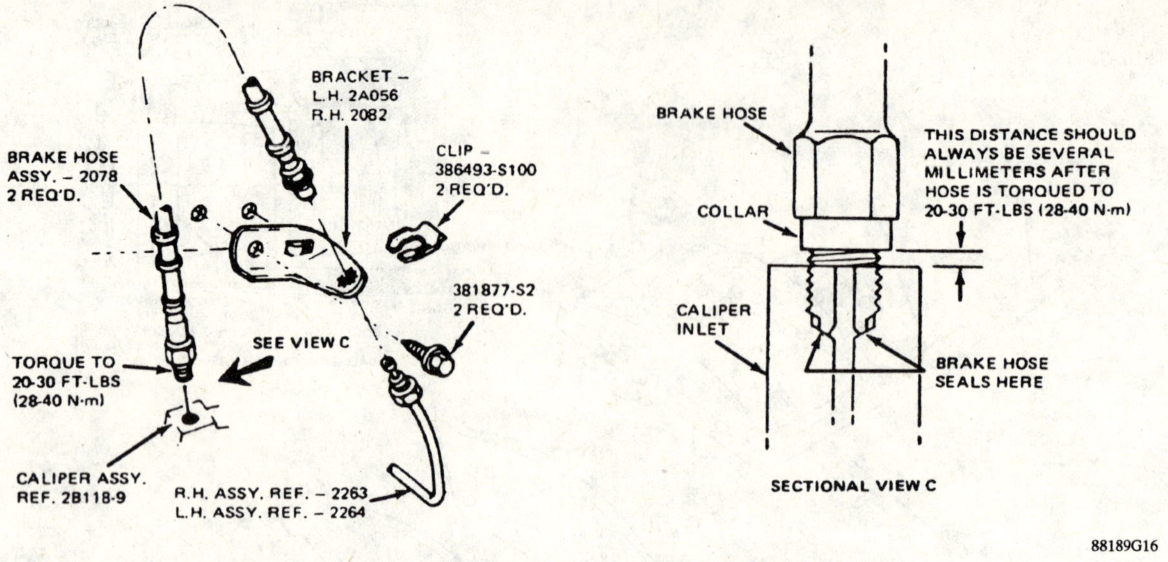

Fig. 22 Brake hose-to-front caliper attachment — 1983-88 vehicles, except 2.3L Turbo Coupe

To install:

6. Make sure that the 2 round torque buttons on the outer shoe are solidly seated in the 2 holes of the outer caliper leg and the shoe is held tightly by the spring clip. Install the caliper on the knuckle, aligning the matchmarks.
7. Lubricate the insulators with 5–7 grams of silicone grease and install them and the locating pins. Make sure the pins are thoroughly clean!

➜ The pins must be easily inserted by hand, and threading must be hand-started to avoid cross-threading.

8. Torque the pins to 30–40 ft. lbs. (41–54 Nm).
9. If detached, uncap and connect the brake hose. Tighten the hose connection to 20–30 ft. lbs. (27–41 Nm).
10. Install the wheel and tire assembly. Hand-tighten the lug nuts.
11. Carefully lower the vehicle, then tighten the lug nuts to 80–105 ft. lbs. (108–142 Nm).
12. Fill the master cylinder to the proper level with DOT 3 brake fluid from a clean, sealed container. If the fluid lines were disconnected, bleed the brake system.
13. Pump the brake pedal to position the pistons.

1985-88 Vehicles

EXCEPT 2.3L TURBO COUPE

➧ See Figure 22

1. Raise and safely support the front end of the vehicle on jackstands.
2. Remove the wheel and tire assembly.
3. Matchmark the caliper and knuckle for installation reference.

➜ If the caliper is being removed for any purpose other than replacement or rebuilding, don't disconnect the brake line. Just suspend the caliper out of the way.

4. If the caliper is being replaced or rebuilt, disconnect the brake hose from the caliper and plug or cap the hose end to prevent fluid loss and contamination.
5. Remove the caliper locating pins and lift the caliper off the rotor.

To install:

6. Install the caliper on the knuckle, aligning the matchmarks made during removal.
7. Lubricate the rubber insulators with 4–8 grams of silicone grease and install them and new locating pins. Make sure the pins are thoroughly clean!

➜ The pins must be easily inserted by hand, and threading must be hand-started to avoid cross-threading.

8. Tighten the caliper pins to 30–40 ft. lbs. (41–54 Nm) on cars through 1987 or to 45–65 ft. lbs. (61–88 Nm) on 1988 models.
9. If detached, uncap and connect the brake hose. Tighten the hose connection to 20–30 ft. lbs. (27–41 Nm).
10. Install the wheel and tire assembly. Hand-tighten the lug nuts.
11. Carefully lower the vehicle, then tighten the lug nuts to 80–105 ft. lbs. (108–142 Nm).
12. Fill the master cylinder to the proper level with DOT 3 brake fluid from a clean, sealed container. If the fluid lines were disconnected, bleed the brake system.
13. Pump the brake pedal to position the pistons.

2.3L TURBO COUPE

➧ See Figures 23 and 24

1. Raise and safely support the front end of the vehicle on jackstands.
2. Remove the wheel and tire assembly.
3. Matchmark the caliper and knuckle for installation reference.

➜ If the caliper is being removed for any purpose other than replacement or rebuilding, don't disconnect the brake line. Just suspend the caliper out of the way.

4. If replacing or rebuilding the caliper, remove the hollow bolt and copper washers attaching the brake hose to the caliper. Discard the washers. Remove the brake hose from the caliper and plug or cap the hose end to prevent fluid loss and contamination.
5. Remove the caliper locating pins and lift off the caliper.

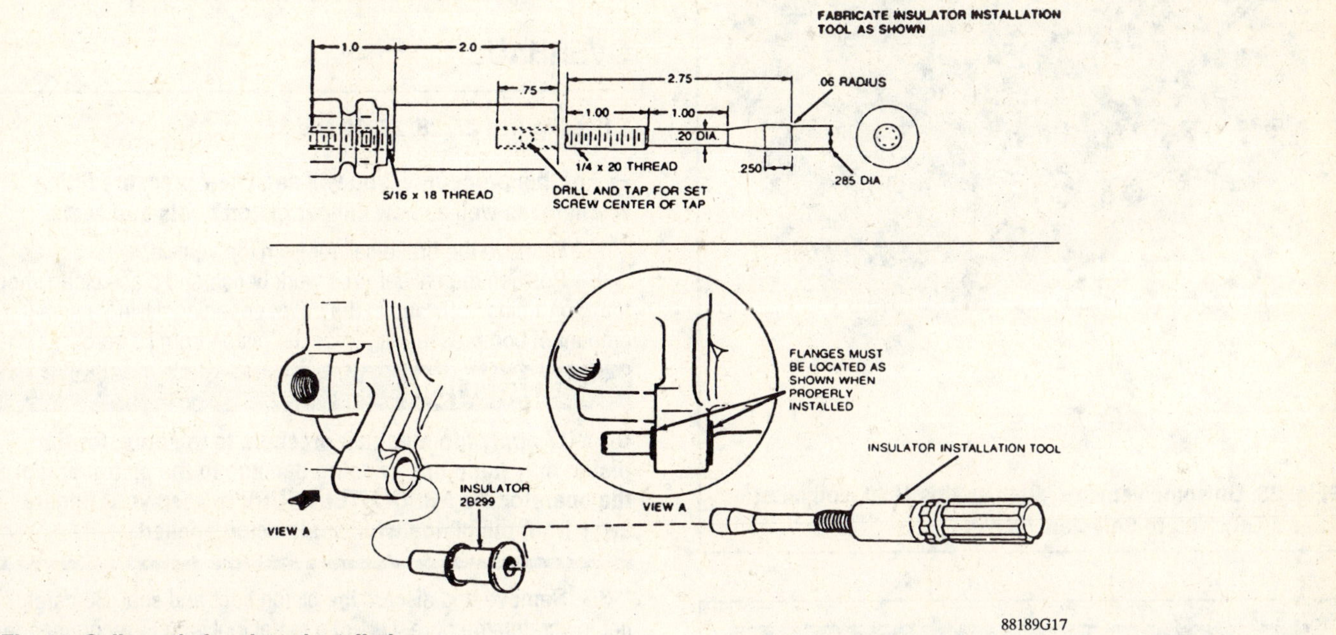

Fig. 23 Caliper pin insulator installation

To install:

6. Install the caliper on the knuckle, aligning the matchmarks.
7. Lubricate the rubber insulators with 4–8 grams of silicone grease and install them and the locating pins. Make sure the pins are thoroughly clean!

➥ The pins must be easily inserted by hand, and threading must be hand-started to avoid cross-threading.

8. Tighten the caliper pins to 45–65 ft. lbs. (61–88 Nm).
9. Connect the brake hose using new copper washers. Tighten the bolt connection to 17–25 ft. lbs. (23–34 Nm).
10. Install the wheel and tire assembly. Hand-tighten the lug nuts.
11. Carefully lower the vehicle, then tighten the lug nuts to 80–105 ft. lbs. (108–142 Nm).
12. Fill the master cylinder to the proper level with DOT 3 brake fluid from a clean, sealed container. If the fluid lines were disconnected, bleed the brake system.
13. Pump the brake pedal to position the pistons.

1989–96 Vehicles

➧ See Figures 24, 25 and 26

1. Raise and safely support the front end of the vehicle on jackstands.
2. Remove the wheel and tire assembly.
3. Matchmark the caliper assembly to be sure it is installed on the correct knuckle during installation.

➥ If the caliper is being removed for any purpose other than replacement or rebuilding, don't disconnect the brake line. Just suspend the caliper out of the way.

4. For vehicles through 1992, remove the caliper locating pins using Torx® Bit D79P–2100–T40 or equivalent. Lift the caliper off the rotor using a rotating motion.
5. If the caliper is being replaced or rebuilt, remove the hollow bolt and disconnect the brake hose from the caliper. Plug the hose to prevent fluid loss and moisture contamination.
6. For 1993–96 vehicles, remove the lower caliper locating pin. Rotate the caliper about 90° away from the caliper anchor plate. Slide the caliper away from the anchor plate until the caliper disengages from the upper caliper locating pin.

To install:

7. For vehicles through 1992, using a suitable C-clamp, retract the piston fully in its bore. Position the caliper above the rotor with the anti-rattle spring (if equipped) under the arm of the knuckle. Install the caliper over the rotor with a rotating motion. Make sure the inner and outer shoes are properly positioned.

➥ Make sure the correct caliper assembly, as marked during removal, is installed on the correct knuckle. The caliper bleed screw should be positioned on top of the caliper when assembled on the vehicle.

➥ The pin threading must be hand-started to avoid cross-threading.

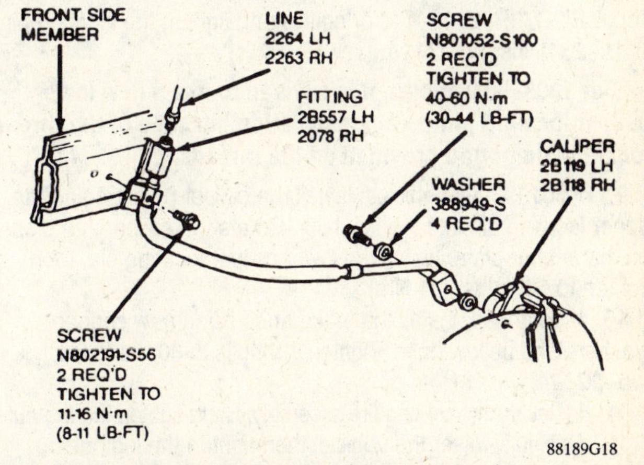

Fig. 24 If the caliper is being replaced, disconnect and cap the brake hose — 1987–88 2.3L and all 1989–96 vehicles

88189P04

Fig. 25 On some vehicles, such as this 1990, you must use a Torx® bit to unfasten, then . . .

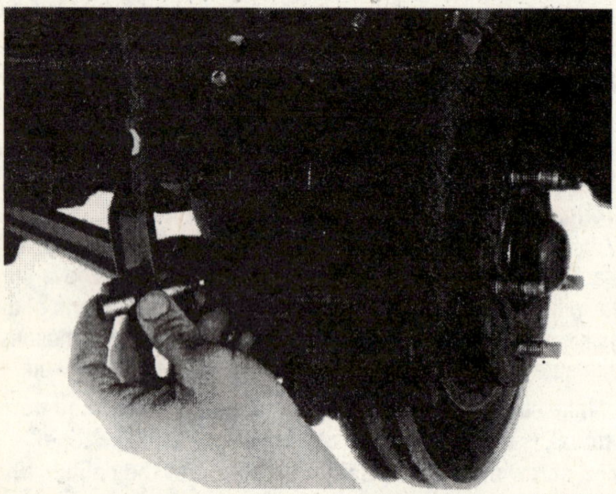

88189P05

Fig. 26 . . . remove the caliper locating pins

8. For vehicles through 1992, lubricate the pins and insulators with a suitable silicone grease and install them. Using Torx® Bit D79P-2100-T40 or equivalent, tighten the locating pin to 19-25 ft. lbs. (25-34 Nm).

➥ For 1993-96 vehicles, it is advised to use a new lower caliper locating pin during installation because of the thread locking compound provided on the threads.

9. For 1993-96 vehicles, install the caliper by engaging the upper locating pin into the insulator. Rotate the caliper into place on the anchor plate. Install the lower caliper locating pin, then tighten to 60 ft. lbs. (81 Nm).
10. If detached, install the brake hose using new copper washers and hollow bolts. Tighten the bolts to 30-44 ft. lbs. (40-60 Nm).
11. Install the wheel and tire assembly. Hand-tighten the lug nuts.
12. Carefully lower the vehicle, then tighten the lug nuts to 80-105 ft. lbs. (108-142 Nm).
13. Fill the master cylinder to the proper level with DOT 3 brake fluid from a clean, sealed container. If the fluid lines were disconnected, bleed the brake system.
14. Pump the brake pedal to position the pistons.

OVERHAUL

➧ See Figures 27, 28, 29, 30 and 31

➥ For this procedure, you will need new pressure fitting washers, as well as new caliper piston boots and seals.

1. Remove the brake caliper from the vehicle.
2. Position the caliper on a work bench and place clean shop towel or a piece of wood in the caliper opening. Using a small amount of compressed air, force the piston from its bore.

✲✲CAUTION

DO NOT apply too much air pressure to the bore, for the piston may jump out, causing damage to the piston and/or the operator. Be ABSOLUTELY SURE to keep your fingers away from the piston while air is being applied.

3. Remove and discard the piston boot and seal. Be careful not to scratch the bore. Use of a metal tool is NOT recommended when removing the boot and the seal because of the possibility of scoring and damaging the bore.

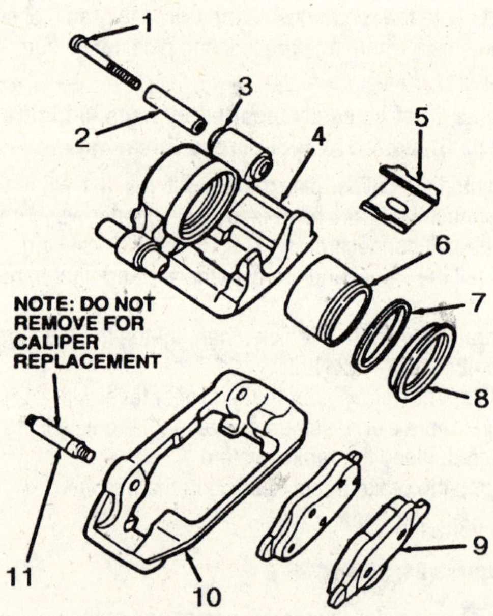

1. Lower caliper brake bolt
 - Tighten to 88 Nm (65 lb. ft.)
2. Front caliper sleeve
3. Insulator
4. Disc brake
5. Disc brake pad anti-rattle clip
6. Caliper piston
7. Piston seal
8. Dust boot
9. Brake shoe and lining
10. Front disc brake caliper anchor plate
11. Disc brake caliper locating pin
 - Tighten to 88 Nm (65 lb. ft.)

88189GA9

Fig. 27 Exploded view of a common caliper assembly

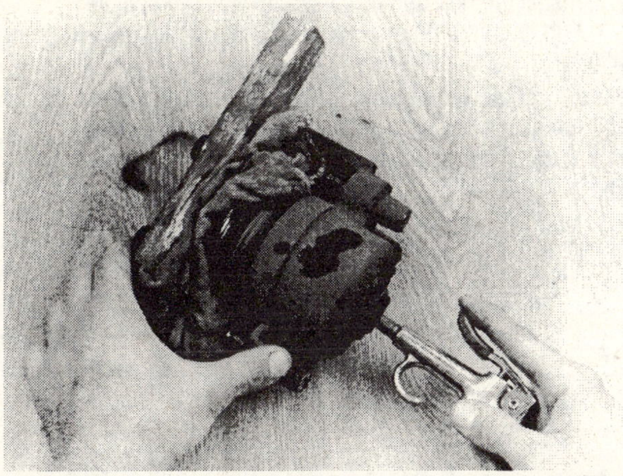

88189P06

Fig. 28 Apply a small amount of compressed air to push the piston out against a clean rag but KEEP YOUR FINGERS CLEAR

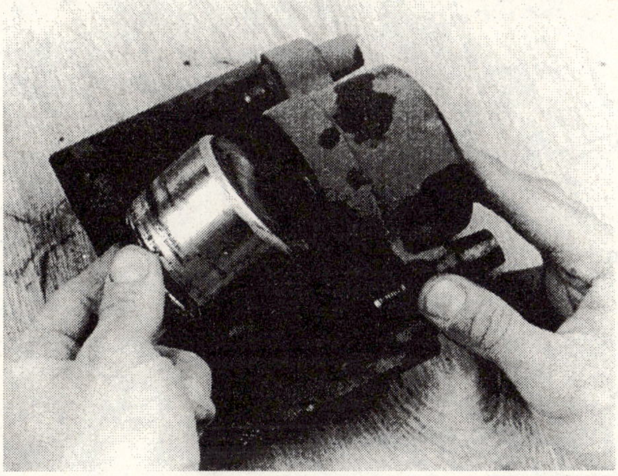

88189P07

Fig. 29 Grasp the piston and remove it from the caliper bore

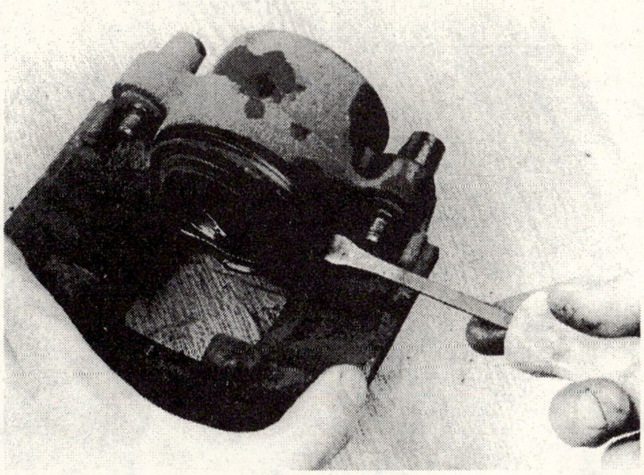

88189P08

Fig. 30 Remove the boot from the caliper housing, taking care not to score or damage the bore

88189P10

Fig. 31 Use EXTREME caution when removing the piston seal; DO NOT scratch the caliper bore

4. Inspect the piston and the caliper bore for damage or corrosion. Replace the caliper and/or the piston (if necessary).
5. Remove the bleeder screw and its rubber cap.
6. Clean all of the parts with non-mineral based solvent and blow dry with compressed air. All rubber parts should be replaced with those in the brake service kit.
7. Inspect the guide pins for corrosion. Replace them if necessary. When installing the guide pins, coat them with a silicone lubricant.

To assemble:

8. Lubricate the piston, caliper and seal with clean brake fluid.
9. Install the seal into the caliper bore making sure it is not twisted in the caliper bore groove.
10. Install the boot onto the piston, then position the piston into the caliper bore.
11. Bottom the piston into the bore, then secure the boot using a suitable piston seal installer tool.
12. Install the caliper on the vehicle and properly bleed the hydraulic brake system.

Brake Disc (Rotor)

REMOVAL & INSTALLATION

1983–88 Vehicles

See Figures 32 and 33

For vehicles through 1988, the rotor is removed with the hub as an assembly.

1. Raise and safely support the vehicle.
2. Remove the wheel and tire assembly.
3. Remove the caliper, as outlined earlier. Suspend the caliper with a suitable piece of wire. Do NOT disconnect the fluid line.
4. Remove the grease cap from the hub. Remove the cotter pin, nut lock, adjusting nut, and flat washer from the spindle. Discard the cotter pin.
5. Remove the outer wheel bearing cone and roller assembly from the hub.

6. Remove the hub and disc assembly from the spindle.

To install:

**WARNING

If a new disc is being installed, remove the protective coating with carburetor degreaser. If the original disc is being installed, make sure that the grease in the hub is clean and adequate, that the inner bearing and grease retainer are lubricated and in good condition, and that the disc breaking surfaces are clean.

7. Install the hub and disc assembly on the spindle.
8. Lubricate the outer bearing and install the thrust washer and adjusting nut.
9. Adjust the wheel bearing, as outlined in Section 8.
10. Install the nut lock, a new cotter pin, and grease cap.
11. Install the caliper assembly, as outlined earlier in this section.
12. Install the wheel and tire assembly and hand-tighten nuts.
13. Carefully lower the vehicle, then tighten the lug nuts to 85–100 ft. lbs. (115–136 Nm).

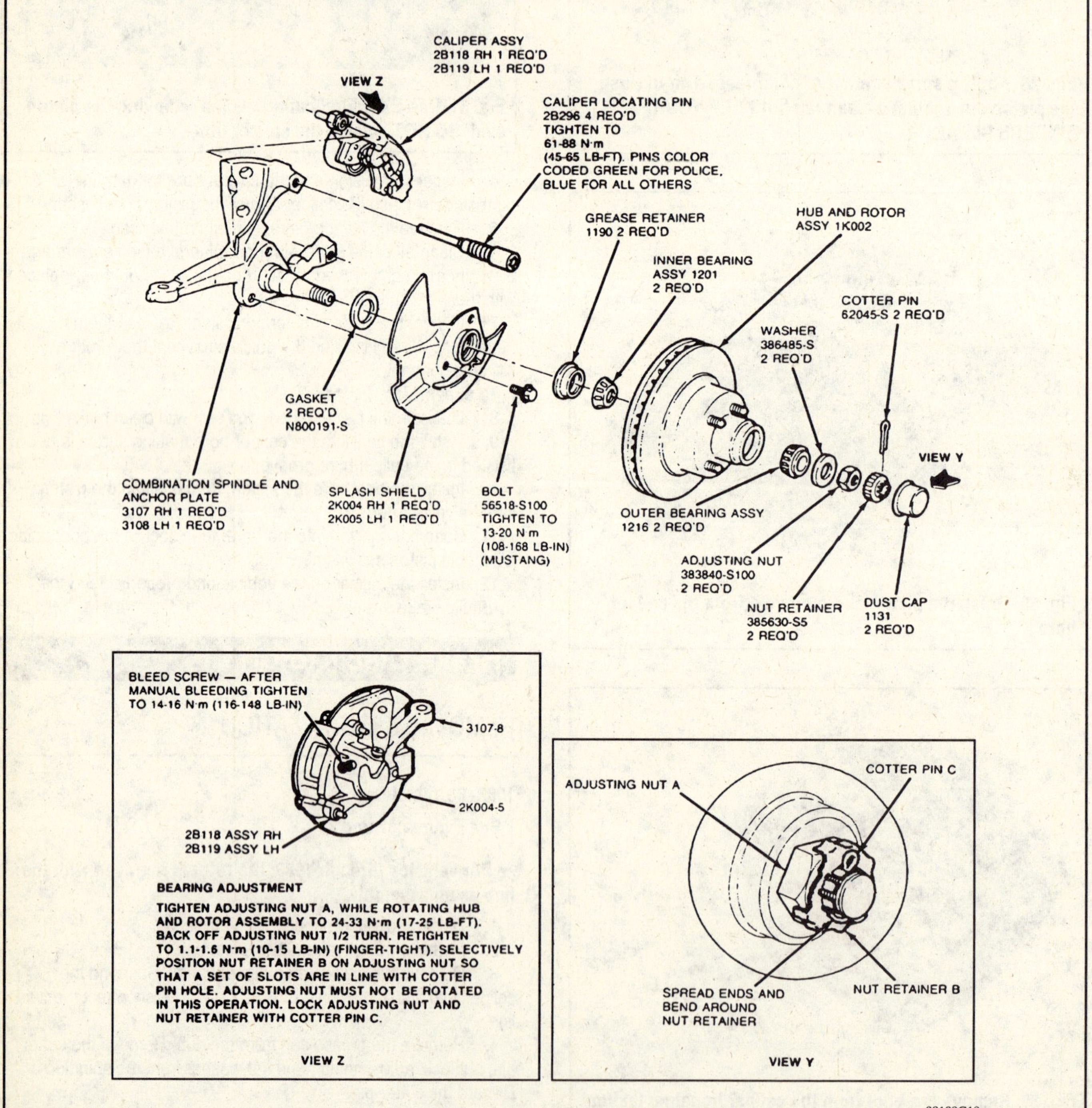

Fig. 32 View of the hub and rotor assembly — 1983–88 vehicles, except 2.3L engine

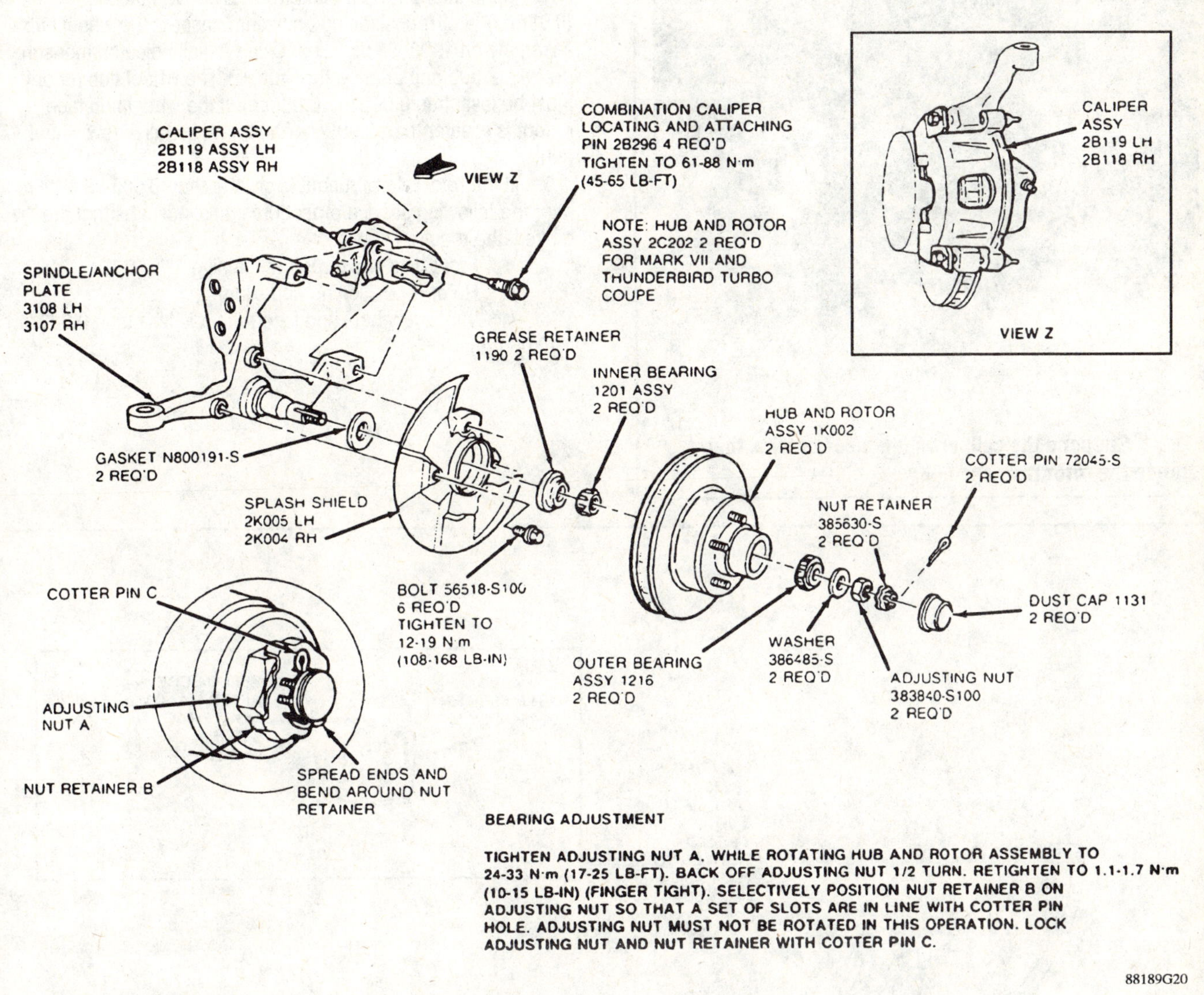

Fig. 33 On 1983–88 vehicles, the rotor and hub are removed as an assembly — 2.3L Turbo engine shown

1989–92 Vehicles

➧ See Figures 34 and 35

1. Raise and safely support the front end of the vehicle on jackstands.
2. Remove the wheel and tire assembly.
3. Remove the caliper and suspend it out of the way with a suitable piece of wire. DO NOT disconnect the brake line.
4. Remove the rotor from the hub.

➥ On high mileage cars the rotor may be rusted to the hub. If so, squirt penetrating oil between the rotor and hub, let it work for a while, and strike the rotor between the lugs with a plastic hammer. If that doesn't work, a 3-jawed puller will be necessary. If excessive force is necessary, the rotor may become distorted.

5. Installation is the reverse of the removal procedure.

➥ If a new rotor is being installed, it will have a protective coating. Remove the coating with carburetor cleaner.

INSPECTION

➧ See Figures 36 and 37

➥ Whenever the rotor has been removed, clean any rust or foreign material from the mating surface on the wheel hub and rotor. Failure to do this may result in increased lateral runout of the rotor and brake pulsation.

1. Visually check the disc for scoring. Minor scores can be removed with fine emery cloth. If it is excessively scored, it must be machined or replaced.
2. Install the rotors, then hold in place using inverted lug nuts and washer to seat the rotors. Tighten the lug nuts to 85 ft. lbs. (115 Nm).
3. Using a suitable dial indicator, measure the rotor lateral runout as shown in the accompanying figure. Center the dial indicator on the braking surface. Rotate the rotor while measuring runout. If the runout is greater than 0.003 in. (0.08mm), reposition the rotor (index) on the hub to obtain the lower possible runout.

Fig. 34 Suspend the caliper with a piece of wire, then remove the rotor from the hub

4. If the lateral runout of the rotor is above 0.003 in. (0.08mm) after repositioning (indexing), inspect the wheel hub assembly on 1993–96 vehicles. Using a dial indicator, measure the wheel hub and bearing face runout. The wheel hub runout must be less than 0.002 in. (0.06mm). If the wheel hub face runout is greater than 0.002 in. (0.06mm), install a new wheel hub.

5. If the rotor lateral runout is greater than 0.003 in. (0.08mm) after the following service procedures, this indicates that the brake lathe requires service:

- Front disc brake rotor machining
- Rotor repositioning (indexing)
- Verifying wheel hub face runout is less than 0.002 in. (0.06mm)

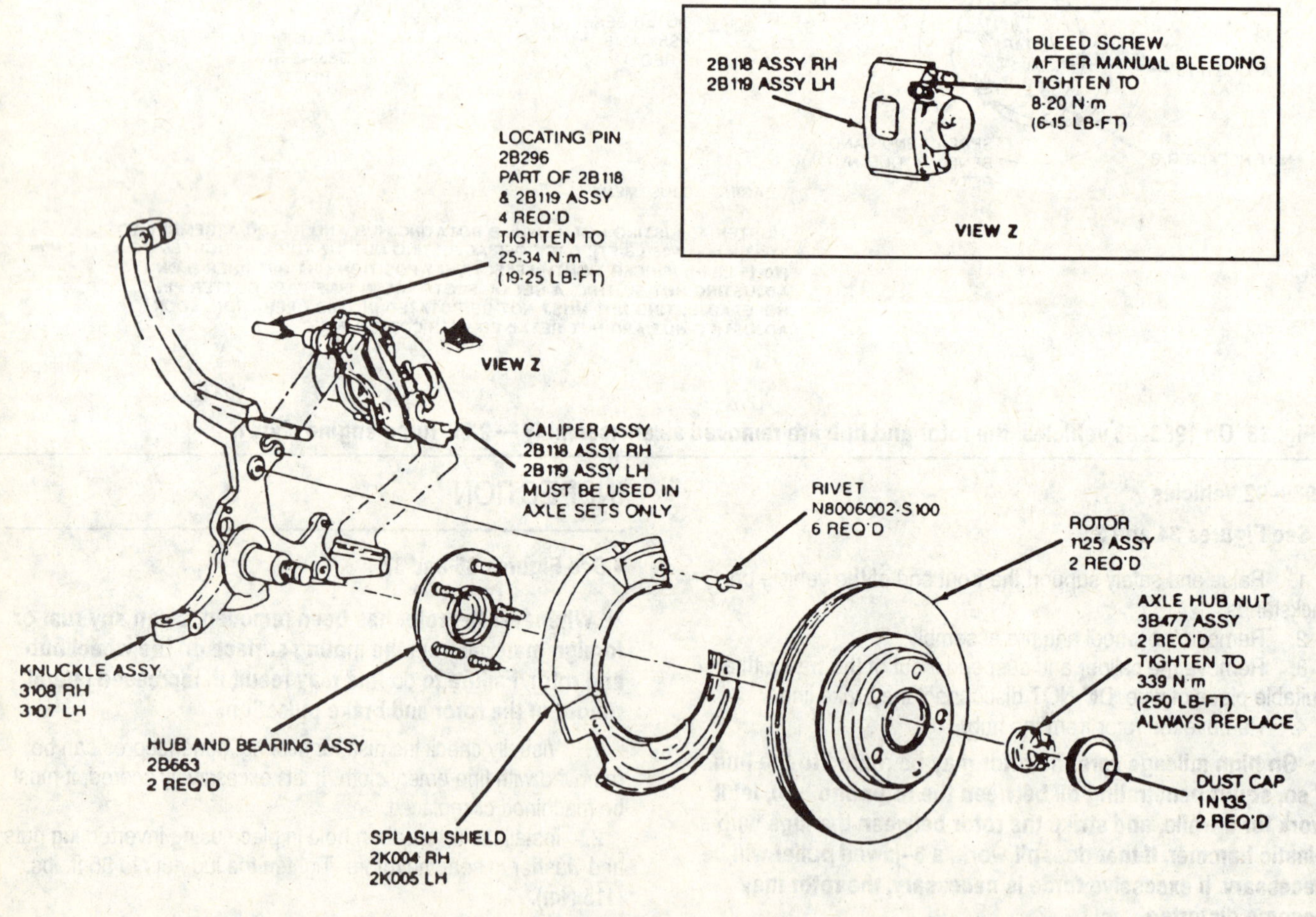

Fig. 35 Exploded view of the rotor and related brake system components

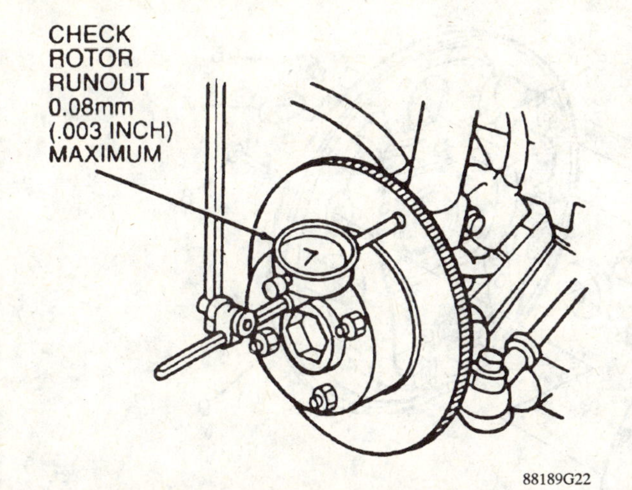

Fig. 36 Use a dial indicator to measure rotor runout — 1995 vehicles shown

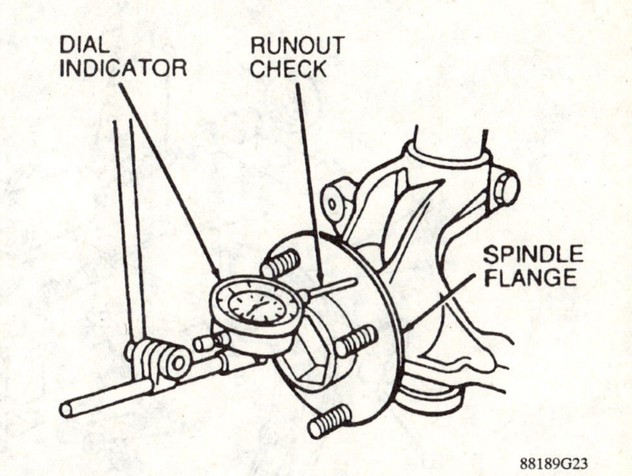

Fig. 37 Checking hub and bearing face runout — 1993–96 vehicles

REAR DRUM BRAKES

➧ See Figure 38

****CAUTION**

Brake shoes contain asbestos, which has been determined to be a cancer causing agent. Never clean the brake surfaces with compressed air! Avoid inhaling any dust from any brake surface! When cleaning brake surfaces, use a commercially available brake cleaning fluid.

Brake Drum

REMOVAL & INSTALLATION

➧ See Figures 39, 40, 41, 42 and 43

1. With the tires on the ground, break loose the lug nuts.
2. Make sure the parking brake is not on, then raise and safely support the rear of the vehicles with jackstands.
3. Remove the wheel cover/and or nuts covers, as applicable.
4. Remove the tire and wheel assembly. If equipped, use a pair of pliers to remove the Tinnerman nuts from the wheel studs.
5. Pull the brake drum of the axle shaft.

****WARNING**

Do not damage the self-adjusting mechanism or it will not function properly.

6. If the drum will not come off, get under the car (make sure you have safety stands under the car to support it) and perform the following
   a. Remove the rubber plug from the brake backing plate. Shine a flashlight into the slot in the plate. You will see the top of the adjusting screw star wheel and the adjusting lever for the automatic brake adjusting mechanism.
   b. To back off on the adjusting screw, you must first insert a small, thin screwdriver or a piece of firm wire (coat hanger wire) into the adjusting slot and push the adjusting lever away from the adjusting screw.
   c. Then, insert a brake adjusting spoon into the slot and engage the top of the star wheel. Lift up on the bottom of the adjusting spoon to force the adjusting screw star wheel downward.
   d. Repeat this operation until the brake drum is free of the brake shoes and can be pulled off.

To install:

7. If installing a new brake drum, remove the protective coating totally and lightly sand the inner brake drum surface.
8. If the brake adjustment was changed to remove the drum, adjust the brakes until the drum will just fit over the brakes. After the wheel is installed it will be necessary to complete the adjustment. See the Brake Adjustment procedure located earlier in this section.
9. Install the brake drum and secure with the retainer nuts, if equipped.
10. Install the tire and wheel assembly. Hand-tighten the lug nuts.
11. Carefully lower the vehicle, them tighten the lug nuts to 85–105 ft. lbs. (115–142 Nm).

INSPECTION

1. Clean the brake drums and remove any grease, brake fluid or other contaminants from the drum using denatured alcohol, or a suitable cleaner.
2. Inspect and measure the brake drum with Rotunda Brake Drum Micrometer 104-00046 or equivalent.
3. Measure the drums with a brake drum micrometer regardless of inspection. The brake drum micrometer is set to the drum diameter and measures the amount and type of ward. Measure the diameter at various point of 45 degrees around the circumference and at the bottom of the deepest groove to determine if the brake drum required replacement.

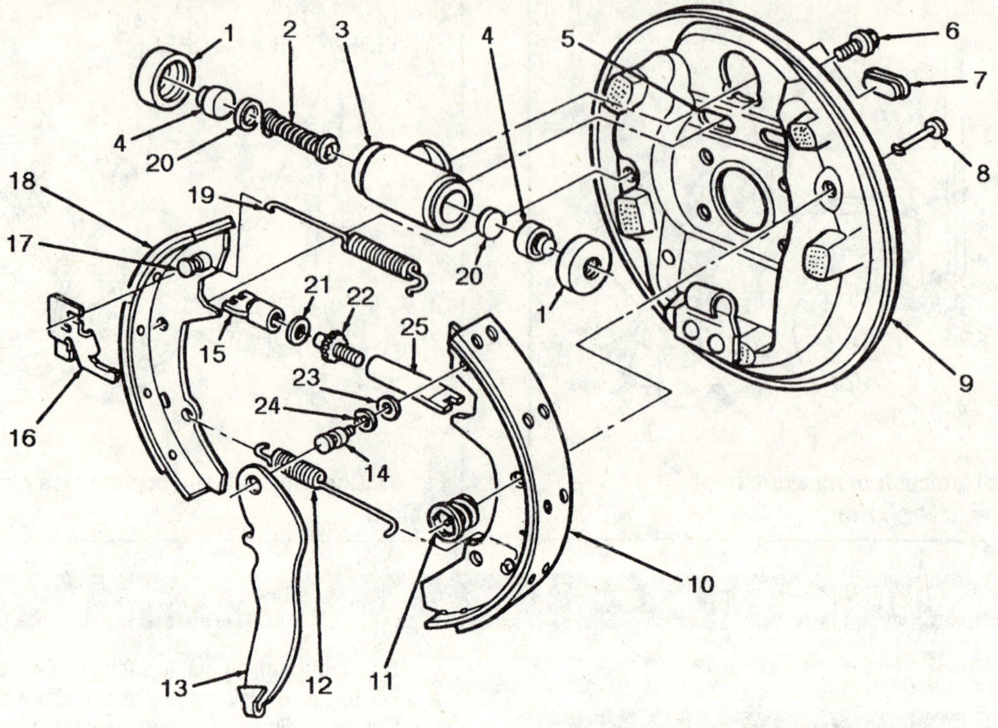

1. Boot
2. Spring expander
3. Rear wheel cylinder
4. Piston and insert
5. Shoe adjustment access hole
6. Wheel cylinder retaining screw (2 req'd) - Tighten to 12-18 Nm (106-159 lb. in.)
7. Brake adjusting hole cover
8. Brake shoe hold down spring pin
9. Brake backing plate
10. Trailing shoe and lining
11. Brake shoe hold down spring
12. Brake shoe retracting spring (lower)
13. Parking brake lever
14. Parking brake lever pin (inner)
15. Brake shoe adjusting screw socket
16. Brake shoe adjusting lever
17. Parking brake lever pin (outer)
18. Leading shoe and lining
19. Brake shoe adjusting screw spring
20. Cup
21. Washer
22. Adjusting screw
23. Washer
24. Parking brake lever pin retainer
25. Adjusting pivot nut

88189G26

Fig. 38 Exploded view of the drum brake assembly — 1995 vehicle shown

88189P12

Fig. 39 Remove the tire and wheel assembly, then . . .

88189P13

Fig. 40 . . . pull the drum off the axle shaft

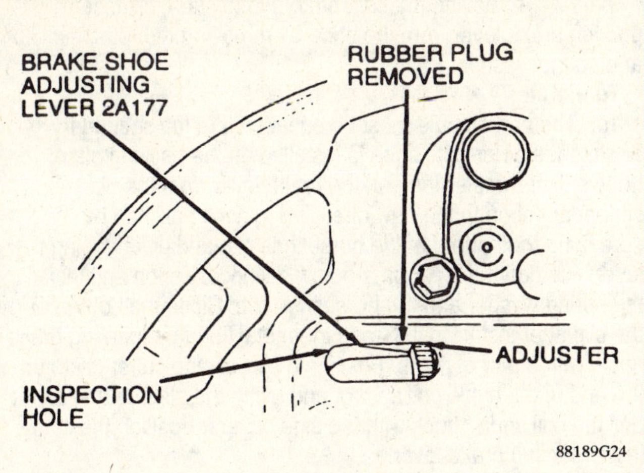

Fig. 41 If the brake drum won't come off, remove the rubber plug from the inspection hole, then . . .

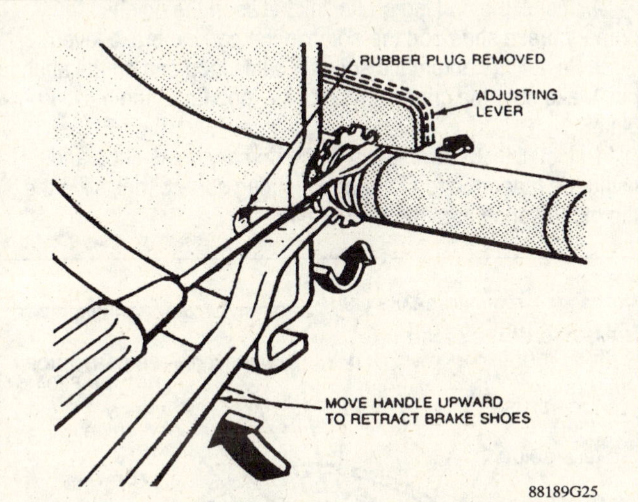

Fig. 42 . . . use a screwdriver to back off the adjusting screw

Brake Shoes

INSPECTION

1. Inspect the rear brake shoes and linings for excessive lining wear or shoe damage. If the lining is damaged or worn within $^1/_{32}$ in. (0.79mm), it must be replaced. Replace any lining that has been contaminated with oil, grease or brake fluid. Replace the linings in axle sets only. Never replace just one rear shoe and lining of a brake assembly. Replace both leading and trailing shoes.

➥ Replace the brake shoe and lining in axle sets only. Never replace just one shoe of a brake assembly.

2. Before replacing the lining, check the brake drum diameter to determine if the brake drum diameter is within specifications. If the braking surface diameter exceeds specifications, the drum must be replaced.

3. Check the condition of the brake shoes and linings, retracting spring, hold-down springs and brake drum for signs of overheating. If the brake shoes and linings have a slight blue coloring, this indicates overheating and retracting. Replace the hold-down springs. If not replaced, overheated springs could lose their tension and allow the new lining to drag and wear prematurely.

REMOVAL & INSTALLATION

➥ If you are not thoroughly familiar with the procedures involved in brake replacement, only disassemble and assemble one side at a time, leaving the other wheel intact as a reference.

1983–88 Vehicles

➧ See Figures 44, 45 and 46

1. Raise and safely support the rear of the vehicle with jackstands.
2. Remove the tire and wheel assembly.
3. Remove the brake drum, as outlined earlier in this section.
4. Place Brake Cylinder Clamp D81L–1103–B or equivalent, over the ends of the brake cylinder.

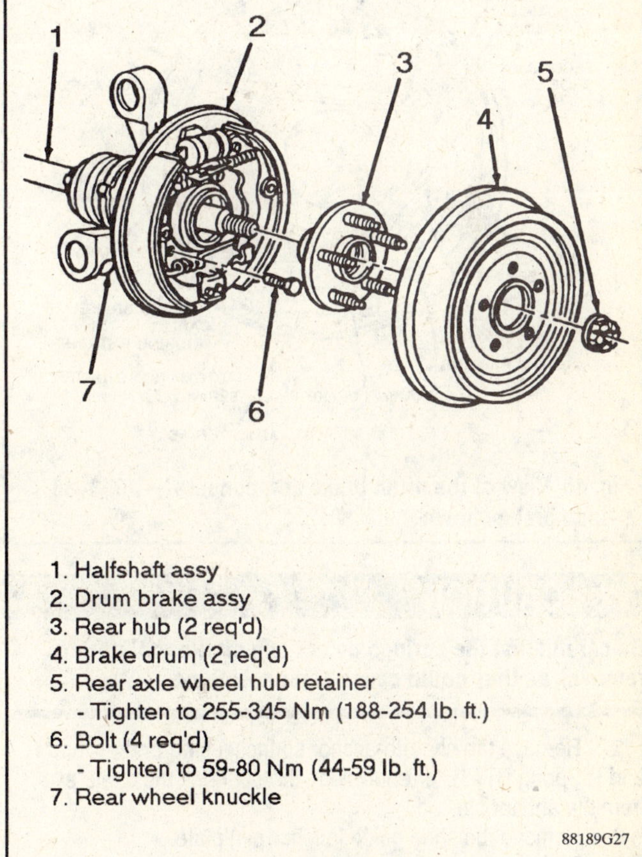

Fig. 43 Exploded view of the brake drum removal — 1995 vehicle shown

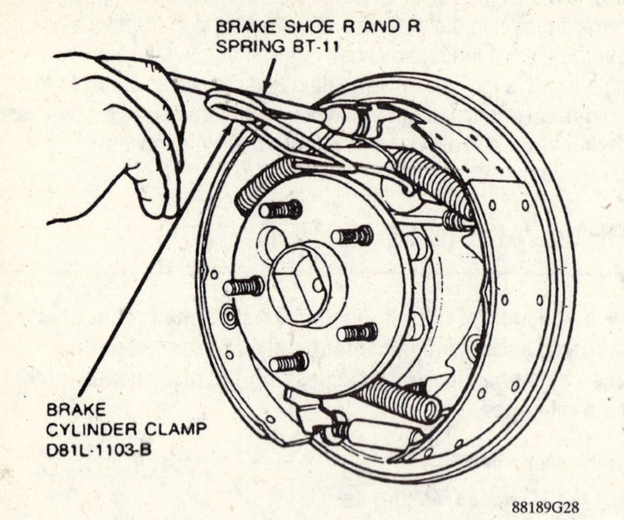

Fig. 44 Place the brake clamp tool over the ends of the wheel cylinder, then remove the shoe-to-anchor springs using the correct tool

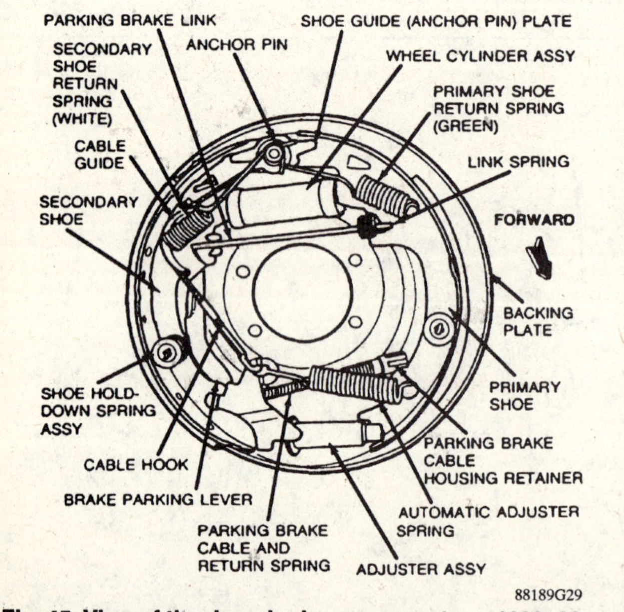

Fig. 45 View of the drum brake components — 1983-88 9-inch brake shown

**CAUTION

Be careful that the springs do not slip off the tool during removal, as they could cause personal injury.

5. Remove the shoe-to-anchor springs, using Brake Shoe R and R Spring BT-11, or equivalent, then unhook the cable eye from the anchor pin.
6. Remove the shoe guide (anchor pin) plate.
7. Remove the shoe hold-down springs, shoes, adjusting screws, pivot nut, socket and automatic adjustment parts.
8. Remove the parking brake link, spring and retainer. Disconnect the parking brake cable from the parking brake lever.
9. After removing the secondary brake shoe, disassembly the parking brake lever from the shoe by removing the retaining clip and spring washer.

To install:

10. The brake cable must be connected to the secondary brake shoe before the shoe is installed on the backing plate. To do this, first transfer the parking brake lever from the old secondary shoe to the new one. This is accomplished by spreading the bottom of the horseshoe clip and disengaging the lever. Position the lever on the new secondary shoe and install the spring washer and the horseshoe clip. Close the bottom of the clip after installing it. Grasp the metal tip of the parking brake cable with a pair of pliers. Position a pair of side cutter pliers on the end of the cable coil spring, and using the plier as a fulcrum, pull the coil spring back with the side cutters. Position the cable in the parking brake lever.
11. Apply a light coating of high temperature grease to the brake shoe contact points on the backing plate. Position the primary brake shoe on the front of the backing plate and install the hold-down spring and washer over the mounting pin. Install the secondary shoe on the rear of the backing plate.
12. Install the parking brake link between the notch in the primary brake shoe and the notch in the parking brake lever.
13. Install the automatic adjuster cable loop end on the anchor pin. Make sure the crimped side of the loop faces the backing plate.
14. Install the return spring in the primary brake shoe and, using the tapered end of the brake spring service tool, slide the top of the spring onto the anchor pin.

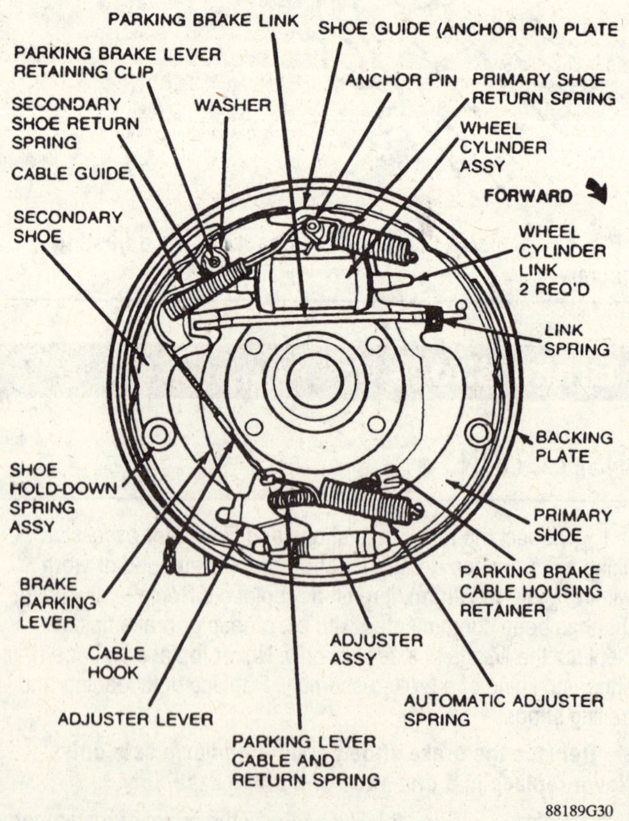

Fig. 46 View of the drum brake components — 1983-88 10-inch brake shown

****CAUTION**

Be careful to make sure that the spring does not slip off the tool during installation, as it could cause injury.

15. Install the automatic adjuster cable guide in the secondary brake shoe, making sure the flared hole in the cable guide is inside the hole in the brake shoe. Fit the cable into the groove in the top of the cable guide.
16. Install the secondary shoe return spring through the hole in the cable guide and the brake shoe. Using the brake spring tool, slide the top of the spring onto the anchor pin.
17. Clean the threads on the adjusting screw and apply a light coating of high temperature grease to the threads. Screw the adjuster closed, then open it $^1/_2$ turn.
18. Install the adjusting screw between the brake shoes with the star wheel nearest to the secondary shoe. Make sure the star wheel is in a position that is accessible from the adjusting slot in the backing plate.
19. Install the short hooked end of the automatic adjuster spring in the proper hole in the primary brake shoe.
20. Connect the hooked end of the automatic adjuster cable and the free end of the automatic adjuster spring in the slot in the top of the automatic adjuster lever.
21. Pull the automatic adjuster lever (the lever will pull the cable and spring with it) downward and to the left and engage the pivot hook of the lever in the hole in the secondary brake shoe.
22. Check the entire brake assembly to make sure that everything is installed properly. Make sure that the shoes engage the wheel cylinder properly and are flush on the anchor pin. Make sure that the automatic adjuster cable is flush on the anchor pin and in the slot on the back of the cable guide. Make sure that the adjusting lever rests on the adjusting screw star wheel. Pull upward on the adjusting cable until the adjusting lever is free of the star wheel, then release the cable. The adjusting lever should snap back into place on the adjusting screw star wheel and turn the wheel one tooth.
23. Expand the brake adjusting screw until the brake drum will just fit over the brake shoes.
24. Install the brake drum and wheel and tire assembly, then adjust the brakes.
25. Carefully lower the vehicle.

1989-96 Vehicles

➧ See Figures 47, 48, 49, 50, 51, 52 and 53

1. Raise and safely support the vehicle.
2. Remove the rear wheel and tire assemblies, then remove the brake drum.
3. Install Brake Cylinder Clamp D81L-1103-B or equivalent, over the ends of the rear wheel cylinder.
4. Disconnect the parking brake cable from the parking brake lever.
5. Remove the 2 brake shoe hold-down retainers, springs and pins.
6. Spread the brake shoes over the piston shoe guide slots. Lift the brake shoes, springs and adjuster off the backing plate as an assembly. Be careful not to bend the adjusting lever.
7. Remove the adjuster spring. To separate the shoes, remove the retracting springs.
8. Remove the parking brake lever retaining clip and spring washer. Remove the lever from the pin.

88189P14

Fig. 47 View of the drum brake assembly with the drum removed

88189P15

Fig. 48 Use a commercially available brake spray to clean the components before removal

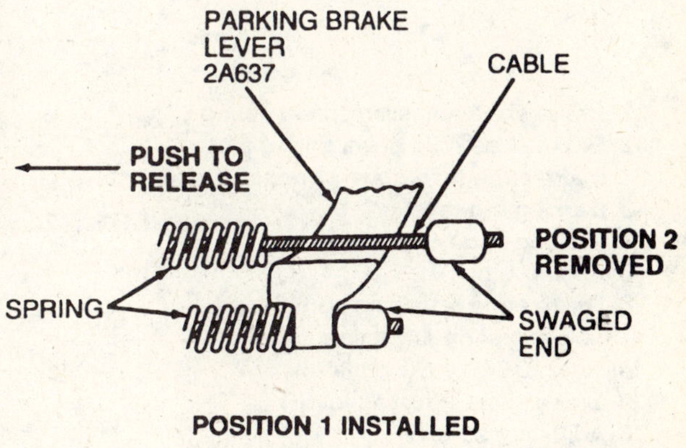

88189G31

Fig. 49 Detach the parking brake cable and conduit from the parking brake lever

88189P16

Fig. 50 Lift the brake shoes, springs and adjuster off the backing plate as an assembly

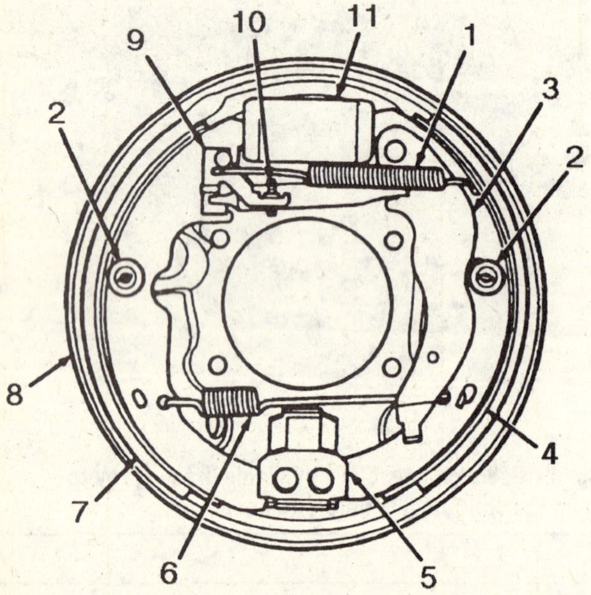

1. Brake shoe adjusting screw spring
2. Brake shoe hold down spring pin/ brake shoe hold down springs
3. Parking brake lever
4. Trailing shoe and lining
5. Anchor block
6. Brake shoe retracting spring
7. Leading shoe and lining
8. Rear brake backing plate
9. Brake shoe adjusting lever
10. Adjusting screw
11. Rear wheel cylinder

88189G32

Fig. 51 Drum brake components — 1995 vehicle shown

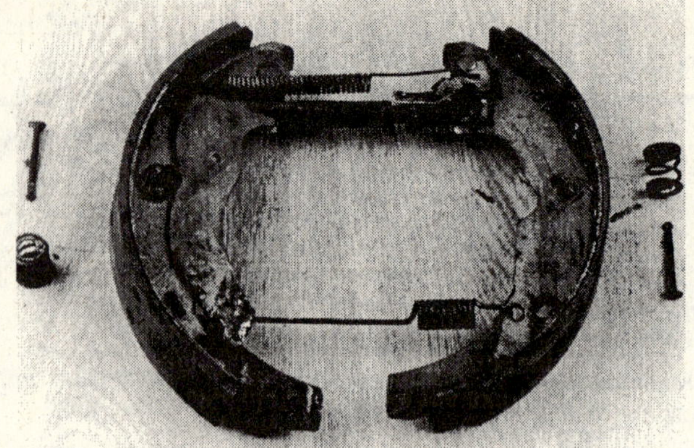

88189P17

Fig. 52 Exploded view of the drum brake components, removed from the vehicle

To install:

9. Apply a light coating of caliper slide grease to the backing plate brake shoe contact areas.
10. Apply a light coat of lubricant to the threaded areas of the adjuster screw and socket. Assemble the brake adjuster with the stainless steel washer. Turn the socket all the way down on the screw, then back off $^1/_2$ turn.
11. Install the parking brake lever to the trailing shoe with the spring washer and a new retaining clip. Crimp the clip to securely retain the lever.
12. Position the trailing shoe on the backing plate and attach the parking brake cable. Position the leading shoe on the backing plate and attach the lower retracting spring to the brake shoes.
13. Install the adjuster assembly to the slots in the brake shoes. The socket end must fit into the wider slot in the leading shoe. The slot in the adjuster nut must fit into the slots in the trailing shoe and parking brake lever.
14. Install the adjuster lever on the pin on the leading shoe and to the slot in the adjuster socket.
15. Install the upper retracting spring in the slot on the trailing shoe and the slot in the adjuster lever. The adjuster lever should contact the star and adjuster assembly.
16. Install the brake shoe anchor pins, springs and retainers. Remove the brake cylinder clamp tool
17. Install the brake drum, wheel and tire assemblies and lower the vehicle.
18. Apply the brakes several times while backing up the vehicle. After each stop, the vehicle must be moved forward.

Wheel Cylinders

REMOVAL & INSTALLATION

➧ **See Figure 54**

1. Raise and safely support the vehicle with jackstands.
2. Remove the tire and wheel assembly.
3. Remove the brake drum and shoes, as outlined earlier in this section.

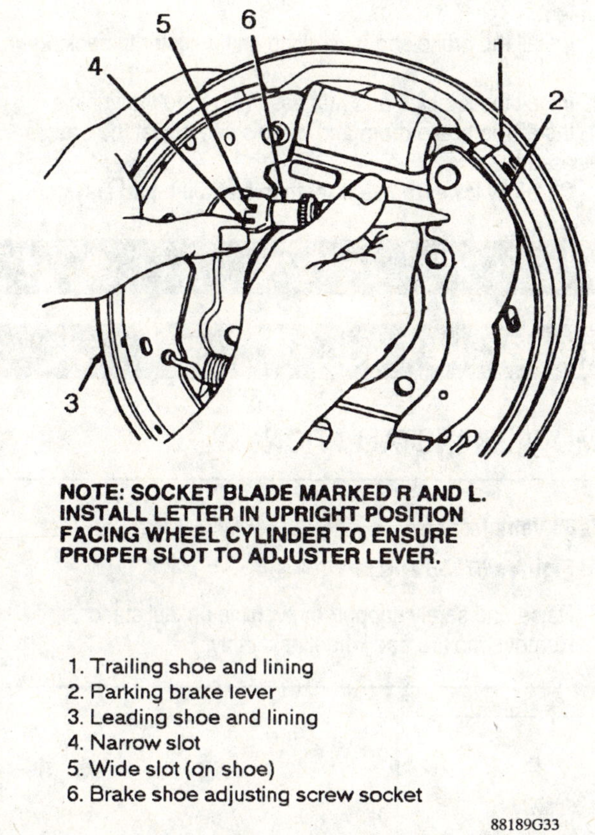

Fig. 53 Install the adjuster assembly in the slots in the brake shoes

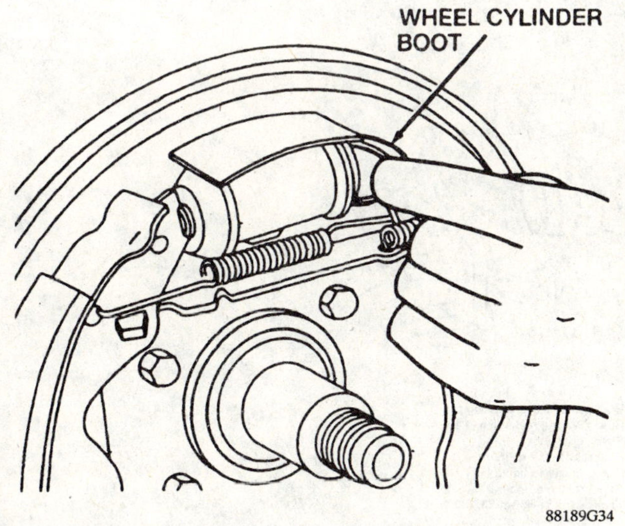

Fig. 54 Wheel cylinder mounting — 1995 vehicle shown

Do not let the brake fluid contact the brake linings or the linings must be replaced.

4. Disconnect and plug the brake tube from the wheel cylinder at the backing plate. The tube will separate from the cylinder when it is removed from the backing plate.
5. Remove the wheel cylinder attaching bolts, then remove the wheel cylinder from the backing plate.

To install:

Before making the fluid line connections, wipe the end(s) of the lines to remove any foreign matter.

6. Position the wheel cylinder on the backing plate, then unplug and finger-tighten the brake line to the cylinder.
7. Secure the wheel cylinder to the backing plate, using the attaching bolts. Tighten the bolts to 10–20 ft. lbs. (14–27 Nm).
8. Tighten the tube nut fitting to 10–14 ft. lbs. (14–18 Nm) using Tube Nut Wrench 1112-144 or equivalent.
9. Install the links 10-inch brakes in the ends of the wheel cylinder, then install the shoes and adjuster assemblies.
10. Adjust the brakes. Install the brake drum and wheel and tire assembly.
11. Carefully lower the vehicle, then bleed the brake system.

Brake Backing Plate

REMOVAL & INSTALLATION

1983–88 Vehicles

1. Raise and safely support vehicle on jackstands.
2. Remove the wheel and tire assembly, then remove the brake drum.
3. Disconnect and plug the brake line from the brake cylinder.
4. Remove the brake shoes, adjuster assemblies and the wheel cylinder.
5. Remove the four bolts retaining the backing plate and the axle shaft to the axle housing and remove the axle shaft and backing plate.

To install:

6. Position the backing plate on the axle housing, install the axle shaft and retaining bolts. Tighten to 20–40 ft. lbs. (27–54 Nm).
7. Install the wheel cylinder and tighten the retaining bolts to 10–20 ft. lbs. (14–27 Nm).
8. Unplug and connect the brake line to the wheel cylinder.
9. Install the brake shoes adjuster assemblies and connect the parking brake lever.
10. Install the brake drums and wheels. Adjust the brakes as necessary.
11. Carefully lower the vehicle.
12. Bleed the brake system and centralize the pressure differential valve.

1989–96 Vehicles

1. Raise and safely support the vehicle with jackstands.
2. Remove the wheels and tire assembly. Remove the brake drum.
3. Remove the knuckle and hub assembly from vehicle.
4. Remove the brake shoes, springs and adjuster from the backing plate.
5. Place the knuckle and hub in a vise. Remove the four bolts retaining the backing plate to the knuckle.

6. Using a 3 jaw puller tool No. D88L-1037-A and step plate No. D80L-630-5 or equivalent, press the hub out from the knuckle.

7. Remove the backing plate.

To install:

8. Install the backing plate assembly using new retaining bolts and tighten to 44-59 ft. lbs. (59-80 Nm).

9. With a hub support tool No. T89P-1104-A or equivalent positioned on a press, position the knuckle assembly on tool.

10. Place hub into position on bearing and press hub into bearing using a hub installer tool No. T83P-1104-AH2 or equivalent.

11. Install the brake shoes, springs and adjuster to backing plate.

12. Install the knuckle and hub assembly onto the vehicle.

13. Install the brake drum and wheels and adjust the brakes as necessary.

14. Carefully lower the vehicle, then bleed the brake system.

REAR DISC BRAKES

➧ See Figures 55 and 56

✱✱CAUTION

Some brake shoes contain asbestos, which has been determined to be a cancer causing agent. Never clean the brake surfaces with compressed air! Avoid inhaling any dust from any brake surface! When cleaning brake surfaces, use a commercially available brake cleaning fluid.

Disc Brake Pads

REMOVAL & INSTALLATION

1987-88 Vehicles

➧ See Figures 57, 58 and 59

1. Raise and safely support the vehicle on jackstands.
2. Remove the tire and wheel assembly.

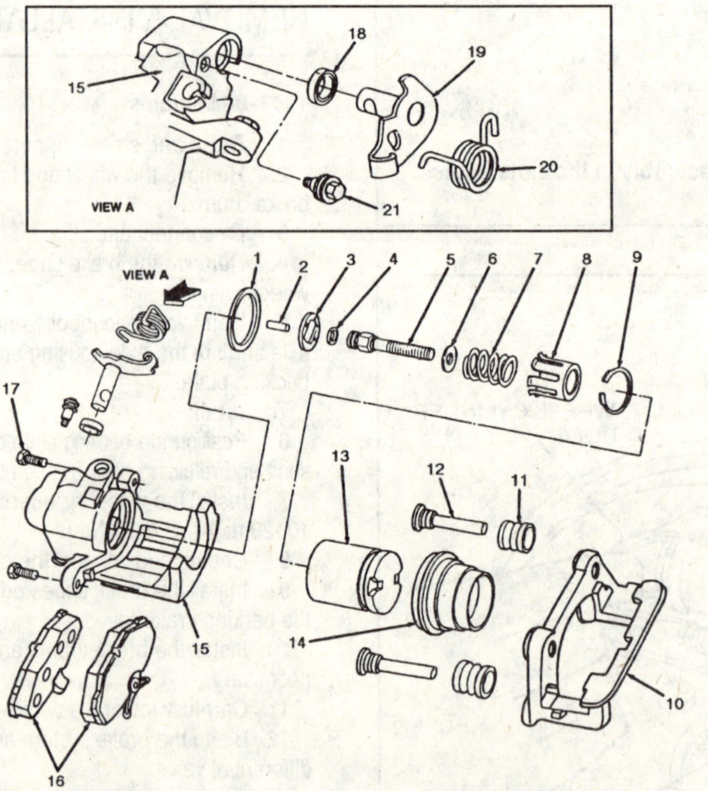

1. Piston seal
2. Pin
3. Locating washer
4. Rear brake caliper piston
5. Push rod
6. Flatwasher
7. Spring
8. Parking brake spring retainer
9. Parking brake lever pin retainer clip (circlip)
10. Rear disc support bracket
11. Slider pin boot seal (2 req'd)
12. Disc brake caliper locating pin
13. Rear disc brake piston and adjuster
14. Piston dust boot
15. Rear disc brake caliper
16. Brake shoe and lining
17. Rear brake pin retainer
 - Tighten to 31-35 Nm (23-26 lb. ft.)
18. Lever shaft seal
19. Rear parking brake cable
20. Parking brake return spring
21. Limiting bolt
 - Tighten to 6-9 Nm (4.5-7.0 lb. ft.)

88189G43

Fig. 55 Rear disc brake caliper and related system components — 1995 vehicle shown

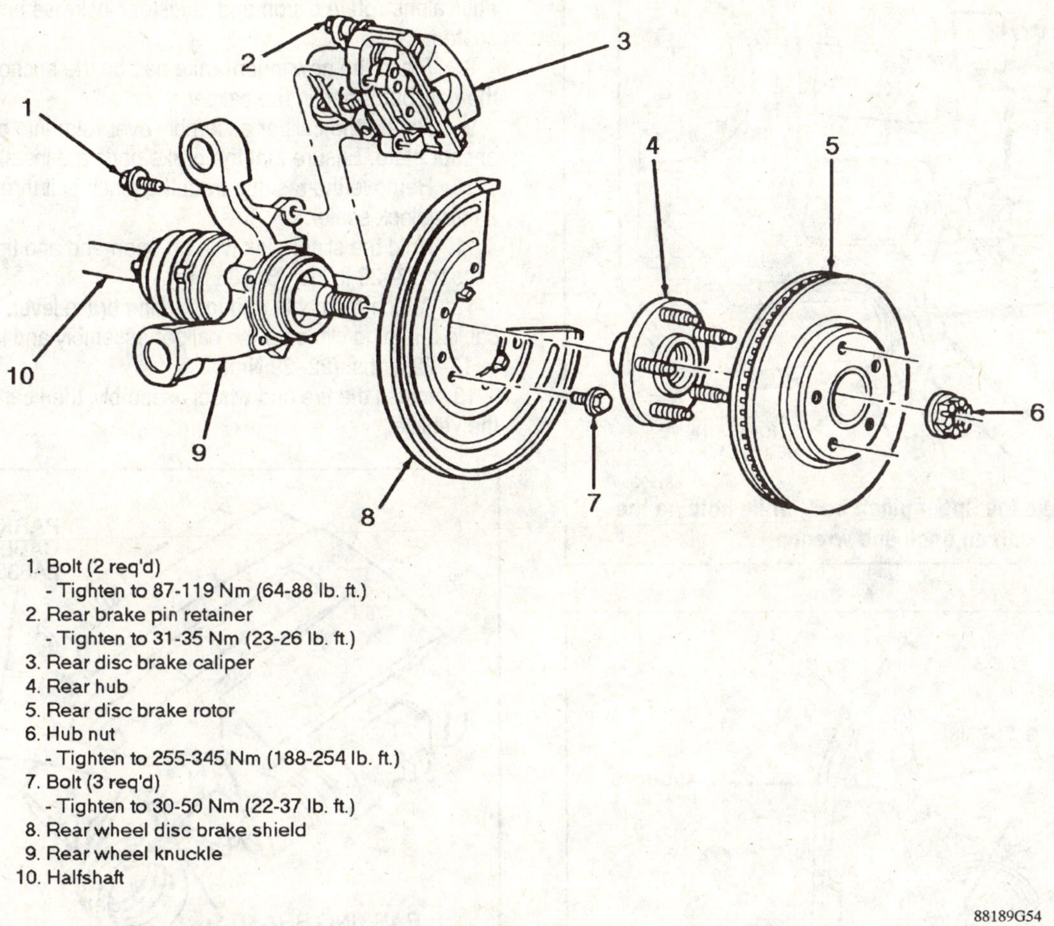

Fig. 56 Rear disc brake system components — 1995 vehicle shown

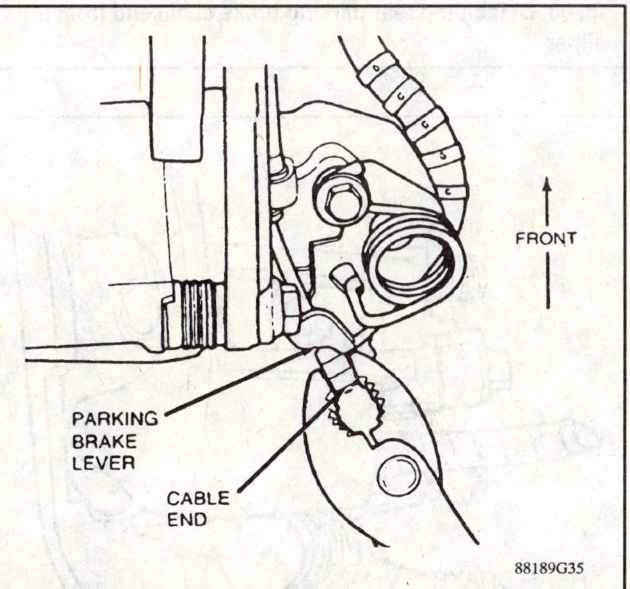

Fig. 57 Detach the parking brake cable end from the lever

3. Remove the screw retaining the brake hose bracket to shock/strut bracket.
4. Remove cable tension, and remove the retaining clip from the parking brake cable at the caliper. Remove the cable end from the parking brake lever.
5. Hold the slider pin hex-heads with an open-end wrench and remove the upper pinch bolt. Loosen, but do not remove the lower pinch bolt.
6. Rotate the caliper away from the rotor.
7. Remove the inner and outer brake pads and the anti-rattle clips from the anchor plate.

To install:

8. Using a piston turning tool T87P-2588-A, or equivalent, rotate piston clockwise until it is fully seated.
9. Place the new inner brake pad on the anchor plate. Place the new outer pad in the caliper.

➥ Ensure that one of the two slots in the piston face is positioned so it will engage the nib on the back of the brake pad.

10. Rotate the caliper assembly over rotor into position on anchor plate. Ensure that the brake pads are installed correctly.
11. Remove the residue from the pinch bolt threads and apply a threadlock sealer E0AZ-19554-A or equivalent.
12. Hold the slider pins with an open-end wrench, and tighten the pinch bolts to 30-35 ft. lbs. (40-47 Nm).
13. Attach the cable end to the parking brake lever. Install the cable retaining clip onto the caliper assembly and tighten screw to 30-37 ft. lbs. (41-50 Nm).
14. Install the tire and wheel assembly, then carefully lower the vehicle.

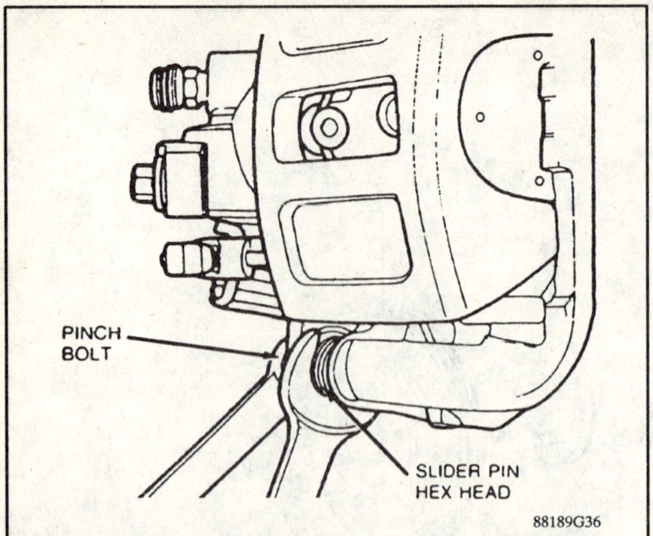

Fig. 58 Remove the upper pinch bolt, while holding the pin hex-heads with an open-end wrench

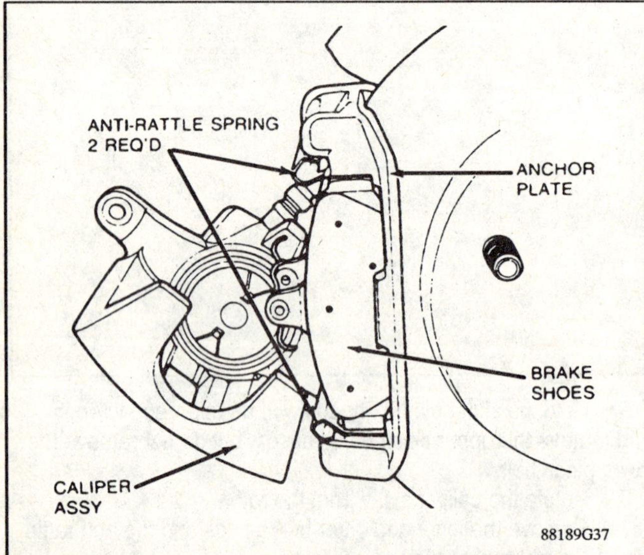

Fig. 59 Removing the brake shoes from the calipers

1989–96 Vehicles

See Figures 60, 61, 62, 63 and 64

1. Raise and safely support vehicle on jackstands.
2. Remove the wheel and tire assembly.
3. Release the parking brake cable tension, and disengage parking brake cable end from the caliper.
4. Remove the rear brake pin retainers. For vehicles through 1992, hold the slider pin hex-heads with an open-end wrench. Remove the upper pinch bolt. Loosen but do not remove the lower bolt.
5. Rotate the caliper away from the rotor.
6. Remove the inner and outer brake pads and the anti-rattle clips from the anchor plate/rear support bracket.

To install:

Ensure that one of the two slots in the piston face is positioned so it will engage the nib on the back of the brake pad.

7. Using Rear Caliper Piston Adjuster T87P-2588-A, or equivalent, rotate piston and adjuster clockwise until it is fully seated.
8. Place the new inner brake pad on the anchor plate. Place the new outer pad in the caliper.
9. Rotate the caliper assembly over rotor into position on anchor plate. Ensure that the brake pads are installed correctly.
10. Remove the residue from the pinch bolt threads and apply a threadlock sealer.
11. Hold the slider pins with an open-end and tighten pinch bolts to 23–26 ft. lbs. (31–35 Nm).
12. Attach the cable end to parking brake lever. Install the cable retaining clip onto the caliper assembly and tighten screw to 16–22 ft. lbs. (22–29 Nm).
13. Install the tire and wheel assembly, then carefully lower the vehicle.

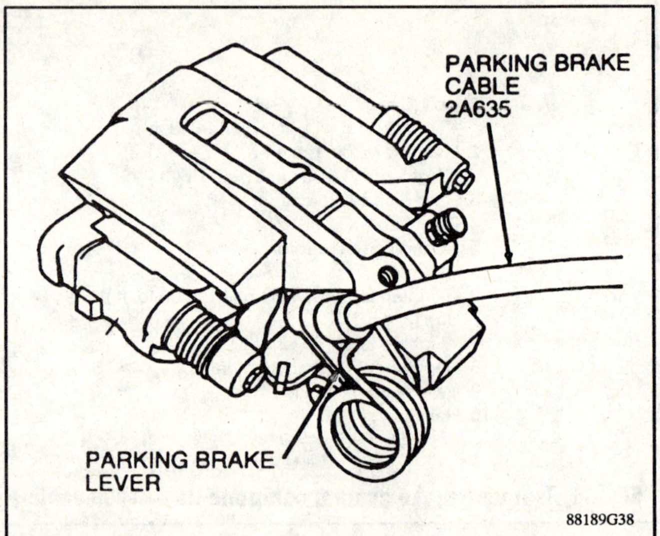

Fig. 60 Detach the rear parking brake cable end from the caliper

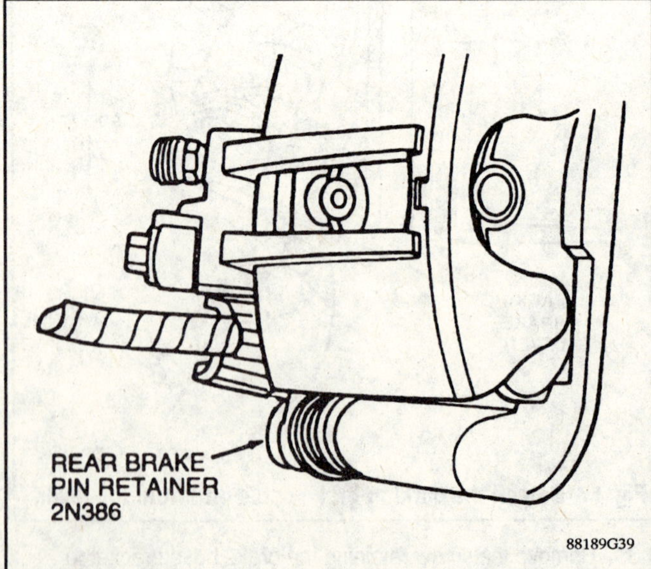

Fig. 61 Rear brake pin retainer locations — 1995 vehicle shown

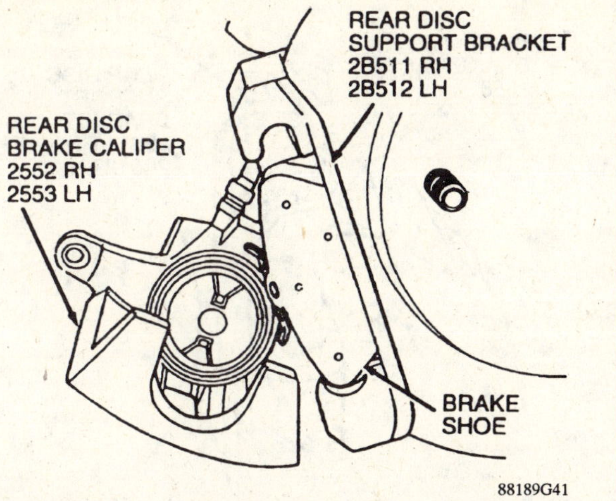

Fig. 62 Rotate the caliper from the rotor, then remove the brake pads

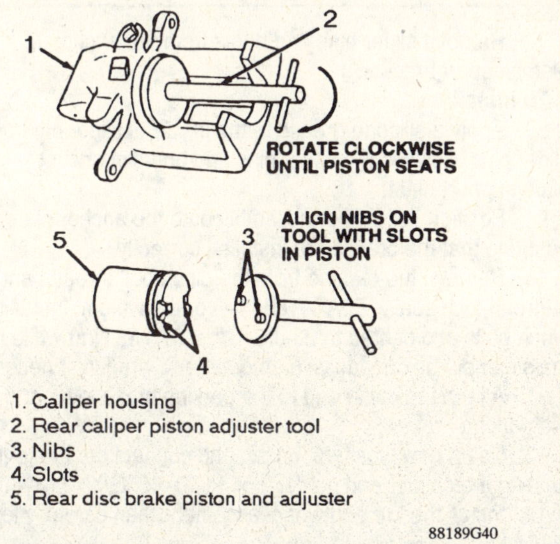

Fig. 63 Rotate the piston and adjuster clockwise until fully seated

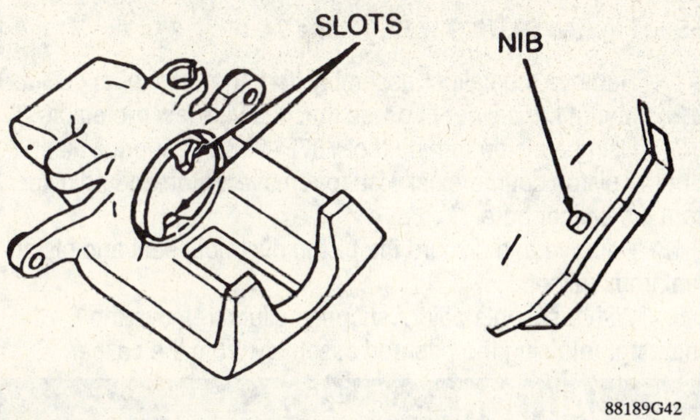

Fig. 64 Install the brake pads, making sure the pads are secure

Caliper

REMOVAL & INSTALLATION

1987-88 Vehicles

➧ See Figures 57, 58 and 65

1. Raise and safely support the vehicle using jackstands.
2. Remove the wheel and tire assembly. Use care to avoid damage or interference with the splash shield.
3. Disconnect the parking brake cable from the lever. Use care to avoid kinking or cutting the cable or return spring.

➥ If the caliper is not being replaced or rebuilt, you do not have to disconnect the fluid line from the caliper.

4. If the caliper is being replaced or rebuilt, detach the brake hose from caliper assembly. Cap the hose to prevent fluid loss and contamination.
5. Hold the slider pin hex heads with an open-end wrench and remove the pinch bolts.
6. Lift the caliper assembly away from the anchor plate.
7. Remove slider pins and boots from the anchor plate.

To install:

8. Apply silicone grease to the inside of slider pin boots and slider pins. Position the slider pins and boots in anchor plate.
9. Position the caliper assembly onto the anchor plate, ensuring that the brakes are installed correctly.
10. Remove the residue from the pinch bolt threads and apply a thread-lock sealer E0AZ-18554-A or equivalent. Install the pinch bolts and tighten to 23-26 ft. lbs. (31-35 Nm) while holding the slider pin hex heads with an open-end wrench.
11. Attach the cable end to the parking brake lever. Install the cable retaining clip on the caliper. Tighten the screw to 16-22 ft. lbs. (22-29 Nm).
12. If detached, using new washers, connect the brake hose to the caliper and tighten bolt to 20-30 ft. lbs. (27-40 Nm).
13. Install the tire and wheel assembly and lower vehicle.
14. If the brake lines were disconnected, Bleed the brake system.

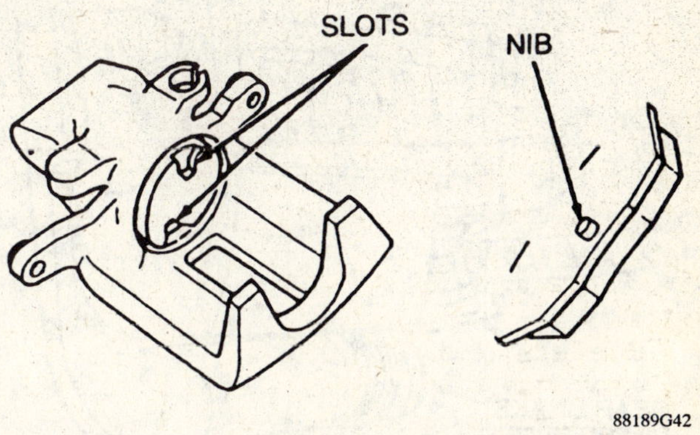

Fig. 65 Caliper removal on 1987-88 vehicles with rear disc brakes

1989–96 Vehicles

➧ **See Figures 66, 67 and 68**

1. Raise and safely support the vehicle with jackstands.
2. Remove the wheel and tire assembly. Use care to avoid damage or interference with the splash shield.

➥ **If the caliper is not being replaced or rebuilt, you do not have to disconnect the fluid line from the caliper.**

3. If the caliper is being replaced or rebuilt, disconnect and cap the brake line from the caliper.
4. Release the rear parking brake cable tension. Detach the cable end from the caliper. Use care to avoid kinking or cutting the cable or return spring.
5. Hold the slider pin hex heads with an open-end wrench and remove the pinch bolts or remove the rear brake pin retainers, as applicable.
6. Lift the caliper assembly away from the anchor plate/support bracket.

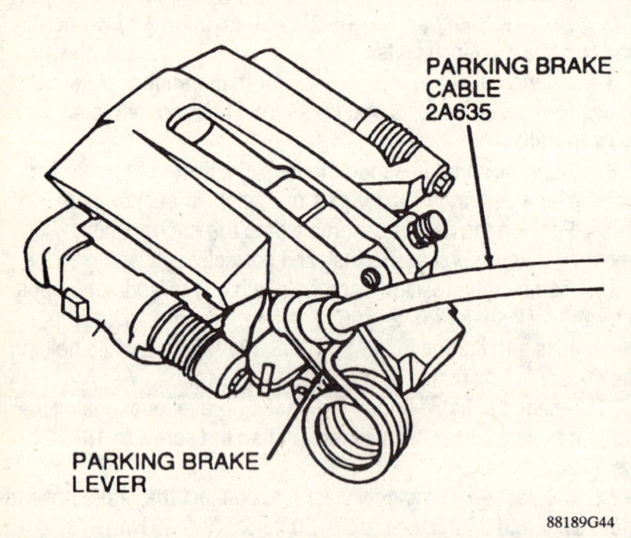

Fig. 66 Detach the parking brake cable from the caliper

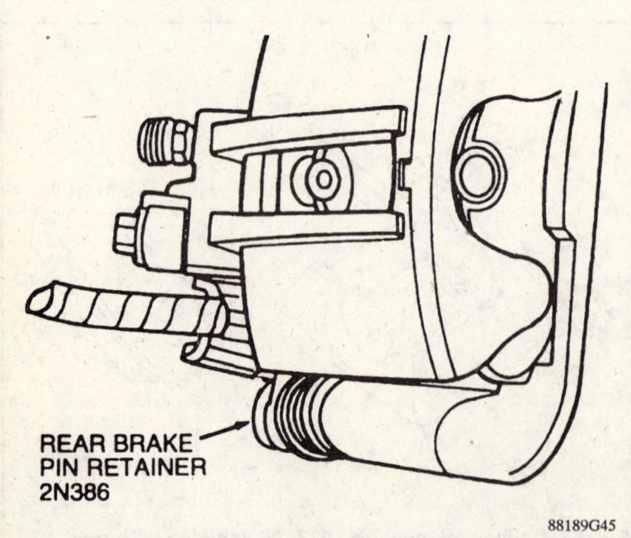

Fig. 67 Rear brake pin retainer location — 1995 vehicle shown

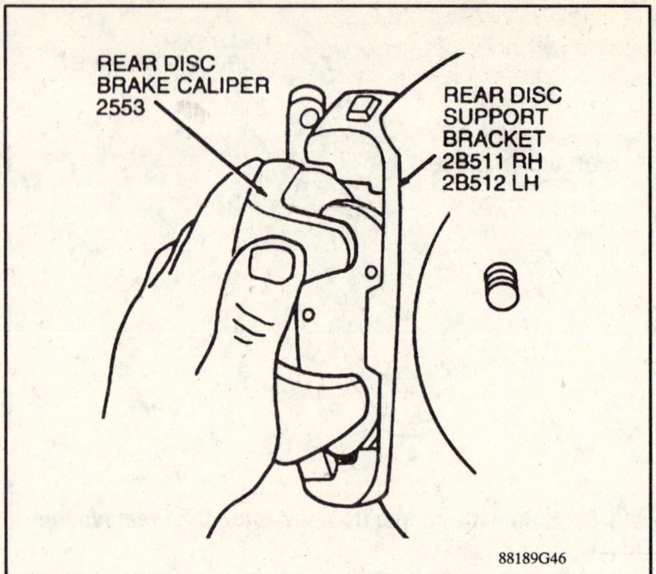

Fig. 68 Position the caliper on the anchor plate/support bracket

7. Remove slider pins and boots from the anchor plate/support bracket.

To install:

8. Apply a silicone grease to the inside of slider pin boots and slider pins. Position the slider pins and boots in anchor plate/support plate.
9. Position the caliper assembly onto the anchor plate, ensuring that the brakes are installed correctly.
10. Remove the residue from the pinch bolt threads and apply a thread-lock sealer E0AZ-18554-A or equivalent. Install the pinch bolts and tighten to 23–26 ft. lbs. (31–35 Nm) while holding the slider pin hex heads with an open-end wrench, if necessary.
11. Attach the cable end to the parking brake lever and adjust the parking brake.
12. Using new washers, uncap and connect the brake flex hose to the caliper and tighten bolt to 30–45 ft. lbs. (40–60 Nm).
13. Install the tire and wheel assembly, then carefully lower vehicle.
14. If the brake hose was disconnected, bleed the brake system.

CALIPER OVERHAUL

➧ **See Figures 69, 70, 71, 72, 73 and 74**

1. Remove the caliper assembly from the vehicle as outlined.
2. Mount the caliper in a vise that has vise jaw protectors.
3. Using a piston turning tool T87P-2588-A or equivalent, turn the piston counterclockwise to remove piston and adjuster from the caliper bore.
4. Remove and discard the piston dust boot seal and piston seal from caliper.
5. With a suitable pair of snapring pliers, remove the snapring, retaining the pushrod assembly, from the caliper.

****CAUTION**

The snapring and spring cover are under spring load, and care should be taken when removing the snapring.

6. Remove the spring cover, spring washer, key plate, and pull out the pushrod and strut pin.
7. Remove and discard the O-ring seal from the pushrod.
8. Remove the parking brake lever return spring, unscrew the parking brake lever stop bolt and pull the parking brake lever out of caliper housing.

Clean all metal parts with isopropyl alcohol. use clean, dry, compressed air to clean out and dry the grooves and passages. Be sure the caliper bore and component parts are completely free of any foreign material. Inspect the caliper bores for damage or excessive wear. Replace the piston assembly if the piston is pitted, scored or plating is worn off.

To install:

9. Lightly grease the parking brake lever bore and lever shaft seal with silicone grease, and press the lever shaft seal into the caliper bore.
10. Grease the parking brake shaft recess and slightly grease the parking brake lever shaft. Insert the shaft into bore in the caliper housing.

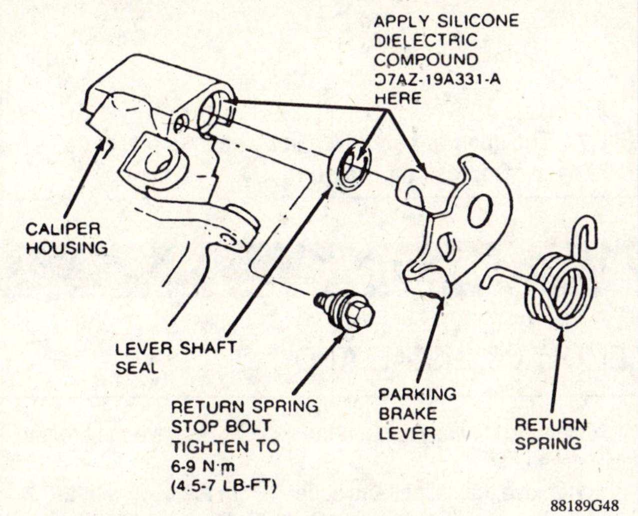

Fig. 69 Parking brake lever installation

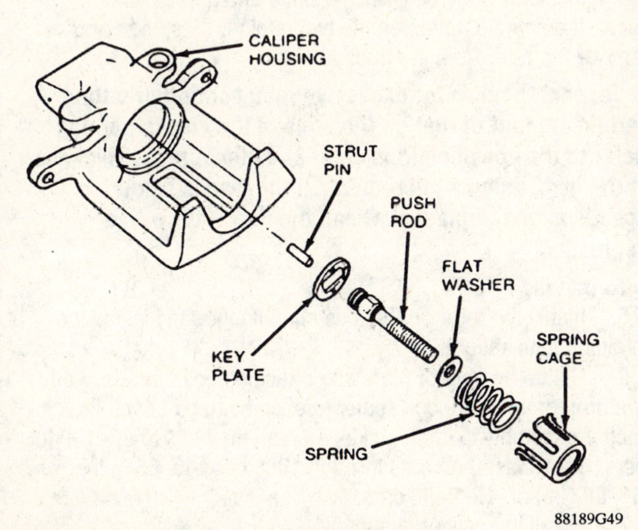

Fig. 70 Parking brake component assembly

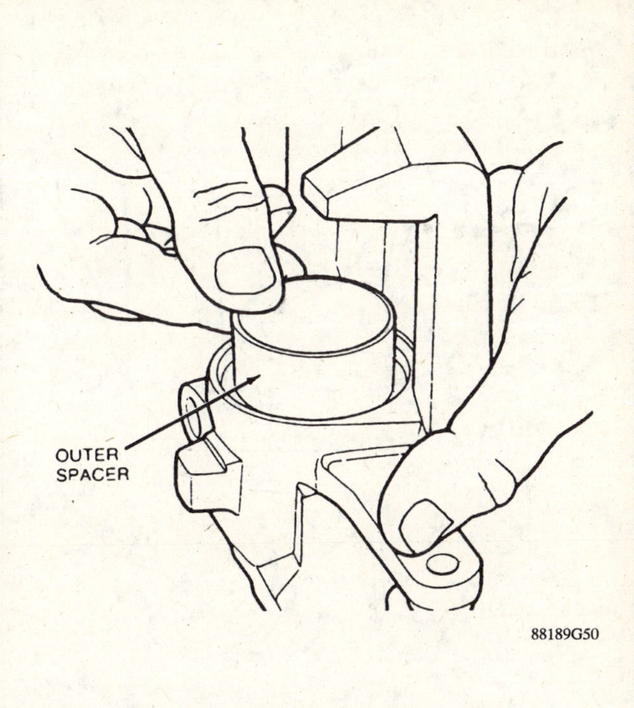

Fig. 71 Spring compressor outer spacer

11. Screw the lever stop bolt into the caliper housing and tighten to 4.5–7 ft. lbs. (6.1 — 9.5 Nm). Attach parking brake lever return spring to the stop bolt and insert free end into the parking brake lever slot.
12. Install a new O-ring seal into the groove of the pushrod. Grease the recess at pushrod end with a silicone grease.
13. Position strut pin into the caliper housing and in the recess of the parking brake lever shaft. Insert pushrod into the pushrod bore of the caliper housing. Ensure the pin is positioned correctly between shaft recess and the recess at end of pushrod.
14. Place key plate over pushrod so that the locating nib fits into the drilled locating hole in caliper housing. Install the flat washer, pushrod spring and spring cover in order.
15. Insert the outer spacer into the piston bore.
16. Insert the inner spacer into the piston bore.
17. Place snapring inside of the inner spacer.
18. Position a spring compressor, screw and cross-block on the pushrod. Lightly screw tool clockwise to compress spring and install the snapring.

The snapring should "click" into place. Do not over-compress the ring.

19. Install a new piston seal in groove in the caliper housing, after lubricating the seal with new brake fluid.
20. Coat the piston and piston dust boot with clean, new brake fluid. Install the dust boot into piston bore of caliper. Spread the dust boot over the piston and seat the dust boot in piston groove. Rotate the piston clockwise with a piston turning tool T87P-2588-A or equivalent, until the piston is fully seated.

Ensure that one slot in piston face is positioned so it will engage in the nib on back of brake pad.

21. Install the caliper assembly, tire and wheel assembly and lower vehicle.
22. Bleed the brake system.

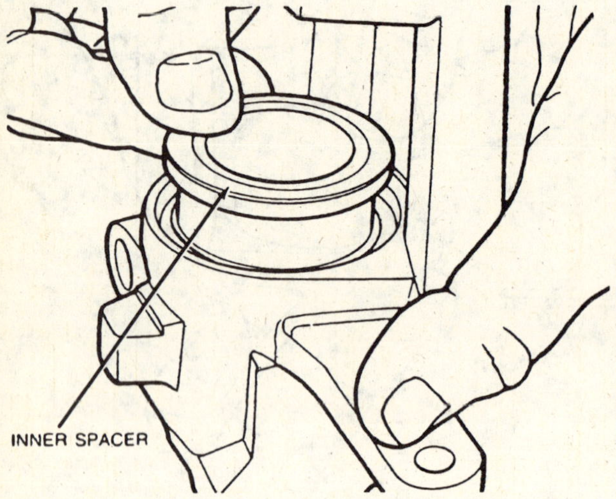

Fig. 72 Spring compressor inner spacer

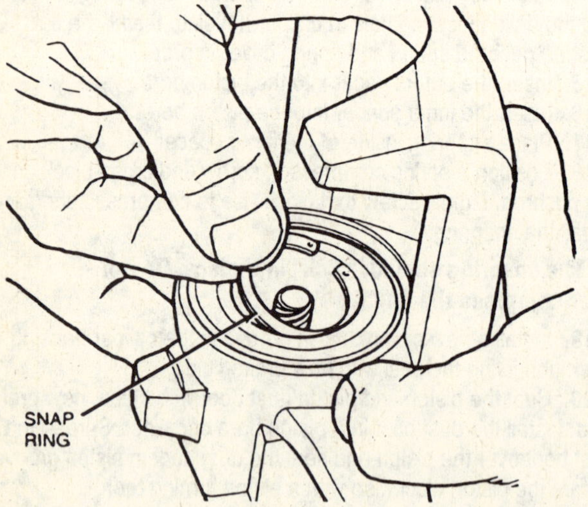

Fig. 73 Snapring positioning

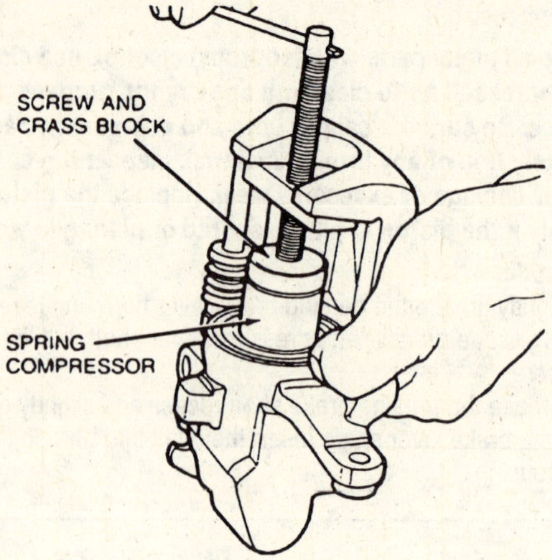

Fig. 74 The snapring should "click" when in place, do NOT over-compress the snapring

Brake Disc (Rotor)

REMOVAL & INSTALLATION

1. Raise and safely support the vehicle. Remove the tire and wheel assembly.
2. Remove the caliper and support from the body with a piece of wire, as outlined earlier. Do NOT disconnect the fluid line.
3. Remove the two bolts that attach the anchor plate to the rear knuckle. Remove the anchor plate and brake pads.
4. If equipped, unfasten the two retainer nuts, then and remove the rotor from the hub.

➥ Inspect the disc for excessive rust, scoring or pitting. A certain amount of rust on the edge of the disc is normal. Refer to the specifications chart and measure the thickness of the disc, using a micrometer. If the disc is below specifications, replace it. Clean the new rotor with a degreaser.

To install:

5. Install the rotor on the axle shaft flange, and install the retaining nuts securely.
6. Clean the anchor plate and attaching bolt threads. Add one drop of a thread-lock sealer to each bolt and attach the anchor assembly to the knuckle. Tighten the bolts to 80–100 ft. lbs. (105–135 Nm) on cars through 1988 or to 45–65 ft. lbs. (61–88 Nm) on 1989–96 cars.
7. Install the caliper assembly.
8. Install the tire and wheel assembly, and lower vehicle.

PARKING BRAKE

Cables

REMOVAL & INSTALLATION

1983-88 Vehicles — Except Thunderbird Turbo Coupes

➧ See Figures 75 and 76

FRONT CABLE

1. Raise and safely support the rear end of the vehicle on jackstands.
2. Remove the adjusting nut at the equalizer and remove the equalizer from the cable.
3. Unfasten the clip that holds the cable to the frame or body bracket.
4. Remove the clip that retains the cable to the parking brake control, inside the car.
5. Disconnect the cable from the control assembly.

➥ Some cars have cables with snap-in fittings. On these cables, compress the tangs, with a 13mm 12-point socket, and remove them from the mounting surface.

6. Pull the cable up through the opening in the dash panel.
7. Installation is the reverse of removal. Adjust the parking brake, as outlined later in this section.

Fig. 75 Parking brake system components used on the 1983-85 Thunderbird, XR-7 and Cougars

INTERMEDIATE CABLE

1. Raise and safely support the rear end of the vehicle on jackstands.
2. Remove the cable adjusting nut.
3. Disconnect the intermediate cable ends from the left rear and the transverse cables.

➛ Some cars have cables with snap-in fittings. On these cables, compress the tangs, with a 13mm 12-point socket, and remove them from the mounting surface.

4. Remove the cotter pin, washer and spring from the pin protruding from the equalizer assembly, and remove the lever.

➛ The intermediate cable cannot be separated from the lever.

5. Installation is the reverse of removal. Adjust the parking brake, as outlined later in this section.

TRANSVERSE CABLE

1. Raise and safely support the rear end of the vehicle on jackstands.
2. Remove the adjusting nut.
3. Remove the transverse cable ends from the right rear and intermediate cables.
4. Remove the hairpin clips or conduit brackets and remove the cable.
5. Installation is the reverse of the removal procedure. Adjust the parking brake, as outlined later in this section.

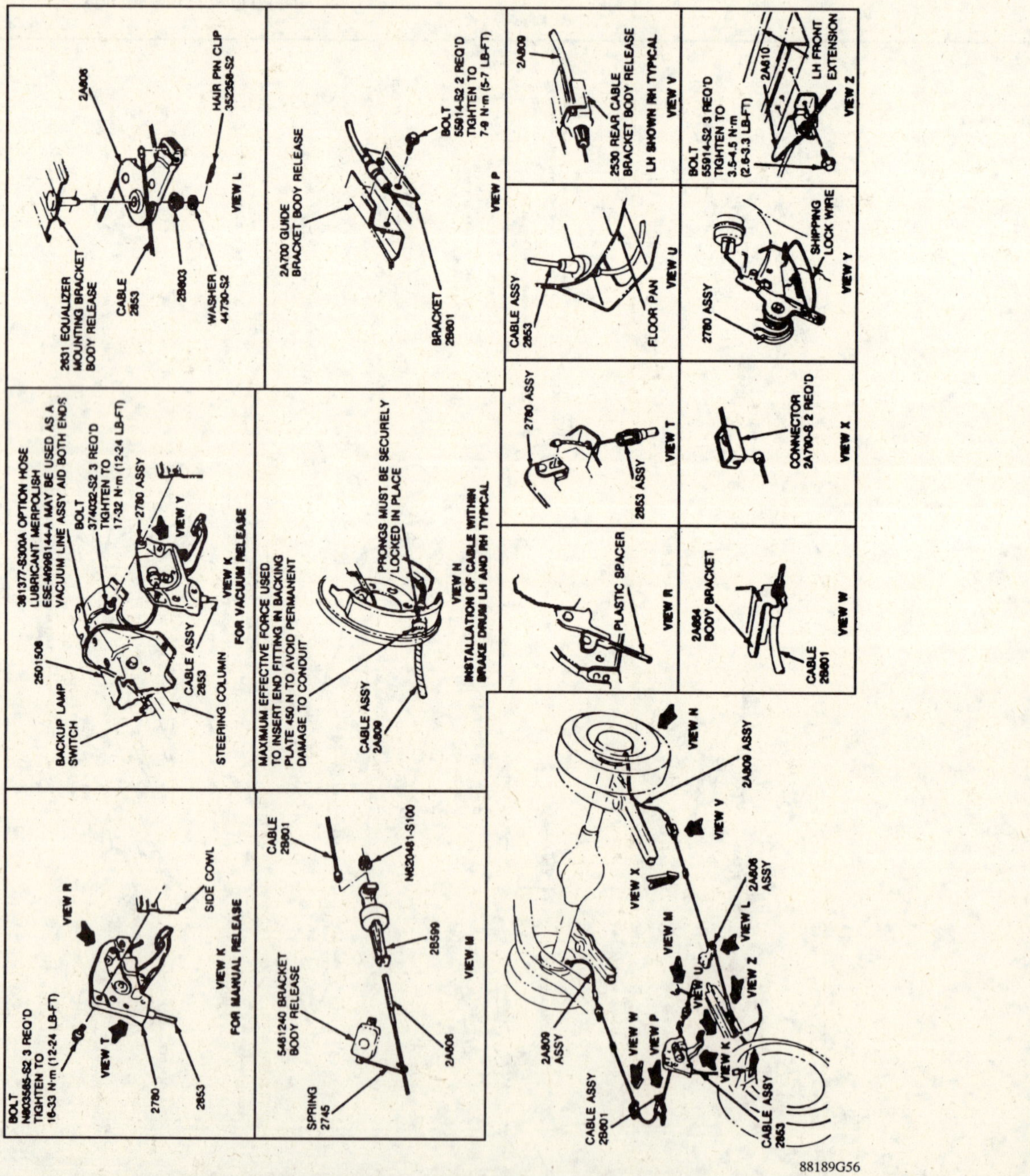

88189G56

Fig. 76 Park brake system components used on the 1986–88 vehicles, except Turbo Coupes

REAR CABLES

1. Raise and safely support the rear end on of the vehicle jackstands.
2. Remove the equalizer adjusting nut and remove the equalizer.
3. Disconnect the rear cables from the right and left rear cable connectors.
4. Remove the cable from the retainer hooks.
5. Remove the hairpin clip retaining the cable housing to the side rail bracket.
6. On cars with rear drum brakes:
    a. Remove the brake drums.
    b. Remove the brake shoes and disconnect the cable end from the self-adjusting lever.
    c. Compress the pronged retainers and remove the cable assembly from the backing plate.
7. On cars with rear disc brakes, remove the clevis pin securing the cable to the caliper actuating arm, then remove the cable.
8. Installation is the reverse of removal. Adjust the parking brake, as outlined later in this section.

Thunderbird Turbo Coupe Through 1988

➧ See Figure 77

FRONT CABLE

1. Raise and safely support the rear end of the vehicle on jackstands.
2. Remove the adjusting nut at the equalizer and remove the equalizer from the cable.
3. Remove the clip that holds the cable to the frame or body bracket.
4. Remove the clip that retains the cable to the parking brake control, inside the car.
5. Disconnect the cable from the control assembly.

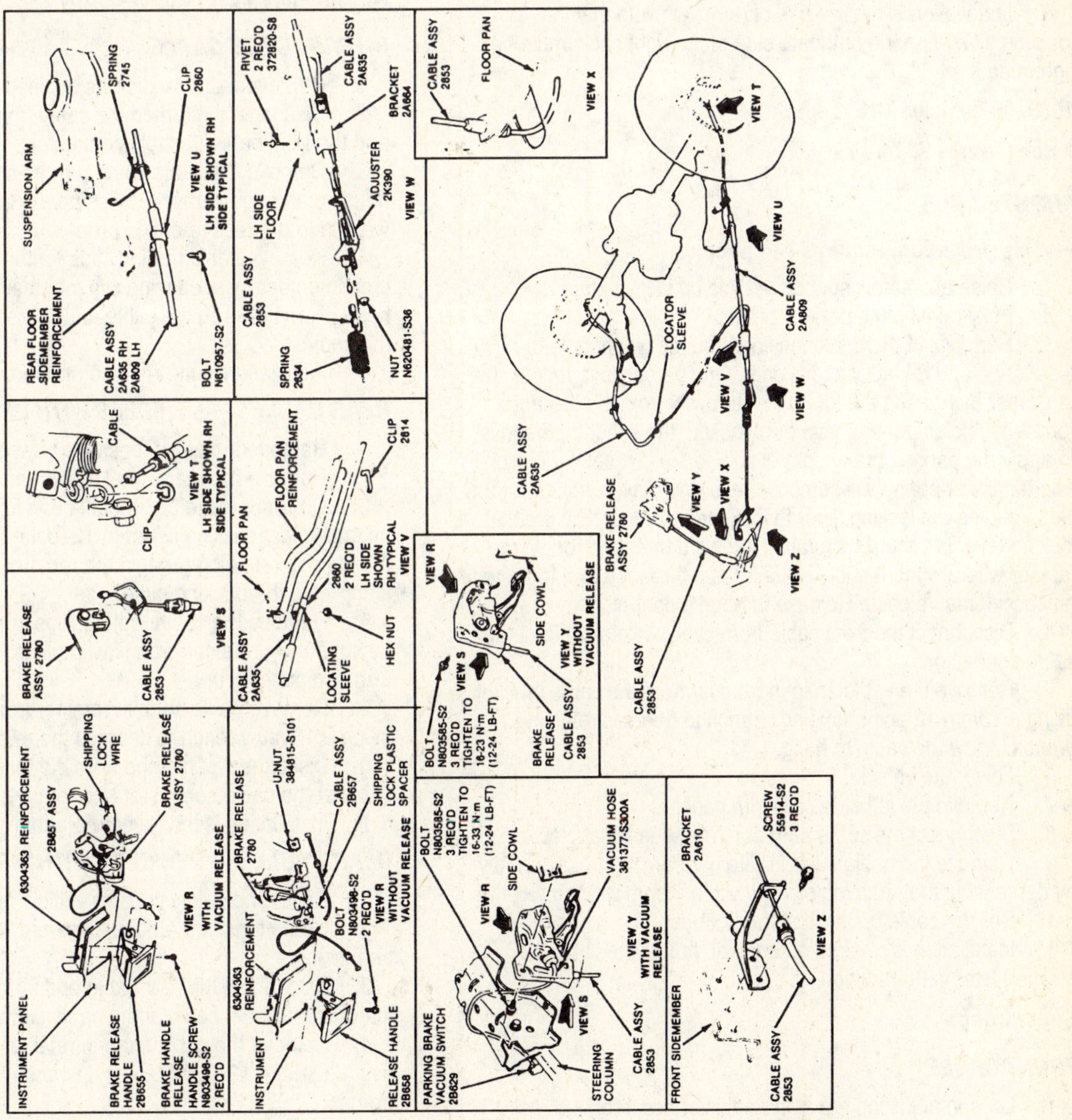

Fig. 77 Parking brake system components used on the 1986–88 Thunderbird Turbo Coupe

➔ Some cars have cables with snap-in fittings. On these cables, compress the tangs and remove them from the mounting surface.

6. Pull the cable up through the opening in the dash panel.
7. Installation is the reverse of removal. Adjust the parking brake, as outlined later in this section.

REAR CABLES

1. Raise and safely support the rear end of the vehicle on jackstands.
2. Remove the adjuster nut.
3. Disconnect the parking brake release spring from the right cable at the equalizer.
4. Detach the right cable from the adjuster and the side rail bracket.
5. Remove all cable retaining brackets.
6. Disconnect the left cable from the equalizer and body side rail bracket.
7. Remove the clips retaining the cables to the calipers and remove the cable ends from the parking brake lever arm.
8. Installation is the reverse of removal. Note that the locating sleeve on the outboard side of the right cable must be tightened first!

1989–96 Vehicles — Except Super Coupe

➧ See Figures 78 and 79

FRONT CABLE

➔ This procedure requires two people.

1. Raise and safely support vehicle on jackstands.
2. Fully release the parking brake.
3. Removal of the cable tension requires two people to disengage and reload the tensioner. One person is to unlock the tensioner by rotating the locking lever away from the threaded rod. While holding the tensioner unlocked, the second person is to apply the parking brake control fully to the last notch position. The tensioner spring will compress allowing cable slack to return. Next release the locking lever to lock the tensioner. Ensure that locking lever is secure by rotating it toward threaded rod. Wrap tape or wire around the locking lever and threaded rod, to prevent any accidental release. Release the brake control.
4. Disconnect the front cable from intermediate cable at the cable connector.
5. Remove the cable snap-in retainer from the cable bracket using a 13mm 12 point box end wrench to depress retaining prongs. Allow the cable to hang.
6. Lower the vehicle.
7. Remove the left side cowl trim panel.
8. Disconnect the cable from control assembly at clevis.
9. Remove the cable snap-in retainer from control assembly by depressing the retaining prongs with a 13mm wrench.
10. Pull the cable up through the floor pan.
11. Installation is reverse of removal. Adjust the cable, as outlined later in this section.

Super Coupe

FRONT CABLE

1. Loosen adjusting nut at the adjuster assembly.
2. Remove the floor console.
3. With hand control assembly in the released position, remove the slotted cable end from control assembly hook. Remove pronged cable retainer from the control assembly using a 13mm 12-point box end wrench.
4. Disconnect front cable from the right rear cable at the cable connector.
5. Remove the cable routing clip from body rear crossmember by squeezing the clip together with a pair of needle nose pliers, between the cable and crossmember. Allow the cable to hang.
6. Carefully lower the vehicle.
7. Remove the rear seat and console.
8. Disconnect cable from the control at clevis hook.
9. Remove the cable snap-in retainer from the hand control assembly by depressing the retaining prongs with a 13mm wrench.
10. Pull the cable and grommet up through the floor pan and out from under the carpet.
11. Installation is reverse of removal. Adjust the cable.

All Models, Except Super Coupe

INTERMEDIATE CABLE

1. Remove cable tension as outlined previously.
2. Disconnect intermediate cable from the right rear cable and the front cable at cable connector.
3. Remove the cable snap-in retainer from the tensioner housing and body bracket by using a 13mm 12-point box end wrench to depress retaining prongs.
4. Remove cable routing clips for the body side rails and rear crossmember by squeezing clip together with a pair of needle nose pliers between the cable and crossmembers, and remove the cable.
5. Installation is the reverse of removal. Adjust the cable.

REAR CABLES — VEHICLES WITH DRUM BRAKES

1. Remove the cable tension as described previously.
2. Remove the rear wheel and drum assembly.
3. Disconnect the brake cable end from the parking brake actuating lever. Using a 13mm 12-point box end wrench, depress the conduit retaining prongs and remove the cable end pronged fitting from the backing plate.
4. Remove the cable routing clips from the lower control arm by squeezing retainer prongs with pliers from under the control arm and pushing up.
5. Remove cable snap-in retainer from the frame bracket using a 13mm wrench to depress the retaining prongs.
6. Disconnect cable end from the tensioner or intermediate cable at the cable connector and remove rear cable.
7. Installation is the reverse of removal. Adjust the cable.

REAR CABLES — VEHICLES WITH DISC BRAKES

1. Raise and safely support vehicle on jackstands.
2. Grasp tensioner and pull forward to compress the spring and lock.
3. Disconnect the rear cable end from tensioner or intermediate/front cable at the cable connector.
4. Remove the cable snap-in retainer from the frame bracket using a 13mm 12-point box end wrench to depress the retaining prongs.

5. Disconnect rear cable end from the caliper housing and remove the cable from the parking brake lever arm on the caliper.
6. Installation is the reverse of removal. Adjust the cable.

ADJUSTMENT

1983–88 Vehicles

WITH REAR DRUM BRAKES

The parking brake should be adjusted for proper operation every 12 months or 12,000 miles and adjusted whenever there is slack in the cables. A cable with too much slack will not hold a vehicle on an incline which presents a serious safety hazard. Usually, a rear brake adjustment will restore parking brake efficiency, but if the cables appear loose or stretched when the parking brake is released, adjust as necessary.

The procedure for adjusting the parking brake on all pedal actuated systems is as follows:

1. Fully release the parking brake.
2. Depress the parking brake pedal one notch from its normal released position. On vacuum release brakes, the first notch is approximately 2 in. (51mm) of travel.
3. Taking proper safety precautions, raise the car and place the transmission in Neutral.
4. Loosen the equalizer locknut and turn the adjusting nut forward against the equalizer until moderate drag is felt when turning the rear wheels. Tighten the locknut.
5. Release the parking brake, making sure that the brake shoes return to the fully released position.
6. Lower the car and apply the parking brake. Under normal conditions, the third notch will hold the car if the brake is adjusted properly.

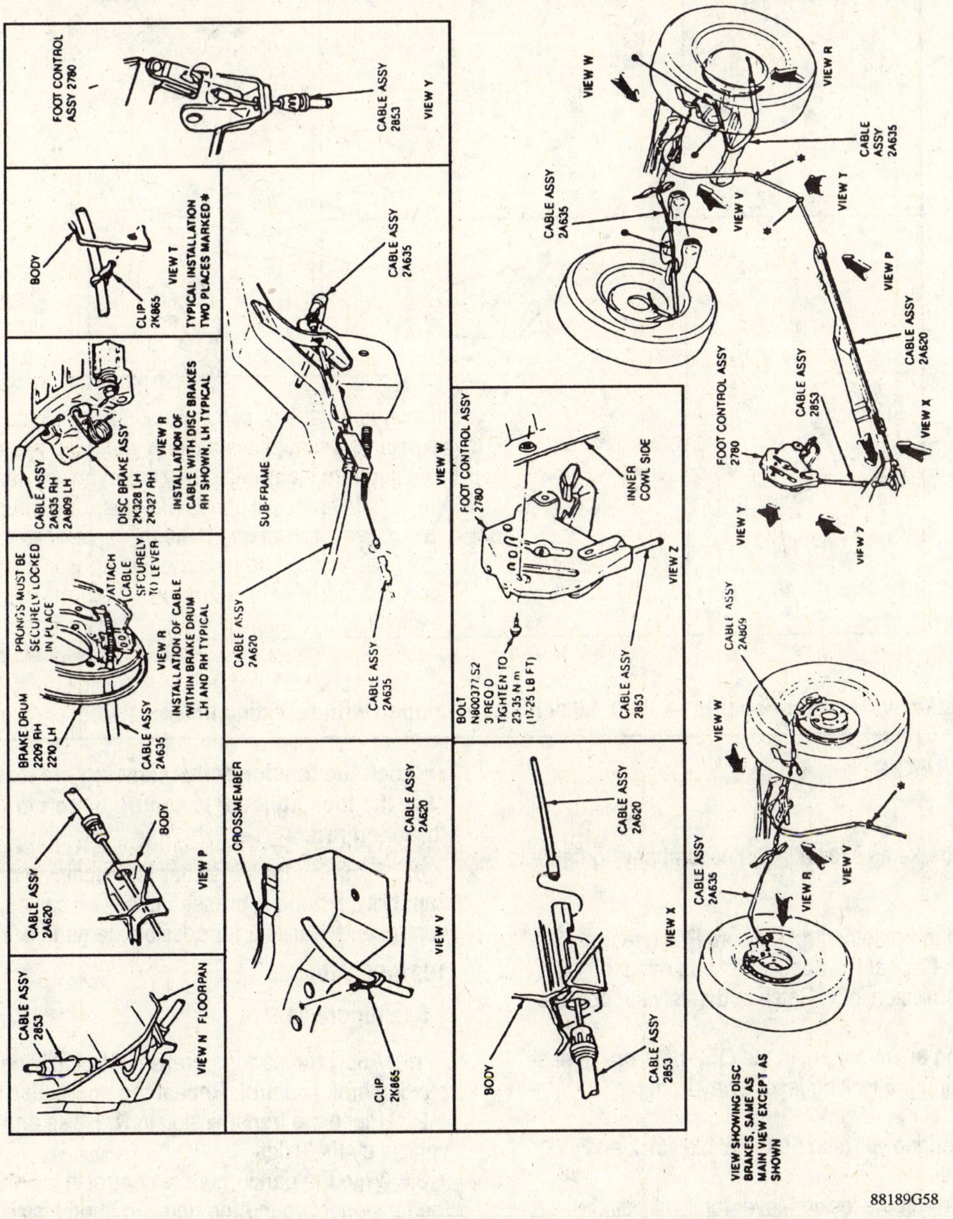

88189G58

Fig. 78 Parking brake system components — 1989–96 vehicles equipped with rear drum brakes

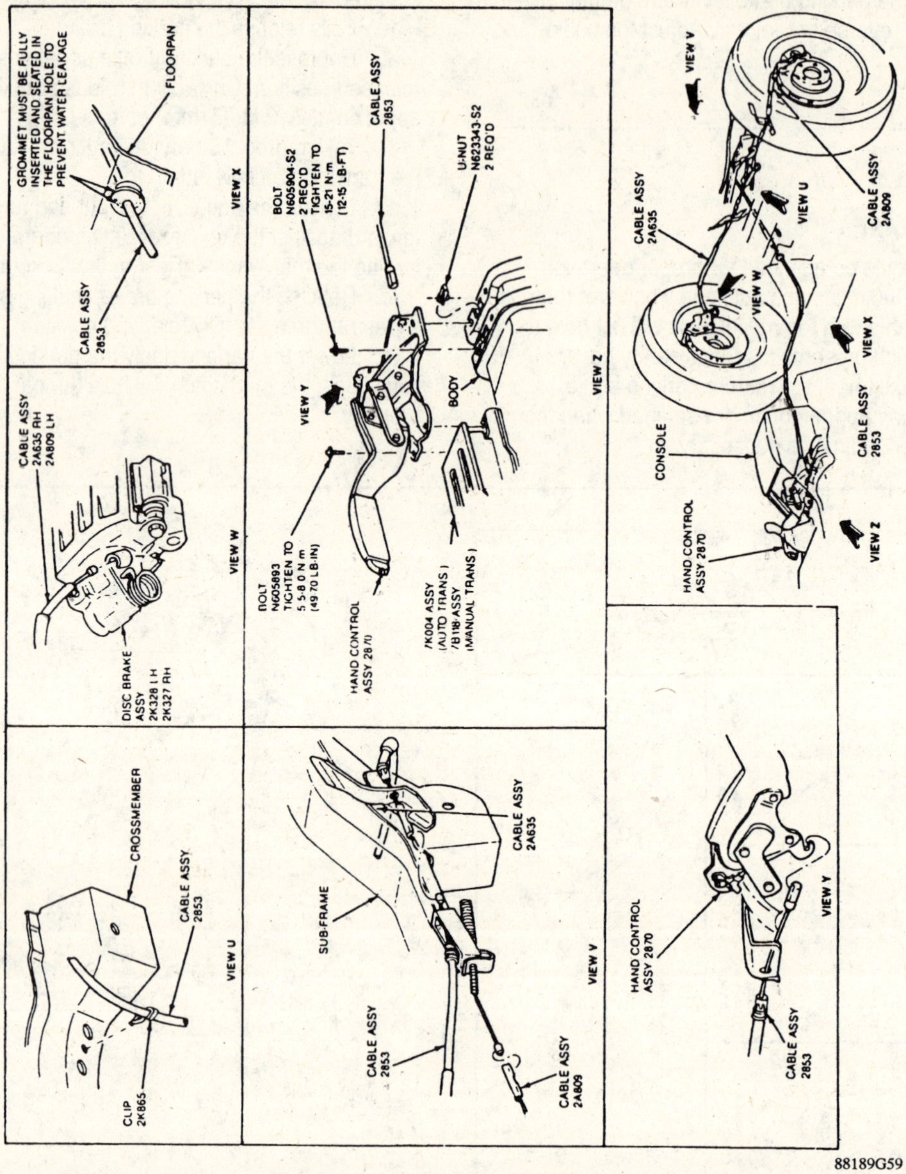

Fig. 79 Parking brake system components — 1989-96 vehicles equipped with rear disc brakes

WITH REAR DISC BRAKES

➧ See Figure 80

Adjust the parking brake as shown in the accompanying figure.

1989-90 Vehicles

1. Apply the parking brake control fully on. Release the parking brake control. Repeat the application and release.
2. Place the transmission in **N**. Raise and safely support the vehicle by the axles.
3. With the parking brake control in the **OFF** position, release the tensioner by rotating the locking lever away from the threaded rod.
4. The tensioner spring will take up the cable slack and preload the cables.
5. Do not pull down on the locking lever for it will pull the cables down and cause the cables to have low tension.

➥ Lock the tensioner by releasing the locking lever. Make sure the locking lever is secure by rotating it toward the threaded rod.

6. Examine the tensioner for remaining cable take up capability. If none is present, check all cables, parking brake control and brackets for possible damage or deflection.

1991-96 Vehicles

➧ See Figure 81

1. Apply the parking brake control fully on. Release the parking brake control. Repeat the application and release.
2. Place the transmission in **N**. Raise and safely support the vehicle by the axles.
3. With the parking brake control in the **OFF** position, grasp the tensioner around the housing, then, using a hook tool, hook the end into the rounded end of the clip between the clip and the housing.

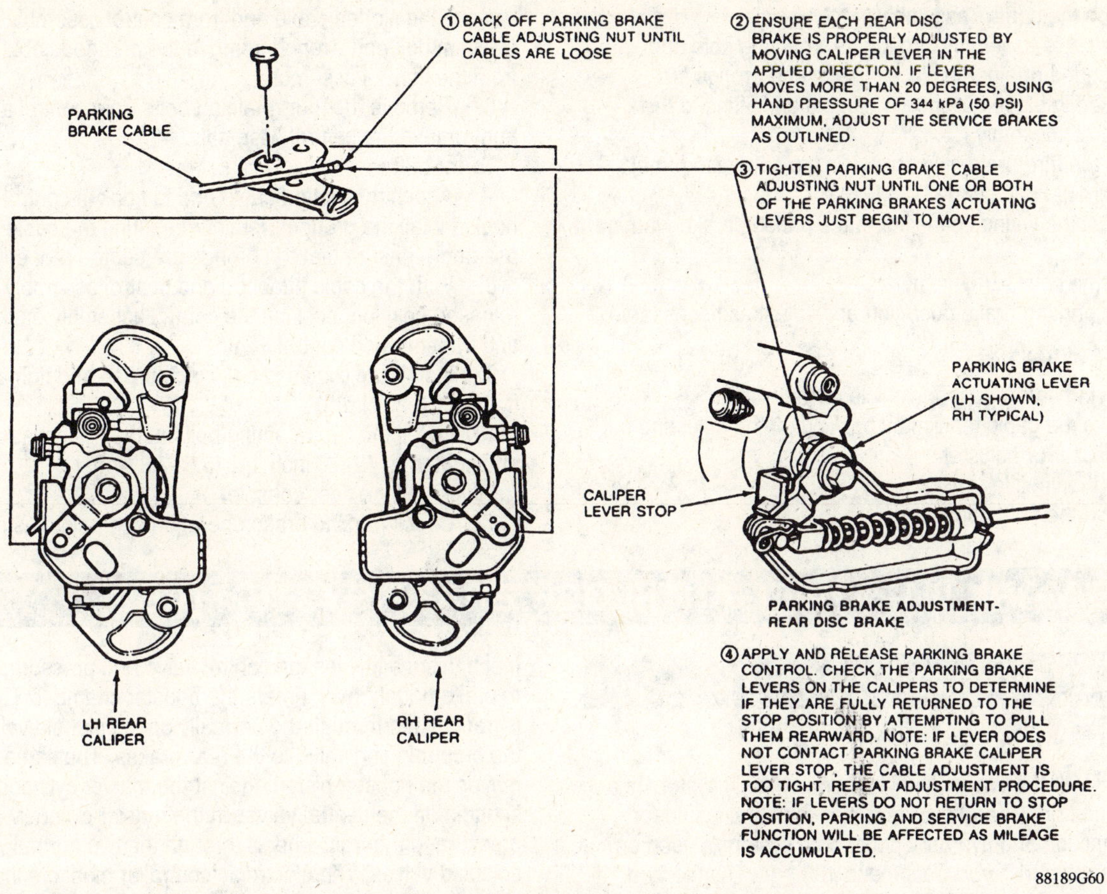

Fig. 80 Parking brake cable adjustment — 1987-88 vehicles with rear disc brakes

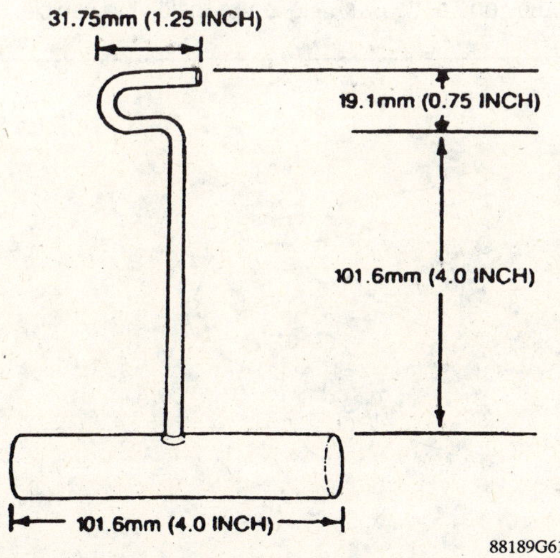

Fig. 81 Parking brake adjustment "hook" tool

4. Unlock the clip by pulling downward with the tool and support tensioner; the tensioner spring will take up cable slack and preload the cables.
5. While holding the tensioner, lock the clip by pushing up on the bottom of the clip. If the clip does not slide up, move the assembly slightly to align the closest groove on the adjuster rod to the clip.
6. Examine the tensioner for remaining cable take up capability. If none is present, check all cables, parking brake control and brackets for possible damage or deflection.

Brake Lever or Pedal

REMOVAL & INSTALLATION

Except Super Coupe

1. Raise and safely support vehicle on jackstands.
2. Remove the cable tension by backing off the adjusting nut from the equalizer or adjuster.
3. Lower the vehicle.
4. Disconnect the wiring connection from the parking brake warning indicator switch.
5. Remove the cowl side trim panel.
6. Remove the cable end from clevis at the brake control.
7. Remove the conduit snap-in filling from the control assembly using a 1/2 in. 12-point bow end wrench to depress the retaining tabs.
8. Remove the three bolts retaining the control to the cowl side panel. Remove the bolt retaining the control to the instrument panel.
9. Remove the control assembly from vehicle. Raise and safely support vehicle on jackstands.

To install:

10. Position the control assembly in the vehicle.
11. Fit the cable assembly through its mounting hole and press the pronged retainer in place. Ensure the prongs are securely locked in place. Connect the cable end fitting to the clevis at control assembly.
12. Install the three retaining screws in the cowl side panel and tighten to 17–25 ft. lbs. (23–34 Nm).
13. Connect the wiring connector to the parking brake warning indicator switch.
14. Install the cowl side trim panel.
15. Check parking brake operation and adjust as necessary.

Super Coupe Models

1. Raise and safely support vehicle on jackstands.
2. Remove the cable tension by backing off the adjusting nut from the equalizer or adjuster.
3. Lower the vehicle.
4. Remove the floor console.
5. With the hand control assembly in the released position, remove the slotted cable end from control assembly hook. Using a 13mm box end wrench, remove the pronged cable retainer from the control assembly.
6. Remove the four retaining bolts from control assembly, and remove the control assembly.

To install:

7. Attach the slotted cable end to hook in control assembly hook. Install the pronged retainer securing the cable to control assembly, ensure that the prongs are seated properly.
8. With the cable attached and control assembly in the released position, position the control assembly on the floorpan and transmission control.
9. Install two retaining bolts in floorpan and tighten to 12–15 ft. lbs. (15–20 Nm).
10. Install the two retaining bolts at the transmission control and tighten to 49–70 inch lbs. (5.5–7.8 Nm).
11. Install the floor console.
12. Check parking brake operation and adjust as necessary.

TEVES MARK II 4-WHEEL ANTI-LOCK BRAKE SYSTEM (ABS)

General Information

See Figure 82

The Teves Mark II 4 Wheel Anti-Lock Brake (ABS) system is a compact integral power brake system that uses brake fluid for both brake function and hydraulic boost. The system is used on 1987–88 Thunderbird Turbo Coupe and 1989–92 Thunderbird Super Coupe and Cougar XR-7 models.

The hydraulic pump maintains between 2,030 to 2,610 psi (13,997–17,996 kpa) pressure in the accumulator which is connected by a high pressure hose to the booster chamber and control valve. When the brakes are applied, a scissor/lever mechanism activates the control valve and pressure, proportional to brake pedal travel, enters the booster chamber. The pressure is transmitted through the normally open solenoid valve through the proportioning valve to the rear brakes. The same pressure moves the booster piston against the master cylinder piston, shutting off the central valves in the master cylinder. This applies pressure to the front wheels through the two normally open solenoid valves. The electronic controller monitors the electro-mechanical components of the system. Malfunction of the anti-lock system will cause the electronic controller to shut off or inhibit the anti-lock system. Normal power assisted braking remains if the anti-lock system shuts off. Malfunctions are indicated by one or two warning lamps inside the vehicle.

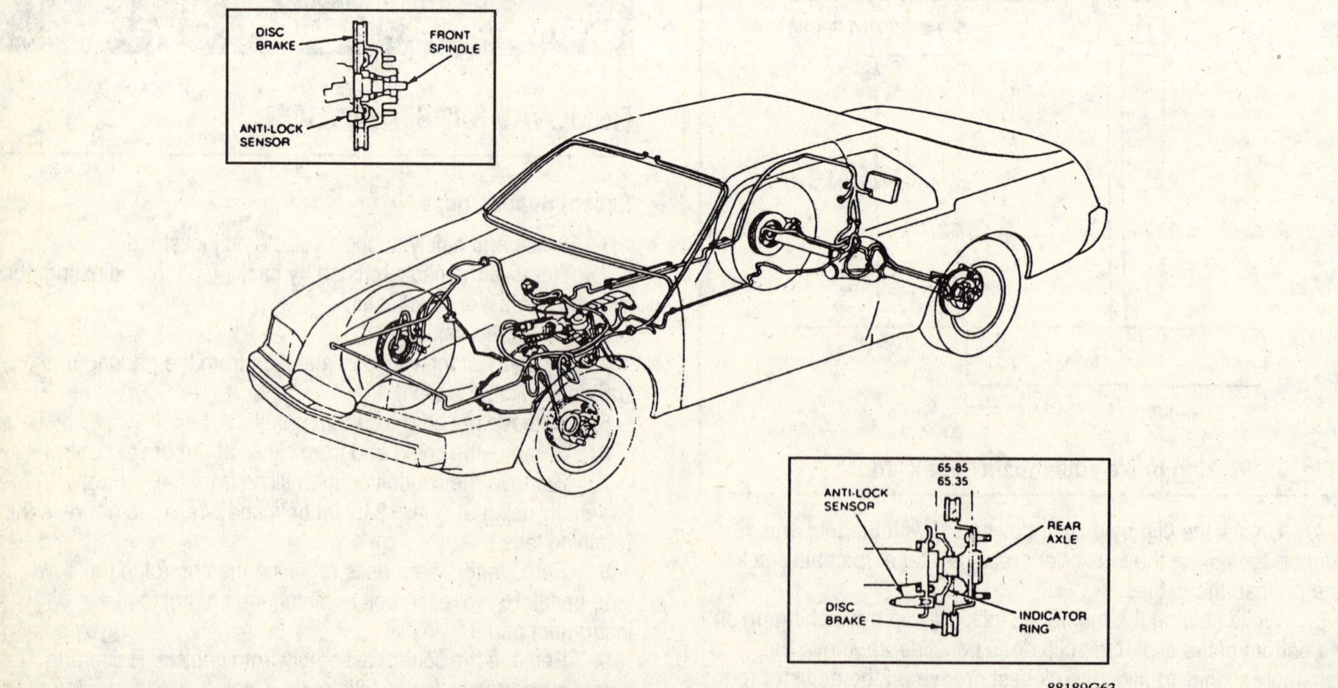

Fig. 82 Teves Mark II ABS system — 1987-88 vehicles shown

The 4-wheel anti-lock system is self-monitoring. When the ignition switch is placed in the Run position, the electronic controller will preform a preliminary self check on the anti-lock electrical system as indicated by a three to four second illumination of the amber Check Anti-Lock Brakes lamp in the overhead console. During vehicle operation, including normal and anti-lock braking operation is continually monitored. Should a problem occur, either the Check Anti-Lock Brakes or the Brake Warning Lamp(s) will be illuminated. The sequence of illumination of these warning lamps, combined with the problem symptoms, can determine the appropriate diagnostic tests to perform. However most malfunctions are stored as a coded number in the controller memory and pinpoint to the exact component needing servicing. Inspection of the system and any necessary repairs should be done before any further vehicle operation.

Individual front wheel brake circuits and a combined rear wheel brake circuit are used. Major components of the system are listed and outlined as follows.

SYSTEM COMPONENTS

Master Cylinder and Hydraulic Booster

➧ See Figures 83 and 84

The master cylinder and brake booster are mounted in the conventional manner. The booster control valve is located in a parallel bore above the master cylinder centerline and is operated by a lever mechanism connected to the brake pedal pushrod.

Electric Pump and Accumulator

A high pressure electric pump runs for short periods at frequent intervals to charge the hydraulic accumulator. The accumulator is a gas filled pressure chamber that is part of the pump and motor assembly. The pump, motor and accumulator are mounted on the master cylinder/booster assembly.

➥ If the pump motor is allowed to run continuously for approximately 20 minutes, a thermal safety switch (inside the motor) will shut off the pump motor. A 2-10 minute cool down period is typical before normal Anti-lock braking can resume. During the cool down period, the brakes will operate under the full power brake lock-up mode.

Valve Body Assembly

The valve body contains three pairs of solenoid valves, one pair for each front wheel and the third pair for both the rear wheels combined. The paired solenoid valves are inlet/outlet valves with the inlet valve normally open and the outlet valve normally closed. The valve body is bolted to the inboard side of the master cylinder/booster assembly.

Reservoir and Fluid Level Warning Switches

A translucent plastic reservoir having two main chambers is connected to the pump assembly and master cylinder by two low pressure hoses. Integral fluid level switches are part of the reservoir cap assembly. The reservoir is mounted on the hydraulic unit with a screw and bracket and a push-in tube outlet that seats in a grommet mounted in the brake booster housing.

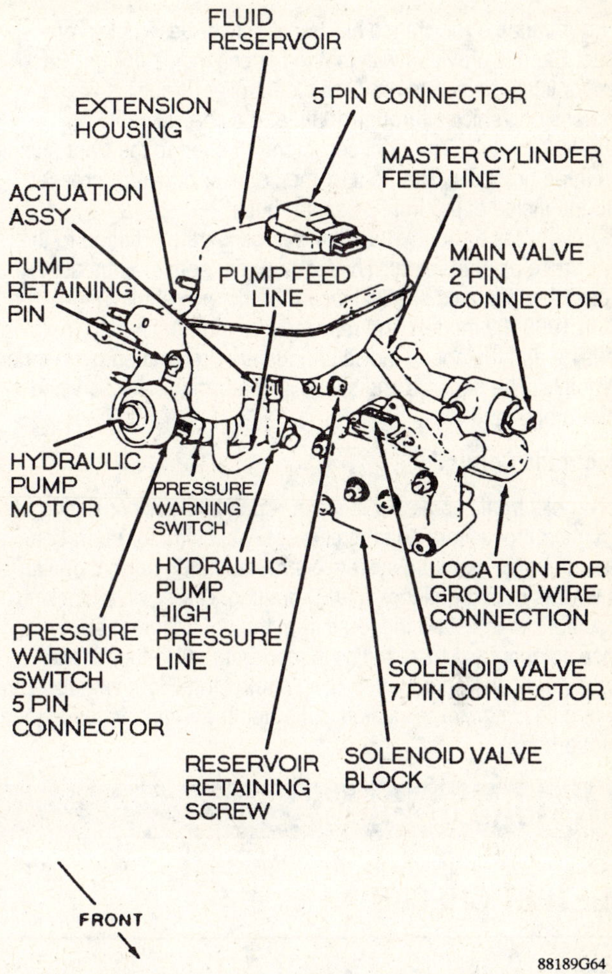

Fig. 83 ABS brake master cylinder — 1987-88 vehicles

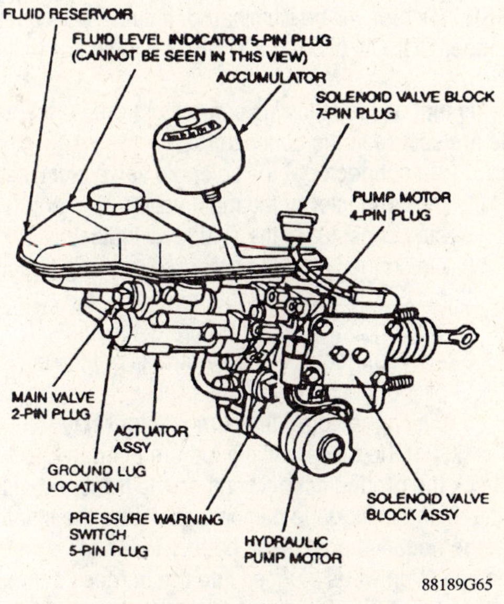

Fig. 84 ABS brake master cylinder — 1989-92 vehicles

Wheel Sensors

Four variable reluctance electronic sensor assemblies are used. Each is provided with toothed speed indicator ring. Each sensor is connected to an electric controller through a wiring harness on vehicles through 1988, and a coaxial cable on 1989-92 models. The front sensors are bolted to the front spindle mounted brackets. The front toothed sensor rings are pressed into the inside of the front disc rotor hubs.

On vehicles through 1988, the rear sensors are bolted to the rear brake axle adapters. The toothed rear sensor rings are pressed on the axle shafts, inboard of the axle shaft flange.

On 1989-92 models, the rear sensors are attached to the axle housing and the speed indicator rings are pressed onto the inner CV joints. The sensors and speed indicator rings are serviced separately.

Electronic Controller

The electronic controller is a non-repairable unit consisting of two microprocessors and the necessary circuitry for operation. The controller monitors system operation during normal driving as well as during anti-lock (panic) braking. Under wheel locking conditions signals are triggered from the controller that open and close solenoid valves resulting in moderate pulsations in the brake pedal and equal anti-locking control to all four wheels. The electronic controller is located in the upper portion of the luggage compartment.

Troubleshooting

PRETEST CHECKS

➧ See Figure 85

The following steps must be checked and done before diagnostic procedures can begin.

1. Verify that the parking brake is fully released.
2. Check the condition of battery, cables and connections.
3. Check the brake fluid level. As brake fluid level falls the red BRAKE indicator will be illuminated. If fluid level continues to fall the amber CHECK ANTI-LOCK BRAKE indicator will illuminate.
4. Verify that all the following connectors are connected and terminals are secure in the connectors:
   - 7-pin connector of the solenoid valve block assembly
   - 2-pin connector of the main valve
   - 5-pin connector of the fluid level indicator
   - 5-pin connector of the pressure warning switch
   - 2-pin connector on all four sensors
   - 4-pin connector on the pump motor
   - 32-pin connector of the electronic controller
   - 5-pin connector of the main relay
   - 5-pin connector of the pump motor relay
5. Check that the fuses and diodes are not damaged.
6. Check the ground connections on the front end of the hydraulic unit and in luggage compartment, and the small black wire from the negative post of the battery to fender apron. Then, check the two main wires plugged into the harness connector.

The anti-lock control module monitors the system operation and stores up to seven different service codes in its memory. However it cannot store two service codes with the same first digit, except for 40's service codes.

Example: The module cannot store a code 25 and code 26 at the same time. It can, however, store a code 25 and code 35. If code 25 were stored first it would have to be serviced before the code 26 can be stored. A valve service code will override any stored service code during self test. The condition must be serviced before any other codes can be displayed.

After all codes have been displayed and serviced, the memory can be cleared by driving the vehicle above 25 mph.

Master Cylinder-Booster Unit/Actuation Assembly

REMOVAL & INSTALLATION

1987-88 Vehicles

➧ See Figure 86

✱✱WARNING

The Anti-lock Brake System must be depressurized before any service is performed. To depressurize the system, turn the ignition OFF and pump the brake pedal at least 20 times, until an obvious increase in pedal pressure is felt.

1. Disconnect the negative battery cable.
2. Tag and detach the electrical connectors from the fluid reservoir cap, main valve, solenoid valve body, pressure warning switch, hydraulic pump motor and the ground connector from the master cylinder.
3. Disconnect and plug the brake lines from the solenoid valve body.
4. Disconnect the booster pushrod from the brake pedal by first disconnecting the spotlight switch wires at the connector on the brake pedal. Then, remove the hairpin connector at the stoplight switch and slide the switch off the pedal pin until the large end of the switch (outer hole) is off of the pin. Remove the switch using a twisting motion. Remove the unit's four retaining nuts at the firewall.
5. Remove the booster from the engine compartment.
6. Installation is the reverse of the removal procedure. Tighten the retaining nuts to 13-25 ft. lbs. (18-34 Nm).
7. Bleed the brake system using the proper procedure located later in this section.

1989-92 Vehicles

➧ See Figure 87

✱✱WARNING

The Anti-lock Brake System must be depressurized before any service is performed. To depressurize the system, turn the ignition OFF and pump the brake pedal at least 20 times, until an obvious increase in pedal pressure is felt.

1. Disconnect the battery ground cable.
2. Remove the air cleaner and ductwork.

SERVICE CODE (COMPONENT)	PINPOINT TEST STEP
11 (Electronic Controller)	AA1
12 (Electronic Controller-Replacer)	AA2
21 (Main Valve)	BB1
22 (LH Front Inlet Valve)	CC1
23 (LH Front Outlet Valve)	CC2
24 (RH Front Inlet Valve)	CC3
25 (RH Front Outlet Valve)	CC4
26 (Rear Inlet Valve)	CC5
27 (Rear Outlet Valve and Ground)	CC6
31 (LH Front Sensor)	DD1
32 (RH Front Sensor)	DD8
33 (RH Rear Sensor)	DD15
34 (LH Rear Sensor)	DD22
35 (LH Front Sensor)	DD1
36 (RH Front Sensor)	DD8
37 (RH Rear Sensor)	DD15
38 (LH Rear Sensor)	DD22
41 (LH Front Sensor)	DD1
42 (RH Front Sensor)	DD8
43 (RH Rear Sensor)	DD15
44 (LH Rear Sensor)	DD22
45 (LH Front Sensor)	DD29
46 (RH Front Sensor)	DD32
47 (RH and LH Rear Sensors)	DD33
48 (Any 3 Sensors missing)	DD34
51 (LH Front Outlet Valve)	EE1
52 (RH Front Outlet Valve)	EE4
53 (Rear Outlet Valve)	EE7
54 (Rear Outlet Valve)	EE10
55 (LH Front Sensor)	DD1
56 (RH Front Sensor)	DD8
57 (RH Rear Sensor)	DD15
58 (LH Rear Sensor)	DD22
61 (FLI and PWS Circuit)	FF1
71 (LH Front Sensor)	EE1
72 (LH Front Sensor)	EE4
73 (RH Rear Sensor)	EE7
74 (LH Rear Sensor)	EE10
75 (LH Front Sensor)	DD1
76 (RH Front Sensor)	DD8
77 (RH Rear Sensor)	DD15
78 (LH Rear Sensor)	DD22
88 (Electronic Controller)	AA1
99 (Electronic Controller)	AA1

88189GA4

Fig. 85 ABS Diagnostic Trouble Code Chart — 1987–92 vehicles

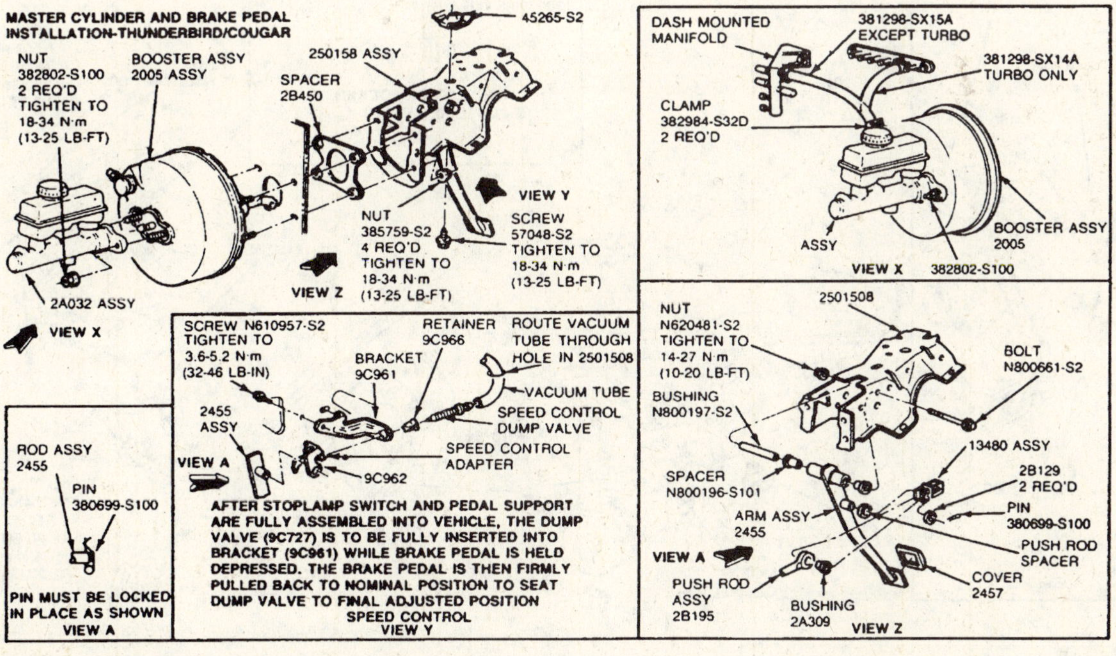

88189G66

Fig. 86 Actuator assembly (master cylinder) removal — 1987–88 vehicles

3. Tag and unplug the electrical connectors at the following components:

- fluid level indicator
- main valve
- solenoid valve block
- pressure warning switch
- hydraulic pump motor
- master cylinder ground

4. Disconnect the 3 brake pipes and immediately plug the openings to prevent fluid loss and contamination.

****WARNING**

Do not allow brake fluid to come in contact with any electrical connection!

5. Remove the steering column trim panel.
6. Disconnect the actuation assembly pushrod from the pedal.
7. Remove the 4 attaching nuts holding the actuation assembly to the pedal support bracket and lift out the assembly.

To install:

8. If a new unit is being installed, transfer the attached parts.
9. Position the new assembly on the mounting bracket and loosely thread on the 4 nuts.
10. Connect the pushrod.
11. Install the trim panel.
12. Tighten the nuts to 13–25 ft. lbs. (18–34 Nm).
13. Unplug and connect the fluid pipes. Tighten the connections to 10–18 ft. lbs. (14–24 Nm).
14. Connect all wiring, as tagged during removal.
15. Install the air cleaner and ductwork.
16. Connect the negative battery cable.
17. Bleed the ABS system, as outlined later in this section.

Hydraulic Accumulator

REMOVAL & INSTALLATION

➧ See Figure 88

****WARNING**

The Anti-lock Brake System must be depressurized before any service is performed. To depressurize the system, turn the ignition OFF and pump the brake pedal at least 20 times, until an obvious increase in pedal pressure is felt.

1. Disconnect the negative battery cable.
2. On 1987–88 models, detach the electrical connector at the hydraulic pump motor.
3. Using an 8mm hex wrench, loosen and unscrew the accumulator. Do not allow any dirt to enter the open port.
4. Loosen and remove the accumulator mounting block, if necessary.

To install:

5. Install in the reverse order using a new O-ring seal coated with clean brake fluid.
6. Tighten the accumulator assembly to 30–34 ft. lbs. (41–46 Nm).
7. Turn the ignition switch to the **ON** position for 1987–88 vehicles, or the **RUN** position for 1989–92 vehicles. Check that the BRAKE warning indicator and Anti-Lock lamps go out after a maximum of one minute. Fill the reservoir as necessary.

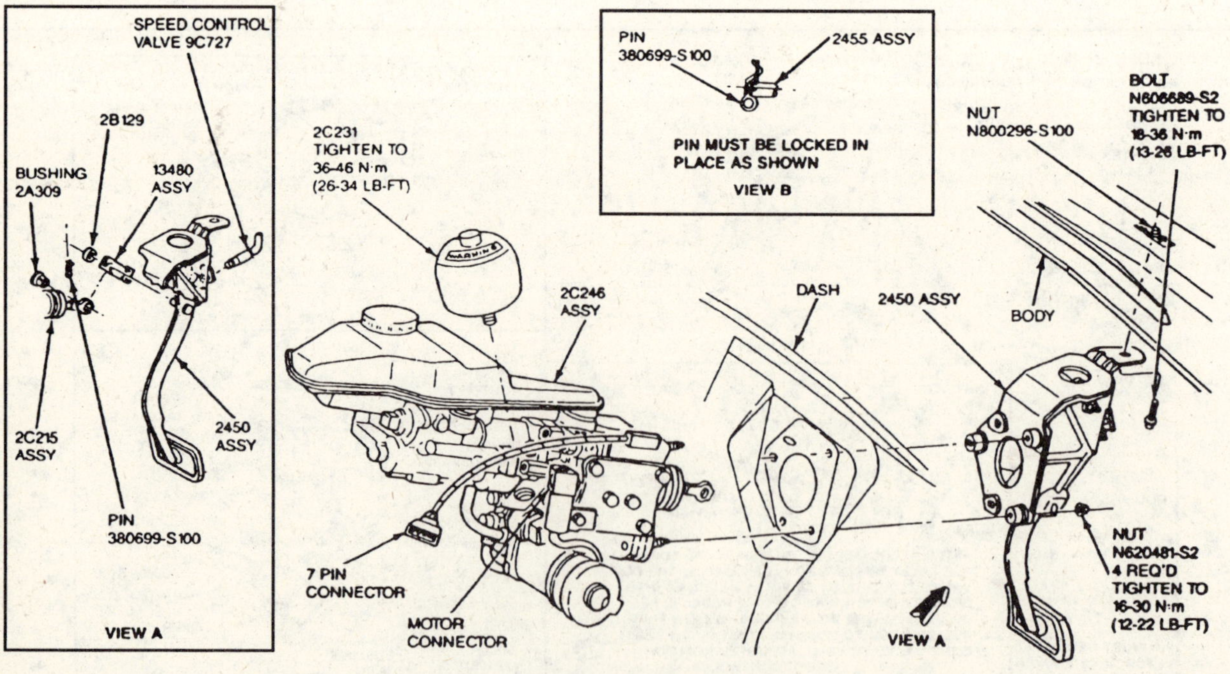

88189G67

Fig. 87 ABS master cylinder (actuator assembly) mounting — 1989–92 vehicles

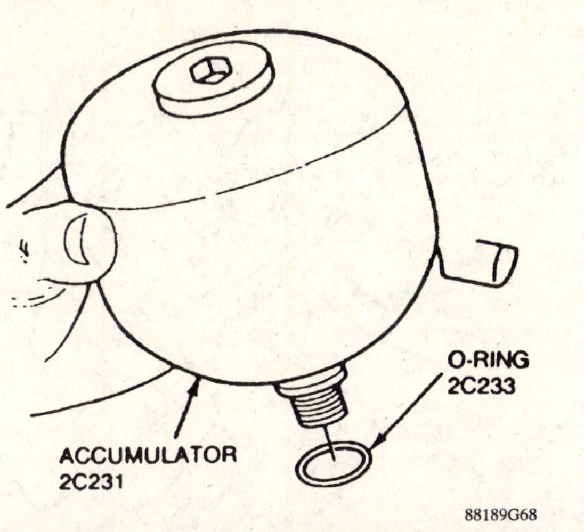

Fig. 88 Hydraulic accumulator assembly mounting

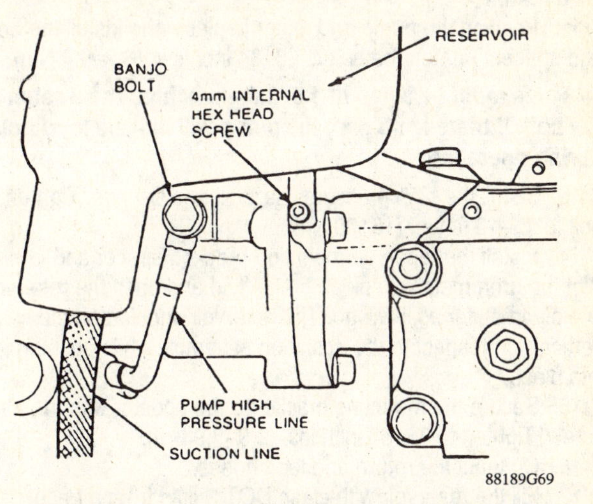

Fig. 89 Reservoir and fluid line — 1987-88 vehicles

Hydraulic Pump Motor

REMOVAL & INSTALLATION

****WARNING**

The Anti-lock Brake System must be depressurized before any service is performed. To depressurize the system, turn the ignition OFF and pump the brake pedal at least 20 times, until an obvious increase in pedal pressure is felt.

1987-88 Vehicles

See Figures 89, 90 and 91

1. Disconnect the negative battery cable.
2. Detach the electrical connections at the hydraulic pump motor, reservoir cap, and pressure warning switch.
3. Using a clean turkey baster or equivalent, drain as much fluid as possible from the reservoir.
4. Remove the suction line between the reservoir and the pump at the reservoir by twisting the hose and pulling.
5. Remove the return line from between the reservoir and master cylinder in the same manner.
6. Unfasten the 4mm hex headed reservoir mounting bolt.
7. Remove the reservoir by gently prying it off with a small prybar.
8. Remove the banjo bolt connecting the high pressure hose to the booster housing, at the housing. Be sure to catch and save the 2 sealing O-rings, one on each side of the banjo bolt head.
9. Using an 8mm allen wrench, remove the accumulator. Make certain no debris falls in the hole!
10. Remove the 6mm allen headed bolt attaching the pump and motor assembly to the extension housing which is located directly under the accumulator. A long extension and universal swivel socket will help reach the bolt.
11. Move the pump assembly toward the engine and remove the retainer pin on the inboard side of the extension housing. Remove the pump and motor assembly.

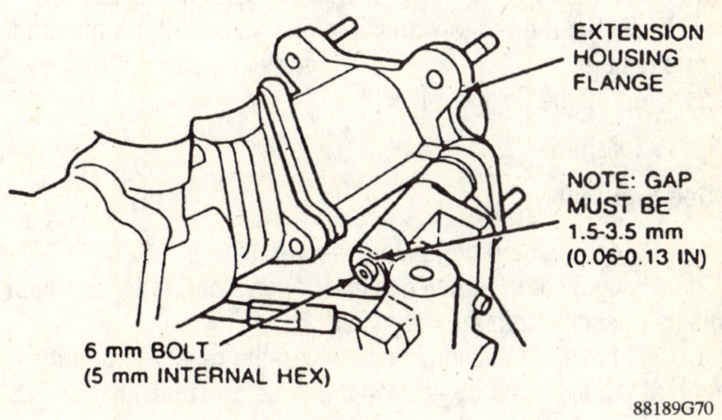

Fig. 90 Check that there is the correct gap between the washer and bracket

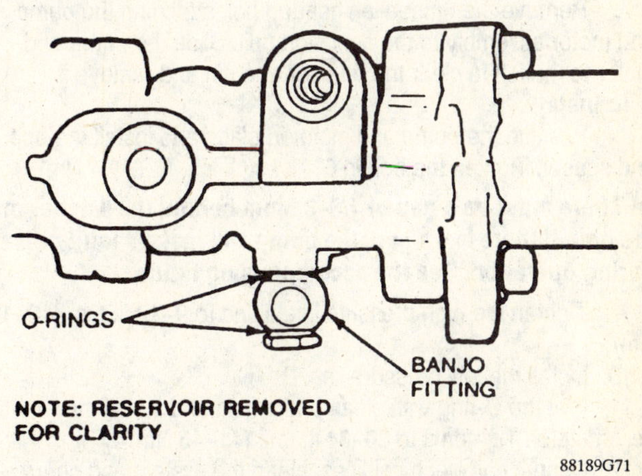

Fig. 91 Banjo bolt installation

To install:

12. Position the pump and motor in place and install the bolt and spacer. Tighten the bolt to 60–84 inch lbs. (6.7–9.4 Nm).

➥ There must be a gap of 1.5–3.5mm behind the washer on the bolt. If there is no gap, the pump will make a loud noise during operation.

13. Install the high pressure line, bolt and O-rings. Tighten the bolt to 12–15 ft. lbs. (16–20 Nm).
14. Install the reservoir mounting bracket, spacer and O-rings. Wet the grommets with clean brake fluid and push the reservoir into place as far as it will go. The reservoir should be held vertically in respect to the actuation assembly while pushing it into place.
15. Secure the mounting bracket to the booster with the allen screw. Tighten to 35–53 inch lbs. (3.9–5.9 Nm).
16. Connect the return and feed hoses.
17. Fill the reservoir with clean DOT 3 fluid from a fresh container.
18. Wet the O-ring with clean brake fluid and install the accumulator. Tighten it to 30–34 ft. lbs. (41–46 Nm).
19. Attach all the electrical connectors and the negative battery cable.
20. Bleed the ABS system, as outlined later in this section, and check that the brake warning lamps go out after a maximum of one minute.
21. Top off the fluid level.

1989–92 Vehicles

➧ See Figure 92

1. Disconnect the negative battery cable.
2. Using a clean turkey baster or equivalent, drain as much fluid as possible from the reservoir.
3. Remove the suction line between the reservoir and the pump at the reservoir by twisting the hose and pulling.
4. Using an 8mm allen wrench, remove the accumulator. Make certain no debris falls in the hole!
5. Loosen the pipe fitting connecting the high pressure hose to the pump housing. Take care to avoid bending the pipe! Disconnect the low pressure line from between the reservoir and suction port.
6. Disconnect the electrical connector from the pump motor and warning switch.
7. Remove the 6mm allen headed bolt attaching the pump and motor assembly to the actuation unit. Slide the pump and motor to the left to clear the retainer and pin and remove it.

To install:

8. Position the pump and motor in place and install the bolt and spacer. Tighten the bolt to 60–84 inch lbs. (6.7–9.4 Nm).

➥ There must be a gap of 1.5–3.5mm behind the washer on the bolt. If there is no gap, the pump will make a loud noise during operation. See the accompanying figure.

9. Tighten the high pressure line fitting to 9–12 ft. lbs. (12–16 Nm).
10. Install the low pressure line.
11. Wet the O-ring with clean brake fluid and install the accumulator. Tighten it to 30–34 ft. lbs. (41–46 Nm).
12. Connect all electrical lines, bleed the system and check that the brake warning lamps go out after a maximum of one minute.
13. Top off the fluid level.

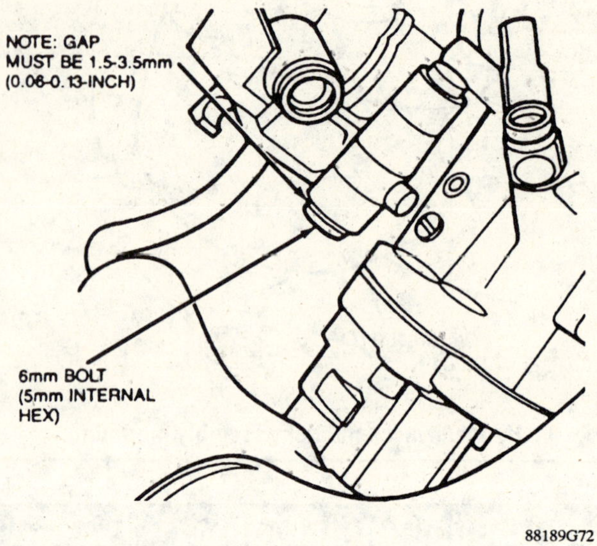

Fig. 92 Check that the gap between the washer and bracket is correct

Reservoir Assembly

REMOVAL & INSTALLATION

✲✲WARNING

The Anti-lock Brake System must be depressurized before any service is performed. To depressurize the system, turn the ignition OFF and pump the brake pedal at least 20 times, until an obvious increase in pedal pressure is felt.

1987–88 Vehicles

➧ See Figure 93

1. Disconnect the negative battery cable.
2. Detach the electrical connectors from the reservoir cap. Unlock and remove the cap.
3. Empty the reservoir of as much fluid as possible using a clean large rubber syringe or suction gun.
4. Remove the line between the pump and reservoir by twisting and pulling the hose from the reservoir fitting.
5. Remove the return line between the reservoir and master cylinder at the reservoir in the same manner as Step 4.
6. Remove the 4mm allen head reservoir mounting screw.
7. Pry the reservoir from the booster housing carefully. Be sure the short sleeve and O-ring are removed from the booster housing.

To install:

8. Install the reservoir mounting bracket in its guide on the bottom of the reservoir. Check to be sure that the short sleeve and O-ring are in position at the bottom of the reservoir. Wet the mounting grommet with brake fluid.

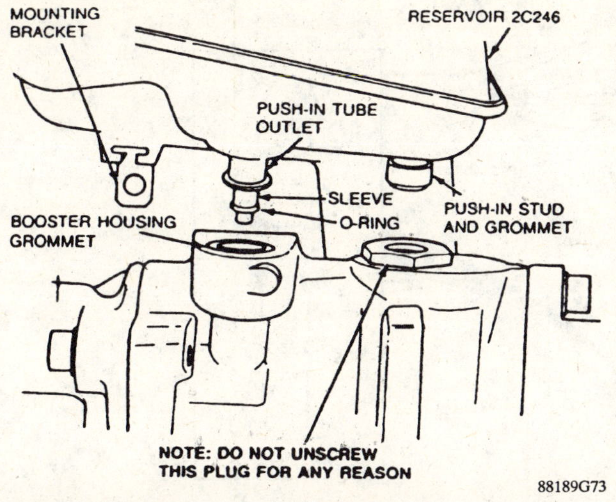

Fig. 93 Reservoir removal and installation — 1987-88 vehicles

9. Insert the reservoir into the grommets on the booster housing, as far as it will go. Make sure the short sleeve and O-ring are in place. The reservoir should be held vertically during installation.

10. The rest of the installation is in the reverse order of removal.

11. Fill the reservoir to the correct level with a charged accumulator. Bleed the system, as outlined later in this section.

1989-92 Vehicles

➧ **See Figure 94**

1. Disconnect the negative battery cable.
2. Remove the electrical connectors from the fluid level indicator.
3. Empty the reservoir of as much fluid as possible using a large rubber syringe or suction gun.
4. Remove the line between the pump and reservoir, from the reservoir by twisting and pulling the hose from the reservoir fitting.
5. Remove the 2 roll pins retaining the reservoir to the master cylinder.
6. Using a small prybar, gently pry the reservoir from the master cylinder.

To install:

7. Lubricate the O-rings, grommets and seals with clean brake fluid.
8. Align the reservoir with the 3 mounting holes and push it firmly into place as far as it will go. Install the roll pins.
9. Connect the hose, wire and battery ground.
10. Fill the reservoir and bleed the system.

Electronic Controller

REMOVAL & INSTALLATION

➧ **See Figures 95 and 96**

The controller is located in the luggage compartment in front of the forward trim panel.

1. Disconnect the negative battery cable.
2. Detach the 32 pin connector from the controller.
3. Remove the three retaining screws holding the controller to the seat back brace and remove the controller. For 1989-92 models, pull the two plastic tabs to remove controller.

To install:

4. Position the controller, then secure with the retaining screws or tabs, as applicable.
5. Attach the 32-pin connector to the controller.
6. Connect the negative battery cable.

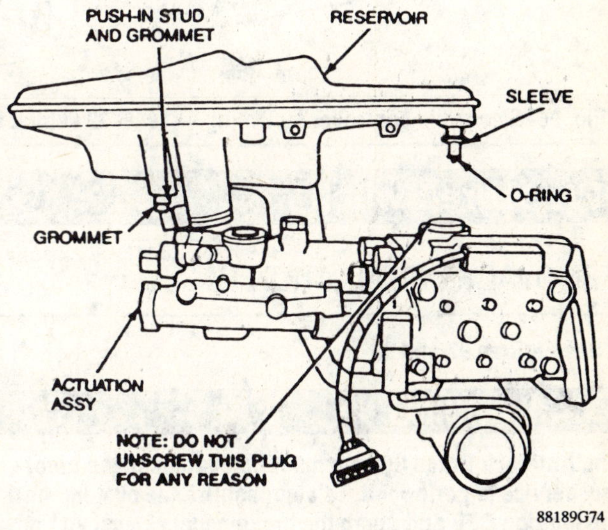

Fig. 94 Removal of the reservoir — 1989-92 vehicles

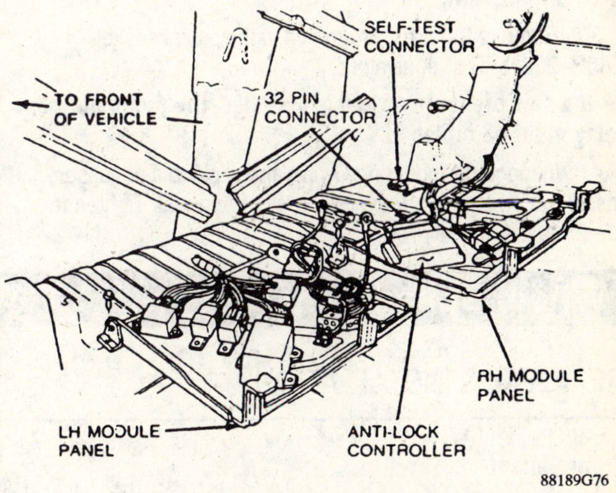

Fig. 95 Electronic controller removal and installation — 1987-88 vehicles

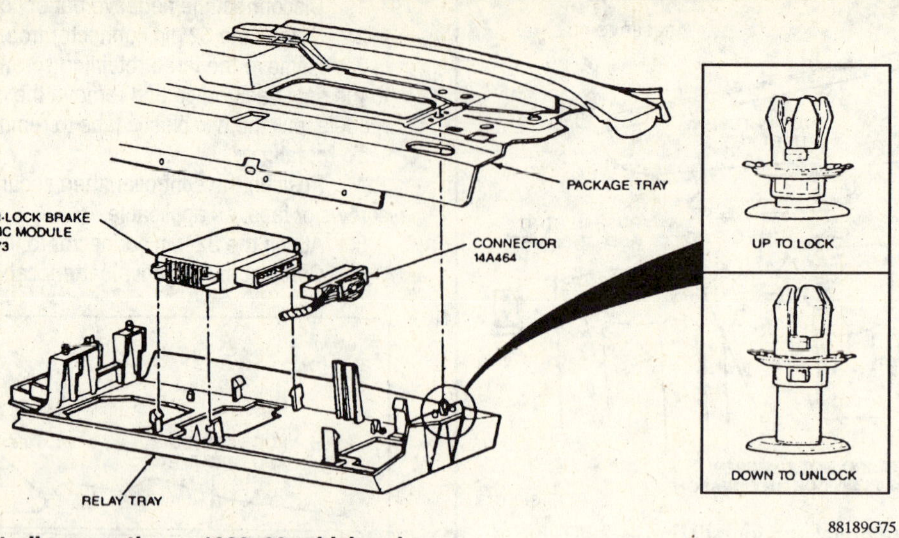

Fig. 96 Electronic controller mounting — 1989-92 vehicles shown

Pressure Switch

REMOVAL & INSTALLATION

➧ **See Figures 97 and 98**

✻✻WARNING

The Anti-lock Brake System must be depressurized before any service is performed. To depressurize the system, turn the ignition OFF and pump the brake pedal at least 20 times, until an obvious increase in pedal pressure is felt.

1. Disconnect the negative battery cable.
2. Detach the valve body electrical connector. Failure to disconnect the connector can result in damage to the connector if struck by removal tool.

➥ **On 1989-92 vehicles, the switch can best be accessed from underneath.**

3. Remove the pressure switch with special socket T85P-20215-B or equivalent.

➥ **If a new pressure switch is installed, the pump motor relay must be replaced.**

4. Inspect the mounting O-ring and replace if necessary. Install the switch in the reverse order of removal. Tighten to 15-25 ft. lbs. (20-34 Nm).

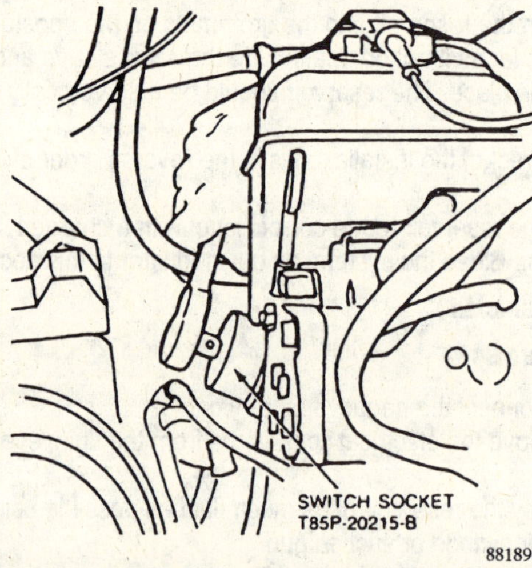

Fig. 97 Pressure warning switch location — 1987-88 vehicles

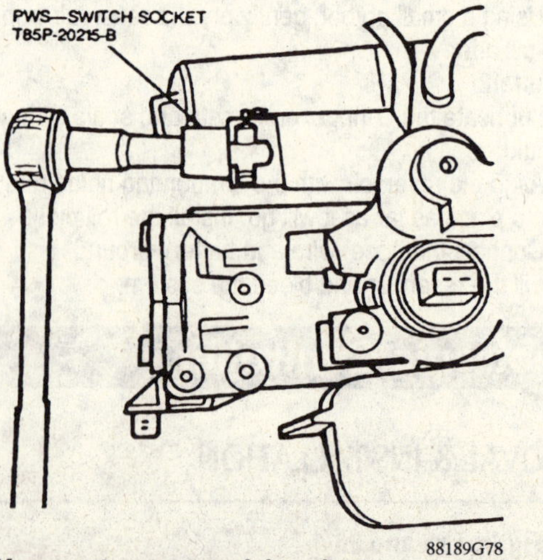

Fig. 98 You must use a special socket to remove the pressure switch — 1989-92 vehicles

Wheel Speed Sensors

REMOVAL & INSTALLATION

Front Sensor

1987-88 VEHICLES

➧ **See Figure 99**

1. Disconnect the negative battery cable.

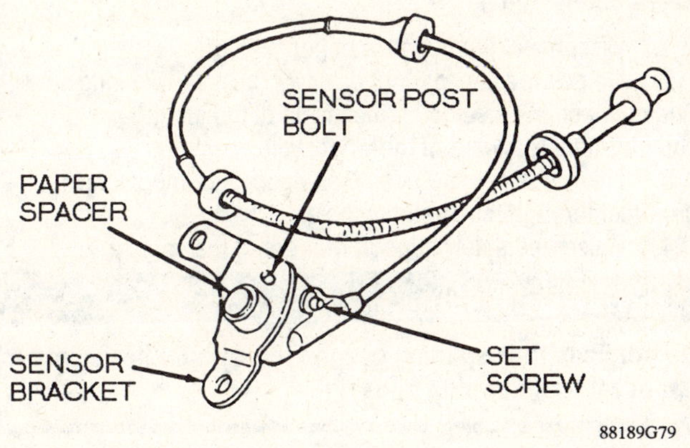

Fig. 99 View of the front wheel speed sensor — 1987-88 vehicles

2. Detach the harness connector on the inside of the engine compartment for either the right or left sensor.
3. Raise and safely support the front end on jackstands.
4. Remove the wheel and tire assembly.
5. Remove the caliper and disc rotor assemblies, as outlined in this section.
6. Disengage the wire grommet at the shock tower and draw the sensor cable carefully through the grommet mounting hole. Remove the harness from the mounting brackets.
7. Loosen the 5mm set screw that holds the sensor to the mounting bracket. Remove the sensor through the hole in the disc brake splash shield.

To install:

8. Clean the sensor face, if reusing the original sensor. Install in the reverse order of removal.
9. Place a new 1.3mm thick paper spacer on the sensor mounting flange before installation.
10. Tighten the post retaining bolt and splash shield bolts to 10–15 ft. lbs. (14–20 Nm). The steel sleeve around the post bolt must be rotated to provide a new, clean surface for the setscrew to indent.
11. Tighten the sensor retaining bolt to 21–26 inch lbs. (2.3–2.9 Nm).
12. Connect the negative battery cable.

1989-92 VEHICLES

See Figure 100

1. Disconnect the negative battery cable.
2. Raise and safely support the front end on jackstands.
3. Detach the sensor connector for either the right or left sensor, located near the radiator support
4. Remove the wiring harness routing clips.
5. Unbolt and remove the sensor from the spindle. If the toothed speed indicator ring appears damaged, replace it.

To install:

6. Position the sensor on the spindle and torque the bolt to 40–60 inch lbs. (4.5–6.7 Nm).
7. Route the wires using the clips, then attach the connectors.
8. Carefully lower the vehicle.
9. Connect the negative battery cable.

Rear Sensor

1987-88 VEHICLES

See Figure 101

1. Disconnect the negative battery cable.
2. Detach the sensor connector for the side requiring service. The connector is located on the inside of the luggage compartment behind the forward trim panel.
3. Lift the carpet and push the sensor wire mounting grommet through the mounting hole.
4. Raise and support the rear of the vehicle. Remove the wheel from the side on which you are working.

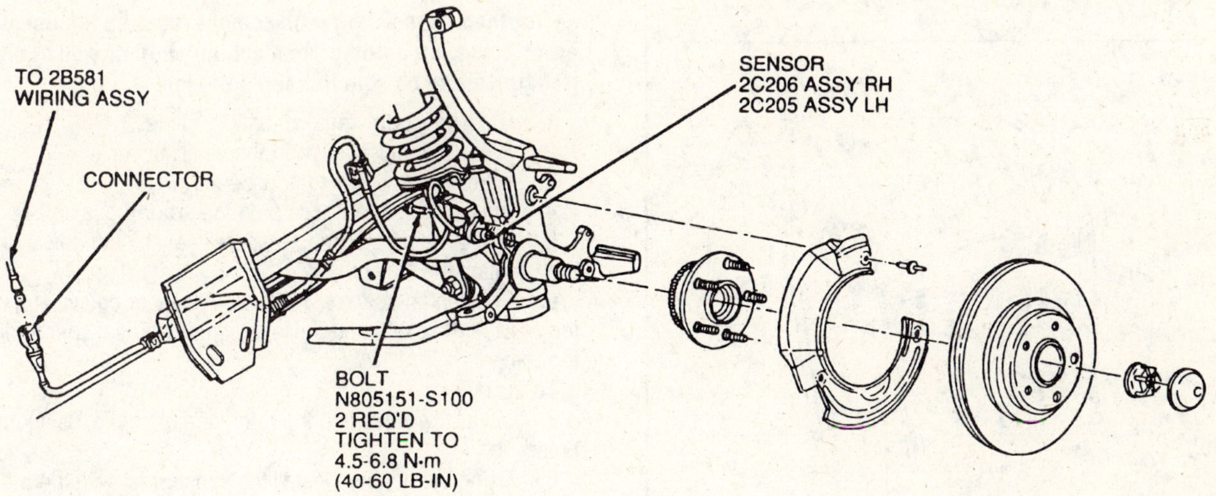

Fig. 100 Front wheel speed sensor mounting — 1989-92 vehicles

5. Remove the wire harness from the retaining brackets and C-clip. Pull rearward on the clip to disengage.

CAUTION

Do not bend the clip any more than is absolutely necessary!

6. Remove the sensor mounting bolt. At this point, inspect the sensor bracket for damage, and replace it if necessary. Inspect the toothed ring and replace it if it appears damaged.

To install:

7. Position the sensor and tighten the bolt to 40–60 inch lbs. (4.5–6.7 Nm).
8. Install the sensor wire in the retainers along the axle housing.
9. Push the connector through the hole in the luggage compartment and seat the grommet in the luggage compartment floorpan.
10. From inside the luggage compartment, attach the wiring connector. Install the carpet as necessary.
11. Connect the negative battery cable and check system operation.

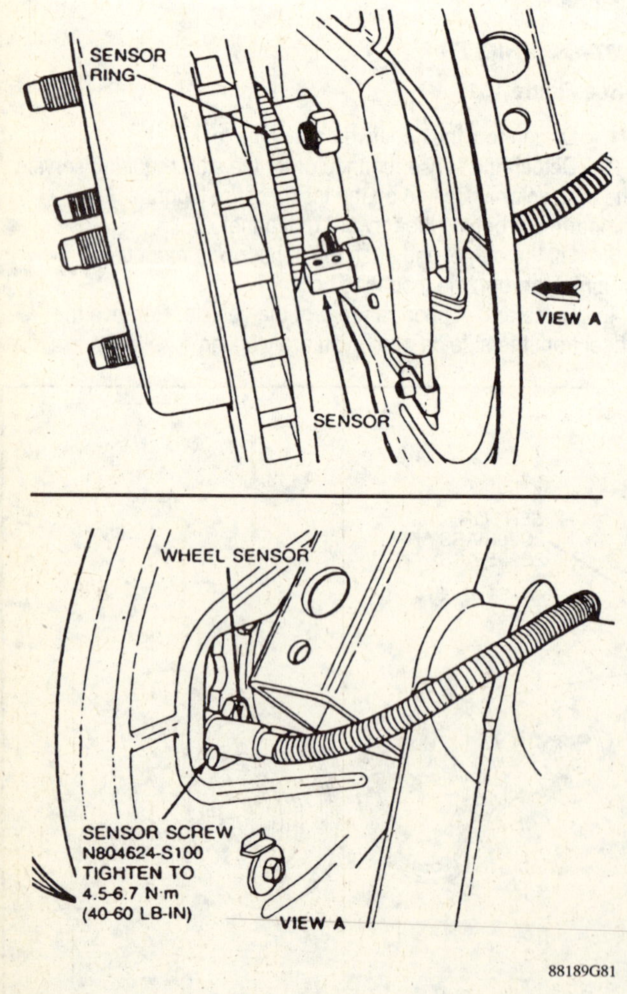

Fig. 101 Rear wheel speed sensor location — 1987–88 vehicles

1989–92 VEHICLES

See Figure 102

1. Disconnect the negative battery cable.
2. Detach the sensor connector for the side requiring service. The connector is located on the inside of the luggage compartment rearward of the wheelwell.
3. Lift the carpet and push the sensor wire mounting grommet through the mounting hole.
4. Raise and safely support the rear of the vehicle.

WARNING

Do not bend the clip open beyond the amount necessary to remove it from the axle housing.

5. Remove the wire harness from the plastic clip.
6. Remove the mounting bolt and sensor.

To install:

7. Align the sensor locating tab and bolt hole with the axle housing and push into position.
8. Position the sensor on the axle, pushing the mounting tab into place. Tighten the bolt to 14–20 ft. lbs. (19–27 Nm).
9. Install the plastic clip retaining the sensor wire to the axle carrier housing and push the connector through the hole in floor into the luggage compartment. Make sure the rubber grommet is proper seated in the hole in the floor.
10. Carefully lower the vehicle.
11. Install and connect the wiring.
12. Connect the negative battery cable, then check the system for proper operation.

Front Wheel Sensor Ring

REMOVAL & INSTALLATION

1987–88 Vehicles

See Figure 103

Toothed sensor ring replacement requires the use of an arbor press. An automotive machine shop or well equipped garage should be able to handle the job.

1. Disconnect the negative battery cable.
2. Raise and safely support the vehicle.
3. Remove the brake rotor assembly.
4. Position the rotor face up on the arbor press bed.
5. Using the proper adapters, press each stud down just until they contact the sensor ring.
6. Position an adapter, T85P-20202-A, or equivalent, on the top of all of the studs and press the studs and sensor ring from the rotor.

To install:

7. Install the studs into the rotor, one at a time, using the press.
8. Using the adapter, install the sensor ring with the press until the ring bottoms in position. MAKE SURE IT IS STRAIGHT!
9. Install the rotor.
10. Carefully lower the vehicle, then connect the negative battery cable.

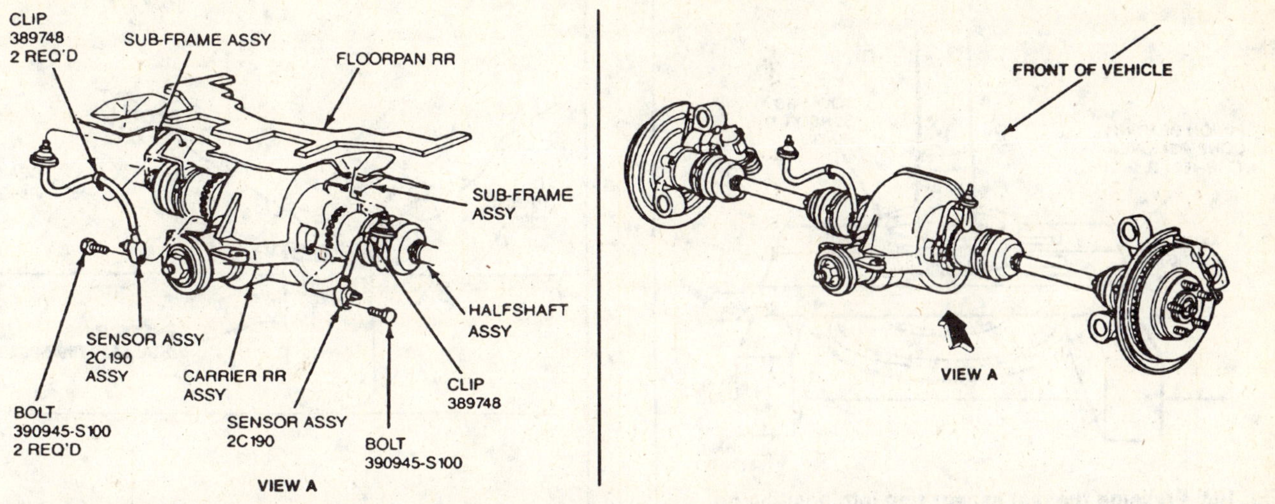

88189G82

Fig. 102 Rear wheel speed sensor location — 1989-92 vehicles

1989-92 Vehicles

1. Raise and safely support the vehicle.
2. Remove the tire and wheel assembly.
3. Remove the brake caliper, rotor and hub assemblies.
4. Using a suitable 3-jawed puller, remove the sensor ring from the hub.

To install:

5. Support the center of the hub so the wheel studs do not rest on the work surface.
6. Position the hub on an arbor press bed, and using a flat plate, press the ring on the hub. MAKE SURE IT IS STRAIGHT!
7. Install the hub, rotor and caliper.
8. Install the wheel and tire assembly, then carefully lower the vehicle.

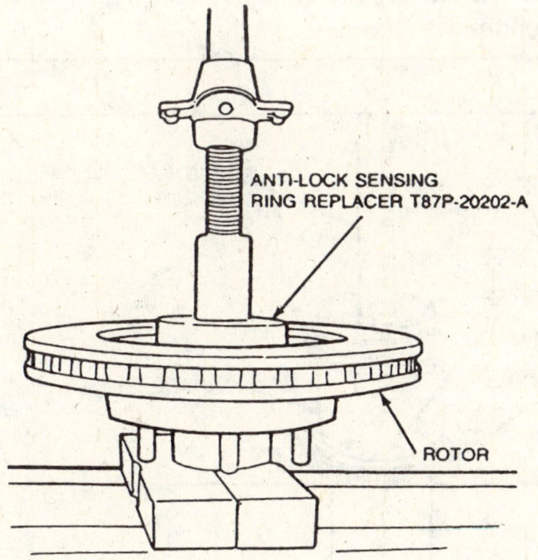

88189G89

Fig. 103 Instating the front sensor ring — 1987-88 vehicles

Rear Wheel Sensor Ring

REMOVAL & INSTALLATION

1987-88 Vehicles

➧ See Figures 104 and 105

1. Raise and safely support the vehicle.
2. Remove the rear axle shaft, as outlined in Section 7.
3. Install a bearing cone remover adapter, such as T71P-4621-B, or equivalent, between the axle shaft flange and sensor ring.
4. Position the axle in an arbor press and remove the sensor ring.

To install:

5. Press the sensor ring into position until a gap of 65.35-85mm between the sensor ring and face of the axle flange is obtained.
6. Reinstall the axle shaft and removed components.

1989-92 Vehicles

➧ See Figures 106, 107, 108 and 109

1. Raise and safely support vehicle on jackstands.
2. Remove the axle halfshaft. Remove the CV-joint assembly from the shaft. See Section 7 for details.
3. Position a 2-jaw puller on the CV-joint inner stub shaft, with the puller jaws under sensor ring. Turn wrench until the ring pulls off.

➥ Brake sensor rings must not be reused. Discard ring after removal and replace with a new one.

To install:

4. Position sensor ring installer T89P-20202-A, or equivalent, on an arbor press bed, with the pilot up.
5. Place the new sensor ring on the installer.
6. Position the CV-joint stub shaft through the sensor ring and allow the joint to rest on the sensor ring.
7. Bottom the press ram in the CV-joint race and press the ring on until it contacts the CV-joint step.

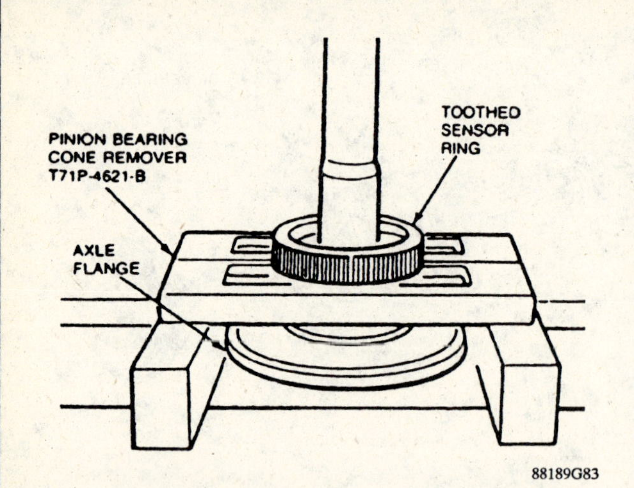

Fig. 104 Pressing the rear sensor ring into position on 1987-88 vehicles

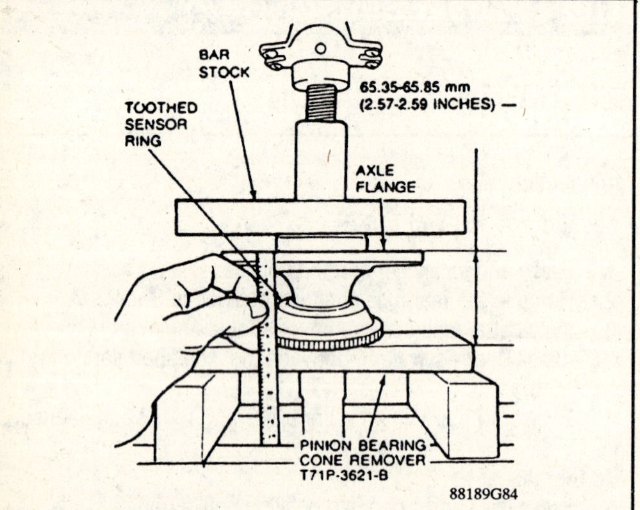

Fig. 105 Measuring the correct installation of rear sensor ring 1987-88 vehicles

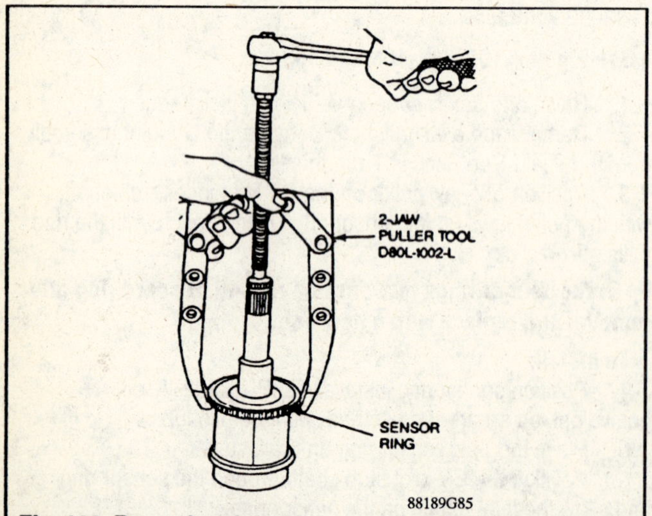

Fig. 106 Removing the rear sensor ring from the CV-joint — 1989-92 vehicles

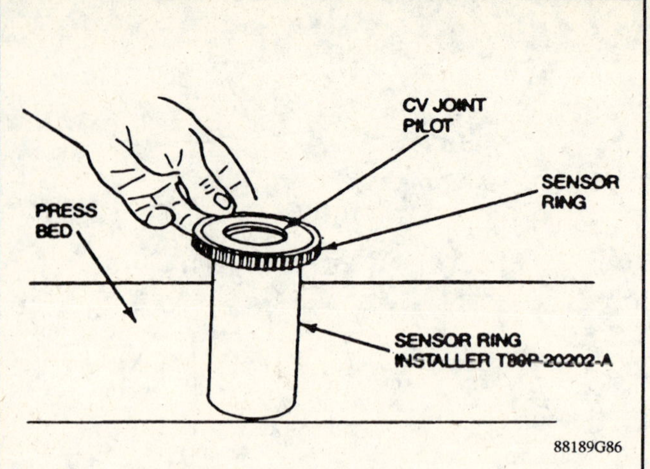

Fig. 107 Placing the sensor ring on the tool

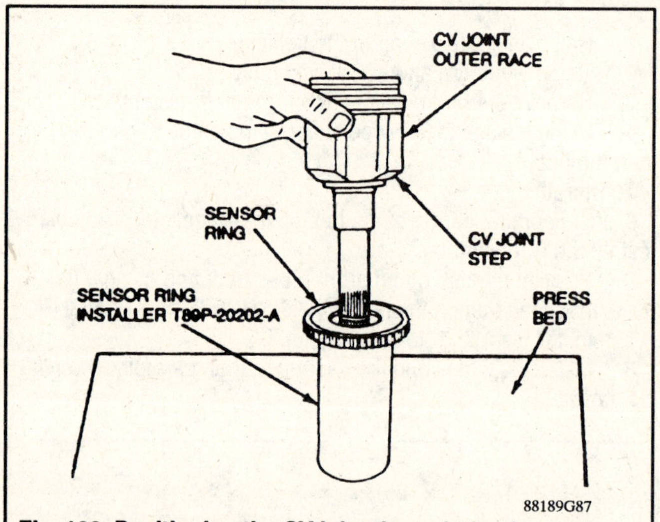

Fig. 108 Positioning the CV-joint through the ring and into the tool

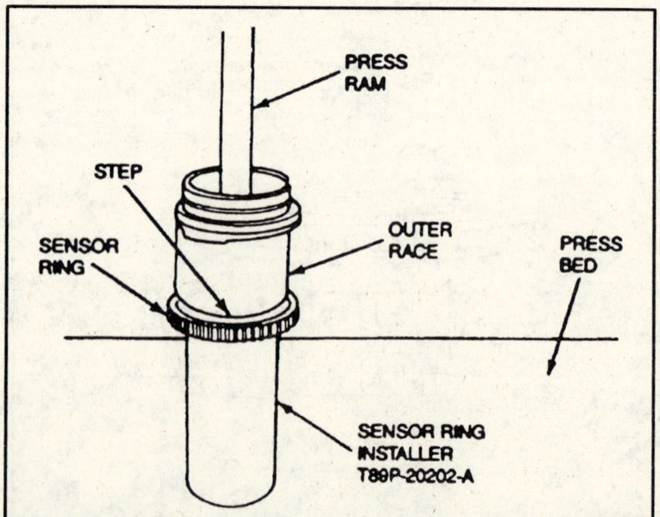

Fig. 109 Pressing the ring onto the CV-joint

Bleeding The ABS System

✻✻CAUTION

The 4-Wheel Anti-Lock brake system is under high accumulator hydraulic pressure most of the time. Before servicing any component which contains high pressure, it is mandatory that the high pressure in the system be discharged.

SYSTEM DISCHARGING (DEPRESSURIZING)

Turn the ignition to the **OFF** position. Pump the brake pedal a minimum of 20 times until an increase in pedal force is clearly felt.

FRONT BRAKE BLEEDING

The front brakes can be bled in the conventional manner, with or without the accumulator being charged. Refer to the previous brake bleeding section at the beginning of this Section for instructions.

REAR BRAKE BLEEDING

A fully charged accumulator is required for successful rear brake system bleeding. Once accumulator pressure is applied to the system, the rear brakes can be bled by opening the rear caliper bleeder screw while holding the brake pedal in the applied position with the ignition switch in the Run position. Repeat the procedure until an air-free flow of brake fluid comes from the bleeder screw. Close the bleeder screw. Add fluid to the master cylinder reservoir until required level is reached.

✻✻CAUTION

Care must be used when opening the bleeder screws. The fluid is under high pressure and could cause injury if splashed into eyes, etc.

BLEEDING THE SYSTEM WITH A FULLY CHARGED ACCUMULATOR

1. Remove the dust cap from the right side rear caliper bleeder fitting. Attach a rubber drain tube to the fitting making sure the end of the tube fits snugly around the fitting.
2. Turn the ignition switch to the **RUN** position. This will turn on the electric pump to charge the accumulator as required.
3. Hold the brake pedal in the applied position. Open the right side rear caliper bleeder fitting for 10 seconds at a time until an air-free stream of brake fluid is observed.

✻✻WARNING

Be very careful when opening the bleeder screws due to the high pressure available from a fully charged accumulator.

4. Repeat the procedure at the left side rear caliper.
5. Pump the brake pedal several times to complete the bleeding procedure and to fully charge the accumulator.
6. Adjust the fluid level in the reservoir to the MAX mark with a fully charged accumulator.

➥ If the pump motor is allowed to run continuously for approximately 20 minutes, a thermal safety switch inside the motor may shut the motor off t o prevent it from overheating. If that happens, a 2–10 minute cool down period is typically required before normal operation can resume.

HYDRAULIC PUMP PRIMING

1. Remove the dust cap from the right side rear caliper bleeder fitting. Attach a rubber drain tube to the fitting making sure the end of the tube fits snugly around the fitting.
2. Turn the ignition switch to the **RUN** position. This will turn on the electric pump.
3. Hold the brake pedal in the applied position. Open the right side rear caliper bleeder fitting for 10 seconds at a time until an air-free stream of brake fluid is observed.
4. Repeat the procedure at the left side rear caliper.

CHECKING FLUID LEVEL AND REFILLING

1. With the ignition switch **ON**, pump the brake pedal until the hydraulic pump motor starts.
2. Wait until the pump shuts off and check the brake fluid level in the reservoir. If the level is below the MAX fill line, add fluid until the line is reached.

✻✻WARNING

Do not overfill! The level may be over the MAX line depending upon the accumulator charge. Perform the above procedure before adding or removing brake fluid.

TEVES MARK-IV ANTI-LOCK BRAKE SYSTEM (ABS)

General Information

➧ See Figures 110 and 111

The Teves Mark-IV Anti-lock Brake System (ABS) is used on 1993–96 models is an electronically operated, all wheel brake control system. Major components include the master cylinder, vacuum power brake booster, ABS Control Module, Hydraulic Control Unit (HCU) and various control sensors and switches.

The brake system is a three channel design. The front brakes are controlled individually and the rear brakes in tandem.

The system is designed to retard wheel lockup during periods of high wheel slip when braking. Retarding wheel lockup is accomplished by modulating fluid pressure to the wheel brake units.

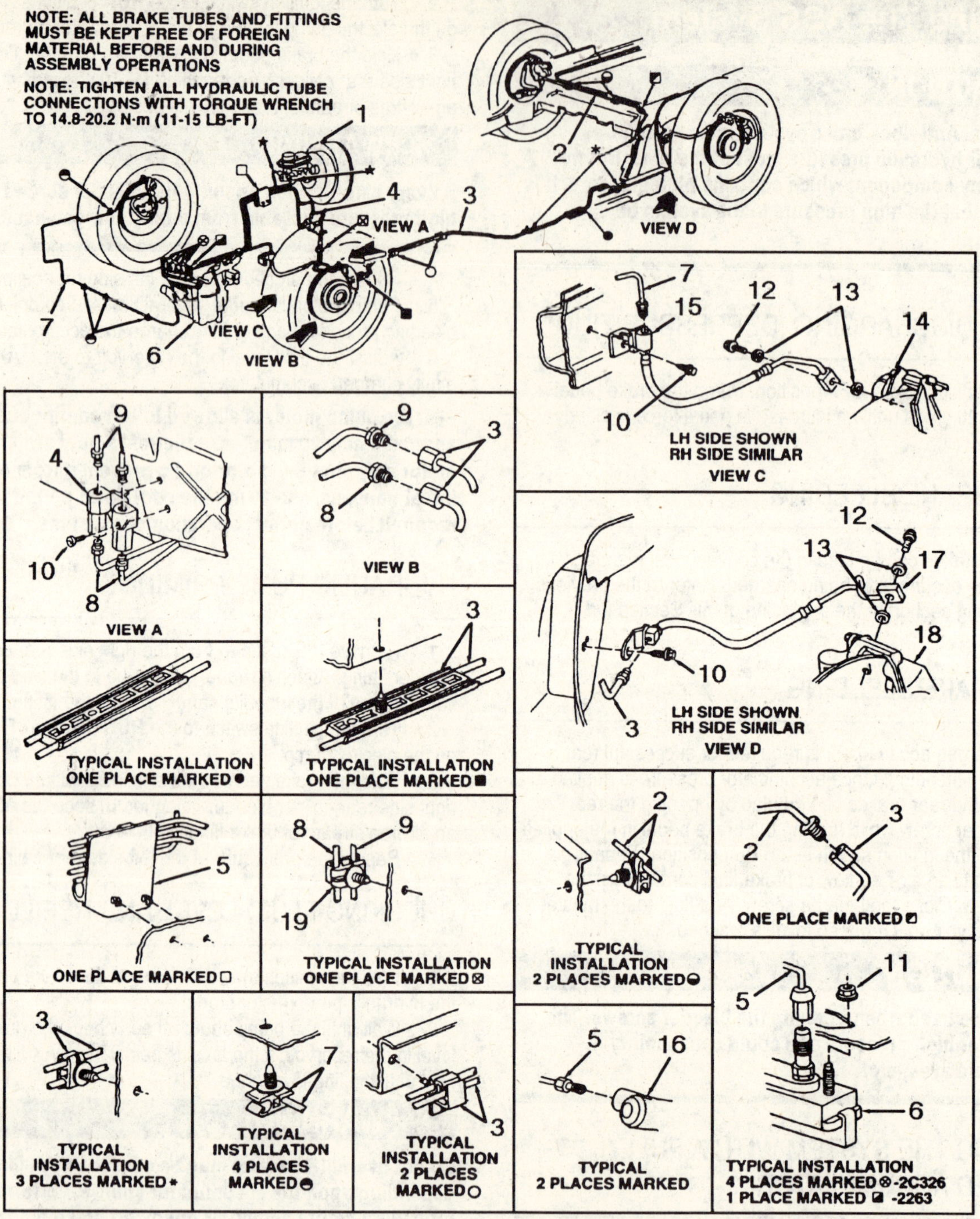

1. Brake booster
2. Rear brake tube assy
3. Brake fluid distribution tube assy
4. Brake pressure control valve assy
5. Tube assy
6. Anti-lock brake control module
7. Front brake tube assy
8. Brake pressure control valve outlet tube assy
9. Brake pressure line
10. Screw
    - Tighten to 11.4-15.6 Nm (8-12 lb. ft.)
11. Nut (2 req'd)
12. Bolt
    - Tighten to 40.3-54.7 Nm (30-40 lb. ft.)
13. Washer (2 req'd)
14. Caliper
15. Flexible brake hose
16. Master cylinder
17. Flexible brake hose
18. Caliper
19. Clip

88189G90

Fig. 110 Exploded view of the Anti-lock Brake System (ABS) components and their locations — 1995 model shown

DTC	CAUSED BY	PINPOINT TEST STEP
11	Generated by a disturbed or defective redundancy channel.	AA1
17	Generated by reference voltage failure, caused by high / low battery voltage, main power relay, main fuse, wire harness.	BB1
18	Generated by open or short circuit-isolation valve # 1, wire harness.	BB26
19	Generated by open or short circuit-isolation valve # 2, wire harness.	BB29
22	Generated by open or short circuit-LH front inlet valve, wire harness.	BB2
23	Generated by open or short circuit-LH front outlet valve, wire harness.	BB5
24	Generated by open or short circuit-RH front inlet valve, wire harness.	BB8
25	Generated by open or short circuit-RH front outlet valve, wire harness.	BB11
26	Generated by open or short circuit-RH rear inlet valve, wire harness.	BB14
27	Generated by open or short circuit-RH rear outlet valve, wire harness.	BB17
28	Generated by open or short circuit-LH rear inlet valve, wire harness.	BB20
29	Generated by open or short circuit-LH rear outlet valve, wire harness.	BB23
31	Generated by open or short circuit-LH front sensor, wire harness.	CC1
32	Generated by open or short circuit-RH front sensor, wire harness.	CC8
33	Generated by open or short circuit-RH rear sensor, wire harness.	CC15
34	Generated by open or short circuit-LH rear sensor, wire harness.	CC22
35	Generated by open or short circuit LH front sensor, wire harness, damaged teeth on indicator ring, sensor air gap too small / large.	CC1
36	Generated by open or short circuit RH front sensor, wire harness, damaged teeth on indicator ring, sensor air gap too small / large.	CC8
37	Generated by open or short circuit RH rear sensor, wire harness, damaged teeth on indicator ring, sensor air gap too small / large.	CC15
38	Generated by open or short circuit LH rear sensor, wire harness, damaged teeth on indicator ring, sensor air gap too small / large.	CC22
41	Generated by missing sensor signal LH front sensor (missing indicator ring).	CC1
42	Generated by missing sensor signal RH front sensor (missing indicator ring).	CC8
43	Generated by missing sensor signal RH rear sensor (missing indicator ring).	CC15
44	Generated by missing sensor signal LH rear sensor (missing indicator ring).	CC22
55	Generated by missing sensor signal LH front sensor (long term failure).	CC1
56	Generated by missing sensor signal RH front sensor (long term failure).	CC8
57	Generated by missing sensor signal RH rear sensor (long term failure).	CC15
58	Generated by missing sensor signal LH rear sensor (long term failure).	CC22
61	Generated by short circuit to ground-FLS # 2 or wire harness.	DD1
62	Generated by short circuit to ground-pedal travel switch or wire harness.	DD1
63	Generated by no pump motor speed sensor signal during initial check@ 31 km / h (19 mph), wire harness or faulty electronic controller.	DD7 FF1
64	Generated by pump unable to build pressure during an ABS stop.	DD22
67	Generated by pump motor running not triggered by ECU.	E1
75	Generated by intermittent missing LH front sensor signal at speeds < 40 km / h (25 mph).	CC1
76	Generated by intermittent missing RH front sensor signal at speeds < 40 km / h (25 mph).	CC8
77	Generated by intermittent missing RH rear sensor signal at speeds < 40 km / h (25 mph).	CC15
78	Generated by intermittent missing LH rear sensor signal at speeds < 40 km / h (25 mph).	CC22

88189G94

Fig. 111 ABS Diagnostic Trouble Code List

SYSTEM COMPONENTS

Power Brake Booster

➧ See Figure 112

The diaphragm-type power brake booster is self contained, and is mounted on the engine compartment side of the dash panel. The booster uses engine intake manifold vacuum and atmospheric pressure for its power. It is serviced as an assembly only, except for the power brake booster check valve.

Brake Master Cylinder

➧ See Figure 112

The brake master cylinder is a tandem master cylinder. The primary (rear) circuit feeds the right side front and left side rear brakes. The secondary (front) circuit feeds the left side front and right side rear brakes. The master cylinder is serviced as a complete assembly.

Brake Pressure Control Valve

➧ See Figure 113

The brake pressure control valve regulates pressure to the rear brakes to create a balance between the front and rear brakes.

Brake Master Cylinder and Brake Fluid Level Switch

The master cylinder reservoir is a clear, translucent plastic container with three main chambers:

- An integral fluid level switch is part of the master cylinder reservoir assembly, with one 3-pin connector.
- A low pressure hose is attached to the master cylinder reservoir which feeds brake fluid to the hydraulic control unit reservoir.
- The brake master cylinder reservoir and brake master cylinder filler cap gasket are serviced separately

Hydraulic Control Unit (HCU)

➧ See Figure 113

The Hydraulic Control Unit (HCU) is located outside of the engine compartment on a bracket which attaches to the outer frame rail. It consists of the following:

- Brake pressure control valve block assembly
- Pump motor
- Hydraulic control unit reservoir which a fluid level indicator assembly

During normal braking, fluid from the master cylinder enters the HCU through two inlet ports located at the rear of the HCU. The fluid then passes through four normally open inlet valve, one to each wheel. The the anti-lock brake control module senses that a wheel is about to lock, the control module closes the appropriate inlet valve. This prevents any more fluid from entering the affected brake.

The anti-lock brake control module then looks at that wheel again. If it is still decelerating, then anti-lock brake control module opens the normally closed outlet valve which decreased the pressure trapped in the line. If equipped, the Traction Assist (TA) valve body contains two isolation valves for traction assist function: one for the primary circuit and one for the secondary circuit. The isolation valves close during traction assist operation to prevent front brake operation.

The following components are serviced separately:

- Brake pressure control valve block
- Pump motor
- Hydraulic control unit reservoir

Anti-Lock Brake Control Module

The anti-lock brake control module is located on the anti-lock brake hydraulic control bracket mounting bracket located outside of the engine compartment attached to the outer frame rail.

The module is an on-board diagnostic non-repairable unit consisting of two microprocessors and the necessary circuitry for their operation. These microprocessors are programmed identically. The anti-lock brake control module monitors system operation during normal driving operation as wheel as during anti-lock braking and traction assist cycling, if equipped.

Under normal driving conditions, the microprocessors produce short test pulses to the solenoid valves that check the electrical system without any mechanical reaction. Impending wheel lock conditions trigger signals from the anti-lock brake control module that open and close the appropriate solenoid valves. This results in moderate pulsations in the brake pedal.

If brake pedal travel exceeds a preset dimension determined by the ABS sensor switch setting, the control module will send a signal to the pump to turn on and provide high pressure to the brake system. When the pump motor starts to run, a gradual rise in pedal height will be noticed. This rise will continue until the anti-lock brake pedal sensor switch closes and the pump motor will shut off until the pedal travel exceeds the sensor switch setting again. During normal braking, the brake pedal feel will be identical to a standard brake system.

Anti-Lock Brake Sensors

➧ See Figures 114 and 115

The anti-lock brake system uses four sets of variable reluctance brake anti-lock sensors to determine the rotational speed of each wheel. The sensors operate on the magnetic induction principle. As the teeth on the sensor rotate past the sensor indicator, a signal proportional to the speed of the rotation is generated and sent to the anti-lock brake control module through a coaxial cable and shielded wiring harness.

The front brake anti-lock sensors are attached to the front wheel spindles, and the front brake anti-lock sensor indicators are pressed onto the wheel hub assembly. The rear brake anti-lock sensors are attached to the rear axle housing and the sensor indicators are pressed onto the inner CV-joints.

The front and rear anti-lock sensors are not adjustable. The rear brake anti-lock sensors and sensor indicators are serviced separately.

Brake Pedal Travel Switch

The anti-lock brake system uses a pedal sensor switch which monitors brake pedal travel and sends this information to the anti-lock brake control module through the wire harness. The anti-lock brake pedal sensor switch adjustment is critical to pedal feel during ABS cycling.

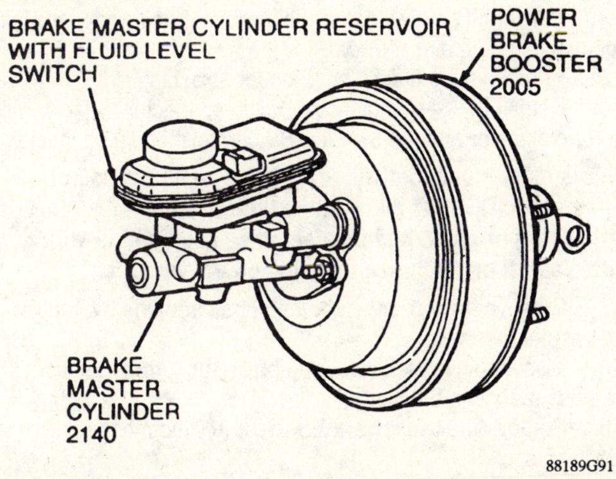

Fig. 112 View of the brake master cylinder, power booster and brake fluid level switch location

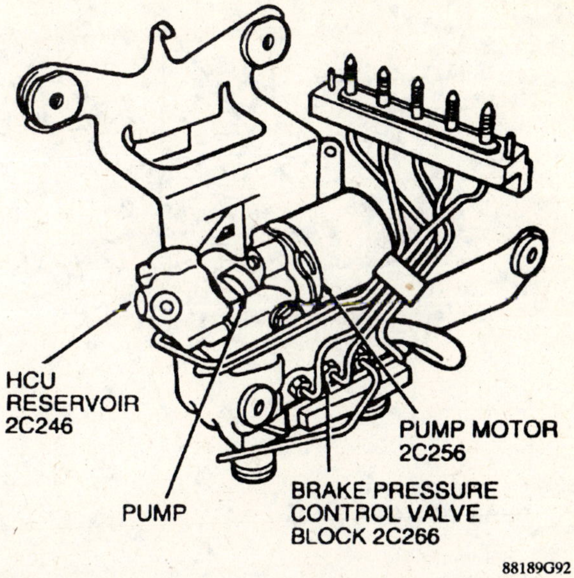

Fig. 113 View of the HCU and components — 1995 vehicle shown

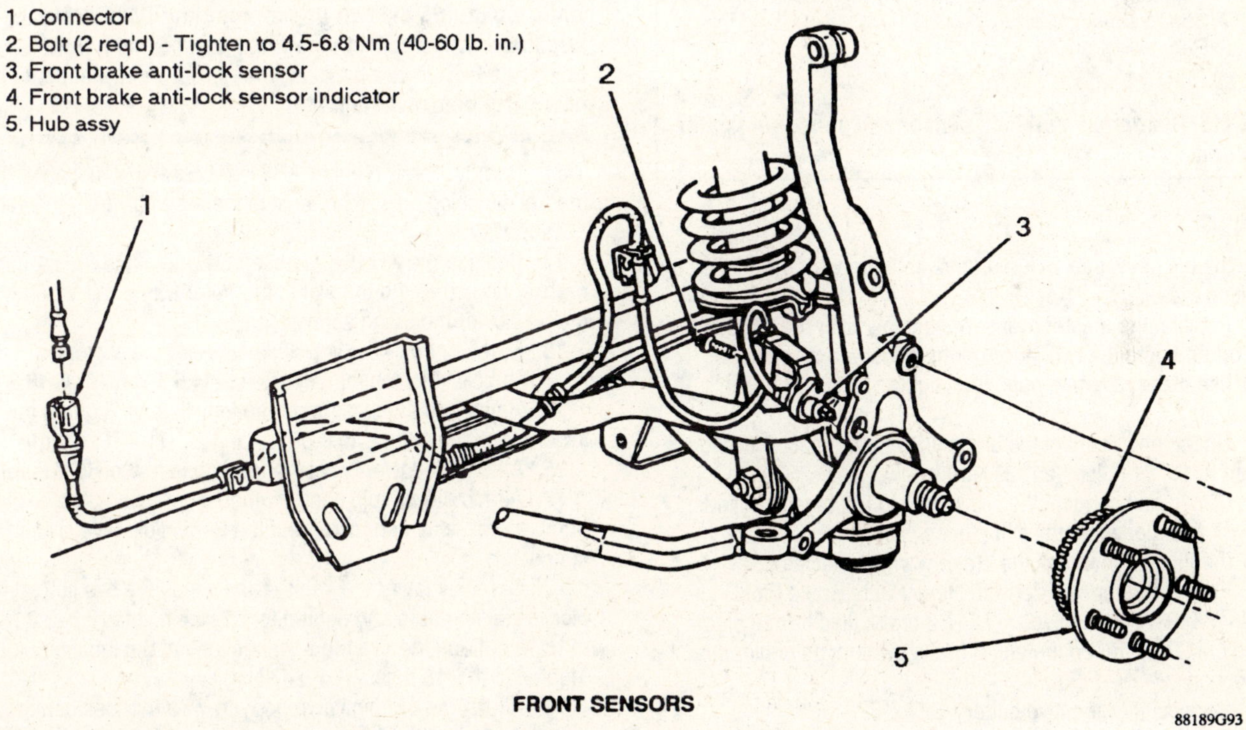

Fig. 114 Front brake anti-lock sensor and sensor indicator locations

Master Cylinder

REMOVAL & INSTALLATION

1. Disconnect the negative battery cable.
2. Apply the brake pedal several times to exhaust all the vacuum in the system.
3. Detach and cap the brake lines from the master cylinder.
4. If equipped, detach the brake warning indicator connector.
5. Disconnect and cap the Hydraulic Control Unit (HCU) supply hose at the master cylinder reservoir and secure in a position to prevent loss of fluid.
6. Unfasten the two nuts and/or lockwashers that attach the master cylinder to the brake booster.
7. Remove the master cylinder from the booster by sliding it forward and upward from the vehicle.

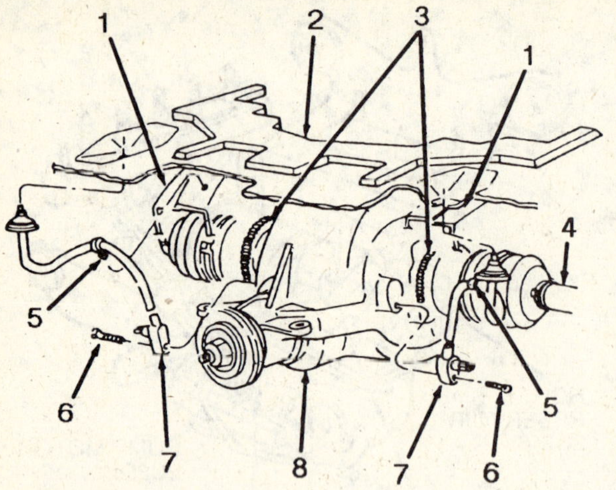

REAR SENSORS

1. Subframe
2. Floorpan
3. Sensor ring
4. Halfshaft assy
5. Clip (2 req'd)
6. Bolt (2 req'd)
   - Tighten to 19-27 Nm (14-20 lb. ft.)
7. Speed sensor
8. Rear axle housing

88189G95

Fig. 115 Rear brake anti-lock sensor and sensor indicator locations

To install:

8. Install a new seal in the groove in the master cylinder mounting face.
9. Position the master cylinder assembly over the booster pushrod and onto the two studs on the booster assembly.
10. Install the retaining nuts, then tighten to 16–21 ft. lbs. (21–29 Nm).
11. Uncap and connect the brake lines to the master cylinder. Tighten to 16–21 ft. lbs. (21–29 Nm).
12. Uncap and connect the HCU hose to the master cylinder reservoir fitting and secure with a hose clamp.
13. If equipped, connect the brake warning indicator.
14. Fill the master cylinder with Heavy Duty Brake Fluid C6AZ-19542-AA or equivalent DOT 3 brake fluid from a clean, sealed container. Bleed the entire brake system, as outlined in this section.
15. Connect the negative battery cable.
16. Operate the brake several times, then check for external hydraulic leaks.

Hydraulic Control Unit (HCU)

REMOVAL & INSTALLATION

See Figure 116

1. Disconnect the negative, then the positive battery cables and remove the battery from the vehicle.
2. Unfasten the power distribution box-to-battery tray attaching bolt, then remove the battery tray.
3. Detach the 16-pin valve body to wire harness connector.
4. Raise and safely support the vehicle, then remove the left front wheel and tire assembly.
5. Remove the left side inner fender splash shield.
6. Detach the 3-pin fluid level switch connector, 4-pin pump motor connector and the 55-pin ABS control module connector.

The master cylinder will drain if the feed hose is not pinched off. DO NOT allow brake fluid to come in contact with wiring or paint. Immediately rinse any paint or wiring with water if brake fluid comes in contact with them.

7. Remove the low pressure feed hose from the hydraulic control unit reservoir.
8. Disconnect the left side front brake tube from the hose at the hose mounting bracket.
9. Remove the two lower ABS assembly mounting bracket attaching screws.
10. Carefully lower the vehicle and disconnect the five brake tube connections at the junction block. Remove the two junction block retaining nuts.

****WARNING**

Do not allow the two upper bushings to turn in the bracket while loosening the two upper mounting bolts. Hold the bushings with a pair of vise grips if necessary. If the bushings turn in the bracket, they must be replaced with new parts before installation.

11. Remove the two upper ABS/HCU assembly mounting bracket attaching bolts, then remove the assembly from the vehicle.

To install:

12. Position the ABS/HCU assembly and place the mounting bracket hook through the slot in the outer frame rail. Hand-start the two lower mounting screws.
13. Carefully lower the vehicle, then install the two upper mounting bolts. Tighten the bolts to 8.5–11.5 ft. lbs. (11.4–15.6 Nm).
14. Raise and safely support the vehicles and tighten the two lower mounting screws to 8.5–11.5 ft. lbs. (11.4–15.6 Nm).
15. Attach the lower pressure feed hose to the HCU reservoir.
16. Attach the 55-pin control module connector, the 4-pin pump motor relay connector and the 3-pin fluid level switch connector.
17. Carefully lower the vehicle and install the two junction block retaining nuts and tighten to 1.7–2.4 ft. lbs. (2.3–3.3 Nm).
18. Reattach the five tube connections at the junction block. Tighten to 10–18 ft. lbs. (14–247 Nm).
19. Attach the 16-pin valve body-to-wire harness connector. Install the battery tray.
20. Install the power distribution box on the battery tray attaching bolt.
21. Install the battery, then connect the positive, then the negative battery cables.
22. Raise and safely support the vehicle. Install the fender splash shield and the tire and wheel assembly.
23. Carefully lower the vehicle. Bleed the brake system as outlined in this section.
24. Test drive the vehicle and test for proper brake operation.

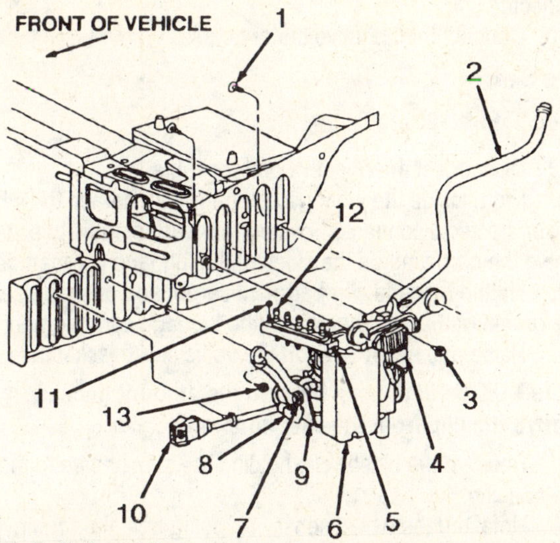

1. Bolt (2 req'd)
 - Tighten to 11.4-15.6 Nm (8.5-11.5 lb. ft.)
2. Low pressure feed hose
3. Pump motor relay screws (2 req'd)
 - Tighten to 7-9 Nm (5-7 lb. ft.)
4. Pump motor relay
5. ABS module mounting screws (3 req'd)
 - Tighten to 7-9 Nm (5-7 lb. ft.)
6. Anti-lock brake control module
7. HCU to mounting bracket bolts (3 req'd)
 - Tighten to 7-9 Nm (5-7 lb. ft.)
8. 4 pin pump motor connector
9. ABS assy
10. 19 pin valve block connector
11. Nuts (2 req'd)
 - Tighten to 2.3-3.3 Nm (1.7-2.4 lb. ft.)
12. Thread savers (5 req'd)
 - Tighten to 12-14 Nm (9-10 lb. ft.)
13. Screws (2 req'd)
 - Tighten to 11.4-15.6 Nm (8.5-11.5 lb. ft.)

88189G96

Fig. 116 View of the HCU and related components mounting — 1995 vehicle shown

Anti-Lock Brake Control Module

REMOVAL & INSTALLATION

➧ See Figure 117

1. Disconnect the negative battery cable.
2. Raise and safely support the vehicle.
3. Remove the wheel and tire assembly and the inner fender shield.
4. Remove the pump motor relay.
5. Detach the 55-pin connector.
6. Unfasten the three screws attaching the control module to the mounting bracket, then remove the module.

To install:

➥ If all three mounting holes in the control module do not line up with the holes in the mounting bracket, the module is incorrectly aligned with the bracket.

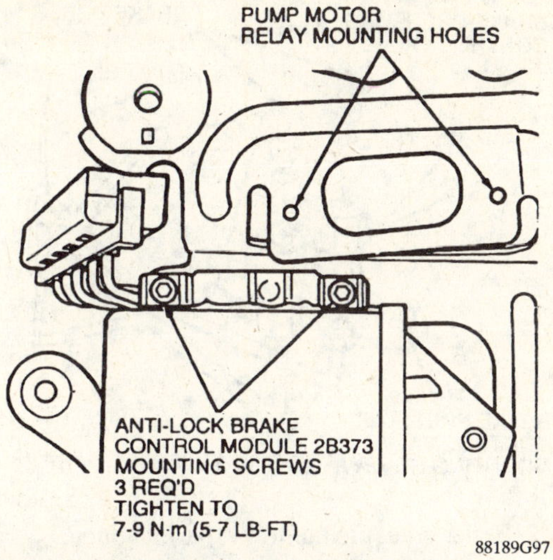

88189G97

Fig. 117 Anti-Lock Brake Control Module mounting — 1995 vehicle shown

7. Align the anti-lock brake control module with the bracket so the connector faces the rear of the vehicle and the locking lever faces up and the side with two mounting holes is flat against the bracket at the top.
8. Install the three retaining screws and tighten to 5–7 ft. lbs. (7–9 Nm).
9. Attach the 55-pin connector by installing the bottom part of the connector into the slots in the control module and pushing the top portion of the connector into the anti-lock brake control module. Then, pull the locking lever completely down to ensure proper installation.
10. Install the pump motor relay. Tighten to 5–7 ft. lbs. (7–9 Nm).
11. Install the inner fender splash shield and the wheel and tire assembly.
12. Carefully lower the vehicle.
13. Test drive the vehicle and verify proper brake operation.

Brake Pressure Control Valve

REMOVAL & INSTALLATION

➧ See Figure 118

1. Disconnect the negative battery cable.
2. Raise and safely support the vehicle.
3. Remove and cap the four brake tubes from the brake pressure control valve.
4. Unfasten the brake pressure control valve mounting screw, then remove the brake pressure control vale.

To install:

5. Position the brake pressure control valve and install the mounting screw.
6. Uncap and connect the four brake tubes to the brake pressure control valve. Tighten the brake tube nuts to 10–18 ft. lbs. (14–24 Nm).
7. Carefully lower the vehicle.
8. Connect the negative battery cable, then bleed the brake system, as outlined in this section.

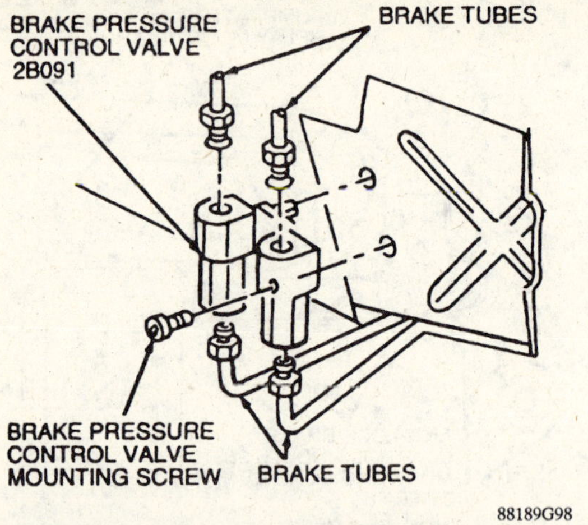

Fig. 118 Brake pressure control valve location

Brake Pedal Travel Switch

REMOVAL & INSTALLATION

1. Disconnect the negative battery cable.
2. Remove the switch retaining ring with a suitable prytool.
3. Pull the travel switch and O-ring from the booster.

To install:

4. Install the travel switch retaining ring into the groove.

➔ Be sure the O-ring is installed on the travel switch.

5. Push the travel switch into the booster until the retaining ring snaps into position.
6. Connect the negative battery cable.

Wheel Speed Sensor

REMOVAL & INSTALLATION

Front Wheel Sensor

➧ See Figure 119

1. Disconnect the negative battery cable.
2. Raise and safely support the vehicle with jackstands.
3. Detach the sensor electrical connector for the right or left front sensor (located near the radiator support).
4. Remove the routing clips along the wiring harness.

➔ If the front brake anti-lock sensor indicator is damaged, replace the front brake sensor.

5. Unfasten the bolt securing the anti-lock sensor to the front wheel spindle.

To install:

6. Install the sensor into the hole in the front wheel spindle. No adjustment is necessary. Install the bolt and tighten to 40–60 inch lbs. (4.5–6.8 Nm).
7. Route the wiring using the clips previously removed. Make sure the wiring is routed proper.
8. Carefully lower the vehicle.
9. Attach the sensor wiring connector to the harness connector.
10. Connect the negative battery cable.

Rear Sensor

➧ See Figure 120

1. Disconnect the negative battery cable.
2. From inside the luggage compartment, detach the wheel sensor electrical connector located rearward of the wheel well, behind the carpeting on the sides of the luggage compartment.
3. Lift the luggage compartment carpet and push the sensor wire grommet through the hole in the luggage compartment floor.
4. Raise and safely support the vehicle with jackstands.

➔ Do NOT bend the clip beyond the amount necessary to remove the clip from the axle housing.

5. Remove the plastic clip holding the sensor wire to the rear axle housing.
6. Unfasten the wheel sensor retaining bolt, then remove the sensor from then vehicle.

To install:

7. Align the sensor locating tab and bolt hole with the rear axle housing, then push into position.
8. Install the sensor retaining bolt and tighten to 14–20 ft. lbs. (19–27 Nm).
9. Install the plastic clip retaining the sensor wire to the rear axle housing and push the electrical connector through the hole in the luggage compartment. Make sure the rubber grommet is properly seated in the hole in the floor.
10. Carefully lower the vehicle.
11. Attach the sensor electrical connector to the connector on the harness.
12. Connect the negative battery cable.

Bleeding The ABS System

The brake system must be bled any time air is permitted to enter the system through loosened or disconnected lines or hoses, or anytime the modulator is removed. Excessive air within the system will cause a soft or spongy feel in the brake pedal.

When bleeding any part of the system, the reservoir must remain as close to full as possible at all times. Check the level frequently and top off fluid as needed.

When any part of the hydraulic system has been disconnected for service, air may enter the system and cause spongy pedal action. Bleed the system after it has been opened to be sure that all air is expelled.

The anti-lock brake system must be bled in 2 steps; both the master cylinder and hydraulic control unit reservoir must be bled using Rotunda Anti-Lock Brake Breakout Box/Bleeding Adapter tool No. T90P-50-ALA or equivalent. If this procedure is not followed, air will be trapped in the hydraulic control unit, and will eventually lead to a spongy brake pedal.

1. Disconnect the 55-pin plug from the electronic control unit/ABS control module, then install Anti-Lock Brake Breakout Box/Bleeding Adapter tool No. T90P-50-ALA or equivalent to the wire harness 55-pin plug.
   a. Place the Bleed/Harness switch in the **BLEED** position.
   b. Turn the ignition to the **ON** position. At this point the red **OFF** light should come **ON**.

c. Push the motor button on the adapter down to start the pump motor. The red **OFF** light will turn **OFF**, and the green **ON** light will turn **ON**. The pump motor will run for 60 seconds after the motor button is pushed. If the pump motor is to be turned off for any reason before the 60 seconds have elapsed, push the abort button to turn the pump motor off.

d. After 20 seconds of pump motor operation, push and hold the valve button down. Hold the valve button down for 20 seconds, then release it.

e. The pump motor will continue to run for an additional 20 seconds after the valve button is released.

2. The brake lines can now be bled in the normal fashion. Bleed the brake system by removing the rubber dust cap from the caliper fitting at the right rear of the vehicle. Place a suitable box wrench on the bleeder fitting and attach a rubber drain tube to the fitting. The end of the tube should fit snugly around the bleeder fitting. Submerge the other end of the tube in a container partially filled with clean brake fluid and loosen the fitting $^{3}/_{4}$ turn.

➥ Brake fluid absorbs moisture from the air. Don't leave the master cylinder or the fluid container uncovered any longer than necessary. Be careful handling the fluid — it will damage the vehicle's paint.

Check the level of the fluid often when bleeding, and refill the reservoirs as necessary. Don't let them run dry, or you will have to repeat the process.

3. Have an assistant push the brake pedal down slowly through its full travel. Close the bleeder fitting and allow the pedal to slowly return to its full release position. Wait 5 seconds and repeat the procedure until no bubbles appear at the submerged end of the bleeder tube. Secure the bleeder fitting and remove the bleeder tube. Install the rubber dust cap on the bleeder fitting.

4. Repeat the bleeding procedure at the left front, left rear and right front (in that order). Refill the master cylinder reservoir after each caliper has been bled, and install the master cylinder cap and gasket. When brake bleeding is completed, the fluid level should be filled to the maximum level indicated on the reservoir.

5. Always make sure the disc brake pistons are returned to their normal positions by depressing the brake pedal several times until normal pedal travel is established. If the pedal feels spongy, repeat the bleeding procedure.

After finishing, there should be no feeling of sponginess in the brake pedal. If there is, either there is still air in the line, in which case the process must be repeated, or there is a leak somewhere, which, of course, must be corrected before the vehicle is moved. After all repairs and service work is finished, road test the vehicle to verify proper brake system operation.

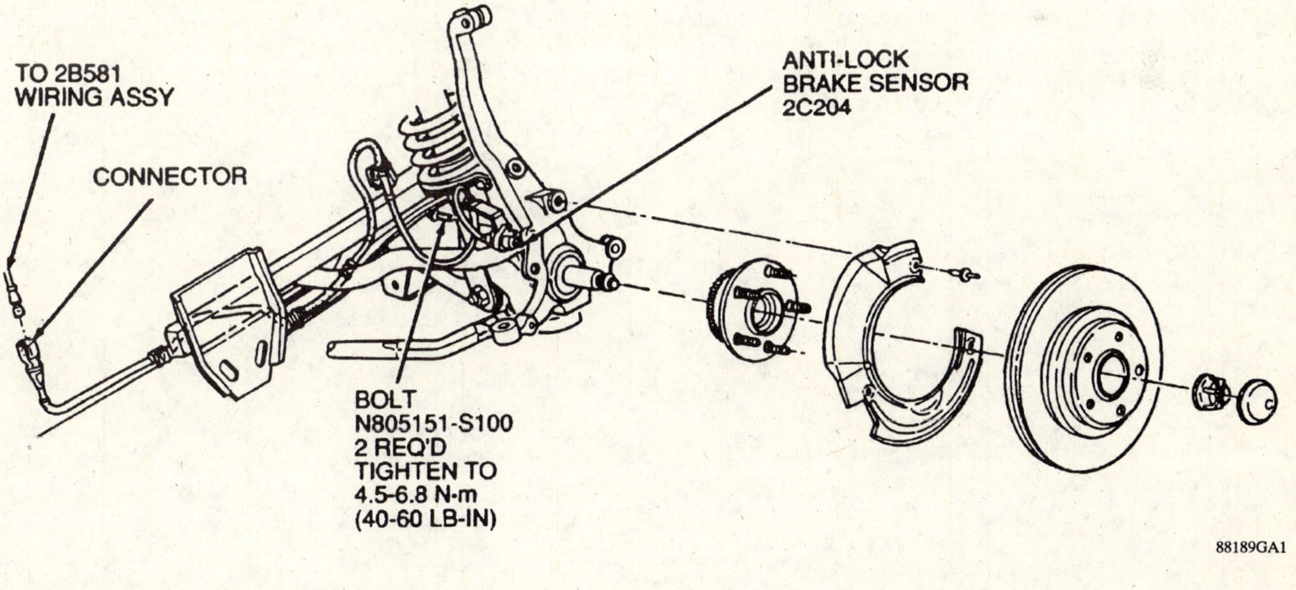

Fig. 119 Front wheel anti-lock brake (wheel speed) sensor location

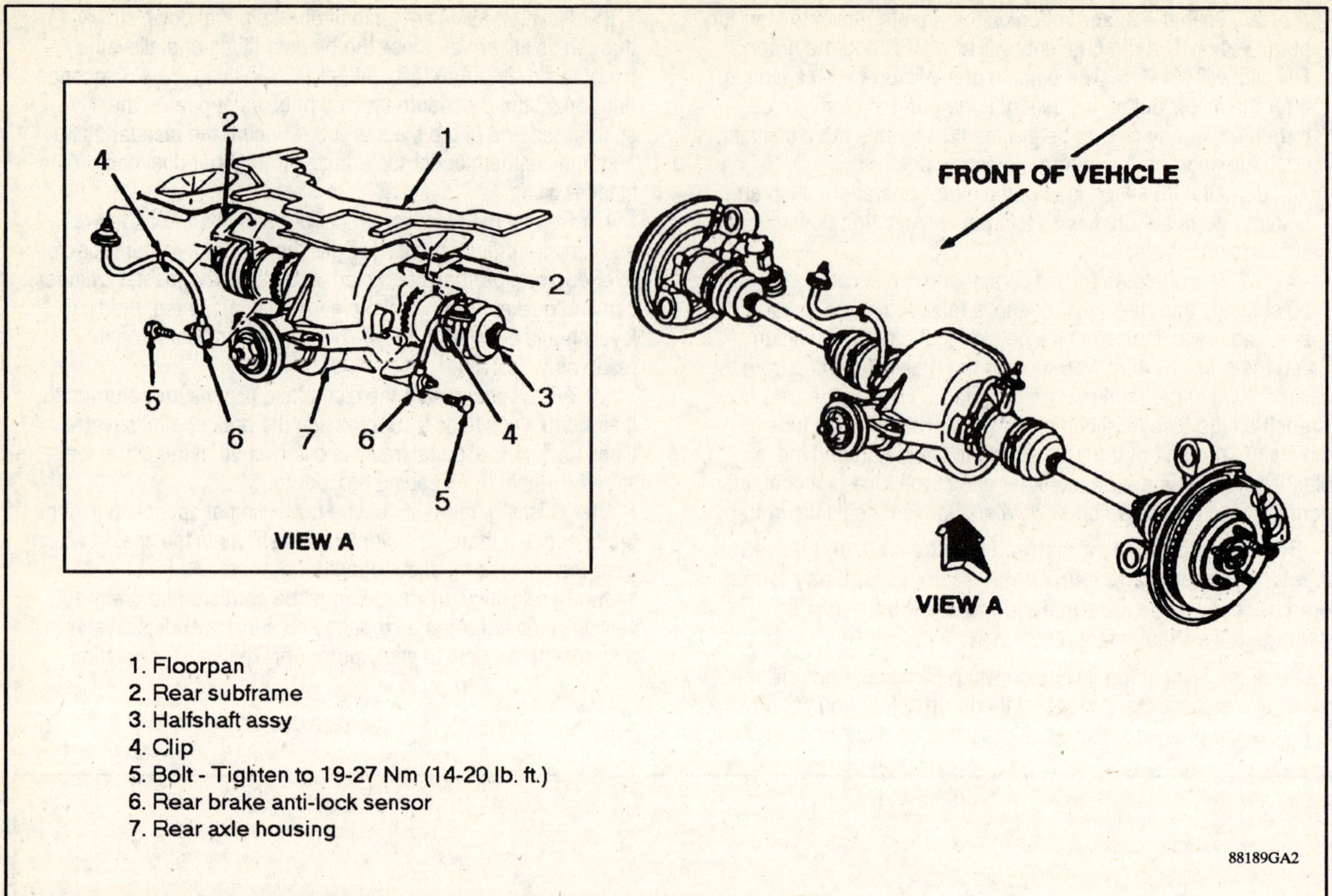

Fig. 120 Rear wheel speed sensor mounting — 1995 vehicle shown

BRAKE SPECIFICATIONS

All measurements in inches unless noted

Year	Model			Master Cylinder Bore	Brake Disc Original Thickness	Brake Disc Minimum Thickness	Brake Disc Maximum Runout	Brake Drum Diameter Original Inside Diameter	Brake Drum Diameter Max. Wear Limit	Brake Drum Diameter Maximum Machine Diameter	Minimum Lining Thickness Front	Minimum Lining Thickness Rear
1985	Cougar	①		0.875	NA	0.810	0.003	9.00	9.09	9.06	0.125	0.030
		②		0.875	NA	0.810	0.003	10.00	10.09	10.06	0.125	0.030
	Thunderbird	①		0.875	NA	0.810	0.003	9.00	9.09	9.06	0.125	0.030
		②		0.875	NA	0.810	0.003	10.00	10.09	10.06	0.125	0.030
1986	Cougar	①		0.875	NA	0.810	0.003	9.00	9.09	9.06	0.125	0.030
		②		0.875	NA	0.810	0.003	10.00	10.09	10.06	0.125	0.030
	Thunderbird	①		0.875	NA	0.810	0.003	9.00	9.09	9.06	0.125	0.030
		②		0.875	NA	0.810	0.003	10.00	10.09	10.06	0.125	0.030
1987	Cougar	①		0.875	NA	0.810	0.003	9.00	9.89	9.06	0.125	0.030
		②		0.875	NA	0.810	0.003	10.00	10.89	10.06	0.125	0.030
	Thunderbird	③		0.875	NA	0.810	0.003	9.00	9.89	9.06	0.125	0.030
		④		0.875	NA	0.810	0.003	10.00	10.89	10.06	0.125	0.030
		⑤		0.875	NA	0.972	0.003	9.00	9.89	9.06	0.125	0.030
		⑥		0.875	NA	0.895	-	-	-	-	-	-
1988	Cougar	①		0.875	NA	0.810	0.003	9.00	9.89	9.06	0.125	0.030
		②		0.875	NA	0.810	0.003	10.00	10.89	10.06	0.125	0.030
	Thunderbird	③		0.875	NA	0.810	0.003	9.00	9.89	9.06	0.125	0.030
		④		0.875	NA	0.810	0.003	10.00	10.89	10.06	0.125	0.030
	Thunderbird	⑥	F	0.875	NA	0.972	0.003	9.00	9.89	9.06	0.125	0.030
		⑥	R	0.875	NA	0.895	0.003	-	-	-	-	-
1989	Cougar	①		0.875	NA	0.810	0.003	9.00	9.89	9.06	0.125	0.030
		②		0.875	NA	0.810	0.003	10.00	10.89	10.06	0.125	0.030
	Thunderbird	⑦		0.875	NA	0.935	0.003	9.80	9.99	9.86	0.125	0.030
		⑧		-	-	0.900	0.003	-	-	-	-	0.123
1990	Cougar	⑦		0.938	1.025	0.974	0.004	-	-	-	0.125	0.030
		⑧		-	0.945	0.896	0.003	9.80	9.89	9.86	-	0.123
	Thunderbird	⑦	F	0.875	NA	0.935	0.003	9.80	9.89	9.86	0.123	0.030
		⑧	R	-	-	0.900	0.003	-	-	-	-	0.123
1991	Cougar	⑦		0.938	1.025	0.974	0.004	-	-	-	0.125	0.030
		⑧		-	0.710	0.657	-	9.80	9.90	9.86	0.123	-
	Thunderbird	⑦	F	0.875	NA	0.935	0.003	9.80	9.89	9.86	0.123	0.030
		⑧	R	-	-	0.900	0.003	-	-	-	-	0.123
1992	Cougar	⑦		0.938 ⑨	1.025	0.974	0.003	-	-	-	0.125	0.030
		⑧		-	0.710	0.657	-	9.80	9.90	9.86	0.123	-
	Thunderbird	⑦	F	0.938 ⑨	1.024	0.974	0.003	9.84	9.90	9.86	0.125	0.030
		⑧	R	-	0.945	0.896	0.003	-	-	-	-	0.123
1993	Cougar	⑦		0.938 ⑨	1.025	0.974	0.003	-	-	-	0.125	0.030
		⑧		-	0.710	0.657	-	9.80	9.89	9.86	0.123	-
	Thunderbird	⑦	F	0.983 ⑨	1.025	0.974	0.003	9.84	9.89	9.86	0.125	0.030
		⑧	R	-	0.945	0.896	0.003	-	-	-	-	0.123

88189c01

BRAKE SPECIFICATIONS

All measurements in inches unless noted

Year	Model		Master Cylinder Bore	Brake Disc Original Thickness	Brake Disc Minimum Thickness	Brake Disc Maximum Runout	Brake Drum Diameter Original Inside Diameter	Brake Drum Diameter Max. Wear Limit	Brake Drum Diameter Maximum Machine Diameter	Minimum Lining Thickness Front	Minimum Lining Thickness Rear
1994	Cougar (7)	F	0.938	1.025	0.974	0.003	9.80	9.89	9.89	0.040	0.030
	(8)	R	-	0.710	0.657	0.003	-	-	-	0.123	-
	Thunderbird (7)	F	0.938 (9)	1.025	0.974	0.003	9.84	9.89	9.89	0.040	0.030
	(8)	R	-	0.709	0.657	0.003	-	-	-	-	0.123
1995	Cougar	F	0.938	1.025	0.974	0.003	-	-	-	0.040	-
		R	-	0.710	0.657	0.003	9.98	NA	9.90	-	(10)
	Thunderbird (7)	F	0.938 (9)	1.025	0.974	0.003	9.84	9.89	9.86	0.040	0.030
	(8)	R	-	0.709	0.657	0.003	-	-	-	-	0.123
1996	Cougar	F	0.938	1.025	0.974	0.003	-	-	-	0.125	-
		R	-	0.710	0.657	0.002	9.80	NA	9.90	-	0.125
	Thunderbird	F	0.938	1.025	0.974	0.002	-	-	-	0.125	-
		R		0.710	0.657	-	9.80	NA	9.90	-	0.125

NOTE: Follow specifications stamped on rotor or drum if figures differ from those in this chart

NA - Not Available

F - Front

R - Rear

1: 9 inch rear

2: 10 inch rear

3: 9 inch rear, except Turbo

4: 10 inch rear, except Turbo

5: Turbo without rear disc

6: Turbo with rear disc

7: Except rear disc

8: With rear disc

9: Without ABS

10: Riveted lining: 0.123
Bonded lining: 0.030

88189c02

10

BODY

EXTERIOR

Doors

REMOVAL & INSTALLATION

➧ **See Figures 1, 2, 3 and 4**

1. Remove the door trim panel.
2. Remove the watershield, and, if a new door is being installed, save all the molding clips and moldings.
3. Remove the wiring harness, actuator and speakers.
4. If a new door is being installed, remove all window and lock components.
5. Mark the location of the hinges on the door and pillar.
6. Support the door and unbolt the hinges from the door.

To install:

7. Position the upper and lower hinges on the door if removed.
8. Position the hinges on the door pillar and partially tighten the hinge bolts.
9. Align the door and tighten the hinge bolts to 18–26 ft lbs. (25–37 Nm).
10. Attach the electrical harness. Install any remaining components if removed.

ADJUSTMENT

1. Determine which door hinge screws must be loosened to move the door in the desired direction.
2. Loosen the hinge screws enough to allow movement of the door with a padded prybar.
3. Move the door the necessary distance. Tighten the hinge screws to 18–26 ft. lbs. (25–35 Nm). Check the door fit ensuring that there is no binding or interference with the adjustment panel.
4. Repeat the procedure until the desired fit is obtained. Check that the door latch striker tapping plate alignment for proper door closing.

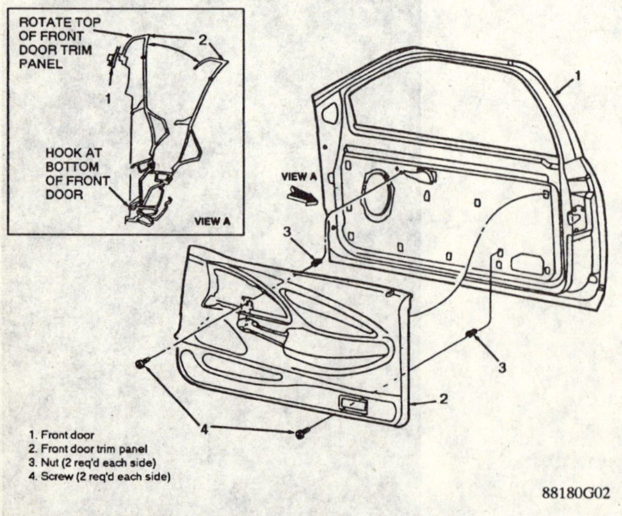

Fig. 1 Assemble the homemade tool as shown

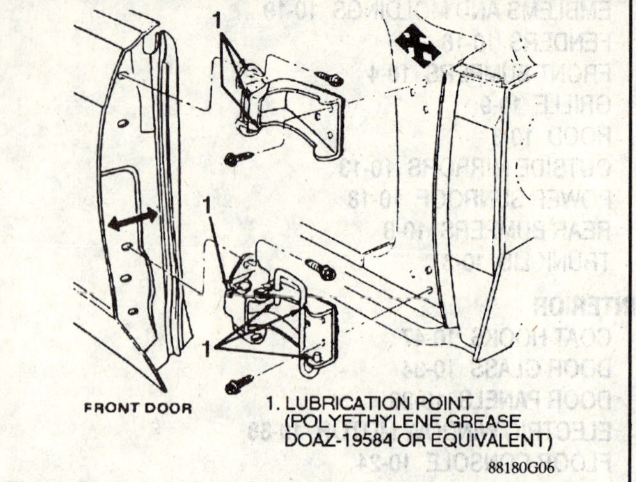

Fig. 2 Exploded view of the door hinges on the 1983–84 models

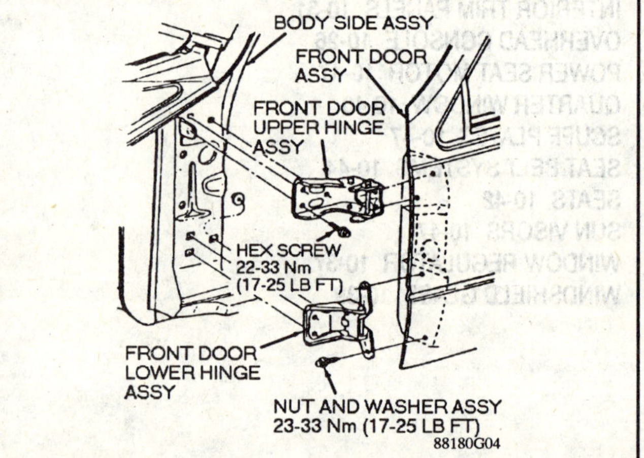

Fig. 3 Exploded view of the door hinges on the 1985–88 models

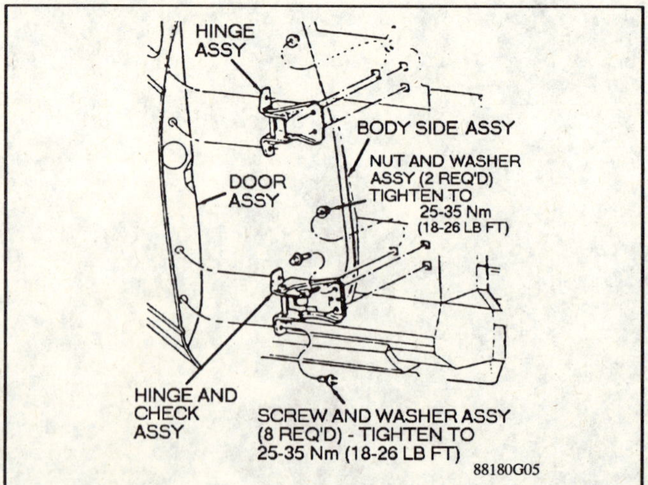

Fig. 4 Exploded view of the door hinges on the 1989–96 models

Hood

REMOVAL & INSTALLATION

➧ **See Figures 5, 6 and 7**

1. Open and support the hood.
2. Matchmark the hood-to-hinge positions.

➥ It is a good practice to cover the fenders with an appropriate covering so as not to scratch or damage the body and paint while removing or installing the hood.

3. Have an assistant support the hood while you remove the hinge-to-hood bolts and disconnect the hood lift/gas supports.
4. Remove the hood, but rest the hood on its side, not on the rear corners.

To install:

5. Position the hood on the hinges.
6. Install the retaining bolts to attach the hood to the hinges.Tighten the bolts to 7–10 ft. lbs. (9–14 Nm).
7. Install the hood lift/gas supports.
8. Install the retaining clip the hood lift/gas supports.
9. Adjust the hood and hood latch.

ALIGNMENT

1. Side-to-side and fore-aft adjustments can be made by loosening the hood-to-hinge attachment bolts and positioning the hood as necessary.
2. Hood vertical fit can be adjusted by raising or lowering the hinge-to-fender reinforcement bolts.
3. To ensure a snug fit of the hood against the rear hood bumpers, it may be necessary to rotate the hinge around the 3 attaching bolts.
4. Front level adjustment is done by adjusting the two front mounted rubbers on the radiator support, either up or down for proper alignment.

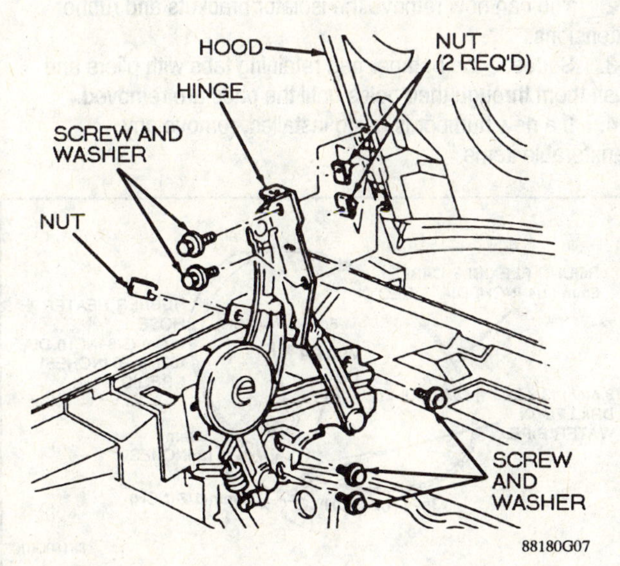

Fig. 5 Hood hinge bolt locations on the 1983–88 models

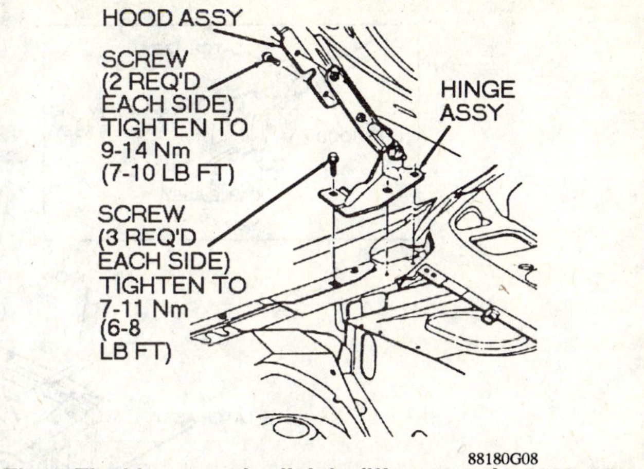

Fig. 6 The hinge type is slightly different on the 1989–96 models

Trunk Lid

REMOVAL & INSTALLATION

1. With the aide of an assistant, remove the hinge-to-trunk lid screws and lift off the lid.

To install:

2. Position the lid on the hinges and loosely tighten the mounting screws.
3. Adjust the trunk lid and tighten the mounting screws to 4–6 ft. lbs. (5–9 Nm).

ALIGNMENT

Trunk Lid

1. Fore-aft fit may be adjusted by loosening the hinge to trunk lid bolts and positioning the lid as necessary.
2. Vertical fit can be adjusted by loosening then tightening the lid hinge screws. Tighten them to 4–6 ft. lbs. (5–9 Nm).

Torsion Bar Loading

➧ **See Figures 8, 9, 10 and 11**

****CAUTION**

Always wear safety glasses when performing this operation!

You'll need the following materials to fabricate an adjusting tool:

- 4 feet (122cm) of $^1/_4$ in. (6mm) diameter flexible steel cable
- One $^1/_4$ in. (6mm) cable clamp
- 2 inch (52mm) length of $^1/_2$ in. (13mm) steel pipe
- 6 inch (152mm) length of $^5/_8$ inch (16mm) rubber heater hose

Assemble the tool as shown in the accompanying illustration.

1. Open the trunk lid and note the pop-up distance. The trunk lid should have finger clearance. If not, the torsion bar tension should be increased. If the trunk lid pops open with more than necessary force, the torsion bar tension should be decreased.

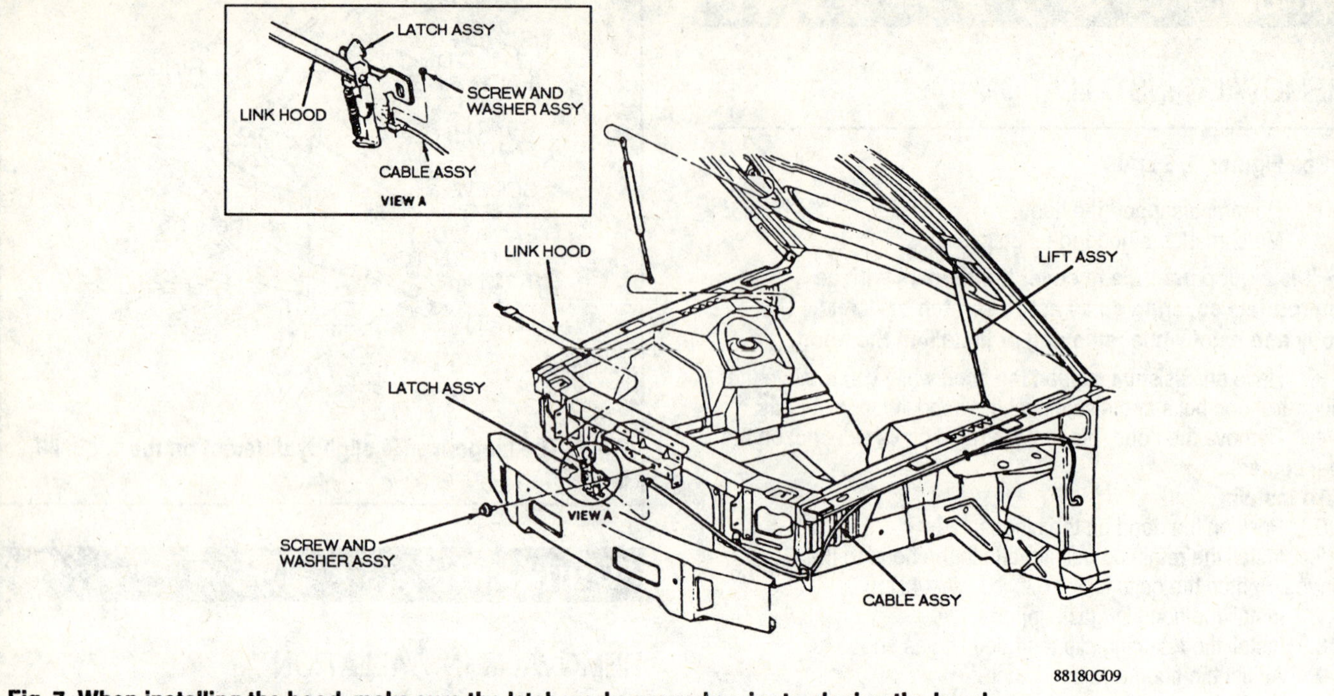

Fig. 7 When installing the hood, make sure the latch works properly prior to closing the hood

****CAUTION**

The torsion bar is under great tension! Be very careful when adjusting it as it can spring out of control with considerable force if not handled properly!

2. Support the trunk lid in the fully open position.
3. Position the homemade tool on one end of the torsion bar. With an assistant, place a long, flat bladed bar over the top of the torsion bar. Pull one end of the torsion bar towards you with the homemade tool, with the assistant holding the flat bladed bar, guide the torsion bar down along the rear edge of the support into the lower groove of the hinge support so the torsion bar can be locked in the lowest outboard adjustment notch.
4. Using the homemade tool, pull the torsion bar towards you and work the bar up the hinge support to the second notch and release it. If further adjustment is necessary, proceed to the next step.
5. Using a $^3/_8$ inch drive with a $^1/_2$ inch deep-well socket and 6 inch (152mm) extension, position the socket over the end of the torsion bar and lift it to unlock the bar. Reposition the torsion bar up the hinge support to the top notch and release it.

Front Bumpers

REMOVAL & INSTALLATION

1983 Thunderbird and XR-7

1. On the XR-7, remove the park and turn signal lamp sockets.
2. Remove the bumper cover assembly from the bumper (8 pushpins and 4 bolts).
3. Remove the 8 bumper retaining bolts, then remove the bumper from the car.
4. If a new bumper is being installed, remove all of the transferable parts.

To install:

5. Fit the bumper on the car, then tighten the bolts snugly.
6. Adjust the bumper height so that the bottom edge of the bumper is $14^{47}/_{64}$ in. $\pm$ $1^1/_2$ in. (374.25mm $\pm$ 38mm) from the ground. Tighten the bolts to 35 ft. lbs. (47 Nm).

1983 Cougar

1. Remove the 3 bolts attaching the bumper reinforcement to each isolator, then remove the bumper. Note the number and position of any shims.
2. You can now remove the isolator brackets and rubber extensions.
3. Squeeze the bumper pad retaining tabs with pliers and push them through their holes until the pads are removed.
4. If a new bumper is being installed, remove any transferable items.

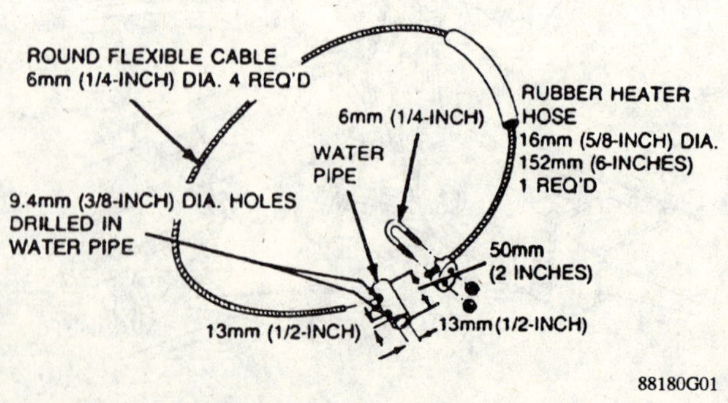

Fig. 8 Assemble the homemade tool as shown

To install:

5. Installation is the reverse of removal. Tighten the mounting bolts snugly.

Adjust the distance between the top edge of the bumper and the ground is 21$^1/_4$ in. + 1$^1/_3$ in. -1$^1/_2$ in. (540mm +34mm -38mm).

Adjust the bumper so that the distance between the front face of the bumper and the front face of the headlight door is 4 $^3/_{64}$ in. + $^3/_8$ in. -$^1/_4$ in. (103mm +10mm -6mm).

Adjust the bumper so that the clearance between the rubber extensions and the fender panels is $^5/_8$ in. ± $^1/_4$ in. (16mm ± 6mm). Tighten the bolts to 35 ft. lbs. (47 Nm).

1984-88 Models

See Figures 12, 13, 14, 15, 16 and 17

1. Remove the park and turn signal lamp sockets.
2. Remove the bumper cover assembly from the bumper.
3. Remove the bumper retaining bolts and remove the bumper from the car.
4. If a new bumper is being installed, remove all transferable parts.

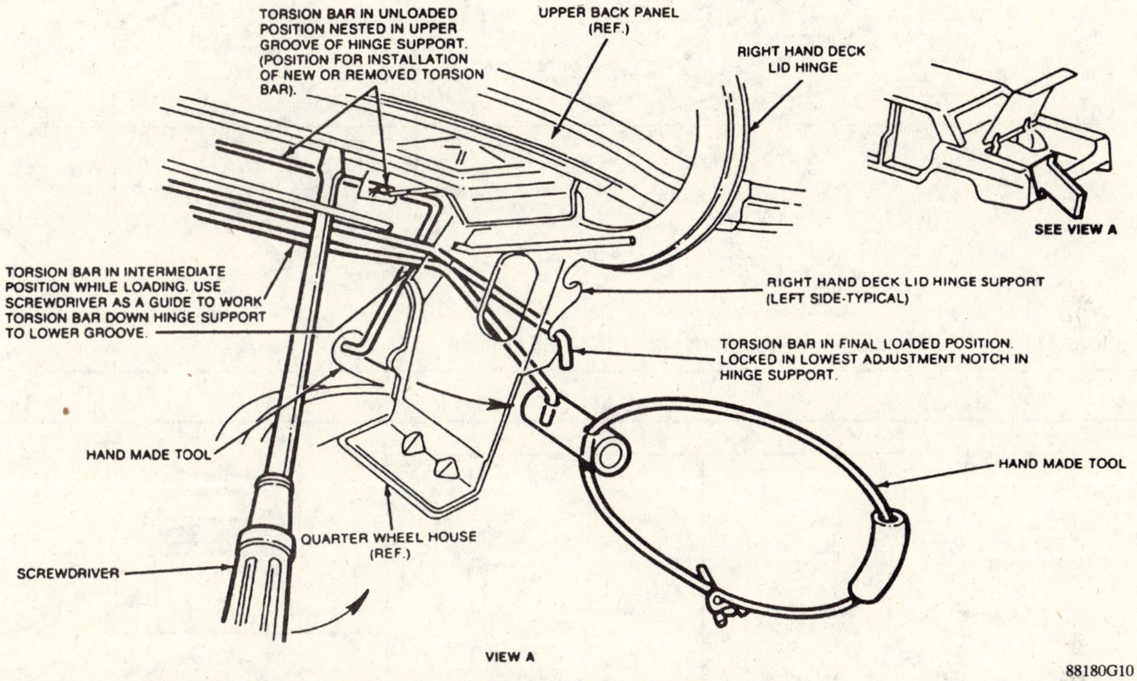

Fig. 9 Using the handmade tool and a flatbladed tool, adjust the torsion bar loading

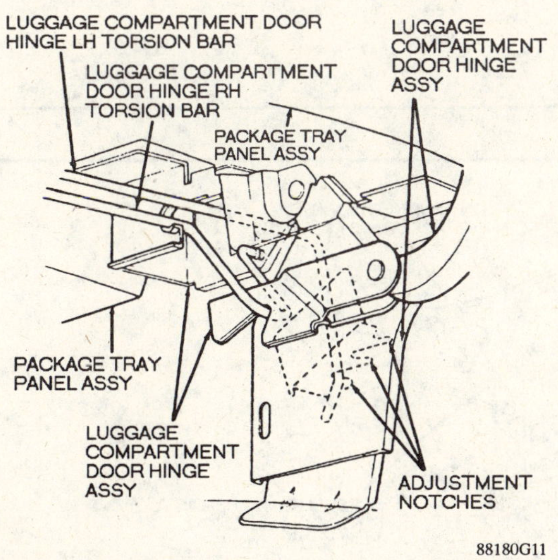

Fig. 10 Cougar trunk lid hinge — 1989-96

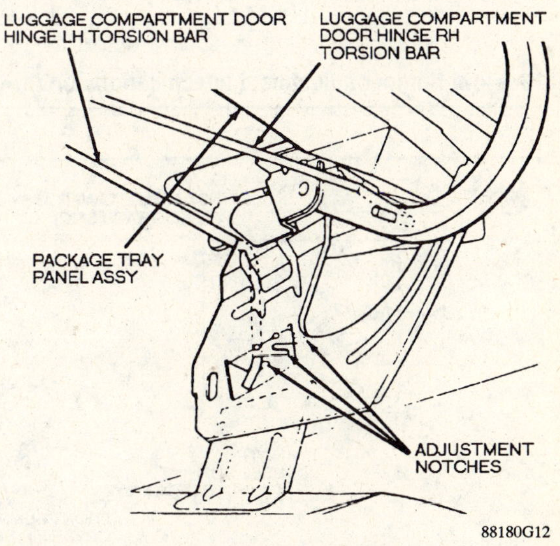

Fig. 11 Thunderbird trunk lid hinge — 1989-96

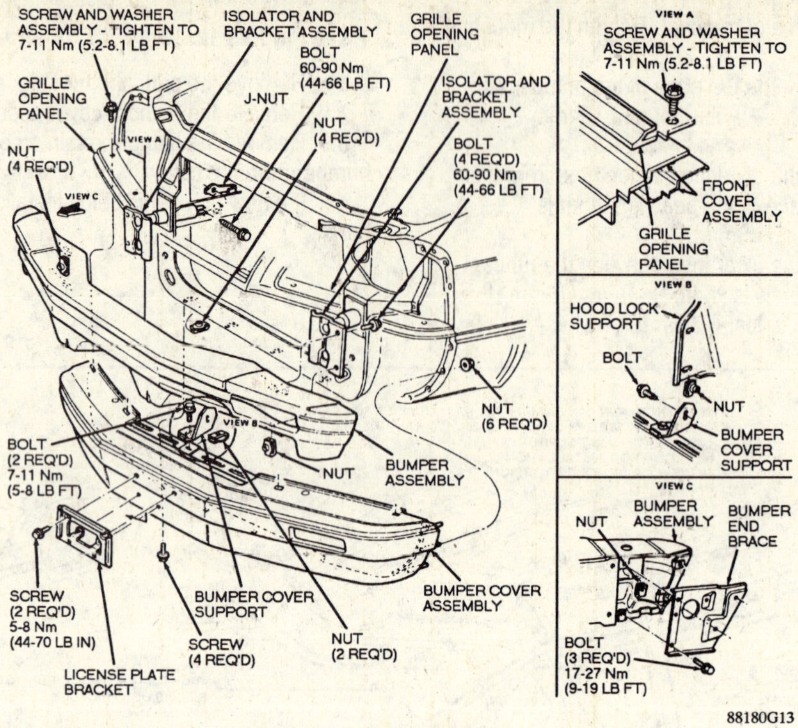

Fig. 12 Exploded view of the front bumper components — 1984–86 models

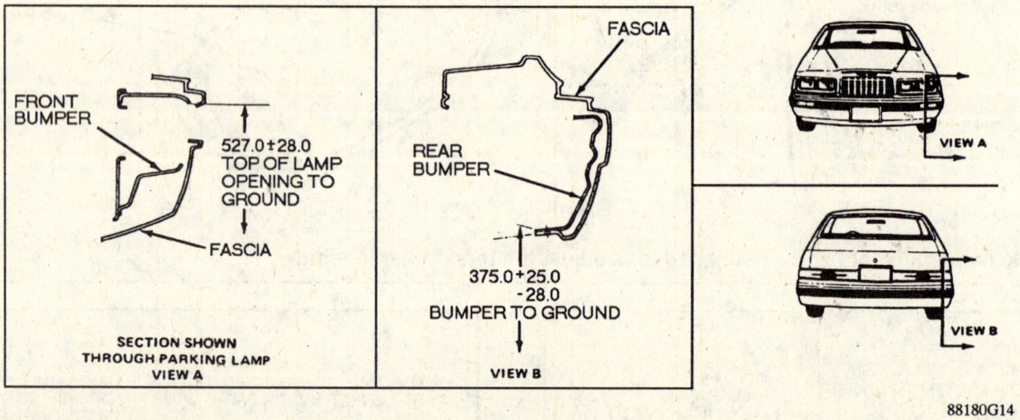

Fig. 13 Front bumper adjustment specifications on the 1984–86 models

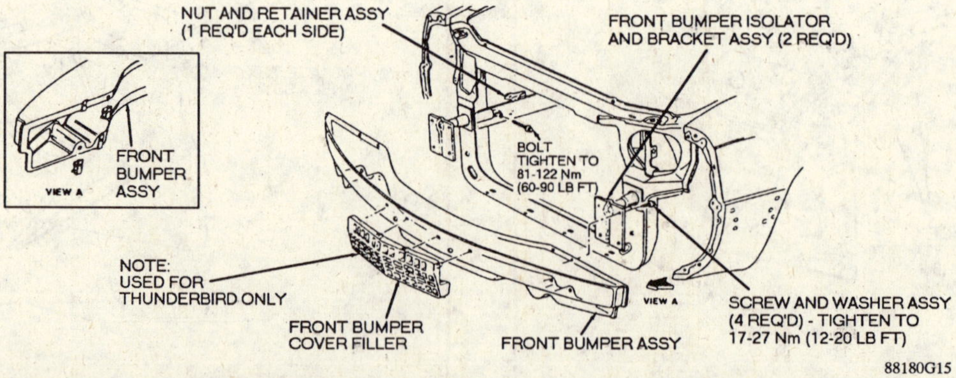

Fig. 14 Front bumper and grille — 1987–88 models

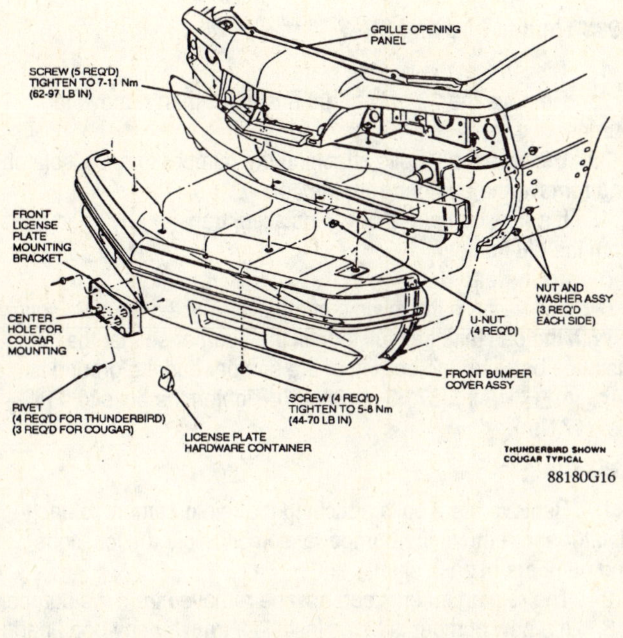

Fig. 15 Front bumper cover components adjustment specifications — 1984-86 models

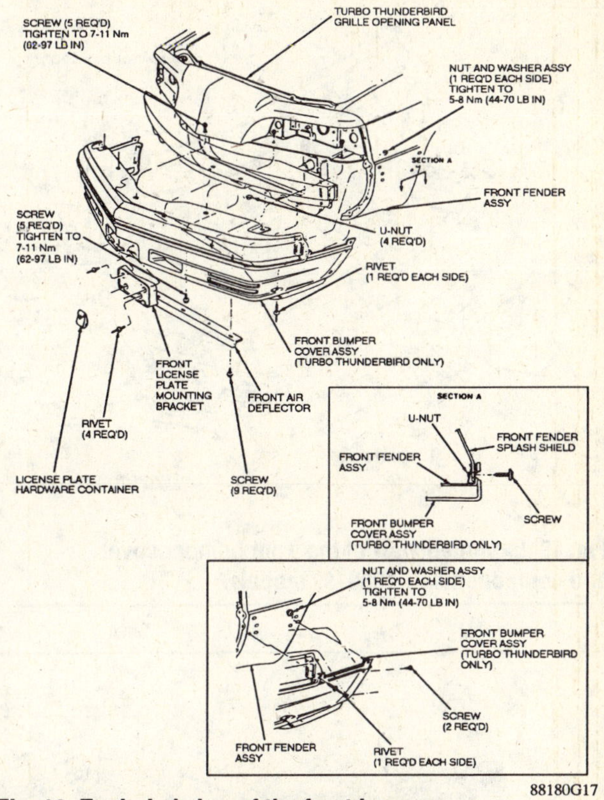

Fig. 16 Exploded view of the front bumper components — 1987-88 Turbo models

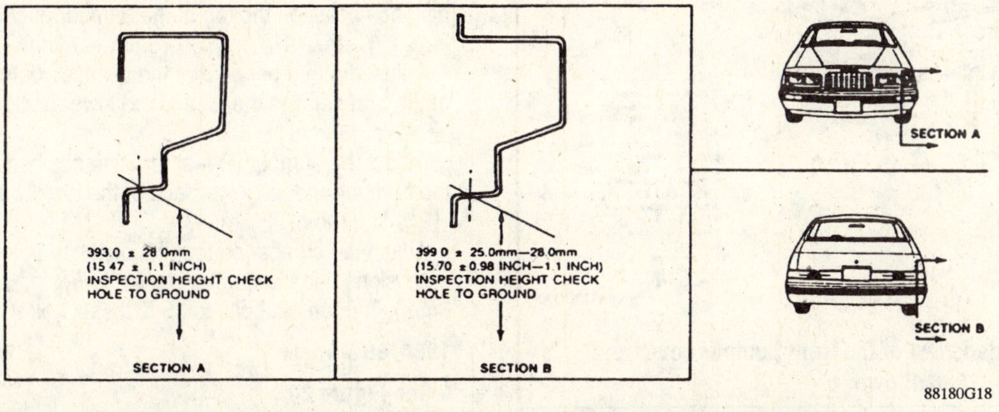

Fig. 17 Front bumper cover components adjustment specifications — 1987-88 models, exc turbo

To install:

5. Fit the bumper to the car and tighten the bolts snugly.

Adjust the bumper height so that the top edge of the bumper is 20 $^{3}/_{4}$ in. ± 1$^{1}/_{8}$ in. (527.05mm ± 29mm) on 1983-86 models and to 15$^{7}/_{16}$ in. ± $^{9}/_{32}$ in. (392.1mm ± 7.1mm) and 1987-88 models from the ground. Tighten the bolts to 66 ft. lbs. (89 Nm).

1989-96 Models

➧ See Figures 18 and 19

The front bumper is an integral part of the welded structure of the front end. Therefore when replacement is necessary it must be installed with the proper tools and welding equipment. The bumper cover and isolator can however be replaced as follows:

1. Remove the park/turn signal and side marker lamps.
2. Unscrew the cover at the front edge of fender.
3. Remove the five plastic retainers, retaining the bottom of cover and air deflector to the bottom of the radiator support.
4. Remove the plastic retainer securing the bracket at center of cover to the bumper beam.
5. Remove four (two on each side) nuts retaining the cover ends to side of front fender.
6. Remove the two (one on each side) screws retaining the ends of the cover to front fenders and splash shield.
7. Remove the cover by sliding the top edge out from slot in grille opening support panel.
8. Drill out the three rivets retaining the isolator to the bumper beam, and remove the isolator. On Cougar, remove isolator insert.

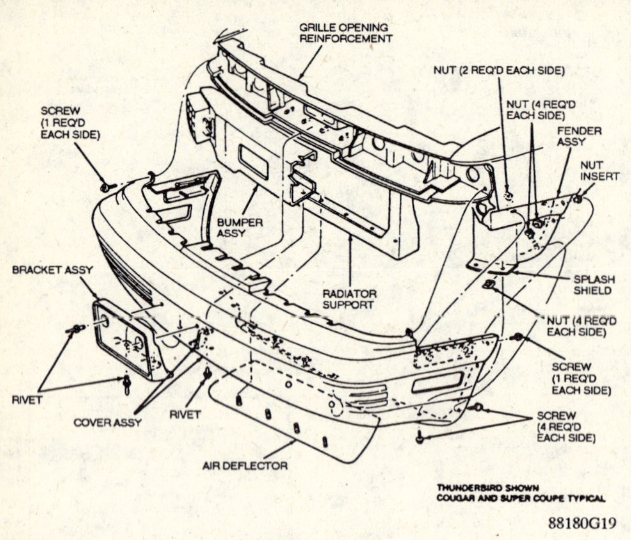

Fig. 18 Exploded view of the front bumper cover and components — 1989-92 models

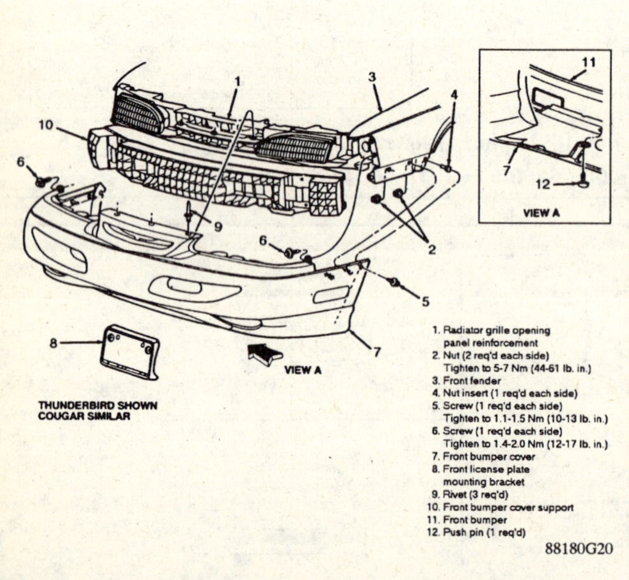

Fig. 19 Exploded view of the front bumper cover and components — 1996 shown

To install:

9. Position the front cover on the vehicle by sliding the top edge into the slot in the grille opening panel reinforcement.
10. Position the four studs on the front cover into the slots located in the side of the fenders.
11. Install the two retaining screws at the front edge of the fender and tighten to 1-2 inch lbs. (5-7 Nm).
12. Install the four nuts to retain the bumper cover ends to the fenders. Tighten to 46-62 inch lbs. (5-7 Nm).
13. Install the three rivets retaining the center of the bumper cover in the grille opening panel reinforcement.
14. Attach the five plastic retainers for the bottom of the cover and air deflector-to-grille opening reinforcement. (Super Coupe only)
15. Install one plastic retainer attaching the cover center bracket to the front bumper.
16. Install the park, turn signal and side marker lamps.

Rear Bumpers

REMOVAL & INSTALLATION

1983 Thunderbird and XR-7

1. Disconnect the license plate light.
2. Remove the 12 nuts and 8 pushpins, then remove the bumper cover.
3. Remove the 3 bolts attaching the bumper to each isolator and remove the bumper from the car.
4. If a new bumper is being installed, transfer any good parts from the old bumper.
5. **To install:**
6. Installation is the reverse of removal. Tighten the bolts snugly.

With the gas tank half full, adjust the bumper so that the distance between the bottom of the bumper and the ground is $14^5/_8$ in. ± $1^1/_2$ in. (371.5 ± 38mm). Tighten the bolts to 35 ft. lbs. (47 Nm).

1983 Cougar

1. Remove the 3 bolts attaching the reinforcement to each isolator and remove the bumper assembly. Note the locations and numbers of each shim.
2. The reinforcements can now be removed from the bumper.
3. If a new bumper is being installed, transfer any good parts from the old bumper.

To install:

4. Installation is the reverse of removal. Tighten the bolts snugly.

With the gas tank half full, adjust the bumper so that the distance between the top of the bumper and the ground is $21^1/_4$ in. + 1 $^7/_{16}$ in. - $1^1/_2$ in. (539.75mm + 37mm - 38mm).

Adjust the bumper so that the distance between the front face of the bumper and the face of the lower back panel is 3 $^{25}/_{64}$ in. ± $^1/_4$ in. (86mm ± 6mm).

Adjust the bumper so that the distance between the top face of the bumper and the lower face of the lower back panel is $^3/_4$ in. ± $^1/_4$ in. (19mm ± 6mm).

Adjust the bumper so that the distance between the rubber extensions and the quarter panels is $^9/_{16}$ in. ± $^1/_4$ in. (14mm ± 6mm). Tighten the bolts to 35 ft. lbs. (47 Nm).

1984-88 Models

➧ **See Figure 20**

1. Remove the 13 nuts and 6 pushpins and remove the bumper cover.
2. Remove the 2-4 bolts attaching the bumper to each isolator and remove the bumper from the car.
3. If a new bumper is being installed, transfer any good parts from the old bumper.

To install:

4. With the gas take half full, adjust the bumper so that the distance between the bottom of the bumper and the ground is $14^3/_4$ in. + $^{63}/_{64}$ in. -$1^1/_8$ in. (374.65mm + 25mm -28.8mm) on the 1984 models. The distance between the bottom of the bumper and the ground is $14^3/_4$ in. + $^1/_4$ in. - $^9/_{32}$ in. (374.65mm + 6mm - 7.1mm) on the 1985-86 models and $15^{11}/_{16}$ in. ± $^9/_{32}$ in. (398.5mm ± 7mm). on the 1987-88 models. Tighten the bolts to 66 ft. lbs. (89 Nm).

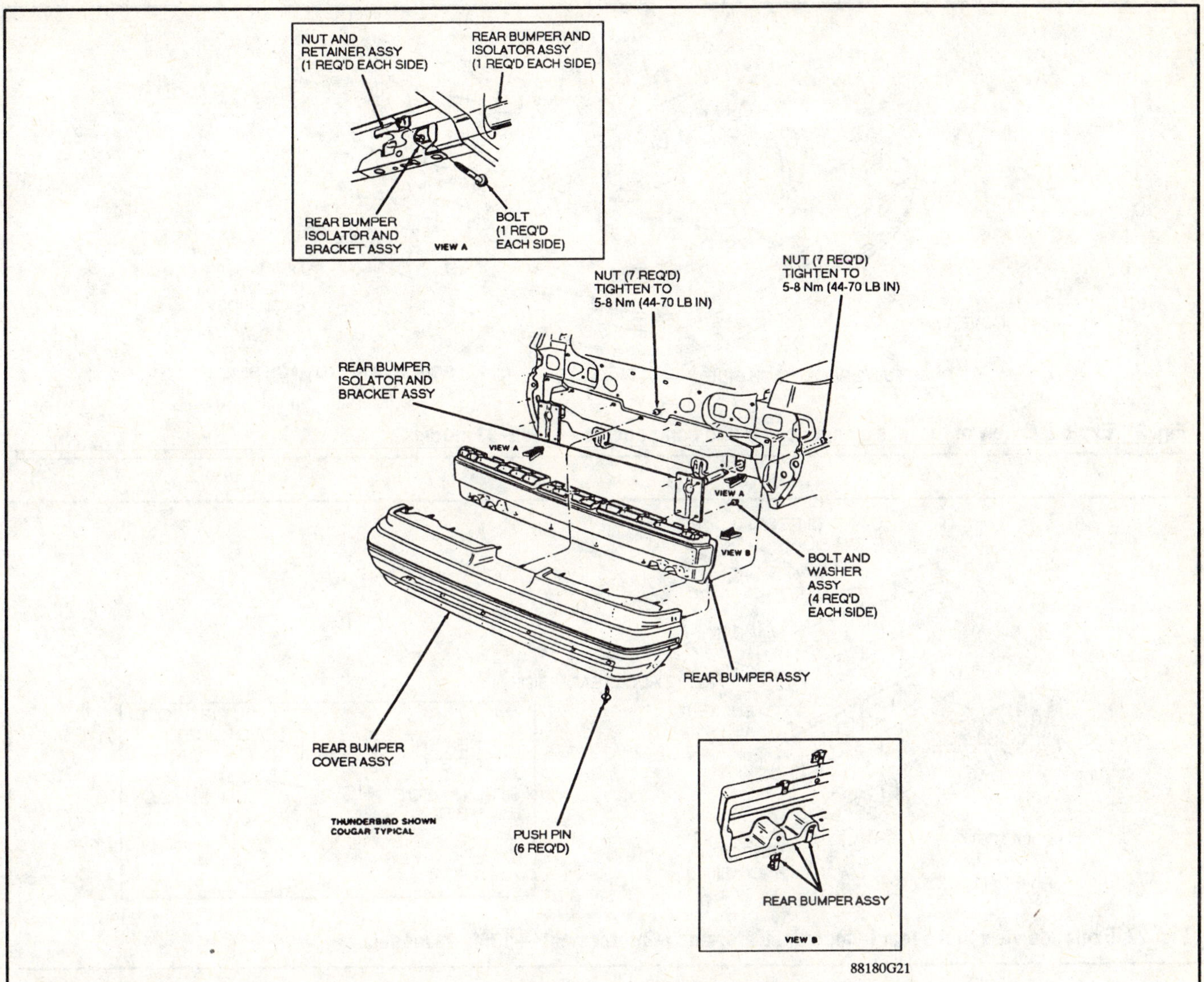

Fig. 20 Exploded view of the rear bumper cover and components — 1987–88 models

1989–96 Models

➧ **See Figures 21, 22 and 23**

1. Remove the plastic retainers, nine on standard models, six on Super Coupe, retaining the bottom of cover to the bumper.
2. Remove the six (three each side) retaining screws attaching the ends of cover to the quarter panels.
3. Working from inside luggage compartment, roll back the trim to gain access to the eight to twelve nuts attaching the cover to the lower back panel. Remove the nuts and pull cover from vehicle.
4. Drill out the eleven rivets retaining the isolator to the bumper, and remove isolator.
5. Remove the two (one each side) inboard studs retaining the bumper to vehicle.
6. Remove the four (two each side) nuts retaining the bumper to vehicle, and remove bumper.

To install:

7. Installation is the reverse of removal. Tighten the rear bumper retaining nuts to 44–62 inch lbs. (5–7 Nm) and the cover ends-to-fender screws to 10–13 inch lbs. (1–2 Nm).

With the gas tank half full, adjust the bumper so that the distance between the bottom of the bumper and the ground is $15^{11}/_{16}$ in. $\pm$ $^{9}/_{32}$ in. (397.1mm $\pm$ 26.5mm).

Grille

REMOVAL & INSTALLATION

1983–88 Models

➧ **See Figures 24, 25, 26 and 27**

1. Open the hood.
2. Remove the screws from front of grille.
3. Separate the grille from the vehicle.

To install:

4. Align the locator pins on grille with the holes in the grille opening panel assembly.
5. Install the screws into the holes in grille assembly.

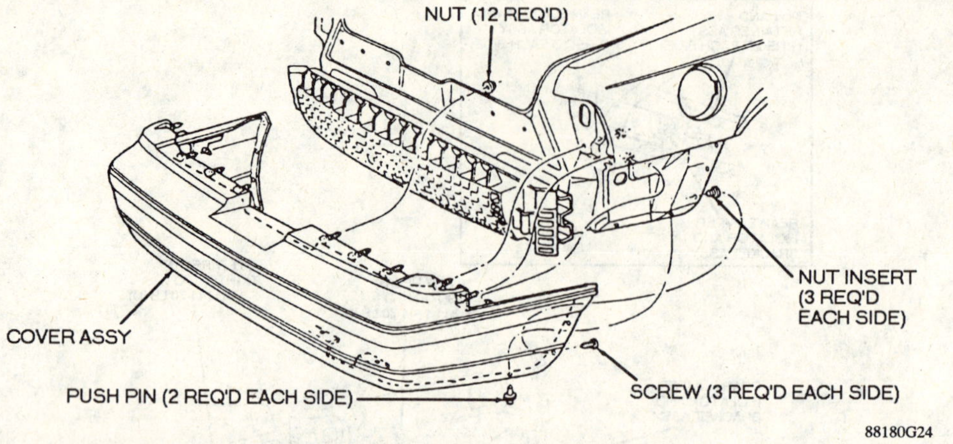

Fig. 21 Exploded view of the rear bumper cover and components — 1989-93 models

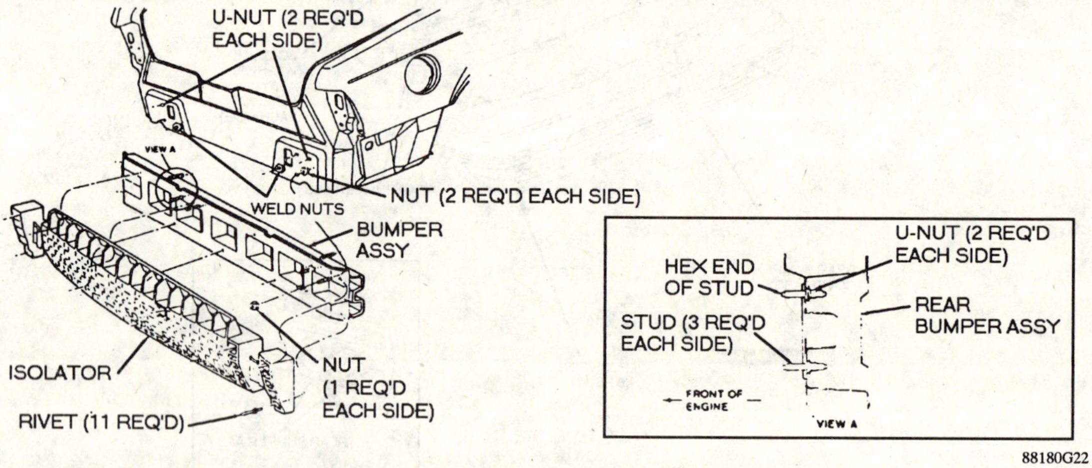

Fig. 22 Exploded view of the rear bumper insulator and reinforcement — 1989-93 models

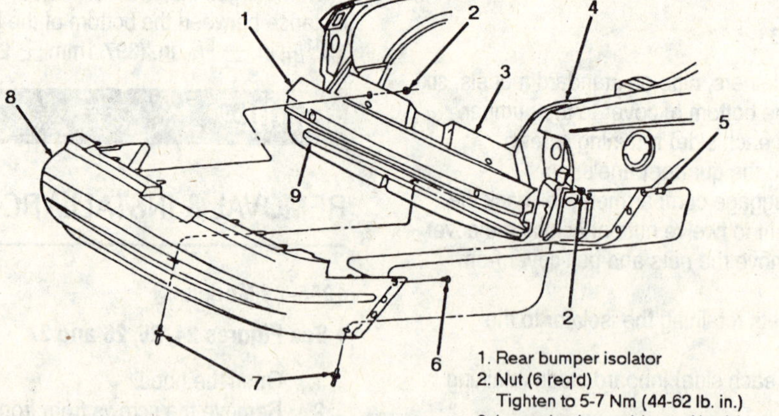

Fig. 23 Exploded view of the rear bumper cover and components — 1996 model shown

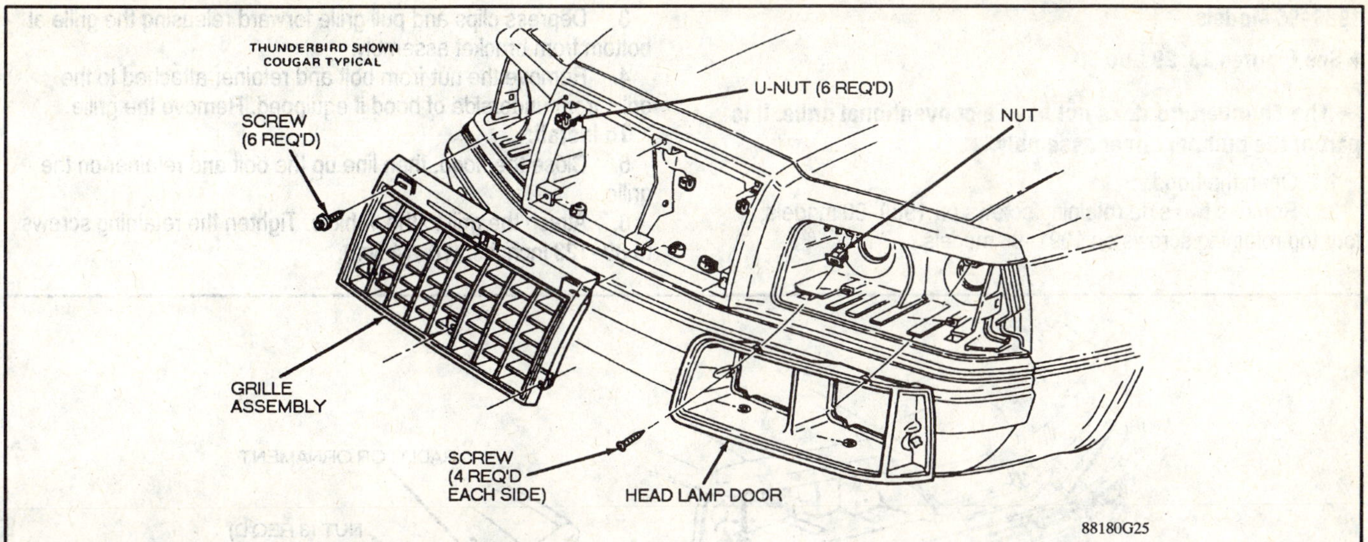

Fig. 24 Exploded view of the grille — 1983-84 Cougar

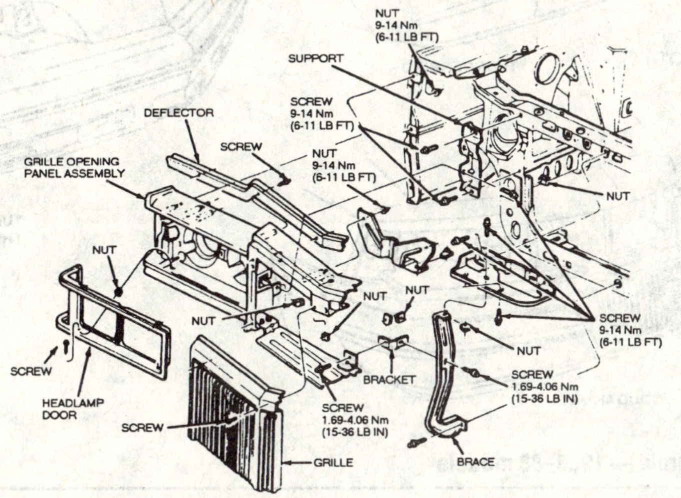

Fig. 25 Exploded view of the grille — 1983-84 Cougar XR-7

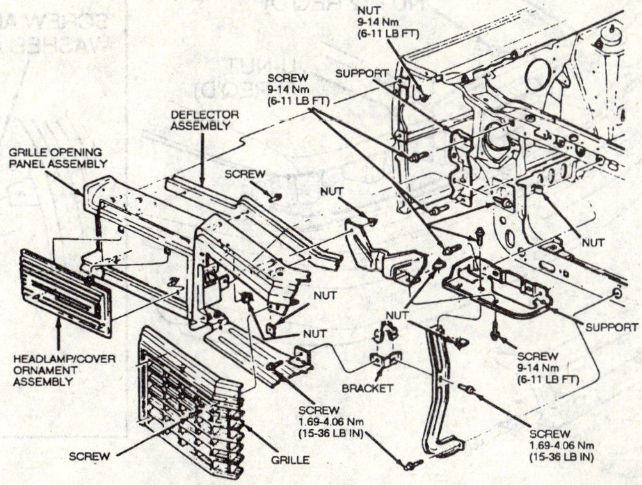

Fig. 26 Exploded view of the grille — 1983-84 Thunderbird

1989-96 Models

➧ **See Figures 28, 29 and 30**

➥ The Thunderbird does not have a conventional grille. It is part of the bumper cover assembly.

1. Open the hood.
2. Remove two side retaining screws on 1989-90 models; four top retaining screws on 1991-96 models.
3. Depress clips and pull grille forward releasing the grille at bottom from bracket assembly.
4. Remove the nut from bolt and retainer attached to the grille from underside of hood if equipped. Remove the grille.

To install:

5. Close the hood, then line up the bolt and retainer on the grille.
6. Attach the grill to the vehicle. Tighten the retaining screws to 89-123 inch lbs. (10-14 Nm).

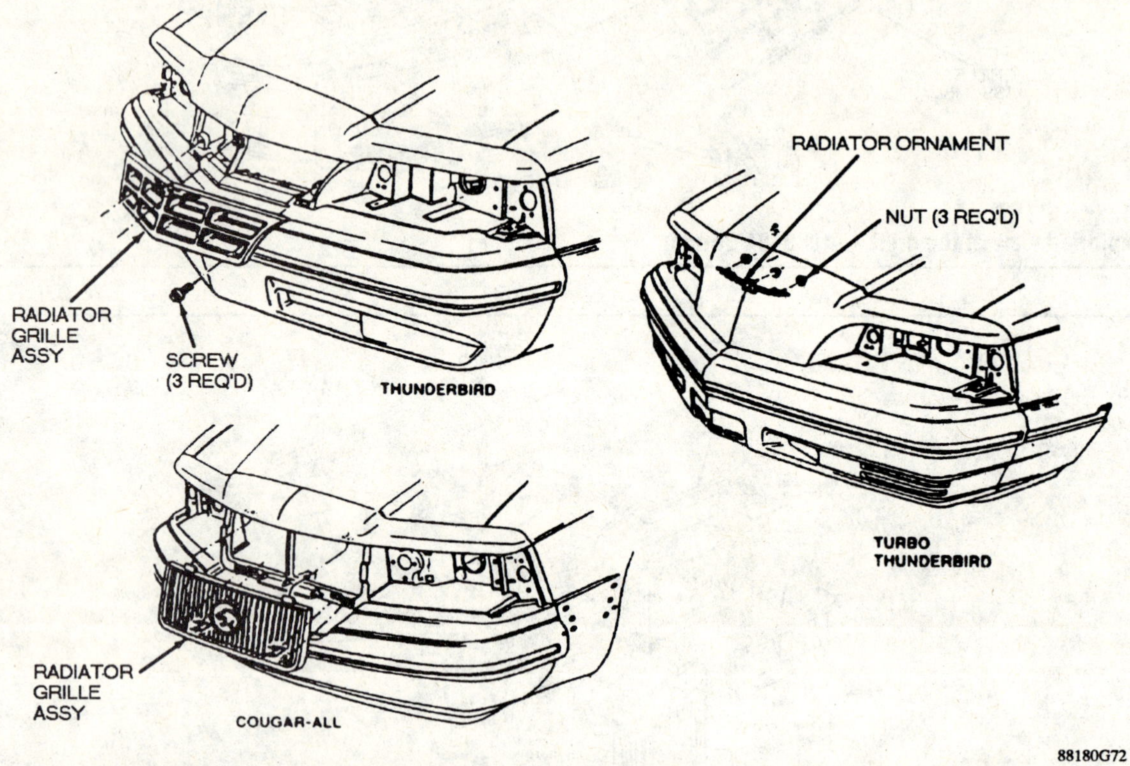

Fig. 27 Exploded view of the grille — 1985-88 models

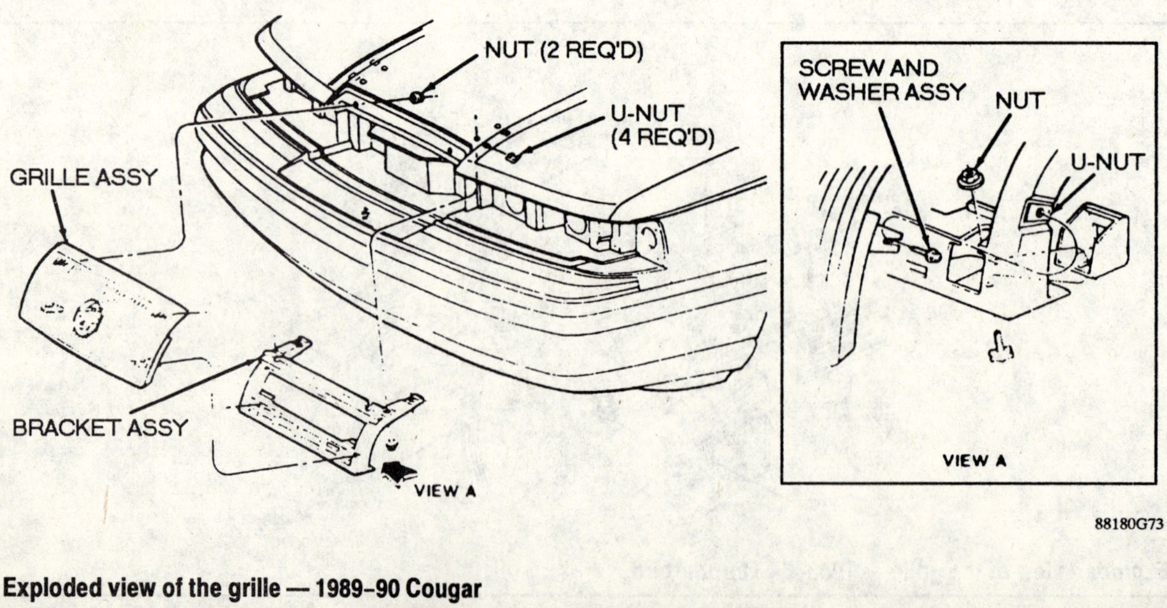

Fig. 28 Exploded view of the grille — 1989-90 Cougar

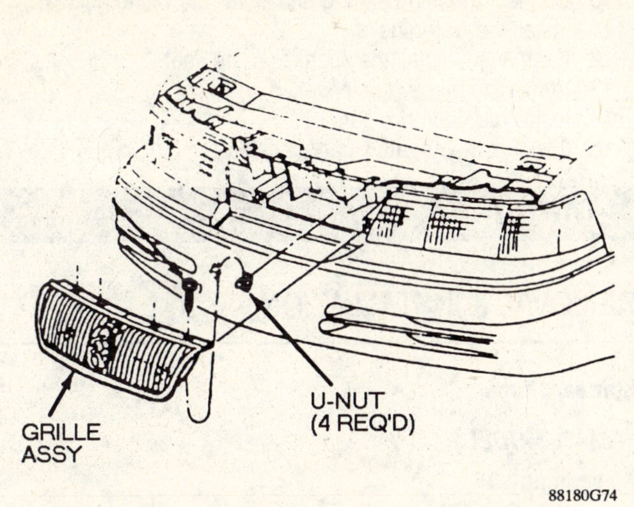

Fig. 29 Exploded view of the grille — 1991-93 Cougar

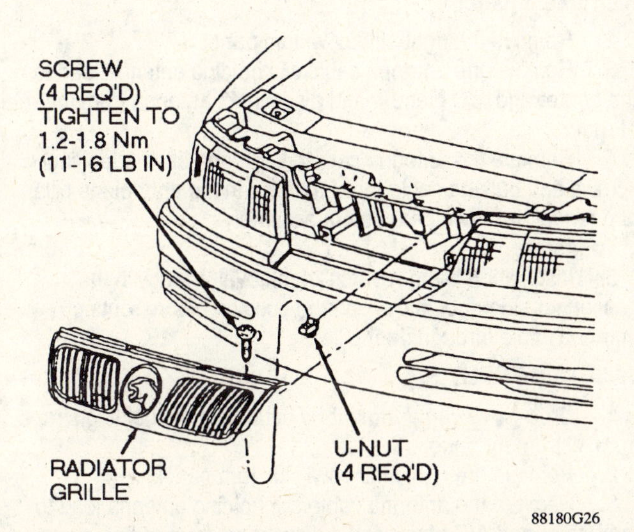

Fig. 30 Exploded view of the grille — 1995-96 Cougar

Outside Mirrors

REMOVAL & INSTALLATION

Standard Manual

COUGAR

See Figure 31

1. Remove the two screws from outside of mirror.
2. Remove the mirror, and gasket. Repeat this for the other side.

To install:

3. Place the gasket on the mirror and attach the mirror to the door.
4. Tighten the mirror screws.

THUNDERBIRD AND XR-7

See Figure 32

1. Remove the inside door trim panel.
2. Remove the two nuts from inside door retaining mirror to the door.
3. Remove the mirror and gasket. Repeat for other side.

To install:

4. Place the gasket on the mirror and attach to the door with the mounting nuts.
5. Install the door interior panel.

Manual Remote

See Figure 33

1. Disconnect the negative battery cable.
2. Remove the inside trim cover retaining screw.
3. Loosen the allen set screw retaining the control to the cover, then remove the cover.
4. Remove the mirror retaining nuts and the mirror.

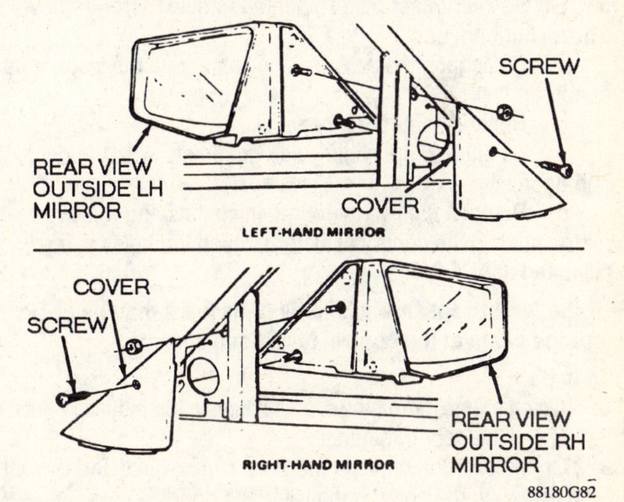

Fig. 31 Manual sail mounted mirrors have a cover on the inside of the vehicle

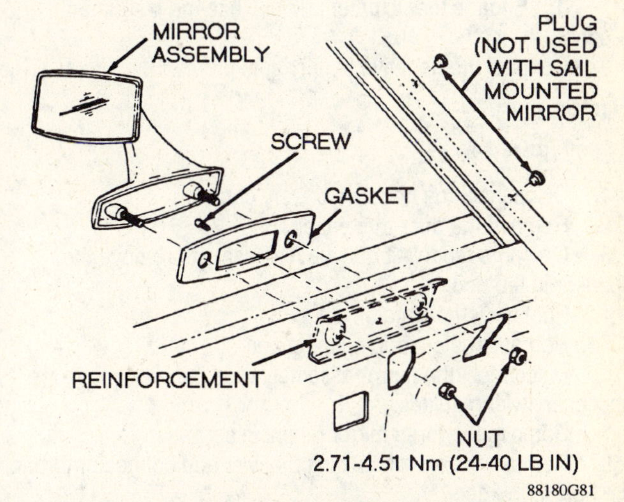

Fig. 32 Standard mirror mounting on the Thunderbird and XR-7

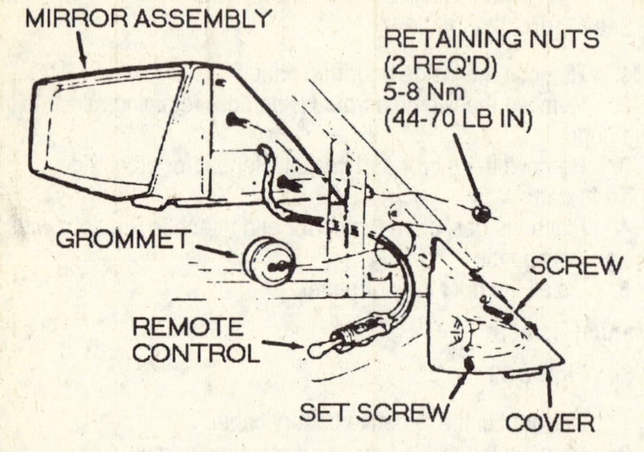

Fig. 33 Manual remote mirrors have a handle to adjust the mirror from inside the car

5. On the instrument panel mounted remote mirror, remove the bezel nut from panel.
 a. Disengage the actuator and cable from the instrument panel.
 b. Remove the door trim panel.
 c. Disengage the cable guide grommets from the door and door pillar.
 d. Remove the two mirror retaining nuts and remove the mirror, guiding the control actuator through the holes in the pillar and door.

➥ If the remote assembly is to be replaced it may be easier to cut the cable at the control to remove control.

To install:

6. Attach the mirror to the bezel and tighten the mounting nuts.
7. Install the door trim panel.
8. On the instrument panel mounted mirror, guide the control actuator through the holes in the pillar and door.
 a. Attach the mirror by the two mounting nuts.
 b. Engage the cable guide grommets to the door and door pillar.
 c. Install the door trim panel.
 d. Engage the actuator and cable to the instrument panel.
9. Connect the negative battery cable.

Electric

➧ See Figure 34

1. Disconnect the negative battery cable.
2. Remove the door trim panel.
3. On some models it may be necessary to remove the speaker in the door.
4. Peel back the watershield.
5. Remove the snap-in mirror cover.
6. Disconnect the mirror assembly wiring, then remove the necessary wiring guides.
7. Remove the three mirror retaining screws.
8. Remove the mirror, guiding the wire and connector through the hole in the door.

To install:

9. Route the connector and wiring through the hole in the door. Install the retaining nuts and tighten to 35–53 inch lbs. (4–6 Nm).
10. Connect the mirror wiring and install the wiring guides.
11. Install the watersheild.
12. If removed, install the speaker in the door.
13. Attach the mirror hole cover.
14. Install the door trim panel.
15. Connect the negative battery cable.

Antenna

REMOVAL & INSTALLATION

Standard Type

1983–88 MODELS

➧ See Figure 35

1. Remove glove compartment.

➥ On Thunderbird and XR-7 models, drop the glove compartment by detaching holding straps from the instrument panel.

2. Remove the right side cowl trim panel.
3. Remove the antenna cable clip holding antenna lead to the heater and A/C plenum and disconnect antenna from the rear of radio.
4. Remove the antenna cap and antenna base attaching screws and pull the cable through holes in the door hinge pillar and fender, remove the antenna assembly.

To install:

5. Installation is the reverse of removal. Start with the passenger side door in the opened position before routing antenna cable through door pillar.

1989–96 MODELS

1. Drop glove compartment by detaching the holding straps from instrument panel.
2. Remove the right side cowl side trim panel.
3. Remove the antenna cable clip holding antenna lead to the heater and A/C plenum and disconnect from radio.

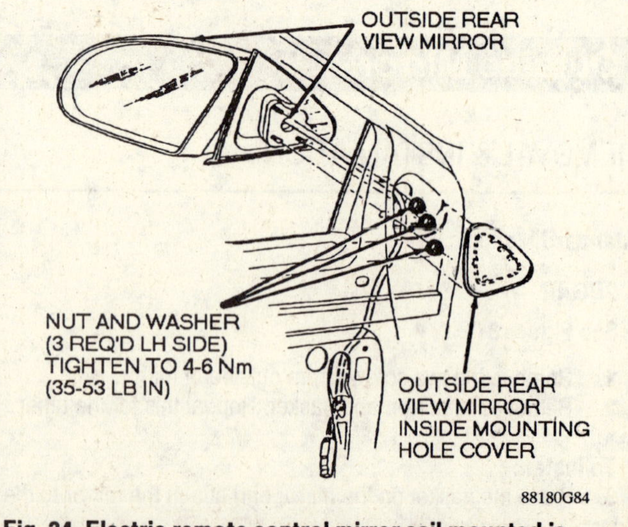

Fig. 34 Electric remote control mirror sail mounted is basically the same design as the manual remote

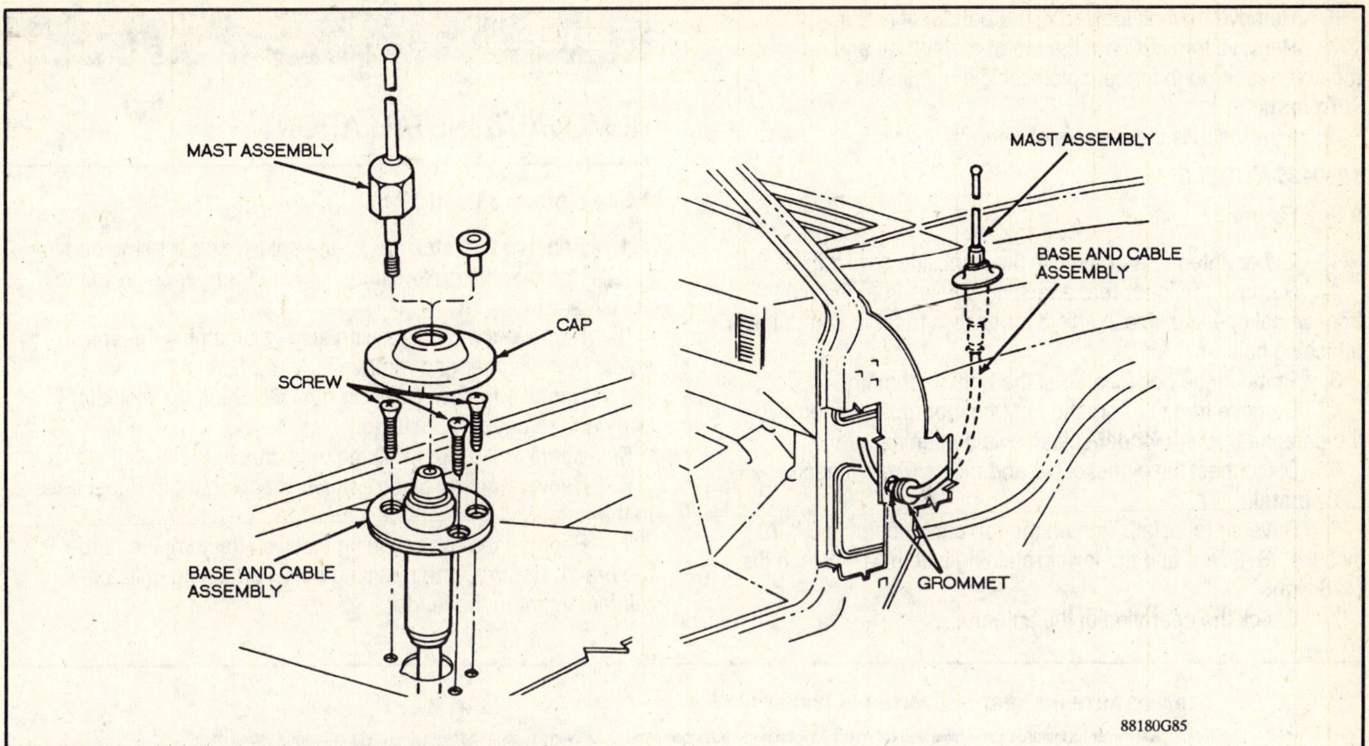

Fig. 35 Standard antenna mounting and wire routing

4. Disconnect the antenna motor wiring at the right side cowl access hole.

5. Remove the inner rear attaching screws of the right front wheel opening splash shield for access to the antenna, if necessary.

6. Remove the antenna cap and the antenna base retaining screws. Pull the cable through the holes in the door hinge pillar and fender and remove the antenna assembly.

To install:

7. With the right front door opened, position the radio antenna base and cable assembly in the fender opening. Place the gasket into position, then install the antenna base to the fender.

8. Pull the antenna lead in cable through the door hinge pillar opening. Seat the grommet by pulling the cable through the hole from the inside of the vehicle.

9. Route the antenna lead in cable behind the heater and evaporator housing. Attach the locating clips.

10. Connect the rear of the radio chassis.

11. Install the cowl side trim panel

12. Install the glove compartment.

Power Type

1983–88 MODELS

➧ See Figure 36

1. Lower antenna and remove the right side cowl trim panel.

2. Drop glove compartment by detaching the holding straps from instrument panel.

3. Remove the antenna cable clip holding antenna lead to the heater and A/C plenum and disconnect from radio.

4. Disconnect the antenna motor wiring at the right side cowl access hole.

5. Remove the inner rear attaching screws from the right front wheel opening splash shield for access to the antenna lower attaching bolt.

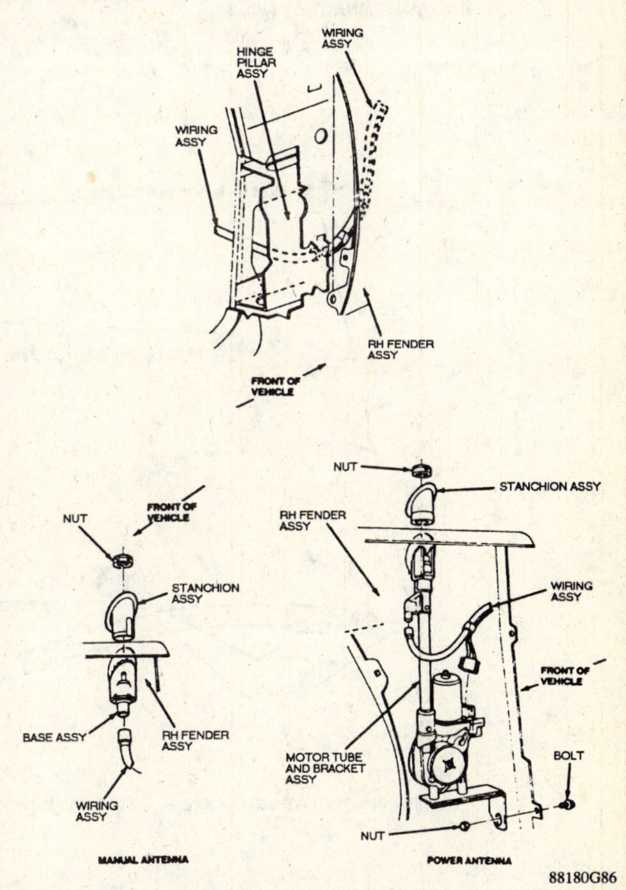

Fig. 36 Power antennas have a motor mounted directly on the unit itself

6. Remove the bolt located at the bottom of motor.
7. Remove trim nut from the top of motor tube and remove the antenna through fender/splash shield opening.

To install:

8. Installation is the reverse of removal.

1989-96 MODELS

➧ See Figure 37

1. Lower antenna and remove the right side cowl trim panel.
2. Remove the inner rear attaching screws from the right front wheel opening splash shield for access to the antenna lower attaching bolt.
3. Remove the bolt located at the bottom of motor.
4. Remove trim nut from the top of motor tube and remove the antenna through fender/splash shield opening.
5. Disconnect the signal cable and motor wire connector.

To install:

6. Reverse to install. Tighten the top antenna nut to 54-70 inch lbs. (6-8 Nm) and the lower retaining bolt to 31-48 inch lbs. (4-6 Nm).
7. Check the operation of the antenna.

Fenders

REMOVAL & INSTALLATION

➧ See Figures 38 and 39

1. Remove the retainers for the splash shield to the body.
2. Remove the screws attaching the bumper cover to the splash shield.
3. Remove the two retaining screws attaching the splash shield to the fender and remove the splash shield.
4. Remove the two push-on nuts attaching the insulator to body and remove the insulator.
5. Remove the two retaining nuts attaching the parking lamp.
6. Remove the retaining screws attaching the bumper cover to the fender.
7. Remove the two retaining screws attaching the fender to the brace. Remove one retaining screw attaching grille opening reinforcement to the fender.

RADIO ANTENNA TEST (ALL ANTENNA TYPES)

With antenna installed on vehicle and cable unplugged from radio, perform the following resistance tests with an ohmmeter. Probes must contact antenna at points specified by arrowheads.

ANTENNA TEST NO. 1

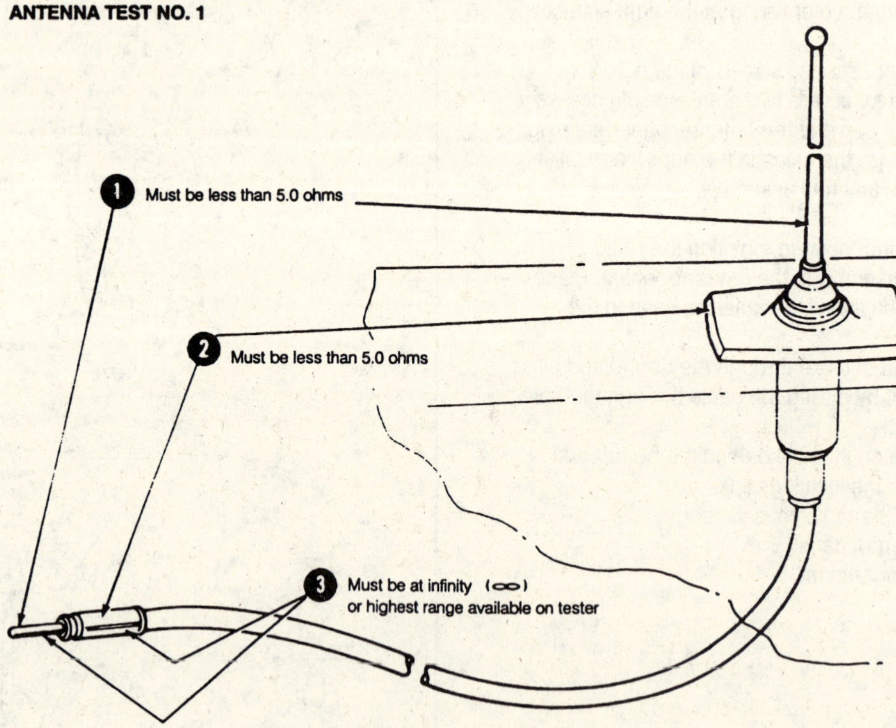

RESULTS

If ohmmeter tests are satisfactory – the antenna is good.

ACTION

If any ohmmeter reading is unsatisfactory:

• Replace the complete antenna and cable assembly.

88180G87

Fig. 37 Testing the antenna for proper operation

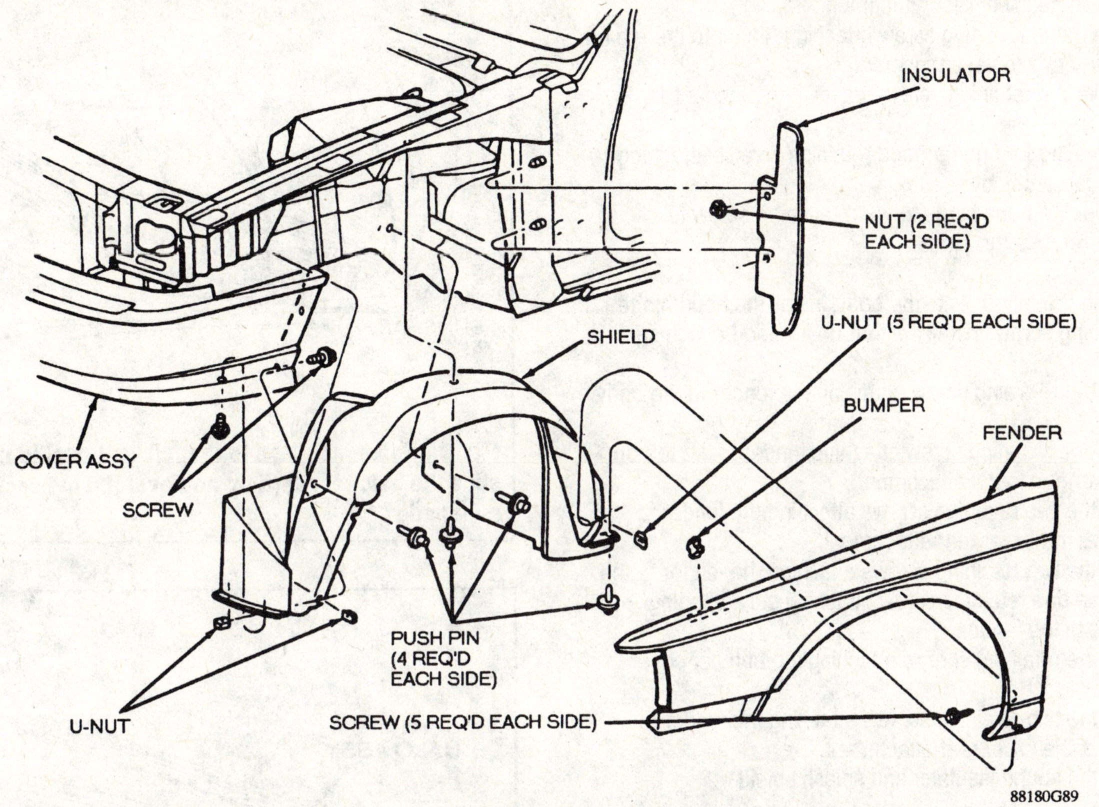

Fig. 38 The splash shield is located under the fender to keep water from rusting the fender

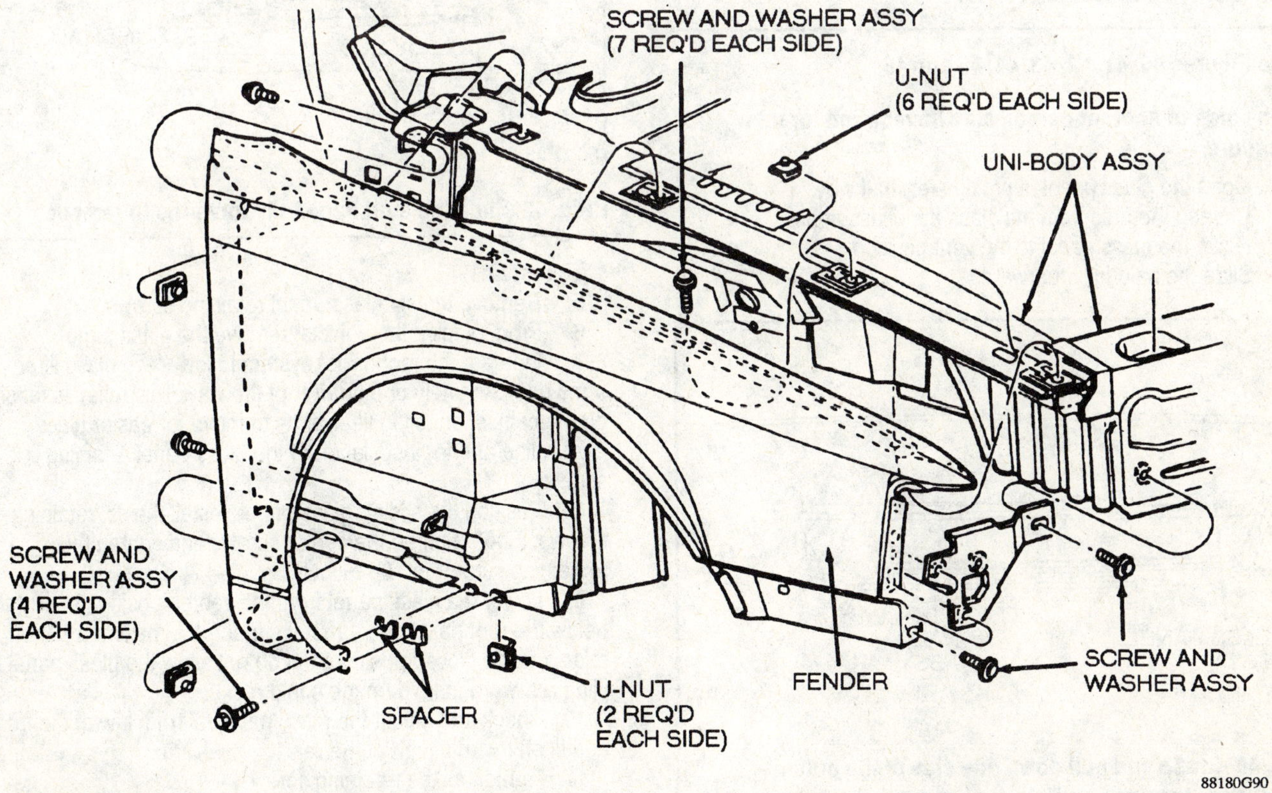

Fig. 39 A fender has many bolts and clips retaining it to the vehicle

8. Remove the two retaining screws attaching the fender to rocker panel at the lower rear attachment.
9. Remove one retaining screw attaching fender to the tab on the body (lower horizontal attachment).
10. Remove the retaining screw attaching the fender to the body tab.
11. Remove the four under hood retaining screws attaching the fender to the uni-body.
12. Remove the hood hinge forward retaining screw to uni-body and remove the fender.

To install:

13. Position the fender onto the body, install the hood hinge forward retaining screw, install the four under hood attaching screws.
14. Install the retaining screw attaching the fender to the body tab.
15. Install one retaining screw attaching fender to the tab on the body (lower horizontal attachment).
16. Install the two retaining screws attaching the fender to rocker panel at the lower rear attachment.
17. Install the two retaining screws attaching the fender to the brace. Remove one retaining screw attaching grille opening reinforcement to the fender.
18. Install the retaining screws attaching the bumper cover to the fender.
19. Install the two retaining screws attaching the fender to rocker panel at the lower rear attachment.
20. Install the sound insulator and splash shield.

Power Sunroof

REMOVAL & INSTALLATION

See Figures 40, 41, 42, 43, 44, 45 and 46

The aide of another person may be required for this procedure.

1. Open the glass panel approximately half way.
2. Unsnap the halo from the glass panel assembly.
3. Raise the glass panel to the vent position.
4. Slide the halo fully rearward.

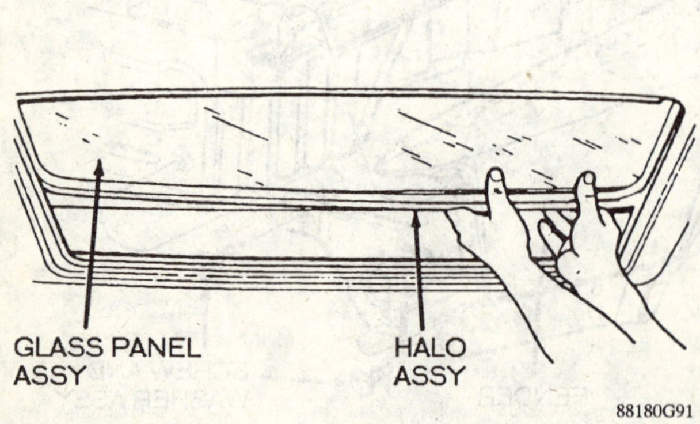

Fig. 40 Grasp and pull down one side of the outside corners of the snap on halo, then remove the halo from the glass panel

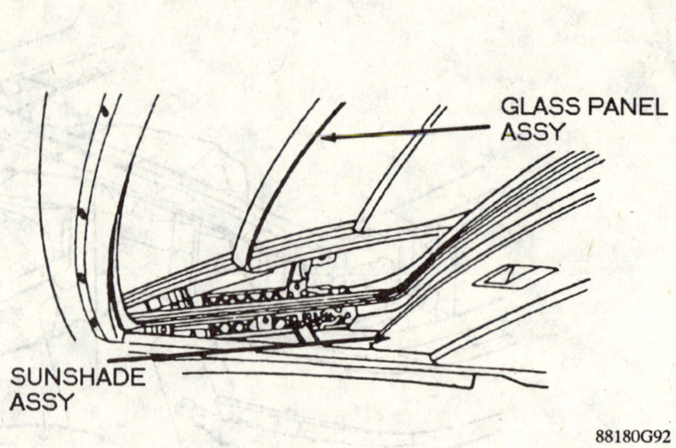

Fig. 41 Raise the glass to the full vent position, then slide the halo rearward up and over the hat section of the sunshade

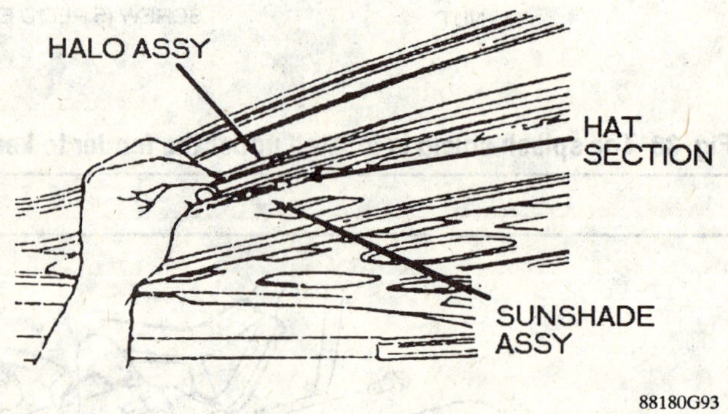

Fig. 42 Slide the sunshade fully forwards to remove

To install:

5. Remove the six glass panel retaining screws.
6. From outside the vehicle, remove the glass panel.
7. Operate the moon roof system to lower the glass lifter arms approximately one quarter of the way. This relieves tension on the cables, enabling lifter arms to move for easier glass positioning and for installation of the glass panel retaining screws.
8. Position the sliding glass panel. Install the six retaining screws. Finger tighten the center screws and tighten the remaining screws to 18–35 inch lbs. (2–4 Nm)
9. Lower the glass panel from the vented position to slightly below the roof panel sheet metal surface ($^1/_2$ maximum), then raise it to the closed position, but do not allow the glass panel to slide rearward, halo damage could result.
10. Check and adjust the glass panel to 1mm low at the front and flush to 1mm high at the rear.
11. Tighten all the retaining screws.
12. Slide the halo forward. Open the moon roof approximately one quarter of the way and install the halo to the glass panel.

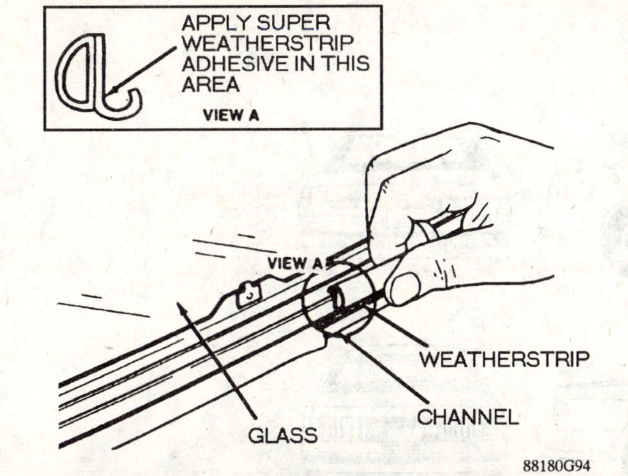

Fig. 43 Locate the butt joint of the weatherstrip on the passenger's side of the glass. Ensure that the bumper insert in the seal is positioned along the front of the glass

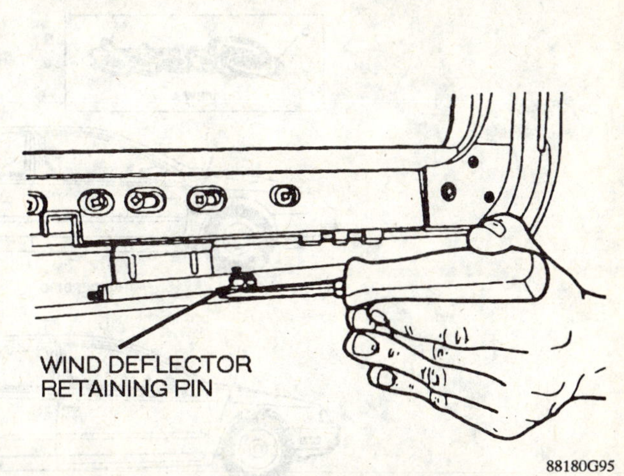

Fig. 44 Fully open the glass to remove the retaining pins on the deflector

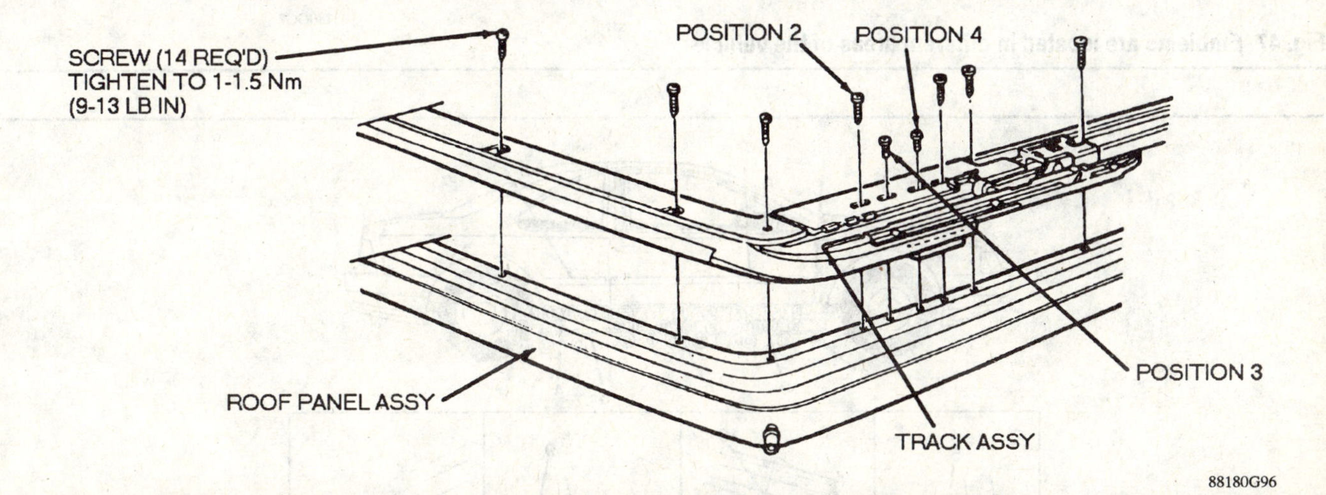

Fig. 45 Remove the module retaining screws except the ones at positions 2, 3 and 4 as shown

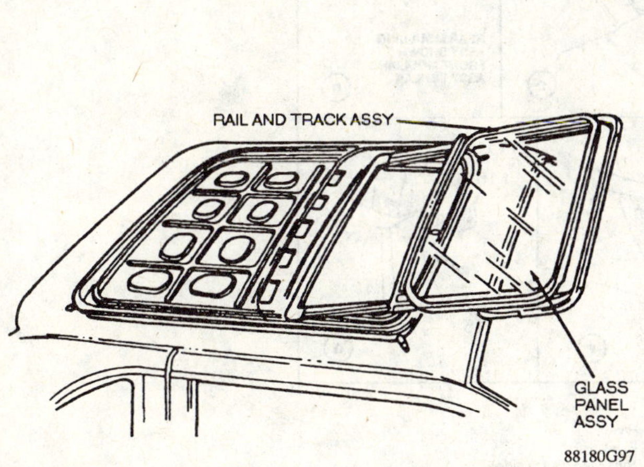

Fig. 46 The sunroof module consists of the complete sliding glass and track assembly

Emblems and Moldings

REMOVAL & INSTALLATION

➧ See Figures 47, 48, 49 and 50

Emblems are located on different areas of your vehicle. They can be mounted with a two sided tape or with clips that hold them in from behind. Either one is a simple job for one to do. The peel-off type of emblem is exactly that, you peel it from the outside of the vehicle, then apply new two sided tape to install it. The other type of emblems have two or more small clips which retaining them to the vehicle. These simply slip off. You may need to purchase new clips to install the emblem once removed. Sometimes the old clips become damaged during removal.

Moldings are usually held in by clips, screws, nuts or pushpins. Be careful not to pry at your moldings, this can cause the moldings to bend and become out of shape. Some moldings may use one or more of the types of retainers such as nuts and pushpins. Look at the item carefully before removing.

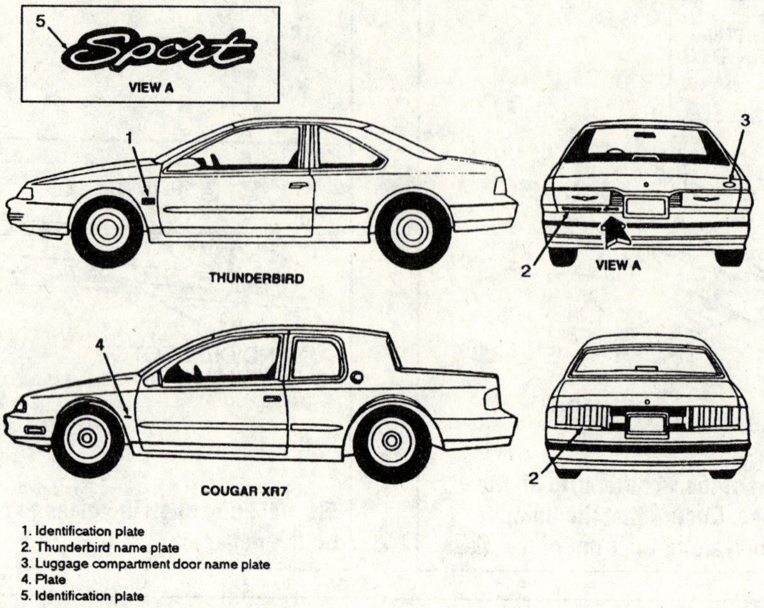

Fig. 47 Emblems are located in different areas of the vehicle

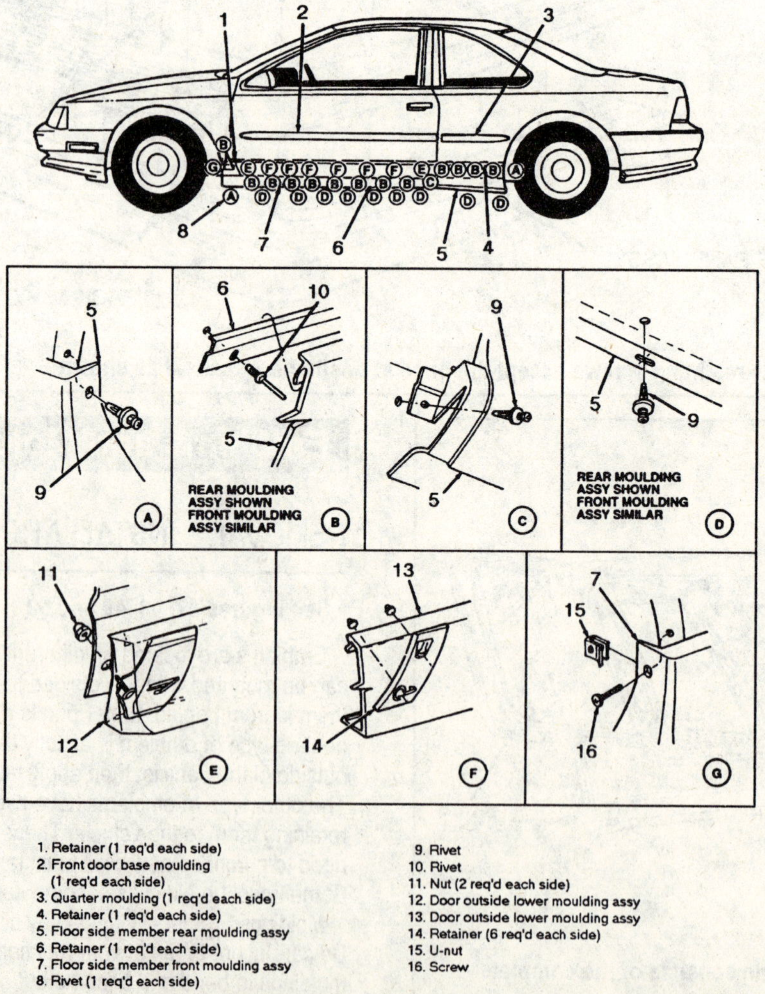

Fig. 48 Body side molding retainer types on the Thunderbirds and Cougars

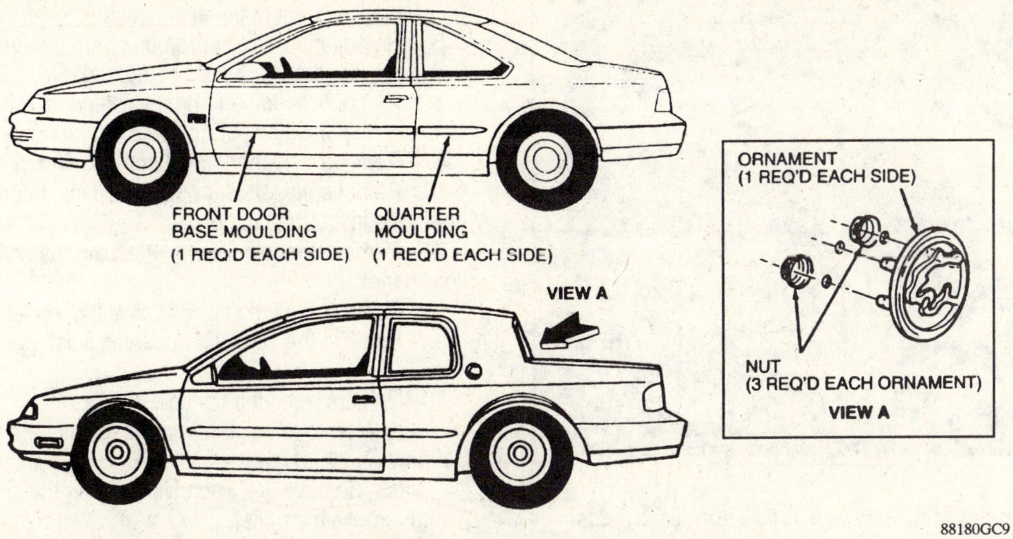

Fig. 49 Body side molding retainer types on the Thunderbirds and Cougars — continued

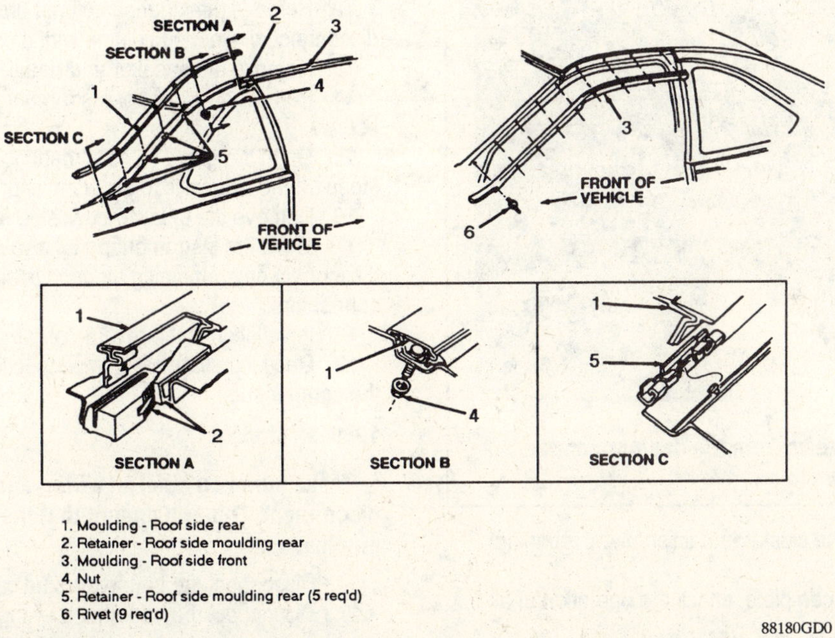

Fig. 50 Roof side molding retainers — Thunderbird shown

INTERIOR

Instrument Panel

REMOVAL & INSTALLATION

➧ See Figures 51 and 52

➝ Make sure you label all wiring and hoses that you disconnect. This will ensure that the installation will be much easier.

1983 Models

1. Remove the cluster and finish panel retaining screws.
2. Remove the instrument panel pad retaining screws in the front and on the ends of the panel.
3. Remove the instrument panel pad retaining screws in the top defroster openings and lift off the pad.

To install:

4. Install the instrument panel pad with the retaining screws, then tighten.

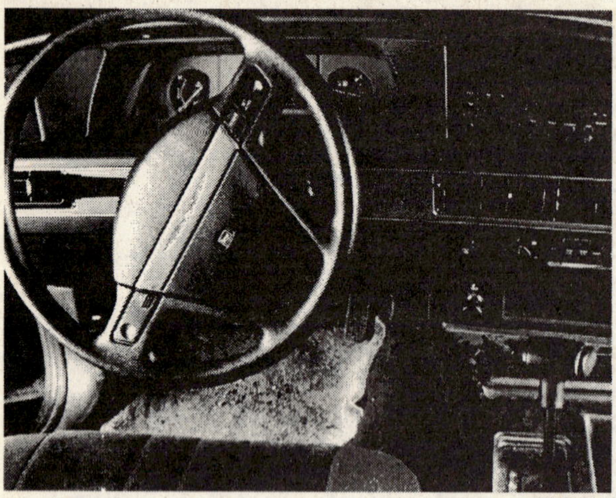

88180P01

Fig. 51 Common overall view of a 1989 Thunderbird dash

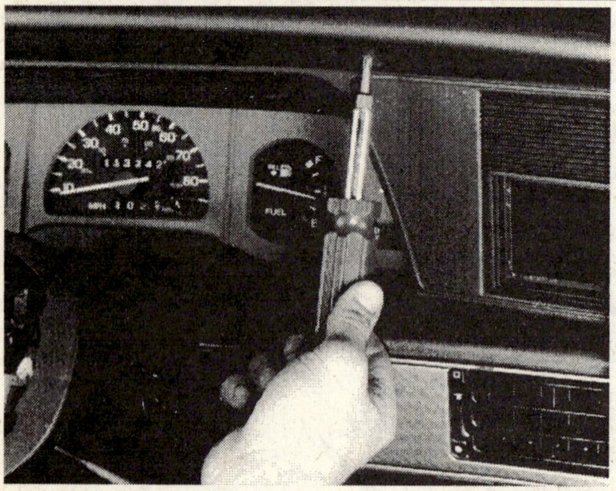

88180P02

Fig. 52 Remove the screws from the dash upper pad. There are several screws to remove

5. Install and tighten the cluster and finish panel retaining screws.
6. Once installation is complete, check the operation of all components in the dash.

1984 Models

1. Remove the 4 front and 2 side instrument panel pad screws.
2. Remove the 4 upper finish panel retaining screws, 2 in each defroster duct opening and lift off the pad and finish panel.
3. Remove the 5 pad-to-panel nuts and separate the pad from the panel.

To install:

4. Attach the instrument pad with the mounting nuts.
5. Install the defroster duct openings on the pad and finish panel.
6. Install and tighten the front and side panel pad screws.
7. Once installation is complete, check the operation of all components in the dash.

1985–88 Models

1. Disconnect the battery ground.
2. In the engine compartment, disconnect all main wiring harness-to-instrument panel connectors.
3. Remove the rubber grommet from the firewall and feed all the wiring into the passenger compartment.
4. Remove the left and right finish panel retaining screws and remove the panels by pulling down on the upper edges.
5. Remove the steering column opening trim cover.
6. Remove the left and right sound insulator assemblies from under the instrument panel.
7. Remove the two screws attaching the hood release to the cowl panel.
8. Remove the left and right cowl trim panels.
9. Remove the 10 cluster opening finish panel retaining screws.
10. On cars without a console:
    a. Remove the ashtray and remove the two outboard screws in the ashtray receptacle.
    b. Remove the 4 screws securing the center finish panel and remove the panel.
11. On cars with a console:
    a. Remove the console front finish panel.
    b. Remove the 4 screws securing the center finish panel and remove the panel.
12. Remove the steering column brace assemblies and disconnect all steering column wiring connectors.
13. Remove the speaker and headlamp dimmer sensor grilles.
14. Remove the 3 upper instrument panel-to-cowl retaining screws.
15. Open the glove compartment door and bend the flexible stops on the sidewalls to allow the liner to swing out.
16. Remove the to lower cowl side retaining screws.
17. Move the instrument panel away from the cowl and disconnect any remaining air conditioning controls and wire connectors.
18. Installation is the reverse of removal.
19. Once installation is complete, check the operation of all of the components.

1989–92 Models

➥ Make sure you label all wiring and hoses that you disconnect. This will ensure that the installation will be much easier.

1. Disconnect the battery ground cable.
2. Disconnect the underhood wiring at the left side of dash panel.
3. Disengage wiring connector from dash panel and push wiring harness into passenger compartment.
4. Remove steering column lower trim cover by removing three screws at bottom, one screw on left side, and pull to disengage five snap-in retainers across top.
5. Remove six screws retaining steering column lower opening reinforcement, and remove from instrument panel.
6. Remove steering column upper and lower shrouds, and disconnect wiring from steering column.
7. Remove shift interlock switch.
8. Disconnect steering column lower universal joint.
9. Support steering column and remove four nuts retaining column to support bracket. Remove column from vehicle.
10. Remove one screw retaining left side of instrument panel to parking brake bracket.

11. Reinstall steering column lower opening reinforcement using only four screws (one in each corner).

➾ Reinforcement prevents instrument panel from twisting when being removed from vehicle.

12. Remove right and left cowl side trim panels.
13. Remove console assembly from vehicle. Refer to Floor Console removal and installation.
14. Remove two nuts retaining center of instrument panel to floor (tunnel).
15. Open glove compartment, squeeze sides of bin and lower to full open position.
16. From underneath the instrument panel and through glove compartment opening, disconnect wiring, heater, A/C vacuum lines and control cables.

➾ Make sure that the vacuum line is disconnected for the boost gauge on supercharged models.

17. Remove two screws at the right and left side retaining the instrument panel to the cowl sides.
18. Remove right and left upper finish panels by pulling up to disengage the snap-in retainers. Three on the right and four on the left sides.
19. Remove four screws retaining the instrument panel to the cowl top. Remove the right and left roof rail trim panel and remove door frame weatherstrip.
20. Carefully pull instrument panel away from the cowl. Disconnect any remaining wiring controls and remove from vehicle.

➾ If instrument panel is being replaced, transfer all components, wiring and hardware to new panel.

21. Installation is reverse of removal
22. Once installation is complete, check the operation of all of the components.

1993-96 Models

♦ See Figures 53, 54 and 55

➾ You will need the help of an aid to perform the following procedure.

➾ Make sure you label all wiring and hoses that you disconnect. This will ensure the installation will be much easier.

1. Disconnect the negative battery cable.
2. Disconnect the positive cable and wait one minute for the air bag diagnostic monitor to deplete the airbag back-up power supply.
3. Loosen the main wiring connector bolt in the engine compartment on the left side of the dash panel, then separate the connectors.
4. Remove the antenna stanchion and disconnect the antenna lead in cable from the lead base of the antenna stanchion.
5. Remove the right and left windshield side garnish moldings.

➾ Do not remove the safety belt retaining bolts.

6. Remove the left and right scuff plates, then remove the door opening weatherstrips from the body flanges.
7. Remove the cowl side trim panels.
8. Remove the screws along the bottom of the steering column cover. Pull on the instrument panel steering column cover to unsnap the clips across the top of the instrument panel steering column cover. Remove the cover.
9. Remove the ignition lock cylinder.
10. Unscrew the steering column shrouds and remove.
11. Install the lock cylinder to prevent the steering wheel from turning.
12. Disconnect the wiring at the multi function switch.
13. Remove the screw and the A/C evaporator register duct from under the column tube.
14. Disconnect the wiring from the bottom of the column tube.
15. Remove the pinch bolt retaining the column tube to the steering column lower yoke, then slightly spread the column lower yoke with a flatbladed tool.
16. While supporting the column tube, remove the four retaining nuts.
17. Remove the interlock cable retaining screws and shift actuator cable fitting.
18. Carefully remove the column tube from the vehicle.
19. Loosen the main wiring connector bolt at the left side of the column opening and separate the connectors.
20. Disconnect the stoplight switch.
21. Disconnect the clutch pedal position switch. (manuals trans.)
22. Pull the carpet back on both sides of the vehicle, then disconnect the window regulator safety relay switch wiring. Next disconnect the PCM harness.
23. Open the glove compartment to the stop, then unsnap the door check from the right side of the glove compartment.
24. Remove the screws from the bottom of the glove box door hinge and box-to-instrument panel. Remove the glove box.
25. Reach through the glove box opening and disconnect the wiring and vacuum hoses from the heater and A/C.
26. Disconnect the main wiring from the speed control amplifier and bracket assembly.
27. Remove the floor console panel.

➾ Protect the instrument panel surface during this procedure.

28. Using a putty knife or similar tool, insert it under the left and right corner of the instrument panel upper finish panel. Pry up on the panel upper finish panel to release the one snap clip.
29. Unsnap the remaining clips by pulling up by hand, then working towards the opposite side of the vehicle.
30. Remove the retaining nuts from the left side of the instrument panel-to-cowl side.
31. Remove the nuts and bolt retaining the panel to the panel console bracket.
32. Remove the retaining nuts on the right side of the instrument panel-to-cowl side.

➾ You will need the help of an aid to proceed.

33. Carefully pull the instrument panel away from the windshield while checking and disconnecting any remaining wiring. Disengage the antenna wire grommet from the sheet metal and pull the antenna lead in cable through the dash panel.
34. If you are replacing the instrument panel, transfer all of the components, wiring and retaining hardware to the new panel as needed.
35. To install, reverse the removal procedure.
36. Once installation is complete, check the operation of all of the components.

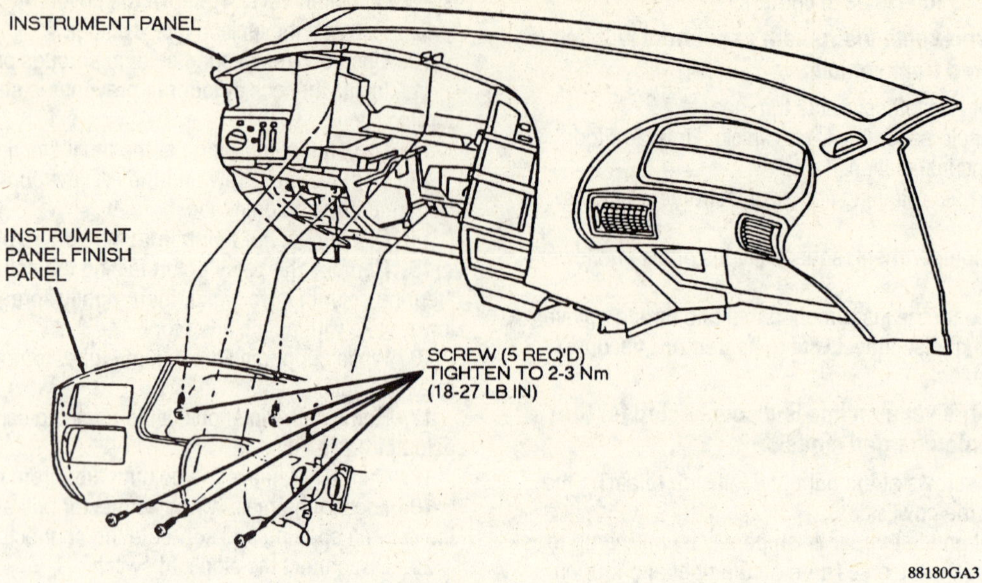

Fig. 53 Exploded view of the instrument panel finish panel mounting screws for the cluster — 1995 shown

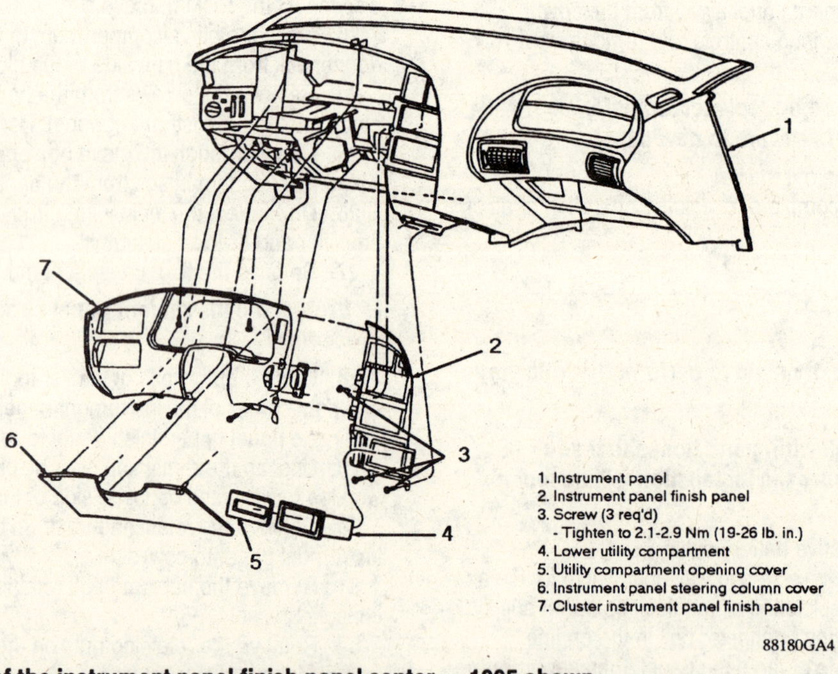

Fig. 54 Exploded view of the instrument panel finish panel center — 1995 shown

Floor Console

REMOVAL & INSTALLATION

1983 Models

1. Open the console glove box door and remove the retaining screws from the bottom of the glove box and the top finish panels.
2. Lift the finish panel and disconnect all wiring at the console.
3. Through the 2 access holes in the front of the console, remove the nuts which attach the console to the instrument panel.
4. Lift up on the back end of the console and slide the console rearward enough to gain access to the wire connectors. Disconnect these wires and ground leads and remove the console.

To install:

5. Attach the wiring to the correct locations.
6. Install the console and tighten the mounting screws.
7. Attach any wring that may still need to be connected.

8. Install the screws to the bottom of the glove box and top finish panels.

1984-88 Models

1. Open the console door and remove the 4 console retaining screws.
2. Remove the ashtray receptacle and the 2 rear finish panel screws.
3. Remove the finish panel and unplug the wiring connectors.
4. Remove the 2 front finish panel screws and lift off the panel.
5. Remove the 2 screws that secure the console to the instrument panel.

On cars with column mounted automatic transmission, remove the two console front support bracket screws and remove the support bracket.

On cars with manual transmission, remove the shifter knob and slide the boot and finish panel up and off of the shifter.

6. Remove the 4 center panel attaching screws: 2 at the top of the panel and 2 under the ashtray receptacle door. Lift off the finish panel and disconnect all wiring.
7. On cars with a manual transmission, remove the support bracket at the ashtray receptacle (4 screws).
8. Pull the two front edges of the console away from the instrument panel to disengage the Velcro® fasteners, and, at the same time, slide the console rearward and upwards to remove it.

To install:

9. Position and attach the console.
10. On cars with a manual transmission, install the support bracket at the ashtray receptacle.
11. On cars with an automatic transmission, attach the console front support bracket.
12. Tighten the console retaining screws to the instrument panel.
13. Attach the front finish panel.
14. Install the ashtray receptacle.
15. Install the screws in the glove box.

1989-92 Models

1. Open console door and remove container and mat to gain access to the two console-to-floorpan retaining screws. Then remove screws.
2. Remove the gear shift knob on manual transmissions only.
3. Remove the two rear finish panel retaining screws. Tilt finish panel forward, disconnect and label the electrical connectors, then remove the panel.
4. Remove the two front console-to-instrument panel retaining screws and remove the console.

To install:

5. Place the console into position, then tighten the two front console-to-panel retaining screws.
6. Attach the electrical connections. Install and tighten the two rear finish panel retaining screws.
7. On cars with a manual transmission, install the gear shift knob.
8. Tighten the remaining screws for the console-to-floor pan, then install the mat and container.

1993-96 Models

➧ **See Figures 56 and 57**

1. Open the glove compartment door to access the screws for the console finish panel.
2. Remove the screws and lift the rear of the console finish panel to unsnap the snap-in retainers.
3. Reach under the finish panel and disconnect the wiring leading to the fog lamp switch, air spring suspension switch and lighter socket and retainer.
4. Lift the rear of the console panel, then slide it rearwards to release the front locating tabs. Remove the console finish panel.
5. Remove the center screws from the console glove compartment, then lift the compartment from the console panel. Disconnect the luggage compartment remote control lock switch and fuel filler door lock switch.

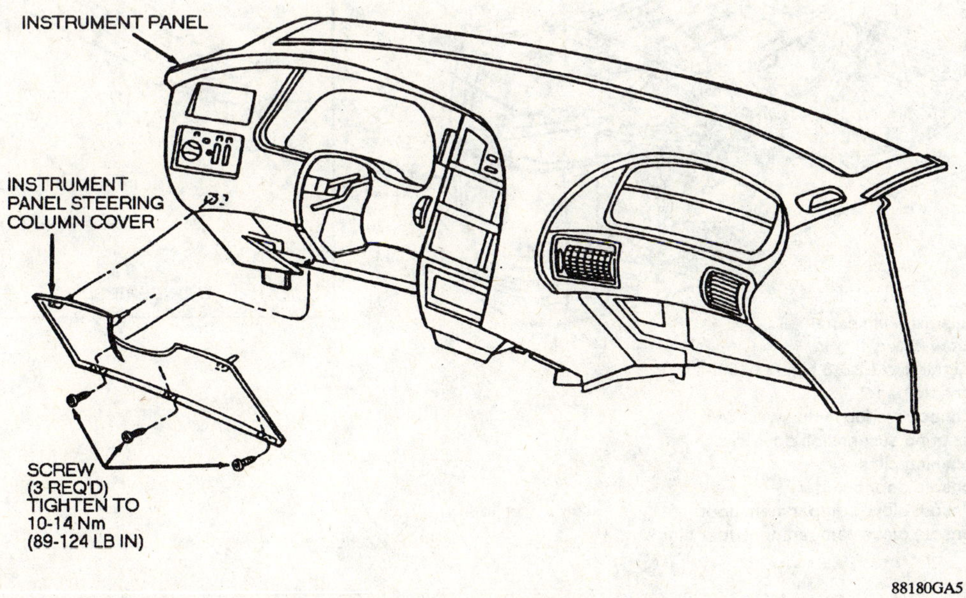

Fig. 55 Instrument panel steering column cover mounting — 1995 shown

6. Remove the screws from the bottom of the console glove compartment to the front floor pan.
7. Remove the two caps and screws, then the floor console panel.
8. Remove the retaining screws from the front of the floor console panel to the instrument panel.
9. Disconnect the main jumper wire and the main wiring. Lift the console from the vehicle.
10. Reverse the procedure to install, tighten all of the components.
11. Check the operation of the switches involved from disconnecting the wiring.

Overhead Console

REMOVAL & INSTALLATION

1986-87 Thunderbird and Cougar

1. Hold one of the map lamps in the switch depressed position and, using a small screwdriver, pop out the lens at the forward edge.
2. Remove the 2 console retaining screws now exposed. Lower the front edge of the console and slide it rearward to disengage the 2 rear clips.
3. Disconnect all wiring and remove the console.

To install:

4. Attach the wiring to the console assembly, then place the console into position.
5. Tighten the mounting screws for the console.
6. Install the lens.
7. Check the operation of the overhead lamp.

Door Panels

REMOVAL & INSTALLATION

1983 Models

➧ **See Figures 58, 59 and 60**

1. Remove the window handle retaining screw and remove the handle.
2. On the Cougar, remove the door latch handle cup retaining screw and remove the cup. The screws are covered by removable appliques.
3. On the Thunderbird and XR-7, remove the inside door handle attaching screw and remove the handle and shield.
4. On the Thunderbird and XR-7, remove the screws from the armrest door pull cup area.
5. On the Cougar, remove the retaining screws from the armrest.
6. On the Thunderbird and XR-7 with power door locks and/or power windows, remove the retaining screws and power switch cover assembly. Remove the screws holding the switch housing.
7. Remove the mirror remote control bezel nut.
8. On the Thunderbird and XR-7, remove the door trim panel retaining screws.
9. With a flat, wood spatula, pry the trim retaining clips from the door panel. These clips can be easily torn from the trim panel, so be very careful to pry as closely as possible to the clips.
10. Pull the panel out slightly and disconnect all wiring.
11. If a new panel is being installed, transfer all necessary parts.
12. Installation is the reverse of removal.

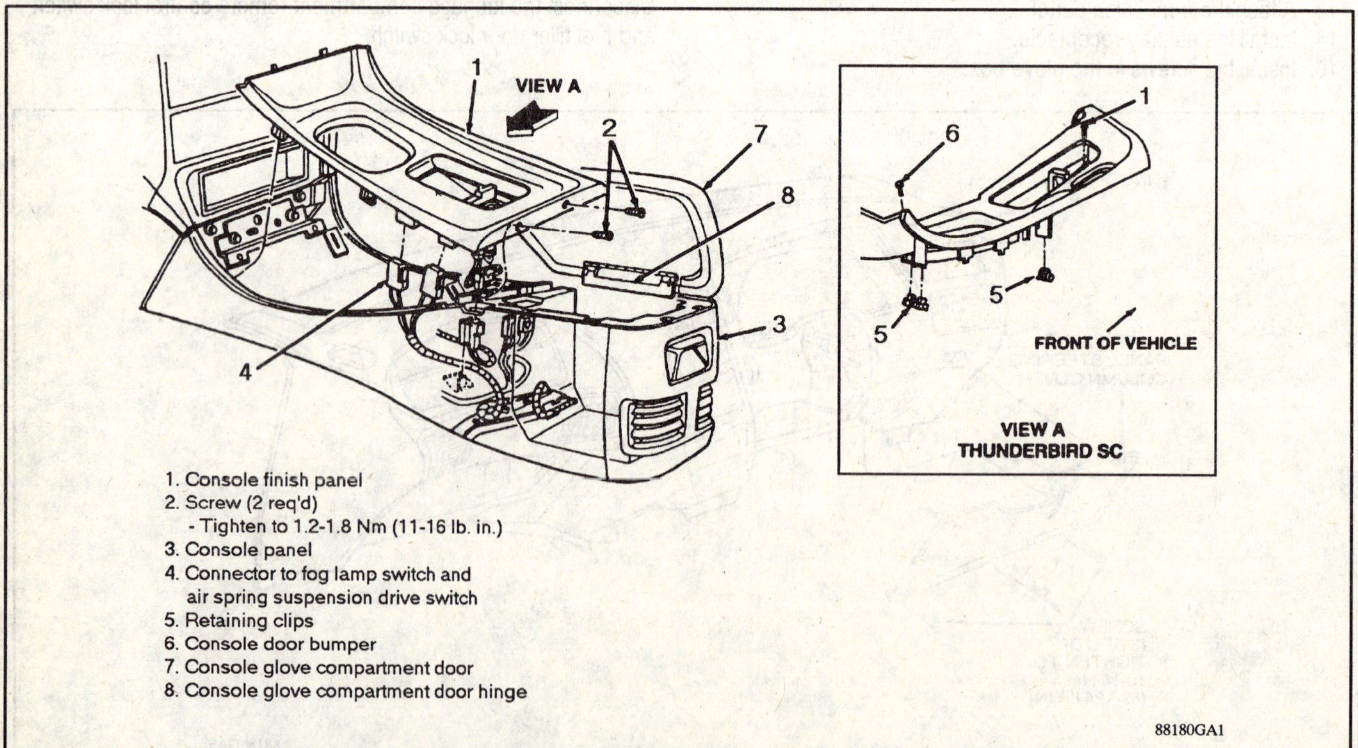

Fig. 56 Exploded view of the floor console assembly — 1995 shown

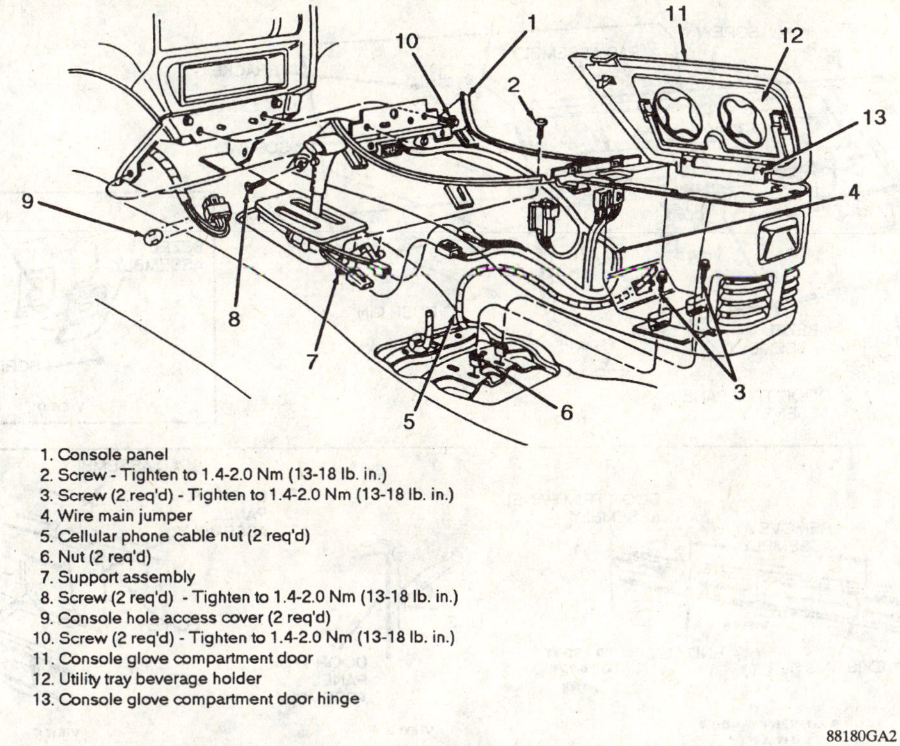

Fig. 57 Exploded view of the floor console assembly — 1995 shown continued

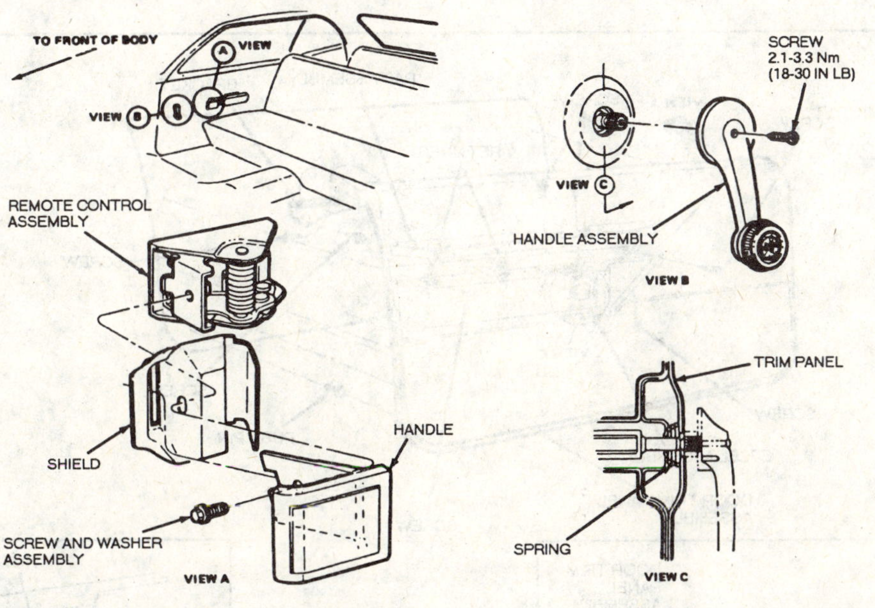

Fig. 58 Door handle removal on the 1983 Thunderbird and XR-7 models

1984–88 Models

➧ See Figure 61, 62, 63 and 64

1. Remove the window handle retaining screw and remove the handle.
2. Remove the retaining screws from the armrest.
3. Remove the mirror remote control bezel nut.
4. Remove the door trim panel retaining screws.
5. With a flat, wood spatula, pry the trim retaining clips from the door panel. These clips can be easily torn from the trim panel, so be very careful to pry as closely as possible to the clips.
6. Pull the panel out slightly and disconnect all wiring.
7. If a new panel is being installed, transfer all necessary parts.
8. Installation is the reverse of removal.

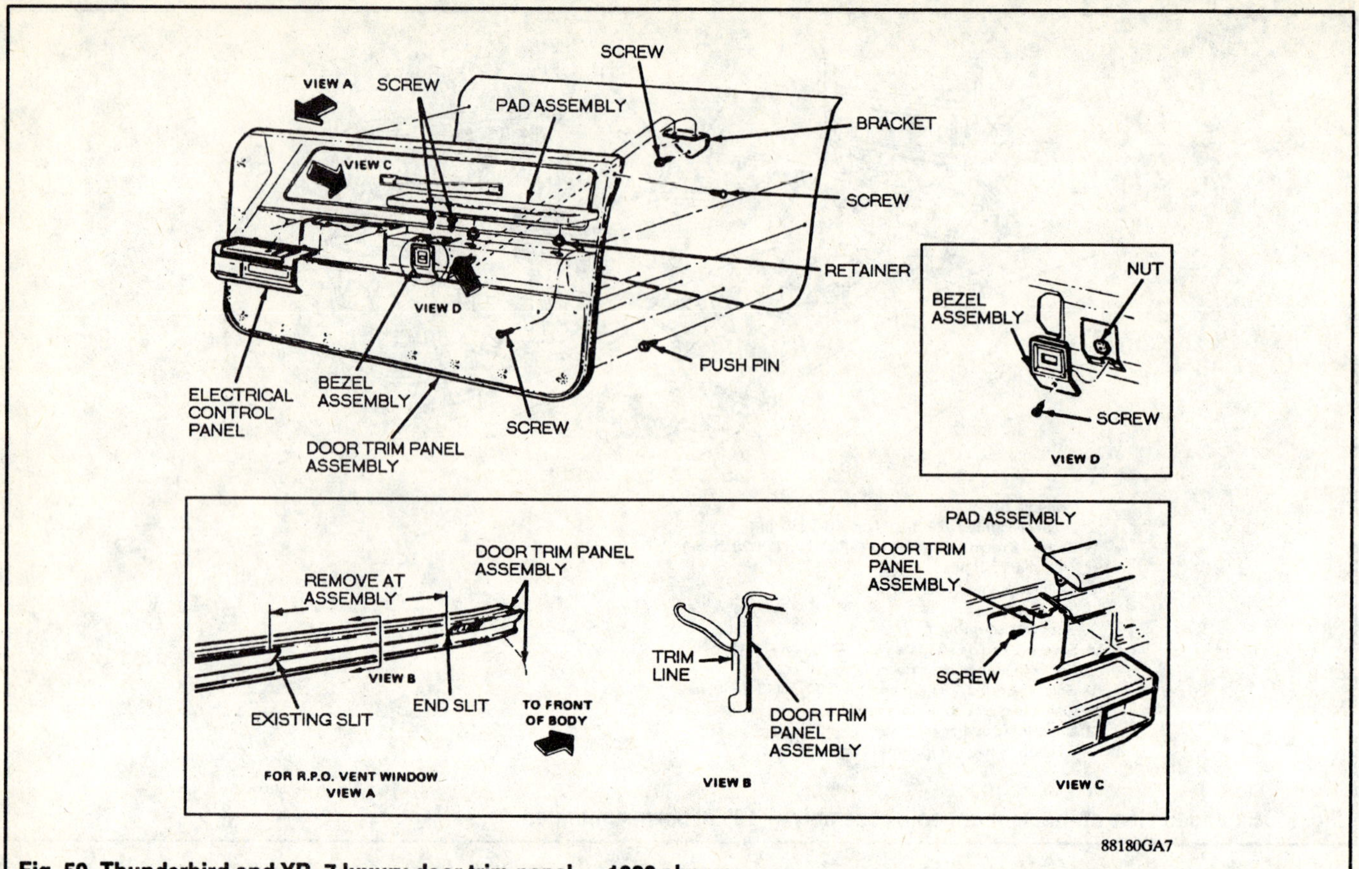

Fig. 59 Thunderbird and XR-7 luxury door trim panel — 1983 shown

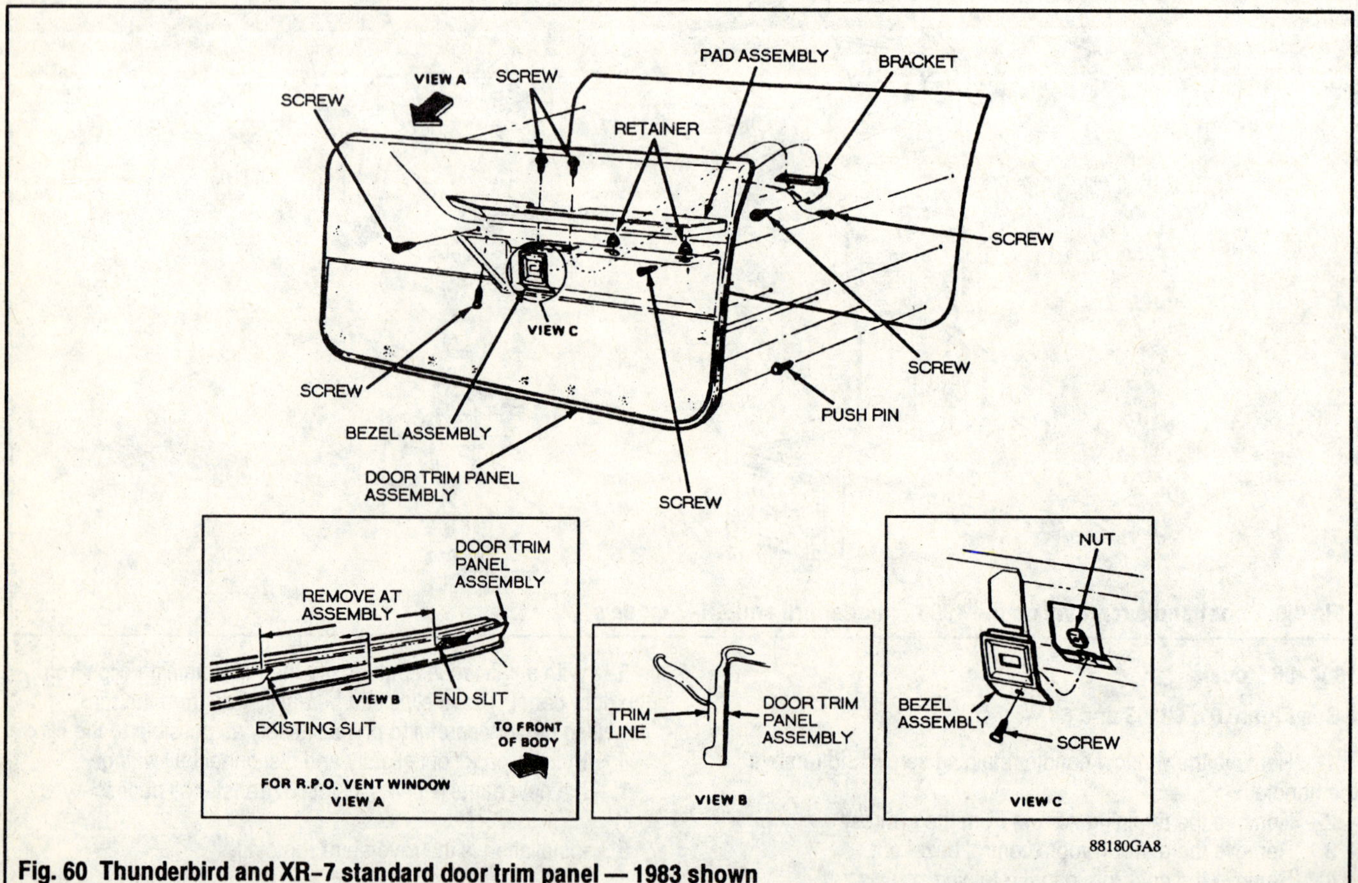

Fig. 60 Thunderbird and XR-7 standard door trim panel — 1983 shown

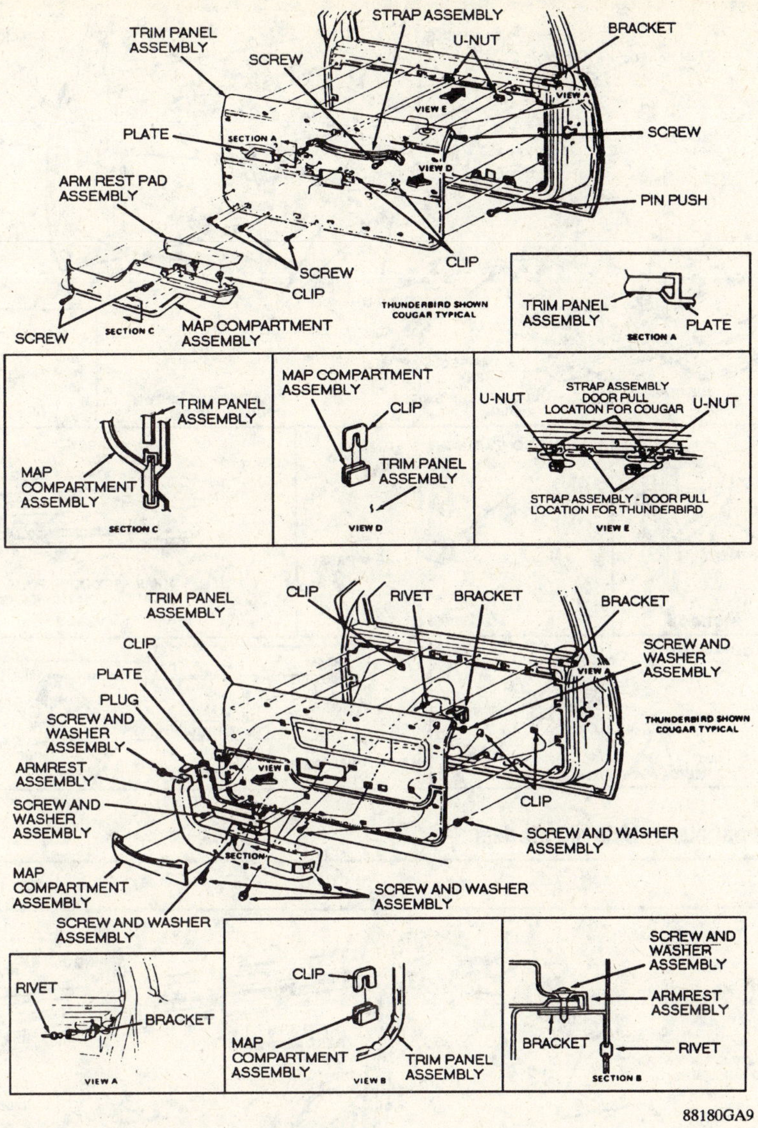

Fig. 61 Thunderbird and Cougar door trim panels — 1984–85

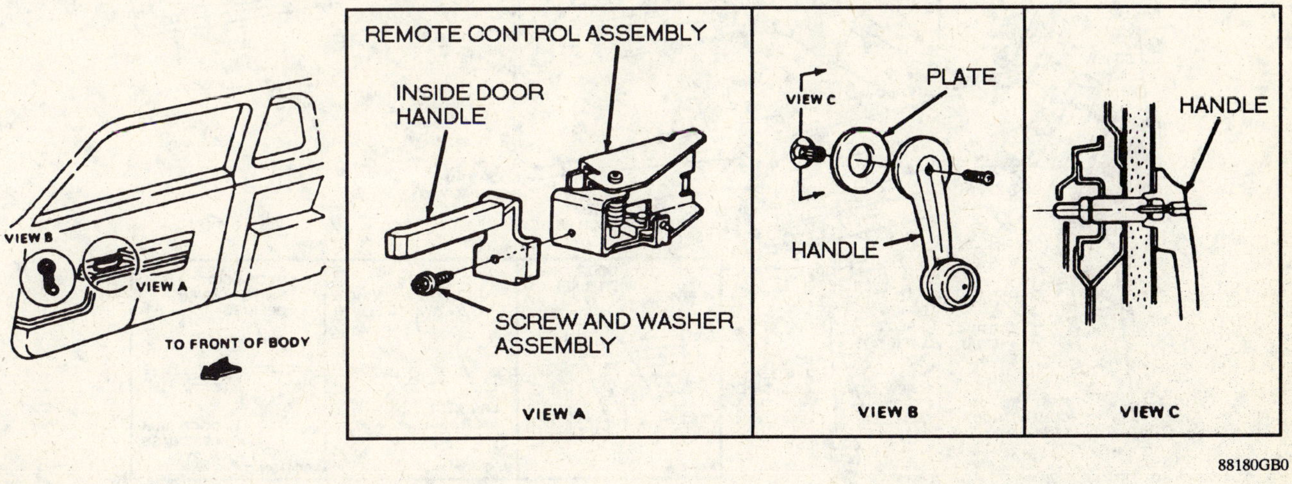

Fig. 62 Door handle removal — 1984–88 models

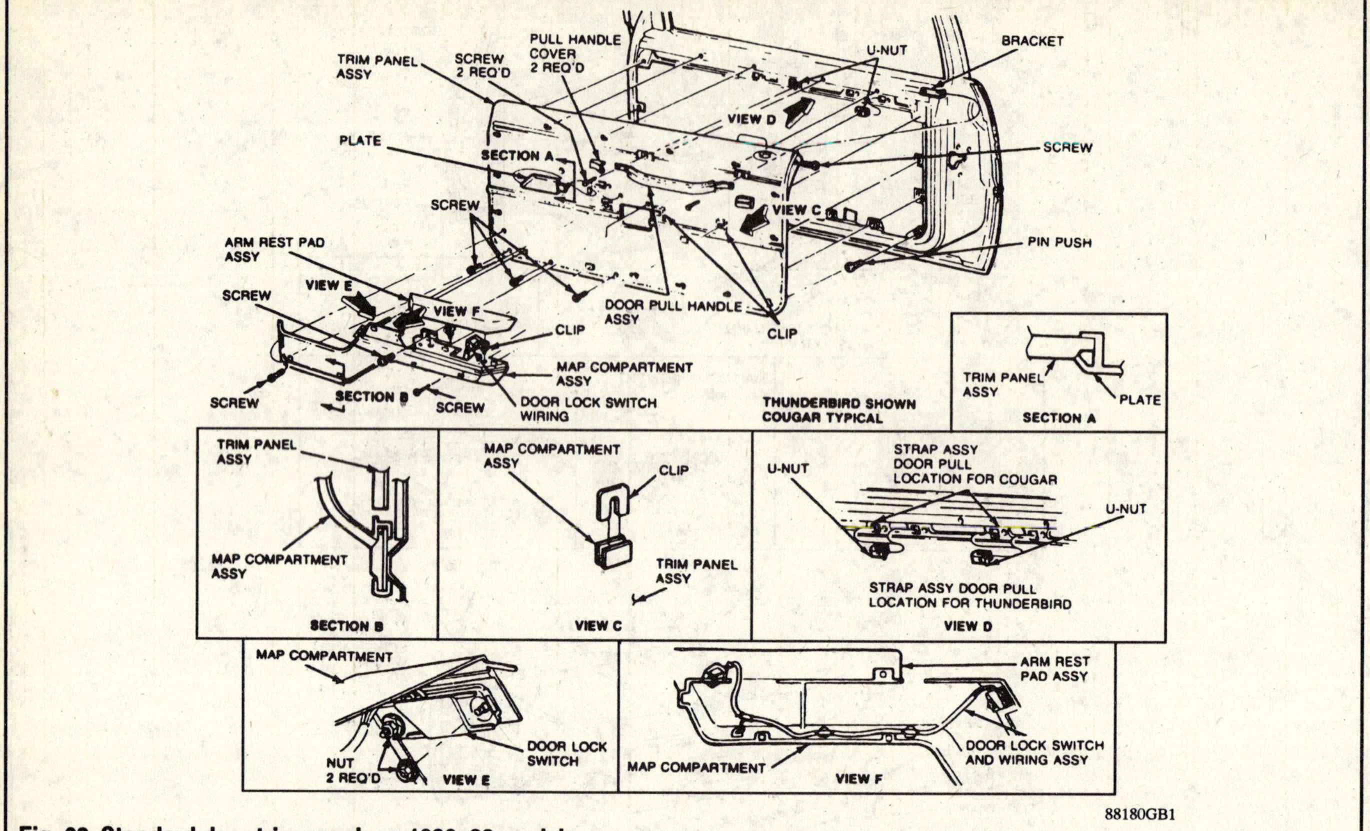

Fig. 63 Standard door trim panels — 1986–88 models

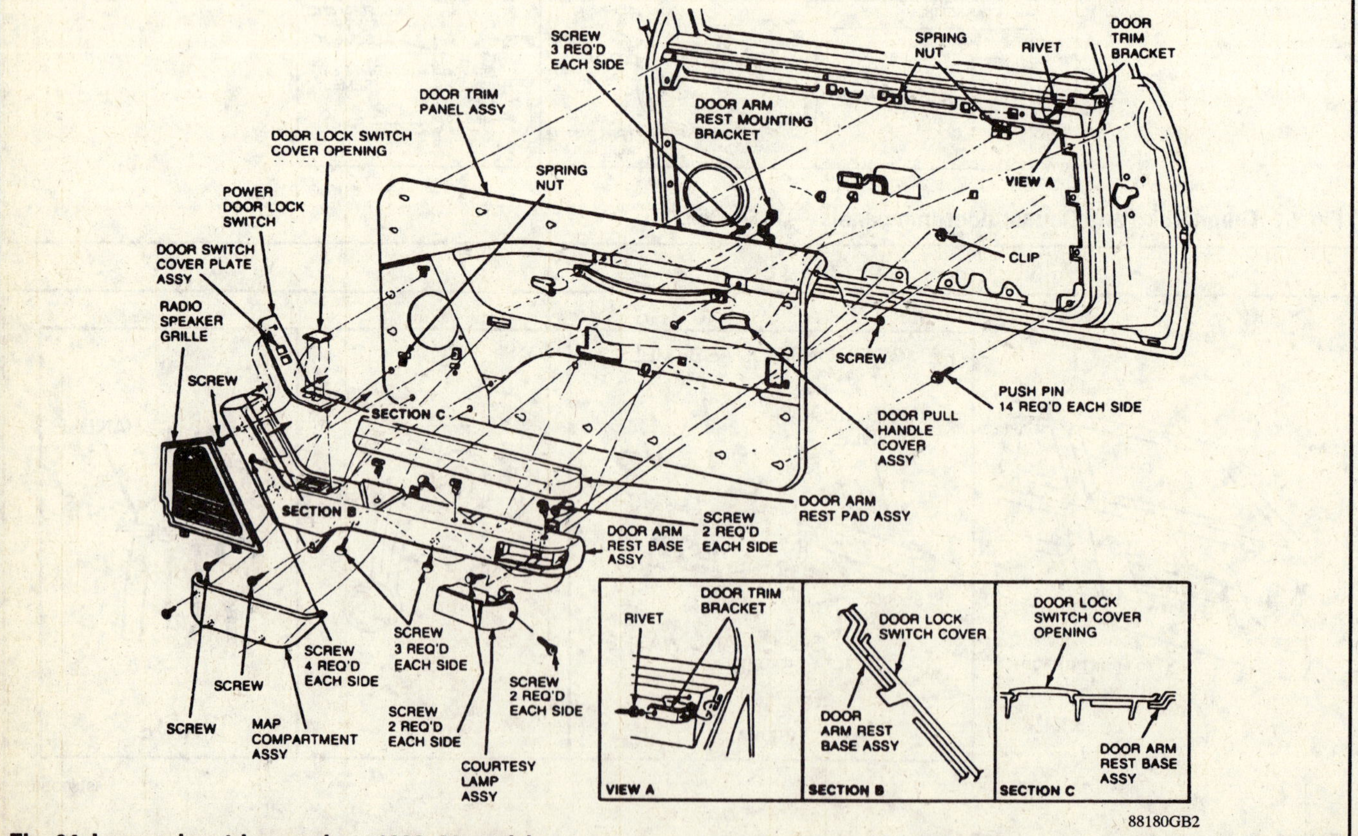

Fig. 64 Luxury door trim panels — 1986–88 models

1989-92 Models

➧ See Figure 65

1. Remove window regulator switch housing.
2. Remove the door inside handle cup (snaps out).
3. Remove the self tapping screw retaining door trim panel upper front extension assembly, and remove assembly.
4. Remove the two self tapping screws retaining door trim panel to the door inner panel.
5. Lift the door trim panel upward and snap out trim panel.
6. Disconnect the wire harness for courtesy lamp.

To install:

7. Attach the wiring harness to the courtesy lamp.
8. Place the door panel into position, then tighten the panel to the inner panel.
9. Attach the upper front extension assembly.
10. Snap the door handle cup on the door assembly.
11. Install the window regulator switch housing.

1993-96 Models

➧ See Figure 66

****WARNING**

Do not pry the door trim panel. Prying the trim panel may break the hook retainers.

1. Disconnect the negative battery cable.
2. Carefully pull the door trim finish panel away from the door trim panel.
3. Disconnect the wiring from the lock switches, outer rear view mirror controls, and regulator controls.
4. If equipped, remove the door trim panel finish panel.
5. Remove the trim panel retaining screw through the door trim panel finish panel opening.
6. Remove the interior lamp lens cover.
7. Remove the screw through the interior lamp opening.
8. Slide the door trim panel upwards to disengage the hooks.
9. Rotate the top of the trim panel away from the door, then lift the bottom hooks from the front door.
10. Disconnect the window regulator jumper wire.
11. Remove the trim panel.

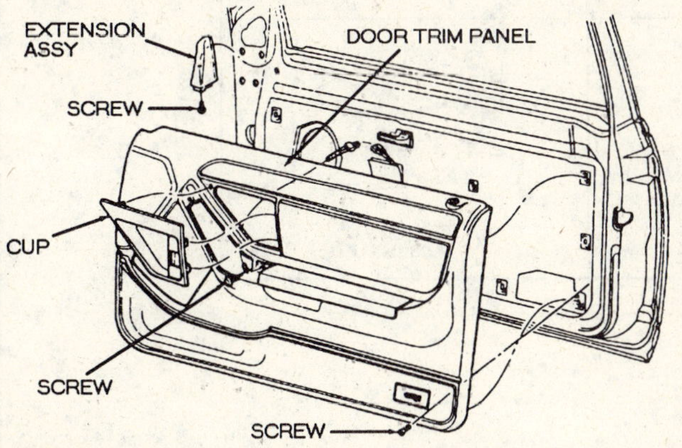

Fig. 65 Door trim panel — 1989-92 models

12. Reverse the procedure to install the components.
13. Connect the wiring, then check the operation of all the components involved.

Interior Trim Panels

REMOVAL & INSTALLATION

1983-92 Models

1. Remove the rear seat, rear seat retractor cover trim and the rear seat retractor.
2. Remove the coat hook and drill point screw at aft end of the panel upper rear.
3. Remove the drill point screw at the passive restraint dog ear.
4. Snap out the quarter trim finish panel cover assembly.
5. Remove the four screws retaining the rear radio speaker opening cover and speaker. Remove the cover and speaker.
6. Remove the push pin at the quarter trim upper panel to quarter trim lower panel.
7. Remove the hidden fasteners from the upper quarter trim panel. Disconnect the lamp, if so equipped.
8. Carefully lift up the panel, so dog ear at the passive restraint track is not damaged and remove the trim panel.

To install:

9. Carefully position the trim panel in vehicle, so the dog ear at the passive restraint track is not damaged.
10. Install the hidden fasteners from the upper quarter trim panel. Connect the lamp, if so equipped.
11. Install the push pin at the quarter trim upper panel to quarter trim lower panel.
12. Install the cover and speaker. Install the four screws retaining the rear radio speaker opening cover and speaker.
13. Snap-in the quarter trim finish panel cover assembly.
14. Install the drill point screw at the passive restraint dog ear.
15. Install the coat hook and drill point screw at aft end of the panel upper rear.
16. Install the rear seat, rear seat retractor cover trim and the rear seat retractor.

1993-96 Models

➧ See Figures 67 and 68

1. Remove the rear seat.
2. Remove the coat hook cover.
3. Carefully pry the quarter trim panel insert from the quarter trim panel.
4. Remove the door scuff plate.
5. Pull the door opening weatherstrip loose at the quarter trim panel area.
6. Remove the rear safety belt retractor and tongue retaining bolt at the quarter panel.
7. Remove the speaker from the panel.
8. Pull the trim panel outwards and release the retaining clips. Feed the safety belt retractor and tongue through the opening in the quarter trim panel.
9. Disconnect the window regulator jumper wire from the interior lamp.
10. Reverse the procedure to install.
11. Check the operation of the speaker and lamp after installation.

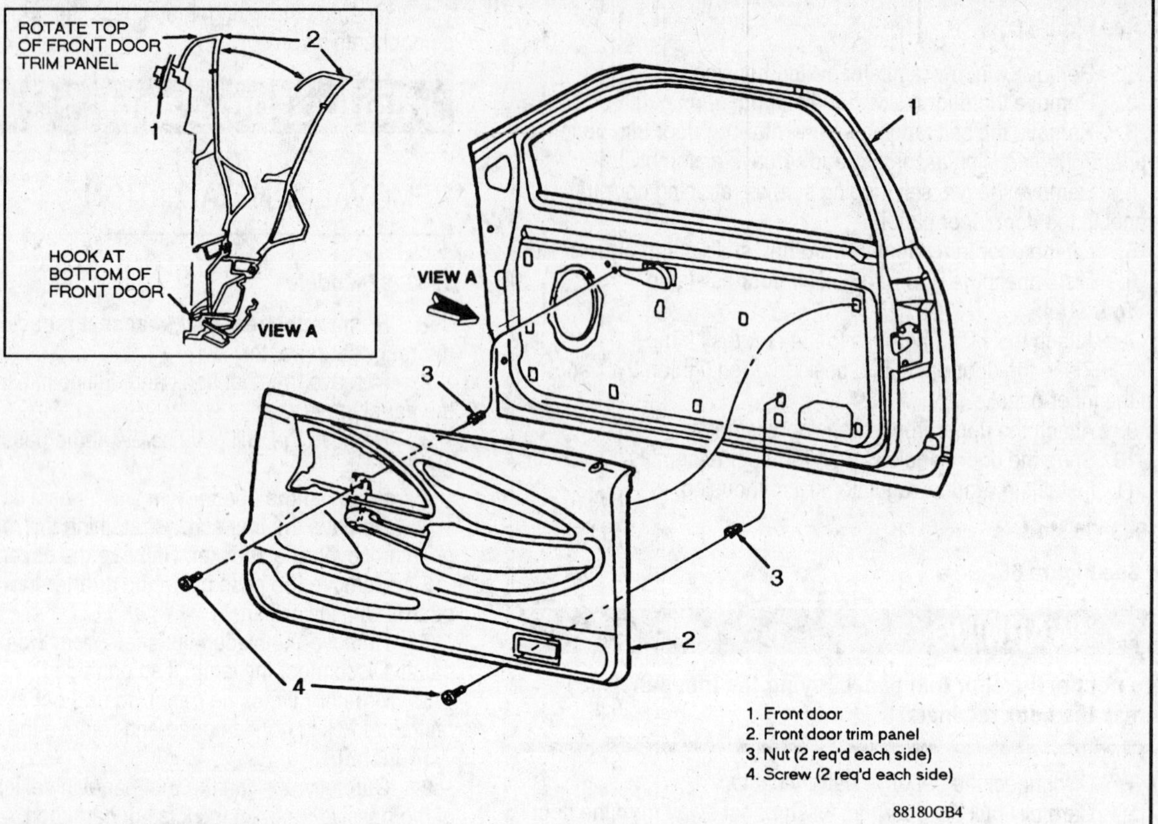

Fig. 66 Door trim panel — 1993–96 models

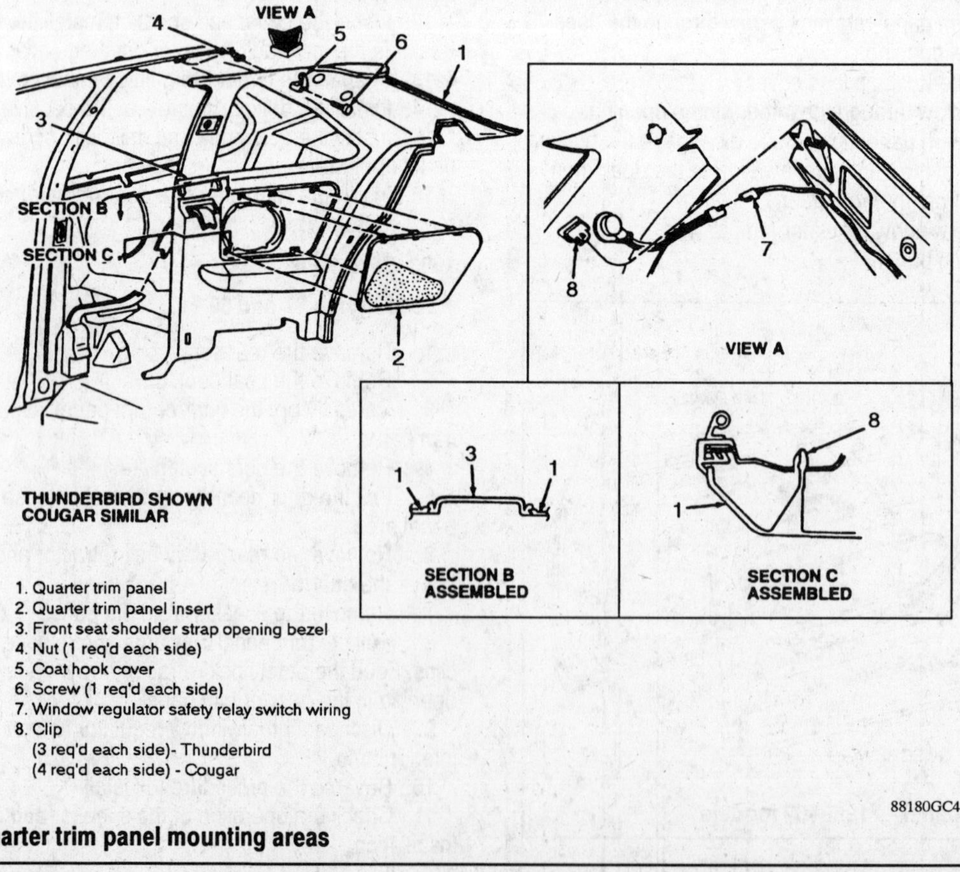

Fig. 67 Upper quarter trim panel mounting areas

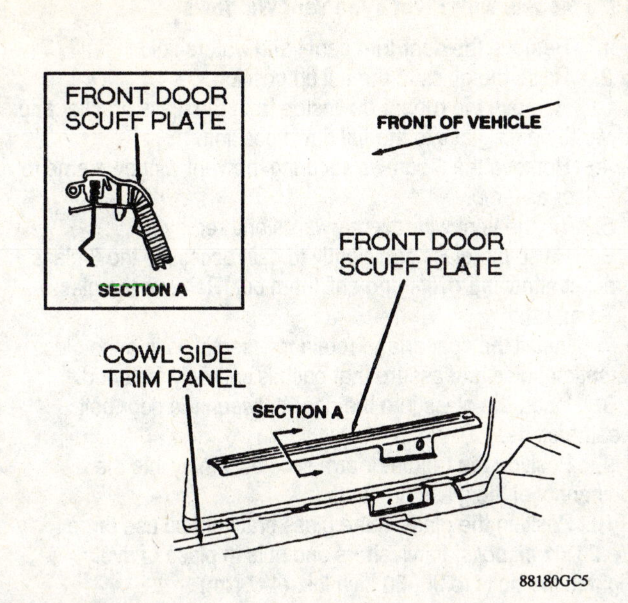

Fig. 68 Scuff plates are located at the opening of the door on the floor edge

Headliner

REMOVAL & INSTALLATION

➧ **See Figures 69, 70 and 71**

1. Remove the sunvisor and bracket assemblies, remove the visor arm clip.
2. Remove all garnish moldings (using tool No. T64P-42006-B and C) and coat hooks.
3. On some models it may be necessary to remove the quarter trim panel.
4. Remove the shoulder belt assembly.
5. Remove the dome lamp and remove the headliner.

To install:

6. Position the headliner in the vehicle and secure it to the roof with push pins.
7. Install the dome lamp.
8. If removed, install the quarter trim panel.
9. Install the garnish moldings, retainers, coat hooks, sunvisors and sun visor clips.
10. Install the shoulder belt assemblies.

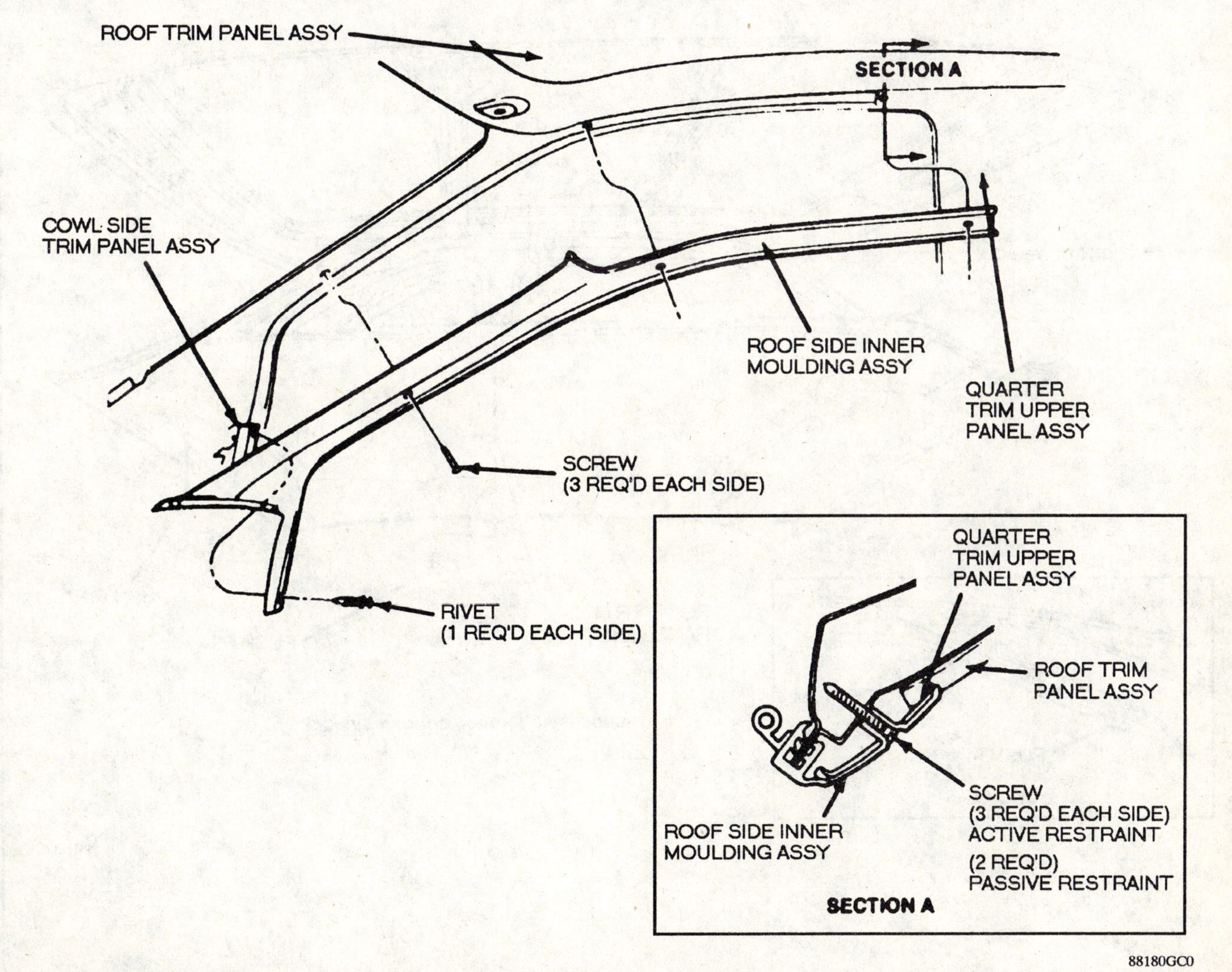

Fig. 69 The roof trim panel may have to be removed to access the headliner

Door Glass

REMOVAL & INSTALLATION

1983 Models without Pivot Type Vent Windows

1. Remove the door panel and watershield.
2. Raise the glass sufficiently to gain access to the 3 glass bracket retaining rivets and drill them out. Never try to pry out the rivets!

****WARNING**

Before removing the rivets you should insert a suitable block support between the door outer panel and the glass bracket, to stabilize the glass during rivet removal.

3. Remove the glass.
4. Installation is the reverse of removal.

1983 Models with Pivot Type Vent Windows

1. Remove the door trim panel and watershield.
2. Raise the glass to the full up position.
3. Remove the rubber downstop from the glass bracket and lower the door glass to the full down position.
4. Remove the 3 screws securing the vent window frame to the door assembly.
5. Tip the vent window rearwards and remove it.
6. Raise the glass sufficiently to gain access to the 3 glass bracket attaching rivets and drill them out. Remove the glass.

To install:

7. Install the spacer and retainer assemblies into the glass retention holes and assure that each is securely fastened.
8. Insert the glass into the door between the door belt weatherstrips.
9. Position the regulator arm slide assembly into the C-channel of the glass bracket.
10. Position the glass in the glass bracket and use three $^1/_4$-20 x 1 in. bolts, flatwashers and nuts in place of rivets. Tighten the bolts to 36–60 inch lbs. (4–7 Nm)

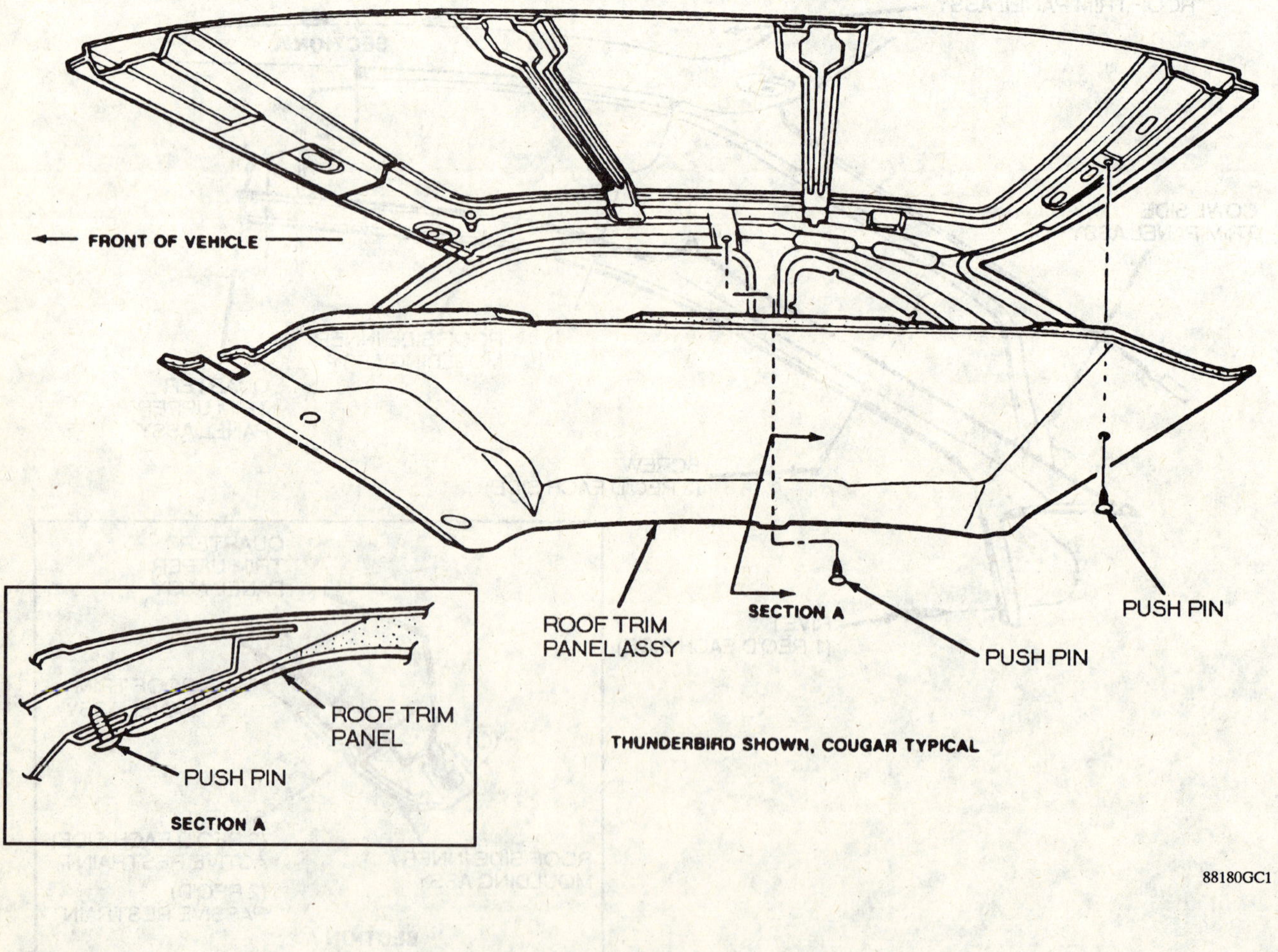

Fig. 70 Install the push pins for the headliner to secure it to the roof

1984-88 Models

1. Remove the door trim panel.
2. Remove the door glass stabilizer.
3. Drill out the two rivets attaching the glass to the glass bracket.
4. Remove the glass. Don't lose the spacers.

To install:

5. Install the glass and attach to the bracket.
6. Replace the rivets with 1/4-20 x 1 in. bolts and nuts.
7. Install the stabilizer and door trim panel.
8. Check the operation of all components.

1989-96 Models

See Figure 72

1. Remove the door trim panel and watershield.
2. Remove the inside door belt weatherstrip assembly.
3. Lower glass to access holes in the door inner panel. Remove the two nuts retaining glass to the glass bracket.
4. Loosen the nut and washer retaining door glass stabilizer.
5. Remove the glass by tipping it forward then removing from between the door belt opening to outboard side of door.

To install:

6. Install the glass into the door at the belt line outside weatherstrip. Make sure the glass is set within the glass run latch side retainers.
7. Position the glass to the door channel bracket.
8. Install the two nuts to secure the glass to the door channel bracket. Tighten the nuts and washers to 8-10 ft. lbs. (10-14 Nm).
9. Install the door belt line inside weatherstrip.
10. Raise the door glass to within 3 inches (75mm) of full-up position, then adjust the door window glass as necessary.
11. Install the door trim panel and door trim shield.

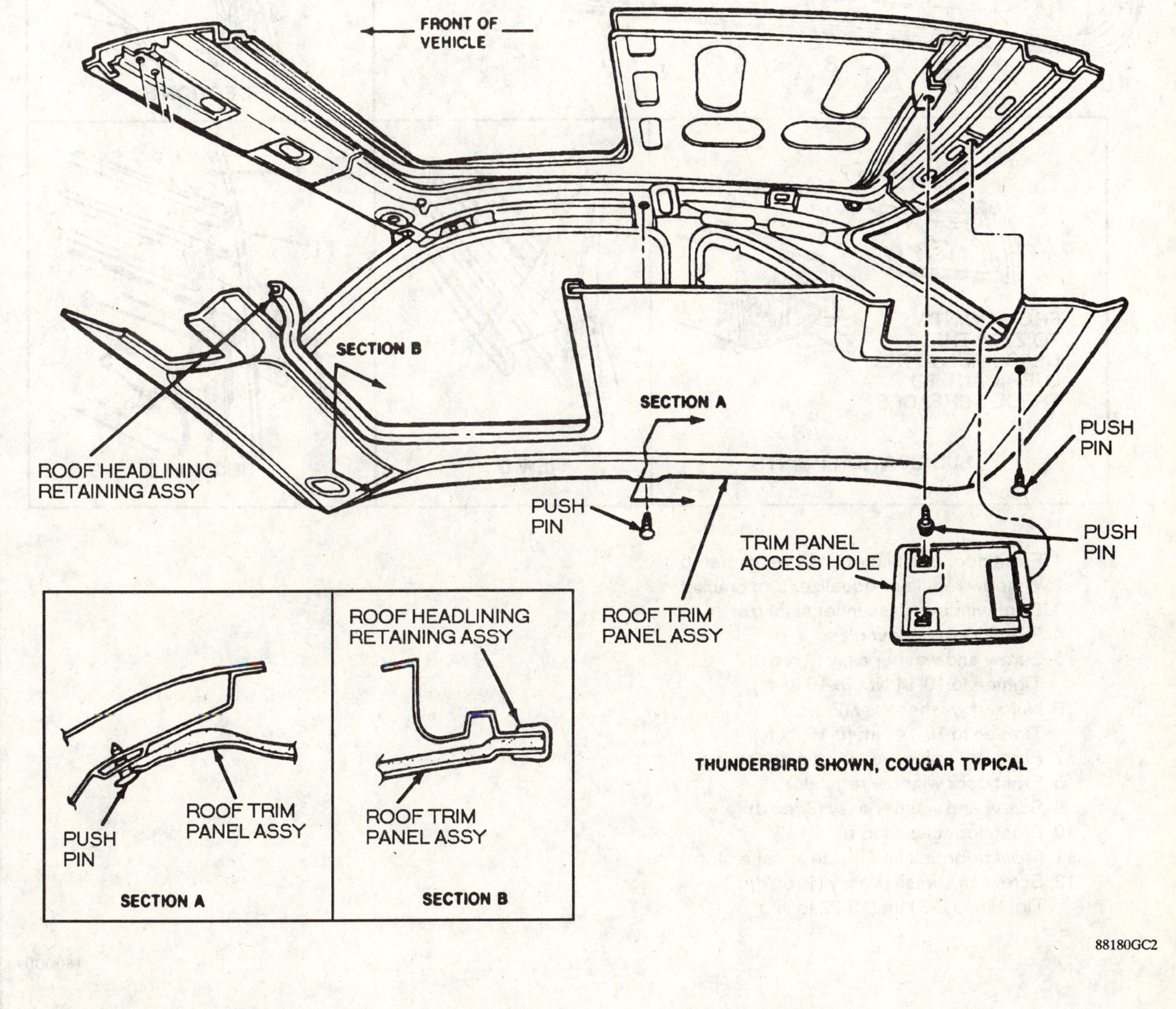

Fig. 71 Headliner installation on a vehicle with a sunroof

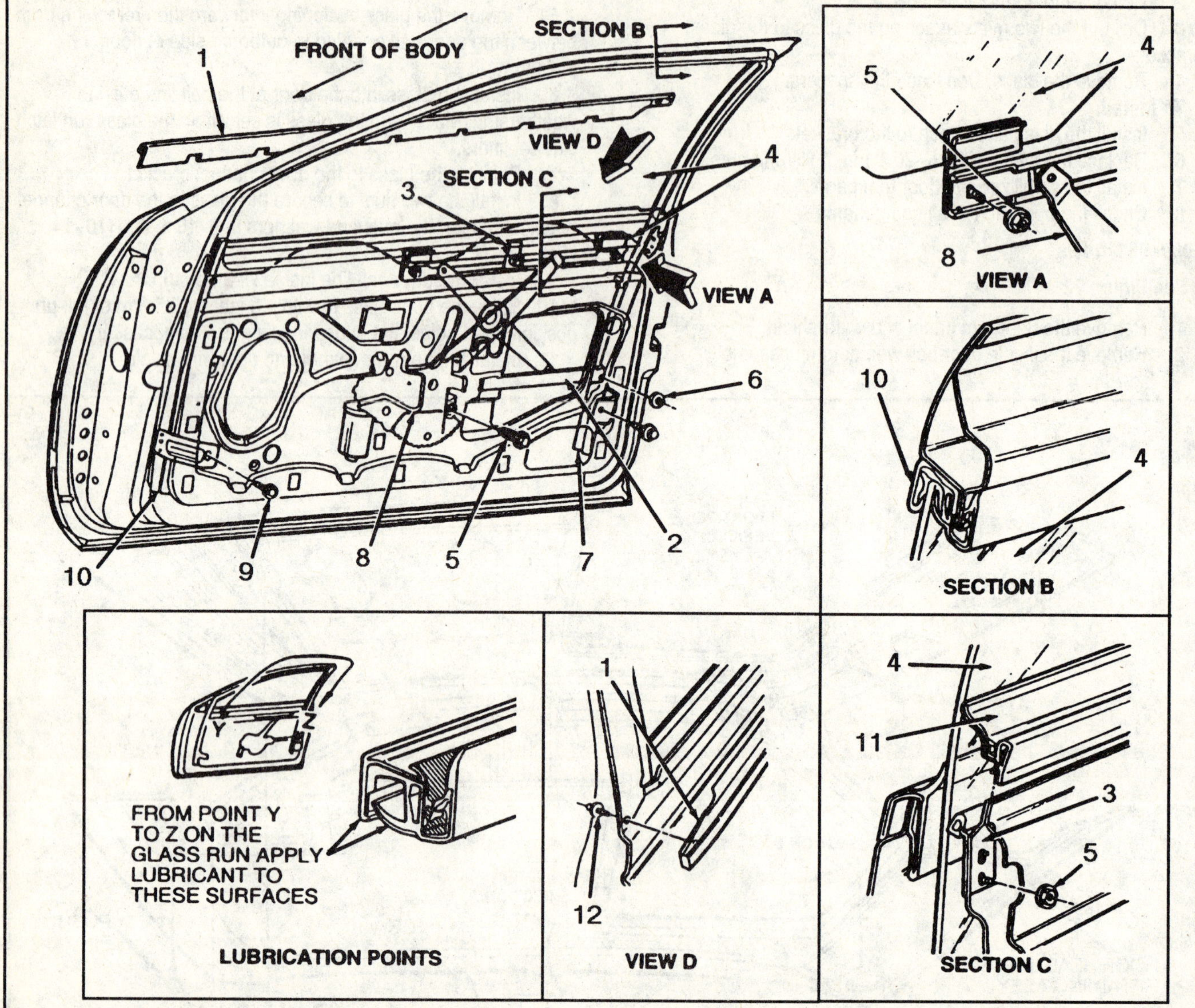

1. Front door belt line outside weatherstrip
2. Window regulator equalizer arm bracket
3. Door window glass inner stabilizer
4. Front door window glass
5. Screw and washer assy (4 req'd)
   Tighten to 10-14 Nm (8-10 lb. ft.)
6. Nut and washer assy (2 req'd)
   Tighten to 10-14 Nm (8-10 lb. ft.)
7. Front door glass run latch side retainer
8. Front door window regulator
9. Screw and washer assy (2 req'd)
10. Front door glass top run
11. Front door belt line inside weatherstrip
12. Screw and washer assy (1 req'd)
    Tighten to 2-3 Nm (13-22 lb. in.)

88180GD9

Fig. 72 Exploded view of the regulator and window glass — 1989–96 models

Window Regulator

REMOVAL & INSTALLATION

1983 Models

➧ **See Figure 73**

1. Remove the door trim panel and watershield.
2. Support the glass in the full up position.
3. On Cougars with power windows, drill out the motor bracket-to-inner panel attaching rivet and remove the rivet. Disconnect the motor wires at the connector. On the Thunderbird and XR-7 with power windows, drill out the regulator attaching rivets and remove the rivets.
4. Disengage the regulator arm from the glass bracket and remove the regulator from the door.
5. If equipped with power windows, secure the regulator in a vise and drill a $\frac{5}{16}$ in. (8mm) hole through the regulator sector gear and the plate. Install a $\frac{1}{4}$ in. (6mm) bolt and nut in the hole to prevent the sector gear from moving when the motor and drive assembly is removed.
6. Remove the motor assembly from the regulator and install it on a new regulator.
7. Installation is the reverse of removal. Replace the rivets with $\frac{1}{4}$-20-$\frac{1}{2}$ in. machine screws. Remove the regulator restraining bolt and nut if the old regulator was re-used.

1984–88 Models

➧ **See Figure 74**

1. Remove the trim panel and watershield.
2. Prop the window glass in the full up position.
3. Disconnect the window motor wiring if so equipped.
4. Drill out the 3 rivets (manual windows) or 4 rivets (electric windows), attaching the regulator to the inner door panel.
5. Remove the upper screw and washer and the lower nut and washer, attaching the run and bracket to the inner door panel. Slide the run tube up between the door belt and glass. It's a good idea to cover the glass with a protective cloth.
6. Remove the regulator slide from the glass bracket and remove the regulator through the door access hole.
7. Installation is the reverse of removal. Replace the rivets with $\frac{1}{4}$-20-1 in. bolts and nuts.

1989–96 Models

****CAUTION**

To avoid personal injury, ensure that the regulator arms are in a fixed position before removing or replacing the regulator counterbalance spring. The spring can unwind violently.

1. Remove the door trim panel and water shield.
2. Lower the glass to access the holes in the door inner panel. Remove the 2 nut and washer assemblies retaining the glass to the glass bracket.

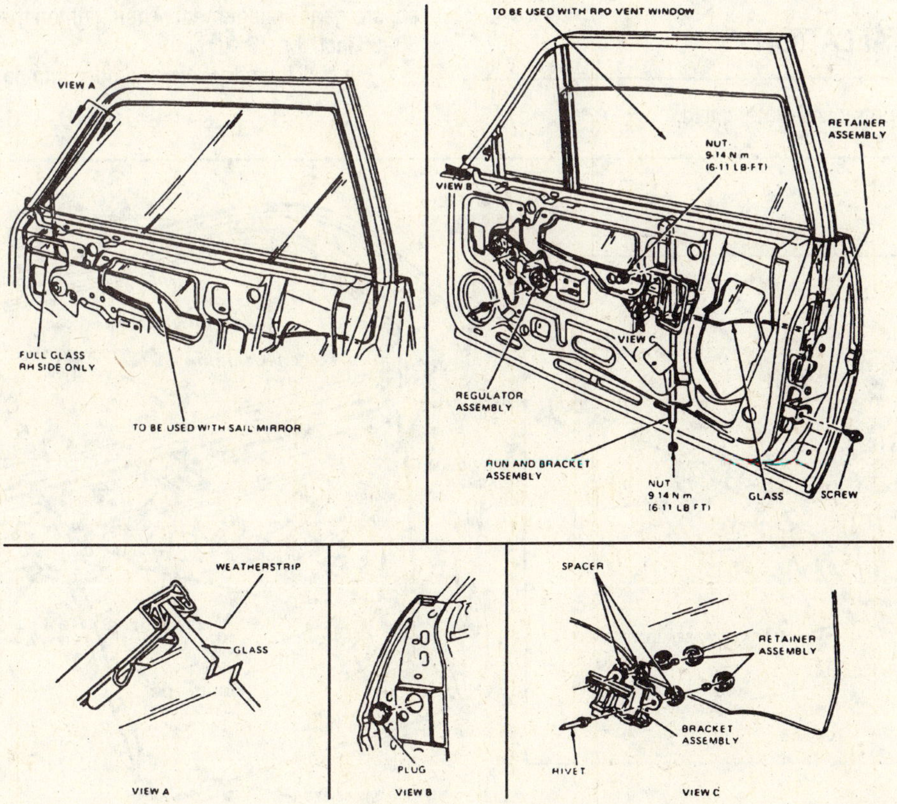

88180GD6

Fig. 73 Thunderbird and XR-7 window mechanism with pivoting vent windows

3. Prop the glass in the full-up position.
4. Disconnect the negative battery cable.
5. Disconnect the electric motor wiring.
6. Remove the 2 nut and washer assemblies retaining the regulator equalizer bracket.
7. Remove the 4 rivets attaching the regulator to the door inner panel, drilling the rivets with a 6mm drillbit.
8. Remove the regulator through the access hole.

To Install:

9. With the glass in the full-up position, install the window regulator through the access hole.
10. Position the regulator base plate to door inner panel and install the 4 rivets.
11. Install the regulator equalizer bracket on the regulator and loosely assemble with the nut and washer assemblies.
12. Install the regulator glass bracket drive channel on the glass and secure with the nut and washer assemblies, torquing to 7–10 ft. lbs. (9–14 Nm).
13. Connect the motor wiring.
14. Connect the negative battery cable.
15. Lower the glass about 3 inches from the full-up position.
16. With the door open, place hands on each side of the glass and pull the glass fully into the door glass run assembly at the B-pillar.
17. Apply a downward pressure on the equalizer bracket and tighten the nut and washer assemblies to 7–10 ft. lbs. (9–14 Nm).
18. Cycle the door glass to ensure proper operation.
19. Install the door trim panel and the watershield.

Electric Window Motor

REMOVAL & INSTALLATION

1. Remove the trim panel and watershield.
2. Remove the speakers.
3. Disconnect the negative battery cable.
4. Disconnect the motor wires and the connector.
5. Using the dimples located on the inner door panel, drill $^3/_4$ in. (19mm) holes for access to the motor.

****WARNING**

When drilling the holes, the glass must be in the up position. The hole saw pilot must not extend more than $^1/_4$ in. (6mm) beyond the hole saw.

****CAUTION**

Secure the regulator in a vise and drill a $^5/_{16}$ in. (8mm) hole through the regulator sector gear and the plate. Install a $^1/_4$ in. (6mm) bolt and nut in the hole to prevent the sector gear from moving when the motor and drive assembly is removed.

6. Working through the holes, remove the 3 motor and drive-to-regulator attaching bolts. Remove the motor and drive from the door.

To install:

7. Clean the chips of metal from the surrounding area. Then coat the bare metal to avoid rust.
8. When installing the motor and drive to the regulator and install the 3 screws just snugly enough to hold it. Remove the regulator restraining bolt and nut if the old regulator was re-used.
9. Connect the negative battery cable.
10. Connect the wires and cycle the glass through its run to ensure gear engagement. Then, tighten the attaching screws to 50–85 inch lbs. (6–10 Nm).
11. Install the speakers and door trim panel with watershield.

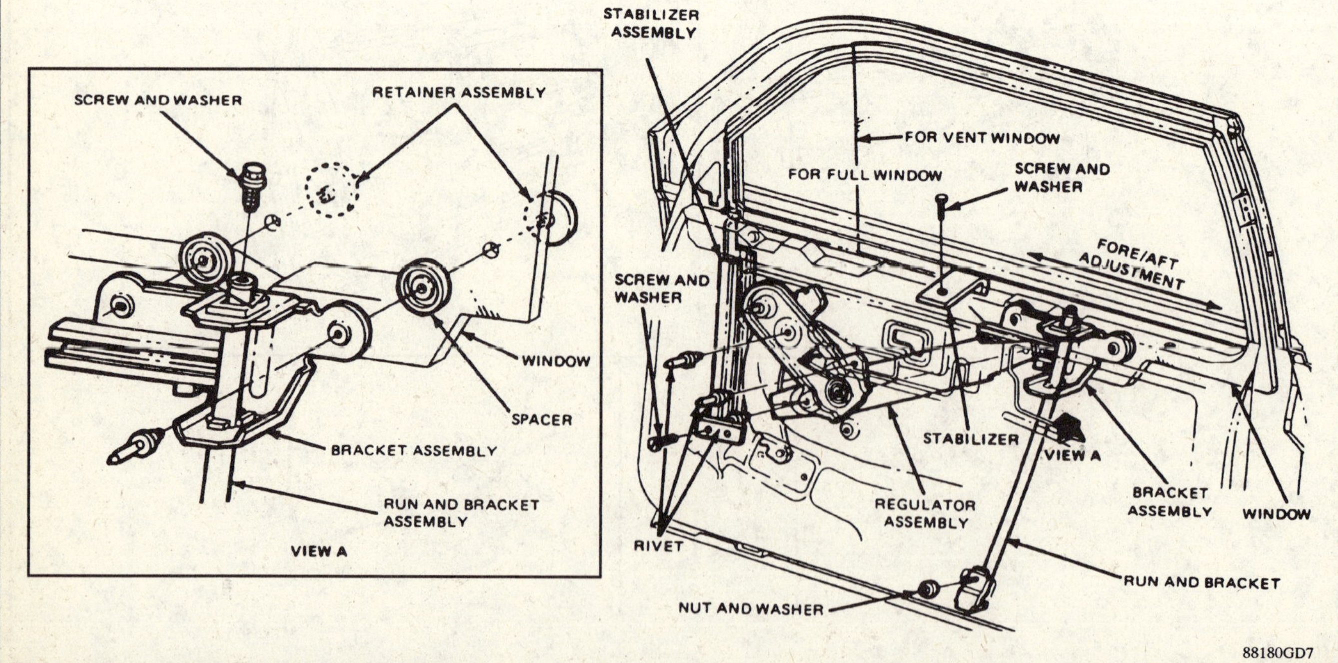

Fig. 74 Door regulator on the 1984–88 models

Windshield Glass

REMOVAL AND INSTALLATION

➧ See Figures 75, 76 and 77

1. Remove the wiper arms and the leaf screen along the cowl for the front windshield. Disconnect the rear defogger on the rear windshield.
2. Remove all moldings, glass stops and retainers.

➥ On the Cougar rear windshield, only the finisher strip of the molding can be removed.

3. Remove the rear view mirror.
4. Using a very thin piano wire or a a special tool called a hot knife, cut through the urethane foam around the edge of glass.

****CAUTION**

To avoid personal injury, wear safety glasses and gloves.

5. Using suction cups or equivalent, carefully remove the glass.
6. Scrape off the urethane left on the window frame until the thickness does not exceed 0.1 inch (2.5mm).

To Install:

7. Using a urethane installation kit, follow the directions to prepare the area and install the glass. As much as 4 hours may be required for the urethane to cure. Apply tape to support the glass as this takes place.
8. Place the windshield on a stable work surface, inside up.
9. Clean the glass, then install the rear view mirror bracket.

➥ Wipe off immediately after application because the primer flash dries.

10. Using a lint free cloth, wipe the outer a ½ in. (13mm) in from the edge. At the bottom of the glass, cover 2 inches (50mm) from the edge. Also apply primer to the leg of the windshield outside molding that is next to the glass. This will ensure the molding to bond to the glass.

****CAUTION**

Allow the glass and parts enough time to cure once installed. If this is not done, the glass may come loose and and/or leak. This could be dangerous.

11. Install a foam dam (with a self adhesive backing) on the pinch weld about 0.35 inch (9mm) from the edge of the windshield. At the bottom of the glass, install a foam dam 2 inches (50mm) from the bottom edge of the glass.
12. Properly align the windshield to the body of the vehicle.
    a. Make sure the lower glass spacers are in place at the bottom of the glass opening.
    b. Place the glass into the opening. Center it on the top and bottom, side-to-side with equal amounts of clearance around the opening.
    c. Using masking tape or crayon, make alignment marks at the points on each of the four sides of both the glass and window opening.
13. Remove the windshield from the vehicle and place it back on the work table.

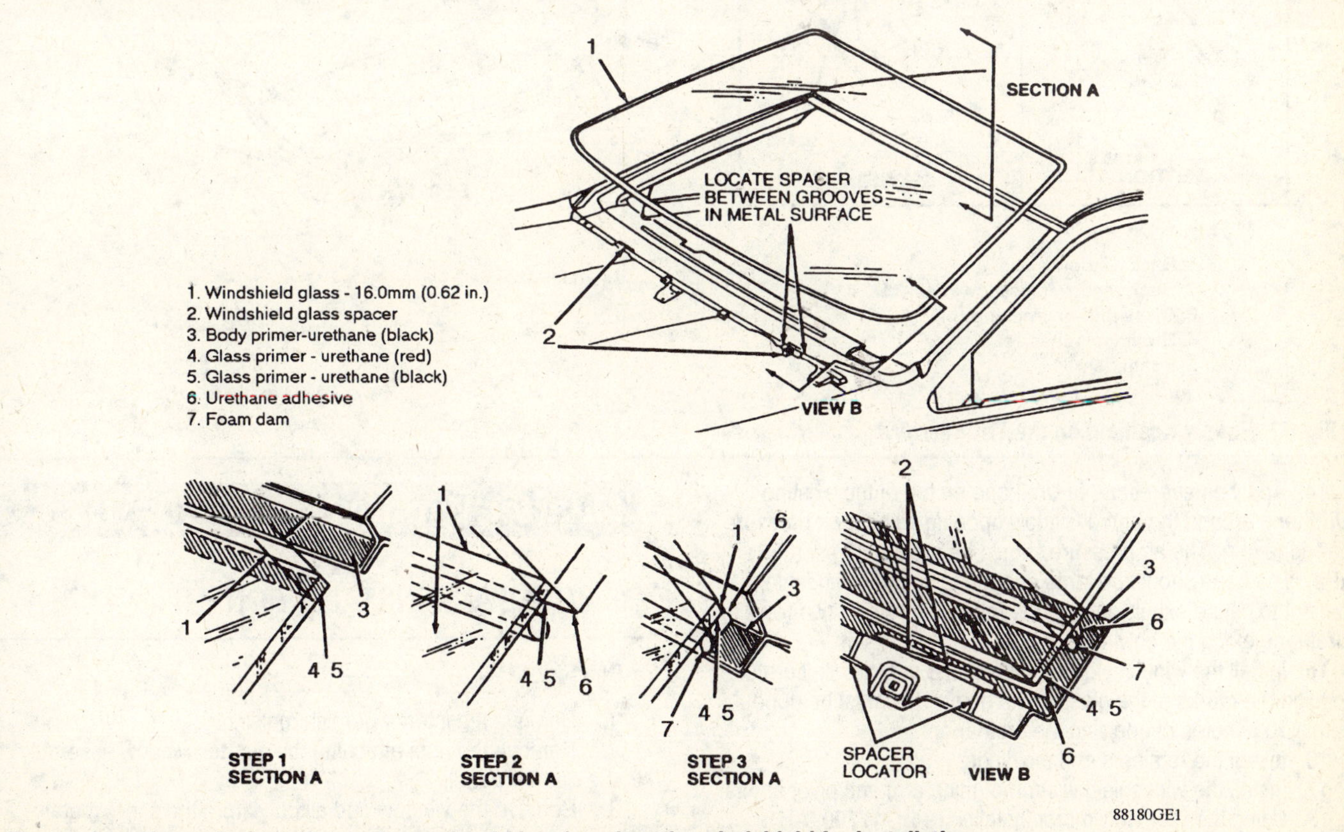

Fig. 75 Locations of where the urethane should be placed on the windshield for installation

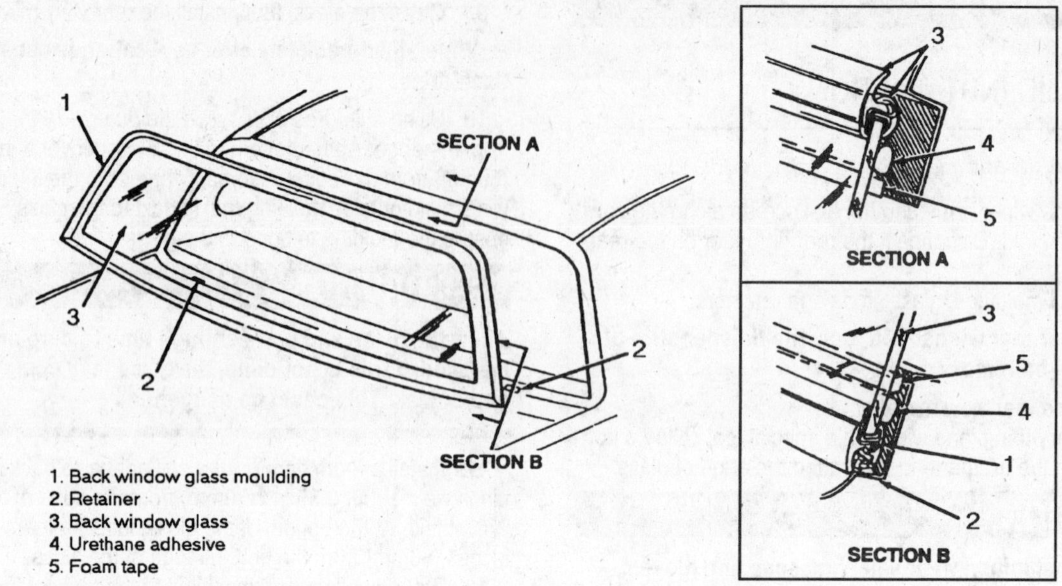

1. Back window glass moulding
2. Retainer
3. Back window glass
4. Urethane adhesive
5. Foam tape

Fig. 76 Rear windshield on the Cougar

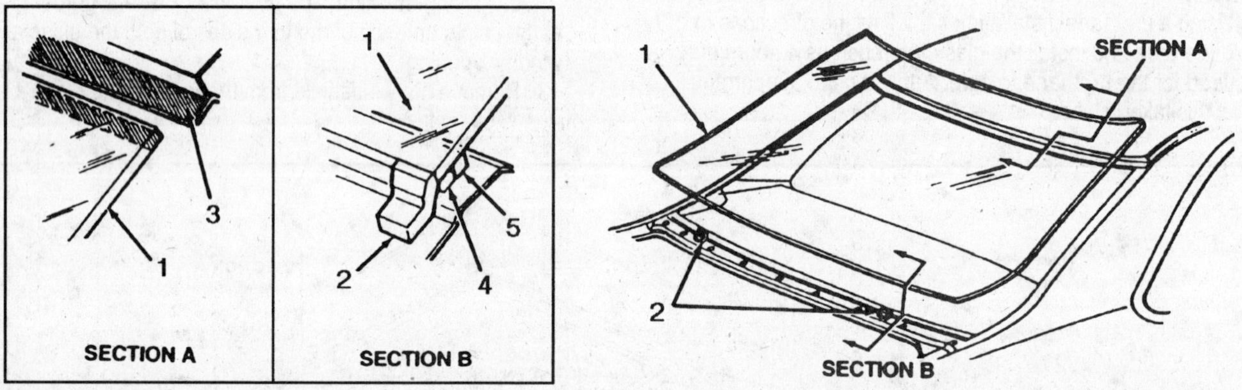

1. Back window glass
2. Back window glass lower spacer
3. Glass primer urethane (black)
4. Urethane adhesive
5. Foam dam

88180GE3

Fig. 77 Rear windshield on the Thunderbird

14. Apply an even bead of Urethane on top of the existing Urethane around the entire window opening using a air pressure cartridge gun. The air pressure should be around 40 psi (276 kPa). The bead should be large enough to seal the windshield but not to cause expulsion over the foam dam. Apply two rows of Urethane along the cowl top.
15. Install the windshield assembly in the vehicle. Be careful to align the marks of the glass to the body. This must be done within 10 minutes of applying the urethane.
16. Install the retainers and moldings.
17. Install the windshield wiper mounting arm and pivot shafts.
18. Using the rear view mirror installer T94P-17700-AH or equivalent, install the mirror on the windshield.

Quarter Window

REMOVAL AND INSTALLATION

➧ See Figure 78

1. Remove the interior garnish moldings.
2. Remove the nuts attaching the quarter window assembly to the quarter panel.
3. Remove the window and all butyl from the sheet metal flange.

To install:

4. Apply foam core butyl service tape to the sealing surface on the back side of the window assembly.
5. Position the window assembly and tighten the nuts to 9–17 inch lbs. (1–2 Nm).
6. Install the interior garnish moldings.

Inside Rearview Mirror

REMOVAL & INSTALLATION

Non Breakaway

1. Loosen the mirror assembly to mounting bracket setscrew.
2. Remove mirror assembly by sliding upward and away from the mounting bracket.
3. If the bracket vinyl pad remains on the windshield, apply low heat from a heat gun until the vinyl softens. Peel vinyl off the windshield and discard.

To install:

4. If necessary, to install a new mounting bracket to windshield, a rearview mirror adhesive kit D9AZ–19554–CA, or equivalent must be obtained. Follow the instructions in the kit for gluing the mounting bracket vinyl to the windshield.
5. Attach the mirror to the mounting bracket.
6. Tighten the mirror mounting bracket setscrew.

Breakaway

➧ See Figures 79, 80 and 81

These breakaway mounts are designed to detach from the rearview mirror bracket during air bag deployment. Any excessive force or excessive up/down, side-to-side adjustment can cause the mirror to detach from the windshield.

➥ It may be necessary to obtain a special service tool to replace the mirror such as T94–17700–AH or equivalent to complete the job.

1. Disconnect the wiring assembly, if equipped with automatic diming outside rearview mirror.
2. Grasp the inside mirror firmly. Use one hand to support one end of the mirror against the windshield. Use the other hand to pull the mirror away from the glass using a sideways movement.

To install:

3. Center the bottom of the mirror mount against the windshield at the top of the mirror bracket.
4. Slide the mirror mount partially onto the bracket, keeping the mount parallel to the windshield.
5. With the use of a special mirror installation tool, T94–17700–AH, complete the installation onto the mirror bracket.

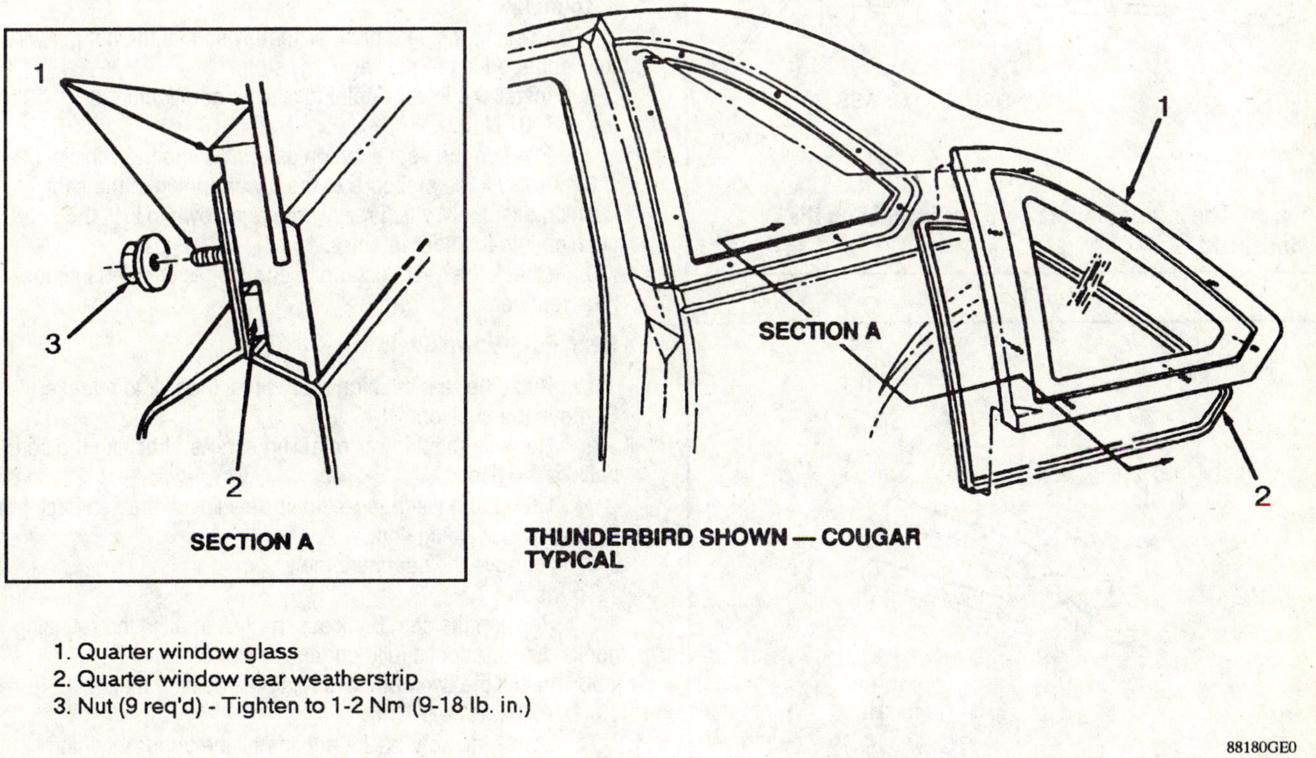

Fig. 78 The quarter window is a stationary glass

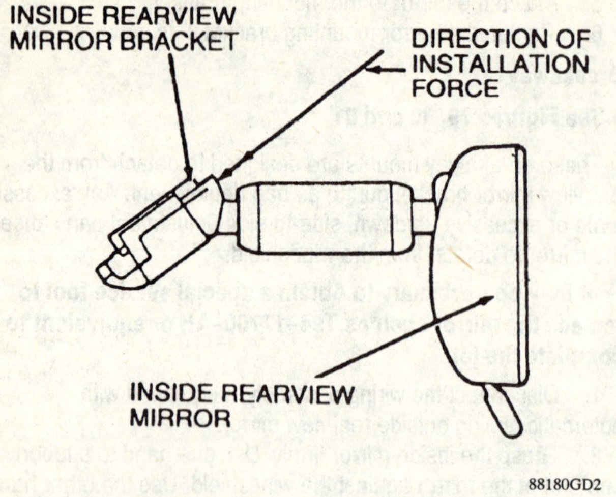

Fig. 79 The breakaway rear view mirror looks the same as a non-breakaway mirror

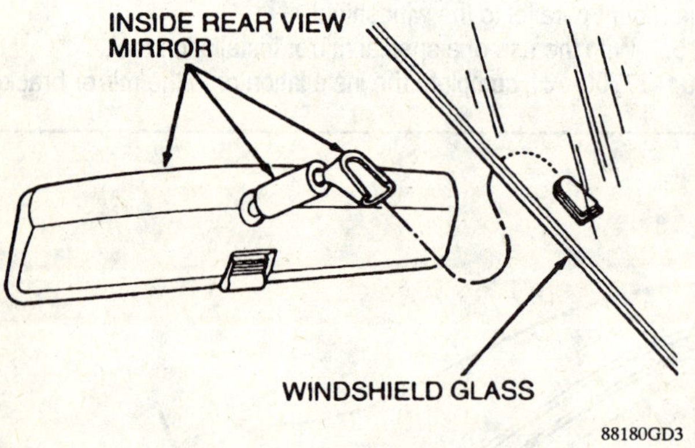

Fig. 80 The mirror mounts onto the bracket on the windshield

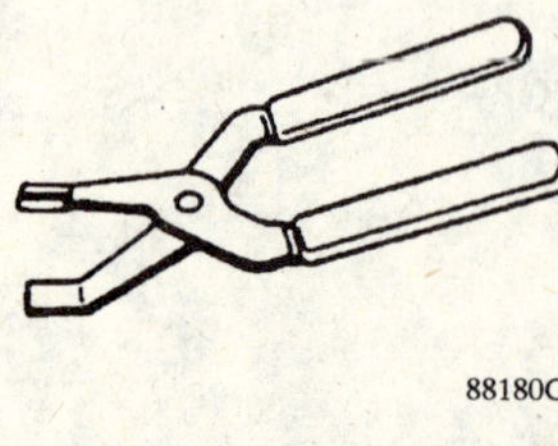

Fig. 81 Installation tool for the mirror — T94-17700-AH

Seats

REMOVAL & INSTALLATION

Front

➧ See Figures 82, 83 and 84

1. Remove the seat track to floor insulators.
2. Remove the seat track bolts and seat belt anchor bolts.
3. On power seats, tilt the seat backward and disconnect the motor wiring prior to lifting the seat from the car.
4. Remove the seat from the vehicle.

To install:

5. Place the seat into position and tighten the seat track and seat belt anchor bolts to 21–31 ft. lbs. (30–43 Nm).
6. Attach the wiring if disconnected.
7. Install the seat track to floor insulators.

Rear Bench

➧ See Figures 85

1. Bearing down with your knee on the rear seat cushion, push the cushion rearward and disengage it from the retaining brackets.
2. Remove the rear seat armrests if applicable.
3. Remove the seatback lower retaining screws and seat belt bolts.
4. Grasp the seatback at the bottom and lift it up to disengage the hanger wire from the retainer brackets.

To install:

5. Position the seat back assembly so that the hanger wire is fully engaged in the package tray slots.
6. Install the lower retaining screws and tighten to 13–19 ft. lbs. (17–37 Nm).
7. Position the seat cushion assembly into the vehicle.
8. Apply knee pressure to the lower portion of the seat cushion assembly. Push rearwards and down to lock the seat cushion into the seat retainer.
9. Check the seat cushion to ensure it is secured into the floor retainer.

Rear, Fold-Down Seats

1. Push the rear cushion rearwards, then lift to release. Remove the cushion.
2. Remove the 2 lower retaining screws attaching the seat back to the floor.
3. Lift up and disengage the upper clips of the seatback from the top of the folding floor.
4. Remove the seat assembly.

To install:

5. Position the seat back assembly and align the retaining hooks. Ensure hooks fully engage in slots.
6. Install the two outboard retaining bolts, then tighten to 13–19 ft. lbs. (17–27 Nm).
7. Lower the seat backs and install the upper retaining screws.
8. Install the lower center retaining screw, tighten to 13–19 ft. lbs. (17–27 Nm).
9. Install the rear seat cushion. Ensure the rear seat cushion front retainers latch properly.

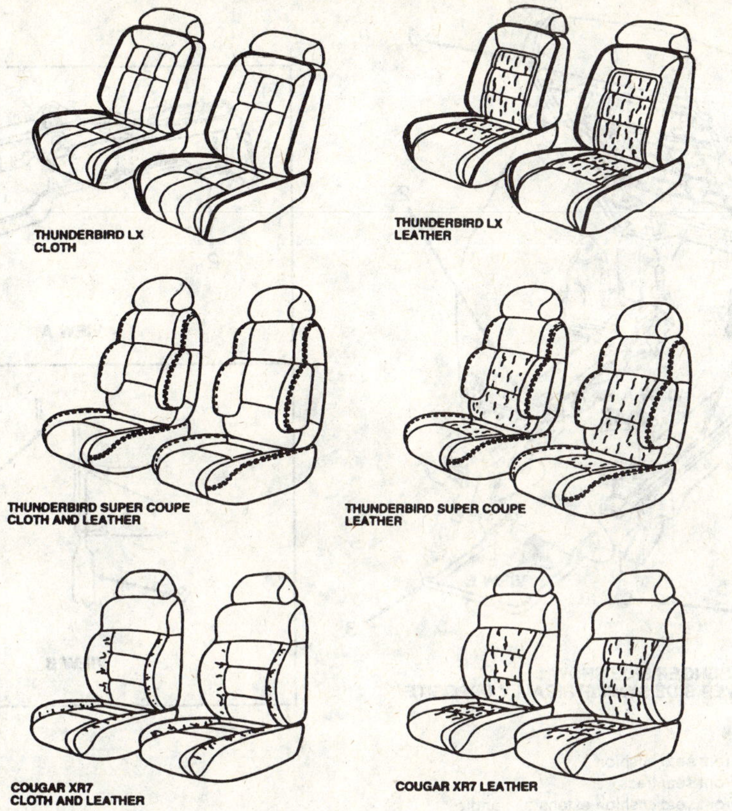

Fig. 82 Front seat designs

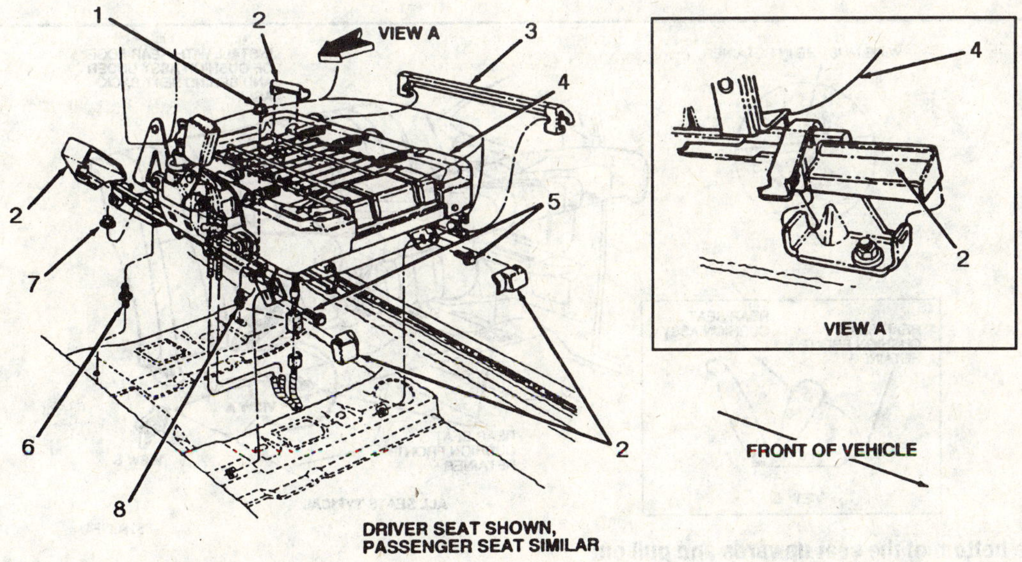

1. Nut and washer (1 req'd) - Tighten to 12-24 Nm (9-18 lb. ft.)
2. Front seat track to floor insulator
3. Front seat track lower shield
4. Front seat cushion assy
5. Screw (2 req'd each seat) - Tighten to 12-24 Nm (9-18 lb. ft.)
6. Stud (1 req'd) - Tighten to 12-24 Nm (9-18 lb. ft.)
7. Nut and washer - Tighten to 68-92 Nm (50-68 lb. ft.)
8. Stud (1 req'd) - Tighten to 12-24 Nm (9-18 lb. ft.)

88180GF1

Fig. 83 Seat track mounting on power seats

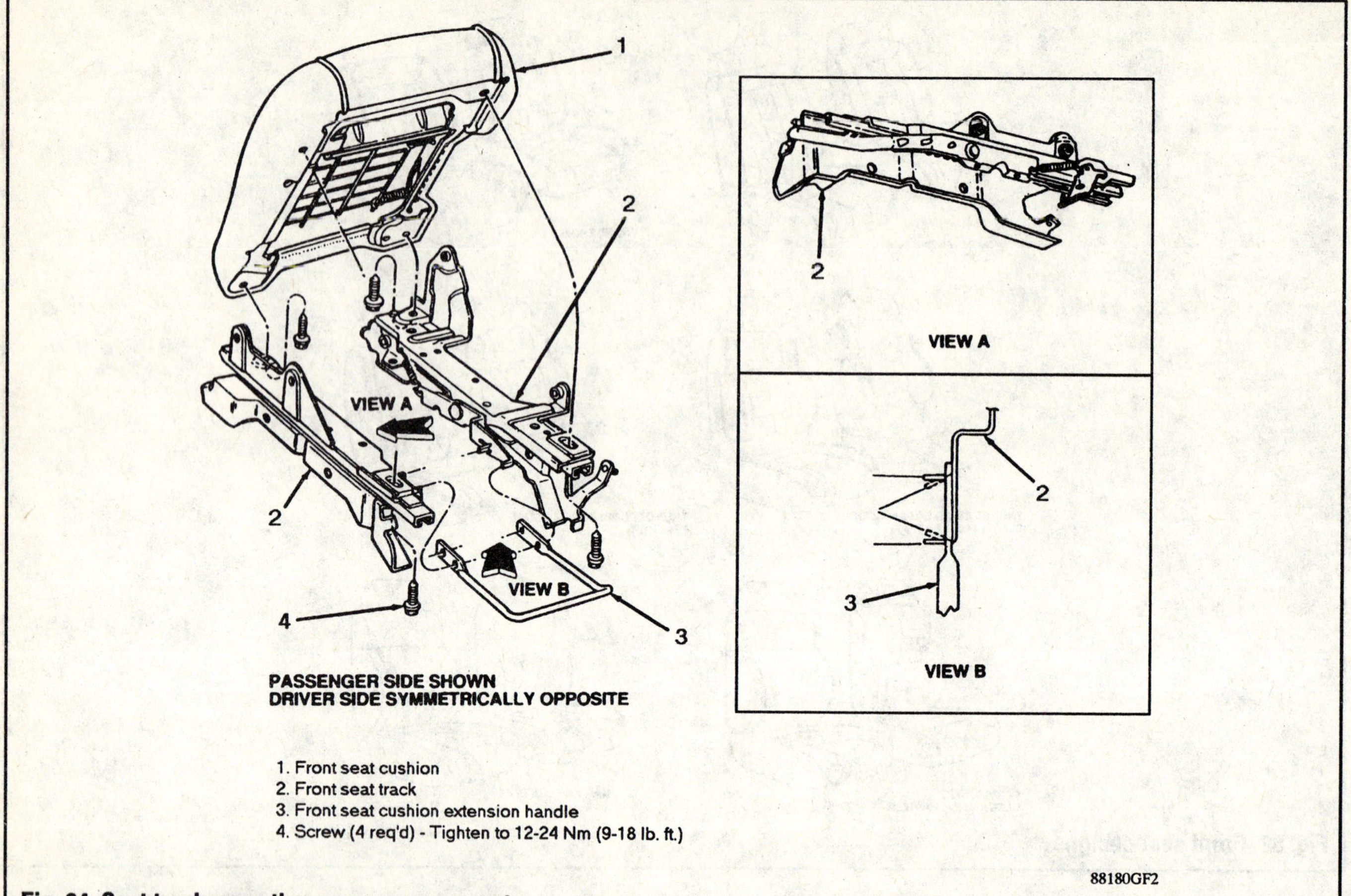

Fig. 84 Seat track mounting on non-power seats

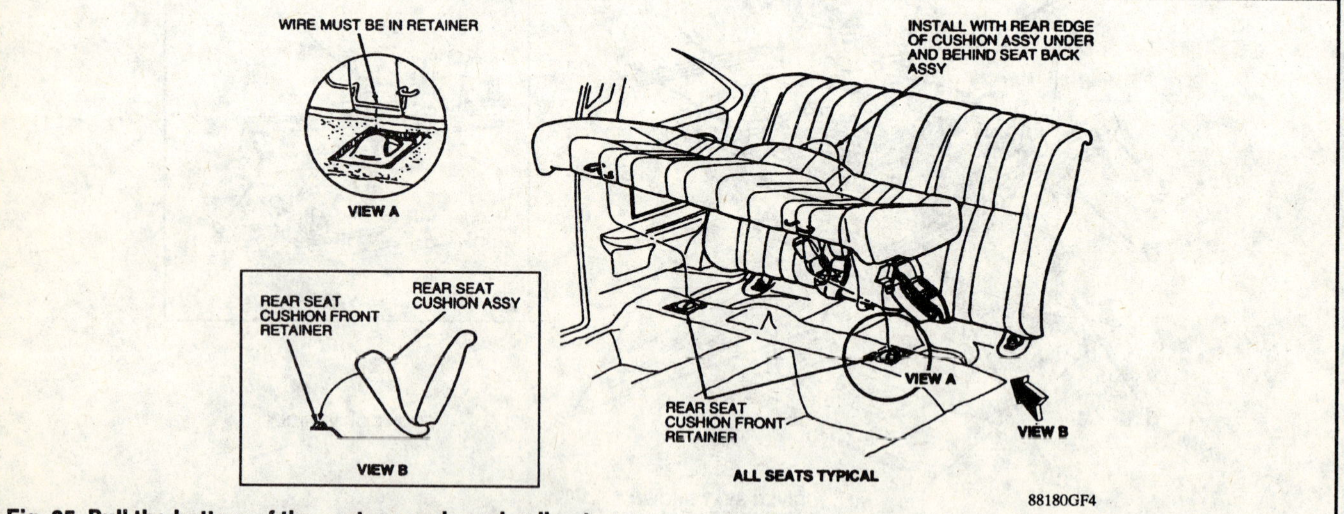

Fig. 85 Pull the bottom of the seat upwards and pull out

Seat Belt Systems

There are two types of restraints available, active and passive. The active restraint system is of a continuous loop, single retractor type available on early U.S models and all Canadian models. The passive restraint system, which operates electrically, restrains the driver and front seat passenger in the vehicle through the use of the automatic shoulder belt, the manual lap belt and knee bolsters. The lap belt must be manually buckled by the driver/passenger and should be snug as low as possible on your hips. The lap and shoulder safety belts are factory installed in their proper locations. If the lap and/or shoulder safety belts are removed for any reason, the vehicle should not be operated until the safety belts are installed in their original positions.

✻✻CAUTION

Children having a seat height greater than 28 inches, which is the maximum height for use of the tot-guard (child seat), should use the safety belts provided with the vehicle. However, the shoulder safety belt should not be used if it contacts the child's face, chin, neck or throat. If the shoulder portion of the safety belt either touches or hangs in front of the child's face, chin, neck or throat, move the child closer to the middle of the center of the vehicle or use a booster seat to help provide a good shoulder belt fit. If the safety belts are not adjusted properly, the child's chances of being injured in a collision increase.

✻✻WARNING

All vehicle occupants, including pregnant women, should wear safety belts for maximum protection in the event of a collision. All vehicle occupants, including pregnant women, should be sure the lap safety belt, or the lap safety belt portion of the lap/shoulder belt, is fitted snugly and as low as possible around the hips, not the waist. Failure to properly use the safety belts may increase the chance and/or the severity of injury in the event of a collision.

REMOVAL & INSTALLATION

Active Type

LAP/SHOULDER BELT RETRACTOR ASSEMBLY

➧ See Figures 86, 87 and 88

➥ A special tool, No. T77L-2100-A or equivalent should be used for removal and installation of all seat belt assemblies.

1. Remove the D-ring cover.
2. Insert the special tool and remove the belt bolt.
3. Remove the safety belt anchor to sill bolt and rubber washer.

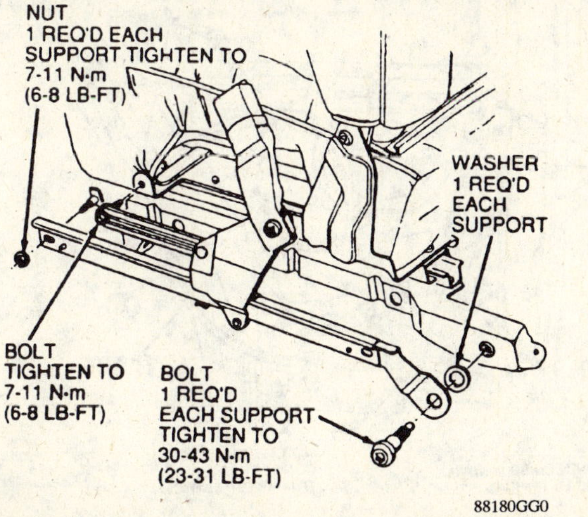

Fig. 86 Seat support assembly with the active restraint system

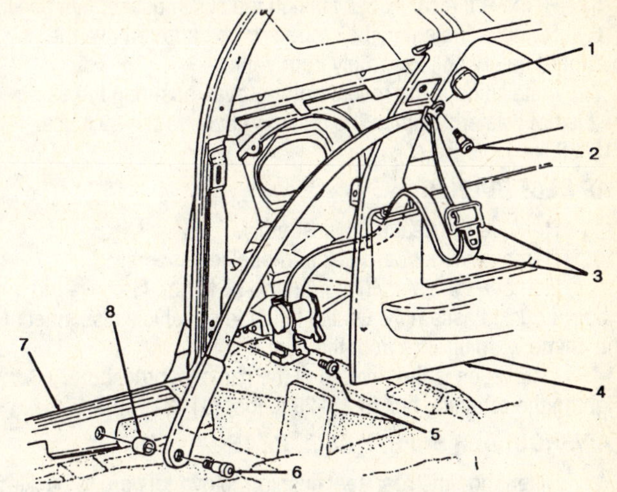

1. Front seat shoulder strap guide cover
2. Bolt - Tighten to 30-40 Nm (23-29 lb. ft.)
3. Front safety belt and retractor assy
4. Panel quarter trim
5. Bolt - Tighten to 30-40 Nm (23-29 lb. ft.)
6. Bolt - Tighten to 30-40 Nm (23-29 lb. ft.)
7. Door scuff plate assy
8. Washer (1 req'd each side)

88180GG2

Fig. 87 Outboard belt assembly on active restraint systems

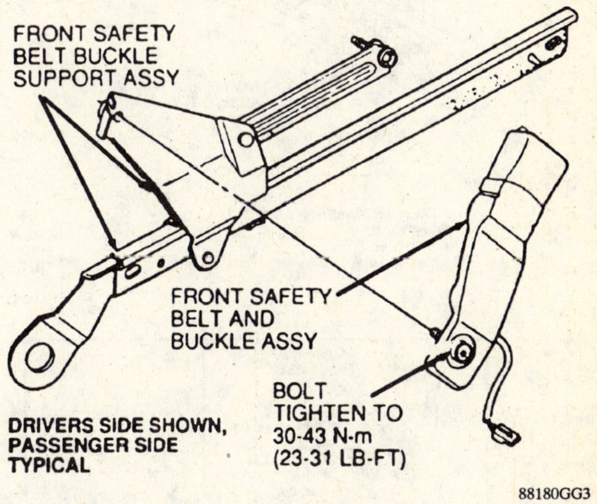

Fig. 88 Inboard belt assembly on active restraint systems

4. Remove the scuff plate/quarter trim panel retaining screws and panel.
5. Remove the safety belt through the slot in quarter trim panel.
6. Remove the safety belt retractor bolt and remove the outboard safety belt assembly from vehicle.
7. Installation is the reverse of removal, ensuring the safety belt is not twisted. Tighten the retaining bolts to 23–29 ft. lbs. (31–39 Nm).

LAP BELT BUCKLE

1. Remove the seat track assembly.
2. Remove the inboard belt and buckle assembly.
3. Remove the safety bolt from the slide bar. Remove the inboard buckle assembly. On the left side of vehicle disconnect the chime warning wire from the connector.
4. Installation is the reverse of the removal procedure. Tighten the retaining bolt to 23–29 ft. lbs. (31–39 Nm).

LAP/SHOULDER SAFETY BELT, REAR

1. Disengage the rear seat cushion. Move forward to buckle end nuts.
2. Remove the buckle end anchor nuts and remove buckle end belts. Remove the seat cushion.
3. Remove the rear back seat.
4. Remove the D-ring cover and attaching bolt.
5. Remove the safety belt anchor-to-sill bolt. Remove the upper and lower quarter trim panels.
6. Remove the push pin retaining the rear safety belt retractor cover assembly. Remove the bezel and cover.
7. Remove the retractor anchor bolt and retractor screw.
8. Remove the anchor end of safety belt through the opening in the quarter trim panel. Remove the outboard safety belt assembly from the vehicle. Repeat procedure for other side.
9. Installation is the reverse of the removal procedure. Ensure that the safety belts are not twisted. Tighten the retaining bolts to 23–29 ft. lbs. (31–39 Nm).

Passive Type

SHOULDER BELT RETRACTOR AND LAP BELT BUCKLE ASSEMBLY

➧ See Figures 89 and 90

1. Cycle the shoulder safety belt to the A-pillar position. Remove the shoulder belt from emergency release buckle of the motor and track carrier assembly, allowing the safety straps to retract into retractor.
2. Disconnect the seat wiring at floor. Remove the front seat and seat track assembly.
3. Remove the support assembly with the belt/retractor assembly, and lap belt buckle/strap assembly still attached. Remove the front retaining hex nut and bolt. Remove the rear Torx® head bolt retaining the support assembly to seat track and remove the support assembly.
4. Remove the Torx® head bolt retaining the lap belt buckle assembly to support assembly, remove the buckle assembly.
5. Remove the nut and washer assembly retaining the shoulder strap retractor assembly to shoulder strap support.
6. Rotate the retractor up away from the support assembly until the hooks disengage and remove retractor from the support assembly by pulling the stud out of hole.
7. Installation is the reverse of the removal procedure, ensure that the straps are not twisted. Tighten the retaining bolt to 23–29 ft. lbs. (31–39 Nm). Tighten the hex nut to 5–8 ft. lbs. (6–10 Nm).

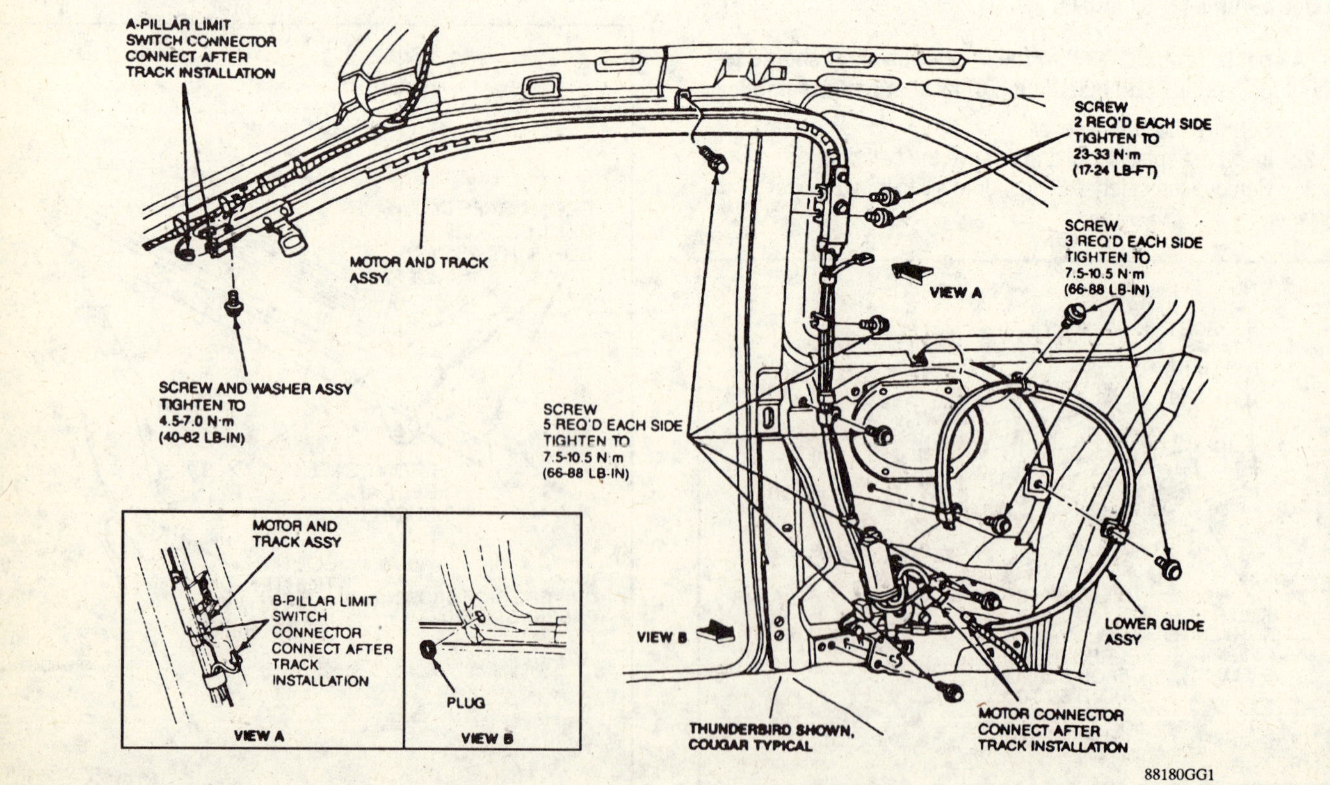

Fig. 89 Passive restraint assembly on all models

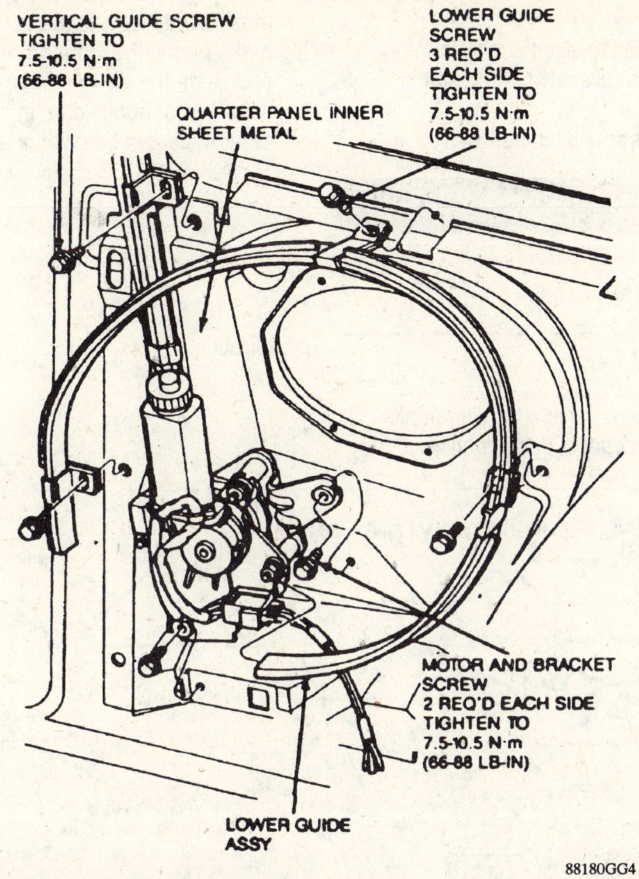

Fig. 90 The passive belt motor is located behind the quarter trim panel

Power Seat Motor

REMOVAL & INSTALLATION

1. Unbolt the seat track and seat belts.
2. Turn the seat over and disconnect the wiring.
3. Remove the seat from the car.
4. Remove the 3 motor mounting bolts.
5. Remove the cable-to-seat track clamps.
6. Open the wire retaining straps and remove the motor and cables from the seat.
7. Installation is the reverse of removal. Tighten the retaining bolt to 23–29 ft. lbs. (31–39 Nm). Tighten the hex nut to 5–8 ft. lbs. (6–10 Nm).

Coat Hooks

REMOVAL & INSTALLATION

1. Remove the retaining screw that attaches the coat hook to the headliner.
2. Remove the coat hook.

To install:

3. Place the coat hook into position, then tighten the retaining screw.

Scuff Plates

REMOVAL & INSTALLATION

1. If necessary, remove the safety belt anchor bolt.
2. On some models, unscrew the scuff plate and remove.
3. On other models, pull up on the scuff plate to release the retaining clips to remove.

To install:

4. Place the scuff plate into position, then attach with either the retaining clips or screws depending on the type you have.
5. If removed, install the safety belt anchor bolt.

Sun Visors

REMOVAL & INSTALLATION

➧ See Figure 91

1. Remove the screws that retain the visor to the roof panel.
2. Disengage the visor from the arm clip holding the visor to the roof panel.
3. Lower the visor.
4. If applicable, disconnect the courtesy or inside lamp switch wiring.

5. Remove the visor.

To install:

6. Attach the wiring if removed to the visor.
7. Attach the visor with the retaining screws, then attach the visor to the arm clip.
8. Check the operation of the visor and lamps.

Floor Mats

REMOVAL & INSTALLATION

➧ **See Figure 92**

The floor mats are a very handy item to have for your vehicle. They can be helpful at keeping the carpet in good condition. The mats must be installed in your vehicle with no folds or rolls. They must be inserted flat as not to get caught up under the gas or brake pedal. Position the mat 1 inch (25mm) away from the pedals on the driver's side. Some models have a pin where the driver's mat hooks onto to keep it from moving while driving. The other mats can be positioned in their appropriate areas.

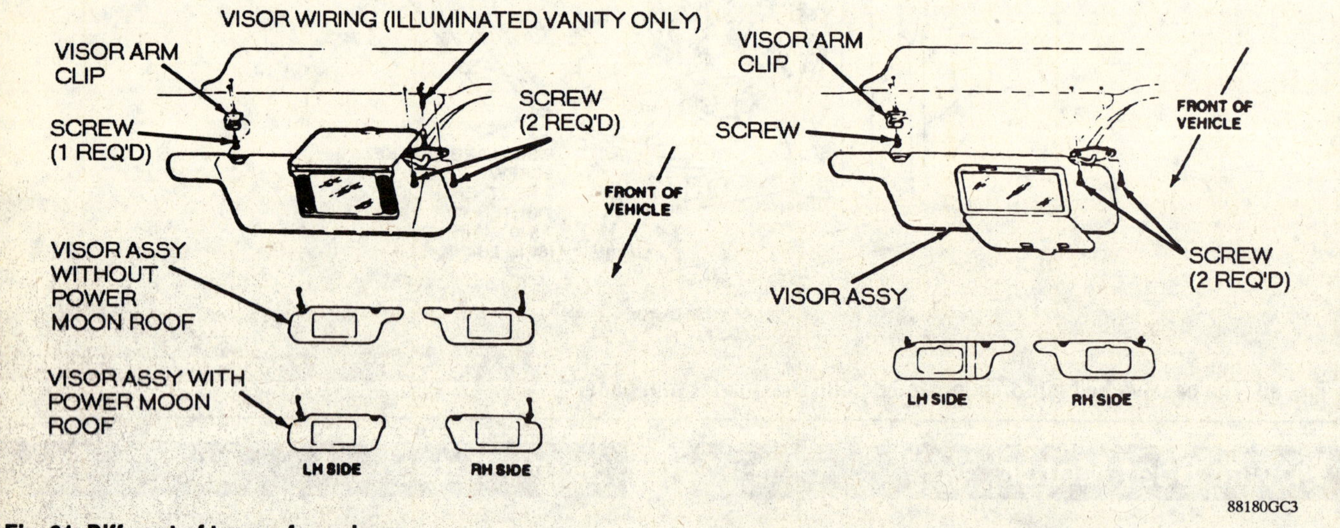

Fig. 91 Different of types of sunvisors

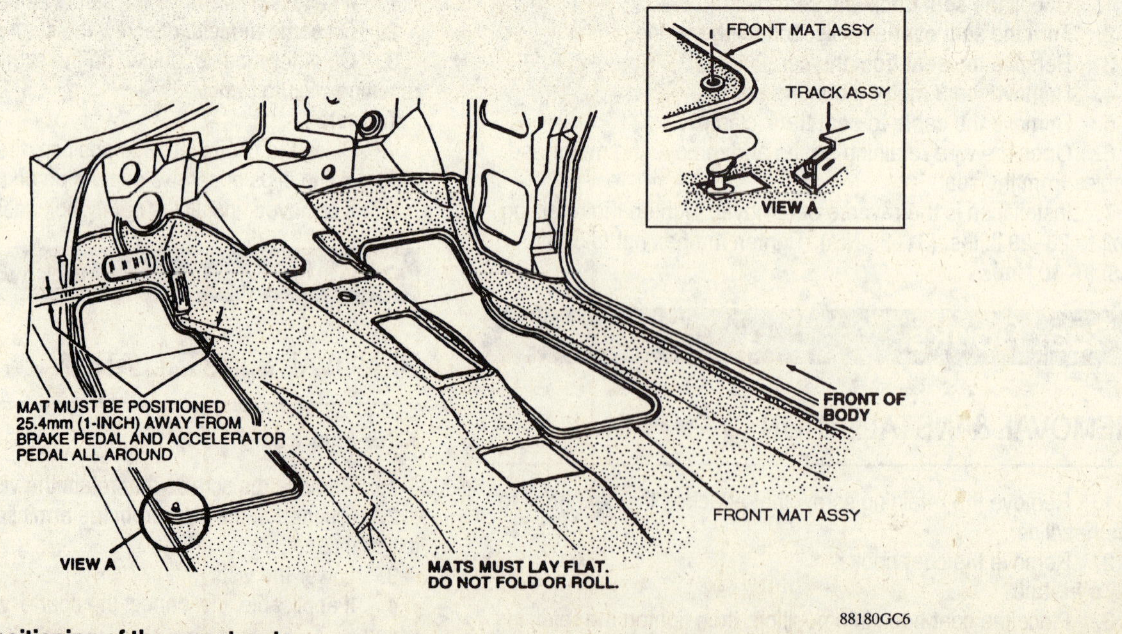

Fig. 92 Common positioning of the carpet mats

GLOSSARY

AIR/FUEL RATIO: The ratio of air-to-gasoline by weight in the fuel mixture drawn into the engine.

AIR INJECTION: One method of reducing harmful exhaust emissions by injecting air into each of the exhaust ports of an engine. The fresh air entering the hot exhaust manifold causes any remaining fuel to be burned before it can exit the tailpipe.

ALTERNATOR: A device used for converting mechanical energy into electrical energy.

AMMETER: An instrument, calibrated in amperes, used to measure the flow of an electrical current in a circuit. Ammeters are always connected in series with the circuit being tested.

AMPERE: The rate of flow of electrical current present when one volt of electrical pressure is applied against one ohm of electrical resistance.

ANALOG COMPUTER: Any microprocessor that uses similar (analogous) electrical signals to make its calculations.

ARMATURE: A laminated, soft iron core wrapped by a wire that converts electrical energy to mechanical energy as in a motor or relay. When rotated in a magnetic field, it changes mechanical energy into electrical energy as in a generator.

ATMOSPHERIC PRESSURE: The pressure on the Earth's surface caused by the weight of the air in the atmosphere. At sea level, this pressure is 14.7 psi at 32°F (101 kPa at 0°C).

ATOMIZATION: The breaking down of a liquid into a fine mist that can be suspended in air.

AXIAL PLAY: Movement parallel to a shaft or bearing bore.

BACKFIRE: The sudden combustion of gases in the intake or exhaust system that results in a loud explosion.

BACKLASH: The clearance or play between two parts, such as meshed gears.

BACKPRESSURE: Restrictions in the exhaust system that slow the exit of exhaust gases from the combustion chamber.

BAKELITE: A heat resistant, plastic insulator material commonly used in printed circuit boards and transistorized components.

BALL BEARING: A bearing made up of hardened inner and outer races between which hardened steel balls roll.

BALLAST RESISTOR: A resistor in the primary ignition circuit that lowers voltage after the engine is started to reduce wear on ignition components.

BEARING: A friction reducing, supportive device usually located between a stationary part and a moving part.

BIMETAL TEMPERATURE SENSOR: Any sensor or switch made of two dissimilar types of metal that bend when heated or cooled due to the different expansion rates of the alloys. These types of sensors usually function as an on/off switch.

BLOWBY: Combustion gases, composed of water vapor and unburned fuel, that leak past the piston rings into the crankcase during normal engine operation. These gases are removed by the PCV system to prevent the buildup of harmful acids in the crankcase.

BRAKE PAD: A brake shoe and lining assembly used with disc brakes.

BRAKE SHOE: The backing for the brake lining. The term is, however, usually applied to the assembly of the brake backing and lining.

BUSHING: A liner, usually removable, for a bearing; an anti-friction liner used in place of a bearing.

CALIPER: A hydraulically activated device in a disc brake system, which is mounted straddling the brake rotor (disc). The caliper contains at least one piston and two brake pads. Hydraulic pressure on the piston(s) forces the pads against the rotor.

CAMSHAFT: A shaft in the engine on which are the lobes (cams) which operate the valves. The camshaft is driven by the crankshaft, via a belt, chain or gears, at one half the crankshaft speed.

CAPACITOR: A device which stores an electrical charge.

CARBON MONOXIDE (CO): A colorless, odorless gas given off as a normal byproduct of combustion. It is poisonous and extremely dangerous in confined areas, building up slowly to toxic levels without warning if adequate ventilation is not available.

CARBURETOR: A device, usually mounted on the intake manifold of an engine, which mixes the air and fuel in the proper proportion to allow even combustion.

CATALYTIC CONVERTER: A device installed in the exhaust system, like a muffler, that converts harmful byproducts of combustion into carbon dioxide and water vapor by means of a heat-producing chemical reaction.

CENTRIFUGAL ADVANCE: A mechanical method of advancing the spark timing by using flyweights in the distributor that react to centrifugal force generated by the distributor shaft rotation.

CHECK VALVE: Any one-way valve installed to permit the flow of air, fuel or vacuum in one direction only.

CHOKE: A device, usually a moveable valve, placed in the intake path of a carburetor to restrict the flow of air.

CIRCUIT: Any unbroken path through which an electrical current can flow. Also used to describe fuel flow in some instances.

CIRCUIT BREAKER: A switch which protects an electrical circuit from overload by opening the circuit when the current flow exceeds a predetermined level. Some circuit breakers must be reset manually, while most reset automatically.

COIL (IGNITION): A transformer in the ignition circuit which steps up the voltage provided to the spark plugs.

COMBINATION MANIFOLD: An assembly which includes both the intake and exhaust manifolds in one casting.

COMBINATION VALVE: A device used in some fuel systems that routes fuel vapors to a charcoal storage canister instead of venting them into the atmosphere. The valve relieves fuel tank pressure and allows fresh air into the tank as the fuel level drops to prevent a vapor lock situation.

COMPRESSION RATIO: The comparison of the total volume of the cylinder and combustion chamber with the piston at BDC and the piston at TDC.

CONDENSER: 1. An electrical device which acts to store an electrical charge, preventing voltage surges. 2. A radiator-like device in the air conditioning system in which refrigerant gas condenses into a liquid, giving off heat.

CONDUCTOR: Any material through which an electrical current can be transmitted easily.

CONTINUITY: Continuous or complete circuit. Can be checked with an ohmmeter.

COUNTERSHAFT: An intermediate shaft which is rotated by a mainshaft and transmits, in turn, that rotation to a working part.

CRANKCASE: The lower part of an engine in which the crankshaft and related parts operate.

CRANKSHAFT: The main driving shaft of an engine which receives reciprocating motion from the pistons and converts it to rotary motion.

CYLINDER: In an engine, the round hole in the engine block in which the piston(s) ride.

CYLINDER BLOCK: The main structural member of an engine in which is found the cylinders, crankshaft and other principal parts.

CYLINDER HEAD: The detachable portion of the engine, usually fastened to the top of the cylinder block and containing all or most of the combustion chambers. On overhead valve engines, it contains the valves and their operating parts. On overhead cam engines, it contains the camshaft as well.

DEAD CENTER: The extreme top or bottom of the piston stroke.

DETONATION: An unwanted explosion of the air/fuel mixture in the combustion chamber caused by excess heat and compression, advanced timing, or an overly lean mixture. Also referred to as "ping".

DIAPHRAGM: A thin, flexible wall separating two cavities, such as in a vacuum advance unit.

DIESELING: A condition in which hot spots in the combustion chamber cause the engine to run on after the key is turned off.

DIFFERENTIAL: A geared assembly which allows the transmission of motion between drive axles, giving one axle the ability to turn faster than the other.

DIODE: An electrical device that will allow current to flow in one direction only.

DISC BRAKE: A hydraulic braking assembly consisting of a brake disc, or rotor, mounted on an axle, and a caliper assembly containing, usually two brake pads which are activated by hydraulic pressure. The pads are forced against the sides of the disc, creating friction which slows the vehicle.

DISTRIBUTOR: A mechanically driven device on an engine which is responsible for electrically firing the spark plug at a predetermined point of the piston stroke.

DOWEL PIN: A pin, inserted in mating holes in two different parts allowing those parts to maintain a fixed relationship.

DRUM BRAKE: A braking system which consists of two brake shoes and one or two wheel cylinders, mounted on a fixed backing plate, and a brake drum, mounted on an axle, which revolves around the assembly.

DWELL: The rate, measured in degrees of shaft rotation, at which an electrical circuit cycles on and off.

ELECTRONIC CONTROL UNIT (ECU): Ignition module, module, amplifier or igniter. See Module for definition.

ELECTRONIC IGNITION: A system in which the timing and firing of the spark plugs is controlled by an electronic control unit, usually called a module. These systems have no points or condenser.

END-PLAY: The measured amount of axial movement in a shaft.

ENGINE: A device that converts heat into mechanical energy.

EXHAUST MANIFOLD: A set of cast passages or pipes which conduct exhaust gases from the engine.

FEELER GAUGE: A blade, usually metal, of precisely predetermined thickness, used to measure the clearance between two parts.

FIRING ORDER: The order in which combustion occurs in the cylinders of an engine. Also the order in which spark is distributed to the plugs by the distributor.

FLOODING: The presence of too much fuel in the intake manifold and combustion chamber which prevents the air/fuel mixture from firing, thereby causing a no-start situation.

FLYWHEEL: A disc shaped part bolted to the rear end of the crankshaft. Around the outer perimeter is affixed the ring gear. The starter drive engages the ring gear, turning the flywheel, which rotates the crankshaft, imparting the initial starting motion to the engine.

FOOT POUND (ft. lbs. or sometimes, ft.lb.): The amount of energy or work needed to raise an item weighing one pound, a distance of one foot.

FUSE: A protective device in a circuit which prevents circuit overload by breaking the circuit when a specific amperage is present. The device is constructed around a strip or wire of a lower amperage rating than the circuit it is designed to protect. When an amperage higher than that stamped on the fuse is present in the circuit, the strip or wire melts, opening the circuit.

GEAR RATIO: The ratio between the number of teeth on meshing gears.

GENERATOR: A device which converts mechanical energy into electrical energy.

HEAT RANGE: The measure of a spark plug's ability to dissipate heat from its firing end. The higher the heat range, the hotter the plug fires.

HUB: The center part of a wheel or gear.

HYDROCARBON (HC): Any chemical compound made up of hydrogen and carbon. A major pollutant formed by the engine as a byproduct of combustion.

HYDROMETER: An instrument used to measure the specific gravity of a solution.

INCH POUND (inch lbs.; sometimes in.lb. or in. lbs.): One twelfth of a foot pound.

INDUCTION: A means of transferring electrical energy in the form of a magnetic field. Principle used in the ignition coil to increase voltage.

INJECTOR: A device which receives metered fuel under relatively low pressure and is activated to inject the fuel into the engine under relatively high pressure at a predetermined time.

INPUT SHAFT: The shaft to which torque is applied, usually carrying the driving gear or gears.

INTAKE MANIFOLD: A casting of passages or pipes used to conduct air or a fuel/air mixture to the cylinders.

JOURNAL: The bearing surface within which a shaft operates.

KEY: A small block usually fitted in a notch between a shaft and a hub to prevent slippage of the two parts.

MANIFOLD: A casting of passages or set of pipes which connect the cylinders to an inlet or outlet source.

MANIFOLD VACUUM: Low pressure in an engine intake manifold formed just below the throttle plates. Manifold vacuum is highest at idle and drops under acceleration.

MASTER CYLINDER: The primary fluid pressurizing device in a hydraulic system. In automotive use, it is found in brake and hydraulic clutch systems and is pedal activated, either directly or, in a power brake system, through the power booster.

MODULE: Electronic control unit, amplifier or igniter of solid state or integrated design which controls the current flow in the ignition primary circuit based on input from the pick-up coil. When the module opens the primary circuit, high secondary voltage is induced in the coil.

NEEDLE BEARING: A bearing which consists of a number (usually a large number) of long, thin rollers.

OHM:(Ω) The unit used to measure the resistance of conductor-to-electrical flow. One ohm is the amount of resistance that limits current flow to one ampere in a circuit with one volt of pressure.

OHMMETER: An instrument used for measuring the resistance, in ohms, in an electrical circuit.

OUTPUT SHAFT: The shaft which transmits torque from a device, such as a transmission.

OVERDRIVE: A gear assembly which produces more shaft revolutions than that transmitted to it.

OVERHEAD CAMSHAFT (OHC): An engine configuration in which the camshaft is mounted on top of the cylinder head and operates the valve either directly or by means of rocker arms.

OVERHEAD VALVE (OHV): An engine configuration in which all of the valves are located in the cylinder head and the camshaft is located in the cylinder block. The camshaft operates the valves via lifters and pushrods.

OXIDES OF NITROGEN (NOx): Chemical compounds of nitrogen produced as a byproduct of combustion. They combine with hydrocarbons to produce smog.

OXYGEN SENSOR: Used with the feedback system to sense the presence of oxygen in the exhaust gas and signal the computer which can reference the voltage signal to an air/fuel ratio.

PINION: The smaller of two meshing gears.

PISTON RING: An open-ended ring which fits into a groove on the outer diameter of the piston. Its chief function is to form a seal between the piston and cylinder wall. Most automotive pistons have three rings: two for compression sealing; one for oil sealing.

PRELOAD: A predetermined load placed on a bearing during assembly or by adjustment.

PRIMARY CIRCUIT: The low voltage side of the ignition system which consists of the ignition switch, ballast resistor or resistance wire, bypass, coil, electronic control unit and pick-up coil as well as the connecting wires and harnesses.

PRESS FIT: The mating of two parts under pressure, due to the inner diameter of one being smaller than the outer diameter of the other, or vice versa; an interference fit.

RACE: The surface on the inner or outer ring of a bearing on which the balls, needles or rollers move.

REGULATOR: A device which maintains the amperage and/or voltage levels of a circuit at predetermined values.

RELAY: A switch which automatically opens and/or closes a circuit.

RESISTANCE: The opposition to the flow of current through a circuit or electrical device, and is measured in ohms. Resistance is equal to the voltage divided by the amperage.

RESISTOR: A device, usually made of wire, which offers a preset amount of resistance in an electrical circuit.

RING GEAR: The name given to a ring-shaped gear attached to a differential case, or affixed to a flywheel or as part of a planetary gear set.

ROLLER BEARING: A bearing made up of hardened inner and outer races between which hardened steel rollers move.

ROTOR: 1. The disc-shaped part of a disc brake assembly, upon which the brake pads bear; also called, brake disc. 2. The device mounted atop the distributor shaft, which passes current to the distributor cap tower contacts.

SECONDARY CIRCUIT: The high voltage side of the ignition system, usually above 20,000 volts. The secondary includes the ignition coil, coil wire, distributor cap and rotor, spark plug wires and spark plugs.

SENDING UNIT: A mechanical, electrical, hydraulic or electromagnetic device which transmits information to a gauge.

SENSOR: Any device designed to measure engine operating conditions or ambient pressures and temperatures. Usually electronic in nature and designed to send a voltage signal to an on-board computer, some sensors may operate as a simple on/off switch or they may provide a variable voltage signal (like a potentiometer) as conditions or measured parameters change.

SHIM: Spacers of precise, predetermined thickness used between parts to establish a proper working relationship.

SLAVE CYLINDER: In automotive use, a device in the hydraulic clutch system which is activated by hydraulic force, disengaging the clutch.

SOLENOID: A coil used to produce a magnetic field, the effect of which is to produce work.

SPARK PLUG: A device screwed into the combustion chamber of a spark ignition engine. The basic construction is a conductive core inside of a ceramic insulator, mounted in an outer conductive base. An electrical charge from the spark plug wire travels along the conductive core and jumps a preset air gap to a grounding point or points at the end of the conductive base. The resultant spark ignites the fuel/air mixture in the combustion chamber.

SPLINES: Ridges machined or cast onto the outer diameter of a shaft or inner diameter of a bore to enable parts to mate without rotation.

TACHOMETER: A device used to measure the rotary speed of an engine, shaft, gear, etc., usually in rotations per minute.

THERMOSTAT: A valve, located in the cooling system of an engine, which is closed when cold and opens gradually in response to engine heating, controlling the temperature of the coolant and rate of coolant flow.

TOP DEAD CENTER (TDC): The point at which the piston reaches the top of its travel on the compression stroke.

TORQUE: The twisting force applied to an object.

TORQUE CONVERTER: A turbine used to transmit power from a driving member to a driven member via hydraulic action, providing changes in drive ratio and torque. In automotive use, it links the driveplate at the rear of the engine to the automatic transmission.

TRANSDUCER: A device used to change a force into an electrical signal.

TRANSISTOR: A semi-conductor component which can be actuated by a small voltage to perform an electrical switching function.

TUNE-UP: A regular maintenance function, usually associated with the replacement and adjustment of parts and components in the electrical and fuel systems of a vehicle for the purpose of attaining optimum performance.

TURBOCHARGER: An exhaust driven pump which compresses intake air and forces it into the combustion chambers at higher than atmospheric pressures. The increased air pressure allows more fuel to be burned and results in increased horsepower being produced.

VACUUM ADVANCE: A device which advances the ignition timing in response to increased engine vacuum.

VACUUM GAUGE: An instrument used to measure the presence of vacuum in a chamber.

VALVE: A device which control the pressure, direction of flow or rate of flow of a liquid or gas.

VALVE CLEARANCE: The measured gap between the end of the valve stem and the rocker arm, cam lobe or follower that activates the valve.

VISCOSITY: The rating of a liquid's internal resistance to flow.

VOLTMETER: An instrument used for measuring electrical force in units called volts. Voltmeters are always connected parallel with the circuit being tested.

WHEEL CYLINDER: Found in the automotive drum brake assembly, it is a device, actuated by hydraulic pressure, which, through internal pistons, pushes the brake shoes outward against the drums.

MASTER INDEX